STATISTICAL REFERENCE INDEX 1984 ANNUAL

A selective guide to American statistical publications from private organizations and state government sources

Abstracts

Congressional Information Service

CIS

Staff

Editorial Director
Susan I. Jover

Director of Statistical Services
Darlene J. Montgomery

Indexing Specialist
Daniel Coyle

Managing Editor
Lynn K. Marble

Assistant Managing Editor, Abstracts
Joseph H. McNally

Assistant Managing Editor, Collection Development
Jeanne Long

Assistant Managing Editor, Index
Jeffrey E. Strandberg

Abstracting and Indexing Staff
Thomas J. Hoffman
Deborah Marlatt Kitchin

Lisette B. Lawson
Jane A. Lean
Mary R. Nolan
Jane Overton Scanlan
James Shields
Thomas A. Stock
Polly Todd
Edie Wett

Accuracy Editor
Katharina C. Wendel

Editorial Assistant
Elizabeth J. Holliday

Acquisitions Editors
Edward Kianka

Diane L. Kinney
Cheryl M. Waldman

Acquisitions Assistant
Gregory Crisostomo

Documents Control
Sally L. MacArthur

Production Coordinator
Dorothy W. Rogers

Production Services Supervisor
Esther R. Aikens

Production Staff
Helene E. Gaffney
Elizabeth Naccarato
Debra Turnell

International Book Number
For the Set: 0-88692-040-X
For Index Volume: 0-88692-041-8
For Abstract Volume: 0-88692-042-6

Congressional Information Service, Inc.
4520 East-West Highway
Bethesda, Md. 20814
(301) 654-1550

This issue of the Statistical Reference Index has been compiled and composed with the aid of SAMANTHA^{TM}, an electronic data processing technique developed by Information and Publishing Systems, Inc. of Bethesda, Md.

SRI 1984 ANNUAL CONTENTS

The Statistical Reference Index 1984 Annual
is published in two volumes, the
contents of which are summarized below.

Abstracts

Index

NOTE: For comprehensive access to U.S. Government statistical publications, consult the American Statistics Index. ASI is published by Congressional Information Service, Inc. and is available in many major libraries. Coverage begins with the early 1960s and is updated monthly.

Detailed Table of Contents: Abstracts Volume

Issuing Sources and SRI Accession Numbers

BUSINESS ORGANIZATIONS

COMMERCIAL PUBLISHERS

INDEPENDENT RESEARCH ORGANIZATIONS

STATE GOVERNMENTS

ALABAMA

ALASKA

ARIZONA

UNIVERSITY RESEARCH CENTERS

USER GUIDE

INTRODUCTION TO SRI

Basic Objectives and Coverage

Each year, thousands of U.S. private organizations and State government agencies prepare and issue countless publications and articles, many of which contain important statistics on business, industry and finance, general economic conditions, government programs and politics, and social trends. These data are typically authoritative, timely, and well-researched, and often present results of original surveys and research. In many cases, they complement or fill important gaps in data prepared and issued by the Federal Government, and also frequently are more current than Federal data.

The *Statistical Reference Index* (SRI) service, which includes printed abstracts and indexes and a companion microfiche collection of source data, is designed to provide a reliable, centralized means of access to this large and significant body of business, financial, and social statistical data, much of which has previously been difficult to locate or obtain for research use.

Specifically, SRI has as its purpose the following functions:

- **Survey and review** current statistical publications issued by major U.S. associations and institutes, business organizations, commercial publishers, independent research centers, State government agencies, and universities.

- **Identify** current publications containing substantial statistical material of general research value.

- **Catalog** the publications in which the data appear, providing full bibliographic data and availability information for each publication.

- **Announce** new publications as they appear.

- **Describe** the contents of these publications fully.

- **Index** this information in full detail for access by subject, category, issuing source, and title.

- **Micropublish** the entire content or the statistical portions of the publications covered. (During 1984, SRI obtained microfilming rights for over 90% of the publications abstracted and indexed.)

SRI data selection criteria, more fully detailed below, have been established with the objectives of covering a wide array of data publishing organizations and subject matter. Criteria also emphasize prompt coverage of currently published sources of statistics and focus on continuing time series data wherever possible. Priority is also given to maintaining coverage of basic social, governmental, economic, and demographic data for each of the 50 States and the District of Columbia.

This 1984 SRI Annual contains abstracts and indexing for more than 1,800 titles, including approximately 1,220 annual or other recurring reports, 240 monographs, 380 periodicals with regularly appearing statistical features, and over 2,000 individual statistical articles. Included are reports from all 50 States and the District of Columbia, and statistical compendia from 30 States.

During 1985, SRI will maintain current coverage of all periodicals, annuals, and other recurring reports covered since its inception in 1980, and will continue to expand that coverage with additional current titles.

Issuing Sources Covered

SRI staff have conducted comprehensive surveys of current sources of data in order to establish a well-rounded sphere of coverage for SRI. Identification and selection of issuing sources currently covered are based on:

- Review of secondary sources, including *Directory of Business and Financial Services, Business Information Sources, Guide to Special Issues and Indexes of Periodicals, Statistical Abstract of the U.S.,* and numerous other bibliographies.

- Review of the Harvard University Baker Library industry statistics file.

- Canvass of national associations with annual budgets over $1 million.

- Canvass of business-oriented periodicals ranked in order of sales in *Folio 400.*

- Canvass of 2,000 State government agencies to identify offices publishing the most comprehensive reports on State administered programs.

- Consultations with librarians who are specialists in information fields such as banking and finance, State documents, and others.

- Follow-up on references cited in current periodicals and other news media.

SRI acquisitions staff are continually reviewing additional publications and canvassing additional sources in an effort to maintain and extend SRI coverage. Within this 1984 Annual, approximately 1,000 issuing source organizations are represented in the following categories:

- **Trade, professional, and other nonprofit associations and institutes,** including those representing manufacturing and nonmanufacturing industries, and academic, occupational, recreational, public interest, and religious groups.

- **Business organizations,** including banks, accounting firms, stock and commodity exchanges, public opinion survey and research firms, and other private companies and corporations.

- **Commercial publishers** of business, trade association, and industry periodical and annual publications, including such major publishers as R. R. Bowker, Chilton Co., Crain Communications, Dun and Bradstreet, Forbes, Lebhar-Friedman, McGraw-Hill, and PennWell Publishing.

- **Independent research organizations,** including public policy, education, demographic, and economic research organizations.

- **State government agencies,** including those with primary responsibility in such areas as State education, employment, health and vital statistics reporting, public assistance, elections, crime and correctional institutions, and the judicial system.

- **Universities and affiliated research centers,** including those focusing on demographic research, and research in the fields of business and industry, agriculture, and economic forecasting.

Criteria for Publication Selection

In selecting publications for coverage, SRI seeks to include:

- Publications presenting business, industrial, financial, and social statistics of general research value, and having national, regional, or statewide breadth of coverage. Where there is redundancy of content among groups or related series of publications, emphasis is placed upon selecting those publications presenting time series or regularly updated statistics, and those with the most comprehensive, detailed coverage.

- Publications containing statistics in subject areas or in geographic detail not well covered by Federal data, and statistics useful for comparison with Federal data.

- Publications presenting data that, while in some respects limited in scope, geographically or otherwise, are the best or most authoritative found for a given subject, or present a unique analysis or statistical base.

SRI coverage excludes:

- Ephemeral or highly localized data of very limited interest.

- Scientific or highly technical data, and instructional handbooks and manuals.

- Publications with very limited or exclusive distribution for which microfiche reproduction rights cannot be obtained, that are thus unlikely to be available to libraries in any form.

- Publications which simply republish Federal data from a single source without analysis or without additional data collected from other sources (comprehensive coverage of Federal data can be found in *American Statistics Index,* published by Congressional Information Service, Bethesda, Md.).

- Publications of municipal and county governments (coverage of this material can be found in the *Index to Current Urban Documents,* published by Greenwood Press, Westport, Conn.).

In addition, SRI excludes coverage of published current securities quotations or price data intended primarily for investment or purchasing reference purposes, as well as coverage of widely publicized and commercially distributed monographs that are already well known and easily accessible.

Selection criteria for inclusion and exclusion are reviewed and refined on a continuing basis. We welcome comments and suggestions from SRI users that will help us in shaping future coverage policies and improving abstracting and indexing procedures.

Types of Statistics Covered

Publications covered by SRI provide users access to the following types of data:

- **National Data** — Production, costs, and earnings in major industries and business sectors; operating and market characteristics of business and commerce; rankings of products and corporations; data related to key areas of social or public interest; professional worker supply and demand; public opinion and salary surveys; demographic data; and national economic trends.

- **Statewide Data** — State statistical compendia, and 10-15 additional periodicals or annual basic reports for each of the 50 States, presenting data on such areas as vital statistics, crime, health, agriculture, business conditions and economic indicators, employment, education, taxation and finance, insurance and other State-regulated industries, the judicial system, corrections, elections, libraries, population, and motor vehicle accidents; and State reports presenting data from the 1980 Census of Population and Housing.

- **Data on Foreign Countries** — World economic and demographic trends; international finance, investment, and trade data; and foreign country social and economic indicators, frequently organized to permit comparison with data for the United States.

- **Local or Otherwise Narrowly Focused Data** — Detail by county and municipality is provided in most State reports selected for inclusion. In addition, selected local or narrowly focused studies or articles, from any source, may be included if the subject matter is judged to have research value beyond the limited area of coverage.

Coverage of SRI Monthly and Annual Editions

SRI indexes and abstracts are issued on a monthly basis except for the combined January/February issue, and are cumulated in an annual edition, published in the spring of the following year.

SRI 1984 Annual. This fifth SRI Annual cumulates the abstracts and indexes originally published in SRI monthly issues January through December 1984, generally covering publications issued October 1983 through September 1984. A selected number of earlier publications are also included, if they retain their value as current research sources. For publications abstracted and indexed prior to 1984, see SRI 1980, 1981, 1982, and 1983 Annuals.

The 1984 Annual provides full descriptions and indexing for all publications covered by SRI during 1984, including "base" descriptions for all periodicals. The SRI 1984 Annual replaces and fully supersedes all 1984 SRI monthly issues.

SRI 1985 Monthly Issues. In general, SRI monthly issues cover periodicals, annuals and other serials, and monographs acquired 8–12 weeks previously. Thus, the SRI monthly issue dated April and shipped in April, for the most part will cover publications acquired during February, the issue dated May will cover March publications, and so forth.

All SRI indexes cumulate monthly during each quarter; that is, the SRI May Index contains all indexing appearing in the April and May issues. Each quarterly issue (March, June, September, December) cumulates all indexing for the quarter. Thus, users need only search the Annuals, the latest monthly SRI index volume, and any previously published quarterly index volumes, in order to search the entire current file. All indexing for the year will be cumulated in the SRI 1985 Annual clothbound issue.

During 1985, in addition to covering new titles, SRI will maintain full current coverage for all new editions of recurring publications, and all new issues of periodicals covered in previous years. Full or "base" abstracts and indexing will be published for all periodicals in the first 1985 SRI monthly issue in which they are covered.

HOW TO USE THE SRI 1984 ANNUAL

ORGANIZATION OF SRI INDEXES

SRI provides access to statistical data through companion volumes of indexes and abstracts. Ordinarily, research will begin with the Index volume. The Index volume contains four basic indexes to lead the user to the information he seeks from a variety of starting points:

- **Index by Subjects and Names**
- **Index by Categories**
- **Index by Issuing Sources**
- **Index by Titles**

Index by Subjects and Names

This index section contains references to specific subjects, places, personal authors, and data source organizations other than issuing sources. Each index entry under a subject term contains a "notation of content," which consists of a brief description of the principal subject matter of the publication as it relates to that term, the date of data coverage or publication, major data breakdowns, and the publication periodicity. These are followed by the SRI accession number identifying the individual document as described in the abstract volume.

Notation of content entries for data of general, national, or international scope are listed first, followed by those for publications limited to individual States and local areas. The initial or key word of these notations of content is selected to provide an added level of specificity under each subject term, and serves, in a general way, to group together entries for similar data under that term.

It should be noted that the notations of content in the *State and local* section of a term (see example below), taken together constitute a unique and useful compilation of the major sources of State data on that subject. (Data in publications not focusing on a particular State, but showing breakdowns *by State*, are most easily accessible through the Index by Categories, under the heading, "By State," as detailed below.)

This index also contains *see* cross references to guide the user to the relevant term formats used in SRI; and *see also* cross references to guide the user to additional material to be found under the related or narrower terms cited.

Subject index terms are assigned for each publication abstracted to represent all subject matter and data that are covered in sufficient depth to have research value. Unusual items or items of special interest that occur in the body of a report or article, or in individual tables or groups of tables, are indexed regardless of whether they are related to the primary focus of the publication at hand.

Subject terms and cross references in the Index of Subjects and Names are based on a controlled hierarchical vocabulary. When indexing a publication to which a hierarchy of vocabulary terms might apply, SRI uses the most specific, generally applicable term or terms, and generally does not also index to broader or narrower terms that, while relevant, do not reflect so well the focus of the publication. In some cases, where the focus of the document is equally upon the more general and the more particular subject term, index references have been placed under both terms.

In general, individual cities and counties, occupations, or other commonly appearing subject breakdowns of data *within* tables are indexed in the Index by Categories and *not* also in the Index by Subjects and Names. Users are urged to review indexed category breakdowns (see section below) and to keep in mind the added depth of coverage provided. A sample search using the Subject Index is illustrated on p. xxx.

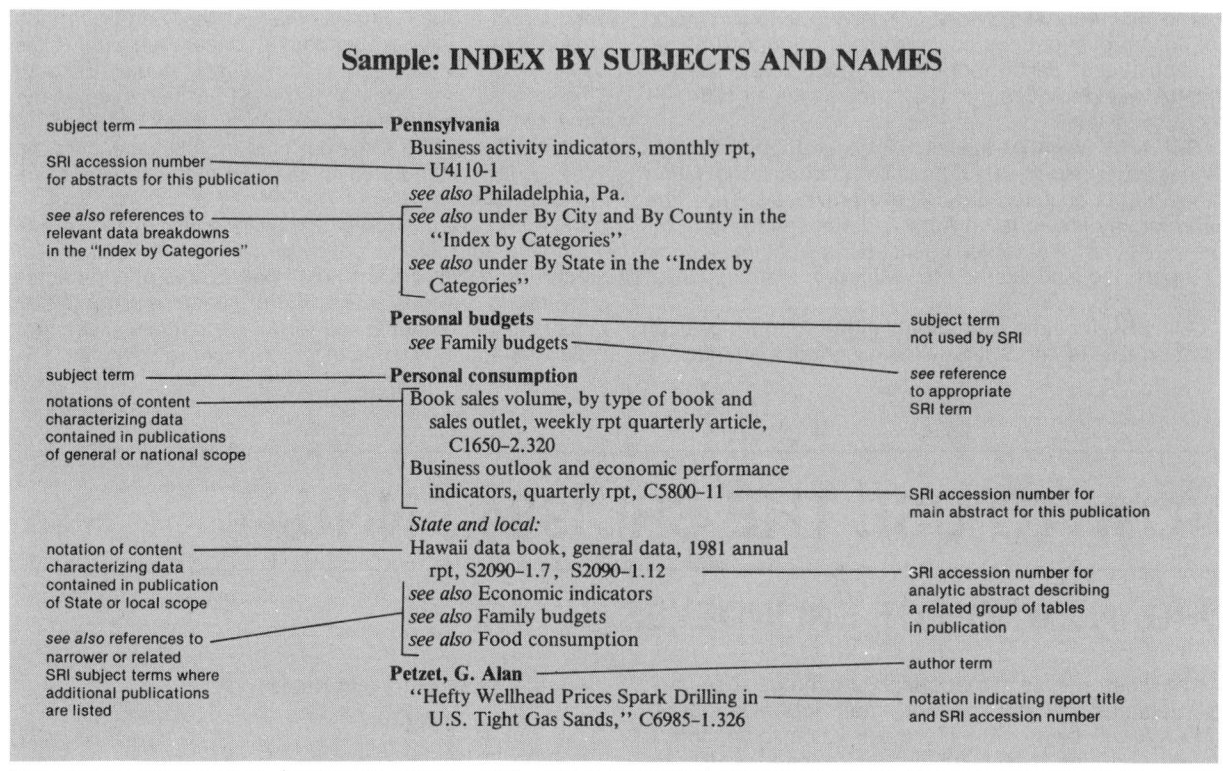

Sample: INDEX BY SUBJECTS AND NAMES

subject term — **Pennsylvania**
Business activity indicators, monthly rpt,
SRI accession number — U4110-1
for abstracts for this publication
see also Philadelphia, Pa.
see also references to — *see also* under By City and By County in the
relevant data breakdowns "Index by Categories"
in the "Index by Categories" *see also* under By State in the "Index by
Categories"

Personal budgets — subject term
see Family budgets — not used by SRI

subject term — **Personal consumption** — *see* reference
notations of content — Book sales volume, by type of book and to appropriate
characterizing data sales outlet, weekly rpt quarterly article, SRI term
contained in publications C1650–2.320
of general or national scope Business outlook and economic performance
indicators, quarterly rpt, C5800–11 — SRI accession number for
main abstract for this publication

State and local:
notation of content — Hawaii data book, general data, 1981 annual
characterizing data rpt, S2090–1.7, S2090–1.12 — SRI accession number for
contained in publication *see also* Economic indicators analytic abstract describing
of State or local scope *see also* Family budgets a related group of tables
see also Food consumption in publication
see also references to —
narrower or related author term
SRI subject terms where **Petzet, G. Alan** —
additional publications "Hefty Wellhead Prices Spark Drilling in notation indicating report title
are listed U.S. Tight Gas Sands," C6985–1.326 and SRI accession number

Index by Categories

This index provides special access to detailed statistical data found in tabular breakdowns and cross classifications. This index includes references to all publications that contain comparative tabular data broken down in any one or more of the following twenty standard categories:

GEOGRAPHIC BREAKDOWNS
By Census Division	By Region
By City	By SMSA or MSA
By County	By State
By Foreign Country or World Area	By Urban-Rural and Metro-Nonmetro

ECONOMIC BREAKDOWNS
By Commodity	By Individual
By Government Agency	Company
By Income	or Institution
By Industry	By Occupation

DEMOGRAPHIC BREAKDOWNS
By Age	By Marital Status
By Disease	By Race
By Educational Attainment	By Sex

For subject searches relating to any of the above breakdowns (e.g., a search for data for a specific city or county, for data on women or income, or on a particular commodity or industry), the Index by Categories is an important access tool. For all categories, this index will generally provide an added depth of coverage beyond that available through the Index by Subjects and Names.

For example, data on individual cities and counties found in detailed breakdowns in State reports will be indexed only in the Index by Categories. In addition, for searches where comparative data are desired (e.g., comparative data for different countries, different companies, different age groups or occupations), the Index by Categories is the most logical starting point.

Within each category in the index, entries are grouped according to subject matter, under one of the following 21 subject headings:

Agriculture and Food
Banking, Finance, and Insurance
Communications
Education
Energy Resources and Demand
Geography and Climate
Government and Defense
Health and Vital Statistics
Housing and Construction
Income
Industry and Commerce
Labor and Employment
Law Enforcement
Natural Resources, Environment, and Pollution
Population
Prices and Cost of Living
Public Welfare and Social Security
Recreation and Leisure
Science and Technology
Transportation and Technology
Veterans Affairs

Definitions and conventions used in assigning these headings are summarized in an introductory section preceding the Index by Categories.

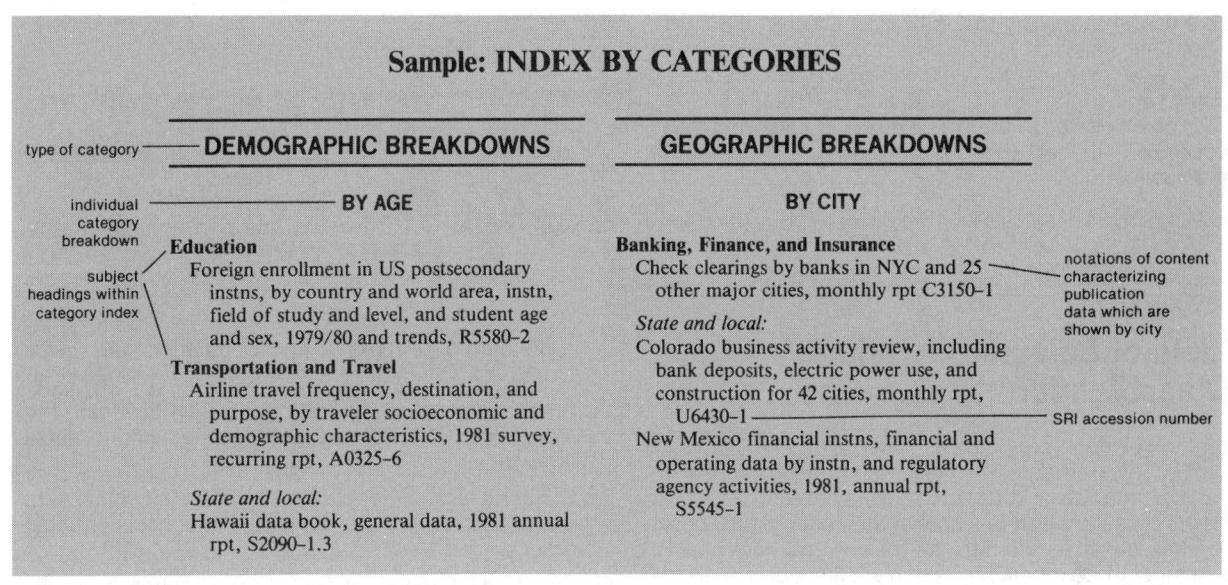

Sample: INDEX BY CATEGORIES

type of category — **DEMOGRAPHIC BREAKDOWNS**

GEOGRAPHIC BREAKDOWNS

individual category breakdown — **BY AGE**

BY CITY

subject headings within category index

Education
Foreign enrollment in US postsecondary instns, by country and world area, instn, field of study and level, and student age and sex, 1979/80 and trends, R5580–2

Transportation and Travel
Airline travel frequency, destination, and purpose, by traveler socioeconomic and demographic characteristics, 1981 survey, recurring rpt, A0325–6

State and local:
Hawaii data book, general data, 1981 annual rpt, S2090–1.3

Banking, Finance, and Insurance
Check clearings by banks in NYC and 25 other major cities, monthly rpt C3150–1

State and local:
Colorado business activity review, including bank deposits, electric power use, and construction for 42 cities, monthly rpt, U6430–1

New Mexico financial instns, financial and operating data by instn, and regulatory agency activities, 1981, annual rpt, S5545–1

notations of content characterizing publication data which are shown by city

SRI accession number

Index by Issuing Sources

This index contains references showing issuing source and publication title for all associations, business organizations, commercial publishers, independent research organizations, State agencies, and university departments or research centers whose publications have been abstracted and indexed by SRI. Periodicity and SRI microfiche status are also shown for each publication title.

Names of issuing sources generally appear in natural word order, with report titles listed below. Where issuing source names have been inverted for purposes of alphabetization by surname (e.g., Best, A.M., Co.), a cross reference from natural word order is provided. University research centers are listed first by university, and secondly by specific center or department issuing the report. In general, titles of State reports are listed under State issuing sources at the Department or highest organizational level, with cross references provided, as necessary, from names of responsible State subagencies. (See example, below.)

Sample: INDEX BY ISSUING SOURCES

name of issuing source — **Metropolitan Life Foundation**
Metropolitan Life Foundation Statistical Bulletin, [Quarterly, SRI/MF/complete], B6045–1

form of issuing source name not used by SRI — **Metropolitan Life Insurance Co.**
see Metropolitan Life Foundation, B6045–1 — cross reference to name form used by SRI

State subagency not used in SRI as issuing source — **Michigan Agricultural Reporting Service**
see Michigan Department of Agriculture, S3950–1 — cross reference to departmental level used in SRI as issuing source

Michigan Department of Agriculture
report title — Michigan Agricultural Statistics, 1982,
report periodicity — [Annual, SRI/MF/complete], — report microfiche status
S3950–1

SRI accession number

Index by Titles

This index lists titles of all publications, including individual reports within a publication series. Titles are listed alphabetically in natural word order, without initial articles (a, an, the), as they appear in the abstracts.

Titles beginning with arabic numerals appear at the end of the index (e.g., 1982 Commodity Year Book), as well as alphabetically under the first key word (e.g., Commodity Year Book, 1982).

Titles of individual articles within a given publication are not generally included in the Title Index, unless the title itself is considered to be sufficiently well known to be a useful searching tool. However, articles or publications that carry an author's name on the title page or otherwise prominently acknowledged, are listed by author in the Index by Subjects and Names.

Each title listed in the Title Index is followed by an SRI accession number, directing the user to the abstract of the publication.

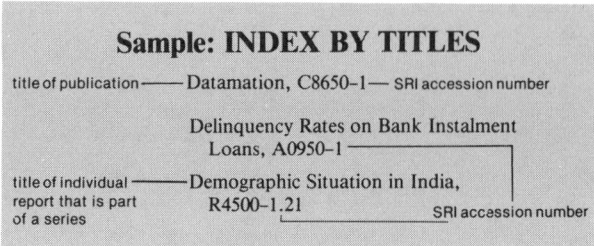

Sample: INDEX BY TITLES

title of publication —— Datamation, C8650–1 —— SRI accession number

Delinquency Rates on Bank Instalment Loans, A0950–1 ———————

title of individual —— Demographic Situation in India, report that is part R4500–1.21 of a series ————— SRI accession number

Lists of Selected Standard Classifications

Statistical data breakdowns indexed in the Index by Categories are frequently presented in accordance with several standard classification systems, and SRI abstracts generally make note of their use. To provide an easily accessible reference for the user, we have printed a number of major classification systems or lists in the "List of Selected Standard Classifications." It includes the following lists:

- Census regions and divisions; outlying areas of the U.S.; Federal Reserve Districts.

- Metropolitan Statistical Areas (MSAs); Consolidated Metropolitan Statistical Areas (CMSAs); cities with population over 100,000; and Consumer Price Index cities.

- Standard Industrial Classification (SIC), providing 1-to 4-digit codes for industry divisions through individual industries.

- Standard Occupational Classification, providing 1- to 4-digit codes for major and minor occupational groups.

- Standard International Trade Classification, a system of 3-digit codes for commodities in world trade, developed by the United Nations, used for foreign trade data, and consistent with the 7-digit codes used for U.S. import-export data.

- List of Part I (Index) and Part II (non-Index) crimes used in Uniform Crime Reporting Systems of the States.

ORGANIZATION OF SRI ABSTRACTS

SRI abstracts are based upon examination of the entire document. Abstracts differ substantially in degree of detail, depending on the type of publication and the kind of data being described. However, all abstracts are written to fulfill certain basic objectives.

These objectives are to describe a publication fully enough to allow the user to determine if it is likely to contain the specific statistical data he seeks; to tell the user where in the publication he can find the data; to provide basic bibliographic data, availability address, price, and other ordering information; and to identify those publications for which SRI provides microfiche reproductions.

This section explains how SRI abstracts are organized in the abstract volume, the internal structure of abstracts, and the special way in which SRI handles periodicals each month.

Accession Numbers

SRI abstracts are organized by accession numbers assigned to each document abstracted and indexed. This accession number identifies not only the individual publication, but also the type of issuing source and the individual organization. It contains four basic elements, illustrated and outlined below.

- **Type of Issuing Source:** The initial letter of an accession number identifies type of issuing source, as follows:

  A – Associations
  B – Business organizations
  C – Commercial publishers
  R – Independent research centers
  S – State agency or subagency
  U – Universities, and affiliated research organizations.

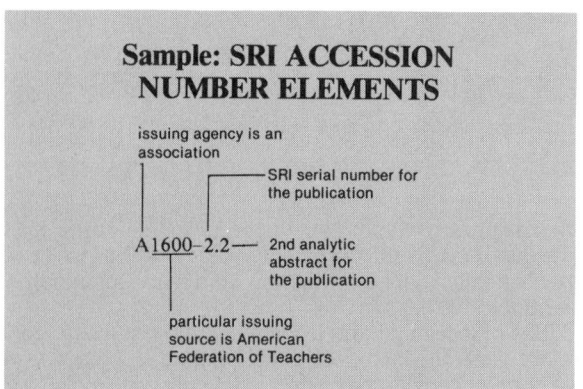

Sample: SRI ACCESSION NUMBER ELEMENTS

issuing agency is an association

———— SRI serial number for the publication

A 1600– 2.2 —— 2nd analytic abstract for the publication

particular issuing source is American Federation of Teachers

- **Individual Issuing Source:** The four digits following the initial letter, up to the hyphen, identify the individual issuing source within the issuing source type.

  (Numbers have been assigned in such a way that individual sources are listed in alphabetical order within a source type.)

- **Sequential SRI Serial Number:** The digits after the hyphen form a unique serial number, sequentially assigned, basically in order of SRI acquisition, so that every publication has its own unique number which can be easily found in the abstracts volume of SRI.

- **Analytic Number:** In many cases, SRI describes publications by using a main abstract in coordination with subordinate or "analytic" abstracts. These analytic abstracts are identified by a decimal number (.1, .2, .3, etc.; or .301, .302, .303, etc.) at the end of the accession number. The analytic abstracts have the following purposes:

  (1) To describe and individually index distinct parts of a large publication, or to identify separate publications in a series. [These analytic abstracts are assigned single digit decimal numbers (A1600-1.1, A1600-1.2, etc.), followed by a heading or title.]

  (2) To describe individual issues of, or specific articles in, current issues of periodicals regularly covered by SRI. [These analytic abstracts are identified by 3-digit decimal numbers (U2735-1.301, U2735-1.302, etc.), followed by cover date of the periodical. A further explanation of periodical abstracts may be found in the section on how SRI handles periodicals, below.]

Generally, once SRI has assigned an accession number to a publication, all successive issues or updates of that publication will receive the same accession number. If the number is changed, cross-references between the old and new numbers are included in the abstracts. This will happen if, for example, the issuing agency of the publication changes.

To use SRI indexes and abstracts effectively, it is not necessary to know how SRI codes and assigns accession numbers, but familiarity with components of the accession number can speed interpretation of entries in the indexes.

Internal Organization of Abstracts

SRI abstracts provide the following information for each publication:

- Title, periodicity, publication date, collation, report number (if assigned by the issuing agency), ISSN or ISBN number and Library of Congress card number (if available), and SRI microfiche coverage information.

- Overview of the publication, including principal subject and purpose, major data topics and breakdowns, geographic areas and time periods covered by data, and data sources.

- Contents summary, with page ranges, covering organization and format of the publication and the number of charts and tables presented.

- Description of statistical content. SRI abstracts present either a summary description of all tables, brief paragraphs describing groups of tables, or a complete listing of individual tables, depending on the level of detail necessary to give a clear picture of the publication's statistical content.

- Complete availability information, including issuing source address for ordering, price, and SRI microfiche coverage.

- For periodicals, cover dates of publications reviewed by SRI, and identification of cover date as either a publication date (P), or as the date of the statistical data presented (D).

Please refer to sample abstracts (p. xxvii-xxix) for illustrations of the above.

Special Handling of Periodicals

SRI observes a few special conventions in describing periodicals. Since most statistical periodicals retain at least some features and tables that are of constant format from issue to issue, it would be redundant to provide full abstracts for each issue. Therefore, a "base" abstract is written for each periodical, to indicate the features common to all issues and to describe tables that appear in each issue or at regular intervals.

For many periodicals, this "base" abstract suffices to describe statistical contents for all issuances during the year, since statistical contents are totally constant in format from issue to issue. However, many periodicals also contain nonrecurring feature articles and special tables, or present recurring tables at irregular intervals. These articles and tables are individually described in analytic abstracts under the heading "Statistical Features."

The "Statistical Features" analytic abstracts use 3-digit analytic numbers and are identified by the cover date of the relevant periodical issue (e.g., A1250-1.201, Nov. 10, 1980 (Vol. 58, No. 45)). For illustration of a typical "Statistical Features" abstract, see sample abstracts, p. xxviii

In composing base abstracts for periodicals, we do not give specific time coverage of the data stated as a specific month or year, but describe it in a general way that will apply to all issues. Similarly, the base abstracts do not include page ranges, which may change from issue to issue.

1985 Monthly Issues

During 1985, SRI will continue covering current issues of periodical titles covered in previous years. The combined January/February issue of SRI contains the initial or "base" abstract for all such periodicals for which issues were received in preceding November or December. For periodicals such as quarterlies which were not received for the 2-month issue, the "base" abstract will be published in the first issue for which they are reviewed in 1985. And, as additional periodicals are included during the year, the initial or base abstract will be provided in the SRI issue in which coverage of that periodical begins.

Throughout the year, whether or not "Statistical Features" abstracts are required to describe particular statistics, each SRI monthly issue will contain both a summary abstract and full indexing of statistical contents for each periodical for which one or more current issues were received during the period of coverage. The monthly summary abstracts will indicate all issues reviewed to date for a periodical, and either present a description of statistics appearing in and indexed for current issues, or refer the user to the SRI issue with the "base" periodical abstract that describes the indexed statistics.

HOW TO ACQUIRE SOURCE PUBLICATIONS

Acquiring Publications from a Library

Many of the publications abstracted in SRI are available in library collections. Ask your librarian for assistance in determining availability of specific titles.

Libraries that subscribe to the SRI Microfiche Library will have source material reproduced on microfiche as indicated in individual abstracts. (See explanation of SRI Microfiche Program, below.)

Requesting or Purchasing Publications from the Issuing Source

Information for requesting or purchasing copies of publications from the issuing source is provided in an Availability section in the SRI abstract for each publication. This information is as current and complete as possible as of SRI date of publication. See sample abstracts (p. xxvii-xxix) and symbols list (p. xxxii) for examples of information provided, and explanation of symbols employed.

The SRI Microfiche Program

Over 90% of the publications covered in SRI are included in the SRI Microfiche Library, available on a subscription basis and included in the collections of many major libraries. An entry in the bibliographic data section of each abstract will describe the microfiche status of that publication in one of the following ways:

- **SRI/MF/complete:** the entire publication is available in the SRI Microfiche Library. (In some series designated SRI/MF/complete, only reports with statistics are abstracted and filmed. Such exceptions are noted in the base description of the series.)

- **SRI/MF/excerpts:** only statistical portions have been filmed and are available on SRI microfiche.

   Many periodicals covered in SRI are less than 50% statistical or have only one or two statistical issues per year, yet each issue averages more than 100 pages collation. Rather than inflate the size and price of SRI Microfiche Library with nonstatistical materials, only the cover, title page, table of contents, statistical content, and any accompanying narrative analysis of the statistical content will be filmed. Issues containing no statistics will not be filmed. A few large directories and calendar handbooks with limited statistical sections will also be filmed in excerpted form for similar reasons. Excerpted portions will be specified in the abstract availability information section.

- **SRI/MF/not filmed:** the publication is copyrighted, and SRI has been unable to obtain permission from the issuing agency to micropublish it.

   SRI will make a continuing effort to obtain reproduction rights to provide as inclusive a microfiche library as possible.

   Publications that have very limited distribution and cannot be micropublished by SRI will not be covered in SRI.

- **SRI/MF/complete, delayed; SRI/MF/excerpts, delayed:** the issuing agency has stipulated that SRI must wait to distribute the microfiche of the publication for a specified period of time as a condition of granting reproduction rights. The delay period will always be stated in the abstract availability section; however, when the delayed microfiche has been shipped by the publication date of the SRI Annual, the bibliographic data section will no longer reflect the "delayed" status.

   Every effort will be made to keep instances of delayed shipment to a minimum.

Microfiche generally are shipped monthly and correspond to abstracts appearing in SRI monthly issues, except for selected periodicals (averaging less than 60 filmed pages) that are shipped on a quarterly basis to minimize waste space in the microfiche collection. Periodicals with quarterly microfiche shipment schedules are identified in the abstract bibliographic information following SRI/MF (e.g., SRI/MF/complete, shipped quarterly; or SRI/MF/excerpts, shipped quarterly).

SRI microfiche are sheets of film that measure 105 × 148 mm (approximately 4″ × 6″), and contain up to 98 document pages. Each has an eye-readable "title header" that identifies the accession number, series title (if any), the document title, issuing organization, and dates of periodical issues, of each publication filmed. Items are filmed separately, and they are plainly sequenced for file integrity and quick retrieval according to SRI accession number.

Automatically updated collections of SRI current publications are available on a subscription basis. Retrospective collections, shipped in their entirety and ready for use, may also be purchased. Collections may be ordered to contain the entire range of SRI publications; or subsets may be ordered to cover only publications issued by State goverments or to cover only publications issued by private organizations and universities.

RELATED CIS SERVICES

American Statistics Index and Index to International Statistics

Since 1973, Congressional Information Service has published the American Statistics Index, a comprehensive monthly abstract and index publication with annual cumulations, covering the thousands of statistical reports and publications prepared and issued by the U.S. Federal Government each year.

Beginning in January 1983, Congressional Information Service initiated publication of the Index to International Statistics, a comprehensive monthly index and abstracting service, covering the statistical publications of international intergovernmental organizations, including UN, OECD, EC, OAS, and approximately 30 other important intergovernmental organizations.

SRI abstracts and indexes are similar to ASI and IIS in many respects, and researchers generally can use SRI,

ASI, and IIS without significantly changing their search methods. However, several differences exist among the abstracts and indexes of the three services that should be noted. Major differences are:

- **Accession Number Periodicity Element**—SRI accession numbers do not indicate periodicity. IIS accession numbers include an indication of periodicity in the first letter after the hyphen, as do ASI accession numbers in the last digit before the hyphen.

- **Issuing Sources Indexing**—SRI and IIS issuing sources are indexed in a separate Index by Issuing Sources. ASI issuing agencies for publications are indexed in the ASI Index of Subjects and Names.

- **Periodicals Indexing in Monthly Issues**—SRI and IIS monthly abstracts and indexing cover all statistical contents of all periodicals received during each month. ASI monthly abstracts and indexing for periodicals cover only articles appearing in current issues, and changes from the "base" description for a periodical in the ASI Annual.

- **Periodical Currency Information in Monthly Issues**—ASI lists current issues of periodicals in a monthly "Periodicals Received and Reviewed" section. SRI and IIS incorporate this information in monthly abstracts for current periodicals.

- **Cumulation Patterns**—IIS indexes and abstracts are cumulated quarterly in the 3rd, 6th, 9th, and 12th issues each year. For ASI and SRI, only indexes are cumulated. ASI indexes are cumulated quarterly on the same schedule as IIS. SRI indexes are cumulated quarterly, but also cumulate throughout the quarter, so that the 2nd issue of a quarter includes indexing from the 1st issue, replacing the earlier monthly index.

All of the documents covered in ASI are included in the ASI Microfiche Library, available on a subscription basis, or through an individual Document on Demand service. The IIS Microfiche Library provides full text availability of over 95% of the publications indexed.

Other CIS Services

Since 1970, Congressional Information Service has published the CIS/Index, a monthly abstract and index publication with annual cumulations, which covers all publications of the U.S. Congress. The CIS/Microfiche Library and CIS/Documents-on-Demand services provide full-text availability of CIS/Index publications.

Through cooperative arrangements with on-line computer services, direct on-line interactive searching of the abstracts and indexing contained in the American Statistics Index and CIS/Index databases is available to the public.

Full details on CIS publications and microform collections are available upon request from the CIS Marketing Department.

ACKNOWLEDGEMENTS

In the development of the Statistical Reference Index, we have had the help and support of so many people that it would be impossible to acknowledge them all individually.

We do wish to thank the hundreds of business organizations, publishers, associations, State government agencies, and research centers that have cooperated in providing us the information to be indexed. We appreciate the many editors, company executives, program and research directors, and State government officials and staff who have shared their expertise and often directed us to other useful sources.

Librarians and information specialists especially have offered useful advice and encouragement as we have discussed with them various aspects of SRI over the years. Our special thanks go to those who have assisted with the development of selection criteria for the publications to be covered: Eleanor C. Au, Head, Special Collections, Thomas Hale Hamilton Library, University of Hawaii at Manoa; Elizabeth Berry, State Documents Librarian, Connecticut State Library; M. Gary Bettis, Documents Librarian, Idaho State Library; Jane Blakey, Documents Librarian, Tennessee State Library and Archives; Vern Buis, Coordinator, Nebraska Publications Clearinghouse, Nebraska Library Commission; Harriet Callahan, Louisiana State Library; Harold L. Chambers, Documents Librarian, Montana State Library; Patricia M. Conley, Reference Librarian, Minnesota State Legislative Reference Library; Lorna Daniells, Harvard University Graduate School of Business Administration, Baker Library; Sandra Faull, Documents Librarian, New Mexico State Library; Jerome B. Frobom, Head of Government Publications Depository, Wyoming State Library; Sue R. Hatfield, Government Documents Librarian, Emporia State University; Clyde Hordusky, Documents Specialist at Ohio State Library; V. Lloyd Jameson, Coordinator for Government Documents, Microtext and Newspapers, Government Documents Department, Boston Public Library; Shirley Johnson, Documents Librarian, Depository Library Center, Iowa State Library Commission; Joan Kerschner, Director, Public Services Division, Nevada State Library; Sims D. Kline, Head of Reference Services and Government Documents, Dupont Ball Library, Stetson University; Nell Laraway, Government Documents Librarian, West Virginia Library Commission; Jack Leister, University of California, Berkeley; Richard Lucas, Reference Librarian, Government Information Services Unit, Michigan State Library; Martha Mashburn, Documents Librarian, Law and Reference Library, Georgia State Library; Patricia Matkovic, State Documents Librarian, Indiana State Library; Edith McCauley, Special Collections Librarian, Portland Public Library, Portland, Maine; John A. McGeachy, Documents Coordinator, Arkansas State Library; Marcia Meister, Reference Librarian for Government Documents, Arizona State University Library; Robert Nedderman, State Documents Librarian, Missouri State Library; John N. Olsgaard, author of *Cumulative Index of South Dakota State Government Publications, 1975-79;* Kathy Pratt, Kentucky Checklist Editor, Division of Archives and Records, Kentucky State Library; Janet D. Pugh, Librarian, Wisconsin Department of Industry, Labor, and Human Relations; Eugenia Rankin, Alabama State Documents Librarian, Department of Archives and History; Jane Rishel, Illinois Documents Coordinator, Illinois State Library; Shirley Rittenhouse, Services Supervisor, Maryland State Law Library; Fran Schell, Reference Librarian, Tennessee State Library and Archives; SLA committee on statistical issues of periodicals; Barbara Smith, Recorder of Documents, Mississippi Library Commission; Lee Steele, Reference Librarian, Delaware Division of Libraries; Alma G. Swann, State Document Reference Librarian, State Library Division, Utah Department of Community and Economic Development; Mary Toll, Documents Librarian, South Carolina State Library; Thomas G. Tyler, Faculty, Graduate School of Librarianship and Information Management, University of Denver; Robert Walton, Texas State Library; Judith Weinrauch, Pennsylvania Documents Librarian, Pennsylvania State Library; Frieda Weise, Reference Librarian, National Library of Medicine; Mary Williamson, Bank Administration Institute, Information Services; and many other State librarians.

The original concept of an SRI data base was developed from suggestions from Jack Leister, Head Librarian at Institute of Governmental Studies, University of California, Berkeley; and Judy Myers, Documents Division of University of Houston Library. Important suggestions in expanding and developing the concept were contributed by Morris Ullman and Ruth Fine.

Sample Abstract—Individual Publication

issuing agency ————

A1325
American
Council of Life Insurance

SRI accession number for publication as a whole ————— A1325-1

1982 LIFE INSURANCE FACT BOOK ————— title

periodicity and date ————— Annual. [1982.] 128 p. ————— collation

LC 47-27134. ————— Library of Congress card number (ISSN or ISBN number also given, if available)

SRI microfiche availability ————— SRI/MF/complete

description of publication as a whole ————

Annual comprehensive fact book on the life insurance industry, including data on life insurance purchases and ownership and benefits payments, and on insurance company reserves, income, assets, obligations, establishments, and employment. Data are current to 1981 with selected historical trends, usually from 1900s.

Data are from American Council of Life Insurance surveys, company annual statements, commercial life insurance statistics publishers, and reports of the Federal Government. ————— data sources

Contains foreword and contents listing (p. 3-4); highlights of the life insurance industry, including 1 summary table and 2 charts (p. 5-8); 84 tables, listed below, accompanied by narrative summaries and occasional illustrative charts (p. 9-105); and directory of State insurance officials, comparative mortality tables, life insurance industry chronology, listing of life insurance industry organizations and assns, glossary, and index (p. 107-128). ————— organization of contents

This is the 37th annual report.

Availability: American Council of Life Insurance, 1850 K St., NW, Washington DC 20006, †; SRI/MF/complete. ————— issuing source address and publication availability
† = free on request
‡ = limited distribution
◆ = copies not available for distribution
$ = price, if available for sale

detailed table listing ————— **TABLES:**
[Historical data prior to approximately 1965 are usually for selected years only. Data by State include District of Columbia.]

SRI accession number for group of related tables within publication ————— **A1325-1.1: Policy Purchases and Ownership**

[All tables except tables [4] and [16] show data for total amount; many include data on number of policies.] ————— note on coverage of tables in report

PURCHASES
[Tables [1-2] and [5] show data exclusive of policy revivals, increases, and dividend additions; tables [1-2] also show data exclusive of reinsurance acquired.]

[1] Purchases of ordinary life insurance by State [1975-81]. (p. 9)

[2] Life insurance purchases [ordinary, group, industrial, and total, 1940-81]. (p. 10)

[3] Analysis of ordinary life insurance purchases [by age, sex, and income of insured, size and detailed type of policy, and payment mode, 1971 and 1981]. (p. 11) ————— annotated titles and page locations of individual tables

[4] Distribution of ordinary life insurance purchases by plan of insurance [1955-81]. (p. 12)

[5] Life insurance purchases in U.S. life insurance companies [ordinary, group, industrial, and total, 1921-81]. (p. 13)

OWNERSHIP SUMMARY DATA

Sample Abstract—Periodical Publication

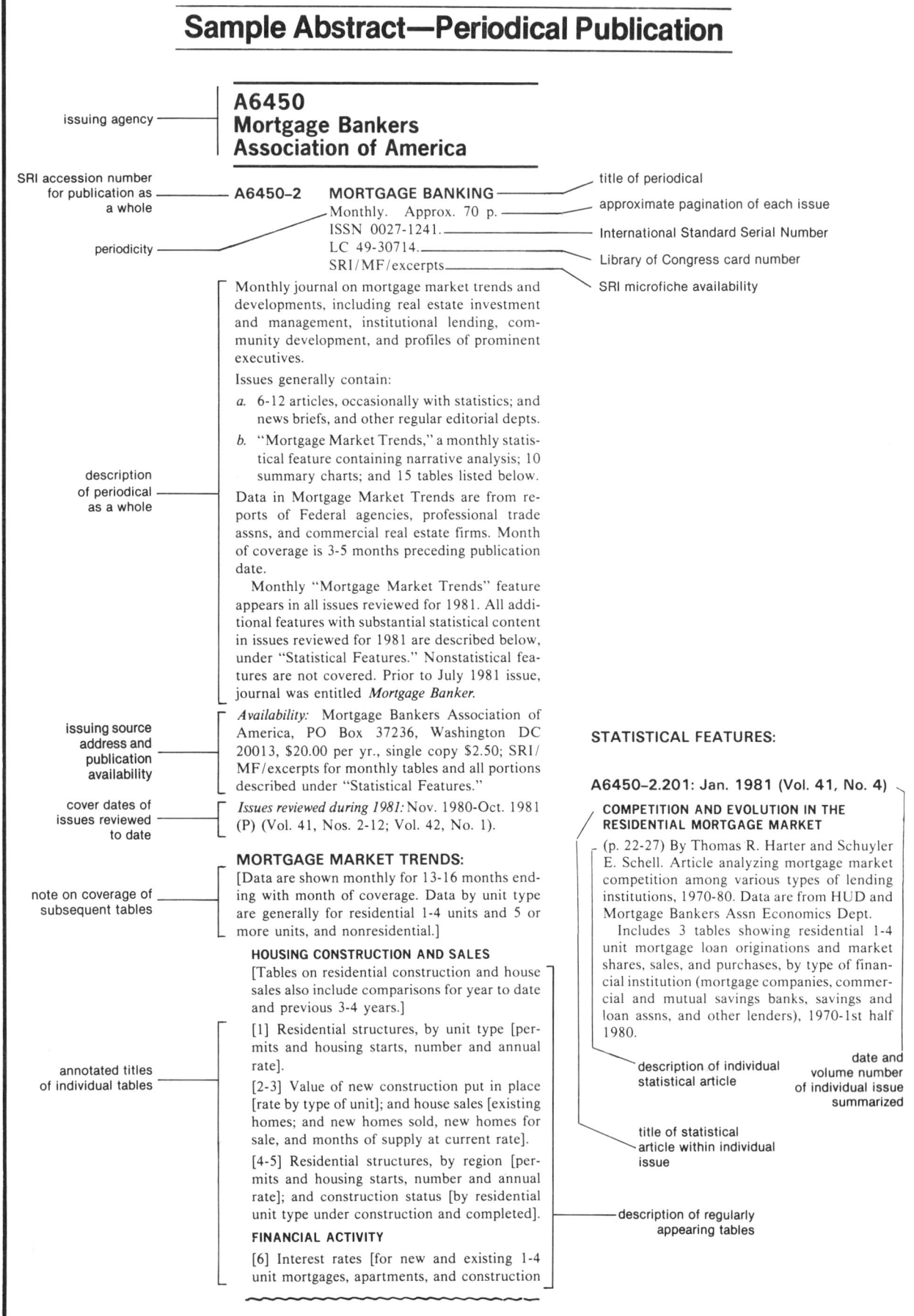

issuing agency

A6450
Mortgage Bankers
Association of America

SRI accession number for publication as a whole

A6450-2 · **MORTGAGE BANKING** — title of periodical

periodicity

Monthly. Approx. 70 p. — approximate pagination of each issue

ISSN 0027-1241. — International Standard Serial Number

LC 49-30714. — Library of Congress card number

SRI/MF/excerpts — SRI microfiche availability

description of periodical as a whole

Monthly journal on mortgage market trends and developments, including real estate investment and management, institutional lending, community development, and profiles of prominent executives.

Issues generally contain:

a. 6-12 articles, occasionally with statistics; and news briefs, and other regular editorial depts.

b. "Mortgage Market Trends," a monthly statistical feature containing narrative analysis; 10 summary charts; and 15 tables listed below.

Data in Mortgage Market Trends are from reports of Federal agencies, professional trade assns, and commercial real estate firms. Month of coverage is 3-5 months preceding publication date.

Monthly "Mortgage Market Trends" feature appears in all issues reviewed for 1981. All additional features with substantial statistical content in issues reviewed for 1981 are described below, under "Statistical Features." Nonstatistical features are not covered. Prior to July 1981 issue, journal was entitled *Mortgage Banker.*

issuing source address and publication availability

Availability: Mortgage Bankers Association of America, PO Box 37236, Washington DC 20013, $20.00 per yr., single copy $2.50; SRI/MF/excerpts for monthly tables and all portions described under "Statistical Features."

cover dates of issues reviewed to date

Issues reviewed during 1981: Nov. 1980-Oct. 1981 (P) (Vol. 41, Nos. 2-12; Vol. 42, No. 1).

MORTGAGE MARKET TRENDS:

note on coverage of subsequent tables

[Data are shown monthly for 13-16 months ending with month of coverage. Data by unit type are generally for residential 1-4 units and 5 or more units, and nonresidential.]

HOUSING CONSTRUCTION AND SALES

[Tables on residential construction and house sales also include comparisons for year to date and previous 3-4 years.]

annotated titles of individual tables

[1] Residential structures, by unit type [permits and housing starts, number and annual rate].

[2-3] Value of new construction put in place [rate by type of unit]; and house sales [existing homes; and new homes sold, new homes for sale, and months of supply at current rate].

[4-5] Residential structures, by region [permits and housing starts, number and annual rate]; and construction status [by residential unit type under construction and completed].

FINANCIAL ACTIVITY

[6] Interest rates [for new and existing 1-4 unit mortgages, apartments, and construction

STATISTICAL FEATURES:

A6450-2.201: Jan. 1981 (Vol. 41, No. 4)

COMPETITION AND EVOLUTION IN THE RESIDENTIAL MORTGAGE MARKET

(p. 22-27) By Thomas R. Harter and Schuyler E. Schell. Article analyzing mortgage market competition among various types of lending institutions, 1970-80. Data are from HUD and Mortgage Bankers Assn Economics Dept.

Includes 3 tables showing residential 1-4 unit mortgage loan originations and market shares, sales, and purchases, by type of financial institution (mortgage companies, commercial and mutual savings banks, savings and loan assns, and other lenders), 1970-1st half 1980.

description of individual statistical article

date and volume number of individual issue summarized

title of statistical article within individual issue

description of regularly appearing tables

Sample Abstract—Publications in Series

U4370
Purdue University:
Credit Research Center

SRI accession number for series as a whole —— **U4370-1** **CREDIT RESEARCH CENTER** —— title of series
WORKING PAPERS
Series. For individual
publication data, see below.
SRI/MF/complete

Continuing series of preliminary drafts of research study reports examining consumer and mortgage credit trends and practices, and their impact on the credit industry, consumers, and government.

description of series as a whole

Reports generally contain narrative analyses with interspersed tables and charts presenting data from government and private published sources, or from original surveys and/or survey analyses.

Recently issued report is described below. For description of previous reports, see SRI 1981 Annual, under this number.

Availability: Purdue University: Credit Research Center, Krannert Graduate School of Management, West Lafayette IN 47907, $1.50 each; SRI/MF/complete. —— availability information for all reports in series

SRI accession number for individual report in series —— **U4370-1.17: Second Mortgage Survey, 1981** —— title of individual report

[Annual. 1982. iii+33 p. Working Paper —— bibliographic data for individual report
No. 43. SRI/MF/complete.]

Annual report, by Richard L. Peterson et al., on a survey of the volume, profitability, and operating policies of the second mortgage lending market, 1980. Data are based on responses of 69 National Second Mortgage Assn members to a 1981 survey.

description of report subject matter

Includes narrative analysis, with 1 table showing survey responses, by institution type; and 10 tables generally showing low, high, average, and/or median, for the following in 1980: —— contents summary

a. Characteristics of second mortgage loans, including number, value, and average size of loans outstanding, extensions, and loan purchases and sales, with selected comparisons to 1979; average size of household and business extensions; ratio of new money to loan extensions; liquidation rates; and loan maturity and equity ratio requirements. Tables 2-5. (p. 6-12)

description of statistical content and page locations of tables

b. Operating ratios, including revenues from interest and other sources, pretax rate of return on equity and average receivables, and ratios of borrowing to receivables, and interest paid to borrowings. Table 6. (p. 14)

c. Delinquency rates by time past due; and chargeoff, foreclosure, and loss allowance ratios. Tables 7-10. (p. 16-20)

d. Comparative data, by lender type, including growth in loans and extensions, selected loan characteristics, operating ratios, delinquency rates, and foreclosures. Table 11. (p. 22)

Previous report, for 1979, was issued as Working Paper No. 39, and is described in SRI 1981 Annual under U4370-1.13. —— cross reference to previous edition of individual report

Sample SRI Search

" How many stores in each of the big convenience food store chains sell gasoline? "

Step 1

Check the SRI Index volume

Start with a "subject" approach, where extensive cross-references will lead to the proper index reference from almost any likely point of entry.

Index by Subjects and Names

Retail trade

Advertising expenditures by media, and sales and stores operated, top 25 retailers and food stores, 1978, annual articles, C2710–1.106

Appliance industry sales trends and forecast, by product type, and economic growth forecast, 1978-85, annual articles, C1885–1.101

State and local:

Wisconsin statistical abstract, general data, 1979 rpt, S8675–1.2

Wyoming retail trade establishments and sales by industry group, and aggregate operating data, by county and selected cities, 1977, U9350–1.102

see also Advertising
see also Agricultural marketing

see also Discount stores
see also Drugstores
see also Food stores
see also Franchises

Convenience stores
see Food stores

Food stores

Bakeries in supermarkets, and sales as percent of store sales, 1980 article, C7900–1.109

Consumer purchases of general merchandise, reasons for choosing supermarkets, drugstores, and discount stores, natl survey, 1980 article, C5150–1.103

Convenience food store chain establishments, profits, total and gasoline sales, stock performance, and operating data for top 13 companies, 1971-79, annual rpt, C8115–1

Gasoline

Agricultural energy use by type of fuel, crop, and farm operation, 1965-80, annual rpt, S2205–1

Consumer expenditures, percent for gasoline by age and household income, monthly rpt special chart, A7475–1.107

Convenience food store chain establishments, profits, total and gasoline sales, stock performance, and operating data for top 13 companies, 1971-79, annual rpt, C8115–1

An alternate approach is through the "Index by Categories." Since you are looking for information about particular firms, you can find it under "By Individual Company or Institution."

Index by Categories

BY INDIVIDUAL COMPANY OR INSTITUTION

Energy Resources and Demand

Auto mileage for 1980 model cars, EPA estimates by size group and model, annual data book, C2700–1.118

Canadian natural gas amounts approved for export to US, by exporting company, 1980-87, article, C7100–1.112

Convenience food store chain establishments, profits, total and gasoline sales, stock performance, and operating data for top 13 companies, 1971-79, annual rpt, C8115–1

Step 2

Go from the index to the data description in the Abstracts Volume

The SRI accession number in the index will lead you to a publication entry that fully describes the document and pin-points the tables containing the statistics you need.

C8115
Roscoe, John F.

C8115-1 NINTH ANNUAL DOLLARS PER DAY SURVEY
Annual. 1979. 107 p.
SRI/MF/complete

Annual report, for 1979, on financial conditions and operations of the 13 largest publicly held convenience store chains in the small food store industry, presented on a dollars per day (DPD) per store basis. Includes profit trends by individual companies, 1971-79; store and gasoline sales, and individual company profiles.

Report is based on the 9th annual survey of company annual reports, proxy statements, or 10-K reports filed with SEC.

Contents:

a. Brief introduction (1-3); and store annual report and DPD analyses, with 36 interspersed tables, listed below (p. 3-26).

b. Historical summaries, 13 companies, each with 1 table showing number of stores, sales per day, DPD sales growth, pre- and after-tax profit DPD, closures, gasoline units, and DPD ranking, 1st-9th surveys, 1971-79. (p. 27-40)

Availability: John F. Roscoe, Dollars Per Day Survey, 391 Castle Crest Rd., Walnut Creek CA 94595, $50.00 1st copy, $5.00 each additional copy; SRI/MF/complete.

TABLES:
[Tables show data for 1979, unless otherwise noted.]

C8115-1.1: Annual Report and DPD Analyses

PROFIT AND SALES

[1-2] Pretax dollars of profit per store per day ranking; and small store industry ranked by profit per store per day [including sales, by company]. (p. 3-5)

[3-5] An aggregate [13 surveyed chains], an annual [average store surveyed]; and average store by day profit and loss statements. (p. 6)

GASOLINE SALES

[21] Number and percentage of stores with gasoline units [by company]. (p. 16)

[22] Gasoline [number of stores, stores with gas units, gas units added, and percent of stores with gas, 1974-79 surveys]. (p. 16)

Step 3

Retrieve the publication

The abstract contains the bibliographic information you need to locate the publication in a library's hardcopy collection or to obtain it from the issuing source, if copies are available.

Alternatively, if you have access to an SRI/Microfiche Library collection, the SRI accession number will lead you directly to the correct microfiche.

Number and Percentage of Stores with Gasoline Units

$DPD Ranking Company	# of Stores	# of Gasoline Units	% of Stores With Gasoline	# of Gasoline Units Added During Year	# of Stores Added During Year
1. Circle K	1,158	681	59%	39	53
2. Shop & Go	379	225	59	--	8
3. Dillon	305	186	61	20	21
4. Southland	6,599	1,857	28	284	242
5. Lil' Champ	130	31	24	6	8
6. National Convenience	806	418	52	[1] 91	81
7. Convenient	316	218	69	[2] 45	31
8. Hop-In	132	108	82	19	20
9. Sunshine Jr.	316	230	73	39	28
10. Li'l General	515	165	32	- 5	- 26
11. UtoteM	934	511	55	21	6
12. Mini Mart	119	11	9	- 2	- 9
13. Munford	1,211	512	42	12	- 140
Totals	12,920	5,153	39.88%	569	323

[1]Purchased 85 when Texas Super Duper Markets were acquired May 1, 1979.
[2]Purchased 15 when gasoline retailing corporation in North Carolina was acquired.

16

A0175
Administrative Management Society

A0175–1 AMS 38th ANNUAL OFFICE SALARIES DIRECTORY: Salary and Benefit Information for Office Employees in the U.S. and Canada
Annual. 1984. 43 p.
ISSN 0731-4434.
LC 82-640803.
SRI/MF/complete

Annual survey report on clerical and word processing salaries and employee benefits provided in the U.S. and Canada, Jan. 1984. Data are shown for 20 job categories by location, and, for U.S. only, by type of business.

Data are primarily from an AMS survey of 5,304 member and nonmember companies employing 338,077 clerical and word processing personnel in 117 cities.

Contains introduction, contents listing, and user guide (p. 3-9); personnel policy summary and highlights, with 1 table showing percent of companies offering selected types of benefits (by region for U.S.), and 1 summary table (p. 10-12); salary statistics, with 5 tables, listed below (p. 13-42); and conversion chart (p. 43).

Availability: Administrative Management Society, 2360 Maryland Rd., Willow Grove PA 19090, members $60.00, nonmembers $100.00; SRI/MF/complete.

SALARY TABLES:
[Data are for 20 job categories, as of Jan. 12, 1984. All tables, except table [3], show average, median, and 1st and 3rd quartile weekly salary, number of companies, and number of employees.]

[1] [Salaries for] total U.S., Canada, and U.S. regions; all types of business. (p. 13)

[2] Salaries by type of business, total U.S. [and regions; for manufacturing/processing, banking/insurance/financial, retail/wholesale sales/distribution, government agencies, and other]. (p. 16-21)

[3] Summary of weekly salary levels, U.S. [number of employees by salary range, by position]. (p. 22)

[4] [Salaries by city: all types of business for 9 Canadian cities, and for major U.S. cities and areas grouped by region.] (p. 24-41)

[5] Chapter salary surveys conducted on dates different than the AMS survey. (p. 42)

A0175–2 TWELFTH ANNUAL GUIDE TO MANAGEMENT COMPENSATION: Salary and Benefit Information for Management Personnel in the U.S. and Canada
Annual. 1984. 44 p.
ISSN 0278-1506.
LC 81-643450.
SRI/MF/complete

Annual report on a survey of salaries paid by U.S. and Canadian companies for 20 middle management staff positions, as of Sept. 16, 1983. Also covers employee benefit policies.

Data are from a survey of 3,039 companies representing 49,064 employees in manufacturing, financial, retail/wholesale trade, utilities, and other industry divisions. Most U.S. data are shown by region.

Contents:

a. Introduction, contents listing, methodology, job titles and descriptions, and summary of company benefit policies, with 3 tables showing U.S. and Canadian payment policies for insurance by type of coverage, profit sharing, stock options, and employee saving plans; pension plan characteristics; and type of salary increases granted. (p. 3-13)

b. Highlights, with 1 table showing U.S. average salary by position, 1982-83. (p. 14)

c. Salary analysis by position, with 10 tables showing average, median, and quartile salaries, and number of employees and companies: for all types of business, U.S. and Canada (p. 15-19); for U.S. by industry division (p. 20-25); and for all types of business in 10 Canadian and 104 U.S. cities and SMSAs (p. 26-43).

d. Salary conversion chart. (p. 44)

Availability: Administrative Management Society, 2360 Maryland Rd., Willow Grove PA 19090, members $60.00, nonmembers $90.00; SRI/MF/complete.

A0175–3 SECOND ANNUAL SYSTEMS AND PROCESSING SALARIES REPORT, 1984
Annual. 1984. 43 p.
SRI/MF/complete

Annual report on a survey of salaries paid by U.S. and Canadian companies for 20 electronic data processing (EDP) positions, as of Sept. 16, 1983. Includes median, average, and quartile salaries; and number of companies and employees represented; shown for Canada, U.S. by region and type of business, and 100 U.S. and 8 Canadian cities and SMSAs, all by position.

Types of business are manufacturing/processing, banking/insurance/financial, retail/wholesale sales/distribution, utilities, data processing service bureaus, and all others.

Also includes summary comparison to 1982; and data on sample characteristics, including distribution of companies by sales and EDP expenditure ranges.

Data are from a survey of 2,585 companies representing 60,218 EDP employees.

Contains introduction, contents listing, methodology, job titles and descriptions, personnel policies and training programs, survey highlights, and 3 summary tables (p. 3-14); and statistical section, with 4 extended tables (p. 15-43).

Availability: Administrative Management Society, 2360 Maryland Rd., Willow Grove PA 19090, members $60.00, nonmembers $90.00; SRI/MF/complete.

A0175–4 1982 AMS OFFICE TURNOVER SURVEY for the U.S. and Canada
Biennial. 1983.
5 p. no paging.
SRI/MF/complete

Biennial report, by Edward G. Thomas, on office employee turnover in the U.S. and Canada, 1982, with selected trends from 1978. Covers employment, terminations, and turnover rate, by U.S. region and for major U.S. and Canadian cities; and U.S./Canadian turnover rates, by type of business, office size, and employee type (exempt and nonexempt). Also includes distribution of employee terminations, by reason and length of service.

Data are from a survey of 2,274 firms in 94 cities, conducted by Administrative Management Society.

Contains narrative report and 8 tables.

SRI coverage of this report begins with the 1982 edition.

Availability: Administrative Management Society, 2360 Maryland Rd., Willow Grove PA 19090, $15.00; SRI/MF/complete.

A0250
Aerospace Industries Association of America

A0250–1 AEROSPACE
Quarterly. Approx. 15 p.
LC 67-5475.
SRI/MF/complete

Quarterly aerospace industry journal, including aerospace economic indicators, and articles on industry sales, employment, R&D, aviation history, commercial and military aircraft design, and space technology and applications. Journal also includes an annual industry review and forecast feature. Indicator data are from the Aerospace Industries Assn.

Issues contain articles, sometimes including statistics; and quarterly aerospace economic indicators table (inside front or back cover) showing the following:

a. Total aerospace sales; and aerospace prime contract awards, and manufacturers' backlog, for Government and other customers.

b. DOD obligations and outlays for aircraft and missiles; and NASA R&D obligations and expenditures.

c. Value of total exports and exports of new commercial transports.

d. Employment for aircraft and missiles/space; and average hourly earnings for production workers.

e. Profit as percent of sales, for aerospace and all manufacturing.

Indicator data are shown for quarter 2-3 quarters prior to cover date, preceding quarter, same period of preceding year, and average 1966-75.

Quarterly indicator table appears in most issues. All additional features with substantial statistical content are described, as they appear, under "Statistical Features." Nonstatistical contents are not covered.

Availability: Aerospace Industries Association of America, 1725 De Sales St., NW, Washington DC 20036, †; SRI/MF/complete.

Issues reviewed during 1984: Fall 1983-Fall 1984 (P) (Vol. 21, No. 3; Vol. 22, Nos. 1-3) [No Summer issues were published in 1983 or 1984].

STATISTICAL FEATURES:

A0250–1.501: Fall 1983 (Vol. 21, No. 3)

NATIONAL BENEFITS OF AEROSPACE EXPORTS

(p. 15-16) Article, with 1 chart showing potential impact of increased aircraft exports on GNP, by sector, 1982-90 period. Data are from Chase Econometrics/Interactive Data Corp.

A0250–1.502: Winter 1984 (Vol. 22, No. 1)

AEROSPACE REVIEW AND FORECAST, 1983/84, ANNUAL FEATURE

(p. 12-17) Annual article presenting summary trends and forecasts for aerospace industry production, sales, and operations, 1968-84. Data are based on company reports and industry assns.

Includes 6 charts, and 1 table showing civil aircraft shipments and value, by type (commercial transport, general aviation, and helicopters), 1968-84.

A0300
Air Conditioning
and Refrigeration Institute

A0300–1   NEWS FROM AIR CONDITIONING AND REFRIGERATION INSTITUTE
Monthly, with annual summaries. Approx. 2 p.
LC 31-35153.
SRI/MF/complete, shipped quarterly

Monthly press release, with annual summaries, on unitary air conditioner/heat pump domestic shipments, by Btu(h) size. Covers equipment used in most residential central installations, plus some commercial and industrial installations using packaged equipment.

Data are from Institute records. Release is issued approximately 2 months after month of coverage.

Contains narrative summary; and 1 table showing total shipments by Btu(h) size and type of condenser.

In addition to the monthly publication, 3 annual summaries are issued, reporting on number and value of residential and commercial installations, and installed value of field-engineered equipment. Annual summaries are described as they are published.

Availability: Air Conditioning and Refrigeration Institute, 1501 Wilson Blvd., Suite 600, Arlington VA 22209, †; SRI/MF/complete, shipped quarterly.

Issues reviewed during 1984: Aug. 1983-Aug. 1984 (D); 1 annual summary for 1982; and 3 annual summaries for 1983.

ANNUAL SUMMARIES:

A0300–1.1: 1982 Installed Value of Field-Engineered Equipment
[Annual. Dec. 12, 1983. 2 p. SRI/MF/complete.]

Annual press release on installed value of field-engineered air conditioning equipment, 1969-82.

Previous report, for 1981, is described in SRI 1982 Annual, under this number.

A0300–1.2: ARI Reports 1983 Residential Installations of Unitary Equipment Increased and Commercial Installations Decreased
[Annual. May 16, 1984. 4 p. SRI/MF/complete.]

Annual press release on shipments of unitary air conditioners, for U.S. residential and commercial installation 1953-83, and for export 1960-83. Includes 1 table.

A0300–1.3: ARI Reports Value of Unitary Air Conditioning Equipment $7.1 Billion During 1983
[Annual. May 16, 1984. 2 p. SRI/MF/complete.]

Annual press release on installed value of unitary residential and commercial air conditioning equipment, 1956-83. Includes 1 table.

A0300–1.4: 1983 Installed Value of Field-Engineered Equipment
[Annual. Sept. 5, 1984. 2 p. SRI/MF/complete.]

Annual press release on installed value of field-engineered air conditioning equipment, 1969-83.

Previous report, for 1982, is described under A0300-1.1, above.

A0325
Air Transport
Association of America

A0325–1   PASSENGER TRAFFIC STATISTICS: U.S. Scheduled Airline Industry
Monthly. Approx. 2 p.
SRI/MF/complete, shipped quarterly

Monthly press release on scheduled airline passenger traffic on domestic and international flights. Release is issued 3-4 weeks after month of coverage. Data are for current month, year to date, and same periods of previous year. Based on reports of approximately 25 commercial carriers.

Contains narrative summary, and 1 table showing revenue passenger miles and available seat miles flown, and passenger load factor.

Availability: Air Transport Association of America, 1709 New York Ave., NW, Washington DC 20006, †; SRI/MF/complete, shipped quarterly.

Issues reviewed during 1984: Oct. 1983-Sept. 1984 (D).

A0325–2   CARGO FLOWN IN SCHEDULED DOMESTIC AND INTERNATIONAL SERVICE: U.S. Scheduled Airline Industry
Monthly. Approx. 2 p.
SRI/MF/complete, shipped quarterly

Monthly press release on scheduled airline freight and mail revenue ton-miles on domestic and international flights. Release is issued 4-5 weeks after month of coverage. Data are for current month, year to date, and same periods of previous year. Based on reports of approximately 25 commercial air carriers.

Contains narrative summary and 1 table showing freight and mail revenue ton-miles, by type of service.

Availability: Air Transport Association of America, 1709 New York Ave., NW, Washington DC 20006, †; SRI/MF/complete, shipped quarterly.

Issues reviewed during 1984: Oct. 1983-Aug. 1984 (D).

A0325–5   AIR TRANSPORT, 1984
Annual. June 1984. 21 p.
LC 70-613485.
SRI/MF/complete

Annual report on finances and operations of scheduled air carriers, 1983 and trends. Includes selected data by individual carrier and for top 30 airports.

Data are based on studies by ATA, Airport Operators Council International, FAA, and other assn and Federal sources.

Contains summary table (inside front cover); 7 charts and 18 tables listed below (p. 2-18); and list of airlines, glossary, and ATA directories (p. 19-21).

Availability: Air Transport Association of America, 1709 New York Ave., NW, Washington DC 20006, †; SRI/MF/complete.

CHARTS AND TABLES:
[Data are shown for 1973 and 1982-83, unless otherwise noted.]

A0325–5.1: Operations, Aircraft, and Finances

[1] 1973-83 highlights, U.S. scheduled airlines [including passengers and average trip length; freight ton-miles; operating revenues, expenses, and profits; aircraft in service; and employees]. (p. 2)

[2-5] Passengers, revenues and losses, cost to fly 1 mile, and discount traffic [and average discount, 1981-83]. [4 charts] (p. 3)

[6] ATA airline statistics [aircraft, employees, passengers, departures, revenue passenger miles, freight ton-miles, total operating revenues, and operating and net profit/loss, by carrier], 1983. (p. 4)

[7] Safety, U.S. air carriers, scheduled service [departures, fatal accidents, and fatalities], 1974-83. (p. 6)

[8] Passengers at top 30 U.S. airports, 1983. (p. 6)

[9] Intercity passenger travel in the U.S. [miles traveled by transport mode]. (p. 7)

[10] Employment [flight and ground personnel, by position]. (p. 7)

[11-12] Passenger and freight yields [for domestic and international flights]. (p. 7)

[13] Aircraft on order [options, and firm orders by delivery date, by aircraft model, aggregated for] ATA airlines, as of Dec. 31, 1983. (p. 8)

[14] Air carrier and general aviation fleets [by aircraft type]. (p. 8)

[15] Operating fleet [by aircraft model, for individual] ATA airlines [no date]. (p. 9)

[16] Principal elements of airline operating expenses [including labor, fuel, and traffic commissions]. (p. 10)

[17-19] Travel agent sales and commissions; interest expense; and fares vs. [CPI; 1981-83]. [3 charts] (p. 11)

[20] Individual airline service [top 30 airlines ranked by passengers, revenue passenger and freight ton miles, and operating revenues], 1983. (p. 12)

[21-24] Traffic [passenger and cargo] and service, operating revenues and expenses, income statement, and balance sheet [all for major, national, and regional carriers, 1982-83]. (p. 14-17)

[25] Domestic all-cargo data (section 418 carriers) [traffic and finances, 1981-83]. (p. 18)

A0325–6   FREQUENCY OF FLYING AMONG THE GENERAL PUBLIC, 1983
Annual. 1983. 21 p.
SRI/MF/complete

Annual report on commercial airline travel frequency, destination, and purpose, 1983, with selected trends from 1962. Data are based on a survey of 4,689 adults conducted June 24-Aug. 8, 1983 by Gallup Organization, Inc.

Contains introduction and summary (p. 1-6); narrative analyses interspersed with 14 tables, described below (p. 7-17); and survey sample composition and design (p. 18-21).

Report previously was issued on an irregularly recurring basis. For description of last previous edition, published in 1981, see SRI 1982 Annual, under this number.
Availability: Air Transport Association of America, 1709 New York Ave., NW, Washington DC 20006, $25.00; SRI/MF/complete.

TABLES:
[Trend data are based on previous surveys, conducted in selected years within year range noted. All data are shown as percent distribution, and are for commercial air travel only.]

a. Frequency: whether ever flown and/or flown in past year, by respondent sex, race, and age group, chief wage earner occupation, and size and region of residence community, 1971-83, and by family income, 1983; and air travel incidence in past year by family income cross-tabulated by age group 1983, by number of trips, 1971-83, and by infrequent, moderate, and frequent flier classifications, 1977-83. 5 tables. (p. 7-11)

b. Destination: whether traveled within the U.S. and/or to Canada, Mexico/Caribbean, or other international points, for all adults surveyed, 1983, and for those who traveled in past year, 1977-83. 2 tables. (p. 12)

c. Purpose: whether traveled for business and/or pleasure or personal reasons and number of trips, for all adults surveyed, and those who traveled in past year, 1971-83; and domestic, international, and total business and pleasure trips during past year, 1977-83. 6 tables. (p. 13-16)

d. Air travel experience: airline travel incidence by traveler sex, age group, occupation, region of residence, and income level, 1962-70. 1 table. (p. 17)

A0400
Aluminum Association

A0400–1   ALUMINUM SITUATION
Monthly.
Approx. 4 p. no paging.
SRI/MF/complete, shipped quarterly

Monthly report on estimated aluminum production, shipments, orders, inventories, and foreign trade. Data are compiled by the Aluminum Assn, primarily from member reports and Dept of Commerce sources. Month of coverage is 1-2 months prior to publication date.

Contains brief narrative interspersed with 3 summary charts, 1 summary table showing shipments for year to date, and 4 monthly tables listed below. Prior to Mar. 1984 issue, report format differs slightly from this description.

Monthly tables appear in all issues; Feb. 1984 issue also includes summary data on shipments and inventories, monthly 1983.
Availability: Aluminum Association, Publications Department, 818 Connecticut Ave., NW, Washington DC 20006, †; SRI/MF/complete, shipped quarterly.

Issues reviewed during 1984: Nov. 1983-Oct. 1984 (P).

MONTHLY TABLES:
[Data are shown for month of coverage and year to date, for current and previous year, unless otherwise noted.]

[1] Net shipments [including mill products by type, ingot, mill product net imports, and total exports].

[2-3] Order receipts [domestic, for mill products by type, ingot, and total exports]; and month-end aluminum inventories, by type of producer [integrated, smelter, and nonintegrated, for current year to date and selected previous periods].

[4] Imports and exports [of mill products, ingot, and scrap].

A0400–2   ALUMINUM STATISTICAL REVIEW for 1983
Annual. [1984.] 64 p.
LC 72-131.
SRI/MF/complete

Annual report on U.S. aluminum ingot and mill product supply, demand, and foreign trade, 1983, with trends from as early as the 1940s. Includes data by end-use market, company, and trading partner. Also includes data on scrap recovery and aluminum plants; and world aluminum supply and demand, by country.

Data are compiled by the Aluminum Assn Statistical and Marketing Research Committee from Commerce Dept, Bureau of Mines, National Assn of Aluminum Distributors, and other sources.

Contains contents listing, and introduction with 1 summary table (p. 1-3); 5 sections, with brief narrative, 5 maps, 7 charts, and 22 tables listed below (p. 4-61); and glossary and list of Aluminum Assn publications (p. 62-64).

This is the 16th annual report.

Availability: Aluminum Association, Publications Department, 818 Connecticut Ave., NW, Washington DC 20006, members $10.00, nonmembers $20.00; SRI/MF/complete.

TABLES:
[Data are for 1973-83, unless otherwise noted.]

A0400–2.1: U.S. Shipments, Markets, and Supply

SHIPMENTS

[1] Total industry shipments [ingots, U.S.-produced and imported mill products, and total domestic and exports]. (p. 5)

[2] Mill products imports [total, and to consumers and aluminum producers, for 3 product categories]. (p. 5)

[3] Net shipments of ingot and mill products (excludes mill product imports to consumers) [by product category], 1946-83. (p. 6-7)

[4] General line distributor shipments [and total U.S. shipments excluding direct mill uses, by mill product category]. (p. 8)

[5] Shipments of castings [by type], 1963-83. (p. 9)

MARKETS

[Major markets are building/construction, transportation, consumer durables, electrical, machinery/equipment, containers/packaging, and other.]

[6] Aluminum net shipments by major market [and exports, 1982-83]. (p. 12)

[7] Product net shipments [for ingot and 14 mill products], by major market [and exports]. (p. 13-17)

[8] Trends in selected markets [shipments of ingot and mill products, by end use]. (p. 18-20)

SUPPLY

[9] Total supply [includes domestic primary production, primary and mill product imports, and secondary recovery from domestic and imported scrap], 1942-83. (p. 23)

[10-11] Suppliers' inventories; and total supply adjusted for [Federal] stockpile. (p. 24)

[12-13] Production of primary aluminum; and primary aluminum capacity [by producer]. (p. 25-26)

[14] Number of plants [by type of aluminum product, 1967, 1977, amd 1982]. (p. 27)

SCRAP

[15-16] Aluminum can reclamation data [weight, number, and percent of cans], 1973-83; and scrap consumption [by secondary smelters, primary producers, and others], and recovery [from new and old scrap], 1946-83. (p. 30-31)

A0400–2.2: U.S. Foreign Trade, and World Production and Consumption

U.S. FOREIGN TRADE

[1] Imports and exports [of ingot, semifabricated products by type, scrap, and dross/skimmings (imports only)]. (p. 36)

[2-3] Imports and exports, by product and country [and world area], 1983. (p. 38-41)

WORLD PRODUCTION AND CONSUMPTION

[4] World primary aluminum production [by country and world area]. (p. 45)

[5-6] Per capita aluminum consumption of selected countries [total, and components used in calculation including primary production, imports, secondary recovery, exports, total consumption, inventory change, and population; by country]. (p. 47-61)

A0600
American Apparel
Manufacturers Association

A0600–2   APPAREL PLANT WAGES SURVEY, 1984
Annual. 1984. 24 p.
ISSN 0275-8873.
LC 81-640459.
SRI/MF/not filmed

Annual report on employment and earnings of apparel plant workers and supervisors, and type of wage plan in use, by region and for 4 southern areas, 1984, with trends from 1978. Data are shown by occupation, and often by type of apparel produced. Also includes survey sample characteristics.

Data are from responses of 155 companies with 453 plants and 117,048 employees to a 1984 AAMA survey.

Contains contents listing and introduction (p. 2-3); and 4 sections with 7 tables, interspersed with narrative summary (p. 3-24).

Availability: American Apparel Manufacturers Association, 1611 N. Kent St., Suite 800, Arlington VA 22209, members $25.00, nonmembers $60.00; SRI/MF/not filmed.

A0600–3   APPAREL SALES/MARKETING COMPENSATION SURVEY, 1984
Annual. 1984. 27 p.
SRI/MF/not filmed

Annual report on apparel industry compensation and employment for sales managers, account executives, and full-time and independent sales representatives, 1983, with summary comparisons to 1981-82. Data are from responses of 65 corporations and divisions employing 2,871 sales and marketing personnel to a 1984 AAMA survey.

Contains contents and table listing, and introduction (p. 1-5); and report, with 5 tables showing survey response described below (p. 6-27).

Availability: American Apparel Manufacturers Association, 1611 N. Kent St., Suite 800, Arlington VA 22209, members $25.00, nonmembers $60.00; SRI/MF/not filmed.

TABLES:
[Most data are shown for 3 corporate and 3 divisional sales value ranges.]

a. Respondent aggregate sales; number of respondents, by type of products manufactured, sales compensation cost as a percent of sales, and type of expenses paid; average annual salary and other compensation for sales personnel by position; respondents and salespersons by type of compensation program; respondents by labor turnover rate; average annual compensation for salespersons with and without paid expenses; and number of salespersons, by annual compensation level. 4 tables. (p. 6-23)

b. Independent sales representatives: number of firms employing, and representatives employed; whether retained by verbal or written agreement; independents as a percent of sales force and of total sales; type of compensation program used; and commissions and average payment. 1 table. (p. 24-27)

A0610
American Association
for Public Opinion Research

A0610–1   PUBLIC OPINION QUARTERLY
Quarterly. Approx. 150 p. cumulative pagination throughout year.
Pub. No. 449380.
ISSN 0033-362X.
SRI/MF/excerpts

Quarterly journal presenting results of scholarly research on problems of communication and public opinion measurement. Includes articles on polling methodology and on implications of public opinion survey results. Publication is editorially sponsored by the Advisory Committee on Communication, Columbia University.

Issues generally contain original articles, frequently including statistics; "The Polls" feature, reporting results of recent opinion surveys by several research organizations on a single topic; and book reviews and reader comments.

Spring 1984 issue was published in 2 parts consisting of a cumulative index of Vols. 1-46 covering 1937-82 (Part A) and the regular quarterly issue (Part B).

Features with substantial statistical content are described, as they appear, under "Statistical Features." Nonstatistical features are not covered.

Availability: Elsevier Science Publishing Co., Inc., Journals Fulfillment Department, 52 Vanderbilt Ave., New York NY 10017, institutions $42.50 per yr., individuals $22.00 per yr., single copy price on request; SRI/MF/excerpts for all portions described under "Statistical Features."

Issues reviewed during 1984: Winter 1983-Fall 1984 (P) (Vol. 47, No. 4; Vol. 48, Nos. 1A-3).

STATISTICAL FEATURES:

A0610–1.501: Winter 1983 (Vol. 47, No. 4)

KNOWLEDGE GAP EFFECTS IN A HEALTH INFORMATION CAMPAIGN

(p. 516-527) By James S. Ettema et al. Article evaluating effectiveness of a cardiovascular health education program. Data are from a study of 250 households in 2 southwestern Minnesota communities.

Includes 6 tables presenting regression analysis of health information test scores before and after the program.

ANONYMOUS vs. IDENTIFIABLE SELF-REPORTS OF ADOLESCENT DRUG ATTITUDES, INTENTIONS, AND USE

(p. 557-566) By Janet H. Malvin and Joel M. Moskowitz. Article examining reliability of identifiable vs. anonymous responses of adolescents surveyed about drug use and attitudes. Data are from a 1979 survey of 8th and 9th grade students in 20 social studies classes in a northern California community.

Includes 2 tables comparing anonymous and identifiable response to questions on drug, alcohol, and cigarette use and attitudes, by sex.

THE POLLS: ETHNIC SOCIAL DISTANCE AND PREJUDICE

(p. 584-600) By Tom W. Smith and Glenn R. Dempsey. Compilation of survey results on public attitudes toward selected ethnic and religious groups. Surveys were conducted by 7 research institutes, various periods 1926-82. Includes distribution of response to 40 questions concerning attitudes toward various groups with regard to the following:

a. Social acceptance in workplace and neighborhood, as immigrants, as guests in home; interracial or interfaith marriage; whether family oriented; overall social standing; and whether good or bad for U.S.

b. Political attitudes: trust in group-endorsed candidates; perceived loyalty or potential threat to U.S.; likelihood of being communistic; perceived power and areas of influence; overrepresentation in population; and acceptability as presidential candidate.

A0610–1.502: Spring 1984 (Vol. 48, No. 1B)

POLITICAL CORRELATES OF TV VIEWING

(p. 283-300) By George Gerbner et al. Article examining the relation between TV viewing and self-designated political ideology. Data are from a study of results of 9 surveys of major polling organizations, conducted 1975-82, representing 14,067 respondents.

Includes 6 tables correlating TV and other media use with political self-designation.

POLITICS FROM THE PULPIT: RELIGIOSITY AND THE 1980 ELECTIONS

(p. 301-317) By Arthur H. Miller and Martin P. Wattenberg. Article analyzing extent to which evangelical Christian religious beliefs influence political attitudes and participation. Data are from a study of 1,614 responses to a 1980 national election survey, conducted by University of Michigan Center for Political Studies.

Includes 6 tables showing interrelation of respondent sociodemographic characteristics, religious beliefs, attitudes on selected national issues, voting for national offices, and election campaign activities.

RELIGIOUS PREFERENCE AND PRACTICE: REEVALUATING THEIR IMPACT ON POLITICAL TOLERANCE

(p. 318-329) By Kathleen Murphy Beatty and Oliver Walter. Article examining the relation of religious denominational preference and church attendance frequency to social tolerance of atheists, communists, homosexuals, militarists, and racists. Data are from a study of 1976-80 General Social Surveys, conducted by National Opinion Research Center. Includes 6 tables.

THE POLLS: GENDER AND ATTITUDES TOWARD VIOLENCE

(p. 384-396) By Tom W. Smith. Compilation of survey results on difference in male and female attitudes toward violence. Surveys were conducted by 6 research institutes, various periods 1936-83. Includes distribution of response to 67 questions on the following subject areas, by sex:

a. War and foreign policy: justification for war and extent of military assistance to selected countries; nuclear weapons use and disarmament; preference for war or Communist domination; and defense spending adequacy.

b. Law enforcement and miscellaneous: capital punishment for murder, treason, rape, and hijacking convictions; justification for striking/hitting and killing by police and others under various circumstances; gun ownership and control; corporal punishment in schools; teenage fighting; amount of TV violence and relation to crime rate; and whether boxing should be legally banned.

A0610–1.503: Summer 1984 (Vol. 48, No. 2)

BALLOT PAPER CUES AND THE VOTE IN AUSTRALIA AND BRITAIN: ALPHABETIC VOTING, SEX, AND TITLE

(p. 452-466) By Jonathan Kelley and Ian McAllister. Article analyzing effect of the position of a candidate's name on the ballot, and candidate's sex and academic or honorary title, on election results in Australia and the UK. Data are from published results of UK general election, Feb. 1974, and Australian Federal elections, 1974, 1977, and 1980. Includes 4 tables.

RACE, GENDER, AND OPINION TOWARD BLACK AND FEMALE PRESIDENTIAL CANDIDATES

(p. 467-475) By Lee Sigelman and Susan Welch. Article, with 2 tables showing voter willingness to cast ballot for female and black presidential candidates, by voter race and sex;

with discriminate coefficient analysis by selected sociodemographic characteristics. Data are based on General Social Surveys conducted by National Opinion Research Center in 1974 and 1978.

YEA-SAYING, NAY-SAYING, AND GOING TO EXTREMES: BLACK-WHITE DIFFERENCES IN RESPONSE STYLES

(p. 491-509) By Jerald G. Bachman and Patrick M. O'Malley. Article analyzing racial differences in response patterns to "agree-disagree" surveys. Data are from annual University of Michigan surveys of senior classes at approximately 130 high schools.

Includes 4 tables showing survey response concerning selected self-perceptions and social attitudes, with correlation and regression analyses of various response patterns, by race, 1982 or 1980-82 period.

WHAT MUST MY INTEREST IN POLITICS BE IF I JUST TOLD YOU 'I DON'T KNOW'?

(p. 510-519) By George F. Bishop et al. Article examining effect of question sequence on survey responses regarding interest in government/public affairs. Data are based on 2 telephone surveys of over 1,500 households, conducted Nov./Dec. 1981 and June 1982.

Includes 3 tables showing response distributions concerning general interest in government/public affairs, and knowledge of U.S. Representative's recent actions and voting record, cross-tabulated by question sequence design, 1981-82.

USE OF BOUNDED RECALL PROCEDURES IN SINGLE INTERVIEWS

(p. 520-524) By Seymour Sudman et al. Article on use of survey bounded recall methods, involving the establishment of a control period to help respondents accurately recall the timing of selected events.

Data are from a 1981 survey of 1,315 Illinois residents concerning recent medical events, and responses of 83 students at the University of Illinois to a 1982 survey on snack food purchases. Includes 2 tables comparing bounded and unbounded survey results.

THE POLLS: REGULATION, PART I

(p. 531-542) By Robert Y. Shapiro and John M. Gillroy. Compilation of survey results on opinions toward government regulation of the economy and private business. Surveys were conducted by 8 research institutes, various periods 1936-83.

Includes distribution of responses to 33 questions on appropriate level of government involvement in economic issues and regulation of business, including imposition of antitrust statutes and other controls, with some detail for various industry groups.

A0610–1.504: Fall 1984 (Vol. 48, No. 3)

PORTRAYAL OF BLACKS IN MAGAZINE ADVERTISEMENTS: 1950-82

(p. 551-563) By Ronald Humphrey and Howard Schuman. Article, with 3 tables showing the following for advertisements in 2-3 individual magazines: number that include blacks; people pictured by occupational activity, by race; and type of interaction (formal or informal) portrayed between whites, and between whites and blacks; various years 1950-82. Data were compiled by the authors.

EFFECTS OF PUBLIC OWNERSHIP ON NEWSPAPER COMPANIES: A PRELIMINARY INQUIRY

(p. 564-577) By Philip Meyer and Stanley T. Wearden. Article analyzing effects of public ownership on newspaper management priorities. Data are based on telephone interviews with 51 security analysts, and a survey of publishers, editors, and staff at 331 newspapers, both conducted by the authors in 1982.

Includes 5 tables showing ratings of importance for selected newspaper performance measures, as reported by security analysts and by personnel of publicly and privately owned newspaper corporations.

SOCIAL CONSERVATISM, NEW REPUBLICANS, AND THE 1980 ELECTION

(p. 592-605) By Jerome L. Himmelstein and James A. McRae, Jr. Article analyzing the attitudes and socioeconomic characteristics of "New Republican" voters (those who voted non-Republican in the 1976 presidential election and Republican in 1980). Data are from 1,039 white eligible voters responding to the 1980 National Election Study.

Includes 8 tables presenting positions on selected social and political issues, socioeconomic profile, and ratings of President Carter's performance, for New Republicans, with comparisons to Old Republicans (those who voted Republican in both elections) and to non-Republicans.

PREELECTION POLLING IN THE 1982 ILLINOIS GUBERNATORIAL CONTEST

(p. 606-614) By Richard Day and Kurt M. Becker. Article examining possible explanations for preelection poll error. Data are based on polls for the 1982 Illinois gubernatorial election, conducted by 4 organizations, Oct.-Nov. 1982. Includes 7 tables showing polling results and selected factors influencing election outcome.

POLL AS A NEWS EVENT IN THE 1980 PRESIDENTIAL CAMPAIGN

(p. 615-623) By James Glen Stovall and Jacqueline H. Solomon. Article, with 4 tables showing number and characteristics of campaign-related newspaper articles appearing during the 1980 presidential election, with focus on articles concerning public opinion polls. Data are from a study of the Sept.-Nov. 1980 issues of 50 newspapers, conducted by the authors.

PASSIVE LEARNING: WHEN THE MEDIA ENVIRONMENT IS THE MESSAGE

(p. 629-638) By Cliff Zukin and Robin Snyder. Article analyzing the relationship between exposure to broadcast media and the incidence of unmotivated ("passive") learning. Data are based on two surveys of 1,000 New Jersey residents of voting age, conducted Sept. 1977 and 1981.

Includes 4 tables showing the effect of exposure to NYC and Philadelphia TV stations on the ability of New Jersey residents to name candidates for NYC mayor and New Jersey Governor, with cross-tabulation by level of interest in the elections.

RECALLING ATTITUDES: AN ANALYSIS OF RETROSPECTIVE QUESTIONS ON THE 1982 GSS

(p. 639-649) By Tom W. Smith. Article on the reliability of survey respondent recall of previous social attitudes. Data are based on responses to 1972-73 and 1982 General Social Surveys.

Includes 2 tables showing actual and recalled responses to three 1972-73 survey questions on selected social issues, with cross-tabulation by educational attainment.

EFFECTS OF AN ADVANCE TELEPHONE CALL IN A PERSONAL INTERVIEW SURVEY

(p. 650-657) By Jane Williams Bergsten et al. Article, with 3 tables comparing response rates for personal interview surveys preceded and not preceded by a telephone call establishing an interview appointment. Data are from Oct.-Nov. 1982 interviews with 1,260 Medicare beneficiaries age 65/over in 3 cities, and are shown separately for each city.

THE POLLS: REGULATION, PART II

(p. 666-677) By Robert Y. Shapiro and John M. Gillroy. Compilation of survey results on opinions toward government regulation of private business. Surveys were conducted by 9 research institutes, various periods 1936-81.

Includes distribution of responses to 29 questions on appropriate level of government involvement in regulation of business, including imposition of controls for environmental and consumer protection, with some detail for various industry groups.

A0612
American Association
of Blood Banks

A0612-1   1983 DIRECTORY OF COMMUNITY BLOOD BANKS
Annual.   1983.   ix+131 p.
SRI/MF/complete

Annual directory, for 1983, presenting profiles of community blood banks, arranged by State and for Puerto Rico. Profiles generally include full- and part-time employees; volunteers; budget; counties, hospitals, and population served; blood draw and outdate rate; and blood products produced by type; primarily 1982.

Contains contents listing (p. v-ix); blood bank profiles (p. 1-121); and 3 appendices, with member lists for 2 major blood bank assns, and directory of American Red Cross blood service offices (p. 123-131).

This is the 3rd edition of the report. SRI coverage begins with this edition.

Availability: American Association of Blood Banks, 1117 N. 19th St., Suite 600, Arlington VA 22209, members $15.00, nonmembers $20.00; SRI/MF/complete.

A0615
American Association
of Colleges of Nursing

A0615-1   REPORT ON NURSING FACULTY SALARIES in Colleges and Universities, 1983/84
Annual.   Jan. 1984.
iii+50 p.   Institutional Data
Series 84-1.
ISSN 0197-8691.
LC SC 80-284.
SRI/MF/complete

Annual report, for academic year 1983/84 and calendar year 1983, on nursing faculty and salaries in baccalaureate and graduate nursing programs, by faculty rank, region, type of school, and size of baccalaureate and masters enrollment. Data are shown for mean, and 25th, 50th, and 75th percentile salaries, for faculty with and without doctorates.

School types include public, secular private, and religious private, with detail for schools in universities and 4-year colleges, on campuses with academic health centers, with baccalaureate programs only, and with master's and doctoral programs.

Data are based on a survey of 312 schools, representing 7,732 full-time positions, by the American Assn of Colleges of Nursing, fall 1983.

Contains contents and table listing (p. i-iii); introduction with 2 summary tables (p. 1-9); table key, and 15 detailed tables repeated for academic and calendar year (p. 10-40); and sample questionnaire, and list of participating schools (p. 41-50).

This is the 6th annual report. Related reports on salaries of deans and administrative faculty are covered in SRI under A0615-2 and A0615-3, respectively.

Availability: American Association of Colleges of Nursing, Institutional Data Systems, 11 Dupont Circle, NW, Suite 230, Washington DC 20036, members $12.00, nonmembers $25.00; ordered with reports on salaries of deans and administrative faculty: members $24.00, nonmembers $40.00; SRI/MF/complete.

A0615-2   REPORT ON SALARIES OF NURSING DEANS in Colleges and Universities, 1983/84
Annual.   Feb. 1984.   ii+24 p.
Institutional Data Series 84-2.
ISSN 0270-8175.
LC 81-643386.
SRI/MF/complete

Annual report on salaries of nursing school deans in colleges/universities, 1983/84, with summary trends from 1978/79. Includes number of deans and salary percentiles for deans continuing in office; and for all deans, by term of appointment (academic and calendar year), region, institutional control and type, presence of academic health center, level of degrees offered, faculty size, and dean's highest degree earned, administrative title, academic rank, and tenure status.

Also includes number of deans, by length of term, whether elected by faculty, and type of formal review process.

Data are from responses of 292 nursing schools to a fall 1983 survey.

Contains contents and table listing (p. i-ii); introduction (p. 1-3); survey results, with narrative analysis, 16 tables, and 2 charts (p. 4-16); and questionnaire facsimile and list of surveyed schools (p. 17-24).

This is the 6th annual report.

Availability: American Association of Colleges of Nursing, Institutional Data Systems, 11 Dupont Circle, NW, Suite 230, Washington DC 20036, members $6.00, nonmembers $10.00; ordered with reports on salaries of faculty and administrative faculty: members $24.00, nonmembers $40.00; SRI/MF/complete.

A0615-3   REPORT ON SALARIES OF ADMINISTRATIVE FACULTY IN NURSING, Excluding Deans, 1983/84
Annual.   May 1984.
iii+23 p.   Institutional Data
Series 84-3.
SRI/MF/complete

Annual report, for 1983/84, on salaries of administrative nursing faculty, excluding deans, in baccalaureate/graduate nursing programs. Data are shown by position title, variously including associate and assistant deans, chairperson, director, head, coordinator, assistant, and other.

Includes data by region, institutional control (public, secular, and religious), faculty size, academic rank, and whether doctorate held. Also includes data for continuing education administrative faculty. Salaries are generally shown at 3-5 percentile levels, sometimes with mean, on both an academic and calendar year basis.

Data cover salaries of 506 administrative faculty, based on responses of approximately 150 institutions to a survey by the American Assn of Colleges of Nursing.

Contains contents and table listing (p. i-iii); introduction and methodology (p. 1-5); 32 tables (p. 6-16); and appendix, including facsimile of questionnaire and list of participating schools (p. 17-23).

This is the 5th annual report.

Availability: American Association of Colleges of Nursing, Institutional Data Systems, 11 Dupont Circle, NW, Suite 230, Washington DC 20036, members $6.00, nonmembers $10.00, plus 30% shipping and handling; SRI/MF/complete.

A0615-4   ENROLLMENT AND GRADUATIONS IN BACCALAUREATE AND GRADUATE PROGRAMS IN NURSING, Public, Private Religious, and Secular, Four Years: 1980-84
Annual.   June 1984.   i+20 p.
Institutional Data Series 84-4.
SRI/MF/complete

Annual survey report, by Marion I. Murphy, on nursing school enrollment and graduates, by degree level, type of institution (public, secular, and religious), and region, 1970/81-1983/84. Includes detail for full- and part-time students, and for students who already are registered nurses vs. other ("generic") students.

Data are from surveys of schools belonging to the American Assn of Colleges of Nursing. Number of schools reporting is specified for each data item. Separate data are presented for a subgroup of schools responding in every survey year.

Contains contents listing (p. i); narrative, with 1 summary table (p. 1-6); and 7 detailed tables (p. 7-20).

This is the 3rd annual report.

Availability: American Association of Colleges of Nursing, Institutional Data Systems, 11 Dupont Circle, NW, Suite 230, Washington DC 20036, members $8.00, nonmembers $12.00, plus 30% shipping and handling; SRI/MF/complete.

A0630
American Association of Colleges of Pharmacy

A0630–2   DEGREES CONFERRED BY SCHOOLS AND COLLEGES OF PHARMACY for the Academic Year 1982/83
Annual. [1984.] iii+20 p.
SRI/MF/complete

Annual report, by Steven H. Chasin, on number of pharmacy degrees conferred, by degree level and field, region, and race/ethnic group (white, black, Hispanic, Native American, Asian, and non-American), all by sex and institution, 1982/83. Data are based on responses of 72 institutions to an American Assn of Colleges of Pharmacy survey.

Contains contents and table listing (2 p.); narrative summary (p. i-iii); and 17 tables (p. 1-20).
Availability: American Association of Colleges of Pharmacy, 4630 Montgomery Ave., Suite 201, Bethesda MD 20814, $5.00; SRI/MF/complete.

A0630–3   ENROLLMENT REPORT ON GRADUATE DEGREE PROGRAMS IN PHARMACY, Fall 1983
Annual. [1984.] iii+28 p.
SRI/MF/complete

Annual report, by Steven H. Chasin, on enrollment in pharmacy graduate programs, by institution, fall 1983. Includes data by degree level; full- or part-time status; discipline; minority group (black, Hispanic, Asian, Native, other minority American, and foreign); sex; geographic origin (same State as institution, other State, Canada, and other foreign country); and State of residence (including Virgin Islands).

Also includes aggregate data on foreign students by country of origin, and summary trends from 1970/71.

Data are based on a survey of 54 pharmacy schools, representing 3,051 graduate students, conducted by the American Assn of Colleges of Pharmacy.

Contains contents/table listing (2 p.); introduction and narrative analysis (p. i-iii); definitions (p. 1); and 20 tables (p. 2-24).
Availability: American Association of Colleges of Pharmacy, 4630 Montgomery Ave., Suite 201, Bethesda MD 20814, $10.00; SRI/MF/complete.

A0630–4   ENROLLMENT REPORT ON PROFESSIONAL DEGREE PROGRAMS IN PHARMACY, Fall 1983
Annual. [1984.] iv+27 p.
SRI/MF/complete

Annual report, by Steven H. Chasin, on fall 1983 full-time enrollment in pharmacy professional degree programs, by year of study, State of residence (including Virgin Islands and Puerto Rico), country of origin, and region. Most data are shown by institution and sex, with selected comparisons to fall 1982.

Also includes data on minority enrollment by institution and in predominantly minority and nonminority schools, by race/ethnicity (black, Hispanic, Native American, Asian, and foreign); and part-time and special enrollments.

Data are based on responses of 72 institutions, comprising all accredited schools of pharmacy, to an American Assn of Colleges of Pharmacy survey.

Contains contents and table listing (1 p.); narrative summary (p. i-iv); 15 tables (p. 5-23); and directory of pharmacy programs, and information on AACP publications (p. 24-27).
Availability: American Association of Colleges of Pharmacy, 4630 Montgomery Ave., Suite 201, Bethesda MD 20814, $10.00; SRI/MF/complete.

A0640
American Association of Community and Junior Colleges

A0640–1   COMMUNITY, TECHNICAL, AND JUNIOR COLLEGE DIRECTORY, 1984
Annual. 1984.
2+108 p.+errata sheet.
ISBN 0-87117-132-5.
SRI/MF/complete

Annual directory, for 1984, of 2-year community, technical, and junior colleges. Presents full- and part-time enrollment and faculty, community education enrollment, professional and administrative staff, and tuition/fees, by institution arranged by State and territory, primarily as of Oct. 1983, with comparisons to 1982, and selected summary trends from 1963.

Data are also shown for AACJC member colleges in British Honduras, Canada, Korea, Panama, Switzerland, and West Germany; and as aggregates for public and independent institutions, by U.S. State and territory.

Data are from a 1983 AACJC survey of all 1,219 regionally accredited 2-year institutions.

Contains contents listing (1 p.); introductory material (p. 1-16); institutional directory, with narrative summary and 5 trend tables, definitions, and 4 detailed tables (p. 17-80); directory of related organizations (p. 81-87); and appendix, including alphabetical list of member colleges (p. 88-108).

Directory has been published annually since 1928. SRI coverage begins with the 1984 directory.
Availability: American Association of Community and Junior Colleges, Publication Sales, 80 S. Early St., Alexandria VA 22304, $20.00; SRI/MF/complete.

A0685
American Association of Engineering Societies

A0685–1   ENGINEERING AND TECHNOLOGY DEGREES, 1983
Annual. For individual publication data, see below.
ISSN 0071-0393.
LC 75-644696.
SRI/MF/complete, delayed

Annual report, issued in 3 parts, on engineering and technology degrees awarded during 1982/83 academic year. Presents data by institution, curriculum, and student ethnic group and sex. Data are based on reports of approximately 300 colleges offering engineering degrees at the bachelor's level or higher, and selected technical institutions offering engineering and technology programs.

Contents:

Part I. By school: summary data by school, curriculum group, and degree level, with 10 tables.

Part II. By minorities: detailed data for minority groups, women, and foreign students, with 58 tables.

Part III. By curriculum: detailed data by curriculum title and accreditation, with 5 tables.

Each part includes contents and table listing and introduction. All tables are listed or described below.
Availability: American Association of Engineering Societies, Publications Department, 345 E. 47th St., New York NY 10017, $200.00 per set; SRI/MF/complete, delayed shipment in Apr. 1985.

PARTS:
[All tables show data for 1982/83. In Parts I and II data by institution include accreditation status and type of control for each institution.]

A0685–1.1: Part I. By School: Summary Data by School, Curriculum Group, and Degree Level
[Annual. 1984. 48 p. Rpt. No. 201 A-83. $75.00. ISBN 0-87615-044-X. SRI/MF/complete, delayed.]

BY INSTITUTION
[Tables [1-8] show number of degrees awarded by institution and State, total and cross-tabulated by 21 curriculum groups, and include summary totals for women, minority groups (black, Hispanic, Asian/Pacific, and American Indian), and foreign students.]

[1-4] Bachelor's, master's, engineer (professional), and doctor's degrees in engineering. (p. 9-30)

[5-8] Certificates, and associate, bachelor's, and master's degrees in engineering technology. (p. 33-45)

SUMMARY
[9-10] Engineering and engineering technology degrees, by curriculum and level. (p. 47-48)

A0685–1.2: Part II. By Minorities: Detailed Data by Minority Groups, Women, and Foreign Students

[Annual. 1984. 162 p. Rpt. No. 201 B-83. $100.00. ISBN 0-87615-054-7. SRI/MF/complete, delayed.]

BY INSTITUTION

[Tables show degrees awarded by institution and State for engineering and engineering technology, by degree level, cross-tabulated by curriculum, for minority groups listed below.]

a. Women. 10 tables. (p. 10-39)

b. Blacks. 10 tables. (p. 42-68)

c. Hispanics. 9 tables. (p. 70-93)

d. Asian/Pacific. 10 tables. (p. 96-120)

e. American Indians. 7 tables. (p. 122-130)

f. Foreign nationals. 10 tables. (p. 132-160)

SUMMARY

g. Engineering and engineering technology degrees, by curriculum and level. 2 tables. (p. 161-162)

A0685–1.3: Part III. By Curriculum: Detailed Data by Curriculum Title and Accreditation

[Annual. 1984. 80 p. Rpt. No. 201 C-83. $75.00. ISBN 0-87615-064-4. SRI/MF/complete, delayed.]

[All tables show number of degrees awarded at each degree level, by specific subfield in each of approximately 25 curriculum groups. Tables [1] and [2] also show degrees awarded women, and black, Hispanic, Asian, American Indian, and foreign students; and accreditation status for each curriculum.]

[1] Engineering curricula by school. (p. 9-40)

[2] Technology curricula by school. (p. 43-60)

[3] Engineering and engineering technology curricula by degree. (p. 63-77)

[4-5] Engineering and engineering technology degrees, by curriculum and level [summary]. (p. 79-80)

A0685–2 ENGINEERING AND TECHNOLOGY ENROLLMENTS, Fall 1982
Annual. For individual publication data, see below.
SRI/MF/complete, delayed

Annual report, published in 2 volumes, on engineering and engineering technology enrollment, fall 1982.

Presents enrollment by institution arranged by State, for all programs and by curriculum. Data are shown for all students and for women, blacks, Hispanics, Asian/Pacific Islanders, American Indians, and (engineering only) foreign nationals.

Engineering data are shown by undergraduate and graduate level and full- and part-time status.

Engineering technology data are shown for associate/pre-engineering and bachelor programs by student year and full- and part-time status, and for postgraduate programs.

Also includes summary trends from 1972. Data are from AAES surveys.

Report volumes are listed below. Each volume contains contents listing, introduction, and table notes; and 14-16 detailed tables.

This is the 15th edition of the report.

Availability: American Association of Engineering Societies, Publications Department, 345 E. 47th St., New York NY 10017; SRI/MF/complete, delayed shipment in Oct. 1984.

REPORT VOLUMES:

A0685–2.1: Part I. Engineering: Engineering Enrollments by School and by Curriculum for All Students Including a Breakdown by Women, Minorities, and Foreign Nationals

[Annual. 1983. 6+320 p. Members $60.00, nonmembers $100.00. ISBN 0-87615-084-9. SRI/MF/complete, delayed.]

A0685–2.2: Part II. Technology: Technology Enrollments by School and by Curriculum for All Students Including a Breakdown by Women and Minorities

[Annual. 1983. 6+200 p. Members $60.00, nonmembers $100.00. ISBN 0-87615-094-6. SRI/MF/complete, delayed.]

A0685–3 ENGINEERS' SALARIES: Special Industry Report, 1983
Annual. 1983.
5+234+App 12 p.
ISBN 0-87615-124-1.
LC 79-8565.
SRI/MF/complete, delayed

Annual report on salaries of supervisory and nonsupervisory professional engineers, by employer size group, major industry, and census division, as of Feb. 1, 1983, with trends from 1960. Data are shown as medians, means, and upper and lower deciles and quartiles, all by educational degree level and years since baccalaureate degree.

Data are based on responses of approximately 1,000 establishments employing 130,128 engineers to a Feb.-May 1983 mail survey conducted by the Engineering Manpower Commission.

Contains contents listing (2 p.); introduction, methodology, effects of inflation on salaries, and definitions, with 5 text tables (p. 1-7); median salary trends, with 12 charts and 1 table (p. 9-22); 4 sections, with salary tables and accompanying charts (p. 23-234); and appendix, with list of participants and sample questionnaire (12 p.).

This is the 17th salary report; during 1958-80 report was published biennially.

Availability: American Association of Engineering Societies, Publications Department, 345 E. 47th St., New York NY 10017, members $135.00, nonmembers $225.00; SRI/MF/complete, delayed shipment in Dec. 1984.

A0685–4 SALARIES OF ENGINEERS IN EDUCATION, 1983
Annual. 1983.
5+66+App 4 p.
ISBN 0-87615-154-3.
LC 75-613272.
SRI/MF/complete, delayed

Annual report, for 1983, on salaries of engineering instructors, professors (assistant, associate, and full), administrators, and researchers employed in engineering and technology schools, by length of contract (9/10 and 11/12 months). Includes breakdowns for engineering schools offering and not offering PhD programs. Data are shown as medians, upper and lower deciles and quartiles, and means, all by years since baccalaureate degree.

Report is based on responses of approximately 17,000 engineers employed in educational institutions, to a Feb.-May 1983 survey.

Contains contents listing (1 p.); introduction, methodology, definitions, and 3 summary tables, including sample distribution (p. 1-8); 3 sections, with detailed salary tabulations and accompanying charts (p. 11-66); and appendix, with questionnaire facsimile (4 p.).

This is the 17th salary report; during 1958-80 report was published biennially.

Availability: American Association of Engineering Societies, Publications Department, 345 E. 47th St., New York NY 10017, members $33.00, nonmembers $55.00; SRI/MF/complete, delayed shipment in Dec. 1984.

A0685–5 PROFESSIONAL INCOME OF ENGINEERS, 1983
Annual. 1983.
5+99+App 15 p.
ISBN 0-87615-135-7.
LC 70-6800.
SRI/MF/complete, delayed

Annual report, for 1983, on salaries of supervisory and nonsupervisory professional engineers, by employer size group, major industry, level of government, and census division. Data are shown as medians, means, and upper and lower deciles and quartiles, all by years since baccalaureate degree.

Report is based on responses of approximately 1,000 businesses, government agencies, and educational institutions, employing 130,128 engineers, to a Feb.-May 1983 survey.

Contains contents listing (1 p.); introduction, methodology, effects of inflation on salaries with 4 text tables, and definitions (p. 1-5); 1 table showing number of engineers represented, by employing sector (p. 7); 5 sections, with salary tabulations and accompanying charts (p. 9-97); and appendix, with list of survey participants and questionnaire facsimile (15 p.).

This is the 17th salary report; during 1958-80 report was published biennially.

Availability: American Association of Engineering Societies, Publications Department, 345 E. 47th St., New York NY 10017, members $42.00, nonmembers $75.00; SRI/MF/complete, delayed shipment in Dec. 1984.

A0685–6 PLACEMENT OF ENGINEERING AND TECHNOLOGY GRADUATES
Annual, discontinued.

Annual report on engineering and technology graduates placement status and starting salaries, discontinued with report covering class of 1982 (for description, see SRI 1983 Annual, under this number).

A0685–8 DEMAND FOR ENGINEERS, 1982
Annual. 1983. 4+62 p.
ISBN 0-87615-113-6.
SRI/MF/complete, delayed

Annual survey report on demand for engineers, covering employment situation as of Oct. 1982 and outlook through Oct. 1983 as perceived by engineers and employers, with comparisons to 1980-81 surveys.

Presents data on engineers' employment and job-seeking status; engineers' expectations for demand in their own companies, local areas, and disciplines; and employers' hiring activity.

Includes varying detail by years since bachelor's degree, highest degree earned, professional society membership, engineering discipline, new vs. experienced engineer, employer type and workforce size, and census division.

Also includes data on median salary, by degree level and society membership.

Data are based on survey responses from 2,592 members of professional societies and 333 employers.

Contains contents and table listings (2 p.); introduction and summary (p. 1-4); 22 tables, interspersed with narrative (p. 5-21); facsimile questionnaires, 5 tables, list of participating societies and employers with 1 table, and 4 tables comparing 1980-82 surveys (p. 27-59); and list of titles available from American Assn of Engineering Societies (3 p.).

Availability: American Association of Engineering Societies, Publications Department, 345 E. 47th St., New York NY 10017, members $65.00, nonmembers $100.00; SRI/MF/complete, delayed shipment in July 1984.

A0700
American Association
of Fund-Raising Counsel

A0700–1 **GIVING USA, 29th ANNUAL ISSUE: A Compilation of Facts and Trends on American Philanthropy for the Year 1983**
Annual. 1984. 105 p.
LC 59-1874.
SRI/MF/complete, delayed

Annual report on philanthropy, covering contributions by type of donor and by subject area (cause), 1983 and trends. Also includes data on tax deductions for contributions, hospital finances and operations, government support for public broadcasting, and volunteers. Selected data are shown by individual institution and/or donor.

Data are compiled from numerous government and private sources, generally identified for each table.

Contents:
a. Listing of contents, tables, and charts; introduction; and summary, with 1 table listed below. (p. 2-9)
b. Analyses of giving by donor type; philanthropy trends; giving by recipient area; and volunteer activity; with 4 charts and 64 tables, listed below. (p. 10-98)
c. Discussion of factors influencing philanthropy; notes on methodology; and definitions. (p. 99-103)

Availability: American Association of Fund-Raising Counsel, 25 W. 43rd St., New York NY 10036, $25.00 (or $55.00 including annual subscription to *Fund-Raising Review*); SRI/MF/complete, delayed shipment in May 1985.

TABLES AND CHARTS:
[Data by source are shown for corporations, foundations, bequests, and individuals, unless otherwise noted. Recipient areas usually include education, social services, health/hospitals, arts/humanities, civic/public, religion, and other.]

A0700–1.1: Sources of Philanthropy

SUMMARY
[1] Philanthropy [contributions by source and recipient area], 1983. (p. 7)

INDIVIDUALS AND BEQUESTS
[2] Giving by individuals [total contributions and personal income, 1970-83]. (p. 11)

[3] 1982 deductions for charitable contributions [by income size, showing number of tax returns and amount of deductions]. (p. 12)

[4] Preliminary itemized deductions [by category and income group], 1982 individual tax returns. (p. 13)

[5] Charitable deduction by itemizers [by income size, showing number of returns and amount of deductions, tax years 1981-82]. (p. 14-15)

[6-7] Giving by bequest [amount, 1970-83]; and large bequests [donor, amount, and recipient], 1983. (p. 16-18)

FOUNDATIONS
[8] Giving by foundations [amount, 1970-83]. (p. 18)

[9] General foundation funding trends [amount, by recipient area, 1980-83]. (p. 19)

[10] Reported [amount and number of] grants designated for special population groups [including aged and handicapped persons, youth, alcohol/drug abusers, criminals, and minorities, no date]. (p. 20)

[11-13] Analysis of grantmaking foundations [number, assets, gifts received, and grants] by asset and grant [size] and type [of foundation, no date]. (p. 21)

[14-15] Distribution of grants [number and value], by subject categories and recipient organization type, 1981-83. (p. 22-25)

[16] Analysis of grantmaking foundations [number, assets, grants, and gifts received], by State [and for Puerto Rico, FY81]. (p. 26-27)

[17] Some leading U.S. private foundations ranked by payment of grants [and including assets and Federal excise tax liability, 1983 with comparison of grant payments for 1982]. (p. 29)

CORPORATIONS
[18] Giving by corporations [total contributions and pretax net income, 1970-83]. (p. 31)

[19] Contributions [and] U.S. pretax net income [by SIC 2-digit industry group], 1982. (p. 32)

[20] Structure of corporate contributions [grants to and contributions by company foundations, and other company contributions, 1980-82]. (p. 33)

[21] Distribution of corporate contributions [by recipient area, 1980-82]. (p. 33)

[22] Corporate contributions, 2 survey years [amount and as percent of income, by recipient area, 1981-82]. (p. 35)

[23] Contibutions dollar [amount, by recipient area 1981-82, and by area subcategory 1982]. (p. 36-37)

[24] Summary of [cash, product, and other] charitable contributions expenditures [of company foundations and direct giving programs, no date]. (p. 39)

A0700–1.2: Total Giving, and Areas of Philanthropic Opportunity

TOTAL GIVING
[1-2] Total giving 1955-83, [and GNP 1968-83]. (p. 40-41)

[3-4] Donors [amount by source] and recipients [amount by area, 1955-83]. (p. 42-44)

RELIGION
[5] Giving to religion [amount, 1970-83]. (p. 47)

[6-7] Religious preferences [distribution of adults by major religion, by selected socioeconomic characteristics], 1983. (p. 48-49)

[8] Church/synagogue attendance [percent of adults attending, by age group, selected years 1958-83]. (p. 49)

[9] Baptized/inclusive membership in selected large religious bodies [1981-82]. (p. 50)

[10] Church/synagogue attendance [percent of population attending, by religion and selected socioeconomic characteristics, 1983]. (p. 51)

[11] Protestant giving in 12 denominations [total and per capita, no date]. (p. 52)

[12] Number of U.S. churches, and of members, by religious groups [no date]. (p. 53)

[13] Some comparative U.S. church statistics [church membership as a percent of population, and change in membership from previous year, 1982-83]. (p. 54)

[14] Church/synagogue attendance [percent of population attending, selected years 1939-83]. (p. 54)

EDUCATION
[15] Giving to education [amount, 1970-83]. (p. 55)

[16-18] Giving to higher education [distribution by source (alumni, nonalumni, foundations, business, religion, and other)]; estimated voluntary support [of higher education], by source and purpose; and estimated total voluntary support; [various years 1972/73-1982/83]. [2 tables and 1 chart] (p. 57-61)

[19] Large gifts to education [donor, amount, and recipient], 1983. (p. 65-66)

HEALTH AND HOSPITALS
[20] Giving to health/hospitals [amount, 1970-83]. (p. 67)

[21-22] Change in general/community and voluntary nonprofit hospitals [number of hospitals, beds, admissions, and outpatient visits; average daily census and length of stay; occupancy rates; total expenses, and expenses per inpatient day; personnel; and payroll; 1978-82]. (p. 68)

[23] National health agencies [contributions and bequests received 1983, and total contributions 1982, by agency]. (p. 70-71)

[24] National health expenditures by type of expenditure and source of funds [private, and Federal and State/local government], 1980-82. (p. 72-73)

[25] Personal health care expenditures by selected 3rd-party payers and type of expenditure, 1980-82. (p. 76-77)

[26] Large gifts to health/hospitals [donor, amount, and recipient], 1983. (p. 77)

SOCIAL SERVICES

[27] Giving to social services [amount, 1970-83]. (p. 78)

[28] Record of United Way campaigns in U.S. [contributions received, 1970-83]. [chart] (p. 81)

[29-30] [Distribution of] sources of United Way support [by type of contributor 1982, and of] services supported with United Way contributions [by type of service 1983]. [charts] (p. 82-83)

[31] Large gifts to social welfare [donor, amount, and recipient], 1983. (p. 86)

ARTS AND HUMANITIES

[32] Giving to arts/humanities [amount, 1970-83]. (p. 87)

[33] Public broadcasting income [of aggregate] public TV and radio systems by source [including State and local government, Federal grant/contract, subscriber, business, and foundation, FY81-82]. (p. 89)

[34] Budget, National Endowment for the Arts [by program, 1983-84]. (p. 91)

[35] Total business support to specific art categories [1981-82]. (p. 92)

[36] State arts agencies [total and per capita] legislative appropriations [by State and territory], FY83-84. (p. 93)

[37] Large gifts to arts/humanities [donor, amount, and recipient], 1983. (p. 94)

CIVIC/PUBLIC, AND VOLUNTEERS

[38-39] Giving to civic/public [amount, 1970-83]; and large gifts to civic/public causes [donor, amount, and recipient], 1983. (p. 94, 96)

[40] Current volunteer strength of 20 national agencies [fund-raising volunteers 1982, and total volunteers 1983]. (p. 98)

A0800
American Association
of University Professors

A0800–1   **ACADEME: The Annual Report on the Economic Status of the Profession, 1983/84**
Bimonthly (selected issue).
July/Aug. 1984. 64 p.
Vol. 70, No. 2.
ISSN 0190-2946.
LC 79-642918.
SRI/MF/complete, delayed

Annual report on college and university faculty compensation and employment, 1983/84, with selected trends from 1972/73.

Includes salary, total compensation, percentile salary rating, benefits as percent of salary, and employment and percent tenured, generally by academic rank and sex, for individual institutions by State, and for Puerto Rico, Guam, Micronesia, and Virgin Islands.

Also includes selected detail for medical schools, aggregate data by institution type and control, and faculty salaries compared to CPI increases and to salaries in similar nonacademic occupations.

Data are based on reports of approximately 2,200 institutions, and were collected and tabulated by Maryse Eymonerie Associates.

Contains contents and table listings (p. 1-2); narrative report with 16 tables (p. 3-16); additional tables available, and data explanation (p. 17-19); and appendices, with 2 detailed tables (p. 20-63).

Report is published as the July/Aug. 1984 issue of the bimonthly *Academe: Bulletin of the AAUP*, and is the only feature of *Academe* covered in SRI.

Availability: American Association of University Professors, Academe, 1012 14th St., NW, Washington DC 20005, members †, nonmembers $25.00 (prepaid); SRI/MF/complete, delayed shipment in Jan. 1985.

A0875
American Automotive
Leasing Association

A0875–1   **ANALYSIS OF COSTS AND RELATED INFORMATION: Non-Finance Leasing (Closed-End), 1982-83**
Annual. [1984.] 12 p.
SRI/MF/complete

Annual report, for 1983, presenting auto nonfinance leasing (closed-end) operating and administrative costs, fleet composition and disposition, and leasing and rental activities, for 16 unnamed firms. Data are from reports to the American Automotive Leasing Assn by member firms.

Contains table listing (1 p.); 1 summary table comparing 1982-83 average per vehicle operating and general/administrative costs (p. 1); and 11 tables, listed below (p. 2-12).

Availability: American Automotive Leasing Association, Heritage Park, 8330 N. Teutonia Ave., Milwaukee WI 53209, †; SRI/MF/complete.

TABLES:
[Tables show data for 16 firms labeled A-P, arranged by fleet size, 1983 with selected comparisons to 1982 average totals. Tables [1-6] show per unit per month costs.]

[1] Analysis of costs [depreciation, repairs/maintenance, insurance, tags/taxes, interest expense, delivery, and general/administrative]. (p. 2)

[2-3] Repairs and maintenance [by item, and including administrative salaries and annual mileage]; and insurance collision/comprehensive and umbrella liability [including salaries]. (p. 3-4)

[4-5] License tags, State/local taxes, and interest expense [including percent of car cost financed, and amortization and average simple interest rates]. (p. 5-6)

[6] General and administrative expenses [including salaries, advertising, travel/promotion, taxes, and insurance]. (p. 7)

[7] Composition of fleets [including distribution of vehicles by model size and make, and percent with air conditioning]. (p. 8)

[8] Type of customer [percent individuals, and fleets by size]. (p. 9)

[9] Used car disposition [percent reconditioned prior to sale and average cost, method of disposition including auctions, and whether sold at home office or on the road]. (p. 10)

[10-11] Leasing and rental activities [whether firm offers 6 selected options]; and record-keeping methods [by hand, mechanical, or electronic]. (p. 11-12)

A0875–2   **ANALYSIS OF COSTS AND RELATED INFORMATION: Finance Leasing (Open-End), 1982-83**
Annual. [1984.] 7 p.
SRI/MF/complete

Annual report, for 1983, presenting auto finance leasing (open-end) interest and administrative costs, fleet composition and disposition, and leasing and rental activities, for 17 unnamed firms. Data are from reports to the American Automotive Leasing Assn by member firms.

Contains table listing (1 p.); and 7 tables, listed below (p. 1-7).

Availability: American Automotive Leasing Association, Heritage Park, 8330 N. Teutonia Ave., Milwaukee WI 53209, †; SRI/MF/complete.

TABLES:
[Tables show data for 17 firms, labeled A-Q, arranged by fleet size, 1983 with selected comparisons to 1982 average totals.]

[1-2] Interest expense [including monthly costs per vehicle, and average monthly loan amortization and simple interest rate]; and general and administrative expenses per unit per month costs [including salaries, advertising, travel/promotion, taxes, and insurance]. (p. 1-2)

[3] Composition of fleets [including distribution of vehicles by model size and make, and percent with air conditioning]. (p. 3)

[4] Type of customer [percent individuals and fleets by size]. (p. 4)

[5] Used car disposition [including average months in operation and mileage per vehicle, percent reconditioned prior to sale and average cost, method of disposition including auctions, and whether sold at home office or on the road]. (p. 5)

[6-7] Leasing and rental activities [whether firm offers 6 selected options]; and record-keeping methods [by hand, mechanical, or electronic]. (p. 6-7)

A0950
American
Bankers Association

A0950–1   **CONSUMER CREDIT DELINQUENCY BULLETIN**
Quarterly.
Approx. 6 p. folder.
SRI/MF/not filmed

Quarterly bulletin on the ratio of delinquent loans to loans outstanding, and on repossession ratios for mobile homes and autos, by State and for Puerto Rico. Loans are considered delinquent if a payment is more than 30 days overdue.

Data are compiled by the American Bankers Assn from member bank reports, and are published 6-12 weeks after quarter of coverage.

Contains brief narrative and 1 summary chart; and 2 tables showing the following data, by State and for Puerto Rico, monthly for quarter of coverage:

a. Delinquency rates for personal, auto, property improvement, home equity/2nd mortgage, mobile home, recreational vehicle, bank card, and revolving credit loans, with accompanying trend charts; (data on home equity/2nd mortgage loans begin with the 1st quarter 1984 issue).

b. Repossession ratios for mobile homes and autos.

Prior to 2nd quarter 1984 issue, report was titled *Delinquency Rates on Bank Instalment Loans.*

Availability: American Bankers Association, Order Processing Department, 1120 Connecticut Ave., NW, Washington DC 20036, members $27.00 per yr., nonmembers $33.00 per yr.; SRI/MF/not filmed.

Issues reviewed during 1984: 3rd Qtr. 1983-2nd Qtr. 1984 (D) (No. 425-428).

A0950–2   1984 RETAIL BANK CREDIT REPORT
Annual. 1984. xiv+95 p.
ABA Pub. No. 201600.
ISSN 0276-9093.
LC 81-641421.
SRI/MF/not filmed

Annual report on bank retail lending activity, by asset size and census division, 1983. Includes data on installment loans, bank cards, other types of lending, employees, overdraft line-of-credit, and credit life insurance.

Most data are based on responses of 591 banks to Feb.-June 1984 survey conducted by American Bankers Assn.

Contains listings of contents, tables, and charts (p. v-xiv); survey background, with 1 map and 3 tables (p. 1-3); and survey findings, presented in 17 sections, with narrative summaries, 4 charts, and 119 tables (p. 4-95).

All tables are listed below.

Annual report series began in 1960.

Availability: American Bankers Association, Order Processing Department, 1120 Connecticut Ave., NW, Washington DC 20036, members $48.00, nonmembers $60.00; SRI/MF/not filmed.

TABLES:

[Unless otherwise noted, data are for 1983. Tables with titles starting "Banks..." generally show data as percent of total banks surveyed. Data are often shown by census division; and most data for 1983 are shown by asset size category (data for previous years are shown by deposit size).]

A0950–2.1: Installment Loans, Other Lending Activity, Loan Income and Expenses, Employees, and Leases

SURVEY BACKGROUND

1-3. Distribution of [respondent and total] banks, and margins of error for percentage survey results. (p. 2-3)

CONSUMER INSTALLMENT CREDIT AND LOAN FUNDS

4-5. Installment credit outstandings [by type of loan and/or lender], 1981-83. (p. 6-8)

6-7. Banks' ratio of total loans to total assets, and of consumer loans to total loans. (p. 10)

PORTFOLIO INFORMATION

8. Selected items of installment loan portfolio [including average loan outstandings and unearned interest]. (p. 12)

9. Installment credit outstandings as a percentage of total assets, 1981-83. (p. 12)

10. Portfolio distribution of loan volume and loan outstandings, by type of loan, 1981-83. (p. 14)

11. Banks having indirect loans. (p. 15)

12. Average percent of total installment loan outstandings in indirect loans. (p. 15)

13. Average gross outstandings per account with open-end credit balances, [year end] 1981-83. (p. 17)

14-15. Average number of accounts per bank in open-end credit plans. (p. 17-18)

16-17. Banks buying and selling portions of their installment loan portfolio from or to other financial institutions, 1981-83. (p. 18-19)

18-20. Banks selling consumer installment loans; average amount outstanding per consumer installment loan sold; and loans sold [distribution by source; all] in the secondary markets. (p. 19-20)

LOAN LOSSES

21-23. Installment credit dollar losses based on outstandings, liquidations, and volume, by type of loan, 1982-83. (p. 21-24)

24-26. Portfolio distribution of gross losses, recoveries from loan losses, and net loan losses, incurred for closed-end credit, by type of loan. (p. 25-27)

27-28. Average amount of gross, recovered and net losses, incurred for closed-end credit and for open-end credit/overdraft/revolving credit plans/personal lines of credit/executive credit. (p. 28-29)

29. Gross losses in check credit/overdraft/revolving credit/personal lines of credit/executive credit plans. (p. 29)

30. Average amount of gross, recovered and net losses, incurred for open-end bank credit card plans. (p. 30)

31-32. Average number of automobile repossessions, and average net dollar losses per repossession, by type of loan, 1981-83. (p. 31-32)

33-34. Average percent of banks' repossessions without losses. (p. 32-33)

35-36. Consumer credit losses due to bankruptcy as a percentage of total consumer credit losses, 1981-83. (p. 34-35)

37. Average number of delinquent loans handled per collector per month. (p. 35)

INCOME AND EXPENSE ELEMENTS

38-39. Average gross income from total bank loans/discounts, and from consumer loans. (p. 37-38)

40. Average gross fee income from various sources. (p. 38)

41. Average gross expense per installment loan. (p. 39)

INSTALLMENT CREDIT EMPLOYEES

42. Average installment lending personnel per bank. (p. 40)

43-44. Average number of loans outstanding per installment credit collection and noncollection employee. (p. 40-41)

45. Banks with centralized [and] decentralized collection depts. (p. 41)

INDIRECT LOANS AND DEALER SERVICE COMPANY PLANS

46-47. Percentage of automobile indirect loans outstanding under various dealer plans. (p. 42-43)

AUTOMOBILE AND SMALL EQUIPMENT LEASES

48-49. Banks engaged in direct/indirect leasing, and [banks by] leasing operation status. (p. 44)

50-51. Banks engaged in direct and indirect automobile leasing, and average amount outstanding per direct and indirect lease. (p. 45)

52-53. Banks leasing small equipment, and average outstandings for leases. (p. 46)

FINANCING TERMS

54. Most common liquidation rate for [new car, mobile home, and home improvement] loans. (p. 47)

55. Percentage of new [direct and indirect] automobile loans financed with various selected maturities. (p. 48)

56. Most common maximum maturity for various loans. (p. 49)

57. Most common annual percentage rate for direct new car loans, by maturity. (p. 50)

58. Average most common interest rate for various loans, by type of loan, 1981-83. (p. 51)

59. Average most common cost of funds charged, 1981-83. (p. 52)

SINGLE-PAYMENT, SIMPLE INTEREST, AND VARIABLE RATE LOANS

60-61. Banks making single-payment consumer loans; and average amount outstanding per single-payment loan; 1981-83. (p. 53)

62-64. Banks not making simple interest loans, 1981-83; percentage of dollar volume and number of loans made on a simple interest basis; and banks paying dealers on a simple interest basis. (p. 54-55)

65. Banks currently offering or planning to offer variable rate installment loans, 1st quarter 1984. (p. 58)

66. Year first offered consumer installment loans on variable rate basis [1983 or 1982/earlier]. (p. 58)

67-68. Average amount outstanding per variable rate loan; and average amount per bank outstanding in variable rate loans. (p. 59)

69-70. Frequency of variable rate change. (p. 60)

71. Banks that installed new computer software package to process variable rate loans. (p. 61)

A0950–2.2: Bank Cards, Overdraft Line-of-Credit, and Other Data

BANK CARD PLANS

72-75. Banks offering bank credit card plans and ATM [automated teller machine] debit/access card plans. (p. 62-64)

76-77. Card agent and card issuing banks carrying card holder receivables [MasterCard, VISA, and Premium/Gold Card]. (p. 64-65)

78-79. Average gross outstandings per bank credit card account, 1981-83. (p. 66)

80. Average bank card deposits from merchants. (p. 67)

81-82. Domestic bank card statistics: VISA and MasterCard [including number of merchant outlets, cardholders, and accounts; average credit line; retail sales and cash advance values; outstandings; delinquencies; and charge-offs; year end] 1981-83. (p. 68-69)

83. Distribution of bank card employees [by function]. (p. 70)

84-85. Extent of profitability for MasterCard and VISA [percent of banks breaking even and with profit and loss]. (p. 71-72)

86. Banks charging fees for credit cards. (p. 73)

87. Type of charging cycle for banks that assess monthly or yearly credit card fees. (p. 73)

88-89. Average yearly fee charged for credit cards. (p. 74)

90. Banks that changed rates of interest charged for outstanding credit card balances. (p. 75)

91. Banks charging the maximum rates of interest allowed by State law for credit card balances. (p. 76)

92. Banks charging variable rates on credit card balances. (p. 76)

93. Average late charges for overdue credit card accounts. (p. 77)

94. Banks using an automated bank card collection process. (p. 78)

95. Average gross fee income per bank from handling of credit card sales drafts for merchants when banks do not carry their own bank card receivables. (p. 78)

BANK CARD LOSSES

96. Bank credit card losses by computational method, 1978-83. (p. 79)

97-98. Average bank credit card losses due to bankruptcy [1983] and to fraud [1981-83], as a percentage of total bank card losses. (p. 80)

99-100. Average bank credit card losses due to fraud as a percentage of bank card outstandings and annual dollar sales volume. (p. 81)

101. [Banks by] mandatory charge-off time. (p. 82)

102. Average delinquent bank card accounts per month handled by 1 collector, 1981-83. (p. 82)

OVERDRAFT LINE-OF-CREDIT SERVICE

103-105. Banks offering a demand deposit account overdraft line-of-credit service; and average number of consumer demand deposit accounts per bank. (p. 83-84)

106-107. Average percentage of all consumer demand deposit accounts approved for overdraft line-of-credit arrangements. (p. 85)

108. Selected ways of accessing overdraft lines of credit [percent of banks using each mode]. (p. 86)

109. Average most common rate of interest charged for overdraft line-of-credit advances, year end 1983. (p. 87)

110-111. Banks offering an executive credit plan separate from check credit/overdraft line of credit. (p. 88)

112. Banks charging fixed or variable rates of interest for executive credit plans, 1981-83. (p. 89)

113. Average amount outstanding per executive credit account. (p. 89)

114-115. Banks offering/planning to offer an equity line of credit secured by a second mortgage; and average amount approved and outstanding per bank. (p. 91)

116-117. Banks charging an origination fee for equity line-of-credit accounts; and average origination fee charged per bank. (p. 92)

118-119. Banks charging a fee to keep equity line-of-credit accounts open; and average fee charged per bank. (p. 93)

CREDIT LIFE INSURANCE AND OTHER DATA

120. Banks having a formal charge made against their installment credit operation for cost of funds used in lending, 1981-83. (p. 94)

121-122. Banks offering credit life insurance to their customers. (p. 95)

A0970
American Bar Association

A0970-1 **REVIEW OF LEGAL EDUCATION IN THE U.S., FALL 1983: Law School and Bar Admission Requirements**
Annual. 1984. vii+88 p.
LC 36-17506.
SRI/MF/complete

Annual report on law school enrollments, degrees, and staff, and State bar admission requirements, 1983, with selected trends from 1963.

Data are compiled by the American Bar Assn (ABA) from law school deans, National Conference of Bar Examiners, and State boards of bar examiners.

Contains contents listing (p. vii); introduction, 8 tables (listed below) presenting law school statistics, and interspersed lists of schools not approved by ABA and of school status changes (p. 1-72); ABA statements, policy, and code (p. 73-78); tabular list of bar admission requirements, by State and for territories (p. 79-85); and directory of State bar examination administrators (p. 86-88).

Availability: American Bar Association, Legal Education and Admissions to the Bar Section, 1155 E. 60th St., Chicago IL 60637, single copy †, additional copies $2.00 each; SRI/MF/complete.

TABLES:
[Data for unapproved schools are only for 12 schools responding to survey.]

[1-3] Law schools and special program on the approved list and law schools not on the approved list of the ABA [showing the following by institution: full- and part-time enrollments by level, including graduate students, fall 1983, and degrees awarded by type, through summer 1983, all for total, female, and minority students; full- and part-time teachers and full-time teaching deans/librarians (total, female, and minority); and tuition/fees, years of college required, weeks and credits required, summer programs, and library holdings], 1983. (p. 4-66)

[4] Law school [full- and part-time] attendance figures for 1983 [total and for women by level, including graduate students, for approved and unapproved schools]. (p. 69)

[5] Number of degrees conferred in 1983 [by type, for total and female part- and full-time students at approved and unapproved schools]. (p. 69)

[6] Number of [total and female full- and part-time] teachers [and teaching deans/librarians] in approved law schools, 1983. (p. 70)

[7] Legal education and bar admission statistics [including enrollment of women, 1st-year enrollment, Law School Admission Test administrations, J.D. (Juris Doctor) or Bachelor of Law degrees awarded, and admissions to the bar], 1963-83. (p. 70)

[8] Survey of minority group students enrolled in J.D. programs in approved law schools [by level, for blacks, Mexican Americans, Puerto Ricans, other Hispanic Americans, American Indian/Alaskan Native, Asian/Pacific Islander, and other, 1971/72-1983/84]. (p. 71-72)

A1015
American
Bowling Congress

A1015-1 **ANNUAL REPORT, Fiscal Year Ended July 31, 1983: American Bowling Congress**
Annual. [1983.] 36 p.
SRI/MF/complete

Annual report of the American Bowling Congress, presenting data on finances, membership, and establishments, FY83. Data are shown by State and for Canada and other regions and areas.

Contains contents listing (inside front cover); narrative review of 88th season activities, with 1 summary table on FY83 awards, legal committee actions, bonding, and sanctioned tournaments (p. 2-3); annual convention minutes, delegate list, and ABC condensed financial report (p. 4-18); and 7 detailed tables, listed below (p. 19-36).

A yearbook of current and historical tournament results and player awards is also published by the issuing agency, but is not covered by SRI.

Availability: American Bowling Congress, 5301 S. 76th St., Greendale WI 53129, ‡; SRI/MF/complete.

TABLES:

MEMBERSHIP
[Tables [1-6] generally also include number of leagues, teams, and assns, and playing strength.]

[1-3] Summary of [membership] dues and [lane] fees, FY83 [for individual assns, by State including D.C., and for Canadian Provinces, 8 outer regions, Europe, Japan, and Pacific area]. (p. 19-35)

[4-6] Membership by [top 25] local assns and by [top 10] States [both based on playing strength, FY83]; and [annual] membership, 1895/96-1982/83. (p. 35-36)

ESTABLISHMENTS AND LANES

[7] Lane certification [including number of establishments and lanes by State, and by 8 foreign countries or outlying areas, including military foreign, FY83; and total establishments and lanes FY82-83, and new FY83]. (p. 36)

A1100
American Bus Association

A1100–1   BUS FACTS: Intercity Bus
Industry
Annual, discontinued.

Annual report on intercity bus industry operations, discontinued with Sept. 1982 report (for description, see SRI 1983 Annual, under this number). Report has been discontinued due to funding restrictions.

A1175
American Cancer Society

A1175–1   CANCER FACTS AND
FIGURES, 1984
Annual. 1983. 31 p.
LC 64-6303.
SRI/MF/complete

Annual report, for 1984, on cancer, covering incidence and mortality, by State, body site, and sex; survival rates by race; death rates by foreign country; developments in prevention, diagnosis, and treatment; and ACS activities and funding.

Data sources are the National Cancer Institute's Surveillance, Epidemiology and End Results Program (1973-79); *World Health Statistics Annual 1980-82;* Census Bureau; NCHS; and ACS.

Contents:

a. Map, contents listing, basic information, and data sources. (p. 1-6)

b. Cancer statistics, with 4 trend charts, and 7 tables listed below. (p. 7-13)

c. Developments pertaining to selected types of cancer, and ACS activities, with text statistics, and 4 tables showing ACS support from crusades and legacies 1973-82, grant amounts requested and funded 1980-83, allocation of funds by function 1982/83, and estimates of 7 cancer-related statistics by community size group 1984. (p. 14-29)

d. Tabular listing of ACS research grants/fellowships awarded, by recipient institution, showing number of grants and total amounts, FY83; and directories of comprehensive cancer centers and ACS divisions. (p. 30-31 and back cover)

Availability: American Cancer Society, 777 Third Ave., New York NY 10017, †; SRI/MF/complete.

CANCER STATISTICS:
[Data are shown by cancer site.]

[1] Trends in survival, by race: cases diagnosed in 1960-63, 1970-73, and in 1973-80. (p. 7)

[2-5] Estimated new cases and deaths: for major sites of cancer; for all sites plus major sites, by State [and Puerto Rico]; and by sex, for all sites; 1984. (p. 7-10)

[6] 25-year trends in age-adjusted cancer death rates per 100,000 population [by sex], 1952-54 and 1977-79. (p. 11)

[7] Cancer around the world [age-adjusted death rates per 100,000 population for all and selected cancer sites; by sex, for 48 countries], 1978/79. (p. 13)

A1225
American Chamber of Commerce Researchers Association

A1225–1   INTER-CITY COST OF
LIVING INDEX
Quarterly. Approx. 25 p. var. paging.
SRI/MF/complete, delayed

Quarterly survey report presenting cost-of-living indexes and average retail prices for selected consumer items in approximately 250 cities. Data are based on reports filed by local chambers of commerce. Report is issued 2-3 months after quarter of coverage.

Contains overview of survey methodology, with accompanying list of consumer items priced; and 3 tables arranged in sections, as follows:

Section 1-2. ACCRA city composite index and cost-of-living index for metro cities [for all and grocery items, housing, utilities, transportation, health care, and miscellaneous goods/services; by city arranged by State and by MSA].

Section 3. Price report [average prices for selected grocery items; apartment rent, and home purchase price and monthly payment; monthly electric, other energy, and telephone bills; bus fare, tire balancing, and gasoline prices; hospital room, doctor and dentist office visits, and aspirin prices; and costs of selected fast food, personal care, clothing, repair, recreation, and alcoholic beverage items; by city arranged by State].

Note that SRI microfiche for this publication begin with the 1st quarter 1983 issue. Coverage of the 1st quarter 1983 issue was originally included in SRI 1983 Annual, but is repeated here due to a change in microfiche status.

Availability: American Chamber of Commerce Researchers Association, Mrs. Alice Klein, c/o Louisville Area Chamber of Commerce, One Riverfront Plaza, Louisville KY 40202, $75.00 per yr.; SRI/MF/complete, delayed until publication of subsequent *Index* issue.

Issues reviewed during 1984: 1st Qtr. 1983-2nd Qtr. 1984 (D).

A1250
American Chemical Society

A1250–1   CHEMICAL AND
ENGINEERING NEWS
Weekly. Approx. 60 p.
ISSN 0009-2347.
LC A41-2413.
SRI/MF/excerpts, shipped quarterly

Weekly publication (except last week in Dec.) reporting U.S. and international developments and trends in research chemistry and the chemicals industry and in related industries using chemical processes for manufacturing purposes. Includes R&D, technology, production, trade, regulation, funding, employment, education, management, and finance.

Issues generally include news features; articles on business, international developments, government, science, technology, and science policy; book reviews; and American Chemical Society (ACS) news.

Statistical features include:

a. "Key Chemicals," usually appearing in 1 or 2 issues each month, providing annual supply, demand, and profitability data for selected chemicals.

b. Quarterly articles analyzing sales and earnings of chemical and allied industries, U.S. and Canada.

c. Semiannual and annual articles including features on capital and R&D spending, plant capacity utilization, profitability, chemistry degrees awarded, employment and earnings, leading chemical firms and chemicals, and worldwide chemical outlook.

d. Annual chemical industry fact book with production, finance, employment, and trade summary for U.S. and foreign chemical and chemical processing industries.

e. Topical articles and features containing statistical material.

All features with substantial statistical content are described, as they appear, under "Statistical Features." Nonstatistical features are not covered.

Availability: American Chemical Society, Director of Financial Operations, 1155 16th St., NW, Washington DC 20036, members †, nonmembers $35.00 per yr., single copy $2.50, annual index $35.00; SRI/MF/excerpts for all portions covered under "Statistical Features;" shipped quarterly.

Issues reviewed during 1984: Nov. 7, 1983-Oct. 29, 1984 (P) (Vol. 61, Nos. 45-51; Vol. 62, Nos. 1-44).

STATISTICAL FEATURES:

A1250–1.501: Nov. 7, 1983 (Vol. 61, No. 45)

FEDERAL DEFICIT MAY HURT CAPITAL SPENDING

(p. 7-10) By William J. Storck. Article examining effects of increased Federal borrowing on the availability of credit for capital investments. Data are from Morgan Guaranty Trust Co. Includes 2 charts showing credit demand value, with distribution by nonfinancial sector, 1981 and 1983.

ENGINEERING PLASTICS HEAD FOR NEW GROWTH

(p. 10) Article, with 1 table showing engineering thermoplastics consumption, by type, 1982 and 1987. Data are from Business Communications, Inc.

ELECTRONICS, CARBON FIBER MARKETS LURE SPECIALTY CHEMICAL MAKERS

(p. 12-14) Article, with 2 charts showing world specialty chemical sales to semiconductor and printed circuit board industries, with market shares for U.S., Japan, and Western Europe, 1982. Data are from SRI International.

NIH FUNDING IS UP ALL-AROUND, DOE GAINS A LITTLE

(p. 27-28) Article, with 2 tables showing NIH and DOE Federal budget appropriations, by program, FY83-84, with Reagan Administration budget requests for FY84.

A1250–1.502: Nov. 14, 1983 (Vol. 61, No. 46)

POLYPROPYLENE: NEW PROCESS IS SIMPLER, CHEAPER

(p. 6-7) Article, with text statistics showing polypropylene capacity and utilization, production volume and value, price, and major end uses, primarily 1982-83.

CHEMICAL EARNINGS ACCELERATE THEIR REBOUND, QUARTERLY FEATURE

(p. 10-15) Quarterly article, by William J. Storck and David Webber, analyzing sales, earnings, and profit margins for major U.S. chemical producing companies, 3rd quarter 1983.

Includes 4 tables showing top 10 chemical companies in sales, earnings, and profitability; sales, earnings, and profit margin, for 30 major chemical, 19 chemical-producing oil/gas, and 26 diversified chemical-producing companies; and petrochemical after-tax earnings for 8 major oil companies; 3rd quarter and first 9 months 1983, with selected comparisons to 1982.

CANADIAN CHEMICAL SALES, PROFITS IMPROVE, QUARTERLY FEATURE

(p. 17) Quarterly report on Canadian chemical industry performance, first 9 months 1983. Includes 1 table showing the following for 4 largest companies: net sales, net income, and profit margin, by company, first 9 months 1983, with comparisons to 1982.

PETROCHEMICAL SURGE FROM DEVELOPING COUNTRIES NEARS

(p. 18-19) Article, with 1 table showing the following for 4 petrochemicals, for U.S. and Western Europe: capacity and percent change in demand, 1974 and 1980; and capacity utilization rate, 1981.

A1250–1.503: Nov. 21, 1983 (Vol. 61, No. 47)

BIOTECHNOLOGY STOCKS: STILL POPULAR, BUT SOME ARE STRUGGLING, RECURRING FEATURE

(p. 4) Recurring article, with 1 table showing stock prices for 21 biotechnology firms, and composite index, as of Nov. 12, 1982 and Nov. 11, 1983.

THERMOSET PLASTICS RIDE DURABLE GOODS RECOVERY: KEY POLYMERS, ANNUAL FEATURE

(p. 7-10) Annual article, by Bruce F. Greek, reporting on supply and demand outlook for 3 thermoset plastics: phenolics, polyesters, and epoxies. Includes text statistics on major end uses, foreign trade, prices, and commercial value, 1983.

For description of previous article, see SRI 1982 Annual, under A1250-1.342.

CHEMICAL DISTRIBUTORS' IMPROVING STATUS

(p. 21-40) By David Webber. Article, with 2 charts showing chemical/allied product shipment and sales values, shipment distribution by type of distributor, and aggregate sales shares for 6 leading chemical firms and other distributors, 1982. Data are from Census Bureau and C&EN estimates.

A1250–1.504: Nov. 28, 1983 (Vol. 61, No. 48)

STUDY UPDATES ACADEME/INDUSTRY RESEARCH

(p. 21) Article, with 1 undated table showing distribution of academic/corporate joint research activity, by type of collaboration. Data are from a recent National Science Board study.

A1250–1.505: Dec. 5, 1983 (Vol. 61, No. 49)

CATALYSTS: A CHEMICAL MARKET POISED FOR GROWTH

(p. 19-26) By Stephen C. Stinson. Article, with 1 table showing catalyst consumption volume and value, by application, 1982 and 1987. Data are from Strategic Analysis, Inc.

A1250–1.506: Dec. 12, 1983 (Vol. 61, No. 50)

CHEMICAL CAPITAL SPENDING STARTS TO REBOUND, ANNUAL FEATURE

(p. 10-12) Annual article, by William J. Storck, on 1984 capital spending plans of the 15 leading U.S. chemical companies. Data are primarily from a C&EN survey. Includes 1 table showing capital spending by company, worldwide 1979-84, and in U.S. 1983-84.

LASER MARKET DUE TO TRIPLE BY 1987

(p. 12) Article, with 2 charts showing laser sales, and market share by laser type and application, 1987. Data are from Predicasts, Inc.

A1250–1.507: Dec. 19, 1983 (Vol. 61, No. 51)

BOOM 1984 FORECAST FOR CHEMICAL INDUSTRY

(p. 5) Article on chemical industry executives' business expectations for 1984. Data are from a Chemical Manufacturers Assn annual survey. Includes 1 chart showing expected percent growth for 6 key chemical industry indicators, 1983/84.

PHENOL, VINYL ACETATE HEAD FOR MODERATE PICKUP IN 1984: KEY CHEMICALS, ANNUAL FEATURE

(p. 7-9) Annual article, by Bruce F. Greek, reporting on supply and demand outlook for 2 major adhesive and coating ingredients: phenol and vinyl acetate. Includes text statistics on major derivatives and end uses, foreign trade, prices, and commercial value, 1983.

For description of previous article, see SRI 1982 Annual, under A1250-1.338.

WORLD CHEMICAL OUTLOOK, ANNUAL FEATURE

(p. 22-50) Annual report, for 1983, on world trends and developments in the chemical industry.

Data are from UN, government agencies, industry assns, and C&EN estimates. Includes 9 articles reporting on industry developments in the U.S. and 7 key countries or world areas. Articles containing substantial statistical content are described below.

U.S.: BUSINESS EXPECTED TO IMPROVE FURTHER FOR CHEMICAL PRODUCERS

(p. 24-26) By David M. Kiefer. Includes 1 table showing production for 34 types of inorganic and organic chemicals, and plastics and synthetic fibers, 1981-84.

FOREIGN TRADE: U.S. SURPLUS IN CHEMICAL TRADE NARROWS AGAIN AS EXPORTS DROP

(p. 27-29) By Earl V. Anderson. Includes 3 tables showing U.S. chemical export and import value, by product and end use categories 1980-83, and by country or world area 1982-83.

JAPAN: CHEMICAL PRODUCERS PUT HOPES FOR REVIVAL ON RESTRUCTURING

(p. 41-43) By Earl V. Anderson. Includes 1 table showing Japan's production of synthetic rubber and 45 types of inorganic and organic chemicals, and plastics, 1982 and first 7 months 1982-83.

CANADA: BUSINESS IS BETTER BUT FEEDSTOCK COSTS CAUSE CONCERN

(p. 44-45) By Earl V. Anderson. Includes 1 table showing Canada's production of 15 chemicals, 1978-83.

USSR/EASTERN EUROPE: SLOW GROWTH CONTINUES IN SOVIET UNION AND EAST EUROPE

(p. 46-47) By Richard J. Seltzer. Includes 2 tables showing production of 6-8 chemicals and products, for Soviet Union and by East European country, various periods 1980-83.

A1250–1.508: Jan. 2, 1984 (Vol. 62, No. 1)

R&D FUNDING OUTLOOK: BATTELLE FORECASTS 9% RISE IN 1984, ANNUAL FEATURE

(p. 6) Annual article forecasting R&D funding and performance, by sector, for 1984. Data are derived from an annual report by Battelle Memorial Institute. Includes 2 charts showing amount of R&D funded and performed by Federal Government, industry, universities, and other nonprofit institutions, 1984.

Full Battelle report is covered in SRI under R3300-1.

A1250–1.509: Jan. 9, 1984 (Vol. 62, No. 2)

LIQUIDITY PROVES TOUGH FOR CHEMICAL FIRMS TO REBUILD

(p. 36-37) By William J. Storck. Article on chemical industry liquid assets, based on a C&EN survey of 23 major companies.

Includes 2 tables showing cash/marketable securities, current and cash ratios, inventories, receivables, accounts payable, and short-term debt, for 13-16 chemical companies and 7 diversified companies, 3rd quarter 1983 with comparisons to 4th quarter 1982.

A1250–1.510: Jan. 16, 1984 (Vol. 62, No. 3)

CHEMICAL FIRMS' R&D SPENDING WILL RISE ONLY MODESTLY IN 1984, ANNUAL FEATURE

(p. 25-26) Annual article, by David Webber, on basic chemical industry planned R&D funding for 1984, based on a C&EN survey of 12 major companies. Includes 1 table showing R&D actual spending 1978-83, planned spending 1983-84, and spending as percent of sales 1982-83, all for 12-15 companies.

INCREASING ENERGY PRODUCTIVITY COULD EASE GREENHOUSE EFFECT

(p. 44-46) Article, with 1 table on relationship between energy values and GDP for the year 2025, as projected under 12 energy supply-demand scenarios. Data are based on an Institute for Energy Analysis model, and are from an NSF study.

A1250–1.511: Jan. 23, 1984 (Vol. 62, No. 4)

U.S. CHEMICAL TRADE: EEC THREATENS HIGHER TARIFFS, QUOTAS

(p. 5-6) Article examining EC limitations on chemical imports from the U.S. Data are from EC. Includes 1 table showing duty and new surcharge rates on methanol and vinyl acetate, 1984-87; and quota (in European currency units) for styrene and for polyethylene sheet by type, as of Mar. 1, 1984.

REINFORCED PLASTICS RECOVERY SEEN FOR 1984

(p. 9) Article, with 1 table showing reinforced plastics demand by major end use, 1974 and 1979-84. Data are from Society of the Plastics Industry.

FUTURE FOR METAL-COATED PLASTICS IS BRIGHT

(p. 10) Article, with 3 tables showing consumption of metal-plated/coated plastics, by plastic type, application, and plating/coating process, quinquennially 1970-90. Data are from Margolis Marketing and Research Co.

BRISK DETERGENT ACTIVITY CHANGES PICTURE FOR CHEMICAL SUPPLIERS

(p. 17-49) By Patricia L. Layman. Article on world supply and demand situation for soap, detergent, and component materials, 1970s-84. Data are from C&EN estimates, USITC, and industry sources. Includes 1 chart and 4 tables showing the following:

a. Distribution of washloads by temperature, 1970 and 1980; detergent formulations; and linear alkylate and fatty alcohol nameplate capacity by company, and aggregate effective capacity and demand, for 3-7 U.S. and Western European producers (no date).

b. Soap and detergent production by world region, 1976, 1980, and 1984; and U.S. production, and sales volume and value, for surface-active agents by type, 1982.

Data corrections appear in Feb. 20, 1984 issue (see A1250-1.514, below).

A1250–1.512: Jan. 30, 1984 (Vol. 62, No. 5)

U.S. FARMING PICKUP HELPS NATURAL GAS-BASED PETROCHEMICALS: KEY CHEMICALS, ANNUAL FEATURE

(p. 10-14) Annual article, by Bruce F. Greek, reporting on supply and demand outlook for 4 natural gas based petrochemicals: ammonia, urea, methanol, and formaldehyde. Includes text statistics on major derivatives and end uses, foreign trade, prices, and commercial value, primarily 1984.

CHEMICALS' LEAD IN STOCK MARKET NARROWS, RECURRING FEATURE

(p. 16) Recurring article, with 1 table showing C&EN chemical stock index compared to 8 major stock indexes, Jan. 20, 1984 and Jan. 21, 1983.

For description of previous article, see SRI 1983 Annual, under A1250-1.446.

SOVIET GAS PIPELINE TO EUROPE STARTS UP

(p. 18) Article, with 1 table showing natural gas imports from USSR, and total consumption, for 4 Western European countries, 1982 and 1990. Data are from International Energy Agency.

EPA PROBES GROUNDWATER POLLUTION THREAT

(p. 20) Article, with 1 table showing number of waste liquid surface storage/treatment/disposal sites and impoundment areas, and sites assessed for safety by EPA, by selected industry group, 1979/80. Data are from EPA.

A1250–1.513: Feb. 13, 1984 (Vol. 62, No. 7)

R&D FUNDING WILL RISE 14% IN 1985 FEDERAL BUDGET, ANNUAL FEATURE

(p. 6-11) Annual article, by Janice R. Long et al., on Federal R&D budget proposal, 1985. Includes 12 tables showing the following for FY83-85:

a. R&D obligations and outlays, by agency, for total R&D, basic research, and R&D facilities.

b. R&D funding for 7 agencies, by subagency, institute, program, or academic discipline, with detail for NSF chemistry funding.

CHEMICAL FIRMS LURED BY THEIR OWN STOCK

(p. 14) Article on chemical companies' repurchase of their own stocks. Data are from the Conference Board. Includes 1 undated table showing number and value of shares repurchased, and reasons for repurchasing, for 10 chemical companies.

CHEMISTRY FACULTIES GAIN WOMEN SLOWLY

(p. 26) Article, with 1 table showing total and female faculty for chemistry depts with 3/more women, and faculty for depts with no women, by PhD-granting institution, 1982/83.

A1250–1.514: Feb. 20, 1984 (Vol. 62, No. 8)

CORRECTIONS

(p. 4) Data correction for article on world soap, detergent, and component material industries (for description, see A1250-1.511, above). Shows corrected data for Western European producers of fatty alcohols.

U.S. SPACE POLICY READY FOR NEXT BIG LEAP

(p. 9-16) By Wil Lepkowski. Article, with 2 charts and 1 table showing proposed NASA budget for FY85, total and for R&D, with distribution by function; and for space science, by detailed program.

CHEMICAL EARNINGS ALMOST DOUBLED IN FOURTH QUARTER, QUARTERLY FEATURE

(p. 18-23) Quarterly article, by William J. Storck, analyzing sales, earnings, and profit margins for major U.S. chemical producing companies, 4th quarter 1983.

Includes 4 tables showing top 10 chemical companies in sales, earnings, and profitability; sales, earnings, and profit margin, for 30 major chemical, 18 chemical-producing oil/gas, and 24 diversified chemical-producing companies; and chemical after-tax earnings for 8 major oil companies; 4th quarter and full year 1983, with selected comparisons to 1982.

MAN-MADE FIBERS RECOVERY TO CONTINUE

(p. 24) Article, with 1 table showing man-made and synthetic fiber production, for total world, U.S., Western Europe, and Japan, 1979-83. Data are from Enka, Netherlands.

CANADIAN CHEMICAL EARNINGS BOUNCED BACK IN 1983, QUARTERLY FEATURE

(p. 25) Quarterly report on Canadian chemical industry performance, 1983. Includes 1 table showing net sales, net income, and profit margin, for 4 largest companies, 1983 and percent change from 1982.

EPA BUDGET INCREASE HIGHEST FOR REGULATORY AGENCIES

(p. 29-30) Article, with 1 table showing Federal budget obligations for EPA, FDA, and OSHA, by function, FY83-85.

A1250–1.515: Feb. 27, 1984 (Vol. 62, No. 9)

WOMEN, MINORITIES MAKE GAINS IN SCIENCE

(p. 8) Article, with 2 tables showing distribution of employed chemists by sex and race, 1982. Data are from NSF report *Women and Minorities in Science and Engineering*.

UPDATE ON SCIENCE AND NATIONAL SECURITY REPORT FINDS LITTLE CHANGE

(p. 15-16) Article, with 1 undated table showing number of research reports generated for DOE/DOD/NASA by DOD labs, industry, universities, and nonprofit organizations, with distribution by security classification (classified, limited, and public).

A1250–1.516: Mar. 5, 1984 (Vol. 62, No. 10)

EARLY RETIREMENT INCENTIVE PLANS REMAIN CONTROVERSIAL

(p. 8-11) By David Webber. Article on corporate payroll cost containment measures, with focus on chemical firms. Data are from 490 major U.S. companies in 12 cities responding to a 1983 Hay Associates survey. Includes 1 table showing percent of respondents offering early retirement incentives, laying off workers, and initiating hiring and wage freezes, for each survey city, late 1981-late 1983 period.

A1250–1.517: Mar. 12, 1984 (Vol. 62, No. 11)

SOCAL TO ACQUIRE GULF: DEAL WILL CREATE BROAD CHEMICALS LINE

(p. 4-5) Article, with 1 table showing top 10 chemical producing oil companies, ranked by chemical sales, 1982.

DRUG PROFITS UP SOLIDLY IN 1983, QUARTERLY FEATURE

(p. 8) Quarterly article, with 1 table showing sales, earnings, and profit margin, for 14 pharmaceutical firms, 4th quarter and full year 1983, with percent change from 1982.

This is the 1st quarterly article.

STUDY CONFIRMS PAUCITY OF CHEMICAL TOXICITY DATA

(p. 12) Article on availability of information regarding potential health hazards of commercial chemicals. Data are from National Research Council. Includes 1 undated table showing number of chemical compounds and availability of toxicity data, for 7 chemical categories.

PETROCHEMICAL REPORT: NATURAL GAS LIQUIDS REMAIN STRONG PETROCHEMICAL FEEDSTOCK

(p. 17-38) By Bruce F. Greek. Article on petrochemical consumption, prices, and feedstocks. Data are from C&EN estimates and various industry and government sources.

Includes 1 chart and 3 tables showing consumption of ethylene and propylene, by end product; prices of basic petrochemicals and feedstocks, and distribution of olefin feedstocks, by type; and light gas oil steam-cracking percent yields for conventional and millisecond furnaces, by product type; various years 1973-90.

A1250–1.518: Mar. 19, 1984 (Vol. 62, No. 12)

UPTURN CONFIRMED IN CHEMICAL CAPITAL FUNDS

(p. 7-8) Article, with 1 table showing capital spending and appropriations for chemicals/allied products industry, quarterly 1983, with percent change from 1982. Data are from the Conference Board.

MORE BIOTECHNOLOGY FIRMS MAKING MONEY, QUARTERLY FEATURE

(p. 11) Quarterly article, with 1 table showing operating and total revenues, and earnings, for 14 biotechnology firms, 4th quarter 1983, with comparisons to 1982.

PROBLEMS BESET CARBOHYDRATE FEEDSTOCKS

(p. 12) Article, with 3 charts showing carbohydrate feedstock output, by end use; and market value of carbohydrate feedstocks used in products developed since 1945, by feedstock type and end use; all for 1983. Data are from L. Hepner and Associates, London.

A1250–1.519: Mar. 26, 1984 (Vol. 62, No. 13)

COMMERCE OUTLINES REAGAN TECHNOLOGY POLICY

(p. 25-26) Brief article, with 1 undated table showing percent of funding from industry sources for 11 university industrial technology centers, by institution. Includes related article (p. 24-25).

OUTLOOK HAZY FOR EMPLOYMENT IN ENERGY R&D

(p. 31-32) Article, with 1 table forecasting effect of Federal and private funding changes on energy R&D employment, by field, for PhD and bachelor/master's degree holders, 1983-88 period. Data are from DOE.

A1250–1.520: Apr. 2, 1984 (Vol. 62, No. 14)

ARCO COMPLETES RETREAT FROM MAJOR POLYOLEFINS

(p. 6) Article, with 1 undated table showing annual polypropylene capacity for 12 manufacturers. Data are from SRI International and industry estimates.

CHLOR-ALKALIES COME BACK STRONG FROM RECESSION: KEY CHEMICALS, ANNUAL FEATURE

(p. 18-21) Annual article, by Bruce F. Greek, reporting on supply and demand outlook for 3 chlor-alkalies: chlorine, caustic soda, and soda ash. Includes text statistics on major derivatives and/or end uses, foreign trade, prices, and commercial value.

UNIVERSITY RESEARCH COSTING CHANGES URGED

(p. 27) Article, with 1 table showing NIH funding for university research, and amount of funding allocated for expenses other than direct research costs, 1972-82. Data are from General Accounting Office.

A1250–1.521: Apr. 9, 1984 (Vol. 62, No. 15)

AAAS R&D ANALYSIS: FEDERAL FUNDING VULNERABLE TO CUTS

(p. 6) Article, with 1 table showing Federal funding for chemistry R&D by agency, with detail by subject area, 1983-85. Data are from American Assn for the Advancement of Science.

ADDITIVES WIDEN REFINERS' OPTIONS IN MAKING GASOLINES

(p. 13-14) Article, with 1 undated table showing costs of using octane-boosting additives for refining/blending gasoline, by additive type and gasoline grade. Data are from Ethyl Corp.

EPA STUDY BACKS CUT IN LEAD USE IN GAS

(p. 18) Article, with 1 table showing costs and benefits of reducing and eliminating leaded additives in gasoline by 1988, including reductions in emissions by type. Data are from EPA's Office of Policy Analysis.

PESTICIDES HEAD FOR RECOVERY

(p. 35-59) By William J. Storck. Article on trends and outlook for the pesticide industry. Data are from Predicasts, Inc. and C&EN estimates. Includes 4 charts showing home/garden pesticide market volume, and pesticide shipment volume and value, with distribution by type of pesticide; and pesticide consumption, with distribution by end use; 1983.

A1250–1.522: Apr. 16, 1984 (Vol. 62, No. 16)

BIOTECHNOLOGY FIRMS' STOCKS HAVE FARED POORLY SINCE LAST FALL, RECURRING FEATURE

(p. 15) Recurring article, with 1 table showing stock prices for 18 biotechnology firms, as of Apr. 6, 1984, and 52-week high and low prices.

CANADIAN CHEMICALS SEE RISING DEMAND, SEMIANNUAL FEATURE

(p. 21) Semiannual article, with 1 table showing Canada's production of 15 chemicals, 1981-83. Data are from Statistics Canada.

A1250–1.523: Apr. 23, 1984 (Vol. 62, No. 17)

WOMEN CHEMISTS MORTALITY STUDY FINDS HIGH SUICIDE RATE

(p. 16-17) Article, with 1 table showing observed and expected deaths by cause, for laboratory, academic, and other women chemists. Data are from a National Cancer Institute study of 347 white women members of the American Chemical Society who died between 1925 and 1979.

JURY STILL OUT ON ADAPTING WESTERN PROCESSES FOR EASTERN SHALE

(p. 25-26) Article examining feasibility of applying western oil shale processing methods to eastern oil shale. Data are from Los Alamos National Laboratory. Includes 1 undated table showing product and operating cost, capital investment, oil production, and by-product income, for eastern shale processing, as estimated for 5 methods currently applied to western shale.

FEEDING THE UNDERDEVELOPED WORLD

(p. 32-39) By John W. Mellor and Richard H. Adams, Jr. Article, with 2 tables showing average annual imports of all major food crops, for developing countries by world region; and fertilizer subsidies and agricultural research funding, for 5 developed and 5 developing countries; various periods 1966-80.

A1250–1.524: Apr. 30, 1984 (Vol. 62, No. 18)

ELASTOMERS FINALLY RECOVER GROWTH

(p. 35-56) By Bruce F. Greek. Article on outlook and trends for the world rubber industry. Data are from International Institute of Synthetic Rubber Producers.

Includes 7 tables showing world synthetic rubber production and capacity by type, and natural and synthetic rubber consumption, with detail by country and world region; and rubber consumption of North American tire industry as percent of total, by rubber type; various years 1973-88.

A1250–1.525: May 7, 1984 (Vol. 62, No. 19)

C&EN's TOP 50 CHEMICAL PRODUCTS AND PRODUCERS, ANNUAL FEATURE

(p. 7-12) Annual report, by David Webber and William J. Storck, on chemical industry production, sales, assets, and earnings, including rankings of 50 leading chemicals and chemical producers, 1983. Data are derived from Federal Government, trade assn, and industry sources, and C&EN estimates.

Includes 2 tables showing top 50 chemicals ranked by production, 1982-83, with average annual change for selected periods 1973-83; and chemical sales, operating profit, profit margin, assets, and return on assets, for top 50 producers ranked by chemical sales, and including comparisons to total sales, profits, and assets, 1983 with comparisons to 1982.

Report on 2nd 50 largest companies is described below, under A1250-1.527.

STOCK MANEUVERINGS ARE RIFE IN CHEMICALS

(p. 18) Article on chemical companies' repurchase of their own stocks. Includes 1 table showing number and value of common or preferred shares repurchased, for 13 chemical companies, primarily 1st 4 months 1984.

URBANA, CHAPEL HILL TOP GRADUATE RANKINGS, ANNUAL FEATURE

(p. 43) Annual article on universities leading in number of chemistry graduates, 1982/83, based on the annual report of the American Chemical Society Committee on Professional Training, described below.

Includes 1 table showing number of chemistry graduates, by degree level and institution, for the 25-28 institutions graduating the most at each degree level, 1982/83.

ACS COMMITTEE ON PROFESSIONAL TRAINING, 1983 ANNUAL REPORT

(p. 44-49) Annual report on number of chemistry and chemical engineering undergraduate and graduate degrees awarded by 570 chemistry and 122 chemical engineering schools in 1982/83.

Includes 4 tables showing ACS-approved graduate programs and enrollment, fall 1982; graduates, by sex, 1983; schools reporting and graduates, 1979-83; and degrees awarded, by institution and/or campus, 1982/83; all by degree level.

Report also summarizes 1983 activities of the ACS Committee on Professional Training.

A1250–1.526: May 14, 1984 (Vol. 62, No. 20)

CHEMICAL INDUSTRY EARNINGS RETAIN VIGOR IN FIRST QUARTER, QUARTERLY FEATURE

(p. 10-13) Quarterly article, by David Webber, analyzing sales, earnings, and profit margins for major U.S. chemical producing companies, 1st quarter 1984.

Includes 4 tables showing top 10 chemical companies in sales, earnings, and profitability; sales, earnings, and profit margin, for 30 major chemical, 16 chemical-producing oil/gas, and 26 diversified chemical-producing companies; and chemical after-tax earnings for 6 major oil/gas companies; 1st quarter 1984, with selected comparisons to 1983.

CONTROVERSY SURROUNDING SYNFUELS CORP. INTENSIFIES

(p. 20-21) By David J. Hanson. Article on operations of U.S. Synthetic Fuels Corp. (SFC). Data are from SFC. Includes 1 table showing production capacity, type of resource under development, and amount and type of SFC assistance, for 11 energy projects, as of early 1984.

A1250–1.527: May 21, 1984 (Vol. 62, No. 21)

RESEARCH INSTRUMENTS: ONE FOURTH OF ACADEME'S ARE OBSOLETE

(p. 4) Article on condition and cost of academic research equipment. Data are from a 1982 NSF inventory of 22,300 pieces of equipment held by 43 universities. Includes 1 table showing distribution of equipment by age, purchase price, and technological status (including obsolete), 1982.

SALES, EARNINGS UP MODERATELY AT MEDIUM-SIZED CHEMICAL FIRMS, ANNUAL FEATURE

(p. 15-19) Annual article, by William J. Storck, on sales, assets, and earnings of the 2nd 50 largest chemical producers, 1983. Includes 1 chart and 3 tables showing the following:

a. Chemical sales, with distribution by company size group and type; and comparisons of 1st and 2nd 50 largest company groups, including financial performance, and number of chemical, petroleum/natural gas, diversified, and foreign owned companies; 1983.

b. Chemical sales, operating profit, profit margin, assets, and return on assets: for 2nd 50 largest chemical producers ranked by chemical sales, with comparisons to total sales, profits, and assets; and for top 100 chemical producers, arranged alphabetically; 1983 and selected comparisons to 1982.

Report on 50 largest producers is described under A1250-1.525, above.

POLYMER OUTPUT RECOUPED MUCH OF 1982's LOSSES, ANNUAL FEATURE

(p. 20-21) Annual article, by David Webber, with 1 table showing production of plastics, and synthetic fibers and rubber, by type, selected years 1973-83.

Previous data were included in the annual reports on top 50 chemical producers; for description of data for 1972-82, see SRI 1983 Annual, under A1250-1.424.

DRUG PROFITS CLIMB 12% OVERALL IN MIXED RESULTS, QUARTERLY FEATURE

(p. 22) Quarterly article, with 1 table showing sales, earnings, and profit margin, for 17 pharmaceutical firms, 1st quarter 1984 with comparison to 1983.

A1250–1.528: May 28, 1984 (Vol. 62, No. 22)

CHEMICAL PLANT CAPACITY USE CONTINUES COMEBACK, SEMIANNUAL FEATURE

(p. 9-13) Semiannual article, by William J. Storck and Bruce F. Greek, analyzing plant capacity utilization of basic chemical and polymer industries, 1st quarter 1984, with comparison to previous periods. Data are based on C&EN estimates, and industry and assn sources.

Includes 2 tables showing nameplate capacity, and nameplate and effective capacity utilization, for principal types of the following: petrochemicals; chlor-alkalies; acids; industrial gases; mineral-based inorganics; plastic, fiber, and adhesive/coating intermediates; pigments; solvents; plastics; and synthetic fibers; 1st and 3rd quarters 1983, and 1st quarter 1984.

CHEMICAL STOCKS FOLLOW MARKET DOWN, RECURRING FEATURE

(p. 20-21) Recurring article, by David Webber, with 2 tables showing C&EN chemical stock index compared to 8 major stock indexes; and stock price including 12-month high and low, price/earnings ratio, annual dividend, and dividend yield, for 29 chemical producers; all for May 18, 1984 with selected comparisons to 1983.

A1250–1.529: June 4, 1984 (Vol. 62, No. 23)

CHEMICAL PROFITABILITY CHANGED LITTLE IN 1983, ANNUAL FEATURE

(p. 17-19) Annual article, by William J. Storck, on profitability of chemical companies in 1983, based on C&EN survey of 36 largest companies.

Includes 4 tables showing profit margins; returns on investment, assets, and stockholders' equity; and rankings; by company, 1982-83.

SPECIALTY CHEMICALS: MIXED BAG FOR GROWTH

(p. 20-23) Article, with 2 tables showing specialty chemical sales, by type, 1983 and 1990, with average annual growth rate, including detail for high-growth chemicals, 1983-90 period. Data are from Strategic Analysis, Inc.

A1250–1.530: June 11, 1984 (Vol. 62, No. 24)

RECOVERY SLOWS FOR LARGE-VOLUME ACIDS: KEY CHEMICALS, ANNUAL FEATURE

(p. 10-12) Annual article, by Bruce F. Greek, reporting on supply and demand outlook for sulfuric and phosphoric acids. Includes text statistics on major end uses, foreign trade, prices, and commercial value, 1984.

PRODUCT SALES BUOY BIOTECHNOLOGY REVENUES, QUARTERLY FEATURE

(p. 13) Quarterly article, with 1 table showing operating and total revenues, and earnings, for 12 biotechnology firms, 1st quarter 1984, with comparisons to 1983.

STUDY INDICATES SOME IMPROVEMENT IN U.S. SCIENCE EDUCATION

(p. 26-28) By James H. Krieger. Article on science knowledge of 5th and 9th grade students. Data are based on achievement test results of 4,867 students for the Second International Science Study (SISS), sponsored by International Assn for the Evaluation of Educational Achievment. Includes 2 tables showing average test results, 1983, with selected comparisons to 1970.

FACTS AND FIGURES FOR THE CHEMICAL INDUSTRY ANNUAL REPORT

(p. 32-74) Annual fact book, for 1983, on U.S. chemical industry production, finances, performance, employment, and trade, with selected data for related industries and foreign countries.

Data are from government agency, trade assn, and manufacturers' reports, and include trends from 1973.

Includes 6 sections, with subsections for foreign countries, each presenting a narrative summary with text statistics, and the tables described below.

This is the 28th annual report.

PRODUCTION

(p. 34-40) "Output Makes a Strong Recovery." Includes 12 tables showing:

a. Production for 50 largest volume chemicals, 1982-83, and average annual percent change, selected periods 1973-83, by chemical ranked by volume. 1 table.

b. Industrial production indexes for manufacturing; nondurable manufacturing; chemicals, synthetic materials, and chemical products, by type; petroleum products; and rubber/plastics products; 1973-83. 1 table.

c. Production and/or consumption of minerals, including iodine and potash imports, and phosphate rock exports; and production of organic and inorganic chemicals, man-made fibers, plastics, and synthetic rubber; by detailed product, 1973-83. 6 tables.

d. Fertilizer supply and demand by type, including imports and exports; and nitrogen and phosphate production, by detailed product; various years 1973-83. 4 tables.

FINANCES

(p. 41-55) "Earnings Rise but Profitability Is Still Low." Includes 13 tables showing:

a. Chemical sales, operating profits, profit margin, assets, and return on assets, for 100 largest chemical producers ranked by sales, 1983 with selected comparisons to 1982 and to total company operations. 1 table.

b. Shipment value for all manufacturing, and selected chemicals/allied products and related industries; and PPI for all commodities, industrial commodities, 8 sectors of chemical/allied products industry, and rubber/plastic products; 1973-83. 2 tables.

c. Chemical industry balance sheet, 1982-83; long-term debt, stockholders' equity, and debt/equity ratio for industrial chemicals/synthetics, chemicals/allied products, and all manufacturing, 1973-83; and cash flow by fund sources and applications, aggregated for 12 major chemical companies, 1979-83. 3 tables.

d. Selected operating ratios for 18 companies with sales over $1 billion and 18 companies with sales less than $1 billion, 1982-83. 1 table.

e. Capital spending, unspent capital funds, and foreign investment, for all manufacturing, and chemical and 2-6 other industries; and chemical industry capital and R&D spending, for 14-15 companies; various years 1973-84. 5 tables.

f. Company financial profiles, including net sales, net income, total assets, plant/equipment value, capital expenditures, net worth, stock data, and selected operating ratios, for 33 chemical and 16 pharmaceutical companies, 1980-83. 1 table.

Data correction for this section appears in Aug. 27, 1984 issue (see A1250-1.540, below).

EFFICIENCY

(p. 56-58) "Productivity Up as Capacity Use Improves." Includes 6 tables showing:

a. Productivity indexes for chemicals/allied products and all manufacturing, and plant utilization rate for chemicals, all manufacturing, and 4 chemical process industries, 1973-83; and plant capacity and utilization rate for 14 organic and 11 inorganic chemicals, selected quarters 1981-1st quarter 1984. 3 tables.

b. Energy use by chemical, fertilizer, and petroleum industries, by energy source, 1972 and 1980-83. 3 tables.

EMPLOYMENT

(p. 59-60) "Little Growth Yet for Chemical Workforce." Includes 4 tables showing:

a. Total employees and production workers, workweek, and wages, for all manufacturing and 10 chemical industries, 1973 and 1981-83; and scientist/engineer employment, total and for 5 chemical industries, 1973-83. 2 tables.

b. Chemical employment for 23 companies, and aggregate sales per employee, 1974-83. 1 table.

FOREIGN TRADE

(p. 61-62) "U.S. Chemical Surplus Continues To Narrow." Includes 5 tables showing U.S. chemical exports and imports by product type; and U.S. and world chemical exports and imports, by country or world area of origin and destination; 1973 and 1981-83.

FOREIGN CHEMICAL INDUSTRIES

Western Europe

(p. 63-65) Includes 4 tables showing:

a. Chemical industry sales, exports, imports, capital spending, production and price indexes, and employment, for 10 countries; man-made fiber production for Benelux and 9 countries; and production by chemical, for 4 countries; various years 1979-83. 3 tables.

b. Major company net sales, net income, profit margin, capital and R&D spending, and employment, for 18 companies in 8 countries, 1980-83. 1 table.

Also includes 1 table showing European currency conversion values, by country, 1979-83.

Japan

(p. 66-67) Includes 4 tables showing the following for Japan:

a. Total and chemical exports and imports; production, shipment, and inventory indexes for all manufacturing, chemicals, and 5 chemical process industries; and production of chemicals and plastics by type, and synthetic dyes and rubber; various years 1980-83. 3 tables.

b. Company sales, net income, profit margin, total assets, and employment, for 23 chemical companies, 1980-83. 1 table.

Canada

(p. 68-69) Includes 7 tables showing the following for Canada:

a. Company sales, net income, profit margin, capital expenditures, and employment, for 5 companies; and chemical production and trade, by chemical or product type; various years 1980-83. 5 tables.

b. Shipments and price indexes, for all manufacturing, chemicals/chemical products, and selected chemical process industries; various years 1980-83. 2 tables.

Mexico

(p. 70) Includes 3 tables showing Mexican chemical production, domestic sales, and imports, by chemical, 1980-83.

Eastern Europe

(p. 71-72) Includes 5 tables showing:

a. Production growth rate for all industries and chemical/rubber industry; and production of man-made fibers, agricultural chemicals, and various other chemical products; for 7 countries, various years 1979-83. 4 tables.

b. Soviet total and chemical exports and imports, 1973-83. 1 table.

Western Pacific

(p. 73-74) Includes 11 tables showing the following, mostly for 1980-83:

a. South Korea production, shipment, and inventory indexes for all manufacturing and for chemicals by product type; chemical production by product; and total and chemical exports and imports. 3 tables.

b. Australia and PRC chemical production, and total and/or chemical exports and imports, by chemical or product type. 5 tables.

c. Taiwan production indexes for all manufacturing and for chemicals by product type, production by chemical, and total and chemical exports and imports.

A1250–1.531: June 18, 1984 (Vol. 62, No. 25)

HOUSE ACTING FAST ON FISCAL 1985 MONEY BILLS

(p. 17-18) By Janice R. Long. Article, with 1 table showing R&D funding for 6 Federal agencies, by subagency, institute, or program, actual FY84 and Administration request and House appropriation for FY85.

ADDITIVES SALES BUOYED BY PVC RECOVERY

(p. 27-52) By Stephen C. Stinson. Article, with 2 tables showing polyvinyl chloride (PVC) consumption by end use, 1984, and PVC plasticizer additive prices by type, 1982. Data are from USITC and other sources.

Also includes 2 tables showing ratings of heat stabilizer suitability and plasticizer performance.

A1250–1.532: June 25, 1984 (Vol. 62, No. 26)

UNIVERSITY/INDUSTRY RESEARCH TIES STILL VIEWED WITH CONCERN

(p. 7-11) By Wil Lepkowski. Article, with 1 table showing 12 universities ranked by total R&D funding and amount supplied by industry, as of FY82. Data are from NSF.

UPSWING CONTINUES IN DEMAND FOR THERMOPLASTICS: KEY CHEMICALS, ANNUAL FEATURE

(p. 13-18) Annual article, by Bruce F. Greek, reporting on supply and demand outlook for 5 major thermoplastics: low- and high-density polyethylene, polyvinyl chloride, polypropylene, and polystyrene. Includes text statistics on major fabricated forms, foreign trade, prices, and commercial value, 1984.

U.S., CANADA WEIGH POSSIBILITY OF PETROCHEMICAL FREE TRADE

(p. 19-21) By Earl V. Anderson. Article, with 1 table showing value of chemical imports from Canada vs. total chemical imports, by type of chemical, 1983. Data are from Census Bureau.

A1250–1.533: July 2, 1984 (Vol. 62, No. 27)

BIOTECHNOLOGY STOCKS STILL FLOUNDERING, RECURRING FEATURE

(p. 9) Recurring article, with 1 table showing stock prices for 17 biotechnology firms, as of June 15, 1984, and 52-week high and low prices.

CONFERENCE MULLS EUROPE'S SPECIALTIES PROSPECTS

(p. 14) Article, with 1 undated table showing chemical sales by category (specialty, fine, pseudo-commodity, and commodity), for Europe, U.S., and all other. Data are from Charles H. Kline and Co.

ALTHOUGH UNEMPLOYMENT DIPS THIS YEAR, SALARY GAINS ARE SLIM, ANNUAL FEATURE

(p. 27-32) Annual article on chemists' employment and earnings as of Mar. 1984, with trends. Data are based on over 10,000 responses to an American Chemical Society member survey.

Includes 10 tables showing employment status of chemical engineers, and of chemists by sex, highest degree, and minority status; chemists' salaries, by degree level, by years since bachelor's degree, sex, type of employer, major manufacturing group, number of subordinates, job function and specialty, and academic rank; and chemists' unemployment rate, by age and most recent type of employer, job function, and specialty; 1984, with selected trends from 1974.

Full ACS survey report is covered in SRI under A1250-4.

A1250–1.534: July 9, 1984 (Vol. 62, No. 28)

EUROPEAN ZEOLITE MAKERS BANK ON CATALYSTS, DETERGENTS

(p. 14-15) By Patricia L. Layman. Article, with 1 table showing European zeolite (water softeners/adsorbents) demand, 1984; and nameplate capacity, with detail by manufacturer (no date); all by type of zeolite. Data are from industry and C&EN estimates.

A1250–1.535: July 16, 1984 (Vol. 62, No. 29)

LARGE-VOLUME FUEL MARKET STILL ELUDES METHANOL

(p. 9-16) By Earl V. Anderson. Article on outlook and trends for the world methanol industry. Data are from Ethyl Corp. and DeWitt and Co.

Includes 1 chart and 3 tables showing costs of using octane-boosting additives for refining/blending gasoline, by additive type and gasoline grade (no date); existing and/or new methanol capacity, by country and U.S. company, various years 1983-85; and distribution of world methanol output from new capacity by destination (domestic use, and export by region), 1986.

MIDDLE EAST WILL BECOME MAJOR ETHYLENE SUPPLIER

(p. 19-20) Article, with 1 table showing ethylene and propylene capacity and/or production and consumption, by country or world region, 1982 and 1990. Data are from Shell International Chemical Co.

BUDGETS SET FOR MANY FEDERAL R&D AGENCIES

(p. 24, 29) Article, with 1 table showing R&D and related funding for 4 Federal agencies, by program category, actual FY84, and Administration request and congressional appropriation for FY85.

A1250–1.536: July 23, 1984 (Vol. 62, No. 30)

ENVIRONMENT COUNCIL REPORT STRESSES R&D

(p. 16) Article, with 1 undated table showing Federal research spending for environmental health, ecological systems and processes, and technology, by agency. Data are from Council on Environmental Quality.

Facts and Figures for Chemical R&D, Annual Feature

(p. 36-68) Annual report, for 1984, on chemical R&D spending and employment in the Federal, industrial, and university sectors.

Most data are from NSF and from C&EN estimates based on Federal Government statistics, and include trends from selected previous years.

Includes introductory article, and 4 statistical sections, described below.

This is the 6th annual report.

SECTION 1: OVERVIEW

(p. 38-41) "R&D Funding To Rise 11% This Year." Includes 5 charts and 10 tables showing the following:

a. Spending for total R&D, basic and applied research, and development, with distribution by sector, 1983; distribution of R&D outlays, by selected Federal functions, and for total nonfederal, 1965-84; and R&D funding and spending by sector, and funding by character of research, in current and constant 1972 dollars, 1974-84. 5 charts and 7 tables.

b. Employed scientists and engineers, by type, 1982; and distribution of research papers in *Chemical Abstracts* by subject field, and number of U.S. patents granted to U.S. and foreign residents, various years 1973-83. 3 tables.

SECTION 2: FEDERAL GOVERNMENT

(p. 44-52) "Defense Wins Most of This Year's Increase." Includes 1 chart and 17 tables showing the following:

a. Federal obligations: for total R&D, basic and applied research (with detail for chemistry and physical science), development, and engineering and chemical engineering research, by dept or agency; and for total research and university total and basic research, by scientific discipline; various years FY78-84. 9 tables.

b. Dept/agency R&D budgets, for DOE, NSF, EPA, NASA, DOD, and NIH, FY82-84, and FY85 appropriation or probable authorization, and Administration request; and Federal Government scientists and engineers, by discipline, 1972-83, with 1983 detail by dept or agency. 1 chart and 8 tables.

SECTION 3: INDUSTRY

(p. 53-56) "Growth Slows a Bit for Industrial R&D." Includes 7 charts and 9 tables showing the following:

a. Federally and company funded industrial R&D; foreign R&D spending by U.S. companies; R&D spending for 15 major chemical companies; and distribution of R&D spending by company employment and R&D budget size; with detail for selected chemical industries; various years 1973-84. 6 charts and 5 tables.

b. R&D scientist/engineer employment, cost per employee, and comparisons to total employment, with detail for selected chemical industries, various years 1971-83; and employment distribution for R&D scientists/engineers in 1983 and chemists in 1984, both by industry sector, with detail by chemists' degree level. 1 chart and 4 tables.

SECTION 4: UNIVERSITIES AND COLLEGES

(p. 65-68) "Growth in Federal Support Slackens." Includes 1 chart and 10 tables showing the following:

a. University R&D spending, by funding source and research type and field, 1973-83; top 12 universities and university R&D centers ranked by R&D spending, with detail by research field, FY82 (table on R&D centers incorrectly reads FY81); and total and full-time university scientists and engineers, by field, 1976-78 and 1980-83. 7 tables.

b. Top 50 universities ranked by chemical R&D spending, and including federally financed spending, 1982 with comparisons to 1979-81; regional distribution of academic physical scientists in 1983 and physical science R&D spending in FY82; chemistry and chemical engineering degrees awarded, by level, 1965/66-1981/82; and total and full-time science and engineering graduate students, by field, 1976-82. 1 chart and 3 tables.

A1250–1.537: July 30, 1984 (Vol. 62, No. 31)

SUPERFUND REWRITE: FIRMS SAY HOUSE TAX BILL OUTRAGEOUS

(p. 4-5) Article on proposed changes in taxes designed to finance Hazardous Waste Re-sponse Trust Fund (Superfund). Includes 1 table showing tax rates on 51 feedstock chemicals, actual 1984 and as proposed in legislation before the House of Representatives, Aug. 1984.

FLAVORS AND FRAGRANCES INDUSTRY FACES SEASON OF CONSOLIDATION

(p. 7-13) By Patricia L. Layman. Article, with 4 charts showing flavor and fragrance material sales, with distribution by end use, and aggregate distribution by type of material and world region, 1984; and flavor/fragrance market shares for synthetics and naturals, 1900, 1970, and 1990. Data are from industry sources.

MINERAL-BASED INORGANICS STRUGGLE OUT OF RECESSION: KEY CHEMICALS, ANNUAL FEATURE

(p. 15-19) Annual article, by Bruce F. Greek, reporting on supply and demand outlook for 4 inorganic chemicals: lime, sulfur, potash, and phosphorus. Includes text statistics on major derivatives and/or end uses, foreign trade, prices, and commercial value, 1984.

A1250–1.538: Aug. 6, 1984 (Vol. 62, No. 32)

WORLD BANK MAY ELIMINATE ITS TECHNOLOGY ADVISORY FUNCTION

(p. 15-17) By Wil Lepkowski. Article, with 1 table showing World Bank loan amounts, by type of project funded, FY83. Data are from World Bank.

A1250–1.539: Aug. 20, 1984 (Vol. 62, No. 34)

CHEMICAL FIRMS POST STRONG GAINS IN SECOND QUARTER, QUARTERLY FEATURE

(p. 12-17) Quarterly article, by William J. Storck, analyzing sales, earnings, and profit margins for major U.S. chemical producing companies, 2nd quarter 1984.

Includes 3 tables showing top 10-11 chemical companies in sales, earnings, and profitability; sales, earnings, and profit margin, for 30 major chemical, 17 chemical-producing oil/gas, and 25 diversified chemical-producing companies; 2nd quarter and 1st half 1984, with selected comparisons to 1983.

PROFITS UP SHARPLY FOR CANADIAN CHEMICALS, QUARTERLY FEATURE

(p. 18) Quarterly report on Canadian chemical industry performance, 1983. Includes 1 table showing net sales, net income, and profit margin, for 4 largest companies, 1st half 1984 with comparisons to 1983.

CUSTOM SYNTHESIS EXPANDING FOR DRUGS AND INTERMEDIATES

(p. 25-60) By Stephen C. Stinson. Article, with 1 table showing value of drug consumption, imports, and exports, by type of drug, 1978-82. Data are from USITC.

A1250–1.540: Aug. 27, 1984 (Vol. 62, No. 35)

CORRECTIONS

(p. 2) Includes correction of June 11, 1984 table on chemical sales, profits, and assets for 100 largest chemical producers. Presents data for 1 company. Original table appears in the Finances section of Facts and Figures Report; for description, see A1250-1.530, above.

DRUG COMPANY EARNINGS ROSE 13% IN SECOND QUARTER, QUARTERLY FEATURE

(p. 9-10) Quarterly article, with 1 table showing sales, earnings, and profit margin, for 17 pharmaceutical firms, 2nd quarter and 1st half 1984 with comparisons to 1983.

HIGHER COSTS IN STORE FOR PIGMENTED PLASTICS

(p. 10) Article, with 1 table showing supply and demand for polyethylene, by type, 1985 and 1988. Data are from Novacor Chemicals, Canada.

A1250–1.541: Sept. 3, 1984 (Vol. 62, No. 36)

SLUMPING SYNTHETIC FIBERS MAY GET HELP FROM IMPORT LIMITS: KEY POLYMERS, ANNUAL FEATURE

(p. 11-14) Annual article, by Bruce F. Greek, reporting on supply and demand outlook for 3 synthetic fibers: polyester, nylon, and acrylic. Includes text statistics on major end uses, foreign trade, prices, and commercial value, 1984.

Also includes 2 charts showing trade volume for man-made fiber apparel, with distribution by country or world region, 1977 and 1983.

A1250–1.542: Sept. 24, 1984 (Vol. 62, No. 39)

PHENOL, VINYL ACETATE FACE TIGHTENING SUPPLY: KEY CHEMICALS, ANNUAL FEATURE

(p. 10-12) Annual article, by Bruce F. Greek, reporting on supply and demand outlook for 2 major adhesive and coating ingredients: phenol and vinyl acetate. Includes text statistics on major derivatives and end uses, foreign trade, prices, and commercial value, 1984.

For description of previous article, for 1983, see A1250-1.507, above.

A1250–1.543: Oct. 1, 1984 (Vol. 62, No. 40)

RECESSION'S HARM TO CHEMICAL EMPLOYMENT DETAILED BY NEW DATA

(p. 10-11) By William J. Storck. Article, with 2 charts and 1 table showing chemical industry employment, total and for women and production workers, by sector, 1979 and 1982-83, with summary comparison to total manufacturing employment, 1983. Data are from Labor Dept.

BIOTECHNOLOGY REVENUES SURGED IN SECOND QUARTER, QUARTERLY FEATURE

(p. 12) Quarterly article, with 1 table showing revenues, earnings, and profit margin, for 15 biotechnology firms, 2nd quarter and 1st half 1984, with comparisons to 1983.

COATINGS INDUSTRY HEADING FOR RECORD YEAR, ANNUAL FEATURE

(p. 51-92, passim) Annual article, by David Webber, on trends and outlook for the paint (coating) industry. Data are from Commerce Dept. Includes 1 chart showing volume and value of paint shipments, with distribution by end use, 1983.

A1250–1.544: Oct. 8, 1984 (Vol. 62, No. 41)

CHEMICAL PLANT CAPACITY USE CONTINUES STEADY RISE, SEMIANNUAL FEATURE

(p. 9-12) Semiannual article, by William J. Storck and Bruce F. Greek, analyzing plant capacity utilization of basic chemical and polymer industries, 3rd quarter 1984, with comparison to previous periods. Data are based on C&EN estimates, and industry and assn sources.

Includes 2 tables showing nameplate capacity, and nameplate and effective capacity utilization, for principal types of the following: petrochemicals; chlor-alkalies; acids; industrial gases; mineral-based inorganics; plastic, fiber, and adhesive/coating intermediates; pigments; solvents; plastics; and synthetic fibers; 3rd quarter 1983, and 1st and 3rd quarters 1984.

A1250–1.545: Oct. 15, 1984 (Vol. 62, No. 42)

VINYL SIDING POISED FOR MAJOR GROWTH

(p. 13) Article, with 1 table showing consumption of home siding by type of material, 1983, 1988, and 1992, with average annual percent change for selected periods 1983-95. Data are from Predicasts, Inc.

A1250–1.546: Oct. 22, 1984 (Vol. 62, No. 43)

1985 EMPLOYMENT OUTLOOK, ANNUAL FEATURE

Annual compilation of articles on career planning and job market outlook for chemical professionals. Includes a brief introduction (p. 29), and the statistical article described below. Feature for 1984 was nonstatistical; for description of feature for 1983, see SRI 1982 Annual, under A1250-1.349.

UNDERGRADUATE STUDIES

(p. 30-38) Article examining chemists' opinions on importance of selected chemistry courses and other disciplines in current undergraduate chemistry programs and in their own undergraduate studies. Data are based on approximately 10,600 responses to an American Chemical Society member survey. Includes 2 tables.

A1250–2   1983 SURVEY REPORT: Starting Salaries and Employment Status of Chemistry and Chemical Engineering Graduates
Annual.   Dec. 1983.
v+67 p.
SRI/MF/complete

Annual report on starting salaries, employment status, and advanced study plans of 1982/83 chemistry and chemical engineering graduates, by highest degree, sex, certification status (for chemists only), and degree or planned study field.

Also includes data by professional experience, employer type, census division, citizenship status, age, number of job offers, race, and ethnicity (American Indian, Asian, and Hispanic); and various cross-tabulations. Salaries generally are shown as medians and means.

Data are from responses of 3,352 graduates to a summer 1983 survey.

Contains contents listing (p. iii); summary with 5 tables (p. 1-11); technical notes and table listing (p. 13-17); survey results, in 6 sections, with 46 tables (p. 18-63); and questionnaire facsimile (p. 65-67).

Availability: American Chemical Society, Distribution Office, 1155 16th St., NW, Washington DC 20036, $10.00; SRI/MF/complete.

A1250–4   SALARIES 1984: Analysis of the American Chemical Society's 1984 Survey of Salaries and Employment
Annual.   July 1984.
iv+118 p.
SRI/MF/complete

Annual report, for 1984, on chemists' and chemical engineers' salaries by years since bachelor's degree and employment status, by highest degree earned.

Chemists' salaries are also cross-tabulated by sex, type of employer (including private industry, government, selected manufacturing group, and colleges/universities by type), census division, selected State and ACS region, number of subordinates, work function (including research, R&D, marketing, forensic, and consulting), field of specialty, and academic rank in college/university.

Chemist employment status data include additional cross-tabulations by age, race and ethnic group (including American Indian, Asian/Pacific Islander, and Hispanic), citizenship, and number of months unemployed.

Data are from 10,644 responses to a Feb.-May 1984 survey of ACS members.

Contains contents listing and introduction (p. iii-iv); summary, methodology, table listing, and technical notes (p. 1-11); 100 report tables (p. 14-114); and facsimile questionnaire (p. 115-118).

Availability: American Chemical Society, Distribution Office, 1155 16th St., NW, Washington DC 20036, $75.00; SRI/MF/complete.

A1275
American
College of Surgeons

A1275–1   SOCIO-ECONOMIC FACTBOOK FOR SURGERY, 1983-84
Annual.   1983.   105 p.
SRI/MF/not filmed

Annual fact book of the surgical profession for 1983, presenting data on surgeon supply, specialties, finances, operative procedures, and education, with comparisons to other medical specialties, various years 1950-82. Also includes data on hospital utilization, health expenditures and insurance, medical costs, and general population characteristics.

Data were compiled by the American College of Surgeons (ACS) Surgical Practice Dept from reports of medical assns, Federal agencies, and related professional sources.

Contains contents/chart/table listing (p. 3-5); statistical sections A-F, with 8 charts and 39 tables, listed below (p. 7-65); and narrative sections G-I, with descriptions of related medical commissions and boards, HHS organization chart, list of congressional committees with health jurisdiction, Federal health legislation, and ACS policy statements (p. 67-105).

Availability: American College of Surgeons, Surgical Practice Department, 55 E. Erie St., Chicago IL 60611, †; SRI/MF/not filmed.

CHARTS AND TABLES:
[Data by surgical specialty are generally shown for colon/rectal, general, neurological, orthopedic, plastic, and thoracic surgery; obstetrics/gynecology; ophthalmology; otolaryngology; and urology. All data are shown for U.S.]

A1275–1.1: Sections A-B: Medical Education and Surgical Manpower

MEDICAL EDUCATION

1-2. Number of operational medical schools, and [total and female] medical students and medical school graduates; and number of filled residency positions [total and foreign medical graduates in primary care, all specialties, and surgical specialties; selected years 1949/50-1982/83]. (p. 8-9)

3-4. Filled 1st year surgical residency positions [by specialty], and filled 1st year primary care residency positions [by type of practice], 1973/74-1982/83. (p. 10-11)

SURGICAL MANPOWER

[Data by major professional activity include office- and hospital-based patient care, medical teaching, administration, research, and other.]

5-6. Number of Federal/non-Federal physicians [chart] and per 100,000 population [total, surgeons, and primary care physicians, various years 1950-81]. (p. 14-15)

7. Federal/non-Federal surgeons by specialty and major professional activity, 1981. (p. 16)

8-11. Active women surgeons and foreign medical graduates by surgical specialty and major professional activity, 1970 and 1980-81. (p. 17-20)

12-13. Annual certificates issued in surgical and nonsurgical specialties, 1973-82. (p. 21-22)

14. Total ACS fellowship [active and retired membership by specialty], Dec. 1982. (p. 23)

15. ACS [active] fellows and initiates [in general surgery and other specialties], 1973-82. (p. 24)

A1275–1.2: Section C: Selected Data on Hospitals and Use of Services

16-18. Total and short-term non-Federal hospitals, beds, and admissions; and short-term non-Federal hospital [outpatient visits, occupancy rate, average length of stay], assets, expenses, and personnel; [selected years 1950-82]. (p. 26-28)

19. Number of patients discharged from short-stay hospitals with and without operation [by patient age group and sex, census region, and hospital bed size group], 1981. (p. 29)

20. Rate of discharges from short-stay hospitals, by diagnostic class and age, 1981. [chart] (p. 30)

21. Ten most frequent operative procedures [and rate per 1,000 population], 1974-81. (p. 32)

22. Cardiovascular operations and procedures [by type], 1980-81. (p. 34)

23. Operative procedures [and rate per 1,000 population, and average length of stay], by patient age, 1974-81. (p. 35)

24. Average length of stay for selected operative procedures [and number performed], 1981. (p. 37)

25. Patient visits to office-based physicians [by specialty], 1981. (p. 38)

26. Settings used by physicians who perform ambulatory surgery [distribution among hospital-based and freestanding ambulatory surgery centers, and physician offices, by type of practice], 1982. (p. 39)

A1275–1.3: Section D: Medical Economics
[Tables and charts 27-33 show data decennially 1950-80 and 1982.]

27-29. National health expenditures: [total, and personal health care portion financed by private and public sources; percent distribution] by object; and as percent of GNP. [1 table and 2 charts] (p. 42-44)

30-31. Percent of Federal budget outlays, by function; and percent of personal spending, by product. (p. 45-46)

32-33. Ratio of personal spending for medical care to disposable personal income and to total personal spending [and total amounts]; and sources of funds for personal health expenditures [direct consumer payments, insurance benefits, public, and other]. [1 table and 1 chart] (p. 47-48)

34-35. CPI for selected and medical care items, [selected years 1950-82]. (p. 49-50)

36. Annual percentage change in CPI [by item, selected years 1960/61-1981/82]. (p. 51)

37. Average net income from medical practice by specialty [selected years 1970-82]. (p. 52)

38. Average physician professional expenses by specialty, 1982. [chart] (p. 53)

A1275–1.4: Sections E-F: Health Insurance and Population Characteristics

HEALTH INSURANCE

39-40. Number of persons with private health insurance protection for hospital and surgical care [under Blue Cross-Blue Shield, commercial insurance, and independent plan coverage]; and benefit payments of private health insurance organizations [Blue Cross-Blue Shield/other plans, and commercial insurance companies; decennially 1950-80 and 1981]. (p. 56-57)

41. Number of persons with private health insurance protection by type of coverage and percent of population covered [for ages under 65 and 65/over], 1981. (p. 58)

42-43. Medicaid recipients and payments, and Medicare enrollment and benefit payments, [selected years 1970-82]. (p. 59-60)

POPULATION CHARACTERISTICS

44. Total resident population, and life expectancy at birth [by sex, decennially 1950-80 and 1981]. (p. 62)

45. Percentage distribution of resident population by age [decennially 1960-80 and 1981]. [chart] (p. 63)

46. Trends in death rates [including infant and maternal, and for 6 leading causes, selected years 1920-81]. (p. 64)

47. Median income for families, and [for] individuals [by sex, decennially 1950-80 and 1981]. [chart] (p. 65)

A1305
American Correctional Association

A1305–1 NATIONAL JAIL AND ADULT DETENTION DIRECTORY, 1983-85
Biennial. 1983. xv+343 p.
ISSN 0172-8228.
ISBN 0-942974-49-2.
LC 79-643153.
SRI/MF/complete, delayed

Biennial statistical directory of jails and adult detention facilities, for 1983. Includes data on jail personnel and salaries, and characteristics of inmates and jails.

Directory lists 3,172 facilities and presents data for 2,775 facilities responding to an ACA survey.

Contains contents listing, user guide, and questionnaire facsimile (p. xi-xvi); directory statistics, described below (p. 1-315); article on jail design and management (p. 318-321); bibliography (p. 323-327); list of State jail inspection officials and agencies (p. 330-331); and ACA information and publications list (p. 333-443).

This is the 3rd edition of the directory. Previous directory, for 1981, is described in SRI 1982 Annual under this number.

Availability: American Correctional Association, 4321 Hartwick Rd., Suite L-208, College Park MD 20740, $25.00; SRI/MF/complete, delayed shipment in May 1984.

DIRECTORY STATISTICS:

Directory shows the following data for 1 Federal detention center, 5 metro correctional centers, and local jails arranged by State:

a. Starting salary range for 5 positions; and total staff.

b. Total and capital budget, FY83; construction appropriations, FY84; year of facility construction and last renovation; security classification; and inmate capacity.

c. Average inmate population, for adults and juveniles by sex, and for whites, blacks, Hispanics, and other.

A1305–3 1984 JUVENILE AND ADULT CORRECTIONAL DEPARTMENTS, INSTITUTIONS, AGENCIES, AND PAROLING AUTHORITIES
Annual. 1984. xxxvi+529 p.
ISBN 0-942974-51-4.
LC 79-1870.
SRI/MF/complete, delayed

Annual statistical directory of U.S. and Canadian correctional facilities, as of July 1983. Includes data on inmates, cost of care, personnel, and death sentences, by facility and/or State. Data are primarily from ACA surveys.

Contents:

a. Foreword, user's guide, and contents listing. (p. v-viii)

b. Information summaries, with 2 charts including State/Federal prisoner trends 1904-83, and 14 tables listed below. (p. x-xxxvi)

c. Directories of correctional facilities and parole services, by agency and type within each jurisdiction, generally including each facility's inmate capacity and average 1983 population, programs available, cost of care, and/or number of employees; grouped by State, U.S. territory, Federal agency including military branches, and for Canada Federal institutions and by Province, as of July 1, 1983. (p. 1-452)

d. Index, and ACA organization and activities. (p. 453-527)

This is the 44th edition of the directory.

Availability: American Correctional Association, 4321 Hartwick Rd., Suite L-208, College Park MD 20740, $35.00 or 20% discount with purchase of any 2 or more Assn. directories; SRI/MF/complete, delayed shipment with SRI 1984 Annual.

TABLES:

[Tables show data as of July 1983, unless otherwise noted. Data by race/ethnicity include Hispanics. Tables show data by sex.

All tables except table [12] show data by State, and variously include D.C., Philadelphia, New York City, Cook County, Ill., Federal Bureau of Prisons, U.S. prison or parole commission, Guam, Puerto Rico, and occasionally other U.S. territories. Tables [1-7] include data for Correctional Services of Canada and/or Canada by Province.]

[1] Fiscal information [adult and juvenile corrections operational budget, capital expenditures, and projects]. (p. x-xi)

[2] Adult inmate population [by race/ethnicity and security level]. (p. xiv)

[3] Juveniles under supervision [in institutions, by race/ethnicity; and in detention, group homes, and day/foster care]. (p. xvi)

[4] Clients on probation and parole or aftercare [adult and juvenile]. (p. xviii)

[5] Offender statistics [number committed but pending in county/other facilities, under 18 in adult systems, in furlough program, on work release, and in State-operated and contract community homes by sex]. (p. xx)

[6] Correctional officers in adult systems [by race/ethnicity, including American Indians/Alaskan Natives]. (p. xxi)

[7] Personnel information [adult and juvenile system employees by race/ethnicity, including American Indians/Alaskan Natives]. (p. xxii)

[8] Characteristics of adult paroling authorities [agency name, whether independent, number of board members, whether serving board full-time, and agency handling field services]. (p. xxiv)

[9] Rate of recidivism [adult and juvenile]. (p. xxvi)

[10] Death sentence survey [whether death sentence exists; number of prisoners sentenced to death, by sex and race/ethnicity, including Asians/Pacific Islanders and American Indians; and intended method of execution; with summary trends from 1978]. (p. xxviii)

[11] Positions of adult and juvenile corrections in State government [State agencies assigned jurisdiction over corrections, and effective date]. (p. xxx)

[12] Prison population and rate of incarceration, [selected years] 1840-1983. (p. xxxiii)

[13-14] Adult and juvenile facilities and programs [listed in directory]. (p. xxxiv-xxxvi)

A1305–4   CORRECTIONAL PERSONNEL COMPENSATION AND BENEFITS: Salary and Related Information

Recurring (irreg.), discontinued.

Recurring report on compensation and benefits provided to correctional personnel, discontinued with report for 1982 (for description, see SRI 1983 Annual, under this number).

Most of the data are now available in *Vital Statistics in Corrections;* for description, see A1305-5 below.

A1305–5   1984 VITAL STATISTICS IN CORRECTIONS

Biennial. 1984. 3+57 p.
ISBN 0-942974-55-7.
SRI/MF/complete, delayed

Biennial report on State corrections depts, including data on budgets, personnel and compensation, and prison inmates and facilities, with detail for adult and juvenile programs, by State, primarily 1983 or 1984, with selected trends from the 1970s and inmate population summary from 1840.

Data are from Dept of Justice, and various ACA and other private surveys, including 110 responses from State corrections agencies to a survey on personnel compensation and benefits.

Contains foreword, and contents listing (2 p.); 4 statistical sections, with brief narratives, and 4 charts and 64 tables described below (p. 1-55); and statement on ACA organizational structure (p. 56-57).

This is the 1st edition of the report. Data on personnel compensation and benefits previously appeared in a recurring ACA report which was discontinued with the 1982 edition; for description of that report, see SRI 1983 Annual, under A1305-4.

Availability: American Correctional Association, 4321 Hartwick Rd., Suite L-208, College Park MD 20740, members $8.00, nonmembers $10.00; SRI/MF/complete, delayed shipment in May 1985.

CHARTS AND TABLES:

[Data by race/ethnicity generally are shown for white, black, and Hispanic, with selected detail for American Indian/Alaskan Native, and Oriental or Asian/Pacific Islander.]

A1305–5.1: State Agencies and Personnel

a. State agencies, services provided, organizational position in State government, operational budgets, capital expenditures, number of new and renovation projects planned, and employees by sex and race/ethnicity, all for adult and juvenile depts; and parole board structures, including number of board members; all by State, as of July 1, 1983. 1 chart and 4 tables. (p. 1-10)

b. ACA total and female members by salary range, years of experience, education, race/ethnicity, and age, and total members by sex and ex-offender status, with detail by position, 1984; correctional officers in adult systems by sex and race/ethnicity, by State, July 1, 1983; and chief administrative officers by title, appointing body or official, and perquisites received, 1979, 1982, and 1984. 12 tables. (p. 13-19)

c. Compensation, including average, high, and low salaries by position, for personnel in parole board and/or adult and juvenile corrections depts, with detail by State; and prevalence of selected incentive pay programs, Civil Service/Merit systems, formal written salary schedules, cost-of-living allowances, and merit increase plans; 1984, with selected trends from 1979. 1 chart and 8 tables. (p. 20-29)

d. Vacation days offered, maximum vacation and sick leave staff may carry forward to next year, and other types of leave provided; and new employee probationary period; 1979, 1982, and 1984. 1 chart and 5 tables. (p. 29-31)

e. Health and disability insurance provisions, including types of coverage and employer vs. employee responsibility for costs, for 9 programs; and characteristics of retirement plans, including mandatory retirement age, benefit calculation methods, credit for employment in other jurisdictions, and period for initial vesting and eligibility; 1979, 1982, and 1984. 20 tables. (p. 32-37)

A1305–5.2: Prison Inmates and Facilities

a. Prison and total U.S. population, selected years 1840-1983; States with 10,000/over inmates, prison population increases of 20%/over and 1,000/over, and incarceration rates of 200/more per 100,000 U.S. population, 1983; and adult and juvenile inmates by race/ethnicity and type of facility, by sex and State, July 1, 1983, with aggregate adult inmates 1979-83. 4 tables. (p. 39-41)

b. Probation and parole population by sex, and rates of recidivism, for adult and juvenile offenders, July 1, 1983; method of sentencing used, including mandatory sentencing (no date); and use of death sentence, number of prisoners sentenced to death by sex and race/ethnicity, and method of execution used, 1983 with aggregate trends from 1978; all by State. 1 chart and 4 tables. (p. 42-47)

c. Prison inmates, and percent requiring maximum security, in facilities with over 1,000 inmates, under age 25, and confined for a violent offense, for Federal/State prisons by date of opening, through 1978; and Federal and State inmates, by type of prison housing, square footage per person, and inmate to staff ratios, 1980. 2 tables. (p. 49-50)

d. Capacities of prisons by State, 1983; States by incidence of court actions involving prison overcrowding, 1983; State prisoners held in local jails because of overcrowding, by State 1981-83, with summary trends from 1976; and actions taken by State administrations to relieve overcrowding (no date). 5 tables. (p. 51-54)

A1315
American
Council for the Arts

A1315-1   GUIDE TO CORPORATE GIVING 3
Recurring (irreg.)   1983.
xxiii+567 p.
ISBN 0-915400-39-1.
LC 82-20732.
SRI/MF/complete

Recurring report presenting profiles of contribution programs of 711 leading corporations, by contribution category, primarily 1981 or 1982. Contribution categories are arts/culture, health/welfare, education, civic, and other, with emphasis on the arts.

Data are from responses of 711 corporations to a survey conducted by American Council for the Arts. Responding companies accounted for over one-third of all corporate giving in 1981.

Contains contents listing and foreword (p. v-vii); introduction, with 17 summary tables described below (p. ix-xiii); user guide and questionnaire facsimile (p. xvii-xxiii); company profiles, also described below (p. 3-501); company indexes, arranged alphabetically and by State, type of activity supported, and type of support given (p. 505-559); and methodological appendix with 1 table, and ACA information (p. 563-567).

Report is intended to help arts groups and other non-profit organizations plan their contributions requests.

This is the 3rd edition of the report. SRI coverage begins with this edition.

Availability: American Council for the Arts, Publications, 570 Seventh Ave., New York NY 10018, $39.95; SRI/MF/complete.

TABLES AND PROFILES:
[Data are for latest available period, primarily 1981 or 1982.]

A1315-1.1: Summary Tables
[All tables include number of reporting companies.]

a. Value of contributions by industry division, with manufacturing detail by company size; distribution of contribution budget; and distribution of companies by size of all contributions and of largest gift; all by contribution category. 9 tables. (p. ix-xi)

b. Distribution of companies by share of contribution budget allocated to home office area and to the arts, by calendar quarter designated for application deadline, and by application processing time; and percent of companies with selected application requirements and evaluation criteria, supporting 13 arts organizations/activities, and providing 6 types of support. 8 tables. (p. xii-xiii)

A1315-1.2: Company Profiles
[Profiles are repeated for each of the 711 companies covered. Each profile contains all or most of the items described below.]

a. Directory information; description of various aspects of company's contribution program, including contact, relevant geographic area, and application requirements; year for which the information pertains; and value of all contributions.

b. Number and value of contributions, largest contribution, and number of requests, by category; and detail for arts support, showing kinds of organizations supported, examples of recent recipients, kinds of support normally considered, and ranking of evaluation criteria by importance.

A1325
American
Council of Life Insurance

A1325-2   PENSION FACTS: 1983 UPDATE
Biennial, with supplementary updates.   [1984.]   17 p.
LC 75-39762.
SRI/MF/complete

Biennial report, with supplementary updates, on private and Government-administered retirement and pension plans, 1982 and trends. Includes data on persons covered, plan assets and reserves, employer and employee contributions, and benefits. Plans covered are private plans funded with life insurance companies, other private plans, Railroad Retirement System, OASDI, and Federal and State/local government employee plans.

Data are from American Council of Life Insurance, Federal agencies, and other specified sources.

Contains foreword (p. 3); and 14 tables listed below (p. 4-17).

A full report, with narrative analysis as well as statistics, is published biennially. An update, with statistics only, is published in intervening years. Current edition is the 1st update; previously, full report was published annually.

Availability: American Council of Life Insurance, Information, Reference, and Statistical Services, 1850 K St., NW, Washington DC 20006-2284, †; SRI/MF/complete.

TABLES:
[Tables 8-9 are omitted. Tables 1-2 show data by type of plan.]

1. Number of persons covered by major pension and retirement programs [selected years 1940-82]. (p. 4)

2. Assets and reserves of major pension and retirement programs [selected years 1950-82]. (p. 5)

3. Pension plans with life insurance companies in force at year end [number of plans, persons receiving and not yet receiving pensions, payments, benefits, and reserves, by type of plan, selected years 1950-82]. (p. 6)

4. Outstanding amounts in IRAs [Individual Retirement Accounts] and Keogh plans with selected [types of] financial institutions, year end [1981-82]. (p. 8)

5. Variable annuity plans [number of plans and persons, variable and other reserves and considerations, persons receiving payments, and annualized income, for group and individual plans], 1982. (p. 9)

6. Life insurance company separate accounts [number of companies, accounts, and participating contracts, and assets held, by type of account, Dec. 31, 1981-82]. (p. 10)

7. Life insurance company separate accounts used solely for group pension contracts [number of accounts and participating contracts, and assets held, by type of investment, Dec. 31, 1981-82]. (p. 11)

10. Federal OASDI program [estimated number of persons with wage credits and insured for retirement benefits, assets, and contributions of employers, employees, and self-employed persons, selected years 1940-82]. (p. 12)

11. Persons receiving OASDI benefits at end of year and amount of benefits during year [shown for retired workers and dependents/survivors, selected years 1940-82]. (p. 13)

12-14. Federal civilian retirement systems [civil service, Federal Reserve Board, Foreign Service, and TVA]; Railroad Retirement System; and State/local government retirement plans; [number of persons receiving and not yet receiving benefits, employer and employee contributions, benefits paid to retired/disabled workers and dependent/survivors, and assets, various years 1930-82]. (p. 14-17)

A1325-3   LIFE INSURANCE BUYING: An Analysis of Ordinary Life Insurance Purchases in the U.S., 1982
Biennial. [1984.] 25 p.
SRI/MF/complete

Biennial report on ordinary life insurance policy purchases in 1982, including characteristics of purchasers. Presents data on distribution of policies and of amount purchased, and average policy size, for males and females, by age, occupational group, marital status, income, policy size and type, and mode of premium payment, with selected cross-tabulations and separate data for adults and all insured.

Data are from a Life Insurance Marketing and Research Assn survey of a representative sample of 32,041 policies issued by 85 companies.

Contains contents listing, narrative highlights and trends, and 1 table on sample distribution (p. 1-3); and 22 tables presenting survey findings (p. 4-25).

Prior to 1982, report was issued annually.

Availability: American Council of Life Insurance, Information, Reference, and Statistical Services, 1850 K St., NW, Washington DC 20006-2284, †; SRI/MF/complete.

A1325-4   DATA TRACK
Series. For individual publication data, see below.
SRI/MF/complete

Series of reports on socioeconomic topics of interest to the life insurance industry. Data are from Federal and private sources, and selected opinion surveys.

Each report covers a single topic, presenting statistical data and discussion of the implications for insurance product development, market analysis, and public relations.

Report reviewed during 1984 is described below.

Availability: American Council of Life Insurance, Social Research Services, 1850 K St., NW, Washington DC 20006-2284, †; SRI/MF/complete.

A1325–4.6: Population Residence and Home Ownership

[Monograph. Dec. 1983. 36 p. Data Track 12. †. SRI/MF/complete.]

Report examining regional and metro-nonmetro population changes, and homeownership trends, various periods 1960-83. Data are from Census Bureau and other Federal and private sources. Includes the following data:

a. Population by census region and division; and net migration for all races and blacks, and selected socioeconomic characteristics of population and households, by census region; various periods 1960-81. Tables 1-3. (p. 7-15)

b. Population and net migration for SMSA central cities and suburbs, and nonmetro areas, with population detail by census region, race, and for Hispanics; population change by size group, for metro counties by census region, and for nonmetro counties; and 10 SMSAs with largest population increase and decrease; various periods 1960-81. Chart G and tables 4-8. (p. 16-24)

c. Preferred residential setting; homeowners and renters, by race and for Hispanics; homeownership status, by age group; profile of home buyers, including median age, household income, purchase price, down payment, and housing expenses by item; attitudes toward ownership; and preferred type of mortgage; various years 1970-83. (p. 26-34)

A1410
American
Council on Education

A1410–1   HIGHER EDUCATION PANEL REPORTS

Series. For individual publication data, see below. SRI/MF/complete

Continuing series of reports, by the Higher Education Panel, on topics of current policy interest to the higher education community and to government agencies.

Reports are based on data drawn from the panel's membership of 760 colleges and universities, stratified by type (university and 4- and 2-year college), public and private control, and size of enrollment. The panel conducts 3-5 surveys per year using the total membership or a subset.

Reports reviewed during 1984 are described below.

Availability: American Council on Education, Higher Education Panel, One Dupont Circle, Washington DC 20036, †; SRI/MF/complete.

A1410–1.14: Student Quality in the Sciences and Engineering: Opinions of Senior Academic Officials

[Monograph. Feb. 1984. x+45 p. HEP Rpt. No. 58. SRI/MF/complete.]

By Frank J. Atelsek. Report on academic officials' opinions on change in the quality of science/engineering undergraduate students and graduate applicants, over the 5-year period ended 1981/82.

Covers perception of quality change and principal indicators of change, for students and applicants; and shift in distribution of most capable students, for science/engineering vs. other disciplines by reason, and within science/engineering by field.

Also includes percent of institutions with foreign applicants for graduate study, and perceived quality of foreign vs. U.S. applicants, 1982.

Data are generally shown for doctorate-granting and other public and private institutions, with some detail for aggregate top 50 and top 100 institutions.

Data are national estimates based on responses of senior academic officials at 685 postsecondary institutions to a Nov. 1982 survey.

Contains listings of contents, charts, and tables (p. iii-vii); highlights (p. ix-x); background, methodology, and findings, with 7 charts and 2 summary tables (p. 1-16); 21 detailed tables (p. 19-35); and 2 appendices, with questionnaire facsimile and technical notes (p. 37-45).

A1410–1.15: Student Quality in the Humanities: Opinions of Senior Academic Officials

[Monograph. Feb. 1984. x+40 p. HEP Rpt. No. 59. SRI/MF/complete.]

By Charles J. Andersen. Report on academic officials' opinions on change in the quality of humanities undergraduate students and graduate applicants, over the 5-year period ended 1981/82.

Covers perception of quality change and principal indicators of change, for students and applicants; and shift in distribution of most capable students, for humanities vs. other disciplines by reason, and within humanities by field.

Data are generally shown for doctorate-granting and other public and private institutions, with some detail for aggregate top 50 institutions.

Data are national estimates based on responses of senior academic officials at 680 postsecondary institutions to a Nov. 1982 survey.

Contains listings of contents, charts, and tables (p. iii- vii); highlights (p. ix-x); background, methodology, and findings, with 9 charts (p. 1-16); 14 detailed tables (p. 18-29); and 2 appendices, with questionnaire facsimile and technical notes (p. 31-40).

A1410–1.16: Financial Aid for Full-Time Undergraduates

[Monograph. Apr. 1984. viii+34 p. HEP Rpt. No. 60. SRI/MF/complete.]

By Charles J. Andersen. Report on higher education financial aid programs for full-time undergraduate students, by institution control and type, fall 1982.

Includes percent of students receiving aid, amount of aid, and Federal program share; family income levels of financially dependent and independent aid recipients; prevalence of financially independent Federal aid recipients; and average expense budget and composition of aid packages, by class level and source of funds (grants/scholarships, student employment, loans, and other); with selected detail by freshman expense budget range.

Also includes institutions with enrollment shortfall, and perceived reasons; use of computers to administer student aid; and basis for determining satisfactory progress standards for Federal aid eligibility.

Data are national estimates based on responses of 557 colleges and universities to a Jan. 1983 survey.

Contains listings of contents, tables, and charts (p. iii-vii); highlights (p. viii); background, summary, and findings, with 14 charts and 7 summary tables (p. 1-13); 30 detailed tables (p. 15-26); and 2 appendices, including questionnaire facsimile and technical notes (p. 28-34).

A1410–1.17: Full-Time Humanities Faculty, Fall 1982

[Monograph. Aug. 1984. viii+56 p. HEP Rpt. No. 61. SRI/MF/complete.]

By Irene L. Gomberg and Frank J. Atelsek. Report presenting data on full-time humanities faculty, by academic rank, tenure and minority status, sex, and highest degree held, by institution type and control and by discipline (English, history, modern languages, and philosophy), with various cross-tabulations, fall 1982 with comparisons to 1979.

Also includes data on new faculty appointments, with estimates for 1983/84.

Data are national estimates based on responses of 504 colleges and universities to an Apr. 1983 survey.

Contains contents, chart, and table listings, and highlights (p. iii-viii); narrative report, with 13 charts and 7 summary tables (p. 1-13); 42 detailed tables (p. 14-45); and appendices, with questionnaire facsimile, and 5 methodological tables (p. 46-56).

A similar report, for 1979, is described in SRI 1981 Annual, under A1410-1.7.

A1475
American Dental Association

A1475–1   DISTRIBUTION OF DENTISTS IN THE U.S., by Region and State

Triennial. [1984.] v+18 p. LC 54-26967. SRI/MF/complete

Triennial report on dentists, by State and census division, 1982. Includes data by age and sex, practicing status, occupational specialty, practice ownership, and full or part-time employment status. Also includes 1982 dental school graduates, and total population.

Data are based on a 1982 survey of members of the American Dental Assn.

Contains contents and table listings (p. iii-v); introduction, methodology, and questionnaire facsimile (p. 1-7); and 7 tables (p. 9-18).

Availability: American Dental Association, Council on Dental Education, Educational Measurements Division, 211 E. Chicago Ave., Chicago IL 60611, †; SRI/MF/complete

A1475–3   1983/84 ANNUAL REPORT:
Dental Education
Annual. [1984.] 29 p.
SRI/MF/complete

Annual report on dental school programs, enrollment, and graduates, by institution, for the U.S. and Canada, 1983/84, with selected trends from 1974.

Also includes data on admission requirements, including policies for transfer/foreign students; and, for U.S. schools, student expenses and financial assistance, type of instruction provided, and faculty positions.

Report is a summary of the 17th annual survey of dental schools conducted for the Council on Dental Education of the American Dental Assn and the American Assn of Dental Schools.

Contains contents and table listing (p. 3); introduction with 2 text tables on enrollment of women, 1982/83-1983/84 (p. 5-7); and 2 charts and 17 tables, listed below (p. 8-30).

Supplements to this report are also published and are covered in SRI under A1475-7.

Availability: American Dental Association, Council on Dental Education, Educational Measurements Division, 211 E. Chicago Ave., Chicago IL 60611, †; SRI/MF/complete.

TABLES AND CHARTS:
[Data are shown for 1983/84 school year, by U.S. and Canadian institution, unless otherwise noted. Data for U.S. include Puerto Rico.]

A1475–3.1: Academic Programs, Enrollment, and Graduates
[Charts 4 and 6 show aggregate U.S. data only.]

1. Dental schools [directory, arranged by State and Province]. (p. 8)

2. Description of academic programs [type and length of term and program, length of academic year, and type of degree granted and institutional support]. (p. 10)

3. Description of admission policies for transfer students/foreign dental graduates [admittance level, and qualifications considered for credit]. (p. 11)

4-5. Level of predental education of 1st-year students, 1974-83 [chart]; and of 1st-year students enrolled, 1983/84. (p. 12-13)

6. Dental school graduates, 1st-year and total enrollment [and number of dental schools], 1974/75-1983/84. [chart] (p. 14)

7. Predoctoral enrollment [by sex and level]. (p. 15)

8-9. Distribution of 1st-year and all predoctoral students [by State of residence; U.S. only]. (p. 16-19)

10. 1st-year enrollment [U.S. only], 1975-83. (p. 20)

11. Dental school [early and late] graduates, 1983. (p. 21)

A1475–3.2: Educational Expenses, Dental School Programs, and Faculty
[Tables show data for U.S. only.]

12. 1st-year tuition [resident and nonresident] and annual related educational expenses [general fees, and other educational costs by student level]. (p. 22)

13. Financial assistance awarded to predoctoral dental students [number applying, qualifying, and receiving assistance; percent of enrollment assisted; and amount requested and awarded]; 1982/83. (p. 23)

14-15. Basic sciences instruction; and advanced education programs conducted. (p. 24-25)

16. Continuing education offered [number of courses, enrollment, and instructors from dental and nondental school faculty; full- or part-time status of director; and percent of part-time director's involvement]; Aug. 1982- July 1983. (p. 26)

17-18. Full- and part-time faculty positions and budgeted faculty vacancies [in biomedical and clinical depts], 1983. (p. 27-28)

19. Full- and part-time faculty positions according to dept [not shown by institution], 1983. (p. 29)

A1475–4   SUPPLEMENTS TO DENTAL EDUCATION, 1982/83
Annual Report
Series. For individual publication data, see below.
SRI/MF/complete

Annual series of supplementary statistical reports, for academic year 1982/83, on dental schools, covering minority enrollment, programs, admission policies and applicants, student attrition, finances, faculty, and related topics. Most reports include data by individual institution.

Series also includes 2 nonstatistical directories of dental school administrators and dept chairmen.

Data are from Commission on Accreditation of Dental Educational Institutions annual survey of all dental schools, conducted during fall 1982.

Statistical reports generally contain table listing, brief narrative summary, and varying number of tables.

Supplement reviewed during 1984 is described below. Base report on 1982/83 survey is described in SRI 1983 Annual under S1475-3. Supplements for 1983/84 are covered under A1475-7.

Availability: American Dental Association, Council on Dental Education, Educational Measurements Division, 211 E. Chicago Ave., Chicago IL 60611, †; SRI/MF/complete.

A1475–4.8: Minority Report, 1982/83
[Annual. Oct. 1983. 25 p. Supplement 3. SRI/MF/complete.]

Annual report on minority enrollments and graduates of dental schools, by sex and race/ethnic group, for 1982/83 academic year. Report covers all accredited dental schools in the U.S. and Puerto Rico.

Contains contents and table listing (1 p.); narrative summary (p. 1-3); and 9 tables, with data by institution, 1982/83, as follows:

a. Dental school minority enrollment by class level, and graduates; all by sex and race/ethnic group (black, Hispanic, American Indian, and Asian). Tables 1-7. (p. 4-10)

b. Minority recruitment program summary, and directory of minority information administrators. Tables 8-9. (p. 11-25)

Previous report, for 1981/82, is described in SRI 1982 Annual, under A1475-7.1.

A1475–5   ANNUAL REPORT: Dental Auxiliary Education, 1983/84
Annual. Apr. 1984. 48 p.
SRI/MF/complete

Annual report, for 1983/84, on dental auxiliary education, including dental assisting, hygiene, and laboratory technology programs. Covers enrollment, graduates, admission requirements, and tuition, by institution. Data are from annual survey of accredited programs.

Contains table listing (1 p.); and 3 charts, and 12 tables listed below (p. 1-48).

Supplements to this report are also published, and are covered in SRI under A1475-8.

Availability: American Dental Association, Council on Dental Education, Educational Measurements Division, 211 E. Chicago Ave., Chicago IL 60611, †; SRI/MF/complete.

TABLES:
[Tables show data for 1983/84, unless otherwise noted. Tables 4-12 show data by institution, arranged by State, including Puerto Rico.]

1-3. 1st-year and total enrollment, and graduates, dental auxiliary programs [by type], 1973-83. (p. 1-2)

4. Institutions conducting dental hygiene education programs. [list] (p. 4-8)

5. Dental hygiene education program admission policies and data [awards granted; term of instruction; number and length of terms; number of summer and inter-sessions; minimum educational requirement; and total cost to in-district, out-of-district, and out-of-State students]. (p. 9-13)

6. Dental hygiene education programs [1st-year capacity, enrollment by year of study, and 1983 graduates by award granted]. (p. 14-18)

7-12. [Tables 4-6 are repeated for institutions conducting dental assisting education programs (p. 19-40) and dental laboratory technology programs (p. 41-48).]

A1475–6   1982 SURVEY OF DENTAL PRACTICE
Recurring (irreg.) [1984.]
ix+77 p.
ISSN 0517-1032.
LC 77-647657.
SRI/MF/complete

Recurring report on operating characteristics and finances of private dental practices, 1981. Includes data by practice type (general and specialist), with detail by census division.

Covers time spent in practice and in specific activities; workload, including patients and visits, patient waiting time, and perceived busyness; auxiliary staff and wages; facility and equipment use, including computer services; practice location and characteristics; number and sources of new patients; net and gross income; and expenses by item.

Also includes distribution by specific specialty and years since graduation.

Data are based on approximately 4,000 responses to two 1982 surveys covering stratified samples of dentists.

Contains contents and table listings (p. iii-ix); introduction and methodology, with 3 tables (p. 1-9); 2 report sections presenting survey findings for solo dentists (p. 13-37) and all independent dentists (p. 41-63), with brief narrative prefaces and 47 tables; and appendix, with questionnaire facsimiles (p. 67-77).

Survey is 13th in a series conducted every 2-3 years since early 1950s. For description of previous survey report, for 1979, see SRI 1982 Annual, under this number.

Availability: American Dental Association, Council on Dental Education, Educational Measurements Division, 211 E. Chicago Ave., Chicago IL 60611, †; SRI/MF/complete.

A1475–7 SUPPLEMENTS TO DENTAL EDUCATION, 1983/84 Annual Report
Series. For individual publication data, see below.
SRI/MF/complete

Annual series of supplementary statistical reports, for academic year 1983/84, on dental schools, covering minority enrollment, programs, admission policies and applicants, student attrition, finances, faculty, and related topics. Most reports include data by individual institution.

Series also includes 2 nonstatistical directories of dental school administrators and dept chairmen.

Data are from Commission on Accreditation of Dental Educational Institutions annual survey of all dental schools, conducted during fall 1983.

Statistical reports generally contain table listing, brief narrative summary, and varying number of tables.

Reports reviewed in 1984 are described below. Base report on 1983/84 annual survey is described under A1475-3, above.

Availability: American Dental Association, Council on Dental Education, Educational Measurements Division, 211 E. Chicago Ave., Chicago IL 60611, †; SRI/MF/complete.

A1475–7.1: Minority Report, 1983/84
[Annual. Mar. 1984. 25 p. Supplement 3. SRI/MF/complete.]

Annual report on minority enrollments and graduates of dental schools, by sex and race, for 1983/84 academic year. Report covers all accredited dental schools in the U.S. and Puerto Rico.

Contains contents and table listing (1 p.); narrative summary (p. 1-3); and 9 tables, with data by institution, 1983/84, as follows:

a. Dental school minority enrollment by class level, and graduates; all by sex and race/ethnic group (black, Hispanic, American Indian, and Asian). Tables 1-7. (p. 4-10)

b. Minority recruitment program summary, and directory of minority information administrators. Tables 8-9. (p. 11-25)

Previous report, for 1982/83, is described above, under A1475-4.8.

A1475–7.2: Trend Analysis, 1983/84
[Annual. Mar. 1984. 23 p.+addendum. Supplement 11. SRI/MF/complete.]

Annual report on dental school applications, enrollment, graduates, tuition, and licensure examinations, by institution or State, 1970s-83, with some earlier trends and enrollment projections through 1988. Also includes data on minority and women student enrollment and graduates. Report covers all accredited dental schools in the U.S. and Puerto Rico.

Contains contents and table listing (1 p.); introduction, with 1 summary text table (p. 1-3); and 18 tables showing the following data, for 1970s-83 unless otherwise noted:

a. Applications, 1st-year enrollment through 1988, public and private nonresidential 1st-year enrollment, predoctoral enrollment, and graduates, all by institution; 1st-year enrollment trends from 1967/68, by level of predental education; and attrition rate by class level, with 1st-year by reason. Tables 1-9. (p. 4-11)

b. Applications by women, 1st-year and total enrollment of women and minority students, and minority graduates, all by institution. Tables 10-15. (p. 12-17)

c. First-year resident and nonresident tuition/fees, by institution; advanced specialty education 1st-year and total enrollment, and graduates, in dental schools and in non-dental-school institutions, by specialty; and graduates passing and failing licensure examination, by State, selected years 1950-82. Tables 16-18. (p. 18-23)

A1475–7.3: Dental School Administrators, 1983/84
[Annual. Oct. 1983. 11 p. Supplement 1. SRI/MF/complete.]

Annual directory of administrators of U.S. dental schools, listed by school, for academic year 1983/84.

A1475–7.4: Financial Report, Fiscal Year Ending June 30, 1983
[Annual. June 1984. 1+32 p. Supplement 4. SRI/MF/complete.]

Annual summary report presenting data on dental school revenues and expenditures by major source and function, with high, low, and mean amounts by enrollment size, all for public, private, and private State-related schools, FY83 with aggregate trends from FY81.

Includes 16 tables.

A1475–7.5: Dental Student Attrition, 1982/83 Academic Year
[Annual. [1984.] 9 p. Supplement 5. SRI/MF/complete.]

Annual report on dental school student attrition, covering withdrawals for personal and academic reasons, and freshman enrollment, by race/ethnicity (including American Indian, Asian/Pacific Islander, and Hispanic), with attrition detail by class level and sex, academic year 1982/83 with selected trends from 1973/74.

Includes 7 tables.

A1475–7.6: Dental School Tuition, 1983/84
[Annual. Dec. 1983. 1+21 p. Supplement 13. SRI/MF/complete.]

Annual report presenting data on dental school undergraduate student expenses, including resident and nonresident tuition, mandatory fees, and costs of instruments, textbooks, and health services, by class level and institution, with selected rankings, academic year 1983/84 and trends from 1979/80.

Includes 15 tables.

A1475–8 SUPPLEMENTS TO THE ANNUAL REPORT, Dental Auxiliary Education
Annual series, discontinued.

Annual series of supplementary statistical reports on dental auxiliary education programs, discontinued with reports for academic year 1981/82 (for description, see SRI 1983 Annual, under this number). Report series has been discontinued because of financial constraints.

Similar data are available in *Annual Report: Dental Auxiliary Education,* covered in SRI under A1475-5.

A1475–9 INCOME FROM THE PRIVATE PRACTICE OF DENTISTRY: Statistical Results from the 1982 Survey of Dental Practice
Recurring (irreg.) Apr. 1983.
vi+28 p.
SRI/MF/complete

Recurring report on net income of dentists in private practice, 1981. Includes data by type of practice (generalist and specialist); ownership status (partner, shareholder, and sole proprietor); age; hours spent in practice per week and year; and census division.

Data are based on over 3,000 responses to two 1982 surveys covering stratified samples of dentists.

Contains contents and table listings (p. iii-vi); introduction, with methodology (p. 1-2); survey findings in 3 sections, with narrative analysis and 24 tables (p. 3-26); and summary of results (p. 27-28).

This is the 1st edition of the report. The Survey of Dental Practice, on which the report is based, has been conducted every 2-3 years since the early 1950s. For description of the survey report, see A1475-6.

Availability: American Dental Association, Council on Dental Education, Educational Measurements Division, 211 E. Chicago Ave., Chicago IL 60611, †; SRI/MF/complete.

A1580
American Federation of State, County and Municipal Employees

A1580–1 STATE OF THE STATES
Recurring (irreg.) Jan. 1984.
203 p. var. paging.
SRI/MF/complete

Recurring report analyzing Reagan Administration changes in Federal aid to State/local governments, for 39 programs, by State and for Puerto Rico, FY82-84.

Presents difference between actual funding and estimated funding needed to maintain FY81 service levels, FY82-84; and per capita totals, rank among the States, and share of Federal spending reduction, for the 3-year period; for each program, by State and for Puerto Rico, with U.S. summary of estimated funding requirements.

Programs are grouped as education/training/human capital investment, health/nutrition, income maintenance/human services, and infrastructure/physical capital investment.

Also includes aggregate U.S. data on change in defense and tax expenditures and net interest cost, FY82-84 period; State/local aid as percent of Federal and State/local spending and of GNP, FY60-85; and household average loss in human resource benefits, and individual tax changes from Reagan Administration tax cut and from inflation/social security tax increases, by income class, various periods FY82-85.

Most data are estimates prepared by Fiscal Planning Services, Inc., for AFSCME.

Contains foreword, and executive summary with 1 chart and 5 tables (20 p.); brief narrative summary and 1 table repeated for each State (156 p.); and appendices, with sources, list of grant programs, 1 table, and methodology (27 p.).

This is the 2nd edition of the report published by AFSCME; SRI coverage begins with this edition. Prior to 1983, less detailed reports were published by Coalition of American Public Employees (now disbanded).

Availability: American Federation of State, County and Municipal Employees, 1625 L St., NW, Washington DC 20036, †; SRI/MF/complete.

A1615
American Financial Services Association

A1615–1   FINANCE FACTS
Monthly, discontinued coverage.

Monthly summary report on consumer finance trends, described in SRI 1983 Annual under this number.

SRI coverage of this report is discontinued in favor of the annual *Finance Facts Yearbook,* covered in SRI under A1615-2.

Availability: American Financial Services Association

A1615–2   1984 FINANCE FACTS YEARBOOK
Annual. [1984.] 77 p.
LC 61-14409.
SRI/MF/complete

Annual report on consumer finance industry lending activity and financial status; and on consumer income and expenditures, including savings and debt; 1970s-83. Also includes data on industrial banking company status in 18-20 States.

Data are derived from annual surveys of 550 AFSA member companies, and nonmember companies; and Federal Reserve Board, Census Bureau, and BLS reports. The most recent AFSA survey, for 1983, drew responses from 106 companies.

Contains foreword, and listings of contents, tables, and charts (p. 2-6); 7 narrative chapters, with 21 charts, and 39 tables listed below (p. 7-74); and references (p. 75-77).

Availability: American Financial Services Association, Publications, 1101 14th St., NW, Washington DC 20005, members, schools, libraries $10.00; others $15.00; SRI/MF/complete.

TABLES:
[Tables show data from middle or late 1970s through 1982 or 1983, unless otherwise noted.]

A1615–2.1: Consumer Characteristics
CONSUMER POPULATION

1-2. Population and number of households [by type]; and population including armed forces abroad, by age and sex; July 1, selected years 1978-2000. (p. 8-10)

3. Labor force participation of the population. (p. 14)

4. Estimated school enrollment [by level]. (p. 15)

5. Employed civilians 16 years/over, by occupational groups, year end 1982-83. (p. 18)

CONSUMER INCOME, SPENDING, AND CAPITAL FORMATION

6-7. Sources and disposition of personal income. (p. 21-22)

8. Selected income characteristics of households [number, and mean and aggregate income, by householder sex, household size, type and tenure status of residence, metro or nonmetro location, and census region], 1982. (p. 24)

9. Distribution of families and unrelated individuals, by total money income in 1982. (p. 25)

10. GNP, by sector [personal consumption expenditures for durable and nondurable goods, and services; and government purchases, domestic investment, and net exports]. (p. 27)

11. Personal income [by source] and its disposition [by object], 1983. (p. 31)

12. Capital formation [by business and consumers; and capital consumption allowances]. (p. 34)

CONSUMER SAVINGS, INVESTMENT, AND DEBT

13. Financing of government by individuals [shows Federal and State/local government receipts, total tax/nontax receipts of all governments, social insurance fund receipts, and personal income from current earnings]. (p. 35)

14. Saving and investment, by households [shows gross, net, and personal saving, and credit from government insurance; capital gains dividends; net durables in consumption; gross investment; capital expenditures; net financial investment; net acquisition of financial assets; net liability increase; and savings/investment discrepancy]. (p. 36)

15. Credit market debt owed, by sector [public, private, and consumer]; and other selected claims [security and trade credit, investment company shares, and other corporate equities]. (p. 37)

16-17. Balance sheet of the household sector; and consumer's asset to debt ratios; end of period. (p. 38-40)

CONSUMER CREDIT
[Credit holders are commercial banks, retailers, gasoline and finance companies, savings/loan assns, credit unions, and mutual savings banks. Installment credit by type is shown for automobile, revolving, mobile home, and other credit.]

18. Consumer installment credit outstanding at year end and net change during year, by type, by holder. (p. 43)

19. Consumer installment credit, by type and holder [year end 1982-83]. (p. 44)

FEDERAL RESERVE BOARD 1977 CONSUMER CREDIT SURVEY

20-21. Annual installment debt payments as a percent of previous year's family income [1977]; and distribution of families reporting installment debt and use of credit cards, 1970 and 1977; [by age of family head and family income level]. (p. 45-46)

22. Loans secured by real estate other than 1st mortgages, nonfarm homeowning families (in percent of number responding) [by use and source of funds, and size of 2nd mortgage extension], 1977. (p. 47)

A1615–2.2: Consumer Finance Industry Operations
LENDING ACTIVITY

23-24. Receivables outstanding and consumer installment credit at finance companies, by [loan] type. (p. 50-51)

25. Growth in 2nd mortgage and other personal loans at a sample group of finance companies. (p. 53)

26. Loan laws under which finance companies operate, by State (no date). [tabular list] (p. 55)

27. Average loan sizes at finance companies, 1981-82. (p. 56)

28-29. Percentage distribution of personal loans made at finance companies by purpose, and by characteristics of borrowers [by annual income level and age group], 1982. (p. 58-59)

30. Percentage distribution of U.S. household population, by annual income level and by age group, 1982. (p. 60)

FINANCES

31. Assets of companies responding to AFSA questionnaire, Dec. 31, 1982. (p. 61)

32-33. Liabilities, capital, and surplus; and gross income, expenses, and net income; of reporting finance companies. (p. 62-63)

34-35. Estimated overall cost of borrowing and return on equity, 1982, for finance companies by size of company [amount of consumer credit outstanding]. (p. 64)

36. Relation of income to outstandings, assets, and equity, for finance companies, 1982. (p. 65)

INDUSTRIAL BANKING COMPANIES
[Tables present data for industrial banking companies in 18-20 States, as of year end 1982 or most recent fiscal year.]

37-39. [Number of companies]; assets [net receivables and other]; and liabilities [deposits and thrift/investment certificates, and other; and total capital]. (p. 68-69)

A1775
American Gas Association

A1775-1   QUARTERLY REPORT OF GAS INDUSTRY OPERATIONS
Quarterly.
Approx. 6 p. folder.
SRI/MF/complete

Quarterly report on natural gas utility industry, with combined income statement for investor-owned companies; and customer, sales, and revenue data for all companies, by census division. Also includes data on average gas prices, and appliance shipments by type and fuel source.

Data are compiled by AGA from company reports and from reports of government and private agencies, including Gas Appliance Manufacturers Assn. Report is issued 3-6 months after quarter of coverage.

Contains narrative analysis, usually with 10-12 trend charts; and 6 quarterly tables, listed below.

Availability: American Gas Association, Order and Billing, 1515 Wilson Blvd., Arlington VA 22209, †; SRI/MF/complete.

Issues reviewed during 1984: 2nd Qtr. 1983-2nd Qtr. 1984 (D).

QUARTERLY TABLES:
[Tables show data for quarter of coverage and/or year to date, with comparisons to previous year.]

[A] Investor-owned gas utility industry income statement [including operating revenues, expenses by type, net income, utility plant value, and accumulated provision for depreciation].

1-2. Gas utility industry customers, sales, and revenues, U.S. and by [census] division [by consuming sector].

[B-C] Average gas prices [by consuming sector, for U.S. and by census division].

[D] Appliance and housing statistics [appliance shipments by type of appliance and fuel source, and total and single family housing starts, private housing completions, and mobile home shipments].

A1775-2   MONTHLY GAS UTILITY STATISTICAL REPORT
Monthly. Approx. 2 p.
SRI/MF/complete, shipped quarterly

Monthly statistical summary of natural gas prices, sales to ultimate consumers, residential appliance shipments, and related economic indicators, compiled by the American Gas Assn for the gas utility industry.

Data are derived from Federal Government and private sources, including the Gas Appliance Manufacturers Assn and BLS; sales data are based on a sample of 69 companies. Report is issued 4-8 weeks after month of coverage.

Contains brief narrative summary, 3 charts, and 4 tables listed below.

Availability: American Gas Association, Order and Billing, 1515 Wilson Blvd., Arlington VA 22209, †; SRI/MF/complete, shipped quarterly.

Issues reviewed during 1984: Sept. 1983-July 1984 (D).

MONTHLY TABLES:

[1] Gas sales to ultimate consumers [Btu by consuming sector, for month of coverage, year to date, and forecast for current year, with comparison to previous year].

[2] Residential appliance shipments [domestic ranges, clothes dryers, warm air furnaces, and boilers, by type (gas, electric, and oil), for month of coverage and same month of previous year].

[3] Economic indicators [including private housing starts; CPI for utility pipe gas, electricity, and fuel oil, and index of total gas sales; and gas utility prices by sector; for month of coverage and same month of previous year].

[4] Average annual gas utility prices [by consuming sector, quarterly for current year through most recent available quarter (1 to 2 quarters prior to current quarter), and annually for preceding 8-10 years].

A1775-3   GAS FACTS 1982: A Statistical Record of the Gas Utility Industry
Annual. 1983. x+218 p.
No. F10182.
LC 72-622849.
SRI/MF/complete

Annual report, for 1982, on natural gas industry, covering utility transmission, distribution, consumption, finances, prices, and personnel. Includes data by State, and trends from 1960s.

Report also covers natural gas reserves, production, supply, underground storage, appliances, and home heating; selected data for petroleum, coal, and electric and nuclear power industries; and foreign gas production, consumption, and trade.

Data are from Uniform Statistical Reports prepared annually by AGA utility company members; reports filed with regulatory commissions; financial publications; and other reports from government and private sources.

Contains contents and chart listings, introduction, and information sources (p. v-x); 17 sections, with 24 summary charts, 16 summary tables, and 155 detailed tables listed below (p. 1-192); 4 appendices, with glossary, conversion table, company listing by type, and 3 tables on gas consumption (p. 193-214); and index (p. 215-217).

Gas Data Book, an annual pocket-sized book containing brief excerpts from *Gas Facts,* is also available from AGA, but is not covered in SRI.

Availability: American Gas Association, Order and Billing, 1515 Wilson Blvd., Arlington VA 22209, members $25.00, nonmembers $30.00; SRI/MF/complete.

DETAILED TABLES:
[Unless otherwise noted, tables present trend data annually or for selected years, from 1960s or 1970s through 1981 or 1982.

Data by State usually are also shown by census division. Data by class of service are shown for total, residential, commercial, industrial, and other users.

Data by type of industry classification are shown for 27-28 industry divisions and major groups. Data by type of company generally are shown for distribution, transmission, integrated, and combination companies; and sometimes for gas holding companies or municipals.]

A1775-3.1: Summary Comparison and Reserves

INDUSTRY SUMMARY COMPARISON

1.1. Comparison of gas utility industry customers, sales, and revenues, by class of service, 1981-82. (p. 4)

U.S. RESERVES

[Tables show data for resources indicated below. Table titles 2.1-2.2, 2.4, and 2.7 begin "Summary of annual estimates of proved reserves..." Table titles 2.3, 2.5, and 2.8 begin "Changes in estimated proved reserves..." and show data by State, with detail for some State regions and districts, including offshore, 1982.]

2.1-2.3. Natural gas. (p. 6-11)

2.4-2.5. Natural gas liquids. (p. 13-15)

2.6. Total estimated remaining identified reserves of coal [anthracite/semianthracite, sub-bituminous, and bituminous] and lignite by State, as of Jan. 1, 1980. (p. 16)

2.7-2.8. Crude oil. (p. 17-19)

CANADIAN RESERVES

[Tables 2.9-2.11 show data for Canada.]

2.9. Summary of annual estimates of reserves of natural gas. (p. 20)

2.10-2.11. Estimated [amount of] and changes in established remaining marketable reserves of natural gas, by Province, 1982. (p. 21)

A1775-3.2: Supply
[Data by type of well generally are for total, gas, oil, dry, and occasionally service wells.]

GENERAL PRODUCTION AND SUPPLY

3.1-3.2. Annual production [Btu and percent] of fossil energy resources [natural gas, crude petroleum, bituminous coal/lignite, and anthracite coal] and electricity from hydropower and nuclear power. (p. 25)

3.3. Supply and disposition of gas [including imports]. (p. 26)

3.4-3.5. Gas utility industry, gas supply and disposition; and maximum and minimum day sendout by source of supply. (p. 27)

PRODUCTION, DELIVERIES, AND FOREIGN TRADE
[Tables 3.6-3.9, 3.11, and 3.14 show data by State.]

3.6-3.8. Gross, net wellhead, and marketed production of natural gas. (p. 28-30)

3.9. Production of natural gas by all interstate natural gas pipeline companies. (p. 31)

3.10. Total offshore production of natural gas and percent State/federally controlled. (p. 32)

3.11. Interstate movements and movements across U.S. borders of natural/supplemental gas, 1981. (p. 33)

3.12. Exports [total, and to Canada, Mexico, and Japan] of natural gas from the U.S. (p. 34)

3.13. Imports [total, and from Canada, Mexico, and Algeria] of natural gas to the U.S. (p. 34)

3.14. Natural gas delivered to consumers. (p. 35)

GASOLINE AND ALLIED PRODUCTS

3.15. Supplemental gas supplies [synthetic natural, propane-air, refinery, and other] by State, 1981. (p. 36)

11.11-11.12. Number of occupied housing units, by type of cooking fuel, 1974-80; and by type of fuel used for water heating and clothes drying, 1970, and for water heating, 1980. (p. 140-141)

A1775–3.8: Finance

INCOME ACCOUNTS

12.1-12.5. Composite income accounts, investor-owned gas utility industry: total industry, distribution companies, transmission companies, and integrated and combination companies. (p. 146-150)

12.6. Investor-owned gas utility industry gas operation and maintenance expenses, by type of company, 1981-82. (p. 151)

BALANCE SHEETS

13.1-13.5. Composite balance sheet accounts, investor-owned gas utility industry [same detail as tables 12.1-12.5]. (p. 155-159)

13.6. Total gas utility industry plant, by type of company [and for total and investor-owned industry], by plant function. (p. 160)

ANALYTICAL RATIOS

14.1-14.5. Selected composite analytical ratios [earnings, expenses, plant, and capitalization], investor-owned gas utility industry [same detail as tables 12.1-12.5]. (p. 163-167)

14.6. Selected analytical ratios relating to investor-owned gas utility industry operating/maintenance expenses. (p. 168)

SECURITY ISSUES

[Table titles 15.1-15.12 begin "Gas utility industry..."]

15.1-15.2. Security issues of distribution/transmission/ holding/combination gas and electric companies, and average percent cost and yield. (p. 171-172)

15.3. Long-term debt issues, [cost, and yield], by Moody's bond rating category, 1982. (p. 173)

COMMON STOCK

15.4. Common stock issues, by type of company. (p. 174)

15.5. Indexes of common stock prices, dividends, yields, and earnings, by type of company. (p. 175)

ISSUES, COST, AND YIELD

[Tables 15.6-15.12 show data by type of company. Tables 15.6-15.11 alternately show amount and number of gas utility industry issues, and average percent cost and yield.]

15.6-15.7. Preferred stock issues. (p. 176-177)

15.8-15.9. Bond issues. (p. 178-179)

15.10-15.11. Debenture issues. (p. 180-181)

15.12. Note issues [amount and number only]. (p. 182)

CONSTRUCTION EXPENDITURES

16.1-16.2. Gas utility industry construction expenditures, by type of facility [total, production/storage, transmission, underground storage, distribution, and general, with forecast through 1986]; and [by purpose for production and storage, transmission, and distribution facilities]. (p. 185-186)

A1775–3.9: Personnel

17.1-17.2. Gas utility industry employees and payroll [total and] by type of payroll [operating, construction, and miscellaneous] and type of company. (p. 189-190)

17.3. Employee accident incident and severity rates of selected industries, 1981. (p. 191)

17.4. Death rates of workers, by [industry division], 1981. (p. 191)

17.5. Employee disabling injury rates, by type of gas utility. (p. 192)

A1775–4   GAS HOUSEHEATING SURVEY: 1982
Annual. 1983. v+61 p.
No. F00083.
SRI/MF/complete

Annual report on natural gas residential heating market, including customers, consumption, and price compared to other fuel types, by utility, State, and census division, 1982, with trends from 1978. Also includes data on anticipated additions of gas househeating units in 1983, housing completions by heating fuel type, conversions to gas from other fuels, and conservation.

Most data are from an American Gas Assn survey of 161 gas utilities serving 89% of all residential customers, and reports of Census Bureau and appliance trade assns.

Contains contents and table listings (iii-iv); executive summary (p. 1-2); analysis of survey findings, with 1 chart on housing start trends and 9 text tables (p. 2-17); and 2 appendices with 2 detailed tables (p. 19-61). All tables are listed below.

This is the 35th annual survey.

Availability: American Gas Association, Order and Billing, 1515 Wilson Blvd., Arlington VA 22209, members $15.00, nonmembers $18.00; SRI/MF/complete.

TABLES:

[Unless otherwise noted, tables show data for 1982.]

TEXT TABLES

1-3. Total U.S. residential housing by heating fuel; regional heating fuels and market shares for residential housing; and residential housing completions by heating fuel type; [for gas, electricity, oil, and other/none], 1978-82. (p. 3-7)

4-5. Residential and househeating customers of gas utilities, and househeating unit additions, by [region, census division, and] State, as of Dec. 31; and househeating conversions to natural gas by type of fuel [oil, propane, electricity, and other, by census division]. (p. 9-11)

6. 1983 anticipated additions of gas househeating units [new housing and conversions, by region, census division, and State]. (p. 12)

7. Manufacturers' shipments of residential heating equipment [gas, oil, and electric warm air furnaces; gas and oil boilers; heat pumps; and wall and floor gas furnaces], 1978-82. (p. 13)

8. Average annual gas consumption/unit by region [for single- and multi-family heating and baseload, with heating degree days compared to 30-year normal]. (p. 15)

9. Average conservation by region [and census division] (percent decline from 1973 baseline [consumption normalized for weather from pre-embargo 1973]). (p. 17)

APPENDIX TABLES

[Both of the following tables show data by gas utility arranged by census division and State.]

1. Househeating data by company [customers, average single-family home consumption, housing unit losses, and unit additions through new construction and conversions, all shown for total residential and househeating-only customers; gas-heated homes' market share; and heating degree days; 1982, with anticipated gas-heated housing unit changes for 1983]. (p. 20-47)

2. Competitive fuel prices [per million Btu, for natural gas, No. 2 fuel oil, electricity, and propane, as of Dec. 31; principal competitive fuel; and average annual gas heating bill]. (p. 50-61)

A1835
American Historical Association

A1835–2   SURVEY OF THE HISTORICAL PROFESSION: Academia, 1981-82, Summary Report
Annual. 1984.
x+62+App 23 p.
SRI/MF/complete

Annual survey report, for 1981/82, on policies and faculty characteristics and compensation of higher education history depts. Covers administrative structure; types of degrees offered; budget; faculty salaries and fringe benefits; travel, paid leave, hiring, promotion, and tenure policies; office staff size; amount and source of research funds; faculty turnover and awards; course offerings and teaching load; and student enrollment, degrees, and postgraduate employment.

Also covers faculty academic rank, tenure status, minority status, salary range, age, experience, and consulting activities outside the university; dept head duties and compensation; and views on most serious problem confronting dept. Faculty data are often shown by sex.

Data are based on 590 responses to a survey of history dept heads in 1,797 schools.

Contains contents and table listings, and introduction (p. iii-x); analysis, with 17 tables (p. 1-39); tabulation of responses to 52 questions (p. 42-62); and narrative appendix (App. 1-23).

Previous report, for 1980/81, is described in SRI 1982 Annual under this number.

Availability: American Historical Association, Publications Department, 400 A St., SE, Washington DC 20003, members $5.00 (prepaid), nonmembers $6.00 (prepaid), $1.00 postage and handling; SRI/MF/complete.

A1865
American
Hospital Association

A1865–1   HOSPITALS

Semimonthly.   Approx. 175 p.
ISSN 0018-5973.
LC 43-4821.
SRI/MF/not filmed

Semimonthly trade publication on topics related to hospital operations, services and staff administration, facilities planning and utilization, and financial management.

Data are from AHA, Federal agencies, and other sources.

Issues include:

a. Recurring article with 1 table on CPI medical care component change for 1- and 12-month periods.

b. Quarterly articles on community hospital finances and operations; and hospital economic forecasts.

c. Annual statistical features, including salary surveys.

d. MULTIs, a separately paginated quarterly magazine on multifacility health system management.

e. Special articles, occasionally with statistics; and regular depts.

All features with substantial statistical content are described, as they appear, under "Statistical Features." Each issue of the journal is reviewed, but an abstract is published in SRI monthly issues only when statistical features appear.

Availability: Hospitals, American Hospital Publishing, Inc., 211 E. Chicago Ave., Chicago IL 60611, $35.00 per yr., single copy $3.00; SRI/MF/not filmed.

Issues reviewed during 1984: Nov. 1, 1983-Oct. 16, 1984 (P) (Vol. 57, Nos. 21-24; Vol. 58, Nos. 1-20).

STATISTICAL FEATURES:

A1865–1.501: Nov. 1, 1983 (Vol. 57, No. 21)

REVENUE GROWTH RATE DROPS, SPENDING RISES, QUARTERLY FEATURE

(p. 38) Quarterly summary, with 2 tables showing community hospital patient days, total and patient revenues and expenses with percent change from 1981, and total and patient revenue margins by census division, 2nd quarter 1982-83.

A1865–1.502: Nov. 16, 1983 (Vol. 57, No. 22)

SLOWER MEDICAL CARE PRICE GROWTH SEEN IN SEPT., RECURRING FEATURE

(p. 25) Recurring article, with 1 table showing 1- and 12-month percent change in CPI medical care components, Sept. 1983.

A1865–1.503: Dec. 1, 1983 (Vol. 57, No. 23)

SURVEY OF HOSPITAL STAFFS: PART 1

(p. 80-84) By Nancie E. Noie et al. Part 1 of a 2-part report on hospital medical staff size, professional characteristics, and administrative practices, 1982 with selected comparisons to 1973. Data are from AHA surveys of short-term hospitals in the contiguous U.S.

Includes text statistics and 1 table showing the following:

a. Average number of staff physicians, with detail for family practitioners, internists, and pediatricians.

b. Percent of hospitals with committees in 8 administrative areas, and including mean committee size (total and physician members) and meetings per year; and percent of governing boards with voting privileges for physician members and hospital chief executive officer.

A1865–1.504: Dec. 16, 1983 (Vol. 57, No. 24)

SURVEY OF HOSPITAL SALARIES, ANNUAL FEATURE

(p. 73-84) Annual article, by Linda I. Collins, on hospital management/supervisory staff compensation. Presents data on mean, median, and 25th and 75th percentile base salaries for 30 supervisory positions, and median salary as a percent of administrator/president's salary for 14 positions, all by bed size category 1982; and percent change in salary increases by position, and in availability of 6 types of benefits, 1982-83.

Also includes occupational profiles for 6 management positions, including compensation, employees supervised, work experience, position tenure, age, educational attainment, and distribution by academic specialization and sex; and correlation findings relating base salary to bed size, revenues/expenses, and supervision exercised.

Data are from 4th annual hospital management compensation survey conducted by Meidinger Inc. in spring 1983. Data cover 145 hospitals. Includes 14 tables.

SURVEY OF HOSPITAL MEDICAL STAFFS: PART 2

(p. 91-94) By Michael A. Morrisey et al. Part 2 of a 2-part report on hospital medical staff size, professional characteristics, and administrative practices, 1982 with selected comparisons to 1973. Data are from AHA surveys of short-term hospitals in the contiguous U.S.

Includes text statistics and 1 table showing the following:

a. Staff physicians: average number of applications; probation period; certification requirements; use of more than 1 hospital; and top admitting physicians' specialty, age, and board certification status.

b. Admitting privileges for nonphysician practitioners; and compensation for administrative and clinical functions, including primary form of compensation for 3 hospital-based specialties.

A1865–1.505: Jan. 1, 1984 (Vol. 58, No. 1)

MEDICAL CARE PRICES RISE AT SLOWEST RATE SINCE 1974, RECURRING FEATURE

(p. 27) Recurring article, with 1 table showing 1- and 12-month percent change in CPI medical care components, Oct. 1983.

BUSINESS EXAMINES HOSPITALS

(p. 61-69) By Glenn Richards. Article on the formation of health care provider and user coalitions concerned with controlling health care cost increases. Data were compiled by AHA for Dunlop Group of Six.

Includes 1 undated chart showing number of coalitions by type of participant, including business, physicians, hospitals, government, commercial insurers, and labor.

CAPITAL: A CRISIS?

(p. 70-74) By Jo Ellen Mistarz. Article on trends in capital sources for the hospital industry. Data were compiled by Jeff G. Goldsmith. Includes 1 chart showing percent of hospital capital attributed to philanthropy, internal reserves, government grants, and debt, 1968 and 1981.

HOSPITAL ECONOMIC FORECAST, QUARTERLY FEATURE

(p. 79-82) Quarterly article, by Kenneth A. Johnson and Clifford Neely, on hospital expenditure and revenue trends and forecasts, 1970s-84. Presents Hospital Inflation Expense Index (HIEI), computed by Merrill Lynch Economics Inc., and based on AHA Market Basket Index.

Includes 1 chart and 2 tables showing HIEI expense component weights; and percent change in HIEI, with detail for wages/salaries and 8 other HIEI components, and comparisons to CPI and other general economic indicators, 1979-84.

A1865–1.506: Jan. 16, 1984 (Vol. 58, No. 2)

TWELVE PERCENT OF U.S. CAN'T AFFORD CARE: REPORT

(p. 17) Article, with 1 chart showing number and percent of all, poor, and unemployed families perceiving it easier or more difficult to obtain medical care, 1982. Data are based on a survey of 7,000 randomly selected individuals, conducted under the auspices of the Robert Wood Johnson Foundation.

MODERATE INCREASES SEEN IN MEDICAL CARE PRICES, RECURRING FEATURE

(p. 25) Recurring article, with 1 table showing 1- and 12-month percent change in CPI medical care components, Nov. 1983.

HALF OF FECs RUN BY NOT-FOR-PROFITS: STUDY

(p. 26) Brief article on operating characteristics of free-standing emergency/primary care centers (FECs). Data are from an American Medical Assn survey of 3,951 nonfederal physicians. Includes 1 chart showing percent of respondents associated with FECs operated by not-for-profit and investor-owned hospitals, and by physician and nonphysician groups, 1983.

A1865–1.507: Feb. 1, 1984 (Vol. 58, No. 3)

HCA HOSPITALS' COSTS, EFFICIENCY STUDIED

(p. 21) Article, with 1 table presenting the following data for Hospital Corporation of America (HCA) and U.S.: discharges per employee, occupancy rate, average case mix index, percent urban beds, and Medicare mix as percent of days, 1981 or FY81. Also compares HCA cost per case to U.S. average. Data are from Health Care Financing Administration and Salomon Bros.

CORPORATE DONATIONS TO HOSPITALS WILL RISE

(p. 33) Article, with 1 chart showing value of nonindividual charitable contributions, and distribution by type of recipient, 1980-88. Data are from American Assn of Fund-Raising Counsel, Inc., and Chemical Bank.

CONTRACT MANAGEMENT: MORE BUYERS, SMARTER SHOPPERS

(p. 53-60) By Lynn Kahn and Mark Harju. Article, with 2 tables showing number and percent of community and multihospital system hospitals under contract management, by type of ownership; with detail for community hospitals by bed size category; 1979-82. Data are from AHA.

DEPARTMENTAL CONTRACT MANAGEMENT UP AS MUCH AS 162 PERCENT

(p. 62-64) By Lynn Kahn. Article, with 1 chart and 1 table showing percent of community hospitals using contract management in 5 service areas, 1982; and number of hospitals using contract management in 9 inpatient clinical areas, 1980-81. Data are from AHA.

A1865–1.508: Feb. 16, 1984 (Vol. 58, No. 4)

MEDICAL CARE, ROOM PRICES CONTINUE TO INCREASE SLOWLY, RECURRING FEATURE

(p. 20) Recurring article, with 1 table showing 1- and 12-month percent change in CPI medical care components, Dec. 1983.

IOWANS NOTE PUBLIC'S ROLE IN CUTTING HEALTH CARE COSTS

(p. 26) Brief article on Iowa public opinion on sector primarily responsible for hospital/health care cost control. Data are from an Oct. 1983 survey of 1,008 Iowa residents, conducted by IMR/Opinion Research for the Health Policy Corp. of Iowa. Includes 1 chart.

3rd QUARTER EXPENSE, REVENUE GROWTH DROP, QUARTERLY FEATURE

(p. 46-48) Quarterly summary, with 3 charts showing total and patient revenue margins of community hospitals, by census division, 3rd quarter 1982-83.

A1865–1.509: Mar. 1, 1984 (Vol. 58, No. 5)

EMPLOYER COST CONTROL ROLE GROWS: STUDY

(p. 27) Article, with 1 table showing percent of corporate health insurance plans providing full coverage of hospital room/board charges, 1979-83. Data are from a study of 250 plans, conducted by Hewitt Associates.

MULTIS WERE FEWER, BUT BIGGER IN 1983

(MULTIs, p. 8-12) Article, with 1 chart and 2 tables showing the following for multihospital systems: number of hospitals and beds, by type of organizational control (Catholic and other church-related, other nonprofit, and investor-owned), and ownership (owned/leased/sponsored and contract-managed); and number of systems by organizational control; 1982-83. Data are from *Directory of Multihospital Systems.*

SECOND ANNUAL MULTIs COMPENSATION SURVEY, ANNUAL FEATURE

(MULTIs, p. 26-43) Annual article, by Linda I. Collins, on compensation of multihospital system executives, as of Sept. 1983. Data are from a survey of 48 systems conducted by Meidinger, Inc.

Includes 15 tables showing summary data on salary increases, and the following for 10 executive/administrative positions and aggregate other 5 highest paid positions: mean, median, and 1st and 3rd quartile salary by type of ownership, bonus, salary grade midpoint, number of owned/managed hospitals, and average bed size and revenues; and types of perquisites received, by salary level.

SPECIAL HOME CARE WRAP-UP

(p. 33-70) Compilation of articles on developments in home medical services. Includes the following statistical articles:

a. "Rapid Growth Pattern Tracked." Includes 1 table showing number of Medicare certified home health care agencies by type, including visiting nurses assns, hospital- and rehabilitation-based agencies, skilled nursing facilities, and proprietary and nonprofit agencies, 1978-83. Data are from National Assn for Home Care. (p. 33-34)

b. "Not-for Profits Lead Growth: Investor-Owneds Gaining." Includes 1 undated chart showing percent of health care institutions with home medical care programs in effect, planned, or not planned, by type of institution (investor- owned and not-for-profit chains and freestanding hospitals, and State/local and Federal hospitals). Data are from American College of Hospital Administrators. (p. 37-38)

c. "Ventilator-Dependent Children Heading Home." By Lynn Kahn. Includes 1 table showing monthly respiratory care cost for ventilator-dependent children, for treatment received in hospitals, and through home care provided by registered nurse and certified home care giver, 1981/82. Data are from Children's Home Health Network of Illinois. (p. 54-55)

THOSE WONDERFUL PEOPLE WHO BROUGHT YOU DRGs

(p. 81-85) By Emily Friedman. Article, with 1 chart showing Federal funding for National Center for Health Services Research, 1970-84. Data are from Assn for Health Services Research.

SURVEY OF HOSPITAL MANAGEMENT INCENTIVE PROGRAMS

(p. 90-94) By Gary S. Whitted and Charles M. Ewell. Article on prevalence and characteristics of incentive compensation programs for hospital managers. Data are from responses of 22 hospitals to a May 1982 Arthur Young and Co. survey.

Includes 1 table with survey responses on number of incentive programs and years in operation; general program goals; type of evaluation criteria, performance measure, and bonus determination method used; maximum bonus relative to salary; and perceived effect of program on managerial decisions and hospital financial performance; all by hospital organizational type.

BUSINESS SPURS UR GROWTH

(p. 96-100) By Glenn Richards. Article on corporations contracting with independent professional standards review organizations (PSROs) to conduct hospital utilization reviews (URs) as a cost containment method. Data are based on a 1983 survey conducted by American Medical Peer Review Assn.

Includes 1 table showing the following by State: number of PSROs reporting receipt of private contracts, reviews conducted, and contractors involved in negotiations.

A1865–1.510: Mar. 16, 1984 (Vol. 58, No. 6)

HMOs' ENROLLMENT LARGEST SINCE 1978

(p. 24) Article, with 1 chart showing annual percent change in HMO membership, 1978-83. Data are from InterStudy's *National HMO Census, June 30, 1983.*

CAPITAL OUTLOOK

(p. 61-64) By Jo Ellen Mistarz. Article on market outlook for hospital bonds and stocks during 1984. Data are from *Bond Buyer,* and Sanford C. Bernstein and Co., Inc. Includes 2 tables showing the following:

a. Value of total and hospital tax-exempt bond issues, and percent refunded, 1980-81 and quarterly 1982-83.

b. Multihospital systems aggregate financial status by type of organizational control, including percent of capital expenditures financed internally, and net debt capital; and ratios of debt coverage, net debt/deferred taxes to capital, and total assets to net revenues; 1982.

TRENDS IN HOSPITAL PHILANTHROPY

(p. 70-74) By Maureen Metz Charhut. Article analyzing trends in charitable contributions to hospitals, 1955-82. Data are from AHA and *Giving USA.*

Includes 1 chart and 2 tables showing value of all charitable contributions and percent given by individuals, contributions as a percent of GNP, and amount contributed to health/hospitals; and percent of hospital construction financed through philanthropy, government, internal reserves, and debt; various years 1955-82.

Giving USA is covered in SRI under A0700-1.

FECs POSE COMPETITION FOR HOSPITAL EDs

(p. 77-83) By Glenn Richards. Article, with 1 chart comparing average medical service charges for 5 common injuries/illnesses at free-standing emergency centers (FECs) and hospital emergency depts (EDs), 1982. Data are from a National Assn of Freestanding Emergency Centers survey.

SURVEY OF PREFERRED PROVIDER ORGANIZATIONS

(p. 85-88) By Kathryn Schroer and Elworth Taylor. Article on the development and structure of preferred provider organizations (PPOs) established by health care providers to facilitate arrangements with buyers of health care services. Data are from responses of 16 PPOs to a 1983 AHA survey.

Includes 2 tables showing survey respondents by year PPO established and by type of provider responsible for establishment; and number of participating hospitals and physicians in each surveyed PPO.

A1865–1.511: Apr. 1, 1984 (Vol. 58, No. 7)

CPI HOSPITAL ROOM PRICES CONTINUE SLOW GROWTH RATE, RECURRING FEATURE

(p. 26) Recurring article, with 1 table showing 1- and 12-month percent change in CPI medical care components, Jan. 1984.

HOSPITALS' SYSTEMS EXPENDITURES SKYROCKET

(p.39) Article, with 1 table showing market value (no date) and projected 1980s growth rate for computerized hospital information systems, by type of use (management, financial, patient care, pharmacy/laboratory). Data are from a 1983 study by William Blair and Co.

RESEARCHERS PREDICT GROWTH IN FINANCIAL SYSTEMS MARKET

(p. 70, 73) Article, with 1 table showing the following for computerized hospital financial systems: sales and number of hospitals using, 1983 and 1986, and major suppliers, all by system type. Data are from a 1983 study by William Blair and Co.

HOSPITAL ECONOMIC FORECAST, QUARTERLY FEATURE

(p. 83-89) Quarterly article, by Clifford Neely, on hospital expenditure and revenue trends and forecasts, 1980-85. Presents Hospital Inflation Expense Index (HIEI), computed by Merrill Lynch Economics Inc., and based on AHA Market Basket Index.

Includes 1 chart and 2 tables showing HIEI expense component weights; and percent change in HIEI, with detail for wages/salaries and 8 other HIEI components, and comparisons to CPI and other general economic indicators, 1980-85.

A1865–1.512: Apr. 16, 1984 (Vol. 58, No. 8)

8 STATE CON LIMITS ABOVE FEDERAL LEVELS

(p. 24) Article on State compliance with federally mandated hospital expenditure limits under certification-of-need (CON) programs. Data were compiled by AHA. Includes 1 table showing CON capital, services, and equipment spending thresholds, by State with comparison to Federal levels, as of Jan. 1984.

HUNGER PROBLEM IS REAL: MEDICAL EXPERTS

(p. 61-63) Article, with text statistics and 1 chart showing incidence of malnutrition and anemia among Massachusetts preschool children from low income families, as of Oct. 1983. Data are based on a Massachusetts Dept of Public Health study of 1,429 children.

DECISIVE DECADE FOR HMOs

Compilation of 3 articles reviewing trends and outlook for HMOs, based primarily on data from HHS. Articles with substantial statistical content are described below.

HEALTH MAINTENANCE ORGANIZATIONS' SLOW START HAS BEEN SUPERSEDED BY RAPID GROWTH AND A MARKET REVOLUTION.

(p. 96-99) By Emily Friedman. Article, with 2 charts and 2 tables showing number of HMOs and enrollment, 1970-83; top 10 States ranked by enrollment, and including number and market penetration of HMOs, 1982 or 1983; and Medicare and Medicaid recipients enrolled in HMOs, FY82.

INVESTOR-OWNEDS ENTER NOT-FOR-PROFITS' BASTION

(p. 100-101) Article, with 1 table showing top 10 HMOs ranked by enrollment, and including number of plans and tax status (not-for-profit or investor-owned), as of Mar. 1983.

A1865–1.513: May 1, 1984 (Vol. 58, No. 9)

COALITION MEMBERS INCREASINGLY DIVERSE

(p. 20) Brief article on composition of health care coalitions, based on responses of 105 coalitions to a survey conducted by Dunlop Group of Six. Includes 1 chart showing percent of respondents reporting participation from business, physician, hospital, insurance, and labor groups, as of Mar. 1984.

CPI's MEDICAL CARE PRICES REINFORCE DOWNWARD TREND, RECURRING FEATURE

(p. 21) Recurring article, with 1 table showing 1- and 12-month percent change in CPI medical care components, Feb. 1984.

FOURTH QUARTER ECONOMIC TRENDS FOLLOW YEAR'S PATTERNS, QUARTERLY FEATURE

(p. 37-40) Quarterly article, with 1 chart showing annualized percent change in selected performance indicators for community hospitals, including expenses, revenues, admissions and length of stay for patients over and under age 65, cost and FTE employees per case, cost index, and labor cost per FTE employee, 4th quarter 1982-83. Data are from AHA National Hospital Panel Survey.

CONTRASTS SEEN AMONG HOSPITALS' RESIDENTS

(p. 65) Article on characteristics of hospitals with residency programs comprised of only U.S. medical school graduates (USMGs) compared to hospitals with both USMGs and foreign medical school graduates (FMGs). Data are from an AHA study. Includes 1 undated table showing distribution of hospitals by census division, for institutions with USMGs only, with FMGs of whom 35% or more are U.S. citizens, and with FMGS of whom 66% or more are not U.S. citizens.

FOCUS ON INFORMATION SYSTEMS

(p. 83-86) By C. L. Packer. First in a series of articles on computer use in hospitals. Data are based on surveys of 4,367 hospitals conducted by Shared Data Research. Includes 1 map, 1 table, and 5 charts presenting survey sample characteristics, and illustrative data concerning computer use and satisfaction and programmer salaries.

A1865–1.514: May 16, 1984 (Vol. 58, No. 10)

HMO ENROLLEES' HOSPITAL USE WISE: STUDY

(p. 17) Article, with 1 table showing number of HMOs by range of inpatient days per 1,000 enrollees, based on 176 responses to InterStudy's *1982 HMO Census.*

UNEMPLOYMENT RATE AMONG HOSPITAL STAFF VARIES: HHS

(p. 22) Article, with 1 table showing unemployment rates for 8 health occupations, with comparisons to all civilian and all hospital employees, 1982-83. Data are from HHS.

STAFF PRIVILEGES FOR NON-MDs OUTLINED BY STATE

(p. 23-25) Article, with 1 undated table indicating whether selected nonphysician health care professionals are allowed hospital access under State law, by State.

CHANGING ECONOMIC PROFILE OF U.S. HOSPITALS, ANNUAL FEATURE

(p. 83-88) Annual article, by Jo Ellen Mistarz, on community hospital cost increases and financial performance, 1983 with selected trends. Data are from AHA Panel Survey and Office of Public Policy Analysis.

Includes 4 charts showing percent change in hospital expenses, costs per case, admissions of patients over and under age 65 by census division, and service units per adjusted patient day; and average length of stay for patients age 65/older; various periods 1967-83.

Data correction appears in the Aug. 1, 1984 issue; for description see A1865-1.519 below.

A1865–1.515: June 1, 1984 (Vol. 58, No. 11)

CPI's MEDICAL CARE PRICES SHOW SIGNS OF LEVELING OFF IN MAR., RECURRING FEATURE

(p. 26) Recurring article, with 1 table showing 1- and 12-month percent change in CPI medical care components, Mar. 1984.

JCAH CITES SHORTCOMINGS IN QUALITY ASSURANCE FUNCTIONS

(p. 60-63) Article, with 1 table showing percent of hospitals not in compliance with 10 types of medical staff quality assurance standards set by Joint Commission of Accreditation of Hospitals (JCAH), 1982. The 10 standards shown are those with the highest rate of noncompliance. Data are from a JCAH survey of 1,155 hospitals.

SYSTEM TIES BOOST SMALL, RURAL ACCREDITATIONS

(MULTIS, p. 6-8) Article, with 5 tables comparing accreditation rates for all community hospitals by bed size, for autonomous vs. system-affiliated small hospitals, and for all vs. system-affiliated rural hospitals, 1982. Tables generally include total hospitals in each category, and number accredited.

Data are from Joint Commission on Accreditation of Hospitals and AHA.

MULTI CEOs ARE YOUNGER, MORE EDUCATED, LESS TENURED: SURVEY

(MULTIs, p. 12-14) Article, with 1 table showing distribution of hospital chief executive officers (CEOs) by age, sex, tenure, and educational degree, for freestanding hospitals and for multihospital systems with hospital-based and separate administrative offices. Data are from 3,451 responses to a recent survey by American College of Hospital Administrators.

INVESTOR-OWNED GROWTH SHIFTS FROM NUMBERS TO NICHE

(MULTIs, p. 16-28) By Kelly F. Guncheon. Article, with 2 charts showing change in number of management company-owned hospitals and beds, by State, 1983 and 1978-83 period. Data are from directories published by American Hospital Publishing, Inc., and Federation of American Hospitals.

Article is the 1st in a 2-part series on growth trends for investor-owned multihospital systems.

MORE WORK NEEDED ON MD/MULTI RELATIONSHIP

(MULTIs, p. 59-64) By Jeffrey A. Alexander and Dorothy L. Cobbs. Article on medical staff participation in policy decisionmaking activities of multihospital systems. Data are based on responses of 160 hospital systems to a May 1983 survey by Hospital Research and Educational Trust.

Includes 5 tables characterizing medical staff policy role, by system age, size, and ownership category.

PREVALENCE OF HOSPITAL-PHYSICIAN CONTRACTS

(p. 75) Article, with 1 chart showing percent of nonfederal patient care physicians with hospital contracts, for anesthesiologists, pathologists, radiologists, and surgeons, 1981. Data are from a survey by American Medical Assn Center for Health Policy Research.

PROFILES OF HOSPITAL EXCLUSIVE-CONTRACT LITIGATION

(p. 78) Article, with 1 chart showing distribution of a sampling of 60 health care antitrust suits pending as of Jan. 1984, by type of case. Data are from National Health Lawyers Assn.

FOUR PRINCIPAL APPROACHES TO DATA PROCESSING AND THE SATISFACTION THEY PROVIDE

(p. 88-93) By C. L. Packer. Second in a series of articles on computer use in hospitals. Data are based on surveys of 4,367 hospitals, conducted by Shared Data Research.

Includes 1 table showing percent of hospitals using computer technology for patient care, financial management, and strategic management, by type of computer system (in-house, turnkey, facilities management, or shared services) and bed-size category. Also includes 5 illustrative charts on satisfaction with each type of system.

SURVEY OF NURSING SERVICE ADMINISTRATORS, PART 1

(p. 94-100) By Myrtle K. Aydelotte. First of 2 articles on compensation and professional characteristics of nursing administrators, 1982 and trends. Data are based on 343 responses to a 1982 membership sample survey by American Society for Nursing Service Administrators.

Includes 7 tables showing distribution of survey respondents by salary range, prior experience in various nursing positions, and highest degree attained, with selected cross-tabulations, detail by hospital bed-size category, and comparisons to 1977 survey.

A1865–1.516: June 16, 1984 (Vol. 58, No. 12)

MARKETING SURGE TIED TO CONSUMERS; DECISIONMAKING MUSCLE BEING FLEXED

(p. 33-34) Article, with 1 undated chart showing percent of nonemergency hospital selections made solely by physicians, solely by patients, and jointly by physicians/patients. Data are from Professional Research Consultants, Inc.

SURVEY OF NURSING SERVICE ADMINISTRATORS, PART 2

(p. 79-80) By Myrtle K. Aydelotte. Second of 2 articles on compensation and professional characteristics of nursing administrators, 1982 and trends. Data are based on 343 responses to a 1982 membership sample survey by American Society for Nursing Service Administrators.

Includes 1 table showing distribution of survey respondents by percent of worktime allocated to 8 types of activities.

A1865–1.517: July 1, 1984 (Vol. 58, No. 13)

M.D., PUBLIC HEALTH ATTITUDES DIFFER: STUDY

(p. 20-21) Article, with 1 undated chart on overall viability of the health care system, as perceived by physicians, hospital administrators, and the general public. Data are from Louis Harris and Associates surveys conducted for Equitable Life Assurance Society of the U.S.

MEDICAL CARE COMPONENT OF CPI REMAINS STABLE, RECURRING FEATURE

(p. 23) Recurring article, with 1 table showing 1- and 12-month percent change in CPI medical care components, Apr. 1984.

WHO'S RESPONSIBLE FOR HOSPITAL EQUIPMENT AND PRODUCT PURCHASING DECISIONS?

(p. 70-71) By Mark Harju. Article, with 1 table showing extent to which hospital administrators, purchasing and financial officers, dept heads, medical staff, and boards are involved in purchasing decisions for 20 equipment/product categories. Data are based on responses of 386 administrators at short-term registered hospitals to a Dec. 1983 survey by Hospital Publishing Inc.

HOSPITAL ECONOMIC FORECAST, QUARTERLY FEATURE

(p. 76-80) Quarterly article, by Clifford Neely, on hospital expenditure and revenue trends and forecasts, 1980-85. Presents Hospital Inflation Expense Index (HIEI), computed by Merrill Lynch Economics Inc.

Includes 1 chart and 3 tables showing HIEI expense component weights; and percent change in HIEI, with detail for wages/salaries and 8 other HIEI components, and comparisons to CPI and other general economic indicators, 1980-85.

WHY HOSPITALS LIKE — OR DISLIKE — THEIR APPROACHES TO DATA PROCESSING

(p. 81-83) By C. L. Packer. Third in a series of articles on computer use in hospitals. Data are based on 1984 surveys of 4,367 hospitals, conducted by Shared Data Research.

Includes 5 charts showing hospitals' satisfaction with their computer systems, and factors determining satisfaction.

A1865–1.518: July 16, 1984 (Vol. 58, No. 14)

AMA COMPILES MEDICARE-PHYSICIAN STATS

(p. 23) Article, with 1 chart showing distribution of physicians, by percent of professional visits covered by Medicare. Data are from a 4th quarter 1983 American Medical Assn survey of 1,202 physicians.

HOSPITAL EXECS CLINCH $100K

(p. 25) Article, with 1 table showing hospital executives' mean and median salary, and percent receiving bonus, for 7 positions, 1983. Data are from responses of 302 hospitals to a survey conducted jointly by AHA and Management Compensation Services.

REPORT TIES MEDICARE LEVELS, BOND RATINGS

(p. 40) Article with 1 table showing baseline data on hospital finances and operations, including median number of beds and occupancy rate, average length of stay, and selected cash flow and balance sheet ratios, 1984. Data are from Moody's Investors Service.

GROWTH IN MEDICAL DIRECTORS SLOW: SURVEY

(p. 66-72) Article, with 1 table showing percent of hospitals employing/considering a medical director, and percent with medical directors serving on joint conference committees, practicing as hospital-based physicians, and subject to periodic performance reviews, 1981 and 1983. Data are from unspecified surveys.

INSURERS IRONING OUT WRINKLES IN LONG-TERM CARE COVERAGE

(p. 110, 113) By Kelly F. Guncheon. Article, with 1 chart showing percent of nursing home and hospital care expenditures covered by Federal/State governments, patients, and insurers, 1982. Data are from Health Care Financing Administration.

STRATEGIES FOR FINANCIAL SUCCESS

(p. FB44, FB50) By Bruce Mansdorf. Article, with 1 chart showing HMO enrollment, 1970-83. Data are from InterStudy's National HMO Census.

CARING FOR THE ELDERLY UNDER PROSPECTIVE PRICING

(p. FB54) By Janet A. Tedesco. Article, with 1 chart showing 1-year percent change in hospital admissions, overall and for patients under and over age 65, by census division, 1983. Data are from AHA *Hospital Panel Surveys*.

A1865–1.519: Aug. 1, 1984 (Vol. 58, No. 15)

GRAPH CORRECTION

(p. 16) Data correction for annual article on community hospital cost increases and financial performance 1983, appearing in May 16, 1984 issue.

For description of original article, see A1865-1.514, above.

STUDY SHOWS RECESSION AFFECTS DEATH RATES

(p. 22-23) Article, with 1 chart showing the estimated effect of a 10% increase in unemployment on total, cardiovascular, and cirrhosis mortality rates, and on number of patients in mental hospitals. Data are from a report prepared for the Joint Economic Committee of Congress.

GROWTH CITED IN EMPLOYERS THAT REQUIRE DEDUCTIBLES

(p. 25) Article, with 1 chart showing employers' average costs for medical insurance claims per covered employee, 1982-84. Data for 1984 are from a Hewitt Associates survey of 1,185 companies.

MEDICAL PRICE INCREASES HOLD STEADY FOR THIRD MONTH, RECURRING FEATURE

(p. 27) Recurring article, with 1 table showing 1- and 12-month percent change in CPI medical care components, May 1984.

FIRST QUARTER TRENDS: CHANGING ENVIRONMENT, QUARTERLY FEATURE

(p. 37-38) Quarterly article, with 4 charts showing annualized percent change in selected performance indicators for community hospitals, including admissions and length of stay for patients over and under age 65, cost per case, and total operating and patient revenue margins, 1st quarter 1981-84. Data are from AHA National Hospital Panel Survey.

AHA SURVEY SHOWS 1983 RN OPENINGS IN HOSPITALS

(p. 60-62) Article, with 1 table showing distribution of hospital full- and part-time staff nurses, by highest degree held, as of Apr. 1983. Data are preliminary findings from a survey by the AHA Division of Nursing.

COMPARISON OF HOSPITAL DATA PROCESSING COSTS

(p. 83-86) By C. L. Packer et al. Fourth in a series of articles on computer use in hospitals. Data are based on 1984 surveys of 4,367 hospitals, conducted by Shared Data Research.

Includes 7 charts showing hospitals' average data processing annual budget and daily cost per patient, by system type (in-house, turnkey, facilities management, or shared service), hospital bed-size category, and level of satisfaction with system.

A1865–1.520: Aug. 16, 1984 (Vol. 58, No. 16)

MEDICAL PRICE INCREASES STEADY FOR FOURTH MONTH

(p. 26) Recurring article, with 1 table showing 1- and 12-month percent change in CPI medical care components, June 1984.

FOOD SERVICES SURVEY SHOWS DELIVERY SHIFT

(p. 61-64) Article on types of patient meal-delivery systems used in NYC hospitals, 1983, with comparison to 1979. Data are from surveys drawing 79 responses in 1979 and 66 responses in 1983. The 1983 sample represents 83% of all NYC short-term general hospitals. Includes 2 tables.

A1865–1.521: Sept. 1, 1984 (Vol. 58, No. 17)

EDUCATION, ARTS GET BIGGER SHARE OF GROWING CHARITY PIE

(p. 36) Brief article, with 1 table showing corporate matching gifts to charitable causes, and number of contributors, by category of recipient including hospitals, biennially 1976-82. Data are from responses of approximately 350 large corporations to annual surveys conducted by Council for Financial Aid to Education.

NATIONAL SURVEY OF MEDICAID REIMBURSEMENT FACTORS

(p. 60-64) By Robert J. Buchanan. Article, with 2 tables showing Medicaid expenditures for total, hospital, and intermediate care, 1975-85; and average payment per stay 1983, and summary of payment limits and methods 1984, by State. Data are from Health Care Financing Administration, and a 1984 survey by Research Institute of Pharmaceutical Sciences of the University of Mississippi.

MAJOR DATA PROCESSING SYSTEMS AND APPLICATIONS

(p. 66-72) By C. L. Packer et al. Fifth in a series of articles on computer use in hospitals. Data are based on 1984 surveys of 4,367 hospitals, conducted by Shared Data Research.

Includes 5 charts showing the following data by type of hospital system (financial management, patient care, and strategic management): use of computer technology by type of data processing (dp) system (in-house, turnkey, facilities management, or shared services) and dp budget size; and dp cost per patient day, and satisfaction level, by number of applications.

A1865–1.522: Sept. 16, 1984 (Vol. 58, No. 18)

MEDICAL CARE COMPONENT OF CPI RISES SLIGHTLY, RECURRING FEATURE

(p. 27) Recurring article, with 1 table showing 1- and 12-month percent change in CPI medical care components, July 1984.

PPS AFTER THE FIRST YEAR

Compilation of articles discussing effects on hospitals of the Medicare prospective pricing system (PPS) designed to contain medical cost increases. Articles with statistical content are described below.

HOSPITALS REDUCE COSTS, LENGTH OF STAY

(p. 37-40) Article, with 1 undated table showing number and percent of discharges from PPS hospitals, for 10 most common diagnostic related groups (medical conditions). Data are from Health Care Financing Administration.

MEDICARE-CERTIFIED HOME HEALTH CARE AGENCIES EXPAND

(p. 78) Article, with 1 table showing number of Medicare-certified home health agencies, by type of sponsoring institution, as of Dec. 31, 1983 and July 1, 1984. Data are from National Assn for Home Care.

HOSPICE GROWTH SLOW DUE TO PAYMENT AND CERTIFICATION REGS

(p. 80) Article, with 1 table showing number of Medicare-certified hospices, by type of sponsoring institution, as of Apr. 1984. Data are from National Assn for Home Care.

Other Articles

PROGRESS REPORT ON HOSPITAL MARKETING

(p. 98-102) By Steven R. Steiber and Joseph A. Boscarino. Article on developments in hospital marketing. Data are from responses of 150 marketers for nongovernment hospitals of 50/ more beds, to a recent telephone survey conducted for *Hospitals*.

Includes 4 charts showing distribution of responses concerning dept and position with primary marketing responsibility, marketers' principal functions and goals, and marketing budget allocations for advertising/promotion, salary, and other.

MALPRACTICE LOSSES ARE BUILDING, AGAIN

(p. 108-115) By Glenn Richards. Article, with 1 chart showing number of jury verdicts awarding $1 million or more for medical malpractice cases, 1973-82. Data are from Jury Verdict Research, Inc.

A1865–1.523: Oct. 1, 1984 (Vol. 58, No. 19)

ILLINOIS HMO ENROLLMENT UP 73 PERCENT

(p. 33) Article, with 1 table showing HMO enrollments nationwide and in Illinois, 1980-Aug. 1984.

SURVEY REFLECTS EMERGENCY CARE CHANGES

(p. 65) Article, with 1 table showing types of physician staffing used for hospital emergency services. Data are based on 3,788 responses to a 1983 survey of all 5,898 nonfederal short-term hospitals, conducted by the Institute for Health Policy Studies, University of California, San Francisco, and the AHA.

HOSPITALS LOOKING TO STANDARD COSTING SYSTEMS

(p. 88-92) By Frederick S. Fink et al. Article on computerized standard costing systems for hospitals. Data are based on 172 responses to a Feb. 1984 survey of hospital financial managers, conducted by Booz-Allen & Hamilton Inc.

Includes 3 tables showing survey response on uses of standard costing information, source of planned system (acquisition or internal development), and expected system cost.

DATA PROCESSING PERSONNEL EXPENSES

(p. 112-118) By C. L. Packer et al. Sixth in a series of articles on computer use in hospitals. Data are based on 1984 surveys of 4,367 hospitals, conducted by Shared Data Research.

Includes 6 charts showing distribution of hospital data processing (dp) personnel and of dp personnel expenses, and average salary, all by job category, with selected detail by dp budget size, region, and system type (in-house, turnkey, facilities management, shared service), and salary comparison to national averages for dp personnel in all economic sectors.

HOSPITAL ECONOMIC FORECAST, QUARTERLY FEATURE

(p. 121-126) Quarterly article, by Clifford Neely, on hospital expenditure and revenue trends and forecasts, 1980-85. Presents Hospital Inflation Expense Index (HIEI), computed by Merrill Lynch Economics Inc.

Includes 1 chart and 3 tables showing HIEI expense component weights; and percent change in HIEI, with detail for wages/salaries and 8 other HIEI components, and comparisons to CPI and other general economic indicators, 1980-85.

A1865–1.524: Oct. 16, 1984 (Vol. 58, No. 20)

HOME CARE COVERAGE: RULE, NOT EXCEPTION

(p. 26) Article on corporate health insurance plan provisions affecting use of hospital services. Data are from a Jan.-Mar. 1984 survey of 1,185 companies, conducted by Hewitt Associates. Includes 1 chart showing percent of companies that have implemented or are considering preadmission testing, mandatory 2nd surgical opinion, and incentives for outpatient surgery.

CLEVELAND, MERRILL LYNCH AT THE TOP IN '83 BOND ISSUES

(p. 46-48) Article on tax-exempt health care bonds issued in 1983. Data are from *Credit Markets* and Securities Data Corp.

Includes 2 tables showing 10 largest bond issues, including issuer and facility name, and bond date, type, amount, net interest charge, quality rating, and underwriting firm; and top 10 underwriters ranked by value of issues underwritten, with total number of issues and number for which firm was senior underwriter; 1983.

WHICH HOSPITALS PAY MOST TOWARD CARE FOR THE INDIGENT?

(p. 109) Brief article, with 1 table showing number of registered community hospitals, and patient revenue, bad debt, and charity care cost, all by type of control (nongovernment/not-for-profit, investor-owned, and State/local government), 1979-82. Data are from AHA.

FUTURE OF HEALTH CARE UNIONS

(p. 121-126) By Daniel A. Richman. Article, with 1 table showing number of health services workers covered under new labor union contracts, by union, 1980-June 1983. Data are from National Labor Relations Board *Election Reports.*

A1865–2   HAS/MONITREND SIX-MONTH NATIONAL DATA BOOK for Period Ending June 30, 1983
Semiannual.   Nov. 1983.
135 p.
AHA Catalog No. 097182.
SRI/MF/not filmed

Semiannual report on median financial and operating performance of short-term hospitals and other health care facilities, Jan.-June 1983. Includes data by facility bed-size group, urban vs. rural location, and census division.

Data are based on a survey of approximately 2,000 institutions participating in the Hospital Administrative Services (HAS) MONITREND program. Explanations of methodology and reporting guidelines are provided in 2 separate publications, *Calculation Reference* and *Guide for Uniform Reporting,* included in the purchase price.

Contains contents listing and introduction (p. 3-5); performance indicator data, arranged in 6 sections (p. 7-128); and listing of States by census division (p. 129).

Performance indicator data are described below.

Availability: AHA Services, Inc., PO Box 99376, Chicago IL 60611 (prepaid); 4444 W. Ferdinand, Chicago IL 60624 (billed), $155.00 (includes *Guide for Uniform Reporting* and *Calculation Reference*); 5-yr. package $175.00; SRI/MF/not filmed.

PERFORMANCE INDICATORS:

[Data are for Jan.-June 1983 period. Data for most sections include 1 table showing number of reporting hospitals, and 1 table showing performance indicators.]

a. General short-term hospitals: approximately 350 median utilization, personnel, expense, and revenue indicators for total hospital and nursing administration, and for individual ancillary depts and support services; presented for total U.S. by bed size group (p. 8-17), and by census division and bed size group (p. 19-69).

b. Urban and rural short-term hospitals: repeats indicators described above, for facilities arranged by Case Mix Index group, based on urban-rural status, bed size, and Medicare case index as assigned by the Health Care Financing Administration. (p. 71-102)

c. Teaching and children's hospitals: repeats indicators described above, for total children's hospitals, and for teaching hospitals by census division. (p. 103-113)

d. Long-term care facilities: includes approximately 130 median financial, utilization, personnel, and service indicators, for within-hospital and separate-building facilities, and by bed size group. (p. 115-119)

e. Rehabilitation facilities: includes approximately 240 median and quartile utilization, personnel, expense, and revenue indicators, for total facility, nursing administration, and individual ancillary depts and support services. (p. 121-128)

A1865–3   AMERICAN HOSPITAL ASSOCIATION GUIDE TO THE HEALTH CARE FIELD, 1984 Edition
Annual. 1984.
628 p. var. paging.
AHA Catalog No. 010084.
ISSN 0094-8969.
ISBN 0-87258-423-2.
LC 72-626765.
SRI/MF/not filmed

Annual directory of hospitals in U.S. and outlying territories, including utilization, expense, and personnel for each hospital, 1983. Also includes listings of AHA members, and of other health-related organizations and agencies in U.S. and elsewhere.

Current data are derived from the AHA 1983 annual survey of hospitals.

Contents:

Contents listing and introduction. (p. iii-vi)

Section A. Health Care Institutions. Includes explanatory notes and definitions; requirements for AHA registration; hospital statistical directory, described below; and directories of U.S. Government hospitals outside the U.S., long-term care facilities, and multihospital systems. (p. A1-A310)

Section B. AHA Members. Includes membership categories, offices, officers, and historical information; and directories of institutional, associate, and personal members. (p. B1-B267)

Section C. Health Organizations and Agencies. Includes directories of international, national, regional, U.S. Government, State, and Canadian provincial agencies and organizations in the health field. (p. C1-C26)

Section D. Index and Abbreviations. (p. D1-D19)

This is the 40th annual guide.

Availability: AHA Services, Inc., PO Box 99376, Chicago IL 60611 (prepaid); 4444 W. Ferdinand, Chicago IL 60624 (billed), members $52.50, nonmembers $72.50; SRI/MF/not filmed.

STATISTICS:

HOSPITAL STATISTICAL DIRECTORY

(p. A10-A260) Directory shows the following data for each hospital, grouped by State and U.S. territory: name and address; types of services and facilities available; classifications; number of beds, admissions, average daily patient census, and occupancy rate; bassinets and births; total and payroll expenses; and FTE personnel; all for 1983.

Hospital classifications include type of control (Federal and other government, nongovernment not-for-profit, investor-owned for-profit, and osteopathic); type of service (general medical/surgical, psychiatric, tuberculosis/other respiratory diseases, children's general, and other specialties); and length of stay (short-term and long-term). Directory includes additional detail for control and service classifications.

A1865–4   HOSPITAL STATISTICS, 1983 Edition
Annual. 1983. xxi+237 p.
AHA No. 082083.
ISSN 0090-6662.
ISBN 0-87258-386-4.
LC 72-626765.
SRI/MF/not filmed

Annual statistical report on hospital capacity, utilization, personnel, finances, facilities, and services, 1982 with trends from 1946. Data are shown by census division, State (including D.C.), SMSA, 100 largest central cities, and outlying territories, cross-tabulated variously by hospital bed size, control, and service classifications.

Current data are derived from responses of 6,-431 hospitals to the AHA 1982 annual survey.

Contents:

a. Contents and table listing; introduction; definitions; analysis of hospital trends, with 15 summary text tables; and technical notes, with 3 tables on survey response distribution. (p. iii-xxi)

b. 25 detailed tables, listed below; index; and sample questionnaire. (p. 1-237)

Availability: AHA Services, Inc., PO Box 99376, Chicago IL 60611 (prepaid); 4444 W. Ferdinand, Chicago IL 60624 (billed), members $35.00, nonmembers $45.00; SRI/MF/not filmed.

DETAILED TABLES:

[Tables showing utilization, personnel, and finances generally include number of hospitals and beds; admissions, inpatient days, occupancy rate, average daily patient census, average stay, and surgical operations; emergency and other outpatient visits; bassinets and births; FTE personnel and trainees, by type; and expenses, including payroll and employee benefits.

Unless otherwise noted, tables show data by hospital classification, generally including type of control (Federal and other government, nongovernment not-for-profit, investor-owned for-profit); major type of service (psychiatric, tuberculosis/other respiratory diseases, and general/other special); and length of stay (short-term and long-term). Many tables include further detail by bed-size and/or other special service categories.

"U.S.-associated areas" refers to 5-6 outlying territories.]

A1865–4.1: Hospital Statistics

TRENDS

1. Trends in utilization, personnel, and finances, for selected years 1946-82. (p. 4)

CURRENT DATA

[Tables 2A-14 show data for 1982 or most recent accounting period.]

2A-2B. Utilization, personnel, and finances in short-term and long-term hospitals. (p. 8-11)

3. Utilization, personnel per census, and finances per inpatient day. (p. 12)

4A-4D. Utilization of and personnel and finances in hospital units and nursing-home-type units operated by hospitals; and by community hospitals, by State [and census division (not shown by hospital classification)]. (p. 14-17)

5A-5E. Utilization, personnel, and finances: in U.S. registered hospitals, in census divisions, in States, in U.S. associated areas [aggregate, including Puerto Rico], and in Puerto Rico. (p. 22-147)

6-7. Utilization, personnel, and finances in community hospitals: by SMSA [grouped by State and census division, with totals for nonmetro areas]; and for the 100 largest central cities; [not shown by hospital classification]. (p. 152-175)

8. Utilization, personnel, and finances in community hospitals affiliated with medical schools [by census division]. (p. 180)

9. Utilization, personnel per census, and finances per inpatient day in accredited hospitals. (p. 184)

10A-10B. AHA membership, approval [accreditation], and affiliation status [cancer program, residency, medical school, nursing school, Council of Teaching Hospitals, Blue Cross, and Medicare, all by hospital classification for U.S., and totals by State and individual associated area]. (p. 186-187)

11. Revenue in community hospitals [inpatient and outpatient revenues in all and nongovernment not-for-profit hospitals, by bed size for U.S., and totals by census division and State]. (p. 188)

12A-12B. Facilities and services [42 detailed types, including abortion, organ transplants, blood banks, genetic counseling, family planning, alcoholism/chemical dependency, computerized tomography scanners, and hospice, by hospital classification for U.S., and totals by census division and State]. (p. 193-204)

13A-13B. Hospitals, units, and beds, by [detailed] inpatient service area [by hospital classification for U.S., and totals by census division and State]. (p. 206-213)

14. Utilization, personnel, and finances in U.S. nonregistered hospitals. (p. 218)

A1865–5 HOSPITAL-BLUE CROSS CONTRACT PROVISIONS, July 1, 1983
Biennial. 1984. v + 105 p.
AHA Catalog No. 073184.
ISBN 0-939450-34-8.
ISSN 0747-8097.
SRI/MF/not filmed

Biennial report on provisions of hospital-Blue Cross contracts in effect as of July 1983. Includes data for individual contracts; and aggregate data for U.S., with comparisons to 1981 and 1979, and selected detail by census division. Most contracts cover all participating hospitals in a single State. Some cover individual cities or other geographic areas.

Includes detailed methods of payment; financial provisions regarding depreciation, debt amortization and interest expense, bad debts, and charity care; provisions for contract termination and amendment; negotiating organization; cost containment and bed reduction incentives; comprehensive health planning, utilization review, generic drug use, and other requirements; appeals procedures; and other contract characteristics.

Also includes data on total non-Federal hospitals in contract area, number participating in conatract, and Blue Cross plan enrollees as percent of total area population, all by location of contract; and number of contracts, and share of U.S. total Blue Cross contract hospitals and plan enrollment, all by census division.

Data are from 1983 AHA survey of State hospital assns, and previous surveys.

Contains contents listing (p. iii); executive summary (p. 1-4); introduction and survey methodology (p. 5-9); national and regional summaries with 9 tables and accompanying narrative (p. 11-37); 3 detailed tables with explanatory notes (p. 39-88); and sample survey questionnaire, definitions, and bibliography (p. 89-105).

This is the 6th edition of the report. For description of the 5th edition, see SRI 1983 Annual, under this number.

Availability: AHA Services, Inc., PO Box 99376, Chicago IL 60611 (prepaid); 4444 W. Ferdinand, Chicago IL 60624 (billed), members $12.00, nonmembers $15.00; SRI/MF/not filmed.

A1875
American Hotel and Motel Association

A1875–1 SALARY AND BENEFIT SURVEY REPORT, Lodging Industry Management Positions
Annual. Oct. 1983.
iii + 38 p.
SRI/MF/complete

Annual report, for 1983, on hotel/motel management compensation and benefits. Covers base salary, bonus, total compensation, and bonus guidelines, for bonus-eligible employees; and total compensation for non-bonus employees; for 11 hotel-related positions by hotel/motel size, and 5 restaurant-related positions by food/beverage revenue level. Data are shown as averages, medians, and 25th and 75th percentiles, and include number of incumbents.

Also includes data on insurance benefits; sick leave, vacation, and holiday policies; and pension and profit-sharing/thrift plans.

Data are from a sample survey of chain-affiliated establishments, conducted in early 1983 by American Hotel & Motel Assn and Peat, Marwick, Mitchell & Co.

Contains contents listing (p. i-iii); introduction and background (p. 1-2); 16 compensation tables (p. 3-18); narrative benefits summary, interspersed with 16 text tables (p. 19-34); and job descriptions (p. 35-38).

This is the 11th survey report. For description of previous report, for 1982, see SRI 1982 Annual under this number.

Availability: American Hotel and Motel Association, Publications Department, 888 Seventh Ave., New York NY 10019, members $40.00, nonmembers $60.00; SRI/MF/complete.

A1875–2 SURVEY OF THE ENERGY AND WATER USE OF SELECTED HOTELS AND MOTELS, 1983
Annual. 1984.
53 p. var. paging.
SRI/MF/complete

Annual report on hotel/motel energy and water use, 1982-83, with trends from 1977. Includes data on total electricity, fossil fuel, and water use, shown for individual hotels/motels identified by State location only. Also includes energy use per square foot; water use per room and per guest; and summary data by property size (number of rooms) and/or region.

Data were compiled by the Technical Services Center from an energy survey of 204 properties in 41 States and D.C., and a water survey of 166 properties in 39 States.

Contains contents and table listings (3 p.); foreword, with 1 table (p. i-iii); narrative report in 2 sections, interspersed with text data and 9 summary tables (p. 1-20); and appendices A-C, with 16 detailed tables (29 p.).

Availability: American Hotel and Motel Association, Publications Department, 888 Seventh Ave., New York NY 10019, $10.00; SRI/MF/complete.

A1875–3 HOTEL/MOTEL WAGE RATES and Other Payroll Costs for Major U.S. Cities
Recurring (irreg.) Mar. 1984.
2 + 41 p.
SRI/MF/complete

Recurring report on wage rates and benefits for hotel/motel employees in 23 major cities, various years 1981-87. Data are based on union contract provisions.

Contains contents listing (1 p.) and the following:

a. 1 table, repeated for 17 occupations, showing hours worked per day, days worked per week, and hourly wage, all by city, various years 1981-87, depending on period covered by labor contract. (p. 1-17)

b. Summaries of holiday, vacation, pension, and health benefits; pay policies for banquet work by food service personnel; and miscellaneous policies, including probationary periods, jury duty, funeral pay, schedule posting requirement, shift differential, and pay for reporting to work; all shown for each city. (p. 18-38)

c. List of data sources, including parties to labor contracts and contract term, for each city. (p. 39-41).

Previous report, issued Aug. 1982, is described in SRI 1982 Annual, under this number.

Availability: American Hotel and Motel Association, Publications Department, 888 Seventh Ave., New York NY 10019, members $15.00, nonmembers $25.00; SRI/MF/complete.

A1880
American Humane Association

A1880–1 HIGHLIGHTS OF OFFICIAL CHILD NEGLECT AND ABUSE REPORTING, 1982
Annual. 1984. 35 p.
LC 78-102260.
SRI/MF/complete

Annual report on cases of child abuse and neglect, with data by jurisdiction, and by characteristics of cases, children, and perpetrators, 1982. Data are from a national study based on State and U.S. Territory official reports of child protective service agencies.

Contains contents listing (1 p.); introduction (p. 1); narrative analysis, with 16 tables, described below (p. 2-24); and appendix, with data items in the national study data base, and 1 table showing data participants by State and territory (p. 25-35).

More detailed data are available from the issuing agency upon request.

Availability: American Humane Association, Child Protection Division, 9725 E. Hampden Ave., Denver CO 80231, $5.00; SRI/MF/complete.

TABLES:
[Data are shown for 1982, unless otherwise noted.]

a. Cases reported: total, 1976-82; and by State, Guam, Puerto Rico, Virgin Islands, and Mariana Islands, 1982. Tables 1-2. (p. 2-4)

b. Case distribution: by case type; source of report; perpetrator and caretaker/household characteristics, including age, sex, race/ethnicity (including Hispanic), number of children in home, and public assistance status; child's age, sex, race/ethnicity, and relationship to caretaker and perpetrator; family stress factors; type of maltreatment; case substantiation and status; and services provided; with various cross-tabulations. Tables 3-16. (p. 5-21)

A1885
American Institute of
Certified Public Accountants

A1885–1   SUPPLY OF ACCOUNTING GRADUATES and the Demand for Public Accounting Recruits, 1984
Annual. 1984. 25 p.
LC 82-21369.
SRI/MF/not filmed

Annual survey report, by Mary McInnes and James H. MacNeill, estimating supply and demand for accounting graduates by degree level, by demographic and selected other characteristics, 1982/83-1983/84 with trends from 1971/72.

Covers accounting graduates by region, sex, and institution's accreditation status with American Assembly of Collegiate Schools of Business (AACSB), and for public and private schools, and minorities (American Indians, Asians, blacks, and Hispanics) in traditionally minority and majority schools; and public accounting firms' employment of new graduates, by sex and minority group; all by degree level.

Also includes percent of new hires expected to hold master's degree, by firm size; and employment plans of graduates, by degree level.

Data are from responses of 379 accredited and nonaccredited AACSB member schools, 73 nonmember schools, and 208 public accounting firms to surveys conducted during 1984.

Contains contents/table listing (2 p.); introduction, summary, and survey results with 32 tables (p. 1-22); and 3 appendices, including questionnaire facsimiles (p. 23-25).

This is the 14th annual report.

Availability: American Institute of Certified Public Accountants, 1211 Ave. of the Americas, New York NY 10036-8775, †; SRI/MF/not filmed.

A1960
American Institute of Physics

A1960–1   EMPLOYMENT SURVEY, 1982
Annual. Oct. 1983. 8 p.
AIP Pub. No. R-282.6.
SRI/MF/complete

Annual report, by Susanne D. Ellis, on employment status of 1981/82 physics and astronomy graduates, by highest degree earned. Covers types of employment and employers, and characteristics of employed graduates and graduates continuing their studies.

Data are from a survey conducted each Dec. as a follow-up to 2 summer surveys reported in *Survey of Physics and Astronomy Bachelor's Degree Recipients* and *Graduate Student Survey.* The 1982 summer survey reports are described in SRI 1983 Annual, under A1960-3 and A1960-4, respectively.

Contains narrative summary, 2 charts, and 10 tables listed below.

Availability: American Institute of Physics, Manpower Statistics Division, 335 E. 45th St., New York NY 10017, †; SRI/MF/complete.

TABLES:
[Data are for 1981/82 degree recipients, unless otherwise noted.

Data on work activity variously include teaching, research, computer science, data analysis, programming, research/development/design, and quality control.

Data on type of employer variously include academic institution, industry, government, and federally funded research center.

Data on occupational status generally include postdoctorate studies/student, full-time employed, part-time employed, unemployed/seeking employment, and sometimes military service.]

I-II. Changes in occupational status of physics and astronomy degree recipients [by degree level] between the summer of 1982 and the following winter. (p. 2-3)

III. Occupational status of experimental and theoretical [doctoral] physicists by type of dissertation research, 1982/83. (p. 3)

IV. Characteristics [sex, age, citizenship, type of research, and subfield] of postdoctoral and full-time employed physics and astronomy doctorate recipients. (p. 4)

V. Subfield mobility of doctoral level physicists [subfield distribution of postdoctoral fellowships and employment, by dissertation subfield]. (p. 5)

VI. Factors influencing the length of postdoctoral fellowships [percent taking less or more than 2 years, by citizenship, subfield, and whether specifically sought postdoctorate], for doctoral level physicists. (p. 6)

VII. Employment with potential permanence accepted by doctorate recipients [by subfield, work activity, whether physics related, and whether interested in a job change; by type of employer]. (p. 6)

VIII-IX. Characteristics of physics masters and bachelors that influence the time required to secure employment [percent requiring various time periods, by sex, age, highest degree granted at institution last attended, type of em-

ployment, type of employer (masters only), school region (bachelors only), and type of work activity]. (p. 7-8)

X. Employment of astronomy bachelors [by work activity and type of employer, with aggregate median monthly salary]. (p. 8)

A1960–2   PHYSICS AND ASTRONOMY ENROLLMENTS AND DEGREES
Annual series. For individual publication data, see below.
SRI/MF/complete

Series of 3 annual reports, by Susanne D. Ellis, on enrollments and degrees awarded in physics and astronomy depts of U.S. colleges and universities.

Reports are based on an annual AIP survey of approximately 800 degree-granting depts.

Series consists of 1 summary analytical report showing aggregate data by institution, student, or dept characteristics; and 2 supplementary reports showing detailed survey data by institution.

Reports are individually described below.

Availability: American Institute of Physics, Manpower Statistics Division, 335 E. 45th St., New York NY 10017, †; SRI/MF/complete.

A1960–2.1: Enrollments and Degrees
[Annual. Mar. 1984. 8 p. AIP Pub. No. R-151.21. SRI/MF/complete.]

Annual summary report on physics and astronomy enrollments and degrees awarded, various academic years 1972/73-1983/84.

Contains narrative analysis, interspersed with 3 trend charts, and 1 chart and 13 tables listed below.

For description of previous report, see SRI 1983 Annual under A1960-2.3.

TABLES AND CHART:
[Data by type of institution are shown by highest degree offered. Data by region are shown for 9 census divisions. Tables II-III and XII show enrollment data through 1983/84 and degree data through 1982/83.]

PHYSICS

I. Institutions, by highest physics degree offered, 1978/79-1983/84. (p. 1)

II-III. Physics enrollments and degrees awarded; and undergraduate and graduate enrollments and degrees, by institution type; 1972/73-1983/84. (p. 2)

IV. Introductory physics enrollments in physics degree-granting institutions, by geographic region, 1979/80-1983/84. (p. 3)

V. Introductory physics enrollments [by major field of study and institution type], 1983/84. (p. 3)

Figure II. Actual and projected number of undergraduate physics majors [by level, for graduating classes of 1984-87]. (p. 4)

VI. Undergraduate physics majors [by level], by geographic region and type of institution, 1983/84. (p. 4)

VII. Trend in entering U.S. and foreign graduate physics students, 1974/75-1983/84. (p. 5)

VIII. Full-time and part-time graduate physics enrollment, by type of institution, 1974/75-1983/84. (p. 5)

IX. Unfilled assistantships for 1st-year graduate physics students [in doctorate- and masters-granting depts, by region], Sept. 1983. (p. 5)

X-XI. Physics degrees, by type of institution and geographic region; and number of physics degrees granted, by sex and minority group status [black, American Indian, Puerto Rican, Mexican American, Hispanic, Oriental, Asian Indian, and Arab]; 1982/83. (p. 6-7)

ASTRONOMY

XII. Trend in astronomy enrollments and degrees, 1975/76-1983/84. (p. 7)

XIII. Astronomy [depts and] enrollments 1983/84, and degrees 1982/83, by type of institution. (p. 8)

A1960–2.2: Data on Physics Enrollments and Degrees: A Supplement

[Annual. Mar. 1984. 20 p. AIP Pub. No. R-151.21A. SRI/MF/complete.]

Annual supplement to AIP survey report, presenting detailed data on physics degrees granted in 1982/83, and enrollments in 1983/84, for approximately 750 individual degree-granting colleges and universities.

Contains 1 table showing physics undergraduates by class, and total and 1st-year graduate students, 1983/84; and degrees granted, by level, 1982/83; all by institution, arranged by State.

For description of previous report, see SRI 1983 Annual under A1960-2.1.

A1960–2.3: Data on Astronomy Enrollments and Degrees: A Supplement

[Annual. Mar. 1984. 6 p. AIP Pub. No. R-151.21B. SRI/MF/complete.]

Annual supplement to AIP survey report, presenting detailed data on astronomy degrees granted in 1982/83, and enrollments in 1983/84, for 68 individual degree-granting colleges and universities.

Contains 1 table showing enrollments in introductory astronomy courses by science and nonscience majors, number of junior and senior undergraduate majors, and total and 1st-year graduate students, 1983/84; astronomy degrees granted, by level, 1982/83; and whether dept is for astronomy only or astronomy/physics combined; all by institution, arranged by State.

For description of previous report, see SRI 1983 Annual under A1960-2.2.

A1960–3   1982/83 SURVEY OF PHYSICS AND ASTRONOMY BACHELOR'S DEGREE RECIPIENTS

Annual. Mar. 1984. 8 p. AIP Pub. No. R-211.15. SRI/MF/complete

Annual report, by Susanne D. Ellis, on a survey of postgraduation plans and characteristics of 1982/83 physics and astronomy bachelor degree recipients.

Includes data on physics bachelors' starting salaries, plans of minority graduates, and anticipated sources for financing graduate study.

Data are from an American Institute of Physics survey, conducted during summer 1983, of 4,795 physics and 138 astronomy baccalaureate recipients, 1982/83 academic year.

Contains narrative summary; 4 charts showing plans of physics and astronomy bachelors, 1982 and selected trends; and 12 tables, listed below.

Availability: American Institute of Physics, Manpower Statistics Division, 335 E. 45th St., New York NY 10017, †; SRI/MF/complete.

TABLES:

[Data by type of employer include some or all of the following: manufacturing and service industries, high school, college/university, government, military, federally funded R&D centers, and other. Data by type of institution are by highest degree offered at institution attended. Data are for academic year 1982/83, unless otherwise noted.]

PHYSICS GRADUATES

I. Postbaccalaureate plans [percent planning physics or other graduate study, civilian employment, military service, and undecided] of successive graduating classes of physics bachelors [and total bachelor's degrees, 1973/74-1982/83]. (p. 1)

II. Characteristics of new physics bachelors [by sex, age, citizenship, minority group (U.S. blacks and other minorities, and foreign minorities), type of institution attended, and whether double major; for graduates planning physics or other graduate study, employment, or undecided]. (p. 2)

III. Comparison between men and women physics bachelors having taken high school physics. (p. 3)

IV. Postbaccalaureate plans [physics or other graduate study, and employment] of U.S. [black, Oriental, and other] and foreign [Oriental and other] minority groups among the physics bachelors of the class of 1983. (p. 3)

V. Selected characteristics [sex, and region and type of institution attended] of minority physics bachelors [black, Mexican American, American and Asian Indian, Hispanic, U.S. and foreign Oriental, and Arab]. (p. 3)

VI. Sources of anticipated support for 1st-year graduate study, biennially 1979-83. (p. 4)

VII. Changes in employment outlook for new physics bachelors [by number of job offers at graduation], 1973-83. (p. 4)

VIII. Initial employment of physics bachelors [by type of employer, 1975/76-1982/83]. (p. 6)

IX. Starting [median] salaries of physics bachelors [by sex and type of employer]. (p. 6)

X. Full-time employment [type of work activity] of new physics bachelors [by type of employer]. (p. 6)

ASTRONOMY GRADUATES

XI. Postbaccalaureate plans [astronomy or other graduate study, employment, and undecided] of successive graduating classes of astronomy bachelors [1975/76-1982/83]. (p. 7)

XII. Characteristics [sex, citizenship, age, type of high school physics and type of institution attended, whether science or arts degree, and double major] of astronomy bachelors. (p. 7)

A1960–4   1982/83 GRADUATE STUDENT SURVEY

Annual. July 1984. 12 p. AIP Pub. No. R-207.16. SRI/MF/complete

Annual report, by Susanne D. Ellis, on physics and astronomy graduate student and degree recipient characteristics and employment opportunities, 1982/83 academic year. Most data are based on responses of 6,442 physics and 494 astronomy graduate students and degree recipients to a summer 1983 survey by the American Institute of Physics.

Contains narrative summary, interspersed with 5 charts showing summary data, and academic background and postdegree employment status of physics terminal master's and physics and astronomy doctorate degree recipients, 1982/83; and 14 tables, listed below.

Survey of physics graduate students has been conducted annually since early 1960s. Astronomy students were added in 1974.

Availability: American Institute of Physics, Manpower Statistics Division, 335 E. 45th St., New York NY 10017, †; SRI/MF/complete.

TABLES:

[Employer types include secondary school, 4-year college, university, industry, government/military, nonprofit organizations, and federally funded research centers. Data are for 1982/83 academic year.]

PHYSICS GRADUATE STUDENTS

I. Characteristics of the graduate physics student population [sex, citizenship, professional society membership, major of bachelor's degree, type of bachelor's and graduate institution, student status, and source of support, for all graduate students, 1st-year students, and terminal master's and doctorate degree recipients]. (p. 2)

II. Characteristics of minority group physics students [sex, degree and student status, professional society membership, FTE years of graduate study, subfield, and graduate degree recipients, for U.S. and foreign black, American Indian, Puerto Rican, Mexican American, other U.S. and foreign Hispanic, Asian Indian, U.S. and foreign oriental, and Arab]. (p. 3)

III. Number of graduate physics students, by subfield and years of graduate study completed. (p. 3)

IV. Sources of support for graduate physics students, by sex and degree status. (p. 4)

V. Number of advanced graduate physics students specializing in selected experimental or theoretical subfields, by years of graduate study completed. (p. 4)

VI. Distribution by subfield and [number of] employment offers, for doctorate [degree] recipients. (p. 5)

VII. Employment of doctoral graduates, by citizenship [for U.S. and foreign employers]. (p. 5)

VIII. Distribution by subfield [and number] of employment offers, for terminal master's [degree recipients]. (p. 7)

IX. Employment characteristics [employer type and work activity] of recipients of master's degrees. (p. 7)

X. Use of physics in potentially permanent employment of graduate degree recipients [percent of doctorate and terminal master's degree recipients reporting extensive, little, or no use of physics training with respect to method and/or subject matter, by type of employer]. (p. 9)

XI. Initial employment with potential permanence for physics doctorate [degree] recipients [by type of employer, including university tenure status, and by type of work activity]. (p. 9)

XII. Median monthly salaries paid by U.S. employers to new physics graduates [by type of employer, for bachelor's, terminal master's, and doctorate degree recipients]. (p. 10)

ASTRONOMY GRADUATE STUDENTS

XIII. Graduate astronomy students, by subfield and years of graduate study. (p. 10)

XIV. Characteristics of the graduate astronomy student population [same detail as in table I]. (p. 11)

A1960–6 1982 SALARIES, SOCIETY MEMBERSHIP SURVEY
Annual. Nov. 1983.
4+28 p. Pub. No. R-311.
ISBN 0-88318-434-6.
SRI/MF/complete

Annual report on salaries of doctoral level physicists, with some data for master's and bachelor's levels, 1982 with comparisons to 1981. Data include means, medians, and quartiles, and are shown by census division, State, selected metro area, employer type, years from degree, work activity, and sex, with selected cross-tabulations. Also includes median age for most categories.

Employer types include universities and colleges (with detail by faculty rank), secondary schools, industry/self employed, government, federally funded R&D centers, and nonprofit organizations.

Work activities include teaching, basic and applied research, development, design/engineering, and administration.

Data are from a spring 1982 random sample survey of American Institute of Physics members.

Contains contents and table listing (1 p.); introduction, with 17 charts and 25 tables (p. 1-26); and appendices with technical notes (27-28).

This is the 1st annual report.

Availability: American Institute of Physics, Manpower Statistics Division, 335 E. 45th St., New York, NY 10017, single copies †, multiple copies on request; SRI/MF/complete.

A2000
American
Iron and Steel Institute

A2000–2 ANNUAL STATISTICAL REPORT, American Iron and Steel Institute, 1983
Annual. 1984. 115 p.
LC 14-3046.
SRI/MF/complete

Annual report, for 1983, on the iron and steel industry, with trends from the 1940s. Includes data on U.S. industry production, finances, employment, shipments, and foreign trade. Also includes selected data for Canada and other foreign countries.

Data are compiled by American Iron and Steel Institute from individual companies and from other foreign and domestic sources, including U.S. Depts of Labor, Commerce, and Interior.

Contains contents listing (1 p.); and 74 tables, listed below.

Availability: American Iron and Steel Institute, 1000 16th St., NW, Washington DC 20036, $15.00 (prepaid); SRI/MF/complete.

TABLES:
[Tables show data for U.S., unless otherwise noted. Data by grade are generally for carbon, alloy, and stainless steel.]

A2000–2.1: Financial and Employment Data

SELECTED HIGHLIGHTS
[Tables 1A-1D show data for 1974-83.]

1A. Shipments, apparent supply, imports [and exports of steel mill products], and employment. (p. 8)

1B. Raw steel data [world and U.S. production, U.S. capability, and percent U.S. production by furnace and cast types]. (p. 8)

1C. Selected financial highlights [including sales, net income, stockholders' equity, working capital ratio, long-term debt, and capital expenditures]. (p. 9)

1D. Source and use of funds [including net income less cash dividends declared, income reinvested, depreciation, change in reserves, total internal sources, external debt/stock, capital expenditures, change in working capital, miscellaneous investment/all other, and total disposition of funds]. (p. 9)

1E. Capital expenditures for environmental facilities [selected periods 1951-75, annually 1976-83, and authorized for 1984/later]. (p. 10)

FINANCIAL AND ECONOMIC STATISTICS

2-3. Income, dividends, [and] return on sales and stockholders' equity [including costs for employment, supplies, and taxes, and number of stockholders, 1974-83]; and steel vs. all other business segments [sales, depreciation/depletion/amortization, operating income, assets, and capital expenditures, 1979-83]. (p. 12-13)

4. Balance sheet [by major item, 1974-83]. (p. 14)

5. BLS: CPI and PPI of steel prices [for steel mill products, other iron/steel products, and total industrial commodities, 1960-83 and monthly 1983]. (p. 15)

EMPLOYMENT AND WAGE DATA
[Tables 6-7 and 10-11 show data for employees engaged in the production of iron/steel products.]

6. Total employment cost per hour worked, wage employees [including regular pay, overtime, and other payroll costs, 1964-83]. (p. 18)

6A. Standard hourly wage rate changes and minimum wage rates (per agreement with the United Steelworkers of America) [effective dates Oct. 1, 1961-Mar. 1, 1983]. (p. 19)

7. Number of employees, hours worked, and payroll cost [for wage and salaried employees, 1964-83]. (p. 20)

8. Collective bargaining agreements with United Steelworkers of America [with effective date of agreement and periods of general steel strikes, 1946-83]. (p. 21)

9. BLS index of output per man-hour in the steel industry (all employees) [1953-83]. (p. 22)

10. Occupational injury/illness [with aggregate man-hours, deaths, and workdays lost, 1979-83]. (p. 23)

11. Wage employees classified by age and by length of service [1981-82]. (p. 23)

A2000–2.2: Shipments, Exports, and Imports
[Most tables show data by product. Data by market classification are shown by industry and/or use.]

SHIPMENTS OF STEEL PRODUCTS

12-13. Shipments of steel mill products, all grades and by grades, 1983. (p. 26-29)

14-15. Net shipments of steel mill products, all grades and by market classifications, [1974-83]. (p. 30-35)

16. Shipments of steel mill products by market classification, all grades, 1983. (p. 36-38)

EXPORTS

17-18. Exports of iron and steel products [with total steel mill exports by grade, various years 1974-83]. (p. 40-43)

19. Exports of steel mill products [by month, 1974-83]. (p. 43)

20-20A. Exports of iron and steel products by countries of destination, 1983. (p. 44-51)

IMPORTS

21-22. Imports of iron and steel products [with total steel mill imports by grade, various years 1974-83]. (p. 52-55)

23. Imports of steel mill products [by month, 1974-83]. (p. 55)

24-25. Imports of iron and steel products, 1983; and of steel mill products [1979-83; all] by countries of origin. (p. 56-63)

26-26A. Imports of iron and steel products, by customs district [and port], 1983. (p. 64-71)

A2000–2.3: Production and Consumption
RAW STEEL PRODUCTION

27-28. Raw steel production: by type of furnace, grade, and cast [1969-83]; and by States [1979-83]. (p. 74-76)

29. Monthly and quarterly raw steel production and capability utilization [1979-83]. (p. 77)

PIG IRON AND FERROALLOYS PRODUCTION

30-32. Blast furnace production [by type of furnace]; pig iron consumption and sales; and pig iron shipments other than for own use [by type; all 1974-83]. (p. 80)

33-34. Production of ferroalloys; and ferroalloy imports for consumption; [both by type, 1979-83]. (p. 81)

35. Materials used by blast furnaces in manufacture of iron (pig/molten), 1983. (p. 82)

BASIC MATERIALS

36. Consumption of coal [by use, 1974-83]. (p. 84)

37. Consumption of fluxes [1978-82, and by use 1983, by flux type]. (p. 84)

38. Production, receipts, consumption, and shipments of coke [1979-83]. (p. 85)

39. Iron ore receipts and consumption [by original source in U.S., Canada, and all other foreign countries], 1983. (p. 86)

40-41. [U.S.] imports of iron ore by countries, and iron ore shipments destined for Great Lakes [by port of origin, 1974-83]. (p. 87-88)

42. Agglomerated products [materials used, products, receipts of foreign production, and consumption in blast and steelmaking furnaces, 1979-83]. (p. 89)

43-44. Scrap: stocks, production, receipts, and consumption [1974-83]; and scrap consumption by grade [including iron scrap, 1982-83]. (p. 90-91)

45. Consumption of scrap and pig iron by types of furnaces [1979-83]. (p. 92)

46-48. Consumption of electric power, oxygen, and fuels [by type, with selected data by use, 1979-83]. (p. 93-95)

49. Imports for [U.S.] consumption of manganese ore, by countries of origin [1974-83]. (p. 96)

A2000-2.4: Canadian and World Production

CANADA

[Tables 50-63 show data for Canada.]

50-51. Income, [costs], dividends, return on sales and stockholders' equity; and balance sheet; (reported by companies comprising 80% of Canadian raw steel production) [1982-83]. (p. 98-99)

52-54. Production of pig iron and ferroalloys; materials consumed by blast furnaces in the production of pig iron; and raw steel production [by type of furnace; 1974-83]. (p. 100-101)

55. Net shipments of rolled steel products [by product, 1974-83]. (p. 102)

56-57. Imports and exports of iron and steel products [by product, 1979-83]. (p. 104-105)

58-60. Consumption of coal, coke, and fuel oil [by use, 1974-83]. (p. 106-107)

61-63. Consumption of fluxes [by type] in steelmaking furnaces [1974-83]; and consumption of oxygen and pig iron [by use,1979-83]. (p. 107-108)

WORLD STATISTICS

64-66. World production of iron ore/concentrates/agglomerates, pig iron, and raw steel, by countries [with totals for world areas, 1979-83]. (p. 110-115)

A2010
American
Iron Ore Association

A2010-1   IRON ORE AND IRON ORE AGGLOMERATES: U.S. and Canada
Monthly.   Approx. 2 p.
SRI/MF/not filmed

Monthly report on U.S. and Canadian iron industry, covering domestic and foreign receipts, consumption, and inventories of ore; and blast furnaces operating. Data are compiled jointly by American Iron Ore Assn and American Iron and Steel Institute. Reports are issued approximately 2 months after month of coverage.

Contains 8 tables showing the following for U.S. and Canada:

a. Great Lakes and other U.S. Canadian ores, and total foreign ores: receipts at iron/steel plants; consumption in blast furnaces, steel furnaces, sintering plants, and miscellaneous processes; and inventory at furnace yards and docks/plants/mines; for month of coverage and/or current year to date, with comparisons to previous year.

b. Blast furnaces: total and number in operation last day of month.

Most U.S. data are also shown by State or region.

Availability: American Iron Ore Association, 1501 Euclid Ave., 514 Bulkley Bldg., Cleveland OH 44115, †; SRI/MF/not filmed.

Issues reviewed during 1984: Sept. 1983-Aug. 1984 (D).

A2010-2   SHIPMENTS OF U.S. AND CANADIAN IRON ORE from Loading Docks Destined to Great Lakes
Monthly.   Approx. 1 p.
SRI/MF/not filmed

Monthly summary of Great Lakes shipments of U.S. and Canadian iron ore, by loading port of origin. Data are compiled by the American Iron Ore Assn and are for month of coverage, current year to date, and same periods of previous year. Reports are issued approximately 1-3 weeks after month of coverage.

Contains 1 monthly table showing shipments in gross tons for U.S., Canada, combined countries, and by individual Great Lake port.

Dec. issue also includes an annual table summarizing shipment trends in 1970s.

Availability: American Iron Ore Association, 1501 Euclid Ave., 514 Bulkley Bldg., Cleveland OH 44115, †; SRI/MF/not filmed.

Issues reviewed during 1984: Oct. 1983-Sept. 1984 (D).

A2010-3   IRON ORE, 1983
Annual.   June 1984.
3+108 p.
LC 59-42154.
SRI/MF/not filmed

Annual report on the iron ore industry in Canada and U.S., 1983, with trends from 1974. Covers production, trade by country of destination and origin, inventories, consumption, receipts, and shipments.

Data were compiled by American Iron Ore Assn from original data collected, and from other sources, including American Iron and Steel Institute, Statistics Canada, and U.S. Dept of Interior.

Contains contents listing (1 p.); definitions (p. 1); 7 sections with explanatory notes, 3 maps, and 51 tables listed below (p. 3-90); and directory of reporting companies, and index (p. 91-108).

Availability: American Iron Ore Association, 1501 Euclid Ave., 514 Bulkley Bldg., Cleveland OH 44115, †; SRI/MF/not filmed.

TABLES:

[Iron ore originating areas are U.S. Great Lakes, western, southern, and northeastern areas; and Canadian Great Lakes, western, and eastern areas. Foreign ores are all iron ores from outside U.S. and Canada.]

A2010-3.1: 1983 Data

[Tables show data for 1983. Data by plant location are for selected groups of States.]

PRODUCTION AND SHIPMENTS

[1-2] Iron ore mine production and total shipments, U.S. and Canada [by originating area and type of ore product, including coarse, fines, pellets, and sinter]. (p. 8-9)

[3-4] Iron ore mined and shipped, U.S. Great Lakes originating area by ranges, and Canada Great Lakes originating area by districts. (p. 10-11)

INVENTORIES, RECEIPTS, AND CONSUMPTION

[5] Domestic/foreign iron ores at iron/steel plants [Jan. 1 and Dec. 31 inventory, and receipts and consumption, for] U.S. [by plant location] and Canada. (p. 12)

[6-11] U.S. and Canada iron ores [by originating area], and foreign iron ores, at iron/steel plants [Jan. 1 and Dec. 31 inventory, and receipts and consumption, for U.S. by plant location and for Canada]. (p. 13-18)

[12-14] Receipts, consumption, and [Dec. 31] inventory of iron ore at U.S. iron/steel plants [by plant location, for U.S. and Canadian Great Lakes and other originating area and for foreign ores]. (p. 19-21)

[15-16] Receipts and consumption at U.S. and Canadian iron/steel plants and inventory at furnace yards and docks/plants/mines [by month]. (p. 22-23)

A2010-3.2: Trends

[Tables show data for 1974-83, unless otherwise noted.]

SHIPMENTS AND TRADE

[1] Iron ore mine production and total shipments, U.S. and Canada [by type of ore product, by originating area], 1979-83. (p. 26)

[2-3] Iron ore in U.S. and Canada [shipments, exports, and imports]. (p. 28-29)

[4] Iron ore exported from U.S. [by country of destination]. (p. 30)

[5-6] Iron ore imports to U.S. by country of origin and by customs districts. (p. 32-35)

[7-8] Iron ore: exported from Canada [by country of destination]; and imports to Canada by country of origin. (p. 36-37)

[9-10] U.S. and Canadian iron ore shipments from loading docks destined to the Great Lakes [annually by port and dock, and total by month]. (p. 38-41)

RECEIPTS, CONSUMPTION, AND INVENTORY

[Tables [11-24] show data by the following iron ore originating areas: Great Lake areas in U.S. and Canada, other U.S. and Canadian areas, and foreign ores. Inventory data are shown as of Dec. 31.]

[11-12] Receipts and consumption of iron ore at U.S. iron/steel plants. (p. 42-43)

[13-15] Consumption of iron ore in U.S. blast and steel furnaces, and sintering plants (located at iron/steel plants). (p. 44-46)

[16-17] Inventory of iron ore at U.S. iron/steel plants, 1974-83; at U.S. docks, 1978-79; and at docks/plants/mines, 1980-83. (p. 47-48)

[18] Receipts of iron ore at Canadian iron/steel plants. (p. 49)

[19-22] Consumption of iron ore at Canadian iron/steel plants, blast and steel furnaces, and sintering plants (located at iron/steel plants). (p. 50-53)

[23-24] Inventory of iron ore at Canadian iron/steel plants, 1974-83; and at docks/plants/mines, 1980-83. (p. 54-55)

WORLD PRODUCTION

[25] World production of iron ore/iron ore concentrates/iron ore agglomerates, by countries. (p. 56-58)

A2010–3.3: Ore Products and Analyses

FURNACES

[1] Number of blast furnaces operating last day of month, U.S. [by State or State group], and Canada, 1983. (p. 60)

PRODUCTS

[Tables [2-6] show data for 1974-83.]

[2-3] Consumption of ore, scrap, mill cinder, limestone, and coke per net ton of pig iron produced in U.S. and Canada. (p. 61-62)

[4] Production of pig iron, U.S. [by State or State group], and Canada. (p. 63)

[5-6] U.S. and Canada steel production [by type of furnace]. (p. 64)

ANALYSES OF ORE

[7-8] Grade names and analyses [of U.S. and Canadian ore] shipped [by originating area]; and of Canada by-product ores, Great Lakes area; [by grade name and mining company], 1983. (p. 66-76)

[9] Grade classification, average analyses [and shipments], U.S. and Canada combined areas, 1979-83. (p. 79-81)

[10] Type of product, average analyses, [and shipments, for run of mine, coarse, fines, pellets, sinter, and other], U.S. and Canada combined areas [and U.S. originating areas], 1979-83. (p. 85-90)

A2050
American
Jewish Committee

A2050–1   AMERICAN JEWISH YEAR BOOK, 1984
Annual. [1984.] xi+417 p.
Vol. 84.
ISBN 0-8276-0235-9.
LC 99-4040.
SRI/MF/excerpts

Annual compilation, for 1984, of articles on characteristics and activities of Israeli, U.S., and world Jewish community. Includes Jewish population estimates, by U.S. State and selected city, 1983, and by country, 1982.

Contains preface (1 p.); list of contributing authors, and contents listing (p. vii-xi); 3 articles on the war in Lebanon (p. 3-116); 3 articles on U.S. issues affecting Jews, and Jewish demography (p. 119-174); 9 articles on Jewish situation in other countries (p. 175-258); and directories, lists, necrology, calendars, and index (p. 261-417).

Articles containing substantial statistics are described below. This is the 84th annual compilation.

Availability: American Jewish Committee, American Jewish Year Book, 165 E. 56th St., New York NY 10022, $23.50; SRI/MF/excerpts for statistical articles described below.

STATISTICAL ARTICLES:

A2050–1.1: Public Opinion Concerning Israeli Activities in Lebanon

U.S. PUBLIC OPINION POLLS AND THE LEBANON WAR

(p. 105-116) By Geraldine Rosenfield. Article on U.S. public opinion concerning Israeli military activities in Lebanon. Data are based on selected polls conducted during period following Israel's incursion into Lebanon (June-Sept. 1982), with comparative data from previous surveys.

Includes 32 tables showing distribution of responses (with occasional detail for Jewish respondents) to questions on impressions of PLO and various Middle Eastern governments; extent of Israeli responsibility for murders in Palestinian refugee camps in Beirut; Israeli military operations in Lebanon and U.S. reaction; policies of Prime Minister Begin; possible increase in antisemitism among Americans; and reactions of U.S. Jews to events in Israel.

A2050–1.2: U.S. Jewry

SOCIAL CHARACTERISTICS OF THE NEW YORK AREA JEWISH COMMUNITY, 1981

(p. 128-161) Article profiling characteristics of the NYC area Jewish population. Data are from a 1981 United Jewish Appeal/Federation of Jewish Philanthropies of New York survey of approximately 4,500 NYC area Jews. Includes 26 tables showing the following, usually as percent or distribution of respondents, by borough and for 3 suburban counties.

a. Population characteristics: actual population and households, with comparison to total NYC area; household size and composition; marital status of household head; population by age with comparison to total

U.S. and NYC area; and population distribution by number of generations since family immigration.

b. Jewish identification: ritual observances; attendance at religious services; Jewish denomination; philanthropic giving; Jewish education of head of household; readership of Jewish newspapers; visit to Israel; and contemplated settlement in Israel.

c. Education, employment, and income: educational attainment; employment status; households by income level; median and 1st and 3rd quartile household income; and households by size, by income level.

d. Neighborhoods: length of residence in neighborhood; satisfaction with safety and cleanliness; outlook for conditions in 3 years; and neighborhood characteristics considered important.

JEWISH POPULATION IN THE U.S., 1983, ANNUAL FEATURE

(p. 162-174) Three annual tables showing U.S. total population and estimated Jewish population, by State, and by census region and division; and Jewish population by city for communities with a Jewish population of 100 or more; 1983.

Tables are accompanied by a brief narrative analysis, with summary table showing distribution of U.S. total population and Jewish population by census region and division, 1974 and 1983.

Data are from census reports, and National Jewish Population Studies.

A2050–1.3: World Jewry

WORLD JEWISH POPULATION, 1982, ANNUAL FEATURE

(p. 247-258) Annual feature with 7 tables showing total population and estimated Jewish population, by continent, world region, and country, 1982, with comparisons to 1980.

A2068
American League of
Professional Baseball Clubs

A2068–1   1984 AMERICAN LEAGUE RED BOOK
Annual. Feb. 21, 1984.
112 p.
LC 72-625050.
SRI/MF/complete

Annual baseball fact book, for 1984, presenting American League personnel profiles, 1983 performance data, and selected historical team and player records. Data are compiled by the league.

Contains introduction, league regulations, and contents listing (p. 1-3); and the following:

a. Team information, including player rosters, with 1983 performance data; directories of administative personnel and scouts; stadium specifications, game times, and admission prices; minor league teams; and brief profile of manager. (p. 4-45)

b. Profiles of rookie prospects; players with college experience; lists of player transactions and free agents; team and player 1983 batting, pitching, and fielding performance data; 1983 leading performances, with historical data from 1893; player awards; team standings; team and player pitching performance vs. opposing clubs; and career records of active pitchers. (p. 46-72)

c. Historical records, including 20-game winners, and total win/loss records by team, 1901-83; top 10 all-time pitchers and batters in selected categories, by team; lifetime batting records and stolen bases of active players; and team performance vs. opposing clubs since 1901. (p. 73-84)

d. 1983 pennant race, by month; box scores of American League championship and World Series games, and World Series results from 1903; 1983 all-star game rosters and box scores; hall-of-fame members; club managers and standings since 1901; and records set and tied in 1983. (p. 85-96)

e. Umpire profiles and years of service; pinch hitting and road game batting performance leaders, 1983; attendance 1982-83, and all-time records, by team; 1983 game lengths; total league attendance, 1901-83; and lists of public relations officials, broadcasters, and press members. (p. 97-107)

f. 1984 spring training and regular season addresses and schedules. (p. 108-112, and back cover)

Availability: Alfred Publishing Co., PO Box 5964, Sherman Oaks CA 91413, $7.95; SRI/MF/complete.

A2072
American
Logistics Association

A2072–1   ALA 1983-84 WORLDWIDE DIRECTORY AND FACT BOOK
Annual. [1983.] 224 p.
ISBN 0-686-40830-6.
SRI/MF/complete

Annual fact book and directory, for 1983/84, of the American Logistics Assn, presenting information of interest to companies that market food and other consumer products to military resale agencies. Includes statistics on sales by product category or dept, for post exchanges and commissaries by military branch, U.S. Army Troop Support Agency, and Veterans Canteen Service, various years FY70s-83.

Also includes sales-inflation comparisons; average sales and profits per square foot, for Army/Air Force Exchange Service; and shelf space allocations by product, for Army Troop Support Agency.

Data are based on reports from individual agencies.

Contains contents listing (p. 1); ALA information and directories, and members of military-related congressional committees (p. 3-138); and information on military resale agencies, including 1-3 tables for most agencies (p. 139-223).

Availability: American Logistics Association, 1133 15th St., NW, Suite 500, Washington DC 20005, corporate members †, individual members $15.00, nonmembers $25.00; SRI/MF/complete.

A2075
American
Management Associations

A2075–4   MIDDLE MANAGEMENT MORALE IN THE '80s
Monograph. 1983. 48 p.
ISBN 0-8144-3147-X.
LC 83-15068.
SRI/MF/complete

By George E. Breen. Survey report on mid-level managers' job and career satisfaction, experience, and expectations. Includes data on the following topics, with selected detail by age and sex:

a. Criteria for success; effect of selected company policies and external factors on morale/job satisfaction; satisfaction with workplace relationships; whether company uses management by objectives; and involvement in civic activities.

b. Most useful graduate school courses; career timetables; number of jobs held; educational attainment; and expectations for the future, including salary level compared to inflation.

Data are based on 1,536 responses to a survey of American Management Assn members in mid-level management positions.

Contains contents listing (p. 5); narrative report in 6 sections, with 15 tables (p. 9-45); and appendix, with 5 tables on sample characteristics (p. 46-48).

Availability: American Management Associations, AMA Membership Publications Division, 135 W. 50th St., New York NY 10020, members: 1st copy †, additional copies $10.00, nonmembers $13.50; SRI/MF/complete.

A2075–5   CHILD CARE INITIATIVES FOR WORKING PARENTS: Why Employers Get Involved
Monograph. 1983. 56 p.
ISBN 0-8144-3149-6.
LC 83-21546.
SRI/MF/complete

By Renee Y. Magid. Report on employer-sponsored child day care program characteristics, users, and finances, 1982. Includes data on features of worksite care centers; organizations reporting programs, by census division and employment size; employees using programs, by occupation, sex, and marital status; types of programs other than worksite centers; and employer reasons for undertaking and closing programs, perceived benefits of programs to employers, and program start-up costs and funding sources.

Report is based primarily on responses of 204 employers to a survey conducted by the author in July 1982. The survey encompassed industry, labor union, government, and health care facility employers with child care programs.

Contains listing of contents, charts, and tables (p. 5); introduction (p. 9-15); 6 chapters covering history of child care programs, survey methodology, and survey findings, with 2 charts and 13 tables (p. 16-45); and questionnaire facsimile, cover letter, and references (p. 46-56).

Availability: American Management Associations, AMA Membership Publications Division, 135 W. 50th St., New York NY 10020, members $10.00, nonmembers $13.50, students $5.00; SRI/MF/complete.

A2075–6   HOW AMERICAN CHIEF EXECUTIVES SUCCEED: Implications for Developing High-Potential Employees
Monograph. 1984. 45 p.
ISBN 0-8144-3150-X.
LC 84-9270.
SRI/MF/complete

By Charles Margerison and Andrew Kakabadse. Report discussing factors of greatest importance for the development of successful executives, as perceived by male and female corporate chief executive officers (CEOs).

Covers personal and professional experiences, attitudes, and abilities with greatest effect on career development; management activities causing the most difficulty and requiring the most time; and management skills that should receive greatest emphasis.

Data are based on responses of 711 CEOs to a recent survey conducted by the authors.

Contains contents and table listings (1 p.); highlights, and methodology with 6 tables on sample characteristics (p. 9-14); report in 3 sections, with 11 tables (p. 15-44); and references (p. 45).

Availability: American Management Associations, AMA Membership Publications Division, 135 W. 50th St., New York NY 10020, members first copy †, additional copies $10.00, nonmembers $13.50; SRI/MF/complete.

A2100
American Meat Institute

A2100–1   MEATFACTS, 1984 EDITION: A Statistical Summary About America's Largest Food Industry
Annual. July 1984. 1+40 p.
SRI/MF/complete

Annual statistical survey, for 1983, of the U.S. meat industry. Includes data on livestock numbers, slaughter, and meat production; farm marketing receipts; meat consumption and prices; foreign meat production, and trade; and meat packing industry financial and operating data; with selected trends from 1925.

Most data are from USDA, Dept of Commerce, and Labor Dept.

Contains contents listing (p. 1); and 41 tables, many with accompanying charts, listed below (p. 2-40).

This is the 14th annual edition.

Availability: American Meat Institute, Communications Department, PO Box 3556, Washington DC 20007, members $5.00, nonmembers $10.00; SRI/MF/complete.

TABLES:

A2100–1.1: Livestock and Meat Production Industry

LIVESTOCK INVENTORIES AND FINANCES

[1] Cattle, sheep, and hogs on farms, Jan. 1; and total U.S. resident population, July 1; [quinquennially 1925-50, and annually 1951-84]. (p. 2)

[2] Cattle/calves and sheep/lambs on farms, Jan. 1, 1984; and hogs, Dec. 1, 1983; by State. (p. 3)

[3] Number of operations with livestock, by State and species [cattle, milk cows, hogs, and sheep], 1982-83. (p. 4)

[4] Number of feedlots and cattle marketed, by feedlot capacity [individually for 7 leading States, and aggregate for 13 leading States], 1983. (p. 5)

[5] Livestock prices received by farmers, U.S. averages for all grades [beef cattle, calves, hogs, and lambs, quinquennially 1925-50, and annually 1951-83]. (p. 6)

[6] Cash receipts from farm marketings of meat animals [cattle/calves, hogs, and sheep/lambs], by State [ranked by total cash receipts], 1983. (p. 7)

SLAUGHTER AND PRODUCTS

[7] Livestock slaughter [by species] and meat production [beef, veal, lamb/mutton, and pork; quinquennially 1925-60, and annually 1961-83]. (p. 8)

[8] Livestock slaughter [number of head and average live weight, by species]; and meat production [dressed weight and average dressed weight, by type; all for federally inspected, other commercial, and farm slaughter]; 1982-83. (p. 9)

[9] Composition of commercial cattle slaughter [steers/heifers, cows, and bulls/stags], 1960-83. (p. 10)

[10] Livestock slaughter shares by firm size [percent of total slaughter accounted for by 4-12 largest firms, and total number of firms], 1972-82. (p. 11)

[11] [Commercial] slaughter and number of [federally inspected] plants, by species and State, 1983. (p. 12)

[12] Number of livestock slaughtering plants, by State, Jan. 1, 1983-84. (p. 14)

[13] Federally inspected slaughter plants [and slaughter], by species and size, 1983. (p. 15)

[14] Large plants, number and slaughter [and percent of federally inspected plants and commercial slaughter, all for cattle and hogs], 1975-83 (p. 15)

[15-16] Steer and hog carcass breakdown [pounds of retail meat, by cut, and other products]. (p. 16-17)

[17] Beef quality and yield graded [and total commercial beef production], 1974-83. (p. 18)

[18] Hamburger and beef: [per capita] consumption and prices, 1971-83. (p. 19)

[19-20] Meat products processed and canned under Federal inspection [by product], 1982-83. (p. 20-22)

[21] U.S. production of edible by-products, edible and inedible tallow, and lard, 1970-83. (p. 23)

[22] Cattlehides: slaughter, prices [at Chicago market], and [volume and value of] exports, 1970-83. (p. 23)

MEAT CONSUMPTION, PRICES, AND EXPENDITURES

[23-24] Per capita disappearance of red meat, carcass and retail weight basis [beef, veal, pork, and lamb/mutton]; and of red meat, poultry, and fish, retail weight basis; 1960-83. (p. 24-25)

[25] Livestock and wholesale meat prices [by species or product], 1976-83. (p. 26)

[26] CPI [for all items, foods, and meats]; and PPI [for total finished goods, all commodities, and meats]; 1976-83. (p. 27)

[27] Average retail meat prices [for beef and pork, by cut, and for poultry by type, quinquennially 1965-80 and annually 1981-83]. (p. 28)

[28] Per capita [disposable] income, and red meat expenditures [amount and as percent of total food expenditures], 1965-83. (p. 29)

[29] Consumer expenditures for meat, poultry, and fish in grocery stores [and total grocery store food/beverage and nonfood/general merchandise sales], 1972 and 1982. (p. 30)

INDUSTRY DATA

[30] Employment, [hourly and weekly] earnings, [and average weekly hours], for meat packing and meat processing industries, compared with all food and all manufacturing [selected years 1965-83]. (p. 31)

[31] Sales, raw materials costs, expenses, and net earnings of the meat packing industry, 1977-82. (p. 32)

[32] Breakdown of meat packers' sales dollar, by species slaughtered [cattle and hogs], 1981-82. (p. 33)

[33] Financial ratios for meat packers compared with all manufacturers, 1982. (p. 33)

A2100–1.2: Meat Foreign Trade and Consumption

[1] Meat animals, meat and meat products: value of U.S. exports and imports [by species], 1981-83. (p. 34)

[2] U.S. imports, exports, and net imports of beef/veal, pork, lamb/mutton, and total meat in relation to domestic production, 1976-83. (p. 35)

[3-4] U.S. imports of selected red meat products; and U.S. exports of selected red meat and livestock products; by major markets, 1982-83. (p. 36-37)

[5] U.S. canned ham imports, by country, 1970-83. (p. 38)

[6] U.S. ham production [by type] and [canned ham] imports, 1970-83. (p. 38)

[7] Per capita meat [beef/veal, pork, lamb/mutton/goat, and poultry] disappearance in selected countries, 1983. (p. 39)

[8] World meat [beef/veal, pork, and lamb/mutton] trade in selected countries, 1983. (p. 40)

A2100–2   ANNUAL FINANCIAL REVIEW of the Meat Packing Industry, 1983

Annual.   Sept. 1984.   30 p.
ISSN 0163-3708.
LC 78-646705.
SRI/MF/complete

Annual report presenting detailed data on meat packing industry finances and processing operations, including slaughter by leading States, 1983, with selected trends from as early as 1910. Data are from a 1983 American Meat Institute (AMI) survey of 148 meat packing and processing companies, USDA, and other Government and trade sources.

Contains contents listing (inside front cover); brief summary, with 1 chart (p. 1); 3 sections on industry and surveyed company finances and industry operations, with 3 charts and 39 tables (p. 2-27); and 3 appendix tables (p. 28-30). All tables are listed below.

This is the 59th annual report.

Availability: American Meat Institute, Communications Department, PO Box 3556, Washington DC 20007, members $7.50, nonmembers $15.00; SRI/MF/complete.

TABLES:

INDUSTRY FINANCES AND EMPLOYMENT

1.1. Financial ratios of the meat packing industry, 1981-83. (p. 3)

1.2. Sales, raw material costs, expenses, and income of the meat packing industry [including depreciation, employee benefit costs by type, rent, and taxes], 1972-83. (p. 4)

1.3-1.6. Commercial meat production [by type]; livestock prices [by species]; meat price indices [by type]; and year-end assets, liabilities, and net worth of the meat packing industry; 1982-83. (p. 6-8)

1.7. Employment and earnings [and weekly hours, for all manufacturing, and meat packing and processing], 1982-83. (p. 8)

SURVEYED COMPANIES FINANCES

[Tables 2.2-2.4 and 2.7-2.22 generally show data by company classification: for meat processing companies, and national, regional, and local meat packing companies. All tables show data for AMI survey participants only.]

2.1. Business structure [number of cooperatives, subsidiaries, and independently incorporated companies; and number of stockholders; for meat packers and processors], 1983. (p. 10)

2.2. Percentage breakdown of the sales dollar, by company classification, 1983. (p. 11)

2.3. Earnings ratios, 1982-83. (p. 12)

2.4. [Percentage] breakdown of the sales dollar, by product category [fresh and processed meat, and non-meat items]; 1983. (p. 12)

2.5a. Breakdown of meat packers' sales dollar by species slaughtered [cattle and hog], 1982-83. (p. 13)

2.5b. Financial ratios for [total, beef, and pork] meat packers compared with all manufacturers, 1983. (p. 13)

2.6. Breakdown of hog packer's 1983 sales dollar by percent of fresh meat sales. (p. 14)

2.7. Percentage breakdown of current assets, 1983. (p. 15)

2.8-2.11. Ratios: current assets to current liabilities; liabilities to net worth; and inventory and receivables to working capital; 1982-83. (p. 15-16)

2.12. Net worth as percent of total assets, 1982-83. (p. 17)

2.13-2.17b. Ratios: fixed assets to net worth; and sales to working capital, net worth, inventory, total assets, and fixed assets; 1982-83. (p. 17-19)

2.18. Average collection period in days, 1982-83. (p. 19)

2.19-2.22. Total selling/administrative, advertising, and repairs/maintenance expenses as percent of total operating expenses; and capital expenditures; 1982-83. (p. 19-20)

PACKER PURCHASES AND SLAUGHTER
[Tables 3.1-3.4 include data by livestock species.]

3.1. Number of [federally inspected and other] livestock slaughter plants [year end; and plants slaughtering during year], 1982-83. (p. 21)

3.2. Federally inspected slaughter as percent of total commercial slaughter [decennially 1910-80 and 1981-83]. (p. 22)

3.3. Number of large plants and percent of commercial slaughter [1975-83]. (p. 22)

3.4. Livestock purchased on a [carcass] grade/weight basis [by all packers and aggregate 10 largest packers], as percent of total purchases, 1971-82. (p. 23)

[3.5-3.8] Cattle, calf, hog, and sheep/lamb slaughter; [direct, terminal market, and auction market] procurement; [and carcass grade/weight purchases as percent of total purchases; by 20 leading States or regions, and for total U.S.]; 1983. (p. 24-27)

APPENDIX DATA

A1. Financial ratios for manufacturing industries [by major industry group], 1982-83. (p. 28)

A2. Financial results of the meat packing industry [including total sales, net worth and income, and income ratios, selected years] 1925-83. (p. 29)

A3. Meat animals processed by the meat packing industry [shows number slaughtered, and live and dressed weight, for cattle, calves, sheep/lambs, and hogs, selected years] 1925-83. (p. 30)

A2200
American
Medical Association

A2200–5   **SOCIOECONOMIC CHARACTERISTICS OF MEDICAL PRACTICE, 1983**
Annual.   Aug. 1983.
xi+156 p.
ISBN 0-89970-165-5.
SRI/MF/complete

Annual compilation of articles and statistics on economic aspects of medical practice, 1973-82. Includes data on physicians' hours, workload, and finances, by medical specialty, type and location of practice, and physician age and employment status.

Data are compiled by the AMA Socioeconomic Monitoring System (SMS) from quarterly telephone surveys of approximately 4,000 physicians.

Contains contents and table listings, foreword, and introduction (p. iii-xi); methodology, with 2 tables (p. 1-9); 8 articles, with 2 charts and 22 tables, described below (p. 11-42); 41 detailed tables, listed below (p. 44-121); and appendices with survey questionnaire, definitions, and computation formulas (p. 123-156).

This is the 1st annual SMS report. It replaces *Profile of Medical Practice,* discontinued with the 1981 edition (for description, see SRI 1982 Annual, under A2200-2).

Availability: American Medical Association, Book and Pamphlet Fulfillment, PO Box 10946, Chicago IL 60610, $12.00+$3.50 shipping and handling (prepaid); SRI/MF/complete.

STATISTICAL ARTICLES AND TABLES:

A2200–5.1: Statistical Articles
[Articles are reprinted from *SMS Report,* a periodically published newsletter.]

PHYSICIANS' FINANCIAL ARRANGEMENTS WITH HOSPITALS

(p. 11-14) Includes 3 tables showing total number of nonfederal physicians, estimated number with hospital financial arrangements, and average annual net income and percent of total income derived from hospital contracts; and distribution of physicians by type of financial arrangement; all by medical specialty, as of 4th quarter 1981.

AMBULATORY SURGERY

(p. 15-18) Includes 3 tables showing share of surgery performed on an ambulatory basis; percent of physicians performing ambulatory surgery currently vs. 2 years ago; and setting used (hospital-based, free-standing center, and physician office); as of 1st quarter 1982.

RECENT TRENDS IN PHYSICIAN LIABILITY CLAIMS AND INSURANCE EXPENSES

(p. 19-22) Includes 2 tables showing physician liability insurance claim rates by practice specialty and type, region, and sex, prior to 1976 and 1976-81 periods; and distribution of physicians by liability insurance expenses, by medical specialty, 1976 and 1981.

CHANGES IN THE USE OF PROCEDURES AMONG PHYSICIANS

(p. 23-26) Includes 3 tables showing distribution of physician responses to questions regarding the adoption and discontinuance of medical procedures, major source of information on new procedures, and reasons for nonadoption; all by major medical specialty practice, as of 1st quarter 1982.

PHYSICIAN UTILIZATION OF ALLIED HEALTH PROFESSIONALS

(p. 27-30) Includes 2 charts and 1 table showing FTE non-physician personnel (allied health professionals, nurses, and clerical workers) per office-based practice and physician, 1975 and 1981; and impact of nurse practitioner/physician assistant utilization on patient visits, fees, and physicians weeks worked and net income.

PHYSICIAN-HOSPITAL RELATIONS

(p. 31-34) Includes 4 tables showing percent of physicians with hospital admitting privileges, 1977 and 1982; and physician administrative concerns, including opinions on hospital staff size, satisfaction with medical director, and representation on hospital governing board; all by major medical specialty, with some detail by region, as of 3rd quarter 1982.

IMPACT OF THE 1981-82 RECESSION ON MEDICAL PRACTICE

(p. 35-38) Includes 3 tables showing average weekly patient visits and physician quarterly net income, by major medical specialty and region, selected periods 2nd half 1981-82; percent of physicians treating patients without health insurance and/or Medicaid coverage, and reducing/suspending fees; and percent of physicians participating in organized "fair share" programs; as of 4th quarter 1982.

PHYSICIAN RESPONSES TO COMPETITION

(p. 39-42) Includes 3 tables showing distribution of response to questions regarding

changes in housecalls, evening office hours, and FTE non-physician staff employment compared to 2 years ago; and use of marketing strategies/techniques, by region and practice characteristics; as of 4th quarter 1982.

A2200–5.2: Detailed Tables
[Tables show data by practice specialty and for solo and nonsolo practice; by census division, metro-nonmetro location and city size, and by physician employment status (self-employed and employee) and age group.

Tables show data for various years 1973-82. Tables showing data for 1982 include detail by demographic and physician characteristics for specific practice specialties.]

WORK HOURS

1-2. Mean number of weeks practiced. (p. 44-47)

3. Mean number of hours in professional activities per week. (p. 48)

4-6. Mean number of hours in [total] and direct patient care activities per week. (p. 50-55)

7-11. Mean number of office hours, hours on hospital rounds, and hours in surgery per week. (p. 56-65)

WORKLOAD

12-17. Mean number of total patient visits, office visits, and visits on hospital rounds per week. (p. 66-77)

18. Mean number of surgical procedures per week. (p. 78)

SPECIALTY WORKLOADS

[Tables 19-22 begin "Mean patient care activities per week" and show number of cases or procedures and hours spent for the specialities noted below.]

19. Psychiatry [sessions with individual patients, and with family/nonfamily groups]. (p. 80)

20. Radiology [film readings, radiodiagnostic procedures, radiotherapy patients, and consultations]. (p. 82)

21. Anesthesiology [patients anesthetized by physician and by nurse anesthetist under physicians' supervision, and preanesthesia/other inpatient visits]. (p. 84)

22. Pathology [surgical consultations, examinations of surgical specimens, laboratory procedures, and autopsies]. (p. 86)

WAITING TIME AND HOSPITAL UTILIZATION

23-24. Mean number of days waiting time to be scheduled for an appointment; and mean number of minutes waiting time by patients arriving for an appointment. (p. 88-91)

25-26. Mean number of patients discharged from the hospital per week; and number of days for hospital stays per patient. (p. 92-95)

FINANCES

27-32. Mean fee for an office visit with an established and a new patient; and for a hospital follow-up visit. (p. 96-107)

33-36. Mean and median professional expenses of self-employed physicians. (p. 108-113)

37. Means of selected components of professional expenses [including non-physician payroll, office expenses, medical supplies and equipment, and professional liability insurance]. (p. 114)

38-41. Mean and median net income from medical practice. (p. 116-121)

A2275
American Music Conference

A2275-1 MUSIC USA: 1984 Review of the Music Industry and Amateur Music Participation
Annual. 1984. 33 p.
ISSN 0197-4173.
ISBN 0-918196-09-4.
LC 80-642143.
SRI/MF/complete

Annual report, for 1984, on music industry. Presents data on retail sales volume and value for musical instruments and accessories, sheet music, and sound equipment, various years 1940-83; and foreign trade of instruments and accessories, 1981-83, with leading trading partner countries for 1983. Instrument data are shown by type.

Also includes data on amateur musicians, by sex and instrument played, 1978 (total) and 1983 (teens); and directory of music assns, with membership data, 1984.

Data are from trade assns; Federal agencies; industry estimates; and a 1978 household survey by the Gallup Organization, and a 1983 survey by Teen-age Research Unlimited, both conducted for AMC.

Contains narrative analysis interspersed with 11 charts and 21 tables.

Availability: American Music Conference, 1000 Skokie Blvd., Wilmette IL 60091, members $2.50, educational profession $10.00, others $25.00; SRI/MF/complete.

A2350
American Newspaper Publishers Association

A2350-1 ANPA NEWS RESEARCH REPORTS
Series. For individual publication data, see below.
ISSN 0195-8585.
LC 79-644433.
SRI/MF/complete

Continuing series of research reports on newspaper production and readership. Reports contain 1-2 studies, some with statistics, on various topics, including writing and reporting trends, socioeconomic characteristics and attitudes of readers, newspaper circulation and format, and business developments in the publishing industry.

Reports are issued 8-10 times a year. All reports are reviewed, but only statistical studies are described in SRI. Reports reviewed during 1984 are described below.

Series is discontinued with Report No. 40.

Availability: American Newspaper Publishers Association, The Newspaper Center, Box 17407, Dulles International Airport, Washington DC 20041, †; SRI/MF/complete.

A2350-1.16: NRC Mining Company Report: Comparisons of Subscribers and Non-Subscribers
[Monograph. Dec. 27, 1983. 11 p. Rpt. No. 39. SRI/MF/complete.]

By Edna Einsiedel. Report comparing characteristics of newspaper subscribers and nonsubscribers. Data were compiled by NRC Mining Co. from 48 studies of 34 markets in U.S. and Canada, conducted 1977-82.

Includes 5 undated tables showing subscribers' and nonsubscribers' TV use and magazine readership, views on attributes of newspapers, demographic characteristics, and political interest and activity, for 1-2 various markets identified by region; and correlation between current subscriber status and childhood exposure to newspapers, by race.

A2350-1.17: Effects of Bad News and Good News on Newspaper and Community Images
[Monograph. Dec. 30, 1983. 7 p. Rpt. No. 40. SRI/MF/complete.]

By Jack B. Haskins. Report analyzing the effect of a newspaper's good news/bad news balance on readers' perceptions of the paper and its community. Presents results of an experiment in which 220 college students recorded their perceptions after reading fictitious newspapers containing varying amounts of good and bad news. Includes 6 undated tables.

A2350-2 PRESSTIME
Monthly. Approx. 50 p.
ISSN 0194-3243.
LC 79-644846.
SRI/MF/complete, shipped quarterly

Monthly trade journal reporting on newspaper publication developments, including technological advances, employee-management relations, and government decisions affecting the news industry.

Issues generally contain:

a. Articles and news briefs, occasionally with statistics; and monthly narrative editorial features.

b. Monthly "Newsprint" section, with 5 monthly tables presenting ANPA survey data on newsprint supply and demand, current to 2-3 months prior to cover date; and 1 quarterly table on paper company net income.

Annual features include articles on ANPA surveys of newspaper prices, capital expenditures, and newsprint consumption; and a report on paper mill labor contract expirations. A semiannual subject index appears in Jan. and July issues.

May 1984 issue contains an annual insert, *'84 Facts About Newspapers,* covered separately in SRI under A2350-4.

Monthly and quarterly tables are listed below; monthly tables appear in most issues. All additional features with substantial statistical content are described, as they appear, under "Statistical Features;" page locations and latest periods of coverage for quarterly table are also noted. Non-statistical features are not covered.

Availability: American Newspaper Publishers Association, Presstime, Box 17407, Dulles International Airport, Washington DC 20041, members †, nonmembers $100.00 per yr.; SRI/MF/complete, shipped quarterly.

Issues reviewed during 1984: Nov. 1983-Oct. 1984 (P) (Vol. 5, Nos. 11-12; Vol. 6, Nos. 1-10).

MONTHLY TABLES:
[All tables show data on newsprint, for month of coverage, sometimes with data for previous 1-3 months; tables [1-4] also show cumulative data for year to date. All tables include comparisons to same periods of previous year.]

[1] Estimated consumption of all U.S. daily newspapers [by region and circulation size].

[2] Estimated consumption of all U.S. users.

[3] Production [U.S. and Canadian].

[4] Shipments [from U.S. and Canadian mills to U.S., Canada, and areas outside North America (export)].

[5] Stocks [and days' supply on hand and in transit; for U.S. publishers and Canadian and U.S. mills].

QUARTERLY TABLE:
[1] Financial report of [13-17 selected] paper companies [net income cumulative for year to date, current to approximately 3-4 months prior to cover date, and for same period of preceding year; (appearance of table is contingent upon availability of data)].

STATISTICAL FEATURES:

A2350-2.501: Nov. 1983 (Vol. 5, No. 11)
THERE'S SATISFACTION OUT THERE FOR JOURNALISM PROGRAMS

(p. 25) By Michael M. Spear. Article on North Carolina journalism school graduates' and newspaper editors' satisfaction with quality of journalism education. Data are based on responses of 416 University of North Carolina graduates and 89 editors to a 1981/82 survey. Includes 1 table showing editors' ratings of journalism graduates in 9 functional areas.

A2350-2.502: Jan. 1984 (Vol. 6, No. 1)
THIS WILL BE A BIG YEAR ON THE LABOR FRONT AT NORTH AMERICA'S NEWSPRINT MILLS, ANNUAL FEATURE

(p. 45) Annual article on U.S. and Canadian paper mill labor contracts due to expire in 1983-88. Data are from American Paper Institute and Canadian Pulp and Paper Assn. Includes 2 tabular lists showing company, location, union, and contract expiration date.

A2350-2.503: Mar. 1984 (Vol. 6, No. 3)
THREE-FOURTHS OF DAILIES COST A QUARTER, BUT A NICKEL WILL STILL BUY A PAPER IN ONE TOWN, ANNUAL FEATURE

(p. 42-43) Annual article on newspaper pricing for 1983. Data are from an ANPA survey of single-copy, street sale (city zone) prices for 1,820 daily and 771 Sunday papers.

Includes 2 tables showing number of daily and Sunday papers, by price, for total U.S., each State, D.C., Canada, Bahamas, Bermuda, Guam, Puerto Rico, and Virgin Islands.

A2350-2.504: Apr. 1984 (Vol. 6, No. 4)
QUARTERLY TABLE

[1] Financial report of 15 paper companies, 1982-83. (p. 68)

A2350-2.505: May 1984 (Vol. 6, No. 5)

CAPITAL EXPENDITURES DROP SHARPLY IN '83, BUT NEWSPAPERS' '84 OUTLAYS COULD SET RECORD, ANNUAL FEATURE

(p. 63-64) Annual article on newspaper industry capital expenditures and outlook, based on responses of 438 U.S. and 22 Canadian newspapers to an ANPA survey. Includes 2 tables showing U.S. and Canadian outlays for plant expansion and modernization, and for new equipment by item, 1983 and estimated 1984.

A2350-2.506: June 1984 (Vol. 6, No. 6)

UNFAIR THIRD-CLASS RATES THREATEN ADVERTISING REVENUES, NEWSHOLE COULD BE NEXT

(p. 30-31) By Otto A. Silha. Article, with 1 undated chart showing 1st- and 3rd-class shares of total USPS mail volume and revenue.

A2350-2.507: Aug. 1984 (Vol. 6, No. 8)

SPECIAL REPORT: MINORITIES

(p. 14-21) By Marcia Ruth. Article, with 1 chart and 2 tables showing minorities as percent of total newsroom employees; and percents of newspapers with minority journalists and without minority news executives, by circulation size; various years 1978-84. Data are from American Society of Newspaper Editors.

CONSUMPTION FOR 1983 UP 3.8%, ANNUAL FEATURE

(p. 58) Annual article, with 2 tables showing newsprint consumption, by State; and number of newspapers and newsprint consumption, by region; 1982-83. Data are based on an ANPA survey of 1,728 daily newspapers.

A2350-2.508: Sept. 1984 (Vol. 6, No. 9)

QUARTERLY TABLE

[1] Financial report of 16 paper companies, for 1st half 1983-84. (p. 62)

A2350-4   '84 FACTS ABOUT NEWSPAPERS

Annual.   Apr. 1984.   25 p.
SRI/MF/complete

Annual report on newspaper publishing industry in the U.S. and Canada, including employment, circulation, advertising revenue, and newsprint consumption, various years 1946-83. Also includes data on ANPA membership. Data are from original studies, *Editor and Publisher,* Commerce Dept, and other sources.

Contains 1983 highlights (p. 1); 16 tables and 7 accompanying charts, described below (p. 2-19); narrative summary with text statistics, including data on readership and delivery (p. 20-21); and description of ANPA organization and services, with 1 table showing membership by newspaper circulation size, as of Apr. 1, 1984 (p. 22-25).

Availability: American Newspaper Publishers Association, Public Affairs Department, The Newspaper Center, Box 17407, Dulles International Airport, Washington DC 20041, †; SRI/MF/complete.

TABLES AND CHARTS:

[Historical data are generally shown for selected years within date ranges noted. Data for newspapers often include breakdowns for morning, evening, and Sunday editions.]

a. Daily newspapers, circulation, single copy sales price, and advertising dollar volume compared to GNP, 1946-83; advertising revenue compared to other media, 1982-83; and ratio of advertising to total content, 1946-82. 3 charts and 7 tables. (p. 2-9)

b. Newsprint consumption and prices, 1970-83; newspaper employment by sex, 1960-83, and compared to U.S. total employment, 1947-83; employment distribution by function, 1978; weekly newspapers and circulation, 1960-84; and circulation of 20 largest newspapers, and daily and Sunday newspapers owned and circulation for 20 largest newspaper companies, both as of Sept. 1983. 4 charts and 6 tables. (p. 10-16)

c. Canada: daily newspapers and circulation, 1946-83; advertising dollar volume compared to GNP, 1962-83; and advertising revenue compared to other media, 1982-83. 3 tables. (p. 17-19)

A2450
American
Optometric Association

A2450-1   1982/83 COE ANNUAL SURVEY OF OPTOMETRIC EDUCATIONAL INSTITUTIONS, Part I

Annual.   Dec. 8, 1983.
23 p. no paging.
SRI/MF/complete

Annual report, for 1982/83, on selected characteristics of optometry school faculty, students, and libraries. Data are based on responses from 15 U.S. schools and 2 Canadian schools to a survey conducted by the Council on Optometric Education.

Contains tabulation of responses to 26 survey questions, described below, presented in 3 sections on faculty, students, and libraries.

Part II presents financial data for optometry schools, and is available to AOA members only. SRI covers only Part I.

For description of previous reports, for 1980/81 and 1981/82, see SRI 1982 Annual, under this number.

Availability: American Optometric Association, 243 N. Lindbergh Blvd., St. Louis MO 63141, †; SRI/MF/complete, Part I.

TABLES:

[Data are shown by school for 1982/83. Minority groups are black, Spanish surname, American Indian, Asian American, and foreign national.]

FACULTY

a. FTE full-time and part-time faculty; and whether full-time faculty allowed optometric practice in and outside school. (2 questions)

STUDENTS

b. Enrollment and degrees: including full-time professional degree students by program year, sex, and minority group; withdrawals/dismissals, by reason and program year; prior educational attainment of 1st-year students; and enrollment by program year, by State or Province of permanent residence. (6 questions)

c. Admissions: including students admitted under State contracts; selected admissions policies; and applications and acceptances to 1st year class. (5 questions)

d. Student finances, including scholarship and loan utilization; percent of students receiving financial aid and loans by program year, and by State and/or Federal source; and resident and nonresident educational expenditures by program year, and average room/board expenditure. (4 questions)

e. Other student enrollment, including part-time/special, graduate, paraoptometric, and residents, by sex. (1 question)

LIBRARIES

f. Library operations: including audiovisual materials, annual losses, bound volumes, serial titles, annual budget by object, and other income. (8 questions)

A2470
American
Osteopathic Association

A2470-1   1983-84 YEARBOOK AND DIRECTORY OF OSTEOPATHIC PHYSICIANS

Annual.   Oct. 1983.   648 p.
LC 81-10637.
SRI/MF/excerpts

Annual American Osteopathic Assn (AOA) yearbook, for 1983, including data on number and location of osteopathic physicians, osteopathic college enrollment and graduates, and physician characteristics, with selected trends and forecasts for 1932-1987/88.

Also includes directories of U.S. and Canadian osteopathic physicians, affiliated organizations, and educational programs; AOA organization and position papers; and related reference material.

Most data are compiled by AOA from a survey of osteopathic colleges.

Contains contents listing (p. 7); and 47 sections, including statistical section (p. 428-442), with 21 tables listed below.

This is the 75th annual yearbook.

Availability: American Osteopathic Association, Order Department, 212 E. Ohio St., Chicago IL 60611, members †, nonmembers $35.00; SRI/MF/excerpts for tables listed below.

TABLES:

[Data by State generally include D.C., and Guam or aggregate U.S. territories.]

OSTEOPATHIC PHYSICIANS

[1] Growth of the osteopathic profession [number of listed AOA members and nonmembers, and new graduates, 1932-83]. (p. 428)

[2-4] Distribution of listed DOs [doctors of osteopathy, AOA members and nonmembers]; and of DOs by age and by occupational status [including patient care by type of setting, intern, resident, other in-training, and retired; all by State, with totals for Canada, foreign, military, and/or U.S. Public Health Service, as of July 1983]. (p. 428-430)

[5] Numbers of current osteopathic certifications [by field, as of July 1983]. (p. 431)

[6] Distribution of DOs by population [size] of community [with total in foreign countries, and unidentified, as of July 1983]. (p. 431)

INTERN AND RESIDENT TRAINING

[7-8] Growth of osteopathic intern training programs [by State]; and interns in Federal training programs [by service branch and for Public Health Service; 1979/80-1983/84]. (p. 432-433)

[9-11] AOA-approved residency positions in osteopathic hospitals, and residents in AOA-approved osteopathic training and nonosteopathic programs, [all by field. 1983/84, most with trend from 1979/80]. (p. 434-436)

COLLEGE ENROLLMENT AND RESEARCH ACTIVITIES

[Tables [14-20] show data by college of osteopathic medicine.]

[12] Women [enrollments and graduates] in colleges of osteopathic medicine [1956/57-1983/84]. (p. 437)

[13] Student AOA membership [and nonmembers by college, as of June 1983]. (p. 437)

[14] Enrollment [1968/69-1987/88]. (p. 438-439)

[15-16] Actual and expected enrollment by class, 1982/83-1983/84. (p. 438-439)

[17] Size of graduating class, 1983 and 1984. (p. 439)

[18-19] Expected enrollment of women and ethnic minorities [by class, and graduates], 1983/84. (p. 440)

[20] Survey of osteopathic research activities [number of studies and funding amounts, by funding source], 1982. (p. 441)

HOSPITAL FACILITIES

[21] Osteopathic hospitals by State [total and AOA-accredited hospitals; hospitals with AOA-approved postdoctoral training programs; total beds, bassinets, and special care beds; and hospitals by number of beds; as of Aug. 1983]. (p. 442)

A2500
American Paper Institute

A2500-2   PAPER, PAPERBOARD, AND WOOD PULP Monthly Statistical Summary
Monthly.
Approx. 12 p.+insert.
ISSN 0003-0341.
LC 76-641204.
SRI/MF/complete, shipped quarterly

Monthly report on wood pulp, paper, and paperboard industry production and trade. Also covers employment, capital expenditures, productivity, prices, inventories, orders, and consumption for selected products.

Data are from American Paper Institute's Pulp, Minerals, and Technology Group; American Pulpwood Assn; Census Bureau; and other government agencies. Data are current to approximately 1-2 months prior to cover date.

Issues contain narrative summary with occasional summary tables; and 18 summary charts, 7 monthly tables including an industry fact sheet insert, and 2 recurring tables.

Monthly and other recurring tables are listed below. Monthly tables appear in all issues; recurring table [8] on sales and earnings appears in July 1984 issue; and recurring table [9] on production, trade, and new supply appears in June 1984 issue.

Availability: American Paper Institute, 260 Madison Ave., New York NY 10016, members †, nonmembers $100.00 per yr.; SRI/MF/complete, shipped quarterly.

Issues reviewed during 1984: Oct. 1983-July 1984 (P) (Vol. 61, Nos. 10-12; Vol. 62, Nos. 1-7).

TABLES:

MONTHLY TABLES

[Data generally are shown for previous 1-2 years, 2-4 most current months available, and current year to date.]

[1] Paper and paperboard statistics: production, shipments, and [new and unfilled] orders [for selected grades].

[2] Wood pulp statistics [production, imports, exports, and new supply of total and market wood pulp, by type].

[3] Fibrous raw materials [consumption at paper/paperboard mills; inventories, by mill type; days supply of chemical paper grade market pulp; and regional receipts, consumption, residues, and inventories].

[4] U.S. trade [imports from and exports to] Canada [by grade].

[5] Pulp, paper, and paperboard imports and exports data [by grade].

[6] PPI [by type of pulp, paper, or paperboard products].

[7] Industry fact sheet [production of paper, paperboard, and wood pulp, by grade; capacity utilization rate; and additional operating data, including employment and production worker earnings; capital expenditures; worker productivity; sales, earnings, and net worth; price and demand indexes; magazine advertising pages; publisher consumption; and total wholesaler sales and inventories].

RECURRING TABLES

[8] Sales and earnings [aggregated for approximately 30 paper and paper/allied product companies, quarterly through most recent quarter of current year, and same quarters of previous year; and occasionally presents additional data on various items, including taxes, equity, and long-term debt].

[9] Paper/paperboard [production, imports, exports, new supply, and real GNP, with selected ratios; quarterly for current year to date and previous year, and annually for 7-9 preceding years].

A2500-3   NEWSPRINT MONTHLY STATISTICAL REPORT
Monthly.
Approx. 11 p.+quarterly inserts.
SRI/MF/complete, shipped quarterly

Monthly report on U.S. and Canadian newsprint production, shipments, inventory, and plant capacity. Also covers U.S. consumption, foreign trade, publishers' stock, and newspaper circulation.

Reports are issued approximately 3-8 weeks after month of coverage. Data are from 16-17

reporting paper companies, API estimates for nonreporting companies, American Newspaper Publishers Assn (ANPA), Canadian Pulp and Paper Assn, Census Bureau, and other sources.

Contains 2 trend charts and 1 summary table; 17 detailed monthly tables, listed below; and 2 quarterly tables, also listed below.

Monthly tables appear in all issues; quarterly table [1] is included in Nov. 1983 and Feb. and June 1984 issues; quarterly table [2] is included in Feb. 1984 issue.

Availability: American Paper Institute, Newsprint Division, 260 Madison Ave., New York NY 10016, members †, nonmembers $25.00 per yr.; SRI/MF/complete, shipped quarterly.

Issues reviewed during 1984: Oct. 1983-June 1984 (D).

MONTHLY TABLES:

PRODUCTION, SHIPMENTS, AND CONSUMPTION

[Data are shown monthly for year to date and 2 previous years, unless otherwise noted.]

[1-6] [Production, shipments, end-of-month inventory, and] distribution of shipments; for North America, U.S., and Canada [including shipments to U.S. from overseas].

[7-8] Total U.S. estimated consumption [by ANPA newspapers and all users, unadjusted and seasonally adjusted; and seasonally adjusted total North American shipments].

[9] ANPA survey of newspapers publishers stock, end of month [unadjusted and seasonally adjusted], and end-of-month days supply [on hand/in transit].

[10] Operating rates [U.S., Canada, and North America].

[11-12] Newsprint shipments by destination [from U.S., Canada, and North America to 8 U.S. census divisions; annually for 1971 to previous year, and quarterly for previous year and current year to date (usually quarter preceding month of publication)].

HISTORICAL AND ECONOMIC DATA

[13] Newsprint historical data [shows selected trends based on tables listed above, plus U.S. newsprint tonnage loss due to newspaper strikes, and U.S. newspaper data, including advertising as percent of total pages, and per-household circulation, all for previous 15-23 years].

[14] GNP and industrial production index [selected estimates and projections, quarterly, current and following year].

[15] Advertising expenditures, by media, percent of total [selected years 1950 to previous year].

[16-17] Annual capacity [actual and projected, 1966 to 1986]; and announced capacity increases [by mill and company, current, previous 3-4, and coming years; both shown for U.S. and Canada].

QUARTERLY TABLES:

[Quarterly tables are issued approximately 3 months after quarter of coverage.]

[1] Exports of newsprint [from the U.S., Canada, and Scandinavia to selected countries and world areas, cumulative quarterly for year to date and same period of previous year; issued approximately 3 months after quarter of coverage].

[2] U.S. news print imports, by country of origin and port of entry [volume and value, for final month of quarter and year to date; table begins in the Feb. 1984 issue].

A2500-4 EXPORTS OF KRAFT LINERBOARD AND CORRUGATING MATERIAL from Major Supplying Countries to World Markets, 1982-83
Annual. May 1984.
33+20 p.
SRI/MF/complete

Annual report on containerboard exports from major supplying countries, by world area and country of destination, 1982-83, with trends from 1970. Includes data for kraft linerboard and corrugating medium.

Supplying countries covered in detail are U.S., Canada, Finland, Sweden, and Norway. Other supplying countries covered are Austria, Portugal, Spain, and Brazil.

Data are derived primarily from reports of Census Bureau, and pulp and paper assns of supplying countries.

Contains narrative analysis, interspersed with 2 illustrative charts and 19 tables (p. 1-29); and appendix and statistical note, with 2 tables (p. 30-33+20 p.).

This is the 20th annual report.

Availability: American Paper Institute, International Department, 260 Madison Ave., New York NY 10016, members †, nonmembers $60.00; SRI/MF/complete.

A2500-5 EXPORTS OF PULP, PAPER, PAPERBOARD, AND CONVERTED PRODUCTS to World Markets, 1983
Annual. May 1984.
30+App 15 p.
SRI/MF/complete

Annual report, for 1983, on volume and value of U.S. paper industry exports, by detailed product category and area or country of destination. Covers pulp, paper, paperboard, and converted products, and includes comparisons to 1982 and trends from 1972.

Areas of destination include Western Europe, Canada, Mexico, Central America/Caribbean area/other islands, South America, Near/Middle East, Africa, Oceania/Far East, Soviet Union/Eastern Europe, Japan, and PRC.

Report is compiled by the American Paper Institute's International Dept, based on Census Bureau data.

Contains narrative analysis, with 2 summary charts and 18 tables (p. 1-29); and 2 appendices with 4 tables (15 p.).

This is the 12th annual report.

Availability: American Paper Institute, International Department, 260 Madison Ave., New York NY 10016, members †, nonmembers $55.00; SRI/MF/complete.

A2500-6 PAPER, PAPERBOARD, WOOD PULP CAPACITY: Fiber Consumption, 1982-85, with Additional Data for 1986
Annual. 1983. 29 p.
SRI/MF/complete

Annual report on U.S. paper, paperboard, and wood pulp industry capacity, by product grade, 1982-86 and trends. Includes data on mills, machinery, and raw material consumption in manufacture, and data by census division. Also includes world capacity data.

Most data are based on responses of over 250 companies, representing approximately 90% of U.S. wood pulp and paper/paperboard production, to a 1983 API survey.

Contains contents listing (p. 1); survey commentary, with 6 summary tables, including capacity growth trends from 1968 (p. 3-7); 4 summary charts, and 19 detailed tables listed below (p. 8-27); and definitions (p. 28 and inside back cover).

Availability: American Paper Institute, 260 Madison Ave., New York NY 10016, members †, nonmembers $225.00; SRI/MF/complete.

DETAILED TABLES:
[Tables show data for U.S., 1982-86, unless otherwise noted. Most data on capacity are shown by grade. Data by census division combine Mountain and Pacific areas.]

CAPACITY DETAIL

[1] Paper and paperboard capacity summary. (p. 8)

[2] Capacity reductions: paper and paperboard mills and machines shut down [selected periods 1970-86]. (p. 9)

[3] Wood pulp capacity summary. (p. 10)

[4-7] Paper, paperboard, construction paper and board, and wood pulp [annual and year-end capacities, and daily rate]. (p. 12-17)

[8] Annual capacity, regional distribution: paper, paperboard, and wood pulp, [by census division], 1982 and 1986. (p. 18)

WORLD DATA

[9] World capacity: wood pulp and paper/paperboard [for total world, and by selected world area and country, mostly 1982 and 1986]. (p. 20)

MILLS AND MACHINES

[10-11] Mill size [paper/board and pulp mills and capacity, by capacity size category]; and capacity in integrated and nonintegrated mills [paper and board capacity of mills that do and do not also produce wood pulp; 1976 and 1982]. (p. 20-21)

[12] Machines operating in 1982 [and percent of capacity, by] year of installation or last major rebuild. (p. 22)

[13] Summary: paper and paperboard machines, [by grade, 1975 and 1982]. (p. 22)

[14-15] [Number of machines and percent of total capacity by machine capacity range], by principal paper and paperboard/other grade produced, [1975 and 1982]. (p. 22-23)

CONSUMPTION

[16-17] Fiber consumption in paper/paperboard manufacture and pulpwood consumption in wood pulp manufacture [by type and census division]. (p. 24-25)

[18] Recyclable paper in paper and paperboard manufacture: actual and planned future consumption [by type and end product grade]. (p. 26)

ANNOUNCED EXPANSIONS

[19] Announced capacity expansion: projects included in survey estimates [with company, location, start-up date, and annual capacity]. (p. 27)

A2575 American Petroleum Institute

A2575-1 WEEKLY STATISTICAL BULLETIN
Weekly. Approx. 10 p.
ISSN 0003-0457.
SRI/MF/complete, shipped quarterly

Weekly report estimating U.S. crude oil and refined product daily average production and imports, and end-of-week stocks, by PAD district. Data are compiled by API from member reports and DOE data, and are issued approximately 1 week after week covered.

Report contains 1 summary table; 7 detailed tables, listed below, of which 6 appear weekly and 1 appears monthly (usually in the 2nd issue of the month); revisions to previous tables; and 3 charts.

For description of API report on monthly estimates of U.S. average daily petroleum supply and demand balance, see A2575-2 below.

Availability: American Petroleum Institute, Publications and Distribution Section, 1220 L St., NW, Washington DC 20005, $50.00 per yr. (includes *Monthly Statistical Report*); SRI/MF/complete, shipped quarterly.

Issues reviewed during 1984: Oct. 28, 1983-Oct. 26, 1984 (D) (Vol. 64, Nos. 43-52; Vol. 65, Nos. 1-43) [Vol. 64, Nos. 47-49, incorrectly read Vol. 63].

TABLES:

WEEKLY TABLES
[All tables show data by PAD district, for week of coverage, with comparisons to previous 1-3 weeks and/or same week of previous year. Tables [1-3] also show data for subdivisions of districts 1-3.

Data on products include motor gasoline, jet fuels (naphtha and kerosene), fuel oils, liquefied petroleum gas (imports only), and other categories.]

[1] Refinery operations [daily averages for total input, crude oil runs to distillation units, input to crude oil distillation units, operable capacity, and percent operated].

[2-3] Refinery output [daily averages], and stocks [end-of-week totals], of selected products.

[4] [Daily average API and DOE latest] estimated domestic production of crude oil (including lease condensate); imports [daily average total and from Canada]; and stocks of crude oil [end-of-week total].

[5] Location of crude oil stocks.

[6] Imports of petroleum products [daily averages].

MONTHLY TABLE

[7] Estimated daily average production of crude oil/lease condensate [by State and Texas district; API data for 2 preceding months, and DOE data for latest 1-2 months available, generally 4-7 months prior to publication date].

A2575-2   MONTHLY STATISTICAL REPORT

Monthly.   Approx. 5 p.
SRI/MF/complete, shipped quarterly

Monthly report on estimated U.S. petroleum supply and demand, compiled by API from member reports and DOE data. Reports are issued 2-3 weeks following month of coverage.

Report regularly includes narrative summary, summary tables and charts, and 1 detailed table showing:

a.   Products supplied and stocks for 8-9 refined products, and exports and total domestic products supplied.

b.   Supply, including domestic production and imports.

c.   Refinery operations, including input to crude oil distillation units, operable capacity, refinery utilization rate, and crude oil runs.

Refined product stocks are shown for current month, previous month, and same month of preceding year. All other items are shown for current month, year to date, and same periods of preceding year. June, Sept., and Dec. issues also include quarterly data for the same items.

Issues also occasionally include statistical articles or special charts. All additional features with substantial statistical content are described, as they appear, under "Statistical Features." Non-statistical features are not covered.

Availability: American Petroleum Institute, Publications and Distribution Section, 1220 L St., NW, Washington DC 20005, $10.00 per yr. (or included in subscription to *Weekly Statistical Bulletin*); SRI/MF/complete, shipped quarterly.
Issues reviewed during 1984: Oct. 1983-Sept. 1984 (D) (Vol. 7, Nos. 10-12; Vol. 8, Nos. 1-9).

STATISTICAL FEATURES:

A2575-2.501: Dec. 1983 (Vol. 7, No. 12)

ESTIMATED U.S. PETROLEUM BALANCE, RECURRING FEATURE

(9 p.) Recurring article summarizing petroleum supply and demand, 1983. Data are from DOE and American Petroleum Institute.

Includes 1 chart and 2 tables showing energy consumption by fuel type; estimated distillate fuel consumption by sector; and distribution of crude oil/refined product imports, by OPEC and non-OPEC country of origin; various periods 1978-83.

A2575-2.502: Feb. 1984 (Vol. 8, No. 2)

ANNUAL IMPORTS DATA

(1 p.) Brief article, with 1 table showing top 10 countries ranked by petroleum exports to U.S., 1982-83.

A2575-2.503: June 1984 (Vol. 8, No. 6)

ESTIMATED U.S. PETROLEUM BALANCE, RECURRING FEATURE

(4 p.) Recurring article summarizing petroleum supply and demand during 1st half 1984. Data are from DOE and American Petroleum Institute.

Includes 1 chart and 1 table showing estimated distillate fuel consumption by sector, 1st half 1983-84; and distribution of crude oil/refined product imports, by country of origin, 1st 4 months 1983-84 and full year 1983.

A2575-3   MONTHLY DRILLING REPORT: Report on Drilling Activity in the U.S.

Monthly.   Approx. 5 p.
SRI/MF/complete, shipped quarterly

Monthly report on exploratory and development oil and gas well drilling in producing States and offshore. Compiled by API from member data, report is issued approximately 3 weeks after month of coverage.

Report regularly contains 1 summary table, and 2 detailed tables listed below.

More detailed and revised data are published quarterly (for description, see A2575-6).

Availability: American Petroleum Institute, Publications and Distribution Section, 1220 L St., NW, Washington DC 20005, $10.00 per yr.; SRI/MF/complete, shipped quarterly.
Issues reviewed during 1984: Oct. 1983-Aug. 1984 (D).

TABLES:

[Tables show number of U.S. wells and footage, onshore and offshore, by State; by district for California, Louisiana, New Mexico, and Texas; and for Federal waters.

Data are for month of coverage, with totals for same month of previous year.]

I.   Total wells drilled [for oil, gas, and service wells; dry holes; and stratigraphic/core tests].

II.   Total exploratory wells drilled [for oil and gas wells and dry holes].

A2575-4   SUMMARY OF OCCUPATIONAL INJURIES AND ILLNESSES in the Petroleum Industry

Annual.   June 1984.
28 p. no paging.
SRI/MF/complete

Annual survey report on occupational injuries and illnesses in the petroleum industry, by function and company, 1983. Presents data on employment; hours worked; recordable injury and illness cases; fatalities; cases involving lost workdays, and number of days away from work and of restricted activity; nonfatal cases without lost workdays; and selected incidence rates; by functional area, for 163 individual companies.

Data are based on company reports to API, and cover only operations subject to OSHA recordkeeping requirements.

Contains introduction (1 p.); 15 tables (21 p.); list of respondents accompanied by identification number used in tables (2 p.); and questionnaire facsimile (4 p.).

Availability: American Petroleum Institute, Publications and Distribution Section, 1220 L St., NW, Washington DC 20005, $5.00; SRI/MF/complete.

A2575-5   LIQUEFIED PETROLEUM GAS REPORT

Monthly.   Approx. 3 p.
ISSN 0024-421X.
LC SC 79-4044.
SRI/MF/complete, shipped quarterly

Monthly report on U.S. inventories of liquefied petroleum and liquefied refinery gases, including ethane, propane, isobutane, normal butane, pentane plus, and other stocks. Report is issued 4-5

weeks after month of coverage and is compiled by American Petroleum Institute from member reports.

Issues contain 2 trend charts, and 1 table showing total end-of-month inventories at plants/terminals/underground/refineries, by product and region; and total underground inventories, by product; for month of coverage, with comparative summary data for previous month, and same month of previous year.

Monthly table appears in all issues. Oct. 1983 issue also includes revised July, Aug., and Sept. 1983 data; Dec. 1983 and June 1984 issues include revised Nov. 1983 and May 1984 data, respectively.

Availability: American Petroleum Institute, Publications and Distribution Section, 1220 L St., NW, Washington DC 20005, $10.00 per yr.; SRI/MF/complete, shipped quarterly.
Issues reviewed during 1984: Sept. 1983-Aug. 1984 (D) [Sept. 1983 issue incorrectly reads Oct. 1983].

A2575-6   QUARTERLY REVIEW OF DRILLING STATISTICS for the U.S.

Quarterly.   Approx. 35 p.
ISSN 0003-5789.
SRI/MF/complete

Quarterly report on oil and gas well drilling in producing States and offshore. Includes data on exploratory and development wells and multiple completions (wells equipped to produce oil and/or gas separately from more than one reservoir).

Data are compiled by API from member reports and incorporate well reclassification information from the American Assn of Petroleum Geologists-Committee on Statistics of Drilling (AAPG-CSD). Reports are issued 2 months after quarter of coverage and have been published by API since 1970.

Contains contents listing and preface; 7 tables, listed below; and 2 appendices listing source agencies for drilling statistics and AAPG-CSD district chairmen.

An annual statistical summary is included in issue for 4th quarter. This issue also includes 2 additional tables showing new-field wildcat wells drilled in the U.S., including number and footage of producing oil and gas wells and dry holes; and total number of year-end suspense wells; all by State and State region, for year of coverage.

Availability: American Petroleum Institute, Publications and Distribution Section, 1220 L St., NW, Washington DC 20005, $20.00 per yr.; SRI/MF/complete.
Issues reviewed during 1984: 3rd Qtr. 1983-2nd Qtr. 1984 (D) (Vol. XVII, Nos. 3-4; Vol. XVIII, Nos. 1-2).

TABLES:

[Tables show number of U.S. wells and footage. Tables I-IV.B generally show data onshore and offshore by State; by district for California, Louisiana, New Mexico, and Texas; and for offshore Federal waters of Pacific Coast and Northern Gulf of Mexico.

Data are shown for quarter of coverage and are repeated for year to date; tables I-IV.B also include summary data for same periods of previous year.]

I.   Total wells drilled [oil, gas, and service wells, dry holes, and stratigraphic/core tests].

II-III. Total exploratory and development wells drilled [oil and gas wells and dry holes].

IV.A-IV.B. Exploratory and development wells completed as multiple completions [wells reported as oil wells, and wells reported as gas wells].

V.A-V.B. Wells drilled by depth intervals [total and exploratory wells, and total onshore and offshore wells, for oil, gas, and dry wells].

A2575–7   U.S. CRUDE OIL DISTILLATION REFINING CAPACITY SURVEY for 1984-85
Annual.   June 1984.   3 p.
SRI/MF/complete

Annual survey report of crude oil distillation refining capacity, Mar. 1984-Mar. 1985, reflecting new refineries and expansions under construction and expected to be completed during survey period. Data are from an API member survey.

Contains 4 tables, listed below.

Availability: American Petroleum Institute, Publications and Distribution Section, 1220 L St., NW, Washington DC 20005, ‡; SRI/MF/complete.

TABLES:
[All tables show barrels per calendar day.]

[1] API crude oil distillation refining capacity survey [total capacities by quarter, Mar. 31, 1984-Mar. 31, 1985; operable capacity shutdown on Mar. 31, 1984; and inoperable refinery capacity, total period Mar. 31, 1983-Mar. 31, 1984; all by PAD district and major subdivision]. (1 p.)

[2-4] New refineries and expansions to crude oil distillation refinery capacity presently under construction and expected to be completed in the quarters ending June 30 and Dec. 31, 1984, and Mar. 31, 1985 [capacity by company arranged by PAD subdivision]. (1 p.)

A2575–8   REPORTED FIRE LOSSES IN THE PETROLEUM INDUSTRY for 1983
Annual.   June 1984.   6 p.
SRI/MF/complete

Annual report on petroleum industry fires and fire loss, 1982-83. Data are shown by class of property affected and class of product.

Data for 1983 are based on reports from 160 companies responding to an annual API survey. Reporting was restricted to fires resulting in losses of $2,500 or more.

Contains 3 tables, listed below, with brief accompanying narrative (p. 1-4); and list of reporting companies (p. 5-6).

This is the 54th annual survey.

Availability: American Petroleum Institute, Publications and Distribution Section, 1220 L St., NW, Washington DC 20005, $5.00; SRI/MF/complete.

TABLES:
[Data by class of property are for exploration/production/gas processing, refining, marketing, pipeline, chemical operations, and miscellaneous.]

1. Current replacement values, fire losses, and fire-loss ratios, by classes of property [revised 1982, and] 1983. (p. 1-2)

2. Number of fires reported for 1982-83 [by class of property for fires originating on and outside oil company property, and for 3 loss size categories]. (p. 3)

3. Tank fire experience, 1982-83: fires originating in tanks resulting in losses of $2,500 or more [by structural type of tank, by class of product (including crude oil and liquefied petroleum gas) and by location]. (p. 4)

A2575–9   1982 JOINT ASSOCIATION SURVEY ON DRILLING COSTS
Annual.   Nov. 1983.
vii+84 p.
SRI/MF/complete

Annual report on 1982 drilling costs for U.S. oil and gas wells and dry holes. Includes number of wells and footage drilled and estimated costs, by State, offshore location, and type of well.

Data are compiled from a Joint Assn Survey (JAS) of operator costs conducted by API, Independent Petroleum Assn of America, and Mid-Continent Oil and Gas Assn; and from the API *Quarterly Review of Drilling Statistics* (QRDS) (for description, see A2575-6).

Contains contents and table listings (p. v-vii), and the following:

a. Summary and survey description, with 3 text tables including summary comparisons to 1981. (p. 1-4)

b. Statistical section, with 53 tables showing number, footage drilled, and drilling cost, by depth interval, for oil and gas wells and dry holes, by State with detail for selected onshore and offshore areas and State districts, and for Appalachian region and Federal waters (total and Gulf of Mexico), 1982. (p. 6-59)

c. Appendix A-C, with survey questionnaire facsimile, and 1 summary table showing QRDS vs. JAS findings. (p. 62-65)

d. Appendix D-F, with 2 tables showing wells, footage, and drilling cost, for exploratory and development oil and gas wells and dry holes, and for single and multiple completion oil and gas wells, 1982; and number of JAS companies and wells, by number of wells drilled, 1978-82. (p. 66-70)

e. Appendix G-H, with 12 maps and survey methodology. (p. 71-84)

Availability: American Petroleum Institute, Publications and Distribution Section, 1220 L St., NW, Washington DC 20005, $15.00; SRI/MF/complete.

A2575–10   NEW CONSTRUCTION AND DEACTIVATION OF SERVICE STATIONS in the Petroleum Industry
Annual.   May 1984.   4 p.
SRI/MF/complete

Annual summary report on gasoline service station construction and deactivation, 1983, based on reports of 33 oil companies.

Contains 2 tables showing total new outlets constructed, and outlets permanently deactivated, 1982-83 (p. 3); and list of reporting companies (p. 4).

Availability: American Petroleum Institute, Publications and Distribution Section, 1220 L St., NW, Washington DC 20005, $5.00; SRI/MF/complete.

A2575–11   REVIEW OF FATAL INJURIES IN THE PETROLEUM INDUSTRY for 1983
Annual.   June 1984.   4 p.
LC 44-37408.
SRI/MF/complete

Annual report, for 1982-83, on petroleum industry accidental deaths, based on reports of 163 oil and gas companies and their subsidiaries.

Contains description of specific accidents, with 1 table showing fatalities by industry function and by cause, 1982-83.

This is the 52nd annual report.

Availability: American Petroleum Institute, Publications and Distribution Section, 1220 L St., NW, Washington DC 20005, $5.00; SRI/MF/complete.

A2575–12   IMPORTED CRUDE OIL AND PETROLEUM PRODUCTS
Monthly.   Approx. 65 p. var. paging.
SRI/MF/complete

Monthly report on U.S. imports of crude oil, residual fuel oil, finished petroleum products, and unfinished oils, by importing company. Within each company, data are further shown by port of entry, country of origin, and, as applicable, recipient company, destination, and type of product. Includes quantity and selected physical properties.

Report is compiled by API from DOE data, and is issued approximately 2 months after month of coverage.

Contains contents listing; 4 tables repeated for PAD Districts I-IV combined and V, and usually for adjusted data for previous months; and list of companies reporting no imports.

Availability: American Petroleum Institute, Publications and Distribution Section, 1220 L St., NW, Washington DC 20005, $200.00 per yr.; SRI/MF/complete.

Issues reviewed during 1984: Aug. 1983-Aug. 1984 (D).

A2575–14   BASIC PETROLEUM DATA BOOK: Petroleum Industry Statistics
3 times per year.
Approx. 300 p. no paging.
ISSN 0730-5621.
LC SN 82-779.
SRI/MF/complete

Compilation of reference statistics, issued 3 times per year, on world oil and gas industry exploration, production, refining, demand, financial condition, prices, and reserves. Data are compiled from API member reports and from numerous Federal Government, trade assn, and commercial publications.

Data are most recent available as of cover date, and include trends from as early as the 1940s. Report format and table topics remain essentially the same from issue to issue. Contents of the current issue are as follows:

Contents and table listings.

Section I. Energy: summary of world supply and demand, with 12 tables.

Section II-IV. Crude oil reserves, exploration, drilling, and production, with 29 tables.

Section V-VI. Financial data and prices, with 25 tables.

Section VII-X. Demand, refining, imports, and exports, with 39 tables.

Section XI-XII. Offshore oil and gas, and transportation, with 1 chart and 23 tables.

Section XIII. Natural gas, with 10 tables.

Section XIV-XV. OPEC, and miscellaneous, with 6 tables.

Each section is preceded by a table listing. Tables and chart are listed below.

Availability: American Petroleum Institute, Publications and Distribution Section, 1220 L St., NW, Washington DC 20005, $40.00 per yr.; SRI/MF/complete.

Issues reviewed during 1984: Jan.-Sept. 1984 (D) (Vol. IV, Nos. 1-3).

TABLES AND CHART:

[Data are shown for U.S., unless otherwise noted.]

A2575-14.1: Energy Supply and Demand

SECTION I: ENERGY SUMMARY

1-2. World energy consumption and fuel shares: history and base scenario midprice projections [by fuel type, by region or country, including U.S., Canada, Japan, Western Europe, Australia/New Zealand, non-OECD, and OPEC, various years 1960-95]. (2 p.)

3-7. Selected economic, demographic, and energy indicators [1947-83]; comparison of [DOE and other] midprice energy supply/demand projections, and projections of energy demand by sector, [by source] for 1990; and total gross consumption and production of energy resources, by major sources [1947-83]. (7 p.)

8-12. Gross consumption by consuming sector; demand for energy inputs in the industrial, household/commercial, and transportation sectors, and for electricity generation by utilities [all by energy source, 1947-83]. (10 p.)

A2575-14.2: Oil Reserves, Exploration, Drilling, and Production

SECTION II: CRUDE OIL RESERVES

1-3. Estimated proved world reserves of crude oil, annually as of Jan. 1 [for U.S., Canada, and 7 world areas, 1948-83; reserves [and production] of U.S. crude oil [1947-82]; and estimated world proven crude oil reserves for 20 leading nations (annually as of Jan. 1) [1975-84]. (7 p.)

4. USGS [U.S. Geological Survey] estimates of [identified and undiscovered recoverable] oil and gas resources [by onshore and offshore petroleum region (no date)]. (1 p.)

SECTION III: EXPLORATION AND DRILLING

1-3. [New-field wildcat and total] exploratory wells and footage, and development and total wells and footage [and service/stratigraphic/core tests, 1947-83]; and wells drilled by depth interval [1959-83]. (7 p.)

4-5. U.S. petroleum geophysical exploration (crew months) [by method, 1951-82]; and Free World exploration [for U.S., Canada, and 5 world areas, 1954-82]. (4 p.)

6-8. Historical record: number of new-field oil, gas, and oil/gas discoveries proved after 6 years to be of significant size [by year drilled, 1947-76]. (6 p.)

9-11. Estimated drilling costs by well classification, onshore and offshore [and total, 1959-82]. (6 p.)

12-13. Free World total and exploratory well completions [by country and world area, 1970-82]. (2 p.)

14-16. Annual average rotary rig activity by State [number in operation, 1949-83]; total [exploratory and development] wells drilled, by State [1967-83]; and rotary rig census [number of contractor and oil company owned rigs, number stacked and active, and number by drilling depth capability and by type, 1967-83]. (9 p.)

17-18. Producing natural gas/condensate wells [1947-82], and oil wells [1947-83], by State (as of Dec. 31). (6 p.)

19-20. Producing oil wells by State and by type [flowing and artificial lift, as of Dec. 31, 1947-83]; and in Free World (as of July 1) [by country and world area, 1970-83]. (9 p.)

SECTION IV: PRODUCTION

1-2. World crude oil production by area [for U.S., Canada, and 6 world areas, 1947-83; and for] 20 leading nations [1974-83]. (6 p.)

3. Stripper wells and stripper well production [1947-82]. (1 p.)

4-5. Crude oil production [total 1947-83], and average per well per day [1947-81], by State. (6 p.)

A2575-14.3: Finance and Prices

SECTION V: FINANCIAL DATA

[Data for "a group of petroleum companies" are aggregates for multinational corporations monitored by Chase Manhattan Bank to determine the financial condition of the petroleum industry.]

1-3. Average hourly earnings, total mining and manufacturing vs. petroleum/natural gas extraction and petroleum refining [1947-83]; number of employees, petroleum/natural gas extraction and petroleum refining [1947-83]; and sources of capital [amount from internal and external funds] of a group of petroleum companies [1947-82]. (3 p.)

4-5. Net income as a percent of net worth: petroleum, other selected industry groups, and total manufacturing, mining, [and trade, 1947-81]; and domestic and foreign net income of a group of petroleum companies [1960-82]. (4 p.)

6-7. World petroleum industry capital and exploration expenditures, U.S. vs. foreign [1947-81]; and sources and uses of working capital of a group of petroleum companies [1947-82]. (4 p.)

8-10. Domestic and foreign capital expenditures [by category] of the world petroleum industry, and estimated U.S. exploration/development expenditures of Chase Manhattan Bank group and all other companies, [1947-81]; and U.S. estimated expenditures for exploration, development, and production [1973-82]. (6 p.)

11. Environmental protection [total, capital, administrative/operating/maintenance, and R&D] expenditures of the petroleum industry [for air, water, and land/other, 1966-82]. (1 p.)

SECTION VI: PRICES

1-2. Average annual wellhead price of crude oil and natural gas, current and constant 1967 dollars or cents [and PPI for all commodities, 1947-83]. (2 p.)

3. Refiner acquisition cost of [domestic and imported] crude oil [1968-83]. (1 p.)

4-5. Trend of wholesale prices of commodities utilized in the production of petroleum; and trend of regular grade gasoline prices vs. prices of other consumer goods and services; [1947-83]. (4 p.)

6-7. Annual average retail price of No. 2 home heating oil [and CPI, 1956-83]; and total dollar value of crude oil and natural gas at the wellhead [including production and price, 1947-82]. (3 p.)

8-9. Average wellhead value of crude oil [1947-80], and natural gas [1947-82], by State. (5 p.)

10-11. Posted and official government selling prices of key foreign crude oils [by type and country, various dates 1970-83]. (4 p.)

12. Average retail gasoline prices [including tax] for [approximately 50] cities [decennially 1920-70, and annually 1971-77]; and [leaded and unleaded] prices for [approximately 30 SMSAs, and for census regions, 1978-83]. (2 p.)

13-14. Average price of natural gas consumed by end-use sector [1967-82]; and cost [and quantity] of petroleum imports [1970-83]. (2 p.)

A2575-14.4: Supply, Demand, Refining, and Trade

SECTION VII: DEMAND

1. Estimated world demand for refined petroleum products by area [for U.S., Canada, and 6 world areas, 1950-83]. (2 p.)

2-6. Total supply and demand for all oils, total and motor gasoline, and distillate and residual fuel oil [including imports and exports, various years 1947-83]. (9 p.)

7-8. Deliveries of distillate and residual fuel oil to electric utilities [1947-82]; and motor gasoline consumption/sales [by State, 1962-83]. (4 p.)

9-12. Sales or deliveries of distillate and residual fuel oils, by State and by uses [1947-83]. (10 p.)

13-17. Total supply and demand [including imports and exports] for naphtha and kerosene type jet fuel [1965-82]; and for kerosene, natural gas liquids/liquefied refinery gases, and lubricants [1947-82]. (8 p.)

SECTION VIII: REFINING

1-2. Estimated worldwide crude oil refining capacity by area, as of Jan. 1 [for U.S. and 6 world areas, 1947-84]; and worldwide crude oil refinery runs [U.S., Canada, Japan, and 8 world areas, 1965-83]. (4 p.)

3-5. Crude oil refining capacity (as of Jan. 1) [1947-84]; percentage yields of refined petroleum products from crude oil [1964-83]; and crude oil refinery runs by PAD district, domestic vs. foreign [1947-82]. (6 p.)

6. Number, and capacity [by process], of [operating and idle] petroleum refineries [by PAD district and State], as of Jan. 1, 1984. (1 p.)

SECTION IX: IMPORTS

1-2. Share of imports in domestic petroleum [refined product] demand, total imports of petroleum [and products], and petroleum [and natural gas liquids] production, [1947-83]. (3 p.)

3-7. U.S. crude oil imports by [world] area and country of origin [1947-83], and by PAD districts [1952-83]; and imports of residual and distillate fuel [1950-83], and of unfinished oils and refined products [1959-83], by PAD districts. (10 p.)

8-9. Total petroleum imports by source [country of origin, 1957-83]; and direct petroleum imports from members of the Organization of Arab Petroleum Exporting Countries, [monthly] Sept. 1973-Apr. 1974. (4 p.)

10. World oil movements [between country or area of origin and destination, 1972-83]. (6 p.)

SECTION X: EXPORTS

1-2. Total domestic production and exports of crude oil and its products [1947-83]; and exports of petroleum to selected areas [by country or world area, 1947-83]. (3 p.)

3-6. Africa and Middle East oil exports to selected areas [U.S., Western Europe, Japan, and other areas, various years 1959-83]; and role of Middle East and African oil in Western European and Japanese consumption and in world exports [1961-83]. (4 p.)

A2575-14.5: Offshore and Transportation

SECTION XI: OFFSHORE

1-2. Estimated worldwide production of crude oil onshore vs. offshore [1969-83]; and estimated worldwide offshore production by area [for U.S., Venezuela, and 6 world areas, 1970-83]. (2 p.)

3. Production and value of crude oil/condensate onshore and offshore [cumulative to 1953, and 1954-83]. (2 p.)

4-5. Estimated worldwide production of natural gas onshore vs. offshore, and estimated worldwide offshore production by area [for U.S. and 6 world areas, 1970-82]. (2 p.)

6-8. Production and value of natural gas onshore and offshore [cumulative to 1953, and 1954-82]; and total offshore wells drilled [by type] 1983, and accumulated production 1982, Federal and State leases [by State and offshore area], all-time to Jan. 1. (4 p.)

9-11. Outer Continental Shelf (OCS) oil/gas lease sales [tracts and acres offered and leased, bonus, 1st-year rental, average and highest bid per acre, and State or area of tract, by sale date, to Nov. 30, 1983]; OCS revenue and production value, percentage cumulative revenue of cumulative production value [1953-82]; and OCS oil/gas sales, total bonus vs. total amount of all bids received, [and State or area of tract, by sale date, to Nov. 17, 1982]. (8 p.)

12-13. Offshore platforms [for] multiwell, single well, and other types [by State, as of] Jan. 1, 1981; and worldwide water depth records [for] exploratory drilling and platforms [and including company and location, various years 1935-83]. [1 table and 1 chart] (2 p.)

14-15. Eight-year OCS blowout experience [including pollution, injuries, and other major damage, total period] 1971-82; and oil spill incidents of 238 or more barrels [and number of structures and annual oil production], OCS, Gulf of Mexico [1964-80]. (2 p.)

16-17. Historical data on leasing continental seabeds adjacent to the U.S. [by region, through Aug. 4, 1981]; and basin ranking [of] 5-year OCS oil/gas leasing program [by resource potential and exploration interest, 1979]. (2 p.)

SECTION XII: TRANSPORTATION

1. Gas utility industry miles of pipeline and main, by type [1947-82]. (1 p.)

2-4. U.S. and world tank ship fleet (actual and T2-SE-A1 equivalents) [number and characteristics, 1947-79]; and age distribution of world tank ship fleet by major flag of registry (as of Dec. 31, 1979) [by year of construction]. (4 p.)

5. Sources of oil spills and [hazardous and] other substances, 1980. (1 p.)

6-7. Total and average consumption of motor fuel, and total and average travel [mileage], by motor vehicles [and including number of vehicles registered, all by vehicle type, 1947-82]. (4 p.)

A2575-14.6: Natural Gas

SECTION XIII: NATURAL GAS

1-3. Estimated proved world reserves of natural gas, annually as of Jan. 1 [for U.S., Canada, and 6 world areas, 1967-84]; and supply of U.S. natural gas and reserves of natural gas liquids [1947-82]. (4 p.)

4-6. World marketed production of natural gas by area [U.S., Canada, and 6 world areas, 1950-83]; salient statistics of natural gas in the U.S. [including production, exports, imports, value at wellhead, consumption, and storage, 1947-82]; and U.S. imports of natural gas by source [Canada, Mexico, and Algeria, 1968-82]. (5 p.)

7-8. Estimated natural gas reserves (as of Jan. 1) [1975-83]; and world natural gas production [1974-83; both for] 20 leading nations. (8 p.)

9-10. Marketed production and consumption of natural gas, by State [1947-82]. (7 p.)

A2575-14.7: OPEC and Miscellaneous

SECTION XIV: OPEC

1-2. OPEC crude oil reserves, annually as of Jan. 1 [1960-84]; and production [per day, 1960-83; all by country]. (2 p.)

3-4. U.S. total petroleum and crude oil imports from OPEC nations [per day, by country of origin, 1960-83]. (2 p.)

SECTION XV: MISCELLANEOUS

1. Estimated average number of employees in [5] important segments of the petroleum industry [by State], 1982. (2 p.)

2. [Conversion tables.] (1 p.)

A2575-15   MONTHLY REPORT OF HEATING OIL AND OTHER MIDDLE DISTILLATES: Sales by States
Monthly.   Approx. 4 p.
SRI/MF/complete, shipped quarterly

Monthly report on nonmilitary sales of kerosene, other heating oils, and diesel oil, by State. Report is issued 1-2 months after month of coverage and is based on reports from approximately 50 companies, accounting for approximately 80% of sales.

Contains 3 tables showing gallons of kerosene, No. 2 oil, and diesel oil sold, by State, for month of coverage, year to date, and same periods of previous year. Also usually includes revisions of previous monthly tables.

Availability: American Petroleum Institute, Publications and Distribution Section, 1220 L St., NW, Washington DC 20005, $16.00 per yr.; SRI/MF/complete, shipped quarterly.

Issues reviewed during 1984: Sept. 1983-Aug. 1984 (D).

A2575-17   SUMMARY OF MOTOR VEHICLE ACCIDENTS IN THE PETROLEUM INDUSTRY for 1983
Annual.   June 1984.
7 p. no paging.
SRI/MF/complete, current & previous year reports

Annual survey report on car and truck accidents in the petroleum industry, 1974-83. Includes number of accidents, fleet size and miles traveled, accident rates per million miles and per 100 vehicles, and number of companies providing data, all shown by petroleum industry sector.

Data are from responses of 147 companies to an API survey.

Contains summary (1 p.); and 4 tables (6 p.).

This is the 51st survey report. The 50th report has also been reviewed and is also available on SRI microfiche under this number [Annual. June 1983. 8 p. no paging. $3.00]. SRI coverage begins with these editions.

Availability: American Petroleum Institute, Publications and Distribution Section, 1220 L St., NW, Washington DC 20005, $5.00; SRI/MF/complete.

A2615
American Planning Association

A2615-1   PLANNERS' SALARIES AND EMPLOYMENT TRENDS, 1983
Recurring (irreg.)   Feb. 1984.
18 p.   PAS Rpt. No. 382.
LC 80-643508.
SRI/MF/complete

Recurring survey report, by James Hecimovich and JoAnn C. Butler, on salary and employment of professional planners in public and private sectors, for U.S. and Canada, 1983. Data are shown by employment-related and demographic characteristics, and include selected comparisons to 1977 and/or 1981.

Covers median salary and number of planners, shown variously by employer type, jurisdiction size and type (for public sector planners), census division, and planners' degree type, years of experience, sex, and race/ethnicity or minority status, with selected detail for directors and staff members.

Employer types include public agency by government level, private consultant, business, college/university, and nonprofit organization. Jurisdiction types are urban, suburban, rural, and mixed. Degree types are B.A., M.A., and law/PhD. Race/ethnicity data include blacks, Hispanics, American Indians, and Asians.

Data are from responses of approximately 7,-440 APA members to a Sept. 1983 survey.

Contains contents and table listings (1 p.); 2 narrative sections, with 21 interspersed tables (p. 1-16); and narrative analysis (p. 17-18).

Previous report, for 1981, is described in SRI 1982 Annual, under this number.

Availability: American Planning Association, Planning Advisory Service, 1313 E. 60th St., Chicago IL 60637, PAS subscribers $8.00, others $16.00; SRI/MF/complete.

A2620
American Psychological Association

A2620-1   **1983/84 FACULTY SALARIES IN GRADUATE DEPARTMENTS OF PSYCHOLOGY**
Annual.   Jan. 1984.
3+37 p. no paging.
SRI/MF/complete

Annual report, by Joy Stapp, on faculty salaries in psychology graduate depts, 1983/84. Covers 9-month salaries in doctoral and master's depts, by faculty academic rank and years in rank, variously cross-tabulated by census division, institution control (public and private), and dept type (including educational psychology, professional school, counseling, and human development). Also includes 12-month salaries for Canadian depts, and trends from 1980/81.

Salaries are variously shown as actual distribution, means, medians, percentiles, and quartiles.

Data are based on responses of 350 graduate depts, with 6,128 full-time faculty, to a fall 1983 survey conducted jointly by American Psychological Assn and Council of Graduate Depts of Psychology.

Contains introduction, methodology, and table listing (p. 1-3); and 21 tables (37 p.).

Availability: American Psychological Association, Human Resources Research, 1200 17th St., NW, Washington DC 20036, †; SRI/MF/complete.

A2625
American Public Power Association

A2625-1   **PUBLIC POWER**
Bimonthly.   Approx. 100 p.
ISSN 0033-3654.
LC 47-36541.
SRI/MF/excerpts, delayed

Bimonthly periodical reporting trends and developments affecting publicly owned electric utilities. Data are compiled from Energy Information Administration and Rural Electrification Administration (REA) reports, and from information provided by American Public Power Assn members.

Issues contain articles, occasionally including statistics; and narrative editorial features. Jan./Feb. issue presents an annual directory of local publicly owned utility systems, including summary statistics. Nov./Dec. issue includes a non-statistical compilation of profiles of innovative public power projects.

Features with substantial statistical content are described, as they appear, under "Statistical Features." Each issue of the journal is reviewed, but an abstract is published in SRI monthly issues only when statistical features appear.

Availability: American Public Power Association, Circulation Manager, Public Power, 2301 M St., NW, Washington DC 20037, $35.00 per yr., single copy $5.00, Directory Issue: members $20.00, nonmembers $40.00; SRI/MF/excerpts for all portions described under "Statistical Features;" delayed shipment 3 months from issue date.

Issues reviewed during 1984: Nov./Dec. 1983-Sept./Oct. 1984 (P) (Vol. 41, No. 6; Vol. 42, Nos. 1-5).

STATISTICAL FEATURES:

A2625-1.501: Nov./Dec. 1983 (Vol. 41, No. 6)

COST OF ELECTRICITY IN MAJOR U.S. CITIES COMPARED

(p. 22-23) Article, with 1 chart and 1 table ranking 30 largest cities by residential electricity cost per kWh, as of Jan. 1, 1983.

FINANCING OPTIONS FOR PUBLIC ELECTRIC SYSTEMS

(p. 62-68) By C. M. Perkins. Article, with text statistics (p. 67) showing value of tax-exempt unsecured promissory notes for 8 public power systems issuing such notes, 1982. Data are from Lehman Brothers, Kuhn Loeb.

A2625-1.502: Jan./Feb. 1984 (Vol. 42, No. 1)

PUBLIC POWER DIRECTORY, 1984, ANNUAL FEATURE

(p. D1-D100) Annual statistical directory of local publicly owned electric utilities. Also includes summary data for other types of electric power organizations, and statistical directories of publicly owned cable communication systems and major Canadian electric utilities.

Data are from American Public Power Assn, Energy Information Administration, Rural Electrification Administration (REA), and other sources.

Contains index (p. D1); and the following:

a. Electric utility summary statistics: number of systems (no date); and customers, revenues, net plant investment, kWh sales, installed capacity, and generation, 1981-82; for local publicly owned systems, private power companies, REA borrowers, and Federal power agencies. 15 charts and 2 tables. (p. D2)

b. Ranking of 20 largest State/local publicly owned electric systems, by number of customers served, plant value, kWh sales, and revenues, 1982. 4 tables. (p. D9)

c. Directory of local publicly owned electric utilities, arranged by State and outlying area, showing address, chief official, meters served, generation and capacity, wholesale power purchases or sales, gross annual revenues, and year established; data are for various years 1980-83, specified for each utility. (p. D10-D72)

d. Directories of organizations representing local publicly owned systems and of American Public Power Assn members. (p. D74-D86)

e. Directory of publicly owned cable communication systems, arranged by State, showing address, chief official, year started, number of subscribers and channels, monthly rate, type of organizational structure and financing, and utility use. (p. D89-D91)

f. Directory of major Canadian electric utilities, by Province, including text statistics on system generating capacity and customers served. (p. D92-D93)

g. Directory of Federal power agencies, with text data on value of REA insured and guaranteed loans, FY83 and cumulative. (p. D94-D96)

h. Editorial index for 1983. (p. D96-D100)

This is the 23rd annual edition of the directory. Corrected data appear in the Mar./Apr. 1984 issue; for description, see A2625-1.503 below.

LOCAL SYSTEMS BUDGET $5.39 BILLION FOR 1984 PLANT WORK, ANNUAL FEATURE

(p. 42-43) Annual article, by Jeannie Kilmer, on capital spending plans of local publicly owned electric utilities for 1984. Data are from an annual *Public Power* survey. Includes 1 table showing expenditures for distribution, transmission, conservation/load management, and generation by fuel type, actual 1983 and projected 1983-84.

A2625-1.503: Mar./Apr. 1984 (Vol. 42, No. 2)

PUBLIC POWER CONTRIBUTES MORE TO LOCAL GOVERNMENTS THAN DO IOUs

(p. 20) By Jeannie Kilmer. Article, with 1 table showing State/local tax payments as a percent of gross electric operating revenue, for public and private utilities by region, 1982. Data are from responses of 653 utilities to an American Public Power Assn (APPA) survey, and include number of respondents for each region.

STREETLIGHTS PROVIDING NEW CHALLENGES, ENERGY SAVINGS

(p. 22-27, 69) By Michael K. Bergman. Article on technological and other developments in streetlighting. Most data are based on responses of 58 public power systems to an APPA survey. Respondents represent 33% of public power system electricity sales.

Includes 4 undated tables showing physical characteristics of 6 types of streetlighting systems, and survey response concerning the following: circuit and lamp types used; energy consumed in lighting production; lighting energy demand, and sales relative to all sales; and lighting system common problems, and replacement and other plans.

PUBLIC POWER BOND ISSUES UP 5%, ANNUAL FEATURE

(p. 70) Annual article reviewing tax-exempt revenue bond issues by local publicly owned electric utilities, 1983. Data were compiled by Lehman Brothers, Kuhn Loeb. Includes 1 chart and 2 tables showing total number of issues, 1977-83 and quarterly 1981-83; and value of issues from individual joint- action power systems, 1975-83 period.

CORRECTION

(p. 92) Data corrections for annual public power directory feature appearing in the Jan./Feb. 1984 issue (for description, see A2625-1.502 above).

A2625-1.504: May/June 1984 (Vol. 42, No. 3)

PUBLIC POWER COSTS LESS, ANNUAL FEATURE

(p. 52-54) Annual article, by Jeannie Kilmer, comparing publicly and privately owned electric utility company sales, expenses, and costs to user. Data are from annual DOE reports.

Includes 4 tables and 4 charts showing the following, for private and public companies: residential and commercial/industrial average annual electricity consumption, revenue per kWh, and bill; and operating and managerial expenses, by type; selected years 1946-82.

A2625–1.505: July/August 1984 (Vol. 42, No. 4)

NATURAL GAS vs. HEAT PUMPS

(p. 30-34) By Arie M. Verrips and Walter A. Canney. Two articles, with 2 tables showing U.S. industrial and residential fuel prices, by type of fuel, 1978-83; and Lincoln, Nebr., residential energy costs by type of heating/cooling system, 1981-87. Data are from DOE, American Gas Assn, and the Lincoln Energy Commission.

HOW PUBLIC POWER SYSTEMS COMMUNICATE

(p. 42-45) By Madalyn Cafruny. Article on public relations depts of public power systems. Data are based on 38 responses to a survey of public relations personnel, conducted by Consumer Dimensions, Inc., for the American Public Power Assn.

Includes 2 tables showing respondent job functions; and public relations dept budget, staff size, and manager salary range, by system size, 1983.

A2625–1.506: Sept./Oct. 1984 (Vol. 42, No. 5)

PUBLIC POWER SALARIES BELOW THOSE OF IOUs, COOPERATIVES

(p. 30-34) By Jeff Tarbert. Article comparing salaries of top executives in public and private electric utilities. Data are from responses of more than 400 utilities to a 1984 survey, conducted by Towers, Perrin, Forster and Crosby.

Includes 5 tables showing number of CEOs, and average and median base salary of CEO and 3-4 other top executives, for public/municipal, investor-owned, and rural cooperative utilities, by revenue size.

IOUs' TAX RECORDS REFUTE THEIR CLAIMS

(p. 44-48) By John Kelly. Article on Federal income tax payments of investor-owned utilities (IOUs). Data are from U.S. Energy Information Administration.

Includes 2 tables showing IOU operating revenue, income before Federal income tax, deferred income tax, investment tax credit, and Federal income tax charged and paid, by utility arranged by State, 1981; and Federal income tax charged and paid, and deferred net tax, for 10 IOUs, 1972-81 period.

A2665
American Rental Association

A2665–1   1983 COST OF DOING BUSINESS SURVEY
Annual. Aug. 1984. 29 p.
SRI/MF/complete

Annual survey report presenting financial data for the equipment rental industry, 1983, with trends from 1980. Includes operating ratios, income by source and operating expenses by item, operating profit, net income before taxes, detailed assets and liabilities, and net worth.

Data are shown variously for all companies; by revenue size, rental share of total revenues, and type of equipment rented; and for 9 U.S. regions and Canada.

Data are based on responses by 363 companies to a 1983 survey, and were compiled for the American Rental Assn by Browne, Bortz, and Coddington, Inc.

Contains contents listing (inside front cover); narrative overview, with text tables and 4 charts (p. 1-3); and 5 sections, with 1 map, 1 chart, and 20 tables (p. 4-29).

Availability: American Rental Association, 1900 19th St., Moline IL 61265, $10.00; SRI/MF/complete.

A2700
American Society
for Engineering Education

A2700–1   ENGINEERING EDUCATION
8 issues per year.
Approx. 60 p. per issue;
cumulative pagination
throughout year.
ISSN 0022-0809.
LC 73-647370.
SRI/MF/not filmed

Monthly journal (Oct.-May) reporting on engineering and technical education, including teaching methods and their evaluation, continuing and nontraditional study, college-industry relations, engineering enrollment, and student and faculty characteristics.

Data are from surveys by American Society for Engineering Education (ASEE) and American Assn of Engineering Societies (AAES), and from studies submitted by individual researchers.

Issues generally contain articles and special features, occasionally including statistics; and narrative editorial depts.

Annual statistical features include reports on engineering and engineering technology enrollment and degrees, and characteristics of faculty and graduate students. The Mar. issue is a special issue presenting statistics on engineering college research and graduate study programs.

May issue includes annual author and subject index.

Features with substantial statistical content are described, as they appear, under "Statistical Features." Each issue of the journal is reviewed, but an abstract is published in SRI monthly issues only when statistical features appear. Generally, statistical data from single-institution samplings are not covered.

Availability: American Society for Engineering Education, 11 Dupont Circle, NW, Suite 200, Washington DC 20036, members †, nonmembers $32.00 per yr., students $15.00 per yr., single copy $3.00, Mar. issue $17.00; SRI/MF/not filmed.

Issues reviewed during 1984: Dec. 1983-Oct. 1984 (P) (Vol. 74, Nos. 3-8; Vol. 75, No. 1).

STATISTICAL FEATURES:

A2700–1.501: Dec. 1983 (Vol. 74, No. 3)

JAPAN'S INTELLECTUAL CHALLENGE: THE STRATEGY

(p. 138-146) By Lawrence P. Grayson. Article on Japanese governmental and industrial policies affecting engineering education since World War II. Data sources include U.S. Labor Dept and Japanese Science and Technology Agency.

Includes 1 chart and 2 tables showing average annual rate of change in number of engineering bachelor's degrees awarded and manufacturing productivity, for U.S. and Japan; and Japanese students in U.S. by discipline, with distribution of student years by engineering field; various periods 1950-1982/83.

Also includes brief inset article, with 2 tables showing Nobel prize recipients by scientific field, 1945-82 period; and patent applications, by nationality of applicant and country of application, 1980; for U.S., Japan, and total world or all foreign countries.

This is the 1st in a series of 3 articles on Japan.

ECONOMICS OF ENGINEERING MANPOWER

(p. 157-162) By Fred Landis. Article on impact of economic factors on demand for engineers. Data sources include independent researchers and College Placement Council surveys.

Includes 3 tables showing value added per engineer and R&D engineer, for 15 major industry groups, 1982; defense budget and defense engineering employment, for procurement, R&D, and military construction, FY82-86; and average salary offers to recent engineering bachelor's degree recipients, by field and industry category, July 1980-83.

Monetary data are shown in current and/or constant dollars.

DECODING AND ENCODING: A BALANCED APPROACH TO COMMUNICATION SKILLS

(p. 163-164) By Cynthia L. Selfe. Article, with 1 table showing importance of selected communications skills for engineering job performance, as rated by corporate college representatives. Data are from a 1982 survey of 100 representatives, conducted by the author.

CAREER PLANNING CHARACTERISTICS OF ENGINEERING STUDENTS

(p. 165-170) By Kevin D. Shell et al. Article, with 1 table showing students' reasons for choosing an engineering education, by sex and race-ethnicity (non-minority, black and Hispanic). Data are based on responses of 1,229 engineering students at 17 schools to the National Engineering Career Development Study survey, conducted spring 1981 by the Purdue Educational Research and Information Systems group.

A2700–1.502: Jan. 1984 (Vol. 74, No. 4)

JAPAN'S INTELLECTUAL CHALLENGE: THE SYSTEM

(p. 210-220) By Lawrence P. Grayson. Article on Japanese educational system, focusing on engineering programs and including comparisons to U.S.

Includes data on classroom time for 8 elementary/secondary school subjects (undated); percent of high school seniors by time spent on homework and by participation in 8 nonacademic activities, by sex, 1980; distribution of engineering degrees, by field and degree level, 1982; and enrollment, tuition, and subject requirements, for engineering bachelor's degree, for 2-3 universities (undated); all for U.S. and Japan.

Also includes data on U.S. degrees granted to U.S./Japanese citizens and all foreign nationals, by degree level, 1982; and number of Japanese national and private universities, with summary operating data, 1982.

Includes 5 tables. This is the 2nd in a series of 3 articles on Japan.

PREDICTING ACADEMIC SUCCESS IN ENGINEERING GRADUATE PROGRAMS

(p. 232-234) By Eric M. Malstrom et al. Article on a model designed to predict academic success of engineering graduate school students. Model was tested using records of 89 University of Cincinnati engineering graduate program enrollees.

Includes 1 tabular list and 1 table showing model variables and predictive accuracy, for students with 3.0 and 3.5 grade point averages.

A2700–1.503: Feb. 1984 (Vol. 74, No. 5)

JAPAN'S INTELLECTUAL CHALLENGE: THE FUTURE

(p. 296-305) By Lawrence P. Grayson. Article on prospects for Japan's economic and educational systems, focusing on engineering education and including comparisons to U.S. Data sources include U.S. Dept of Education.

Includes 1 chart and 1 table, showing distribution of Japanese Government budget for science/technology by agency, FY83; and university engineering research expenditures, with percent from government and nongovernment sources, for total U.S. and national and private Japanese universities, 1980 or 1982.

This is the 3rd in a series of 3 articles on Japan.

A2700–1.504: Mar. 1984 (Vol. 74, No. 6)

ENGINEERING COLLEGE RESEARCH AND GRADUATE STUDY, ANNUAL FEATURE

(p. 332-616) Annual full-issue report on engineering college research and graduate study programs, based on a 1983 survey of 218 engineering colleges and schools belonging to the American Society for Engineering Education.

Contains foreword (p. 332); narrative article on industry support for university R&D, list of institutions responding, questionnaire, and data summary (p. 337-350); summaries for individual institutions (p. 351-588); and indexes to graduate study fields and research areas (p. 589-616).

Each institution summary includes text data and 1-6 tables showing most or all of the following, for 1982/83 or fall 1983:

a. Names of officers, total number of faculty and undergraduates, graduate degree requirements, and off-campus extension centers.

b. Number of faculty, and enrollment and degrees granted by level, by degree program; appointments made to graduate students; and topics of accepted doctoral theses.

c. Personnel engaged in separately budgeted research; research expenditures, by source of support; separately budgeted research expenditures, by engineering college unit; and number of projects and expenditures for engineering-related research outside the engineering college, by type.

This is the 18th annual survey report.

A2700–1.505: Apr. 1984 (Vol. 74, No. 7)

ENGINEERING DEGREES GRANTED, 1983, ANNUAL FEATURE

(p. 640-645) Annual article, by Paul Doigan, on engineering degrees awarded in 1983. Data are from an annual American Assn of Engineering Societies (AAES) survey of 287 engineering schools.

Includes 6 tables showing degrees by level, by curriculum, minority group (black, Hispanic, American Indian, Asian/Pacific, female, and foreign national), and institution; women's bachelor degrees by curriculum; and top 5 States and 10 institutions ranked by number of degrees by level; 1983.

Full AAES survey report is covered in SRI under A0685-1.

A2700–1.506: May 1984 (Vol. 74, No. 8)

TRENDS IN ENGINEERING TECHNOLOGY EDUCATION

(p. 703-707) By Michael T. O'Hair. Article comparing selected characteristics of 4-year higher education programs in education technology, 1978 and 1982. Characteristics include administrative structure, relative popularity of various engineering fields, teaching loads, faculty hiring problems and degree requirements, laboratory requirements, placement situation and average starting salaries of graduates, and 10-year projected enrollment.

Data are from surveys by Purdue University, drawing responses from 71 schools in 1978 and 76 schools in 1982.

Includes 11 tables.

WOMEN AND MEN IN ENGINEERING TECHNOLOGY: SHAPING THE FUTURE

(p. 716-721) By Diane Tarmy Rudnick. Article comparing characteristics of female vs. male engineering technology students, 1978 and 1982. Characteristics include reasons for college and career choice, academic achievements and expectations, extracurricular activities, attitudes toward role of women, field of study, and expected career interruptions.

Data are from American Society for Engineering Education surveys of over 2,000 1st-year engineering technology students. The 1978 survey was limited to Wentworth Institute of Technology. The 1982 survey covered Wentworth and 4 other institutions.

Includes 5 tables.

ENGINEERING TECHNOLOGY PROFESSION: FUTURE DIRECTIONS

(p. 722-726) By Lawrence J. Wolf. Article, with 1 table and 2 charts showing selected trends in engineering, as follows: number of engineers, and percent with 4 years/more higher education, census years 1960-80 or 1960-70; and distribution of mechanical engineering programs at major universities by focus of curriculum, selected years 1955-82. Data are from Census Bureau, and the author's studies of curricula at 4-9 universities.

ENGINEERING TECHNOLOGY ENROLLMENTS, 1982, ANNUAL FEATURE

(p. 727-731) Annual article, by Patrick J. Sheridan, reporting on the annual engineering technology enrollment survey conducted by the Engineering Manpower Commission of the American Assn of Engineering Societies, 1982.

Includes 4 tables showing engineering technology enrollment by academic level, and number of schools, fall 1972-82; and enrollment detail by curriculum, by institution arranged by State, and for women and minorities (black, Hispanic, Asian/Pacific Islander, and American Indian), fall 1982. Most tables include detail for full-time and part-time students.

Full survey report by Engineering Manpower Commission is published in 2 parts and is covered by SRI under A0685-2.

ENGINEERING TECHNOLOGY DEGREES, 1983, ANNUAL FEATURE

(p. 732-735) Annual article, by Patrick J. Sheridan, on engineering technology degrees awarded in 1983. Data are from an annual survey of 285 engineering schools, conducted by the Engineering Manpower Commission of the American Assn of Engineering Societies (AAES).

Includes 2 tables showing degrees by curriculum and by institution arranged by State, all by degree level, 1983.

Full AAES survey report is covered in SRI under A0685-1.

A2700–1.507: Oct. 1984 (Vol. 75, No. 1)

ENGINEERING ENROLLMENTS, FALL 1983, ANNUAL FEATURE

(p. 45-49) Annual article, by Patrick J. Sheridan, reporting on the 16th annual engineering enrollment survey conducted by the Engineering Manpower Commission of the American Assn of Engineering Societies.

Includes narrative summary and 4 tables showing engineering enrollment by academic level, and number of schools, fall 1974-83; and enrollment detail by curriculum, and by institution arranged by State, and for women, minorities (black, Hispanic, Asian/Pacific Islander, and American Indian), and foreign nationals, fall 1983.

Full survey report by Engineering Manpower Commission is published in 2 parts and is covered by SRI under A0685-2.

ASEE SURVEY OF ENGINEERING FACULTY AND GRADUATE STUDENTS, FALL 1983, ANNUAL FEATURE

(p. 50-55) Annual article, by Paul Doigan, on engineering faculty shortage and graduate student and faculty characteristics as of fall 1983. Data are from responses of 186 engineering school deans to a 1983 ASEE survey, and from a similar 1982 survey. Reporting schools represent approximately 80% of all engineering enrollment in 1983.

Includes 16 tables showing the following, for 1983 unless otherwise noted, mostly with detail for public and private schools and comparisons to 1982:

a. Full-time faculty positions and vacancies, by engineering field; vacancies as a percent of positions, and share of vacancies unfilled since previous year, by academic rank; and perceived change in faculty recruiting/retention ability, effects of recruiting/retention inability on research and teaching arrangements, and factors in improved recruiting/retention ability.

b. Faculty mobility between academic and government/industry employment, with detail by tenure status and academic rank for faculty joining from industry/government, 1982/83.

c. Factors limiting PhD production; share of U.S. students among all graduate students, by category (teaching and research assistants, fellows, and other), and by engineering field for masters and doctoral candidates 1981-83; stipends for graduate teaching and research assistants, by academic level; and level of change in section size of junior/senior classes.

d. Authorized faculty positions, and faculty shortage, relative to total faculty needed to maintain/restore quality in engineering programs, by academic rank.

A2900
American Society of Association Executives

A2900-4   POLICIES AND PROCEDURES OF ASSOCIATIONS, 1982
Quadrennial. 1983. 79 p.
SRI/MF/complete

Quadrennial survey report on association policies and practices regarding finances, personnel, and organizational structure and activities, by member type (individuals, companies, or other assns) and geographic scope (national, State/regional, and local), 1981.

Presents data on dues and membership; investments and other financial practices, including tax-exempt status; personnel, including staff turnover rates, paid holidays, retirement and insurance plans, and other benefits; governing structure; office operations, including computer use, building ownership or rental fees, and non-member services; and other activities, including lobbying, publishing, and scholarship programs.

Also includes distribution of survey sample by budget, annual income, and staff size.

Data are based on responses of 1,692 assns to a 1982 ASAE survey.

Contains foreword, contents/table listing, and introduction (p. 2-7); and 9 sections, with brief narrative summaries and 157 tables (p. 9-79).

This is the 3rd quadrennial survey report. SRI coverage begins with the 3rd report.

Availability: American Society of Association Executives, 1575 Eye St., NW, Washington DC 20005, members $20.00, nonmembers $30.00; SRI/MF/complete.

A3000
American Soybean Association

A3000-1   SOYA BLUEBOOK '84
Annual. 1984.
238 p.+Foldout.
ISSN 0275-4509.
LC 81-640171.
SRI/MF/complete

Annual bluebook, with data on U.S. soybean production, processing, prices, utilization, and foreign trade, with comparisons to other oils, oilseeds, meals, and fats, various years 1925-84. Also includes some world, Brazilian, Argentine, and Canadian data. Data are compiled from USDA and other sources, identified for each table.

Contains contents listing (p. 7); directories of soybean-related trade assns, government agencies, and companies, and buyer's guide to products and services (p. 10-168); statistical section with contents listing, 2 maps, 12 trend charts, and 32 tables described below (p. 170-218); and glossary, soybean standards, and indexes (p. 219-238).

Availability: American Soybean Association, Circulation and Sales Department, 777 Craig Rd., PO Box 27300, St. Louis MO 63141, $25.00; SRI/MF/complete.

TABLES:
[Data are for U.S., unless otherwise noted. Data are usually shown for 1983 or 1983/84, generally with trends from the 1970s or earlier, including selected trends from as early as 1925. Some tables include detail by month.]

a. Soybean acreage, yield, and production, total and by State; and soybean planting and harvesting dates, by State. 3 tables. (p. 172-175)

b. Brazilian soybean harvested area, yield, and production, by State; Canadian soybean acreage, yield, production, farm price and value, foreign trade, processing, and products; and world soybean harvested area and production, by country. 4 tables. (p. 179-183)

c. Supply and disposition data for soybeans and soybean meal and oil, including acreage, yield, stocks, production, and trade; for U.S., Brazil, and Argentina. 4 tables. (p. 187-192)

d. Soybean prices; price support operations, including Commodity Credit Corp. (CCC) activities; crop value, total and for major producing States; distribution of farm marketings by month; product yields, prices, and value, with spread between product value and soybean price received by farmers. 6 tables. (p. 193-198)

e. Products: soybean meal and soy oil prices; supply and disposition data for soybean meal, soy and 3 other types of oilseed cakes/meals, and soy oil, including stocks, production, foreign trade, and domestic disappearance; world fat and oil production, by detailed type; and soy oil utilization by product type;. 8 tables. (p. 199-207)

f. Foreign trade: soybean and product exports; imports and exports of soy and other types of cakes/meals; soybean exports by port; soy and cottonseed oil exports, by type (commercial or Public Law 480) and method of payment; and Brazilian soybean and product

exports; generally with export detail by country or area of destination. 7 tables. (p. 208-218)

A3025
American Supply Association

A3025-1   1984 OPERATING PERFORMANCE OF THE P-H-C-P WHOLESALER INDUSTRY
Annual. 1984. 166 p.
SRI/MF/complete

Annual report on performance of plumbing/heating/cooling/piping (P/H/C/P) product wholesalers, 1983. Presents numerous financial and operating ratios, and other performance indicators.

Includes net sales and change from 1982; average lines per invoice and invoice value; per-employee sales, profit, compensation, and benefit value; number of days average inventory carried; use of last in/first out (LIFO) inventory method; average collection period for accounts receivable; and receivable dollars and accounts distribution, and average accounts balance, by days past due.

Also includes data on change in total, hardware/plumbing/heating/cooling, and P/H/C/P wholesale sales, and change in P/H/C/P price index, various years 1973-83; and summary ratio comparisons to 1981-82.

Most data are shown for typical case and as middle range, as follows: by primary type of product sold, by sales size and for high-profit firms; and for New York State excluding NYC, Michigan excluding upper Michigan, Chicago/northern Illinois, and 10 regions.

Report is intended to enable individual wholesalers to compare their performance with industry averages.

Data are primarily based on 286 responses to the American Supply Assn annual member survey, conducted by Industry Insights, Inc. and Management Horizons, Inc.

Contains introduction and contents listing (p. 3-6); overview, discussion of data application, and executive summary, with 7 charts and 5 tables (p. 7-29); detailed survey tabulations (p. 33-151); and appendix with methodology, definitions, and sample survey form (p. 155-166).

Availability: American Supply Association, 20 N. Wacker Dr., Suite 2260, Chicago IL 60606, members $30.00, nonmembers $60.00; SRI/MF/complete.

A3075
American
Trucking Associations

A3075–1   MONTHLY TRUCK
TONNAGE REPORT
Monthly.   Approx. 2 p.
SRI/MF/complete, shipped
quarterly

Monthly press release summarizing truck freight tonnage carried, and comparing tonnage indexes with production, sales, and price indexes. Data are based on approximately 200 responses to a monthly survey of Class I and II motor carriers of general freight, representing approximately one-half of tonnage moved. Report is issued approximately 2 months after cover date.

Contains narrative, and 3 monthly tables as follows:

[1] Indexes and comparisons [showing tonnage index, industrial production index, retail store sales index, PPI, CPI, and total tonnage carried, for current month, previous 2 months, and same month of previous year].

[2] Adjusted monthly truck [tonnage] index, historical [current year to date and 5 previous years].

[3] Three-month moving average of adjusted truck tonnage index [monthly, for current year to date through month prior to month of coverage, and 1-2 previous years].

Monthly tables appear in all issue; Apr. 1984 issue includes 2 additional tables showing revised truck tonnage index data, monthly 1979-83, with seasonal/trading day adjustment factors for 1984.

Report price includes *Weekly Truck Tonnage Report,* not covered by SRI.

Availability: American Trucking Associations, Statistical Analysis Department, 2200 Mill Rd., Alexandria VA 22314, $35.00 per yr.; SRI/MF/complete, shipped quarterly.

Issues reviewed during 1984: Sept. 1983-Aug. 1984 (D).

A3075–4   FINANCIAL ANALYSIS OF
THE MOTOR CARRIER
INDUSTRY
Annual, discontinued.

Annual report on Class I and II motor carrier finances, discontinued with 1983 report (for description, see SRI 1983 Annual, under this number). Report has been discontinued due to funding constraints.

Data are available on request from American Trucking Associations, Statistical Analysis Dept, 1616 P Street, NW, Washington DC 20036.

A3075–6   INTERSTATE
INFORMATION REPORT:
Truck Taxes and Highway
Finance
Recurring (irreg., selected issue).   May 31, 1984.
10 p. no paging.
SRI/MF/complete

Annual report on trucking industry's share of State and Federal highway taxes, 1982. Presents the following data for trucks compared to all motor vehicles: registrations, and State and Federal highway user taxes paid, by State, with U.S. totals by tax type and trends from 1957.

Also includes data on highway user fees and tax rates; and capital outlay and maintenance and total expenditures for State-administered highways.

Contains narrative summary, 1 chart, and 10 tables.

Interstate Information Report is a generally nonstatistical newsletter published approximately 4 times each year. The annual issue on truck taxes, usually published in the spring, is the only feature covered in SRI.

Availability: American Trucking Associations, Department of Interstate Cooperation, 2200 Mill Rd., Alexandria VA 22314, †; SRI/MF/complete.

A3150
American
Waterways Operators

A3150–1   1981-82 INLAND
WATERBORNE COMMERCE
STATISTICS
Annual.   [1984.]   55 p.
ISSN 0157-581X.
LC 77-642119.
SRI/MF/complete

Annual report, for 1981-82, of the barge and towing industry, presenting data on principal commodities transported and ton-miles moved on U.S. navigable inland and intracoastal waterways, generally excluding the Great Lakes. Data are compiled primarily from Army Corps of Engineers reports and include selected trends from 1940.

Contains contents listing (2 p.); and introduction and report, with 2 summary charts, 47 tables listed below, and centerfold map with accompanying table showing navigable lengths of individual waterways and lengths authorized by Congress for improvement (p. 1-55).

Availability: American Waterways Operators, 1600 Wilson Blvd., Suite 1000, Arlington VA 22209, †; SRI/MF/complete.

TABLES:

[Tables show data for 1982, unless otherwise noted. Data on traffic generally show net tons and ton-miles.]

A3150–1.1: National Data

[Traffic data in tables [3] and [6-8] are shown as net tons only.]

[1] Commercially navigable waterways of the U.S. by lengths and depths [by group or system]. (p. 2)

[2] Freight ton-miles by mode [air carrier, oil pipeline, rail, highway, and inland waterway], 1981-82. (p. 3)

[3] Barge traffic and key economic indicators [GNP and industrial production index, 1970-82]. (p. 4)

[4-5] Number [and horsepower or cargo capacity] of towing vessels and barges of the U.S. operated for the transportation of freight [by waterway system], as of May 1, 1982, and [annual totals] 1977-80 and 1981/82. (p. 5-6)

[6] Domestic barge traffic [by commodity], 1970-82. (p. 8)

[7-8] Mississippi river system net inland traffic, and Ohio River system internal and local traffic [by commodity], 1980-82. (p. 9-10)

[9] Traffic transported on inland waterways of U.S. (exclusive of Great Lakes) [1940 and 1965-82]. (p. 11)

[10] Coastal/coastwise traffic [1958 and 1965-82]. (p. 12)

[11] Principal [52] commodities transported on the inland waterways of the U.S. (exclusive of the Great Lakes) in net tons of 2,000 pounds, 1980-82. (p. 13)

A3150–1.2: Individual Waterways

[1-36] [Annual traffic and principal commodities carried by waterways, generally showing waterway section and length; controlling depth; total annual traffic, 1971-82; and commodities carried, 1982; arranged alphabetically by waterway.] (p. 15-55)

A3225
Association for
Education in Journalism
and Mass Communication

A3225–1   JOURNALISM EDUCATOR
Quarterly (selected issue).
Winter 1983.   (p. 3-52).
Vol. 37, No. 4.
ISSN 0022-5517.
SRI/MF/excerpts

Annual feature, "J-School Enrollments Hit Record 91,016," by Paul V. Peterson, on college/university enrollment and degrees awarded for journalism/mass communications programs, 1982 with trends from 1968.

Includes enrollment and degrees awarded by level, by institution and campus; with various institutional rankings and selected detail by sex and specialization. Also includes graduate degrees awarded to minorities by sex, for 16 institutions reporting 25 or more minority graduates.

Data are based on 216 responses to a 1982 survey of colleges and universities.

Contains survey report article, with 9 tables (p. 3-10); 1 table on 15-year enrollment trends (p. 17); and 2 additional tables presenting detailed data by institution and 10-year trends (p. 44-52).

Journalism Educator is a primarily narrative periodical on developments in journalism/mass communication education. Survey report on enrollment and degrees awarded is the only feature covered in SRI.

SRI coverage begins with the 1982 survey.

Availability: Association for Education in Journalism and Mass Communication, University of South Carolina, College of Journalism, Columbia SC 29208, $15.00 per yr., single copy $5.00; SRI/MF/excerpts for all portions presenting survey results.

A3235
Association for Library and Information Science Education

A3235-1 **LIBRARY AND INFORMATION SCIENCE EDUCATION Statistical Report, 1984**
Annual. 1984.
275 p. var. paging.
ISSN 0739-506X.
SRI/MF/complete, delayed

Annual report, for 1984, on U.S. and Canadian library/information science school faculty, students, finances, and curricula, by school, 1982/83 academic year, with some data for 1983/84 and selected trends from 1946. Includes data on faculty salaries, student aid, funding by source, and continuing education.

Data are based on approximately 70 responses to a member survey by ALISE, and generally are shown separately for institutional members (accredited by American Library Assn) and associate institutional members (not accredited). Number of schools reporting varies and usually is specified in table titles or accompanying text.

Contains listings of contents and tables (p. iii + xiii); introduction (p. 1-3); and 5 sections with narrative analyses and 165 tables, listed below, on faculty (p. F1-F86), students (p. S1-S70), curriculum (p. C1-C41), income and expenditures (p. FIN1-FIN17), and continuing education (p. CE1-CE32). Also includes a narrative summary and analysis, with 1 table (p. SCA1-SCA13).

This is the 5th annual report.

Availability: Association for Library and Information Science Education, 471 Park Lane, State College PA 16803, $25.00; SRI/MF/complete, delayed shipment in July 1985.

TABLES:
[Data by ethnic origin are shown for American Indian/Alaskan Native, Asian/Pacific Islander, black, Hispanic, and white.]

A3235-1.1: Faculty
[Data are for 1983/84 academic year, or as of Jan. 1, 1984, unless otherwise noted. Data by term of appointment are for academic and fiscal year appointments. There are no tables numbered I.16 and I.33.]

MEMBER SCHOOLS

I.1-I.2. Average faculty size, 1974-84; and variation in the number of full-time faculty, including deans and directors per school, Jan. 1, 1984. (p. F3)

I.3-I.4. Male/female ratio of full-time faculty; and changes in ratio [by academic rank; various years 1975/76-1983/84]. (p. F4-F5)

I.5-I.7c. Titles, disciplines of the doctorates held, and age categories divided by sex, of heads of schools, Jan. 1, 1984; and average salary of deans/directors [by sex, 1975/76-1983/84]. (p. F7-F11)

I.8. Year of appointment of heads of schools [1965-84]. (p. F12)

I.9. Faculty holding administrative titles [by title and academic rank], 1983/84. (p. F13)

I.10-I.11. Ratio of new faculty appointments to total faculty [1975/76-1983/84], and rank and sex of new faculty appointed [during 1983], exclusive of deans and directors. (p. F15)

I.11a. New assistant professors: academic year appointments [and average salary by sex, 1976/77-1983/84]. (p. F17)

I.12. Distribution of salaries for 25 [individual] new assistant professors [Canada and U.S., by term of appointment and sex]. (p. F18)

I.13-I.14a. Faculty salaries [average and median]; average salary for faculty divided by region [and for Canada]; average salaries, U.S. compared to Canada; and improvement in salaries and percentage of improvement; [all by academic rank and term of appointment, various years] 1979/80-1983/84. (p. F19-F22).

I.15. Male and female faculty salaries [by rank and term of appointment]. (p. F23)

I.17-I.18. Ethnic background and age categories of full-time faculty [by rank]. (p. F24)

I.19-I.20. Year of initial appointment and appointment/promotion to their present rank, of full-time faculty in their respective schools [by rank and sex, various years 1946-84]. (p. F25-F27)

I.21-I.21a. Faculty promotions [1979/80-1983/84], and number of years as a full-time faculty member in their respective schools of the individuals promoted in 1983/84, [by rank to which promoted and sex]. (p. F27-F28]

I.22-I.22a. Earned doctorates held by faculty [in and outside library/information science, by sex and rank, Jan. 1, 1984; and percentage of full-time faculty with earned doctorates, by sex], 1977-84. (p. F28-F29)

I.23-I.24. Earned doctorates outside library/information science held by full-time faculty [by discipline], and [number of schools by] percentage of faculty having doctorates. (p. F30-F31)

I.25. Percentages of tenured faculty [1976/77-1983/84]. (p. F31)

I.26-I.26a. [Number of schools by] percentage of tenured faculty, and tenure status by rank and sex. (p. F32)

I.27. Salaries of full-time faculty [by rank, for 9/10- and 11/12-month appointments]. (p. F34-F38)

ASSOCIATE MEMBER SCHOOLS

I.28. Titles of heads of schools. (p. F40)

I. 29-I.31. Organizational status, and number, rank, and sex of full-time faculty. (p. F40-41)

I.31a-I.32. Age categories of full-time heads of schools, Jan. 1, 1984; and year of appointment of heads of schools [1971-83]. (p. F42)

I.34. Faculty salary comparisons, member schools and associate member schools [average and median salaries, by rank and term of appointment]. (p. F43)

I.35. Average faculty salaries [by sex, rank, and term of appointment]. (p. F43)

1.36. Age categories of full-time faculty [by rank]. (p. F44)

I.37. Earned doctorates outside library science held by faculty members [by discipline]. (p. F45)

I.38-I.39. [Tables I.19-I.20 are repeated for associate member schools.] (p. F45-F47)

I.40. [Table I.27 is repeated for associate member schools.] (p. F48-F50)

DATA BY SCHOOL
[Data are shown by individual member and associate member school, for 1982/83 academic year, unless otherwise noted.]

I.41-I.44. Full- and part-time faculty [fall, winter, spring, and summer terms]. (p. F52-F59)

I.45-I.46. Average percentage of and basis for salary improvement for full-time faculty. (p. F59-F61)

I.47-I.47c. Faculty replacement appointments; unfilled, funded, full-time faculty positions; and positions lost and created/funded; among member schools. (p. F62-F66)

I.48. Percentage value in relationship to faculty salaries of fringe benefits, member schools, 1979/80-1982/83. (p. F67-F69)

I.49-I.50. Support for faculty travel [faculty members receiving travel funds, and average amount]. (p. F69-F73)

I.51. Member schools where faculty received sabbatical/study leaves [number of faculty, length of leave, and percent of salary received]. (p. F73-F74)

I.52-I.55. Support staff [full- and part-time by position], and use of students as part-time support staff [by position]. (p. F77-F86)

A3235-1.2: Students
[Data are shown for member and associate member schools, unless otherwise noted. Tables show data for fall term 1983, unless otherwise noted.]

ENROLLMENT

II.1a-II.1f. Student [full- and part-time] enrollment, by [degree] program and sex to determine FTE [summary, and by school]; and undergraduate library science majors enrolled full- and part-time, by sex [by school]. (p. S3-S16)

II.2a-II.2b. Number of classes or sections of classes, by number of students enrolled [by school]. (p. S18-S20)

DEGREE PROGRAM
[Tables II.3a-II.4d show data by sex and ethnic origin; tables II.3a-II.3e also include data for foreign students.]

II.3a-II.3b. Degrees and certificates awarded [by degree level], 1982/83. (p. S21)

II.3c. Member schools: bachelor's degrees awarded [by school], 1982/83. (p. S21)

II.3d-II.3e. Degrees and certificates awarded [by degree level and school], 1982/83. (p. S22-S29)

II.4a-II.4d. Number of students [by degree program level; summary, and by school]. (p. S30-S41)

RESIDENCY STATUS, FOREIGN STUDENTS, AND AGE DISTRIBUTION

II.5a-II.5b. Number of in-State/Province and out-of-State/Province students enrolled, including foreign students [by school and degree program level]. (p. S42-S45)

II.6a-II.6d. Number of foreign students enrolled [by sex and degree program level; summary, and by school]. (p. S45-S50)

II.7. Countries of origin [according to visas] and number of foreign students enrolled, by country and [degree] program level [for U.S. and Canadian member and total associate member schools]. (p. S51)

II.8a-II.8b. Students enrolled, by [degree program level], age, and sex, as of Jan. l, 1984. (p. S54)

II.9a-II.9b., II.10a-II.10b. [Information not requested for 1982/83 survey.] (p. S55)

STUDENT AID, COSTS, AND GRADUATE SALARIES
[Tables show data by school. Tables II.11a-II.12b show data for FY83.]

II.11a-II.11b. Scholarship aid awarded/accepted by all graduate library science students, by amount, sex, and level of program of recipient. (p. S56-S59)

II.12a-II.12b. Number of assistantships awarded by the library school, by level of program, sex, amount of award per year, and average number of hours of work per week required of an individual. (p. S61-S65)

II.13a-II.13b. Total tuition and fee cost for complete programs (full-time), for in-State/Province and out-of-State/Province students and tuition per credit [by degree program level]. (p. S67-S70)

A3235–1.3: Curriculum
[Most tables show data for member and associate member schools. All data are for 1982/83 academic year.]

GENERAL PROGRAM STRUCTURE

III.1-III.2. Academic year division; and number of weeks per term [by school]. (p. C1-C3)

III.2a-III.2f. Degree requirements: in hours [for] undergraduate, masters, post-masters, doctoral, joint program, and all programs [all by school]. (p. C4-C14)

III.3a-III.4. Minimum and maximum time for completion of programs [summary and by school], and status of courses after maximum time [all by degree level]. (p. C15-C19)

COURSES AND CREDIT HOURS
[Tables III.5-III.14 generally show data by degree level. No table is numbered III.17.]

III.5. Required course work by number of hours. (p. C20-C21)

III.6-III.8. [Availability of] exemption of required courses; and methods of exempting, and credit gained through exemption of required courses. (p. C21-C22)

III.9. [Maximum allowable] credit hours transferred. (p. C23)

III.10a-III.10b. Number of schools, by [required or optional] thesis; and hours of thesis credit, by schools. (p. C24-C26)

III.11a. Number of schools offering field work for credit. (p. C26)

III.12. Special requirements for graduation [comprehensive exam and foreign language]. (p. C27)

III.13. Prerequisites for entering program [by type]. (p. C27)

III.14. Courses offered away from main campus [by school]. (p. C28-C29)

III.15-III.16. Courses listed in catalog by level taught last academic year, and courses cross-listed with other units of instruction, [by school]. (p. C30-C32)

III.18-III.19. Curriculum committee members, and curriculum changes considered, by category. (p. C40-C41)

A3235–1.4: Income and Expenditures
[Data are for FY83, unless otherwise noted. Tables IV.1-IV.12a are for member schools.]

IV.1-IV.5. Five-year funding levels [total and average income, FY79-83]; percentage of increase/decrease and frequency distribution of total income [FY83]; sources of funds [parent institution, Federal Government, and other], FY79-83; frequency distribution of income from parent institution [FY83]; and average Federal funding, FY79-83. (p. FIN1-FIN5)

IV.6-IV.7a. [Mean income] for schools with and without library support; sources of funds for schools with and without doctoral programs; and regional distribution of total average income [by source]. (p. FIN6-FIN7)

IV.8. Expenditures over 7 major categories. (p. FIN8)

IV.9. Allocation of salaries/wages [by personnel category]. (p. FIN8)

IV.10-IV.10b. Categories of expenditures; [and mean, high, and low] computing and travel costs; for schools with and without doctoral programs. (p. FIN9-FIN10)

IV.11-IV.12. Total income and source, and total expenditures [by object]. (p. FIN11-FIN14)

IV.12a. Institutional benefits. (p. FIN15)

IV.13-IV.14. [Tables IV.11-IV.12 are repeated for associate member schools.] (p. FIN16-FIN17)

A3235–1.5: Continuing Education
[Data are for 1982/83 academic year, for continuing education (CE) in member schools, unless otherwise noted.]

MEMBER SCHOOLS

V.1-V.5. Number, duration, and enrollment of CE events [by school]; and 5-year comparison [1978/79-1982/83] and 1982/83 summary by type of activity. (p. CE1-CE7)

V.6-V.9. Summary of number of hours of instruction and enrollment, 1982/83; and comparison of enrollments [1978/79-1982/83]; by type of event. (p. CE7-CE9)

V.10. Number of programs offering CEUs [continuing education units] and number of CEUs awarded [by school, by type of activity]. (p. CE11)

V.11-V.12. Summary of credit course offerings [by length of course; and offerings by school]. (p. CE14-CE15)

V.13-V.14. Summary of geographic target groups [local, State/Province, regional, and national; and groups by school]. (p. CE16-CE18)

V.15-V.16. Summary of sources of financial support [institutional, Federal, fees, contracts/grants; and sources by school]. (p. CE18-CE20)

V.17-V.18. Methods of determining compensation for program faculty [summary, and by school, for in-school faculty and outside instructors]. (p. CE21-CE24)

V.19-V.20. Summary of sources of faculty for instruction [showing use of regular and visiting library science faculty, other faculty, and practitioners; and sources by school]. (p. CE25-CE28)

V.21-V.22. Methods of administration and coordination of CE activities [summary; and by school]. (p. CE29-CE31)

V.23-V.24. Number, duration, and enrollment of CE events [by school]; and summary [by type of event]; for associate member schools. (p. CE32)

A3245
Association for School, College and University Staffing

A3245–1   TEACHER SUPPLY/DEMAND, 1984: A Report Based upon an Opinion Survey of Teacher Placement Officers
Annual. Jan. 1984.
6 p. no paging.
SRI/MF/not filmed

Annual report, by James N. Akin, presenting supply/demand ratings for elementary/secondary school teachers by academic field, for contiguous U.S. 1976-84, and by region and for Alaska and Hawaii 1984.

Also includes average starting salaries of special education and elementary/secondary school teachers with bachelors and masters degrees, by region and for Alaska and Hawaii, 1981/82-1983/84.

Data are based on 61 responses to an Oct. 1983 survey of teacher placement officers, and previous surveys.

Contains survey background and summary (2 p.); and 3 tables (4 p.).

SRI coverage of this report begins with the 1984 edition.

Availability: Association for School, College and University Staffing, PO Box 4411, Madison WI 53711, †; SRI/MF/not filmed.

A3255
Association for University Business and Economic Research

A3255–1   UNIVERSITY RESEARCH IN BUSINESS AND ECONOMICS: A Bibliography of 1982 Publications
Annual. 1983. vii+270 p.
Vol. XXVII.
ISSN 0066-8761.
ISBN 0-89527-082-X.
SRI/MF/complete, delayed

Annual bibliography listing approximately 2,000 journal articles and monographs published in 1982 by university business and economics schools and research organizations. Covers only institutions that are members of the Assn for University Business and Economic Research (AUBER) or the American Assembly of Collegiate Schools of Business.

Contains preface and contents listing (p. iii-vii); bibliography arranged by subject area (p. 3-128) and by institution and publication (p. 131-246); and author index (p. 249-269).

Availability: Association for University Business and Economic Research, Bureau of Business

Research, College of Business and Economics, West Virginia University, PO Box 6025, Morgantown WV 26506, $25.00; SRI/MF/complete, delayed shipment in Oct. 1984.

A3273
Association of American Medical Colleges

A3273–2   REPORT ON MEDICAL SCHOOL FACULTY SALARIES, 1983/84
Annual. Jan. 1984. ii+94 p.
LC 78-648234.
SRI/MF/complete

Annual report, by William C. Smith, Jr., on compensation of medical school full-time faculty, 1983/84 academic year, with selected comparisons to 1982/83. Includes data by dept; region; degree (MD, other doctoral, and nondoctoral); academic rank; public or private institution control; and type of compensation (base compensation only and base/supplemental compensation); with selected cross-tabulations.

Data are shown variously as total, percentile, and mean compensation values, generally with number of faculty represented.

Data are from a survey of 122 of 127 accredited medical schools and represent 34,187 filled positions. Data are current as of Sept. 1983.

Contains contents listing (p. i-ii); scope and definitions, questionnaire facsimile, and list of participating schools (p. 1-6); and 32 tables, with accompanying key (p. 7-94).

This is the 19th annual report.

Availability: Association of American Medical Colleges, Membership and Subscriptions, One Dupont Circle, NW, Suite 200, Washington DC 20036, $8.75 (book rate), $10.00 (1st class) (prepaid); SRI/MF/complete.

A3273–3   1983 COTH SURVEY OF HOUSESTAFF STIPENDS, BENEFITS, AND FUNDING
Annual. Jan. 1984.
v+113+App 14 p.
SRI/MF/complete

Annual report, for 1983/84 academic year, on teaching hospital house staff (interns/residents and clinical fellows) stipends, benefits, and expenditures, by region, and hospital affiliation status, ownership, and bed size.

Stipend data are shown as median, mean, and 25th and 75th percentiles amounts, by post-MD year; and also include detail for 26 cities, comparisons to 1982/83, and national trends from 1969/70.

Also includes funding distribution by source of revenue, moonlighting policies, and minorities as a proportion of house staff.

Data are from 315 responses of Council of Teaching Hospitals member institutions to Assn of American Medical Colleges survey.

Contains contents and table listings (p. i-v); introduction, and 3 chapters with narrative summaries, 7 charts, and 89 tables (p. 1-113); and 7 appendices with sample questionnaire and 6 tables (14 p.).

Availability: Association of American Medical Colleges, Membership and Subscriptions, One Dupont Circle, NW, Suite 200, Washington DC 20036, $6.00 (prepaid); SRI/MF/complete.

A3273–4   COTH DIRECTORY 1984: Educational Programs and Services
Annual. [1984.] xiv+229 p.
SRI/MF/complete

Annual directory, for 1984, of teaching hospital members of the Council of Teaching Hospitals (COTH) of the Assn of American Medical Colleges. Includes data on hospital education programs, services, and operating characteristics, for institutions in States, D.C., Puerto Rico, and Beirut, Lebanon.

Data are from a COTH annual survey of member hospitals, American Hospital Assn, and Accreditation Council on Graduate Medical Education.

Contains contents listing, introduction, listings of officers and representatives, and directory data codes and abbreviations (p. i-xiv); 1 directory table, described below, presenting teaching member hospital characteristics (p. 2-217); address directory of corresponding members (p. 218-220); and index (p. 222-229).

This is the 16th annual directory.

Availability: Association of American Medical Colleges, Membership and Subscriptions, One Dupont Circle, NW, Suite 200, Washington DC 20036, $7.00; SRI/MF/complete.

DIRECTORY TABLE:

[The following items are shown for each hospital listed in the directory, arranged by State and city.

Types of government and nonprofit control include State, county, city, city-county, and hospital district/authority (nonfederal); church operated and other nonprofit; and Air Force, Army, Navy, PHS, VA, Dept of Justice, and other Federal.]

a. Hospital administrator and address; and accreditation/approval and facilities/services provided, indicated by number code.

b. Type of government or nonprofit control; specialty service provided; whether average stay is short- or long-term; inpatient beds, births, and admissions; emergency room and outpatient visits; total and payroll expenses; and number of personnel.

c. Medical school affiliation; foreign medical graduates and other residents in training, 1st post-M.D. year and total; and approved graduate/undergraduate educational program residencies, by specialty.

A3273–8   JOURNAL OF MEDICAL EDUCATION
Monthly. Approx. 85 p.
cumulative pagination throughout year.
ISSN 0022-2577.
LC 52-64044.
SRI/MF/excerpts, shipped quarterly

Monthly journal reporting on issues and developments in medical education, including medical school curriculum, instruction, research, applications, enrollments, and characteristics of faculty, students, and graduates.

Issues include articles and research news briefs, many with statistics; and "Datagram," recurring statistical feature usually analyzing time series data on selected topics.

Special issues on selected topics are published occasionally, as part 2 of regular issues.

Features with substantial broad-based statistical content are described, as they appear, under "Statistical Features." Nonstatistical features and analyses based on experience of single institutions are not covered. Each issue of the journal is reviewed, but an abstract is published in SRI monthly issues only when features with broad-based statistics appear.

Availability: Association of American Medical Colleges, Membership and Subscriptions, One Dupont Circle, NW, Suite 200, Washington DC 20036, $27.50 per yr., students $22.50 per yr., single copy $3.00, supplements $5.00; SRI/MF/ excerpts for all portions described under "Statistical Features;" shipped quarterly.

Issues reviewed during 1984: Nov. 1983-Oct. 1984 (P) (Vol. 58, Nos. 11-12; Vol. 59, Nos. 1-10).

STATISTICAL FEATURES:

A3273–8.501: Nov. 1983 (Vol. 58, No. 11)
TRENDS IN TEACHING SYSTEMS COURSES IN AMERICAN MEDICAL SCHOOLS, 1975-83

(p. 899-901) By Charles G. Atkins. Article on U.S./Canadian medical schools' use of traditional curricula vs. curricula organized around specific organ systems. Data are from AAMC *Curriculum Directory.*

Includes 1 table showing number of medical schools by type of curriculum, including traditional, systems, and combined and integrated approaches, 1975/76-1982/83.

DATAGRAM: RELATIONSHIP BETWEEN MCAT SCIENCE SCORES AND UNDERGRADUATE SCIENCE GPA

(p. 908-911) Article, with 1 table showing mean score and standard deviation for 4 science sections of the Medical College Admission Test (MCAT) by undergraduate science grade-point average (GPA), and MCAT/GPA correlation, all by selectivity level of undergraduate institution, 1981/82.

Data are based on performance of 32,271 medical college applicants.

A3273–8.502: Dec. 1983 (Vol. 58, No. 12)
FAMILY MEDICINE HOME VISIT PROGRAMS IN U.S. AND CANADIAN MEDICAL SCHOOLS

(p. 934-940) By Linda Z. Nieman and James G. Jones. Article, with 1 table showing number of U.S./Canadian medical schools teaching selected patient care skills through use of home visit programs. Data are from responses of 37 schools with home visit programs to a summer 1982 survey.

CLINICAL PROBLEM-SOLVING SKILLS OF INTERNISTS TRAINED IN THE PROBLEM-ORIENTED SYSTEM

(p. 947-953) By David Babbott and William D. Halter. Article comparing problem-solving skills of internists trained under University of Vermont problem-solving system with those of other candidates for American Board of Internal Medicine (ABIM) certification, 1978-80.

Includes 4 tables showing mean scores, standard deviations, and/or faculty evaluation for the true-false and patient-management sections of the ABIM certification test, for candidates from the University of Vermont, and from Northeast and national pools, 1978-80.

DATAGRAM: FINANCIAL ASSISTANCE FOR MEDICAL STUDENTS, 1982/83

(p. 973-975) Article, with 2 tables showing number and value of scholarships, loans, and work study grants awarded to medical students, by general source and type, 1981/82-1982/83; and total value of aid, 1973/74-1982/83.

A3273–8.503: Jan. 1984 (Vol. 59, No.1)

TEACHING OF CANCER MEDICINE BY EDUCATIONAL OBJECTIVES

(p. 24-32) By Richard F. Bakemeier and W. P. Laird Myers. Article on characteristics of medical school cancer education programs. Data are primarily based on responses of 1,311 faculty members and 1,757 clinical students to an American Assn for Cancer Education 1978 survey.

Includes 2 tables showing percent of faculty desiring increased curriculum hours in 7 cancer subjects, by dept, 1978; and percent of 1978 students seeing none and 6/more cancer patients, and number of 1983 new cancer cases, by cancer site.

DATAGRAM: NET PATIENT REVENUE AT UNIVERSITY-OWNED TEACHING HOSPITALS, 1981, ANNUAL FEATURE

(p. 65-68) Annual article on university-owned teaching hospitals' funding trends, FY75-81. Data are based on responses of 64 hospitals to the 1982 12th annual survey conducted for Council of Teaching Hospitals.

Includes 4 tables showing distribution of State-funded teaching hospitals by proportion of operating revenues received from State appropriations, FY75-81; and aggregate net patient revenue of teaching hospitals, by source, for hospitals receiving and not receiving State appropriations, and for inpatient and outpatient care, FY80-81.

For description of article covering the 1981 survey, see SRI 1982 Annual, under A3273-8.313.

A3273–8.504: Feb. 1984 (Vol. 59, No. 2)

TRACKING STUDY OF 1977 MEDICAL GRADUATES THROUGH GRADUATE MEDICAL EDUCATION IN ONTARIO

(p. 107-111) By A. I. Rothman. Article analyzing postgraduate training paths of students graduated from Ontario (Canada) and other medical schools in 1977, and serving internships/residencies in the Ontario postgraduate system during 1977/78-1981/82. Data are from the postgraduate registry of the Ontario Physician Manpower Data Centre and cover 683 trainees.

Includes text statistics, and 5 tables showing distribution of Ontario and other medical school graduates in Ontario's postgraduate system, by enrollment status and program area, with detail for non-Ontario Canadians/landed immigrants and non-Canadians with visas, 1977/78-1981/82.

DATAGRAM: TRENDS IN TEACHING HOSPITAL CONSTRUCTION FUNDING, 1969-81

(p. 143-147) Article analyzing changes in the relative importance of Federal and State/local grants, philanthropic contributions, internal operations, and debt financing for teaching hospital construction funding, 1969-81. Data sources include American Hospital Assn annual surveys based, in part, on member reports from Council of Teaching Hospitals (COTH).

Includes 3 tables showing total and average (per institution) funding by source for COTH nonfederal hospitals, selected years 1969-81; and for COTH State/local government, non-government/nonprofit, and total nonfederal/nonprofit hospitals, with comparison to all hospitals in each category, 1981.

A3273–8.505: Mar. 1984 (Vol. 59, No. 3)

RESPONSE OF FACULTY MEMBERS TO MEDICAL STUDENTS' PERSONAL PROBLEMS

(p. 180-187) By James C. Brown and John M. Barnett. Article, with 3 tables showing medical educators' perceptions of problems facing medical students, and of their own responses to those problems. Data are based on survey responses of 96 faculty members at 12 medical schools.

USE OF ANONYMOUS STUDENT EVALUATIONS OF FACULTY MEMBERS IN U.S. MEDICAL SCHOOLS

(p. 196-197) By Stephen R. Smith and Leslie J. Paulen. Article, with 1 table showing number of medical schools with regular and written student evaluations of faculty, number requiring students to identify themselves on the evaluation form, and number using evaluations in tenure/promotion/salary decisions. Data are from responses of 120 medical schools to a telephone survey conducted June-Aug. 1983.

A3273–8.506: Apr. 1984 (Vol. 59, No. 4)

ENROLLMENT AND DEMOGRAPHIC CHARACTERISTICS OF PHYSICIAN'S ASSISTANT STUDENTS

(p. 316-322) By Reginald Carter et al. Article, with 3 charts and 2 tables showing enrollment in physician assistant programs, by sex, race, age, prior academic training, and previous military and other health care experience, various periods 1967-82. Data were compiled by Assn of Physician Assistant Programs.

FACTORS AFFECTING THE CHOICE OF ANESTHESIOLOGY BY MEDICAL STUDENTS FOR SPECIALTY TRAINING

(p. 323-330) By Phool Chandra and Mark Hughes. Article on factors influencing medical students' selection of anesthesiology as their residency specialty. Data are from National Resident Matching Program (NRMP), and responses of 63 teaching hospitals to a 1980 survey.

Includes 2 charts and 3 tables showing mean ratio of residency applications to positions, by medical specialty; staffing patterns of anesthesiology depts; and correlation between the number of medical students specializing in anesthesiology and selected operational characteristics of anesthesiology depts; various periods 1978-83.

PRACTICE PATTERNS OF GRADUATES OF NEW COMMUNITY-BASED MEDICAL SCHOOLS

(p. 345-347) By William D. Marder. Article, with 1 table showing the following for patient care physicians graduated from older medical schools and from new community-based and other schools during 1970-75 period: distribution by sex and medical specialty, and percent practicing in same State in which medical school was located, as of 1981. Data are from Physician Masterfile.

GENDER COMPOSITION OF MEDICAL SCHOOLS AND SPECIALTY CHOICES OF GRADUATES

(p. 347-349) By Carol S. Weisman. Article with 1 table presenting multiple regression findings relating sex of medical students with selection of pediatrics as their 1st-year residency specialty, 1970-75. Data are from American Medical Assn.

A3273–8.507: May 1984 (Vol. 59, No. 5)

DATAGRAM: RESULTS OF THE NRMP FOR 1984, ANNUAL FEATURE

(p. 441-443) Annual article reporting on National Resident Matching Program (NRMP) participation, 1984. Includes 2 tables showing number of matched applicants and positions offered, by specialty; and unmatched participants and withdrawals; most by applicant type (U.S. senior medical students, other U.S./Canadian citizens, and foreign graduates of foreign medical schools).

A3273–8.508: June 1984 (Vol. 59, No. 6)

VALIDITY OF THE MCAT IN PREDICTING PERFORMANCE IN THE FIRST TWO YEARS OF MEDICAL SCHOOL

(p. 455-464) By Robert F. Jones and Maria Thomae-Forgues. Article comparing ability of Medical College Admission Test (MCAT) scores and undergraduate grade point averages to predict medical students' performance as measured by course grades and National Board of Medical Examiners test scores, with detail by subject area.

Data are from the MCAT Interpretive Studies Program, and are based on reports for 1978/79 entering classes at 20 medical schools.

Includes 5 tables, primarily presenting results of correlation analysis.

DATAGRAM: MCAT SCORES AND STUDENT PROGRESS IN MEDICAL SCHOOL

(p. 527-531) Article, with 2 tables correlating medical students' performance on the Medical College Admission Test (MCAT) with their progress in medical school. Tables show total medical school entrants in 1978/79 and number graduating on time, with delayed graduation, and withdrawn/dismissed, by MCAT chemistry and reading score.

Data are based on Assn of American Medical colleges records for 32,354 students entering 126 schools in 1978/79.

A3273–8.509: July 1984 (Vol. 59, No. 7)

PROGRAM RELATIONSHIPS OF COMMUNITY HOSPITALS AND MEDICAL SCHOOLS IN CME

(p. 553-558) By Robert H. Younghouse and William H. Young. Article on cooperation between medical schools and community hospitals in cosponsoring continuing medical education (CME) programs for hospital staff. Data are based on responses of 92 medical school deans/continuing education directors to a Nov. 1982 survey. Includes 2 tables showing respondents' views on benefits and important characteristics of cosponsored CMEs.

A3273–8.510: Aug. 1984 (Vol. 59, No. 8)

UNDERGRADUATE MEDICAL EDUCATION IN PREPAID HEALTH CARE PLAN SETTINGS

(p. 615-624) By Joseph C. Isaacs and Morton A. Madoff. Article, with 1 table showing number of medical schools providing undergraduate training in prepaid health care plan (PHCP) facilities, and including enrollment range, and type and duration of educational activities, by academic level, 1982.

Data are from responses of 26 medical schools with PHCP programs to a July 1982 AAMC survey, and responses of 44 PHCP facilities to a Sept. 1982 Tufts University survey.

PARTICIPATION IN CONTINUING MEDICAL EDUCATION OF GENERAL PRACTITIONERS IN NEW ZEALAND

(p. 649-654) By Philip M. Barham and John Benseman. Article, with 2 tables showing the following for general practice physicians in New Zealand: level of participation in professional conferences and continuing education groups, and use of 4 types of professional publications, 1982. Data are from 1982 interviews with 305 general practitioners.

A3273–8.511: Sept. 1984 (Vol. 59, No. 9)

CURRICULUM EVALUATION, EDUCATION FINANCING, AND CAREER PLANS OF 1983 MEDICAL SCHOOL GRADUATES

(p. 691-698) By Maria Thomae-Forgues et al. Article discussing academic experiences and career plans of medical school seniors, 1983. Data are from responses of 10,481 seniors to a 1983 AAMC survey.

Includes 7 tables showing survey response concerning participation in selected medical school educational activities; opinion on amount of instruction offered in selected curriculum areas; level of premedical and medical school debt; scholarship receipts by source; residency plans by specialty area; and career plans, by specialty and by type of practice or activity (including administration, research, and teaching).

TEACHING OF LIBERAL ARTS IN INTERNAL MEDICINE RESIDENCY TRAINING

(p. 714-721) By Gail J. Povar and Karla J. Keith. Article, with 2 tables showing percent of internal medicine residency programs offering courses that incorporate social science and liberal arts subjects, and range of instructional hours allotted, for 12 course areas; and prevalence of selected problems encountered in establishing the courses.

Data are based on 102 responses to a survey of directors of internal medicine programs, conducted by AAMC during 1982-83.

A3273–8.512: Oct. 1984 (Vol. 59, No. 10)

HEALTH CARE INSTITUTIONS: SURVIVAL IN A CHANGING ENVIRONMENT

(p. 773-782) By Karen W. Tyson and Jeffrey C. Merrill. Article, with 1 table showing expenditures for total and personal health care and for hospital and physician care, 1982, 1990, and 2000, with average annual real growth rate for 1970-82 and 1982-2000 periods. Data are from Georgetown University Center for Health Policy Studies.

ACADEMIC ORIGINS OF MEDICAL SCHOOL APPLICANTS AND ENTRANTS, 1980-82

(p. 825-828) By Gwendolyn L. Lewis. Article, with 1 table showing distribution of bachelor degree recipients 1979-81 period, and medical school applicants and matriculants 1980-82 period, by type of public and private under-

graduate institution. Data are from AAMC and National Institute of Independent Colleges and Universities.

FACULTY DEVELOPMENT IN FAMILY MEDICINE: A SURVEY OF NEEDS AND RESOURCES

(p. 831-833) By S. R. Frisch and Yves Talbot. Article, with 1 table showing importance of faculty development training in 11 medical and teaching skill areas, as rated by heads of university-affiliated family practice depts. Data are from 115 responses to a 1982 survey of U.S. and Canadian family practice departments.

A3273–9   MINORITY STUDENT OPPORTUNITIES IN U.S. MEDICAL SCHOOLS, 1984/85

Biennial.   1984.   xii + 307 p.
ISSN 0085-3488.
LC 79-640963.
SRI/MF/complete

Biennial report on medical school minority applicants, enrollments, and graduates, by race/ethnicity, sex, and institution, 1981/82-1983/84. Also includes data on Medical College Admission Test (MCAT) scores and faculty. Based on a survey of 127 medical schools, and other sources.

Data by racial/ethnic group are shown for black Americans, American Indians, Mexican Americans/Chicanos, and mainland Puerto Ricans, unless otherwise noted.

Contents:

a. Contents listing, alphabetical and geographical listings of medical schools, list of appendix tables, and foreword. (p. v-xii)

b. Institution profiles for 127 medical schools, arranged by State, each with program description and, generally, 2 tables showing minority applicants, admissions, and 1st-year and total enrollments, by sex and State residency, 1981/82-1982/83; and minority graduates, 1981/82-1983/84; both by race/ethnic group. (p. 2-298)

c. 4 appendix tables, listed below. (p. 300-307)

This is the 8th biennial report. Previous report, issued in 1982, is described in SRI 1982 Annual, under this number.

Availability: Association of American Medical Colleges, Membership and Subscriptions, One Dupont Circle, NW, Suite 200, Washington DC 20036, $5.00; SRI/MF/complete.

APPENDIX TABLES:

1. Summer and yearly motivational and enrichment programs [tabular lists of participating institutions, by program type]. (p. 300)

2. Medical school graduates by [institution and] selected racial/ethnic groups, 1981/82-1983/84. (p. 302-306)

3. Mean MCAT score for MCAT areas of assessment, by racial/ethnic groups [includes whites and total examinees], 1981-82 examinations. (p. 307)

4. Distribution of [total] medical school faculty by ethnic origin [includes Asian, other Hispanic, Caucasian, and unknown], and degree, 1982. (p. 307)

A3273–10   MEDICAL SCHOOL ADMISSION REQUIREMENTS, 1985/86, U.S. and Canada

Annual.   1984.   xiv + 365 p.
LC 51-7778.
SRI/MF/complete

Annual report on medical school programs, applicants, admissions, enrollment, and fees in the U.S. and Canada, 1983/84. Report is designed to assist premedical students and their advisers. Most data are from reports to the Assn of American Medical Colleges by 127 U.S. (including 3 Puerto Rican) and 16 Canadian medical schools, and are current as of Feb. 1984. Includes trends from 1975/76 and estimates for 1984/85.

Contains contents and table listings, and alphabetical and geographical listings of medical schools (p. v-xiv); foreword (p. 1-2); and the following chapters:

U.S.

Chapter 1-2. Overview of medical education process; and premedical curriculum planning guidelines, with 2 tables showing undergraduate subjects required by 10 or more medical schools, 1985/86; and total and accepted applicants, by undergraduate major, 1983/84. (p. 3-11)

Chapter 3. Factors in deciding whether and where to apply to medical school, with 7 tables showing applicants/acceptees, by undergraduate grade average and Medical College Admission Test (MCAT) score; State residency status and sex of 1st-year entrants, by individual institution; acceptance rates, by age and sex; applicants and acceptees by sex and minority group (black, American Indian, Mexican American, and Puerto Rican), and women entrants; and total and 1st-year enrollment, by racial/ethnic category including minority groups noted above, Asian/Pacific Islanders, other Hispanics, and other foreign students; various years 1979/80-1983/84. (p. 12-26)

Chapter 4-6. Information on MCAT and American Medical College Application Service; explanation of the medical school application and selection process, with 1 table (p. 33) showing applicants, applications, and new entrants, 1979/80-1983/84; and financial information, with 1 table (p. 42) showing private and public school average expenses for 1st-year students, 1983/84. (p. 27-47)

Chapter 7-9. Minority student assistance, with 3 tables showing 1st-year and total enrollment, 1975/76-1983/84, and by individual institution, fall 1983, for the 4 minority groups noted above; alternatives for applicants not admitted to medical school; and planning information for high school students. (p. 48-74)

Chapter 10. Profiles of 127 medical schools, each covering curriculum, entrance requirements, selection factors, and financial aid, with 3 tables showing application timetable, 1st-year class 1985/86; and resident and nonresident expenses, applicants, and entrants, 1st-year class 1983/84. (p. 75-329)

CANADA

Chapter 11. Information about Canadian medical schools, including 2 summary tables showing subjects required by 3 or more schools for entering class 1985/86, and expenses for 1st-year students 1983/84; and profiles of 16 individual institutions, similar to those described above for U.S. schools. (p. 330-365)

This is the 35th edition of the report.

Availability: Association of American Medical Colleges, Membership and Subscriptions, One Dupont Circle, NW, Suite 200, Washington DC 20036, $7.50 (prepaid, book rate), $9.00 (prepaid, 1st class); SRI/MF/complete.

A3274
Association of
American Publishers

A3274–2   **1983 INDUSTRY
STATISTICS**
Annual. 1984.
103 p. var. paging, looseleaf.
LC 72-625115.
SRI/MF/complete, delayed

Annual report on publishing industry finances and operations, by publisher type and sales size, 1983, with selected data by book subject area or type, customer category, and comparisons to 1982. Covers trade/religious, technical/science, business/other professional, medical, mass market paperback, book club, mail order, and textbook publishers.

Includes data on volume and value of sales and returns; other income by source; expenses by detailed item; inventory; operating ratios; overdue accounts and bad debt losses; and foreign sales, usually with detail for world regions and UK and/or Canada.

Not all data are shown for every type of publisher. Data for textbook publishers are shown separately for elementary/high school and college, and also for audiovisual, test, and other materials.

Also includes data on book publishing industry sales trends from 1972; book club membership; and textbook sales by State and for aggregate U.S. possessions, with trends from 1966 and comparisons to enrollment.

Most data are based on survey responses of 88 publishers, and are shown as total, average, and/or mid-range amounts. Sales trends are industrywide estimates based on the 1977 Census of Manufactures and preliminary 1982 census data. Textbook data by State include both actual sales by surveyed publishers, and industrywide estimates.

Report is intended to enable individual publishers to compare their performance with that of the industry.

Contains contents and table listing, foreword, and introductory material (p. iii-x); list of respondents, introduction, and industry summary with 2 charts and 1 table (p. xi-xvii); and 6 statistical sections paginated separately and organized by publisher type, with 17 charts and 101 tables (86 p.).

Availability: Association of American Publishers, One Park Ave., New York NY 10016, members †, nonmembers $250.00 (prepaid); SRI/MF/complete, delayed shipment in May 1985.

A3275
Association of
American Railroads

A3275–1   **RAILROAD REVENUES,
EXPENSES, AND INCOME:
Class I Railroads in the U.S.**
Quarterly. Approx. 4 p.
SRI/MF/complete

Quarterly report on Class I railroad freight and passenger revenues, expenses, and income, including data by railroad company and district. Data are compiled from railroad reports to the ICC and are issued 3-6 months after quarter of coverage.

Usually contains 5 tables, listed below.

Availability: Association of American Railroads, Information and Public Affairs Office, 1920 L St., NW, Washington DC 20036, $20.00 per yr., single copy $5.00; SRI/MF/complete.

Issues reviewed during 1984: 2nd Qtr. 1983-2nd Qtr. 1984 (D) (No. 714-718).

QUARTERLY TABLES:
[Most tables exclude switching and terminal companies.]

[1] Railroad revenues, expenses, and income [by account item, with selected ratios, for quarter of coverage, year to date, and same periods of previous year].

[2] Rate of return on property investment [eastern, southern, and western districts, year to date and same period of previous year].

[3-4] Railroad [freight and operating] revenues, [operating] expenses, net [operating] income, [and ordinary income; by district and individual railroad, for quarter of coverage, year to date, and same periods of previous year].

[5] Total operating revenues, expenses, ordinary income, net railway operating income, revenue ton-miles, and capital expenditures [by quarter, year to date and previous 4-5 years].

A3275–2   **TRENDS: Carloadings of
Major Railroads**
Weekly. Approx. 2 p.
SRI/MF/complete, shipped
quarterly

Weekly press release on estimated major railroad freight traffic, by commodity. Data are compiled by Assn of American Railroads from reports submitted to ICC. Week of data coverage is approximately 1 week prior to publication date.

Contains narrative summary with text statistics on piggyback carloadings, and 1 table showing:

a. Carloadings by approximately 20 commodity groups, for week of coverage, with change from same week of previous year and preceding week.

b. Total cars loaded, for current and preceding years to date.

c. Estimated revenue ton-miles, for week of coverage and year to date of current and preceding years.

Jan. 6, 1984 issue also includes a table showing carloading and revenue ton-mile trends, 1982-83.

Availability: Association of American Railroads, Information and Public Affairs Office, 1920 L St., NW, Washington DC 20036, †; SRI/MF/complete, shipped quarterly.

Issues reviewed during 1984: Nov. 3, 1983-Oct. 25, 1984 (P).

A3275–3   **TRENDS: Freight Cars and
Locomotives Ordered and
Delivered**
Monthly. Approx. 2 p.
SRI/MF/complete, shipped
quarterly

Monthly press release on railroad and private car line freight cars and locomotives ordered and delivered, and backlog, compiled by Assn of American Railroads and American Railway Car Institute. Data are current to 3-6 weeks prior to publication date.

Contains narrative summary, and 1 table showing:

a. New and rebuilt freight cars ordered and delivered, and locomotives delivered, for month of coverage, year to date, same periods of preceding year, and previous month.

b. Backlog orders of new and rebuilt freight cars and locomotives, usually as of 1st of cover date month, same month of previous year, and previous month, with annual averages for current and preceding year.

Table shows data for freight cars built in railroad shops and by car builders.

Availability: Association of American Railroads, Information and Public Affairs Office, 1920 L St., NW, Washington DC 20036, †; SRI/MF/complete, shipped quarterly.

Issues reviewed during 1984: Nov. 21, 1983-Oct. 25, 1984 (P) [Jan. 25 and Feb. 22, 1984 issues incorrectly read 1983].

A3275–4   **STATISTICS OF RAILROADS
OF CLASS I in the U.S.,
Years 1972-82**
Annual. Oct. 1983.
17 p. Oversized.
Statistical Summary 67.
ISSN 0091-4894.
LC A-25-749.
SRI/MF/complete

Annual summary report on Class I line-haul railroad finances and operations, 1972-82, with detail on National Railroad Passenger Corp. (Amtrak). Most data are from ICC summaries of reports of 38 Class I railroads, and Assn of American Railroads records.

Contains contents listing (1 p.); and 17 tables, listed below (p. 1-17).

Availability: Association of American Railroads, Information and Public Affairs Office, 1920 L St., NW, Washington DC 20036, (included with *Analysis of Class I Railroads, 1982,* $75.00); SRI/MF/complete.

TABLES:
[Tables show data for 1972-82, unless otherwise noted. Tables [1-15] show data for Class I line-haul railroads.]

FINANCIAL STATEMENTS

[1] Operating income account [by item]. (p. 1)

[2] Net railway operating income, property investment, shareowner's equity, net working capital, dividends, and capital expenditures. (p. 2)

[3] Revenues, expenses, and income by primary account, 1982: freight and passenger service. (p. 3)

EMPLOYMENT AND OPERATIONS

[4-5] Employees and their compensation [including hours worked and health/welfare benefits/pensions], 1972-82; and average number of employees and average compensation, by occupational classification, 1982. (p. 5)

[6] Freight traffic [revenue tons by commodity]. (p. 6)

[7] Cars of revenue freight loaded [by quarter and by commodity]. (p. 7)

VEHICLES

[8-9] Locomotives and freight train cars. (p. 8-9)

[10] Passenger train cars, company service cars, and passenger traffic [gross ton-miles; includes Amtrak]. (p. 10)

[11] Locomotive mileage, train mileage, and car mileage. (p. 11)

MISCELLANEOUS

[12] Distribution of railway operating revenues [for salaries and benefits, taxes, equipment, depreciation, loss, and rent]. (p. 12)

[13] Railway tax accruals. (p. 13)

[14] Freight and passenger service operating statistics [mileages, yard switching service, and motive power and car equipment; includes Amtrak]. (p. 14)

[15] Fuel consumed by locomotives, average cost of railroad fuel, and rail and ties laid. (p. 15)

AMTRAK

[16-17] Statistics of the National Railroad Passenger Corp. (Amtrak) [including property investment, shareowner's equity, net working capital, operating income account, gross capital expenditures, passengers and passenger revenue (including commuters), mileage, employment and compensation, and equipment]. (p. 16-17)

A3275-6   ECONOMIC ABZ's OF THE RAILROAD INDUSTRY
Annual. 1983.
103 p. no paging.
SRI/MF/complete

Annual compilation of statistics on railroad finances and operations, shown primarily for 1972-82, with selected earlier trends. Includes data by railroad company and commodity, with comparisons to other transportation modes.

Data are compiled by the Economics and Finance Dept primarily from railroad annual reports, and quarterly reports to the ICC.

Contains preface and chart/table listing (7 p.); 7 statistical sections with 2 charts and 79 tables, described below (79 p.); and 1 section presenting brief profiles of 9 industry assns and organizations (9 p.).

Availability: Association of American Railroads, Information and Public Affairs Office, 1920 L St., NW, Washington DC 20036, members: † to previous subscribers, $5.00 to new subscribers; nonmembers: $5.00 to previous subscribers, $25.00 to new subscribers; SRI/MF/complete.

CHARTS AND TABLES:
[Data are shown for railroads, 1972-82, unless otherwise noted.]

A3275-6.1: Industry Overview and Capital Investments

INDUSTRY OVERVIEW

a. Railroad contributions to general economy, 1981 or 1982; total intercity ton-miles, by transportation mode, 1982; number of Class I and other line-haul railroads, and switching/terminal companies, quinquennially 1920-80 and 1983; list of railroad mergers and consolidations, 1957-83; operating revenues by company and subsidiary, 1982; and description of intermodal transport arrangements involving railroads. Tables I.1-I.5.

CAPITAL INVESTMENTS

b. Capital expenditures on rolling stock and roadway/structures; leased locomotive and freight car expenditures and installations; total locomotive installations; locomotives in service, by type; and age distribution of locomotive fleet in 1982. Tables II.1-II.6.

c. Freight car installations; total freight cars, by type; 1969-82; age distribution of freight cars, Jan. 1983; new rail and crossties laid, and line-owned railroad track mileage, 1971-82; and freight car deliveries by car type, and total cars rebuilt, 1977-82. Tables II.7-II.13.

d. Locomotive engine installations, by horsepower class, 1982; track mileage by rail weight group, Dec. 1981; service life and percent salvage value by freight car type, 1977; and description of equipment financing methods. Tables II.14-II.17.

A3275-6.2: Cost of Operations

a. Operating expenses by type; freight service costs and revenue ton-miles; average hourly wages; fringe benefit expenses for payroll taxes and health/welfare; diesel fuel prices; and fixed charges, by type. Tables III.1-III.5.

b. Freight loss/damage claims; and interest rates on equipment obligations, and new diesel locomotive and freight car costs, various years 1950-82. Tables III.6-III.8.

A3275-6.3: Demand and Traffic

a. GNP, Index of Industrial Production, and total intercity ton-miles; railroad ton-miles and tons originated; shares of intercity freight traffic, by transport mode; regulated carrier revenues, by mode, selected years 1969-81; railroad tons originated, by commodity, 1969-82; index of quarterly carloadings; and revenue shares, by commodity, 1982. Tables IV.1-IV.8.

b. Coal tons originated, for 6 largest railroads, and all others, 1982; total coal production and tons transported by rail; average coal prices per ton, and rail rates and real revenue per ton-mile; piggyback carloadings, selected years 1957-82, with detail by service plan for 1971-82; grain and motor vehicle shipments, by transport mode, various years 1972-82; and nonstatistical table showing types of freight cars used for various commodities. Tables IV.9-IV.17.

A3275-6.4: Energy and Financial Performance

ENERGY USE

a. Energy consumption shares, by transport mode, 1980; railroad energy efficiency, by type of service with comparisons to other transport modes, 1982; revenue ton-miles and fuel consumed in freight service; diesel fuel consumption; and coal production, and use by Class I railroads, selected years 1920-82. Tables V.1-V.5.

FINANCIAL PERFORMANCE

b. Operating revenues; revenue margin; net operating income, current and adjusted for inflation; and return on net investment and shareholder equity, with 1975-82 comparisons to other industries. Tables VI.1-VI.6.

c. Long-term debt, capital, and ratio; equipment debt; income coverage of fixed charges; current assets, liabilities, and net working capital; daily operating costs and days of coverage; operating revenues, property investment, and capital turnover rate; and income, depreciation, capital expenditures, and cash flow ratio. Tables VI.7-VI.14.

d. Class I railroad bond ratings, 1975-Sept. 1983; and common stock dividend yield, earnings per share, and price/earnings ratio, 1977-82; all by company. Tables VI.15-VI.16.

A3275-6.5: Resource Availability and Utilization

a. Diesel locomotive units in service and average horsepower; average freight train load, car load, and cars per train; number and capacity of freight cars; total freight revenue ton-miles and tonnage carried, and average haul length; and freight revenue ton-miles per locomotive, car, and mile. Tables VII.1-VII.6.

b. Employment in Class I railroads excluding Amtrak, selected years 1920-82; freight revenue ton-miles per employee and employee hour paid; nonstatistical table showing labor unions representing various categories of employees; number of overheated journals compared to freight car miles; and average freight car trips per year, by car type, 1971-82. Tables VII.7-VII.11.

A3275-7   ANALYSIS OF CLASS I RAILROADS, 1982
Annual. Sept. 1983.
ii+204 p. Series No. 5.
ISSN 0091-4894.
LC 73-643888.
SRI/MF/complete

Annual report on Class I freight and passenger railroads, covering finances, operations, and employment, by railroad company and district, 1982.

Contains contents listing and index to companies (p. i-ii); 14 line items showing financial summary data (p. 1-6); 764 line items, described below, showing detailed data (p. 7-168); 11 charts and 22 tables ranking companies by selected measures (p. 169-187); and index and data sources (p. 189-204).

Report price also includes *Statistics of Railroads of Class I in the U.S., 1972-82,* described above under A3275-4.

This is the 5th annual report.

Availability: Association of American Railroads, Information and Public Affairs Office, 1920 L St., NW, Washington DC 20036, $75.00; SRI/MF/complete.

DETAILED TABLES:
[Data are shown for total U.S., 3 railroad districts, and 33 companies, for 1982.]

a. Income statement and balance sheet: operating revenues and other income, fixed charges, income taxes, assets including road and equipment, current and noncurrent liabilities, shareholders' equity, and net working capital. Lines 15-99. (p. 7-24)

b. Cash and stock dividends, investments and rate of return, sources and applications of working capital, operating and freight service expenses by function and object, railway taxes, equipment rents, and financial ratios. Lines 100-300. (p. 25-66)

c. Resources and railway operations: average employment, and total and average annual compensation, all by job function; hours worked and paid, including overtime and vacation/holiday; mileage operated; ties and rail laid; capital expenditures; locomotives and freight cars in service, owned and leased, installed, and retired; and summary of operations. Lines 301-532. (p. 67-114)

d. Traffic and operations: carloads and tons originated and gross freight revenue, all by commodity group; and operations characteristics, including loaded and empty freight car miles by car type, switching data, operating ratios, and fuel consumption and costs by fuel type and function. Lines 533-778. (p. 115-168)

A3350
Association of
Home Appliance
Manufacturers

A3350–1   MAJOR HOME APPLIANCE FACTORY SHIPMENTS
Monthly.   Approx. 2 p.
SRI/MF/complete, shipped quarterly

Monthly press release on factory shipments of major home appliances, including room air conditioners, dehumidifiers, dishwashers, disposers, compactors, refrigeration units, electric ranges, microwave ovens/ranges, and laundry appliances. Data are based on appliance manufacturer reports to Assn of Home Appliance Manufacturers, and are generally issued 2-3 weeks after month of coverage.

Contents:

a. Narrative summary; and 1 monthly table showing shipments by appliance type, for month of coverage, year to date, and same periods of previous year, with quarterly summary.

b. 1 recurring table usually showing 12-year trends and forecasts for appliance shipments by type.

Monthly table appears in all issues; recurring table appears in Dec. 1983 and Sept. 1984 issues.

Availability: Association of Home Appliance Manufacturers, 20 N. Wacker Dr., Chicago IL 60606, †; SRI/MF/complete, shipped quarterly.
Issues reviewed during 1984: Oct. 1983-Sept. 1984 (D).

A3350–2   APPLIANCE SALES BY DISTRIBUTORS, States, 1983
Annual.   1984.
6 p. var. paging.
SRI/MF/complete

Annual report, for 1983, on distributors' sales of home laundry, refrigeration, and kitchen appliances, by State and product type. Also includes number of households, by State, 1980. Data are from AHAM and Census Bureau.

Contains 3 tables.

Availability: Association of Home Appliance Manufacturers, 20 N. Wacker Dr., Chicago IL 60606, †; SRI/MF/complete.

A3354
Association of
Information Systems
Professionals

A3354–1   TENTH ANNUAL SALARY SURVEY RESULTS, 1984
Annual.   1984.   115 p.
SRI/MF/complete

Annual report, for 1984, on a survey of 15 word processing (wp) position salaries in effect Feb. 1984 in the U.S. and Canada. Includes data by U.S. zip code region, and for selected U.S. and Canadian metro areas and industries.

Data are based on a mail survey of 22,888 wp employees in 2,391 U.S. and Canadian companies.

Contains contents listing, survey methodology, job title definitions, and map of zip code regions (p. 2-7); and 1 table showing the following for each of 15 positions: number of companies and employees surveyed; weekly average, high, low, median, and modal salaries; and total average weekly hours for each location or industry. Table is repeated for:

a. U.S., 10 zip code regions, 36 metro areas, and total nonmetro. (p. 8-55)

b. Canada, 5 metro areas, and total nonmetro. (p. 56-62)

c. 31 U.S. industries. (p. 63-93)

d. 22 Canadian industries. (p. 94-115)

Availability: Association of Information Systems Professionals, 1015 N. York Rd., Willow Grove PA 19090, members $25.00, nonmembers $40.00; SRI/MF/complete.

A3360
Association of
Physical Plant Administrators
of Universities and Colleges

A3360–1   ENERGY COST AND CONSUMPTION REPORT, 1980-81 AND 1981-82
Biennial.   1983.   v+308 p.
ISBN 0-913359-21-1.
LC 81-71815.
SRI/MF/complete

Biennial report on energy consumption and costs of higher education facilities in U.S. and Canada, by fuel type and institution, FY81-82.

Includes data on campus size and student enrollment; heating and cooling degree days; percent of campus air-conditioned; presence of central plant; purchased and self-generated energy costs and/or use, by fuel type; coal sulfur content and mine location; and electricity source (city or institution).

Data are shown by individual institution code, arranged variously by State and Province, campus size, and energy consumption.

Data are based on 800 responses to a 1983 mail survey of institutions.

Contains contents listing (1 p.); introduction and definitions (p. iii-v); sample questionnaire (p. 1-17); index of reporting institutions (p. 21-28); and 8 extended tables (p. 31-308).

For description of previous report, covering FY80, see SRI 1983 Annual, under this number.

Availability: Association of Physical Plant Administrators of Universities and Colleges, 1446 Duke St., Alexandria VA 22314-3492, members $15.00, nonmembers $21.00; SRI/MF/complete.

A3360–2   1982/83 COMPARATIVE COSTS AND STAFFING REPORT for College and University Facilities
Biennial.   1984.   vi+87 p.
ISSN 0742-7476.
ISBN 0-913359-25-4.
SRI/MF/complete

Biennial report, for 1982/83, on higher education physical plant maintenance/operating costs and employment, by institution. Includes data on enrollment, building square footage maintained, cost, and employees, by maintenance function; and employees, whether unionized, and wage/salary level, by position. Data are shown for individual institutions arranged by region and square footage.

Data are from responses of 757 institutions to a survey of 1,900 members of Assn of Physical Plant Administrators and National Assn of College and University Business Officers. Sample includes institutions in U.S., Canada, and selected other countries.

Report is intended to enable administrators to compare their physical plant costs with those of other institutions.

Contains contents listing, and explanatory material (p. iii-vi); index of institutions (p. 1-17); unit cost and wage/salary data, with 2 computer printout tables (p. 18-62); and appendices, including questionnaire facsimile (p. 63-87).

For description of report for 1980/81, see SRI 1982 Annual, under this number.

Availability: Association of Physical Plant Administrators of Universities and Colleges, 1446 Duke St., Alexandria VA 22314-3492, members $25.00, nonmembers $35.00; SRI/MF/complete.

A3365
Association of
Research Libraries

A3365–1   ARL STATISTICS, 1982-83
Annual. 1984.
72 p.+errata sheet.
ISSN 0147-2135.
LC 77-647280.
SRI/MF/complete

Annual report, compiled by Carol A. Mandel and Alexander Lichtenstein, on research library holdings, expenditures, and staff, 1982/83. Presents data for 104 university and 13 other research libraries.

Covers total and added volumes, microform holdings, and current serials; interlibrary loan activity; operating expenditures by function, including salaries/wages; and FTE staff; all with rank order, by institution.

Also includes university aggregate operating ratios; and library size indexes, PhD degrees awarded, and fall 1982 student enrollment, by institution.

Data are from an annual survey of ARL members.

Contains contents listing (p. 3); introduction, with 1 summary table and trend chart, references, and library code guide (p. 5-9a); 4 tables, library size index, and 14 ranking tables (p. 10-47); and facsimile questionnaire, footnotes, and list of ARL statistical compilations (p. 48-72).

Availability: Association of Research Libraries, 1527 New Hampshire Ave., NW, Washington DC 20036, members $8.00, nonmembers $10.00; SRI/MF/complete.

**A3365–2   ARL ANNUAL SALARY
SURVEY, 1983**
Annual. Feb. 1984.
49 p.+errata sheets.
ISSN 0361-5669.
LC 76-640547.
SRI/MF/complete

Annual survey report, by Gordon Fretwell, on salaries at university and nonuniversity member libraries of Assn of Research Libraries (ARL), FY84 with selected trends from FY74.

Includes median and beginning salaries, and professional staff, for 12 nonuniversity libraries; filled positions, average years of experience, and average, median, and beginning salaries, for approximately 100 university libraries; university and nonuniversity librarians by salary range; and university librarians and average salary, by minority status, sex, position, years of experience, institutional control, staff size, census division, and for Canada.

Also includes salary index comparisons to CPI; data on number of libraries; and number of librarians by census division and race/ethnicity (black, Hispanic, Asian, and American Indian/Alaskan Native).

Contains contents and table listing (p. 3-4); introduction and explanatory notes, with 2 text

tables (p. 5-7); 19 detailed tables (p. 10-32); and list of participating universities, questionnaire facsimiles, and footnotes. (p. 33-49)

Availability: Association of Research Libraries, 1527 New Hampshire Ave., NW, Washington DC 20036, members $8.00, nonmembers $10.00; SRI/MF/complete.

A3370
Association
of Schools and
Colleges of Optometry

**A3370–1   JOURNAL OF OPTOMETRIC
EDUCATION**
Quarterly. Approx. 30 p.
ISSN 0098-6917.
LC 76-646768.
SRI/MF/excerpts

Quarterly journal of the Assn of Schools and Colleges of Optometry, containing feature articles and statistics on student, applicant, and school characteristics, and various academic and professional issues.

Each issue contains regular depts and feature articles. Features with substantial statistical content are described, as they appear, under "Statistical Features." Each issue of the journal is reviewed, but an abstract is published in SRI monthly issues only when statistical features appear.

Availability: Association of Schools and Colleges of Optometry, 600 Maryland Ave., SW, Suite 410, Washington DC 20024, members †, nonmembers $10.00 per yr.; SRI/MF/excerpts for all portions covered under "Statistical Features."

Issues reviewed during 1984: Fall 1983-Summer 1984 (P) (Vol. 9, Nos. 2-4; Vol. 10, No. 1).

STATISTICAL FEATURES:

A3370–1.501: Fall 1983 (Vol. 9, No. 2)
**ASSESSMENT OF THE NEED FOR OPTOMETRIC
EDUCATION IN PUERTO RICO**

(p. 8-28) By Edwin C. Marshall. Report on optometric service supply and demand in Puerto Rico. Includes data on population, vision care service utilization, and optometrists, by age and health region, various dates 1977-82; and projected impact of Inter American University (IAU) School of Optometry on optometric manpower supply through 2000.

Data are from Puerto Rico Dept of Health, Puerto Rico Planning Board, HHS, Colegio de Optometras de Puerto Rico, and IAU.

Contains 3 sections, with text data, 2 maps, 2 charts, 10 tables, and bibliographical references.

A3370–1.502: Winter 1984 (Vol. 9, No. 3)
**ANNUAL SURVEY OF OPTOMETRIC
EDUCATIONAL INSTITUTIONS, 1982/83**

(p. 24-29) Annual survey report, for 1982/83 academic year, on optometry school student enrollment characteristics and financial aid. Data are from a survey of 16 schools, conducted by the Council on Optometric Education of the American Optometric Assn.

Includes 7 tables showing the following, by institution, 1982/83:

a. Entering class grade point averages and number of students; and previous higher educational attainment of 1st-year students (years of study completed or degree earned).

b. Enrolled students by sex and minority group (black, Spanish surname, American Indian, Asian American, and foreign national); percent of students receiving financial aid and student loans; and annual student expenditures; mostly by student year level.

c. Number of students by location of permanent residence, with data by State and Canadian Province, and for Puerto Rico, and aggregates for U.S. possessions, Canadian territories, and other countries.

A3372
Association of
Schools of Public Health

**A3372–3   SCHOOLS OF PUBLIC
HEALTH EDUCATIONAL
DATA REPORT, 1982/83**
Annual. Oct. 1983. v+30 p.
SRI/MF/complete

Annual report, by Susan H. Klein and Judith H. Magee, on characteristics of applicants, accepted and enrolled students, and graduates, for accredited schools of public health, 1982/83 with some trends from 1958/59.

Includes selected detail by sex, U.S. vs. foreign citizenship, race, ethnicity (American Indian/Alaskan Native, Asian/Hawaiian, and Hispanic), full- and part-time enrollment status, age, area of specialization, highest previous degree, and degree earned or planned; and enrollments by institution.

Also includes data on school expenditures by object, and for Federal and other grants by type and for student aid, by individual unidentified institution, 1981/82.

Data were compiled by ASPH Data Center from reports of all 23 accredited schools of public health.

Contains contents/table listing (1 p.); preface (p. i-v); 5 report sections, with 6 tables (p. 1-20); and appendices with 9 tables (p. 22-30).

Previous edition included more detail by institution.

Availability: Association of Schools of Public Health, 1015 15th St., NW, Suite 404, Washington DC 20005, ‡, price upon request; SRI/MF/complete.

**A3372–4   SCHOOLS OF PUBLIC
HEALTH EDUCATIONAL
DATA REPORT on 1982-83
Graduates and 1982-83
Expenditures**
Annual. June 1984. i+15 p.
SRI/MF/complete

By Judith H. Magee. Report on graduates and expenditures of accredited schools of public health, 1982/83.

Includes graduates by sex, U.S. vs. foreign citizenship, race/ethnicity (including American Indian, Asian, and Hispanic), area of specialization, degree earned (including joint degrees), and highest previous degree, with various cross-tabulations; and masters and doctoral degrees awarded, by institution.

Also includes school expenditures by object, and for Federal and other grants by type and for student aid, by individual unidentified institution.

Data were compiled by ASPH Data Center from reports of all 23 accredited schools of public health.

Contains contents/table listing (p. i); acknowledgments and explanatory notes (p. 1-4); and 26 tables (p. 5-15).

This report covers the period from July 1, 1982 to the end of each school's 1982/83 academic year. Report supplements the edition of *Schools of Public Health Educational Data Report* which presents financial data for 1981/82 and academic data for the year ended June 30, 1983 (for description see A3372-3, above). Issuing agency has changed the reporting period for these data and has issued this supplemental report to allow statistical continuity.

Availability: Association of Schools of Public Health, 1015 15th St., NW, Suite 404, Washington DC 20005, ‡, price on request; SRI/MF/complete.

A3377
Association of University Programs in Health Administration

A3377–1   BACCALAUREATE HEALTH ADMINISTRATION GRADUATES: A Decade Review
Monograph. 1983.
viii + 155 p.
LC 83-70723.
SRI/MF/complete

Report on graduates of baccalaureate programs in health administration, 1970/71-1980/81. Presents data on personal characteristics, including race, sex, marital status, years since graduation, and age at graduation; academic background; detailed work experience, including current employment status, position, type of employer, and salary; and perceptions of skills/knowledge needed on the job.

Includes selected cross-tabulations, and multivariate statistical analyses identifying factors related to career patterns and earnings.

Also includes data on number of programs and graduates by census division and in Canada; and number of programs, by State.

Data are based on 1,170 responses to a Sept. 1981 survey of graduates, and 100 responses to a Dec. 1980 survey of college/university health administration programs. There were an estimated 5,603 total graduates at the time of the 1981 survey.

Contains contents and table listings and preface (p. i-viii); introduction and methodology, with 7 tables (p. 1-16); narrative analysis in 4 sections, interspersed with 34 tables (p. 17-79); and 8 appendices with questionnaire facsimiles, 26 tables, definitions, listing of institutions offering health administration programs, AUPHA membership criteria, and bibliography (p. 81-155).

Availability: Association of University Programs in Health Administration, 1911 N. Fort Myer Dr., Suite 503, Arlington VA 22209, $10.00 (prepaid) or $12.50; SRI/MF/complete.

A3425
Bank Administration Institute

A3425–1   1982 SURVEY OF THE CHECK COLLECTION SYSTEM
Annual. 1983. ix + 115 p.
No. 6282.
LC 77-77478.
SRI/MF/complete, delayed

Annual survey report, by Stanley E. Miltko and Kathleen Sandri, analyzing commercial bank check collection and processing system performance and labor productivity, 1982, with comparisons to 1979-81.

Covers system performance measures, including incidence of rejected items, transit returns and holdovers, and free/lost, missent/miscoded, and exception items; labor productivity measures for various check collection/processing activities; and performance of electronic processing systems and check truncation methods.

Also includes dollar value analysis of return and exception items.

Data are generally shown for 16 regions, each identified by a major city, and include separate totals for banks that participated in the 1st performance survey conducted by Arthur D. Little, Inc. (ADL) in 1970.

Data are based on responses of 170 banks to a Bank Administration Institute survey covering the week of Nov. 15-19, 1982. Respondents include 38 banks that also participated in the 1970 ADL survey.

Contains contents and table listings (p. v-ix); analysis and discussion of survey results, with 64 tables (p. 1-89); and appendices, with survey questionnaire facsimile, and selected respondent comments (p. 91-115).

This is the 12th annual survey.

Availability: Bank Administration Institute, 60 Gould Center, Rolling Meadows IL 60008, members $16.00, nonmembers $24.00; SRI/MF/complete, delayed shipment in Feb. 1985.

A3425–2   U.S. BANK PERFORMANCE PROFILE
Annual. 1984.
124 p. no paging.
Rpt. No. 1203.
SRI/MF/complete, delayed

Annual report presenting 63 financial and operating performance ratios for banks, by bank asset size and State, 1983. Data are based on periodic reports filed with Federal regulatory authorities by 14,592 insured banks. Number of reporting banks is specified for each asset size category and State.

Contains introduction and methodology, 5 trend charts, and ratio definitions (10 p.); 1 profit distribution table showing data as bottom and top percentiles, median value, and lower and upper quartiles, repeated for 6 asset size classes, all banks, and each State, and 1 additional table repeated for each State identifying median bank performance for each asset size class (109 p.); and appendix, with ratio formulas (5 p.). Both tables show the following:

a. Operating performance: 15 ratios, including interest and noninterest income and expenses, salaries/benefits, and return on assets and equity, all as percent of total assets.

b. Yields and rates: 9 ratios, including tax-equivalent yields on earning assets and investment securities; break-even and loan yields; loan loss provision and charge-off rates; and deposit and total interest fund rates.

c. Capital position: 4 ratios, including effective tax rate and cash dividends as percent of operating income; capital formation ratio; and equity capital as percent of total assets.

d. Productivity: 6 ratios, including personnel expense per employee, employees per million assets, and noninterest income as percent of salaries.

e. Asset/liability management, use of funds: 9 ratios, including investment securities, Federal funds sold, loan loss reserve, and 5 types of loans, all as percent of earning assets.

f. Asset/liability management, source of funds: 14 ratios, including demand, savings, and time deposits; money market certificates of deposit; foreign deposits; and borrowings; all as percent of earning assets.

g. Growth statistics: 6 ratios, including 1- and 5-year percent changes in income and assets.

This series began in 1973. Customized analyses of operating ratios for individual or groups of banks may be ordered from the issuing agency but are not covered in SRI.

Availability: Bank Administration Institute, 60 Gould Center, Rolling Meadows IL 60008, $35.00; SRI/MF/complete, delayed shipment in Oct. 1985.

A3425–3   1982 SURVEY OF THE ELECTRONIC FUNDS TRANSFER TRANSACTION SYSTEM
Annual. [1984.] vii + 72 p.
Rpt. No. 6472.
LC 80-67016.
SRI/MF/complete, delayed

Annual report, by Marjolijn van der Velde and Kathleen Sandri, on banking industry use of electronic funds transfer, 1982. Report focuses on automated clearinghouses (ACH), which move debit and credit transactions among financial institutions, and automated teller machines (ATM).

Data are from a Nov. 1982 survey of electronic transactions at 157 banks, with selected comparisons to 1978-81 surveys.

Contains contents and table listings (p. v-vii); introduction (p. 3); ACH and ATM findings, with 17 tables, listed below (p. 5-39); and appendices A-C, with sample questionnaire, map of geographic regions, respondent comments, and 1 table showing respondents by region, 1978-82 (9 p., p. 55-72).

This is the 5th annual survey.

Availability: Bank Administration Institute, 60 Gould Center, Rolling Meadows IL 60008, members $24.00, nonmembers $36.00; SRI/MF/complete, delayed shipment in May 1985.

TABLES:

[Tables generally show data by 16 regions, each identified by a major city. All data are shown for 1982; most tables include annual trends from 1978 or 1979.]

ACH TRANSACTIONS
[All tables begin "Percent of..."]

1-3. ACH debits and credits sent and received, and items sent vs. received. (p. 6-8)

4-5. ACH items returned of items sent and received. (p. 10-11)

6-7. ACH debit transactions sent and received, by type of transaction [insurance premiums, home mortgages, telephone bill payments, and corporate and other payments]. (p. 12-15)

ATM TRANSACTIONS
[ATM transaction types include cash withdrawals from checking, savings, and credit cards; checking and savings deposits; and generally bill payments. Locations are main offices, branches, and off-premise. Installation types include lobby, vestibule, through-the-wall, drive-up, freestanding, shopping center, and hospital.]

8-9, [A], and 10. Percent of ATM transactions; average dollar value; total dollar value [not by region]; and average weekly transactions per ATM unit; all by type [of transaction]. (p. 18-26)

11. Number of weekly transactions per ATM unit [by] location [and installation type]. (p. 27)

12-13. ATM units [percents by type of unit and location]. (p. 30-33)

14-15. ATM unit installation plans [percents by location and installation type]. (p. 34-38)

16. On-line vs. off-line ATM units. (p. 39)

A3425–4   1983 BAI BANK OFFICER CASH COMPENSATION SURVEY
Annual. 1983.
208 p. no paging.
Rpt. No. 413..
ISSN 0194-0759.
SRI/MF/complete, delayed

Annual report, by Andrew M. Mosko, on bank employee salaries, by bank asset size and census division, 1983. Includes mean and median base salary, salary range, and number of reporting banks and incumbents, for 89 officer-level and other positions.

Also includes officers' mean age, years of service and in present position, employees supervised, and salary comparison to 1981.

Data are based on 1,239 responses to an Apr. 1983 survey of Bank Administration Institute member banks, ranging in asset size from under $20 million to over $1 billion.

Contains contents listing and introduction (5 p.); and 1 table repeated for all banks by asset size, and by census division and asset size (203 p.).

This is the 10th survey. Prior to 1983, surveys were conducted biennially, and issued in 3 separate volumes (for description of 1981 report, see SRI 1982 Annual, under this number).

Availability: Bank Administration Institute, 60 Gould Center, Rolling Meadows IL 60008, members $50.00, nonmembers $75.00; SRI/MF/complete, delayed shipment in Dec. 1984.

A3445
Battery Council International

A3445–1   1984 BATTERY COUNCIL INTERNATIONAL STATISTICS ANNUAL
Annual. 1984. 2+46 p.
SRI/MF/complete

Annual report, for 1984, of the storage battery manufacturing industry. Includes data on U.S. and world production of batteries and motor vehicles, lead supply and demand, and U.S. motor vehicle registration by State, 1983, with trends from as early as 1939.

Data are primarily from Federal agencies and industry assns.

Contains contents listing (1 p.); narrative review (p. 1-3); 17 summary charts, and 43 tables listed below (p. 4-42); and an index (p. 43-46).

Availability: Battery Council International, Research and Statistics Department, 111 E. Wacker Dr., Chicago IL 60601, members $15.00, nonmembers $50.00; SRI/MF/complete.

TABLES:
[Data are for U.S., unless otherwise noted.]

A3445–1.1: Batteries

[1-2] Total shipments of SLI [starting/lighting/ignition] batteries, and breakdown of [replacement, original equipment, and export] battery shipments, 1939-83. (p. 4-5)

[3-4] Automotive replacement batteries, quarterly shipments and 12-month moving totals [1973-83]. (p. 8-9)

[5-7] Battery shipments, replacement and original equipment: shares by product category [1979-83]. (p. 10-11)

[8-11] Automotive replacement battery shipments to channels of distribution [by type of retail outlet and distributor channel, with detail for] private brands vs. manufacturer's own [various years 1965-83]. (p. 12-15)

[12-15] Automotive replacement and original equipment battery production and inventories [1982-83]. (p. 17-19)

[16-17] Quarterly production of Australian SLI batteries, and 12-month moving totals [1973-83]. (p. 20)

[18] Canadian automotive replacement battery shipments, 12-month moving totals [1976-83]. (p. 21)

[19-20] Japanese [automobile and motorcycle] lead-acid [and] original equipment vs. replacement battery shipments, [various years] 1967-83. (p. 22-23)

[21] Global Western European starter battery market [home market sales, exports, imports, and production], 1977-83. (p. 24)

A3445–1.2: Lead
[Unless otherwise noted, the following tables show data for 1979-83.]

[1] World refined production and consumption of lead [1978-83]. (p. 25)

[2] Consumption of lead by product category. (p. 26)

[3-4] Primary lead smelted and refined and secondary lead recovered [by source and type]. (p. 27)

[5-6] Stocks of lead at smelters, and consumer/secondary stocks of lead [by lead type]. (p. 28)

[7] Shipments of storage battery oxides [monthly]. (p. 29)

[8] Imports and exports of lead [by type]. (p. 29)

[9] Australian lead prices, f.o.b. Port Pirie per metric ton, expressed in Australian dollars [monthly 1978-83]. (p. 30)

[10-12] Canadian pig lead prices, London metal exchange lead prices, and U.S. producer lead prices, U.S. cents per pound [monthly 1978-83]. (p. 31-32)

[13] Lead used in production of industrial type batteries [1964-83]. (p. 32)

A3445–1.3: Motor Vehicles

[1-2] World motor vehicle production [by vehicle type and country, various years 1979-83]. (p. 33-35)

[3] Vehicles in use [1947-83]. (p. 36)

[4] Motor vehicle registrations [by State, 1978-83]. (p. 37)

[5] Growth of cars in use [percent increase, selected years 1950-83]. (p. 38)

[6-7] New car registrations [1946-83; and by State and for Federal Government, 1980-83]. (p. 39-40)

[8] Growth of trucks in use [percent increase, selected years 1950-83]. (p. 41)

[9] New truck registrations [1946-83]. (p. 42)

A3470
Bicycle Manufacturers Association of America

A3470–1   1983 BICYCLE MARKET IN REVIEW
Annual. [1984.] 10 p.
SRI/MF/complete

Annual report, for 1983, on domestic shipments and imports of bicycles, by type. Data are from Bicycle Manufacturers Assn of America. Contains 9 charts and 1 table showing the following:

a. Domestic and import market shares; imports from top 4 and all other countries of origin; domestic orders and shipments, and imports, by quarter; import and domestic lightweight bicycle market shares; and domestic shipments by hub type (coaster, and 3-, 5-, and 10-speed); 1982-83. (p. 2-8)

b. Market shares: for factory and private brand bicycles, 1983; and for national distributors, retailers, wholesalers/jobbers, regional chains, and discount houses, 1982-83. (p. 9-10)

Availability: Bicycle Manufacturers Association of America, 1055 Thomas Jefferson St., NW, Washington DC 20007, †; SRI/MF/complete.

A3675
Building Owners and Managers Association International

A3675–1   1984 BOMA EXPERIENCE EXCHANGE REPORT: Income/Expense Analysis for Office Buildings
Annual. 1984. 428 p.
LC 79-649602.
SRI/MF/complete, delayed

Annual report on U.S. and Canadian private sector and government office building income and expenses per square foot, by city and building characteristics, 1983. Covers income by source, including office and retail space rental; and expenses by detailed item, including utilities and payroll. Also covers space per tenant and worker, occupancy rate, and year-end rent.

Data are shown as median, average, and/or ranges, for major cities, with detail by building square footage and type of location (downtown or surburban). Also included are national analyses by building square footage, height, age, and type of location; comparisons for buildings surveyed 1979-83; and analyses for all-electric, single-purpose, medical, agency-managed, and financial buildings.

Report also includes detailed survey data on office building occupancy, by region and city, as of May 1, 1983.

Financial data are from a 1984 survey of 2,432 private and 543 government office buildings; other data are from an occupancy survey of 6,121 buildings.

Purpose of report is to permit building owners and managers to compare their operations with those of similar size and location.

Contents:

a. Foreword, contents listing, and highlights, with 2 charts and 4 tables. (p. 3-8)
b. User information; methodology; articles on applications of report data, including sample charts of accounts for major building ownership/operations/management groups; and Building Owners and Managers Assn activities. (p. 9-64)
c. 4 statistical sections, each preceded by contents listing, with tabulations covering U.S. and Canadian private sector and government office buildings. (p. 65-403)
d. Appendixes, including facsimile of survey questionnaire, building area measurement methodology, and 1 table presenting results of office building occupancy survey. (p. 405-428)

This is the 64th annual report.

Availability: Building Owners and Managers Association International, 1250 Eye St., NW, Washington DC 20005, members $65.00, nonmembers $150.00, $5.00 shipping and handling; SRI/MF/complete, delayed shipment in Feb. 1985.

A3710
Business/Professional Advertising Association

A3710–1   1984 B/PAA SALARY/JOB SURVEY
Biennial. [1984.]
12 p. Pocket size.
SRI/MF/complete

Biennial survey report, for 1984, on salaries of members of the Business-Professional Advertising Assn (B/PAA). Includes data on positions held, salaries by census division and for Canada, and advertiser budget size; and comparisons to previous surveys from 1968.

Data were compiled by Business Marketing Research from 1,094 responses to a Mar. 1984 survey of B/PAA members.

Contains contents listing, introduction, and methodology with 1 table on survey sample (p. 2-4); and survey findings, with 20 tables, described below, each with brief narrative (p. 4-12).

Previous report, for 1982, is described in SRI 1982 Annual, under this number.

Availability: Business/Professional Advertising Association, 205 E. 42nd St., New York NY 10017, members †, nonmembers $10.00; SRI/MF/complete.

TABLES:
[Tables show data for 1984, with selected comparisons to 1982, 1980, and 1968 surveys. Types of employer are advertiser, agency, and publishing.]

a. Median salaries for advertising professionals, total and by type of employer and census division, and for Canada; percent of B/PAA members receiving additional compensation, and median amount, by type of employer; and median salaries, by age group. Tables 1-4. (p. 4-6)
b. Median salary for Certified Business Communicator (CBC) and others, by type of employer; percent of B/PAA members with CBC certification, by age group; median age of B/PAA members, and median years with present company, by type of employer; and median salaries, by size of company advertising expenditures and agency billings. Tables 5-10. (p. 6-7)
c. Level of change in advertiser appropriations and agency billings over past 2 years; and anticipated change in advertising expenditures and personnel over next 2 years, by census division and for Canada. Tables 11-14. (p. 8-9)
d. Distribution of advertising expenditures by detailed media type, and of publishers by industry sector; and distribution of B/PAA members by highest degree held, and by type of employer by job title, years with present title, and dept. Tables 15-20. (p. 9-12)

A3750
California Fig Institute

A3750–1   STATISTICAL REVIEW OF THE CALIFORNIA DRIED FIG INDUSTRY, 1983
Annual. [1983.]
20 p. no paging.
SRI/MF/complete

Annual report on California fig production, acreage, yield, shipments, utilization, farm value, and prices, 1982, with selected trends from 1943. Data are shown variously for fresh and/or dried figs, and include detail by variety and for merchantable and substandard production. California produces all commercial U.S. figs.

Also includes data on U.S. imports and consumption of dried figs and fig paste, by country of origin.

Data are primarily from California Crop and Livestock Reporting Service, California Dried Fig Advisory Board, and U.S. Dept of Commerce.

Contains foreword and contents listing (2 p.); and 18 tables (18 p.).

Availability: California Fig Institute, 1205 E. Olive, PO Box 709, Fresno CA 93712, †; SRI/MF/complete.

A3800
Carpet and Rug Institute

A3800–1   CARPET AND RUG INSTITUTE INDUSTRY REVIEW, 1982
Annual. 1984. 17 p.
SRI/MF/complete

Annual report on the carpet and rug industry, presenting data on shipments, PPI, materials consumed, and foreign trade, 1982 and trends. Most data are from industry sources and Census Bureau.

Contains preface, highlights, and contents listing (2 p.); 18 charts showing industry trends, mostly from the 1970s, with PPI trends from 1950 (p. 2-6); and 13 appendix tables, listed below (p. 7-17).

Availability: Carpet and Rug Institute, PO Box 2048, Dalton GA 30720, members $3.00, nonmembers $10.00; SRI/MF/complete.

TABLES:
[Most tables show quantity; dollar value is also frequently included. Tables show data for 1976-82, unless otherwise noted.]

1-2. Total industry shipments [by carpet type]. (p. 7)
3. Total industry shipments, quarterly analysis. (p. 8)
4-5. Total industry and broadloom shipments [1962-82]. (p. 9)
6. Carpet/rug fiber shipments [by type of material, 1980 and quarterly 1981-82]. (p. 10)
7. Carpet/rug exports and imports. (p. 10)
8. Carpet and total textiles balance of trade. (p. 11)
9-10. 1982 exports and imports of carpet/rugs by type [by country of destination and origin]. (p. 12-15)

11-12. Primary and secondary backing consumed [by carpet and material types]. (p. 16)

13. Housing starts and [shipments of] tufted roll goods/rugs larger than 6'x9' [1963-82]. (p. 17)

A3840
Chamber of
Commerce of the U.S.

A3840–1   EMPLOYEE BENEFITS, 1982
Annual.   1984.   35 p.
ISSN 0194-3499.
ISBN 0-89834-049-7.
LC 54-2030.
SRI/MF/complete

Annual report on employee benefits by type and industry group, 1982. Covers employer share of legally required and voluntary payments, payments for time not worked, other payments such as profit-sharing and bonuses; and employee payroll deductions for insurance and pension plans.

Data are from survey responses of 1,507 employers, Chamber estimates, and Commerce Dept. Survey is generally limited to employees who are covered by the Fair Labor Standards Act. Data are not shown for individual companies.

Contains contents listing, introduction and summary (p. 3-5); survey analysis interspersed with 3 charts, and 21 tables listed below (p. 6-30); and survey methodology and facsimile of survey questionnaire (p. 31-35).

This is the 21st edition of the report.

Availability: Chamber of Commerce of the U.S., Survey Research Center, Economic Policy Division, 1615 H St., NW, Washington DC 20062, $12.00 (prepaid); SRI/MF/complete.

TABLES:
[Unless otherwise noted, data are for 1982. Most data are expressed as percent. Tables 3 and 5-18 show data by major industry group. Generally, data "by type of benefit" show:

a. Employer share of: payments for OASDHI, unemployment compensation, workers' compensation, and Railroad Retirement Tax/other legally required payments; and pension, insurance, and 6 other agreed-upon types of payments.

b. Payments for rest/lunch/other nonworking periods at the job, vacations, holidays, sick leave, and National Guard/jury duty/time lost due to death in family.

c. Profit-sharing payments, contributions to employee thrift plans, bonuses, employee education expenditures, and special court-ordered wage/union steward/other payments.]

BENEFITS DISTRIBUTION
1-2. Distribution and 5 levels of employee benefits [by percent of payroll, cents per payroll hour, and dollars per year per employee]. (p. 6)

3. Distribution of employee benefits as percent of payroll. (p. 7)

4. Employee benefits, by type of benefit [as percent of payroll for all companies, total manufacturing, and total nonmanufacturing]. (p. 8)

INDUSTRY, REGIONAL, AND COMPANY SIZE COMPARISONS
5. Major types of employee benefits. (p. 9)

6-8. Employee benefits as percent of payroll, cents per payroll hour, and dollars per year per employee; [all] by type of benefit. (p. 11-13)

9-10. Employee benefits as percent of payroll, by region and by size of company. (p. 14-15)

PENSION, INSURANCE, AND COMPANY PAYMENTS
11-12. Pension and insurance payments. (p. 16-17)

13. Insurance payments, by type of insurance [life and health]. (p. 18)

14. Employee payroll deductions for pensions and insurance. (p. 19)

15-16. Percent of companies paying employee benefits; and average benefit costs as percent of payroll for companies paying employee benefits; [by type of benefit]. (p. 21-22)

GENERAL DATA
17. Payroll deductions for employee benefits. (p. 23)

18. Wage data [average hourly earnings as percent of payroll and as cents per hour]. (p. 25)

19. Estimated total employee benefit payments [and wages/salaries, by industry division]. (p. 27)

20-21. Growth of employee benefits [as percent of wages/salaries, by type of payment]; and supplements to wages/salaries [by type of benefit and industry division; selected years] 1929-82. (p. 28-29)

A3840–2   ANALYSIS OF WORKERS' COMPENSATION LAWS, 1984
Annual.   1984.   viii+46 p.
U.S. Chamber Pub. No. 6707.
ISSN 0191-118X.
ISBN 0-89834-019-5.
LC 60-36379.
SRI/MF/complete

Annual report, for 1984, presenting detailed information on workers' compensation laws, by State, outlying area, and Canadian Province. Includes type of law (mandatory or elective), insurance requirements (including penalties for failure to insure), coverage, benefits, and claims administration.

Data are from legislative reporting services, insurance companies, and various government agencies.

Contains contents and table listing, and introduction (p. iii-viii); 3 parts, with 15 tables and directory of workers' compensation administrators (p. 1-46); and abbreviations and methodology (p. 46).

Availability: Chamber of Commerce of the U.S., Data Processing, 1615 H St., NW, Washington DC 20062, $12.00; SRI/MF/complete.

A3840–3   1983 INTERIM SURVEY OF LOCAL CHAMBERS OF COMMERCE
Biennial.   [1984.]   4+46 p.
SRI/MF/not filmed

Biennial interim survey, alternating with biennial *Survey of Local Chambers of Commerce,* to provide data on income, salary, and benefits, 1983.

Report is intended to enable individual organizations to compare their operations with averages for other chambers in localities of similar income size and population. Data are from survey responses of 689 organizations.

Contents:

Part I. 5 tables, listed below. (p. 1-13)

Part II. Management salaries by total income, including the following data repeated by income size group: average, median, highest, and lowest total and membership income, payroll, employees, and salaries; top 10 salaries of chief executives; and percent of organizations offering each of 10 specific benefits. Data on salaries and benefits are shown by management position. (p. 16-43)

List of organizations represented in 1983 survey. (3 p.)

Alternate biennial survey report includes additional detail on finances, organizational structure, facilities, and programs. Previous interim report for 1981 and biennial report for 1982 are described in SRI 1982 and 1983 Annuals respectively, under this number.

Availability: Chamber of Commerce of the U.S., Office of Chamber of Commerce Relations, 1615 H St., NW, Washington DC 20062, $20.00; SRI/MF/not filmed.

PART I TABLES:
[All tables show 1983 averages by population size group, and include number of organizations reporting. For selected items, separate averages for top 10 organizations are included.]

[1] Income: sources and average amount [including total and membership income, 5 special project sources, and special funds]. (p. 1)

[2] Income from government, services [and publications], foundations, and reserve funds [by source]. (p. 2)

[3] Salaries and [10] fringe benefits for [34 positions of] management level personnel [with average percent increase in salary]. (p. 3-11)

[4] Payroll, staff, and personnel procedures [including salary review, holidays, vacation, and sick leave]. (p. 12)

[5] Finance and membership [including membership rates, number and average value of membership accounts, cost of service per member, percent of accounts lost, and revenue lost due to lost accounts]. (p. 13)

A3840–6   ECONOMIC OUTLOOK: Chamber of Commerce of the U.S.
Monthly.   Approx. 20 p.
SRI/MF/complete

Monthly report (with occasional combined issues) presenting forecasts and/or recent trends for approximately 50 economic indicators. Data are from U.S. Chamber of Commerce Forecast Section.

Issues generally contain narrative summary and/or feature articles on economic outlook, often with illustrative charts or tables, and occasionally with more substantial data; and 2 monthly economic indicator tables, accompanied by forecast assumptions.

Monthly tables are described below and appear in all issues. All additional features with substantial statistical content are described, as they appear, under "Statistical Features." Nonstatistical features are not covered.

Availability: Chamber of Commerce of the U.S., Forecast Section, 1615 H St., NW, Washington DC 20062, $60.00 per yr., single copy $7.50; SRI/MF/complete.

Issues reviewed during 1984: Oct./Nov. 1983-Oct. 1984 (P).

MONTHLY TABLES:

[Table 1 shows most data as percent change, annually for previous, current, and 2-3 coming years, and quarterly for 7-10 consecutive quarters, usually through 1-2 coming years. Data through quarter ending 2-4 months prior to cover date are actual; other data are forecasts.

Table 2 shows data for current and previous month or quarter, specified for each indicator, and same period of preceding year. Data for most indicators are current to 1-2 months prior to cover date.

Table numbers and indicators may vary from issue to issue.]

1. U.S. economic outlook [GNP, consumption, investment, exports, imports, and Federal purchases; inventory change; new car sales and housing starts; unemployment rate; compensation, productivity, and unit labor costs; consumer prices, GNP deflator, and prime interest rate; corporate profits; and Federal receipts, outlays, and deficit (annually only)].

2. Trends in commerce [including population, GNP, and money supply; personal income, savings rate, and consumption expenditures; employment and earnings; CPI; retail sales; manufacturing capacity utilization rate; business failures; new incorporations; PPI; merchandise export and import value; indexes of industrial production, business labor and nonlabor costs, aggregate leading indicators, and Federal spending; and Federal debt outstanding].

STATISTICAL FEATURES:

A3840-6.501: Oct./Nov. 1983

INTERNATIONAL DEBT PROBLEM REVISITED: THE CASE OF LATIN AMERICA

(p. 12-19) By Rajni Bonnie Ohri. Article on external debt situation for Latin America, 1970s-83. Data are from World Bank, Inter-American Bank, and IMF. Includes 3 tables showing the following, with some detail by Latin American country:

a. External debt held by financial institutions and official agencies/bondholders, and debt as a percent of exports and GNP, for Latin America and all other developing countries, mid-1982; and Latin America export prices for 12 commodities, 1978-82.

b. Interest payment, amortization, and total debt service, all as percent of exports, for Latin America and all non-oil developing countries, 1978-83.

A3840-6.502: Dec. 1983/Jan. 1984

CONTINUED ECONOMIC EXPANSION BODES WELL FOR EMPLOYMENT GROWTH

(p. 8-12) By Graciela Testa Ortiz and Rajni Bonnie Ohri. Article, with 1 table showing employment change by industry division and manufacturing group, for July 1981-Nov. 1982 recession period and Nov. 1982-83 recovery period. Data are from U.S. Chamber of Commerce Forecast Section.

A3840-6.503: May 1984

WORLD OIL MARKETS: WHAT NOW?

(p. 3-8) By Graciela Testa-Ortiz. Article, with 1 table showing world oil demand, OPEC and non-OPEC supply, and net exports of centrally planned economies, 1973, 1979, and 1983. Data are from Data Resources Inc.

A3840-6.504: June 1984

WHAT NEW MANUFACTURING JOBS MEAN TO A COMMUNITY

(p. 5, 7-10) By Martin Lefkowitz. Article analyzing effect of increased manufacturing employment on the overall economy of a community. Data are based on a Chamber of Commerce study of a group of nonmetro counties with increased manufacturing employment during 1970-80 and a similar group of counties with no such increase.

Includes 2 undated tables showing the impact of new manufacturing jobs on non-manufacturing jobs by industry division and on retail sales by type of business.

REGIONAL SURVEY

(p. 10-17) By Rajni Bonnie Ohri. Article, with 3 tables showing personal income per capita, retail sales change, and manufacturing and nonmanufacturing share of total employment, by region and for total U.S., various periods 1982-84.

GOOSE AND THE GOLDEN EGG: INCENTIVES DO MATTER

(p. 17-21) By William Orzechowski. Article analyzing effects of Federal income tax cuts of 1981. Data are from Treasury Dept and Congressional Budget Office (CBO).

Includes 2 tables showing tax revenues, 1981-82; and CBO forecasts of changes in 1982-85 tax revenues resulting from Economic Recovery Tax Act (ERTA)/Tax Equity and Fiscal Responsibility Act (TEFRA); all by income bracket.

A3840-6.505: July 1984

STEADY AS SHE GOES

(p. 1-5) By Richard W. Rahn. Article, with 2 charts showing government sector deficit as a percent of GNP, for U.S. 1982-86, and for 6 other countries 1984.

INVESTMENT IN THE CURRENT RECOVERY

(p. 5-9) By Martin Lefkowitz. Article, with 2 tables showing gross private savings, by component, 1983; and nonfinancial corporate cash flow summary, 4th quarter 1982-1st quarter 1984.

REAGAN TAX CUT SOAKS THE RICH

(p. 15) Brief article, with 1 chart showing 1-year percent change in tax collections, by income bracket, 1982.

A3840-6.506: Aug./Sept. 1984

DELUSIVE TRADE DEFICIT

(p. 9-12) By Rajni Bonnie Ohri. Article, with 1 chart showing percent increase in real exports during 5 economic recovery periods, 1958-83. Data are from Commerce Dept.

A3840-6.507: Oct. 1984

MASTERS OF OUR DESTINY? WHY SUSTAINED RAPID ECONOMIC GROWTH IS POSSIBLE

(p. 1-3) By Richard W. Rahn and Ronald D. Utt. Article, with 1 table showing GNP, Federal budget receipts and outlays, unemployment rate, 3-month Treasury bill rate, and GNP deflator, projected under high growth assumptions, 1984-89. Data are based on Data Resources, Inc., econometric model simulation.

ELECTION YEAR ECONOMY

(p. 4-7) By Graciela Testa-Ortiz. Article, with 1 table showing annual percent change in GNP by component and in selected other economic indicators, for 2nd quarter of presidential election years 1972-84.

INTERNATIONAL PERSPECTIVES ON TAX POLICY AND ECONOMIC GROWTH

(p. 7-9) By William Orzechowski. Article comparing economic growth of countries with differing tax burdens. Data are from OECD, Data Resources, Inc., and World Bank.

Includes 3 tables showing real GNP growth rate and/or tax receipts as percent of GNP, for U.S., Japan, European OECD, and 17 OECD countries; and GDP and labor productivity growth rates, and gross domestic investment share of GDP, for selected high-tax and low-tax countries with similar per capita income; various periods 1960-84.

IMMIGRATION: HOW IT BENEFITS US

(p. 9-12) By Rajni Bonnie Ohri. Article, with 1 chart and 1 table showing legal immigration into the US, 1976-82, with distribution of immigrants by world area of origin, 1977-79 period. Data are from Select Commission on Immigration and Refugee Policy, and *Population Trends and Public Policy*.

NATIONAL SECURITY: THE MISUNDERSTOOD CONSUMER GOOD

(p. 12-16) By Chris Plato. Article, with 1 table comparing defense expenditures for FY82-86, as proposed by Carter and Reagan Administrations. Data sources include DOD and OMB.

INTERNATIONAL TRANSACTIONS OF THE U.S.

(p. 19) Article, with 1 table showing U.S. assets abroad, foreign assets in U.S., and percent of Federal debt held by foreigners, 1980-83 and 1st quarter 1984. Data are from Federal Reserve Bank of St. Louis.

A3840-7   CONSUMER OPINION SURVEY

Quarterly, discontinued.

Quarterly survey report on consumer attitudes regarding personal financial situation, discontinued with Aug. 1983 issue (for description, see SRI 1983 Annual under this number). Report has been discontinued due to budgetary constraints.

A3870
Child Welfare
League of America

A3870–4 CHILDREN AS PARENTS:
Final Report on a Study of
Childbearing and Child
Rearing Among 12- to
15-Year Olds
Monograph. 1983.
xvi+117 p. Stock No. 2040.
ISBN 0-87868-204-X.
LC 83-5284.
SRI/MF/not filmed

By Shelby H. Miller. Survey report on teenage
mothers' personal characteristics, and attitudes
and practices regarding child rearing and related
topics. Includes survey findings on the following:

a. Incidence of delivery problems; self-esteem
and other personal assessments, including
child care competence; frequency of sexual
intercourse; knowledge of fertility cycle; contraceptive use; views on acceptability of abortion; sources of child development/parenting
information; and assessment of child's condition, including incidence of specific health
and behavioral problems.

b. Persons involved in child care decisions; contact with and educational status of child's father; housing and money problems; income
sources including public support; child care
arrangements; use and need of support services; educational goals; attitude toward marriage; desired family size; and expected living
arrangements.

Survey data are based on 184 interviews with
teenage mothers conducted June 1979-Jan.
1980, and 144 follow-up interviews conducted
Oct. 1980-Feb. 1981. Survey group was composed of mothers age 12-15 in contact with 13
social service agencies in Chicago, Cleveland,
and Minneapolis/St. Paul.

Also includes NCHS data on births and birth
rates for mothers under age 20, by age group,
race, and/or marital status, selected years 1950-
77.

Contains contents and table listings, and acknowledgments (p. ix-xvi); introduction, with 2
tables (p. 1-4); 12 chapters, with narrative analysis and 32 interspersed tables (p. 5-112); and
references (p. 113-117).

Availability: Child Welfare League of America,
CN 3103, 300 Raritan Center Pkwy., Edison NJ
08818, $9.95+$1.50 postage and handling
(prepaid); SRI/MF/not filmed.

A3880
Clothing Manufacturers
Association of the U.S.A.

A3880–1 SPECIAL STATISTICAL
REPORT ON PROFIT,
PRODUCTION, AND SALES
TRENDS IN THE MEN'S
AND BOYS' CLOTHING
INDUSTRY
Annual. Oct 1984. 21 p.
SRI/MF/not filmed

Annual report on men's and boys' clothing industry. Covers profitability; production volume by
wholesale price range and fabric, value of shipments, and foreign trade, all by type of garment;
number of production plants and workers; and
average hourly wage; various years 1963-83, with
employment and wage projections for May 1984.

Also includes results of a consumer survey on
men's clothing purchases by type, by price paid,
various periods 1981-84; and male population
projections, by age group, selected years 1985-
2080.

Data are from Commerce Dept and BLS; Dun
& Bradstreet, Inc.; and 30,000 responses to
household surveys conducted during 1982-84 by
NFO Research, Inc.

Contains contents listing (1 p.); introduction
(p. 1); and 19 tables interspersed with narrative
(p. 2-21).

Availability: Clothing Manufacturers Association of the U.S.A., 1290 Ave. of the Americas,
New York NY 10104, $20.00; SRI/MF/not
filmed.

A3900
College and
University Personnel
Association

A3900–1 1983/84 ADMINISTRATIVE
COMPENSATION SURVEY
Annual. Feb. 1984.
xi+130 p.
LC 77-83796.
SRI/MF/complete, delayed

Annual survey report, by Forest C. Benedict et
al., on salaries for 99 higher education administrative positions, 1983/84. Salaries are generally
shown as 1st and 3rd quartiles and/or medians,
by position.

Shows salaries for universities and 2- and 4-
year colleges, by institutional control (public and
private), enrollment size, and budget size; and for
private independent and religious institutions,
theological seminaries, medical schools/centers,
traditionally black institutions, and 2-year technical institutes.

Also includes salaries for inside vs. outside
hire; salaries and years of service by minority
status and by sex; salary trends, 1980/81-1983/
84; and distribution of salary ranges.

Data are based on responses from 1,515 of
2,856 institutions surveyed by the College and
University Personnel Assn, and reflect salaries in
effect during fall 1983.

Contains contents and table listings (p. ii-v);
introduction, with sample characteristics, me-

thodology, and definitions (p. vi-xi); 85 tables (p.
1-85); and 5 appendices, with 1 table, list of responding institutions, questionnaire facsimile,
position descriptions, and special study order
form (p. 87-130).

This is the 7th annual survey. Prior to 1977,
surveys were conducted biennially.

Availability: College and University Personnel
Association, 11 Dupont Circle, Suite 120, Washington DC 20036, members $25.00, nonmem-
bers participating in study $75.00, others
$150.00; SRI/MF/complete, delayed shipment
in Feb. 1985.

A3900–4 CUPA 1983-84 NATIONAL
FACULTY SALARY SURVEY
BY DISCIPLINE AND RANK
in Private Colleges and
Universities
Annual. Jan. 1984. ii+28 p.
SRI/MF/complete, delayed

Annual report, by Richard D. Howe et al., on
faculty salaries in private colleges and universities, 1983/84. Presents average, high, and low
salaries, and number of faculty and institutions
represented, by academic rank, for 48 disciplines.

Data are from responses of 355 private institutions, representing approximately 30,000 faculty,
to a survey conducted by CUPA in conjunction
with Appalachian State University.

Contains contents listing (p. ii); introduction
and survey methodology (p. 1-6); and appendices, with listings of disciplines and participating institutions, and 1 table repeated for each
discipline (p. 7-28).

This is the 2nd annual survey. For description
of a related report on State colleges and universities, see A3900-5 below.

Availability: College and University Personnel
Association, 11 Dupont Circle, Suite 120, Washington DC 20036, members $10.00, nonmem-
bers $20.00; SRI/MF/complete, delayed
shipment in May 1985.

A3900–5 CUPA 1983-84 NATIONAL
FACULTY SALARY SURVEY
BY DISCIPLINE AND RANK
in State Colleges and
Universities
Annual. Feb. 1984. ii+27 p.
SRI/MF/complete, delayed

Annual report, by Richard D. Howe et al., on
faculty salaries at State colleges and universities,
1983/84. Presents average, high, and low salaries, and number of faculty and institutions represented, by academic rank, for 48 disciplines.

Data are from responses of 215 public institutions, representing approximately 47,000 faculty,
to a survey conducted by CUPA in conjunction
with Appalachian State University.

Contains contents listing (p. ii); introduction
and survey methodology (p. 1-6); and appendices, with listings of disciplines and participating institutions, and 1 table repeated for each
discipline (p. 7-27).

This is the 2nd annual survey. For description
of a related report on private colleges and universities, see A3900-4 above.

Availability: College and University Personnel
Association, 11 Dupont Circle, Suite 120, Washington DC 20036, members $10.00, nonmem-
bers $20.00; SRI/MF/complete, delayed
shipment in May 1985.

A3940
College Placement Council

A NOTE ABOUT CPC SALARY SURVEY

The *CPC Salary Survey* reports, covered by SRI under A3940-1 and A3940-2, track starting salaries and jobs offered to graduating college students over a 12-month period beginning in Sept. Data are based on a survey of 187 placement offices at 162 colleges and universities.

Each report includes the following data, presented in 4-5 tables: number of job offers and average salary offered, and 10th, 50th, and 90th salary percentiles, by field of study and type of employer for bachelor and master degree candidates, and by field of study for doctoral candidates. Data for bachelor candidates are also shown by job function. Data for master degree candidates include selected detail for candidates with and without employment experience.

Employer types include business (3 categories), manufacturing/industrial (12 categories), Federal and State/local government, and non-profit/educational institutions.

A3940-1   CPC SALARY SURVEY: National and Regional Interim Reports
Annual series.   7 p. (national reports), approx. 20 p. (regional reports).
ISSN 0196- 1044 (national).
ISSN 0196- 1004 (regional).
LC 79-4046.
SRI/MF/complete

Annual set of 3 national interim reports issued in Feb., Apr., and May; and interim reports for 7 regions issued 5 times per year in Feb., Mar., Apr., May, and June. Data are shown for job and salary offers made during interim period since preceding report and cumulatively from Sept. 1 through 1st or 2nd week of publication month.

Each report contains the data described in the note above. Regional data are presented in 7 regional issues, which also include comparisons to national data, and lists of survey schools in each region.

Recently issued reports are listed below.

Issuing agency also publishes preliminary and formal national job and salary offer reports, and an annual report on employer plans for hiring college graduates, described in SRI under A3940-2 and A3940-3, respectively.

Availability: College Placement Council, 62 Highland Ave., Bethlehem PA 18017, members and subscribers to the salary survey package: national issues $10.00 each, regional issues $15.00 each; others inquire at issuing agency; SRI/MF/complete.

REPORTS:

A3940-1.1: National Reports
Issues reviewed during 1984: Feb.-May 1984 (P) (Nos. 1-3).

A3940-1.2: Eastern College Personnel Officers
Issues reviewed during 1984: Feb.-June 1984 (P) (Nos. 1-5).

A3940-1.3: Middle Atlantic Placement Association
Issues reviewed during 1984: Feb.-June 1984 (P) (Nos. 1-5).

A3940-1.4: Midwest College Placement Association
Issues reviewed during 1984: Feb.-June 1984 (P) (Nos. 1-5).

A3940-1.5: Rocky Mountain College Placement Association
Issues reviewed during 1984: Feb.-June 1984 (P) (Nos. 1-5).

A3940-1.6: Southern College Placement Association
Issues reviewed during 1984: Feb.-June 1984 (P) (Nos. 1-5).

A3940-1.7: Southwestern Placement Association
Issues reviewed during 1984: Feb.-June 1984 (P) (Nos. 1-5).

A3940-1.8: Western College Placement Association
Issues reviewed during 1984: Feb.-June 1984 (P) (Nos. 1-5).

A3940-2   CPC SALARY SURVEY: A Study of 1983-84 Beginning Offers, Preliminary and Formal Reports
Annual series.   Approx. 8 p.
ISSN 0196-1004.
LC 79-4046.
SRI/MF/complete

Annual set of 5 national reports on job and salary offers to graduating college students. Set includes a preliminary report issued in Dec.; formal reports issued in Jan., Mar., and July; and summer supplement issued in Oct.

Preliminary and formal reports show data for offers made from Sept. 1 through 1st or 2nd week of publication month (prior month for July report). Summer supplement shows data for offers made from early June through late Sept. All reports include comparisons to previous year.

Each report contains the data described in the note above A3940-1, accompanied by brief narrative analysis. July 1984 formal report also includes the additional data described below.

Subscription price includes an annual report on employer plans for hiring college graduates, covered by SRI under A3940-3. Issuing agency also publishes interim national and regional job and salary offer reports, covered under A3940-1.

Availability: College Placement Council, 62 Highland Ave., Bethlehem PA 18017, members †, nonmembers $105.00 (includes *Recruiting*); SRI/MF/complete.

Issues reviewed during 1984: Summer supplement (for 1982/83 graduates): Oct. 1983 (P).

Issues reviewed during 1984: Preliminary report (for 1983/84 graduates): Dec. 1983 (P).

Issues reviewed during 1984: Formal reports (for 1983/84 graduates): Jan., Mar., and July 1984 (P) (Nos. 1-3).

Issues reviewed during 1984: Summer supplement (for 1983/84 graduates): Oct. 1984 (P).

ADDITIONAL DATA:

A3940-2.501: July 1984 (Formal Report No. 3)

DATA BY SEX

(p. 4-5) Regular tables and illustrative chart on job and salary offers to bachelor's degree candidates by field of study and job function show data by sex, for Sept. 1983-June 8, 1984 period.

A3940-3   RECRUITING '84
Annual.   Oct. 1983.   8 p.
ISSN 0272-2259.
LC SN 80-13783.
SRI/MF/complete, delayed

Annual report on employer plans for hiring 1984 college graduates, by field, degree level, and type of employer. Also includes actual hires of 1983 graduates, recruiting interview schedules, and Federal Government job openings.

Data are from survey responses of 443 private sector employers to a July 1983 survey, and from U.S. Office of Personnel Management.

Contains narrative summary, with 4 tables listed below (p. 1-7); and employer classification definitions (p. 8).

Report has been published since 1970/71. It is available separately or as part of a package that also includes an annual series of survey reports on jobs and salaries offered to graduates, described above, under A3940-2.

Availability: College Placement Council, 62 Highland Ave., Bethlehem PA 18017, members †, nonmembers $10.00 (or $105.00 included in *CPC Salary Survey*); SRI/MF/complete, delayed shipment in Apr. 1984.

TABLES:

[Tables 1-3 show actual/anticipated data for 1983/84 and actual data for 1982/83. Employer types include business (3 categories), manufacturing/industrial (12 categories), and nonprofit/educational institutions.]

1. Number of hires and percentage change by curricular groupings and degree levels. (p. 2)

2. Number of hires by curricular group and type of employer [cross-tabulated by degree level]. (p. 3)

3. Number of hires and number of interview schedules and campuses scheduled for recruiting visits [and number of employers, all by type of employer]. (p. 6)

4. Public sector: number of hires and percentage change [by degree level and type of Federal Government career entry level position, FY83-84]. (p. 7)

A3940-4   INFLATION AND THE COLLEGE GRADUATE
Quinquennial, with annual supplements.   For individual bibliographic data, see below.
LC 82-119504.
SRI/MF/complete

Quinquennial report, with annual supplements, on average actual and inflation-adjusted salary offers to new college graduates in selected fields, for current recruiting year and trends. Covers detailed business, science, and engineering fields for bachelor's and master's degree candidates, and humanities and other social sciences for bachelor's candidates. Also includes CPI trends.

Data are from College Placement Council's *Salary Survey* reports, covered in SRI under A3940-1 and A3940-2. Inflation adjustments are based on CPI changes.

Annual supplements update all tables in the quinquennial report. Most recent supplement is described below.

Availability: College Placement Council, 62 Highland Ave., Bethlehem PA 18017, $15.00 (for base report and annual updates through 1985); SRI/MF/complete.

A3940-4.4: Inflation and the College Graduate, 1982-83 Update

[Annual. [1984.] 4 p. SRI/MF/complete.]

Contains 1 extended table showing data for recruiting year 1982/83.

A4175
Copper
Development Association

A4175-1   ANNUAL DATA, 1984: Copper, Brass, Bronze; Copper Supply and Consumption, 1963-83
Annual. [1984.] 20 p.
SRI/MF/complete

Annual report on supply and consumption of copper and copper alloys in the U.S., 1963-83. Includes the following data:

a. Production, for copper mines by State, smelters, and refined copper; stocks and/or foreign trade, for ore, blister and refined copper, and scrap; and copper recovery from scrap.

b. Consumption of refined copper, scrap, metals, and alloying metals; and product supply, consumption by end use market, and foreign trade; shown variously for brass mills, wire rod mills, foundries, powder plants, and aggregate other industries.

Also includes data on copper mine production and brass mill product supply, by foreign country.

Data are from Bureau of Mines, Commerce Dept, American Bureau of Metal Statistics, and other sources, identified in each table.

Contains preface, table listing, and 1 schematic chart on the flow of copper in the U.S. economy (p. 1-5); and 24 tables, arranged in 4 groups (p. 6-20).

Availability: Copper Development Association, Greenwich Office Park 2, Box 1840, Greenwich CT 06836-1840, †; SRI/MF/complete.

A4325
Council for
Financial Aid to Education

A4325-1   CORPORATE SUPPORT OF HIGHER EDUCATION, 1982
Annual. Jan. 1984. 1+21 p.
ISSN 0270-4501.
LC 80-644000.
SRI/MF/complete

Annual report on corporate contributions to higher education, 1982 and trends. Includes data by industry and marketing area, and comparisons to total corporate contributions, education contributions from all sources, and corporate earnings and assets.

Most data are based on responses of 534 corporations to a CFAE survey.

Contains contents listing and highlights (p. 1); report, with narrative analysis, 3 charts, and 14 tables listed below (p. 2-18); and appendix with data notes (p. 19-20).

Availability: Council for Financial Aid to Education, 680 Fifth Ave., Suite 800C, New York NY 10019, $6.00 (prepaid); SRI/MF/complete.

TABLES:
[Data are for 1982, unless otherwise noted. Tables V-VII, IX-X, and XIV show data by major industry group.]

I. National trends in corporate pretax net income and [total and education] contributions [1967-82]. (p. 2)

II. Corporate support of colleges/universities in relation to total voluntary support and institutional expenditures [1966/67-1982/83]. (p. 4)

III. Distribution [and amount] of corporate contributions [to education, health/human services, culture/art, civic activities, and other, 1980-82]. (p. 5)

IV. Structure of corporate contributions [to company foundations and others, and from company foundations; and number of companies with foundations; 1974-82]. (p. 5)

V-VII. Percentage of reporting companies with corporate foundations; foundation cash flow [payments in, earnings, and grants made]; and changes in market value of corporate foundation assets. (p. 6-8)

VIII. Total contributions and support of education in relation to worldwide and U.S. only pretax net income and assets [1977-82]. (p. 9)

IX. Support of education, 2 survey years (442 companies participating in both surveys) [1981-82]. (p. 10)

X. Total contributions and support of education in relation to worldwide pretax net income and assets. (p. 12-13)

XI. Contributions by manufacturing companies, by size of worldwide pretax net income and assets. (p. 14)

XII. Support of education, [total contributions, and worldwide pretax net income, by 21] major marketing areas. (p. 15)

XIII. Support of education by purpose [1980 and 1982]. (p. 17)

XIV. Percentage distribution of purposes of educational support. (p. 18)

A4325-2   VOLUNTARY SUPPORT OF EDUCATION, 1982/83
Annual. May 1984.
73 p. Oversized.
ISSN 0363-3683.
LC 81-641373.
SRI/MF/complete

Annual survey report on voluntary support to educational institutions, 1982/83, with comparisons to 1981/82 and selected summary trends from as early as 1949/50. Covers amounts of voluntary support by source, purpose, and form of giving; and enrollments, total expenditures, and endowment market value; all by institution.

Sources of voluntary support include alumni, nonalumni individuals, foundations, corporations/businesses, religious denominations, and other, with detail for corporation matching gift giving and gifts-in-kind. Forms of giving include bequests and annuities/life contracts/insurance. Also includes detail for levels of annual fund support, including number of alumni on record and solicited, and number of donors.

Purposes shown are current operations and capital purposes, with summary detail by institution type for unrestricted, physical plant, research, student aid, faculty compensation, and other purposes.

Types of institutions covered are private universities and men's, women's, and coeducational colleges; professional/specialized schools; public 4-year institutions; public and private 2-year institutions; and private secondary/elementary schools.

Also includes comparisons to CPI and Higher Education Price Index; alumni solicitation effectiveness rate and average gift, by higher education institution type; and rankings for top 10 private elementary/secondary schools and top 20 colleges/universities, based on 2-5 measures of voluntary support.

Data are primarily based on responses from 1,617 institutions, 1982/83, and previous surveys. Enrollment data not directly supplied by the institutions are from NCES. Voluntary support data do not include income from endowments and investments or aid from government agencies.

Contains contents listing and preface, with 1 table on survey sample (p. 1-2); report, with 18 tables (p. 3-67); and appendix, with 6 tables (p. 68-72, and inside back cover).

This is the 24th edition.

Availability: Council for Financial Aid to Education, 680 Fifth Ave., Suite 800C, New York NY 10019, $20.00; SRI/MF/complete.

A4325-3   PROFILE OF CORPORATE CONTRIBUTIONS
Monograph. Apr. 1983.
46 p.
SRI/MF/complete

By Hayden W. Smith. Report on corporate charitable contributions, primarily 1970 and 1977, with trends from as early as 1936 and summary data through 1981.

Covers value of corporate contributions, with detailed comparisons to corporate profits, receipts, assets, and net income; and number of total and contributing corporations; variously shown by asset and contribution size, contributions as percent of net income, and industry division and manufacturing group, with some detail for corporations taxed as partnerships and corporations reporting net income and losses.

Also includes data on contributions from bequests, foundations, and individuals filing itemized and non-itemized tax returns.

Most data are from IRS records.

Contents:

a. Highlights (inside front cover); contents listing, foreword, and introduction (p. 1-6); and report, with 4 charts and 16 tables. (p. 7-23)

b. Appendices, including discussion of IRS data collection and quality, with 1 table; and reprint of a similar 1977 report, with 11 tables. (p. 24-46)

Availability: Council for Financial Aid to Education, 680 Fifth Ave., Suite 800C, New York NY 10019, $10.00 (prepaid); SRI/MF/complete.

A4375
Council of
State Governments

A4375–1   BOOK OF THE STATES, 1984-85
Biennial.   Apr. 1984.
x+545 p.   Vol. 25.
ISBN 0-87292-049-6.
LC 35-11433.
SRI/MF/complete

Biennial source book, for 1984-85, providing detailed comparisons of State government structures, finances, and activities for the 50 States, D.C., and U.S. territories. Includes intergovernmental relations, public services, and governmental developments.

Data are primarily for 1982-84, with selected historical trends from the 1950s or earlier. Most data are compiled from State and Federal sources.

Contents:

Contents and table listings, and foreword. (p. iv-x)

Section I-VIII. 57 topical reports on intergovernmental affairs, governors/executive branch, legislatures, judiciary, constitutions, legislation, elections, administration, finance, and services. Most reports have supporting tables. Reports with statistical data, as well as other tabular information such as laws, provisions, and rates, are described below. (p. 1-505)

Section IX. Tabular listings of historical data and selected government officials, by State/territory; and 1 table (p. 510-511) showing the following for each State, territory, and for Federated States of Micronesia, Marshall Islands, Northern Mariana Islands, and Belau: population of entire State/territory and of capital and largest city, and land area, density, and number of representatives in Congress, 1980. (p. 506-540)

Indexes. (p. 541-545)

This is the 25th edition of the report. For description of 24th edition, see SRI 1982 Annual, under this number.

Availability: Council of State Governments, Publications, Iron Works Pike, PO Box 11910, Lexington KY 40578, $42.50; SRI/MF/complete.

REPORTS:
[Data are generally shown by State and territory. Most data are current as of 1983; exceptions and trends are noted.]

A4375–1.1: Section I. Intergovernmental Affairs

Interstate Organizations
INTERSTATE COMPACTS

(p. 11-14) Includes 1 undated table showing interstate compact participation, by pact.

Intergovernmental Relations
FEDERAL-STATE RELATIONS

(p. 18-20) By Jane F. Roberts. Includes 1 table showing Federal aid to States, FY78-82.

GENERAL REVENUE SHARING

(p. 24-29) By Kent A. Peterson. Includes 3 tables showing Federal revenue sharing payments to State and local governments, by entitlement period, 1972-83.

STATE AID TO LOCAL GOVERNMENT

(p. 30-37) By Maurice Criz. Report on State intergovernmental expenditure and program administration, FY82. Includes 7 tables showing the following:

a. Direct aid to local governments as percent of State general expenditure, selected years FY64-82; and State receipts from Federal Government FY82, and payments to Federal and local governments in selected years FY42-82, generally by function.

b. State intergovernmental expenditures: total and per capita, biennially 1976-82, with detail by function and type of receiving government, 1982.

A4375–1.2: Section II. Governors and the Executive Branch

EXECUTIVE BRANCH: ELECTIVE OFFICIALS AND ORGANIZATION

(p. 44-46) By Thad L. Beyle. Includes 1 table showing number of separately elected State officials by office, 1965 and 1984.

EXECUTIVE BRANCH: ISSUES

(p. 47-77) By Thad L. Beyle. Report on executive branch functions and authority, and major structural changes occurring during 1981-83. Includes 18 tables showing the following:

a. Governors' political party, term, qualification requirements, salary and benefits, support staff, legislated powers, and transition provisions.

b. Qualification requirements, duties, salaries, selection methods, and other provisions, for other State officials.

A4375–1.3: Section III. Legislatures
STATE LEGISLATURES

(p. 79-140) By William T. Pound. Includes 28 tables showing the following:

a. Legislative bodies and convening places; number of legislators, length of term, party affiliation, and qualification requirements; legislative leadership positions and method of selection; and compensation, benefits, and membership turnover in 1982 elections.

b. Number of sessions, bills and resolutions introduced and enacted, and governor

vetoes, 1981-82; and legislative procedures, number of standing committees during 1983 session, and appropriations process.

c. Legislator support staff; content and distribution of fiscal notes; legislative regulatory powers; State agency sunset legislation; data processing systems use; and lobbyist registration procedure and definition.

A4375–1.4: Section IV. Judiciary
STATE OF THE JUDICIARY

(p. 142-163) By Daina Farthing-Capowich. Includes 7 tables showing appellate and major trial court judges, salaries, qualification requirements, and selection and removal methods; and court administrative officer salaries.

A4375–1.5: Section V. Legislation, Elections, and Constitutions

Legislation
TRENDS IN STATE LEGISLATION: 1982-83

(p. 165-172) By Elaine Stuart Knapp. Includes 5 tables showing legislative initiative provisions and referendum procedures, provisions for recall of State officials, legal age for specified activities, and types of legalized gaming.

UNIFORM STATE LAWS

(p. 173-179) By John M. McCabe. Description of 11 uniform and model acts drafted by National Conference of Commissioners on Uniform State Laws. Includes 1 table showing State legislative action on uniform acts.

Elections and Constitutions
ELECTION LEGISLATION

(p. 180-210) By Richard G. Smolka. Includes 12 tables showing the following:

a. Campaign finance laws, public funding of State elections, voter registration regulations, polling hours, State officers to be elected in 1984-85, nomination methods, and dates and purpose of primaries.

b. Registered voters, voting age population, and turnout, biennially 1972-82; and Republican and Democratic votes cast in gubernatorial elections, mostly 1982.

STATE CONSTITUTIONS: 1982-83

(p. 211-213) By Albert L. Sturm and Janice C. May. Includes 1 table showing State constitutional changes proposed and adopted, by method of initiation, 1970/71, 1980/81, and 1982/83.

STATE CONSTITUTIONAL CHANGES

(p. 214-217) By Albert L. Sturm and Janice C. May. Includes 1 table showing substantive State constitutional changes proposed and adopted, by subject area, 1970/71, 1980/81, and 1982/83.

SOURCES ON STATE CONSTITUTIONS

(p. 218-229) By Albert L. Sturm and Janice C. May. Includes 6 tables showing State constitution history including number of amendments proposed and adopted, and methods of revision.

A4375–1.6: Section VI. Administration

Administrative Activities

STATE FINANCIAL ADMINISTRATION

(p. 231-240) By Kay T. Pohlmann. Includes 3 tables showing State cash management policies, and accounting, reporting, and auditing procedures.

BUDGETING IN THE 1980s

(p. 242-249) By Robert P. Kerker. Includes 3 tables showing budgetary practices and State financial organization.

STATE INFORMATION MANAGEMENT

(p. 253-260) By Lorraine Amico. Includes 4 tables showing State statistical activities, number of States performing top 15 statistical functions, and types of official State projections available.

STATE INFORMATION SYSTEMS

(p. 261-264) By Carl W. Vorlander. Covers growth of governmental computer use. Includes 3 tables showing information system external and internal problems, 1979-83; and security measures used.

STATE LIBRARY AGENCIES

(p. 265-269) By Lester L. Stoffel. Includes 2 tables showing State library agency structure and appropriations FY84, and functions.

Employment

STATE GOVERNMENT EMPLOYMENT

(p. 271-278) By Alan V. Stevens. Includes 10 tables showing Federal, State, and local government employment and payroll, 1970, 1980, and 1982; State and local government employment and payroll, by function, various years 1970-82; and State education and total employment, payroll, and average earnings, 1952-82.

FINANCES OF STATE-ADMINISTERED PUBLIC EMPLOYEE RETIREMENT SYSTEMS

(p. 279-287) By Maurice Criz. Includes 6 tables showing number, membership, benefits, and finances, for State-administered employee retirement systems, various years 1962-82.

DEVELOPMENTS IN STATE PERSONNEL SYSTEMS

(p. 288-297) By Keon S. Chi. Includes 4 tables showing State personnel system organization and collective bargaining policies; State employee compensation provisions and selected benefits, including paid holidays; and use of employee evaluation systems.

A4375–1.7: Section VII. Finances

Revenue, Expenditure, and Debt

STATE AND LOCAL GOVERNMENT FINANCES IN 1981-82

(p. 299-313) By Maurice Criz. Includes 9 tables showing State/local government indebtedness, and revenues and expenditures per $1,000 personal income; and Federal, State, and local government total and per capita revenues by source and expenditures by function; FY82, with State and local revenue and expenditure trends from FY78.

STATE FINANCES IN 1982

(p. 314-326) By Maurice Criz. Includes 6 tables showing State revenues by source, expenditures by function and object, and outstanding debt, FY82 with summary trends from FY60.

Taxation

RECENT TRENDS IN STATE TAXATION

(p. 327-339) By John Gambill. Covers State legislation on sales, income, fuel, and excise taxes, 1982-83. Includes 6 tables showing tax-administering agencies, tax rates, and exemptions, as of Jan. 1, 1984.

STATE TAX COLLECTIONS IN 1983

(p. 341-352) By Maurice Criz. Includes 7 tables showing State tax revenues by tax type, 1983 with summary comparisons to 1981-82 and trends from 1957; population, 1982-83; personal income, 1982; and State portion of State/local tax revenue, FY82.

A4375–1.8: Section VIII. Major State Services

Education

POSTSECONDARY EDUCATION

(p. 359-375) By Nancy M. Berve and Gordon Van de Water. Includes 14 tables showing the following:

a. State support and enrollment for elementary/secondary and higher education; elementary/secondary education revenues by source; teachers and average salaries; course requirements for high school graduation; and competency testing use; mostly 1980/81 and 1982/83.

b. Higher education: public and private enrollment, institutions, and faculty salaries by academic rank; State appropriations for operating expenses; State financial aid to students; and institutions with occupational programs by institution type; various periods 1973/74-1983/84.

Transportation

TRANSPORTATION IN THE 1980s

(p. 376-389) Includes 8 tables showing rural and urban road/street mileage, and State highway receipts and disbursements, 1982; Federal highway aid apportionment, FY83; motor vehicle license and insurance laws; and motor vehicle registrations, licenses, and fees, 1982.

Health and Human Services

FOOD STAMPS, MEDICAID, SOCIAL SERVICES, AND AGING

(p. 392-402) Includes 7 tables showing recipients and payments for AFDC and food stamp programs, and SSI total, aged, blind, and disabled programs, 1982 or 1983; Medicaid expenditures, FY81; AFDC and non-AFDC child support enforcement collections, expenditures, and caseload, FY82; and Federal social services allotments to States under Social Security Act, FY81-84.

STATE HEALTH AGENCY PROGRAMS

(p. 403-413) By Jeffrey L. Lake and James T. Dimas. Includes 4 tables showing health agency responsibilities; and public health expenditures, sources of funds, and persons served, by program area; FY82.

Safety and Public Protection

CORRECTIONS, COURTS, AND CRIMINAL JUSTICE

(p. 415-419) By Edward D. Feigenbaum. Includes 2 tables showing method of execution, and women and total persons on death row, as of Dec. 1983; and prison population, 1980-81.

STATE REGULATION OF OCCUPATIONS AND PROFESSIONS

(p. 420-423) By Frances Stokes Berry and R. Douglas Roederer. Description of licensure boards and their authority over selected occupations, including 1 table showing occupations for which mandatory continuing education is a condition for relicensing, as of Feb. 1984.

STATE POLICE AND HIGHWAY PATROLS

(p. 424-426) By R. H. Sostkowski. Includes 1 table showing sworn and civilian law enforcement employees, by sex, 1982.

DEVELOPMENTS IN PUBLIC UTILITIES REGULATION

(p. 427-432) By James E. Suelflow. Includes 3 tables showing public utility commission employment, commissioners and term length, and regulatory functions; and average electric and gas bills, by consuming sector, 1981.

Development and Housing

HOUSING AND COMMUNITY DEVELOPMENT

(p. 436-439) By Carol H. Hartwell. Includes 1 table showing State housing finance agency bond issues, and cumulative loans by type.

BUSINESS AND INDUSTRIAL DEVELOPMENT

(p. 440-448) Includes 3 tables showing types of industry financial assistance available, tax incentives, and special services provided.

Natural Resources

ENVIRONMENTAL MANAGEMENT: EMERGING ISSUES

(p. 450-457) By Jon Grand. Includes 3 tables showing State environmental agencies; regulations for hazardous waste facility siting; and number of waste disposal impoundments, and sites on EPA priority list.

STATE PARKS AND OUTDOOR RECREATION

(p. 458-461) By John Karel. Includes 1 table showing State parks, acreage, attendance, income generated, and operating and capital outlay budgets, FY83.

STATE AGRICULTURE

(p. 463-471) By Edward H. Glade, Jr. and Mae Dean Johnson. Includes 7 tables showing cash receipts from livestock, crops, and government payments; farm income and production cost; farms, acreage, and value; production by crop type; livestock and poultry inventory; and total and foreign privately owned agricultural acreage; 1982.

STATE FORESTRY ADMINISTRATION AND MANAGEMENT

(p. 472-481) By Leslie Cole. Includes 7 tables showing the following:

a. Forest acreage by type of ownership, 1982; average annual forest fires and acreage burned, 1978-82 period; and Federal and State expenditures, and acreage covered, for fire prevention and forest development programs, 1982 or FY83.

b. Insect/disease management expenditures, State forestry personnel, and State nursery program seedlings produced and acreage, FY83; State forest administration agencies; and taxes applied to forest lands, 1982.

SOIL AND WATER CONSERVATION

(p. 482-487) By Neil Sampson and Eugene Lamb. Includes 4 tables showing State and local funding for soil conservation programs, selected years 1957-83; soil and water conservation program provisions; and conservation districts, farms and acreage covered, and employees.

Labor Relations

LABOR LEGISLATION: 1982-83

(p. 488-505) By Richard R. Nelson. Includes 7 tables showing the following:

a. Workers compensation benefits available and payments, various periods 1980-83; status of State occupational safety and health act plans, and child labor standards, as of Dec. 1983; and nonfarm minimum wage rates, selected years 1965-84.

b. Unemployment insurance claims, beneficiaries, average duration, payments, and available funds, and employers covered and contribution rate, 1982; and unemployment and rate, 1976-81.

A4375–6   STATE TREASURY ACTIVITIES AND FUNCTIONS

Monograph. 1983. iv+68 p.
C-18.
ISBN 0-87292-043-7.
SRI/MF/complete

Report on operations of State treasurers' offices in 46 States and Puerto Rico, 1982. Covers organization, functions, investment and cash management policies and practices, and other activities.

Includes statistics on employment and salaries; budget; percent of State funds under treasurer's jurisdiction; portfolio composition by maturity and type of instrument; number of banks and/or savings and loan assns holding time and demand deposits; rate of return on investments; and volume of checks/warrants and electronic funds transfers.

Data are from a fall 1982 survey conducted by the Council of State Governments.

Contains contents and table listings (p. iii); introduction (p. 1); 6 report sections, with 39 tables and accompanying notes (p. 2-63); and appendices, with survey questions and directory of State treasurers' offices (p. 64-68).

Availability: Council of State Governments, Publications, Iron Works Pike, PO Box 11910, Lexington KY 40578, $10.00; SRI/MF/complete.

A4375–7   COMPARATIVE DATA REPORT SERIES I

Series. For individual publication data, see below.
SRI/MF/complete

Continuing series of reports on topics related to State government management. Reports are intended to aid in decisionmaking processes among State legislators and other government officials.

SRI coverage of this series begins with the reports described below.

Availability: Council of State Governments, Publications, Iron Works Pike, PO Box 11910, Lexington KY 40578; SRI/MF/complete.

A4375–7.1: State Revenues: Eastern Region

[Monograph. 1983. 2+35 p. Rpt. C-14. $7.50. SRI/MF/complete.]

Report on State and local government tax revenues, for 10 eastern States, 1981-82, with selected trends from 1977. Also includes data on government expenditures, population, and personal income.

Includes the following data, for 10 eastern States:

a. Population, 1980; personal income, 1981; State excise tax rate and enactment date for sales/gross receipt and cigarette and motor fuel taxes, and State tax revenue by type of tax, 1982; and total State tax revenue, 1980-82.

b. State and local general tax revenue, with detail for sales, property, and income taxes; State general revenue by level of government and tax revenue by type of tax, total amount and/or per capita and per $1,000 of personal income; and State expenditures per $1,000 of personal income, with detail for education, higher education, public welfare, and highways; 1981 with some comparisons to 1980.

c. State/local: tax revenue per capita and per $1,000 of personal income, and revenue from property, sales, and income taxes; and general revenue from own sources and own/Federal sources; 1977-81.

Data are primarily from Commerce Dept.

Contains foreword and contents listing (2 p.); introduction and narrative report in 4 sections, interspersed with 5 charts and 27 tables (p. 1-33); and conclusion (p. 34-35).

A4375–7.2: State Revenues: Midwestern Region

[Monograph. 1983. 2+32 p. Rpt. C-15. $7.50. SRI/MF/complete.]

Report on State and local government tax revenues, for 12 midwestern States, 1981-82, with selected trends from 1977. Also includes data on government expenditures, population, and personal income.

Data content and periods of coverage are the same as those in the report on eastern States (for description see A4375-7.1, above).

Contains foreword and contents listing (2 p.); introduction and narrative report in 4 sections, interspersed with 5 charts and 27 tables (p. 1-31); and conclusion (p. 32).

A4375–7.3: State Revenues: Western Region

[Monograph. 1983. 2+36 p. Rpt. C-16. $7.50. SRI/MF/complete.]

Report on State and local government tax revenues, for 13 western States, 1981-82, with selected trends from 1977. Also includes data on government expenditures, population, and personal income.

Data content and periods of coverage are the same as those in the report on eastern States (for description see A4375-7.1, above).

Contains foreword and contents listing (2 p.); introduction and narrative report in 4 sections, interspersed with 6 charts and 28 tables (p. 1-34); and conclusion (p. 34-36).

A4425
Council of the
Great City Schools

A4425–1   STATISTICAL PROFILES OF THE GREAT CITY SCHOOLS, 1970-82

Biennial. 1983. 3+54 p.
SRI/MF/complete

Biennial report on public elementary/secondary school enrollment, staff, and finances in 32 major city school systems, various years 1970/71-1982/83.

Includes public school enrollment by race/ethnicity (including Hispanic, Asian, and total minority); students with limited English proficiency and in special education; school board size and organization; number of days with teachers on duty; number of schools; professional staff by position; and school system revenue by level of government, with detail for Federal programs including school lunch/milk program.

Also includes land area, population (with detail for blacks and Hispanics), school-age children below poverty level, private school enrollment, municipal and school bond ratings, and selected comparisons to total U.S.

Contains listings of contents, tables, and charts (3 p.); 4 statistical sections, with 18 charts and 18 tables (p. 1-45); and educational program section, with listings of desegregation activities, educational testing score summary, and graduation requirements (p. 46-54).

This is the 1st biennial report.

Availability: Council of the Great City Schools, 1413 K St., NW, 4th Floor, Washington DC 20005, members †, nonmembers $10.00; SRI/MF/complete.

A4530
CPC Foundation

A4530–2   CAREER PLANNING AND PLACEMENT OFFICE: IMPLICATIONS FOR THE FUTURE

Monograph. 1983. 3+74 p.
ISBN 0-914885-04-9.
SRI/MF/complete

By Gary J. Scott. Report on the organization and activities of career planning/placement offices in colleges, 1981. Includes data on types of services offered at public and private institutions, by enrollment size; other campus offices offering planning/placement services; and planning/placement office research activity, mission in 1981 compared to 1975, reporting structure, and 1980-81 budget trend.

Also includes views of planning/placement administrators and/or other campus officials on viability of planning/placement, most important activities, problems, appropriateness of various services, and budget priority relative to other programs.

Data are based on survey responses of 711 college placement directors, 182 college presidents, 257 chief academic officers, and 324 chief student affairs officers.

Contains preface and contents listing (3 p.); 8 narrative sections, with 1 table (p. 1-49); appendices with 17 tables and interspersed narrative (p. 50-69); and bibliography (p. 70-74).

Availability: CPC Foundation, 62 Highland Ave., Bethlehem PA 18017, $8.95; SRI/MF/ complete.

A4575
Credit Union
National Association

A4575–1   CREDIT UNION REPORT, 1983
Annual. [1984.]
7 p. no paging.
SRI/MF/complete

Annual report on credit union finances and operations, 1983 and trends. Includes selected data by State and for Puerto Rico. Covers the following:

a. Total credit unions, membership, and value of shares/deposits, loans outstanding, reserves, and assets, selected years 1935-83; credit union distribution, types of services offered, operating ratios, and employment, all by asset size, 1983; and credit union distribution by common bond (association, occupation by industry division, and residential), 1983.

b. Data by State: credit unions by type of charter (State or Federal), membership and ratio to population, and value of savings, loans, reserves, assets, share drafts, real estate loans, individual retirement acounts, and money market accounts, 1983.

c. State and federally insured credit unions, and value of insured savings, Dec. 1983; credit union share composition (regular, certificates, drafts) and average dividend on savings, by quarter, 4th quarter 1980-83; credit union installment loans, auto loans, and savings, compared to other types of institutions, Dec. 1982-83; and interest rates for personal and auto loans, by credit union asset size, Dec. 1980-83.

Contains brief narrative, 15 tables, and directory of credit union leagues.

Availability: Credit Union National Association, PO Box 431, Madison WI 53701, †; SRI/ MF/complete.

A4650
Distilled Spirits
Council of the U.S.

A4650–1   ANNUAL STATISTICAL REVIEW, 1983/84, Distilled Spirits Industry
Annual. Aug. 1984.
vi+62 p.
ISSN 0066-4367.
LC 54-17193.
SRI/MF/complete

Annual report on the production and distribution operations of the distilled spirits industry, 1983. Also includes data on public revenues, retail prices, and operations in license and control States, with selected historical data from 1933.

Data are from Bureau of Alcohol, Tobacco and Firearms; Census Bureau; Internal Revenue Service; and other Federal, State, and local government and industry sources.

Contains preface, foreword, and contents listing (p. iii-vi); 55 tables, listed below, with brief summaries and 14 accompanying maps and charts (p. 1-57); and glossary and bibliography (p. 58-62).

This is the 44th annual report.

Availability: Distilled Spirits Council of the U.S., Economics and Statistics Division, 1250 Eye St., NW, Washington DC 20005, †; SRI/ MF/complete.

TABLES:
[Classes of distilled spirits include whiskey, brandy, rum, gin, vodka, and others. Trends from the 1930s to the 1960s generally are shown for selected years; other trends are shown annually.]

A4650–1.1:   Distillation,   Shipments, Stocks, and Withdrawals
DISTILLATION AND SHIPMENTS

1-2. Distillation of whiskey, brandy, and rum, 1934-83; and by month, 1982-83. (p. 3-4)

3. Direct distillation (partial production) of gin and vodka, 1934-83. (p. 4)

4-5. Whiskey distillation, by [selected] State, 1982-83, and by month, 1972-83. (p. 5)

6-7. Grain/grain products used by the distilled spirits industry: by type of grain, [monthly] 1983; and selected years 1946-83. (p. 6)

8. Production of distillers' dried grains, 1946-83. (p. 7)

9. Shipments of whiskey barrels in the U.S., [annually] 1933-83. (p. 7)

10. Fruit/fruit products used by the distilled spirits industry, 1955-83. (p. 7)

STOCKS AND WITHDRAWALS

11-12. Stocks of distilled spirits at distilleries, by class, year end 1934-83; and apparent whiskey stocks, distillation, and usage; 1935-83. (p. 9)

13-14. Stocks of distilled spirits in bonded storage at distilleries, by class, month end; and whiskey stocks in bonded storage, year end, by [selected] State, 1982-83. (p. 10)

15-16. Taxable withdrawals from bonded premises at $10.50 per [proof] gallon [by month]; and tax-free withdrawals of distilled spirits, by usage, 1982-83. (p. 11)

A4650–1.2: Bottling, Sales, and Shipments
BOTTLING
[Tables 17-21 begin "Bottling of..."]

17-18. Distilled spirits: by class, 1940-83; and by class [and month], 1982-83. (p. 13-14)

19-20. Whiskey and other distilled spirits, by [selected] State, 1983; and whiskey by type, 1939-83. (p. 15)

21. Distilled spirits, by class and type, 1982-83. (p. 17)

SALES AND SHIPMENTS

22-23. Sales of distilled spirits [gallons] and percentage distribution: retail sales in control States, and supplier shipments in license States (shipments by distillers/rectifiers/bottlers/importers), by class and type, 1983. (p. 18-21)

24-25. Estimated distilled spirits [domestic and imported] entering U.S. trade channels, including bottled exports: by class and type, 1974-83; and [for] domestic and foreign bottling, by class and type, 1982-83. (p. 22-24)

26-27. Red and green strip stamps used by the distilled spirits industry, by bottle size; and distilled spirits volume represented by strip stamps, by bottle size and stamp color; FY74-83. (p. 25-26)

A4650–1.3: Foreign Trade

28. U.S. commercial exports of distilled spirits [by class], 1934-83. (p. 27)

29. U.S. commercial exports of [whiskey and other] distilled spirits, by [country of] destination, 1982-83. (p. 28)

30-31. U.S. shipments of distilled spirits to Puerto Rico and U.S. Virgin Islands: [by class and container type], 1982-83; and by class, 1974-83. (p. 30)

32-34. U.S. dutiable imports of distilled spirits for consumption, by class: 1934-83; and by country of origin, and bottled and bulk, 1982-83. (p. 31-36)

35. Shipments of [rum and other] distilled spirits to U.S. from Puerto Rico and U.S. Virgin Islands, 1935-83. (p. 37)

A4650–1.4: Apparent Consumption, and Public Revenues
APPARENT CONSUMPTION

36. Apparent consumption of distilled spirits: in license and control States [includes wine and per capita gallons; number of States allowing sale of distilled spirits, 1934-83; and aggregate resident and adult population and per capita consumption, 1969-83]. (p. 38)

37-39. Apparent consumption of distilled spirits: by month, 1982-83; by State, 1974-83; and by State, total and per capita, 1982-83. (p. 39-41)

40-41. Adult per capita consumption of distilled spirits, wine, and beer, by State; and apparent consumption of distilled spirits, wine, and beer, by State, total and per capita; 1983. (p. 42-43)

PUBLIC REVENUES

42. Public revenues from distilled spirits of Federal, State, and local governments, 1961-83. (p. 45)

43. U.S. Federal tax collections from distilled spirits, by tax class, 1982-83. (p. 45)

44. Federal and license State excise taxes on distilled spirits [for 31 States and D.C.], 1933-84. (p. 46)

45. Import duties on distilled spirits [by class and type], 1958-84. (p. 48)

A4650–1.5: Miscellaneous
ECONOMIC DATA

46. Value added per employee-hour, distilled spirits and all manufacturing, [and] supplier price [index] and CPI, 1967-83. (p. 49)

47. Retail prices of selected brands of distilled spirits inclusive of statewide sales tax, [and tax rate, by] license and control States, 1st quarter 1984. (p. 51)

48. Estimated U.S. retail expenditures on alcohol beverages by type, 1949-83. (p. 52)

49. Alcohol beverage expenditures for personal and business consumption, 1959-83. (p. 53)

50. Percentage of on- and off-premise spirit sales in control States, [by State], 1982-83. (p. 53)

STATE AND LOCAL CONTROLS

[Unless otherwise noted, tables show data by State, 1983. Tables 53-54 arrange data for license and control States.]

51. Wet and dry population for consumption of distilled spirits. (p. 54)

52. Legal age to purchase distilled spirits; and number of counties or other political subdivisions permitting and prohibiting sale. (p. 55)

53. Number of retail outlets/licenses issued for the sale of distilled spirits; number of outlets/licenses per 1,000 population; and number of persons per outlet/license; [all for on- and off-premise]. (p. 56)

54. Legal minimum age for purchases of distilled spirits, Jan. 1984; and legal age population, [as of] July 1983. (p. 57)

55. Summary of local option changes [wet and dry status changes, and counties gained for legal sales, for 5 States]. (p. 57)

A4650–2   1982/83 PUBLIC REVENUES FROM ALCOHOL BEVERAGES

Annual.   Apr. 1984.
viii+86 p.
ISSN 0148-0863.
LC 77-642153.
SRI/MF/complete

Annual report on Federal, State, and local revenues from the sale, taxation, or regulation of alcoholic beverages, by State, beverage type, and revenue source, 1982, with comparisons to 1981 and selected trends from 1933. Includes data on tax rates, import duties by world area of origin, and State alcoholic beverage revenue share of total tax revenues.

Also includes alcoholic beverage consumption, by State; Federal excise tax revenue collections, and tax rates as percent of sales value, by type of commodity or service; and list of State exemptions from excise taxes on alcoholic beverages.

Data are from State and local alcoholic beverage regulatory units, and other sources.

Contains preface, foreword, and contents listing (p. iii-viii); Parts I-III, with brief narrative summaries, 12 charts, and 21 tables (p. 1-33); and Part IV, with introductory summary and chart, and individual State profiles each with 1 table and accompanying text (p. 35-86).

Availability: Distilled Spirits Council of the U.S., Economics and Statistics Division, 1250 Eye St., NW, Washington DC 20005, †; SRI/MF/complete.

A4700
Edison Electric Institute

A4700–1   STATISTICAL YEARBOOK OF THE ELECTRIC UTILITY INDUSTRY, 1982

Annual.   Oct. 1983.
v+97 p.+errata sheet.
No. 50.
ISSN 0361-3607.
LC 82-641051.
SRI/MF/complete, delayed

Annual report presenting electric utility industry financial and operating data, 1982 with selected trends from 1962. Most data are shown by State and census division for total and investor-owned electric utilities.

Covers electricity production and capacity by type of prime mover and fuel; fossil fuel consumption and cost for electric generation; customers, sales, revenues, and average bills, by consuming sector; investor-owned electric utility construction and other expenditures, assets, liabilities, and employment; and overhead electric line circuit miles.

Also includes electricity production and capacity of top 15 countries; U.S. exports and weekly output index of electric power; energy supply and disposition, by type of energy; public utility taxes and long-term financing and yield, by financing method; CPI and PPI trends; and industrial electric power cost as percent of product shipment value, by SIC 2-digit industry.

Data are from Energy Information Administration, and various other government and private sources.

Contains contents listing, narrative review, and 1 summary table (p. iii-v, 1-5); 10 statistical sections, with 15 charts and 90 tables (p. 6-94); and index and 2 maps (p. 95-97).

Availability: Edison Electric Institute, Publishing Department, 1111 19th St., NW, Washington DC 20036-3691, $27.50, members 20% discount; SRI/MF/complete, delayed shipment when next edition is published.

A4700–2   1983 ELECTRIC POWER ANNUAL REPORT

Annual.   [1984.]   42 p.
SRI/MF/complete, delayed

Annual report on electric power industry capacity, requirements, scheduled expansions, and heavy equipment manufacture, 1983, with selected trends, and projections to 1993. Data are shown for contiguous U.S., by regions of the North American Electric Reliability Council (NERC) or by utility ownership.

Data are based on electric power system reports to DOE, NERC reports, and an EEI semiannual survey of electric power equipment manufacturers.

Contains survey contributor and contents listings, map of NERC regions, foreword, and summary (p. 1-5); 3 sections, with 28 tables listed below (p. 6-39); and abstracts of EEI publications (p. 40-42).

Report incorporates data from *Annual Electric Power Survey,* which was discontinued with the 1983 edition (for description, see A4700-3 below).

Prior to 1983, *Electric Power Annual Report* was entitled *Year-End Electric Power Survey.*

Availability: Edison Electric Institute, Publishing Department, 1111 19th St., NW, Washington DC 20036-3691, $10.00, members 20% discount; SRI/MF/complete, delayed shipment until next edition is published.

TABLES:

A4700–2.1: Electric Power Supply

[Tables 1-5 and 10-14 show data by NERC region.]

PERFORMANCE TRENDS

1-2. Summer and winter capabilities, peak loads, and installed and percent capacity margins [1979-1983/84]. (p. 7-8)

3. Summer peak loads expressed as percentage of peak load for the following winter [various years 1968-1983/84]. (p. 9)

4-5. Annual [megawatthour] requirements and load factor [1979-83]. (p. 10)

6A-6B. Changes in scheduled operation date of nuclear and fossil fired steam turbine-generators, 300 megawatts or larger, removed from schedule, and delayed a year or more between, Jan. 1, 1983-Jan. 1, 1984 [by company or system, with location and net expected capability]. (p. 11-12)

7-8. 1983 additions to electric generating capability [includes name and type of unit, type of ownership, net expected capability, and use of fossil fuels, by company or system grouped by NERC region]. (p. 13-16)

9. Nuclear power units in operation in the contiguous U.S. as of Jan. 1, 1984 [summer and winter capability, location, and date placed in commercial operation, by company or system]. (p. 17-18)

PERFORMANCE PROJECTIONS

10-11. [Data in tables 1-2 are repeated for 1984-1993/94.] (p. 20-22)

12. [Data in table 3 are repeated for 1984/85-1993/94.] (p. 23)

13-14. [Data in tables 4-5 are repeated for 1984-93.] (p. 24)

15. Number and aggregate capability of steam turbine-generators in the expansion program, grouped according to size range, as of Jan. 1, 1984. (p. 25)

16-17. Scheduled additions to electric generating capability [to 1998] based on scheduled dates of commercial operation as of Jan. 1, 1984 [repeats data in tables 7-8, and also includes scheduled date of operation]. (p. 26-32)

A4700–2.2: Equipment Manufacture

18. Capacities of [heavy electric power] equipment ordered by U.S. electric power systems from domestic/foreign manufacturers [total by type of equipment, 1979-83]. (p. 33)

19-26. Manufacture of electric generating equipment [1 table repeated for 10 types of equipment including nuclear, showing number and capacity for units shipped and new orders placed, 1983, and for units scheduled for shipment, generally 1984-85/later, for U.S. electric power systems, U.S. industrials, and for exports; some tables also show shipments and orders to foreign manufacturers]. (p. 34-39)

A4700–3   1983 ANNUAL ELECTRIC POWER SURVEY

Annual. [1983.] 42 p.
Rpt. No. 04-82-06.
ISSN 0190-5600.
LC 79-4783.
SRI/MF/complete

Final annual report on electric power industry capacity, requirements, scheduled expansions, and equipment manufacture, presenting latest available data as of Apr. 1, 1983, with trends from 1948 and projections to 1993. Data are for contiguous U.S., and are often shown for regions of the North American Electric Reliability Council (NERC) and by type of source fuel and equipment.

Data are based on electric power system reports to DOE, NERC report *Electric Power Supply and Demand, 1983-92,* and on an EEI Apr. 1983 survey of electric power equipment manufacturers.

Contents:

Map of NERC regions, contents listing, foreword, and definitions. (inside front cover and p. 1-4)

Part I-II. Electric power supply and equipment manufacture, with 5 charts including power supply and demand trends from 1948, and 22 tables listed below. (p. 5-36)

Appendix, with list of electric generating capacity scheduled additions as of Apr. 1, 1983, by power system grouped by NERC region, showing expected net capability, ownership and equipment type, and scheduled operation date. (p. 37-42)

Separate publication of this report has been discontinued with the edition presenting data available as of Apr. 1983. Data have been incorporated in the *Electric Power Annual Report,* covered in SRI under A4700-2.

Availability: Edison Electric Institute, Publishing Department, 1111 19th St., NW, Washington DC 20036-3691, $10.00, members 20% discount; SRI/MF/complete.

TABLES:

A4700–3.1: Electric Power Supply

[Tables I-VII and IX-X show data by NERC region.]

PEAK CAPABILITIES, LOADS, REQUIREMENTS, AND MARGINS

[Data are shown for total industry.]

I-II. Summer and winter capabilities, peak loads, and reserve margins [1981-1992/93]. (p. 6-9)

III. Summer peak loads expressed as percentage of peak load for the following winter [1975-92]. (p. 12)

IV-V. Annual kWh requirements, and annual load factors, [1981-92]. (p. 14-16)

FUEL REQUIREMENTS

VI. Net [kWh] generation by source: fuels [by type, including nuclear] and hydro [1982-92]. (p. 18)

VII. Fossil [coal, oil, and gas] requirements for electric generation in physical units [1982-92]. (p. 20)

GENERATING CAPACITY EXPANSION, AND NUCLEAR UNITS

VIII. Number and aggregate capacity of thermal units in expansion program grouped according to size range as of Apr. 1, 1983, in terms of manufacturers' ratings of the units. (p. 21)

[A] Nuclear and conventional steam turbine-generators, 300 MW [megawatts]/larger, removed from schedule and delayed 1 year or more between Jan. 1 and Apr. 1, 1983 [number and total capacity of units]. (p. 21)

IX-X. Additions to electric generating capacity during 1st 3 months of 1983; and scheduled additions based on scheduled dates of commercial operation as of Apr. 1, 1983, in terms of manufacturers' ratings of the units; [both showing number and capacity of new units, by type of unit and ownership]. (p. 22-23)

XI. Nuclear power units in the contiguous U.S. as of Apr. 1, 1983 [summer and winter capability, location, reactor type, and date placed in commercial operation, by company or system]. (p. 24-25)

A4700–3.2: Equipment Manufacture, and Scheduled Expansions

PRODUCTION SUMMARY

XII. Capacity of new heavy power equipment placed on order with manufacturers during 1982 and 1st 3 months of 1983, and total capacity on order/scheduled for shipment as of Apr. 1, 1983 to U.S. electric power systems [by equipment type]. (p. 26)

PRODUCTION DETAIL

[Tables show number and capacity for units shipped in 1982 and 1st quarter and last 9 months 1983, scheduled for shipment 1983-88/later, and new orders placed 1st quarter 1983; generally for U.S. electric power systems, U.S. industrials, and outside U.S. Some tables also show orders to foreign manufacturers.]

XIII-XVIII. Manufacture of electric generating equipment, steam/hydraulic units; steam turbine-generators [total], conventional, and nuclear; generators for hydraulic turbines; conventional steam generators; hydraulic turbines; and combustion turbine-generators. (p. 27-34)

XIX. Manufacture of power transformers [includes estimated open manufacturing capacity for additional production, 1983-88/later]. (p. 35)

XX. Manufacture of nuclear reactors [shown for U.S. electric power sytems and outside U.S. only]. (p. 36)

A4700–4   ELECTRIC PERSPECTIVES

Quarterly. Approx. 50 p.
ISSN 0364-474X.
LC 80-645213.
SRI/MF/complete

Quarterly publication reporting on business, regulatory, and technological developments concerning electric utilities. Data sources include Edison Electric Institute (EEI) and Federal agencies.

Issues contain feature articles, occasionally statistical; and regular editorial depts, including the following:

a. "Financial Review" section, occasionally statistical, including quarterly data on investor-owned utility finances.

b. "Statistical Review" section, with data on varying topics including utility costs and sales, and residential energy costs.

c. "Regulatory Review" section, including recurring data on rate change actions compiled through surveys by EEI's Rate Regulation Dept.

All features with substantial statistical content are described, as they appear, under "Statistical Features." Nonstatistical features are not described.

Availability: Edison Electric Institute, Electric Perspectives, 1111 19th St., NW, Washington DC 20036-3691, members $22.00 per yr., nonmembers $27.50 per yr.; SRI/MF/complete.

Issues reviewed during 1984: Winter 1983-Summer 1984 (P).

STATISTICAL FEATURES:

A4700–4.501: Winter 1983

REGULATORY PROCESS IN NUCLEAR PROGRAMS

(p. 11-17) By Suzanne R. Phelps. Article on impact of NRC regulations on nuclear power plant construction costs and delays. Data are based on 62 responses to an Aug. 1982 survey of EEI member plants. Includes 1 chart and 2 tables showing average time elapsed between issuance of construction permit and operating license 1970-83, and the following:

a. Initial capital cost (total and per kilowatt); and modification costs imposed by NRC, imposed by NRC following Three Mile Island incident, voluntarily committed by utilities, and anticipated for near future; all by plant, for 41 unnamed plants licensed during 1970-78.

b. Time elapsed between issuance of construction permit and operating license, and total and per kilowatt initial capital cost, estimated at receipt of permit and actual or estimated at licensure, by plant, for 21 unnamed plants licensed during 1980-83.

FINANCIAL REVIEW

In the 2 articles described below, data are national estimates based on unaudited reports from investor-owned electric utilities accounting for approximately 95% of industry assets and revenues.

ELECTRIC UTILITY OPERATING INCOME UP 10.2 PERCENT; EARNINGS PER SHARE UP 6.9 PERCENT, QUARTERLY FEATURE

(p. 29-30) Quarterly article, with 1 table showing investor-owned electric utility income by source, operating expenses by type, net income, stock dividends, and earnings and dividends per share, 3- and 12-month periods ended June 30, 1982-83.

EQUITY INCOME AND SHARES OUTSTANDING INCREASE, QUARTERLY FEATURE

(p. 29, 31) Quarterly article, with 1 table showing investor-owned electric utility assets and liabilities, by type, as of June 30, 1982-83.

Other Article

STATISTICAL REVIEW: REDUCTIONS IN PLANNED NEW CAPACITY CONTINUE, ANNUAL FEATURE

(p. 34-35) Annual article, with 1 table showing electric power system capacity ordered, removed from schedule, installed, and backlog at year end, for fossil, nuclear, combustion turbine, and hydropower units of the electric utility industry, 1975-82. Data are from EEI *Electric Power Survey.*

A4700–4.502: Spring 1984

WHAT HAPPENED TO 40 PERCENT?

(p. 28-31) Article on changes in selected economic and energy use indicators, 1960s-82. Data are based on a report by Data Resources, Inc.

Includes 1 table showing average annual percent change in GNP, disposable income, electricity price, inflation, population, labor force, electricity consumption by sector, and energy efficiency improvements in new household electric appliances, for 1960-72 and 1973-82 periods.

STATISTICAL REVIEW: 1983 ELECTRIC OUTPUT

(p. 32-34) Article, with 1 table showing quarterly electric output, 1982-83. Data are from Edison Electrical Institute (EEI).

FINANCIAL REVIEW: ELECTRIC OPERATING REVENUES UP 11.2 PERCENT; ANNUALIZED GROWTH OF CWIP SLOWS TO 10 PERCENT THROUGH THIRD QUARTER, QUARTERLY FEATURE

(p. 34-37) Quarterly article, with 2 tables showing investor-owned electric utility income by source, operating expenses by type, net income, preferred stock dividends, earnings per share, and assets and liabilities by type, for 12- and/or 3-month periods ended Sept. 30, 1982-83.

Data are national estimates based on unaudited reports from investor-owned utilities accounting for over 90% of industry assets and revenues.

FORECAST COMPARISONS

(p. 42-44) Article, with 1 table showing average annual growth rates for GNP, and consumption of primary energy, electricity, and end-use energy, as forecast by 12 organizations, various periods 1979-2000. Data were compiled by EEI.

A4700–4.503: Summer 1984

CLEAN AIR ACT AND ACID RAIN

(p. 2-11) By Eugene M. Trisko. Article on impact of proposed clean air legislation on the electric utility industry. Data are from a July 1983 Office of Technology Assessment study. Includes 1 table showing percent change in electric rates with and without imposition of fees designed to offset costs associated with acid rain prevention, for 7 States.

ELECTRICITY SALES AND THE BUSINESS CYCLE

(p. 28-33) By Michael L. Hays. Article examining impact of business cycles on electricity consumption. Data are from *Business Conditions Digest,* Federal Reserve Board, EEI, and Data Resources, Inc.

Includes 2 tables showing percent change in coincident indicator and industrial production indexes, and electricity sales to ultimate customers, selected years 1954-82; and share of industrial production and electricity sales (no date), and percent change in production during 1981-83 recessionary and recovery periods, for 5 electricity-intensive industries.

STATISTICAL REVIEW: ENERGY OUTLOOK

(p. 34-35) Article, with 2 tables showing GNP and GNP deflator; electricity sales; and energy consumption and prices by type of energy, and consumption by end-use sector with detail for electricity, various periods 1983-2000. Data are from DOE.

FINANCIAL REVIEW: ELECTRIC OPERATING INCOME UP 11.8 PERCENT IN 1983; CWIP GROWTH RATE SLOWS SIGNIFICANTLY, QUARTERLY FEATURE

(p. 36-39) Quarterly article, with 2 tables showing investor-owned electric utility income by source, operating expenses by type, net income, stock dividends, earnings per share, and assets and liabilities by type, for 12- and/or 3-month periods ended Dec. 31, 1982-83.

Data are national estimates based on unaudited reports from investor-owned electric utilities accounting for over 90% of industry assets and revenues.

A4725
Electronic
Industries Association

A4725–1 ELECTRONIC MARKET DATA BOOK, 1984 Edition

Annual. 1984.
xiii + 182 p. + errata sheet.
LC 72-627504.
SRI/MF/not filmed

Annual data book on electronic industry production, sales, R&D, foreign trade, and other operating statistics, by product, generally 1974-83, with selected trends from as early as 1953. Also includes data on DOD, DOE, DOT, and NASA budgets by program, FY81-85. Data are compiled from reports of Federal agencies, and EIA estimates.

Contains foreword, and listings of contents, tables, and charts (p. iii-xiii); introduction and summary, with 2 charts, and 1 table showing factory sales by industry group, 1974-83 (p. 1-4); and 6 chapters, with 41 charts and data maps, and 100 tables (p. 5-177).

All chapter tables, and selected maps and charts with substantial statistics not included in tables, are described below.

Availability: Electronic Industries Association, Marketing Services Department, 2001 Eye St., NW, Washington DC 20006, $60.00 (prepaid); SRI/MF/not filmed.

TABLES AND CHARTS:

[Unless otherwise noted, sales and shipment data are shown for factory sales volume/and or value, and factory shipments.]

A4725–1.1: Consumer Electronics

a. Consumer electronic product sales, and number in use, by product type, 1974-83. 2 tables. (p. 5-6)

b. Video equipment and related data, including TV broadcast stations; production and/or sales of TV receivers, projection TVs, videocassette recorders, blank videocassettes, color video cameras, and videodisc players; videocassette recorder imports; and distribution of TV receiver and video-

cassette recorder sales to dealers by census division; various years 1974-84. 3 maps and 15 tables. (p. 6-16)

c. Audio equipment, including home and auto radio sales; audio system sales, by type; portable tape equipment sales, and player and recorder imports; and blank cassette tape sales; various years 1974-83. 6 tables. (p. 20-23)

d. Foreign trade in consumer electronics, by product type, 1974-83; and CPI for 3 consumer electronic products and all items, 1967-83. 3 tables. (p. 29-33)

e. Estimates of sales to dealer volume and factory sales value of home computers and software, programmable video games, video game cartridges, video discs, compact disc players, and telephones and answering devices; and percent of households with various types of electronic products; various years 1980-84. 6 tables. (p. 35)

A4725–1.2: Communications and Industrial Electronics

COMMUNICATIONS

a. General, including communications equipment shipment summary, by type; and communications and communications carrier equipment shipments, by class and/or detailed type; 1974-83. 4 tables. (p. 37-41)

b. Telephone installed base or instrument market for private branch exchange (PBX), key, and Centrex systems, by type of telephone company ownership, various years 1978-87. 4 tables. (p. 46-51)

c. Broadcasting, including TV and radio stations, by type and operating status; total TV households, and cable TV systems, subscribers, and market penetration; citizens band (CB) stations by State; and public safety and special service radio stations in use, by type; various years 1965-84. 5 tables. (p. 56-65)

d. Foreign trade in communications equipment, by type, 1982-83. 1 table. (p. 69)

INDUSTRIAL ELECTRONICS

e. Computer and peripheral equipment shipments, and industrial electronic equipment shipments and sales, all by type; 1974-83. 2 tables. (p. 71-73)

f. Industrial equipment, including control and processing equipment shipments, by type; industrial robot shipments, by type; robot exports, production capacity, and capacity utilization rates; and shipments of testing and measuring equipment, nuclear radiation detection and monitoring instruments, and electromedical equipment, by type; various years 1974-83. 9 tables. (p. 100-113)

g. Automotive electronic system sales, by type; and new car sales; selected years 1967-95. 1 table. (p. 116)

h. Miscellaneous, including industrial electronic equipment foreign trade; miscellaneous electronic systems and equipment shipments; and percent of laser industry parent companies, manufacturing, and consumption located in Japan, Europe, North America, and other areas; various years 1974-83. 1 chart and 2 tables. (p. 117-121)

A4725–1.3: Government Electronics

a. DOD budget total obligational authority and outlays, by function and program, with detail for R&D and procurement, various years FY81-85. 1 chart and 6 tables. (p. 129-134)

b. NASA, DOT, and DOE budgets, by function, various years FY83-85. 2 charts and 2 tables. (p. 132-134)

A4725–1.4: Electronic Components

a. Summary of component sales by type, 1974-83. 1 table. (p. 136)

b. Electron tubes, including TV picture tube sales volume and value, and foreign trade, with detail for color TV tube imports by country of origin; receiving tube sales and exports; power/special purpose tube sales; and electron tube foreign trade; generally by type, various years 1973-83. 11 tables. (p. 136-144)

c. Solid state product shipments and sales, including domestic and export shipments by market, and foreign trade, all by type, various years 1976-83. 3 tables. (p. 146-148)

d. Electronic parts and other components, including resistor consumption; sales of capacitors, passive networks, and TV/FM radio accessories; shipments of switches, connectors, quartz crystals, filters, coils and transformers, and wires and cables; and foreign trade; all by type, various years 1969-83. 12 tables. (p. 151-158)

A4725–1.5: General Information

a. Foreign trade in electronic products, by industry sector and country of origin and destination, with detail for major trading partners; various years 1979-83. 6 tables. (p. 160-166)

b. Employment in electronic industries, including employment by occupational group; total and female employment; and production worker employment, average earnings, and average hours and overtime hours; generally by SIC 3- to 4-digit industry; various years 1979-83. 4 tables. (p. 167-170)

c. R&D funding from Federal, industry, and academic sources, selected years 1953-84; and total employment of scientists/engineers, with distribution by sector, 1983. 1 chart and 1 table. (p. 172-175)

A4725–2   ELECTRONIC MARKET TRENDS

Monthly.   Approx. 30 p.
SRI/MF/not filmed

Monthly report on electronics industry market developments in the consumer, commercial, government, and foreign sectors. Covers new products and applications; and trends in employment, price indexes, sales, and foreign trade.

Data are compiled by the Electronic Industries Assn (EIA) from industry publications, and reports of U.S. Dept of Commerce, other Federal sources, trade assns, and research firms.

Issues generally contain:

a. Feature articles, occasionally with statistics, usually on selected product categories, market sectors, or foreign markets.

b. Monthly EIA Statistics, with 7 tables on sales, employment, general and industry economic indicators, and foreign trade. Month of data coverage is 3 months prior to cover date.

Monthly tables are listed below and appear in all issues. All additional features with substantial statistical content are described, as they appear, under "Statistical Features." Nonstatistical features are not covered.

Availability: Electronic Industries Association, Marketing Services Department, 2001 Eye St., NW, Washington DC 20006, $150.00 per yr., single copy $15.00, combined subscription with *Electronics Foreign Trade* $225.00 per yr.; SRI/MF/not filmed.

Issues reviewed during 1984: Nov. 1983-July 1984 (P).

MONTHLY TABLES:

[Tables generally show data for month of coverage and year to date, often with comparison to previous year. Tables [1-3] include 5-year trends.]

1-2. Electronic industries trends by industry group [consumer electronics, communications equipment, computers or computers/industrial products, and electronic components]: factory sales [and production workers and total] employment.

3. Government economic performance indicators: GNP; prices [CPI for TV, sound equipment, and all items]; production [PPI for intermediate materials and electronic components, and industrial production index]; and interest rates.

4. Factory sales of selected electronic products [home video equipment and electron tubes, by type].

5-6. Balance of trade, [and value of] bilateral trade [with 10] major trade partners, by [electronic] product group; [bilateral data begin with the Apr. 1984 issue].

7. [Value of] imports and exports of electronic products [by type].

STATISTICAL FEATURES:

A4725–2.501: Nov. 1983

AUTOSOUND SHIFTS TO HIGH GEAR

(p. 1-5) Article on characteristics of the car audio equipment market. Data are from an Apr. 1983 EIA consumer survey.

Includes 2 tables showing the following for car audio equipment purchased during past 2 years, by equipment type: percent of households buying and items bought as separate components, buyers' sex and median income and age, and distribution of buyers by metro area size and for nonmetro areas.

DEFENSE AND ECONOMY: MAJOR FACTORS IN 1984 NATIONAL R&D EXPENDITURES

(p. 6-8) Article, with 2 tables showing average annual rates of change for GNP in constant dollars; and for Federal and non-Federal R&D expenditures in current and constant dollars; 1969-75, 1975-83, and 1983-84 periods. Data are from NSF.

CAPACITOR MARKET TRENDS

(p. 9-12) Article, with 2 tables showing sales volume and value for electronic capacitors, by type, various years 1968-82. Data are from EIA Marketing Services Dept.

A4725–2.502: Dec. 1983

SCIENCE AND ENGINEERING STUDENT QUALITY

(p. 1-3) Article, with 1 table showing opinions of graduate school deans about trends in quality of science/engineering students over 5-year period ending 1982, by institution type and control. Data are from a panel survey of deans, sponsored by NSF and American Council on Education.

TRADE AND TARIFF: EQUIPMENT FOR MAKING, BREAKING, PROTECTING, OR CONNECTING CIRCUITS

(p. 12-18) Article, with 9 tables showing the following for electronic equipment for making/breaking/protecting/connecting circuits: import and export values by country of origin and destination, and value of total shipments and apparent consumption, with detail for selected equipment types, 1978-82. Data were compiled by USITC from Commerce Dept statistics.

A4725–2.503: Jan. 1984

FACSIMILE: AN EFFECTIVE COMMUNICATIONS MODE

(p. 6-10) Article on market for facsimile (electronic mail) technologies. Data are from Venture Development Corp. Includes 1 chart showing share of facsimile terminal shipments, for domestic models and for imports marketed by U.S. and foreign companies, 1981.

TECHNICAL EMPLOYMENT GROWTH IN NONMANUFACTURING INDUSTRIES

(p. 15-18) Article, with 1 table showing nonmanufacturing employment for scientists, engineers, and technicians, total and for 3 industry categories, 1981 with percent change from 1978. Data are from NSF.

A4725–2.504: Feb. 1984

1984 FEDERAL R&D GROWTH

(p. 1-3) Article, with 1 table showing Federal R&D funding by budget function, 1974-84.

GREAT SCOT! IT'S SILICON GLEN

(p. 4-9) Article on electronics industry in Scotland. Data are from the Scottish Development Agency and Universities Central Council on Admissions.

Includes 2 tables showing number of electronics companies in Scotland subcontracting from original equipment manufacturers, by equipment type (undated); and university enrollment, total and for engineering, mathematics, and physics fields, Dec. 1980.

COMPETITIVE POSITION OF U.S. ROBOTICS

(p. 10-16) Article, with text statistics and 4 tables showing U.S. industrial robot domestic shipments by type, export volume and value, and production capacity and utilization, 1979-83; and number of robots in 6 major consuming countries, 1981, 1985, and 1989.

A4725–2.505: Apr. 1984

LARGEST INCREASE IN FEDERAL R&D FUNDS FOR 1984 SINCE MIDSIXTIES

(p. 17-19) Article, with 1 table showing Federal R&D obligations by type of funded organization, 1974 and 1982-84. Data are from NSF.

A4725–2.506: July 1984

COMPANIES' R&D FUNDING INCREASED 13% DURING 1982

(p. 1-4) Article, with 1 table showing total or Federal and corporate R&D funds, ratio of total and corporate R&D funds to net sales, and R&D scientists/engineers, for 5 industry groups and all others, various periods 1981-83. Data are from NSF.

SOVIET MILITARY RESEARCH AND DEVELOPMENT

(p. 14-19) Article, with 2 tables showing USSR deliveries of military equipment to 4 world areas, by equipment type, 1978-83 period; and number of Soviet military and economic advisers in Africa, 1964 and 1984.

A4725–3   ELECTRONICS FOREIGN TRADE

Monthly.   Approx. 65 p.
ISSN 0146-9231.
SRI/MF/not filmed

Monthly report presenting data on foreign trade in electronic products, by detailed product classification and foreign country. Data are compiled by EIA Marketing Services Dept mainly from U.S. Dept of Commerce reports. Report is issued approximately 6 weeks after month of data coverage.

Contains contents listing, notes, and 8 monthly tables listed below. Tables [3-8] begin with the Jan. 1984 issue. Prior to Jan. 1984, report included 2 tables showing detail by product classification for imports under provisions 806.30 and 807.

Availability: Electronic Industries Association, Marketing Services Department, 2001 Eye St., NW, Washington DC 20006, $150.00 per yr., single copy $15.00, combined subscription with *Electronic Market Trends* $225.00 per yr.; SRI/MF/not filmed.

Issues reviewed during 1984: Sept. 1983-Aug. 1984 (D).

MONTHLY TABLES:

[Tables show data for month of coverage and/or year to date. Product groups are electronic parts; electron tubes; consumer electronics; and communications, industrial, and solid state products. Detailed import and export data are shown by USITC and Dept of Commerce product classifications, respectively.]

[1] Balance of trade for electronic products [value of imports, exports, and trade balance, by product group].

[2] [Import and export detail by product classification: value and unit volume.]

[3] Bilateral trade [value] by product group, major U.S. trade partners.

[4-6] Imports and exports [value] by product group, major country suppliers and markets [with value and unit volume detail by product classification].

[7-8] 806.30/807 and Generalized System of Preferences (GSP) imports, by product group, major country suppliers [shows value of imports under provisions 806.30/807 (manufactured in U.S., further processed abroad, and reimported for completion, or assembled abroad from U.S. components); and under GSP (duty free products from designated beneficiary countries)].

A4725–4   CONSUMER ELECTRONICS ANNUAL REVIEW, 1984 Edition: Industry Facts and Figures

Annual.   [1984].   62 p.
SRI/MF/not filmed

Annual report on consumer electronics industry developments, including production, factory sales, and trade, by product type, 1970s-83. Data are from the Marketing Services Dept of the Electronic Industries Assn.

Contains foreword, and contents listing (p. 1-4); overview and history, with 2 trend charts, and 2 tables described below (p. 5-13); narrative report, interspersed with 3 maps and 36 tables, also described below (p. 14-50); and industry chronology, lists of available publications and trade assns, and glossary (p. 51-62).

Availability: Electronic Industries Association, Marketing Services Department, 2001 Eye St., NW, Washington DC 20006, † with stamped, self-addressed envelope; SRI/MF/not filmed.

MAPS AND TABLES:

[Data are shown for 1973-83, unless otherwise noted.]

a. Overview: factory sales, totals 1973-83, and by product 1974-83. 2 tables. (p. 5-6)

b. Video: TV production and sales to dealers, for color and monochrome portable and console sets; distribution of sales to dealers by region, for color and monochrome TV sets and videocassette recorders, 1983; projection TV production, factory sales, and sales to dealers, and video cassette recorder, color video camera, videodisc player, blank videocassette, and videodisc factory sales and/or sales to dealer, various years 1978-83; and TV stations in operation, 1960-84. 3 maps and 14 tables. (p. 14-28)

c. Audio: factory sales of portable/table, compact, component, and console audio systems, 1974-83; imports of audio tape equipment; audio tape equipment and cassettes, and car sound equipment sales to dealers and/or factory sales, various years 1980-83; radio production, including FM-AM/FM table, clock, portable, and car units, 1973-83; and AM and FM broadcasting stations in operation, 1960-84. 10 tables. (p. 29-38)

d. Computers, video games, and telecommunications: sales to dealers and factory sales of home computers and software, programmable video games, video game cartridges, telephone answering devices, and cordless, corded, and total telephones, various years 1980-83. 8 tables. (p. 41-43)

e. Foreign trade and product use: imports and exports of color and monochrome TVs, home and car radios, phonographs, and audio and video tape equipment, and imports of car tape players; and products in use, and household penetration as of year end 1983, of consumer electronics by product type. 4 tables. (p. 47-50)

A4875
Fibre Box Association

A4875–1   FIBRE BOX INDUSTRY 1983 ANNUAL REPORT

Annual.   1984.   16 p.
LC 72-624847.
SRI/MF/complete

Annual report on fiber box industry trends, 1960-83. Includes data on shipments by geographic area and end-use industry, production, materials consumption, prices, employment, earnings, and productivity. Data are from industry reports, American Paper Institute, and BLS.

Contains contents listing (inside front cover); introduction (p. 1); statistical section with 20 illustrative charts, and 15 tables described below (p. 2-15); and definitions (p. 16).

This is the 43rd annual report.

Availability: Fibre Box Association, 5725 N. East River Rd., Chicago IL 60631, $10.00; SRI/MF/complete.

TABLES:

a. Corrugated and solid fiber container shipment value and volume, sheet and converting plants and shipments, 1960-83; and monthly and quarterly total container shipment volume (actual and seasonally adjusted), and shipment distribution by SIC 2- or 3-digit end-use industry, 1981-83. 6 tables. (p. 2-7)

b. Corrugated production by type of board, and total container shipment volume by geographic area, 1960-83, with shipment quarterly and monthly detail for 1981-83. 3 tables. (p. 8-11)

c. Containerboard production for domestic use, and consumption by box plants, 1960-83; and inventory and weeks of supply at box plants and mill sites, monthly Jan. 1982-84; all by type of board. 3 tables. (p. 12-13)

d. Corrugated container quarterly price index, compared to PPI 1960-83, and by area 1980-83; and industry employment, hours, earnings, and productivity ratios, 1960-83. 3 tables. (p. 14-15)

A4950
Food Marketing Institute

A4950–2   FACTS ABOUT STORE DEVELOPMENT, 1983

Annual.   1984.
iii+27+App 4 p.
ISSN 0732-233X.
LC 82-642410.
SRI/MF/complete, delayed

Annual report on supermarkets opened, remodeled, and closed, in U.S. and Canada, 1983. Includes data on average new store size and cost, remodeling capital investments, incorporation of specialty depts, new and existing store ownership status, and lease arrangements. Most data are shown by region, other location characteristics, store type and size, and company sales range.

Data are from responses of 187 companies, representing more than 7,500 supermarkets, to a Jan. 1984 FMI survey.

Contains contents listing (p. iii); survey report, with 26 tables listed below (p. 1-27); and appendix, with questionnaire facsimile (p. 29-33).

Availability: Food Marketing Institute, Research Division, 1750 K St., NW, Washington DC 20006, members $7.50, nonmembers $15.00; SRI/MF/complete, delayed shipment in Oct. 1985.

TABLES:

[Tables 4-15 show data by some or all of the following: company sales range; store location in 8 U.S. regions and Canada; store size; store type (conventional, superstore, combination, limited assortment, and warehouse); and location type (community/regional, neighborhood, free standing, and other).

Data are for 1983, unless otherwise noted.]

1-2. Percentage of stores opened, closed, or remodeled, 1979-83; and percentage of store activity [new and closed stores] in 1983, by type of store. (p. 1-2)

3. Type and average age of supermarkets in operation on Dec. 31, 1983. (p. 2)

4-8. Average total square feet for new stores; average building, store equipment/fixtures/ decorations, and total construction costs per square foot; and average number of months from construction to breakeven; [showing median, middle range, and number of stores]. (p. 3-7)

9A-9D. Profile of new store construction: number of stores and medians. (p. 8-9)

10A-10B. Percent and base number of stores with specialty depts [bakery, service deli, floral, and snack bar/restaurant]. (p. 10-11)

11A-15. Number of supermarkets owned and leased; and mean rent and ownership/lease arrangement for new and existing stores [minimum rent, overages as percent of sales, expected total rent after 5 years, services provided by landlord, and store size]. (p. 12-25)

16-19. Years from 1st opening and last major remodeling to present remodeling, and capital investment per supermarket and per square foot for major remodeling [median, middle range, and number of stores, by company sales range]. (p. 26-27)

A4950–3   TRENDS: CONSUMER ATTITUDES AND THE SUPERMARKET, 1984
Update
Annual. 1984. vi+51 p.
ISSN 0163-4488.
LC 78-646718.
SRI/MF/complete, delayed

Annual survey report, for 1984, on consumer practices and attitudes affecting the supermarket industry, including general economic concerns, views on supermarket industry performance and practices, and shopping patterns. Also includes comparative data from previous surveys, Nov. 1974-Jan. 1983.

Current data are from a national telephone sample survey conducted by Louis Harris and Associates in Jan. 1984, and are based on responses from 1,008 heads of household who had shopped for groceries recently. The sample was weighted to a 80% female-20% male ratio.

Contains contents and table listings (p. iii-vi); introduction and highlights (p. 1-4); 7 chapters presenting survey findings, with 44 tables, de-

scribed below (p. 5-47); and methodology, with 2 tables showing sample demographic profiles, weighting, and sampling error (p. 49-51).

This is the 13th report in the FMI attitude survey series.

Availability: Food Marketing Institute, Research Division, 1750 K St., NW, Washington DC 20006, members $15.00, nonmembers $30.00; SRI/MF/complete, delayed shipment in May 1985.

SURVEY FINDINGS:

[Tables show distribution of responses to questions in the areas noted below. Selected tables show data by sociodemographic breakdowns, including family type and size; income; region; race (white, black, and Hispanic); rural or urban residence; age; sex, including data for working women; marital status; and education.]

a. General outlook, and prices: assessments of trends and outlook for economy, unemployment, and personal financial situation; and prices of utilities, housing, gasoline, and other basic consumer items. Tables 1-6. (p. 5-9)

b. Supermarkets: views on supermarket responsibilities and services. Tables 7-10. (p. 12-16)

c. Methods of economizing: use of various shopping methods to lower food bills and to save time in the supermarket. Tables 11-16. (p. 17-22)

d. Shopping patterns: weekly grocery expenditures; number of different stores visited; shopping frequency and preferred time of day; and preferred outlet type for selected food and nonfood items. Tables 17-26. (p. 23-30)

e. Consumer activism: willingness to participate in various personal and organized consumer protest activities, and actions taken in past year. Tables 27-29. (p. 31-32)

f. Nutrition and product safety: concern about food nutritional content; behavior and views regarding food safety; reliance on self, government, or private organizations to ascertain product safety; concern about tampering with nonprescription drugs; and awareness of contaminated food recalls. Tables 30-40. (p. 34-42)

g. Consumer group comparisons: responses of shoppers by marital status and household type to selected questions noted above. Tables 41-44. (p. 44-47)

A4950–4   OPERATING RESULTS OF INDEPENDENT SUPERMARKETS, 1983
Annual. 1984. ix+125 p.
SRI/MF/complete, delayed

Annual report presenting detailed sales and operating ratios for independent supermarkets, 1983. Data are shown separately for conventional, super, warehouse, combination, and superette stores, with detail for most and least profitable stores in 3 of the store categories, and by region (conventional stores only) and sales size (conventional and super stores only).

Includes sales distribution, gross margin, and inventory turnover, by dept; sales change from 1982; average transaction size; operating expenses by category, and pretax profit, expressed as percent of sales; personnel productivity ratios, including payroll and benefits per labor hour; and store area, checkouts, and space productivity ratios.

Data are shown as typical (median or mean) amounts and middle ranges, and are based on responses of 150 companies to a spring 1984 survey of FMI members in U.S. and Canada. Respondents represent 241 stores; number of stores reporting is shown for each data item.

Report is intended to enable individual stores to compare their performance with that of similar stores.

Contains contents listing, foreword, and summary, with 1 table (p. iii-ix); 5 statistical sections, with 4 basic tables repeated for each store category (p. 1-109); and appendix, with definitions, survey form facsimile, and order forms (p. 112-124).

Prior to issue presenting data for 1983, report was published in 5 separate volumes.

Availability: Food Marketing Institute, Research Division, 1750 K St., NW, Washington DC 20006, members $25.00, nonmembers $50.00; SRI/MF/complete, delayed shipment in July 1985.

A4950–5   FOOD MARKETING INDUSTRY SPEAKS, 1984
Annual. For individual publication data, see below.
ISSN 0190-504X.
LC 79-640398.
SRI/MF/complete, delayed

Annual survey report on food marketing industry wholesale and retail operations, sales, and productivity, for U.S. and Canada, 1983. Report is issued in 2 volumes: a narrative summary report, with 18 illustrative charts and 25 summary tables; and a statistical volume of 223 detailed tables. Contents of individual volumes are described below.

Data are from Food Marketing Institute surveys, and various business and Federal Government publications.

Availability: Food Marketing Institute, Research Division, 1750 K St., NW, Washington DC 20006, 2 volume report: members $15.00, nonmembers $30.00; summary only: members $7.50, nonmembers $ 15.00; SRI/MF/complete, delayed shipment in Oct. 1985.

A4950–5.1: Narrative Summary
[Annual. 1984. 16 p. SRI/MF/complete, delayed.]

Contains 1 table showing typical store performance (p. 2); contents listing (p. 3); and narrative analysis with 18 charts and 24 tables, presenting summary and trend data on current economic conditions and food marketing industry financial performance and operations (p. 4-16).

Most data in charts and tables are based on the detailed tabulations described below.

A4950–5.2: Detailed Tabulations
[Annual. 1984. xiv+155 p. SRI/MF/complete, delayed.]

Contains foreword and contents and table listings (p. iii-xiv); 223 tables, listed below (p. 1-136); and glossary and survey questionnaire facsimiles (p. 137-155).

TABLES:

[Data are for 1983, unless otherwise noted. Data by region are shown for 8 U.S. regions and Canada. Data by affiliation are shown for chain and independent retailers, and/or for cooperative, voluntary, and unaffiliated wholesalers.]

Wholesale Operations

[Tables 1-5 show data by wholesale sales size class, and usually by type of affiliation.]

1. Geographic region of wholesale headquarters. (p. 1)

2A-2B. Average percent change in wholesale sales [also shows data by region and number of supermarkets served], 1983 vs. 1982. (p. 2)

3. Percentage of annual sales volume attributed to [independent food stores, corporately owned stores, other food chains, convenience stores, restaurants, hospitals, schools, and other], summary table of means. (p. 3)

4. Average sales per retail store served, in millions of dollars. (p. 3)

5. Services provided to membership [including private and generic label, advertising, engineering, accounting, education/training, discount, and space allocation programs]. (p. 4)

Distribution Center Operations

SAMPLE DESCRIPTIONS

6. Profile of companies [geographic region of headquarters, for retailers and by type of wholesale affiliation]. (p. 4)

7A-7B. Distribution centers [includes average and longest distance between centers and stores served, for wholesalers and retailers, by region]. (p. 5)

8-12B. Proportion of fleet owned vs. leased; type of trailers/tractors; truck fleet [data, including miles traveled and fuel purchases and expenditures]; number of [full- and part-time company and hired service] drivers employed in typical week per company; and percentage of inbound truck loads delivered by [type of carrier and region; all shown for wholesale and/or retail operations, with selected detail by sales or fleet size]. (p. 6-9)

DRY GROCERY

[Tables 13-29 show data for dry grocery distribution center/section, usually by square footage range. Some data are shown for retail and wholesale operations, and by automation status.]

13-16. Average total area in square feet, number of employees, and number of supermarkets served per center/section; and type of selection method. (p. 10-11)

17-21. Average number of cases shipped per week, per direct and total labor hour; and cases selected and stored/replenished per direct labor hour. (p. 11-12)

22-24. Average number of inbound truck loads and rail cars, and outbound vehicle loads, per week. (p. 13)

25A-26. Average number of items available, and of inventory turns. (p. 14-15)

27. Current scratch rate. (p. 15)

28A-28C. Average number of orders processed weekly. (p. 16)

29. Shifts per day, days per week of operation, and unionization. (p. 17)

REFRIGERATED FOODS

30-145. [Data from tables 13-29 are repeated for various refrigerated produce, meat, dairy, and delicatessen distribution center/sections.] (p. 18-60)

Retail Operations

[Most tables show data by geographic region of retailer's headquarters, sales size class, and type of retail affiliation.]

SAMPLE DESCRIPTIONS

146. Geographic region of retailers headquarters. (p. 61)

147. Average percentage of operations supplied by outside wholesalers and direct vendor deliveries. (p. 62)

148. Number of supermarkets company operates [by region only]. (p. 62)

149A-149B. Percentage of operation supplied by [own warehouse; direct vendor deliveries; and voluntary, cooperative, and unaffiliated wholesalers]. (p. 63)

RETAIL SALES

150-152B. Retail sales [omits data by affiliation], 1983; and average percent change in retail sales [totals and identical stores], 1982-83. (p. 64-66)

153. Average weekly sales per supermarket. (p. 67)

154. Trends in sales distribution [percent of store sales in grocery, meat, and produce depts, totals only, 1976-83]. (p. 67)

155A-155B. Profile by store type [average weekly sales, productivity, size, item prices, and number of items carried; for conventional, super, combination, and warehouse stores only]. (p. 68)

PRODUCTIVITY

156A-159B. Average weekly sales per square foot of selling area and per checkout; average sale per customer transaction; and average sales per labor hour for store employees. (p. 69-72)

160. Sales per labor hour and hourly wage rates [by dept only, 1976-83]. (p. 73)

INDUSTRY ACTIVITY

161. Store development [new, remodeled, and closed supermarkets, as percent of all supermarkets; totals only]. (p. 73)

162. Total size of typical supermarket. (p. 74)

163A-164B. Average number of items and average price of each item carried by a typical supermarket. (p. 75)

165A-165B. Credit cards [percent of stores accepting credit cards for groceries and other items]. (p. 76)

166A-166C. Percentage of sales accounted for by general merchandise, tobacco, and HABA (health and beauty aids). (p. 77-79)

167A-167B. Specialty depts and services offered by supermarkets. (p. 80-81)

MERCHANDISING TRENDS

168A-168B. Average supermarket advertising costs as a percent of sales. (p. 82)

168C-168D. Percentage of advertising dollars spent [by media]. (p. 83)

SCANNING AND BULK FOODS

169A-170B. Companies that will be 100% scanning by end of 1983, and companies with person responsible for scanning; and current uses of scanning POS [point-of-sale] data. (p. 84-85)

171. Scanning installation update [by manufacturer and State, 1983, and summary, 1974-1st quarter 1984]. (p. 86)

172A-174B. Percentage of supermarkets selling bulk food items [total and by type of item], and average number of items. (p. 87-89)

PRODUCE DEPT

175-178B. Produce dept, and change in produce dept, as a percent of total selling area and total sales. (p. 90-93)

179-182B. Average number of employees in produce dept, and average sales per labor hour; and percentage of companies including certain items in produce sales, and operating fresh orange juice machines. (p. 94-97)

183A-186B. Store [produce] display techniques, and pricing [methods]; average number of fresh produce items carried; and produce-related services available to customers. (p. 98-101)

187A-189B. Percentage of companies with produce identification program available for employees, and training and retraining employees; and position or dept responsible for produce identification training. (p. 102-104)

190A-194B. Salad bar: sales as a percent of produce dept; percentage of stores [providing], and having eating area available; number of items carried; and store employees responsible. (p. 105-109)

MEDICAL BENEFITS

195A-198B. Percentage of companies: providing health programs, medical services, and certain medical health plans to employees [by type of program or service]; and which encourage employees to use [ambulatory surgery, home health care, HMOs, and home professional nursing]. (p. 110-112)

199A-199B. [Percent of companies increasing family and individual] deductions, and [with employee-paid] deductibles. (p. 113)

200A-200B. Percentage of companies which educate employees to [ask questions before surgery, and ask for written estimate]; and who ask employees to obtain a second opinion [with detail for whether company or employee paid]. (p. 114-115)

201A-202B. Change in medical benefits costs during the past 2 years; and percentage of companies considering [selected] alternatives for lowering medical benefits costs. (p. 116-117)

ELECTRONIC FUNDS TRANSFER

[Data in tables 206-217B refer to Automatic Teller Machines (ATMs).]

203A-205B. Percentage of companies and supermarkets with ATM/other electronic banking services; and location of ATMs. (p. 118-120)

206-209B. Typical number of transactions per week per machine; owners [including banks and other financial institutions]; reimbursement for nonsupermarket-owned equipment; and [type of] system. (p. 121-124)

210-213B. Customer use and access; mixture of transactions [including cash dispensing and deposits; customer or clerk] system operation; and rating [of machine use and selected operations]. (p. 125-128)

214A-217B. Effect on check and cash volume; personnel/agencies receiving customer complaints; and anticipated services in next 5 years. (p. 129-132)

218A-219B. Percentage of companies expecting to install [an ATM or other electronic banking] system within next 2 years; and companies which have been approached by a bank to install [systems]. (p. 133-134)

External Factors

[Tables 220-222 show data for 1976-83; tables 222-223 incorrectly read 223-224, respectively.]

220. Operating results [profit and expense percentages]. (p. 135)

221. Percent of disposable income spent on food [at home and away from home]. (p. 135)

222. CPI [all items, food at home, and food away from home]. (p. 136)

223. Historical data [average percent change in retail sales and in retail sales for identical stores, weekly store sales and sales per square foot, sales per transaction, and number of items in supermarket; various years 1974-83]. (p. 136)

A4950-6   1983-84 MANAGEMENT COMPENSATION STUDY for Wholesalers and Large Retailers
Annual. 1984. 367 p.
SRI/MF/complete, delayed

Annual report, prepared by Sibson and Co., on salary and bonus compensation for 47 senior executive, staff, merchandising, and store operations positions in the food marketing industry, for the year ended Mar. 31, 1983. Includes data by sales size and region. Also includes summary data on benefit programs.

Report is based on survey responses of 83 food marketers and is intended to enable individual companies to compare their compensation levels with industry averages.

Contains contents listing, introduction, and index (1 p., p. 1-5); and the following parts:

Part I. Participant profile, with 3 tables showing number of respondents by sales and employment size, and region; and list of responding companies. (p. 6-10)

Part II. Compensation program information, with summary analysis, and 14 tables showing types of bonus and benefit plans offered with detail for health care programs; basis for bonus awards; and bonus as percent of salary; with detail by sales size, region, and position. (p. 11-26)

Part III. Percent change in compensation, with 1 table showing average change in compensation by bonus and nonbonus companies for 47 positions. (p. 27-29)

Part IV. Pay levels for survey positions, with explanation of data (p. 31-38); and 1 detailed table, further described below, usually with accompanying chart, presenting compensation data for 47 positions nationally (p. 40-257), and for 4-10 merchandising and store operations positions in 5 regions (p. 261-355).

Appendix. Survey position descriptions. (p. 359-367)

Availability: Food Marketing Institute, Research Division, 1750 K St., NW, Washington DC 20006, members $250.00, nonmembers $500.00; SRI/MF/complete, delayed shipment in Oct. 1985.

PART IV TABLE:

Table shows average bonus and/or salary, and salary range, for each position. Data are grouped by sales size, number of stores, or purchasing expenditures, as appropriate for each position. Table also shows number of incumbents; selected detail by position reported to; and, for national and/or regional data on store and meat dept managers, average weekly days, nights, and hours worked, annual Sundays worked, and Sunday and holiday pay policies.

A4950-8   MANAGEMENT COMPENSATION STUDY FOR INDEPENDENT SUPERMARKETS
Annual, discontinued.

Annual report on salary and bonus compensation for independent supermarket executives, discontinued with 1982 report (for description, see SRI 1982 Annual, under this number). Report has been discontinued due to budgetary constraints.

A4950-12   SUPERMARKET ENERGY USE AND EXPENSE: A Tool for Identifying Where Each Supermarket Stands
Monograph. 1982. iii+22 p.
SRI/MF/complete

By Todd S. Mann. Report on supermarket energy consumption and costs, 1981. Includes data on electricity and fossil fuel consumption, by store square footage and climate region, with detail for all-electric stores; total energy cost per square foot; and electricity and fossil fuel prices; all shown as median and selected percentile levels.

Also includes data on types, cost, and evaluation of store energy management systems; and store variations from average energy consumption, by type of lighting, type of frozen food cases, use of energy management system, store age and hours, and other factors.

Data are from responses of over 150 companies representing 300 stores in U.S., Puerto Rico, and Canada. Report is intended to enable individual stores to compare their energy use with that of similar stores.

Contains summary (p. iii); listings of contents, charts, and tables (1 p.); introduction, report description with 2 charts, methodology and profile of survey sample, and user guide (p. 1-7); and 15 tables (p. 8-22).

Availability: Food Marketing Institute, Research Division, 1750 K St., NW, Washington DC 20006, members $10.00, nonmembers $20.00; SRI/MF/complete.

A4950-14   ADVERTISING FUNCTION AND ACTIVITIES IN THE FOOD MARKETING INDUSTRY
Monograph. Jan. 1983.
v+19 p.
Special Research Rpt. No. 33.
SRI/MF/complete

Report on advertising practices in the food marketing industry, 1982. Presents data for retail and wholesale companies, with detail for retailers by number of stores.

Covers advertising dept organizational structure and employees; advertising budget composition, budget size compared to 1981, and

budgeting methods; types of advertising functions performed in-house and elsewhere; media use; regular use of advertising agency; and methods for measuring advertisement effectiveness.

Data are from a fall 1982 survey of 1,096 FMI member companies. Response rate was 30%.

Contains summary and contents listing (p. iii-v); introduction and methodology (p. 1); report in 3 sections, with narrative analysis and 27 interspersed tables (p. 2-16); and facsimile of survey questionnaire (p. 17-19).

Availability: Food Marketing Institute, Research Division, 1750 K St., NW, Washington DC 20006, members $2.50, nonmembers $5.00; SRI/MF/complete.

A4950-15   INVENTORY SHORTAGE IN FOOD RETAILING AND WHOLESALING
Monograph   Dec. 1983.
v+47 p.
Special Research Rpt. No. 34.
SRI/MF/complete, delayed

Report on inventory shortage in food retail and wholesale operations due to theft, breakage, and other loss, 1982, and strategies for reducing shortage. Covers shortage levels and calculation methods, inventory and audit procedures, security systems, cash register types or billing methods, and delivery procedures; shown for retail and wholesale companies, with selected detail by commodity category (grocery, nonfood, produce, and meat) and by number of retail stores.

Data are from responses of 217 food marketing companies to a summer 1983 survey.

Contains summary and contents listing (p. iii-v); introduction and methodology, with 1 table (p. 1-2); and 62 tables, with accompanying narrative, covering retailers (p. 3-30) and wholesalers (p. 31-47).

Availability: Food Marketing Institute, Research Division, 1750 K St., NW, Washington DC 20006, members $2.50, nonmembers $5.00; SRI/MF/complete, delayed shipment in Dec. 1984.

A4950-16   LOSS PREVENTION IN THE SUPERMARKET
Monograph.   Apr. 1984.
v+33 p.
Special Research Rpt. No. 35.
SRI/MF/complete, delayed

Report on retail food store policies and procedures for reducing losses from employee, customer, and vendor theft.

Presents data on person responsible for loss prevention; methods used for stress measurement and/or loss prevention training of security and other personnel; use of pre-employment testing; education and prior work experience of guards; responsibilities of loss prevention personnel and interaction with other depts; prosecution policies, and conviction rate; employment and arming of selected security personnel; and loss prevention and parking lot security methods in use.

Also includes data on loss prevention budget relative to sales, and incidence of loss through theft vs. other occurrences.

Most data are shown by company size.

Data are from responses of 142 FMI member companies to a winter 1983/84 survey.

Contains executive summary and contents listing (p. iii-v); narrative report with 32 tables (p. 1-27); and appendix presenting tables of contents for 3 related FMI studies (p. 29-33).

A companion report, *Inventory Shortage in Food Retailing and Wholesaling,* is described under A4950-15, above.

Availability: Food Marketing Institute, Research Division, 1750 K St., NW, Washington DC 20006, members $2.50, nonmembers $5.00; SRI/MF/complete, delayed shipment in Apr. 1985.

A4957
Footwear Industries of America

A4957–1   FOOTWEAR MANUAL, 1984
Annual. 1984. 6+319 p.
ISSN 0095-1048.
LC 74-647881.
SRI/MF/complete

Annual report on footwear production, employment, foreign trade, consumption, marketing, finance, and raw material supply and demand, primarily for U.S. and OECD countries, by product type, various years 1970s-82, with selected trends from the 1950s and some data for 1983.

Includes U.S. data by SIC 2- to 4-digit industry, State, and company; OECD data by country; and selected world data for other countries. Data are from agency's own records; U.S. Depts of Commerce and Agriculture, BLS, and USITC; OECD; and other sources.

Contains general contents listing and highlights (5 p.); and 293 tables, described below, grouped in 8 sections, each prefaced with its own contents listing (p. 1-319).

Report price includes subscription to quarterly *Statistical Reporter,* covered in SRI under A4957-2.

Availability: Footwear Industries of America, Publications, 3700 Market St., Philadelphia PA 19104, members $55.00, nonmembers $265.00, educational institutions/libraries $130.00 (all prices include subscription to *Statistical Reporter*); SRI/MF/complete.

TABLES:
[Data are for U.S., unless otherwise noted. Production data by State are generally shown for 5-21 major footwear producing States.]

A4957–1.1: Section I: Manufacturing

a. Nonrubber footwear production: by month, State and region, quantity and value of shipments, and types of construction, upper, and sole; and domestic and imported nonrubber and rubber canvas footwear consumption; mostly by footwear type, various periods 1958-82. Tables 1-15. (p. 1-23)

b. Shoes/slippers with sole vulcanized to fabric upper, by month and by product type, and rubber and plastic protective footwear by type: production and shipment value and/or volume, various years 1972-82. Tables 16-19. (p. 24-27)

c. General industry statistics, including companies and/or establishments, employ-

ment, payroll, hours, wages, material costs, capital expenditures, end-of-year inventories, and operating ratios, with selected detail by State; capacity utilization rate, by footwear type; shipment values, by product class and State; and material consumption and cost by kind; all by SIC 4-digit industry and 5-digit product code; various years 1967-82. Tables 20-28. (p. 28-38)

d. Industry concentration data, including establishments and employees by employment size range, share of shipment value represented by top 4-50 companies, and manufacturer and production distribution by production size range; with selected detail by footwear type; various years 1967-81. Tables 29-31. (p. 39-41)

e. OECD countries: production of nonrubber footwear by type and of total rubber footwear, all by country, various years 1974-81. Tables 32-38. (p. 42-48)

A4957–1.2: Sections II-IV: Labor, Exports, and Imports

SECTION II: LABOR

a. Employment in footwear and related industries, by SIC 2- to 4-digit code; and nonrubber and rubber footwear industries' total and women employed, average weekly and overtime hours, earnings, and labor turnover, with selected detail by product type and month; various years 1971-82. Tables 1-21. (p. 55-67)

b. Leather/leather products, leather tanning/finishing, and nonrubber footwear industries' employment, earnings, and hours, by State; leather/leather products and nonrubber footwear industries' quarterly unemployment rates; nonrubber footwear indexes of output, employee hours, employment, and output ratios; and footwear industry hourly wage and production, unit labor cost, and average unit price; various years 1960-82. Tables 22-29. (p. 68-74)

c. World data: production worker hourly earnings and compensation in footwear-related industries, for 8 countries, 1972-81. Table 30. (p. 75)

d. Footwear industry wage and benefit survey: production workers and/or earnings, by sex, footwear type, metro and nonmetro status, establishment employment size, earnings size range, and detailed occupation; and worker distribution by method of payment, scheduled weekly hours, paid annual holidays, length of paid vacations, and benefits by type; all by region, Apr. 1980. Tables 31-41. (p. 76-89)

e. Occupational injury/illness and injury incidence rates, by case type and industry division, with detail for selected SIC 2- to 4-digit footwear and other industries, and by employment size group, 1980 and/or 1981. Tables 42-44. (p. 90-92)

SECTION III: U.S. EXPORTS

f. Footwear exports classification, 1981; and volume and value, for nonrubber footwear by product type, month, type of upper, and country of destination, and for rubber fabric footwear by country of destination, various years 1972-82. Tables 1-24. (p. 96-122)

SECTION IV: U.S. AND OECD IMPORTS

g. U.S. imports: TSUSA for footwear, 1983; and import volume and value, by product type, type of upper, and country of origin, for nonrubber, rubber-soled, protective, and other types of footwear, with selected data by month, various years 1971-82. Tables 1-34. (p. 127-175)

h. OECD imports: volume and value of imports, by footwear type or material, including rubber, for total OECD and 16-17 member countries, 1974-75 and/or 1976-81. Tables 35-43. (p. 176-184)

A4957–1.3: Section V: Marketing

a. New footwear market supply, including domestic production and imports; and consumption and import share, by price range; all by footwear type, including type of upper, various years 1972-82. Tables 1-9. (p. 191-202)

b. Population: families and unrelated individuals, by income, 1977-82; and population by age and sex, various years 1970-2000. Tables 10-12. (p. 203-205)

c. Nonrubber footwear domestic production and foreign trade, per capita consumption of footwear by type, personal consumption expenditures for footwear and selected other expenditure groups in current and constant 1972 dollars, and footwear buying index by State and SMSA, various years 1947-82; and list of SMSA component areas, 1977. Tables 13-18. (p. 206-217)

d. Total retail sales, seasonally adjusted and unadjusted, by month and retail outlet type, including shoe stores; monthly distribution of total and chain shoe store sales; and number of establishments retailing footwear, and footwear sales, both by retail outlet type; various years 1963-82. Tables 19-26. (p. 218-225)

e. Footwear sales and retail outlet share, by State, 1967 and 1972; sales by census division, 1967, 1972, and 1982; PPI and CPI for all commodities and footwear by type, with PPI also for hides/skins and leather goods, and some data by month, various years 1963-82; foot size and width of survey respondents 13 years/older by sex, 1974; and distribution of men's and women's shoe purchases by size, 1982. Tables 26A-41A. (p. 226-241)

f. OECD countries: total and per capita consumption of footwear by type, by country, selected years 1974-81. Tables 42-47. (p. 242-247)

A4957–1.4: Sections VI-VIII: Finance; Raw Materials; and World Production, Trade, and Consumption

SECTION VI: FINANCE

a. Plant closings and openings, with closings by State; footwear manufacturing, wholesaling, and retailing failures and liabilities; and operating ratios for shoe manufacturers, shoe retailers, and shoe stores; various years 1960-82. Tables 1-9. (p. 253-260)

b. By production size group: net sales, assets, stockholders' equity, long-term debt/stockholders' equity, and selected expense and profit ratios, for a sample of producers; and industry operating and pretax profit margins; various years 1970-82. Tables 10A-14. (p. 261-266) *c.* Financial and/or operating ratios: for non-rubber footwear manufacturing establishments, by asset size group, with sample size and total receipts, FY78-80; and for shoe stores by type, including single- vs. multi-unit, sales size group, type of shoe sold, and traditional vs. concept store, 1980-81. Tables 15-24. (p. 267-276)

d. By company: sales, stockholders' equity, net profit as percent of sales and equity, operating profit, and footwear shares of sales and profit, all for 9-19 selected retailers, manufacturers, and suppliers; number of total and footwear outlets for retailers; and sales and operating profits for top 5 retailers and top 5 manufacturers ranked by sales; various years 1979-82. Tables 25-30. (p. 277-282)

SECTION VII: RAW MATERIALS
[Tables frequently include data by month.]

e. Hide supply and demand including exports, and prices; cattle on farms by type and weight class; federally inspected and other wholesale/retail cattle slaughter; and wettings of hides/skins, and leather production, by use category; various years 1970-83. Tables 1-5. (p. 286-290)

f. U.S. cattlehide exports, by world area and country of destination, and total imports; Chicago packer cattlehide monthly prices; and PPI of hides/skins and leathers by type, natural and synthetic rubber, rubber heels and soles, and footwear cut stock; and leather WPI; various years 1972-82. Tables 6-19. (p. 291-302)

g. OECD countries: production and consumption of cattlehides and calfskins, sole/industrial leather, leather for uppers/other purposes, and sheep/goat leather, by OECD country, 1971-81. Tables 20-29. (p. 303-312)

SECTION VIII: WORLD PRODUCTION, TRADE, AND CONSUMPTION

h. Footwear production, exports, imports, consumption, and, often, population, by country, for 5 world regions, 1981. Tables 1-5. (p. 316-319)

A4957-2   STATISTICAL REPORTER: Quarterly Report
Quarterly.   Approx. 18 p.
SRI/MF/complete

Quarterly statistical report on the footwear industry. Covers quantity and/or value of footwear production, shipments, and trade by country of origin and destination, with detail by footwear type and material. Also covers industry employment, hours, earnings, and labor productivity; and PPI, CPI, retail sales, and personal consumption expenditures, for footwear and selected other categories.

Data are primarily from Commerce and Labor Depts, and generally are shown for quarter of coverage, year to date, and selected previous periods. Report is published 3-9 months after quarter of coverage.

Contains 8 highlight tables and 25 detailed tables.

Report updates and supplements annual *Footwear Manual,* covered in SRI under A4957-1. A summary report is also issued, but is not covered by SRI.

Availability: Footwear Industries of America, Publications, 3700 Market St., Philadelphia PA 19104, members †, nonmembers $15.00 per yr. (or † with purchase of *Footwear Manual*); SRI/MF/complete.
Issues reviewed during 1984: 1st-4th Qtrs. 1983 (D).

A4965
Foreign Policy Association

A4965-1   GREAT DECISIONS '84 NATIONAL OPINION BALLOT REPORT
Annual.   June 1984.
6 p. Foldout.
SRI/MF/complete

Annual report presenting results of an opinion survey on selected foreign policy topics. Data for each topic are based on responses of 2,400-5,000 participants in the Great Decisions program, a series of nationwide foreign policy seminars.

Contains summaries of survey findings, and distribution of responses to questions regarding:

a. U.S.-USSR relations: military vs. conciliatory approach in dealing with USSR; and use of economic sanctions to influence Soviet policy.

b. Latin America: U.S. policy regarding insurgency-threatened governments with alleged human rights violations, leftist governments, and illegal immigration from Mexico.

c. U.S. security: nuclear force build-up, freeze, or reduction as best means of strengthening security; and U.S. nuclear missile deployment in Europe.

d. South Africa: U.S. economic, race-related, and military policies toward South Africa, and efforts to bring about independence for Namibia.

e. International debt crisis: increase of U.S. lending resources for IMF, appropriateness of IMF's terms for conditional loans, and relative importance of various factors in resolving the debt crisis.

f. Middle East: U.S. role in Middle East peace efforts, and military cooperation with Saudi Arabia and Jordan.

g. PRC-U.S. relations: U.S. stance in relations with PRC, and sale of arms to PRC and Taiwan.

h. International drug traffic: U.S. actions to gain foreign cooperation in combating drug traffic; and foreign supply reduction vs. domestic law enforcement as means of reducing U.S. drug use.

Availability: Foreign Policy Association, 205 Lexington Ave., New York NY 10016, †, 10 or more copies $0.50 each (prepaid); SRI/MF/complete.

A5025
Fraternal Order of Police

A5025-1   SURVEY OF SALARIES AND WORKING CONDITIONS of the Police Departments in the U.S.
Annual, discontinued.

Annual report on police salaries, staffing, hours, and benefits, discontinued with Mar. 15, 1983 report (for description, see SRI 1983 Annual, under this number).

Report has been discontinued in favor of a computerized data base, available to members only.

A5040
Futures Industry Association

A5040-1   VOLUME OF FUTURES TRADING, 1958-83
Annual.   [1984.]
8 p. no paging.
SRI/MF/complete

Annual report on commodity futures contracts trading volume for farm products, metals and raw materials, securities, and foreign currencies, by commodity and exchange, 1983, with detailed trends from 1979 and summary trends from 1958. Also includes option contracts traded, Oct.-Dec. 1982 and Jan.-Dec. 1983.

Contains 1 chart and 5 tables.

Report is an annual summary of a weekly report available to members only, and not covered in SRI.

Availability: Futures Industry Association, 1825 Eye St., NW, Suite 1040, Washington DC 20006, members †, nonmembers ◆; SRI/MF/complete.

A5040-2   MONTHLY VOLUME REPORT: Futures Contracts Traded
Monthly.   Approx. 3 p.
SRI/MF/complete, shipped quarterly

Monthly summary of a weekly bulletin on volume of commodity futures contracts traded on approximately 10 exchanges, by commodity and exchange. Report, compiled by the Futures Industry Assn, is issued approximately 2 weeks after month of coverage.

Contains the following tables:

[1] Futures contracts traded [by commodity and exchange, for month of coverage, year to date, and same periods of previous year; and total contract volume for same periods of preceding 4 years].

[2] [Commodities having] contracts with [volume] changes of 20,000/over in [month of coverage from same month of previous year, showing increase and decrease in number of contracts].

[3] Options contracts traded [by commodity and exchange, for month of coverage, year to date, and same periods of previous year].

[4] Futures/options [by exchange, for month of coverage; table begins with the Jan. 1984 issue].

Availability: Futures Industry Association, 1825 Eye St., NW, Suite 1040, Washington DC 20006, members †, nonmembers ◆; SRI/MF/complete, shipped quarterly.

Issues reviewed during 1984: Oct. 1983-Sept. 1984 (D).

A5100
Gas Appliance Manufacturers Association

A5100–1   STATISTICAL HIGHLIGHTS
Monthly, with annual summary. Approx. 13 p. SRI/MF/complete, shipped quarterly

Monthly report on shipments of gas and electric appliances and heating equipment. Data are compiled from member reports to GAMA, and releases from Assn of Home Appliance Manufacturers, and are issued approximately 1 month after month of coverage.

Contains contents listing, and 12 monthly tables listed below.

An annual 10-year summary table generally is included with the Mar. or Apr. issue.

Availability: Gas Appliance Manufacturers Association, 1901 N. Fort Myer Dr., Arlington VA 22209, †; SRI/MF/complete, shipped quarterly.

Issues reviewed during 1984: July 1983-Aug. 1984 (D); and 1974-83 annual summary.

TABLES:
[Tables show total industry shipments, monthly and by quarter for current year to date and previous year, unless otherwise noted.]

[1-2] Residential gas and electric ranges [by type].

[3] LP-Gas (liquefied petroleum gas) ranges [with and without ovens] for recreational vehicles, not expanded.

[4] Residential gas and electric storage water heaters, not expanded.

[5] Commercial [gas and electric] water heaters, not expanded.

[6] Central heating [gas, oil, and electric warm air] furnaces.

[7] Heating equipment [gas boilers; and oil boilers, not expanded].

[8] Gas residential [vented and direct vent system] wall furnaces.

[9] Other heating equipment, not expanded [gas recreational vehicle heating systems and gas floor furnaces].

[10] Gas unit heaters [propeller fan and blower types] and duct furnaces.

[11] Gas and electric clothes dryers.

[12] Gas grills [annual totals only, for previous 2 years].

A5120
General Aviation Manufacturers Association

A5120–1   GENERAL AVIATION AIRPLANE SHIPMENT REPORT
Monthly, with annual summary. Approx. 4 p. SRI/MF/complete, shipped quarterly

Monthly report, with annual summary, on general aviation aircraft shipments and billing prices, by manufacturer and model. Report excludes helicopters, gliders, and military contracts; but, as of Jan. 1984, includes separate data for shipments of "off-the-shelf" aircraft to the military.

Data are compiled by General Aviation Manufacturers Assn, and are shown for month of coverage, previous month, and current year to date. Report is issued 2-3 weeks after month of coverage.

Contains 1 extended table.

An annual summary accompanies the Dec. or Jan. issue.

Availability: General Aviation Manufacturers Association, Suite 801, 1400 K St., NW, Washington DC 20005, †; SRI/MF/complete, shipped quarterly.

Issues reviewed during 1984: Oct. 1983-Sept. 1984 (D); and annual summary for 1983.

A5120–2   GENERAL AVIATION STATISTICAL DATABOOK, 1984 Edition
Annual. [1984.] 29 p. SRI/MF/complete

Annual report on general aviation operations, 1983. Covers aircraft production and active fleet, pilots and other aviation personnel, landing facilities, accidents, and fuel use, with selected trends from 1946 and forecasts to 1995. Selected data are shown by State. Data are from original studies, FAA, and National Transportation Safety Board.

Contains foreword and contents listing (p. 1-2); report in 5 sections, with 2 charts and 21 tables (p. 4-27); and directory of GAMA members, and index (p. 28-29). All tables, and 1 chart presenting data not found in the tables, are listed below.

An additional annual report, *Industry Reports,* containing forecast data on aircraft shipments, is also published by issuing agency, but is not covered by SRI.

Availability: General Aviation Manufacturers Association, 1400 K St., NW, Suite 801, Washington DC 20005, $3.00; SRI/MF/complete.

TABLES AND CHART:
[Data are for U.S. general aviation, unless otherwise noted. Data by type or class of certificate include airline transport, helicopters, and gliders.]

A5120–2.1: Aircraft

[1] Annual shipments of new aircraft, by units shipped, number of companies reporting, and factory net billings [1946-83]. (p. 4)

[2-3] Aircraft shipments, by type of aircraft and by month [1962-83]. (p. 6-7)

[4] Aircraft exports [units and billings, 1965-83]. (p. 8)

[5] Type and primary use of active aircraft, 1982. (p. 10)

[6] Active aircraft, by region and State (as of Dec. 31, 1981-82). (p. 11)

[7] Estimated hours flown, by type of aircraft [as of Dec. 31, 1976-82]. (p. 12)

[8] Active aircraft and average hours annually flown per aircraft, by type [1978-82]. (p. 12)

A5120–2.2: Pilots
[All tables except table [3] show data as of Dec. 31. Data on personnel are for all types of aviation.]

[1] Active pilot [and nonpilot aviation-related] certificates held [by type of certification, 1971-82]. (p. 14)

[2] Active pilots [by type] and flight instructors, by FAA region and State (1982). (p. 15)

[3] Student pilot certificates processed, by month [1971-83]. (p. 16)

[4-5] Estimated total and instrument rated pilots, 1976-82; and estimated instrument ratings held, by class of certificates, 1981-82. (p. 17)

[6] Women actively engaged in aviation [by type of certificate, 1970-82]. (p. 18)

A5120–2.3: Miscellaneous
[Tables 1-4 show data as of Dec. 31.]

[1] Civil/joint-use airports/heliports/stolports/seaplane bases on record, by type of ownership [and by whether paved and lighted, all by FAA region and State], 1983. (p. 20)

[2] FAA air route facilities and services [by type, including air traffic control towers and centers, instrument landing systems, and radar], 1972-82. (p. 22)

[3-4] Estimated active aircraft by type of aircraft [1978-94]; and forecast active pilots by type of certificate [1983-94]. (p. 24-25)

[5-6] Forecast hours flown and estimated fuel consumed, by type of aircraft; [FY79-95]. (p. 26)

[7] Accident rates [for total and fatal accidents], 1972-83. [chart] (p. 27)

[8] Fuel consumed, by type of aircraft, 1982. (p. 27)

A5135
German American Chamber of Commerce

A5135–1   GATN: GERMAN-AMERICAN TRADE NEWS
Quarterly. Approx. 35 p. ISSN 0192-0103. LC 67-5453. SRI/MF/complete

Quarterly journal promoting trade and business relations between the U.S. and the Federal Republic of Germany. Includes reporting on investment trends, industries or individual companies, financing, and trade legislation or regulation.

Most data are current to 3-6 months prior to cover date. Data sources include IMF, U.S. and German Government agencies, and Deutsche Bundesbank.

Issues generally contain feature articles, some with statistics; news briefs and trade fair calendar; and 1 recurring economic review table, described below.

Recurring table generally appears in alternate issues. All additional features with substantial statistical content are described, as they appear, under "Statistical Features." Nonstatistical features are not covered.

Prior to the Oct. 1984 issue, journal was published bimonthly.

Availability: German American Chamber of Commerce, 666 Fifth Ave., New York NY 10103, $9.00 per yr., single copy $2.50; SRI/MF/complete.

Issues reviewed during 1984: Nov./Dec. 1983-July/Aug. 1984 (bimonthly); Oct. 1984 (quarterly) (P) (Vol. 37, No. 6; Vol. 38, Nos. 1-5) [July/Aug. 1984, Vol. 38, No. 4 incorrectly reads May/June 1984, Vol. 38, No. 3].

RECURRING TABLE:

Table shows the following for U.S. and for Germany:

a. Foreign trade and U.S./German trade, including imports, exports, and balances.

b. Industrial production changes, total and for 7 industries; and labor market profile, including labor force, unemployment, and gross hourly wages in manufacturing.

c. Prices (annual change in CPI, PPI, and terms of trade); and currency exchange rates (U.S. dollar/German mark).

d. National accounts components, including GNP, current account balance, monetary reserves, and total and foreign direct investment (total and U.S.-Germany).

All data are shown annually for 2 preceding years. National accounts data are also shown for 2-4 consecutive quarters through quarter ending 2-5 months prior to issue date. All other data are also shown for 3 consecutive months through month 3-5 months prior to publication date.

STATISTICAL FEATURES:

A5135–1.501: Nov./Dec. 1983 (Vol. 37, No. 6)

NEW GERMAN MEDIA

(p. 9-13) Article, with 2 tables showing the following for 14 West European countries: population, and number of licensed TVs and percent color, (no date); and households, and cable and master antenna TV subscribers, Dec. 1981. Data sources include *EBU Review, TV/Radio Age International,* and Frost and Sullivan.

A related article appears on p. 17-22.

A5135–1.502: Jan./Feb. 1984 (Vol. 38, No. 1)

SPECIAL TABLES

[The following rankings are for individual companies in West Germany, 1982 with comparisons to 1981. Data are from *Die Grossen 500.*]

[1-2] Top 100 industrials and top 75 trading firms [ranked by sales, and also showing employment]. (p. 16-17)

[3] Top 50 banks [ranked by balance totals]. (p. 18)

Similar data, for 1980-81, were published in the Jan./Feb. 1983 issue (for description, see SRI 1983 Annual, under A5135-1.403.)

A5135–1.503: Mar./Apr. 1984 (Vol. 38, No. 2)

MACHINE BUILDERS AT THE CROSSROADS

(p. 5-10) Article on Germany's machinery industry. Data are from German Assn of Machine Builders. Includes 2 tables showing value of German machinery exports to developing countries, 1980-83; and world machinery output, by country, 1983; all in German Marks.

A5135–1.504: July/Aug. 1984 (Vol. 38, No. 4)

[Issue contents page incorrectly reads May/June 1983, Vol. 38, No. 3.]

EFFECTS OF EXCHANGE RATE UNCERTAINTY ON GERMAN AND U.S. TRADE

(p. 19-26) By M. A. Akhtar and R. Spence Hilton. Article, with 2 tables estimating the effects of exchange rate variability on multilateral trade in manufactures, for West Germany and U.S. Estimates are based on statistical analysis of trade and exchange rate data for 1970s-81.

A5135–2   U.S.-GERMAN ECONOMIC SURVEY, 1983
Annual. Jan. 1984. 210 p.
ISSN 0147-4421.
LC 77-649637.
SRI/MF/complete

Annual compilation of articles and comparative statistics on West German and U.S. commercial and economic trends and policies, 1960s-83. Includes data on socioeconomic conditions, industrial production, energy, finance, trade, GNP, and prices. Data are primarily from U.S. Commerce and Labor Depts, and Statistisches Bundesamt.

Contents:

a. Contents listing; preface; and 16 feature articles on investment, trade, energy consumption, auto industry, technology, banking, and insurance, with German-language summaries. (p. 7-146)

b. Narrative profiles of companies, States, German cities, and trade fair organizations purchasing advertising space. (p. 148-185)

c. Statistical review section, with 2 maps, 20 charts, and 39 tables; and information sources and index of advertisers. (p. 187-210)

Articles with statistics, and statistical review tables and charts, are described below.

This is the 9th annual edition.

Availability: Manhattan Publishing Co., PO Box 650, Croton-on-Hudson NY 10520, $12.50; SRI/MF/complete.

STATISTICAL FEATURES:

A5135–2.1: Statistical Articles

VIEW FROM BONN

(p. 11-20) By Gerhard Stoltenberg. Article discussing world economic situation. Includes 5 charts showing German long-term capital exports and imports by type and world region, 1979-82 period; and structure of German enterprises' direct investment abroad, including form of organization and foreign participation, 1981.

GERMAN INDUSTRIAL INVESTMENTS IN THE USA

(p. 49-54) By Karl W. Brandt and Dieter Elsner. Article, with 2 tables showing German investments in U.S., selected years 1972-82; and U.S. affiliates of 14 German companies, including company ownership share, and value of turnover, 1981. Data are from Bundesbank, *Forbes,* and *Wirtschaftswoche.*

GERMAN ENERGY OUTLOOK

(p. 64-70) By Rudolf von Bennigsen-Foerder. Article, with 1 chart showing total German energy consumption (in hard coal tons equivalent), selected years 1979-2000.

U.S. ECONOMIC AND PETROLEUM CONDITIONS

(p. 73-78) By Tor Meloe. Article, with 3 charts showing U.S. petroleum demand trends by type of product, various periods 1978-90; and OPEC crude oil production and capacity, 1983 and trends.

A5135–2.2: Statistical Review Tables and Charts

[All data are shown for U.S. and West Germany.]

a. Population by sex, age, and State or Province; households and land area; labor force and unemployment; manufacturing, farm, government, and other employment; hourly earnings in manufacturing and 6 major industry groups; and CPI and PPI, by major component; various years 1960-82. 2 maps, 2 charts, and 10 tables. (p. 188-191)

b. Industrial production, including index trends, value of shipments (total and for 7 industry groups), and production of 8 commodities, various years 1960-82. 2 charts and 4 tables. (p. 192-193)

c. Manufacturing productivity and labor costs, including hourly output and compensation indexes, and production worker compensation amounts, generally 1975-82. 2 charts and 4 tables. (p. 194-195)

d. Trade, including trends from 1960; and imports and exports by commodity group, percent distribution for 5 leading countries of origin and destination, and U.S. exports to and imports from Germany by detailed commodity, 1980-82. 6 charts and 5 tables. (p. 196-199)

e. Foreign investment, including U.S.-German investment trends from 1960; and direct investment abroad and foreign investment in U.S. and Germany, by industry and country, 1976-82. 2 charts and 4 tables. (p. 200-201)

f. GNP, including personal and government consumption, private domestic investment, and net exports, at current and constant prices, 1960 and 1970-82. 2 charts and 4 tables. (p. 202-203)

g. Finance, including monetary reserves, current account balance for 3 sectors, and currency exchange rates; and number of households by income level, family budgets at 3 levels by item, and percent of households owning 6 types of durable goods; various periods 1960-June 1983. 4 charts and 8 tables. (p. 204-207)

A5145
Gold Institute

A5145-1   MODERN GOLD COINAGE, 1983

Annual. [1984.] 30 p.
ISSN 0149-4279.
LC 77-643382.
SRI/MF/complete, delayed

Annual report on gold coins issued as money in 65 countries or world areas, 1983. Includes number, gold content, and physical characteristics of coins, for 181 coin issues grouped by country. Also includes mint where coins were struck, total gold used, and total face value of coins in local currency, for each country.

Data are from ministries of finance, central banks, government and private mints, and numismatic experts.

Contains introduction (p. 1); 1 summary table (p. 2-3); 1 detailed table repeated for each country (p. 4-29); and directory of mints (p. 30).

Availability: Gold Institute, 1001 Connecticut Ave., NW, Washington DC 20036, $7.00; SRI/MF/complete, delayed shipment in Mar. 1985.

A5145-2   WORLD MINE PRODUCTION OF GOLD, 1982-86

Annual. Jan. 1984. 10 p.
SRI/MF/complete

Annual report on gold mine production from underground/surface/alluvial sources in 57 countries, 1982-86. Data are from approximately 250 mining enterprises.

Contains brief narrative (p. 1); 2 tables showing gold production by country, 1982, estimated 1983, and projected 1984-86 (p. 2-3); and list showing name and location of participating companies, arranged by country (p. 4-10).

Availability: Gold Institute, 1001 Connecticut Ave., NW, Washington DC 20036, †; SRI/MF/complete.

A5160
Guttmacher, Alan, Institute

A5160-1   FAMILY PLANNING PERSPECTIVES

Bimonthly. Approx. 50 p.
cumulative pagination
throughout year.
ISSN 0014-7354.
LC 72-620943.
SRI/MF/not filmed

Bimonthly journal devoted to family planning medical and policy issues, including contraception and abortion.

Each issue contains articles, some with statistical content; a news digest section summarizing recent developments in family planning; and book reviews. Annual subject and author indexes appear in Nov./Dec. issue.

Features with substantial statistical content are described, as they appear, under "Statistical Features." Each issue of the journal is reviewed, but an abstract is published in SRI monthly issues only when statistical features appear. Features presenting solely clinical data are not covered.

Availability: Alan Guttmacher Institute, 360 Park Ave. S., New York NY 10010, members $9.25, nonmembers $18.50; SRI/MF/not filmed.

Issues reviewed during 1984: Sept./Oct. 1983-July/Aug. 1984 (P) (Vol. 15, Nos. 5-6; Vol. 16, Nos. 1-4).

STATISTICAL FEATURES:

A5160-1.501: Sept./Oct. 1983 (Vol. 15, No. 5)

CONTRACEPTIVE CONTINUATION AMONG ADOLESCENTS ATTENDING FAMILY PLANNING CLINICS

(p. 211-217) By Frank F. Furstenberg, Jr. et al. Article evaluating interview methods used to assess contraceptive practices among teenagers. Data are from a study of 445 female adolescents using 9 federally funded family planning clinics in Philadelphia, Pa., Jan. 1980-Sept. 1981.

Includes text statistics and 2 tables showing percent of patients reporting contraceptive use according to 3 methods of analyzing interview data, with multiple regression analysis and detail by sexual history, and demographic and educational characteristics.

YOUNG AMERICAN WOMEN DELAYING MOTHERHOOD; 25 PERCENT MAY REMAIN PERMANENTLY CHILDLESS

(p. 224-225) Article, with 1 table estimating mother's average age and standard deviation in age at 1st birth, and percent of women ever giving birth, by age group, as derived from 1976 National Survey of Family Growth, 1978 National Longitudinal Survey, and 1980 Current Population Survey.

RISK OF PID 5X GREATER FROM DALKON SHIELD THAN FROM OTHER IUDs

(p. 225-226) Article, with 1 table showing risk of contracting pelvic inflammatory disease (PID), for contraceptive users relative to nonusers, by contraceptive type (including 5 types of intrauterine device), 1976-78 period. Data are based on a 1976-78 study of 622 women aged 18-44 who were hospitalized for PID and 2,369 women who acted as controls.

POTENCY OF ESTROGEN, PROGESTIN CAN AFFECT LEVELS OF CHOLESTEROL

(p. 228-229) Article, with 2 tables showing estrogen and progestin composition of 8 oral contraceptives; and level of high- and low-density lipoprotein cholesterol for women using hormones by type and for nonusers, by age group (20-44 and 45-65 years) and menstrual status.

Data are from a 1971-76 survey of 1,744 white women, age 20 years and older, participating in the Lipid Research Clinics Program sponsored by NIH.

ABORTION ISSUE IN THE 1980 ELECTIONS

(p. 231-238) By Donald Granberg and James Burlison. Article on impact of abortion issue on 1980 elections. Most data are based on pre- and post-election interviews with 1,614 persons of voting age, conducted by University of Michigan Center for Political Studies. Most political action committee (PAC) data are from *Congressional Quarterly* election reports.

Includes 12 tables showing the following for 1980 election, unless otherwise noted:

a. Presidential election: respondent distribution by preferred candidate, by respondent's position on abortion and belief that candidate shares that position, and perceived importance of abortion and other issues; and correlation coefficients showing impact of selected issues (including abortion) and demographic characteristics on candidate selection.

b. Respondent distribution by perception of abortion position of Federal Government, major political parties, and presidential candidates.

c. Congressional elections: correlation coefficients showing impact of selected issues (including abortion) on Senate elections; and voting distribution for House and Senate elections involving candidates backed by pro- and anti-abortion PACs, by candidate, with some detail by respondent's abortion position, 1980 and 1982.

EFFECTS OF VAGINAL SPERMICIDES ON PREGNANCY OUTCOME

(p. 244-250) By Theresa O. Scholl et al. Article, with text statistics and 1 table showing possibility ratios for giving birth to a female infant and for losing fetus, for women using vaginal spermicides before and after conception relative to former users and nonusers, Jan. 1973-Sept. 1976 period. Data are from the National Survey of Family Growth conducted by NCHS.

A5160-1.502: Nov./Dec. 1983 (Vol. 15, No. 6)

SECOND PREGNANCIES AMONG TEENAGE MOTHERS

(p. 268-272) By Kathleen Ford. Article on contraceptive use and pregnancy risk among sexually active teenage mothers during year after 1st birth. Data on use and risk levels are shown variously by race, income as percent of poverty level, marital status and age at 1st pregnancy and/or birth, months since 1st birth, and whether 2nd pregnancy was planned.

Data are based on responses of 483 teenage women interviewed during the 1976 National Survey of Family Growth. Includes 3 tables.

FAMILY PLANNING CLINIC SERVICES IN THE U.S., 1981

(p. 272-278) By Aida Torres and Jacqueline Darroch Forrest. Article on family planning provider services and patients, 1981 and trends. Data are primarily based on the Alan Guttmacher Institute most recent survey of the family planning clinic network. Includes 7 tables showing the following:

a. Providers: distribution of agencies, and average number of women served, by type of facility (hospitals, health depts, Planned Parenthood affiliates, and other); and clinics and women served, by region and State; various years 1969-81.

b. Pregnancy risk: women at risk for unintended pregnancy, by age group and poverty status; and low-income and teenage women at risk, with percent obtaining family planning services from clinics and private physicians, by region and State; 1981.

c. Clinic patients: distribution by age (over and under 20), race, number of previous births, and contraceptive method used before and after 1st visit to clinic, various years 1969-81.

PUBLIC SUPPORT FOR LEGAL ABORTION CONTINUES, ALTHOUGH POLLS SHOW CONFLICTING TRENDS IN 1983

(p. 279-281) Article, with 1 table showing percent of adults approving of legal abortions under 6 specific circumstances and under any circumstance, selected periods 1965-83. Data are based on a 1983 survey of 1,599 adults conducted by National Opinion Research Center (NORC), and earlier NORC surveys.

FAMILY SIZE AND ECONOMIC WELFARE

(p. 289-294) By Thomas J. Espenshade et al. Article analyzing impact of family size on economic well-being. Data are based on responses of 4,136 households selected from 10,106 households responding to the 1973 Consumer Expenditure Survey.

Includes 6 tables showing the following by number of children and household head's age group and education: number of households; total and food expenditures; earnings of husband, wife, and children; percent of income spent on current consumption; percent of households receiving welfare and food stamps; and home size, market value, and monthly rent.

A5160–1.503: Jan./Feb. 1984 (Vol. 16, No. 1)

SOURCES OF PRESCRIPTION CONTRACEPTIVES AND SUBSEQUENT PREGNANCY AMONG YOUNG WOMEN

(p. 6-13) By Melvin Zelnik et al. Article on prescription contraceptive use and subsequent pregnancies among adolescent women, with some comparison to users of nonprescription contraceptives. Data are based on a 1979 probability sample survey of urban women aged 15-19.

Includes 2 tables presenting regression analyses; and 8 tables showing survey response for the following, generally by race and prescription source (clinic and private physician):

a. First use of contraceptive by whether prescription or nonprescription; and 1st prescription method used, and frequency of prior use of nonprescription contraceptives.

b. Prescription contraceptive users: age at 1st use and 1st intercourse; parental education and family stability; reason for medical visit at which prescription obtained; reason for choosing method; and incidence of premarital pregnancy by number of months since 1st prescription use.

CHARACTERISTICS OF WOMEN WHO STOP USING CONTRACEPTIVES

(p. 14-18) By Charles R. Hammerslough. Article examining socioeconomic characteristics of currently married women who discontinued contraceptive use after 1 year. Data are from the 1973 and 1976 National Surveys of Family Growth, conducted by NCHS.

Includes 3 tables presenting discontinuance probability ratios and respondent distributions, variously tabulated for former contraceptive method used, and respondent race, income, age, education, and religion.

AVAILABILITY OF SEX EDUCATION IN LARGE CITY SCHOOL DISTRICTS

(p. 19-25) By Freya L. Sonenstein and Karen J. Pittman. Article on elementary and secondary school sex education. Data are from responses of 179 school districts representing 161 cities with populations over 100,000 to a 1982 Urban Institute survey.

Includes 6 tables showing percent of elementary, junior high, and high schools citing selected reasons for initiating sex education programs, and number of schools with programs by program enrollment and annual hours of instruction; and aggregate response concerning major goals and content of sex education classes.

PUBLIC HEALTH EFFECTS OF LEGAL ABORTION IN THE U.S.

(p. 26-28) By Christopher Tietze. Article, with 3 tables showing birth-related mortality rates; abortion-related mortality rate for legal, illegal, and spontaneous abortions; and abortion rate for psychiatric, rubella, and other patients, for New York City and U.S.; various periods 1958-80. Data are from NCHS and Centers for Disease Control.

NSFG 1982: STERILIZATION USE UP, PILL USE DOWN AMONG MARRIED WOMEN

(p. 37-38) Article, with 1 chart showing distribution of all and currently married women aged 15-44 who have ever had sexual intercourse, by current contraceptive method. Data are from Cycle III of the 1982 National Survey of Family Growth (NSFG), conducted by NCHS.

U.S. WOMEN UNHAPPY WITH THE CURRENT CHOICE OF BIRTH CONTROL METHODS

(p. 41-42) Article, with 1 table comparing 3 contraceptive methods as rated by all women and users of each method. Data are from responses of 155 women aged 18-45 to a 1982 Yankelovich, Skelly and White, Inc. survey.

FERTILITY OF WHITE, BUT NOT OF BLACK, CATHOLICS STILL SOMEWHAT HIGHER THAN THAT OF PROTESTANTS

(p. 42) Article, with 1 table showing fertility rate, births expected, and wanted pregnancies, for women aged 15-44, by religion and race, and for Hispanic Catholics. Data are from the 1973 and 1976 National Surveys of Family Growth, conducted by NCHS.

A5160–1.504: Mar./Apr. 1984 (Vol. 16, No. 2)

REPEAT ABORTION: IS IT A PROBLEM?

(p. 70-75) By Charlene Berger et al. Article characterizing Canadian first- and repeat-abortion patients. Data are from Statistics Canada, and responses of 580 abortion patients at Montreal General Hospital to a 1977-78 survey conducted by the authors. Includes 3 tables showing the following:

a. Survey respondent distribution by age, marital and economic status, educational attainment, religious affiliation and strength of beliefs, number of children, and whether contraceptive was being used during month of conception (with detail by type of contraceptive for users), all for first- and repeat-abortion patients, 1977/78.

b. Canadian and Quebecois abortion patients by age, marital status, and whether obtaining first or repeat abortion, 1978.

Also includes 1 table showing summary coefficient analysis.

OBSERVATION: CONTRACEPTIVE METHOD USE FOLLOWING AN ABORTION

(p. 75-77) By Stanley K. Henshaw. Article on contraceptive use among abortion patients. Data are from 1970 National Fertility Study, and a Minnesota Dept of Health study of 22,-070 first and 8,374 repeat abortion patients 1981/82.

Includes 1 table showing contraceptive failure rates, 1970; and distribution of women at risk of and obtaining first and repeat abortions, 1981/82; all by contraceptive method.

SEX, CONTRACEPTION, AND PARENTHOOD: EXPERIENCE AND ATTITUDES AMONG URBAN BLACK YOUNG MEN

(p. 77-82) By Samuel D. Clark, Jr., et al. Article examining attitudes of black urban adolescent males regarding sexual activity and contraception, based on 663 responses to a Sept. 1981 survey of students from 2 schools in Baltimore, Md. Includes 5 tables showing the following:

a. Distribution of respondents by sexual activity and contraceptive use, by age.

b. Percent of respondents rating 8 contraceptive methods as very good; and responses concerning contraceptive acceptability, responsibility, practices, and availability; all by respondent sexual experience and contraceptive use.

PRIVATE PHYSICIANS AND THE PROVISION OF CONTRACEPTIVES TO ADOLESCENTS

(p. 83-86) By Margaret Terry Orr. Article, with 3 tables on physicians' policies toward adolescents seeking contraceptives. Tables show how physicians respond to requests for contraceptives, types of contraceptives prescribed, and fee charged (by metro status and region), all by physician specialty. Data are from responses of 1,207 private physicians in 37 counties to a 1982-83 Alan Guttmacher Institute survey.

OUT-OF-WEDLOCK BIRTHRATE RISING AMONG WHITES, FALLING AMONG BLACKS; OVERALL FERTILITY DECLINING

(p. 90-91) Article, with 2 tables showing number of births, and fertility rate by age, for all and unmarried women by race, 1980-81. Data are from NCHS.

USING AN IUD FOR FIVE OR MORE YEARS MAY LEAD TO AN INCREASED RISK OF SEVERE PELVIC INFECTION

(p. 93-94) Article on possible relationship between use of intrauterine devices (IUDs) and incidence of pelvic inflammatory disease (PID). Data are based on a study of 690 PID and 2,569 control group patients conducted by Women's Health Study in 16 hospitals in 9 cities, 1976-78. Includes 1 table showing patient distribution by severity of PID and duration of IUD use, with relative risk of contracting PID for each group of patients.

A5160–1.505: May/June 1984 (Vol. 16, No. 3)

ABORTION SERVICES IN THE U.S., 1981-82, ANNUAL FEATURE

(p. 119-127) Annual article, by Stanley K. Henshaw et al., on abortion service availability and use, 1981-82. Data are from the 8th annual survey of health institutions and private physicians providing abortion services, conducted by Alan Guttmacher Institute in 1983.

Includes 11 tables showing the following, for various years 1980-83, with selected trends from 1973:

a. Metro and nonmetro abortions and facilities, and abortions and rate by State and census division; percent of metro and nonmetro counties with no abortion facilities and with no facilities reporting more than 400 abortions, and percent of women aged 15-44 living in those counties; and hospitals providing abortions by caseload and type, and hospital abortions by caseload.

b. Nonhospital abortion facilities by caseload and percent providing selected services to nonabortion patients, and nonhospital abortions, by facility type; distribution of abortion facilities by type, by maximum gestation accepted; and average charges for nonhospital abortions by facility type and caseload.

c. Distribution of HMOs by type of abortion services provided; and percent of abortion facilities accepting State reimbursement for abortions for Medicaid-eligible patients, by type of facility and selected State.

Data corrections appear in July/Aug. issue (see A5160-1.506, below).

For description of previous article, see SRI 1982 Annual, under A5160-1.303.

PUBLIC FUNDING OF CONTRACEPTIVE, STERILIZATION, AND ABORTION SERVICES, 1982

(p. 128-133) By Barry Nestor and Rachel Benson Gold. Article on publicly funded contraceptive services and abortions, FY82. Data are from various Federal and private sources.

Includes 4 tables showing contraceptive service and sterilization expenditures by funding source, and number of sterilizations, by State; and abortion expenditures and number of publicly funded abortions by funding source, by State arranged by type of abortion available; FY82 with summary comparisons to FY81.

EFFECTS OF FEDERAL FUNDING CUTS ON FAMILY PLANNING SERVICES, 1980-83

(p. 134-138) By Aida Torres. Article examining effects of Federal and State funding cuts on family planning services. Data are from 327 responses to a 1982 Alan Guttmacher Institute survey of agencies providing family planning services, and from a 1983 follow-up survey.

Includes 5 tables showing survey response on the following: agencies receiving funds and experiencing funding reductions, by type of agency and funding source; and agencies providing selected family planning services, with detail by funding source; 1980 and 1983.

WORLD POPULATION: WIDE REGIONAL VARIATIONS IN FERTILITY, MORTALITY RATES

(p. 145-146) Article, with 1 table showing world population by region, selected years 1950-2000. Data are from Census Bureau.

A5160–1.506: July/Aug. 1984 (Vol. 16, No. 4)

OUT-OF-WEDLOCK BIRTHS, PREMARITAL PREGNANCIES, AND THEIR EFFECT ON FAMILY FORMATION AND DISSOLUTION

(p. 157-162) By Martin O'Connell and Carolyn C. Rogers. Article examining effects of out-of-wedlock pregnancies and births on subsequent marriages. Data are from Census Bureau. Includes 7 tables showing the following for various 4-year periods (cohorts), 1925-81:

a. Firstborn babies conceived out-of-wedlock (total and as percent of all 1st births), by mother's age, race, and marital status at baby's birth; and percent of women whose firstborn was conceived out-of-wedlock who married before and after baby's birth, by race and age; all by birth cohort of baby.

b. Women married by age 18 and 21, by race, birth cohort, and whether they gave birth prior to 1st marriage; and women separating from their husbands within 5 years and 1st married in 1980/81, shown variously by fertility status and age at marriage, race, marriage cohort, and marital status, with detail by selected socioeconomic characteristics.

Article updates a previous study on legitimacy status of 1st births covering 1939-78 period, described in SRI 1980 Annual under A5160-1.103.

FAMILY COMMUNICATION AND TEENAGERS' CONTRACEPTIVE USE

(p. 163-170) By Frank F. Furstenberg, Jr., et al. Article on prevalence and openness of mother-daughter discussions regarding sex and birth control, and the possible relationship to effective use of contraceptives among teenage women. Data are based on responses of 290 teenage women visiting family planning clinics in southeastern Pennsylvania to 1980-81 surveys conducted by the authors.

Includes 3 tables showing survey response and selected respondent characteristics.

MEDICAID CUTOFF AND ABORTION SERVICES FOR THE POOR

(p. 170-180) By Stanley K. Henshaw and Lynn S. Wallisch. Article on effects of Federal restrictions on Medicaid funding for abortions. Data are based on records of an inner-city abortion clinic in St. Louis, Missouri, and responses of 197 abortion patients at the clinic to an Oct. 1982-Feb. 1983 survey conducted by the authors.

Includes 7 tables showing the following, generally by Medicaid eligibility, 1977 and/or 1982, with summary comparisons to U.S., 1980:

a. Distribution of abortion patients by age, education, marital status, race, number of lifetime births and prior abortions, and source of funds for abortion.

b. Mean gestation of terminated pregnancies; mean length of selected intervals between last menstrual period and abortion; and percent of abortion patients delayed in obtaining pregnancy test and abortion by reason for delay, and percent receiving abortion information from 8 sources.

ADOLESCENT SEXUAL ATTITUDES AND BEHAVIOR: ARE THEY CONSISTENT?

(p. 181-185) By Laurie S. Zabin et al. Article comparing sexual attitudes and behavior of urban teenagers. Data are based on responses of 3,534 inner-city high school students to a 1981/82 survey.

Includes 8 tables showing survey response on the following, generally by sex, race, age, and sexual experience: best age for 1st intercourse, and best age cited vs. current age and age at 1st intercourse; views on premarital sex; most appropriate relationship for initiating intercourse, and relationship cited vs. relationship with partner at most recent intercourse; and contraceptive use at most recent intercourse.

CORRECTION

(p. 200) Correction to article on abortion service availability and use appearing in May/June 1984 issue. Includes corrected data on abortions in South Dakota, 1982.

For description of original article, see A5160-1.505, above.

A5160–2   ABORTION SERVICES in the U.S., Each State, and Metropolitan Area, 1979-80
Recurring (irreg.) 1983.
9+ii+102 p.
LC 81-69082.
SRI/MF/not filmed

Recurring report, edited by Stanley K. Henshaw, on abortions, 1980, with trends from 1973. Includes data on patient characteristics; and abortions performed and facilities providing abortions, by SMSA, State, census division, and nonmetro area.

Data are from approximately 3,300 responses to the 1981 Abortion Provider Survey conducted by the Alan Guttmacher Institute (AGI), and previous Institute surveys; and from the Centers for Disease Control.

Contains list of survey staff, acknowledgements, and contents and table listings (7 p.); introduction (p. i-ii); 7 articles, with numerous charts and tables (p. 1-49); 11 detailed tables, preceded by narrative introduction (p. 53-91); and methodology and facsimile questionnaires. (p. 94-102)

Detailed tables are described below. Articles were originally published in the AGI *Family Planning Perspectives* and are described in SRI 1982 and 1983 Annuals under A5160-1.

Availability: Alan Guttmacher Institute, 360 Park Ave., S., New York NY 10010, $10.00; SRI/MF/not filmed.

TABLES:

A5160–2.1: Detailed Tables

a. Abortions: number, rate, and as percent of pregnancies, by age, race, and marital status; and abortions by number of previous abortions and live births, weeks of gestation, and method; 1973-80. Tables 1-4. (p. 55-58)

b. Abortions, providers, and women age 15-44 years, by SMSA and for all nonmetro areas by State; abortions and providers, by facility type (public and private hospitals, nonhospital clinics, and physician's offices), by State; and hospital and nonhospital providers, and percent of abortions performed in hospitals, by SMSA; various years 1978-80. Tables 5-8. (p. 59-81)

c. Providers performing 50-499 and 500/ more 2nd trimester abortions, by census division, State, and SMSA, 1980; and abortions and rate, by census division and State, 1973-80. Tables 9-11. (p. 82-91)

A5173
Health Insurance
Association of America

A5173–2   SOURCE BOOK OF HEALTH INSURANCE DATA, 1982-83, 1984 Update
Biennial. [1984.]   30 p.
LC 60-187.
SRI/MF/complete

Biennial interim report, for 1984, providing updated information for selected tables appearing in the biennial *Source Book of Health Insurance Data, 1982-83*. Presents data on health insurance coverage, benefit payments, premium income, and health care expenditures and costs, various years 1935-84.

Data are compiled from insurance company, health insurance plan, government agency, and hospital and medical assn reports. Data source is noted on each table.

Contains foreword and 1 trend table (p. 1-2); 26 updated chapter tables from the *Source Book*, listed below (p. 3-26); 2 appendix tables showing number of persons covered, by type of coverage and insurer, 1982 (p. 27-28); and listings of additional updated tables available, and tables not updated (p. 29-30).

This report alternates with the biennial source book. Prior to 1984, full source book was published annually. For description of 1982-83 source book, see SRI 1983 Annual under this number.

Availability: Health Insurance Association of America, Order Fulfillment, 1850 K St., NW, Washington DC 20006, †; SRI/MF/complete.

UPDATED CHAPTER TABLES:
[Table numbers correspond to those published in the 1982-83 source book.]

A5173–2.1: Health Insurance
[Data shown by type of insurer generally include all insurers, all insurance companies, Blue Cross/Blue Shield and other plans.
  Data by type of policy are for group policies and individual/family policies.]

EXTENT OF COVERAGE
[Tables 1.1-1.8 begin "Number of persons..." Tables 1.1-1.6 include 1982 detail for persons under 65 and 65/over.]

1.1. With health insurance protection, by type of coverage [hospital, surgical, physician, major medical, and dental expense, and short- and long-term disability income, selected years 1940-82]. (p. 3)

1.2-1.5. With hospital insurance, and surgical, physician's, and major medical expense protection, by type of insurer [and policy, various years 1940-82]. (p. 4-7)

1.6. With major medical expense protection with insurance companies, by type of policy [selected years 1951-82]. (p. 8)

1.7. With disability income protection, by type of [insurance] program [and policy, including formal paid sick leave], selected years 1946-82. (p. 9)

1.8. With dental expense protection, by type of insurer [1967-82]. (p. 10)

BENEFIT PAYMENTS
[Tables 2.1-2.2 begin "Health insurance benefit payments..." Data by type of coverage include medical and dental expenses, and loss of income.]

2.1. By type of insurer and by type of coverage [selected years 1950-82]. (p. 11)

2.2. Of insurance companies [by type of coverage, by type of policy, selected years 1945-82]. (p. 12)

PREMIUM INCOME
[Tables begin "Health insurance premiums..."]

3.1. And ratio to disposable personal income [by type of insurer, selected years 1940-82]. (p. 13)

3.2. Of insurance companies, by type of policy and by type of protection [loss of income and hospital/medical expenses, selected years 1935-82]. (p. 14)

A5173–2.2: Medical Care Costs
[Types of expenditure include personal health care expenses, program administration/net cost of insurance, government public health activities, research, and construction.]

NATIONAL AND PERSONAL HEALTH CARE EXPENDITURES

5.1. Estimated national health expenditures, by type of expenditure, and source of funds [public or private], 1983. (p. 15)

5.2. Comparison of [amount and] growth rates of GNP and national health expenditures [selected years 1950-83]. (p. 15)

5.5. National health care expenditures, by type of expenditure [including personal health spending for hospital and nursing home care, physician and dental services, and drugs/medical sundries, by] source of funds [consumer, other private, Federal, and State/local], 1982-83. (p. 16)

5.9. Personal health care expenditures, by source of payment [including direct payments, and private health insurance, government, and philanthropy/industry payments, 1966-82]. (p. 17)

PERSONAL CONSUMPTION AND CPI

5.10. Personal consumption expenditures, by type of product, 1982. (p. 18)

5.11. Ratio of personal consumption expenditures for medical care to disposable personal income and to total personal consumption expenditures [selected years 1950-82]. (p. 19)

5.13. CPI for medical care items [by item, selected years 1947-83]. (p. 20)

HOSPITAL AND OTHER COSTS

5.19. Average cost to community hospitals per patient day and per patient stay [and] average length of stay in community hospitals [selected years 1946-82]. (p. 21)

5.20. Community hospital statistics [average hospital cost per day, and average length of stay, by State], 1982. (p. 22)

5.21. Comparison of hospital semi-private room charges, by State, July 1983 and Jan. 1984, and percent change. (p. 23)

5.22-5.23. Average surgeon's and dental fees [by procedure], selected [metro and nonmetro] areas, 1983. (p. 24-25)

5.24. Median office-visit fees, by type of physician, 1981-83. (p. 26)

5.25. Regional variations in median physician fees [by type of visit, for general practitioners, and all surgical and all nonsurgical specialists], 1983. (p. 26)

A5173–3   HEALTH AND HEALTH INSURANCE: The Public's View
Annual.   1984.   39 p.
SRI/MF/complete

Annual survey report on public attitudes toward health care service and costs, cost containment, medical malpractice, health insurance companies, and bioethical issues, 1983. Includes selected comparisons from previous surveys, 1977-83.

Data are based on 1,508 responses to a sample survey conducted Mar. 21-May 5, 1983, by Yankelovich, Skelly, and White, Inc.

Contains foreword, contents listing, highlights, and overview, with 3 summary charts (p. 3-11); 8 sections discussing survey results, with 4 charts and 28 tables described below (p. 12-30); narrative analysis contrasting opinions of politically aware/active (influential) respondents and general public, with 1 table showing demographic characteristics of the 2 subsamples (p. 31-33); and technical appendix, questionnaire facsimile, and list of related publications (p. 34-39).

Availability: Health Insurance Association of America, Order Fulfillment, 1850 K St., NW, Washington DC 20006, †; SRI/MF/complete.

CHARTS AND TABLES:
[Data are shown for 1983, often with trends from previous surveys, sometimes from as early as 1977. Tables and charts show distribution of responses to questions on topics described below, with selected detail by region and educational attainment.]

a. Costs and use: increases compared to general inflation; perceived ability to pay for major illness; nonuse of medical services due to cost; and satisfaction with health care. 2 charts and 4 tables. (p. 12-14)

b. Public policy and individual initiatives: institution/group responsible for rising health care costs, and possible solutions; and willingness to pay higher insurance deductible, to be treated by nurse rather than physician, to use clinic rather than private physician, to limit use of expensive technology, and to give up right to sue for malpractice. 2 charts and 5 tables. (p. 15-20)

c. Physicians and medical malpractice: whether physicians and hospitals should advertise; decisions influencing physician choice; patient requests for less expensive treatment; and awareness of malpractice suits, perceived causes, and possible solutions. 6 tables. (p. 21-24)

d. Health insurance: whether patients/physicians would cut costs if insurance paid less; whether insurance should pay for unnecessary, preventive, and routine health care; insurance company encouragement of physician vs. hospital use, and role in reducing medical costs; perceived fairness in claim handling; and legitimacy of insurance company profits. 9 tables. (p. 25-28)

e. Bio-ethical issues: right of family to request removal of life support systems from unconscious, terminally ill patient; physician euthanasia of incurably ill patient at patient's request; whether test tube method of conception should be available to childless couples; and whether parents should be able to select sex of child. 4 tables. (p. 29-30)

A5185
Hearing Industries Association

A5185–1   QUARTERLY REPORT
Quarterly.   Approx. 5 p.
SRI/MF/complete

Quarterly report on domestic and foreign manufactured hearing aid unit sales, by type and State. Also includes exports by country or world region of destination (with detail for Canadian Provinces), and hearing aids issued to VA clinics. Report is issued approximately 6 weeks after quarter of coverage. Data are from HIA participating companies and Federal agencies, and are compiled by Hauck & Associates, Inc.

Contains 8 quarterly tables, listed below.

Availability: Hearing Industries Association, 1800 M St., NW, Washington DC 20036, †; SRI/MF/complete.

Issues reviewed during 1984: 3rd Qtr. 1983-2nd Qtr. 1984 (D).

QUARTERLY TABLES:

[Tables A-C show data annually for preceding 2-6 years. Tables [1-2] and D-E show data for current year through quarter of coverage and preceding 1-4 years. Data are shown as cumulative totals, unless otherwise noted. Types of hearing aids are eyeglass, behind and inside the ear, and convertible. Sequence of tables may vary.]

[1]   Unit sales: by States, domestic; and export [to Canada and other].

A.   Import statistics [hearing aid units and value and parts value].

B.   Veterans Administration [hearing aids issued to VA clinics by the Federal Prosthetics Distribution Center; fiscal year data].

C.   Cros [contralateral routing of offside signals] and bicros, by type [except convertible; units of domestic and foreign manufactured hearing aids sold].

D.   Tinnitus maskers [unit shipments].

E.   Gross exports of completed hearing aid units, by destination [Japan and 5 world regions].

[2]   Units sold, by type and [domestic and foreign] origin [quarterly].

F.   Canadian [unit sales of U.S. companies] by Province [for current year through quarter of coverage; table begins with the 1st quarter 1984 issue].

A5200
Highway
Loss Data Institute

NOTE ABOUT HIGHWAY LOSS DATA INSTITUTE PUBLICATIONS:

Highway Loss Data Institute (HLDI) is a nonprofit organization supported by the Insurance Institute for Highway Safety. Publications are based on motor vehicle noncommercial insurance loss data supplied by major insurance firms, standardized for proportion of youthful operators and deductible amounts of coverage.

HLDI publications include 1 annual series on collision coverage (A5200-1); 2 annual reports on automobile theft and personal injury insurance loss experiences (A5200-2 and A5200-3); and a continuing series of special reports analyzing particular vehicles or safety features (A5200-4).

Annual reports show data by make and model series for each model year by passenger car size group (small and other subcompact and compact, and large), and body style (2-door, 4-door, station wagon, and sports/specialty); or for multipurpose vehicles by type (van, pickup, and utility).

A5200–1   AUTOMOBILE INSURANCE LOSSES: Collision Coverages
Annual series.   For individual publication data, see below.
SRI/MF/complete

Annual series of reports comparing collision coverage claim frequencies and amounts for motor vehicles damaged during their 1st 1-3 years of operation, by vehicle type.

Reports reviewed during 1984 are described below.

Availability: Highway Loss Data Institute, Watergate 600, Washington DC 20037, †; SRI/MF/complete.

A5200–1.1: Insurance Losses, Collision Coverages: Passenger Cars, Vans, Pickups, and Utility Vehicles. 1983 Models During Their First Year, 1982 Models During Their First Two Years, 1981 Models During Their First Three Years
[Annual. Jan. 1984. viii+51 p. Research Rpt. HLDI R83-2. ISSN 0093-0466. SRI/MF/complete.]

Annual report presenting standardized insurance claim frequencies and loss experiences for 1981-83 model passenger cars and other noncommercial vehicles, by make and series, during their 1st 1-3 years of operation.

Contains summary, and listings of contents, charts, and tables (p. v-viii); introduction and discussion of results, with 2 summary charts, and 10 tables listed below (p. 1-36); 2 appendices, with lists of vehicle classifications and definitions (p. 37-49); and list of HLDI publications (p. 50-51).

TABLES:

PASSENGER CARS

1-3. Relative average loss payments per insured vehicle year for 1981-83 model year cars with the best and worst collision coverage loss experience. (p. 4-7)

4. Distribution of collision coverage exposure [by car size, 1981-83 models]. (p. 8)

5-7. Insurance losses, collision coverages, 1981-83 models, passenger cars [shows total insured vehicle years, relative claim frequency, and relative average loss payment per claim and per insured vehicle year, by make and model grouped by body style and size]. (p. 9-28)

OTHER NONCOMMERCIAL VEHICLES

8-10. [Tables 5-7 generally are repeated for 1981-83 model vans, pickups, and utility vehicles.] (p. 32-36)

A5200–1.2: Automobile Insurance Losses, Collision Coverages: Initial Results for 1984 Models
[Annual. June 1984. viii+25 p. Research Rpt. HLDI R84-1. ISSN 0196-2663. SRI/MF/complete.]

Annual report on insurance claim frequency and average loss payment for 1984 model passenger cars during their initial 6 months of operation, from Oct. 1983 through Feb. 1984. Includes data by size class, make, and series, with summary comparison to 1983 models.

Contains summary and listings of contents, chart, and tables (p. v-viii); introduction and discussion of results, with 1 chart and 2 tables (p. 1-9); appendices, with data sources, methodology, definitions, and vehicle specifications (p. 10-23); and list of other HLDI publications (p. 24-25).

A5200–2   INSURANCE LOSSES, THEFT COVERAGES: Passenger Cars, Vans, Pickups, and Utility Vehicles. 1983 Models During Their First Year, 1982 Models During Their First Two Years, 1981 Models During Their First Three Years
Annual.   May 1984.
viii+50 p.
Research Rpt. HLDI T83-1.
ISSN 0276-4997.
SRI/MF/complete

Annual report on theft insurance claims and payments for 1981-83 model automobiles and noncommercial vans, pickups, and utility vehicles. Shows claim frequency, and average payment per claim and per insured vehicle year, by vehicle size class and/or body style, make/series, and model year.

Data are based on claims filed with 11 insurers under comprehensive coverage, which generally excludes such electronic equipment as tape decks and citizens' band radios. Data are adjusted for differences in operator age groups and deductible amounts.

Contains summary, and listings of contents, charts, and tables (p. v-viii); narrative report with 2 charts and 12 tables (p. 1-35); and appendices with vehicle series designations, definitions, and HLDI publications list (p. 36-50)

Availability: Highway Loss Data Institute, Watergate 600, Washington DC 20037, †; SRI/MF/complete.

A5200–3 **INSURANCE LOSSES, PERSONAL INJURY PROTECTION COVERAGES: Passenger Cars, Vans, Pickups, and Utility Vehicles, 1981-83 Models**
Annual. Sept. 1984.
viii+30 p.
Research Rpt. HLDI I83-1.
ISSN 0734-9017.
SRI/MF/complete

Annual report on personal injury insurance claim frequencies for 1981-83 model passenger cars, vans, pickup trucks, and utility vehicles, by domestic and foreign make and series, shown for all medical claims, and claims exceeding $250, $500, and $1,000, for the period from model's introduction through Dec. 1983.

Report is based on claims for medical expenses made under personal injury protection (PIP) coverages provided in 19 "no-fault" States. Frequency analyses are presented for all vehicles in each claim size category, and data may not be comparable for all vehicles.

Contains summary, and listings of contents, charts, and tables (p. v-viii); introduction and narrative analysis, with 2 summary charts, and 5 tables listed below (p. 3-17); appendices A-D, including list of PIP States, methodology, definitions, and list of model vehicle series designations (p. 18-28); and list of HLDI publications (p. 29-30).

Availability: Highway Loss Data Institute, Watergate 600, Washington DC 20037, †; SRI/MF/complete.

TABLES:
[All tables show years of exposure and claim frequency by size of PIP claim, for 1981-83 model vehicles. Tables [2-5] show data by make, series, and total years produced.]

1. Claim frequencies [per 1,000 insured vehicle years; for each passenger car model year]. (p. 3)

2-3. Passenger cars with the best and worst [at least 35% better or worse than average] injury loss experience: relative injury claim frequencies. (p. 5)

4-5. Relative claim frequency [for passenger cars by body style, vans, pickup trucks, and utility vehicles, most by vehicle-size group]. (p. 6-12, 16-17)

A5200–4 **AUTOMOBILE INSURANCE LOSSES: Special Analyses**
Series. For individual publication data, see below.
SRI/MF/complete

Continuing series of special reports analyzing particular aspects of loss experiences in collision, personal injury, and comprehensive insurance coverage for passenger cars, often relating to specific models, model years, features, and/or size classes.

Reports reviewed during 1984 are described below.

Availability: Highway Loss Data Institute, Watergate 600, Washington DC 20037, †; SRI/MF/complete.

A5200–4.12: Insurance Losses, Personal Injury Protection Coverages: Injury Claim Frequencies for Volkswagen Rabbits with Automatic and Manual Seat Belts, 1981 and 1982 Models

[Monograph. Apr. 1984. viii+10 p. Research Rpt. HLDI A-21. SRI/MF/complete.]

Report comparing personal injury insurance claim frequency for 1981-82 Volkswagen Rabbit autos equipped with manual seat belts and with automatic seat belts. Includes detail for 2-door and 4-door models.

Contains summary, and contents and table listings (p. v-viii); introduction and discussion of results, with 4 tables (p. 1-6); and methodology, definitions, and list of HLDI publications (p. 7-10).

A5200–4.13: Insurance Losses, Collision Coverages: An Analysis of Salvage Credits, 1977 Through 1982 Model Year Cars

[Monograph. July 1984. viii+9 p. Research Rpt. HLDI A-22. SRI/MF/complete.]

Report analyzing trends in frequency with which crash-damaged autos are sold for salvage rather than repaired, based on collision insurance claim data for 1977-82 model year autos. Includes percent of claims involving salvage credits, by body style and size class, and distribution of all insured autos by size class, for each model year.

Contains summary, and listings of contents, charts, and tables (p. v-viii); introduction and discussion of results, with 2 charts and 2 tables (p. 1-6); and definitions and list of HLDI publications (p. 7-9).

A5370
Idaho Library Association

A5370–1 **IDAHO LIBRARIAN**
Quarterly. Approx. 20 p. per issue; cumulative pagination throughout year.
ISSN 0019-1213.
LC SN 78-355.
SRI/MF/excerpts

Quarterly journal of Idaho library activities and operations. Covers library administration and services, technological developments, and librarian education.

Issues are primarily narrative and generally contain editorial depts and feature articles. Annual tables on academic and public library operations are included in the Jan. and Apr. issues, respectively.

Features with substantial statistical content are described, as they appear, under "Statistical Features." Each issue of the journal is reviewed, but an abstract is published in SRI monthly issues only when annual tables or other features with substantial statistical content appear.

Availability: Idaho Library Association, Editor, Idaho Librarian, University of Idaho Library, Moscow ID 83843, members †, nonmembers $10.00 per yr., single copy $2.50; SRI/MF/excerpts for all portions described under "Statistical Features."

Issues reviewed during 1984: Jan.-Oct. 1984 (Vol. 36, Nos. 1-4).

STATISTICAL FEATURES:

A5370–1.501: Jan. 1984 (Vol. 36, No. 1)

STATISTICS FOR IDAHO ACADEMIC LIBRARIES, ANNUAL FEATURE

(p. 5) Annual table showing Idaho academic library holdings by type, hours of operation, professional and nonprofessional staff, and expenditures of State/institution and Federal funds, all by individual institution, as of July 1, 1983.

A5370–1.502: Apr. 1984 (Vol. 36, No. 2)

PUBLIC LIBRARY STATISTICS: 1983, ANNUAL FEATURE

(p. 47-52) Annual feature consisting of 2 tables showing Idaho public library income by source, expenditures by object, population served, borrowers, holdings, and circulation, all by library grouped by county and region, FY83.

A5425
Independent Petroleum Association of America

A5425–1 **PETROLEUM INDEPENDENT: The Oil and Gas Producing Industry in Your State, 1984**
7 times per year (selected issue). Sept. 1984. 128 p.
LC 41-10748.
SRI/MF/complete

Annual report presenting detailed petroleum industry data for the U.S. and by producing State, 1983, with trends from the 1970s or earlier. Covers exploration and development, production, reserves, prices, and industry finances and employment. Also includes data on U.S. energy consumption.

Data are compiled from reports of industry assns and Federal and State agencies, and from other published materials.

Contains contents listing, introduction with 5 summary charts, data sources, energy conversions, and abbreviations (p. 3-13); national and State 1983 statistical profiles, described below, (p. 16-99); 2 charts and 27 tables, listed below, primarily presenting trend data by State (p. 102-124); and glossary (p. 126).

Report is published as the Sept. issue of *Petroleum Independent,* a periodical issued 7 times a year. The periodical does not usually contain substantial statistics. This annual issue is the only feature covered by SRI.

Availability: Petroleum Independent Publishers, Inc., Statistics Department, 1101 16th St., NW, Washington DC 20036, $5.00; SRI/MF/complete.

STATISTICS:

A5425–1.1: Profiles

(p. 16-99) The following 4 tables, plus 2 trend charts and 1 map showing oil and/or gas producing areas, are repeated for total U.S. and 33 producing States.

Tables include data for crude oil, natural gas, and natural gas liquids, as appropriate.

TABLES:

[1] Historical information [including producing States or counties and acreage, and percent

of acreage leased; 1st year of production; year and amount of peak production; deepest well drilled; total wells drilled as of Dec. 1983; and cumulative production and reserves, as of Dec. 1982].

[2] Value of oil and gas [including average field price and wellhead value of production; all-time high wellhead value; severance/ production taxes paid; and production employment; 1983].

[3] 1983 industry statistics [including seismic crew months worked; average rotary rigs active; wildcat and development wells and footage drilled; producing wells; and average daily production].

[4] 1982 latest data [including new reserves added, and total proved reserves; producing and abandoned stripper wells; stripper well production and reserves; and drilling costs].

A5425–1.2: Trends
[All tables except [12-13] and [22-27] show data by State.]

[1] Seismic exploration activity [crew months worked, 1974-83; also includes data for marine and undesignated land areas]. (p. 102)

[2] Acreage under lease [1979-83]. (p. 103)

[3] Rotary rigs active [1974-83]. (p. 104)

[4] New field wildcat wells drilled [1974-83; also includes data for Federal waters]. (p. 105)

[5] Value of U.S. fossil fuel production [for crude oil, natural gas, coal/lignite, and anthracite, 1977-83]. (p. 106)

[6] Energy consumption [of crude oil/natural gas liquid, natural gas, and total energy, 1949-83]. (p. 106)

[7] Drilling costs [total, per well, and per foot, 1964-82]. (p. 107)

[8] Cost indices [for oil field machinery and wages, oil well casing, and carbon line pipe, 1964-83]. (p. 107)

[9] Drilling summary [including wells and footage drilled, total cost, and average depth, for oil wells, gas wells, and dry holes], 1982. (p. 107)

[A] U.S. energy [production and consumption, by energy type]. [chart] (p. 108)

[B] Consumption of energy by end-use sector. [chart] (p. 108)

[10-11] Exploratory and total wells drilled [1974-83; also includes data for Federal waters]. (p. 110-111)

[12] World crude oil reserves [for 8 world regions, 1974-83]. (p. 112)

[13] Crude oil production by Chase Group of companies [aggregate compared to all other production; 1949-82, and excluding North Slope, 1977-82]. (p. 113)

[14] Cost of drilling and equipping wells [including wells and footage drilled, and cost and depth per well, with detail for onshore and offshore locations, Texas districts, selected other State subareas, and 4 Federal water areas], 1982. (p. 114)

[15-16] Stripper well crude oil production, and number of producing stripper wells, [1973-82]. (p. 115)

[17-18] Crude oil and natural gas production [1974-83, with U.S. average daily oil production]. (p. 116-117)

[19] Number of petroleum industry employees [for mining, manufacturing, transportation, wholesale, and retail sectors], 1983. (p. 118)

[20] Severance/production taxes paid [1979-83]. (p. 119)

[21] Consumption of petroleum products [by type], 1983. (p. 120)

[22] Peak year milestones [for selected petroleum industry indicators]. (p. 121)

[23] Financial data [including rates of return for oil/gas companies compared to all manufacturing companies, and exploration/development outlays for larger oil/gas companies and independents, 1961-82]. (p. 121)

[24] Gasoline retail prices [excluding taxes, tax amount, and pump price, 1964-83]. (p. 121)

[25-26] Wholesale petroleum prices [total and east of California, by product type, 1935-83]. (p. 122-123)

[27] Statistical summary of the petroleum producing industry [including production, imports, exports, reserves, prices, wells and footage drilled, and earnings, with selected detail for crude oil, natural gas, natural gas liquids, and refined products, 1954-83]. (p. 124)

A5425–2   **U.S. PETROLEUM STATISTICS, 1984 Revised**
Annual. Sept. 1984.
10 p. no paging, pocket size foldout.
SRI/MF/complete

Annual report on U.S. oil and gas industry trends, 1964-83, including supply and demand, prices, and finances. Data are compiled by the Independent Petroleum Assn of America from member data and reports of Federal and other industry sources.

Contains 1 table showing peak year data for 17 supply indicators, and 15 other tables listed below.

Availability: Independent Petroleum Association of America, Statistics Department, 1101 16th St., NW, Washington DC 20036, †; SRI/ MF/complete.

TABLES:
[Tables show data for 1964-83.]

A5425–2.1: Supply and Demand

1. Exploration activity [crew months worked, total acres leased, active rotary rigs, and total, dry, and new field wildcat wells].

2. Drilling [oil, gas, dry, and service well completions; and total footage drilled].

3. New reserves added [crude oil, gas liquids, and natural gas; and amount of crude oil and natural gas per new well].

4. Proved reserves [of crude oil, gas liquids, and natural gas; and reserve/production ratios for crude oil, total liquids, and natural gas; as of Dec. 31].

5. Petroleum supply [domestic production of crude oil and gas liquids; and total imports and other supply].

6. Petroleum consumption [domestic petroleum demand and exports, and percent of U.S. energy consumption in petroleum and natural gas].

7. Total oil imports [including crude oil, residual fuel oil, and light products].

8. Imports by origin [OPEC, Arab OPEC, and Western and Eastern Hemispheres].

A5425–2.2: Prices and Finance

9. Natural gas [production, imports, exports, and domestic supply; and current and constant 1983 prices].

10. Composite value and prices [crude oil and natural gas wellhead value, natural gas price per barrel, and composite oil/gas price per barrel in current and constant 1983 dollars].

11. Wholesale oil prices [per gallon for motor gasoline, kerosene, and distillate and residual fuel oil; and aggregate price per barrel].

12. Prices [for crude oil wellhead in current and constant 1983 dollars, and motor gasoline including and excluding retail fuel taxes]; and wages [for oil/gas and all manufacturing industries].

13. Drilling costs and indices [for oil field machinery, well casings, and oil field wages; and total, per well, and per foot drilling costs].

14. Financial data [rate of return for oil and all manufacturing companies, and exploration/ development outlays for larger companies and independents].

15. General economic data [GNP, PPI, and CPI].

A5435
Independent Sector

A5435–1   **DIMENSIONS OF THE INDEPENDENT SECTOR: A Statistical Profile**
Annual. 1984. vii+79 p.
SRI/MF/complete

Annual report, by Virginia Ann Hodgkinson and Murray S. Weitzman, on finances, employment, and operations of independent not-for-profit organizations (the "independent sector"), 1970s-80, with trends from 1955 and some data for 1981-82. Includes detail by organization type, and comparisons to other private not-for-profit entities and to business and government sectors.

The independent sector is comprised of not-for-profit, tax-exempt voluntary organizations, churches, private schools, company-sponsored and other foundations, and social welfare and civic assns.

Data are from various private and government sources, and are specified in each table.

Contains listings of contents and tables (p. v-vii); highlights and introduction (p. 1-6); 3 narrative sections, interspersed with 22 charts, and 51 tables listed below (p. 7-66); afterword (p. 67-69); report notes, with 2 text tables showing number of tax-exempt organizations by type, and churches by denominational group, various years 1952-82 (p. 70-78); and bibliography (p. 79).

This is the 1st edition of the report.

Availability: Independent Sector, 1825 L St., NW, Washington DC 20036, $35.00; SRI/MF/ complete.

TABLES:
[Data are for 1974, 1977, and 1980, unless otherwise noted.]

A5435–1.1: Overview and Data by Sector

[Tables 1.0-1.5 and 1.7 show data for private not-for-profit, business, and government sectors. Data for private not-for-profit sector are generally shown for independent and other organizations.]

1.0. Selected [economic] indicators [summary]. (p. 9)

1.1-1.2. National income [generated]; and national income including assigned values for volunteers and unpaid family workers. (p. 11)

1.3. Earnings from work: wages/salaries, self-employment income, and assigned values for volunteers and unpaid family workers. (p. 12)

1.4-1.5. Estimates of total employment, and of employment by type of employment [paid employees, self-employment, volunteers, and unpaid family workers]. (p. 12-13)

1.6. Number of active not-for-profit entities, including estimated number of churches [selected years 1974-82]. (p. 14)

1.7. Number of entities operating [with government detail by level, and business detail for farms, forestry/fisheries, and services]. (p. 15)

1.8-1.9. Private not-for-profit organizations: estimated current [and constant] operating expenditures [with comparison to population], 1960-82; and estimated current and per capita operating expenditures, including assigned dollar values for volunteers. (p. 16-17)

1.10. Comparison of per capita expenditures: [for] personal consumption [of goods and services], and [among] private not-for-profit organizations, in current and constant (1972) dollars, selected years 1960-82. (p. 17)

A5435–1.2: Finances and Volunteers

PRIVATE CONTRIBUTIONS

2.0. Private donor contributions compared with current operating expenditures for all private not-for-profit organizations, [and with] national income and population, 1955-82. (p. 22)

2.1. Private donor contributions by source to all sectors of the economy, [and total per capita contributions in current and constant 1972 dollars], 1955-82. (p. 23)

2.2-2.3. Individual donor contributions [and number of households, with distribution] by household income, 1973 and 1981. (p. 24)

2.4. Percent [of] givers by personal characteristics [occupational group, employment status, education, and age], 1978 and 1981. (p. 25)

VOLUNTEERS

2.5. Selected characteristics of volunteers [distribution of population and volunteers by sex, race, education, and income, various periods 1973-81]. (p. 26)

2.6. Proportion of population volunteering, by selected characteristics [sex, age, race, education, and income, year ended Mar.] 1981. (p. 27)

FOUNDATIONS

[Foundation types are independent, operating, company-sponsored, and community.]

2.7-2.8. [Number of] foundations, [and value of] grants [made], gifts [received], and assets, [total] 1975-81, and by asset [size] category 1980. (p. 29)

2.9. 15 largest foundations of each type of foundation ranked by assets, [with value of] grants [made], 1980. (p. 30)

2.10-2.11. Foundations in *The Foundation Directory*, 9th edition: [number of foundations, and value of] grants [made], gifts [received], and assets, by type of foundation, and by decade established and by asset [size] category, [1981]. (p. 31)

CORPORATE CONTRIBUTIONS

2.12. [Value of] corporate contributions for charitable purposes, [and number and assets of corporations; with distribution, and contributions as percent of pretax net income], by asset [size] category; 1977. (p. 32)

2.13. Corporate contributions for charitable purposes, [and] corporations with net income, by industry [division], 1977. (p. 33)

2.14. First-time summary for those companies reporting corporate assistance expenditures not taken as charitable contributions [companies and expenditures by assistance type], 1982. (p. 33)

FINANCES AND OPERATIONS

2.15-2.16. Total sources of support, and dollar assigned values for volunteer services, [for the] independent sector. (p. 34)

2.17-2.18. Total use of resources [expenditures by function, and] assigned value of volunteer services, [for the] independent sector. (p. 36)

2.19. Number and wages/salaries of employees on nonagricultural payrolls by employment universe [all employees, and employees of not-for-profit entities and independent sector], selected years 1972-82. (p. 37)

2.20. Contributions and current operating expenditures for all private not-for-profit organizations, and personal disposable income and consumption expenditures (in per capita 1972 dollars) [selected years 1960-82]. (p. 38)

2.21-2.22. Assets, [tax returns filed, receipts, liabilities], and net worth of private not-for-profit organizations filing Federal tax returns, [with detail for those] classified as schools/colleges and in health services, 1977-78 and/or 1975. (p. 39-40)

A5435–1.3: Profiles by Sub-Sector

[Sub-sectors generally include health services, education/research, religious organizations, social services, civic/social/fraternal organizations, arts/culture, foundations, and legal services. "Components" are various types of organizations within sub-sectors.]

INCOME AND EXPENDITURES

[All tables, except table 3.5, show data for independent sector only.]

3.0-3.1. Annual sources of support and percentage distribution, by sub-sector and [private and government] source. (p. 44-45)

3.2. Givers: illustrative distribution patterns by type of donor [corporations, foundations, individuals, and bequests], by sub-sector, 1980. (p. 46)

3.3-3.4. Annual resource [expenditures] and percentage distribution, by sub-sector and function. (p. 48-49)

3.5. Current operating expenditures for [independent sector and for other] private not-for-profit organizations [by type, selected years 1974-80]. (p. 51)

3.6. Current operating expenditures by sub-sector and components [selected years 1974-80]. (p. 52)

EMPLOYEES AND WAGES

3.7-3.8. All employees on nonagricultural payrolls and wages/salaries: total, [independent sector, and other] private not-for-profit organizations [by type, selected years 1972-82]. (p. 53-54)

3.9-3.10. Independent sector: employees and wages/salaries by sub-sector and components, [selected years 1972-82]. (p. 54-55)

3.11. Percent and annual rates of change for all employees on nonagricultural payrolls and in the independent sector, and for selected components, selected periods 1972-82. (p. 57)

3.12-3.16. Independent sector, [by sub-sector] and components: current operating expenditures, wages/salaries, number employed, and selected relationships. (p. 59-66)

A5600
Institute of
Real Estate Management

A5600–1   INCOME/EXPENSE
ANALYSIS: APARTMENTS,
1983 Edition
Annual. 1983. 224 p.
ISSN 0194-1941.
ISBN 0-912104-72-4.
LC 79-643863.
SRI/MF/not filmed

Annual report on apartment building income and expense ratios for U.S. and Canada, 1982, with trends primarily from 1979. Covers income by source, vacancy/rent loss, and expenses by detailed item, all shown as percent of total possible income and as amount per square foot; and tenant turnover rate.

Data are shown as medians and/or ranges, by building type, for selected U.S. and Canadian metro areas, by U.S. region, and for total U.S. and Canada.

Building types are furnished and unfurnished elevator, low-rise (12-24 units and 25/more units), and garden-type. Income and expense data for unfurnished buildings also are shown by building age.

Also includes summary trends for percent of buildings with utilities/services included in rent, and for heating costs by type of fuel; and distribution of buildings by heating fuel type and region.

Data are from a 1983 survey of 6,042 apartment buildings. Report is intended as an aid in comparing operations of similar apartment properties.

Contains contents listing, user guidelines, and map (p. 3-10); trend analysis with narrative summary, 4 charts, and 28 tables (p. 12-42); detailed tabulations of survey results, arranged by building type, with accompanying summary chart and tables (p. 44-215); and survey form facsimile, worksheet, sample characteristics, and index (p. 216-224).

Availability: Institute of Real Estate Management, Publications, 430 N. Michigan Ave., Chicago IL 60611, $61.95; SRI/MF/not filmed.

A5600-2   INCOME/EXPENSE ANALYSIS: OFFICE BUILDINGS, DOWNTOWN AND SUBURBAN, 1983 Edition
Annual. 1983. 224 p.
ISSN 0146-9630.
ISBN 0-912104-73-2.
LC 77-649065.
SRI/MF/not filmed

Annual report on downtown and suburban office building income and expenses for U.S. and Canada, 1982, with trends from 1971. Covers income by source, vacancy/rent loss, and expenses by detailed item, shown as medians and ranges, per square foot of building area and rentable office space; year-end vacancy level; percent of buildings that contract cleaning services; and average tenant alteration allowances.

Data are shown for downtown and suburban buildings, for selected U.S. and Canadian metro areas, by U.S. region, and for total U.S. and Canada, with U.S. detail by building size, age group, rental range, and number of stories.

Also includes analyses of leasing commissions, and energy consumption and cost by fuel type, by U.S. city and region, and for Canada.

Data are from a 1983 survey of 2,057 office buildings. Report is intended as an aid in comparing operations of similar office building properties.

Contains contents listing (p. 3); trend analysis and summary, with 3 charts and 18 tables (p. 4-11); user guidelines and map (p. 12-18); detailed tabulations of survey results, arranged by location (p. 20-206); 4 summary charts (p. 207-208); leasing and energy analyses, with detailed tabulations (p. 210-215); and survey form facsimile, worksheet, participating cities and sample characteristics, and index (p. 216-224).

Availability: Institute of Real Estate Management, Publications, 430 N. Michigan Ave., Chicago IL 60611; $61.95; SRI/MF/not filmed.

A5600-3   EXPENSE ANALYSIS: CONDOMINIUMS, COOPERATIVES, AND PLANNED UNIT DEVELOPMENTS, 1983 Edition
Annual. 1983. 152 p.
ISBN 0-912104-74-0.
LC 79-642606.
SRI/MF/not filmed

Annual report on expenses of condominiums, cooperatives, and planned unit developments (PUDs) in U.S. and Canada, by detailed item, 1982. Data are shown as medians and ranges per unit and per square foot of floor area, by building type, grouped for selected metro areas, by building age and price range, and by U.S. region and total Canada. Building types are high-rise, low-rise, townhouse, and combination.

Also includes data on monthly owner assessments; and percent of projects furnishing utilities and recreational facilities, by type.

Data are from a survey of 985 condominiums, 74 cooperatives, and 133 PUDs. Report is intended as an aid in comparing operations of similar properties.

Contains contents listing, summary with 2 charts and 13 tables, and user guidelines (p. 3-13); detailed tabulation of survey results for condominiums (p. 16-96), cooperatives (p. 98-118),

and PUDs (p. 120-143); and survey form facsimile, worksheet, sample characteristics, and index (p. 144-152).

Availability: Institute of Real Estate Management, Publications, 430 N. Michigan Ave., Chicago IL 60611, $44.95; SRI/MF/not filmed.

A5625
Institute of
Scrap Iron and Steel

A5625-1   FACTS, 40th EDITION, 1982 Yearbook
Annual. 1983.
12 p.+errata sheet.
ISSN 0163-3899.
LC 78-646697.
SRI/MF/complete

Annual report on ferrous scrap metal, covering production, consumption, prices, shipments, and foreign trade, 1982, with selected trends from 1962. Includes data by furnace type and grade of scrap.

Data are from American Iron and Steel Institute, *Iron Age,* Bureau of Mines, and other Federal agencies.

Contains contents listing (p. 2); and 6 summary charts, and 16 tables listed below, interspersed with brief narrative (p. 3-12).

Availability: Institute of Scrap Iron and Steel, 1627 K St., NW, Washington DC 20006, $5.00; SRI/MF/complete.

TABLES:

PRODUCTION, CONSUMPTION, AND RECEIPTS

[1] Facts summary [selected years 1962-82]. (p. 3)

[2-5] Ferrous scrap consumption, purchased scrap receipts, and home scrap production; and raw steel production, and steel mill and foundry castings shipments; [1973-82 and monthly 1980-82]. (p. 4-5)

[6] Trend of U.S. steel production by [type of] furnace [1973-82]. (p. 5)

[7] Purchased scrap receipts, home scrap production, and ferrous scrap consumption, by grade [1980-82]. (p. 6)

[8] U.S. consumption of ferrous scrap and blast furnace iron, by type of furnace [1973-82]. (p. 6)

[9] Iron ore [consumption, imported for consumption, and mined domestically, monthly 1980-82]. (p. 7)

FOREIGN TRADE

[10-12] U.S. exports: of carbon steel/iron scrap [monthly 1980-82]; and of ferrous scrap by country and grade [1978-82]. (p. 8-9)

[13] U.S. imports of ferrous scrap, iron ore, pig iron, and steel products [1973-82]. (p. 9)

PRICES

[14-16] No. 1 heavy melting steel scrap, No. 2 bundles, and finished steel composite prices [monthly 1973-82]. (p. 10)

A5650
Insurance
Information Institute

A5650-1   INSURANCE FACTS, 1983-84 Edition
Annual. Nov. 1983. 112 p.
LC 73-2557.
SRI/MF/complete

Annual report on the property/casualty insurance industry, including data on number of policies and value of premiums written for various types of insurance, industry financial data, and data on insurance losses from disasters, accidents, property crimes, and health and other claims, 1982, with trends from 1957, and selected data from as early as 1871.

Data are compiled from Federal and State government and private sources, particularly A. M. Best Co., National Safety Council, and National Fire Protection Assn. Data source is noted under each table.

Contents:

a.   1 table showing property/casualty insurers' aggregate operating results, 1980-82 (inside front cover); and contents listing (p. 3-4).

b.   6 narrative sections, with 6 trend charts, and 2 other charts and 91 tables listed below. (p. 5-93)

c.   2 sections of background reference, with 1 table showing auto financial responsibility limits by State and Canadian Province; lists of States with "no-fault" auto insurance, and insurance regulatory agencies and officials; glossary; and lists of insurance service organizations, and Insurance Information Institute officials and offices. (p. 94-112, and inside back cover)

Availability: Insurance Information Institute, 110 William St., New York NY 10038, member companies and insurance agents $3.00; others $6.00; SRI/MF/complete.

CHARTS AND TABLES:

A5650-1.1: Overview

COMPANIES, EMPLOYMENT, AND COVERAGE

[1] Property/casualty insurance companies [home offices], by State, 1983. (p. 11)

[2] Employment in insurance, 1976-82 (annual averages). (p. 12)

[3] Auto insurance coverage reported by U.S. car owners [distribution of car owners with and without insurance by age group and residence (urban, suburban, and rural)], 1981. (p. 13)

[4] Insurance coverage reported by U.S. households [fire and household contents insurance, for renters and owners], 1981. (p. 13)

WORLD INSURANCE INDUSTRY

[5] Growth of world private insurance premiums [value, by world area, 1965, 1975, and 1981]. (p. 15)

[6] World's [10] leading insurance countries [ranked by total premium value, with value of life and non-life premiums], 1981. (p. 15)

A5650-1.2: Industry Finances and Premiums

OPERATING RESULTS AND INVESTMENTS

[1] Net premiums written, by line, 1981-82. (p. 16)

[2] Assets and policyholders' surplus, industry aggregates, property/casualty insurance, 1958 and 1982. [chart] (p. 17)

[3] Consolidated assets and policyholders' surplus, 1978-82. (p. 18)

[4] Where the premium dollar goes [distribution for property/casualty premiums by expenditure type, 1982]. [chart] (p. 18)

I-III. Underwriting results, investment income, and combined net income before taxes: property/casualty insurance business, 1958-82. (p. 19-20)

[5] Average annual rates of return on net income after taxes as percent of net worth, selected industries [1973-82]. (p. 22)

[6] Investments of property/casualty insurers [distribution of bonds, common and preferred stocks, and other, 1972, 1977, and 1982]. (p. 23)

PREMIUMS

[7] Total net premiums written by property/casualty insurance companies [accident/health and all other], 1973-82. (p. 24)

[8] Purchases of property/casualty insurance [premiums paid by commercial and individual purchasers, by type of insurance], 1982. (p. 24)

[9-23] [Premiums written for] auto liability and physical damage; fire and allied lines; homeowner, commercial, and farmowner multiple peril; crop-hail; general liability; medical malpractice; workers' compensation; surety; fidelity; burglary/theft; boiler/machinery; glass; inland and ocean marine; and nuclear insurance; [various periods 1957-82]. (p. 25-34)

[24-26] Direct written premiums [for all and 23] selected lines, and premium taxes, by State, 1982. (p. 35-40)

GUARANTY FUNDS

[27] Guaranty fund assessments by State [and Puerto Rico], 1969-82 [period]. (p. 41)

A5650–1.3: High Risk Insurance and Factors Affecting Insurance Costs

HIGH RISK INSURANCE

[Tables [1-5] show data by State. Selected tables include data for Guam, Virgin Islands, and/or Puerto Rico.]

[1] Private passenger cars insured through voluntary market [1981] and shared market [1981-82] mechanisms. (p. 43)

[2-3] Insurance provided by FAIR [Fair Access to Insurance Requirements] plans; and by beach/windstorm plans; [1982]. (p. 44-45)

[4] Flood insurance in the U.S. [number of communities, and number and value of residential and commercial policies in force; as of June 30, 1983]. (p. 46)

[5] Federal crime insurance [residential and commercial policies and value of insurance in force, at year end], 1982. (p. 48)

INSURANCE COSTS AND COST OF LIVING

[6] Price indices for property and auto insurance and related items, and annual rates of change, 1973-82 (base: 1967 = 100). (p. 49)

[7] Cost of operating autos [by size] and vans, cents per mile, 1982. (p. 51)

[8] Composition of median monthly housing expense [1979 and 1981]. (p. 51)

LIABILITY LAWSUITS

[9] Product liability cases commenced in Federal district courts [by State and outlying area, FY82-83]. (p. 53)

HEALTH CARE COSTS

[10] Hospital semiprivate room rates [by State and for Puerto Rico], Jan. 1982-83. (p. 54)

A5650–1.4: Losses

FIRES

[1-2] U.S. fire losses, [selected years] 1875-1982; and fire deaths per 100,000 [by age group], 1973-82. (p. 56)

[3-4] Causes of reported [residential and non-residential] fires, and incendiary/suspicious fires in structures, [number or distribution of fires, injuries and/or deaths, and dollar loss], 1981 or 1982 estimate. (p. 57-58)

[5-6] Structural fires and civilian fire deaths, by property use, 1982 estimates. (p. 59)

[7-8] 1982 fires resulting in 10 or more deaths [by type of property], and 10 worst multiple-death fires in the U.S.; [date, place, and/or type of structure, and number of deaths]. (p. 60)

[9-10] U.S. fires causing property damage of $5 million or more, 1982, and 15 most costly fires; [date, place, type of property, and estimated loss]. (p. 61-62)

CIVIL DISORDERS AND DISASTERS

[Data for "most costly" events include dates, location, and estimated losses.]

[11] 10 most costly U.S. civil disorders. (p. 62)

[12] Catastrophe record [date, place and estimated loss], 1982. (p. 63)

[13] 10 most costly U.S. earthquakes. (p. 65)

[14-15] Hurricanes [and resulting deaths] in the U.S., 1958-82; and 10 most costly insured hurricanes. (p. 66)

[16-17] Tornadoes [and resulting deaths] in the U.S., 1958-82; and 5-year totals, tornadoes [and resulting deaths and injuries] by State [and Puerto Rico], 1978-82. (p. 67)

ACCIDENTAL DEATHS

[18-19] Accidental deaths [4 types], 1981-82; and numbers and types of home accident deaths, 1973-82. (p. 68)

MOTOR VEHICLE ACCIDENTS AND INSURANCE CLAIMS

[20-21] Motor vehicle accidents [deaths, injuries, and economic loss], 1981-82; and traffic deaths [and rates], 1973-82. (p. 69)

[22] Summary of societal costs [medical, productivity and property loss, and other] of motor vehicle accidents, 1980. (p. 70)

[23] Measures by States to curb drunk driving [as of Aug. 1, 1983]. (p. 72)

[24] Sex of drivers involved in [all and fatal] accidents, 1973-82. (p. 74)

[25] Motor vehicle deaths and injuries, by type of accident, [for urban and rural locations], 1982. (p. 75)

[26] Countrywide average paid claim costs [for bodily injury and property damage], liability insurance, private passenger cars [1973-82]. (p. 75)

[27] [Total number of drivers, and drivers in fatal and total] accidents, by age of drivers, 1982. (p. 76)

[28] Cost of replacing selected [auto] parts, 1975 and 1983. (p. 77)

[29-30] Front- and rear-end crash test results, damage repair costs, [selected 1982-83 model cars]. (p. 78)

[31] Collision coverages: loss payment summary by model year, [by] years since introduction [claim frequency, and loss per claim and per insured vehicle year], 1980-82 model year passenger cars. (p. 79)

[32] Relative average loss payments per insured vehicle year for 1982 model year cars with the best and worst collision coverage loss experience [by make, series, and body style]. (p. 80)

[33-34] 1979-81 passenger cars with best and worst loss experience, relative injury claim frequencies, personal injury protection coverages [by make series, and body style]. (p. 82)

[35] Loss experience summary by vehicle size and model year, theft losses [claim frequency, and loss per claim and per insured vehicle year, 1981-82]. (p. 83)

[36] 1982 model year cars with the lowest and highest relative frequency of theft claims. (p. 84)

WORK ACCIDENTS AND PROPERTY CRIMES

[37-38] Work fatalities and injuries [and rates], and economic losses from work accidents, [selected years] 1960-82. (p. 85)

[39-40] Crimes against property and motor vehicle registrations and thefts, 1973-82. (p. 86-87)

[41] Motor vehicle thefts, by States, 1981-82. (p. 87)

[42] Arrests, distribution by age [and crime], 1982. (p. 88)

AIRCRAFT AND BOATING ACCIDENTS

[43-44] 1982 aircraft accidents [by type]; and accidents, scheduled airlines, 1978-82; [both showing hours flown, total and fatal accidents, and fatalities]. (p. 89)

[45] Boating accidents [fatalities, injuries, and property damage] by State [and for Puerto Rico and Virgin Islands], 1982. (p. 90)

HEALTH INSURANCE AND HOSPITAL COSTS

[46] [Health insurance benefits paid, for private insurers, Blue Cross/Blue Shield, other plans, Medicare, and Medicaid, 1980-81.] (p. 92)

[47] Cost of hospitalization [per day and average length of stay] and health insurance benefits paid by private insurers [by State and outlying area], 1981. (p. 92-93)

A5750
International Association of Ice Cream Manufacturers

A5750–2   LATEST SCOOP, 1984 Edition: Facts and Figures on Ice Cream and Related Products
Annual.   Aug. 1984.
4+38 p.
ISSN 0732-0620.
LC 82-641843.
SRI/MF/complete

Annual report on U.S. and foreign production of ice cream and related products, 1983 and trends. Includes data by U.S. State and region, Canadian Province, and foreign country. Also includes data on U.S. industry operations.

Data are from the Census Bureau, USDA, International Assn of Ice Cream Manufacturers surveys and estimates, and other sources.

Contains contents listing (1 p.) general information (p. 1-5); and 29 tables, listed below, with interspersed narrative (p. 6-38).

Also includes 4 text tables showing selected highlights for U.S. (p. 4) and Canada (p. 29), including preliminary ice cream production for Jan.-May 1984.

Availability: International Association of Ice Cream Manufacturers, 888 16th St., NW, Washington DC 20006, members $1.00, nonmembers $5.00; SRI/MF/complete.

TABLES:

A5750–2.1: U.S. Data

OPERATING DATA AND PRICES

[1-2] Employees, wages, and value of shipments; and capital expenditures for new plants and equipment; [selected years] 1947-82. (p. 6-7)

[3] "Real" price of ice cream [average production worker wages, average retail price, and minutes of labor required to purchase a half-gallon of ice cream], 1973-83. (p. 8)

PRODUCTION

[Production data generally are shown for ice cream, ice milk, sherbet, and mellorine type products, and sometimes for water ices and other frozen dairy products. Tables [4-12] show combined data for hard frozen/soft serve products.]

[4-6] Total and per capita production, [selected years] 1859-1983; and production by States and regions, and 10 leading States, 1983. (p. 9-11)

[7-8] Monthly production, 1981-83; and [aggregate monthly production of all products] as a percent of annual average, 1963 and 1983. (p. 12-13)

[9-10] Production by regions, 1983; and per capita production by regions, [selected years] 1960-83. (p. 14-15)

[11] Production of mix for frozen products, by States and regions, 1983. (p. 16)

[12] Number of plants [including and excluding counter freezers for ice cream], 1960-83. (p. 17)

[13-19] Production [total and per capita, shown separately for hard frozen and soft serve products, 1983, with detail by region and trends from 1955]. (p. 18-24)

MISCELLANEOUS

[20] Performance of selected [dairy and other] products in the supermarket: sales, gross profits, margins, and assortment of items/brands/sizes/ at warehouse, 1983. (p. 26)

[21] Food service [number of units (no date), and sales value 1981-82, for 5 types of food service establishments including ice cream/custard stands]. (p. 26)

[22] Ice cream consumed in a 3-day period, by age groups and sex, 1977/78. (p. 27)

[23] Estimated wholesale value of [4 selected] ice cream products, 1981-83. (p. 27)

[24] Flavors: ice cream, ice milk, and sherbet, 5-10 top flavors [1978]. (p. 28)

A5750–2.2: Canadian and International Data

CANADA

[1-2] Production, 1971-83; and monthly production, 1983; of ice cream and related products. (p. 30-31)

[3-4] Per capita production of ice cream, [selected years] 1970-83; and hard and soft production of ice cream, 1981-83; by Provinces. (p. 32-33)

INTERNATIONAL

[5] [Total and per capita production of ice cream and related frozen products, by type, for 55 countries, various years 1975-83]. (p. 34-38)

A5785
International Business Forms Industries

A5785–2   PERSPECTIVE 84: The Present and Future of the Forms Industry
Annual.   1984.   3+34 p.
SRI/MF/complete

Annual report on the business form industry, presenting data on shipment value by product type, 1983, with comparisons to 1982 and projections through 1988.

Also includes data on form industry retail vs. shipment values, paper supply-demand situation, and profitability, mostly 1983; estimated number of desktop computers, and related demand for forms, 1982-87; and number of form companies, plants, and employees, selected years 1958-77.

Also includes shipment value trends, various years 1958-82, for the following: all business forms by type, forms manufactured by the forms industry and by other industries, and products other than forms made by the forms industry.

Data are from IBFI member firms, and other industry and government sources.

Contains listings of contents, tables, and charts (2 p.); narrative report, interspersed with 14 charts and 19 tables (p. 1-29); and 6 appendices, with 2 charts and 4 tables (p. 30-34).

Availability: International Business Forms Industries, 1730 N. Lynn St., Arlington VA 22209, members $125.00, nonmembers $250.00; SRI/MF/complete.

A5785–3   1983-84 ANNUAL RATIO STUDY
Annual.   1984.   iii+54 p.
SRI/MF/complete

Annual report, compiled by Feddeman and Lesche, Inc., presenting detailed balance sheet, income and expense, and operating ratios for the business forms industry, 1983. Report is intended for use by individual companies in comparing their performance to industry averages.

Ratios are shown primarily by company sales size, market (direct and indirect), product type (continuous custom, unit sets, and mixed), and average order size, with separate data for industry leaders.

Also includes absolute data on industry sales, production value, pretax net income, assets, and employment.

Data are based on survey responses from 75 International Business Forms Industries members, for year ended Dec. 31, 1983.

Contents:

a. Contents listing (1 p.); introduction and summary (p. i-iii); ratio analysis, with illustrative statistics (p. 1-9); and absolute data, with 1 table (p. 13).

b. Ratio tabulations (p. 14-32); key ratio analysis, including ranges and cause-effect relationships for selected ratios (p. 33-42); and standard account classifications and sample questionnaire (p. 43-54).

Availability: International Business Forms Industries, 1730 N. Lynn St., Arlington VA 22209, members $150.00, nonmembers $300.00; SRI/MF/complete.

A5800
International City Management Association

A5800–1   MUNICIPAL YEAR BOOK, 1984
Annual.   Jan. 1984.
xx+419 p. Vol. 51.
ISSN 0077-2186.
ISBN 0-87326-959-4.
LC 34-27121.
SRI/MF/not filmed

Annual source book, for 1984, of urban data and developments, for U.S. and Canadian cities. Includes information on local government structure, public services, and intergovernmental relations.

Data are based on International City Management Assn (ICMA) surveys of local officials of 6,603 cities with over 2,500 population and 373 areas under 2,500 population; reports of the Federation of Canadian Municipalities; Census Bureau reports; and other sources. Data are primarily for 1983, with some trends from the 1970s.

Contains contents listing (3 p.) and the following:

Introduction. Includes 4 tables showing U.S. and Canadian municipalities by ICMA region; number of U.S. Federal, State, and local governments, by type; and U.S. municipalities and counties by population size, region, metro status, and form of government. (p. xi-xx)

Part A. Municipal Profiles. Annual statistical report, described below. (p. 3-70)

Part B-D. 9 annual and special reports, described below. (p. 73-223)

Part E. Directories of the following: State and/or Canadian Province municipal and county leagues and assns, councils of governments, and professional organizations; local government officials in Canadian municipalities with over 10,000 population; and U.S. county and municipal officials, with 4 tables (p. 242, 282) showing number of officials by sex, race/ethnicity (including white, black, Asian, American Indian, Mexican-American, and other), and position. (p. 227-374)

Part F. References. (p. 377-398)

Biographical sketches of authors, and index. (p. 401-419)

Availability: International City Management Association, 1120 G St., NW, Washington DC 20005, $58.75, nonmembers must prepay; SRI/MF/not filmed.

STATISTICAL REPORTS:

A5800–1.1: Part A. Local Government Profiles

PROFILES OF INDIVIDUAL CITIES AND COUNTIES

(p. 3-70) Annual report, by Sherman Landau, on the population characteristics, and government structure, employment, and finances of 2,576 municipalities with 10,000 or more population, and 1,358 counties with 25,000 or more population, according to the 1980 census.

Includes 23 tables (p. 3-13) showing summary data on city and county population, finances, and employment, by population size group and census division; and 2 extended tables (p. 14-69) showing the following for individual cities and counties, grouped by State:

a.   Government form; metro status; 1980 population, and percent change from 1970; and educational attainment of population.

b.   Local governments located within county, by type (counties only); and public debt (cities only).

c.   Revenues, and percent of revenue from intergovernmental sources, property and other taxes, and charges and miscellaneous sources.

d.   Expenditures, and percent of expenditures for operations, capital, and selected functions; and personnel by administrative sector.

A5800–1.2: Part B. The Intergovernmental Dimension

FEDERAL ACTIONS AFFECTING CITIES: IN THE SHADOW OF RECOVERY

(p. 73-84) By Frank Shafroth. Report, with 1 table showing estimates of annual expenditures on new and repair public works projects, and Federal share, by type of project, 1983-90 period. Data are from Congressional Budget Office.

SIGNIFICANT STATE ACTIONS AFFECTING LOCAL GOVERNMENTS

(p. 84-96) By Dennis M. Kouba. Report on State-local relations. Includes 3 tables showing number of States with legislative limits on local

government taxing and spending powers, as of Jan. 1983; and number with direct/indirect and development aid programs for local governments, 1982.

ANNEXATIONS AND CORPORATE CHANGES: 1970-79 AND 1980-83

(p. 96-101) By Joel C. Miller and Richard L. Forstall. Report on municipal annexation and incorporation activity. Data are from Census Bureau's *Boundary and Annexation Survey.* Includes 13 tables showing the following, for various periods 1970-83:

a.   Municipal annexations and detachments and resulting changes in population and land area, with detail by city, population size group, and census region and division.

b.   States with most new municipal incorporations and with greatest population in newly incorporated places, by State; and population of newly incorporated places with over 10,000 population, and year incorporated, by place.

Report appeared annually in 1975-79 issues of the *Year Book.* For description of report for 1979, see SRI 1980 Annual, under A5800-1.2.

NEW ENGLAND TOWN MEETING: PURE DEMOCRACY IN ACTION?

(p. 102-106) By Joseph F. Zimmerman. Report, with 4 tables showing town meeting average attendance, acceptance of finance committee recommendations, and establishment of special committees; for 5 New England States, generally by town population size, 1982.

A5800–1.3: Part C. Personnel Issues

SALARIES OF MUNICIPAL OFFICIALS FOR 1983

(p. 109-133) Annual report, by Ross H. Hoff, on salaries of municipal officials, as of Jan. 1, 1983. Presents data for 26 positions, based on responses of 5,169 cities to an ICMA survey. Includes 1 table on survey sample characteristics, and 3 tables showing:

a.   Average salaries for 24 positions, 1978-83; and for 4 positions in central cities and suburban areas of 20 SMSAs, Jan. 1, 1983.

b.   Mean, median, and 1st and 3rd quartile salaries for 26 positions, by city size category, with varying detail by region, city type, and form of government, Jan. 1, 1983.

For description of report for 1984, see A5800-2.55, below.

SALARIES OF COUNTY OFFICIALS FOR 1983

(p. 133-144) Report on salaries of county officials, as of July 1, 1983. Report was also published in *Baseline Data Reports;* for description, see A5800-2.52, below.

POLICE, FIRE, AND REFUSE COLLECTION AND DISPOSAL DEPARTMENTS: PERSONNEL, COMPENSATION, AND EXPENDITURES

(p. 145-192) Annual report, by Gerard J. Hoetmer, on employment, compensation, and expenditures of police, fire, and refuse collection/disposal depts of 1,424 cities with over 10,000 population, as of Jan. 1, 1983. Includes 13 summary tables showing data by city size, with detail for personnel by census division and form of government; and 1 extended table, listing cities by size and showing the following for each dept:

a.   Uniformed and total personnel, weekly hours, entrance and maximum salaries, maximum longevity pay, and number of years to maximum.

b.   Expenditures for salaries/wages, contributions to employee retirement/insurance, capital outlay, and other.

A5800–1.4: Part D. Management Issues and Trends

MICROCOMPUTERS: A SURVEY OF LOCAL GOVERNMENT USE

(p. 195-202) By Donald F. Norris and Vincent J. Webb. Report examining municipal government microcomputer ownership, use, programming sources, and related services. Data are from responses of 2,433 cities to an ICMA 1982-83 survey.

Includes 1 table on sample characteristics, and 5 charts and 10 tables showing survey response for the following, generally by city size, census region, metro status, and form of government:

a.   Microcomputer ownership/leasing, offices using, plans to purchase, and reasons for not purchasing; microcomputers in use by make, and users by employee category; user problems and negative and positive impact, by type; and staff reaction.

b.   Microcomputer detailed applications by programming source, and use in conjunction with mini and mainframe computers.

MUNICIPAL MANAGEMENT CAPACITY: PRODUCTIVITY IMPROVEMENT AND STRATEGIES FOR HANDLING FISCAL STRESS

(p. 206-214) By Theodore H. Poister and Robert P. McGowan. Report on municipal use of various managerial strategies for budgeting, information management, and productivity. Data are from responses of 456 cities to a 1982 survey conducted by the authors. Includes 1 table on sample characteristics, and 10 tables showing distribution of survey response for the following:

a.   Use and perceived effectiveness of 8 managerial strategies; cities using strategies, by size, census region, and form of government; and selected strategies applied to contracted services.

b.   Impact of various strategies on municipal productivity and finances.

A5800–2   BASELINE DATA REPORTS
Series.   For individual publication data, see below.
LC 76-5644.
SRI/MF/not filmed

Continuing series of reports on municipal government activities and management. Each report covers one selected topic, including finance, employment, and government functions and structures.

Data are based on surveys of municipal officials by the International City Management Assn (ICMA), Census Bureau studies, and other sources. Many of the reports are also included in *Municipal Yearbook,* covered in SRI under A5800-1.

Reports reviewed during 1984 are described below.

Availability: International City Management Association, 1120 G St., NW, Washington DC 20005, $225.00 per yr., single report $13.75; SRI/MF/not filmed.

A5800–2.51: City Employment and Payrolls

[Monograph. Nov. 1983. 16 p. Vol. 15, No. 11. SRI/MF/not filmed.]

Report on city government employment and payrolls, as of Oct. 1982. Data are from a Census Bureau survey covering all cities with populations over 25,000 and a sampling of smaller cities. Includes 4 tables showing:

a. Summary: FTE and total employment, and total payroll, by detailed municipal function; and employment and payroll summary data by city size.

b. By city: population; total and FTE employment; total payroll; and payroll and FTE employment, by selected non-school function; for individual cities with population over 25,000, arranged by State.

A5800–2.52: Salaries of County Officials for 1983

[Monograph. Dec. 1983. 13 p. Vol. 15, No. 12. SRI/MF/not filmed.]

Report on salaries of county officials, as of July 1, 1983. Presents data for 12 positions, based on responses of 1,801 counties to an ICMA survey. Includes 2 summary tables; and 1 detailed table showing mean, median, and 1st and 3rd quartile salaries for 12 positions by county size category, with varying detail by region, county type (metro and nonmetro), and form of government (with and without administrator).

Also includes 1 table on survey sample characteristics.

A5800–2.53: Infrastructure

[Monograph. Jan. 1984. 10 p. Vol. 16, No. 1. SRI/MF/not filmed.]

Report presenting highlights of a National League of Cities/U.S. Conference of Mayors report on municipal capital investment decisions to meet infrastructure needs, based on a Dec. 1982-Feb. 1983 survey. Includes selected summary data on infrastructure conditions; and improvement priorities, cost estimates, financing ability, and sources of finances.

Full survey report, *Capital Budgeting and Infrastructure in American Cities: An Initial Assessment,* is described in SRI 1983 Annual, and is available on SRI microfiche, under A9330-5.

A5800–2.54: Characteristics of City Populations

[Monograph. Feb. 1984. 16 p. Vol. 16, No. 2. SRI/MF/not filmed.]

Compilation of demographic and socioeconomic data on cities with populations over 25,-000, 1980. Data are from 1980 Census of Population and Housing, Summary Tape File 3A. Includes brief introductory narrative, and 1 extended table showing the following for each city, arranged by State, generally as of Apr. 1, 1980:

a. Population, with percent change from 1970 and distribution by race/ethnicity (including Native American, Asian/Pacific Islander, and Hispanic); percent of persons under 18 and over 65 years; and distribution of persons 16/over by educational attainment and industry division for employed persons.

b. Median family income, 1979; percent of persons working in same city as residence; and means of transportation and travel time to work.

A5800–2.55: Salaries of Municipal Officials, 1984

[Annual. Mar. 1984. 27 p. Vol. 16, No. 3. SRI/MF/not filmed.]

Annual report, by Ross H. Hoff, on salaries of municipal officials, as of Jan. 1, 1984. Presents data for 26 positions, based on responses of 5,106 cities to an ICMA survey. Includes 3 tables showing:

a. Average salaries for 24 positions, 1979-84; and for 4 positions in central cities and suburban areas of 26 SMSAs, Jan. 1, 1984.

b. Mean, median, and 1st and 3rd quartile salaries for 26 positions, by city size category, with varying detail by region, city type, and form of government, Jan. 1, 1984.

Also includes 1 table on survey sample characteristics.

A5800–2.56: Local Government Assistants, 1983

[Monograph. Apr. 1984. 54 p. Vol. 16, No. 4. SRI/MF/not filmed.]

Report on characteristics of local government assistant managers. Data are from responses of 3,073 assistant managers employed by 1,291 cities, counties, and councils of governments to a summer 1983 ICMA survey.

Includes 1 table showing survey response on principal job responsibilities by position; and 2 detailed tables presenting the following respondent characteristics, with various cross-tabulations:

a. Sex, race/ethnicity (including Hispanic, Asian, and American Indian), salary range, position title, population size and type of jurisdiction where employed, and educational attainment.

b. Average age, salary by region, years of experience, and number of positions held, governments worked for, and years in current position.

Also includes detailed directory of assistant managers responding to survey, including population and form of government for jurisdiction where employed, and respondent job title, highest level of education completed, and years of local government service, all by jurisdiction arranged by State.

A5800–2.57: Characteristics of Housing Units: Cities with a Population of 25,000 or More

[Monograph. May 1984. 17 p. Vol. 16, No. 5. SRI/MF/not filmed.]

Compilation of data on housing unit financial and structural characteristics for cities with population over 25,000 in 1980. Data are from 1980 Census of Population and Housing, Summary Tape File 3M. Includes brief introductory narrative, and 1 extended table showing the following for each city, arranged by State, 1980:

a. Population; number of housing units, with percent rental units; and percent of units built before 1940 and since 1969, connected to public/private sewer system, and with selected types of heating equipment and fuels.

b. Distribution of mortgaged, nonmortgaged, and rental units by monthly owner costs or rent; and distribution of all units by period householder moved in.

A5800–2.58: Intergovernmental Service Arrangements and the Transfer of Functions

[Monograph. June 1984. 10 p. Vol. 16, No. 6. SRI/MF/not filmed.]

By Lori M. Henderson. Report examining local government delivery of public services through the use of intergovernmental agreements. Data are from responses of chief administrative officers of 1,654 cities and 435 counties to a summer 1983 survey conducted by ICMA and the Advisory Commission on Intergovernmental Relations (ACIR).

Includes 1 summary table, and 3 tables repeated for 3 types of intergovernmental service agreement (service contracts and transfers, and joint agreements), showing survey response of cities and counties for the following:

a. Number with agreements, by population size, census region, metro status, and form of government.

b. 10 services most frequently arranged; and number of agreements, by type of service and cooperating jurisdiction or organization (including other cities and counties, school and special districts, State, regional and nonprofit organizations, and private firms).

Also includes 1 table on survey sample characteristics; and 1 table presenting summary data on cities' use of private contracting services, based on 1972 and 1982 ACIR surveys.

A5800–3 SALARIES $35,000 AND OVER FOR LOCAL GOVERNMENT MANAGERS, COUNTY MANAGERS/CHIEF ADMINISTRATIVE OFFICERS, AND REGIONAL COUNCIL DIRECTORS, as of Jan. 1, 1984.

Annual. [1984.]
26 p. var. paging.
SRI/MF/not filmed

Annual compilation of data on salaries $35,000 and over paid chief appointed officials in cities, counties, and regional councils, as of Jan. 1, 1984. Data are compiled from reports submitted to Municipal Data Service of the International City Management Assn.

Contains 1 extended table showing annual salary paid and population for each municipality or area, ranked by salary, for local government managers (16 p.), county managers/chief administrative officers (2 p.), and regional council directors (6 p.).

Availability: International City Management Association, Municipal Data Service, 1120 G St., NW, Washington DC 20005, †; SRI/MF/not filmed.

A5900
International Ladies Garment Workers Union

A5900–1   CONDITIONS IN THE WOMEN'S GARMENT INDUSTRY
2 issues per year.
Approx. 15 p.
SRI/MF/complete

Recurring report, published 2 times a year, on sales, production, imports, employment, and earnings in the women's and children's garment industry.

Data are from Census Bureau, BLS, and ILG-WU Research Dept, and are current to 2-3 months prior to cover date.

Contains narrative analysis of industry and general economic developments, interspersed with 5 tables showing the following:

a. Retail sales of women's/children's clothing/accessories by type of outlet; unit production of selected women's/misses' garments, and value of output; and employment, man-hours, and payroll of production workers, by garment type; all for various periods of current and previous year, and annually for 11-13 previous years. 3 tables.

b. Imports of selected women's and children's garments, by type of fabric, for year to date, same period of previous year, and annually for 5 prior years; and average hourly earnings, women's garment industry sectors and other selected industries, month of coverage and same month of 6 previous years. 2 tables.

An annual table, showing unit production and net value of shipments for women's and children's garments by detailed product, for approximately 10 previous years, is included when data become available.

All regular tables appear in both issues; annual table is included in the Sept. 12, 1984 issue.

Availability: International Ladies Garment Workers Union, Research Department, 1710 Broadway, New York NY 10019, †; SRI/MF/complete.

Issues reviewed during 1984: Mar. 12 and Sept. 12, 1984 (P).

A6025
Investment Company Institute

A6025–1   1984 MUTUAL FUND FACT BOOK
Annual. [1984.] 104 p.
ISSN 0077-2550.
LC 80-647954.
SRI/MF/complete

Annual fact book, for 1984, on the mutual funds industry, presenting data on industry growth, performance, holdings, and transactions, various years 1952-83. Selected data are shown by State and census division. Also includes 1983 survey data on demographic characteristics of mutual fund shareholders and individual retirement account (IRA) owners. Data are compiled by the Investment Company Institute.

Contains contents listing (p. 3); narrative report interspersed with 33 charts and 18 tables (p. 5-52); glossary (p. 53-55); statistical appendix, with 39 tables (p. 57-98); and index (p. 99-104).

All tables and selected charts are listed below.

Availability: Investment Company Institute, Research Department, 1600 M St., NW, Washington DC 20036, $2.00; SRI/MF/complete.

CHARTS AND TABLES:
[Investment objectives include aggressive growth, growth, growth/income, balanced, income, bond and municipal bond, option income, and money market funds.]

A6025–1.1: Text Charts and Tables

PERFORMANCE TRENDS AND PORTFOLIO COMPOSITION

[1-2] Dividends and reinvestment [1971-83], and capital gains and dividends distributions to shareholders [1975-83], all types of mutual funds. (p. 13)

[3-4] Money market funds asset composition; and portfolio composition of equity/bond/income funds; year end or Dec. 1983. (p. 18)

[5-6] Diversification of mutual fund portfolios, percent of total common stock and [market value of] common stock holdings, by [industry group, selected years 1973-83]. (p. 19-20)

ACCOUNTS, ASSETS, SALES, AND REDEMPTIONS

[7-9] Number and shareholder accounts, and assets of mutual funds [various years 1940-83]. [charts] (p. 23-24)

[10-12] Sales, redemptions, and assets: equity/bond/income funds; money market mutual funds; and short-term municipal bond funds [various years 1971-83]. (p. 25)

[13-14] Percent of equity and bond/income funds sales and redemptions [by investment objective, 1976 and 1983]. (p. 27)

[15-16] Mutual fund assets and sales classified by investment objective, [1982-83]. (p. 28)

[17] Net exchanges [transfer of investment funds] by investment objective, 1983. [chart] (p. 30)

INVESTOR NEEDS SURVEY, AND INVESTMENT PERFORMANCE

[18-19] Household ownership of mutual funds, and distribution of households within fund owner and nonowner groups, classified according to income and [respondent] age [all by type of fund; based on a national sample of 1,500 respondents with incomes of $30,000/more]. (p. 37)

[20] Comparative equity investment performance [of mutual funds, bank funds, and S&P 500; 5- and 10-year returns; through Dec. 31, 1983]. [chart] (p. 43)

MUTUAL FUND AND IRA OWNERS

[21] Characteristics of households with incomes of $30,000/more classified according to mutual fund and IRA ownership [including number of households, and data on income, median age, and prevalence of higher education degrees, 1983]. (p. 48)

[22] [Distribution of] mutual fund owners with household income of $30,000/more [by age, higher education attainment, and income], classified by IRA ownership [1983]. (p. 49)

[23] Estimated value of IRA plans outstanding [by type of institution holding funds and for self-directed accounts], Dec. 1982 and Dec.1983. (p. 50)

A6025–1.2: Appendix Tables
[Fund characteristics include distribution methods (broker/dealer, direct selling, no-load, and other), and investment objectives.]

ACCOUNTS, ASSETS, SALES, AND REDEMPTIONS

[1-2] Shareholder accounts, total net assets, and cash position, 1965-83; and distribution of mutual fund assets [by type of investment], 1966-83; [for] equity/bond/income funds. (p. 59-60)

[3-4] Total net assets and cash position by fund characteristics, year end [1980-83]; and total net assets by investment objective, within method of distribution, 1976-83. (p. 61-62)

[5-7] Type of shareholder accounts [regular, contractual accumulation and single payment, and withdrawal], 1971-83; capital changes, 1965-83; and annual repurchase (redemption) rate, 1952-83; [all for] equity/bond/income funds. (p. 63-65)

[8-9] Mutual fund net new money flow related to net new money flow from individuals to savings and investment vehicles [selected years 1960-83]; and distributions to shareholders, 1965-83, equity/bond/income funds. (p. 66-67)

[10] Sales and reinvested dividends, by fund characteristics, 1980-83. (p. 68)

[11] Sales and redemptions of equity/bond/income funds by fund characteristics [and by type of sale and redemption, 1981-83]. (p. 70)

[12-13] Sales and redemptions of mutual funds by investment objective within method of distribution, 1976-83. (p. 71-72)

GEOGRAPHIC DISTRIBUTION OF SALES

[14-15] Investor purchases of equity/bond/income fund shares by States and geographical regions [census divisions, U.S. territories/possessions, Canada, and other countries], by method of distribution, 1983. (p. 73-76)

PORTFOLIO TRANSACTIONS

[16-18] Total purchases, total sales, and net purchases of portfolio securities, common stocks, and securities other than common stocks, by mutual funds, 1963-83. (p. 77-79)

[19-22] Portfolio purchases and sales by fund characteristics [1980-83]; and sales, redemptions, and net sales due to exchanges, by investment objectives, 1981-83. (p. 80-81)

MUNICIPAL BOND FUNDS

[23] Limited maturity municipal bond funds [sales, redemptions, net sales, number of funds, accounts outstanding, and net assets, 1980-83]. (p. 82)

MONEY MARKET FUNDS
[Tables [24-27] begin "Money market fund..."]

[24] [Sales, redemptions, net sales, number of funds, accounts outstanding, average maturity, and net assets, 1974-83.] (p. 83)

[25-26] Assets [1978-83]; and shareholder accounts [1981-83; shown monthly, by type of fund]. (p. 84-86)

[27] Asset composition year end 1978-83. (p. 87)

IRA AND KEOGH ACCOUNTS

[28-29] IRA and Keogh assets and accounts [managed by mutual funds], by investment objective, year end 1983. (p. 88)

FIDUCIARY, BUSINESS, AND INSTITUTIONAL INVESTORS

[Tables [30-38] begin "Fiduciary, business, and institutional investors of..."]

[30] Mutual funds excluding money market and short-term municipal bond funds [reported assets, institutional accounts in force, and value of institutional holdings, 1954-83]. (p. 89)

[31-38] Equity/bond/income funds; money market funds [total and by type of fund (general purpose, broker/dealer, and institutional)]; and short-term municipal bond funds; [all showing] number of accounts and value of holdings [by type of investor including corporations, employee pension/profit sharing plans, insurance companies/other financial institutions, unions, churches/religious organizations, schools/colleges, and foundations, various years 1981-83]. (p. 90-97)

[39] Assets of major institutions and financial intermediaries [aggregated for commercial and mutual savings banks, credit unions, savings and loan assns, fire/casualty and life insurance companies, bank trusts, closed-end investment companies, mutual funds, and private and government pension funds, 1976-83]. (p. 98)

A6025–5   **TRENDS IN MUTUAL FUND ACTIVITY**
Monthly. Approx. 10 p. no paging.
SRI/MF/complete, shipped quarterly

Monthly report presenting statistics on mutual fund sales, assets, and investments, by investment objective. Also includes data on short-term (money market and limited maturity municipal bond) funds. Report is issued 1-2 months after cover date.

Data are compiled from reports of approximately 700 mutual funds, 90 municipal bond funds, and 300 money market funds.

Issues contain 8 monthly tables, listed below.

Issuing agency also publishes a less detailed monthly news release covering mutual fund activities. News release is not covered in SRI.

Availability: Investment Company Institute, Research Department, 1600 M St., NW, Washington DC 20036, †; SRI/MF/complete, shipped quarterly.

Issues reviewed during 1984: Oct. 1983-Sept. 1984 (D).

MONTHLY TABLES:
[All data are shown for cover date month, previous month, and same month of preceding year. Tables 1-4 exclude data on short-term funds.

Methods of distribution are broker-dealer, direct selling, no-load, and other. Investment objectives are aggressive growth, growth, growth/income, balanced, income, corporate bond, long-term municipal bond, and option/income.]

1. Monthly statistics of open-end companies [total and new sales, reinvested dividends, sales due to exchanges, share redemptions, cash/short-term security holdings, net assets, liquid asset ratio, common stock and other security purchases and sales, and number of funds].

2-2A. Sales and redemptions, and exchanges into and out of the funds, classified by method of distribution and investment objective.

3. Total assets, liquid assets, and liquidity ratios, classified by method of distribution and investment objective.

4. Portfolio activity [common stock and other security purchases and sales], classified by investment objective.

A. Monthly statistics [of] limited maturity municipal bonds [total net assets and change during month, regular sales of shares, investment income reinvested, total redemptions, sales and redemptions due to exchanges, and number of funds].

B. Monthly statistics of money market funds [total net assets and change during month; composition of assets (including Treasury bills and other U.S. securities, repurchase agreements, 3 types of certificates of deposit, commercial paper, bankers' acceptances, and cash reserves); average portfolio maturity; and number of accounts outstanding and funds].

C. Sales and redemptions of money market funds [regular sales of shares, investment income reinvested, total redemptions, and sales and redemptions due to exchanges].

A6125
Labor Institute
for Human Enrichment

A6125–1   **WORKING AND NOT WORKING IN THE PERFORMING ARTS: A Survey of Employment, Underemployment, and Unemployment Among Performing Artists in 1980**
Monograph. [1983.]
iv+294+App 8 p.
SRI/MF/complete

Survey report on employment and earnings experience of performing artists, by union affiliation and profession, 1980, with some comparisons to 1979 and 1976.

Covers survey responses to questions on the following topics: type and extent of employment in arts and other fields, and reasons for employment choices; number of different performing arts employers; periods of unemployment, and applications for and collection of unemployment compensation; and earnings from performing arts and other jobs, with comparisons to all professional/technical workers and all households.

Other topics include time and money spent on continuing training, and training sources and effects; participation in CETA and other federally supported employment and training programs; job information sources; career counseling needs and preferences; and plans to change careers, including reasons and expected age at change.

Also includes selected data by sex; and survey sample demographic characteristics.

Data are from over 3,000 responses to a spring/summer 1981 sample survey of members of the 5 principal performing arts unions, conducted by Ruttenberg, Friedman, Kilgallon, Gutchess and Associates, Inc. The study was sponsored by the Labor Institute for Human Enrichment, in cooperation with the AFL-CIO Dept for Professional Employees.

Contains contents listing (p. i-iv); overview and methodology, with 2 tables (p. 1-31); narrative analysis in 8 sections, interspersed with 150 tables (p. 32-294); and facsimile questionnaire (8 p.).

Availability: Labor Institute for Human Enrichment, 815 16th St., NW, Washington DC 20006-4182, $25.00; SRI/MF/complete.

A6225
Life Insurance Marketing
and Research Association

A6225–1   **MONTHLY SURVEY OF LIFE INSURANCE SALES in the U.S. and Canada**
Monthly, with annual supplement. Approx. 6 p.
SRI/MF/complete, shipped quarterly

Monthly report, with annual supplement, on trends in life insurance policy sales in U.S. and Canada. Presents data on reported sales of ordinary and group life insurance policies, aggregated for approximately 140 U.S. and 40 Canadian companies. Report is issued approximately 2 months after month of coverage.

Issues generally contain data explanation, with 1-2 summary tables; and 5 monthly tables showing U.S. and Canadian life insurance sales results, and summary of interest rate ranges.

Sales results include annualized premium, and/or number and face value of policies, and are shown monthly and cumulatively for current year through month of coverage, with comparisons to previous year. Interest rates are shown for month of coverage and previous month.

Data for ordinary policy sales include detail for company categories based on amount of insurance in force, and further U.S. detail for ordinary and combination companies/depts and universal life policies.

Annual supplement, usually issued with the Jan. report, is a list of reporting companies.

Prior to the Jan. 1984 issue, report did not include data on universal life policies, interest rates, and group insurance.

Availability: Life Insurance Marketing and Research Association, PO Box 208, Hartford CT 06141, †; SRI/MF/complete, shipped quarterly.

Issues reviewed during 1984: Sept. 1983-Aug. 1984 (D); and 1984 annual supplement.

A6325
Manufactured Housing Institute

A6325–1 MANUFACTURING REPORT

Monthly. Approx. 8 p.
SRI/MF/complete, shipped quarterly

Monthly report on mobile/manufactured home production and estimated shipments, by State and region, and manufacturer inventory. Data are from reports to National Conference of States on Building Codes and Standards. Reports are issued approximately 2 months after month of coverage.

Contains brief analysis, and 7 monthly tables listed below.

Availability: Manufactured Housing Institute, 1745 Jefferson Davis Hwy., Suite 511, Arlington VA 22202, members †, nonmembers $55.00 per yr.; SRI/MF/complete, shipped quarterly.

Issues reviewed during 1984: Sept. 1983-Aug. 1984 (D).

MONTHLY TABLES:

[1-2] Mobile/manufactured home production and estimated shipments [monthly and cumulatively for present year to date and previous year].

[3] Manufacturer inventory [total homes, and as percent of production, monthly for present year to date and previous year].

[4-5] Mobile/manufactured home production and shipments [by State and region, for month of coverage and year to date for present and previous year].

[6] Year-to-date product mix [shipments and production of single- and multi-section homes, by State and region].

[7] Shipments of [total, and single- and multi-section] mobile/manufactured homes, by State, ranked from highest to lowest [for month of coverage].

A6325–2 MANUFACTURED HOME FINANCING IN 1983, 33rd Annual Survey

Annual. May 25, 1984.
2+23 p.
SRI/MF/complete

Annual report on mobile home consumer financing, by type of lending institution, loan characteristics, and methods of repayment, 1983 and trends. Also includes data on manufacturer shipments, by State, 1979-83.

Data are from responses of 542 lending institutions to a Jan. 1984 survey sponsored by MHI; and from National Conference of States on Building Codes and Standards, Federal Reserve Board, and Jon Whitney Associates, Inc.

Contains contents listing (1 p.); survey portion, with background, summary, 8 charts, and 25 tables listed below (p. 1-19); and appendix, with 2 charts and 3 tables also listed below (p. 20-23).

Availability: Manufactured Housing Institute, 1745 Jefferson Davis Hwy., Suite 511, Arlington VA 22202, members †, lenders, educational institutions, and investment analysts ‡, others inquire at issuing agency; SRI/MF/complete.

TABLES AND APPENDIX CHARTS:

A6325–2.1: Survey Data

[Tables show data by type of institution: banks, savings and loan assns, finance companies, mortgage bankers, service companies, and credit unions. Data are for 1983, unless otherwise noted.]

SUMMARY

[1-2] Gross dollar value of manufactured [home] retail paper outstanding and number of accounts of reporting institutions; and number of loans made; [1980-83]. (p. 4-5)

FINANCING ARRANGEMENTS, PROFITABILITY, AND PLANS

[3] Financing of other types of housing/construction [including conventional homes/tracts, manufactured home/modular subdivisions, and manufactured home parks]. (p. 6)

[4] Profitability of manufactured home lending compared to real estate loan programs. (p. 6)

[5-6] Plans for manufactured home financing [start or discontinue financing, and degree of change in portfolio size]; and approximate dollar volume lenders plan to commit for manufactured home loans; in 1984. (p. 7)

[7-9] Institutions currently active in manufactured home financing, number of financial locations represented, and number of States operating. (p. 8)

[10-12] Minimum acceptable down payment, and average/typical and maximum maturity, on manufactured home loans [for new and existing single- and multi-section homes]. (p. 9-11)

REPAYMENT OF LOANS

[13] Average turnover for manufactured home retail loans. (p. 12)

[14-15] Manufactured home loans paid off by repayment/prepayment, and by repossession. (p. 12)

[16-17] Manufactured home consumer loan delinquencies; and repossessions on hand/in process, as of Dec. 31; [1980-83]. (p. 13-14)

[18] Percentage of loans outstanding recovered in selling a repossessed manufactured home. (p. 15)

[19] When repossession proceedings begin. (p. 16)

[20] Manufactured home portfolio protection methods [6 types, including FHA insurance and VA guaranty]. (p. 16)

INSTITUTIONS AND WHOLESALE FINANCING

[21] Number of years experience in manufactured home financing. (p. 16)

[22] Manufactured home loan net activity [loans advanced, repayment and repossession liquidations, and accounts outstanding at beginning and end of year, 1980-83]. (p. 17)

[23] Dollar amounts outstanding of manufactured housing wholesale financing. (p. 18)

[24] Manufactured housing dealers/distributors represented in wholesale portfolio. (p. 18)

[25] Regional distribution of manufactured housing lenders [by region and State]. (p. 19)

A6325–2.2: Appendix Data

SHIPMENTS

[1] Manufactured home shipment and dollar volume trends [1970-83]. (p. 20)

[2] Change in manufactured home product mix: multisection manufactured home shipments [and share of total shipments, 1970-83]. (p. 20)

[3] Manufactured home shipments to States [by region and State, and for export/government, 1979-83]. (p. 21)

FINANCES

[4] Percent of manufactured homes purchased with financing [1978-83]. [chart] (p. 22)

[5] Federal Reserve estimates of 1983 value of manufactured home retail outstandings [by type of institution, except mortgage bankers and service companies]. [chart] (p. 23)

A6375
Menswear Retailers of America

A6375–1 1983 ANNUAL BUSINESS SURVEY, Men's Store Operating Experiences

Annual. June 25, 1984.
59 p.
MRA Business Newsletter Section II.
SRI/MF/complete

Annual survey report on men's wear retailer operating and financial performance, 1983. Report covers firms handling men's wear only and firms also handling women's wear, and includes data by sales volume, metro population size group, and geographic region. Most data are shown as ratio medians and ranges.

Data are based on survey responses from 185 men's wear retailers, compiled by Tyson Belzer and Associates, Inc. Report is intended to permit individual retailers to compare their operations with those of similar retailers.

Contains contents listing, definitions, and sample characteristics (p. 1-9); analyses of survey data, with 4 trend charts, and 18 tables described below (p. 10-22); and 8 sections, with 39 tables also described below (p. 23-56).

Availability: Menswear Retailers of America, National Clothier Corporation Division, 2011 Eye St., NW, Suite 600, Washington DC 20006, $35.00, members 20% discount; SRI/MF/complete.

TABLES:

[Data are for 1983, unless otherwise noted.]

SPECIAL ANALYSES

a. Sales distribution, initial markup, and markdown, by men's wear category, 1979-83. 3 tables. (p. 10)

b. Key business ratios, by firm sales volume, region, and metro size class. 4 tables. (p. 12-15)

c. Star performers: data for selected financial performance criteria, aggregated for firms in the upper 25% of performance criterion, by sales volume and region. 2 tables. (p. 17)

d. Number of store employees by function, by sales volume; and employee productivity and sales productivity measures, by sales volume, metro size, and region. 7 tables. (p. 18-21)

e. Compensation of store owners and alteration/tailoring personnel, by sales volume, region, and metro size. 2 tables. (p. 22)

MERCHANDISING AND OPERATING DATA

[Most tables show data for all firms, firms handling men's wear only, and firms also handling women's wear.]

f. Operating experiences, including profit levels; initial markup and shrinkage by major dept; leased dept sales as percent of total sales; and selected merchandising, productivity, and financial ratios. 5 tables. (p. 23-26)

g. By merchandise classification: distribution of sales, average inventory, and ending inventory; sales change from 1982; markdowns as percent of sales; and inventory turnover. 7 tables. (p. 27-33)

h. Stock/sales ratio at the beginning of each month; advertising expenditure distribution by media; composite operating statement; and monthly sales/publicity cost ratios. 6 tables. (p. 34-38)

i. Detailed merchandising, operating, productivity, and financial data, generally expressed as percent of sales or other ratio, by sales volume, metro size, and region, with some comparisons to 1982. 21 tables. (p. 39-56)

A6376
Metal Treating Institute

A6376-1　ANALYSIS OF NATIONAL BILLINGS: COMMERCIAL HEAT TREATERS
Monthly.
Approx. 6 p. no paging.
SRI/MF/complete, shipped quarterly

Monthly press release on commercial metal heat treatment industry billings, by region. Heat treatment involves use of high temperatures to alter the properties of metals.

Data are reported by approximately 200 companies belonging to the Metal Treating Institute (MTI), accounting for approximately 10% of the heat treatment industry. Release is issued 6 weeks after month of coverage.

Contains brief narrative with 1 summary table; 1-9 charts with monthly and cumulative trends; and 2 tables showing number of member companies and billings, for Michigan and 8 MTI districts, for month of coverage, year to date, and same periods of previous year. Also occasionally includes revisions for previous issues.

Availability: Metal Treating Institute, 1311 Executive Center Dr., Suite 200, Tallahassee FL 32301, participating members †, others inquire at issuing agency; SRI/MF/complete, shipped quarterly.

Issues reviewed during 1984: Sept. 1983-Sept. 1984 (D).

A6400
Morris, Robert, Associates

A6400-1　REPORT ON DOMESTIC AND INTERNATIONAL LOAN CHARGE-OFFS
Annual.　1984.　47 p.
SRI/MF/not filmed

Annual report on domestic and international loan charge-offs and recoveries by banks in 1983. Includes data by Federal Reserve district, bank asset size, and borrower type, industry, and country. Data are from a survey of over 1,000 Robert Morris Associates member banks.

Contains contents and table listing, and preface (p. 3-4); and 2 sections, with explanatory notes and 21 tables listed below (p. 5-47).

This is the 13th annual report.

Availability: Robert Morris Associates, Order Department, 1616 Philadelphia National Bank Bldg., Philadelphia PA 19107, members $10.00, nonmembers $15.00; SRI/MF/not filmed.

TABLES:

[Data are for 1983, unless otherwise noted.]

DOMESTIC LOAN CHARGE-OFFS

[Tables 1-11 present data by bank asset size group and Federal Reserve district.]

1. Base data gathered from banks responding to the survey [number of banks, total assets, loans outstanding, and dollars charged off and recovered]. (p. 9)

2. Charge-off and recovery experience in percentage form [including gross and net charge-offs as percent of average loan portfolio, and recoveries as percent of charge-offs, 1981-83]. (p. 10)

3. Loan charge-offs compared to average loan portfolio in median and quartiles. (p. 11)

4-11. Reported loan and charge-off experience, by type of loan [real estate, financial institutions, securities, farming, commercial/industrial, individuals, and all other]. (p. 12-34)

12-16. Ranking of high-loss industries nationwide: by number of times SIC [number] is cited, by bank size groupings, by Federal Reserve districts, and by dollars charged off, 1983; and by probability of charge-offs in 1984. (p. 35-41)

INTERNATIONAL LOAN CHARGE-OFFS

[Tables 1-2 show data by asset and international loan portfolio size groups.]

1. Base data gathered from banks responding to the survey [number of banks, total assets, international loans/deposits outstanding and charged off, and total dollars recovered]. (p. 44)

2. Charge-off and recovery experience in percentage form [gross and net charge-offs as percent of international loans/deposits outstanding, and recoveries as percent of charge-offs, 1982-83]. (p. 44)

3-5. International charge-offs: by country of borrower; by type of borrower; and by type of borrower, further broken down by country of borrower. (p. 45-47)

A6400-2　JOURNAL OF COMMERCIAL BANK LENDING
Monthly.　Approx. 75 p.
ISSN 0021-986X.
LC 75-648976.
SRI/MF/not filmed

Monthly journal on developments and issues in commercial bank lending, including analyses of lending practices and characteristic risks for selected industries, project financing, international finance, and loan sharing. Also includes reports on legislation affecting commercial lending, and on management methods.

Issues generally include contents listing; and several articles, usually by bank executives, occasionally including statistics.

Features with substantial statistical content are described, as they appear, under "Statistical Features." Each issue of the journal is reviewed, but an abstract is published in SRI monthly issues only when statistical features appear.

Availability: Robert Morris Associates, Order Department, 1616 Philadelphia National Bank Bldg., Philadelphia PA 19107, associates $12.25 per yr., others $24.50 per yr., single copy $3.00; SRI/MF/not filmed.

Issues reviewed during 1984: Nov. 1983-Oct. 1984 (P) (Vol. 66, Nos. 3-12; Vol. 67, Nos. 1-2).

STATISTICAL FEATURES:

A6400-2.501: Feb. 1984 (Vol. 66, No. 6)

ANALYSIS OF THE AIRLINE INDUSTRY

(p. 18-28) By Craig A. Schmutzer. Article, with text statistics and 4 tables showing selected composite financial data for the airline industry, including operating margin, value of net operating capital, percent change in retained earnings, passenger revenue, expenses, and net income; and aggregate debt/equity ratio, and return on equity and assets, for major and national airlines; primarily 1978-81. Data are from CAB records as borrowed by Standard & Poor's Corp.

ASSESSING THE QUALITY OF REPORTED EARNINGS IN THE OIL AND GAS INDUSTRY: SOME GUIDANCE FOR CREDIT ANALYSIS

(p. 29-38) By Kenneth R. Ferris and M. Edgar Barrett. Article on petroleum industry accounting practices, and their effect on company returns as reflected in financial statements. Data are from a survey of 21 largest U.S.-based petroleum companies.

Includes 3 tables showing reported value and percent of earnings for before-tax interest capitalization, and after-tax LIFO (last-in, first-out) inventory liquidation, by company, 1981-82; and hypothetical data illustrating impact of cost center definition on income statements.

A6400-2.502: Apr. 1984 (Vol. 66, No. 8)

COOPERATIVES VS. COMMERCIAL BANKS: THE UNEASY COMPETITION IN AG LENDING

(p. 49-54) By Robert W. Wyatt et al. Article on role of commercial banks in the agricultural credit system. Data are from USDA and 2 Federal Intermediate Credit Banks.

Includes 3 tables showing the following for non-real estate farm loans: debt outstanding, and percent held by banks, Product Credit Assns (PCAs), Farmers Home Administration, and Commodity Credit Corp.; bank share of total bank/PCA loans in 4 midwestern States; and interest rates charged by banks and PCAs; various periods 1960-82.

A6400-2.503: Sept. 1984 (Vol. 67, No. 1)
MATERIALITY: ARE BANKERS MORE CONCERNED THAN CPAs?

(p. 14-27) By Philip M. J. Reckers et al. Article, with 4 tables comparing views of bankers and certified public accountants on dollar thresholds for corporate disclosure of selected items in financial statements. Items include inventory write-downs due to obsolescence, pending litigation, gain from forced sale of land, product line discontinuation, and sensitive payments to foreign governments.

Data are based on responses of 65 bankers and 50 CPAs to a recent survey.

ANALYSIS OF FINANCE COMPANY RATIOS IN 1983, ANNUAL FEATURE

(p. 46-55) Annual article, by David P. Tomick and David H. Curtis, with 2 tables showing detailed financial and operating ratios aggregated for consumer (direct cash lending) and diversified finance companies, Dec. 31, 1980-83. Tables also show total loan volume and amount outstanding. Data are compiled by First National Bank of Chicago.

A6400-3   RMA '84 ANNUAL STATEMENT STUDIES, Fiscal Year Ends June 30, 1983-Mar. 31, 1984
Annual. Sept. 1984. 416 p.
LC 72-626355.
SRI/MF/not filmed

Annual report presenting composite financial ratios and performance data for over 300 manufacturing, wholesaling, retailing, service, and contractor SIC 4-digit industries, for fiscal years ending between June 30, 1983-Mar. 31, 1984, and trends from FY80.

Most data are based on financial statements of companies with assets less than $100 million, as reported by Robert Morris Associates member banks, and may not be representative of a given industry. Report is designed for commercial bankers and others who make lending and business decisions.

Contents:

Contents listing, introduction, definition of ratios, and descriptions of industries covered. (p. 3-40)

Part I. Manufacturing. Financial statements for individual industries, showing the following for each industry: number of statements received; distribution of itemized assets, liabilities, and income; 17 financial and operating ratios (upper and lower quartiles, and median); and value of net sales and total assets. Ratios include sales/receivables, cost of sales/inventory and payables, sales/working capital and total assets, debt/worth, and officer compensation/sales. Data are for 4 asset size categories, FY83 or FY84, and 4 categories combined, FY80-84. (p. 41-184)

Part II. Wholesaling industries. Presents data as described above for Part I. (p. 185-242)

Part III. Retailing, services, and industries not elsewhere classified. Presents data as described above for Part I. (p. 243-369)

Part IV. Contractor industries. Repeats data as described above for Part I, with the following variations: data are shown for 4 contract revenue size categories, with no upper limit, FY83 or FY84, and 4 categories combined, FY82-84; total contract revenues are shown in place of net sales; and statements present 14 financial and operating ratios. (p. 371-390)

Part V. Finance industry supplement. Consumer finance and diversified finance company composite lending and financial ratios, as of Dec. 31, 1981-83. Data were compiled by the First National Bank of Chicago. 2 tables. (p. 391-394)

Part VI. Sources of composite financial data: bibliography; indexes; and survey form facsimile. (p. 395-416)

This is the 62nd annual report.

Availability: Robert Morris Associates, Order Department, 1616 Philadelphia National Bank Bldg., Philadelphia PA 19107, members $10.00, nonmembers $29.50 (prepaid); SRI/MF/not filmed.

A6450
Mortgage Bankers Association of America

A6450-1   NATIONAL DELINQUENCY SURVEY
Quarterly.
Approx. 6 p. folder.
SRI/MF/complete

Quarterly report on 1- to 4-unit residential mortgage loans with overdue installments, by State, including conventional, VA, and FHA loans. Report is issued approximately 3 months after quarter of coverage. Data are based on a survey by the Mortgage Bankers Assn Economics Dept of approximately 500 financial institutions holding over 8 million mortgage loans.

Contains narrative summary; 1 summary trend chart; and 3 tables showing percent of all, conventional, VA, and FHA loans past due 30, 60, and 90 or more days, and percent in foreclosure, as follows:

a. Quarterly for year to date and 2 previous years; and by State (including Puerto Rico), and census division and region, for quarter of coverage (also shows total loans serviced).

b. Change from previous quarter and from same quarter of previous year, by census region.

Most tables include detail for FHA 235/237 and 245 loans.

Availability: Mortgage Bankers Association of America, Economics Department, 1125 15th St., NW, Washington DC 20005, members †, nonmembers $25.00 per yr.; SRI/MF/complete.

Issues reviewed during 1984: 3rd Qtr. 1983-2nd Qtr. 1984 (D).

A6450-2   MORTGAGE BANKING
Monthly. Approx. 100 p.
ISSN 0027-1241.
LC 49-30714.
SRI/MF/excerpts, shipped quarterly

Monthly journal (with additional buyer's guide issue) on mortgage market trends and developments, including real estate investment and management, institutional lending, community development, and profiles of prominent executives.

Issues generally contain:

a. Feature articles, occasionally with statistics; and news briefs, and other regular editorial depts.

b. "Mortgage Market Trends" monthly statistical feature, with narrative analysis, 2-4 summary charts, and 14 tables listed below.

Data in "Mortgage Market Trends" are from reports of Federal agencies, professional trade assns, and commercial real estate firms. Month of coverage is 3-5 months preceding publication date.

An Annual index to articles appears in the Jan. issue.

Most monthly "Mortgage Market Trends" tables appear in all issues. All additional features with substantial statistical content are described, as they appear, under "Statistical Features." Nonstatistical features are not covered.

Availability: Mortgage Banking, PO Box 37236, Washington DC 20013, $29.00 per yr., single copy $2.75; SRI/MF/excerpts for monthly tables and all portions described under "Statistical Features;" shipped quarterly.

Issues reviewed during 1984: Nov. 1983-Oct. 1984 (P) (Vol. 44, Nos. 2-13; Vol. 45, No. 1) [Vol. 44, No. 13 incorrectly reads No. 12].

MORTGAGE MARKET TRENDS:
[Data are shown monthly for 13 or more months ending with month of coverage. Data by unit type generally are shown for residential 1-4 units, 5 or more units, and nonresidential.]

HOUSING CONSTRUCTION AND SALES
[Tables on residential construction and house sales also include comparisons for year to date and previous 3-4 years.]

[1] Residential structures, by unit type [permits and housing starts, number and annual rate].

[2-3] Value of new construction put in place [rate by type of unit]; and house sales [existing homes; and new homes sold, available for sale, and months of supply at current rate].

[4-5] Residential structures, by region [permits and housing starts, number and annual rate]; and construction status [units under construction and completed, by type].

FINANCIAL ACTIVITY

[6] Interest rates [for new and existing 1-4 unit conventional mortgages, apartments, and construction loans] and yields [for FNMA, GNMA, Aaa utility, Federal Government, and prime commercial paper securities; and selected basis point spreads].

[7] Long-term mortgage loans closed [by type of lending institution and type of unit].

[8] Long-term commitment activity [amount outstanding and issued during month, by institution type].

[9] Mortgage insurance [applications received, and units and amounts insured, for FHA, VA, and private mortgages].

[10] Secondary market activity [FNMA, Federal Home Loan Mortgage Corp. (FHLMC), and GNMA].

[11] Mortgage bankers construction and land loan activity [disbursements during month and construction loans closed, including detail by type of unit].

MORTGAGE BANKING ACTIVITY

[Tables [12-14] generally show data by unit type. Tables [12-13] include selected detail for FHA, VA, and conventional mortgages.]

[12] Long-term mortgage loans closed [seasonally adjusted and unadjusted].

[13] Commitment activity: long-term mortgage loans [commitments made and outstanding to borrowers from investors; outstanding inventory; coverage; and servicing volume].

[14] Construction and land loan activity [disbursements, construction loans closed, inventory, commitments to borrowers, and notes payable].

STATISTICAL FEATURES:

A6450–2.501: Dec. 1983 (Vol. 44, No. 3)

INTEREST RATES: HIGHER BUT STABLE

(p. 17-22) By Daniel T. Van Dyke and Michael S. Salkin. Article, with 1 table showing mortgage rates and originations, housing starts, and existing home sales, 1975-84. Data sources include Bank of America.

MOVE TOWARD MORTGAGE SECURITIZATION

(p. 25-28) By Michael A. Smilow. Article on secondary mortgage market trends, with 1 table showing value of mortgages converted into securities by private organizations and Federal Government agencies, 1976-82 and first 8 months 1983. Data are from FNMA and Salomon Brothers, Inc.

MORTGAGE SECURITIES

(p. 47-54) By Scott M. Pinkus and Evan B. Firestone. Article discussing methods of estimating mortgage prepayment rates in determining the value of mortgage securities. Data are from Merrill Lynch Capital Markets, Debt Strategy Group, Mortgage-Backed Securities Research.

Includes 2 tables primarily showing prepayment rates for selected GNMA single-family mortgage security coupons, monthly Sept. 1982-Aug. 1983, with detail by year of issuance for 8% coupons.

A6450–2.502: Jan. 1984 (Vol. 44, No. 4)

MULTI-FAMILY MORTGAGES: ON THE BLOCK

(p. 29-34) By Audrey Hinton. Article on HUD multi-family mortgage sales. Includes 1 table showing number and value of mortgage offerings and sales, net proceeds, and average price as percent of unpaid principal; and number of sales to project owners, HUD-approved mortgagees, and with and without insurance; for 5 auctions held Mar. 1982-July 1983.

A6450–2.503: Feb. 1984 (Vol. 44, No. 5)

PROBING THE DEPTH OF MORTGAGE POOLS

(p. 11-23, 72-75) By Kenneth R. Scott and James E. Monsma. Article comparing 4 prepayment models for estimating yield and price of GNMA mortgage-backed securities pools comprised of mortgages other than typical FHA or VA 30-year loans.

Includes several charts and tables presenting methodological background; and 8 tables estimating security price under each model, at selected yield and net rate levels.

ENJOYING EQUITY WITH SECOND MORTGAGE LOANS

(p. 25-34) By David A. Olson. Article estimating size of the market for second mortgages (loans secured by junior liens on 1-4 family residential properties or condominiums). Data are from a variety of public and private sources.

Includes 4 tables showing alternate estimates of value of junior mortgages outstanding 1981, and second mortgage originations 1978-83, both by type of lender; and value of second mortgages outstanding at 5 large investment houses, 1983.

HEDGING GNMA PASS-THROUGHS

(p. 54-63) By Glenn Picou. Article examining futures trading in GNMA pass-through certificates, and the risk of using these securities as a hedging vehicle. Includes 3 tables showing issue date, and pool speed (unscheduled principal prepayments/scheduled repayments) as percent of FHA experience, for 8 GNMA pools, various periods 1983; and net gain/loss in 2 hypothetical hedging operations.

A6450–2.504: June 1984 (Vol. 44, No. 9; Special Issue)

CMOs AND HOW THEY GREW

(p. 9-15) By Richard M. Hamecs. Article on investment features of collateralized mortgage obligations (CMOs), bonds backed by mortgage loans or mortgage-backed pass-through securities. Data are from various financial publications and institutions.

Includes 6 tables showing number and value of CMOs sold, by issuer; distribution of CMO sales by type of purchasing institution and CMO maturity class; detailed price and yield data for selected CMO series; and yield spreads and comparisons for Treasury, GNMA, AAA-corporate, and AAA-utility bonds; various periods, primarily mid-1983 to Feb. 1984.

A6450–2.505: June 1984 (Vol. 44, No. 10)

CROWDING OUT?—AN ANALYSIS OF CREDIT SUPPLY AND DEMAND

(p. 35-46) By Bernard M. Markstein III. Article projecting credit supply-demand situation through 1986. Based on data from Chase Econometrics Associates, and Federal Reserve Bank of New York. Includes 6 tables showing the following:

a. GNP; domestic nonfinancial credit supply, and credit demand by sector; and private credit availability relative to Federal funding needs, under 3 alternative credit growth assumptions; quarterly 1984-86.

b. Credit market funds raised, by borrower sector (Federal and State/local government, household, corporate business, and noncorporate business), 1973-83; and personal and business savings as percents of GNP, with percent available for net new private investment, decennial periods 1961-80 and projected 1985.

MORTGAGE MARKETS AND MORTGAGE-RELATED SECURITIES: DEVELOPMENTS AND IMPLICATIONS

(p. 55-68) By Frederick E. Flick. Article, with 3 tables showing the following for 1- to 4-family nonfarm mortgage loans: value and market share of originations, by type of lender; and total sales on the secondary market; 1970-83. Data are from HUD.

A6450–3   FINANCIAL STATEMENTS AND OPERATING RATIOS for the Mortgage Banking Industry, 1982

Annual. Sept. 1983. 37 p.
Trends Rpt. No. 32.
ISSN 0095-9308.
LC 75-640703.
SRI/MF/complete

Annual report presenting mortgage banking industry aggregate financial and operating data, 1982. Covers income and expenses, assets and liabilities, and selected operating ratios and activity indicators, by volume and type of lending activity and type of ownership.

Data are based on responses of 160 mortgage banking firms to a Mortgage Bankers Assn survey. Report is intended to permit individual firms to compare their performance with industry averages.

Contains preface, contents and table listing, and narrative summary, with 1 trend table (p. 1-5); 25 tables, listed below (p. 8-36); and notes (p. 37).

This is the 19th annual report. (Previous abstract mistakenly identified the 1981 report as the 20th report.)

Availability: Mortgage Bankers Association of America, 1125 15th St., NW, Washington DC 20005, members $30.00, nonmembers $50.00; SRI/MF/complete.

TABLES:

[Each of the tables listed below is repeated for the following breakdowns:

.01-.02. By millions of dollars of mortgage loans closed and serviced.

.03-.04. By percent of income property loans closed and serviced to total loans closed and serviced.

.05. By type of ownership (bank holding company controlled, savings and loan/other controlled, and independent company).

Tables show data for 6 size groups, except those tables showing data by type of ownership. All data are for 1982.]

1.01-1.05. Comparative income statement [distribution]. (p. 8-12)

2.01-2.05. Income statement, average firm [amounts]. (p. 14-18)

3.01-3.05. Comparative balance sheet [distribution]. (p. 20-24)

4.01-4.05. Balance sheet, average firm [amounts]. (p. 26-30)

5.01-5.05. Selected ratios [12 profitability ratios, 5 leverage ratios, 12 banking activity and operating ratios, and 10 liquidity ratios]. (p. 32-36)

A6450–4   LOANS CLOSED AND SERVICING VOLUME for the Mortgage Banking Industry, 1982

Annual. Sept. 1983. 29 p.
Trends Rpt. No. 33.
ISSN 0363-1710.
LC 76-644814.
SRI/MF/complete

Annual report on loans closed and serviced in the mortgage banking industry, 1982, with trends from 1975. Includes data by type of loan and investor, and also by service and origination volume.

Data are from approximately 200 member firms, FHLBB, Federal Reserve Board, and HUD.

Contains preface, contents and table listing, and narrative summary with 1 trend table (p. 1-6); 4 sections with 7 illustrative charts, and 17 tables listed below (p. 7-28); and notes (p. 29).

Availability: Mortgage Bankers Association of America, 1125 15th St., NW, Washington DC 20005, members $20.00, nonmembers $35.00; SRI/MF/complete.

TABLES:

[Tables show data for 1982, unless otherwise noted. Most tables with data by property type are for 1-4 unit and multiunit residential, and nonresidential; and data by loan type generally include FHA, VA, and conventional. Tables 9-10, 13-14, and 17 also include data for construction, land development, 2nd mortgage, mobile home, and other non-1st mortgage loan types.

Data by investor or institution generally include life insurance companies, mutual savings banks, commercial banks, savings and loan assns, Federal and/or federally sponsored credit agencies, and State finance agencies.]

MORTGAGE BANKERS' SHARE OF THE MARKET

[Data by institution include mortgage bankers and omit State finance agencies.]

1. Total mortgage originations [value and distribution], by 6 institutions [and by type of property and loan]. (p. 8)

2. Originations by mortgage bankers as a percent of originations [aggregate for] 6 institutions [for residential property by loan type], 1975-82. (p. 9)

3. Servicing by mortgage bankers as a percent of mortgage debt outstanding [by type of property and loan], 1975-82. (p. 10)

MORTGAGE BANKING HISTORICAL TRENDS

[Tables 4-8 show total value and distribution of loans, 1975-82, and begin "Mortgage bankers'..."]

4. Originations by type of loan. (p. 12)

5. Loans originated, by purchasing investor. (p. 13)

6. Originations of non-1st mortgage loans [construction, land development, 2nd mortgage, and other nonmortgage loans]. (p. 14)

7-8. Servicing: by investor, and by property and loan type. (p. 15-16)

AVERAGE SIZE LOAN

9-10. Mortgage bankers' average size loan originated and serviced, by loan type and by origination or servicing volume [loan size group]. (p. 18-19)

11. Mortgage bankers' average size loan originated for investor [types], by origination volume. (p. 20)

LOANS CLOSED AND SERVICED

12. Mortgage loans originated by type of investor by size of origination volume for mortgage bankers [and type of property and loan]. (p. 22)

13-14. Loans originated and loans serviced by mortgage bankers [by size of origination volume and by size of servicing portfolio; both by type of loan and investor]. (p. 24-25)

15. Share of mortgage bankers' originations by type of loan, 1977-82, by size of servicing portfolio. (p. 26)

16. Percent of mortgage loans originated, 1978-82, by type of purchasing investor, by size of mortgage bankers' servicing portfolio. (p. 27)

17. Mortgage bankers' activity, average firm [by type of loan and investor], 1976-82. (p. 28)

A6475
Motor Vehicle Manufacturers Association of the U.S.

A6475–1   MVMA MOTOR VEHICLE FACTS AND FIGURES '84
Annual. 1984.
96 p.+addenda.
ISSN 0272-3395.
LC 76-649119.
SRI/MF/not filmed

Annual compilation of data on the motor vehicle manufacturing industry, 1983, with selected trends from 1900. Includes U.S. and world data on motor vehicle production, sales, registration, ownership and use, and industry economic impact.

Data are from Motor Vehicle Manufacturers Assn, R. L. Polk and Co., American Trucking Assns, FHA, and other Federal and commercial sources, identified for each table.

Contains contents listing (p. 1); narrative overview (p. 2-3); 56 charts, 5 maps, and 134 tables listed below (p. 4-93); and index (p. 94-96).

A 4-page supplement, with additional data on new car price trends, has also been received.

Availability: Motor Vehicle Manufacturers Association of the U.S., Communications Department, 300 New Center Bldg., Detroit MI 48202, $7.50; SRI/MF/not filmed.

TABLES:

[Tables show data for U.S., unless otherwise noted. Most tables show separate data for passenger cars and trucks/buses. Corresponding charts accompany many tables.]

A6475–1.1: Production, Sales, Registrations, and Foreign Trade

PRODUCTION AND SALES

[1-5] Highest annual production years and retail sales years; record production and retail sales by month; and production milestones; [various years from 1906]. (p. 4)

[6-7] Annual motor vehicle production, factory sales, and [total and domestic new car and truck] retail sales [various years 1900-83]. (p. 6-7)

[8] U.S. and Canada motor vehicle production [by manufacturer and make], 1981-83. (p. 8-9)

[9-10] Factory sales [total and domestic] of trucks/buses and diesel trucks by gross vehicle weight (GVW) [various years 1965-83]. (p. 10-11)

[11] Annual motor vehicle factory sales from U.S. and Canadian plants [selected years 1965-83]. (p. 11)

[12] Truck and bus factory sales by body type [1977-83]. (p. 12)

[13] Recreational vehicle shipments [travel trailer, truck camper, motor home, and camping trailer, 1964-83]. (p. 12)

[14] Motor vehicle assemblies by State [and specific plant location, 1983]. (p. 13)

RETAIL SALES

[15] Retail sales of passenger cars [domestic and imports, by domestic manufacturer], 1978-83. (p. 14-15)

[16] Retail passenger car sales [domestic; imports from Japan, Germany, and other countries; and U.S.-sponsored imports; 1971-83]. (p. 16)

[17] New car retail sales [distribution] by [size] class [1971-83]. (p. 16)

[18] Retail sales of new trucks by franchised dealers of U.S. manufacturers [by GVW and type 1978-83]. (p. 17)

[19] Total retail sales of new trucks [domestic, by GVW; and imports, total and from Japan; 1972-83]. (p. 17)

REGISTRATIONS

[Tables [20] and [22-25] show data by State.]

[20] New registrations [1982-83]. (p. 18)

[21] Historical total [privately and privately/publicly owned] motor vehicle registrations [selected years 1900-83]. (p. 19)

[22-23] Total motor vehicle registrations, 1982-83; and [privately and privately/publicly owned] truck registrations [1979-82]. (p. 20-21)

[24-25] Motor bus [including commercial, federally owned, and school buses], trailers, truck tractors, light truck registrations, 1982. (p. 22-23)

OPERATING AND RETIRED VEHICLES

[26-29] Average age of passenger cars and trucks in use [selected years 1941-83]; and passenger cars and trucks in use by age (as of July 1) [1970, 1975, 1980, and 1983]. (p. 24-25)

[30] Cars in operation, by model year (as of July of each year) [1971-83]. (p. 26)

[31] Motor vehicles retired from use [selected years 1955-83]. (p. 26)

[32] Trucks in operation, by model year (as of July of each year) [1971-83]. (p. 27)

[33] Passenger car and truck survival rates [by vehicle age], 1979-82 [period]. (p. 27)

WORLD PRODUCTION AND TRADE

[34] World vehicle production (in descending order of 1982 total vehicle output) [by manufacturer, with world region summary, 1981-82]. (p. 28)

[35-36] World motor vehicle production [for 25 countries], 1982-83; [and for U.S., Canada, Europe, Japan, and others, selected years 1950-83]. (p. 29)

[37] New passenger car exports by country of destination, 1983. (p. 30)

[38] Automotive exports by product, 1983. (p. 30)

[39] Automotive imports by country of origin, 1983. (p. 31)

[40] Imports of new assembled passenger cars [from 8 countries and all others, selected years 1965-83]. (p. 31)

[41] Automotive imports by product, 1983. (p. 31)

[42] Exports and imports of motor vehicles [and exports as percent of production; all for U.S. and 25] selected countries, 1982. (p. 32)

[23] Voluntary truck/bus fuel conservation program (millions of gallons) [for selected fuel efficiency options, 1974-82]. (p. 74)

[24] Gas guzzler tax, Energy Tax Act of 1978 [by MPG, 1980-86]. (p. 75)

[25] Federal and [8] State motor vehicle noise standards (required of manufacturers) [1982-86]. (p. 75)

TAXES AND HIGHWAY EXPENDITURES

[Tables [26-33] show data on taxes or fees, by type.]

[26-27] State and Federal motor vehicle taxes, and special State and Federal truck taxes [receipts for selected years 1930-83]. (p. 76)

[28] State highway user tax revenues, by States, 1983. (p. 77)

[29-30] Federal automotive excise taxes, and truck taxes, by States, 1982. (p. 78-79)

[31-32] State highway user taxes and Federal Highway Trust Fund receipts [from all motor vehicles and trucks], 1982. (p. 79)

[33] Motor use tax revenues by States, 1983. (p. 80)

[34] Receipts and disbursements for highways [1977-84]. (p. 81)

[35-36] Highway Trust Fund receipts and disbursements [FY60 and FY64-83]. (p. 82)

HIGHWAYS AND STREETS

[37-38] Interstate/defense highway system mileage by States, 1983; and national system [1970 and 1983; including mileage open, under construction, and planned]. (p. 83)

[39] 3.9 million miles of roads/streets [surfaced and nonsurfaced, by type of control], 1982. (p. 84)

[40] Rural and urban road mileage [by State], 1982. (p. 84)

AIR POLLUTANTS AND CONTROLS

[41] Sources of air pollutants, 1982. (p. 85)

[42-43] Cars in operation with emission controls [by type of control, and without emission controls, selected years 1967-83]. (p. 86)

[44-46] Automobile and light- and heavy-duty truck exhaust emissions reduction progress, Federal 49-State standards [by type of emission and model year]. (p. 87)

TRAFFIC ACCIDENTS AND SAFETY

[47] Federal motor vehicle safety standards. [tabular list] (p. 88)

[48] Traffic fatality rate [and deaths] by causes [5-year averages 1913-47 and annually 1949-83]. (p. 89)

[49] Traffic fatality rates [and deaths], by States [1981-82]. (p. 90)

[50] Motor vehicle fatalities and injuries, by highway systems [rural and urban], 1982. (p. 91)

[51-52] Traffic fatality rate and deaths in [U.S. and 13] selected countries [various years 1970-82]. (p. 92)

[53] Countries [and Canadian Provinces] with safety belt use laws [and effective date]. (p. 92)

MOTOR VEHICLE THEFT

[54-55] Motor vehicle registrations and thefts, 1969-82; and thefts by State, 1981-82. (p. 93)

A6475–2   WORLD MOTOR VEHICLE DATA, 1983 Edition
Annual. 1983. 346 p.
ISSN 0085-8307.
LC 73-640507.
SRI/MF/complete, delayed

Annual report on motor vehicle industry world production, trade, sales, and registrations, by country, mostly 1982, and trends. Data are compiled primarily from foreign government agencies, trade assns, private services, and the press.

Data are generally shown by type of vehicle, variously including passenger cars, trucks, tractors, buses, and commercial vehicles. Production, sales, and registrations are generally shown by manufacturer and occasionally by model. Some foreign trade data are shown by country of origin or destination.

Also includes some data on vehicles in use and scrappage.

Contents:

a. Contents listing. (p. 5)

b. World summary. 30 tables on total and diesel production, by country; 30 leading world manufacturers; and diesel sales and registrations, and total exports, imports, registrations, scrappage, and demand, all by country; various years 1900-90. (p. 7-52)

c. Country data. 1-28 tables showing production, assemblies, exports, imports, sales, and/or registrations, various years 1900-82, repeated as applicable for 47 countries and 4 country groups, arranged by continent, as indicated below. (p. 53-346)

Report has been published since 1964. This is the 20th edition.

Availability: Motor Vehicle Manufacturers Association of the U.S., Communications Department, 300 New Center Bldg., Detroit MI 48202, $35.00; SRI/MF/complete, delayed shipment in July 1984.

COUNTRY TABLES:

A6475–2.1: Country Data

a. Africa: total continent, Morocco, and South Africa. 6 tables. (p. 54-61)

b. Asia: India, Israel, Japan, South Korea, Kuwait, Malaysia, Philippines, Saudi Arabia, and Taiwan. 48 tables. (p. 64-110)

c. Europe: Austria, Belgium, Denmark, EC, Finland, France, West Germany, Greece, Ireland, Italy, Luxembourg, Netherlands, Nordic countries, Norway, Portugal, Spain, Sweden, Switzerland, Turkey, and UK. 140 tables. (p. 112-250)

d. Eastern Europe: Czechoslovakia, East Germany, Hungary, Poland, Soviet Union, Yugoslavia, and Eastern bloc countries (including Bulgaria, Romania, and China). 27 tables. (p. 252-268)

e. Oceania: Australia and New Zealand. 13 tables. (p. 270-282)

f. Western Hemisphere: Argentina, Brazil, Canada, Chile, Colombia, Latin American Free Trade Association countries (including Uruguay), Mexico, Peru, Puerto Rico, U.S., and Venezuela. 47 tables. (p. 284-346)

A6485
Motorcycle Industry Council

A6485–1   1984 MOTORCYCLE STATISTICAL ANNUAL
Annual. 1984. 46 p.
ISSN 0149-3027.
LC 77-643309.
SRI/MF/complete

Annual report on the composition, growth, and retail sales of the motorcycle market, and on motorcycle usage, cost of operation, accidents, and registrations, 1983 and trends from 1945. Also includes a socioeconomic profile of motorcycle owners.

Data are compiled by the Motorcycle Industry Council from member dealers and from public sources, identified in each table. Most data are shown by State.

Contains introduction and contents listing (p. 1-4); 43 charts and tables, listed below, each accompanied by a narrative summary with text statistics (p. 6-43); and listings of national and State motorcycle assns, and index (p. 44-46).

Availability: Motorcycle Industry Council, Research and Statistics Department, 3151 Airway Ave., Bldg. P-1, Costa Mesa CA 92626, members †, nonmembers $25.00, educational institutions, students and motorcycle dealers $10.00; SRI/MF/complete.

TABLES AND CHARTS:
[Data are for 1983, unless otherwise noted.]

A6485–1.1: Motorcycle Market and Marketing

MOTORCYCLE MARKET

[1-2] Estimated motorcycle population: model type, engine displacement, and year [sold new]; and model type by engine displacement; [1982-83]. (p. 6-7)

[3-4] Estimated motorcycle population and penetration, by region [chart], and by State. (p. 8)

[5-6] Total motorcycle registrations, [selected years] 1945-83; and by State, 1974-83. (p. 9-10)

[7] Estimated annual economic value of the motorcycle retail marketplace [and new motorcycle retail sales volume and value], by State. (p. 11)

[8] New motorcycle unit sales summary: imports, [U.S. production], wholesale and retail sales, and inventories, 1969-83. (p. 12)

[9-10] U.S. motorcycle imports [and value], by country [Japan, Europe, and all others], and by engine displacement, 1977-83. (p. 13)

[11-12] New motorcycle wholesale sales: [total volume and value; and volume by model, engine type, and engine displacement, and for] 10 leading States; 1979-83. (p. 14)

[13-14] New motorcycle registrations: by State, and 10 leading brands by market share, 1978-83. (p. 15-16)

MANUFACTURERS AND DISTRIBUTORS

[15] Profile of [5] major motorcycle manufacturers and distributors [brand name, address of manufacturer and distributor, year of incorporation, and other products sold]. (p. 18)

[16] Other 1984 motorcycle manufacturers/distributors [for 31 brands, primary U.S. manufacturer/distributor, and country of manufacture]. (p. 19-20)

RETAIL MARKETPLACE

[Data are shown for franchised and nonfranchised outlets.]

[17] Motorcycle retail outlets, employees, and payroll [by State, 1984]. (p. 22)

[18-19] Estimated retail sales by motorcycle outlets [new and used motorcycles, parts/accessories, service, and other], and distribution of motorcycle outlets by retail sales. (p. 23)

[20-21] Motorcycle retail outlet profile [employees, payroll, years at same location and under current ownership, advertising expenditures, new and used motorcycle sales, and number of new brands carried]; and distribution of motorcycle related sales [by type] per outlet [chart]. (p. 24)

A6485–1.2: Usage and Ownership

MOTORCYCLE USAGE

[1-2] Motorcycles used on- and off-highway [by model type and] by State. (p. 26)

[3] Public land and off-highway motorcycle statistics, by State [total acreage; Federal and State public land acreage; and off-highway motorcycle data, including sales, number in use, economic value of market, and market penetration]. (p. 27)

[4-6] 11.7 billion motorcycle miles traveled, on- and off-highway mileage, by model type. [charts] (p. 28-29)

[7-9] Average annual [motorcycle] mileage traveled [by model type; distribution of on- and off-highway mileage] by season and riding area and for weekends and daylight; and motorcycle commuting [number used, and average days per month and roundtrip mileage]. (p. 30)

[10-11] Motorcycles retired from use/scrapped; and operability rate [probability of operation 6 months to 11.5 years after sale, by model type; with accompanying chart]. (p. 31)

[12-13] Energy use per passenger mile [for selected transportation modes and uses, chart]; and 1984 motorcycle fuel economy figures [by model type and engine displacement]. (p. 32)

[14] Annual operating and ownership costs [by type], automobile vs. motorcycle. (p. 33)

[15-17] State motorcycle rider education programs [including number of rider education sites, graduates, and instructors, and State and Federal funding]; and 1984 State motorcycle operator licensing programs and procedures; [all by State]. (p. 35-37)

[18] Motorcycle accident statistics [including registrations, accidents reported, fatalities, and rates; all by State, 1983, with U.S. totals 1982-83]. (p. 38)

[19-20] State motorcycle equipment requirements, May 1984; and off-highway motorcycle requirements, June 1984; [both by State]. [charts] (p. 39-40)

MOTORCYCLE OWNERS

[21-22] Motorcycle owner profile: number of owners and riders, [1983; and distribution by] sex, marital status, age, education, occupation, income, and motorcycle ownership [years of regular riding, and total motorcycles ever owned, mostly for 1980]. (p. 42-43)

A6490
Motorcycle Safety Foundation

A6490–1   CYCLE SAFETY INFO: State Motorcycle Operator Licensing, 1984
Annual. [1984.]   4 p.
SRI/MF/complete

Annual report presenting motorcycle licensing requirements, and number of testing sites and examiners, as of Sept. 1983; and number of licensed drivers and motorcycle operators, as of Dec. 31, 1982; all by State.

Data were compiled by the Motorcycle Safety Foundation from a survey of State licensing authorities.

Contains narrative summary (1 p.); and 3 tabular lists (3 p.).

This is the 8th annual report.

Availability: Motorcycle Safety Foundation, National Headquarters, PO Box 5044, Costa Mesa CA 92628, †; SRI/MF/complete.

A6520
National Association for State Information Systems

A6520–1   1983-84 NASIS REPORT: Information Systems Technology in State Government
Annual. 1984.
421 p. var. paging.
SRI/MF/complete

Annual report on State government computer systems, including inventory, uses, personnel, funding, management, and intergovernmental relations, 1983, with trends for 1970s. Data are based on annual State surveys conducted by National Assn for State Information Systems (NASIS), and also encompass various Canadian Provinces and Pacific territories.

Report is intended primarily to assist States in management and development of information systems resources.

Contents:

Contents and table/chart listings, foreword, and NASIS description. (p. iii-vii)

Chapter 1-2. Introduction and observations. (p. 3-7)

Chapter 3. Responses of reporting States, with narrative, text tables on information processing salaries and funding sources, and 24 tables and 1 chart listed below. (p. 11-35)

App. A-D. Application inventory and description, computer installations, communications and data entry equipment, and off-line peripheral equipment; with extended tabular lists presenting detailed information on computer uses, equipment specifications, and monthly costs, all shown by government branch and agency (excluding higher education), arranged by State (variously also including Trust Territory of Pacific Islands, Guam, Ontario, Saskatchewan, and/or Quebec).

App. E. NASIS prime contact directory. (p. E3-E10)

This is the 14th annual report.

Availability: National Association for State Information Systems, Iron Works Pike, PO Box 11910, Lexington KY 40578, $50.00; SRI/MF/complete.

CHART AND TABLES:

[Unless otherwise noted, tables show 1983 survey results. Tables 2, 6, 15, and 21 include data for Northern Mariana Islands, Saskatchewan, and/or Quebec.]

A6520–1.1: State Responses

COORDINATION AND INVENTORY

1-2. State agencies control summary, 1981-83; and coordination and control [by State, 1983; both showing scope of centralized authority information system functions]. (p. 11-12)

3. Computers by size, 1975-83. (p. 14)

4-5. Method of procurement of computer systems [summary], 1972-83, and by size, 1980-83. (p. 14)

6. Trend of computer inventories [by State], 1972-83. (p. 15)

PERSONNEL AND TRAINING

7. State agency personnel summary, 1971-83. (p. 17)

8. Personnel distributions [by occupation]. (p. 17)

9. Consultant expenditures [and projects, by area of computer application], 1983-84. (p. 18)

10. Instructional methods and number of personnel attending [training programs]. (p. 20)

11. Percentage distribution of trainees, by type, 1973-83. (p. 20)

12. Cost of training, 1983-84. (p. 20)

MANAGEMENT AND INTERGOVERNMENTAL RELATIONS

13-14. External and internal problems related to information systems, 1979-83. (p. 22)

15. Formalized documentation: State plans and standards [by State]. (p. 24)

16. State responsibility for liaison with local governments on information systems/computerization. (p. 26)

17. State agency control over local government information systems [by local government function]. (p. 26)

18. Federal assistance in State information systems development [by area of computer application, as of July 1983]. (p. 26)

19. Use of software packages in information systems function (exclusive of utility programs) [number of States by type of package]. (p. 28)

20. Characteristics of management reporting systems internal to the information systems function. (p. 28)

FUNDING, SECURITY, AND TRANSFER PROJECTS

21. Financial structure [percent of information system funds from direct appropriations and from revolving/working capital funds or applied receipts, by State]. (p. 30)

22. Basis of billing for computer hardware costs, 1977-83. (p. 31)

23. State EDP (electronic data processing) spending [distribution by object]. [chart] (p. 31)

24. Security [number of States with physical and data security plans]. (p. 32)

25. Systems and programs transferred to or from other States [by State, including type of application and product, year transfer began, and status as of July 1981-83]. (p. 33-35)

A6600
National
Association of
Barber-Styling Schools

A6600-1   RESEARCH REPORTS
Series. For individual publication data, see below.
SRI/MF/complete

Continuing series of reports presenting data on barbers, barber shops, barber schools and students, licensing laws, and requirements, all by State and for Puerto Rico. Data are compiled by the National Assn of Barber-Styling Schools.

Report reviewed during 1984 is described below.

Issuing agency name has changed from National Assn of Barber Schools.

Availability: National Association of Barber-Styling Schools, 304 S. 11th St., Lincoln NE 68508, †; SRI/MF/complete.

A6600-1.1: State Barber Laws; and Barber School, Barber Students, and Barber Statistics
[Annual. Apr. 1, 1984. 2 p. Research Rpt. No. 3A/6A. SRI/MF/complete.]

Two annual tables showing the following by State and for Puerto Rico, as of Apr. 1, 1984:

a. Barber laws: summary of education, residence, apprenticeship, and other requirements for barber certification, and costs of barber and apprentice license and other fees.

b. Barber schools and barbers: number of barber schools (private, vocational, and penal), students enrolled and graduating, barber shops, registered and apprentice barbers, and barber/population ratio.

For description of tables for 1983, see SRI 1983 Annual under A6600-1.1 and A6600-1.2.

A6635
National
Association of Broadcasters

A6635-1   1983 RADIO FINANCIAL REPORT
Annual. 1983. 123 p.
SRI/MF/complete, delayed

Annual report presenting median financial and employment data for radio broadcasting stations, by type of station, market size, and revenue size, 1982 with summary trends from 1975. Data are from 1,238 responses to a survey of all 7,983 commercial stations operating for the full calendar year 1982.

Report is intended to enable radio broadcasters to compare their operations with industry medians.

Most data are shown for all stations and by the following station categories: full-time AM, AM/FM, daytime, FM, and class 1A 50 kw.

Contents:

Contents and table listing, and introduction. (p. 1-3)

Part I. Nationwide summary. Median station revenues by source, expenses by object, profit margin, and full- and part-time employment, 1982 and summary trends 1975-83. 6 charts and tables 1-2. (p. 4-9)

Part II. Selected financial and employment data. Operating and productivity ratios, median and middle range of employment, advertising agency/representative commissions as percent of advertising revenue, and percent of revenue from national vs. regional advertising, with detail by revenue and/or market size. Tables 3-6. (p. 10-14)

Part III-IV. Financial yardsticks. Data in Part I are repeated with detail for profit-only stations, and additional detail by market and revenue size, and station format type. Tables 7-112. (p. 15-122)

Definitions. (p. 123)

Availability: National Association of Broadcasters, Publications, 1771 N St., NW, Washington DC 20036, members $20.00, nonmembers $60.00; SRI/MF/complete, delayed shipment in Dec. 1984.

A6635-2   1983 TELEVISION FINANCIAL REPORT
Annual. 1983. 116 p.
SRI/MF/complete, delayed

Annual report presenting median financial and employment data for TV broadcasting stations, by type of station, market size, and revenue size, 1982 with summary trends from 1975. Data are from 440 responses to a survey of all 774 commercial stations operating for the full calendar year 1982.

Report is intended to enable TV broadcasters to compare their operations with industry medians.

Most data are shown by census division, and for all stations and the following station categories: affiliate, independent, UHF, UHF and VHF independent, UHF affiliate, satellite, primary and secondary market, and 1 and 2 station market.

Contents:

Contents and table listing, and introduction. (p. 1-3)

Part I. Nationwide summary. Median station revenues by source, expenses by object, profit margin, and full- and part-time employment, 1982 and summary trends 1975-83. 6 charts and tables 1-2. (p. 4-9)

Part II. Selected financial and employment data. Median, and middle range of employment, productivity and operating ratios, advertising agency/representative commissions as percent of advertising revenue, and percent of revenue from national vs. regional advertising, with selected detail by market and revenue size. Tables 3-6. (p. 10-17)

Part III. Financial yardsticks. Data in Part I are repeated with detail for profit-only stations, and additional detail by market and revenue size. Tables 7-102. (p. 18-114)

Listing of areas of dominant influence grouped by market size, and definitions. (p. 115-116)

Availability: National Association of Broadcasters, Publications, 1771 N St., NW, Washington DC 20036, members $20.00, nonmembers $60.00; SRI/MF/complete, delayed shipment in Dec. 1984.

A6635-5   IMPACT OF CABLE AND PAY CABLE TELEVISION ON LOCAL STATION AUDIENCES
Monograph. Oct. 1982.
108 p.
SRI/MF/complete

By James G. Webster. Report comparing TV viewing habits in households with broadcast-only, basic cable, and pay cable TV reception, based on viewing diaries compiled in 24 Arbitron areas of dominant influence (ADIs) during Feb. 1982. The purpose of the comparison is to assess the impact of cable TV on broadcast audiences.

Includes the following data for each TV reception category:

a. Number of households and individual viewers; average age of household head, by sex; age distribution of viewers; average weekly viewing hours; and average weekly channels viewed; shown for each ADI.

b. Market shares by program source, aggregated by ADI market type and by ADI market size group.

Program sources include VHF and UHF local affiliate and independent stations, local educational stations, distant stations (not licensed within the ADI), pay cable channels, and other cable-only channels. Market types are 8 classifications based on the number and mix of VHF and UHF stations in the ADI.

Market share data include detail for selected viewing times (prime time, early and late evening news, and prime time access) and demographic groups (men and women age 18-49, and all adults age 50/over). Prime time access market shares also are shown by program type (off network, 1st run syndication, and locally produced), within each demographic group.

The report was prepared by the Broadcast Research Center, Ohio University, for the National Assn of Broadcasters.

Contains contents and table listings (3 p.); summary, methodology, and definitions, with 2 tables (p. 1-20); and narrative analysis, with 69 tables (p. 21-108).

Availability: National Association of Broadcasters, Publications, 1771 N St., NW, Washington DC 20036-2898, members $15.00, nonmembers $30.00; SRI/MF/complete.

A6635-6 RADIO TODAY AND TOMORROW
Monograph.   Oct. 1982.
viii+75 p.
SRI/MF/complete

By Paul I. Bortz and Harold Mendelsohn. Survey report on radio listening patterns, 1982. Covers listening habits, including frequency, reasons, time of day, location, favorite program format, use of public radio, random vs. specific program choice, and radio as focus of attention vs. background, with selected cross-tabulations.

Also covers the following characteristics, most cross-tabulated with selected listening habits: interests, activities, and entertainment tastes; use of other media, including frequency and reasons; cable TV subscription, costs, and satisfaction; radio ownership; current and planned ownership of selected home electronic products; self-perceptions, including modern vs. traditional; and demographic characteristics, including age, education, and marital status.

Includes a detailed comparison of listening habits, interests, and activities, for housewives vs. single female heads of household.

Data are based on 1,433 responses to a telephone survey of a national sample of 1,506 persons, conducted during June/July 1982 under the direction of Browne, Bortz, and Coddington, Inc.

Contains contents and table listings, introduction, and summary (p. ii-viii); narrative report in 2 sections, interspersed with 10 tables (p. 1-26); and appendices, with methodology, sample questionnaire, tabulated responses to questions, and 23 tables showing selected cross-tabulations (p. 38-75).

Availability: National Association of Broadcasters, Publications, 1771 N St., NW, Washington DC 20036-2898, members $20.00, nonmembers $60.00; SRI/MF/complete.

A6635-7 RADIO IS . . .
Monograph.   [1983.]   48 p.
SRI/MF/complete

Compilation of summary data on radio industry and audiences, various periods 1950-82. Includes radio station employment, sets in use and unit sales, audience size and listening habits, and advertising revenue and cost-per-thousand, with varying detail by audience socioeconomic characteristics and selected comparisons to other media.

Most data are from NAB and other industry sources.

Contains contents listing (p. 3), chronology of major radio events, glossary, and acronym list (p. 5-13); 43 charts and 22 tables interspersed with brief narratives (p. 13-46); and references (p. 47-48).

Availability: National Association of Broadcasters, Publications, 1771 N St., NW, Washington DC 20036-2898, members $1.00, nonmembers $3.00; SRI/MF/complete.

A6635-8 1983 RADIO EMPLOYEE COMPENSATION AND FRINGE BENEFITS REPORT
Biennial.   1984.   48 p.
SRI/MF/complete, delayed

Biennial report on radio station personnel compensation, employment, and benefits, 1983. Includes annual compensation, full- and part-time employment, turnover rate, and compensation methods for sales personnel, by position or function, by station type, market size, and revenue size.

Also includes data on fringe benefit plans by whether company or employee paid, types of bonuses, paid sick and vacation leave, and number of paid holidays, by station employment size.

Data are based on 854 responses to a Sept.-Oct. 1983 NAB survey of AM and FM commercial radio stations. Data are shown as medians and/or averages with detail for lowest and highest responses, or as response distributions.

Contains contents listing (p. 2); introduction and methodology (p. 3-4); 31 tables on employment and compensation (p. 5-35); detailed listing of compensation methods for sales personnel (p. 36-42); and 6 tables on employee benefits (p. 43-48).

This is the 3rd edition of the biennial report. SRI coverage begins with this edition.

Availability: National Association of Broadcasters, Publications, 1771 N. St., NW, Washington DC 20036, members $20.00, nonmembers $60.00; SRI/MF/complete, delayed shipment in Aug. 1985.

A6635-9 1983 TELEVISION EMPLOYEE COMPENSATION AND FRINGE BENEFITS REPORT
Biennial.   1984.   32 p.
SRI/MF/complete, delayed

Biennial report on TV station personnel compensation, employment, and benefits, 1983. Includes annual compensation, full- and part-time employment, turnover rate, and compensation methods for sales personnel, by position or function, for affiliate and independent stations by market size.

Also includes data on fringe benefit plans by whether company or employee paid, types of bonuses, paid sick and vacation leave, and number of paid holidays, by station employment size.

Data are based on 288 responses to a Sept.-Oct. 1983 NAB survey of commercial TV stations. Data are shown as medians and/or averages with detail for lowest and highest responses, or as response distributions.

Contains contents listing (p. 2); introduction and methodology (p. 3-4); 15 tables on employment and compensation (p. 5-19); detailed listing of compensation methods for sales personnel (p. 20-26); and 6 tables on employee benefits (p. 27-32).

This is the 3rd edition of the biennial report. SRI coverage begins with this edition.

Availability: National Association of Broadcasters, Publications Manager, 1771 N St., NW, Washington DC 20036, members $20.00, nonmembers $60.00; SRI/MF/complete, delayed shipment in Aug. 1985.

A6650
National Association of Business Economists

A6650-2 NABE NEWS: National Association of Business Economists 1983 Annual Meeting Membership Survey
Bimonthly (selected issue).
Nov. 1983.   (p. 1-8).   No. 42.
SRI/MF/excerpts

Annual *NABE News* feature, by A. Nicholas Filippello, presenting economic forecasts and policy views of business economists, based on a 1983 sample survey of 407 NABE members. Includes narrative analysis and 5 tables showing the following:

a. Economic outlook: forecast and recent performance of GNP, GNP components, and selected economic and financial indicators, various periods 1982-85.

b. Long-term outlook: year of next recession; GNP, inflation, productivity change rate, and Federal budget deficit, through 1987, with comparisons to previous forecasts and actual rates; and change in current business conditions.

c. Policy: views on selected economic measures, adequacy of current monetary and fiscal policy, and likely impact of a balanced budget amendment to the Constitution.

The survey feature appears annually in the Nov. issue of *NABE News* and is the only feature of this publication covered in SRI.

Availability: National Association of Business Economists, 28349 Chagrin Blvd., Suite 201, Cleveland OH 44122, members †, nonmembers $7.50 per issue; SRI/MF/excerpts, for annual NABE survey.

A6705
National Association of College and University Business Officers

A6705-1 COMPARATIVE FINANCIAL STATISTICS for Public Community and Junior Colleges, 1982/83
Annual.   Feb. 1984.
ix+90 p.
SRI/MF/complete

Annual report, by Nathan Dickmeyer and Anna Marie Cirino, on finances and other characteristics of 2-year public community/junior colleges, FY83, with trends from FY79. Covers revenues by source, expenditures by function, and staff by function, all shown as percent distribution and as amount per student.

Also includes course distribution by class size; building replacement value, scholarships/Pell grants, and service area population, all shown as ratios to enrollment; and computer service sources, and types of computer systems used.

Data are shown for 4 enrollment size groups and for primarily vocational/technical schools. Most data are shown as median and 1st and 3rd quartile.

Data are from a sample survey of 520 colleges, conducted by NACUBO in cooperation with Assn of Community College Trustees, American Assn of Community and Junior Colleges, and NCES. Report is intended primarily to enable individual colleges to compare their financial performance with national norms for similar institutions.

Contains contents and table listings and preface (p. iii-ix); report, in 4 chapters, with 37 tables (p. 1-67); and 4 appendices, including methodology, facsimile questionnaire, definitions and listing of participating colleges (p. 69-90).

This is the 6th annual report.

Availability: National Association of College and University Business Officers, One Dupont Circle, Suite 500, Washington DC 20036-1178, members $25.00, nonmembers $30.00; SRI/MF/complete.

A6705–2 RESULTS OF THE 1983 NACUBO COMPARATIVE PERFORMANCE STUDY and Investment Questionnaire

Annual. 1984. vi+157 p.
SRI/MF/complete

Annual survey report, by Bruce M. Dresner, analyzing college/university investment pool performance and endowment fund characteristics, FY83, with selected trends from FY71. Report is intended to aid administrators in evaluating their investment pools.

Presents data on investment pool rates of return and asset composition, including aggregates by pool asset size and investment objective; comparisons to Higher Education Price Index and other indexes; and detail for individual institutions, nontraditional investments (foreign securities and venture capital), and stock and bond turnover.

Also includes data on endowment fund size (total, per student, and per faculty), life income fund size, and funds held in trust, all for individual institutions; and selected aspects of investment pool and endowment fund management.

Individual institutions are identified by name for fund size data, but only by code for investment pool data.

Data are based on a survey of 195 institutions representing over 200 endowment/life income funds with a market value of approximately $25.2 billion.

Contains preface and contents listing (p. iii-vi); 2 report sections, with narrative analysis, 6 charts, and 67 tables (p. 1-76); 6 supplemental exhibits, including indexes of investment managers and endowment custodians (p. 77-147); and 3 appendices, with methodology and definitions (p. 148-157).

Report has been published annually since 1971.

Availability: National Association of College and University Business Officers, One Dupont Circle, Suite 500, Washington DC 20036-1178, members $30.00, nonmembers $50.00 (prepaid); SRI/MF/complete.

A6752 National Association of Employers on Health Care Alternatives

A6752–1 1982 SURVEY OF NATIONAL CORPORATIONS ON HEALTH CARE COST CONTAINMENT

Biennial. 1983.
67 p. var paging.
SRI/MF/not filmed

Biennial report, for 1982, on employer strategies for controlling health care costs. Includes data on health plan costs 1979-81, hospital utilization, participation in health care coalitions, arrangements with HMOs, and cost containment and health promotion/wellness programs.

Data are based on a survey of 308 major employers (53.9% response rate), and generally are shown separately for NAEHCA members and nonmembers.

Also includes reprint of a report presenting results of a similar 1979 survey.

Contains contents listing (1 p.); table listing (p. i-ii); introduction and summary of findings (p. 1-5); survey report in 9 sections, with 20 tables (p. 6-34); and appendices, including reprint of 1979 report with 14 tables, and questionnaire facsimile (23 p. var. paging).

This is the 3rd biennial report. Previous reports were published by NAEHCA's predecessor, the National Association of Employers on Health Maintenance Organizations. SRI coverage begins with the 3rd report.

Availability: National Association of Employers on Health Care Alternatives, 1134 Chamber of Commerce Bldg., 15 S. Fifth St., Minneapolis MN 55402, $25.00; SRI/MF/not filmed.

A6755 National Association of Fleet Administrators

A6755–1 NAFA BULLETIN: The Magazine for Fleet Administrators

Monthly. Approx. 40 p.
SRI/MF/excerpts, shipped quarterly

Monthly periodical reporting on topics of concern to automobile fleet administrators, including fleet management, energy trends and developments, and automobile efficiency, maintenance, and safety. Data are based on National Assn of Fleet Administrators (NAFA) surveys and other sources.

Issues contain editorial depts and feature articles. Features include annual surveys of fleet administrators regarding operating expenses; new car acquisition costs and plans; and personal use of fleet cars, and reimbursement for company use of personally owned cars.

Features with substantial statistical content are described, as they appear, under "Statistical Features." Each issue of the journal is reviewed, but an abstract is published in SRI monthly issues only when statistical features appear.

Availability: National Association of Fleet Administrators, 295 Madison Ave., New York NY 10017, members †, nonmembers $24.00 per yr.; SRI/MF/excerpts for all portions described under "Statistical Features;" shipped quarterly.

Issues reviewed during 1984: Nov. 1983-Sept. 1984 (P).

STATISTICAL FEATURES:

A6755–1.501: Nov. 1983

ILLINOIS STUDY INDICATES ROOF LIGHTS DON'T HELP POLICE

(p. 22-26) Article reporting police officers' opinions on the use and effectiveness of roof-mounted emergency lights on patrol cars. Data are from a 1983 Illinois State Police study. Includes text statistics.

A6755–1.502: Dec. 1983

RUNZHEIMER'S "PROFILE" OF TODAY'S FLEET CAR

(p. 17, 22) Article, with 5 tables on fleet composition and operations, including auto and engine sizes, auto accessories and body styles, and anticipated operational problems. Data are shown for U.S. and Canadian business and U.S. Government fleets, and are derived from a 1983 Runzheimer and Co. survey of 775 fleets.

Also includes 1 table showing current and 1984 expected auto production distribution by type (large, small, sporty, specialty), based on Chase Econometrics data.

A6755–1.503: Jan. 1984

FLEET MANAGEMENT IS COMPLEX BUT 'UNAPPRECIATED' JOB

(p. 21-29, 42) Article on job responsibilities of fleet managers as perceived by 200 managers responding to a survey of NAFA members. Includes text statistics showing degree of managers' control over various fleet operations, and number of respondents by educational level.

A6755–1.504: Feb. 1984

NAFA PERSONAL USE SURVEY, ANNUAL FEATURE

(p. 6-22) Annual survey on personal use of company fleet cars and business use of personally owned cars. Data are based on responses of 401 U.S. and Canadian fleets to a 1983 NAFA survey.

Includes 5 tables showing distribution of responses as follows:

a. Reimbursement rate for business use of personal car, and chargeback rate for personal use of fleet cars, 1980-83, for U.S. commercial fleet cars.

b. Number of fleets, total cars, company-owned cars, and leased cars; and policies and limitations governing personal use of fleet cars; shown for 8 industry groups, public utilities, and government (all U.S. only), and for Canada, 1983.

A6755–1.505: Mar. 1984

AVERAGE SERVICE LIFE 29 MONTHS/56,000 MILES; FEW FLEETS PLANNING TO CHANGE CYCLE FOR 1984, ANNUAL FEATURE

(p. 6-19) Annual article on marketing of used fleet autos. Data are from responses of 257 fleet managers to the 1983 NAFA Used-Car Marketing Survey. Respondents represent 166,409 autos.

Includes 3 tables showing changes in auto replacement criteria (months and miles of service) for 1984; and number of owned and leased autos in fleet, used autos sold in 1983 by model year and marketing method, and average miles and months of service at time of sale, for 9 industry sectors, utilities and government, and Canadian fleets.

A6755–1.506: Apr. 1984

FLEET OPERATING COSTS FALL BELOW 8 CENTS A MILE, ANNUAL FEATURE

(p. 8-14) Annual article on fleet operating expenses in U.S. and Canada. Data are from a NAFA survey of 85 fleets operating over 75,-000 passenger autos.

Includes 1 chart and 3 tables showing U.S. composite fleet operating, incidental, and standing expenses, by item, and personal use credits; and operating expenses by item, and average miles per month and per gallon, by auto size class for U.S., and total for Canada; mostly 1981-83.

1983 DOMESTIC 4-DOOR MODELS HAD LOWEST COLLISION LOSS EXPERIENCE

(p. 20-24) Article, with 1 table showing index of collision coverage loss per insured vehicle year, for selected 1983 model year autos with best and worst coverage loss. Data are from Highway Loss Data Institute.

LEASING HELPS CREATE NEW JOBS; STIMULATES BUSINESS INVESTMENT

(p. 32-36) Article, with 2 tables showing business fixed investments for structures and durable equipment, and investment funds by source, 1980-83; and total capital expenditures, and expenditures for leased equipment, for 6 industries, 1982. Data are from Brimmer and Co.

A6755–1.507: May 1984

ELIMINATION OF INCENTIVE PROGRAMS POSES SERIOUS THREATS TO ECONOMY

(p. 26-29) Article reporting auto fleet managers' opinions on proposed Federal legislation that would limit direct sales incentives offered by auto manufacturers. Data are from responses of 332 fleets representing 287,714 autos to a Jan. 1984 NAFA survey.

Includes 1 table showing managers' position on legislation; respondent fleet composition by owned or leased status; new auto acquisitions planned for 1984; respondent participation in incentive programs, including average per auto cost and value of benefits realized from incentives, 1983; and probable response to elimination of incentives.

A6755–1.508: June 1984

MAINTENANCE IS AN IMPORTANT ASPECT OF YOUR DAILY OPERATION

(p. 20-21) Article, with 2 charts showing motor vehicle service establishments by type (dealers, service stations, fleet service, independent shops), 1981; and cost per mile of operating a new car, with distribution by item (no date). Data are from *Motor Service*.

A6755–1.509: July 1984

'THIRD EYE' AUTO TAILLIGHT ON REAR DECK REDUCES REAR-END COLLISIONS BY 50 PERCENT

(p. 18-23) Article comparing the effectiveness of 4 taillight designs in reducing passenger car rear-end collisions. Data are from an Essex Corp. study covering 2,100 taxicabs in Washington, D.C., during an unspecified 12-month period. Includes 1 chart showing number of rear-end collisions involving study vehicles equipped with each of the 4 taillight designs.

A6755–1.510: Aug. 1984

HERE'S WHAT LEASING COMPANIES RECOMMEND FOR 1985 MODEL YEAR

(p. 10-21) Article, with 1 undated table showing new car acquisition cost, operating cost per mile, and resale value, for selected 1985 model year passenger cars, by model arranged by size class. Data are from Gelco Corp.

Also includes lists of vehicle specifications, and model recommendations of selected leasing companies.

A6755–1.511: Sept. 1984

FOR 1985, SHIFT TO MID-SIZE UNITS CONTINUING, ANNUAL FEATURE

(p. 6-20, 62-63) Annual survey on new auto acquisition plans of commercial fleets. Data are based on responses of 197 fleets operating 149,365 vehicles to a 1984 NAFA survey.

Includes 5 tables showing the following:

a. Composite fleet summary, by auto size class, 1980-84; and distribution of new auto orders, by body style.

b. Fleet size, composition by owned or leased status and auto size class, and new auto acquisitions, 1984; planned new auto acquisitions by size class, 1985; and number of fleets ordering 12 items of optional equipment, by auto size class; all for 7 industry sectors, with optional equipment data also shown for government and utility fleets.

COMPACTS COST 3 CENTS LESS PER MILE TO OPERATE THAN LARGE CARS

(p. 44-50) Article, with 5 tables showing the following for 1984 model year autos by size class: total and per mile operating costs by item, and total ownership cost, for 1st, 2nd, and 3rd year of operation, based on specified annual mileage for each year. Data are from Federal Highway Administration.

A6755–2   NAFA's ANNUAL REFERENCE BOOK, 1984
Annual. 1983. 116 p.
SRI/MF/excerpts

Annual automobile fleet administrator's reference book, for 1983, presenting manufacturer sales and service representative directory, service recommendations for 1981-84 automobile makes, and features on topics of interest to fleet administrators, including vehicle fuel efficiency and specifications, emission controls, safety, operating expenses, State and Canadian Province regulations and taxes, and tire quality.

Data sources include National Assn of Fleet Administrators surveys, and Government reports.

Features with substantial statistical content are described below.

NAFA's Annual Reference Book is included in monthly *NAFA Bulletin* subscription price. *NAFA Bulletin* is covered in SRI under A6755-1.

Availability: National Association of Fleet Administrators, 295 Madison Ave., New York NY 10017, members †, nonmembers $15.00; SRI/MF/excerpts for portions described under "Statistical Features."

STATISTICAL FEATURES:

A6755–2.1: Vehicle Information, Safety Survey, and Fleet Finances

a. Fuel efficiency: EPA estimated miles per gallon (MPG) for 1984 automobile models grouped by size class, with selected specifications. 1 table. (p. 6-12, 77)

b. "Fog, Spit and Spray." Article on emission control technology. Includes 1 table showing U.S. and California emission control standards for passenger cars, model years 1960 and 1978-83. (p. 24-28)

c. Canada: average fleet operating costs per mile, including running, standing, and incidental expenses, and gas prices, 1979-82 and 1st half 1983. 1 table. (p. 32)

d. Finances and safety: composite fleet per car operating, incidental, and standing expenses by item, credits, and average miles per month, 1980-82, with operating expense trends from 1963; and highway accident summary aggregated for 377 fleets, including miles driven, preventable and nonpreventable accidents, injuries, and value of vehicle damage, 1983. Text data and 2 tables. (p. 68-70)

A6835
National Association of Independent Schools

A6835–1   NAIS MEMBER SCHOOL TUITION FEES, TEACHERS' SALARIES, ADMINISTRATIVE SALARIES, 1983/84
Annual. 1983. 20 p.
ISSN 0161-1097.
LC 77-646697.
SRI/MF/not filmed

Annual report on private elementary and secondary school average tuition fees, and teacher and administration salaries, 1983/84. Presents data by type of school and by grade and U.S. region, with selected data for Canada and Virgin Islands/Puerto Rico/Guam.

Data are based on responses from 780 NAIS member schools.

Contains 9 tables, listed below, with brief accompanying analysis.

A companion annual report on school operations and enrollment is also published by the issuing agency; for description, see A6835-2.

Availability: National Association of Independent Schools, 18 Tremont St., Boston MA 02108, members $5.00, nonmembers $50.00; SRI/MF/not filmed.

TABLES:

[Data generally are shown for girls', boys', and coeducational day and boarding schools, 1983/84. Most tables include median and range. Several include data for Canada and Guam/Puerto Rico/Virgin Islands.]

TUITION FEES

1-3. Tuition fees [by region and grade, with percent change from 1982/83]. (p. 3-7)

FACULTY SALARIES

1. Cash salaries for beginning teachers with no teaching experience. (p. 8)

2. Teachers' salaries by area [with detail for experienced and new teachers]. (p. 8-10)

3. Teachers' salaries [including percent increase since 1978/79]. (p. 11)

ADMINISTRATIVE SALARIES

1-3. Salary ranges for administrative officers [by position, by enrollment size of school]. (p. 12-20)

A6835–2   NAIS MEMBER SCHOOL OPERATIONS, 1982/83; NAIS Membership, 1983/84
Annual. 1984.
14 p.+errata sheet.
ISSN 0160-8282.
LC 77-641437.
SRI/MF/not filmed

Annual report on private elementary and secondary school finances, and minority enrollment and faculty, by type of school, various years 1979/80-1983/84. Also includes data on NAIS membership.

Data are based on responses to an Sept. 1983 survey from approximately 600 schools belonging to NAIS.

Contains introduction, contents listing, glossary, and 1 summary table (p. 1-2); and 5 sections, with narrative summaries, and 18 tables, described below (p. 3-14).

Availability: National Association of Independent Schools, 18 Tremont St., Boston MA 02108, members $5.00, nonmembers $50.00; SRI/MF/not filmed.

TABLES:

[Most data are shown for girls', boys', and coeducational day and/or boarding schools, frequently with further detail for elementary and secondary levels. Data are for 1982/83, unless otherwise noted.]

a. Financial aid: distribution of income by source, including tuition, endowments, and gifts; schools reporting total financial aid income from single source; and students aided, amounts granted, and financial aid share of total enrollment and operating budget. Tables 1-2. (p. 3)

b. Racial data: minority student enrollment by region and for Puerto Rico/Virgin Islands and Hawaii/Guam, and teachers, all by race-ethnicity (including Hispanic, Asian, and Native American, and occasionally Pacific Islander), 1983/84, with selected trends from 1979/80. Tables 3-8. (p. 4-5)

c. Operations: number of schools where income exceeded and equaled expense, and expense exceeded income; student/teacher and teacher/other personnel ratios; and expense and income per student, by detailed item. Tables 9 and 10A-C. (p. 6-11)

d. NAIS membership analysis: number of member schools and enrollments, with summary data by membership status (active, affiliate, and new school services), and detail for active members/new school services, as of Sept. 1983; and schools and enrollment, 1979/80-1983/84. 5 tables. (p. 12-13)

A6840
National Association
of Insurance Commissioners

A6840–1   NAIC REPORT ON PROFITABILITY by Line and by State for the Year 1982
Annual. Apr. 27, 1984.
99 p.
SRI/MF/complete, current & previous year reports

Annual report presenting property and liability insurance industry premiums and underwriting ratios, by line of coverage, State, and territory, 1982. Data are from annual exhibits filed by individual insurers.

Contents:

a. Contents listing. (1 p.)

b. Transmittal letter, with methodology. (p. 1-5)

c. NAIC position statement on financial data, and detailed table, described below, repeated for U.S., each State, and American Samoa, Guam, Puerto Rico, and Virgin Islands. (p. 6-64)

d. Premium tax rates by line of coverage and State, 1983; and guaranty fund assessment or return rates for individual insolvent companies, 4th quarter 1982-83. 2 tables. (p. 65-77)

e. Supplemental information: data specifications, and list of companies not included in report. (p. 78-99)

This is the 10th annual edition. Previous edition, for 1981, was also reviewed by SRI during 1984, and is also available on SRI microfiche under this number [Annual. May 1983. 9+85 p. $100.00]. Previous report was substantially similar in format and content, but omitted data on American Samoa and guaranty fund rates by company, and included aggregate comparative data for 4 other industries.

Report for 1980 is described in SRI 1982 Annual, under this number.

NAIC data also are available on computer tape.

Availability: National Association of Insurance Commissioners, 1125 Grand Ave., Kansas City MO 64106, $100.00; SRI/MF/complete.

DETAILED TABLE:

Table shows premiums earned; and losses incurred, loss adjustment expense, general and sales expenses, taxes/licenses/fees, policyholder dividends, investment gain, Federal income taxes, and underwriting and operating profits, all as percent of premiums earned; by line of coverage, 1982.

Lines of coverage include private and commercial automobile physical damage and liability, homeowners, farmowners, commercial multiple peril, ocean/aircraft, fire/allied lines, medical malpractice, other liability, workers compensation, accident/health (group, credit, and other), fidelity/surety, and credit.

A7000
National
Association of Realtors

A7000–1   OUTLOOK FOR THE ECONOMY AND REAL ESTATE
Monthly. Approx. 7 p.
SRI/MF/complete, shipped quarterly

Monthly report, by Jack Carlson, on current and projected economic conditions and trends affecting the residential, commercial, and industrial real estate markets, with detailed forecasts of housing sales and prices. Data are derived from a model developed by the National Assn of Realtors (NAR), and Data Resources, Inc.

Each issue contains narrative analysis, occasionally including statistics; and 2 tables showing the following data for quarter 1-3 quarters prior to cover date, 7 subsequent quarters, current year, and 2-3 previous and 1-2 coming years:

a. Aggregate economy, including GNP and percent change in selected components; manufacturing capacity utilization rate; auto sales; percent change in industrial production in Japan and European Common Market; employment and unemployment rate; household income, taxes, and net worth; percent change in CPI, PPI, hourly compensation, productivity, and labor and capital costs; corporate profits; and Federal tax receipts and expenditures.

b. Real estate markets and prices, including new and existing single-family home sales and median prices; mortgage new commitments and debt outstanding; homeowners' equity; housing inventory; private single- and multi-family housing starts; mobile home shipments; rental, office, and industrial vacancy rates; and percent change in new commercial and industrial building construction.

c. Financial markets, including percent change in money supply; personal savings and rate; business and State/local government savings; foreign current account deficits; change in consumer installment debt, and commercial/industrial loans; and interest rates by type.

Monthly tables appear in all issues. All additional features with substantial statistical content are described, as they appear, under "Statistical Features." Nonstatistical features are not covered.

Availability: National Association of Realtors, Economics and Research Division, 777 14th St., NW, Washington DC 20005, †; SRI/MF/complete, shipped quarterly.

Issues reviewed during 1984: Nov. 1983-Oct. 1984 (P) [No Dec. 1983 issue was published].

STATISTICAL FEATURES:

A7000–1.501: Nov. 1983

RELATIONSHIP BETWEEN FEDERAL DEFICITS AND INTEREST RATES

(p. 5-10) Article, with 2 tables showing impact of Federal Reserve monetary policy, Federal debt, and inflation and market expectations on Aaa corporate bond interest rate, annually 1970-82 and quarterly 1983-85, with detail for impact of Three-For-All Program, 3rd quarter 1983-4th quarter 1988.

Three-For-All Program is an NAR legislative proposal to decrease interest rates by slowing Federal spending and reversing trend toward personal income tax reductions.

A7000–1.502: Jan. 1984

MONETARY POLICY AND INTEREST RATES

(p. 3-4) Article, with 1 table showing the following for M-1, M-2, and M-3 money supply: compound annual growth rates, July-Nov. 1983; Federal Reserve Board targeted rate, various periods 1982-83; and forecast rate for 1984.

A7000–1.503: May 1984

U.S. ECONOMIC AND REAL ESTATE OUTLOOK

(p. 1-6) Article, with 4 tables showing distribution of GNP by component, 1976-80 and 1981-85 periods; yield on selected Treasury securities, and compound annual growth rate for money supply categories, various months Nov. 1983-Apr. 1984; and square footage of retail, office, and industrial building contracts, 1981-85.

A7000–1.504: July 1984

U.S. ECONOMIC AND REAL ESTATE OUTLOOK

(p. 1-3) Article, with 2 tables showing the following:

a. Interest rates for Federal funds and selected Treasury bills and securities, Jan.-June 1984.

b. Impact of a tax law revision extending the cost recovery period for depreciable real estate on the following: investment and square footage cost for commercial, industrial, and rental residential structures; GNP; and employment; 1984.

A7000–1.505: Aug. 1984

U.S. ECONOMIC AND REAL ESTATE OUTLOOK

(p. 2-5) Article, with 1 table showing percent change in GNP by component, 4th quarter 1982-2nd quarter 1984 period, with comparison to 3 preceding recovery periods.

A7000–1.506: Sept. 1984

OUTLOOK FOR THE ECONOMY AND REAL ESTATE

(p. 2-5) Article, with 2 tables showing selected interest rates, Jan.-Aug. 1984; and square footage of retail, office, and industrial building contracts, 1981-85.

A7000–1.507: Oct. 1984

EMPLOYMENT AND INFLATION

(p. 1-2) Article, with 1 table showing percent change in employment, household income, consumption, and private investment in residential and nonresidential construction, with percent shares of GNP, for current recovery period compared to average of 5 preceding recovery periods.

A7000–2   EXISTING HOME SALES, Monthly Report

Monthly. Approx. 15 p.
SRI/MF/complete, shipped quarterly

Monthly report on sales of existing homes. Covers single family home sales volume and value and price range by region, and median price in selected metro areas; apartment condominium/cooperative sales by region; and total sales by State. Also includes housing affordability index.

Most data are compiled by NAR from reports of over 220 local boards of realtors and multiple listing systems. Month of coverage is month prior to publication date.

Report regularly includes narrative introduction, with text statistics and summary tables; 1 table showing U.S. summary trends, including homes available for sale; and 12 detailed tables, listed below, some with corresponding charts.

Availability: National Association of Realtors, Economics and Research Division, 777 14th St., NW, Washington DC 20005, members $36.00 per yr., nonmembers $48.00 per yr.; SRI/MF/complete, shipped quarterly.

Issues reviewed during 1984: Nov. 1983-Sept. 1984 (P).

TABLES:

[Tables [1-6] and [9-10] usually show data for total U.S. and by census region. Tables [1-3] and [8-12] show data for month of coverage or quarter ending in month of coverage, with monthly or quarterly trends for preceding 12 months or 4 quarters, and annual trends mostly from 1970s.]

[1-2] Existing single family home sales and dollar volume of existing single family home sales [seasonally adjusted and unadjusted].

[3] Sales price of existing single family homes (not seasonally adjusted) [median and mean].

[4-5] Sales of existing single family homes, by price class (percentage distribution) [for month of coverage and same month of previous 4 years; also shows median price].

[6] Sales of existing single family homes, by number of bedrooms (percentage distribution) [for month of coverage].

[7] Median sales price of existing single family homes for the U.S., by number of bedrooms [for month of coverage and same month of previous 4 years].

[8] Housing affordability [existing home median price, mortgage rate, monthly principal/interest payment and payment as percent of income, median family income, qualifying income, and affordability index; total U.S. only].

[9-10] Apartment condo/co-op sales; and total existing home sales, single family/apartment condos/co-ops (seasonally adjusted annual rates).

[11] Total existing home sales for each State, single family/apartment condos/co-ops.

[12] Median sales price of existing single family homes [in each of 31] metro areas (not seasonally adjusted).

A7000–4   EXISTING HOME SALES, 1983

Annual. 1984. 17 p.
ISSN 0161-5882.
LC 78-641508.
SRI/MF/complete

Annual report on the market for existing homes, 1983, with trends from as early as 1968. Includes number and/or value of single-family homes and condominium/cooperative apartments sold, by region and State; price data for single-family homes, including sales distribution by price class, and median price nationwide and in 31 metro areas; and selected sales and price detail by number of bedrooms and by month and quarter.

Also includes number of homes on the market; and housing affordability index and components, including average mortgage rate, monthly payment (amount and as percent of income), and qualifying income.

Data are compiled by NAR from reports by approximately 275 boards of realtors and multiple listings systems, representing over 1,180,000 single-family home sales during 1983.

Contains survey description (inside front cover); narrative summary (p. 1-3); and 16 tables (p. 4-17).

Availability: National Association of Realtors, Economics and Research Division, 777 14th St., NW, Washington DC 20005, included in subscription to monthly *Existing Home Sales,* or sold separately $10.00; SRI/MF/complete.

A7015
National Association of Regulatory Utility Commissioners

A7015–1   1982 ANNUAL REPORT ON UTILITY AND CARRIER REGULATION

Annual. Nov. 16, 1983.
xvii+910 p.
LC 76-644813.
SRI/MF/complete, delayed

Annual report, for 1982, presenting detailed data on the activities, jurisdiction, finances, and employment of U.S. and Canadian Government agencies regulating the public and private utility and transportation industries. Includes data by regulated company on rates, revenues, expenses, and operations.

Industry coverage includes electric, gas, telephone, telegraph, water, and sewer utilities; pipelines and cable TV services; and air, bus, motor, and railroad carriers.

Data are compiled by the National Assn of Regulatory Utility Commissioners from reports submitted by 11 Federal, State, territorial, and provincial and national Canadian agencies.

Contents:

Preface, and contents and table listing. (p. iii-xvii)

Part I. Agency profiles and history, generally with 1 organization chart, and 1-5 tables for each agency on personnel and/or receipts and expenditures, volume of proceedings, and consumer complaints. Agencies are arranged alphabetically. (p. 1-301)

Part II. Rate cases, with 1 extended table showing rate increases requested and granted, profitability allowed, projected revenues and expenses, and capital structure and costs allowed, by company, 1982. Data are arranged by type of utility and carrier, and by individual regulatory agency. (p. 302-420)

Part III. Utility regulation, with 93 tables on scope of agency jurisdiction and operations of regulated utilities, by type of utility. (p. 421-745)

Part IV. Transportation regulation, with 26 tables on scope of jurisdiction, by type of carrier. (p. 746-798)

Part V. Miscellaneous regulatory information, with 25 lists and tables on agency employment, salaries, budget, and administrative procedures. (p. 799-901)

Index. (p. 902-910)

Tables in Parts III-V are described below.

Availability: National Association of Regulatory Utility Commissioners, 1102 Interstate Commerce Commission Bldg., Constitution Ave. and 12th St., NW, PO Box 684, Washington DC 20044, $40.00; SRI/MF/complete, delayed shipment in Dec. 1984.

PARTS III-V TABLES:

[Data are generally shown by regulatory agency, and are for 1982 unless otherwise noted. Data by State generally include Canadian Provinces and/or U.S. territories.]

A7015–1.1: Regulatory Data

UTILITY REGULATION

a. Number of utilities and pipelines under agency jurisdiction, by State; utilities by type and ownership; scope of rate regulation; method of determining rate base, cost of service allowances, and depreciation policies; rate of return allowed and earned; and accounting, auditing, and report requirements. Tables 1-33. (p. 423-523)

b. Corporate transactions regulated; competitive bidding requirements; computer use and plans; safety and service requirements; certificates, licenses, and permits; interstate compacts affecting hydroelectric developments; environmental standards; income tax provisions; billing practices; and energy conservation activities. Tables 34-50. (p. 525-590)

c. Cable TV activities regulated, 1982; and industry finances and subscribers, FY81; both by State, with national trends from 1977. Tables 51-52. (p. 592-595)

d. Communications utilities and activities regulated, including telephone rates and subscriber privacy; Bell System intrastate rate increases, 1970-82; regulated telephone utility telephones in service, and average customers and residential bill; plant value, revenues, and expenditures for regulated telephone utilities, by agency, and for Bell System by company; State taxation of telecommunications services; and telephone directory advertising revenues. Tables 53-70. (p. 597-674)

e. Electricity, gas, and water and sewerage utility regulation, and plant value, revenues, expenses, customers, consumption, average bills, and plant investment; gas companies adding new customers; gas pipeline safety activity and expenses; average gas and competing fuel prices, selected cities; and States with higher gas prices than oil prices. Tables 71-93. (p. 676-745)

TRANSPORTATION REGULATION

f. Scope of regulation, by type of carrier; motor carriers regulated and enforcement activity; and railroads regulated, and safety program participation and expenses. Tables 94-119. (p. 747-798)

MISCELLANEOUS REGULATORY DATA

g. Other functions performed by agencies, and other businesses under agency jurisdiction; terms of commissioners; time requirements for rate decisions and appeals; and commission officials and staff, including number of full-time employees and salary for key positions, 1983. Tables 120-128. (p. 801-851)

h. Costs of regulation, including agency receipts by source and expenditures by object; legal status of agencies; use of administrative law examiners; public information services; freedom of information statutory requirements; and directory of State consumer and energy offices. Tables 129-144. (p. 853-901)

A7040
National Association of Schools of Art and Design

A7040–1 **ANNUAL REPORT, National Association of Schools of Art and Design**
Annual, discontinued.

Annual report on art school enrollment, faculty, operations, and students, for private independent art schools and public and private colleges/universities, discontinued with 1981/82 edition (for description, see SRI 1982 Annual, under this number).

Report has been discontinued, because issuing agency is computerizing its data collection operations. Information on data availability may be obtained from National Association of Schools of Art, 11250 Roger Bacon Dr., No. 5, Reston VA 22090.

A7055
National Association of Schools of Music

A7055–1 **MUSIC IN HIGHER EDUCATION**
Annual, discontinued.

Annual report on music school enrollment, degrees, faculty, and operations, in public and private institutions of higher education, discontinued with 1981/82 edition (for description, see SRI 1982 Annual, under this number).

Publication has been discontinued, because issuing agency is computerizing its data collection operations. Information on data availability may be obtained from National Association of Schools of Music, 11250 Roger Bacon Dr., No. 5, Reston VA 22090.

A7085
National Association of Secondary School Principals

A7085–1 **MOOD OF AMERICAN YOUTH**
Monograph. 1984.
viii+64 p.
ISBN 0-88210-155-2.
SRI/MF/not filmed

Report examining high school students' opinions and attitudes concerning various aspects of their own lives and of society in general. Data are from a 1983 survey of 1,500 students in grades 7-12, sponsored by National Assn of Secondary School Principals.

Contains contents listing, foreword, and introduction (p. iii-viii); and 5 narrative chapters, interspersed with 30 tables showing survey response on the topics described below (p. 1-64).

Availability: National Association of Secondary School Principals, Publications Sales, 1904 Association Dr., Reston VA 22091, $5.00+$2.00 postage and handling; SRI/MF/not filmed.

SURVEY TOPICS:

[Most data are shown by sex.]

a. Reasons for liking school, characteristics of worst teachers, importance ratings for 18 courses, reasons for not liking courses, participation in school-related activities, and opinions on the value of student government. 6 tables.

b. Extracurricular and leisure activity participation, including volunteer community services, sports, music, hobbies, and reading; importance of leisure activities; most common forms of transportation; and average expenditures of own money, by item. 9 tables.

c. Parental rules; family members with whom students can discuss problems; agreement with parental attitudes, by topic; worst influences on young people; most important national and world problems; views on selected national issues; and immediate, career, and life goals, including salary and marital expectations. 15 tables.

A7105
National Association of Securities Dealers

A7105–1 **1983 NASDAQ FACT BOOK**
Annual. [1984.] 112 p.
LC 82-21228.
SRI/MF/complete

Annual report on trading volume and price performance of 4,467 over-the-counter securities on the NASDAQ national list and national market systems, 1983, with aggregate trends from 1974. Data are compiled by NASD.

Includes number of shares traded, and high, low, and closing bid prices, by security, with summary data by industry division, detail for 50 most active securities and market value leaders, and trading comparisons to NYSE and AMEX markets.

Also includes selected financial data for a typical NASDAQ company; number of NASDAQ companies and market makers (registered brokers), by State; listing of market makers; data for American Depositary Receipts (ADRs) and foreign securities traded on NASDAQ, including share and dollar volume for leading securities, and number of issuers by country; listing of newspapers and other media covering NASDAQ; and number of NASDAQ computer terminal installations, including detail by country.

Contains contents listing (p. 1); and report, with narrative analysis, 4 charts, and 26 tables (p. 2-112).

Availability: National Association of Securities Dealers, 1735 K St., NW, Washington DC 20006, †; SRI/MF/complete.

A7130
National Association of State Racing Commissioners

A7130–1   PARI-MUTUEL RACING, 1983
Annual.   [1984.]
23 p.+errata sheets
SRI/MF/complete

Annual report, for 1983, on pari-mutuel horse racing in U.S., Canada, and Puerto Rico. Also covers greyhound racing and jai alai in U.S. Includes data on revenue, total races and games, attendance, and purse distribution, by State and Province.

Data are based on information provided by members of the National Assn of State Racing Commissioners, and the Canadian Ministry of Agriculture.

Contains 4 sections, with 17 tables listed below. Each section on the U.S. also includes a brief summary of related tax methods, by State.

Availability: National Association of State Racing Commissioners, Box 4216, Lexington KY 40504, $10.50; SRI/MF/complete.

TABLES:
[Tables show data for 1983, unless otherwise noted. Revenues by category are for track and/or occupational licenses, pari-mutuel taxes, breakage, admission taxes, miscellaneous, and, for jai alai only, franchise fees.]

A7130–1.1: Horse Racing

U.S.
[Tables [2-8] show data by State, for thoroughbred, harness, quarter horse, and mixed races.]

[1] Racing revenue to States by years (1934-83). (p. 2)

[2] Total horse racing days and total races. (p. 3)

[3] Attendance and daily average attendance. (p. 4)

[4] Pari-mutuel and daily average handle. (p. 5)

[5-6] Total revenue to government; and revenue to government by category. (p. 6-9)

[7] Simulcasting/telephone betting in the U.S. [pari-mutuel handle and total revenue to government; includes data for greyhound racing]. (p. 10)

[8] Stakes/purse distribution. (p. 11)

CANADA AND PUERTO RICO
[Tables present data by Canadian Province and for Puerto Rico, for thoroughbred/quarter horse and harness races.]

[9] Horse racing in Canada and Puerto Rico [racing days, number of races, attendance, and daily average attendance]. (p. 16)

[10] Handle [pari-mutuel and daily average], total revenue, and stakes/purse distribution. (p. 17)

A7130–1.2: Greyhound Racing and Jai Alai in U.S., and Legal Age Summary

GREYHOUND RACING
[1-2] Greyhound racing in the U.S. [total performances, number of races, attendance, daily average attendance, and pari-mutuel and daily average handle]; and revenue to government [by category], and stakes/purse distribution; [all by State and for 2 Alabama counties]. (p. 18)

[3-4] Greyhound racing revenue and total greyhound/horse racing revenue to the States (1959-83). (p. 21)

JAI ALAI
[Tables show data for Connecticut, Florida, and Rhode Island.]

[5-6] Jai alai [number of performances and games played, attendance, daily average attendance, and pari-mutuel and daily average handle]; and revenue to government [by category]. (p. 22)

LEGAL AGE
[7] Legal age to attend and wager at race track [by State]. (p. 23)

A7140
National Association of State Scholarship and Grant Programs

A7140–1   NASSGP 15TH ANNUAL SURVEY REPORT, 1983/84 Academic Year
Annual.   Dec. 1983.
ii+121 p.
SRI/MF/complete

Annual report on State-administered student aid for higher education, 1983/84. Includes data on number and value of awards, and characteristics of recipients, with detail by program, State, and territory. Data were compiled by NASSGP, and are based primarily on reports of member agencies.

Contains contents/table listing (p. i-ii); report, with narrative summary, and 26 tables and lists presenting the statistics described below and also including summaries on application criteria (including actions taken to verify Selective Service registration by aid applicants), eligible institution and program types, and agency and program administration (p. 1-111); and NASSGP directory (p. 112-121).

SRI coverage begins with the report for 1983/84.

Availability: Pennsylvania Higher Education Assistance Agency, Attention: Research and Statistics, 660 Boas St., Harrisburg PA 17102-1398, $5.00; SRI/MF/complete.

STATISTICS:
[Data are estimates for 1983/84, unless otherwise noted. Most data are shown by detailed aid program, arranged by State and territory.]

a. Totals: number and value of need- and non-need based awards to undergraduate and graduate students, with comparisons to 1982/83; and awards, appropriation, and selection criteria, for other awards from NASSGP member agencies, and for awards from nonmember agencies (also shows administering agency). (p. 9-31)

b. Need-based undergraduate awards: number and value of awards with competitive and attendance conditions; award and award value distributions by type of institution (in-State public and private, and out-of-State); and value of State Student Incentive Grant (SSIG) program awards, with 1982/83 comparison to amount awarded and amount returned to Federal Government. (p. 32-41)

c. Program characteristics: number of applicants, recipients, and rejections due to lack of need or funds; and program starting year, maximum allowable award, and average, low, and high awards. (p. 46-60)

d. Recipients of need-based undergraduate awards, and value of awards, by selected recipient characteristics, including type of school or program attended, citizenship and residency status, whether financially independent, sex, race/ethnicity (including American Indian, Oriental, and Spanish American), age, and family income. (p. 111)

A7150
National Association of State Universities and Land-Grant Colleges

A7150–3   APPROPRIATIONS OF STATE TAX FUNDS for Operating Expenses of Higher Education, 1983/84
Annual.   Oct. 1983. 25 p.
LC 75-617890.
SRI/MF/complete

Annual report, by M. M. Chambers, on State appropriations for higher education, by institution and function, FY84. Includes appropriations for operating expenses of colleges and universities, coordinating and governing boards, student financial aid, and community colleges and vocational/technical schools. Excludes appropriations for capital outlay.

Data are collected by Dept of Educational Administration and Foundations, Illinois State University. This is the 25th edition of the report.

Contains introduction (p. 1-4); 1 table showing appropriations by State, FY74, FY82, and FY84, and percent gains over the past 2- and 10-year periods (p. 6); and 1 table repeated for each State showing FY84 appropriations, by institution and function (p. 7-25).

Availability: National Association of State Universities and Land-Grant Colleges, Office of Communications Services, One Dupont Circle, NW, Suite 710, Washington DC 20036, †; SRI/MF/complete.

A7150–4 1983/84 STUDENT CHARGES AT STATE AND LAND-GRANT UNIVERSITIES
Annual. [1984.] 1+22 p.
SRI/MF/complete

Annual report on State and land-grant university student charges, 1983/84. Covers resident and nonresident tuition/fees, room, and board; and includes data for individual institutions. Data are from survey responses of 195 institutions in the 50 States, D.C., Guam, Puerto Rico, and Virgin Islands.

Contains table listing (1 p.); and narrative analysis with 18 tables, listed below (p. 1-22).

Availability: National Association of State Universities and Land-Grant Colleges, Office of Communications Services, One Dupont Circle, NW, Suite 710, Washington DC 20036, †; SRI/MF/complete.

TABLES:

[Data are for 1983/84, unless otherwise noted. Most data are shown for undergraduate residents and nonresidents. Tables 1-17 are based on a subsample of 146 respondents with 4-year campus, PhD program, and room/board.]

1. Comparison of median charges [tuition/fees, room, and board, 1982/83-1983/84]. (p. 1)

2. Regional comparison of median tuition/fees. (p. 3)

3. Comparison of median tuition/fees for graduate and professional [law, medicine, veterinary medicine, and dentistry] students, [1982/83-1983/84]. (p. 4)

4-9. Ranges, and range of increases, for tuition/fees and total charges. (p. 5-8)

10-11. 19-year trend of median charges for tuition/fees, [1965/66-1983/84]; and 15-year trend of median total charges, 1969/70-1983/84]. (p. 9-10)

12-17. Highest and lowest charges for tuition/fees and total charges; and largest and smallest increase in tuition/fees [ranked for 10 universities]. (p. 11-14)

18. Full-time student charges [tuition/fees, room, and board; by institution, grouped by State or territory]. (p. 16-22)

A7310
National
Association of Wheat
Growers

A7310–1 WHEAT GROWER: 1984
Wheat Facts
Monthly (selected issue).
Aug. 1984. (p. 17-38).
Vol. 7, No. 8.
SRI/MF/excerpts

Annual report, for 1984, by *Wheat Grower* journal, on wheat production, consumption, and foreign trade in U.S. and other major wheat growing countries. Includes data on production costs, prices received by farmers, and government wheat support programs, 1960s-84 and selected previous years.

Data are from USDA, Chase Econometrics, and other sources.

Contains chronology of major events affecting wheat growers, 3 charts and 19 tables, lists of wheat testing weight and quality requirements, harvest seasons and statistical crop years by country, measurement conversions, and explanation of wheat classes, and list of State wheat assns. All tables, and a chart presenting data not covered in tables, are listed below.

Wheat Grower is a monthly periodical reporting trends and developments in the wheat growing industry, and normally contains only narrative articles. This annual report is the only feature covered in SRI.

This is the 7th annual report.

Availability: National Association of Wheat Growers, 415 Second St., NE, Suite 300, Washington DC 20002, $3.50; SRI/MF/excerpts for annual Wheat Facts section.

TABLES AND CHART:

U.S. DATA

[1] Annual wheat production, [acreage, and yield, 1960-84]. (p. 20)

[2] Wheat production [and yield in 16] NAWG States [1981-83]. (p. 20)

[3] Marketing year wheat supply and disappearance [including beginning and ending stocks, trade, production, and domestic use, 1965/66-1984/85]. (p. 21)

[4] Wheat by classes: supply and disappearance [for 5 varieties, 1983/84-1984/85]. (p. 21)

[5] Wheat supply and use [acreage, yield, production, trade, domestic use, and carryover, selected years] 1930/31-1984/85. (p. 22)

[6] White pan bread marketing spreads [includes baking and ingredient costs and wholesale and retail prices, per pound, Apr.-June 1983 period]. [chart] (p. 22)

[7] Use of wheat [domestic food, feed/seed/industrial, trade, and reseed/farmer-owned reserve, 1960-84]. (p. 23)

[8] Monthly prices received by farmers: all wheat [for 20 States, 1982-83, and total U.S., 1978-83]. (p. 24)

[9] Wheat program summary I [production; national average support/target price and price to farmers; direct payments; loan rate; farm value; and government payments; 1960-85]. (p.25)

[10] Cost of production [by item, with selected ratios, 1976-83]. (p. 25)

[11] Wheat program summary II [participating farms, acreage allotment, acreage diversion/set aside, diversions/special grazing and hay program payments, and marketing certificate/deficiency payments, 1960-83]. (p. 26)

[12] Wheat parity prices [selected annual averages 1950-83, and monthly average Jan. 1983-June 1984]. (p. 26)

[13] Rate of [farm] income return to equity, by debt/asset ratio and interest rate [no date]. (p. 27)

[14] Debt distribution by farm size [as of Jan. 1, 1984]. (p. 27)

FOREIGN DATA AND U.S. EXPORTS

[15] Wheat: world production, consumption, and net exports [for major exporters and importers, residual, and world; 1982/83-1984/85]. (p. 30)

[16] Wheat inspected for export by class, region, and port area [for U.S., June 1983-May 1984 period]. (p. 31)

[17] U.S. wheat exports by [country or area of] destination [1978/79-1983/84]. (p. 31)

[18-19] USSR and PRC wheat and coarse grain imports [by country or area of origin, various years 1974/75-1983/84]. (p. 32)

[20] Wheat supply and disappearance: major U.S. competitors [Canada, Australia, Argentina, and EC, 1973/74-1984/85]. (p. 33)

A7330
National
Automobile Dealers
Association

A7330–1 NADA DATA FOR 1984:
Economic Impact of America's New Car and Truck Dealers
Annual. [1984.] 20 p.
SRI/MF/complete

Annual report on franchised new car and truck dealer sales, operations, and employment, by State, 1983. Includes data on domestic and import sales, advertising, scrappage, and vehicle registrations, 1970s-84.

Data are compiled by the NADA Industry Analysis Dept from original research, and from reports of Federal agencies and *Ward's Automotive Reports*.

Contains contents listing (inside front cover); introduction (p. 1); 5 charts, and 42 tables arranged in 15 table sections, each usually accompanied by brief analysis (p. 2-19); and list of NADA officials, and 1 tabular listing of industry operating highlights for 1983 (p. 20).

Sections are listed below, and tables within each section are described.

Availability: National Automobile Dealers Association, Industry Analysis Department, 8400 Westpark Dr., McLean VA 22102, $5.00; SRI/MF/complete.

TABLE SECTIONS:

[1] Average dealer profile [sales, gross, expense, and net worth; net pre-tax profit in current and constant 1967 dollars; new and used vehicle and service/parts sales; and average new vehicle selling price; 1977-83]. (p. 2)

[2] NADA optimism index [dealer profit expectation index, quarterly Jan. 1979-Jan. 1984]. (p. 3)

[3] Number of franchised new car dealerships [for dual and exclusive domestic and imported makes, 1975-84; and total dealerships by State, as of Jan. 1, 1984]. (p. 4)

[4] Total dealership sales dollars [total and average franchised dealer sales, 1973-83, and by State, 1983; and number of franchised dealers and dealer sales, payroll, and employees, as percent of retail totals, by State]. (p. 5-6)

[5] New vehicle dept [new domestic and imported car sales volume, 1974-83; total sales by month with seasonally adjusted annual rates, 1982-83; sales and market shares for 8 domestic and foreign manufacturers and all other imports, average new car sales per dealer and

vehicle selling price, and domestic and imported new car inventories and days supply, various years 1973-83]. (p. 7-8)

[6] Used vehicle dept [wholesale and retail used vehicle sales volume, and average retail selling price of used cars, for franchised dealers, 1974-83]. (p. 9)

[7] Service and parts depts [aggregate market value by type of service establishment, 1978-83; number of auto repair facilities by type, 1983; and franchised dealer labor and parts sales by type, 1982-83]. (p. 10)

[8] Employment and payrolls [franchised dealership employees by occupation, 1983; total and average dealership employment, 1973-83, and by State, 1983; and total and average annual or weekly payroll and earnings, various years 1974-83, and by State, 1983]. (p. 11-12)

[9] Advertising and the franchised dealership [local advertising expenditures, including total amounts, averages per dealer and per new vehicle sold, and ratios to sales, with detail by media type and sales volume, various years 1976-83]. (p. 13)

[10] Consumer credit [average finance rate on new car loans at finance companies and banks, average prime rate, and total consumer and auto installment credit outstanding; and auto credit outstanding by type of lending institution; 1973-83]. (p. 14)

[11] Vehicles in operation and scrappage [cars and trucks/buses in operation, as of Jan. 1, 1974-84; population and cars in operation, selected years 1910-2005; and car and truck/bus scrappage, number and as percent of cars and trucks/buses in operation and new cars and trucks/buses registered, 1974-83]. (p. 15)

[12] Total registrations [cars and trucks/buses, by State, 1983, and totals, 1975-83]. (p. 16)

[13] Franchised new truck dealer [new truck sales by gross vehicle weight, 1982-83]. (p. 17)

[14] Truck inventories [and days supply, by weight class, 1982 and monthly 1983]. (p. 18)

[15] Truck dealership profile [total sales value by dept (new and used vehicle and service/parts), and new unit sales by weight class, 1982-83; and NADA American Truck Dealers Division membership by primary make and State, and for selected metro areas, Puerto Rico, and Canada, as of Apr. 1984]. (p. 18-19)

A7350
National
Business Aircraft Association

A7350-1 **NBAA BUSINESS FLYING**
Series. For individual publication data, see below.
SRI/MF/complete

Series of reports on business aircraft ownership and use. Data generally are drawn from annual FAA reports and privately commissioned surveys or studies.

1-3 reports are issued each year, including an annual report on general and business aviation.

Report reviewed during 1984 is described below.

Availability: National Business Aircraft Association, One Farragut Sq., S., Washington DC 20006, not available by subscription, member single copy $1.00, nonmember single copy $2.00, minimum charge $10.00; SRI/MF/complete.

A7350-1.15: Business Aviation Statistics —Past, Present, and Future
[Annual. June 1984. 12 p. SRI/MF/complete.]

Annual report on general aviation trends, including fleet size and composition, flight hours, avionics use, and fuel consumption, various years 1978-88. Data are from FAA and National Business Aircraft Assn surveys. Includes introduction, contents listing, definitions, and 3 charts and 14 tables showing:

a. General aviation fleet size and hours flown, 1979-88, and by aircraft type and primary use (corporate, business, personal, instructional, aerial application and observation, commuter carrier, air taxi, rental, and other), 1982; and average hours flown by aircraft type, 1978-82.

b. Avionics equipment inventory and percent of aircraft using, 1982, with percent growth in equipment used by aircraft type, 1977-81 period, all by equipment type; and hours flown by weather and light conditions, 1982; all for general aviation.

c. Pilots active by type of certificate (student, private, commercial, airline transport, helicopter, glider, and other), and number with instrument rating, 1979-88; and total mechanics and dispatchers, 1978-82.

d. Fuel consumed in general aviation, 1979-88, and consumption rates, 1982, both by aircraft type, with detail for aviation gasoline and jet fuel; and civil/joint-use airports on record with FAA by type, characteristics, type of ownership, and length of longest runway, and reported abandonments, various years 1978-83.

e. Aviation activity indicators: revenue passenger enplanements and miles, fleet size, and hours flown; and air traffic control center aircraft and instrument operations, instrument flight rated aircraft handled, and flight services (pilot briefs, flight plans, aircraft contacts); with varying detail for airline and commuter carriers, general aviation, and military aircraft; selected years 1979-85, with growth rates to 1995.

A7375
National
Catholic Educational
Association

A7375-1 **U.S. CATHOLIC ELEMENTARY AND SECONDARY SCHOOLS, 1983/84**
Annual. Feb. 14, 1984.
18 p.
SRI/MF/complete

Annual report, by Frank H. Bredeweg, on Catholic elementary and secondary schools, enrollment, teachers, and student characteristics, with some data for other types of schools, primarily 1983/84, with trends from 1960s and projections to 1990.

Includes Catholic schools and enrollment by region; schools by type of parish affiliation, urban and rural location, and enrollment size category; enrollment distribution for Catholics and non-Catholics; top 10 States and 20 dioceses ranked by enrollment; enrollment by race/ethnicity (black, Hispanic, Asian, American Indian, and other); pupil/teacher ratio; religious teachers by sex; and lay teachers.

Also includes public and private school enrollment projections to 1990; and private school enrollment, with detail by religious affiliation.

Most data are shown for elementary and secondary schools.

Data are primarily from NCES and reports of 166 diocesan offices to National Catholic Educational Assn.

Contains introduction (1 p.); and report highlights and narrative, with 27 tables (p. 1-18).

Availability: National Catholic Educational Association, Publication Sales, Suite 100, 1077 30th St., NW, Washington DC 20007, $5.00 (prepaid), members 10% discount; SRI/MF/ complete.

A7400
National Coal Association

A7400-2 **INTERNATIONAL COAL, 1983**
Annual. 1984.
125 p. var. paging.
ISSN 0146-3845.
LC 77-648257.
SRI/MF/not filmed

Annual statistical report on world coal industry, covering production, reserves, consumption, trade, and employment, by country, 1978-82 and selected historical trends. Also includes data on world energy resources. Data are compiled from reports of U.S. and foreign government agencies and private assns.

Contains contents listing (2 p.); 4 summary tables (p. i); 3 statistical sections, with 1 chart, 144 tables, and articles on Canada and Japan (p. I.1-III.59); and 2 appendices, with 1 table, 2 charts, and membership directory of U.S. Coal Exporters Assn (p. IV.1-IV.3). All tables are described below.

Availability: National Coal Association, Publications Department, 1130 17th St., NW, Washington DC 20036-4677, members †, nonprofit organizations $75.00, others $125.00; SRI/MF/not filmed.

TABLES:

[Tables generally show data for 1978-82, with selected data for 1983 and trends from as early as 1925. Data by coal type are shown for bituminous, anthracite, and, occasionally, coke, lignite, and briquets.]

A7400-2.1: World and U.S. Data

a. World data: coal reserves and production, by type; coal vs. industrial production indexes; crude oil, natural gas, and raw steel production; energy consumption, by source; and mineral fuel shipments through Panama Canal, by trade route, with detail for coke/coal; generally shown by country. 15 tables. (p. I.1-I.21)

b. U.S. coal supply and demand summary; number of mines, employment, and productivity, by mine or coal type; and bituminous/lignite consumption, by sector. 3 tables. (p. II.1)

c. U.S. trade: export and import volume and/or value, by coal type, country of destination or origin, and U.S. customs district; monthly bituminous trade; bituminous exports by use (metallurgy or steam) and by port of exit, both by destination; and quantity, cost, Btu value, and sulfur content of imported coal delivered to electric utilities, by country of origin and utility. 30 tables. (p. II.2-II.32)

d. Rail rates from mine to port of exit for U.S. export coal, by coal type, mine district, and port; U.S. rail dumpings of bituminous coal for export, by Atlantic port and railroad company; coal shipments to U.S. military forces in West Germany, by type; and ocean freight rates for selected routes. 4 tables. (p. II.33-II.35)

A7400-2.2: Data for Selected Countries

[Data for each country or area noted below include 3-8 tables, usually showing coal production, consumption by sector, trade volume and value by country of origin and/or destination, and, often, number of mines, year-end stocks, productivity, and employment, with selected detail by coal type. Substantial additional data and exceptions are indicated below.]

a. Australia; Belgium; Canada, also including energy consumption by source, capacity of British Columbia coal export terminals, electricity trade with U.S. with detail for selected U.S. regions or States, and coal imports from U.S. by transport mode; and Colombia, also including electric generating capacity by fuel source projected to 1990, and coal reserves. 31 tables. (p. III.1-III.23)

b. France; Federal Republic of Germany; Italy; Japan, also including energy demand and electric generation by fuel source projected to 1995, and crude steel output; Netherlands, showing only trade data; and Poland. 40 tables. (p. III.26-III.49)

c. South Africa, showing only summary coal production, domestic sales, and export volume and/or value; Spain and Sweden, both showing only coal import volume and/or value, by country of origin; UK,

also including coal mines closed, and energy consumption by source; and USSR, showing only coal production, and summary consumption and trade volume and value. 21 tables. (p. III.51-III.59)

d. EC, showing coal production, employment, colliery stocks, imports from 3rd-party countries, and deliveries. 1 table. (p. IV.1)

A7400-3   INTERNATIONAL COAL REVIEW

Semimonthly. Approx. 15 p. SRI/MF/not filmed

Semimonthly journal reporting, in alternate issues, on U.S. and foreign coal trade. U.S. data are primarily from U.S. Dept of Commerce. International data are primarily from EC, Statistics Canada, Australian Joint Coal Board, and International Iron and Steel Institute.

U.S. coal trade issue includes 18 monthly tables, listed below. Month of coverage for most tables is 2 months prior to month of publication.

Foreign coal trade issue usually includes 4 monthly tables, also listed below; and occasional special tables, generally focusing on individual countries, often Poland and South Africa. Month of coverage is 2-6 months prior to month of publication.

Issue dates vary considerably depending upon availability of data.

Most monthly tables appear as explained above. All additional features with substantial statistical content, including special tables, are described, as they appear, under "Statistical Features."

Availability: National Coal Association, Publications Department, 1130 17th St., NW, Washington DC 20036-4677, members †, nonmembers $100.00 per yr.; SRI/MF/not filmed.

Issues reviewed during 1984: U.S. trade issues: Nov. 3 and Dec. 5, 1983; Jan. 9, Feb. 2, Mar. 5, Apr. 3, May 2, June 5, July 5, Aug. 6, Sept. 5, and Oct. 3, 1984 (P).

Issues reviewed during 1984: Foreign trade issues: Nov. 29, 1983; Jan. 25, Feb. 16, Mar. 13, Apr. 30, May 30, June 14, July 24, Aug. 15, Sept. 27, and Oct. 26, 1984 (P).

MONTHLY TABLES:

A7400-3.1: U.S. Coal Trade

[Tables [3-16] show value and/or quantity, for month of coverage and/or year to date and generally for same periods of previous year, for U.S.]

1-2. Summary of U.S. bituminous coal exports and export prices [to Canada and overseas, by month for year to date and previous year].

3-8. Exports of metallurgical and steam coal [by country of destination].

9-11. Exports of anthracite, lignite, and coke [by country of destination].

12-14. Exports of metallurgical and steam coal, by country of destination, by customs district of exit.

15. Imports of bituminous coal, coke, and briquets [by country of origin].

16. Imports of bituminous coal and coke, by country of origin, by customs district of entry.

17. Single-trip ocean freight rates per long ton of coal [for selected world routes; as of date of publication or up to 6 weeks prior to publication date].

18. Foreign exchange rates [for approximately 40 currencies vs. U.S. dollar, for month of coverage, previous 2 months, and same month of previous year].

A7400-3.2: Foreign Coal Trade

[Table sequence and format may vary.]

[1] Australian coal exports [by country of destination and/or type, generally for fiscal year to date through month of coverage, and selected prior periods].

[2] Canadian coal and coke production [by type], exports [by country of destination], and imports [by type; for month of coverage and year to date, and same periods of previous year].

[3] Crude steel production [by country and world area; for month of coverage and year to date, and same periods of previous year].

[4] Coal production [by region and method], stocks [by region, domestic] consumption [by sector], and exports [by country of destination and port of exit], for New South Wales, Australia [for year to date through month of coverage, and same period of previous year].

STATISTICAL FEATURES:

A7400-3.501: Nov. 29, 1983 (Foreign Coal Trade Issue)

SPECIAL TABLES

[Data are from UN and *Mineral Commodity Profiles 1983*.]

[A] Iron and steel supply-demand relationships [U.S. and rest of world raw steel production; and U.S. steel mill and iron and steel foundry shipments, iron/steel foreign trade, and iron/steel demand by sector], 1972-82.

[B] Steel exports by country [or world area of origin] and destination, 1981.

[C] World raw steel production 1982, and capacity 1982 and 1985 [by country or world area].

A7400-3.502: Jan. 25, 1984 (Foreign Coal Trade Issue)

SPECIAL TABLE

[A] [Metallurgical and steam] coal exports from South Africa [1st 3 quarters 1983; data are from H. Clarkson and Co.]. (p. 2)

A7400-3.503: Mar. 13, 1984 (Foreign Coal Trade Issue)

SPECIAL TABLE

[A] Japanese [metallurgical and steam] coal imports [by country of origin, 1982-83; data are from Japanese Ministry of Finance]. (p. 6)

A7400-3.504: Apr. 30, 1984 (Foreign Coal Trade Issue)

SPECIAL TABLES

[A] South African [bituminous and anthracite] coal production [and] exports [1980-83; data are from South African Dept of Mineral and Energy Affairs]. (p. 2)

[B] Polish coal exports to the West [by world area of destination, 1982-83; data are from H. Clarkson and Co.]. (p. 2)

A7400–3.505: June 14, 1984 (Foreign Coal Trade Issue)

SPECIAL TABLES

[A] Polish [metallurgical and steam] coal production, [and aggregate] exports [to market and nonmarket economies, 1983 and 1st 4 months 1984, with 1984 annual targets; data are from the Polish Embassy]. (p. 3)

[B] UK coal supply and demand [production, domestic consumption, exports, imports, and stocks, 1980-83 and Jan.-Feb. 1983-84]. (p. 5)

A7400–3.506: July 24, 1984 (Foreign Coal Trade Issue)

SPECIAL TABLE

[A] 1983 Canadian imports of bituminous coal from the U.S., by Province, [by transportation method, with comparisons to 1982; data are from the Canadian Energy, Mines and Resources Dept]. (p. 3)

A7400–3.507: Aug. 15, 1984 (Foreign Coal Trade Issue)

SPECIAL TABLES

[A] Canadian imports of bituminous coal from the U.S., by Province [by transportation method, 1st quarter 1984 with comparisons to 1st quarter 1983; data are from the Canadian Energy, Mines and Resources Dept]. (p. 3)

[B] Coal production, exports from South Africa [for anthracite, and bituminous by type, Jan.-Apr. 1984; data are from South African Dept of Minerals and Energy Affairs]. (p. 4)

A7400–3.508: Sept. 27, 1984 (Foreign Coal Trade Issue)

SPECIAL TABLES

[A] Coal exports from Poland [by country of destination, with aggregate coking and steam coal exports to Communist and non-Communist world areas, 1982-83; data are from *Polish Coal Review*]. (p. 3)

[B] Coal production [and] exports from South Africa [for anthracite, and bituminous by type, 1st quarter and Apr.-May, 1984; data are from South African Dept of Minerals and Energy Affairs]. (p. 5)

A7400–3.509: Oct. 26, 1984 (Foreign Coal Trade Issue)

SPECIAL TABLE

[A] Coal production [and] exports from South Africa [for anthracite, and bituminous by type, 1st quarter and Apr.-June 1984; data are from South African Dept of Minerals and Energy Affairs]. (p. 4)

A7400–4   COAL TRAFFIC, 1982

Annual. 1984.
55 p. var. paging, foldouts.
ISSN 0069-4916.
LC 75-641344.
SRI/MF/not filmed

Annual report on transportation of coal by rail, water, truck, and pipeline, 1978-82 with selected trends from 1900. Also includes data on origin and destination of shipments, and railroad equipment and carloadings.

Data are from Federal Government sources and private assns.

Contains foreword and contents listing, with 1 summary table (5 p.); 6 statistical sections with 4 charts, and 63 tables described below (p. I.1-VI.3); section on rail transportation contracts (p. VII.1-VII.23); and 5 appendices, including rail rate data, definitions, and Bureau of Mines coal producing districts (p. VIII.1-VIII.10).

Availability: National Coal Association, Publications Department, 1130 17th St., NW, Washington DC 20036-4677, members †, nonprofit organizations $50.00, others $75.00; SRI/MF/not filmed.

TABLES:

[Tables generally show data for various years 1978-82, with selected trends from as early as 1900.

Data by coal district are shown for 23-24 Bureau of Mines producing districts. Data by consumer use are generally shown for coke/gas plants, electric utilities, other industrial, and residential/commercial.

Data sources are shown for each table.]

A7400–4.1: Shipments

(p. I.1-I.5) Includes 6 tables showing coal shipments as follows:

a. Total, and by consumer sector, district of origin, and destination State; for rail, water (often including breakdowns for river, Great Lakes, and Tidewater), truck, and tramway/conveyor/slurry pipeline.

b. By district of origin by destination State, with detail for Canada and overseas.

A7400–4.2: Railroad Traffic

[Data by rail district are shown for the 3 Class I railroad districts.]

a. Summary: rail shipments by destination State, consumer sector, and coal district of origin; and average revenue, freight carload, and haul for bituminous/lignite, and for total carload traffic. 5 tables. (p. II.1-II.4)

b. Class I and individual railroads: total and coal revenue freight originated and revenue received, 1963-82; average coal revenue per ton by railroad district, 1973-82; volume carried and average revenue, by railroad, 1981-82; and revenue freight originated and terminated, total traffic, and gross revenue, by Class I railroad, 1982. 5 tables. (p. II.5-II.9)

c. Freight cars and carloadings: aggregate weekly carloadings; coal and total commodity carloadings, by railroad; freight cars and/or general service hopper cars, including ownership, capacity, number, utilization, installed and on-order, and new/rebuilt, variously shown by railroad, Class I railroad, or major coal-hauling railroad; and number of locomotives owned by Class I railroads, by locomotive type and serviceability; various years 1956-83. 15 tables. (p. II.10-II.19)

d. Coal dumpings at Atlantic ports, by railroad, destined for New England, abroad, and inside capes; various years 1978- 82. 2 tables. (p. II.20)

e. Indexes: for total and coal railroad freight, PPI, and coal by month; 1973-82. 2 tables. (p. II.21)

A7400–4.3: Water Traffic

[Data for waterborne traffic are shown for 1977-81. Data by traffic type are shown for coastwise, lakewise, internal, and local traffic.]

a. Domestic inland waterway: tons of coal shipped, by shipping and receiving areas, and by origin by destination; and tons originated, terminated, and carried, by major coal-hauling river system. 4 tables. (p. III.1-III.3)

b. Coal water traffic: domestic ton-miles of water movement of coal and all commodities by carrier type; average haul total and over inland waterways, with inland waterway tonnage; tonnage, by coal district of origin, and for imports, exports, and domestic shipments; coal share of all waterborne commerce; and tonnage shipped by barge; all generally by traffic type. 8 tables. (p. III.4-III.6)

A7400–4.4: Truck, Great Lakes, and Pipeline Traffic

a. Truck shipments: by destination State, consumer sector, and coal district of origin. 4 tables. (p. IV.1-IV.3)

b. Great Lakes: coal tonnage and total bulk freight, 1900-82; bituminous shipments by month, by lake, with detail for shipments to U.S. and Canadian ports from Lake Erie, by loading ports and destination; railroad coal dumpings at Lake Erie ports, by port and railroad; and State of origin of Lake Erie coal. 10 tables. (p. V.1-V.5)

c. Coal slurry pipelines: pipeline systems existing and planned, showing each system's length, annual capacity, and current status. 2 tables. (p. VI.1-VI.3)

A7400–5   COAL DATA 1981/82

Annual. 1983.
127 p. var. paging.
ISSN 0145-417X.
LC 76-648911.
SRI/MF/not filmed

Annual report on coal industry, including production, value, consumption, distribution, stocks, employment, safety, and machinery, with data by coal district and State, 1981-82 and trends. Also covers total energy production, reserves, and use; and coke production and consumption.

Data are from DOE and other Federal Government and private sources.

Contents:

a. Foreword, contents listing, and 1 summary table. (4 p., p. i)

b. 3 statistical sections, with 175 tables, described below. (p. I.1-III.3)

c. 4 appendices, covering pay provisions; wage classifications showing standard daily wage rates under National Bituminous Coal Wage Agreement for 1981, by class of labor, by quarter June 1981-June 1984; conversion factors; and definitions of Bureau of Mines coal producing districts. (p. IV.1-IV.16)

Report has been published since 1935.

Availability: National Coal Association, Publications Department, 1130 17th St., NW, Washington DC 20036-4677, members †, nonprofit organizations $35.00, others $50.00; SRI/MF/not filmed.

TABLES:

[Tables generally show data for 1978-82; monthly data for 1981-82, as noted; and occasionally, historic trends from as early as 1922. Data by State generally are shown for only the relevant resource-bearing States; data by region generally are shown for east and west of the Mississippi River.

Data by method of mining are shown for underground or surface mining. Major consuming sectors shown are residential/commercial, industrial, and transportation, often with detail for industrial users (electric utilities, coke plants, and other).

Data by coal type are generally shown for bituminous, sub-bituminous, lignite, and anthracite/semianthracite. Each table includes extensive footnotes.]

A7400–5.1: Energy Statistics

a. Reserves: coal resources, by source and coal type; reserve bases of coal by type, method of mining, and region, with detail for sulfur content, volatility, and coal on Indian reservations; federally leased coal reserves and production by region; and reserves and discoveries in new and old fields of crude oil, natural gas liquids, and natural gas; all by State. 15 tables. (p. I.1-I.11)

b. Supply and demand: energy production, consumption by consuming sector, and net imports, by type of energy source and month; detailed industrial use of natural gas; sales of distillate and residual fuel oil, by end use; and petroleum imports by type, month, and from OPEC and non-OPEC countries. 15 tables. (p. I.12-I.19)

A7400–5.2: Bituminous Coal

[Data by district are shown for 23 coal production districts defined by Bureau of Mines. Footnotes for each table define the occasional inclusion of shipments to Canada or Mexico.]

a. National summary data: bituminous supply and demand components, 1922-82; industrial production and productivity indexes, PPI, and average weekly earnings, for bituminous and other selected industries; bituminous production by method of mining and region; total production value; and number of mines, average annual output per mine, employment, productivity, number of days worked, and price indicators, all by method of mining. 12 tables. (p. II.1-II.5)

b. Coal production: production of 50 largest bituminous/lignite mines, by company; production, weekly 1980-82, and for peak weeks 1920-82; production by month, district, State, mining method, and mining equipment type; captive production for selected industries; number of mines and production by size of output and mining method; production, by coal type and volatility, coalbed and overburden thickness, and major coalbed; and surface mining acres mined and reclaimed. 25 tables. (p. II.6-II.23)

c. Number of mines, employment, output per person per day, and days worked: all by State, district, and method of mining. 24 tables. (p. II.24-II.35)

d. Safety: fatal, nonfatal with and without days lost, disabling, and nondisabling injuries and incidence rates, by method of mining and type of mine or other mine-related operation; with detail for fatalities by cause. 6 tables. (p. II.36-II.38)

e. Prices: average price per ton by method of mining and for coal sold in the open market, by State and district. 8 tables. (p. II.39-II.42)

f. Plant and equipment: units of equipment, by type, by method of mining, with selected State data; cleaning plant operations and methods, and clean coal as percent of total production with number of plants by State. 9 tables. (p. II.43-II.46)

g. Supply and demand, for bituminous or bituminous/lignite: consumption by month; stocks and days supply at end of year, and by month; distribution, by district of origin and by census division and State of destination, and by mode of transportation; exports by country of destination and imports by country of origin; and shipments by mode of transportation, and by State and district, with detail for average sulfur content; generally by consuming sector with detail for industrial users. 17 tables. (p. II.47-II.63)

A7400–5.3: Electric Utilities, Coke, Iron and Steel, and Anthracite

a. Electric utilities: electricity production by energy source, census division, and State; fuel consumption at electric utilities and fuel deliveries at steam electric plants, by type of fuel; and electricity generated by coal and coal consumed at electric utilities, by month. 7 tables. (p. II.64-II.69)

b. Steam electric plants: average fuel delivery price, average heating and/or sulfur content quality of fuels delivered, and fuel utilization efficiency, by fuel type; average quality of coal delivered, by census division; average coal delivery price and volume, by type of purchase (contract or spot), method of mining, and census division and State. 8 tables. (p. II.70-II.78)

c. Coke, iron, and steel: coke imports and exports, and production by coke and plant type, and State; coke consumption and sales by user type; iron/steel industry coal and coke consumption, and production of pig iron/ferroalloys; characteristics of coal used at coke plants, including State and country of origin; coke stocks by plant type and month; monthly raw steel production and capability utilization; and selected production ratios. 19 tables. (p. II.79-II.84)

d. Anthracite: exports and stocks; production by method, and consumption by end use; number of mines, days worked, employees, and output per person-day; equipment use by mine type; shipments by mode of transportation; distribution by destination State; and end-of-month stocks by industrial consumer class. 10 tables. (p. III.1-III.3)

A7400–6   FACTS ABOUT COAL

Annual, discontinued coverage.

Annual fact book presenting summary data on coal reserves, production, consumption, manpower, transportation, and trade, described in SRI 1983 Annual under this number.

SRI has discontinued coverage of the fact book in favor of a more detailed annual report, *Coal Data*, described under A7400-5, above. The fact book continues to be available from the issuing agency, at the address noted in A7400-5.

A7400–7   STEAM ELECTRIC PLANT FACTORS, 1984

Annual. 1984. iv+137 p.
ISSN 0090-3884.
LC 73-641171.
SRI/MF/not filmed

Annual report on steam electric plant operations and fuel use, 1983. Presents detailed data on capacity; generation; and fuel deliveries, consumption, quality, origins, and cost; by fuel type, shown variously by plant, utility, State, census division, and North American Electric Reliability Council region.

Also includes selected summary trends from 1977; capacity of plants scheduled to come on stream through 1993; plant construction delays; and capacity, generation, and status of coal conversion plants.

Contains foreword, and listing of contents and tables (p. i-iv); 1 chart and 17 tables (p. 1-128); lists of holding companies, jointly-owned companies, and utilities (p. 129-134); and 2 maps (p. 135-136).

Previous report, for 1983, was also reviewed by SRI during 1984 [Annual. 1983. iv+119 p. Members †, nonmembers $100.00, nonprofit organizations $75.00]. SRI coverage of this report begins with the 1983 edition.

Availability: National Coal Association, Publications Department, 1130 17th St., NW, Washington DC 20036-4677, members †, nonmembers $100.00, nonprofit organizations $75.00; SRI/MF/not filmed.

A7400–8   STEAM ELECTRIC MARKET ANALYSIS

Monthly. Approx. 40 p. var. paging.
SRI/MF/not filmed

Monthly report presenting operating data for individual steam electric plants, arranged by State. Data are compiled by the National Coal Assn. Reports are issued 2 months after month of coverage.

Contains 3 monthly tables, listed below. SRI coverage of this report begins with the Aug. 1983 issue.

Availability: National Coal Association, Publications Department, 1130 17th St., NW, Washington DC 20036-4677, members †, nonmembers $300.00 per yr.; SRI/MF/not filmed.

Issues reviewed during 1984: Aug. 1983-Aug. 1984 (D).

MONTHLY TABLES:

[Tables show data by individual plant, arranged by operating utility and State. Data are shown for month of coverage, generally with comparisons to same month of previous year.]

[1] Fuel consumption [for coal, oil, and gas] and [coal] stockpiles at electric utility plants.

[2] Generation at steam electric plants capable of burning coal [with distribution by fuel type].

[3] Generation at nuclear steam electric plants.

**A7400–9   POWER PLANT COAL
DELIVERIES**
Monthly.   Approx. 60 p. var.
paging.
SRI/MF/not filmed

Monthly report on volume, cost, and quality of coal delivered to power plants, by census division, State, and plant. Also includes source mine. Data are compiled by National Coal Assn. Reports are issued 3 months after month of coverage.

Contains 4 monthly tables, listed below. SRI coverage of this report begins with the July 1983 issue.

Availability: National Coal Association, Publications Department, 1130 17th St., NW, Washington DC 20036-4677, members †, nonmembers $500.00 per year; SRI/MF/not filmed.

Issues reviewed during 1984: July 1983-July 1984 (D).

MONTHLY TABLES:

[Tables [2-4] show data for month of coverage. Quality measures variously include average Btu per pound, sulfur and ash content as percent of coal weight, and sulfur content range.]

[1] Steam coal [volume and] prices [for contract, spot, surface, and underground coal deliveries, for month of coverage and same month of previous year; table begins with the Nov. 1983 issue].

[2-3] Summary: [volume], cost, and quality of contract, surface, underground, and spot coal deliveries, by State and census [division].

[4] [Volume], cost, and quality of coal delivered to electric utilities [with source mine type and location, and selected summaries for contract and spot coal deliveries, all by individual plant, arranged alphabetically by operating utility and also indicating State].

A7440
National
Collegiate Athletic
Association

**A7440–1   REPORT NUMBER SIX ON
THE INTERCOLLEGIATE
ATHLETIC, PHYSICAL
EDUCATION, AND
RECREATIONAL
PROGRAMS of the Member
Institutions of the National
Collegiate Athletic
Association**
Quinquennial.   Feb. 1984.
59 p.   Rpt. No. 6.
SRI/MF/complete

Quinquennial report on college and university sports and recreational programs for 1981/82 school year, with selected trends from 1957. Includes data on intercollegiate and intramural sports, physical education courses, and informal recreation programs and clubs. Also includes data on facilities, personnel, and finances.

Data are estimates for the 753 active member institutions of National Collegiate Athletic Assn (NCAA), based on responses from 436 institutions surveyed. NCAA member institutions are

classified into 7 groups (Class A-G) based on level of competition (Divisions I-III) and dominance of football or basketball.

Contains foreword (p. 2); contents listing (p. 3); 5 charts and 20 tables, described below, with brief accompanying narrative (p. 4-57); and conclusions (p. 58-59).

Previous report, for 1976/77, is described in SRI 1980 Annual under this number.

Availability: National Collegiate Athletic Association, Nall Ave. at 63rd St., PO Box 1906, Mission KS 66201, †; SRI/MF/complete.

TABLES AND CHARTS:

[Data are for 1981/82, with trends as noted. Data generally are shown by institution class. Tables showing sports or activities generally include number of institutions and student participants, for 20-50 individual sports.]

a. Men's and women's intercollegiate sports, with participation trends from 1956/57 (men) and 1966/67 (women), and number of contests (varsity, junior varsity, freshman, and average per institution). 6 tables, 4 charts. (p. 4-23)

b. Intramural sports; required physical education, with trend from 1957; and physical education activities; with selected detail by sex. 5 tables, 1 chart. (p. 25-35)

c. Recreational club and informal recreation activities, including student participants by sex and other participants. 4 tables. (p. 37-44)

d. Facilities, personnel, and finances: institutions and units, by facility type, with trends from 1961/62; value of indoor and outdoor facilities; facility use by nonstudent groups; full- and part-time personnel, by position; coaches, by sport; and operating costs for intercollegiate and intramural sports, physical education, and clubs. 5 tables. (p. 46-57)

A7460
National Conference
of Catholic Charities

**A7460–1   NCCC ANNUAL SURVEY,
1982**
Annual.   Oct. 1983.
viii+47 p.
ISSN 0161-4894.
LC 78-643453.
SRI/MF/complete

Annual report, for 1982, on activities and operations of the National Conference of Catholic Charities, including personnel, funding, and services. Report is based on survey responses from agencies in 120 dioceses.

Contains listings of contents, tables, and charts (4 p.); introduction (p. vii-viii); narrative report in 5 parts, with 9 charts, and 23 tables listed below (p. 1-33); reports from 3 national assns, with text statistics (p. 35-41); and appendix, with list of participating agencies (p. 43-47).

This is the 5th annual survey.

Availability: National Conference of Catholic Charities, 1346 Connecticut Ave., NW, Washington DC 20036, $7.50; SRI/MF/complete.

TABLES:

[Tables show data for 1982, unless otherwise noted.]

A7460–1.1: Administrative Information
ORGANIZATION AND PERSONNEL

1. Organizational structure [of reporting diocesan agencies]. (p. 1)

2-3. Categories of personnel [religious and lay staff by sex]; and personnel by ethnic group [white, black, Hispanic, Asiatic, and other; all by position]. (p. 2-3)

4-5. CETA-sponsored personnel; and volunteer activities [number of volunteers]. (p. 5)

FINANCES

6-7. Income sources [and trends from 1978]; and expenditures; [by category]. (p. 6)

A7460–1.2: Services and Activities
SERVICES

[Tables show number of agencies offering services and number of persons served. Tables 8-12 show services by category, including counseling, foster family and group home and day care, emergency shelter and financial assistance, homemaker and adoption services, and other specified services as applicable.]

8-10. Services to families/children, youth, and the aging. (p. 9-12)

11. Services to the physically ill/handicapped, mentally ill/retarded, and drug abusers/alcoholics. (p. 13-14)

12. Services to population at high risk: unmarried parents, abused children and adults, divorced/separated persons, prisoners/probationers, military families, Native Americans, refugees/other immigrants [Cuban, Southeast Asian, European, Western Hemisphere, and other], and chronically homeless [by sex]. (p. 15-20)

13. Health, education, recreation, employment, legal, and housing services. (p. 22-23)

LEGISLATIVE AND COMMUNITY ACTIVITIES

14-15. Legislative action [by type of issue]; and influencing public policy implementation, general policy and Title XX comprehensive annual services plan, [by type of action; generally showing number of dioceses involved at national, State, and local levels]. (p. 24-25)

16-17. Community organizing [groups involved, by type of issue]; and community program development. (p. 25-26)

18-19. Convening issues [participants and convenings, by type of issue and group]. (p. 27)

PARISH PROGRAMS

20. Deployment of personnel in parish programs. (p. 28)

21. Parish social ministry programs: parish, social service, and community organization/constituency development [activities]. (p. 29-30)

FAMILY LIFE PROGRAM AND RESEARCH

22. Family life [program] relationship: directors, and implementation of Bishop's Plan [shows diocesan organization and activities]. (p. 32)

23. Research [includes agencies employing research directors; administering research programs, by funding source; and participating in external projects, by type of conducting organization]. (p. 33)

A7485
National Cotton Council of America

A7485-1   COTTON COUNTS ITS CUSTOMERS: The Quantity of Cotton Consumed in Final Uses in the U.S., Revised 1981-82 and Preliminary 1983

Annual. 1984. vi+110 p.
SRI/MF/not filmed

Annual report on cotton and other material consumption in textile product manufacture, by end use, 1981-83. Covers 92 detailed product categories in apparel, home furnishing, and industrial sectors.

Data are from textile manufacturers and Census Bureau.

Contains foreword and contents listing (p. iii-vi); 2 summary tables, including rankings of 92 major end-use product categories by cotton consumption, 1983 (p. 1-19); and 1 detailed table showing production, gray cotton material requirement, and total and cotton material consumption, by detailed end use within each product category, 1981-83 (p. 20-110).

Availability: National Cotton Council of America, Economic Services, PO Box 12285, Memphis TN 38112, members †, nonmembers $50.00, 40% discount to public and educational institution libraries; SRI/MF/not filmed.

A7485-2   ECONOMIC OUTLOOK FOR U.S. COTTON, 1984

Annual. Feb. 1984.
28 p.+App 72 p.
SRI/MF/not filmed

Annual report on cotton economic performance and outlook, including production, consumption, foreign trade, acreage, crop value, prices, and production costs, various years 1950s-85. Includes data on other fibers, cottonseed and cottonseed products, and world supply and demand.

Contains contents listing (1 p.); narrative report, with 32 text tables and charts, including some projections for 1984/85 (p. 1-28); and appendix, with table listing, and 69 tables described below (72 p.).

Availability: National Cotton Council of America, Economic Services, PO Box 12285, Memphis TN 38112, †; SRI/MF/not filmed.

TABLES:
[Data are for U.S., unless otherwise noted.]

a. General economic indicators, including retail sales for apparel stores and CPI for apparel/upkeep; and textile industry indicators, including mill inventory/shipment ratio and inventory/unfilled order ratio for cotton gray goods, and textile mill and apparel/other textile employment and average hours; various periods 1964-83. Tables A.1-A.14 and B.1-B.5. (19 p.)

b. Mill fiber consumption, for cotton, wool, silk/wool, and man-made fibers by type; man-made fiber-producing capacity, by fiber type; denim and corduroy production and related cotton consumption; and textile imports, exports, and balance for man-made fiber, cotton, and wool; various periods 1959-85. Tables C.1-C.7 and D.1-D.9. (16 p.)

c. World and foreign fiber consumption, by fiber type; foreign cotton acreage and production, for importing and exporting countries; and U.S. and foreign cotton stocks, production, consumption, and trade; various years 1974-83. Tables E.1-E.3 and F.1-F.2. (5 p.)

d. Cotton planting intentions, by region or State, for 1984/85 crop year; and cotton planted and harvested acreage, production, and yield, by State and/or region, and value and harvested acreage compared to selected other crops, various years 1964/65-1983/84. Tables G.1-G.9. (9 p.)

e. Raw cotton exports by country of destination; cotton price index; mill-delivered prices of staple cotton, polyester, and rayon; spot cotton prices; and upland cotton prices received by farmers; various periods 1972/73-1983. H.1-H.2 and I.1-I.4.(6 p.)

f. Cottonseed and cottonseed product data, including production (with detail by State for seed), seed consumption and crushings, prices, value, and yield; and cotton production costs, including average gasoline prices paid by farmers in Cotton Belt States; various periods 1964-83. J.1-J.10 and K.1-K.4. (14 p.)

A7505
National Council for US-China Trade

A7505-1   CHINA BUSINESS REVIEW

Bimonthly. Approx. 75 p.
ISSN 0163-7169.
LC 74-643476.
SRI/MF/not filmed

Bimonthly journal reporting commercial and economic information of special interest to exporters and importers engaged in U.S.-China trade. Covers developments in China's economy, U.S. Government regulations, and news of scientific, technical, and other exchanges or agreements between China and other countries.

Data are from U.S. and Chinese Government publications, press releases, private industry, and other sources.

Journal includes feature articles and editorial depts, some with statistics; and "China Business" and "China Data" sections, described below, with recurring data on China foreign business arrangements and trade, and key domestic socio-economic indicators.

"China Business" section appears in all issues. "China Data" section appears when data are available. Additional features with substantial statistical content are described, as they appear, under "Statistical Features;" page location and latest period of coverage for "China Data" section are also noted. Nonstatistical contents are not covered.

Availability: China Business Review, 1050 17th St., NW, Suite 350, Washington DC 20036-5559, $90.00 per yr., academic libraries $60.00, faculty/students $48.00, single copy $15.00; SRI/MF/not filmed.

Issues reviewed during 1984: Nov./Dec. 1983-Sept./Oct. 1984 (P) (Vol. 10, No. 6; Vol. 11, Nos. 1-5).

STATISTICAL SECTIONS:

CHINA BUSINESS
["China Business" section consists of tabular lists describing recently reported foreign business arrangements, as noted below, current to approximately 4-6 weeks prior to cover date. Lists include nature, value, and status of each arrangement, and parties involved. Lists of sales and negotiations appear in every issue. Lists of joint ventures and other arrangements appear when data are available.]

a. China's imports and exports: sales and negotiations, by type of industry or commodity.

b. Direct investment/processing/countertrade: includes joint ventures, compensation trade, licensing, coproduction, leasing, and/or processing/assembly.

CHINA DATA
["China Data" section consists of 1 extended table showing all or some of the following data, generally for 4-6 preceding years, sometimes with projections for current year. Table content may vary, depending on data availability.]

a. Key indicators, including GNP, population, and industrial and agricultural output; official price index; State budget revenues and expenditures; and currency in circulation.

b. Output by detailed commodity, for industry consumer goods, and agriculture.

c. Foreign trade, total and with principal trading partners; and total, foreign exchange, and gold reserves.

STATISTICAL FEATURES:

A7505-1.501: Nov./Dec. 1983 (Vol. 10, No. 6)

FISCAL RELATIONS

(p. 25-27) By Audrey Donnithorne. Article on China Central Government fiscal problems, including provincial subsidies and military expenditures, 1957-80. Data are from World Bank, and China Ministry of Finance and State Statistical Bureau.

Includes 3 tables showing total and per capita subsidies (in domestic and U.S. currency) 1980, and population 1979, for 11 Provinces; and central government revenues, and total and defense expenditures (overt and CIA estimates), various years 1957-80.

A7505-1.502: Jan./Feb. 1984 (Vol. 11, No. 1)

CHINA DATA, RECURRING FEATURE

(p. 52-53) Most data are shown for 1977-83; for data description, see A7505-1 above.

CHINAMAGS

(p. 18-19) By Carol S. Goldsmith. Brief article, with 1 table comparing the publishing histories of 27 Chinese language trade journals issued by U.S. publishers during 1981-84. Includes the following for each publication, grouped by subject category: publisher and year established; advertising cost, as of Jan. 1984; and circulation and periodicity (including discontinued), as of Oct. 1981 and Jan. 1984.

Data are from PennWell Publishing Co. and *China Business Review.* Data provide updated information for a similar article published in the Sept./Oct. 1981 issue (for description see SRI 1981 Annual, under A7505-1.206).

INSURING THE CHINA TRADE

(p. 20-21) By D. C. Chan Wai-Kown et al. Article on insurance coverage of U.S. companies doing business in China. Data are based on responses of approximately 180 U.S. corporations with current or planned China operations, to a June-Aug. 1983 survey conducted by China America Insurance Company, Ltd.

Includes 2 charts showing percent of respondents involved in selected types of business activity, and percent covered by 11 types of insurance.

WAY AHEAD

(p. 34-37) By John Stuermer. Article on the outlook for China's balance of payments through 1988. Data sources include author's estimates based on IMF, U.S. Government, and other reports.

Includes 3 charts and 2 tables showing foreign trade of China and 3 other Asian countries; China trade and current account balances, and capital flows, with detail by commodity or financial item; international reserves by type, for China, U.S., and 12 other countries; and U.S.-China trade levels; various years 1978-88.

WORLD BANK LOANS TO CHINA

(p. 38-39) Table on World Bank loans to China, showing the following for each transaction completed or under negotiation, FY82-85: project name, actual or expected approval date, loan amount, and products to be purchased. Also includes list of projects planned for FY86.

Table is accompanied by a related article (p. 40-45).

A7505–1.503: Mar./Apr. 1984 (Vol. 11, No. 2)

FOREIGN INVESTMENT DELAYS

(p. 4) Brief article, with 1 table showing number of approved Chinese-foreign joint equity ventures in China, inside and outside special economic zones, 1980-83.

FIVE YEARS OF U.S.-CHINA TRADE

(p. 18-19) By Jeffrey L. Lee and JeNelle Matheson. Article, with 2 tables showing value of U.S. exports to and imports from China, by commodity, 1979-83. Data are from Dept of Commerce.

BUSINESS REGISTRATION IN CHINA

(p. 24-35, passim) By Jamie P. Horsley. Article, with 1 table and 1 chart showing office rental costs in Beijing, by hotel. Also includes inset article, with 1 table showing minimum, average, and deluxe office budgets, by item, for foreign companies in Beijing; and list of foreign businesses with offices in Beijing and Shanghai. No data dates are provided.

Data are from National Council for U.S.-China Trade and other sources.

A7505–1.504: May/June 1984 (Vol. 11, No. 3)

CONFERENCE FACILITIES IN CHINA

(p. 12-15) By Rudy Wright and Sarah Wright. Article, with list of major conference centers in 6 Chinese cities, generally showing the following for each center: completion and/or renovation date; rooms and rates; meeting rooms and seating capacity; restaurants; other features/services; and quality rating.

Data are from Convention and Conference Consultants, Inc.

CHINESE LABOR

(p. 16-25) By Jamie P. Horsley. Article on China labor costs and practices. Data are from Chinese government sources. Includes 3 charts showing labor costs per worker for typical State-owned enterprise and typical foreign joint equity venture, 1983; and average annual wage in State-owned enterprises, by region and industry sector, 1982.

MICROCOMPUTERS IN CHINA

(p. 26-29) By James B. Stepanek. Article, with two charts showing China's inventory of domestic and imported microcomputers and mini/mainframe computers, and number of units produced or imported annually, 1977-85.

Data sources include China Ministry of Electronics Industry and Chinese media reports.

INSTRUMENT SALES

(p. 40-46) By Erin McGuire Endean. Article, with 1 table showing U.S. exports of scientific instruments to China, by type of instrument, 1979-83. Data are from National Council for U.S.-China Trade, U.S. Commerce Dept and industry sources, and *Japan Economic Journal*.

Also includes list of China-foreign joint venture agreements for the manufacture of scientific instruments, with names of partners and date of agreement.

CIVIL AVIATION'S GROWING PAINS AND OPPORTUNITIES

(p. 50-55) By Madelyn C. Ross. Article, with 1 chart and 1 table showing number and type of runways and navigational aids, and airports available for substitute use, for China's 7 international and 8 alternate airports (no date); and U.S. exports of aircraft/engine parts to China, 1973-83.

Data are from International Civil Aviation Organization, U.S. Dept of Commerce, and National Council for US-China Trade.

CHINA'S RISING DEMAND FOR HELICOPTERS

(p. 56-57) by Madelyn C. Ross. Article, with 1 table showing the following for U.S.-manufactured helicopters used in China for geophysical and petroleum related activities: number, type, air base, and owner and operator, 1984. Data are from U.S. industry representatives, and National Council for US-China Trade.

EXPORT CONTROLS: WHERE CHINA FITS IN

(p. 58-62) By Madelyn C. Ross. Article, with 1 table showing number and value of China export licenses approved by Dept of Commerce, and number denied and returned without action, 1981-84; and number and value of licenses approved for 7 Commodity Control List (CCL) restricted categories, 1st quarter 1984. Data are from U.S. Commerce Dept.

A7505–1.505: July/Aug. 1984 (Vol. 11, No. 4)

CHINA IN SPACE

(p. 12-24) By Bradley Hahn. Article on development of China's aerospace program. Data sources include Hahn Associates International.

Includes 3 tables showing purpose, date placed in service, operating authority, and

specifications, for marine vessels in space support fleet; launch date and carrier system, specifications, orbital parameters, and decay date, by spacecraft; and launch date, purpose, specifications, and orbital parameters, for planned spacecraft; all as of early 1984.

DEFENSE MODERNIZATION

(p. 40-45) By Christopher M. Clarke. Article, with 1 table showing China's defense budget in yuan and U.S. dollars, and as a percent of total national budget, 1977-84. Data are author's estimates.

A7640
National Education Association

A7640–1 ESTIMATES OF SCHOOL STATISTICS, 1983/84
Annual. Apr. 1984. 43 p.
LC 59-914.
SRI/MF/complete

Annual report estimating enrollment, attendance, instructional staff, and finances of public elementary and secondary schools, by State, for 1983/84 school year, with revised estimates for 1982/83 and trends from 1973/74. Also includes data on school districts.

Report is compiled by NEA Research Division from Dec. 1983 estimates of State education officials.

Contains contents and table listing, foreword, and 2 summary tables (p. 1-7); narrative report, with text tables showing trends from 1973/74 (p. 9-25); 11 detailed tables, listed below, with explanatory notes (p.26-40); and glossary (p. 41-43).

This is the 42nd edition of the report.

Availability: National Education Association, NEA Professional Library, PO Box 509, West Haven CT 06516, members $4.95 (Order No. 3090-7-40), nonmembers $12.95 (Order No. 3090-7-50); SRI/MF/complete.

TABLES:

[Tables show revised estimates for 1982/83 and preliminary estimates for 1983/84 for public elementary/secondary schools, by State and region. Data on enrollment and classroom teachers are shown separately for elementary and secondary schools.]

1. Number of basic administrative units [operating and nonoperating school districts]. (p. 30)

2. Fall enrollment. (p. 31)

3-4. Average daily membership and average daily attendance in public elementary/secondary day schools, and number of public high school graduates. (p. 32-33)

5-6. Number of instructional staff members, by type of position [and, for classroom teachers, by sex]. (p. 34-35)

7. Average annual salaries of total instructional staff and of classroom teachers. (p. 36)

8-9. Revenue and nonrevenue receipts [from Federal, State, and local/other sources]. (p. 37-38)

10-11. Expenditures [total and per pupil current expenditures for schools, current expenditures for other programs, capital outlay, and interest on school debt]. (p. 39-40)

A7640–3 SALARIES SCHEDULED FOR FACULTY IN HIGHER EDUCATION, 1982/83
Annual. May 1984. 23 p.
SRI/MF/complete

Annual report on higher education faculty salary schedules for academic year 1982/83. Based on NEA survey of 1,048 private and public 2- and 4-year degree-granting institutions utilizing faculty salary schedules.

Report presents data on high, low, median, mean, and 1st and 3rd quartile minimum and maximum scheduled salaries, by faculty rank and degree attainment; by public and private institution type and enrollment size. Also includes aggregate data on salary percent increase from 1981/82.

Contains contents listing (p. 1); narrative analysis, with 6 text tables (p. 5-10); table listing (p. 11); and 12 detailed tables (p. 12-23).

Availability: National Education Association, NEA Professional Library, PO Box 509, West Haven CT 06516, members $2.50 (Order No. 1671-8-20), nonmembers $6.95 (Order No. l671-8-30); SRI/MF/complete.

A7640–5 PRICES, BUDGETS, SALARIES, AND INCOME
3 issues per year, discontinued.

Recurring report on public higher education and elementary/secondary teacher salaries, discontinued with Feb. 1983 report (for description, see SRI 1983 Annual, under this number).

NEA is currently establishing a computerized data bank, including compensation statistics. Information on the availability of statistics can be obtained from local NEA offices.

A7640–6 NATIONWIDE TEACHER OPINION POLL, 1983
Annual. Sept. 1983. 15 p.
SRI/MF/complete

Annual survey report on public school teachers' views regarding education-related issues. Topics include the following:

a. Educational issues: quality of public education; job satisfaction; student truancy, discipline, and violence; computers in education; censorship; reductions in teaching personnel; performance evaluation; appropriate uses for standardized tests; and differential compensation policies, including salary supplements for outstanding teachers.

b. Political and legislative issues: nonteaching duties in compliance with Federal legislation; community support for legislation affecting education funding; importance of political candidates' position on public education; tuition tax credits for parents of children in non-public schools; influence of selected public interest groups; and President Reagan's performance.

Also covers teachers' demographic, socioeconomic, and professional characteristics.

Data are based on responses of 1,490 teachers to a 1983 survey.

Contains foreword and contents listing (p. 1-2); and narrative report with text data, 5 charts, and 5 tables (p. 3-15).

This is the 24th annual survey.

Availability: National Education Association, NEA Professional Library, PO Box 509, West Haven CT 06516, members $2.50 (Stock No. 3082-6-20), nonmembers $4.75 (Stock No. 3082-6-30); SRI/MF/complete.

A7640–7 RANKINGS OF THE STATES, 1984
Annual. July 1984. 71 p.
ISSN 0077-4332.
LC 74-176052/R76.
SRI/MF/complete

Annual report presenting State rankings pertaining to public education, including school enrollment, faculty, and finances; and population, income, and general government finances; various periods 1980-1983/84, with some trends from the 1970s. Report focuses on elementary/secondary education, but also includes some data on higher education.

Data are from NEA research, Federal agencies, and *Sales and Marketing Management, Survey of Buying Power.*

Contains foreword, and contents listing (2 p.); 9 statistical sections, with notes and narrative summaries, and 124 tables described below (p. 6-64); and bibliography, glossary, and table index (p. 65-71).

This is the 27th annual report.

Availability: National Education Association, NEA Professional Library, PO Box 509, West Haven CT 06516, members $6.00 (Order No. 3092-3-40), nonmembers $14.95 (Order No. 3092-3-50); SRI/MF/complete.

TABLES:
[All tables show rankings of States, with U.S. total or average, by the items noted below. Data are for public elementary/secondary schools, unless otherwise noted. Tables on revenue and expenditures include comparisons to per capita income in addition to the data noted. Abbreviations: ADA (average daily attendance) and ADM (average daily membership).]

a. Population, including total, change from 1973, detail by age group, and density; and live births; various periods 1973-83. 12 tables. (p. 7-10)

b. Enrollment and attendance, including number of school districts, enrollment number and as percent of school age population, ADA, ADM, private school enrollment share, and percent of public/private school pupils participating in Federal school lunch program, various periods 1980-1983/84; percent change in high school graduates, 1978/79-1983/84 period; and higher education total enrollment and percent women, fall 1982, with total change from 1981. 14 tables. (p. 12-16)

c. Faculty, including FTE instructional and noninstructional staff in local schools and public higher education institutions, Oct. 1982; pupil/teacher ratios, fall 1983; percent male teachers, 1983/84; and average salaries for teachers and instructional staff 1982/83-1983/84, and for higher education faculty at 2- and 4-year public institutions 1982/83, with selected trends from 1973/74. 25 tables. (p. 19-27)

d. General financial resources, including total and per capita personal and disposable income; personal income per school age child and per pupil in ADA; government enterprise personal income as percent of total income; farm income; and effective buying income and retail sales per household; 1982, with selected comparisons to 1972 and 1981. 16 tables. (p. 30-35)

e. Government revenue, including State and/or local government per capita general revenue, and total and property tax revenue and/or collections; 1981/82. 12 tables. (p. 38-41)

f. School revenue, including amount per pupil; and percent from local, State, and Federal sources; 1982/83-1983/84. 11 tables. (p. 43-46)

g. Government expenditures and debt, including State and/or local government expenditures for all functions, public welfare, health/hospitals, police and fire protection, and highways; and capital outlay, interest on debt, and long-term debt outstanding; all shown per capita, mostly for 1981/82. 10 tables. (p. 49-52)

h. School expenditures, including State and/or local government per capita expenditures for higher education and local schools, and for education as percent of total expenditures, 1981/82; and per pupil expenditures, 1982/83-1983/84, with percent change from 1973/74. 17 tables. (p. 54-59)

i. Miscellaneous, including Federal Government civilian employees; ratio of government employees to population and as percent of employees in nonagricultural establishments; physician- and dentist-population ratios; and crime rate; 1981 or 1982. 7 tables. (p. 62-64)

A7680
National Electrical Contractors Association

A7680–1 OPERATION OVERHEAD, 1982
Triennial. 1983. 44 p.
SRI/MF/complete

Triennial report on finances of electrical contractors, FY82. Presents industry averages for 12 financial ratios; sales and profits; and expenses by category, with detail for overhead expenses by item. Includes data by payroll size, shown by U.S. region and for Canada.

Also includes average capital investment as percent of sales, trends in sales and after-tax profit from FY69, and survey sample characteristics.

Data are from 648 responses to an NECA membership survey.

Report is intended to enable individual contractors to compare their financial performance with that of similar contractors.

Contains introduction, 1 chart, and contents listing (p. 1-3); user guide, with 5 tables (p. 4-5); 2 statistical sections, with 1 chart and 35 tables (p. 6-42); and 2 self-evaluation forms (p. 43-44).

This is the 28th edition. SRI coverage begins with this edition.

Availability: National Electrical Contractors Association, 7315 Wisconsin Ave., Bethesda MD 20814, $10.00 (prepaid); SRI/MF/complete.

A7800
National Farm and
Power Equipment
Dealers Association

A7800-1   EQUIPMENT DEALERS 1983 COST OF DOING BUSINESS STUDY: Agricultural, Industrial, Lawn and Garden
Annual. [1984.] 15 p.
SRI/MF/complete

Annual report presenting U.S./Canadian agricultural, industrial, and lawn/garden equipment dealers' average operating and financial data, 1983, with summary comparisons to 1982. Report is intended to enable individual dealers to compare their performance with industry averages.

Includes sales and margins for new and used equipment, parts, service, other lines, and rental/lease income; expenses by item; assets and liabilities; inventory by type; personnel by function; and financial and productivity ratios; shown for each type of dealer, with detail by region and/or sales volume for agricultural equipment dealers.

Additional data for agricultural equipment dealers include inventory turnover; investment in fixed assets by type; and average sales and profit, by selected State and region and for Ontario.

Data are based on 1,240 responses to an NFPEDA survey of approximately 11,000 U.S. and Canadian agricultural and industrial equipment dealers, and selected U.S. lawn/garden equipment dealers.

Contains 6 trend charts (cover, p. 7); methodology and analysis, with 6 summary tables (p. 2-6); 5 tables (p. 8-14); and explanation of terms (p. 15).

Availability: National Farm and Power Equipment Dealers Association, 10877 Watson Rd., St. Louis MO 63127, $7.50; SRI/MF/complete.

A7815
National Federation
of Independent Business

A7815-1   NFIB QUARTERLY ECONOMIC REPORT for Small Business
Quarterly. Approx. 30 p.
ISSN 0362-3548.
LC 76-642389.
SRI/MF/not filmed

Quarterly report on the expectations of small business firms concerning economic conditions affecting their own business and business in general. Data are from a survey of NFIB members, conducted quarterly since 1973. Report is issued approximately 4 months after date of coverage.

Contains contents listing; narrative report with trend and summary charts, and generally 25-30 tables on survey topics described below; and appendices, with 4 tables showing characteristics of responding firms, and facsimile survey questionnaire.

Report data are also available on computer tape; for information, contact Faculty Associates, Inc., Box 181, Redwood Valley CA 95470.

Availability: National Federation of Independent Business, Research and Education Foundation, Capital Gallery East, Suite 695, 600 Maryland Ave., SW, Washington, DC 20024, †; SRI/MF/not filmed.

Issues reviewed during 1984: Oct. 1983-Apr. 1984 (D) (Nos. 41-43).

TOPICS:
[For each topic noted below, 2 or more tables and/or charts are presented, showing response for current survey, usually with comparison to selected earlier surveys and occasionally with detail by industry or census division.]

a. Sales and earnings levels compared to prior quarter; expected sales level for next quarter; and reasons for higher or lower earnings.

b. Employment change, current job openings, and expected net labor force changes for next quarter.

c. Price and compensation levels compared to prior quarter, and planned changes for next quarter; (compensation data begin with the Apr. 1984 issue).

d. Inventory change during prior quarter, current adequacy, and planned change for next quarter.

e. Capital expenditures, including whether made in last 6 months, by type of expenditure; distribution, by size of expenditure; and whether expected in next 3-6 months.

f. Credit conditions and accounts receivable, including interest rate on short-term loans; interest rate and loan availability compared to prior quarter; and expected credit availability for next quarter.

g. Outlook: expected general business conditions over next 3-6 months, and climate for small business expansion in next quarter; and most important problem (such as taxes, inflation, interest rates, and government regulation).

A7815-2   CREDIT, BANKS, AND SMALL BUSINESS
Monograph.   May 1983.
1+55 p.+errata sheet.
SRI/MF/not filmed

Survey report on participation by small businesses in financial markets, 1982, with comparisons to 1980 and selected trends from 1970s. Includes data by sales, asset, and employment size; years in business; industry; census division; urban vs. rural location; and State bank branching law status. Covers the following topics:

a. Sources of financing, including detail for new businesses; use of government assistance programs; and borrowing frequency, with trends.

b. Characteristics of most recent loan, including amount, maturity, year obtained, purpose, and collateral requirements; preapproved lines of credit, and compensating balance requirements; and interest rates, with trends.

c. Credit availability, including whether credit needs have been met; satisfaction with loan terms; reasons for loan refusals; and comparison of firms whose loan applications were accepted and rejected.

d. Banking relationships, including whether bank solicited business; perceived changes in bank competition; important factors in banking relationship; and assessment of own bank's performance.

e. Comparison of borrowing and nonborrowing firms, including trend in earnings, sales, prices, capital expenditures, and employment.

Data are based primarily on an Apr. 1982 NFIB membership survey, drawing 2,349 responses; and on a similar survey conducted in 1980.

Contains narrative analysis interspersed with 33 tables.

Availability: National Federation of Independent Business, Research and Education Foundation, Capital Gallery E., Suite 695, 600 Maryland Ave., SW, Washington DC 20024, †; SRI/MF/not filmed

A7830
National
Federation of State
High School Associations

A7830-1   NATIONAL FEDERATION HANDBOOK, 1983/84
Annual. 1983. 115 p.
LC 77-648224.
SRI/MF/complete

Annual yearbook of the National Federation of State High School Assns, whose members govern athletic competition and other interscholastic activities. Includes data on sports participation of member schools, by State, for 1982/83.

Contents:

a. Contents listing; and Federation information, including constitution and bylaws, history, programs, recommended athletic eligibility standards, and awards. (p. 2-72)

b. Athletic competition optional limitations; types of nonathletic competition sponsored; and types of athletic competition in which State championships are determined, for boys and girls; all by State. 3 tables. (p. 73-76)

c. Sports participation survey results, showing number of schools and participants, for boys and girls, by type of sport (total and by State and D.C.), and for 10 most popular sports, 1982/83 school year; and total sports participants by sex, 1971-1982/83. 6 tables. (p. 77-90)

d. Federation officers, staff, and committee members; and membership directory, including number of schools and students represented by each State, Canadian, and U.S. outlying area and military base assn. (p. 91-113)

Availability: National Federation of State High School Associations, Order Department, 11724 Plaza Circle, PO Box 20626, Kansas City MO 64195, $2.00+$2.00 handling; SRI/MF/complete.

A7830-2   NATIONAL HIGH SCHOOL SPORTS RECORD BOOK, 1984 Edition
Annual. 1984. 255 p.
ISSN 0192-978X.
LC 79-643196.
SRI/MF/complete

Annual compilation of all-time record scores and achievements for 15 interscholastic high school sports, often shown separately for boys and girls, current through 1982/83 school year. Also includes data on high school sports participation, by State. Data are from National Federation of State High School Assns members, representing approximately 89% of public/private high schools.

Contains contents listing and foreword (p. 3-4); record statistics, arranged alphabetically by sport (p. 6-240); participation survey results, with 2 summary tables, and 3 tables showing number of schools and students participating, by sex, sport, and State, 1982/83 (p. 242-251); and photo and other credits (p. 253-255).

This is the 6th edition of the *Record Book*.

Availability: National Federation of State High School Associations, Order Department, 11724 Plaza Circle, PO Box 20626, Kansas City MO 64195, $3.95+15% shipping and handling; SRI/MF/complete.

A7838
National Fire
Protection Association

A7838–1   FIRE FACTS
Annual, discontinued.

Annual report on fires and fire losses, and fire fighting developments, discontinued with 1982 edition (for description, see SRI 1982 Annual, under this number).

Report publication has been discontinued in favor of annual *Fire Almanac*, described under A7838-2, below.

A7838–2   1984 FIRE ALMANAC
Annual. 1983. vi+805 p.
NFPA No. FSP-62A.
ISSN 0736-6027.
ISBN 0-87765-263-5.
SRI/MF/complete, current & previous year reports

Annual report on fires and fire deaths, injuries, and economic losses, with data by type of property, cause of fire, and major incident, 1970s-83, with historical trends from as early as 1835. Also includes fire fighter employment, summary data for foreign countries, and extensive narratives on fire incidence and fire fighting developments and organizations.

Data are from National Fire Protection Assn and other specified sources.

Contains contents listing (p. iii-v), and the following:

Year in Review. Includes descriptions of significant world fires, 1982-83 (p. 4-23); 1 table (p. 13) showing U.S. fires with losses of more than $500,000 for which wood shingle/shake roof covering was contributing factor, 1972-83; and 1 map (p. 16) showing number of houses burned and deaths during Australia's "Ash Wednesday" bushfires, Feb.-Mar. 1983. (p. 1-42)

Organizations and People. Includes 1 table (p. 77-84) showing hospitals with burn care services, and number of burn care beds. (p. 43-130)

Fire Statistics. Includes 17 charts and 29 tables, described below. (p. 131-196)

Fire Service and Careers in the Fire Service. Includes 12 tables, described below. (p. 197-371)

Fire Fighter Safety and Problem of Arson. Includes 8 charts and 9 tables, described below. (p. 372-404)

Emergency Medical Service, Fire Service References, and Public Fire Safety Education. Includes 2 tables (p. 448-470) showing characteristics of emergency communication systems for selected U.S. and Canadian cities and counties, with resident population and land area. (p. 405-511)

Fire Protection in Business and Industry. Includes 8 charts and 13 tables, described below. (p. 512-566)

Fire Protection Standards, National Fire Protection Assn, and Hazardous Materials. Includes 1 table (p. 636-650) profiling hazardous material services offered by individual fire depts (arranged by State), with land area and population served. (p. 567-695)

International Fire Protection. Includes 6 charts (p. 697-703) showing fire loss per capita, per fire, and as percent of GNP; and fire incidence and death rates; for U.S. and 12 other countries, various periods 1965-80. (p. 696-713)

Legends and Lore, Reference, and Index. Includes 1 table (p. 780-781) showing chronology of major incidents involving fireworks, with deaths, injuries, and property loss, 1978-83. (p. 714-805)

Most sections include directories of fire fighter and fire safety organizations, suppliers of fire fighting equipment, or Federal and State agencies with fire interests.

This is the 2nd annual edition. Previous report, for 1983, has also been reviewed and is also available on SRI microfiche under this number [Annual. 1983. vi+792 p. NFPA No. FSP 62. ISBN 0-87765-247-3. $9.95]. Previous report is similar in format and content.

Prior to 1983, similar data were published in *Fire Facts;* for description of the final (1982) edition of that report, see SRI 1982 Annual, under A7838-1.

Availability: National Fire Protection Association, Batterymarch Park, Quincy MA 02269, $9.95; SRI/MF/complete.

STATISTICAL SECTIONS:

A7838–2.1: Fire Statistics

(p. 131-196) Contains 17 charts and 29 tables. Includes number of fire dept responses to non-fire incidents; fires, property loss, and civilian deaths and injuries, shown variously by type of property and fire, community size, region, cause, time of occurrence, and city (with population); and multiple-death and residential fires and characteristics; various years 1971-82.

Also includes chronology of major fires, with number of deaths, 1900-83; distribution of smoke detector owners and nonowners, by race, income, and education, 1982; and Maryland fire deaths, by age group, blood alcohol level, and medical cause, 1972-77 period.

Also includes the following data on forest fires: distribution by cause, by region, 1978; number by cause, with aggregate damages and acres burned, for 11 western States, 1981; and Bureau of Land Management fire protection services, 1981.

A7838–2.2: Fire Service and Careers in the Fire Service

a. Fire depts, equipment, stations, and budgets; area and population protected; emergency medical service operations; and career and volunteer fire fighters; shown variously by size of protected population by region, and for 96 metro areas with population over 200,000 or with at least 400 career fire fighters (no dates). 3 tables. (p. 198-207)

b. Fire station construction costs by component; and construction labor, material, and average costs, for approximately 500 U.S. and Canadian cities, 1983. 1 table. (p. 209-214)

c. Entrance and maximum fire fighter salaries, by city arranged by region and population size, 1982. 1 table. (p. 221-223)

d. Typical residential construction cost for single-family wood houses, and typical value of furnished rooms, by type of house or room, 1982. 2 tables. (p. 286-287)

e. Federal Government fire fighters, by agency and military service (no dates); and capacity and characteristics of fire fighter training facilities, by facility arranged by State (no dates). 5 tables. (p. 315-316, 364-371)

A7838–2.3: Fire Fighter Safety and the Problem of Arson

a. Fire fighter deaths in line of duty, by cause and type of injury, age, type of duty and property, rank, and years of service, with detail for volunteer vs. career personnel, various years 1975-82; and injuries and/or rates, by type of duty and injury, cause, community size, and region, with comparisons to number of fires, mostly 1981. 8 charts and 6 tables. (p. 374-385)

b. Civilian deaths and property loss in structure fires of incendiary and suspicious origin, with number of fires, 1978-82. 3 tables. (p. 396-397)

A7838–2.4: Fire Protection in Business and Industry

LARGE LOSS FIRES

a. Loss in specific fires, 1835-1982; and fires and property loss, with detail by loss size category, in constant and 1978 dollars, 1978-82. 2 charts and 6 tables. (p. 513-517)

b. Fires and property loss by type of property, 1978-82; distribution of fires and loss by cause, for storage, store, and manufacturing properties, 1973-82 period; and distribution of fires by time of occurrence, operating status of property at time of fire, and method of fire detection, 1982. 6 charts and 5 tables. (p. 518-523)

ARSON

c. Loss in structure fires of incendiary and suspicious origin, with number of fires, 1978-82. 2 tables. (p. 525)

A7850
National
Food Processors Association

A7850–1   CANNED FOOD PACK
STATISTICS, 1982-83
Annual.   Jan. 1984.   2+61 p.
ISSN 0069-018X.
LC 55-40089.
SRI/MF/not filmed

Annual report on canned vegetable and fruit production and shipments, mostly 1973-82, with some data for 1983, and selected trends from as early as 1899. Includes carryover, pack production, stocks, and shipments by commodity, with pack production detail for fruit juices, and by container size and producing State or area.

Also includes data on acreage and yield, and per capita consumption, for selected commodities; and salmon pack production by species.

Data are compiled by the National Food Processors Assn, and include data from the *Almanac of the Canning, Freezing, Preserving Industries,* USDA, and other Federal and private sources.

Contains foreword and contents listing (2 p.); 2 tables showing container and case specifications and conversion factors (p. 1-3); and 35 illustrative charts and 121 tables (p. 4-61).

Availability: National Food Processors Association, Economics and Statistics Division, 1401 New York Ave., NW, Washington DC 20005, $20.00; SRI/MF/not filmed.

A7870
National Forest
Products Association

A7870–1   FINGERTIP FACTS AND
FIGURES
Monthly, with quarterly
supplements.   Approx. 4 p.
ISSN 0470-0384.
SRI/MF/complete

Monthly report, with quarterly supplements, on lumber industry production, consumption, sales, employment, foreign trade, and related economic indicators, compiled by Copeland Economics Group for the National Forest Products Assn.

Data are from original studies and Census Bureau. Monthly data are current to 2 months prior to issue date. Quarterly data are issued 2-5 months after quarter of coverage.

Monthly report contains 7 tables, listed below, accompanied by 1 trend chart. Quarterly supplement contains 4 tables, also listed below. Monthly data appear in all issues; quarterly supplement accompanies the Feb., May, and Nov. issues.

Report is discontinued with the May 1984 issue. Selected data are continued in *Monthly Statistics for the Wood Products Industry,* described under A7870-2, below.

Availability: National Forest Products Association, 1619 Massachusetts Ave., NW, Washington DC 20036, $15.00 per yr.; SRI/MF/complete, shipped quarterly.

Issues reviewed during 1984: Oct. 1983-May 1984 (P) (Nos. 305-312); and 3rd Qtr. 1983-1st Qtr. 1984 supplements.

TABLES:
[All tables except table [E] show data for softwood and hardwood lumber. Tables [A-B], 1-2, and 4 show data by lumber region, defined by species (generally including southern and western pine, Douglas fir, California redwood, southern and Appalachian hardwood, and other).

Tables [D-F] show data for month of coverage, year to date, and percent change from previous month and same periods of preceding year. Table order may vary.]

MONTHLY TABLES

[A] Current monthly domestic production and trade statistics: estimated industry totals [production, shipments, and orders received, for month of coverage; and unfilled orders and gross stocks as of end of month; table includes data for flooring and structural panels].

[B] Seasonally adjusted [production and shipment] annual rates [for month of coverage, and percent change from previous month and same month of previous year].

[C] Year-to-date domestic lumber production and trade statistics [shipments and orders received; includes data for same period of previous year].

[D] International trade statistics [imports and exports, total and to and from Canada].

[E] Construction and housing statistics [new construction value, housing starts, building permits authorized, and mobile home shipments].

[F] Lumber consumption.

[G] Economic indicators [employment in lumber, furniture, all manufacturing, and total industries; and PPI for 18 construction materials, including selected lumber species; for latest quarter or month available, with percent change from previous period and same period of previous year].

QUARTERLY TABLES

[Data are shown quarterly for current year to date and 2 previous years, and annual averages for 6-8 earlier years.]

1. Estimated total regional lumber production, shipments, and new orders.

2. Estimated regional sources of domestic consumption of lumber (net imports allocated).

3. Imports and exports of lumber [by species].

4. Estimated gross mill stocks of lumber and estimated unfilled orders for lumber.

A7870–2   MONTHLY STATISTICS FOR
THE WOOD PRODUCTS
INDUSTRY
Monthly.   2 p.
SRI/MF/complete, shipped
quarterly

Monthly report on lumber industry production, consumption, shipments, new and unfilled orders, gross stocks, and foreign trade, compiled by Copeland Economics Group for the National Forest Products Assn. Report is issued approximately 2 months after month of coverage.

Contains 5 monthly tables, listed below.

Report begins with Apr. 1984 issue. Similar monthly data, with quarterly supplements, were published in *Fingertip Facts and Figures,* discontinued with May 1984 issue. For description, see A7870-1, above.

Availability: National Forest Products Association, 1619 Massachusetts Ave., NW, Washington DC 20036, members $5.00 per issue, nonmembers $10.00 per issue; SRI/MF/complete, shipped quarterly.

Issues reviewed during 1984: Apr.-Aug. 1984 (D).

MONTHLY TABLES:
[Data are shown for softwood and hardwood lumber, with additional detail as noted. Lumber producing regions are defined by species.

Tables [3-4] show data for month of coverage and year to date, with percent change from previous month and/or same period of preceding year.]

[1] Estimated industry totals [production, shipments, orders received, and end-of-month unfilled orders and gross stocks, by lumber] producing region [with aggregate data on flooring and structural panels, for month of coverage, with summary comparisons to previous month and same month of preceding year].

[2] Year-to-date domestic lumber production, and trade statistics [shipments and orders received, for current and previous year].

[3] International trade statistics [imports and exports, with detail for railroad ties and for trade with Canada].

[4] Lumber consumption.

[5] Seasonally adjusted annual rates [of production and shipments, with softwood detail by lumber producing region, for month of coverage with percent change from previous month and same month of preceding year].

A7900
National Funeral Directors
Association of the U.S.

A7900–1   STATISTICAL ABSTRACT
OF FUNERAL SERVICE
FACTS AND FIGURES of the
U.S., 1983 Edition
Annual.   Sept. 22, 1983.
6+108 p.
SRI/MF/complete

Annual survey report, by Vanderlyn R. Pine, on funeral home operators' income, expenses, and service price ranges, FY82. Report is based on a 1983 survey of 836 operators reporting 125,819 funerals.

Contains a preface with survey questionnaire facsimile, and contents listing (6 p.); and 2 maps, and 129 detailed tables listed below (p. 1-108).

Previous report, for FY81, is described in SRI 1982 Annual, under this number.

Availability: National Funeral Directors Association of the U.S., 135 W. Wells St., Suite 600, Milwaukee WI 53203, nonprofit and educational institutions $10.00, others $50.00; SRI/MF/ complete.

TABLES:

[Tables show data for the U.S. and by census division, FY82, unless otherwise noted. Most data are percentages or averages. Table numbers begin with 2.]

A7900–1.1: Characteristics and Income Sources of Reporting Firms

2-3A. Source of survey data: [number of firms participating and number of funerals reported, by State]; and percentage of firms reporting, average number and percentage of all services conducted, and total number for firms reporting, per volume category. (p. 2-3)

4. Form of ownership [individual proprietorships, partnerships, and public and private corporations]. (p. 4)

5. Collection procedures [allowing cash discounts, charging interest, and using sales contracts and finance plans]. (p. 4)

6. Personnel [percent of licensees among employees and owners, and firms with retirement and profit-sharing plans]. (p. 5)

7. Motor equipment [percent operating ambulance service, owning and renting all or part of motor equipment, and pooling equipment with others]. (p. 5)

8. [Average] investment [per funeral, by category]. (p. 6)

9-11. Charges as a percent of gross sales for total adult services; [average] charges and [casket] cost; and average funeral charges per firm. (p. 6-8)

12. Interment receptacle [percent usage, and average sale and cost]. (p. 8)

A7900–1.2: Operating Income, Expenses, and Price Ranges

[Table titles beginning "Operating service income" generally show percent of total reported funerals and charges, and average funeral charge and casket cost, all by service category: child, welfare-adult, partial-adult (not all services provided by funeral home), and total-adult (all services provided by funeral home) by funeral charge dollar range.]

13-13.9. Operating service income. (p. 9-18)

14-14.9. Average funeral service operating expenses [for 8 items, including automobile, personnel, promotion, and taxes, by service category]. (p. 19-28)

14S. Selected expenses [employee and owner compensation, automobile, and building]. (p. 29)

15. Average margins (all services). (p. 30)

16-16.9. Funeral service operating income, operating expenses, and investment patterns by size category (average per services). (p. 32-41)

17-17.9. Selected findings [including ownership, personnel, compensation, investment, and collection data]. (p. 42-51)

18-18.9. Average and percentage per service income and expense statement for all services. (p. 52-61)

19-19.9. Ranges in prices of services offered. (p. 62-66)

20A-20J. Operating service income: nonveterans; all veterans; noneligible and eligible veterans; [veterans, by period of conflict; and] other eligible veterans; [U.S. totals only]. (p. 67-76)

21-24. Charges and [casket] costs for firms using single bi-, tri-, and multi-unit pricing. (p. 77-79)

25A-25B. Operating service income [by sex of deceased; U.S. totals only]. (p. 80-81)

26A-26C. Operating service income, by age [and sex of deceased. U.S. totals only]. (p. 82-84)

27. Operating service income, by arrangement status [non- and prearranged; U.S. totals only]. (p. 85)

28-28.9. Operating service income, partial-adult services. (p. 86-90)

29-30D. Average values, by competition category and by market area [population size] category [including operating income and expenses, merchandise costs, investments, and charges per funeral; U.S. totals only]. (p. 91-96)

31A-31D. Funeral service operating income, operating expenses, and investment patterns, by size category for firms using single, bi-, tri-, and multi-unit pricing (average per all services) [U.S. totals only]. (p. 97-100)

32A-32E. Charges and [casket] costs for funerals with final disposition burial, cremation, entombment, scientific donation, and other. (p. 101-103)

33-33.9. Balance sheet. (p. 104-108)

A7945
National Golf Foundation

A7945–1   STATISTICAL PROFILE OF GOLF in the U.S.
Annual. [1984.] 13 p.
Rpt. No. ST-1.
SRI/MF/complete

Annual report on golf facilities, presenting statistics on courses and golfers, 1983 and trends. Data are compiled by National Golf Foundation.

Contains contents listing (p. 1); and 7 charts and 11 tables described below (p. 2-13).

Availability: National Golf Foundation, 200 Castlewood Dr., North Palm Beach FL 33408, $20.00; SRI/MF/complete.

TABLES:
[Data are for 1983, unless otherwise noted. Types of facilities are private, daily fee, and municipal.]

a. Golfer profile, including average age, income, college education, rounds played annually, average score, and annual golf expenditure, by sex and public or private course; and golfer expenditure distribution by item.

b. Rounds played annually, by census division, and for men, women, juniors, and seniors, by facility type; 1983, with trends from 1957.

c. Facilities by type, selected years 1931-83; and regulation, executive, and par-3 golf facilities and 9- and 18-hole courses, by facility type, State, and census division.

d. Ratio of golf courses (total and public 18-hole) to population, by State and census division; men, women, and junior frequent and total occasional golfers, by type of facility, 1979-83; and statistical highlights, including number of electric and gasoline carts in use, and total golf course acreage and maintenance expenditures.

A7945–2   NATIONAL GOLF FOUNDATION 1983 MUNICIPAL SURVEY: Summary of Results
Biennial. [1983.] 4 p.
Rpt. No. MU-5.
SRI/MF/complete

Biennial report, for 1983, on municipal golf facilities, fees, operations, and finances.

Contains brief narrative; 3 tables and 1 map showing municipal courses by size of facility, average course acreage, and number of facilities by State and region, as of Jan. 1, 1983; and 1 detailed table showing the following for 18-hole courses by region and for all 9-hole courses, for 1982:

a. Playable days; rounds played by men and women; green fees, with increase for 1983-84; courses offering special rates; season tickets sold, and rates; and golf cart fuel types, rental rates, and use.

b. Income, and expenses including payroll and course maintenance; number of employees and percent unionized; salaries for golf pro and course superintendent; percent of pro shops and food/beverage services operated by city and concessions; and leasing activity.

Previous report, for 1981, is described in SRI 1981 Annual, under this number.

Availability: National Golf Foundation, 200 Castlewood Dr., North Palm Beach FL 33408, $1.50; SRI/MF/complete.

A7955
National Governors' Association

A7955–2   FISCAL SURVEY OF THE STATES, 1984
Annual. June 1984. 29 p.
ISSN 0198-6562.
LC 80-641033.
SRI/MF/complete

Annual report, for 1984, on financial condition of State governments. Includes general fund revenues, expenditures, and balances, by State and for Puerto Rico, FY83-85. Data are actual for FY83 and estimates for FY84-85, and are based on a spring 1984 survey of State budget officers.

Also includes aggregate trends in fund balances from 1979; and data on budget-balancing and austerity measures undertaken, including layoffs and hiring restrictions.

Contains contents listing (1 p.); narrative analysis, with text statistics, 2 charts, and 1 table (p. 1-10); and appendix, with 9 detailed tables (p. 12-29).

This is the 10th annual report.

Availability: National Governors' Association, Public Affairs Office, Hall of the States, 444 N. Capitol St., NW, Washington DC 20001, $7.00; SRI/MF/complete.

A7980
National Housewares Manufacturers Association

A7980–1   SURVEY OF ATTITUDES AND PURCHASE HABITS OF CONSUMERS OF HOUSEWARES PRODUCTS

Recurring (irreg.) July 1983.
60 p.
SRI/MF/complete

Recurring report on consumer attitudes and purchasing habits for housewares products, 1983, with comparisons to 1979 and 1974.

Includes importance of product price, color/design, size, brand name, selection, and warranty; perception of product quality and cost; purchasing habits, including purchases by retail outlet type, and amount spent for gifts; and sources of new product information; all for kitchen tools/gadgets, cooking/bakeware items, serving/buffet products, bathroom accessories, small electrical appliances, and outdoor products.

Also includes opinion on responsiveness to consumer needs, for housewares and 5 other consumer good industries; ownership of selected product types, with detail for microwave ovens and barbecue grills; expected durability of small appliances; types of kitchen decor, and kitchen and bathroom color selections; and purchasing frequency for food away from home.

Some data include detail for single households.

Data are from 1,940 responses to a 1983 survey conducted by B. Angell and Associates, Inc., and from 2 previous surveys.

Contains contents listing (p. 2); introduction, methodology, and overview (p. 3-8); survey results, in 6 sections, interspersed with 14 charts and 45 text tables (p. 11-57); and 1 table showing population distribution by selected sociodemographic characteristics (p. 60).

This is the 3rd edition of the report. For description of previous report, for 1979, see SRI 1980 Annual, under this number.

Availability: National Housewares Manufacturers Association, Publication Orders, 1324 Merchandise Mart, Chicago IL 60654-1273, †; SRI/MF/complete.

A7980–2   SEVENTEENTH ANNUAL MARKETING RESEARCH STUDY of Housewares Manufacturers, 1983

Annual. Apr. 1984. 16 p.
SRI/MF/complete

Annual report summarizing houseware manufacturers' sales and marketing activities, 1983, with some forecasts for 1984 and trends from 1966.

Includes data on manufacturers and sales by sales range and product category, sales to retailers and wholesalers by outlet type, consumer color preferences by product category, price changes and reasons for change, incidence of manufacturing within and outside U.S., prevalence of immediate order fulfillment, duration of accounts receivable, and anticipated economic and operational problems.

Data are from responses of 611 manufacturers participating in the 1983 NHMA International Housewares Expositions, to a survey conducted by B. Angell and Associates, Inc.

Contains methodology, and highlights with text statistics (p. 1-3); and survey report, with 5 charts and 12 tables (p. 4-16).

Availability: National Housewares Manufacturers Association, Publication Orders, 1324 Merchandise Mart, Chicago IL 60654-1273, †; SRI/MF/complete.

A8000
National Institute of Independent Colleges and Universities

A8000–2   FEDERAL STUDENT ASSISTANCE PROGRAMS: Research Materials for the Eighth Annual Meeting

Recurring (irreg.) Jan. 1984.
vii+55 p.
SRI/MF/complete

Recurring report on funding of Federal student assistance programs in higher education, FY80-84. Presents funding amount for 20 undergraduate, graduate, and professional programs, generally by State with detail by type of institutional control.

Undergraduate programs include: Pell, Supplemental Educational Opportunity, and State-Student Incentive Grants; College Work-Study program; National Direct Student, Guaranteed Student, PLUS, and Nursing Student Loans; Social Security Student Benefits, and Indian Higher Education Grants; and veterans education benefits, including Vocational Rehabilitation and Dependents/Survivors Educational Assistance programs.

Graduate and professional programs include: Graduate and Professional Opportunities, and Legal Training for the Disadvantaged programs; Health Education Assistance Loans; Health Professions Student Loan Program; National Health Service Corps Scholarships; and Scholarships for First-Year Students of Exceptional Financial Need.

Also includes higher education revenue distribution by source; average tuition/fees, and full-time enrollment, by State and type of institution; and data on State matching funds.

Report, distributed as background for discussions during the 8th annual meeting of National Assn of Independent Colleges and Universities/National Institute of Independent Colleges and Universities, is based primarily on Federal Government sources and is intended to serve as a reference guide to Federal student assistance programs.

Contains contents listing, introduction, and 1 summary table (p. iii-vii); 17 report sections, with narrative and 49 tables (p. 1-49); and appendices, with 2 charts and 2 tables (p. 51-55).

Report previously was issued annually and also included funding data for Federal categorical aid programs in postsecondary education. For description of prior report, issued in 1981, see SRI 1982 Annual, under this number.

Availability: National Institute of Independent Colleges and Universities, 1717 Massachusetts Ave., NW, Suite 601, Washington DC 20036, $10.00; SRI/MF/complete.

A8000–4   SUPPLEMENT TO OPENINGS, CLOSINGS, MERGERS AND ACCREDITATION STATUS OF INDEPENDENT COLLEGES AND UNIVERSITIES, Winter 1970 Through Summer 1979

Recurring (irreg.) 1983.
18 p.
SRI/MF/complete

Recurring report, by Julianne Still Thrift and Gerald Harrington, on independent college and university transitions, 1970-79, covering openings, closings, mergers, shifts to public control, and attainment of accreditation. Includes data on enrollment and other institution characteristics.

Data are from a survey of State postsecondary agencies and State assns of independent colleges and universities, *Education Directory,* and *Accredited Institutions of Postsecondary Education.*

Contents:

a. Highlights and methodology. (p. 1)

b. 5 tables showing openings, closings, mergers, shifts to public control, and accreditations, for 2-year, 4-year, and specialized schools, 1970-79. (p. 2-4)

c. 4 detailed tables listing institutions and branches undergoing transitions mentioned above, arranged by State and Puerto Rico, and showing the following for each institution: year entered in *Education Directory;* year founded; type and affiliation; whether single sex or coed; accreditation status as of Dec. 1979; and enrollment, 1978 or as noted. (p. 6-18)

Report supplements 3 other reports presenting cumulative data on the status of independent schools in the 1970s. Supplement contains selected information previously unreported, including data for the final 6 months of 1979, information on Puerto Rico, and new findings for selected institutions. The last previous report was issued in 1980 and is described in SRI 1980 Annual, under this number. Future reports will be published on an irregularly recurring basis.

Availability: National Institute of Independent Colleges and Universities, Suite 601, 1717 Massachusetts Ave., NW, Washington DC 20036, $5.00; SRI/MF/complete.

A8010
National League for Nursing

A8010–1   NLN NURSING DATA BOOK, 1983-84

Annual. 1984. xv+160 p.
Pub. No. 19-1954.
ISBN 0-88737-058-6.
LC 79-103040.
SRI/MF/complete, delayed

Annual report on registered and practical/vocational nursing (RN and PN) public and private education programs, students, and staff, by State, 1982 or 1981/82, with some data for 1982/83 and trends from as early as the 1960s. Includes data on program tuition and fees, and employment follow-up data for newly licensed nurses.

Data are from periodic surveys conducted by the NLN Division of Research.

Contains preface, contents and table listing, and explanatory notes (p. iii-xv); and 171 tables, interspersed with narrative, described below (p. 1-160).

This is the 6th edition of the report.

Availability: National League for Nursing, Publications Division, Ten Columbus Circle, New York NY 10019, $15.95, members 10% discount; SRI/MF/complete, delayed shipment in Dec. 1984.

TABLES:

[Data "by jurisdiction" are generally shown by region and by State and U.S. territory, including Guam, Puerto Rico, U.S. Virgin Islands, and, often, American Samoa. Most data are shown for 1982 or 1981/82; tables usually include trends for various years, from as early as 1962/63.

Data by program support source are for programs primarily funded publicly and privately. Data for minority students are for blacks, Hispanics, and American Indians/Orientals, and are generally for 1980/81 or Oct. 1981 only. Data by ethnic background are for American Indian/Alaskan Native, Asian/Pacific Islander, black, Hispanic, and white.]

A8010–1.1: Basic RN Education

[Data by type of nursing program are for baccalaureate, associate degree, and diploma programs, unless otherwise noted.]

BASIC RN PROGRAMS

[Most data are shown by type of nursing program.]

a. Basic RN programs by jurisdiction and number of schools; programs by support source, size of student enrollment by region, and NLN-accreditation status by jurisdiction; and number of baccalaureate nursing schools with and without basic nursing programs, by accreditation status. Tables 1-12. (p. 1-12)

b. Median annual tuition and additional mandated fees for full-time resident students, by program support source, cross-tabulated by jurisdiction and by size of student enrollment by region, 1982/83. Tables 13-20. (p. 13-20)

c. Admissions, by program support source and by jurisdiction, by NLN-accreditation status by jurisdiction, and for men and minority students by jurisdiction; and fall admission applications, disposition by program support source, vacancies, and number on waiting list, mostly by region. Tables 21-35. (p. 21-36)

d. Graduations: total and from NLN-accredited programs, by program support source and by jurisdiction; for men and minority students, by jurisdiction; from baccalaureate schools with and without basic and State-approved generic nursing programs; and from baccalaureate programs, by jurisdiction and by previous graduations from diploma and associate degree nursing programs. Tables 36-55. (p. 37-55)

e. Enrollments: by program support source; by NLN-accreditation status and for men and minority students, both by jurisdiction; in baccalaureate nursing schools with and without State-approved generic and basic nursing programs, and for baccalaureate

students by previous graduation from other program types, mostly by full- and part-time status; and net retention of students, by program support source and length, by region. Tables 56-72. (p. 56-72)

HIGHER DEGREE NURSING EDUCATION

[Some tables include data for 1982/83.]

f. Doctoral nursing programs, enrollments, and graduations, all by jurisdiction for nursing education depts. Tables 73-77. (p. 73-77)

g. Master's nursing programs, enrollments by jurisdiction and region, and graduations, with detail by NLN-accreditation status, functional area of study, and nursing content area; full-time enrollments in programs preparing for teaching and advanced clinical practice, by nursing content area; and ratio of master's to baccalaureate program graduations. Tables 78-91. (p. 78-87)

A8010–1.2: RN Faculty

[Most data are shown by RN program type, usually baccalaureate/higher degree, associate degree, and diploma.]

a. Full- and part-time nurse faculty and unfilled budgeted positions; and full-time nurse and non-nurse faculty by teaching status, by region. Tables 92-94. (p. 88-91)

b. Full-time nurse faculty: by highest earned credential and NLN-accreditation status; with master's and baccalaureate degrees, by nursing or non-nursing major; assigned exclusively to baccalaureate and/or higher degree programs; and by ethnic background; most by region. Tables 95-100. (p. 92-97)

c. Students and weekly teaching hours per faculty member for clinical and classroom setting, and by program support source, all by region. Tables 101-102. (p. 98-99)

d. Part-time nurse faculty: by highest earned credential and NLN-accreditation status; with master's and baccalaureate degrees, by nursing or non-nursing major; and by ethnic background; most by region. Tables 103-106. (p. 100-103)

e. Nursing education administrators, and full- and part-time nurse faculty by jurisdiction, both by highest earned credential; unfilled budgeted nurse faculty positions, by nursing content area; and ratio of vacancies to full-time faculty. Tables 107-111. (p. 104-108)

A8010–1.3: RN Student Follow-Up

[Tables show newly licensed RNs 6-8 months after Feb. or July 1982 licensure.]

a. By census division and State of residence at licensure, and by nursing program: by employment status, main reason for unemployment, length of time to find a job, full- or part-time employment status, type of employer and position, and annual salary for full-time work. Tables 112-125. (p. 109-120)

b. By nursing program: by age, sex, and marital status. Tables 126-128. (p. 121-122)

A8010–1.4: Basic PN Education

[Data by type of administrative control are for programs in secondary and trade/technical/vocational schools, junior and senior colleges, hospitals, and independent and government agencies.]

a. Basic PN programs by type (adult, high school, and high school extended); number of programs by jurisdiction, program support source, region, and type of administrative control; and median annual tuition and additional mandated fees for full-time resident students, by program support source, by jurisdiction and by size of student enrollment and region, 1982/83. Tables 129-134. (p. 124-129)

b. Admissions, graduations, enrollments, and fall admissions: by jurisdiction, program support source, and type of administrative control by region; and, except for fall admissions, for men and minority students by jurisdiction. Tables 135-153. (p. 130-148)

c. Applications, number on waiting list, vacancies, and disposition of applications, by region. Tables 154-155. (p. 149-150)

A8010–1.5: PN Faculty

a. Full-time nurse faculty: by whether teaching; by highest earned credential; with master's and baccalaureate degrees by nursing or non-nursing major; by ethnic background; and unfilled budgeted positions by specialization; most by region. Tables 156-162. (p. 151-154)

b. Students and weekly teaching hours per faculty member for clinical and classroom settings, by program support source and region. Tables 163-164. (p. 155)

c. Part-time nurse faculty: by highest earned credential; with master's and baccalaureate degrees by nursing or non-nursing major; and by ethnic background; most by region. Tables 165-168. (p. 156-158)

d. Administrators by highest earned credential; and full- and part-time nurse faculty by highest earned credential, and unfilled budgeted positions, both by jurisdiction. Tables 169-171. (p. 158-160)

A8010–2   EMPLOYMENT, MOBILITY, AND PERSONAL CHARACTERISTICS OF NURSES NEWLY LICENSED IN 1981: State Summaries, Volume 1
Annual. 1983.
319 p. var. paging.
Pub. No. 19-1934.
SRI/MF/complete, delayed

Annual report presenting detailed data on registered and practical nurses (RNs and PNs) newly licensed in 1981, by State. Covers demographic characteristics; type of education program completed; year of graduation; geographic mobility; employment status, including reasons for unemployment; salary; miles traveled to work; type of nursing employer and position; job search experiences; job market perceptions; and satisfaction with current job.

Demographic characteristics include age, sex, race/ethnic group, marital status, and household composition.

Data are from an NLN survey of all 76,910 RNs and 42,554 PNs licensed in 48 States (excludes Iowa and Colorado) and D.C., 1981. Response rates were 73% for RNs and 67% for PNs. Survey was conducted approximately 6 months after time of licensure.

Contains contents and table listings (p. v-viii); introduction (p. 1-7); Parts A-C, presenting survey findings in 9-18 tables repeated by State of residence at time of licensure (p. A1-A50) and time of survey (p. B1-B100), and State of employment at time of survey (p. C1-C100); and appendix, with 45 summary tables (50 p.)

This report is part of the 5th edition of a series that also includes reports on individual States (Volumes 2-50) showing similar data by health service area and county. The State reports are available from the issuing agency on microfiche only, and are not covered by SRI.

Availability: National League for Nursing, Publications Division, Ten Columbus Circle, New York NY 10019, nonmembers $30.00, members 10% discount; SRI/MF/complete, delayed shipment with the SRI 1984 Annual.

A8010-3   **NURSING AND HEALTH CARE**
Monthly. Approx. 55 p. cumulative pagination throughout year.
ISSN 0276-5284.
LC SC 82-684.
SRI/MF/excerpts, shipped quarterly

Monthly journal (except July and Aug.) reporting on topics of interest to nurses, primarily developments in nursing service, education, and research.

Issues contain feature articles, occasionally with statistics; and regular editorial depts.

Features with substantial statistical content are described, as they appear, under "Statistical Features." Each issue of the journal is reviewed, but an abstract is published in SRI monthly issues only when statistical features appear.

Availability: Nursing and Health Care, Technomic Publishing Co., 851 New Holland Ave., PO Box 3535, Lancaster PA 17604, members †, nonmembers $17.00 per yr., libraries and institutions $25.00 per yr.; SRI/MF/excerpts for all portions described under "Statistical Features;" shipped quarterly.

Issues reviewed during 1984: Nov. 1983-Oct. 1984 (P) (Vol. 4, Nos. 9-10; Vol. 5, Nos. 1-8).

STATISTICAL FEATURES:

A8010-3.501: Nov. 1983 (Vol. 4, No. 9)

WILL YOUR COMPUTER MEET YOUR CASE-MIX INFORMATIONAL NEEDS?

(p. 493-497) By Jane Fedorowicz. Article on computerized coordination of data for hospital services, administration, and finances. Data are from a survey of 77 hospitals in the Chicago, Ill., area, conducted by Hospital Financial Management Assn.

Includes 1 table showing hospital computer use or plans in selected administrative and patient care applications.

NURSES, POLITICAL PARTICIPATION, AND ATTITUDES TOWARD REFORMS IN THE HEALTH CARE SYSTEM

(p. 504-507) By Elisabeth Moore and Deborah Oakley. Article on nurses' political attitudes and participation, based on a July 1980 survey of 153 nurses, conducted by National League for Nursing and University of Michigan.

Includes 4 tables showing distribution of response to questions on nurses' role in politics;

voter registration, voting, and campaign activity; and changes needed in health care services, costs, and insurance.

CLINICAL LADDER

(p. 510-514) By Leah I. Aleksandrowicz and Sandra G. Dickau. Article, with 4 tables showing hypothetical costs for registered nurse recruitment and orientation, and implementation of a clinical nursing career advancement program, FY83-86. Data are from Greater Baltimore Medical Center.

A8010-3.502: Dec. 1983 (Vol. 4, No. 10)

FY84 APPROPRIATIONS BILL SIGNED

(p. 553) Brief article, with 1 text table showing HHS appropriations for nursing education and research, actual FY83-84 and Reagan Administration request FY84.

A8010-3.503: Apr. 1984 (Vol. 5, No. 4)

CONGRUENCE AMONG PRIMARY NURSES IN THEIR PERCEPTION OF THEIR NURSING FUNCTIONS

(p. 213-217) By Gwen Marram Van Servellen and Carl Joiner. Article on nurses' perceptions of the importance, time requirements, and proportion of patients involved, for 7 major nursing functions. Data are based on survey responses of 91 nurses and aides in 3 hospitals. Includes 5 undated tables.

A8010-3.504: June 1984 (Vol. 5, No. 6)

UPDATE: NURSING EDUCATION FUNDS, NIN, DRGs, AND EDUCATION

(p. 302-303) By Sally B. Solomon. Article, with 1 table showing congressional appropriations and/or funding authorizations, for selected nursing education programs, FY84-85.

A8010-3.505: Sept. 1984 (Vol. 5, No. 7)

GRADUATE EDUCATION IN GERONTOLOGICAL NURSING REVISITED

(p. 390-395) By H. Terri Brower. Article on status of graduate programs in gerontological nursing, based on 47 responses to a spring 1982 survey of 51 programs.

Includes 4 tables showing data on indicators of curriculum quality, relationship of student employment and traineeship support, and regional comparisons of enrollment characteristics including full-time vs. part-time, with selected detail for State and private schools.

A8010-3.506: Oct. 1984 (Vol. 5, No. 8)

USE OF GRADUATE ASSISTANTS IN NURSING EDUCATION

(p. 441-443) By Aloise Anne Zasowska and Lillian C. Solomon. Article, with 1 table showing criteria used by graduate nursing programs in selecting graduate assistants. Data are based on 67 responses to a national survey of 80 programs. No survey date is given.

A8010-4   **STATE-APPROVED SCHOOLS OF NURSING: R.N., 1984**
Annual. 1984. xiii+125 p.
Pub. No. 19-1961.
ISBN 0-88737-075-6.
SRI/MF/complete, delayed

Annual statistical directory of institutions with State-approved nursing programs. Includes data

on programs preparing students for licensure as registered nurses (RNs) and/or offering baccalaureate degrees for RNs previously graduated from associate degree or diploma programs. Data include enrollments as of Oct. 1983; admissions and graduations, Aug. 1982-July 1983; and fall admissions, Aug.-Dec. 1983; by institution, arranged by State or territory.

Also includes summary data on new and closed programs, Oct. 1982-83 period, with detail for graduates from closed programs, Aug. 1982-July 1983.

Programs covered are diploma; associate, baccalaureate, and master's degree; and doctor of nursing.

Data are from annual NLN survey of all nursing schools, conducted Aug. 1982-Dec. 1983, and cover approximately 1,450 schools offering 1,466 programs.

Contains preface, contents listing, and key to abbreviations and jurisdictions (p. v-xiii); directory of schools offering initial programs (p. 3-83) and offering baccalaureate degrees to RNs (p. 87-115); 2 summary tables (p. 119-121); and directory of nursing boards (p. 123-125).

This is the 42nd edition of the report.

Availability: National League for Nursing, Publications Division, Ten Columbus Circle, New York NY 10019, $11.95, members 10% discount; SRI/MF/complete, delayed shipment in May 1985.

A8010-5   **STATE-APPROVED SCHOOLS OF NURSING: L.P.N./L.V.N., 1984**
Annual. 1984. vi+81 p.
Pub. No. 19-1962.
ISBN 0-88737-093-4.
SRI/MF/complete, delayed

Annual statistical directory of institutions with State-approved programs preparing students for licensure as practical and/or vocational nurses (LPN and LVN), 1983. Includes data on enrollment as of Oct. 1983; admissions and graduations, Aug. 1982-July 1983; and fall admissions, Aug.-Dec. 1983; by institution.

Also includes summary data on number of schools, programs by type (adult, high school, and extended high school), admissions, enrollment, and graduations, by State and for U.S. territories; and lists of new and closed schools.

Data are from annual NLN survey of all schools offering LPN/LVN programs as of Oct. 15, 1983.

Contains preface and contents listing (p. iii-vi); key to abbreviations and jurisdictions (p. 2); directory of institutions (p. 3-69); 3 summary tables (p. 73-75); and directory of nursing boards (p. 79-81).

This is the 26th edition of the report.

Availability: National League for Nursing, Publications Division, Ten Columbus Circle, New York NY 10019, $10.95, members 10% discount; SRI/MF/complete, delayed shipment in May 1985.

A8010-6   **REGISTERED NURSES FIFTEEN YEARS AFTER GRADUATION: A Report of the Nurse Career-Pattern Study**
Monograph. 1983. x+85 p.
Pub. No. 19-1919.
SRI/MF/complete

Survey report on nurses' demographic characteristics, employment, education, geographic mobility, and career developments, 1960s-81. Includes data by type of degree, years since graduation, and other personal and professional characteristics.

Data are from the Nurse Career-Pattern Study of 6,983 registered nurses (RNs). Study participants were surveyed upon entering nursing programs in 1962, at graduation, and then at intervals through 1981.

Contains contents and table listings (p. v-x); introduction (p. 1-6); report, in 7 chapters, with 59 tables described below (p. 7-76); and appendix with questionnaire facsimile (p. 77-84).

Availability: National League for Nursing, Publications Division, Ten Columbus Circle, New York NY 10019, $9.95; SRI/MF/complete.

SURVEY RESULTS:

[Data show respondent distribution, usually by type of degree and years since graduation, and include numerous additional cross-tabulations among the data described below. Degree types are associate, diploma, and baccalaureate.]

a. Demographics: marital status, race (including Oriental), age, family income, whether primary or secondary wage earner in family, when marriage occurred, number of children, age of youngest child, husband's occupation, and index of husband's career success. Tables 1-12. (p. 8-15)

b. Labor force participation: years of nursing employment, full- and part-time nursing vs. other employment, reasons for not working in nursing and in any field, child care provisions, year of most recent nursing employment search, ease of finding any and desired nursing job, and reasons desired job was difficult to find. Tables 13-32. (p. 17-34)

c. Employment and further education: number of nursing employers during career, types of nursing employers, and nursing position and clinical field; and degree earned or program entered, and financing methods, for education following 1st nursing degree. Tables 33-45. (p. 37-49)

d. Geographic mobility and professional developments: residential changes, fulfillment of nursing expectations, RN licensure, organizational membership, planned vs. actual nursing employer and position, and satisfaction with choice of nursing program. Tables 46-59. (p. 52-66)

A8015
National League of Professional Baseball Clubs

A8015–1   NATIONAL LEAGUE GREEN BOOK, 1984
Annual.   1984.   1+112 p.
ISBN 0-88284-228-5.
SRI/MF/excerpts

Annual fact book, for 1984, presenting detailed information on National League baseball club teams and players, including performance statistics and game attendance for 1983 and past seasons, and performance records. Data are compiled by the National League.

Contains city franchise dates and other league information (inside front cover); contents listing (p. 1); team administrative personnel (p. 2-3); and the following:

a. Team information, including stadium specifications and game times, uniforms, player rosters and 1983 season performance data, manager biographies, past managers, rookie profiles, and players with college experience; and umpire information. (p. 4-41)

b. Comprehensive performance statistics for 1983 season, with trends for past seasons since early 1900s, including team and individual player performance, World Series games, 1983 and all-time records, award winners, player contract sales/trading, and league rules. (p. 42-104)

c. Attendance trends, 1901-83; attendance records; 1982-83 attendance at home and away games; and 1984 ticket prices, by team. (p. 105)

d. Press and public relations directories; 1984 schedules for regular season away games and for spring training games; and team headquarters during out-of-town games. (p. 106-112)

e. Home game schedule for 1984 season. (back cover)

Availability: Alfred Publishing Co., PO Box 5964, Sherman Oaks CA 91413, $7.95; SRI/MF/excerpt, p. 105 (attendance and ticket prices).

A8050
National Machine Tool Builders' Association

A8050–1   INDUSTRY ESTIMATES: Machine Tool Orders and Shipments
Monthly.   Approx. 10 p.
SRI/MF/complete, shipped quarterly

Monthly press release on value of machine tool industry domestic and foreign orders, shipments, and cancellations, for metal cutting and metal forming tools. Data are derived from reports submitted to the National Machine Tool Builders' Assn, and are issued 1 month after month of coverage.

Each issue contains narrative analysis; and 4 tables showing net and gross new orders, order

backlog, shipments, and cancellations, monthly and cumulatively for current year through month of coverage, with selected comparisons to previous year.

Issue for last month of each quarter usually includes an additional table showing quarterly orders and shipments for current and previous 5-7 years, generally with 3 accompanying charts showing trends from 1956. Three annual summary tables appear in the Jan. issue.

Availability: National Machine Tool Builders' Association, Publications, 7901 Westpark Dr., McLean VA 22102, $25.00 per yr. (or $40.00 per yr. with *Economic Handbook*); SRI/MF/complete, shipped quarterly.

Issues reviewed during 1984: Oct. 1983-Sept. 1984 (D).

A8050–2   1983-84 ECONOMIC HANDBOOK OF THE MACHINE TOOL INDUSTRY
Annual.   Aug. 1983.
325 p. var. paging.
ISSN 0070-8550.
LC 73-646105.
SRI/MF/complete

Annual compilation of data on the machine tool industry, 1982, with selected trends from 1950s and earlier. Report covers U.S. and world machine tool production, trade, employment, finance, and use; and also includes U.S. and world general economic data.

Data are compiled by National Machine Tool Builders' Assn from various Federal, international, and industry sources, identified in each table.

Contains 9 chapters with brief narrative reviews, 49 summary charts, and 245 detailed tables, described below (p. 1-265); and abbreviations, explanation of terms, and index (53 p.).

Report is 15th annual edition.

Availability: National Machine Tool Builders' Association, Publications, 7901 Westpark Dr., McLean VA 22102, members $14.00, nonmembers $25.00; SRI/MF/complete.

TABLES:

[Machine tool industry data often are shown separately for the metal cutting and metal forming sectors. Most production, shipment, and foreign trade data are shown as value and units.]

A8050–2.1: Economic Trends

U.S. DATA

a. Economic indicators, including GNP compared to all manufacturing and machine tool shipments, government receipts by level, and private investment; price deflators; corporate profits and tax liability; and Federal budget. 10 tables. (p. 4-11)

b. Balance of trade for machine tools/parts and all merchandise; U.S. direct foreign investment, by country or area; and capital investment of machinery industry and all manufacturing for foreign affiliates of U.S. companies, by country or area. 3 tables. (p. 12-14)

c. Plant and equipment investments, with machine tool share; manufacturing total and equipment purchases, depreciation, net investment, and net value; new and unspent capital appropriations; total and machinery/equipment depreciable assets gross book value; and property/plant/equipment net value; with selected detail for major machine tool-consuming industries. 8 tables. (p. 15-22)

d. Business loan interest rates; manufacturing capacity utilization, production indexes, inventories, new and unfilled orders, and shipments, for machine tool and/or major consuming industries; business cycle leading indicators, and troughs and peaks since 1854; PPI for machine tools and components; and national defense purchases and price deflators, by type. 25 tables. (p. 23-42)

WORLD DATA

e. GNP, fixed capital investment as percent of GNP, U.S. foreign investment, production and price indexes, export value index, foreign trade, balance of trade and payments, production worker earnings, and manufacturing productivity indexes, by selected country; Soviet Union trade with Communist and non-Communist countries; and U.S. trade with Communist countries. 14 tables. (p. 44-55)

f. Capital cost recovery allowances; and tax revenues as percent of GNP, by tax type, with detail for social security tax revenues; all by selected country. 3 tables. (p. 56-58)

A8050–2.2: U.S. Machine Tool Industry

a. Establishments, employees, value added, and shipment value, by region and State; establishments and employees, by employment size group; materials cost and consumption; inventories of finished products, work in process, and materials; and value of primary and secondary products. 14 tables. (p. 62-74)

b. Domestic and foreign shipments, new orders, and cancellations; unfilled orders; shipments, by machine average value and detailed type including numerically controlled/automated; and value of shipments by SIC 4-digit industry, and of military prime contract awards, both by type of machine. 31 tables. (p. 77-120)

c. Foreign trade, including imports as percent of domestic consumption, by machine type; total production, trade, and domestic consumption; and imports and exports, by country of origin or destination and detailed machine type. 29 tables. (p. 126-160)

A8050–2.3: World Machine Tool Industry

a. Summary world production, consumption, and trade, by country; export market shares of major producing countries; imports and exports of EC countries, by SITC 6-digit machine tool classification; and import share of domestic consumption for U.S., Japan, UK, and West Germany. 16 tables. (p. 163-184)

b. Detailed machine tool production and/or trade for West Germany, Japan, UK, Spain, France, Italy, Sweden, Switzerland, Netherlands, Canada, Argentina, Czechoslovakia, and Soviet Union.

Also includes employment for Germany, Japan, UK, Spain, and France; productivity for Germany; shipments and orders for UK and France; hours and earnings for France; companies and employment for

Sweden; and comparisons to other industrial production for Argentina and Soviet Union. 55 tables. (p. 186-228)

c. Production for PRC and for East Europe by country, with comparisons to U.S.; and Communist bloc imports by major non-Communist country of origin, and exports by area of destination. 4 tables. (p. 229-232)

A8050–2.4: Machine Tool Employment, Finances, and Use

[Data are for U.S., unless otherwise noted.]

a. Employment and payroll; production workers, hours, earnings, overtime, and work injury rates, with selected comparisons to other industries; labor turnover; female employment; earnings, by occupation and selected city; productivity; and earnings and/or supplemental labor costs in U.S. and 6-7 foreign countries. 20 tables. (p. 235-249)

b. Finances, including financial ratios, with comparisons to other industries; gross book value of depreciable assets; capital investments; and indexes of sales, profit, depreciation, stock value, and working capital. 5 tables. (p. 253-257)

c. Use of machine tools, including number in metalworking industries, by equipment type and age, industry, and selected city; total in other industries, training, and storage/surplus; and number in 6 foreign countries. 8 tables. (p. 260-265)

A8050–3   U.S. FOREIGN TRADE IN MACHINE TOOLS

Monthly.   Approx. 15 p. var. paging.
SRI/MF/complete, shipped quarterly

Monthly report on volume and value of U.S. machine tool imports and exports, by country of origin and destination, by type of machine. Data are from U.S. Dept of Commerce and National Machine Tool Builders' Assn, and are issued 2-4 months after month of coverage.

Each issue contains brief narrative analysis with 2-3 charts and 1 summary table; and 4 detailed tables showing trade data by specific type of machine tool (as defined in Tariff Schedules of the U.S.) for major trading partners, and by general category (metal cutting and forming) for other countries, for month of coverage, with selected year-to-date totals.

June and Dec. issues include additional summary tables, and 4 additional detailed tables presenting trade data for the 1st half and full year, respectively. Issues for the last month of each quarter include summary data for the quarter.

Availability: National Machine Tool Builders' Association, Publications, 7901 Westpark Dr., McLean VA 22102, $36.00 per yr. (prepaid); SRI/MF/complete, shipped quarterly.

Issues reviewed during 1984: Aug. 1983-July 1984 (D).

A8060
National Mass Retailing Institute

A8060–2   SECURITY AND SHRINKAGE: Annual Study of Inventory Shrinkage Control and Security Procedures in Retailing
Annual. Dec. 1983. 54 p.
LC 77-151334.
SRI/MF/complete

Annual report on retail industry inventory "shrinkage" and control measures, including use of security personnel, programs, and devices. Data are based on a 1983 Arthur Young & Co. survey of 86 mass merchandisers, 36 department stores, and 58 specialty stores, with operations in more than 36,000 locations. Also includes data on food retailers.

Contains contents listing and introduction (p. 3-5); narrative report in 12 sections, with 8 charts, and 37 tables described below (p. 6-47); and appendices I-II, with 3 tables on food retailers' shrinkage and control measures, and a loss prevention checklist (p. 48-54).

This is the 5th annual report.

Availability: National Mass Retailing Institute, 570 Seventh Ave., New York NY 10018, members $30.00, nonmembers $45.00; SRI/MF/complete.

TABLES:
[Most data are shown for 1982, generally as distributions for mass merchandisers, department stores, specialty stores, and all other respondents.]

a. Inventory shrinkage and sample characteristics: sample companies by sales size, number and urban-suburban location of stores, and shrinkage as percent of sales, with total shrinkage rate by region. Tables 1-5. (p. 6-9)

b. Shoplifting: apprehensions of employees by job category, total apprehensions, convictions as percent of apprehensions and prosecutions, and whether management policy and company expenditures emphasize apprehension or loss prevention. Tables 6-9. (p. 16-20)

c. Security practices: sample companies by security expenditure/sales ratio, and number of full-time security personnel; and security devices used on selling floor, with ratings of most and least effective methods. Tables 10-15. (p. 21-26)

d. Personnel practices: screening methods and prior experience deemed important in hiring security personnel; methods used to screen nonsecurity personnel; categories of employees given polygraph and psychological stress evaluator tests, and reasons for not administering tests; and whether polygraphs administered by employee or outsider. Tables 16-23. (p. 27-30)

e. Training and rewards: training programs used for security and nonsecurity personnel, and reward policies for improved loss prevention, by type. Tables 24-25. (p. 31-32)

f. Shrinkage comparisons: low vs. high shrinkage companies by sales size, security expenditure/sales ratio, use of security and nonsecurity personnel training programs, and security devices used on selling floor. Tables 26-37. (p. 36-47)

A8060–4   CONSUMER REBATE OFFERS from the Viewpoint of the Retailer, the Manufacturer, the Consumer
Monograph.   May 1983.
67 p.
SRI/MF/complete

Report on merchandise rebate programs, covering perceptions and practices of retailers, manufacturers, and consumers. Data are from responses of 46 retailers and 90 manufacturers to mail surveys of National Mass Retailing Institute members, and personal interviews conducted in Dec. 1982 with 1,129 consumers. All data were collected by Ralph Head & Affiliates.

Contains contents listing (1 p.); introduction and foreword (p. 1-2); summary (p. 3-20); details, with distribution of responses to survey questions on the topics described below (p. 21-66); and demographic characteristics of interviewed consumers (p. 66-67).

Availability: National Mass Retailing Institute, 570 Seventh Ave., New York NY 10018, members 1st copy †, additional copies $30.00 each; nonmembers $45.00; certified educational institutions $15.00; postage and handling $3.50; SRI/MF/complete.

SURVEY TOPICS:
[Data pertain to rebate programs, unless otherwise noted.]

RETAILERS

a. Adequacy of manufacturers' lead time, notification methods, and point-of-sale materials; coupon distribution methods and location in store; problems in signing and presentation of coupons by consumers; coupon outages; consumer complaints; characteristics of successful and unsuccessful programs; and general advantages and problems; most with respondents' recommendations for improvements. (p. 21-37)

MANUFACTURERS

b. Past and current use; types of products rebated, with rebate value; use of out-of-house rebate service; advertising methods; percent of applications received incomplete, and response; factors preventing rebate delivery; usual time between mailing application and receiving rebate; consumer complaints; and consumer fraud problem. (p. 39-44)

c. Lead time, notification, promotional materials, and cooperative advertising provided for retailers; consumer- and retailer-directed incentives; methods of determining number of coupons issued per store and evaluating program; coupon redemption rate, and redemptions by new users of products; programs with high and low redemption rates; problems with retailers, and solutions; and past use of rebates by product type. (p. 44-52)

CONSUMERS

d. Rebate use and plans, and reasons; and characteristics of rebate product purchases, including product type and price, whether impulse purchase, whether 1st use of product, type of outlet, source of information on rebate, rebate value, whether applied for rebate, and reasons for not applying. (p. 53-61)

e. Quality of rebated vs. other products; problems with rebates; response to lack of rebate coupons at store; preferred source of information on rebates; whether rebate/coupon

magazine subscriber or club member; and non-rebate coupon use and problems. (p. 61-66)

A8110
National
Office Products Association

A8110–1   NOPA DEALER OPERATING RESULTS, 1983
Annual.   1983.   68 p.
SRI/MF/not filmed

Annual report presenting median financial and operating data for office product dealers, 1982, with summary trends from 1972. Most data are shown by sales volume, region, and major product (office supplies or furniture).

Includes detailed balance sheet, income and expenses, and other financial and operating ratios; average sales and profit per employee and per square foot; average inventory turns; and distribution of companies by community size, number of stores, profitability, personnel structure, type of business organization, service personnel and average salary, and selected operating characteristics.

Report is based on data from 522 NOPA members, and is intended to permit individual dealers to compare their operations with industry averages.

Contents:

a. Contents listing; and introduction, methodology, and summary, with 2 charts and 3 tables. (p. 2-5)

b. 3 basic tables, generally repeated for all dealers, by sales volume, and for dealers with branch stores (p. 6-19); by region (p. 20-35); and by major product (p. 36-50).

c. 14 important financial ratios, with definitions and 3 tables. (p. 51-59)

d. Chart of accounts and worksheet. (p. 60-68)

This is the 54th annual report.

Availability: National Office Products Association, 301 N. Fairfax St., Alexandria VA 22314, price on request; SRI/MF/not filmed.

A8140
National
Paper Trade Association

A8140–2   PAPER MERCHANT PERFORMANCE for the Year 1983
Annual.   1984.
77 p. var. paging.
SRI/MF/complete

Annual report presenting average financial and operating performance measures for paper merchants, 1983, with trends from 1973. Covers approximately 40 ratios and other measures of sales, profitability, and management performance, including employee productivity, for printing, industrial, and dual paper merchants. Includes detail by sales volume; sales emphasis (direct, indirect, warehouse); profitability category; and NPTA region.

Also includes trends in printing PPI, and sample median and total sales.

Data are based on 226 responses to a 1984 survey of NPTA members, conducted by Management Foresight, Inc. Report is intended to permit individual firms to compare their operations to industry averages.

Contains contents listing (1 p.); introduction, and narrative report in 4 chapters interspersed with 24 text tables (p. 2-27); summary table list (p. 28); 12 summary tables (12 p.); and 7 appendices, including 1 table on sample characteristics, methodology, definitions, and facsimile questionnaire (34 p.).

Availability: National Paper Trade Association, 111 Great Neck Rd., Great Neck NY 11021, 1st copy $125.00, additional copies $35.00; SRI/MF/complete.

A8140–3   NPTA MANAGEMENT NEWS
Monthly.   Approx. 16 p.
ISSN 0739-2214.
SRI/MF/complete, shipped quarterly

Monthly report on industrial and printing paper wholesale business activity, with monthly sales data for 7 regions, and NYC, Chicago, and Los Angeles metro areas. Month of data coverage is 2 months prior to cover date.

Contains several regular editorial depts and 1 or more feature articles, occasionally with statistics, primarily reporting on industry news, management methods, and regulatory developments; and monthly "Paper Merchant Sales Report" section, containing 6 trend charts, and 1 table described below.

Monthly charts and table appear in all issues. All additional features with substantial statistical content are described, as they appear, under "Statistical Features." Nonstatistical features are not covered.

Availability: National Paper Trade Association, 111 Great Neck Rd., Great Neck NY 11021, $50.00 per yr.; SRI/MF/complete, shipped quarterly.

Issues reviewed during 1984: Nov. 1983-Oct. 1984 (P) (Vol. XXIV, Nos. 11-12; Vol. XXV, Nos. 1-10) [Mar. 1984 issue incorrectly reads Mar. 1983].

MONTHLY TABLE:
[Data are shown for industrial and printing papers, by region and for 3 metro areas.]

a. Percent change in sales activity per selling day, for month of coverage compared to previous month and to same month of previous year, and for year to date compared to same period of previous year.

b. Days outstanding for accounts/notes receivable at close of month of coverage, and calendar days' cost of ending inventory for month prior to month of coverage, both with comparisons to same month of previous year.

STATISTICAL FEATURES:

A8140–3.501: Nov. 1983 (Vol. XXIV, No. 11)

WAREHOUSING OPPORTUNITIES IN THE MID-EIGHTIES

(p. 7) Article on paper industry inventory management. Data are from NPTA's annual industry performance study, based on a member survey.

Includes 1 table showing warehouse performance indicators for printing, industrial, and dual paper merchants, 1982.

Full study report is covered in SRI under A8140-2.

A8140-3.502: Dec. 1983 (Vol. XXIV, No. 12)

QUARTERLY SALES AND PROFITS

(p. 7) Table showing sales and net income for 18 paper manufacturers, 3rd quarter 1983. Data are from *New York Times* and company reports.

GROSS PROFIT PER EMPLOYEE, THE KEY TO COMPENSATION

(p. 6) Article reporting on paper industry employee compensation practices. Data are from NPTA's annual financial ratio study, based on a member survey.

Includes 1 table showing the following for printing, industrial, and dual paper merchants: payroll, compensation, and fringe benefit value, per employee and as percent of gross profit; and gross profit per employee; 1982.

Full study report is covered in SRI under A8140-2.

A8140-3.503: Jan. 1984 (Vol. XXV, No. 1)

MILL CAPACITY IS ON THE RISE

(p. 9) Article, with 1 table showing mill capacity, start-up date, location, and paper grade, by company, for actual and planned mill expansions, 1982-86. Data are from American Paper Institute.

A8140-3.504: Feb. 1984 (Vol. XXV, No. 2)

RECENT TRENDS IN MERCHANT SALES AND INVENTORY

(p. 10-11) Article, with 3 tables showing sales and inventories of all, nondurable goods, and paper/paper products merchant wholesalers, with distribution by type of ownership; and distribution of merchant wholesalers by method of inventory valuation used; various years 1981-83. Data are from U.S. Dept of Commerce.

A8140-3.505: Mar. 1984 (Vol. XXV, No. 3)

INDUSTRIAL PAPER PRICE TRENDS BY COMMODITY TYPE

(p. 5) Table showing percent change in PPI for industrial paper by type, Dec. 1983 vs. Dec. 1982. Data are from BLS.

FEDERAL SPENDING ON SOCIAL PROGRAMS

(p. 15) Table showing Federal spending on social programs by program or agency, 1982-83. Data are from National Assn of Wholesaler-Distributors.

A8140-3.506: May 1984 (Vol. XXV, No. 5)

STUDY SHOWS INDUSTRIAL PAPER PRODUCTS SOLD BY DISTRIBUTORS OF SANITARY SUPPLIES AND EQUIPMENT

(p. 5) Article, with 1 undated table showing distribution of sanitary/maintenance paper product supplier sales, by product type. Data are from *Maintenance Supplies*.

LEANER INVENTORIES: A FUNDAMENTAL CHANGE IN OPERATIONS FOR THE 1980s

(p. 6, 12) Article on trends in paper industry inventories. Data are from Dept of Commerce and NPTA.

Includes 3 tables showing stock/sales ratio for paper/paper products and all wholesalers; inventory turnover, and gross margin return on inventory, for industrial, printing, and dual paper wholesalers; and calendar days cost of ending inventory for industrial and printing paper; various periods 1974-84.

INSURANCE COVERAGE: IS WHAT YOU HAVE RIGHT FOR YOUR COMPANY?

(p. 16) Article, with 1 undated table showing average sales, number of locations and employees, and insurance premiums by type, for all and paper wholesalers. Data are from National Assn of Wholesaler-Distributors.

A8140-3.507: July 1984 (Vol. XXV, No. 7)

[Data for the following articles are from NPTA's 1983 *Paper Merchant Performance* report; full report is covered in SRI under A8140-2.]

MERCHANTS RECOVER WITH STRONG SALES GAINS

(p. 6-9) Article, with 5 tables showing median sales, profitability, inventory turnover, and selected other performance measures, for printing, industrial, and dual paper merchants, 1982-83.

SALES PERSONNEL PRODUCTIVITY TRENDS

(p. 9-10) Article, with 1 table showing selected productivity measures for sales depts, outside representatives, and service personnel, for printing, industrial, and dual paper merchants, 1982-83.

A8140-3.508: Aug. 1984 (Vol. XXV, No. 8)

MEASURE YOUR ROTA! ANNUAL FEATURE

(p. 7) Annual article, with 1 table showing expense/gross profit ratios for 8 expense items, for printing, industrial, and dual paper merchants with high and low return on assets, 1983.

Data are from NPTA's annual financial ratio study, based on a member survey. Full study report is covered in SRI under A8140-2.

A8140-3.509: Sept. 1984 (Vol. XXV, No. 9)

RECENT CENSUS BUREAU STUDY RESULTS GOOD NEWS FOR INDUSTRIAL PAPER MERCHANTS

(p. 10-11) Article, with 4 tables showing the following for industrial/personal service paper wholesalers: sales distribution by product type; top 10 States ranked by total sales and by sales per establishment and employee, with U.S. totals, and per employee comparison by NPTA region; and percent change in sales, with comparisons to printing and dual firms, and CPI; various years 1977-83.

Data are from the Census Bureau, NPTA, and BLS.

MERCHANT INVENTORY CONTROL

(p. 40) Article, with 1 table showing selected inventory performance measures for industrial and printing paper merchants, with detail for merchants with high and low return on assets, 1982-83.

Data are from NPTA's annual financial ratio study, based on a member survey. Full study report is covered in SRI under A8140-2.

A8140-3.510: Oct. 1984 (Vol. XXV, No. 10)

SALES DEPARTMENT PERFORMANCE

(p. 7-8) Part 1 of a 2-part article on the performance of paper merchant sales depts. Data are from NPTA's annual industry performance study, based on a member survey.

Includes 1 table showing the following for printing, industrial, and dual paper merchants: median sales, pay/travel expenditures, profit, and inside sales service employees, all per outside sales representative, 1981-83.

Full study report is covered in SRI under A8140-2. Part 2 of the article will be published in the Nov. 1984 issue.

NAPL SURVEY FINDS PRINTERS 'NERVOUS ABOUT PAPER'

(p. 16) Article, with 1 table showing average order backlog for printing companies by type, as of 1st day of 1st 3 quarters 1984, with comparison to record high backlog during 1980-2nd quarter 1984 period. Data are from National Assn of Printers and Lithographers.

A8145
National Paperbox
and Packaging Association

A8145-1   59th ANNUAL FINANCIAL SURVEY OF THE RIGID PAPER BOX INDUSTRY
Annual. [1984.] 29 p.
SRI/MF/complete

Annual report, by Robert D. Landel, on rigid paper box industry finances and operations, 1983, with trends from 1967. Includes data on billings, sales, price and production indexes, pretax profits, financial and operating ratios, inventory and labor turnover rates, billing collection period, employment, user industries, and new and used equipment purchases, with detail by region and sales size category.

Also includes selected U.S. economic indicators.

Data are based on reports from National Paperbox and Packaging Assn members, and are intended to permit individual companies to compare their performance with that of similar companies.

Contains 1 section on the general economy (p. 1-10) and 2 sections on the paperbox industry (p. 11-29), with narrative analysis, 4 charts, and 16 tables.

Availability: National Paperbox and Packaging Association, 231 Kings Hwy., E., Haddonfield NJ 08033, members $25.00, nonmembers $50.00; SRI/MF/complete.

A8175
National Planning Association

A8175–5   1983 NATIONAL ECONOMIC PROJECTIONS SERIES

Annual series. For individual publication data, see below.
SRI/MF/not filmed

Annual series of 3 reports presenting long-term national economic trends and projections based on data from Federal agencies and NPA growth model.

The series provides continuously revised projections of major indicators for the economy as a whole and for industry divisions. The same indicators are covered each year, but the distribution of the data among the reports and the analytical focus may vary.

The 2nd volume of the 1983 series is described below. Volume 1 has not yet been published. The first 2 volumes of the 1982 series are described in SRI 1983 Annual under A8175–9; volume 3 is described below, under the same number.

Availability: National Planning Association, Center for Socio-Economic Analysis, 1616 P St., NW, Washington DC 20036, $900.00 per 3-volume set, $2000.00 joint subscription with Regional EPS series and all NPA publications, 50% discount for university and public libraries; SRI/MF/not filmed.

A8175–5.1: Sectoral Projections of the U.S. Economy, 1983-2000

[Monograph. Jan. 1984. vii+67 p. Rpt. No. 83-N-2. SRI/MF/not filmed.]

By Nestor E. Terleckyj and Martin K. Holdrich. Report presenting long-term economic trends and projections for industry divisions. Includes economic growth, labor productivity, employment, earnings, GNP, and hours, by industry division, 1947-2000.

Contains contents/table listing and preface (p. v-vii); narrative report, interspersed with 7 tables (p. 1-18); and statistical section, with 24 tables (p. 20-67).

A8175–6   1983 REGIONAL ECONOMIC PROJECTIONS SERIES

Annual series. For individual publication data, see below.
ISSN 0090-9262.
LC 73-641587.
SRI/MF/not filmed

Annual series, by Martin K. Holdrich, issued in 3 volumes, presenting regional, State, and local trends and projections for major economic and demographic indicators. Data are NPA estimates based on reports from Bureau of Economic Analysis (BEA), other Federal agencies, and the University of Georgia Institute for Behavioral Research.

Volumes I-III of the 1983 series are described below. Volume I of the 1982 series is described in SRI 1983 Annual, under A8175–10; volumes II and III of the 1982 series are described below, under the same number.

Data in this series also are available from the issuing agency on computer tape and in computer printout form.

Availability: National Planning Association, Center for Socio-Economic Analysis, 1616 P St., NW, Washington DC 20036, $1600.00 per 3-volume set, $2000.00 joint subscription with National EPS series and all NPA publications, 50% discount for university and public libraries; SRI/MF/not filmed.

A8175–6.1: Regional Economic Growth in the U.S., 1982-2000. Volume I: Population, Employment, and Income Detail for Nation, Regions, States, SMSAs; Projection Summaries for States, Counties

[Annual. Feb 1984. vii+412 p. Rpt. No. 83-R-1. SRI/MF/not filmed.]

Presents the following data: population, employment and earnings by industry division, and personal income by source, by region, State, and SMSA; and population, employment, and personal income, by State and county; all quinquennially 1970-2000. Earnings and income data are in 1972 dollars.

Also includes personal consumption expenditure index, 1967-81.

Contains contents listing and preface (p. v-vii); overview and methodology, with 2 charts and 10 summary tables (p. 1-36); 2 detailed tables (p. 38-347); and appendix, with list of counties comprising Bureau of Economic Analysis economic areas and SMSAs (p. 349-412).

A8175–6.2: Regional Economic Growth for States, Regions, and Economic Areas, 1982-2000. Volume II: Population, Employment, and Income Detail for Nation, Regions, States, Economic Areas

[Annual. Feb. 1984. xi+192 p. Rpt. No. 83-R-2. SRI/MF/not filmed.]

Presents the following data: population, employment and earnings by industry division, and personal income by source, by region, State, and BEA economic area, quinquennially 1970-2000. Earnings and income data are in 1972 dollars.

Contains contents listing and preface (p. v-xi); 1 detailed table (p. 1-127); and appendix, with list of counties comprising BEA economic areas (p. 129-192).

A8175–6.3: Regional Demographics in the U.S., 1982-2000. Volume III: Population by Age, Sex, and Race for U.S., Regions, States, BEAs, SMSAs

[Annual. Mar. 1984. vii+350 p. Rpt. No. 83-R-3. SRI/MF/not filmed.]

Presents the following data: total and white population by age and sex, by region, State, BEA economic area, and SMSA, 1970 and quinquennially 1980-2000.

Contains contents listing and preface (p. v-vii); methodology (p. 1-3); 1 detailed table (p. 5-286); and appendix, with list of counties comprising BEA economic areas and SMSAs (p. 287-350).

A8175–9   1982 NATIONAL ECONOMIC PROJECTIONS SERIES

Annual series. For individual publication data, see below.
SRI/MF/not filmed

Annual series of 3 reports presenting long-term national economic trends and projections based on data from Federal agencies and NPA growth model.

The series provides continuously revised projections of major indicators for the economy as a whole and for industry divisions. The same indicators are covered each year, but the distribution of the data among the reports and the analytical focus may vary.

The 3rd volume of the 1982 series is described below. For description of the 1st 2 volumes, see SRI 1983 Annual, under this number.

Availability: National Planning Association, Center for Socio-Economic Analysis, 1616 P St., NW, Washington DC 20036, $850.00 per 3-volume set, $1750.00 joint subscription with Regional EPS series and all NPA publications, 50% discount for university and public libraries; SRI/MF/not filmed.

A8175–9.3: Sectoral Projections II: Earnings and Prices, 1982-2000

[Monograph. Sept. 1982. vii+52 p. Rpt. No. 82-N-3. SRI/MF/not filmed.]

By Nestor E. Terleckyj and Martin K. Holdrich. Report presenting long-term economic trends and projections for industry divisions. Includes private business sector output, output and earnings per worker, and implicit output deflator, selected years 1948-2000; and total earnings, earnings per worker, and output price indexes, by industry division, 1947-2000. Earnings are in 1972 dollars.

Contains contents listing and preface (p. v-vii); and narrative report, interspersed with 12 tables (p. 1-52).

A8175–10   1982 REGIONAL ECONOMIC PROJECTIONS SERIES

Annual series. For individual publication data, see below.
ISSN 0090-9262.
LC 73-641587.
SRI/MF/not filmed

Annual series, by Martin K. Holdrich, issued in 3 volumes, presenting regional, State, and local trends and projections for major economic and demographic indicators. Data are NPA estimates based on reports from Bureau of Economic Analysis (BEA), other Federal agencies, and the University of Georgia Institute for Behavioral Research.

Volumes II and III of the 1982 series are described below; for description of Volume I, see SRI 1983 Annual, under this number. For description of 1981 series, see SRI 1983 Annual, under A8175–6.

Data in this series also are available from the issuing agency on computer tape and in computer printout form.

Availability: National Planning Association, Center for Socio-Economic Analysis, 1616 P St., NW, Washington DC 20036, $1400.00 per 3-volume set, $1750.00 joint subscription with National EPS series and all NPA publications, 50% discount for university and public libraries; SRI/MF/not filmed.

A8175–10.2: Long-Term Economic Outlook for the States, Regions, and Economic Areas of the U.S. Volume II: Population, Employment, and Income Detail for Nation, Regions, States, Economic Areas

[Annual. Apr. 1983. xi+171 p. Rpt. No. 82-R-2. SRI/MF/not filmed.]

Presents the following data: population, employment and earnings by industry division, and personal income by source, by region, State, and BEA economic area, quinquennially 1970-2000. Earnings and income data are in 1972 dollars.

Contains contents listing and preface (p. v-xi); 1 detailed table (p. 1-127); and appendix, with list of counties comprising BEA economic areas (p. 129-171).

A8175–10.3: Projection of Demographic Trends in the Regional Economies of the U.S., 1981-2000. Volume III: Population by Age, Sex, and Race for U.S., Regions, States, BEAs, SMSAs

[Annual. Aug. 1983. vii+352 p. Rpt. No. 82-R-3. SRI/MF/not filmed.]

Presents the following data: total and white population by age and sex, by region, State, BEA economic area, and SMSA, 1970 and quinquennially 1980-2000.

Contains contents listing and preface (p. v-vii); overview and methodology (p. 1-7); 1 detailed table (p. 9-289); and appendix, with list of counties comprising BEA economic areas and SMSAs (p. 291-352).

A8175–11   U.S. ECONOMIC POLICIES AFFECTING INDUSTRIAL TRADE: A Quantitative Assessment

Monograph. 1983. x+130 p.
CIR Rpt. No. 13, NPA Rpt. No. 200.
ISBN 0-89068-068-X.
LC 83-60013.
SRI/MF/complete

By Peter Morici and Laura L. Megna. Report quantifying protection afforded U.S. industries by Government nontariff measures that affect foreign trade, 1970s-80s. Presents tariff-equivalent estimates and other indicators of protection, by specific measure and industry. Covers the following measures:

a. Import-limiting practices that affect producer and consumer prices, including quantitative restrictions on imports of specific products, customs valuation and Government procurement activities, excise taxes, and product standards.

b. Domestic production subsidy programs, including loans, loan guarantees/insurance, technical assistance, R&D incentives, oil and gas price regulation, and industrial revenue bonds.

c. Export-promoting practices, including export credits through Export-Import Bank, loans and loan guarantees through Overseas Private Investment Corp., tax incentives for domestic international sales corporations, and bilateral foreign aid programs.

Also includes analysis of overall tariff and nontariff protection structure, by industry; and comparisons to protection measures in other industrial countries.

Data sources include International Trade Commission, Depts of Commerce and Labor, scholarly articles, and others. Sources are shown for each table.

Contains contents and table listings (p. iii-vi); introduction (p. 1-3); 5 chapters with narrative analysis and 46 interspersed tables (p. 4-104); 4 appendices on data sources and methodology,

with text data and 5 tables (p. 105-127); and NPA description, officers, and publications (p. 128-130, inside back cover).

Availability: National Planning Association, Center for Socio-Economic Analysis, 1616 P St., NW, Washington DC 20036, $12.00; SRI/MF/complete.

A8195
National Regulatory
Research Institute

A8195–1   ELECTRIC AND GAS UTILITY RATE AND FUEL ADJUSTMENT CLAUSE INCREASES, 1978-79

Monograph. Sept. 1981.
iv+188 p.
SRI/MF/complete

Report on electric and gas utility rate increases and fuel adjustment clause (FAC) revenues, 1978-79 and trends. Presents data on rate increases requested, granted, and pending with State public utility commissions; allowed and actual rates of return; total and FAC revenues; and FAC charges incorporated into basic rates; by utility and State, including D.C. and Virgin Islands, primarily 1978-79 with some data for 1980 and FAC revenue trends from mid-1970s.

Data are based on responses of 40 State public utility commissions to a 1980 National Regulatory Research Institute survey.

Contains contents listing (p. iv); 3 narrative sections interspersed with 11 summary tables (p. 1-39); and 2 appendices with questionnaire facsimile and 4 detailed tables (p. 43-188).

Similar reports, covering 1974-77, were issued by the Senate Committee on Governmental Affairs, and are covered in *CIS/Index.*

Availability: National Regulatory Research Institute, Publications Office, 2130 Neil Ave., Columbus OH 43210, $13.50; SRI/MF/complete.

A8200
National
Restaurant Association

A8200–1   NRA NEWS

Monthly. Approx. 40 p.
ISSN 0465-7004.
LC SN 78-5535.
SRI/MF/complete, shipped quarterly

Monthly trade journal (combined June/July issue) reporting on food service industry trends and developments. Covers retail sales, employment, customer characteristics, food prices, government regulation, and other topics of interest to food service executives.

Data are from the National Restaurant Assn (NRA) and Federal and private sources.

Each issue contains several feature articles and editorial depts, occasionally with statistics; and "Foodservice Trends" section, with the following statistical features:

a. Commodity price index, with 1 recurring table showing percent change in wholesale prices of approximately 15 food commodities, and in NRA food cost index and PPI (all food), for various periods current to 2-3 months prior to cover date.

b. Food service economic indicators, with 1-3 recurring tables showing percent change in selected indicators including CPI for food at home and away from home; food service average weekly earnings and hours; and sales for total food service industry, and commercial and eating place segments; for latest available period, with comparisons to previous periods.

c. Quarterly CREST (Consumer Reports on Eating-Out Share Trends) survey article, with 4 charts showing percent change in customer traffic, industry sales, and check size, by restaurant type, for quarter ending approximately 3 months prior to cover date, with comparison to previous periods; based on data compiled by NPD Research, Inc., from records maintained by a panel of 10,000 families and 2,800 nonfamily households.

Annual statistical features include franchise restaurant sales and establishments; food service sales trends and outlook; and review of industry operations.

Articles with substantial statistical content are described, as they appear, under "Statistical Features;" page locations and latest periods of coverage for recurring tables and CREST charts are also noted. Nonstatistical features are not covered.

Availability: NRA News, Publications Department, 311 First St., NW, Washington DC 20001, members †, nonmembers $125.00 per yr.; SRI/MF/complete, shipped quarterly.

Issues reviewed during 1984: Nov. 1983-Oct. 1984 (P) (Vol. 3, Nos. 10-11; Vol. 4, Nos. 1-9).

STATISTICAL FEATURES:

A8200–1.501: Nov. 1983 (Vol. 3, No. 10)

QUARTERLY CREST CHARTS

a. Restaurant customers, sales, and average check size, for summer 1983. (p. 36-39)

AMERICANS SHOW HEALTHY PREFERENCE FOR NUTRITIONAL FOODS

(p. 30-31) Article, with 2 tables showing percent of consumers reporting changed eating habits at home and in restaurants, by sex, age, educational attainment, income, and women's employment status; and by type of change, for restaurant dining.

Data are from responses to a survey conducted for NRA by the Gallup Organization.

EATING AND DRINKING PLACE FAILURE TRENDS

(p. 34-35) Article, with 2 tables showing number of business failures for eating/drinking places, selected periods 1940-82; and failure rate per 10,000 operating concerns, by type of retail business, 1981. Data are from Dun and Bradstreet.

A8200–1.502: Dec. 1983 (Vol. 3, No. 11)

**GLOWING YEAR AHEAD:
1984 NRA FORECAST,
ANNUAL FEATURE**

Annual compilation of articles on food service sales trends and outlook, with final data for 1981-82, revised estimates for 1983, and forecasts for 1984. Unless otherwise noted, data are prepared by NRA in consultation with Malcolm M. Knapp, Inc. Individual articles are as follows:

INDUSTRY SALES WILL TOTAL $157 BILLION IN 1984

(p. 11-21) Annual article forecasting food/drink sales for commercial, institutional, and military food services in 1984. Includes 3 charts and 3 tables showing sales for each food service segment and by detailed eating place type, various years 1981-84.

Also includes 1 chart (p. 16) showing 17 ethnic food types ranked by popularity in restaurants, with detail for patron ordering frequency. Data are from an NRA telephone survey of 800 adults, conducted in Aug.-Sept. 1983.

REGIONAL AND STATE-BY-STATE FORECAST

(p. 22-28) Annual article forecasting eating place sales, by State, 1983-84. Includes 2 tables, repeated for each census division, showing percent change in manufacturing and nonmanufacturing employment and in total personal income; and eating place sales, by State; 1983-84.

Employment and income data are from Commerce Dept, National Planning Assn, and the Conference Board.

FOOD AND DRINK PURCHASES PROJECTED TO REACH $65.2 BILLION IN 1984

(p. 29) Annual article forecasting food/drink purchases for commercial, institutional, and military food services in 1984. Includes 1 table showing purchases by detailed eating place type, 1984.

INDUSTRY SALES REACH $144.2 BILLION IN 1983

(p. 30) Annual article, with 1 table showing food/drink sales, by eating place type, 1982-83.

CONSUMERS WANT TO EAT OUT MORE OFTEN

(p. 31-32) Annual article comparing consumers' current and desired levels of eating-out activity, by sex, income, household size, and age. Data are from a Sept. 1983 NRA-sponsored Gallup poll of 1,181 adults, with comparisons to Sept. 1982 poll. Includes 2 charts.

A8200–1.503: Jan. 1984 (Vol. 4, No. 1)

RECURRING TABLE

a. Commodity price index, for Oct. 1983. (p. 34)

STARTING ON THE ROAD TO SUCCESS

(p. 19-20) Article analyzing characteristics of successful restaurants. Data are from NRA. Includes 1 undated table showing distribution of restaurant customers by reason for eating out, for patrons of fast food, family, and all restaurants.

5,000 PERSONS WITH IMPAIRMENTS PLACED IN FOODSERVICE

(p. 29) Article, with 1 table showing number of persons with impairments placed in food service jobs, for top 9 States in placements, FY83. Data are from 290 responses to an NRA Projects with Industry program survey of vocational rehabilitation services/agencies/training facilities in 49 States.

1984 FOOD COSTS SHOULD TRAIL INFLATION, ANNUAL FEATURE

(p. 32-34) Annual article, with 1 table showing percent change in wholesale food prices for 12 commodity groups, and in NRA food cost index and PPI (all food), 1976-Oct. 1983. Data are from BLS and NRA.

AMERICANS EXPECTED TO EAT SLIGHTLY LESS FOOD IN 1984, ANNUAL FEATURE

(p. 35) Annual article on projected food consumption in 1984. Data are from USDA. Includes 1 table showing per capita consumption for all food and 9 commodities, 1981-84.

ANNUAL CREST REPORT SHOWS TRAFFIC UP FOR THIRD YEAR IN A ROW, ANNUAL FEATURE

(p. 36-37) Annual article analyzing trends in restaurant customer traffic. Data are from CREST surveys by NPD Research, Inc. Includes 3 charts showing percent change in sales, per person check size, and customer traffic, 12-month periods ending Aug. 1980-83.

NRA PUBLISHES THREE NEW CONSUMER ATTITUDE STUDIES

(p. 39) Article reporting on consumer expectations regarding restaurant food, for customers who eat out frequently and those with income over $35,000, and for male and single customers, all by type of restaurant. Data are from NRA surveys. Includes 3 tables.

A8200–1.504: Feb. 1984 (Vol. 4, No. 2)

QUARTERLY CREST CHARTS

a. Restaurant customers, sales, and average check size, for fall 1983. (p. 36-39)

ARE CUSTOMERS GETTING THE SERVICE THEY EXPECT?

(p. 29-31) Article on consumer attitudes regarding restaurant service. Data are from telephone surveys of approximately 1,000 adults conducted in Aug. 1982 by NRA and in Sept. 1983 by Gallup Organization.

Includes 2 tables showing consumer expectations for various aspects of restaurant service by type of restaurant, and perceptions of service received by meal period.

LOOK AT THE MARKET POTENTIAL OF HOLIDAYS

(p. 32-35) Article on consumer eating out patterns on holidays. Data are from NPD Research, Inc. Includes 5 tables showing the following for selected holidays: percent of families dining out, average check per person, and percent of customers using incentive promotions, 1977-83.

A8200–1.505: Mar. 1984 (Vol. 4, No. 3)

FRANCHISE RESTAURANT SALES $34.2 BILLION IN 1982, ANNUAL FEATURE

(p. 28-39) Annual compilation of 4 articles, by Cecelia Niepold, on franchise restaurant companies, sales, and establishments. Data are from Commerce Dept's *Franchising in the Economy, 1982-84.*

Includes 2 maps and 18 charts showing the following for the franchise industry:

a. Sales and units, with sales comparison to total eating place industry, various years 1969-84; establishments by census division and for selected States, and companies and sales by firm size, 1982; companies by type of food and service offered, 1981-82; and sales for hamburger franchises, 1981-84.

b. Companies with international operations, and number of establishments by country or world area, 1981 and/or 1982.

A8200–1.506: Apr. 1984 (Vol. 4, No. 4)

RECURRING TABLE

a. Commodity price index, for Jan. 1984. (p. 39)

WHO IS SPENDING WHAT ON DINING OUT?

(p. 31-34) By Cecelia Niepold. Article, with 1 chart and 2 tables showing average weekly consumer expenditures for food away from home and for all food, by age group; and spending for food away from home, per capita and as percent of total food budget, by income and household size; 1980/81, with selected comparisons to 1960/61 and 1972/73.

Data are from BLS.

SUMMER EATING PATTERNS

(p. 35-36) Article, with 1 chart showing percent of restaurant customers ordering selected foods during the summer vs. average for entire year, 1983. Data are based on CREST surveys of 12,800 households conducted in 1983 by NPD Research, Inc.

A8200–1.507: May 1984 (Vol. 4, No. 5)

RECURRING TABLES

a. Commodity Price Index, for Feb. 1984. (p. 38)

b. Food service economic indicators, various periods 1981-84. (p. 38-39)

QUARTERLY CREST CHARTS

a. Restaurant customers, sales, and average check size, for winter 1984. (p. 41-43)

BREAKFAST BUSINESS IS BOOMING

(p. 33-36) By Cecelia Niepold. Article, with 4 charts showing distribution of restaurant breakfast customers, by type of establishment and customers' age; and change in breakfast and total restaurant customer traffic and in wholesale prices for foods served at breakfast; various years 1978-83.

Most data are from CREST surveys by NPD Research, Inc.

A8200–1.508: June/July 1984 (Vol. 4, No. 6)

GROWING INTEREST IN FOOD SAFETY AND SULFITES

(p. 27-28) Article, with 1 table showing consumer views on relative safety of 6 substances contained in foods. Data are from a 1984 survey conducted by Louis Harris and Associates for the Food Marketing Institute (FMI).

Full FMI survey report is covered in SRI under A4950-3.

FOODSERVICE INDUSTRY: 1982 IN REVIEW, ANNUAL FEATURE

(p. 29-44) Annual report on the size, scope, and growth of the food service industry, 1981-82. Data are from Malcolm M. Knapp, Inc., and industry and government sources.

Includes 2 charts and 12 tables showing food service industry food/drink sales and purchases, 1981-82, and number of units (no date), all by detailed industry segment; and alcoholic beverage sales by type of eating/drinking place, and changes in selected economic indicators, 1982.

This is the 15th annual report.

A8200–1.509: Aug. 1984 (Vol. 4, No. 7)

QUARTERLY CREST CHARTS

a. Restaurant customers, sales, and average check size, with detail for family households, spring 1984. (p. 40-44)

REVISED 1984 FORECAST

(p. 38) Article, with 1 table showing revised estimates of 1982-84 food/drink sales, for commercial food service by segment, and for institutional and military food services. Data are from NRA and Malcolm M. Knapp, Inc., and are based on Federal reports.

For description of original 1984 forecast, see A8200-1.502, above.

1984 ANNUAL OPERATING RATIO REPORT NOW AVAILABLE

(p. 39) Article highlighting NRA's *Restaurant Industry Operations Report '84*. Data are from a Laventhol and Horwath analysis of survey responses from 705 NRA members. Includes 1 table showing distribution of restaurant revenues by source and expenses by type, 1982-83.

Full report is covered in SRI under A8200-3.

A8200–1.510: Sept. 1984 (Vol. 4, No. 8)

RECURRING TABLE

a. Commodity price index, for June 1984. (p. 44)

ELUSIVE TEENAGE MARKET

(p. 11-14) By Kathy Boyle. Article, with 2 tables showing teenage weekly allowance/earnings and spending for food/snacks, by age group and sex (no date); and consumer dining-out frequency by age group and meal period, 1981. Data are from Rand Youth Poll and NRA.

HOW MUCH TIME DO CUSTOMERS SPEND IN YOUR RESTAURANT?

(p. 36-37) Article, with 1 chart and 3 tables showing restaurant customer estimates of time spent in restaurants, with detail by age, restaurant type, and meal period. Data are from a Mar. 1984 NRA-sponsored Gallup poll of approximately 1,000 adults.

CREST DATA PROVIDES INFORMATION ON VISIT FREQUENCY, MARKET PENETRATION

(p. 38-40) Article reporting on consumer restaurant patronage. Data are derived from a model developed by GDR/CREST Enterprises for NPD Research, using information supplied by the CREST survey panel during the year ended Aug. 1983.

Includes 1 chart and 2 tables showing eating out frequency and percent of respondents eating out at least once a year, by age and type of restaurant, with detail by income and meal period.

RETAIL CENSUS REPORT: SALES AND ESTABLISHMENT DATA NOW AVAILABLE

(p. 41-43) Article, with 1 table showing sales for food service establishments with and without table service, by census division and State, 1977 and 1982, and average annual percent change 1977-82 period. Data are from NRA and the 1977 and 1982 Census of Retail Trade.

A8200–1.511: Oct. 1984 (Vol. 4, No. 9)

CUSTOMER SATISFACTION ON THE RISE

(p. 40-42) Article, with 4 tables showing customer ratings of price/value at most recent restaurant meal, by restaurant type, customer age and sex, and meal period, 1981 and 1984. Data are from 2 NRA-commissioned Gallup surveys of approximately 1,000 adults, conducted Dec. 1981 and June 1984.

A8200–2   FRANCHISE RESTAURANTS: A Statistical Appendix to Foodservice Trends

Annual. Feb. 1984. 39 p.
SRI/MF/complete

Annual report, for 1984, on the franchise restaurant industry, including data on establishments, sales, services, employment, and ownership. Most data are for 1973-84, with selected trends from 1969. Data are from *Franchising in the Economy,* published by U.S. Dept of Commerce.

Contains table listing (1 p.); and 6 statistical sections with 37 tables, described below.

Availability: National Restaurant Association, Publications Department, 311 First St., NW, Washington DC 20001, members $12.50, nonmembers $25.00; SRI/MF/complete.

TABLES:

[Franchise types are chicken, hamburger/franks/roast beef, pizza, Mexican, seafood, pancakes, steak/full menu, and sandwich/other.]

a. Total industry: companies surveyed, by franchise type, 1973-82; company- and franchisee-owned establishments and sales, 1969-84; chains, by type of service provided (self-service/drive-in/drive-thru and waiter/waitress), by franchise type, 1979-82; and chains, establishments, and sales, by 6 size groups based on number of establishments, 1973-82. 7 tables. (p. 1-7)

b. Franchise types: including company- and franchisee-owned establishments and sales, by franchise type, 1973-84. 9 tables. (p. 8-17)

c. Establishments (company- and franchisee-owned), by State and census division, 1974-82. 9 tables. (p. 18-26)

d. Other data: company- and franchisee-owned restaurant employment; minority ownership (black, Spanish surname, Oriental, and American Indian); ownership changes; franchise establishments repurchased; and renewals and terminations; various years 1971-82. 5 tables. (p. 27-31)

e. Donut shops and ice cream stores: companies and employment, 1977-82; and establishments and sales (company- and franchisee-owned), 1977-84. 3 tables. (p. 33-35)

f. International franchising: establishments, by country or world region; and U.S. companies in international franchising; both by franchise type, various years 1973-82. 4 tables. (p. 36-39)

A8200–3   RESTAURANT INDUSTRY OPERATIONS REPORT '84 for the U.S.

Annual. 1984. 80 p.
LC SN 82-20267.
SRI/MF/complete, current & previous year reports

Annual report presenting detailed financial and operating ratios for restaurants, 1983. Includes data by type of establishment, urban-rural location, region, sales size, and profit-loss status.

Data are based on reports submitted by 705 National Restaurant Assn members, compiled and analyzed by Laventhol and Horwath accountants. Report is intended to enable individual restaurant owners to compare their performance with that of the industry.

Contents:

a. Listings of contents, tables, and charts; introduction; explanatory notes; and analysis, with 2 trend charts. (p. 1-6)

b. Survey results, with 2 charts showing sales and costs per seat, and income and expense distribution of restaurant industry dollar, 1983 with comparisons to 1982; and 26 tables, listed below; all repeated for food-only restaurants (p. 8-39) and for food/alcoholic beverage restaurants (p. 40-69).

c. Comments on restaurant business situation in 22 metro areas, explanation of terms, and worksheet. (p. 70-80)

Previous report, for 1982, was also reviewed in 1984, and is also available on SRI microfiche, under this number [Annual. 1983. 79 p. Members $15.00, nonmembers $30.00].

Availability: National Restaurant Association, Publications Department, 311 First St., NW, Washington DC 20001, members $17.50, nonmembers $35.00; SRI/MF/complete.

TABLES:

[In the listing below, the 1st page number is for food-only restaurants, the 2nd for food/alcoholic beverage restaurants.

All data are for 1983. Tables 2-5 and 17-26 show median, upper quartile, and lower quartile levels. Tables 4 and 9-26 show data as amount per seat and as ratio to total sales.

Restaurant types variously include full menu/tableservice, limited menu/tableservice, limited menu/no tableservice, cafeteria, coffee shop, and other. Data by location are for urban, suburban, and rural. Types of affiliation are single-unit/independent, multi-unit/company-operated, and multi-unit/franchise-operated.]

1. Composition of participating restaurants [including distribution by years in business, restaurant type, region, location, affiliation, types of meals served, sales size class, profit vs. loss, owned or leased land/building, type of ownership, and menu theme]. (p. 9, 41)

2-3. Average check, and average daily seat turnover [by years in business, location, types of meals served, menu theme, and region, with additional detail by restaurant type for food-only restaurants]. (p. 10-11, 42-43)

4. Net income differential [selected financial and operating data for restaurants reporting profit vs. loss]. (p. 12, 44)

5. Earnings ratio [by lease or ownership of land/building, occupancy in attached or detached building, and type of restaurant]. (p. 14, 46)

6. Cost per dollar of sales [total cost of sales and payroll, with additional detail for cost of food and beverages for food/beverage restaurants, by restaurant type, location, profit vs. loss, ownership, and menu theme, and for food-only restaurants by types of meals served]. (p. 14, 46)

7. Analysis of employee data [full- and part-time employees per restaurant; FTE employees per restaurant and per 100 seats and average daily covers; sales and payroll per FTE employee; and productivity index; by restaurant type, location, and profit vs. loss]. (p. 15, 47)

8. Occupancy costs [rent, property and other taxes, and insurance], interest, and depreciation, amount per seat [by restaurant type, location, and region]. (p. 16, 48)

9-16. Cross-tabulation of profit before occupation costs and of restaurant profit, by franchise [or independent ownership] and [single- and multi-unit] organization; by location and type of restaurant; by sales [size class] and age of operation; and by menu theme and sales [size class] or region. (p. 16-19, 48-51)

17-26. Statement of income and expenses [by restaurant type, years in business, location, affiliation, sales size class, region, and menu theme]. (p. 20-39, 52-69)

A8200–8 CONSUMER ATTITUDE AND BEHAVIOR STUDIES
Series. For individual publication data, see below.
SRI/MF/complete

Continuing series of reports analyzing restaurant user characteristics and attitudes, based on results of consumer surveys. Reports are intended to aid the restaurant industry in marketing decisions.

Reports reviewed during 1984 are described below.

Availability: National Restaurant Association, Publications Department, 311 First St., NW, Washington DC 20001; SRI/MF/complete.

A8200–8.3: Consumer Expectations with Regard to Dining at Atmosphere Restaurants
[Monograph. Nov. 1983. 118 p. members $15.00, nonmembers $30.00. SRI/MF/complete.]

Report analyzing consumer expectations about dining in fast food, family, and atmosphere restaurants, with focus on atmosphere restaurants. Includes restaurant patrons' expectations about food, service, cleanliness, and atmosphere, by selected socioeconomic characteristics; and reasons for eating out, preferred meal, and frequency of eating out; with detail for atmosphere restaurants.

Data are from an Aug. 1982 survey of 1,001 recent restaurant patrons, conducted by Porter, Novelli and Associates.

Contains contents listing (1 p.); report objectives, notes, and summary (p. 1-9); 2 chapters with narrative analysis and 54 tables (p. 10-100); and methodology, with 7 tables and questionnaire facsimile (p. 101-118).

A8200–8.4: Consumer Preferences for Ethnic Foods in Restaurants

[Monograph. Mar. 1984. 86 p. members $15.00, nonmembers $30.00. SRI/MF/complete.]

Report analyzing consumer practices and attitudes regarding ethnic foods in restaurants, 1983. Includes detailed data on ordering frequency and other topics, for specific types of ethnic food, by consumer age, sex, household composition, income, and dining out frequency.

Data are from an Aug.-Sept. 1983 survey of approximately 800 recent restaurant patrons, conducted by Burke Marketing Research.

Contains contents listing (1 p.); report objectives, methodology, notes, and summary, with 1 table (p. 1-6); 2 sections with narrative analysis, 3 charts, and 51 tables (p. 7-57); 9 detailed tables (p. 59-80); and facsimile of survey questionnaire (p. 82-85).

A8275
National
Retail Hardware Association

A8275–1 FINANCIAL OPERATING REPORTS
Annual series. For individual publication data, see below.
SRI/MF/complete

Annual series of 3 reports on average financial and operating data of retail hardware stores, home centers, and lumber/building material outlets, 1982.

Reports are based on annual spring mail surveys of retailers and include analysis of results by sales volume category.

General format:

a. Contents listing, introduction, highlights, and monthly sales: includes 2 tables showing annual net sales and increase over previous year, margin, net profit on sales and on investment, and stock turns, for all retailers and by sales volume size and selected other store categories; and industry average percent of sales by month.

b. Average operating results: includes income statement, balance sheet, and financial and operating ratios, for all retailers and high and low profit retailers, and by sales volume and sales floor size groups; and income statement and operating ratios only, by trade area size, store location, whether single or multiple store business, and selected other store categories.

c. Strategic profit model, with 1 chart showing computation of average rate of return on net worth for high profit store category.

d. Departmental sales and productivity: including departmental share of net sales, sales area, inventory, and cost of goods sold, for handling firms and average store; departmental sales per square feet for handling firms only; and average store gross margin return on inventory investment (GMROI), by dept.

e. New store feasibility analysis, with 1 illustrative table.

Survey size and additional breakdowns, as applicable, are described below.

Availability: National Retail Hardware Association, Research Services Department, 770 N. High School Rd., Indianapolis IN 46224; SRI/MF/complete.

A8275–1.1: 1983 Management Report for Retail Hardware Stores
[Annual. 1983. 22 p. $20.00. SRI/MF/complete.]

Presents data for retail hardware stores, 1982, based on survey responses from 815 dealers. Income statement and operating ratios are also shown by type of ownership and by census division.

A8275–1.2: 1983: The Bottom Line for Retail Home Centers
[Annual. 1983. 21 p. $20.00. SRI/MF/complete.]

Presents data for retail home center outlets, for 1982, based on survey responses from 192 dealers. Income statement and operating ratios are also shown by type of origin (originally hardware, lumber/building material, or home center dealer).

A8275–1.3: 1983 Lumber/Building Materials Financial Report
[Annual. 1983. 19 p. $20.00. SRI/MF/complete.]

Presents data for retail lumber/building material outlets, for 1982, based on survey responses from 265 dealers. Income statement and operating ratios are also shown by outlet orientation (contractor or consumer).

A8300
National
Retail Merchants Association

A8300–2 FINANCIAL AND OPERATING RESULTS OF DEPARTMENT AND SPECIALTY STORES of 1982
Annual. 1983. 122 p.
ISSN 0547-8804.
LC 72-92812.
SRI/MF/not filmed

Annual report, for 1982, on department and specialty store average sales, earnings, and expenses, by sales volume size, with trends from 1972. Also includes sales change by census division and in selected States and cities.

Data are based primarily on a survey of 141 companies operating 2,334 stores, and are for the fiscal year ending nearest to Jan. 31, 1983.

Contents:

Contents listing. (1 p.)

Part I. Summary financial operating results, methodology, and selected performance analyses, with 2 charts and 19 tables. (p. 1-36)

Part II. Typical and middle range operating data and ratios by store sales volume category, with 2 extended tables. (p. 38-122)

All tables are listed or described below.

Availability: National Retail Merchants Association, Book Order Division, 100 W. 31st St., New York NY 10001, members $37.50, nonmembers $69.50; SRI/MF/not filmed.

TABLES:
[Unless otherwise noted, data are shown separately for department and specialty stores, by 2-8 sales volume categories.]

A8300–2.1: Part I, Summary

FINANCIAL AND OPERATING TRENDS

[1-4] Department and specialty stores 10-year financial operating results [aggregate sales, gross margin, net expense, earnings from merchandising operations, other income/deductions, pretax earnings in current and 1967 constant dollars, and CPI], 1972-82. (p. 1-5)

[5] Number of reporting companies [including aggregate and average sales volume for owned and leased departments, 1982]. (p. 7)

[6-7] Annual financial and operating trends [aggregate] department and specialty stores with annual total company sales over $1 million [including percent changes and ratios for total sales; ratios for retail departments' sales, gross margin, profits, operating costs, pretax earnings, and sales by terms of sale; and actual stock turns, and sales per square foot]; 1973-82. (p. 14-17)

[8] Performance guidelines [including ratios for sales, merchandising, earnings, expenses by function, sales and buying payroll, and selected financial operating items, 1982]. (p. 20-23)

SELECTED PERFORMANCE TABLES

I. Sales and inventory price trends [aggregate department and specialty store annual percent change in sales, and percent change from prior year for department store inventory price index], 1973-82. (p. 26)

II-VI. Pretax earnings, percent of total store sales and of capital/surplus; stock shortage, percent of net owned retail sales; and net operating expenses and credit sales, percent of total company sales; 1973-82. (p. 26-28)

VII. Distribution of sales and sales promotion expenditures by month [aggregate all stores, for newspaper, display, radio/TV, and total], percent of total year's expenses [1982]. (p. 29)

VIII. Inward transportation [typical and middle range] percent of cost purchases [1978-82]. (p. 30)

IX. Balance sheet data, ratios [1982]. (p. 31)

SALES CHANGE BY GEOGRAPHIC DIVISION

[X-XI] Estimates of monthly retail sales [percent change from previous year for GAF stores (stores which specialize in department store type merchandise) in 18 States and 5 cities; and for department and GAF stores by census division; 1981-82]. (p. 35-36)

A8300–2.2: Part II, Operating Results

Two tables generally showing typical, middle range, and prior year typical sales, merchandising, earnings, and expense ratios. Tables are repeated for sales volume categories of department stores (p. 38-102), and specialty stores (p. 104-122).

Ratios include sales per employee, salespeople as percent of total employees, and, for stores over $1 million, additional itemization of expenses by detailed retail accounting classification.

A8375
National Safety Council

A8375–1   TRAFFIC SAFETY
Bimonthly.   Approx. 30 p.
ISSN 0041-0721.
LC L 38-35.
SRI/MF/not filmed

Bimonthly publication reporting developments in traffic safety programs and trends in accident and fatality statistics.

Data are from State traffic authorities, the National Safety Council, R. L. Polk and Co., NCHS, and other sources. Month of data coverage is 3-6 months preceding publication date.

Issues contain feature articles and editorial depts, occasionally with statistics, including an annual analysis of traffic fatalities; and 4 bimonthly tables presenting traffic accident data.

Bimonthly tables are listed below; most appear in all issues. All additional features with substantial statistical content are described, as they appear, under "Statistical Features." Nonstatistical features are not covered.

Availability: Traffic Safety Magazine, PO Box 11933, Chicago IL 60611, members $12.55 per yr., single copy $2.90; nonmembers $15.75 per yr., single copy $3.65; SRI/MF/not filmed.

Issues reviewed during 1984: Jan./Feb.-Sept./Oct. 1984 (P) (Vol. 84, Nos. 1-5).

BIMONTHLY TABLES:

[All tables except [2] show cumulative data for current year to date, and include comparisons to the previous year or 2 years.]

[1] [Traffic fatality] reductions at the end of [month of coverage; for States and cities with year-to-date improvement in death rate compared to same period of previous year].

[2] Motor vehicle deaths and changes, total U.S. [by month for current year to date and previous 3 years].

[3-4] Traffic deaths [and rates for major cities in 9 population size classes; and by State, with some data for U.S. possessions and Canadian Provinces].

STATISTICAL FEATURES:

A8375–1.501: Mar./Apr. 1984 (Vol. 84, No. 2)

A LOOK AT WHAT'S CONTAINED IN THE NEW STATE CHILD RESTRAINT LAWS

(p. 10-13) By Nancy Berk. Article, with tabular description of State laws requiring use of child restraint devices in motor vehicles, for 43 States, as of Jan. 1984.

A8375–1.502: May/June 1984 (Vol. 84, No. 3)

1983 TRAFFIC DEATHS: THE DOWNWARD TREND CONTINUES, ANNUAL FEATURE

(p. 18-22) Annual analysis, by Barbara Carraro, of motor vehicle fatalities, including location, circumstances, and victim age, 1983 and trends. Includes text statistics, and 8 tables showing the following:

a. Motor vehicle deaths, injuries, costs, mileage, death rates, and registrations, and total population, 1983; and percent change in motor vehicle deaths, by region, 1973-83 and 1982-83 periods.

b. Motor vehicle deaths, by urban population size group, rural road type, accident type, and victim age group, 1983, with change from 1973 and 1982.

c. National accident fatality toll, for motor vehicle accidents, public non-motor-vehicle accidents, and accidents at home and at work, 1982-83.

d. States and cities (over 200,000 population) reporting decreases in traffic fatalities, and percent decrease, 1983.

A8375–1.503: July/Aug. 1984 (Vol. 84, No. 4)

NOW YOU SEE IT! NEW TAILLIGHT REQUIREMENT AIMS TO CUT REAR COLLISIONS

(p. 6-7, 27-29) Article comparing the effectiveness of 4 taillight designs in reducing passenger car rear-end collisions. Data are from an Essex Corp. study covering 2,100 taxicabs in Washington, D.C., during an unspecified 12-month period. Includes 1 chart showing number of rear-end collisions involving study vehicles equipped with each of the 4 taillight designs.

A8375–2   ACCIDENT FACTS, 1983
Edition
Annual.   1983.   97 p.
Stock No. 021.63.
ISBN 0-87912-012-6.
LC 28-14389.
SRI/MF/not filmed

Annual report on accidental deaths and disabling injuries, 1982, with trends from 1865. Covers accidents occurring in the workplace, traffic, public areas, home, in schools, and on farms; with selected data for cities, States, and foreign countries. Includes analysis of accident circumstances, victim demographic characteristics, and value of economic loss.

Data are compiled from numerous government and private sources, specified for each table.

Contains contents listing (p. 1); 7 sections with brief narrative analyses interspersed with 19 charts and 95 tables, described below (p. 2-93); index (p. 94-96); and definitions (inside back cover).

This is the 62nd edition. Previous report, for 1981, is described in SRI 1982 Annual, under this number.

Availability: National Safety Council, Order Department, 444 N. Michigan Ave., Chicago IL 60611, members $8.50, nonmembers $10.75 (prepaid); SRI/MF/not filmed.

CHARTS AND TABLES:

[Tables show data for 1982, unless otherwise noted. Most tables include rates for accidents or deaths. Accidents by class are mostly for motor vehicle, work, home, and public place accidents.]

A8375–2.1: Summaries

a. Summaries by class of accident, including average annual accidental deaths and disabling injuries; costs and cost components of accidents; deaths by type of accident and victim age; leading causes of accidental and other deaths, by sex and age, 1979; and accident incidence rates. 3 charts and 8 tables. (p. 2-11) *b.* Accidental deaths, by International Classification of Diseases category, 1979. 1 table. (p. 12)

c. Accidental deaths: by class, age, and type, selected periods 1903-82; by age, sex, month, and type, 1979; by month, 1982; by class and selected cities and counties, 1981-82; by class and State, 1982; and State totals, 1977-79. 1 chart and 8 tables. (p. 13-19)

d. Fires and property loss, by property use; distribution of lightning deaths and injuries by location, 1959-82 period and 1982; and deaths from specific major disasters, by location and date, 1865-1982. 4 tables. (p. 20-21)

e. World accidental deaths: for Canadian Provinces by cause, 1981; and totals for 32 countries, latest available year, 1979-81. 2 tables. (p. 22)

A8375–2.2: Work Accidents

a. Summaries of deaths and injuries by industry division; time lost because of injuries; work accident costs; on and off job accidental deaths and injuries, quinquennially 1945-65 and annually 1966-82; parts of body injured; and work accident deaths, rates, and disabling injuries, by cause, industry division, and/or occupation, various years 1979-82, with selected trends from 1933. 2 charts and 10 tables. (p. 23-29)

b. Occupational injury/illness, lost work days, and rates, by SIC 1- to 4-digit industry, various periods 1980-82; industrial safety awards, by industry group and leading company; and work deaths and injuries compensated, 1982, and total compensation payments, 1980, by State and Canadian Province. 1 chart and 7 tables. (p. 30-39)

A8375–2.3: Motor Vehicle Accidents

a. Summary, including deaths, disabling injuries, costs, mileage, registered vehicles, and licensed drivers; fatal, injury, and property damage accidents, and drivers involved; deaths and/or injuries, by accident type, day or night, urban/rural location, and victim age; deaths and fatal accidents, by turnpike, 1981-82; and pedalcycle use, and deaths by age, 1940-82. 4 charts and 6 tables. (p. 40-45)

b. Vehicle movement analysis and urban and rural accidents, various periods 1980-82; accidents, deaths, and injuries, by city population size and rural road type; types of improper driving; Washington State fatal and injury accident distribution, by vehicle defect; and world traffic fatalities, by country, various years 1975-81. 7 tables. (p. 46-49)

c. Accidents, by day and hour; deaths by day, 1982, and month, 1973-82; legal drinking age, by State and beverage; effective dates of child passenger restraint laws by State and D.C.; accidents, by driver age, 1982, and sex, 1966-82. 1 chart and 7 tables. (p. 50-54)

d. Pedestrian deaths/injuries, by age and action, 1979; North Carolina fatal and injury accident distribution, by condition of pedestrian and driver; number of vehicles involved in accidents, and occupant

fatalities, by vehicle type; motorcycle rider deaths, 1963-82; deaths on holidays, 1971-82; and Washington State accident severity by vehicle size, 1980. 6 tables. (p. 55-57)

e. Deaths by type of accident and victim age, and accident costs, various periods 1913-82; distribution of accidents by driver State residence status; deaths by urban and rural location and accident type, selected periods 1943-82, and by age, 1982; motor vehicle deaths, and mileage rates, by State, various years 1977-82; and fleet accident rates, by vehicle type, various periods 1959-82. 3 charts and 9 tables. (p. 58-64)

f. Traffic deaths for specific cities, 1981-82; and average days between deaths, 1977-82; both by population size group. 2 tables. (p. 65-71)

A8375–2.4: Other Accidents

PUBLIC ACCIDENTS

a. Public accidental deaths, by type and victim age; deaths, by public accident type, 1950 and 1955-82; sports participation, fatalities, and injuries, by type of sport; civil and general aviation accidents and deaths, 1973-82; railroad crossing accidents, selected years 1943-82; and railroad accident deaths and injuries, selected years 1933-82. 1 chart and 5 tables. (p. 72-78)

HOME ACCIDENTS

b. Home urban and farm accidental deaths and disabling injuries; deaths by type of accident and victim age; poisoning deaths by type, age, and sex, 1979; and deaths by type of accident, 1950 and 1955-82. 2 charts and 3 tables. (p. 79-84)

FARM ACCIDENTS

c. Farm resident accidental deaths and disabling injuries, by class; farm work injury rates, by region, age, sex, and type and size of farm; tractor accident fatality rates, by type of accident, 1969-82; accidental deaths, by class, 1963-82; and nontransport deaths, by type of accident, 1960-79. 1 chart and 6 tables. (p. 85-88)

SCHOOL ACCIDENTS

d. Accidental deaths by class, aged 5-14 age group; deaths by age group, 1969-79; student accident rates, kindergarten-grade 12, by activity and location, by sex, 1980/81; and school bus accidents by type, and injuries, by State. 5 tables. (p. 89-93)

A8450
National Sheriffs Association

A8450–1   **STATE OF OUR NATION'S JAILS, 1982**
Recurring (irreg.)   Aug. 1982.
233+14 p.
SRI/MF/complete

Recurring survey report, by Kenneth E. Kerle and Francis R. Ford, on characteristics of county and larger city jails, 1982. Presents data on administration policies and operations, facilities, personnel, inmate population, programs, and services, by jail bed-size category.

Report defines a jail as a facility used to confine both arrestees awaiting trial or pretrial release and inmates serving sentences.

Data are based on 2,664 responses to a National Sheriffs' Assn survey of local sheriffs and jail administrators, conducted Sept. 1981-Apr. 1982.

Contains contents listing (1 p.); summary, introduction, and survey description, with selected text data from 1978 Census of Jails (p. 3-27); survey findings, with narrative commentary and 51 tables, described below (p. 31-232); and questionnaire facsimile (14 p.).

This is the 1st edition of the report.

Availability: National Sheriffs' Association, 1450 Duke St., Suite 320, Alexandria VA 22314, $12.00; SRI/MF/complete.

TABLES:

[Tables show survey response, by jail bed-size category, as of 1982 unless otherwise noted.]

a. **General and legal:** including level of government running jail; use of National Institute of Corrections Jail Center services; whether ever or currently under State or Federal court order, by reason; and whether a State or Federal lawsuit is pending. 6 tables. (p. 33-57)

b. **Administration:** including average operating budget, 1979-81; daily cost per inmate; existence of policy/procedure manual; and jail replacement/renovation bond issues proposed over past 3 years, outcome, and bond issues currently pending or proposed. 4 tables. (p. 59-73)

c. **Facilities:** including number of beds (total, male, female, and juvenile) in use and originally designed; decade built; whether jail is in separate building or shares building with other agencies; number and size of cells, by type; occupancy rate of largest dormitory; availability of space for various activities; whether jail has ever undergone major renovation/expansion; and use of scheduled evacuation drills. 8 tables. (p. 75-109)

d. **Staffing:** including total, supervisory, part-time, and volunteer staff; applicant screening procedures; presence of union; training source; services contracted out; presence of full-time cook; whether female officer on duty when females detained; inmate supervision by officers of opposite sex; whether 24-hour supervision is provided; shift practices; starting salaries of jail and patrol officers, by union status; and jail-patrol officer duty rotations. 14 tables. (p. 111-154)

e. **Inmates:** average daily male, female, and juvenile inmates; percent pretrial and sentenced inmates, and average length of detention, 1980; policies on housing inmates from other jurisdictions (including fee charged), handling special inmate problems, housing inmates for weekends only, contracting inmates to other jurisdictions, separating adults and juveniles, and housing work release inmates; and inmate suicide occurrence. 10 tables. (p. 155-192)

f. **Programs, services, and problems:** education programs and counseling services provided; use of chaplain; medical staff hours and services; inmate recreation hours per week; use of trustees; visitation policies; presence of detoxification center and alternative program to incarceration in community; and ranking of major problems. 9 tables. (p. 193-232)

A8460
National Society
of Professional Engineers

A8460–1   **PROFESSIONAL ENGINEER INCOME AND SALARY SURVEY, 1984**
Annual. Apr. 1984. 64 p.
NSPE Pub. No. 0004.
LC A55-10041.
SRI/MF/complete

Annual survey report on compensation of professional engineers, 1983. Includes data by experience, degree level, engineering field, job function, professional registration status, level of professional and managerial responsibility, industry or service of employer, organization size, annual service billings for consulting firms, region, and selected metro area, with various cross-tabulations.

Compensation data are shown as means, medians, 1st and 9th deciles, and 1st and 3rd quartiles.

Also includes data on vacation policy; and pension plans, including coverage, vesting provisions, and employer contributions.

Data are based on responses of 14,108 NSPE members to a Jan. 1984 mail survey conducted by Abbott, Langer and Associates.

Contains introduction, contents listing, highlights, definitions, and methodology (p. 2-5); report, with 1 map, 12 charts and 19 tables (p. 6-21); and 2 appendices including sample survey form and detailed income cross-tabulations, with 22 tables (p. 22-64).

This is the 18th survey report.

Availability: National Society of Professional Engineers, 2029 K St., NW, Washington DC 20006, members $30.00, nonmembers $55.00; SRI/MF/complete.

A8485
National
Sporting Goods Association

A8485–1   **COST OF DOING BUSINESS for Retail Sporting Goods Stores, 1983-84 Financial Survey**
Biennial. 1984. 59 p.
ISSN 0736-0703.
SRI/MF/complete, delayed

Biennial report, for 1983/84, presenting average financial and productivity ratios and selected operating characteristics for sporting goods dealers, by size, type of business, and region. Data are based on an Apr. 1983 survey of approximately 4,000 National Sporting Goods Assn (NSGA) members. Of the 1,047 responses received, 320 included FY82 income statements.

Report is intended to permit dealers to compare their operations with industry averages.

Contains contents listing and introduction (p. 3-5); income statements and productivity ratio tables, described below, interspersed with 8 additional tables primarily showing summary comparisons to 1980 (p. 6-49); worksheets (p. 51-58); and accounting classifications (p. 59).

Previous report, for 1981/82, is described in SRI 1982 Annual, under this number.

Availability: National Sporting Goods Association, 1699 Wall St., Mt. Prospect IL 60056, members $15.00, nonmembers ◆; SRI/MF/complete, delayed shipment in Dec. 1984.

TABLES:

A8485–1.1: Income Statements and Productivity Ratios
[Tables are repeated by sales size group (p. 13-16), profit as percent of sales (p. 19-22), number of stores (p. 24-28), selling space (p. 30-32), geographic region (p. 34-39), type of store (full line or specialty) (p. 41-44), and percent team business (p. 46-49). Data are for FY82.]

a. Income statements: cost of goods sold, operating and administrative expenses, gross and net profit, and income before taxes, all as a percent of sales.

b. Productivity ratios: average FTE employees and selling floor area; sales and profits per employee and square foot; and inventory turnover.

A8485–2   **SPORTING GOODS MARKET in 1984**
Annual. 1984. 70 p.
ISSN 0736-0703.
SRI/MF/complete, delayed

Annual report estimating consumer purchases of sporting goods, by detailed type of product, Oct. 1982-Sept. 1983 for spring/summer products, and Jan.-Dec. 1983 for fall/winter products. Covers clothing, footwear, and equipment.

Includes volume, value, and average price of purchases, with selected detail by type of outlet and trends from 1976; distribution of purchases, by census division, age of user, household income, and education of household head; and product rankings within each census division and income group, by share of all purchases.

Also includes forecasts of sporting goods and recreational transport product sales for 1984.

Most data are projections based on a survey of approximately 80,000 households on the National Family Opinion, Inc., consumer panel. Survey response rate was 74%. Study was conducted by Irwin Broh and Associates, Inc.

Contains contents listing (p. 3); introduction (p. 4-5); 1 summary table (p. 6-7); 3 basic tables repeated for each product category or type (p. 8-45); 3 additional tables, with accompanying notes (p. 47-70); and inserted order form for brand share reports on individual product types, also available from the issuing agency but not covered in SRI.

Availability: National Sporting Goods Association, 1699 Wall St., Mt. Prospect IL 60056, members $25.00, nonmembers $95.00; SRI/MF/complete, delayed shipment in May 1985.

A8510
National Urban League

A8510–1   **STATE OF BLACK AMERICA, 1984**
Annual. Jan. 19, 1984.
6+vii+185 p.
ISSN 0148-6985.
ISBN 0-87855-937-X.
LC 77-647469.
SRI/MF/complete

Annual compilation of papers, for 1984, on selected social, political, and economic events and conditions affecting black Americans. Papers were prepared at the invitation of the National Urban League. Most data were compiled from Federal sources and are current to 1981-82, with trends from 1970s or earlier.

Contains contents listing (1 p.); overview (p. i-vii); 6 papers, most with substantial statistics (p. 1-141); conclusions and recommendations, and 1983 chronology of events with implications for race relations (p. 143-167); and statistical appendix (p. 169-181).

Papers with substantial statistics and appendix tables are described below.

Availability: National Urban League, Communications Department, Equal Opportunity Bldg., 500 E. 62nd St., New York NY 10021, $15.00; SRI/MF/complete, delayed shipment in Dec. 1984.

A8510–1.1: Papers

ECONOMIC STATUS OF BLACK AMERICA: IS THERE A RECOVERY?

(p. 1-23) By Denys Vaughn-Cooke. Includes 11 tables (p. 18-23) showing the following data by race, various years 1955-83: unemployment and labor force participation rates by age and/or sex; persons below poverty level by age; and median family income by census region, with detail for individuals and full-time workers by sex.

HIGH-TECH REVOLUTION AND ITS IMPLICATIONS FOR BLACK EMPLOYMENT

(p. 25-42) By Charles L. Betsey and Bruce H. Dunson. Includes 8 tables (p. 35-42) showing the following data:

a. Dislocated workers (workers unemployed due to structural changes in their industry), by age, previous year's income, educational attainment, race/ethnicity (including Hispanic), and sex; as of 1980.

b. Employment in selected high-technology industry groups, by race, 1982 and 1995; black employment in each of top 10 high-technology employment States, 1980; and high-technology employment in 3 States, with detail for top 5 SMSAs, Sept. 1982.

c. Black population in 5 SMSAs, percent residing in the central city, percent using public transportation, and percent of labor force working in central city, 1980.

d. Education: percent of persons age 25/over with 4/more years of high school, by sex and race, 1970 and 1981; and number of black college degree recipients, with detail for 6 fields of study and black share of total degree recipients, 1978/79.

PROFILE OF THE BLACK SINGLE FEMALE-HEADED HOUSEHOLD

(p. 43-67) By James D. McGhee. Report on sociodemographic characteristics of black female-headed households with no husband present. Data are from Census Bureau, and the Black Pulse survey of 3,000 black heads of households, conducted by the National Urban League in 1979 and 1980. Includes 18 tables (p. 56-67) showing the following data, various periods 1960-80:

a. Families and median family income, by family type (married couple families by wife's employment status, and female householder), by race; black female and all other black household head distribution by marital status; and divorced persons per 1,000 married with spouse present, by race and sex.

b. Black female household head distribution by educational attainment, employment status and sector (with detail for unemployment reasons), selected disease incidence, income source, and gross weekly earnings level.

c. Median income of husband-wife and female-headed families by race; and average monthly rent and food expenditures of black and other female household heads.

d. Social and opinion data, including perceived reasons child care services needed; distribution of types of school attended by children of black female and other black household heads, and parental visits by reason; crime victimization incidence, by offense; and participation in informal support systems.

BLACK VOTE: THE SLEEPING GIANT

(p. 69-93) By Dianne M. Pinderhughes. Includes 10 tables (p. 85-93) showing the following data:

a. Electoral votes, black share of voting age population, unregistered black voters, and Reagan victory margin over Carter, and over Carter/Anderson, for 20 States and D.C.; number of congressional districts with large black populations, by black share of total and voting age population; and population of voting age in 10 major cities, by race/ethnicity including Hispanic; 1980.

b. Black city officials, by office; voting data for mayoral elections involving a black candidate in 4 cities; black vs. white political attitudes as measured by Gallup Polls; and voting population age 18-24 and 25/over, and percent of population under age 25 registered and voting, by race; various periods 1973-83.

c. Share of black and white presidential vote going to Democratic Party candidate; and voting age population and percent voting in congressional and presidential elections, by region (North/West vs. South) and race; various election years 1952-82.

A8510–1.2: Appendix

AMERICA'S BLACK POPULATION: 1970 TO 1982, A STATISTICAL VIEW

(p. 171-179) Excerpts from Census Bureau publication. Includes 3 charts and 1 table showing black population distribution by metro-nonmetro status; median family income by family type and race; black professional/skilled labor force, by sex and detailed occupation; and black families by family type; various years 1970-82.

EDUCATION DATA

(p. 180-181) Includes 2 tables showing public elementary/secondary school enrollment, by race and ethnic group (including Hispanic, Asian/Pacific Islander, and American Indian/Alaskan Native), by State; and average reading performance of students at 3 specified ages, by race and census region.

A8600
Newspaper Advertising Bureau

A8600–5   1983 DAILY NEWSPAPER READERSHIP DEMOGRAPHIC TABLES for Total U.S., Top 100 Metros, and Top 100 DMAs
Annual. [1983.] i+31 p.
SRI/MF/complete

Annual report, for 1983, on socioeconomic characteristics of daily newspaper readers, aggregated for total U.S., top 100 MSAs, and top 100 designated market areas. Shows total adult population, and average weekday newspaper audience, gross impressions, and gross rating points, by sex, cross-tabulated by age, education, household income and size, employment and marital status, occupation, race, census region, and locality type (metro central city, suburban, nonmetro).

Data are from a 1983 Simmons Market Research Bureau study.

Contains contents listing (1 p.), table explanation (p. i), and 31 tables (p. 1-31).

Availability: Newspaper Advertising Bureau, Research Department, 1180 Ave. of the Americas, New York NY 10036, $3.00; SRI/MF/complete.

A8600–6   1984 SUNDAY/WEEKEND NEWSPAPER READERSHIP DEMOGRAPHIC TABLES for Total U.S., Top 100 Metros, and Top 100 DMAs
Annual. [1984.] i+34 p.
SRI/MF/complete, current & previous year reports

Annual report, for 1984, on socioeconomic characteristics of Sunday/weekend newspaper readers, aggregated for total U.S., top 100 MSAs, and top 100 designated market areas. Shows total

adult population, and average Sunday/weekend newspaper audience, gross impressions, and gross rating points, by sex, cross-tabulated by age, education, household income and size, employment and marital status, occupation, number of employed adults in household, race, census region, and locality type (metro central city, suburban, nonmetro).

Data are from a 1984 Simmons Market Research Bureau study.

Contains contents listing (1 p.), table explanation (p. i), and 34 tables (p. 1-34).

Availability: Newspaper Advertising Bureau, Research Department, 1180 Ave. of the Americas, New York NY 10036, $3.00; SRI/MF/complete.

A8600–7   NEWSPAPER READERSHIP PROJECT RESEARCH REPORTS
Series. For individual publication data, see below.
SRI/MF/complete

Continuing series of marketing research reports analyzing aspects of newspaper readership and production, including personnel profiles, management practices, and consumer behavior. Reports are intended to promote circulation and readership.

Data are based on surveys conducted or sponsored by NAB's Newspaper Readership Project, and often include breakdowns by sex, age, education, income, and other sociodemographic characteristics.

Reports have been published since 1977. SRI coverage begins with the reports described below, and includes only those reports with broad-based statistical content.

Availability: Newspaper Advertising Bureau, Research Department, 1180 Ave. of the Americas, New York NY 10036; SRI/MF/complete.

A8600–7.1: World of the Working Journalist

[Monograph. Sept. 1982. vii+155 p. NRP 82-07. $5.50. SRI/MF/complete.]

By Judee K. Burgoon et al. Report on journalists' perceptions of their jobs, newspaper readers, and the future of journalism. Includes opinions on "news" definition and perceived journalist role, job satisfaction, beliefs about reader media use and sophistication, and own research and media use.

Data are from a study of approximately 500 journalists employed at 10 daily newspapers, sponsored jointly by Newspaper Readership Project and American Society of Newspaper Editors.

Contains contents listing (p. v-vii); introduction and report, interspersed with 41 tables (p. 1-117); and 3 appendices, with respondent characteristics table, methodology, and questionnaire facsimiles (p. 121-155).

A8600–7.2: Circulation and Home Delivery Patterns

[Monograph. Nov. 1983. xvii+52 p. $3.75. SRI/MF/complete.]

Report on consumer use of home delivery vs. single-copy purchases to obtain newspapers, 1982. Covers prevalence of delivery and purchases; demographic characteristics of subscribers and purchasers; delivery methods, and satisfaction with delivery service; subscription solicitations, and reasons for not subscribing; and purchase frequency and outlet preferences.

Includes selected detail for morning and evening papers, for Sunday and weekday editions, and by market metro-nonmetro status and region.

Also includes correlation between newspaper readership and home delivery, with detail for children.

Data are based on a May 1982 survey of adults in 1,979 households, conducted by Audits & Surveys, Inc.

Contains preface, listings of contents and tables, introduction, and highlights (p. v-xvii); narrative analysis, interspersed with 29 tables (p. 1-42); appendix on sample characteristics, with 3 tables (p. 43-49); and methodological note (p. 51-52).

A8600–7.3: Newspaper Inventory: Summary Tables and Findings (Weekday Editions), 1983

[Recurring (irreg.)   Nov. 1983.   v+39 p. $2.75. SRI/MF/complete.]

Recurring report on content, layout, and other characteristics of daily newspapers, by circulation size, 1983, with selected comparisons to 1979. Includes types of regular features carried; sources of features (local or syndicated); pages devoted to news/editorial items; space devoted to photographs/other illustrations; number of separate sections; use of color; advertising positioning policies; and weekdays most food and general merchandise advertising appear.

Also includes home delivery percent of total circulation; and participation in Newspaper in Education programs.

Data for 1983 are based on responses from 1,310 daily newspapers to a survey conducted by the Newspaper Advertising Bureau. The survey covered all daily and Sunday/weekend newspapers in U.S. and Canada. Similar surveys were conducted in 1967, 1974, and 1979.

Contains introduction and table listing (p. i-v); and 29 tables, with accompanying narrative (p. 1-39).

A similar report on Sunday/weekend papers is described below, under A8600-7.4.

A8600–7.4: Newspaper Inventory: Summary Tables and Findings (Sunday/Weekend Editions), 1983

[Recurring (irreg.)   Dec. 1983.   iii+25 p. $2.75. SRI/MF/complete.]

Recurring report on content, layout, and other characteristics of Sunday/weekend newspapers, by circulation size, 1983. Includes number of separate sections; types of regular features carried, with comparison to daily newspapers; volume of department store and other general merchandise advertising; use of mail order feature; use of color; and home delivery percent of total circulation.

Data are based primarily on responses from 572 Sunday/weekend newspapers to a 1983 survey conducted by the Newspaper Advertising Bureau. The survey covered all daily and Sunday/weekend newspapers in U.S. and Canada. Similar surveys were conducted in 1967, 1974, and 1979.

Contains introduction and table listing (p. i-iii); and 16 tables, with accompanying narrative (p. 1-25).

A similar report on weekday newspapers is described above, under A8600-7.3.

A8600–7.5: Meeting Readers' Multiple Needs: Content and Readership of News and Features in the Daily Press

[Monograph. Mar. 1984. xvii+68 p. $3.50. SRI/MF/complete.]

Report on editorial content of daily newspapers, and newspaper reading habits of consumers, 1982, with content trends from 1971. Includes data on types of features presented, by size and location in paper; types of features and advertising read, by consumer demographic characteristics; reading methods (browsing vs. specific section/page); time spent reading; and relationship between feature readership and selected factors, including number of pages in paper, whether morning or evening edition, feature location, and presence of photographs.

Data are based primarily on a May 1982 survey of adults in 1,979 households, conducted by Audits & Surveys, Inc.

Contains preface, listings of contents and tables, and highlights (p. iii-xvii); narrative analysis in 4 chapters, with 27 interspersed tables (p. 1-56); and appendix, with codes and 8 tables (p. 57-68).

A8600–7.6: Newspaper Pages, Ads, and Readers

[Monograph.   May 1984.   v+26 p. $3.25. SRI/MF/complete.]

Report on content and readership of display advertisements in daily newspapers, 1982. Includes data on distribution of ads by type of product or service and by ad size; and ad exposure (number of page-openings by readers), readership, and interest, shown variously by reader demographic characteristics, ad characteristics (subject, size, and location), and newspaper circulation and page size; with selected detail for retail and national ads and for black-and-white and color ads.

Data are based on a May 1982 survey of adults in 1,979 households, conducted by Audits & Surveys, Inc.

Contains preface, table listing, and highlights (p. ii-v); narrative report (p. 1-7); and 19 tables (p. 8-26).

A8600–8   RESEARCH REPORT SERIES
Series.   For individual publication data, see below. SRI/MF/complete

Continuing series of marketing research reports analyzing aspects of newspaper readership, advertising effects, and consumer behavior, either generally or in relation to a particular industry. Reports are directed to newspapers and their advertisers, and are intended to help individual companies use newspaper advertising effectively.

Data are based on surveys conducted or sponsored by NAB, and usually include breakdowns by age, sex, education, income, and other sociodemographic characteristics.

SRI covers only those reports with broad-based statistical content. Reports reviewed during 1984 are described below.

Availability: Newspaper Advertising Bureau, Research Department, 1180 Ave. of the Americas, New York NY 10036; SRI/MF/complete.

A8600–8.12: Readership of Newspaper Pages and Sections: Demographic Segments, SMRB SMM–1983

[Recurring (irreg.)   Dec. 1983.   i+23 p. $2.00. SRI/MF/complete.]

Recurring report on daily newspaper readership, with data on percent of weekday audience reading entire paper and specific sections, and estimated average weekday audience, by reader sociodemographic characteristics.

Data are from *1983 Study of Media and Markets,* a Simmons Market Research Bureau report derived from interviews with a multistage area probability sample of over 19,000 adults.

Contains contents listing (p. i); introduction (p. 1-4); and 19 tables (p. 5-23).

For description of previous report, with 1981 study results, see SRI 1982 Annual under A8600-8.4.

A8600–8.13: Demographic Characteristics of Frequent Movie-Goers

[Monograph. Jan. 1984. 19 p. var. paging. $1.50. SRI/MF/complete.]

Report on characteristics of persons who frequently attend movies. Includes distribution by age group, locale type (urban, suburban, or rural) and population level, census region, income, and TV viewing and newspaper reading habits, with detail for teenagers and adults.

Data are from Simmons Market Research Bureau surveys of over 19,000 randomly selected adults and an unspecified number of teenagers. No survey dates are indicated.

Contains contents listing and introduction (p. ii-iv); summary (p. 1-2); and 12 tables with accompanying narrative analyses (13 p.).

A8600–8.14: Key Facts About Newspapers and Advertising, 1984

[Annual. Feb. 1984. vii+41 p. price on request. SRI/MF/complete.]

Annual report describing services available from NAB and presenting data on aspects of newspaper readership and advertising, with selected comparisons to other media. Includes the following data, shown primarily for 1982 or 1983, often with trends from 1970s:

a. Sociodemographic characteristics of newspaper audience; number and circulation of newspapers, by type; consumer spending on newspapers; how newspapers are obtained (subscription, single-copy purchases, other); and newspaper reading habits.

b. Availability of color newspaper ads; ad readership; reader response to ads, including enjoyment and believability compared to other media; advertising influence on purchases, by media; and coupon data, including distribution by media and consumer use.

c. Advertising expenditure/sales ratio for selected retail and service industries; newspaper vs. TV ad costs in selected markets; national and local/retail advertising expenditures, by media; newspaper classified ad expenditures; and volume of newspaper preprint and insert ads.

Data are from a variety of sources, specified for each table.

Contains contents listing (p. iii-vii); 1 chart and 33 tables with interspersed narrative (p. 1-34); and list of NAB reports (p. 35-41).

A8600–8.15: Estimating Daily Newspaper Reach and Frequency for Major Demographic Segments

[Monograph. June 1984. iii+29+App 3 p. $3.00. SRI/MF/complete.]

Report discussing a methodology for estimating newspaper reach among various demographic sectors, based on audience turnover rates.

Includes data on average turnover rate by region, by selected demographic characteristics; and readership net reach, average frequency, and gross rating points, estimated for 2-5 consecutive issues at selected turnover rates.

Data are derived from 1982-83 studies conducted by Scarborough Research Corp. and Simmons Market Research Bureau, covering over 100 daily newspapers.

Contains contents listing and introduction (p. i-iii); 2 narrative sections interspersed with 4 tables (p. 1-14); statistical section with 15 tables (p. 15-29); and appendix, with methodological note and list of newspapers studied (3 p.).

A8600–8.16: Frequent Fliers and Airline Ads

[Monograph. Aug. 1984. ii+25+App 32 p. $4.00. SRI/MF/complete.]

Report examining effectiveness of newspaper airline advertising among frequent airline customers, with focus on customers' responses to general image vs. specific promotion advertising. Includes data on customers' reactions to both types of ads, including influence on airline selection, likelihood of examining the ad, and impact of the ad's main theme.

Data are shown variously for selected demographic groups, and by travel characteristics including flights per year, reason for travel, whether respondent or secretary/travel officer makes arrangements, and participation in airline bonus programs.

Data are from interviews with 604 frequent air travelers, conducted in 3 major airports during Feb. 1984.

Contains contents and table listings (p. i-ii); introduction, and narrative report in 3 chapters (p. 1-25); and a separately paginated appendix, with 15 tables, and facsimile ads and interview forms (p. 1-32).

A8600–8.17: Real Estate in the Eighties: A Study of Home Buyers and Sellers

[Monograph. Sept. 1984. xiii+52 p. $4.00. SRI/MF/complete.]

Report discussing economic and general market aspects of home buying and selling, and presenting consumers' opinions regarding realtors, primarily 1984 with trends from the 1970s. Includes the following data, often shown for both buyers and sellers and by sociodemographic characteristics:

a. Median sales price of new and existing homes, and of homes purchased by 1st-time and repeat buyers; sales distribution by price, and median square footage, for new one-family homes; percent increase in major CPI components; and median family income.

b. Newspaper readership among realtor clients; main reasons for moving; recall of real estate advertising, with detail by media;

time spent looking for a house to buy, and number of realtors contacted; ratings of realtor performance of selected services; future housing plans of sellers; and frequency of checking home listings in newspaper classified section.

c. Ratings of honesty/ethical standards of realtors and 5 other occupations; advantages of dealing with local independent realtor and large organization; most desirable investment, reasons real estate is considered most desirable, and perceived changes in value of real estate as an investment; and perceived market value of housing relative to inflation.

d. Interest in and source of information for keeping up with real estate trends; perceived importance of real estate to national economy; willingness to make arrangements through a realty firm for mortgage financing and homeowner insurance and for investment in a real estate development; and principal advantages of buying vs. renting.

Most data are based on responses of 382 home buyers and sellers, mainly in North Central and Pacific census divisions, to a spring 1984 telephone survey.

Contains contents and table listings, highlights, and introduction (p. i-xiii); report in 3 sections, with 32 tables interspersed with narrative (p. 1-47); and appendix, with 4 tables (p. 48-52).

A8610
Newsprint
Information Committee

A8610–1   NEWSPAPER AND NEWSPRINT FACTS at a Glance, 1983-84
Annual. [1984.] 29 p.
SRI/MF/complete

Annual report on U.S. and Canadian newsprint and newspaper industry, 1984, with selected trends from 1933. Covers newsprint production, trade, capacity by mill, consumption, and prices. Also includes data on U.S. consumption by State and major newspaper, and world production and consumption.

Data are from Canadian Pulp & Paper Assn, American Paper Institute, American Newspaper Publishers Assn, Audit Bureau of Circulations, and other sources.

Contains introduction, and 12 tables listed below (p. 3-15); highlights of Newsprint Information Committee research surveys on advertising, consumer habits, and other topics, with text statistics (p. 16-25); and newsprint specifications, assn meeting information, and index (p. 26-29). This is the 26th edition.

Availability: Newsprint Information Committee, 420 Lexington Ave., New York NY 10017, media/research organizations †, others $2.50; SRI/MF/complete.

TABLES:

NORTH AMERICA

[1] 1984 newsprint capacity, by producers [by Canadian and U.S. mill]. (p. 3)

[2] North American newsprint capacity, production, consumption, [and] sources of supply [selected years 1964-84]. (p. 6)

[3] Flow of North American newsprint [Canadian and U.S. production, consumption, and exports, and U.S. imports], 1983. (p. 7)

OTHER FOREIGN

[4] Canada leads world in newsprint production [production and percent of world total, for 10 countries, 1983]. (p. 8)

[5] U.S. is world's leading consumer of newsprint [consumption and percent of world total, for 11 countries, 1983]. (p. 8)

U.S.

[6] Price of newsprint, 1933-83. (p. 9)

[7] Newsprint as an element of total publishing cost [for daily newspapers, by circulation size, 1982-83]. (p. 9)

[8] U.S. newsprint consumption, 1953-83. (p. 10)

[9] Data on U.S. newspapers [including circulation, average pages printed, and advertising revenue, 1973 and 1982-83]. (p. 12)

[10] Largest [10] U.S. dailies [ranked by circulation, as of Mar. 31, 1984, with 1983 newsprint usage]. (p. 13)

[11] Largest [10] U.S. newspaper companies (ranked by daily circulation) [and with Sunday circulation, average for 6-months ended Sept. 30, 1983; also shows number of daily and Sunday papers]. (p. 13)

[12] Newspaper newsprint consumption, by States [and census division, 1982-83]. (p. 14-15)

A8630
North American
Electric Reliability Council

A8630–2   ELECTRIC POWER SUPPLY AND DEMAND, 1984-93
Annual. 1984. 175 p.
SRI/MF/complete

Annual report presenting detailed forecasts of U.S. and Canadian electricity supply and demand, by NERC region and subregion, various years 1983-93. Covers summer and winter peak demand; total electricity requirement; load factor (average/peak demand ratio); generating capacity and net generation, by energy source; and fossil fuel requirements, by type of fuel.

Also includes lists of planned generating unit additions by energy source, unit conversions from oil to coal, and unit retirements, all with production capacity and scheduled service date, by utility; and existing and planned transmission line mileage.

Data are based on reports of NERC regional councils.

Contains contents listing, highlights with 3 summary/trend charts, and introduction (p. 2-7); and 23 tables, arranged in 16 sections, with brief narrative summaries and illustrative charts (p. 8-175).

Availability: North American Electric Reliability Council, Research Park, Terhune Rd., Princeton NJ 08540, †; SRI/MF/complete.

A8640
North American Telecommunications Association

A8640-2   1983-84 TELECOMMUNICATIONS SOURCE BOOK
Annual.   [1983.]   314 p.
SRI/MF/excerpts

Annual telecommunications industry source book, including trends, product development, and directories; and statistics on telephone equipment installations and other industry operations, 1982 and trends. Data are from FCC, other Federal Government, and telephone industry sources.

Statistical section of this report was previously issued as a separate publication, under the title *Telecommunications Equipment Industry Statistical Review.* For description of report for 1982, see SRI 1983 Annual, under A8640-1.

Contains contents listing (2 p.); narrative industry overview, trends, and products sections (p. 1-100); statistical review section, with 4 charts, and 18 tables described below (p. 103-140); and directory and resource listings (p. 143-314).

Availability: North American Telecommunications Association, 2000 M St., NW, Suite 550, Washington DC 20036, members $25.00, nonmembers $50.00; SRI/MF/excerpts for "Statistical Review" section.

STATISTICAL REVIEW SECTION:
[Data sources are noted beneath each table.]

a.   Telephones in use, number and share for Bell or regional operating companies, independents, interconnect, and AT&T; and telephone shipment value and volume for Western Electric and independents; repeated for key, Private Branch Exchange (PBX), and centrex markets, 1978-87. 8 tables. (p. 109-118)

b.   PBX lines and systems installed by line size, with centrex totals; Bell PBX/centrex instruments installed and removed by State; and Bell and interconnect PBX market shares, and PBX systems by line size, by city; various years 1981-86. 4 tables. (p. 119-122)

c.   Sales volume and value, and other revenues, for PBX and key markets, 1982-87; and retail telephone sales volume, value, and average price, by telephone type, 1982. 2 tables. (p. 124-125)

d.   Residential and business carrier telephones in use; subscriber access lines and revenues, by type of service, for AT&T, Southern New England & Cincinnati Bell, and independents; and residential, business, and main telephones, and telephones per 100 population, for approximately 450 urban areas; various years 1970-82. 3 tables. (p. 126-138)

e.   Export and import values for telephones, and switching/switchboard and other equipment, by country or world area, 1982. 1 table. (p. 139)

A8670
Pacific Area Travel Association

A8670-1   ANNUAL STATISTICAL REPORT, 1982
Annual.   [1983.]   vi+105 p.
SRI/MF/not filmed

Annual report on visitor arrivals in Pacific Area Travel Assn (PATA) countries, by visitor travel mode, nationality, residence, sex, and purpose of visit, all by PATA country, 1982 with selected trends from 1972.

Also includes data on number of hotel rooms and average occupancy rates, rooms under construction and planned (with forecasts to 1987), average length of stay, visitor expenditures, and national tourist organization budgets by function and market area, all by PATA country; and outbound travel of PATA country residents by country of destination.

Data are from reports submitted by PATA countries based on tourist embarkation/debarkation cards.

Contains contents and table listing (2 p.); introduction, summary, and table notes (p. i-vi); 6 sections, with 3 charts and 26 tables (p. 2-100); and listing of tourism R&D projects, by country, 1982-83 (p. 101-104).

This is the 15th annual report.

Availability: Pacific Area Travel Association, 228 Grant Ave., San Francisco CA 94108, members $35.00, nonmembers $60.00; SRI/MF/not filmed.

A8680
Phi Delta Kappa

A8680-1   PHI DELTA KAPPAN
10 issues per year.
Approx. 100 p. paginated consecutively from beginning of volume year.
ISSN 0031-7217.
LC 46-35485.
SRI/MF/excerpts, shipped quarterly

Monthly professional journal (published Sept.-June) presenting research results and essays on issues, trends, and policies in education and the teaching profession. Covers testing, curriculum development, teacher education, enrollment, school finance and administration, and other topics of interest to the profession. A Gallup Poll on public attitudes toward public schools appears annually.

Issues contain feature articles and essays, occasionally with supporting statistics; and regular narrative editorial features.

Features with substantial statistical content are described, as they appear, under "Statistical Features." Each issue of the journal is reviewed, but an abstract is published in SRI monthly issues only when statistical features appear.

Availability: Phi Delta Kappan, Director of Administrative Services, 8th and Union, PO Box 789, Bloomington IN 47402, $20.00 per yr., single copy $2.50; SRI/MF/excerpts for all portions described under "Statistical Features;" shipped quarterly.

Issues reviewed during 1984: Nov. 1983-Oct. 1984 (P) (Vol. 65, Nos. 3-10; Vol. 66, Nos. 1-2).

STATISTICAL FEATURES:

A8680-1.501: Nov. 1983 (Vol. 65, No. 3)
BIG DISTRICTS AND THE BLOCK GRANT: FIRST-YEAR FISCAL IMPACTS

(p. 199-203) By Richard Jung and Michael Tashjian. Article analyzing urban school districts' Federal funding under the Education Consolidation and Improvement Act (ECIA). Most data are based on a study of 28 large school districts.

Includes 3 tables showing the following data by district: ECIA block grant receipts, including formula amount and discretionary grants, FY82; total funding under pre-ECIA programs, FY80-81; and ranking by percent funding change FY81/82, with actual funding under Emergency School Aid Act FY81.

A8680-1.502: Jan. 1984 (Vol. 65, No. 5)
ANTI-DEMOCRATIC ATTITUDES OF HIGH SCHOOL SENIORS IN THE ORWELL YEAR

(p. 327-332) By Stanley M. Elam. Article comparing political attitudes of high school students graduating in 1952 and 1984. Data are based on 634 responses to the 1951 Purdue Youth Opinion Poll, and on 425 responses to a similar survey conducted by the author in 1983.

Includes 4 tables showing response distribution for both surveys concerning attitudes toward various aspects of the U.S. Bill of Rights, marxism, and fascism; and knowledge of selected well-known political figures and events.

GROWING IMBALANCE BETWEEN EDUCATION AND WORK

(p. 342-346) By Russell W. Rumberger. Article on increased educational attainment of the labor force compared to job opportunities requiring advanced schooling. Data are from *Monthly Labor Review* and other sources.

Includes 2 tables showing percent of all and young workers with 4 or more years of college, proportion of high level jobs in the economy, and percent of young college graduates in high level jobs by sex, decennially 1960-90; and increase in jobs, for 10 occupations with highest relative and absolute growth, 1978-90 period.

1983 SAT SCORES AND THEIR LINK TO NUCLEAR FALLOUT

(p. 372-374) By Ernest J. Sternglass and Steven Bell. Article hypothesizing a relationship between Scholastic Aptitude Test (SAT) scores in the 1980s and the effects of fallout from nuclear tests in the 1960s. Includes 1 chart showing SAT verbal score changes for selected northern and central States, 1982-83.

A similar article was published in the Apr. 1983 issue (for description, see SRI 1983 Annual under A8680-1.406).

A8680-1.503: Mar. 1984 (Vol. 65, No. 7)
SEX EDUCATION: AN OVERVIEW OF CURRENT PROGRAMS, POLICIES, AND RESEARCH

(p. 491-496) By Asta M. Kenney and Margaret Terry Orr. Article, with 4 tables showing teenage pregnancies, births, illegitimate births, abortions, and miscarriages; sexually active teenagers as percent of all urban teenagers, by age and sex; public approval of sex education in schools; and frequency of inclusion of selected topics in public secondary school sex education programs; various years 1965-82.

Data are from Federal sources and various private studies and surveys.

A8680–1.504: May 1984 (Vol. 65, No. 9)

TESTING TEACHERS IN LOUISIANA: A CLOSER LOOK

(p. 626-628) By Donald Kauchak. Article on Louisiana employment trends for black teachers, and the possible effects of basing certification on National Teacher Examination (NTE) results. Includes 1 table showing number of Louisiana college graduates taking NTE, by race, 1978-82.

TITLE I TALE: HIGH READING/MATH GAINS AT LOW COST IN KANSAS CITY, KANSAS

(p. 632-634) By Ruth Weinstock. Article, with 1 table showing achievement gains in reading and mathematics, and total per pupil cost, for grades 3-6 in Kansas City programs funded under Title I of the Elementary and Secondary Education Act, 1977/78-1980/81.

WRITING FOR PROFESSIONAL PUBLICATION: WAYS TO INCREASE YOUR SUCCESS

(p. 635-637) By Kenneth T. Henson. Article, with 1 table showing selected editorial practices and characteristics of 40 education journals, including manuscript acceptance rate and preferred length, articles and issues published per year, and university personnel as a percent of contributors. Data are based on responses to a fall 1983 survey conducted by the author.

A8680–1.505: Sept. 1984 (Vol. 66, No. 1)

16th ANNUAL GALLUP POLL OF THE PUBLIC'S ATTITUDES TOWARD THE PUBLIC SCHOOLS

(p. 23-38) Annual survey article, by George H. Gallup, on public opinion concerning public schools. Survey covered 1,515 adults and was conducted May 18-27, 1984. Includes 5 charts and 38 tables showing survey responses related to the following:

a. Education's importance to America's future; ratings of public schools, staff, and officials, and of students' parents; tax increases to support education; 1984 presidential candidates' support for education; lengthening of school day and year; student workloads; course requirements for college-bound and other students; special instruction and extracurricular activities; examination-based graduation; and raising college entrance requirements.

b. Teacher examinations and career ladders; teacher compensation, including adequacy of current levels, higher salaries for math/science/vocational teachers, and merit pay; teaching as career for own child; school prayer; schools without traditional grade level systems; credit for community service; school problems, including student discipline; education goals; and responsibility for determining school curriculum.

Many tables show data by whether respondent has child in school and/or in public or nonpublic school; and by respondent sex, race, age, community size, education, and region. Selected tables also include comparisons to previous years, from as early as 1969.

A8680–1.506: Oct. 1984 (Vol. 66, No. 2)

GALLUP POLL OF TEACHERS' ATTITUDES TOWARD THE PUBLIC SCHOOLS

(p. 97-107) By Alec Gallup. First part of a 2-part article on teachers' attitudes concerning the public school system and various education-related issues. Data are based on 813 responses to an Apr./May 1984 Gallup/Phi Delta Kappa survey. Includes 6 charts and 30 tables showing responses related to the following:

a. Ratings of own and local schools, local teachers and school officials, students' parents, and own educational training; 1984 presidential candidates' support for education; school prayer amendment; own school's difficulty in attracting and retaining good teachers; and reasons teachers leave education profession.

b. Compensation adequacy; higher salaries for science/math/technical/vocational teachers; and merit pay, including reasons for support or opposition, percent of teachers warranting, and responsibility and criteria for awarding.

c. School problems, including discipline; standard examinations for grade promotion and graduation; remedial instruction; raising college entrance requirements; and teacher examinations.

Many tables show separate responses for elementary and high school teachers, and include comparisons with attitudes of the general public. Part 2 of the survey is scheduled to appear in the Jan. 1985 issue of *Phi Delta Kappan*.

BETTER TEACHERS FOR THE YEAR 2000: A PROPOSAL FOR THE STRUCTURAL REFORM OF TEACHER EDUCATION

(p. 116-120) By David L. Clark. Article, with 1 table showing number of States considering selected actions for reforming teacher education and certification, 1983. Data are from *Education Week*.

TEACHER RECERTIFICATION: A SURVEY OF THE STATES

(p. 123-126) By Madlyn Levine Hanes and Michael D. Rowls. Article, with 1 table showing State regulations for teacher recertification, including recertification period, and semester hours of continued education required, by State, primarily 1982. Data are based on surveys of education depts in State governments and major universities, conducted by the authors.

A8695
Photo Marketing
Association International

A8695–1   **COST OF DOING BUSINESS SURVEY for Photo Retailers, Photo Finishers, and Specialty Professional Labs**
Annual.   May 1984.   40 p.
SRI/MF/not filmed

Annual report presenting average operating ratios for photography-based firms, by firm type and sales range, 1983. Covers photo retail and photofinishing firms, single-unit independent mini labs, and specialty professional labs.

Includes itemized sales, cost of goods sold, operating expenses and profit, pretax income, assets, and liabilities, all expressed as percent of sales. Also includes liquidity, leverage, profitability, and other operating ratios.

Data are from a 1983 Photo Marketing Assn survey of member firms. Report is intended to permit companies to compare their operations with industry averages.

Contains contents listing, introduction, and foreword (p. 3-8); 12 tables arranged in 4 sections (p. 9-28); and definitions and ratio formulas (p. 29-40).

Availability: Photo Marketing Association International, 3000 Picture Pl., Jackson MI 49201, members $50.00, nonmembers $60.00; SRI/MF/not filmed.

A8720
Potash and
Phosphate Institute

A8720–1   **STATISTICAL REPORT: Potash Sales**
Monthly.
Approx. 5 p. Oversized.
SRI/MF/complete, shipped quarterly

Monthly report on U.S., State, and Canadian Province potash sales by producers, including U.S. and Canadian exports. Report is issued 3-6 weeks after month of coverage, and is one of a series on potash production and disposition (see A8720-2 through A8720-5).

An errata for selected tables in the Jan. 1984 issue has also been received and is available on SRI microfiche under this number.

Contains 7 tables, listed below.

Availability: Potash and Phosphate Institute, 2801 Buford Hwy., NE, Suite 401, Atlanta GA 30329, †; SRI/MF/complete, shipped quarterly.

Issues reviewed during 1984: Sept. 1983-July 1984 (D).

TABLES:

[Tables [2-7] show data for current month. Potash types shown are standard, coarse, granular, and soluble muriates; and sulphates.]

[1] Total potash sales [agricultural by State and Canadian Province, and total exports; nonagricultural total U.S., Canada, and exports; and total by type; usually for current month, fertilizer year (July-June) to date, and same periods of previous year].

[2-4] North American, Canadian, and U.S. producers potash sales [agricultural by State and Province of destination, and agricultural exports; and nonagricultural sales in U.S. and Canada, and exports; all by type].

[5-7] North American, Canadian, and U.S. producers [agricultural and nonagricultural] potash exports [by type and country of destination; prior to the Jan. 1984 issue, data were shown for North America only].

A8720-2   STATISTICAL REPORT: Potash Production, Inventory, Disappearance, and Sales
Monthly, with quarterly and annual summaries.
Approx. 5 p. Oversized.
SRI/MF/complete, shipped quarterly

Monthly report, with quarterly and annual summaries, on total potash production tonnage, inventories, disappearance, and agricultural and nonagricultural sales and exports by U.S. and Canadian producers. Report is issued monthly, with separate quarterly summaries, and annual summaries for the calendar and fertilizer (July-June) years. Report is usually issued 4-6 weeks after the period covered, and is one in a series on potash production and disposition (see A8720-1 through A8720-5).

Contains 4-13 tables, listed below.

Availability: Potash and Phosphate Institute, 2801 Buford Hwy., NE, Suite 401, Atlanta GA 30329, †; SRI/MF/complete, shipped quarterly.

Issues reviewed during 1984: Monthly Reports: Oct. 1983-Aug. 1984 (D).

Issues reviewed during 1984: Quarterly Summaries: July/Sept. 1983-Apr./June 1984 (D).

Issues reviewed during 1984: Annual Summaries: calendar year 1983 and fertilizer year 1983/84.

TABLES:
[Monthly tables [1-4] show data for U.S. and Canadian producers, for month of coverage and same month of previous year. Tables [1-4] also appear in quarterly and annual summaries, showing data for current period of coverage and same period of previous year. Quarterly tables [5-7] also appear in fertilizer year annual summary, showing data for current year of coverage.

Tables [8-13] appear in annual reports only, and show tonnages for the fertilizer or calendar year.]

MONTHLY TABLES
[1] Potash report summary [tonnage; also including cumulative tonnage and monthly inventories, for previous and current fertilizer year to date].

[2-4] Report of potash production, inventory, disappearance, and [agricultural and nonagricultural] sales [and exports; for 6 types of muriates, and sulphates].

QUARTERLY TABLES
[5-7] North American, Canadian, and U.S. producers [agricultural and nonagricultural] potash exports [by country of destination, for current quarter of coverage; tables begin in Jan./Mar. 1984 quarterly summary].

ANNUAL TABLES
[8-13] North American, Canadian, and U.S. producers domestic potash sales [by State and Province of destination, and total exports]: agricultural and nonagricultural.

A8720-3   STATISTICAL REPORT: Potash Exports
Quarterly, with annual summaries. Approx. 2 p.
SRI/MF/complete

Quarterly report on potash exports of North American producers, by type and country of destination, with annual summaries issued at the end of the calendar and fertilizer (July-June) years. Report is issued 5-6 weeks after period covered, and is one in a series on potash production and disposition (see A8720-1 through A8720-5).

Contains 1 table showing North American producers' potash exports, agricultural and nonagricultural, for muriates by type, and sulphates, by country of destination, for quarter of coverage.

Reports subsequent to Oct./Dec. 1983 were not available for review.

Availability: Potash and Phosphate Institute, 2801 Buford Hwy., NE, Suite 401, Atlanta GA 30329, †; SRI/MF/complete.

Issues reviewed during 1984: July/Sept.-Oct./Dec. 1983; and annual summary for calendar year 1983 (D).

A8720-4   STATISTICAL REPORT: Potash Imports
Quarterly, with annual summaries. Approx. 1 p.
SRI/MF/complete

Quarterly report, with annual summaries, on U.S. potash imports, by State and by country of origin. Report is issued 4-9 weeks after period covered, with annual summaries at the end of the calendar and fertilizer (July-June) years.

Contains 1 table showing data for muriate and sulphate potash and potash product, for quarter of coverage.

Report is part of a series on potash production and disposition (see A8720-1 through A8720-5).

Availability: Potash and Phosphate Institute, 2801 Buford Hwy., NE, Suite 401, Atlanta GA 30329, †; SRI/MF/complete.

Issues reviewed during 1984: July/Sept. 1983-Apr./June 1984; and annual summaries for calendar year 1983 and fertilizer year 1984 (D).

A8720-5   STATISTICAL REPORT: Press Release, Potash Sales
Quarterly. Approx. 2 p.
SRI/MF/complete

Quarterly press release on total U.S. and Canadian sales, exports, and imports of potash muriates and sulphates, with annual summaries included at the end of the calendar and fertilizer (July-June) years. Report is issued 5-6 weeks after quarter covered, and is one of a series on potash production and disposition (see A8720-1 through A8720-4).

Contains brief narrative summary, and 1 quarterly table showing U.S. and Canadian agricultural and nonagricultural sales and combined exports, and total overseas imports into U.S., by potash type, for current quarter and same quarter of previous year.

Availability: Potash and Phosphate Institute, 2801 Buford Hwy., NE, Suite 401, Atlanta GA 30329, †; SRI/MF/complete.

Issues reviewed during 1984: July/Sept. 1983-Apr./June 1984 (D) (Nos. E.261-E.264).

A8740 Printing Industries of America

A8740-3   1981-82 PRODUCTION MANAGEMENT COMPENSATION SURVEY
Recurring (irreg.) 1982.
375 p.
SRI/MF/complete

Recurring report on compensation and characteristics of production management personnel in U.S. and Canadian printing industries, 1981 with summary comparisons to 1978. Includes data on salaries, bonuses, supervisory responsibilities, and average age and years in position, for 26 production management positions.

Also includes data on salary reviews and raises; and vacation, insurance, and retirement benefits.

Most data are shown by U.S. region and for Canada, and by type of business, shop labor union status, and sales size category.

Data are based on 486 responses to a 1981 survey of printing companies.

Contains contents listing (1 p.); 2 narrative summary sections interspersed with text data and 17 tables (p. 1-25); 26 statistical sections, each covering 1 management position, with 182 tables (p. 26-363); and questionnaire facsimile and position descriptions (p. 364-375).

Most recent previous survey was conducted in 1978. Issuing agency plans to update survey every 2-4 years.

Availability: Printing Industries of America, Publications Division, 1730 N. Lynn St., Arlington, VA 22209, members $90.00+postage, nonmembers $140.00+postage; SRI/MF/complete.

A8770 Public Relations Society of America

A8770-1   PUBLIC RELATIONS JOURNAL
Monthly. Approx. 50 p.
ISSN 0033-3670.
LC 49-23911.
SRI/MF/excerpts, shipped quarterly

Monthly journal (semimonthly in Sept.) reporting on public relations practices and developments in business, nonprofit organizations, and government.

Issues generally contain articles, occasionally with statistics, and editorial depts. An annual survey of business and assn advertising costs appears in Nov. issue. Additional Sept. issue is a directory of members, not included in subscription for nonmembers.

Features with substantial statistical content are described, as they appear, under "Statistical Features." Each issue of the journal is reviewed, but an abstract is published in SRI monthly issues only when statistical features appear.

Availability: Public Relations Society of America, 845 Third Ave., New York NY 10022, members †, nonmembers $28.00 per yr., single copy $3.00, directory issue $95.00 to nonmember subscribers; SRI/MF/excerpts for all portions described under "Statistical Features;" shipped quarterly.

Issues reviewed during 1984: Nov. 1983-Oct. 1984 (P) (Vol. 39, No. 11-12; Vol. 40, Nos. 1-10).

STATISTICAL FEATURES:

A8770–1.501: Nov. 1983 (Vol. 39, No. 11)

WHAT HAPPENS WHEN CORPORATE AD BUDGETS ARE CUT?

(p. 25-31) By Thomas F. Garbett. Article on reasons for corporate reductions in advertising budgets. Data are from *Barron's Regular Investor Confidence Tracking Study.* Includes 1 table showing investor confidence ratings by industry group, 4th quarter 1981-82.

CORPORATE ADVERTISING, ANNUAL FEATURE

(p. 32-38) Annual survey report on business and assn advertising expenditures, by media, 1976-1st half 1983, with detail for 20 leading advertisers, 1982-1st half 1983. Data are compiled by Leading National Advertisers from Publishers Information Bureau, Broadcast Advertising Reports, and Institute of Outdoor Advertising. Includes 6 tables. This is the 12th annual survey.

A8770–1.502: Jan. 1984 (Vol. 40, No. 1)

STUDY SHOWS THAT PUBLIC INFORMATION CAMPAIGNS WORK

(p. 8-9) Article presenting survey results on the impact of a public service announcement program promoting crime prevention. Data are from national and local surveys reaching 2,249 respondents. Surveys were conducted by Roper Organization and were funded through a Justice Dept grant.

Includes 1 table comparing respondents' crime prevention activities before and after the program.

A8770–1.503: Mar. 1984 (Vol. 40, No. 3)

NEW PROFESSIONALS: A PROFILE

(p. 26-29) By Frederick Teahan. Article on first-job experiences of 1983 public relations graduates. Data are based on 65 responses to a Jan. 1984 survey of 200 former members of Public Relations Student Society of America.

Includes 3 tables showing average starting salary by sex, by State, Public Relations Society of America district, and business sector, for bachelor and master degree graduates.

For description of similar article on 1980 public relations graduates, see SRI 1982 Annual under A8770-1.302.

A8770–1.504: May 1984 (Vol. 40, No. 5)

NOT-FOR-PROFIT COMPENSATION

(p. 23-26) Article on executive compensation in not-for-profit organizations. Data are from responses of 178 organizations to a 1983 survey conducted by Towers, Perrin, Forster, and Crosby, Inc., representing 1,446 employees in 23 surveyed positions.

Includes 3 tables showing high, low, median, and mean salaries of top executives, by position function, years in position, and organization type, budget, and employment size, 1983 with selected comparisons to 1982.

A8770–1.505: Aug. 1984 (Vol. 40, No. 8)

SURVEY BY ORC REVEALS PRACTITIONERS' VIEWS ON MAJOR ISSUES

(p. 29-30) Article on corporate performance on key issues of national importance, as rated by public relations executives, other executives in major and mid-sized companies, and leaders of the Washington, D.C. establishment. Data are based on 1,350 responses to a survey conducted by Opinion Research Corp.

Includes 1 undated table showing percent of each group surveyed giving business excellent/good ratings for each issue.

A8770–1.506: Sept. 1984 (Vol. 40, No. 9)

COMPLAINT STUDY ENDORSES CONSUMER-AFFAIRS FUNCTION IN BUSINESS

(p. 6-7) Article on consumer complaints to Better Business Bureaus. Data are from a Council of Better Business Bureaus annual report. Includes 4 undated tables showing 15 industries receiving most complaints, top 10 complaint categories, and 14-15 industries with highest and lowest complaint settlement rates.

A8775
Public
Securities Association

A8775–1   STATISTICAL YEARBOOK OF MUNICIPAL FINANCE: The New Issue Market in 1983

Annual. 1984. 128 p.
ISSN 0740-5790.
LC SC83-7396.
SRI/MF/complete, delayed

Annual report, for 1983, on municipal securities sales, yields, and underwriting activity, by region. Includes data on long- and short-term volume, ranking of leading underwriters, sales by State and use of proceeds, and sales trends, 1966-83.

Data are from the data base maintained by the Municipal Finance Study Group at the State University of New York at Albany.

Contains contents listing and introduction (p. 2-5); and 5 sections, with 97 tables, listed below (p. 7-128).

Availability: Public Securities Association, One World Trade Center, New York NY 10048, members $40.00, nonmembers $60.00; SRI/MF/complete, delayed shipment in Sept. 1985.

TABLES:

[Data are for 1983, unless otherwise noted.

Data by use of proceeds include education by level, transportation, utilities/conservation, social welfare, industrial aid for pollution control and other, public services, recreation, and miscellaneous. Data by issuer include State, municipality, county, and other statutory authorities.]

A8775–1.1: General Municipal Market Statistics and National Underwriting Activity

GENERAL MARKET STATISTICS

[Tables [1-5] also include data for 1982.]

[1] Municipal market summary [amount and number of long- and short-term issues, by month]. (p. 8)

[2A-2B] Long-term volume by type of security [includes unlimited and limited tax, and other general obligation issues, and utility, user charge, special tax, lessee revenue, and other revenue issues; by month]. (p. 8)

[3] Short-term volume by type of security [for 6 types, including urban renewal, by month]. (p. 9)

[4] Municipal bond sales summary, by use of proceeds. (p. 9)

[5] Long-term municipal volume by type of offering [negotiated, competitive, and/or private placement, by Moody's ratings]. (p. 10)

[6] Percent distribution of long-term volume, by size and type [general obligation and revenue] of issue. (p. 12)

[7-8] New yields on general obligation and revenue [by Moody's ratings and length of maturity, by month]. (p. 12-13)

[9-11] General obligation and revenue bond sales, competitive and negotiated sales, and municipal bond sales by type of issuer, for each of the 50 States. (p. 14-17)

[12] Tax exempt/taxable yield ratio [short-term, and long-term by rating; by month, 1981-83]. [Table is numbered 9 in the publication.] (p. 18)

NATIONAL UNDERWRITING ACTIVITY

[13-26] Leading underwriters [top 100 firms, all issues; and top 50 firms for general obligation, revenue, competitive and negotiated offerings, negotiated revenue, all housing, single- and multi-family housing, industrial development bonds for pollution control and other, health care revenue, public power, and refunding bonds; all ranked by amount underwritten, and showing number of issues]. (p. 20-34)

A8775–1.2: Regional Activity and Historical Trends

REGIONAL MARKET AND UNDERWRITING ACTIVITY

[1] Summary of the regional markets, by type of security and type of offering [by region]. (p. 36)

[2-8] New England: municipal bond sales [amount and number] summary, by use of proceeds, 1982-83; and leading underwriters [ranked by amount underwritten, with number of issues, for all, general obligation, revenue, competitive, negotiated, and negotiated revenue issues]. (p. 37-43)

[9-50] [Tables [2-8] are repeated for each of 6 regions.] (p. 44-85)

NATIONAL AND REGIONAL LARGEST ISSUES

[Tables [51-54] include issuer, issue type, State, 2 ratings of issue, initial and 2nd bid cost of issue, total amount of issue, reoffer yield, purpose, security type, and underwriters.]

[51-52] 20 largest competitive and negotiated issues [U.S.]. (p. 88-95)

[53-54] New England: 10 largest competitive and negotiated issues. (p. 96-99)

[55-66] [Tables [53-54] are repeated for each of 6 regions.] (p. 100-123)

HISTORICAL TRENDS

[Tables show data for 1966-83, unless otherwise noted. Data by type of issue or security are for all issues, and general obligation and revenue bonds.]

[67-68] Long-term volume, by type of security, and by offering [competitive, negotiated, privately placed, and other]. (p. 125)

[69] Percent distribution of long-term volume, by size and type of issue, 1969-83. (p. 126)

[70] New issue reoffering yields yearly average [at 5, 10, and 15 years of maturity] for Moody's AA/AA-1 rated bonds [by type of security]. (p. 128)

A8789
Radio Advertising Bureau

A8789–1   RADIO FACTS
Annual. 1984. 44 p.
SRI/MF/complete

Annual statistical compilation, for 1984, on radio ownership, listenership, and advertising revenues and effectiveness, with selected comparisons to other media. Data generally are current to 1983, with selected trends from 1960. Report is intended as a reference tool for radio advertising salespersons.

Data are from media research firms, advertising agencies, and trade assns.

Contains contents listing (p. 2-3); 15 sections, with 26 charts and 37 tables described below, and list of acronyms (p. 4-35); radio history and glossary (p. 36-41); and list of data sources (p. 42-44).

Availability: Radio Advertising Bureau, 485 Lexington Ave., New York NY 10017, member stations †, others ‡; SRI/MF/complete.

TABLES AND CHARTS:
a. Trends in radios sold and in use, and households with radios, various years 1970-83. 2 charts and 1 table. (p. 4-5)

b. Radio audience reach and listening habits, including data on average hours spent listening; time of day, location, and seasonality of listening; and types of radios used; with selected detail for men, women, and teenagers. 8 charts and 19 tables. (p. 5-16)

c. Radio audience comparisons to TV, newspapers, and other media, including use as 1st news source, advertising awareness, time between media exposure and day's largest purchase, shares of daily time spent with media, and audience reach, with selected detail for age groups, college graduates, professional men, working women, other demographic groups, and users of specific products and services (no dates); and change in radio advertising cost vs. selected other media, 1967-83 period. 15 charts and 4 tables. (p. 17-25)

d. Radio advertising: expenditures of top 25 spot and network advertisers, by company, 1983; rankings of business categories by shares of 1983 spot and network expenditures, and by share of local radio expenditures with detail by market size; and spot, local, and network advertising revenues, 1979-83 with aggregate trends from 1960. 1 chart and 5 tables. (p. 26-30)

e. Radio stations, and AM and FM station distribution, by program format, primarily 1984; and AM and FM radio sales volume (with detail for car radios), stations operating, advertising revenue, and average commercial minutes and spots per hour and newscast length, various years 1980-83. 8 tables. (p. 32-35)

A8790
Recreation Vehicle
Industry Association

A8790–1   RV FINANCIAL FACTS
Quarterly.   Approx. 6 p.
SRI/MF/complete

Quarterly newsletter on recreational vehicle (RV) industry market developments and general economic conditions affecting RV industry outlook. Data are from issuing agency and American Bankers Assn.

Issues contain brief narrative articles; 1 illustrative chart showing RV shipment trends; and 1 other chart showing delinquency rates on 8-10 types of bank installment loans, for quarter 2 quarters prior to cover date.

Availability: Recreation Vehicle Industry Association, Publications, 14650 Lee Rd., PO Box 204, Chantilly VA 22021, †; SRI/MF/complete.
Issues reviewed during 1984: Fall 1983-Summer 1984 (P) (Vol. 9, Nos. 3-4; Vol. 10, Nos. 1-2).

A8790–3   RVs, AMERICA'S FAMILY
CAMPING VEHICLES: A
Year-End Report, 1983
Annual.   1984.   19 p.
SRI/MF/complete

Annual report on recreational vehicle (RV) shipments and deliveries, by vehicle type, State, and census division, 1983, with trends from 1970. Also includes data on retail value of shipments. Data are from annual RVIA surveys of RV manufacturers.

Contents:

a. Contents listing and introduction. (p. 2-3)

b. Manufacturer survey results, with 6 charts and 7 tables showing shipments, retail value, distribution of shipments and deliveries by State and census division, and market shares by vehicle length, all by vehicle type, various years 1970-83. (p. 4-13)

c. Narrative analysis of consumer survey results; and appendix, with 3 economic indicator trend charts, description of vehicle categories, and text data on wholesale and retail value by vehicle type 1976-83. (p. 15-19)

Availability: Recreation Vehicle Industry Association, Publications, 14650 Lee Rd., PO Box 204, Chantilly VA 22021, members one copy †, all others $5.75; SRI/MF/complete.

A8790–4   RECREATION VEHICLE
FINANCING, 1984 Survey
Annual.   1984.   2+31 p.
ISSN 0733-530X.
LC 82-644156.
SRI/MF/complete

Annual report on new and used recreational vehicle (RV) financing practices of banks, savings and loan assns, finance companies, and credit unions, 1983. Covers retail and wholesale RV loans. Also includes data on other loans, delinquency rates, and RV shipments.

Data are based primarily on 299 responses, representing 6,051 operating locations, to a Jan. 1984 RVIA Finance Committee survey of financial institutions.

Contains contents listing (1 p.); narrative summary, with 1 text table (p. 1-4); 14 charts and 50 tables, described below (p. 5-25); and appendix, with descriptions and average prices of RV types, questionnaire facsimile, and 3 economic indicator trend charts (p. 26-31).

This is the 5th annual survey.

Availability: Recreation Vehicle Industry Association, Publications, 14650 Lee Rd., PO Box 204, Chantilly VA 22021, $5.75; SRI/MF/complete.

CHARTS AND TABLES:
[Unless otherwise noted, data are for 1983. Tables show number of respondent banks, savings and loan assns, sales installment/finance firms, and credit unions for the areas noted below.]

a. Lender characteristics: value of all and RV loans outstanding; profitability of RV loans vs. auto and other secured loans; future plans for RV financing; number of financing locations; years making RV loans; and methods used to determine loan values. 1 chart and tables 1-6. (p. 5-7)

b. RV retail direct and indirect loans: number and value of loans outstanding, and made in 1983; percent of portfolio invested in RVs; interest accounting methods; minimum down payment required; maximum maturity, percent early payoffs, and average turnover; and additional items and vehicle types financed. 1 chart and tables 7-29. (p. 8-14)

c. RV wholesale financing (floor planning): value of loans and percent of manufacturer's invoice financed; renewal terms; percent of units financed wholesale that became retail loans; percent of wholesale portfolio invested in RVs; portfolio protection methods; and number of RV manufacturing firms and dealerships represented in portfolio. 1 chart and tables 30-36. (p. 16-17)

d. Defaults and other loans: RV loan defaults by time in arrears; repossession activities; number and value of all direct and indirect loans outstanding; value of all wholesale loans; and financing availability for autos, airplanes, boats, motorcycles, and snowmobiles. Tables 37-44. (p. 18-21)

e. Bank loan delinquency rates by type of loan; and percent of RVs purchased with trade-in and credit, by vehicle type. 4 charts. (p. 23)

f. RV shipments, by vehicle type, 1970-83. 6 charts and 6 tables. (p. 24-25)

A8800
Robotic Industries Association

A8800–1   WORLDWIDE ROBOTICS SURVEY AND DIRECTORY
Annual.   1983.   40 p.
LC 83-060843.
SRI/MF/complete

Annual worldwide robotics industry survey and directory, 1982. Includes data on number and value of robots in operation, year end 1982, and of robot production, 1983-85 and 1990; applications and capabilities of robots; robot price ranges; and status of robotics industry standards; all shown for 11-18 countries.

Also includes information on multinational robotics industry agreements (including joint ventures and mergers); and directory of robot manufacturers, suppliers, and systems houses, with brief profiles for RIA members.

Data are based primarily on responses from representatives of 25 robotics-related organizations in 19 countries to an RIA survey.

Contains contents listing (1 p.); introduction, with 1 chart (p. 1); survey findings, with 6 tables (p. 2-5); robotics agreements (p. 6-7); directory (p. 8-38); and list of survey respondents (p. 39-40).

This is the 2nd edition of the survey/directory; SRI coverage begins with this edition. Note that, prior to 1984, issuing agency name was Robot Institute of America.

Availability: Robotic Industries Association, PO Box 1366, Dearborn MI 48121, members $25.00 (prepaid), nonmembers $30.00 (prepaid), $1.00 shipping and handling; SRI/MF/complete.

A8810
Rubber Manufacturers Association

A8810–1   MONTHLY TIRE AND INNER TUBE REPORT
Monthly.   Approx. 2 p.
SRI/MF/not filmed

Monthly report on tire shipments, production, inventories, and exports; and inner tube shipments. Data are compiled from Commerce Dept and approximately 25 tire manufacturer reports, and Rubber Manufacturers Assn estimates, and are published irregularly, generally 3 months after month of coverage.

Contains narrative summary and 1 table showing the following: tire shipments (original equipment, replacements, and exports), production, and inventory; and inner tube shipments; all by vehicle type, for month of coverage and year to date, and same periods of preceding year.

Prior to June 1983 issue, report was titled *Monthly Tire Shipments and Production Report.*

Availability: Rubber Manufacturers Association, Management Information Services, 1400 K St., NW, Washington DC 20005, selected institutions †, others $100.00 per yr.; SRI/MF/not filmed.

Issues reviewed during 1984: July 1983-Aug. 1984 (D).

A8810–2   INDUSTRY RUBBER REPORT
Monthly.   Approx. 4 p.
SRI/MF/not filmed

Monthly report on rubber industry production, trade, consumption, and stocks. Data are compiled from Commerce Dept and reports submitted to RMA by rubber manufacturers, and are published approximately 2 months after month of coverage.

Includes 1 table showing data, as applicable, for new, natural, and synthetic rubber, by SIC 7-digit product code, for month of coverage and previous month, same month of previous year, and cumulatively for current and previous year.

Availability: Rubber Manufacturers Association, Management Information Services, 1400 K St., NW, Washington DC 20005, selected institutions †, others $100.00 per yr.; SRI/MF/not filmed.

Issues reviewed during 1984: Aug. 1983-July 1984 (D).

A8818
Scientific Manpower Commission

A8818–1   SALARIES OF SCIENTISTS, ENGINEERS, AND TECHNICIANS: A Summary of Salary Surveys, Eleventh Edition
Biennial.   Nov. 1983.
v+185 p.
ISSN 0146-5015.
LC 77-641787.
SRI/MF/complete

Biennial compilation, by Eleanor L. Babco, of detailed salary data for scientists, engineers, and technicians, with some comparative data for other professions. Data are primarily for 1982 or 1983 with selected trends from 1961. Data are derived from assn, Federal, and private surveys.

Salaries, and usually number employed, generally are shown by academic or professional field, degree level, years of experience, years since bachelor's degree, type of employer or institution, sex, census division, and selected States.

Also includes data by race for scientists, engineers, and college faculty; by age for scientists; by age and metro area for engineers; and by academic rank for faculty.

Contains contents listing and introduction (p. i-v); starting salaries, with 2 charts and 34 tables (p. 1-30); experienced personnel, 2 charts and 74 tables (p. 31-86); engineers, 1 chart and 43 tables (p. 87-117); technicians and technologists, 7 tables (p. 118-123); Federal employees, 6 tables (p. 124-136); faculty, 45 tables (p. 137-178); and bibliography and index (p. 179-185).

Each section is preceded by a brief narrative. Data source is listed on each table.

For description of previous report, for 1980-81, see SRI 1982 Annual, under this number.

Availability: Scientific Manpower Commission, 1776 Massachusetts Ave., NW, Washington DC 20036, $30.00 (prepaid); SRI/MF/complete.

A8818–2   PROFESSIONAL WOMEN AND MINORITIES: A Manpower Data Resource Service, Fifth Edition
Annual.   Aug. 1984.
vi+280 p.
ISSN 0190-1796.
LC 75-324671.
SRI/MF/complete, delayed

Annual compilation, by Betty M. Vetter and Eleanor L. Babco, of education and labor force statistics for women and minorities in professional fields, 1980s and trends. Includes data on higher education enrollment and degrees, and employment by sector, all by detailed field. Data are primarily for 1970s-83, with some trends from as early as 1870 and labor force projections to 2000.

Data are compiled from approximately 200 published and unpublished Federal Government, professional assn, and other private sources, individually identified on each table. Report is intended as a resource for manpower planners and affirmative action personnel.

Contains contents listing (i-vi); foreword and introduction (p. 1-4); 10 chapters, each preceded by contents listing, with a total of 337 tables described below (p. 5-265); and bibliographies and index (p. 266-280).

Availability: Scientific Manpower Commission, 1776 Massachusetts Ave., NW, Washington DC 20036, $70.00; SRI/MF/complete, delayed shipment in Aug. 1985.

TABLES:

[Tables generally show data by sex, or for total and women. Data by race or minority group are shown for various categories, including white, black, Hispanic, American Indian/Alaskan Native, Asian/Pacific Islander, and foreign. Data generally are shown for 1982 or 1983, with various trends 1950s-81; major exceptions are noted below.]

A8818–2.1: Education

POPULATION

a. Births, 1933-81. 1 table. (p. 6)

ENROLLMENT

b. Secondary education, including math and science assessment results, by age and race; graduates, projected to 1990/91; Scholastic Aptitude Test (SAT) scores and examinees, by race; high school curricula; and probable majors of college-bound seniors. 8 tables. (p. 7-12)

c. Undergraduate education, including minority share of enrollment, and enrollment status of persons age 16-24 by race; freshman probable majors and career choices; and enrollment, by race, type of institution, degree level, and field of study. 10 tables. (p. 13-20)

d. Graduate education, including entrance exam scores, by race and undergraduate major, with detail for Hispanic students; and science and engineering dept enrollment, by level, field of study, citizenship, type of institution, race, and source of financial support. 7 tables. (p. 21-27)

DEGREES

e. Doctoral degrees awarded, including women recipients by field of study, since 1920; women's share of degrees by level, since

1870; science and engineering degree recipients, by field of study and citizenship status; and U.S. citizen/permanent resident recipients, by race, field of study, and source of financial support. 9 tables. (p. 29-35)

f. Degrees awarded by level, including recipients by field of study and race, various periods 1940-82; degree attainment rates; and science and engineering degrees projected to 1989. 11 tables. (p. 37-51)

PROFESSIONAL FIELDS

g. Education summary, including percent of women and minorities enrolled, graduating, and working in professional fields; doctorate recipients by field of study since 1920; and first professional degree recipients and enrollment, by field of study and race. 7 tables. (p. 53-59)

h. Architecture, including degrees awarded by level; total registered architects; American Institute of Architects (AIA) members by race; and total, woman-owned, and minority-owned architecture firms in AIA. 2 tables. (p. 60)

i. Accounting and business, including accounting firm professional employment, total and for certified public accountants (CPAs), by race; job placement of accounting graduates from black/minority colleges; business school graduates, by degree level; and business faculty, by race. 5 tables. (p. 61-62)

j. Law, including degrees awarded by level; law school faculty by teaching load and race; and 1st-year and total enrollment, and Federal employment in detailed legal occupations, by race. 5 tables. (p. 63-65)

A8818–2.2: Employment

GENERAL WORKFORCE

a. Labor force summary, including population, labor force, and professional/technical workers variously cross-tabulated by occupation, labor force status, educational attainment, race, and age; and labor force projected to 1990 and 18-year olds by race projected to 2000. 9 tables. (p. 67-80)

SCIENCE, ENGINEERING, AND HUMANITIES

b. Doctoral population by field, cross-tabulated by race and citizenship status, with detail for scientists and engineers by employment status, years of experience, employment sector, and work activity; and science/engineering labor force participation and utilization rates. 18 tables. (p. 81-99)

c. Miscellaneous, including highest degree of scientists and engineers by field and race; employment status of recent science and engineering master's and bachelor's degree recipients, by field and race, with participation and utilization rates; and science and engineering bachelor's degrees granted compared to workforce. 6 tables. (p. 100-105)

d. Physically handicapped scientists and engineers, total and with PhDs, by field, race, age, employment status, employing sector, and work activity. 1 table. (p. 106)

ACADEMIC WORKFORCE

e. Doctoral academic employment, including doctorates by field, academic rank, race, year of degree, age, and tenure status; academic employment share of all employed doctorates, by graduate field; and faculty tenure rates by academic rank and type of institution. 11 tables. (p. 108-118)

f. Scientists and engineers, including academic employment by field, full- or part-time status, and type of institution; total and women full-time employment at top 25 institutions ranked by women scientists/engineers employed, and at top 50 public and top 50 private institutions ranked by total scientists/engineers employed; and total and foreign postdoctorates, and non-faculty doctoral research staff, by field. 8 tables. (p. 119-126)

g. Faculty summary, including women's share of full-time faculty employment, by academic rank and type of institution; elementary, secondary, and postsecondary education staff, by race; postsecondary faculty, by field and race; and total postsecondary institutions and faculty since 1869/70. 5 tables. (p. 127-131)

h. College administration, including women college presidents by type of institution. 1 table. (p. 132)

i. Elementary and secondary education staff, including percent of men teachers since 1948; distribution of women teachers and principals since 1928; distribution of public school teachers, by race; distribution of mathematics, science, and social studies teachers, by grade range; and vocational school staff by type of institution and position. 4 tables. (p. 133-134)

A8818–2.3: Detailed Professions

[Tables on detailed professions generally show proportion of women and minorities in the field; degrees awarded by level and race, with detail for doctorates by citizenship status, and subfield since 1920; academic and nonacademic employment, by race; and Federal employment by occupation and race.

These data, together with the additional data described below, are arranged by specific field under the major headings indicated below.]

a. Physical, mathematical, and computer sciences, including American Chemical Society (ACS) member characteristics, and employment by specialty and work function; distribution of tenured chemists; institutions with and without women on chemistry faculty; characteristics of astronomy, physics, and geosciences students; women on physics faculty, by rank and institution; physicists in industrial labs, by company; mathematics faculty, by rank and tenure status; and mathematics/statistics and computer science degrees, by level, projected to 1989. 57 tables. (p. 136-168)

b. Engineering, technology, and technicians, including leading engineering schools granting degrees to women and minorities; engineering enrollment, compared to high school graduates and to freshman and total college enrollment; B.S. degree completion rates; and enrollment by level and race, for total and nuclear engineering, health physics/radiation protection, and engineering technology. 29 tables. (p. 170-198)

c. Agricultural, biological, medical, and health sciences, including agricultural and biological science degrees by level, projected to 1989; health sciences enrollments and graduates, by race and field; medical schools, applicants, and students repeating academic year; women physicians, by specialty and major activity; physician residencies by specialty; dental school applicants, and faculty, by race; American Veterinary Medicine Assn members; and registered nurse characteristics. 64 tables. (p. 200-239)

d. Social and behavioral sciences, including anthropology, sociology, psychology, and economics faculty; women economist characteristics; previous activity of newly-hired economics faculty and current activity of faculty not rehired; and political science graduate enrollments and doctorates job placement. 32 tables. (p. 241-260)

e. Arts, humanities, and education. 6 tables. (p. 262-265)

A8825
Securities
Industry Association

A8825–1   SECURITIES INDUSTRY TRENDS: An Analysis of Emerging Trends in the Securities Industry
6-8 issues per year.
Approx. 20 p. var. paging.
ISSN 0276-2749.
LC 79-3918.
SRI/MF/complete, shipped quarterly

Periodical issued approximately 6-8 times per year, presenting summary analyses of the securities industry. Includes data on securities trading activity, yields, prices, and underwriting; and revenues and expenses of securities firms.

Month of data coverage is 1-4 months prior to publication. Data are from SEC studies and reports by securities firms and other Federal and commercial sources.

Report regularly includes special feature articles, usually with statistics; securities industry statistics section, with 7 recurring tables, listed below; and book and periodical reviews.

Recurring tables appear in most issues. All additional features with substantial statistical content are described, as they appear, under "Statistical Features." Nonstatistical features are not covered.

Availability: Securities Industry Association, Research Department, 120 Broadway, New York NY 10271, members $30.00 per yr., nonmembers $48.00 per yr.; SRI/MF/complete; shipped quarterly.

Issues reviewed during 1984: Oct. 31, 1983-July 30, 1984 (P) (Vol. IX, Nos. 5-6; Vol. X, Nos. 1-4).

RECURRING TABLES:

[Tables show data for month of coverage and same month of previous year, unless otherwise noted. Tables [1], [4], and [5] also show data for year to date for current and previous year. Table sequence may vary.]

TRADING DATA

[1] [Average daily share] volume [and value of shares traded by major stock exchange, odd-lot shares purchased and sold on NYSE, and contracts traded].

[2] [Corporate and municipal bond] yields (monthly averages) [and Bond Buyer Index].

[3] [End of month] prices [averages/indices for 6 major reporting authorities].

[4] Underwriting [value and/or volume of gross new corporate stock and debt and municipal note and bond issues].

[5] Mutual funds [net sales, net purchase of common stock and other securities, and cash position].

[6] Margin debt [outstanding, net change, and percent of accounts with equity under 40%].

NYSE FIRMS FINANCIAL DATA

[7] [Aggregate] financial data for NYSE firms doing a public business [revenue, expenses, net income before taxes, and percent of firms showing loss; quarter ending 3-5 months prior to cover date, usually year to date, and same periods of previous year].

STATISTICAL FEATURES:

A8825–1.501: Oct. 31, 1983 (Vol. IX, No. 5)

TAX COMPLIANCE TRENDS: REVIEW AND OUTLOOK

(p. 1-17) By Carolyn Hildebrandt. Article on Tax Equity and Fiscal Responsibility Act (TE-FRA) income reporting provisions, with estimates on Federal revenue losses from incorrect reporting (tax gap). Data are from IRS. Includes 5 tables showing the following estimates for various years 1973-81:

a. Tax gap by source: illegal sector; corporations; individual nonfilers, and filers' unreported income, overstated business expenses and personal exemptions, and mathematical errors; and employers' underwithholding.

b. Individual unreported and reported income, and unreported income marginal tax rate, by type of income.

A8825–1.502: Nov. 25, 1983 (Vol. IX, No. 6)

FIRST HALF OF 1983: IF ONLY IT COULD CONTINUE! SEMIANNUAL FEATURE

(p. 1-26) Second article of a 2-part semiannual feature, by Jeffrey M. Schaefer and Ira Epstein, reviewing securities industry financial developments and trading activities, 1982-1st half 1983.

Contains analysis, with text statistics and 12 tables showing the following data primarily for 1982-1st half 1983, with selected quarterly detail and trends from 1979:

a. Securities industry finances: aggregate after-tax equity returns; revenues and trading profits by source; value of underwriting by type of security, and of initial public offerings; and expenses by function.

b. Discounters: NYSE discounters' revenues by source and net pretax income; and NYSE/National Assn of Securities Dealers discounters' commissions and revenue share.

c. Industry concentration: aggregate equity returns, revenues, commissions, and capital shares, for top 10, next 15, and all other firms.

d. Selected interest rates and inflation indexes; average daily transaction volume for 3 major stock exchanges; and NYSE customer margin debit and free credit balances, and customer margin and broker call rates.

First article is described in SRI 1983 Annual, under A8825-1.404.

A8825–1.503: May 14, 1984 (Vol. X, No. 2)

SOME OBSERVATIONS ON INDUSTRY PROFITABILITY, SEMIANNUAL FEATURE

(p. 1-16) Semiannual article, by Edward I. O'-Brien, reviewing securities industry financial developments and trading activities, 1979-83.

Includes 12 charts and 11 tables showing security industry trading volume for selected new financial products; growth rates for revenues by source and expenses by item; after-tax equity return, by type of firm; net income; and capital; primarily 1983 with selected quarterly detail and trends from 1979.

A8825–1.504: June 14, 1984 (Vol. X, No. 3)

FLAT RATE TAX: PROS AND CONS

(p. 1-19) By Carolyn Hildebrandt. Article discussing possible benefits of a flat rate income tax system as compared to the current progressive rate structure. Data are from various Federal and private sources. Includes 6 tables showing the following:

a. Current tax structure: average and marginal individual tax rate at 4 income levels, selected years 1965-84; estimated revenue losses from selected exemptions, exclusions, and deductions, 1983-84, with distribution by adjusted gross income (AGI) class 1982; and net long-term capital gains in excess of short-term losses, by AGI class, 1977-81.

b. Tax payment under flat rate tax of 15% with $5,000 exemption, for 4 income levels; and savings, savings/consumption of fixed capital, and gross total and non-residential fixed capital formation, each as a percent of GDP, for U.S. and 5 other industrial countries, 1972-81 period.

A8825–1.505: July 30, 1984 (Vol. X, No. 4)

SECURITIES INDUSTRY PERFORMANCE 1983 AND 1st HALF 1984, SEMIANNUAL FEATURE

(p. 1-19) First article of a 2-part semiannual feature, by Jeffrey M. Schaefer et al., reviewing securities industry financial developments and trading activities, 1983-1st half 1984.

Contains analysis, with text statistics and 17 tables showing the following primarily by quarter for 1983, with some data for 1st-2nd quarter 1984, and trends from 1979:

a. Industry-wide finances: after-tax return on equity; key ratios; revenue by source; underwriting value and volume by type of security, with aggregate market shares for largest companies; broker call rate and rate charged to margin customers; expenses by function; and capital assets by type.

b. Discounters' finances: revenues, expenses, pre-tax net income, after-tax return on equity, pre-tax profit margin, commissions, and market shares, for NYSE/National Assn of Securities Dealers discounters.

A8825–2 FOREIGN ACTIVITY: An Analysis of Foreign Participation in the U.S. Securities Markets
Quarterly. Approx. 9 p.
SRI/MF/complete

Quarterly report on foreign investor purchases and sales of U.S. Treasury and corporate securities. Includes analysis of activity by Canadian, European, Mideastern, Latin American, and Asian investors, with related domestic or international economic developments, and net purchases of foreign stocks by U.S. investors.

Data are current through quarter 3-4 months prior to cover date.

Contains narrative highlights and analysis sections, interspersed with 4 tables, listed below; and, occasionally, summary or recent trend tables.

Availability: Securities Industry Association, Research Department, 120 Broadway, New York NY 10271, members $30.00 per yr., nonmembers $48.00 per yr.; SRI/MF/complete.

Issues reviewed during 1984: Nov. 9, 1983-July 2, 1984 (P) (Vol. VI, No. 4; Vol. VII, Nos. 1-3).

QUARTERLY TABLES:

[Tables show data by world region and selected country. Data are generally for quarter of coverage and preceding quarter. Table sequence and titles may vary.]

I. Gross activity/transactions in and net purchases of U.S. equities.

II. Gross activity/transactions and net purchases of U.S. corporate bonds.

III. Net foreign purchases and total foreign holdings of U.S. Treasury notes and bonds.

IV. Gross activity/transactions in and net purchases of foreign stocks by U.S. investors.

A8900
Shipbuilders
Council of America

A8900–2 STATISTICAL QUARTERLY
Quarterly.
Approx. 8 p. no paging.
SRI/MF/complete

Quarterly report on civilian and naval shipyard employment, civilian shipyard hours and earnings, and index of steel vessel construction materials. Also occasionally presents data on naval shipyard wages, merchant fleet status, construction contract awards, finished steel shipments, and tonnage and value of U.S. waterborne trade.

Reports are issued approximately 6-9 months after quarter of coverage. Data are from BLS, Maritime Administration, and other sources.

Issues generally contain 5 quarterly tables, and 2-6 additional tables and charts. Quarterly tables are listed below; most appear in all issues. All additional tables and charts are described, as they appear, under "Statistical Features."

Availability: Shipbuilders Council of America, 1110 Vermont Ave., NW, Suite 1250, Washington DC 20005-3553, †; SRI/MF/complete.

Issues reviewed during 1984: 3rd-4th Qtr. 1983 (D) [No issue was published for 2nd Qtr. 1983].

QUARTERLY TABLES:

[Tables [1] and [3] show data monthly for 15-27 months through quarter of coverage with annual averages from 1970s or earlier.]

[1] Naval shipyard employment [total and by region of base].

[2] Index of straight-time hourly earnings for selected shipyards, all regions [monthly for current year to date and preceding 5 years].

[3] Average hours and earnings for selected industries [total private, durable goods, and shipbuilding/repair].

[4-5] CPI (large cities), and Material Index for NAVSEA [Naval Sea Systems Command] steel vessel contracts [monthly for current year to date and preceding 6 years].

STATISTICAL FEATURES:

A8900–2.501: 3rd Qtr. 1983

SPECIAL TABLES

[A] Merchant ships [tonnage] on order in world [by country, selected dates Dec. 1973-Sept. 1983; data are from *Lloyd's Register Shipbuilding Returns*].

[B] Merchant fleets of the world: oceangoing steam and motor ships of 1,000 gross tons and over as of Jan. 1, 1983 [number and tonnage of combination passenger/cargo ships, freighters, bulk carriers, and tankers, by country, with detail for U.S. by type of ownership]. (Excludes ships operating on the Great Lakes and inland waterways; special types such as channel ships, icebreakers, cable ships, etc.; and merchant ships owned by any military force.)

[C] Naval combatant and auxiliary vessels contracted for with private U.S. shipyards [including vessels, contract yards, tonnage, and initial contract value, 1960-83].

A8900–2.502: 4th Qtr. 1983

SPECIAL TABLES AND CHARTS

[A] Mobile oil rig orderbook [rigs under construction/on order in foreign and U.S. shipyards, Jan. 1973-84]. [chart]

[B-F] New naval and merchant type vessels (1,000/over light displacement or gross tons) in U.S. private shipyards: [number and tonnage] under construction or on order [by vessel type, Jan. 1980-84 with summary trends from 1964; and delivered, 1964-83]. [tables and charts]

A8900–3 **ANNUAL REPORT, Shipbuilders Council of America**
Annual, discontinued coverage.

Annual report on shipbuilding industry, described in SRI 1983 Annual, under this number. Because this report no longer includes statistics, SRI coverage will not be continued.

Selected data on marine construction, repair, and conversion will be included in *Statistical Quarterly,* also issued by Shipbuilders Council of America. *Statistical Quarterly* is covered in SRI under A8900-2.

A8902
Silver Institute

A8902–1   **MINE PRODUCTION OF SILVER IN 1982 with Projections for 1983-86**
Annual. Nov. 1983. 9 p.
SRI/MF/complete

Annual report on silver mine production, worldwide and by country, 1982-83, with projections to 1986. Presents data for 48 designated International Trade Countries arranged by production size group, and for 9 Communist countries, all ranked by actual 1982 production.

Data are from U.S. Bureau of Mines, foreign government depts, and 233 mining enterprises headquartered in 31 countries.

Contains brief narrative (p. 1); 1 table (p. 2-3); and list of participating companies (p. 4-10).

Previous report, issued in 1981, is described in SRI 1981 Annual, under this number. No report was issued in 1982 due to lack of funding.

Availability: Silver Institute, 1001 Connecticut Ave., NW, Suite 1138, Washington DC 20036, †; SRI/MF/complete.

A8902–2   **MODERN SILVER COINAGE, 1983**
Annual. [1984.] 40 p.
ISSN 0149-7707.
LC 78-640559.
SRI/MF/complete, delayed

Annual report on silver coins issued as money in 77 countries, 1983. Includes number, silver content, and physical characteristics of coins, for 264 coin issues grouped by country. Also includes mint where coins were struck, total silver used, and total face value of coins in local currency, for each country.

Data are from ministries of finance, central banks, government and private mints, and numismatic experts.

Contains introduction (p. 1); 1 summary table (p. 2-3); 1 detailed table repeated for each country (p. 4-38); and list of mints issuing coins in 1983 (p. 39-40).

This is the 12th annual edition.

Availability: Silver Institute, 1001 Connecticut Ave., NW, Suite 1138, Washington DC 20036, $7.00; SRI/MF/complete, delayed shipment in Jan. 1985.

A8902–3   **SILVER INSTITUTE LETTER: Information on Silver for Industry**
Bimonthly.   Approx. 4 p.
ISSN 0730-8132.   LC 82-717.
SRI/MF/complete

Bimonthly newsletter reporting on worldwide refined silver production, disposition, and stocks; uses of silver; and Silver Institute activities. Data are from reports of approximately 50 silver refineries to the institute.

Contents:

a. Brief articles, occasionally with substantial statistics; and a recurring table on industrial silver consumption in Japan.

b. 2 bimonthly tables showing "999" silver production by source (primary ores/concentrates, coins, and old and new scrap), disposition (converted in plant, and shipped out), and stocks, for U.S. and foreign refiners.

Bimonthly data are shown for month 1-2 months prior to publication date, previous 1-3 months and years, and current and previous years to date. Foreign data are aggregated for all known refiners in Australia, Canada, Mexico, Peru, South Africa, Sweden, and West Germany, and some other refiners in Europe and Asia.

Bimonthly tables appear in all issues; Apr. 1984 issue also includes an additional table showing average monthly silver use, by U.S. and non-U.S. Silver Conversion Series participants, 1980-84. Recurring table and all additional features with substantial statistical content are described, as they appear, under "Statistical Features." Nonstatistical features are not covered.

Availability: Silver Institute, 1001 Connecticut Ave., NW, Suite 1138, Washington DC 20036, †; SRI/MF/complete.

Issues reviewed during 1984: Dec. 1983-Oct. 1984 (P) (Vol. 13, No. 6; Vol. XIV, Nos. 1-5).

STATISTICAL FEATURES:

A8902–3.501: Dec. 1983 (Vol. 13, No. 6)

ONLY 4% ANNUAL GROWTH IN WORLD SILVER MINE PRODUCTION

(p. 1-2) Article, with 1 table showing scheduled silver mine production, for 9 countries, 1983. Data are from the Silver Institute's *Mine Production of Silver, 1982-86.*

JAPAN INDUSTRY MONTHLY SILVER USE RUNNING NEARLY 10% AHEAD OF LAST YEAR, RECURRING FEATURE

(p. 4) Recurring table showing Japanese average monthly silver consumption, by industrial end use, 1982 and 1st 8 months 1983. Data are from Japan Mining Industry Assn reports.

A8902–3.502: June 1984 (Vol. XIV, No. 3)

JAPAN PRODUCTS USE MORE SILVER, RECURRING FEATURE

(p. 4) Recurring table showing Japanese silver consumption, by industrial end use, 1982-83. Data are from Japan Mining Industry Assn reports.

A8902–3.503: Oct. 1984 (Vol. XIV, No. 5)

KEY SPEECH ON SILVER TO AMERICAN MINING CONGRESS

(p. 3-4) Article on nonindustrial demand for silver, with 1 table showing silver average price, and volume of nonindustrial meltdown/disinvestment and acquisition/investment, 1977-83.

Data are from a speech by Carl E. Peterson of Engelhard Corp.

A8912
Society of Exploration Geophysicists

A8912–1 MONTHLY SEISMIC CREW COUNT
Monthly.   Approx. 2 p.
SRI/MF/complete, shipped quarterly

Monthly press release on number of seismic land crews and marine vessels exploring for oil/gas in the U.S. and Canada. Data are compiled by the Society of Exploration Geophysicists and are issued approximately 2 weeks after month of coverage.

Contains brief narrative summary, 3 charts with trends from the 1930s, and 2 tables showing number of seismic crews and vessels, and number of sponsors, all by type of sponsor (contractors, oil companies, and/or government).

Data for the U.S. are shown for the current and preceding month, and same month of 6 preceding years; and for Canada for the current and preceding month.

Availability: Society of Exploration Geophysicists, Headquarters Office, PO Box 702740, Tulsa OK 74170-2740, †; SRI/MF/complete, shipped quarterly.

Issues reviewed during 1984: Oct. 1983-Sept. 1984 (D).

A8912–2 INTERNATIONAL SEISMIC CREW COUNT
Quarterly.   Approx. 2 p.
SRI/MF/complete

Quarterly press release on seismic land crews and marine vessels exploring for oil/gas, by world area. Data are compiled by the Society of Exploration Geophysicists, and are issued approximately 5 months after quarter of coverage.

Contains brief summary, with 1 trend chart; and 2 tables showing number of seismic crews and vessels, and number of sponsors, all by type of sponsor (contractors, oil companies, and governments), in U.S., Canada, Mexico, Central/South America, Europe, Middle East, Africa, and Far East, for last month of current and previous quarters.

Availability: Society of Exploration Geophysicists, Headquarters Office, PO Box 702740, Tulsa OK 74170-2740, †; SRI/MF/complete.

Issues reviewed during 1984: 3rd Qtr. 1983-lst Qtr. 1984 (D).

A8912–3 SPECIAL REPORT: GEOPHYSICAL ACTIVITY IN 1983
Annual.   July 1984.   21 p.
ISSN 0016-8030.
LC 60-37909.
SRI/MF/complete

Annual report, by Russell J. Senti, on geophysical exploration activity for energy resources, research, and other purposes in the non-Communist world, 1983. Includes data on costs, miles surveyed, survey methods, and crew months, by world area.

Data are compiled by the Geophysical Activity Committee from questionnaires sent to more than 500 institutions and companies.

Contains narrative, 7 charts, and 19 tables listed below.

Report is reprinted from the July 1984 issue (Vol. 3, No. 7) of *Geophysics: The Leading Edge of Exploration,* and is paginated from that issue.

Availability: Society of Exploration Geophysicists, Headquarters Office, PO Box 702740, Tulsa OK 74170-2740, $3.00; SRI/MF/complete.

TABLES:
[Tables show data for 1983. Expenditure data are shown in U.S. dollars. Data by area are for 6 world areas, U.S., Canada, and Mexico.

Survey objectives generally include petroleum, minerals, engineering, geothermal, groundwater, oceanography, and research. Survey types include land, marine, airborne, and drill hole.

Seismic and other exploration activities include acquisition cost, line-miles, crew-months, and various operating ratios.]

1-2. Total worldwide expenditures by survey type and area, by survey objective. (p. 49-51)

3-6. Worldwide petroleum land and marine seismic activity, and seismic line-miles by energy source [including dynamite, all by area]. (p. 52-53)

7. Worldwide average unit costs [and exploration activities] for petroleum surveys [by area, survey type, and method]. (p. 55-58)

8-10. Petroleum seismic [land and marine] activity [in U.S. and Canada by State, Province, and offshore region; and in Mexico]. (p. 59-60)

11-12. Total worldwide expenditures on gravity/magnetic and airborne surveys [by survey objective and area]. (p. 60-61)

13A-14B. Western and Eastern Hemisphere airborne and land mining activity [by survey method]. (p. 61-62)

15-16. Worldwide groundwater/engineering and geothermal activity [by survey method]. (p. 62-63)

17. Worldwide average unit costs [and exploration activity], by survey objective, type, and method. (p. 63-68)

A8916
Society of Industrial Realtors

A8916–1 INDUSTRIAL REAL ESTATE MARKET SURVEY
Semiannual.
Spring/Summer 1984.
vii+196 p.
ISSN 0730-0131.
LC 81-649990.
SRI/MF/complete, Fall/Winter 1983 & Spring/Summer 1984 reports

Semiannual survey report, for spring/summer 1984, on industrial real estate market conditions and outlook, including sales, construction costs, prices, and financing, by region and metro area. Also includes data for Canada and France. Based on a spring 1984 survey of 141 specialists in 83 metro areas.

Contains users' guide, glossary, contents listing, and roster of survey participants (p. iii-vii); national analysis, with 9 summary charts and tables (p. 1-7); 9 basic tables, listed below, repeated for 77 U.S. cities or metro market areas grouped by region (each regional section also includes 5 charts showing summary data for the region), and 3 Canadian and 3 French cities (p. 10-193); and questionnaire facsimile (p. 194-196).

This is the 9th semiannual survey. Previous report, for fall/winter 1983, was also reviewed in 1984 and is also available on SRI microfiche under this number [Semiannual. Fall/Winter 1983. vii+213 p. $50.00]. Previous report is substantially similar in format and content, but also includes data for 6 additional U.S. cities and 1 city in England.

Availability: Society of Industrial Realtors, 777 14th St., NW, Washington DC 20005, $50.00 per yr.; SRI/MF/complete.

BASIC TABLES:
[The following tables are repeated for 14 northeastern cities or metro market areas (p. 12-39); 20 north central cities (p. 44-83); 28 southern cities (p. 88-143); 15 western cities or metro market areas (p. 148-177); Hamilton, Montreal, and Toronto, Canada (p. 180-185); and Lille, Lyon, and Paris, France (p. 188-193).

Data by category are shown for manufacturing, warehousing/distribution, and high technology.]

[1] Industrial market characteristics [square footage of available space and area vacant, for central city and suburbs].

[2] Dollar volume of sales and leases compared to a year ago [by category].

[3] Gross sales and lease prices of prime industrial buildings and sites [for central city and suburbs, price per square foot, and change from previous year].

[4] Rate of new construction compared to a year ago [by category].

[5] Construction cost of prime industrial buildings [cost per square foot, and change from previous year].

[6] Vacancy situation [and average shelf life] for prime industrial properties [by property size].

[7] Composition of absorption [of available space, by category; and inside and outside industrial parks].

[8] Mortgage financing for industrial properties [most important source, most prevalent interest rates, and money supply availability].

[9] Outlook for industrial real estate activity for next 12 months [sales and lease prices and dollar volume, construction costs, and absorption].

A8920
Society of the
Plastics Industry

A8920-1   FACTS AND FIGURES OF THE U.S. PLASTICS INDUSTRY, 1984 Edition
Annual.   Sept. 1984.
3+130 p.+foldout.
ISSN 0740-8420.
LC SC83-8335.
SRI/MF/complete, current & previous year reports

Annual report, for 1984, on the plastics industry, covering production, sales, markets, and foreign trade, by resin type; and industry financial and operating characteristics. Includes data by company. Most data are for 1983, with some forecasts for 1984 and trends from 1979 or earlier.

Data sources, identified for each table, include monthly statistical reports of the Society of the Plastics Industry (SPI), compiled by Ernst & Whinney from company surveys; other SPI reports; and government and private sources.

Contains contents listing (2 p.); report, with 51 charts and 110 tables, interspersed with narrative (p. 1-123); and list of other sources of information (p. 124-130).

All tables are listed below. Most charts illustrate or provide long-term trends for data contained in tables; however, 1 chart (p. 23) shows plastics processing industry hourly wage index, 1968-83.

Previous report, for 1983, was also reviewed in 1984 and is also available on SRI microfiche under this number [Annual. Oct. 1983. 3+138 p.+foldout. Members $45.00, nonmembers $90.00]. Previous report is substantially similar in format and content, but omits data on State rankings, and includes data on energy savings and use, and employment and operations for approximately 20 foreign countries and for chemicals and related industries.

Availability: Society of the Plastics Industry, Statistical Department, 355 Lexington Ave., New York NY 10017, members $55.00, nonmembers $110.00; SRI/MF/complete.

TABLES:
[Data "by major market" are generally shown for transportation, packaging, building/construction, electrical/electronic, furniture/furnishings, consumer/institutional, industrial/machinery, adhesives/inks/coatings, exports, and other.]

A8920-1.1: Industry Overview

TRENDS

[1] Introduction of plastics resins [with date and example of use, 1868-1982]. (p. 3)

[2-3] 1983 in review: production and sales/captive use [by resin]; and distribution of sales/captive use, by major market; [1982-83]. (p. 4)

[4-5] Total U.S. production and sales/captive use of plastics resin [total and by resin, various years 1958-83]. (p. 5-7)

[6] Plastics resins domestic merchant sales [quantity and value by resin, 1982-83]. (p. 9)

[7] Apparent U.S. consumption of selected plastics resins [also showing production, imports, and exports, by resin for 1983, and totals for 1976-82]. (p. 10)

[8] Plastics materials/resins: value of shipments [compared to other chemical categories and other commodities, 1979-83]. (p. 11)

[9-10] Plastics materials/resins (SIC 2821) and miscellaneous products (SIC 3079): [shipment value, employment, production workers and earnings, capital spending, production and/or PPI, and trade; selected years 1972-84]. (p. 12)

GENERAL ECONOMIC STATISTICS

[11] Commodity, balance of trade [for plastics/resins and 6 other commodity categories, 1979-83]. (p. 14)

[12] PPI [for plastics resins/materials and 5 other commodity groups, 1968-83]. (p. 17)

[13] Profile of 50 biggest [SIC 4-digit] manufacturing industries [ranked by value of shipments, and including number of plants, 1983 with comparison to 1982]. (p. 18)

[14] Industry financial performance [median return on sales, changes in sales and profits, sales and assets per employee, return to investors, and return on stockholders' equity, for rubber/plastics products, chemicals, and selected other major industry groups, 1983, with selected comparisons to 1982 or 1973-83 period]. (p. 19-20)

[15] [Plastics, chemicals, and total] sales of major plastics producing companies [1982-83, with company rankings by plastics sales for 1983]. (p. 22)

[16] Top 10 States of the plastics industry [ranked by establishments, employment, value of shipments, new capital expenditures, and payroll], 1982. (p. 25)

[17] Plastic processing industry: [detailed financial and operating ratios] by sales group, 1982. (p. 26a-c)

FEEDSTOCKS AND ADDITIVES

[18-20] Plastics derived from major feedstocks [1982-83]; plastics consumption of feedstocks, 1983; and selected plastics precursors [1982-83; showing total feedstock or precursor production and portion used to manufacture plastics]. (p. 28)

[21] Consumption of additives [by type, 1979-83]. (p. 30)

A8920-1.2: Individual Resins
[Most data are shown for 1979-83, with selected trends from 1973. Tables [1-18], [25-28], [33-38], and [42-71] generally include the following data for the individual resins noted: production and sales/captive use, share of total plastics sales/captive use, domestic consumption by end use, and distribution by major market.

Lists of companies providing data are included for most resin types.]

THERMOSETTING RESINS

[1-18] Epoxy, phenolic, unsaturated polyester, urea, and melamine. (p. 37-47)

[19] Miscellaneous thermosets [production and sales, by resin]. (p. 49)

[20-21] Polyurethane foam: distribution of sales/use by major market; and domestic sales/captive use [by end use; all for flexible/semiflexible and rigid foam]. (p. 50)

[22-24] Isocyanates, polyether polyols, and polyester polyols [production and sales/captive use]. (p. 51)

THERMOPLASTIC RESINS

[Tables [33-38] and [42-71] include capacity utilization rates, 1974-83; and manufacturing capacity estimates, by company, as of Dec. 31, 1983-84.]

[25-28] ABS [acrylonitrile-butadiene-styrene] and SAN [styrene-acrylonitrile]. (p. 53-54)

[29-31] Engineering thermoplastic resins [types manufactured, by company; production and sales/captive use; and distribution of major market]. (p. 57)

[32] Sales of fluoropolymer resins (granular type only). (p. 58)

[33-38] High density polyethylene. (p. 60-61)

[39-41] Latex materials [production distribution by product type and end use; and production, and sales/captive use by end use, for styrene butadiene/other styrene based latexes]. (p. 63)

[42-71] Low density polyethylene, nylon, polypropylene, polystyrene, and polyvinyl chloride. (p. 64-77)

[72] Polyvinyl acetate [sales/captive use of vinyl acetate monomer for polyvinyl acetate, by end use]. (p. 79)

[73] Polyvinyl alcohol [production, and domestic and export sales/captive use]. (p. 79)

[74] Other vinyl resins [production and sales/captive use]. (p. 80)

[75] Miscellaneous thermoplastics [production and sales, by type of resin]. (p. 80)

[76] Domestic sales/use of selected thermoplastics, by process grade. (p. 81-82)

A8920-1.3: Products, Markets, and Machinery
[Data are for 1979-83, unless otherwise noted.]

FABRICATED PLASTICS PRODUCTS

[1] Reinforced plastics shipments, by market [1979-84]. (p. 85)

[2-6] Shipments of thermoplastic pipe/tube/conduit and plastic fittings, by material and application. (p. 87-91)

MAJOR MARKETS

[7-9] Comparison of 1983 data to prior years: 5-year comparison of resin [unit] sales/use, and comparative percentage distribution, [1979-83]; and percentage change in sales/use, [selected periods 1978-83; all] by major market. (p. 95-96)

[10] 1983 distribution of plastic resin sales/use (captive), by major market [with detail by product category, by resin type]. (p. 114-117)

MACHINERY

[11-13] Dollar sales of plastics machinery [by type]; and shipments of single screw extrusion machinery, and of injection molding machinery [domestic and export]. (p. 122-123)

A8920-2   1983 ANNUAL LABOR SURVEY, Plastics Processing Companies
Annual.   Jan. 15, 1984.
42 p.
SRI/MF/complete

Annual report, for 1983, on employees in the plastics processing industry. Includes data on labor union representation, benefits, earnings, and employment. Most data are shown by region.

Data are based on responses to a Sept. 1983 survey of 286 companies employing approximately 27,200 workers.

Contains contents listing (1 p.); highlights and 26 tables, listed below (p. 1-27); and list of participants, job classifications, and facsimile of survey questionnaire (p. 28-42).

This is the 45th edition of the report.

Availability: Society of the Plastics Industry, Statistical Department, 355 Lexington Ave., New York NY 10017, members $50.00, nonmembers $100.00; SRI/MF/complete.

TABLES:
[Tables show data by region for 1983, unless otherwise noted. Most tables include summary comparative data for 1982.]

A8920–2.1: Employees in the Plastics Industry

HIGHLIGHTS AND PLANT STATISTICS

[1-4] Highlights of the survey [number of companies, by region and State, 1983; industry wage index, 1968-83; and summary of 1983 increases in hourly and salaried wages]. (p. 1-2)

[5] Plant statistics [including employees; plants by employee size group; and low, average, and high hours worked per week]. (p. 3)

[6] Union statistics [number of companies unionized; and distribution by length and expiration date of contract, existence of wage reopener clause and cost-of-living increase, and maximum increase per hour]. (p. 3)

[7] [Names of] unions representing workers in the plastics processing industry [shows number of companies for each union]. (p. 4)

BENEFITS AND TURNOVER

[8-13] Rest period, lunch and other [piecework and sick leave] payment policies; premiums paid for afternoon and midnight shifts; and fringe benefits [total and] by type, as percent of hourly rate. (p. 6-8)

[14-17] Number of paid holidays; vacation and [Christmas] bonus statistics; and other fringe benefits [including life and health insurance, pensions, and profit sharing]. (p. 9-11)

[18-19] Turnover statistics [for] hourly employees; and shift statistics [including number and average length of shifts]. (p. 11-12)

[20-22] Christmas bonus practices, profit sharing and other incentive plans, and overtime pay provisions; [all for] salaried employees. (p. 13-14)

EARNINGS AND NUMBER OF EMPLOYEES

[Tables 23-26] show data by job classification.]

[23-24] Comparison of median hourly wages of hourly employees, and of median monthly salaries of salaried employees [aggregate for all regions]. (p. 15-16)

[25-26] Labor survey, hourly and salaried employees [median and 1st and 3rd quartiles]. (p. 17-27)

A8920–4   FINANCIAL AND OPERATING RATIOS, Survey No. 22, 1983: Plastics Processing Companies
Annual.   June 30, 1984.
2+vi+35 p.   Survey No. 22.
SRI/MF/complete

Annual report presenting plastics processing industry financial and operating ratios, 1983. Data are from a 1984 survey of 183 companies. Report is intended to enable individual companies to compare their performance with industry medians.

Data show itemized median income and expenses as percent of net sales, assets, liabilities as percent of total assets, and selected operating and productivity ratios, by sales size class arranged by major company activity, and by product end use, generally for firms with less profitable, median, or more profitable operations.

Contains contents and table listings (1 p.); summary highlights, with 18 charts and 6 tables on respondent characteristics (p. i-vi); 3 extended survey result tables (p. 1-21); definitions (p. 22-23); list of survey participants (p. 24-27); and questionnaire facsimiles (p. 29-35).

Availability: Society of the Plastics Industry, Statistical Department, 355 Lexington Ave., New York NY 10017, members $50.00, nonmembers $100.00; SRI/MF/complete.

A8920–5   MONTHLY STATISTICAL REPORT, RESINS: Production and Sales, and Captive Use of Thermosetting and Thermoplastic Resins
Monthly, with quarterly and annual summaries.
Approx. 10 p.
SRI/MF/complete, shipped quarterly

Monthly report, with quarterly and annual summaries, on plastic resin production and sales/captive use, by detailed resin type and end use including exports, for month of coverage, year to date, and same periods of previous year.

Data are compiled from approximately 110 companies by Ernst and Whinney, Inc., for the SPI Committee on Resin Statistics. Report is issued approximately 3 months after month of coverage.

Each monthly issue contains 1 summary trend chart and 4 tables. Issues occasionally also include a tabular list of reporting companies, showing types of resins produced by each company.

Annual summary presents all report data by month for the full calendar year. Quarterly summaries contain 1 table showing domestic polyester resin summary data for quarter of coverage, year to date, and same periods of previous years; and, occasionally, revised data for previous periods. Summary for 4th quarter also includes quarterly data by month for the full year.

Availability: Ernst and Whinney, Trade Association Service Department, 153 E. 53rd St., New York NY 10022, members $300.00 per yr., nonmembers $400.00 per yr.; SRI/MF/complete, shipped quarterly.

Issues reviewed during 1984: Monthly Reports: Aug. 1983-Aug. 1984 (D) (1983 Nos. 8-12; 1984 Nos. 1-8).

Issues reviewed during 1984: Quarterly Summaries: 3rd-4th Qtrs. 1983 (D).

Issues reviewed during 1984: Annual Summary: calendar year 1983.

A8920–6   MONTHLY STATISTICAL REPORT, PIPE AND FITTINGS: Shipments of Thermoplastics Pipe, Tube, Conduit, and Fittings
Monthly, with annual summary.   Approx. 12 p.
SRI/MF/complete, shipped quarterly

Monthly report, with annual summary, on thermoplastic pipe/tube/conduit and fittings shipment volume, by type of material and application, for month of coverage, year to date, and same periods of previous year. Also includes shipment value for fittings.

Data are compiled from approximately 80 companies by Ernst and Whinney, Inc., for the SPI Committee on Resin Statistics. Reports are issued approximately 3 months after month of coverage.

Contains 6 tables; and usually a tabular list of reporting companies, showing types of products manufactured by each company.

Annual summary accompanies the Jan. issue and presents monthly data for the year.

Availability: Ernst and Whinney, Trade Association Service Department, 153 E. 53rd St., New York NY 10022, members $50.00 per yr., nonmembers $100.00 per yr.; SRI/MF/complete, shipped quarterly.

Issues reviewed during 1984: Sept. 1983-Aug. 1984; and annual summary for 1983 (D).

A8945
Southern
Regional Education Board

A8945–1   FACT BOOK ON HIGHER EDUCATION IN THE SOUTH, 1983 and 1984
Biennial.   1984.   v+93 p.
ISSN 0191-1643.
LC 79-642573.
SRI/MF/complete

Biennial fact book, compiled by Michael M. Myers, on higher education enrollment, degrees awarded, institutional and student finances, and faculty salary levels in 14 Southern Regional Education Board (SREB) States, 1983-84. Also includes comparative national data, and data on population, income, and tax revenues.

Data are from NCES, State higher education agencies, and other sources. Data are for various years, 1970-84, with selected trends from 1960s, and population projections through 2000.

Contains foreword and contents listing (p. iii-v); SREB State profiles and highlights, with 1 summary table (p. 1-4); 6 statistical sections, preceded by summaries, with 8 charts and 62 numbered tables (p. 5-81); and appendix with definitions of institutional categories, directory of State education agencies and officials, bibliography, and index (p. 83-93). All numbered tables, and selected charts showing data not covered in tables, are listed below.

Previous report, for 1981-82, is described in SRI 1982 Annual, under this number.
Availability: Southern Regional Education Board, 1340 Spring St., NW, Atlanta GA 30309, $4.50; SRI/MF/complete.

CHARTS AND TABLES:

[Most tables show data for total U.S. and by SREB State: Alabama, Arkansas, Florida, Georgia, Kentucky, Louisiana, Maryland, Mississippi, North and South Carolina, Tennessee, Texas, Virginia, and West Virginia. Data by institutional control are for public and private. Data by institutional type are for 2- and 4-year schools, unless otherwise noted.]

A8945–1.1: Population and Economy

1. Total resident population, 1982; past and projected percent change in population, [selected periods] 1972-2000; and percent metro population, 1970 and 1980. (p. 7)

2. Resident 18-24 year-old population, 1982; and past and projected percent change in 18- to 24-year-old population, [selected periods] 1970-2000. (p. 8)

3. Educational attainment of the population aged 25 and above, 1980. (p. 9)

4. Per capita personal income, in dollars and as a percent of U.S. [1960, 1970, and 1982]. (p. 10)

5. State/local tax revenues as a percent of total tax collections, by source, FY82. (p. 11)

A8945–1.2: Enrollment, Institutions, and Projections

SUMMARY

6. Number of institutions of postsecondary education by type and control, fall 1982. (p. 15)

7. Total enrollment in higher education, [selected years] 1950-82. (p. 16)

8. Total college enrollment, by control of institution, fall 1982; and percent public, fall 1960, 1970, 1976, and 1982. (p. 17)

9. Total college enrollment by institutional control and and type; and 2-year enrollment as a percent of total enrollment, by control; fall 1982. (p. 18)

10. Total college enrollment by level, all institutions, fall 1982. (p. 19)

11. Graduate enrollment, 1982; percent change, 1970-75 and 1976-82 [periods]; and percent of total enrollment, 1970, 1976, and 1982. (p. 20)

12. U.S. institutions with enrollment of over 30,000, fall 1982. (p. 21)

13. FTE enrollment, public 4-year institutions in the South [doctoral, master's, baccalaureate, and specialized], fall 1983. (p. 22)

14. New doctoral programs in public universities in the South, by State and by program, 1971-83 [period]. (p. 23)

15-16. Part-time enrollment as a percent of total enrollment, by control of institution; and women as a percent of total enrollment; fall [various years 1965-82]. (p. 24-25)

HISPANIC AND BLACK ENROLLMENT

17-18. Total Hispanic and black enrollment, 1982; percent change, 1980-82 [period]; percent by level, 1982; and percent population Hispanic and black, 1980. (p. 26-27)

19. Black enrollment, by institutional control and type, fall 1982. (p. 28)

20. Black undergraduate enrollment; percent change [for period]; and percent in predominantly black institutions; 1976 and 1982. (p. 29)

MEDICAL AND ENGINEERING ENROLLMENTS

21. Medical school enrollment [by sex, and number of 1st-year students]; State residents entering medical school [total, per 100,000 population, and per 1,000 bachelor's degrees awarded]; and interns/residents; 1982/83. (p. 30)

22. Undergraduate and graduate engineering enrollments, fall 1975 and 1981. (p. 31)

HIGH SCHOOL GRADUATES AND HIGHER EDUCATION ENROLLMENT

23. High school graduates, 1981/82; and past and projected percent change, [selected periods] 1977-97. (p. 32)

24. Participation in higher education, by 18-24 year-old population, 1970, 1980, and 1982. (p. 33)

A8945–1.3: Degrees

[Data by sex are shown for 1981/82, with percent change for 1970-75 and 1975-82 periods. Data for black students and selected fields are shown for 1980/81, unless otherwise noted.]

25. Associate degrees and other awards below the baccalaureate, by length and type of curriculum, 1981/82; and percent change, 1974-82 [period]. (p. 37)

26-27. Bachelor's degrees awarded: by sex; and to black students [total, and] percentage in selected fields. (p. 38-39)

28-29. First professional degrees awarded: by sex; and to black students in selected fields [with percent of total awarded]. (p. 40-41)

30-31. Master's degrees awarded: by sex; and to black students [total, and] percentage in selected fields. (p. 42-43)

32-33. Doctoral degrees awarded: by sex; and in selected fields [total, and] percent awarded to black students. (p. 44-45)

34-37. Bachelor's, master's, doctoral, and 1st professional degrees awarded in selected fields, 1981/82 and percent change 1971-82 [period]. (p. 46-49)

38-39. Degrees awarded in engineering and engineering technology [by degree level], 1981/82 and percent change, [various periods] 1971-82. (p. 50-51)

A8945–1.4: Institutional and Student Finances

INSTITUTIONAL FINANCES

[A] State appropriations for operating expenses of higher education: [percent increase, 1982-84 period; and amount per $1,000 of personal income], 1983/84. [chart] (p. 53)

40. Appropriations of State tax funds for operating expenses of higher education, 1973/74, 1981/82, and 1983/84; and appropriations per capita, 1983/84. (p. 55)

41. State appropriations for higher education as a percent of State taxes, 1976/77-1981/82. (p. 56)

42. Education/general appropriations, and appropriations per FTE student [by level of institution], public 4-year institutions, 1983/84. (p. 57)

43-44. Sources of current funds revenues; and current funds expenditures [by function]; percentage distribution, public institutions, 1981/82. (p. 58-59)

45-46. Total current funds revenues and expenditures, public and private institutions, 1982; and percent change 1978-80 and 1980-82 [periods]. (p. 60-61)

47. Federal obligations to universities/colleges, by agency [DOD, Dept of Education, HHS, NSF, and other], 1981/82. (p. 62)

48. Federal obligations for R&D to universities and colleges receiving the largest amounts [leading 10 in U.S. and leading 22 from SREB States, by institution], 1981/82. (p. 63)

LIBRARIES

49. Large college and university libraries in the South: collections, expenditures, and [FTE] staff [by institution], 1982/83. (p. 64)

STUDENT FINANCES

[B] Estimated student aid [percent of total], by source, 1983/84 academic year, U.S. [chart] (p. 65)

50. Annual tuition/required fees for resident undergraduates and public institutions [by level of institution], 1983/84. (p. 67)

51. Basic Educational Opportunity (Pell) Grants: allocations by type of institution [public, private, and proprietary], 1983/84, and percent change 1980-84 [period]. (p. 68)

52. Federal campus-based student financial aid programs [by type], amounts allotted, 1983/84, and percent change 1982-84 [period]. (p. 69)

53. Estimated number of student awards for Federal campus-based student financial aid programs [by type], 1983/84; and percent change 1982-84 [period]. (p. 70)

54. Federal financial aid programs in the health professions [including loan amounts for 4 programs], 1983/84. (p. 71)

55. Comprehensive State scholarship/grant programs for student financial aid [award amount, 1983/84; percent change, 1980-82 and 1982-84 periods; and number and average amount of awards, 1982/83]. (p. 72)

A8945–1.5: Faculty

56. Average salaries and rankings for full-time faculty, public 4-year institutions, [selected years] 1971/72-1983/84. (p. 75)

57. Average faculty salaries in land-grant universities for selected disciplines, all ranks, U.S. and [aggregate for] selected southern States, 1983/84; and percent change 1982-84 [period]. (p. 76)

58-61. Average salaries of full-time faculty: public doctoral, master's, baccalaureate, and 2-year institutions [by academic rank, with] percent change, 1983/84. (p. 77-80)

62. Student-faculty ratios for 4-year public institutions [by level of institution], 1983/84. (p. 81)

A8945–2 DEGREES AWARDED IN THE NATION AND THE SOUTH, BY RACE, 1980/81

Annual. 1983. vi+76 p.
LC 76-620757.
SRI/MF/complete

Annual report, by Michael M. Myers, enumerating academic degrees conferred by postsecondary institutions in 14 southern States and total U.S., by degree level, field of study, and race, with detail for public and private institutions, 1980/81 and selected trends from 1970/71.

Data are compiled by SREB based on earned degree data collected by NCES.

Contains foreword and table listing (p. iii-vi); introduction and narrative analysis, with 2 charts, and 20 tables showing summary data and trends (p. 1-27); and 3 detailed tables (p. 29-76).

This is the 9th annual report. Reports for school years beginning with odd-numbered years present data by sex; those for school years beginning with even-numbered years present data by race.

Availability: Southern Regional Education Board, 1340 Spring St., NW, Atlanta GA 30309, $5.50; SRI/MF/complete.

A8945–3   COMPARATIVE INFORMATION ON HIGHER EDUCATION, 1983
Annual. Oct. 1983. 2+41 p.
SRI/MF/complete

Annual report, by Michael M. Myers, on public higher education financing, faculty compensation, enrollment, and degrees awarded in 14 Southern Regional Education Board (SREB) States, 1982/83 and trends. Data are primarily from SREB surveys.

Contains contents listing, introduction, and definitions (3 p.); 6 sections, with 2 charts and 25 tables described below (p. 2-34); and "Educational Quality" section with summaries of testing practices and graduation requirements for secondary schools, and requirements for college admission and participation in teacher education programs, by SREB State (p. 35-41).

Previous report, for 1980/81, is described in SRI 1982 Annual under this number. This report supplements biennial *Fact Book on Higher Education in the South* (covered in SRI under A8945-1).

Availability: Southern Regional Education Board, 1340 Spring St., NW, Atlanta GA 30309, $3.00; SRI/MF/complete.

TABLES:
[Unless otherwise noted, data are shown for the following SREB States: Alabama, Arkansas, Florida, Georgia, Kentucky, Louisiana, Maryland, Mississippi, North Carolina, South Carolina, Tennessee, Texas, Virginia, and West Virginia. Some tables include U.S. comparisons. Institution types are based on degree levels offered.]

a. State appropriations: percent increase for operating expenses; general appropriations by institution type; tax fund appropriations as percent of total taxes; and appropriations per FTE student, by institution type; various years 1970/71-1982/83. Tables 1-4. (p. 3-6)

b. Tuition and fees: average annual tuition and required fees for resident and nonresident graduate and undergraduate students, by type of institution, 1982/83. Tables 5-6. (p. 8-9)

c. Faculty compensation: average salaries of full-time faculty, by institution type and faculty rank, with State rankings; and average faculty salaries by discipline (not shown by State); 1982/83, with selected data for 1981/82. Tables 7-12. (p. 11-16)

d. Enrollment and degrees: FTE undergraduate and graduate enrollment, by institution type, fall 1982; and degrees awarded by level, for selected fields, 1980/81 with comparisons to 1970s. Tables 13-21. (p. 18-27)

e. Health professions education: graduates by field, and percent increase in State appropriations, for total SREB, various periods 1960-82; enrollment by field, including internships/residencies, fall 1982; and medical school entrants, graduate programs and residents, and student fees and resident and nonresident tuition by institution, various years 1974-1982/83. Charts 1-2 and tables 22-25. (p. 29-34)

A8945–6   STATE AND LOCAL TAX PERFORMANCE
Annual, suspended.

Annual report analyzing State/local government use of ability to collect taxes, suspended with 1982 report (for description, see SRI 1983 Annual, under this number). Report publication has been suspended indefinitely due to budgetary constraints.

Data on State/local tax effort are available from Southern Regional Education Board, 1340 Spring St., NW, Atlanta GA 30309.

A8945–7   MEASURING EDUCATIONAL PROGRESS IN THE SOUTH: Student Achievement
Monograph. 1984. iv+44 p.
SRI/MF/complete

Report on assessment of student achievement in 14 southern States. Includes descriptions of elementary and secondary educational testing programs; and selected test results, by subject matter and grade level, primarily for school year 1982/83, with some data for 1983/84 and trends from 1978/79.

Data are based on information supplied by each State's dept of education.

Contains foreword (p. iii-iv); narrative report on elementary/secondary testing (p. 1-5); State profiles, generally with text data and 1-3 tables and/or charts for each (p. 6-33); and narrative report on higher education testing (p. 35-44).

Availability: Southern Regional Education Board, 1340 Spring St., NW, Atlanta GA 30309, $4.00; SRI/MF/complete.

A8955
Spain-U.S. Chamber of Commerce

A8955–1   SPAIN-U.S. TRADE BULLETIN
Bimonthly. Approx. 40 p.
ISSN 0561-5313.
SRI/MF/complete

Bimonthly journal promoting U.S./Spanish trade relations. Includes reporting on business activities, recent legislation, trade regulations, tourism, and areas of investment opportunity in both countries. Some articles are in Spanish.

Data are from U.S. Dept of Commerce, the Spanish Ministry of Commerce and Tourism, and other sources.

General format:

a. Feature articles and news brief sections, occasionally with statistics, including annual trade reviews; and bimonthly summary of Spanish legislation published officially during the previous 2 months.

b. Bimonthly table on Spanish exports to U.S., for approximately 70 products grouped under 10 industry sectors, for current year through month 2-3 months prior to publication date, with change from previous year.

Bimonthly table appears in all issues. All additional features with substantial statistical content are described, as they appear, under "Statistical Features." Nonstatistical features are not covered.

Beginning with the Mar./Apr./May 1984 issue, journal temporarily is published on a quarterly schedule.

Availability: Spain-U.S. Chamber of Commerce, 500 Fifth Ave., New York NY 10110, members †, others $25.00 per yr., single copy $5.00; SRI/MF/complete.

Issues reviewed during 1984: Sept./Oct. 1983-June/July/Aug. 1984 (P) (Nos. 130-134).

STATISTICAL FEATURES:

A8955–1.501: Nov./Dec. 1983 (No. 131)

NOTA SOBRE EL COMERCIO ENTRE ESPAÑA Y LOS ESTADOS UNIDOS DURANTE EL PRIMER SEMESTRE DE 1983, ANNUAL FEATURE

(p. 7-10, 18) Annual article, by Antonio Llanos, summarizing Spain-U.S. trade trends in the 1st half of 1983. Includes 6 tables showing total trade value, balance, and index (in pesetas); and trade value (in dollars) by commodity; 1st half 1978-83. Article is in Spanish.

A8955–1.502: June/July/Aug. 1984 (No. 134)

EL COMERCIO ENTRE ESPAÑA Y LOS ESTADOS UNIDOS EN 1983, ANNUAL FEATURE

(p. 22-28) Annual article, by Antonio Llanos, discussing Spain/U.S. trade activity during 1983, with comparisons from 1979. Article is in Spanish.

Includes 9 tables showing trade value, balance, and index (in pesetas and dollars); and trade value by commodity, with detail for U.S. imports of footwear, olives, and sherry; 1979-83.

A8965
Special Libraries Association

A8965-1   SLA TRIENNIAL SALARY SURVEY
Triennial, with annual updates.
1983.   vi+74 p.
ISBN 0-87111-302-3.
LC 83-595.
SRI/MF/complete

Triennial survey report on salaries of special librarians in the U.S. and Canada, as of Apr. 1982. Presents number of respondents and mean, median, and percentile salaries, variously cross-tabulated by the following:

a. Sex, census division (U.S. only), SMSA, type of employer, primary work responsibility, number of supervised employees by type, highest degree in any field and in library science, and field of highest degree.

b. Years of professional library and other experience, years with current employer, total number of employers, race/ethnicity (including Asian/Pacific Islander and Hispanic), age, job title, and organization's budget size.

Also includes summary data on unemployment, and salary trends from 1967 with comparisons to CPI.

Data are from responses of 3,255 SLA members to an Apr.-May 1982 survey.

Contains table listing (p. v-vi); narrative report on survey scope and findings (p. 1-8); 78 tables (p. 9-70); and questionnaire facsimile (p. 71-74).

This is the 6th triennial survey report. SRI coverage begins with this report. Previous survey results were published in *Special Libraries*, a quarterly journal. Annual summary updates for this triennial report will also be published in *Special Libraries* (for description see A8965-2, below).

Availability: Special Libraries Association, Order Department, 235 Park Ave. S., New York NY 10003, $20.00; SRI/MF/complete.

A8965-2   SPECIAL LIBRARIES: SLA 1983 Salary Survey Update
Quarterly (selected issue).
Oct. 1983.   (p. 390-391).
Vol. 74, No. 4..
ISSN 0038-6723.
SRI/MF/excerpts

Annual article on salaries of special librarians in U.S. and Canada, 1983. Data are from responses of 1,158 SLA members to a May 1983 survey. Includes 2 tables showing mean, median, and percentile salaries, by U.S. census division and for Canada, as of Apr. 1983 with comparisons to 1982.

Data provide a partial update for detailed salary statistics presented in *SLA Triennial Salary Survey* (for description see A8965-1, above).

Special Libraries is a primarily narrative periodical reporting on management, research, and other professional topics of interest to special librarians. Annual salary update is the only feature covered in SRI.

SRI coverage begins with the 1983 update.

Availability: Special Libraries Association, Circulation Department, 235 Park Ave. S., New York NY 10003, members $12.00 per yr., nonmembers $36.00 per yr., single copy $9.00; SRI/MF/excerpts for annual survey article.

A8990
Steel Service Center Institute

A8990-2   BUSINESS CONDITIONS
Monthly, in 2 parts.
Approx. 8 p. no paging.
SRI/MF/not filmed

Monthly report, in 2 parts, on steel service center business conditions, including orders, shipments, inventories, work force, and dependence on foreign steel. Service centers distribute steel products to manufacturers and fabricators.

Data are from ongoing member surveys of the Steel Service Center Institute (SSCI) and the National Assn of Purchasing Management (NAPM) Steel Committee. The SSCI sample accounts for 30-40 percent of total industrial steel shipments.

Report is published in 2 parts, described below. Parts I and II are issued during the 1st and 3rd weeks of the month, respectively. Prior to Jan. 1984 issue, Part I was issued quarterly.

Part II is accompanied by a narrative summary, not covered in SRI.

Availability: Steel Service Center Institute, 1600 Terminal Tower, Cleveland OH 44113-2229, ‡; SRI/MF/not filmed.

Issues reviewed during 1984: Part I: Jan. 6-Oct. 4, 1984 (P).

Issues reviewed during 1984: Part II: Nov. 17, 1983-Oct. 19, 1984 (P).

REPORT PARTS:
[Data are from SSCI member surveys, unless otherwise noted.]

PART I
[Most data are shown monthly for current year through month of publication and previous year.]

a. General business conditions: expectations for general economy in next 3 months. 1 table.

b. Own business: shipment levels and customer payment promptness compared with 3 months ago; expected order levels in next 3 months; adequacy of current order levels; and whether work force is on short time/layoff. 5 tables.

c. Inventories: current inventory levels compared with 3 months ago; number of months inventory would cover current shipping levels; adequacy of current inventory levels; current receipts compared with shipments; and expected receipt and inventory levels and specific product shortages in next 3 months. 7 tables.

d. Foreign steel: foreign mills' prices compared with domestic prices, and activity in seeking U.S. business compared with 3 months ago; and expected dependence on foreign steel in next 6 months. 3 tables.

PART II
[Data are current to month prior to month of publication, unless otherwise noted.]

e. Tonnage shipments and inventories, for flat roll, stainless, and other steel, for 3 or more consecutive quarters through most current full quarter, and monthly for current year to date. 1 table.

f. NAPM survey: purchasing managers' expected steel order, backlog, and receipt levels in next 3 months, and inventory level in next 6 months; and number of months inventory would cover current shipping levels; monthly for current year through month of publication and previous year. 5 tables.

g. Number of months' shipments on hand, and shipment and inventory summary trends, monthly for current year to date and 2 previous years. 1 table.

A9025
Teachers Insurance and Annuity Association

A9025-1   LESSONS ON RETIREMENT: A Statistical Report of the 1982-83 Survey of Retired TIAA-CREF Annuitants
Monograph.   1984.   82 p.
SRI/MF/complete

Survey report on the experiences and opinions of retired persons receiving annuity income from the Teachers Insurance and Annuity Assn-College Retirement Equities Fund (TIAA-CREF), 1982.

Covers responses to survey questions on retirement reasons and preparation; age at retirement; retirement finances, housing, activities, health, and health insurance coverage; personal views about retirement; and demographic and socioeconomic characteristics; variously cross-tabulated.

Data are based on 1,794 responses to an Oct. 1982 TIAA-CREF random sample survey of 2,-200 annuitants, and include summary comparisons from a similar survey conducted in 1972. Most survey respondents were former college faculty, administration, and support staff members. Some respondents were former faculty and administration members in private elementary/secondary schools, or held other technical or professional positions.

Contains listings of contents, tables, and charts (p. 3-5); introduction and summary (p. 7-11); narrative report in 8 sections, with text data and 42 tables (p. 12-63); and appendices, with discussion of methodology, 1 table, and questionnaire facsimile with response totals (p. 64-82).

Availability: Teachers Insurance and Annuity Association, Educational Research Division, 730 Third Ave., New York NY 10017, ‡; SRI/MF/complete.

A9055
Television
Bureau of Advertising

A9055-1   TV BASICS 27: The Television Bureau of Advertising's Report on the Scope and Dimensions of Television Today
Annual.   [1984.]
10 p. no paging.
SRI/MF/complete

Annual report on TV ownership, use, perceived credibility, and advertising investment, with comparisons to other media types, various years 1950-84. Most data are compiled from private media research organizations.

Contains 23 tables showing the following data:

a. Color, multiset, and total TV homes, Jan. 1984; total and per home average daily viewing hours, 1983; daily viewing hours, by region and demographic characteristics, Feb. 1984; and UHF and VHF commercial TV stations, and total and summer daily viewing hours, various years 1950-84. 5 tables.

b. Advertisers and brands using network and spot TV; TV penetration and daily viewing hours, by sex, and for teenagers and children; distribution of time spent with 4 types of media; network and spot TV billings, and TV share of total billings, for top 10 TV advertising agencies; and expenditures of top 10 types of business using local TV advertising; various years 1982-84. 5 tables.

c. Cable TV operating systems and subscribers, selected years 1960-84; cable and noncable household weekly viewing hours of over-the-air and cable stations, Feb. 1984; and total, national, and local advertising expenditures, by media, 1982-83. 5 tables.

d. Color TV households and percent penetration; color and black and white TV set sales; advertising media judged most authoritative, creative, and influential; media judged most credible and source of most news; and distribution of network and non-network TV commercials by time length; various years 1959-84. 6 tables.

e. Local TV advertising revenue, and rank; and distribution of commercials by day part, length, and month; for top 40 types of business advertisers, 1983. 1 table.

f. Network and spot TV advertising expenditures, for top 100 companies ranked by total TV advertising expenditures, 1983. 1 table.

Availability: Television Bureau of Advertising, Creative Department, 485 Lexington Ave., New York NY 10017, $0.25; SRI/MF/complete.

A9055-2   GNP, AD VOLUME, AND TV AD VOLUME, 1960-90
Recurring (irreg.) Mar. 1984.
3 p. no paging.
SRI/MF/complete, Nov. 1983
& Mar. 1984 reports

Recurring report showing trends in total and TV advertising expenditures and GNP for 1960-90. Data are from Commerce Dept and McCann-Erickson advertising agency, with estimates by TV Bureau of Advertising.

Contains 3 tables showing GNP, and value of all advertising and of network, spot, and local TV advertising, 1960-90.

Report is issued irregularly, as sufficient new data become available. Previous report, issued in Nov. 1983, was also reviewed in 1984 and is also available on SRI microfiche under this number [Recurring (irreg.) Nov. 1983. 3 p. no paging. ‡].

Availability: Television Bureau of Advertising, Research Department, 485 Lexington Ave., New York NY 10017, ‡; SRI/MF/complete.

A9055-3   ADVERTISING VOLUME IN THE U.S., 1948-84
Semiannual. Aug. 1984. 6 p.
SRI/MF/complete, Jan. and
Aug. 1984 reports

Semiannual report on national and local advertising expenditures in 8 major media, 1948-84. Data are from McCann-Erickson, Inc.

Contains 1 table showing value of all advertising in newspapers; magazines; farm publications; network, spot, and local TV and radio; direct mail; business papers; outdoor; and miscellaneous; with national and local totals for selected media; 1948-84.

Previous report, issued in Jan. 1984, was also reviewed in 1984 and is also available on SRI microfiche, under this number [Semiannual. Jan. 1984. 6 p. ‡].

Availability: Television Bureau of Advertising, Research Department, 485 Lexington Ave., New York NY 10017, ‡; SRI/MF/complete.

A9055-4   TRENDS IN TELEVISION, 1950 to Date
Semiannual. Mar. 1984.
13 p.
SRI/MF/complete

Semiannual report on trends in TV ownership, usage, advertising expenditures, and stations, various years 1950-84. Most data are from media research organizations.

Contains contents listing (p. 1); and 12 tables, listed below (p. 2-13).

Previous report, issued in Mar. 1983, is described in SRI 1983 Annual, under this number.

Availability: Television Bureau of Advertising, Research Department, 485 Lexington Ave., New York NY 10017, ‡; SRI/MF/complete.

TABLES:

[1-2] TV households [and total households]; and multiset and color TV households [1950-84]. (p. 2-3)

[3] TV sets [in home, and average number per household and per multiset household, 1950-84]. (p. 4)

[4] Time spent viewing, per TV home, per day [1950-83]. (p. 5)

[5] TV set sales (domestic/imports) [monochrome and color, 1950-83]. (p. 6)

[6] Commercial [UHF and VHF] TV stations [1950-84]. (p. 7)

[7-8] Advertising [dollar] volume in the U.S. [total and TV]; and TV advertising [dollar] volume [network, spot, and local; 1950-84]. (p. 8-9)

[9] Station time sales [network compensation, spot, and local, 1950-83]. (p. 10)

[10-11] Non-network and network TV commercial activity, by length of commercial [1965-83]. (p. 11-12)

[12] Number of advertisers and brands using [spot and network] TV [1970-83]. (p. 14)

A9065
Theatre Communications Group

A9065-1   THEATRE FACTS 83: A Statistical Guide to the Finances and Productivity of the Nonprofit Professional Theatre in America
Annual. 1984. 13 p.
Vol. 10.
ISBN 0-930452-37-2.
SRI/MF/complete, delayed

Annual report on nonprofit professional theater finances and operations, 1979-83. Data are from Theatre Communications Group (TCG) 1983 survey of 189 member theaters.

Contents:

a. Foreword and methodology, with 1 table showing the following for the total sample: earned, contributed, and total income; total expenses and deficit; attendance; subscribers, performances, and productions; and artistic, administrative, and technical staff; 1983. (p. 1-2)

b. Narrative trend analysis, with 9 tables and accompanying charts showing the following for a subsample of 32 theaters: earned and contributed income by source, and expenses by category, 1979-83. (p. 3-11)

c. Lists of TCG board of directors and participating theaters. (p. 12-13)

This is the 10th annual survey.

Availability: Theatre Communications Group, Publications Department, 355 Lexington Ave., New York NY 10017, $2.50; SRI/MF/complete, delayed shipment in Dec. 1984.

A9095
Toy Manufacturers of America

A9095-1   NATIONAL STATISTICS PROGRAM: Shipments, 1982 vs. 1983
Annual. Feb. 1984.
4 p.+insert.
SRI/MF/complete

Annual report on toy shipment volume and value, by type of toy, 1982-83. Also includes factory sales of home computers and software, 1982-84, and video games and game cartridges, 1980-84.

Data are from survey responses of 65 toy companies, accounting for 60% of industry shipments in 1983; and from Electronic Industries Assn and other sources. Data were compiled by The NPD Group, in conjunction with Toy Manufacturers of America.

Report consists of 2 tables.

Availability: Toy Manufacturers of America, 200 Fifth Ave., New York NY 10010, †; SRI/MF/complete.

A9095–2   MONTHLY MARKET TREND REPORTS
Monthly.   Approx. 3 p.
SRI/MF/complete, shipped quarterly

Monthly summary of toy shipment and order values. Data are compiled by Locker, Greenberg, and Brainin, P.C., from surveys of approximately 50 toy manufacturers. Reports are issued approximately 6 weeks after month of coverage.

Contains list of participating companies, and 2 tables showing value of toy shipments, and orders received, canceled, and on hand, monthly and cumulatively through month of coverage, for current and previous 1-2 years.

Availability: Toy Manufacturers of America, 200 Fifth Ave., New York NY 10010, †; SRI/MF/complete, shipped quarterly.

Issues reviewed during 1984: Sept. 1983-Aug. 1984 (D).

A9095–3   TOY MANUFACTURERS OF AMERICA 1982 Financial and Operating Ratio Report
Annual.   [1983.]   19 p.
SRI/MF/complete, current & previous year reports

Annual report presenting toy industry financial and operating ratios, 1982, with selected trends from 1978. Also includes sales trends, advertising expenditure distribution by media type, and sales distribution by outlet type.

Most data are shown by company sales size, and for all and high-profit companies.

Data are compiled by Profit Planning Group from survey responses of 42 toy manufacturers.

Contains executive summary and contents listing (p. 1-2); introductory profit analysis, with 2 charts and 2 tables (p. 3-6); and survey analysis and results, with 2 charts and 8 tables (p. 7-19).

Previous report, for 1981, was also reviewed in 1984 and is also available on SRI microfiche under this number [Annual. [1982.] 2+13 p. Participants †, nonparticipating members $75.00, others $100.00]. Previous report was compiled by Touche Ross and Co. and is substantially similar in content, but omits data on industry sales and advertising, and for high-profit companies.

Availability: Toy Manufacturers of America, 200 Fifth Ave., New York NY 10010, participants †, nonparticipating members $75.00, others $100.00; SRI/MF/complete.

A9275
U.S. Brewers Association

A9275–1   BREWING INDUSTRY IN THE U.S.: Brewers Almanac, 1983
Annual.   1983.   vi+106 p.
LC 45-51432.
SRI/MF/not filmed

Annual report presenting detailed brewing industry financial and operating data, 1982, with trends from as early as 1862, and some data for 1983. Selected data are shown by State and census division. Most data are from Treasury Dept, Census Bureau, BLS, and State alcohol beverage control agencies.

Contains listing of contents, tables, and charts (p. iii-vi), and the following:

Chapter 1-2. Industry overview, with 1 map, and 1 text table (p. 1) showing 1982 brewery production in 22 countries. (p. 1-5)

Chapter 3-6. Industry data, with 11 summary charts, 1 summary table, and 75 detailed tables listed below; each chapter includes a brief introduction. (p. 6-97)

Chapter 7. Local option and State controls as of July 1, 1983; and directory of State alcohol beverage control agencies. (p. 98-106)

Availability: U.S. Brewers Association, 1750 K St., NW, Washington DC 20006, members †, nonmembers $50.00; SRI/MF/not filmed.

DETAILED TABLES:
[Most fiscal year data are shown for year ended June 30.]

A9275–1.1: Production and Withdrawals (Brewery Sales)

1-2. Production, withdrawals, and per capita consumption of malt beverages, [various fiscal years] 1903-82. (p. 7)

3. Production, removals [taxable and tax-free withdrawals], losses, and stocks on hand June 30, and breweries operated, FY41-82. (p. 8)

4. Production of malt beverages, by States, FY74-82. (p. 9)

5-7. Tax removals of packaged beer, draught beer, and malt beverages, by States [FY74-82]. (p. 10-12)

8. Taxpaid withdrawals of malt beverages, by [census] division, FY73-82. (p. 13)

9. Malt beverage sales by States: taxable removals, by State and combination groupings, 1982. (p. 14)

10. Production, draught and packaged sales, and total taxpaid withdrawals of malt beverages, 1935-82. (p. 14)

11. Production and withdrawals of malt beverages [by month] 1971-82, with percent change from same month of previous year. (p. 15)

12. Taxpaid packaged removals of malt beverages by type of container, 1975-82. (p. 18)

13. Number of breweries operated, by States, FY71-82. (p. 18)

14. Seasonal index of production and withdrawals, [monthly] 1983. (p. 19)

15. Production and withdrawals adjusted for seasonal variation, [monthly] 1978-82. (p. 22)

16. [Brewing] consumption of agricultural products [by commodity], FY56-82. (p. 25)

17-18. Shipments and production of [returnable and nonreturnable] beer bottles [monthly] 1973-82. (p. 26)

19. Estimated production of beer cans, 1953-82. (p. 26)

A9275–1.2: Census of Manufactures Data
[Data are from Census of Manufactures and interim 1981 Annual Survey of Manufactures.]

20. General statistics for malt beverage industry [employees and payroll; number, man-hours, and wages of production workers; value added; material cost; value of shipments; and new capital expenditures, 1949-81]. (p. 27)

21. Selected general statistics, by size of establishment [establishments, employees, payroll, value added, value of shipments, and new capital expenditures, for malt and malt beverages], 1977. (p. 28)

22. Value of manufacturers' inventories [malt and malt beverages], 1972 and 1977. (p. 28)

23-24. Malt beverages: selected operating ratios [1967-72 and 1977]; and materials consumed, by kind, 1972 and 1977. (p. 28-29)

25. Quantity and value of shipments by all producers [by product], 1972 and 1977. (p. 29)

26. General statistics [same breakdowns as in table 20, plus number of establishments, 1977; and employees and value added, 1972], by geographic areas [for] malt beverages. (p. 30)

27. Malt, general statistics [same breakdowns as in table 20, plus number of establishments, gross value of fixed assets, end-of-year inventories, specialization ratio, and coverage ratio], 1963-81. (p. 30)

A9275–1.3: Financial Data; Employment, Hours, and Earnings; and Price Indexes
FINANCIAL DATA

[A] Percent of net profit (after Federal income taxes) to gross sales and receipts from operations for the brewing industry and all manufacturing, 1953-80. (p. 31)

28-29. Comparative profit and loss statement and comparative balance sheet, for breweries submitting balance sheets [1975-80]. (p. 32-33)

30-38. Number of returns; current, other, and total assets; liabilities; net worth; gross sales/gross receipts from operations; and net profit or loss before and after Federal income/excess profits taxes; all by total assets classes for breweries submitting balance sheets [1971-80]. (p. 34-42)

EMPLOYMENT, HOURS, AND EARNINGS

39. Employment, hours, and earnings for production workers in the malt beverage, all food, and all manufacturing industries, 1965-82. (p. 43)

PRICE INDEXES

40. Wholesale and retail price indexes for malt beverages, 1962-82. (p. 44)

A9275–1.4: Shipments and Consumption

41-42. Shipments of malt beverages: by States, 1975-82; and by [census] divisions, 1973-82. (p. 46-47)

43. 1982 consumption and per capita consumption of malt beverages, distilled spirits, and wines, by [census division]. (p. 47)

44-49. Shipments 1975-82, and per capita consumption 1972-82, of malt beverages, distilled spirits, and wine; all by States. (p. 48-53)

50. 1982 population and malt beverage consumption [total and per adult and per capita, by State]. (p. 54)

51. Malt beverage shipments by States, barrels per month in 1982, with percent change from same month in 1981. (p. 55-71)

52. State per capita [malt beverage] consumption by rank, 1980-82. (p. 72)

53-54. Shipments of malt beverages [total and] adjusted for seasonal variation, by months 1976-82. (p. 73)

55. Consumer expenditures for alcohol beverages [1960-81]. (p. 74)

56. Seasonal index of shipment of malt beverages [by month], 1983. (p. 74)

A9275–1.5: Foreign Trade

57-60. U.S. exports of malt beverages (exclusive of shipments to armed forces overseas), malt extracts, malt, and hops [by country or world area of destination, various years 1972-82]. (p. 76-79)

61. U.S. exports of malt beverages, by months, 1965-82. (p. 80)

62-64. U.S. imports of malt beverages, barley malt, and hops [by country or world area of origin, various years 1972-82]. (p. 81-82)

65. Imports of malt beverages, by months, 1974-82. (p. 83)

A9275–1.6: Taxes

FEDERAL TAX

66. History of Federal excise tax on beer [1862-present]. (p. 84)

67. Internal revenue paid to U.S. Government by the distilling and brewing industries [FY01-82]. (p. 85)

68. Federal internal revenue collections from the malt beverage industry [FY34-82]. (p. 85)

69. Internal revenue collections by principal sources [alcohol, corporation income/profits, individual income, employment, estate/gift, tobacco, manufacturer's excise, and all other taxes], FY51-82. (p. 86)

STATE TAX

70. Average State tax per barrel, 1955-82. (p. 91)

71-72. Methods of tax collection, by States [rate, method of payment, and by whom paid]; and State taxes on malt beverages, expressed by rate; July 1, 1983. (p. 92-94)

73. Federal tax collections on malt beverages, distilled spirits, and wines, by States, FY82. (p. 95)

74. History of State excise/license tax collections, 1973-82. (p. 96)

BEER PROHIBITION

75. Post-Prohibition population in areas dry for beer, by States, 1973-82. (p. 97)

A9300
U.S. Catholic Mission Association

A9300–1   MISSION HANDBOOK, 1984-85
Annual. [1984.]   47 p.
ISSN 0095-2036.
LC 74-648018.
SRI/MF/complete

Annual handbook on U.S. Catholic clerical and lay missionaries serving abroad, by country and sponsoring religious order or organization, 1984, with trends from 1956. Includes data for Alaska, Hawaii, and selected U.S. territory missions; and directories of Catholic missionary organizations. Data are compiled by the U.S. Catholic Mission Assn.

Contains contents listing, and description of assn purpose and activities (p. 3-8); mission inventory, with 6 tables, described below (p. 10-41); and directories of Catholic mission-sending groups, mission institutes and seminars, and other assistance organizations (p. 45-47).

Availability: U.S. Catholic Mission Association, 1233 Lawrence St., NE, Washington DC 20017, $1.50; SRI/MF/complete.

TABLES:
[Tables show data for U.S. Catholic personnel, 1984, unless otherwise noted.]

[1] Personnel serving abroad: religious priests, brothers, and sisters; diocesan priests; and lay personnel [showing number of missionaries sent abroad in each category by country served, alphabetically by sponsor]. (p. 11-23)

[2] Overseas missionaries [same personnel types as above, plus seminarians; selected years] 1956-84. (p. 23)

[3-4] U.S. Catholic mission fields abroad: [ranking of 113 countries by missionary population, with accompanying map]; and countries abroad served by U.S. Catholic personnel [by sex, showing number of religious missionaries by sponsor and total lay missionaries, listed alphabetically by country]. (p. 24-38)

[5] Field distribution by [world] areas, [selected years] 1956-84. (p. 39)

[6] Field distribution abroad of missionaries [by sex and country, arranged by world region]. (p. 40-41)

A9330
U.S. Conference of Mayors

A9330–4   FEDERAL BUDGET AND THE CITIES: A Review of the President's Budget for FY85
Annual.   Feb. 3, 1984.
vi+95 p.
SRI/MF/complete

Annual report analyzing the potential impact on urban areas of the Reagan Administration's Federal budget proposal for FY85. Includes data on past and proposed budgets for selected programs and agencies, mostly FY80-85.

Budget areas covered include Administration on Aging programs; National Endowments for the Arts and Humanities; HUD community development and assisted housing programs; DOD; Economic Development Administration assistance programs; Labor Dept employment and training programs; selected DOE and EPA programs; and Interior Dept urban parks, land/water conservation, and historic preservation programs.

Additional areas covered include selected HHS programs, including Medicare and Medicaid, Centers for Disease Control, and community action, social services, and income security programs; NSF; DOT public transportation and Federal highway programs; and major VA program areas.

Report also includes data on Federal budget outlay distribution trends, including percent for individuals and State/local government aid, and forecasts for selected economic indicators, various years FY80-87; summary data on FY85 deficit, including effects of DOD spending, unemployment, and individual income tax cut; and grants-in-aid outlays to State/local governments, FY80-85.

Data are primarily from *U.S. Budget,* Federal agency budget highlight reports and briefing papers, and U.S. House of Representatives reports.

Contains contents listing, preface, and overview, with 1 table (1 p., p. i-vi); narrative analysis in 20 sections, interspersed with 25 tables (p. 1-90); and glossary (p. 91-95).

Availability: U.S. Conference of Mayors, Office of Information and Member Communications, 1620 Eye St., NW, Washington DC 20006, $10.00; SRI/MF/complete.

A9350
U.S. League of Savings Institutions

A9350–1   HOMEOWNERSHIP: Celebrating the American Dream
Biennial. 1984. vii+146 p.
SRI/MF/complete

Biennial report on 1983 home buyers, including buyer socioeconomic characteristics, type and location of purchased homes, and financing, with selected comparisons from 1977.

Covers home buyer age, marital status, and household size and income (including 2nd income as percent of total); home price and age, and new and existing home size; monthly housing expense; housing expense/buyer income ratio; and downpayment as percent of purchase price; for all buyers, repurchasers and 1st-time buyers, and buyers by region and city size.

Also includes summary statistical profiles for unmarried, 1st-time, and condominium buyers, by city size and region; buyers using FHA vs. conventional mortgages; and buyers in 75 SMSAs.

Also includes data on mortgage types used and interest rate charged; frequency of mortgage rate and payment adjustments; and trends in Federal deficits and personal and business savings.

Most data are from a weighted random sample of over 13,000 conventional single-family home mortgage loans made by 371 savings assns during 2nd quarter 1983.

Contains contents and table listings (p. iii-vii); introduction and summary (p. 1-5); analysis of housing market trends and economic policy, with 1 table (p. 6-13); 4 chapters, with 51 tables (p. 16-58); summary statistical profiles (p. 61-144); and methodology (p. 145-146).

This is the 4th biennial report. For description of previous report, for 1981, see SRI 1982 Annual, under this number.

Availability: U.S. League of Savings Institutions, Order Processing, 111 E. Wacker Dr., Chicago IL 60601, members $10.00, nonmembers $25.00; SRI/MF/complete.

A9350–2   '84 SAVINGS INSTITUTIONS SOURCEBOOK
Annual. 1984. 80 p.
LC 55-37094.
SRI/MF/complete

Annual sourcebook on savings institutions' lending activities and financial condition, 1983, with trends from 1960. Includes data on savings, mortgage lending, housing trends, savings institution operations, and Federal agencies.

Data are compiled by the U.S. League of Savings Institutions from the Federal Reserve Board, Dept of Commerce, FHLBB, and other government and private sources.

Contains contents listing, preface, and narrative review (p. 3-19); 101 tables, listed below (p. 21-70); and glossary and index (p. 71-80).

This is the 1st edition of *Savings Institutions Sourcebook.* Report continues data series previously published in *Savings and Loan Sourcebook,* described in SRI 1983 Annual under this number.

Availability: U.S. League of Savings Institutions, Order Processing, 111 E. Wacker Dr., Chicago IL 60601, †; SRI/MF/complete.

TABLES:
[Tables show data for 1960, 1965, and annually 1970-83, unless otherwise noted. Data for savings institutions generally are shown for savings assns and savings banks.]

A9350–2.1: Savings

1. Distribution of total personal income [including taxes, disposable income, outlays, and savings]. (p. 21)

2. Allocation of household funds [1980-83]. (p. 22)

3-4. Annual change in financial assets of households [by type of financial institution, life insurance and pension fund reserves, credit/equity instruments, and money market fund shares]; and over-the-counter savings [by type of financial institution]. (p. 22-23)

5. Average annual yield on selected investments [including savings deposits and State/local, Federal, and corporate bonds]. (p. 23)

6-7. Total savings, and number and size of accounts at all savings institutions. (p. 24)

8. Average interest rate on savings at assns [by month, 1981-83]. (p. 24)

9. Savings flows at all savings institutions. (p. 25)

10-11. Savings deposits, year end 1983; and quarterly change in savings deposits, 1983; at FSLIC-insured institutions, by type of account [including passbook and money market certificate]. (p. 26)

12. Net new savings flows at savings institutions [quarterly 1976-83]. (p. 27)

A9350–2.2: Mortgage Lending

13. Growth in selected types of credit [including residential and commercial mortgages, corporate/foreign bonds, government obligations, consumer credit, and Federal debt, 1960 and 1983]. (p. 28)

14-15. Mortgage loans outstanding: by type of property [residential (1- to 4-family and multi-family), commercial, and farm]; and by type of property and lender, year end 1983. (p. 28-29)

16. Residential mortgage loans outstanding and savings institutions' share, 1983. (p. 29)

17. Annual change in [Federal] agency-supported residential debt. (p. 30)

18-19. 1- to 4-family and multi-family mortgage loans outstanding, by [type of] lender. (p. 30-31)

20. Long-term interest rates [for conventional loans on new homes, and yields on new utility issues and corporate bonds, 1965 and 1970-83]. (p. 31)

21. Effective interest rates on conventional home mortgage loans closed [for savings institutions and all major lenders, monthly 1983-June 1984]. (p. 32)

22. Terms on conventional mortgage loans [and average purchase price, for new and existing single-family homes, Dec. 1980-83]. (p. 32)

23. Mortgage portfolio [including value of loans oustanding for 1- to 4-family homes and other properties, total number of loans, and average balance], all savings institutions. (p. 33)

24-25. Mortgage lending activity [loans outstanding and acquired, portfolio inflows, and turnover ratio], of all savings assns; and all savings banks [1970-83]. (p. 34)

26-27. Mortgage loans acquired [including loans closed, and loans/participations purchased], all FSLIC-insured assns; and all savings banks [1970-83]. (p. 35)

28-29. Mortgage portfolio inflows [including repayments, and loans/participations sold] at FSLIC-insured assns and all savings banks [1970-83]. (p. 36)

30-31. Mortgage loans made, by purpose of loan [home purchase, home construction, and other]; and 1- to 4-family [new and existing] homes financed; all assns. (p. 37)

32. Mortgage loans made [and distribution of loans closed] by FSLIC-insured institutions, by purpose of loan [1982-83]. (p. 37)

33. Private and government mortgage insurance [and insurance as percent of home mortgage debt]. (p. 38)

34. Mortgage foreclosures by FSLIC-insured assns [including number and rate for conventional and FHA/VA loans, 1965 and 1970-83]. (p. 38)

A9350–2.3: Housing

35-36. Private and public housing starts; and private housing starts, by regions. (p. 39)

37-38. Private housing starts, by months [1981-83]; and subsidized housing starts [1965 and 1970-83]. (p. 39)

39. Annual dollar volume of [public, private, and private residential] new construction; [and GNP and private domestic investment; 1979-83]. (p. 40)

40. Private housing starts, by number of family units. (p. 40)

41. Private starts of apartments [buildings and units, 1965 and 1970-83]. (p. 41)

42-43. New 1-family homes sold, by price [1973-83]; and [number, dollar volume, and median price of] new and existing 1-family homes sold [1970-83]. (p. 41)

44. Inventory of unsold speculatively built 1-family homes, and number of months required to clear inventory [by month 1981-83]. (p. 42)

45. Mobile home shipments. (p. 42)

46. Residential construction costs and consumer prices [percent change, and Boeckh index of residential construction costs]. (p. 42)

47. Homeownership [owner- and renter-occupied units, selected years] 1890-1981. (p. 43)

48. Number of families and households. (p. 43)

49. Apartment absorption rates [quarterly 1970-3rd quarter 1983]. (p. 44)

50. Rental and homeowner vacancy rates. (p. 44)

A9350–2.4: Savings Institution Operations
[Tables show data for all savings institutions, unless otherwise noted.]

51. Total assets of financial intermediaries at year end [by type of financial institution, selected years 1960-83]. (p. 44)

52-54. Number and assets: by State [and for U.S. territories] Dec. 31, 1983; [for] savings assns, by [Federal and State] charter; and [for] savings banks, by insurance status [FDIC, FSLIC, and State funds]. (p. 45-47)

55. Distribution of assns by asset size, Dec. 31, 1983. (p. 48)

56. Permanent stock assns [number and assets, for California, Texas, Florida, Ohio, and other States, Dec. 31, 1982-83]. (p. 48)

57. Mergers. (p. 48)

58-65. Statement of operations; total operating income and expense [distribution by source and object]; and income and expense ratios [1981-83]; all for FSLIC-insured institutions and FDIC-insured savings banks. (p. 49-51)

66. Selected significant ratios [asset utilization, profit margin, and return on equity and on average assets], for [all] federally insured savings institutions. (p. 52)

67. Minimum liquidity requirements for FHLB members [short-term and overall, selected dates 1950-80]. (p. 52)

68. Number of offices, [and branches]. (p. 53)

69. Personnel [total and per $1 million of assets]. (p. 53)

70-75. Condensed statement of condition of FSLIC-insured savings institutions and FDIC-insured savings banks, as of Dec. 31, 1983; and total assets and liabilities [by item]. (p. 54-56)

A9350–2.5: Federal Agencies

76. FHLB districts. (p. 57)

77. Membership of the FHLB system [including number of federally- and State-chartered assns, savings banks, and life insurance companies, by bank district], year end 1983. (p. 57)

78. Selected operating factors of the FHLB system [including average cost of obligations, weighted average rate on advances, and number of borrowers at month end, by month 1982-83]. (p. 58)

79. FHLBB consolidated obligations issued [date, amount, maturity, and coupon rate], 1983. (p. 58)

80. FHLB lending activity [including advances made, repaid, and outstanding]. (p. 59)

81. FHLB capital stock, member deposits, and obligations. (p. 59)

82-83. Weighted rate on advances, and dividend rates paid, by FHLB district, 1981-83. (p. 59)

84-85. FHLB combined statement of condition, and combined operating statement, 1981-82. (p. 60)

86-87. Number of FSLIC and FDIC member institutions; and FSLIC [primary and secondary] reserves, and FDIC deposit insurance fund [both as percent of insured liability]. (p. 61)

88-89. FSLIC comparative statement of condition, and comparative operating statement, 1981-82. (p. 62)

90-91. FDIC comparative statement of condition, and comparative operating statement, 1982-83. (p. 63)

92. FDIC regions. (p. 64)

93. Federal Home Loan Mortgage Corp. activity [mortgage purchases and sales, and FHA/VA and conventional loans, 1970-83]. (p. 64)

94. VA guaranteed home mortgage loans made [number and amount]. (p. 64)

95. FHA insured mortgage and other loans made. (p. 65)

96. FHA interest rate ceilings [on 1-family homes and apartments, selected dates 1970-83]. (p. 65)

97. FNMA activity [loan purchases and sales, and total portfolio]. (p. 66)

98-99. GNMA loan portfolio, by function [special assistance and management/liquidation, 1965 and 1970-83]; and GNMA mortgage-backed security program [value of pass-through security applications and issues, and of bonds sold, 1970-83]. (p. 66)

100-101. Major Federal laws [1932-83] and major regulatory changes [1983] affecting savings institutions. (p. 67-70)

A9360
U.S. Telephone Association

A9360–1   HOLDING COMPANY REPORT
Annual.   May 1984.
23 p. var. paging.
SRI/MF/complete

Annual report, for 1983, on finances and operations of 10 major independent telephone holding companies reporting to the U.S. Telephone Assn and controlling 242 of the 1,400 operating independent companies in the U.S., and 79% of the independent access lines.

Includes data by company on stockholders, employment, facilities, revenue, plant investment, and construction expenditures. Also includes selected data for the top 25 holding companies or groups.

Contains introduction, and the following:

a. 1 table showing aggregate operating and financial data for the 10 major holding companies. (1 p.)

b. Statistics for each holding company, with address and lists of officers and operating companies; number of stockholders, and operating company access lines, exchanges, States of operation, total plant investment, operating revenues, and employment, as of Dec. 1983; and construction expenditures, 1983 and estimated 1984-85. (p. 1-10a)

c. 1 table showing access lines and total operating revenues of top 25 telephone holding companies or groups, as of Dec. 1983. (1 p.)

Previous reports are described in SRI under A9340-1. Issuing agency name has changed from U.S. Independent Telephone Assn.

Availability: U.S. Telephone Association, 1801 K St., NW, Suite 1201, Washington DC 20006, †; SRI/MF/complete.

A9360–2   STATISTICS OF THE INDEPENDENT TELEPHONE INDUSTRY, 1983
Annual.   For individual publication data, see below.
LC 56-19815.
SRI/MF/complete, delayed

Annual report on independent telephone company finances and operations, covering income and expenses, assets and liabilities, employment, and equipment, 1983 and trends. Includes data by

FCC classification based on annual operating revenues. Also includes comparisons to the Bell System, and data for the Rural Electrification Administration (REA).

Most data are from reports submitted to the U.S. Telephone Assn by 678 companies; and from American Telephone and Telegraph Co.

Report is issued in 2 volumes as follows:

Vol. I. Presents aggregate data for the 678 independent reporting companies, other independents, and Bell System; with data on REA activities.

Vol. II. Presents data for each of the 678 independent reporting companies.

Both volumes are described below.

For description of previous report, see SRI 1983 Annual, under A9340-2. Issuing agency name has changed from U.S. Independent Telephone Assn.

Phone Facts '84 containing summary highlights is also available from the assn, but is not covered by SRI.

Availability: U.S. Telephone Association, 1801 K St., NW, Suite 1201, Washington DC 20006; SRI/MF/complete, delayed shipment in Jan. 1985.

A9360–2.1: Volume I
[Annual. July 1984. 3+33 p. $10.00. SRI/MF/complete, delayed.]

Contains contents listing (p. 1); 1 summary table described below (p. 2-5); narrative highlights (p. 7); and 7 charts, and 22 tables also described below (p. 8-33). All tables show aggregate data.

TABLES:

a. Industry summary including number of access lines, companies, and exchanges; total investment in plant, operating revenues, and employment; and daily average number of conversations; generally for independent reporting and nonreporting companies, and the Bell System, 1974-83. 1 table. (p. 2-5)

b. Independent companies: top 100 companies ranked by number of access lines, and including operating revenues, 1983; construction expenditures, 1964-83; and companies and access lines, by State, 1983. 3 tables. (p. 8-13)

c. Reporting companies' financing by type of security; assets and liabilities, with detail for investment in plant; income and expenses, with detail for operating revenues and taxes; access lines by type; average daily calls and toll messages; central offices by number of lines and type of equipment; financial ratios; employment by sex and occupation; payroll; and operating ratios; various years 1974-83. 15 tables. (p. 14-29)

d. Comparisons for reporting companies grouped by revenue class, including number of companies and access lines; capitalization by type of investment, value of plant in service and depreciation reserve; and revenues, expenses, and net operating income, per access line; 1979-83. 3 tables. (p. 30-32)

e. REA and Rural Telephone Bank loan activities, and REA borrowers and subscribers by type, various years 1973-83. 1 table. (p. 33)

A9360–2.2: Volume II

[Annual. July 1984. 15+170 p. Reporting companies $10.00, nonreporting member companies $15.00, others $35.00. SRI/MF/complete, delayed.]

Contains foreword and explanation of codes (2 p.); alphabetical listing of independent reporting companies, with revenue class, location, and ranking based on 1983 operating revenues (13 p.); and 1 detailed table (p. 1-170), showing the following for each of the 678 independent reporting companies, arranged in rank order, 1982-83:

a. Value of plant in service; depreciation/amortization reserves; number of exchanges and access lines; and capitalization including funded debt (bonds and other), stock, retained earnings, and maturity of long-term debt/short-term notes.

b. Revenue from local and toll service and other sources; expenses including taxes; net income; deductions including interest; and dividends.

A9385
Western
Interstate Commission
for Higher Education

**A9385–1   WICHE STUDENT
EXCHANGE PROGRAM,
Academic Year 1983/84**
Annual. Dec. 1983. 15 p.
Pub. No. 2A131.
SRI/MF/complete

Annual report on student exchange programs in the 13 western member States of WICHE, 1983/84. Includes data on enrollments, on support fees paid by States to enable resident students to enroll in professional and graduate programs in other States when not available in their own home States, and on other exchange programs.

Contains narrative description of programs, interspersed with 7 tables listed below (p. 2-15).

Availability: Western Interstate Commission for Higher Education, Publications, PO Drawer P, Boulder CO 80302, †; SRI/MF/complete.

TABLES:
[Unless otherwise noted, data are for academic year 1983/84. Tables 1-2 and 5 include out-of-region data.]

PROFESSIONAL STUDENT EXCHANGE PROGRAM
[Table titles begin "Professional student exchange program..."]

1. Summary of enrollment and fees for purposes of comparison [by field; and participating programs receiving and prepared to receive students; 1982/83-1983/84]. (p. 3)

2. Student and fee totals, all fields [students sent and fees paid, and received in public and private programs, by State]. (p. 4)

3-4. Enrollment and fees; and student distribution [by receiving school] and fee payments; [all by sending State and field]. (p. 4-7)

5. Receipt of support fees by States and institutions [by field]. (p. 8-9)

OTHER PROGRAMS

6. Community college student exchange program: nonresident tuition waivers granted [by State and institution]. (p. 12-13)

7. Scholars program: [listing, showing field of study and institution, by State]. (p. 15)

**A9385–3   TUITION AND FEES IN
PUBLIC HIGHER
EDUCATION IN THE WEST,
1983/84**
Annual. Feb. 1984.
viii+74 p. Pub. No. 2A128.
SRI/MF/complete

Annual report on public higher education tuition/fees in the 13 western member States of WICHE, 1983/84, with change from 1982/83 and 1979/80. Data are shown by individual institution, for resident students at 2-year colleges, and for resident and nonresident graduate and undergraduate students at 4-year schools. Also includes summary data by WICHE State and comparisons to selected institutions in 7 other States.

Data are from State higher education executive officers, and from *The College Cost Book, 1983-84.*

Contains contents listing and foreword (p. iii-viii); 3 narrative chapters, with 4 charts and 8 tables (p. 1-20); and appendices, with 5 tables, and descriptions of State policies for determining tuition/fees (p. 23-74).

Availability: Western Interstate Commission for Higher Education, Publications, PO Drawer P, Boulder CO 80302, $5.00 (prepaid); SRI/MF/complete.

**A9385–4   HIGH SCHOOL
GRADUATES: Projections
for the Fifty States
(1982-2000)**
Recurring (irreg.) Jan. 1984.
2+33 p. Pub. No. 2A129.
SRI/MF/complete

Recurring report, by William R. McConnell and Norman Kaufman, projecting high school graduates, by State, 1983-2000. Also includes actual graduates, 1975-82; and summary projections by region. Data cover public/nonpublic schools for 22 States, and public schools for 28 States and D.C.

Report was compiled by WICHE, in cooperation with the Teachers Insurance and Annuity Assn and the College Board. Projections are based primarily on enrollment and graduate data provided by State education agencies.

Contains listing of contents, charts, and tables, and foreword (2 p.); introduction (p. 1-2); report, with narrative, 63 charts, and 1 detailed table (p. 1-20); and methodology, with 2 tables (p. 30-33).

This is the 2nd edition of the report; the 1st edition was published in 1979. SRI coverage begins with the 2nd edition. Also available from the issuing agency are reports for individual States ($2.00 each) and regions ($15 each or $50 for set of 4); these reports are not covered in SRI.

Availability: Western Interstate Commission for Higher Education, Publications, PO Drawer P, Boulder CO 80302, $7.00; SRI/MF/complete.

A9395
Western Wood
Products Association

**A9395–1   1983 STATISTICAL
YEARBOOK OF THE
WESTERN LUMBER
INDUSTRY**
Annual. Aug. 1984.
2+33 p.
ISSN 0195-931X.
LC 82-640405.
SRI/MF/not filmed

Annual report, for 1983, on western region lumber production and sawmill operating characteristics, and lumber industry export and import trends, including data by species cut, State, county, and region; and trends from 1971.

Data are from various Federal and private sources.

Contains brief introduction (inside front cover); map of the 12-State western lumber region, and contents listing (2 p.); 24 tables, described below (p. 1-32); and additional reference sources (p. 33).

Availability: Western Wood Products Association, Economic Services Department, 1500 Yeon Bldg., Portland OR 97204, $10.00; SRI/MF/not filmed.

TABLES:

a. State commercial forest acreage and sawtimber volume, and distribution of public and private ownership, Jan. 1, 1977; lumber production volume and value, 1975-83; employment, 1982-83; and State sawmill operating profile, including timber source by ownership, species cut, processing, transport, markets, and distribution channels, 1982. 2 tables, repeated for 10 States and California/Nevada combined. (p. 1-11)

b. Western region commercial forest acreage and sawtimber net volume, and ownership, for region excluding and including Alaska/Hawaii, and for total U.S., Jan. 1, 1977; western region, excluding Alaska/Hawaii, lumber production and value, 1975-83, and employment, 1982-83; and regional western sawmill operating profiles, including most data described above for States, by annual production size class, 1982. 5 tables. (p. 12-15)

c. Coastal and inland region production summaries, including new and unfilled orders, shipments, and stocks, by month, 1982-83; production by region and species, 1975-83; production by State, county, and species, 1983; and total annual production by State and county, and by State and species, 1975-83. 8 tables. (p. 16-25)

d. California redwood region lumber production, by species and county, 1975-83; comparison of soft and hardwood production in U.S., and western regions, 1971-83; and lumber production, for 29 States, 1974-82. 4 tables. (p. 26-27)

e. Exports of softwood logs and lumber to all countries and Japan from 4 States, 1974-83; lumber exports, by destination and by species, 1975-83; lumber imports from all countries and Canada, by species, 1975-83; softwood consumption, by type of demand and supply region, 1978-83; and housing starts and mobile home shipments, by U.S. region and type of structure, 1975-83. 5 tables. (p. 28-32)

A9398
Wheat Industry Council

A9398–1 FOOD, NUTRITION, AND DIETING: A Comprehensive Study of American Attitudes, Habits, Perceptions, and Myths
Monograph. Oct. 1983.
242 p. var. paging.
SRI/MF/complete

Report on consumer perceptions and attitudes regarding wheat-based and other food products, nutrition and dieting, and related topics, 1983. Includes data on shopping habits, awareness of and attitudes toward product labeling and nutrition/ingredient information, price/value perceptions, food consumption, health and dieting, meal consumption patterns, and exercise, all by respondent sociodemographic characteristics.

Also includes cross-tabulations for selected nutritional concerns and eating habits; and data on microwave oven ownership and use.

Data are based on 3,368 responses to a 1983 survey sponsored by the Wheat Industry Council. The report was prepared by Riter Marketing Research in conjunction with Market Facts.

Contains contents listing (2 p.); summary, introduction, and methodology (p. i-xvi, 1-4); 6 sections presenting survey results, interspersed with 45 charts and 85 tables (p. 5-199); notes on methodology (7 p.); and 2 appendices, with questionnaire facsimile and sample characteristics (18 p.).

A summary report and *Special Baker's Supplement* are also available from the issuing agency, but are not covered in SRI.

Availability: Wheat Industry Council, 1333 H St., NW, Suite 1200, Washington DC 20005, price on request; SRI/MF/complete.

A9415
Women's International Bowling Congress

A9415–1 WOMEN'S INTERNATIONAL BOWLING CONGRESS ANNUAL REPORT, 1982-83
Annual. [1983.] 68 p.
ISSN 0162-7147.
LC 80-643765.
SRI/MF/complete

Annual report of the Women's International Bowling Congress (WIBC). Includes data on WIBC members and leagues, by city, State, outlying area, Canadian Province, and selected foreign country and city, July 31, 1983. Also includes data on WIBC charitable contributions.

Contains contents listing (inside front cover); review of WIBC activities, with 2 tables (p. 1-36); WIBC delegates by State, scores, and prizes (p. 37-54); membership statistics (p. 55-65); and WIBC financial report and personnel rosters (p. 66-69).

Availability: Women's International Bowling Congress, 5301 S. 76th St., Greendale WI 53129, †; SRI/MF/complete.

A9600
Zinc Institute

A9600–1 U.S. MARKETS FOR ZINC DIE CASTING, 1978-82
Annual. [1983.]
10 p. no paging.
SRI/MF/complete

Annual report on zinc die casting consumption, by end-use market, 1978-82. Also includes total die casters, and number reporting sales in each market.

Data are based on Zinc Institute surveys of die casters. The 1982 survey drew 419 responses.

Contains narrative analysis, 2 summary charts, and 2 charts repeated for each end use.

This is the 9th annual report. Previous report, for 1977-81, is described in SRI 1982 Annual, under this number.

Availability: Zinc Institute, 292 Madison Ave., New York NY 10017, †; SRI/MF/complete.

A9600–2 1977-83 U.S. AUTOMOTIVE MARKET FOR ZINC DIE CASTING
Annual. [1983.] 2 p.
SRI/MF/complete

Annual report on auto industry use of zinc die castings, 1977-83. Includes data on average weight of castings per auto, by auto size class; and casting market shares, by auto manufacturer.

Contains narrative analysis and 12 charts.

Previous report, for 1982, is described in SRI 1982 Annual, under this number.

Availability: Zinc Institute, 292 Madison Ave., New York NY 10017, †; SRI/MF/complete.

A9600–4 1982 SHIPMENTS OF HOT DIP AFTER FABRICATION GALVANIZED STEEL by End-Use Industries
Annual. 1983. 5 p. foldout.
SRI/MF/complete

Annual report on shipments of hot dip after fabrication galvanized steel, by end-use industry, 1982, with trends from 1980. Data are based on surveys of U.S. and Canadian galvanizers. The 1982 survey drew 44 responses.

Contains narrative and 4 tables.

For description of report for 1981, see SRI 1982 Annual, under this number.

Availability: Zinc Institute, 292 Madison Ave., New York NY 10017, †; SRI/MF/complete.

A9600–5 U.S. AUTOMOTIVE MARKET FOR ZINC COATINGS, 1983
Annual. [1983.] 3 p.
SRI/MF/not filmed

Annual report on auto industry use of zinc coatings, 1982-83. Includes data on amount and types of zinc-coated steel used, with detail by auto size class and by auto manufacturer. Also includes zinc content (coated metals and paint) of a typical car.

Contains narrative analysis, 5 charts, and 2 tables.

This is the 2nd annual report.

Availability: Zinc Institute, 292 Madison Ave., New York NY 10017, †; SRI/MF/not filmed.

Business Organizations

B0125
Advance Mortgage Corp.

B0125-1 U.S. HOUSING MARKETS
Quarterly. Approx. 10 p.
ISSN 0502-9716.
SRI/MF/not filmed

Quarterly report on housing markets in 17 SMSAs, covering permits, construction, completions, vacancies, mortgage and loan activity, and market area employment. Includes selected data for 1- and 2- to 4-family units, walkup and elevator apartments, and mobile home shipments and prices.

Data are compiled from reports of private organizations and of State, local, and Federal government agencies, including U.S. Census Bureau. Report is issued approximately 2-3 months after quarter of coverage.

General format: contents listing, and narrative introduction with text statistics and 1 semiannual summary table; 8 quarterly tables, accompanied by 1-2 summary charts; 7 semiannual tables, including data on mortgages; and 1 annual table on market absorption of housing.

Subscription to *U.S. Housing Markets* also includes prepublication and special releases which are primarily narrative and are covered in SRI only when they include substantial statistics.

Quarterly tables are listed below; most appear in all issues. All additional features with substantial statistical content are described, as they appear, under "Statistical Features."

Availability: U.S. Housing Markets, Circulation Department, 404 Penobscot Bldg., Detroit MI 48226, $130.00 per yr., sample issue $24.95; SRI/MF/not filmed.

Issues reviewed during 1984: 3rd Qtr. 1983-1st half 1984 (D).

QUARTERLY TABLES:
[Tables show data for most recent quarter available or final month of period of coverage, with selected comparisons to previous quarters, months, or years. Table sequence may vary.]

PERMITS AND COMPLETIONS
[1] Private housing permits: dwelling units in permits issued [1-family and 2- to 4-family units, and highrise and/or total apartments, for U.S. and 17 SMSAs; includes U.S. housing starts].

[2] Multifamily completions: units in [walkup and elevator and/or total] buildings of 2 or more units [and units under construction; U.S. and 17-27 SMSAs].

VACANCIES
[3] Distribution of U.S. vacancies [percent of housing for rent and for sale in central cities, suburbs, and outside metro areas].

[4] Vacancies in multiple units [percent of units for rent and for sale in structures with 2 or more and 5 or more units].

[5] Vacancy rates: estimated vacancies [and/or vacancy rates] in total available housing supply [for U.S. and 19-24 urban and suburban areas].

EMPLOYMENT
[6] Employment trends [total and manufacturing employment, and unemployment rate, by region and 17 SMSAs].

MANUFACTURED HOUSING
[7] U.S. [single- and multi-wide] mobile home shipments [and total placements; and total and multisection shipments for 12 States].

[8] Average price of mobile homes placed for residential use [U.S. and by region].

STATISTICAL FEATURES:

B0125-1.501: 2nd Half, 1983
SEMIANNUAL TABLES
[1] Housing starts and permits [1-family and multifamily, for total U.S., 4 regions, 8 divisions, and 17 SMSAs], 1983 vs. 1982. (p. 14)

[2] Other significant markets: housing permits [for 1-family and multifamily units], and employment growth [for 20 SMSAs, various periods 1981-83]. (p. 22-23)

[3-6] Mortgage rates: bond yields [Aaa corporate new issues and U.S. long term]; insured mortgage yields [rate, private market GNMA average, and FNMA mandatory]; conventional loan secondary markets [Federal Home Loan Mortgage Corp. and FNMA mandatories]; and conventional loan rates [for 80%, 90%, and 75% loans, including FHLBB effective fixed rates, for 17 SMSAs; all mortgage rates are shown as of selected dates, Nov. 1982-Feb. 1984]. (p. 25-26)

[7] Insured loan activity [FHA and VA applications and homes insured, for new 1-family and existing homes, U.S. and 17 SMSAs, quarterly 3rd quarter 1982-4th quarter 1983, and annually 1981-83]. (p. 27-29)

B0125-1.502: 1st Qtr. 1984
ANNUAL TABLE
[1] Estimates of market absorption [single- and multi-family units completed, change in occupancy, total absorbed, and building permits issued, for U.S. and 11 metro areas, 1981-83 and 5-year average. U.S. data also show mobile home placements]. (p. 11)

B0125-1.503: 1st Half, 1984
SEMIANNUAL TABLES
[1] Housing starts and permits [1-family and multi-family, for total U.S., 4 regions, 8 divisions, and 17 SMSAs], 1st half 1984 vs. 1st half 1983. (p. 14)

[2] Other significant markets: housing permits [for 1-family and multi-family units], and [total] employment, [for 20 SMSAs, various periods 1981-84]. (p. 22-23)

[3-6] Mortgage rates: long-term bond yields [Aaa corporate new issues and U.S. long term]; insured mortgage yields [rate, private market GNMA average, and FNMA mandatory]; conventional loan secondary markets [Federal Home Loan Mortgage Corp. and FNMA fixed and adjustable rate]; and conventional loan rates [for 80%, 90%, and 1-year adjustable loans, including FHLBB effective fixed rates, for 17 SMSAs; all mortgage rates are shown as of selected dates, May 1983-Aug. 1984]. (p. 25-26)

[7] Insured loan activity [FHA and VA applications for new 1-family and existing homes, and FHA and VA total 1-family homes insured, U.S. and 17 SMSAs, quarterly 1st quarter 1983-2nd quarter 1984, and annually 1981-83]. (p. 27-29)

B0350
American Telephone and Telegraph Co.

B0350-1 WORLD'S TELEPHONES: A Statistical Compilation as of Jan. 1, 1982
Annual. [1983.] 144 p.
LC 12-16862.
SRI/MF/complete

Annual report on world telephone operations, covering the number of telephones in service, by type, country, and city, as of Jan. 1, 1982. Also includes selected trends, and data on telephone lines and conversations. Data are from survey responses of telephone administrations and operating companies in 135 countries.

Contains contents/table listing, introduction, notes, and description of international telephone world numbering zones (p. 3-12); 34 charts and 15 tables (p. 13-94); and listing of nonreporting countries, table notes, definitions, and index (p. 95-144). All tables, and selected charts presenting substantial data not covered in tables, are listed below.

For description of report for 1981, see SRI 1982 Annual under this number.

Availability: AT&T, Reuben H. Donnelly, 550C Amsterdam Ave., NE, Atlanta GA 30306, Attention: The World's Telephones, †; SRI/MF/complete.

TABLES AND CHARTS:
[Tables show data as of Jan. 1, 1982, unless otherwise noted. Tables 7-15 show data for individual countries grouped by international telephone world numbering zone.]

1-3. Telephones by the international world numbering zone plan [total, per 100 population, privately operated, and automatic, all as of Jan. 1, 1982; and total as of Jan. 1, 1977]. (p. 13)

[A-B] World population as of July 1, and reported world telephones as of Jan. 1, [selected years 1925-82]. [charts] (p. 14)

4-6. Countries which have reported 1,000,000 or more telephones [number in service, including total, per 100 population, business, residence, automatic with electromechanical (EMSS) and electronic (ESS) switching systems, main, and extension/private branch exchange (PBX), for 37 countries]. (p. 16-20)

7. Total telephones [and number per 100 population, percent automatic EMSS and ESS, and number government and privately operated]. (p. 21-23)

8. Main and [extension/PBX] telephones. (p. 25)

9. Business and residence telephones [and extensions as percent of total]. (p. 28-29)

10. [PBX/associated extension] telephones [business and residence]. (p. 34)

11. Coin box and public telephone stations [total and number capable of originating international calls]. (p. 37)

12. Telephone subscriber lines (business and residence). (p. 40)

13. Reported [pulse-metered and all other] conversations (local, long distance, and international with percent [international subscriber dialing]). (p. 43)

14. Reported telephone conversations [listing of countries most frequently called]. (p. 46-55)

15. Total and main telephones [and population] in the world's principal cities. (p. 57-94)

B0525
Arbitron Ratings Co.

B0525–3   1983-84 UNIVERSE ESTIMATES SUMMARY
Annual. 1983. 5+149 p.
SRI/MF/complete

Annual report, for 1983/84, on TV markets, presenting data on the number and geographic distribution of all contiguous U.S. households and households owning TVs, by census division, State, Area of Dominant Influence (ADI), non-ADI market, and county. ADI data are for Arbitron-defined TV market areas, and include detail by age and sex.

Data are from Market Statistics, Inc.; Advertising Research Foundation; Census Bureau; and Arbitron surveys.

Contains contents and table listing (1 p.); introduction, methodology, and explanatory notes (4 p.); 10 tables, described below (p. 1-146); and calendar showing market survey dates and number surveyed (1 p.).

Availability: Arbitron Ratings Co., 1350 Ave. of the Americas, Suite 1105, New York NY 10019, †; SRI/MF/complete.

TABLES:
[Data are for 1983/84.]

a. ADI and non-ADI markets: rankings by number of TV households, and alphabetic listings; with additional data for ADI markets on total households, percent TV penetration, and percent of U.S. total TV households. 4 tables. (p. 1-8)

b. Counties in ADI markets: including TV households and population size group for individual counties, grouped by ADI market. 1 table. (p. 9-31)

c. Population in TV households: by age group and sex, for each ADI market arranged alphabetically; and by ADI market, arranged alphabetically and by ADI ranking, for each age group and sex category. 3 tables. (p. 32-95)

d. By county, State, and census division: total and TV households and percent TV penetration; with population size category and ADI market assignment for each county. 2 tables. (p. 96-146)

B0600
Atlas Van Lines

B0600–1   ATLAS VAN LINES 17th ANNUAL SURVEY OF CORPORATE MOVING PRACTICES
Annual. Apr. 1984.
9 p. no paging.
SRI/MF/complete

Annual survey report on corporate employee transfers, and relocation policies, assistance, and costs, 1983 and trends. Includes the following data, shown for 1983 unless otherwise noted:

a. Number and percent of employees moved in 1983, with change from 1982, reasons for change, and expected trend in 1984; average move frequency per employee; percent of transferred employees who are women; effect of spouse employment status on employee relocation; and employees declining relocation, with trend, reasons, and career effect.

b. Company moving policies and practices, including carrier selection and evaluation criteria; reimbursement level and types of assistance provided transferred employees; and use of relocation and special transportation services.

c. Cost of average relocation, total and for van line packing/transport only; most useful provisions of 1980 Household Goods Transportation Act; and use of contract services for employee relocation and for transport of products and general commodities.

Also includes selected comparisons to previous surveys, 1978-82.

Data for 1983 are based on responses of 677 corporate executives to a Jan. 1984 survey.

Contains narrative analysis, with 4 summary trend charts (3 p.); and response distribution for 45 survey questions (6 p.).

Availability: Atlas Van Lines, 1212 St. George Rd., PO Box 509, Evansville IN 47703, ‡; SRI/MF/complete.

B0650
Bank of America

B0650–1   ECONOMIC OUTLOOK: CALIFORNIA 1984
Annual. Dec. 1983. 8 p.
SRI/MF/complete

Annual report forecasting California's economic growth, 1984, with comparisons to 1982-83.

Covers selected economic indicators, including GSP, retail sales, employment, new jobs by industry division, labor force, personal and farm income, inflation, housing starts, and unemployment rate.

Also includes data on California population growth by region, 1980-83 period.

Forecasts are prepared by the Bank of America, using information available as of Nov. 5, 1983.

Contains overview and narrative analysis, 1 map, 4 charts, and 1 table.

Availability: Bank of America, Corporate Communications Planning and Administration No. 3401, PO Box 37000, San Francisco CA 94137, †; SRI/MF/complete.

B0650–2   ECONOMIC OUTLOOK: WORLD 1984
Annual. Dec. 1983. 11 p.
SRI/MF/complete

Annual report on 1984 world economic outlook, presenting Bank of America forecasts of GDP and inflation for selected countries, world regions, and country groupings, 1982-84, based on data available as of Oct. 28, 1983.

Contains narrative report with 6 trend charts, 1 summary table, and 7 tables showing 1983 GDP level, and percent change in GDP and CPI 1982-84, for 29 countries grouped by world region.

Availability: Bank of America, Corporate Communications Planning and Administration No. 3401, Box 37000, San Francisco CA 94137, †; SRI/MF/complete.

B0650–3   ECONOMIC OUTLOOK: U.S. 1984
Annual. Nov. 1983. 8 p.
SRI/MF/complete

Annual report on 1984 U.S. economic outlook, presenting Bank of America trends and forecasts based on data available as of Nov. 5, 1983. Includes new car sales and housing starts, unemployment rate, and percent change in GNP, personal consumption, business and residential investment, and foreign trade, 1982-84; and Federal deficit, and deficit as percent of GNP and of net new funds raised by final users, 1973-84.

Contains narrative analysis, with 1 chart and 2 tables.

Availability: Bank of America, Corporate Communications Planning and Administration No. 3401, Box 37000, San Francisco CA 94137, †; SRI/MF/complete.

B0650–4   CALIFORNIA OUTLOOK: Agriculture 1984

Annual. May 22, 1984. 8 p.
SRI/MF/complete

Annual report on financial outlook for California's agricultural sector in 1984. Includes data on farm cash receipts, with detail for 4 crop categories and livestock/livestock products; value of agricultural exports; and farm income and production expenses; 1978-84.

Data are prepared by Bank of America.

Contains narrative overview and analysis, with 2 charts and 2 tables.

Availability: Bank of America, Banking Divisions Public Relations No. 3402, Box 37000, San Francisco CA 94137, †; SRI/MF/complete.

B0900
Bankers Trust Co.

B0900–1   ECONOMIC BENCHMARKS

Periodic report, with quarterly data. Approx. 4 p.
SRI/MF/complete

Periodic report showing quarterly data on approximately 44 economic indicators for the U.S., including GNP, CPI, consumer spending, investment, exports and imports, government expenditures, sales, personal income, savings rate, profits, housing starts, industrial production index, and unemployment rate.

Data are compiled by the Economics Dept of Bankers Trust Co. Report is published approximately 3 times per year.

Contains narrative summary on the state of the economy, and 2 tables showing the following for each indicator:

a. Quarterly data (actual, projected, and, occasionally, estimated) for previous, current, and following years.

b. Annual data (actual and projected), for 3-4 years, generally ending coming year, with annual and 4th quarter to 4th quarter percent changes.

Availability: Bankers Trust Co., Economics Department, PO Box 318, Church St. Station, New York NY 10015, †; SRI/MF/complete.

Issues reviewed during 1984: Oct. 27, 1983-Feb. 29, 1984 (P).

B0900–2   CREDIT AND CAPITAL MARKETS, 1984

Annual. Jan. 20, 1984.
14+30 p.
SRI/MF/complete

Annual report forecasting 1984 credit expansion and capital formation activities in long- and short-term financial markets, with data on sources and uses of funds raised through corporate, government, and financial instruments of credit, 1978-84. Also discusses investment practices of financial institutions, insurance companies, pension funds, and investment companies.

Data are compiled from Federal agency reports, professional assns, Alfred M. Best Co., and *The Daily Bond Buyer.*

Contains contents listing (1 p.); narrative summary, interspersed with 11 trend charts, and 1 text table (p. 1) showing interest rate changes during economic recoveries for 10 types of securities, Mar. 1975-76 and Dec. 1982-83 (p. 1-11); table listing and notes (p. 13-14); and 30 detailed tables listed below (p. T1-T30).

Revised data on credit and capital markets and corporate finance are issued by Bankers Trust Co. approximately 6 months after this report. Revised forecasts are covered in SRI under B0900-3.

Availability: Bankers Trust Co., Economics Department, PO Box 318, Church St. Station, New York NY 10015, †; SRI/MF/complete.

TABLES:
[Tables show data for 1978-84; 1983 data are estimated and 1984 data are projected.]

SUMMARY
[Tables [1-14] generally show amount of funds raised by type of marketable instrument, and funds supplied by life insurance companies, pension funds, thrift institutions, investment companies, banks, business corporations, government, and foreign and individual investors.]

[1-3] Summary of financing: total, investment, and short-term funds. (p. T1-T3)

[4-6] U.S. Government and agency securities. (p. T4-T6)

[7-8] Corporate bonds and stocks. (p. T7-T8)

[9] State/local government obligations. (p. T9)

[10-12] Total, home, multi-family, commercial, and farm mortgages. (p. T10-T12)

[13-14] Open market paper and consumer credit. (p. T13-T14)

SOURCES AND USES OF FUNDS
[Tables [15-27] begin "Sources and/or uses of funds..." and show origin of funds and amount invested by type of marketable instrument.]

[15-27] Life insurance companies, private noninsured pension funds, State/local governments [retirement and general funds], fire/casualty [insurance] companies, savings and loan assns, mutual savings banks, credit unions, investment companies, other financial intermediaries [finance companies and real estate investment trusts], commercial banks, and business corporations. (p. T15-T27)

[28] Funds supplied: U.S. Government agencies. (p. T28)

[29] Foreign activity in U.S. credit and capital markets [sources of funds (net sales of securities, loans from commercial banks, and open market paper) and uses of funds]. (p. T29)

[30] Individual [investors] and others [funds supplied]. (p. T30)

B1530
Board of Trade of
Kansas City, Missouri

B1530–1   ANNUAL STATISTICAL REPORT, 1983, The Board of Trade of Kansas City, Missouri, Inc.

Annual. [1984.] 46 p.
ISSN 0193-4376.
LC 79-3226.
SRI/MF/complete

Annual report on Kansas City Board of Trade grain market activity, Jan.-Dec. 1983. Includes futures volume and prices, daily cash prices, and grain storage, receipts, and shipments, 1983; U.S. grain production by State, 1981-83; and selected trends from 1956.

Contains contents listing (p. 1); 23 tables, listed below (p. 4-45); and grain freight rate and metric conversion tables (p. 46).

Availability: Board of Trade of Kansas City, Missouri, 4800 Main St., Kansas City MO 64112, current edition †, prior year reports $3.00; SRI/MF/complete.

TABLES:
[Tables on "grain" generally include detail for wheat, corn, sorghum, oats, rye, barley, and soybeans. Data are for 1983, unless otherwise noted.]

FUTURES VOLUME AND PRICES

[1-3] Volume of wheat futures trading [bushels and contracts, monthly 1982-83 and annually 1972-81]; and Kansas City wheat futures [high and low prices and dates set, by month of delivery, 1983]. (p. 4)

[4-5] Jan.-Dec. daily wheat futures prices [open, high, low, and close, by month of delivery]; and daily cash grain prices [low and high, by grain]. (p. 5-20)

[6-7] Volume of Value Line futures contracts [by month]; and Kansas City Value Line futures contract high and low prices and dates set [by month of delivery]. (p. 21)

[8] Jan.-Dec. [daily] Value Line stock index futures [open, high, low, and settle, by month of delivery]. (p. 22-33)

[9-10] Volume of mini Value Line futures contracts [by month, July-Dec.]; and Kansas City mini Value Line futures contract high and low prices and dates set [by month of delivery]. (p. 34)

[11] July [29]-Dec. [daily] mini Value Line stock index futures [open, high, low, settle, by month of delivery]. (p. 35-39)

U.S. GRAIN PRODUCTION

[12-15] Wheat and corn production [by State]; and soybean and sorghum production of leading States; [1981-83, with harvested acres and yield for 1983]. (p. 40-42)

[16] Grain crop production of U.S. [1956-83]. (p. 42)

GRAIN STORAGE, RECEIPTS, AND SHIPMENTS

[17] Mills, grain elevators, and operators in Kansas City, storage capacity of elevators, and daily capacity of mills, as of Dec. 31, 1983. (p. 43)

[18-19] Receipts of grain [bushels by month, and carloads by individual railroad]. (p. 44)

[20] Shipments of grain, bran/shorts, and flour [by month]. (p. 44)

[21] Stocks of grain in store, Jan. 1 and Dec. 31, 1983; receipts and shipments in bushels during the year [by transport mode]; and average bushels per [rail] carload. (p. 45)

[22-23] Receipts and shipments of grain at Kansas City in bushels for past 15 years [1969-83]. (p. 45)

B1582
Boeing
Commercial Airplane Co.

B1582–1 WORLD JET AIRPLANE INVENTORY at Year-End 1983
Annual.   May 1984.   88 p.
Doc. No. Z12645.
SRI/MF/complete

Annual report on world commercial jet aircraft fleet, 1983 and trends. Presents detailed data by aircraft model, including announced deliveries to and orders from U.S. and non-U.S. customers, various years 1947-83; and inventories at year end 1983, by age of aircraft, individual owner/operator, equipment type and series, and world region.

Also shows jet planes leased out by airlines at year end, including lessee and lessor.

Owner/operator categories are airlines, government agencies, manufacturers/brokers/leasing companies, and private operators.

Data are from Boeing's JETTRACK computerized information system containing reports from plane manufacturers and operators, governments, trade publications, and other sources.

Contains contents and table listing (p. 1); introduction and abbreviations (p. 2-3); and 47 tables, arranged in 7 sections (p. 5-88).

This is the 6th annual report.

Availability: Boeing Commercial Airplane Co., Marketing Department, PO Box 3707, Mail Stop 76-77, Seattle WA 98124, †; SRI/MF/complete.

B1900
Chase Manhattan Bank

B1900–2 PETROLEUM SITUATION
Recurring (irreg.)
Approx. 6 p.
SRI/MF/complete

Recurring report on petroleum and energy industry developments. Issues generally consist of a feature article analyzing trends or outlook for a specific energy source or industry sector.

Features with substantial statistical content are described, as they appear, under "Statistical Features." All issues are reviewed and filmed, and an abstract appears in SRI monthly issues regardless of statistical content.

Prior to May 1984 issue, report was issued 3-4 times a year and contained recurring tables.

Availability: Chase Manhattan Bank, Energy Economics, One Chase Manhattan Plaza, New York NY 10081, †; SRI/MF/complete.

Issues reviewed during 1984: May 1984 (P) (Vol. 7, No. 3).

STATISTICAL FEATURE:

B1900–2.501: May 1984 (Vol. 7, No. 3)
CHANGING STRUCTURE OF THE U.S. NATURAL GAS INDUSTRY
(6 p.) Article, with 3 tables showing percent change in energy demand by consuming sector, various periods 1973-90; and natural gas reserves and actual and desired production, for contiguous U.S., 1982-86.

B1900–3 FINANCIAL ANALYSIS OF A GROUP OF PETROLEUM COMPANIES, 1982
Annual.   Apr. 1984.   32 p.
ISSN 0193-8940.
LC SC 79-3306.
SRI/MF/complete, current & previous year reports

Annual report, by Rantch Isquith et al., summarizing the aggregate financial performance of 24 multinational petroleum companies, 1982, with trends from 1971.

Data are compiled primarily from annual company reports to stockholders and to the SEC.

Contains listing of companies and foreword (p. 2-3); narrative report, interspersed with text tables and 23 illustrative charts (p. 4-20); and statistical section, with 18 detailed tables, listed below (p. 21-32).

Previous report, for 1981, has also been received, and is also available on SRI microfiche, under this number [Annual. [1983.] 32 p. †]. Report for 1980 was published as a special issue of *Petroleum Situation* (see SRI 1982 Annual, under B1900-2.302).

Availability: Chase Manhattan Bank, Energy Economics, One Chase Manhattan Plaza, New York NY 10081, †; SRI/MF/complete.

TABLES:

B1900–3.1: Detailed Tables
HISTORICAL DATA
[Tables A-E show data for 1971-82.]

A. Income statement [includes taxes, write-offs, and net income in the U.S. and rest of world]. (p. 22)

B. Rates of return [on average shareholders' equity, for U.S. and rest of world; and on capital employed, total assets, and gross fixed assets]. (p. 22)

C. Source and use of working capital [by fund source or expenditure category]. (p. 22)

D. Expenditures for fixed assets [U.S. and rest of world, for crude oil/natural gas, natural gas liquids plants, pipelines, marine and other transportation, refineries/chemical plants, marketing, and other]. (p. 24)

E. Balance sheet [by item]. (p. 24)

CURRENT DATA
[Tables show data for 1981 and/or 1982, unless otherwise noted.]

1-2. Source of crude oil, and refinery crude runs [barrels per day, for U.S., Canada, Venezuela, other Western Hemisphere, and 4 Eastern Hemisphere regions]. (p. 26)

3-4. Income statement; and distribution of total revenue dollar; [both by item]. (p. 27)

5. Rates of return [and earnings, for average capital employed, shareholders' equity, total assets, and gross operating profit; and average gross fixed assets]. (p. 28)

6. Source and use of working capital [by fund source or expenditure category]. (p. 28)

7. Expenditures for fixed assets [for same categories as in table D, 1982; and aggregate for U.S., Canada, Venezuela, other Western Hemisphere, and 4 Eastern Hemisphere regions, 1979-82]. (p. 29)

8. Capital and exploration expenditures [U.S. and other countries, by function]. (p. 29)

9-10. Balance sheet [by item]; and earnings reinvested and employed. (p. 30)

11-12. Net assets [U.S. and aggregate other countries]; and working capital (p. 31)

13. Investments in fixed [gross and net] assets, [for same breakdowns as in table 7]. (p. 32)

B1900–4 1981 CAPITAL INVESTMENTS OF THE WORLD PETROLEUM INDUSTRY
Annual.   [1983.]   20 p.
LC 72-621455.
SRI/MF/complete

Annual report, by Richard S. Dobias and Norma J. Anderson, on oil and gas industry capital and exploration expenditures, by non-Communist country or world area, 1971-81. Data are estimates based on Chase Manhattan's review of the financial performance of major oil companies and on surveys of investor-owned and government-owned operators.

Contains foreword and narrative summary, with 4 summary charts (p. 3-9); and statistical appendix, with contents listing, and 5 tables listed below (p. 11-20).

Availability: Chase Manhattan Bank, Energy Economics Division, One Chase Manhattan Plaza, New York NY 10081, †; SRI/MF/complete.

TABLES:
[Tables 1-4 show data for crude oil/natural gas and natural gas liquids production, and pipelines, tankers, refineries, chemical plants, marketing, and other capital expenditures, for U.S., Canada, Venezuela, and 5 world areas. Tables 1 and 4 also include data for geological/geophysical expense/lease rentals.]

1. Capital and exploration expenditures, 1981. (p. 12)

2-3. Gross and net investment in fixed assets, Dec. 31, 1981. (p. 12)

4. Capital and exploration expenditures [and total foreign flag tankers, 1971-81]. (p. 14-19)

5. Exploration and development expenditures, U.S. (excludes natural gas liquids plants) [for on- and offshore lease acquisitions, producing wells, dry holes, geological/geophysical expense, and lease rentals], 1971-81. (p. 20)

B1900–5   COAL SITUATION
Quarterly. Approx. 4 p.
LC SN 82-20018.
SRI/MF/complete

Quarterly review of U.S. and world coal industry developments. Issues usually contain 1 article with statistics.

Features with substantial statistical content are described, as they appear, under "Statistical Features." All issues are reviewed and filmed, and an abstract is published in SRI monthly issues regardless of statistical content.

Prior to the Nov. 1983 issue, report included 2 quarterly tables on U.S. and EC coal supply-demand.

Availability: Chase Manhattan Bank, Global Mining and Metals Division, Coal Situation, 33rd Floor, One Chase Manhattan Plaza, New York NY 10081, †; SRI/MF/complete.

Issues reviewed during 1984: Nov. 1983-June 1984 (P) (Vol. 3, No. 4; Vol. 4, Nos. 1-3).

STATISTICAL FEATURES:

B1900–5.501: Nov. 1983 (Vol. 3, No. 4)
OUTLOOK FOR THE U.S. DOMESTIC METALLURGICAL COAL MARKET

(p. 1-4) Article, with 8 tables showing the following U.S. data for various periods 1963-82, with forecasts as noted:

a. Metallurgical coal consumption, exports, and production, with consumption forecast to 1990.

b. Steel total supply and imports; and raw steel and pig iron production, with forecast to 1990.

c. Blast furnace coke and supplemental fuel consumption rates; coal received at coke plants; and number, average age, and capacity of coke ovens by operational status.

Includes low, medium, and high forecasts.

B1900–5.502: Mar. 1984 (Vol. 4, No. 2)
INTERNATIONAL COAL TRADE 1984, ANNUAL FEATURE

(4 p.) Annual article analyzing factors affecting world coal trade through 1984. Includes 5 tables showing metallurgical and thermal coal (hard coal) imports and exports, 1982-83, and forecast 1984 under 3 economic growth assumptions; and EC hard coal imports from third party countries, 1981-83; all by country or world area.

B1900–5.503: June 1984 (Vol. 4, No. 3)
WORLD COAL MARKETS: THE PAST 10 YEARS

(3 p.) Article, with 1 table showing average annual percent change in coal consumption, for non-Communist world, with detail by country or country group, selected periods 1973-83.

B2120
Chicago Board of Trade

B2120–1   1983 INTEREST RATE AND METALS FUTURES STATISTICAL ANNUAL
Annual. 1984. 421 p.
SRI/MF/current report delayed, previous report complete

Annual compilation of statistics on futures trading in fixed-interest rate securities and precious metals on Chicago Board of Trade (CBT), Jan.-Dec. 1983, for delivery to 1986. Covers GNMA Collateralized Depository Receipts (CDRs), long-term Treasury bonds, Treasury bond options, 2 year and 6.5-10 year Treasury notes, silver, and gold.

For each type of future, highlights of trading conditions are presented, together with the following trading data: 1983 deliveries against commitments, by delivery day; 1983 opening, high, low, and closing prices or premiums, and volume of sales and open contracts, by trading day and delivery month; and monthly price ranges since year first traded, by trading and delivery month.

Contents:

a. Introduction and discussion of factors affecting futures prices, with 5 trend charts; record futures contract prices, for 1982-83 delivery and all-time, by contract month and trading date; date of highest volume of sales and open contracts for 24 commodities, including 90-day commercial paper and 8 types of futures noted above; and sales volume, monthly 1982-83 and annually 1975-83, and deliveries against commitments, monthly 1983, for 15-18 commodity contracts. (p. 1-12)

b. GNMA-CDR futures contracts: trading data, covering deliveries through Mar. 1986 and price ranges since 1975; registrations, monthly 1977-83; applications and securities issued, monthly 1976-83; 8% and 9% contract prices and yields, daily 1983; and FNMA portfolio activities, monthly 1982-83. (p. 13-48)

c. Treasury bond futures contracts: trading data, covering deliveries through Sept. 1986 and price ranges since 1977; and cash market quotes, and 9% contract prices and yields, daily 1983. (p. 49-80)

d. Treasury bond futures call and put options: trading data, covering deliveries through Sept. 1984 and premium ranges 1982/83-1983/84. (p. 81-300)

e. Treasury 2-year and 6.5-10 year note futures contracts: trading data, covering deliveries through Dec. 1984 and price ranges since 1981/82. (p. 301-324)

f. Silver (5,000 ounce) futures contracts: trading data, covering deliveries through Oct. 1983 and price ranges since 1972/73. (p. 325-344)

g. New silver (1,000 ounce) futures contracts: trading data, covering deliveries through Apr. 1985 and price ranges since 1980/81. (p. 345-374)

h. Gold (100 ounce) futures contracts: trading data, covering deliveries through June 1983 and price ranges since 1978/79. (p. 375-386)

i. Kilo gold futures contracts: trading data, covering deliveries through Feb. 1985 and price ranges since 1982/83. (p. 387-409)

j. Miscellaneous data: yields/rates for 8 types of financial instruments; prime rate; selected commodity wholesale prices; silver consumption by end use; monthly gold and silver imports, exports, production, and futures contracts registrations; CPI by expenditure category; monthly money supply; and quarterly GNP; various years 1973-83. (p. 410-415)

k. Index. (p. 417-421)

Previous report, for 1982, was also reviewed in SRI during 1984 and is available on SRI microfiche, under this number [Annual. 1982. 299 p. same price as current report]. Previous report was substantially similar in format and content, but omitted data on kilo gold futures, and included data on certificates of deposit.

For description of CBT companion volume, see B2120-2, below.

Availability: Chicago Board of Trade, Education Publications, LaSalle at Jackson, Chicago IL 60604, members and educators $16.00, others $17.00; set of both 1983 CBT annuals: members and educators $25.00, others $30.00; postage and handling $2.50 each, $3.00 per set; SRI/MF/complete, delayed shipment in Dec. 1984.

B2120–2   STATISTICAL ANNUAL, 1983, CHICAGO BOARD OF TRADE: Grains, Forest Products, Energy
Annual. 1984. 7+378 p.
ISSN 0163-5409.
LC 78-648247.
SRI/MF/current report delayed, previous report complete

Annual report on grain, grain product, plywood, gasoline, and crude and heating oil futures traded on the Chicago Board of Trade (CBT) Jan.-Dec. 1983, for delivery to 1985.

Includes futures prices, volume, and open contracts, selected trading data for other exchanges, cash prices, and selected agricultural commodity shipment and disposition information, various years 1970-84.

Data are from CBT and other exchanges, USDA, and private research services.

Contains contents listing and introduction (8 p.); 4 statistical sections, described below (p. 1-359); and index (p. 361-378).

Previous report, for 1982, was also reviewed in SRI during 1984 and is also available on SRI microfiche, under this number [Annual. 1982. 6+338 p. same price as current report]. Previous report was substantially similar in format and content, but omitted data on crude and heating oil trading.

For description of CBT companion volume, see B2120-1, above.

Availability: Chicago Board of Trade, Education Publications, LaSalle at Jackson, Chicago IL 60604, members and educators $16.00, others $18.00; set of both 1983 CBT annuals: members and educators $25.00, others $30.00; plus postage and handling $2.50 each, $3.00 per set; SRI/MF/complete, delayed shipment in Dec. 1984.

STATISTICAL SECTIONS:

B2120–2.1: Futures Prices, Sales, and Open Contracts

SUMMARY

a. CBT: futures highest and lowest prices for 1982-83 delivery, and for all-time, and highest 1-day volume of sales and open contracts, all by commodity and trading date; dates trading began, by commodity; contract sales volume, by commodity, monthly 1982-83, and annually 1975-83; and monthly deliveries against futures commitments, by commodity, 1983. (p. 2-6)

DAILY PRICES AND VOLUME

[Data shown for each commodity futures are: deliveries against futures commitments, daily 1983; and opening, high, low, and closing prices, and volume of sales and open contracts, by trading day Jan.-Dec. 1983 for delivery through the month noted.]

b. Wheat for delivery to Mar. 1985 (p. 7-24); corn for delivery to May 1985 (p. 25-49); oats for delivery to Dec. 1984 (p. 51-64); soybeans for delivery to Mar. 1985 (p. 65-90); soybean oil for delivery to Jan. 1985 (p. 91-116); and soybean meal for delivery to Mar. 1985 (p. 117-142).

c. New plywood for delivery to Jan. 1984 (p. 143-160); unleaded gasoline for delivery to Dec. 1983 (p. 161-179); crude oil for delivery to Apr. 1984 (p. 181-199); and heating oil for delivery to Feb. 1984 (p. 201-214).

MONTHLY PRICE RANGES

d. Monthly high and low prices for wheat, corn, oats, soybeans, soybean oil and meal, new plywood, unleaded gasoline, and crude and heating oil, by various trading years 1972/73-1983/84, and various delivery years 1974-85. (p. 215-253)

B2120–2.2: Cash Prices

RECORD PRICES

a. CBT record highest and lowest cash grain prices, with occurrence date, by commodity. (p. 255)

DAILY AND MONTHLY PRICES

b. Daily cash prices at selected commodity exchanges for wheat, corn, soybeans, soybean oil and meal, coconut and cottonseed oil, and palm oil, 1983. (p. 256-277)

c. Monthly cash prices at selected commodity exchanges for crude soybean oil, palm oil, wheat, corn, grain sorghum, oats, barley, cottonseed and linseed meal, soybean meal, soybeans, and plywood; and price ratios for hog/corn, steer/corn, and broiler/feed; by crop years 1974-83. (p. 278-283)

d. Monthly range of cash prices at selected commodity exchanges for loose lard, corn oil, and coconut, by crop year 1975-83. (p. 284)

HISTORICAL PRICES

e. Record highest and lowest cash prices for wheat, corn, and oats, 1893-1983, and for soybeans, 1947-83, including month of occurrence. (p. 285-288)

B2120–2.3: Receipts, Shipments, Exports, and Imports

RECEIPTS AND SHIPMENTS

a. Grain receipts and shipments at CBT and primary markets, by type of grain, weekly and monthly 1983, and annually 1974-83. (p. 290-293)

b. CBT receipts and shipments, by transport mode and grain type, 1974-83; shipments to Canadian and overseas ports, by grain type, 1983; lake shipments, largest 1-day receipts, and crop year receipts and shipments, by grain type, 1974-83; and St. Lawrence Seaway official opening and closing dates, 1974-83. (p. 294-297)

c. Western grain center receipts and shipments by center, 1981-83; CBT and U.S. grain stocks, weekly 1983, and monthly 1970-83; and total and deliverable weekly stocks, for CBT and 3 grain centers, 1983; all by grain type. (p. 298-304)

EXPORTS AND IMPORTS

d. CBT exports by grain type, weekly 1983, and annually 1974-83; and U.S. grain exports by country of destination, for wheat, barley, oats, corn, sorghum, soybeans and cottonseed, and soybean and cottonseed meal and oil, various periods 1978-83. (p. 305-310)

e. U.S. exports and imports of flour, and grain by type, monthly 1983, and annually 1979-83; and exports of flour, and types of grain, oilseed, oil, and meal, including peanuts, crop years 1974/75-1982/83. (p. 311-312)

f. Grain inspected for export from U.S. and Canada by grain type, by country of destination 1981, and by U.S. region and port area 1982/83. (p. 313-315)

B2120–2.4: Supply, Disposition, and Miscellaneous

GRAINS, LIVESTOCK, AND PLYWOOD

a. Supply, disposition, and price summary for wheat, soybean oil, soybeans, and soybean meal; feed grain supply and disposition, and quarterly consumption; soybean product volume and value-price spread; and soybean crushings and capacity utilization; various years 1971-84. (p. 318-331)

b. U.S. carry-over grain on and off farms by crop year, 1976-83; quarterly grain stocks, by grain type, 1975-83; and monthly Chicago registrations for soybean oil and meal, 1974-83, and for western plywood, 1982-83. (p. 332-334)

c. U.S. oil seeds monthly crushings, production, and stocks, by seed, with palm oil imports, 1974/75-1983/84; monthly prices received by farmers and parity prices, by type of grain, 1974-83; and U.S. grain price support quantities, rate, and average farm prices, by grain, 1980/81-1982/83. (p. 335-341)

d. U.S. grain harvested acreage, yield, and production, by grain type, total 1974-83, and by State 1983; world grain production by grain type, by country and world area, 1981/82-1982/83; U.S. cattle/calf, hog, and chicken inventory, total 1974-83, and by State 1983 or 1984; and U.S. livestock inventory by detailed class, 1981-84. (p. 342-348)

e. Plywood inventory, production, exports, imports, new orders, and shipments, monthly 1976-83; private housing permits, starts, and completions, and mobile home shipments, monthly 1983, and annually 1974-82. (p. 349-350)

FACILITIES

f. Listings of public grain elevators, and CBT nongrain storage facilities, by commodity, showing operator, location, and capacity; and U.S. and Canada commercial grain storage capacity, by principal grain center. (p. 351-353)

TARIFF RATES, DUTIES, AND WEATHER

g. Carload tariff rates, from Chicago to 11 cities, Jan. 1984; annual precipitation, by State, 1971-83; last killing frost and freezing temperature dates, 4 midwestern States, 1982-83; and U.S. tariff duties on cereal and farm product imports, and Canadian tariff duties on imports from U.S., by commodity, as of Jan. 1, 1979. (p. 354-357)

MISCELLANEOUS

h. Domestic and metric measures equivalents and conversion factors; recommended seed planting dates, by U.S. region; and harvest months by foreign country. (p. 358-359)

B2130
Chicago Mercantile Exchange

B2130–1   INTERNATIONAL MONETARY MARKET Year Book, 1982

Annual. [1983.] 598 p.
ISSN 0195-9980.
LC 79-644317.
SRI/MF/complete

Annual report on International Monetary Market (IMM) futures contracts trading in gold, U.S. silver coins, Treasury bills and notes, certificates of deposit, and 8 foreign currencies, 1982 and trends. Includes trading volume and price trends, and selected economic indicators for U.S. and 8 foreign countries. Data are compiled by the Statistical Dept of the Chicago Mercantile Exchange (CME).

Contains contents listing (p. 1); introduction, with 27 tables showing IMM membership sales, trading history and price range trends, and trading summary, various periods 1972-84 (p. 3-82); 4 statistical sections, with 359 tables, described below (p. 83-546); 1 chart section, with 35 trend charts (p. 547-583); and index (p. 585-598).

Availability: Chicago Mercantile Exchange, Office Services, 30 S. Wacker Dr., Chicago IL 60606, $10.00; SRI/MF/complete.

TABLES:

[Foreign countries and currencies covered are: UK, Canada, West Germany, Netherlands, France, Japan, Mexico, and Switzerland.]

FUTURES

a. Contract daily price ranges, settlement prices or indexes, volume, and open interest, for contracts traded in 1982, for delivery as far as Dec. 1984, by commodity, as follows: 90-day Treasury bills (p. 85-118); 3-month domestic certificates of deposit (p. 119-134); 3-month Eurodollar time deposits (p. 135-151); gold bullion (p. 152-188); U.S. silver coins (p. 189); and 8 foreign currencies (p. 190-296). 13 tables. (p. 85-296)

b. Trading volume and interest: CME, IMM, and Index and Option Market monthly trading volume, and IMM daily volume and open interest, 1982; and IMM volume, volume high, open interest, open interest high, and contracts delivered, by month, various years 1972-82; all by commodity. 98 tables. (p. 299-349)

CASH MARKET PRICES

c. Treasury bill auction market yields, for 13-, 26-, and 52-week bills; Federal debt, and gross public debt; daily cash market price ranges, for Treasury bills, certificates of deposit, Eurodollar, and Federal funds; Federal Reserve interest rates; Federal Reserve Bank of New York open-market operations; and average money market rates; various periods 1968-82. 16 tables. (p. 353-381)

d. Gold and silver bullion average prices, London market, 1800s-1982; and daily prices for bullion and Krugerrands, by market 1982. 11 tables. (p. 382-405)

e. Foreign currency: high, low, and last spot prices, monthly 1972-82 and daily 1982; and closing against U.S. dollar, forward rates, and London Euro deposit daily closings (including U.S. dollar), daily 1982; all by currency. 40 tables. (p. 406-501)

ECONOMIC INDICATORS AND FUNDAMENTALS

f. Gold: New York and Chicago depository holdings and movements, weekly 1982; world gold bullion supply and demand, 1948-81; U.S. production, imports, and exports, monthly 1976-82; non-Communist world production, and fabrication by product, by country, 1970-81; and Federal Reserve open market transactions. 13 tables. (p. 505-515)

g. U.S. and 8 foreign countries: selected indicators, variously including GNP, national income, international transactions, and reserves (all with detail by item for U.S.); construction activity (U.S. only); population; balance of trade; government finances; personal income; money supply; production, price, sales, and earnings indexes; interest rates and bond yields; and others; shown monthly, quarterly, or annually, various years 1967-82. 168 tables. (p. 516-546)

B2320
Columbian Chemicals Co.

B2320–1 **QUARTERLY CONSUMPTION REPORT: Carbon Black and Dry Rubber Hydrocarbons**
Quarterly. Approx. 4 p.
SRI/MF/complete

Quarterly report on carbon black, and dry rubber hydrocarbon, supply and demand. Reports are issued 3-6 months after quarter of coverage.

Issues include narrative summary, and 1 table and 1 chart showing carbon black production and shipments, by grade; and dry rubber hydrocarbon and carbon black domestic consumption, by type or grade; for quarter of coverage, with comparisons to selected previous quarters.

Issue for 4th quarter also includes additional long-term trends. Prior to 1st quarter 1984 issue, report includes 1 table showing styrene butadiene (SBR) black rubber production, by type.

Availability: Columbian Chemicals Co., 3200 W. Market St., PO Box 5373, Akron OH 44313, †; SRI/MF/complete.

Issues reviewed during 1984: 2nd Qtr. 1983-1st Qtr. 1984 (D).

B2360
Commercial
Service Systems, Inc.

B2360–1 **21st ANNUAL REPORT: Shoplifting in Supermarkets, Drug Stores, Discount Stores**
Annual. Mar. 15, 1984.
21 p.
SRI/MF/complete

Annual report, by Roger Griffin, on shoplifters apprehended in supermarkets, drugstores, and discount stores, 1983, with selected trends from 1972. Also includes shoplifter characteristics and circumstances, and type and value of recovered merchandise. Data are from a study of 31,081 shoplifting apprehensions at 1,001 stores located in Southern California and other western States.

Contains table index (1 p.); introduction, with text table showing survey sample, 1983 (p. 1-2); formulas for estimating shoplifting losses for individual retailers (p. 3-5); 21 tables, listed below (p. 6-18); sample apprehension report form (p. 19); and narrative summary (p. 20-21).

Availability: Commercial Service Systems, Inc., PO Box 3307, Van Nuys CA 91407, †; SRI/MF/complete, except sample apprehension report form.

TABLES:
[Most tables show data for supermarkets, drugstores, and discount stores, 1983.]

[1-4] Average number of items and value of merchandise recovered per apprehension [all cases, and for adults and juveniles by sex]. (p. 6-7)

[5-6] Number of cases in which 1 to 25 items were recovered; and value range [of] merchandise recovered. (p. 8-9)

[7-8] Shoplifters referred to police [adults prosecuted and juveniles referred, by sex]. (p. 10)

[9-14] When apprehension occurred [time of day, month, and day of week]; sex of shoplifter [adults and juveniles]; age of shoplifter; and [percent of] shoplifters under 30 years of age. (p. 11-13)

[15] Increase in cigarette thefts [cigarette item recoveries as percent of all cases and of all merchandise value, for 8 unnamed companies, 1982-83]. (p. 14)

[16-17] Value of merchandise recovered [total and cigarettes]; and categories of merchandise recovered. (p. 15)

[18] Methods of concealment. (p. 16)

[19-21] Shoplifting [summary] data [various years 1972-83]. (p. 17-18)

B2380
Commodity Exchange, Inc.

B2380–1 **COMEX 1983 STATISTICAL YEARBOOK**
Annual. For individual publication data, see below.
ISSN 0162-4970.
LC 78-645223.
SRI/MF/complete, current and previous year reports

Annual statistical yearbook of futures trading on the Commodity Exchange, Inc. (COMEX) during 1983. Covers gold, silver, copper, aluminum, and gold options. Data are compiled by COMEX.

Yearbook is issued in 2 volumes, covering metals futures and gold options. Volumes are individually described below.

Prior to the 1983 edition, the yearbook was issued in a single volume.

Previous yearbook, for 1982, was also reviewed in 1984 and is also available on SRI microfiche, under this number [Annual. 1982. 176 p. $11.50]. The 1982 yearbook does not include data on aluminum options.

Availability: Commodity Exchange, Inc., Public Information Department, Four World Trade Center, New York NY 10048, $15.00+$1.50 postage and handling per volume; SRI/MF/complete

B2380–1.1: Metals Futures Data, 1983
[Annual. 1984. 135 p. SRI/MF/complete.]

Annual report on COMEX futures trading during 1983, for delivery through Oct. 1985. Covers gold, silver, copper, and aluminum contracts.

Contents:

a. Introduction, contents listing, trading summary, contract specifications, 1 trend chart, 1 summary table, and abbreviations key. (p. 3-10)

b. Trading data for gold (p. 12-44), silver (p. 48-79), copper (p. 82-113), and aluminum (p. 116-120), with 5-7 tables for each category, showing opening, high, low, closing, and settlement prices; volume traded; open interest; and (except for aluminum) depository or warehouse stocks, and deliveries; by trading day and delivery month.

c. Metals prices, with 7 tables showing London bullion fixing, and Handy and Harman base prices, for gold and silver; and copper prices for U.S. producers cathode, refiners scrap No. 2, and New York dealers spot cathode; all by trading day. (p. 124-134)

B2380–1.2: Gold Options Data, 1983
[Annual. 1984. 165 p. SRI/MF/complete.]

Annual report on COMEX trading in gold put and call options during 1983, for delivery through Dec. 1984.

Contents:

a. Introduction, contents listing, trading summary, contract specifications, 1 trend chart, 1 summary table, and abbreviations key. (p. 3-11)

b. Trading data for gold put and call options, with 10 tables showing opening, high, low, closing, and settlement prices, volume traded, and open interest, by trading day and delivery month. (p. 14-163) *c.* Options exercised, with 1 table showing 1983 put and call options exercised during contract life and at expiration, by strike price and trading month. (p. 164)

B2535
Conlon, Thomas R., and Associates

B2535–1   EXECUTIVE COMPENSATION STUDY, 1984
Annual. 1984. 46 p.
SRI/MF/complete

Annual report on corporate executives' incentive compensation and perquisites, 1984. Includes data on average incentive compensation amount and perquisite costs, for selected executive positions; and average cost, number of companies providing, and number of executives eligible and receiving, for specific types of perquisites; with comparisons to average base salary and company sales volume.

Also includes methods of determining incentive compensation eligibility, generating compensation funds, and allocating awards.

Data are from responses of 186 companies to a 1984 survey by Thomas R. Conlon and Associates.

Contains contents listing (1 p.); preface (p. 1-3); and survey report in 4 sections, with text data and 23 tables (p. 4-46).

For description of previous report, for 1982, see SRI 1982 Annual, under this number. No report was issued in 1983.

Availability: Thomas R. Conlon and Associates, 93 Pine St., Deer Park NY 11729, $95.00; SRI/MF/complete.

B2975
Deutsch, Shea and Evans

B2975–1   HIGH TECHNOLOGY RECRUITMENT INDEX
9-12 per year. Approx. 2 p.
SRI/MF/complete, shipped quarterly

Recurring press release (9-12 per year) presenting index of demand for engineers/scientists based on recruitment advertising in approximately 40 major newspapers and technical journals (1961=base year).

Includes brief narrative, and 1 table showing high technology recruitment index for month of coverage and/or 3-month running average, current to 1-2 months prior to publication date, with comparisons to previous 11-12 months.

Availability: Deutsch, Shea and Evans, Research Department, 49 E. 53rd St., New York NY 10022, ◆; SRI/MF/complete, shipped quarterly.

Issues reviewed during 1984: Nov. 28, 1983-Oct. 25, 1984 (P).

B3075
Douglas Aircraft Co.

B3075–1   OUTLOOK FOR COMMERCIAL AIRCRAFT, 1984-98
Annual. June 1984. i+31 p.
SRI/MF/complete

Annual report projecting world airline traffic and aircraft requirements to 1998, with trends from 1971. Includes passenger traffic; seat capacity and load factors; and aircraft retirements, orders, options, requirements, deliveries, and new and used aircraft availability, by generic class. Selected traffic data are shown by type of service, world region, and/or U.S. and non-U.S. area.

Projections are derived from econometric models for 32 International Air Transport Assn regions, based on data from 77 individual airlines.

Contains contents listing (p. i); introduction, and 4 report sections, with 20 charts and 2 tables (p. 1-23); and appendices, with definitions, and 5 tables (p. 26-31).

Availability: Douglas Aircraft Co., Marketing Strategic Plans (18-70), 3855 Lakewood Blvd., Long Beach CA 90846, ‡; SRI/MF/complete.

B3370
Exxon Corp.

B3370–1   TURBINE-ENGINED FLEETS OF THE WORLD'S AIRLINES, 1984
Annual. 1984. 42 p.
SRI/MF/complete, current & previous year reports

Annual report on world air carrier turbine fleets, covering aircraft in service and on order as of Mar. 31, 1984. Data are compiled by Aviation Data Service, Inc., from a survey of 766 airlines, including local service/commuter airlines.

Contains narrative highlights (p. 1); 2 tables showing turbine-powered aircraft and helicopters in service and on order as of Mar. 31, 1984, by manufacturer and model, arranged by propulsion type, and arranged alphabetically by airline, with airline country of operation, aircraft engine specifications, and remarks on options and leases (p. 2-41); and glossary (p. 42).

Report is issued each year as a supplement to *Air World Survey,* a narrative report not covered in SRI.

Previous report, for 1983, was also reviewed in SRI during 1984 and is also available on SRI microfiche, under this number [Annual. 1983. 39 p. †].

Report for 1982 is described in SRI 1982 Annual, under this number.

Availability: Exxon International Co., Commercial Department, Air World Survey, 200 Park Ave., Florham Park NJ 07932, †; SRI/MF/complete.

B3500
First Hawaiian Bank

B3500–1   ECONOMIC INDICATORS, Hawaii
Bimonthly, with annual summary. Approx. 8 p.
ISSN 0015-2757.
SRI/MF/complete

Bimonthly report, with annual summary, reviewing Hawaii business activity, employment, population, and personal income changes. Data are compiled by the Research Dept of First Hawaiian Bank.

Period of coverage is 2-4 months prior to publication, and is specified for each data series covered. Some data are reprinted the following issue if more recent figures are not available.

Each issue contains feature articles, usually with trend charts; and 6 bimonthly tables listed below. An annual summary accompanies a spring issue (usually Mar./Apr.).

Availability: First Hawaiian Bank, Research Department, PO Box 3200, Honolulu HI 96847, †; SRI/MF/complete.

Issues reviewed during 1984: Sept./Oct. 1983-July/Aug. 1984 (P); and annual summary for 1982-83.

BIMONTHLY TABLES:
[All tables include percent change from preceding period and from same period of previous year. Some data are reported cumulatively from Jan. Tables are repeated in annual summary, showing data for previous 2 years.]

[1] U.S. economic indicators [shows 3-4 general business indicators, and banking and credit, construction, employment, CPI, and PPI].

[2] Business activity [tourism (includes visitors, accommodations, and hotel occupancy rate, all by county, and meeting attendance); defense expenditures; sugar production and price; pineapple shipments; crop and livestock production and prices for selected commodities; construction (total put in place, private single- and multi-family residential and non-residential permits authorized by county, public contracts awarded by level of government and county, and cost indexes); housing sales and prices, by county; business sales (gross receipts, sales in 5 industry sectors, and Oahu new car sales); public utilities (electricity generated, gas sales, and telephone lines in service); and Honolulu CPI].

[3] Population [by county, and for military and foreign immigration]; and personal income [by industry division and type, and per capita by county].

[4] Employment and unemployment [by county; number of jobs in 16 industry sectors, including sugar and pineapple industries and government; and unemployment insurance claims and payments].

[5] Public assistance [recipients and payments, by type of service].

[6] Banking and finance [including bank total and demand deposits by county, and loans outstanding by type; savings and loan assn deposits and loans; and tax collections by county].

B3500-2 NEIGHBOR ISLAND PROFILES
Series. For individual publication data, see below.
SRI/MF/complete

Annual series of reports on socioeconomic conditions in Hawaii, for Hawaii, Kauai, and Maui Counties, 1979-1st quarter 1984. Data are prepared by the research division of First Hawaiian Bank.

Each report covers a single county and contains narrative analysis and 1 table showing the following data:

a. Population, per capita personal income, civilian labor force by employment status, and number of jobs.

b. Tax collections, bank deposits and debits to demand deposits, private construction permits by type of unit, and public contracts awarded by level of government.

c. Tourism, including number of westbound visitors with intended length of stay, and hotel inventory and occupancy.

d. Telephone access lines, and motor vehicle registration.

e. Sugar production, and value of livestock and crops.

Data for Honolulu County are not covered in this series, but are presented in bimonthly *Economic Indicators* (described in SRI under B3500-1).

No reports were published during 1983; for description of 1982 reports, see SRI 1983 Annual, under this number. Series title has changed from *Hawaii Counties Report*.

Report reviewed in 1984 is listed below.

Availability: First Hawaiian Bank, Research Department, PO Box 3200, Honolulu HI 96847, †; SRI/MF/complete.

REPORT:

B3500-2.1: Hawaii County in 1984
[Annual. July/Aug. 1984. 8 p. SRI/MF/complete.]

B3700
First National Bank of Chicago

B3700-1 CONSUMER FINANCE (DIRECT CASH LENDING) COMPANY RATIOS
Annual. [1984.] 3 p.
SRI/MF/complete

Annual report presenting aggregate lending ratios and other financial data for consumer finance companies involved in direct cash lending, Dec. 1980-83. Data are based on a mail survey, conducted by Robert Morris Associates, of a cross-section of national and regional loan companies.

Contains 1 table showing 41 items as of Dec. 31, 1980-83, including numerous financial and lending ratios, lending volume for year, total amount outstanding, average loan size and balance, and percent delinquent accounts by days past due.

Report has been published since 1948.

Availability: First National Bank of Chicago, Group D, One First National Plaza, Suite 0084, Chicago IL 60670, †; SRI/MF/complete.

B3700-3 DIVERSIFIED FINANCE COMPANY RATIOS
Annual. [1984.] 3 p.
SRI/MF/complete

Annual report presenting aggregate lending ratios and other financial data for diversified finance companies, Dec. 1980-83. Data are based on a mail survey, conducted by Robert Morris Associates, of a cross-section of national and regional diversified finance companies.

Contains 1 table showing 56 items as of Dec. 31, 1980-83, including numerous financial and lending ratios, lending volume for year, total amount outstanding, and analysis of retail auto lending.

Report has been published since 1935.

Availability: First National Bank of Chicago, Group D, One First National Plaza, Suite 0084, Chicago IL 60670, †; SRI/MF/complete.

B3900
First
Security Bank of Idaho

B3900-1 IDAHO CONSTRUCTION REPORT: Authorized Building Permit Construction, 54 Major Locations
Monthly. Approx. 5 p.
SRI/MF/complete, shipped quarterly

Monthly report on Idaho construction activity, by location. Data are compiled by First Security Bank of Idaho. Reports are issued approximately 1 month after month of coverage.

Contains brief narrative; 1 summary table; and 4 detailed tables showing housing units constructed, building permits issued, value of new residential and nonresidential construction, and value of alterations/repairs, in 54 Idaho cities and counties, for month of coverage, year to date, and same periods of previous year.

Availability: Dr. Kelly K. Matthews, First Security Co., PO Box 30006, Salt Lake City UT 84125, †; SRI/MF/complete, shipped quarterly.

Issues reviewed during 1984: Oct. 1983-Sept. 1984 (D) (Vol. 30, Nos. 10-12; Vol. 31, Nos. 1-9).

B4000
Grant, Alexander, and Co.

B4000-1 FIFTH STUDY OF GENERAL MANUFACTURING BUSINESS CLIMATES of the Forty-Eight Contiguous States of America
Annual. 1984. 112 p.
SRI/MF/not filmed

Annual report ranking the manufacturing business climate in 48 contiguous States and 8 regions, 1983. Covers 22 factors in the areas of government fiscal policy, State regulated employment costs, labor availability and productivity, energy costs, environmental control, and population.

Report is intended to assist manufacturers in site selection. Data are derived from Federal Government reports, U.S. Chamber of Commerce, Insurance Technical and Actuarial Consultants Corp., and other sources.

Contains contents listing (1 p.) and the following:

a. Introduction/executive summary, with 1 map and 3 tables; background and methodology, with 2 tables on factor weighting; and regional analyses. (p. 1-17)

b. 22 tables on individual factors, listed below. (p. 19-63)

c. State analyses, each with the following data: national and regional composite rank for all, government, and nongovernment factors; and rank, factor value, and national average, for each factor; all for 1983. (p. 64-112)

Availability: Business Climates Study, Alexander Grant and Co., Prudential Plaza, 6th Floor, Chicago IL 60601, $20.00; SRI/MF/not filmed.

MEASUREMENT FACTOR TABLES:
[All tables show factor value and national and regional rank, by State, with regional averages, 1983.]

FISCAL POLICY, UNEMPLOYMENT INSURANCE, AND WORKERS' COMPENSATION

A1-A5. State/local taxes per $1,000 of personal income, and percentage change over 3 years; government general expenditure vs. general revenue growth over 3 years; and government debt and public welfare expenditure per capita. (p. 20-29)

B1-B4. Average unemployment compensation benefits paid per year, and net worth of State unemployment compensation trust fund, per covered worker; maximum weekly payment for temporary total disability under workers' compensation insurance; and weighted average workers' compensation levels [aggregated] for manufacturing classifications. (p. 30-37)

LABOR COSTS, AVAILABILITY, AND PRODUCTIVITY

C1-C4. Annual average hourly manufacturing wage, and percentage change over 3 years; and total private sector, nonagricultural union membership per 100 workers, and percentage change over 2 years. (p. 38-45)

D1-D5. Vocational educational enrollment as a percentage of population; percentage of population 25 years old/over who have completed 4 years of high school; average percent of estimated nonagricultural working time lost due to work stoppages over 2 years; value added by manufacturing employees per dollar of production payroll; and annual average hours worked per week. (p. 46-55)

OTHER FACTORS

E1-E4. Fuel/electric energy costs per million Btu(s) for manufacturers; State expenditure on environmental control as a percentage of total State expenditures; population density per square mile; and absolute change in population over 3 years. (p. 56-63)

B4050
Grimm, W. T., and Co.

**B4050–1   MERGERSTAT REVIEW,
1983**
Annual. 1984. 3+152 p.
SRI/MF/excerpts

Annual report on business mergers, acquisitions, and divestitures, 1983, with trends from 1963. Covers announced transfers of ownership involving at least 10% of a company's assets or equity, and divestitures with a minimum purchase price of $500,000.

Includes data on number of transactions and dollar value paid; largest transactions, with participants and price paid; methods of payment; transactions involving foreign buyers and sellers, with detail by country; outcomes of tender offers; leveraged buyouts; acquisitions of public and private companies; premiums (over market price) and price/earnings ratios paid; and terminated transactions.

Other data include transaction volume and characteristics for specific industries; and rankings of industries, companies, States, and regions by various indicators of acquisition and/or divestiture activity.

Also includes a roster of 242 individual transactions in 1983, showing date, participants, seller's line of business and annual sales, price paid, payment method, and selected other financial aspects of each transaction.

Data are from W. T. Grimm and Co. research, and other private sources.

Contains introduction and contents listing (3 p.), and the following:

Section I. Statistical Review and Discussion. Includes 74 tables. (p. 1-98)

Section II-III. Historical Data Checklist, and Industry Analysis. Includes 3 tables. (p. 99-105)

Section IV. Transaction Roster. (p. 106-146)

Section V. Index of Company Names. (p. 147-152)

This is the 4th annual report.

Availability: W. T. Grimm and Co., 135 S. La Salle St., Chicago IL 60603, $125.00; SRI/MF/ excerpts for all sections except transaction roster.

B4300
Handy and Harman

**B4300–1   SILVER MARKET, 1983,
68th Annual Review**
Annual. 1984. 28 p.
ISSN 0361-2732.
LC 81-649254.
SRI/MF/complete

Annual report on silver market activity in the U.S. and non-Communist world, including stocks, consumption by end use, foreign trade, and prices, 1970s-83. Data are compiled from reports by government and private sources, and U.S. Bureau of Mines *Mineral Industry Surveys.*

Contents:

a. Highlights, contents listing, and market review for world, U.S., UK, West Germany, France, Canada, Mexico, Japan, and India, 1983; with text statistics, 3 U.S. trend charts, and 1 table showing Japan industrial silver consumption by end use, 1982-83. (p. 2-17)

b. Summary of world stocks and outlook, with 1 table showing private and U.S. Government stocks by depository, estimated total foreign government stocks, and conjectural U.S. and foreign stocks, 1982-83. (p. 18-21)

c. Statistical section, with 6 detailed tables listed below. (p. 24-28)

Availability: Handy and Harman, Advertising Department, 850 Third Ave., New York NY 10022, †; SRI/MF/complete.

TABLES:
[Data are for 1979-83, unless otherwise noted. Most data for 1983 are preliminary.]

[1-2] World silver consumption and supplies (excluding Communist-dominated areas) [including industrial uses, coinage, new production, and secondary supply sources, mostly with detail for U.S. and selected other countries]. (p. 24-25)

[3] U.S. industrial consumption of silver, by end use. (p. 26)

[4-5] Imports of silver into and exports from the U.S. [by country]. (p. 27)

[6] Silver quotations [high, low, and average New York (Handy and Harman) and London daily fixing prices, 1974-83]. (p. 28)

B4490
Heidrick and Struggles

B4490–2   PROFILE SERIES
Series. For individual
publication data, see below.
SRI/MF/complete

Continuing series of reports on selected characteristics and attitudes of corporate executives. Most data are from Heidrick and Struggles' surveys of executives in the largest U.S. industrial corporations and selected nonindustrial sectors.

General format: introduction and narrative summary of findings; and 1-22 tables presenting survey response data.

Reports are updated either irregularly or annually. Reports reviewed during 1984 are described below.

Availability: Heidrick and Struggles, 125 S. Wacker Dr., Suite 2800, Chicago IL 60606; SRI/ MF/complete.

B4490–2.9: Changing Board: 1984 Profile of the Board of Directors

[Annual. 1984. 12 p. $20.00. SRI/MF/complete.]

Annual board profile series update, for 1983, presenting survey findings on the composition, compensation, and policies of corporate boards of directors.

Data are based on a late 1983 survey of 500 largest industrial companies and 500 leading nonindustrial companies. Survey response rate was 39.3%.

Includes 22 tables showing the following data, generally for all companies, all industrials, industrials by sales size, and all nonindustrials:

a. Board members: chairman's role in management; board size and number of meetings; board composition by whether independent or company-affiliated, and by sex and race; and number of board committees, and prevalence and composition by purpose.

b. Director compensation amount and basis; outside director perquisites, retirement policy, and expected time commitment; board procedures for evaluating chief executive officer; and primary board concerns.

c. Chairmen's views on selected aspects of board operations.

This is the 9th survey.

B4490–2.10: Profile of a Chief Executive Officer

[Recurring (irreg.) 1984. 12 p. $20.00. SRI/ MF/complete.]

Survey report on the background, job characteristics, and opinions of chief executive officers (CEOs), 1984, with selected comparisons to 1980.

Data are based on a survey of the 500 largest industrial and 500 leading nonindustrial corporations. Survey response rate was 32%.

Includes 22 tables showing the following data, generally for all companies, all industrials, industrials by asset size, and all nonindustrials:

a. Job and personal characteristics, including CEO's title, years in present post, immediate previous position, cash compensation and perquisites, age, religion, highest educational attainment, years with present company, employers during career, experience prior to present position, relocations, weekly hours devoted to business, weeks of vacation, and board seats held. (p. 3-8)

b. Opinions of CEOs, including whether own views on public policy issues should be made known to constituents, sufficiency of time for personal activities, personal priorities, work enjoyment compared to executives at other levels, planned retirement age, most effective CEOs in U.S., measures to improve American competitiveness in world market, and trend and outlook for CEO role. (p. 9-11)

B4500
Hertz Corp.

B4500–2   NEW CAR OPERATING COSTS SURVEY, 1983
Annual. Jan. 23, 1984.
5+6 p.
SRI/MF/complete

Annual press release presenting Hertz Corp. estimates, for 1983, of the per mile cost of owning and operating new U.S. model cars. Includes estimates for 1983 models, and comparative estimates from 1972-82 model years, by size category and use duration.

Contains narrative summary with text statistics (p. 1-5); 6 tables, listed below (4 p.); and methodology (2 p.).

Availability: Hertz Corp., Public Affairs Department, 660 Madison Ave., New York NY 10021, †; SRI/MF/complete.

TABLES:

[Operating costs are expressed in cents per mile. Current data may not be comparable to earlier data due to car size group changes. Car size groups are subcompact, compact, midsize, intermediate, and standard.]

I. Estimates of 1983 model new passenger car ownership and operating costs [averages for various average annual mileages and years of use, by car size group].

[IA] Historical comparisons: new intermediate-size car [3- and 10-year use operating costs for various annual average mileages, selected years 1925-83].

[IB] Current 1983 data: compact car expenses [by 1-10 years of usage, for constant and declining annual mileage].

II. Cents per mile breakout of ownership and operating cost estimates for selected cars at 10,000 miles per year [including depreciation, insurance/licenses/fees, interest, maintenance, and gasoline/other service station expenses; by purchase price and years owned, for 1972-83 model intermediate cars and 1979-83 model compact cars].

III. Yearly and lifetime costs: intermediate-size car bought new in 1973, driven 10,000 miles per year and scrapped in 1982 [similar cost breakdowns as shown in table II].

IV. 10-year summary of domestic auto size changes [price, wheelbase, overall length, and weight; by car size group, 1973-83 model years].

B4500–7   CAR AND TRUCK LEASE-RENTAL STUDY
Annual. Aug. 31, 1984.
6+7 p.
SRI/MF/complete

Annual press release on the passenger car and truck lease-rental industry, including revenues, vehicles, mileage, and fuel consumption, 1983 and trends. Also presents general data on vehicle sales for personal vs. nonpersonal use, and mileage and fuel consumption by purpose of travel. Data are Hertz Corp. estimates.

Contents:

a. Narrative analysis, with text statistics. (p. 1-6)

b. 1 table showing the following for passenger cars and/or trucks: lease and rental units and revenues, with detail for lease units by whether fleet vs. individual car or full service vs. financed truck; new units into lease/rental service; vehicles on the road; lease/rental units' fuel consumption and mileage; and fleet cars on the road and mileage; with selected comparisons to all vehicles, selected years 1950-83. (3 p.)

c. 2 tables showing domestic and imported fleet and individual new car sales; and mileage travelled and fuel used, for trucks and for passenger cars by purpose of travel; various years 1950-83. (3 p.)

d. 1 table showing new and used domestic and imported cars sold for personal and nonpersonal use, 1983. (1 p.)

Availability: Hertz Corp., Public Affairs Department, 660 Madison Ave., New York NY 10021, †; SRI/MF/complete.

B4675
Hughes Tool Co.

B4675–1   INTERNATIONAL ROTARY DRILLING RIG REPORT
Monthly. Approx. 7 p.
SRI/MF/complete, shipped quarterly

Monthly report on number of rotary drilling rigs in operation in 6 world areas, by country, excluding the U.S. and Canada. Data are compiled by the Hughes Tool Co. Report is issued approximately 6 weeks after month of coverage.

Contains 2 tables showing total rig count, for 6 non-Communist world areas and offshore PRC; and land and offshore rig counts for approximately 85 countries, arranged by world area; for month of coverage, previous month, and same month of preceding year.

Availability: Hughes Tool Co., PO Box 2539, Houston TX 77001, ◆; SRI/MF/complete, shipped quarterly.

Issues reviewed during 1984: Oct. 1983-Sept. 1984 (D).

B4750
Irving Trust Co.

B4750–1   FINANCIAL MARKETS
Weekly. Approx. 2 p.
SRI/MF/complete, shipped quarterly

Weekly report, with narrative summary and 1 table presenting Irving Trust Co. prime lending rate; Federal Reserve Bank discount rate; and market yields for Federal funds, repurchase agreements, U.S. Treasury issues, negotiable certificates of deposit, bankers' acceptances, Eurodollar deposits, prime commercial paper, AA corporate utility bonds, and tax-exempt project notes and AAA bonds.

Data are current as of publication date, and are also shown for same day of previous week and year. Yields are shown for varying maturity periods as applicable.

Report is discontinued with the July 27, 1984 issue.

Availability: Irving Trust Co. customer representatives, ‡; SRI/MF/complete, shipped quarterly.

Issues reviewed during 1984: Oct. 28, 1983-July 27, 1984 (D).

B4750–2   ECONOMIC OUTLOOK
Monthly. Approx. 2 p.
SRI/MF/complete, shipped quarterly

Monthly report analyzing major consumer, business, industrial, and government economic performance indicators. Actual data are current to 2-4 months prior to publication date.

Contains narrative analysis; and 1 table presenting actual percent changes for most recent quarter or months and year, and forecast annual or quarterly percent changes over the following year, for approximately 30 price and industry indicators.

Both actual and forecast data are revised for each monthly report to incorporate latest available data.

Availability: Irving Trust Co. customer representatives, ‡; SRI/MF/complete, shipped quarterly.

Issues reviewed during 1984: Nov. 1983-Oct. 1984 (P).

B4790
Johnson and Higgins

B4790–2   EXECUTIVE REPORT ON LARGE CORPORATE PENSION PLANS, 1983
Annual. 1983. 49 p.
ISSN 0192-222X.
LC 79-644875.
SRI/MF/complete

Annual report on corporate pension plan costs and benefit funding status, by industry, 1982, with comparisons to 1981. Data are based on annual reports to shareholders of 660 companies listed in *Fortune* magazine's rankings of top industrial and nonindustrial companies.

Contains contents listing (1 p.) and the following:

Introduction and summary, with 3 text tables; and methodology. (p. 1-5)

Section 1-10. Sample characteristics and analysis of survey findings, with 9 summary charts and tables, and 10 detailed tables listed below. (p. 6-43)

App. A-B. Additional survey findings, with 1 table on unfunded vested benefits at various interest rate assumptions, and list of surveyed corporations. (p. 44-49)

This is the 6th annual report. Previous reports were entitled *Funding Costs and Liabilities of Large Corporate Pension Plans, Executive Report.*

Availability: Johnson and Higgins, National Benefits Office, 95 Wall St., New York NY 10005, †; SRI/MF/complete.

DETAILED TABLES:

[Data are for 1981-82, unless otherwise noted. Tables show data for 5 *Fortune* 500 industrial ranking groups, 26 manufacturing industry groups, and 4 nonmanufacturing industry sectors. Most tables show average percentages and/or amounts, totals on which averages are based, and sample distribution by percentile range.]

1. Survey participants, 1982. (p. 7)

2-3. Change in pension cost, and pension cost as a percent of pretax profits. (p. 10-15)

4. Change in pension cost per employee. (p. 18-19)

5. Pension cost as a percentage of compensation. (p. 22-23)

6-7. Funded ratios: vested and total accumulated benefits [compared to plan assets], 1982. (p. 26-31)

8-9. Unfunded vested benefits (UVB) and unfunded total accumulated benefits (UTAB) as a percentage of net worth, 1982. (p. 34-39)

10. Effect of interest assumption on UVB benefits, 1982. (p. 42-43)

B4940
Kelly Services

B4940–4 KELLY REPORT ON PEOPLE IN THE ELECTRONIC OFFICE III: THE SECRETARY'S ROLE
Monograph. 1984. 65 p.
SRI/MF/complete

Survey report on secretaries' attitudes toward their profession and own job, including the impact of word processing (wp) use. Includes data for U.S. and Canadian secretaries, and selected detail by age and other characteristics.

Data are from interviews with 507 secretaries and administrative assistants of companies randomly selected from Dun and Bradstreet's *Million Dollar Directory,* and with 106 similar employees of top 500 Canadian companies. Interviews were conducted Oct.-Nov. 1983.

Contains contents listing (1 p.); introduction (p. 1); and the following:

Chapter 1. Conflicts and Contrasts: Ambitions vs. Reality. Includes 1 chart and 20 tables showing professional and job satisfaction with detail by type of position held; career goals; views on advancement possibilities (including impact of male vs. female manager and college education), and whether own child should become a secretary; perceptions of new positions open to secretaries with wp/equipment skills, and effect of wp skills on salary and on time spent doing various tasks. (p. 2-18)

Chapter 2. Job Stress and Physical Ailments. Includes 14 tables showing perceived stressfulness of job, with detail by age, marital status, and circumstance including situations associated with wp use; effect of stress on personal life by age and education, and on job satisfaction; and incidence of various physical ailments and relation to wp use. (p. 19-30)

Chapter 3. Secretaries and Word Processing. Includes 16 tables showing general attitude toward wp, with detail by time spent using equipment; concern about wp effect on job permanence; ability to program computer, and perceived expectations for secretaries;

perceptions of own and boss's productivity; and wp equipment use in own office, including effect on size and status of secretarial staff, impact on office relations, percent of staff using and time spent with equipment, incidence of equipment sharing, and own wp experience. (p. 31-40)

Chapter 4. A New Breed of Secretary. Includes 14 tables repeating selected responses on wp use and skills and career satisfaction and goals, and also showing views on factors most likely to influence salary increase decision, and secretarial skills considered most important, all by age. (p. 41-55)

Sample Profile and Methodology. (p. 56-62)

Appendix. Includes 3 tables showing distribution of respondents by industry group; satisfaction with secretarial career by income, age, length of employment, and education; and concern about electronic equipment causing job elimination, by age. (p. 63-65)

For description of *Kelly Report on People in the Electronic Office* and *Kelly Report on People in the Electronic Office II: How Office Workers View Automation,* see SRI 1983 Annual, under B4940-2 and B4940-3, respectively.

Availability: Kelly Services, Public Relations Department, GPO Box 1179, Detroit MI 48266, †; SRI/MF/complete.

B4950
Kent Economic and Development Institute, Inc.

B4950–1 KEDI ECONOMIC SURVEY
Monthly. Approx. 30 p.
SRI/MF/complete, delayed

Monthly report forecasting quarterly changes in national income and product account components, employment and unemployment, and financial sector activity, over a 10-12 quarter period. Also includes actual data for varying prior periods.

Report is based on a large-scale economic model developed by the Kent Economic and Development Institute (KEDI). Forecasts are made approximately 6 weeks preceding publication.

Issues generally contain:

a. Contents and table listing; and overview of current economic conditions, and explanation of forecast assumptions, with 1 highlights table showing KEDI forecasts for 15 economic indicators, usually for current, preceding, and 2 selected future years.

b. 11 monthly forecast tables, listed below, each accompanied by narrative summary, with occasional text tables.

c. 1 table comparing accuracy of forecasts made by KEDI and various other major forecasters for 1 or more economic indicators, selected each month; and 1 table showing historical data series sources.

Text tables presenting substantial data on topics not covered in monthly tables are described, as they appear, under "Statistical Features."

An annual assessment of the accuracy of forecasts made by major forecasters for selected previous periods, usually 3 prior years, is published separately, but is not covered by SRI.

Prior to Nov. 1983 issue, report is covered in SRI under U2635-1. KEDI, Inc., is now an independent company and is no longer affiliated with Kent State University.

Availability: KEDI Economic Survey, PO Box 99, Tallmadge OH 44278, $500.00 per yr.; SRI/MF/complete, delayed shipment 3 months from issue date.

Issues reviewed during 1984: Nov. 1, 1983-Oct. 1, 1984 (P) (Vol. 9, Nos. 5-12; Vol. 10, No. 1) [Vol. 9, Nos. 5, 6, and 11 have been used twice; no issue is numbered 7].

MONTHLY FORECAST TABLES:
[Data usually are shown quarterly and annually for current, preceding, and following years (Jan.-May issues), or for current and 2 following years (June-Dec. issues), with additional annual totals.]

1.11-1.12. Selected indicators of real growth [including industrial production index, capacity utilization rate, housing starts, and auto sales]; and real GNP [including personal consumption expenditures, private domestic investment, net exports, and Federal and State/local purchases].

1.21-1.22. Prices and nominal GNP [including CPI, PPI, and GNP price deflators].

1.30. Employment and labor [including labor force, total and farm employment, and unemployment rate].

1.41. Housing [including starts, building permits, home prices, and mobile home shipments].

1.42. Automobiles [shows passenger car domestic and import sales, dealer inventories, and factory shipments; and light-duty truck sales].

1.50. Federal and State/local budgets [shows personal and corporate income tax revenues, and budget surplus/deficit].

1.60. Income [including personal income and savings, corporate profits, and average weekly earnings].

1.70. Money and credit [including currency/demand deposits, time deposits, consumer credit, bank business loans, and savings and loan assn mortgages outstanding].

1.80. Interest rates, yields, and securities prices [shows prime, conventional mortgage, and Aaa corporate bond rates; 90-day Treasury bill and 20-year Government bond yields; and Standard & Poor's 500 average].

STATISTICAL FEATURE:

B4950–1.501: Jan. l, 1984 (Vol. 9, No. 7)
[Issue incorrectly reads No. 5.]

SPECIAL TABLE

(p. 10) Table showing industrial production index, by industry group, selected periods 1981-85.

B5000
Korn/Ferry International

B5000-3 BOARD OF DIRECTORS ANNUAL STUDY

Annual series. For individual publication data, see below.
LC 78-643541.
SRI/MF/complete

Annual series of 5 reports on corporate board of director composition, compensation, and practices, 1983, with comparisons to 1979 and/or 1982. Data are presented for all boards and for those of retail and insurance companies, companies with revenues over $1 billion, and financial institutions.

Reports generally include number of inside and outside directors; director occupational and sociodemographic characteristics, including detail for women and minorities; types of committees; director compensation amounts and increases, benefits, and time spent on board matters; meeting frequency; various board policies and practices; addition of new directors; and views on relative importance of various board-related issues; with selected detail by company revenue size.

Data are from responses of 603 major U.S. corporations to a 1983 Korn/Ferry International survey.

Each report contains narrative summary with text statistics, and 14-29 tables. Individual reports are listed below.

This is the 11th edition of the report series.

Availability: Korn/Ferry International, 237 Park Ave., New York NY 10017, $12.00 each; SRI/MF/complete.

REPORTS:

B5000-3.1: Board of Directors Eleventh Annual Study
[Annual. Feb. 1984. 24 p. SRI/MF/complete.]

B5000-3.2: 1984 Annual Board of Directors Study of Retail Companies
[Annual. [Feb. 1984.] 20 p. no paging. SRI/MF/complete.]

B5000-3.3: Board of Directors Eleventh Annual Study: Billion Dollar Corporations, Supplement 1984
[Annual. [Feb. 1984.] 16 p. SRI/MF/complete.]

B5000-3.4: 1984 Annual Board of Directors Study of Insurance Companies
[Annual. [Feb. 1984.] 18 p. no paging. SRI/MF/complete.]

B5000-3.5: Board of Directors Eleventh Annual Study: Banks and Other Financial Institutions, Supplement 1984
[Annual. [Feb. 1984.] 16 p. SRI/MF/complete.]

B5050
Laventhol and Horwath

B5050-1 WORLDWIDE LODGING INDUSTRY, 1983 EDITION: Thirteenth Annual Report on International Hotel Operations

Annual. 1983. 108 p.
ISSN 0361-218X.
LC 76-640982.
SRI/MF/complete

Annual report on international hotel median operating and financial performance, 1982. Includes data on occupancy, income, expenses, assets, and liabilities, with detail on sales and payroll by hotel dept.

Data are shown by world regions, and are based on responses from 652 hotels to a Dec. 1982 survey.

Contents:

a. Listings of contents and exhibits; foreword; and discussion of tourism trends in various countries and world regions, with 1 table on U.S. hotel sales and occupancy rates, by region and selected hotel characteristics, as of Apr. 1983, and percent change from 1982. (p. 1-23)

b. Worldwide summary, with 5 tables, listed below; and 1 summary chart. (p. 24-29)

c. Regional sections, each with narrative and 18 tables, listed below, showing data for the region and usually for its composite subregions and/or countries, as follows: Africa/Middle East (p. 30-44), Asia/Australasia (p. 45-59); North America (p. 60-73); Europe (p. 74-87); and Latin America (p. 88-99).

d. Currency conversion tables and definitions. (p. 100-105)

A digest of the annual report and a narrative midyear commentary are also issued, but are not covered by SRI.

Availability: Laventhol and Horwath, Publications, 1845 Walnut St., Philadelphia PA 19103, $50.00; SRI/MF/complete.

TABLES:
[Data are for 1982, unless otherwise noted. Most data are shown as mean or median figures.]

B5050-1.1: Summary

1-2. General profile of typical contributor based on various measures of central tendency; and highlights, all hotels. (p. 25)

3. Market data [percent domestic, foreign, and repeat business; distribution of government, business, tourist, conference, and other sources of business; percent advance reservations, and distribution by type; and ratio of travel agent commissions to room sales]; 5-year trend, all hotels [1978-82]. (p. 26)

4. [Data in table 3 are repeated, with detail for Africa/Middle East, Asia/Australasia, North America, Europe, and Latin America, 1982.] (p. 28)

5. Nationality of guests [percents and rankings for 17 countries or regions of guest origin, with detail for each of the hotel regions noted in table 4, and ranking comparisons to 1981]. (p. 29)

B5050-1.2: World Regions

AFRICA AND MIDDLE EAST

[All tables show data for the total region. Tables I.3-I.18 include detail for Northern Africa, Southern Africa, and the Middle East.]

I.1-I.2. General profile of typical contributor based on various measures of central tendency; and highlights. (p. 30)

I.3-I.4. Market data and nationality of guests [with same breakdowns as in tables 3 and 5 above]. (p. 32-33)

I.5. Comparison of sales and profitability [sales, income before fixed charges, and net income, all per available room; ratios of income before fixed charges to room and total sales; and number of times average room rate was earned; 1981-82]. (p. 33)

I.6. Occupancy, double occupancy, [and] room rates. (p. 34)

I.7. Composition of sales [percent rooms, food, beverages, telephone, minor operated dept, and rental/other]. (p. 34)

I.8. Minor operated depts and other income [and expenses] amounts per room and ratios to [total] sales. (p. 35)

I.9. Food and beverage statistics [sales, shown variously per room, per seat, and per guest; with detail by type of facility and for room service, selected ratios, average check size, and covers served per seat]. (p. 36-37)

I.10. Cash payroll, employee benefits, total payroll, and employment statistics [including sales per employee, productivity index for 1981-82, and FTE employees per 100 available rooms by dept]. (p. 38)

I.11. Analysis of undistributed operating expenses [amounts and ratios to sales, for administrative/general, marketing, energy, and property operation/maintenance, with comparative ratios for 1981]. (p. 39)

I.12. Energy costs per occupied room per day [by energy source; credit for energy sales; and net energy costs, 1981-82]. (p. 40)

I.13. Method of payment for hotel services [percent cash, credit card, travel agent/tour operator, and other credit]. (p. 41)

I.14. Credit card commission annual cost per occupied room [and ratio to sales]. (p. 41)

I.15. Fixed charges [rent, property taxes, insurance, interest, and depreciation/amortization] amounts per room and ratio to total sales. (p. 41)

I.16. Balance sheet statistics—liquidity ratios [current assets/liabilities ratio; accounts receivable per room, and ratio to sales; and food, beverage, and operating supplies turnover and/or inventories per room]. (p. 42)

I.17. Statement of income and expenses—per available room. (p. 43)

I.18. Ratio to total sales [for each income and expense item]. (p. 44)

ASIA AND AUSTRALASIA

II.1-II.18. [Tables I.1-I.18 are repeated for Asia/Australasia, with detail for Asia, Far East, and Pacific Islands.] (p. 45-59)

NORTH AMERICA AND CARIBBEAN

III.1-III.18. [Tables I.1-I.18 are repeated for North America, with detail for Canada, U.S., and Caribbean.] (p. 60-73)

EUROPE

IV.1-IV.18. [Tables I.1-I.18 are repeated for Europe, with detail for Continental Europe, Scandinavia, and UK.] (p. 74-87)

LATIN AMERICA

V.1-V.18. [Tables I.1-I.18 are repeated for Latin America, with detail for Mexico and Central/South America.] (p. 88-99)

B5050-2   U.S. LODGING INDUSTRY, 1983 EDITION: 51st Annual Report on Hotel and Motor Hotel Operations
Annual. 1983. 82 p.
ISSN 0361-2198.
LC 76-640984.
SRI/MF/complete

Annual report, by John D. Lesure et al., on median operating results of the U.S. lodging industry, 1982, with comparisons to 1981. Also includes data on composition and sources of lodging demand.

Data are shown as the ratio of itemized operating expenditures to total and departmental revenues, and as costs and income per available room, by geographic region, urban location, and establishment size, rate group, and occupancy ratio.

Report is based on a study of hotel and motel operations, conducted by Laventhol and Horwath.

Contains contents listing (1 p.) and the following:

a. Industry summary and outlook, with 6 charts, 1 text table, and 2 tables showing occupancy percent and room sales per occupied room, by establishment affiliation, location, size, region, and city, 1982 and 1st 6 months 1983, with percent change from 1981 or 1982; and narrative comment, with some text data, on 1982 lodging market in 48 cities or areas. (p. 2-33)

b. Study results, with narrative analysis, 2 charts showing income and expense distributions for 1982, and 34 tables listed below. (p. 34-79)

c. Explanation of terms. (p. 81-82)

Availability: Laventhol and Horwath, Publications, 1845 Walnut St., Philadelphia PA 19103, $50.00; SRI/MF/complete.

TABLES:
[Data are shown for 1982, unless otherwise noted. Most data are shown as medians or arithmetic means.

Data by establishment type are shown for some or all of the following: property age, size, room rate group, occupancy, and restaurant operation, including ratio of food/beverage sales to room sales.

Data by location are generally shown for center city, airport, suburban, highway, and resort. Data by region are shown for Northeast, Southeast, North and South Central, and Western regions. Data by market are for convention and other.]

B5050-2.1: General and Sales Data

MARKETS

1-2. General profile of typical contributor [hotel], based on various measures of central tendency; and [financial and occupancy] highlights. (p. 35)

3. Market data [percent domestic, foreign, and repeat business; distribution of government, business, tourist, conference, and other sources of business; percent advance reservations, and distribution by type; and ratio of travel agent commissions to room sales; all by location and market types]. (p. 38)

4. Nationality of guests [by region, U.S. and international, including ratios of 15 foreign nationalities to total international]. (p. 39)

PERFORMANCE MEASUREMENTS
[Tables 5-9 include medians for all establishments.]

5. Comparison of sales and profitability by selected criteria [by establishment type; for total sales, income before fixed charges, and net income before tax, 1981-82]. (p. 40)

6. General statistics [by establishment type; ratio of income before fixed charges to room and total sales, and number of times average rate was earned, 1981-82]. (p. 41)

7. Return on total assets [turnover, earnings ratio, and 1981-82 rates of return or loss, by total sales categories and establishment type]. (p. 42)

8. Return on investment [capital and equity, by establishment type; includes aggregate medians for 1981]. (p. 43)

9. Occupancy, double occupancy, and average rate [by establishment type, region, and total sales category; 1981-82]. (p. 44)

10. Net income differential [by dept and balance sheet item for lodging facilities reporting net income and loss, and percent change in net income]. (p. 45)

11-12. Independent and chain affiliated [1982], and comparison of data by location, 1981-82 [ratio or amounts by dept and balance sheet item]. (p. 46-47)

SALES ANALYSIS

13. Composition of sales [percent share by dept, by establishment type and location, with reported net income and loss]. (p. 48-49)

14. Sales per guest day [by dept, by location, market, and reported net income and loss]. (p. 48)

15-16. Rooms dept: median [revenue and expense] amounts per room and ratios to sales [by establishment size]; and expenses per occupied room per day, by occupancy. (p. 50-51)

B5050-2.2: Restaurant Operations and Minor Operated Depts
[Tables 17-19 include food/beverage sales ratios to room sales.]

17. Restaurant operations, by selected criteria [occupancy rate, establishments reporting net income and loss, and convention market, for sales and sales costs, 11 types of departmental expenses, income, and productivity index]. (p. 53)

18. Food and beverage statistics, by selected criteria [establishments size and location, and convention market; for food and beverage sales by facility, with amount per available room and per seat; and for average food check, and covers, and room service sales per occupied room and per guest]. (p. 54)

19. Restaurant operations, cost of sales/cash payroll [1981-82]. (p. 56)

20. Minor operated depts and other income, median amounts per room, and ratios to sales [by establishment size, location, and market; includes rental income and telephone costs]. (p. 58)

B5050-2.3: Payroll and Other Expenses

EMPLOYEES, PAYROLL, AND ROOM EXPENSES

21. Staffing levels and employee productivity, all establishments [employees per 100 available and occupied rooms, and sales per employee, by dept]. (p. 59)

22. Cash payroll, employee benefits, total payroll, and employment statistics, by selected criteria [by establishment type, dept, and reported net income and loss, and including 1981-82 productivity index]. (p. 60-61)

23. Payroll/related expenses per occupied room per day, by [dept and] occupancy. (p. 62)

UNDISTRIBUTED OPERATING EXPENSES
[Tables 26-28 include means for all establishments.]

24. Analysis of undistributed operating expenses, by selected criteria [costs per room, and ratios to room and total sales, for administrative/general, marketing, energy costs, and property operation/maintenance, by establishment type]. (p. 62-63)

25. Management fees, all establishments [amount per room and ratio to total sales, in lower and upper quartiles and median, 1981-82]. (p. 64)

26. How the marketing dollar was spent [payroll, sales, advertising, merchandising, public relations/publicity, fees/commissions, other sales/promotions, and marketing cost index, by location and convention market]. (p. 64)

27. Energy costs per occupied room per day, by location [4 energy types and credit for sale, 1982, and net cost, 1981-82]. (p. 65)

28. How the property operation and maintenance dollar was spent, by [establishment] age [by 9 expense categories]. (p. 65)

B5050-2.4: Credit, Fixed Charges, and Balance Sheets
[Tables 29-31 include medians or means for all establishments.]

CREDIT AND COLLECTION

29. Method of payment for services [by establishment type and location]. (p. 66)

30. Credit card commissions, annual cost per occupied room [and ratio to total sales, by establishment type and location, 1981-82]. (p. 67)

FIXED CHARGES

31. Fixed charges, median amounts per room, and ratio to total sales, by selected criteria [by establishment age, size, region, and location]. (p. 68-69)

BALANCE SHEET DATA

32. Balance sheet statistics, liquidity ratios, all establishments [accounts receivable, and food and beverage inventories, 1981-82]. (p. 68)

SUMMARY

[33-34] Statement of income and expenses, median amounts per available room; and ratios to total sales; [both by establishment type, including sales volume category, and region]. (p. 70-79)

B5050–4   NATIONAL TREND OF BUSINESS: Lodging Industry
Monthly.   Approx. 6 p.
SRI/MF/complete, shipped
quarterly

Monthly report on hotel and motel room sales, occupancy rates, and food and beverage sales and costs, by affiliation, region, location, size, and type. Data are based on a monthly survey of approximately 2,000 hotels and motels, and are published approximately 10 weeks after month of coverage.

Report consists of a brief narrative analysis, with 2 tables showing occupancy rate projections for 3 coming months, and seasonally adjusted occupancy rates for month of coverage; and 6 detailed tables showing the following data by hotel/motel affiliation, region, type of location, and lodging size and type, for month of coverage, year to date, and 12-month period ending in month of coverage, with comparisons to same periods of previous year:

a. Room and food/beverage sales change; total and double occupancy rates; and room and total sales per occupied room.

b. Food/beverage sales per occupied room, and average receipt per cover; food and beverage costs per dollar of sales; food/beverage payroll per dollar of sales and per cover; and change in number of covers served.

Report also includes 1 annual table, appearing in Dec. issue, showing occupancy rates and room sales per occupied room, by region, with detail for selected States and urban areas, 1982-83.

A similar report, *National Trend of Business: Economy Lodging Industry,* is also available from issuing agency, but is not covered by SRI.

Availability: Laventhol and Horwath, Publications, 1845 Walnut St., Philadelphia PA 19103, †; SRI/MF/complete, shipped quarterly.

Issues reviewed during 1984: Aug. 1983-July 1984 (D).

B5050–6   THIRD ANNUAL STUDY OF FINANCIAL RESULTS AND REPORTING TRENDS IN THE GAMING INDUSTRY, 1983
Annual.   1983.   27 p.
SRI/MF/complete

Annual report presenting financial data for casino/hotel operations of 15 corporations, 1982, with comparisons to 1981. Data are shown by corporation, with detail for individual casino/hotels in Atlantic City.

Data are compiled from corporate reports to shareholders and the SEC, New Jersey Casino Control Commission records, and a survey of corporations with gaming operations. The report sample represents 70% of all gaming revenues, and 100% of revenues in Atlantic City.

Contains contents listing and introduction (p. 1-3); and narrative report, with 8 tables listed below (p. 4-27).

Availability: Laventhol and Horwath, Publications, 1845 Walnut St., Philadelphia PA 19103, $35.00; SRI/MF/complete.

TABLES:
[Tables B-H show data by corporation, 1981-82, unless otherwise noted.]

A. Corporations included in this study [square footage and number of guest rooms, by individual casino/hotel]. (p. 4-5)

B. Consolidated corporate operating results [total revenue, income from operations, net income, and casino/hotel revenue]. (p. 10-11)

C. Gross operating profit [and casino and hotel/other revenue] of gaming operations. (p. 16-17)

D. Promotional allowance as a percentage of casino revenue. (p. 18)

E. Gaming gross operating profit as a percentage of identifiable gaming operation assets. (p. 19)

F. Corporate interest expense and depreciation/amortization. (p. 21)

G. Total corporate assets, shareholders' equity, return on shareholders' equity, and debt-to-equity ratio [1982]. (p. 23)

H. 1982 Atlantic City summary [itemized income and expenses, including table game and slot machine revenues, income taxes, and casino labor expenses; and casino revenue and income per square foot; for 9 casino/hotels]. (p. 26-27)

B5165
Lilly, Eli, and Co.

B5165–1   LILLY DIGEST, 1983
Annual.   1983.   55 p.
LC 50-19446.
SRI/MF/complete

Annual report presenting average operating and financial statistics for a cross-section of independent community pharmacies and their prescription depts, 1982. Includes analysis by store sales volume category, and by census division, with selected trends from 1960s.

Data are based on responses of 1,528 pharmacies to a Lilly Co. annual survey. Report is intended for use by stores in comparing their operations with industry averages.

Contains foreword and contents listing (p. 1-3); report, with 5 charts and 30 tables, interspersed with narrative analyses (p. 4-54); and survey form facsimile (p. 55).

All tables are listed below. For description of last previous report, see SRI 1982 Annual, under this number.

Availability: Eli Lilly and Co., Lilly Digest, 307 E. McCarty St., Indianapolis IN 46285, †; SRI/MF/complete.

TABLES:
[Tables show data for 1982, unless otherwise noted. Tables 1-3, 7-8, 10-15, and 19-20 include averages per pharmacy for most or all of the following operating items:

a. Prescription, other, and total sales; cost of goods sold; gross margin; 15 types of expenses, including heat/light/power; net profit before taxes; total income of self-employed proprietor; value of inventory at cost and as percent of sales; and annual inventory turnover rate.

b. Size of area and sales per square foot; sales and net profit per dollar invested in inventory; number of new and renewed prescriptions dispensed; prescription charge; and hours per week pharmacy was open, worked by proprietor, and worked by employed pharmacist.]

OPERATIONS AND SALES

1-2. Current trends in pharmacy and prescription dept operations [1981-82]. (p. 5)

3. Summary of sales volume [by sales size class, and number of pharmacies in each class]. (p. 8-11)

4. Average prescription charge index compared with [5] standard price indices [1967-82]. (p. 13)

5. Averages of pharmacy operations [for selected operating items], 1973-82. (p. 14-15)

PRESCRIPTION DEPT ANALYSIS

6. Average community pharmacy break-even data [required months and percent of total sales], 1973-82. (p. 16)

7. Summary by number of prescriptions dispensed daily. (p. 18)

8. Summary of prescription income [by ratio of prescription income to sales]. (p. 20)

9. Prescription trends in *Lilly Digest* pharmacies [for sales, ratio of prescription sales to total sales, number of prescriptions, percent renewals, prescription charge, prescription inventory, and prescription sales per dollar of prescription inventory, 1963-82]. (p. 22)

HEART OF THE LILLY DIGEST

10-15. [Operating data by annual sales size class and by number of daily prescriptions.] (p. 24-35)

NET PROFIT AND TURNOVER

16. Net profit according to sales size [1982, with totals 1981]. (p. 36)

17. Turnover comparison (percent of sales) [for selected operating items, for fast and slow inventory turnover pharmacies]. (p. 36)

REGIONAL VARIATIONS, LOCATION, AND RENT

18. Geographic summary of average prescription charge and net profit [by census division]. (p. 37)

19-20. Summary [of averages per pharmacy for detailed operating items] by [census division], and according to location [downtown, neighborhood, shopping center, and medical office building]. (p. 38-41)

21-22. Rental percentages, by sales size; and rent correlated with various factors [average sales, rent, and square footage, by annual sales volume, prescription percent of total sales, prescriptions dispensed daily, years pharmacy has been in operation, and census division]. (p. 42-43)

BALANCE SHEET AND FINANCIAL RATIOS

23-24. Current trends in balance sheet information [as of Dec. 31, 1981-82]; and current financial ratios, by pharmacy age. (p. 46)

25-28. Balance sheet and finanical ratios by pharmacy age [for 4 sales sizes] as of Dec. 31, 1982. (p. 47-50)

29. 10-year trends [in balance sheet items, 1973-82]. (p. 51)

30. Summary of [selected] operating figures in pharmacies reporting 2 years and 1 year [1981 and/or 1982]. (p. 52)

**B5165–2   1983 NACDS-LILLY DIGEST:
A Survey of Chain Pharmacy
Operations for 1982**
Annual. 1983. 40 p.
ISSN 0092-8410.
LC 74-640605.
SRI/MF/complete

Annual report presenting operating and financial statistics for chain drugstores and their prescription depts, by store characteristics and location, 1982 with selected trends from 1973.

Includes data on prescription and other sales; cost of goods sold; gross margin; 11 types of expenses; net profit before taxes; warehouse fee; value of prescription and other inventory at cost and as percent of sales; and annual inventory turnover rate.

Also includes data on size of prescription and other area, and sales per square foot; prescription and other sales and total net profit per dollar invested in inventory; number of new and renewed prescriptions dispensed; prescription charge; and weekly hours open and hours worked by manager and employed pharmacists.

Data are shown by sales size, prescription volume, prescription income as percent of sales, number of units in chain, location (downtown, neighborhood, shopping center, medical building), and census division.

Data are based on responses of 1,228 pharmacies to an Eli Lilly and Co. annual survey.

Contains foreword and contents listing (p. 1-3); and report, with narrative analysis, 10 charts, and 16 tables (p. 4-40).

This is the 13th edition of the *Digest.*

Availability: Eli Lilly and Co., NACDS-Lilly Digest, 307 E. McCarty St., Indianapolis IN 46285, †; SRI/MF/complete.

B5275
Manpower, Inc.

**B5275–1   MANPOWER, INC.
Employment Outlook Survey**
Quarterly.
Approx. 6 p.+insert.
SRI/MF/complete

Quarterly report on employer hiring intentions, by industry division and region. Data are from a survey of over 11,000 public and private employers in approximately 350 cities. Survey is conducted by telephone approximately 5 weeks prior to quarter of coverage, and report is issued 1-2 weeks before the beginning of the quarter.

Contains 5 sections, covering U.S. and 4 regions, each with brief analysis, 1 trend chart, and 1 table showing distribution of employers by hiring plans (increase, no change, decrease, or undecided) for quarter of coverage, by industry division.

Report also usually includes an insert sheet, with narrative and 1 table showing comparative summary data for selected quarter or quarters of previous year.

Availability: Manpower, Inc., International Research Department, International Headquarters, 5301 N. Ironwood Rd., PO Box 2053, Milwaukee WI 53217, ‡; SRI/MF/complete.

Issues reviewed during 1984: 1st-4th Qtrs. 1984 (D).

B5350
Manufacturers
Hanover Trust Co.

B5350–2   FINANCIAL DIGEST
Weekly. Approx. 4 p.
SRI/MF/complete, shipped
quarterly

Weekly report (biweekly in July and Aug.) on money and securities markets and banking activity. Most data are current to within approximately 1 week of cover date and are compiled by Manufacturers Hanover Trust Co.

Contains narrative analysis of selected aspects of the economy, usually including charts or other text statistics, and occasionally including tables or charts with substantial statistical content; and 7 regularly appearing tables showing selected weekly totals or averages for the following activities:

a. Selected Federal Reserve transactions; the New York money market; and business indicators (most recent quarter or month).

b. Short-term paper outstanding (certificates of deposit and commercial paper), commercial/industrial bank loans, security markets, and international Eurodollar and foreign exchange rates.

All tables except table on New York money market include comparisons to selected previous periods including same period of the previous year.

Weekly tables appear in all issues. All additional features with substantial statistical content are described, as they appear, under "Statistical Features." Nonstatistical features are not covered.

Availability: Manufacturers Hanover Trust Co., Economics Department, Financial Digest, 270 Park Ave., 17th Floor, New York NY 10017, †; SRI/MF/complete, shipped quarterly.

Issues reviewed during 1984: Nov. 7, 1983-Oct. 29, 1984 (P) (Vol. XX, Nos. 40-47; Vol. XXI, Nos. 1-38).

STATISTICAL FEATURES:

B5350–2.501: Mar. 19, 1984 (Vol. XII, No. 11)

FOR ORGANIZED LABOR, IT COULD BE ANOTHER YEAR OF SMALL WAGE RAISES

(3 p.) Article, with 1 chart showing aggregate percent wage increase for major collective bargaining settlements, by industry division, 1981 and 1983.

B5350–2.502: Apr. 2, 1984 (Vol. XXI, No. 13)

MARKETING TAKES THE BIGGEST BITE OF OUR FOOD DOLLARS

(3 p.) Article, with 1 chart showing farm production value vs. food marketing cost, 1973 and 1983.

B5350–2.503: Apr. 16, 1984 (Vol. XXI, No. 15)

TAX TIME HEIGHTENS INTEREST IN STATE AND LOCAL SECURITIES

(3 p.) Article, with 1 chart showing value of new municipal bond issues, and Bond Buyer Index as percent of new AA utility rate, 1979 and 1984.

B5350–2.504: Apr. 23, 1984 (Vol. XXI, No. 16)

US TRADE DEFICITS STEM FROM SEVERAL CAUSES AND IMPROVEMENT WILL BE SLOW

(3 p.) Article, with 1 chart showing U.S. merchandise trade balance, with detail for Western Europe and Latin America, 1981-83.

B5350–2.505: Sept. 17, 1984 (Vol. XXI, No. 32)

PROCESS OF REPAIRING CORPORATE BALANCE SHEETS HITS A SNAG

(3 p.) Article, with 1 chart showing corporate short-term debt, and short-term liabilities as a percent of all liabilities, various quarters 1982-84.

B5350–3   ECONOMIC REPORT
Monthly. Approx. 4 p.
SRI/MF/complete, shipped
quarterly

Monthly report (except July and Aug.), by Irwin L. Kellner, commenting on U.S. economic developments and presenting quarterly economic forecasts.

Contains narrative articles, occasionally with substantial statistics; and 1 recurring table showing annual and quarterly levels for GNP components and selected indicators, including consumption, investment, net exports, government purchases, final sales, CPI, personal income, savings rate, employment rate, industrial production index, housing starts, domestic automobile sales, corporate profits, and net cash flow.

Table shows actual data for quarter preceding cover date month and 2-4 previous quarters, and projections for 3-5 succeeding quarters.

Each issue of the report is reviewed, but an abstract is published in SRI monthly issues only when recurring table or other statistical features appear. Recurring table appears in Oct. 1983 and Feb., June, and Oct. 1984 issues. Articles with substantial additional statistics are described, as they appear, under 'Statistical Features.'

All issues are filmed, but microfiche is shipped only when an issue is abstracted.

Availability: Manufacturers Hanover Trust Co., Economics Department, 270 Park Ave., New York NY 10017, †; SRI/MF/complete, shipped quarterly.

Issues reviewed during 1984: Oct. 1983-Oct. 1984 (P).

STATISTICAL FEATURES:

B5350–3.501: Apr. 1984

DEBT BOMB DEFUSED?

Article analyzing trends in external debt of developing Latin American countries. Data are from International Monetary Fund, and Commodity Research Bureau, Inc.

Includes 4 tables showing merchandise trade and current account balances, interest payments, export earnings, total reserves, average monthly imports, and import cover; all for 6 high-debt Latin American countries; and worldwide price indexes for raw industrials, agricultural products, and metals, and prices for selected commodities; various periods 1981-84.

B5350–3.502: Sept. 1984

WHO'S RIGHT?

Article, with 2 tables comparing OMB and Congressional Budget Office outlook for selected economic indicators including Federal budget deficit, interest outlays, and interest outlays as percent of total expenditures and of personal income tax revenues, 1984-89; with comparisons to actual performance, 1983.

B6025
Merrill Lynch
Relocation Management

B6025–1 **STUDY OF EMPLOYEE
RELOCATION POLICIES
Among Major U.S.
Corporations, 1984**
Annual. 1984. xv+272 p.
SRI/MF/complete

Annual report on employee relocation practices of U.S. corporations, presented by major industry group, 1983. Includes data on reimbursement policies for transferred homeowners, problems encountered, and expenses covered.

Data are based on telephone interviews with administrative personnel in 607 firms, conducted Jan.-Feb. 1984.

Contains contents listing (1 p.); introduction with 2 tables showing survey sample by industry and by number of transferred homeowners, 1979-83 (p. i-iii); summary of findings, with 13 tables including selected comparisons from previous surveys as early as 1975 (p. iv-xv); and statistical section with 87 tables, described below (p. 1-272).

This is the 12th edition of the report. A separately published summary of this edition, a reprint of p. i-xv, is also available from the issuing agency for $10.00, but is not covered separately in SRI.

Availability: Merrill Lynch Relocation Management, Marketing Department, Four Corporate Park Dr., White Plains NY 10604, $25.00; SRI/MF/complete.

TABLES:

[All tables show data for 20 major industry groups and all others, and by number of transferred renters or homeowners (under 25 to 500 or more). Tables show data for 1983, unless otherwise noted.]

a. Total and women employees transferred, expected transfers in 1984, and homeowners transferred. Tables 1-4. (p. 1-12)

b. Company policies for disposing of transferred employee's former living quarters and purchase of new house, including expenses reimbursed, limitations, and equity loans/advances; problems experienced; and aid given employees to get mortgage financing. Tables 5-27. (p. 13-81)

c. Firms having difficulties with employees accepting transfers into high cost-of-living areas, and incentives used; mortgage interest differential allowances (MIDA), including adjustable rate mortgage provisions; mortgage buy-downs and refinancing; assistance to offset additional tax liability; job placement assistance for working spouses; renter

transfer assistance; reimbursement for househunting trips, temporary quarters, household goods shipments, and incidental expenses; and firms use of outside relocation services. Tables 28-68. (p. 82-206)

d. Eligibility of new professional and new college graduate hires for same relocation benefits as current employees, and type of assistance given; domestic and international short-term transfers, and average length of stay; and provision and administration of property management assistance, for employees on short-term assignments. Tables 69-77. (p. 207-235)

e. Companies relocating groups of employees; average homeowner relocation cost; and average cost per transferred employee for MIDA/cost-of-living/mortgage assistance/tax adder allowances. Tables 78-80. (p. 236-244)

f. Firms requiring relocation expense reimbursement if transferred employee leaves firm within 1 year; firms offering to move employees to another location, if original move is unsuccessful; firms with flexible benefit programs for transferred employees; and recent changes in relocation policy and anticipated changes in 1984. Tables 81-87. (p. 245-272)

B6045
Metropolitan
Life Insurance Co.

B6045–1 **STATISTICAL BULLETIN,
Metropolitan Life Insurance
Co.**
Quarterly. Approx. 20 p.
ISSN 0741-9767.
LC 31-30794.
SRI/MF/complete, delayed

Quarterly report on health and demographic topics of interest to the insurance industry, including trends in life expectancy, mortality, accidents, disease and disability, and population growth. Most data are from Census Bureau, NCHS, and other Federal agencies.

Issues contain several articles, usually statistical. Fourth quarter issue includes an index and contents list for the year.

Features with substantial statistical content are described, as they appear, under "Statistical Features."

Availability: Metropolitan Life Insurance Co., Statistical Bulletin, One Madison Ave., New York NY 10010, non-profit organizations $20.00 per yr., others $50.00 per yr.; SRI/MF/complete, delayed shipment 3 months after abstract is published.

Issues reviewed during 1984: Jan./Mar.-Oct./Dec. 1984 (P) (Vol. 65, Nos. 1-4); [No issues were published for 3rd-4th Qtrs. 1983].

STATISTICAL FEATURES:

**B6045–1.501: Jan./Mar. 1984 (Vol. 65,
No. 1)**

ALCOHOL AND OTHER DRUG ABUSE AMONG
ADOLESCENTS

(p. 4-13) Article on prevalence of cigarette smoking and alcohol and other drug use among adolescents, 1970s-82. Data are from National Institute on Drug Abuse.

Includes 3 charts and 4 tables showing the following for cigarette smoking, and use of alcohol and of other drugs by substance or type: frequency of use among high school seniors and among adolescents age 12-17, and distribution of high school seniors by grade level at 1st use, various years 1972-82.

U.S. POPULATION OUTLOOK

(p. 16-19) Article, with 1 table showing total population, and female population per 100 males, by age group, selected years 1970-2050. Data are from Census Bureau.

MEASUREMENT OF OVERWEIGHT

(p. 20-23) Article on relationship between body weight and life expectancy, by sex and height, with detail by body build, 1959 and 1983. Data are based on Metropolitan Life height/weight tables. Includes 4 tables.

**B6045–1.502: Apr./June 1984 (Vol. 65,
No. 2)**

RECREATIONAL BOATING FATALITIES: 1978-82

(p. 2-6) Article, with 1 chart and 1 table showing average annual death rate from water transport accidents, for males by age, 1969/70 and 1979/80; and number of fatalities from recreational boating accidents, by accident type, 1978-82. Data are from NCHS and U.S. Coast Guard.

PROJECTIONS OF POPULATION GROWTH AT
THE OLDER AGES

(p. 8-12) Article, with 2 tables showing the following for persons aged 65/older, by age group and sex: population, selected years 1970-2050; and distribution by race, and by marital, family, and labor force status, Mar. 1982. Data are from Census Bureau and Labor Dept.

HOW CHILDREN AND ADOLESCENTS PERCEIVE
ALCOHOL AND OTHER DRUG ABUSE

(p. 16-21) Article, with 1 chart and 2 tables showing high school seniors' perceptions of the harmfulness and availability of drugs, as follows: potential harm by frequency of use, and prevalence of use among friends, by substance (including alcohol and cigarettes); and whether drugs are easily available, by substance; primarily 1975-82.

Data are from survey results published by National Institute on Drug Abuse.

ACCIDENT DEATH TOLL CONTINUED TO
DECLINE IN 1983, ANNUAL FEATURE

(p. 22-23) Annual article, with list of disasters resulting in 25 or more deaths, including date and place of occurrence, and number of fatalities, 1979-83.

**B6045–1.503: July/Sept. 1984 (Vol. 65,
No. 3)**

DRINKING AND DRIVING

(p. 2-6) Article, with 1 chart and 2 tables showing percent of driver fatalities by blood alcohol level, share of all fatal accidents, number of fatalities, and accidents per 100 million vehicle miles by driver age, all for alcohol-related motor vehicle accidents, primarily 1980-82; and distribution of population and of motor vehicle accident fatalities, by age, 1980.

Data sources include National Highway Traffic Safety Administration, Census Bureau, and NCHS.

REGIONAL VARIATIONS IN MORTALITY FROM DISEASES OF THE HEART

(p. 8-14) Article, with 3 charts and 4 tables showing mortality rates from heart disease for white men and women aged 35-74 by age group, by census division and State, with rankings of 4-5 States with highest and lowest rates, 1980. Data are based on NCHS statistics.

GAINS IN U.S. LIFE EXPECTANCY, ANNUAL FEATURE

(p. 18-23) Annual article, with 2 tables showing life expectancy at selected ages, by sex, selected periods 1900-83; and life expectancy and mortality rate, by age, sex, and race, 1980. Data are from NCHS, and Metropolitan Life Insurance Co.

B6045–1.504: Oct./Dec. 1984 (Vol. 65, No. 4)

GROWTH OF SCHOOL-AGE POPULATION

(p. 2-10) Article, with 2 charts and 3 tables showing school-age population distribution by educational level, 1983 and 2000; and population aged 5-19 by census region and division and by State, and total population aged 4-17, all by age group, various periods 1970-2050. Data are from Census Bureau.

DRUG THERAPY IN OFFICE VISITS TO PHYSICIANS

(p. 12-19) Article, with 3 charts and 2 tables showing number of office visits to physicians, visits involving use of medication, number of medications used, and distribution of visits by number of medications used, all by diagnosis or purpose of visit; and distribution of medication used by whether generic or brand name, prescription or nonprescription, single or multiple ingredient, and controlled or not controlled by DEA; 1980. Data are from National Ambulatory Medical Care Survey, conducted by NCHS.

REGIONAL VARIATIONS IN MORTALITY FROM CIRRHOSIS OF THE LIVER

(p. 22-28) Article, with 3 charts and 4 tables showing mortality rates from cirrhosis of the liver for white men and women aged 35-74 by age group, by census division and State, with rankings for 5 States with highest and lowest rates, 1980. Data are based on NCHS statistics.

B6110
Minneapolis Grain Exchange

B6110–1   ONE HUNDRED AND FIRST STATISTICAL ANNUAL, Year Ending Dec. 31, 1983, Minneapolis Grain Exchange
Annual. [1984.]   120 p.
SRI/MF/complete

Annual report, for 1983, on the grain market in northwestern States served by the Minneapolis Grain Exchange (MGE). Includes data on grain production and MGE carlot receipts, for Minnesota, North and South Dakota, and selected other States; and movement, storage, and prices; all by type of grain, with selected trends from 1912.

Data are from MGE, USDA, and Western Weighing and Railroad Inspection Bureau.

Contains contents listing, foreword, and definitions (p. 5-7); 34 tables listed below, accompanied by 3 summary charts (p. 8-119); and measurement conversion tables (p. 120).

Availability: Minneapolis Grain Exchange, 150 Grain Exchange Bldg., 400 S. Fourth St., Minneapolis MN 55415, $20.00+$1.35 postage, supply limited; SRI/MF/complete.

TABLES:

[Tables showing data by commodity generally include wheat, corn, oats, barley, rye, flaxseed, soybeans, and sunflower seed.

Data are shown by month for 1983, unless otherwise noted. Tables often also include totals for 1982-83.]

B6110–1.1: Production and Futures Market

[1-2] Spring wheat futures, 1st trade and life-of-the-contract highs and lows to Dec. 31, 1983; and cash commodities highs and lows [by commodity] during 1983. (p. 8)

[3] Crop production [harvested acreage, and yield per acre, by commodity, in Minnesota, North and South Dakota, and selected other States, annually 1977-83, and for U.S. 1982-83]. (p. 9)

[4] Daily Minneapolis futures opening, high, low, close, open contracts, and volume of trading, spring wheat. (p. 14-26)

B6110–1.2: Storage and Movement

[Tables [3-11] and [13-15] show data by commodity.]

[1-2] Elevator capacity within Duluth-Superior and Minneapolis-St. Paul switching districts [by company and elevator]. (p. 29)

[3-9] Volume of grain handled by Minneapolis-St. Paul/Red Wing/Winona and Duluth-Superior area elevators as reported to the MGE, by rail, truck, and barge or vessel; and trucks received in Minneapolis-St. Paul area terminals (including Hastings/Savage/New Ulm). (p. 30-37)

[10] Navigation season comparative final report, vessel clearances of grain out of Duluth-Superior to domestic, Canadian, and overseas ports [annually 1981-83]. (p. 37)

[11] Historic lake shipments [annually] 1951-83. (p. 39)

[12] Summary of primary wheat exports from Pacific Northwest/California ports. (p. 40)

[13-14] Weekly stocks of grain and sunflower seed in stores in Minneapolis-St. Paul licensed public elevators; and weekly stocks of grain, sunflower seed, and flaxseed in stores in Duluth-Superior licensed public elevators. (p. 41-44)

[15] [Weekly] stocks of grain at selected elevator/terminal sites in the U.S. [omits data for flaxseed and includes sorghum]. (p. 45)

[16] [Weekly] spring wheat stocks in a deliverable position, Minneapolis-St. Paul/Duluth-Superior/Red Wing switching districts. (p. 46)

B6110–1.3: Call and Cash Markets

[Tables [10-14] show data by commodity.]

CALL MARKET

[1] Call session trades [quantity, quality, delivery, shipment, and price terms, for selected commodities, various dates Jan.-June 1983]. (p. 50-52)

CASH MARKET

[2] Daily Minneapolis cash wheat prices, local and diversion prices. (p. 55-66)

[3-4] Minneapolis [monthly] cash wheat high and low, 1912-83; and daily Minneapolis cash durum prices as reported by the USDA *Grain Market News.* (p. 67-69)

[5] Daily prices reported for Mineapolis cash coarse grain, barley, flaxseed, soybeans, and sunflowers (includes local and diversion points). (p. 71-82)

[6] Monthly average cash grain prices [for No. 1 dark northern spring wheat, No. 2 yellow corn, No. 1 yellow soybeans, No. 2 heavy oats, No. 1 flaxseed, and No. 2 rye, Minneapolis 1971-83; and for oil sunflower seed, Minneapolis and Duluth 1975-83]. (p. 83)

[7-9] Daily basis: 14% protein wheat, delivered Minneapolis/Duluth; and No. 2 yellow corn and No. 1 yellow soybean, delivered Minneapolis. (p. 85-89)

CARLOT RECEIPTS AND SHIPMENTS

[10-11] Daily carlot receipts handled by MGE sampling dept [for Minnesota and North and South Dakota]; and monthly summary of rail cars and amounts handled [includes screenings, buckwheat, milo, and millet]. (p. 92-104)

[12-13] Daily carlot shipments reported by Western Weighing and Railroad Inspection Bureau; and monthly summary of rail cars and amounts shipped from Minneapolis-St. Paul; [includes data for screenings, flour, millstuffs, and various oils and meals]. (p. 106-118)

[14] Receipts and shipments (by rail, in bushels), 1950-83 [annually; omits data for soybeans and sunflower seeds]. (p. 119)

B6200
Morgan Guaranty
Trust Co. of New York

B6200–1   MORGAN GUARANTY
SURVEY
Monthly
Approx. 15 p.
SRI/MF/complete, shipped
quarterly

Monthly report on current U.S. and international business, economic, and financial topics, such as energy, credit markets, the Federal Reserve Board, government regulation, inflation, and productivity. Data are compiled by the Morgan Guaranty Trust Co.

Issues usually contain:

a. Feature articles, including "Economy Watch" analysis, often with statistics.

b. "Economic Projections" monthly table (usually appearing with "Economy Watch" analysis) showing percent change in GNP, business capital outlays, consumer prices and spending, and disposable personal income; and saving rate, housing starts, auto sales, and unemployment rate; actual or forecast for 5 consecutive quarters, usually through quarter ending 5-7 months after cover date (data are continuously revised).

c. Recurring economic and/or monetary indicator trend charts.

Monthly "Economic Projections" table appears in all issues. All additional features with substantial statistical content are described, as they appear, under "Statistical Features." Nonstatistical features are not covered.

Publication is discontinued with the Jan. 1984 issue.

Availability: SRI/MF/complete.

Issues reviewed during 1984: Nov. 1983-Jan. 1984 (P).

STATISTICAL FEATURES:

B6200–1.501: Nov. 1983

ECONOMY IN 1984 AND BEYOND

(p. 1-15) Article, with trend charts, and 2 tables showing percent of growth accounted for by consumer expenditures, residential construction, business investment, net exports, inventory investment, and government purchases, during current (4th quarter 1982-3rd quarter 1983) compared to "typical" recovery; and percent change in actual and cyclically adjusted productivity, 1970-84.

B6200–1.502: Dec. 1983

ECONOMY WATCH

(p. 1-3) Article, with 1 table showing percent change in unemployment rate, employment, labor force, working age population, and labor force participation rate, during 3 economic recovery periods beginning in 1958, 1975, and 1982.

INFLATION BAROMETER: ROUGHER WEATHER AHEAD

(p. 6-7) By Geoffrey H. Moore and Stanley Kaish. Article forecasting 1984 inflation rate, based on recent trends in Morgan Guaranty's leading inflation index.

Includes 1 table showing dates of troughs and peaks for leading inflation index and for actual inflation rate; and changes in leading inflation index, index-based estimate of inflation rate, and actual inflation rate, for expansionary periods; 1949-83.

TUG-OF-WAR OVER 'FLOAT'

(p. 11-14) Article, with 1 table showing estimated value of outstanding checks ("float"), and value of interest associated with outstanding checks, for 4 stages of the clearance/payment process, as of late 1983.

B6200–1.503: Jan. 1984

BEHIND THE DECLINE IN UNEMPLOYMENT

(p. 3, 5-6) Article analyzing causes of decline in unemployment rate during 1983. Includes 2 tables showing annual rate of change in labor force, employment, unemployment rate, population, and labor force participation rate by sex, 1975-79 period compared to 1983.

COLLECTIVE BARGAINING IN 1984

(p. 4-5) Article, with 1 table showing workers covered under labor contracts due to expire in 1984, by month and industry.

CREDIT MARKETS IN 1984, ANNUAL FEATURE

(p. 7-12) Annual article forecasting credit conditions in 1984. Includes 2 tables showing credit demand by type (including government and corporate securities, mortgages, and consumer credit), and supply by source, 1979-84.

B6200–2   WORLD FINANCIAL
MARKETS
Monthly.   Approx. 20 p.
ISSN 0190-2083.
LC 78-2438.
SRI/MF/complete, shipped
quarterly

Monthly report on foreign exchange market developments and rates, and domestic and international economic issues affecting financial markets.

Most monthly data are current to month preceding cover date, with some data current to cover date month. Data are compiled by Morgan Guaranty Trust Co. from various private and government sources.

Issues generally contain:

a. 1-2 feature articles, with statistics, on selected aspects of the world economy.

b. Statistical appendix section, with 16 detailed monthly tables, listed below; and irregularly recurring index key to data.

Most monthly appendix tables appear in all issues. All articles with substantial statistical content are described, as they appear, under "Statistical Features." Nonstatistical features are not covered.

Availability: Morgan Guaranty Trust Co. of New York, 23 Wall St., New York NY 10015, ‡; SRI/MF/complete, shipped quarterly.

Issues reviewed during 1984: Nov. 1983-Sept. 1984 (P).

MONTHLY APPENDIX TABLES:

[Tables generally show data for month prior to cover date, with various trends, usually including data for several recent months and for 3-4 previous years (full year or as of Dec. 31).

Tables [1-2] and [9-16] show data for U.S. and 13-33 other countries. Table sequence and format may vary.]

[1] Nominal effective exchange rates [also includes weekly detail for cover date month and preceding month].

[2] Real effective exchange rates.

[3] Eurocurrency deposit rates [prime banks' bid rates in London, for 6-9 Eurocurrency denominations by duration of deposit].

[4-5] [New] international bond issues: by currency [of denomination; and] by country of borrower [with totals for industrial and centrally planned countries, developing countries by world area, and international organizations].

[6] International bond yields [on long-term issues for U.S. companies and European governments].

[7] Eurocurrency bank credits by country of borrower [with totals for industrial and centrally planned countries, developing countries by world area, and international organizations].

[8] Eurocurrency market size [estimated liabilities to nonbanks, central banks, and other banks; and Eurodollars as a percent of gross liabilities in all Eurocurrencies].

[9] Central bank discount rates.

[10-12] Day-to-day money rates, Treasury bill rates, and representative money market rates.

[13-16] Commercial bank deposit rates and lending rates to prime borrowers, and domestic government and corporate bond yields.

STATISTICAL FEATURES:

B6200–2.501: Nov. 1983

CANADA: RECENT DEVELOPMENTS AND PROSPECTS

(p. 1-9) Article, with 1 table showing value of Canadian current account components, 1982-84.

B6200–2.502: Dec. 1983

EUROPE'S ECONOMIC WOES

(p. 1-7) Article reviewing European economy for 1983, and presenting short-term outlook for 1984. Includes 11 tables showing the following, generally for EC, 4 EC countries, U.S., and Japan:

a. Export value and share of GDP; percent of exports to industrial, developing, and socialist countries (with some regional detail); and general government budget balance and discretionary spending as percent of GDP; various periods 1981-83.

b. Government spending, and total capital investment, both as percent of GDP, various periods 1960-83.

c. Current account balance; and percent change in real GDP, consumer prices, labor force, and employment; various periods 1975-84.

B6200–2.503: Mar. 1984

KOREA: ADJUSTMENT MODEL FOR THE 1980s?

(p. 1-9) Article discussing South Korean economic performance, 1983 and trends. Includes 6 tables showing the following for South Korea:

a. Population, GNP, military-related expenditures as percent of GNP, merchandise export value, and debt to commercial banks, 1983; and average growth rate for real GNP, 1963-75 and 1976-83 periods; all compared to North Korea.

b. Current account changes, by component; merchandise export shares, by country or world area of destination and by product; and short- and long-term external debt, and international reserves, by type; various periods 1973-83.

B6200–2.504: Apr. 1984
DOLLAR: CORRECTION OR PLUNGE?

(p. 1-9) Article, with 6 tables showing the following:

a. Selected exchange rates in terms of U.S. dollar; percent change in U.S. merchandise exports and imports, by selected country and world area of origin and destination; U.S. current account; and percent change in GNP or GDP and consumer prices, for U.S., 6 other industrialized countries, and Western Europe; various periods 1982-84.

b. U.S. balance of payments; and, for banks in U.S., claims on and liabilities to foreigners, including foreign offices and unaffiliated foreign banks; 1982-83.

B6200–2.505: May 1984
MEXICO: PROGRESS AND PROSPECTS

(p. 1-11) Article, with 3 tables showing the following for Mexico: targeted vs. actual values for selected components of central bank economic adjustment program, quarterly 1983; balance of payments components, 1982-84; and components of net borrowing requirements, with percent change in external debt and ratio of debt to exports, selected periods 1983-90.

B6200–2.506: June 1984
JAPAN'S FINANCIAL LIBERALIZATION AND YEN INTERNATIONALIZATION, ANNUAL FEATURE

(p. 1-11) Annual article analyzing Japan's financial strength in international markets, and current policy options. Includes 5 tables showing the following for Japan, various periods 1970-84:

a. Trade balance, with detail for selected countries and world areas, and comparative data for U.S.

b. Distribution of corporate and personal financial assets by financial instrument, and of corporate liabilities and stock issues by type by currency (Yen and foreign).

c. Domestic and Eurocurrency capital market holdings by type, with selected detail relative to GNP, and comparison to U.S. and West Germany.

Also includes 1 table showing distribution of world official foreign exchange reserves by currency, 1975, 1980, and 1982.

B6200–2.507: July 1984
STABILIZATION POLICIES IN BRAZIL

(p. 1-11) Article on Brazil's economic policy trends and outlook. Includes 7 tables showing the following for Brazil:

a. Petroleum consumption, production, and net imports; total exports by country or

world area of destination; foreign trade and current account balances; change in fiscal, monetary, and wage policy indicators; and public-sector borrowing as percent of GDP; various years 1977-84.

b. Balance of payments outlook, including external debt, 1984-85 and 1986-90 average.

B6200–2.508: Aug. 1984
CURRENCY DIVERSIFICATION FOR LDC EXTERNAL DEBT

(p. 1-6) Article on currency diversification as a method for controlling external debt, with focus on developing countries.

Includes 4 tables showing 6-month London inter-bank offered rate (LIBOR) for 5 currencies, selected periods 1974-84; currency composition of public sector external debt of 8 countries, various periods 1982-83; and potential benefits of currency diversification for a hypothetical 8-year loan, under 3 assumptions of dollar exchange rates.

B6200–2.509: Sept. 1984
STRENGTHENING U.S. COMPETITIVENESS

(p. 1-13) Article summarizing trends in U.S. foreign trade. Includes 4 tables showing the following, various periods 1973-1st 7 months 1984:

a. U.S.: non-OPEC trade distribution, by country or world area; trade balance with industrial, developing, and socialist countries, with detail by country or country group; and change in components of trade and current account balances.

b. Foreign: exports to U.S. as percent of GNP, and percent change in exports to other areas, for 11 countries.

B6625
New York Stock Exchange

B6625–1   FACT BOOK 1984
Annual.   June 1984.   i+90 p.
LC 56-10699.
SRI/MF/complete

Annual fact book, for 1983, on NYSE activity. Includes securities trading volume, stock prices, credit data, and investor and member firm characteristics, with historical trends from as early as 1875. Also includes selected data for other U.S. exchanges and for foreign exchanges. Data are from government and private sources, and NYSE.

Contains contents listing (p. 1); narrative analysis in 10 sections, interspersed with 7 summary charts, and 89 tables described below (p. 2-68); historical section, with list of significant dates, and 24 tables listed below (p. 69-86); and index and list of NYSE publications (p. 87-90).

This is the 29th edition.

Availability: New York Stock Exchange, Publications Department, 11 Wall St., New York NY 10005, $3.70; SRI/MF/complete.

TABLES:

B6625–1.1: Text Tables
[In addition to the topics described below, tables present additional 1983 detail, including monthly trading data, for topics covered in historical section tables.]

MARKET ACTIVITY AND FUTURES EXCHANGE
[Most data are shown for 1983, with selected trends from 1970s.]

a. NYSE activity, including new records set; trading days and hours; most active stocks; trading volume for AT&T and 7 regional holding companies; market quality indicators; and shares offered by special methods. 20 tables. (p. 5-15)

b. Trading of NYSE-listed stocks on other exchanges and over-the-counter markets; Intermarket Trading System activity; and comparison of trading on NYSE vs. American Stock Exchange (ASE). 7 tables. (p. 17-20)

c. Warrant and bond market volume on NYSE, and most active bonds; NYSE common stock yield and price/earnings ratio indexes, with comparison to selected other types of securities; and New York Futures Exchange futures and options trading. 7 tables. (p. 21-29)

NYSE STOCK PRICES, LISTED COMPANIES, AND MARKET CREDIT

d. Price changes, 1979-82; and high and low prices by month for industrial, transportation, utility, and finance stocks, 1983. 4 tables. (p. 30-33)

e. Cash dividends on common stocks, by industry, 1983; common stock yields, 1979-83; longevity of dividend records for all common stocks; and companies paying annual dividends since 19th century. 4 tables. (p. 34-35)

f. Listing requirements, selected years 1961-84; listed securities and market value, by industry and type, 1983; and foreign securities listings and market value, by world region, 1983. 6 tables. (p. 38-40)

g. 50 leading companies in number of stockholders and in market value of stock, Dec. 31, 1983; stock list net increase, stock dividends and splits, new listings, and removals, 1974-83; and rosters of companies with new common stock listings, mergers and consolidations, name changes, listing removals, and stock splits in 1983. 11 tables. (p. 41-49)

h. Securities market credit, including initial margin rate requirements, selected periods 1934-74; and net equity status of stock margin accounts, Dec. 1982-83. 5 tables. (p. 50-53)

INVESTORS, EXCHANGE COMMUNITY, AND FOREIGN MARKETS

i. Shareholder characteristics, including highlights of 7 NYSE shareowner surveys; shareowner distribution by State, demographic characteristics, and portfolio size; and estimated holdings of selected types of institutional investors; various years 1955-83. 4 tables. (p. 54-57)

j. Public transaction study highlights, including volume distribution by type of investor, shown for NYSE and/or other markets, various periods 1971-80. 6 tables. (p. 58-60)

k. Exchange community, including NYSE seat sales, 1983; securities industry personnel in U.S., New York State, and NYC, 1974-83; NYSE member offices and registered representatives, by State, 1982-83; NYSE disbursements for customer assistance, 1963-83; Securities Investor Protection Corp. assessments and advances, 1971-83; and new securities issues, by type, 1974-83. 12 tables. (p. 61-66)

l. Foreign purchases from and sales to Americans, for U.S. and foreign stocks, 1973-83; and foreign stock exchange data, including listed companies, market value, trading activity, and stock price index, by exchange, 1983, with price index trends from 1980. 3 tables. (p. 67-68)

B6625-1.2: NYSE Activity: Trends

[Tables generally show recent trends annually and historical trends for selected years within the date range noted. Many tables note record highs and lows.]

[1] Reported volume, turnover rate, and reported trades, [1900-83]. (p. 72)

[2] Daily reported share volume: average, high, and low days [1900-83]. (p. 73)

[3] Total volume in round and odd lots, average prices [1930-83]. (p. 74)

[4] NYSE large block transactions [total and daily average, number of shares, and shares as percent of reported volume, 1965-83]. (p. 74)

[5] Reported share volume records [years, months, days, quarters, weeks, and 1st hour, 1972-Mar. 30, 1984]. (p. 75)

[6] Largest block transactions [in NYSE history, through Mar. 30, 1984]. (p. 75)

[7] NYSE member purchases and sales in round lots [1937-83]. (p. 76)

[8] Odd-lot volume [purchase and sales shares and value, 1920-83]. (p. 76)

[9-10] [Number and] market value of shares sold on [NYSE, ASE, and other] registered exchanges [1935-83]. (p. 77)

[11] Bond volume (par value) [total, daily average, and high and low day, 1900-83]. (p. 78)

[12] NYSE common stock index (closing prices) [high and low day, and year end, 1939-83]. (p. 79)

[13] Cash dividends and yields [common and preferred stocks, 1929-83]. (p. 80)

[14] Listed companies' financial data [all U.S. vs. NYSE companies, and assets, sales or revenues, and net income, 1962-82]. (p. 81)

[15-16] All NYSE listed stocks and bonds [number of companies or issuers, issues, market or par value, and average price, 1924-83]. (p. 82)

[17] Securities industry credit [margin accounts and debt, securing collateral, credit balances, and potential purchasing power, year end 1965-71 and quarterly 1972-83]. (p. 83)

[18] Short sales [round lots for members and nonmembers, and odd lots, 1940-83]. (p. 84)

[19] Short interest [high, low, and year end, 1931-83]. (p. 84)

[20] [Partnership and corporation] member organizations, sales offices, and personnel [1899-1983]. (p. 85)

[21] Membership prices [high and low, 1875-1983]. (p. 85)

[22-23] Income and expenses and balance sheet of NYSE member firms [1971-83]. (p. 86)

[24] NYSE communication services [number of tickers/displays, and last sale and bid/ask interrogation devices, 1975-83]. (p. 86)

B6625-2   SHAREOWNERSHIP 1983: The 10th National Survey

Biennial.   Apr. 1984.   33 p.
ISSN 0278-1514.
LC 81-643413.
SRI/MF/complete

Biennial report on shareowners of publicly owned corporations, covering shareowner geographic and socioeconomic characteristics, mid-1983 with comparisons to mid-1981. Data are estimates based on a mid-1983 Chilton Research Services sample survey of 1,537 shareowners and 3,012 nonowners. Survey was conducted for the NYSE, but was not confined to shares traded exclusively through NYSE.

Contains contents listing (inside front cover); introduction and narrative report, with 17 summary charts, and 1 chart and 27 tables described below (p. 1-31); and survey methodology (p. 32).

This is the 10th in a series of surveys begun in 1952. For description of 9th survey, see SRI 1982 Annual, under this number. Additional data based on the 1983 survey are available from Survey Research Dept of the NYSE.

Availability: New York Stock Exchange, Publications Department, 11 Wall St., New York NY 10005, $3.70, NY residents $4.00; SRI/MF/ complete.

CHART AND TABLES:

[Tables show number of shareholders, for mid-1983 compared to mid-1981, unless otherwise noted.]

a. Shareowners: total and as percent of population, selected years 1952-83; and by type of security (NYSE and other exchange listed, over-the-counter, and stock mutual funds) and participation basis (multi-market or exclusive market). 1 chart and 2 tables. (p. 3-4)

b. Characteristics of shareowners: by age, sex, educational attainment, occupation, income, portfolio size, and method of 1st stock acquisition, including company bonus and individual retirement account/Keogh plan. 7 tables. (p. 6-12)

c. Geographic detail: number of shareowners by size of metro area and aggregate nonmetro; in top 25 metro areas; and by census division and State, with comparison to 1983 total household population. 12 tables. (p. 14-24)

d. Shareowner profiles, including value of assets and recent stock transactions, issues owned, portfolio size, age, income, marital status, stock acquisition methods, and willingness to take risks, shown variously for the following shareowner groups: all adults, new (since mid-1981) and veteran owners, men and women, persons under and over age 65, brokerage account owners, and stock investors in individual retirement accounts/Keogh plans. 6 tables. (p. 26-31)

B6625-3   PEOPLE AND PRODUCTIVITY: A Challenge to Corporate America

Monograph.   1982.   53 p.
SRI/MF/complete

Report comparing U.S. and Japanese approaches to labor productivity improvement, and analyzing U.S. corporate use of productivity improvement techniques as of 1982. Presents data on prevalence, types, effectiveness, and age of U.S.

productivity programs in 2 categories: human resource programs, designed to improve the quality of work life; and gain sharing programs, linking a portion of workers' income to productivity or profits. Includes selected detail by company employment size, and for manufacturing and non-manufacturing companies.

Also includes data on percent high school and college graduates by sex, and corporate use of selected management techniques, for U.S. and Japan; and math and science test scores of school children in U.S. and 9-13 foreign countries. Most of these data are for mid-1970s.

Data are primarily from an NYSE Office of Economic Research Mar.-Apr. 1982 survey drawing responses from 1,158 U.S. corporations with 100 or more employees.

Contains contents listing, preface, and introduction (p. 1-6); 3 narrative sections interspersed with 6 charts and 7 tables (p. 8-40); 2 appendices, including 11 tables and methodological notes (p. 42-50); and bibliography (p. 51-53).

Availability: New York Stock Exchange, Publications Department, 11 Wall St., New York NY 10005, †; SRI/MF/complete.

B6670
Nielsen, A. C., Co.

B6670-1   1984 NIELSEN REPORT ON TELEVISION

Annual.   1984.   17 p.
SRI/MF/complete

Annual chartbook on TV viewing patterns, audience size, and leading programs, 1983, with selected trends from 1950. Data are from various Nielsen indexes.

Contains narrative, and 13 charts and 3 tables, described below.

This is the 29th edition of the report.

Availability: A. C. Nielsen Co., Nielsen Business Services, Nielsen Plaza, Northbrook IL 60062, †; SRI/MF/complete.

CHARTS AND TABLES:

a. TV households, distribution by number of stations and channels received, and percent with color and multiple sets; and persons in TV households, by age and sex; various periods 1950-83. 3 charts. (p. 2-4)

b. TV usage, including average daily hours, 1965/66-1982/83; and average weekly hours, by household size, income, whether cable subscriber, and presence of nonadults, and by viewer age and sex, by day-part, Nov. 1983. 4 charts. (p. 5-9)

c. Prime time audience by half-hour segment and evening audience by program type, both by viewer age and sex, Nov. 1983; prime time audience, by night of week, Nov. 1975 and 1983; source of prime-time viewing (cable, pay cable, network, and other), by cable subscription status 1982-83, and change in cable subscriptions, 1981/82-1982/83. 4 charts. (p. 10-13)

d. TV viewership of Democratic and Republican national conventions during presidential election years, including percent of households viewing, average hours viewed, and network hours aired, 1968-80. 1 chart. (p. 14) *e.* Ratings of top 10 prime-time TV programs in 6 cities, top 20 syndicated programs, and top 15 regularly scheduled network programs by audience sex and age; Nov. 1983. 2 tables. (p. 15-17)

B6785
Norwest Corp.

B6785–1   ECONOMIC INDICATORS
Bimonthly.   Approx. 6 p.
SRI/MF/complete

Bimonthly report on economic trends and developments, focusing on upper Midwest region and Minnesota.

Issues generally contain 1 feature article, often with statistics, on U.S., international, or regional economic topics; and 8 charts showing trends in selected economic indicators for Minnesota, Minneapolis-St. Paul, and U.S.

Report also includes a semiannual survey of upper Midwest bankers' expectations for regional economic conditions; and a recurring feature on trends and outlook for selected U.S. economic indicators.

Trend charts appear in most issues. All additional features with substantial statistical content are described, as they appear, under "Statistical Features." Nonstatistical features are not described.

Issues reviewed during 1984: Nov. 10, 1983-Sept. 21, 1984 (P).

Availability: Norwest Corp., Economic Indicators, 1200 Peavey Bldg., Minneapolis MN 55479, †; SRI/MF/complete.

STATISTICAL FEATURES:

B6785–1.501: Nov. 10, 1983

FALL 1983 REGIONAL ECONOMIC SURVEY, SEMIANNUAL FEATURE

Semiannual report on survey of Upper Midwest bankers' expectations for regional economic conditions in 1984. Data are from responses of approximately 700 bankers in 7 States to an Oct. 1983 survey, and are generally shown separately for banks in agricultural areas by State, and/or for banks in Minnesota's Twin Cities and northeastern areas and in western Montana.

Includes tabulation of responses to 29 questions on respondents' bank credit operations and opinions on general business conditions; and 1 chart with survey response trends from 1976.

This is the 15th semiannual survey.

B6785–1.502: Jan. 18, 1984

WHAT'S AHEAD FOR 1984? RECURRING FEATURE

Recurring article analyzing economic outlook for 1984. Includes 5 tables showing selected economic indicators including unemployment rate, car sales, housing starts, and Federal deficit; percent change in GNP, urban CPI, profit margins, commodity prices, and wages; and distribution of Federal debt; various periods 1982-84.

B6785–1.503: May 10, 1984

SPRING 1984 REGIONAL ECONOMIC SURVEY, SEMIANNUAL FEATURE

Semiannual report on survey of Upper Midwest bankers' expectations for regional economic conditions in 1984. Data are from responses of approximately 600 bankers in 7 States to an Apr. 1984 survey, and are generally shown separately for banks in agricultural areas by State, and/or for banks in Minnesota's Twin Cities and northern Minnesota/Wisconsin.

Includes tabulation of responses to 28 questions on respondents' bank credit operations and opinions on general business conditions; and 1 chart with survey response trends from 1976.

This is the 16th semiannual survey.

B6785–1.504: July 13, 1984

LATIN AMERICAN DEBT

Article, with 6 tables showing the following for 5 Latin American countries: real GDP change, inflation rate, and current account balance, 1983-84; and outstanding debt, with comparison to aggregate Latin American and developing nations (no date).

B6785–1.505: Sept. 21, 1984

ECONOMY SLOWING, BUT EXPANSION NOT OVER YET, RECURRING FEATURE

(p. 1-2) Recurring article analyzing economic outlook for 1985. Includes 1 table showing auto sales volume, housing starts, and Federal deficit; and change in GNP, CPI, and corporate profits; selected periods 1983-85.

REGIONAL RECOVERY NOT STRONG FOR ALL

(p. 2, 4) Article, with 1 table showing employment in upper Midwest region as of July 1984, with change from previous year and from employment peak prior to most recent recessionary period, for 7 States, with detail for Minnesota twin cities area and rest of State, and comparisons to U.S.

B6790
Nuclear Assurance Corp.

B6790–1   UPDATE: A Bimonthly Review of the Nuclear Industry
Bimonthly.   Approx. 25 p.
SRI/MF/not filmed

Bimonthly report reviewing trends and developments in the nuclear power industry worldwide, and presenting data on nuclear reactor and fuel cycle operations. Most data are from NAC's Fuel-Trac computerized information service.

Each issue includes contents listing and the following sections:

a. "Industry Overview and Status," with articles on selected topics including nuclear generating capacity, and fuel conversion, fabrication, and reprocessing.

b. "Statistical Digest," with tables presenting selected data based on Fuel-Trac and on government and private sources.

c. "Focus on" special feature article.

Features with substantial statistical content are described, as they appear, under "Statistical Fea-

tures." Each issue of the report is reviewed, but an abstract is published in SRI monthly issues only when features with substantial nontechnical statistics appear.

SRI coverage of this report begins with Oct. 1983 issue.

Availability: Nuclear Assurance Corp., 5720 Peachtree Pkwy., Norcross GA 30092, $250.00 per yr., single copy $80.00; SRI/MF/not filmed.

Issues reviewed during 1984: Oct. 1983-Aug. 1984 (Nos. 20-25).

STATISTICAL FEATURES:

B6790–1.501: Oct. 1983 (No. 20)

GNP AND ELECTRICITY GROWTH COUPLING; HISTORICAL TREND COMPARISONS AND FUTURE PROJECTIONS

(p. 2-4) Article, with 3 tables on electric utilities' planned new capacity, planned plant retirements, and additional capacity required to maintain 3% economic growth, showing coal and nuclear units and generating capacity for each category, various years 1983-2000. Data sources include North American Electric Reliability Council, DOE, and NAC.

OIL COMPANY INVOLVEMENT IN THE URANIUM INDUSTRY

(p. 5-6) Article, with 1 table showing owners and ownership shares, for uranium production facilities with at least one-third oil company ownership, by facility, Oct. 1983.

STATISTICAL DIGEST, RECURRING FEATURE

(p. 10-13) Includes 2 recurring tables on licensing and construction status of U.S. nuclear power plants, showing the following:

a. Nuclear reactor units licensed for commercial operations, construction permits granted and pending, reactor units on order and announced, and total units and design capacity, annually 1973-82 and monthly Jan.-Apr. 1983.

b. Listing of nuclear generating plants under construction or planned, including utility, reactor type, planned startup date and capacity, percent complete, and licensing status (no date).

FOCUS ON: FUEL FABRICATION INDUSTRY

(p. 14-20) Article, with 3 charts and 2 tables showing light water reactor nuclear fuel market shares, for selected individual fabricators, all Japanese fabricators, and others, 1982 and quinquennially 1985-2000. Data are shown for worldwide, U.S., and non-U.S. markets, and include projections under 2 sets of assumptions regarding market developments.

Also includes 6 charts illustrating selected fuel fabrication supply-demand trends and projections.

Data are from NAC.

B6790–1.502: Dec. 1983 (No. 21)

NUCLEAR GENERATION CAPACITY AND NATIONAL/REGIONAL FUEL CYCLE FACILITIES

(p. 2-3) Article, with 1 table comparing planned domestic nuclear generating capacity, and capacity that could be serviced by planned domestic fuel cycle facilities, for 27 countries, Free World, OECD, EC, Europe, and Asia, 1990. Includes detail by facility type (uranium production, conversion, enrichment, fuel element fabrication, and reprocessing).

STATISTICAL DIGEST, RECURRING FEATURE

(p. 12-18) Includes 1 recurring undated table presenting fuel cycle data for all light water nuclear reactors operating/under construction in the non-Communist world. Table shows technical data (initial core and equilibrium cycle parameters) and generating capacity for individual reactors, arranged by nuclear steam system supplier.

FOCUS ON: JAPAN'S NUCLEAR POWER PROGRAM

(p. 19-22) Article, with 2 tables and 1 chart showing utility, generating capacity, type, startup date, and/or construction status, for Japan's nuclear reactors in operation, under construction, and planned, by reactor, Dec. 1983; and source country shares of Japanese uranium supply commitments through 2000.

Data sources include Japan's Ministry of International Trade and Industry.

B6790–1.503: Feb. 1984 (No. 22)

U308 COMMITMENT STATUS AND HISTORICAL PRICE LEVELS

(p. 2-4) Article, with 1 text table showing percent change in worldwide and U.S. uranium enrichment forward contract commitments, uncommitted demand, and year-end inventory levels, 1982-83.

NATURAL UF6 STORAGE IN EUROPE

(p. 5-6) Article, with 1 table showing Europe's cumulative inventory and available storage capacity for natural UF6, 1982-1990.

OVERVIEW OF THE LWR FUEL FABRICATION INDUSTRY

(p. 6-11) Article, with 1 chart and 2 tables on light water reactor nuclear fuel fabrication facilities in non-Communist world, showing the following: fabrication capacity distribution by country; and location, capacity by type, and comments on operations, for individual facilities in U.S. and other countries; Feb. 1984.

SPENT-FUEL STORAGE SITUATION AT EUROPEAN REPROCESSORS

(p. 12-14) Article, with 3 tables showing nuclear reactor spent oxide fuel committed from Europe and Japan, quantity unreprocessed through May 1983, potential cumulative reprocessing capability, and name of reprocessor, all by European country and for USSR; and spent fuel projected storage capacity and facility operating status for 2 reprocessors. Fuel commitment, reprocessing capability, and storage capacity data are through 1990.

STATISTICAL DIGEST, RECURRING FEATURE

(p. 15-23) Includes 3 recurring tables on U.S. and non-U.S. nuclear power plant capacity factors, showing the following:

a. U.S. reactors licensed, nuclear-based electricity generation capacity, nuclear share of total electricity generation, maximum dependable generation capacity, and capacity factor (capacity utilization percent), annually 1973-1981 and monthly 1982-July 1983.

b. Capacity factor and cumulative generation for individual U.S. and non-U.S. light water reactors, various periods 1960s-83.

FOCUS ON: U.S. URANIUM PRODUCTION LEVEL PROJECTIONS

(p. 24-26) Article, with 1 text table showing number of uranium mines and mills shut down/on standby/deferred, by previous operational status (operational, under construction, and in planning stage), 1984.

B6790–1.504: Apr. 1984 (No. 23)

NUCLEAR MEGAWATT FORECASTS THROUGH THE YEAR 2000

(p. 2-3) Article, with 1 table showing nuclear generating capacity as of Apr. 1984, and projected capacity quinquennially 1985-2000, for 25 individual countries and others. Includes utility-based and Nuclear Assurance Corp. projections.

CONVERTER PROFILES

(p. 6-8) Article, with 1 table showing location and capacity of 8 U.S. and foreign companies that perform uranium conversion services, Apr. 1984.

STATISTICAL DIGEST, RECURRING FEATURE

(p. 10-13) Includes 2 recurring tables on licensing and construction status of U.S. nuclear power plants, showing the following:

a. Nuclear reactor units licensed for commercial operations, construction permits granted and pending, reactor units on order and announced, and total units and design capacity, annually 1973-82 and monthly Jan.-Oct. 1983.

b. Listing of nuclear generating plants under construction or planned, including utility, reactor type, planned startup date and capacity, percent complete, and licensing status (no date).

FOCUS ON: FINLAND

(p. 14-16) Article, with 1 chart showing distribution of Finland's uranium supply by source, 1983.

B6790–1.505: June 1984 (No. 24)

EFFECT OF REGULATION AND COST INCREASES ON NUCLEAR POWER CONSTRUCTION

(p. 2-5) Article, with 2 tables showing capacity, percent completion, and date canceled and/or ordered, for light water nuclear reactors canceled and at risk of cancellation, by reactor arranged by utility, as of June 1984.

CONVERSION INDUSTRY OUTLOOK

(p. 6-7) Article, with 1 undated table showing capacity and country, for individual uranium conversion companies.

VARIABLE TAILS WITH THE UTILITY SERVICES ENRICHMENT CONTRACT

(p. 8-9) Article comparing 2 DOE uranium enrichment contract arrangements allowing customer to select optimum tails assays (uranium concentration in waste products).

Includes 1 table showing distribution of DOE separative work unit deliveries committed under adjustable fixed-commitment contracts, by tails assay level selected, FY84-89, as of June 1984.

STATISTICAL DIGEST, RECURRING FEATURE

(p. 11-17) Includes 1 recurring undated table presenting fuel cycle data for all light water nuclear reactors operating/under construction in the non-Communist world. Table shows technical data (initial core and equilibrium cycle parameters) and generating capacity for individual reactors, arranged by nuclear steam system supplier.

B6790–1.506: Aug. 1984 (No. 25)

CURRENT STATUS OF U.S. URANIUM SUPPLY

(p. 2-5) Article, with 2 tabular lists showing uranium producers with mills in operation and with mills on standby or shutdown, and generally including capacity utilization or date removed from operation and contract commitment status for individual mills, 1984.

STATISTICAL DIGEST, RECURRING FEATURE

(p. 12-21) Includes 3 recurring tables on U.S. and non-U.S. nuclear power plant capacity factors, showing the following:

a. U.S. reactors licensed, nuclear-based electricity generation capacity, nuclear share of total electricity generation, maximum dependable generation capacity, and capacity factor (capacity utilization percent), annually 1973-1983 and monthly Jan.-Mar. 1984.

b. Capacity factor and cumulative generation for individual U.S. and non-U.S. light water reactors, various periods 1960s-84.

B6800
NUEXCO

B6800–1   NUEXCO MONTHLY REPORT ON THE NUCLEAR FUEL MARKET
Monthly.
Approx. 25 p.+addendum.
SRI/MF/complete, shipped quarterly

Monthly report on U.S. and worldwide uranium marketing and procurement activities, and other industry trends and developments. Includes data on uranium supply, demand, trade, and prices; market for uranium conversion and enrichment services; and material and labor costs relevant to uranium production in selected countries.

Data are prepared as a broker service, and are compiled from industry and government sources. Data are current to 1-4 months prior to publication date.

Contents:

a. Insert, with executive summary, "Figures of the Month" summary, and index to previous issue.

b. Contents listing.

c. Several narrative sections, and occasional special inserts, discussing developments in the uranium market, and including world regional analyses with detail for specific countries; some with statistics.

d. Statistical sections, with 23 monthly tables listed below.

Occasionally also includes tables showing current cost of enriched uranium and optimum tails assay (concentration of uranium in waste products) at various feed and work unit cost levels.

Subscription also includes occasional special reports.

Monthly tables appear in all issues. All additional features and special reports with substantial statistical content, except uranium cost and optimum tails assay tables, are described, as they appear, under "Statistical Features." Nonstatistical features are not covered.

Availability: NUEXCO, R. Wesley Miller, 3000 Sand Hill Rd., Menlo Park CA 94025, subscription price on request; back issues $25.00 each; SRI/MF/complete, shipped quarterly.

Issues reviewed during 1984: Nov. 1983-Oct. 1984 (P) (Nos. 183-194); and Nov. 1983 Special Report.

MONTHLY TABLES:

[Market data are current to month prior to cover date. Government data are current to 1-4 months prior to publication. Sequence of tables may vary from issue to issue.]

CURRENT MARKET DATA

[Tables [1-5] are often combined as 1 table. Tables [10-16] show number of pounds or separative work units (SWUs), and delivery period, by NUEXCO reference number.]

[1] Exchange value [price at which transactions for significant quantities of natural uranium concentrates could be concluded].

[2] Transaction value [weighted average price of uranium in recent transactions].

[3] Loan use charge rate [annual interest rate at which uranium loans could be concluded].

[4] Conversion value [price at which spot and/or near-term transactions for significant quantities of conversion services could be concluded].

[5] SWU value [price at which transactions for significant quantities of SWU could be concluded; with detail by delivery period and whether DOE or other origin].

[6-9] Exchange, transaction, conversion, and SWU value, expressed in selected producer/consumer currencies.

[10] Recent transactions [uranium sales and loans, and secondary market conversion and enrichment services; also includes price as percent of current exchange, conversion, or SWU value, and country or world area of seller/lender and buyer/borrower group].

[11-12] Uranium supply [available for sale] and demand [inquiries to purchase].

[13] Loan supply [available for loan] and demand [inquiries to borrow].

[14] Conversion supply [available for sale] and demand [inquiries to purchase].

[15-16] SWU supply [available for sale] and demand [inquiries to purchase].

HISTORICAL MARKET DATA

[17] Historical exchange values [monthly from Aug. 1968].

[18] Historical transaction values [monthly from May 1976].

[19] Historical conversion values [monthly from Jan. 1981].

GOVERNMENT STATISTICS

[Most data are shown monthly for month of coverage and previous 10-20 months, with annual average for previous year. Occasionally, additional tables are included showing monthly data for several previous years.]

[20] Australia [price index for materials used in manufacturing industry, and mining wage index].

[21] Canada [industry selling price index for manufacturing, and average hourly earnings for uranium and metal mining, mines/quarries/oil wells, primary nonferrous metal, and chemicals/chemical products industry groups;

a notation concerning coverage and format for this table appears in the Feb. 1984 issue, for description see B6800-1.505, below].

[22] Republic of South Africa [average declared working costs per metric ton of gold ore milled, CPI, PPI, and mining/quarrying industry employment and wages/salaries].

[23] U.S. [PPI for industrial and all commodities; CPI; GNP implicit price deflator; and gross average hourly earnings of production or nonsupervisory workers for metal mining, primary nonferrous metals, chemicals/allied products, and electric/electronic equipment industry groups].

STATISTICAL FEATURES:

B6800–1.501: Nov. 1983 (No. 183)

JAPAN, RECURRING FEATURE

(p. 17) Recurring article, with 1 table showing Japanese electric power plant construction and generation costs, by energy source, as of Oct. 1983. Data are from Japan's Ministry of International Trade and Industry.

Data for 1982 are described in SRI 1983 Annual, under B6800-1.401.

REPUBLIC OF SOUTH AFRICA, QUARTERLY FEATURE

(p. 17-18) Quarterly article on uranium-related developments in South Africa. Includes text statistics, and 1 table showing uranium production at 13 mining operations, 3rd quarter and 1st 9 months 1983.

B6800–1.502: Nov. 1983 Special Report

[Report presents material excerpted from an Oct. 21, 1983, hearing of the Conservation and Power Subcommittee of the U.S. House of Representatives Energy and Commerce Committee.]

SECONDARY MARKET FOR ENRICHMENT SERVICES

(p. 1-26) Report examining the secondary market for uranium enrichment services, with focus on DOE enrichment service contracts. Includes 9 tables primarily illustrating market impacts of DOE contract policy changes.

Article consists of testimony and accompanying exhibits as presented by J. R. Wolcott of Nuexco.

STATEMENT OF Dr. ROBERT CIVIAK

(p. 29-32) Article on projected worldwide uranium enrichment market, 1983-95.

Includes 3 tables showing existing and planned uranium enrichment capacity, and process used, by supplier country or organization; total enrichment demand; and "most likely" nuclear power plant capacity to be supplied by DOE enrichment services, by country, with total enrichment requirements; various years 1983-95.

Article is a statement prepared by Robert Civiak of the Congressional Research Service.

B6800–1.503: Dec. 1983 (No. 184)

FREE WORLD URANIUM PRODUCTION FORECAST, RECURRING FEATURE

(p. 16) Table presenting revised forecast for recurring data on uranium production, by country or world area, 1983-92.

Original forecast appeared in Oct. 1983 issue, and is described in SRI 1983 Annual, under B6800-1.413.

FORECAST OF SWU CONSUMPTION

(p. 20) Article, with 1 table showing non-Communist world separative work unit (SWU) consumption, by buyer group (U.S., Europe, Far East, and other), 1983-90.

WEST GERMANY

(p. 21-26) Article discussing West German nuclear power industry developments and uranium supply-demand outlook. Includes 5 tables showing the following, for West Germany:

a. Output, utility, reactor type, and completion status and/or start-up date, for commercial nuclear power stations in operation, under construction, and planned, by unit, as of 1983; and total possible nuclear capacity in 1991.

b. Companies with interests in foreign uranium production projects, showing project and percent of involvement (no date).

c. Uranium and SWU purchases from U.S. to offset dollar flow associated with maintenance of U.S. military personnel.

d. Uranium enrichment contracts with DOE, showing SWUs contracted, utility, and type of contract, by reactor, FY84-89; and utilities' uranium supply and demand, including years of supply in beginning inventory, 1983-92.

B6800–1.504: Jan. 1984 (No. 185)

IMPORTANCE OF BY-PRODUCT URANIUM TO PHOSPHATE ROCK PRODUCERS

(4 p. special insert) By M. J. Reaves. Article, with 1 table showing plant capacity for uranium recovery from phosphoric acid, by company, with plant location and operating status, as of Jan. 1980. Data are from Nuexco.

ITALY

(p. 19) Article, with 1 table showing distribution of electricity generation, by type of source fuel, for Italy's state electric utility (ENEL), 1983 and planned 1995. Data are from ENEL.

NUCLEAR POWER IN THE UK

(p. 25-28) Article, with 2 tables showing the following for UK: number of nuclear reactors, reactor capacity and type, operating entity, actual or planned operational date, and completion status, for individual commercial nuclear stations (no date); and estimated uranium consumption, 1983-90. Data are from Nuexco.

Data corrections appear in the Feb. 1984 issue; for description, see B6800-1.505 below.

JAPAN'S NUCLEAR POWER INDUSTRY INFRASTRUCTURE

(p. 29-32) Article on Japan's nuclear power industry. Data sources include the Electrical Industry Survey Institute. Includes 4 undated tables showing electric utility customers, employees, plants, and capacity, with detail for 11 largest utilities; composition of nuclear industrial groups; and capacity and other characteristics of 1st 4 commercial nuclear reactors and of 3 nuclear fuel fabrication companies.

Data corrections appear in the Feb. 1984 issue; for description, see B6800-1.505, below.

B6800–1.505: Feb. 1984 (No. 186)

NATURAL URANIUM AND CONVERSION: 1983 REVIEW, ANNUAL FEATURE

(p. 1-6) Annual article compiling world uranium current market data reported in 1983 issues of *Nuexco*. Includes 6 tables showing uranium exchange and conversion values, loan use charge rates, inquiries to purchase and sell, supply and demand for secondary market conversion and natural uranium loans, number of transactions by buyer and seller groups, and value and quantity of transactions, monthly 1983; and conversion and loan transaction summary, 1983.

FEDERAL REPUBLIC OF GERMANY

(p. 22) Article discussing effects of possible design problem in nuclear power "convoy" units in West Germany. Data sources include German utility industry. Includes 1 undated table showing capacity, expected startup date, completion status, primary utility owner, and unit type, for convoy units planned or under construction.

CORRECTIONS TO PREVIOUS REPORTS

(p. 23) Presents data corrections for articles on nuclear power in the UK and Japan, originally appearing in the Jan. 1984 issue (for descriptions, see B6800-1.504, above).

Also includes notation concerning expanded coverage and format correction for monthly government statistics table [21] for Canada; for base description of monthly tables, see B6800-1, above.

1983 ANNUAL REVIEW

(p. 24-38) Compilation of articles on world uranium industry developments, 1983. Articles are described below.

CANADA

(p. 24-25) Article, with 1 table showing capacity, completion status, expected startup date, and utility owner, for Canadian nuclear reactors in operation, under construction, or planned, as of early 1984.

JAPAN

(p. 26-29) Article on Japan's nuclear power industry, 1983. Data sources include Japanese Ministry of International Trade and Industry.

Includes 1 text table showing Oct. 1983 revisions of official targets for installed nuclear generating capacity, FY90, FY95, and FY2000; and 2 tables showing capacity, startup date, utility owner, and reactor type, for nuclear reactors in operation, under construction, or undergoing testing or licensing, as of year-end 1983.

REPUBLIC OF SOUTH AFRICA, QUARTERLY FEATURE

(p. 29-31) Quarterly article on uranium-related developments in South Africa. Includes text statistics, and 1 table showing uranium production at 13 mining operations, quarterly 1983.

UNITED STATES

(p. 31-34) Article, with 3 tables showing capacity, utility owner, reactor type, and status, for nuclear units delayed, deferred, cancelled, entering or nearing commercial operation, or under construction/on order, in 1983. Data sources include utility forecasts.

U.S. URANIUM ACTIVITIES

(p. 35-37) Article, with 1 tabular list showing mine and plant closings and other events/announcements related to U.S. uranium industry, with company or agency involved, by month, 1983.

WORLD URANIUM PRODUCTION, ANNUAL FEATURE

(p. 38) Annual article on uranium production of non-Communist world, 1982-84. Includes 3 tables showing actual and forecast production, by country or world area, various years 1982-84, with detail by U.S. State, 1983.

B6800-1.506: Mar. 1984 (No. 187)

SECONDARY MARKET ENRICHMENT SERVICES: 1983 REVIEW

(p. 2-5) Article, with 2 tables summarizing separative work unit (SWU) values, monthly 1983 with Oct.-Dec. detail for DOE and non-DOE origin; and number and volume of secondary market SWU transactions; all by delivery period, primarily FY83-85/later.

1983 U.S. CONSUMPTION vs. U.S. PRODUCTION

(p. 22-23) Article, with 1 table showing uranium consumption, production, imports, exports, and inventory change, 1983. Data are from *Nuexco* and DOE estimates.

FRANCE

(p. 24-30) Article on nuclear power industry in France. Data sources include *Nuclear News* and utility reports.

Includes 4 tables showing nuclear reactor capacity, type, actual or expected commercial operation date, and (as applicable) completion status, for units in operation or under construction/on order as of 1983; operator and estimated output of uranium mills, by unit, 1983; and Eurodif ownership share for 1 French and 4 other nuclear power entities (no date).

Data corrections appear in June 1984 issue; for description, see B6800-1.509, below.

B6800-1.507: Apr. 1984 (No. 188)

SPAIN

(p. 19) Article discussing Spanish Government's new nuclear energy plan. Includes 1 table showing utility, reactor type, capacity, and date of commercial operation, for individual nuclear power plants currently operating, approved, and indefinitely deferred (with percent completion), 1984.

U.S. NUCLEAR POWER PLANT BACKLOG

(p. 20-21) Article, with 4 tables showing utility, capacity, reactor type, and percent completion, for indefinitely delayed nuclear power units; and utility, and percent completion as of Jan. 1982 and Jan. 1984, for backlogged nuclear power units; all based on early 1984 status. Data sources include *Nuclear News*.

Data correction appears in May 1984 issue; for description, see B6800-1.508, below.

EURODIF

(p. 26-29) Article on operations of Eurodif, an enrichment services consortium formed by European nuclear fuel companies. Includes 1 table showing headquarters country, and share in Eurodif ownership, by company, for original (1973) and current (1984) Eurodif owners.

B6800-1.508: May 1984 (No. 189)

SOUTH AFRICA'S ROLE IN THE URANIUM MARKET

(8 p. special insert) By Chris I. Von Christierson. Article discussing history and outlook for South African uranium marketing. Article was originally presented at the Atomic Industrial Forum Fuel Cycle Conference, held in Atlanta, Ga., Apr. 2, 1984. Data sources include *Nuexco* estimates.

Includes 4 tables showing selected economic indicators related to South African gold/uranium industry, 1973 and 1982; South African uranium production commitments, by world area including U.S., 1984; and South African uncommitted uranium production, and U.S. unfilled uranium requirements, with comparisons to total non-Communist world, 1984-92.

Data corrections appear in June 1984 issue; for description, see B6800-1.509, below.

JAPAN

(p. 15) Article on results of price negotiations between Japanese utilities and their major uranium suppliers, with 1 table showing negotiated price compared to *Nuexco* exchange values, FY81-85.

REPUBLIC OF SOUTH AFRICA, QUARTERLY FEATURE

(p. 16-17) Quarterly article on uranium-related developments in South Africa. Includes text statistics, and 1 table showing uranium production at 13 mining operations, 4th quarter 1983-1st quarter 1984.

Data corrections appear in June 1984 issue; for description, see B6800-1.509, below.

CORRECTION

(p. 18) Data correction for article on U.S. nuclear power plant backlog appearing in the Apr. 1984 issue; for description, see B6800-1.507, above.

NON-U.S. NUCLEAR POWER PLANT BACKLOG

(p. 19-24) Article discussing progress on backlogged nuclear power units in foreign countries outside the Soviet bloc, as of early 1984. Data sources include *Nuclear News*. Includes 3 summary tables, and 3 tables showing the following:

a. Individual units: percent completion as of Jan. 1982 and Jan. 1984, for backlogged units; and percent completion as of Jan. 1982, and date commercial operation began, for units beginning operation between Jan. 1982 and Jan. 1984; all by unit (with capacity and utility for each), arranged by country.

b. Country data: units and capacity in commercial operation and under construction as of Jan. 1984, and average progress on backlog since Jan. 1982, by country, with comparative data for U.S.

B6800-1.509: June 1984 (No. 190)

FINLAND

(p. 16-18) Article on nuclear power industry in Finland. Data sources include *European Energy Review*. Includes 2 tables showing distribution of energy consumption by source, 1973 and 1983; and capacity, capacity factor, supplier, commercial operation date, type of reactor, and utility, for 4 individual nuclear power units, 1983.

FRENCH URANIUM INDUSTRY STRUCTURE

(p. 19-20) Presents data corrections for article on nuclear power in France, originally appearing in the Mar. 1984 issue (for description, see B6800-1.506, above).

CORRECTIONS

(p. 19) Presents data corrections for article on history and outlook for South African uranium marketing, and for quarterly feature on South Africa, both originally appearing in the May 1984 issue (for description, see B6800-1.508, above).

B6800–1.510: July 1984 (No. 191)

SECONDARY MARKET ENRICHMENT SERVICES

(p. 1-2) Article discussing separative work unit (SWU) buyers' responses to DOE offer of the Utility Services Enrichment Contract (USEC). Includes 1 table showing aggregate generating capacity of U.S., European, Japanese, and other buyers, by USEC conversion status and former contract type, as of July 1984.

URENCO

(p. 16-20) Article on operations of Urenco, a federation of gas centrifuge uranium enrichment companies from UK, West Germany, and the Netherlands. Data are *Nuexco* estimates. Includes 1 chart and 1 table showing Urenco SWU delivery commitments to UK, Germany, and other countries, 1983-90; and ownership shares in Urenco, by company (no date).

JAPAN

(p. 21-22) Article, with 2 tables showing total and nuclear generating capacity and actual generation, for each of Japan's 9 regional electric power companies, FY83; and nuclear reactors operating in Japan, with average capacity factors, 1974-83.

CENTRAL AFRICA

(p. 23-25) Article, with 2 undated tables showing ownership shares, by company, for 3 uranium mining/milling consortiums in Gabon and Niger.

B6800–1.511: Aug. 1984 (No. 192)

CHANGING ROLE OF BROKERS

(p. 12-13) Article, with 1 table showing share of nuclear fuel market transactions involving a broker, by type of transaction, 1983. Data are from Nuexco.

REPUBLIC OF SOUTH AFRICA, QUARTERLY FEATURE

(p. 14) Quarterly article on uranium-related developments in South Africa. Includes text statistics, and 1 table showing uranium production at 13 mining operations, 1st-2nd quarters 1984.

B6800–1.512: Sept. 1984 (No. 193)

SECONDARY MARKET ENRICHMENT SERVICES

(p. 1-3) Article discussing separative work unit (SWU) buyers' responses to DOE offer of the Utility Services Enrichment Contract (USEC). Includes 1 table showing aggregate generating capacity of U.S., European, Japanese, and other buyers, by USEC conversion status and former contract type, as of Aug. 31, 1984.

ENRICHED URANIUM SALES: EFFECT ON URANIUM SUPPLY INDUSTRY

(p. 14-20) By Richard K. Andersen. Article, with 1 table showing Nuexco estimates of change in uranium demand due to DOE offer of Utility Services Enrichment Contract, and to secondary market sales of low-enriched uranium, 1983-91 period. Data are from a pre-

sentation at the Uranium Institute's 9th Annual Symposium, held in London, Sept. 7, 1984.

U.S. AND EUROPEAN UTILITY URANIUM PURCHASES, 1979-84

(p. 21-24) Article, with 2 tables showing number of transactions and quantity involved in U.S. and European utility purchases of uranium for longer term (2 years/over) and nearer term delivery, by producer country or world area, transaction years (Feb.-Jan.) 1979-83 and Feb.-Aug. 1984 period. Data are from Nuexco reports.

SOUTH AFRICA

(p. 25-26) Article, with 1 table showing South Africa's official assessment of reasonably assured and estimated additional uranium resources, by principal deposit or district, as of Jan. 1, 1981 and 1983. Data are from Nuclear Development Corp. of South Africa.

UNITED KINGDOM

(p. 27) Article, with 1 table showing operating entity, capacity, completion status, and actual or planned operational date, for advanced gas-cooled nuclear reactors in the UK, as of mid-1984.

UNITED STATES

(p. 28-30) Article, with 1 table showing operating utility, start-up or licensing date, reactor type, and capacity, for nuclear reactors beginning commercial operation, receiving full power operating licenses, and receiving fuel loading/low power testing licenses, 1st 8 months 1984.

KOREA

(p. 31) Article, with 1 table showing capacity, reactor type, actual or planned operational date, and completion status, for nuclear reactors in South Korea, as of mid-1984.

TAIWAN

(p. 33-34) Article, with 1 table showing capacity, reactor type, actual or planned operational date, and completion status, for nuclear reactors in Taiwan, as of mid-1984.

B6800–1.513: Oct. 1984 (No. 194)

ENRICHED URANIUM AND SWUs

(p. 2-4) Article, with 1 table on DOE's loss of uranium enrichment service business due to contract cancellations and lost new sales, 1979-Mar. 1984 period. Table shows value of loss and name of replacement supplier, for individual reactors arranged by country.

JAPAN'S NUCLEAR FUEL FABRICATORS

(p. 14-15) Article, with 1 undated table showing current and projected capacity, type of fuel, ownership shares, and location, for Japanese nuclear fuel fabrication plants, arranged by company.

JAPAN

(p. 16-18) Article on Japan's nuclear power industry, as of mid-1984. Data sources include Japanese Ministry of International Trade and Industry.

Includes 1 text table showing official targets for installed nuclear generating capacity, FY90, FY95, and FY2000; and 2 tables showing capacity, startup date, utility owner, and reactor type, for nuclear reactors in operation, under construction, or undergoing licensing, as of mid-1984.

Article updates a report appearing in the Feb. 1984 issue; for description see B6800-1.505, above.

SWITZERLAND

(p. 19) Article, with 1 table showing utility owner, capacity, reactor type, and actual or planned operational date, for nuclear reactors in Switzerland, as of fall 1984.

B7100
Pannell Kerr Forster

B7100-1   TRENDS IN THE HOTEL INDUSTRY, 1983
International Edition
Annual. 1983. 92 p.
ISSN 0278-3983.
LC 81-643956.
SRI/MF/not filmed

Annual report on operating results of international hotel industry, 1982, with comparisons to 1981. Includes data for payroll, food, beverages, casino operations, fuel and telephone use, laundry/dry cleaning, and other income and expense items. Data are shown as the ratio of itemized operating expenses to total and departmental revenues, and as costs per available room per year, by world region and selected country.

Also includes average rooms per establishment, occupancy rates, room charges, and selected comparisons to U.S. hotel/motel industry; exchange rates in terms of U.S. dollar, by country arranged by world area, as of Dec. 31, 1982; and summary trends from 1976.

Report is based on a survey of 500 international hotels, conducted by Pannell Kerr Forster.

Contains contents and table listings (p. 1); and report, with 3 charts and 38 tables (p. 2-92).

This is the 10th annual report. Previous report, issued in 1982, was also received in 1984 [Annual. 1982. 80 p. $50.00].

Availability: Pannell Kerr Forster, Publications, 420 Lexington Ave., New York NY 10170, $50.00; SRI/MF/not filmed.

B7100-2   TRENDS IN THE HOTEL INDUSTRY, USA Edition, 1983
Annual. 1983. 75 p.
LC A40-3316.
SRI/MF/not filmed

Annual report on operating results of the U.S. hotel and motel industry, 1982, with comparisons to 1981 and trends from 1963.

Data are shown by specific operating item, and are presented for transient and resort hotels, and motels with and without restaurants, by geographic region, rate group, and size classification. Report is based on a survey of 1,000 hotels and motels, conducted by Pannell Kerr Forster.

Contains listing of contents, tables, and charts (p. 1); narrative analysis (p. 2-11); and 47 tables and charts, arranged by hotel and motel type (p. 12-75). All tables and charts are listed below.

This is the 47th annual report.

Previous report, presenting data for 1981, has also been reviewed by SRI [Annual. 1982. 75 p. $50.00]. For description of report for 1980, see SRI 1982 Annual, under this number.

Availability: Pannell Kerr Forster, Publications, 420 Lexington Ave., Suite 2420, New York NY 10170, $50.00; SRI/MF/not filmed.

TABLES AND CHARTS:

[Tables showing "selected revenue and expense items, 20-year trend" generally include revenues, costs, expenses, and income per available room; ratios to total post-property-tax/insurance income, property taxes/insurance, payroll/related costs, and rooms, food, beverage, and other revenues; food and beverage costs per dollar of sales; and occupancy and room rates; all for selected years 1963-82.]

B7100–2.1: Operations Summary: 1,000 Hotels and Motels

1. How hotels and motels performed [number and percent showing decrease or increase in rooms sold; guests accommodated; rooms, food, beverage, and total revenues; and post-tax/insurance income]; 1981-82. [chart] (p. 12)

2. Statistical highlights [occupancy percent, average room rate, revenues and income per available room per year, and ratio of income to revenues, of 350 transient and 100 resort hotels, and 375 motels/motor hotels with, and 175 motels/motor hotels without, restaurants; average for top 25%, large and small city setting, and by geographical division, size classification, and rate group], 1982. (p. 13)

3. Source and disposition of the industry dollar. [chart] (p. 15)

4-5. Condensed statement of operations [revenues, departmental costs and expenses, undistributed operating expenses, and property taxes and insurance]; and comparative results of operations, percentage distribution of revenues and expenses; [all by item], 1981-82. (p. 16-17)

6. Payroll costs, 1981-82 [and ratios to total payroll and revenues, all by item]. (p. 18)

7. Payroll and related costs percentage distribution and dollars per room [total payroll/cost variations for 1982 based on 1981; ratios of cash payrolls, employees' meals, and payroll taxes/employee benefits to total revenues; ratio of employees' meals/payroll taxes, etc. to cash payrolls; and total payroll/related costs per occupied and available room; by hotel and motel classification, including top 25% based on income, geographical area, size, and rate group]; 1982. (p. 19)

8. Management fees, franchise fees, and provision for doubtful accounts [ratios based on total revenues and amounts per available room per year for 4 types of hotels and motels, by geographic division], 1982. (p. 20)

9. Monthly occupancy rates in selected cities and States, 1982 vs. 1981 [and 1st quarter 1983].

10. Selected revenue and expense items, 20-year trend. (p. 23)

B7100–2.2: Operations by Hotel and Motel Type

[Data for each hotel and motel type are shown for all, average for top 25%, and by geographic division and hotel size classification. Data for transient hotels only are also shown by rate group, large and small city setting, and hotel age; data for motels with and without restaurants are also shown by rate group. All additional data in tables are described below.]

350 TRANSIENT HOTELS

11. Expenses and income per available room [1963-82]. [chart] (p. 27)

12. Selected revenue and expense items, 20-year trend. (p. 28)

13-15. Ratios to total revenues [including revenues by source, departmental costs and expenses, undistributed operating expenses including energy costs, and property taxes and insurance, all by major item; with occupancy and room rates and average number of rooms], 1982. (p. 29-31)

16-21. Ratios to departmental revenues and dollars per available room [for rooms and food/beverage depts net revenues and expenses by item, including salaries, laundry, and payroll taxes/employee benefits], 1982. (p. 32-37)

22-25. Summary: dollars per available room [for same breakdowns as tables 13-15], 1981-82. (p. 38-42)

100 RESORT HOTELS

26-30. [Data described for tables 11-21 are repeated for resort hotels.] (p. 46-50)

31. Summary: dollars per guest day [revenues, departmental costs and expenses, undistributed operating expenses, and property taxes and insurance], 1981-82. (p. 51)

32. Summary: dollars per available room [for same breakdowns as tables 13-15], 1981-82. (p. 53)

375 MOTELS WITH RESTAURANTS

33-42. [Data described for tables 11-25 are repeated for motels with restaurants.] (p. 57-67)

175 MOTELS WITHOUT RESTAURANTS

43. Selected revenue and expense items, 20-year trend. (p. 70)

44-47. Ratios to total and rooms revenues, 1982; and summary: dollars per available room [shows same breakdowns as tables 13-15 and includes rooms dept revenue and expenses], 1981-82. (p. 71-75)

B8130
Salmon, Kurt, Associates

B8130–1   KSA PERSPECTIVE FOR TEXTILE MANAGEMENT: KSA's 1983 Financial Performance Profile of Public Textile Companies
Annual.   May 1984.   12 p.
Rpt. No. 35.
SRI/MF/complete

Annual report presenting financial performance data for 46 publicly owned textile manufacturers, in 5 industry segments, FY83 and trends. Includes sales, net income, and 9 financial and operating ratios, all by company, FY83, with rankings for each indicator, comparisons to FY82, and top performers over FY79-83 period.

Industry segments covered are finished consumer products, knitted/woven fabrics, spun/textured yarn, diversified companies, and other (converters/printers/nonwovens/miscellaneous).

Also includes sales and net income of 2 multi-industry conglomerates with textile sales comprising less than half of total business; and balance sheets for total industry and 1 representative company, FY79-83.

Data are derived from annual reports to SEC and to company stockholders.

Contains narrative analysis interspersed with 7 charts and 6 tables.

Report is excerpted from detailed profile of industry finances, a computer print-out of approximately 400 pages, available from the issuing agency for $300.00, but not covered by SRI.

Availability: Kurt Salmon Associates, 350 Fifth Ave., New York NY 10118, †; SRI/MF/complete.

B8130–2   KSA PERSPECTIVE FOR APPAREL MANAGEMENT: KSA's 1983 Financial Performance Profile of the Apparel Industry
Annual.   May 1984.   8 p.
Rpt. No. 32.
SRI/MF/complete

Annual report presenting financial performance data for 64-81 publicly owned apparel manufacturers in 4 industry segments, FY83 and trends.

Includes sales, net income, and 9 financial and operating ratios, all by company, FY83, with rankings for each indicator, comparisons to FY82, and top industry performers over FY79-83 period.

Industry segments covered are women's/children's wear, men's/boys' wear, diversified, and associated fashion products.

Also includes sales and net income of 17 multi-industry conglomerates with apparel sales comprising less than half of total business.

Data are derived from annual reports to SEC and to company stockholders.

Contains narrative analysis interspersed with 2 charts and 6 tables.

Data on footwear, previously included in this report, are now published separately. For description see B8130-3, below.

Report is excerpted from detailed profiles of industry finances, a computer print-out of approximately 400 pages, available from the issuing agency for $300.00, but not covered by SRI.

Availability: Kurt Salmon Associates, 350 Fifth Ave., New York NY 10118, †; SRI/MF/complete.

B8130–3   KSA PERSPECTIVE FOR FOOTWEAR MANAGEMENT: KSA's 1983 Financial Performance Profile of the Footwear Industry
Annual.   June 1984.
4 p. no paging.
SRI/MF/complete

Annual report presenting financial performance data for 30 publicly owned footwear manufacturers and retailers, in 3 industry segments, 1983 and trends.

Includes sales, net income, and 9 financial and operating ratios, with rankings for each indicator, all by company, 1982-83; and industry top performers.

Industry segments covered are manufacturers, retailers, and miscellaneous/multi-industry companies.

Data are derived from annual reports to SEC and to company stockholders.

Contains narrative analysis interspersed with 3 charts and 3 tables.

This is the 1st edition of the report. Prior to the 1983 report, data were included in the apparel industry report, covered in SRI under B8130-2.
Availability: Kurt Salmon Associates, 350 Fifth Ave., New York NY 10118, †; SRI/MF/complete.

B8150
Seafirst Corp.

B8150–1   PACIFIC NORTHWEST INDUSTRIES: Seafirst Corporation Annual Review
Annual.   June 1984.   15 p.
SRI/MF/complete

Annual report, for 1984, on economic and industrial trends and outlook for Pacific Northwest region; with detailed data on Washington State business indicators, employment, and production, 1935-83.

Data are from Census Bureau and other specified government and private sources.

Contains narrative section, with 2 charts and 1 table (p. 1-6, 10-15); and statistical supplement, primarily for Washington State, with 8 tables (p. 7-9).

All tables are listed below.

Availability: Seafirst Bank, Economic Research Department, PO Box 3977, Seattle WA 98124, †; SRI/MF/complete.

TABLES:
[Unless otherwise noted, data are shown for Washington, quinquennial averages 1935-74, and annually 1975-83.]

[1] A decade of growth [Pacific Northwest region population, per capita personal income, and nonagricultural employment, for 16 metro areas and for total nonmetro area and U.S.; 1980, with change from 1970. (p. 3)

[2] Population and [total and per capita] personal income. (p. 8)

[3] Basic indicators of business and industrial activity [value of construction contracts, adjusted building index, gross business income, retail sales, foreign trade, Seattle-Everett CPI, personal consumption and building implicit deflator indexes, and electric energy production]. (p. 8-9)

[4] Labor force data [including unemployment, and employment in manufacturing, non-manufacturing, aerospace, and forest products industries]. (p. 8)

[5] Food products [production of canned fruits/berries and vegetables in Pacific Northwest; frozen fruits/berries and vegetables in Washington/Oregon; canned salmon in Alaska, Washington, and Oregon; and wheat flour in Washington]. (p. 9)

[6] Forest products [production of lumber in Washington and Oregon, pulp in Washington, and plywood in Pacific Northwest region]. (p. 8)

[7] Agricultural production [by commodity; and value of farm production and cash receipts]. (p. 8-9)

[8] Manufacturing gross income [by SIC 3-digit food and forest products and other industries, and for aerospace industry, year ending Sept. 30, 1983]. (p. 9)

[9] Value of farm products [by commodity, 1983]. (p. 9)

B8250
Security Pacific
National Bank

B8250–1   ECONOMIC REPORT: OUTLOOK SERIES
Series. For individual publication data, see below.
SRI/MF/complete

Series of 3 annual reports analyzing the economic outlook for California, the U.S., and world regions. Most data are based on Security Pacific Economics Dept analyses of State and Federal sources, or international statistical sources such as the OECD.

U.S. report is published in spring/summer. The California edition, which also includes data on near-term U.S. outlook, is published in fall. The international edition usually is published in winter; however, no international edition was issued for winter 1983/84.

Reports received during 1984 are described below.

Availability: Security Pacific National Bank, Economics Department, H8-13, PO Box 2097, Terminal Annex, Los Angeles CA 90051, †; SRI/MF/complete.

B8250–1.3: California Economic Outlook and U.S. Economic Update
[Annual. Fall 1983. 37 p. SRI/MF/complete.]

Annual report on California economic trends and outlook, 1976-84; and U.S. outlook, through 1984.

Contains 4 sections, with 19 tables as follows:

California

a. Near-term outlook: GSP; total, disposable, and per capita income; labor force, unemployment, and employment by industry division; population and net migration; and taxable retail sales and CPI; quarterly 1983-84 and/or annually 1982-84. (p. 1-5)

b. Industry trends: bank loans and deposits by type, and loan/deposit ratio; new housing permits by type, and residential and non-residential construction value by type, 1982-84; and imports and exports, for 10 leading trading countries and 5 leading product categories, Jan.-May 1983. (p. 8-12)

c. Regional trends: selected economic indicators for 3 State regions, 1976-82. (p. 19-23)

U.S. Near-Term Outlook

d. GNP and deflator, 1982-84; Federal budget receipts, defense and nondefense outlays, and deficit, 1981-84; and forecasts for selected economic and business indicators, including capital spending, corporate profits, and inflation, quarterly 1983-84 and/or annually 1982-84. (p. 26-37)

Fall 1982 report is described in SRI 1982 Annual, under this number.

B8250–1.4: Long-Term U.S. Outlook Edition
[Annual. Spring/Summer 1984. 28 p. No. 71. SRI/MF/complete.]

Annual report on U.S. economic outlook through 1989, presenting forecasts of GNP components, industrial growth, labor force, unemployment, corporate profits, inflation, interest rates, and other economic indicators.

Contains contents listing (p. 1); summary and policy overview (p. 2-3); and narrative report in 3 sections, with 3 trend charts and 7 tables (p. 4-28). Tables show the following, primarily for various periods 1973-89:

a. U.S. economic forecast: projections and/or annual growth rates for GNP, unemployment, inflation, hours per worker, labor force, productivity, hourly compensation, personal consumption expenditures, gross private domestic investment, government purchases, net exports, interest rates, and corporate profits, with selected comparisons in current and 1972 dollars.

b. Inflation and currency growth rates, postwar annual averages, for U.S. and 5 South American and 4 Western European countries.

c. Industry outlook: annual industry production and employment growth rates, for 23 high, medium, and low growth industries; and annual compound growth rate comparisons, for 65 industry groups.

B8400
Sibson and Co.

B8400–1   ANNUAL STUDY, 1984: EXECUTIVE COMPENSATION
Annual.   1983.   7+132 p.
LC 81-642136.
SRI/MF/not filmed

Annual report on top management compensation and related corporate policies, 1983. Includes data on salary and bonus levels; performance measures used for compensation packages; prevalence and characteristics of stock option and other long-term incentive plans, and of other perquisites including retirement and insurance plans; and employment contract components and use.

Also includes selected detail by position or management level, and summary trends from 1979. Data are often shown by company sales size and/or type of industry.

Most data are from a 1983 survey of approximately 1,000 companies with sales of $10 million-$30 billion.

Contains foreword, and contents and exhibits listings (6 p.); highlights (p. 1-6); report, with 5 charts and 67 tables (p. 7-121); and appendix, with list of companies participating in survey (p. 123-132).

This is the 19th annual report. Additional comprehensive reports covering insurance and financial industries in detail, and cluster reports tailored to meet participant's specifications, are also available from the issuing agency, but are not covered by SRI.

Availability: Sibson and Co., 777 Alexander Rd., Princeton NJ 08540, $175.00; SRI/MF/not filmed.

B8400–2   1985 ANNUAL SALARY PLANNING SURVEY
Annual. Aug. 1984.
1+17 p.
SRI/MF/not filmed

Annual survey report on corporate salary increase plans for 1985, with detail by employee group and comparisons to 1984.

Includes data on average salary range revisions and merit increases, by region and industry sector; competitive salary objectives, factors influencing merit budget, and variable compensation policies; prevalence of written job descriptions and methods used for job evaluation; use of geographic differential and of salary investment and flexible benefit plans; and salary program information available to employees.

Most data are shown for exempt and nonexempt employees and for officers/executives.

Data are from 875 company responses to a 1984 survey.

Contains introduction (1 p.); contents listing, profile of participants with 1 table, and summary (p. 1-3); report with brief narrative analyses and 14 tables (p. 4-15); and appendix listings of industry sector components and geographic regions (p. 16-17).

This is the 11th annual survey report.

Previous report, for 1984, was also received in 1984 [Annual. 1983. 1+17 p. †]. Previous report presents data on incidence of salary postponements/freezes and use of economic adjustments; merit pay and variable compensation policies; and salary range revisions and merit increases; with detail by employee group and industry sector.

Availability: Sibson and Co., 777 Alexander Rd., Princeton NJ 08540, participants †, others ‡; SRI/MF/not filmed.

B8560
Sunkist Growers, Inc.

B8560–1   CITRUS FRUIT INDUSTRY Statistical Bulletin, 1984
Annual. 1984.
4+61 p.+errata sheet.
ISSN 03262-014X.
LC 76-641810.
SRI/MF/complete

Annual report on California/Arizona citrus fruit production, acreage, shipments, utilization, consumption, marketing, production costs, prices, and trade, by type of fruit and processing, 1973/74-1982/83.

Also includes comparisons to Florida, Texas, and selected foreign countries; and data on orange auction sales, consumption and/or production of deciduous and other fruits by type, volume of U.S. imports and exports by origin and destination, tariffs for fresh and processed products, and summary trends from 1953/54.

Data, compiled by Sunkist Growers Inc., are derived from Federal and State government reports, and industry sources including California/Arizona Citrus League.

Contains table listing (2 p.); and 36 summary charts and 61 tables (p. 1-61).

Availability: Sunkist Growers, Inc., Information Systems Department, PO Box 7888, Van Nuys CA 91409, †; SRI/MF/complete.

B8935
Towers, Perrin,
Forster and Crosby

B8935–2   1984 EXECUTIVE COMPENSATION STUDY: The Industrial 100 and the Service 100
Annual. [1984.] 24 p.
SRI/MF/complete, current & previous year reports

Annual report, for 1984, on executive compensation practices of large industrial and service corporations. Data are from statements filed with SEC by the leading 100 industrial and 100 service companies as ranked in the *Fortune 500* listings.

Contains contents and chart listing (p. 1); introduction, and study results, with 12 charts listed below, interspersed with brief narrative (p. 2-18); and appendix, with definitions, and 2 lists showing short- and long-term incentive plans used by each company (p. 19-24).

Prior to the 1984 edition, report covered industrial companies only, and also included data for companies ranked 401-500 on the *Fortune 500* list. Previous report, for 1983, has also been received, and is also available on SRI microfiche, under this number [Annual. [1983.] 21 p. ‡].

Availability: Towers, Perrin, Forster and Crosby, 600 Third Ave., New York NY 10016, ‡; SRI/MF/complete.

CHARTS:
[Data are for 1983, unless otherwise noted. Most data are shown separately for industrial and service companies; data for service companies often include detail for diversified service, commercial banking, diversified financial, retailing, and transportation companies. Abbreviation: CEO, chief executive officer.]

1-2. Financial statistics [median profits, equity, assets, and sales or revenues, 1982-83]; and median total annual shareholders return [1973-83 period, and 1983]. (p. 3-6)

3. Total compensation mix, CEO median [salary, annual and long-term incentive, and benefit shares of total compensation]. (p. 7)

4. Prevalence of major compensation elements [selected short- and long-term incentives, and executive benefits]. (p. 8)

5-6. Median percentage increase in cash compensation for CEOs; and senior executive compensation as a percentage of CEO pay. (p. 9-10)

7-9. Total cash compensation statistics; percentage of companies offering short-term incentives; and annual incentive award as a percentage of base salary; [with detail for CEO and 2nd-5th highest paid executives]. (p. 11-13)

10-11. Prevalence of short- and long-term incentives [number of companies using short-term, current and/or deferred, and cash and/or stock awards; and long-term awards, including stock options and appreciation rights, performance units and shares, stock grants/restricted stock, phantom stock, and dividend units]. (p. 14-15)

12. Prevalence of executive benefits [number of companies using ERISA (Employee Retirement Income Security Act) excess plans,

SERPs (supplemental executive retirement plans), death and medical benefits, and long-term disability and accidental death/dismemberment benefits]. (p. 17)

B9300
United Van Lines

B9300–1   UNITED VAN LINES MIGRATION STUDY
Annual. Feb. 17, 1984. 5 p.
Rpt. No. 14-84.
SRI/MF/complete

Annual press release reporting 1983 interstate population migration patterns, as indicated by over 150,000 household goods shipments handled by United Van Lines.

Contains narrative analysis; 1 table showing outbound and inbound household goods shipments, by State; and 1 map illustrating migration patterns.

Availability: United Van Lines, One United Dr., Fenton MO 63026, †; SRI/MF/complete.

B9550
Young, Arthur, and Co.

B9550–1   EXECUTIVE COMPENSATION, The Eleventh Edition
Annual. 1983. 187 p.
LC 77-156190.
SRI/MF/complete

Annual report, by Edwin S. Mruk and James A. Giardina, on corporate executive salary and bonus levels as of Dec. 31, 1981-82 or Apr. 1983. Includes data by position, industry, corporation sales volume or asset size, and region, with detail for bonus and nonbonus companies, separate data for parent companies and subsidiaries/divisions, and trends from 1977.

Data are from survey responses of approximately 1,400 Financial Executives Institute member corporations and other companies, and represent approximately 13,700 executives in 22 top executive and senior financial management positions.

Most data are shown separately for bonus and nonbonus companies. Data by industry group are shown for manufacturing (durable and nondurable goods), nonmanufacturing, and financial services industries; and data by industry are shown for 26 SIC 2- or 3-digit industries.

Contains listings of contents and tables (p. 3-4); foreword, methodology, and highlights (p. 5-10); and the following:

Part I: Parent Companies

a. Overview, including average compensation increases, 1982. Table 1. (p. 11-15)

b. Chief executive officer compensation rank and index, 1981-82, and average compensation increase, and bonus as percent of base salary, 1982, by industry; and average compensation, increases, and bonuses, by company sales volume or asset size, region, and industry group, 1982. Tables 2-21. (p. 15-25)

c. Top executive compensation, including compensation increase, 1982, and bonus level trends, 1977-82, by industry; compensation index, by sales volume or asset size, by region and industry group, with selected detail for 11 specific positions, and comparisons to chief executive officer salaries, 1982; and compensation increase for each position, by industry and region, 1982. Tables 22-53. (p. 26-48)

d. Senior financial management compensation, including bonus and salary increases, bonus as percent of base salary, compensation index, and comparison to top financial officer's compensation, all for 10 specific positions; and compensation index, by industry group, sales volume or asset size, and region. Tables 54-61. (p. 49-53)

e. Industry group and detailed industry tables, including average base salary and/or bonus, by sales volume or asset size, for approximately 20 positions in each industry group, and as available for 12 top executive positions in each industry, 1982-83. Tables 62-398. (p. 55-151)

Part II: Subsidiaries and Divisions

f. Selected data for subsidiaries/divisions, including compensation increase, by position, industry group, and region, and average compensation compared to parent company average, 1982; and industry group tables, showing average base salary and/or bonus, by sales volume or asset size, for 13-20 positions in each industry group, 1982-83. Tables 399-474. (p. 153-178)

g. App. I-II, with job descriptions and industry definitions. (p. 179-187)

Availability: Arthur Young Executive Resource Consultants, PO Box 5806, Grand Central Station, New York NY 10017, $175.00; SRI/MF/complete.

B9550–4   EXECUTIVE DEMAND INDEX
Quarterly.   Approx. 6 p.
SRI/MF/complete

Quarterly report presenting indexes of demand for executives, based on employment advertising in major business publications (1978=base year). Reports are issued 1-3 weeks after quarter of coverage.

Issues usually include narrative summary, definitions, and 1 chart and 7 tables showing demand index by executive function, industry sector, and region, for quarter of coverage and year to date, with comparisons to same periods of previous year, and summary trends for previous 12-24 quarters.

Data by region are shown for 5 U.S. regions and total international. Data by industry sector are shown for manufacturing, general services, and financial services.

Availability: Edwin S. Mruk, Arthur Young Executive Resource Consultants, 277 Park Ave., New York NY 10172, †; SRI/MF/complete.

Issues reviewed during 1984: 4th Qtr. 1983-3rd Qtr. 1984 (D).

B9550–5   ORGANIZATION AND COMPENSATION OF BOARDS OF DIRECTORS
Biennial.   1983.   40 p.
SRI/MF/complete

Biennial report, by Edwin S. Mruk and James A. Giardina, on organization and compensation of corporate boards of directors, 1983. Covers the following topics:

a. Primary responsibilities and degree of influence.

b. Organization: number of directors, company executives serving on board, average number of board meetings and hours spent by directors on board business, type of information provided to board, types of committees, average committee composition and meetings per year, and sources of new directors.

c. Compensation: method and average amount paid, with detail for committee chairmen and nonmanagement directors by committee type; and provision for reimbursement of expenses, 5 types of insurance benefits, stock purchase and stock option plans, deferred compensation and pension plans, and college matching gifts.

Most data are shown separately for management and nonmanagement directors in manufacturing, nonmanufacturing, and financial service sectors, often by sales or asset size, and with some detail for selected industry groups.

Data are from responses of over 600 publicly held corporations to a 1983 Arthur Young survey.

Contains contents and table listings (2 p.); foreword, study scope and method, and overview with 2 tables (p. 5-13); and narrative results, with 36 tables (p. 14-40).

For description of 1981 study, see SRI 1982 Annual, under this number.

Availability: Arthur Young Executive Resource Consultants, PO Box 5806, Grand Central Station, New York NY 10017, $75.00; SRI/MF/complete.

Commercial Publishers

C0105
Abingdon Press

C0105-1 YEARBOOK OF AMERICAN AND CANADIAN CHURCHES, 1984

Annual. 1984. v+297 p.
ISSN 0195-9043.
ISBN 0-687-46639-3.
LC 16-5726.
SRI/MF/excerpts

Annual report on U.S. and Canadian churches, presenting data on denominations, membership, attendance, clergy, finances, and theological seminary enrollment. Most data are for 1982 or 1983, with selected trends for 1970s and historical comparisons from as early as 1890. Also includes directories of religious organizations and publications.

Data are compiled by National Council of the Churches of Christ in the U.S.A. from 219 U.S. and 83 Canadian religious bodies, Census Bureau, Gallup surveys, and other sources.

Contents:

Introduction and contents listing. (p. iii-v)

Chapter I. Calendar for church use. (p. 1-3)

Chapter II. Directories of U.S. and Canadian national, regional, and local religious organizations; international confessional, interdenominational, and cooperative agencies; Christian conferences; theological seminaries and church-related colleges; religious periodicals; and service agencies. (p. 5-228)

Chapter III. Statistical and historical section, with narrative, 2 charts and 47 tables described below, and list of depositories of historical materials in U.S. and Canada. (p. 229-288)

Index. (p. 289-297)

This is the 52nd edition of the report.

Availability: Abingdon Press, Yearbook of American and Canadian Churches, 201 Eighth Ave. S., PO Box 801, Nashville TN 37202, $17.95; SRI/MF/excerpts for statistical portions of Chapter III.

CHAPTER III STATISTICS:

C0105-1.1: Churches, Membership, and Finances

CHURCHES AND MEMBERSHIP

a. Churches, membership, pastors, total clergy, and Sunday/Sabbath schools and enrollment, shown for 219 U.S. and 83 Canadian denominations/religious bodies, 1983 or most current year reported; and percent of U.S. population with church membership, and change in membership, 1982-83. 5 tables. (p. 231-243)

b. Churches and members of major U.S. religions; churches, membership, and pastors, for religious bodies comprising National Council of the Churches of Christ in the

U.S.A., 1983 or most current year reported; U.S. membership in 30 denominations, selected years 1940-82; and total membership, selected years 1890-1982. 4 tables. (p. 244-248)

FINANCES

c. Total and per member contributions and donations, for 40 U.S. and 30 Canadian Protestant denominations, 1983 or most current year reported; total U.S. charitable contributions, by donor type 1982, and by function 1955-82; Canadian per taxpayer charitable contributions, by Province, 1980; selected characteristics of U.S. and Canadian personal and family income and expenses, various years 1979-83; and denominational per member contributions, in current and constant 1967 dollars, 1961-82. 2 charts and 11 tables. (p. 250-259)

C0105-1.2: Canada Data, Seminaries, and Selected Survey Results

a. Canada: top 6-7 religious groups ranked by membership as percent of total population, for Canada and by Province and territory; and membership distribution among major religions; various years 1951-81. 2 tables. (p. 261-264)

b. Salary survey: clergy, salary, and total income, in 12 U.S. Protestant denominations variously cross-tabulated by denomination, sex, age, position, and education, 1982. 8 tables. (p. 265-269)

c. U.S./Canadian theological seminaries and FTE enrollment, and U.S. and Canadian full/part-time enrollment; and U.S. seminary enrollment of women, blacks, Hispanics, and Pacific/Asian Americans, various years 1970-83. 6 tables. (p. 270-272)

d. U.S. survey responses to questions in the following areas: religious preference (Protestant, Catholic, Jewish, other, and none); church/synagogue membership and attendance; confidence in organized religion; importance of religion in society and for the individual; religious beliefs, experiences, and practices; and interfaith tolerance and relations; various years 1958-83. 8 tables. (p. 274-279)

e. Church/synagogue attendance: percent of U.S. adults attending in average week for selected years 1939-82, with 1982 detail by region, major religion, and selected demographic characteristics. 2 tables. (p. 282-283)

f. Construction value of new religious buildings in current and constant 1977 dollars, 1968-82. 1 table. (p. 284)

C0175
American Banker, Inc.

C0175-1 AMERICAN BANKER

5 per week. Approx. 30 p.
Oversized.
ISSN 0002-7561.
LC SN 78-4624.
SRI/MF/excerpts

Daily (Mon.-Fri.) journal of the financial service industry. Covers news concerning banks and related financial institutions. Includes detailed statistics on the financial performance of individual institutions and bank investment funds.

Issues contain numerous newspaper-style news and feature articles; and several recurring depts, including statistics on recent investment market and bank stock performance.

Statistical features include the following:

a. Annual rankings of individual financial institutions, including top commercial banks and thrift institutions, holding companies, credit unions, finance companies, and foreign-owned banks, by various criteria; and leading institutions in correspondent banking, holiday savings fund activity, trust activity, mortgage and commercial/industrial lending, and executive compensation.

b. Occasional special tables and statistical articles.

Major annual and special statistical features are described, as they appear, under "Statistical Features." Each issue of the journal is reviewed, but an abstract is published in SRI monthly issues only when such features appear. Nonstatistical features are not covered.

Availability: American Banker, Inc., One State St. Plaza, New York NY 10004, $395.00 per yr., single copy $2.75; SRI/MF/excerpts for all portions covered under "Statistical Features."

Issues reviewed during 1984: Nov. 1, 1983-Oct. 31, 1984 (P) (Vol. CXLVIII, Nos. 215-255; Vol. CXLIX, Nos. 1-217).

STATISTICAL FEATURES:

C0175-1.501: Nov. 8, 1983 (Vol. CXLVIII, No. 220)

$69 BILLION INVESTED IN IRAs

(p. 3, 12) By Alice Arvan. Article analyzing individual retirement account (IRA) investment trends. Data are from Investment Co. Institute. Includes 3 tables showing number and asset value of IRAs, by type of financial institution, various periods Dec. 1981-Apr. 1983.

C0175-1.502: Nov. 14, 1983 (Vol. CXLVIII, No. 223)

SAVINGS AND LOAN ASSN HOLDING COMPANIES, ANNUAL FEATURE

(p. 28) Annual table ranking 50 largest savings and loan assn (S&L) holding companies by asset size, as of Dec. 31, 1982, and also showing:

total assets and deposits, Dec. 1981-82; asset rank for 1981; net income of parent company and S&L subsidiaries, 1982; and number of S&Ls. Data were compiled by *American Banker*.

This is the 3rd annual ranking. Table is accompanied by a related article (p. 1, 14).

TOP PERSONAL TRUST BANKS

(p. 44) Table ranking 90 largest personal trust banks by value of total discretionary assets administered, and also showing value of personal trust and estate assets, all as of Dec. 31, 1982. Data were compiled by Carner and Associates, Ltd.

Table is accompanied by a related article (p. 2, 43).

C0175–1.503: Nov. 15, 1983 (Vol. CXLVIII, No. 224)

TOP 100 U.S. COMMERCIAL BANKS IN FARM LENDING

(p. 20) Table ranking 100 largest banks in agricultural lending, 1982, and also showing value of farm loans as of Dec. 31, 1981-82, with 1982 detail by type of farm loan and comparison to total loans.

Data were compiled by Automatic Data Processing, Inc. Network Services Division, and are accompanied by a related article (p. 3).

C0175–1.504: Nov. 28, 1983 (Vol. CXLVIII, No. 232)

AMERICAN BANKER RANKS THE TOP CORRESPONDENT BANKS, ANNUAL FEATURE

(p. 34, 44-48) Annual compilation of 6 tables on correspondent balances of commercial banks, showing deposit data for 100 largest banks in demand deposits due all and domestic banks, and 53 largest banks in demand deposits due foreign banks, with detail for Edge Act subsidiaries.

Deposit data are shown as of June 30, 1982-83, with aggregate trends from 1950. Some tables include detail for demand and time/savings deposits, comparisons of correspondent and total deposits, and number of banks reporting.

Data are from an annual *American Banker* survey. Tables are accompanied by a related article (p. 1, 34-36).

C0175–1.505: Dec. 5, 1983 (Vol. CXLVIII, No. 237)

PROBLEM LATIN LOANS HIT 7% LEVEL

(p. 1, 3, 39) By Karen Slater. Article, with 1 table showing the following for 10 largest U. S. banks: value of total and nonperforming loans to each of 5 Latin American countries, and Latin American loans as percent of equity, Sept. 30, 1983. Data are from SEC reports.

C0175–1.506: Dec. 8, 1983 (Vol. CXLVIII, No. 240)

TOP 100 CREDIT UNIONS IN THE U.S., ANNUAL FEATURE

(p. 16) Annual table ranking 100 largest credit unions by assets as of June 30, 1983, and also showing the following: assets and rank for Dec. 1982; value of member savings and share draft accounts, number of share draft and regular share accounts, and dividend rates, as of June 1983; and type of insurance.

Data are from an *American Banker* annual survey, and the Credit Union National Assn. Table is accompanied by related articles (p. 1, 17, 23).

C0175–1.507: Dec. 16, 1983 (Vol. CXLVIII, No. 246)

LARGEST BANKS IN EEC COUNTRIES

(p. 20-23) Table ranking largest banks in each of 10 EEC countries by deposits as of Dec. 31, 1982. Number of banks ranked ranges from 2 to 35. Data were compiled by *American Banker*.

C0175–1.508: Dec. 23, 1983 (Vol. CXLVIII, No. 251)

AMERICAN BANKER STATISTICAL GUIDE TO THE TOP 100 BANK HOLDING COMPANIES IN THE U.S., ANNUAL FEATURE

(p. 8-10) Annual compilation of 6 tables on bank holding companies, showing the following data mostly for 1981-82 or Dec. 1981-82:

a. Alphabetical list of 100 largest companies, including assets, operating income, equity capital, return on assets and equity capital, deposits, business and foreign loan volume, total and foreign offices, and number of branches and employees; with selected rankings.

b. Rankings of top 10 companies by assets, executive remuneration, correspondent balances, earnings, and return on assets.

C0175–1.509: Jan. 6, 1984 (Vol. CXLIX, No. 4)

NO IMMEDIATE DROPOFF SEEN IN FAILURE RATE

(p. l-23, passim) By Lisa J. McCue. Article, with 1 table showing number of failed banks and savings and loan assns, 1979-83; and 2 listings of commercial bank failures and thrift institution closures, with deposit or asset value and name of acquiring or assuming institution for each, 1983.

AMERICAN BANKER RANKS THE TOP HOLIDAY CLUB INSTITUTIONS, ANNUAL FEATURE

(p. 7-16) Annual compilation of 7 tables showing holiday savings club accounts, payouts, rate offered, and major account type, for individual commercial and savings banks, savings and loan assns, and credit unions, grouped by State, 1982-83; with top 25 institutions, commercial banks, and thrift institutions ranked by 1983 payouts.

Data are from responses of 372 institutions to an *American Banker* annual survey. Tables are accompanied by a related article (p. 1, 23) with 1 table ranking top 10 credit unions by 1983 payouts.

C0175–1.510: Jan. 9, 1984 (Vol. CXLIX, No. 5)

RACE FOR THE IRA MARKET

(p. 1) Table showing Individual Retirement Account (IRA) aggregate balances, Dec. 1981 and June 1983; and share of new IRA funds, 1st 6 months 1983; all by type of financial service. Data are from *IRA Reporter*.

Table is accompanied by 2 related articles (p. 1, 8-10).

C0175–1.511: Feb. 9, 1984 (Vol. CXLIX, No. 28)

TOP 10 TRUST REVENUE PRODUCERS

(p. 12) Table ranking top 10 banks/trust companies by trust revenue, 1983, with comparison to 1982 and 4th quarter 1982-83.

C0175–1.512: Feb. 23, 1984 (Vol. CXLIX, No. 38)

AMERICAN BANKER RANKS THE FOREIGN BANKS IN THE U.S., ANNUAL FEATURE

(p. 1A-23A) Annual compilation of data on large foreign banks with U.S. affiliates (branches, agencies, commercial bank subsidiaries, Edge Act corporations formed by U.S. banks to engage in foreign banking, and New York investment company subsidiaries). Includes 10 tables and 1 list showing the data described below, as of June 1983, most with comparisons to 1982. Loan data are shown for commercial/industrial loans outstanding.

a. Loans, assets, and deposits or deposits/credit balance: for banks with more than $1 billion in loans at U.S. affiliates, with number of branch/agency offices and subsidiaries; summary, by type of affiliate and for 10 leading countries; for 61 commercial bank subsidiaries and 27 Edge Act corporations ranked by loan size, and 8 New York investment company subsidiaries, with name of parent company; and for affiliates of all types, grouped by parent company and country, with parent's Dec. 1983 assets.

b. Top 10 U.S. cities ranked by total foreign banking offices, with number of offices by type; and lists of agencies, branches, and representative offices, grouped by city and State (including Guam, Puerto Rico, and Virgin Islands), with agency and branch loans.

Data were compiled by *American Banker* from Federal Reserve Board reports.

Tables are accompanied by a related article (p. 1, 8, 10).

C0175–1.513: Feb. 27, 1984 (Vol. CXLIX, No. 40)

100 SMALLEST INSURED COMMERCIAL BANKS IN THE U.S.

(p. 6) Table ranking 100 smallest insured commercial banks by value of deposits, and also showing assets, equity capital, net loan value, profitability ratios, and 5-year deposit growth, all as of June 30, 1983. Also shows year established.

Data are from Carner and Associates, based on bank reports submitted to Federal Government regulators. Table is accompanied by a related article with 1 summary table (p. 1, 18-19).

C0175–1.514: Feb. 28, 1984 (Vol. CXLIX, No. 41)

TOP 300 THRIFTS IN THE U.S., ANNUAL FEATURE

(p. 23-27, 30-34) Annual compilation of data on large thrift institutions, including savings banks and savings and loan assns. Based on findings from *American Banker* annual survey.

Includes 6 tables showing the following data as of Dec. 1983, most with comparisons to 1982: deposit and asset value, net worth, and type of charter and insurance, for top 300 thrifts, 100 savings banks, and 100 savings and loan assns, with rankings by deposit size and groupings by State; and top 300 thrifts ranked by assets.

Tables are accompanied by a related article with 2 summary tables, and 2 tables showing top 10 thrift institutions ranked by net income and by ratio of net worth to total assets, 1983 (p. 1, 48).

C0175–1.515: Feb. 29, 1984 (Vol. CXLIX, No. 42)

AMERICAN BANKER RANKS THE TOP CORRESPONDENT BANKS, ANNUAL FEATURE

(p. 1A-23A, passim) Annual compilation of 9 tables on correspondent balances of commercial banks, showing deposit data for 317 largest banks in demand deposits due all banks; 300 largest banks in demand deposits due domestic banks; 54 largest banks in demand deposits due foreign banks, with detail for Edge Act subsidiaries; and 349 largest banks in total deposits due all banks.

Deposit data are shown as of June 1983, with selected comparisons to 1982, rankings, aggregate trends from 1950, and data grouped by Federal Reserve district and State (includes Puerto Rico). Some tables include detail for demand and time/savings deposits, comparisons of correspondent and total deposits, and number of banks reporting.

Data are from an annual *American Banker* survey.

C0175–1.516: Mar. 16, 1984 (Vol. CXLIX, No. 54)

AMERICAN BANKER RANKS THE TOP 300 BANKS IN THE U.S., ANNUAL FEATURE

(p. 31-42, passim) Annual compilation of 4 tables ranking top 300 commercial banks by deposits and by assets, and including the following for top 300 in deposits: groupings by State and for Puerto Rico, and amount of capital, surplus/undivided profits, and, where applicable, supplemental capital in use; as of Dec. 31, 1983 with comparisons to 1982.

Also includes related article, with 1 table showing summary deposit trends for various subgroups of the top 300, and deposit comparisons to all other commercial banks and to all savings banks, selected years 1960-83 (p. 1, 66).

Commercial bank data have been compiled annually since 1921 by *American Banker* in cooperation with *Polk's Bank Directory*. Savings bank summary data are from National Council of Savings Institutions.

C0175–1.517: Mar. 26, 1984 (Vol. CXLIX, No. 60)

GROWTH OF BANK HOLDING COMPANIES

(p. 2) Table showing number of bank holding companies and number of banks owned by bank holding companies, selected years 1956-82. Data are from Assn of Bank Holding Companies.

Table is accompanied by a related article (p. 2, 27).

AMERICAN BANKER REVIEWS THE ACQUISITIONS OF THE TOP 300 BANKS, ANNUAL FEATURE

(p. 17-19) Annual list of 1983 merger/acquisition activities and name changes among top

300 banks in deposits, including name and location of participants, type and date of transaction, and, where applicable, value of merged deposits as of Dec. 1983.

Data were compiled by *American Banker* in cooperation with *Polk's Banking Directory*.

List is accompanied by a related article with 1 table showing number of acquiring and acquired banks, and deposits in acquired banks, by State and for Puerto Rico, 1983 (p. 1, 26-27).

C0175–1.518: Mar. 30, 1984 (Vol. CXLIX, No. 64)

AMERICAN BANKER RANKS THE TOP BANK HOLDING COMPANIES BY ASSETS AND EARNINGS, ANNUAL FEATURE

(p. 13-18, 24) Annual compilation of 3 tables showing top 200 bank holding companies ranked by assets, and including deposits, and number of banks and branches; and top 100 banks/bank holding companies ranked by net income, and including adjusted net income (with value of items used in adjustments), and returns on assets and equity; as of Dec. 1983 with comparisons to 1982.

Data were compiled by *American Banker*.

Tables are accompanied by a related article with 1 table showing number of bank holding companies and aggregate assets, by State, Dec. 1982-83 (p. 1, 25-26).

C0175–1.519: Apr. 9, 1984 (Vol. CXLIX, No. 70)

TOP DEPOSIT TAKERS AMONG COMMERCIAL BANKS AND THRIFTS

(p. 17-25) Compilation of 6 tables presenting data on size and characteristics of deposits in 300 largest commercial banks and 300 largest thrift institutions. Tables show the following data, as of Dec. 1983:

a. Deposit size and national rank, and value of negotiable order of withdrawal (NOW), super NOW, money market demand, and individual retirement accounts (IRA), for top 300 banks and 300 thrift institutions arranged by State and for Puerto Rico, and including commercial bank branches and employees, and thrift institution net income during preceding year.

b. Rankings of top 25 deposit-taking institutions by value of all and IRA deposits, and of top 25 banks and 25 thrift institutions by value of IRA deposits.

Data were compiled by *American Banker*. Tables are accompanied by 2 related articles, with 2 summary tables (p. 1, 30, 38).

C0175–1.520: Apr. 20, 1984 (Vol. CXLIX, No. 79)

TOP 100 BANKS IN THE U.S. IN TOTAL CAPITAL FUNDS

(p. 12) Table showing top 100 commercial banks ranked by capital funds (shareholders' equity/subordinated debt), and including assets value, capital/assets ratio, and rank number based on deposits, as of Dec. 1983 with comparisons to 1982. Data were compiled by *American Banker*.

Table is accompanied by a related article, with 1 summary table (p. 1, 13, 19).

C0175–1.521: Apr. 23, 1984 (Vol. CXLIX, No. 80)

AMERICAN BANKER RANKS THE TOP 5,000 BANKS IN THE U.S.A., ANNUAL FEATURE

(p. 27-55) Annual table showing top 5,000 commercial banks ranked by deposit value, as of Dec. 1983 with comparisons to 1982. Data are arranged by State and for Guam and Puerto Rico, with subgroupings for major cities.

Data were compiled by *American Banker* in cooperation with *Polk's Bank Directory*. Table is accompanied by 2 related articles (p. 1, 55, 62).

C0175–1.522: May 7, 1984 (Vol. CXLIX, No. 90)

TOP 100 MORTGAGE SERVICERS IN THE U.S., ANNUAL FEATURE

(p. 22-27) Annual table showing top 100 mortgage servicers ranked by value of permanent real estate serviced, and including number of loans and investors, and notes on corporate affiliations, 1983 with comparative rank for 1982. Data were compiled by *American Banker*.

Table is accompanied by an additional table showing top 25 mortgage servicers ranked by value of mortgages serviced by all subsidiaries, and including number of subsidiaries, 1983 (p. 27). Data are accompanied by a related article, with 1 summary table (p. 1, 38).

C0175–1.523: May 11, 1984 (Vol. CXLIX, No. 94)

AMERICAN BANKER RANKS THE TOP 50 BANKING COMPANIES IN EXECUTIVE PAY

(p. 15-23) Annual table showing top 50 banking companies ranked by aggregate compensation of 2 highest paid executives, and including each organization's earnings and assets, and each executive's age, position, and compensation, 1983 with comparisons to 1982. Data were compiled by *American Banker*.

Table is accompanied by 2 related articles (p. 1, 24-25, 27) with 1 summary chart; 1 table showing compensation, age, and position, for 2 highest paid executives at 16 nonbank financial institutions, 1983; and listing of the top 50 banking companies by location.

C0175–1.524: June 15, 1984 (Vol. CXLIX, No. 119)

AMERICAN BANKER RANKS THE TOP 100 FINANCE COMPANIES, ANNUAL FEATURE

(p. 17-20) Annual compilation of 6 tables showing the following data for finance companies, mainly as of Dec. 31, 1983, with selected comparisons to Dec. 31, 1982:

a. Capital funds rankings of top 100 companies, also showing capital/surplus, net and acquired receivables, total assets, net and deferred income, and bank credit available/in use; and capital funds rankings for top independent/affiliated, bank-related, and captive companies.

b. Receivables of top 10 companies in consumer, commercial/industrial, bank-related and nonbank industrial/equipment leasing, and factoring sectors; and net income ranking for top 50 companies.

Data are from an annual *American Banker* survey. Tables are accompanied by related articles, with 1 summary table and glossary (p. 1, 16, 21-22).

C0175-1.525: June 21, 1984 (Vol. CXLIX, No. 123)

AMERICAN BANKER RANKS THE TOP LENDERS, ANNUAL FEATURE

(p. 19-22) Annual table ranking top 300 banks by total commercial/industrial lending volume, as of Dec. 31, 1982-83; and also showing value of commercial/industrial loans to foreign and domestic borrowers, total gross loans, and total assets, by institution, as of Dec. 31, 1983.

Data were compiled by Data Resources, Inc., from call reports submitted to Federal agencies. Table is accompanied by a related article, with summary table (p. 1, 23-24).

C0175-1.526: June 22, 1984 (Vol. CXLIX, No. 124)

AMERICAN BANKER RANKS THE TOP PERFORMING BANKING COMPANIES, ANNUAL FEATURE

(p. 21-23) Annual compilation of 3 tables ranking 71 commercial banking companies with assets over $5 billion, by return on average assets and equity, percent change in earnings per share, stock market-to-book value, and year-end assets, mostly for 1983.

Companies are ranked within the following categories: money center institutions, and other institutions with assets of $10 billion/more and $5-$10 billion. Tables also show each company's stock market-to-book value ratio, price/earnings multiple, and dividend yield, as of Jan. 31, 1983.

Data are from Cates Consulting Analysts, Inc. Tables are accompanied by a related article (p. 1, 24-25).

C0175-1.527: June 29, 1984 (Vol. CXLIX, No. 129)

TOP 100 BANKS AND TRUST COMPANIES, ANNUAL FEATURE

(p. 20-24) Annual compilation of 3 tables on top bank and trust companies, showing the following data, by company, 1983, with selected comparisons to 1982:

a. Top 100 companies ranked by market value of discretionary assets, and also showing deposit rank, trust income rank, number of trust subsidiaries, and discretionary assets of individual subsidiaries.

b. Top 100 companies ranked by trust income, and also showing total operating income and market value of trust assets.

Data are from American Banker annual survey. Tables are accompanied by related articles (p. 1, 19).

Data addenda are described under C0175-1.528, below.

C0175-1.528: July 13, 1984 (Vol. CXLIX, No. 138)

SAVINGS AND LOAN INDUSTRY IS THREATENED BY RISING INTEREST RATES; MUTUALS HIT HARDEST

(p. 1, 9, 14-16) By David LaGesse. First of 2 articles assessing financial viability of the thrift industry, including calculations based on GAAP (regulatory net worth minus net worth of certificates and appraised equity capital).

Data are from an American Banker survey, and private studies based on Federal Reserve and Federal Home Loan Bank statistics.

Includes 1 chart and 3 tables showing the following:

a. FSLIC-insured institutions: aggregate tangible net worth as a percent of assets, and number of institutions, by institution type; distribution of institutions by size of GAAP/asset ratio; and value of assets, GAAP components, and tangible net worth; various years 1981-83.

b. Savings and loan assns with GAAP/asset ratio of 1% or less: ranking of 204 assns by GAAP/asset ratio, with GAAP worth, regulatory net worth, and assets, as of Dec. 1983.

Second article appears in July 24, 1984 issue; for description, see C0175-1.530, below.

CORRECTION

(p. 8) Notice of omission in annual compilation of tables on top bank and trust companies. For description of annual compilation, see C0175-1.527, above.

C0175-1.529: July 23, 1984 (Vol. CXLIX, No. 144)

AS FALL ELECTIONS APPROACH, VOTING RECORDS EYED CLOSELY BY POLITICAL ACTION COMMITTEES

(p. 3, 22) By Lee J. Miller. Article, with 2 tables showing number and amount of contributions from political action committees to members of the House Banking, Finance and Urban Affairs Committee, by recipient and donor, for an unspecified period ended Mar. 31, 1984. Data were compiled by American Banker from Federal Election Commission reports.

C0175-1.530: July 24, 1983 (Vol. CXLIX, No. 145)

RISING RATES THREATEN SAVINGS BANKS

(p. 1, 22, 24) By Lisa J. McCue. Second of 2 articles assessing financial viability of the thrift industry, including calculations based on GAAP (regulatory net worth minus net worth of certificates and appraised equity capital). Data were compiled by Data Resources Inc. from Federal Reserve Board statistics.

Includes 1 table ranking mutual savings banks by GAAP/asset ratio, with GAAP worth, regulatory net worth, and assets, for 36 institutions with GAAP/asset ratio of 3% or less, as of Dec. 1983.

First article appears in July 13, 1984 issue; for description, see C0175-1.528, above.

C0175-1.531: July 30, 1984 (Vol. CXLIX, No. 149)

AMERICAN BANKER RANKS THE WORLD'S TOP 500 BANKS BY DEPOSITS, ANNUAL FEATURE

(p. 41-55) Annual compilation of 11 tables on foreign and U.S. banks with largest deposits, showing the following data as of Dec. 1983 with selected comparisons to 1982:

a. World's top 900 banks ranked by deposits, with the following detail for the top 500: deposits in domestic currency, ranking within each country and U.S. State, aggregate deposits and number of banks by country, and alphabetical listing with deposit and asset rank.

b. Top 9-10 banks ranked by 1-year deposit gain and loss; and savings banks ranked by deposits; for banks listed among the top 500.

Data were compiled by American Banker.

Tables are accompanied by 2 related articles, with 1 chart and 2 tables showing distribution of deposits in top 500 banks, currency exchange rates, and number of banks in the top 500 by quintile, all by country, 1982 and/or 1983 (p. 1, 10-14).

C0175-1.532: July 31, 1984 (Vol. CXLIX, No. 150)

AMERICAN BANKER RANKS THE WORLD'S TOP 500 BANKS BY ASSETS, ANNUAL FEATURE

(p. 45-51, 62-64) Annual compilation of 6 tables on foreign and U.S. banks and bank companies with largest assets, showing the following data as of Dec. 1983 with selected comparisons to 1982:

a. World's top 500 banks ranked by assets, with number of branches and employees; and top 83 banks or bank holding companies ranked by assets, and alphabetical list of top 500 banks, both with asset and deposit rank among the top 500.

b. Top 10 banks (among the 500) ranked by 1-year assets increase; and assets and number of banks aggregated for U.S., foreign countries, and 5 countries with greatest number of banks among the 500.

Data were compiled by American Banker.

Tables are accompanied by a related article, with 3 charts and 1 table showing distribution of assets and deposits in top 500 banks, and number of banks in the top 500 by quintile, all by country, 1982 and/or 1983 (p. 1, 8-12).

C0175-1.533: Aug. 8, 1984 (Vol. CXLIX, No. 156)

AMONG TROUBLED DEBTOR NATIONS, 12 OWE 90% OF TOTAL BORROWINGS

(p. 2, 15) Article, with 1 table showing guaranteed and unguaranteed foreign debt, for 33 countries that interrupted their international debt service during 1982-84, and aggregated for 154 other countries, as of Dec. 1983. Data are from OECD and Bank for International Settlements.

C0175-1.534: Aug. 15, 1984 (Vol. CXLIX, No. 161)

GUIDE TO ON-LINE SECURITIES BROKERS

(p. 3) Table showing the following for 7 retail on-line brokerage firms: location, hours of operation, number of on-line accounts, commission rates and minimum fee, and types of service provided.

Table is accompanied by a related article (p. 1, 3, 7).

C0175-1.535: Aug. 21, 1984 (Vol. CXLIX, No. 165)

AMERICAN BANKER RANKS THE TOP 300 THRIFTS IN THE U.S., ANNUAL FEATURE

(p. 29-35) Annual mid-year ranking of top 300 thrift institutions by deposit size, as of June 30, 1984. Covers mutual and stock savings and loan assns and savings banks. Data are from American Banker mid-year survey.

Includes 9 tables showing top 300 thrift institutions ranked by deposits, and including net worth, net worth/assets ratio, and charter and insurance type, with groupings by State and for Puerto Rico, and detail for 10 institutions with greatest deposit gain and loss and with largest and smallest net worth/assets ratio; and summary of top 300 institutions by type of charter and insurer; all as of June 1984 with comparisons to June and Dec. 1983.

Tables are accompanied by a related article (p. 1, 37).

For description of year-end rankings for 1983, see C0175-1.514, above.

C0175–1.536: Aug. 24, 1984 (Vol. CXLIX, No. 168)

AMERICAN BANKER RANKS THE TOP 300 BANKS IN THE U.S., ANNUAL FEATURE

(p. 31-38) Annual mid-year ranking of top 300 commercial banks by deposit size as of June 30, 1984. Data are from *American Banker* mid-year survey. Includes 8 tables showing the following:

a. Top 300 banks ranked by deposits, with groupings by State, detail for 10 banks with greatest deposit gain and loss, and detail for banks involved in acquisitions (including deposits of merged banks); and top 25 banks ranked by assets; primarily as of June 1984 with comparisons to June and Dec. 1983.

b. Deposits of aggregate 1st, 2nd, and 3rd 100 largest banks, as of June for selected years 1965-84.

Tables are accompanied by a related article (p. 1, 47).

For description of year-end rankings for 1983, see C0175-1.516, above.

C0175–1.537: Oct. 15, 1984 (Vol. CXLIX, No. 203)

AMERICAN BANKER RANKS THE TOP 300 MORTGAGE COMPANIES IN THE U.S., ANNUAL FEATURE

(p. 26-32) Annual table ranking top 300 mortgage companies by value of mortgages serviced, and including number of investors by type (GNMA pools and others) and mortgages serviced, for year ended June 30, 1984 with comparisons to previous year.

Data are from the 18th *American Banker* survey of the mortgage industry. Table is accompanied by a related article, with 2 summary tables (p. 1, 42-43).

C0175–1.538: Oct. 16, 1984 (Vol. CXLIX, No. 204)

TOP 100 COMMERCIAL BANKS IN SERVICING OF PERMANENT MORTGAGES, ANNUAL FEATURE

(p. 12) Annual table ranking top 100 commercial banks by value of mortgages serviced for investors, and including number of investors by type (GNMA pools and others), number of mortgages serviced for investors, and value of all mortgages serviced and owned, as of June 30, 1984, with comparative rank for June 1983.

Data are from an annual *American Banker* survey of commercial bank mortgage activity. Table is accompanied by a related article, with 2 summary tables, and 1 table ranking top 25 institutions by value of mortgages serviced for investors (table is a combined ranking of mortgage companies and commercial banks) (p. 3, 28, 30).

C0175–1.539: Oct. 18, 1984 (Vol. CXLIX, No. 206)

BANKS AND THRIFTS ELIGIBLE FOR THE GOVERNMENT MINORITY BANK DEPOSIT PROGRAM

(p. 11-14) Compilation of 5 tables on banks and thrift institutions with at least 50% of ownership held by minorities (including women.) Tables show the following data, as of Dec. 1983, with selected comparisons to 1982:

a. Assets, net income, and value of deposits and/or loans, for individual minority-owned banks and thrifts arranged by State.

b. Rankings of minority-owned institutions: top 10 institutions by assets and net income; top 3-5 commercial banks by assets by type of minority owner (Asian Americans, blacks, Hispanics, Native American/Eskimo/Aleuts, and women); and top 75 commercial banks by return on assets, with return on equity, and ratios of loans and Government deposits to total deposits.

c. Financial profile of average minority and non-minority bank, including selected asset, liability, and equity capital items, operating income and expenses by type, and employment, all by asset size aggregated for banks under and over 3 years old.

Data are from 1st *American Banker* survey of minority-owned financial institutions, and are accompanied by related articles with 1 summary table (p. 1, 8-10, 15, 22).

C0175–1.540: Oct. 19, 1984 (Vol. CXLIX, No. 207)

GUIDE TO ON-LINE SECURITIES BROKERS

(p. 6) Table showing the following for 6 retail on-line brokerage firms: location, hours of operation, number of on-line accounts, commission rates and minimum fee, and types of service provided. Data are from a recent *American Banker* survey.

Table is accompanied by a related article (p. 3, 6).

A similar table appeared in Aug. 15, 1984 issue (for description, see C0175-1.534, above).

C0175–1.541: Oct. 24, 1984 (Vol. CXLIX, No. 212)

AMERICAN BANKER SURVEYS U.S. BANKS ABROAD, ANNUAL FEATURE

(p. 22-34) Annual compilation of 7 tables presenting data on foreign activity of U.S. banks including Edge Act companies (nationally chartered organizations established to engage only in international banking and investment). Tables show the following data, as of Dec. 1983, unless otherwise noted:

a. 100 largest U.S. bank holding companies, listed alphabetically, with asset rank, and total and foreign assets and offices; and foreign offices by type, for U.S. banks arranged by country and world area; all by institution.

b. Top 10 Edge Act banking systems ranked by assets, and including number of offices, with comparisons to Dec. 1982; and aggregate Edge bank offices and assets by location (13 cities, all other U.S., and foreign), Dec. 1980-83, and (for offices only) June 1984.

c. Edge Act bank corporations, listed alphabetically, with each office's location, assets, deposits, clearing balances, business loans, and opening date; and geographic listing of Edge offices, arranged by State, city, and foreign location, and showing each office's assets; with comparisons to Dec. 1982.

Data are from *American Banker* survey of top 100 bank holding companies, and 5th annual survey of Edge Act banking. Tables are accompanied by related articles, with 2 summary tables (p. 2, 16-17, 35)

Corrected data appear in the Oct. 25, 1984 issue; for description see C0175-1.542, below.

C0175–1.542: Oct. 25, 1984 (Vol. CXLIX, No. 213)

U.S. BANKING ACTIVITIES ABROAD

(p. 19) Data correction for annual compilation of 7 tables on foreign activity of U.S. banks. For description of tables, see C0175-1.541, above.

C0175–1.543: Oct. 29, 1984 (Vol. CXLIX, No. 215)

SAVINGS INSTITUTIONS' HOLDING COMPANIES, ANNUAL FEATURE

(p. 22) Annual table ranking 50 largest savings banks/savings and loan assn holding companies by asset size, and also showing deposits, net income of parent company, and number and net income of savings institution subsidiaries, primarily as of Dec. 1983 with comparisons to 1982.

Data are from *American Banker* 4th annual survey of savings institution holding companies, and are accompanied by a related article (p. 12, 24).

Previous table, for 1982, is described under C0175-1.502, above.

C0200
American Demographics, Inc.

C0200–1   INTERNATIONAL DEMOGRAPHICS
Monthly. Approx. 12 p.
ISSN 0731-5414.
LC SN 82-940.
SRI/MF/complete, shipped quarterly

Monthly report on current topics related to international demography, with statistics on population size and characteristics for various countries, and analyses of related economic and social factors.

Data are from foreign government agencies and statistical yearbooks, U.S. Census Bureau, UN, and private sources.

Issues generally contain:

a. Several articles and brief news items, occasionally with statistics.

b. "Country Profile" monthly feature, focusing on a different country each month, with 1 table showing population by age group and sex, with illustrative chart; a varying number of trend charts; and often 1 or more additional tables.

c. "Regions" recurring feature, often with statistics, including updated or corrected census data for countries previously profiled in *International Demographics*.

d. Listings and descriptions of new publications and available data sources.

An annual cumulative index is published in the Dec. issue.

"Country Profile" and all other features with substantial statistical content are described, as they appear, under "Statistical Features." Nonstatistical features are not covered.

Availability: International Demographics, PO Box 68, Ithaca NY 14851, $148.00 per yr.; SRI/MF/complete, shipped quarterly.

Issues reviewed during 1984: Nov. 1983-Oct. 1984 (P) (Vol. 2, Nos. 11-12; Vol. 3, Nos. 1-10) [Vol. 3, No. 7 incorrectly reads No. 6].

STATISTICAL FEATURES:

C0200–1.501: Nov. 1983 (Vol. 2, No. 11)
COUNTRY PROFILE: SCANDINAVIA

(p. 1, 4-10) Profiles of Norway, Denmark, Sweden, and Finland. Data sources include ILO, statistical yearbooks of each country, and private publications.

Includes 8 tables showing the following, various years 1979-81:

a. For each country except Finland: population for cities over 100,000; population by age and sex; and employment and women's share, by industry division.

b. For each country: households by type; average household size; fertility rate; percent of population in urban areas, over age 65, and under age 15; life expectancy, population density, and per capita GNP; and percent of households owning selected consumer appliances, TVs, and autos.

Finland's population for 1980 was profiled in Feb. 1983 issue, described in SRI 1983 Annual under C0200-1.411.

PAKISTAN FOCUSES ON WOMEN'S DEVELOPMENT

(p. 3) Article discussing Pakistan's *Sixth Five Year Plan*. Includes 1 table showing percent of girls enrolled in school, percent of villages with electricity, and rates of infant mortality, live births, and fertility, actual 1983 and goals for 1988.

REGIONS, RECURRING FEATURE

(p. 11-15) Includes 3 tables showing percent of UK households owning selected appliances, TVs, telephones, autos, and central heating, selected years 1972-82; population by age and sex, for 10 Latin American countries, 1980, 1985, and 1990; and Burundi population by Province, 1979.

Data are from 1982 UK general household survey, July 1983 *Boletin Demografica*, and 1979 Burundi census.

PROJECTING THE WORLD AUTO MARKET

(p. 16) Article, with 2 tables on automobile demand, showing projected annual growth rate and demand volume, by world area, various periods 1970-2000. Data are from OECD.

C0200–1.502: Dec. 1983 (Vol. 2, No. 12)

COUNTRY PROFILE: KINGDOM OF THAILAND

(p. 4-9) Profile of Thailand. Includes 4 tables showing population by age and sex, and distribution of active labor force by occupational group and sex with detail for metropolitan Bangkok, 1980; and population of major cities, and percent of urban and rural households owning selected consumer durables, 1979.

Data sources include Thailand 1980 census, UN, and Chulalongkorn University.

C0200–1.503: Jan. 1984 (Vol. 3, No. 1)
COUNTRY PROFILE: REPUBLIC OF COSTA RICA

(p. 1, 4-7) Profile of Costa Rica. Includes 3 tables showing population by age and sex, 1980; population by Province and capital city, as of Jan. 1, 1983; and labor force by industry and occupational group, for Costa Rica and metropolitan San Jose, 1981. Data sources include UN and Costa Rican publications.

MID-1983 POPULATION ESTIMATES: WHOSE ARE THE BEST?

(p. 3, 8-11) Article, with 1 table comparing UN and U.S. Census Bureau world population estimates by country, grouped by world region, for mid-1983.

C0200–1.504: Feb. 1984 (Vol. 3, No. 2)
IN EUROPE, THE SEXES WORK ALIKE

(p. 1-2) Article, with 1 chart showing ratio of female to male labor force participation in 8 European countries, 1970 and 1981. Data are from OECD.

WORLD'S LARGEST METRO AREAS

(p. 3, 11-12) Article, with 1 table showing the following data for 30 world metro areas with 5 million/over population: total population and rank, and population of largest central city, 1984, with annual change rate for area. Data are from Rand McNally.

COUNTRY PROFILE: KINGDOM OF SRI LANKA

(p. 4-9) Profile of Sri Lanka. Includes 3 tables showing population by age and sex; population, average growth rate since 1971, and male to female ratio, by district; and labor force by industry division and occupational group; 1981. Data sources include Sri Lanka Dept of Census and Statistics, and ILO.

C0200–1.505: Mar. 1984 (Vol. 3, No. 3)
WORLD'S TELEPHONES

(p. 1-3) Article, with 1 table showing telephones, total and per 100 population, by country arranged by world area, as of Jan. 1982. Data are from AT&T.

Full AT&T report is covered in SRI under B0350-1.

COUNTRY PROFILE: TAIWAN

(p. 4-8) Profile of Taiwan. Includes 3 tables showing population by age and sex, population of capital cities, and employment by occupational group and sex, 1981. Data are from *Statistical Yearbook of the Republic of China*.

REGIONS, RECURRING FEATURE

(p. 10-13) Includes 3 tables showing census counts and updated official population estimates for Europe, by country, as of various dates 1980-83; population projections for England by region, selected years 1986-2001, with 1981 base population; and Australian population, vital statistics, and labor force status indicators, often by sex, as of mid-1981.

Data sources include Office of Population Censuses and Surveys (London) and *Australian Statistical Yearbook, 1983*.

TRACKING CANADA'S BABY-BOOM GENERATION

(p. 14-15) Article, with 3 tables showing Canada population projections by age group with focus on groups aged 20-39, various years 1981-2001; and projected births, immigration, and population, under 6 fertility and immigration rate assumptions, 2001. Data are from *The FutureLetter*.

C0200–1.506: Apr. 1984 (Vol. 3, No. 4)
POPULATION SHIFTS IN WAR-TORN LEBANON

(p. 3, 10) Article, with 2 tables showing population of Lebanon, city and suburbs of Beirut, and 5 other major urban centers, by age and sex, mid-1982. Data are from estimates by Robert H. Weller.

COUNTRY PROFILE: REPUBLIC OF IRELAND

(p. 4-9) Profile of Ireland. Includes 4 tables showing population by age and sex; population and households, by Province and county or borough; and employment by occupation and industry, by sex; 1981, with some comparisons to 1971. Data are from Ireland's Central Statistics Office.

C0200–1.507: May 1984 (Vol. 3, No. 5)
MEXICO'S DEMOGRAPHIC TRENDS AND EMPLOYMENT PROSPECTS

(p. 3, 10-11) Article, with 3 tables showing the following for Mexico: labor force by sex, and agricultural and nonagricultural labor force, various years 1970-2000; and population, quinquennially 1950-2010. Data are from U.S. Census Bureau.

COUNTRY PROFILE: REPUBLIC OF ARGENTINA

(p. 4-8) Profile of Argentina. Includes 2 tables showing population by age and sex; and housing units, and population by sex, by Province; 1980 with selected comparisons to 1970. Data are from Argentina National Census of Population and Housing, 1980.

WORLD POPULATION GROWTH: WHOSE BUSINESS?

(p. 8-9) Article, with 1 table showing world population distribution by area, selected years 1950-2025. Data are from UN.

IMPLICATIONS OF CHINA'S ONE-CHILD POLICY

(p. 11-12) Article, with 1 table showing births by sex, for selected areas of Anhui Province in China, various years 1979-81. Data are from *People's Daily*.

C0200–1.508: June 1984 (Vol. 3, No. 6)
IN THE SPRING, A YOUNG BELGIAN'S FANCY...

(p. 1-2) Article presenting selected findings from 1982 EC survey of approximately 4,000 Europeans age 15-24. Includes 1 table showing distribution of student, working, unemployed, and other youth age 15-19 and age 20-24, by living arrangements, 1982.

COUNTRY PROFILE: REPUBLIC OF SOUTH AFRICA

(p. 4-11) Profile of South Africa. Includes 4 tables showing population by age, sex, and Province, by race or racial category (white, black, coloured, and Asian), 1980 with provincial growth rates from 1970; population of principal cities, 1980; and population by occupational group, by sex and racial category, 1960, 1970, and 1980.

Data are from U.S. Census Bureau and *Bulletin of Statistics.*

REGIONS, RECURRING FEATURE

(p. 12-15) Includes 4 tables showing average number of children ever born per ever-married woman, by age, education, and occupation, for Thailand, 1981; selected population characteristics for Bangladesh, including literacy rates by sex, 1981; and selected marriage pattern data for Sudan, by urban-rural status, region, and educational attainment, 1979.

Data sources include a Thailand contraceptive prevalence survey, *Asian and Pacific Census Forum,* and a Sudan fertility survey.

C0200-1.509: July 1984 (Vol. 3, No. 7)

[Issue incorrectly reads Vol. 3, No. 6.]

COUNTRY PROFILE: SWITZERLAND

(p. 1, 4-8) Profile of Switzerland. Includes 5 tables showing population by age and sex and by Canton (State), and population of 17 principal cities, 1983; percent of households owning various types of consumer durable goods, 1980; and labor force by industry group, 1982.

Data sources include U.S. State Dept and the *Statistical Yearbook of Switzerland.*

POPULATION REDISTRIBUTION IN NIGERIA

(p. 9-10) Article, with 3 tables showing Nigerian population by region and regional capital, and by State and State capital, with land area by State, selected years 1963-81. Data are from Nigerian census, UN, and *West Africa.*

C0200-1.510: Aug. 1984 (Vol. 3, No. 8)

COUNTRY PROFILE: THE METROPOLITAN AREA OF SAO PAULO, BRAZIL

(p. 1, 4-11) Profile of Sao Paulo, Brazil, metro area. Data are from the Brazilian census bureau, and the Statistical Division of the State Planning Agency. Includes 4 tables showing the following:

a. Sao Paulo municipal and metro area population by age and sex; and metro area employment by industry division and sex; 1980.

b. Population, population density, and median income relative to minimum wage, 1980; population growth rate, 1970-80 period; and infant mortality rate, 1982; all by metro area municipality.

c. Households, and percent of households with electricity and owning selected consumer durables, for selected metro area municipalities and Sao Paulo districts, 1980.

NEW UNESCO YEARBOOK REVEALS GROWTH IN ELECTRONIC MEDIA

(p. 15) Article, with 1 table showing the following for 56 countries: radios and TVs in use per 1,000 population, primarily 1979 and 1981; and per capita cinema attendance, various years 1977-81. Data are from UNESCO.

C0200-1.511: Sept. 1984 (Vol. 3, No. 9)

SCHOOL TRENDS

(p. 1-2) Article, with 1 chart and 1 table showing births, 1982; and change in primary, secondary, and higher education enrollment, 1970-80 period; for 19-23 OECD countries. Data are from OECD.

COUNTRY PROFILE: FRANCE

(p. 4-11) Profile of France. Includes 3 tables showing population by age and sex; population of principal cities; and population and population density by region and dept; 1982. Data are from France's National Institute of Statistics and Economic Studies (INSEE).

REGIONS, RECURRING FEATURE

(p. 12-13) Includes 1 table showing number and percent of Japan's population age 20/over participating in 27 athletic activities, 1982. Data are from *Look Japan.*

C0200-1.512: Oct. 1984 (Vol. 3, No. 10)

COUNTRY PROFILE: CHINA

(p. 4-12) Profile of PRC. Data sources include the 1982 PRC census, various PRC publications, and the World Bank. Includes 4 tables showing population by age and sex 1982, and the following:

a. Administrative units: capital city; land area; population, birth and death rates, and sex ratio, 1982; percent of population in urban areas, 1979; per capita output value (in yuan), 1981; population per hospital bed and per "barefoot" doctor, 1979; and life expectancy, 1973-75 period; all for total PRC and by administrative unit.

b. Family structure: distribution of families by type, for 1 village, 1936 and 1981.

c. Socioeconomic data: urban and rural income and living space; consumption of grain, vegetable oil, pork, cloth, and other consumer goods; bicycles and buses; savings; TVs, radios, newspapers, and books/magazines; educational enrollment rate; university students; hospital beds and doctors; number of persons supported by each employee; and number of retail/catering/service shopping units and employees; generally shown per capita or per 100 or 10,-000 persons, 1979 and 1982.

C0250
American Paint Journal Co.

C0250-1   DECORATIVE PRODUCTS WORLD: Retailer Survey Results
Bimonthly (selected issue).
Mar. 1984.   (p. 22-31).
Vol. 76, No. 5.
ISSN 0199-4328.
LC 82-643606.
SRI/MF/excerpts

Annual feature on retail operations of decorative product dealers, 1983, based on responses of 350 *Decorative Products World* subscribers to a 1984 survey.

Covers decorative product sales and merchandising of lumber/building supply and hardware stores, home centers, independent and paint manufacturer-owned specialty stores, and other dealer types.

Includes 12 tables showing survey response on the following, by dealer type, for 1983 unless otherwise noted:

a. Sales of decorative products, with change from 1982; anticipated change in sales and in cost of goods sold, 1984; average product dis-

play space and staff size; percent of dealers employing a decorator; average inventory value and gross margin, by product type; sales distribution by dept and customer category; and assessment of business climate.

b. Paint depts: average number of product lines carried, with detail for national, regional, and private labels; gross margin; and inventory value, with anticipated change in 1984.

c. Wallcovering depts: percent of dealers selling from sample books, stock, and self-displays; and average number of sample books, and investment and gross margin for samples and stock.

d. Dealer types perceived as chief competition; percent of stores carrying selected product types; and plans to open new stores, remodel, expand, or relocate, 1984.

Survey is an annual feature of the monthly publication *Decorative Products World,* which generally contains only narrative articles. Annual survey is the only feature covered by SRI.

Availability: Decorative Products World, 2911 Washington Ave., St. Louis MO 63103, $18.00 per yr., single copy $2.50, Buyers' Guide $15.00; SRI/MF/excerpts for annual survey article.

C0500
Army Times Publishing Co.

C0500-1   MILITARY MARKET
Monthly.
SRI now covers this publication under C8910-1.

C0875
Bankers Monthly, Inc.

C0875-1   BANKERS MONTHLY: 24th Annual Finance Industry Survey
Monthly (selected issue).
May 15, 1984.   (p. 12-19).
Vol. CI, No. 5.
ISSN 0005-5476.
SRI/MF/not filmed

Annual *Bankers Monthly* analysis of commercial finance company earnings performance, interest rates, balance sheet characteristics, credit losses, and mergers, 1983. Data sources include Federal Reserve System and annual finance company reports to shareholders.

Includes text data, and 2 tables showing aggregate earnings statements for 4 unnamed large and small finance companies, and aggregate assets and liabilities for all companies (p. 12-16); and roster of major finance companies, showing capital/surplus funds, subordinated debentures, outstanding net receivables, and net earnings, for 41 companies ranked by total capital size, Dec. 31, 1983, with selected comparisons to 1982 (p. 16-19).

Bankers Monthly is a monthly trade journal covering trends and developments in community banking and finance company management. Issues generally contain narrative articles, and 1 monthly table on bank stock trends. Annual survey article is the only feature covered by SRI.

Availability: Bankers Monthly, Inc., 601 Skokie Blvd., Northbrook IL 60062-2858, $18.00 per yr., single copy $3.00; SRI/MF/not filmed.

C1050
Best, A. M., Co.

C1050-1 BEST'S REVIEW: PROPERTY/CASUALTY INSURANCE EDITION
Monthly. Approx. 150 p.
ISSN 0161-7745.
LC 73-613400.
SRI/MF/not filmed

Monthly trade journal reporting on property/casualty insurance industry marketing trends and developments, management topics, current events, regulation, and finance.

General format:

a. Regular departmental features, including data on insurance company stocks; and "World Insurance Forum," often with statistics on foreign insurance industries.

b. Articles, often with substantial statistics, including annual data on property/casualty underwriting business by individual company, line of business, and State.

Features with substantial statistical content are described, as they appear, under "Statistical Features." Each issue of the journal is reviewed, but an abstract is published in SRI monthly issues only when statistical features appear.

Availability: Best's Review: Property/Casualty Insurance Edition, Subscription Department, Oldwick NJ 08858, $14.00 per yr., single copy $1.50; SRI/MF/not filmed.

Issues reviewed during 1984: Nov. 1983-Oct. 1984 (P) (Vol. 84, Nos. 7-12; Vol. 85, Nos. 1-6).

STATISTICAL FEATURES:

C1050-1.501: Nov. 1983 (Vol. 84, No. 7)
1982 P/C BOND HOLDINGS

(p. 10) Article, with 1 chart and 1 table showing property/casualty insurance industry bond, short-term investment, and cash holdings, and total assets, 1981-82; and bond distribution by maturity period, 1982. Data are from industry annual convention statements.

WORKERS' COMPENSATION, INLAND MARINE, AND BOND MARKETING, 1982, ANNUAL FEATURE

(p. 12-24, 120-126) Annual article, for 1982, on marketing trends in workers' compensation, inland marine, and fidelity and surety bonding insurance lines. Data are from *Best's Executive Data Service.* Includes 4 text tables on market share of national and regional companies and direct writers, for each line, 1978-82; and 8 tables showing the following for each line:

a. By State: direct premiums written, and change from 1981; loss ratio; and market shares of national and regional companies, direct writers, and each of 3 leading companies; 1982.

b. For 20 leading writers: total direct premiums written, 1982, and change from 1981; market share, 1979-82; and loss ratio, 1980-82.

Report for 1981 on workers' compensation insurance is described in SRI 1982 Annual, under C1050-1.311; report for 1981 on inland marine and fidelity and surety bonding insurance is described in SRI 1983 Annual, under C1050-1.401.

C1050-1.502: Dec. 1983 (Vol. 84, No. 8)
FINANCIAL SECURITY OR FRATRICIDE?

(p. 64-70) By Donald J. Greene and Kim Hoyt Sperduto. Article discussing capital/surplus standards established by National Assn of Insurance Commissioners for approved surplus lines insurers. Data are based on analysis of 94 companies.

Includes 1 chart showing percent of companies increasing and decreasing capital/surplus holdings since 1976, by company capital/surplus level, 1981.

C1050-1.503: Jan. 1984 (Vol. 84, No. 9)
REVIEW AND PREVIEW, ANNUAL FEATURE

(p. 28-32, 91-98) Annual article, by John C. Burridge, on property-casualty insurance industry financial performance and operating results, by company type and line of coverage, 1979-83.

Data are based on information supplied by property/casualty companies representing approximately 88% of the industry.

Includes 1 table showing net premiums written; and loss/loss adjustment expense, underwriting expense, and combined pre-dividend and post-dividend ratios, and underwriting gain or loss after dividend; generally for stock, mutual, reciprocal, and all companies, 1979-83. Table is repeated for the following lines:

a. All property/casualty; and auto, including commercial, private passenger, physical damage, and liability.

b. Fire, allied, homeowners, commercial multiple peril, inland marine, workers' compensation, miscellaneous liability, medical malpractice, and other liability.

Also includes 2 text tables showing property/casualty industry 1983 surplus status, and 1977-83 underwriting cash flow; and brief in-set article with 1 table showing distribution of property/casualty industry investment funds by source, 1951-83.

WORLD INSURANCE FORUM: MANILA, ANNUAL FEATURE

(p. 62-64) Annual article, by K. S. Bang, on Philippine non-life insurance industry developments. Includes 5 tables showing number of domestic and foreign life, non-life, and professional reinsurance companies, and number of ordinary agents, insurance brokers, and reinsurance brokers, 1980-82; and non-life insurance premiums written and loss ratios by insurance line, and investments by type, 1980-81.

For description of previous article, see SRI 1982 Annual, under C1050-1.310.

OFFSHORE LOSSES MOUNTING

(p. 99) Article, with 1 table showing UK insurance industry premiums and claims, for offshore construction projects, 1974-82.

C1050-1.504: Feb. 1984 (Vol. 84, No. 10)

1983 INSURANCE STOCK TRENDS, ANNUAL FEATURE

(p. 12-15, 102) Annual article, by John H. Lafayette, on the insurance stock performance of 81 major property/casualty, multiple line, life/health, and broker/agent companies, 1983. Includes 2 tables showing market value, dividend, and yield, 1983; year-end prices, 1978-83; and 5-year high and low prices; by company, with indexes for total companies included in *Best's Insurance Industry Stock Indexes,* and price comparisons to 6 major securities market indexes.

COLLISION COURSE

(p. 30-36, 92-94) By Henry T. Tillman, III. Article on financial institutions' involvement in insurance business. Most data are from the FHLBB, *1982 Service Corporation Directory,* and Federal Reserve Bank of Chicago.

Includes 4 tables showing number of companies with insurance business involvement, for small town bank holding companies and for service corporations associated with Federal savings and loan assns in top 10-11 States housing such institutions, with summary trends for savings and loan assns including commission income earned; and outstanding mortgage loans and installment/revolving credit for top 15 consumer lenders; as of Dec. 31, various years 1975-82.

Also includes text table (p. 94) showing consumer reasons for not using discount brokerage services offered by financial institutions. Data are from a Mar. 1983 *Unidex Reports* survey of 1,936 households.

TOO MUCH OF A GOOD THING

(p. 40-42, 95) By Sean F. Mooney. Article on property/casualty insurance industry "excess capacity" (surplus capital). Data are from the Insurance Information Institute.

Includes 2 tables showing property/casualty industry growth rate for all premiums, commercial lines, and workers' compensation, with comparison to GNP, 1978-82 period; and profit margin, premium/surplus ratio, and rate of return, 1978 and 1982.

C1050-1.505: Mar. 1984 (Vol. 84, No. 11)
E&S MARKET OF THE FUTURE

(p. 62-68) By Thomas E. Corless. Article on developments in the excess and surplus (E&S) insurance industry (companies that handle business not acceptable to other insurers). Data are from NATESCO Underwriters and *Insuranceweek.*

Includes text data and 8 tables showing E&S premiums written, with detail for 5 leading States, top 20 domestic companies, leading non-U.S. broker groups, and selected national companies operating in 3 western States; premiums earned and losses incurred for 6 States with high loss ratios, and for all States; and capital/surplus for 10 major E&S companies and New York Insurance Exchange; various years 1970-83.

CORPORATE CHANGES, 1983, ANNUAL FEATURE

(p. 76-82, 119-121) Annual article on property/casualty insurance company formations, retirements (including mergers), and name and ownership changes, 1983. Includes descriptive listing of actions taken by individual companies; and 1 table showing number of new companies, ownership changes, and retirements, all by type of company, 1983.

C1050–1.506   Best, A. M., Co.

C1050–1.506: Apr. 1984 (Vol. 84, No. 12)

WORLD INSURANCE FORUM: PANAMA

(p. 77) By Daniel A. Pagenta, Jr. Article on Panama insurance industry developments. Includes 1 table showing gross premiums for 10 leading Panamanian insurers and for 5 leading foreign insurers, 1983.

WORLD INSURANCE FORUM: ZURICH, ANNUAL FEATURE

(p. 80, 99) Annual article, by K. G. Fletcher, on Swiss insurance industry developments. Includes 1 table showing top 10 companies ranked by value of premiums written (in Swiss francs), 1982 with comparison to 1981.

For description of article for 1983, see C1050-1.512 below.

C1050–1.507: May 1984 (Vol. 85, No. 1)

1983 UNDERWRITING RESULTS—AN UPDATE

(p. 16-20) By John C. Burridge. Article on underwriting results for the property/casualty insurance industry, 1983. Data are based on information supplied by property/casualty companies representing approximately 99.5% of the industry.

Includes text data and 2 tables showing property/casualty premiums written and earned, losses incurred, underwriting expense and gain or loss, policyholder dividend and surplus, operating and net investment income, and pure loss and selected other financial ratios, 1983 with 4th quarter detail, and comparisons to 1978 and 1982. Data include some detail by line of coverage and for 5 major insurers and stock, mutual, and reciprocal companies.

Lines of coverage include fire, allied, homeowners and commercial multiple peril, inland marine, workers' compensation, medical malpractice, other liability, and auto liability and physical damage.

REFUTING THE DEATH KNELL

(p. 32-34, 108) By Dennis H. Pillsbury. Article discussing market outlook for independent insurance agencies. Data are from *Best's Executive Data Service*. Includes 2 tables showing independent agency market shares, 1978-82; and acquisition expense/net premiums ratios aggregated for top 5 independent agency companies and for top 4 direct writers, 1982; all by line of insurance.

Lines of insurance include homeowners, commercial multiple peril, workers' compensation, general liability, and various types of auto liability.

WORLD INSURANCE FORUM: ATHENS

(p. 92-94) By John D. Polites. Article on Greek insurance industry developments. Includes 1 table showing insurance premium revenue (in drachmas) for Greek and foreign companies by line of coverage, 1982.

WORLD INSURANCE FORUM: TEL AVIV

(p. 94-96) By Shlomo Jannai. Article on Israeli non-life insurance industry developments. Data are from the Israeli insurance commissioner's office, and are shown in shekels.

Includes 1 table showing non-life insurance premiums written by Israeli and foreign companies/Lloyd's, fees retained by Israeli insurers, foreign reinsurers share of Israeli companies' business, and premiums written by Israeli reinsurers, 1982.

C1050–1.508: June 1984 (Vol. 85, No. 2)

200 LEADING PROPERTY/CASUALTY COMPANIES AND GROUPS, ANNUAL FEATURE

(p. 24-28) Annual article on 200 largest insurance companies in property/casualty premium income, 1983. Data are from Best's Executive Data Service. Includes text statistics and 2 tables ranking companies by property/casualty premiums, 1983, with comparison to 1978 and 1982. Tables also show 1983 accident/health, life, and total premiums, and total premium rank, for top 100 companies.

ECONOMIC FACTORS IN PROPERTY/LIABILITY INSURANCE CLAIMS COSTS, ANNUAL FEATURE

(p. 68, 70) Annual article, by Norton E. Masterson, on economic factors affecting insurance claim settlement costs. Includes 2 tables showing CPI (total and for auto body work), and indexes of physician fees, hospital room rates, and auto crash part costs, Dec. 1981-83; and claim settlement cost indexes for 14 lines of property and liability insurance coverage, 1975-84.

C1050–1.509: July 1984 (Vol. 85, No. 3)

INSURANCE PREMIUM DISTRIBUTION, 1983, ANNUAL FEATURE

(p. 14-16) Annual article, by John C. Burridge, analyzing property/casualty insurance premiums written in the U.S. in 1983, including leading insurers and distribution of premiums by line of business and State.

Data are from Best's Executive Data Service, and cover more than 1,600 companies representing 98% of total U.S. business.

Includes 4 tables as follows:

[1] Percent of property/casualty market [for national and regional agency, and direct writer insurers, 1974-83].

[2] Leading insurers and their market share [ranked by premiums written in 1983, showing change from 1982, and market share, 1982-83, for each of 20 companies].

[3] Premium distribution by line [showing for each line of business: premiums written in 1983; change from 1982; loss ratio, 1982-83; and 3 leading writers and their share of total premiums for the line, with the line's share of the top writer's total premiums, 1983].

[4] Insurance premium distribution and leading writers by State [showing for each State: rank order, direct premiums, percent of U.S. total, loss ratio, change in premiums from 1982, and 3 leading writers and their share of State market, all for 1983].

WORLD INSURANCE FORUM: AMSTERDAM, ANNUAL FEATURE

(p. 70) Annual article, by F. Schreuder, on Dutch insurance industry developments, 1984. Data are from the Dutch Chamber of Insurance. Includes 2 tables showing the following for supervised Dutch companies: premiums (in guilders) by line of insurance, 1978-82; and technical balance (minus expenses), interest/other income, result, and solvency margin, all as percent of gross premiums, 1977-82.

C1050–1.510: Aug. 1984 (Vol. 85, No. 4)

AUTO INSURANCE, 1983, ANNUAL FEATURE

(p. 14-16, 68-69) Annual article, by Pamela Loos, analyzing the distribution and profitabil-

ity of auto insurance premiums written in 1983. Includes 3 text tables on market shares of national, regional, and direct writers, 1979-83; and the following data:

a.   20 leading companies in all types of auto insurance, and in private passenger and commercial auto insurance, showing for each company: premiums written, 1983 and change from 1982; market share, 1980-83; loss ratios, 1981-83; and auto insurance share of company's total premiums, 1983. 3 tables.

b.   State distribution of 1983 auto insurance business, showing for each State: premiums written, change from 1982, and national rank; loss ratio; and State market shares for national, regional, and direct writers, and for 3 leading companies. 1 table.

IS THE END IN SIGHT?

(p. 42-47) By Dennis H. Pillsbury and Peter van Aartrijk, Jr. Article on commercial insurance market conditions. Data are based on approximately 600 responses to a 1984 membership survey by Independent Insurance Agents of America.

Includes 2 tables showing percent of respondents reporting a firming of premium rates, by commercial insurance line; and percent reporting various indicators of rate firming.

ROBOTIC SAFETY: A POTENTIAL CRISIS

(p. 74-77, 95) By Robert Van Deest. Article, with 1 undated table showing distribution of occupational injuries from industrial robot use, by cause.

C1050–1.511: Sept. 1984 (Vol. 85, No. 5)

GAME HAS CHANGED

(p. 16-20, 118-126) By Peter B. Walker. Article discussing property/casualty underwriting profitability. Most data are from A. M. Best Co. and McKinsey and Co. Includes 4 charts showing trends in property/casualty surplus holdings, with detail for surplus components, and comparisons to UK; and net premiums written/surplus ratio; various periods 1951-83.

This is the 1st of 2 articles.

PROPERTY INSURANCE MARKETING, 1983, ANNUAL FEATURE

(p. 24-26, 130-138) Annual article, by Pamela Loos, analyzing property/casualty insurance marketing data, by State and leading company, for homeowners, commercial multiple peril, fire, and allied lines, 1983 and trends. Data are from A. M. Best Co.

Includes 8 tables showing the following for each line of insurance:

a.   For each State: direct premiums, rank, and gain; loss ratio; and market shares for national, regional, and direct writers, and for 3 top companies; 1983.

b.   For each of 20 leading companies: direct premiums, gain, and share of company's total premiums, 1983; company's market share, 1980-83; and loss ratio, 1981-83.

ALIVE AND WELL

(p. 78-82) By Samuel H. Weese and Gary E. Frohn. Article reporting on the surplus lines insurance market. Data are from responses of 30 wholesale brokers to a Nov. 1983 survey conducted by Gary E. Frohn. Includes 1 table showing respondents' expectations for short-, intermediate-, and long-term profits.

INSURING MAN'S BEST FRIEND

(p. 90-95) By Timothy L. Swiecki. Article on marketing of health insurance for household pets. Data are from a 1981 telephone survey conducted by Grey Advertising, Inc. Includes 2 charts showing number of dogs and cats in households; percent of households with dogs only, cats only, and both; and number of households with dogs or cats; 1981. Also includes listing of exclusions for all and 4 major pet insurance plans.

KEMPER ISSUES MID-1984 REPLACEMENT COST STUDY, ANNUAL FEATURE

(p. 97-98) Brief annual article, with 1 table showing percent change in replacement costs for machinery/equipment by type of industry and for industrial buildings by region, semiannually 2nd half 1981-1st half 1984. Data are from Kemper Group biennial surveys of over 300 North American manufacturers.

WORLD INSURANCE FORUM: BOMBAY, ANNUAL FEATURE

(p. 100-101) Annual article, by R. M. Solanki, on insurance industry developments in India. Includes 4 tables showing gross direct and net premium income (in rupees), and claims ratios, by line of coverage and company, 1982-83.

C1050–1.512: Oct. 1984 (Vol. 85, No. 6)

GAME HAS CHANGED

(p. 22-24, 137-143) By Peter B. Walker. Article discussing property/casualty underwriting profitability. Data are from industry annual convention statements. Includes 1 chart showing 25 companies ranked by insurance operating and premium/surplus ratios, by return on equity from insurance and from investments, and by total return on equity, 1979-83 period.

This is the 2nd of 2 articles.

CAN WE SAY GOODBYE TO UNDERWRITING PROFIT?

(p. 32-34, 62-78) By Klaus Gerathewohl. Article analyzing factors in property/casualty insurance industry profitability. Includes 1 chart showing property/casualty industry underwriting loss and investment income, 1979-83.

GENERAL LIABILITY/MEDICAL MALPRACTICE INSURANCE MARKETING, 1983, ANNUAL FEATURE

(p. 92-94, 146-148) Annual article analyzing general liability and medical malpractice insurance marketing data, by leading company and State, 1983 and trends. Includes 1 text table showing market shares for national, regional, and direct writers of liability insurance, 1979-83; and 5 detailed tables showing:

a. 20 leading companies in general liability and medical malpractice insurance and in both lines of insurance combined, showing for each company: premiums written in 1983, and change from 1982; market share, 1980-83; loss ratios, 1981-83; and liability insurance share of company's total premiums, 1983.

b. State distribution of 1983 general liability and medical malpractice insurance business, showing for each State: ranking; premiums written, and change from 1982; loss ratio; and State market shares for national, regional, and direct writers, and for 3 leading companies.

WORLD INSURANCE FORUM: ZURICH, ANNUAL FEATURE

(p. 115-116) Annual article, by K. G. Fletcher, on Swiss insurance industry developments. Data are from company annual reports, and are shown in Swiss francs. Includes 1 table showing top 8 companies ranked by value of premiums written, 1983, with change from 1982.

For description of previous article, for 1982, see C1050-1.506 above.

C1050–2   BEST'S REVIEW: LIFE/HEALTH INSURANCE EDITION
Monthly.   Approx. 125 p.
ISSN 0005-9706.   LC 80-175.
SRI/MF/not filmed

Monthly trade journal reporting on life/health insurance industry marketing trends and developments, management topics, current events, regulation, and finance.

General format:

a. Articles, often with substantial statistics, including annual data on underwriting activity and finances of individual companies.

b. Regular departmental features, including data on insurance company stocks.

c. Monthly feature, appearing in "Marketing Facts and Ideas" section, comparing life insurance policies of major insurers.

Monthly feature is described below and appears in all issues, beginning in Nov. 1983. All other features with substantial statistical content are described, as they appear, under "Statistical Features." Nonstatistical contents are not covered.

Availability: Best's Review: Life/Health Insurance Edition, Subscription Department, Oldwick NJ 08858, $14.00 per yr., single copy $1.50; SRI/MF/not filmed.

Issues reviewed during 1984: Nov. 1983-Oct. 1984 (P) (Vol. 84, Nos. 7-12; Vol. 85, Nos. 1-6).

MONTHLY POLICY COMPARISON

Monthly feature comparing life insurance policies of major insurers. Data generally are based on analysis of policies issued by 200 companies with at least $500 million in ordinary life insurance business during 1-2 previous years.

Each issue covers 1 type of policy, with updates usually appearing semiannually. Types of policies include universal life and interest sensitive whole life, participating whole life, graded premium whole life, indeterminate premium whole life and renewable term, flexible premium retirement annuities, and variable life.

Feature contains brief narrative and 1 table showing detailed characteristics of policies, including minimum issue amount, charges or premiums, policy loan rate, and cash value; all by company.

STATISTICAL FEATURES:

C1050–2.501: Nov. 1983 (Vol. 84, No. 7)

1982 EXPENSE/PREMIUM RATIOS

(p. 12) Brief article, with 1 text table showing expense/premium ratio aggregated for top 100 life insurance companies, 1979-82.

1982 LIFE/HEALTH BOND HOLDINGS, ANNUAL FEATURE

(p. 12) Annual article, with 1 chart and 1 table showing life/health insurance industry bond, short-term investment, and cash holdings, and total assets, 1981-82; and bond distribution by maturity period, 1982. Data are from industry annual convention statements.

For description of article for 1983, see C1050-2.511 below.

ACCIDENT AND HEALTH PREMIUMS, 1982, ANNUAL FEATURE

(p. 92-96) Annual article on accident/health insurance underwriting results, 1982. Includes 2 tables showing percent change in premiums written and earned 1978-82, and the following data shown for each of 300 largest companies: premiums written and earned, loss and expense ratios, and underwriting change, 1982; and company rank, 1981-82.

For description of article for 1983, see C1050-2.511 below.

C1050–2.502: Dec. 1983 (Vol. 84, No. 8)

ANNUITY INTEREST RATES

(p. 12) Article, with 1 chart showing insurance annuity median interest rates for qualified and nonqualified single premium deferred annuities and flexible premium retirement annuities, as of Aug. 1, 1981-83.

Data are from *Best's Insurance Management Reports,* and are based on analysis of interest rates offered by 118 life insurance companies with annuity sales over $10 million in 1982.

EXCLUSIVE AGENTS: END OF AN ERA?

(p. 22-25, 82-86) By James O. Mitchel. Article discussing trend in life insurance agents' placement of business with one vs. several companies. Data are from Life Insurance Marketing and Research Assn (LIMRA) biennial Survey of Agency Opinion, 1976-80; and surveys of exclusive agents for 8 unnamed companies, conducted by the companies during 4th quarter 1981-2nd quarter 1983 period.

Includes 4 tables showing LIMRA survey findings on percent of U.S. and Canadian agents placing all business with their primary company, by type of agent, selected years 1976-80; and 8-company survey findings on extent of exclusive agents' business placement with other companies, with detail by type of policy.

10-YEAR DIVIDEND COMPARISONS, ANNUAL FEATURE

(p. 62-72) Annual article comparing actual and 1973-scale dividend payments for average $25,000 life insurance policies issued in 1973 to males aged 35, by 71 leading life insurance companies, 1974-83. Data are from *Best's Flitcraft Compend.* Includes 2 tables showing the following for 1974-83:

a. Top 10 insurers ranked by average yearly payment and difference, and interest-adjusted payment and surrender cost indexes, for total period.

b. Actual and 1973-scale annual and total premiums, total dividends per $1,000 of insurance and net payments, 10th-year cash value and term dividend, and payment and surrender cost indexes and rankings; by insurer.

20-YEAR DIVIDEND COMPARISONS, ANNUAL FEATURE

(p. 73-80) Annual article comparing actual and 1963-scale dividends for average $10,000 life insurance policies issued in 1963 to males aged 35, by 70 leading life insurance companies. Data are from *Best's Flitcraft Compend.* Includes 2 tables showing the following for 1964-83:

a. Top 10 insurers ranked by average yearly payment and difference, and interest-adjusted payment and surrender cost indexes, for total period.

b. Actual and 1963-scale annual and total premiums, total dividends per $1,000 of insurance and net payments, 20th-year cash value and term dividend, and payment and surrender cost indexes and rankings; by insurer.

Data corrections appear in the Jan. 1984 issue (see C1050-2.503, below).

C1050–2.503: Jan. 1984 (Vol. 84, No. 9)

CORRECTION

(p. 104) Corrected data for article on 20-year life insurance dividend comparisons for policies issued in 1963, appearing in Dec. 1983 issue; for description, see C1050-2.502 above.

C1050–2.504: Feb. 1984 (Vol. 84, No. 10)

1982 ORDINARY BENEFITS

(p. 12) Article, with 1 chart showing total benefits paid, and distribution by benefit category, aggregated for top 100 life insurance companies, 1980-82.

1983 INSURANCE STOCK TRENDS, ANNUAL FEATURE

(p. 58-61, 108) Annual article, by John H. Lafayette, on the insurance stock performance of 81 major property/casualty, multiple line, life/health, and broker/agent companies, 1983. Article also appears in property/casualty insurance edition of *Best's Review,* and is described under C1050-1.504, above.

C1050–2.505: Mar. 1984 (Vol. 84, No. 11)

YEAR END RESULTS

(p. 12) Brief article on financial results for life/health insurance industry, based on performance of 130 mutual and 1,354 stock companies, 1982. Data are from *Best's Industry Composite of Life/Health Companies.* Includes 1 chart showing net operating gain from previous year for all mutual/stock companies, 1976-82.

LIFE INSURANCE COMPANY CHANGES, 1983, ANNUAL FEATURE

(p. 46-52, 103-106) Annual article on life insurance company transitions, 1983 and trends.

Includes lists of company formations, name changes, and mergers, 1983; and 2 tables showing number of new and retired companies 1974-83, and new, retired, and total companies, by State, 1983, with comparisons to 1982.

C1050–2.506: May 1984 (Vol. 85, No. 1)

ANNUITY INTEREST RATES PRESENTED

(p. 12) Article, with 1 table showing insurance annuity median interest rates for qualified and nonqualified single premium deferred annuities and flexible premium retirement annuities, as of Feb. and Aug. 1981-83 and Feb. 1984.

Data are based on analysis of interest rates offered by 111 life insurance companies with annuity sales over $10 million.

C1050–2.507: June 1984 (Vol. 85, No. 2)

INDIVIDUAL AND GROUP ANNUITY PREMIUMS IN 1983, ANNUAL FEATURE

(p. 74-80) Annual article on annuity premium income of 218 companies with annuity writings of at least $10 million in 1983. Includes text statistics, and 1 table showing individual and group direct and total premiums and annuity fund deposits, by company, ranked by total annuity funds, 1983.

C1050–2.508: July 1984 (Vol. 85, No. 3)

ON-LINE REPORTS ISSUES FIRST OF MAJOR INDUSTRY STATISTICAL STUDIES

(p. 12) Article, with 1 chart and 1 table showing life/health insurance issued and in force, and industry assets, actual 1982-83, and growth rate 1980-83. Data were compiled by A. M. Best Co.

UNIVERSAL LIFE AND BILLING SYSTEMS

(p. 25-28, 104) By John G. Metz. Article reporting on insurance industry administration of universal life insurance business. Data are based on a study of 110 universal life policies reissued during May-Aug. 1983 due to policyholder request for increased coverage.

Includes 1 chart and 4 tables showing the following for policy reissues resulting from policyholder request for coverage increase and from policyholder acceptance of company 10% coverage increase offer: distribution of policyholders by age, with comparison to all policyholders offered 10% coverage increase; and average value of premium and coverage increase per policy.

1983 SALES RESULTS OF THE LEADING LIFE COMPANIES, ANNUAL FEATURE

(p. 58-62) Annual ranked lists, with accompanying narrative analysis, of leading U.S./Canadian life insurance companies, 1983. Includes 3 tables showing leading 100, 50, and 25 companies in sales of ordinary, group, and industrial life insurance, respectively, ranked by insurance issued and in force, and gain in insurance in force, 1983 with comparisons to 1982.

LEADING LIFE COMPANIES IN THREE CATEGORIES, ANNUAL FEATURE

(p. 65-68) Annual article, with 3 tables showing 100 leading U.S./Canadian life insurance companies ranked by assets and insurance issued and in force; and 100 leading U.S. mutual and stock life companies ranked by assets and insurance in force; 1983 with comparisons to 1982.

500 LEADING LIFE COMPANIES IN TOTAL PREMIUM INCOME, ANNUAL FEATURE

(p. 76-79) Annual article, with 1 table showing 500 leading U.S/Canadian life/health insurance companies ranked by premium income, 1983, and including percent change from 1982, comparative 1982 and 1973 rank, and growth rate for 1973-83 period.

C1050–2.509: Aug. 1984 (Vol. 85, No. 4)

DIRECT PREMIUM VOLUME BY LINE

(p. 12) Article, with 1 chart showing distribution of life/health insurance direct premiums written, by type of policy and line of coverage, 1983. Data are from A. M. Best Co.

UNIVERSAL LIFE INSURANCE, 1983

(p. 88-92) Annual article, by Carole King, with 1 table showing universal life insurance direct and net premiums, and insurance issued and in force, for each of 242 companies, 1983, with comparisons to 1982. Data are based on responses of over 1,600 life insurance companies to a survey by A. M. Best Co.

C1050–2.510: Sept. 1984 (Vol. 85, No. 5)

SURVIVING IN A NEW ENVIRONMENT

(p. 16-20, 152-153) By Rebecca M. Hurtz and Mona J. Gardner. Article analyzing effect of financial institutions' deregulation on the life insurance industry. Data are from responses of 34 life insurance companies to an Apr. 1984 survey of top 53 companies based on 1982 assets.

Includes 3 tables showing survey response on use of checks for funds transfer, and of wire and electronic fund transfers; whether increase is planned in use of electronic fund tranfers, and in range of insurance products offered, over next 5 years; importance of selected securities in investment portfolio; whether deregulation will increase investment options; use of financial futures as a risk management tool; and types of insurance offered to policy holders.

HMOs: INJECTION OF COMPETITION

(p. 54-56, 157) By Stephen J. Kaufmann and Vickie A. Verwey. Article, with 1 table showing number of HMOs and enrollees, June or Dec. 1974-84.

LIFE INSURANCE COMPANY ASSETS, 1983, ANNUAL FEATURE

(p. 148-151) Annual article, by Carole King, on asset allocation and investment yields of 125 leading U.S. and Canadian life insurance companies, 1983. Includes 3 tables showing the following:

a. Asset allocation among bonds, preferred and common stock, mortgages, real estate, policy loans, cash, separate accounts, and other assets, 1983; and net yield on invested assets before Federal income tax, 1979-83; by company, ranked by total assets.

b. Aggregate asset allocation, 1979-83; and investment yield by asset type, aggregated for all, stock, and mutual life insurance companies, 1982-83.

C1050–2.511: Oct. 1984 (Vol. 85, No. 6)

LIFE/HEALTH INDUSTRY BOND HOLDINGS, ANNUAL FEATURE

(p. 12) Annual article, with 1 chart showing distribution of life/health insurance industry bond holdings by maturity period, 1983, with detail for maturity periods showing exceptional change in size of holdings since 1982.

For description of previous article, for 1982, see C1050-2.501 above.

1983 LAPSE RATIOS ON INDIVIDUAL BUSINESS, ANNUAL FEATURE

(p. 118-119) Annual article, by Carole King, on lapse ratios for individual life insurance policies of the 150 companies with most ordinary life insurance in force at year end 1983. Data are compiled by A. M. Best Company. Includes 1 table showing for each company: ratios, 1979-83; and average policy issued, 1983.

ACCIDENT AND HEALTH PREMIUMS, 1983, ANNUAL FEATURE

(p. 120-124) Annual article, by Carole King, on accident/health insurance underwriting results, 1983. Includes text table showing percent change in premiums written and earned 1979-83; and 1 detailed table showing the following data for each of 300 largest companies: premiums written and earned, loss and expense ratios, and underwriting change, 1983; and company rank, 1982-83.

For description of previous article, for 1982, see C1050-2.501 above.

C1200
Bill Communications

C1200–1   SALES AND MARKETING MANAGEMENT

Monthly, and special annual issues. Approx. 130 p.
ISSN 0163-7517.
LC 75-649980.
SRI/MF/excerpts, shipped quarterly

Monthly trade journal, with 4 additional annual survey issues, reporting on corporate sales and marketing management activities in industrial and consumer markets. Covers marketing strategies and problems; sales force performance, motivation, and compensation; analysis of market composition; selected company profiles; and personnel changes.

Data are from the Federal Government, private assns and research firms, individual companies, and the journal's own research.

Journal is published monthly, except semi-monthly in Feb., Apr., July, and Oct. These 4 additional issues are annual surveys of selling costs, industrial purchasing power, and consumer buying power (2 issues).

General format:

a. News briefs on sales or marketing topics, occasionally statistical; including a recurring S&MM Barometer table or chart on selected economic indicators, with brief accompanying narrative.

b. Feature articles, some with statistics, including annual surveys of sales meeting practices, employee incentive programs, and executive compensation; and narrative monthly depts.

c. S&MM Marketgraph, recurring market analysis feature, usually with charts and tables on sales and marketing opportunities in specific markets.

d. Recurring S&MM Salesgraph, usually presenting 1 table, with brief accompanying narrative, on sales or shipments of specific products.

All features with substantial statistical content are described, as they appear, under "Statistical Features." Nonstatistical features or issues are not covered.

Availability: Sales and Marketing Management, Subscription Service Department, PO Box 588, King of Prussia PA 19406, $36.00 per yr., single copy $5.00, special issue prices vary; SRI/MF/excerpts for all portions described under "Statistical Features;" shipped quarterly.

Issues reviewed during 1984: Nov. 14, 1983-Oct. 29, 1984 (P) (Vol. 131, Nos. 7-8; Vol. 132, Nos. 1-8; Vol. 133, Nos. 1-6).

STATISTICAL FEATURES:

C1200–1.501: Nov. 14, 1983 (Vol. 131, No. 7)

COMPUTERS IN SCHOOLS

(p. 19) Table showing percent of public schools with microcomputers, by level, 1981/82. Data are from the NCES.

ROSIER FORECASTS—SORT OF

(p. 20) Article, with 1 table showing 21 SIC 2- to 4-digit industries, ranked by estimated value of 1983 shipments (in constant 1972 dollars), and also showing revised and original percent growth forecasts for 1982/83. Data are from Bureau of Industrial Economics.

HOW CORPORATE TRAVEL COSTS ARE CHANGING

(p. 22) Article, with 1 table showing average monthly expenditures per person for various aspects of corporate travel, 1981-82 and 1st 8 months 1983. Data are from PHH Group.

S&MM MARKETGRAPH

(p. 41) "Clustering Takes on an Hispanic Flavor." Shows Hispanic population distribution by State or State group and country of origin, and percent of families with children under 18 by race and for Hispanics, 1980. Data are from the Census Bureau.

MEETINGS CARRY THE MESSAGE, ANNUAL FEATURE

(p. 66-76) Annual survey article, by Rayna Skolnik, on sales meeting practices. Data are based on 235 responses to an Aug. 1983 survey of S&MM corporate subscribers. Includes 12 tables showing response distribution for the following:

a. Company annual sales, size of sales force, use of own sales force vs. independent representatives, and use of distributors and their involvement in sales meetings.

b. Company annual sales meeting budget and whether reduced from last year, agenda items and preparation, actual and planned use of teleconferences, and meeting sites and selection factors.

C1200–1.502: Dec. 5, 1983 (Vol. 131, No. 8)

STAYING ALIVE

(p. 22) Article, with 1 table showing consumer expenditures for hospital, physician, and nursing home care, 1978 and 2003. Data are from NCHS.

C1200–1.503: Jan. 16, 1984 (Vol. 132, No. 1)

MARKETERS CHOOSE THEIR WEAPONS, RECURRING FEATURE

(p. 70-76) Recurring article, by Steven Mintz, on audiovisual (AV) equipment use in company sales presentations. Data are from responses of 153 sales/marketing executives to a 1983 S&MM survey, and from responses to a similar 1981 survey. Includes 1 table and 6 charts showing distribution of responses to questions on AV equipment uses, budget, and purchase plans.

For description of 1981 survey results, see SRI 1981 Annual, under C1200-1.204.

C1200–1.504: Feb. 6, 1984 (Vol. 132, No. 2)

S&MM MARKET HIGHLIGHT: FASTEST-GROWING SERVICES

(p. 16) News brief, with 1 table showing consumer expenditures for 5 types of services, 1982 with percent change from 1981. Data are from the Census Bureau.

S&MM BAROMETER

(p. 21) Shows total and manufacturing employment by region, Oct. 1983 with percent change from Oct. 1982. Data are from BLS.

S&MM MARKETGRAPH

(p. 34) "Where You'll Find Discretionary Dollars." Shows number of households with discretionary income and amount of discretionary income, by pre-tax income category, with demographic detail for "typical" discretionary income households, various periods 1980-81. Data are from the Conference Board and Census Bureau.

PCs AND MARKETERS FORGE A PRODUCTIVE ALLIANCE

(p. 35-39) By Norman Wiener. Article, with 1 undated table showing personal computer applications ranked by sales managers' ratings of importance. Data are from an Alexander Hamilton Institute survey of sales managers.

C1200–1.505: Feb. 20, 1984 (Vol. 132, No. 3)

[Special issue price is $35.00.]

1984 SURVEY OF SELLING COSTS ANNUAL FULL-ISSUE FEATURE

(p. 11-135) Annual survey issue, for 1984, on trends in the component costs of selling, including costs in 86 major metro areas; compensation levels; sales meetings, training, and support; and transportation. Also includes selling costs in 6 Canadian metro areas.

Data are from S&MM survey research, Federal Government, private corporations and research firms, and trade assns.

Contents:

Section I, features and highlights, with 4 charts and 17 tables. (p. 11-43)

Sections II-VI, covering individual sales cost components, with 5 charts and 43 tables. (p. 45-134)

All charts and tables are listed below.

CHARTS AND TABLES:

[Data are shown for 1983, unless otherwise noted. Data by industry are shown for various major industry groups.]

SECTION I. SURVEY FEATURES

[Tables and charts [1-2] and [7] show data for the following cost components: food/drink, lodging, and auto rental. Types of salesperson are account representative, detail salesperson, sales engineer, industrial products salesperson, and service salesperson.]

[1-2] S&MM's projection of 1984 [U.S.] selling cost index; and U.S. selling cost index [1972-83]. [table and chart] (p. 12-13)

[3-4] Increases in Canadian field selling costs [1982-83]; and S&MM's Canadian selling cost index [1974-83; for food/drink and lodging]. [table and chart] (p. 14)

[5] S&MM's 1984 cost per call: inching up [1979-83]. [chart] (p. 14)

[6] Fluctuations in cost per sales call [by type of salesperson, 1983 median and trends from 1974]. (p. 17)

[7] Changes in U.S. selling cost index components [1981-83]. (p. 17)

[8] S&MM's regional and national selling cost averages and per diem indexes. (p. 19)

[9] High-cost markets and low-cost markets [top and bottom 10-13 SMSAs ranked by per diem sales cost index]. (p. 21)

[10] Where sales costs are rising the fastest [9 SMSAs, annual percent change 1981-83]. (p. 28)

[11] Evening dining costs in [15] major cities. (p. 32)

[12] Selling expense index [1972-83]. [chart] (p. 36)

I.1-I.4. Typical salespeople's call patterns [average calls per day and per year, and days in field per year]; direct sales costs of salesperson's calls; direct sales costs per salesperson's call; and cost per call by effective call days per week; [all by type of salesperson]. (p. 39)

I.5-I.9. [Tables illustrate computation of sales call efficiency indexes]. (p. 42-43)

SECTION II. METRO SALES COSTS: U.S. AND CANADA

II.1-II.2. Selling costs in 86 major U.S. markets and in [6] major Canadian markets [for lodging; meals; per diem total, with increase from 1982 and index; cost of 2 drinks; airport to downtown by taxi and limousine; and per diem auto rental]. (p. 46-56)

II.3. Meal and lodging tax rates by metro market [for each market included in tables II.1-II.2]. (p. 57)

SECTION III. COMPENSATION

III.1. Salespeople's annual compensation [salary and incentive pay for consumer and industrial products sectors, by salesperson level, 1982-83]. (p. 60)

III.2. Sales force selling expenses as a percentage of sales in major industries [compensation, and travel/entertainment, 1982-83]. (p. 60)

III.3. Total selling expenses as a percentage of company sales [by industry, 1982-83]. (p. 61)

III.4. Compensation of sales trainees by industry [middle 50% range, median, and average]. (p. 61)

III.5. Total compensation [of salespeople] by experience level and type of plan [1981 and 1983]. (p. 61)

III.6. Alternative sales compensation and incentive plans [distribution of companies by type of plan used, for consumer and industrial products and other industries, with total industry comparison to 1982]. (p. 61)

III.7.-III.8. How compensation for salespeople and sales-support personnel is growing [by level of authority or experience, 1977-83]. [charts] (p. 62-63)

III.9. Manufacturers' representatives' commissions [average high and low rates, by industry]. (p. 66)

III.10. Compensation for three types [experience levels] of salesperson by industry [with percent change 1981-83]. (p. 66)

III.11. Turnover rates by industry [for resignations, discharges, retired, and other]. (p. 67)

III.12-III.14. Starting salaries [offered to] trainees with college degrees [1982-83], [and to] college graduates to be hired [from classes of 1983-84]; and median starting salaries paid to college graduates [1983; all shown for bachelor's degrees and master of business administration (MBA) degrees or candidates, by sales function and/or field]. (p. 68)

III.15. Salary statistics for MBA graduates entering industrial marketing [average salary and range, classes of 1982-83]. (p. 68)

SECTION IV. SALES MEETINGS AND SALES TRAINING

[Tables IV.1-IV.3 show data by type of company: industrial products, consumer products, and services.]

IV.1. Average cost of sales training per salesperson [training/salary cost and median training period, 1982-83]. (p. 72)

IV.2. Sites most frequently used for sales training [and median length of training time]. (p. 72)

IV.3. Length of training period for new salespeople [1982-83]. (p. 73)

IV.4. Sales meetings costs [for 30 cities: lodging, food/beverage, hospitality functions, and meeting rooms]. (p. 76-90)

IV.5. Conference centers: learning away from it all [facilities and rates for 12 centers]. (p. 92-95)

IV.6. Selected resort hotels: combining learning with luxury [facilities, and rates by season, for 27 hotels]. (p. 96-103)

IV.7-IV.8. Selected airport hotels [for 20 cities] and budget motel chains [for 8 cities; facilities and rates]. (p. 104-109)

SECTION V. SALES SUPPORT AND INCENTIVES

V.1. Selected incentive travel destinations: locations for motivation [air fare, lodging, meal, and group activity costs for 19 U.S. and foreign locations]. (p. 112-114)

V.2. Expected increases in 1984 trade show exhibition costs [by component]. (p. 114)

V.3-V.4. Audiovisual equipment purchase and rental costs [by type of equipment, 1982-83]. (p. 116)

V.5. Typical trade show exhibit costs [by component]. (p. 116)

V.6. Expected 1984 advertising costs: up a hair [cost index by media, 1980-84]. (p. 118)

V.7. Use of commission dollars by [manufacturers' representative] agencies [distribution by function]. [chart] (p. 118)

V.8. Estimated advertising percentages [of net sales] in selected industries [1982-84, and percent change from 1981]. (p. 120)

SECTION VI. TRANSPORTATION

VI.1-VI.2. Fleet car operating costs, by region [no date]; and 5-year forecast of fleet car costs [by component, 1984 and 1989]. (p. 124)

VI.3. Automobile fleet purchase costs [for selected models, by engine size, 1983-84]. (p. 124)

VI.4. Auto mileage reimbursement plans [distribution of consumer and industrial products companies and other companies, by type of plan used, 1982-83]. (p. 127)

VI.5. Breakdown of fleet car operating costs [1983, and percent change from 1982]. (p. 127)

VI.6. Average annual travel expenses by [manufacturers' representative] agencies [by agency type, 1982-83]. (p. 127)

VI.7. Annual operating costs for selected 1984 model cars [annual variable and fixed costs by make and model]. (p. 127)

VI.8. Auto rental companies used by manufacturers' [representatives]. [chart] (p. 127)

VI.9. Sources of autos used by salespeople [company and employee owned and leased, 1978-83]. [chart] (p. 128)

VI.10. Fuel cost and consumption by car size [1984 models]. (p. 130)

VI.11. Average cost of 15 frequently made moves [between metro areas, 1983 and percent change from 1982]. (p. 130)

VI.12. Air fares for the 25 most traveled routes [1982-83]. (p. 130)

VI.13. Average cost of moving between selected cities. (p. 132)

VI.14. Standard and economy car rental rates [by region and city/metro area] (p. 134)

C1200–1.506: Mar. 12, 1984 (Vol. 132, No. 4)

FOR IBM, THE BEST IS YET TO COME

(p. 13-16) Article, with 1 chart showing homes with personal computers (total and as a percent of TV homes), 1982, 1985, and 1990. Data are from The Yankee Group.

S&MM MARKET HIGHLIGHT: TOGETHERNESS ON THE FARM

(p. 16) News brief, with 2 charts showing distribution of farm and nonfarm women by marital status, 1982. Data are from the Census Bureau.

S&MM BAROMETER

(p. 18) "A Banner Year for Industrial Sellers." Shows percent change in real shipments, 1982/83 and 1983/84, and percent change from peak year to 1984, for 10 SIC 3- and 4-digit manufacturing industries. Data are from Bureau of Industrial Economics.

S&MM MARKETGRAPH

(p. 61) "Families: What's Traditional?" Shows number of households, families as a percent of households, and distribution of families by household type, 1960, 1970, and 1983. Data are from Census Bureau.

C1200–1.507: Apr. 2, 1984 (Vol. 132, No. 5)

S&MM MARKET HIGHLIGHT: A SURPRISE IN 'GROWTH' STATES

(p. 25) News brief, with 1 table showing population percent change 1980-83 period, and population 1983, for 5 States with greatest and least change. Data are from Census Bureau.

WHO'S MINDING THE SALES FORCE?

(p. 35-36) Article, with 1 undated table showing frequency and types of reports that sales managers require from their manufacturer representatives. Data are from a Dartnell Management Research Panel survey of 55 companies.

GOOD TIMES OR BAD, MOTIVATORS RAGE ON, ANNUAL FEATURE

(p. 80-86) Annual article, by Al Urbanski, on use, costs, and types of employee incentive programs in sales organizations. Data are based on 313 responses to a Jan. 1984 survey of S&MM subscribers.

Includes 1 chart and 3 tables showing distribution of responses to questions on line of business, annual sales, use of incentives or formal recognition programs, user program budgets and plans for 1984, and non-user reasons and future incentive plans if any; and incentive spending trends for sales force and dealer merchandise and travel awards, 1979-83.

FORGET ABOUT A PC SHAKEOUT

(p. 160) Brief article, with 1 chart showing number of personal computer marketers, 1979-84. Data are from International Data Corp.

C1200–1.508: Apr. 23, 1984 (Vol. 132, No. 6)

1984 SURVEY OF INDUSTRIAL AND COMMERCIAL BUYING POWER, ANNUAL ISSUE

Annual survey of 1983 industrial and commercial activity, as indicated by number of establishments, employment, and shipment values, with industry concentration measures, and selected trend and outlook data.

Presents data for detailed nonagricultural industries, including data by leading county for SIC 4-digit industries. Survey is intended primarily as a guide for industrial marketing.

Most data are from Trinet, Inc.; other data sources include the Commerce Dept.

Contents:

a. Contents listing. (p. 5)

b. Highlights, including narrative articles with 10 interspersed survey highlight charts and tables, listed below. (p. 6-28)

c. Statistical section, with user guides, and 2 detailed tables also listed below. (p. 47-111)

TABLES AND CHARTS:

[Tables show data for 1983, unless otherwise noted. Total plants or establishments generally include only units with 20 or more employees. Large plants or establishments are units with 100 or more employees. Leading counties are counties with 1,000 or more employees in the applicable SIC 4-digit industry.]

HIGHLIGHTS TABLES

[1] Average plant totals: the Southwest is hot [average manufacturing shipment value per plant, by region]. [chart] (p. 7)

[2] 50 leading metro markets in manufacturing activity [ranked by shipment value, and also showing share of U.S. shipments, and number of plants]. (p. 8)

[3] Summary of 2-digit major groups in this year's SICBP [total and large establishments, employment, shipments/receipts, and percent of shipments produced in large plants]. (p. 10)

[4] Top 50 counties in [number of] manufacturing plants [and including share of U.S. shipments]. (p. 11)

[5] Nation's largest employers: 8062 is the big winner [top 6 SIC 4-digit manufacturing and nonmanufacturing industries ranked by total employment]. (p. 14)

[6] Regional manufacturing: Who's got the biggest slice? [distribution of manufacturing shipments by region]. [chart] (p. 17)

[7] Survey vs. the Bureau: [comparison of] 1983 shipment totals as reported by [Trinet, Inc. and Census Bureau, for selected SIC 2-digit manufacturing industries]. (p. 21)

[8] Regional and State summaries of manufacturing markets [total and large plants, shipment value, share of U.S. shipments, plant index, and percent of shipments produced in large plants, 1982-83]. (p. 22)

[9] Top 50 counties in manufacturing activity [ranked by shipment value, and including plants, leading SIC industry and shipment value, shipments of leading SIC industry as percent of U.S. total for that SIC and of the county's all-manufacturing total, and comparisons to 1982]. (p. 23)

[10] Profile of the 50 biggest manufacturing industries [ranked by shipment value, and including plants, shipment index, percent of shipments produced in large plants, and comparisons to 1982]. (p. 24)

BY SIC 4-DIGIT INDUSTRY

[11] U.S. establishment and shipments/receipts totals for 4-digit SIC industries [total and large establishments, employment, shipments/receipts, and percent of shipments produced in large plants]. (p. 50-53)

STATE AND COUNTY DATA

[12] State and county totals for manufacturing and nonmanufacturing industries surveyed [total and large establishments, shipment value, share of U.S. shipments, and percent of shipments produced in large plants, by State and county, with SIC 4-digit industry detail for leading counties]. (p. 54-111)

C1200–1.509: May 14, 1984 (Vol. 132, No. 7)

GRAY MATTERS

(p. 20) Article, with 1 table showing top 10 metro areas ranked by percent of population over 50 years old. Data are from S&MM.

S&MM BAROMETER

(p. 25) "Heeding the Need for Plants and Equipment." Shows planned capital outlays, 1984 with percent change from 1982-83; and anticipated percent change in sales, 1984 vs. 1983; by industry division and major manufacturing industry group. Data are from Commerce Dept.

S&MM MARKETGRAPH

(p. 56) "New York, NY: Going Down, but Still Tops." Shows top 5 TV markets ranked by population and including share of U.S. population for each, with some additional demographic data for NYC. Data sources include A. C. Nielsen Co.

D(ECISION) DAY NEARS FOR SALESPEOPLE

(p. 106) By Thayer C. Taylor. Brief article, with 1 undated table estimating operating cost and direct and indirect savings of computerized ordering, for grocery industry distributors, brokers, and manufacturers. Data are from Arthur D. Little, Inc.

C1200–1.510: June 4, 1984 (Vol. 132, No. 8)

59 MILLION TV DINNERS

(p. 16) Article, with 1 undated table showing total and single-person households, for 6 States with highest proportion of single-person households. Data are from S&MM.

SOFTWARE'S DISTRIBUTION CHANNELS

(p. 22) Brief article, with 1 table showing personal computer software sales by distribution method, 1983 and 1988. Data are from Future Computing, Inc.

LESS FEM-LIB

(p. 26-27) Article, with 1 table showing percent of women marketers involved in selected business activities, 1980 and 1984. Data are from a Schoonmaker Associates survey.

C1200–1.511: July 2, 1984 (Vol. 133, No. 1)

HOW THE AFFLUENT GET THEIR KICKS

(p. 16) Article, with 1 table showing median household effective buying income (EBI) and percent of population aged 18-49, for 10 metro areas with EBI over $30,000 and 18-49 population of over 45%. Data are from S&MM's *1983 Survey of Buying Power.*

S&MM SALESGRAPH

(p. 26) "Consumers Pick Their Product." Table showing percent of consumers planning to buy personal computers and videocassette recorders, by family income; age of household head; whether purchase is 1st time, replacement, or extra; and type of household (family, and single male and female); 1984. Data are from an Industrial Marketing Research survey of 5,500 households.

COMPUTERVISION FIGHTS TO STAY NO. 1

(p. 43-46) Article, with 2 charts showing sales of computer-aided design/computer-aided manufacturing industry, and market share for top 5 companies, 1980 and 1983-84. Data are from Daratech, Inc.

C1200–1.512: July 23, 1984 (Vol. 133, No. 2)

[Issue price is $65.00.]

1984 SURVEY OF BUYING POWER, PART I, ANNUAL ISSUE

Annual survey of population, effective buying income, and retail sales of U.S. and Canadian markets, 1983. Most data are from S&MM calculations, 1980 Census of Population and Housing, other Census Bureau reports, Dept of Labor, and Statistics Canada.

Contents:

Contents listing. (p. A5)

Section A. Feature articles on marketer use of buying power survey, and Federal reclassification of metro areas, with interspersed survey and market highlights charts and tables; and S&MM Marketgraphs. (p. A7-A56)

Section B-C. National, regional, and State summaries, and metro area rankings; and metro area, county, and city data. (p. B1-B55, C1-C214)

Section D. Canadian Survey of Buying Power. (p. D1-D18)

Statistical portions of sections are described below.

SURVEY SECTIONS:

[Data are for 1983, unless otherwise noted. Data reflect Federal reclassification of metro statistical areas.

Abbreviations: EBI (effective buying income) and BPI (buying power index).]

SECTION A: HIGHLIGHTS AND MARKETGRAPHS

Highlights Charts and Tables

[1] Shoulder to shoulder: [10] metros with the highest population density. (p. A8)

[2] Consolidated area losses: Midwest exodus and one surprise [population for 6 consolidated MSAs, 1982-83]. (p. A9)

[3] Retail store sales, survey vs. Census Bureau [by selected kind of business, 1983 and percent change from 1982]. (p. A10)

[4-5] For richer or for poorer: median household EBI for the top 10 and bottom 10 metros. (p. A19)

[6-7] Threads and bread: the Nation's biggest apparel markets and their respective income levels, and the situation reversed [apparel/accessory sales and median household EBI, for 10 metro areas with highest apparel/accessory sales and highest EBI]. (p. A19)

[8] The top 25: leading black metros [top 25 metro areas ranked by black population, and including blacks as a percent of total metro population]. (p. A28)

[9] Nuances of regional growth [population, 1983 and percent change from 1980; and share of U.S. population, 1970, 1980, and 1983; by census division and State]. (p. A34)

[10] Consolidated metropolitan statistical areas [population and rank]. (p. A50)

S&MM Marketgraphs

(p. A52) "The Hispanic Market: Talk About Concentration!" 1 chart and 2 tables showing top 5 States ranked by Hispanic population, with share for largest country of origin; top 25 metro markets ranked by Hispanic population, with Hispanics as a percent of total population; and distribution of Hispanics by country of origin; various years 1980-83.

(p. A54) "Rural Trends: What's Going on Out There?" 2 charts and 2 tables showing top 25 nonmetro counties ranked by median household EBI; percent increase in metro and nonmetro retail sales, for 12 States; and metro and nonmetro median household income, and household distribution by income category; various periods 1979-83.

(p. A56) "Households: Reversing the Flow." 2 charts and 2 tables showing top 25 metro markets ranked by number of single-person households; top 10 States ranked by household growth; and number of households with distribution by size, and householder distribution by age group; various periods 1980-83.

SECTION B: U.S., REGIONAL, AND STATE SUMMARIES; METRO MARKET RANKINGS

(p. B1-B55) Contains table listing, 28 tables listed below, and alphabetical listing of over 300 metro markets covered. Tables [1-3] show data by census division and State; titles begin "Regional and State summaries of..."

[1] Population [median age, population by age group, and households]. (p. B3)

[2] EBI [total, per capita, average and median household EBI; and households by EBI group]. (p. B5)

[3] Retail sales [total, per household, and by kind of business; and indexes of sales activity, buying power, and quality]. (p. B7)

[4-28] Metro market ranking: [by total], suburban, black, and Spanish-origin population; children under 6 and 6-17, and population 35-49 years old; households; EBI; suburban EBI; median household EBI; households with EBI $50,000/over; BPI; total and per household retail sales; [sales for 9 kinds of business]; and one-person households. (p. B9-B50)

SECTION C: METRO AREA, COUNTY, AND CITY DATA LISTED BY STATES

(p. C1-C214) Contains table listing, user guide, glossary, and the following data for each metro area, county, and city arranged by State: population (total population, median age, population distribution by age group, and households); retail sales (total and by kind of business); and EBI (total and median household EBI, household distribution by EBI group, and BPI).

SECTION D: CANADA: A WAIT-AND-SEE ATTITUDE

(p. D1-D18) Contains introductory article; and population, retail sales, and EBI data comparable to that described in Section C, shown by Province, S&MM and census metro area, city, and county. No population age data are presented for Canada.

C1200–1.513: Aug. 13, 1984 (Vol. 133, No. 3)

S&MM SALESGRAPH

(p. 21) "Coming Up: Another Good Year." Chart showing housing starts and new car sales, and percent change in real GNP, industrial production, disposable personal income, and nonresidential fixed investment, 1984-85. Data are from Eggert Economic Enterprises, Inc.

S&MM MARKET HIGHLIGHT: WORKING WIVES DON'T PROSPER IN SALES

(p. 24) News brief, with 1 chart comparing mean earnings of husbands vs. wives, by occupational group, 1981. Data are from Census Bureau.

CORPORATE TRAVEL: HIGH COST OF EATING

(p. 30) Brief article, with 1 table showing meals purchased and average cost, for corporate travelers dining alone, 1980-84. Data are from PHH Group.

UNEXPECTED 11% RAISE A TREND? ANNUAL FEATURE

(p. 45-54) Annual article reporting on 1983 compensation of 105 sales and marketing executives of 104 companies in 24 industry groups. Data are based on an S&MM annual survey.

Includes 1 table showing salaries/fees/bonuses/commissions, and long-term gain realized, for each executive, with company name, sales, profit/loss, and industry group, 1983 and selected changes from 1982; and 1 table showing summary data for top 10 executives.

S&MM MARKETGRAPH

(p. 54) "Wired Home: New Insights into the Electronic Mix." Shows number and percent of households with cable TV, video game console, videocassette recorder, and home computer, with detail for cable TV subscribers and home computer owners; and percent of households purchasing each product within the past year; 1983.

Data are based on a recent survey of 4,237 households, conducted by International Data Corp.'s Link Resources.

C1200–1.514: Sept. 10, 1984 (Vol. 133, No. 4)

S&MM SALESGRAPH

(p. 36, 39) "Harbinger of a Merry Christmas." Chart showing percent increase in shipments of 6 major consumer items, 1st half 1983-84. Data are from Assn of Home Appliance Manufacturers and Electronic Industries Assn.

WHAT MARKETERS LOVE AND HATE ABOUT THEIR MANUFACTURERS' REPS

(p. 60-65) By Earl Hitchcock. Survey article on company satisfaction with independent sales representatives and distributors, based on 200 responses to a recent S&MM survey.

Includes 6 tables showing survey response concerning types of representatives and distributors used, satisfaction with their performance, reasons for lack of satisfaction, and types of training and marketing support most needed by sales representatives.

SALES COMPENSATION: IT'S UNFAIR

(p. 202) Article, with 1 table showing employment and earnings of nonretail sales workers, by sex and race (including Hispanic), 1979 or 1980. Data are from Census Bureau.

C1200–1.515: Oct. 8, 1984 (Vol. 133, No. 5)

LADY MEANS BUSINESS

(p. 19) Brief article, with 1 chart showing percent of business/management degrees awarded to women, by degree level, 1970/71 and 1981/82 academic years. Data are from NCES.

S&MM SALESGRAPH

(p. 26) "Working Couples Back in Style." Three charts showing number and weekly earnings of working couples, 2nd quarters 1982 and 1984; and working couples as percent of married-couple families, by race and for Hispanics, 2nd quarter 1984. Data are from BLS.

SPECIAL SECTION: FLEET CARS, ANNUAL FEATURE

Annual compilation of articles on developments affecting commercial car fleets. Data are from Runzheimer International. Articles with statistics are described below.

Feature published in 1983 was nonstatistical. For description of previous statistical feature, see SRI 1982 Annual, under C1200-1.315.

CARS THAT ARE HERE TO STAY

(p. 70-83) Article, with 1 undated table showing average operating cost per mile, ownership cost per month, and total annual cost, for typical fleet car, U.S. and 9 cities.

DEALERS REV UP THE WAR ON FLEET INCENTIVES

(p. 84-86) By Al Urbanski. Article with 1 table showing fleet car annual costs by type, and value of benefit to salesperson from use of car, 1973-84.

C1200–1.516: Oct. 29, 1984 (Vol. 133, No. 6)

[Issue price is $35.00.]

1984 SURVEY OF BUYING POWER, PART II, ANNUAL ISSUE

Part II of a special annual survey of population, effective buying income (EBI), and retail sales of U.S. markets, 1983 and 1988, with summary population projections to 2080. Most data are from S&MM calculations and Census Bureau reports.

Contents:

Contents listing. (p. 5)

Section A. Narrative features and survey and market highlights, with 10 tables. (p. 7-38)

Section B-F. Merchandise line sales; metro area market projections; and newspaper, TV, and zip code markets; with 25 tables. (p. 41-174)

Tables are listed below.

For description of Part I, see C1200-1.512 above.

TABLES:

[Abbreviations: EBI (effective buying income); ADI (area of dominant influence); BPI (buying power index).]

SECTION A. SURVEY HIGHLIGHTS

[1] Metro market outlook through 1988 [metro and nonmetro population, households, EBI, retail sales, and BPI; 1988 projections, and percent change for 1983-88 period]. (p. 8)

[2] Top 50 markets in 1988 [ranked by population, 1988, with percent change from 1983, and 1983 rank]. (p. 9)

[3-4] Tomorrow's fastest growing and negative-growth markets [top 25 metro markets ranked by greatest population growth and loss, 1983-88 period, with population for 1988]. (p. 10)

[5] Reaching for households: the biggest ADIs and how they rate [top 25 ADIs ranked by population; with households, EBI, total retail sales, and rankings; 1983]. (p. 13)

[6] Most affluent markets of 1988: suburban metros hold the big bucks [top 50 metro markets ranked by per household EBI, 1988, with percent increase from 1983, and growth index]. (p. 14)

[7] 100 years and 83 million: what the Census Bureau says [population by age group, selected years 1980-2080]. (p. 16)

[8] How good are the survey's projections? [1983 population (actual and as projected by 1979 Survey of Buying Power), by census division, and for most populated States and metro areas]. (p. 22)

[9] Retail sales outlook, 1984-86 [sales by kind of business]. (p. 24)

[10] Where the Money's Going: 1988 average household EBI by State [1988, with percent increase from 1983]. (p. 29)

SECTION B. MERCHANDISE LINE SALES

[Tables [11-18] show 1983 data for the following merchandise lines: groceries/other foods, health/beauty aids, women's/girls' clothing, men's/boys' clothing, footwear, major household appliances, and furniture/sleep equipment.]

[11] Summary of merchandise line sales by [census division] and State [sales for all stores, and by store type (food, drug, apparel, department, or furniture/home furnishings/appliance stores, as applicable), for each merchandise line]. (p. 43)

[12-18] Metro market ranking [by sales, for each merchandise line]. (p. 44-50)

SECTION C. 1988 PROJECTIONS FOR U.S. METRO MARKETS

[Tables [19-20] show population, households, EBI, retail sales, and BPI, in indicated geographic detail, 1988 with comparisons to 1983.]

[19] Summary of projections by [census division] and State. (p. 52-53)

[20] Metro area projections [by State, SMSA, and selected smaller cities and metro counties]. (p. 54-94)

SECTIONS D-E. NEWSPAPER AND TV MARKETS

[Store groups are food, general merchandise, furniture/furnishings/appliances, automotive, and drugs.]

[21] Newspaper market ranking [by number of] households [1983]. (p. 97)

[22] Survey of newspaper markets [population; households; EBI; retail sales, total and by store group; and newspaper circulation related to number of households; by metro market, grouped by State, 1983]. (p. 98-148)

[23] Alphabetical listing of TV markets [showing each county's share of households in the ADI]. (p. 152-155)

[24] Survey of TV markets [population by age, households, black and Hispanic population, EBI, retail sales, and BPI, by TV ADI market grouped by State, 1983]. (p. 156, 162-170)

[25-29] Arbitron TV market (ADI) ranking [by] population, households, EBI, total retail sales, and BPI, [1983]. (p. 157-161)

SECTION F. ZIP CODE MARKETS

[30-35] [Top 50 zip code areas ranked by number of] children age 0 to 5 years; households with income of $75,000 and over; persons employed in manufacturing industries; Asian/Pacific Islander population; households with 6 or more persons; and households in mobile homes/trailers/boats/etc. (p. 171-174)

C1200–2 SURVEY OF BUYING POWER DATA SERVICE, 1983

Annual. 1983.
910 p. var. paging, looseleaf.
LC 79-643867.
SRI/MF/complete

Annual survey of consumer buying power, 1982, presenting detailed market, population, household, and retail sales data, by location. Includes market data projections for 1987, population comparisons to 1980, and retail sales comparisons to 1977. Data are shown for total U.S. and by census division, State, MSA, county, and TV area of dominent influence (ADI), with selected MSA and ADI rankings.

Data are from *Sales and Marketing Management* calculations, and Census Bureau reports, including 1977 Census of Retail Trade.

Market data generally include population and density, percent white population, households, effective buying income (EBI), retail sales, buying power index (BPI), and BPI for economy-, moderate-, and premium-priced products.

Population data include population by age and sex, and median age by sex.

Household data generally include number of households by age of householder, size, and EBI group; average household size; median and average household EBI; and per capita EBI.

Retail sales are shown by kind of business and selected merchandise line. Businesses generally include all food stores, supermarkets, eating/drinking places, general merchandise and department stores, apparel/accessory stores, furniture/home furnishings/appliance stores, automotive dealers, gasoline service stations, building materials/hardware dealers, and drugstores. Merchandise lines generally include groceries/other foods, drugs, health/beauty aids, major household appliances, TV, audio equipment/musical instruments and supplies, furniture/sleep equipment, men's/boy's clothing, women's/girl's clothing, and footwear.

Contains user's guide (p. 1-12); contents listing, definitions, and addenda (p. A1-A14); and 21 separately paginated sections arranged in 3 volumes, as follows:

Volume I: Market, Population, and Household Data

Section 1-2. Maps and selected summary MSA data (105 p.); and market, population, and household data, by census division and State (5 p.).

Section 3-7. MSA rankings, by selected market and household data (14 p.); and market, population, and household data, by MSA and county, arranged by State (367 p.).

Volume II: Retail Sales

Section 8-10. Retail sales by kind of business and merchandise line, by census division and State (7 p.); metro market rankings by retail sales, by kind of business (14 p.); and retail sales by kind of business, by MSA and county, arranged by State (145 p.).

Section 11-12. MSA rankings by retail sales, by merchandise line (11 p.); and retail sales by merchandise line, by MSA and aggregate for nonmetro areas, arranged by State (43 p.).

Volume III: Market Data Projections and ADI Data

Section 13-15. Market data projections, by census division, State, MSA, and county, with selected MSA rankings. (84 p.)

Section 16-21. ADI data, including market data and projections, and retail sales by kind of business and merchandise line, with ADI rankings. (66 p.)

Portions of this report, along with comparable data for Canada, appear in the 2nd July and Oct. issues of *Sales and Marketing Management*, covered by SRI under C1200-1.

Availability: Bill Communications, Sales and Marketing Management, Sales Builder Division, 633 Third Ave., New York NY 10017, $259.95; SRI/MF/complete.

C1200–3 SURVEY OF BUYING POWER FORECASTING SERVICE

Annual, discontinued.

Annual forecast of consumer buying power, discontinued with 1983 report (for description, see SRI 1983 Annual, under this number).

Data are no longer published, but are available on computer tape from: Bill Communications, Sales and Marketing Management, Sales Builder Division, 633 Third Avenue, New York NY 10017.

C1200–4   INCENTIVE MARKETING

Monthly. Approx. 150 p.
ISSN 0019-3364.
LC 52-41302.
SRI/MF/excerpts, shipped quarterly

Monthly journal reporting on the sales and consumer incentives market. Covers merchandise and travel incentives for salespeople and dealers; and coupons, premiums, gifts, sweepstakes/contests, and other types of consumer promotions.

Most data are from *Incentive Marketing* reader surveys covering companies that use incentive programs.

Issues generally contain several feature articles, occasionally with statistics; and numerous editorial depts. Annual statistical features include survey reports on incentive spending by industry. Nonstatistical travel and buyer's guides usually appear in Jan. and Feb.

Features with substantial statistical content are described, as they appear, under "Statistical Features." Each issue of the journal is reviewed, but an abstract is published in SRI monthly issues only when statistical features appear.

Prior to the Nov. 1983 issue, journal was described in SRI under C4425-2.

Availability: Bill Communications, Circulation Department, 633 Third Ave., New York NY 10017, $32.00 per yr., single copy $3.00, Dec. Facts issue $15.00; SRI/MF/excerpts for all portions described under "Statistical Features;" shipped quarterly.

Issues reviewed during 1984: Nov. 1983-Oct. 1984 (P) (Vol. 157, Nos. 11-12; Vol. 158, Nos. 1-10).

STATISTICAL FEATURES:

C1200–4.501: Nov. 1983 (Vol. 157, No. 11)

MAIL-IN PRICES UP AGAIN IN EARLY 1983, SEMIANNUAL FEATURE

(p. 46-47) Semiannual article reporting on consumer premium promotion trends, 1st half 1983. Data are from analyses of 190 promotions, and previous promotion studies. Includes 2 tables showing distribution of mail-in promotions by premium price, and of all promotions by sponsoring industry, 1st half 1982-83 and 2nd half 1982.

For description of previous article, see SRI 1983 Annual under C4425-2.404.

C1200–4.502: Dec. 1983 (Vol. 157, No. 12)

1982: A TOUGH YEAR FOR INCENTIVES, ANNUAL FEATURE

(p. 48-93) Annual survey report on incentive market trends. Covers merchandise and travel incentives for salespeople and dealers, and various types of consumer promotions.

Includes detailed data on incentive expenditures by type and industry, 1981-82, and summary trends from 1967.

Also includes cost per sales and dealer incentive award; travel incentive expenditures

on domestic vs. foreign trips, and trip costs; and relative effectiveness of 6 types of supermarket product promotions; various years 1977-82.

Data are from the 16th annual census survey, and previous surveys, of *Incentive Marketing* readers.

Contains 5 articles, with 16 charts and 6 tables, presenting overview (p. 48-74); and sales, dealer, travel, and consumer incentive reports (p. 75-93).

C1200–4.503: Feb. 1984 (Vol. 158, No. 2)

1983 REPORT: A CAUTIOUS YEAR, AS BUYERS WAIT FOR THE RECOVERY, ANNUAL FEATURE

(p. 13-34) Annual survey report on incentive market trends, by industry, 1982-83. Covers merchandise and travel incentives for salespeople and dealers, and consumer mail-in promotions and other premiums. Data are from annual census survey of *Incentive Marketing* readers.

Includes 3 charts and 2 tables showing detailed data on incentive expenditures by type and industry, and summary trends for trading stamp and business gift expenditures, 1982-83.

C1200–4.504: Mar. 1984 (Vol. 158, No. 3)

INSURANCE INCENTIVES: PLANNERS SEEK MORE BANG FOR THEIR INCENTIVE BUCKS, ANNUAL FEATURE

(p. 29-33) Annual article on insurance industry use of sales incentives. Data are from responses of 140 insurance marketing executives to a 1984 survey by *Incentive Marketing.* Includes 5 charts showing types of incentives used; reasons for using incentives; and spending distribution, median cost, and length of promotion period, for travel and merchandise awards.

C1200–4.505: Apr. 1984 (Vol. 158, No. 4)

EXECS' OPTIMISM FOLLOWS LAST YEAR'S SPURT OF ACTIVITY, ANNUAL FEATURE

(p. 32-38) Annual article on dealer incentive programs. Data are from a 1984 survey of 169 executives, and from previous surveys.

Includes text data and 5 charts showing sales gain with use of incentives, and incentive costs as percent of sales gain; average cost per award and spending plans, for merchandise and travel programs; dealer incentive objectives; types of incentives used most often and considered most effective; and means of obtaining and delivering awards; various years 1980-84.

C1200–4.506: May 1984 (Vol. 158, No. 5)

RECOVERY SPURS SOLID GAINS IN CONSUMER PREMIUM USAGE, SEMIANNUAL FEATURE

(p. 41-48) Semiannual article reporting on use of consumer premiums, 1983, based on responses of 179 companies to a 1984 survey by *Incentive Marketing.*

Includes 1 chart and 1 table showing consumer premium expenditures of top 10 user industries, with aggregate share of all spending for consumer premiums; and types of premiums considered most effective in achieving various objectives; 1983.

C1200–4.507: July 1984 (Vol. 158, No. 7)

WORLD TRAVEL SURVEY: THE LURE OF TRAVEL, ANNUAL FEATURE

(p. 51-62) Annual article on corporate use of travel incentives for salespeople, dealers, and distributors. Data are from 133 responses to a May 1984 survey of companies that use travel incentives, and from previous surveys.

Includes 5 charts and 2 tables showing top 10 industry groups ranked by incentive travel expenditures, 1983; and travel budget allocations, trip costs, sales gain with use of incentives, incentive costs as percent of sales, trip starts by month, and trip arrangement methods and destination preferences, generally 1984 with selected comparisons to 1982-83.

C1200–4.508: Aug. 1984 (Vol. 158, No. 8)

BUSINESS GIFTS WRAP-UP, ANNUAL FEATURE

(p. 21-28) Annual article reporting on business gift-giving practices. Data are based on 185 responses to a 1984 reader survey. Includes text data, and 6 tables showing gift sources and delivery and presentation methods, use of personalized gifts, and most popular gifts.

C1200–4.509: Oct. 1984 (Vol. 158, No. 10)

SALES INCENTIVES '84: BATTLING THE 'BLAHS'

(p. 57-66) Article reporting on use of incentive programs for salespeople. Data are from responses of 132 sales incentive users to a 1984 survey, and from previous surveys.

Includes text data and 6 charts showing sales incentive objectives, sales gain with use of incentives, percent of sales force earning awards, sales incentive expenditures of top 10 user industries, methods of obtaining awards, incentive campaigns launched by month, and incentive costs as percent of sales, various years 1977-84.

C1200–5   RESTAURANT BUSINESS

18 issues per year.
Approx. 200 p.
ISSN 0097-8043.
LC 74-644389.
SRI/MF/excerpts, shipped quarterly

Trade journal (published 18 times a year) of the restaurant and food service industry, including company and market profiles, and articles on product line merchandising and promotion, equipment, and management.

Most data are from the journal's own research, Federal Government, and private research assns.

Issues generally contain narrative special features or articles; and regular editorial depts, including "Trade Quotes" section presenting selected stock data for approximately 80 food service companies.

Annual statistical features include franchise restaurant operations summary; restaurant advertising expenditures; and restaurant growth index.

Features with substantial statistical content are described, as they appear, under "Statistical Features." Each issue of the journal is reviewed, but an abstract is published in SRI monthly issues only when statistical features appear.

Prior to the Nov. 1, 1983 issue, journal was described in SRI under C8075-1; issuing agency has changed from Restaurant Business, Inc. Prior to the Jan. 1, 1984 issue, journal was published monthly.

Availability: Restaurant Business, 633 Third Ave., New York NY 10017, qualified subscribers †, others $63.00 per yr.; SRI/MF/excerpts for all portions described under "Statistical Features;" shipped quarterly.

Issues reviewed during 1984: Nov. 1, 1983-Oct. 10, 1984 (P) (Vol. 82, Nos. 14-15; Vol. 83, Nos. 1-15).

STATISTICAL FEATURES:

C1200–5.501: Nov. 1, 1983 (Vol. 82, No. 14)

WEST GERMANY: MARKET OFFERS POTENTIAL FOR U.S. INVESTORS

(p. 176-177, 279) Article, with 1 table showing top 20 West German food service companies ranked by 1982 sales, with number of units and franchises as of Dec. 31, 1982, type of operation, names of affiliated chains, and sales and unit detail for selected affiliates.

Data are from *Fast Food Praxis.*

C1200–5.502: Feb. 10, 1984 (Vol. 83, No. 3)

PIZZA TURNS CHIC AS SALES SOAR

(p. 134-154) Article, with 1 chart showing number of pizza restaurants and market share of all restaurants, by census division, 1983. Data are from Restaurant Consulting Group.

C1200–5.503: Mar. 20, 1984 (Vol. 83, No. 5)

FRANCHISING: MATURING MENUS AND MARKETS ANNUAL FEATURE

Annual compilation of articles on restaurant franchising. Statistical features are described below. Data are from Commerce Dept's *Franchising in the Economy, 1982-84,* and *Restaurant Business.* Data generally are shown separately for company- and franchisee-owned operations. This is the 19th annual feature on franchising.

ICE CREAM STORES AND DONUT SHOPS, ANNUAL FEATURE

(p. 160, 163) Two annual tables showing ice cream and donut store units and sales,1982-84. Tables are accompanied by related articles.

RESTAURANT FRANCHISING IN THE ECONOMY, ANNUAL FEATURE

(p. 167-182) Annual article analyzing developments in franchising generally and for restaurants and other specific industries. Includes text data, and 1 chart and 9 tables showing the following:

a. Franchise companies, units, and sales, by type of food served, 1978 (units and sales only) and 1982-84; and franchisor sales of products/services to franchisees, by sales category, 1982-84.

b. Top 30 franchise systems in sales and units, 1982-83; and franchise and all other restaurant sales, 1978 and 1983.

c. Franchise units, by State; and companies with international franchises, and units by country or world area, by type of food served; 1982.

C1200–5.504: Apr. 10, 1984 (Vol. 83, No. 6)

MEXICAN MENUS INVADE AMERICAN MARKETS

(p. 144-166) By Jacque W. Kochak. Article, with 1 table and 2 charts showing the following for Mexican food restaurants: top 10 chains ranked by 1983 sales, with number of units as of Feb. 1984; industry total units by census division, 1983; and number of franchise units, 1978 and 1983.

Data are from *Restaurant Business* estimates, Restaurant Consulting Group, and Commerce Dept.

C1200–5.505: June 10, 1984 (Vol. 83, No. 9)

TOP 15 TV AND RADIO ADVERTISERS, ANNUAL FEATURE

(p. 94-100) Annual article, with 2 tables showing network and local TV advertising expenditures and total radio advertising expenditures, 1982-83, for top 15 restaurant advertisers in each medium ranked by 1983 expenditures.

Data are from Radio Advertising Bureau and TV Bureau of Advertising, based on Broadcast Advertisers Reports.

ORIENTAL MARKET POISED FOR EXPLOSIVE CHAIN GROWTH

(p. 154-174) By Jacque W. Kochak. Article, with 1 table and 2 charts showing the following for restaurants serving Oriental food: units and sales for 1983, type of service, and growth outlook, for 6 major chains; total units by census division, 1983; and change in customer traffic compared to all restaurants, 1981-82.

Most data are from Restaurant Consulting Group and National Restaurant Assn.

C1200–5.506: July 20, 1984 (Vol. 83, No. 11)

WONDERFUL NEW TAX ANIMAL

(p. 74-76) By Irving L. Blackman. Article, with 1 table showing percent of tax returns audited by IRS, for individuals and noncorporate businesses by income class, and for corporations by asset size, 1983.

C1200–5.507: Aug. 10, 1984 (Vol. 83, No. 12)

BARBECUE: THE ACCENT IS ON REGIONAL GROWTH

(p. 108-130) By Jacque W. Kochak. Article, with 1 table and 1 chart showing the following for barbecue food restaurants: top 11 chains ranked by 1983 sales, with number of units as of mid-1984, and expansion plans; and industry total units by census division, 1983.

Data are from *Restaurant Business* estimates and Restaurant Consulting Group.

MERGERS AND ACQUISITIONS

(p. 147-173) Article, with 1 table showing the following for selected mergers or acquisitions involving food service industry companies, Feb. 1979-June 1984: companies involved and FY83 revenues, and date and value of transaction.

Data are from *Restaurant Business* and The Food Institute.

C1200–5.508: Sept. 20, 1984 (Vol. 83, No. 14)

17th ANNUAL RESTAURANT GROWTH INDEX, ANNUAL FEATURE

(p. 119-216) Annual report on food service sales, by major market segment, 1982-83, with projections to 1988. Also includes selected demographic data; and restaurant sales, and restaurant activity and growth indexes (RAI and RGI), by geographic area.

Major market segments are separate eating/drinking places, hotel/motel, retail, business/industrial, transportation, health care, student, and leisure. Geographic breakdowns include census divisions, States, MSAs, and TV areas of dominant influence (ADIs).

RAI is based on an area's eating place-food store sales ratio. RGI is a measure of restaurant supply-demand in an area.

Data are from RBI Research, Malcolm M. Knapp Inc., and the Census Bureau.

Contents:

a. Summary article, with 2 tables showing food service industry sales, sales growth rate, and purchases, for commercial/contract, institutional/internal, and military markets, and by major market segment, 1982-83, with sales and growth rate projections to 1988. (p. 119-121)

b. Major market segment analyses, each with 1 table showing the sales, growth rate, and purchase data described above, for the total segment and 3-8 subsegments. (p. 122-153)

c. "17th Annual Restaurant Growth Index," by Jeffrey Hall. Article with narrative analysis, definitions, explanation of RGI computation, and 2 tables showing 25 largest cities ranked by 1982 population, with 1970 population, and median family income change during 1970-80; and distribution of households by income, 1967 and 1982. (p. 157-164)

d. List of MSAs covered in RGI. (p. 168-174)

e. 3 tables showing population, average household size, sales of eating/drinking and eating places, sales and market share of fast food establishments and restaurants, RAI, and RGI, all by census division, State, MSA, nonmetro portion of State, and ADI, 1983. (p. 178-211)

f. 4 tables ranking top 100 MSAs and ADIs, by restaurant and fast food sales, RAI, and RGI, 1983. (p. 212-216)

C1200–5.509: Oct. 10, 1984 (Vol. 83, No. 15)

SUPERMARKETS CATER CONVENIENCE TO ONE-STOP SHOPPER

(p. 190-206) By Rona Gindin. Article, with 1 table showing supermarket sales and number of stores, and percent of stores offering selected special services including delicatessens, bakeries, salad and snack bars, and sit-down restaurants, 1973-83. Data are from *Progressive Grocer.*

C1560
Boating Industry, Inc.

C1560-1   BOATING INDUSTRY
Monthly.   Approx. 100 p.
ISSN 0006-5404.
SRI/MF/excerpts, shipped
quarterly

Monthly trade journal of the recreational boating industry, reporting on sales trends, marketing strategies, trade shows, new products, and other topics of interest to marine product dealers and manufacturers, and marinas. Covers power boats and sailboats; boat motors, materials, and accessories; and water skis and other water sports equipment.

Data are from industry sources, Federal agencies, and *Boating Industry* surveys.

Issues generally contain feature articles, occasionally with statistics; and numerous regular depts.

Annual features include boating industry statistics (Jan.); overview of the sailing industry market (May); and marine buyers guide (Dec.).

A 2nd issue published in Feb. is a nonstatistical annual supplement sponsored by Marine Retailers Assn of America.

Features with substantial statistical content are described, as they appear, under "Statistical Features." Journal is reviewed every month but an abstract is published in SRI monthly issues only when features with substantial statistical content appear.

Availability: Boating Industry, Circulation Department, PO Box 1076, Skokie IL 60076, qualified subscribers $20.00 per yr., single copy $4.00, Buyer's Guide $20.00, Jan. issue $5.00; SRI/MF/excerpts for all portions described under "Statistical Features;" shipped quarterly.

Issues reviewed during 1984: Nov. 1983-Oct. 1984 (P) (Vol. 46, Nos. 11-12; Vol. 47, No. 1-10).

STATISTICAL FEATURES:

C1560-1.501: Jan. 1984 (Vol. 47, No. 1)
OCCUPATIONS OF UPPER INCOME BOAT BUYERS

(p. 21) Table showing distribution of upper-income boat buyers by occupational category and income (undated). Data are from National Marine Manufacturers Assn.

BOATING BUSINESS, 1983, ANNUAL FEATURE

(p. 45-60) Annual compilation of recreational boating industry statistics, 1983 and trends. Data sources include *Boating Industry* surveys, trade assns, U.S. Coast Guard, and U.S. Chamber of Commerce.

Includes text statistics, 15 charts, and 7 tables, with substantial data for the following:

a. Retail sales: total, outboard boat and motor, inboard/outdrive boat, and trailers, with average values, various years 1976-83.

b. Boat export and import value, 1974-82; market shares for top 10 countries of destination and top 8 competing countries, 1982; and top 6 countries of destination ranked by U.S. export growth rate, 1978-82 period.

c. Outboard boat sales and average length; and boating accidents, boats involved in accidents, fatalities, nonfatal injuries, and fatality rate; various years 1968-83.

d. Registered boats, population, inland water area, miles of coastal shoreline, and 1982 effective buying income, by State and outlying territory; and registered boats by region.

e. Water ski and trailer sales; average trailer retail cost; and sailboat sales and average retail cost (non-powered, and auxiliary-powered by size); various years 1972-83.

C1560-1.502: July 1984 (Vol. 47, No. 7)
MARINE MONEY MARKETS SPUR SALES, BUT WORRY DEALERS

(p. 19-20) By Peter Morton Coan. Article, with 2 tables showing average interest rate, downpayment, and maximum term, for new boat loans, mid-year 1983-84; and primary credit sources, and average sales, credit maximum, and interest rate, for marine product dealers, mid-1984; all by region. Data sources include a *Boating Industry* survey of 25 leading dealers.

C1575
Bobit Publishing Co.

C1575-1   SCHOOL BUS FLEET
Bimonthly.   Approx. 80 p.
ISSN 0036-6501.
LC SN 79-9218.
SRI/MF/excerpts

Bimonthly periodical on school bus fleet management and operating trends and developments. Periodical is primarily narrative, but occasionally includes features with substantial statistical content, including an annual compilation of data, appearing in the annual factbook issue (Dec./Jan.).

Features with substantial statistical content are described, as they appear, under "Statistical Features." Each issue of the journal is reviewed, but an abstract is published in SRI monthly issues only when statistical features appear.

Availability: School Bus Fleet, Subscription Department, 2500 Artesia Blvd., Redondo Beach CA 90278-3296, qualified subscribers †, others $12.00 per yr., single copy $2.00, Fact Book $10.00; SRI/MF/excerpts for all portions covered under "Statistical Features."

Issues reviewed during 1984: Dec. 1983/Jan. 1984-Oct./Nov. 1984 (P) (Vol. 28, No. 6; Vol. 29, Nos. 1-5).

STATISTICAL FEATURES:

C1575-1.501: Dec. 1983/Jan. 1984 (Vol. 28, No. 6)
SCHOOL BUS INDUSTRY STATISTICS, ANNUAL FEATURE

(p. 87-92) Annual compilation of statistics on school bus pupil transportation, accidents, and costs, by State, selected years 1960/61-1981/82. Data are from reports of the National Safety Council, National Assn of State Directors of Pupil Transportation Services, State education and highway depts, and other sources. Includes the following tables:

[1] School transportation [pupils transported at public expense, vehicles used by type and ownership, buses, and transportation expenditures including capital outlay, all by State and for Manitoba, Guam, Puerto Rico, and Saipan], 1981/82. (p. 87)

[2] School bus accidents by State [includes mileage, accidents by type, and total and pupil injuries, primarily 1981/82]. (p. 91)

[3] Growth of school transportation in the U.S. [pupils transported, vehicles used, and expenditures, 1960/61-1981/82]. (p. 92)

Feature is part of the annual factbook issue.

C1575-1.502: Feb./Mar. 1984 (Vol. 29, No. 1)
SHOULD PUPILS BE BELTED?

(p. 12-15) By Cliff Henke. Article on installation of safety belts in school buses, with 1 chart showing school bus occupant fatalities, 1974-82. Data are from the National Safety Council.

C1575-1.503: June/July 1984 (Vol. 29, No. 3)
USED BUS PRICES

(p. 11) Table showing the following for 3 size classes of used school buses: base wholesale value for gas and diesel models; and add-on value for automatic transmissions, air brakes, and handicap lifts; biennially 1976-82. Data are from *Yellow School Bus Book*.

C1575-1.504: Aug./Sept. 1984 (Vol. 29, No. 4)
DEATH ZONES OR SEAT BELTS: WHICH IS MORE IMPORTANT

(p. 24-30) By Roscoe G. Bernard. Article, with 1 table showing number of children killed during school bus loading/unloading, 1979-82. Includes deaths caused by school buses and by other vehicles. Data are from Kansas Dept of Transportation, and cover total U.S.

C1575-2   AUTOMOTIVE FLEET
Monthly.   Approx. 100 p.
ISSN 0005-1519.
LC 68-2155.
SRI/MF/excerpts, shipped
quarterly

Monthly report on trends and developments in automobile and light truck fleet management and operations, with data on fuel prices and used car auction prices.

Issues generally contain feature articles, occasionally statistical; editorial depts, including news columns and industry personnel developments; and 2 monthly tables, listed below.

Prior to the Jan. 1984 issue, journal also included 1 monthly chart on airport auto rental revenues and market shares for 4 major and all other companies.

Monthly tables appear in all issues. All additional features with substantial statistical content (except vehicle specifications) are described, as they appear, under "Statistical Features." Nonstatistical features are not covered.

Availability: Automotive Fleet, Subscription Manager, 2500 Artesia Blvd., Redondo Beach CA 90278, qualified subscribers †, others $18.00 per yr., single copy $2.00, Fact Book $20.00; SRI/MF/excerpts for monthly data and all portions covered under "Statistical Features;" shipped quarterly.

Issues reviewed during 1984: Nov. 1983-Oct. 1984 (P) (Vol. 23, Nos. 1-12).

MONTHLY TABLES:

[1] Gas prices [for unleaded gasoline full- and self-serve in approximately 15 cities, as of a selected date during month 1-2 months prior to cover date; data are from Runzheimer and Co.].

[2] Used cars [average auction prices by year, make, and model, by region, usually for week 1-4 weeks prior to cover date; data are from *Automotive Market Report*].

STATISTICAL FEATURES:

C1575–2.501: Dec. 1983 (Vol. 23, No. 2)

LIGHT TRUCK PLANNED PURCHASING SURVEY RESULTS, ANNUAL FEATURE

(p. 21-22) Annual article on light truck fleet plans for purchasing/leasing 1984 models, based on 258 responses to an *Automotive Fleet* 1983 survey.

Includes 1 chart and 4 tables showing respondents by sector and method of acquiring trucks; current fleet size and composition, including whether equipment owned or leased and domestic or import, number of vehicles by truck body type, and actual 1983 and planned 1984 vehicles bought/leased, all by gross vehicle weight; and average annual mileage and replacement life.

LIGHT TRUCK STATISTICS, ANNUAL FEATURE

(p. 31-37) Annual compilation of statistics on light truck/van fleets, sales, and registrations. Includes 2 charts and 6 tables showing the following:

a. Top 25 business/commercial and utility light truck/van fleets, ranked by number of vehicles, 1983; and light truck total and fleet sales or registrations, by domestic and import manufacturer, 1975-83.

b. Light truck factory sales, by gross vehicle weight, with detail for domestic factory sales by body type and for diesel trucks, various years 1969-82.

C1575–2.502: Jan. 1984 (Vol. 23, No. 3)

FLEET MANAGERS AND THEIR ENVIRONMENT

(p. 64-75) By Barry Mitnick and Donna J. Wood. Article, with 1 table showing demographic characteristics of 200 fleet managers responding to a National Assn of Fleet Administrators membership survey, spring 1983. Includes number of U.S. and Canadian respondents, and respondents by sex, age, and salary.

C1575–2.503: Mar. 1984 (Vol. 23, No. 5)

FLEET MANAGERS MOVING TO COMPUTERIZATION

(p. 23) Brief article on auto fleet maintenance program control. Data are from a Runzheimer and Co. survey of approximately 600 U.S. and Canadian fleet managers. Includes 1 undated table showing respondents' planned methods for gaining greater control of fleet maintenance programs.

AUTOMOTIVE FLEET'S FIFTH ANNUAL TOP 100, ANNUAL FEATURE

(p. 27-45) Annual *Automotive Fleet* ranking of 100 largest corporate auto and light truck/van fleets, 1984. Includes 1 table showing the following for each company, ranked by total fleet size: headquarters and fleet contact person;

whether vehicles are owned or leased, and name of lessor or use of in-house leasing; number of autos and trucks/vans; and comparative rank order for 1983.

HERTZ' AUTO EXPENSE ESTIMATES

(p. 100-103) Article, with 2 tables showing average compact auto purchase price; and ownership/operating cost per mile by auto size, with detail by cost item for compact autos; 1978 and 1982-83. Data are from Hertz Corp.

NAFA PERSONAL USE SURVEY, ANNUAL FEATURE

(p. 109-119) Annual survey article on personal use of company fleet cars and business use of personally owned cars. Data are based on responses of 401 U.S. and Canadian fleets to a 1983 National Assn of Fleet Administrators (NAFA) survey.

Includes 4 tables showing survey response for the following:

a. Number of fleets, and company-owned and leased cars, shown for 7 industry groups, public utilities, and government (all U.S. only), and for Canada, 1983.

b. Reimbursement rate for business use of personal car, and chargeback rate for personal use of fleet cars, 1980-83, for U.S. commercial fleets.

For description of full NAFA survey report, see A6755-1.504, above.

C1575–2.504: April 1984 (Vol. 23, No. 6)

AUTOMOTIVE FLEET'S EIGHTH ANNUAL FLEET DEALER AWARDS, ANNUAL FEATURE

(p. 52) Annual tabular list of *Automotive Fleet* fleet dealer award recipients, showing national sales manager, dealership name and location, and number of units sold, for top 3 dealers for each of 13 makes, 1983.

Previous tables, for 1981-82, were both published under the title "seventh annual awards."

CAR MARKETING SURVEY

(p. 56-68) Article on auto fleet vehicle use and disposition, 1983. Data are from responses of 257 fleet managers to the 1983 Used-Car Marketing Survey conducted by National Assn of Fleet Administrators. Respondents represent 166,409 autos.

Includes 1 table (p. 59) showing number of owned and leased autos in fleet; used autos sold in 1983, by model year and marketing method; and average miles and months of service at time of sale; for 9 industry sectors, utilities and government, and Canadian fleets.

C1575–2.505: May 1984 (Vol. 23, No. 7)

RUNZHEIMER REPORTS COSTS PER MILE, EXPENSE BREAKDOWN

(p. 14-16) Article, with 1 table showing average operating and ownership costs, by item, for typical 1984 model year compact and intermediate autos. Data are from Runzheimer and Co.

ANNUAL FACT BOOK

Annual *Automotive Fleet* fact book presenting data on fleet car and light truck registrations, make and size of cars, types of ownership and leasing arrangements, and operating costs.

Data are from *Automotive Fleet* Research Dept, American Automotive Leasing Assn (AALA), National Assn of Fleet Administrators (NAFA), and other sources.

Contents:

a. Statistical section, with 17 tables and 4 charts, listed below. (p. 27-44, 222)

b. Fleet directories, including fleet sales and marketing personnel, by motor vehicle manufacturer and selected makes (p. 47-70); lease/rental companies (p. 73-136); and fleet dealers by make, disposal/salvage companies, and consultants (p. 138-171).

c. Fleet auto guide, including State no-fault insurance specifications; *Automotive Fleet* editorial index, 1981-May 1984; directories of National Auto Auction Assn members and tire industry fleet experts; vehicle management computer software buyers guide; 1984 model year auto and truck specifications, by make and model; and State auto insurance, registration, and tax requirements. (p. 172-225)

Only the statistical section is available on SRI microfiche.

TABLES AND CHARTS:

[Types of fleets include business fleets, by ownership or leasing arrangement; and government, utilities, police, taxi, daily rental, and driver school fleets.]

[1] Fleet figures by type and size [and selected data for leasing by individuals, and trucks in rental and leasing], as of Jan. 1, 1984. (p. 27)

[2-3] Daily rental market profile [number of cars, 1983 revenue, and 1982-83 airport market shares, for each of top 4 companies and all others; with 1 chart showing average age of cars at replacement, revenue per month, and yearly mileage, selected years 1976-82]. (p. 28)

[4] Fleet registrations by month and year [1974-83]. (p. 29)

[5] Cars in fleets by type of business [and individually leased cars, other fleets by type, and selected leasing data for trucks in rental, 1974-83]. (p. 30)

[6] New fleet vehicles registered [cars and trucks: renting/leasing, commercial, and government, 1974-83]. (p. 30)

[7] 1983 model year registrations, fleet vs. retail [by model]. (p. 32)

[8] Fleet registrations [by make], 1977-83 model years. (p. 34)

[9] Net change of fleet sales, by [motor vehicle] manufacturer, 1981-83 model years. [chart] (p. 34)

[10] Size and model cars purchased, by major leasing companies [distribution], 1982 vs. 1983. (p. 36)

[11] AALA fleet costs survey [monthly operating costs, by item, 1982-83; and total monthly costs, average months in operation, and average annual mileage, 1976-83]. (p. 38)

[12] Composition of the AALA fleet [distribution by size and make, and percent with air conditioning, 1976-83]. (p. 38)

[13] [AALA] used car disposition [distribution to dealers, auctions, and lessee employees; and percent and average expenditure of AALA members doing reconditioning; 1976-83]. (p. 38)

[14] Fleet car operating costs by region [no date]. (p. 40)

[15] Composition of *Automotive Fleet* fleet/leasing market [by fleet type, with average annual mileage and trade-in time, no date]. [chart] (p. 41)

[16] Personal use reimbursement [distribution of U.S. commercial fleets by reimbursement rates for business use of personal car, 1980-83]. (p. 42)

[17] Used fleet-car marketing data [including percent of autos sold in 1983, with distribution by model year and marketing method; and average miles and months in service at time of sale; for U.S. commercial fleets and sample leased and owned fleets]. (p. 42)

[18-20] NAFA survey of operating expenses [by item, composite and by auto size class; with summary personal use credits, and average miles per month and per gallon; 1981-83. Includes summary chart.] (p. 44)

[21] 1984 EPA ratings [miles per gallon, by car model]. (p. 222)

C1575–2.506: June 1984 (Vol. 23, No. 8)

FLEET OPERATING COSTS FALL

(p. 39-43) Article on fleet operating expenses in U.S. and Canada. Data are from a National Assn of Fleet Administrators (NAFA) survey of 85 fleets operating over 75,000 passenger autos.

Includes 1 chart and 2 tables showing composite fleet operating, incidental, and standing expenses, by item, and personal use credits; and operating expenses by item, and average miles per month and per gallon, by auto size class; 1981-83.

Tables and chart are reprinted from *Automotive Fleet* annual fact book issue, described in C1575-2.505, above.

C1575–2.507: Sept. 1984 (Vol. 23, No. 11)

USED CAR PRICES, MILEAGE, AND AGE ALL RISE IN '83

(p. 94-97) Article comparing new and used car prices and operating cost, 1983. Data are from Hertz Corp. Includes 1 table showing the following for a compact car driven 10,000 miles per year: purchase price, and ownership/operating cost per mile for car kept 4 years and kept until scrapped, for new cars and for used cars by age at purchase, 1983.

C1575–2.508: Oct. 1984 (Vol. 23, No. 12)

NAFA's SURVEY OF FLEETS' NEW-CAR ACQUISITIONS, ANNUAL FEATURE

(p. 74-84) Annual article on corporate auto fleet composition in 1984, and planned acquisition of 1985 models. Data are based on responses of 197 fleets operating 149,365 vehicles to a 1984 National Assn of Fleet Administrators (NAFA) survey.

Includes 2 tables showing fleet composition by owned or leased status and auto size class, and new car acquisitions, 1984; and planned acquisitions by auto size class, 1985; for 7 industry sectors, with selected composite trends from 1980.

For description of complete NAFA survey, see A6755-1.511 above.

RUNZHEIMER'S ANALYSIS OF CHANGES IN PERSONAL-USE CHARGEBACKS

(p. 92-110) Article on corporate chargebacks to employees for personal use of company fleet cars. Data are from Runzheimer and Co.

Includes 2 charts and 2 tables showing distribution of companies using monthly and per mile chargeback methods, by chargeback rate, 1975/76 and 1983/84; and typical company

fleet car annual operating and ownership costs, and fringe benefit value to employees at selected levels of personal use, 1973-84, with detail for 3 cities, 1984.

C1575–3   METROPOLITAN: Fact Book
Bimonthly (selected issue).
Sept. 1983. 150 p.
Vol. 79, No. 5.
ISSN 0162-6221.
SRI/MF/excerpts

Annual fact book issue of *Metropolitan,* presenting funding and employment data for urban mass transit systems, generally for 1965-Sept. 1982 period. Issue also includes directory of equipment and service suppliers. Data are from American Public Transit Assn and Urban Mass Transportation Administration (UMTA).

Issue includes 3 charts and 3 tables, listed below.

Metropolitan is a bimonthly periodical reporting on trends and developments in the mass transport industry. Journal does not usually contain substantial statistics. Only the annual fact book and an annual feature on the top 50 urban bus transit systems are covered by SRI.

Previous fact book, published Sept./Oct. 1982, is described in SRI 1982 Annual, under this number.

For description of urban transit system feature, see C1575-4, below.

Availability: Metropolitan, Subscription Department, 2500 Artesia Blvd., Redondo Beach CA 90278, qualified subscribers †, others $12.00 per yr., single copy $2.00, Fact Book $20.00; SRI/MF/excerpts for statistical portions described below.

TABLES AND CHARTS:
[Unless otherwise noted, data are for 1965-Sept. 1982 period.]

[1] UMTA capital grant approvals to urbanized areas with multi-modal systems [for bus, rapid transit, commuter rail, and miscellaneous, all by urban area]. (p. 139)

[2] Trend of transit employment [selected years 1940-82]. (p. 140)

[3] Direct employment impacts on major industry group from transit capital investments [for new rail starts, rail modernization, and buses/garages; no date]. [chart] (p. 141)

[4] UMTA funded transit vehicles [by type]. (p. 143).

[5] Cumulative Federal capital grants by mode [rail transit, bus, commuter rail, and boat/other]. [chart] (p. 143)

[6] Capital grant funding for [advanced fixed guideways, ferry boat transportation, and cable cars/inclines/railroads]. [chart] (p. 143)

C1575–4   METROPOLITAN: TRANSIT'S TOP 50
Bimonthly (selected issue).
Sept. 1984. (p. 51-63)
Vol. 80, No. 5.
ISSN 0162-6221.
SRI/MF/excerpts

Annual feature ranking top 50 urban bus transit systems by fleet size, and including number of articulated buses and buses over and under 35 feet in length, and average age of buses, 1984 with comparisons to 1983. Data are from 267

responses to an American Public Transit Assn member survey, and Bobit Publishing Research.

Includes brief narrative and 1 extended table. This is the 1st annual feature.

Metropolitan is a bimonthly periodical reporting on trends and developments in the mass transport industry. Journal does not usually contain substantial statistics. Only the top 50 fleet feature and the annual fact book are covered by SRI.

For description of annual fact book issue, see C1575-3, above.

Availability: Metropolitan, Subscription Manager, 2500 Artesia Blvd., Redondo Beach CA 90278, $12.00 per yr., single copy $2.00, Fact Book $20.00; SRI/MF/excerpts for annual top 50 fleet feature.

C1650
Bowker, R. R., Co.

C1650–1   LIBRARY JOURNAL
Semimonthly.
Approx. 130 p. per issue;
cumulative pagination
throughout year.
ISSN 0363-0277.
LC 76-645271.
SRI/MF/not filmed

Semimonthly trade journal (monthly in Jan., July, and Aug.) of the library and information services professions, focusing primarily on public libraries. Covers book, periodical, and equipment selection; government activities affecting libraries; information technology; facilities design; and personnel, salaries, and professional development topics.

Most data are from the journal's own research, or are based on news and research reported by library systems and individuals.

Issues generally contain news briefs; feature articles, some with statistics; and narrative depts. Annual statistical features cover automated circulation systems, periodical prices, placements and salary levels of library school graduates, and public and academic library construction projects.

Features with substantial statistical content are described, as they appear, under "Statistical Features." Each issue of the journal is reviewed, but an abstract is published in SRI monthly issues only when statistical features appear.

Availability: R. R. Bowker Co., Library Journal, Subscription Department, PO Box 1427, Riverton NJ 08077, $59.00 per yr., single copy $3.50, Spring and Fall Announcement Issues $4.95; SRI/MF/not filmed.

Issues reviewed during 1984: Nov. 1, 1983-Oct. 15, 1984 (P) (Vol. 108, Nos. 19-22; Vol. 109, Nos. 1-17).

STATISTICAL FEATURES:

C1650–1.501: Dec. 1, 1983 (Vol. 108, No. 21)

LIBRARY BUILDINGS IN 1983, ANNUAL FEATURE

(p. 2209-2218) Annual feature, by Bette-Lee Fox et al., on academic and public library construction and renovation. Includes 8 tables showing cost, size, and book and seating capacity of individual projects, FY83, with selected aggregate trends for academic libraries from FY73 and for public libraries from FY78.

Individual project data are shown by institution or community, and include projects in Canada. Public library data also include funding by source.

TWO-YEAR COLLEGE LRC BUILDINGS, BIENNIAL FEATURE

(p. 2219-2221) Biennial report, by D. Joleen Bock, on learning resource center (LRC) construction activity at public and independent 2-year colleges, July 1, 1981-June 30, 1983.

Includes 4 tables showing number of new buildings and average costs, various periods 1965-83; number of colleges providing selected services via LRC facilities built, FY82/83; and enrollment size, and project costs, area, and seating capacity, by college arranged by State and territory, for new and remodeling LRC construction, FY82/83.

For description of FY80/81 report, see SRI 1982 Annual, under C1650-1.302.

C1650-1.502: May 1, 1984 (Vol. 109, No. 8)

COMPETITION AND CHANGE: THE 1983 AUTOMATED LIBRARY SYSTEM MARKETPLACE, ANNUAL FEATURE

(p. 853-860) Annual article, by Joseph R. Matthews, on the library market for automated systems, 1983. Includes 2 charts and 5 tables showing total and new turnkey automated systems in operation, by vendor and system size (number of terminals), 1983 with summary trends from 1973; and library- and vendor-developed microcomputer systems available and software price.

C1650-1.503: Aug. 1984 (Vol. 109, No. 13)

PRICE INDEXES FOR 1984: U.S. PERIODICALS AND SERIAL SERVICES, ANNUAL FEATURE

(p. 1422-1425) Annual article, by Norman B. Brown and Jane Phillips, on trends in library subscription prices for periodicals and serial services, 1977-84. Data are based on a study of 3,731 periodical titles and 1,537 serial services.

Includes 5 tables showing number of titles, average price, and price index, for total periodicals and serial services, and by subject category, 1977-84.

This is the 24th annual survey.

C1650-1.504: Oct. 1, 1984 (Vol. 109, No. 16)

PLACEMENTS AND SALARIES 1983: CATCHING UP, ANNUAL FEATURE

(p. 1805-1811) Annual report, by Carol L. Learmont and Stephen Van Houten, on placements and salaries for 1983 graduates of accredited library school programs in U.S. and Canada. Data are from survey responses of 60 schools.

Includes 13 tables showing placements and salary averages and ranges, by region, graduating school, and type of employing library, with selected historical trends from the 1950s; and comparative salary data for graduates with and without previous experience. Most data are shown by sex; data by region include totals for Canada.

This is the 33rd annual report.

C1650-2 PUBLISHERS WEEKLY

Weekly. Approx. 60 p.
ISSN 0000-0019.
LC 1-15589.
SRI/MF/not filmed

Weekly trade journal (except last week in Dec.) reporting on U.S. and foreign publishing and bookselling, marketing, design, manufacturing, and foreign trade. Occasionally includes data on business and finance, and on book sales, production, and consumer expenditures. Data are based on original surveys and other commercial and Federal sources.

General format:

a. Narrative features and editorial depts, including book reviews and bestseller lists; and annual articles reporting book trade statistics.

b. Irregularly recurring table, entitled "A Look at the Books," showing quarterly financial performance of 1-10 selected publishing companies, with comparisons to same quarter of previous year.

c. Monthly "Gallup Survey," by Leonard A. Wood, on book purchasing habits and consumer characteristics; based on surveys of approximately 1,000-1,500 adults, conducted by the Gallup Organization.

d. Quarterly article on book publishing industry sales and consumer expenditures on books, based on data from Book Industry Study Group, Census Bureau, and other sources.

A semiannual index is published in Feb. and Aug. issues.

All features with substantial statistical content are described, as they appear, under "Statistical Features;" page locations and latest periods of coverage for recurring table are also noted. Non-statistical features and issues are not covered.

Availability: R. R. Bowker Co., Publishers Weekly, Subscription Department, PO Box 1428, Riverton NJ 08077, $78.00 per yr., single copy $2.00, announcement issues $4.95; SRI/MF/not filmed.

Issues reviewed during 1984: Nov. 4, 1983-Oct. 26, 1984 (P) (Vol. 224, Nos. 19-26; Vol. 225, Nos. 1-26; Vol. 226, Nos. 1-17).

STATISTICAL FEATURES:

C1650-2.501: Nov. 4, 1983 (Vol. 224, No. 19)

GALLUP SURVEY, MONTHLY FEATURE

(p. 20) Monthly survey article, with 4 tables showing distribution of responses to questions on subject categories of books purchased as gifts, relationship of recipient to purchaser, and whether gift was specifically requested, mostly by sex. Survey was conducted Sept. 10-18, 1983.

1982 BOOK PURCHASES: A HARD YEAR, ANNUAL FEATURE

(p. 22) Annual article, by John P. Dessauer, presenting revised book industry sales data, 1981-82. Data are from Book Industry Study Group.

Includes 2 tables showing estimated volume and value of consumer expenditures on books, by type of book and sales outlet, 1981-82.

C1650-2.502: Nov. 11, 1983 (Vol. 224, No. 20)

RECURRING TABLE

(p. 13) Look at the books, for quarter and 6 or 9 months ended Sept. 30, 1983.

C1650-2.503: Nov. 25, 1983 (Vol. 224, No. 22)

RECURRING TABLE

(p. 24) Look at the books, for quarter and 9 months ended Sept. 30 or Oct. 2, 1983.

C1650-2.504: Dec. 2, 1983 (Vol. 224, No. 23)

GALLUP SURVEY, MONTHLY FEATURE

(p. 30) Monthly survey article, with 3 tables showing distribution of responses to questions on book purchasing habits of women with and without college degrees, including subject categories and sales outlet types. Survey was conducted Jan.-July 1983.

C1650-2.505: Dec. 23, 1983 (Vol. 224, No. 26)

THIRD QUARTER SALES: THE BIG REBOUND, QUARTERLY FEATURE

(p. 31) Quarterly article, by John P. Dessauer, on book industry sales in 3rd quarter 1983. Includes 2 tables showing estimated net sales quantity and value by type of book, and consumer expenditures on books by type of sales outlet, 3rd quarter and first 9 months 1982-83.

C1650-2.506: Jan. 6, 1984 (Vol. 225, No. 1)

GALLUP SURVEY, MONTHLY FEATURE

(p. 28) Monthly survey article, with 3 tables on book purchasing trends during the Christmas shopping season, 1983. Tables show distribution of responses to questions on book purchase locations and prices paid, Nov./Dec. 1983.

LONGEST-RUNNING HARDCOVER AND PAPERBACK BESTSELLERS FOR 1983, ANNUAL FEATURE

(p. 38-39) Two annual lists of bestselling books in rank order, showing title, publisher, price, number of weeks on the 1982 and 1983 bestseller lists, and date published, for fiction and nonfiction hardcover, and mass market and trade paperback books.

C1650-2.507: Jan. 13, 1984 (Vol. 225, No. 2)

RECURRING TABLE

(p. 31) Look at the books, for quarter and 6 or 9 months ended Sept. 30 or Oct. 31, 1983.

C1650-2.508: Feb. 3, 1984 (Vol. 225, No. 5)

STUDY SHOWS BOOK PUBLISHERS TRAIL OTHER COMMUNICATIONS GROUPS

(p. 292) Article on publishing industry growth compared to the total communications industry, 1978-82. Data are from a survey of 29 book publishing companies extracted from a larger survey of communications companies, conducted by Veronis, Suhler, and Associates.

Includes 5 tables ranking top 10 book publishers by revenue, operating income, and operating margin, 1982; and by revenue and operating income growth rates, 1978-82 period; with comparisons to communications industry average.

GALLUP SURVEY, MONTHLY FEATURE

(p. 300) Monthly survey article, with 3 tables showing distribution of responses to questions on paperback and hardcover book purchasing, by subject category, 1983.

C1650–2.509: Feb. 10, 1984 (Vol. 225, No. 6)

MAJOR FORCES IN THE SOFTWARE INDUSTRY

(p. 43-52) By Robert S. Jones and Franklyn L. Jones. Article profiling the largest computer software companies. Data are from research by Future Computing, Creative Strategies International, and International Resource Development.

Includes 2 tables showing the 3 companies' forecasts of microcomputer software sales, various years 1983-88; and revenues of the top 5 microcomputer software firms, 1983.

MASS MARKET RAZOR/BLADE SELL

(p. 81-89) By Martin Brochstein. Article, with 1 chart showing microcomputer software sales by sales outlet type (computer specialty store, software store, mass merchandise, mail order, and electronic), 1983 and 1988. Data are from Future Computing, Inc.

C1650–2.510: Feb. 24, 1984 (Vol. 225, No. 8)

FICTION SWEEPS BRITAIN'S 1983 100 BESTSELLING PAPERBACKS

(p. 73) Article, with 1 text table showing sales volume for top 10 bestselling paperback books in the UK, 1983. Data are from the *Guardian*.

C1650–2.511: Mar. 2, 1984 (Vol. 225, No. 9)

RECURRING TABLE

(p. 23) Look at the books, for quarter and year or 9 months ended Nov. 30 or Dec. 31, 1983.

GALLUP SURVEY, MONTHLY FEATURE

(p. 28) Monthly survey article, with 3 tables showing distribution of responses to questions on whether books are purchased at full or discount prices, by sex and education. Survey was conducted Jan. 13-16, 1984.

C1650–2.512: Mar. 9, 1984 (Vol. 225, No. 10)

RECURRING TABLE

(p. 26) Look at the books, for quarter and year or 9 months ended Dec. 31, 1983 or Jan. 31, 1984.

C1650–2.513: Mar. 16, 1984 (Vol. 225, No. 11)

RECURRING TABLE

(p. 22) Look at the books, for quarter and year or 9 months ended Dec. 31, 1983 or Jan. 31, 1984.

THE YEAR 1983 IN REVIEW, ANNUAL FEATURE

Annual collection of articles reviewing publishing industry trends, for 1983. Articles containing substantial statistics are described below.

HARDCOVER TOP SELLERS, ANNUAL FEATURE

(p. 27-30) Annual article, by Daisy Maryles, with 1 list showing title, publisher, and copies sold, for top 15 fiction and 15 nonfiction hardcover bestsellers, 1983. Covers books published in 1982 or 1983.

PAPERBACK TOP SELLERS, ANNUAL FEATURE

(p. 31-37) Annual article, by Sally A. Lodge, with 3 lists showing title, publisher, and copies in print, for mass market paperbacks with over 1 million copies in print; mass market titles reissued in conjunction with TV or movie productions; trade paperbacks with shipments of over 50,000 copies; and almanacs, atlases, and annuals; 1983. Covers paperbacks published or reprinted in 1982 or 1983.

TITLE OUTPUT AND AVERAGE PRICES: 1983 PRELIMINARY FIGURES, ANNUAL FEATURE

(p. 46-49) Annual article, by Chandler B. Grannis, on book production and average retail prices per volume, by book type, in 23 subject areas, 1983 and trends. Data are derived from computer analysis of listings in *Paperbound Books in Print* and *Weekly Record,* published by R. R. Bowker.

Includes 8 tables showing hardbound and paperbound new books and new editions published, imported titles, total value, and average price, by subject area or Dewey Decimal classification, various years 1977-83.

Data corrections appear in the Apr. 6, 1984 issue; for description, see C1650-2.516 below.

C1650–2.514: Mar. 23, 1984 (Vol. 225, No. 12)

SURVEYS OF SOFTWARE USERS

(p. 50) Article, with 1 table showing software sales by computer type (mainframe, minicomputer, and personal computer), 1983-84. Data are from responses of 2,000 businesses to a 4th quarter 1983 survey conducted by *Software News.*

C1650–2.515: Mar. 30, 1984 (Vol. 225, No. 13)

RECURRING TABLE

(p. 18) Look at the books, for quarter and/or year ended Dec. 31, 1983.

GALLUP SURVEY, MONTHLY FEATURE

(p. 22) Monthly survey article, with 2 tables showing distribution of responses to questions on awareness of hardcover book prices, by size and subject category. Survey was conducted Jan. 13-16, 1984.

4th QUARTER SALES, 1983: A STRONG FINISH, QUARTERLY FEATURE

(p. 31) Quarterly article, by John P. Dessauer, on book industry sales in 4th quarter 1983. Data corrections appear in May 18, 1984 issue; for description, see C1650-2.520 below.

Includes 2 tables showing estimated net sales quantity and value by type of book, and consumer expenditures on books by type of sales outlet, 4th quarter and full year 1982-83.

C1650–2.516: Apr. 6, 1984 (Vol. 225, No. 14)

CORRECTION

(p. 15) Corrections for data in annual article on book title output and prices, appearing in Mar. 16, 1984 issue (p. 46-49). For description, see C1650-2.513 above.

C1650–2.517: Apr. 13, 1984 (Vol. 225, No. 15)

RECURRING TABLE

(p. 18) Look at the books, for quarter and 9 months ended Feb. 28, 1984.

C1650–2.518: Apr. 20, 1984 (Vol. 225, No. 16)

RANKING THE TOP 100 SOFTWARE PUBLISHERS

(p. 56-57) Article excerpted from *Soft•Letter*, with 1 table showing top 100 computer software companies ranked by sales, 1983. Data are from individual companies, industry analysts, and other sources.

C1650–2.519: May 11, 1984 (Vol. 225, No. 19)

GALLUP SURVEY, MONTHLY FEATURE

(p. 174) Monthly survey article, with 4 tables showing book purchasing trends, by type of book, sales outlet, and price, Jan.-Mar. 1984.

C1650–2.520: May 18, 1984 (Vol. 225, No. 20)

CORRECTION

(p. 31) Corrections for data in quarterly article on book industry sales, appearing in Mar. 30, 1984 issue. For description, see C1650-2.515 above.

AUTOMATED CRYSTAL BALLS

(p. 84-90) By Franklyn L. Jones. Article, with 1 table comparing microcomputer software sales projections of 10 market research firms, 1982-88.

C1650–2.521: May 25, 1984 (Vol. 225, No. 21)

BOOK READING 1955-84: THE TREND IS UP

(p. 39) Special Gallup survey article, by Leonard A. Wood, with 1 table showing distribution of responses to a question on book reading habits, by sex, age, educational attainment, and region, 1955 and 1984.

C1650–2.522: June 8, 1984 (Vol. 225, No. 23)

RECURRING TABLE

(p. 23) Look at the books, for quarters ended Dec. 31, 1983, Feb. 29, 1984, or Mar. 31, 1984.

GALLUP SURVEY, MONTHLY FEATURE

(p. 28) Monthly survey article, with 1 table showing distribution of responses to questions on source of most recently read books, by type of book and selected reader characteristics. Survey was conducted Apr. 6-15, 1984.

C1650–2.523: June 22, 1984 (Vol. 225, No. 25)

BOOK SALES RISE 9.5% TO $8.6 BILLION IN 1983

(p. 34) Brief article, with 1 table showing book publishing industry sales revenues, by type of publisher, 1972, 1977, and 1982-83. Data are from Assn of American Publishers (AAP).

Full AAP report, *Industry Statistics,* is covered by SRI under A3274-2.

STRONG BOOKSELLER PRESENCE IS THE BOTTOM LINE AT UPBEAT WASHINGTON SHOW

(p. 50-52) Article, with 1 table showing attendance of booksellers, exhibitors, and others at American Booksellers Assn annual conventions, 1982-84.

C1650–2.524: June 29, 1984 (Vol. 225, No. 26)

RECURRING TABLE

(p. 18) Look at the books, for quarter ended Mar. 31, 1984, or quarter and year ended Apr. 30, 1984.

C1650–2.525: July 6, 1984 (Vol. 226, No. 1)

FIRST QUARTER 1984 SALES: MOSTLY SOLID AND STABLE, QUARTERLY FEATURE

(p. 34) Quarterly article, by John P. Dessauer, on book industry sales in 1st quarter 1984.

Includes 2 tables showing estimated net sales quantity and value by type of book, and consumer expenditures on books by type of sales outlet, 1st quarter 1983-84.

C1650–2.526: July 13, 1984 (Vol. 226, No. 2)

GALLUP SURVEY, MONTHLY FEATURE

(p. 24) Monthly survey article, with 1 table showing distribution of responses to question on subject areas browsed during bookstore visits. Survey was conducted Feb. 11-20, 1984.

C1650–2.527: Aug. 3, 1984 (Vol. 226, No. 5)

RECURRING TABLE

(p. 16) Look at the books, for quarter and/or 6 or 12 months ended Apr. 30, May 31, or June 30, 1984.

C1650–2.528: Aug. 17, 1984 (Vol. 226, No. 7)

RECURRING TABLE

(p. 16) Look at the books, for quarter and 6 months ended June 30, 1984.

GALLUP SURVEY, MONTHLY FEATURE

(p. 20-21) Monthly survey article, with 4 tables showing distribution of responses concerning frequency of bookstore shopping, by sex, age, number of recent purchases, and interest in selected subject categories. Survey was conducted Feb. 11-20, 1984.

C1650–2.529: Aug. 24, 1984 (Vol. 226, No. 8)

RECURRING TABLE

(p. 17) Look at the books, for quarter and 6 months ended June 30, 1984.

C1650–2.530: Aug. 31, 1984 (Vol. 226, No. 9)

SECOND QUARTER SALES: GENERALLY GOOD, WITH SOME WEAKNESSES, QUARTERLY FEATURE

(p. 322) Quarterly article, by John P. Dessauer, on book industry sales in 2nd quarter 1984.

Includes 2 tables showing estimated net sales quantity and value by type of book, and consumer expenditures on books by type of sales outlet, 2nd quarter and 1st 6 months, 1983-84.

C1650–2.531: Sept. 7, 1984 (Vol. 226, No. 10)

GALLUP SURVEY, MONTHLY FEATURE

(p. 32) Monthly survey article, with 3 tables showing distribution of responses concerning recent book purchases, by sex (with employ-ment status detail for women), age, education, income, region, and book subject category, 1st half 1983-84.

U.S. BOOK TITLE OUTPUT AND AVERAGE PRICES: FINAL FIGURES FOR 1983, ANNUAL FEATURE

(p. 44-47) Annual article, by Chandler B. Grannis, on book production and prices, 1983 and trends. Data are derived from *Paperbound Books in Print* and *Weekly Record,* published by R. R. Bowker Co.

Includes 8 tables showing hardbound and paperbound new books and new editions published, and total and average prices, by subject area or Dewey Decimal classification, with selected detail for mass market and trade paperbacks, and imported titles, various years 1977-83.

C1650–2.532: Sept. 14, 1984 (Vol. 226, No. 11)

U.S. EXPORTS, IMPORTS, UNESCO REPORTS, ANNUAL FEATURE

(p. 116-118) Annual article, by Chandler B. Grannis, on U.S. book exports and imports, and world book production, 1983 and trends. Data are from Commerce Dept, UNESCO, and R. R. Bowker Co.

Includes 4 tables showing volume and/or value of U.S. book exports and imports, by book category and principal country; and title output, by country; various years 1979-83.

C1650–2.533: Sept. 21, 1984 (Vol. 226, No. 12)

BOOK PAGE EDITOR BLUES

(p. 28-30) By Robert Wyatt. Article discussing concerns of newspaper book page editors. Data are from responses of 167 book editors representing over 65% of newspapers with circulation above 100,000, to a survey conducted by the author.

Includes 4 undated tables showing ratings of book selection criteria and subject categories, and the following by newspaper circulation size: number of respondents; and mean or median weekly book reviews, percent of reviews written locally, page allotments, publicity materials (press releases and review copies) received, author interviews conducted, and percent of materials and interviews that are useful.

C1650–2.534: Oct. 5, 1984 (Vol. 226, No. 14)

GALLUP SURVEY, MONTHLY FEATURE

(p. 34) Monthly survey article, with 5 tables showing distribution of responses to questions on purchases of biographies/autobiographies, Aug. 1983-July 1984 period. Includes data on price paid, whether paperback or hardback, place of purchase, and whether purchased as gift, with selected detail by purchaser age and sex.

C1650–3   BOWKER ANNUAL OF LIBRARY AND BOOK TRADE INFORMATION, 29th Edition, 1984

Annual. 1984. xii+683 p.
ISSN 0068-0540.
ISBN 0-8352-1680-2.
LC 55-12434.
SRI/MF/not filmed

Annual compilation of articles and statistics relating to library, book trade, and information industry activities during 1983. Also includes directories of library and related organizations. Data are from R. R. Bowker Co., NCES, *American Library Directory,* library assns, and other Federal and private research services.

Contents:

Contents listing and preface. (p. v-xii)

Part 1. Reports from the Field. 25 articles on industry news, library services, Federal agencies and libraries, and activities of national assns. (p. 3-190)

Part 2. Legislation, Funding, and Grants. 15 articles on legislation affecting information science and publishing; and on Federal and foundation funding to libraries. (p. 193-275)

Part 3. Library Education, Placement, and Salaries. 4 articles on placement and salaries of librarians, and lists of accredited library schools, and library scholarship sources and awards. (p. 279-334)

Part 4. Research and Statistics. 21 articles and statistics on number and types of libraries, library building construction, and book publishing and distribution. (p. 337-450)

Part 5-6. Reference Information and Directory of Organizations. Includes bibliographies; 1983 book awards and best sellers, directory of library, book trade, and related organizations; calendar of 1984/85 library activities; and index. (p. 453-683)

Articles with statistics are described below.

Availability: R. R. Bowker Co., 1180 Ave. of the Americas, New York NY 10036, $60.00; SRI/MF/not filmed.

STATISTICAL ARTICLES:

[Data by State generally include D.C. and outlying areas.]

C1650–3.1: Part 1: Reports from the Field

a. "Public Libraries," by Ann E. Prentice. Includes 1 table showing average salaries for beginning librarian, dept head, and library director, compared to library budget percent increase and CPI; selected years 1970-83. (p. 62-66)

b. "School Libraries and Media Centers," by Eliza T. Dresang. Includes 2 tables showing titles of school library media center statistical reports; and average book and audiovisual material expenditures per student; selected years 1954-83. (p. 67-74)

c. "College and University Libraries," by Richard J. Talbot. Includes 1 table showing academic library expenditures vs. general higher education expenditures, selected years 1950-80. (p. 74-82)

d. "National Agricultural Library," by Eugene M. Farkas. Includes 1 table showing additions to collection, and technical and service activities, 1983. (p. 130-135)

e. "National Library of Medicine," by Robert B. Mehnert. Includes 1 table showing holdings, titles received and cataloged, circulation and interlibrary loan transactions, and computer searching activities, FY83. (p. 135-138)

C1650–3.2: Part 2: Legislation, Funding, and Grants

LEGISLATION

a. "Legislation and Regulations Affecting Librarianship in 1983," by Eileen D. Cooke and Carol C. Henderson. Includes 2 tables showing appropriations for Federal library and library-related programs, FY83-84; and status of library legislation, as of Nov. 18, 1983. (p. 193-204)

FUNDING AND GRANTS

b. "Council on Library Resources, Inc.," by Jane A. Rosenberg. Includes listing of grants awarded to CLR supported projects, showing amount, recipient, and type of program, FY83. (p. 221-229)

c. "Library Services and Construction Act," by Nathan Cohen et al. Includes 2 tables showing major urban resource library funding, by government level, FY79-81; and Federal and State/local funding for library construction projects under the Appalachian Regional Development Act funds, by project, FY82. (p. 231-240)

d. "Higher Education Act, Title II-A, College Library Resources," by Beth Phillips Fine. Includes 2 tables showing number of Title II-A grants and obligations, by State, FY83; and total Title II-A appropriations, obligations, and grants by type, FY66-83. (p. 241-243)

e. "Higher Education Act, Title II-B, Library Career Training," by Frank A. Stevens and Janice Owens. Includes 3 tables showing number of library career training fellowship recipients and amounts, by institution, 1983/84; categories of minority groups recruited for fellowship program; and total institutions offering fellowships, and recipients by degree level, 1966/67-1983/84. (p. 243-247)

f. "Higher Education Act, Title II-B, Library Research and Demonstration Program," by Yvonne B. Carter. Includes 1 table showing library research/demonstration projects and obligations, FY67-83. (p. 247-249)

g. "Higher Education Act, Title II-C, Strengthening Research Library Resources," by Louise V. Sutherland and Janice Owens. Includes 4 tables showing program funding summary, FY77-84; applications and number funded, by type of recipient institution, FY83; and grant awards, by institution and program type, FY83. (p. 250-257)

h. "Education Consolidation and Improvement Act of 1981, Chapter 2: A Follow-Up Report," by Phyllis Land Usher. Includes 1 table showing ECIA Chapter 2 appropriations, by State, FY83. (p. 257-259)

i. "National Endowment for the Humanities Support for Libraries, 1983." Includes 1 table showing amount, institution, and subject of 7 NEH library awards, FY83. (p. 260-265)

j. "Analysis of Foundation Grants to Libraries, 1983." Includes 3 tables showing number and amount of grants awarded by 10 leading library funders; and largest grants to libraries and leading recipients, 1980-82. (p. 272-275)

C1650–3.3: Part 3: Library Education, Placement, and Salaries

a. "Library Labor Market: A Study of Supply and Demand," by Nancy K. Roderer. Includes 1 table showing library employment, job openings, and library school graduates and other entrants to library labor force, quadrennial periods 1978-90. (p. 283-290)

b. "Placements and Salaries, 1982: Slowing Down," by Carol L. Learmont and Stephen Van Houten. Includes 13 tables showing the following data, by sex, for 1982 graduates of library schools in U.S. and Canada: employment status as of spring 1983, by U.S. region; placements and salary ranges, by placing school, type of library, and U.S. region, with summary trends from 1950s; special placements, by type; and salaries with and without previous experience. (p. 307-321)

c. "Library Scholarship and Award Recipients, 1983." List of awards showing amount, purpose, donor, and recipient, by award name. (p. 327-334)

C1650–3.4: Part 4: Research and Statistics

LIBRARY RESEARCH AND STATISTICS

a. "Selected Characteristics of the U.S. Population," by W. Vance Grant. Table showing resident population in U.S. and outlying areas, and armed forces serving abroad; population by age, education, and metro-nonmetro and employment status; total and private school enrollment, by level; and higher education faculty and students; 1983 or latest available date. (p. 345-346)

b. "Number of Libraries in the U.S. and Canada." Table showing number of libraries in the U.S., U.S.-administered areas, and Canada, by detailed type, 1983. (p. 347-348)

c. "U.S. College and University Library Statistics in Series," by Frank L. Schick. Includes 1 table showing academic library surveys conducted and reports published, various periods 1960-84. (p. 356-359)

d. "Survey of Federal Libraries, FY78," by Anne Heanue. Includes 5 tables showing Federal library holdings, services, automation status, expenses, and employment; number of libraries, by governmental branch, library type, and type of location; and percent of employees who are female, by library classification and salary grade; FY78. (p. 359-367)

e. "Expenditures for Resources in School Library Media Centers, FY83," by Marilyn L. Miller and Barbara B. Moran. Includes 17 tables showing school library media center expenses, holdings, media specialist average experience and salary, and volunteer assistance, variously by school level and type (public and private), enrollment, region, and school district population; method of budget preparation and use of advisory committee, by presence of district-level coordinator; average Federal funds by object; and microcomputer uses and expenses. (p. 367-383)

f. "Public and Academic Library Acquisition Expenditures, 1982/83." Includes 2 tables showing public and college/university library acquisition expenditures by type, and number of libraries, by State, 1982/83. (p. 384-388)

g. "Price Indexes for School and Academic Library Acquisitions," by Kent Halstead. Includes 2 tables showing average prices and price indexes for elementary and secondary, and college/university library materials, by type, 1974-82. (p. 389-394)

h. "College and University Libraries, 1978/79 and 1981/82: Three Years of Change," by Robert A. Heintze. Includes 5 tables showing college/university library holdings and acquisitions, by type of material; expenses by object, and Federal receipts; FTE staff by level and sex, and student assistance hours; and services, 1978/79 and 1981/82. (p. 394-397)

i. "Library Buildings in 1983," by Bette-Lee Fox et al. Includes 7 tables showing new construction and renovation costs, square footage, capacity, and architect, for public libraries by city (arranged by State and Canada Province), and academic libraries by institution, with funding by government level for public libraries; FY83 and summary trends from 1973. (p. 397-406)

j. "Two-Year College Library Resource Center Buildings," by D. Joleen Bock. Includes 4 tables showing number of new buildings and average costs, various periods 1965-83; size, cost, and seating capacity of new and remodeled library resource centers, by college (arranged by State), FY82/83; and services available in new centers. (p. 406-410)

BOOK PUBLISHING STATISTICS

k. "Book Title Output and Average Prices, 1983 Preliminary Figures," by Chandler B. Grannis. Includes 8 tables showing number of domestic and imported new books and editions, paperback titles, and average hardcover and paperback prices, mostly by subject, various years 1977-83. (p. 411-418)

l. "Book Sales Statistics: Highlights from Assn of American Publishers Annual Survey, 1982," by Chandler B. Grannis. Includes 1 table estimating book publishing sales, by industry segment, selected years 1972-82. (p. 419-421)

m. "U.S. Consumer Expenditures on Books, 1982," by John P. Dessauer. Includes 2 tables showing unit and dollar expenditures, by type of book and channel of distribution, 1981-82. (p. 422-424)

n. "Prices of U.S. and Foreign Published Materials," by Dennis E. Smith. Includes 13 tables showing average prices and/or price indexes for U.S. periodicals and serial services, hardcover books, paperbacks, nonprint materials, library microfilm, and newspapers; and for books published in UK, Germany, and 26 Latin American countries and areas; with selected detail by subject area, various years 1977-83. Many tables also show quantity published or purchased by major U.S. libraries. (p. 425-438)

o. "U.S. Book Exports and Imports and International Title Output," by Chandler B. Grannis. Includes 5 tables showing quantity and/or value of U.S. book imports and exports, by type and country; book production, by country; and book translations from 25 original languages; various years 1976-82. (p. 439-443)

p. "British Book Production, 1983." Includes 3 tables showing UK book title output, by subject, 1982-83, with summary trends from 1947. (p. 444-448)

q. "Number of Book Outlets in the U.S. and Canada." Includes 2 tables showing bookstores by type, and general and paperback wholesalers, for the U.S. and Canada, 1983. (p. 448-449)

r. "Book Review Media Statistics." Table showing number of books reviewed by specific publications, 1982-83. (p. 450)

C1750
Broadcasting Publications

C1750–1 BROADCASTING
Weekly. Approx. 100 p.
ISSN 0007-2028.
LC 33-14221.
SRI/MF/excerpts, shipped quarterly

Weekly trade journal (combined issue at year end) of the radio and TV broadcasting industry, containing news, feature articles, and statistics on broadcaster financial condition, network and program ratings, advertising investment, Government regulation, broadcast journalism, and technological and production developments.

Data are from Federal Government, private research firms, advertising agencies, individual companies, and the journal's own research.

Each issue contains narrative articles, occasionally with statistics; and numerous editorial depts, including stock and earnings data for broadcasting-related companies. Recurring statistical features include the following:

a. Weekly table on TV program ratings, usually in "Programming" section, showing network, rating, and share, for all prime time TV programs for week ended 1 week preceding publication.

b. Weekly "Summary of Broadcasting" table, usually in "For the Record" section, showing stations licensed/on the air and with construction permits, and total authorized, by type of station, for most recent date reported by FCC; data for same month frequently appear in more than 1 weekly issue.

c. Other features, including recurring articles on prime time audience of commercial TV networks, and spot radio advertising billings; and numerous annual features, including advertising billings and expenditures, and broadcasting industry finances.

Weekly tables appear in most issues. All additional features with substantial statistical content are described, as they appear, under "Statistical Features." Nonstatistical features are not covered.

Availability: Broadcasting, 1735 DeSales St., NW, Washington DC 20036, $60.00 per yr., single copy $2.00, special issues $3.50; SRI/MF/ excerpts for weekly tables and all portions covered under "Statistical Features;" shipped quarterly.

Issues reviewed during 1984: Nov. 7, 1983-Oct. 29, 1984 (P) (Vol. 105, Nos. 19-25; Vol. 106, Nos. 1-26; Vol. 107, Nos. 1-18).

STATISTICAL FEATURES:

C1750–1.501: Nov. 21, 1983 (Vol. 105, No. 21)

STUDY COMPARES WHITE vs. NONWHITE TV VIEWING

(p. 44) Article, with 1 table showing rank and audience share among white and nonwhite viewers, for top 25 regular prime time programs in nonwhite households, Jan./Feb. 1983. Data are from A. C. Nielsen Co.

C1750–1.502: Dec. 12, 1983 (Vol. 105, No. 24)

FOCUS ON PROGRAMING AS CABLE GATHERS ON WEST COAST

(p. 31-32) Article on cable TV industry, with 1 table showing total systems (no date), and subscribers in May 1982 and Dec. 1983, for individual basic cable, pay cable, and pay-per-view programming services.

CABLE TV's AUDIO ANCILLARIES

(p. 58) Table showing systems, subscribers, and subscriber cost per month, for 10 cable TV audio programming services (no date).

GOOD YEAR FOR TV STATIONS, ANNUAL FEATURE

(p. 112-113) Annual article on finances of a typical TV station, 1982. Data are based on responses of 447 commercial TV stations to a National Assn of Broadcasters survey. Includes 1 table showing typical revenues and expenses by item, pretax profit, and profit margin, by type of TV station.

For description of article on 1980-81 survey results, see SRI 1982 Annual, under C1750-1.331.

C1750–1.503: Jan. 9, 1984 (Vol. 106, No. 2)

CHANGING HANDS 1983: RADIO-TV STATION SALES TOP $2.8 BILLION; CABLE SYSTEM TRANSACTIONS HIT $1 BILLION, ANNUAL FEATURE

(p. 71-105) Annual report on broadcasting ownership changes in 1983. Contains narrative summary of individual transactions, including stations, owners, and dollar amounts involved; and 1 table (p. 74) showing total transaction value and number of stations involved in ownership changes, for radio, TV, and combined radio/TV, 1954-83.

C1750–1.504: Jan. 16, 1984 (Vol. 106, No. 3)

SORTING OUT THE DBS PROPOSALS, RECURRING FEATURE

(p. 48) Recurring article on direct broadcast satellite (DBS) system proposals of 8 corporations receiving provisional FCC authorization in 1982. Includes 2 tables showing proposed number of satellites, transponders per satellite, geographic coverage, and channels by orbital slot, all by corporation.

C1750–1.505: Jan. 23, 1984 (Vol. 106, No. 4)

BROADCASTING'S TOP 50 AGENCIES, ANNUAL FEATURE

(p. 47-60) Annual report on top 50 advertising agencies ranked by broadcast billings, 1983. Data are based on a *Broadcasting* survey.

Contains narrative summary; brief profile of each agency; and 1 table showing each agency's broadcast billings (total, for cable TV, and for network and spot TV and radio), and broadcast billings as percent of all billings, 1983 with selected comparisons to 1982.

This is the 32nd annual article. Corrected data appear in the Feb. 6, 1984 issue, for description see C1750-1.507, below.

C1750–1.506: Jan. 30, 1984 (Vol. 106, No. 5)

NAB FINDS 'TYPICAL' RADIO STATION HAD $50,000 PROFIT IN '82, ANNUAL FEATURE

(p. 60-61) Annual article on finances of a typical radio station, 1982. Data are based on responses of 1,238 radio stations to a National Assn of Broadcasters survey.

Includes 1 table showing advertising sales, and revenue and expenses, by item; and pretax profit, profit margin, and full- and part-time employment; for typical radio station, 1982.

Preliminary survey results were published in the Sept. 12, 1983 issue (for description, see SRI 1983 Annual, under C1750-1.440). Full survey report is covered in SRI under A6635-1.

C1750–1.507: Feb. 6, 1984 (Vol. 106, No. 6)

ERRATA

(p. 26) Data corrections for annual feature on top 50 advertising agencies, appearing in Jan. 23, 1984 issue (for description, see C1750-1.505, above.)

C1750–1.508: Feb. 13, 1984 (Vol. 106, No. 7)

NOV. LOCAL TV SWEEPS: TOO CLOSE TO CALL BETWEEN ABC, CBS, RECURRING FEATURE

(p. 174-186) Recurring article, with 1 table comparing prime time audience of the 3 commercial TV networks, by Arbitron area of dominant influence (ADI), Nov. 1983. Table shows results of Arbitron sweep reports as compiled by 2 of the networks.

C1750–1.509: Feb. 27, 1984 (Vol. 106, No. 9)

BASEBALL: 1984, ANNUAL FEATURE

(p. 45-52) Annual article on payments by radio and TV networks and stations for the rights to broadcast major league baseball games. Includes 2 tables showing TV and radio rights holders, number of affiliates, and broadcast rights payments for 1983-84, by baseball team, arranged by league and division; and total payments to the major leagues, 1975-84.

C1750–1.510: Mar. 5, 1984 (Vol. 106, No. 10)

1983 SPOT RADIO

(p. 16) Brief article, with 1 table showing spot radio advertising expenditures for 27 product categories, 1983. Data are based on reports by leading advertising firms and local radio stations to Radio Expenditure Reports, Inc.

NAB PRESENTS: THE RETURN OF THE FINANCIAL FIGURES

(p. 40-42) Article, with 2 tables showing TV station financial data, including network compensation, national/regional and local advertising revenue, trade-outs/barter value, net revenues, expenses, and pre-tax profit, for 67-81 market areas, 1981-82. Also includes number of stations reporting in each market.

Data are from National Assn of Broadcasters. More detailed data were compiled by the FCC through 1980. FCC 1980 data appeared in the Aug. 10, 1981 issue (for description, see SRI 1981 Annual, under C1750-1.240).

TVB NUMBERS, SEMIANNUAL FEATURE

(p. 58) Semiannual article, with 1 table showing top 25 network TV advertisers ranked by 1983 expenditures, with comparison to 1982. Data are from TV Bureau of Advertising, based on Broadcast Advertisers Reports data.

C1750–1.511: Mar. 12, 1984 (Vol. 106, No. 11)

JANUARY SALES, RECURRING FEATURE

(p. 14) Recurring article, with 1 table showing spot radio advertising billings, by market size, Jan. 1983-84. Data are from Radio Expenditure Reports, Inc.

BUSINESS YEAR IN REVIEW: MIXED ACTION IN BOTTOM LINE

(p. 42, 46) Article, with 1 table showing total and broadcasting revenue and income, and earnings per share, for 12 broadcasting companies, 1982-83. Data are from individual company reports.

C1750–1.512: Mar. 19, 1984 (Vol. 106, No. 12)

SPOT NUMBERS, SEMIANNUAL FEATURE

(p. 16) Semiannual article, with 1 table showing top 25 national/regional spot TV advertisers ranked by 1983 expenditures, with comparison to 1982. Data are from TV Bureau of Advertising, based on Broadcast Advertisers Reports data.

C1750–1.513: Mar. 26, 1984 (Vol. 106, No. 13)

LOCAL/RETAIL TV GROWS, ANNUAL FEATURE

(p. 10) Annual article, with 1 table ranking top 25 local retail TV advertisers by expenditures, 1983 with comparison to 1982. Data are from TV Bureau of Advertising, based on Broadcast Advertisers Reports data.

POST-NATPE PROGRAM MARKETPLACE

(p. 47-48, 52) Article, with listing of new TV programs and off-network series available for the 1984 fall season, including number of episodes, program length and type, and distributor. Data are from NATPE International.

BATES PREDICTS SLIGHT RISE IN C-P-M, ANNUAL FEATURE

(p. 56-57) Annual article on media advertising price trends and forecast. Data are from Ted Bates Advertising. Includes 1 table showing CPI; and advertising cost and national expenditure indexes, for network and spot TV, magazines, newspapers, spot and/or network radio, and outdoor advertising; various years 1975-84.

C1750–1.514: Apr. 2, 1984 (Vol. 106, No. 14)

ABC WINS FEB. SWEEPS, RECURRING FEATURE

(p. 36-37) Recurring article, with 1 table comparing prime time audience of the 3 commercial TV networks, by Arbitron area of dominant influence (ADI), Feb. 1984. Table shows results of Arbitron sweep reports as compiled by CBS.

C1750–1.515: Apr. 9, 1984 (Vol. 106, No. 15)

NATIONAL SPOT, RECURRING FEATURE

(p. 18) Recurring article, with 1 table showing spot radio advertising billings, Jan.-Feb. 1983-84, and by market size Jan./Feb. 1983-84. Data are from Radio Expenditure Reports, Inc.

AFTER 10 YEARS OF SATELLITES, THE SKY'S NO LIMIT, RECURRING FEATURE

(p. 43-68) Recurring article, with 1 table and 1 tabular list showing number of satellites, transponders per satellite, geographic coverage, channels of service, and orbital slot, for 8 corporations with direct broadcast satellite (DBS) systems provisionally approved by FCC; and owner/lessee by transponder, for 4 principal satellites. No dates are given.

C1750–1.516: Apr. 16, 1984 (Vol. 106, No. 16)

TOP 100 COMPANIES IN ELECTRONIC COMMUNICATIONS, ANNUAL FEATURE

(p. 51-61) Annual report on revenues and earnings of 100 largest publicly owned companies in broadcasting and related electronic communication fields, 1983. Data are from *Broadcasting*.

Includes 1 table showing the following, by company: total revenues and earnings, profit margin, earnings per share, price/earnings ratio, electronic communication share of total revenues, and rankings for total and electronic communication revenues, 1983 with selected comparisons to 1982.

Also includes text data on earnings of top executives of 14 companies.

RTNDA RELEASES SALARY SURVEY

(p. 95) Brief article, with 1 table showing median and mean weekly salaries for news dept personnel at TV and radio stations, by occupation, 1983. Data are from responses of 432 commercial TV and 371 commercial radio stations to a summer 1983 survey conducted by Radio-TV News Directors Assn.

C1750–1.517: May 7, 1984 (Vol. 106, No. 19)

EASTMAN SURVEY

(p. 52) Two tables showing the following for spot radio advertisers: percent of advertising spots requested, by age group and type of market targeted, and by length of campaign, quarterly 1983-1st quarter 1984; with some undated detail by region. Data are from Eastman Radio.

C1750–1.518: May 14, 1984 (Vol. 106, No. 20)

SPOT RADIO EXPENDITURES, RECURRING FEATURE

(p. 86) Recurring article, with 1 table showing spot radio advertising billings, Jan.-Mar. 1983-84, and by market size Mar. 1983-84. Data are from Radio Expenditure Reports, Inc.

C1750–1.519: May 21, 1984 (Vol. 106, No. 21)

KEEPING UP WITH THE DILLERS

(p. 39-42) Article on compensation of top executives at broadcasting/entertainment companies, 1983. Data are from proxy statements and 10-K financial reports filed with the SEC. Includes 1 table showing compensation of 174 executives at over 60 companies, 1983 with some comparisons to 1979.

C1750–1.520: June 4, 1984 (Vol. 106, No. 23)

BROADCASTING'S CABLE PROGRAMING NUMBERS

(p. 64) Brief article, with 1 table showing cable TV systems and subscribers, for basic and pay services, as of Dec. 1983 and May 1984.

BROADCASTING'S TOP 50 MSOs, ANNUAL FEATURE

(p. 81) Annual table on the top 50 cable multiple system operators (MSOs), showing the following for each operator: basic subscribers, homes passed, basic penetration, pay subscriptions, and total homes in franchised areas, mostly as of Apr. 30, 1984.

June 11 and 25, 1984 issues contain data corrections; for description see C1750-1.521 and C1750-1.523, below.

MAJOR RADIO ADVERTISERS SPEND CLOSE TO $400 MILLION

(p. 82-84) Article, with 3 tables showing national spot and network radio advertising expenditures of top 20 advertisers, ranked by total radio advertising expenditures; top 12 radio advertising agencies, ranked by billings; and spot, local, and network TV advertising expenditure rankings for top 25 product categories; 1983 with comparison to 1982.

Data are from Radio Advertising Bureau and TV Bureau of Advertising, based on data from Broadcast Advertisers Reports.

C1750–1.521: June 11, 1984 (Vol. 106, No. 24)

ERRATA

(p. 30) Includes corrected data for annual table on top 50 cable TV multiple system operators, described above under C1750-1.520.

C1750–1.522: June 18, 1984 (Vol. 106, No. 25)

NATIONAL SPOT RADIO CONTINUES CLIMB, RECURRING FEATURE

(p. 63) Recurring article, with 1 table showing spot radio advertising billings, Jan.-Apr. 1983-84. Data are from Radio Expenditure Reports, Inc.

C1750–1.523: June 25, 1984 (Vol. 106, No. 26)

ERRATA

(p. 24) Includes corrected data for annual table on top 50 cable TV multiple system operators, described above under C1750-1.520.

INTV REVEALS INDIES' SHARE OF NATIONAL SPOT, RECURRING FEATURE

(p. 64-65) Recurring article, with 3 tables showing independent TV stations' share of spot advertising expenditures, for top 20-25 advertisers and product categories ranked by total spot advertising expenditures, and for top 25 advertisers ranked by expenditures with independent stations, 1st quarter 1984.

ARBITRON AND NIELSEN RANK CABLE PENETRATION

(p. 71-72) Article, with 1 table comparing Arbitron vs. Nielsen estimates of cable TV penetration in approximately 200 market areas, as of May 1984.

C1750–1.524: July 9, 1984 (Vol. 107, No. 2)

MARKET-BY-MARKET SWEEPS: IT'S ABC, NBC, AND CBS, RECURRING FEATURE

(p. 66-68) Recurring article, with 1 table comparing prime time audience of the 3 commercial TV networks, by Arbitron area of dominant influence (ADI), May 1984. Table shows results of Arbitron sweep reports as compiled by CBS.

C1750–1.525: July 23, 1984 (Vol. 107, No. 4)

NETWORK RADIO BUSINESS: CLIMBING TO A PLATEAU, ANNUAL FEATURE

(p. 56-64) Annual article, with 1 table listing satellites and transponders used, and also showing number of affiliates, for 14 major radio networks, 1984.

PROCTER AND GAMBLE REMAINS TOP ADVERTISER, ANNUAL FEATURE

(p. 108-109) Annual table ranking top 100 advertisers by total TV advertising expenditures, with detail for spot and network expenditures, 1983 with comparison to 1982. Data are from TV Bureau of Advertising, based on Broadcast Advertisers Reports.

C1750–1.526: July 30, 1984 (Vol. 107, No. 5)

HOW WILL MARKET REACT TO NEW LIMITS?

(p. 29-30) Article on potential effects of a July 1984 FCC ruling increasing the number of broadcasting stations which may be owned by 1 company. Includes 1 undated table showing number of AM, FM, and TV stations owned, for companies operating a full complement of stations in at least 1 category prior to the July FCC ruling.

C1750–1.527: Aug. 6, 1984 (Vol. 107, No. 6)

SPECIAL REPORT: FOOTBALL 1984, ANNUAL FEATURE

(p. 40-50) Annual article on payments and rights to broadcast collegiate and professional football games on radio and TV, 1984.

Includes text data on payments and rights; and 2 tabular lists showing National Football League local/regional coverage by team, including broadcast originator, number of stations, games scheduled, and rights holder, for radio broadcasts of preseason and regular season games and for TV broadcast of preseason games; 1984.

C1750–1.528: Aug. 13, 1984 (Vol. 107, No. 7)

PUTTING A PRICE ON FIFTH ESTATE FIRMS IS ELUSIVE BUSINESS

(p. 58-59) Article, with 1 table showing the following for 6 publicly traded broadcasting companies which returned to private control during May 1983-June 1984: transaction date and price, offer per share, premium over trading price, transaction type (outside acquisition or leveraged buyout), and percent of holdings controlled by "insiders."

C1750–1.529: Sept. 3, 1984 (Vol. 107, No. 10)

FALL SYNDICATED PROGRAMMING: A HORN OF PLENTY

(p. 33-35) Article, with 1 table showing the following for 20 syndicated TV programs premiering in fall 1984: syndicator and producer, number of original and repeat episodes, number of TV markets carrying the program and share of TV households, and premiere date.

CURTAIN FALLING ON THEATRICAL FILMS ON TV

(p. 42-44) Article, with 1 table showing audience rating and share, for top 5 theatrical and made-for-TV motion pictures broadcast on network TV during the 1983/84 season.

INDEPENDENT TV TAKES 54% SPENT BY TOP 25 SPOT ADVERTISERS, ACCORDING TO INTV, RECURRING FEATURE

(p. 57) Recurring article, with 3 tables showing independent TV stations' share of spot advertising expenditures, for top 20-25 advertisers and product categories ranked by total spot advertising expenditures, and for top 25 advertisers ranked by expenditures with independent stations, 1st half 1984. Data were compiled by Assn of Independent TV Stations.

C1750–1.530: Sept. 17, 1984 (Vol. 107, No. 12)

ADULT CONTEMPORARY RULES THE RATINGS, ANNUAL FEATURE

(p. 68-80) Annual table showing program format and average listening audience of the 10 most popular radio stations in the top 50 markets, based on Arbitron spring 1984 survey. Includes brief accompanying article.

Data correction appears in Sept. 24, 1984 issue; for description, see C1750-1.531, below.

C1750–1.531: Sept. 24, 1984 (Vol. 107, No. 13)

ERRATA

(p. 26) Includes correction for annual table on top 10 radio stations in top 50 markets; for description, see C1750-1.530, above.

RATINGS SERVICES MAKE MARKET CHANGES, RECURRING FEATURE

(p. 92-94) Recurring article, with 2 tables showing 205-211 Nielsen and Arbitron market areas ranked by number of TV households, 1984/85 TV season, with comparative Arbitron rank for 1983/84.

Data correction appears in Oct. 1, 1984 issue, for description see C1750-1.532, below. For description of last previous Arbitron data, see SRI 1983 Annual under C1750-1.445; for Nielsen data, see SRI 1982 Annual under C1750-1.343.

C1750–1.532: Oct. 1, 1984 (Vol. 107, No. 14)

ERRATA

(p. 26) Includes correction for recurring article on Nielsen and Arbitron market rankings.

For article description, see C1750-1.531, above.

FORMAT LIST, ANNUAL FEATURE

(p. 58) Annual table ranking top 18 radio formats by number of stations using format full-time, as of Sept. 1, 1984. Data are from the Radio Information Center.

C1750–1.533: Oct. 15, 1984 (Vol. 107, No. 16)

DBS RANKS CUT IN HALF, RECURRING FEATURE

(p. 75-76) Recurring article, with 1 undated table showing number of satellites, transponders per satellite, geographic coverage, channels of service, and orbital slot, for 4 corporations with direct broadcast satellite (DBS) systems receiving final FCC approval in 1984.

C1750–2   BROADCASTING/CABLE-CASTING YEARBOOK, 1984
Annual.   1984.
1270 p. var. paging.
LC 71-649524.
SRI/MF/excerpts, delayed

Annual broadcasting industry directory and statistical source book, 1984. Covers regulation, station ownership and operations, broadcast markets, cable TV (CATV), advertising agencies and other broadcast-related businesses, equipment, professional awards and assns, and broadcast education.

Most data are from Federal agencies and private research firms.

Contents:

Preface, editorial and advertiser indexes, and glossaries. (p. i-xvi)

Section A. Fifth Estate. Includes history of radio, TV, and educational broadcasting; broadcast finance and operation highlights (p. A2); FCC staff and technical regulations; and owners of multiple station and cross-media holdings. (p. A1-A62)

Section B. Radio. Includes U.S. and Canada station directory, showing affiliations, personnel, programming format, and advertising rates; nearby foreign and U.S. international stations; U.S. market populations; stations, by call letters and frequency; world radio and TV facilities, including number of receivers and transmitters, by country; and broadcasting growth; with 1 table. (p. B1-B400)

Section C. TV. Includes U.S. and Canada station directory, showing affiliations, personnel, and advertising rates; nearby foreign, low power, Spanish-language, experimental, and subscription stations; stations, by call numbers and channel; channel assignments by city; station applications; ownership transfers; and market characteristics; with 4 tables. (p. C1-C208)

Section D. Cable. Includes regulations and current developments; operation and finance highlights (p. D3); directory of U.S. and Canadian CATV systems, by State, U.S. territory, Province, and city, with data on personnel, area served, subscribers and charges, homes passed, stations carried, advertising revenue, and ownership; and directory of U.S. and Canadian multiple system operators (MSOs), including number and locations of systems operated; with 4 tables. (p. D1-D320)

Section E-F. Satellites and Programming. Includes satellite owners, operators, programmers, networks, cable program services, and superstations (stations transmitting via satellite or microwave), often with number of cable systems and subscribers served; production and distribution services; broadcasting awards; radio and TV networks, staff, and station affiliates; news services; and radio program formats. (p. E1-E8, F1-F96)

Section G-I. Advertising, Marketing, Technology, and Professional Services. Includes advertising agencies and representatives; radio and TV ownership, usage, and audience composition; equipment manufacturers and distributors; teletext and videotext operations; land line and microwave carriers; broadcasting growth; TV and radio sales; buyers guide; professional services and assns; broadcast schools; and broadcasting bibliography; with 7 tables. (p. G1-G16, H1-H72, I1-I72)

U.S. directories generally include U.S. territories. All tables are listed below.

Availability: Broadcasting Publications, 1735 DeSales St., NW, Washington DC 20036, $65.00 (prepaid), $75.00 (if billed); SRI/MF/excerpts, for text statistics, Section D, and tables listed below; delayed shipment in Dec. 1984.

TABLES:

C1750-2.1: Broadcasting Data

RADIO AND TV MARKETS

[B1] Radio city of license, with county or market population [alphabetical list by State]. (p. B317-B331)

[C1] ADI market atlas [for 1983/84, for each of 209 markets listed alphabetically, showing: rank; TV households in ADI, by county; TV stations; and accompanying map]. (p. C126-C200)

[C2] Markets ranked by size [number and percent of U.S. total TV households, and men, women, teens, and children, by ADI]. (p. C201-C204)

[C3] TV markets by Nielsen Marketing Research Territory [TV households, percent of region and U.S., and rank, by region and SMSA]. (p. C204-C205)

[C4] How network delivery varies by market [TV households, percent of U.S. TV households, and audiences as percent of U.S. TV index by network, by ADI]. (p. C205-C208)

CABLE TV

[D1] Cable penetration [and households, by Nielsen market area, as of July 1983]. (p. D318-D319)

[D2] Top 50 designated market areas ranked by % cable penetration. (p. D319)

[D3] Cable penetration and projected households [in top 50 designated market areas]. (p. D319)

[D4] Top 50 MSOs [ranked by number of basic subscribers, with numbers of homes passed, unpassed homes in franchise area, pay subscriptions, projected basic subscribers, and percent penetration]. (p. D320)

AUDIENCE

[G1] Trend of radio and TV ownership [for 1949-83]. (p. G16)

[G2] TV usage per home per week in hours and minutes [by time of day for weekday periods, Saturdays, and Sundays, Feb. 1983]. (p. G16)

[G3] TV audience composition [percent of homes using TV, number of viewers per 1,000 viewing homes, and percent of audience comprised of men, women, teens, and children, by day-part, Feb. 1983]. (p. G16)

[G4] Types of [prime-time] network TV shows and their audiences [number of programs, percent of average audience, and percent share of programming, for mystery/suspense, situation comedy, general drama, feature films, adventure, and all regular programs], Feb. 1983. (p. G16)

RADIO AND TV TRENDS AND SALES

[H1] Growth in broadcasting stations [TV and AM and FM radio stations authorized and operating; AM stations licensed and under construction; and experimental FM stations; various years or periods 1922-84]. (p. H55)

[H2-H3] TV receiver and radio set sales [volume and value, by type, 1958-1981]. (p. H56)

C1800
Business News Publishing Co.

C1800-1   **AIR CONDITIONING, HEATING, AND REFRIGERATION NEWS: 1984 Statistical Panorama**
Weekly (selected issue).
Apr. 2, 1984. 144 p.
Vol. 161, No. 14, Serial No. 2870.
ISSN 0002-2276.
SRI/MF/complete

Annual heating/cooling industry review and outlook issue, by Gordon D. Duffy and Thomas A. Mahoney, presenting data on shipments of air conditioning, refrigeration, home heating, and related products, 1983, with selected forecasts for 1984 and trends. Also includes energy use patterns, and cost projections, new housing characteristics, and selected foreign trade data; and 1980 housing and market profiles by metro area.

Data sources include Census Bureau, Air Conditioning and Refrigeration Institute, National Assn of Home Builders, and an *Air-Conditioning and Refrigeration Wholesalers* member survey.

Contains contents listing (p. 5); and numerous brief articles and metro area market profiles as follows:

a. 1984 forecasts and perspective, with 6 charts showing various air conditioning, heating, and refrigeration product shipments, 1982; and annual percent change in shipments of selected products, and in housing starts and passenger car sales, various years 1963-83. (p. 8-20)

b. Shipments of air conditioning, refrigeration, heating, and related products, including air pollution control equipment; with 23 charts and 4 tables showing shipments of 23 products, and distribution of selected products by type and/or capacity, various years 1976-83. (p. 20-37, 98-106)

c. Market profiles, with 1 table repeated for 188 metro areas, showing number of housing units, distribution by type of heating system and fuel used, and percent of housing units with central or room air conditioning; and distribution of single-family homes by age of heating system, or 10-year growth in single- and multi-family homes with detail by type of heating and cooling system; 1980. (p. 38-96)

d. Housing and construction characteristics, with 3 tables and 1 chart showing average residential heating costs by fuel type, 1983-93; percent of air conditioning equipment with selected energy efficiency ratios, by product type, 1976-83; number of single- and multi-family homes completed, by type of heating system and/or space-heating fuel, and by presence of air conditioning, all shown by region, 1982-83; and conventional housing starts, selected years 1974-83. (p. 107-125)

e. International trade, with 1 table and text data showing value of air conditioning/refrigeration equipment exports to Canada and 6 world areas; and imports and exports by product type, with detail for major countries of origin or destination; various years 1979-83. (p. 126-128)

f. Wholesalers, with 2 tables showing air conditioning and refrigeration equipment unit shipments by detailed product type, 1973-82; and results of a wholesaler survey, showing expectations for sales change by product, by U.S. region and for Canada, 1983-84. (p. 128-133)

Air Conditioning, Heating, and Refrigeration News is a weekly publication reporting trends and developments in the heating/cooling industry, and normally contains only limited statistical data. The annual statistical panorama is the only feature of ACH&RN covered by SRI.

This is the 19th annual statistical panorama report.

Availability: Business News Publishing Co., PO Box 2600, Troy MI 48007, $15.00; SRI/MF/complete.

C1850
Cahners Publishing Co.

C1850–1   PACKAGING

Monthly. Approx. 100 p.
ISSN 0746-3839.
SRI/MF/not filmed

Monthly trade journal (semimonthly in Mar.) reporting on developments and trends in the packaging industry. Covers manufacturing, R&D, marketing, and consumption. Most data are from Cahners Economics Dept, U.S. Dept of Commerce, and individual company reports.

General format:

a. Feature articles, occasionally with statistics, and narrative depts, placed throughout.

b. Quarterly "Packaging Economics" feature, with 1 table showing PPI for approximately 25 container types, for quarter ending 3 months prior to cover date, previous quarter, and same quarter of previous year; occasionally with charts forecasting trends for selected packaging materials, or additional tables.

c. Annual *Packaging Encyclopedia,* published as 2nd issue in Mar., containing material and process information, technical specifications, and industry statistics.

Oct. issue usually is a nonstatistical buyer's guide.

Features with substantial statistical content are described, as they appear, under "Statistical Features;" page location and latest period of coverage for quarterly table are also noted. Each issue of the journal is reviewed, but an abstract is published in SRI monthly issues only when quarterly table or other statistical features appear.

Availability: Packaging, 270 St. Paul St., Denver CO 80206, qualified subscribers †, others $45.00 per yr., single copy $4.00, Packaging Encyclopedia $25.00, Annual Buyers Guide $20.00; SRI/MF/not filmed.

Issues reviewed during 1984: Nov. 1983-Oct. 1984; and Packaging Encyclopedia 1984 (P) (Vol. 28, Nos. 12-13; Vol. 29, Nos. 1-11).

STATISTICAL FEATURES:

C1850–1.501: Dec. 1983 (Vol. 28, No. 13)

PACKAGING ECONOMICS, QUARTERLY FEATURE

(p. 17) PPI, for 3rd quarter 1983. For data description, see C1850-1 above.

C1850–1.502: Jan. 1984 (Vol. 29, No. 1)

PACKAGING MATERIALS OUTLOOK: MOST SUPPLIES ASSURED

(p. 98-100) Article, with 1 chart showing worldwide operating rate for styrene-butadiene-styrene (SBS) paperboard, biennially 1976-88.

C1850–1.503: Mar. 1984 (Vol. 29, No. 3)

PACKAGING ECONOMICS, QUARTERLY FEATURE

(p. 19) PPI, for 4th quarter 1983. For data description, see C1850-1 above.

C1850–1.504: Packaging Encyclopedia 1984 (Vol. 29, No. 4)

STATISTICS OF PACKAGING, ANNUAL FEATURE

(p. 334-339) Annual article, by Susan Rich Friedman, on container and packaging material production and marketing, 1983, with selected trends 1960-87. Data sources include Charles H. Kline and Co., Commerce Dept, and Chemical Specialties Manufacturers Assn.

Includes 15 tables showing:

a. Shipments and/or market share and growth rate, for paperboard, metal, plastic, paper, glass, wood, and textile packaging materials, selected years 1973-87.

b. Consumption of films and plastics for packaging, by material type; end-use distribution of polyethylene film and extrusion coatings, cellophane, and aerosol containers; and shipments of blow-molded plastic bottles; various years 1960-83.

c. Packaging material value, by detailed container or material type; production, by consumer and shipping container types; and end-use distribution, by container type; various years 1960-83.

C1850–1.505: May 1984 (Vol. 29, No. 6)

GROWING SOFTWARE FIELD DEMANDS PACKAGE VARIETY

(p. 45-51) By H. Guy Lee. Article, with 1 table showing typical costs for packaging computer software, by package type and order size. Data are author estimates.

C1850–1.506: June 1984 (Vol. 29, No. 7)

PACKAGING ECONOMICS, QUARTERLY FEATURE

(p. 19) PPI, for 1st quarter 1984. For data description, see C1850-1 above.

C1850–1.507: Aug. 1984 (Vol. 29, No. 9)

PLASTIC PRICES RISING SLOWLY

(p. 15) Brief article, with 1 table showing PPI forecast for 9 plastic materials and products used in packaging, 1st quarter 1984-1st quarter 1985. Data are from BLS.

C1850–1.508: Sept. 1984 (Vol. 29, No. 10)

PRICE HIKES FOR PAPER PRODUCTS

(p. 18) Brief article, with 1 table showing PPI for 9 paper materials and products used in packaging, 1st quarter 1984-1st quarter 1985. Data are from BLS and Cahners Economics.

C1850–2   ELECTRONIC BUSINESS

Semimonthly. Approx. 140 p.
ISSN 0163-6197.
LC 78-648318.
SRI/MF/not filmed

Semimonthly trade journal (issued 19 times per year) reporting on U.S. and world business trends in the electronics industry, including marketing, new products, management, and other nontechnical industry topics. Data are based on Cahners Economic Dept forecasts, BLS and Commerce Dept studies, individual company reports, and other sources.

Issues contain semimonthly "Business Barometer" and monthly "Leadtime Index" and "Leadtime Forecast" statistical depts, described below; other regular depts; and feature articles, often with statistics.

Semiannual statistical features include electronic components/equipment market forecasts,

and rankings of top 100 and 2nd 100 electronics companies. Annual statistical features include data on leading companies in various electronics industry sectors, leading European electronics companies, military electronics market, and salaries of electronics executives.

Semimonthly "Business Barometer" appears in all issues, monthly "Leadtime Index" and "Leadtime Forecast" usually appear in alternate issues. All additional features with substantial statistical content are described, as they appear, under "Statistical Features." Nonstatistical features are not covered.

Prior to the Apr. 1, 1984 issue, journal was published monthly (semimonthly in May), and all statistical depts appeared in each issue.

Availability: Electronic Business, 270 St. Paul St., Denver CO 80206, qualified subscribers †, others $40.00 per yr., single copy $4.00, plant site issue $10.00; SRI/MF/not filmed.

Issues reviewed during 1984: Nov. 1983-Mar. 1984 (monthly); Apr. 1-Oct. 15, 1984 (semimonthly) (P) (Vol. 9, Nos. 12-13; Vol. 10, Nos. 1-16).

STATISTICAL DEPTS:

SEMIMONTHLY DATA

a. "Business Barometer," including narrative analysis with several charts, most showing trends and outlook for various electronics industry indicators.

MONTHLY DATA

b. "Leadtime Index," with 1 table indicating number of weeks required to build/ship orders, by detailed type of electronic component and subsystem, as of publication month.

c. "Leadtime Forecast," including narrative analysis, usually with 1-2 charts, on leadtime trends and outlook for a selected electronics product category each month.

STATISTICAL FEATURES:

C1850–2.501: Nov. 1983 (Vol. 9, No. 12)

WE HAVE SEEN THE FUTURE, AND IT IS AI

(p. 36-42) By Frank Kashner. Article, with 1 chart showing sales of computer software applications of artificial intelligence (AI) and market share by type, 1982 and 1990. Data are from DM Data, Inc.

HARD TIMES FOR U.S. ROBOT MANUFACTURERS

(p. 44-46) Article, with 1 chart showing industrial robot shipment value, and market share by manufacturer, 1983. Data are from Prudential-Bache Securities.

TWO NEW ENTRANTS JOIN AN EMERGING WAFER-TESTER MARKET

(p. 71-72) Article, with 1 chart showing world market value for parametric semiconductor-wafer test equipment, selected years 1979-87. Data are from VLSI Research, Inc.

OUTLOOK DIM FOR TAAP, AN AID PROGRAM FOR SMALL BUSINESSES

(p. 74) Article, with text data and 1 chart showing number of U.S. electronics companies certified for aid under the Commerce Dept's Trade Adjustment Assistance Program since 1975, and distribution by product line. Data are from New England Trade Adjustment Center.

JAPAN: 4, U.S.: 1 IN THE U.S. LCD WORLD SERIES

(p. 92) Article on Japan-U.S. competition for the liquid-crystal display (LCD) market. Data are from Stanford Resources. Includes 1 chart showing value of U.S. LCD consumption, and market share by application, 1982 and 1990.

CAPACITORS 1983: ON THE REBOUND, ANNUAL FEATURE

(p. 136-140, passim) Annual article, by Mary Ann Murphy, on capacitor market developments and leading manufacturers, 1982. Data are from Electronic Industries Assn and Gnostic Concepts, Inc.

Includes 1 chart and 1 table showing capacitor domestic sales and foreign trade volume and value, by type, 1981-82; and top 10 capacitor manufacturers, ranked by U.S. shipment value, 1982.

U.S. FAX MARKET TAKES OFF, WITH JAPANESE ENGINES

(p. 164-166) Article, with 1 chart and 1 table showing facsimile equipment installed base by type, and market share by manufacturer, various years 1979-84. Data are from Creative Strategies International.

HOT COMPETITION TO AUTOMATE DESIGN OF CIRCUIT BOARDS

(p. 174-179) Article, with 1 chart showing computer-aided-design equipment sales for use in printed circuit board manufacture, selected years 1982-87. Data are from Dataquest, Inc.

ELECTRONIC BUSINESS SECOND 100, SEMIANNUAL FEATURE

(p. 186-196) Semiannual article on financial performance of 2nd 100 largest electronics companies, ranked by electronics sales during most recent fiscal year. Data are from company financial reports, and are shown for fiscal years ending in various months, June 1982-May 1983 (mostly Dec. 1982).

Includes 1 detailed table showing each company's electronics sales and rank; total sales and net income, with amounts per employee and 5-year growth rates; and selected financial and operating ratios. Also includes 1 summary table showing top 4-11 companies in per-employee sales in 7 industry segments.

DISPLAY DIAGNOSIS: GOOD NEWS FOR A FLAT BUSINESS

(p. 222-226) Article, with 1 chart showing sales of displays for computer monitors, and market share by type, 1981 and 1986. Data are from Gnostic Concepts, Inc.

C1850–2.502: Dec. 1983 (Vol. 9, No. 13)

REINCARNATION: CP/M IS DEAD, LONG LIVE CP/M

(p. 28-30) By Mary Jo Foley. Article, with 1 chart showing 16-bit computer operating system shipments, and market share by type, 1983 and 1987. Data are from Creative Strategies, Inc.

GOING UP: CHIP MAKERS SEE CONTINUED GOOD TIMES

(p. 54) Article, with 1 table showing semiconductor shipment value, by selected world area and product type, 1982-86. Data are from Semiconductor Industry Assn.

SOFTWARE GENERATORS: SEND IN THE CLONES

(p. 58) Article, with 1 chart showing worldwide revenues of U.S. independent software suppliers, 1982 and 1987. Data are from International Data Corp.

LOT'S NEW AT GDC, INCLUDING PROFITABILITY

(p. 108-110) By Tim Mead. Article, with 1 chart showing modem and multiplexer shipment values, and market share by manufacturer, 1982. Data are from Kidder, Peabody and Co.

MILITARY ELECTRONICS, ANNUAL FEATURE

Annual collection of articles on the military market for electronics products. Includes the following statistical articles:

BOOM TIMES? MILITARY BUDGET HAS BOTH GOOD AND BAD NEWS, ANNUAL FEATURE

(p. 132-134) Annual article on Electronic Industries Assn forecast of military spending for electronic products. Includes 1 chart showing value of electronics portion of DOD budget, FY84-93.

TESTING THE DEFENSE: IE FINDS A MILITARY SUCCESS

(p. 147-148) Article, with 1 chart showing value of automatic test equipment shipments to the military market, by contract type, 1983 and 1987. Data are from Frost and Sullivan, Inc.

BY THE NUMBERS: WHERE THE $$ ARE HEADED FOR ELECTRONICS

(p. 150) Article, with 2 tables showing value of military purchases of electronic components and production of military electronic equipment, by type, 1983-85. Data are from Henderson Ventures.

Other Articles

MARKET SIZZLE: FAST TIMES ON MEMORY LANE, ANNUAL FEATURE

(p. 166-173) Annual article, by William F. Arnold, on memory integrated circuit market developments and outlook. Data are from Semiconductor Industry Business Service and Intel Corp. Includes 1 chart and 1 table showing market value for memory integrated circuits, by product group, 1982-86.

AIRCRAFT PURCHASES HEAD UP STRONG MILITARY MARKET

(p. 182) Brief article on U.S. military procurement market and international arms sales, based on data from Henderson Ventures.

Includes 1 chart showing military equipment export value, by country of destination and equipment type, 1982.

BRITISH TELECOMMUNICATIONS: SOUNDS LIKE THE U.S., BUT...

(p. 186) Brief article, with 1 table showing UK market value for telecommunications equipment, by type, 1983 and 1985. Data are from International Resource Development, Inc.

EVOLUTIONARY CHIPS: A NEW ROUND OF SIGNAL PROCESSORS

(p. 188-189) Article, with 1 chart showing market value for digital-signal-processing integrated circuits, by type, 1983-84. Data are from Integrated Circuit Engineering Corp.

C1850–2.503: Jan. 1984 (Vol. 10, No. 1)

STILL GREEDY AFTER ALL THESE YEARS

(p. 38-40) Article, with 2 charts showing high-technology companies receiving venture capital investments, value of investments, and distribution by general purpose, 1981-82. Data are from *Venture Capital Journal*.

SPIES: YOU AIN'T SEEN NOTHIN' YET

(p. 76-78) Article on Customs Dept efforts to curtail illegal high-technology transfers to Eastern Bloc countries. Includes 1 chart showing number and value of Customs Dept electronics seizures, 1982-83.

KOREA: A SLEEPING GIANT STARTS TO STIR

(p. 90-93) Article, with 1 chart and 2 tables showing the following for South Korea: sales and net income of top 12 electronics companies; and value of domestic and export electronics shipments, by application; 1st half 1983, with comparisons to 1982. Data are from Dong Suh Securities Co., Ltd., and *Electronic Business*.

MIXING ELECTRONICS ASSEMBLY AND FOREIGN POLICY IN THE CARIBBEAN

(p. 110-111) By Nancy Henderson. Article, with 1 data map showing value of electronics exports to the U.S. by type, for 7 Central American and Caribbean countries or islands, 1981. Data are from Commerce Dept.

OUTLOOK 1984, ANNUAL FEATURE

Annual compilation of articles forecasting market trends for electronics equipment and components, 1984. Articles with substantial statistical content are described below.

ON THE PERIPHERY: TERMINALS, DISKS AND PRINTERS TO TOP $20B

(p. 166-168) Article on computer peripherals market, with 1 chart showing printer revenues by printer type, 1983-84. Data are from Venture Development Corp.

BYE RECESSION AND OLD AT&T; HI RECOVERY, BOCs AND UNCLE SAM

(p. 172-176) Article, with 3 charts showing construction spending of regional holding companies created from American Telephone and Telegraph Co. (AT&T) reorganization; and production value of all and military electronic communications equipment; 1983-84. Data are from AT&T, Gnostic Concepts, Inc., and Henderson Ventures.

TEST AND MEASUREMENT SALES GET A FAST GROWTH TRACK

(p. 181-182) Article, with 2 charts showing world sales of electronic test/measurement equipment, and growth by type, 1983-84. Data are from Prime Data, Inc.

SEMI-EQUIPMENT COMPANIES BRACED FOR DEMAND SURGE

(p. 188-193) Annual article, with 1 table showing electronics equipment purchasing plans of electronics manufacturers, 1984. Data are from an *Electronic Business* survey of purchasing managers.

IN THE CHIPS: 1984 PROMISES CONTINUED GOOD TIMES FOR ICs

(p. 196-198) Article, with 1 chart showing world semiconductor production value, 1983-84. Data are from Integrated Circuit Engineering, Inc.

FORECAST OF U.S. OEM ELECTRONIC-COMPONENT PURCHASES

(p. 200-219) Annual article, with 28 tables showing value of original equipment manufacturer (OEM) purchases of electronic components, by detailed product type and application, 1982-84, and expected change in unit prices, 1984 vs. 1983. Data are from an *Electronic Business* survey of purchasing managers.

Other Articles

LITHIUM LIGHTS UP A FAST-GROWING BATTERY MARKET

(p. 244-246) Article, with 1 undated chart showing market share and price range of lithium batteries, by application. Data are from Catalyst Research Corp.

FIXED DISK-DRIVE SALES UP 16%; REMOVABLE LOOK 'BLEAK'

(p. 248-250) Article, with 1 chart showing disk drive revenues, and market share by type, 1982 and 1986. Data are from *1983 DISK/ TREND Report*.

CMOS DEVICES HEAD UP WORLD USE IN GROWING SEMI MARKET

(p. 250) Brief article, with 1 table showing value of world consumption of U.S. manufactured complementary-metal-oxide semiconductors, by application, biennially 1982-90. Data are from L. O. Brown Associates.

C1850–2.504: Feb. 1984 (Vol. 10, No. 2)

NEW LCD MARKET STUDY

(p. 28) Brief article, with 1 chart showing value of liquid-crystal display (LCD) market in Japan and U.S., 1985 and 1990. Data are from Stanford Resources, Inc.

STAYING ALIVE IN '85 WITH THE IBM PC-COMPATIBLE

(p. 42-46) By Geoff Lewis. Article on market growth for manufacturers of IBM-compatible microcomputers. Includes 1 chart showing total microcomputer shipment value, and market share of IBM and IBM-compatible microcomputers, 1983 and 1988. Data are from Future Computing, Inc.

PACKET-SWITCHING MARKET SWITCHES INTO HIGH GEAR

(p. 56-58) Article on market growth of packet-switching equipment used in data communications. Data are from International Data Corp. Includes 1 chart showing shipment value for packet-switching equipment, by type, 1982 and 1987.

ARCHIVE, CIPHER AND CO. CROWD INTO THE TAPE MARKET

(p. 77) Article, with 1 chart showing world cartridge-tape computer memory drive shipments, by size, 1981 and 1987. Data are from Freeman Associates.

FROM DESERT TO MOUNTAINTOP: THE U.S. SEMI-EQUIPMENT BOOM

(p. 85) Article, with 1 table showing worldwide capital investments for semiconductor production equipment, by type, 1982-88. Data are from VLSI Research, Inc.

WILL KOREA OPEN ITS PC MARKET TO U.S. VENDORS?

(p. 98) Article, with 1 undated table showing volume and value of South Korean computer and peripheral production, domestic sales, and exports, by type. Data are from Electronic Industries Assn of Korea.

IT TAKES VISION TO SELL VISION

(p. 170-174, passim) Article, with 1 chart showing electronic vision system sales, and market share by application, 1984. Data are from Prudential-Bache Securities, Inc. and General Electric Co.

POWER PLAY: MOSFETs CHALLENGE THE BIPOLARS

(p. 199-200) Article, with 2 charts showing worldwide shipment value for metal-oxide semiconductor field-effect transistors (MOSFETs), by end-use market and selected country or world area, 1982 and 1990. Data are from L. O. Brown Associates.

NEXT WAVE? KEEPING YOUR COMPUTER IN A BRIEFCASE

(p. 202-208) Article, with 2 charts showing sales volume and retail revenue, for world and U.S. portable computer market, and for U.S. total personal computer market, 1983-84 and 1987. Data are from Future Computing, Inc.

ALPHANUMERIC CRTs HEADLINE TERMINAL GROWTH

(p. 219) Brief article, with 1 chart showing computer terminal shipment value, and market share by type, 1984. Data are from Venture Development Corp.

HOT SPOTS SHINE FORTH IN A $201 BILLION INDUSTRY, SEMIANNUAL FEATURE

(p. 227-236) Semiannual article on financial performance of top 100 electronics companies, ranked by electronics sales during most recent 4 quarters for which data were available, primarily Oct. 1982-Sept. 1983. Data are from annual company financial reports and other sources.

Includes 4 charts showing aggregate trends, FY80-83; and 1 detailed table showing each company's electronics sales and rank, total revenues, and net income or loss, FY83, with comparative sales rankings for FY82.

Also includes 1 summary table showing percent change in electronics sales and profits of 2-12 leading companies in 6 industry segments, FY82-83.

DECADE OF PRODUCTIVITY

(p. 266) Article, with 1 chart showing capital spending of all manufacturing vs. electrical machinery industry, 1981-83. Data are from Commerce Dept.

C1850–2.505: Mar. 1984 (Vol. 10, No. 3)

VOICE-RECOGNITION GEAR: SAY IT AGAIN, SAM

(p. 44, 48) Article, with 2 charts showing value of voice-recognition device market, and market share by type and application, 1984 and 1986. Data are from Strategic Inc.

DEC's VT200s SPAWN A COPYCAT MARKET

(p. 56) Article on market growth of Digital Equipment Corp. (DEC) competitors manufacturing DEC-compatible computer terminals. Data are from Advanced Resources Development. Includes 1 chart showing shipments of DEC/DEC-compatible terminals and market share by manufacturer, 1982.

CHIP KINGS: CHANGING STRATEGIES IN A HOT MARKET, ANNUAL FEATURE

(p. 86-90) Annual article, by William F. Arnold, on world semiconductor market performance, 1983. Data are from Integrated Circuit Engineering Corp.

Includes 4 charts and 1 table showing world semiconductor and integrated circuit production value, consumption, and/or sales, by leading manufacturer and/or for U.S., Europe, Japan, and rest of world, various years 1982-84.

TAKE ASPIRIN, A CAT SCAN—NO NMR, X-RAY OR ULTRASOUND

(p. 164-168) Article, with 1 chart and 1 table showing market value of image-producing medical equipment by type, 1982-83, and major manufacturers of each. Data are from Cable House and Ragan.

HONG KONG: BUSINESS AS USUAL IN THE MIDST OF UNCERTAINTY

(p. 172-176) By Vonnie Bishop. Article, with 1 chart showing Hong Kong electronics industry market value, and market share by product group, 1981. Data are from Hong Kong Dept of Industry.

C1850–2.506: Apr. 1, 1984 (Vol. 10, No. 4)

ROBOTICS: I CAN ASEA CLEARLY NOW

(p. 26-27) Article, with 1 chart showing total industrial robot sales, and market share by manufacturer, 1983. Data are from Prudential Bache Securities, Inc.

OCR IMAGE PROCESSING: HIGH HOPES FOR THE HIGH END

(p. 28) Article, with 1 table showing market value for optical character recognition equipment, by selected industry division or sector, 1984 and 1992. Data are from International Resource Development.

MERGERS AND ACQUISITIONS CONTINUE AT A RAPID CLIP

(p. 34) Article, with 1 table showing number and value of mergers/acquisitions in the computer software/services industry, and median transaction value, 1981-83. Data are from Broadview Associates.

EUROPEAN TARIFFS: LOVE 'EM OR LEAVE 'EM

(p. 37) Article, with 1 undated table showing EC tariff rates on computer, TV, and video cassette recorder parts and equipment.

CENTRONICS: THE ONCE AND FUTURE(?) PRINTER KING

(p. 82-84) By Michael Seither. Article, with 1 chart showing computer printer shipments by manufacturer, and total shipment value, 1982. Data are from International Data Corp.

REVAMPED CONNECTOR FIRMS PLUG INTO A $3B BUSINESS, ANNUAL FEATURE

(p. 108-112) Annual article, by Mary Ann Murphy, on market performance of electronic and telecommunication connectors and interconnection devices, 1983. Data are from Gnostic Concepts, Inc. and Merrill Lynch Capital Markets Group.

Includes 3 charts and 1 table showing sales of top 11 connector/interconnection suppliers, connector/socket production value, and value of connector demand by application, various years 1982-84.

MICROMINIS TO DOMINATE $25B COMPUTER MARKET BY 1987

(p. 121-122) Article, with 1 chart and 1 table showing world minicomputer sales, by computer size category, 1982-87. Data are from Electronic Trend Publications.

FABRICATION TO TEST: PROBERS BRIDGE GAP

(p. 126-127) By Andy Santoni. Article, with 1 chart showing market growth of wafer probers (semiconductor testing devices) by type, biennially 1984-88. Data are from VLSI Research, Inc.

RECOVERY PLUS NEW PRODUCTS EQUALS BOOM TIMES FOR SUPPLIERS

(p. 131-133) Article on consumer electronics market conditions. Data are from Electronics Industries Assn.

Includes 5 tables showing factory sales value and percent growth for various categories of computers, electronic games, video equipment, telephones, and audio equipment including auto audio, 1984.

C1850–2.507: Apr. 15, 1984 (Vol. 10, No. 5)

OPEN UP THEM GOLDEN GATES: TAIWAN'S DISK-DRIVE INVASION

(p. 30-32) By Mike O'Connor. Article, with 1 chart and 1 table showing volume and value of Taiwan's magnetic disk exports, for top 10 countries of destination and all others, 1983. Data are from Taiwan Board of Foreign Trade.

WHERE VENTURE CAPITAL FEARS TO TREAD: R&D PARTNERSHIPS

(p. 60-62) Article, with 1 chart showing value of publicly offered R&D limited partnerships, 1982-83. Data are from Robert A. Stanger & Co.

DEDICATED STRATEGY TO KEEP INTEL NO. 1

(p. 76-83) By Mary Ann Murphy. Article, with 2 charts showing world sales of microprocessor development systems, and of test/measurement equipment by type, various years 1980-84. Data are from Prime Data. Also includes 1 table summarizing Intel Corp. finances.

DATA COMMUNICATIONS, SPECIAL REPORT

Special compilation of articles on market condition for data communications equipment. Statistical articles are described below.

MARKETING BURSTS AHEAD AS KEY LINK TO SUCCESS

(p. 89-91) By Tim Mead. Article, with 5 tables and 5 charts showing sales of network processors and management products, gateways, modems, and multiplexers, with detail by type, 1984 and 1987, and compounded annual growth rate. Data are from Strategic, Inc.

IVDTs LINK UP WITH GROWTH AFTER COSTLY MISCONNECTIONS

(p. 94-95) By Mary Jo Foley. Article, with 1 chart showing shipment volume and value for integrated voice/data terminals, 1984, 1987, and 1990. Data are from International Resource Development, Inc.

NEW PROTOCOL FOR SUPPLIERS: CONVERTING BITS INTO BUCKS

(p. 96-97) By Tim Mead. Article on market growth of protocol converters, electronic devices that link microcomputers and mainframe computers. Data are from International Resource Development, Inc. Includes 1 chart showing protocol converter market value, by type, 1984, 1987, and 1990.

C1850–2.508: May 1, 1984 (Vol. 10, No. 6)

CELLULAR RADIO: NO JAPANESE NEED APPLY

(p. 40) Article, with 1 chart showing market value of cellular radio (mobile telephone) equipment, by type, 1983 and 1985. Data are from Frost and Sullivan, Inc.

GATESVISION: THE MACRO STRATEGY AT MICROSOFT

(p. 82-91) By Mary Jo Foley. Article, with 1 chart and 1 table showing microcomputer software sales volume and value, by type; and sales, income, R&D and marketing as percent of sales, profit margin, and employees, for 5 software manufacturers; various years 1983-86. Data are from Software Access, Inc., and *Electronic Business*.

RECOVERY RELEASES DEMAND FOR AUTOMATION, ANNUAL FEATURE

(p. 106-114) Annual article, by Cindy Thames, on market performance of semiconductor production equipment, 1983. Data are from VLSI Research, Inc.

Includes 2 charts showing worldwide sales of wafer processing, test, and assembly equipment, for use in semiconductor production, by type, with shares for 2-3 leading manufacturers of each type, 1983; and top 11 manufacturers ranked by semiconductor equipment revenue, 1983 with comparisons to 1982.

FINE LINES: VLSI PUSHES PRODUCTION-EQUIPMENT MAKERS

(p. 118-120) By Nowlan Ulsch. Article, with 1 chart showing shipment value of application-specific integrated circuit (ASIC) chips; and ASIC and standard shares in captive and merchant markets; 1985 and 1990. Data are from Dataquest, Inc.

FULL MEASURES: MARKETS WIDEN FOR OPTO TEST

(p. 137-141) By Norman Alster. Article, with 1 undated chart showing sales distribution for laser/electro-optic test equipment, by end-use sector. Data are from Frost and Sullivan, Inc.

FAULTLESS MARKET DRAWS MANY NEW CONTENDERS

(p. 142-150) By Sarah Glazer. Article, with 1 chart showing market value of fault-tolerant computer systems, and market share by manufacturer, 1982. Data are from International Development, Inc.

ROBOTICS TAKES OFF: $2B MARKET BY 1990

(p. 154-155) Article, with 2 charts showing industrial robot sales, and market share by manufacturer and/or application, 1983 and 1988. Data are from The Yankee Group.

C1850–2.509: May 15, 1984 (Vol. 10, No. 7)

METAL-OXIDE SEMICONDUCTORS: THE MARKET GATHERS MOMENTUM

(p. 43-44) Article, with 1 chart showing metal-oxide semiconductor memory market value, by type, 1984 and 1989. Data are from Montgomery Securities, Inc.

LATEST PERIPHERAL IS AT YOUR FINGERTIPS

(p. 112-116) By Sarah Glazer. Article, with 1 chart showing computer keyboard market value, and share by type, 1987. Data are from Venture Development Corp.

REACTIVE-ION ETCHING TO DOMINATE WAFER PROCESSING

(p. 174) Brief article, with 1 chart showing market value of semiconductor dry etching equipment, and share by type, 1988. Data are from Strategic, Inc.

C1850–2.510: June 1, 1984 (Vol. 10, No. 8)

HOW I LEARNED TO STOP WORRYING AND LOVE GALLIUM ARSENIDE

(p. 24-26) By Jack Cushman. Article, with 1 chart showing market value for gallium arsenide integrated circuits, and market shares by end-use industry, 1984, 1988, and 1992.

COMING SHAKEOUT IN THE MICRO UNIX MARKET

(p. 50-51) Article, with 1 chart showing market volume and value for computers compatible with Unix (an AT&T developed multiuser, multitasking computer operating system), and market share by product or product group, 1983. Data are from Yates Ventures.

IBM: MANAGEMENT

(p. 88-91) Article, with 3 tables showing revenue and net income for International Business Machines Corp. (IBM) and 10 other computer manufacturers; assets, and R&D and capital spending, for IBM vs. American Telephone and Telegraph Co.; and selected income and earnings detail for IBM; 1983.

TEUTONIC ANALYSIS: DOLCH AIMS AT A LOGICAL CHOICE

(p. 94-102) By Mary Ann Murphy. Article, with 1 chart showing logic-analyzer world sales, and market share for Tektronix/Hewlett-Packard and all others, 1983. Data are from Prime Data, Inc.

C1850–2.511: June 15, 1984 (Vol. 10, No. 9)

WHERE HAVE ALL THE WORD PROCESSORS GONE?

(p. 28-30) By Anne Hyde. Article, with 1 chart showing number of word processors installed in offices and number of office workstations with personal/desktop computers, 1983 and 1988. Data are from Dataquest, Inc.

NO STANDSTILL: KIERULFF SPEEDS INTO NEW MARKETS

(p. 78-82) By Tim Mead. Article, with 2 tables showing average annual percent change in sales and net income, and average number of inventory turns per year, for 9-10 electronic distributors, 1978-83 period; and selected financial data for Kierulff Electronics, 1981-83. Data are from Hambrecht and Quist, Inc.

IBM ADD-ONS ADD UP TO A MULTIBILLION-DOLLAR MARKET

(p. 118-122) By Geoff Lewis. Article, with 1 chart showing market value for personal computer hardware, and market share for add-ons, 1984-86 and 1989. Data are from Future Computing, Inc.

UNLOCKING THE EMBEDDED MARKET OF SILICON SOFTWARE

(p. 124-128) By Mary Jo Foley. Article, with 1 chart showing value of microprocessor world shipments, with distribution by application, 1983. Data are from Integrated Circuit Engineering Corp.

WINCHESTER WARS TIGHTEN MARGINS FOR DISK MAKERS

(p. 130-132) By Geoff Lewis. Article, with 2 charts showing world shipments of disk drives, with distribution by drive size, 1984 and 1986; and world shipments of 5.25 inch Winchester-type disk drives, 1984-86. Data are from *1983 Disk/Trend Report.*

SONY SALLIES INTO THE OEM BUSINESS

(p. 140-144) By Jessica Schwartz. Article, with 1 chart showing world sales of microfloppy disk drives, 1983-86. Data are from *1983 Disk/Trend Report.*

CAPITAL IDEA? ARROW'S LEVERAGED STRATEGY

(p. 152-154) Article, with 2 tables showing long-term debt, shareholders' equity, and capitalization, for 4 electronic distributors, 1984; and selected financial data for Arrow Electronics, Inc., 1982-83.

C1850–2.512: July 10, 1984 (Vol. 10, No. 10)

CHIPS: YOU GOTTA SPEND MONEY TO MAKE MONEY

(p. 28-32) By John Eckhouse. Article, with 2 tables showing R&D and capital spending summary for 3 semiconductor manufacturers; and U.S./European semiconductor shipments, by type; various years 1980-86. Data are from company reports, *Electronic Business,* and Semiconductor Industry Assn.

EUROPE'S NOT THE HAPPY HUNTING GROUND IT SEEMS

(p. 37) Article, with 1 chart showing installed microcomputer units in Europe, and market share by company, 1983. Data are from Logica UK Ltd.

MOTOROLA: MOVING HEAD-ON INTO CELLULAR SERVICE

(p. 48-51) Article, with 1 chart showing cellular system (mobile telephone) sales, and market share by company, 1983. Data are from Frost and Sullivan, Inc.

MMM...MODEM MARKET MAKES MANUFACTURERS MUCH MONEY

(p. 58-60) Article, with 2 charts showing microcomputer modem installed base and market share by company, 1983; and percent of microcomputers with modems, biennially 1984-88. Data are from Creative Strategies International.

JOCKEYING FOR POSITION IN THE KOREAN CHIP RACE

(p. 72-74) Article, with 1 table showing value of Korean production, exports, and domestic shipments, for integrated circuits and other semiconductors, 1982-83. Data are from Electronic Industries Assn of Korea.

200 ELECTRONIC BUSINESS, SEMIANNUAL FEATURE

(p. 93-130) Semiannual collection of articles on financial performance of top 200 electronics companies, ranked by electronics sales during 1983. Data are primarily from company financial reports.

Includes 1 detailed table (p. 100-109) showing each company's electronics sales and rank; total sales and net income, with amounts per employee and 5-year growth rates; and selected financial and operating ratios.

Also includes 1 chart showing electronics industry share of GNP, 1980-85; and 15 summary tables showing the following for 1983: aggregate data for top 200 companies; top 5-17 companies in 8 industry segments ranked by sales per employee, with selected financial ratios; and top 10 and bottom 5 companies ranked by selected measures covered in detailed table.

Previously, separate semiannual articles reported performance of top 100 and 2nd 100 companies.

FAT CATS FEAST ON RECOVERY; STRAY CATS LAP UP NICHES, ANNUAL FEATURE

(p. 135-141) Annual article, by Mary Ann Murphy, with 1 chart and 2 tables showing sales distribution by product, operating profit as percent of sales, sales per employee, number of stocking locations, and field sales employment, for top 15 industrial electronics distributors ranked by total sales, and for 10 unranked distributors, calendar or fiscal year 1983 with comparisons to 1982; and aggregate sales of top 15 distributors, 1980-83.

Data are from *Electronic Business.*

TAKE A SALESPERSON TO LUNCH

(p. 161-164) By Bill Meserve. Article, with 1 chart showing market growth for electronics distributors, decennially 1970-90.

PORTABLES CARRY WEIGHT: MARKET PULLS TECHNOLOGY

(p. 194-197) By Norman Alster. Article, with 3 charts showing world portable computer sales, and market share by size and end-use sector, various years 1983-88. Data are from InfoCorp and Creative Strategies International.

HARD COMPETITION SPARKS A COLORFUL MARKET BATTLE

(p. 204-206) By Edward S. Foster. Article, with 1 chart showing market value for computer printers with color capability, and market share by application, 1986. Data are from International Data Corp.

BATTLE FOR IC-DESIGN DOLLARS

(p. 214-225) By Andy Rappaport. Article, with 2 charts showing semicustom integrated circuit (IC) market value, and shares by type, 1982 and 1991; and market shares for IC process technology, by type, 1982-83. Data are from *EDN* magazine and Dataquest.

AUTOMATION COMPETITION RISES AS USERS DRIVE THE MARKET

(p. 260-262) Article, with 1 chart showing value of industrial automation equipment market, and share by type or application, 1988. Data are from Harbor Research.

C1850–2.513: Aug. 1, 1984 (Vol. 10, No. 11)

JUMP BALL: ROLM, AT&T AND NT VIE IN THE PBX TOURNAMENT

(p. 34-36) By Anne Hyde. Article, with 1 chart showing shipments of private branch exchange (PBX) lines, with market share by manufacturer, 1983 and 1988. Data are from Hambrecht and Quist Inc.

MITCH KAPOR: MAKING SUCCESS LOOK AS EASY AS 1-2-3

(p. 78-80) By Mary Jo Foley. Article, with 1 chart showing revenue of microcomputer integrated software industry, with market share by software package, 1983. Data are from Creative Strategies International.

MATERIAL WEALTH: DuPONT DOMINATES A CHANGING MARKET

(p. 86-93) By Norm Alster. Article, with 3 charts showing market shares for dry film photoresist products and thick film materials used in the electronics industry, by manufacturer, with detail for DuPont, primarily 1983. Data are from Strategic Analysis, Inc.

FIGHT FOR EUROPE, ANNUAL FEATURE

Compilation of features on financial performance of major electronics companies operating in Europe. Articles with substantial statistical content are described below.

TOGETHER, EUROPE STANDS; DIVIDED EFFORTS FAIL

(p. 105-109) By Keith Jones. Article, with 1 chart showing sales of computer equipment, components, communications equipment, and consumer electronics, in Europe, 1982 and 1987. Data are from Mackintosh International.

ANNUAL TABLE

(p. 112-115) Annual table showing sales, assets, and profits per employee; selected financial and operating ratios; and headquarters country; for top 100 electronics companies operating in Europe, ranked by electronics sales; for most recently completed fiscal year as of mid-1983, with comparison to rank in previous year.

EUROPEAN CHIP SCENE

(p. 127) Chart showing value of European integrated circuit production and consumption, and trade with U.S., Japan, and all others, 1983. Data are from Integrated Circuit Engineering Corp.

COST OF AN OFFICE ON THE CONTINENT

(p. 130) By William F. Arnold. Brief article analyzing costs of operating a European sales office, for U.S. companies. Data are from Mentor International. Includes 1 undated table showing typical expenditures by item, including personnel and travel.

Other Articles

FIBER-OPTIC HEADLINES RUN BIGGER THAN COMPONENT ORDERS

(p. 139) Article, with 1 chart showing compound annual growth rate for fiber-optic market, with detail by product category, 1983-88 period. Data are from Frost and Sullivan, Inc.

NUMBER CRUNCHERS ENJOY A SUPERCHARGED MARKET

(p. 144-146) By William F. Arnold. Article, with 1 chart showing sales of computer array processors, for 11 vendors, 1982. Data are from Star Technologies, Inc.

SEMI MARKET HITS 10-YEAR HIGH: 1984 PRODUCTION TOPS $32B

(p. 149) Article, with 1 table showing semiconductor production value, for North America, Japan, Western Europe, and rest of world, 1983-85. Data are from Henderson Ventures.

C1850–2.514: Aug. 15, 1984 (Vol. 10, No. 12)

TURNING THE SCREWS ON THE U.S. PRODUCTION-EQUIPMENT MARKET

(p. 28-29) By John Eckhouse. Article, with 1 chart showing world semiconductor sales, with market share for U.S., Japanese, and all other manufacturers, 1979-83. Data are from VLSI Research, Inc.

ETA: FROM THE FOLKS WHO BROUGHT YOU THE CYBER SERIES

(p. 30-33) Article, with 1 chart showing U.S. and foreign installations of high-speed computers, by U.S. vendor, as of Dec. 1983. Data are from International Data Corp.

JOHN IMLAY'S AMAZING SOFTWARE MACHINE

(p. 82-85) By Mary Jo Foley. Article, with 1 chart showing world packaged software revenues, by vendor, 1983. Data are from International Data Corp. Also includes 1 table showing financial and operating data for Management Science America Inc.

PRIVATE USERS AND DIGITAL SYSTEMS CREATE MACROWAVES

(p. 117) Article, with 1 table showing shipment value for commercial microwave-communications equipment, by type, 1982 and 1987, with compound annual growth. Data are from International Data Corp.

COMPUTERS COME TO DOMINATE WORLDWIDE CMOS APPLICATIONS

(p. 140) Chart showing world market value for complementary metal oxide semiconductors (CMOS), by application, 1993. Data are from Strategic, Inc.

C1850–2.515: Sept. 1, 1984 (Vol. 10, No. 13)

BUDDY, CAN YOU SPARE $10 MILLION? HARD TIMES IN SILICON VALLEY

(p. 36-38) Article, with 1 chart showing total number of initial public stock offerings, with percent offered by computer hardware/software and high-technology manufacturing companies, 1982-83 and 1st half 1984. Data are from *Going Public: The IPO Reporter.*

IBM RAISES THE PRESSURE IN THE 3270-TERMINAL MARKET

(p. 51-54) Article, with 1 chart showing shipments of data entry terminals compatible with the IBM 3270 computer, with distribution by manufacturer, 1983. Data are from International Data Corp.

DAISY GOES IBM PC WITH CAE SOFTWARE

(p. 62) Article, with 1 table showing number of installed sites, systems, and workstations, for electrical/electronic design sector of computer-aided-design/computer-aided-manufacturing market, by supplier or supplier group, 1982. Data are from International Data Corp.

BIG...BIGGER...MATURE: BOARD MAKERS GROW UP

(p. 148-150) By David Card. Article on market outlook for printed circuit board (PCB) industry. Data are from Gnostic Concepts Inc. and Kirk-Miller Associates.

Includes 3 charts showing PCB production value by type, 1983 and 1988; top 10 independent PCB manufacturers ranked by sales, 1983 with projections for 1984; and value of PCB consumption, by industry group, 1984 and 1988.

(ARTIFICIAL) EYES HAVE IT

(p. 154-162) By John Kerr. Article on market outlook for automated optical inspection (AOI) equipment used to examine printed circuit boards. Data are from *Electronic Business.*

Includes 1 table and 1 chart showing AOI vendors, cumulative value and volume of installations, and value of shipments, by application, 1990.

BOARD REAL ESTATE SHRINKS, BUT BOARD MATERIALS GROW

(p. 174) Article, with 2 charts showing market value for materials used in printed circuit board (PCB) production, by end use, 1983; and PCB consumption of 3 raw materials, 1980 and 1988. Data are from Strategic Analysis, Inc. and International Technology Group.

HOT PLOTS: ELECTROSTATICS CHALLENGE THE PEN PLOTTERS

(p. 178-180) By John Kerr. Article on market outlook for electrostatic and other plotting devices used in the computer graphics industry. Data are from *Electronic Business* and Machover Associates Corp.

Includes 3 charts showing market values for the following: wide-format graphics devices in computer-aided-design systems, with market share by application, 1984; computer graphics devices by type, 1984 and 1989; and electrostatic plotters, with market share for Japanese companies and/or by U.S. vendor, 1984 and 1990.

SEMICONDUCTOR CONSUMPTION: 1984 MARKET WILL TOP $32B

(p. 188-190) Article, with 1 chart showing value of worldwide semiconductor consumption, with distribution by end use and world area, 1985. Data are from Henderson Ventures.

MICROCOMPUTER AFTERMARKETS WORTH $53.9B BY 1989

(p. 190) Brief article, with 1 chart showing sales of microcomputer parts/supplies, with market share by type, 1983 and 1989. Data are from Business Communications Co.

C1850–2.516: Sept. 15, 1984 (Vol. 10, No. 14)

STOPPING THE FLOW

(p. 128-129) Article on Government efforts to stop shipments of advanced technology to unfriendly nations. Data are from Dept of Commerce and U.S. Customs Service.

Includes 2 charts showing export licensing applications processed, pre-licensing investigations, cases referred to Justice Dept, and convictions; and number and value of export seizures, and number of detentions; various periods 1982-1st 5 months 1984.

SUPERMINIS CROSS THE LINE TO THE MAINFRAME WORLD

(p. 152-157) By Geoff Lewis. Article, with 1 chart and 1 table showing superminicomputer market shares, by manufacturer (with detail for 1 company), 1983. Data sources include Quantum Science Corp.

C1850–2.517: Oct. 1, 1984 (Vol. 10, No. 15)

EXECS PAY SPURRED IN '83 BY THE BOTTOM LINE BONANZA, ANNUAL FEATURE

(p. 120-140) Annual article, by John Halbrooks, with 2 tables on compensation of electronics industry executives, 1983. Tables show cash compensation, position, and company, for 50 highest paid executives, and for 5-6 top executives in over 100 companies, with company sales rankings.

AUTOMATIC TEST EQUIPMENT

Collection of articles on automatic test equipment (ATE) industry outlook, including data on market performance, manufacturers, and materials. Statistical articles are described below.

TEST RESULTS SHOW PATIENT HEALTHY BUT UNDER STRESS, ANNUAL FEATURE

(p. 164-167) Annual article, by Mary Ann Murphy, on ATE market developments, and financial performance of leading manufacturers, 1983. Data are from Prime Data, Inc. Includes 4 charts showing ATE total revenue; top 11 manufacturers ranked by revenue; and market shares and growth rate by product type; 1983, with selected comparisons to 1982.

ON TARGET: BOARD TESTERS AIM AT PCs AND EXOCETS

(p. 170-172) By Alberto Socolovsky. Article on testers for bus-structured circuit boards used in microcomputers and missiles. Data are from Logical Solutions Inc. Includes 1 chart showing world market value of testers for bus-structured and other boards, 1983-84.

IT WAS IN FRONT OF THEM ALL THE TIME

(p. 176-179) By Douglas Greenwood. Article, with 1 chart showing world sales of dedicated/focused ATE for semiconductors, by type (logic, memory, and linear), 1983 and 1988. Data are from VLSI Research Inc.

Other Articles

STEADY GROWTH FOR LASERS: $2.8B WORLD MARKET IN '84

(p. 198-200) Article, with 1 table showing laser industry revenue, by end use, 1984. Data are from International Resource Development Inc.

WORLDWIDE OFFICE-PC MARKET WILL HIT $55B BY 1989

(p. 200) Brief article, with 1 chart showing value of office microcomputer market, and market shares for software, biennially 1983-89. Data are from Future Computing Inc.

C1850–2.518: Oct. 15, 1984 (Vol. 10, No. 16)

WHAT'S BIG AND BRIGHT? THE ANSWER IS ARTIFICIAL

(p. 52-53) Article on the artificial intelligence (AI) industry. Data are from D. M. Data Inc. and Knowledge Analysis Inc. Includes 3 charts showing AI market value by type of system, with detail by end use for expert systems; and AI expenditures, by user sector; 1984.

CMOS: IT'S NOT JUST FOR PORTABLES ANYMORE

(p. 64-66) Article, with 1 chart showing value of complementary-metal-oxide-silicon semiconductor sales worldwide for 4 manufacturers and others, 1983. Data are from Dataquest Inc.

PHONE WARS TAKE THEIR TOLL AS UPSTART MCI BATTLES AT&T

(p. 79-95) By Anne Hyde. Article on competition between AT&T and MCI in the communications industry. Data are from Eastern Management Group and industry sources.

Includes 1 table and 3 charts showing long-distance market value, with shares for AT&T and others, 1983 and 1987; capital equipment investments for MCI, 1982-85, and for AT&T and GTE, 1985; and selected MCI financial and operating data.

MINORITIES: A MAJOR CHALLENGE FOR THE ELECTRONICS INDUSTRY

Compilation of articles on the employment of women and minorities in the electronics industry. Statistical articles are described below.

ELECTRONIC MINORITY: KNOCKING ON HIGH TECH DOOR

(p. 102-106) By Mary Jo Foley. Article, with 6 undated charts showing women/minorities as percent of total management, clerical, and blue-collar employees, for electronics, banking, education, health, retail, and social service employers. Data are from Equal Employment Opportunity Commission.

ELECTRONICS FIRMS SCURRY FOR MINORITY AND WOMEN CANDIDATES

(p. 114-116) By Michael Seither. Article, with 1 chart showing women and minorities as percent of total employees at Hewlett-Packard and IBM, 1981-83. Data are from the companies.

WOMEN: MOST UNDERREPRESENTED MINORITY IN ELECTRONICS

(p. 120-122) By Mary Jo Foley. Article, with 1 chart showing total electrical/computer science engineering degrees (bachelors, masters, and PhD), and percent awarded to women, 1974, 1978, and 1983. Data are from American Assn of Engineering Societies.

C1850–3 RESTAURANTS AND INSTITUTIONS

Biweekly. Approx. 150 p.
ISSN 0273-5520.
LC 81-641204.
SRI/MF/not filmed

Biweekly trade journal of the food service industry, reporting on finances and operations, customer attitudes and characteristics, marketing techniques, food preparation, and individual companies and establishments. Includes data on sales, costs, employment, salaries, and menus. Covers full-service and fast-food restaurants, and hotel, school, retail store, transportation, health care, military, and employee dining facilities.

Data are primarily from the journal's own or other private research.

Issues generally contain:

a. Articles, some with statistics.

b. "Reconnaissance" section with several regular depts, including monthly charts or tables on food service sales and profits, managerial and hourly job openings, labor and food cost indexes, and prices of selected menu items; and recurring chart on food service equipment dealer sales.

Annual statistical features include industry trends and outlook; leading independent restaurants; jobs report covering personnel developments; report on employee training; menu census; top 400 food service operations; growth chains; alcoholic beverage consumption survey; and consumer eating out patterns.

Journal also includes an annual buyer's guide; and several full-issue cookbooks.

Substantial monthly statistics are described below. All additional features with substantial statistical content are described, as they appear, under "Statistical Features." Nonstatistical features are not covered.

Prior to the Jan. 18, 1984 issue, journal was published semimonthly.

Availability: Restaurants and Institutions, 270 St. Paul St., Denver CO 80206, qualified subscribers †, others $70.00 per yr., single copy $4.00, Feb. 15 Buyers Guide $20.00, other special issue prices vary; SRI/MF/not filmed.

Issues reviewed during 1984: Nov. 1-Dec. 28, 1983 (semimonthly); Jan. 18-Oct. 24, 1984 (biweekly) (P) (Vol. 93, Nos. 9-12; Vol. 94, Nos. 1-21) [only 1 issue was published in Jan. 1984].

MONTHLY STATISTICS:

[Data on profits, managerial openings, and food cost index generally appear within one issue; remaining data appear in the alternate issue.

Data for profits, sales, and job openings are based on surveys of food service operators, conducted 2-3 months prior to cover date.]

PROFITS AND SALES

Two charts showing change in food service profits and sales, for survey month and 6-month outlook, in commercial and institutional establishments. Charts appear in "Business Confidence Index" dept.

JOB OPENINGS

Two charts showing change in food service job openings for managerial and hourly positions, for survey month compared to previous year average. Chart appears in "Human Resources" dept.

FOOD COST INDEX

Table showing wholesale prices for approximately 20 food items, for month prior to cover date, previous month, same month of prior year, and selected other months.

LABOR COST INDEX

Table showing salaries for 7-8 food service industry positions, by region and for commercial and institutional establishments, for current month. Data are based on a monthly survey of 160 food service operators. Table appears in "Human Resources" dept.

MENU SELLING PRICES

Table showing average selling price for selected menu items, by census region and type of restaurant, generally for month 1-2 months prior to cover date. Data are based on surveys of approximately 75 restaurants. Table appears in "Menu Concepts" dept.

STATISTICAL FEATURES:

C1850–3.501: Nov. 1, 1983 (Vol. 93, No. 9)

COSTING OUT

(p. 171-172) Article reporting on annual "Creative Use of Frozen Foods Competition" sponsored by *Restaurants and Institutions* and 2 industry assns, spring 1983. Data were compiled by competition entrants from Michigan State University.

Includes 2 tables comparing cost and profit for restaurant dinners prepared with fresh vs. frozen ingredients.

C1850–3.502: Nov. 15, 1983 (Vol. 93, No. 10)

GROWTH CHAINS, ANNUAL FEATURE

(p. 89-141) Annual feature on food service organizations with outstanding growth prospects, 1983. Data are from *Restaurants and Institutions* and company estimates.

Includes 1 table (p. 132-141) showing the following for 70 such organizations grouped by type: headquarters, type of operation, establishments as of July 1983, food/drink sales, and summary of current activities and outlook.

C1850–3.503: Dec. 1, 1983 (Vol. 93, No. 11)

TASTES OF AMERICA, ANNUAL FEATURE

(p. 105-158P) Annual feature on consumer eating out practices and preferences, 1983, with comparisons to 1981-82, and detail by type of food service operation, region, and various consumer characteristics.

Data are based on responses of approximately 1,400 households to the 4th annual *Restaurants and Institutions* consumer survey, conducted May-June 1983 by NFO Research, Inc. Contains 6 sections with the following statistics:

a. "Eating Out." Includes expectations for buying power and eating out frequency; weekly eating out occasions by meal period and type of food service operation; type of restaurant patronized in past month, with detail for weakest and strongest regional markets; perceived value of eating out, and restaurant vs. home entertaining preferences; and past month purchases of food for consumption away from purchase place, by type of operation. 1 chart and 4 tables. (p. 106-112)

b. "Choice of Chains." Includes popularity rankings of top 65 chains, with selected detail by chain type, region, and customer characteristics, familiarity with chains, and patronage, and with comparisons to 1981-82; and chains most likely to succeed in 1984, based on customer eating out intentions. 2 charts and 12 tables. (p. 116-133)

c. "Best Customers." Includes the following for consumers who spend heavily on food away from home, combine business and eating out, and who are most likely to try new restaurants: average weekly spending on meals away from home, compared to 1982; factors influencing decision to try new restaurant; and complaints about restaurants. 5 charts and 2 tables. (p. 136-145)

d. "Food Trends." Includes types of food ordered in past month, by region; and growth index for selected food items, with comparisons to 1982. 2 tables. (p. 148-154)

e. "Liquid Assets." Includes percent of consumers ordering alcoholic beverages in restaurants, by selected characteristics. 4 charts. (p. 158A-158H)

f. "Lifestages." Includes distribution of households; average weekly spending on food away from home; factors influencing decision to try new restaurant; weekly eating out by type of food service operation; purchases of food for consumption away from purchase place, by type of operation; and use of discount coupons; variously by income level, type of household, and age of head of household. 3 charts and 7 tables. (p. 158L-158P)

C1850–3.504: Jan. 18, 1984 (Vol. 94, No. 1)

1984 ANNUAL REPORT

(p. 86-167) Annual report, for 1984, on food service industry trends and outlook. Presents data on food and alcoholic beverage sales, number of establishments, employment, and food sales market shares, 1982-84, with total 1973 sales; all by detailed industry segment.

Industry segments covered include full-service and fast food restaurants, health care, schools, business/industry, hotel/motel, retail, military, recreation, and transportation.

Also presents data on selected aspects of, and conditions affecting, the food service industry and individual segments, including recession-to-recovery changes in industry share of total food dollar, 1957-58, 1973-74, and 1980-82 periods; and percent change in customer traffic and share of industry sales for full-service restaurants by type, 3 month periods Sept. 1982-Aug. 1983.

Data sources include Cahners Bureau of Foodservice Research, USDA, GDR/CREST Enterprises, and other sources.

Contains overview and 11 segment reports, with narrative analysis, 5 charts, and 15 tables. This is the 9th annual report.

C1850–3.505: Feb. 1, 1984 (Vol. 94, No. 2)

DINING DYNASTIES OF AMERICA, ANNUAL FEATURE

(p. 103-130) Annual article, with text data profiling the top 61 restaurants with independent owners, ranked by total annual sales. Also includes listing of top 83 restaurants with independent owners and annual sales between $1 million and $3 million. Data are compiled by *Restaurants and Institutions.*

C1850–3.506: Feb. 15, 1984 (Vol. 94, No. 3)

HERE COME THE TOURISTS

(p. 20) Article, with 1 table showing foreign visitor expenditures in the U.S., by country or world area of residence, 1983-84. Data are from U.S. Travel and Tourism Administration.

C1850–3.507: Mar. 14, 1984 (Vol. 94, No. 5)

1984 JOB$ SURVEY, ANNUAL FEATURE

(p. 97-125) Annual feature on food service industry personnel developments, focusing on executives' characteristics, salaries, and attitudes; and tip-reporting practices.

Data are from responses of more than 2,500 food service executives to a *Restaurants and Institutions* 1984 survey, and from reports filed with the SEC.

Contains 4 articles with the following statistics:

a. "JOB$." Includes executives' average salary by position and sex; and views on adequacy of salary level and last raise, reasons for food service industry difficulty in attracting young employees, use of robots in food service, presidential candidate preference by sex, and main sources of irritation on and off the job. 4 charts and 4 tables. (p. 97- 104)

b. "Salaries at the Top." Includes compensation and company for 14 highest paid food service chain executives, generally 1982; turnover rates for 6 positions in fast food and total food service industry; and profile

of average chain vice president including demographic characteristics, salary, work experience, company annual sales, and personal and career concerns and interests. 1 chart and 2 tables. (p. 109-111)

c. "Effects of Tip Reporting." Includes extent of compliance with tip reporting regulations, and reasons for noncompliance; frequency of non-tipping customers; and employee and employer reactions to regulations. 5 charts and 2 tables. (p. 115-118)

d. "Portrait of a Restaurant Owner, and the Institutional Manager." Includes profiles of average restaurant owner, school food service director, and dietitian, generally repeating characteristics described above for average chain vice president; and educational attainment of average institutional food service manager, health care manager, and dietitian. 1 chart and 3 tables. (p. 119-125)

FRANCHISING: ALIVE AND WELL IN FOODSERVICE

(p. 145-147) Article on franchise restaurant companies, establishments, and sales. Data are from Commerce Dept's *Franchising in the Economy, 1982-84.*

Includes 3 charts and 2 tables showing restaurant franchise companies and sales by type of food served, company- and franchisee-owned total establishments and sales, and franchisor sales of products/services to franchisees by sales category; and total sales of all franchised businesses; various years 1973-84.

C1850–3.508: Mar. 28, 1984 (Vol. 94, No. 6)

DEALERS SALES FOR THE 3 MONTHS ENDED DEC. 31, 1983, RECURRING FEATURE

(p. 70) Recurring chart showing percent change in dealer sales of 4 types of food service equipment, 4th quarter vs. 3rd quarter, 1983. Data are from *Foodservice Equipment Specialist* Dealer Business Index.

UPDATE: THE RECOVERY GAINS STRENGTH

(p. 119-121) Article presenting revised forecast for food service industry sales, 1984. Data are from Cahners Bureau of Foodservice Research, National Restaurant Assn, and Technomic Consultants. Includes 2 tables showing each organization's forecast of foodservice sales and real growth, by industry segment, 1984, with detail for Cahner's original and revised forecasts, 1983-84.

For description of original forecast, see C1850-3.504 above.

RESTAURANT CRITICS: THE POISON OF THE PEN?

(p. 165-182) Article discussing restaurant critics' impact on industry business. Data are from *Restaurants and Institutions* annual Tastes of America survey of over 1,400 households (described under C1850-3.503, above).

Includes 1 chart showing percent of consumers reading a review before visiting a new restaurant, 1982-83.

C1850–3.509: Apr. 11, 1984 (Vol. 94, No. 7)

OPERATORS SAY 'YES' TO LOW-COST HOME COMPUTERS

(p. 50) Article reporting on microcomputer use by food service operators. Data are from a

fall 1983 *Restaurants and Institutions* survey. Includes 2 charts showing distribution of respondents by brand of computer personally owned; and percent of commercial and institutional operators using various types of computer software programs.

C1850–3.510: May 9, 1984 (Vol. 94, No. 9)

COMPUTER INTERFACE: A REVIEW OF MICROCOMPUTER SOFTWARE FOR RESTAURATEURS

(p. 63, 66) Article, with 1 chart and 1 table showing types of food service-related software programs most desired by commercial and institutional food service operators; and percent of restaurant executives who have written programs, by industry sector and for those using own or company-owned equipment.

Data are from a fall 1983 *Restaurants and Institutions* survey. For description of other data from survey, see C1850-3.509 above.

APPEALING SNACKS BRING SALES REWARDS

(p. 238R-238T) Article, with 1 chart showing snack food sales change from previous year, by type of snack food, 1982-83. Data are from the Snack Food Assn.

C1850–3.511: May 23, 1984 (Vol. 94, No. 10)

DEALER SALES FOR THE 3 MONTHS ENDED FEB. 29, 1984, RECURRING FEATURE

(p. 76) Recurring chart showing percent change in dealer sales of 4 types of food service equipment, for 3 month period ended Feb. 1984 vs. preceding 3 month period. Data are from *Foodservice Equipment Specialist* Dealer Business Index.

EXECUTIVE SALARIES: THEY'VE FOUND THE BEEF

(p. 187-192) Brief article, with list showing compensation of top 2-5 food service/lodging executives in 47 companies, 1982 or 1983. Data are from reports filed with the SEC.

C1850–3.512: June 6, 1984 (Vol. 94, No. 11)

TIPS REPORTED TO THE IRS MORE THAN DOUBLED IN 1983

(p. 22) Article, with 1 table showing amount of restaurant tips reported to IRS, quarterly 1982-83. Data are based on employer reports filed with the IRS.

FOR THE FIRST TIME, MOST SCHOOL LUNCHES GO TO THE NEEDY

(p. 22) Article, with 1 table showing the following for the National School Lunch Program: percent of students served full-price lunches and reduced-price/free lunches, number of lunches served, and enrollment for schools that participate in program; biennially FY79-83. Data are from the General Accounting Office and Dept of Agriculture.

FOODSERVICE TRAINS ITS SIGHTS ON THE FUTURE, ANNUAL FEATURE

(p. 101-110) Annual article, by Elizabeth Faulkner, on food service employee training, 1983. Data are from responses of 80 training directors to a *Restaurants and Institutions* survey.

Includes 3 charts showing directors' average salary by type of food service operation, educational background, and company annual sales volume; changes in training budget and staffing levels; and training budget as percent of gross sales, and role of training director or dept in company operations, by company relative growth level; 1983.

C1850–3.513: June 20, 1984 (Vol. 94, No. 12)

MENU CENSUS 1984, ANNUAL FEATURE

(p. 95-128) Annual article, for 1984, reporting on food service menu survey. Presents detailed data on popularity of individual food and beverage menu items, including percent of food service operators offering each item, and percent rating each item a good seller by region, with additional detail by type of food service operation.

Data are from responses of 2,616 food service operators to a *Restaurants and Institutions* survey.

Contains narrative analyses with text data, and 9 charts and 18 tables.

C1850–3.514: July 18, 1984 (Vol. 94, No. 14)

CHAIN RESTAURANTS TUNE IN TO YOU ON THE RADIO

(p. 12) Article, with 1 table showing radio advertising expenditures, 1982-83, for top 15 restaurant advertisers ranked by 1983 expenditures. Data are from Radio Advertising Bureau.

HOUSE ACTS ON MINIMUM DRINKING AGE INCENTIVE

(p. 30) Article, with 2 tables showing changes in minimum legal drinking age, by State, 1983-84; and number of States with various minimum drinking age laws, 1984.

DEALER SALES FOR THE 3 MONTHS ENDED APR. 30, 1984, RECURRING FEATURE

(p. 76) Recurring chart showing percent change in dealer sales of 4 types of food service equipment, for 3-month period ended Apr. 30, 1984 vs. preceding 3-month period. Data are from *Foodservice Equipment Specialist* Dealer Business Index.

C1850–3.515: Aug. 1, 1984 (Vol. 94, No. 15)

'400' PART I: BUSINESS AND FINANCE, ANNUAL FEATURE

(p. 89-257) Annual ranking of top 400 food service/lodging organizations based on food service sales in 1983 with comparison to 1982, and including headquarters location, industry segment, and number of units as of Jan. 1, 1983-84.

Also includes data on total sales for the food service industry and for the "400" by industry segment, and sales growth in current and constant dollars for the "400," with trends from 1964; top 25 organizations based on total food service/lodging sales, and on food service sales growth; stock price trends for all industrials and for food service industry with detail for 45 companies, various periods 1976-84; leading organizations in each industry segment; room sales, and number of properties and guest rooms for top 100 lodging organizations; and ranking of top 50 restaurant chains.

Industry segments covered include fast food and full-service restaurants, franchise and diversified operations, schools, employee feed-

ing, colleges, military, transportation, health care, retail, recreation, lodging, and government institutions.

Data are from a Mar.-May 1984 survey conducted by *Restaurants & Institutions.*

Contains analysis, with 2 charts (p. 89-103); ranked listing of the "400" (p. 104-122); profiles of companies and industry segments, interspersed with 2 charts and 5 tables (p. 124-235); ranked listings of top lodging organizations and restaurant chains, with narrative summaries (p. 236-250); and alphabetical listing of the top "400" (p. 252-257).

This is Part I of the 20th annual report.

C1850–3.516: Aug. 15, 1984 (Vol. 94, No. 16)

'400' PART II: CONCEPTS AND OPERATIONS, ANNUAL FEATURE

(p. 105-235) Annual report on operations of top 400 food service/lodging organizations grouped by concept or market segment, and including number of units, and ranking based on food service sales, 1983.

Concepts and market segments covered include various food themes, coffee shops/family restaurants, retail and recreation, theme and dinner houses, cafeterias, transportation, lodging, schools, and franchise operations.

Also includes data on expansion plans; alcoholic beverage sales; increases in menu prices and food and labor costs; distributor services desired by food service operators, types of distributors used, and types of products purchased from specialty distributors; and advertising expenditures and projected budgets; all shown for various individual organizations or by type of operation.

Also presents data on top 25 international food service organizations ranked by total number of units, with number of units and ranking excluding U.S. operations, 1983; and number of foreign units operated by U.S. franchise companies, by country or world area and type of operation, 1982.

Data are from a Mar.-May 1984 survey conducted by *Restaurants & Institutions,* and from *Hotels and Restaurants International.*

Contains analyses interspersed with company profiles and 3 charts and 6 tables (p. 105-223); summary of international food service organizations, with 2 tables (p. 224-225); ranked listing of the "400," by census division (p. 226-229); and alphabetical listing of the "400" (p. 230-235).

This is Part II of the 20th annual report.

C1850–3.517: Aug. 29, 1984 (Vol. 94, No. 17)

1984 GROWTH CHAINS, ANNUAL FEATURE

(p. 101-144) Annual feature, by Elizabeth Faulkner et al., on food service organizations with outstanding growth prospects, 1984. Data are from *Restaurants & Institutions* and company estimates.

Includes profiles of 88 such organizations grouped by type, presenting headquarters location, establishments as of July 1984, food/drink sales for 1983 or 1984, owners and/or top executives, and summary of current activities and outlook.

Also includes company index.

For description of previous article, for 1983, see C1850-3.502, above.

C1850–3.518: Sept. 12, 1984 (Vol. 94, No. 18)

DE NOBLE VIEW OF MERGERS, ACQUISITIONS

(p. 24) Article, with 3 tables showing the following aggregate data for 47 firms that acquired restaurant companies, 1976-81 period: distribution of acquiring companies by share of revenues earned from restaurant operations prior to acquistion, reason for acquisition, and type of acquisition (horizontal, vertical, concentric, and conglomerate).

Data are from a survey conducted by Alex De Noble in conjunction with a doctoral dissertation presented at Virginia Polytechnic Institute.

DEALER SALES FOR THE THREE MONTHS ENDED JUNE 30, 1984, RECURRING FEATURE

(p. 68) Recurring chart showing percent change in dealer sales of 4 types of food service equipment, for 3-month period ended June 30, 1984 vs. preceding 3-month period. Data are from *Foodservice Equipment Specialist* Dealer Business Index.

C1850–3.519: Oct. 24, 1984 (Vol. 94, No. 21)

UNDERSTANDING MATURE U.S. MARKET AIDS MENU PLANNING

(p. 82) Article, with 2 undated charts showing percent of meals skipped and share of total calories obtained from snacks, for men aged 19-50 and 50/over. Data are from General Mills Inc. and Market Research Corp. of America.

1984 ALCOHOLIC BEVERAGES SURVEY, ANNUAL FEATURE

(p. 115-118) Annual article, by Hilary Green, reporting on alcoholic beverage consumption in restaurants. Data are from a *Restaurants and Institutions* 1984 survey of restaurant/hotel operators. Includes 11 charts showing survey response concerning the following:

a. Sales change by type of operation and detailed liquor type, and for wines and speciality drinks; and market share for beer, wine, and spirits, for domestic vs. imported beer, and for light beer (with comparison to 1982).

b. Operators serving free snacks with drinks, and conducting employee training programs related to drunk-driving awareness campaigns, by type of operation; and leading seasonal drinks, and most popular drinks by meal period.

R&I GIANTS: A REPORT ON THE NATION'S LARGEST SINGLE-UNIT INSTITUTIONAL OPERATIONS

(p. 183-196) By Elizabeth Faulkner. Article on leading single-unit food service operations in military, college, employee feeding, health care, and airline catering market segments, as ranked by value of food purchases, 1984. Data are from *Restaurants and Institutions* and company estimates.

Includes 1 table showing the following for top 10 operations in each market segment: value of food purchases, 1984-85; number of meals served per day (no date); and summary of operating activities.

C1865
Cash Management Institute

C1865-1   DONOGHUE'S MUTUAL FUNDS ALMANAC, 15th

Annual Edition
Annual. 1984. 130 p.
ISSN 0737-0369.
ISBN 0-913755-01-X.
LC 72-622174.
SRI/MF/complete

Annual mutual fund reference book, presenting background information for investors on the characteristics, objectives, and financial performance of over 850 mutual funds, 1983, with trends from 1974. Data are compiled from company annual reports to shareholders, and financial and government publications.

Contains contents listing (1 p.), and the following:

a. Narrative overview, with 3 tables showing assets of mutual funds, and taxable and tax-free money funds, Dec. 1980-83; 1983 assets and 1979-83 investment performance for 10 top-performing funds permitting switching; and yield equivalents for tax-free vs. taxable money fund investments, by tax bracket, 1984. (p. 1-22)

b. Statistical section, with 5 tables listed below (p. 23-122); and appendices, with lists of mutual fund name changes, mergers, stock splits, and liquidations, and glossary (p. 123-130).

Availability: Donoghue's Mutual Funds Almanac, PO Box 540, Holliston MA 01746, $23.00; SRI/MF/complete.

TABLES:

1-2. Alphabetical listings of all open-end funds and of fund families. (p. 23-45)

3. Listing of open-end funds by objective [taxable and tax-exempt money market funds, and bond, balanced, income, growth/income, and growth funds, showing the following: percent gain or loss per share, 1974-83; growth of $10,-000 investment over 5- and 10-year periods ending 1983; date organized; minimum purchase requirements; total assets, 1982-83; and availability of checking and wire redemption services, exchange privileges, and IRA and Keogh Plans, with minimum check amount and wire fee; all by fund]. (p. 48-119)

4. 1983 top 10 general purpose, institutional, Government-only, and tax-free money funds ranked by 12-month performance [assets and yields, 1983]; and top 10 performing bond, income, balance, growth/income, and growth funds [yields], 1983. (p. 120)

5. Top 50 funds, 1974-83, based on what $10,-000 grew to in 5-year and 10-year period. (p. 122)

C1865-2   DONOGHUE'S MONEY FUND DIRECTORY

Annual, discontinued.

Annual directory of money market funds, discontinued with 1983 report (for description, see SRI 1983 Annual, under this number).

Data on money market funds are available in *Donoghue's Mutual Funds Almanac,* covered in SRI under C1865-1.

C2000
Chase, Dana, Publications

C2000-1   APPLIANCE

Monthly. Approx. 100 p.
ISSN 0003-6781.
LC 78-1694.
SRI/MF/not filmed

Monthly trade journal of the appliance industry. Covers trends and developments in production, engineering, purchasing, and management, for producers of consumer, commercial, and business appliances.

General format:

a. Feature or special report articles, occasionally with statistics; and regular narrative depts, placed throughout.

b. Monthly "Appliance Statistics" table showing factory unit shipments for approximately 40 appliances, including major appliances, air conditioner and heating systems, TVs, and video recorders, for month 3 months prior to cover date, same month of preceding year, and year to date for current and preceding years.

Major annual features include statistical forecast of appliance sales and shipments, and industry purchasing directory (Jan. issue); 10-year statistical review of appliance shipments (Apr. issue); and industry portrait with directories (Sept. issue).

Monthly table appears in all issues. All additional features with substantial statistical content are described, as they appear, under "Statistical Features." Nonstatistical contents are not covered.

Availability: Appliance, Circulation Department, 1000 Jorie Blvd., CS 5030, Oak Brook IL 60521, qualified subscribers †, others $30.00 per yr., single copy $3.00, Jan. issue $15.00; SRI/MF/not filmed.

Issues reviewed during 1984: Nov. 1983-Oct. 1984 (P) (Vol. 40, Nos. 11-12; Vol. 41, Nos. 1-10) [Nov. 1983, Apr. 1984, July 1984, and Sept. 1984 issues are published in 2 sections].

STATISTICAL FEATURES:

C2000-1.501: Dec. 1983 (Vol. 40, No. 12)

PILOT STUDY OF DISHWASHER USERS

(p. 13) Article, with 1 undated table showing operating characteristics of automatic dishwashers ranked by importance to consumers, and by consumer satisfaction. Data are from a consumer study conducted by Longview Marketing Services, Inc.

C2000-1.502: Jan. 1984 (Vol. 41, No. 1)

[Issue price is $15.00.]

APPLIANCE 32nd ANNUAL FORECASTS

Annual *Appliance* forecast report, for 1984, consisting of articles analyzing the outlook for appliance industry sales and shipments in the 1980s. Articles with substantial statistical content are described below.

YEAR OF FINE PROSPECTS! ANNUAL FEATURE

(p. 41-45) Annual article, by David E. Simpson and Christopher Prout, forecasting appliance sales and industry developments in the 1980s. Data for 1982 are from Commerce Dept; other data are *Appliance* forecasts.

Includes 2 tables showing unit shipments of major appliances, and of water heating, comfort conditioning, electric housewares, and business and/or outdoor appliances; and distributor unit sales of consumer electronic products; all by detailed product type, 1982-89.

ANTICIPATING CONTINUED GROWTH IN '84, ANNUAL FEATURE

(p. 47) Annual article, by Harry Paynter, presenting Gas Appliance Manufacturers Assn industry forecast for 1984. Includes 1 table showing unit sales of 10 gas appliances, 1982-84.

C2000-1.503: Feb. 1984 (Vol. 41, No. 2)

STUDY OF ELECTRONIC CONTROLS

(p. 21) Brief article, with 1 table showing electronically controlled appliances as percent of total appliances in each of 12 categories, 1983-84 and 1988. Data are from an *Appliance* survey of 162 engineering employees at appliance companies.

C2000-1.504: Mar. 1984 (Vol. 41, No. 3)

COMPUTER GRAPHICS IN EUROPE ON THE INCREASE

(p. 13) Brief article, with 1 table showing computer graphics market value in Europe, by market segment, 1984-86. Data are from Technology and Business Communications, Inc. and JJ+J Consultants.

C2000-1.505: Apr. 1984 (Vol. 41, No. 4)

[Issue is published in 2 parts.]

PART 1

LEARNING EXPERIENCE, ANNUAL FEATURE

(p. 24-27) Annual article, by James Stevens, on Domotechnica (an international appliance exhibition) and appliance marketing trends and outlook in Europe. Includes 1 table showing the following for West Germany: production, exports, and imports, for major appliances and electric housewares by type, 1982.

31st ANNUAL APPLIANCE STATISTICAL REVIEW

(p. 29-32) Annual *Appliance* 10-year review of unit shipments for major, comfort conditioning, consumer electronic, personal care, electric houseware, outdoor, and business appliances; vending machines; and plumbing appliances/fixtures; 1974-83.

Data are from trade assns, *Appliance* estimates, *Merchandising,* and Commerce Dept.

Contains 1 summary table, and 9 detailed tables showing shipments of specified products in each of the categories noted above, 1974-83. (Table for consumer electronics shows distributor unit sales, rather than shipments.)

PART 2

STRONG GROWTH EXPECTED IN SMALL d.c. MOTORS

(p. 25) Brief article, with 2 charts showing market value for small direct current permanent magnet motors/ motor controls, and market distribution by application, 1982 and 1987. Data are from the Electronicast Corp.

C2000-1.506: May 1984 (Vol. 41, No. 5)

CHARTING THE WORLD'S APPLIANCE PRODUCTION

(p. 21) Brief article, with 1 table showing production of 7 major appliances, by country, 1982. Data are from *Officiel de L'equipment Menager.*

C2000–1.507: June 1984 (Vol. 41, No. 6)

BALANCE OF TRADE IN COMPUTERS AND BUSINESS EQUIPMENT DECLINING

(p. 21) Article, with 1 table showing computers/business equipment imports and exports, 1979-83. Data were compiled by the Computer and Business Equipment Manufacturers Assn from Census Bureau statistics.

PERSPECTIVE 40

Compilation of articles on trends in the appliance industry during the past 40 years. Includes the statistical articles described below.

FOUR DECADES IN REVIEW

(p. 44-55) By Dana Chase, Jr. Article, with 1 table showing unit production for 7 types of appliances, generally 1953 and 1983.

GROWTH

(p. 69-71) By James Stevens. Article, with 3 tables showing selected U.S. economic indicators, including industrial production index, population, households, housing starts, employment, GNP, personal consumption expenditures, nonresidential fixed investment, and inflation; world population and households; and world demand for 7 types of major appliances, and for radios, TVs, and room air-conditioners; various years 1950-95.

Data are from McGraw-Hill Economics, Predicasts Inc., and Federal sources.

C2000–1.508: Aug. 1984 (Vol. 41, No. 8)

APPLIANCE PRODUCTION FOR AUSTRALIA

(p. 13) Table showing Australian production of household appliances, by type, for year ended June 30, 1981-83. Data are from Australian Bureau of Statistics.

C2000–1.509: Sept. 1984 (Vol. 41, No. 9)

[Issue is published in 2 parts.]

PART 1

WORLD PRODUCTION OF RADIO AND TV SETS

(p. 21) Table showing world production of car and other radios, and black-and-white and color TV sets, by country, 1981-82. Data are from *L'Officiel de L'Equipement Menager.*

PORTRAIT OF THE U.S. APPLIANCE INDUSTRY, 1984, ANNUAL FEATURE

(p. 49-68) Annual article presenting overview of appliance industry. Data are from *Appliance* surveys and estimates, and other sources. Includes:

a. 4 tables showing the following, by appliance type: percent of homes with various appliances, selected years 1963-83; low, high, and average life expectancy, and number of units to be replaced in 1984-85; and retail market value and shares held by top manufacturers, 1983.

b. Directory of U.S. appliance companies and principal executives, with types of appliances produced.

c. Revenues/net sales and earnings/net income of selected appliance manufacturers (no date).

C2130
Chicago Sun-Times

C2130–1   POCKET GUIDE TO THE CHICAGO MARKET, 1984
Annual. [1984.]
115 p. Pocket-size.
SRI/MF/complete

Annual compilation of statistics on population, income, economic, and retail trade characteristics of the Chicago market. Data are shown primarily for 1980-82, with selected trends from 1935 and projections to 2000. Data sources include Federal Government, *Sales and Marketing Management* magazine, private assns and research firms, and *Chicago Sun-Times* research.

The Chicago market is defined variously as Chicago city, Northeastern Illinois Counties Area (NICA, formerly the Chicago SMSA), Chicago city/retail trading zone, Chicago-Gary-Lake County Consolidated Metropolitan Statistical Area (CMSA), Chicago Area of Dominant Influence, and NICA/Gary-Hammond Primary Metropolitan Statistical Area.

Report is designed to present a comprehensive overview of the Chicago market. Extensive socioeconomic, demographic, and geographic breakdowns are shown, as applicable, for most topics. These breakdowns include component community, county, commodity, income, industry, age, marital status, and sex. Comparisons to other U.S. metro areas are also occasionally included.

Contains contents and table listing (p. 3); and 3 sections, with 46 tables described below, interspersed with brief narrative highlights, and lists of Chicago area zip codes (p. 5-115).

Availability: Chicago Sun-Times, National Advertising, 401 N. Wabash Ave., Chicago IL 60611, †; SRI/MF/complete.

TABLE SECTIONS:

C2130–1.1: Section 1: Understanding and Defining the Chicago Market

(p. 5-24) Contains 11 tables. Includes population, households, effective buying income (EBI), and retail sales, projected to 1993; housing units by tenure and household size; employment; newspaper circulation; gross metropolitan product; personal income; wages/salaries; bank clearings; manufactured products gross sales; industrial activity index; electric power sales; steel production; industrial building/land investment; and air traffic.

C2130–1.2: Section 2-3: Measuring and Selling the Chicago Market

(p. 25-115) Contains 35 tables. Includes U.S. population by CMSA and Metropolitan Statistical Area (MSA), including inside and outside central cities; and 42 MSAs ranked by EBI.

Also includes Chicago population and households, projected to 2000; median household income; marriages, births, and deaths; new car sales; housing permits; median home value and contract rent; weather averages and extremes; retail establishments and sales, with sales comparisons to Cook County and State; and NICA vs. New York area population, households, EBI, and retail sales.

Also includes PPI, CPI, and food prices; size and location of regional shopping centers;

---

comparison of Chicago *Sun-Times* and *Tribune* newspapers, including net reach and advertising costs per selected reader group; selected appliance ownership; and adults purchasing clothes in past year.

C2140
Child and Waters

C2140–1   TRAVEL INDUSTRY WORLD YEARBOOK: The Big Picture, 1984
Annual. 1984. 136 p.
Vol. 28.
ISBN 0-9611200-1-0.
ISSN 0738-9515.
SRI/MF/not filmed

Annual report, by Somerset R. Waters, for 1984, on U.S. and world tourist travel trends and markets. Includes data on travel industry, travel destinations, accommodations, and transportation. Data are generally for 1982-83, with selected trends from early 1950s and projections to 1990.

Data are from various sources, including Federal Government, OECD, private companies, foreign governments, World Tourism Organization (WTO), and other trade organizations.

Contains contents listing and geographic index (p. 2-3); narrative analysis interspersed with 1 map, 10 charts, and 53 tables, described below (p. 4-124); 12 supplemental tables, also described below (p. 125-134); and glossary and references (p. 135-136).

This is the 28th annual edition.

Availability: Child and Waters, 516 Fifth Ave., New York NY 10036, $47.00+$3.00 postage; SRI/MF/not filmed.

TABLES AND CHARTS:

[Data sources are noted beneath each table and chart.]

C2140–1.1: World Tourism Summary

a. Travel trends: tourist arrivals, receipts, and/or expenditures, by country or world region, various years 1981-83; change in visitor arrivals for U.S. and 4 world areas, decennial periods 1950-80; comparison of U.S. and world tourism and selected economic indicators, before and after oil embargo of 1973; and revenues generated from U.S. and world tourism, compared with GNP and world gross product and trade, 1982 and 1990. 5 tables. (p. 5-11)

b. Top 10 cities ranked by museum attendance (no date); passenger expenditures by transportation mode, 1980-81; and top 4 retail businesses ranked by receipts, and travel/tourism spending and direct/indirect jobs generated, 1982. 2 charts and 4 tables. (p. 15-20)

C2140–1.2: U.S. Domestic and International Travel

a. Travel summary: change in U.S. travel receipts by kind of business, traffic by mode, national park use, and gasoline demand, 1st 8 months 1983 vs. 1982; State tourist office budgets, by State, FY83; and top 10 cities ranked by convention meetings and attendance, 1982. 3 tables. (p. 22-26)

b. Domestic trip characteristics, including person-trips, -miles, and -nights, shown by transportation mode, reason, distance, duration, region and/or area of origin and destination, number and household composition of persons traveling, and demographic characteristics, 1977. 2 tables. (p. 32-35)

c. Top 10 cities ranked by average daily meal/lodging cost (no date); and distribution of conventions, by State and for Puerto Rico, 1982. 2 tables. (p. 43-50)

d. International travel: U.S. citizen total and air departures by foreign destination, various periods 1977-83; foreign visitors to U.S., with detail by country or world area of origin, 1981-84; and U.S. citizen foreign travel expenditures, and U.S. receipts from foreign visitors, by country or world region, 1979-82. 3 charts and 6 tables. (p. 52-59)

C2140–1.3: World Regional Travel Summary

a. Canadian tourist arrivals in U.S., 1981-84; and stayover tourist arrivals in the Caribbean, by country or region of origin and destination, various periods 1970-83. 1 chart and 3 tables (p. 61-66)

b. Western Europe: change in international and U.S. arrivals in Europe, selected periods 1950-82; and GNP increase and share of world goods/services production, for Western Europe and selected countries or other world areas, various periods 1950-85. 3 tables. (p. 68-69)

c. International tourism changes in arrivals, nights of accommodation, and receipts, by industrial nation or world area, 1980-82; share of international tourism receipts, by world area, 1972-82; room and meal costs at moderately priced hotels or restaurants in 7 European cities, 1980 and 1983; and U.S. citizen direct business and pleasure travel, and total border entries, to Soviet Union, 1972-83. 5 tables. (p. 73-79)

d. Mexican visitors to U.S., 1981-84; Japanese overseas travelers, 1971-82; percent change in destination patterns of Japanese tourists, selected periods 1978-83; and Africa per capita income, by country, 1980; 1 map, 2 charts, and 1 table. (p. 83-101)

C2140–1.4: Travel Agents, Hotels, and Food Service

a. Number of travel agency locations for top 10 States ranked by percent change in number of locations, and total locations by census region and State, 1970 and 1983; ATC-accredited travel agencies located within corporations, 1978-82 and 1st quarter 1983; and travel agencies and population per agency by State, and travel agent share of bookings by travel mode and for hotels, (no date). 5 tables (p. 103-106)

b. Hotels: top 50 world hotel/motel chains ranked by number of rooms, and including number of establishments; and percent change in foreign hotel occupancy, daily room rate, revenue, operating cost/expense, and income, by country and world region; 1982 compared to 1981. 2 tables. (p. 108-110)

c. Food service industry sales by type of establishment, 1983; and distribution of expenses for food-only restaurants, by expense category, 1981-82. 1 chart and 1 table. (p. 113-114)

C2140–1.5: Transportation

a. Passenger car registrations, for selected countries, 1970 and 1981; and U.S. rental car fleet size and rental locations, by company, 1981-83. 1 chart and 2 tables. (p 115-117)

b. World airline passenger traffic 1973-82, with detail for North Atlantic route 1979-82; passenger traffic, revenue, and profit or loss, for aggregate U.S. airlines and for selected individual U.S. and Canadian airlines, various years 1977-84; world's top 20 airlines ranked by total, international, and domestic passenger traffic, 1982; and world's top 50 airports ranked by passenger traffic, and International Air Transport Assn (IATA) member airlines' passenger traffic and load factors, 1982. 9 tables. (p. 118-124)

C2140–1.6: Supplemental Data

a. Passports recipients, by object of travel, occupation, sex and age, selected SMSA, and State and region of residence, various years 1977-82. 5 tables. (p. 125-128)

b. U.S. citizen air departures by country and world region, 1982; Federal Government per diem foreign travel allowance by country or city, 1982-83; selected dollar exchange rates, 1980-82; U.S. air passenger arrivals and departures for top 20 countries of origin and destination, various periods 1981-83; visitor expenditure in selected Asian/South Pacific countries or areas, 1981-82; and population and auto registrations, by world area and country, 1981 with aggregate trends from 1960. 7 tables. (p. 129-134)

C2150
Chilton Co.

C2150–1   CHILTON'S DISTRIBUTION for Traffic and Transportation Decision Makers
Monthly. Approx. 100 p.
ISSN 0273-6721.
LC 80-643825.
SRI/MF/excerpts, shipped quarterly

Monthly trade journal on technical, regulatory, and financial aspects of the physical distribution of industrial goods, including management of inventory control, materials handling, and traffic.

General format:

a. Editorial depts; and feature articles, occasionally with statistics.

b. "Dialogue" feature, usually with statistics, based on results of reader surveys.

c. Quarterly "Forecast" section, with 5 tables and 1 chart.

July issue is an annual nonstatistical index to transportation and distribution services. Dec. issue includes annual editorial index.

Prior to the Jan. 1984 issue, quarterly "Forecast" feature appeared monthly, and contained 2 tables on distribution indexes and transportation indicators.

Quarterly forecast tables and chart are listed below. All additional features with substantial statistical content are described, as they appear, under "Statistical Features;" page locations and latest period of coverage for quarterly tables and chart are also noted. Nonstatistical features are not covered.

Availability: Chilton's Distribution, PO Box 1438, Riverton NJ 08077, qualified subscribers †, others $25.00 per yr., single copy $2.00, Distribution Guide $20.00; SRI/MF/excerpts for monthly tables and all portions described under "Statistical Features;" shipped quarterly.

Issues reviewed during 1984: Nov. 1983-Oct. 1984 (P) (Vol. 82, Nos. 11-12; Vol. 83, Nos. 1-10) [Vol. 83, No. 5 incorrectly reads No. 4].

QUARTERLY FORECAST TABLES AND CHART:
[Data are forecasts for quarter following month of publication, with comparisons to various previous periods. Tables [2] and [4-6] begin in the June 1984 issue.]

[1] General economic indicators [including GNP, car sales, housing starts, interest rates, and PPI; table begins in Mar. 1984 issue].

[2] Diesel [full- and self-serve] fuel prices.

[3] Distribution index shipper forecast [truck, rail, air, and water shipments; warehouse space utilization; and inventory valuation; based on survey responses of approximately 100 shippers/warehousers].

[4] Purchasing managers' composite index [of purchasing activity]. [chart]

[5-6] Transportation tonnage and cost indexes [for rail, truck, and barge traffic].

STATISTICAL FEATURES:

C2150–1.501: Nov. 1983 (Vol. 82, No. 11)
DIALOGUE: ETHICS, A MATTER OF COURSE

(p. 7-8) Article reporting shippers' opinions on questions of business ethics. Includes 1 table.

DISTRIBUTION CAREERS, 1983, ANNUAL FEATURE

(p. 44-47) Annual survey article, by Bernard J. La Londe and David E. Lloyd, for 1983, on industrial distribution executives' career patterns, work responsibilities, and industry outlook. Data are based on responses from 171 National Council of Physical Distribution Management members to a summer 1983 survey conducted by Ohio State University Logistics Research Group.

Includes 11 charts and 3 tables showing respondents' organizational position, job functions, educational background and needs, age distribution, compensation, and expectations for the 1980s, including computer use, impact of deregulation, and economic outlook.

C2150–1.502: Dec. 1983 (Vol. 82, No. 12)
DIALOGUE: AN ENDLESS DATA PROCESS

(p. 13) Article reporting shippers' opinions on computerization in the distribution industry. Includes 1 table showing percent of respondents computerized, by distribution function.

HEADHUNTERS LEAD YOU THROUGH THE JUNGLE

(p. 62-66) By Nancy Entwisle. Article, with 1 chart showing high, medium, and low salaries for 10 managerial positions in the distribution industry. Data are from a *Distribution* 1983 survey of employment placement firms.

AIR FREIGHT: STILL HAVING ITS UPS AND DOWNS

(p. 77-79) By Thomas A. Foster. Article on trends and outlook for the air freight industry. Data are from Air Transport Assn (ATA) and International Air Transport Assn (IATA). Includes text statistics and 6 tables showing the following for air freight carriers:

a. Top 30 carriers ranked by freight ton miles; sales and profits for 15 carriers and total industry; and top 6 carriers ranked by freight revenues, with debt-to-equity ratio and after-tax profit margin; various periods 1982-83.

b. Value of freight ton-miles, freight revenue, profit and income, and return on investment, for aggregate scheduled airlines, 1972-82.

c. Traffic and financial data for domestic all-cargo carriers, 1981-82; cargo ton miles and operating and net profit/loss for 29 U.S. and 2 Canadian ATA airlines, 1982; and world air freight percent change, 1982-85, and market shares, 1982, for most active regions and region-region or region-country pairs, with world total freight change.

C2150-1.503: Jan. 1984 (Vol. 83, No. 1)

DIALOGUE: INTERNATIONAL DISTRIBUTION

(p. 7-8) Article reporting on shippers' involvement in international distribution, and opinions on factors affecting foreign trade. Data are from a reader survey. Includes 1 table.

C2150-1.504: Feb. 1984 (Vol. 83, No. 2)

DIALOGUE: GETTING A FULL MEASURE

(p. 7-8) Article reporting on criteria used by shippers to measure success in meeting corporate objectives. Data are from a reader survey. Includes 1 table.

C2150-1.505: Mar. 1984 (Vol. 83, No. 3)

QUARTERLY FORECAST FEATURE

(p. 19) For 2nd quarter 1984. For data description, see C2150-1 above.

DIALOG: IT'S A SUPERCARRIER!

(p. 7-8) Article reporting shippers' opinions on multimodal transportation companies providing "supercarrier" service. Data are from a reader survey. Includes 1 table.

SUPER (MARKET) STRATEGIES: THE BOXCAR'S NEW ROLE

(p. 33-38) By Nancy Entwisle. Article on food manufacturer use of railroads for food shipments. Data are from Herbert W. Davis and Co. Includes 1 table showing food distribution costs as a percent of manufacturer sales, by type, 1983.

WHO'S WHAT IN BROKERING

(p. 40-55) By Bruce Heydt and Joseph V. Barks. Article presenting a directory of transportation brokering operations. Data are from a survey of Transportation Brokers Conference of America members.

Includes 1 extended table showing the following for approximately 100 transportation brokers, arranged by region: types of services provided, number of carriers and shippers using services, total movements and tonnage, employment, and whether computerized, 1983.

C2150-1.506: Apr. 1984 (Vol. 83, No. 4)

DIALOGUE: HAZARDOUS MATERIALS

(p. 7-8) Article reporting shippers' opinions on regulations covering shipment of hazardous materials. Data are from a reader survey. Includes 1 table.

STATE TAXES AND HIGHWAY REGULATIONS, ANNUAL FEATURE

(p. 27-35) Annual feature, for 1984, summarizing State taxes, fees, highway regulations, and other State data of interest to distributors. Includes 1 extended table showing the following, by State: summary of taxation methods and tax capacity; average manufacturing wage and hours; labor force (manufacturing and for-hire transportation); motor fuel and corporate income tax rates; average State/Federal user fees paid per truck; highway motor vehicle size and weight limits. No data dates are provided.

Data were compiled by *Distribution* from a variety of specified sources.

C2150-1.507: May 1984 (Vol. 83, No. 5)

[Issue incorrectly reads No. 4.]

DIALOGUE: LABOR'S FACE

(p. 7-8) Article reporting shippers' opinions on labor unions and labor/management relations in the transportation industry. Data are from a reader survey. Includes 1 table.

C2150-1.508: June 1984 (Vol. 83, No. 6)

QUARTERLY FORECAST FEATURE

(p. 58-59) For 3rd quarter 1984. For data description, see C2150-1 above.

DIALOGUE: PLENTY TO DECLARE

(p. 7-8) Article reporting on shippers' opinions regarding effect of transportation industry deregulation on loss/damage claims. Data are from a reader survey. Includes 1 table.

1983 MOTOR CARRIER FINANCIAL PROFILE: THE GULF WIDENS, AND THE TABLES TURN, ANNUAL FEATURE

(p. 48-56) Annual article, by Kurt C. Hoffman, with 1 table on the financial performance of freight trucking companies, showing the following: operating revenues and income, net income, revenue tons hauled, operating ratio, and return on equity, for each of 100 largest Class I carriers, arranged by district, 1982-83.

C2150-1.509: Aug. 1984 (Vol. 83, No. 8)

DIALOGUE: ONLY IF THE PRICE IS RIGHT

(p. 7-8) Article reporting shippers' opinions on private carrier operations and outlook. Data are from a reader survey. Includes 1 table.

1983 RAIL FINANCIAL PROFILE: HAULING A HEAVY LOAD, ANNUAL FEATURE

(p. 46-50) Annual article, by Thomas A. Foster, with 5 tables showing the following for individual Class I railroads, by district: operating revenues and income, income before extraordinary items, net income, freight revenue ton-miles, and return on net investment, with selected rankings, 1982-83.

C2150-1.510: Sept. 1984 (Vol. 83, No. 9)

QUARTERLY FORECAST FEATURE

(p. 27-29) For 4th quarter 1984. For data description, see C2150-1 above.

DIALOGUE: GETTING A HANDLE ON INBOUND

(p. 7-8) Article reporting shippers' opinions on inbound materials management. Data are from a reader survey. Includes 1 table.

C2150-1.511: Oct. 1984 (Vol. 83, No. 10)

DIALOGUE: INTERNATIONAL TRADE

(p. 7-8) Article reporting shippers' opinions on problems associated with international distribution. Data are from a reader survey. Includes 1 table.

RENOVATIONS FOR JAPAN'S TRADING HOUSES

(p. 17-25) By Roger Schreffler. Article, with 1 table showing sales, profits, and net income (all in yen) for 9 Japanese trading companies, various periods 1981-85. Data are from company reports and forecasts by International Business Information, Inc., Tokyo.

MORE TRENDS IN INTERNATIONAL DISTRIBUTION, ANNUAL FEATURE

(p. 56-66) Annual article on international business practices of U.S. companies, focusing on international distribution functions. Data are from an undated *Distribution* survey of 126 companies involved in international business.

Includes 12 charts showing survey response distribution for the following: type of international business activity; value of corporate sales, imports, and exports; annual export freight bill; organization of international distribution activities, and number of professional employees involved; export consignees, by type; and methods of payment for exports, and terms of import and export sales.

This is the 2nd annual survey.

C2150-2   CHILTON'S IRON AGE: Metals Producer

Semimonthly. Approx. 100 p.
ISSN 0747-6329.
LC 80-642133.
SRI/MF/excerpts, shipped quarterly

Semimonthly trade journal of metalworking management, reporting on trends and developments in metal producing and metalworking industries. Covers materials availability and prices, production, technology, marketing, and industry general economic setting.

Most data are from American Iron and Steel Institute, company annual reports and other industry sources, *Iron Age* research, and the Federal Government.

Issues contain news and feature articles, some with statistics; regular editorial depts; and 4 semimonthly and 3 monthly tables, listed below.

Annual statistical features include a forecast of metalworking orders and shipments in 29 industries, updated quarterly; a review of metals prices and production; and financial and operating data for individual metals companies. A quarterly sales and earnings summary for metals companies is also included.

Beginning with the Jan. 2, 1984 issue, journal is published in separate "Metals Producer" and "Manufacturing Management" editions. Both editions contain all regularly recurring statistics. SRI covers only the "Metals Producer" edition. Prior to Jan. 1984, the single edition was titled *Chilton's Iron Age.*

Semimonthly tables appear in all issues. Articles with substantial statistical content are described, as they appear, under "Statistical Features;" page locations and latest periods of coverage for monthly tables are also noted. Nonstatistical features are not covered.

Availability: Chilton's Iron Age: Metals Producer, Circulation Manager, PO Box 2040, Radnor PA 19089, qualified subscribers †, selected others $42.00 per yr., single copy $2.50; SRI/MF/excerpts for semimonthly and monthly tables and all portions described under "Statistical Features;" shipped quarterly.

Issues reviewed during 1984: Nov. 7, 1983-Oct. 15, 1984 (P) (Vol. 226, Nos. 27-30; Vol. 227, Nos. 1-20).

SEMIMONTHLY TABLES:

[Tables [1-4] generally show data as of week 2-4 weeks prior to cover date. Tables [1-3] include selected comparisons to prior periods.]

[1] Price and production data [steel production by district, and prices for iron ore at Lake Superior].

[2] Steel production, composite prices [net production, capability utilization rate, selected composite prices, and scrap prices; also includes year-to-date data].

[3] Nonferrous prices [for primary metal, Straits tin, and scrap by type].

[4] Ferrous scrap prices [by type, in 17 cities].

MONTHLY TABLES:

[1] Steel prices [by product type and producer, and by product type in 24 steel service center cities; for month prior to cover date].

[2] Metalworking order trends [capital expenditures for manufacturing and mining, for quarter ending 1-3 months prior to cover date, or projected for current or next quarter; and durable goods new orders, shipments, inventories, and unfilled orders, and metalworking new orders by industry group, for month 2 months prior to cover date; all with comparative data for selected previous periods].

[3] Metalworking price trends [price indexes for approximately 20 metalworking product lines including equipment, automobiles, trucks, and containers; for month 2 months prior to cover date, with change from previous month and year].

STATISTICAL FEATURES:

C2150–2.501: Nov. 7, 1983 (Vol. 226, No. 27)

MONTHLY TABLES

[1] Steel prices [Oct. 1983]. (p. 93, 97)

[3] Metalworking price trends [Sept. 1983]. (p. 36)

STEEL READY TO SHAKE LOOSE MONEY FOR MILL EQUIPMENT

(p. MP7-MP10) By George J. McManus. Article, with 1 table showing steel industry capital investments and spending for material supply services, 1973-82. Data are from American Iron and Steel Institute.

C2150–2.502: Nov. 25, 1983 (Vol. 226, No. 28)

MONTHLY TABLE

[2] Metalworking order trends [3rd quarter or Sept. 1983]. (p. 60)

BUYING BACK THEIR OWN STOCK USUALLY WORKS WELL FOR COMPANIES

(p. 35) Brief article, with 1 table showing number of companies buying back their own stocks, and shares bought, 1980-81 and 1st 10 months 1982. Data are from the Conference Board.

STEEL/NONFERROUS BEGIN TO SEE SOME DAYLIGHT, QUARTERLY FEATURE

(p. 37-42) Quarterly article, by George J. McManus and Robert J. Regan, with 2 tables showing earnings/loss and sales for 19 steel and 19 nonferrous companies, 3rd quarter 1982-83. Also shows earnings per share rate for 6 companies (no date).

$100B TRADE SHORTFALL POSSIBLE IN THE 1980s

(p. 51-59) By Edwin W. Bowers. Article, with 1 chart and 1 table showing U.S. trade deficit, Jan.-Sept. 1983; and value of world machine tool production, exports, and imports, for U.S. and 19 foreign countries, 1982.

PLANT OUTLAYS SHIFT IS CRITICAL TO METALWORKING

(p. 63-66) By John D. Baxter. Article, with 1 table showing percent change in basic industrial and high technology capital investment, total and by type of equipment, 1960-70 and 1970-80 periods. Data are from Morgan Stanley and Co.

C2150–2.503: Dec. 5, 1983 (Vol. 226, No. 29)

MONTHLY TABLES

[1] Steel prices [Nov. 1983]. (p. 96-97)

[3] Metalworking price trends [Oct. 1983]. (p. 100)

VIENNA REPORT: STEEL IN 1990

(p. MP7-MP11) By Gene Beaudet. Article on production and consumption trends and outlook for world steel industry. Data are from International Iron and Steel Institute. Includes 2 tables showing world apparent steel consumption and liquid steelmaking capacity, by world region or economic grouping, with detail for U.S. and Japan, various years 1974-90.

HOW COMPANIES ARE PUTTING WASTE OIL BACK TO WORK

(p. 61-67) By Keith W. Bennett. Article on recycling of lubricating oil and grease. Data are from DOE. Includes 2 tables showing sales volume of new oil and estimated volume recycled, by type of oil, 1978; and cost of new vs. recycled oil at an unnamed steel mill, 1979/80-82 and 1st 9 months 1983.

C2150–2.504: Dec. 14, 1983 (Vol. 226, No. 30)

MONTHLY TABLE

[2] Metalworking order trends [4th quarter or Oct. 1983]. (p. 76)

PERSONAL COMPUTERS LOOK FOR ROOM ON THE FACTORY FLOOR

(p. 51-54) By Robert E. Harvey. Article, with 2 charts showing value of personal computer market, with market share by type, 1983 and 1988. Data are from Future Computing, Inc.

C2150–2.505: Jan. 2, 1984 (Vol. 227, No. 1)

PAYDIRT! AFTER A LONG WAIT, ANNUAL FEATURE

(p. 27-61) Annual article, by John D. Baxter, presenting *Iron Age* forecast of business conditions for 29 metal-intensive industries, 1984.

Includes 5 charts showing selected general economic indicators, various years 1981-86; and 29 charts showing shipment levels, sales, or orders, by metal-intensive industry, 1980-84.

ANNUAL STATISTICAL REVIEW

(p. 95-106) Annual statistical review, for 1983, of metal prices and production, with selected trends from 1952. Contains 29 tables, listed below:

Steel Production

[1] World steel production [by country, 1973-83]. (p. 95)

[2] U.S. yearly raw steel production [by method, 1952-82, and total 1983]. (p. 95)

[3] U.S. monthly raw steel production, net tons [1958-83]. (p. 96)

[4] U.S. raw steel production, rate of capability utilization [monthly, 1965-83]. (p. 96)

Steel Prices

[5-6] Composite prices by periods [1977-83]; and *Iron Age* finished steel composite price [monthly 1964-83]. (p. 96)

[7-15] Hot-rolled sheet and strip, tinplate, galvanized and cold-rolled sheets, structural steel shapes, special quality bars, steel plates, and composite pig iron price [monthly prices, various years 1970-83]. (p. 98-99)

Steel Scrap

[16-17] Scrap composites: [prices at Philadelphia, Pittsburgh, and Chicago]; and average *Iron Age* scrap prices, Pittsburgh/Chicago/Philadelphia [for No. 1 scrap or heavy melting, and No. 2 bundles, monthly 1978-83]. (p. 101-102)

Nonferrous Prices and Production

[18-24] U.S. production of primary aluminum, refined copper, slab zinc, and refined lead; [and prices for] aluminum 99.5% ingot, electrolytic copper, and Straits tin [monthly, various years 1972-83]. (p. 102-103)

Iron Ore

[25] Pig iron, production [by type 1972-82, and total 1983]. (p. 104)

[26] Supply of iron ore in the U.S. [domestic shipments, exports, and imports, 1975-83]. (p. 104)

Nonferrous Prices

[27-29] [Prices for] common grade lead, zinc, and electrolytic nickel [most shown monthly, various years 1972-83]. (p. 106)

C2150–2.506: Jan. 16, 1984 (Vol. 227, No. 2)

MONTHLY TABLE

[2] Metalworking order trends [3rd quarter or Nov. 1983]. (p. 30)

COMPUTER COURSES ADVANCE CAREERS

(p. 19) By Patricia Aiman. Article on management career advancement trends, based on a University of Michigan Graduate School of Business Administration 1983 survey of 1,459 newly promoted executives. Includes 1 chart showing distribution of respondents by reasons for seeking corporate advancement.

COUNTRY-BY-COUNTRY ANALYSIS

(p. 38-47) Article, with 1 table showing crude steel production for 29 countries or world areas, 1980-84. Data are from U.S. and foreign industry assns.

DATA CORRECTION

(p. 87) Data correction for semimonthly table [4] on ferrous scrap prices. Shows corrected data for Hamilton, Ont., effective Dec. 12, 19, and 27, 1983.

C2150–2.507: Feb. 6, 1984 (Vol. 227, No. 3)

MONTHLY TABLES

[1] Steel prices [Jan. 1984]. (p. 71-73)

[3] Metalworking price trends [Dec. 1983]. (p. 76)

SPANISH STAINLESS STEEL MAKERS FACE DUMPING SUIT

(p. 14) Article, with 1 table showing stainless steel imports from Spain, total and as percent of all stainless steel imports, 1980-83. Data are from Specialty Steel Industry of the U.S.

COOL PRICES IN A HOT MARKET

(p. 23-28) By George J. McManus. Article, with 1 table showing domestic and import steel rod and wire/wire product shipments, 1967-82. Data are from American Iron and Steel Institute and Commerce Dept.

C2150–2.508: Feb. 20, 1984 (Vol. 227, No. 4)

MONTHLY TABLE

[2] Metalworking order trends [4th quarter or Dec. 1983]. (p. 100)

WORLD STEEL FINANCING

(p. 26-31) By George J. McManus. Article on steel industry finances. Data are from American Iron and Steel Institute. Includes 3 tables showing steel industry changes in long-term debt, and internal financing and capital expenditures, 1970-82.

Also includes 1 table on factors considered by steel companies in evaluating investments, by world area and for Japan. Table is based on a recent International Iron and Steel Institute survey covering 63 companies in 29 countries.

C2150–2.509: Mar. 5, 1984 (Vol. 227, No. 5)

MONTHLY TABLES

[1] Steel prices [Feb. 1984]. (p. 80-81)

[3] Metalworking price trends [Jan. 1984]. (p. 84)

STEEL TAKES ITS LUMPS; NONFERROUS RECOVERING, QUARTERLY FEATURE

(p. 34-40) Quarterly article, by George J. McManus and Robert J. Regan, with 2 tables showing earnings/loss and sales for 18 steel and 21 nonferrous companies, full year and/or 4th quarter 1982-83.

C2150–2.510: Mar. 19, 1984 (Vol. 227, No. 6)

MONTHLY TABLE

[2] Metalworking order trends [4th quarter 1983 or Jan. 1984]. (p. 84)

INDUSTRY STRENGTHENS ITSELF THROUGH PEOPLE POWER

(p. 43-49) By John D. Baxter. Article, with 1 chart and 1 table showing percent of major corporations with selected human resource programs, and employee perceptions of selected factors affecting job motivation and satisfaction, (no dates). Data are from NYSE, NSF, and Public Agenda.

IRON ORE UPDATE: BATTERED, BRUISED, BUT NOT BEATEN

(p. 50-55) By George A. Weimer. Article, with 3 charts showing iron ore consumed per ton of crude steel produced and percent of raw steel produced in electric furnaces, 1953, 1982, and 1990; North American current iron ore capability and capacity; and average annual iron ore pellet demand, 1983-90 period. Data are from Hanna Mining and American Iron and Steel Institute.

DETROIT FORCES THE ISSUE IN GALVANIZING

(p. 57-59) By George J. McManus. Article, with 2 tables showing shipments of hot-dipped galvanized steel sheet, 1972-83; and shipments of galvanized sheet/strip to auto industry, 1972- 82. Data are from American Iron and Steel Institute.

COAL PRODUCERS FORESEE SLOW, BUT STEADY GROWTH

(p. 80) Brief article, with 1 table forecasting coal consumption by end use, and total production, under 3 economic growth assumptions, 1985. Data are from National Coal Assn.

C2150–2.511: Apr. 2, 1984 (Vol. 227, No. 7)

MONTHLY TABLES

[1] Steel prices [Mar. 1984]. (p. 80-81)

[3] Metalworking price trends [Feb. 1984]. (p. 84)

QUARTERLY FORECAST: INDUSTRY ON A ROLL, QUARTERLY FEATURE

(p. 24-50) First and 2nd quarter 1984 update of *Iron Age* annual forecast of business outlook for 29 metal-intensive industries. Most data are from industry assns and Commerce Dept. Includes 3 charts on general economic indicators; and 29 charts showing quarterly trends in shipments, sales, or orders, by industry, 1st quarter 1983-2nd quarter 1984.

C2150–2.512: Apr. 16, 1984 (Vol. 227, No. 8)

MONTHLY TABLE

[2] Metalworking order trends [4th quarter 1983 or Feb. 1984]. (p. 124)

TOP 50 WORLD STEEL PRODUCERS

(p. 100-107) By James B. Pond. Article on production and operations of world's 50 largest steel producers, 1983. Data are from an *Iron Age: Metals Producer* survey.

Includes 5 summary tables ranking top 7-10 producers by labor productivity, production gain, and employment increase and decrease; and 1 extended table showing top 50 producers ranked by crude steel production, and including maximum capability, exports as percent of shipments, employment, labor productivity, and capital expenditures, primarily 1983 with comparisons to 1982.

C2150–2.513: May 7, 1984 (Vol. 227, No. 9)

MONTHLY TABLES

[1] Steel prices [Apr. 1984]. (p. 77-79)

[3] Metalworking price trends [Mar. 1984]. (p. 82)

ANNUAL STEEL/NONFERROUS FINANCIAL ANALYSIS

(p. 27-32) Annual article, by Michael Marley and Robert J. Regan, presenting financial data for 21 steel and 16 nonferrous metals companies, 1982-83.

Includes 2 tables showing the following for each company, 1982-83: net sales/revenues, profit, invested and working capital, funded/other long-term debt, capital expenditures, stockholders' equity and outstanding stock, earnings and dividends per share, and selected operating ratios. Tables also show:

a. For steel companies: production, shipments, employment costs, depreciation/depletion/amortization, provision for Federal income taxes, net income, interest expense on funded debt, common stock value and price range, and stock price/earnings ratio.

b. For nonferrous metals companies: U.S./foreign income tax, extraordinary income, and net and retained earnings.

SERVICE CENTERS AHEAD OF 1983's PACE, SEE FURTHER GAINS THIS YEAR

(p. 69) Brief article, with 1 table showing steel service center average daily shipments of flat-rolled products, Sept. 1983-Mar. 1984. Data are from Steel Service Center Institute.

C2150–2.514: May 21, 1984 (Vol. 227, No. 10)

MONTHLY TABLE

[2] Metalworking order trends [1st quarter or Mar. 1984]. (p. 100)

STEEL: WILL IT EVER BE THE SAME?

(p. 35-42) By George J. McManus. Article, with 2 tables showing steel consumption, imports and exports, production, and consumer and mill inventories; and steel production and shipments for 9 companies; various years 1976-84. Data are from industry sources.

FIRST QUARTER EARNINGS: STEEL SHOWS LIFE; NONFERROUS EDGES UP, QUARTERLY FEATURE

(p. 61-67) Quarterly article, by George J. McManus and Robert J. Regan, with 2 tables showing earnings/loss and sales for 19 steel and 19 nonferrous companies, 1st quarter 1983-84. Also shows earnings per share rate for 12 steel companies, 1984.

C2150–2.515: June 4, 1984 (Vol. 227, No. 11)

MONTHLY TABLES

[1] Steel prices [May 1984]. (p. 80-81)

[3] Metalworking price trends [Apr. 1984]. (p. 84)

LIVING OVERSEAS GETS CHEAPER

(p. 26) By Patricia S. Aiman. Article, with 1 table showing annual living cost for U.S. executives in 8 major foreign cities, Jan. and Dec. 1983. Data are from Conference Board.

FACTORY 2000

(p. 27-58) By Robert E. Harvey. Article on factory automation developments and outlook. Data sources include a National Electrical Manufacturers Assn membership survey, and Predicasts, Inc. Includes 1 chart and 2 tables showing the following:

a. Percent of electrical manufacturing firms citing selected obstacles to implementing automated manufacturing (no date); and percent of labor force employed in manufacturing, selected years 1947-2000.

b. GNP; value of manufacturing new plants/equipment; manufacturing index; and factory automation system sales, including minicomputers and mainframes, computer-aided-design/computer-aided-manufacturing systems, machine tools and controls, and industrial robots by application; selected years 1967-95.

WARNING: A COKE SHORTAGE JUST AROUND THE CORNER

(p. 59-65) By George J. McManus. Article, with 1 table showing iron/steel industry coke receipts, consumption at blast furnaces, and consumption per ton of iron produced, 1972-83. Data are from American Iron and Steel Institute.

C2150–2.516: June 18, 1984 (Vol. 227, No. 12)

MONTHLY TABLE

[2] Metalworking order trends [1st quarter or Apr. 1984]. (p. 100)

SPECIALTY STEEL'S NEW APPROACH: CUT PRICES

(p. 30-40) By George J. McManus. Article, with 3 tables showing stainless steel sheet/strip exports, imports, and domestic shipments; sheet/strip and consumer durable goods production indexes; and stainless and tool steel imports and/or total shipments; various periods 1973-Mar. 1984.

Data are from Allegheny Ludlum Steel Corp. and American Iron and Steel Institute.

MANAGEMENT CHALLENGE: U.S. INDUSTRY FIGHTS BACK IN WORLD TRADE

(p. 43-53) By John D. Baxter. Article on trends in U.S. balance of trade. Data are from Morgan Stanley and Co. and Federal government sources.

Includes 3 charts and 2 tables showing U.S. exports as a percent of world exports; index of dollar value in world trade; U.S. balance of trade for all items, all manufacturing, and 7 metals/metalworking industries; and percent change in U.S. manufacturing wages/compensation, and in manufacturing unit labor costs for U.S. and 11 other countries; various periods 1965-84.

C2150–2.517: July 2, 1984 (Vol. 227, No. 13)

MONTHLY TABLES

[1] Steel prices [June 1984]. (p. 72-73)

[3] Metalworking price trends [May 1984]. (p. 76)

QUARTERLY FORECAST: A HOT RECOVERY COOLS DOWN, QUARTERLY FEATURE

(p. 28-54) By John D. Baxter. Third quarter 1984 update of *Iron Age* annual forecast of business outlook for 29 metal-intensive indus-

tries. Most data are from industry assns and Commerce Dept. Includes 3 charts on general economic indicators; and 29 charts showing quarterly trends in shipments, sales, or orders, by industry, 2nd quarter 1983-3rd quarter 1984.

STEEL LICKS THE POLLUTION PROBLEM, FOR NOW

(p. 56-60) By George J. McManus. Article, with 1 table showing steel industry capital expenditures for air and water pollution control, 1974-83. Data are from American Iron and Steel Institute.

BEACON OF HOPE COULD BE SNUFFED OUT

(p. 61-63) By Edwin W. Bowers. Article, with 1 table showing number of workers certified for Trade Adjustment Assistance (a program designed to aid workers unemployed due to imports), by industry, Apr. 1975-Sept. 1983 period. Data are from Labor Dept.

C2150–2.518: July 16, 1984 (Vol. 227, No. 14)

MONTHLY TABLE

[2] Metalworking order trends [1st quarter or May 1984]. (p. 76)

WORLD CONTINUOUS CASTING REPORT: NEW PROJECTS ON THE HORIZON

(p. 49-58) By Keith W. Bennett and George A. Weimer. Article, with 1 table showing continuously cast raw steel production, total and as a percent of all steel production, by country and for EC, 1981-83. Data are from International Iron and Steel Institute.

C2150–2.519: Aug. 6, 1984 (Vol. 227, No. 15)

MONTHLY TABLES

[1] Steel prices [July 1984]. (p. 61-63)

[3] Metalworking price trends [June 1984]. (p. 68)

C2150–2.520: Aug. 20, 1984 (Vol. 227, No. 16)

MONTHLY TABLE

[2] Metalworking order trends [2nd quarter or June 1984; title incorrectly reads price trends]. (p. 84)

PUTTING TIGHT CONTROL ON STEELMAKING

(p. 31-47) By George J. McManus. Article, with 1 table showing number of hot strip and slabbing mills, blast furnaces, and coke batteries, and percent using computer process control (with detail by plant type), 1981 and 1985. Data are from International Iron and Steel Institute.

SECOND QUARTER EARNINGS: STEEL STALLED; NONFERROUS GAINS SLIGHTLY, QUARTERLY FEATURE

(p. 53-54) Quarterly article, by George J. McManus and Robert J. Regan, with 2 tables showing earnings/loss and sales for 20 steel and 19 nonferrous companies, 2nd quarter 1983-84. Also shows earnings per share for 17 steel companies, 1984.

C2150–2.521: Sept. 3, 1984 (Vol. 227, No. 17)

MONTHLY TABLES

[1] Steel prices [Aug. 1984]. (p. 72-73)

[3] Metalworking price trends [July 1984]. (p. 76)

FIRST ANNUAL FINANCIAL SCOREBOARD

(p. 26-46) By John D. Baxter. Annual article on financial performance of 275 companies in 14 metal producing and metalworking industry groups, 1983. Data are primarily from company annual reports.

Includes 1 table repeated for each industry group showing the following, by company: revenues, operating profits, and net earnings, FY83; and average annual percent change in revenues, operating profits, net earnings, and return on invested capital, equity, and sales, FY79-83 period.

Companies are ranked within each industry group by average annual return on invested capital, FY79-83 period.

AMERICA'S INDUSTRIAL HEART AND SOUL

(p. 49-54) By Edwin W. Bowers. Article, with 2 tables showing employment in 5 metalworking industries and all manufacturing, for 5 North Central States, 1979-83.

2nd QUARTER EARNINGS: STEEL STALLED; NONFERROUS GAINS SLIGHTLY, QUARTERLY FEATURE

(p. 54A4-54A8) Quarterly article, by George J. McManus and Robert J. Regan, with 2 tables showing earnings/loss and sales for 20 steel and 19 nonferrous companies, 2nd quarter 1983-84. Also shows earnings per share rate for 17 steel companies, 1984.

Tables are reprinted from Aug. 20, 1984 issue (for description, see C2150-2.520 above), but are accompanied by a more extensive narrative analysis.

C2150–2.522: Sept. 17, 1984 (Vol. 227, No. 18)

MONTHLY TABLE

[2] Metalworking order trends [2nd quarter or July 1984]. (p. 92)

WORLD STEEL OUTPUT UP IN FIRST HALF; U.S. AND LATIN AMERICA POST BEST GAINS

(p. 21) Brief article, with 1 table showing steel production for EC, U.S., Japan, and other producers, 1st half 1983-84. Data are from International Iron and Steel Institute.

JAPAN: AISI CRITIQUE OF CBO REPORT INACCURATE

(p. 27) Article, with 1 table showing U.S. steel imports, total and from Japan, June 1983 and May-June 1984. Data are from American Iron and Steel Institute (AISI).

AISI: CBO ANALYSIS FLAWED BY INACCURACIES

(p. 30) Article, with 1 table showing U.S. steel imports, by country or world region of origin, 1st half 1983-84. Data are from AISI.

HOW CAPITAL SPENDING IS MAKING STEEL MORE COMPETITIVE

(p. 32-54B4) By George J. McManus and Cynthia Stueber. Article on steel industry plant expansions and shutdowns. Data are from industry sources. Includes text data on capital spending (generally by type of equipment) and capacity for new facilities installed or planned, and capacity of facilities shut down or divested, for 17-31 steel companies by facility, various years 1982-86.

C2150–2.523: Oct. 1, 1984 (Vol. 227, No. 19)

MONTHLY TABLES

[1] Steel prices [Sept. 1984]. (p. 84-85)

[3] Metalworking price trends [Aug. 1984]. (p. 88)

4th QUARTER FORECAST: MORE MUSCLE THAN EXPECTED, QUARTERLY FEATURE

(p. 19-56) By John D. Baxter. Fourth quarter 1984 update of *Iron Age* annual forecast of business outlook for 29 metal-intensive industries. Most data are from industry assns and Commerce Dept. Includes 3 charts on general economic indicators; and 29 charts showing quarterly trends in shipments, sales, or orders, by industry, generally for 3rd quarter 1983-4th quarter 1984.

C2150–2.524: Oct. 15, 1984 (Vol. 227, No. 20)

MONTHLY TABLE

[2] Metalworking order trends [2nd quarter or Aug. 1984]. (p. 108)

WHAT VOLUNTARY QUOTAS MEAN TO WORLD STEEL

(p. 52-56) By George McManus. Article, with 1 chart showing imports as a percent of steel supply, 1976-85.

C2150–3 CHILTON'S AUTOMOTIVE INDUSTRIES

Monthly. Approx. 150 p.
ISSN 0273-656X.
LC 80-644280.
SRI/MF/excerpts, shipped quarterly

Monthly trade journal of the automotive and automotive supplier industries, presenting news and analyses of manufacturing, materials, and supply and demand trends and developments.

Issues are primarily narrative, but occasionally present articles with substantial statistics. Annual features include a compilation of vehicle engine specifications (Apr.) and a supplier directory (June).

Beginning with the July 1983 issue, journal incorporates *Chilton's Truck and Off-Highway Industries* as a separately paginated bimonthly insert covering the heavy-duty truck and off-highway equipment industry. *Truck and Off-Highway Industries*, which contains articles, specifications, and occasional statistics, previously was published separately, and was covered by SRI under C2150-5.

All features with substantial statistical content, except vehicle and equipment specifications, are described, as they appear, under "Statistical Features." Each issue of the journal is reviewed, but an abstract is published in SRI monthly issues only when statistical features appear.

Availability: Chilton's Automotive Industries, Circulation Department, PO Box 1441, Riverton NJ 08077-0455, qualified subscribers †, others price on request; SRI/MF/excerpts for all portions described under "Statistical Features;" shipped quarterly.

Issues reviewed during 1984: Nov. 1983-Oct. 1984 (P) (Vol. 163, Nos. 11-12; Vol. 164, Nos. 1-10).

STATISTICAL FEATURES:

C2150–3.501: Nov. 1983 (Vol. 163, No. 11)

[Includes *Truck and Off-Highway Industries.*]

Automotive Industries

CYCLE TURNS RAG

(p. 36) Brief article, with 1 table showing domestic and imported new car sales volume, 1983-88. Data are from Citibank.

C2150–3.502: Dec. 1983 (Vol. 163, No. 12)

DOES AMERICA SUBSIDIZE ITS IMPORTS?

(p. 29-30) By John McElroy. Article analyzing effect of value added taxes (VATs) on import and export auto prices and U.S. tax revenues. Data are based on Dept of Commerce statistics. Includes 3 tables showing auto import effects on U.S. tax revenues 1982, effects of Japanese VATs on U.S. auto prices (no date), and European auto VAT rates by country (no date).

QUALITY: THE NEW YARDSTICK

(p. 47-48) By John McElroy. Article, with 1 chart showing 25 domestic and imported auto makes ranked by customer satisfaction index, 1983. Data are from J. D. Power and Associates.

INDUSTRY ANALYSTS: WELCOME TO EASIER TIMES, RECURRING FEATURE

(p. 62-63) Recurring article, by Andrew M. Andrews, with 1 table showing auto and light truck production and import/domestic sales forecasts of 12 research organizations, 1984.

C2150–3.503: Jan. 1984 (Vol. 164, No. 1)

[Includes *Truck and Off-Highway Industries.*]

Automotive Industries

GM PRODUCTIVITY SHOWS RECENT JUMP

(p. 24) Brief article, with 1 table showing domestic new car retail sales volume by manufacturer, and total import sales, 1982-84. Data are from Goldman Sachs Research, Inc.

DRI EYES WORLD MARKET

(p. 24) Brief article, with 1 table showing auto production and sales volume, by country and world region, 1983-84 and 1988. Data are from DRI Europe Ltd.

Truck and Off-Highway Industries

CE EXPORTS: DIGGING OUT?

(p. 18-20) By Lance A. Ealey and Douglas Williams. Article on outlook for U.S. construction equipment (CE) exports. Data are from Census Bureau and Construction Industry Manufacturers Assn. Includes 1 table showing CE total and export sales, by equipment type, 1979 and 1982, and percent change, 1983-84.

C2150–3.504: Apr. 1984 (Vol. 164, No. 4)

AI's TOTAL CAR COEFFICIENT, ANNUAL FEATURE

(p. 70-71) Annual article, by Lance A. Ealey, on total car coefficient (TCC), a measurement of auto quality based on interior volume, gas mileage, acceleration capability, and price. Includes 1 table showing auto models ranked by TCC, grouped by price range.

U.S. PASSENGER CAR PRODUCTION

(p. 83) Table showing quarterly auto production, 1965-83. Data are from Motor Vehicle Manufacturers Assn.

U.S. PASSENGER CARS, 1983 MODEL YEAR FACTORY INSTALLATION OF OPTIONAL EQUIPMENT

(p. 89) Table showing factory installations of air conditioning, and transmission, engine, power accessory, and selected other options, for 1983 model year autos, by auto model. Data are shown as a percent of auto model production.

C2150–3.505: May 1984 (Vol. 164, No. 5)

[Includes *Truck and Off-Highway Industries.*]

Automotive Industries

AMERICAN STEEL FIGHTS BACK!

(p. 37-40) By George J. McManus. Article, with 1 table showing steel shipments to the automotive industry, 1973-83. Data are from American Iron and Steel Institute.

C2150–3.506: June 1984 (Vol. 164, No. 6)

ANALYSTS SEE CONTINUED UPSWING AND PROBABLE STRIKE, RECURRING FEATURE

(p. 84-85) Recurring article, by Neil M. Szigethy, with 1 table showing auto and light truck production and import/domestic sales forecasts of 12 research organizations, 1984. Table also shows each organization's opinion on whether United Auto Workers will strike in fall 1984, and against which manufacturer.

C2150–3.507: July 1984 (Vol. 164, No. 7)

[Includes *Truck and Off-Highway Industries.*]

Automotive Industries

WORLD GROWTH SEEN IN PASSENGER CARS

(p. 9) Brief article, with 1 table showing auto production and sales volume, by country or world region, 1983-84 and 1990. Data are from Data Resources International.

WHAT IF?

(p. 17-22) By John McElroy. Article examining potential effects of expiration of auto trade restraint agreement between U.S. and Japan. Includes 1 table showing motor vehicle production per employee, for 3 U.S. and 6 Japanese manufacturers, primarily 1977-83; and list of Japanese auto models not sold in U.S. market.

Truck and Off-Highway Industries

DIESELIZATION: IS THE MEDIUM THE REAL MESSAGE?

(p. T13-T15) By Douglas Williams. Article, with 1 table showing factory sales volume for medium (Class 5-7) trucks, and percent diesel powered, 1974-83. Data are from Motor Vehicle Manufacturers Assn.

C2150–3.508: Aug. 1984 (Vol. 164, No. 8)

HOW TO MAKE RECORD PROFITS

(p. 8) By Joseph M. Callahan. Article, with 1 chart showing profit/loss for 4 major auto manufacturers, 1981-83.

COMPETITION HOT IN EUROPE

(p. 17-18) By Peter J. Mullins. Article, with 1 table showing European auto market shares for 10 manufacturers and for Japanese cars sold in Europe, 1982-83. Data are from UEA Motor Industry Database.

NON-UNION WORKERS CRY 'FOUL'

(p. 33-37) By Lance A. Ealey. Article, with 1 chart and 1 table showing summary characteristics of white-collar worker benefit plans, including medical and life insurance, savings/stock investment plans, and vacation, and number of workers on bonus roll (no date); and salaried/nonbonus employment, 1979 and 1984; all for 4 major auto manufacturers.

HOW WORK PRACTICES SEND PRODUCTIVITY SOARING

(p. 39-43) By John McElroy. Article comparing productivity of newest U.S. and Japanese auto plants. Data are from *Automotive Industries* and Harbour and Associates.

Includes 2 undated tables showing plant size, production rate, employment and wages, productivity, absenteeism rate, inventory, and number of robots, for General Motors Lake Orion plant, Suzuki Kosai plant, and Mazda Hofu plant; and Japanese manpower savings in 9 production-related areas.

C2150-3.509: Sept. 1984 (Vol. 164, No. 9)

[Includes *Truck & Off-Highway Industries*.]

Automotive Industries

DETROIT GOES PSYCHO!

(p. 44-48) By Elizabeth A. Capelli. Article on lifestyle and demographic categorization of potential car buyers, based on the Values and Life Styles (VALS) program developed by SRI International, and the Potential Rating Index Zip Market (PRIZM) system developed by Claritas Corp. Includes 2 tables showing percent of population or households by VALS or PRIZM group (no dates), with percent of domestic full-size cars bought by 19 PRIZM groups, 1982.

WORLD AUTOMOTIVE OUTLOOK

(p. 97) By Thomas F. O'Grady. Article, with 1 table showing passenger car demand in industrial and developing countries, 1980, 1985, and 1990.

C2150-4   CHILTON'S COMMERCIAL CARRIER JOURNAL

Monthly. Approx. 100 p.
ISSN 0734-1423.
LC 82-4905.
SRI/MF/excerpts, shipped quarterly

Monthly trade journal on commercial truck and other vehicle fleet management, maintenance, finances, and operations. Most data are from industry sources and Federal agencies.

Issues generally contain feature articles, occasionally with statistics; and narrative editorial depts and columns. Annual features include non-statistical fleet reference guide (Apr. issue) and buyers' guide (Oct.); and a statistical review of industry financial and operating performance (July).

Features with substantial statistical content are described, as they appear, under "Statistical Features." Each issue of the journal is reviewed, but an abstract is published in SRI monthly issues only when statistical features appear.

Availability: Chilton's Commercial Carrier Journal, Circulation Department, PO Box 2045, Radnor PA 19089, qualified subscribers †, others $30.00 per yr., single copy $3.50, special issues $6.00; SRI/MF/excerpts for all portions described under "Statistical Features;" shipped quarterly.

Issues reviewed during 1984: Nov. 1983-Oct. 1984 (P) (Vol. 140, Nos. 11-12; Vol. 141, Nos. 1-10).

STATISTICAL FEATURES:

C2150-4.501: Feb. 1984 (Vol. 141, No. 2)

ICC SURVEY SHOWS TRUCKLOAD CARRIERS ARE PURCHASING NEW TRAILERS DESPITE ECONOMY

(p. 20) Survey article, with 1 table showing new trailer purchases/orders, and net trailer additions after trade-ins, by type, for carriers with annual revenues of $12 million or more, and less than $12 million, 1983. Data are based on responses of 110 truckload carriers to an Interstate Carriers Conference survey.

C2150-4.502: July 1984 (Vol. 141, No. 7)

1983's TOP 100: TRUCKING INDUSTRY BEGINS TO SEE A FEW LONG-DISTANCE SWIMMERS, ANNUAL FEATURE

(p. 65-80) Annual article, by Carl Glines and Dorothy DiNunzio, on the financial and operating performance of 100 largest for-hire general freight carriers, and financial performance of 2nd 100 largest carriers, 1983 and trends. Data were compiled by Trinc Transportation Consultants from company reports.

Includes 2 tables showing the following data by company, 1983, with selected comparisons to 1982 and aggregate trends from 1981:

a. Top 100: operating revenue and rank, expenses, and net aftertax income; trucks, tractors, and trailers owned; equipment expenditures; maintenance employment and tire/tube expenditures; intercity shipments, tons carried, and owned and rented vehicle mileage; rail/water mileage; average load tonnage and distance hauled; and operating ratio and rank.

b. 2nd 100: operating revenue and rank, expenses, net aftertax income, and operating ratio.

INDUSTRY TRENDS AND STATISTICS, ANNUAL FEATURE

(p. 82-90) Annual compilation of trucking industry statistics, including number of carriers, carrier finances, and truck factory sales, 1983 and trends. Data are from Motor Vehicle Manufacturers Assn, carrier reports filed with ICC, and other sources. Includes 8 tables showing the following:

a. For-hire carriers, by ICC class, 1977-83; and Class I/II common carriers, operating revenues, expenses by type, net income and profit margin, and operating ratio, 1982-83.

b. Factory sales of trucks, with domestic detail by gross vehicle weight and for diesel trucks, and by truck and diesel engine make; and trailer shipments, by type; various periods 1969-83.

DRIVE TO SURVIVE: WHERE ARE THEY NOW?

(p. 95-100) By Leo Abruzzese. Article profiling finances of 7 major trucking companies. Includes 1 table showing the following for each company: operating revenues, expenses, net aftertax income, and operating ratio, 1982-83.

PRIVATE FLEETS, ANNUAL FEATURE

(p. 105-122) Annual statistical compilation, by Rich Cross, on characteristics of vehicle fleets

operated by businesses and government agencies, various years 1981-83. Data are from a journal census of fleets, GSA, and responses of 443 private fleets to an A. T. Kearney, Inc. survey sponsored by Private Truck Council of America. Includes 18 tables showing the following:

a. Total fleets, and vehicles by type, both by fleet size and operator category, including common/contractor carriers, lease/rental companies, governments, 7 industry categories, schools, and bus operators, 1984.

b. Private fleet survey findings, including fleet mileage, number of drivers and vehicles, union status, operating costs, driver and mechanic wages, and selected ratios; response to questions on single-source and trip leasing, transportation subsidiaries, and intercorporate hauling; and private fleets with and applying for authority to also operate as for-hire carriers; generally shown for straight truck/van, mixed, and tractor/trailer fleets, 1982-83.

c. Fleet vehicles, by type, for individual large fleet operators, including 251 food, utility, lease/rental, petroleum, and other companies, and 32 State and 55 city governments, 1984, and 16 Federal agencies, 1983, with mileage and leased vehicles for most operators.

C2150-4.503: Aug. 1984 (Vol. 141, No. 8)

TEAMSTER'S VIEW OF SAFETY

(p. 59-65) By Leo Abruzzese. Article on results of roadside truck inspections conducted by DOT's Bureau of Motor Carrier Safety. Includes 3 tables showing total and "out of service" violations by type of defect, by type of carrier, 1982 and May 2-5, 1983.

C2150-6   CHILTON'S FOOD ENGINEERING

Monthly. Approx. 150 p.
ISSN 0193-323X.
SRI/MF/excerpts, shipped quarterly

Monthly trade journal of the food and beverage product manufacturing industry. Covers processing methods and equipment, packaging, new products, industry finances, Federal Government regulation, and related topics.

Data are from journal surveys, Federal Government, and other sources.

Issues contain regular editorial depts; and feature articles, occasionally with substantial statistics.

Annual statistical features include a "state-of-the-industry" report, with sales and profit data for individual companies; and reports on plant construction, new products, capital spending, and management salaries.

Features with substantial statistical content are described, as they appear, under "Statistical Features." Each issue of the journal is reviewed, but an abstract is published in SRI monthly issues only when statistical features appear.

Availability: Chilton's Food Engineering, Circulation Department, Chilton Way, Radnor PA 19089, qualified subscribers $24.00 per yr., academic community/college students $12.00 per yr., others $36.00 per yr., single copy $3.00; SRI/MF/excerpts, for all portions described under "Statistical Features;" shipped quarterly.

Issues reviewed during 1984: Nov. 1983-Oct. 1984 (P) (Vol. 55, Nos. 11-12; Vol. 56, Nos. 1-10) [Vol. 56, No. 10 contents page incorrectly reads Vol. 55].

STATISTICAL FEATURES:

C2150–6.501: Nov. 1983 (Vol. 55, No. 11)

CAPITAL SPENDING REPORT, ANNUAL FEATURE

(p. 75-89) Annual article on 50 leading food/beverage manufacturers' capital expenditures. Data are from journal's survey.

Includes 1 table ranking companies by capital expenditures, 1982 with comparisons to 1979-81; and 1 table repeated for each company, showing capital expenditures, and net sales and earnings, generally 1981-82, with estimated spending for 1983.

This is the 5th annual survey.

C2150–6.502: Dec. 1983 (Vol. 55, No. 12)

1983 SALARY SURVEY, ANNUAL FEATURE

(p. 55-59) Annual article on salaries of food/beverage manufacturing company management employees, based on approximately 1,600 responses to a 1983 journal survey of employees.

Includes 7 tables showing median salary, by job function, company employment size, product specialty, years of experience, region, and educational attainment; and salary range, by job function.

C2150–6.503: Feb. 1984 (Vol. 56, No. 2)

TAKING THE MYSTERY OUT OF PROCESS CONTROLS

(p. 75-83) Article on computer process control systems for the food industry. Data are from a Frost and Sullivan market survey. Includes 1 table showing food processing company ratings of various factors affecting purchasing decisions for digital process control systems.

C2150–6.504: May 1984 (Vol. 56, No. 5)

CHEMICAL RESIDUES CONCERN CONSUMERS

(p. 37-38) Brief article on issues of concern to consumers regarding food safety and nutrition. Data are from a Jan. 1984 telephone survey of 1,008 consumers conducted by Louis Harris and Associates for the Food Marketing Institute (FMI). Includes 1 table showing respondents' perceptions of 6 substances as a 'serious hazard' in the food supply.

Full FMI survey report is described in SRI under A4950-3.

LOW-SALT: WILL IT SELL?

(p. 109-110) Article, with 3 charts showing percent of food shoppers who read ingredients lists on products, with detail for those avoiding salt/sodium, sugar, and preservatives, 1978 and 1982; grocery store sales volume for light salt/salt substitutes, 1980-83; and number of new low/no sodium products introduced, selected periods 1979-83.

Data sources include FDA consumer surveys.

FOOD SPENDING UP; RETAILERS POST GAINS

(p. 242) Article, with 1 table showing grocery store sales, by census region, 1983 with percent change from 1982. Data are from The Food Institute.

C2150–6.505: June 1984 (Vol. 56, No. 6)

SEVEN-UP COMPANY CITES RECENT SALES GROWTH

(p. 42) Article, with 1 table ranking 5 major soft drink companies by change in sales, 1983. Data are from Seven-Up Co.

CONFLICT OVER COLOR CONTROL

(p. 95-98) Article reporting on outlook for synthetic food color industry. Data are from International Life Sciences Institute. Includes 1 table showing number of synthetic food colors in use in 25 countries, 1984, with change from 1980.

C2150–6.506: July 1984 (Vol. 56, No. 7)

BLT: HOLD THE CARCINOGENS

(p. 69-71) Article reporting on consumer concerns regarding nutrition and food ingredients. Data are from a survey by the Wheat Industry Council. Includes 1 undated table showing percent of respondents expressing concern about selected eating habits and health issues, by sex.

Full Wheat Industry Council survey report is described under A9398-1.

$370,000 QUESTION

(p. 73-76) Article comparing costs of ultrafiltration and conventional food clarification systems. Data are from plant installations. Includes 2 undated tables.

C2150–6.507: Aug. 1984 (Vol. 56, No. 8)

STATE OF THE FOOD INDUSTRY: BUSINESS, ANNUAL FEATURE

(p. 87-92) Annual article presenting financial performance data for food/beverage manufacturing companies, 1983. Data sources include Profit Press Inc. and The Food Institute.

Includes 2 tables showing food/beverage sales and net profits, for 90 leading companies, 1983, with comparisons to 1981-82; and U.S. vs. foreign sales, profits, assets, and margins, for 18 companies, FY83, with selected comparisons to FY82.

Also includes list of major mergers or acquisitions involving food companies, 1st half 1984.

This is the 5th annual report.

C2150–6.508: Sept. 1984 (Vol. 56, No. 9)

NEW FOOD PLANTS: WHO'S BUILDING WHAT AND WHERE? ANNUAL FEATURE

(p. 65-80) Annual listing, for 1984, of new construction and expansion projects involving food plants, generally showing the following for each project: company, location, primary product, square footage, estimated cost, employees, and planning/completion status and date.

This is the 7th annual listing. Includes brief accompanying article.

FANCY FOODS FARE WELL

(p. 83-86) Article, with 1 table showing value of imports for 16 categories of specialty foods, 1981. Data are from the National Assn of the Specialty Food Trade and British Trade Development Office.

BARRIER MATERIALS RESHAPE PACKAGING

(p. 96) Article reporting on impact of high barrier multilayer plastic packaging on the food packaging industry. Data are based on a survey

commissioned by DuPont Co. Includes 1 chart showing market share for 6-9 types of rigid packaging, 1981 and 1991.

C2150–6.509: Oct. 1984 (Vol. 56, No. 10)

[Contents page incorrectly reads Vol. 55.]

INDUSTRY IN TRANSITION

(p. 68-69) By LeRoy H. Doar, Jr. Article, with 1 table showing value of U.S. packaging machinery exports and imports, with detail for major trading countries, 1st quarter 1984. Data are from the Commerce Dept and Package Machinery Manufacturers Institute.

NEW PRODUCTS ANALYSIS, ANNUAL FEATURE

(p. 73-96) Annual article, by Dianne L. Taylor, with 3 tables on introduction of new food products. Tables show top 50 food companies ranked by number of products introduced, and number of introductions by food category, July 1983-June 1984 period, with comparisons to July 1982-June 1983; and 11 companies ranked by number of new products earning over $40 million during 1972-82, with 1982 retail sales for these products. Data are from *Food Engineering* and Selling Areas Marketing Inc.

Also includes 1 chart showing Nielsen National Scantrack data on fruit drink market shares by type of packaging used, 1983.

This is the 4th annual analysis.

C2175
Chronicle of
Higher Education, Inc.

C2175–1   CHRONICLE OF HIGHER EDUCATION

Weekly.   Approx. 80 p.
Oversized.
ISSN 0009-5982.
LC 80-1055.
SRI/MF/excerpts, shipped quarterly

Weekly journal (except last 2 weeks in Aug. and Dec.) presenting news and opinion articles on trends and developments in higher education in the U.S. and foreign countries; and including data on higher education enrollment, funding levels and sources, and student and faculty characteristics.

Data are from various Federal and State agencies, private organizations, and surveys conducted for the journal by John Minter Associates.

Issues generally contain:

a. Articles, generally narrative, but occasionally including substantial statistics.

b. "Fact-File" and "Chronicle Survey" sections, each usually containing 1 or more tables and accompanying article on varying subjects.

c. Regular editorial depts, including weekly listings of grant awards, gifts, and bequests; notes on status of Federal legislation affecting education; Federal agency rulings; and recurring current awareness tables or charts illustrating trends in stock market performance of endowment or faculty pension funds, faculty pay compared to CPI, and best selling titles in campus bookstores.

Last issue of each volume includes an article index.

All features with substantial statistical content, including "Fact-File" and "Chronicle Survey" sections, are described, as they appear, under "Statistical Features." Nonstatistical features are not covered.

Availability: Chronicle of Higher Education, Subscription Department, PO Box 1955, Marion OH 43305, $45.00 per yr., single copy $1.75; SRI/MF/excerpts for all portions described under "Statistical Features;" shipped quarterly.

Issues reviewed during 1984: Nov. 2, 1983-Oct. 31, 1984 (P) (Vol. XXVII, Nos. 10-24; Vol. XXVIII, Nos. 1-24; Vol. XXIX, Nos. 1-10).

STATISTICAL FEATURES:

C2175-1.501: Nov. 9, 1983 (Vol. XXVII, No. 11)

FACT-FILE: CHANGES IN FALL ENROLLMENT AT PRIVATE INSTITUTIONS, 1982-83, ANNUAL FEATURE

(p. 18) Annual table showing percent change in private institution enrollment, and distribution of schools by level of enrollment change, for all students, freshmen, undergraduates, and part-time and FTE students, all by institution type and region.

Data are from responses of 1,184 of the 1,547 U.S. private institutions to a survey conducted by National Institute of Independent Colleges and Universities. Includes accompanying article (p. 1, 18).

FACT-FILE: FOREIGN STUDENTS IN U.S. INSTITUTIONS, ANNUAL FEATURE

(p. 21) Three annual tables showing 70 institutions ranked by number of foreign students, with percent of total enrollment, 1982/83; 50 foreign countries, ranked by number of students in U.S. colleges, 1982/83; and number of foreign students, by discipline, 1981/82-1982/83. Data are from Institute of International Education. Includes accompanying article.

C2175-1.502: Nov. 16, 1983 (Vol. XXVII, No. 12)

BENEFITING FROM STOCK BOOM: COLLEGE ENDOWMENTS RETURN A RECORD 42 PCT. IN ONE YEAR, ANNUAL FEATURE

(p. 1, 14) Annual article, by Jack Magarrell, with 1 chart showing investment return rate for higher education institutions' endowment funds, FY74-83. Data are from preliminary results of a recent survey of 172 investment funds of 144 postsecondary institutions and earlier surveys, conducted by the National Assn of College and University Business Officers (NACUBO).

Full NACUBO survey report is covered in SRI under A6705-2.

C2175-1.503: Nov. 23, 1983 (Vol. XXVII, No. 13)

ENROLLMENT UP 1 PCT. THIS FALL, SURVEY FINDS

(p. 2) Article, with 1 table showing 1-year percent change in enrollment, by level and for all students and 1st-time freshmen, with detail for full- and part-time and FTE students, all by type of institution, 1983.

Data are based on 2,240 responses to a fall 1983 survey of higher education institutions, conducted by the Assn Council for Policy Analysis and Research.

CORRECTIONS

(p. 3) Article, with 2 tables, correcting and amending Oct. 26, 1983 "Fact-File" report on State appropriations for higher education. For description of original tables, see SRI 1983 Annual, under C2175-1.443.

CHRONICLE SURVEY: FACULTY VIEWS OF TRENDS IN THEIR DEPTS, 1980 TO 1982

(p. 20) Table showing faculty perceptions concerning trends in their depts, including faculty quality, course offerings, enrollment, library services, and budget, all by dept's field of study.

Data are based on 4,235 responses to a sample survey of faculty members teaching during fall 1980-82 period. Includes accompanying article (p. 19).

C2175-1.504: Nov. 30, 1983 (Vol. XXVII, No. 14)

MATCH-UPS FOR THIS YEAR'S FOOTBALL BOWL GAMES, ANNUAL FEATURE

(p. 21) Annual table estimating payments to college football bowl participating teams, by game, 1983 season.

C2175-1.505: Dec. 7, 1983 (Vol. XXVII, No. 15)

FACT-FILE: ENROLLMENT, STIPENDS, AND DEGREES AT 243 GRADUATE SCHOOLS, ANNUAL FEATURE

(p. 18) Annual table showing total and 1st-time graduate enrollment; applications received; graduate assistants and fellows; chemistry, economics, electrical engineering, and English dept teaching assistant stipends; and master's and PhD degrees awarded; all by institution type and/or control, fall 1983 and change from fall 1982.

Data are from Council of Graduate Schools and Graduate Record Examinations Board. Includes accompanying article (p. 1, 18).

C2175-1.506: Dec. 14, 1983 (Vol. XXVII, No. 16)

EDUCATION GIFTS FORECAST TO RISE 9 PCT. A YEAR

(p. 2) Article, with 1 chart showing value of charitable contributions, total and for education, 1980-88. Data are from Chemical Bank.

GRADUATES' JOB OUTLOOK IMPROVES BY 5 PCT.

(p. 3) Article, with text statistics forecasting average starting salary for graduates with bachelor's degrees, by field, 1984. Data are from responses of 617 employers to a survey conducted by Michigan State University's Placement Services.

C2175-1.507: Jan. 4, 1984 (Vol. XXVII, No. 17)

FACT-FILE: ESTIMATED STATE STUDENT AID, 1983-84, ANNUAL FEATURE

(p. 13) Annual table showing number and value of undergraduate and graduate/professional student aid awards for needy and non-needy students, by State and aggregated for 5 territories, 1983/84. Includes accompanying article.

Data are based on a survey conducted by the National Assn of State Scholarship and Grant Programs.

C2175-1.508: Jan. 11, 1984 (Vol. XXVII, No. 18)

FACT-FILE: EARNED DEGREES CONFERRED IN 1981/82 BY U.S. COLLEGES AND UNIVERSITIES

(p. 18) Table showing higher education degrees conferred, by field, sex, and level, for public and private institutions, 1981/82. Data are from NCES.

TELEVISION RATINGS OF COLLEGE FOOTBALL HIT ALL-TIME LOW

(p. 25-26) Article, with 1 table showing number of TV households and percent viewing college football games, 1968-83. Data are from the National Collegiate Athletic Assn.

C2175-1.509: Jan. 18, 1984 (Vol. XXVII, No. 19)

FACT-FILE: AVERAGE FACULTY SALARIES, BY RANK AND SEX, FOR 1982/83

(p. 21-30) Two tables showing average 9-month faculty salaries, by academic rank and institution, and aggregated for top 3 ranks; all by sex, by State and selected territory, 1982/83. Includes accompanying article (p. 20), with 1 table showing summary data for total U.S.

Data are from a John Minter Associates analysis of an NCES survey of over 2,700 institutions. Data corrections appear in Feb. 8, 1984 issue (see C2175-1.512, below).

C2175-1.510: Jan. 25, 1984 (Vol. XXVII, No. 20)

COMPANIES' GIFTS TO COLLEGES UP OVER 20 PCT. IN 1982, DESPITE SAG IN PROFITS, SURVEY FINDS, ANNUAL FEATURE

(p. 11) Annual article, with 1 table showing corporate contributions to higher education (amount, as percent of pretax net income, and as percent of total giving), 1967-82.

Data are from an annual report of the Council for Financial Aid to Education. Full report is covered in SRI under A4325-1.

FACT-FILE: SOURCES OF STUDENT AID

(p. 16) Two tables showing value of higher education student aid in current and constant 1982 dollars, by program; and distribution of Pell Grant and campus-based aid, by type of institution; various years 1963/64-1983/84.

Includes accompanying article (p. 1, 16), with 1 chart. Data are from the College Board.

C2175-1.511: Feb. 1, 1984 (Vol. XXVII, No. 21)

FACT-FILE: FRESHMAN CHARACTERISTICS AND ATTITUDES, ANNUAL FEATURE

(p. 13-14) Two annual tables presenting data on college freshman characteristics, activities, and attitudes, based on a fall 1983 survey of over 254,000 freshmen at 489 2- and 4-year colleges. Data are from *American Freshman: National Norms for Fall 1983* (for description of full report, see U6215-1, below).

Tables show response distributions for questions on students' socioeconomic background; academic and career plans; methods of financing education; and work- and recreation-related activities, political views, attitudes on a variety of current issues, and personal objectives, with detail by sex and by type of school including Catholic, Protestant, and predominantly black colleges.

Includes accompanying article (p. 12).

C2175–1.512: Feb. 8, 1984 (Vol. XXVII, No. 22)

MORE UNIVERSITIES BACKING ANTI-NUCLEAR MEASURES AT STOCKHOLDER MEETINGS

(p. 11-12) By Jack Magarrell. Article, with text statistics ranking top 20 public corporations by value of Federal contracts for primary nuclear warfare systems, FY81. Data are from DOD and DOE.

REAGAN BUDGET SEEKS INCREASES FOR RESEARCH, ASKS PARENTS TO BEAR MORE OF COLLEGE COSTS

(p. 13-17) Article, with 1 table showing the following by family income, with and without enactment of Reagan Administration proposals for FY85: higher education costs financed through student aid, student earnings, and family contributions, at low, medium, and high cost institutions. Data are from Dept of Education.

FACT-FILE: HIGHER EDUCATION FUNDS IN PRESIDENT REAGAN'S 1985 BUDGET, RECURRING FEATURE

(p. 18) Recurring table showing FY83 actual, FY84 estimated, and FY85 requested Federal funds for higher education programs in Education Dept and other Federal agencies, by detailed program.

FACT-FILE: AVERAGE FACULTY SALARIES, BY RANK AND SEX, FOR 1982/83, CORRECTED DATA

(p. 21-30) Correction of Jan. 18, 1984 "Fact-File" on faculty salaries by rank, sex, and institution, 1982/83. For description of original table, see C2175-1.509, above.

FOOTBALL FATALITIES LAST YEAR INCLUDED 3 COLLEGE PLAYERS

(p. 32) Article, with 1 table showing high school and college football player deaths directly and indirectly attributable to participation in football, 1977-83. Data are based on a survey sponsored by the National Collegiate Athletic Assn, American Football Coaches Assn, and National Federation of State High School Assns.

C2175–1.513: Feb. 22, 1984 (Vol. XXVII, No. 24)

TOP STUDENTS MOVE TO SCIENCE STUDIES, LEAVE HUMANITIES

(p. 1, 11) By Jean Evangelauf. Article, with 1 table showing distribution of senior academic officers perceiving improvement, decline, and no change in quality of humanities and science/engineering students, by academic level, 1976/77-1981/82 period.

Data are based on American Council on Education surveys of officers at 486 colleges/universities.

Full survey report is described in SRI under A1410-1.

STUDENTS COULD HANDLE LARGER DEBTS IF GIVEN 15 YEARS TO REPAY COLLEGE LOANS, STUDY FINDS

(p. 13, 15) By Donna Engelgau. Article, with 1 table showing amount of "manageable" student loans under 10- and 15-year repayment schemes with graduated and/or equal installment options, by degree level and field for students entering college in 1985. Data are from an Educational Testing Service report, *Student Loan Limits.*

FACT-FILE: MEDIAN SALARIES OF ADMINISTRATORS, 1983/84, ANNUAL FEATURE

(p. 18) Annual table showing median salaries for college/university administrators in approximately 90 positions, by position and type of institution, 1983/84, with percent change from 1982/83 for all institutions. Data are from responses of 1,515 institutions to a College and University Personnel Assn survey. Includes accompanying article (p. 17).

Full survey report is covered in SRI under A3900-1.

C2175–1.514: Feb. 29, 1984 (Vol. XXVIII, No. 1)

FACT-FILE: AVERAGE FACULTY SALARIES BY RANK IN SELECTED FIELDS, 1983/84, ANNUAL FEATURE

(p. 17) Annual table showing higher education faculty average salary at public and private institutions, by academic rank and detailed discipline, 1983/84. Data are from a College and University Personnel Assn survey of 570 public and private institutions. Includes accompanying article (p. 15).

Corrected table headings appear in Mar. 7, 1984 issue (see C2175-1.515, below).

NCAA WEIGHS PLANS TO DIVVY UP MONEY FROM A TV-RICH BASKETBALL TOURNAMENT

(p. 23) By N. Scott Vance. Article on plans of National Collegiate Athletic Assn (NCAA) regarding distribution of TV revenues from 1985-87 NCAA tournament. Data are from NCAA. Includes 1 chart showing tournament TV revenues payed to each of the 4 finalist teams, 1971 and 1982-85.

ACADEMIC PROGRAM FOUND MOST IMPORTANT IN RECRUITING FOOTBALL PLAYERS

(p. 24) Article, with text statistics showing percent of freshman college football players citing selected factors as important in college selection. Data are based on responses of 666 players at 30 universities to an Aug. 1983 College Football Assn survey.

C2175–1.515: Mar. 7, 1984 (Vol. XXVIII, No. 2)

CORRECTION

(p. 3) Corrected table headings for Fact-File feature on average faculty salaries, appearing in Feb. 29, 1984 issue (for description, see C2175-1.514, above).

CHRONICLE SURVEY: ESTIMATED FACULTY SALARIES FOR 1983/84, ANNUAL FEATURE

(p. 28) Annual table showing average faculty salaries by academic rank, by institution type and control, and academic discipline, 1983/84 and change from 1982/83. Data are based on responses of 2,100 faculty members to a sample survey. Includes accompanying article (p. 28).

C2175–1.516: Mar. 14, 1984 (Vol. XXVIII, No. 3)

FACT-FILE: PROJECTED CHANGES IN GRADUATES BY STATE, FROM 1981 TO 2000

(p. 15) Table showing graduates from public or public/private high schools, by State, 1980/81, and projected for selected years 1983/84-1999/2000. Data are from a report of the Western Interstate Commission for Higher Education (WICHE).

Includes accompanying article (p. 15). Full WICHE report is covered in SRI under A9385-4.

C2175–1.517: Mar. 21, 1984 (Vol. XXVIII, No. 4)

MATTER OF CHOICE: COLLEGE EMPLOYEES WEIGH OPTIONS FOR RETIREMENT SAVINGS

(p. 17-19) By Robert L. Jacobson. Article, with 1 undated table showing the amount of money a college employee would accumulate for retirement at age 65 from tax-sheltered salary reductions of $1,000 per year, and from after-tax savings of $660 per year. Data are shown by the age of the employee when savings start, and for selected earnings/savings rates. Data are from Georgetown University.

5.7-Pct. RAISES REPORTED FOR 'CONTINUING' FACULTY, ANNUAL FEATURE

(p. 17, 20) Annual article, by Jean Evangelauf, with 1 table showing average percent increase in salary for faculty working at same college/university in 1983/84 as in 1982/83, by institution type and control and academic rank, 1983/84.

Data are from responses of 1,389 institutions to an annual survey by American Assn of University Professors. Full survey report is covered in SRI under A0800-1.

C2175–1.518: Mar. 28, 1984 (Vol. XXVIII, No. 5)

CHRONICLE SURVEY: ESTIMATED FACULTY SALARIES FOR 1983/84, ANNUAL FEATURE

(p. 26) Annual table showing average faculty salaries by sex, tenure status, and age, cross-tabulated by academic discipline and/or institution type and control, 1983/84 and change from 1982/83. Data are based on responses of 2,100 faculty members to a sample survey. Includes accompanying article (p. 21, 26).

C2175–1.519: Apr. 4, 1984 (Vol. XXVIII, No. 6)

FACT FILE: REVENUES AND EXPENDITURES OF COLLEGES AND UNIVERSITIES, 1981/82

(p. 14) Brief article, with 1 table and 2 charts showing public and private higher education revenues by source and expenditures by category, all by type of institution, 1981/82. Data are from NCES, and are based on financial reports of 3,294 institutions.

1982/83 NCAA CHAMPIONSHIPS: HOW MUCH THEY COST

(p. 28) Brief article, with 1 table showing National Collegiate Athletic Assn (NCAA) receipts and disbursements for Division I, II, and III championship tournaments, by sport, 1982/83. Data are from NCAA.

C2175–1.520: Apr. 11, 1984 (Vol. XXVIII, No. 7)

GIVING BY WEALTHIEST DOWN 30 Pct.; DROP IN TAX BREAK CITED

(p. 1, 22) By Jack Magarrell. Article, with 1 text table showing percent change in average size of gifts reported as itemized deductions on Federal income tax returns, by income level, 1982 vs. 1981. Data are from Independent Sector, Inc.

TEXAS UNIVERSITIES SCRAMBLE TO SIGN UP MERIT SCHOLARS

(p. 1, 19-21) By Lawrence Biemiller. Article, with 1 table showing top 40 universities ranked by number of National Merit Scholarship winners in freshman class, and including number of scholarships sponsored by each institution, fall 1983. Data are from National Merit Scholarship Corp.

C2175–1.521: Apr. 18, 1984 (Vol. XXVIII, No. 8)

LACK OF HIGH-SCHOOL MATH SEEN HINDERING WOMEN, MINORITIES IN SCIENCE

(p. 14) By Jean Evangelauf. Article, with 1 text table showing percent of college freshmen choosing quantitative majors (math/science/engineering/economics), by whether a parent attended college, for all students and by race/ethnicity (including American Indian, Asian American, Chicano, and Puerto Rican), fall 1981. Data are from Rockefeller Foundation.

C2175–1.522: May 9, 1984 (Vol. XXVIII, No. 11)

FACT-FILE: VOLUNTARY SUPPORT FOR HIGHER EDUCATION, 1982/83, ANNUAL FEATURE

(p. 15) Three annual tables showing higher education voluntary support, by type of institution and purpose and source of support, 1982/83; and enrollment, CPI, higher education price index, and total and per student institutional expenditures and voluntary support, selected years 1949/50-1982/83. Data are from Council for Financial Aid to Education.

Includes accompanying article, with 1 table ranking top 20 institutions by voluntary funds received, with data for 2 multiple-unit systems, 1982/83.

Full survey report is covered in SRI under A4325-2.

FACT-FILE: VALUE OF 202 ENDOWMENTS ON JUNE 30, 1983, ANNUAL FEATURE

(p. 16) Annual table showing market value of endowments of 202 higher education institutions, as of June 30, 1982-83. Data are from National Assn of College and University Business Officers (NACUBO).

Includes accompanying article, with 1 table showing average return rates of college endowments vs. return rates for selected equities and bonds, and CPI and Higher Education Price Index (p. 17).

Detailed annual NACUBO report is covered in SRI under A6705-2.

C2175–1.523: May 23, 1984 (Vol. XXVIII, No. 13)

2-YEAR COLLEGES FACE A DECLINE IN ENROLLMENT

(p. 1, 16) By Beverly T. Watkins. Article, with 1 table showing 2-year college enrollment by State, 1983/84 and percent change from 1982/83. Data are from American Assn of Community and Junior Colleges.

FACT-FILE: 1982/83 HOLDINGS OF RESEARCH LIBRARIES IN U.S., CANADA, ANNUAL FEATURE

(p. 11) Annual table showing U.S. and Canadian university library total and added volumes, current serials, and spending for materials and salaries, by institution, 1982/83. Data are from Assn of Research Libraries report described in SRI under A3365-1.

CHRONICLE SURVEY: FACULTY MEMBERS' SUMMER-SCHOOL EARNINGS, 1983

(p. 22) Table showing percent of faculty members teaching summer school, and summer school average earnings and earnings as percent of base salary, by discipline, academic rank, and institution type and control, 1983. Data are based on responses of 2,100 faculty members to a weighted sample survey of faculty teaching courses in fall 1983. Includes accompanying article (p. 21-22).

C2175–1.524: May 30, 1984 (Vol. XXVIII, No. 14)

FACT-FILE: BENEFITS AND COMPENSATION OF COLLEGE PRESIDENTS, 1983/84

(p. 22) Compilation of data on compensation and benefits of college and university chief executives. Data are from Assn of Governing Boards of Universities and Colleges, and College and University Personnel Assn.

Includes 2 tables showing number of institutions and average salary of chief executives, by institution type, control, and operating budget and enrollment size; and number of reporting institutions by type, with distribution by selected characteristics of chief executive, and whether selected benefits are offered; 1983/84.

Also includes accompanying article (p. 21).

C2175–1.525: June 6, 1984 (Vol. XXVIII, No. 15)

FACT-FILE: GIFTS TO EDUCATION ROSE 7.1 Pct. IN 1983, STUDY FINDS, ANNUAL FEATURE

(p. 9) Two annual tables showing grants awarded, 1982-83, and assets, 1983, for top 55 foundations ranked by 1983 grants; and amount, donor, and recipient, for 89 largest gifts/bequests to higher education institutions, 1983. Data are from American Assn of Fund-Raising Counsel (AAFRC). Includes brief article.

Full AAFRC report, *Giving USA,* is covered in SRI under A0700-1.

C2175–1.526: June 20, 1984 (Vol. XXVIII, No. 17)

FACT-FILE: AVERAGE FACULTY SALARIES BY RANK AND TYPE OF INSTITUTION, 1983/84, ANNUAL FEATURE

(p. 18) Annual table showing average faculty salary, by academic rank and institution type (including church-related institutions), 1983/84 and percent change from 1982/83. Data are from American Assn of University Professors annual survey. Also includes accompanying article with summary chart showing annual changes in faculty salaries, 1973/74-1983/84 (p. 1).

Full survey report is covered in SRI under A0800-1.

C2175–1.527: June 27, 1984 (Vol. XXVIII, No. 18)

FACT-FILE: U.S. FUNDS FOR COLLEGES AND UNIVERSITIES, ANNUAL FEATURE

(p. 12) Annual table ranking top 100 higher education institutions by Federal funding obligations, total and for R&D, FY82. Data are from NSF. Includes brief article.

C2175–1.528: July 5, 1984 (Vol. XXVIII, No. 19)

BIG BUCKS OF TELEVISED FOOTBALL

(p. 23) Chart showing National Collegiate Athletic Assn (NCAA) contract values for televised football games, by TV network, 1975-85. Data are from NCAA.

Includes related articles (p. 1, 22-28).

C2175–1.529: July 18, 1984 (Vol. XXVIII, No. 21)

FACT-FILE: AVERAGE 1983/84 SALARIES FOR FULL-TIME FACULTY MEMBERS AT MORE THAN 1,900 U.S. COLLEGES AND UNIVERSITIES, ANNUAL FEATURE

(p. 15-19) Annual table showing higher education average faculty salaries, by academic rank, for 1,972 institutions arranged by State (and including Guam, Puerto Rico, and Virgin Islands), with summary percentile data by type of institution, 1983/84. Data are from American Assn of University Professors (AAUP).

Additional data appear in Aug. 8, 1984 issue (see C2175-1.531, below).

Last previous table presented data for 1981/82; for description, see SRI 1982 Annual, under C2175-1.339. Full AAUP report is covered in SRI under A0800-1.

C2175–1.530: Aug. 1, 1984 (Vol. XXVIII, No. 23)

FACT-FILE: UNIVERSITIES RANKED AMONG THE TOP 500 DEFENSE CONTRACTORS IN FY83, ANNUAL FEATURE

(p. 14) Annual table showing value of defense contracts and rank among top 500 defense contractors, for 88 colleges/universities, FY83. Data are from DOD.

FACT-FILE: UNDERGRADUATE STUDENT-AID RECIPIENTS: WHERE THEIR COLLEGE MONEY COMES FROM

(p. 16) Table showing the following for dependent and independent postsecondary students receiving financial aid during 1983/84: average expenses and amount covered by student and parent contributions, grants, student employment, loans, and other aid; and remaining need; shown for private and public institutions. Data are from a survey sponsored by 4 higher education assns of 13,200 students at 324 colleges and universities.

Includes accompanying article with 1 table showing distribution of student-aid recipients by family income, 1983/84.

C2175–1.531: Aug. 8, 1984 (Vol. XXVIII, No. 24)

ADDENDA

(p. 3) Additional data for July 18, 1984 table on higher education average faculty salaries. Includes data for 8 institutions.

For description of original table, see C2175-1.529, above.

C2175–1.532: Aug. 29, 1984 (Vol. XXIX, No. 1)

966,000 ARE TAKING FOREIGN LANGUAGES, UP 4.5 Pct. IN 4 YEARS

(p. 1, 23) Article, with 1 table showing enrollment in foreign language courses, by language, fall 1983, with percent change from 1980. Data are from a survey of 850 2-year and 1,521 4-year higher education institutions conducted by Modern Language Assn.

TUITION AND STUDENT FEES AT 2,660 COLLEGES AND UNIVERSITIES, 1984/85, ANNUAL FEATURE

(p. 15-22) Annual table showing tuition/fees 1983/84-1984/85, and added out-of-State tuition 1984/85, for 2,660 institutions, arranged by State and for Puerto Rico.

Includes accompanying summary chart, and 1 map showing selected data aggregated by region (p. 1, 17). Also includes accompanying article with 1 table and 1 chart showing types of institutions parents of college bound students would prefer and expect their children to attend; and average tuition/fees, room/board, and other student expenses, by institution type, 1984/85 (p. 15).

Most data were compiled by the College Board.

Additional data appear in Oct. 17, 1984 issue (see C2175-1.538, below).

C2175–1.533: Sept. 5, 1984 (Vol. XXIX, No. 2)

FACT-FILE: FOREIGN STUDENTS IN U.S. INSTITUTIONS, 1983/84, ANNUAL FEATURE

(p. 21) Three annual tables showing 75 institutions ranked by number of foreign students, with percent of total enrollment, 1983/84; number of foreign students, by discipline, 1982/83-1983/84; and 63 foreign countries, ranked by number of students in U.S. colleges, 1983/84. Data are from Institute of International Education. Includes accompanying article.

For description of previous article, for 1982/83, see C2175-1.501 above.

NCAA TO SPEND $41.6 MILLION THIS YEAR; BUDGET BALANCED BY SHIFTING SURPLUS, ANNUAL FEATURE

(p. 34) Annual article, with 1 table showing National Collegiate Athletic Assn (NCAA) budgeted revenues by source and expenses by function/object, 1983/84-1984/85. Data are from NCAA.

C2175–1.534: Sept. 12, 1984 (Vol. XXIX, No. 3)

FACT-FILE: A PROFILE OF 1982/83 RECIPIENTS OF DOCTORATES, ANNUAL FEATURE

(p. 20) Annual table showing characteristics of 1982/83 recipients of doctoral degrees, including sex, race, ethnicity (American Indian, Asian, Puerto Rican, Mexican American, other Hispanic), citizenship, marital status, median age and years since bachelor's degree, and planned postdoctoral study and planned employment by region, all by field of study. Data are from a National Research Council annual survey.

Includes accompanying article.

C2175–1.535: Sept. 19, 1984 (Vol. XXIX, No. 4)

FACT-FILE: INCOME AND EXPENDITURES OF PUBLIC 2-YEAR COLLEGES, 1982/83

(p. 12) Table showing median student expenditures by function/object and revenues by source, for public 2-year colleges by enrollment size and for vocational institutions, 1982/83 with summary comparisons to 1981/82. Data are from a report by National Assn of College and University Business Officers (NACUBO). Includes accompanying article.

Full NACUBO report is covered in SRI under A6705-1.

C2175–1.536: Sept. 26, 1984 (Vol. XXIX, No. 5)

SAT SCORES RISE 3 POINTS IN MATH, 1 ON VERBAL TEST

(p. 1, 11) By Lawrence Biemiller. Article, with 1 table showing average verbal and mathematics Scholastic Aptitude Test scores, with percent of students taking test, by State, 1983/84. Data are from College Board.

MORE THAN 84 Pct. OF 1983 MEDICAL GRADUATES HAD DEBTS FOR EDUCATION COSTS, SURVEY FINDS

(p. 16) Article on college debts and career plans of senior medical students. Data are from responses of approximately 10,500 medical school seniors to a 1983 Assn of American Medical Colleges (AAMC) survey.

Includes 3 tables showing survey response on the following: premedical and medical school debts; career plans, including careers in medical research, private and clinical practice, and administration; and choice of specialization, by specialty type.

Full AAMC survey report appears in the Sept. 1984 issue of *Journal of Medical Education;* for description see A3273-8.511, above.

CHRONICLE SURVEY: VIEWS OF ACADEMIC OFFICERS ON FACULTY QUALITY AND PERFORMANCE

(p. 28) Table showing higher education chief academic officers' perceptions of change in selected faculty working conditions, attitudes, performance measures, and in percent of faculty with PhDs, by type of institution, 1983/84 compared to 1982/83. Data are from responses of officers at 162 public and 177 private institutions to a recent *Chronicle* survey conducted by John Minter Associates.

Includes accompanying article (p. 25). A similar feature, covering the 1981/82 academic year, is described in SRI 1983 Annual under C2175-1.434.

BETTER MEDICAL EQUIPMENT AND PERSONNEL SAID TO HELP CURB FOOTBALL INJURIES AND DEATHS

(p. 31-32) Article, with 1 text table showing deaths and permanent cervical cord injuries related to football, for high school/college players, 1977-83. Data are from University of North Carolina researchers.

For description of similar data, for 1977-82, see SRI 1983 Annual, under C2175-1.424.

C2175–1.537: Oct. 10, 1984 (Vol. XXIX, No. 7)

CHRONICLE SURVEY: VIEWS OF CHIEF ACADEMIC OFFICERS ON CHANGES AMONG STUDENTS, 1982/83-1983/84

(p. 17) Table showing distribution of higher education chief academic officers' perceptions of students' academic preparation and attitudes, trends in instruction, and student services, all by type of institution and detailed area, 1983/84 change from 1982/83.

Data are based on responses from officers of 69% of a stratified random sample of 162 public and 177 private schools. Includes accompanying article (p. 16).

A similar feature, covering the 1981/82 academic year, is described in SRI 1983 Annual under C2175-1.430.

C2175–1.538: Oct. 17, 1984 (Vol. XXIX, No. 8)

ADDITIONAL TUITION AND FEE DATA FOR 1984/85 REPORTED BY THE COLLEGE BOARD

(p. 11) Additional data for Aug. 29, 1984 annual table on tuition/fees at 2,660 higher education institutions. Includes data for 324 institutions.

For description of original table, see C2175-1.532, above.

C2175–1.539: Oct. 24, 1984 (Vol. XXIX, No. 9)

POLL FINDS 63 Pct. WANT MORE AID FOR COLLEGES

(p. 3) By Jean Evangelauf. Article, with 1 table showing public attitudes on funding levels for federally financed programs, including aid to higher education and needy college students. Data are based on 1,006 responses to a fall 1984 survey conducted by Group Attitudes Corp. under the sponsorship of 3 national education organizations.

FACT-FILE: FEDERAL APPROPRIATIONS FOR HIGHER EDUCATION IN FY85, RECURRING FEATURE

(p. 20) Recurring table showing FY84 actual and FY85 requested and appropriated Federal funds for higher education programs in Education Dept and other Federal agencies, by detailed program.

C2175–1.540: Oct. 31, 1984 (Vol. XXIX, No. 10)

FACT-FILE: STATE APPROPRIATIONS FOR HIGHER EDUCATION IN 1984/85 AND CHANGES OVER 2 YEARS, ANNUAL FEATURE

(p. 16-18) Two annual tables showing State higher education appropriations, by institution and for student aid, arranged by State, 1984/85 and 2-year percent change; and State rankings by 1984/85 appropriation total amount, amounts per capita and per $1,000 personal income, and 2- and 10-year percent change with and without inflation.

Data were compiled by M. M. Chambers for the National Assn of State Universities and Land-Grant Colleges. Tables are accompanied by a related map (p. 1) and article (p. 1, 18).

Full report is covered in SRI under A7150-3.

C2400
Commodity Research Bureau

C2400–1   **1983 COMMODITY YEAR BOOK**
Annual. May 1983. 385 p.
ISBN 0-910418-15-2.
LC 39-11418.
SRI/MF/complete

Annual yearbook, through Apr. 1983, on trends in basic commodities of world commerce, including production, consumption, supply, foreign trade, and prices. Includes data by country, State, and end use.

Data are compiled from government, commodity exchange, trade assn, and other private agency reports.

Contents:

a. Introduction and contents listing; 1982-83 price trend analysis, with illustrative charts and a futures price index, monthly 1980-Apr. 1983; and 4 papers, with illustrative statistics, discussing commodity price forecasting methods, impact of 1981 Agriculture and Food Act on prices, commodity options trading strategies, and stock index futures market. (p. 2-44)

b. Futures trading highlights, with 1 trend chart and 2 tables showing exchange volume rankings, 1981-82; and total contracts traded, by commodity and exchange, 1978-82. (p. 45-47)

c. Commodity sections for more than 110 individual commodities, arranged alphabetically, most with brief narrative analysis, price trend charts, and 2-35 tables described below. (p. 48-384)

d. Measurement conversion factors. (p. 385)

Data are updated in Oct., Jan., and Apr. following publication of *Commodity Year Book*. Updates are covered by SRI as they appear, under C2400-2. For description of *1982 Commodity Yearbook*, see SRI 1982 Annual, under C2400-1.

Availability: Commodity Research Bureau, 75 Montgomery St., Jersey City NJ 07302, $35.95; SRI/MF/complete.

COMMODITY TABLES AND CHARTS:

C2400–1.1: Commodities

Data are generally shown for 1970s-82, and occasionally through Apr. 1983. U.S. data frequently include monthly detail.

Data for each commodity usually include production by country or world area; spot, average, and/or wholesale prices in selected countries, world areas, and/or cities; and U.S. detail, including stocks, consumption by end use, foreign trade, sales/shipment volume and value, futures trading, supply, disappearance, acreage, yield, prices, and taxes.

Also includes U.S. data on livestock slaughter; pasture and range condition; coal industry employment, days worked, and productivity; crop price support; industrial capacity or utilization; government loan program; fuel consumption for electric power generation; and natural gas reserves.

Other U.S. data include cold storage holdings; lead recovered from scrap; PPI; CPI; money supply; GNP; futures trading for Treasury bonds and bills, stock indexes, and GNMAs; residential construction contracts; motor vehicle registrations; and selected production, consumption, and livestock data by State.

C2425
Communication Channels

C2425–1   PENSION WORLD
Monthly. Approx. 70 p.
ISSN 0098-1753.
LC 75-642816.
SRI/MF/excerpts, shipped quarterly

Monthly journal on pension fund and employee benefit plan investment and administration, including articles on pension fund investment strategies, regulatory compliance, and legislative developments, and profiles of corporate benefit plans and prominent benefit administration firms.

Issues include feature articles, occasionally with industry survey statistics; and editorial depts.

Annual statistical features include data on assets of State employee retirement systems, and real estate investing by pension funds; and statistical directories of real estate investment management companies, and master and directed trust services.

Issues also include 2 nonstatistical annual directories of professional benefit administration firms and insurance company services for employee benefit plans; and an annual index to articles (Jan. issue).

Features with substantial statistical content are described, as they appear, under "Statistical Features." Each issue of the journal is reviewed, but an abstract is published in SRI monthly issues only when statistical features appear.

Availability: Pension World, Circulation Department, 6255 Barfield Rd., Atlanta GA 30328, $39.00 per yr., single copy $3.50; SRI/MF/excerpts for all portions described under "Statistical Features;" shipped quarterly.

Issues reviewed during 1984: Nov. 1983-Oct. 1984 (P) (Vol. 19, Nos. 11-12; Vol. 20, Nos. 1-10).

STATISTICAL FEATURES:

C2425–1.501: Dec. 1983 (Vol. 19, No. 12)
REAL ESTATE AGAIN EXCEEDS INFLATION

(p. 38) Article with 1 table showing Frank Russell Co. index of property investment rates of return, by region and component property type, 1st half 1983 and annual average 1978-83 period.

8th ANNUAL DIRECTORY OF MASTER AND DIRECTED TRUST SERVICES

(p. 57-83) Annual directory, for 1983, of banks and trust companies offering master and/or directed trust services.

Includes 1 table showing the following for 77 firms: address and principal contact; number of separate master and directed trust clients; value of master, directed, and custodial and total employee benefit assets managed; number of portfolios maintained; average account workload of managers and supervisors; and selected operating characteristics, including type of accounting system and short-term instruments used, reporting and credit timeliness, types of services provided, and fee structure.

C2425–1.502: Jan. 1984 (Vol. 20, No. 1)
1984 SALARY BUDGETS REFLECT CAUTION

(p. 45) Article with 1 table showing planned salary increase for corporate exempt employees in selected major industries, 1984. Data are based on responses of 550 companies in 50 industries to a survey by Wyatt Co.'s Executive Compensation Service.

C2425–1.503: Feb. 1984 (Vol. 20, No. 2)
UPDATED GUIDE FOR SCREENING MANAGERS

(p. 22-24) By Brian Rom. Article presenting performance criteria for selecting pension fund investment managers. Data are from Peat, Marwick, Mitchell and Co.

Includes 9 tables showing median return rates established by Peat Marwick as screening criteria for U.S. equity and fixed-income managers and for international equity and bond managers, various periods 1978-83; and number of managers passing a sample screening for each type of investment, with detail for U.S. managers by firm type and size.

S&Ls CONTINUE EXPERTISE IN MORTGAGE LENDING

(p. 27-29) By Dallas Bennewitz. Article, with 3 tables showing net new savings, interest credited to accounts, and value of mortgage loans, for FSLIC-insured savings institutions, 1976-83, with 1982 monthly detail for net new savings. Data are from U.S. League of Savings Institutions and Federal Home Loan Bank Board.

C2425–1.504: Mar. 1984 (Vol. 20, No. 3)
STATE AND LOCAL PENSION PLAN ASSETS UP

(p. 49) Article, with 1 table showing value of assets and benefit payments, and number of active and retired participants, in private pension plans 1978, and in State/local and Federal plans FY82. Data were compiled by Employee Benefit Research Institute from Commerce and Labor Dept reports.

C2425–1.505: May 1984 (Vol. 20, No. 5)
REAL ESTATE INVESTMENT CONTINUES UPWARD TREND

(p. 14) Article, with 1 table showing real estate investment rates of return, by region, 1st 9 months 1983 and annual average 1978-83 period. Data are from Frank Russell Co. and National Council of Real Estate Investment Fiduciaries.

CHANGING PATTERN OF SOCIAL SECURITY SPENDING

(p. 48) Article, with 1 table comparing government social spending with GDP, for 7 OECD countries, various periods 1960-81. Data are from OECD.

C2425–1.506: June 1984 (Vol. 20, No. 6)
WHAT EMPLOYERS ARE SAYING ABOUT LUMP-SUM DISTRIBUTIONS

(p. 45-48) By Thomas J. Cook. Article on lump-sum distribution provisions in corporate defined-benefit pension plans. Data are based on 366 responses to a survey of *Fortune* 500 largest industrial corporations, conducted by Teachers Insurance and Annuity Assn/College Retirement Equities Fund during Dec. 1983-Feb. 1984.

Includes 4 tables showing survey response on availability of lump-sum distribution for salaried and hourly employees terminating employment prior to and at retirement age, and on payment limitations and conditions.

C2425–1.507: July 1984 (Vol. 20, No. 7)

TUCS SHOWS MARKETS OUTPACED MANAGERS

(p. 12) Article, with 1 table showing median rate of return for balanced, equity, and fixed-income funds included in Trust Universe Comparison Service database of over 3,300 investment portfolios, with comparison to 2 major indexes, for 3-month, and 1-, 3-, and 5-year periods ending Mar. 1984.

SWITZERLAND BRACES FOR NEW PENSION LEGISLATION

(p. 55-56) Article, with 2 tables showing the following for Swiss pension plans: earnings coverage by age and sex, under legislation effective Jan. 1, 1985; and rate of return for funds managed by typical insurance companies and banks, compared to domestic inflation rate, 1979-83.

C2425–1.508: Aug. 1984 (Vol. 20, No. 8)

11th ANNUAL SURVEY OF STATE RETIREMENT SYSTEMS

(p. 35-47) Annual article reporting on the portfolio composition and investment advisors of State retirement funds as of various reporting dates 1983-84. Data are from an Apr. 1984 *Pension World* survey.

Includes 1 table showing the following for 62 funds grouped by State: fund name, address, and principal contact; value of total assets, common/preferred stock, Government securities, corporate bonds, mortgages, other real estate, cash/short-term securities, and other holdings; reporting date; and investment advisor.

C2425–1.509: Sept. 1984 (Vol. 20, No. 9)

REAL ESTATE INVESTING BY PENSION FUNDS, 1984, ANNUAL FEATURE

(p. 24-32) Annual article on corporate/public pension fund managers' real estate equity investment attitudes and experiences, 1981-84. Data are from responses of 279 senior fund investment officers to a survey conducted in May 1984 by Money Market Directories, Inc., and from previous surveys. Respondents for 1984 represent 26% of total assets for 1,400 largest funds.

Contains narrative analysis, interspersed with 19 text tables showing survey findings as follows, various years 1981-84:

a. Summary of pension fund current real estate ownership and purchase plans for next 3 years.

b. Perceived responsiveness of real estate industry to pension fund investment requirements; perceived contribution of real estate investments to fund performance; minimum acceptable cash yield and expected annual appreciation for investments; and projected fund asset composition in 1995.

c. Participation in direct ownership and commingled (pooled) real estate investment, including current ownership and purchase plans by type of property or sponsor; use of outside investment management, type of management organization used, and acceptable management fees; and property development activity, alone and by type of partner organization.

d. Current and planned investment in mortgages and real estate financing, by investment type; and classification of 6 types of investment as real estate, fixed income, or other.

This is the 8th annual survey.

7th ANNUAL REAL ESTATE PORTFOLIO MANAGER DIRECTORY

(p. 65-85) Annual directory, for 1984, of 93 companies providing real estate investment management services for pension funds. Companies listed responded to a 1984 survey of 638 U.S. and Canadian firms offering some form of real estate service.

Includes the following information for each company: name, address, contact person, value of all and pension fund real estate assets under management, number of pension fund real estate clients, composition of real estate holdings, type of participation offered, geographical diversification, minimum investment, return on investment, and fee.

C2425–1.510: Oct. 1984 (Vol. 20, No. 10)

MORE PLANS ARE ADDRESSING THE REAL RATE OF RETURN ISSUE

(p. 54-56) By Eugene B. Burroughs. Article, with 1 table showing rates of return for 14 types of tangible and financial investments, compared to CPI change, for 15-year period ended May 31, 1984. Data are from Salomon Bros., Inc.

C2425–2 TRUSTS AND ESTATES

Monthly. Approx. 100 p.
ISSN 0041-3682.
LC 76-646521.
SRI/MF/excerpts, shipped quarterly

Monthly journal (semimonthly in Dec.) of professional trust fund administration and estate planning services. Includes analyses of trends in portfolio management, investment in selected industries or equities, and outlook for the general economy.

Issues contain feature articles, occasionally with statistics; and editorial depts. Additional Dec. issue is an annual directory of trust institutions.

Features with substantial statistical content are described, as they appear, under "Statistical Features." Each issue of the journal is reviewed, but an abstract is published in SRI monthly issues only when statistical features appear.

Availability: Trusts and Estates, Circulation Department, 6255 Barfield Rd., Atlanta GA 30328, $47.00 per yr., single copy $3.75, Directory issue $24.50; SRI/MF/excerpts for all portions described under "Statistical Features;" shipped quarterly.

Issues reviewed during 1984: Nov. 1983-Oct. 1984 (P) (Vol. 122, Nos. 11-12; Vol. 123, Nos. 1-10); and 1984 Directory of Trust Institutions (Dec. 15, 1983).

STATISTICAL FEATURES:

C2425–2.501: Nov. 1983 (Vol. 122, No. 11)

INTERMARKET TRADING SYSTEM: CORNERSTONE OF THE NATIONAL SECURITIES MARKET

(p. 33-37) By Albert J. Fredman et al. Article on Intermarket Trading System (ITS), a telecommunications network linking major U.S. stock exchanges. Data are from SEC and ITS Operating Committee.

Includes 2 tables showing ITS trading volume, 1978-82; and distribution of ITS trade by originating and receiving exchange, Feb. 1983.

C2425–2.502: 1984 Directory of Trust Institutions (Dec. 15, 1983)

1984 DIRECTORY OF TRUST INSTITUTIONS

(p. 47-219) Annual directory of trust institutions. Presents list of over 5,000 bank trust depts in the U.S. (arranged by State and city, and including Puerto Rico and Virgin Islands) and Canada (arranged by Province and city), with the value of managed trust assets, year end 1982, shown for most institutions.

This is the 22nd annual directory.

C2425–2.503: Jan. 1984 (Vol. 123, No. 1)

TRUST OFFICERS DIVIDED OVER DEREGULATION

(p. 16-17) By Philip Bolton. Article presenting views of bank trust officers regarding banking deregulation. Data are based on a recent *Trusts and Estates* survey of 170 officers.

Includes 6 charts showing distribution of responses to questions on further deregulation, disclosure, and higher required capital/loan ratios for banks; changes in attorney/trust officer relations; and whether bank trust dept offers discount brokerage service, and considered/implemented dept name change.

C2425–2.504: Feb. 1984 (Vol. 123, No. 2)

SYNERGY AND LONG-TERM PROFIT: THE ADVANTAGES OF PURSUING FUTURE FEE BUSINESS

(p. 74-78) By Lawrence H. Budner and Daryl W. Hendrix. Article, with 5 tables comparing bank trust dept income from current fees (derived from asset management) and future fees (from estate planning), 1979-82. Data are from a 1983 survey of 10 banks with over $500 million in managed assets.

C2425–2.505: Mar. 1984 (Vol. 123, No. 3)

AUTOMATION PRACTICES OF TRUST DEPARTMENTS: A SURVEY

(p. 30-32) Article on data processing operations of bank trust depts. Data are based on a 1983 survey of 210 banks, conducted by Fast-Tax.

Includes 1 table showing survey response regarding dept asset and staff size, and current trust acounting system; brand of automated equipment in use; tax preparation methods, including manual, computerized service, inhouse software, and trust system vendor; input method and trend in computer use; and person responsible for automation decisions; with selected detail by type and number of tax returns processed.

C2425–2.506: July 1984 (Vol. 123, No. 7)

BANKS LOSE GROUND TO INVESTMENT COUNSELORS IN '83, ANNUAL FEATURE

(p. 30-32) Annual article, by Martin McKerrow, comparing performance and market share of equity portfolios managed by bank/trust companies and investment counselors, with detail by management concept, various periods 1979-83. Data are based on analysis of 3,500 tax-exempt funds comprising SEI Corp.'s Funds Evaluation Services data base. Includes 7 tables.

HOME MORTGAGES LEARN TO COMPETE IN THE CAPITAL MARKETS

(p. 35-37) By Leland C. Brendsel. Article reporting on the issue and sale of collateralized mortgage obligations (CMOs), bonds backed by pools of mortgage loans or mortgage-backed pass-through securities. Data are from Federal Home Loan Mortgage Corp. (Freddie Mac).

Includes 2 tables showing sales distribution for a selected group of Freddie Mac CMO issues, by type of purchasing institution (no date); and number and value of CMO issues, by type of issuer (Freddie Mac, builder bonds, and private conduits), with number of issuers for builder bond and private conduit sectors, as of May 1984.

C2425–3   AMERICAN CITY AND COUNTY
Monthly.   Approx. 70 p.
ISSN 0149-337X.
LC 75-647619.
SRI/MF/excerpts, shipped quarterly

Monthly journal for local government officials, reporting on trends and technological developments in public works engineering and management.

Issues contain articles, occasionally with statistics; regular editorial depts; and "Municipal Cost Indexes" section, with 1 chart and 2 tables showing the following data:

a. Cost indexes for approximately 60 types of equipment, construction materials, fuel, and other products used by local governments; CPI and PPI; and *American City and County* municipal cost and construction aggregate cost indexes; for month of publication, with comparison to previous month and year.

b. Municipal finance trends, including total receipts; Federal grants; expenditures by category; budget surplus; and employment; for most recent available quarter, with comparison to previous periods.

"Municipal Cost Indexes" section appears in most issues. All additional features with substantial nontechnical statistical content are described, as they appear, under "Statistical Features." Nonstatistical and technical specification features are not covered.

Availability: American City and County, Circulation Department, 6255 Barfield Rd., Atlanta GA 30328, qualified subscribers †, others $39.00 per yr., single copy $3.50; SRI/MF/excerpts for monthly cost indexes and all portions described under "Statistical Features;" shipped quarterly.

Issues reviewed during 1984: Oct. 1983-Oct. 1984 (P) (Vol. 98, Nos. 10-12; Vol. 99, Nos. 1-10).

STATISTICAL FEATURES:

C2425–3.501: Nov. 1983 (Vol. 98, No. 11)

DATA PROCESSING SURVEY SHOWS USE IS MULTIPLYING

(p. 42-44) Article on local government use of data processing (DP) systems, 1982-83. Data are from responses of 743 local governments to an *American City and County* survey.

Includes 4 tables showing survey response concerning use of in-house or any DP system, with detail by application; DP budget; and manufacturer of in-house system; for townships and municipalities, and by population size, 1982 with some estimates for 1983.

C2425–3.502: Jan. 1984 (Vol. 99, No. 1)

EXPANDING ECONOMY SHOULD SPUR GROWTH

(p. 60-61) By Jeff Atkinson. Article, with 1 chart showing PPI, CPI, and *American City and County* construction and municipal cost indexes, 4th quarter 1982-84.

C2425–3.503: July 1984 (Vol. 99, No. 7)

AC&C's 1984 SALARY AND BENEFITS SURVEY

(p. 32-34, 40) By Ken Anderberg. Article on salaries and benefit plans for local government employees. Data are from responses of 560 city/county financial officers to a spring 1984 survey conducted by *American City and County*.

Includes 6 charts showing survey response on frequency of employee performance reviews; prevalence of supervisory and non-supervisory employee medical, dental, and life insurance coverage, and retirement and pension plans, by type (fully or partially paid by employer, employee paid, or no program); and salary levels for 5 key positions, by population size and region.

C2500
Congressional Quarterly, Inc.

C2500–2   CONGRESSIONAL QUARTERLY ALMANAC: 98th Congress, 1st Session, 1983
Annual.   1984.
1068 p. var. paging.
Vol. XXXIX.
ISBN 0-87187-314-1.
LC 47-41081.
SRI/MF/not filmed

Annual review of the organization and major legislative actions of the Congress, covering the 98th Congress, 1st session, 1983. Includes data on committee, floor, and conference activities; Administration budget requests and final appropriations; and member characteristics and voting records.

Contents:

Contents listing; glossary; and description of the legislative process. (p. vii-xxviii)

Chapter 1. 98th Congress, 1st Session. Overview of organization and activity, with 4 tables. (p. 3-106)

Chapter 2. Foreign Policy, with 2 tables. (p. 109-170)

Chapter 3. Defense, with 2 tables. (p. 171-214)

Chapter 4. Economic Policy, with 1 table. (p. 217-283)

Chapter 5. Law Enforcement/Judiciary, with 2 tables. (p. 285-324)

Chapter 6. Environment/Energy. (p. 325-372)

Chapter 7. Agriculture. (p. 373-388)

Chapter 8. Health/Education/Welfare, with 1 table. (p. 389-421)

Chapter 9. Budget and Appropriations, with 2 charts and 25 tables. (p. 422-542)

Chapter 10. Transportation/Commerce/Consumers. (p. 543-562)

Chapter 11. Congress and Government, with 1 table. (p. 563-604)

App. A-F, including special reports; political report and voting studies, with 44 tables; lobby registrations; presidential messages, with 2 tables; and public laws enacted. (p. 1A-10F)

App. S and H. Senate and House Roll-Call Votes. (p. 1S-148H)

Index. (32 p.)

All charts and tables noted above are described below. Report also includes scattered text tables or less substantial tables; these are not described. Most described tables showing final budget authorizations or appropriations also include amount passed by the House and Senate and/or requested by the Administration.

Availability: Congressional Quarterly, Inc., Order Division, 1414 22nd St., NW, Washington DC 20037, $125.00; SRI/MF/not filmed.

CHARTS AND TABLES:

C2500–2.1: Legislative Action

98th CONGRESS, 1st SESSION

a. Public laws enacted, 1968-83; vetoes cast by President Reagan, 1981-83; Senate cloture votes, 1983; and House and Senate recorded vote totals, 1971-83;. 4 tables. (p. 4-12)

FOREIGN POLICY

b. State Dept authorizations, by program, FY84-85; and military and economic aid to El Salvador, FY81-84. 2 tables. (p. 146, 162)

DEFENSE

c. Authorizations for DOD and military construction, by program, FY84. 2 tables. (p. 176, 194)

ECONOMIC POLICY

d. Federal budget receipts, outlays, and surplus or deficit, FY24-83. 1 table. (p. 232)

LAW ENFORCEMENT/JUDICIARY

e. Female, black, and Hispanic judicial nominees as percent of all nominees for U.S. court of appeals and district court, for Reagan Administration and 4 preceding Administrations; and refugee admissions, by world region of origin, FY81-84. 2 tables. (p. 303-305)

HEALTH/EDUCATION/WELFARE

f. Federal food assistance budget, participants, benefit, and eligibility criteria, by program, FY83. 1 table (p. 414-415)

BUDGET AND APPROPRIATIONS

g. Budget authority, outlays, revenues, and deficit, by resolution stage; and budget totals; various years FY78-86. 1 chart and 2 tables. (p. 424-427)

h. Reagan Administration: assumptions for selected economic indicators and Federal pay raises, 1981-88; estimated savings from 4-point savings plan, FY84-88; and budget authority and outlays, by function and agency, FY82-84. 1 chart and 4 tables. (p. 428-434)

i. Congressional targeted budgets, deficit reduction, and conference agreements compared to Reagan proposals, FY83-86, with detail for FY84 targets by program; and supplemental jobs funding appropriations, by function, FY83. 3 tables. (p. 440-449)

j. Appropriations for military construction, Federal depts, and independent agencies, by detailed agency and/or program, FY84; 2nd supplemental bill provisions, FY83; and foreign aid appropriations by program, FY84, with detail for security assistance to 16 countries, FY83-84. 16 tables. (p. 459-532)

CONGRESS AND GOVERNMENT

k. Censure proceedings in the House, and dispositions, 1798-1983. 1 table. (p. 581)

APPENDICES

l. Election returns for gubernatorial and special House and Senate races, by party, candidate, and State, 1983. 10 text tables. (p. 3B-7B)

m. Annual analysis of congressional voting support of President, including annual percent of presidential victories in voting, 1953-83; composite Democratic and Republican presidential support and opposition scores, for House and Senate, total and by region, 1982-83; and outcome of recorded votes on which President took a position, highest congressional scores in support of and opposition to President, and score of each member, House and Senate, 1983. 12 tables. (p. 12C-25C)

n. Annual analyses of party unity, member voting participation, and conservative coalition voting, by party and region; with highest, lowest, and individual scores, 1983 with selected trends from 1964. 22 tables. (p. 27C-42C)

o. Reagan budget message to Congress 1983, including budget summary FY82-86; and estimated deficit reduction, FY84-88. 2 tables. (p. 9E-11E)

C2700
Crain Automotive Group

C2700–1   AUTOMOTIVE NEWS

Weekly.   Approx. 50 p.
Oversized.
ISSN 0005-1551.
LC 77-618337.
SRI/MF/excerpts

Weekly trade journal of the automotive industry, presenting news and statistics on motor vehicle production, sales, registrations, R&D, dealership and promotional developments, and related industry topics.

Most data are from journal staff surveys, motor vehicle manufacturer and trade assns, R. L. Polk & Co. Motor Statistical Division, and Data Resources Inc. Period of coverage is 2-10 days prior to cover date for weekly data, 1-3 months prior to cover date for monthly data.

General format:

a. Newspaper style articles and news briefs, occasionally with statistics; and special topic inserts, appearing several times each year, usually including some statistics.

b. 28 regularly recurring weekly, monthly, and quarterly tables, each usually accompanied by a summary article with text statistics.

c. Quarterly *Automotive News* World Outlook feature, with varying motor vehicle trend and forecast data by country and region.

A special additional market data book issue is published in Apr.

Regularly recurring tables are listed below. All additional features with substantial statistical content, including quarterly World Outlook feature, are described, as they appear, under "Statistical Features;" page locations and latest periods of coverage for recurring tables are also noted. Nonstatistical features and features presenting only vehicle technical or specification data are not covered.

Availability: Automotive News, Circulation Department, 740 Rush St., Chicago IL 60611, $40.00 per yr., single copy $1.00, Market Data Book $20.00; SRI/MF/excerpts for all portions covered under "Statistical Features."

Issues reviewed during 1984: Nov. 7, 1983-Oct. 29, 1984 (P) (Nos. 4994-5046).

TABLES:

WEEKLY TABLES

[1-2] Auction averages: model breakdown [average price for 8 model years, for month of coverage, and previous 2 months]; and used car sales [average price for month of coverage, previous month, and same month of previous year].

[3-6] U.S. and Canadian truck and car production [by manufacturer, with U.S. car detail by make and model, for week of cover date, previous week, and current month and year to date, with selected comparisons to previous year].

[7] Domestic car sales [by make and manufacturer, for 10-day period ended approximately 2 weeks prior to cover date, current and previous years. Table presenting data for 3rd period of each month also shows data for entire month and year to date, and includes detailed breakdown by model. Table appears approximately 3 times a month].

MONTHLY TABLES

[Tables show data for month 2-3 months prior to month of publication and year to date of the current and previous year, unless otherwise noted.]

[8] Big 3 truck sales [by manufacturer and model, for month prior to month of publication and year to date of current and previous years].

[9-10] Truck and heavy-duty registrations [number and market shares, by make; cumulative for current and previous years to date].

[11] New truck registrations [or sales], by make and GVW [gross vehicle weight] class.

[12] Auto market in [month prior to month of publication, sales by size group and total import sales].

[13] New car stocks [days supply, by manufacturer, make, and model, for month of publication, previous month, and same month of preceding year].

[13A] Import stocks [days supply, by manufacturer with totals for Japanese, German, and other car models; and days supply of imported trucks by manufacturer; for month of publication, previous month, and same month of preceding year; table begins in the Mar. 19, 1984 issue].

[14] New car market shares in U.S. [registrations and market share by domestic make and manufacturer, and total imports].

[15] *Automotive News* analysis of new car registrations [by detailed model].

[16] Market shares [by domestic and import make, and total registrations, year to date of current and previous years].

[17] Import registration shares in U.S. [number and market share by make. Accompanying article usually includes text tables showing import registrations by country of origin, and imported truck registrations by make].

[18] Service index [percent change in profits, repair orders written, and sales of labor, shop parts, and all parts/accessories].

[19-20] Imported car sales, and U.S. car sales by marketing unit [both by make only, for month prior to month of publication and year to date of current and previous years].

[21] Import sales by nameplate [model].

[22] Top cars [number of registrations by make, ranked for year to month of coverage, present and previous years.].

[23-24] Overseas production and registrations [for cars and/or trucks/buses, by make, for year through varying months, for selected countries including France, UK, Spain, Japan, Argentina, Switzerland, and West Germany].

QUARTERLY TABLES

[25] U.S. car outlets [number of dealerships active as of 1st day of current and selected preceding quarters, by domestic manufacturer].

[26] U.S. franchises [number of domestic franchises active as of 1st day of current and selected preceding quarters, by make].

[27] Auto makers' financial results [sales and/or net profits/loss for 4 largest U.S. manufacturers, for quarter ending 1-2 months prior to month of publication and usually year to date of current and previous year].

STATISTICAL FEATURES:
[Page numbers for recurring tables include accompanying articles.]

C2700–1.501: Nov. 7, 1983 (No. 4994)

WEEKLY TABLES

[1-2] Auction averages, for Nov. 1983. (p. 41)

[3-6] Production, for week ended Nov. 5, 1983. (p. 55)

[7] Domestic car sales [by model], for Oct. 21-31, 1983. (p. 2, 54)

MONTHLY TABLES

[12] Auto market, for Oct. 1983. (p. 2, 54)

[19-20] Import sales, and U.S. car sales by marketing unit, for Oct. 1983. (p. 2, 54)

[23] Overseas production in France, through Aug. 1983; Japan, through July 1983; and UK and Spain, through June 1983. (p. 31)

[24] Overseas registrations in UK and Sweden, through Sept. 1983; West Germany, Austria, and Denmark, through Aug. 1983; Japan, through July 1983; and France and Belgium, through June 1983. (p. 31)

QUARTERLY TABLES

[25-26] U.S. car outlets and franchises, for Oct. 1, 1983. (p. 1, 50)

PEUGEOT PREPARES FOR THE FUTURE

(p. 29, 32) By Richard Feast. Article, with 1 table showing European new auto market size, and shares by manufacturer, 1979-82 and 1st 6 months 1982-83.

WEST GERMAN EXPORTS DROP IN FIRST HALF

(p. 31) Article, with 2 tables showing West German motor vehicle exports, by world region and for top 18 countries of destination, 1st half 1983, with comparisons to 1982. Data are from VDA, Frankfurt.

OUTPUT RISES FOR '83 MODEL YEAR, ANNUAL FEATURE

(p. 33) Annual article, by Mary Beth Mayer, on domestic car production trends for 1983 model year. Includes 1 table showing production by manufacturer, make, and model, 1982-83 model years.

C2700–1.502: Nov. 14, 1983 (No. 4995)

WEEKLY TABLES

[1-2] Auction averages, for Nov. 1983. (p. 71)

[3-6] Production, for week ended Nov. 12, 1983. (p. 84)

[7] Domestic car sales, omitted.

MONTHLY TABLES

[13] New car stocks, for Nov. 1, 1983. (p. 1, 80)

[16] Market shares, for 1st 8 months 1983. (p. 56)

[17] Import registration shares, for Aug. 1983. (p. 32)

[18] Service index, for Sept. 1983. (p. 2)

[22] Top cars, through Aug. 1983. (p. 56)

DOMESTIC MAKERS OPEN '84 WITH 286 MODELS, DOWN 10, ANNUAL FEATURE

(p. 1, 79) Annual article, by John K. Teahen, Jr., reviewing 1984 domestic car body styles. Includes 3 tables showing number of 1984 models offered, by manufacturer, model, and size class, all by body style, with summary comparisons to 1983; and total models offered, 1942 and annually 1946-84.

CANADIAN AUTOMOTIVE MARKET

(p. 30) Table on the motor vehicle industry in Canada, showing: sales volume and revenue, after-tax profits, assets, shareholders' equity, capital expenditures, and employment, all for individual Canadian manufacturers and Japanese manufacturers operating in Canada; and export volume for 4 Canadian manufacturers; 1977-82. Data are from Chrysler Canada, Ltd.

U.S. CUTS LEAD OF JAPANESE IN AUTO PRODUCTION

(p. E48) Article, with 1 table showing auto and commercial vehicle production and exports for U.S. and 5 foreign countries, 1st 6 months 1982-83. Data are from CSCA, Paris.

AUTOMOTIVE AFTERMARKET, 1981-88

(p. 62) Table showing retail sales of auto aftermarket goods and services, by type of product including fuel, 1981 and 1988. Data are from Frost and Sullivan, Inc.

C2700–1.503: Nov. 21, 1983 (No. 4996)

WEEKLY TABLES

[1-2] Auction averages, for Nov. 1983. (p. 52)

[3-6] Production, for week ended Nov. 19, 1983. (p. 56)

[7] Domestic car sales, for Nov. 1-10, 1983. (p. 2)

MONTHLY TABLES

[8] Truck sales, for Oct. 1983. (p. 52)

[14-15] New car market shares and registrations, for Sept. 1983. (p. 7, 36)

[21] Import sales by nameplate, for Aug. 1983. (p. 22)

JAPANESE TO TOP MILLION IN EUROPE

(p. 32) By Richard Feast. Article, with 1 table showing new car registrations and market shares for Japanese cars sold in Europe, by country, 1st 9 months 1983.

C2700–1.504: Nov. 28, 1983 (No. 4997)

WEEKLY TABLES

[1-2] Auction averages, for Nov. 1983. (p. 45)

[3-6] Production, for week ended Nov. 26, 1983. (p. 57)

[7] Domestic car sales, omitted.

MONTHLY TABLES

[9-11] Truck and heavy-duty registrations, and new truck registrations, through Sept. 1983. (p. 10, 18, 30, 42)

[16] Market shares, for 1st 9 months 1983. (p. 54)

[17] Import registration shares, for Sept. 1983. (p. 4)

[22] Top cars, through Sept. 1983. (p. 4)

C2700–1.505: Dec. 5, 1983 (No. 4998)

WEEKLY TABLES

[1-2] Auction averages, for Dec. 1983. (p. 49)

[3-6] Production, for week ended Dec. 3, 1983. (p. 62)

[7] Domestic car sales, omitted.

MONTHLY TABLES

[21] Import sales by nameplate, for Sept.-Oct. 1983. (p. 38, 57)

[23] Overseas production in France, through Sept. 1983; Spain and Japan, through Aug. 1983; and UK, through July 1983. (p. 36)

---

[24] Overseas registrations in UK and Sweden, through Oct. 1983; Italy, West Germany, Holland, Belgium, Austria, and Denmark, through Sept. 1983; and Switzerland and Japan, through Aug. 1983. (p. 36)

FIBERGLASS COMPOSITES ON THE RISE

(p. D1-D2) Article on consumption and applications of glass fiber composites in the North American motor vehicle industry. Data are from Owens-Corning Fiberglas Corp.

Includes 8 tables showing car and truck production, and consumption of glass fiber composites, by vehicle component and size class, and by composite manufacturing process, 1982-88.

REGISTRATIONS BOOM IN UK

(p. 35-36) By Richard Feast. Article, with 2 tables showing new car registrations in Europe, for 6 manufacturers and 16 countries, 1st 9 months 1983, with selected comparisons to 1982.

ANNUAL COSTS TO OPERATE '83 WAGONS VARY WIDELY

(p. 49) Article, with 1 table showing engine size and operating and ownership expenses for ten 1983 station wagon models. Data are from Runzheimer and Co.

C2700–1.506: Dec. 12, 1983 (No. 4999)

WEEKLY TABLES

[1-2] Auction averages, for Dec. 1983. (p. 49)

[3-6] Production, for week ended Dec. 10, 1983. (p. 62)

[7] Domestic car sales [by model], for Nov. 21-31, 1983. (p. 6, 58)

MONTHLY TABLES

[12] Auto market, for Nov. 1983. (p. 6, 58)

[13] New car stocks, for Dec. 1, 1983. (p. 1, 3)

[18] Service index, for Oct. 1983. (p. 1, 8)

[19-20] Import sales, and U.S. car sales by marketing unit, for Nov. 1983. (p. 6, 58)

AUTOMATIC 5-SPEEDS MADE GAINS, ANNUAL FEATURE

(p. 28) Annual article, by Joseph Bohn, with 1 table showing transmission installations on 1983 model year autos, by transmission type and auto manufacturer, make, and model. Includes number of installations, and percent of total auto output.

'AUTOMOTIVE NEWS' WORLD OUTLOOK, QUARTERLY FEATURE

(p. E2) Table showing auto and truck/van production and registrations, by selected countries and/or world regions, 1981-88. Data are from Data Resources, Inc. Includes accompanying article (p. E1-E4).

U.S. MODEL YEAR SALES

(p. E2) Table showing 1983 model year auto sales volume, with 1984 forecast, by manufacturer, make, and model.

SUMMARY BY MANUFACTURERS OF CAR AND COMMERCIAL WORLD VEHICLE PRODUCTION IN 1981 AND 1982

(p. 38) Table showing world auto and commercial vehicle production, for top 40 manufacturers and all others, and for North American, Japanese, and Western and Eastern European companies, 1981-82. Data are from Motor Vehicle Manufacturers Assn.

C2700–1.507: Dec. 19, 1983 (No. 5000)

WEEKLY TABLES

[1-2] Auction averages, for Dec. 1983. (p. 29)

[3-6] Production, for week ended Dec. 17, 1983. (p. 42)

[7] Domestic car sales, for Dec. 1-10, 1983. (p. 8)

MONTHLY TABLE

[8] Truck sales, for Nov. 1983. (p. 16)

AIR CONDITIONING IS STILL A STAPLE, ANNUAL FEATURE

(p. 28) Annual article, by Joseph Bohn, with 1 table showing air conditioning unit installations on 1982-83 model year autos, by auto manufacturer, make, and model. Includes number of installations, and percent of total auto output.

TURBOS, FUEL INJECTION GROWING FAST, ANNUAL FEATURE

(p. 28) Annual article, by Joseph Bohn, with 1 table showing turbo charged and fuel injected engine installations in 1983 model year autos, by auto manufacturer, make, and model. Includes number of installations, and percent of total auto output.

C2700–1.508: Dec. 26, 1983 (No. 5001)

WEEKLY TABLES

[1-2] Auction averages, for Dec. 1983. (p. 20)

[3-6] Production, for week ended Dec. 24, 1983. (p. 35)

[7] Domestic car sales, omitted.

MONTHLY TABLES

[9-11] Truck and heavy-duty registrations, and new truck registrations, through Oct. 1983. (p. 14, 29, 30)

DECADE OF ITALIAN AUTO OUTPUT

(p. 28) Table showing auto production in Italy by manufacturer, with detail for Fiat makes, 1973-82 and 1st 6 months 1983. Data are from ANFIA.

C2700–1.509: Jan. 2, 1984 (No. 5002)

WEEKLY TABLES

[1-2] Auction averages, omitted.

[3-6] Production, omitted.

[7] Domestic car sales, for Dec. 11-20, 1983. (p. 3)

MONTHLY TABLES

[23] Overseas production in France, through Oct. 1983; Japan and Spain, through Sept. 1983; and UK, through Aug. 1983. (p. 26)

[24] Overseas registrations in UK and Sweden, through Nov. 1983; West Germany, Austria, and Denmark, through Oct. 1983; Switzerland and Japan, through Sept. 1983; and France, through Aug. 1983. (p. 26)

POWER BRAKES AND STEERING CONTINUE TO GAIN POPULARITY, ANNUAL FEATURE

(p. 22) Annual article, by Joseph Bohn, with 1 table showing power equipment installations on 1983 model autos, by equipment type and auto manufacturer, make, and model. Includes number of installations, and percent of total auto output.

MODEST RECOVERY FOR EUROPEAN TRUCK OUTPUT

(p. 25) Article projecting market for European commercial vehicles. Data are from DRI Europe. Includes 2 tables showing medium/heavy and light commercial vehicle production and demand, by country, selected years 1980-90.

CAR PRICING IS A MAJOR CONCERN IN EUROPE

(p. 25-26) By Richard Feast. Article, with 1 table showing price index for 10 European auto models in France, West Germany, and UK, as of Oct. 25, 1983. Data are from a European Bureau of Consumers' Unions (BEUC) survey.

ELECTRONIC OPTIONS GAIN ON '83 CARS, ANNUAL FEATURE

(p. 37) Annual article, by Joseph Bohn, with 1 table showing installations of digital clock, electronic instrument panel, and steering wheel tilt and tilt/telescope options in 1983 model autos, by auto manufacturer, make, and model. Includes number of installations, and percent of total auto output.

ENGINE OPTIONS ON 1983 U.S. MODELS, ANNUAL FEATURE

(p. 38) Annual table showing engine installations by engine type, by auto manufacturer, make, and model, for 1983 model cars. Includes number of installations, and percent of total auto output.

C2700–1.510: Jan. 9, 1984 (No. 5003)

WEEKLY TABLES

[1-2] Auction averages, omitted.

[3-6] Production, for week ended Jan. 7, 1984. (p. 68)

[7] Domestic car sales [by model], for Dec. 21-31, 1983. (p. 1, 65)

MONTHLY TABLES

[12] Auto market, for Dec. and full year 1983. (p. 1, 65)

[14-15] New car market shares and registrations, for Oct. 1983. (p. 6, 63)

[19-20] Import sales, and U.S. car sales by marketing unit, for Dec. 1983. (p. 1, 65)

TIRE OPTIONS ON 1983 U.S. MODELS, ANNUAL FEATURE

(p. 32) Annual table showing tire installations on 1983 model autos, by tire type and auto manufacturer, make, and model. Includes number of installations and percent of total auto output.

WORLD CAR AND COMMERCIAL VEHICLE PRODUCTION BY MANUFACTURER

(p. 40-41) Table showing world passenger car and commercial vehicle production, by major manufacturer and subsidiary, 1981-82. Data are from Motor Vehicle Manufacturers Assn.

C2700–1.511: Jan. 16, 1984 (No. 5004)

WEEKLY TABLES

[1-2] Auction averages, for Jan. 1984. (p. 45)

[3-6] Production, for week ended Jan. 14, 1984. (p. 58)

[7] Domestic car sales, omitted.

MONTHLY TABLES

[13] New car stocks, for Jan. 1, 1984. (p. 53)

[18] Service index, for Nov. 1983. (p. 2)

AUTO MARKET LOOKS GRIM IN CHILE

(p. 42) By Vicki Carpenter. Article on motor vehicle market in Chile. Data are from Derco S.A. Includes 2 tables showing sales of 4-wheel drive vehicles, and autos and utility vehicles by engine size; and motor vehicle market shares; all by manufacturer, 1st 10 months 1983.

C2700–1.512: Jan. 23, 1984 (No. 5005)

WEEKLY TABLES

[1-2] Auction averages, for Jan. 1984. (p. 41)

[3-6] Production, for week ended Jan. 21, 1984. (p. 54)

[7] Domestic car sales, for Jan. 1-10, 1984. (p. 1, 50)

MONTHLY TABLE

[8] Truck sales, for Dec. 1983. (p. 2)

SPENDING PLANS TRIMMED BY AUTO MAKERS

(p. E2-E3) By Kathleen Hamilton et al. Article, with 3 tables showing motor vehicle industry capital spending, sales, and profits, for 4 U.S. and 5 foreign manufacturers, various periods 1979-85. Data are from manufacturers and other sources.

CAD MARKET CAPERS

(p. E8) Article, with 2 charts showing computer-aided-design (CAD) equipment market value, and market shares by application, 1982 and 1987. Data are from the Yankee Group, Inc.

EXPANDING ELECTRONICS ROLE

(p. E10) Article, with 1 chart showing automotive electronic device market shares, by application, 1982 and 1988. Data are from Frost and Sullivan, Inc.

C2700–1.513: Jan. 30, 1984 (No. 5006)

WEEKLY TABLES

[1-2] Auction averages, for Jan. 1984. (p. 71)

[3-6] Production, for week ended Jan. 28, 1984. (p. 87)

[7] Domestic car sales, for Jan. 11-20, 1984. (p. 6)

MONTHLY TABLES

[9-10] Truck and heavy-duty registrations, through Nov. 1983. (p. 14, 71)

[11] New truck sales, for Nov. 1983. (p. 80)

[16] Market shares, for 1st 10 months 1983. (p. 64)

[17] Import registration shares, for Oct. 1983. (p. 64)

[22] Top cars, through Oct. 1983. (p. 64)

CUTLASS SUPREME TOPS '83 SALES

(p. 87) Table showing top 10 auto models ranked by sales volume, 1983.

C2700–1.514: Feb. 6, 1984 (No. 5007)

WEEKLY TABLES

[1-2] Auction averages, for Feb. 1984. (p. 245)

[3-6] Production, for week ended Feb. 4, 1984. (p. 252)

[7] Domestic car sales, omitted.

MONTHLY TABLES

[18] Service index, for Dec. 1983. (p. 2)

[21] Import sales by nameplate, for Nov. 1983. (p. 166, 186)

ENGINE OPTIONS ON 1983 U.S. MODELS, ANNUAL FEATURE

(p. 66) Annual table showing engine installations on domestic 1983 model year autos, by engine type and auto manufacturer, make, and model. Includes number of installations, and percent of total auto output.

GAINS SEEN FOR SYNTHETIC RUBBER

(p. 76) Article, with 1 table showing North American consumption of synthetic rubber by type, and of natural and tire rubber, 1982-88. Data are from International Institute of Synthetic Rubber Producers, Inc.

CHEMICAL INDUSTRY LISTS GAINS IN '83

(p. 188) Article on trends in chemical industry operations and finances, 1970s-83. Data are from various Federal agencies.

Includes 1 table showing the following for chemical/allied products industry, 1973-83: value of shipments, corporation sales, net income, assets, capital expenditures, R&D funds, exports, and imports; PPI and production index; operating rate; employment; and average weekly wage for production workers.

C2700–1.515: Feb. 13, 1984 (No. 5008)

WEEKLY TABLES

[1-2] Auction averages, for Feb. 1984. (p. 33)

[3-6] Production, for week ended Feb. 11, 1984. (p. 47)

[7] Domestic car sales [by model], for Jan. 21-31, 1984. (p. 6, 41)

MONTHLY TABLES

[12] Auto market, for Jan. 1984. (p. 6)

[13] New car stocks, for Feb. 1, 1984. (p. 8, 47)

[14-15] New car market shares and registrations, for Nov. 1983. (p. 29-30)

[19-20] Import sales, and U.S. car sales by marketing unit, for Jan. 1984. (p. 6, 41)

[21] Import sales by nameplate, for Dec. 1983. (p. 20, 22)

QUARTERLY TABLES

[25-26] U.S. retail car outlets [exclusive and multiple dealerships] and franchises, for Jan. 1, 1984 [data are combined in a single table and are shown by manufacturer and make]. (p. 1, 46)

DOMESTIC DEALER TOTAL UP FOR FIRST TIME SINCE 1955

(p. 1, 46) By John K. Teahen, Jr. Article, with text statistics and 1 table showing number of auto dealerships handling domestic makes, Jan. 1, 1947-84, and quarterly Jan. 1, 1983-Jan. 1, 1984. Data are from *Automotive News*.

C2700–1.516: Feb. 20, 1984 (No. 5009)

WEEKLY TABLES

[1-2] Auction averages, for Feb. 1984. (p. 45)

[3-6] Production, for week ended Feb. 18, 1984. (p. 59)

[7] Domestic car sales, for Feb. 1-10, 1984. (p. 3)

MONTHLY TABLES

[8] Truck sales, for Jan. 1984. (p. 16, 22)

[16] Market shares, for 1st 11 months 1983. (p. 12)

[17] Import registration shares, for Nov. 1983. (p. 12, 45)

[22] Top cars, through Nov. 1983. (p. 12)

C2700–1.517: Feb. 27, 1984 (No. 5010)

WEEKLY TABLES

[1-2] Auction averages, for Feb. 1984. (p. 59)

[3-6] Production, for week ended Feb. 25, 1984. (p. 62)

[7] Domestic car sales, for Feb. 11-20, 1984. (p. 1, 4)

MONTHLY TABLES

[23] Overseas production in France and UK, through Dec. 1983. (p. 36)

[24] Overseas registrations in West Germany, UK, Holland, Italy, Belgium, Sweden, Austria, and Norway, through Dec. 1983. (p. 36)

85 IMPORT DEALERS ADDED DURING 1983; 1st GAIN SINCE 1977, SEMIANNUAL FEATURE

(p. 1, 58) Semiannual article, by Kathleen Hamilton, reviewing import auto dealership trends. Includes 4 tables showing import franchises by make and nationality, and outlets handling imports only (exclusives and duals) and import-domestic duals, Jan. 1, 1983-84; and total and import outlets, Jan. 1, 1957-84.

AUTO PROFITS FOR 1983 ARE RECORD $6 BILLION

(p. 2) By Kathleen Hamilton. Article, with 1 table showing sales and net income for 4 major motor vehicle manufacturers, 1982-83.

C2700–1.518: Mar. 5, 1984 (No. 5011)

WEEKLY TABLES

[1-2] Auction averages, for Mar. 1984. (p. 47)

[3-6] Production, for week ended Mar. 3, 1984. (p. 63)

[7] Domestic car sales, omitted.

SALES PER DEALER RISE IN '83; JAPAN SEIZES TOP FOUR SPOTS, SEMIANNUAL FEATURE

(p. 1, 60) Semiannual article, by Jenny L. King, reviewing auto dealer sales volume in 1983. Includes 3 tables showing sales per outlet, by make, 1974-83; and by model nameplate for 5 size groups, 1982-83.

C2700–1.519: Mar. 12, 1984 (No. 5012)

WEEKLY TABLES

[1-2] Auction averages, for Mar. 1984. (p. 43)

[3-6] Production, for week ended Mar. 10, 1984. (p. 59)

[7] Domestic car sales [by model], for Feb. 21-29, 1984. (p. 4, 54)

MONTHLY TABLES

[12] Auto market, for Feb. 1984. (p. 54)

[13] New car stocks, for Mar. 1, 1984. (p. 58)

[19-20] Import sales, and U.S. car sales by marketing unit, for Feb. 1984. (p. 4, 54)

[21] Import sales by nameplate, for Jan. 1984. (p. 24)

DIESEL HERE TO STAY DESPITE SETBACK, RECURRING FEATURE

(p. 1, 37-40) Recurring article, by Richard Johnson, reviewing diesel auto sales trends. Includes 2 tables showing diesel sales, total and as percent of all sales, for 13 diesel auto makes, 1982-83.

IMPORT MODEL COUNT CLIMBS TO 199, ANNUAL FEATURE

(p. E4) Annual article, by John K. Teahen, Jr., reviewing 1984 imported auto body styles offered in U.S. Includes text statistics and 1 table showing number of 1984 models offered by 30 import manufacturers as of Mar. 1984, for 4 body styles, with summary comparisons to 1983; and total import models offered, Mar. 1978-82.

IMPORT SALES BY NAMEPLATE, ANNUAL FEATURE

(p. E4) Annual table showing imported auto sales, by make and model, 1982-83.

IMPORT PENETRATION INTO U.S. CAR MARKET

(p. E4) Table showing sales of domestic autos, and total, Japanese, and domestic-sponsored import autos, 1970-83. Data are from Motor Vehicle Manufacturers Assn.

PRICE INCREASE AVERAGES $163.25

(p. E14-E18) By John K. Teahen, Jr. Article, with 1 table showing average new car transaction price, for domestics and imports, 1960-83. Data are from U.S. Bureau of Economic Analysis.

Also includes accompanying text data showing prices for new imports by detailed model, as of Mar. 1, 1984.

FOREIGN FIRMS GAIN TIRE FOOTHOLDS

(p. E20-E22) By Roger Rowand. Article, with 1 table showing tire sales volume, and market share for all-season and radial tires, all for original equipment and aftermarket tires, 1983-84 and 1987.

PRODUCTION UP IN JAPAN, RECURRING FEATURE

(p. E34) Recurring article, with 5 tables showing the following for Japan: auto, truck, and bus production, new registrations, and exports to U.S. and all countries; and auto production by size class; 1982-83. Data are from Japan Mini-Vehicle Assn, Japan Automobile Dealers Assn, and Japan Automobile Manufacturers Assn.

EXCLUSIVE IMPORTER

(p. E48) By John A. Russell. Article reviewing import auto dealership trends. Includes 3 tables showing import franchises by make and nationality, and outlets handling imports only (exclusives and duals) and import-domestic duals, Jan. 1, 1983-84; and import outlets, Jan. 1, 1957-84.

Data also appeared in semiannual feature described under C2700-1.517, above.

IMPORTS HIKE TV OUTLAYS

(p. E50) By Joseph Bohn. Article, with 1 table showing network and spot TV advertising expenditures of 12 foreign auto/truck manufacturers, 1982-83. Data are from TV Bureau of Advertising based on Broadcast Advertisers Reports.

HIGHER SALES PER DEALER

(p. E52) By Jenny L. King. Article, with 1 table showing new car sales per outlet, by make, 1974-83. Data also appeared in semiannual feature described above, under C2700-1.518.

C2700–1.520: Mar. 19, 1984 (No. 5013)

WEEKLY TABLES

[1-2] Auction averages, for Mar. 1984. (p. 63)

[3-6] Production, for week ended Mar. 17, 1984. (p. 78)

[7] Domestic car sales, for Mar. 1-10, 1984. (p. 3)

MONTHLY TABLES

[8] Truck sales, for Feb. 1984. (p. 60)

[9-11] Truck and heavy-duty registrations, and new truck registrations, through Dec. 1983. (p. 16, 58, 60)

[13A] Import stocks, for Mar. 1, 1984. (p. 1, 77)

[14-15] New car market shares and registrations, for Dec. 1983. (p. 6, 57)

[18] Service index, for Jan. 1984. (p. 3)

FWD FLAWS NOT EXCESSIVE, FLEET REPAIR SURVEY FINDS

(p. 20, 52) By Francis J. Gawronski. Article on auto fleet maintenance problems associated with front-wheel drive cars. Data are from responses of 402 fleet managers representing 265,000 cars to a recent survey conducted by Runzheimer and Co. Includes 2 tables showing percent of respondents citing abnormal maintenance with front-wheel drive cars, for selected 1980-83 models and selected maintenance categories.

FLEET-CAR SERVICE LIFE IS 29 MONTHS

(p. E4) Article summarizing auto fleet vehicle use and disposition, 1983. Data are from responses of 257 fleet managers to the 1983 Used-Car Marketing Survey conducted by National Assn of Fleet Administrators. Respondents represent 166,409 cars.

Includes 1 table showing number of owned and leased autos in fleet; used autos sold in 1983, by model year and marketing method; and average miles and months of service at time of sale; for 9 industry sectors, utilities and government, and Canadian fleets.

FRONT-DRIVE CUTS COSTS

(p. E8) Article, with 1 table showing average operating and ownership costs, for selected 1984 model year autos, arranged by size class. Also includes engine size and drivetrain type (rear- or front-wheel drive) for each model. Data are from Runzheimer and Co.

COST OF CAR OWNERSHIP GOES DOWN

(p. E13) By Francis J. Gawronski. Article, with 2 tables showing average auto ownership/operating cost, by auto size and cost item, 1978 and 1982-83. Data are from Hertz Corp.

CALL ME A 'MANAGER'

(p. E20) Article, with 1 undated table showing executives with auto fleet responsibility, by position and salary range. Data are from responses of 489 executives to a recent Runzheimer and Co. survey.

LEASING AS FINANCIAL TOOL

(p. E20) Article, with 1 table showing total capital expenditures, and expenditures for leased equipment, for 6 industries, 1982. Data are from Brimmer and Co.

DECORATIVE ROOF OPTIONS ON 1983 U.S. MODELS, ANNUAL FEATURE

(p. 51) Annual table showing decorative roof option installations on 1983 model year autos, by option type and auto manufacturer, make, and model. Includes number of installations, and percent of total auto output.

SOUND-EQUIPMENT OPTIONS INSTALLED ON 1983 U.S. MODELS, ANNUAL FEATURE

(p. 75) Annual table showing sound equipment installations on 1983 model year autos, by equipment type and auto manufacturer, make, and model. Includes number of installations, and percent of total auto output.

'AUTOMOTIVE NEWS' WORLD OUTLOOK, QUARTERLY FEATURE

(p. 77) Quarterly table showing auto and truck production and registrations, by selected country and/or world region, 1983-90. Data are from Data Resources, Inc. Includes accompanying article (p. 1, 77).

C2700–1.521: Mar. 26, 1984 (No. 5014)

WEEKLY TABLES

[1-2] Auction averages, for Mar. 1984. (p. 63)

[3-6] Production, for week ended Mar. 24, 1984. (p. 66)

[7] Domestic car sales, omitted.

MONTHLY TABLES

[23] Overseas production in West Germany and Japan, through Dec. 1983. (p. 35)

[24] Overseas registrations in Japan, Switzerland, Denmark, and Norway, through Dec. 1983. (p. 35)

U.S. MODEL COUNT CLIMBS TO 305 AS GM C-CARS BOW, ANNUAL FEATURE

(p. 1, 65) Annual article, by John K. Teahen, Jr., reviewing 1984 domestic car body styles. Includes 3 tables showing number of 1984 models offered by body style and model, by manufacturer and size class, with summary comparisons to 1983; and total models offered, 1942 and 1946-84.

JAPAN SETS EUROPEAN MARK, SEMIANNUAL FEATURE

(p. 36) Semiannual article, with 2 tables showing Japanese motor vehicle exports, by world region and for top 20 importing countries, 1983, with comparisons to 1982. Data are from Japan Automobile Manufacturers Assn.

C2700–1.522: Apr. 2, 1984 (No. 5015)

WEEKLY TABLES

[1-2] Auction averages, for Mar. 1984. (p. 35)

[3-6] Production, for week ended Mar. 31, 1984. (p. 51)

[7] Domestic car sales, for Mar. 11-20, 1984. (p. 14)

MONTHLY TABLE

[21] Import sales by nameplate, for Feb. 1984. (p. 49)

C2700–1.523: Apr. 9, 1984 (No. 5016)

WEEKLY TABLES

[1-2] Auction averages, for Apr. 1984. (p. 44)

[3-6] Production, for week ended Apr. 7, 1984. (p. 59)

[7] Domestic car sales [by model], for Mar. 19-30. (p. 8, 56)

MONTHLY TABLES

[12] Auto market, for Mar. 1984. (p. 8)

[16] Market shares, for 1983. (p. 26)

[17] Import registration shares, for Dec. 1983. (p. 26)

[19] Import sales, for Mar. 1984. (p. 56)

[22] Top cars, through Dec. 1983. (p. 26)

C2700–1.524: Apr. 16, 1984 (No. 5017)

WEEKLY TABLES

[1-2] Auction averages, for Apr. 1984. (p. 56)

[3-6] Production, for week ended Apr. 14, 1984. (p. 71)

[7] Domestic car sales, omitted.

MONTHLY TABLES

[12] Auto market, totals for 1st quarter 1984. (p. 52)

[13] New car stocks, for Apr. 1, 1984. (p. 1, 67)

[18] Service index, for Feb. 1984. (p. 1, 69)

[20] U.S. car sales by marketing unit, for Mar. 1984. (p. 52)

C2700–1.525: Apr. 23, 1984 (No. 5018)

WEEKLY TABLES

[1-2] Auction averages, for Apr. 1984. (p. 46)

[3-6] Production, for week ended Apr. 21, 1984. (p. 50)

[7] Domestic car sales, for Apr. 1-10. (p. 3)

MONTHLY TABLES

[8] Truck sales, for Mar. 1984. (p. 16, 31)

[9-11] Truck and heavy-duty registrations, and new truck registrations, through Jan. 1984. (p. 16-17, 22)

[13A] Import stocks, for Apr. 1, 1984. (p. 1, 47)

[23] Overseas production in Brazil, through Jan. 1984; and Spain, through Dec. 1983. (p. 30)

[24] Overseas registrations in Sweden, Italy, and Austria, through Feb. 1984. (p. 30)

EUROPEAN MARKET TURNS TOPSY-TURVY, RECURRING FEATURE

(p. 1, 45) Recurring article, by Richard Feast, on new auto sales in Western Europe. Includes 2 tables showing sales by country and manufacturer, 1st quarter 1984.

For description of previous article, see SRI 1983 Annual, under C2700-1.443.

NISSAN FIRST IN EUROPE

(p. 27-28) Article, with 1 table showing sales and market share for Japanese cars sold in Europe, by country and manufacturer, 1983.

RENAULT REIGNS IN 1983 NEW-CAR SALES

(p. 28-30) By Richard Feast. Article, with 1 table showing new car market volume, and market share by manufacturer and for all Japanese imports, for 16 European countries, 1982-83. Data are from *Automotive News* and are based primarily on government statistics.

VW GOLF IS TOP SELLER, ANNUAL FEATURE

(p. 30) Annual article, by Richard Feast, with 1 table showing top 10 auto models ranked by sales, and total auto sales, for 14 European countries, 1983 (with comparative rank for 1982). Data are from an *Automotive News* survey.

C2700–1.526: Apr. 25, 1984 (No. 5019)

WEEKLY TABLES

[1-7] Omitted.

1984 MARKET DATA BOOK ISSUE

Annual auto industry market data book, covering production, sales, registrations, prices, option installations, manufacturers, dealers, and selected other topics, 1983 and trends. Also includes detailed specifications for 1984 model autos and trucks. Book focuses on U.S. auto industry, but also presents data on imports and on production in Canada and other countries.

Data are from original surveys, and reports of Motor Vehicle Manufacturers Assn, R. L. Polk & Co., and other industry sources.

Includes contents listing (p. 1); 9 statistical sections, with 3 charts and 108 tables interspersed with narratives and text data, and industry directories (p. 3-196); and index (p. 198).

Tables, charts, and substantial text data are described below. Industry directories (p. 93-192) are not included on SRI microfiche.

TABLES, CHARTS, AND TEXT DATA:

[Data are for U.S., unless otherwise noted. Most data are shown for various periods 1983, generally with comparison to 1982 or trends from 1970s. Also includes selected historical trends from as early as 1946 and projections to 1990.]

a. Production: world motor vehicle production, for autos and trucks by region and country, and for top 12 manufacturers; U.S. and Canadian auto and truck production by manufacturer, with detail by make and/or model; and U.S. factory sales (domestic and export) of special trucks by type, and auto production by size class and State. 19 tables. (p. 3-18)

b. Sales/registrations: auto and truck sales and registrations, total and per outlet, with detail by domestic and import manufacturer, make, and model, and by size class; auto and truck registrations, by State and for Federal Government, and total mobile home registrations, by manufacturer and selected make; and auto registrations in 11 foreign countries, by make. 2 charts and 23 tables. (p. 19-40)

c. Specifications, prices, and options: detailed specifications for domestic and import autos and trucks, number of domestic models offered by body style, and domestic and import auto retail prices, all for 1984 models; domestic and import retail auto sales, with detail for Japanese and domestic sponsored imports; number of option installations on 1983 domestic models, by detailed option type; and diesel auto sales; with detail by manufacturer, make, and model. Text data and 23 tables. (p. 41-72)

d. Manufacturers: net sales, profit/loss, and selected other financial and operating data, for 4 major manufacturers; and expenditures on new plants/equipment, production value and index, employment, and capacity utilization, for motor vehicle and parts industries, with comparisons to all manufacturing. Text data and 12 tables. (p. 73-78)

e. Dealers: domestic and import auto and truck retail outlets and auto franchises, by make and manufacturer; auto operating costs; used vehicle sales by new auto/truck dealers; commercial fleet personal use chargeback rates; capital and leased equipment expenditures, for 6 industries; aver-

age dealership financial performance trends; sales and net income for 4 domestic manufacturers; and Japanese motor vehicle exports, by country and world region. 17 tables. (p. 79-84)

f. Suppliers: shipments of reinforced plastic, by end use; amount of zinc coatings and aluminum in typical auto; machine tool orders and shipments; magnesium production by world region; North American rubber consumption by type; tire production and shipments by type; chemical/allied products industry operating and financial data; metal-plated/coated plastic production, and consumption by type and end use; and auto electronic device market shares by application. Text data, 1 chart, and 4 tables. (p. 87-92)

g. Et Cetera: auto and truck production and registrations to 1990, by selected country and/or world region; network and spot TV advertising expenditures, by domestic and import manufacturer; auto operating/ownership costs by auto size; new auto inventory and days supply; used auto average auction prices; U.S. and Canada cross-border shipments, by manufacturer, make, and model; and autos and trucks in use and scrapped. 10 tables. (p. 193-196)

C2700–1.527: Apr. 30, 1984 (No. 5020)

WEEKLY TABLES

[1-2] Auction averages, for Apr. 1984. (p. 39)

[3-6] Production, for week ended Apr. 28, 1984. (p. 51)

[7] Domestic car sales, for Apr. 11-20, 1984. (p. 8)

MONTHLY TABLES

[14-15] New car market shares and registrations, for Jan. 1984. (p. 4, 47)

[16] Market shares, for Jan. 1984. (p. 22)

[17] Import registration shares, for Jan. 1984. (p. 22)

[22] Top cars, through Jan. 1984. (p. 22)

C2700–1.528: May 7, 1984 (No. 5021)

WEEKLY TABLES

[1-2] Auction averages, for May 1984. (p. 53)

[3-6] Production, for week ended May 5, 1984. (p. 67)

[7] Domestic car sales [by model], for Apr. 21-30, 1984. (p. 3, 66)

MONTHLY TABLES

[12] Auto market, for Apr. 1984. (p. 3, 66)

[19-20] Import sales, and U.S. car sales by marketing unit, for Apr. 1984. (p. 3, 66)

[21] Import sales by model, for Mar. 1984. (p. 40)

QUARTERLY TABLE

[27] Auto makers' financial results, for 1st quarter 1984. (p. 3)

BROCK TOUCHES OFF A FUROR ON QUOTA; PANIC SUBSIDES

(p. 1, 7) Article discussing executive compensation in the motor vehicle industry and the possible impact on Federal policies concerning import quotas. Includes 2 tables showing income of top 5 executives for 4 leading U.S. manufacturers, with aggregate data for all top executives of each company, including compensation per vehicle and per employee, 1982-83.

C2700–1.529: May 14, 1984 (No. 5022)

WEEKLY TABLES

[1-2] Auction averages, for May 1984. (p. 49)

[3-6] Production, for week ended May 12, 1984. (p. 62)

[7] Domestic car sales, omitted.

MONTHLY TABLES

[9-11] Truck and heavy-duty registrations, and new truck sales, through Feb. 1984. (p. 16, 36, 44)

[13] New car stocks, for May 1, 1984. (p. 1, 61)

[13A] Import stocks, for May 1, 1984. (p. 61)

[18] Service index, for Mar. 1984. (p. 1, 60)

C2700–1.530: May 21, 1984 (No. 5023)

WEEKLY TABLES

[1-2] Auction averages, for May 1984. (p. 60)

[3-6] Production, for week ended May 19, 1984. (p. 74)

[7] Domestic car sales, for May 1-10, 1984. (p. 8)

MONTHLY TABLES

[8] Truck sales, for Apr. 1984. (p. 16, 56)

[23] Overseas production in Japan and France, through Feb. 1984; UK, through Jan. 1984; and Belgium through Dec. 1983. (p. 42)

[24] Overseas registrations in West Germany, Italy, UK, Austria, and Sweden, through Mar. 1984; Japan, through Feb. 1984; France, through Jan. 1984; and Ireland and Finland, through Dec. 1983. (p. 42)

QUARTERLY TABLES

[25-26] U.S. car outlets and franchises, for Apr. 1, 1984. (p. 1, 73)

STUDY NOTES COST PENALTY FOR TURBO

(p. 52) By Francis J. Gawronski. Article, with 1 table comparing operating and ownership expenses of turbocharged vs. standard versions of four 1984 auto models. Data are from Runzheimer and Co.

C2700–1.531: May 28, 1984 (No. 5024)

WEEKLY TABLES

[1-2] Auction averages, for May 1984. (p. 46)

[3-6] Production, for week ended May 26, 1984. (p. 60)

[7] Domestic car sales, for May 11-20, 1984. (p. 2)

MONTHLY TABLES

[9-11] Truck and heavy-duty registrations, and new truck sales, through Mar. 1984. (p. 16, 44, 58)

[14-15] New car market shares and registrations, for Feb. 1984. (p. 24, 28)

C2700–1.532: June 4, 1984 (No. 5025)

WEEKLY TABLES

[1-2] Auction averages, for June 1984. (p. 37)

[3-6] Production, for week ended June 2, 1984. (p. 51)

[7] Domestic car sales, omitted.

MONTHLY TABLES

[16] Market shares, for 1st 2 months 1984. (p. 32)

[17] Import registration shares, for Feb. 1984. (p. 32)

[22] Top cars, through Feb. 1984. (p. 32)

C2700–1.533: June 11, 1984 (No. 5026)

WEEKLY TABLES

[1-2] Auction averages, for June 1984. (p. 64)

[3-6] Production, for week ended June 9, 1984. (p. 70)

[7] Domestic car sales [by model], for May 20-31, 1984. (p. 2, 65)

MONTHLY TABLES

[12] Auto market, for May 1984. (p. 2, 65)

[14-15] New car market shares and registrations, for Mar. 1984. (p. 3, 53)

[18] Service index, for Apr. 1984. (p. 1, 65)

[19-20] Import sales, and U.S. car sales by marketing unit, for May 1984. (p. 2, 65)

[21] Import sales by model, for Apr. 1984. (p. 67)

NUMBER OF PARTS STORES UP

(p. 20, 22) By Francis J. Gawronski. Article, with 1 chart showing percent change in number of retail outlets handling automotive supplies vs. all retail outlets, by type of outlet, 1980-83 period. Data are from Automotive Parts and Accessories Assn.

ANALYST: IMPORTS HIKE ALL CAR PRICES

(p. 51-52) Article, with 1 table showing average auto purchase price and workweeks necessary to finance purchase, compared to import share of auto market, 1970-83. Data are from Commerce Dept and BLS.

'AUTOMOTIVE NEWS' WORLD OUTLOOK, QUARTERLY FEATURE

(p. 66) Quarterly table showing auto and truck production and registrations, by selected country and/or world region, 1983-90. Data are from Data Resources, Inc. Includes accompanying article (p. 1, 66).

C2700–1.534: June 18, 1984 (No. 5027)

WEEKLY TABLES

[1-2] Auction averages, for June 1984. (p. 50)

[3-6] Production, for week ended June 16, 1984. (p. 63)

[7] Domestic car sales, for June 1-10, 1984. (p. 2)

MONTHLY TABLES

[8] Truck sales, for May 1984. (p. 18, 46)

[13] New car stocks, for May 1984. (p. 1, 60)

[13A] Import stocks, for June 1, 1984. (p. 1, 59)

[23] Overseas production in France, through Mar. 1984; and UK and Spain, through Feb. 1984. (p. 36)

[24] Overseas registrations in West Germany, UK, Italy, Sweden, and Austria, through Apr. 1984; Switzerland, Norway, and Denmark, through Mar. 1984; and France, Feb. 1984. (p. 36)

HOT SAE SESSIONS IN THE CAPITAL

(p. 22, 43) By Roger Rowand. Article, with 1 table showing National Highway Traffic Safety Administration expenditures on motor vehicle safety research, by category, actual FY84 and requested FY85.

C2700–1.535: June 25, 1984 (No. 5028)

WEEKLY TABLES

[1-2] Auction averages, for June 1984. (p. 52)

[3-6] Production, for week ended June 23, 1984. (p. 64)

[7] Domestic car sales, omitted.

MONTHLY TABLES

[16] Market shares, for 1st 3 months 1984. (p. 30)

[17] Import registration shares, for Mar. 1984. (p. 30)

[21] Import sales by model, for May 1984. (p. 28)

[22] Top cars, through Mar. 1984. (p. 30)

ENGINE TREND REVERSED; V-8s STAGE COMEBACK

(p. 1, 8) By Keith Gave. Article, with 1 table showing production of 4-, 6-, and 8-cylinder engines, for 1979-83 model autos.

SALES FORECASTS FOR THIS YEAR ARE COMPARED

(p. 18) Brief article, with text statistics showing auto sales forecasts of 6-7 econometric firms, 1983-84.

C2700–1.536: July 2, 1984 (No. 5029)

WEEKLY TABLES

[1-2] Auction averages, for June 1984. (p. 35)

[3-6] Production, for week ended June 30, 1984. (p. 50)

[7] Domestic car sales, for June 11-20, 1984. (p. 49)

MONTHLY TABLES

[14-15] New car market shares and registrations, for Apr. 1984. (p. 3, 36)

C2700–1.537: July 9, 1984 (No. 5030)

WEEKLY TABLES

[1-2] Auction averages, for July 1984. (p. 56)

[3-6] Production, for week ended July 7, 1984. (p. 70)

[7] Domestic car sales [by model], for June 21-30, 1984. (p. 1, 67)

MONTHLY TABLES

[9-11] Truck and heavy-duty registrations, and new truck sales, through Apr. 1984. (p. 16, 48, 53)

[12] Auto market, for June 1984; and totals for 1st half 1984. (p. 1, 67)

[19-20] Import sales, and U.S. car sales by marketing unit, for June 1984. (p. 1, 67)

FORD, GM FAIL ON '83 CAFE

(p. 1, 66) By Jake Kelderman. Article, with 1 table showing corporate average fuel economy (CAFE) vs. fuel economy standard assigned by the National Highway Traffic Safety Administration, for 1983 model autos and trucks, by vehicle manufacturer and type.

INDUSTRY IS VULNERABLE, COMMERCE DEPT SAYS

(p. 2, 66) By Jake Kelderman. Article, with 4 tables showing auto industry aggregate revenues and net income, 1977-83; and long-term debt/equity and current and quick asset/liability ratios, for 4 major manufacturers, as of Dec. 31, 1978-83. Data are from Commerce Dept.

95 DEALERSHIPS ADDED IN CANADA; TOTAL IS 3,449

(p. 44) Brief article, with 1 table showing number of Canadian auto dealerships, by manufacturer, Mar. 1983-84. Data are from Federation of Automobile Dealer Assns of Canada.

C2700–1.538: July 16, 1984 (No. 5031)

WEEKLY TABLES

[1-2] Auction averages, for July 1984. (p. 51)

[3-6] Production, for week ended July 14, 1984. (p. 67)

[7] Domestic car sales, omitted.

MONTHLY TABLES

[8] Truck sales, for June 1984. (p. 16, 49)

[13] New car stocks, for July 1, 1984. (p. 1, 8)

[16] Market shares, for 1st 4 months 1984. (p. 30)

[17] Import registration shares, for Apr. 1984. (p. 30, 34)

[22] Top cars, through Apr. 1984. (p. 30)

LOOKING FOR TRUCK REVIVAL, ANNUAL FEATURE

(p. 37) Annual article on European truck market. Data are from DRI Europe. Includes 2 tables showing medium/heavy truck production and demand, by country, 1980, 1983-85, and 1990.

C2700–1.539: July 23, 1984 (No. 5032)

WEEKLY TABLES

[1-2] Auction averages, for July 1984. (p. 47)

[3-6] Production, for week ended July 21, 1984. (p. 62)

[7] Domestic car sales, omitted.

MONTHLY TABLES

[9-11] Truck and heavy-duty registrations, and new truck sales, through May 1984. (p. 16, 38)

[13A] Import stocks, for July 1, 1984. (p. 2)

[14-15] New car market shares and registrations, for May 1984. (p. 8, 56, 60)

[18] Service index, for May 1984. (p. 1)

SERVICE PROFITS, ANNUAL FEATURE

Annual compilation of articles on auto dealer service and parts business. Includes the annual statistical articles described below.

SERVICE MOOD IS UPBEAT AT DEALERSHIPS

(p. E1-E4) Annual survey article, by Al Fleming, on auto dealer service dept operations and profit outlook, based on responses of service managers to a 1984 *Automotive News* survey. Includes 1 table showing survey response on the following, 1983-84:

a. Sales outlook for dealer and auto industry; dealer's best-selling and other auto makes carried, and auto sales in past 12 months; and area population.

b. Dealer service dept: profit potential, advertising/promotion adequacy, responsibility for hiring mechanics and buying service equipment, new service equipment buying plans, hours open per week, number of employees, most and least profitable service operations, and profitability of new auto warranty work and extended service.

c. Respondent characteristics: age, previous job, years in current position, and compensation level and composition.

SERVICE BUSINESS BOOMING

(p. E6) Annual article, by Francis J. Gawronski, on trends in auto dealer service/parts dept business, with 1 chart showing *Automotive News* service index, 1970-Apr. 1984.

DEALERS REAP $25 BILLION

(p. E18-E22) Annual article, by Francis J. Gawronski, on auto dealer parts and service sales. Data are from the National Automobile Dealers Assn.

Includes 3 tables showing value of service/parts market, 1978-83, and number of auto repair facilities, 1983, by type of service establishment; and franchised new auto dealer labor and parts sales, by type, 1982-83.

C2700–1.540: July 30, 1984 (No. 5033)

WEEKLY TABLES

[1-2] Auction averages, for July 1984. (p. 35)

[3-6] Production, for week ended July 28, 1984. (p. 51)

[7] Domestic car sales, for July 11-20, 1984. (p. 8)

MONTHLY TABLES

[21] Import sales by model, for June 1984. (p. 29)

IMPORT-DEALER TOTAL RISES, SEMIANNUAL FEATURE

(p. 1, 50) Semiannual article, by Kathleen Hamilton, reviewing import auto dealership trends. Includes 3 tables showing import franchises by make and nationality, and outlets handling imports only (exclusives and duals) and import-domestic duals, Jan. 1 and July 1, 1984; and import outlets, Jan. 1, 1957-84 and July 1, 1984.

C2700–1.541: Aug. 6, 1984 (No. 5034)

WEEKLY TABLES

[1-2] Auction averages, for Aug. 1984. (p. 55)

[3-6] Production, for week ended Aug. 4, 1984. (p. 62)

[7] Domestic car sales, omitted.

MONTHLY TABLES

[16] Market shares, for 1st 5 months 1984. (p. 41)

[17] Import registration shares, for May 1984. (p. 41)

[22] Top cars, through May 1984. (p. 41)

QUARTERLY TABLES

[25-26] U.S. car outlets and franchises, for July 1, 1984. (p. 1, 57)

[27] Auto makers' financial results, for 2nd quarter 1984. (p. 8)

U.S. AUTO EXECS' COMPENSATION SOARS 40 Pct. IN 1983, ANNUAL FEATURE

(p. 1, 58-59) Annual article, by Michelle Krebs, on motor vehicle industry executive compensation, with comparisons to Japan, 1983. Includes 3 tables showing total compensation or income of 1-2 top executives of 4 U.S. and 4 Japanese auto manufacturing companies; and salary/bonus of 172 most highly paid executives of vehicle manufacturing and supplier companies in U.S.; 1983 with comparisons to 1982.

U.S. data are from company proxy statements.

C2700–1.542: Aug. 13, 1984 (No. 5035)

WEEKLY TABLES

[1-2] Auction averages, for Aug. 1984. (p. 47)

[3-6] Production, for week ended Aug. 11, 1984. (p. 51)

[7] Domestic car sales [by model], for July 20-31, 1984. (p. 6, 44)

MONTHLY TABLES

[12] Auto market, for July 1984. (p. 6, 44)

[13] New car stocks, for Aug. 1, 1984. (p. 1, 49)

[19-20] Import sales, and U.S. car sales by marketing unit, for July 1984. (p. 6, 44)

[23] Overseas production in France, through Apr. and May 1984; Japan, through Apr. 1984; and UK and Spain, through Mar. and Apr. 1984. (p. 30)

[24] Overseas registrations in UK, Italy, Austria, Sweden, and Denmark, through May and June 1984; Belgium, through Mar. and June 1984; Ireland, Japan, and Switzerland, through Apr. 1984; France, Finland, and Holland, through Mar. 1984; and West Germany, through May 1984. (p. 29-30)

HONDA LEADS IN FIRST-HALF SALES PER DEALER, SEMIANNUAL FEATURE

(p. 1, 50) Semiannual article, by Jenny L. King, reviewing auto dealer sales volume in 1st half 1984. Includes 3 tables showing sales per outlet, by make, 1st half 1974-84; and by model nameplate for 5 size groups, 1st half 1983-84.

FIGHT FOR FIRST IN EUROPE, RECURRING FEATURE

(p. 28) Recurring article, by Richard Feast, on new auto sales in Western Europe. Includes 2 tables showing sales by country and manufacturer, and for all Japanese autos sold in Europe, 1st half 1983-84.

ABSENTEEISM CONTINUES AS PLANK, ANNUAL FEATURE

(p. 44) Annual article, by Marjorie Sorge, on absenteeism and costs in the auto industry. Data are from company reports. Includes 1 table showing absentee rates, by manufacturer, 1974-84.

C2700–1.543: Aug. 20, 1984 (No. 5036)

WEEKLY TABLES

[1-2] Auction averages, for Aug. 1984. (p. 33)

[3-6] Production, for week ended Aug. 18, 1984. (p. 46)

[7] Domestic car sales, for Aug. 1-10, 1984. (p. 6)

MONTHLY TABLES

[8] Truck sales, for July 1984. (p. 18, 28)

[13A] Import stocks, for Aug. 1, 1984. (p. 1, 43)

[18] Service index, for June 1984. (p. 1, 43)

EUROPE SWELLS U.S. TRADE DEFICIT

(p. 1, 43) By Jake Kelderman. Article, with 1 table showing value and volume of U.S. automotive trade deficit with Canada, Japan, 6 EC countries, and all others, 1983. Data are from USITC.

WITH SALES UP, DEALER PROFITS CLIMB UPWARD

(p. E1-E2) By Colleen Belli. Article on profit expectations of new car/truck dealers. Data are from National Automobile Dealers Assn surveys. Includes 1 table showing percent of dealers expecting increased, decreased, and unchanged profits, and profit expectation index, quarterly Jan. 1979-Jan. 1984.

C2700–1.544: Aug. 27, 1984 (No. 5037)

WEEKLY TABLES

[1-2] Auction averages, for Aug. 1984. (p. 51)

[3-6] Production, for week ended Aug. 25, 1984. (p. 67)

[7] Domestic car sales, for Aug. 11-20, 1984. (p. 3)

MONTHLY TABLES

[14-15] New car market shares and registrations, for June 1984. (p. 61)

[21] Import sales by model, for July 1984. (p. 40)

C2700–1.545: Sept. 3, 1984 (No. 5038)

WEEKLY TABLES

[1-2] Auction averages, for Aug. 1984. (p. 41)

[3-6] Production, for week ended Sept. 1, 1984. (p. 55)

[7] Domestic car sales, omitted.

MONTHLY TABLES

[9-11] Truck and heavy-duty registrations, and new truck sales, through June 1984. (p. 18, 31, 34)

C2700–1.546: Sept. 10, 1984 (No. 5039)

WEEKLY TABLES

[1-2] Auction averages, for Sept. 1984. (p. 49)

[3-6] Production, for week ended Sept. 8, 1984. (p. 62)

[7] Domestic car sales [by model], for Aug. 21-31, 1984. (p. 58)

MONTHLY TABLES

[12] Auto market, for Aug. 1984. (p. 58)

[18] Service index, for July 1984. (p. 2)

[19-20] Import sales, and U.S. car sales by marketing unit, for Aug. 1984. (p. 58)

[23] Overseas production in France, through June 1984; and Japan, UK, and Spain, through May 1984. (p. 35)

[24] Overseas registrations in UK and Sweden, through July 1984; West Germany, Netherlands, and Norway, through June 1984; Switzerland, through May 1984; France, through Apr. 1984; and Greece, through Mar. 1984. (p. 35-36)

GM SETS SIGHTS ON SALES LEADERSHIP

(p. 34) By Richard Feast. Article, with 1 table showing auto sales volume in Europe, with detail for 3 leading models, 1979-83.

PROBLEMS PLAGUE FRENCH

(p. 34-35) By Richard Feast. Article, with 1 table showing French auto and commercial vehicle production, exports, and registrations, with registration detail by auto model and for imports, 1979-83. Data are from CSCA, Paris.

C2700–1.547: Sept. 17, 1984 (No. 5040)

WEEKLY TABLES

[1-2] Auction averages, for Sept. 1984. (p. 45)

[3-6] Production, for week ended Sept. 15, 1984. (p. 59)

[7] Domestic car sales, for Sept. 1-10, 1984. (p. 3)

MONTHLY TABLES

[8] Truck sales, for Aug. 1984. (p. 16, 41)

[13-13A] New car and import stocks, for Sept. 1, 1984. (p. 1, 57)

[16] Market shares, for 1st half 1984. (p. 26)

[17] Import registration shares, for June 1984. (p. 26, 40)

[22] Top cars, through June 1984. (p. 40)

C2700–1.548: Sept. 24, 1984 (No. 5041)

WEEKLY TABLES

[1-2] Auction averages, for Sept. 1984. (p. 49)

[3-6] Production, for week ended Sept. 22, 1984. (p. 62)

[7] Domestic car sales, omitted.

MONTHLY TABLES

[9-11] Truck and heavy-duty registrations, and new truck sales, through July 1984. (p. 16, 44)

[21] Import sales by model, for Aug. 1984. (p. 46)

DEVELOPMENT OF ELECTRIC CAR TRACED

(p. 22, 32) Article, with 1 chart showing average daily petroleum consumption, with distribution by transportation mode, 1980 and 2000. Data are from DOE.

MORE RESPECT, MORE BUCKS, ANNUAL FEATURE

(p. E1, E4) Annual article, by Joseph Bohn, analyzing domestic automobile industry advertising expenditures in 1983. Data are from *Advertising Age* and other industry sources. Includes 1 table showing expenditures by manufacturer, by media 1983, and total 1982.

PANEL PREDICTS RISING SALES IN 1985, ANNUAL FEATURE

(p. E2) Annual survey article, by Michelle Krebs, reporting on new car sales projections by 9 market analysts. Includes 1 table showing new car and truck sales projections by each analyst, 1984-87.

SPLIT-PERSONALITY STATE

(p. E6) Article on California car market. Data are from J. D. Power and Associates. Includes 2 undated tables showing summary demographic characteristics, and distribution of present and planned car ownership by body style, for northern and southern California.

SPENDING DESPITE QUOTAS, ANNUAL FEATURE

(p. E38) Annual article, by Joseph Bohn, on advertising expenditures in U.S. by major car importers in 1983. Data are from *Advertising Age,* Leading National Advertiser reports, and other industry sources. Includes 1 table showing expenditures by manufacturer, by media 1983, and total 1982.

C2700–1.549: Oct. 1, 1984 (No. 5042)

WEEKLY TABLES

[1-2] Auction averages, for Sept. 1984. (p. 37)

[3-6] Production, for week ended Sept. 29, 1984. (p. 51)

[7] Domestic car sales, for Sept. 11-20, 1984. (p. 6)

EPA MILEAGE RATINGS FOR '85 MODELS, ANNUAL FEATURE

(p. 47-48) Annual tabular listing of EPA fuel economy mileage estimates for all 1985 model year passenger cars, pickup trucks, vans, and specialty vehicles sold in U.S., by model arranged by size group.

C2700–1.550: Oct. 8, 1984 (No. 5043)

WEEKLY TABLES

[1-2] Auction averages, for Oct. 1984. (p. 66)

[3-6] Production, for week ended Oct. 6, 1984. (p. 72)

[7] Domestic car sales, for 1984 model year; [and by model], for Sept. 21-30, 1984. (p. 1, 70)

MONTHLY TABLES

[12] Auto market, for Sept. 1984. (p. 70)

[14-15] New car market shares and registrations, for July 1984. (p. 36, 67)

[19-20] Import sales, and U.S. car sales by marketing unit, for Sept. 1984. (p. 70)

C2700–1.551: Oct. 15, 1984 (No. 5044)

WEEKLY TABLES

[1-2] Auction averages, for Oct. 1984. (p. 50)

[3-6] Production, for week ended Oct. 13, 1984. (p. 65)

[7] Domestic car sales, omitted.

MONTHLY TABLES

[8] Truck sales, for Sept. 1984. (p. 16, 60)

[13-13A] New car and import stocks, for Oct. 1, 1984. (p. 1, 3, 62)

[18] Service index, for Aug. 1984. (p. 3)

[23] Overseas production in Japan, UK, and Brazil, through June 1984. (p. 38)

[24] Overseas registrations in UK and Sweden, through Aug. 1984; West Germany and Austria, through July 1984; Japan, through June 1984; and France, through May 1984. (p. 38)

LOTSA LADAS

(p. 36) Brief article, with 1 table showing sales volume for Soviet-made Lada/other autos in 12 Western European countries, with total European market share, 1980-1st half 1984. Data are from national assns, Lada Cars, and Automotive Industry Data (UK).

'AUTOMOTIVE NEWS' WORLD OUTLOOK, QUARTERLY FEATURE

(p. 60) Quarterly table showing auto and truck production and registrations, by selected country and/or world region, 1983-90. Data are from Data Resources, Inc. Includes accompanying article (p. 1, 60).

C2700–1.552: Oct. 22, 1984 (No. 5045)

WEEKLY TABLES

[1-2] Auction averages, for Oct. 1984. (p. 45)

[3-6] Production, for week ended Oct. 20, 1984. (p. 62)

[7] Domestic car sales, omitted.

THE JAPANESE, ANNUAL FEATURE

Annual compilation of features on Japanese motor vehicle production, sales, registrations, and exports, and industry financial performance. Features with substantial statistical content are described below.

JAPANESE AUTO COMPANY PROFILES

(p. E8) Table showing the following for 9 Japanese motor vehicle manufacturers: employment, with detail for body assembly, engine/transmission, and overseas plants and main subsidiaries/affiliated companies (no date); and production of cars and commercial vehicles or trucks/buses, 1983.

JAPANESE CAR MAKERS ARE IN THE MONEY, ANNUAL FEATURE

(p. E16) Annual article, by Michelle Krebs, analyzing financial performance of Japanese motor vehicle industry. Includes 1 table showing sales and net income (in yen and dollars), and sales volume, for 6 manufacturers, various 12-month periods 1983-84, with percent change from previous period.

BIG-VEHICLE WAVE MOVING IN FROM JAPAN

(p. E20) Article, with 1 chart showing diesel engine sales in North American heavy vehicle/equipment markets (industrial, construction, and agriculture) and for class 6-8 trucks/buses, with aggregate market shares for leading manufacturers (including Japanese firms), 1983.

LABOR'S A MIXED BAG FROM NATION TO NATION

(p. E28) Article, with 2 tables showing base hourly wages by skill category, and contractual and actual working hours, for Japanese auto manufacturers and their foreign subsidiaries, by company, 1983. Data are from International Metalworkers Federation.

MOST EXPORTS IN THREE YEARS, SEMIANNUAL FEATURE

(p. E30) Semiannual article, with 2 tables showing Japanese motor vehicle exports, by world region and for top 10 importing countries, 1st half 1984, with comparisons to 1983. Data are from Japan Automobile Manufacturers Assn.

C2700–1.553: Oct. 29, 1984 (No. 5046)

WEEKLY TABLES

[1-2] Auction averages, for Oct. 1984. (p. 45)

[3-6] Production, for week ended Oct. 27, 1984. (p. 61)

[7] Domestic car sales, for Oct. 1-10 and 11-20, 1984. (p. 3, 14)

MONTHLY TABLES

[9-11] Truck and heavy-duty registrations, and new truck sales, through Aug. 1984. (p. 16, 32, 36)

[16] Market shares, for 1st 7 months 1984. (p. 26)

[17] Import registration shares, for July 1984. (p. 26)

[22] Top cars, through July 1984. (p. 26)

C2710
Crain Communications

C2710-1   ADVERTISING AGE

Semiweekly, and special annual issues. Approx. 135 p.
Oversized.
ISSN 0001-8899.
LC 42-47059.
SRI/MF/excerpts

Semiweekly trade journal of the advertising and marketing industry. Includes data on advertising expenditures, finances of advertising agencies and media companies, magazine advertising pages, consumer awareness of advertisements, and other advertising/marketing-related topics. Most data are from individual company reports, trade assns, and private research or consulting firms.

Two special annual issues, presenting data on leading advertising agencies and advertisers, are published in Mar. and Sept., respectively.

General format:

a. Numerous news briefs and feature articles, some with statistics, including 2 weekly charts (beginning with the Aug. 1984 issues) showing stock performance trends for aggregate leading advertisers and media companies; and weekly special section, occasionally with separate pagination, focusing on a selected topic, and usually containing some statistics.

b. 2 monthly tables and 1 quarterly table on advertising expenditures and pages; and 1 irregularly recurring table on newspaper advertising linage, based on data from Media Records; all listed below.

c. Monthly "adWatch" feature, by Scott Hume, measuring consumer recall of advertising, based on a monthly random survey of approximately 1,250 adults by SRI Research Center, Inc.; usually with text data, and 1-4 tables or charts.

Monthly "adWatch" feature and all articles with substantial statistical content are described, as they appear, under "Statistical Features;" page locations and latest periods of coverage for monthly, quarterly, and other recurring tables are also noted. Nonstatistical features are not covered.

Prior to the Apr. 23, 1984 issue, journal was published weekly.

Availability: Advertising Age, Circulation Department, 740 Rush St., Chicago IL 60611, $52.00 per yr., single copy $1.25, special issue prices vary; SRI/MF/excerpts for all portions covered under "Statistical Features."

Issues reviewed during 1984: Nov. 7, 1983-Oct. 29, 1984 (P) (Vol. 54, Nos. 47-54; Vol. 55, Nos. 1-73) [Cover date of Aug. 23, 1984 issue incorrectly reads Aug. 27].

RECURRING TABLES:

MONTHLY TABLES

[Monthly tables appear on a space available basis; data for a sequential month may occasionally be omitted. Data are current to 1-3 months preceding publication.]

[1] Flash Report: newspaper advertising investment [by 16 product or service categories; month of coverage and same month of previous year].

[2] Advertising pages for U.S., Canadian, and [other] foreign consumer publications [by publication; for month of coverage and year to date, and same periods of previous year].

QUARTERLY TABLE

[1] Ad pages in [U.S. and Canadian] farm publications [by publication, for quarter ending 1 month prior to cover date, year to date, and same periods of previous year].

IRREGULARLY RECURRING TABLE

[Data are current to 3-5 months preceding publication.]

[1] Newspaper ad linage [for selected newspapers in approximately 60 cities, for month of coverage and same month of previous year; table begins with the Oct. 1, 1984 issue.]

STATISTICAL FEATURES:

C2710-1.501: Nov. 7, 1983 (Vol. 54, No. 47)

NEXT YEAR'S COST INCREASES MAY AVERAGE ONLY 6%, ANNUAL FEATURE

(p. M10-M11, M20) Annual article, by Robert J. Coen, on advertising media price trends. Data are from McCann-Erickson, Inc. Includes 2 charts and 3 tables showing indexes of cost per 1,000 exposures and per unit, by media, 1980-84, with comparison to selected other economic indicators, 1979-83.

'LAUNCH FEVER' STILL LIVES IN THE MAGAZINE GAME

(p. M38-M41) By Stuart J. Elliott. Article, with 1 table ranking 33 magazine format categories by advertising revenue, 1982, with comparative 1981 ranking. Data are from Folio Publishing Corp.

WHY MARKETERS LIKE THE SALES PROMOTION GAMBIT

(p. M52-M54) By Don E. Schultz. Article, with 1 chart comparing expenditures for advertising and sales promotion, 1975-83. Data are from Russell D. Bowman of John Blair Marketing.

DALLAS, DETROIT PAPERS SHOW GAINS

(p. 86) By Robert Reed. Article, with 2 tables ranking top 10 daily and Sunday newspapers by average circulation, Apr.-Sept. 1983, with comparison to same period 1982. Data are from the Audit Bureau of Circulations.

C2710-1.502: Nov. 14, 1983 (Vol. 54, No. 48)

WOMEN CHECKING OUT 'HOTEL,' RECURRING FEATURE

(p. 10) Recurring article, by James P. Forkan, with 1 table showing Nielsen ratings for top 10 prime time TV series, for men and women aged 18-34 and 25-54, Sept./Oct. 1983.

FROM APPLE TO WANG, COMPUTERS MEAN BUSINESS

(p. M9-M11) By Udayan Gupta. Article, with 2 charts showing computer shipment volume and value, by computer type, 1982 and 1987. Data are from International Data Corp.

SOFTWARE PROGRAMS PICK UP POWER

(p. M36) By Betsy Gilbert. Article, with 1 table showing top 10 independent software suppliers ranked by software revenue, with comparison to total revenue, 1982. Data are from a survey of software product and service companies conducted by International Computer Programs.

C2710-1.503: Nov. 21, 1983 (Vol. 54, No. 49)

MONTHLY TABLE

[2] Advertising pages for U.S., Canadian, and other foreign consumer publications, Oct. or Nov. 1983. (p. 55-56) [For corrected data, see C2710-1.506 and C2710-1.507, below.]

PUBLIC SHOPS HOLD THEIR OWN IN QUARTER, QUARTERLY FEATURE

(p. 30-32) Quarterly article, by Christy Marshall, on finances of publicly owned advertising agencies. Data are from agency reports. Includes 1 table showing net income and revenues for 8 public advertising agencies, 3rd quarter and first 9 months, 1982-83.

WHERE AMERICANS RUN TO EAT

(p. M11) By John C. Maxwell, Jr. Article on consumer fast-food purchasing habits. Data are from Commerce Dept and Lehman Brothers, Kuhn Loeb Research. Includes 2 tables showing top 10 fast-food chains ranked by sales, with comparison to total fast-food sales, 1980-82; and types of fast food ranked by sales, 1981-83, with number of companies for each type.

C2710-1.504: Nov. 28, 1983 (Vol. 54, No. 50)

MONTHLY 'adWATCH' FEATURE

(p. 3, 80) "Burgers Burn in Memory." Covers Oct. 1983 survey. Includes text data on awareness of advertising for fast food and 4 other industry categories; and listing of top 10 products recalled.

CIGARET SALES IN DOWNSPIN, ANNUAL FEATURE

(p. 37) Annual article, by John C. Maxwell, Jr., on cigarette production and consumption, by brand and company, 1982-83. Data are from Lehman Brothers, Kuhn Loeb.

Includes 3 tables showing domestic and export production and domestic market share, by company; production and market share for 10 leading brands; and low-tar cigarette consumption and market share, by company; 1982-83.

MARKETING'S STEPCHILD COMES INTO ITS OWN

(p. M9-M10, M64, M66) By Lori Kesler. Article on trends in direct marketing sales and advertising expenditures. Data are from Direct Marketing Assn, and Robert Coen of McCann Erickson. Includes 3 tables showing direct marketing advertising expenditures by medium, 1977-83; and direct marketing sales, 1975-82.

TELEMARKETERS START GROUP

(p. M65) By Eddy Christman. Article, with 1 table showing telemarketing expenditures for residential and business originated local and toll calls, 1982 with percent change from 1981. Data are from M. J. Sheehan of AT&T Communications.

C2710-1.505: Dec. 5, 1983 (Vol. 54, No. 51)

MONTHLY TABLE

[1] Flash Report: newspaper advertising investment for Sept. 1983. (p. 86)

100 LEADING MARKETS, TRIENNIAL FEATURE

(p. M3-M61) Triennial report profiling recent economic and business developments in the top 100 metro market areas ranked by 1980 population. Data are from U.S. Census Bureau, Marketing Economics Institute, and other private sources.

Includes profile index and introductory article; and market profiles arranged by census division, interspersed with 16 tables showing the following:

a. 100 markets: population 1980, and personal income and retail sales (total and for 9 product groups) 1982, for each market.

b. Top 10-11 markets among the 100 ranked by TV households, population and retail sales growth, ratio of retail sales to disposable income, household income, Fortune 500 headquarter offices, building construction value, rural percentage of metro area, Hispanic population, quality-of-life rating, suburban population, airport passengers, and services employment, various periods 1977-83.

For description of last previous report, see SRI 1980 Annual under C2710-1.112.

C2710–1.506: Dec. 12, 1983 (Vol. 54, No. 52)

NEWSPAPERS ACTIVELY SEEKING POLITICIANS' 'VOTE' FOR AD BUYS

(p. 3, 68) By Stuart Emmrich. Article, with 1 table showing political advertising expenditures for newspapers and network/spot TV, 1976, 1980, and 1984. Data are from Television Bureau of Advertising and Newspaper Advertising Bureau.

CORRECTIONS AND CLARIFICATIONS

(p. 6) Includes corrected data for monthly table [2] on advertising pages in consumer publications, described under C2710-1.503, above.

STAGE AND SCREEN PUT TO THE TEST

(p. M9-M10) By Louis Weisberg. Article on marketing developments for films and Broadway stage productions. Data are from *Variety*. Includes 1 table showing top 10 movies ranked by rental income, as of July 1983.

42nd STREET SINGS THE BLUES

(p. M20-M23) By Barry H. Slinker. Article on developments in Broadway production planning. Data are from League of New York Theatres and Producers. Includes 1 table showing top 10 Broadway productions ranked by number of performances, as of Dec. 1983.

C2710–1.507: Dec. 19, 1983 (Vol. 54, No. 53)

MONTHLY TABLE

[2] Advertising pages for U.S., Canadian, and other foreign consumer publications, Nov. or Dec. 1983. (p. 35-36)

AD SPENDING SEEN CLIMBING 13.8%, ANNUAL FEATURE

(p. 3, 56) Annual article, by Christy Marshall, on advertising sales trends and outlook by media. Data are from Robert Coen of McCann-Erickson. Includes 1 table showing national and local advertising revenue forecast for 1984, with detail for national print and broadcast.

CORRECTIONS AND CLARIFICATIONS

(p. 6) Includes corrected data for monthly table [2] on advertising pages in consumer publications, described under C2710-1.503, above.

C2710–1.508: Dec. 26, 1983 (Vol. 54, No. 54)

MONTHLY 'adWATCH' FEATURE

(p. 3, 19) "United's Awareness Hitting Lofty Heights." Covers Nov. 1983 survey. Includes text data on awareness of advertising for airlines and 5 other industry categories.

C2710–1.509: Jan. 2, 1984 (Vol. 55, No. 1)

UP AND DOWN THE LADDER: AVERAGE HIGHS AND LOWS OF AD AGENCY SALARIES

(p. M17) Table showing average high and low salaries for advertising agency personnel, by position, primarily 1981 and 1983. Data are from Jerry Fields Associates, Judd-Falk, and Simmy Sussman, Inc.

MEDIA OUTLOOK FOR '84

(p. 31) Table showing advertising revenue by detailed media, 1983-84. Data are from Robert Coen of McCann-Erickson, Inc.

C2710–1.510: Jan. 16, 1984 (Vol. 55, No. 3)

QUARTERLY TABLE

[1] Ad pages in U.S. and Canadian farm publications, 4th quarter 1983. (p. 50).

Corrected data appear in the Jan. 30, 1984 issue; for description see C2710-1.512, below.

BEER MARKETING: SATISFYING A THIRST FOR IMAGES

(p. M9-M11) By Robert Reed. Article, with 1 chart and 1 table showing advertising expenditures for each of top 10 beer brewers and aggregate top 15 brewers, and share of advertising expenditures by market segment; 1979-82. Data are from Impact Databank and other sources.

PEOPLE'S CHOICE

(p. M10) Brief article on consumer beer preferences, based on a survey of 1,000 adults conducted by R. H. Bruskin Associates. Includes 3 tables and 1 chart showing respondent distribution regarding alcoholic beverages recently consumed, and type of beer preferred, by sex; beer consumption by age group, and brand preferences; and awareness of beer brand advertising.

WINE MARKETING: IS WINE HANGING UP ITS TUXEDO IMAGE?

(p. M31-M33) By Richard Paul Hinkle. Article, with 1 table showing top 5 and 3 other wine companies ranked by advertising expenditures, with detail by brand, 1st half 1983 with comparison to 1st half 1982. Data are from Leading National Advertisers, Inc. and Impact Databank.

CHOOSING THE RIGHT MEDIUM: IT'S NO MEAN FEAT

(p. M34-M36) By James Suckling. Article, with 1 table showing wine industry advertising expenditures by media, 1st half 1982-83. Data are from Leading National Advertisers, Inc. and Impact Databank.

C2710–1.511: Jan. 23, 1984 (Vol. 55, No. 4)

MONTHLY TABLE

[2] Advertising pages for U.S., Canadian, and other foreign consumer publications, Dec. 1983 or Jan. 1984. (p. 67-68)

Corrected data appear in the Jan. 30, 1984, and Mar. 5, 1984 issues; for descriptions see C2710-1.512 and C2710-1.517, below.

RATING THE CITIES

(p. 16-18) Article, with 1 undated table showing 7 major cities rated for various business and life style factors. Data are from *The Comparative Costs of Doing Business in Seven Cities*, prepared by Julien J. Studley, Inc.

MOLTING SEASON FOR COMPANY LOGOS

(p. M22-M23) Article, with 1 table showing number of company name changes, by industry group, 1982-83. Data are from Anspach Grossman Portugal.

C2710–1.512: Jan. 30, 1984 (Vol. 55, No. 5)

MONTHLY 'adWATCH' FEATURE

(p. 3, 77) "Beverages, Fast-Food Tops in Ad Awareness." Summarizes monthly 1983 surveys. Includes text data on awareness of advertising for various product categories.

CORRECTIONS AND CLARIFICATIONS

(p. 6) Includes corrected data for quarterly table [1] on advertising pages in U.S. and Canadian farm publications, and for monthly table [2] on advertising pages in consumer publications, described under C2710-1.510 and C2710-1.511, respectively.

URUGUAY: LATIN AMERICA'S FAVORITE TEST MARKET

(p. 52) By Marina Specht. Article, with 1 table showing top 5 advertising agencies in Uruguay, ranked by 1983 billings. Data are from *Advertising Age*.

LIQUOR SALES KEPT STAGGERING THROUGH '83, ANNUAL FEATURE

(p. 68) Annual article, by John C. Maxwell, Jr., on liquor sales trends. Data are from Lehman Brothers, Kuhn Loeb. Includes 1 table ranking 36 leading brands by case sales, 1982-83. Table also shows company for each brand.

C2710–1.513: Feb. 6, 1984 (Vol. 55, No. 6)

MARKETERS' TIE-INS PAYING OFF ALREADY

(p. 1, 60) By Scott Hume. Article on consumer awareness of advertising for sponsors of the Olympic games. Data are based on responses of 1,253 consumers to a Dec. 1983 SRI Research Center, Inc. survey. Includes text data and 1 chart.

An accompanying list groups 1984 Winter Olympic sponsors by the amount of their network TV advertising expenditures during Feb. 7-19, 1984. List is from American Broadcasting Co.

LUCRATIVE FORMULA YIELDS SUPPLY OF SUCCESS

(p. M12-M13) By Mark Wolf. Article profiling TV program syndicators. Data are from Ronald Krueger of TelCom Associates. Includes 1 table showing distributor and number of half-hour and hour episodes available, for selected syndicated TV programs, 1984-88.

LUCY'S LEGEND LEAVES LOTS OF LOOT

(p. M18) By William Mahoney. Article on broadcasting history of the "I Love Lucy" TV program. Data are from A. C. Nielsen Co. Includes 1 table showing rank and network for 5 top rated TV programs, 1951/52-1956/57 TV "seasons."

C2710–1.514: Feb. 13, 1984 (Vol. 55, No. 7)

BEER MAKERS TRY NEW TACKS

(p. 2, 70) By Robert Reed. Article, with 1 chart showing shipments for 5 leading beer brewers, 1982-83. Data are from individual brewers.

FINANCIERS TRADE KID GLOVES FOR BOXING GLOVES

(p. M10-M11) By Kurt C. Hoffman. Article on advertising of financial service companies. Data are from Leading National Advertisers and Radio Advertising Bureau. Includes 1 table showing advertising expenditures by media, for top 10 financial service companies ranked by total expenditures, 1st half 1983.

OLE! PINSTRIPES PLAY MATADOR IN A NEW FIGHT

(p. M22-M23) By Bob Mahlburg. Article on marketing of brokerage services available through banks. Data are from Leading National Advertisers and Radio Advertising Bureau. Includes 1 table showing top 10 banking corporations ranked by advertising expenditures, 1st half 1983.

BROKERS: BULLDOZING COMPETITORS OR DOZING BULLS?

(p. M24) By Mark Liff. Article on marketing practices in the brokerage industry. Data are from Leading National Advertisers and Radio Advertising Bureau. Includes 1 table showing top 10 brokers ranked by advertising expenditures, 1st half 1983.

VIDEOGAME REBOUND SEEN

(p. 74) Article, with 1 table showing video game cartridge sales volume, for 6 manufacturers and all others, 1983. Data are from Goldman, Sachs and Co.

C2710–1.515: Feb. 20, 1984 (Vol. 55, No. 8)

MONTHLY TABLE

[2] Advertising pages for U.S., Canadian, and other foreign consumer publications, Jan. or Feb. 1984. (p. 57-58)

HOW IT'S DONE

(p. M11) Article on test marketing techniques. Data are based on a spring 1983 survey of 183 consumer goods/service companies, conducted by Market Facts. Includes 2 tables showing response distribution regarding use of test marketing for new products, 1978-82 period; and test market techniques most frequently used, 1978 and 1983.

A similar article, "Many Hesitate To Simulate," is described below.

EUROPEAN TEST PATTERNS

(p. M36-M38) Collection of brief articles on test marketing practices in 7 European countries. Data are from *European Media & Marketing Guide*.

Includes 7 maps and 13 tables generally showing the following for West Germany, Netherlands, Italy, Spain, France, UK, and Greece: population of principal cities and Nielsen marketing regions; and advertising expenditures for selected product categories, in domestic currency; primarily 1982.

MANY HESITATE TO SIMULATE

(p. M42-M43) Article on use of simulated test marketing for new product development. Data are based on a spring 1983 survey of 183 con-

sumer goods/service companies, conducted by Market Facts. Includes 1 table showing percent of respondents using selected marketing techniques within the past year, 1978 and 1983.

A similar article, "How It's Done," is described above.

UK BEER MARKET CHANGES ITS TASTE

(p. 42, 47) By Sean Milmo. Article, with 1 chart showing share of UK beer market, by beer type, 1973 and 1981. Data are from *Advertising Age*.

B&B MOVES TO STOP DOWNWARD SPIRAL IN GERMANY

(p. 44) By Dagmar Mussey. Article, with 1 table showing gross income 1983, and billings 1982-83, for top 10 advertising agencies operating in West Germany. Data are from *Horizont/Advertising Age Deutschland*.

WALL STREET KEEPS UP CONFIDENCE IN SHOPS, QUARTERLY FEATURE

(p. 72) Quarterly article, by Pat Sloan, on finances of publicly owned advertising agencies. Data are from agency reports. Includes 1 table showing income and revenues for 7 agencies, 4th quarter and full year 1982-83.

C2710–1.516: Feb. 27, 1984 (Vol. 55, No. 9)

MONTHLY adWATCH FEATURE

(p. 3, 73) "Apple and 'Beef' Big Hits on Ad Recall Menu." Covers Jan. 1984 survey. Includes 4 tables on consumer awareness of corporate advertisers in personal computers, home electronics, apparel, and financial institution categories; and text data on top 10 advertisements recalled.

NEW STRATEGIES REVIVE THE ROSE'S FADING BLOOM

(p. M9-M11, M44) By Bess Gallanis. Article on marketing of fragrances for women. Data are from Leading National Advertisers and Business Trend Analysts. Includes 1 table showing top 10 perfume/toilet water brands ranked by advertising expenditures (actual amount and as percent of industry), with manufacturer for each; and list of top 5 fragrances distributed through dept stores; 1982.

MEN'S FRAGRANCE ADS: THERE'S LUST IN THEIR SPOTS

(p. M10-M11, M44) By Hortense Leon. Article, with 1 table showing top 10 men's toiletry brands ranked by advertising expenditures (actual amount and as percent of industry), with manufacturer for each, 1982. Data are from Leading National Advertisers.

HIGH-TECH MAGAZINES STILL FLYING HIGH, SEMIANNUAL FEATURE

(p. 67) Semiannual article, by Stuart J. Elliott, with 1 table showing top 10 magazines ranked by circulation, 2nd half 1982-83. Data are from Audit Bureau of Circulations.

C2710–1.517: Mar. 5, 1984 (Vol. 55, No. 10)

PRODUCT CLAIMS NOT BELIEVABLE, RECURRING FEATURE

(p. 1, 32) Recurring article, by Nancy Millman, on consumer attitudes toward advertising, based on a Nov. 1983 survey of 1,250 consumers conducted by SRI Research Center, Inc. for *Advertising Age*. Includes 2 charts

showing response rates for questions on product claim credibility and quality of TV advertising.

CORRECTIONS AND CLARIFICATIONS

(p. 6) Includes corrected data for monthly table [2] on advertising pages in consumer publications, described under C2710-1.511, above.

COMPUTER MARKETING: NO LONGER FUN AND GAMES

(p. M11-M13, M16) By Daniel Burstein. Article, with 1 chart and 1 table showing number of home/office personal computers installed, by 6 manufacturers, as of Dec. 1983; and personal computer market shares for top 6 and all other manufacturers, 1980-83. Data are from Future Computing and Dataquest.

TIMING TROUBLES CHIP INTO SALES

(p. M18-M24) By Richard Edel. Article on marketing of personal computers, with 3 tables showing shipment volume, and software and hardware shipment values, various years 1980-88. Data are from Dataquest and Future Computing.

MAGAZINES FACE TERMINAL ILLNESS

(p. M60-M62) By Craig Endicott. Article, with 1 table showing advertising revenue and pages, 1982-83, and publisher, for top 10 magazines directed to microcomputer users ranked by 1983 advertising revenue. Data are from Adscope, Inc.

C2710–1.518: Mar. 12, 1984 (Vol. 55, No. 11)

FLAT SALES FORCE WINERY CHANGES

(p. 3, 66) By Ruth Stroud. Article, with 1 chart showing shipments and market shares for top 5 and all other California wine marketers, 1982-83. Data are from Impact, Inc.

NETWORK RADIO RATINGS

(p. 30) Table showing top 15 radio networks ranked by adult (age 25-54) audience, spring-fall 1983 period, with comparison to fall-spring 1982/83 period. Data are from Radio All-Dimension Audience Research (RADAR) surveys, prepared by Statistical Research, Inc.

TOP-RATED MOVIES ON TV

(p. 42) Table showing 20 top rated motion pictures broadcast on TV during Sept. 26, 1983-Feb. 27, 1984 period, and also showing audience share, whether made-for-TV or theatrical production, and network. Data are from A. C. Nielsen Co.

C2710–1.519: Mar. 19, 1984 (Vol. 55, No. 12)

MONTHLY TABLES

[1] Flash Report: newspaper advertising investment for Dec. 1983. (p. 41)

[2] Advertising pages for U.S., Canadian, and other foreign consumer publications, Feb. or Mar. 1984. (p. 67-68)

HARDEE'S JUMPS INTO NET TV FRAY, RECURRING FEATURE

(p. 1, 78) Recurring article, by Scott Hume, with 1 table showing network and local TV advertising expenditures, 1982-83, for top 15 fast food chains ranked by 1983 expenditures and for total fast food industry. Data are from TV Bureau of Advertising and Broadcast Advertisers Reports. Corrected data appear in the Mar. 26, 1984 issue; for description, see C2710-1.520, below.

MARKETING TO HISPANICS: MAKING THE MOST OF MEDIA

(p. M9-M11, M40) By Craig Endicott. Article, with 2 tables showing Hispanic market advertising expenditures by media; and TV, radio, and print advertising expenditures in top 10 Hispanic markets; 1983. Data are from *Hispanic Business*.

C2710–1.520: Mar. 26, 1984 (Vol. 55, No. 13)

MONTHLY adWATCH FEATURE

(p. 3, 72) "It's Everywhere, It's Everywhere." Covers Feb. 1984 survey. Includes text data on top advertisements recalled, for fast food and 2 other product categories.

CENSUS STUDY SHOWS MAJOR AGENCY GROWTH

(p. 3, 76) Article, with 1 table showing number of advertising agencies with payroll, and agency receipts, employment, and receipts per employee, for U.S. and top 10 States in each category, 1982 with comparison to 1977. Data are from Census Bureau.

CORRECTIONS AND CLARIFICATIONS

(p. 6) Includes corrected data for table on fast-food chains' TV advertising expenditures; for description, see C2710-1.519, above.

C2710–1.521: Mar. 28, 1984 (Vol. 55, No. 14)

[Issue price is $3.00.]

U.S. ADVERTISING AGENCY PROFILES, 1984 EDITION (ANNUAL ISSUE)

(p. 1-112) Annual special issue on income, accounts, and employees of 816 advertising agencies, 1983. Includes narrative profiles of each agency, grouped by income, each showing most or all of the following data: U.S. and international gross income; U.S. and foreign billings, with U.S. detail by type and media; subsidiaries; accounts lost and gained; and number of employees and offices, 1983, with comparisons to 1982.

Also includes profiles of 3 major holding companies (p. 6) whose subsidiaries are principally advertising agencies, with 1 table showing income and billings for each company compared to top individual agencies, 1983.

Issue also contains the following tables, all showing data by agency, in rank order:

[1-4] Top 10 agencies in world income, U.S. income, non-U.S. income, and world billings [1982-83]. (p. 1)

[5-6] Agencies with gross income of more than $15 million and of $5-15 million [shows world and U.S. gross income and billings, U.S. capitalized fees, and total employees, 1982-83]. (p. 12-16)

[7-8] Agencies with gross income of $1-5 million and under $1 million [1982-83]. (p. 16-20)

This is the 40th annual feature. Corrected data appear in the Apr. 23, 1984 issue; for description, see C2710-1.524, below.

C2710–1.522: Apr. 2, 1984 (Vol. 55, No. 15)

WOMEN WHO WORK

(p. M22) Table showing distribution of working women by age, occupational group, and income, 1984. Data are from 713 responses to a *Newsweek* survey of working women.

C2710–1.523: Apr. 16, 1984 (Vol. 55, No. 17)

QUARTERLY TABLE

[1] Ad pages in U.S. and Canadian farm publications, lst quarter 1984. (p. 73)

NESTLE, HILLS COFFEE DEAL GOOD NEWS, BAD NEWS

(p. 1, 82) By Gay Jervey and Jennifer Pendleton. Article, with 1 chart showing soluble and ground coffee market shares, by company, 1983. Data are from Lehman Brothers, Kuhn Loeb.

DIRECT MARKETERS OUTLINE GOALS, TROUBLES

(p. M10, M64) Article, with 2 tables showing top 25 companies ranked by sales generated through direct marketing, 1983 with comparison to 1982; and direct marketing advertising expenditures by media, 1977-83. Data are from Direct Marketing Assn.

SEEKING CREATIVITY AMONG THE TEASER ENVELOPES

(p. M11, M64-M66) By M. Howard Gelfand. Article on developments in direct response advertising. Data are from Direct Marketing Assn. Includes 1 table showing top 28 direct response advertising agencies ranked by gross billings, 1983 with comparison to 1982.

BROKERS MAKING LISTS AND CHECKING THEM TWICE

(p. M34-M39) By Eileen Norris. Article on mailing list brokers and the use of established mailing lists for direct marketing. Data are from Kobs and Brady Advertising. Includes 1 chart showing volume of direct marketing mail, 1982-83, with detail for 1st and 3rd class postage and nonprofit-sponsored mailings, 1983.

BARBECUE GRILL SALES BY OUTLET

(p. 78) Table showing distribution of barbecue grill sales, by retail outlet type (no date). Data are from Radio Advertising Bureau and *Merchandising*.

C2710–1.524: Apr. 23, 1984 (Vol. 55, No. 18)

MONTHLY TABLE

[2] Advertising pages for U.S., Canadian, and other foreign consumer publications, Mar. or Apr. 1984. (p. 97-98)

LAWYERS SEEN EASING TV USE

(p. 3, 103) By Maurine Christopher. Article, with 1 table showing top 10 law firms ranked by TV advertising expenditures, and indicating market areas for each, 1983 with comparison to 1982. Data are from TV Bureau of Advertising, based on data from Broadcast Advertisers Reports, Inc.

CORRECTIONS AND CLARIFICATIONS

(p. 6) Includes corrected data for advertising agency profiles issue; for description, see C2710-1.521, above. Correction covers accounts lost/gained at 2 agencies.

OVERSEAS LICENSING GROWING

(p. 55-56) By Dennis Chase. Article, with 1 undated table showing circulation and/or countries of actual or planned circulation, for licensed foreign editions of 13 U.S. magazines. Data are from *Advertising Age*.

FOREIGN AGENCY INCOME REPORT, ANNUAL FEATURE

(p. 57-80) Annual report, by Dennis Chase, on income, billings, and employees of 895 advertising agencies in 75 foreign countries. Data are from a 1983 *Advertising Age* survey.

Includes 3 tables showing world's top 15 agency groups and top 50 agencies ranked by gross income, with billings, 1983; and individual foreign agency gross income and billings in dollars and local currency, employment, and number of offices, arranged by country, 1983, with selected comparisons to 1982.

Corrected data appear in the Apr. 30, May 14, and July 16, 1984 issues; for descriptions, see C2710-1.526, C2710-1.530, and C2710-1.546, below.

C2710–1.525: Apr. 26, 1984 (Vol. 55, No. 19)

MARKETING PHENOMENON

(p. M6-M8) By Charlene Canape. Article on trends and outlook for the marketing/advertising industry. Data are from *Advertising Age* and American Assn of Advertising Agencies.

Includes 2 charts and 1 table showing advertising expenditures of aggregate top 100 and individual top 10 advertisers, various years 1954-82; and advertising agency employment, selected years 1967-2000.

BUSINESS PRESS: RESPONDING TO NEEDS IN A SPECIALIZED WAY

(p. M15-M17) By John Maes. Article, with 4 tables showing top 10 business magazines ranked by advertising pages, advertising revenue, total revenue, and circulation, 1982. Data are from Folio Publishing Corp.

C2710–1.526: Apr. 30, 1984 (Vol. 55, No. 20)

MONTHLY adWATCH FEATURE

(p. 2, 66) "Jackson Good, But Clara Stands Out." Covers Mar. 1984 survey. Includes 1 chart on advertisers with the greatest increase or decrease in consumer awareness; and text data on awareness of advertising for computer, tea, and beer categories.

CORRECTIONS AND CLARIFICATIONS

(p. 6) Includes corrected data for foreign agency income feature, described under C2710-1.524, above.

COFFEE MARKET STILL COOL, ANNUAL FEATURE

(p. 14) Annual article, by John C. Maxwell, Jr., with 1 table showing regular and instant coffee market shares, by company and brand, 1979-83. Data are from Lehman Brothers, Kuhn Loeb.

C2710–1.527: May 3, 1984 (Vol. 55, No. 21)

GOURMET POPCORN BUSINESS POPPING

(p. M52-M53) By Hortense Leon. Article, with 1 table showing popcorn sales volume, 1968 and 1983; and sales value and consumption (no date). Data are from Popcorn Institute.

C2710–1.528: May 7, 1984 (Vol. 55, No. 22)

CENSUS SEES STEEP RISE IN SHOP GROWTH

(p. 68) Brief article on advertising agency growth, with 4 tables showing number of agencies, receipts, employment, and payroll, selected years 1939-82. Data are from Census Bureau.

100,000-PLUS CIRCLE

(p. 74-75) Table ranking cities with over 100,-000 population, by population as of July 1, 1982, with comparison to July 1, 1980. Data are from Census Bureau.

C2710–1.529: May 10, 1984 (Vol. 55, No. 23)

[Data for the following articles are from an *Incentive Marketing* survey. For description of complete survey results, see C1200-4.503.]

PREMIUMS AND PROMOTIONS: WITHOUT A PLAN, THE CARROTS JUST DANGLE

(p. M15-M17, M48) By Ed Fitch. Article, with 1 table showing marketer expenditures for consumer premiums, by type, 1983 with percent change from 1982.

COMPANIES FIND A WINNER IN DEALER INCENTIVES

(p. M42-M44) By Mary McCabe English. Article, with 2 tables showing top 10 industries ranked by expenditures for dealer travel and merchandise incentives, 1983; and total corporate expenditures for travel and merchandise incentives for salespeople and dealers, 1982-83.

C2710–1.530: May 14, 1984 (Vol. 55, No. 24)

FINAL FIGURES: ADVERTISING SURGED IN '83, ANNUAL FEATURE

(p. 62-63) Annual article, by Robert J. Coen, with 2 tables showing actual value and monthly index of advertising expenditures by media, 1982 and/or 1983. Data are from McCann-Erickson, Inc.

Corrected table appears in the May 28, 1984 issue; for description, see C2710-1.533, below.

FOREIGN AGENCY ISSUE ADDENDA

(p. 76) Corrected data for annual feature on foreign advertising agencies. For description, see C2710-1.524, above.

C2710–1.531: May 17, 1984 (Vol. 55, No. 25)

MARKETING THE OLYMPICS: FEWER SPONSORS, BUT GREATER IMPACT

(p. M6) Article, with 1 undated chart showing top 10 corporate sponsors of the 1984 summer Olympic games, ranked by value of contributions. Data are from *Advertising Age*.

RESEARCH BUSINESS REVIEW: THE NATION'S TOP 35 MARKET RESEARCH COMPANIES, ANNUAL FEATURE

(p. M15-M39, passim) Annual report, by Jack J. Honomichl, on marketing/advertising research industry. Data are from *Advertising Age*.

Includes 1 chart and 2 tables showing top 35 research companies ranked by research revenue, and total worldwide and U.S. revenues for aggregate top 35 research companies and 35 advertising agencies, 1983 with comparisons to 1982; and research industry nominal and real revenue growth trends, 1975-83.

Also includes brief profile of each ranked company, including business description and employment data.

SKYROCKETING REVENUES

(p. M40) By Jack J. Honomichl. Article, with 1 table showing top 10 marketing/advertising research organizations ranked by revenue growth, 1979-83 period. Data are from *Advertising Age*.

C2710–1.532: May 21, 1984 (Vol. 55, No. 26)

MONTHLY TABLE

[2] Advertising pages for U.S., Canadian, and other foreign consumer publications, Apr. or May 1984. (p. 69-70)

SUNBELT CITIES LEAD GROWTH

(p. 40) Article, with 1 table showing top 50 MSAs ranked by population, July 1, 1982, with comparison to Apr. 1, 1980. Data are from Census Bureau.

C2710–1.533: May 28, 1984 (Vol. 55, No. 28)

MONTHLY adWATCH FEATURE

(p. 3, 49) "Eastern, IBM Ads Are Catching On." Covers Apr. 1984 survey. Includes text data on top advertisements recalled, for computers, airlines, and 3 other product categories.

CEREAL MILKS '83 GAINS, ANNUAL FEATURE

(p. 32) Annual article, by John C. Maxwell, Jr., with 2 tables showing share of cold cereal market volume and value, by company and brand, 1981-83. Data were compiled by the author.

U.S. ADVERTISING VOLUME

(p. 50) Corrected table for annual feature on advertising expenditures by media, described under C2710-1.530, above.

SEVERAL SHOPS OFF TO FAST '84 START, QUARTERLY FEATURE

(p. 59) Quarterly article, by Stewart Alter, on finances of publicly owned advertising agencies. Data are from agency reports. Includes 1 table showing income and revenues for 9 agencies, 1st quarter 1983-84.

Corrected data appear in the June 25, 1984 issue, for description, see C2710-1.541, below.

C2710–1.534: May 31, 1984 (Vol. 55, No. 29)

AD QUALITY GOOD; BELIEVABILITY LOW, RECURRING FEATURE

(p. 3, 54) Recurring article on consumer attitudes toward advertising, based on a Feb. 1984 survey of approximately 1,200 consumers conducted by SRI Research Center, Inc. for *Advertising Age*. Includes 2 tables showing response rates for questions on quality of advertising, with detail for TV advertising and comparisons to previous surveys.

NETWORKS STAKE SURVIVAL ON AD REVENUES

(p. 30-38) By Jack Myers. Article on cable TV as an advertising medium. Data are from Cabletelevision Advertising Bureau and Paul Kagan Associates. Includes 2 tables showing top 10 cable TV advertisers ranked by expenditures, 1st 9 months 1983; and top 10 cable networks/superstations ranked by advertising revenues, 1983-84.

C2710–1.535: June 4, 1984 (Vol. 55, No. 30)

FROZEN FISH TREAD WATER, SAMI SAYS

(p. 42) Article, with 1 table showing frozen fish sales shares by product type, 1979 and 1983. Data are from Selling Areas Marketing, Inc.

U.S. WINE INDUSTRY UNCORKS SALES HIKE, ANNUAL FEATURE

(p. 50) Annual article, by John C. Maxwell, Jr., with 1 table showing wine shipments and market shares for 34 leading domestic wine companies, all other domestic companies, and total imports, 1981-83, with 1982-83 rankings. Data were compiled by the author.

C2710–1.536: June 7, 1984 (Vol. 55, No. 31)

PERSONAL COMPUTER MARKETING GOES GLOBAL

(p. 8-9) By Daniel Burstein. Article, with 1 table showing microcomputer sales volume in 4 European countries, 1982 and 1986. Data are from Intelligent Electronics Europe.

CONSUMER ELECTRONICS: NEW TECHNOLOGIES GRAB FOR CONSUMER ATTENTION

(p. 15-17) By Udayan Gupta. Article, with 1 table showing sales of consumer electronics by product type, 1974-83. Data are from Electronic Industries Assn.

C2710–1.537: June 11, 1984 (Vol. 55, No. 32)

PET FOODS SEE SALES GAINS, ANNUAL FEATURE

(p. 49) Annual article, by John C. Maxwell, Jr., with 4 tables showing pet food sales by brand and product type, and sales and market share by manufacturer, 1982-83. Data were compiled by the author.

C2710–1.538: June 14, 1984 (Vol. 55, No. 33)

POSTAL RATE INCREASES DELIVER LATEST SKIRMISH

(p. 30-32) By Gary M. Levin. Article, with 1 table showing U.S. post office mail volume, weight, and revenues, by class, 1983. Data are from Mail Advertising Service Assn, and USPS.

C2710–1.539: June 18, 1984 (Vol. 55, No. 34)

MONTHLY TABLE

[2] Advertising pages for U.S., Canadian, and other foreign consumer publications, May or June 1984. (p. 81-82)

C2710–1.540: June 21, 1984 (Vol. 55, No. 35)

DEFENDING DEALER ADVERTISING

(p. 26-28) Article, with 1 table showing top 10 auto dealers ranked by TV advertising expenditures, 1983 with comparison to 1982. Data are from TV Bureau of Advertising, based on data from Broadcast Advertisers Reports, Inc.

STATES FINDING LOTTERIES ARE GOOD GAMBLES

(p. 48) Article, with 1 table showing advertising budgets for State lotteries by State, with advertising agency used, 1983/84. Data are from *Advertising Age*.

C2710–1.541: June 25, 1984 (Vol. 55, No. 36)

MONTHLY adWATCH FEATURE

(p. 4, 113) "BK Ads Trigger Awareness Gain." Covers May 1984 survey. Includes 1 table showing 7 advertisers with the greatest increase or decrease in consumer awareness during past month; and text data on awareness of advertising for fast food, and 3 other product categories.

CORRECTIONS AND CLARIFICATIONS

(p. 6) Includes corrected data for quarterly feature on finances of publicly owned advertising agencies. For description, see C2710-1.533, above.

INTERNATIONAL AGENCY/CLIENT REPORT

(p. 54-71) Article profiling 27 advertising agencies with mulinational clients accounting for over $3 million of business. Data are compiled by *Advertising Age*, from individual company reports.

Includes text data on agencies' total and non-U.S. gross income and billings, and number of affiliated agencies, 1983 with comparison to previous years. Each profile also includes tabular list of multinational clients, showing countries in which they advertise.

C2710–1.542: June 28, 1984 (Vol. 55, No. 37)

100 LEADING MEDIA COMPANIES, ANNUAL FEATURE

(p. 5-83) Annual report on finances and activities of the 100 companies with highest revenues from media properties, 1983. Data are from individual company reports and *Advertising Age* estimates.

Contents:

a. Introductory article (p. 8-10); and 1 table ranking top 100 companies by media revenues, and also showing total revenues, 1982-83 (p. 12-15).

b. Company profiles, including lists of media properties owned, interspersed with 4 tables showing the following data by profiled company: newspaper, broadcast, magazine, and cable TV revenues, 1982-83; and circulation of company's top newspaper, number of radio and TV stations owned by type, advertising revenues for company's top magazine, and cable subscribers, 1983 (p. 16-83).

Also includes a summary of broadcast and print property purchases by top 100 companies during 1983-84, including buyer, seller, property, and price (p. 48).

This is the 4th annual report. Corrected data appear in the Aug. 13, 1984 issue; for description, see C2710-1.551, below.

C2710–1.543: July 2, 1984 (Vol. 55, No. 38)

BIG FAST-FOOD CHAINS GLUTTONS ON SPENDING, RECURRING FEATURE

(p. 3, 37) Recurring article, by Scott Hume, with 1 table showing network and local TV advertising expenditures, for top 15 fast food chains ranked by network/local expenditures, and for total fast food industry, 1st quarter 1984 with comparison to 1st quarter 1983. Data are from TV Bureau of Advertising and Broadcast Advertisers Reports.

C2710–1.544: July 5, 1984 (Vol. 55, No. 39)

LATIN AMERICAN MEDIA BREAKDOWN

(p. 22) Table showing advertising expenditures, and distribution by media; ownership structure for TV, newspapers, and radio; and advertising commission rates and structure; all for 7 Latin American countries, 1983. Data are from *Advertising Age*.

C2710–1.545: July 9, 1984 (Vol. 55, No. 40)

MONTHLY TABLE

[1] Flash Report: newspaper advertising investment for Apr. 1984. (p. 50)

SMOKELESS TOBACCO MARKET EVENING OUT, ANNUAL FEATURE

(p. 56) Annual article, by John C. Maxwell, Jr., with 2 tables showing smokeless tobacco sales volume by product type, by company and brand, 1981-83. Data are from A. G. Becker Paribas.

For similar data on cigars, see C2710-1.546, below.

C2710–1.546: July 16, 1984 (Vol. 55, No. 42)

QUARTERLY TABLE

[1] Ad pages in U.S. and Canadian farm publications, 2nd quarter 1984. (p. 62)

CORRECTIONS AND CLARIFICATIONS

(p. 6) Includes corrected data for annual feature on foreign advertising agencies.

For description of feature, see C2710-1.524, above.

SMOKE SEEMS TO CLEAR FOR CIGAR INDUSTRY, ANNUAL FEATURE

(p. 30) Annual article, by John C. Maxwell, Jr., with 1 table showing sales volume for large/small and little cigars, by company and brand, 1981-83. Data were compiled by the author.

For similar data on smokeless tobacco, see C2710-1.545, above.

C2710–1.547: July 23, 1984 (Vol. 55, No. 44)

MONTHLY TABLE

[2] Advertising pages for U.S., Canadian, and other foreign consumer publications, June or July 1984. (p. 73-74)

C2710–1.548: July 26, 1984 (Vol. 55, No. 45)

LIQUOR MARKETING: BURSTING THROUGH THE CLUTTER

(p. 15, 17) Article, with 3 tables showing top 10 liquor brands and companies ranked by advertising expenditures, and including rank order based on sales for top brands, 1983 with comparison to 1982; and ranking of liquor types by market share, 1983 with comparison to 1975. Data are from Impact, Inc.

DISTILLERS TRY TO STIR UP INTEREST IN PREMIX MARKET

(p. 41-42) By Eileen Norris. Article, with 1 table showing top 10 types of premixed cocktails ranked by sales volume, 1st 11 months 1983 with percent change from same period of 1982. Data are from *U.S. News and World Report*.

C2710–1.549: July 30, 1984 (Vol. 55, No. 46)

MONTHLY adWATCH FEATURE

(p. 3, 58) "Pepsi Ads Top List in Ad Awareness." Covers June 1984 survey. Includes 1 chart showing 9 advertisers with the greatest increase or decrease in consumer awareness; and text data on top 10 advertisements recalled, and awareness of advertising in 22 product categories.

C2710–1.550: Aug. 9, 1984 (Vol. 55, No. 49)

MASS MERCHANDISERS MOVING UP

(p. 12) By Belinda Hulin-Salkin. Article, with 1 chart showing retail sales for 10 types of business, 1982-83, with percent change from 1981. Data are from Dept of Commerce.

NEWCOMERS TO WATCH: 'V,' 'LOST LOVES,' AND 'MURDER'

(p. 27) Article, with 1 chart showing advertising agencies' predictions of audience shares for prime time TV network programs, 4th quarter 1984. Data were compiled by *Advertising Age*.

C2710–1.551: Aug. 13, 1984 (Vol. 55, No. 50)

CORRECTIONS AND CLARIFICATIONS

(p. 6) Includes corrected data for annual feature on 100 leading media companies.

For feature description, see C2710-1.542, above.

MERGER SIDETRACKS MAJOR NEWSPAPER WAR IN SINGAPORE

(p. 38, 42) By Jack Burton. Article, with 1 undated table showing circulation and advertising rates for Singapore's 7 newspapers. Data are from *Advertising Age*. Corrected data appear in the Oct. 1, 1984 issue; for description see C2710-1.563, below.

AD-TO-SALES RATIOS LISTED BY INDUSTRY, ANNUAL FEATURE

(p. 44) Annual article, with 1 table showing advertising expenditure growth rates, and expenditures as percent of sales and of gross margin, for 258 industries (primarily SIC 4-digit), 1983. Data are from an annual study by Schonfeld and Associates, based on over 5,000 10-K Reports filed with the SEC.

C2710–1.552: Aug. 16, 1984 (Vol. 55, No. 51)

SHOPS' 2nd QUARTER STRONG, BUT 'GOOFY,' QUARTERLY FEATURE

(p. 2, 65) Quarterly article, by Stewart Alter, on finances of publicly owned advertising agencies. Data are from agency reports. Includes 1 table showing income and revenues for 8 agencies, 2nd quarter and 1st half 1983-84.

C2710–1.553: Aug. 20, 1984 (Vol. 55, No. 52)

MONTHLY TABLES

[1] Flash Report: newspaper advertising investment for May 1984. (p. 66)

[2] Advertising pages for U.S., Canadian, and other foreign consumer publications, July or Aug. 1984. (p. 69-70)

C2710–1.554: Aug. 23, 1984 (Vol. 55, No. 53)

[Issue cover incorrectly reads Aug. 27, 1984.]

FOR THE RICH, HOME IS WHERE THE HEART IS

(p. 12-13) By B. G. Yovovich. Article, with 1 table ranking top 10 counties by per capita income, 1980. Also includes list of top 10 SMSAs based on income. Data are from Census Bureau.

NEIGHBORHOODS TELL LIFE STYLE

(p. 12-13) Article, with 1 table showing top 20 central city neighborhoods with population 25,000/over ranked by per capita income, and including number of households, population per household, percent of adults with college degree, and percent of workers employed in downtown area, 1980. Data are from Census Bureau.

C2710–1.555: Aug. 27, 1984 (Vol. 55, No. 54)

MONTHLY adWATCH FEATURE

(p. 4, 60) "While Others Broil or Beef, Big Mac Stays on the Top." Covers July 1984 survey. Includes 1 chart showing 6 advertisers with the greatest increase or decrease in consumer awareness; and text data on awareness of advertising in fast food and 7 other product categories.

HIGH-TECH MAGAZINES COOL OFF, SEMIANNUAL FEATURE

(p. 54) Semiannual article, with 1 table showing top 10 magazines ranked by circulation, 1st half 1983-84. Data are from Audit Bureau of Circulations.

C2710–1.556: Aug. 30, 1984 (Vol. 55, No. 55)

POLLED RETAILERS STAMP APPROVAL ON DIRECT MAIL

(p. 8) Article, with 1 undated chart showing distribution of retailers by preferred advertising medium. Data are based on interviews with approximately 400 retail store executives, conducted by Aaron Cohen Marketing Services.

HOME IMPROVEMENT MARKETING

(p. 11-14) Compilation of articles, with 2 tables and 1 chart showing top 10 home improvement retailers ranked by sales, and including number of stores, 1983; home improvement sales for total and do-it-yourself markets, quinquennially 1970-90; and distribution of home improvement consumers by preferred retail outlet type, 1984.

Data are from *Building Supply and Home Centers,* Do-It-Yourself Research Institute, and *National Home Center News.*

C2710–1.557: Sept. 10, 1984 (Vol. 55, No. 58)

NESTLE UPS ANTE FOR FOOD MERGERS

(p. 1, 100) By Nancy Giges and Gay Jervey. Article, with 1 chart showing world's top 6 food marketers ranked by sales, 1983. Data are from *Fortune* magazine.

C2710–1.558: Sept. 13, 1984 (Vol. 55, No. 59)

[Data for the following 3 articles are from Radio Advertising Bureau.]

RADIO: MEDIUM IS ALIVE AND WELL IN THE AGE OF VIDEO

(p. 11-13) By J. Fred MacDonald. Article, with 1 chart showing radio advertising revenues, selected years 1960-83.

TV TESTS TRIED AND TRUE SPOTS

(p. 13) By Marie Spadoni. Article, with 1 table showing top 15 spot radio advertisers ranked by expenditures, 1983.

BROADCAST MEDIUM FILLS VOIDS IN ADVERTISING

(p. 28) By Karrie Jacobs. Article, with 1 chart showing top 10 network radio advertisers ranked by expenditures, 1983.

C2710–1.559: Sept. 14, 1984 (Vol. 55, No. 60)

**100 Leading
National Advertisers
(Annual Issue)**

Special annual issue on 1983 media expenditures of the 100 largest U.S. advertisers, including summary firm profiles. Each profile includes 1983 data and 1982 comparisons for most or all of the following: sales, earnings, and advertising expenditures by media. Data are based on reports from individual companies, statistical services, and trade assns.

Issue contains an analytical summary article; 100 profiles, arranged alphabetically; and 12 tables and 1 chart listed below, interspersed throughout the issue .

TABLES AND CHART:

[1] Leading advertisers by rank, [top 100 ranked by total advertising expenditures, 1983]. (p. 1)

[2] Advertising expenditures as a percentage of U.S. sales, [and value of U.S. advertising expenditures, U.S. and worldwide sales, and worldwide earnings, for top 100 advertisers, grouped by type of product or service, 1983]. (p. 8)

[3] Analysis of media spending by 100 leading national advertisers [for newspapers, magazines, farm publications, spot and network TV and radio, outdoor, and all other media, all by company, 1982-83]. (p. 16-17)

[4-12] Top 25 advertisers in newspapers (p. 28); magazines (p. 44); farm publications (p. 66); spot TV (p. 78); network TV (p. 86); spot radio (p. 114); network radio (p. 122); outdoor (p. 132); and cable TV (p. 136); [all showing advertising expenditures, by company, 1982-83].

[13] 100 leading national advertisers' share of measured advertising expenditures [aggregate expenditures of 100 leading and all other national advertisers, for 8 media, 1982-83]. [chart] (p. 144)

C2710–1.560: Sept. 17, 1984 (Vol. 55, No. 61)

MONTHLY TABLE

[2] Advertising pages for U.S., Canadian, and other foreign consumer publications, Aug. or Sept. 1984. (p. 59-60) [Corrected data appear in the Oct. 8, 1984 issue, for description, see C2710-1.564, below.]

OLYMPIC LINKS PROVE BARGAINS

(p. 3, 80) By Scott Hume. Article on consumer awareness of advertising for sponsors of the 1984 Winter and Summer Olympic games. Data are based on responses of 1,255 consumers to a Aug. 1984 SRI Research Center, Inc. survey. Includes text data and 1 chart.

C2710–1.561: Sept. 24, 1984 (Vol. 55, No. 63)

MONTHLY TABLE

[1] Flash Report: newspaper advertising investment for June 1984. (p. 90)

C2710–1.562: Sept. 27, 1984 (Vol. 55, No. 64)

MONTHLY adWATCH FEATURE

(p. 3, 62) "Summer Ads Portend Active Fall." Covers Aug. 1984 survey. Includes 1 chart showing advertisers with the greatest increase or decrease in consumer awareness; and text data on awareness of advertising in 7 product categories.

GROCERY MARKETING: POPULARITY OF PREMIUM DESSERTS, SWEETS SOARS

(p. 11-13) By Mary McCabe English. Article, with 3 tables showing percent of women purchasing dessert/sugar-related products by type (no date); and supermarket shoppers' concern about food nutritional content, with detail for specific ingredients/food qualities, 1983-84; all with detail by various sociodemographic characteristics.

Data are from Simmons Market Research Bureau, and an annual Food Marketing Institute (FMI) survey of food shoppers. Full FMI survey report is covered in SRI under A4950-3.

C2710–1.563: Oct. 1, 1984 (Vol. 55, No. 65)

IRREGULARLY RECURRING TABLE

[1] Newspaper ad linage, May 1984. (p. 66)

CORRECTIONS AND CLARIFICATIONS

(p. 6) Includes corrected data for article on Singapore's newspapers.

For article description, see C2710-1.551, above.

C2710–1.564: Oct. 8, 1984 (Vol. 55, No. 67)

IRREGULARLY RECURRING TABLE

[1] Newspaper ad linage, June 1984. (p. 76)

CONSUMERS VOTE FOR POINT-OF-SALE, RECURRING FEATURE

(p. 3, 104) Recurring article on consumer attitudes toward advertising, based on a July 1984 survey of 1,252 consumers conducted by SRI Research Center, Inc. for *Advertising Age.*

Includes 2 tables showing consumer reliance on advertising for major and daily purchases, by media, with comparison to previous surveys; and text data on attitudes toward advertising quality.

SENTIMENTAL SPOTS PAYING OFF FOR PEARLE

(p. 4, 92) By Sarah Stiansen. Article, with 1 chart ranking top 5 eyecare/eyewear retail chains by revenues, and including number of outlets, 1983. Data are from Eppler, Guerin and Turner.

CORRECTIONS AND CLARIFICATIONS

(p. 6) Includes corrected data for monthly table [2] on advertising pages in consumer publications.

For table description, see C2710-1.560, above.

C2710–1.565: Oct. 11, 1984 (Vol. 55, No. 68)

DIRECT TACTICS GET POLITICIANS' VOTES

(p. 50-53) By Richard Edel. Article, with 1 table showing political campaign revenue, total for 1984 election, and by source (including political organizations, House/Senate races, and Republican and Democratic Parties) for 1980 and 1982 elections. Data are from Federal Election Commission.

C2710–1.566: Oct. 15, 1984 (Vol. 55, No. 69)

IRREGULARLY RECURRING TABLE

[1] Newspaper ad linage, July 1984. (p. 82)

QUARTERLY TABLE

[1] Ad pages in U.S. and Canadian farm publications, 3rd quarter 1984. (p. 92)

C2710–1.567: Oct. 18, 1984 (Vol. 55, No. 70)

MAGAZINES: GETTING A READING ON THE BABY BOOM

(p. 11-13) By B. G. Yovovich. Article, with 1 table ranking top 25 magazines by total revenue, and including advertising revenue and pages, and average circulation, 1983 with comparison to 1982. Data are from Folio Publishing Corp.

WOMEN KEEP REPUBLICANS ON THEIR TOES

(p. 54) By Peter Francese. Article, with 1 chart showing number of working women per 100 working men, in 4 income groups, 1983. Data are from American Demographics.

C2710–1.568: Oct. 22, 1984 (Vol. 55, No. 71)

MONTHLY TABLE

[2] Advertising pages for U.S., Canadian, and other foreign consumer publications, Sept. or Oct. 1984. (p. 83-84)

C2710–1.569: Oct. 25, 1984 (Vol. 55, No. 72)

SEEING THAT SPECIAL EVENTS MEASURE UP

(p. 20-24) By Mary McCabe English. Article, with 1 table and 1 chart showing advertising and sales promotion shares of marketing expenditures, 1976 and 1979-83; and distribution of sales promotion expenditures by type, 1983. Data are from Russell D. Bowman of John Blair Marketing.

C2710–1.570: Oct. 29, 1984 (Vol. 55, No. 73)

MONTHLY adWATCH FEATURE

(p. 12, 82) "Fast-Food's Favorites Fire Fast, Furious Flurries." Covers Sept. 1984 survey. Includes 1 chart and text data showing awareness of advertising in fast food and 9 other product categories.

ALDA STAYS ON TOP OF HIS 'Q'

(p. 72) By James P. Forkan. Article on popularity of TV performers, based on viewer preference/familiarity ratings ("Q" scores). Data are from a survey conducted by Marketing Evaluations. Includes 1 table showing "Q" scores for top 12 performers overall, with comparisons to scores among black and Hispanic viewers, 1984.

C2710–2   PENSIONS AND INVESTMENT AGE

Biweekly.   Approx. 55 p.
Oversized.
ISSN 0273-5466.
LC 74-648522.
SRI/MF/excerpts, shipped quarterly

Biweekly journal reporting on trends and developments in the management and investment of institutional pension, employee benefit, profit-sharing, and other tax-exempt funds. Covers corporate, State and local government, Taft-Hartley, and other major funds.

Data are from Pensions & Investments Performance Evaluation Report (PIPER), original surveys, and Computer Directions Advisors and other investment research firms.

Issues include numerous news and feature articles, occasionally with statistics; summaries of new security issues and corporate cash management funds; and narrative editorial depts. Recurring statistical features include the following:

a. Quarterly review of performance of bank and insurance company pooled equity and fixed-income funds, described below.

b. Quarterly feature on performance of pooled special equity funds; and semiannual article on cash/short-term holdings of Fortune 100 corporations.

c. Annual features, including ranking of 1,000 largest employee benefit funds (Jan.); analysis of pension fund and financial data for Fortune 100 companies (Aug.); and profiles of U.S., Canadian, and international investment advisors.

Features with substantial statistical content are described as they appear, under "Statistical Features;" page location and latest period of coverage for quarterly review of pooled equity and fixed-income funds are also noted. Each issue of the journal is reviewed, but an abstract is published in SRI monthly issues only when statistical features appear.

Availability: Pensions and Investment Age, Circulation Department, 740 Rush St., Chicago IL 60611, $67.00 per yr., single copy $3.50, special issue prices vary; SRI/MF/excerpts for all portions covered under "Statistical Features;" shipped quarterly.

Issues reviewed during 1984: Oct. 31, 1983-Oct. 29, 1984 (P) (Vol. 11, Nos. 22-26; Vol. 12, Nos. 1-22).

QUARTERLY REVIEW:

POOLED EQUITY AND FIXED-INCOME FUNDS

Quarterly review of bank and insurance company pooled equity and fixed-income funds' investment performance through quarter ending 2-3 months prior to publication date. Data are from PIPER which ranks the performance of approximately 230 funds.

Includes 2 charts and 4 tables showing rates of return for equity and fixed-income funds, as follows: high, low, median, and 1st and 3rd quartile rates; and rates for individual funds in top quartile and for top 10 funds in each of 4-8 asset size groups; with selected comparisons to Salomon Brothers, Standard & Poor's 500, and Lehman Brothers, Kuhn Loeb Government/Corporate Indexes; generally for 3-month and 1-, 3-, 5-, and 10-year periods ending with last month of quarter of coverage.

Feature for 4th quarter includes 2 additional tables showing rates for all funds.
Also includes 1-3 accompanying articles.

STATISTICAL FEATURES:

C2710–2.501: Oct. 31, 1983 (Vol. 11, No. 22)

WHO OWNS CORPORATE AMERICA?

(p. 23-68, passim) By Pavan Sahgal. Article analyzing trends in stock market participation by pension funds and other institutional investors. Data sources include Computer Directions Advisors, Inc.; NYSE; and Federal Reserve System Board of Governors. Includes 1 chart and 4 tables showing the following:

a. Average daily NYSE large block transactions, selected years 1965-83; date, stock traded, and size, for 10 largest NYSE transactions all-time and in 1st 9 months 1983; and top 20 stocks ranked by percent institutional ownership, year end 1981.

b. Top 50 financial management companies ranked by market value of equity, with number of stocks held (no date); and aggregate assets of households, foreign investors, mutual funds, insurance companies, private and government pension funds, and savings institutions, selected years 1960-2000.

ASSET GROWTH SOARS IN DECADE

(p. 31) Article on corporate pension fund asset growth, with 1 table showing assets of 10 largest funds, 1972 and 1982.

INSTITUTIONS WRESTLE FOR LION'S SHARE OF MARKET

(p. 47-48) By Richard J. Gillespie. Article, with 2 charts comparing financial management market shares of banks, insurance companies, and investment management firms, 1975 and 1981.

C2710–2.502: Nov. 14, 1983 (Vol. 11, No. 23)

THIRD QUARTER TOP PERFORMERS FOR EQUITY AND FIXED INCOME, QUARTERLY FEATURE

(p. 13-80, passim) For quarter ended Sept. 30, 1983. For data description, see C2710-2, above. Also includes data for top quartile special equity funds.

SUN MAY BE RISING ON SES

(p. 49) By Graham Bamping. Article on Stock Exchange of Singapore Ltd. (SES). Data are from InterSec Research Corp. Includes 1 table and 1 chart showing Capital International Singapore index compared to Standard & Poor's 500 stock index, 1973-82; and exchange rate trends for Singapore vs. U.S. dollar, 1976-82.

C2710–2.503: Nov. 28, 1983 (Vol. 11, No. 24)

LARGEST INDUSTRIALS' CASH HOLDINGS GREW, SEMIANNUAL FEATURE

(p. 17, 19) Semiannual article on cash holdings (cash/short-term investments) among Fortune 100 largest industrial companies, as of June 30, 1983. Data are compiled by Wright Investors' Service.

Includes 3 tables showing holdings as of June 1982-83 for 10 companies with largest current holdings, and with largest increases and decreases.

MERGERS, ACQUISITIONS NUMBER 677 IN 3rd QUARTER; NEAR RECORD

(p. 33, 36) Article, with 1 table showing number of divestitures, and acquisitions of publicly traded, privately held, and foreign companies, Jan.-Sept. 1982-83. Data are from W. T. Grimm and Company.

C2710–2.504: Dec. 12, 1983 (Vol. 11, No. 25)

SURVEY SHOWS 1 OF 6 CITIZENS A SHAREHOLDER

(p. 3, 55) By Pavan Sahgal. Article, with 1 chart showing number of individuals directly holding corporate stocks, selected years 1952-83. Data are from NYSE.

C2710–2.505: Jan. 23, 1984 (Vol. 12, No. 2)

TOP 1,000 FUNDS, ANNUAL FEATURE

Annual compilation of articles, profiles, and tables on the investment activities and performance of major nonfederal employee benefit funds, including pension, profit-sharing, and thrift plans, for year ended Sept. 1983, with summary comparisons to 1982. Covers corporate, public, union, and miscellaneous plans.

Data are from Money Market Directories Inc. and surveys by *Pensions and Investment Age.*

Contents:

a. "Assets Surge to $806 Billion." Article, with 1 chart showing aggregate asset mix of top 200 funds by type of fund, 1982-83. (p. 3, 14)

b. "Contributions to Top Funds Drop for 2nd Year," by Kimberly Blanton. Article, with 2 charts showing aggregate asset mix of top 200 funds, 1982-83; and aggregate asset value of top 1,000 funds, and of top 200 by type of fund, 1981-83. (p. 13)

c. Top 1,000 funds/sponsors, ranked by asset size, 1983. 2 tables. (p. 16-20)

d. Profiles of the top 200 funds, each with 1 table showing asset value by type of plan, employer contributions, and benefit payments, 1983; and brief description of investment portfolio and management. (p. 22-76)

e. Asset size and rank, 1983, for: top 10-25 corporate, public, union, and miscellaneous funds; funds with equity real estate, international equity, and fixed income investments; top 25 profit sharing and 25 pension plans; sponsors of internally managed plans (also shows asset mix); and pension funds with guaranteed income contracts (GIC) from life insurance companies, and with indexed and dedicated assets. 13 tables. (p. 28-68, passim)

f. Aggregate assets for top 25-1,000 funds and top 200 pension funds, and for funds with in-house management, indexing, and 4 types of investments; and number of sponsors with 8 types of investments; 1982-83. 1 table. (p. 32)

g. Listings of funds investing in venture capital, and oil/gas. 2 tables. (p. 46, 72)

C2710–2.506: Feb. 6, 1984 (Vol. 12, No. 3)

SALOMON BROS. LEAD UNDERWRITER IN 1983

(p. 13-16) By Pavan Saghal. Article on securities underwriting activity by brokerage houses, 1983. Data are from Securities Data Corp.

Includes 11 tables showing aggregate value of capital raised by type of security underwritten, 1981-83; and top 15 brokerage houses ranked by value of all, common stock, straight debt, initial public offering, and shelf registered underwritings, each including number of shares involved and shown for underwritings credited to managers/co-managers and to lead managers only, 1983.

C2710–2.507: Feb. 20, 1984 (Vol. 12, No. 4)

FIRMS TURN TO BASICS IN SLACK BOND MARKET: POOLED EQUITY AND FIXED-INCOME FUNDS, QUARTERLY FEATURE

(p. 17-25) For quarter ended Dec. 31, 1983. For data description, see C2710-2 above. Also includes rates for all funds.

C2710–2.508: Mar. 5, 1984 (Vol. 12, No. 5)

FUNDS HAVE GOOD YEAR DESPITE TECHNOLOGY DROP, QUARTERLY FEATURE

(p. 13-14) Quarterly article, by Barry B. Burr, with 1 chart and 2 tables showing rates of return for bank and insurance company pooled special equity funds, as follows: high, low, median, and 1st and 3rd quartile rates; and rates for 100 individual funds, with rankings for top quartile funds, and comparisons to Standard and Poor's 500; generally for 3-month, and 1, 3, 5, and 10-year periods ended Dec. 1983.

Data are from *Pensions and Investments Performance Evaluation Report (PIPER).*

This is the first quarterly article.

C2710–2.509: Mar. 19, 1984 (Vol. 12, No. 6)

FINDING THE DOLLARS AND THE DEALS

(p. 29-41) Profiles of 44 investment banking firms and 22 banks handling corporate equity and debt financings, mergers/acquisitions, leveraged buyouts, private placements, and other financing transactions, primarily 1983. Data are from a *Pensions and Investments Age* survey.

Each profile includes most or all of the following: volume and value of financing activity, by type; services offered; total and excess capital (investment banking firms); assets, legal lending limit, and/or outstanding loans (banks); and number of employees and offices. Also includes brief introductory article.

HOW TO TRANSLATE OVERSEAS RETURNS

(p. 48) By Rick Nelson. Article, with 1 table comparing changes in selected foreign and U.S. stock exchange indexes, 1972-82 period.

C2710–2.510: Apr. 2, 1984 (Vol. 12, No. 7)

INTERNATIONAL MARKETS PROVE FRUITFUL SHOPPING

(p. 3, 42) By Rose Darby. Article, with 1 table showing value of foreign investments for 17 large corporate pension funds, 3rd quarter 1982-83. Data were compiled by *Pensions & Investment Age.*

Data correction appears in the Apr. 16, 1984 issue; for description, see C2710-2.511, below.

C2710–2.511: Apr. 16, 1984 (Vol. 12, No. 8)

CORRECTIONS

(p. 4) Data correction for article on foreign investments of pensions funds, appearing in the Apr. 2, 1984 issue; for description, see C2710-2.510, above.

FINANCING HITS JAN. RECORD, SETTLES

(p. 10) Article on State/local bond market developments, with 1 table showing top 50 underwriters of State/local governments ranked by underwriting value, 1980-83. Data are from Public Securities Assn.

C2710–2.512: Apr. 30, 1984 (Vol. 12, No. 9)

[Special issue price is $4.00.]

TOTAL ASSETS INCREASE TO MORE THAN $1 TRILLION, ANNUAL FEATURE

(p. 15-106) Annual article profiling assets and operations of 648 investment management organizations, including commercial banks, insurance companies, and investment counselors, as of Jan. 1, 1984.

Data are from a survey by *Pensions and Investment Age.*

Contents:

a. Narrative summary, with 5 charts showing aggregate data on asset size and mix of top 100 organizations, and asset mix of top 200 organizations, with selected comparisons to Jan. 1982-83. (p. 15-16)

b. Ranking of all organizations by tax-exempt assets managed (and also showing total assets managed), and of top 100 organizations by total assets managed. 2 tables. (p. 20-24)

c. Profiles of individual organizations, each with 1 table showing total, tax-exempt, and fully discretionary tax-exempt assets managed; minimum and types of accounts managed; number of tax-exempt clients, portfolio managers, and research personnel; and, where applicable, size of real estate, master trust and custody, and international assets managed. (p. 26-106)

d. Summary data, including average number of stocks followed, and number of managers using options, stock index futures, and fixed-income futures; and top 25 banks/trust companies, insurance companies, investment counselors, master trust banks, and real estate and international managers, ranked by assets managed. 7 tables. (p. 30-52, passim)

e. List of organizations by location. (p. 42, 46)

C2710–2.513: May 14, 1984 (Vol. 12, No. 10)

DEFENSIVE STRATEGIES CAPTURE TOP RETURNS: POOLED EQUITY AND FIXED-INCOME FUNDS, QUARTERLY FEATURE

(p. 13-17) For quarter ended Mar. 31, 1984. For data description, see C2710-2 above.

C2710–2.514: May 28, 1984 (Vol. 12, No. 11)

MASTER TRUST DIRECTORY, ANNUAL FEATURE

(p. 19, 22-33) Annual feature profiling 42 U.S. and Canadian master trust/master custodial banks controlling $300 million or more in master trust/custodial assets. Data are compiled by *Pensions & Investment Age* from survey responses of approximately 170 pension fund executives.

Profiles include all or most of the following data: value of master trust, master custodial, and other assets; number of clients; smallest and largest clients' asset size; type of services offered; accounting and reporting practices; and fee structure.

Also includes related article (p. 19, 33) with 2 tables ranking master trust/master custodial assets of the banks profiled.

RECOVERY BOOSTS '83 CASH HOLDINGS, SEMIANNUAL FEATURE

(p. 39) Semiannual article on cash holdings (cash/short-term investments) among *Fortune* 100 largest industrial companies, as of Dec. 31, 1983. Data are compiled by Wright Investors' Service.

Includes 3 tables showing holdings as of Dec. 1982-83, for 10 companies with largest current holdings, and with largest increases and decreases.

REPUBLICBANK DALLAS LEADS SPECIAL EQUITY, QUARTERLY FEATURE

(p. 45) Quarterly article, with 1 chart and 1 table showing rates of return for bank and insurance company pooled special equity funds, as follows: high, low, median, and 1st and 3rd quartile rates; and rates for top quartile individual funds, with rankings and comparison to Standard & Poor's 500; generally for 3-month, and 1-, 3-, 5-, and 10-year periods ended Mar. 31, 1984.

Data are from *Pensions & Investments Performance Evaluation Report (PIPER).*

C2710–2.515: June 11, 1984 (Vol. 12, No. 12)

ADDENDUM

(p. 24-25) Addendum to annual article profiling assets and operations of investment management organizations. Addendum presents profiles of 11 additional organizations. For description of annual article, see C2710-2.512 above.

C2710–2.516: June 25, 1984 (Vol. 12, No. 13)

INTERNATIONAL DIRECTORY, ANNUAL FEATURE

(p. 25-47) Annual profiles of approximately 100 U.S.- and foreign-based investment management firms controlling more than $14.6 billion in international market investments by U.S. tax-exempt institutions, as of Jan. 1, 1984. Data are from a *Pensions and Investment Age* survey.

Profiles generally include text statistics on all or some of the following: amount invested in international markets, and countries of investment concentration; total assets managed; number of clients; and investment approach.

Also includes related articles (p. 26, 47) with 3 tables showing top 25 international management firms ranked by U.S. tax-exempt assets, 1984; top 10 firms ranked by increase in international assets, 1982-83; and average portfolio weightings for top 10 countries, 1984.

C2710–2.517: July 9, 1984 (Vol. 12, No. 14)

CANADIAN DIRECTORY, ANNUAL FEATURE

(p. 21-28) Annual feature, for 1984, on Canadian investment management firms. Includes 1 table ranking top 10 firms by tax-exempt assets under management, and profiles of 60 firms, each generally showing: name and address; value of total, tax-exempt, fully discretionary, and real estate assets; minimum separate account size; number of tax-exempt clients, portfolio managers, and research staff; and distribution of tax-exempt assets by type of security.

C2710–2.518: July 23, 1984 (Vol. 12, No. 15)

SALOMON BROS. TROUNCES COMPETITION, RECURRING FEATURE

(p. 25-26) Recurring article, by Kimberly Blanton, with 3 tables showing net underwriting proceeds for common and preferred stocks, and bonds, 1st half 1983-84; and top 10 investment management firms ranked by volume of domestic debt and equity underwritings, 1st half 1984. Data are from Securities Data Corp.

C2710–2.519: Aug. 6, 1984 (Vol. 12, No. 16)

ASSET GROWTH EXCEEDED LIABILITIES IN 1983, ANNUAL FEATURE

(p. 3, 36-37, 62) Annual article, by Kimberly Blanton, analyzing pension fund and corporate financial data for *Fortune* 100 companies, 1983. Data were compiled by Wright Investors' Service from company annual financial reports.

Includes 1 detailed table showing the following for each company: pension fund total and vested benefits, assets, vested funding status, and expenses; rate of return assumed in computing pension benefits; corporate net worth, assets, and operating income; and selected ratios; 1983, with selected comparisons to 1982.

Also includes 3 summary tables ranking top 5 companies by 3 selected indicators of pension fund financial condition.

This is the 2nd annual article.

DIRECTORY OF CONSULTANTS, ANNUAL FEATURE

(p. 39-48) Annual feature, for 1984, profiling 69 investment management consulting firms, generally including the following for each firm: types of services offered, number of clients, and size of professional staff.

Data are from a *Pensions and Investment Age* survey.

Also includes 3 related articles (p. 39, 48-50).

C2710–2.520: Aug. 20, 1984 (Vol. 12, No. 17)

POOLED EQUITY AND FIXED-INCOME FUNDS, QUARTERLY FEATURE

(p. 3, 15-21) For quarter ended June 30, 1984. For data description, see C2710-2 above.

CASH MANAGEMENT: SURVEY FINDS 4 FAVORITES

(p. 35, 38) By Richard J. Gillespie. Article, with 1 table showing the following for 23 large cash management banks: asset value, and equity/asset, primary capital/asset, profitability, liquidity, and excess problem loan ratios, as of Dec. 31, 1983. Also includes lists of 2-6 banks with highest performance ratings in 12 cash management areas.

Data are from a 1984 *Pensions and Investment Age* survey of 180 cash managers representing the largest U.S. corporations, and from Veribanc Inc.

RETURNS BETTER OVERSEAS

(p. 41) Article, with 1 table showing estimated overall equity returns for investments in U.S. and 17 foreign countries, 1st half 1984. Data are from Phillips & Drew International Ltd.

C2710–2.521: Sept. 3, 1984 (Vol. 12, No. 18)

ERISA: ERODING OR HOLDING ITS GROUND?

(p. 3, 75-76) By Joel Chernoff. Article on corporate pension plan developments under the Employee Retirement Income Security Act (ERISA). Data are from company reports and American Council of Life Insurance.

Includes 1 chart and 2 tables showing number of private pension plans and participants, and value of assets, for defined contribution and benefit plans, 1975-83.

GLUT OF OFFICE BUILDINGS FLATTENS RENTAL INCOME

(p. 5, 101) By Steve Hemmerick. Article, with 1 table showing vacancy rates for downtown office buildings in 26 U.S cities and Toronto, Canada, as of June 1984. Data are from Coldwell Banker.

REPUBLICBANK DALLAS FUND LEADS SPECIAL EQUITY POOLS, QUARTERLY FEATURE

(p. 17, 99) Quarterly article, by Rose Darby, with 1 chart and 1 table showing rates of return for bank and insurance company pooled special equity funds, as follows: high, low, median, and 1st and 3rd quartile rates; and rates for top quartile individual funds, with rankings and comparison to Standard & Poor's 500; for 3-month, and 1-, 3-, 5-, and 10-year periods ended June 30, 1984.

Data are from *Pensions & Investments Performance Evaluation Report (PIPER).*

REAL ESTATE DIRECTORY, ANNUAL FEATURE

(p. 21-44) Annual feature, for 1984, profiling 109 real estate investment advisors. Includes data on value of investments managed for U.S. pension funds/other tax-exempt clients, and for foreign pension funds. Data are from *Pensions and Investment Age* annual survey. Contains the following:

a. Brief article, with 4 tables showing top 10 real estate equity, mortgage, and foreign fund advisors, ranked by tax-exempt assets managed; and top 10 advisors ranked by new tax-exempt asset commitments; with number of clients for real estate equity and new commitment categories.

b. Profiles of 109 firms, most including amount and types of investments managed and committed, number and types of clients, and types of investment instruments and services offered.

BANK SIZE, SHARE OF MARKET LINKED

(p. 49, 51) By Richard J. Gillespie. Article relating bank deposit size to cash management activities, 1983. Data are from Arthur Young and Co.

Includes 5 charts showing average monthly transactions and/or average transaction price for wholesale lockboxing, money transfer, and account reconciliation and cash concentration services, for 5 groups of banks aggregated in order of their deposit rank, Oct. 1983.

C2710–2.522: Sept. 17, 1984 (Vol. 12, No. 19)

GOLDMAN TOPS BROKERAGE SURVEY, ANNUAL FEATURE

(p. 3, 19) Annual article, by Kimberly Blanton, on investment managers' evaluations of brokerage firms, based on responses of 85 investment firms to a *Pensions and Investment Age* survey, 1983. Includes 2 tables showing the following:

a. Aggregate brokerage commission payments; high, median, and low commission payment, number of brokers used, and trading cost per share; and top 5 brokers ranked by fees received from respondents; 1983.

b. Best regional brokerage firms; stock market technicians; Wall Street economists; and national brokerage firms in equity and fixed-income research and trading or execution; as cited by respondents.

PORTFOLIO DEDICATIONS ESTIMATED AT $10 BILLION

(p. 5, 72) By Barry B. Burr. Article on use of bond portfolio dedications and immunizations to enhance pension fund profitability during periods of high interest rates. Includes 1 table showing investment strategy, and portfolio value and manager, for 15 corporate pension fund portfolios dedicated or immunized in 1984.

SDC: 'OLIGOPOLY' CORNERS SHELF MARKET

(p. 21-23) By Marci Baker. Article on concentration of underwriting business for shelf-registered securities (company securities registered in one lot but sold over a 2-year period). Data are from Securities Data Corp.

Includes 1 table showing volume and value of syndicated and nonsyndicated shelf offerings underwritten by top 10 and all other investment firms, with aggregate comparison to total securities offerings, 1st half 1984.

C2710–2.523: Oct. 1, 1984 (Vol. 12, No. 20)

DIRECTORY: DISKS AND DATA

(p. 15-43) Directory of approximately 190 investment service data bases and software systems offered for microcomputers, showing for each system: address, background, access requirements, and occasionally number of clients, data base size, and access fees.

Data are from a recent *Pensions and Investment Age* survey. Also includes brief article (p. 16) on computerized pension fund portfolio management.

C2710–2.524: Oct. 15, 1984 (Vol. 12, No. 21)

PERFORMANCE NUMBERS UP

(p. 13, 24-25) By Mark Westerbeck. Article, with 1 chart and 1 table showing total giving by 10 largest independent foundations, ranked by assets, generally for 1983. Data are from the Foundation Center.

SCHOOLS DIVIDED ON INTERNATIONAL

(p. 13, 24) By Rose Darby. Article, with 1 table ranking tax-exempt assets of 10 largest university endowments, 1983. Data are from the National Assn of College and University Business Officers.

DREXEL BURNHAM ADVANCES TO 2nd IN DEBT UNDERWRITING, RECURRING FEATURE

(p. 33, 36) Recurring article, by Kimberly Blanton, with 3 tables showing net underwriting proceeds for common and preferred stocks, and bonds, 3rd quarter and 1st 9 months 1984; and top 15 investment management firms ranked by volume of domestic debt and equity underwritings, 1st 9 months 1984. Data are from Securities Data Corp.

C2710–2.525: Oct. 29, 1984 (Vol. 12, No. 22)

9% DECLINE REPORTED IN CASH STANCE, SEMIANNUAL FEATURE

(p. 19, 21) Semiannual article, by Richard G. Gillespie, on cash holdings (cash/short-term investments) among *Fortune* 100 largest industrial companies, as of June 30, 1984. Data are compiled by Wright Investors' Service.

Includes 3 tables showing holdings as of June 1983-84, for 10 companies with largest current holdings, and with largest increases and decreases.

C2825
Daily Racing Form, Inc.

C2825–1   1983 SURVEY ON SPORTS ATTENDANCE
Annual. [Apr. 1984.]
8 p. no paging.
SRI/MF/complete

Annual report on attendance at horse races and other spectator sports, 1983, with trends from 1940. Data are from sports assns and publications.

Includes 4 tables showing thoroughbred and harness/trotting race attendance, compared to 10 other sports nationwide and to major league baseball in 8 cities, 1983 with change from 1982; and thoroughbred racing days and/or attendance, annually 1940-83, and by State for 1983.

Availability: Daily Racing Form, Inc., Ten Lake Dr., PO Box 1015, Hightstown NJ 08520, †; SRI/MF/complete.

C2950
Decisions Publications

C2950–3   MARKETING AND MEDIA DECISIONS
Monthly, and special annual issues. Approx. 175 p.
ISSN 0195-4296.
LC 80-640244.
SRI/MF/excerpts, shipped quarterly

Monthly journal, with 2 annual special issues, covering topics related to advertising media selection. Includes recurring data on advertising costs and expenditures, by media and/or brand.

Data are from private research firms, advertising agencies, Federal Government, and individual companies.

Issues generally contain:

a. Feature articles, often with statistics; and editorial depts.

b. "Media Cost Index" monthly feature, with 9-11 charts on costs of purchasing specified units of advertising time or space, for nighttime and daytime network TV, spot TV, spot and network radio, national supplements, consumer magazines, daily newspapers, business publications, and outdoor advertising.

Data are excerpted from industry published sources (identified for each chart), and are shown monthly for current year through month 2-3 months prior to cover date, and previous year.

c. "Brand Report" feature article, evaluating recent advertising expenditures and strategies of selected products or industries, usually including 1-3 tables.

Annual statistical features include surveys of advertising expenditures by leading brands, top marketing successes, and media costs.

Monthly "Media Cost Index" feature appears in all regular issues. All additional features with substantial statistical content are described, as they appear, under "Statistical Features." Nonstatistical features are not covered.

Availability: Marketing and Media Decisions, 1140 Ave. of the Americas, New York NY 10036, qualified subscribers †, others $40.00 per yr., single copy $3.00; SRI/MF/excerpts for cost index charts and all portions covered under "Statistical Features;" shipped quarterly.

Issues reviewed during 1984: Nov. 1983-Oct. 1984 (P) (Vol. 18, Nos. 13-14; Vol. 19, Nos. 1-13). [No issue was numbered Vol. 18, No. 12; Vol. 19, Nos. 8 & 10 incorrectly read Vol. 18].

STATISTICAL FEATURES:

C2950–3.501: Nov. 1983 (Vol. 18, No. 12)
[Issue incorrectly reads No. 13.]

WHO'S GOT THE CABLE SUBSCRIBERS?

(p. 49) Brief article, with 1 undated table showing number of basic cable TV subscribers for top 10 multiple system operators ranked by market shares. Data are from Paul Kagan Associates.

POSITIVE OUTLOOK FOR INTERNATIONAL MARKETS

(p. 54) Brief article, with 1 table showing Gross World Product, and GNP for selected countries and world areas, 1982, 1987, and 1995. Data are from Predicasts, Inc.

CONGRESSIONAL SEATS BY REGION: 1980 AND 1990

(p. 56) Table showing number of congressional seats by census region, 1980 and projected 1990. Also includes accompanying article. Data are from *American Demographics* magazine and Census Bureau.

ABCs OF VIDEOTEX/TELETEXT

(p. 64-65, 112-114) By Vivienne Vilardi. Article on outlook for the home electronic information market. Data sources include Link Resources. Includes 2 charts and 1 table showing home electronic information market households and revenues, 1995; and North American text/graphics segment revenues from users, advertisers, and order fulfillment charges, 1984-88.

MAGAZINE SELECTION AND LIFESTYLE

(p. 92-98) By Tom Johnson. Article on truck buyer demographic characteristics. Includes 1 undated table showing median buyer age and income, and percents with white-collar occupation and college background, by market segment (standard and compact pickup, utility van, and sport utility).

BRAND REPORT 92: HEROES TAKE ROLE IN TOYS AND GAMES

(p. 163-172) Includes 2 tables showing toy/game advertising expenditures for 11 leading brands, by media; and unit sales distributions by type of retail outlet and recipient age, percent planned purchases, and sales volume and value, for child and family board and action games; 1982.

Data are from Leading National Advertisers and *Playthings* magazine.

Data corrections appear in the Jan. 1984 issue; for description, see C2950-3.503 below.

C2950–3.502: Dec. 1983 (Vol. 18, No. 13)
[Issue incorrectly reads No. 14.]

TV ALTERNATIVES IN FOCUS

(p. 36, 38) Article presenting views of advertising executives and media representatives on the future of TV as an advertising medium. Data are based on a Vitt Media survey. Includes text statistics, and 1 undated chart showing distribution of respondents by importance attributed to quality TV programming.

YOU CAN'T BUY CABLE BY THE NUMBERS

(p. 58-59, 139-142) Article on problems in cable TV audience measurement. Data are from A. C. Nielsen Co. Includes 1 table showing TV viewership distribution for top 3 commercial networks, independent and public TV, and advertiser-supported and pay cable TV, by household type (all TV, and non-cable, cable, and pay cable TV households), 2nd quarter 1983.

VALUE OF A LOYAL AUDIENCE

(p. 88-92) By Chet Bandes. Article examining the relationship between advertising effectiveness and audience loyalty for various media. Data are from recent market research studies. Includes 11 text tables.

SPANISH SPOKEN HERE?

(p. 99-108) Article on the social and economic characteristics of the Hispanic American consumer market. Data are from the Census Bureau, *Hispanic Business* magazine, and various market research studies.

Includes 2 charts and 5 tables showing: auto ownership of Hispanic vs. general population, and Hispanic advertising expenditures and population as percent of total in top 10 market areas, 1980; consumption indexes for selected products for Hispanic vs. all adult population, and Spanish language advertising expenditures by media, 1983; and employment distribution by occupation and sex, and political party preferences, for Mexican Americans, Puerto Ricans, Cuban Americans, other Hispanics, and total population, 1981.

BRAND REPORT 93: APPAREL

(p. 111-120) Includes 1 undated table showing advertising expenditures by media ranked for top 8 clothing retailer and manufacturer advertisers. Data are from Leading National Advertisers, Media Records, and Radio Expenditure Reports.

C2950–3.503: Jan. 1984 (Vol. 19, No. 1)

CORRECTION

(p. 32) Correction to text material for Brand Report 92 on toy and game industry, originally appearing in Nov. 1983 issue (for description, see C2950-3.501 above).

AUDIENCE SEGMENTATION HITS HOLLYWOOD

(p. 64-66, 117-118) Article, with 1 chart and 1 table showing the following for 6-7 film production companies: boxoffice revenue distribution, 1983; and advertising expenditures by media, 1981-82. Data are from *Variety* and other industry sources.

BRAND REPORT 94: OFFICE AUTOMATION

(p. 103-110) Includes 3 tables and 1 chart showing advertising expenditures by media, for 6 office automation companies; white collar workers and work stations with electronic keyboards; value of shipments by type of office machine; and manager and employee perceived fears of office automation; various years 1981-87.

Data are from International Data Corp., Honeywell, Inc., and Leading National Advertisers.

C2950–3.504: Feb. 1984 (Vol. 19, No. 2)

REGARDLESS OF SIZE BARTER WILL BOOM

(p. 64-65, 166-167) Article on potential TV revenues from barter programming. (In a barter arrangement, a station exchanges commercial time for syndicated programs, rather than paying the syndicator a license fee.) Data are from a Nov. 1983 Blair TV report.

Includes 2 tables showing potential barter revenue, and barter vs. network advertising rates for selected programs, 1983.

DO YOU KNOW YOUR CONSUMERS?

(p. 76-78, 142-144) Article on changes in consumer attitudes and effect on marketing strategy. Data are from the American Council of Life Insurance, the Health Insurance Assn of America, and Dancer Fitzgerald Sample.

Includes 1 chart and 2 tables showing consumer attitudes on family responsibilities and other social issues (no date); and average new product introductions, monthly, 1980-83 and 1964-79 period.

CABLE AD SCORECARD, ANNUAL FEATURE

(p. 126-131) Article profiling the top 20 agencies in cable TV advertising, 1983-84. Data are from individual company reports. Includes 20 agency profiles, with data on cable TV billings by agency, 1983-84.

BRAND REPORT 95: SOFT DRINKS

(p. 135-141) Includes 1 table showing advertising expenditures, by media, for 11 leading soft drink brands, 1982. Data are from industry sources.

C2950–3.505: Mar. 1984 (Vol. 19, No. 3)

LOCAL METER MEASUREMENT EXPANDING

(p. 36, 44) Article, with 1 undated chart showing population distribution of U.S. and of total Arbitron meter-monitored TV markets, by socioeconomic category. Data are from Arbitron Ratings.

HOW TOP CABLE NETS WIN ADVERTISERS

(p. 76-78, 104-106) Article, with 1 table showing local TV advertising expenditures of individual pay/basic cable programming services, and network expenditures of 2 services, 1st 9 months 1982-83. Data were compiled by TV Bureau of Advertising from Broadcast Advertisers Reports.

HOW TO AVOID NEW PRODUCT BLUES

(p. 98-100) By Lance P. Nelson. Article, with 2 tables showing number of new food products introduced since 1970, and number currently remaining on market by sales range; and top 10 new food products ranked by 1982 retail sales, with percent of households using each. Data are from industry sources.

BRAND REPORT 96: COSMETICS

(p. 129-136) Article, with 1 table showing top 10 cosmetic manufacturers ranked by advertising expenditures, with detail by media, 1982. Data sources include Leading National Advertisers.

C2950–3.506: Apr. 1984 (Vol. 19, No. 4)

COMMUNICATIONS INDUSTRIES BOOM

(p. 26) Article, with 1 table ranking top 5-6 communications companies, by operating margin 1982, and by cumulative revenue and pre-tax income growth rates 1978-82, and also showing market segment for each. Data are from Veronis, Suhler and Associates.

CABLE HITS 39% PENETRATION

(p. 44) Brief article, with 1 table showing percent of households with cable TV, for 15 largest areas of dominant influence, Oct. 1983. Data are from Arbitron Ratings.

FEWER COUPONS BEYOND REDEMPTION

(p. 48) Brief article, with 1 table showing percent of coupons issued in/on product and through selected media, with detail for newspapers, 1981-83. Data are from the A. C. Nielsen Clearing House.

GET READY FOR THE VIDEO GENERATION

(p. 59-61, 116-120) Article on market outlook for electronic media, 1980s-2000. Data are from industry sources.

Includes 5 charts showing year various electronic media will penetrate 25% of the market; percent of households with computers and selected types of electronic media equipment and services; and percent of time spent with selected media; various years 1980-2000.

BRAND REPORT 96: JEWELRY AND WATCHES

(p. 123-139) Includes 8 tables showing advertising expenditures by media, for 6 watch/jewelry companies with some detail by brand; watch/jewelry retail sales outlook by product line; distribution of watch sales, and of jewelry sales by type, by retail outlet type; and jewelry/watch sales compared to other retail sales; various periods 1975-84.

Data are from Leading National Advertisers, Broadcast Advertisers Reports, and other industry sources.

C2950–3.507: May 1984 (Vol. 19, No. 6)

CABLE TO HIT $5.5 BILLION BY 1994

(p. 26) Brief article, with 1 table projecting cable TV advertising revenue, 1983-94. Data are from Paul Kagan Associates.

BRAND LOYALTY AIN'T WHAT IT USED TO BE

(p. 44) Brief article, with 1 undated table showing importance of selected factors in consumer purchases of nationally advertised product brands. Data are from a Gallup Organization survey of 1,104 users of national brands.

MEN'S COSMETICS A GROWTH PROSPECT

(p. 46) Brief article, with 1 table showing total consumer spending, and cosmetic/toiletry shipment value by product type and aggregate price index, selected years 1967-95. Data are from Predicasts, Inc.

TED BATES 5% 'CABLE' SOLUTION, UPDATE

(p. 102-108) By Barry Kaplan. Article comparing household penetration for cable and broadcast TV. Data are primarily from Nielsen Cable Status Report.

Includes 5 tables showing percent of TV households with pay and basic cable TV service, Nov. 1979-83 and Dec. 1983; primetime share of pay cable and noncable households, by type of cable TV service and/or broadcast TV station, Nov.-Dec. 1982-83; and index of pay cable relative to all TV households, by income, family size, and age of householder and children (no date).

SEGMENTATION APPROACH TO THE MARKET

(p. 134-136) Article, with 1 undated table showing purchases by black and Hispanic consumers relative to white consumers, for 9 product categories. Data are from the Wellington Group.

BRAND REPORT 97: AUTOMOTIVE

(p. 145-162) Includes 4 tables showing the following for the motor vehicle industry: advertising expenditures by media, for 8 manufacturers, with some detail by model; passenger car sales; market share by U.S. manufacturer, and for Japanese and European imports; and sales for 6 leading manufacturers; various periods 1983-87.

Data are from Leading National Advertisers, Broadcast Expenditure Reports, Chase Econometrics, J. D. Power & Associates, and Data Resource, Inc.

C2950–3.508: Spring 1984

15 TOP MARKETING SUCCESSES OF 1983, ANNUAL FEATURE

Annual special issue profiling most successful marketing campaign in each of 15 industries with greatest national media use, 1983. Selection was based in part on a survey of *Marketing and Media Decisions* readers, and on discussions with marketing experts and others.

Issue is primarily narrative, with interspersed data for selected companies and brands. Data sources include Leading National Advertisers/Broadcast Advertiser Reports, Media Records, Radio Expenditure Reports, and *Business Week*.

Includes 1 chart and 7 tables (p. 28, 37, 50, 62, 68, 79, 91, 104) showing advertising expenditures by media for 3 of the selected companies; travel industry advertising expenditures by transport mode; and product sales by company division, model, or brand, for 5 selected companies; various years 1975-84.

This is the 3rd annual special Spring issue on top marketing successes.

C2950–3.509: June 1984 (Vol. 19, No. 8)
[Issue incorrectly reads Vol. 18, No. 8.]

HORSE RACING LOSES THE HORSE RACE

(p. 38) Article, with 1 table showing spectator attendance at 11 major sports, with selected detail for professional and collegiate leagues/teams, 1983 with change from 1982. Data are from the 37th annual survey conducted by *Daily Racing Form*. Full report is covered in SRI under C2825-1.

WNTD: MKTG VP W/PCKG GDS. EXPER.

(p. 50-52) Article on the demand for corporate marketing executives. Data are from a 1984 Heidrick and Struggles' survey of 1,000 chief executives. Includes 1 table showing distribution of chief executives by previous career position, by company type and size (no date).

For description of full survey report, see B4490-2.10.

FOREIGN CIRCULATION

(p. 100-102) By Deborah Solomon. Article, with 2 tables showing foreign circulation of U.S. magazines with over 10% or 15,000 copies in foreign circulation, percent of total circulation, and whether foreign circulation is included in advertising rate base, 2nd half 1983. Data are from the Audit Bureau of Circulations Publishers Statements of 108 major consumer magazines.

1983 BRAND LEADERS IN NEWSPAPERS, ANNUAL FEATURE

(p. 117-138) Annual article on national newspaper advertising expenditures, by service or product type and leading brands and companies, 1983 and trends. Data are primarily from Media Records.

Includes 5 tables showing national newspaper advertising expenditures for the following:

a. Automobile companies, top 25 makes, with detail for factory, dealer, local, and pickup/camper ads; and cigarette companies, with detail for top 20 brands; 1983.

b. 100 leading advertisers, 1982-83; 3 leading brands or companies in selected product/service categories, 1979-83; and by detailed product/service category, 1982-83.

Detailed survey report is available for $1,050 from Media Records, 370 Seventh Ave., New York NY 10001. Individual product reports are also available, for $110-$305.

C2950–3.510: July 1984 (Vol. 19, No. 9)

UNDER SIEGE, CIGARETTE MARKETERS FIGHT BACK

(p. 34-37, 175-177) Article, with 1 table showing major generic cigarette group and top 10 cigarette brands ranked by market volume, and including market share and manufacturer for each, 1st quarter 1984 with comparison to 1st quarter 1983. Data are from Lehman Brothers, Kuhn Loeb.

13th ANNUAL REPORT: THE TOP 200 BRANDS

(p. 49-158) Annual report on advertising expenditures, by media, for top 200 advertised brands, 1983 and trends. Data are from various media research organizations, including Leading National Advertisers Inc., Media Records, Broadcast Advertisers Reports, and Radio Expenditure Reports. Includes the following:

a. Index of brand profiles; narrative summary; 1 chart showing aggregate advertising expenditures for top 100 and 200 brands, 1977-83; and 1 chart comparing media distribution of advertising budgets for CBS, Inc. and Sprite, 1982-83. (p. 52-54)

b. 1 table showing top 200 brands ranked by advertising expenditures, 1983 with comparisons to 1980-82. (p. 56-66)

c. Summaries for top 200 advertised brands, each including parent company; marketing and advertising executives; advertising agencies and executives; and 1 table showing advertising expenditures, by media, 1982-83. (p. 70-158)

C2950–3.511: Aug. 1984 (Vol. 19, No. 10)
[Issue incorrectly reads Vol. 18.]

PEERING AT AN AGING AMERICA: THE MARKET FOR EYEWEAR

(p. 28) Article, with 1 undated table showing percent of adults wearing contact lenses, by sex, age, income, and region. Data are based on a recent survey of 1,000 adults age 18/over, conducted by R. H. Bruskin Associates.

CABLE'S TROUBLES PALE NEXT TO DBS AND MDS

(p. 51-53, 82-84) Article on developments and outlook for cable, direct broadcast satellite (DBS), and other pay TV industries. Data are from Titsch Communications, Inc., and Link Resources, Inc.

Includes 1 chart analyzing the potential market for DBS service, including total TV households, and households with cable TV, videocassette recorders, and other programming services, 1985; 2 tables showing cable TV subscribers, and cable share of TV households, 1984-90, as estimated on Dec. 31, 1983 and Mar. 30, 1984; and a listing of cable franchising status for top 15 TV markets.

BRAND REPORT 101: PHARMACEUTICALS

(p. 87-97) Includes 1 chart and 3 tables showing consumer expenditures for non-prescription health products, with distribution by product type, 1982; and advertising expenditures by media, for 5-10 leading analgesic, cough/cold remedy, and digestive product brands, 1983. Data sources include *Drug Topics*.

C2950–3.512: Sept. 1984 (Vol. 19, No. 11)

MORE SPORTSCASTS, LOWER RATINGS

(p. 26) Article, with 1 table showing the following for network sports broadcasts: number and hours of telecasts; number of viewers, viewers per viewing household, and ratings of audience size, for men 18/over; and ratings for households; 1979-83. Data are from BBDO International, Inc.

VCRs: OGRE OR OPPORTUNITY?

(p. 48-50, 108-110) Article, with 1 table showing video cassette recorder sales volume, installed base, and household market penetration, 1984-88. Data are from Link Resources and Electronic Industries Assn.

SEAGRAM BLANKETS THE WINE SPECTRUM

(p. 54-58, 122-123) Article, with 3 charts showing market share for 7 major California wine brands and all others, selected years 1970-83; and share of shipments and retail sales for 1983, and estimated average price per bottle (no date), all for 10 leading wine marketers and all others. Data are from *Impact*.

OUTLOOK REMAINS BULLISH FOR INDEPENDENT TV

(p. 62-63, 116-118) Article, with 3 tables showing spot TV advertising expenditures of top 25 advertisers and top 20 industries, ranked by expenditures at total and independent stations, 1st quarter 1984. Data are from the TV Bureau of Advertising and Broadcast Advertisers Reports.

TOWARD BETTER TV RESEARCH ESTIMATES

(p. 104-105) By John S. McSherry. Article comparing various systems for estimating TV reach levels. Includes 2 tables showing reach level comparisons for 4 time-sharing systems and a proprietary system, by day part, 1983; and for Nielsen Co., a proprietary system, and a time-sharing system, for viewers aged 18-49, by sex (no date).

Also includes 4 tables illustrating factors influencing estimates of reach levels.

C2950–3.513: Fall 1984 (Vol. 19, No. 12)

MEDIA COSTS ISSUE

Special issue on media advertising costs. Includes the statistical features described below.

1985's SIGNAL: STILL GREEN, BUT SOME FLASHES OF YELLOW, ANNUAL FEATURE

(p. 8-10) Annual feature on media cost outlook for 1985, based on a *Marketing and Media Decisions* survey of media directors. Includes 3 tables showing actual and anticipated changes in media unit cost, audience, and cost-per-thousand, by media, various years 1980-85.

This is the 14th annual forecast.

ECONOMY IS SHOWING SIGNS OF SLOWING DOWN. THE QUESTION IS, HOW MUCH?

(p. 12-19) Article, with 1 table showing forecasts of 5 economists for 4 economic indicators, 2nd half 1984-1st half 1985.

MEDIA COST-PER-THOUSAND TRENDS 1975-84, ANNUAL FEATURE

(p. 27-32) Annual feature on media cost trends, 1975-84. Data are from Ted Bates Advertising/New York. Includes 6 tables showing advertising cost-per-thousand indexes, and total and national advertising expenditures, with detail by media and comparisons to CPI and GNP, various years 1975-84.

TV COSTS EXPECTED TO RISE REFLECTING STRONG DEMAND FOR MEDIUM

(p. 35-38, 42) Article, with 3 tables showing change in network and spot TV ad revenues, Jan.-May 1983-84; network and spot TV advertising expenditures of the top 10 TV advertisers ranked by total expenditures for TV advertising, 1983; and average daily viewing time per TV household by region, and viewer education and household size, Feb. 1984.

Data are from McCann-Erickson, TV Bureau of Advertising analysis of Broadcast Advertisers Reports data, and A. C. Nielsen Co.

COSTS UP BUT CABLE IS STILL A GOOD BUY

(p. 45-52, 117) Article on developments in cable TV advertising. Data are from Paul Kagan Associates, Inc. and Cable Advertising Bureau. Includes 3 tables and 1 chart showing the following:

a. Homes with TVs, and cable TV homes available to advertising-supported cable networks, both with adjustments for number of homes actually viewing TV; and revenues for major broadcast networks and advertising-supported cable networks; 1980-93.

b. Advertising cost estimates for top 10 cable networks ranked by number of subscribers, with ratings per number of households, cost-per-thousand, and cost per 30-second spot, for daytime and by type of programming (no date).

c. Broadcast network affiliate share trends for cable and non-cable households, for daytime, primetime, and total day, 1979/80-1982/83; and cable TV advertising expenditures, 1982-83, of the top 10 cable advertisers ranked by 1983 expenditures.

RADIO SETS ITS DIAL TO STRONG SALES AND MORE NETWORKS

(p. 53-56, 117) Article, with 3 charts and 2 tables showing comparisons for radio and other media cost-per-thousand changes, 1967-83 period, and for share of time spent with each media type, by user characteristics (no date); top 10 radio advertisers ranked by spot and network advertising expenditures, 1983; and radio reach, by day part, for listeners 12 years/ over (no date).

Data are from Radio Advertising Bureau, Inc.

CONSUMER MAGAZINES ASK FOR 7% RATE HIKE, ANNUAL FEATURE

(p. 59-68) Annual article on consumer magazine advertising and rate setting, 1984. Most data are from James B. Kobak and Co. Includes 7 tables showing the following:

a. Consumer magazine advertising, subscription, and single copy shares of total revenue, and expenses and profit as percent of revenues; and advertising rate indexes, advertising rate increases compared to other media, and circulation prices and indexes, all with comparisons to CPI; various periods 1970-84.

b. Consumer magazines published, advertising pages and dollars, and circulations, selected years 1960-83; and magazine paper usage distributed by weight category, 1981-83.

BOOMING BUSINESS PRESS PLANS SMALL COST PUSH, ANNUAL FEATURE

(p. 73-80, 119) Annual article on business magazine advertising and rate setting, 1984. Data are from James B. Kobak and Co. and other industry sources. Includes 7 tables showing the following:

a. Business magazine operating cost indexes, selected years 1974-86; advertising rate indexes with comparison to CPI, advertising and subscription shares of total revenues, and yearly subscription increases, selected

years 1970-84; and magazines published, advertising pages and dollars, and circulation, selected years 1960-83.

b. Business magazine aggregate advertising revenues of 100 publications for 6-month period 1983-84, and expected change in use of advertising pages in 1984-85, all by publication category; and indexes of ad pages and revenues, 1983-86.

NEWSPRINT WILL UP THE COST OF NEWSPAPERS BY 8%

(p. 83-86) Article, with 1 table showing newspaper advertising general rate index, monthly 1981-June 1984. Data are from Newspaper Advertising Bureau.

OUTDOOR: TRYING TO HOLD DOWN PRICES, WHILE LABOR, PAPER, AND LAND COSTS RISE, ANNUAL FEATURE

(p. 89-92) Annual article on outdoor advertising costs. Data are from the Institute of Outdoor Advertising. Includes 2 tables showing rates for unilluminated and illuminated advertising boards in 9 areas, 1984; and poster panel costs aggregated for top 50 metro markets, monthly 1979-June 1984.

CATALOGUERS FACE EXPENSE EXPLOSION

(p. 101-106) Article on direct marketing costs. Data are from Direct Marketing Assn Inc., BLS, and a Decisions Publications' survey. Includes 2 tables showing direct mail advertising costs for 2 quantity categories, for 10 cost components, 1981-83; and price increases for 4 operating costs, 1985.

C2950–3.514: Oct. 1984 (Vol. 19, No. 13)

DIET FOOD DEMAND SPURS FLAVORS AND FRAGRANCES MARKET

(p. 42) Article, with 1 table showing flavoring and fragrance market value by type of substance, and market volume by end use, 1983, 1988, and percent change for 1988-95 period. Data are from Predicasts and Frost & Sullivan.

RETAILERS HIGH ON DIRECT MAIL

(p. 44) Brief article, with 1 undated chart showing retailers' plans regarding continued use of direct mail advertisements. Data are from a survey of 400 retail businesses, conducted by Aaron Cohen Marketing Services.

BIRTH & MARRIAGE DATA

(p. 54) Table showing selected birth and marriage trends and projections, including total marriages, 1st marriages as percent of total, divorces/annulments, total and 1st births, and births of 3rd/higher order as percent of total, quinquennial periods 1961-90. Data are from *American Baby*. Includes brief accompanying article.

CABLE AT ITS BEST

(p. 114-116) By Beverly O'Malley. Article on cable and broadcast TV coverage of the 1984 Democratic Convention. Data are from NHI. Includes 3 tables showing Cable News Network (CNN) and ABC/NBC/CBS audience rating or share for 4 convention nights; and Tuesday-night shares for broadcast networks, CNN, ad-supported and pay cable networks, and superstations/independents.

1984's MAGAZINE CIRCULATION PICTURE

(p. 148-155) Article, with 2 tables showing magazine circulation index, by type of content, 1979-83 period; and 1984 audience, and percent change from 1983, for 27 selected magazines including 10 with greatest percent gain over 1983. Data are from Audit Bureau of Circulation's *1984 Magazine Trend Report,* and Simmons Market Research Bureau.

BRAND REPORT 103: PERSONAL COMPUTERS

(p. 157-174) Includes 1 table showing advertising expenditures by media, for 5 personal computer manufacturers, 1983. Data are from Leading National Advertisers, Radio Advertising Bureau, and Newspaper Advertising Bureau.

C3150
Dun and Bradstreet

**C3150–1   MONTHLY BANK
            CLEARING REPORT**
Monthly. Approx. 3 p.
ISSN 0027-0199.
SRI/MF/complete, shipped
quarterly

Monthly report on bank check clearings in NYC and 25 other major cities, compiled from Federal Reserve Bank records. Report is usually issued 1-3 months after month of coverage.

Contains narrative summary, and 2 tables showing the following:

a. Comparisons of clearings, by city, for current month, preceding month, and same month of preceding year.

b. Total clearings for 26 cities, NYC, and 25 cities excluding NYC, monthly for year to date and preceding 3 years.

Availability: Dun and Bradstreet, Business Economics Division, 299 Park Ave., New York NY 10171, price on request; SRI/MF/complete, shipped quarterly.

Issues reviewed during 1984: Sept. 1983, Dec. 1983, Jan.-May 1984, July 1984 (D) [Oct.-Nov. 1983 and June 1984 issues not yet available for review].

**C3150–3   MONTHLY NEW
            INCORPORATIONS**
Monthly. Approx. 2 p.
SRI/MF/complete, shipped
quarterly

Monthly report on new business incorporations, by census division and State. Report, compiled by the Business Economics Division, is issued 3-5 months after month of coverage, earlier if State data are available.

Contains narrative summary; and 2 tables showing unadjusted new business incorporations by census division and State, for month of coverage, year to date, and same periods of previous year. Also shows seasonally adjusted totals for month of coverage and selected prior periods.

Availability: Dun and Bradstreet, Economic Analysis Department, 99 Church St., New York NY 10007, $18.00 per yr.; SRI/MF/complete, shipped quarterly.

Issues reviewed during 1984: July-Dec. 1983 (D).

C3150–4   BUSINESS EXPECTATIONS
Quarterly. Approx. 5 p.
SRI/MF/complete

Quarterly press release on business executives' expectations for sales, profits, selling prices, inventory levels, new orders, and employment. Shows percent of executives expecting increase, decrease, and no change in each indicator for current quarter compared with same quarter of previous year. Includes detail for durable and nondurable goods manufacturers, wholesalers, and retailers.

Data are from surveys of approximately 1,400 businessmen conducted approximately 6 weeks prior to quarter of coverage. Report is issued 2-4 weeks after beginning of quarter covered.

Contains narrative summary of survey findings, with 1-2 trend charts and 1 table.

Availability: Dun and Bradstreet, Economic Analysis Department, 99 Church St., New York NY 10007, $23.00 per yr.; SRI/MF/complete.

Issues reviewed during 1984: 1st-2nd Qtrs. 1984 (D).

C3165
Duncan, James H., Jr.

**C3165–1   AMERICAN RADIO: Spring
            1984 Report**
Semiannual. Aug. 1984.
292 p. var. paging.
Vol. IX, No. 1.
SRI/MF/complete, Fall 1983 &
Spring 1984 reports

Semiannual report, by James H. Duncan, Jr., on radio broadcast industry, spring 1984, presenting detailed data on station formats and audiences, broadcast market characteristics, and broadcast-related businesses, with selected trends from as early as 1975.

Includes numerous station and market rankings based on various listenership measures, with detail by station type (including public/noncommercial stations), and program format; station trading activity, including transaction price; leading music syndicators/consultants and radio representatives based on listeners and/or stations covered; station and listenership measures for leading ownership groups; and audience characteristics, including age and sex composition, for individual stations grouped by format.

Also includes Arbitron and other market reports for over 170 individual market areas, with data on population, consumer spendable income, and retail sales; aggregate radio revenue; FM market share; average audience and audience shares for individual stations and program formats; and other station data, including audience age and sex composition, market share trends from 1982, frequency, power authorization, and advertising rates.

Data are from Arbitron Co. and other private research firms, Birch monthly reports, *Broadcasting Yearbook,* and original research.

Contains introduction, highlights, and index (6 p.); section A, with rankings, broadcast-related data, and format detail (p. A1-A62); and section B, with market report data (224 p.).

Report generally is issued in Feb. (fall edition) and Aug. (spring edition). This is the 17th edition.

Previous report, for fall 1983, was also reviewed in 1984 and is also available on SRI microfiche under this number [Semiannual. Feb. 1984. 278 p. var. paging. Vol. VIII, No. 2. $50.00].

Availability: James H. Duncan, Jr., Duncan Media Enterprises, Inc., Box 2966, Kalamazoo MI 49003, $55.00; SRI/MF/complete.

C3250
Editor and Publisher Co.

**C3250–1   1984 EDITOR AND
            PUBLISHER MARKET GUIDE**
Annual. 1983.
610 p. var. paging.
ISBN 9-9916233-1-0.
LC 45-44873.
SRI/MF/complete, delayed

Annual market guide, for 1984, presenting detailed sociodemographic and economic characteristics for MSAs, counties, and communities with a daily newspaper, in the U.S., Puerto Rico, and Canada.

Includes location, population, disposable income and other household characteristics, transportation, principal industries, utilities, and retail sales and outlets. Also includes summary State and Province data.

Report is based on *1977 Census of Retail Sales,* 1980 U.S. census, and other U.S. Government agency reports; Statistics Canada censuses; *Editor and Publisher* estimates; and other sources.

Retail sales data by kind of business are shown for lumber/hardware, general merchandise, food, automotive dealers, gasoline stations, apparel, furniture, eating/drinking places, and drugstores.

Contents:

Section I. Introduction: index, definitions, and notes; alphabetical listing of MSAs and Consolidated Metropolitan Statistical Areas; market rankings of MSAs and leading counties and cities, 1984, in terms of population, disposable personal income, total retail and food sales, and disposable income per household; and directory of newspaper representatives in U.S. and Canada. 5 tables. (p. I.1-I.44)

Section II-III. Surveys of daily newspaper cities: city profiles with text data, described below, arranged by State, including Puerto Rico, and Canadian Province. (p. II.1-II.388, III.1-III.21)

Section IV. Population, income, and retail sales tables: population, 1980 or 1981, and estimated Jan. 1, 1985; number of households, 1985; disposable personal income, 1980 and 1984; income per capita and per household, 1984; number of farms, and crop and livestock values, 1978 or 1982; total retail sales, 1971 or 1977, and 1983-84: and number of stores, 1977, and/or estimated sales, 1984, by kind of business; all by State, Province, MSA and Canadian metro area, county, and city, with U.S. and Canadian totals. 2 tables. (p. IV.1-IV.151)

Index to advertisers. (1 p.)

Market guide has been published annually since 1924.

Availability: Editor and Publisher Co., 575 Lexington Ave., New York NY 10022, $50.00 (prepaid); SRI/MF/complete, delayed shipment in Dec. 1984.

NEWSPAPER MARKET SURVEYS:

C3250–1.1: Text Data

a. For each State and Province: population by age group, and retail sales by kind of business, various years 1970-84. 2 tables.

b. For each metro area: location; transportation facilities by type; population; households; number of financial institutions and deposits, including commercial banks, savings and loan assns, and occasionally credit unions; passenger autos; electric and gas utility meters; principal industries, generally with employment and worker weekly earnings; climate; tap water characteristics; shopping centers and retail outlets; and newspaper circulation.

C3320
Energy Publications

C3320–1   PIPELINE AND GAS JOURNAL
Monthly.

SRI now covers this publication under C4385-1.

C3320–2   PETROLEUM ENGINEER INTERNATIONAL
Monthly.

SRI now covers this publication under C4385-2.

C3400
Fairchild Publications

C3400–1   FAIRCHILD FACT FILE
Series. For individual publication data, see below.
SRI/MF/complete

Series of fact file reports presenting production and retail marketing data for selected consumer goods industries, including apparel, home textiles, major household appliances, and home electronic products. Series also includes special additional reports on aspects of manufacturing and marketing and the U.S. economy.

Reports are generally updated annually or biennially and are compiled by the Market Research Division from sources such as consumer surveys, BLS, BEA, Census Bureau, trade assns, Target Group Index, and *Sales and Marketing Management.*

General format for reports on specific industries includes a narrative summary of industry and market trends, and the following data:

a. General industry statistics, including companies, establishments, total and production employment, hours and earnings, payroll, value added, shipments value, and capital expenditures; establishments and employment, by employment size and leading State; and industry concentration and financial data, including key business ratios; all for 1-10 SIC 4-digit industries.

b. Production and shipments data, generally including quantity and/or value by item, fabric/material, and leading State; raw materials consumption; production indexes and/or PPI; and selected wholesale price data.

c. Foreign trade, including quantity and value of imports by product type and leading country of origin, and exports by item.

d. Retail market, including product target market population by sex and/or age group projected to 2000; stores, product sales, and operating ratios for selected outlet types, including department stores; newspaper advertising linage monthly distribution; CPI; and, occasionally, monthly sales distribution.

e. Consumer buying habits, variously including selection criteria; expenditure data; selected survey results; and purchase distributions by price level, type of outlet, month, and individual item.

Reports that basically follow the general format are described briefly, as they appear; periods of coverage, data omissions, and additional data are noted. Reports issued in special format are described in detail, as they appear.

Availability: Fairchild Fact Files, Book Division, Seven E. 12th St., New York NY 10003; SRI/MF/complete.

C3400–1.56: Major Appliances and Electric Housewares

[Biennial. 1983. 50 p. $12.50. ISBN 87005-464-3. SRI/MF/complete.]

Biennial report on household appliances. Report basically follows general format and covers various periods 1977-83, with some trends from as early as 1972 and household projections through 1995.

Omits data on employment by company employment size, establishments and employment by leading State, producer business ratios, production, raw materials consumption, wholesale prices, imports by country of origin, population projections, and consumer purchase distribution.

Additional data include value added by leading State; domestic consumption; leading companies ranked by market share; new homes by type of appliance included in sale, by region and home price; years average household keeps appliance; housing starts and permits; distribution of households by age of householder, income, and region; top 25 SMSAs ranked by retail appliance sales; and consumer purchasing plans.

Most data are shown by appliance type. Includes 55 tables.

Report updates a 1981 report; for description, see SRI 1982 Annual, under C3400-1.34.

C3400–1.57: Textile/Apparel Industries

[Biennial. 1983. 49 p. $12.50. ISBN 87005-463-5. SRI/MF/complete.]

Biennial report on textile and apparel industries, various periods 1972-83. Report basically follows general format for sections on general industry statistics, production and shipments, and foreign trade, but omits data on production and shipments for leading States, raw materials consumption, wholesale prices, and imports by country of origin. Report also omits sections on retail market and consumer buying habits.

Additional data include leading SIC 2-digit industries ranked by value added and shipment value; leading fiber, textile, and apparel companies ranked by sales, with net income; establishments, employment, and value added, by census division and/or leading State; fiber consumption; textile mill capital expenditures and equipment; and textile machinery industry statistics; various years 1972-82.

Includes 46 tables.

Report updates a 1981 report; for description see SRI 1982 Annual, under C3400-1.32.

C3400–1.58: Department Store Sales

[Annual. 1983. 57 p. $12.50. ISBN 87005-465-1. SRI/MF/complete.]

Annual report summarizing data on retail sales of department stores and leading apparel specialty stores, 1982. Data are based on company financial statements and trade source estimates.

Report, which varies from the general format for the series, contains introduction (p. 1) and the following tables, generally showing data for 1982 or the latest available fiscal year:

[1] Summary of available sales [revenues] for department stores [by headquarters location]. (p. 2-38)

[2] Department store volume leaders [ranking by sales value, with location and parent company]. (p. 39-44)

[3] Major national/regional chains [sales, by company]. (p. 45-47)

[4] Traditional department stores and apparel stores operated by conglomerate corporations [listing, with 1982-83 status changes]. (p. 48-54)

C3400–1.59: Consumer Market Developments

[Annual. 1983. 61 p. $12.50. ISBN 87005-466-X. SRI/MF/complete.]

Annual report presenting demographic and economic data relevant to consumer market conditions, various periods 1970-2000. Most data are from Census Bureau, BLS, and Commerce Dept.

Contains contents listing (1 p.) and 12 sections, with narrative analysis and the following tables:

a. Economic projections, with quarterly percent change in 10 indicators, 4th quarter 1983-84. 1 table. (p. 2)

b. Births and fertility rates, by race, 1972-82; distribution of births, and fertility rate, by age of mother, various periods 1978-82; monthly births, 1981-82; and women age 18-44 years, with percent childless, and births per 1,000 women, all by census division, year ended June 1982. 5 tables. (p. 3-6)

c. Population, by age, sex, census division and region, State, and mobility status, various periods 1970-83, with selected projections to 2000; urban/rural population by race and for Hispanics, 1980; and distribution of population and personal income, by census division, 1990 and change from 1980. 9 tables. (p. 6-17)

d. Marriages and rates; and distribution of single (never married) population, by age group and sex; various years 1970-83. 2 tables. (p. 18)

e. Households by composition, with distribution by metro status, census region, race/ethnicity (includes Hispanics), age of householder, and presence of children; living arrangements for youths, by race and for Hispanics; and unmarried-couple households by sex and age of householder, and presence of children; various periods 1970-83. 4 tables. (p. 20-23)

f. Education trends, including school enrollment by academic level, and college enrollment by sex and age group, 1970, 1975, and 1981; and educational attainment of adults age 25/over, by age, sex, and race, and for Hispanics, 1970 and 1981. 3 tables. (p. 23-27)

g. Labor force, by employment status; unemployment rates by race, for Hispanics, and by occupation; and employment by industry division, major manufacturing group, and full- and part-time status; with selected detail by sex and age group, various periods 1977-83 with selected projections to 1995. 10 tables. (p. 28-36)

h. Earnings by industry division; median weekly earnings by occupation and sex; wage/salary workers age 15/over and distribution by income level, with aggregate mean and median income, by sex and race, and for Hispanics; and households and median and mean earnings, and median family income, by number of earners; various periods 1980-2nd quarter 1983. 5 tables. (p. 36-39)

i. Personal income trends including income disposition and sources; population age 15/over and median income, by race and for Hispanics, and by sex, relationship to householder, age, and occupation; top 15 SMSAs in per capita income; and total and per capita income by region and State; various periods 1979-83, with selected trends from 1959. 6 tables. (p. 40-46)

j. Profile of top wealth holders including population with gross assets over $300,000, and value of assets, by sex, with detail by age group and type of asset, 1981. 1 table. (p. 47)

k. Household income trends including households and average income by census division; households by income level; and total households and households with discretionary income, and value of discretionary income, by age of householder; various years 1980-82. 4 tables. (p. 48-50)

l. Family income trends including families and unrelated individuals by income level, and median and mean income, by race; and families and median income, by farm and metro status, census region, and family size; various years 1979-82. 3 tables. (p. 51-52)

m. Consumer assets and liabilities; urban CPI by category; personal consumption expenditures, by product type; and Consumer Expenditure Survey findings on average weekly expenditures of urban consumers; various periods 1972-83. 6 tables. (p. 53-58)

C3400–1.60: Household Furniture and Bedding (Mattresses and Dual-Purpose Sleep Furniture)

[Biennial. 1984. 41 p. $12.50. ISBN 87005-479-1. SRI/MF/complete.]

Biennial report on household furniture and bedding industries, various periods 1972-85. Report basically follows general format, but omits data on establishments and production for leading States, employment by employment size, raw materials consumption, wholesale prices, imports by country of origin, and population projections.

Additional data include value added by leading State; new orders; households by type, and average size; housing starts, permits, and sales; total and furniture/bedding personal consumption expenditures; top furniture and bedding retailers, and top department stores in furniture sales; and trends in furniture marketing by material and style.

Includes 41 tables.

Report updates a 1982 report; for description, see SRI 1982 Annual, under C3400-1.36.

C3400–1.61: Toiletries, Cosmetics, Fragrances and Beauty Aids

[Biennial. 1984. 37 p. $12.50. ISBN 87005-480-5. SRI/MF/complete.]

Biennial report on perfumes, cosmetics, and toilet preparations industry, various periods 1972-84, with population projections to 2000. Report basically follows general format, but omits data on establishments, employment, and production, by leading State; production and shipment quantity; raw material consumption; wholesale prices; foreign trade by product/item and country of origin; number of stores by outlet type; and newspaper advertising linage.

Additional data include shipment value and value added, by leading State; latest 5-year average profitability ratios and sales growth, ranked for top 9 firms; industry concentration and PPI, by product type; export-to-shipment and import-to-new-supply ratios; advertising expenditures ranked for top 10 perfume and men's toiletries brands; and survey detail for consumer use of specified product types.

Includes 40 tables.

Report updates a 1982 report; for description, see SRI 1982 Annual, under C3400-1.38.

C3400–1.62: Hosiery/Legwear (Men's, Women's, and Children's)

[Biennial. 1984. 37 p. $12.50. ISBN 87005-481-3. SRI/MF/complete.]

Biennial report on hosiery and legwear industry, various periods 1972-83, with population projections to 2000. Report basically follows general format, but omits data on employment and establishments by leading State; production index, PPI, and wholesale prices; imports by country of origin; and stores by outlet type, newspaper advertising linage, and CPI.

Additional data include advertising expenditures by media; shipment value by class of customer; sales rankings for leading athletic sock and bodywear/exercise apparel manufacturers; seasonal shipment patterns; per capita consumption of hosiery; and pantyhose retail price trends by outlet type.

Includes 44 tables.

Report updates a 1982 report; for description, see SRI 1982 Annual, under C3400-1.39.

C3400–1.63: Men's Sportswear, Casual Wear and Jeans

[Biennial. 1984. 42 p. $12.50. ISBN 87005-484-8. SRI/MF/complete.]

Biennial report on men's sports and casual wear industries, various periods 1978-83, with population projections to 2000. Report basically follows general format, but omits data on key business ratios by industry, raw materials consumption, wholesale prices, and consumer expenditures.

Additional data include sales rankings for leading sportswear manufacturers; percent of men age 15/over participating in selected sports; male population age 18-74, by height and weight; and consumer purchase distributions by fabric.

Includes 65 tables.

Report updates a 1982 report; for description, see SRI 1983 Annual, under C3400-1.43.

C3400–1.64: Footwear (Men's, Women's, Boys', and Girls')

[Annual. 1984. 45 p. $15.00. ISBN 87005-483-X. SRI/MF/complete.]

Annual report on footwear industry, various years 1972-84, with population projections to 2000. Report basically follows general format, but omits data on employee hours, establishments and employment by leading State, raw material consumption, wholesale prices, imports by country of origin, newspaper advertising linage, and consumer selection criteria and purchases by price and month.

Additional data include plant closings and openings, employment and payroll by region, monthly production, sales in 10 leading metro markets, top 10 athletic footwear manufacturers ranked by sales, purchase distribution by region, and teenage girls' purchasing patterns.

Includes 47 tables.

C3400–1.65: Sportswear, Casual Wear, Separates, and Jeans (Women's, Misses', and Juniors')

[Biennial. 1984. 46 p. $12.50. ISBN 87005-485-6. SRI/MF/complete.]

Biennial report on women's sports and casual wear industries, various periods 1977-84, with population projections to 2000. Report basically follows general format, but omits data on establishments by leading State, industry concentration and finances, and raw materials consumption.

Additional data include value added by leading State; leading sportwear manufacturers ranked by sales; women age 18-64, by height and weight; percent of women age 15/over participating in selected sports; consumer intentions to purchase sportwear, by sex, age, income, and region; purchase distributions by fabric; and teenage girls purchasing, and number and value of purchases.

Includes 64 tables.

Report updates a 1982 report; for description, see SRI 1983 Annual, under C3400-1.42.

C3400–1.66: Sports/Fitness/Leisure Markets

[Biennial. 1984. 50 p. $15.00. ISBN 87005-482-1. SRI/MF/complete.]

Biennial report on sporting/athletic equipment and clothing, various periods 1972-84, with population projections to 2005. Report basically follows general format, but omits data on production and shipments by leading State, raw materials consumption, wholesale prices, and imports by country of origin.

Additional data include shipment value by leading State; leading manufacturers and sporting good retailers ranked by sales, with detail for selected product categories; households, and total and discretionary income, by age of household head; and sports participation and attendance, by sport, with detail by sex.

Includes 56 tables.

Report updates a 1982 report; for description, see SRI 1982 Annual, under C3400-1.37.

C3400–2 FAIRCHILD'S FINANCIAL MANUAL OF RETAIL STORES, 1983

Annual. 1983. 6+239 p.
ISBN 87005-443-0.
LC 59-4791.
SRI/MF/complete, delayed

Annual report presenting financial and operating data for approximately 320 publicly owned retail chains, by company, various years 1977-83. Most data are from annual company reports to shareholders.

Contents:

a. Summary statistics for 86 leading general merchandise, food, drug, and shoe chains, showing the following for each company: sales, net and pretax income, and shareholders' equity, and ratios, 1981-82; and aggregate trends from 1973. 12 tables. (4 p.)

b. Individual firm organizational and financial data, including number of stores; net sales and income; common stock shares outstanding, earnings per share, equity, and cash and stock dividends; income, assets, and liabilities, by type; and statistical summary (working capital, shareholders' equity, and 3-5 operating ratios); various years 1977-83. (p. 1-222)

c. Index of chain companies and subsidiaries. (p. 223-239)

This is the 56th annual edition.

Availability: Fairchild Books, Department SK, Seven E. 12th Street, New York NY 10003, $60.00; SRI/MF/complete, delayed shipment in Oct. 1984.

C3400–4 ELECTRONIC NEWS FINANCIAL FACT BOOK and Directory, 1983

Annual. 1983. 4+526 p.
ISBN 87005-441-4.
LC 62-19605.
SRI/MF/complete, delayed

Annual directory of approximately 620 publicly owned electronic companies, with business and financial information, various years 1977-83. Data are from annual company reports to shareholders and *Electronic News.*

Contents:

a. Summary data for 51 leading companies in electronic sales, showing for each company: total and electronic sales, 1983; stock prices, June 30, 1982-83; and earnings per share, price/earnings ratio, and sales, 1982-83. 2 tables. (2 p.)

b. Individual firm organizational and financial data, generally including divisions and sub-

sidiaries; number of employees; plant area; net sales and income; revenues by line of business; common stock shares outstanding, earnings per share, equity, and cash and stock dividends; income, assets, and liabilities; and working capital, shareholders' equity, and 4-5 operating ratios; various years 1977-83. (p. 1-502)

c. Index of electronic companies and subsidiaries. (p. 503-526)

This is the 22nd annual edition.

Availability: Fairchild Books, Seven E. 12th St., New York NY 10003, $100.00; SRI/MF/ complete, delayed shipment in Oct. 1984.

C3400–5 FAIRCHILD'S TEXTILE AND APPAREL FINANCIAL DIRECTORY, 1983

Annual. 1983. 4+182 p.
ISBN 87005-442-2.
SRI/MF/complete, delayed

Annual directory of approximately 200 publicly owned textile and apparel companies, with business and financial information, various years 1977-83. Most data are from annual company reports to shareholders.

Contents:

a. Summary statistics for 56 leading fiber/textile and apparel manufacturers, showing for each company: sales, net and pretax income, shareholders' equity, and ratios of net income to sales and to shareholders' equity, 1981-82. 2 tables. (2 p.)

b. Individual firm organizational and financial data, including business activities; divisions and subsidiaries; net sales and income; revenues by line of business; common stock shares outstanding, earnings per share, equity, and cash and stock dividends; income, assets, and liabilities, by type; and statistical summary (working capital, shareholders' equity, and 2-5 operating ratios); various years 1977-83. (p. 1-148)

c. Indexes of textile trademarks, and divisions and subsidiaries. (p. 149-182)

This is the 10th annual edition.

Availability: Fairchild Books, Seven E. 12th St., New York NY 10003, $50.00; SRI/MF/ complete, delayed shipment in Oct. 1984.

C3400–6 SN DISTRIBUTION STUDY OF GROCERY STORE SALES, 1984

Annual. 1984. 4+311 p.
ISBN 87005-472-4.
SRI/MF/complete, delayed

Annual report, for 1984, on sales, store units, and market shares of food store chains, voluntary/cooperative groups, convenience stores, and independents, for 300 metro markets in U.S. and Canada. Data are from various newspaper organizations, Federal agencies, Food Marketing Institute, and *Sales & Marketing Management.*

Contents:

Overview, contents listing, and introduction. (4 p.)

Section 1. Statistical profiles of the top 50 SMSAs ranked by supermarket sales, showing the following: number of stores, market share, and principal supplier, for leading stores arranged by type; and retail food store

and supermarket sales, number of food stores, households by size, population by age of household head, net effective buying income (EBI), and households by EBI group, all for total SMSA, central city, and U.S.; 1982, with EBI changes projected to 1987. (p. 1-101)

Section 2. Other markets' retail grocery store profiles, showing number of stores, market share, and principal supplier, for leading stores grouped by type, and arranged alphabetically by State, SMSA or city, and Canadian Province and city. (p. 103-263)

Section 3. Profiles of 31 leading publicly owned food chains, including number of stores, market areas covered, and retail sales; with 1 table (p. 266) showing sales, net and pretax income, and shareholder's equity, by chain, 1981-82. (p. 265-285)

Section 4. Grocery store statistical profile, with 15 tables listed below. (p. 287-299)

Section 5. Calendar of industry conventions and annual meetings for 1984, and directories of food assns and newspapers/representatives. (p. 301-311)

Availability: Fairchild Books, Seven E. 12th St., New York NY 10003, $40.00; SRI/MF/complete, delayed shipment in Mar. 1985.

SECTION 4 TABLES:

[Data are for grocery stores, unless otherwise noted.]

[1] Firms, [stores, and sales], by sales size, 1977. (p. 288)

[2] Concentration of sales, [stores, and payroll] among [4-50] major firms, 1977. (p. 288)

[3] Firms, number of stores operated, and sales [by store units per firm], 1977. (p. 289)

[4-5] Stores [and sales] by sales size; and stores with payroll and sales, by type of merchandise; 1972 and 1977. (p. 290-291)

[6-7] [Total and chain] grocery stores and supermarkets: estimated number of stores and sales, 1972-82. (p. 292)

[8-9] Distribution of sales and per capita sales, by geographic region [1979-82]. (p. 293)

[10] Sales by months, 1978-82. (p. 294)

[11] Distribution of the U.S. resident population, personal income, and supermarket sales, by State and [census division], 1982. (p. 295)

[12] Per capita consumption of major food commodities [by commodity, 1979-81]. (p. 297)

[13] CPI [1979-82]. (p. 298)

[14] Supermarkets: trends in operating results, 1976-80. (p. 298)

[15] Estimated sales of merchant wholesalers [by type], 1976-80. (p. 299)

C3475
Fieldmark Media

C3475–1   SUPERMARKET BUSINESS

Monthly.   Approx. 50 p.
Oversized.
ISSN 0196-5700.
LC 79-649274.
SRI/MF/excerpts, shipped
quarterly

Monthly trade journal of the retail and wholesale grocery industry, covering product sales and merchandising, technology, store operations and design, finance, advertising and sales promotion, and personnel management. Most data are from Federal Government, Selling Areas Marketing Inc., and journal surveys of industry executives and individual companies.

General format:

a. Feature articles, occasionally with statistics; regular narrative depts; and scattered news briefs and analyses of current grocery trends.

b. Monthly table, with accompanying article, showing percent change in health/beauty aids sales in food stores, by product type, for 2-3 consecutive 4-week periods ended approximately 6 weeks prior to cover date, compared to same periods of previous year.

c. Annual features, including report on consumer use of supermarket products (June); study of household spending for products sold through grocery stores (Sept.); supermarket chain sales and income report (Oct.); directory of equipment suppliers (Nov.); and subject index (Dec.).

Journal occasionally includes *Instore Business* or other separately paginated supplements.

Monthly table appears in most issues. All additional features with substantial statistical content are described, as they appear, under "Statistical Features." Nonstatistical features are not covered.

Availability: Fieldmark Media, Supermarket Business, 25 W. 43rd St., New York NY 10036, industry subscribers †, nonindustry subscribers $32.00 per yr., single copy $3.50, Sept. issue $20.00; SRI/MF/excerpts for monthly table and all portions covered under "Statistical Features;" shipped quarterly.

Issues reviewed during 1984: Nov. 1983-Oct. 1984 (P) (Vol. 38, Nos. 11-12; Vol. 39, Nos. 1-10).

STATISTICAL FEATURES:

C3475–1.501: Dec. 1983 (Vol. 38, No. 12)

REPORT ON RETAILING FOR 80s EXAMINES MARKET STRATEGIES

(p. 12) Article, with 1 table showing grocery store sales, 1977-86. Data are from Dun and Bradstreet.

C3475–1.502: Jan. 1984 (Vol. 39, No. 1)

STUDY EXAMINES AMERICAN SHOPPING PATTERNS

(p. 10) Article, with 1 undated chart showing distribution of white bread purchases, by retail outlet type. Data are from the Wheat Industry Council.

C3475–1.503: Mar. 1984 (Vol. 39, No. 3)

HOW INDEPENDENT RETAILERS RATE THEIR WHOLESALERS

(p. 25-28) Article on the relationship between independent grocery retailers and their wholesalers. Data are from responses of over 500 randomly selected store owners/operators to a Feb. 1984 survey.

Includes 4 tables showing retailers' responses regarding voluntary and cooperative warehouse wholesalers, as follows: ratings for selected performance criteria; and availability, use, and performance rating, for selected services.

ETHNIC HBA: GAINS BRING GROWING PAINS

(p. 53-54, 72-74) By Sarah Lum. Article, with 2 charts showing sales distribution of hair care products for blacks, by outlet type, 1982; and recommended shelf allocation as a percent of total footage for ethnic hair care product categories. Data are from National Research Organization and American Health and Beauty Aids Institute.

GM/HBA PRACTICES IN FOOD RETAILING

(p. 65-70) Article on food store sales and marketing of general merchandise (GM) and health and beauty aid (HBA) products. Data are from a Willard Bishop Consulting Economists, Ltd. study of 60 companies operating approximately 8,230 stores. Study results were released in Jan. 1984.

Includes 4 charts showing GM and HBA sales and gross profit margin as percent of total sales, and shelf allocation as percent of total shelf space, by type of food store.

C3475–1.504: Apr. 1984 (Vol. 39, No. 4)

BEST FOOD DAY ADS SHOW MAJOR SHIFT

(p. 8) Article, with 1 chart showing distribution of food store advertising, by day of week, 1981-83. Data are from a Majers Corp. study of 24 product categories in 24 markets.

C3475–1.505: May 1984 (Vol. 39, No. 5)

IS SCANNING INSTALLATION RATE SLOWING?

(p. 11) Brief article, with 1 table showing number of supermarkets with checkout scanning devices, 1974-83. Data are from the Food Marketing Institute.

VIDEOCASSETTE RECORDERS AS TRAINING DEVICES IN THE GROCERY INDUSTRY

(p. 56-60) By Mel Bomprezzi et al. Article on use of videocassettes for in-store training of grocery industry personnel. Data are from a survey of 300 employees and interviews with training personnel and store managers at 4 grocery chains in Southern California.

Includes 1 table on sample characteristics; and 3 tables showing survey response concerning requirements, practices, and perceived effectiveness of videocassette training programs.

LOOKING AT NUTRITIONAL FACTS ABOUT MEAT

(p. 92, 101) By John Francis. Article, with 3 tables showing the following for red meat: per capita consumption by meat type, 1982; and average daily per capita consumption by meat type, and nutritional contribution by nutrient type, with detail for consumer groups based on frequency of meat consumption, primarily 1983. Data sources include USDA and Yankelovich, Skelly, and White.

C3475–1.506: June 1984 (Vol. 39, No. 6)

FIRST ANNUAL PRODUCT PREFERENCE STUDY

(p. 19-81 passim) First annual feature, by Robert Dietrich, presenting consumer use data for supermarket products in 10 major Areas of Dominant Influence (ADIs), with comparison to U.S., 1983. The 10 ADIs represent approximately 32 percent of the total U.S. population.

Data are based on Mediamark Research Inc. survey of over 40,000 adults, approximately 20,000 of whom live in the 10 ADIs. Feature is intended to enable retailers to evaluate product preference data for markets demographically similar to their own.

Contents:

a. Introduction, methodology, and user guide, with 3 tables showing the following: list of product categories, including number of products in each category; total males, females, and female homemakers, for each of the 10 ADIs; and demographic composition of female homemakers for aggregate 10 ADIs compared to U.S. (p. 19, 22-23)

b. Product index: alphabetical listing of approximately 300 products, including percent of U.S. consumers using each product, consumer group on which use percent is based (female householders for most products), and product category. (p. 24-25, 78, 81)

c. ADI profiles: each with narrative commentary; 1 table showing ADI homemaker demographic characteristics that differ most from U.S. norms (with percent difference for each characteristic); and 1 chart for each of 18 product categories, showing products with unusually high and low use in ADI compared to U.S. (with percent difference for each product). (p. 27-66)

C3475–1.507: July 1984 (Vol. 39, No. 7)

SECOND ANNUAL OPERATIONS REPORT

(Supplement, p. 1A-16A) Annual article on supermarket deli and fresh bakery dept operations, 1983. Data are based on a *Supermarket Business* survey drawing responses from industry executives responsible for over 10,000 supermarkets.

Includes deli and bakery sections, with a total of 17 charts and 24 tables showing survey response on the following:

a. Number and percent of supermarkets with depts; dept size and sales, with comparison to total store, and sales change from 1982 and expected for 1984; number of employees; labor costs as percent of sales; gross margins; and sales per square foot and per employee.

b. Types of equipment, suppliers, and promotional methods used; sales shares, by product type; percent of store customers who shop dept, and average amount spent; preferred location for dept; items most frequently added/increased; and preparation methods, by product (bakery only).

C3475–1.508: Aug. 1984 (Vol. 39, No. 8)

CONSUMER SPENDING WAS UP IN 1983

(p. 7) Article, with 1 chart showing per capita expenditures in food stores, by census division, 1983, with percent change from 1982. Data are from an American Institute of Food Distribution analysis of Commerce Dept data.

C3475–1.509: Sept. 1984 (Vol. 39, No. 9)

37th ANNUAL CONSUMER EXPENDITURES STUDY

(p. 36-174) Annual report on consumer expenditures for food and selected nonfood items in grocery stores, by product and store type, 1983, with trends from 1963. Also includes comparisons of grocery store vs. total market, by product type. Data are from Federal Government and *Supermarket Business* research.

Contents:

a. Contents listing, and narrative report and methodology, with 5 charts and 14 tables listed below. (p. 36-50)

b. Highlights: 5 tables showing value of consumption, expenditures in grocery stores, share of store sales, and grocery share of total market, 1982-83; percent change in grocery tonnage, 1983 vs. 1982; and expenditures in supermarkets, share of supermarket sales, and supermarket dollar and percent margins, 1983; all for perishables, dry groceries, household, pet, and tobacco products, and general merchandise and health/beauty aids, by detailed product type. (p. 55-78)

c. Product category profiles: narrative sales review, and generally 1 chart showing sales index and amount for grocery stores and/or all outlets, mostly 1974-83, presented for 20 product categories; with 7 interspersed tables showing general merchandise and health/beauty aid sales trends by product, mostly 1982-83. (p. 82-174)

Report Charts and Tables:

[1] Total grocery store sales [distribution by product type, 1983 with comparison to 1982]. [chart] (p. 38)

[2] Weekly spending in grocery stores per household and per capita [by product type, 1982-83]. (p. 40)

[3] How an average household doles out its dollars in grocery stores each week [by detailed product type, 1982-83]. (p. 40)

[4-9] Categories that increased and decreased in sales in 1983 [shows 10-20 product categories with largest increases and decreases in dollar sales, and includes percent change in sales, sales share of total store volume, and selected detail on percent change in retail price and tonnage, 1983 vs. 1982]. (p. 43)

[10] Some significant shifts over 20 years [market share by product category, 1963 and 1983]. [chart] (p. 45)

[11] 15-year perspective on how food products sell in grocery stores [total sales, with shares by detailed product type, selected years 1968-83]. (p. 45)

[12] Most stable prices in years [percent change in aggregate food store prices, 1974-83]. [chart] (p. 46)

[13-14] Food store sales by size of store and affiliation [1982-83]. (p. 46)

[15] Service and size pull in shoppers [market share by food store type, 1983 with comparison to 1982]. [chart] (p. 49)

[16] The year supermarket prices leveled off [percent price change by detailed product type, 1982-83]. (p. 49)

[17] Dining out still beats eating at home [share of food dollar 1982-83, and percent

change in dollar sales, prices, and tonnage, 1983 vs. 1982, for restaurants and grocery stores]. [chart] (p. 50)

[18] Grocery store [and selected other kinds of business] sales [1983 with percent change from 1982]. (p. 50)

[19] Grocery store sales trends [number of grocery stores and sales, with detail by sales size and for chain stores], 1983. (p. 50)

C3475–1.510: Oct. 1984 (Vol. 39, No. 10)

50 TOP CHAINS, ANNUAL FEATURE

(p. 26-28, 40) Annual article, by Norman Bussel, on sales and profitability of the 50 leading publicly owned supermarket chains, 1983, based on an analysis of company annual reports.

Includes 7 tables showing sales, net income, and stores operated, for top 50 chains ranked by sales; with additional groupings for top 10 chains ranked by profit margin and growth in sales and earnings, and 15 chains with earnings decline; 1983 with comparisons to 1982.

WHAT INVESTORS CAN EXPECT FROM SUPERMARKET STOCKS, ANNUAL FEATURE

(p. 32-36) Annual article, by Norman Bussel, on supermarket chains rated as best investment opportunities in *Value Line Investment Survey* from Value Line, Inc. Includes 1 table showing price/earnings ratio, and earnings and dividend yields, for 24 publicly owned supermarket chains, generally 1st 9 months 1984.

C3935
Folio Publishing Corp.

C3935–1   FOLIO: The Magazine for Magazine Management
Monthly.   Approx. 125 p.
ISSN 0046-4333.
LC 72-626840.
SRI/MF/excerpts, shipped quarterly

Monthly trade journal (2 issues in Oct.) of the magazine publishing industry, reporting developments in management techniques, circulation, advertising, sales, graphics, and production. Includes announcements of new magazines, mergers and acquisitions, and closings.

Data are from Audit Bureau of Circulations, trade assns, private sources, and the journal's own research.

Includes:

a. Editorial sections and feature articles, occasionally with statistics; and regular editorial depts.

b. Annual Folio 400 ranking of top consumer and trade magazines (2nd Oct. issue).

c. Other annual features, including data on advertising revenue, and profits; article index (Feb.); and a nonstatistical directory of suppliers (May).

d. Other recurring statistics, including top 10 rankings for circulation, overseas sales, and advertising revenues; and a quarterly table evaluating delivery time by selected city.

Quarterly table is described below. Other features with substantial statistical content are described, as they appear, under "Statistical

Features;" page locations and latest periods of coverage for quarterly table are also noted. Each issue of the journal is reviewed, but an abstract is published in SRI monthly issues only when quarterly table or other statistical features appear.

Availability: Folio, PO Box 4006, 125 Elm St., New Canaan CT 06840-4006, $58.00 per yr., single copy $5.00, May issue $10.00, Folio 400 issue $25.00, back issues $8.00; SRI/MF/excerpts for all portions covered under "Statistical Features;" shipped quarterly.

Issues reviewed during 1984: Nov. 1983-Oct. 1984 (P) (Vol. 12, Nos. 11-12; Vol. 13, Nos. 1-10) and Folio 400 Issue [May 1984 issue is published in 2 parts; July 1984 issue omits volume number].

QUARTERLY TABLE:

[1] Publication delivery box score: ordinary 2nd class and controlled circulation publications [shows percent of publications delivered early, on-time, and late in relation to USPS service standard, by selected city, for quarter ending 4-5 months prior to cover date].

STATISTICAL FEATURES:

C3935–1.501: Nov. 1983 (Vol. 12, No. 11)

QUARTERLY TABLE

[1] Publication delivery, by selected city, 2nd quarter 1983. (p. 38)

SMRB READERS-PER-COPY FIGURES CONSISTENT; RESEARCH EXECS PLEASED

(p. 28-30) Article, with 1 table showing top 10 magazines ranked by number of readers per copy, 1983 with comparison to 1982. Data are from Simmons Market Research Bureau.

BLEED ADS ATTRACT 21% MORE ATTENTION: MCGRAW-HILL STUDY

(p. 30) Article, with 1 chart showing reader attention score indexes for corporate and product bleed and non-bleed advertisements. (Bleed ads are borderless and fill the page.)

Data are from McGraw-Hill Research and are based on 3,406 ads.

62% OF CONSUMER MAGAZINES GAIN CIRC IN 1st HALF OF 1983, SEMIANNUAL FEATURE

(p. 32) Semiannual article on magazine circulation, 1st half 1983. Data are from Audit Bureau of Circulations. Includes 1 table showing top 10 magazines ranked by average circulation per issue, 1st half 1983 with comparison to 1st half 1982.

53% OF 'TIME-VALUE' PUBLICATIONS DELIVERED IN TIME, RECURRING FEATURE

(p. 36) Recurring table on USPS delivery efficiency for weekly priority publications. Data are from Red Tag News Publications Assn, Inc. Table shows percent of on-time, 1 day late, and later deliveries in approximately 40 cities, 1st half 1983.

For description of last previous article, see SRI 1982 Annual, under C3935-1.312.

55% OF MAGAZINES REPORT 1st HALF SINGLE-COPY DECLINES, SEMIANNUAL FEATURE

(p. 41-42) Semiannual article on single copy magazine sales, 1st half 1983. Data are from Audit Bureau of Circulations. Includes 1 table showing top 10 magazines ranked by single copy sales, 1st half 1983 with comparison to 1st half 1982.

C3935-1.501 Folio Publishing Corp.

CAN SUPERMARKET SCANNER DATA IMPROVE SINGLE-COPY SALES?

(p. 43, 54) Article, with 1 chart showing number of supermarkets with check-out scanners, 1974-1st quarter 1983. Data are from Food Marketing Institute.

C3935-1.502: Jan. 1984 (Vol. 13, No. 1)

POSTAL RATE INCREASE COULD TAKE EFFECT BY OCT. 1984

(p. 7-8) Article, with 1 table showing proposed postal rate changes, by mail category, filed with Postal Rate Commission by U.S. Postal Service, Nov. 1983.

5% MORE PAPER TO BE USED IN 1984: MPA PAPER SURVEY, ANNUAL FEATURE

(p. 26-28) Annual article forecasting magazine publishing industry paper demand through 1984. Data are based on responses by 93 publishers to a spring 1983 Magazine Publishers Assn survey. Includes 2 tables showing paper demand by paper grade; and distribution of basis weight and printing process used; 1982-84.

For description of 1982 survey, see SRI 1982 Annual, under C3935-1.312.

DATABASE & SOFTWARE OPPORTUNITIES: FINALLY THE TIME IS RIGHT

(p. 63-69) By Haines B. Gaffner. Article, with 1 table showing worldwide revenues of 3 types of U.S. personal computer software suppliers, 1981-87. Data are from LINK Resources Corp., a division of International Data Corp.

1984 PRODUCTION TRENDS SURVEY

(p. 82-83) By Barbara Love. Article on magazine production developments, based on a fall 1983 *Folio* survey of 253 production managers.

Includes 16 charts showing distribution of response to questions on paper supply, in-house operations, typesetting methods, electronic editing system use, printer efficiency, advertising materials and reproduction quality, quality control methods, binding needs, information sources, and management support.

Article updates a similar survey report appearing in Jan. 1981 issue, and includes text statistics comparing selected responses from the 2 surveys. For description of previous report, see SRI 1981 Annual, under C3935-1.204

FORBES 400: PUBLISHERS AT THE TOP

(p. 94-95) By James B. Kobak. Article on the wealthiest individuals and families in publishing. Data are based on *Forbes* ranking of 400 wealthiest persons and families, 1983.

Includes tabular list of wealthiest families and individuals in publishing, showing 1982-83 estimated worth, source of wealth, age, and family members; and 3 tables showing total individuals and families ranked among wealthiest, by industry source of wealth, with detail for those with inherited wealth and with founder still active.

C3935-1.503: Feb. 1984 (Vol. 13, No. 2)

QUARTERLY TABLE

[1] Publication delivery, by selected city, 3rd quarter 1983. (p. 26)

AD PAGES TO INCREASE 8% TO 10% IN 1984, COEN PREDICTS, ANNUAL FEATURE

(p. 16, 19) Annual article on magazine advertising pages and revenue. Data are from Robert Coen of McCann-Erickson, Inc. Includes 1 chart and 2 tables showing percent change in magazine advertising pages, 1976-1st 10 months 1983; and national advertising revenue by media, 1982-83, and forecast for 1984 (with total for local advertising revenue).

CORRECTIONS TO THE FOLIO 400/1983

(p. 43-44) Article presenting corrections and additions to 1983 Folio 400 annual ranking of the magazine publishing industry, described in SRI 1983 Annual under C3935-1.412.

C3935-1.504: Mar. 1984 (Vol. 13, No. 3)

MAGAZINE PUBLISHERS INCLUDED AMONG INC.'s FASTEST-GROWING FIRMS

(p. 8, 17-20) Article, with 1 table showing sales revenues of 8 leading small privately held magazine publishers, 1978 and 1982. Data are from INC. magazine.

CONSUMER MAGAZINES: GROWING SLOWLY, BUT HOLDING MARGINS

(p. 12-14) Article, with 1 table ranking top 10 publicly held consumer magazine publishers by sales revenues, pre-tax income, and operating margin, 1982, and by compound annual revenue growth, 1978-82. Data are from Veronis, Suhler and Associates.

1983 REVENUES, PAGES SHOW HEALTHIEST GAINS SINCE 1978, RECURRING FEATURE

(p. 23, 29) Recurring article on advertising revenues and pages of Publishers Information Bureau magazines for 1983. Includes text summary data, and 2 tables ranking top 10 magazines in advertising pages and revenues, 1983, with comparisons to 1982.

MAGAZINES' PRODUCTIVITY AT RETAIL SURPASSES OTHER CATEGORIES BY FAR

(p. 32-34) Article, with 1 undated table showing inventory turnover and gross margin, for magazines, tobacco, candy, and greeting cards carried in retail stores (no date). Data are from Periodicals Institute.

TOP 10 AMERICAN MAGAZINES IN ANNUAL FOREIGN SALES, SEMIANNUAL FEATURE

(p. 32) Semiannual article on U.S. magazines with highest single copy sales overseas. Data are full-year 1983 estimates from Boarts International, Inc., based on Audit Bureau of Circulations report for June 30, 1983.

Includes 1 table ranking top 10 magazines by foreign sales value, and showing foreign and U.S. issues sold, cover price, and issue frequency, 1983.

C3935-1.505: Apr. 1984 (Vol. 13, No. 4)

QUARTERLY TABLE

[1] Publication delivery, by selected city, 4th quarter 1983. (p. 30)

BUSINESS MAGAZINES' ANNUAL GROWTH RATE OVER FIVE YEARS: 11%

(p. 10) Article, with 1 table ranking top 9 publicly held business magazine publishers by revenue and operating margin and income, 1982, and by compound annual revenue growth, 1978-82, with comparisons to total communications industry. Data are from Veronis, Suhler and Associates.

'83 CORPORATE ADVERTISING IN MAGAZINES REMAINED AT RECESSION YEAR LEVEL

(p. 42-44) Article, with 1 table showing advertising expenditures by media, for 10 leading corporate advertisers, 1st half 1983. Data are from *Public Relations Journal.*

C3935-1.506: May 1984 (Vol. 13, No. 5)

67% OF CONSUMER MAGAZINES GAIN CIRC IN 2nd HALF OF 1983, SEMIANNUAL FEATURE

(p. 20-24) Semiannual article on magazine circulation, 2nd half 1983. Data are from Audit Bureau of Circulations. Includes 1 table showing top 10 magazines ranked by average circulation per issue, 2nd half 1983 with comparison to 2nd half 1982.

18 MAGAZINES OVERSTATE FOURTH QUARTER CIRCULATION, RECURRING FEATURE

(p. 22) Recurring brief article, with 1 table showing publisher vs. Audit Bureau of Circulations (ABC) estimates of circulation, for U.S. and Canadian magazines for which the 2 estimates vary by more than 2%. Data are from ABC audit report for 4th quarter 1983.

49% OF 'TIME-VALUE' PUBLICATIONS DELIVERED LATE, RECURRING FEATURE

(p. 26) Recurring table on USPS delivery efficiency for weekly priority publications. Data are from Red Tag News Publications Assn, Inc. Table shows percent of on-time, 1 day late, and later deliveries in approximately 40 cities, 2nd half 1983. Table is accompanied by a related article (p. 20, 25-27).

COST OF MAKING PRINT AD UP 12% AFTER 2-YEAR LULL, ANNUAL FEATURE

(p. 34) Annual brief article, with 1 table showing costs of producing 6 types of print advertisements, 1979-83. Data are from Trout and Ries Advertising.

SEVERE PAPER SHORTAGE WORRYING PUBLISHERS AND DRIVING PRICES UP

(p. 38-39) Article, with 1 chart showing production capacity for coated groundwood paper, 1979-86.

55% OF MAGAZINES REPORT SINGLE-COPY SALES DECLINES, SEMIANNUAL FEATURE

(p. 46) Semiannual article on single copy magazine sales, 2nd half 1983. Data are from Audit Bureau of Circulations. Includes 1 table showing top 10 magazines ranked by single copy sales, 2nd half 1983 with comparison to 2nd half 1982.

ESTIMATED TOTAL SALES VOLUME FOR PUBLICATIONS BY INDUSTRY, 1982

(p. 49) Chart showing value of magazine/paperback book sales, for supermarkets, and drug, convenience, and discount stores, 1982. Data sources include *Chain Store Age* and *Publisher's Weekly.* Chart is accompanied by 2 related articles (p. 48-50).

COLLEGE STORE MARKET FOR MAGAZINES GROWING, SURVEY INDICATES, ANNUAL FEATURE

(p. 50) Annual article on college bookstore market for magazines. Data are from responses of over 100 college bookstore managers to a 1984 *College Store Executive* survey. Includes text data, and 1 table showing 10 most popular magazine titles in college stores.

C3935–1.507: June 1984 (Vol. 13, No. 6)

INDIVIDUAL MAGAZINES RATED FOR FIRST TIME BY MRI 'PAGE EXPOSURE'

(p. 21-22) Article, with 2 tables showing top 15 magazines ranked by total and average page exposures (number of days an average issue page is viewed by a different reader), spring 1984. Data are based on Mediamark Research, Inc., interviews with 20,000 magazine readers.

CIRCULATION BATTLE PLAN

(p. 66-75) By David H. Foster. Article, with 11 tables illustrating circulation management strategies of selected magazines. Tables show circulation, audience, and/or advertising page and revenue trends for various periods 1978-83. Data are from Mediamark Research, Inc., and other sources.

REMARKABLE PERCEPTIONS

(p. 186, 170) By James B. Kobak. Article summarizing publishing industry rankings based on recent surveys. Includes 6 tables showing the following:

a. *Fortune* survey on most admired corporations: rankings for 25 industries, 10 publishing/printing companies, and 10 most admired companies.

b. *Inc.* list of 500 fastest growing private companies, 1978-82 period: rankings for 17 publishing companies on list.

c. *Forbes* 5-year management performance survey of 1,000 large public companies: rankings based on sales growth, return on equity, and other financial ratios, for top 10 industries in return on equity, and for 12 publishing companies.

C3935–1.508: July 1984 (Vol. 13, No. 7)

[Issue omits volume number.]

QUARTERLY TABLE

[1] Publication delivery, by selected city, 1st quarter 1984. (p. 28)

PUBLISHING COSTS TO RISE 34.4% FROM 1983 TO 1986

(p. 5-6) Article, with 1 table showing specialized business magazine publishing costs, by type, 1983-86. Data are from American Business Press.

AVERAGE BASE SALARIES FOR CIRCULATION EXECS HOLD STEADY SINCE 1983, ANNUAL FEATURE

(p. 26, 31-33) Annual article, with 1 table showing salary ranges, and top salaries paid by leading firms, for trade and consumer magazine circulation directors and managers, and for magazine fulfillment managers, by years of experience, 1984. Data are from Crandall Associates.

15 MAGAZINES OVERSTATE CIRCULATION, RECURRING FEATURE

(p. 33) Recurring brief article, with 1 table showing publisher vs. Audit Bureau of Circulations (ABC) estimates of circulation, for 16 U.S. and French magazines with estimate variances exceeding 2%. Data are from ABC audit report for 1st quarter 1984.

WOMEN IN PRODUCTION AVERAGE SALARY UP 26% SINCE 1982

(p. 36) Article, with 1 table showing mean and median salaries of women professionals in the publishing industry, by position, Dec. 1983. Data are based on 195 responses to a member-

ship survey conducted by Women in Production, Inc. (WIP). Nearly all WIP members are in the New York metro area.

C3935–1.509: Aug. 1984 (Vol. 13, No. 8)

MAGAZINE FREELANCE POLICIES VARY WIDELY, 'WRITER'S DIGEST' REVEALS

(p. 22, 25) Article on best magazines for freelance writers, based on *Writer's Digest* criteria. Data are from a *Writer's Digest* survey of several hundred magazines. Includes 1 undated table showing minimum and maximum word rate, percent of payment made for stories commissioned but not used, and whether author is shown galleys, for 10 best magazines.

A similar article, based on a previous *Writer's Digest* survey, is described in SRI 1982 Annual under C3935-1.306.

SELLING COSTS RISING FASTER THAN AD COSTS, MCGRAW-HILL REPORTS, BIENNIAL FEATURE

(p. 29) Biennial article, with 1 chart showing average cost of an industrial sales call, biennially 1973-83. Data are from McGraw-Hill Research.

For description of previous article, see SRI 1982 Annual, under C3935-1.311.

MICROCOMPUTER AD PAGES DOWN 1% IN FIRST QUARTER

(p. 32) Article, with 1 table showing advertising pages in 17 microcomputer magazines, 1st quarter 1983-84. Data are from Adscope, Inc.

C3935–1.510: Sept. 1984 (Vol. 13, No. 9)

PRE-TAX PROFITS REACH 10.89% IN 1983, MPA/PW SURVEY REVEALS, ANNUAL FEATURE

(p. 5, 17) Annual article on magazine publishing revenues and expenses, 1983. Data are from responses of 154 magazines to a 1983 survey conducted by Price Waterhouse for Magazine Publishers Assn, and from previous surveys.

Includes 3 tables showing aggregate revenues by source, costs by item, and pre-tax profits, all as percent of total revenues, 1981-83, with 1983 pre-tax profit detail by circulation size and advertising revenue range.

PAPER USE JUMPS 8% WITH STRONG ECONOMY, MPA STUDY REVEALS, ANNUAL FEATURE

(p. 21-23) Annual article forecasting magazine publishing industry paper demand through 1985. Data are based on responses of 83 publishers to a 1984 Magazine Publishers Assn survey. Includes 2 tables showing paper demand by grade, with distribution by basis weight and printing process, 1983-85; and summary data on inventory levels and planned roll size changes, 1984.

For description of 1983 survey, see C3935-1.502, above.

FOLIO 400 PREVIEW: PER COPY ANALYSIS

(p. 92-111) Article presenting per copy advertising and circulation analyses for top consumer and business magazines, 1983. Data were compiled by the magazines and analyzed by *Folio,* and are intended for use in conjunction with the annual *Folio 400* report.

Includes 144 tables showing rankings by advertising revenue and pages and circulation revenue per copy, for top 80-100 consumer and business magazines overall, top 2-29 consumer magazines in 29 market segments, and top 2-15 business magazines in 18 market segments, 1983.

For description of *Folio 400* report, see C3935-1.512 below.

C3935–1.511: Oct. 1984 (Vol. 13, No. 10)

QUARTERLY TABLE

[1] Publication delivery, by selected city, 2nd quarter 1984. (p. 34)

15 MAGAZINES OVERSTATE CIRCULATION, RECURRING FEATURE

(p. 28) Recurring brief article, with 1 table showing publisher vs. Audit Bureau of Circulations (ABC) estimates of circulation, for U.S. and Canadian magazines for which the 2 estimates vary by more than 2%. Data are from ABC audit report for 2nd quarter 1984.

49% OF 'TIME-VALUE' PUBLICATIONS DELIVERED LATE, RECURRING FEATURE

(p. 31) Recurring table on USPS delivery efficiency for weekly priority publications. Data are from Red Tag News Publications Assn, Inc. Table shows percent of on-time, 1 day late, and later deliveries in approximately 40 cities, 1st half 1984.

COEN SEES A 15% RISE IN MAGAZINE AD REVENUE IN '84: MPA SEES MORE

(p. 45-49) Article updating 1984 forecast of advertising revenue, prepared by Robert J. Coen of McCann-Erickson, Inc. Includes 2 tables showing national advertising revenue, by media (with total for local advertising revenue), 1984 with comparison to 1983; and percent change in advertising expenditures by product category, for 3 media, 1st quarter 1983-84.

For description of original forecast, see C3935-1.503 above.

AD REPRODUCTION No. 1 QUALITATIVE FACTOR IN ADVERTISER'S MAG CHOICE

(p. 50) Article, with 2 charts showing 10 most and 5 least important non-cost factors influencing decision to buy magazine advertising space. Data are from a Folio Publishing Corp. survey of 190 senior marketing executives, covering 1983 magazine advertising.

C3935–1.512: Folio 400/1984

(484 p., special issue) Annual ranking of top 400 magazines for 1983, based on revenues, advertising pages, and circulation. Covers consumer and trade publications, and includes data on multipublication companies. Data are compiled by the magazines and analyzed by *Folio.*

Contents:

a. Contents listing (p. 8-12); and introductory material, including user's guide (p. 16-33).

b. Overview, with 5 summary charts, including 1979-83 performance summary for the Folio 400. (p. 37-47)

c. Folio 400 table. (p. 49-73)

d. Sections on consumer magazines, with 8 charts, 61 tables, and magazine profiles (p. 74-344); magazine networks, with profiles of 22 networks (p. 345-354); and trade magazines, with 2 charts, 4 summary tables, 38 tables, and magazine profiles (p. 357-446).

e. Indexes. (p. 449-484)

Folio 400 table, consumer and trade magazine tables, and magazine and network profiles are described below.

This is the 6th annual ranking. A Folio 400 preview article, presenting per copy analyses, appears in the Sept. 1984 issue; for description, see C3935-1.510 above.

TABLES AND PROFILES:

FOLIO 400

(p. 49-73) Table shows the following for each of the top 400 magazines, ranked by total revenue: total, advertising, subscription, and newsstand revenues; percent revenue growth; advertising pages; and average subscription and newsstand circulation; 1983, with 1982 total revenue ranking.

CONSUMER AND TRADE MAGAZINE TABLES

(p. 74-344, 357-446) Tables show 1983 rankings of magazines by numerous performance criteria, including items in the Folio 400 table, plus subscription prices, types of pages per copy, other ratios, and growth categories.

Rankings are shown for top magazines overall, for fastest growing and/or new magazines, and for magazines grouped by detailed market segment, including various industry, occupation, consumer interest, humanities and science, and demographic groups.

MAGAZINE AND NETWORK PROFILES

(p. 115-446, passim) Profiles of individual magazines and magazine networks include publisher directory information, and summary of editorial content or focus. Network profiles also include some or all of the following: summary of market/subscriber research available, advertising discount structure, circulation of network magazines, page distribution of major advertising categories, and selected reader/subscriber demographic data.

C3950
Forbes, Inc.

C3950–1   **FORBES**
Biweekly.   Approx. 300 p.
ISSN 0015-6914.   LC 76-149.
SRI/MF/excerpts, shipped quarterly

Biweekly journal, with 2 additional issues, reporting on domestic and foreign business and investment trends. Presents articles on corporate developments, money and securities markets, taxes, banking, Government policies, and investment strategies.

Includes occasional articles with substantial data on securities, corporations, or industry sectors, grouped for analytical purposes. Also includes annual features presenting stock performance forecasts and reviews; financial data on major corporations, banks, and mutual funds; results of a corporate executive compensation survey; and profiles of 400 wealthiest persons/families.

Issues contain feature articles, occasionally with substantial statistics; regular editorial depts; and the following biweekly statistical features:

a. "Forbes Index," with 9 charts showing trends in *Forbes* composite economic index since 1969; and 8 component economic indicators for latest 13-14 months, ending 2-3 months prior to cover date.

b. "Forbes/Wilshire 5000 Review," prepared by Wilshire Associates, with 11 charts and 3 tables showing trends in Wilshire 5000 equity index since early 1970s; selected other stock performance indexes, including percent change by industry sector for 2- and 52-week periods ending approximately 4 weeks prior to cover date; and securities analysts' current estimates of annual earnings per share by industry sector, with rankings based on recent changes in estimates.

Biweekly "Forbes Index" and "Forbes/Wilshire 5000 Review" appear in all issues. All additional features with substantial statistical content are described, as they appear, under "Statistical Features." Nonstatistical features are not covered.

Availability: Forbes, Subscription Services Manager, 60 Fifth Ave., New York NY 10011, $42.00 per yr., single copy $3.00, special issues $4.00; SRI/MF/excerpts for "Forbes Index" and "Forbes/Wilshire 5000 Review," and for all portions covered under "Statistical Features;" shipped quarterly.

Issues reviewed during 1984: Nov. 21, 1983-Oct. 22, 1984 (P) (Vol. 132, Nos. 12-14; Vol. 133, Nos. 1-14; Vol. 134, Nos. 1-10).

STATISTICAL FEATURES:

C3950–1.501: Nov. 21, 1983 (Vol. 132, No. 12)

PICK A NAME

(p. 42) By Richard L. Stern. Article, with 1 table showing number of initial public stock offerings underwritten by each of 18 leading investment firms in 1983, with average percent gain or loss per share from offering to Oct. 1983 compared to Standard & Poor's 500. Data are from Abrahamsen and Co.

HAPPY DAYS ARE HERE AGAIN?—ANNUAL FEATURE

(p. 212-246) Annual article, by Steve Kichen and Leslie Pittel, forecasting 1984 stock performance for Forbes 500 companies. Data are from Lynch, Jones, and Ryan's Institutional Brokers Estimate System, which gathers earnings estimates from over 1,300 securities analysts.

Includes 1 extended table showing the following for each stock: recent price; earnings per share, 1982 and estimated 1983-84; and estimated price/earnings ratio for 1984, with number of analysts contributing estimates, and confidence factor indicating level of agreement among analysts.

C3950–1.502: Dec. 5, 1983 (Vol. 132, No. 13)

GAMES BANKERS PLAY

(p. 172-186) By Norman Gall. Article on reasons for Brazil's current external debt situation. Data are from banks; Keefe, Bruyette & Woods; and Institute for International Economics.

Includes 1 table showing total loans and loans to Brazil, Dec. 31, 1982; and loan loss reserves and stockholders' equity, Sept. 30, 1983; for 5 U.S. banks with largest loans to Brazil.

C3950–1.503: Dec. 19, 1983 (Vol. 132, No. 14)

WHERE THE SMART MONEY WANTS TO GO

(p. 38-39) By Priscilla S. Meyer and Robert McGough. Article on leveraged buyouts of company stock by management. Includes 2 tables showing acquisition price and transaction participants, for 36 leveraged buyouts, 1978-83.

WHAT'S AN MBA REALLY WORTH?

(p. 176) By Maria Fisher. Article on costs and benefits of obtaining a Masters in Business Administration (MBA) degree. Includes 1 table showing: median starting salary of MBA graduates, spring 1978 and spring 1983; and applicants, admissions, incoming class distribution by sex and percent with 1 or more years of work experience, and estimated student expenses, 1983; for 14 business schools.

C3950–1.504: Jan. 2, 1984 (Vol. 133, No. 1)

36th ANNUAL REPORT ON AMERICAN INDUSTRY

(p. 38-290) Annual feature presenting "Forbes Yardsticks 1983," on the profitability, growth, and stock market performance of 1,008 publicly owned corporations with revenues in excess of $450 million. Includes comparisons of capital and equity returns, sales and earnings, and financial and operating ratios, for individual firms, overall and within industry groups.

Contains brief introduction and alphabetical index of companies covered, with summary rankings (p. 38-50); industry summaries and company rankings within each industry group, with 48 tables (p. 55-252); and profitability, growth, and stock performance rankings, with 3 tables and accompanying narrative (p. 254-290).

All tables are described below.

TABLES:

COMPANY RANKINGS WITHIN EACH INDUSTRY

[For each industry sector noted below, tables show 5-year average and latest 12-month returns on equity and total capital, 5-year average percent growth in sales and earnings per share, debt/equity ratio, net profit margin, and 5-year ranks within the industry, by company, with industry medians.]

a. Finance and energy: financial services; banks; thrift institutions; life/accident, fire/casualty, and multiple line insurance companies; brokerage companies; energy companies, including international oils, other oil/gas, and coal; natural gas producers, pipeliners, and distributors; oilfield drillers/services; and electric utilities by region. 9 tables. (p. 55-94)

b. Transportation: auto suppliers, including tire/rubber and parts makers; truckers and other surface transportation shippers; auto/truck manufacturers; airlines; aerospace/defense; and railroads. 6 tables. (p. 99-151)

c. Resources and capital goods: steel; nonferrous metals; forest products; diversified and specialized chemicals; electronics; computers; office equipment and services; construction, mining, and rail equipment; industrial production equipment, specialty equipment/materials, and services; electrical equipment; building materials and equipment; and contractors in heavy construction and homebuilding. 12 tables. (p. 154-203)

d. Consumer goods and services: household goods, including appliances, housewares/furnishings, and housekeeping products; food processors, including meatpackers and agricultural commodities; diversified and specialized branded foods; alcoholic beverages and soft drinks; health care; drugs; apparel, including clothing, textiles, and shoes; toiletries/cosmetics; and tobacco. 9 tables. (p. 204-224)

e. Distribution and leisure: packaging; food distributors and other wholesalers; supermarket chains; specialty retailers, including drug and fast food chains and other specialists; general retailers, including department and discount/variety stores; hotels/gambling, entertainment, and recreation. 6 tables. (p. 224-236)

f. Communications and diversified companies: telecommunications; broadcasting; publishing; and diversified companies and conglomerates. 5 tables. (p. 237-248)

g. Industry median summary. 1 table. (p. 249-252)

OVERALL RANKINGS

[The following tables show data by individual company.]

h. Profitability and growth rankings, showing returns on equity and capital, 5-year average and latest 12 months, and percent growth in sales and earnings per share, 5-year average, and latest 12 months vs. average 1980-82, for companies ranked by 5-year averages. 2 tables. (p. 254-272)

i. Stock market performance rankings, showing recent price, 5-year change, and range 1979-83; book value per share and recent price/book value ratio; latest 12-month earnings per share, and price/earnings ratio; and indicated annual dividend and current yield; for companies ranked by 5-year price change, 1982-83. 1 table. (p. 274-290)

C3950–1.505: Jan. 16, 1984 (Vol. 133, No. 2)

LAWYERS VERSUS THE MARKETPLACE

(p. 73-77) By Richard Greene. Article on supply and demand trends for lawyers. Includes 2 undated charts showing number of lawyers per 1,000 population in U.S. and 4 other industrial countries; and distribution of lawyers by work status (private practice, industry, government, judiciary, inactive/retired, and other). Data are from the American Bar Foundation and other sources.

C3950–1.506: Jan. 30, 1984 (Vol. 133, No. 3)

ALONE ON A WIDE, WIDE SEA

(p. 98) Article, with 1 undated table showing the following for 9 shipping companies formed since 1979 by stock spinoffs from parent companies: year of transaction, sales and net income for most recent fiscal year, recent stock price, and number of shares issued per share of parent company stock.

CONVERTIBLES ARE BACK IN STYLE

(p. 127-128) By Leslie Pittel. Article on the investment potential of newly issued preferred stocks that are convertible into common shares. Data are from Lipper Analytical Services, Zacks Investment Survey, and *Forbes*.

Includes 1 table showing the following for 55 convertible preferred stock issues carrying higher yields than their underlying common stock: preferred stock price, dividend, and yield, and conversion rate, value, and premium; and common stock price, yield, and earnings per share (latest 12-month and 1984 estimate).

C3950–1.507: Feb. 13, 1984 (Vol. 133, No. 4)

CAR WARS

(p. 84-87) By Rosemary Brady. Article, with 1 chart showing share of European auto market for 10 European manufacturers, including Ford and General Motors of Europe, and for all others, 1983.

VALIANT EFFORTS

(p. 131-138) By Barbara Rudolph. Article assessing mutual funds' investment performance, 2nd half 1983. Data are from Computer Directions Advisors, and *Forbes*.

Includes 2 tables showing total returns, performance rank, and year-end assets, for 313 open-end stock and balanced mutual funds; and for 19 closed-end funds, also showing percent premium/discount, and price, at beginning and end of period; 2nd half 1983.

FLICKERS OF EXCITEMENT?

(p. 168-170) By Leslie Pittel. Article on recent performance of natural gas distribution company stocks. Data are from Business Information Systems and *Forbes*.

Includes 1 table showing the following data for 37 natural gas distribution utilities: location and Standard & Poor rating; recent stock price and revenues; latest 12-month earnings and 5-year earnings growth rate; and book value, dividend, and yield, per share.

C3950–1.508: Feb. 27, 1984 (Vol. 133, No. 5)

CLASS STRUGGLE

(p. 73-76) By Pamela Sherrid. Article on corporate practice of issuing stock with restricted voting privileges in order to limit corporate control to a selected group. Includes 1 table listing 11 companies issuing restricted voting stock, and showing the following for each: control mechanism and group, and percent of voting stock held by controlling group.

ROAD TO RECOVERY

(p. 186-188) By Leslie Pittel. Article on pharmaceutical industry stock performance and outlook. Data are from Business Information Systems; Lynch, Jones & Ryan; and *Forbes*.

Includes 1 table showing the following data for 19 drug manufacturers: recent stock price, 52-week range, and performance compared to market; latest 12-month price/earnings ratio and 5-year range; and dividend, return on equity, and latest 12-month and estimated 1984 earnings per share.

SWITCH IN MOOD

(p. 188) By Barbara Rudolph. Article on the performance of income-and-capital preservation mutual funds, with 1 table showing 1- and 5-year returns and *Forbes* rating in up and down markets for 40 such funds.

C3950–1.509: Mar. 12, 1984 (Vol. 133, No. 6)

NEW WAY TO SPOT BARGAINS

(p. 202-208) By Steve Kichen. Article on stock price/sales ratio as basis for investment decisions. Data are from Media General Financial Services Inc., Business Information Systems, Wilshire Associates, and *Forbes*.

Includes 2 tables showing the following for 61 companies with low price/sales ratios, and 61 companies with high ratios: price/sales ratio; recent price; lastest 12-month price/earnings ratio and earnings per share; sales (no date); 5-year sales growth; current ratio; and debt/equity ratio.

C3950–1.510: Mar. 26, 1984 (Vol. 133, No. 7)

UP THE DOWN STAIRCASE, ANNUAL FEATURE

(p. 226-236) Annual lists, with accompanying analysis by Steve Kichen and Leslie Pittel, of 79 companies predicted by security analysts to post significant earnings gains or losses during 1984, and of 92 companies with earnings estimates revised substantially since Aug. 1983.

Data are from Lynch, Jones, and Ryan's Institutional Brokers Estimate System, representing estimates by approximately 1,800 security analysts.

Includes 4 tables showing the following data for each company: recent stock price; earnings per share, 1983 and estimated 1984; price/earnings ratio based on 1984 estimates; number of estimates received; and level of agreement among estimates. Tables on companies with revised estimates include both Aug. 1983 and current estimates.

C3950–1.511: Apr. 9, 1984 (Vol. 133, No. 8)

SMARTER AND RICHER

(p. 62-68) By Paul B. Brown. Article, with 1 table showing the following for the 3 largest retail computer chains: date founded and whether franchisor; number of sales centers, Dec. 31, 1983-84; and projected sales, revenues, and pretax earnings, 1984.

PEOPLE ARE GOING TO GET BURNED

(p. 98) By Jessica Greenbaum. Article, with 1 table showing the following for 12 restaurant chains with theme concepts: stock price (recent, and latest offering); latest earnings per share; 12-month price/earnings ratio; revenues; market value; and price sales/ratio.

1984 ANNUAL BANKING SURVEY

Annual survey of the financial performance of the 100 largest bank holding companies, 50 largest bank trust depts, and 25 largest savings and loan assns, ranked by assets, 1983. Contains 2 statistical features, as follows.

THERE'S NO SUCH THING AS A FREE CHECK, ANNUAL FEATURE

(p. 117-122) Annual article, by Ben Weberman, analyzing financial condition of the banking industry. Includes 3 tables showing:

a. Financial performance measures for 4 highest and 4 lowest performing banks, compared to industry medians, 1979-83 period or 1983.

b. Financial profile of 100 largest bank holding companies, including assets, deposits, loans, loan loss reserve as percent of loans, investments, standby letters of credit, capital, operating and net income, noninterest revenues, and long-term debt as a percent of capital, 1983; assets, equity, and earnings per share, dividends, and return on equity, 4-year average and/or 1983 vs. 1982; and selected profitability/cost and stock performance measures.

c. Trust assets market value, and trust dept revenues and percent of total bank operating revenues, for 50 largest bank trust depts, 1983 with change from 1982.

A THRIFT IS STILL A THRIFT, ANNUAL FEATURE

(p. 126-128) Annual article, by Jinny St. Goar, on savings and loan industry developments. Includes 2 tables showing:

a. Financial performance measures for 4 highest and 4 lowest performing thrift institutions, compared to industry medians, 1979-83 period or 1983.

b. Financial profile of 25 largest savings and loan assns, including assets, savings deposits, loans receivable, investment securities, advances from FHLB, revenues, and net income, 1983, with selected 4-year averages and comparisons to 1982; and yield on earning assets, cost of funds, and spread, as of Dec. 31, 1983.

Other Article

FOREST RICH WITH GAME

(p. 192-196) By Leslie Pittel. Article discussing the 1984 investment potential of stocks with low price/earnings ratios. Data are from Wilshire Associates and Institutional Brokers Estimate System.

Includes 1 table showing the following data for 89 such stocks: earnings per share and price/earnings ratio, for latest 12 month period and estimated for 1984; recent stock price and 52-week range; and dividend and yield per share.

C3950–1.512: Apr. 23, 1984 (Vol. 133, No. 9)

NO-OVERHEAD HOSPITAL

(p. 76) By Anne Bagamery. Article, with 1 table showing the following for 5 home health care companies: sales, FY83; earnings per share, shares outstanding, and stock price (recent, and 52-week high and low).

MYTHS OF EMPLOYEE OWNERSHIP

(p. 108-111) By William Baldwin. Article, with 1 table showing the following for 9 employee-owned companies: sales; employees; and per-employee surplus, funded debt, equity, appraised value, and pension assets; primarily for FY82. Data are from Labor Dept and SEC.

C3950–1.513: Apr. 30, 1984 (Vol. 133, No. 10)

[Issue price is $4.00.]

FORBES 500s, ANNUAL FEATURE

(p. 170-328) Annual feature, for 1983, ranking the top 500 publicly owned corporations by selected measures, and presenting detailed stock market data for each ranked company. Data are from Forbes, and Media General Financial Services, Inc.

Contains brief overview, with 1 summary table (p. 244-245); and 8 detailed tables, most with brief accompanying narrative and summary data, as follows:

a. Top 500 companies in sales (p. 173-178); net profits and cash flow (p. 180-189); assets (p. 190-194); market value (p. 196-203); and employment, and per-employee sales, profits, and assets (p. 204-216); with data and rankings for 1983, and selected comparisons to 1982. 5 tables.

b. Alphabetical list of all 808 ranked companies, with financial data and rankings repeated for each company. 1 table. (p. 218-242)

c. Stock market data for each ranked company, including prices (recent, 5-year and 12-month high and low, latest 12-month change); performance index relative to overall industry and market; price/earnings ratio (5-year high and low, latest 12 month, and 1984 estimate); price/sales ratio; per-share earnings, 1982-84; dividends (indicated rate, yield, payout ratio, and 5-year growth); net profit margin; debt/equity ratio; and shares outstanding, trading volume, and bank/mutual fund share of holdings. 1 table. (p. 244-285)

d. Directory of ranked companies, including address, telephone number, chief executive, stock ticker symbol, and industry group. 1 table. (p. 287-328)

This is the 16th annual feature on the Forbes 500.

THAT NEW KID ON THE BLOCK

(p. 346) By Stanley W. Angrist. Article, with 1 table showing aluminum production and consumption in Western vs. Communist bloc countries, and producers' stocks, 1980-84. Data are from Shearson/American Express' Metal Research Division.

C3950–1.514: May 7, 1984 (Vol. 133, No. 11)

PENSION FUNDS AS PROFIT CENTERS

(p. 35-36) By Thomas O'Donnell. Article, with 1 chart showing percent of large industrial companies with underfunded vs. overfunded vested benefit liabilities, 1975-83. Data are from Johnson and Higgins.

BOUTIQUE IN YOUR LIVING ROOM

(p. 86-94) By Richard Greene. Article, with 1 table ranking 12 largest mail order catalog retailers by direct sales, 1983, with percent change from 1982. Data are from Direct Marketing Assn.

WHEN IS OUR 1916?

(p. 117, 120) By Pamela Sherrid. Article, with 1 table ranking 4 largest publicly held insurance brokers by 1983 sales revenues, and also showing each broker's percent noninsurance business, 1983 net profit, and 1983 profit change from 1980-82 average.

C3950–1.515: May 21, 1984 (Vol. 133, No. 12)

BARGAINS BELOW $5

(p. 246) Article, with 1 undated table showing the following for 25 low-priced (below $5) stocks judged to have potential value exceeding their current price: recent price, latest 12-month earnings per share and price/earnings ratio, current and debt/equity ratios, 4-year earnings growth, sales, and return on equity. Data are from ISYS Corp. and Forbes.

SELLING HIGH

(p. 248-249) By Steve Kichen and Leslie Pittel. Article on investment potential of companies deemed likely candidates for leveraged stock buyouts by management. Data are from ISYS Corp. and Forbes.

Includes 1 undated table showing the following for 31 such companies with sales of $20 million-$5 billion: recent stock price and 52-week range; sales; latest 12-month earnings per share and price earnings ratio; yield; debt/equity, current, and cash flow/debt ratios; and asset turnover.

For description of a related article, see C3950-1.516, below.

WHERE THE ACTION IS

(p. 256-257) By Thomas P. Murphy. Article, with 1 table showing distribution of venture capital investment, for top 9 and all other industries, 1981-82. Data are from Venture Economics Inc.

C3950–1.516: June 4, 1984 (Vol. 133, No. 13)

WHO GETS THE MOST PAY, ANNUAL FEATURE

(p. 96-146) Annual article, by John A. Byrne, on compensation paid to chief executive officers (CEOs) of 805 corporations, 1983. Includes 1 table showing the following data by company: chief executive's name, age, tenure with firm (total and as CEO), background, and compensation (salary/bonus, stock gains, and other), with overall and industry compensation rank.

CRASH OF 1984?

(p. 152) By Subrata N. Chakravarty. Article, with 1 undated table showing volume of replacement oil available from selected countries and U.S. Strategic Petroleum Reserve in the event of a Persian Gulf oil supply disruption. Data are from International Energy Agency, CIA, and private research firms.

WRONG NUMBERS?

(p. 154-155) By Kevin McManus. Article on mobile cellular radiotelephone industry, with 1 undated table showing the following for 22 companies: amount of investment in cellular telephone business; company location; and status and location of cellular telephone activity.

GOOD AMNESTY OR POOR ENFORCEMENT?

(p. 174-175) By Jill Andresky. Article on State amnesty programs for uncollected taxes. Includes 1 table showing revenue collections, number of individual and business participants, and effective dates, for tax amnesty programs in 7 States.

UP & COMERS: BARGAIN HUNTER

(p. 177-178) Article, with 1 undated table showing the following for 8 paint companies: sales, earnings per share, margin, return on equity, price/earnings ratio, and stock price.

WITH A LEVER LONG ENOUGH...

(p. 220) Article on investment potential of large companies deemed likely candidates for leveraged stock buyouts by management. Data are from ISYS Corp. and Forbes.

Includes 1 undated table showing the following for 24 such companies with sales of $4 billion/more: recent stock price and 52-week range; sales; latest 12-month earnings per share and price/earnings ratio; yield; debt/equity, current, and cash flow/debt ratios; and asset turnover.

For description of a related article, see C3950-1.515, above.

STICKS AND STONES AND MOBILE HOMES

(p. 222, 224) By Leslie Pittel. Article, with 1 table showing the following for 46 potential growth stocks in the housing industry: company name and business; sales; recent stock price and 52-week range; dividend yield; price/earnings and debt/equity ratios; and earnings per share, for latest 12 month period, and estimated 1984-85. Data are from Institutional Brokers Estimate System, ISYS Corp., and *Forbes*.

C3950–1.517: June 18, 1984 (Vol. 133, No. 14)

HIGH-RISK DIVIDENDS

(p. 194-196) By Steve Kichen. Article, with 1 undated table showing the following for 27 companies with dividend growth despite earnings decline: 5-year dividend and earnings growth rates, indicated dividend, yield, stock price (recent and 52-week range), latest 12-month earnings per share, company sales, current ratio, and debt/equity ratio.

Data are from ISYS Corp., Wilshire Associates, and *Forbes*.

C3950–1.518: July 2, 1984 (Vol. 134, No. 1)

TOMORROW THE WORLD

(p. 104-108) By Marcia Berss. Article reporting on world stock market developments and trends in international trading.

Includes 1 chart and 2 tables showing top 5 publicly-held companies ranked by sales or assets, for 6 industries in U.S. and worldwide (no date); share of world equity market for NYSE, 10 foreign exchanges, and all others (no date); and transaction date, acquired company and purchaser, percent of stock purchased, price paid, and price/book value ratio, for foreign acquisitions of 7 major U.S. brokerage houses.

SPECIAL REPORT: SPOTLIGHT ON INTERNATIONAL BUSINESS, ANNUAL FEATURE

(p. 116-140) Annual report, by Carol E. Curtis, on international business, with 3 tables presenting selected financial data for the largest 125 foreign investments in the U.S., 125 U.S. multinational corporations, and 200 foreign companies, primarily 1983. Rankings include the following:

a. Foreign investors ranked by total revenues from U.S. companies owned; foreign and U.S. companies involved; and each U.S. company's foreign ownership share, revenue, net income, assets, and primary industry.

b. U.S. multinational corporations ranked by foreign revenue, and including total revenue, and foreign and total operating profit and assets.

c. Foreign companies ranked by revenue, and including net income, assets, market value of common stock, corporate headquarters, industry, and employees.

STOCKS WITH A FOREIGN ACCENT, ANNUAL FEATURE

(p. 184-188) Annual article, by Leslie Pittel, on investment potential of foreign companies listed on U.S. stock exchanges. Data are from *Forbes,* and *Wilshire Associates.*

Includes 1 table showing the following data for 95 stocks and American Depositary Receipts traded widely in the U.S.: exchange on which traded, primary industry, and headquarters country; and recent price and 52-week range, latest 12-months earnings, price/earnings ratio, dividend, and yield.

C3950–1.519: July 16, 1984 (Vol. 134, No. 2)

WHITHER OIL PRICES?

(p. 32-33) By Allan Dodds Frank. Article, with 1 table showing crude oil average monthly production, and installed, maximum, and available capacity; and production during all-time peak month; for total world and 11 countries or country groups, generally as of Feb. 1984. Data are from CIA, DOE, *Petroleum Intelligence Weekly,* and Georgetown Univerity Center for Strategic and International Studies.

SHAKEOUT

(p. 67-70) By James Cook. Article discussing the investment potential of companies producing industrial robots and similar automated equipment. Data sources include Prudential-Bache Securities Inc.

Includes 1 table showing the following data for 9 smaller robot manufacturers: total sales, and earnings per share, 1983 and percent change from 1980; industrial robot/related equipment sales, 1983-84; and recent stock price, price/earnings and debt/equity ratios, and 5-year average return on equity.

WHERE THE AISLES AREN'T CROWDED

(p. 166-167) By Steve Kichen. Article discussing stock performance and outlook for companies listed on AMEX. Data are from ISYS Corp., Wilshire Associates, and *Forbes.*

Includes 2 tables showing some or most of the following for 11 AMEX companies likely to outperform the market in the future, and for 20 AMEX companies that outperformed the market during 1st half 1984: recent stock price and 52-week range; latest 12-month earnings (and 4-year growth rate), price/earnings ratio, yield, and book value, all per share; and sales, current and debt/equity ratios, and increase in market capital.

C3950–1.520: July 30, 1984 (Vol. 134, No. 3)

SMART DARTS AND OTHER GAMES

(p. 95-99) By Steve Kichen. Article comparing performance of randomly selected stocks with performance of portfolios based on specified selection criteria. Data sources include *Forbes* and Institutional Brokers Estimate System. Includes 6 tables showing the following:

a. Current value (generally 1984) for $1,000 invested in 28 stocks chosen at random in June 1967.

b. Recent stock price, latest 12-month earnings per share (EPS) and price/earnings ratio, yield, EPS estimated for 1985, 4-year sales and EPS growth, and price/book value and debt/equity ratios, all for 25 companies in each of the following categories: lowest price/earnings and price/book value ratios, highest proven and anticipated composite performance, and no specified criteria (random selection).

Periodic updates on the status of these companies are planned by the author.

SEARCH FOR EXCELLENCE

(p. 112-114) By Ben Weberman. Article on characteristics of top performing companies in the Southeast. Data are from the Federal Reserve Bank of Atlanta.

Includes 2 tables showing age and employment for top 22 companies, and the following data for the top 12 nonfinancial companies: sales and pretax income, 1983 and 5-year growth rate; latest 12-months earnings per share; indicated dividend; quarterly net income during most recent period and 1 year ago; and recent stock price and 52-week range.

DIFFERENT KINDS OF BIG

(p. 144-145) By Ben Weberman. Article, with 1 table ranking top 30 banks by stock market value as of June 1984, and including shares outstanding; recent price; and asset, deposit, and net income value and comparative rank. Data are from MicroScan and *Forbes.*

C3950–1.521: Aug. 13, 1984 (Vol. 134, No. 4)

LIFE ON THE FAST TRACK

(p. 62-63) By Richard Phalon. Article, with 1 table showing the following for 4 smaller pharmaceutical firms manufacturing generic drugs compared to 4 larger pharmaceutical firms: sales, and return on equity, 1983; recent stock price; and earnings per share, net income as percent of sales, and price/earnings ratio (no dates).

HIDDEN ASSETS

(p. 127-128) By Leslie Pittel. Article, with 2 undated tables showing the following for 20 companies with overfunded pension plans and 20 companies with underfunded plans: amount of overfunding or underfunding, and ratio of excess or deficit to market capitalization and equity; interest coverage; cash flow/debt ratio; recent stock price; earnings per share for latest 12-months; yield; and price/earnings ratio. Companies are ranked by ratio of pension excess or deficit to market capitalization.

Data are from Oppenheimer & Co., ISYS Corp., and *Forbes.*

WHY GLAMOUR DOESN'T PAY

(p. 133) By Kenneth L. Fisher. Article, with 1 table showing the following for 10 California-based companies with best stock performance in 1983: stock price, and price/sale and price/earnings ratios, as of Jan. 1, 1983; and sales, and percent gain in stock price, 1983. Data are from *California Business.*

C3950–1.522: Aug. 27, 1984 (Vol. 134, No. 5)

1984 ANNUAL MUTUAL FUND SURVEY

(p. 68-119) Annual feature on mutual fund performance, with investment results for approximately 900 funds, as of June 30, 1984. Fund types covered are load, no load, and closed-end stock, balanced, and bond/preferred stock funds; and municipal bond, foreign investment, exchange, dual purpose, and money market funds. Data are from Computer Directions Advisors, Inc.

Includes 3 tables showing:

a. Summary data for 25 most consistently high-performing funds; and number of funds rated and composite rating, for 15 multiple fund marketers offering at least five funds each.

C3950–1.522   Forbes, Inc.

b. By fund, grouped by type: *Forbes* ratings in rising and declining markets; average annual total return, 1974-84, and return (total and from income dividends) in latest 12 month period; assets as of June 30, 1984, with percent change from 1983; annual expenses per $100 investment and maximum sales charge, as applicable; and minimum investment and portfolio maturity (for money market funds).

For data correction, see C3950-1.524 below.

HOW TO PULL A CHRYSLER

(p. 120) By William Baldwin. Article, with 1 chart showing distribution of mutual fund individual retirement account assets, by fund type (money market, bond/income, and equity), year end 1983. Data are from Investment Company Institute.

HOG TIDE EBBS

(p. 164) By Stanley W. Angrist. Article, with 1 table showing hog/pig inventories for breeding and available for market, and number of hogs bred, 1982-84. Data are from USDA.

C3950–1.523: Sept. 10, 1984 (Vol. 134, No. 6)

SAAB, MERCEDES, VOLVO, BMW, JAGUAR, WATCH OUT!

(p. 41-48) By Lawrence Minard. Article on Japanese auto marketing in U.S. Data are from auto industry publications. Includes 1 chart and 2 tables showing export sales distribution by auto size class, for 6 Japanese manufacturers, 1st half 1984; Japanese domestic and export auto production, 1978-83; and current resale price as percent of original price, for selected 1980-83 Japanese, European, and U.S. model autos.

OILFIELD SERVICE—WHY ACQUISITORS ARE ON THE PROWL

(p. 88-90) By Robert H. Bork, Jr. Article, with 1 table showing the following data for 16 oilfield service companies ranked by excess cash flow for 1984/85: earnings per share, 1981 and 1984; year end 1980 and recent stock prices; percent change in employment since Jan. 1981; and cash flow, dividends, and capital spending per share, 1983. Data are from company disclosures and other sources.

SECOND TIME AROUND

(p. 112) By Thomas O'Donnell. Article, with 1 table showing external debt of 7 East European countries, and percent held by U.S. banks, as of Dec. 31, 1980 and Mar. 31, 1984. Data are from Wharton Econometric Forecasting Associates.

CHEAPER THAN THEY LOOK?

(p. 206-210) By Steve Kichen. Article on the investment potential of stocks currently selling at a price less than 7.5 times estimated 1985 earnings, as of Aug. 1984. Data are from Institutional Brokers Estimate System and *Forbes*.

Includes 1 table showing the following data for 93 such stocks: recent prices; indicated yield; and earnings per share and/or price/earnings ratio, 1983-85.

IDLE CASH, THE INVESTOR'S PLAYGROUND?

(p. 212) By Leslie Pittel. Article on the investment potential of stocks in companies with large cash holdings. Data are from Standard & Poor's Corp. and *Forbes*.

Includes 1 undated table showing the following data for 11 such companies: recent stock price and 52-week range; book value and earnings per share; price/earnings; cash/price, debt/eqity, and current ratios; and sales.

C3950–1.524: Sept. 24, 1984 (Vol. 134, No. 7)

SMART? OR JUST LUCKY?

(p. 242-244) By Leslie Pittel and Barbara Kallen. Article on the investment potential of 92 stocks with market price below book value, and positive earnings growth. Data are from ISYS Corp.

Includes 3 undated tables showing the following data by company grouped by trading exchange: recent stock price and 52-week range; compound 4-year earnings growth; earnings, book value, and yield per share; price/earnings, price/book value, and debt/equity ratios; and sales.

CORRECTION

(p. 249) Data correction for 1984 annual mutual fund survey, appearing in Aug. 27, 1984 issue.

For description of original article, see C3950-1.522, above.

C3950–1.525: Oct. 1, 1984 (Vol. 134, No. 8)

[Issue price is $4.00.]

FORBES 400, ANNUAL FEATURE

(p. 69-208) Annual feature, by Richard Behar et al., profiling the 400 wealthiest persons and/or families in the U.S., 1984. Data are based on *Forbes* research.

Includes introductory articles, and individual profiles presenting most or all of the following: name, age, locality, history, and lifestyle of individual or family; total net worth; type and source of earnings/assets including inheritance; and charitable activities and/or contributions.

Profiles are arranged in descending order according to net worth.

Also includes profiles of 44 former *Forbes* 400 members not on 1984 list, and 7 individuals who nearly made the list; and an alphabetical index.

Also includes text tables on *Forbes* 400 members' educational attainment (p. 119), top 10 colleges/universities attended (p. 133), top 10 metro areas of residence (p. 134), marital status (p. 146), and top 5 States of residence (p. 148).

C3950–1.526: Oct. 8, 1984 (Vol. 134, No. 9)

SHORT CIRCUIT?

(p. 250-256) By Leslie Pittel. Article, with 1 table showing the following for 65 electronics stocks: recent price and 52-week range, book value, and yield; earnings per share in latest 12 months, with estimates for 1984-85 and 5-year growth rate; and estimated price/earnings ratio, 1985. Data are from ISYS Corp. and *Forbes*.

C3950–1.527: Oct. 22, 1984 (Vol. 134, No. 10)

GREAT LEMMING RACE

(p. 264) By Thomas P. Murphy. Article, with 1 table showing number of computer disk

manufacturers receiving venture capital backing, 1978-83. Data, shown separately for manufacturers of floppy and hard disks, are from Capital Publishing Co.

C3975
Freeman, Miller, Publications

C3975–1   FOREST INDUSTRIES
Monthly.   Approx. 60 p.
ISSN 0015-7430.
LC 63-26965.
SRI/MF/excerpts, shipped quarterly

Monthly trade journal reporting developments and trends in logging, pulpwood and forest management, and manufacture of lumber, plywood, board, and pulp. Occasionally includes data on U.S. and Canadian lumber mill capital investment, plant capacity, and production. Data are from USDA, forestry assns, lumber companies, and other sources.

Issues contain articles, occasionally with statistics; and regular editorial depts.

Features with substantial statistical content are described, as they appear, under "Statistical Features." Each issue of the journal is reviewed, but an abstract is published in SRI monthly issues only when statistical features appear.

Availability: Forest Industries, Circulation Department, 500 Howard St., San Francisco CA 94105, qualified subscribers †, others $35.00 per yr., single copy $3.50; SRI/MF/excerpts for all portions described under "Statistical Features;" shipped quarterly.

Issues reviewed during 1984: Nov. 1983-Oct. 1984 (P) (Vol. 110, Nos. 11-12; Vol. 111, Nos. 1-10).

STATISTICAL FEATURES:

C3975–1.501: Jan. 1984 (Vol. 111, No. 1)
AMERICAN TREE FARM SYSTEM CONTINUES TO FLOURISH

(p. 26) Article, with 1 table showing tree farm reinspections needed and completed, 1975-83. Data are from American Forest Institute, which conducts the inspection program.

C3975–1.502: Apr. 1984 (Vol. 111, No. 4)
1984 PANEL REVIEW, ANNUAL FEATURE

Annual review feature for the panel sector of the lumber industry, including the following statistical articles:

STRUCTURAL PANELS, MDF SET PRODUCTION RECORDS

(p. 24-25) Annual article, by David A. Pease, on wood panel market activity, 1983. Includes 1 table showing panel production by grade, 1973-83.

MARKET EXPANSION FORECAST FOR RECONSTITUTED BOARDS

(p. 40-43) By William H. Pennington. Article on market growth of structural panel sector of reconstituted board industry.

Includes 2 tables showing U.S. and Canada waferboard capacity, selected years 1957-81; and structural panel consumption, production, and trade compared to construction activity and housing starts, 1984-90.

C3975–1.503: July 1984 (Vol. 111, No. 7)

1984 ANNUAL LUMBER REVIEW: LUMBER FIRMS ENJOYED '83, BUT '84 OUTLOOK IS DIMMER

(p. 14-21) Annual article on U.S. and Canadian lumber production and mills, 1983 and trends. Data are from National Forest Products Assn; Statistics Canada; and responses of 408 U.S. and Canadian firms, representing approximately 86% of production, to a survey conducted by *Forest Industries.* Includes 5 tables showing the following:

a. U.S. softwood and hardwood consumption, and production by region; Canadian softwood/hardwood production, for British Columbia and other Provinces; and production, mills, and number of companies producing over 1 billion board feet, aggregated for top 100 producers; 1974-83.

b. Production ranking of 408 leading companies, with headquarters location and number of mills, 1983 with production comparison to 1982.

C3975–1.504: Oct. 1984 (Vol. 111, No. 10)

SAWMILLERS CAN PROFIT BY KNOWING MARKET TRENDS

(p. 20-23) By Stuart U. Rich. Article, with 1 table showing softwood lumber consumption, by market sector including residential (conventional and factory-built) and nonresidential construction, repair/remodeling, and industrial, 1983.

C3975–2   PULP AND PAPER
Monthly. Approx. 225 p.
ISSN 0033-4081.
LC 79-6885.
SRI/MF/excerpts, shipped quarterly

Monthly trade journal (semimonthly in Nov.) reporting on U.S. and Canadian paper, pulp, and board manufacturing industries, including production, engineering/maintenance, management, and marketing.

Most data are from U.S. Dept of Commerce, the American Paper Institute, Paperboard Packaging Council, and Canadian Pulp and Paper Assn.

General format:

a. "Month in Statistics" section, with 1 chart and 1 table, described below.

b. "News Roundup" section, including occasional statistical items, and 1 quarterly table on income results (sales and earnings) of approximately 40 U.S. and Canadian paper/forest product companies, for quarter ending 3 months prior to cover date, with percent change from previous year.

c. "Grade Profile" section, appearing in most issues, providing annual data on a selected industry sector or product type, with text statistics on outlook and prices, and 2 tables showing total production, capacity, and consumption, and frequently capacity utilization rate and foreign trade, for current and previous 2 years for that sector or product, and current annual capacities and capacity share for major producing companies; for U.S. and occasionally for Canada.

d. "Chemical Markets" section, appearing in most issues, providing annual data on a selected chemical used in the paper industry, with text statistics on major producers, availability, market outlook, and prices; and 1-2 tables generally showing production, capacity, foreign trade, and demand for that chemical, for current or preceding year and previous 3-4 years; for U.S. and Canada.

e. Editorial depts and feature articles, some with statistics, including annual statistical features on industry outlook and capital spending plans (Jan.); world production and marketing developments (Aug.); and a chemical supply survey (Oct. or Nov.).

The additional Nov. issue is a nonstatistical buyers guide. An annual index is included in the Dec. issue.

"Month in Statistics" section appears in all issues. Articles with substantial nontechnical statistical content are described, as they appear, under "Statistical Features;" page locations, topics, and latest periods of coverage for "Grade Profile" and "Chemical Markets" sections and quarterly "News Roundup" table are also noted. Nonstatistical features are not covered.

Availability: Pulp and Paper, Circulation Department, 500 Howard St., San Francisco CA 94105, industry subscribers †, others $45.00 per yr., single copy $4.00, Buyers Guide $22.50; SRI/MF/excerpts for "Month in Statistics" and all portions covered under "Statistical Features;" shipped quarterly.

Issues reviewed during 1984: Nov. 1983-Oct. 1984 (P) (Vol. 57, Nos. 11-13; Vol. 58, Nos. 1-10).

MONTH IN STATISTICS:

Includes U.S. paper and paperboard production, by type; woodpulp production, and wastepaper and pulpwood consumption; corrugated box shipments, and containerboard inventories; total paper imports, and imports of Canadian newsprint; and exports of paper, linerboard, and wood pulp.

Also includes Canadian newsprint and wood pulp shipments and operating rates, and Canadian newsprint inventories held by U.S. consumers.

Data are shown for month 3 or 4 months prior to cover date, and year to date, with comparisons to previous year.

STATISTICAL FEATURES:

C3975–2.501: Nov. 1983 (Vol. 57, No. 11)

EQUITY FINANCING RUNNING AT RECORD PACE

(p. 23) Brief article, with 1 table showing value of equity-linked financing and type of security involved, for the paper/forest products industry, by company, 1983. Data are from Morgan Stanley and Co.

STRONG U.S. DOLLAR HURTS PULP PRICES...AND LINERBOARD IN OVERSEAS MARKETS

(p. 31) Article, with 2 tables showing price of northern bleached softwood kraft, and volume and value of U.S. exports of unbleached kraft linerboard, all by selected country, various periods 1983. Data are from Commerce Dept.

FAO SURVEY SEES SLOWDOWN FOR 1982-87

(p. 35) Brief article, with 1 table showing woodpulp and paper/paperboard capacity, by country or world area, 1982 and 1987. Data are from UN Food and Agriculture Organization.

WOODPULP CONSUMPTION SEEN RISING

(p. 37) Brief article, with 1 table showing world paper/paperboard production, and woodpulp, wastepaper, and other fiber consumption, 1981, 1985, and 1995. Data are from Predicasts, Inc.

CHEMICAL PULP BLEACHING: SURVEY OF U.S. BLEACH PLANT OPERATIONS, ANNUAL FEATURE

(p. 53-57) Annual article, by Michael J. Ducey, on chemical use in pulp bleaching plants, based on a 1982 *Pulp and Paper* survey of 83 mills/bleach plants.

Includes 4 tables showing sample characteristics; and average use of 4 chemicals in the bleaching process, by region, end use, and bleaching sequence.

This is the 1st annual survey report.

PULP/PAPER CHEMICAL USE, PRICES TO STRENGTHEN SLOWLY IN 1983-84, ANNUAL FEATURE

(p. 75-84) Annual *Pulp and Paper* surveys, by Barry Shockett, of U.S. and Canadian chemical producers, listing some or all of the following for 27 major chemicals used in the pulp and paper industry: uses, availability, demand, sources, and prices, various years 1978-83, and market forecast 1984. Includes text data and 4 charts.

C3975–2.502: Dec. 1983 (Vol. 57, No. 13)

MONTHLY SECTIONS

Grade Profile: Newsprint

(p. 13) Presents industry data for 1982-84, and company capacity data for 1983.

Chemical Markets: Titanium Dioxide

(p. 161) Presents industry data for 1980-83.

NEWS ROUNDUP QUARTERLY TABLE

(p. 21) Paper/forest products income results, 3rd quarter 1983.

SALARY SURVEY: IS YOUR PAY UP TO PAR? ANNUAL FEATURE

(p. 48-55) Annual article, by Kenneth E. Smith, on salaries and benefits of pulp/paper professionals, based on a Sept. 1983 survey of an unspecified number of *Pulp and Paper* readers.

Includes 3 charts and 16 tables showing survey response concerning type and value of employee benefits; and compensation level, by employer type and sales size, job function, supervisory responsibility, years of experience, number of jobs held, years with current employer, degree level and field, and age.

This is the 1st annual survey.

DYNAMIC PUMP SEALS REDUCE MILL'S BEARING LOSSES, MAINTENANCE COSTS

(p. 68-70) By Bruce Hoffenbecker. Article, with 3 undated tables showing annual operating costs of titanium dioxide, paper stock, and process pumps using packed stuffboxes and dynamic seals. Data are from Weyerhaeuser Co.

C3975–2.503: Jan. 1984 (Vol. 58, No. 1)

MONTHLY SECTIONS

Grade Profile: Linerboard

(p. 13) Presents industry data for 1982-84, and company capacity data for 1983.

Chemical Markets: Chlorine

(p. 197) Presents industry data for 1980-83.

CASH WOES SLOW CAPACITY GAINS—API

(p. 33, 35) Article, with 2 tables showing paper/paperboard and pulp capacity changes for 3- and 16-year periods ending 1986, with detail by region. Data are from American Paper Institute.

OUTLOOK '84, ANNUAL FEATURE

Annual compilation of articles on paper industry outlook in U.S. and Canada for 1984, based on American Paper Institute and Canadian Pulp and Paper Assn estimates, and other sources. Includes 4 articles with substantial statistics, as follows:

STRONG U.S. PULP AND PAPER INDUSTRY RECOVERY SEEN CONTINUING IN 1984, ANNUAL FEATURE

(p. 74-81) Includes 2 tables showing changes in real GNP and in paper industry production, operating rates, prices, costs, and profits, as predicted by 10 analysts, 1984; and operating rates by paper grade, 1982-84.

CANADIAN INDUSTRY: LIGHT AT END OF TUNNEL MAY BE REAL FOR CANADIAN MILLS IN '84 AFTER ALL, ANNUAL FEATURE

(p. 82-88) Includes 2 tables showing newsprint operating rates for U.S. and Canada, 1983-84; and world consumption of white paper and pulp, and North American/Scandinavian white pulp shipments, 1981-85.

LABOR: BARGAINING TO FOCUS ON EASTERN CANADA, ANNUAL FEATURE

(p. 90-91) Includes 1 table showing major contracts on U.S. paper industry bargaining calendars, including companies, mill locations, unions, contract expiration dates, and number of employees affected, by region, 1984. Also includes related narrative information for Canada.

ENERGY: MORE MODERATION EXPECTED IN FUEL COSTS, ANNUAL FEATURE

(p. 93) Includes 1 table showing pulp/paper/paperboard industry distribution of purchased and self-generated energy use, by fuel type, 1st 6 months, 1972, 1982, and 1983.

Other Articles

PERSONAL COMPUTER SYSTEM PROVES COST-EFFECTIVE TOOL FOR MB MILL

(p. 105-107) By David L. DeGroot. Article, with 2 undated tables showing costs/benefits of installing a computer system in the technical services dept of a paper mill. Data are from MacMillan Bloedal, Inc.

NAVAL STORES INDUSTRY IN A SLUMP DESPITE WORLD ECONOMIC RECOVERY, ANNUAL FEATURE

(p. 112-114) Annual article, by Kenneth E. Smith, reporting on outlook for world naval stores industry. Data are from industry estimates. Includes 3 tables showing U.S. production of wood, tall oil, and gum rosins; gum and tall oil rosin foreign trade; and crude tall oil, and tall oil rosin and fatty acid inventories; various periods 1964-84.

CAPITAL SPENDING, ANNUAL FEATURE

(p. 123-130) Annual article, by Stephanie Pollitzer, on U.S. and Canadian pulp and paper firms' capital spending plans through 1986. Data are from an annual survey by *Pulp and Paper*. Includes the following data, generally shown for U.S. and Canada:

a. Capital expenditures for production and environmental quality: trends 1978-84; and by State, Province, type of facility, and U.S. census division or Canadian region, total 1983-85 or later.

b. Capital expenditures for individual companies spending $100 million or more, 1982-84 and 1983-85 periods; and "greenfield" mills and new paper machines (including capacity and startup date), and major modernization/expansion project expenditures, by mill.

The complete survey results are available from *Pulp and Paper* for $75.00.

C3975–2.504: Feb. 1984 (Vol. 58, No. 2)

MONTHLY SECTION

Grade Profile: Tissue

(p. 13) Presents industry data for 1982-84, and company capacity data for 1984.

PRODUCTIVITY GAINS CONSOLIDATED

(p. 35) Brief article, with 1 table showing employment, production worker average earnings, and labor productivity index, for paper and allied products industry by sector, June 1983 and Sept. 1982-83. Data are from BLS and American Paper Institute.

CAUTION, STUDY ARE KEYS FOR ENTERING THE UNCOATED GROUNDWOOD MARKET

(p. 94-96) By David R. Allan. Article, with 2 tables showing groundwood specialties/newsprint operating rates in U.S. and Canada, 1982-85; and projected paper shipments to the business forms industry, by grade, 1990. Data are from Brian Topp, Jones Heward & Co. and Hunt Harris, Star Forms, Inc.

C3975–2.505: Mar. 1984 (Vol. 58, No. 3)

MONTHLY SECTION

Grade Profile: Coated Free-Sheet Papers

(p. 13) Presents industry data for 1982-84, and company capacity data for 1984.

NEWS ROUNDUP QUARTERLY TABLE

(p. 23) Paper/forest products income results, full year 1983.

B.C. INDUSTRY IDLED BY LOCKOUT

(p. 25) Article, with 1 table showing capacity for British Columbia (Canada) pulp and paper mills affected and not affected by a Feb. 1984 lockout of union workers. Data are from *Pulp and Paper Week*.

WASTEPAPER STAGES SHARP RECOVERY: PRICES ARE STRONG, DEMAND STABLE

(p. 132-135) By Debra A. Adams. Article on market outlook for wastepaper to 2000. Data are from Data Resources, Inc., and Franklin Associates, Ltd.

Includes 7 tables showing wastepaper recovery, prices, and domestic and foreign demand, by region and wastepaper grade; with export demand by selected country; various years 1970-2000.

C3975–2.506: Apr. 1984 (Vol. 58, No. 4)

MONTHLY SECTIONS

Grade Profile: Uncoated Printing/Writing Papers

(p. 13) Presents industry data for 1982-84, and company capacity data for 1984.

Chemical Markets: Sodium Hydroxide

(p. 235) Presents industry data for 1980-83.

NEWS ROUNDUP QUARTERLY TABLE

(p. 23) Paper/forest products income results (Canada data only), 4th quarter and full year 1983.

WHEN IS A CONCESSION AN ADVANCE?

(p. 43) Article, with 1 chart showing percent increase in wages (with and without cost-of-living adjustments) for paper industry, compared with all manufacturing and all industry, 1983. Data are from BLS and American Paper Institute.

YOU CAN SAVE ENERGY ON YOUR OLDER LINERBOARD OR NEWSPRINT MACHINES

(p. 122-125) By Richard Reese and Hannu Paulapuro. Article, with 5 undated tables showing investment requirements, and potential energy and monetary savings, for newsprint and linerboard machines modified for energy efficiency.

CPPA TECHNICAL MEETING FEATURES COMPREHENSIVE, BALANCED PROGRAM

(p. 143-145) By John C. W. Evans and David R. Allan. Article, with 2 tables showing Canadian pulp and paper shipments and operating rate by grade, and shipments by destination (domestic, U.S., and overseas), 1982-84. Data are from Canadian Pulp and Paper Assn.

UNSEEN SIDE OF COMPUTER'S IMPACT ON THE PAPER INDUSTRY: THE PLUS SIDE

(p. 150-155) By Norman Wiener. Article on impact of computers on the paper industry, including paper consumption by computer printers and computer-related publications.

Includes 2 undated tables showing circulation and number of computer magazines by end-use market, and circulation and average paper use of 10 leading computer magazines.

C3975–2.507: May 1984 (Vol. 58, No. 5)

MONTHLY SECTIONS

Grade Profile: Coated Groundwood Papers

(p. 13) Presents industry data for 1982-84, and company capacity data for 1984.

Chemical Markets: Alum

(p. 205) Presents industry data for 1980-83.

LOCKOUT TIGHTENS PULP MARKETS

(p. 27) Brief article, with 1 table showing chemical paper-grade pulp inventories of North American/Scandinavian producers, Oct. 1983-Feb. 1984. Data are from American Paper Institute.

STRIKE NOTICE GIVEN IN U.S. TALKS

(p. 29) Brief article, with 1 table showing production capacity of pulp/paper mills in the Pacific Northwest involved in labor negotiations with Assn of Western Pulp and Paper Workers, by mill arranged by company (no date).

U.S. PRODUCERS REVEAL AMBITIOUS PLANS

(p. 37) Brief article, with 1 table showing capital spending plans of 12 U.S. and Canadian paper companies, 1982-83. Data are from individual company reports.

COATING, FILLER PIGMENTS: PRICES ARE STEADY BUT AVAILABILITY IS TIGHTENING, ANNUAL FEATURE

(p. 56-57) Annual article, by Susan S. Taylor, on supply and demand for clays and other coating and filling pigments used in the paper industry. Data are from *Pulp and Paper*. Includes 1 table showing availability and prices of 8 major pigments, 1983-84.

BENEFITS OF RECOVERY BOILER COMPUTER CONTROL SEEN AT 13 MILLS IN FINLAND

(p. 95-98) By Pertti Valkamo and Ossi Pantsar. Article on potential benefits to the pulping industry from recovery boiler computerization. Data are from a presentation made at International Recovery of Chemicals in the Wood and Pulp Industry Conference.

Includes specifications and 1 table showing recovery boiler control systems and production capacity of 13 Finnish mills, 1983.

HIGH PRODUCTION LEVELS CONTINUE INTO 1984, API PAPER WEEK TOLD

(p. 118-121, 123) Article, with 3 tables showing coated paper production vs. GNP; bleached board consumption by end use; and wastepaper exports and mill consumption by grade; various years 1978-87. Data are from American Paper Institute and Morgan Stanley Research.

JAPANESE PULP AND PAPER INDUSTRY STRUGGLES AGAINST IMPORT THREAT

(p. 135-137) By Richard S. Thorn. Article, with 1 table showing paper and paperboard production in Japan, for 10 leading companies and all others, 1982. Data are from Japan Paper Assn.

C3975–2.508: June 1984 (Vol. 58, No. 6)

MONTHLY SECTION

Grade Profile: Corrugating Medium

(p. 13) Presents industry data for 1982-84, and company capacity data for 1984.

NEWS ROUNDUP QUARTERLY TABLE

(p. 23) Paper/forest products income results (U.S. data only), 1st quarter 1984.

C3975–2.509: July 1984 (Vol. 58, No. 7)

MONTHLY SECTIONS

Grade Profile: Recycled Paperboard

(p. 13) Presents industry data for 1982-84, and company capacity data for 1984.

Chemical Markets: Sodium Hydrosulfite

(p. 205) Presents industry data for 1981-84.

NEWS ROUNDUP QUARTERLY TABLE

(p. 29) Paper/forest products income results (Canada data only), 1st quarter 1984.

PACIFIC RIM THE HOTTEST GROWTH AREA; EUROPE "MATURE"

(p. 62-63) By David R. Allan. Article, with 2 tables showing European demand for printing/writing paper and southern U.S. pine pulp, various years 1978-87. Data are from BIS Marketing Research Ltd.

CORRUGATED SHIPMENTS SEEN RISING 7% IN 1984: RECORD FIRST QUARTER

(p. 138-141) By Willard E. Mies. Article, with 3 tables showing selected general economic indicators; fiber box production and shipments; and unbleached paperboard production, export volume, capacity, and operating rate; various years 1982-85. Data sources include American Paper Institute.

SURVEY EXAMINES THE TYPICAL ENGINEER

(p. 165-166) By Matt Coleman. Article comparing perceptions of engineers and others regarding selected educational, professional, and personal characteristics of paper industry engineers. Data are from a May 1984 *Pulp and Paper* reader survey. Includes 3 tables.

C3975–2.510: Aug. 1984 (Vol. 58, No. 8)

MONTHLY SECTIONS

Grade Profile: Bleached Paperboard

(p. 13) Presents industry data for 1982-84, and company capacity data for 1984.

Chemical Markets: Sodium Sulfate

(p. 187) Presents industry data for 1981-84.

MERGER MARKETPLACE IS LIVELY

(p. 23) Article, with 1 table showing sales and earnings, 1983 with percent change from 1982, for 3 lumber companies involved in merger/acquisition activities in mid-1984.

GROUNDWOOD PAPERS TO LEAD EXPANSION, ANNUAL FEATURE

(p. 29) Annual article, with 1 table showing Canada pulp and paper/paperboard capacity, by grade, 1983-86. Data are from Canadian Pulp and Paper Assn.

U.S. PAPERMAKERS TO BOOST 1984 OUTLAYS, ANNUAL FEATURE

(p. 35) Annual article, with 1 table showing paper industry capital spending compared to all manufacturing, for U.S. and Canada, 1982-84. Data are from Commerce Dept, McGraw-Hill, and Statistics Canada.

ENVIRONMENTAL SPENDING MAY CLIMB

(p. 35) Article, with 1 table showing paper industry expenditures for pollution control, by type of pollution and as a percent of total capital expenditures, 1982-84. Data are from Commerce Dept.

WORLD REVIEW, ANNUAL FEATURE

Annual compilation of articles, interspersed throughout the issue, reviewing world developments in the pulp and paper industry. Includes the following statistical articles:

WORLD PULP AND PAPER INDUSTRY: STRONG RECOVERY SETS NEW RECORDS, ANNUAL FEATURE

(p. 53-62) Annual article, by Peter Sutton et al., reviewing world pulp and paper/paperboard capacity, production, and consumption, 1983. Data were compiled by *Pulp and Paper International*. Includes 4 tables showing the following, generally for pulp and paper/paperboard:

a. Production, by continent, 1960, 1970, and 1980-83; and production and per capita consumption for 20 leading producing and consuming countries, 1983 with percent change from 1982.

b. Mills, capacity, production, and total and per capita consumption, for 147 countries and 9 world areas; and summary profiles, including capacity, operating rate, production, imports, and exports, with chemical woodpulp production and trade detail, for 26 leading producing countries; 1982 and/or 1983.

WORLD PULP MARKETS STRENGTHEN IN U.S., STILL SLOW IN EUROPE, JAPAN

(p. 89-92) By John C. W. Evans. Article, with 1 table showing world location, startup date, capacity, and products, for market pulp mills initiating operations in 1984-85.

WORLD TiO2 PIGMENT SUPPLY SEEN TIGHTENING THROUGH THIS DECADE

(p. 106-108) By Fred Montanari. Article analyzing the world market for titanium dioxide pigment. Includes 2 tables and 3 charts showing the following:

a. U.S.: growth rates for GNP, and for titanium dioxide and selected end-use industries, during recessionary and recovery periods 1981-83.

b. U.S., Western Europe, and all others: growth rates, and distribution of titanium dioxide consumption, for selected end-use industries; and titanium dioxide consumption, capacity, and foreign trade; various years 1979-88.

Other Article

READER SALARY SURVEY: TELL US ABOUT YOUR SALARY AND BENEFITS

(p. 76-77) By Kenneth E. Smith. Article presenting summary data from a 1983 *Pulp and Paper* reader survey, and including 2 charts showing distribution of respondents by income and years of experience.

For description of full survey results, see C3975-2.502, above.

C3975–2.511: Sept. 1984 (Vol. 58, No. 9)

MONTHLY SECTIONS

Grade Profile: Uncoated Groundwood Paper

(p. 13) Presents industry data for 1982-84, and company capacity data for 1984.

Chemical Markets: Sodium Carbonate

(p. 315) Presents industry data for 1980-83.

NEWS ROUNDUP QUARTERLY TABLE

(p. 31, 33) Paper/forest products income results, 2nd quarter 1984.

GEORGIA-PACIFIC WILL INSTALL UNCOATED FREE-SHEET MACHINE AT PORT HUDSON MILL

(p. 35) Article, with 1 table showing paper mill free-sheet capacity, 1984; and new capacity, and year added or planned, for individual mills arranged by company, 1983-89; U.S. and Canada. Data are from *Pulp and Paper*, American Paper Institute, and Canadian Pulp and Paper Assn.

JAMES RIVER APPROVES NAHEOLA MACHINE

(p. 37) Article, with 1 table showing company owner, capacity, and startup date, for new paper tissue machinery announced/proposed as of 1984, by mill.

MILLS OF THE '80s, SPECIAL REPORT

Compilation of articles on market outlook for U.S. and foreign pulp/paper industries. Statistical articles are described below.

AFTER PULP MARKET'S DRAMATIC FIRST-HALF JUMP: WHAT'S NEXT?

(p. 96-97) Article on market developments for the northern bleached kraft pulp industry. Data are from American Paper Institute and Mead Pulp Sales Inc. Includes 2 tables showing North American and Scandinavian pulp market capacity, potential production, and demand, 1982-85; and softwood or hardwood pulp production costs, by item, for 4 countries, 1984.

STRONG BOX DEMAND BOOSTS RECOVERY IN CONTAINERBOARD

(p. 140-141) Article, with 1 table showing the following for the containerboard industry: box shipments; linerboard exports; and production, capacity, utilization rate, and prices, for linerboard and for semichemical and recycled corrugating medium; 1982-84. Data are from American Paper Institute, Commerce Dept, and *Pulp and Paper.*

UNCOATED FREE SHEET WEAKENS AFTER STELLAR PERFORMANCE

(p. 170-171) Article, with 1 table showing uncoated free-sheet shipments, by end use, 1st 5 months 1984 with percent change from 1st 5 months 1983. Data are from *Pulp and Paper.*

C3975-2.512: Oct. 1984 (Vol. 58, No. 10)

MONTHLY SECTIONS

Grade Profile: Paper-Grade Chemical Market Pulp

(p. 13) Presents industry data for 1982-84, and company capacity data for 1984.

Chemical Markets: Hydrogen Peroxide

(p. 219) Presents industry data for 1981-84.

FAO CAPACITY SURVEY SHOWS GROWTH

(p. 33) Article, with 3 tables showing world woodpulp and paper/paperboard capacity, by grade and by country or world area, various periods 1973-88. Data are from the UN Food and Agriculture Organization.

WIDE ACCEPTANCE OF NEW BLEACHING EQUIPMENT AND TECHNOLOGY REVEALED, ANNUAL FEATURE

(p. 56-61) Annual article, by Michael J. Ducey, on chemical use in pulp bleaching plants. Data are based on responses of 69 mills/bleach plants to a 1984 *Pulp and Paper* survey.

Includes 3 tables showing sample characteristics; summary of chlorine dioxide substitution benefits; and capacity, designed bleaching sequence, wood species, startup date, and company owner, for displacement bleach plants in operation or planned as of 1984.

For description of survey results published in 1983, see C3975-2.501 above.

FINISHING AND CONVERTING UPGRADES REFLECT CHANGING MARKET DEMANDS

(p. 98-99) By Matt Coleman. Article, with 4 tables showing fine/coated and boxboard/industrial paper converting machinery, by type and region; paperboard and fine/printing paper-grade production; and capacity, startup date, and owner, for individual fine/printing paper mills; various years 1979-84.

WASTEPAPER OUTLOOK GOOD FOR '84, NARI ROUNDTABLE SPEAKERS REPORT

(p. 100-101) By Debra A. Adams. Article, with 1 table showing wastepaper exports, by country or world area of destination, 1st 5 months 1980 and 1984. Data are from National Assn of Recycling Industries, based on Commerce Dept reports.

FAVORABLE SUPPLY/DEMAND EQUATION ADDS UP TO FIRM U.S. MARKETS AHEAD

(p. 142-145) By Carl Espe. Article on market outlook for world pulp and paper industries. Data are from American Paper Institute, Mead Pulp Sales Inc., and Weyerhaeuser Co.

Includes 4 tables showing chemical paper-grade market pulp capacity, production, and demand; production costs by item, for bleached kraft paper-grade market pulp (softwood and hardwood); and kraft liner or linerboard supply and demand, including foreign trade; all for total world and/or selected countries or regions, various years 1982-85.

C4040
Gallup Poll

C4040-1   GALLUP REPORT

Monthly.   Approx. 30 p.
ISSN 0731-6143.
LC SC 81-3017.
SRI/MF/not filmed

Monthly report on opinion surveys conducted by the Gallup Poll concerning contemporary political, social, or economic issues, trends, or policies. Data are generally current to 2 weeks prior to publication date. Report usually is issued several months after publication date.

Most issues contain survey results on approximately 6 topics, each with narrative summary of survey background and response, text summary tables, and 1-5 tables showing survey response, by detailed sociodemographic breakdowns. Survey results for some topics may also include additional tables on responses to follow-up questions, and text statistics on opinion trends from previous surveys.

Issues also generally contain description of polling and survey interpretation techniques, with 2-4 tables showing sample size and methodology for estimating sampling error. A table on national election prediction accuracy since 1936 is included on a space available basis.

Sociodemographic breakdowns are based on a sample size of at least 1,500 persons, and show response distribution by sex, race, educational attainment, region, age, income, political affiliation, religious preference, occupation, city size, and labor union status.

All features with substantial statistical content are described, as they appear, under "Statistical Features." Nonstatistical contents are not covered.

Availability: Gallup Reports, PO Box 628, Princeton NJ 08542, $75.00 per yr., single copy $10.00, June/July issue $25.00; SRI/MF/not filmed.

Issues reviewed during 1984: July 1983-July 1984 (P) (Nos. 214-226).

STATISTICAL FEATURES:

C4040-1.501: July 1983 (No. 214)

Special July 1983 issue presenting results of a recurring survey on public perception of honesty/ethical standards of persons in 25 occupations, as follows:

a. Clergy, druggists/pharmacists, dentists, physicians, engineers, college teachers, police, bankers, TV reporters/commentators, journalists, newspaper reporters, funeral directors, and lawyers. (p. 5-17)

b. Stockbrokers, Senators and Congressmen, State and local political officeholders, business executives, building contractors, realtors, labor union leaders, insurance salesmen, advertising practitioners, and car salesmen. (p. 18-29)

Poll was conducted May 20-23, 1983, with summary trends from 1976. For description of previous poll, see SRI 1982 Annual, under C4040-1.302.

C4040-1.502: Aug. 1983 (No. 215)

Opinion and attitude polls covered in the Aug. 1983 issue are as follows:

a. Handguns: support for laws restricting or banning handgun sales; whether stricter handgun laws would reduce crime, deaths caused by family disputes, and accidental deaths; and personal gun ownership. Conducted May 13-16, 1983; with 9 tables, and trends from 1972. (p. 3-12)

b. Acquired Immune Deficiency Syndrome (AIDS): likelihood of researchers finding a cure within next 2 years, and likelihood of disease reaching epidemic proportions. Conducted June 10-13, 1983; with 2 tables. (p. 13-15)

c. Abortion: support for Supreme Court ruling, and whether abortion should be legal under all circumstances. Conducted June 24-27, 1983; with 2 tables, and trends from 1969. (p. 16-18)

d. Presidential election 1984: Democratic and Independent voters' preferences among Democratic candidates; preferences for Reagan vs. 3 Democratic candidates; and likelihood of Reagan running for reelection. Conducted various periods May-Aug. 1983; with 9 tables, and trends from 1981. (p. 19-30)

C4040-1.503: Sept. 1983 (No. 216)

POLL RESULTS

Opinion and attitude polls covered in the Sept. 1983 issue are as follows:

a. Central America: awareness of El Salvador situation, support for sending additional U.S. military advisors, and likelihood of a U.S. Vietnam-like involvement; and support for sending military aid to Central American governments. Conducted July 29-Aug. 1, 1983; with 5 tables, and trends from 1981. (p. 3-8)

b. Presidential election: likelihood of voting for Catholic, Jewish, female, Atheist, or homosexual presidential candidate. Conducted Apr. 29-May 2, 1983; with 5 tables, and trends from 1937. (p. 9-14)

c. General indicators: satisfaction with national and personal condition. Conducted Aug. 5-8, 1983; with 2 tables, and trends from 1979. (p.15-17)

SPECIAL SURVEY: 15th ANNUAL GALLUP POLL OF THE PUBLIC'S ATTITUDES TOWARD THE PUBLIC SCHOOLS

(p. 19-31) Special reprint of annual survey article reviewing trends in public opinion concerning public schools. Article was originally published in the Sept. 1983 issue of *Phi Delta Kappan.* Survey covered 1,540 adults and was conducted May 13-22, 1983. Includes 5 charts and 33 tables showing survey responses related to the following:

a. Public school problems and ratings; reasons for discipline problems; tax increases to improve education; and voucher system of Government allotment for each child's education at school of parent's choice.

b. Examination-based promotion; national student achievement tests; student workloads; lengthening of school day and year; course requirements for college-bound and other students; foreign language requirements; student access to computers; public involvement with local schools; and importance of college education.

c. Teaching as career for own child; desirable personal attributes of teachers; teacher compensation, including adequacy of current levels, higher salaries for math/science/vocational teachers, and merit pay; report by President's National Commission on Excellence in Education; and education system outlook for year 2000.

Many tables show data by whether respondent has child in school and/or in public or nonpublic school; and by respondent sex, race, age, education, community size, and region. Selected tables also include comparisons to previous years, from as early as 1969.

Article is also described in SRI 1983 Annual, and is available on SRI microfiche, under A8680-1.407.

C4040–1.504: Oct. 1983 (No. 217)

Opinion and attitude polls covered in the Oct. 1983 issue are as follows:

a. Societal institutions: ratings of public confidence in church/organized religion, military, banks/banking, Supreme Court, public schools, newspapers, Congress, big business, organized labor, and television. Conducted Aug. 5-8, 1983; with 11 tables, and trends from 1973. (p. 3-14)

b. Education: support for voucher system for educational funding, and proposed constitutional amendment allowing school prayer; and preferred environment for children's religious training. Conducted June 24-27 and July 22-25, 1983; with 4 tables, and selected trends from 1970. (p. 15-20)

c. Presidential candidate personality profiles and opinion ratings; and political party perceived best for peace and prosperity. Conducted Aug. 12-15 and Sept. 6-9, 1983; with 8 tables, and party rating trends from 1939. (p. 21-30)

C4040–1.505: Nov. 1983 (No. 218)

Opinion and attitude polls covered in the Nov. 1983 issue are as follows:

a. Economy: expected timing of economic downturn; perceived threats to recovery including high interest rates, inflation, international trade problems, budget deficits, and taxes; and whether taxes should be raised to reduce deficit. Conducted Sept. 16-19, 1983; with 7 tables. (p. 3-10)

b. Illegal aliens: whether hiring illegal aliens should be illegal; support for mandatory identification cards; and whether illegal aliens should be eligible for permanent resident status after 6 years. Conducted Oct. 21-24, 1983; with 3 tables, and trends from 1977. (p. 11-14)

c. UN: performance ratings of UN; whether U.S. should withdraw membership; and whether UN should remove headquarters from U.S. Conducted Oct. 7-10, 1983; with 3 tables, and trends from 1951. (p. 15-18)

d. Presidential veto: whether President should be able to veto line items of congressional bills. Conducted Oct. 21-24, 1983; with 1 table, and trends from 1945. (p. 19-20)

e. Presidential election 1984: Democratic and Independent voters' preferences among Democratic candidates; and preferences for Reagan vs. 4 Democratic candidates. Conducted Oct. 7-10 and Oct. 21-24, 1983; with 8 tables, and Democratic candidate trends from 1955. (p. 21-30)

C4040–1.506: Dec. 1983 (No. 219)

Dec. 1983 issue includes opinion and attitude polls, and tabular listings, as follows:

a. National problem perceived as most important, including unemployment, fear of war, inflation, foreign relations, moral decline, government spending, Reagan Administration budget cuts, economy, dissatisfaction with government, and crime; and likelihood of nuclear war and effect of Reagan Administration defense policies. Conducted Nov. 18-21, 1983; with 3 tables, and national problem trends from 1935. (p. 3-8)

b. Ten most admired men and women, 1946-83. 3 annual tabular lists. (p. 9-13)

c. President Reagan: approval of general performance and handling of the economy, foreign policy, Soviet relations, nuclear disarmament, and situations in Lebanon, Central America, and Grenada. Conducted Nov. 18-21 and Dec. 9-12, 1983; with 10 tables, and trends from 1981. (p. 14-29)

C4040–1.507: Jan./Feb. 1984 (Nos. 220/221)

Opinion and attitude polls covered in the Jan./Feb. 1984 issue are as follows:

a. Quality of life: satisfaction with general personal and national conditions. Conducted Feb. 10-13, 1984; with 2 tables, and trends from 1979. (p. 3-5)

b. President Reagan: approval of general performance and handling of the economy, budget deficit, unemployment, foreign policy, Soviet relations, and situations in Lebanon and Central America; whether U.S. made mistake in sending troops to Lebanon, and support for troop withdrawal; 1984 presidential candidate perceived best for prosperity and peace; and whether world is safer now than before Reagan took office. Conducted Jan. 27-30 and Feb. 10-13, 1984; with 13 tables, and trends from 1981. (p. 6-21)

c. Cost of living: adequacy of family income for food, clothing, health care, and general family needs. Conducted Jan. 27-30, 1984; with 4 tables, and trends from 1974. (p. 22-26)

d. National problem perceived as most important, including unemployment, government spending, fear of war, inflation, foreign relations, moral decline, social program budget cuts, economy, crime, dissatisfaction with government, and nuclear arms race; and political party best able to handle major problem. Conducted Feb. 10-13, 1984; with 2 tables, and trends from 1945. (p. 27-31)

e. International: annual world report on public expectations for 1984, including general conditions, labor disputes, peace, prosperity, unemployment, and chance of world war in next 10 years. Conducted Nov.-Dec. 1983 in 31 countries; with 2 charts and 7 tables, including responses by country, demographic detail for U.S., and summary U.S. trends from 1960. (p. 32-43)

f. Orwell's "1984": world report on chances of losing freedom as visualized by George Orwell, including likelihood of privacy loss, poor people's reliance on winning lottery to get ahead, severe government propaganda programs and suppression of critics, war, financial rift between officials and the public, government support for artificial insemination, and dictatorial rule; and perceived freedom in specified countries. Conducted Dec. 9-12, 1983 in 6 countries; with 15 tables, including responses by country and demographic detail for U.S. (p. 44-60)

C4040–1.508: Mar. 1984 (No. 222)

Special Mar. 1984 issue features full reprint of annual *Religion in America, 1984.* Report is covered in SRI under R8780-2, and is also available on SRI microfiche under that number.

C4040–1.509: Apr. 1984 (No. 223)

Opinion and attitude polls covered in the Apr. 1984 issue are as follows:

a. Cost of living: annual survey of perceived income needs for family of 4 and respondent's own family. Conducted Jan. 13-16 and Jan. 27-30, 1984; with 1 table, and trends from 1937. (p. 3-4)

b. Finances: personal financial situation, expected change for next year and perceived change from 1 year ago; and awareness of Reagan Administration FY85 budget proposal, opinion on adequacy of budget and whether budget deficit will affect economic recovery, and preferred areas for budget cuts. Conducted Feb. 10-13 and Mar. 16-19, 1984; with 8 tables, and selected trends from 1976. (p. 5-13)

c. Central America: support for military aid, and approval of Reagan Administration policies. Conducted Apr. 11-15, 1984; with 2 tables, and trends from 1983. (p. 14-16)

d. Presidential election 1984: political party perceived best for prosperity and peace; Democratic and Independent voters' preferences among Democratic candidates; preferences for Reagan vs. 2 Democratic candidates; and perceived campaign styles and personal traits of Hart and Mondale. Conducted Mar. 16-19 and Apr. 6-9, 1984; with 10 tables, and trends from 1951. (p. 17-30)

C4040–1.510: May 1984 (No. 224)

Opinion and attitude polls covered in the May 1984 issue are as follows:

a. President Reagan: reasons for voting against and for Reagan, and opinion on whether Reagan's trip to PRC will improve relations. Conducted Apr. 6-9 and May 3-5, 1984; with 3 tables. (p. 3-8)

b. Elections: voter registration, with detail by race; political party supported in congressional elections; preferences for Reagan vs. 2 Democratic candidates; Democratic and Independent voters' preferences among Democratic presidential candidates; and presidential candidate opinion ratings. Conducted various periods Nov. 1983-May 1984; with 16 tables, and trends from 1966. (p. 9-27)

c. Affirmative action: support for special treatment of women/minorities in hiring and college placement, and approval of Reagan Administration civil rights record. Conducted Jan. 27-30, 1984; with 2 tables, and trends from 1977. (p. 28-30)

C4040–1.511: June 1984 (No. 225)

Opinion and attitude polls covered in the June 1984 issue are as follows:

a. Economy: expected timing of economic downturn; and perceived threats to recovery, including high interest rates, inflation, budget deficits, international trade problems, and taxes. Conducted May 18-21, 1984; with 6 tables, and trends from 1983. (p. 3-9)

b. President Reagan: approval of general performance and handling of the economy, foreign policy, situation in Central America, and Soviet relations. Conducted May 18-21, 1984; with 5 tables, and trends from 1983. (p. 10-15)

c. Presidential election 1984: preferences for Reagan/Bush vs. Mondale/Hart tickets, and for Reagan vs. 2 Democratic candidates; and perceived capability of Mondale vs. Hart in handling foreign affairs, disarmament, situation in Central America, unemployment, conditions of minorities, threats of war, inflation, the economy, women's rights, and environmental problems. Conducted Apr. 23-May 6 and May 18-21, 1984; with 13 tables, and trends from 1981. (p. 16-29)

C4040–1.512: July 1984 (No. 226)

Opinion and attitude polls covered in the July 1984 issue are as follows:

a. Auto safety: support for national legal drinking age of 21, and for withholding of Federal highway funds from States with legal age below 21; seat belt use, and support for law fining nonusers; and support for laws requiring air bags and automatic seat belts in new autos. Conducted various periods May 18-July 2, 1984; with 6 tables, and selected trends from 1973. (p. 2-8)

b. Jogging/exercise: participation in jogging and physical exercise. Conducted May 7-13, 1984; with 2 tables, and trends from 1961. (p. 9-11)

c. Presidential election 1984: preferences for Reagan/Bush vs. Mondale/Ferraro tickets, and for Reagan vs. Mondale. Conducted July 13-16, 1984; with 3 tables, and trends from 1981. (p. 12-15)

d. National problem perceived as most important, including threat of war, international tensions, defense, unemployment, inflation, budget deficit, moral decline in society, Reagan Administration budget cuts, economy, crime, and dissatisfaction

with government; and political party best able to handle major problems. Conducted June 22-25, 1984; with 4 tables, and trends from 1945. (p. 16-21)

e. Electoral reform: support for national primary for determining presidential candidates, and for regional presidential primaries. Conducted June 22-25, 1984; with 2 tables, and trends from 1952. (p. 22-24)

f. Foreign policy: likelihood of U.S. involvement in Central America becoming similar to involvement in Vietnam; and whether U.S. should withdraw from UNESCO. Conducted May 18-21, 1984; with 2 tables. (p. 25-27)

C4125
Geyer-McAllister
Publications, Inc.

C4125–1   GEYER'S DEALER TOPICS: 1983 Dealer Profile
Monthly (selected issues).
For individual publication data, see below.
ISSN 0016-948X.
SRI/MF/not filmed

Set of 2 *Geyer's Dealer Topics* articles on office product dealer operations, sales, and merchandise, based on a survey conducted July 1983. Includes comparisons to surveys conducted in 1972, 1977, and 1981. Articles are further described below.

Geyer's Dealer Topics is a primarily narrative periodical on office equipment and supply dealerships. Only the dealer survey, which is conducted every 2-5 years, is covered in SRI. Previous survey report, for 1981, is described in SRI 1982 Annual, under this number.

Availability: Geyer-McAllister Publications, Inc., PO Box 1129, Dover NJ 07801, $16.00 per yr., single copy $3.50; SRI/MF/not filmed.

SURVEY ARTICLES:

C4125–1.1: Dealer Profile 1983, Part 1
[Oct. 1983 (Vol. 148, No. 10). (p. 27-33)]

Article reporting on office product dealers' operations, sales, and merchandise. Includes text data and 9 charts showing the following:

a. Median and mean sales; percent of dealers handling selected types of office equipment, with detail for data/word processing supplies; and percent of office machine dealers targeting specific markets by market type.

b. Sales to businesses as percent of total; mean and median profitability of dealer machine service depts as percent of gross service revenues; and percent of dealers using and planning to use computerized management information, and planning facility expansion and remodeling.

C4125–1.2: Dealer Profile 1983, Part 2
[Nov. 1983 (Vol. 148, No. 11). (p. 19-26)]

Article reporting on office product dealers' purchasing and marketing patterns, and competition. Includes text data and 6 charts showing survey response rates for the following:

a. Dealers offering open plan systems furniture; extent of contractual sales; importance of various purchasing decision makers; and importance of purchasing manager by product category.

b. Existence of business development plans, and equipment/supply sources by type and product category, by sales size; strength of competitors by type and product category; and furniture sales by price class.

C4170
Gordon Publications

C4170–1   MART
Monthly.   Approx. 50 p.
Oversized.
ISSN 0025-4061.
LC 58-40314.
SRI/MF/excerpts, shipped quarterly

Monthly trade journal reporting on marketing developments and trends of interest to retailers of consumer electronic products and home appliances. Covers sales, management, new products, store operations, promotional techniques, and consumer buying attitudes.

Data are primarily from manufacturers and trade assns, and from the journal's own research.

Issues generally contain sections on appliances, consumer electronics, retail management, and housewares, with news briefs, regular depts, and articles. Articles occasionally present sales or consumer survey statistics for a selected product category. Annual statistical features include consumer electronics market trends and outlook, and a survey of videocassette recorder purchasers.

Features with substantial statistical content are described, as they appear, under "Statistical Features." Each issue of the journal is reviewed, but an abstract is published in SRI monthly issues only when original consumer surveys, or other features with statistics not already described and filmed in other sources, appear.

Journal was previously published by Morgan-Grampian Publishing Co.; issues prior to Aug. 1983 issue are described under C6185-3.

Availability: Mart, Circulation Manager, PO Box 1952, Dover NJ 07801-0952, qualified subscribers †, others $30.00 per yr., single copy $3.00; SRI/MF/excerpts for all portions covered under "Statistical Features;" shipped quarterly.

Issues reviewed during 1984: Nov. 1983-Oct. 1984 (P) (Vol. 30, Nos. 3-12; Vol. 31, Nos. 1-2).

STATISTICAL FEATURES:

C4170–1.501: Jan. 1984 (Vol. 30, No. 5)
GAS-GRILLS SALES HEAT UP IN SECOND QUARTER: MART SURVEY

(p. 31) Article on gas grill sales performance. Data are from a 1983 *Mart* survey of gas grill retailers. Includes 5 tables showing respondent distribution by most popular price category, percent change in sales from last year, average profit margin, and whether accessories are also sold.

BLANK TAPE SALES OUTLOOK IS ROSY, SAY
SUPPLIERS AT ITA UPDATE

(p. 44) Article, with 1 table showing distribution of videocassette recorders, by price category, 1982-84. Data are from Sony Consumer Products.

C4170–1.502: Feb. 1984 (Vol. 30, No. 6)

AUDIO '84: VERY ALIVE, VERY WELL

(p. 21, 23) Article, with 1 table showing factory sales of separate audio components, 1979-84. Data are from Electronic Industries Assn/Consumer Electronics Group.

COMPUTER CROWD IS BULLISH ON
PROSPECTS FOR '84

(p. 21, 24) Article, with 2 tables on sales of home computers and related software, showing volume of sales to dealers and value of factory sales, 1982-84. Data are industry estimates.

1984 'THE YEAR OF THE SPECIALIST:' CES
PANEL

(p. 22) Article, with 1 table on telephone sales, showing volume of sales to dealers and value of factory sales, 1982-84.

MORE PROMOS THAN NEW PRODUCTS IN
AUDIO TAPE AT WINTER CES

(p. 29) Article, with 1 table on sales of blank audio cassettes, showing volume of sales to dealers and value of factory sales, 1981-84. Data are from Electronic Industries Assn/Consumer Electronics Group.

C4170–1.503: Mar. 1984 (Vol. 30, No. 7)

WHAT CONSUMERS PLAN TO BUY IN '84

(p. 5) Article, with 1 table showing percent of consumers intending to purchase selected major appliances and electronic products in 1984. Data are from an Industrial Marketing Research survey of 4,225 households, conducted during 4th quarter 1983.

GAS-GRILL SALES SEEN NEARING 3-MILLION
MARK BY 1987: ARKLA, ANNUAL FEATURE

(p. 18) Annual article on gas barbecue grill industry growth, with projections to 1987. Data are from Arkla Industries, Inc.

Includes text statistics on gas grill sales, with data by retail outlet type, price range, and region; and 1 chart showing distribution of all barbecue grill sales by grill type, 1983-87.

CD SUPPLIERS POOL RESOURCES TO
PROMOTE CONSUMER AWARENESS

(p. 43-44) Article, with 1 table on compact disc player sales, showing volume of sales to dealers and value of factory sales, 1983-84. Data are from Electronics Industries Assn/Consumer Electronics Group.

C4170–1.504: June 1984 (Vol. 30, No. 10)

ARE YOU PAYING YOUR SALES STAFF TOO
MUCH . . . OR TOO LITTLE?

(p. 10-12) Article, with 3 undated tables showing average salary for salespeople and 3-5 other positions in consumer electronic, appliance/TV, and specialty stores, by store sales size. Data are from a *Mart* survey of 1,000 owners, presidents, and managers of retail stores.

RECREATION SOFTWARE FIGHTS BACK TO
STIMULATE MARKET GROWTH

(p. 49) Article on developments in the computer recreational software market. Data are based on responses of 280 home computer owners to a Feb. 1984 LINK Resources Corp. survey. Includes 1 table showing number of respondents using home computers for 11 applications.

WATCH OUT FOR THE APPLES AND LEMONS:
HERE COMES THE '84 COMPUTER
REVOLUTION

(p. 50-51) Article analyzing home computer market in 1984. Data are based on responses of 280 home computer owners to a Feb. 1984 LINK Resources Corp. survey. Includes 2 tables showing percent of respondents owning 4 types of peripherals and using computers for 7 applications, by computer price category.

APPLIANCE EXECS ARE EYEING RECORD YEAR

(p. 63, 72) Article, with 1 table showing factory shipments of major appliances, by type, 1984-85. Data are from Assn of Home Appliance Manufacturers.

C4170–1.505: July 1984 (Vol. 30, No. 11)

ELECTRONICS '84,
ANNUAL FEATURE

[The following articles are part of an annual report on market trends and outlook for selected consumer electronics sectors. Each article includes 1 table showing volume of sales to dealers, and value of factory sales, for the product categories and dates shown below. Data are from Electronic Industries Assn.]

PHONE SUPPLIERS MIXED ON CORDLESS
OUTLOOK

(p. 33-35) Data cover telephones, 1982-85.

BIG CES NEWS IN VIDEO? IT'S AUDIO!

(p. 33, 36-37) Data cover videocassette recorders, 1980-85.

SALES TURN TO DIGITAL AND AV FOR TOTAL
ENTERTAINMENT, SOUND REPRODUCTION

(p. 39) Data cover one-brand audio component systems, 1980-85.

WHERE'S THE MICRO? DIGITAL DROUGHT AT
CES

(p. 43) Data cover home computers, 1982-85.

COMPUTER-SOFTWARE INDUSTRY MOVES
TOWARD EDUCATION, 'EDUTAINMENT'

(p. 33, 44) Data cover home computer software, 1982-85.

C4170–1.506: Aug. 1984 (Vol. 30, No. 12)

VHS TAPES PACE '83 CASSETTE GAINS

(p. 23) Article, with 1 table showing sales value and volume for blank video-tapes by type, 1983, with percent change from 1982. Data are from International Tape/Disc Assn.

C4170–1.507: Oct. 1984 (Vol. 31, No. 2)

TV/APPLIANCE STORES GAIN IN VCR SALES:
MART SURVEY, ANNUAL FEATURE

(p. 39-41) Annual article presenting results of a 1984 *Mart* survey of approximately 2,000 videocassette recorder (VCR) purchasers.

Includes 24 tables showing distribution of responses to questions in the following areas:

a. Importance of selected factors in VCR model selection; place of purchase (type of retail outlet); most common use of VCR; and whether salesperson attempted also to sell tapes/camera at time of VCR purchase.

b. Number of blank and pre-recorded tapes bought at time of VCR purchase and after; use of rental tapes, participation in rental tape club, and number of rentals per month; software bought/rented, by type of content and retail outlet; and video camera and disc player ownership and purchasing plans.

c. Income, marital status, sex, educational attainment, and age.

This is the 7th annual survey.

C4200
Gralla Publications

C4200–1   MERCHANDISING
Monthly.   Approx. 100 p.
Oversized.
ISSN 0362-3920.
LC 76-641228.
SRI/MF/excerpts, shipped
quarterly

Monthly trade journal reporting on marketing developments and trends in consumer electronics, housewares, and major appliances. Covers retail sales, consumer buying attitudes, store operations, new products, and promotional techniques.

Data are based on original surveys of consumers and retailers, and manufacturer reports of shipment estimates.

Issues generally contain regular narrative depts, and special features. Recurring statistical features include the following:

a. Prerecorded videocassette industry news, with 1 monthly table showing the following rankings: top 30 videocassettes in rentals; and top 10 videocassettes, top 5 laserdiscs, and top 5 capacitance electronic disc (CED) videodiscs, in sales; all for current and previous month, and indicating number of months included among top.

b. Retail opinion file, a survey of retailer attitudes, practices, or expectations regarding varying topics.

c. Annual statistical and marketing reports on sales, retail value, and trade of consumer electronics, housewares, and major appliances; and an annual national consumer attitude survey.

Monthly table appears in all issues. All additional features with substantial statistical content are described, as they appear, under "Statistical Features." Nonstatistical features are not covered.

Prior to the Mar. 1984 issue, journal included an additional monthly table on top 10 video game software titles.

Availability: Merchandising, Circulation Department, Rm. 930, 1501 Broadway, New York NY 10036, qualified subscribers †, others $33.00 per yr., single copy $4.00, Mar. and July issues $15.00 each; SRI/MF/excerpts for monthly tables and all portions covered under "Statistical Features;" shipped quarterly.

Issues reviewed during 1984: Nov. 1983-Oct. 1984 (P) (Vol. 8, Nos. 11-12; Vol. 9, Nos. 1-10).

STATISTICAL FEATURES:

C4200-1.501: Nov. 1983 (Vol. 8, No. 11)

9th ANNUAL MAJOR APPLIANCE STATISTICAL AND MARKETING REPORT

(p. 15-22) Annual feature on retail sales of cooking, cleanup, air treatment, refrigeration, and laundry appliances, 1983. Contains narrative and 51 tables generally showing total factory shipments, percent of shipments by model characteristics (including price range and size for some appliances), and percent of sales by type of outlet, for the following:

a. Electric, gas, and smoothtop ranges, and microwave ovens. 9 tables. (p. 16)

b. Built-in and portable dishwashers, food waste disposers, and trash compactors. 9 tables. (p. 18)

c. Room air conditioners (also includes shipments by energy efficiency ratio), air cleaners, and dehumidifiers. 8 tables. (p. 20)

d. Refrigerators and freezers. 16 tables. (p. 20-21)

e. Washers and dryers. 9 tables. (p. 22)

GEAR SELECTION TO SALESPERSON'S CAPACITY TO GIVE INFORMED PITCH ON SOFTWARE STOCKED

(p. 60, 62) By Howard S. Rauch. Article, with 1 chart showing personal computer software sales, and distribution by outlet type, 1983 and 1988. Data are from Future Computing, Inc.

C4200-1.502: Dec. 1983 (Vol. 8, No. 12)

RETAIL OPINION FILE: STORES TO BEEF UP SKUs TO REAP 25-40 MARGINS ON SOFTWARE, PERIPHERALS

(p. 29, 32-33) By Lee Rath. Report on retailers' computer sales and future expectations, based on responses of 214 retailing companies to a 1983 survey. Includes 6 tables showing the following for typical department, discount, and computer specialty store chains, and radio/TV, consumer electronics, and radio/TV/personal electronics stores:

a. Number of stores (for chains only), date computer sales began, and computer selling space and brands carried; and sales value and profit margin distribution, for hardware, software, and peripherals, primarily 1983-84.

b. Distributions of sales by quarter, software volume by program type, and software purchases from publishers and local distributors; and percent of sales made in "packages."

C4200-1.503: Mar. 1984 (Vol. 9, No. 3)

62nd ANNUAL STATISTICAL AND MARKETING REPORT

(p. 15-36) Annual report on shipments and retail sales, including foreign trade, of major household appliances, consumer electronic products, and housewares, 1979-83. Also includes market profiles by State for 1983. Data are from Federal and private sources.

Contains narrative analysis, and 78 tables showing:

a. Shipments and retail value, 1979-83, and unit sales highlights, 1982-83, by product, for major appliances (p. 16-20), home and auto electronic products (p. 22-26), and housewares (p. 28-32). 67 tables.

b. Export and import shipments and manufacturer's value/freight/insurance, by product, 1980-83. 10 tables. (p. 33-35)

c. Market profiles: residential and farm residential electrified homes, total housing permits, and personal income, by census division and State, 1983, with percent change from 1982. 1 table. (p. 36)

C4200-1.504: Apr. 1984 (Vol. 9, No. 4)

MASS MERCHANDISERS TO GET MORE COMPUTER PIE

(p. 41, 43-44) By Michele Tomasik. Article on consumer computer purchasing patterns. Data are from a Jan. 1984 *Merchandising* survey.

Includes 1 chart and 17 tables showing survey response concerning preferred outlet for purchase, average price paid, purchasing and spending plans, household income, number of persons and children in household, and computer peripherals use and purchasing plans, generally for owners of computers valued over and under $1,000, with some comparisons to non-owners.

61% OF MASS MERCHANTS POLLED CARRY OR PLAN TO CARRY COMPUTERS

(p. 46, 48) By Michele Tomasik. Part 1 of a 3-part article on computer merchandising plans of retailers. Data are from responses of 406 retailers, representing 1,378 stores, to a 1984 *Merchandising* survey.

Includes 11 tables showing survey response concerning plans to carry computer merchandise; expected change in sales and inventory, and inventory value, for computer hardware, software, and peripherals; software titles by type; software and hardware sales by price range; and present and future inventory of peripherals by type; all for mass merchandisers and electronics single- and multi-unit retailers, various periods 1983-85.

C4200-1.505: May 1984 (Vol. 9, No. 5)

RETAILERS PLEASED WITH VENDORS OF PERIPHERALS, SOFTWARE, BUT FAULT HARDWARE MANUFACTURERS

(p. 16) By Frank Cavaliere. Part 2 of a 3-part article on computer merchandising plans of retailers, with focus on retailer/vendor relations. Data are derived from responses of 406 retailers, representing 1,378 stores, to a 1984 *Merchandising* survey.

Includes 5 tables showing survey response concerning perception of software, peripheral, and hardware manufacturers' awareness of retail marketing needs; causes of consumer resistance to home computer purchasing; and whether home computer market has been overstated.

C4200-1.506: June 1984 (Vol. 9, No. 6)

MOST RETAILERS POLLED BUY SOFTWARE FROM LOCAL DISTRIBUTOR COMPANIES

(p. 78, 82) By Frank Cavaliere. Part 3 of a 3-part article on computer merchandising plans of retailers, with focus on software. Data are from responses of 406 retailers, representing 1,378 stores, to a 1984 *Merchandising* survey.

Includes 6 tables showing software sources (direct purchase, or local or national distributor), stock balancing program participation, display arrangement (subject or manufacturer) and physical layout, employee training methods, and importance of demonstration tapes/videos in selling computer products; for all mass merchandisers, and for single- and multi-unit electronics outlets.

C4200-1.507: July 1984 (Vol. 9, No. 7)

TWELFTH ANNUAL CONSUMER SURVEY

(p. 13-31) Annual report on consumer ownership and purchase plans, for 28 types of electronic products, major appliances, and housewares, 1984. Data are from an Apr.-May 1984 survey of 1,733 consumers.

Includes 132 tables showing respondent distribution, by some or all of the following, for each type of product: current ownership, purchase plans, reasons for not purchasing, place of purchase, product preference, and price range.

Also includes 9 tables showing respondent characteristics.

MULTI-FEATURE UNITS REPLACING LEASED PHONES

(p. 48A, 52) By Marilyn Sibirski. Article, with 2 charts showing telephone sales and unit market share, by type, 1984. Data are from AT&T Consumer Products.

C4200-1.508: Aug. 1984 (Vol. 9, No. 8)

FROM VCRs TO COMPUTERS, '84 IS A BANNER YEAR

(p. 12-15) By Lee Rath. Article, with 1 table showing volume of sales to dealers, for consumer electronics by product type, 1984 with percent change from 1983. Data are from Electronics Industries Assn/Consumer Electronics Group.

C4200-1.509: Sept. 1984 (Vol. 9, No. 9)

HOME HEALTHCARE HEADS LIST OF STRONG SELLERS

(p. 15-16) By Michael Garry. Article, with 1 table showing volume of housewares sales to dealers, by product type, 1984 with percent change from 1983. Data are from housewares manufacturers.

C4200-1.510: Oct. 1984 (Vol. 9, No. 10)

MICROWAVES, AIR CONDITIONERS PUSH MAJAPS TO WHAT SHOULD BE THE BEST SALES YEAR EVER

(p. 38, 53) By Nancy Markov. Article, with 1 table showing volume of household appliance sales to dealers, by product type, 1984 with percent change from 1983. Data are from the Assn of Home Appliance Manufacturers and Gas Appliance Manufacturers Assn.

C4215
Graves, Earl G.,
Publishing Co.

C4215–1   BLACK ENTERPRISE
Monthly.   Approx. 100 p.
ISSN 0006-4165.
LC 74-25061.
SRI/MF/not filmed

Monthly journal reporting on topics of interest to blacks, including career opportunities, black-owned businesses, and economic, social, and political issues. Data sources include Federal agencies and the journal's own research.

General format:

a. Feature articles and regular narrative depts.

b. "Facts and Figures" section, with 1-3 charts or tables often including data on various indicators of black socioeconomic standing.

Annual statistical features include financial performance of top 100 black-owned businesses and of black-owned financial institutions; and economic outlook for black Americans.

Features with substantial statistical content are described, as they appear, under "Statistical Features." Each issue of the journal is reviewed, but an abstract is published in SRI monthly issues only when statistical features appear.

Availability: Black Enterprise, Circulation Department, PO Box 5500, Bergenfield NJ 07621, $15.00 per yr., single copy $1.75, June issue $3.00; SRI/MF/not filmed.

Issues reviewed during 1984: Dec. 1983-Nov. 1984 (P) (Vol. 14, Nos. 5-12; Vol. 15, Nos. 1-4).

STATISTICAL FEATURES:

C4215–1.501: Dec. 1983 (Vol. 14, No. 5)
PLAGUED BY AIDS SCARE

(p. 24) Article reporting on discrimination against Haitians since their inclusion on the U.S. Public Health Service list identifying acquired immune deficiency syndrome (AIDS) high-risk groups. Data are from the Centers for Disease Control and *Statistical Abstract of the U.S., 1981.*

Includes 1 undated chart showing AIDS cases per million persons, for total and Haitian-American population, with detail for males and homosexuals/bisexuals.

FACTS AND FIGURES

(p. 47) Includes 2 tables showing median family income for blacks and whites and distribution of black families, both by type of family structure, various years 1970-82. Data are from the Census Bureau.

C4215–1.502: Jan. 1984 (Vol. 14, No. 6)
FACTS AND FIGURES

(p. 27) Includes 1 chart showing distribution of commuters by transportation mode, for blacks and all others, 1972. Data are from the Census Bureau.

FIRST ANNUAL ECONOMIC OUTLOOK FOR BLACK AMERICA: 1984

(p. 28-39) Annual article summarizing views of leading black economists serving on *Black Enterprise* Board of Economists. Also includes 3 tables showing the following:

a. Population and income, 1982-84; and median income, by sex and educational attainment, for all workers and year-round full-time workers, 1982; all by race.

b. General, Federal, and State revenues for 4 major cities with black mayors, FY62, FY72, and FY77.

Data are from Commerce Dept, Brimmer and Company Inc., and Data Resources Inc.

C4215–1.503: Feb. 1984 (Vol. 14, No. 7)
FACTS AND FIGURES

(p. 35) Includes 2 charts showing population distribution by labor force status, by race and sex; and law school enrollment, for blacks, Hispanics, Native Americans, and Asians; various periods 1965-83. Data are from BLS and Law School Admission Council.

SUITE SUCCESS

(p. 48-54) Article on career opportunities for blacks in hotel chains. Includes 1 undated table showing the following for 7 major hotel chains: number of hotels and black general managers, total and percent black employment, and black managers as percent of all managers.

C4215–1.504: Mar. 1984 (Vol. 14, No. 8)
FACTS AND FIGURES

(p. 35) Includes 2 tables on black voters, showing the following:

a. Unregistered black voting-age population, and Reagan 1980 victory margin over Carter, in 15 key States.

b. 15 cities with largest black population: total and black population, 1980; and total and registered voting-age blacks, for State in which city is located, 1982.

Data are from the Joint Center for Political Studies, Census Bureau, and the National Coalition on Black Voter Registration.

POWER OF THE BLACK VOTE: ELECTION 1984

(p. 36-45) Article, with 1 table showing the following by congressional district or State for 1984 congressional election contests in which black support could affect the outcome: incumbent (and whether black, possibly facing black challenger, or retiring), with party affiliation, year first elected, victory margin in last election, and *Black Enterprise* rating of voting record on issues of concern to blacks; and black percent of voting age population, principal city, and date of 1984 primaries.

BRINGING UP BABY

(p. 67-68, 76) Article reporting on maternity and infant rearing costs. Data are from Health Insurance Assn of America. Includes 1 table showing detailed expenses including loss of mother's salary during maternity leave, and costs of pregnancy, childbirth, and infant furniture and equipment; and obstetrical fees in 7 major cities; 1982.

C4215–1.505: Apr. 1984 (Vol. 14, No. 9)
FACTS AND FIGURES

(p. 35) Includes 1 chart showing divorce ratio for women, 1970 and 1982; and combined ratio for men and women, 1982; by race. Data are from Census Bureau.

C4215–1.506: May 1984 (Vol. 14, No. 10)
FACTS AND FIGURES

(p. 39) Includes 1 chart showing percent increase in owner-occupied and renter-occupied housing units, by race of householder, 1970-80 period. Data are from the Census Bureau.

BLOOD, SWEAT, AND STEEL

(p. 40-48) Article reviewing the position of blacks in the construction industry. Data are from BLS, and labor union reports filed with the Equal Employment Opportunity Commission. Includes 2 tables showing construction industry total and minority or black employment, and black membership as percent of total union membership, with detail by occupation or trade, various years 1960-83.

C4215–1.507: June 1984 (Vol. 14, No. 11)
FACTS AND FIGURES

(p. 75) Includes 1 chart showing distribution of all and minority-owned businesses by type of ownership (sole proprietorship, partnership, and corporation), 1977. Data are from SBA.

EXPANSION: SEEKING NEW FRONTIERS, ANNUAL FEATURE

(p. 81-166) Annual feature on black-owned businesses and financial institutions, including lists of the top 100 businesses ranked by 1983 sales, and of all banks, savings and loan assns, and insurance companies, ranked by 1983 assets. Lists also show location, year started, chief executive, employment, and the following: type of business and 1982 sales rank, for top 100; deposits and loans, for banks and savings and loan assns; and insurance in force, and premium and net investment income, for insurance companies.

Top 100 list is accompanied by an analytical article, with 2 charts and 3 tables showing company distribution and sales by industry group, top 10 companies in sales growth and employment, and companies new to list, 1983; and aggregate number and sales of auto dealerships on list, 1974-83. Financial institution lists also are accompanied by analytical articles, each with 1 table showing aggregate employment and financial data for 1982-83.

Feature also includes articles on outstanding companies. This is the 12th presentation of the annual lists.

C4215–1.508: July 1984 (Vol. 14, No. 12)
FACTS AND FIGURES

(p. 33) Includes 4 undated charts showing distribution of whites, blacks, Hispanics, and Asian/Pacific Islanders by occupation. Data are from the Census Bureau.

C4215–1.509: Sept. 1984 (Vol. 15, No. 2)
FACTS AND FIGURES

(p. 33) Includes 1 chart and 1 table showing percent of population aged 25-34 completing high school, by race, 1970 and 1982; and higher education full-time undergraduate enrollment for black students seeking degrees, with blacks as percent of total enrollment, biennially 1970-80. Data are from Census Bureau and Dept of Education.

C4215–1.510: Oct. 1984 (Vol. 15, No. 3)

FACTS AND FIGURES

(p. 39) Includes 1 undated chart showing the following for black, white, and Hispanic families: number, median income, and incidence of poverty, for all families, and for families with no wage earners and with 1 and 2/more earners (with detail by whether earnings are from husband, wife, others, or various combinations). Data are from Census Bureau.

C4215–1.511: Nov. 1984 (Vol. 15, No. 4)

FACTS AND FIGURES

(p. 47) Includes 2 tables showing the following:

a. Selected data for 29 States in which blacks could affect outcome of 1984 elections, including number of electoral votes, blacks as percent of voting-age population, and congressional districts with black candidates.

b. Voter turnout (percent of population reporting that they voted) in congressional and presidential elections, by race and region, 1964-82 election years.

Data are from *Black Enterprise,* Joint Center for Political Studies, and the Census Bureau.

AUTO DEALERS REV UP FOR RECORD SALES

(p. 71-75) By Jay Koblenz and Edmund Newton. Article, with 1 chart and 1 table showing number of auto dealerships included in *Black Enterprise* list of top 100 black-owned businesses, with aggregate sales, 1974-83; and black-owned dealerships of 3 major automakers, 1974-84. Data are from *Black Enterprise* and National Assn of Minority Automotive Dealers.

C4300
Hanley-Wood

C4300–1   BUILDER

Monthly. Approx. 100 p.
ISSN 0744-1193.
SRI/MF/excerpts, shipped quarterly

Monthly journal of the National Assn of Home Builders (NAHB), reporting on housing construction and market developments. Covers construction and remodelling activities, design, marketing techniques, financing, new products, and economic and governmental developments affecting the housing industry.

Issues contain news and feature articles, some with statistics; and regular editorial depts, including "Outlook" section, by Michael Sumichrast, presenting the following:

a. 5-7 monthly charts showing summary housing trends; and 3 monthly charts showing builder ratings for present new housing sales and 6-month sales outlook.

b. 1-2 additional tables or charts, including a recurring chart showing 6-month sales outlook by region.

Annual features include a survey of prospective homebuyer characteristics, and ranking of top 100 builders.

Monthly "Outlook" charts appear in all issues beginning with Jan. 1984. All other statistical features, and additional "Outlook" tables and charts with substantial statistical content, are described, as they appear, under "Statistical Features."

Availability: Circulation, Builder Magazine, PO Box 1434, Riverton NJ 08077, NAHB members †, key employees of NAHB members $15.00 per yr., others $25.00 per yr., single copy $3.00; SRI/MF/excerpts for monthly "Outlook" feature, and all portions described under "Statistical Features;" shipped quarterly.

Issues reviewed during 1984: Nov. 1983-Oct. 1984 (P) (Vol. 6, Nos. 11-12; Vol. 7, Nos. 1-10).

STATISTICAL FEATURES:

C4300–1.501: Nov. 1983 (Vol. 6, No. 11)

STARTS: A PLEASANT SURPRISE

(p. 12) By Michael Sumichrast. Article with 1 table showing estimated housing starts, by State, 1983-84. Data were compiled by NAHB.

FIRMS RUSH TO GO PUBLIC WHILE MARKET IS HOT

(p. 29-30) Article, with 1 table showing the following for 5 home building companies making initial public stock offerings during June-Sept. 1983: date and share volume of initial offer, and price per share at offering and as of Oct. 1983.

NAHB ACTION: IN SPITE OF RATES, BUILDERS STILL OPTIMISTIC

(p. 93) Article, with 1 chart and 1 table showing homebuilders' opinions regarding impact of higher interest rates on housing sales, by region, based on a membership survey conducted by NAHB during Sept. 1983.

C4300–1.502: Dec. 1983 (Vol. 6, No. 12)

FORECASTERS SEE FLAT BUT EVEN YEAR AHEAD

(p. 36) Article, with 1 table showing single- and multi-family housing starts, by region, 1983-84. Data are from NAHB and Census Bureau.

C4300–1.503: Jan. 1984 (Vol. 7, No. 1)

OUTLOOK

(p. 11-14) Includes 1 table showing housing starts in U.S. and top 20 SMSAs, 1983-84; and recurring chart on builder 6-month expectations for new single-family housing sales, by region. Data are from NAHB.

BUILDERS LOOK AHEAD, SEE A GOOD YEAR

(p. 46-56) Article, with 1 chart showing forecasts of 7 economists for housing starts and 30-year fixed-rate mortgage interest rates, 1984.

HOUSING MAY (OR MAY NOT) FOLLOW POPULATION TRENDS

(p. 96-98) Article, with 1 table showing population of 38 metro areas designated SMSAs since the 1980 census. Data are from Census Bureau.

C4300–1.504: Feb. 1984 (Vol. 7, No. 2)

OUTLOOK

(p. 11-14) Includes 1 table showing private expenditures for nonresidential and residential building, 1978-82 and Oct. 1983; and recurring chart on builder 6-month expectations for new single-family housing sales, by region. Data are from Census Bureau and NAHB.

C4300–1.505: Mar. 1984 (Vol. 7, No. 3)

OUTLOOK

(p. 13-16) Includes recurring chart on builder 6-month expectations for new single-family housing sales, by region. Data are from NAHB.

HOUSING WAS MORE AFFORDABLE LAST YEAR

(p. 46) Article on housing affordability, with 1 table showing ratio of conventionally financed mortgage payments to average household income in 15 major SMSAs, 1982-83. Data are from Advance Mortgage Corp.

ARMs MAKE GAINS

(p. 50) Article, with 1 chart showing distribution of adjustable rate mortgages, by duration, 1983. Data are from Federal Home Loan Mortgage Corp.

C4300–1.506: Apr. 1984 (Vol. 7, No. 4)

OUTLOOK

(p. 11-14) Includes recurring chart on builder 6-month expectations for new single-family housing sales, by region. Data are from NAHB.

DEMAND SURGES FOR DETACHED HOUSES

(p. 58) Article, with 1 table showing distribution of housing sales by type, 1982-83. Data are from Chicago Title Insurance Co.

WHAT BUYERS WANT, ANNUAL FEATURE

(p. 64-79) Annual article, by George A. Fulton et al., on new-home shopper characteristics and buying attitudes, 1984. Data are from 2,-176 responses to a recent survey of prospective buyers in 6 metro areas, conducted by George A. Fulton Research and Consulting.

Includes 8 tables showing buyer characteristics and purchasing plans, including household composition, income, home ownership, and housing value, equity, or rent, with detail by type of housing preferred; and interest in selected options and motivations for buying by buyer type (1st-time, move-up, and empty-nester).

This is the 2nd annual survey.

C4300–1.507: May 1984 (Vol. 7, No. 5)

FIRST-TIME BUYERS CLAIM RECORD MARKET SHARE

(p. 45, 48) Article, with 1 table showing distribution of conventionally financed home purchases, by price range, and median purchase price, biennially 1977-83. Data are from U.S. League of Savings Institutions.

RENTAL STARTS TO PLUNGE

(p. 60) Article, with 1 table showing rental housing vacancy rates, by region, year end 1982-83. Data are from Advance Mortgage Corp.

WATCH OUT FOR ACCIDENTS ON THE JOB

(p. 72, 76) Article, with 1 table showing housing construction accident distribution, by type, 1980. Data are from BLS.

HOUSES ARE GETTING BIGGER AND BETTER

(p. 76) Article, with 1 table showing percent of new single-family homes with selected features, including central air conditioning, 1982-83. Data are from Census Bureau.

SAN DIEGO BUILDER PARES WASTED SPACE

(p. 87) Article presenting results of a study comparing cost and use for specific rooms of single-family homes. Data are from a W. R. Effinger and Co. survey of 5,000 homeowners in southern California. Includes 1 chart.

AMERICAN DREAM HASN'T CHANGED

(p. 87, 92) Article, with 1 table showing residents' satisfaction with the size of specific rooms in their homes. Data are from a 1983 survey of 4,300 households conducted by the Harvard-MIT Joint Center for Urban Studies.

CALIFORNIA BOASTS THE BIGGEST S&Ls

(p. 112) Article, with 1 table showing top 10 savings and loan assns ranked by assets, 1983. Data are from U.S. League of Savings Institutions.

BUILDER 100, ANNUAL FEATURE

(p. 124-145) Annual ranking of top 100 home construction companies based on 1983 production, showing the following for each company: whether public or privately held; top executives; housing production (total, detached and attached for-sale, and rental), 1983; gross revenues; principal State markets, and diversified enterprises.

Also includes narrative summary, profiles of selected companies, and 8 summary tables.

Data are from CMR Associates and other sources.

C4300–1.508: June 1984 (Vol. 7, No. 6)

OUTLOOK

(p. 11-14) Includes 1 table showing monthly inventory of unsold new homes for selected end-of-recovery period years, 1976-Feb. 1984.

RISING INTEREST RATES SHADOW 1985

(p. 34-35) Article, with 1 chart showing NAHB forecast for 30-year fixed-rate mortgage interest rates, quarterly 1984-85.

ECONOMISTS EXPECT 1985 HOUSING DOWNTURN

(p. 35-38) Article, with 1 table showing single- and multi-family housing starts by region, and total mobile home shipments, 1983-85. Data are from Census Bureau and NAHB.

PROPERTY INDEX GUIDES PENSION INVESTMENTS

(p. 50) Article describing FRC (Frank Russell Co.) Property Index of investment return rate for real estate owned by institutions. Index is based on data from the National Council of Real Estate Investment Fiduciaries. Includes 1 table showing index by region and type of property, 1st 9 months 1983.

ECONOMISTS PICK THE HOT SPOTS FOR 1984

(p. 64, 68) Article, with 1 table showing housing starts for top 20 SMSAs, 1984 with change from 1983. Data are from Census Bureau and NAHB.

NAHB REPORT: HBA LEADERS RANK DEFICIT AS NUMBER ONE PROBLEM

(p. 123-124) Article reporting on home builder assn leaders' outlook for the general economy and the housing industry. Data are based on a Feb.-Mar. 1984 survey by NAHB. Includes 2 tables showing perceived effects of legislation permitting greater involvement of savings/loan assns in home building industry, and views on 1984 vs. 1983 economic climate for housing starts/sales.

C4300–1.509: July 1984 (Vol. 7, No. 7)

RECESSION HURT MID-SIZE BUILDERS THE MOST

(p. 42-44) Article, with 2 tables showing distribution of builders and share of total new housing units built, by builder size group, 1978 and 1982; and number of building firms by region, 1972, 1977, and 1982. Data are from NAHB and Census Bureau.

COMPUTERS ARE COMING, COMPUTERS ARE COMING

(p. 66-85) By Deborah V. Woodcock. Article, with 3 charts and 2 tables showing percent of homebuilders using computers, by function, computer size, and cost of hardware, all by company size group, 1983. Data are from a recent survey of 547 builders, conducted by Inter-Media Marketing.

Also includes directory of software suppliers, including number of builder users.

NAHB REPORT: COLLEGE STUDENTS WANT TO BUY DETACHED HOMES

(p. 116) Article on homebuying aspirations of college students. Data are from a recent NAHB survey of 1,324 students at 9 universities. Includes 1 undated table showing perceived obstacles to buying a home.

C4300–1.510: Aug. 1984 (Vol. 7, No. 8)

SINGLE-FAMILY HOMES ARE GETTING BIGGER

(p. 64) Article, with 1 table showing average square footage of single-family homes sold, by price range, 1983-84. Data are based on approximately 50 responses to a survey of large-volume builders, conducted by RAMS Marketing, Inc.

NEARLY HALF THE NAHB BUILDERS DO REMODELING

(p. 64) Article, with 1 table showing builders' ratings of remodeling market conditions (good, fair, or poor), by region, 1st quarter and 1st 9 months 1984. Data are based on a survey of 186 remodelers, conducted by NAHB Remodelors Council.

C4300–1.511: Sept. 1984 (Vol. 7, No. 9)

OUTLOOK

(p. 11-14) Includes 1 table showing top 10 States ranked by housing starts, 1983-84. Data are from NAHB.

HOUSING IS HEADED FOR ANOTHER RECESSION

(p. 40-41) Article, with 1 chart showing new single-family home sales and mortgage interest rates, Jan.-July 1984. Data are from FHLBB.

ARE JOINT VENTURES A NECESSARY EVIL?

(p. 56) Article, with 1 chart showing distribution of builders involved in joint ventures with financial institutions, by type of project (for-sale housing, income-producing property, and other), 1983. Data are from a recent NAHB survey of 170 builders, 14% of whom participated in joint ventures during 1983.

DOORS ARE CLOSING FOR LOW-INCOME HOUSEHOLDS

(p. 64) Article, with 1 undated table showing average months waited for public housing and HUD Section 8 housing assistance, by household type. Data are from a recent survey of low-income housing in 66 cities, conducted by the U.S. Conference of Mayors.

C4300–1.512: Oct. 1984 (Vol. 7, No. 10)

OUTLOOK

(p. 11-14) Includes 1 table showing percent change in GNP and components, 4th quarter 1980-2nd quarter 1984 period. Data were compiled by NAHB from Dept of Commerce and other sources.

BUILDER VIEWPOINT: NATIONAL SURVEY

(p. 38-39) Article, with 2 tables showing builders' opinions on the impact of 3 legislative issues affecting the housing industry, and on the effectiveness of the housing lobby. Data are from a 1984 telephone survey of 508 builders, conducted by Inter-Media Marketing.

BANKS SUPPLY MOST CONSTRUCTION LOANS

(p. 90) Brief article on real estate development financing. Data are based on a survey of loans received for 287 projects, conducted by Urban Land Institute. Includes 1 table showing distribution of construction and permanent development loans, by type of lender, 4th quarter 1983-1st quarter 1984 period.

TOP 20 CITIES BY MULTIFAMILY STARTS

(p. 102) Table ranking top 20 cities by multi-family housing starts, 1984. Data are from NAHB.

C4380
Harcourt Brace Jovanovich

C4380–1   **QUICK FROZEN FOODS**
Monthly.   Approx. 75 p.
ISSN 0033-6408.
LC 44-46818.
SRI/MF/not filmed

Monthly trade journal of the frozen food industry. Covers retail and food service sales, storage and transportation developments, Government regulation, processing, and merchandising and promotion. Data are primarily from the journal's own or other private research.

Issues generally contain feature articles and narrative depts; and recurring "Data File" feature, with 1-2 tables variously showing frozen food production, consumption, exports, and cold storage holdings, by product type.

Annual statistical features include refrigerated warehouse and trucking surveys; and expansion plans for supermarkets and frozen food distributors and packers. Issues also include "Regional Reports" (occasionally titled "SAMI Survey"), a series of articles on frozen food sales and consumption in specific market areas.

Recurring "Data File" tables, and all articles with substantial statistical content, are described as they appear, under "Statistical Features." Each issue of the journal is reviewed, but an abstract is published in SRI monthly issues only when statistical features appear.

Availability: Quick Frozen Foods, Circulation Department, One E. First St., Duluth MN 55802, $20.00 per yr., single copy $2.00; SRI/MF/not filmed.

Issues reviewed during 1984: Nov. 1983-Oct. 1984 (P) (Vol. 46, Nos. 4-12; Vol. 47, Nos. 1-3).

STATISTICAL FEATURES:

C4380–1.501: Nov. 1983 (Vol. 46, No. 4)

FF TOPS $30 BILLION IN 1982, FOODSERVICE PROVIDES PUSH, ANNUAL FEATURE

(p. 16-32, 46-48) Annual article, by Ross Chamberlain, on frozen food production. Includes 2 tables on frozen food volume and value, showing retail and institutional production, by product type, 1982 and change from 1981; and total and per capita production, 1942-82.

REGIONAL REPORT: PHOENIX/TUCSON SHOPPERS OPT FOR ETHNIC FROZEN FOODS

(p. 42-45, 49) Sixteenth in a series of articles on frozen food sales and consumption, by product type, in specific market areas. Data are from Selling Areas Marketing Inc. (SAMI).

Current article covers Phoenix/Tucson, Ariz., and includes 4 tables showing per household consumption indexes for product types with highest and lowest indexes, including Phoenix/Tucson's rank among 42 SAMI markets, for an unspecified period.

C4380–1.502: Dec. 1983 (Vol. 46, No. 5)

SAMI SURVEY: JACKSONVILLE/TAMPA—DESSERT PIES, MIXED FRUIT REIGN SUPREME

(p. 26-30) Seventeenth in a series of articles on frozen food sales and consumption, by product type, in specific market areas. Data are from Selling Areas Marketing Inc. (SAMI).

Current article covers Jacksonville/Tampa, Fla., and includes 4 tables showing per household consumption indexes for product types with highest and lowest indexes, including Jacksonville/Tampa's rank among 42 SAMI markets, for an unspecified period ended June 24, 1983.

Seventh article in this series also covered Jacksonville/Tampa, Fla. (for description, see SRI 1983 Annual under C4380-1.401).

DATA FILE, RECURRING FEATURE

(p. 40-41) Includes the following tables:

[1] Cold storage holdings [frozen fruits, juices, vegetables, poultry, eggs, fish, and shellfish, all by type, June and Sept. 1982, and Apr.-Sept. 1983].

[2] Pack: frozen green beans [by cut, 1981-83].

[3] Spring pack: frozen [leaf and chopped] spinach [retail and institutional volume and value, 1982 and 1st half 1982-83].

SAMI SURVEY: AS SAMI SEES SAN ANTONIO

(p. 42-46) Eighteenth in a series of articles on frozen food sales and consumption, by product type, in specific market areas. Data are from Selling Areas Marketing Inc. (SAMI).

Current article covers San Antonio/Corpus Christi, Tex., and includes 4 tables showing per household consumption indexes for product types with highest and lowest indexes, including San Antonio/Corpus Christi's rank among 45 SAMI markets, for an unspecified period ended June 24, 1983.

C4380–1.503: Jan. 1984 (Vol. 46, No. 6)

SAMI SURVEY: SAN FRANCISCO SAMI MARKET

(p. 38-42) Nineteenth in a series of articles on frozen food sales and consumption, by product type, in specific market areas. Data are from Selling Areas Marketing Inc. (SAMI).

Current article covers San Francisco, Calif., and includes 4 tables showing per household

consumption indexes for product types with highest and lowest indexes, including San Francisco's rank among 45 SAMI markets, for an unspecified period ended June 24, 1983.

DATA FILE, RECURRING FEATURE

(p. 43) Includes the following table:

[1] Per capita [retail and institutional] poundage and value of [all] frozen foods [and of frozen prepared foods, seafoods, vegetables, poultry, meat, beverages, and fruits], 1972-82.

C4380–1.504: Feb. 1984 (Vol. 46, No. 7)

JUICE OUTLOOK FAVORABLE DESPITE LATE '83 FREEZE, ANNUAL FEATURE

(p. 34, 36, 42, 51) Annual article on Florida citrus industry conditions, with data on frozen concentrated orange juice (FCOJ) sales. Data are from Florida Citrus Processors Assn, Florida Citrus Mutual, and *Quick Frozen Foods*.

Includes 2 tables showing Florida FCOJ retail, institutional, and bulk sales value and volume, 1959/60-1982/83.

NORTHWEST IS MECCA FOR FROZEN CONCENTRATES

(p. 35, 38-41) Article, with 1 undated table showing sales index and market share for frozen concentrated beverages by type, in 45 market areas. Data are from Selling Areas Marketing Inc.

DATA FILE, RECURRING FEATURE

(p. 66) Includes the following tables:

[1] Cold storage holdings [frozen vegetables, potatoes, fish and other seafood, fruits, juices, poultry, and eggs, all by type, Sept.-Nov. 1983 with comparison to 1981 or 1982].

[2] Pack: frozen corn [cut corn and corn on the cob, by region, 1981-83].

C4380–1.505: Mar. 1984 (Vol. 46, No. 8)

FF DISTRIBUTORS STEP UP WAREHOUSE CONSTRUCTION, ANNUAL FEATURE

(p. 24-31) Annual survey report on frozen food distributors' expansion plans for 1984. Includes 2 charts and 3 tables showing percent of distributors planning construction or renovation for warehouse, office, and other areas; and percent planning purchases of equipment and warehouse insulation, by type, with ranking for top 7 equipment items; 1984, and various trends 1981-83.

PACKERS SIDESTEP CONSTRUCTION TO BUY PROCESSING EQUIPMENT, ANNUAL FEATURE

(p. 43-49, 62-64) Annual survey report on frozen food packers' expansion plans for 1984. Includes 2 charts and 5 tables showing percent of packers planning purchases of equipment and supplies by detailed type, with ranking for top 15 equipment items; and percent planning construction or renovation for plant, warehouse, office, and other areas; 1984, and various trends 1981-83.

DATA FILE, RECURRING FEATURE

(p. 66) Includes the following table:

[1] California vegetable fall pack: frozen broccoli [by cut], cauliflower, and brussels sprouts, [retail and institutional volume, 2nd half 1982-83.] (p. 66)

C4380–1.506: Apr. 1984 (Vol. 46, No. 9)

DATA FILE, RECURRING FEATURE

(p. 32LL) Includes the following tables:

[1] Cold storage holdings [frozen vegetables, potatoes, fish and other seafood, fruits, juices, poultry, and eggs, all by type, selected months Dec. 1982-Jan. 1984].

[2] Frozen catfish [retail and institutional volume and value, 1981-83].

FLA. CITRUS DAMAGE ESTIMATES SOAR WHILE COUNT CONTINUES

(p. 40-45, 63) Article discussing effects of freeze losses on Florida's orange crop, 1970s-84. Data are from Florida Citrus Processors Assn and State agencies. Includes 3 tables showing Florida orange and frozen concentrate orange juice (FCOJ) production, and loss due to freezes, 1976/77 and 1980/81-1983/84 seasons, with FCOJ detail for 1983/84 season.

REGIONAL REPORT: MEMPHIS/LITTLE ROCK SURVEY

(p. 56-60) Twentieth in a series of articles on frozen food sales and consumption, by product type, in specific market areas. Data are from Selling Areas Marketing Inc. (SAMI).

Current article covers Memphis, Tenn./Little Rock, Ark., and includes 4 tables showing per household consumption indexes for product types with highest and lowest indexes, including Memphis/Little Rock's rank among 45 SAMI markets, for the year ended Dec. 9, 1983.

C4380–1.507: May 1984 (Vol. 46, No. 10)

FF DEPARTMENTS BUILDING UP: RETAILERS COOL NEW OPENINGS, ANNUAL FEATURE

(p. 18-32) Annual article on anticipated supermarket chain business and expansion plans, with emphasis on frozen foods (FF), 1984. Data are from surveys of food retailers.

Includes 8 tables showing survey response for the following: planned new store openings and FF dept expansions; number of stores served; FF case buying plans, by type of case; FF warehouse construction, expansion, and renovation plans; FF-related equipment purchase plans, by type of equipment; and FF products with greatest growth and decline; 1984 with comparisons to 1983.

Data are shown for corporate chains, voluntaries, and cooperatives.

DATA FILE, RECURRING FEATURE

(p. 77) Includes the following tables:

[1] Cold storage holdings [frozen vegetables, potatoes, fruits, juices, poultry, eggs, and fish and other seafood, all by type, Feb. 1983 and Jan.-Feb. 1984].

[2] Frozen strawberries [retail and institutional volume and value, 1982-83].

REGIONAL REPORT: HARTFORD AREA MARKET FAVORABLE TO FROZENS

(p. 78-82) Twenty-first in a series of articles on frozen food sales and consumption, by product type, in specific market areas. Data are from Selling Areas Marketing Inc. (SAMI).

Current article covers Hartford and New Haven, Conn./Springfield Mass., and includes 4 tables showing per household consumption indexes for product types with highest and lowest indexes, including Hartford/New Haven/Springfield's rank among 45 SAMI markets, for an unspecified 12-month period.

C4380-1.508: June 1984 (Vol. 46, No. 11)

ANNUAL WAREHOUSING SURVEY:
ZERO-DEGREE STORAGE LEADS 1984 NEW
WAREHOUSE PLANS

(p. 24-27) Annual survey article on public refrigerated warehouse construction and equipment purchase plans, and services provided, 1984.

Includes 3 tables showing percent of respondents planning equipment purchases, by type, 1982-84; percent planning new warehouse construction, additions, or renovation, 1980-84; and percent providing fast freezing service, rental space for food processing and offices, and distribution as well as storage, 1984.

REFRIGERATED STORAGE IS UP: BUT IT'S
COOLERS, NOT FREEZERS; BIENNIAL FEATURE

(p. 32-36, 64) Biennial article highlighting a USDA study on refrigerated warehouse capacity, 1983 and trends.

Includes 3 tables showing the following for refrigerated warehouses: capacity of public, private/semi-private, and meat packing facilities, biennially 1941-83; and gross space and net piling space, for public and private/semi-private general storage facilities and apple houses biennially 1977-83, and by State and census division 1983.

For description of article presenting data through 1981, see SRI 1982 Annual, under C4380-1.307.

NEW FROZEN FISH ITEMS SLOW BUT TONNAGE
MOVING ON UP

(p. 39-42, 66) Article on marketing trends for frozen fish products, 1980-84. Data are from Selling Areas Marketing, Inc.

Includes 2 charts and 2 tables showing frozen fish price per pound, new products introduced, and private label and generic market shares, 1980-83; and frozen fish brands and items offered, introduced, and discontinued, for 3 markets with high and low frozen fish consumption, year ended Mar. 2, 1984.

REFRIGERATED TRUCKLINES SURVEY: CATCH
22 ON THE ROAD. . . BUT THEY'RE ROLLING
ANYWAY, ANNUAL FEATURE

(p. 46-49, 65) Annual survey article on refrigerated trucking industry equipment buying and leasing plans and frozen food haulage, 1982-84.

Includes 2 tables showing percent of respondents with plans to buy or lease selected types of equipment, 1983-84; and percent with frozen food haulage increase and decrease, existing refrigerated storage facilities, and plans to build/add and rent more refrigerated storage space, 1982-84.

C4380-1.509: July 1984 (Vol. 46, No. 12)

NATIONAL PREFERENCES SHIFT AS PIZZA
SLICES OFF THE FAIRWAY, ANNUAL FEATURE

(p. 20-27) Annual article, with 1 chart showing frozen pizza market shares, by topping, for 7 leading market areas, and for total U.S. with detail for private label products, 1983. Data are from Selling Areas Marketing Inc.

Article appearing in 1983 contained no statistics. For description of last previous statistical article, see SRI 1982 Annual, under C4380-1.308.

DATA FILE, RECURRING FEATURE

(p. 42) Includes the following table:

[1] Cold storage holdings [frozen vegetables, potatoes, poultry, eggs, fruits, juices, fish, and shellfish, all by type, Feb.-Mar. 1984, and Mar. 1982-83].

FISH STICKS MOVE IN BATTER, BREADED
PORTIONS DO BETTER, ANNUAL FEATURE

(p. 46-51) Annual article on production of frozen fish sticks and fish portions, 1979-83. Data are from Commerce Dept and *Quick Frozen Foods.*

Includes 3 charts and 2 tables showing fish portion and fish stick production quantity and value, by product type, 1979-83, with detail for retail and institutional markets, 1982-83.

REGIONAL REPORT: CINCINNATI, RED HOT FOR
FROZENS IT'S NOT

(p. 52-55) Twenty-second in a series of articles on frozen food sales and consumption, by product type, in specific market areas. Data are from Selling Areas Marketing Inc. (SAMI).

Current article covers Cincinnati/Dayton/Columbus, Ohio, and includes 4 tables showing per household consumption indexes for product types with highest and lowest indexes, including Cincinnati/Dayton/Columbus' rank among 45 SAMI markets, for an unspecified period.

C4380-1.510: Aug. 1984 (Vol. 47, No. 1)

AMERICA STILL SWEET ON DESSERTS, BUT PIE
IN THE SKY IS TRADE'S CRY, ANNUAL
FEATURE

(p. 30-32, 35-40) Annual article, by Ross Chamberlain, with 1 chart showing market shares for frozen sweet goods and/or pies, by type, in 7 leading market areas, 1983. Data are from Selling Areas Marketing Inc.

Article appearing in 1983 contained no statistics. For description of last previous statistical article, see SRI 1982 Annual, under C4380-1.309.

NMFS: COOKED SHRIMP SHRINKS AS RAW
BOOSTS TOTAL SALES, ANNUAL FEATURE

(p. 46-47) Annual article, with 1 table showing frozen shrimp production volume and value, by product type, for retail and institutional markets, 1982-83. Data are from Commerce Dept and *Quick Frozen Foods.*

REGIONAL REPORT: SPOKANE, A GLIMPSE
INTO SMALL-TOWN USA

(p. 48-51) Twenty-third in a series of articles on frozen food sales and consumption, by product type, in specific market areas. Data are from Selling Areas Marketing Inc. (SAMI).

Current article covers Spokane, Wash., and includes 4 tables showing per household consumption indexes for product types with highest and lowest indexes, including Spokane's rank among 45 SAMI markets, 1983.

DATA FILE, RECURRING FEATURE

(p. 52) Includes the following tables:

[1-2] U.S. exports, frozen foods [volume and value, for meat, poultry, fish, other seafood, vegetables, fruits, and fruit juices, all by type, 1979-83 and Jan. 1984].

C4380-1.511: Sept. 1984 (Vol. 47, No. 2)

REGIONAL REPORT: MIAMI, VEGETABLES
SPROUT BIG PROFITS

(p. 42-45) Twenty-fourth in a series of articles on frozen food sales and consumption, by product type, in specific market areas. Data are from Selling Areas Marketing Inc. (SAMI).

Current article covers Miami, Fla., and includes 4 tables showing per household consumption indexes for product types with highest and lowest indexes, including Miami's rank among 48 SAMI markets, for an unspecified period.

DATA FILE, RECURRING FEATURE

(p. 46-47) Includes the following tables:

[1] Cold storage holdings [frozen vegetables, potatoes, poultry, eggs, fruits, juices, fish, and shellfish, all by type, May-June 1983, and Mar.-June 1984].

[2] U.S. exports of frozen foods [meat and poultry, fish and seafoods, vegetables, fruits and berries, and fruit juice concentrates, all by type, Feb.-Apr. and year-to-date 1984].

C4380-1.512: Oct. 1984 (Vol. 47, No. 3)

REGIONAL REPORT: MILWAUKEE SHOPPERS
PICK PIZZA, ONION RINGS TO GO WITH BEER

(p. 50-53) Twenty-fifth in a series of articles on frozen food sales and consumption, by product type, in specific market areas. Data are from Selling Areas Marketing Inc. (SAMI).

Current article covers Milwaukee, Wis., and includes 4 tables showing per household consumption indexes for product types with highest and lowest indexes, including Milwaukee's rank among 48 SAMI markets, for year ended June 22, 1984.

C4380-2   HOME AND AUTO
Monthly. Approx. 50 p.
Oversized.
ISSN 0162-8801.
LC 70-612942.
SRI/MF/not filmed

Monthly trade journal (semimonthly in July) of the automotive aftermarket industry, reporting on do-it-yourself (DIY) sales, marketing, and product trends and developments. Data are primarily from the journal's own research.

Issues generally contain news and feature articles, occasionally with statistics; and regular depts, including price comparisons for selected automotive products in various chains and locations, and, sometimes, stock exchange averages for selected retail chains.

Annual statistical features include car care survey of automotive aftermarket sales (Apr.), nonautomotive chain aftermarket sales survey (June), and automotive DIY survey (Aug. or Sept.). The 2nd July issue is an annual buyer's guide.

Features with substantial statistical content are described, as they appear, under "Statistical Features." Each issue of the journal is reviewed, but an abstract is published in SRI monthly issues only when features with substantial statistical content appear.

Prior to Nov. 15, 1983 issue, journal was published semimonthly.

Availability: Home and Auto, Circulation Department, One E. First St., Duluth MN 55802, $24.00 per yr., single copy $2.00, July Buyer's Guide $8.00; SRI/MF/not filmed.

Issues reviewed during 1984: Nov. 15, 1983-Oct. 1, 1984 (P) (Vol. 93, Nos. 8-9; Vol. 94, Nos. 1-10).

STATISTICAL FEATURES:

C4380–2.501: Nov. 15, 1983 (Vol. 93, No. 8)

TV, RADIO TAKING BIGGER CHUNK OUT OF CHAIN ADVERTISING $

(p. 8) Article, with 1 table ranking top 10 retail chains by percent increase in TV advertising expenditures, 1st half 1983 compared to 1st half 1982. Data are from Television Bureau of Advertising.

C4380–2.502: Mar. 1, 1984 (Vol. 94, No. 3)

FACE IT: LONGER DAYS AHEAD

(p. 1, 39) Article on hours of operation for automotive aftermarket chain stores. Data are from a recent *Home and Auto* survey. Includes 4 text tables showing distribution of chains by opening and closing time on weekdays, Saturdays, and Sundays.

C4380–2.503: Apr. 1, 1984 (Vol. 94, No. 4)

CAR CARE CENTER, ANNUAL FEATURE

(p. 21-59) Annual survey report on auto aftermarket retail sales, 1983, with selected trends from 1979. Data are based on a survey of 46 retail aftermarket chains representing approximately 25,000 outlets in the U.S. and Canada.

Contains sections on 19 auto repair and maintenance product groups, each with narrative analysis including 1984 sales projections, and 5 charts showing aftermarket sales, annual turns, average gross margin, and car care promotion's share of sales, for retail chains; and total aftermarket sales; various years 1979-83.

This is the 10th annual survey.

C4380–2.504: May 1, 1984 (Vol. 94, No. 5)

SOFT GOODS SALES SOLID

(p. 1, 22-24) Article, with 5 tables showing sales, inventory turns, and gross margins, for selected nonmechanical automobile accessories, 1983-84 with some quarterly sales detail. Data are from *Home and Auto.*

C4380–2.505: June 1, 1984 (Vol. 94, No. 6)

DRUG CHAINS, HOME CENTERS SHOW THE WAY TO 9.5% GAINS, ANNUAL FEATURE

(p. 1, 21-23) Annual article on auto aftermarket sales by nonautomotive retailers. Data are from a survey of 50 retail chains.

Includes 3 charts and 1 table showing the following for nonautomotive retail chains: distribution of aftermarket sales, and sales as percent of total aftermarket sales, by product group; and aftermarket sales by food, drug, hardware, and home center chains; 1979-83.

Also includes text data on nonautomotive retailers' average gross margins 1982-83, and sales change 1983-84, by outlet type.

ALARMS SPUR HIGH-TECH SALES

(p. 28, 32) Article profiling auto electronics aftermarket sales, with 6 tables showing: inventory turns and gross margins, and retail sales, with distributions by season and for automotive chain and other outlets, for 4-5 auto electronics products, 1983-85. Data are from *Home and Auto 1984 Car Care Center* survey.

C4380–2.506: July 1, 1984 (Vol. 94, No. 7)

HEALTHIER ECONOMY BOOSTS WHEELS, COVERS, TIRES

(p. 1, 16-17, 20) Article on retail sales trends and outlook for tires, wheels, and wheel accessories. Data are from a *Home and Auto* survey of auto aftermarket retailers and manufacturers.

Includes 5 charts and 1 table showing retail sales and percent of retailers planning increased display space, 1984, with sales distribution by season (no date) and annual percent change 1983-85, for tires, wheels, and wheel covers and accessories; wheel care chemical sales, 1984; and distribution of wheel cover and replacement wheel sales by type of outlet (no date).

CHAINS INCH CLOSER TO INTEGRATED MERCHANDISING, ANNUAL FEATURE

(p. 23-26) Article on import merchandising practices of auto aftermarket chain stores, with import auto market trends. Data are from automotive industry sources, and a *Home and Auto* survey of 297 aftermarket chains. Includes 5 charts and 2 tables showing the following:

a. Import share of new auto sales, selected years 1968-83; and domestic and import shares of auto registrations by State, and import market shares by make, 1982-83.

b. Aftermarket chain survey findings, including percent of respondents selling import parts and using various merchandising practices, 1983-84.

This is the 2nd annual survey.

C4380–2.507: Aug. 1, 1984 (Vol. 94, No. 8)

WHO WILL DO THE BRAKE WORK?

(p. 1, 9) Article on auto brake do-it-yourself (DIY) repair activity and aftermarket sales trends. Data are from a recent *Home and Auto* survey of auto aftermarket retailers.

Includes 6 charts showing DIY and commercial service bay share of brake repairs, and percent of DIY persons performing drum and disc brake overhauls; and aftermarket brake product sales and average gross margin by product type, and sales distribution by season; various years 1979-84.

C4380–2.508: Sept. 1, 1984 (Vol. 94, No. 9)

PRICE CUTS BRIGHTEN HALOGENS

(p. 1, 15-17) Article on auto aftermarket sales of replacement headlights and auxiliary fog/driving lights, including sales distribution by product or outlet type (no date), and retailer average margins and turns for 1983-84. Most data are from a recent *Home and Auto* survey of retailers and manufacturers. Includes 4 charts.

DIY UNIVERSE STABILIZES BUT EXPERTISE EXPLODES, ANNUAL FEATURE

(p. 33-43) Annual survey report, for 1984, on automotive do-it-yourself (DIY) activity in U.S. and Canada, with trends from 1980. Data are based on over 15,000 responses by DIY customers to questionnaires distributed by retail chains.

Includes 3 charts and 11 tables showing distribution of under hood, under chassis, electri-

cal, and cosmetic DIY activity, by specific type of work; and DIYer profile, including level of experience, age, reasons for doing own work, sources of assistance and advertising, auto repair schooling, type of retail outlet preferred, unplanned purchases, and number of vehicles owned; all for U.S. and Canadian respondents, various years 1980-84.

This is the 10th annual survey.

C4380–2.509: Oct. 1, 1984 (Vol. 94, No. 10)

SURVEY: APPLICATION DATA IS TOP PACKAGING REQUIREMENT

(p. 115-116) Article on automotive aftermarket retailers' views on product packaging. Data are from responses of merchandising executives of 35 aftermarket chains, representing over 1,700 outlets, to a summer 1984 survey by *Home and Auto.*

Includes 2 charts showing views on importance of selected packaging characteristics, and importance of packaging vs. other factors in product line selections.

C4385
Harcourt Brace Jovanovich: Energy Publications

C4385–1   PIPELINE AND GAS JOURNAL
Monthly. Approx. 85 p.
ISSN 0032-0188.
LC 76-612862.
SRI/MF/excerpts, shipped quarterly

Monthly trade journal (semimonthly in Apr. and July) reporting developments in international pipeline and natural gas utility design, construction, and operations.

Issues generally contain regular news and editorial depts; and feature articles, occasionally with statistics.

Annual statistical features include reports on pipeline construction, finances and operations of 500 largest gas distribution utilities and pipeline companies, distribution utilities' capital expenditures, and supplemental (peakshaving) gas supplies.

Apr. 15 issue is a nonstatistical *Handbook and Buyers Guide.*

The journal's quarterly report on oil and gas company finances has been discontinued with the Mar. 1984 issue (see C4385-1.504 below).

Features with substantial statistical content are described, as they appear, under "Statistical Features." Each issue of the journal is reviewed, but an abstract is published in SRI monthly issues only when features with substantial statistical content appear.

Prior to Nov. 1983 issue, journal was described in SRI under C3320-1.

Availability: Pipeline and Gas Journal, PO Box 1589, Dallas TX 75221-1589, industry subscribers $12.00 per yr., nonindustry subscribers $40.00 per yr., single copy $3.00, Apr. 15 issue $10.00; SRI/MF/excerpts for all portions covered under "Statistical Features;" shipped quarterly.

Issues reviewed during 1984: Nov. 1983-Oct. 1984 (P) (Vol. 210, Nos. 13-14; Vol. 211, Nos. 1-12) [Vol. 211, No. 9 incorrectly reads Vol. 212].

STATISTICAL FEATURES:

C4385-1.501: Nov. 1983 (Vol. 210, No. 13)

CAPACITY INCREASES SLIGHTLY, INDUSTRY READY FOR WINTER, ANNUAL FEATURE

(p. 28-39) Annual article, by Dean Hale, on winter 1983/84 supplemental (peakshaving) gas supply available from underground storage fields and propane-air and LNG plants, based on a P&GJ gas industry survey.

Includes 1 table on underground gas storage operations, showing fields, wells, miles of storage lines, and storage compressor stations and horsepower, by company, 1983.

C4385-1.502: Dec. 1983 (Vol. 210, No. 14)

MAINTENANCE HIKES 1984 OUTLAY TO $3.76 BILLION, ANNUAL FEATURE

(p. 18-19) Annual article, by Jim Watts, forecasting gas distribution utilities' expenditures for expansion and maintenance in 1984, based on P&GJ 18th annual survey of over 350 gas utilities. Includes 3 charts showing expenditures for new/replacement mains/services and distribution system maintenance, and miles of new/replacement main and service line installations, actual 1983 and planned 1984.

PLASTIC PIPE MAKES BIG MOVE IN 1983, ANNUAL FEATURE

(p. 20) Annual article on plastic pipe installation for gas distribution systems, 1983, based on P&GJ 18th annual piping survey. Includes 1 undated chart showing distribution of plastic pipe used by gas utilities, by type of use.

C4385-1.503: Jan. 1984 (Vol. 211, No. 1)

MODEST CONSTRUCTION YEAR SEEN FOR U.S., CANADA PIPELINES, ANNUAL FEATURE

(p. 28-34) Annual report, by Dean Hale and Jim Watts, on U.S. and Canadian pipeline projects planned or under construction, for 1984, based on P&GJ annual construction survey.

Includes 2 tables showing U.S. and Canadian pipeline mileage planned/proposed and expected to be completed, by type, 1984; and tabular list of pipeline projects by type and company, showing mileage, size, points of origin and destination, and status for most projects, and cost, contractor, and/or expected completion date for some projects.

EQUIPMENT OWNERSHIP REFLECTS CHANGING REQUIREMENTS

(p. 40-42) By Dean Hale. Article on construction practices and equipment ownership of gas distribution utilities, 1982. Data are from responses to P&GJ Construction Equipment Survey.

Includes text table showing distribution of gas utility pipe by diameter, selected years 1961-82; and 3 tables showing average miles of main per unit for selected types of equipment, and response distribution to questions on whether company or outside contractors install gas mains and service lines, and on excavation methods.

ENERGY MANAGEMENT: QUARTERLY FINANCIAL REPORT

(p. EM3-EM5) "Oil Companies Post Higher Earnings." Summarizes survey of oil and gas companies' profits for 3rd quarter 1983. Includes 2 quarterly tables showing revenues,

earnings, and profit margin, for approximately 100 oil and 30 gas companies, for 3- and 9-month periods ended Sept. 30, 1982-83.

C4385-1.504: Mar. 1984 (Vol. 211, No. 3)

ENERGY MANAGEMENT: QUARTERLY FINANCIAL REPORT

(p. EM3-EM4) "Substantial Drop in Net Income Reported." Summarizes survey of oil and gas companies' profits for 4th quarter 1983. Includes 2 quarterly tables showing revenues, earnings, and profit margin, for approximately 100 oil and 30 gas companies, for 3- and/or 12-month periods ended Dec. 31, 1982-83.

This is the final appearance of the quarterly financial report.

C4385-1.505: May 1984 (Vol. 211, No. 6)

COMPRESSOR STATION MODERNIZATION: THE KEY IS CUTTING FUEL COSTS

(p. 17-20) By Dean Hale. Article on factors affecting modernization of gas pipeline compressor stations. Data were compiled by P&GJ, and include responses from a seminar attended by representatives of 6 large compressor station operating companies.

Includes 3 tables showing total horsepower, and stations by type, for 20 largest compressor station companies (no date); representative costs for various sizes and types of gas compressor stations; and aggregate station and unit modernization and replacement plans for 6 companies, 1984 and next 3 years.

C4385-1.506: June 1984 (Vol. 211, No. 7)

PUMP STATION MODERNIZATION

(p. 22-26) By Dean Hale. Article on liquids pipeline pump station replacement and modernization. Data were compiled by P&GJ, and are based in part on responses from a seminar attended by representatives of 7 major liquids pipeline companies.

Includes 2 tables showing replacement and modernization plans, for all liquids pipelines and aggregated for 7 major companies, 1984 and 1985-87 period, with 1984 planned expenditures.

C4385-1.507: July 1984 (Vol. 211, No. 8)

TIME TO RENEW

(p. 14-21) By Dean Hale. Article discussing age and condition of gas pipeline systems, by region, 1983. Data sources include recent P&GJ analyses of 300 leading gas distribution companies, and 100 top gas and 100 top liquids pipeline companies. Includes 9 tables showing the following:

a. Pipeline mileage by type of gas and oil line, by region; and distribution of gas system leaks by installation period and/or cause and location, and distribution of systems by construction material, pipe size, and installation period, shown variously for gas main and service systems and transmission and gathering lines.

b. Distribution of gas systems within 6 regions, by installation period by type (main and service systems, and transmission and gathering lines).

INDUSTRY LEADERS

(p. 22-32) By Jim Watts. Article profiling 4 of the first gas utility companies, as of 1983. Includes 4 text tables generally showing the following for each utility: date operations began, service area, number of meters and employees, suppliers, gas sales volume, operating revenue, net income, and capital expenditures, 1983.

C4385-1.508: Aug. 1984 (Vol. 211, No. 10)

4th P&GJ 500: DIMENSIONS OF 500 LEADING ENERGY PIPELINE COMPANIES, ANNUAL FEATURE

(p. 12-32) Annual article, by Denise Luttrall et al., presenting data on the finances and operations of the 500 largest gas distribution utilities, gas transmission/gathering pipelines, and liquids (crude oil and products) pipeline companies, 1983. Data are from a P&GJ industry survey.

Contains review of survey findings, with 14 summary tables ranking top 10 companies in each category (including some separate rankings for integrated gas and combination gas/electric utilities) by value of plant additions, revenues, sales, miles of mains or pipelines, deliveries, and/or number of customers, 1983 (p. 12-14); and 3 detailed tables, listed below (p. 14-32).

All tables show comparative rank order for previous year.

TABLES:
[Tables show operating revenues, net income, value of plant additions and/or property, and additional data noted below, by company, 1983.]

[1] 300 leading gas distribution utilities [ranked by number of customers, and including sales and miles of mains and services].

[2] 100 leading gas pipelines [ranked by total pipeline miles, and including sales, and miles of transmission, field/gathering, and storage pipelines].

[3] 100 leading liquid pipelines [ranked by total delivery volume, and including delivery volume of crude oil and products, and miles of gathering and crude and products trunk pipelines].

C4385-1.509: Oct. 1984 (Vol. 211, No. 12)

INTERNATIONAL PIPELINES, ANNUAL FEATURE

(p. 16-23) Annual article, by Dean Hale, on pipeline construction mileage planned or underway outside the U.S., 1984. Data are from a P&GJ survey.

Includes 4 tables showing pipeline mileage planned and under construction, by country or world area, and mileage completed during 1984, all by type of pipeline, as of Oct. 1984.

C4385-2   PETROLEUM ENGINEER INTERNATIONAL
Monthly. Approx. 140 p.
ISSN 0031-6466.
SRI/MF/excerpts, shipped quarterly

Monthly trade journal (semimonthly in Mar., July, and Nov.) reporting trends and developments in world oil and gas drilling activity and production technology. Also includes data on industry finance. Recurring rig data are from Hughes Tool Co. reports; most financial data are from company reports.

Journal includes feature articles and recurring editorial depts, occasionally with statistics; and the following regularly appearing statistical features:

a. Monthly rotary rig drilling activity feature (p. 3), with 1 table showing number of rigs in operation by State (including land and offshore totals for some States), Texas district, and land and offshore Canada, for week 2-3 weeks prior to cover date and 3 preceding weeks.

b. Recurring international rotary rig report, with 1 table showing total and offshore rotary rigs in operation, by country and world region; for month 3 months prior to cover date, previous month, and same month of preceding year.

c. Semiannual lists of land and offshore contract drilling rigs, by State subregion, Canadian Province, and foreign country.

d. Annual deep well drilling report, usually in Mar. issue; and annual article on well servicing activity.

The journal's quarterly report on oil and gas company finances has been discontinued with the Mar. 1984 issue (see C4385-2.504 below).

Monthly drilling activity feature appears in most issues. Recurring international rig report appears in Nov.-Dec. 1983 issues, and in Jan., Apr., and June 1984 issues. All additional features with substantial statistical content are described, as they appear, under "Statistical Features." Nonstatistical features and technical data are not covered.

Prior to Nov. 1983 issue, journal was described in SRI under C3320-2.

Availability: Petroleum Engineer International, PO Box 1589, Dallas TX 75221-1589, qualified subscribers $18.00 per yr., others $50.00 per yr., single copy $3.00; SRI/MF/excerpts for monthly and recurring tables and for all portions covered under "Statistical Features;" shipped quarterly.

Issues reviewed during 1984: Nov. 1983-Oct. 1984 (P) (Vol. 55, Nos. 13-15; Vol. 56, Nos. 1-12).

STATISTICAL FEATURES:

C4385–2.501: Dec. 1983 (Vol. 55, No. 15)

1983 DRILLING COSTS DOWN MORE THAN 17%

(p. 76) Article, with 1 table showing onshore drilling costs index 1981-83, and actual costs 1983, by well depth. Data are from DOE.

C4385–2.502: Jan. 1984 (Vol. 56, No. 1)

U.S. DRILLING COSTS DOWN DRAMATICALLY IN '83

(p. 85) Article discussing drilling trends and outlook. Includes 1 table showing tubular goods supply including exports and imports, rotary rig activity, and wells and footage drilled, 1973-82 and Jan.-July 1983. Data are from Independent Petroleum Assn of America.

U.S. STRIPPER WELL PRODUCTION UP BY 15 MILLION BARRELS

(p. 86) Article, with 1 table showing number, production volume, and abandonments of

stripper wells, 1973-82. Data are from most recent edition of *National Stripper Well Survey.*

ENERGY MANAGEMENT: QUARTERLY FINANCIAL REPORT

(p. EM3-EM5) "Oil Companies Post Higher Earnings." Summarizes survey of oil and gas companies' profits for 3rd quarter 1983. Includes 2 quarterly tables showing revenues, earnings, and profit margin, for approximately 100 oil and 30 gas companies, for 3- and 9-month periods ended Sept. 30, 1982-83.

C4385–2.503: Feb. 1984 (Vol. 56, No. 2)

RIG UTILIZATION RISES AS OFFSHORE DRILLING MAKES SPOTTY RECOVERY

(p. 23-27) By Harrison T. Brundage. Article discussing world offshore drilling outlook for 1984. Data sources include Offshore Data Services, Inc., and Sonat Offshore Drilling, Inc.

Includes 5 tables showing operator, world location, and well and water depth, for selected recent discoveries; Gulf of Mexico lease acreage for 1983 and cumulative, and rigs required, by water depth; total and idle offshore rigs for Gulf of Mexico, Europe/Mediterranean, and worldwide, late 1982-83; Gulf of Mexico exploration plans by company, as of Dec. 1983; and all-time water depth records.

SPRING 1984 INTERNATIONAL OFFSHORE RIG LOCATOR, SEMIANNUAL FEATURE

(p.R4-R11) Semiannual tabular list showing operating specifications and status for offshore contract drilling rigs, by contractor arranged by foreign country and U.S. State subregion, with contractor directory, spring 1984.

C4385–2.504: Mar. 1984 (Vol. 56, No. 3)

ANNUAL DEEP WELL REPORT

Annual report, by Rich McNally and Laura Jacobus, on deep oil/gas well drilling activities in the U.S., 1981-83, presenting data on wells drilled to 15,000 feet or deeper. Data are derived from various industry sources, including contract drilling and operating companies and Petroleum Information Corp.

Contains 2 statistical articles, described below; and 2 foldouts (p. 37-40), with list of deep well operators, 1 map, and 5 charts showing selected deep well drilling trends, 1977-83.

This is the 40th annual report.

DEEP DRILLING IN U.S. DECLINES BY 52% IN 1983, ANNUAL FEATURE

(p. 21-30) Annual article on drilling activity for wells drilled to 15,000 feet or deeper, 1981-83 and trends. Includes 7 tables showing:

a. Number of wells; average well depth and cost, mud cost, and number of bits; average tubular goods tonnage and cost; total, wildcat, and development well success ratios; total costs for mud, drilling, and completion; and total costs and footage; 1981-83, repeated for U.S. and 13 States, with land and offshore detail for selected States.

b. Total, exploratory, and producing wells completed; average number of bits, and mud and well costs; footage drilled; and record depths; 1938-83.

ULTRADEEP DRILLING FALLS TO 16-YEAR LOW, ANNUAL FEATURE

(p. 32-34) Annual article on characteristics of wells drilled to 20,000 feet or deeper, 1981-83.

Includes 3 tables repeating data described in paragraph a. of preceding article, for ultradeep well completions in U.S. and 5 States, 1981-83.

Other Features

EXPENDITURES INCREASE IN 1982 DESPITE DECLINE IN COMPLETIONS, ANNUAL FEATURE

(p. 64-68) Annual article on oil and gas well drilling costs, 1982, based on a joint industry assn survey. Includes 2 tables showing the following for oil and gas wells, and dry holes: number and average depth and cost, by depth interval, 1982; and number, footage, and cost, 1981-82.

U.S. RESERVES CONTINUE TO DROP

(p. 68-71) Article, with 2 tables showing domestic and worldwide proved reserves of oil/gas, with revisions, additions, production, and purchases and sales of reserves in-place, aggregated for 300 companies surveyed by Arthur Andersen and Co., 1980-82.

ENERGY MANAGEMENT: QUARTERLY FINANCIAL REPORT

(p. EM3-EM4) "Substantial Drop in Net Income Reported." Summarizes survey of oil and gas companies' profits for 4th quarter 1983. Includes 2 quarterly tables showing revenues, earnings, and profit margin, for approximately 100 oil and 30 gas companies, for 3- and/or 12-month periods ended Dec. 31, 1982-83.

This is the final appearance of the quarterly financial report.

SPRING 1984 INTERNATIONAL LAND RIG LOCATOR, SEMIANNUAL FEATURE

(p. R1-R37) Semiannual tabular list showing operating specifications for contract rotary land drilling rigs, by contractor, arranged by State, Canadian Province, and country arranged by world region; with contractor directories, spring 1984.

C4385–2.505: June 1984 (Vol. 56, No. 7)

INTERNATIONAL DEEP DRILLING COSTS APPROACH $2 BILLION, ANNUAL FEATURE

(p. 21-26) Annual article, by Harrison T. Brundage, on non-U.S. drilling activity for wells drilled to 15,000 feet or deeper, 1983. Data are from a recent *Petroleum Engineer International* survey.

Includes 14 tables showing the following by country and/or world area, with selected detail for Soviet Union by area or field: new wells completed, wells drilling, average depth and number of bits, average total and mud costs, exploratory and development well success ratios, total costs by type, and total footage, 1983.

C4385–2.506: July 1984 (Vol. 56, No. 8)

WELL SERVICING ACTIVITY DROPS FROM PREVIOUS HIGHS, ANNUAL FEATURE

(p. 21-34) Annual article, by Steven D. Moore, presenting detailed data on oil and gas well servicing activities, 1983. Data are based on a *Petroleum Engineer International* survey of over 200 independent and integrated companies.

Includes 3 maps and 3 tables showing the following, for total U.S. and 11 oil/gas producing regions:

a. Total wells, well completions/recompletions, artificial lifts, lift installations and repairs, tubular repairs, fracturing/acid stimulations, and servicing budget, 1983; and estimated servicing budget, 1984.

b. Total oil and gas wells, new oil and gas exploration and development wells completed, wells recompleted in same and new zone, and abandoned wells, as of Jan. 1, 1984.

c. Service jobs, by type, 1983.

DRILLING/EXPLORATION ACTIVITIES: PRODUCTION COSTS DECREASE IN 1983

(p. 104-108) Article, with 1 table showing equipment costs for primary oil recovery, 1983, and composite production cost indexes, 1981-83, all by well depth for 4 States and west and south Texas. Data are from DOE.

C4390
Harcourt Brace Jovanovich: Magazines for Industry

C4390–1   BEVERAGE INDUSTRY, 1984 Annual Manual
Annual. 1983. 298 p.
ISSN 0148-6187.
SRI/MF/excerpts

Annual directory and statistical compilation for the beverage industry, 1982, with selected trends from as early as 1849. Covers soft drinks, coffee, milk, powdered drinks, tea, wine, beer, fruit juice, liquor, and bottled water. Includes data on sales, consumption, and operations.

Most data are from Federal Government, private research organizations, and *Beverage Industry* research.

Contents:

Contents listing. (p. 3-5)

Section 1. Annual Statistics. Narrative articles, with 6 charts and 67 tables, including data on consumption, market shares, production, sales, advertising, foreign trade, packaging, and vending machines; and descriptive listing of restrictive packaging and litter/recycling laws. (p. 7-121)

Section 2. New Products, Services, Literature. Includes narrative descriptions. (p. 123-146)

Section 3. Manual of Operations. Includes cost calculation charts, and industry production and formula specifications; and directory of industry assns, manufacturers, brand names, franchise companies, and manufacturers representatives. (p. 147-210)

Section 4. Comprehensive Buyer's Guide. Includes 2 directories, arranged alphabetically and by product, of companies that supply products and services to the soft drink industry. (p. 211-297)

All tables, and selected charts with substantial data not included in tables, are described below.

Prior to this edition, publication was described in SRI under C5250-1.

Availability: Book Sales, HBJ Publications, One E. First St., Duluth MN 55802, $45.00; SRI/MF/excerpts for all statistical tables described below and accompanying articles.

TABLES AND CHARTS:

Volume 5, Number 1-12

C4390–1.1: Beverage Consumption and Soft Drink Sales Trends

a. Beverage consumption by type, including imputed water consumption; tea sales; and domestic and imported wine consumption; various years 1964-82. 4 tables. (p. 11-12)

b. Population projections by region for 3 under-34 age groups, selected years 1980-90. 2 tables. (p. 14)

c. Isotonic beverage sales by sector (retail, institutional, and industrial); and advertising expenditures by media, by isotonic beverage brand and type; various years 1977-85. 5 tables (p. 18-20)

d. Soft drink total and per capita consumption, and market shares by flavor; consumption by company and brand, with detail for top 10 brands; 13 companies with highest sales growth; plants, production, and wholesale sales value, by region and sales size group; and plants by State; various years 1940-82, with selected production and consumption trends from 1849. 1 chart and 9 tables. (p. 24-40)

C4390–1.2: Alcoholic Beverages

a. Beer production by company and brand, tax-free exports/military, imports, and total consumption, various years 1976-82; and 1982 year-end capacity by company. 2 tables. (p. 43-44)

b. Alcoholic beverage wholesalers and producers for beer, wine, and distilled spirit categories, with aggregate market shares for top 3 companies in each; various years 1948-82. 4 tables. (p. 46)

c. Beer sales volume by type; wholesaler sales volume and/or establishments by sales size group and company; Simmons market beer drinker index by sex and age group; production and market share of top 10 domestic beer brands; and sales volume and market share of leading imported beer brands; various years 1963-90. 12 tables. (p. 46-51)

C4390–1.3: Packaging and Fruit Juice Market

a. Packaging: shipments, sales, and/or gallonage contained, by container type and end-use market, with detail for New York State one-way glass and can shipments; beer packaging shares by type in 5 mandatory deposit States; and packaging share of GNP; various years 1971-83. 1 chart and 6 tables. (p. 61-63, 67)

b. Fruit juice and drink sales volume and shares by type, including frozen and ready-to-serve by container type, 1981-82. 1 table. (p. 79)

C4390–1.4: Sweeteners and Bottled Water

a. Sweetener usage levels for sucrose and high fructose corn syrup (HFCS), by beverage company and brand; low calorie sweetener world production, wholesale price, and sweetness and use as compared to sugar, by sweetener; domestic sugar and HFCS consumption; and liquid and dry HFCS capacity by company; various years 1970-84. 4 tables. (p. 82-86)

b. Bottled water sales by company, and domestic and imported shares by region;

market gallonage by type, including imports; and sales by domestic brand; various years 1976-82. 4 tables. (p. 89-90)

C4390–1.5: Miscellaneous

a. Tax rate and maximum for Federal highway use tax on heavy vehicles, with some detail for 2-axle truck-trailers by weight class, various periods FY84-88/later. 2 tables. (p. 93-94)

b. Vending machine sales distribution and sales per machine, by product; vending profit analysis by sales size class; shipment volume and value and number of manufacturers for all vending machines, and for beverage machines by type; and soft drink packaged and bulk sales volume, and total wholesale value; various years 1965-82. 4 tables. (p. 102-106)

c. Drink mixes: institutional sales volume for powdered mixes by brand and for syrups; and retail sales volume for instant breakfast and other powdered mixes by brand; with aggregate data on sales value; various years 1974-82. 3 tables. (p. 107-109)

d. Liquor consumption by class and type, including imported and bottled abroad; and top 40 distilled liquor brands ranked by 9-liter cases sold; 1982 with comparisons to 1981. 2 tables. (p. 120-121)

C4390–2   BEVERAGE INDUSTRY
Monthly. Approx. 60 p.
Oversized.
ISSN 0148-6187.
LC 73-640297.
SRI/MF/excerpts, shipped quarterly

Monthly journal of the beverage industry, reporting on trends in marketing, sales, consumption, and product/equipment development for soft drinks, beer, bottled water, juice, wine, beverage powders, and spirits.

Most data are from National Soft Drink Assn (NSDA) and other industry sources, the Federal Government, and *Beverage Industry* research.

Contents:

a. News and feature articles, including coverage of beverage market trends; company profiles; and annual features with data on beer production and market conditions, liquor sales, soft drink sales and consumption, and other topics.

b. "Beverage Business Indicators" monthly feature, with 3 tables and 3 charts, generally showing the following: shipments of closures by type; beverage CPI and PPI by beverage type; and imports and domestic removals of beer, wine, and spirits; for various months ranging from 4-10 months prior to cover date, with comparison to prior month and previous year; (prior to Sept. 1984 issue, feature includes additional tables with data on glass container shipments, sweetener wholesale prices, and plastic bottle production).

Monthly "Beverage Business Indicators" feature appears in all issues. All additional features with substantial statistical content are described, as they appear, under "Statistical Features." Non-statistical features are not covered.

Prior to Nov. 1983 issue, journal was covered in SRI under C5250-2.

Availability: Beverage Industry, One E. First St., Duluth MN 55802, qualified subscribers †, others $35.00 per yr., single copy $2.00; SRI/MF/excerpts for "Beverage Business Indicators" and all portions covered under "Statistical Features;" shipped quarterly.

Issues reviewed during 1984: Nov. 1983-Oct. 1984 (P) (Vol. 74, Nos. 18-19; Vol. 75, Nos. 1-10; Whole Nos. 978-989).

STATISTICAL FEATURES:

C4390–2.501: Nov. 1983 (Vol. 74, No. 18, Whole No. 978)

70% OF BEVERAGE FIRMS PLAN CAPITAL EXPANSION

(p. 69-70) Article on beverage industry plant expansion plans, based on a 1983 *Beverage Industry* survey. Includes 6 tables showing response distribution for the following, by beverage type:

a. Planned capital expenditures by amount; planned equipment expenditures, change over 1983, and for new equipment by amount and equipment type; and planned filling line expansions by number of lines and size of package; 1984.

b. Cost increases in 4 expense categories, 1983.

POPULATION SHIFTS TO NEGATIVELY AFFECT SOFT DRINK CONSUMPTION BY 1990: STUDY

(p. 144-147) By Holly Klokis. Article, with 3 tables showing soft drink packaged gallonage, by package type and region 1981, and for regular and diet drinks 1970-82; and bulk and packaged gallonage by region, 1982.

Data are based on a 1983 Beverage Marketing Corp. survey of approximately 1,550 industry executives and managers.

C4390–2.502: Dec. 1983 (Vol. 74, No. 19, Whole No. 979)

272 MEGA-FIRMS OPERATE HALF OF U.S. BOTTLING PLANTS

(p. 1, 34-35) By Holly Klokis. Article on soft drink industry concentration, 1982. Data are from Beverage Marketing Corp.

Includes 3 tables showing number of companies, manufacturing and distributing plants, and sales, by company sales size, for headquarter companies (multi-plant owners); and manufacturing plants by wholesale sales size, for headquarter and other companies; 1982.

C4390–2.503: Jan. 1984 (Vol. 75, No.1, Whole No. 980)

[Annual beer industry articles, described below, were presented as a single feature in 1983. Data for all beer industry articles are from Lehman Brothers Kuhn Loeb Research.]

BOTTLERS FLOOD ASEPTIC MARKET

(p. 1, 51-54) Article on beverage industry use of aseptic packaging (flexible containers that do not require refrigeration). Data are from *Beverage Industry.* Includes 6 undated charts showing total, filling, handling/storage, processing, packaging, and distribution/retail costs per 1,000 gallons of juice/juice drink packaged in aseptic, glass, and can containers.

BEER INDUSTRY HAS MODEST BOUNCEBACK, UP 1% IN '83, ANNUAL FEATURE

(p. 1, 15-17) Annual article, with 3 tables showing top 10 beer brands ranked by market share, 1983; production by brewer and brand, 1977-83; and malt liquor sales volume for 10 brands and all others, 1972-83.

NON-SPARKLING WATER AT 76.1% OF U.S. BOTTLED WATER MARKET, ANNUAL FEATURE

(p. 4, 9, 20) Annual article, by Holly Klokis, with 3 tables showing bottled water gallonage by type (including imported), and per capita consumption, 1976-83. Data are from Beverage Marketing Corp.

FASTER, MORE AUTOMATIC UNITS BEING SOUGHT

(p. 12-13) Article on development trends for beverage industry palletizing and depalletizing equipment. Data are from a *Beverage Industry* survey of major equipment suppliers. Includes 2 undated tables showing response distribution to questions concerning major problems and desired characteristics in palletizers/depalletizers.

TOP TEN: LIGHT BEERS MAKE BIG STRIDES IN '83

(p. 15) Article, with 1 table showing top 9 and all other light beer brewers ranked by market share, 1980-83.

IMPORTED BEER OUTLOOK POSITIVE WITH 8% VOLUME GROWTH IN '83, ANNUAL FEATURE

(p. 16-17, 60) Annual article, with 3 tables showing beer market volume by type, including imported, 1981-83; production 1971-83, and year-end capacity 1983, for 9 brewers and all others; tax-free exports, total imports, and consumption, 1971-83; and import gallonage for 28 leading brands and all others, 1979-83.

C4390–2.504: Feb. 1984 (Vol. 75, No. 2, Whole No. 981)

WARM WEATHER, NEW PRODUCTS BOOST SOFT DRINK TOTALS

(p. 1, 27, 30) Article on beverage consumption, 1983 and trends. Data are from various Federal and private sources. Includes 1 chart and 3 tables showing per capita consumption by beverage type, 1965-83; sales volume for iced and hot tea, 1978-83; and per capita consumption of domestic and imported wine, 1977-83.

BI STUDY: SPEED, EFFICIENCY TOP BUYERS' EQUIPMENT REQUIREMENTS

(p. 4-55, passim) By Craig Fintor. Article on beverage industry equipment requirements and problems, based on a survey of industry executives conducted by Infometrics National Research Center of Harcourt Brace Jovanovich Publications.

Includes 3 tables showing response distribution concerning major machinery problems, desired equipment capabilities, and expected base period for and factors affecting return on capital investment, all by beverage type.

SPEED AND EFFICIENCY SOUGHT BY BOTTLERS

(p. 48-49) Article on development trends for beverage industry casing and uncasing equipment. Data are from a *Beverage Industry* survey of major equipment suppliers. Includes 2 undated tables showing response distribution concerning significance of selected improvements and problems with casers/uncasers.

C4390–2.505: Mar. 1984 (Vol. 75, No. 3, Whole No. 982)

PRIMARY CONTAINERS SHOW 3.2% GAIN FOR SDs IN '83

(p. 1, 32-33, 36) By Gary A. Hemphill. Article, with 2 charts and 2 tables showing soft drink and beer total sales volume, and packaged sales volume by container type, 1982-84. Data are from Arthur M. Stupay of Prescott, Ball and Turben.

STUDY: BOTTLED WATER SALES TO REACH $1.7 BILLION BY '90

(p. 4, 22) Article, with 2 tables showing sales of bottled water by type, various years 1979-90. Data are from FIND/SVP.

SECONDARY PACKAGES GOING MORE GENERIC

(p. 4, 36) Article on developments in beverage industry secondary packaging (packaging used to hold together several containers). Includes 2 undated tables showing distribution of soft drink and beer containers, by type of secondary packaging material.

SPEED, SIMPLICITY TOP PRIORITY FOR CODERS/IMPRINTERS/LABELERS

(p. 10-11, 79) Article on development trends for beverage industry coding/imprinting and labeling equipment. Data are from a *Beverage Industry* survey of major equipment suppliers. Includes 1 undated table showing response distribution concerning significance of selected problems with coders/imprinters.

DISTILLED SPIRITS DOWN 1.6% IN '83, ANNUAL FEATURE

(p. 52) Annual article, with 2 tables showing case sales and producing company, for top 36 distilled spirit brands; and consumption of distilled spirits by type, with detail for domestic and imported Canadian and Scotch whiskey; 1982-83. Data are from Lehman Brothers, Kuhn Loeb.

C4390–2.506: Apr. 1984 (Vol. 75, No. 4, Whole No. 983)

SD SALES VAULT 4.5% IN '83, ANNUAL FEATURE

(p. 1, 13-19) Annual article, by Gary A. Hemphill, on soft drink sales and market shares, by company and brand, 1983 and trends. Data are from Lehman Brothers, Kuhn Loeb.

Includes 1 chart and 5 tables showing soft drink consumption by company and brand, and market share by flavor, with detail for top 10 brands and for diet drinks and caffeine-free cola/pepper drinks, various years 1970-83; and total and per capita consumption, 1963-83.

BULK GROWTH CONTINUES TO OUTPACE SD INDUSTRY, ANNUAL FEATURE

(p. 4, 58-59) Annual article, by Craig Fintor, with 1 table showing volume of bulk soft drink sales, 1972-83. Data are from National Soft Drink Assn.

TOP FOUR REMAIN THE SAME; NEWCOMERS CRACK BI CHART

(p. 19, 53) Article, with 2 tables showing top 10-20 soft drink brands ranked by sales volume, and including market share, 1973 and 1983. Data are from *Beverage Industry.*

PROMOTIONS JUST AS VITAL AS PRICES FOR FOOD CHAINS

(p. 74-76) Article, with 1 table showing number of franchisee-owned restaurants and value of sales, by type of food served, 1983-84. Data are from *Franchising in the Economy, 1982-84*.

C4390-2.507: May 1984 (Vol. 75, No. 5, Whole No. 984)

HFCS SUPPLIERS GEARING TO MEET DEMAND

(p. 1, 40-46) Article, with 2 charts showing share of per capita sweetener consumption, for sugar, high fructose corn syrup (HFCS), and other products, 1975 and 1983; and HFCS price relative to sugar, selected months 1981-83. Data are from USDA.

CMI REPORT REFLECTS 8.1% CAN INCREASE

(p. 1, 14) Article, with 1 table showing percent change in soft drink sales through food stores, by container type or size, for the 2 States most recently enacting mandatory deposit legislation, full year or Oct./Nov. 1983 vs. 1982. Data are from Can Manufacturers Institute.

C4390-2.508: June 1984 (Vol. 75, No. 6, Whole No. 985)

HIGHER DISTRIBUTION COSTS LIKELY IN '84

(p. 1, 16-20) Article on distribution costs and operations of 4 major beverage industry sectors. Data are based on responses from 299 beer distributors, soft drink plants, soft drink warehouses, and bottled water plants to a recent survey conducted by SRCH Statistical Research Center for *Beverage Industry*.

Includes 1 chart and 7 tables showing responses of each survey group concerning the following:

a. Distribution cost per case, distribution cost changes and cost shares by component, and computer use by application, mostly 1983-84.

b. Distribution fleet characteristics, including vehicles by type, average annual mileage, percent of vehicles owned and leased, average vehicle age and mileage per gallon, and average number of deliveries per vehicle per day.

TOTAL ADVERTISING EXPENDITURES BY MAJOR BREWERS

(p. 4) Table showing advertising expenditures of 12 major beer brewers, 1978-82. Data are from Business Trend Analysts, Inc.

ROUTE PERSONNEL ACCOUNT FOR 62% OF UNIFORM SALES

(p. 28) Article, with 1 undated table showing distribution of sales of employee uniforms to the beverage industry, by occupational category. Data are from a *Beverage Industry* survey of major suppliers.

HAND TRUCK SALES GROW OVER LAST SIX MONTHS

(p. 29, 71) Article, with 1 undated table showing importance of selected hand truck features, as perceived by beverage industry equipment suppliers. Data are from a survey of suppliers conducted by SRCH Statistical Research Center for *Beverage Industry*.

C4390-2.509: July 1984 (Vol. 75, No. 7, Whole No. 986)

RETAIL SHIFT: BOTTLERS DIVERSIFY SD SALES

(p. 1, 54) Article, with 1 chart showing distribution of bottlers' soft drink sales among food stores, convenience stores, vending, and other retail outlets, 1974 and 1984. Data are from a *Beverage Industry* survey.

C4390-2.510: Aug. 1984 (Vol. 75, No. 8, Whole No. 987)

SURVEY REVEALS TOP EXECUTIVE SALARY LEVELS

(p. 1, 30-32) By Paul E. Mullins. Article, with 1 chart and 4 tables showing average or median salary for beverage industry executives/managers, as follows: by management level; by position, by company employment size; and by position, education, and years experience, with detail for soft drink plants, breweries, and beer distributors.

Data are from 1,167 responses to a recent survey conducted by SRCH Statistical Research Center for *Beverage Industry*.

CONSOLIDATION OF INDUSTRY REFLECTED IN FEWER, BUT LARGER BEVERAGE FIRMS

(p. 1, 10-11) Article on industry concentration among soft drink plants and beer wholesalers. Data are from Beverage Marketing Corp. Includes 1 chart and 4 tables showing soft drink plants, 1980-83; soft drink plants and sales volume and value, and beer wholesalers and sales volume, by sales size group, 1982-83; and sales volume, for top 12 brewers and all others, 1971 and 1977-83.

POWDERED DRINK REPORT: NUTRASWEET CALLED FACTOR IN 14% SALES JUMP IN '83

(p. 4, 35) Article, with 1 table showing the following for powdered drink mixes, 1974-83: sales value; and sales volume, by company and brand, and for private label/others. Data are from Lehman Brothers, Kuhn Loeb.

MICROBREWERY PRODUCTION EXPECTED TO MAKE GAINS

(p. 8) Article, with 1 table showing number of breweries with annual production capacity of 10,000 barrels or less, and aggregate sales volume, 1977-84. Data are from Malt Beverage Research International, California State Board of Equalization, and *Modern Brewery Age*.

COST OF FLEET OPERATION RISES 2% TO $1.29/MILE

(p. 14) Article, with 1 chart showing private tractor/trailer fleet average operating cost per mile, for administration, drivers, and equipment, 1981-83. Data are from responses of 443 private fleets to a 1983 survey sponsored by Private Truck Council of America, Inc., and A. T. Kearney, Inc., and from previous surveys.

BLOW MOLDED USAGE COULD EXPAND 17%

(p. 21) Article, with 1 table showing shipments of blow molded plastic containers, for soft drinks, fluid milk, and alcoholic beverages, 1982, 1985, and 1987. Data are from Frost and Sullivan, Inc.

POOR WEATHER HURTS JAPAN'S SD SALES

(p. 29) Article, with 1 table showing soft drink shipments in Japan, by type, for 13 major suppliers, 1982. Data are from Yamasaki International.

C4390-2.511: Sept. 1984 (Vol. 75, No. 9, Whole No. 988)

VENDING SHIPMENTS UP 30% IN '83, ANNUAL FEATURE

(p. 4) Annual article, with 1 table showing shipment volume and value of beverage vending machines, and number of companies, by beverage and/or machine type, 1982-83. Data are from Dept of Commerce.

SURVEY REVEALS SYSTEMS A NECESSITY, NOT A LUXURY

(p. 45-47) Article on computer use in the beverage industry. Data are from a survey of major computer hardware and software suppliers, conducted for *Beverage Industry*.

Includes 3 undated charts showing distribution of beverage industry market among major computer hardware suppliers; and survey responses concerning type of beverage manufacturer/distributor supplied, and importance of selected equipment concerns.

C4390-2.512: Oct. 1984 (Vol. 75, No. 10, Whole No. 989)

WORKING WOMEN: 80% USE SD's ONCE A WEEK

(p. 4, 29) Article, with 2 tables showing percent of working women consuming selected beverages, by education and age, 1984. Data are based on a Jan.-Feb. 1984 telephone survey of 713 working women age 21-65, conducted by Mathematica Policy Research for *Newsweek* magazine.

SWEETENER FIRMS SHOW UNITY AT 1st SYMPOSIUM

(p. 4, 34) Article, with 1 table showing consumption of sweeteners by type, 1983 and 1992. Data are from USDA.

TOTAL DOLLAR VALUE UP FOR LIQUID BASES

(p. 30) Article, with 1 table showing shipment value and volume, and number of producers with shipments of $100,000/over, for liquid beverage base products by type, 1977 and 1982. Data are from Dept of Commerce.

C4390-3   PAPERBOARD PACKAGING
Monthly. Approx. 100 p.
Oversized.
ISSN 0031-1227.
LC 62-38067.
SRI/MF/excerpts, shipped quarterly

Monthly trade journal reporting on trends and developments in the paperboard packaging industry, including production, marketing, technological developments, international news, and management. Data are from National Paperbox and Packaging Assn, American Paper Institute, industry reports, and other sources.

General format:

a. Monthly "Industry Statistics" feature, with news briefs and 3 charts showing average weekly paperboard production, fiber box shipments, and composite tube/core sales, for month 2 months prior to cover date with cumulative year-to-date totals and averages.

b. Feature articles and regular editorial depts, occasionally with statistics.

Annual statistical features include an industry buying forecast (Jan.) and trend review (Sept.).

Monthly "Industry Statistics" feature appears in all issues. All additional features with substantial nontechnical statistical content are described, as they appear, under "Statistical Features." Nonstatistical features are not covered.

Prior to Nov. 1983 issue, journal was described in SRI under C5250-3.

Availability: Paperboard Packaging, One E. First St., Duluth MN 55802, $18.00 per yr., single copy $2.00; SRI/MF/excerpts for monthly charts and all portions described under "Statistical Features;" shipped quarterly.

Issues reviewed during 1984: Nov. 1983-Oct. 1984 (P) (Vol. 68, Nos. 11-12; Vol. 69, Nos. 1-10) [Vol. 69, No. 9 incorrectly reads No. 8].

STATISTICAL FEATURES:

C4390-3.501: Jan. 1984 (Vol. 69, No. 1)

1984 BUYING FORECAST ANNUAL FEATURE

Annual compilation of articles forecasting paperboard packaging industry purchases of equipment, materials, and supplies for 1984, with selected operating trends from 1972. Data are primarily from Census Bureau, Bureau of Industrial Economics, and individual company reports.

Includes nonstatistical introductory article (p. 24-25), and the statistical articles described below.

CORRUGATED BOXMAKERS ALL AGREE: SALES WILL BE UP

(p. 25-33) Article, with 2 tables showing the following for the corrugated/solid fiber box industry (SIC 2653):

a. Shipment value in current and constant 1972 dollars, total employment, production workers and earnings, capital expenditures, PPI, unit shipments, and foreign trade, various years 1972-84.

b. Equipment unit purchases, and expenditures on materials and supplies, by item, all by census division, 1984.

FOLDING CARTON INDUSTRY FACES TOUGH COMPETITION

(p. 33-46) Article on folding paperboard box industry (SIC 2651), with 2 tables showing data similar to those described for preceding article on corrugated/solid fiber box industry.

RIGID BOX INDUSTRY IS IN MATURE PHASE

(p. 46-48) Article, with 1 table showing rigid box sales distribution, by end use, 1974-82.

CONVERTERS ARE FINALLY STARTING TO SIGN CHECKS

(p. 48-52) Article on machinery purchase plans of corrugating/sheet and folding carton plants, 1984. Data are from a *Paperboard Packaging* survey. Includes 8 tables showing response distribution concerning planned expenditures for new equipment and for replacement and improvement of existing equipment, planned purchases by equipment type, and significant machinery problems.

CANADIAN OUTLOOK FOR 1984

(p. 52-56) Article, with 2 tables showing equipment unit purchases, by item, for Canadian corrugated container and folding carton industries, 1984.

C4390-3.502: July 1984 (Vol. 69, No. 7)

CENSUS '84 SHOWS BUYING IS BRISK, ANNUAL FEATURE

(p. 20-26) Annual article on major equipment and materials purchasing plans of corrugated and folding carton converting sectors of the paperboard packaging industry, 1984. Data are from surveys of operations at 1,415 corrugated converting plants and 679 folding carton plants in the U.S. and Canada, conducted by Infometrics.

Includes 17 charts and 3 tables showing number of plants planning major equipment purchases within next year, by equipment type; distribution of adhesives and cutting dies used, by type; average and total expenditures for selected materials, 1983-84; and in-house vs. outside production of printing plates (for folding carton plants only).

This is the 1st annual article.

C4390-3.503: Aug. 1984 (Vol. 69, No. 8)

WILL MARKETING BE PREPRINT'S ACHILLES' HEEL?

(p. 16-20) By Mark Arzoumanian. Article on market outlook for preprinted linerboard. Data are from responses of 6 major preprinted linerboard suppliers to a 1984 survey conducted by Schiffenhaus Packaging Corp.

Includes 2 tables and 1 chart showing the following for preprinted linerboard: sales volume, required machine hours for preprinting, and market distribution by end-use industry, 1983 and 1990; and 1990 sales volume to be met by presses on hand, on order, and planned, as of 1983.

C4390-3.504: Sept. 1984 (Vol. 69, No. 9)
[Issue incorrectly reads Vol. 69, No. 8.]

HOW LONG WILL GOOD TIMES LAST? ANNUAL FEATURE

(p. 18-46) Annual report, by Fred Sharring, reviewing paperboard packaging industry trends, 1943-83. Data are from Commerce Dept, American Paper Institute, Fibre Box Assn, and other sources. Includes narrative overview; and analyses of 9 industry sectors, with the following data, generally for 1973-83, with various trends from as early as 1943 and some data for 1984:

a. Paper and paperboard total and per capita production; average annual and daily paperboard packages used, by type; and converted paperboard shipment value, by product type. Tables A1-A4. (p. 21-22)

b. Pulp production, foreign trade, and net supply, by grade; pulp consumption for board/paper and other uses; and North American pulp prices, by grade. Tables B1-B3. (p. 22-26)

c. Paperstock mill receipts, trade, recovery and ratio, and consumption by end use; paperstock consumption in board/paper production compared to other materials; and paperstock prices, by grade and region. Tables C1-C3. (p. 27-33)

d. Paperboard mill production, by grade; board mill capacity and utilization; and capacity outlook, by paperboard grade, through 1985. Tables D1-D3. (p. 33-36)

e. Fiber box production, and fiber shipment volume and value, all for corrugated and solid fiber; corrugated board production,

and corrugated and solid fiberboard consumption, by grade; and fiber box plants, equipment, companies, capital investment, and employment. Tables E1-E5. (p. 36-38)

f. Folding boxboard production by grade, and shipment volume and value; and folding carton plants, equipment, companies, capacity, employment, and capital investment. Tables F1-F3. (p. 42-44)

g. Composite fiber can and other product production. Table G. (p. 45)

h. Fiber drum production, value, and average price. Table H. (p. 46)

i. Rigid box sales, and distribution by end use. Tables I1-I1. (p. 46)

C4390-3.505: Oct. 1984 (Vol. 69, No. 10)

PAPERBOARD PACKAGING EQUIPMENT AND MATERIALS CENSUS

(p. 35-38) Compilation of charts, with brief accompanying narrative, presenting operational data for the corrugated container industry. Data are from a survey of combiner and sheet plants, conducted by the Infometrics division of Harcourt Brace Jovanovich.

Includes 17 undated charts showing survey responses concerning the following:

a. Containerboard consumption, by weight range; use of single, double, or triple wall; corrugator running speeds; considerations in machinery maintenance/purchasing and overall cost planning; factors affecting starch consumption; prevalence of in-line corrugated and out-of-line process printing, and of display work; and use of color coatings.

b. Most troublesome operational factors; use of flexo and letterpress ink rolls, and of functional and graphic coatings; likelihood of purchasing and producing preprinted linerboard in 3 years; seriousness of speed limitations due to linerboard/medium; presence of unionized workers; and employment and wages for selected occupations.

Feature is included with the 1st annual "State of the Corrugated Industry Report."

C4425
Hartman Communications

C4425-2   INCENTIVE MARKETING
Monthly.

SRI now covers this publication under C1200-4.

C4485
Hayden Publishing Co.

C4485–1   COMPUTER DECISIONS

Monthly.   Approx. 250 p.
ISSN 0010-4558.
LC 70-9210.
SRI/MF/excerpts, shipped
quarterly

Monthly journal (semimonthly in Mar., June, and Sept.) reporting on data processing management trends and developments, including outlook for new products, user evaluation of equipment, personnel practices, and activities of top manufacturers.

Issues contain articles, occasionally presenting statistics; and editorial depts, including coverage of new data processing products on the market, and tabular summaries of product specifications and prices.

Annual statistical features include a survey of data processing managers' salaries and benefits, and a report on the financial performance of the top 100 data processing vendors. An annual index is included in the Jan. issue.

Features with substantial statistical content other than product specifications and prices are described, as they appear, under "Statistical Features." Each issue of the journal is reviewed, but an abstract is published in SRI monthly issues only when statistical features appear.

Availability: Computer Decisions, PO Box 1417, Riverton NJ 08077, qualified subscribers †, others $40.00 per yr., single copy $3.00; SRI/MF/excerpts for all portions described under "Statistical Features;" shipped quarterly.

Issues reviewed during 1984: Nov. 1983-Oct. 1984 (P) (Vol. 15, Nos. 12-13; Vol. 16, Nos. 1-13).

STATISTICAL FEATURES:

C4485–1.501: Nov. 1983 (Vol. 15, No. 12)

USERS RATE INTERACTIVE TERMINALS

(p. 202-210) By John J. Hunter. Article, with 4 tables ranking 50 interactive computer terminals by user ratings for overall performance, reliability/vendor support, ergonomics (user comfort), and display/editing/formatting features. Data are from responses of over 2,000 users to a June-July 1983 Data Decisions Inc. survey.

C4485–1.502: Dec. 1983 (Vol. 15, No. 13)

AND THE RACE GOES ON, PART I, ANNUAL FEATURE

(p. 94-96) Annual article rating 38 office-automation equipment vendors' likelihood of surviving as suppliers to large companies through 1989, with comparisons to a 1982 forecast of vendor survival through 1988. Data are based on responses of 36 Office Automation Society International members to a 1983 *Computer Decisions* survey, and on 22 responses to a 1982 survey. Includes 1 table.
This is the 1st of 2 articles.

C4485–1.503: Jan. 1984 (Vol. 16, No. 1)

ARE CORPORATE MICROS UNDERUSED?

(p. 14) Article, with 1 table showing corporate use of microcomputers and hours saved, by type of application. Data are based on re-

sponses of 100 corporate information system managers and 200 other employees to an Aug. 1983 survey conducted by Penn and Schoen Associates for Control Data Corp.

USERS RATE SMALL SYSTEMS

(p. 18) Article on user ratings of service provided by small computer system vendors. Data are from a summer 1983 Input Corp. survey of 251 users of small computer systems.

Includes 1 table showing the following for 14 vendors: user ratings for overall service, software service, and ability to diagnose problems.

SONY HEADS UP WP HONOR ROLL

(p. 26-30) Article on top 12 word processing systems, based on ratings of over 4,800 users responding to a Datapro Research Corp. survey. Includes 1 table showing number of respondents using, and overall and lowest ratings, for top 7 stand-alone and top 5 multi-terminal systems.

AND THE RACE GOES ON, PART II, ANNUAL FEATURE

(p. 68-70) Annual article rating 38 office-automation equipment vendors' likelihood of surviving as suppliers to small (single computer) companies through 1989, with comparisons to a 1982 forecast of vendor survival through 1988.

Data are based on responses of 36 Office Automation Society International members to a 1983 *Computer Decisions* survey, and on 22 responses to a 1982 survey. Includes 1 table.
This is the 2nd of 2 articles.

C4485–1.504: Feb. 1984 (Vol. 16, No. 2)

SALARY-STATUS SURVEY, PART I: WHERE THE DOLLARS ARE, ANNUAL FEATURE

(p. 114-122) Annual article, by David Whieldon, reporting on compensation of management information system/data processing (MIS/DP) managers, 1983. Data are from a survey of 1,529 *Computer Decisions* readers, conducted in Aug. 1983 by Abbot, Langer and Associates.

Includes 7 charts and 1 table showing the following:

a. Median salaries of top MIS/DP officers and of data processing managers: by region and for selected metro areas and States; by industry division, with selected detail by company annual sales volume and asset size; by company MIS/DP budget size and employment size; and by number of employees supervised.

b. Median salary for 9 MIS/DP manager specialized positions.

This is the 1st of 2 articles reporting survey findings.

C4485–1.505: Mar. 1984 (Vol. 16, No. 3)

SALARY-STATUS SURVEY, PART II: BENEFIT$, YOUR HIDDEN PAY, ANNUAL FEATURE

(p. 90-96) Annual article, by David Whieldon, reporting on benefits, perquisites, and incentives of management information system/data processing managers, 1983. Data are from responses of 1,529 *Computer Decisions* readers to an Aug. 1983 survey conducted by Abbott, Langer and Associates.

Includes 6 charts showing percent of managers receiving selected types of benefits and perquisites, with detail for managers at 2 specified salary levels.

This is the 2nd of 2 articles reporting survey findings.

C4485–1.506: Mar. 15, 1984 (Vol. 16, No. 4)

25 MANAGERS RATE MAJOR MICROS

(p. 108-121) By Jordan Gold. Article on corporate managers' ratings of selected microcomputer models and related services and equipment. Ratings are from a *Computer Decisions* poll of 25 managers. Includes 3 tables.

C4485–1.507: May 1984 (Vol. 16, No. 6)

THE VOGUE IN OA IS FORMALITY

(p. 96) Article reporting managers' views on purchasing office automation systems. Data are based on a survey of approximately 850 managers, conducted by Omni Group Ltd. Includes 1 chart showing percent of respondents citing selected objectives for purchasing office automation systems, by company size.

C4485–1.508: June 1984 (Vol. 16, No. 7)

MORE ADVISE THAN CONSENT ON MICROS

(p. 14) Article on corporate use of microcomputers. Data are from responses of 155 executives to a survey conducted by Newton-Evans Research Co. Includes 1 undated chart showing survey response regarding preferred microcomputer manufacturer.

TOP 100 IN DP, ANNUAL FEATURE

(p. G1-G42) Annual article, by William Cappelli, analyzing performance of leading data processing (dp) vendors, 1983. Data are from the Gartner Group. Includes 12 tables showing the following dp rankings for 1983, with selected comparisons to 1981-82:

a. Top 100 companies, by revenues; top 20, by revenue growth rate; bottom 20, by revenue growth rate; and aggregate revenues of top 100 by product segment.

b. Top 10-20 companies: by revenue increase, operating margin, revenues per employee (with number of employees), operating income, and domestic and foreign revenues.

c. Top companies with less than 25 percent of revenues from dp.

Also includes index to ranked companies. A more detailed report is available from the Gartner Group, 72 Cummings Point Rd., Stamford CT 06902.

C4485–1.509: Aug. 1984 (Vol. 16, No. 10)

OA FOR SMALL SHOPS

(p. 80-82) By Randy J. Goldfield and David Culver. Article, with 1 undated chart showing corporate executive or dept responsible for policies on office automation, by company size. Data are from a recent survey by The Omni Group Ltd.

C4485–1.510: Sept. 1984 (Vol. 16, No. 11)

USERS RATE HP NUMBER ONE

(p. 16-20) Article on user ratings of large-system computer manufacturers. Data are from responses to a recent survey of approximately 2,800 users, conducted by Stuart Kirkland. Includes 4 charts ranking 11-12 computer vendors by users' overall ratings, and by ratings on quality of service and reliability of hardware and software.

C4590
Hitchcock Publishing Co.

C4590–1   INFOSYSTEMS: The Magazine for Information Systems Management

Monthly. Approx. 120 p.
ISSN 0364-5533.
LC 72-625717.
SRI/MF/excerpts, shipped quarterly

Monthly trade journal reporting developments and trends in the data processing and information systems management industries. Journal is primarily narrative, but occasionally contains statistical articles, including annual features on micrographics use, and data processing employment, salaries, and budgets.

Features with substantial statistical content are described, as they appear, under "Statistical Features." Each issue of the journal is reviewed, but an abstract is published in SRI monthly issues only when statistical features appear.

Availability: Hitchcock Publishing Co., Circulation Department, Infosystems, PO Box 1000, Wheaton IL 60189-1000, qualified subscribers †, others $60.00 per yr., single copy $5.50; SRI/MF/excerpts for all portions covered under "Statistical Features;" shipped quarterly.

Issues reviewed during 1984: Nov. 1983-Oct. 1984 (P) (Vol. 30, Nos. 11-12; Vol. 31, Nos. 1-10) [June 1984 issue is published in 2 parts].

STATISTICAL FEATURES:

C4590–1.501: Dec. 1983 (Vol. 30, No. 12)

PROTECTING THE INVESTMENT

(p. 64-68) By Wendy Lea McKibbin. Article on environment control systems for computer installations. Data are from Frost and Sullivan. Includes 1 chart showing market value for environment control systems, by type of equipment or function, 1982.

C4590–1.502: Feb. 1984 (Vol. 31, No. 2)

COMPUTER PROFESSIONALS PLEASED WITH JOBS

(p. 14) Article, with 2 charts showing computer professionals' satisfaction with career advancement, and perceptions of work environment intensity level. Data are from responses of 301 computer professionals to a survey conducted by Research and Forecasts Inc. for John Dewar and Sons, Ltd.

PCs NOW UNDER THE WING OF MIS?

(p. 72) Brief article on Management Information Systems (MIS) dept role in coordinating use of personal computers (PCs). Data are based on responses to a Future Computing, Inc. 1983 survey of companies randomly selected from the 2,000 largest U.S. corporations.

Includes 1 chart and 1 table showing companies with and without designated group/dept for PC management, dept responsible, and role of MIS and data processing depts in multiple group management settings.

C4590–1.503: Mar. 1984 (Vol. 31, No. 3)

'MYTHICAL' DATACOMM MANAGER

(p. 28-30) By Wayne L. Rhodes Jr. and Perry S. True. Article reporting on the data communications roles of management information systems/data processing (MIS/DP) managers. Data are from nearly 1,600 responses to a Jan. 1984 Hitchcock Research Services survey of 4,000 MIS/DP managers.

Includes 8 tables showing survey response concerning the following: position title of supervisor and person responsible for data communications, degree of intergration of data and voice communications, job title and role in purchase of data communications equipment/services, and current and planned geographic extent of data base system (local, metro, and long distance) and use of selected products and services.

C4590–1.504: Apr. 1984 (Vol. 31, No. 4)

DOES IBM GET HELP FROM MIS IN 'SELLING' TO TOP CORPORATIONS?

(p. 10) Article on corporate use of personal computers (PCs). Data are from a Sept. 1983 survey of 2,000 large corporations, conducted by Future Computing, Inc. Includes 2 charts showing survey response regarding preferred PC manufacturer, and manufacturer of PCs currently in use.

DATACOMM MARKET MAY SOON SEE SOME 'FUNDAMENTAL DISLOCATIONS'

(p. 16) Article, with 2 charts showing share of telecommunications market, for AT&T, independent equipment suppliers, independent telephone companies, spun-off Bell operating companies, and other, 1984 and 1988. Data are from Strategic Inc.

MIS COMMAND GROWS, ANNUAL FEATURE

(p. 52-56) Annual survey article, by Karen G. Beagley and Wendelin J. Colby, on micrographics use by businesses. Data are based on 1,969 responses to a Dec. 1983 survey conducted by Hitchcock Marketing and Research Services.

Contains narrative analysis, and 13 tables showing distribution of survey responses on the following:

a. Dept or staff supervising micrographic operations, designing systems, recommending equipment, and approving expenditures; and expenditures on micrographics in the next and past years.

b. How micrographics are used and their planned usage in next year; how micrographics needs are handled (in-house vs. service organization); types of micrographics services used; use of in-house computer-output-micrographics and computer-assisted retrieval systems; and other methods used for document storage.

This is the 14th annual survey.

C4590–1.505: June 1984 (Vol. 31, No. 6, Part 1)

26th ANNUAL DP SALARY SURVEY: ON THE RISE AGAIN

(p. 26-34) Annual article, by Karen Beagley and Raymond S. Winkler, on salaries of data processing (DP) staff by detailed position. Data are from a 1984 *Infosystems* survey of 972 firms reporting salaries for 10,581 employees. Includes 1 chart and 5 tables showing:

a. Distribution of dp budget by function; average total and DP employees, by DP equipment rental range; and ranked list of DP personnel sources.

b. Average weekly salary, by census division, equipment rental range, and industry; and lowest, highest, quartile, average, median, and mean weekly salaries; all by detailed DP position, as of Mar. 1984 with summary comparisons to 1983.

C4590–1.506: July 1984 (Vol. 31, No. 7)

NOVEL DISTRIBUTION CHANNELS MAY EMERGE FOR MICROCOMPUTERS

(p. 12) Article, with 1 chart showing world market value for microcomputers, and market share by end use (business, education, and consumer), 1981-86. Data are from Strategic Inc.

C4590–1.507: Aug. 1984 (Vol. 31, No. 8)

88% OF WHITE-COLLAR WORKERS REPORT THEY ARE COMPUTER LITERATE

(p. 20) Article, with 2 charts showing computer use and knowledge among corporate middle management. Data are based on responses of 464 middle managers to a 1983 survey conducted by Exxon Office Systems.

C4590–1.508: Sept. 1984 (Vol. 31, No. 9)

INFORMATION REVOLUTION MOVING TOO FAST FOR COMPANIES TO ASSESS

(p. 18-19) Brief article comparing corporate managers' attitudes and abilities regarding computer systems as perceived by the managers and by computer trainers. Data are from surveys of 100 computer trainers and 5,000 middle managers, conducted by Omni Group in conjunction with Exxon Office Systems. Includes 2 undated charts.

C4590–1.509: Oct. 1984 (Vol. 31, No. 10)

FAILURE TO PROVIDE PROPER WORK ENVIRONMENT REAL SOURCE OF ILLS

(p. 17) Brief article on health problems associated with the use of video display terminals (VDTs). Data are from a survey of 351 data entry operators and 140 clerical workers, conducted by Data Entry Management Assn. Includes 1 undated table showing percent of respondents reporting selected health problems.

C4670
Huebner Publications

C4670–1 PURCHASING WORLD
Monthly. Approx. 125 p.
ISSN 0093-1659.
LC 73-642852.
SRI/MF/excerpts, shipped
quarterly

Monthly trade journal of industrial purchasing management, reporting trends and developments in wholesale purchasing, commodity prices and availability, economic indicators, and purchasing strategies.

Data are from journal surveys of industrial corporations; private research organizations, including Data Resources, Inc. (DRI); BLS and other Federal Government sources; the National Assn of Purchasing Managers; and industry trade assns. Data in regular statistical features are presented for trend purposes rather than for currency, but are usually current to 1-2 months prior to cover date.

Journal includes feature articles, occasionally with statistics, including surveys of purchasing managers' views on business conditions; DRI and Wharton economic forecasts; narrative editorial depts; and the following regular statistical sections:

a. "PW Predicts" section covering market, supply and demand, and price outlook for approximately 15 varying commodities, with narrative analysis and text statistics, and trend charts or tables for 4 or more selected commodities, some including price projections for next 6 months.

b. "Business Datatrak" section, with monthly charts and tables, described below, occasional special charts or tables, and accompanying narrative analyses.

"PW Predicts" and monthly "Datatrak" statistics appear in all issues. All additional features with substantial statistical content are described, as they appear, under "Statistical Features." Nonstatistical features are not covered.

Prior to Nov. 1983 issue, journal was described in SRI under C8650-2. Issuing agency has changed from Technical Publishing Co.

Availability: Purchasing World, 6521 Davis Industrial Pkwy., Solon OH 44139, qualified subscribers †, others $46.00 per yr.; SRI/MF/excerpts for monthly statistical sections, and all portions covered under "Statistical Features;" shipped quarterly.

Issues reviewed during 1984: Nov. 1983-Oct. 1984 (P) (Vol. 27, Nos. 11-12; Vol. 28, Nos. 1-10) [Vol. 28, No. 3 incorrectly reads Vol. 29].

BUSINESS DATATRAK:

[1] Key economic trends [with 3 or more charts showing selected economic indicator trends, varying in each issue; and 1 chart showing National Assn of Purchasing Managers (NAPM) "business barometer"].

[2] Current prices [with 3 or more charts, and 1 table showing price levels for approximately 50 industrial products, for month 2-3 months prior to cover date, and percent change from previous month and year].

[3] Steel scene [with 6 charts showing selected steel industry trends, including comparison of import and domestic steel prices, based on sur-

veys by the NAPM Steel Buyers Committee and the Steel Service Center Institute; may not appear in every issue].

[4] Procurement status [with 4 charts showing selected business purchasing indicator trends; and 1 table showing leadtimes for selected commodities in 8 industry sectors, in Chicago, Cleveland, Houston, Los Angeles, Philadelphia, and Pittsburgh, for month of coverage, previous month, and month 6 months previously].

[5] Raw material price barometer [with 1 trend chart, and 1 table showing spot market prices for materials in 8 categories including scrappage, for month of coverage, previous month, and same month of previous year].

STATISTICAL FEATURES:

C4670–1.501: Nov. 1983 (Vol. 27, No. 11)
PROFILE OF THE PURCHASING PROFESSIONAL, 1983, BIENNIAL FEATURE

(p. 54-55) Biennial article on purchasing manager characteristics and job functions, based on a survey of approximately 1,300 *Purchasing World* readers. Includes 3 charts showing purchasing dept responsibilities, and in-house committee membership and previous work experience of purchasing managers.

Previous survey is described in SRI 1981 Annual, under C8650-2.212.

EXPECT HEAVY SPENDING FOR POLLUTION CONTROL AND SAFETY EQUIPMENT

(p. 68) Article, with 1 table showing expenditures for safety/health and pollution control equipment as a percent of expected total capital spending, by selected industry group, 1983. Data are from McGraw-Hill and Occupational Safety and Health Administration.

PACKAGING BUYERS SEE STABLE MARKET

(p. 94) Article on purchasing manager's outlook for packaging price trends, 1983-84, based on a survey of *Purchasing World* readers. Includes 2 charts.

C4670–1.502: Dec. 1983 (Vol. 27, No. 12)
PRICE INCREASES REVISED DOWNWARD, QUARTERLY FEATURE

(p. 54) Quarterly article, with 1 chart showing revised freight shipping rate increases, 1977-85. Data are from Wharton Econometric Forecasting Associates, Inc.

WIDESPREAD DISCOUNTING CONTINUES

(p. 74) Article on discount price trends, based on a *Purchasing World* reader survey. Includes 2 undated charts showing frequency of discounting activity and average discount obtained.

C4670–1.503: Jan. 1984 (Vol. 28, No. 1)
UPSWING CONTINUES, ANNUAL FEATURE

Annual compilation of economic forecast articles. Those with substantial statistics are described below.

GREAT EXPECTATIONS, ANNUAL FEATURE

(p. 63, 66) Annual article presenting 1984 economic predictions of members of National Assn of Purchasing Management's Business Survey Committee. Includes text statistics and 4 charts showing expected trends in prices, business conditions, capital spending, and operating rates.

FEW BIG GAINS IN PRICES, QUARTERLY FEATURE

(p. 66-67) Quarterly DRI economic forecast article presenting price forecasts for basic industrial commodities into 1985. Includes 1 table comparing 4th quarter prices for 31 commodities grouped as raw materials/energy, metals, components, construction supplies, and machinery, shown as annual percent change, 1982/83-1984/85.

BRIGHT YEAR AHEAD, ANNUAL FEATURE

(p. 70-71) Annual article, with 1 table comparing 4 major econometric consulting firms' forecasts for real GNP, industrial production, GNP price deflator, PPI, CPI, prime interest rate, and unemployment rate, 1983-85.

BUYERS ACCENT THE POSITIVE, ANNUAL FEATURE

(p. 71-72) Annual article on purchasing managers' business outlook for 1984, based on a survey of *Purchasing World* readers. Includes text statistics and 4 charts showing respondents' expectations about price trends, demand, inventories, and order lead times, 1984.

LABOR NEGOTIATIONS IN 1984

(p. 72) Table showing collective bargaining agreement expirations, and workers and major industries affected, monthly 1984. Data are from BLS.

C4670–1.504: Feb. 1984 (Vol. 28, No. 2)
DEMAND TO SUPPORT HIGHER PAPER PRICES

(p. 49-50) Article, with 2 tables showing percent change in paper prices and value of demand, 1980-85. Data are from Wharton Econometric Forecasting Associates.

DIP IN FREIGHT RATES HAS ENDED, SEMIANNUAL FEATURE

(p. 68) Semiannual article reporting on purchasing/transportation executives' perceptions of direction and degree of change in overall freight costs, 1983-84. Data are based on a *Purchasing World* survey. Includes 3 charts.

C4670–1.505: Mar. 1984 (Vol. 28, No. 3)
[Issue incorrectly reads Vol. 29.]

BUYERS KEEPING INVENTORIES TIGHT, SEMIANNUAL FEATURE

(p. 44) Semiannual article on purchasing managers' views of inventory conditions for purchased material, based on a survey of *Purchasing World* readers. Includes 1 chart showing respondents' opinions on current inventory status and expected change in 6 months, and expected change in order lead-times, 1984.

C4670–1.506: Apr. 1984 (Vol. 28, No. 4)
INDUSTRIAL PRICE TRENDS, QUARTERLY FEATURE

(p. 14) Quarterly DRI economic forecast article presenting price forecasts for basic industrial commodities into 1985. Includes 1 table comparing 4th quarter prices for 26 types of materials, components, equipment, and other commodities, shown as annual percent change, 1983/84-1984/85.

CARRIERS CAUGHT IN COST-PRICE SQUEEZE, QUARTERLY FEATURE

(p. 56) Quarterly article, with 1 chart showing revised freight shipping rate increases, 1977-85. Data are from Wharton Econometric Forecasting Associates.

BUYERS PLAN MORE IMPORT ACTIVITY

(p. 83) Article on purchasing manager plans for importing activity, based on a survey of *Purchasing World* readers. Includes 2 undated charts showing change in importing activity and perceived import price advantage.

C4670-1.507: May 1984 (Vol. 28, No. 5)

PACKAGING MARKETS: PURCHASING FEELS THE PRESSURE

(p. 47-51) By Robert S. Reichard. Article, with 8 charts summarizing packaging industry trends and outlook, including market shares by type of packaging material (no date). Data sources include Frost and Sullivan, Inc.

C4670-1.508: June 1984 (Vol. 28, No. 6)

RATE HIKES, YES; DOUBLE DIGIT, NO! QUARTERLY FEATURE

(p. 63) Quarterly article, with 1 chart showing revised freight shipping rate increases, 1978-86. Data are from Wharton Econometric Forecasting Associates.

PW OUTLOOK SURVEY: PRICES, ANNUAL FEATURE

(p. 126) Annual article, with 3 charts showing purchasing managers' outlook for change in industrial prices, overall and in 5 sectors, through mid-1985. Data are from *Purchasing World* national survey.

C4670-1.509: July 1984 (Vol. 28, No. 7)

MIDYEAR APPRAISAL, ANNUAL FEATURE

Annual compilation of mid-year economic forecast articles. Those with substantial statistics are described below.

ECONOMETRIC FORECASTS COMPARED, ANNUAL FEATURE

(p. 56-58) Annual article, with 1 table comparing 4 major econometric consulting firms' forecasts for GNP, GNP price deflator, industrial production, PPI, CPI, prime interest rate, and unemployment rate, 1984-85.

BUYERS ARE STILL OPTIMISTIC, ANNUAL FEATURE

(p. 60-62) Annual article on purchasing managers' business outlook for 1984, based on surveys of *Purchasing World* readers and members of National Assn of Purchasing Management's Business Survey Committee. Includes 6 charts showing respondents' expectations regarding market growth, price trends, inventory strategies, and capital outlays, 1984.

DETAILED PRODUCT BY PRODUCT PRICE FORECAST, QUARTERLY FEATURE

(p. 62-64) Quarterly DRI economic forecast article presenting price forecasts for basic industrial commodities into 1986. Includes 1 table comparing 2nd quarter prices for 29 commodities grouped as raw materials/energy, metals, components, construction supplies, and machinery, shown as annual percent change 1983/84-1985/86.

C4670-1.510: Aug. 1984 (Vol. 28, No. 8)

CHEMICALS BUOYANT, PRICES LESS SO

(p. 64-65) Article, with 1 chart showing percent change in aggregate chemical prices, 1981-86. Data are from Wharton Econometrics.

CHEMICAL OUTLOOK IS BRIGHT FOR BUYERS

(p. 66-71) By Thomas F. Dillon. Article, with 1 undated chart showing distribution of chemical industry sales between final and intermediate users. Data are from Commerce Dept.

PW SURVEY: TRANSPORTATION, SEMIANNUAL FEATURE

(p. 74) Semiannual article reporting on purchasing managers' perceptions of direction and degree of change in overall freight costs, mid-1983 to mid-1985. Data are based on a *Purchasing World* survey. Includes 3 charts.

C4670-1.511: Sept. 1984 (Vol. 28, No. 9)

POLLUTION CONTROL

(p. 18) Article, with 1 chart showing pollution control equipment spending change by selected industry, and spending distribution for air, water, and solid waste, 1984. Data are from McGraw-Hill.

NON-FERROUS REPORT

(p. 54-60, 70-72) Compilation of 2 articles on market trends and outlook for nonferrous metals. Most data are from Bureau of Mines. Includes text data, and 18 charts showing summary price change trends, 1980-84; consumption distribution by end-use market, for each of 11 metals (no dates); and changes in prices and in consumption or shipments, for copper and aluminum, primarily 1980-85.

NO NEW BUILD-UP SOON, SEMIANNUAL FEATURE

(p. 86) Semiannual article on purchasing managers' views of inventory conditions for purchased material, based on a survey of *Purchasing World* readers. Includes 1 chart showing respondents' opinions on current inventory status and expected change through early 1985.

FREIGHT BARGAINS END BUT HIKES TO BE MODERATE, QUARTERLY FEATURE

(p. 104-107) Quarterly article, with 1 chart showing revised freight shipping rate increases, 1978-86. Data are from Wharton Econometric Forecasting Associates.

C4670-1.512: Oct. 1984 (Vol. 28, No. 10)

PW's BUSINESS DATA FILE, ANNUAL FEATURE

(p. 51-64) Annual article, for 1984, presenting buyers guide to office equipment. Data are from company reports.

Includes 1 extended table showing model names, specifications, and prices; company annual sales; and number of sales and service locations; all by company, for electronic typewriters, copiers, and facsimile equipment.

This is the 1st of 2 features comprising the 1984 buyers guide. Part 2, covering microcomputers, is scheduled for the Nov. 1984 issue and will be described when received.

C4680
Hunter Publishing Co.

C4680-1 NATIONAL PETROLEUM NEWS
Monthly. Approx. 70 p.
ISSN 0149-5267.
LC 55-3942.
SRI/MF/excerpts, shipped quarterly

Monthly publication (semimonthly in June or July) reporting on U.S. petroleum product marketing, R&D, sales, regulation, and finance. Includes data on oil jobbers, service stations, convenience stores with gasoline sales, and fuel oil and liquefied petroleum gas dealers. Also presents periodic data on gasoline prices, petroleum product stocks, and oil company earnings.

Issues generally contain brief articles on regional and general developments and trends, and topical articles and features, occasionally with statistics; and monthly editorial features.

Regular statistical features include:

a. 2 monthly tables on gasoline prices and petroleum stocks ("Marketplace at a Glance").

b. 1 quarterly table on oil company earnings (article title varies).

c. Annual NPN Factbook issue (mid-June or July), and annual outlook feature for marketers (Dec.).

Monthly tables are listed below and appear in all issues except the annual Factbook. All additional features with substantial statistical content are described, as they appear, under "Statistical Features." Nonstatistical features are not covered.

Availability: National Petroleum News, Circulation Department, 950 Lee St., Des Plaines IL 60016, qualified subscribers $42.00 per yr., others $56.00 per yr., single copy $4.50, Fact Book $35.00; SRI/MF/excerpts for monthly tables and all portions described under "Statistical Features;" shipped quarterly.

Issues reviewed during 1984: Nov. 1983-Oct. 1984 (P) and NPN Fact Book Issue (Vol. 75, Nos. 11-12; Vol. 76, Nos. 1-10).

MONTHLY TABLES:

[1] Average gasoline prices in the U.S. [by grade of gasoline and region, with U.S. city average, generally for month 2-3 months prior to cover date; data are from BLS].

[2] Stocks [total and unleaded gasoline, jet kerosene, distillates, and residual fuels, generally as of 4-7 weeks prior to cover date, and for same date of previous year; data are from American Petroleum Institute].

STATISTICAL FEATURES:

C4680-1.501: Nov. 1983 (Vol. 75, No. 11)

C-STORE TIE-IN ON RISE, BUT STATION STILL TOPS

(p. 30) Article discussing types of retail gasoline outlets. Data are from *Lundberg Letter,* and industry assns. Includes 1 table showing retail gasoline outlets, by type, 1977 and 1982.

OCTANE RATINGS DOWN, BUT OUTLOOK IS UP, RECURRING FEATURE

(p. 32) Recurring article on gasoline octane ratings. Data are from DOE. Includes 2 tables showing octane ratings for leaded and unleaded gasoline by method of measurement, for summer and winter 1981-1982/83, and by region for winter 1982/83.

Previous articles are described in SRI 1983 Annual, under C4680-1.401 and C4680-1.409.

EROSION CONTINUES IN LUBRICANT SALES, RECURRING FEATURE

(p. 33) Recurring article, with 1 table showing automotive and industrial lubricant sales volume by type, 1978-82. Data are from National Petroleum Refiners Assn.

GASOLINE YIELDS RISE, BUT RESID DIPS

(p. 34) Article, with 1 table showing distribution of product yield from crude oil, by 16 product categories, 1979-82. Data are from American Petroleum Institute and DOE.

RESTROOM, PHONE, FUEL HEAD DRIVER WISH LIST, MIDWEST SURVEY SAYS

(p. 72) Brief article on a 1982 survey of what motorists want from a fuel stop. Survey was conducted at 7 midwestern fuel stops, by Lester B. Knight and Associates. Includes 1 table showing percent of respondents desiring 10 services.

AGA STUDY: OIL-TO-GAS CONVERSIONS STILL DOWN

(p. 74) Article, with 1 table showing number of households by type of heating energy used, by census region, 1982. Data are from American Gas Assn.

WILL YOUR TAX RETURN BE AUDITED?

(p. 100) Article, with 2 tables showing percent of tax returns audited by IRS, for noncorporate businesses and individuals by income class, and for corporations by asset size, 1982. Data are from IRS.

C4680–1.502: Dec. 1983 (Vol. 75, No. 12)

PROJECTED MARKETING EXPENDITURES PUSHING RECORD TOTALS AMID MARKET SHARE BATTLES

(p. 27-28) Article, with 1 table showing petroleum industry capital spending, by function, 1981-85. Data are from McGraw-Hill Economics Dept.

THIRD QTR. EARNINGS IMPROVE FOR TOP GLOBAL COMPANIES, QUARTERLY FEATURE

(p. 28) Quarterly article on trends in oil company earnings. Includes 1 table showing earnings for 21 companies, 3rd quarter and 1st 9 months 1982-83.

DECLINE IN U.S. OIL RESERVES EXPECTED TO CONTINUE FOR '83

(p. 30) Article, with 1 table showing discoveries, production, and proved reserves, for crude oil and natural gas, 1978-82, and for natural gas liquids, 1979-82. Data are from DOE.

1984: A YEAR OF DECISIONS, ANNUAL FEATURE

(p. 38-43) Annual article, by J. Richard Shaner, on oil industry marketing outlook, for 1984. Data are from the Independent Petroleum Assn of America and McGraw-Hill Economics Dept. Includes 2 charts and 2 tables showing the following:

a. Retail prices and/or supply, for motor gasoline, distillate and residual fuel oil, and other petroleum products, 1982-84 and quarterly 1983-84.

b. Domestic demand for 6 petroleum products; total exports; domestic production of crude oil and natural gas liquids; required imports for crude oil and 6 products; other supply; closing stocks for 6 products, unfinished oils, natural gas liquids, and crude oil; and crude runs to stills; 1983 and quarterly 1984.

c. Capital spending in oil industry, by function, 1983-85.

MARKETER COUNT DROPS A LITTLE BIT, BUT OVERALL EMPLOYMENT INCHES UP

(p. 49) Article, with 1 table showing petroleum industry employment, with detail for wholesale petroleum/petroleum products and retail gasoline service station segments, by State, 1981-82.

Data are from 1982-83 editions of *The Oil Producing Industry in Your State*. Full report is covered in SRI under A5425-1.

C4680–1.503: Jan. 1984 (Vol. 76, No. 1)

FAST MONEY REVOLUTION

(p. 38-46) By Tim Grace. Article on instant credit approval systems as alternatives to conventional payment methods for gasoline purchases. Data are from Atalla Corp. Includes 1 undated table showing gasoline purchase transaction cost by payment method including cash, credit cards, check, and debit card.

1984 OUTLOOK BRIGHTENS FOR OIL HEAT

(p. 54-55) Article, with 1 table showing expected unit sales of central heating equipment and water heaters, by type, 1982-84. Data are from Gas Appliance Manufacturers Assn.

BATTERY MARKET CHANGING: BETTER DAYS AHEAD?

(p. 62) Article, with 1 table showing shipments of motor vehicle replacement batteries, monthly 1982-Oct. 1983. Data are from Battery Council International.

C4680–1.504: Feb. 1984 (Vol. 76, No. 2)

TEXACO/GETTY SCORES COUP, IF DEAL AVOIDS ANTITRUST

(p. 22) Article on Texaco buy-out of Getty Oil, with 1 undated table showing number of gasoline stations operated by each company in 27 States. Data are from oil industry.

POST-EMBARGO STATION SHAKEOUT CONTINUES; OPTIMAL LEVEL ESTIMATED SAME AS IN 1930s, ANNUAL FEATURE

(p. 36-37) Annual article reporting on U.S. Dept of Commerce forecasts of establishments and sales for gasoline service stations, auto product/service (aftermarket) stores, and convenience stores, 1984. Includes 3 tables showing number and sales of company- and franchisee-owned establishments in each category, 1982-84.

MARKET FACES TRIALS IN MATURING YEARS

(p. 56-59) Article on trends in petroleum product marketing. Includes 1 table showing number of jobber and agent distributors for 16 major oil companies, 1972 and 1983.

HOW PETROLEUM PRODUCTS GOT MOVING

(p. 80-82) By Tim Grace. Article reviewing developments in petroleum transportation. Data are from Hertz Corp. Includes 1 table showing CPI, and tractor/trailer annual and per mile transport costs, 1967-81.

HEATING OIL SURVIVES FIGHT WITH GAS; SULFUR LAWS, EMBARGO BLUDGEON RESID

(p. 84-88) By J. Richard Shaner. Article discussing trends in the fuel oil industry. Data sources include American Petroleum Institute and *Petroleum Facts & Figures*. Includes 3 tables showing consumption of distillate and residual fuel oil, with detail by consuming sector, various years 1926-82, and projections for 1983 and 1990.

C4680–1.505: Mar. 1984 (Vol. 76, No. 3)

CATCHING UP

(p. 13) Compilation of brief news items on petroleum products industry, including 1 table showing owner, location, capacity, and years of operation, for oil refineries closed during 1st 10 months of 1983. Data are from Energy Information Administration.

SURVEY SHOWS DRAMATIC RETAIL DIVERSITY

(p. 31) Article, with 1 chart showing distribution of gasoline service stations by marketing method (full-serve only, split island, and self-serve only), for aggregate major and nonmajor gasoline retailers, and individually for 16 leading companies. Data are from a Jan. 1984 survey of 16,810 service stations, conducted by Lundberg Survey, Inc.

C-STORES SOLD 12% OF '82 'GAS;' LOOK FOR 20% BY 1985: ROSCOE, ANNUAL FEATURE

(p. 32) Annual article on convenience store gasoline marketing, 1982. Data are from 13th annual John F. Roscoe survey of 10 top publicly owned chains.

Includes 1 table showing the following for each surveyed chain: number of units selling gasoline, gallons sold, average number of gallons sold per day per unit, profit margin per gallon, and gasoline sales as percent of total sales, 1982.

Full survey report is covered in SRI under C8115-1.

LATE '83 DEMAND HIKES YEAR-END PROFITS, QUARTERLY FEATURE

(p. 33) Quarterly article on trends in oil company earnings. Includes 1 table showing earnings for 21 companies, 4th quarter and full year 1982-83.

REPORT SAYS 207,000 PLACES SELL MOTOR FUEL; 234,000 TANKS ARE MORE THAN 21 YEARS OLD

(p. 33) Article, with 1 table showing number of motor fuel tanks at service stations, by tank age, 1982. Data are from an informal survey sponsored by National Petroleum Council.

GASOHOL PENETRATES 8.1% OF FUEL MARKET, DESPITE TAX SETBACKS, ANNUAL FEATURE

(p. 35) Annual article on fuel ethanol and methanol sales. Data are from Information Resources, Inc. Includes 1 table showing fuel ethanol sales volume and share of total gasoline sales, for 5 States with highest sales, 1983.

DAWN OF A NEW ERA? SUPER-MARKETERS ARISE FROM FUEL OIL RANKS

(p. 38-42) Article discussing recent trends in retail heating oil industry. Data are from annual survey by *Fuel Oil News*.

Includes 1 undated table showing the following, for the average fuel oil dealer: number of residential and commercial/industrial accounts; sales volume of distillate and residual fuel; and number of employees; by region, and for total U.S.

Full report on fuel oil survey is covered in SRI under C4680-2.

C4680–1.506: Apr. 1984 (Vol. 76, No. 4)

MERGER FRENZY: SUPPLIER FALLOUT BEGINS TO SHAKE THE INDUSTRY

(p. 20-25) Article discussing effects of mergers in the petroleum industry. Data are from company annual reports, and Lundberg Survey. Includes text data showing top 4 petroleum companies after 1984 mergers ranked by 1983 assets, and 3 tables showing the following:

a. Top 21 petroleum corporations ranked by assets, with domestic and foreign crude oil and natural gas reserves, 1982.

b. Market share in 12 States, refineries, retail outlets, jobbers, and employees, for 2-4 companies involved in mergers as of early 1984, various periods 1982-84.

TEXACO'S $90-M SPINOFF MAKES POWER TEST AWESOME ATLANTIC FORCE, NO. 1 U.S. INDIE

(p. 25-27) Article, with 2 tables showing number of gasoline stations operated by Getty Oil and Power Test Corp. in 12 States; and acquiring and acquired company, cost, and date, for 6 petroleum industry mergers, July 1981-Mar. 1984.

WHY C-STORES LEAD GASOLINE MARKETS

(p. 34-39) Article on development of retail outlets combining convenience stores (C-stores) and gasoline marketing. Data are from oil company executives, and *Dollars per Day Survey*. Includes 2 tables showing oil company outlets and number with C-stores, and C-store company outlets and number selling gasoline, both with average store sales and gallonage per month, by company, primarily 1982.

C4680–1.507: May 1984 (Vol. 76, No. 5)

OIL FUTURES: A GROWING FACTOR IN PRICING

(p. 36-40) By J. Richard Shaner. Article, with 1 table showing volume of futures contracts traded on New York Mercantile Exchange, for heating oil and gasoline 1981-83, and for crude oil 1983.

LOWER '83 FUEL PRICES HELPED DAMPEN COST OF OPERATING AUTOMOBILES

(p. 50) Article, with 1 table showing average per mile operating cost of a typical new compact car, for 20 cities, 1982-83. Data are from Hertz Corp.

Full Hertz Corp. report is covered in SRI under B4500-4.

C4680–1.508: June 1984 (Vol. 76, No. 6)

MAJORS' 1st-QTR. EARNINGS SUPPORTED BY DOWNSTREAM, QUARTERLY FEATURE

(p. 35) Quarterly article on trends in oil company earnings. Includes 1 table showing earnings for 21 companies, 1st quarter 1983-84.

INDIE MARKETERS TRIMMING DOWN: SIGMA STUDY, ANNUAL FEATURE

(p. 35-36) Annual article on trends in service station operations among members of Society of Independent Gasoline Marketers of America (SIGMA). Includes 2 tables showing the following for SIGMA members: distribution of gasoline purchases by type of supplier, 1983, and of outlets by type of service provided, 1982-83.

MOST MAJORS MARKET SOME ALCOHOL FUEL, SAYS RESEARCH FIRM

(p. 38) Article, with 1 table showing alcohol fuel blend share of total gasoline sales, for 14 major oil companies. Data are from a Nov. 1983-Apr. 1984 study by Information Resources, Inc.

TUNEUP MARKET SHOWS INCREASES, BUT SERVICE STATION SHARE WEAKENS

(p. 66) Article, with 1 table showing distribution of automobile tune-ups by type of provider, 1973, 1978, and 1983. Data are from surveys by Champion Spark Plug Co.

C4680–1.509: 1984 Fact Book Issue (Vol. 76, No. 6a)

NPN FACT BOOK ISSUE

Annual fact book presenting detailed petroleum industry statistics and related directories. Covers finances, supply and demand, marketing, prices, and employment, including data by product, company, and State, various years 1950-84. Also includes selected data for Canada and other foreign countries, and data on vehicle registrations and sales of tires, batteries, and accessories.

Data are compiled from NPN surveys and numerous Government and industry sources, identified for each table.

Contains introduction, contents listing, and index (p. 4-12); statistical sections, generally including narrative summaries, with 38 maps and charts, and 140 tables (p. 15-160); and directories of trade assns, oil marketing companies and executives, and Federal energy-related officials (p. 161-212).

All tables, and charts presenting data not covered in tables, are listed below.

Addenda appear in Sept. and Oct. 1984 issues; for description, see C4680-1.512 and C4680-1.513 below.

TABLES AND CHARTS:

ANNUAL REPORTS

[1] Ranking the top [21 major oil] marketing companies [by total assets, net income, and net sales among *Fortune* 500 companies, 1982-83]. (p. 15)

[2] Oil company annual reports [gross sales, net income, and total assets, 1982-83, with percent change from 1978; net income as percent of average stockholder equity, crude oil and refined product imports, net domestic and foreign crude oil production and refinery runs, and domestic refined product sales, 1982-83; for 23 companies]. (p. 16-17)

[3-4] Quarterly and full year earnings, 1983 vs. 1982; and how they fared in 1982 vs. 1981; [for 22 major oil companies]. (p. 18)

ADVERTISING

[5] How oil companies split their [advertising] budgets [expenditures by media, for 3 major companies, various years 1977-82]. (p. 20)

[6-7] Network and spot TV spending [on advertising, for 15-20 oil companies, 1982-83]. (p. 20)

AUTOMOTIVE

[8] Current automotive registrations [of cars, trucks/buses, and motorcycles, 1982 and/or 1983, by State]. (p. 24)

[9] Estimated licensed drivers, by sex and State, 1982-83. (p. 25)

[10-13] Automotive trends: fuel and oil consumption [average annual mileage, and gasoline and oil consumption, 1965 and 1970-83]; U.S. passenger car compression ratios [1965 and 1970-84]; vehicle ownership by households and licensed drivers [1980]; and passenger car use of premium [gasoline, 1970, 1972, and 1974-84]. (p. 26)

[14] 1982 relationships by population and drivers [population; licensed drivers and registered motor vehicles per 1,000 persons; fuel consumption per vehicle; and miles per gallon of gas, per vehicle, and per driver; all by State]. (p. 27)

BRAND NAMES

[15] Brand names of gasoline and motor oil [by company]. (p. 28-30)

CAPITAL SPENDING

[16] Capital spending in the oil industry: almost $500 billion in 35 years [by function, 1951-85]. (p. 33)

DISTRIBUTION, OUTLETS, AND EMPLOYMENT

[17] How oil companies handle product distribution [total branded retail outlets, number of States where gasoline brand is marketed, and detail for branded service stations, branded jobbers, commission agents, bulk plants, and terminals; for over 200 oil companies and jobbers, 1984]. (p. 34-42)

[18] Branded retail outlets [by State, for approximately 250 companies, 1984]. (p. 44-51)

[19] Average number of employees [in oil mining, manufacturing, transportation, wholesale, and retail, by State], as of Jan. 1, 1983. (p. 53)

FUEL OIL

[20-22] How distillates, residual [oils], and kerosene were used [1981-82]. (p. 55)

[23] How new homes are heated [1981, and by census region 1982]. (p. 55)

[24] Gas: who uses it for heat [residential usage, by census division, 1982]. (p. 55)

[25] Gas heat equipment shipments [by type, 1982-83]. (p. 55)

[26-28] Distillate, kerosene, and residual fuel oil sales, by categories and uses [by State and PAD district, 1981-82]. (p. 56-63)

[29-30] Sales of distillate and residual fuel oil, by uses [selected years 1960-82]. (p. 64)

INTERNATIONAL

[31-34] World oil production, crude oil reserves and refining capacity, and natural gas production, by area [most shown for U.S., Canada, and by world area, 1975-82 or 1976-83]. (p. 65)

[35-36] Estimated crude oil reserves [1982-83] and production [1981-82] in 20 leading nations. (p. 66)

CANADA

[Tables 37-49] show data for Canada.]

[37-39] Refined product sales [by product, 1983]; gasoline outlets [undated]; and premium ratios [Dec. 1982-83; all by Province] (p. 69)

[40] Oil companies: how distribution is organized [shows breakdowns similar to table [17] for 18 companies, various years 1981-84]. (p. 70-71)

[41] Brand names of gasoline and motor oils [by company, various years 1982-84]. (p. 70)

STORAGE CAPACITY

[127] Primary storage capacity [in operation, under construction, and idle but available, by product, Mar. 31, 1978 and/or Mar. 31, 1983]. (p. 136)

[128] Primary minimum operating inventories, 1979 [and for PAD Districts 1-4 and 5, 1983, by product]. (p. 136)

[129-133] Estimated storage capacity and inventory in the petroleum distribution system; [for primary system]; for secondary system [with detail for] bulk plants and for retail motor fuel outlets; [and for] tertiary storage system [with detail by end-use sector; generally by product], as of Mar. 31, 1983. (p. 138)

TAXES

[134-135] 1983 tax collections: [by] State [from motor fuel taxes, 1982-83, with 1983 gasoline tax rates per gallon]; and Federal [collections from gasoline, diesel/special fuels, and lube oil taxes, 1969-83]. (p. 140)

TIRES, BATTERIES, AND ACCESSORIES (TBA) AFTERMARKET

[136-137] Outlook for tires and batteries at stations [shipments, and total and per-station unit sales]; and battery shipments improve [replacement and original equipment; primarily 1970 and 1973-83]. (p. 143)

[138] Where batteries are sold [private and manufacturer brand shipments, by distribution channel, 1982-83]. (p. 143)

[139-140] Auto, truck, and farm tire shipments [original equipment, replacement, and export, by vehicle type, 1982-83]. (p. 144)

[141] Where consumers get tune-ups [distribution among service stations, car dealers, repair shops, and do-it-yourselfers, 1980-83]. [chart] (p. 144)

[142-143] Ethylene glycol-base antifreeze sales [civilian and government bulk and packaged], 1982-83. (p. 144)

[144] Automotive products/services [establishments and sales, for company- and franchisee-owned establishments, 1982-84]. (p. 145)

[145-147] 1984 crankcase drain intervals and recommended oil; chassis lubrication intervals; and automatic transmission drain intervals and recommended fluids; [by manufacturer]. (p. 145)

VEHICLE SERVICE JOB ANALYSIS

[148] Service job analysis [number of jobs performed in service stations by repair cost category and by type of service, and percent of stations performing each type of service, for approximately 50 services, 1983]. (p. 146)

PETROLEUM PRODUCT YIELDS

[149] Average annual yields from 1 barrel of crude oil [by product, 1982]. (p. 148)

REFINERIES

[Tables [150-153] show data by company.]

[150] Refineries and capacities, by States (crude oil operable capacity on Jan. 1, 1983) [also includes detail by State region, and for Puerto Rico, Virgin Islands, and Guam]. (p. 151-153)

[151] Lubricating oil and wax capacities of U.S. [and Canadian] refineries [1983]. (p. 153)

[152] Refineries and capacities, by companies [ranked by total capacity, with individual breakdowns for each refinery location] (in descending order as of Jan. 1, 1983). (p. 154-158)

[153] Refinery closings [and resulting capacity reduction, by PAD district with refinery owner and location], 1981-83. (p. 160)

C4680–1.510: July 1984 (Vol. 76, No. 7)

SECONDARY STORAGE IS SURPRISINGLY HIGH, QUITE UNDERUSED, BUT FLEXIBLE, SAYS NPC

(p. 30-31) Article, with text data and 1 table showing petroleum industry storage capacity and inventory, by product, for the following distribution segments: primary storage; secondary storage, with detail for bulk plants and retail outlets; and tertiary storage, also shown by end-use sector; all as of Mar. 31, 1983. Data are based on a study by the National Petroleum Council.

C4680–1.511: Aug. 1984 (Vol. 76, No. 8)

[Data for the following articles are from DOE's *Petroleum Supply Annual.*]

'83 REFINERY UNIT COUNT, WITH 7 UP AND 18 DOWN, IS LOWEST IN U.S. HISTORY, ANNUAL FEATURE

(p. 31) Annual article, with 2 tables showing owner, location, and years of operation and/or capacity, for refineries closed and for refineries reactivated during 1983, grouped by PAD district.

KEROSINE DEMAND FALLS; ASTM MULLS STANDARDS

(p. 32-33) Article, with 1 table showing kerosene deliveries by consuming sector, by State arranged by PAD district, 1982-83.

'83 HOME HEATING OIL DIPPED 9-MILLION Bbl., ANNUAL FEATURE

(p. 71) Brief annual article, with 1 table showing distillate and residual fuel oil deliveries by consuming sector (including on-highway diesel and/or military), 1979-83.

C4680–1.512: Sept. 1984 (Vol. 76, No. 9)

FACTBOOK ADDENDUM

(p. 9) Correction to directory information for American Petroleum Institute, originally appearing in annual fact book issue.

For description of fact book, see C4680-1.509, above.

OHIO'S '83 FUEL DEMAND HALTS FIVE-YEAR SLIDE

(p. 20-21) Article, with 1 table showing top 20 motor fuel marketing companies operating in Ohio, ranked by market share, 1983. Data are from Ohio Petroleum Marketers Assn.

2nd QUARTER EARNINGS DAMPENED BY POOR MARKETS AND MARGINS, QUARTERLY FEATURE

(p. 32) Quarterly article on trends in oil company earnings. Includes 1 table showing earnings for 25 companies, 2nd quarter and 1st half 1983-84.

C4680–1.513: Oct. 1984 (Vol. 76, No. 10)

HIGHWAY OIL OMITTED, FACTBOOK ADDENDUM

(p. 9) Addendum to annual fact book issue. Shows number of outlets and States supplied by Highway Oil, Inc.

For description of fact book, see C4680-1.509 above.

OCTANE FINDINGS LOWER DESPITE 'GUTSY GAS' INTROS, RECURRING FEATURE

(p. 43) Recurring article on gasoline octane ratings. Data are from National Institute for Petroleum and Energy Research. Includes 1 table showing octane ratings for leaded and unleaded gasoline, for summer and winter 1981-1983/84, and by region for winter 1983/84.

'83 INDUSTRIAL LUBE SALES THE BEST IN FIVE YEARS, RECURRING FEATURE

(p. 85) Recurring article, with 1 table showing automotive/industrial oil and grease sales volume, 1980-83. Data are from National Petroleum Refiners Assn.

C4680–2   FUEL OIL NEWS: 1984 Source Book

Monthly (selected issue).
Dec. 1983. 50 p.
Vol. 48, No. 12.
SRI/MF/excerpts

Annual fuel oil dealers' source book, presenting directories of suppliers of products and services, and 1983 survey data on dealers' fuel and heating/cooling equipment operations. Survey was conducted by *Fuel Oil News*.

Contains contents listing (p. 4), and the following:

a. Directories of petroleum trade assns and suppliers, interspersed throughout publication.

b. Table showing highlights from surveys conducted by North Carolina Oil Jobbers Assn, selected years 1971-83 (p. 26).

c. Survey report in 4 parts, with 27 tables listed below.

Source book is a special industry review issue of the monthly trade journal, *Fuel Oil News,* which does not regularly contain statistical data and is not otherwise covered in SRI. This is the 6th annual source book.

Source book was previously described in SRI under C8025-1.

Availability: Fuel Oil News, PO Box 360, Whitehouse NJ 08880, $19.00 per yr., single copy $2.00; SRI/MF/excerpts for survey report.

TABLES:

[Tables show data by region, mostly as percents or averages.]

C4680–2.1: Part I-II: Fuel Sales, Futures Trading, Computer Use, and Truck Fleets

FUEL SALES AND FUTURES TRADING

1. Type of petroleum sold [fuel oil and gasoline]. (p. 24)

2. Average size of business [number of residential fuel oil accounts and customers; distillate, residual, and gasoline volumes; and employees]. (p. 24)

3. Sources of business income [retail and bulk fuel oil and gasoline sales]. (p. 24)

4. Petroleum products sold [No. 2 fuel oil, gasoline, and other product categories]. (p. 25)

5. Annual heating oil sales by types of customers [private homes, apartments, and educational, hospital, commercial, and industrial facilities]. (p. 25)

6. Average drop [delivery] in gallons [for 275 and 550 gallon tanks]. (p. 25)

7. Percent of dealers trading on the futures markets. (p. 25)

COMPUTERS AND TRUCKS

A. Percent of fuel oil dealers using [selected] computer services. (p. 31)

B. Trucks per dealer [average number and capacity, and type of engine used and preferred]. (p. 31)

C. Average age of trucks [oldest and newest, and percent buying in 1983]. (p. 32)

D. Truck tanks by type [steel and aluminum, use and dealer preference]. (p. 32)

E. Percent [of dealers] using 2-way radios. (p. 32)

C4680-2.2: Part III: Heating and Cooling Equipment Operations

I. Percent of fuel oil dealers that sell/install/service all types of heating/cooling equipment. (p. 37)

II. Trends of equipment sales past 12 months [for residential and commercial sales]. (p. 37)

III. Sources of business income [percent income from wholesale and retail sales of heating equipment]. (p. 37)

IV-VI. Percent of fuel oil dealers that sell/install/service selected heating and cooling equipment [residential and commercial, by type of equipment]. (p. 37-38)

VII. Average number of units installed in past 12 months [residential and commercial burners, boilers, and furnaces]. (p. 38)

VIII. Service dept [percent of dealers with depts; percent with profitable depts; and average calls per year, parts/inventory value, and number of technicians]. (p. 38)

C4680-2.3: Part IV: Conversions to Gas, and Miscellaneous

a-b. Percent of dealers: losing customers to gas heat [and average number of customers lost]; and indicating gas conversions are a major threat to their business, [taking steps to combat conversions, and making conversions from oil to gas]. (p. 41)

c. Percent indicating [selected] factors in brand selection. (p. 41)

d. Brand name specifications (percentage of dealers who recommend equipment replacements by brand), [percent of customers following recommendations, and percent of dealers offering on-site home energy audits]. (p. 42)

e-f. Percent recommending furnace/boiler replacement under [selected] conditions; and indicating involvement in selected products/markets. (p. 42)

(1) Industry publication most helpful to dealers in operating their fuel oil business. (p. 42)

C4687
Inc. Publishing Co.

C4687-1   INC.
Monthly. Approx. 150 p.
ISSN 0162-8968.
LC 79-643168.
SRI/MF/excerpts, shipped quarterly

Monthly journal reporting trends in business activity and management of smaller corporations. Covers company finance, accounting, marketing, regulatory developments, personnel practices, and prominent firms and executives.

Issues generally contain feature articles, occasionally with substantial statistics; and editorial depts, including monthly "Investing in Growth Companies" section presenting selected stock market data for small corporations.

Annual statistical features include rankings of fastest growing privately and publicly held small corporations; survey of executive or management compensation at small corporations; and analysis of States' small business conditions, with ratings.

Features with substantial statistical content are described, as they appear, under "Statistical Features." Each issue of the journal is reviewed, but an abstract is published in SRI monthly issues only when statistical features appear.

Availability: INC. Magazine, PO Box 2538, Boulder CO 80322, $24.00 per yr., single copy $3.00; SRI/MF/excerpts for all portions described under "Statistical Features;" shipped quarterly.

Issues reviewed during 1984: Dec. 1983-Oct. 1984 (P) (Vol. 5, No. 12; Vol. 6, Nos. 1-10).

STATISTICAL FEATURES:

C4687-1.501: Dec. 1983 (Vol. 5, No. 12)

INC. 500: America's Fastest-Growing Private Companies, Annual Feature

Annual compilation of articles and statistics on the fastest growing small privately held companies. The INC. private 500 companies had sales of $100,000 to $25 million in 1978, and are ranked by 1978-82 sales growth. Includes the statistical features described below.

INSIDE THE INC. 500

(p. 68-69) By Curtis Hartman. Narrative analysis, with composite profile of the INC. private 500, and 3 tables ranking top 10 companies by total and per-employee sales, 1982; and by number of new employees, 1978-82 period. Includes accompanying introduction (p. 67).

AMERICA'S FASTEST GROWING PRIVATE COMPANIES

(p. 71-124, passim) Ranked listing of INC. private 500, showing the following for each company: sales growth 1978-82, and rank; sales, profit range, and employees, 1978 and 1982; number of acquisitions during 1978-82; business description; and founding date.

Data are from individual companies, and are accompanied by selection criteria (p. 124) and alphabetical index (p. 146).

This is the 3rd annual ranking.

INDUSTRY BY INDUSTRY... BY THE NUMBERS

(p. 138) Table showing the following for 22 industries: number of INC. private 500 companies; average 1978-82 sales and employment growth rates and 1982 sales per employee, with rankings; and 1982 profit ranking.

C4687-1.502: Jan. 1984 (Vol. 6, No. 1)

THAT DARING YOUNG MAN AND HIS FLYING MACHINES

(p. 42-52) By Lucien Rhodes. Article on People Express airline. Includes 1 table showing operating expense per available seat mile, revenue per passenger mile, and load factor, for People Express and 4 other airlines, 1982 and 1st half 1983.

ACCOUNTING FOR GROWTH

(p. 75-82) By Donna Sammons. Article on major accounting firms' competition for small business clients. Data are from INC. and American Institute of Certified Public Accountants.

Includes 3 undated tables showing the following for 15-21 national accounting firms: percent of gross fees from management advisory, accounting/auditing, and tax services; number of INC. 500 clients, compared to all other accounting firms; and professional staff size, and number of partners, employees, offices, and SEC clients, with rankings.

C4687-1.503: Feb. 1984 (Vol. 6, No. 2)

SURPRISE! SURPRISE!

(p. 36) Article on unemployment tax surcharge on employers imposed by U.S. Dept of Labor in jurisdictions with delinquent Federal unemployment compensation loans. Data are from U.S. Chamber of Commerce.

Includes 1 table showing surcharge per worker in 19 States, D.C., Puerto Rico, and Virgin Islands, 1983-84.

C4687-1.504: May 1984 (Vol. 6, No. 5)

SHOW AND SELL

(p. 64-76) By Susan Buchsbaum and Mark K. Metzger. Article on trade show marketing developments, with 1 table showing top 10 trade shows ranked by exhibit space, and including attendance and location for each, 1983. Data are from *Trade Show Week.*

SUGAR BABY

(p. 85-92) By John F. Persinos. Article, with 2 charts showing revenues for 5 major chocolate bar manufacturers, 1983; and candy bar market share for 3 major manufacturers and all others, 1982.

INC: 100, ANNUAL FEATURE

(p. 155-166) Annual article on the 100 fastest growing publicly held companies with sales of $100,000-$25 million in 1979, ranked by percent increase in sales, 1979-83. Data sources include company annual reports and SEC disclosure forms, business publications, and journal telephone surveys.

Contains analysis of findings and description of survey methodology; index of companies; and the following statistics:

a. Composite profile table; 4 tables ranking top 10 companies by total and per employee sales, employment growth, and net income compared to sales, 1983; and 1 table showing number of INC. 100 companies by selected State, 1983-84.

b. Ranked list of top 100 companies, showing the following for each: type of business and date incorporated; sales, net income, and employment, 1979 and 1983; equity value, 1983; and number of acquisitions during 1979-83 period.

c. Industry summary: list of top 100 companies within 11 industry sectors, with aggregate 1979-83 sales growth for each sector.

This is the 6th annual survey.

YEAR OF THE FAST-GROWTH BEAR, ANNUAL FEATURE

(p. 169-170) Annual article analyzing the stock performance of the 1984 INC. 100 fastest growing publicly held small companies. Includes 2 tables showing INC. 100 companies ranked by Mar. 1984 value of a $100 investment made in Mar. 1983; and including stock price for each company, and comparison to industrial averages of 4 major stock indexes, Mar. 1983-84.

C4687–1.505: July 1984 (Vol. 6, No. 7)

INVESTING FOR COLLEGE

(p. 140) Article, with 1 undated table showing projected cost of a 4-year private and public college education in 5, 10, 15, and 18 years, with current investment in 12% zero-coupon bonds required to defray cost. Data are from T. Rowe Price Associates, Inc.

C4687–1.506: Aug. 1984 (Vol. 6, No. 8)

HIGH-TECH DREAM WON'T COME TRUE

(p. 13-14) By Seymour Melman. Article, with 1 table showing foreign-manufactured products' share of U.S. consumption, for 18 products, 1979/80.

C4687–1.507: Sept. 1984 (Vol. 6, No. 9)

TAKE AT THE TOP, ANNUAL FEATURE

(p. 44-56) Annual article, by Ellen Wojahn, analyzing executive compensation in small/medium sized companies, 1984. Covers chief executive, operating, financial, and marketing officers.

Data are from responses by 1,016 companies to a Mar.-Apr. 1984 survey of INC. subscribers, conducted by INC. and Peat, Marwick, Mitchell and Co.

Includes 6 charts and 3 tables showing characteristics of respondent companies and their chief executive officers; methods used to improve compensation; average salary by sales volume, industry, and region, and typical perquisites, all by position; bonus practices; types of companywide benefits offered; and use of long-term stock incentives.

This is the 6th annual compensation survey.

C4687–1.508: Oct. 1984 (Vol. 6, No. 10)

REPORT ON THE STATES, ANNUAL FEATURE

(p. 108-113) Annual report, by Bruce G. Posner, rating States according to social, economic, and governmental conditions affecting small business activity. Data are primarily from Federal and State agencies.

Includes 1 table showing the following indicators for 50 States, ranked by overall rating:

a. Bank loans as percent of bank assets; commercial/industrial loans per capita; Small Business Investment Co. investments per 1,000 population, availability of direct

loans, loan and bond guarantees, and venture capital; average weekly wage; percent of labor force unionized and high school graduates; and value added per worker.

b. Taxes per $1,000 personal income; types of small business support programs and agencies available; population, employment, and personal income percent change, various periods 1980-83; business units per 1,000 population; and number of INC. 100 companies, 1979-84 period.

The trend periods noted are the only data dates provided. Accompanying narrative analysis includes rankings of top 10 States for selected indicators.

This is the 4th annual report.

C4710
Information for Industry

C4710–1   MERGERS AND ACQUISITIONS: The Journal of Corporate Venture
Quarterly. Approx. 120 p.
ISSN 0026-0010.
LC 66-9930.
SRI/MF/excerpts

Quarterly journal, with annual "Index and Almanac," on corporate mergers and acquisitions. Data are compiled by Information for Industry. Quarter of data coverage is 2 quarters prior to cover date.

General format:

a. Regularly recurring features, including reports on recent merger, divestiture, and joint venture activity; and articles, occasionally with statistics.

b. Quarterly "Rosters" section, with narrative review of selected transactions; and 3 tables and 3 rosters.

Annual "Almanac and Index" issue is usually published in spring, and includes "Profile" section with annual summary of quarterly data; cross-index of acquiring and acquired companies; and previous year article index.

Quarterly tables and rosters are listed below. All additional features with substantial statistical content are described, as they appear, under "Statistical Features."

Availability: Mergers & Acquisitions, 229 S. 18th St., Philadelphia PA 19103, $95.00 per yr.; SRI/MF/excerpts for quarterly tables and rosters and portions described under "Statistical Features."

Issues reviewed during 1984: Fall 1983-Summer 1984 (P) (Vol. 18, Nos. 3-4; Vol. 19, Nos. 1-2); and Almanac and Index 1984.

QUARTERLY TABLES AND ROSTERS:
[All tables and rosters show data for quarter of coverage. Table [2] also includes data for 3-4 previous quarters.]

TABLES

[1] Top 25 transactions by dollar volume [shows value of transaction, acquiring and acquired/merged companies, and investment advisors].

[2] Merger and acquisition activity [number of U.S. and foreign mergers/acquisitions by U.S. companies, and number of U.S. mergers/acquisitions by foreign companies].

[3] [Number of acquisitions by] most active acquirers.

ROSTERS

[1-3] U.S. mergers and acquisitions, foreign investment in U.S., and U.S. investment abroad [arranged by SIC 2- or 3-digit industry, showing the following for each transaction: company name and location, sales or revenues, net income or loss, terms, and effective date].

STATISTICAL FEATURES:

C4710–1.501: Fall 1983 (Vol. 18, No. 3)

DO MERGERS MAKE MONEY?

(p. 40-48) By J. Fred Weston and Kwang S. Chung. Article reviewing theories and research concerning corporate merger motives and impact of mergers on investment performance of participating companies' stocks. Includes 3 tables summarizing sample characteristics and findings for 15 studies of stock performance impact of merger and tender offers. The studies were conducted during 1973-82 and cover various periods 1929-78.

C4710–1.502: Winter 1984 (Vol. 18, No. 4)

TOMBSTONE TALLY 1983, ANNUAL FEATURE

(p. 24) Annual article, with 1 table ranking investment companies involved in 10 or more corporate mergers/acquisitions/related transactions, and including number of transactions of $100 million or more for each, 1983. Data were compiled from *Wall Street Journal* advertisements.

This is the 1st annual ranking.

BUYING ABROAD: WHERE THE MONEY IS

(p. 57-63) By Paul Foster and Sheldon Novack. Article assessing potential benefits of foreign mergers or acquisitions by U.S. corporations. Data are based on return/risk analyses covering securities of a sample of 522 companies in 17 industries in 10 countries.

Includes text statistics and 3 tables showing sample company distribution, and average total and annual returns, by industry and country, 1973-81 period.

C4710–1.503: Almanac and Index 1984

1983 PROFILE, ANNUAL FEATURE

(p. 21-44) Third annual compilation of charts, lists, and tables profiling merger activity in the U.S. and by U.S. firms abroad, 1983. Data are from quarterly tables and rosters. Includes the following data, shown for 1983 unless otherwise noted:

a. Merger/acquisition completions and transaction value by SIC 2-digit industry, for U.S. and foreign acquisitions in the U.S. and for U.S. acquisitions abroad, with summary comparison to 1982, and aggregate completions for 1974-83; 10 most active acquirers ranked by number of transactions; and 100 largest transactions ranked by purchase price. 5 lists and tables.

b. Transactions and divestitures, by form of payment and/or price range; 10 most active industries ranked by number and value of transactions; and 25 largest divestitures ranked by value. 1 chart and 5 lists and tables.

c. 25 largest foreign acquisitions in the U.S. ranked by value; number of transactions for 10 countries most active in U.S. acquisitions and for 9 industries attracting foreign buyers; 25 largest merger cancellations, ranked by price and including reason; and number of acquired companies by sales range. 5 lists and tables.

C4710-1.504: Spring 1984 (Vol. 19, No. 1)
TENDER OFFER UPDATE: 1984, ANNUAL FEATURE

(p. 63-65) Annual article, by Douglas V. Austin and Michael J. Jackson, analyzing tender offer activity, 1978-83. Data are from SEC filings.

Includes 6 tables showing number of offers, by type, success level, contested or uncontested status, and premium level, with selected cross-tabulations and aggregate offer value, 1978-83; and premium level and buyer and target company, for 5 tender acquisitions with premiums of over 100% and 6 acquisitions with negative premiums, 1983.

Data correction appears in Summer 1984 issue; for description, see C4710-1.505, below.

C4710-1.505: Summer 1984 (Vol. 19, No. 2)
WASHINGTON UPDATE

(p. 19-20) Article, with 1 table showing value and market share of imports, for 20 product categories subject to substantial import competition, 1983. Data are from Commerce Dept.

CORRECTION

(p. 20) Data correction for annual article analyzing tender offer activity, 1978-83, appearing in Spring 1984 issue.

For description of original article, see C4710-1.504, above.

C4725
Intertec Publishing Corp.

C4725-1   IMPLEMENT AND TRACTOR
Monthly. Approx. 75 p.
ISSN 0019-2953.
LC 46-31380.
SRI/MF/excerpts, shipped quarterly

Monthly trade journal (semimonthly in Jan. and Mar.) reporting trends and developments in the farm and industrial equipment industry, covering retail and wholesale management and operations, engineering and product information, foreign trade, and news of meetings, expositions, and other industry events.

The 2nd Jan. issue is a nonstatistical directory of dealers, product brand names, equipment distributors, and exporters/importers, with subject index to articles published in the previous year; the 2nd Mar. issue (Red Book) presents equipment specifications and performance data.

Data are from the Farm and Industrial Equipment Institute (FIEI), Food and Agriculture Organization, dealer reports, original surveys, and Commerce Dept.

General format:

a. Editor's introduction, usually with text statistics on recent or forecast production, sales, or export trends.

b. Articles, usually focusing on aspects of tractor or large equipment distribution operations, frequently with statistics, including an annual market statistics report in the Nov. issue.

c. "Manufacturers Edition" section, with articles and features aimed at manufacturers of farm, construction, and lawn/garden equipment, occasionally including statistics; section is separately paginated and only included in industry subscriptions.

d. 2 monthly tables and 1 irregularly recurring table, listed below, on used equipment auction prices and equipment retail sales.

Monthly tables appear in most issues. All additional features with substantial statistical content are described, as they appear, under "Statistical Features;" page locations and latest periods of coverage for irregularly recurring table are also noted. Nonstatistical features are not covered.

Availability: Implement and Tractor, Circulation Department, PO Box 12901, Overland Park KS 66212-0930, qualified subscribers $10.00 per yr., others $34.00 per yr., single copy $2.00, Annual Statistical Number $4.00, Product File and Red Book issues $5.00; SRI/MF/excerpts for monthly tables and all portions covered under "Statistical Features;" shipped quarterly.

Issues reviewed during 1984: Nov. 1983-Oct. 1984 (P) (Vol. 98, Nos. 13-14; Vol. 99, Nos. 1-12).

RECURRING TABLES:
MONTHLY TABLES

[1] Unit retail sales [text table showing summary totals for farm 2- and 4-wheel-drive tractors by horsepower, combines, balers, forage harvesters, and mower conditioners, for month 2 months prior to cover date, year to date, and same periods of previous year; table occasionally includes data for Canada].

[2] Auction prices of used equipment [showing equipment manufacturer, model, and condition, and prices paid, at national wholesale auctions of selected dealers conducted during month 2-3 months prior to cover date].

IRREGULARLY RECURRING TABLE

[3] Retail sales of selected farm equipment [combines, corn heads, hay balers, windrowers, grinder-mixers, forage harvesters, and mower conditioners; by State, and for Federal Government purchases, for year to date ending 3 months prior to cover date, and same period of previous year].

STATISTICAL FEATURES:

C4725-1.501: Nov. 1983 (Vol. 98, No. 13)
46th ANNUAL STATISTICS ISSUE

(p. 20-54) Annual compilation of farm equipment market statistics. Most data are from Farm and Industrial Equipment Institute and dealer reports, or from Commerce Dept and Census of Agriculture reports. Includes 12 tables, as follows:

a. Motor vehicles and specified machines on farms; wheel tractors' wholesale prices; and principal machines on farms, by State and region; various years 1927-83. 2 tables. (p. 20-32)

b. Retail sales volume for farm wheel tractors, by horsepower, and for self-propelled combines and 8 other types of equipment, all by State and for Federal Government purchases and miscellaneous, 1982. 2 tables. (p. 34-36)

c. Farm equipment imports and exports quantity and/or value, by country of origin or destination and by product type, with detail for wheel tractor imports, various periods 1978-1st half 1983. 5 tables. (p. 38-46)

d. Shipment value for wheel tractors, farm machinery, and garden equipment, including attachments and parts; and unit shipments of farm machines and equipment; all by type of unit, 1978-82. 3 tables. (p. 48-54)

C4725-1.502: Dec. 1983 (Vol. 98, No. 14)
IS PARTS SERVICE TOO GOOD?

(p. ME2-ME7) By Scott R. Nesbitt. Article on cost of supplying service parts for farm and industrial equipment. Data are from responses of 31 member firms to a 1982 Farm and Industrial Equipment Institute survey.

Includes 2 tables showing total and parts sales; parts returns, warranty claims, and discounts/allowances, all as percent of sales; and costs for parts distribution, administration, and marketing, also as percent of sales; for firms supplying farm equipment, fixed farmstead items, and industrial/construction equipment.

C4725-1.503: Feb. 1984 (Vol. 99, No. 3)
BIG FORECAST OF 1984-85, SEMIANNUAL FEATURE

(p. 8-12) Semiannual article, by Bill Fogarty, forecasting farm equipment retail sales through 1985. Forecast is based on a Farm and Industrial Equipment Institute (FIEI) survey, conducted in Dec. 1983; forecast was presented at the Jan. 1984 FIEI Marketing and Management Conference.

Includes 14 tables showing actual and/or forecast unit retail sales or percent change in retail dollar volume, all by equipment type, various years 1982-85.

SOUTHWEST CONNECTION

(p. 16, 18) By Richard A. Edwards. Article on computer use by farm equipment dealers in the Southwest. Data are from a survey of 252 dealers in Texas, Oklahoma, and New Mexico, conducted by Texas A&M University's Agricultural Economics Dept, Sept.-Oct. 1983.

Includes 3 tables showing distribution of dealers by type of computer system used, applications, and reasons for not buying a computer.

W. GERMAN TRACTOR SALES UP DESPITE SLOWER 2nd HALF

(p. 19) Article, with 1 table showing West German tractor sales and market share for 6 companies, 1982-83.

PARTS DEPARTMENT PERFORMANCE REVIEW: HOW ARE DEALERS DOING?

(p. 20-21) Brief article, with 5 tables showing farm equipment dealer parts dept inventory value and turnover; sales and gross margins; and personnel, salaries, and sales productivity; various years 1974-82.

Data are from a cost-of-doing-business study conducted by the National Farm and Power Equipment Dealers Assn.

C4725–1.504: Mar. 1984 (Vol. 99, No. 4)

SOUTHWEST CONNECTION: SURVEY FINDS MANY DEALERS READY TO BUY COMPUTERS

(p. 20, 22, 52) By Richard A. Edwards. Article on computer ownership among farm equipment dealers in the Southwest. Data are from a survey of 252 dealers in Texas, Oklahoma, and New Mexico, conducted by Texas A&M University's Agricultural Economics Dept, Sept.-Oct. 1983.

Includes 2 tables showing percent of dealers using and owning in-house computer systems, by sales size; and distribution of noncomputerized dealers by planned expenditure level for computerization.

C4725–1.505: Mar. 31, 1984 (Vol. 99, No. 5)

NEBRASKA TRACTOR TESTS, ANNUAL FEATURE

(p. 325-391) Annual report on results of tractor performance tests conducted fall 1982-fall 1983, under University of Nebraska direction, to verify advertising claims of new tractors offered for sale. Tests show power take-off and drawbar performance, fuel consumption, and sound level, by manufacturer and model, under specified test conditions.

Contains contents listing (p. 325); explanation of test law and test conditions (p. 326); results of approximately 50 tests, 1982-83 (p. 327-383); and summary of 1973-83 tests, by tractor manufacturer and model (p. 384-391).

Report is included in 68th annual *Implement & Tractor Red Book Issue,* which presents detailed specifications for agricultural tractors and equipment, hydraulic components, and ground loading transport equipment.

C4725–1.506: Apr. 1984 (Vol. 99, No. 6)

IRREGULARLY RECURRING TABLE

[3] Retail sales of selected farm equipment, 1983. (p. 30)

SMALL TRACTORS BY STATE! SHIFTING DEMAND FOR BIG UNITS! ANNUAL FEATURE

(p. 37-39) Annual article, by Bill Fogarty, on 2- and 4-wheel drive farm tractor retail sales, 1983. Data are from Farm and Industrial Equipment Institute. Includes 2 summary tables, and 1 table showing unit sales by horsepower, by State and to the Federal Government.

C4725–1.507: May 1984 (Vol. 99, No. 7)

REVIEWING MAJOR INVENTORIES

(p. 12-14) By Bill Fogarty. Article, with 2 tables showing industry inventory and sales volume for tractors (with inventory detail by horsepower size) and for self-propelled combines, various periods 1978-83. Data are from Farm and Industrial Equipment Institute.

MARKET SHARE TAKES A BIG JUMP

(p. 16, 45) By Scott R. Nesbitt. Article, with 1 table showing sales of front-wheel assist tractors as a percent of all tractor sales, by horsepower, 1978, 1980, and 1983. Data are from manufacturer estimates.

C4725–1.508: June 1984 (Vol. 99, No. 8)

DEALER ATTRITION

(p. 10-11, 14) By Bill Fogarty. Article, with 1 table showing number of closings of retail farm equipment outlets, by company, 1st and 2nd half 1981-83. Data are from a Farm Equipment Manufacturers Assn member survey.

FIEI SALES FORECAST IS DOWNSCALED, SEMIANNUAL FEATURE

(p. 24) Semiannual article, by Bill Fogarty, forecasting farm equipment retail sales through 1985. Forecast is based on a Farm and Industrial Equipment Institute (FIEI) survey conducted in Mar. 1984; forecast was presented at the May 1984 FIEI Marketing and Management Conference.

Includes 2 tables showing actual and/or forecast unit retail sales or percent change in sales, by equipment type, various periods 1983-85.

C4725–1.509: Sept. 1984 (Vol. 99, No. 11)

ADDING A PRODUCT LINE

(p. 16-18) By George Freshwater. Article, with 1 undated table showing types of farm equipment added to and dropped from dealers' product lines. Data are from responses of 464 dealers to a survey by *Implement and Tractor.*

C4725–2   LAWN AND GARDEN MARKETING

10 issues per year.
Approx. 100 p.
ISSN 0091-4665.
LC 73-643478.
SRI/MF/excerpts, shipped quarterly

Periodical, published 10 times per year, reporting on trends and activities in the lawn and garden industry.

Journal is primarily narrative, but also includes a quarterly statistical report on product seasonal movements, annual market data articles, and other annual and special statistical features. Annual article index appears in Nov./Dec. issue.

Features with substantial statistical content are described, as they appear, under "Statistical Features." Each issue of the journal is reviewed, but an abstract is published in SRI monthly issues only when statistical features appear.

Availability: Lawn and Garden Marketing, PO Box 12901, Overland Park KS 66212-0930, qualified subscribers †, others $24.00 per yr., single copy $2.00, back issues $3.00, plus postage and handling; SRI/MF/excerpts for portions described under "Statistical Features;" shipped quarterly.

Issues reviewed during 1984: Nov./Dec. 1983-Oct. 1984 (P) (Vol. 22, No. 10; Vol. 23, Nos. 1-9).

STATISTICAL FEATURES:

C4725–2.501: Nov./Dec. 1983 (Vol. 22, No. 10)

TOP TEN FAVORITE OUTDOOR ACTIVITIES

(p. 26) Table showing number of households participating in 10 leading outdoor leisure activities, July 1983. Data are from a Gallup Organization survey conducted for Gardens for All, the National Assn for Gardening.

1983 INVENTORY FIGURES DOWN, ANNUAL FEATURE

(p. 26) Annual article presenting American Assn of Nurserymen summary data on level of 1983 spring purchases and fall carryovers of plants compared to 1982. Data are based on survey responses of an unidentified number of retailers. Includes 1 table.

SMALL DECLINE IN 1983 L&G SHIPMENTS, ANNUAL FEATURE

(p. 36) Annual article on lawn and garden power equipment industry shipments, 1982-83. Data are from Outdoor Power Equipment Institute. Includes 1 table showing shipment volume and value for walk-behind power mowers, lawn tractors/riding mowers, riding garden tractors, and rotary tillers, 1982-83.

C4725–2.502: Jan. 1984 (Vol. 23, No. 1)

GFA COMPARES GALLUP, SIMMONS DATA

(p. 12) Article comparing surveys on home gardening, conducted by Gallup Organization and Simmons Market Research Bureau.

Includes 2 tables and text data showing Gallup results on percent of households with a vegetable garden 1972-82, and on participation in 5 gardening activities 1980-81; and Simmons results on households with a vegetable garden and whether seeds or plants were purchased, 1982.

C4725–2.503: Feb. 1984 (Vol. 23, No. 2)

PORTABLE POWER SALES CURVE

(p. 12-14) By Wendall J. Burns. Article on market for portable lawn/garden power equipment. Data are from Echo Inc., and *Lawn and Garden Marketing* research.

Includes 1 chart and 2 tables showing spin trimmer market shares, by price range and purchase reasons (no date); and leaf blower/vacuum sales trend, by region, 1982-83.

PRODUCT MOVEMENT REPORT, AUTUMN 1983, QUARTERLY FEATURE

(p. 36) Quarterly article on lawn and garden product seasonal retail sales. Data are from a *Lawn and Garden Marketing* survey of retailers.

Includes 1 table showing percent of retailers reporting increased, steady, and decreased sales, by product type and census region; and chain saw median inventory; fall 1983.

C4725–2.504: Mar. 1984 (Vol. 23, No. 3)

LAWN SERVICE CONTRACTING: THREAT OR OPPORTUNITY FOR RETAILERS?

(p. 24-26) By Steven Trusty. Article on market for professional lawn care services, including impact on retail garden products industry. Data are from 1982-83 surveys conducted by Mobay Chemical Corp. and *Lawn & Garden Marketing.*

Includes 1 table and 2 charts showing percent of retail garden product centers offering lawn care services; distribution of persons responsible for lawn care decisions, by sex; and summary profile of lawn care customers, including income and use of lawn service.

NESDA SURVEYS PROMOTIONAL PRACTICES

(p. 44) Brief article reporting opinions of power equipment servicing dealers regarding sales promotions sponsored by manufacturers. Data are from responses of approximately 250 servicing dealers to an Aug.-Sept. 1983 survey conducted by National Equipment Servicing Dealers Assn. Includes 1 table.

C4725-2.505: Apr./May 1984 (Vol. 23, No. 4)

GARDENING HOUSEHOLDS, A STATISTICAL PROFILE

(p. 6-8, 12) By Bruce Butterfield. Article, with 1 table ranking various leisure activities, including lawn care and gardening, by percent of households participating, 1983. Data are from Gardens for All.

PRODUCT MOVEMENT REPORT, QUARTERLY FEATURE

(p. 36) Quarterly article on lawn and garden product seasonal retail sales. Data are from a *Lawn and Garden Marketing* survey of retailers.

Includes 1 table showing percent of retailers reporting increased, steady, and decreased sales, by product type and census region; and kerosene heater median inventory; winter 1983/84.

BIRDS ARE BIG BUSINESS

(p. 54-58) By Steven Trusty. Article, with 1 chart showing number of people who feed birds and maintain bird feeders, by region, 1980. Data are from Interior Dept.

C4725-2.506: June 1984 (Vol. 23, No. 5)

SELLING POWER PRODUCTS FOR WINTER LIVING

(p. 22, 24, 26) By Wendall J. Burns. Article, with 2 undated tables showing the following for saws with new technology chains and saws with low-kickback guidebars: number of models, and share of all saw models and sales, by cubic inch displacement category. Data are from the Portable Power Equipment Manufacturers Assn and the Consumer Product Safety Commission.

SNOW AND SALES

(p. 32) Brief article, with 1 table showing snowfall in 15 cities, historical average and 1979. Data are from Toro Co.

C4725-2.507: Aug. 1984 (Vol. 23, No. 7)

PRODUCT MOVEMENT REPORT, SPRING 1984, QUARTERLY FEATURE

(p. 34) Quarterly article on lawn and garden product seasonal retail sales. Data are from a *Lawn and Garden Marketing* survey of retailers.

Includes 1 table showing percent of retailers reporting increased, steady, and decreased sales, by product type and census region; and walk-behind mower median inventory; spring 1984.

MOWERS TO RETURN TO 5 MILLION MARK, ANNUAL FEATURE

(p. 42-53, 72) Annual article presenting the Outdoor Power Equipment Institute industry forecast for 1985. Data are from a survey of 25 manufacturers.

Includes 6 charts showing shipments of walk-behind rotary-powered mowers, rear-engine riding mowers, front-engine lawn tractors, garden tractors, and walk-behind tillers and snow throwers, 1980-85.

C4725-2.508: Sept. 1984 (Vol. 23, No. 8)

SIMMONS AND GALLUP DATA PRESENTED TO EXECUTIVE FORUM: THE GROWING MARKET

(p. 34-44) Article examining the market for lawn and garden products. Data are from Simmons Market Research Bureau and Gallup Organization Inc.

Includes 9 tables showing distribution of seed and fertilizer purchases, by selected type and price range; lawn fertilizer purchaser profile; lawn/garden equipment ownership, with trends for garden tiller owners; lawn/garden retail sales, by product category; and percent of households involved in lawn/garden activity, by type of activity and selected sociodemographic characteristics; various periods 1980-83.

C4725-2.509: Oct. 1984 (Vol. 23, No. 9)

LAWN FERTILIZER UPDATE: RETAILERS SWITCH BRANDS, STRATEGIES TO HOLD MARKET SHARE

(p. 6-12) Article, with 1 undated chart showing percent of retailers adding and dropping lawn fertilizer and chemical product lines, by type of outlet. Data are from a summer 1984 *Lawn and Garden Marketing* survey.

C4740
Irving-Cloud Publishing Co.

C4740-1   JOBBER TOPICS: Fiftieth Anniversary Marketing Directory Issue
Monthly (selected issue).
July 1984. (p. 60-65, 1S-48S).
Vol. 126, No. 6.
SRI/MF/excerpts

Annual marketing directory issue, for 1984, presenting automotive parts wholesale industry directories and statistics, including data on wholesaler financial performance, motor vehicle production and registrations, and related topics. Data are compiled from numerous trade assns and other sources, identified for each table.

Issue includes the following annual statistical features:

a. "Study Shows Optimism; Aftermarket Moving to Higher Ground." By Bill Ellis. Survey article on jobber business conditions in 1984. Includes 6 tables showing survey response on trends in unit and dollar sales, cash position, and collections; retail trade group most responsible for improved sales; and general economic trends; all by region, 1984. (p. 60-65)

b. "Automotive Statistics" section, with index, and 1 map, 5 charts, and 60 tables described below. (p. 1S-48S)

Jobber Topics is a monthly magazine, generally narrative in content, but also including monthly survey statistics on jobber business conditions, and Dept of Commerce data on automotive equipment wholesaler sales and inventories. Monthly issues also include occasional original survey articles. The 2 annual features noted above are the only features covered in SRI.

The annual marketing directory issue also includes directories of trade assns, warehouse distributors, parts remanufacturers, manufacturers' agents, jobbers, and parts manufacturers; and a buyer's guide.

Availability: Irving-Cloud Publishing Co., 7300 N. Cicero Ave., Chicago IL 60646, $20.00 per yr., single copy $2.50, directory $20.00; SRI/MF/excerpts for business conditions survey article and "Automotive Statistics" section.

AUTOMOTIVE STATISTICS SECTION:
[Data are primarily shown for 1983, with selected trends from 1970s or earlier.]

C4740-1.1: Automotive Statistics

a. Branches, sales personnel, and shops of 41 largest automotive wholesalers; automotive service establishments, including motor vehicle and parts manufacturers, service and repair firms, new and used car dealers, fleets, farm/garden equipment wholesalers, and trade assns; service/parts market value, by retail outlet type; and vehicle registrations and dealers, parts/supplies wholesalers, service stations, and repair shops, by State.

b. Financial and operating performance of automotive wholesalers, including income, expenses, balance sheets, inventory turnover, and operating ratios; sales and labor productivity; battery shipments; wholesaler trade assn membership, by State or region; certified mechanics by type of employer, and certification/testing activities; average employment per wholesaler by occupation; shipments of passenger car tires; and distribution of jobber advertisements by media.

c. Parts sales, by product line; Canada vehicle registrations, wholesale parts sales, and vehicle and parts trade with U.S.; wholesaler distribution by type of location; production of top 12 vehicle manufacturers worldwide; fleet purchase considerations and preferred sources for replacement parts; warehouse distributor financial performance; bus, truck, and trailer registrations, by State; and selected publicly owned auto parts companies ranked by revenues, income, profit margin, and return on capital.

d. Heavy duty distributor financial performance, sales and labor productivity, and preferred sources for replacement parts by industry; motor vehicle factory sales; new import car sales, by manufacturer; average mileage, by vehicle type; auto production, by manufacturer and model; trade show exhibitors and attendance since 1933; auto ownership and operating costs; wholesaler bankruptcies and liabilities; service labor and parts sales of franchised dealers; and auto and truck scrappage.

C4775
Jobson Publishing Corp.

C4775–1   LIQUOR HANDBOOK, 1983

Annual. 1983. 324 p.
SRI/MF/not filmed

Annual report, for 1983, on liquor industry production, finances, and marketing; consumer characteristics; and government regulation and taxation. Also includes data on illegal liquor activity, foreign trade, and summary population characteristics. Data are generally current to 1982, with selected trends from as early as 1922, and projections to 2000.

Data were compiled by Gavin-Jobson Associates, Inc., from Federal agencies, Distilled Spirits Council of the U.S., original estimates, and other sources.

Contains contents listing and foreword (p. 8-12); 52 charts, 14 maps, and 321 tables with accompanying narrative, arranged in 4 sections, described below (p. 17-320); and indexes (p. 321-324).

This is the 30th annual edition of the report. SRI coverage begins with this edition.

Availability: Jobson Publishing Corp., 352 Park Ave., S., New York NY 10010, $39.95; SRI/MF/not filmed.

TABLE SECTIONS:
[Data are shown for distilled spirits, unless otherwise noted. Data sources are noted beneath each table. Product types include whiskey varieties, gin, rum, brandy, cordials and liqueurs, vodka, prepared cocktails, and miscellaneous.]

C4775–1.1: Section 1: National Liquor Market

MARKET SUMMARY

a. Consumption and/or sales, by product type, State, census division, and month, with selected comparisons to beer and wine; sales of 67 leading brands; gallonage entering retail trade channels; consumption per capita and as percent of income, by State; and consumption and sales compared to total population, purchasing power, and total personal consumption. 12 charts, 1 map, and 22 tables. (p. 17-70)

b. Population and socioeconomic trends; estimated population of legal drinking age, by State; sales of top 50 metro areas and top 10 States; average alcohol content (proof), by product type; sales projected to 1992, by product type, census division, and State; and non-whiskey gallonage bottled. 10 charts and 20 tables. (p. 72-98)

REGULATION AND PRICES
[Distribution of distilled spirits is regulated either by State monopoly (control States) or by tier system of licensing (license States).]

c. Distribution trends, including wholesalers/importers/distributors, by license State and beverage type; licensed manufacturers and suppliers, by type; retail licenses for on- and off-premise consumption, by license and control State; distribution of sales in 6-7 price classes, by product type; mark-up on delivered cost, and applicable Federal tax, by control State; and number of counties permitting, restricting, and prohibiting sales, by State. 7 tables. (p. 99-104)

d. Taxation, including Federal tax revenue from alcoholic beverages, by type; Federal excise rates; and State tax rates since repeal of Prohibition. 3 tables. (p. 105)

e. Illegal activity and law enforcement, including federally seized stills; production, capacity, and estimated days of operation of seized stills; and tax revenue loss to U.S. Treasury. 2 charts and 1 table. (p. 106)

f. Prices and industry finances, including sales margin compared to manufacturing; retail prices of 9 leading brands, by control and license State; sales, profit margin, and earnings per share for 8 selected distilling companies; and list of State couponing laws. 4 tables. (p. 107-110)

CONSUMER CHARACTERISTICS

g. Socioeconomic profiles of drinking population; drinking and purchasing habits including brand loyalty and selection, with detail for women, affluent adults, college students, and blacks; summary population trends; and liquor store owner/manager opinions on consumers and best-selling premium brand sales trends and outlook. 6 charts, 1 map, and 32 tables. (p. 111-138)

C4775–1.2: Section 2: Distillery Operations

a. Production by product type; whiskey used in redistillation, by selected State; whiskey production, and distillery and bottling operations, by State; whiskey barrel shipments, strip stamp use on domestic and import products, by container size; and grain and malt consumption at distilleries, by commodity. 1 chart and 7 tables. (p. 139-143)

b. Storage and use, including stocks, by product type and age, and selected State; Kentucky whiskey stocks, by distiller; whiskey consumption by product age; and tax-paid withdrawals by product type, with detail for whiskey by month and selected State. 11 tables. (p. 144-147)

c. Bottling trends, including gallonage bottled by month, product type, and major State; cost of carrying bulk whiskey and case goods; and rectified spirits production and materials used. 7 tables. (p. 148-151)

C4775–1.3: Section 3: Market for Major Distilled Spirit Types

a. Whiskey sales and consumption trends by variety, shown variously by month, census division, State, metro area, and price class; whiskey gallonage bottled and rectified; and whiskey advertising expenditures by media and brand. 4 charts, 3 maps, and 49 tables. (p. 152-180)

b. Foreign trade by product type and country of origin or destination; used bourbon barrel exports; production of top 10 producing countries; per capita consumption of leading countries, with trends for all alcoholic beverages; U.S. customs duties and duty reductions; and U.S. bourbon import duties of selected countries. 2 charts and 14 tables. (p. 182-192)

c. Imports and market trends for Scotch, Canadian, and Irish whiskey, including consumption by month, census division, State, metro area, and price class; and advertising expenditures by media and brand; and sales restrictions placed on grocery, drug, and liquor stores regarding alcoholic and nonalcoholic beverages and accessories, by license and control State. 3 charts, 2 maps, and 34 tables. (p. 194-222)

d. Nonwhiskey sales and consumption trends by product type, shown variously for same breakdowns as shown for whiskey; with additional data on imports by country of origin; gin and brandy production, withdrawals, stocks, bottling, and use; cordial flavor preferences; and top 20 cocktail recipes. 9 charts, 7 maps, and 86 tables. (p. 225-284)

C4775–1.4: Section 4: Advertising and Promotion

a. Magazine and newspaper distilled spirits advertising expenditures, by product type, month, company, and brand, with detail for top 10 brands; circulation of top 25 daily and Sunday newspapers; and households and circulation of top 25 newspaper groups. 3 charts and 18 tables. (p. 285-303)

b. Outdoor advertising expenditures, by product type and company, with detail for top 10 brands; and transportation display expenditures, by company and brand. 5 tables. (p. 315-318)

c. December holiday packaging/promotion market share of total annual sales. 1 table. (p. 319)

C4825
Journal Publications

C4825–3   SEAFOOD BUSINESS REPORT: Pacific Packers' Report, Annual Feature

Bimonthly (selected issue).
Spring 1984. (p. 51-88).
Vol. 3, No. 2.
ISSN 0733-0464.
LC SN 82-4231.
SRI/MF/excerpts

Annual issue of *Seafood Business Report* on Pacific Coast seafood industry, 1983, with selected trends from 1940. Most data are shown for Alaska, Washington State, Oregon, California, and/or British Columbia.

Covers landings; processing, including canned packs and fresh and frozen poundage and/or values, with some detail by company; and prices; shown variously for salmon, shellfish, bottomfish, and/or tuna, by species.

Also includes data on Alaska salmon harvest forecasts for 1984, and joint venture and foreign bottomfish catch; U.S. tuna packs, including data for selected non-Pacific Coast areas, and imports of frozen tuna; and salmon hatchery releases, by agency, including data for Idaho.

Data are compiled from reports of State, Federal, and Canadian agencies responsible for fisheries management, and industry trade assns.

Includes 31 tables (p. 51-88).

Seafood Business Report is a bimonthly, generally narrative periodical reporting trends and developments in the seafood industry. Prior to 1982, "Pacific Packers' Report" was published as a separate semiannual report; report was incorporated into *Seafood Business Report* as an annual feature in spring 1982, and is the only feature of the periodical covered in SRI.

Availability: Seafood Business Report, Circulation Department, 21 Elm St., Camden ME 04843, qualified subscribers †, others $12.00 per yr.; SRI/MF/excerpts for annual feature described.

C4850
Judge, Edward E., and Sons

C4850-1   ALMANAC OF THE CANNING, FREEZING, PRESERVING INDUSTRIES, 1984
Annual. 1984. 662 p.
LC 72-622383.
SRI/MF/excerpts

Annual almanac, for 1984, of the food processing industries. Includes detailed data by commodity on fruit and vegetable crops, and frozen and canned food packs and international trade, 1970s-83, with selected historical trends. Also includes detailed data on food processing company operations, taken from the 1977 Census of Manufactures; various technical, regulatory, and other information pertaining to food processing industries; and a buyer's guide.

Most data are from USDA, Commerce Dept, National Food Processors Assn, and other industry assns and publications.

Contents:

Index to contents, and list of assn presidents and convention cities since 1890. (p. 3-15)

Section I-II. Assn and FDA Personnel; and Food Law and Regulations. (p. 16-84)

Section III. Labeling and Packaging. Includes 3 tables (p. 158-160) showing can prices, by type and size, 1931-83; metal can shipments, by product category, 1976-83; and glass container shipments, by type, 1974-82. (p. 85-164)

Section IV-V. Emergency Permits, Unavoidable Contaminants, and Good Manufacturing Practice Regulations; and Food and Drug Standards of Identity, Quality, and Fill. (p. 165-329)

Section VI. USDA Quality Grade Standards: Canned, Glass, and Frozen Foods. (p. 330-482)

Section VII. Raw Product Statistics. Contains 77 tables generally showing harvested acreage, yield, production, and value for 15 vegetable crops (including prices and sales for mushrooms), by State, various years 1972-83; and 14 tables generally showing utilized production, use, price, and value for apples and 8 other fruit crops, by State and type, various years 1974-83. (p. 483-525)

Section VIII. U.S. Pack Statistics. Includes 153 tables on commodity packs, described below; and 1977 Census of Manufactures industry and product statistics, with 9 tables, also described below. (p. 526-590)

Section IX. International Trade and World Packs. Includes 9 tables showing quantity and/or value for the following: U.S. canned and frozen food exports and imports, by product; U.S. exports of canned fruits and vege-

tables, by country or area of destination; world canned fruit and vegetable imports, by importing country and country of origin; and world fruit and vegetable packs, by country and commodity; various years 1974-83. (p. 591-608)

Section X. Canned Food Prices. Contains 1 table showing high and low canner spot selling prices for canned vegetables, fruits, and fish, by commodity, 1977/78-1983/84. (p. 609-615)

Section XI. Appendix. Includes 12 tables (p. 619-624) showing Government canned and frozen food purchases for military and for child nutrition and domestic feeding programs, various years 1974-84; and civilian per capita consumption of canned, fresh, and frozen products, various periods 1909-82; all by commodity. (p. 616-626)

Section XII. Buyer's Guide for Machinery, Supplies, and Services. (p. 627-661)

Index to advertisers. (p. 662)

This is the 69th annual edition. A detailed directory of companies and assns is also available from the issuing agency, but is not covered by SRI.

Availability: Edward E. Judge and Sons, PO Box 866, Westminster MD 21157, $29.50; SRI/MF/excerpts for nontechnical statistical tables in Sections III and VII-XI.

TABLES:

C4850-1.1: U.S. Pack and Industry Statistics

a. Canned vegetables, fruit, and juice, by commodity: total packs, various years 1899-1977; and packs by region or State and by container size, with detail for some commodities on pack by product style, and on carryover, stock, shipments, exports, and Government purchases, various years 1972-83. 106 tables. (p. 527-558)

b. Canned seafood: per capita consumption, by type; pack and value, total and by State and type; salmon and tuna packs, by State or area, variety, and/or container size; and packing plants, by State and type; mostly 1974-83, with summary pack trends from 1927. 9 tables. (p. 558-562)

c. Salad dressing, mayonnaise, and canned and frozen specialty products by type, pack and value, selected years 1963-77; and canned meat pack, by type, 1974-83. 3 tables. (p. 562-565)

d. Frozen vegetables and fruit, by commodity: total packs, various years 1942-77; and packs by State or region, and by container size and/or product style, mostly 1973-83. 33 tables. (p. 566-578)

e. Frozen citrus juice concentrate production, by type; and noncitrus concentrate/juice production; various years 1948-83. 2 tables. (p. 579)

f. Industry data: number of companies and establishments, employees, payroll, production workers, hours of labor, and wages; value added by manufacture; cost of materials; production value; capital expenditures; value of fixed assets; inventories; fuels, electricity, and materials consumed; and selected operating ratios; all for 8 SIC 4-digit industries, with selected detail by employment size, mostly 1977 with some data for 1981, and selected trends from 1958. 9 tables. (p. 582-590)

C4950
Kenedy, P. J., and Sons

C4950-1   OFFICIAL CATHOLIC DIRECTORY, 1984
Annual. 1984. 1614 p.
LC 1-30961.
SRI/MF/excerpts

Annual directory, for 1984, on the Catholic Church, listing Vatican officials and offices; U.S. dioceses and archdioceses, national organizations, territorial and foreign missions, religious orders, churches, institutions, clergy, and deceased hierarchy and clergy; and Canada and Mexico dioceses and officials. Includes data on churches, institutions, clergy, and religious orders for dioceses in U.S. and territories.

Contains contents listing and general information (p. iii-viii); directory listing for Vatican (p. ix-xvi); directory listings for U.S., Canada, and Mexico, including statistical summaries for dioceses and religious orders (p. xvii-xxxii, 1-1486); and 1 extended table (4 p. oversized foldout) showing the following items by census division, State, archdiocese, and diocese, 1984, with totals for 1974 and 1983:

OFFICIALS, CLERGY, AND CHURCHES

a. Cardinals, archbishops, bishops, abbots, diocesan and religious priests, total priests, permanent deacons, total brothers, and total sisters.

b. Parishes, resident and nonresident pastors, missions, stations, and chapels.

SEMINARIES

c. Diocesan and religious seminaries and students, diocesan students in other seminaries, and total seminarians.

SCHOOLS, STUDENTS, AND TEACHERS

d. Colleges/universities, diocesan/parochial and private high schools and elementary schools, and protective institutions, with number of students for each type of institution; released-time high school and elementary pupils; and total students under Catholic instruction.

e. Teaching priests, scholastics, brothers, and sisters; lay teachers; and total teachers.

HOSPITALS, NURSING HOMES, AND INSTITUTIONS

f. General and special hospitals, with bed capacity and patients treated annually for each type of hospital; and schools for nurses, with number of students.

g. Orphanages/asylums, with number of resident children; children in foster homes; total dependent children; and homes for the aged, with number of guests.

MISCELLANEOUS STATISTICS

h. Infant baptisms, converts, total baptisms, marriages, deaths, Catholic population, and total population (as of Jan. 1).

Availability: P. J. Kenedy and Sons, 866 Third Ave., New York NY 10022, $77.20; SRI/MF/excerpts for oversized foldout table.

C5150
Lebhar-Friedman

C5150–2   DRUG STORE NEWS

Biweekly, and annual special
issue.   Approx. 55 p.
Oversized.
ISSN 0191-7587.
LC 79-642712.
SRI/MF/excerpts

Biweekly trade journal (monthly in Dec. and an
additional annual issue in Apr.) of the retail and
wholesale drug industry, covering drugstore operations and finances, wholesale distribution,
Government regulation, and pharmaceutical and
health/beauty aid (H&BA) sales, manufacture,
and merchandising. Data are from private research firms, individual companies, and the journal's own research.

Issues contain news articles; "Financial" section with 1-3 tables showing stock market performance and financial position of leading drugstore
chains and drug manufacturers; "Merchandiser"
section on product merchandising and management; and the following recurring statistical features:

a. Recurring "Pharmacy" articles, usually pre-
    senting data on market shares and retail mar-
    gins for a particular type of drug.
b. Recurring article on local TV advertising ex-
    penditures of top drug chain advertisers.
c. Annual features, including pharmacy practice
    reference, with marketing data for selected
    prescription drugs; drugstore pharmacy oper-
    ations; consumer characteristics and shop-
    ping habits; chain drug industry financial
    performance and marketing operations; "Tri-
    ple A Product Study" on sales of leading
    drugstore products; and retailer and wholes-
    aler sales and operations.

Stock market performance feature appears in all
issues. All additional features with substantial
statistical content are described, as they appear,
under "Statistical Features." Nonstatistical features are not covered.

Availability: Drug Store News, Subscription
Department, 99 Park Ave., New York NY
10157, $15.00 per yr., single copy $2.00, selected
articles are also available as reprints; SRI/MF/
excerpts for stock performance feature and all
portions described under "Statistical Features."
Issues reviewed during 1984: Oct. 31, 1983-Oct.
29, 1984 (P) (Vol. 5, Nos. 23-26; Vol. 6, Nos.
1-23) [Vol. 6, No. 20, incorrectly reads No. 17].

STATISTICAL FEATURES:

C5150–2.501: Oct. 31, 1983 (Vol. 5, No. 23)

DRUG WHOLESALERS: COMPUTERS, HOSPITALS SPUR GROWTH IN '83

(p. 61-62) By Allen Mundth. Article, with 2
tables showing net sales distribution for all and
general line drug wholesalers, by customer
type and product category, 1977-82. Data are
based on 1982 survey of drug wholesalers conducted by the National Wholesale Drug Assn.

C5150–2.502: Nov. 14, 1983 (Vol. 5, No. 24)

CHAIN DRUG STORES: A NATURAL NICHE FOR NATURAL PRODUCTS

(Special insert section) Compilation of features on natural product sales and marketing.
Features with substantial statistical content
are described below.

NUTS: EVERYTHING THEY'RE CRACKED UP TO BE

(2 p.) Article, with 1 table showing per capita
consumption of nuts by type, 1970-82. Data
are from Almond Board of California.

NATURAL CENTERS SPUR VITAMIN SALES GROWTH

(2 p.) Article, with 2 charts showing vitamin/
supplement sales by store or distribution type,
and vitamin sales by type, 1981-82. Data are
from Center for Responsible Nutrition.

WHO'S DOING WHAT WITH NATURAL PRODUCTS

(1 p.) Tabular listing of leading drugstore
chains, showing number of stores, number and
typical size of natural product depts, and types
of products carried (no date).

Other Feature

SPECIAL REPORT: Rx OPERATIONS SURVEY, ANNUAL FEATURE

(p. 47-53) Annual compilation of articles
based on a 1983 *Drug Store News* survey of
drugstore chains operating 2,246 pharmacy
depts. Includes 5 interspersed tables showing
the following averages for drugstore pharmacies, 1982-83:

a. Prescriptions: volume and value per hour,
    and per pharmacist per week; value, total
    and per dept square foot; new and refill
    volume; and retail price and profit margin.
    3 tables.
b. Pharmacist productivity at 6 unnamed
    chains with large and limited numbers of
    computers; and pharmacist salaries, num-
    ber of pharmacists and technicians per
    dept, sales and dollar margin per pharma-
    cist, and hours of operation per week. 2
    tables.

Corrected data appear in the Jan. 9, 1984 issue;
for description, see C5150-2.505, below.

C5150–2.503: Nov. 28, 1983 (Vol. 5, No. 25)

DRUG STORE H&BA MARKET SHARE DOWN 2%

(p. 4) Article, with 1 chart showing distribution of health/beauty aid sales among food,
drug, and mass merchandise stores, July/Aug.
1982-83. Data are from A. C. Nielsen Co.

BUYERS EXPECT SUNGLASS RECOVERY IN '84, ANNUAL FEATURE

(p. 29, 37) Annual article, by Jim Ricchiuti,
with 2 tables and 2 charts showing the following for sunglasses: retail sales average price,
1983-87, and by outlet type (with number of
outlets), 1982; and sales distribution by price
group and lens type (no date). Data are from
Bausch and Lomb, Corning Glass Works, and
Packaged Facts.

C5150–2.504: Dec. 12, 1983 (Vol. 5, No. 26)

PHARMACY: GENERICS CAPTURE 26% OF DIURETICS MARKET, ANNUAL FEATURE

(p. 17, 20) Annual article on market performance of diuretic drugs. Data are from Decision Data, Inc. Includes 1 table showing retail
market share, average quantity and price per
prescription, and percent retail margin, for top
25 products and all others, July 1982-83. Also
shows manufacturers for top products.

For description of previous article, see SRI
1982 Annual, under C5150-2.323

3rd ANNUAL CONSUMER STUDY

(p. 27-28, 49-70) Annual compilation of articles on drugstore consumer characteristics and
shopping habits, based on a Sept. 1983 survey
of 750 consumers conducted by Lebhar-Friedman Research.

Includes text data, and 22 charts showing
frequency of impulse purchases; average expenditure per shopping trip; prescription and
other product purchase distribution for chain
and independent stores; generic drug awareness and requests; and purchase distribution
for 17 product categories, by retail outlet type;
various years 1981-83.

C5150–2.505: Jan. 9, 1984 (Vol. 6, No. 1)

CORRECTION

(p. 34) Corrected data on pharmacist average
salary, originally included in annual feature on
pharmacy operations (for description, see
C5150-2.502, above).

C5150–2.506: Jan. 23, 1984 (Vol. 6, No. 2)

EXECUTIVES: ECONOMIC UPTURN TO SPUR DRUG STORE CONSTRUCTION

(p. 2, 57) Article, with 1 table showing new
stores built or planned, for 4 drugstore chains,
1983-84. Data are from *Drug Store News*.

FOOD STORES GAIN IN H&BA SHARE

(p. 2, 58) Article, with 1 chart showing sales
for aggregate 25 health/beauty aid products, in
food stores, drugstores, and mass merchandise
stores, Sept./Oct. 1982-83. Data are from A.
C. Nielsen Co.

ADS, COUNSELING BOOST SALES OF EXTENDED WEAR LENS AIDS

(p. 36) Brief article on contact lens merchandising. Data are from Pipeline Research, Inc.
and *Drug Store News*. Includes profile of typical lens wearer; list of top 16 eye care products
based on unit movement; and 1 table showing
percent change in sales of lens care products,
by type, 1983.

C5150–2.507: Feb. 6, 1984 (Vol. 6, No. 3)

NEW SUNCARE ITEMS TO STRESS COSMETICS

(p. 33-34) By Jim Ricchiuti. Article, with 1
chart showing distribution of sun protection
product sales among supermarkets, mass merchandisers, and drug stores, Mar.-Oct. period
1982-83. Data are from A. C. Nielsen Co.

SUNGLASS MARKET DEMANDS HEAVY PROMOS

(p. 33, 36) Article, with 1 chart showing sales
distribution of nonprescription sunglasses
among supermarkets, mass merchandisers,
and drug stores, Mar.-Oct. period 1982-83.
Data are from A. C. Nielsen Co.

C5150–2.508: Feb. 20, 1984 (Vol. 6, No. 4)

MOST CHAINS STICK TO BASICS IN TOYS

(p. 11, 45) Article, with 1 chart showing toy/game sales volume, and market share by type, 1981-82. Data are from NPD Research.

REAPING THE REWARDS

(special insert section) Compilation of articles on sales and marketing of greeting cards, stationery products, and school and home office supplies. Includes 2 articles, described below, presenting data based on 86 responses to a recent Lebhar-Friedman survey of home office supply buyers for leading drug, discount, general merchandise, and supermarket chains.

RETAILERS PREDICT LONG-TERM GROWTH

(2 p.) Article, with 2 undated charts showing average number of stock keeping units and average gross margin for home office/school supplies by type.

YEAR-ROUND DEMAND STIMULATES SALES

(1 p.) Article, with 1 undated chart showing average annual inventory turns for home office/school supplies by type.

Other Feature

PHARMACY: '83 SCRIPT SALES SOAR, BUT MARGINS REMAIN STAGNANT

(p. 57-58) Article, with 1 undated table showing average retail price and retailer margin for 7 leading drugs. Data are from *1984 Reference for Pharmacy Practice,* prepared by *Drug Store News.*

C5150–2.509: Mar. 5, 1984 (Vol. 6, No. 5)

PHARMACY: RETAILERS AWAIT TRIPHASIC BIRTH CONTROL PILL DEBUT, RECURRING FEATURE

(p. 14) Recurring article on market performance of leading oral contraceptive drugs. Data are from Decision Data, Inc. Includes 1 table showing retail market share, percent of prescriptions that are refills, average price per prescription, and percent retail margin, for 14 leading brands and all others, Aug. 1980 and/or Sept. 1983. Also shows manufacturers for top products.

For description of previous article, see SRI 1983 Annual, under C5150-2.402.

RXMEN CAN CLEAR UP ALLERGY CONFUSION

(p. 33, 36) By Jim Ricchiuti. Article, with 1 undated list showing 12 top selling over-the-counter products containing antihistimines. Data are from *Drug Store News.*

C5150–2.510: Mar. 19, 1984 (Vol. 6, No. 6)

GENERICS, 'FANCY BRANDS' BOOST TOBACCO SALES

(p. 33-39) Article, with 2 tables showing production of tobacco products by type, and cigarette market shares by company and brand, 1982-83. Data are from USDA and Lehman Brothers Kuhn Loeb Research.

BEST-SELLING OTCs: CHARTING THE TOP 100 OTC PRODUCTS

(p. 59-67) Article on over-the-counter (OTC) health product sales, based on an undated *Drug Store News* study of warehouse withdrawal data from major retail drug chains.

Includes 17 lists showing rank order for top 100 OTC products in unit and dollar sales (with breakdowns for 6 product categories), and for top 10 private label products in unit sales; and 1 table showing average prices for 5 analgesic products.

C5150–2.511: Apr. 2, 1984 (Vol. 6, No. 7)

PHARMACY: SPECIAL REPORT, HOW AMERICANS USE OTC PRODUCTS

(p. 16-18) Compilation of articles on consumer health care practices, including use of over-the-counter (OTC) remedies. Data are based on 2,062 responses to a recent survey sponsored by the Proprietary Assn.

Includes 5 undated tables showing survey responses concerning satisfaction with OTC remedies by health problem, most frequently experienced problems, problems most likely to be referred to doctor/dentist or treated with self-medication/nonprescription product, and treatment methods most frequently used.

MINI-ELECTRONICS MAKE SMALL-SIZED BATTERIES BIG

(p. 29) Article, with 1 chart showing distribution of battery sales among food, drug, and mass merchandise stores, 1982-83. Data are from A. C. Nielsen Co.

C5150–2.512: Apr. 1984 Special Issue (Vol. 6, No. 8)

1984 REFERENCE FOR PHARMACY PRACTICE, ANNUAL FEATURE

Annual special issue presenting detailed business and clinical reference information for pharmacists, including supplier directories, and marketing data for selected prescription drugs. Data are from Decision Data, Inc., Market Measures, and journal's own research.

Includes the following marketing data:

a. Product rankings for 200 leading prescription drugs in number of prescriptions, dollar value, and dollar margin; arranged in rank order and alphabetically by manufacturer, Oct. 1983. 2 tables. (p. 8-14)

b. Dispensing profiles for selected prescription drug brands, generally showing average retail price and quantity dispensed per prescription, average prescriptions per month per pharmacy, and the following data by quantity dispensed per prescription: percent of total prescriptions dispensed, percent of prescriptions that are refills, average percent gross margin, and contribution of quantity to gross margin. 35 charts and 34 tables. (p. 15-23)

c. Bulk buying guide for 100 leading prescription drugs, showing manufacturer, size and price for small and bulk purchases, and savings by buying in bulk. 1 table. (p. 24-25)

d. Top 20 generic drugs based on number of new prescriptions, 1983, with comparative rank for 1981-82 and percent change in volume of new and total prescriptions from 1982; distribution of pharmacist substitutions by drug category, Sept. 1983; and new and refill prescription volume, 1983 with percent change from 1982. 1 chart and 2 tables. (p. 40)

C5150–2.513: Apr. 16, 1984 (Vol. 6, No. 9)

MERCHANDISING STYLE TRANSLATES INTO SALES $$

(p. 6, 116) Article on consumer shopping and purchasing habits in drugstores. Data are based on preliminary findings from 1983 interviews with 12,131 shoppers at 258 drugstores in 40 markets, conducted by Point-of-Purchase Advertising Institute/Du Pont. Includes 1 table showing unplanned purchases as a percent of total, by major product category.

C5150–2.514: Apr. 30, 1984 (Vol. 6, No. 10)

1984 ANNUAL REPORT OF THE CHAIN DRUG INDUSTRY

(p. 47-143) Annual compilation of articles on chain drugstores' financial performance and marketing operations, including sales, stores, product merchandising, and industry concentration, various years 1974-84.

Data are from *Drug Store News,* A. C. Nielsen Co., Chain Store Guides, Commerce Dept, Media General, and company reports.

Contains contents listing (p. 48) and the following sections:

a. Performance: news articles and features, with 22 tables on drugstore finances and operations, listed below. (p. 47-77)

b. Products: introduction, with 1 summary table; prescription dept summary, with 2 tables showing sales volume and value and number of stores with prescription depts (for all and chain drugstores) 1982-83, and new and refill prescriptions for total drugstore industry 1983; and 12 additional dept summaries, each with 2 tables showing dept sales by product category with percent change from 1982, share of total chain drug sales, typical gross margin, gross profit yield, and average number of turns, 1983. (p. 78-111)

c. Profiles: for 23 leading drugstore chains, each with narrative analysis and generally 1-2 charts, mostly showing sales and earnings trends, various periods 1979-84. (p. 115-143)

PERFORMANCE SECTION TABLES:

[Tables show data for 1983, unless otherwise noted.]

[1-3] 10-year sales, sales share, [and number of stores, for chain and independent stores, 1974-83]. (p. 48-49)

[4] Top 50 drug chains [ranked by sales, with number of stores]. (p. 51)

[5] How the chain drug industry has changed [showing chain companies and stores operated, by chain size group, 1974 and 1983]. (p. 51)

[6] 10-year drug store share trends [chain and independent shares of total stores, 1974-83]. (p. 52)

[7] Top 50 chains [ranked by] store totals. (p. 52)

[8] Average sales per store [for total, chain, and independent stores]. (p. 57)

[9] Breakout of multiunit [companies and] stores by unit size. (p. 57)

[10] Chain drug stock performance [high, low, and last stock prices, and percent change, 1983; year-end price/earnings ratios, 1982-83; and price as of Apr. 9, 1984; by company]. (p. 57)

[11] Top drug chains in warehousing [ranked by total warehouse square footage, with number of facilities, 1983 with comparison to 1982]. (p. 59)

[12-19] [Top 19-20 drug chains ranked by] total sales, sales per store, gross margin, net income, net-to-sales ratio, return on investment, expense ratio, and drug stores, [1983 with comparisons to 1979-82]. (p. 60-61)

[20] Pharmacy computer installations [1981-83, and number of stores with pharmacies, 1983, by chain]. (p. 66)

[21] Leading drug chains operating home health care centers [and number of centers operated, as of early 1984]. (p. 69)

[22] Chains join the ranks of deep discounters [owner, major market, and number of franchised and total stores, by deep-discount drugstore company]. (p. 70)

Other Feature

POPAI/DU PONT 1983 MERCHANDISING STUDY

(p. 144-147) Compilation of articles on consumer shopping and purchasing habits in drugstores. Data are based on preliminary findings from 1983 interviews with 12,131 shoppers at 258 drugstores in 40 markets, conducted by Point-of-Purchase Advertising Institute/Du Pont.

Includes 1 chart and 8 tables showing percent of purchases planned and unplanned, with detail for unplanned purchases by product category; advertising methods influencing store choice; distribution of shoppers by sex; shopping habits, including average shopping time, expenditures per trip and month, and purchases per trip by region; and percent of drugstores featuring selected product categories, and using 3 advertising methods.

C5150–2.515: May 14, 1984 (Vol. 6, No. 11)

TOP CHAINS HIKE TV AD SPENDING 25%, RECURRING FEATURE

(p. 32) Recurring article, with 1 table showing local TV advertising expenditures for top 15 drug chain local TV advertisers, 1983 with comparison to 1982. Data are from TV Bureau of Advertising.

FDA GIVES GO-AHEAD FOR CONSUMER Rx ADS

(p. 37-38) Article, with 1 chart showing consumer opinions regarding consumer-oriented advertising for prescription drugs. Data are from Nov.-Dec. 1983 FDA surveys of approximately 1,500 persons in 4 cities.

FLOOD OF NEW SHAMPOOS POSES RISKS

(p. 55-56) Article, with 1 undated chart showing distribution of shampoo sales among food, drug, and mass merchandise stores. Data are from A. C. Nielsen Co.

DRUG STORE SHARE SLIPS IN PERMS, COLORS, SPRAYS

(p. 58) Article, with 1 undated chart showing distribution of hair coloring product sales among food, drug, and mass merchandise stores. Data are from A. C. Nielsen Co.

SPECIAL REPORT ON ETHNIC PRODUCTS

(p. 61-69) Compilation of articles, with 2 undated charts and 1 undated table showing sales distribution for ethnic-oriented personal care products among chain and independent drugstores, supermarkets, and mass merchandise stores; Hispanic share of population over age 12 in 19 metro areas with high Hispanic penetration; and distribution of personal care products marketed for blacks, by product type.

Also includes listing of 25 top-selling ethnic-oriented personal care products. Data are from National Research Organization, Strategy Research, Business Trend Analysis, and Judith Lynn Sales, Inc.

C5150–2.516: May 28, 1984 (Vol. 6, No. 12)

LILLY STUDY: BELT TIGHTENING PAYS OFF FOR INDEPENDENTS

(p. 13, 17) Article, with 1 chart showing prescription share of sales in independent drugstores, 1982-83. Data are from a 1983 Eli Lilly and Co. survey of 860 independent drugstores.

C5150–2.517: June 11, 1984 (Vol. 6, No. 13)

OTC CONVERTS LEAD COUGH/COLD

(p. 33) Article, with 2 lists of top 20 cough/cold remedies based on sales volume and value, 1983. Data are from a *Drug Store News* survey of chain drugstores.

C5150–2.518: June 25, 1984 (Vol. 6, No. 14)

WHOLESALER SALES RISE, PROFITS SLIP

(p. 2, 53) Article, with 1 table showing drug wholesaler average sales, gross profit, stock turnover rate, collection period, and selected financial and operating ratios, 1982-83. Data are based on preliminary results from a survey conducted by National Wholesale Drug Assn.

BUYING FLAIR FUELS COSMETICS SALES, ANNUAL FEATURE

(p. 22-24) Annual article, by Faye Brookman, with 1 chart showing distribution of cosmetic sales among food, drug, and mass merchandise stores, 1979-83. Data are from A. C. Nielsen Co.

C5150–2.519: July 9, 1984 (Vol. 6, No. 15)

WAXMAN BLASTS PATENT-BILL CRITICS; BITTER BATTLE LOOMS

(p. 13-14) Article, with 1 table showing 1982 sales, and patent expiration date, for 19 drug brands with patents expiring during 1976-84. Data are from Generic Pharmaceutical Industry Assn.

LEADING COMBO STORE OPERATORS

(p. 37) Table showing number of combination food and drug stores, and headquarters location, for 7 leading combination store companies (no date). Data are from *Drug Store News*.

C5150–2.520: July 23, 1984 (Vol. 6, No. 16)

PHARMACY: GENERICS PLAY SMALLER ROLE IN AMOXICILLIN/AMPICILLIN FIELD, ANNUAL FEATURE

(p. 37) Annual article on market performance of leading ampicillin/amoxicillin drugs. Data are from PharmAssist.

Includes 1 table showing retail market share, average quantity and price per prescription, and percent retail margin, for 24 leading brands and all others, Dec. 1982 and/or Mar. 1984. Also shows manufacturer for leading products.

MERCHANDISER: TRIPLE A PRODUCT STUDY, ANNUAL FEATURE

(p. 47-66) Annual article on top-selling products in chain drugstores. Data are based on a 1984 *Drug Store News* survey.

Includes 41 tables showing top 9-10 product categories and top 100 products, based on sales volume and value and on profitability; and top 2-14 products in each of 11 categories, based on some or all of the following: unit movement, profitability, and sales volume and value. Tables are listings only and do not include actual values for the rankings.

Corrected data appear in Sept. 3, 1984 issue; for description, see C5150-2.523, below.

C5150–2.521: Aug. 6, 1984 (Vol. 6, No. 17)

DRUG STORES LOSE GROUND TO OTHER OUTLETS ON H&BAs

(p. 3, 58) Article, with 1 table showing sales growth index for health and beauty aids (total and for 25 product types), at drug, food, and mass merchandise stores, Jan. 1, 1977-84 period. Data are from A. C. Nielsen Co.

CREATING A COSMETICS DEPT FOR TODAY'S SHOPPER

(p. 24-25) Article on women's shopping patterns for cosmetics. Data are based on a survey of 1,000 women comprising the *Better Homes and Gardens* consumer panel.

Includes 2 charts and 5 tables showing survey response concerning influence of advertising, action taken when preferred product not found in store, expenditure per shopping trip, brand loyalty, sales service and retail outlet preferences, and use of body care products (no dates).

C5150–2.522: Aug. 20, 1984 (Vol. 6, No. 18)

DRUG INDUSTRY PACs SET FUND-RAISING RECORD

(p. 8, 11) By Laura Woda. Article, with 2 tables showing the following for 10 political action committees (PACs) sponsored by drugstore chains or related trade assns: funds remaining from 1982 election; and number and value of contributions to Federal candidates by party, value of collections for 1984 campaign, contributions to State candidates and other industry PACs, and administrative costs, late 1982-mid 1984 period.

Data are from reports filed with the Federal Election Commission.

PHARMACY: TOP 100 Rx PRODUCT MOVEMENT SURVEY

(p. 31-44) Article, with 30 tables showing top 100 prescription drugs, and top 2-16 drugs in each of 11 categories, generally based on number of prescriptions dispensed, sales value, and gross profit. Also includes rankings of drug categories based on number of products in the top 100. Tables are listings only and do not include actual values for the rankings. Data are from Decision Data, Inc.

C5150–2.523: Sept. 3, 1984 (Vol. 6, No. 19)

CORRECTION

(p. 4) Contains data correction for annual triple A product study feature.

For feature description, see C5150-2.520, above.

NIELSEN REVIEW OF RETAIL DRUGSTORE TRENDS, 1984, ANNUAL FEATURE

(p. 15-34) Annual review of aggregate drugstore sales and merchandising trends, various years 1975-86. Data were compiled by A. C. Nielsen Co. from various sources.

Includes illustrative data on effects of product promotion, and 7 charts and 23 tables showing the following:

a. Sales by kind of retail business, CPI by item, disposable income, and change in cost-of-living index; sales for chain and independent drugstores, with detail by chain store size; and total drugstore sales, with share for chain stores, for 10 Nielsen regions; various years 1975-83.

b. Health and beauty aid products in drugstores: percent change in sales, prices, inventories, and stock turns; market shares; and sales per foot of shelf space, and shelf space allocations and inventory turnover, for chain and independent stores; all with detail by product category, and comparisons to food and mass merchandise stores; various years 1978-83.

c. Food stores with computerized checkout scanners, and scanning stores' share of total sales, with detail by major marketing area, various years 1977-86.

This is the 48th annual review.

OTC BUYER SURVEY

(p. 94-98) Compilation of articles based on a recent survey of drugstore buyers responsible for over-the-counter (OTC) drug products. Data are based on 90 telephone interviews with buyers from independent drugstores, and from drugstore chains among the top 100 and the 2nd 100 in 1983 sales, conducted by Lebhar-Friedman.

Includes 1 chart and 1 table showing survey responses concerning frequency of visits from manufacturers' representatives, and types of new product information desired, for buyers from each type of drugstore.

C5150–2.524: Sept. 17, 1984 (Vol. 6, No. 20)

[Issue incorrectly reads Vol. 6, No. 17.]

SPECIAL REPORT: PHARMACY COMPUTERS AND POS SYSTEMS

(p. 1, 39-49) Compilation of articles on drugstore pharmacy use of computers and point-of-sale (POS) computerized management systems, 1984. Data are from *Drug Store News* surveys of drugstore executives and pharmacists.

Includes 5 undated tables showing drugstore chains testing computer/POS systems, with number of total and system-equipped stores; system specifications by manufacturer; drug wholesalers with computer systems, and total and system-equipped customers; and importance of computer features as ranked by pharmacists.

Correction appears in the Oct. 29, 1984 issue; for description, see C5150-2.527 below.

CONVENIENCE, QUALITY ARE PHOTO DEPT ASSETS

(p. 13-14) Article, with 1 chart showing photo processing market shares by retail outlet type, 1983. Data are primarily from Photo Marketing Assn.

C5150–2.525: Oct. 1, 1984 (Vol. 6, No. 21)

FASHION BOOSTS OFF-SEASON SUNGLASS SALES

(p. 13, 16) Article, with 1 undated chart showing sales distribution of nonprescription sunglasses among supermarkets, mass merchandisers, and drugstores. Data are from A. C. Nielsen Co.

VENDOR DEBUTS LOWER-PRICED HALOGEN FLASHLIGHTS

(p. 40) Article, with 1 chart showing distribution of flashlight sales by retail outlet type, 1982 and 1985. Data are from NFO Research, Inc.

C5150–2.526: Oct. 15, 1984 (Vol. 6, No. 22)

AUTO PART ADS RENEWED AS USER PROFILE CHANGES

(p. 9-10) Article, with 1 table showing manufacturers' sales of auto aftermarket products by type, 1983. Data are from C. H. Kline and Co.

STUDY FINDS MANUFACTURERS LAX IN BRIEFING RxERS ON SIDE EFFECTS

(p. 13, 21) Article on pharmacists' knowledge of prescription drug side-effects. Data are based on a recent survey of over 1,000 consumers age 45/over, conducted by American Assn of Retired Persons.

Includes 2 undated tables showing responses concerning frequency of receiving information from pharmacists about prescription drug side-effects, and consumer sources of drug information.

1984 STORE DETAILING STUDY, ANNUAL FEATURE

(p. 19-22) Annual compilation of articles on pharmacists' satisfaction with pharmaceutical manufacturers' services. Data are from 575 responses to a *Drug Store News* survey of chain and independent pharmacists.

Includes 3 tables showing responses concerning visits from manufacturers' representatives for 6 new drug brands, and actual and desired frequency of representatives' visits (no date); and average daily number of prescriptions filled, 1981 and 1984; all for total and/or chain and independent stores.

C5150–2.527: Oct. 29, 1984 (Vol. 6, No. 23)

1984 ANNUAL REPORT OF THE WHOLESALE DRUG INDUSTRY

(p. 15-30) Annual compilation of articles on wholesale drug industry finances and operations, 1984. Data are from National Wholesale Druggists' Assn, and a 1984 *Drug Store News* survey of 107 drug wholesalers operating 321 distribution facilities.

Includes profiles of 7 leading wholesalers, generally including 1 chart showing sales trends; and 1 chart and 7 tables showing the following:

a. Sales from drug wholesaling, for top 20 firms, including wholesale share of total company sales, for most current fiscal year (specified for each company), with comparison to previous year; and number of wholesale distribution centers, by company, 1983-84. (p. 17)

b. Operating ratios, including profit, expense, and return on net worth; sales shares, and expected future growth in sales, by customer type; and sales or sales distribution, by product type and for sales to retail drugstores; various years 1977-84. (p. 21-24)

This is the 1st annual report.

PHARMACY: GENERICS TAKE BIGGER BITE FROM Rx INDUSTRY PIE

(p. 49-50) Article, with 1 chart showing sales of branded and generic prescription drugs, 1978, 1983, and 1990. Data are from A. D. Little and Co.

CORRECTION

(p. 53) Correction for compilation of articles on drugstore pharmacy use of computers. Presents corrected system specifications for 1 manufacturer.

For description of original articles, see C5150-2.524, above.

PHARMACY: CHAINS STAKING CLAIM IN HOME-HEALTH MARKET

(p. 57, 60) Article, with 3 tables showing number of home health care centers operated by 13 leading retail drug chains, 1984; population (total and age 65/over), and expenditures per capita for home health care among persons age 65/over, 1983, 1988, and 1995; and consumer expenditures for home health care services, equipment, and supplies, 1983, 1988, and 1990.

Data are from Predicasts, Inc. and *Drug Store News*.

C5150–3   DISCOUNT STORE NEWS

Biweekly.   Approx. 100 p.
Oversized.
ISSN 0012-3587.
LC 63-52555.
SRI/MF/excerpts

Biweekly journal of the full-line and specialty discount department store industry, covering financial and marketing developments, merchandise line sales and profitability, and consumer and economic trends. Journal is published every 3rd week in Sept.-Oct., and once in Dec.

Data are from industry sources, including store chains, wholesalers, and National Mass Retailing Institute; media research firms; and the journal's own research. Data are current to 3-6 months preceding publication date.

General format:

a. News articles, occasionally with statistics; and narrative editorial depts.

b. Irregularly appearing features on stock price and earnings trends for discount store chains and retailers; and on advertised prices for varying brand name products sold by discount chains.

c. Recurring Product Movement Audit (PMA) feature, with narrative and usually 1 table, based on data from a leading wholesale distributor, presenting unit movement and average retail price for top-selling products in selected categories, for 3-week to 12-month periods.

Annual features include a discount store census (July issue) presenting store sales and earnings by department, with selected data by company, State, and metro area.

All articles with substantial statistical content are described, as they appear, under "Statistical Features;" page locations and period of coverage for recurring PMA tables are also noted. Non-statistical features are not covered.

Availability: Discount Store News, Subscription Department, 99 Park Ave., New York NY 10157, retailers $12.00 per yr., others $20.00 per yr., single copy $2.00, census issue $20.00; SRI/MF/excerpts for all portions covered under "Statistical Features."

Issues reviewed during 1984: Oct. 31, 1983-Oct. 29, 1984 (P) (Vol. 22, Nos. 21-24; Vol. 23, Nos. 1-21).

STATISTICAL FEATURES:

C5150-3.501: Oct. 31, 1983 (Vol. 22, No. 21)

NEW AUDIO PACKAGES UP HOME-SOUND BIZ

(p. 3, 18) Article, with 1 table showing radio and audio entertainment equipment sales, and audio reproduction equipment sales by type, selected years 1977-95. Data are from Predicasts, Inc.

C5150-3.502: Nov. 14, 1983 (Vol. 22, No. 22)

LADIES' WEAR LEAD NAME-BRAND GROWTH, ANNUAL FEATURE

(p. 19-76) Annual compilation of articles on market penetration of national brand name products in the discount store industry. Data are from a 1983 survey of store managers conducted by Leo J. Shapiro and Associates. Includes 10 charts and 52 tables showing respondent distribution to questions on the following:

a. Depts with greatest increase in name brands, reasons for increase in name brand sales, and expected sales gain, by discounter type (conventional and upscale); and managers expecting name brands to increase 1983 business, by region and store size group.

b. Top-selling brands by region and/or discounter type and leading chain, repeated for 16 product categories; and increase in brands carried by region, by selected product category, 1982/83.

This is the 1st annual feature. A related article appears on p. 1.

C5150-3.503: Dec. 12, 1983 (Vol. 22, No. 24)

STORES PROSECUTE THIEVES MORE, BOOST CONVICTION RATE, ANNUAL FEATURE

(p. 3, 88) Annual article on discount store theft losses and measures taken to prevent theft, or inventory "shrinkage." Data are from responses of 180 retailers to a 1982 survey conducted by Arthur Young and Co. for National Mass Retailing Institute. Includes 1 table showing use of various methods for training security and nonsecurity personnel in shrinkage control, by type of store.

C5150-3.504: Jan. 9, 1984 (Vol. 23, No. 1)

CLOSEOUT STORES MULTIPLY, GIVE BIRTH TO AN 'INDUSTRY'

(p. 1, 77) By Arthur Markowitz. Article on "closeout" retailers, those specializing in surplus or salvage merchandise. Data are from *Discount Store News.* Includes 1 table showing sales for 1983, and number of stores and projected store openings in 1984, for 19 closeout chains.

PROFITS OF DISCOUNTERS, OLD-LINERS SHRINK IN LATEST FISCAL YEAR, ANNUAL FEATURE

(p. 2, 66) Annual article comparing discount and department store merchandising performance by product category. Data are from National Mass Retailing Institute (NMRI) *Operating Results of Self-Service Discount Department Stores, 1982-83* and National Retail Merchants Assn (NRMA) *Department Store and Specialty Store Merchandising and Operating Results of 1982.*

Includes 1 table showing markup, markdown, stock shortage, gross margin, stock turns, and percent of total sales, for 15 product categories in discount and department stores.

Full NMRI and NRMA reports are covered in SRI under U1380-1 and A8300-1, respectively.

PHONE SALES SEEN GETTING HOTTER; AT&T UPS PLANS

(p. 23, 77) Article, with 1 table showing population, households, residential telephones in use, telephone answering machines per 1,000 households, and telephone and answering machine sales volume and value, selected years 1972-95. Data are from Predicasts, Inc.

HOME VIDEO HOT; SHIPMENTS OF VCRs TO STORES MORE THAN DOUBLED IN 1983

(p. 50) Article, with 1 table showing sales of TVs by type, videocassette recorders, and color video cameras, Nov. and 1st 11 months 1982-83. Data are from Electronic Industries Assn.

NEWER ITEMS TO HELP TUNE UP CE MARKET TO $58B BY 1995

(p. 52-53) Article, with 3 charts showing sales of consumer electronics by product type, with detail for audio and video equipment, 1982 and 1995. Data are from Predicasts, Inc.

C5150-3.505: Jan. 23, 1984 (Vol. 23, No. 2)

DISCOUNTERS INCREASE 5 KEY PERKS FOR EXECS, BUT WHITTLE 3 OTHERS

(p. 2, 33) Article, with 1 table showing percent of discount chains offering 8 types of perquisites, by management level, 1983. Data are from a National Mass Retailing Institute survey.

DISCOUNTLAND APPAREL: KIDS' WEAR IS SHOPPED THE MOST

(p. 31) Article on apparel purchasing habits of discount shoppers. Data are from a Nov./Dec. 1983 consumer survey conducted by Leo J. Shapiro and Associates. Includes 1 table showing percent of respondents most apt to buy selected clothing items in discount, off-price, and factory outlet stores.

C5150-3.506: Feb. 6, 1984 (Vol. 23, No. 3)

PRODUCT MOVEMENT AUDIT (PMA) TABLE

(p. 27-29) Hardware, Nov. 1983.

CONSUMERS STILL PREFER DISCOUNTERS FOR HARD GOODS

(p. 14) Article on consumers' discount or "off-price" store shopping practices. Data are based on a Dec. 1983 survey of approximately 1,000 consumers conducted by Leo J. Shapiro and Associates for *Discount Store News.* Includes 3 tables showing survey response concerning shopping practices for 30 product categories, with some detail by outlet type.

SALES OF BLANK AUDIO AND VIDEO TAPES KEEP CLIMBING

(p. 19) Article, with 2 tables showing unit sales to dealers and factory sales value, for blank video cassettes 1982-84, and blank audio cassettes 1981-84. Data are from Electronic Industries Assn, Consumer Electronics Group.

SALES PER SQUARE FOOT KEEP RISING

(p. 51) Brief article, with 1 table showing discount store toy dept average size, annual turns,

sales per square foot, percent markup, and gross margins, selected years 1971-83. Data are from *Discount Store News.*

C5150-3.507: Feb. 20, 1984 (Vol. 23, No. 4)

PRODUCT MOVEMENT AUDIT (PMA) TABLE

(p. 39, 43) Automotive supplies, Dec. 1983.

DIFFERENTLY PRICED CIGGIES DRAWING MIXED RESULTS

(p. 3, 44) Article, with 2 tables showing production of tobacco products by type, 1980-83; and national brand and generic cigarette production, 1981-83. Data are from USDA and Gary Tobacco.

C5150-3.508: Mar. 5, 1984 (Vol. 23, No. 5)

1983 SALES JUMPED FOR TOP DISCOUNTERS

(p. 6, 68) Article, with 1 table showing sales for 15 major discount chains or parent companies, Jan. 1983-84 and FY83-84. Data are from company reports.

No. 1 MARSHALLS IS EN ROUTE TO $1.3B IN 1984

(p. 27-29) Article on off-price apparel merchandising industry. Data are from *Discount Store News.* Includes 1 table showing number of stores, sales, and average store size, for 16 leading off-price apparel merchandisers, various periods 1983-84.

BUG KILLERS, CHAIN SAWS, MOWERS HOT

(p. 50) Article, with 1 table showing consumer purchasing plans for 12 outdoor power equipment products, with distribution by family status, age of householder, and purchase type (first, replacement, and extra). Data are from responses of 4,225 consumers to a 3rd quarter 1983 survey conducted by Industrial Marketing Research, Inc.

C5150-3.509: Mar. 19, 1984 (Vol. 23, No. 6)

WRITING-INSTRUMENT INNOVATIONS HYPO GROWTH; COST TRENDS VARY

(p. 47) Article, with 1 table showing shipments of writing instruments by type, selected years 1955-82. Data are from Writing Instruments Manufacturers Assn.

C5150-3.510: Apr. 2, 1984 (Vol. 23, No. 7)

PROFIT GAINS OUTDO SALES RISES AS DISCOUNTERS REPORT BIG '83, SEMIANNUAL FEATURE

(p. 1, 4) Semiannual article, with 1 table showing sales and earnings of 21 major discount chains or parent companies, 1982-83. Data are from company reports.

10th ANNUAL PRODUCT MOVEMENT AUDIT

(p. 29-74, passim) Annual Product Movement Audit of leading items sold in 8 discount store depts, 1983. Data are based on reports from wholesale distributors.

Includes 8 tables showing sales rank, 1982 and/or 1983; and unit movement, average retail price, and total sales value, 1983; for top-selling items in stationery, hardware, automotive, housewares, health and beauty aids, consumer electronics, toys, and sporting goods depts.

C5150–3.511: Apr. 16, 1984 (Vol. 23, No. 8)

PRODUCT MOVEMENT AUDIT (PMA) TABLES

(p. 47-106, passim) Housewares, 1983 with 1982 rankings; and health and beauty aids, 1983. Corrected data for housewares appear in May 14, 1984 issue; for description see C5150-3.513, below.

DROPS IN CONSUMPTION OF COFFEE CONTINUE FOUR-YEAR DOWNTREND, ANNUAL FEATURE

(p. 38) Annual article on coffee consumption trends, based on a winter 1983 survey conducted by the International Coffee Organization. Includes 1 chart and 2 tables showing distribution of coffee consumption, by coffee type, 1983; cups consumed per person per day, selected years 1962-83; and percent of consumers using 7 coffee-making products, selected years 1975-83.

VACS GRAB LEAD IN BIG-APPLIANCE INTENT-TO-BUY POLL

(p. 70) Article, with 1 table showing percent of consumers intending to buy 12 major appliances, with distribution by family status, age of household head, type of purchase, and income. Data are from 4,225 responses to a 3rd quarter 1983 survey conducted by Industrial Marketing Research, Inc.

DISCOUNTERS SWELL LEAD AMONG HOUSEWARES OUTLETS, ANNUAL FEATURE

(p. 72) Annual article, with 2 tables showing houseware manufacturers' sales, by retail outlet type and to wholesalers 1981-83, and by product category 1982-83. Data are based on 611 responses to the 17th annual National Housewares Manufacturers Assn survey of manufacturers.

SALES KEEP RISING, BUT TURNOVER SLIPS

(p. 91) Brief article, with 1 table showing the following for discount store houseware depts: total sales, and average sales per store, dept size, annual turns, initial markup, and gross margin, 1973 and 1978-83. Data are from *Discount Store News*.

C5150–3.512: Apr. 30, 1984 (Vol. 23, No. 9)

DISCOUNTERS AMONG FASTEST-GROWING H&BA OUTLETS: POLL

(p. 16, 23) Article, with 2 tables showing sales of cosmetics and toiletries, by retail outlet type, selected years 1967-82; and PPI for cosmetics and toiletries by product type, with comparison to total CPI, selected years 1967-95. Data are from Predicasts, Inc.

C5150–3.513: May 14, 1984 (Vol. 23, No. 10)

CORRECTION

(p. 4) Correction for Housewares PMA table, described under C5150-3.511, above.

ZAPPING (SWITCHING OFF) COMMERCIALS SEEMS ON RISE

(p. 63) Article, with 1 chart showing distribution of TV households by TV service (pay and basic cable, and noncable), and by presence of remote control device, Mar. 1983. Data are from A. C. Nielsen Co.

MOST CHAINS' TV-AD OUTLAY SOARS IN 1983, ANNUAL FEATURE

(p. 68, 72) Annual compilation of articles on TV advertising expenditures of discount store chains. Data are from TV Bureau of Advertising, based on Broadcast Advertisers Reports.

Includes 4 tables showing expenditures of top 10 discount department store chains in single market spot advertising, of top 15 discount chains in spot advertising, and of top 15 off-price advertisers; and network and spot expenditures of 4 major chains; 1982-83.

MICROCOMPUTERS' BACKROOM USE IS AN EMERGING TREND

(p. 106, 123) Article, with 1 undated table on microcomputer use in retailing, including interaction with main data processing system, average number in use, and primary applications, by sales size and outlet type. Data are from Arthur Young and Co.

DISCOUNTER PACs ARE ARMED FOR CONGRESSIONAL RACES

(p. 116) Article, with 2 tables showing the following for 6-8 political action committees (PACs) sponsored by discount chains or related trade assns, primarily 1983: number and value of contributions to Federal candidates, by party; and value of collections for 1984 campaign, funds remaining from 1982 election, contributions to State candidates and other industry PACs, and administrative costs.

Data are from reports filed with the Federal Election Commission.

C5150–3.514: June 11, 1984 (Vol. 23, No. 12)

L/F UNVEILS 1st QUARTERLY RETAIL INDEX, QUARTERLY FEATURE

(p. 2) Quarterly article, with 1 table showing retail sales, and sales distribution by outlet type or retailer group for durable and nondurable goods, 1st quarter 1980 and 1983-84. Data are from Lebhar-Friedman research and Dept of Commerce.

This is the 1st quarterly article.

GIANTS EVOLVING AMONG CE DISCOUNT CHAINS

(p. 3, 55) Article, with 2 tables showing top 10 consumer electronics discount chains ranked by total and consumer electronics sales for most recently completed fiscal year, and including number of stores as of Jan. 1983-85, and average store size. Data are from *Discount Store News*.

TV AD USE IN 1983 BALLOONED FOR MANY LEADING CE CHAINS

(p. 57) Article, with 1 table showing top 10 consumer electronics discount chains ranked by TV advertising expenditures, 1983 with comparison to 1982. Data are from TV Bureau of Advertising, based on Broadcast Advertisers Reports.

C5150–3.515: June 25, 1984 (Vol. 23, No. 13)

AUTO CHAINS' GROWTH PLANS SHIFT INTO HIGH

(p. 3, 32) Article, with 1 table showing top 10 automotive chains ranked by sales for most recently completed fiscal year, and including number of stores as of Jan. 1, 1984-85. Data are from *Discount Store News*.

PARTS STORES SOAR TO 38,000 FROM 1980 TO 1983: APAA

(p. 37) Article, with 2 tables showing number of outlets and percent of retailers selling auto parts/supplies, by retail outlet type, 1980 and 1983. Data are from Automotive Parts and Accessories Assn.

C5150–3.516: July 9, 1984 (Vol. 23, No. 14)

DISCOUNTLAND GARNERS 37% OF CUT-PRICE BIZ

(p. 1, 5) Article on consumer shopping habits for discount-priced products. Data are based on a survey of 1,688 households, conducted by Leo J. Shapiro & Associates.

Includes 6 undated tables showing percent of consumers paying less than full price, and expecting or seeking discounted prices, for selected product categories, with detail by retail outlet type; and perceived disadvantages of sales.

C5150–3.517: July 23, 1984 (Vol. 23, No. 15)

1984-85 DISCOUNT STORE CENSUS, ANNUAL FEATURE

(p. 1, 15-119, passim) Annual statistical feature on discount store sales and productivity by dept, and stores and sales by company, State, and metro area, 1984, with selected projections for 1985 and trends from 1962.

Data are from the journal's own research; *Sales and Marketing Management* magazine; and other sources.

Contains contents listing (p. 1); industry summaries, interspersed with 1 chart, and 8 tables described below (p. 15-36); individual discount chain activities (p. 38-62); and merchandising profiles for 17 depts, interspersed with 2 summary tables, and 17 detailed tables also described below (p. 67-119).

TABLES:

a. Top 100 chains ranked by general merchandise sales, with net earnings, for most recent fiscal year with comparison to previous fiscal year; and stores and square footage, Jan. and Dec. 1984, and scheduled additions, 1985. 1 table. (p. 17)

b. Historical trends: full-line discounter sales, stores, square footage, dollars per square foot, average sales per store, and average store size, 1962-84. 1 table. (p. 18)

c. Stores and square footage, by region, Dec. 1984; and stores by square footage range, Dec. 1983-84. 2 tables. (p. 21, 25)

d. Stores, square footage, and sales, for total and full-line discounters, in top 50 metro market areas and by State; population, households, and effective buying income, for top 50 metro market areas; and total retail sales by State; primarily 1984. 2 tables. (p. 26, 31)

e. Specialty discount chains: top 25 ranked by sales, FY83 with comparison to FY82, with stores and square footage as of Jan. and Dec. 1984, and scheduled additions, 1985. 1 table. (p. 34)

f. Catalog showroom chains: top 20 ranked by sales, with net profit, for most recent fiscal year with comparison to previous fiscal year; and showrooms, Jan. and Dec. 1984, and scheduled openings, 1985. 1 table. (p. 36)

g. Merchandising profiles showing the following for 17 depts: sales, for full-line and specialty discounters, and catalog showrooms; and full-line discount stores total sales, sales per store and square foot, average dept size, annual turns, initial markup, and gross margin, 1984. 17 tables (p. 68-112)

C5150–3.518: Aug. 6, 1984 (Vol. 23, No. 16)

SHOPPERS' LOYALTY STRONGLY IMPACTED BY PL: SURVEY

(p. 2, 33) Article on consumer opinions regarding national brand vs. private label products. Data are based on 1,104 responses to a consumer survey conducted by Gallup Poll. Includes 2 undated tables showing factors rated as very important in choosing national or store brand, and interest in selected store brand promotional activities.

DISCOUNT BOOK CHAINS CHANGING THE SHAPE OF AN $8B INDUSTRY

(p. 3-4) By Larry Carlat. Article, with 1 table showing the following for retail book chains: sales 1983, stores as of Jan. 1984-85, and average store size, for 2 full-margin and 6 discount chains; and discount rate on hardcover and paperback best-sellers and new releases, for 6 discount chains. Data are from *Discount Store News*.

C5150–3.519: Aug. 20, 1984 (Vol. 23, No. 17)

PRODUCT MOVEMENT AUDIT (PMA) TABLE

(p. 45-46, 51) Hardware, Feb. 1-June 30, 1984 period.

8.4% ANNUAL SALES BOOST PROJECTED FOR POWER TOOL CONSUMABLES, ACCESSORIES

(p. 24) Article, with 1 table showing sales of portable power tool accessories/consumables to do-it-yourself consumers, by product type, 1983 and 1988. Data are from Frost and Sullivan, Inc.

'84 OUTLOOK: FEWER CHAINS, MORE SALES

(p. 55, 61) Article, with 1 table showing top 11 discount toy chains ranked by sales in FY83, and including stores Jan. 1983-85, and average store size. Data are from *Discount Store News*.

A summary article and table are also included (p. 1).

TOYS 'R' US AND CHILD WORLD SHRANK TV AD OUTLAYS IN 1983

(p. 62) Article, with 1 table ranking top 4 discount toy chain companies by TV advertising expenditures, 1983, with detail for subsidiaries and comparisons to 1982. Data are from TV Bureau of Advertising, based on Broadcast Advertisers Reports.

C5150–3.520: Sept. 3, 1984 (Vol. 23, No. 18)

CHAINS SEE SALES COOLING ONLY A BIT, SEMIANNUAL FEATURE

(p. 1, 58) Semiannual article, with 1 table showing sales and earnings of 19 major discount chains or parent companies, 1st half 1983-84. Data are from company reports.

TOP 50 OPERATORS TO OPEN 87 NEW SHOWROOMS IN '84, ANNUAL FEATURE

(p. 3, 29) Annual article, with 1 table showing the following for top 50 catalog showroom chains ranked by sales: sales and net profit for most recent fiscal year, with comparison to previous fiscal year; and number of showrooms as of Jan. and Dec. 1984, and openings planned for 1985. Data are from *Discount Store News*.

AUTO CHEMICALS' WHOLESALE BIZ SEEN SOARING TO $2.4B IN 1987

(p. 45) Article, with 1 chart on sales of chemical-related automotive care products, showing distribution of wholesale sales through retail outlets by product type, 1982. Data are from C. H. Kline and Co.

C5150–3.521: Sept. 17, 1984 (Vol. 23, No. 19)

SPORTING GOODS CHAINS EYE $1B

(p. 2, 77) Article, with 1 table showing top 10 discount sporting goods chains ranked by sales, FY83, and including number of stores, Jan. 1983-85, and average store size. Data are from *Discount Store News*.

DISCOUNTERS LEAD IN SALES OF BASIC SPORTING GOODS

(p. 23, 68) Article, with 1 table showing sales of sporting equipment, and athletic clothing and shoes, all by type, 1982-84. Data are from National Sporting Goods Assn.

BUYERS SEE GAS MODELS CONTINUING TO IGNITE GRILL AREA

(p. 42) Article, with 1 table showing distribution of barbecue grill sales, by retail outlet type, 1977 and 1983. Data are from Barbecue Industry Assn.

C5150–3.522: Oct. 8, 1984 (Vol. 23, No. 20)

PRODUCT MOVEMENT AUDIT (PMA) TABLES

(p. 58-123, passim) Housewares, various periods Jan.-Aug. 1984; and automotive accessories, Feb.-July 1984 period.

FULL-LINE DISCOUNT STORES AGAIN LEAD GEN. MDSE. RETAILERS, QUARTERLY FEATURE

(p. 2, 5) Quarterly article, with 1 chart showing retail sales, and sales and market shares by outlet type or retailer group, for general merchandise nondurable goods, primarily 2nd quarter and 1st 6 months, 1983-84. Data are from Lebhar-Friedman research and Dept of Commerce.

C5150–3.523: Oct. 29, 1984 (Vol. 23, No. 21)

WHOLESALE MEMBERSHIP CLUBS SEEN EXPLODING BY 50% IN '85

(p. 1, 30) Article on wholesale membership clubs (companies offering wholesale-priced goods to retailers in exchange for a membership fee and marketing bulk goods slightly above wholesale prices to private groups). Data are from *Discount Store News*.

Includes 1 table showing sales, number of stores, and markets covered, for 14 wholesale membership clubs, various periods 1984-85.

C5150–4   CHAIN STORE AGE, EXECUTIVE

Monthly. Approx. 100 p.
ISSN 0193-1199.
LC 45-30011.
SRI/MF/excerpts, shipped quarterly

Monthly trade journal of the retail chain store and shopping center industries. Retail chain types include department store, discount, general merchandise, specialty, drug, and supermarket operations. Covers merchandising, finances, new construction, technology, store design, Federal Government regulation, and economic developments that affect retail trade.

Data are from Federal Government, store chains, private research assns, and the journal's own research.

Issues contain articles, occasionally with statistics; and regular editorial depts, including a descriptive list of new stores and shopping centers.

Annual statistical features include reports on capital expenditures of leading retail chains; chain store expansion and physical support systems; and activities of chains with sales over $100 million.

Some issues are published in 2 sections. The 2nd section usually focuses on retail technology.

Features with substantial statistical content are described, as they appear, under "Statistical Features." Each issue of the journal is reviewed, but an abstract is published in SRI monthly issues only when statistical features appear.

Availability: Chain Store Age, Executive, Subscription Department, 99 Park Ave., New York NY 10157, $20.00 per yr.; SRI/MF/excerpts for all portions described under "Statistical Features;" shipped quarterly.

Issues reviewed during 1984: Nov. 1983-Oct. 1984 (P) (Vol. 59, Nos. 11-12; Vol. 60, Nos. 1-10) [May and Oct. issues are published in 2 sections].

STATISTICAL FEATURES:

C5150–4.501: Nov. 1983 (Vol. 59, No. 11)

BIG BUILDERS DRAFT 1983 BLUEPRINT AT $4.7 BILLION, ANNUAL FEATURE

(p. 20-57) Annual feature on expansion and capital expenditures of leading retail chains. Data are from individual chains, and *Chain Store Age Executive* estimates. Includes the following:

a. Summary, with 3 tables showing top 25 chains ranked by capital expenditures, and gross and net square footage added, 1983 with comparison to 1982. (p. 20-23)

b. Profiles of 20 chains' capital expenditures, each with 1 table showing stores in operation at end of year, stores and square footage added, stores closed, and total capital expenditures, 1982-83. (p. 23-57)

ELECTRONICS MAKE A SPLASH IN THE TYPING POOL

(p. 74-77) Article on retailer use of electronic typewriters, based on a Lebhar-Friedman survey of 200 major retailers. Includes 1 undated chart showing brands of electronic typewriter used.

C5150–4.502: Dec. 1983 (Vol. 59, No. 12)

MANAGEMENT'S DESKTOP PCs KEEP EXECS ON TOP OF BUSINESS

(p. 41-43) Article on retailer use of personal computers, based on a Lebhar-Friedman survey of 200 major retailers. Includes 3 undated charts showing expected change in annual expenditures, favorite personal computer manufacturer, and brand of computer used.

C5150–4.503: Jan. 1984 (Vol. 60, No. 1)

LIFO SURVEY SHOWS IT'S HERE TO STAY

(p. 32-33) Article on retailers' use of the LIFO (last-in, first-out) inventory valuation method. Data are from BLS and from a Lebhar-Friedman survey of 120 major retail chains.

Includes 3 tables showing length of time LIFO used, and factors influencing size of LIFO reserves, by chain type and/or sales size; and percent change in department store inventory price indexes, by merchandise category, for 6- and 12-month periods ended July 1983.

1984 FORECAST: RECOVERY'S TEMPO QUICKENS

(p. 39-42) Article, with 2 charts showing percent change in CPI, general merchandise prices, and consumer spending for durables, nondurables, and services, 1980-84. Data are from Morgan Stanley Research.

WORDS, WORDS, WORDS. . .AN OFFICE DILEMMA

(p. 48-50) Article on retailer use of office automation equipment. Data are based on a *Chain Store Age* survey of 200 major retail chains. Includes 1 undated chart showing retail store use of word processors, by manufacturer.

DEVELOPERS GET BACK TO BUSINESS

(p. 83-90) Article reporting on construction plans of shopping center developers, 1984. Data are based on a *Chain Store Age* survey.

Includes 5 charts showing expected increase in gross leasable area, number of new centers planned, estimated costs for expansion and new construction, and main sources of financing.

C5150–4.504: Feb. 1984 (Vol. 60, No. 2)

PRIVATE TO PUBLIC: IS THE WINDOW CLOSING?

(p. 21-24) Article on retail companies making initial public stock offering during 1983. Data are from Daniel Barry of Kidder, Peabody and Co. Includes 1 table showing stock price and price/earnings ratio for each company, at date of offer and at year end, 1983.

C5150–4.505: Mar. 1984 (Vol. 60, No. 3)

DEVELOPERS TRACK THE DATA

(p. 80-83) Article on shopping center developers' use of market analysis data. Includes 2 charts and 1 table showing population share and per capita disposable income, by region and selected SMSA; and per capita retail sales growth rate by census division; various periods 1982-88. Data are from A. C. Nielsen Co. and Management Horizons.

C5150–4.506: Apr. 1984 (Vol. 60, No. 4)

STORE REMODELING: HOW PROFITABLE CAN IT BE?

(p. 17-20) Article, with 1 chart and 1 table showing retail chain distribution by remodel-ing cost per square foot, and average percent increase in sales and profits after remodeling, for discount/mass merchandise, department and drug store, and supermarket chains (no date). Data are from a Lebhar Friedman survey of 120 retail chains.

C5150–4.507: May 1984 (Vol. 60, No. 5)

SECTION 1

INCENTIVES SERENADE SUPERMARKET SHOPPERS

(p. 35-38) Article on perceptions and use of purchasing incentives among supermarket shoppers. Data are from *Chain Store Age Executive* surveys of consumers in 4 major cities.

Includes 1 chart and 6 tables showing survey response on frequency of coupon use, reasons for using, and perception of stores offering double couponing; media used to find purchasing incentives; store characteristics with greatest influence on shopping; and incentives most frequently used; with detail by shopper sex and marital status, and for selected shopping patterns and individual survey cities.

MANAGEMENT AND UNIONS: A SUPERMARKET TUG OF WAR

(p. 38-41) Article, with 1 chart showing number of United Food and Commercial Workers Union (UF&CW) members covered by contracts expiring in 1984, by industry. Data are from UF&CW.

SECTION 2

OCR-A: BECAUSE IT'S NOT PEAS

(p. 7) Article, with 2 charts showing percent of retailers planning to implement use of OCR-A (merchandise tags combining machine- and eye-readable inventory and price information) and Universal Product Code machine-readable labels by 1987, by outlet type. Data are from National Retail Merchants Assn.

C5150–4.508: June 1984 (Vol. 60, No. 6)

CAPITAL EXPENDITURES ON THE RISE

(p. 15-19) Article on distribution operations and costs of retail chain stores. Data are based on 180 responses to a *Chain Store Age, Executive* survey of chain executives in 6 retail sectors. Includes 8 charts showing survey findings on the following, generally by sector:

a. Average number and square footage of distribution centers, stores served per center, distribution trips and mileage per week, cost per mile, and age of equipment.

b. Transportation methods (owned vs. leased equipment, own operators vs. common carriers); computer use for various distribution functions; distribution share of total capital expenditures, 1983-85; and transportation equipment share of total distribution expenditures.

Except for the 1983-85 data noted, no data dates are given.

EYEWEAR ABOUT TO MAKE A SPECTACLE OF ITSELF

(p. 23-29) Article, with 1 chart showing eyewear market distribution among retail chains, optometrists, ophthalmologists, and opticians, 1973 and 1984. Data are from Pearle Health Services.

C5150–4.509: July 1984 (Vol. 60, No. 7)

INDUSTRY PROFILES AND PHYSICAL SUPPORT SYSTEMS, ANNUAL FEATURE

(p. 29-88) Annual report, for 1984, on developments in retail chain expansion and physical support systems (store equipment). Data are from *Chain Store Age, Executive* research.

Contains narrative reports, interspersed with 1 chart and 32 tables showing the following:

a. Profiles of 6 types of chains, each with 1 table showing median and/or mean total and selling space for existing stores and those opening in 1983/84, and mean shell construction costs within previous 12-month period. (p. 29-42)

b. Profiles of 13 support system categories, most with 1-3 undated tables primarily showing equipment costs and life span, by type of chain. (p. 45-88)

Corrected data appear in Aug. 1984 issue; for description, see C5150-4.510 below.

C5150–4.510: Aug. 1984 (Vol. 60, No. 8)

CORRECTION

(p. 10) Corrected data on mean store size, originally appearing in annual feature on chain expansion and physical support systems.

For feature description, see C5150-4.509, above.

SENIOR CITIZEN MARKETING: SHATTERING STEREOTYPES

(p. 17-20) Article, with 1 chart showing population age 55/over, decennially 1980-2020. Data are from Dept of Commerce.

$100 MILLION CLUB, ANNUAL FEATURE

(p. 31-48) Annual feature on retail chains with sales of $100 million or more, 1983. Data are from companies, and *Chain Store Age, Executive* estimates.

Includes 2 tables showing the following for 323 chains ranked by sales: sales, earnings, return on equity, and number of stores, 1983 with selected comparisons to 1982; and stores to be added in 1984; with selected detail for divisions of conglomerate chains. Also includes alphabetical index of companies covered.

STRUGGLE TO POST SALES GAINS

(p. 57-58) Article, with 1 chart showing supermarket sales per square foot, 1974 and 1980-83. Data are from Food Marketing Institute.

C5150–4.511: Sept. 1984 (Vol. 60, No. 9)

RETAILERS DEVELOPING METHODS TO GAUGE PRODUCTIVITY

(p. 23-25) Article on retailer methods for measuring productivity. Data are based on a recent *Chain Store Age, Executive* survey of retailers.

Includes 5 tables showing survey response concerning sales per labor hour and per net and gross square foot, 1983; and methods used to measure and improve productivity (no date); all by retail outlet type.

Corrected data appear in the Oct. 1984 issue; for description, see C5150-4.512 below.

ON THE TRACK WITH EXPLOSIVE STARTS

(p. 29-38) Article, with 1 chart and 1 table showing 1983 sales and earnings, return on equity, number of stores, average store size, annual inventory turns, and advertising budget as a percent of sales, for 7 specialty retail chains with high sales growth during 1983. Data are from *Chain Store Age, Executive.*

SURVEY SAYS SALES STILL STRONG

(p. 60-66) Article on retailer sales productivity in shopping centers. Data are based on a recent *Chain Store Age, Executive* survey of shopping center owners/managers.

Includes 7 tables showing responses concerning sales per square foot of gross leasable area (GLA), and retail outlet types producing highest sales, with detail by region and shopping center size and type; types of shopping centers owned/managed; and shopping center sizes with greatest expected increase in sales; mostly for 1984, with comparison to 1983.

C5150–4.512: Oct. 1984 (Vol. 60, No. 10)

SECTION 1

CORRECTION

(p. 10) Includes corrected data for article on retailer methods for measuring productivity; for description, see C5150-4.511 above.

C5150–5   NATION'S RESTAURANT NEWS

Weekly.   Approx. 100 p.
Oversized.
ISSN 0028-0518.
LC SN 78-6256.
SRI/MF/excerpts, shipped quarterly

Weekly trade journal (no issues published last 2 weeks in Dec.) reporting on financial and marketing trends in the food service industry. Covers sales, construction and expansion, promotion, menu development, food trends, and government activities and other general news of interest to the food service industry.

Data are from the journal's own research, trade assns, company reports, Dept of Commerce, and other government and private sources.

Issues contain mostly news articles, occasionally with statistics; narrative editorial depts; and the following weekly statistical features:

a. "Chain Stock Analysis" table showing recent stock price and earnings trends, and last fiscal year financial position, for approximately 100 leading food service chains, with 3 accompanying tables (beginning with the Aug. 13, 1984 issue) presenting trading volume data for 10 most active stocks and for 5 stocks with greatest increase and decrease in price.

b. "Price Movement at a Glance" table, with brief accompanying narrative, showing prices for 5-11 food commodities usually for a selected date 2-4 weeks prior to cover date, and same day of previous month and year.

Journal also includes "NRN Focus," containing articles on a selected food service-related topic, frequently with statistics. Annual statistical features include a forecast of food service industry sales and market developments, and a detailed report on top 100 food service chains.

Prior to the Oct. 8, 1984 issue, journal was published biweekly, and included "Chain Stock Analysis" in each issue and "Price Movement" in alternate issues. Prior to the Oct. 22, 1984 issue, journal included an additional table in each issue showing recent revenues for 4-32 food service chains.

Recurring features appear in issues as noted above. All other features with substantial statistical content are described, as they appear, under "Statistical Features." Nonstatistical features are not covered.

Availability: Nation's Restaurant News, Subscription Department, 99 Park Ave., New York NY 10157, $18.00 per yr., single copy $1.00; SRI/MF/excerpts for weekly tables, and all portions covered under "Statistical Features;" shipped quarterly.

Issues reviewed during 1984: Nov. 7, 1983-Sept. 24, 1984 (biweekly); Oct. 8-Oct. 29, 1984 (weekly) (P) (Vol. 17, Nos. 23-25; Vol. 18, Nos. 1-20; Vol. 18, Nos. 21-24) [Nov. 7, 1983 and Mar. 26 and July 2, 1984 issues are published in 2 sections].

STATISTICAL FEATURES:

C5150–5.501: Nov. 7, 1983 (Vol. 17, No. 23)

GOING AFTER BUSINESS: MARKETING YOUR BAR OPERATIONS, ANNUAL FEATURE

(Insert, p. 5-14) Annual article reporting on trends in restaurant alcoholic beverage sales. Data are from a 1983 NRN survey of alcoholic beverage operations. Includes 5 charts showing sales share, with comparison to 1982; change in sales from 2 years ago; profitability ratings; and average price per serving; all by type of beverage. Most data are shown separately for independent, chain, and all operations.

Article is included in "Bar Management" insert section of issue.

C5150–5.502: Jan. 2, 1984 (Vol. 18, No. 1)

NRN FOCUS: FORECAST '84, ANNUAL FEATURE

Annual feature forecasting food service industry sales and market developments for 1984. Includes the following statistical features:

LATE '83 REBOUND TO CONTINUE?

(p. 61, 64) Article, with 1 chart showing sales for total food service industry, and for commercial and limited menu (fast food) establishments, 1982-84. Data are from the National Restaurant Assn.

MONTHLY STORE SALES OF MAJOR CHAINS

(p. 64) Table showing percent change in store sales, menu prices, and real sales, for 17 major food service chains, generally Oct. 1982-83 period. Data are from *Restaurant Trends.*

Includes accompanying article (p. 5, 64).

C5150–5.503: Jan. 16, 1984 (Vol. 18, No. 2)

HOSPITALITY SEEN GROWING IN '84

(p. 24) Article, with 1 table forecasting median salary range for restaurant/food service and lodging industry executives, by position, 1984. Data are from Roth Young Personnel Service, Inc. *1984 U.S. Salary Outlook Survey.*

C5150–5.504: Jan. 30, 1984 (Vol. 18, No. 3)

RESTAURANT COMPANIES SCRAMBLING TO GO PUBLIC

(p. 11) By Rick Telberg. Article, with 1 table showing the following for food service companies making initial public stock offering (IPO)

in 1983: headquarters location, type of food service, number of stores at time of IPO, revenues for FY prior to IPO, date of IPO and amount raised, and percent change in per share price since IPO.

Data are from *Nation's Restaurant News, Going Public* magazine, and company reports.

C5150–5.505: Feb. 13, 1984 (Vol. 18, No. 4)

PUBLIC CONCERN SPURS DECLINE IN LIQUOR SALES

(p. 1, 27) Article on restaurant/bar operators' reactions to strengthened drunk driving laws, including perceived effect on liquor sales. Data are from responses of 60 chain and 40 independent restaurant/bar operations to a survey conducted by Lebhar-Friedman Research. Includes text data and 1 chart.

C5150–5.506: Mar. 12, 1984 (Vol. 18, No. 6)

[Issue cover incorrectly reads Vol. 18, No. 5.]

INDEPENDENTS FIGHT SEAFOOD SHORTAGES

(p. 5, 245) By Charles Forman. Article, with 1 table showing per capita consumption of 3 types of seafood, selected years 1960-82; and consumption share for fresh seafood, 1980-82. Data are from the Commerce Dept and National Fisheries Institute.

INDUSTRY PACs STOCKPILING '84 ELECTION FUNDS

(p. 17-18) Article, with 1 table showing the following for 26 political action committees (PACs) sponsored by food service companies or related assns, 1983: collections for 1984 campaign, funds remaining from 1982 elections, administrative costs, and contributions to Federal and State candidates and other industry PACs.

Data are from reports filed with the Federal Election Commission.

U.S. FOOD SERVICE SALES TRIPLE BETWEEN '72-'82

(p. 22) Article, with 1 table showing sales, employment, and average hourly earnings, for eating/drinking places, various years 1972-84. Data are from Federal Government sources.

NRN FOCUS: 2nd TIER CHAINS

(p. 113-153) Compilation of articles on sales and marketing strategies of regional restaurant chains. Data are from NRN research. Includes 1 table, repeated for 16 chains, and generally showing the following: sales or revenues, profit or loss, number of units, average check size, and menu price percent change, various periods 1980-84.

PER CAPITA CONSUMPTION OF MEAT PRODUCTS

(p. 162) Table showing per capita consumption for red meat by type and for poultry, 1976-83. Data are from USDA. Table is accompanied by 2 related articles.

ALCOHOLIC BEVERAGE INDUSTRY GROWTH STYMIED

(p. 225, 228) Article, with 2 tables showing shipment value, price index, and share of alcohol market, for malt beverages, wine/brandy, and distilled spirits, various years 1972-84.

C5150-5.507: Mar. 26, 1984 (Vol. 18, No 7)

FRANCHISING IN THE 80's, PART 1

(p. 36-39) First of 2 features on franchise restaurant companies, establishments, and finances. Data are from Commerce Dept's *Franchising in the Economy, 1982-84.*

Includes 3 tables showing company-owned and franchisee-owned restaurant sales and units, 1969-84; and number of restaurant franchise companies and company-owned and franchisee-owned units, by type of food served, various years 1982-84.

CONCERN MOUNTS OVER DRUNK-DRIVING LIABILITY

(Insert, p. 4-12) Article discussing effect of anti-drunk driving campaign on restaurants. Data are from an NRN survey of restaurant/bar operators.

Includes 3 charts and 1 table showing percent of operators reporting liquor sales decrease and liability insurance rate change due to campaign; and operators' views on restricting liquor advertising and on restaurant industry role in drunk-driving issue. No data date is given.

Article is included in "Bar Management" insert section of issue.

DETERMINING ACCOUNTABILITY UNDER DRAM SHOP LAWS

(Insert, p. 15-18) Article, with 1 undated list presenting minimum drinking age and characteristics of statutes related to drunken driving, including blood alcohol content level used to determine intoxication, by State. Data are from National Alcoholic Beverage Control Assn, Inc., and property/casualty insurance industry.

Article is included in "Bar Management" insert section of issue.

C5150-5.508: Apr. 9, 1984 (Vol. 18, No. 8)

CHAINS ESCALATE TV AD SPENDING 24% IN 1983

(p. 11) Article, with 1 table showing network and local TV advertising expenditures, for top 15 restaurant chains ranked by total TV advertising expenditures, 1983 with comparison to 1982. Data are from TV Bureau of Advertising, based on Broadcast Advertisers Reports.

FRANCHISING IN THE 80's: PART 2

(p. 27-28) Second of 2 features on franchise restaurant companies, establishments, and finances. Data are from Commerce Dept's *Franchising in the Economy, 1982-84.*

Includes 2 tables showing company-owned and franchisee-owned restaurants, by State, 1982; and number of restaurant franchise companies 1983, and sales for company-owned and franchisee-owned restaurants 1983-84, by type of food served.

NRN FOCUS: ENERGY COST CONTROLS

(p. 41-43) By Rick Telberg. Article reporting on restaurant energy costs and conservation measures. Data were compiled by Charles Claar of Pennsylvania State University. Includes 1 chart showing distribution of restaurant energy dollar, by energy end use, 1984.

C5150-5.509: Apr. 23, 1984 (Vol. 18, No. 9)

NRN FOCUS: WINE AND SPIRITS

Compilation of articles on restaurant alcoholic beverage merchandising practices. Data are from industry sources. Includes the following statistical features:

DRINK MERCHANDISING FOR PROFITS

(p. 47, 53) By Charles Forman. Article, with 4 charts showing liquor consumption and sales, various years 1980-83; distribution of wine consumption, by type of wine, selected years 1972-82; and distribution of beer consumption by whether on- or off-premises (no date).

BEER, WINE, AND DISTILLED SPIRITS REGULATIONS

(p. 77) Chart showing minimum legal drinking age by State and type of alcoholic beverage (no date).

C5150-5.510: May 21, 1984 (Vol. 18, No. 11)

DOMESTIC LODGING REPORTS FIRST YEAR-TO-YEAR RISE SINCE 1979

(p. 22) Article, with 1 table showing hotel occupancy rates in 28 cities or areas, 1983 with change from 1982. Data are from Laventhol and Horwath.

C5150-5.511: July 2, 1984 (Vol. 18, No. 14)

PANELISTS PUSH ALL-SUITES VIABILITY

(p. 3, 65) By Susan Spedalle. Article reporting on hotels that offer suite accommodations only. Data are from NRN Research and 6th Annual National Hospitality Industry Investment Conference. Includes 1 table showing the following for 4 all-suite hotel chains: number of hotels operating, under construction, and planned by year end; turnkey cost per room; average occupancy and room rate; and whether franchised; as of mid-1984.

MULTIUNIT TRENDS: ANALYZING INDUSTRY TRENDS BRINGS ANSWERS

(p. 11) First in a series of articles on recent developments in restaurant chain operations. Data are based on responses to monthly Restaurant Trends questionnaires distributed to a stratified sample of units in major restaurant chains.

Includes 2 tables showing average monthly percent change in prices and nominal sales relative to previous year, and in real sales relative to previous year and preceding 3-month period, for 18 restaurant chains and aggregate eating/drinking places and food stores, Feb.-Apr. 1984 period; and percent of stores participating in 39 cent hamburger promotion campaign of 2 fast food chains, with relative performance of participating vs. nonparticipating units, Jan.-Apr. 1984.

NEW TECHNOLOGIES GENERATE CONTINUING CHANGE

(Insert, p. 5-14) By Charles Forman. Article on computer use in the restaurant industry. Data are based on responses to an NRN survey of restaurant operators who use computers in their business. Includes 8 undated tables and 4 undated charts showing the following:

a. Type of computer system used (point of sale/electronic cash register (POS/ECR) or other); length of time establishments have been computerized, and mean number of months required to regain invest-

ment; factors affecting decision to acquire computer; reduction in selected operating costs due to computer use; and views on positive and negative aspects of computer usage; all by type of restaurant.

b. POS/ECR computer functions available and in use by operators; incidence of POS/ECR and other system interface; and use of non-POS/ECR systems for interunit communication.

Article is included in "Restaurant Technology" insert section of issue.

REGULATING THE USAGE OF MANPOWER

(Insert, p. 21, 24) By Charles Forman. Article on employee time accounting systems. Data are from American Payroll Assn. Includes 2 undated tables showing potential costs to employer for 5 minutes of lost work time, and for timecard auditing errors.

Article is included in "Restaurant Technology" insert section of issue.

C5150-5.512: July 16, 1984 (Vol. 18, No. 15)

MULTIUNIT TRENDS: WAR'S HELL, EXCEPT TO ACCOUNTANTS

(p. 12) By Charles Forman. Second in a series of articles on recent developments in restaurant chain operations. Data are based on responses to monthly Restaurant Trends questionnaires distributed to a stratified sample of units in major restaurant chains.

Includes 3 tables showing average monthly percent change in nominal and real sales and in prices, for 18 restaurant chains and aggregate eating/drinking places and food stores, with real sales detail by type of restaurant, various periods 1981-84; and menu price change activity of major chains, 1979-83.

NRN FOCUS: WAGE AND BENEFITS STUDY

(p. 49-61) Compilation of articles reporting on food service industry executive compensation. Data are based on telephone interviews with 120 executives of major chains and on company annual reports. Includes 6 tables showing the following:

a. Top 25 executives ranked by total compensation, with age, position and company, shares of company stock owned (total and as percent of outstanding shares), and value of various types of compensation received, FY83 or FY84.

b. Executive average annual salary and bonus, and percent of executives receiving annual bonuses, by position; and methods for calculating bonuses, and types of benefits provided; all by type of restaurant chain; (no dates).

C5150-5.513: July 30, 1984 (Vol. 18, No. 16)

MULTIUNIT TRENDS: BREAKFAST BECOMES A STRATEGIC MEAL

(p. 12) By Charles Forman. Third in a series of articles on recent developments in restaurant chain operations. Data are based on responses to monthly Restaurant Trends questionnaires distributed to a stratified sample of units in major restaurant chains.

Includes 4 tables showing restaurant breakfast sales as percent of total sales, and breakfast average check size, for the following: hamburger and coffee shop segments and all chains, by census region, Apr. 1983-Mar. 1984 period; and 3-4 major hamburger and coffee shop chains, quarterly 1983-1st quarter 1984.

C5150–5.514: Aug. 13, 1984 (Vol. 18, No. 17)

MULTIUNIT TRENDS: IN SEARCH OF THE GOLD McNUGGETS— SHREWD McD MARKETING PAYS OFF

(p. 18-20) By Charles Forman. Fourth in a series of articles on recent developments in restaurant chain operations. Data are based on responses to monthly Restaurant Trends questionnaires distributed to a stratified sample of units in major restaurant chains.

Includes 2 tables showing average monthly percent change in nominal and real sales and in prices, for 18 restaurant chains and aggregate eating/drinking places and food stores, with aggregate real sales detail by type of restaurant; and 3 tables on marketing trends for a major product of McDonald's restaurant chain; various periods 1981-84.

CHAIN ANALYSIS PART I: THE TOP 100, ANNUAL FEATURE

(p. 71-146) Annual report on financial and operating results of top 100 food service chains and top 100 chain companies ranked by estimated sales or revenue, primarily FY84. Data are from NRN Research, and are shown for fiscal years. Includes the following:

a. Narrative overview, with index of the top 100 chains; and summary of food service companies' diversification activities. (p. 71-76)

b. Top 100 chains ranked by estimated sales for current year, and including sales for 2 previous years, share of industry sales and number of new units for current year, total units for previous year, and type of chain and name of parent company. 1 table. (p. 78-79)

c. Top 100 chain companies ranked by estimated revenue for current year, and including revenue for 2 previous years, headquarters location, and types or names of chains owned. 1 table. (p. 80-81)

d. Chain profiles, grouped by industry segment, most with 1 table generally showing sales and/or revenues, profit, average store sales and check size, number of units, and menu price increase over previous year; various years FY82-85. (p. 84-146)

A highlights article, with 1 summary table, is also included (p. 5, 218).

C5150–5.515: Aug. 27, 1984 (Vol. 18, No. 18)

MULTIUNIT TRENDS: NEW PRODUCTS—WHY SOME SUCCEED, OTHERS FAIL

(p. 11) By Charles Forman. Fifth in a series of articles on recent developments in restaurant chain operations. Data are based on responses to monthly Restaurant Trends questionnaires distributed to a stratified sample of units in major restaurant chains.

Includes 4 tables showing price, and share of sales, for 1-4 products at 4 major restaurant chains, various quarters 1982-1st quarter 1984.

FOOD SERVICE POLITICAL ACTION COMMITTEES: CANDIDATES MAY NET $1M FROM INDUSTRY COFFERS

(p. 53-55) By Laura Woda. Article, with 2 tables showing the following for 16-28 political action committees (PACs) sponsored by food service companies or related trade assns, primarily 1984: number and value of contributions to Federal candidates, by party; and value of collections for 1984 campaign, funds remaining from 1982 election, contributions to State candidates and other industry PACs, and administrative costs.

Data are from reports filed with the Federal Election Commission.

CHAIN ANALYSIS PART II, ANNUAL FEATURE

(p. 63-79) Annual report on food service chain finances, customer characteristics, and menu items, 1984, with trends from 1979. Data are from NRN Research. Contains 14 tables showing the following:

a. CPI for food away from home, and WPI for food, monthly 1979-June 1984.

b. Burger and family restaurant/coffee shop chains: average check size, sales per unit, cost/sales ratios, profit margin, and menu price increase, 1981-84; food and labor cost increases, customer age and income distribution, and sales distribution by meal period, 1982-84; average weekly sales, items sold, and prices, by menu item, 1983-84; and cost distributions, for food, supplies, labor, and 7 other items, 1983-84.

C5150–5.516: Sept 10, 1984 (Vol. 18, No. 19)

MULTIUNIT TRENDS: TAKE-OUT FOODS SATISFY NEW, CHANGING LIFESTYLES

(p. 9-11) By Charles Forman. Sixth in a series of articles on recent developments in restaurant chain operations. Data are based on responses to monthly Restaurant Trends questionnaires distributed to a stratified sample of units in major restaurant chains.

Includes 4 tables showing restaurant takeout and drive-through business as percent of total sales, with detail by census region, for 6-7 chains; and average weekly phone orders, and monthly sales change, for a major pizza chain; various periods 1983-84.

NRN FOCUS: OVERSEAS INVESTMENTS FINALLY PAY OFF FOR SOME U.S. CHAINS, ANNUAL FEATURE

(p. 31, 37) By Joe Edwards. Annual article, with 1 table ranking 18 major restaurant chains by number of foreign units, with some detail by country, 1983. Data are from NRN Research.

C5150–5.517: Oct. 8, 1984 (Vol. 18, No. 21)

U.S. CHAINS: SUCCESS POSSIBLE, BUT ELUSIVE

(p. 203-204) By Elizabeth J. Block. Article, with 1 table showing top 20 food service companies operating in Japan ranked by FY83 sales, with number of units and type of operation. Data are from *Japan Economic Journal.*

C5150–5.518: Oct. 15, 1984 (Vol. 18, No. 22)

MORE JOBS SPURRED BY UNITS OPENING DURING RECESSION

(p. 16) Article, with 1 table showing number of restaurant establishments by employment size, 1980 and 1982. Data are from SBA.

C5150–5.519: Oct. 29, 1984 (Vol. 18, No. 24)

PILLSBURY, PEPSICO LEAD CONGLOMERATE SURGE

(p. 1, 76) By Charles Bernstein. Article, with 1 table showing pretax operating profit from restaurant operations for 4 major conglomerates, latest available fiscal period ending May-Sept. 1984, with change from same period of previous year.

C5150–6   NATIONAL HOME CENTER NEWS

Biweekly.   Approx. 40 p.
Oversized.
ISSN 0192-6772.
LC 79-6811.
SRI/MF/excerpts

Biweekly journal (monthly in Dec.) of the home center (retail building materials/hardware/home improvement) industry. Covers financial and marketing developments, merchandise line sales, store expansion, sales promotion, lumber and construction industry trends, and relevant legislation and government activities.

Data are from industry sources, including store chains and trade assns; private research firms; Federal sources; and the journal's own research.

Issues contain numerous news articles and regular depts, some with statistics; and the following regularly recurring statistics:

a. Recent advertised prices of selected brand-name products in various individual stores, and stock prices for leading chains.

b. Sales and earnings for 2-12 varying home center firms, for most recent 1- to 12-month period (specified for each firm) and same period of previous year.

c. Lumber report, generally including 1-2 charts showing 4-year quarterly price trends for total or selected types of lumber and plywood, through quarter of cover date, or previous quarter; 1 table showing futures trading activity; and occasional additional charts showing trends in lumber inventory and/or production.

d. "Home-Building Activity" feature with text data, 4 charts, and 1 table showing total and single family housing starts and permits for month 2 months prior to cover date and selected previous months, with detail by region.

e. "Existing Single Family Home Sales" feature with text data and 4 charts showing trends in existing single-family home sales, including median sale price by census region for month 2 months prior to cover date and 3 previous months.

Annual statistical features include an industry census, consumer home improvement survey, and brands report.

Most recurring features appear in at least 1 issue each month. Annual features and other articles with substantial statistical content are described, as they appear, under "Statistical Features." Nonstatistical features are not covered.

Availability: National Home Center News, Subscription Department, 99 Park Ave., New York NY 10157, qualified subscribers †, others $20.00 per yr., single copy $2.00; SRI/MF/excerpts for recurring sales/earnings table, lumber report, "Home Building Activity" feature, existing single family home sales feature, and all portions covered under "Statistical Features."

Issues reviewed during 1984: Oct. 24, 1983-Oct. 22, 1984 (P) (Vol. 9, Nos. 22-25; Vol. 10, Nos. 1-22) [Vol. 9, No. 22 incorrectly reads No. 21].

C5150–6.501: Jan. 2, 1984 (Vol. 10, No. 1)

NHCN's 1984 METRO MARKET OUTLOOK, ANNUAL FEATURE

(p. 27-42) Annual compilation of articles on housing construction and building materials/hardware sales trends in leading metro markets. Data are from *Sales and Marketing Management,* National Assn of Home Builders, and National Assn of Realtors.

Includes 1 table showing top 100 SMSAs ranked by retail building material/hardware sales, 1982; and profiles of 8 SMSAs, each with 3 tables showing summary demographics, total retail and building material/hardware sales, total and single-family housing starts, and median sales price of existing single-family homes, various periods 1977-1987.

DIY INDUSTRY TV SPENDING RISING AT 62% CLIP, QUARTERLY FEATURE

(p. 45) Quarterly article, with 1 table showing top 15 home center chains ranked by TV advertising expenditures, with detail for selected subsidiaries, 1st 9 months 1983, with comparison to 1st 9 months 1982. Data are from TV Bureau of Advertising analysis of Broadcast Advertisers Reports data.

C5150–6.502: Jan. 16, 1984 (Vol. 10, No. 2)

POLL: LUMBERYARDS ATTRACT MORE ENERGY PRODUCT BUYERS

(p. 3) Article, with 2 undated tables showing distribution of consumer planned and/or actual purchases of energy-related products, by product type and by retail outlet type or leading company. Data are based on 1,602 responses to a reader survey conducted by *New Shelter* magazine.

C5150–6.503: Jan. 30, 1984 (Vol. 10, No. 3)

NATIONAL SURVEY TRACKS RENT COSTS

(p. 43) Article, with 1 undated table showing top 32 metro areas ranked by median monthly rent for an 850 square foot apartment. Data are from a survey conducted by Institute of Real Estate Management. Full survey results are covered in SRI under A5600-1.

C5150–6.504: Feb. 13, 1984 (Vol. 10, No. 4)

HOME CONSTRUCTION TOPS $142B IN '83

(p. 1) Chart showing private housing starts, 1978-84. Data are from U.S. Dept of Commerce and National Assn of Home Builders. Corrected data appear in the Mar. 12, 1984 issue, for description see C5150-6.505, below.

SURGE OF FIRST-TIME HOME BUYERS CAPS BUILDING INDUSTRY RECOVERY

(p. 2, 4) Article, with 1 table showing States ranked by housing starts, 1983-84. Data are from National Assn of Home Builders.

C5150–6.505: Mar. 12, 1984 (Vol. 10, No. 6)

CLARIFICATION

(p. 12) Data correction for chart on private housing starts appearing in the Feb. 13, 1984 issue (for description, see C5150-6.504, above).

WHY HOME CONSTRUCTION IN THE 80s WILL FALL SHORT OF EXPECTATIONS

(p. 45-48) By Wyatt Kash. Article, with 2 charts showing distribution of new home construction by type of locale (SMSA central cities and suburbs, and non-SMSA areas); population and household growth rates by region; net housing loss; and total new home construction; various periods 1960-90. Data are from Census Bureau, and Joint Center for Urban Studies of Massachusetts Institute of Technology and Harvard University.

CHARCOAL BEST SELLING BUT GAS LEADS IN $ VALUE

(p. 66-68) Article, with 4 tables and 3 charts showing barbecue grill sales volume and value by type, and sales distribution by region and month; and gas grill volume distribution by price range, and sales distribution by retail outlet type and grill size; various years 1970-83. Data are from Barbecue Industry Assn, Census Bureau, and Arkla Industries.

UPSWING IN DIY SALES TO BOOST FUTURE ECONOMY

(p. 102-104) Article, with 1 chart showing growth rate for per capita retail sales, by census division, 1983-88 period. Data are from Management Horizons, Inc.

C5150–6.506: Mar. 26, 1984 (Vol. 10, No. 7)

PROFITABLE YEAR FOR DIY CHAINS SPURS SHUFFLING IN TOP 10 RANKING

(p. 1-2, 90) By Greg Puchalski. Article, with 1 table showing top 10 home center chains ranked by do-it-yourself (DIY) sales, 1983 with comparison to 1982. Also includes number of stores and total sales, 1983. Data are from *National Home Center News* and company reports.

PAYLESS PACES DIY CHAINS IN '83 TV AD EXPENDITURES, QUARTERLY FEATURE

(p. 3, 90) Quarterly article, with 1 table showing top 15 home center chains ranked by TV advertising expenditures, 1983 with comparison to 1982. Data are from TV Bureau of Advertising analysis of Broadcast Advertisers Reports data.

INDUSTRY PACs MAP STRATEGY FOR '84 ELECTION

(p. 12) Article, with 1 table showing the following for 10 political action committees (PACs) sponsored by home center industry corporations or housing-related trade assns: collections, contributions to Federal and State candidates and other PACs, and administrative costs, primarily 1983; funds remaining from 1982 election; and funds available for 1984 campaign.

Data are from reports filed with the Federal Election Commission.

AGGRESSIVE TRADE PAC's COFFERS FULL FOR '84

(p. 19) Article, with 1 table showing number and value of political campaign contributions by party, for 9 political action committees sponsored by home center industry corporations or housing-related trade assns, primarily 1983.

STUDY: RETAIL ADHESIVE SALES OUTPACED INDUSTRY

(p. 35) Article, with 1 table showing sales volume of adhesives and sealants for home and auto use, with detail by adhesive type, selected years 1967-95. Data are from Predicasts, Inc.

U.S. EXISTING HOME SALES LEAP 37.2% IN '83

(p. 72-74) Article, with 2 tables showing existing home sales volume by State, and median prices for single-family existing homes in 30 SMSAs, various periods 1980-83. Data are from National Assn of Realtors.

MORE AMERICANS CAN AFFORD TO PURCHASE HOUSING AS INCOME QUALIFICATIONS DROP

(p. 74) Article, with 1 table presenting data on housing market conditions, including housing starts, interest rates, median single-family home prices and price index, and per capita disposable income, 1978-83. Data are from various Federal sources.

C5150–6.507: May 7, 1984 (Vol. 10, No. 10)

TOP 100's TOTAL SALES EXCEED $14.6 BILLION

(p. 1, 4) By Wyatt Kash. Article on performance of top 100 home improvement retail chains, with comparative data for the entire industry, 1983. Data are from Commerce Dept. Includes 1 chart and 1 table showing home improvement industry retail sales, by census region, 1978-83; and consumer spending for residential maintenance/repair and improvement, by type, 1981-83.

NHCN ANNUAL REPORT ON THE HOME CENTER INDUSTRY, ANNUAL FEATURE

(p. 1, 33-98) Annual compilation of articles on home center industry, including sales trends, stores, company rankings, operating and marketing developments, and employee compensation, 1983. Data sources include company reports, industry assns, journal's own research, and Commerce Dept.

Includes 3 charts and 22 tables showing the following:

a. Summary retail sales trends, 1975-85; and number of warehouse stores, by chain, 1983-84. 2 charts. (p. 33, 35)

b. Company rankings: top 100 companies ranked by do-it-yourself (DIY) and total sales, with number of stores (including forecast for 1984) and/or selling area; and top 25 companies ranked by DIY and total sales growth, total and new stores, DIY sales per store, and selling area; 1983 with selected comparisons to 1982. 10 tables. (p. 43-48, 57-71)

c. Product marketing: average sales per square foot, share of total sales, floor space allotment, gross margin, sales-to-inventory ratio, and gross margin return on investment, for 9 product lines, 1983. 9 tables. (p. 73-88)

d. Buying cooperatives: top 18 hardware/lumber/building material cooperatives ranked by sales, and including dealer stores and home centers, employment, warehouses, inventory value and volume, and employment; and top 7 wholesaler cooperatives ranked by sales, and including warehouses, inventory volume and value, employment, advertising expenditures, and number of wholesalers, affiliated dealers, and customers; 1983 with comparisons to 1982. 2 tables. (p. 91-92) *e.* Employee compensation: home center employee average salary, percent of home center companies awarding bonuses, average bonus, and percent of employees receiving bonuses over $10,000, all by position, 1984. 1 chart and 1 table. (p. 97-98)

This is the 10th annual report. Corrected data appear in the June 4, 1984 issue; for description see C5150-6.508, below.

C5150–6.508: June 4, 1984 (Vol. 10, No. 12)

CORRECTIONS

(p. 4) Includes data corrections for annual feature on the home center industry (for description, see C5150-6.507, above). Corrections cover buying cooperatives' sales.

C5150–6.509: July 16, 1984 (Vol. 10, No. 15)

NHCN's 1984 CONSUMER ATTITUDE SURVEY: THE ANATOMY OF CONSUMER BUYING DECISIONS, ANNUAL FEATURE

(p. 1, 17-69) Annual compilation of articles on consumer home improvement activity, spending, and plans, 1984 with selected comparisons to 1983.

Includes data on planned purchases, projects, and expenditures; and factors affecting buying decisions, including importance of brand label and store, outlet preferences, and selected product characteristics; all by type of product.

Also includes views on retail store advertisements and price variations, and customer demographic characteristics, by outlet type; popularity of various types of projects; incidence of do-it-yourself vs. contracted projects; and percent of projects completed by women.

Data are based on an Apr.-May 1984 telephone survey of approximately 2,000 households, conducted by Leo J. Shapiro and Associates; and a recent NHCN study of the Phoenix market.

Includes 15 charts and 38 tables.

TOP TV ADVERTISING BUYERS SPEND $4.9M IN FIRST QTR., QUARTERLY FEATURE

(p. 3, 81) Quarterly article, with 1 table showing top 15 home center chains ranked by TV advertising expenditures, with detail for selected subsidiaries, 1st quarter 1984, with comparison to 1st quarter 1983. Data are from TV Bureau of Advertising analysis of Broadcast Advertisers Reports data.

C5150–6.510: Aug. 13, 1984 (Vol. 10, No. 17)

RETAILERS OPT FOR ALTERED EUROPEAN CABINET LOOK

(p. 56, 160) Article, with 1 table showing kitchen cabinet production distribution by type of material, for new construction and repair/remodeling markets, 1979 and 1984. Data are from National Kitchen Cabinet Assn.

HOME CENTERS LEAD OTHER TYPES OF CHAINS IN COMPUTERIZED RECEIVE-SHIPPING

(p. 146) Article, with 1 undated chart showing percent of large retail chains using computers for 5 distribution center functions, by type of chain. Data are based on responses from 30 of the top 100 chains in 6 retail categories, to a survey conducted by Lebhar-Friedman Research for *Chain Store Age, Executive.*

For description of complete survey results, see C5150-4.508, above.

C5150–6.511: Oct. 8, 1984 (Vol. 10, No. 21)

1984 NHCN BRANDS REPORT, ANNUAL FEATURE

(p. 19-67) Annual compilation of articles on retailer preferences and marketing patterns regarding national brand and private label products in the home center industry. Data are from 291 responses to a 1984 survey of home center chains operating 1,342 stores, and a consumer survey, both conducted by Leo J. Shapiro and Associates. Includes 6 charts and 44 tables showing responses concerning the following:

a. Home center stores carrying more national brands than during 1983; brand importance as rated by retailers and consumers, and retailer opinion on number of brands that should be carried; incidence of retailer emphasis on decorative products, with detail for large home centers and home centers in large metro areas; and planned changes in space allocations, with detail by store size; all with detail by product category. (p. 19-20)

b. Private label use by region, metro-nonmetro location, company sales size, and store size; private label product pricing, and importance of private labels, by product category; and product categories cited as traffic and profit catalysts. (p. 22-24)

c. Brands cited as best-selling by retailers, with detail by company sales size and store size, repeated for 17 product categories. (p. 29-67)

This is the 2nd annual feature.

C5150–6.512: Oct. 22, 1984 (Vol. 10, No. 22)

EIGHTEEN CHAINS TOP $300,000 IN HALF-YEAR ADVERTISING FIGURES, QUARTERLY FEATURE

(p. 3, 43) Quarterly article, with 1 table showing top 18 home center chains ranked by TV advertising expenditures, with detail for selected subsidiaries, 1st half 1984, with comparison to 1st half 1983. Data are from TV Bureau of Advertising analysis of Broadcast Advertisers Reports data.

RESIDENTIAL CONSTRUCTION SPURS HOME EXPANSION

(p. 52-54) Article, with 5 tables showing total and single-family building permits issued, by census region and State, with selected rankings, 1st half 1983-84. Data are from Census Bureau.

C5150–7   CHAIN STORE AGE, GENERAL MERCHANDISE EDITION

Monthly. Approx. 100 p.
ISSN 0193-1350.
LC SN 79-4345.
SRI/MF/excerpts, shipped quarterly

Monthly trade journal of the general merchandise retail chain industry. Chain types covered include general merchandise discount, department, variety, and catalogue stores; and apparel and other specialty stores. Includes reporting on

finances and operations, merchandise lines, consumer trends, management development, and new products.

Most data are from industry sources and the journal's own research.

Issues contain news and feature articles, some with statistics; and regular departmental features, including "Financial News" section, with the following recurring tables:

a. Retail chain sales: monthly table showing sales for approximately 25 general merchandise chains, for month 2 months prior to cover date, cumulative year to date, and same periods of previous year; and number of stores in each chain, for current and previous year.

b. Retail chain earnings: quarterly table showing earnings or loss for approximately 25 general merchandise and specialty chains, generally for quarter ending 4-5 months prior to cover date, cumulative year to date, and same periods of previous year.

Journal also includes annual features on financial performance of leading retail chains, consumer buying intentions, and departmental sales and productivity.

Monthly table appears in all issues. All additional features with substantial statistical content are described, as they appear, under "Statistical Features;" page locations and latest period of coverage for quarterly table are also noted. Non-statistical features are not covered.

Prior to Nov. 1983, selected issues were published in 2 sections. Second section, covering apparel merchandising, is now issued as a separate publication (for description, see C5150-8 below).

Availability: Chain Store Age, General Merchandise Edition, Subscription Department, 99 Park Ave., New York NY 10157, retailers $12.00 per yr., others $20.00 per yr., single copy $2.00; SRI/MF/excerpts for monthly table, and for all portions covered under "Statistical Features;" shipped quarterly.

Issues reviewed during 1984: Nov. 1983-Oct. 1984 (P) (Vol. 59, Nos. 11-12; Vol. 60, Nos. 1-10).

STATISTICAL FEATURES:

C5150–7.501: Nov. 1983 (Vol. 59, No. 11)

NARROWING THE GENDER GAP

(p. 34-36) Article on women in the retail industry. Data are from BLS. Includes 1 chart showing women working in retailing, and total working women with distribution by major occupational group, Aug. 1983.

DEPARTMENT STORES BOAST STRONG INCREASES

(p. 67-72) Article, with 2 charts showing retail inventory turns of domestic products by type, 1982-83; and distribution of promotion frequency for total, department, discount, and variety stores (no date). Data are based on responses of 75 retailers to a 1983 survey conducted by Lebhar-Friedman Research.

SALES STAGE SET FOR RECORD COMEBACK

(p. 80, 84) Article, with 1 chart showing record/tape sales, 1978-84. Data are from Recording Industry Assn.

C5150–7.502: Dec. 1983 (Vol. 59, No. 12)

CONSUMER BUYING INTENTIONS STUDY, ANNUAL FEATURE

(p. 11-84) Annual survey report on consumer buying practices. Covers 1983 purchases and/or 1984 buying intentions by detailed product category, with cross-tabulations by type of outlet and census division, and selected comparison to previous surveys.

Also includes types of outlets preferred, and reasons; prevalence of outlet and brand preference by product category; and price expectations and additional market analyses for individual product categories, including data by selected consumer sociodemographic characterisitics.

Data by type of outlet also are shown for 4 individual major chains.

Data are from a 1983 survey of approximately 8,500 households conducted for *Chain Store Age* by Leo Shapiro and Associates.

Contains article profiling 3 consumer types, with 1 table (p. 11-14); market overview, with 13 tables (p. 19-27); and reports on 10 product categories, with 14 charts and 20 tables (p. 29-84).

This is the 3rd annual survey.

C5150–7.503: Jan. 1984 (Vol. 60, No. 1)

QUARTERLY TABLE

(p. 96) Retail chain earnings, 3rd quarter 1983.

OUTLOOK '84: SPREADING THE WEALTH IN '84, ANNUAL FEATURE

(p. 25) Annual article analyzing outlook for consumer retail spending. Data are from *Levine Reports*. Includes 1 table showing sales change from previous year for 14 product categories, 1982-84.

BUYERS LAUD SUPERIORS, CRITICIZE FIELD PERSONNEL

(p. 27-30) Article on retail store merchandise buyers' views concerning company policies and own job. Data are based on responses from 122 buyers for 15 product lines and 6 types of stores to a *Chain Store Age* survey.

Includes 1 chart showing selected characteristics of the average buyer, and 1 chart and 5 tables showing the following, generally for department and discount store buyers and hard line and soft line product buyers: likes, dislikes, and perceptions about own job; major responsibilities; percent receiving training, and ratings of program; and base salary distribution, and mean salary.

RISKY BUSINESS: IN SEARCH OF THE OLYMPIC DOLLAR

(p. 39-43) Article reporting on outlook for sales of 1984 Summer Olympics merchandise. Data are from an Aug. 1983 *Chain Store Age/Better Homes and Gardens* consumer survey.

Includes 1 chart showing percent of consumers interested in purchasing selected Olympic-related products.

CONSUMER ELECTRONICS

Compilation of articles reporting on consumer electronics market. Includes the statistical articles described below, with data from surveys conducted for *Chain Store Age* by Leo Shapiro and Associates, unless otherwise noted.

RETAILERS BRACE FOR DYNAMITE YEAR

(p. 55) Article, with 1 undated table showing outlet preference of consumers with family income over $35,000 for purchases of home computers and software and all consumer electronics. Data are from a *Chain Store Age/Better Homes and Gardens* survey.

CONSUMERS RATE SHOPPING ABILITIES

(p. 58) Article, with 1 undated table showing consumer ratings of own shopping ability for purchases of color TV and stereo equipment.

SMART TV SHOPPERS LOOK TO QUALITY

(p. 58-59) Article, with 3 undated tables showing consumers' color TV purchase factors, and outlet and brand preferences.

DEMAND FOR HIGH-END CAR AUDIO COMING IN LOUD AND CLEAR

(p. 78) Article, with 1 table showing consumer purchase price expectations for car stereo equipment, 1983-84.

Other Article

SPORTING GOODS/HEALTH CARE

(p. 83-87) Article reporting on market for physical fitness equipment and health care products. Data are from a *Chain Store Age/ Better Homes and Gardens* survey.

Includes 2 undated tables showing percent of consumers owning and interested in purchasing health care products and fitness equipment, by presence of children in household; and consumer age and income profile; all by type of product or equipment.

C5150–7.504: Feb. 1984 (Vol. 60, No. 2)

MARKET STABILIZING FOR HOME COMPUTERS

(p. 14) Article, with 1 table showing microcomputer hardware and software retail sales, for home use, 1982-86. Data are from Future Computing, Inc.

SHOPKO: SERVING MIDDLE AMERICA

(p. 34-36) Article on ShopKo discount chain store operations. Includes 1 table showing sales and operating income per gross square foot for ShopKo and 5 other discount chains, 1982, with percent change from 1978. Data are from *Chain Store Age*.

SHOULD GMers DO BUSINESS WITH BUSINESS?

(p. 59-63) Article on general merchandise store involvement in business-oriented microcomputer merchandising. Data are from Future Computing, Inc. Includes 2 charts showing microcomputer software total sales, with distribution by type of outlet, and revenues from microcomputer sales (excluding those for home use) by outlet type; 1983 and 1988.

CONSUMERS LIMIT TOY BUDGETS

(p. 83-84) Article on toy purchasing practices. Data are from a *Chain Store Age/Better Homes and Gardens* survey. Includes 3 charts and 1 table showing distribution of respondents by outlet choice by household size, and by current and planned spending levels; and factors influencing outlet choice for all respondents and for households with children.

REAPING THE REWARDS

(p. 99-118) Compilation of articles on sales and marketing of greeting cards, stationery products, and school and home office supplies. Articles also appear in *Drug Store News,* and are described above under C5150-2.507

REPLACEMENT BIZ SWEEPS VACUUM CLEANER SALES

(p. 135) Article on vacuum cleaner market. Data are from a *Chain Store Age/* Leo Shapiro and Associates consumer survey. Includes 1 chart showing percent of respondents choosing store brand or nationally advertised brand, or with no brand preference.

C5150–7.505: Mar. 1984 (Vol. 60, No. 3)

BIG CITY STATS IN SMALL TOWN FLATS

(p. 31) Article reporting on discount stores that operate in nonmetropolitan areas. Data are from Lehman Brothers Kuhn Loeb and *Chain Store Age*. Includes 1 table showing growth in sales and profit, 1978-82 period; and return on assets and on investment, 1980-82 period; for 5 chains with nonmetro stores and aggregate for all publicly held retailers.

SPENDING 'HIGH' FOR FANS COOLS OFF

(p. 45) Article, with 1 chart showing consumers' outlet choices for purchases of electric fans. Data are from a 1983 survey by Leo Shapiro and Associates and *Chain Store Age*.

LICENSING BY THE NUMBERS

(p. 49) Brief article, with 1 table showing distribution of licensed product sales, by product category, 1982-83. Data are from *The Licensing Letter*.

WHO WILL ATTRACT NEW HOME SEWERS?

(p. 51, 54) Article, with 1 chart showing age distribution of home sewers intending to purchase clothing patterns, 1983-84. Data are from a 1983 survey by Leo Shapiro and Associates and *Chain Store Age*.

HEALTHY OUTLOOK FOR MOISTURIZERS

(p. 61-62) Article, with 1 chart and 1 table showing consumers' outlet choices and spending expectations for facial moisturizers. Data are from a 1983 survey by Leo Shapiro and Associates and *Chain Store Age*.

WOMEN MAKE STRIDES IN RETAILING

(p. 74) Article, with 1 table showing total and female executives in 3 key positions, aggregated for 56 unnamed department stores, 1973 and 1983. Data are from a 1983 study by Thorndike Deland Associates.

C5150–7.506: Apr. 1984 (Vol. 60, No. 4)

GOURMET LIFESTYLE HAS SALES COOKING

(p. 55-62) Article reporting on gourmet cookware market. Data are from a Feb. 1984 *Chain Store Age/* Leo Shapiro and Associates consumer survey. Includes 3 charts and 2 tables showing extent of interest in purchasing gourmet cookware by age and income, and for buyers of gourmet food; cookware material preferences; price awareness; brand name familiarity; and outlet choice for gourmet cookware purchase.

CUTLERY EDGES OUT GOURMET MACHINES

(p. 65) Article reporting on consumer interest in buying selected housewares. Data are from a Feb. 1984 *Chain Store Age/* Leo Shapiro and Associates survey. Includes 1 chart showing percent of respondents familiar with selected brands of cutlery.

OLD RELIABLES SCORE STRONG SALES

(p. 84) Article on licensed character products. Data are from a 1983 *Chain Store Age/Better*

Homes and Gardens consumer survey. Includes 1 table showing consumer familiarity with 15 characters.

BRIGHT PROFITS FOR PRICEY FLASHLIGHTS

(p. 92) Article, with 1 table showing flashlight sales, by product price category (premium, medium, low-end), 1982-85. Data are from RAYOVAC, Inc.

PHOTO/CAMERA

(p. 95-100) Compilation of articles, with 4 undated tables showing sales distribution for camera lenses by type and for camera cases and disc cameras by brand; and stock turns and gross margins for 5 categories of photography equipment; all by retail outlet type. Data are from a *Chain Store Age*/Lebhar-Friedman survey of photo/camera buyers from department, discount, and variety stores.

SOFT GOODS INCREASES SALES PERCENTAGE

(p. 120) Article, with 1 table showing LIFO (last-in first-out) department store inventory index and percent change adjusted for inflation, by merchandise category, Jan. 1983-84. Data are from BLS.

C5150–7.507: May 1984 (Vol. 60, No. 5)

QUARTERLY TABLE

(p. 80) Retail chain earnings, 4th quarter 1983.

C5150–7.508: June 1984 (Vol. 60, No. 6)

OFF-PRICERS LEAD WAY IN TV ADS

(p. 16) Brief article, with 1 table showing top 15 off-price retail chains ranked by TV advertising expenditures, 1983 with comparison to 1982. Data are from TV Bureau of Advertising, based on Broadcast Advertisers Reports.

STATE OF THE INDUSTRY, ANNUAL FEATURE

(p. 35-49) Annual compilation of articles on financial performance of leading retail chains, 1983. Data are from *Chain Store Age* and company reports. Includes 2 charts and 6 tables showing the following:

a. Change in earnings and sales, aggregated for top 15 retail chains, 1978-83; and sales and earnings of top 15 retail chains, and sales and number of stores for top 20 specialty chains, 1982-83, ranked by 1983 sales.

b. Discount vs. department store chains: sales and operating income percent change and value per square foot, average sales per store, and selected profitability ratios, 1983; and compound sales and operating income percent change, 1978-83 period; all for 24 major chains.

c. Sales and number of stores, 1982-83, for top 100 retail chains ranked by 1983 sales (with detail for subsidiaries); and aggregate sales distribution by type of outlet, 1983.

CSA OUTLOOK, ANNUAL FEATURE

(p. 51-98) Annual compilation of articles analyzing financial performance of 30 leading retail chain stores. Data are from *Chain Store Age*. Each article covers an individual chain and includes 1 table showing sales, profits, and number of stores, 1979-83.

AUTO DEALERS LEAD CAR STEREO SALES

(p. 107, 110) Article, with 1 undated chart showing factors influencing consumer choice of car stereo·brand. Data are from Venture Development Corp.

CASSETTES OUTPLAY RECORD SALES

(p. 114) Article, with 1 chart showing market share for albums, cassettes, 8-track tapes, single records, and compact discs, 1982-83. Data are from Recording Industry Assn of America.

CALCULATORS ADD UP AND DIVIDE MARKET

(p. 129) Article, with 1 chart showing sales for programmable and nonprogrammable calculators, 1982-84. Data are from Aurora Impex Corp.

C5150–7.509: July 1984 (Vol. 60, No. 7)

QUARTERLY TABLE

(p. 98) Retail chain earnings, 1st quarter 1984.

GMMs: WELL-PAID, OPTIMISTIC, OVERWORKED

(p. 20-33) Article on chain store general merchandise managers' views concerning company policies and own job. Data are based on responses from 120 managers of 5 types of chains to a *Chain Store Age* survey.

Includes 6 tables showing the following, generally by type of chain: selected characteristics of the average manager; major responsibilities; attitudes about retail business; salary distribution, and mean salary; ratings of own company on selected measures; and desire for greater training in selected skills for managers and buyers.

CONSUMERS CITE LACK OF RESPONSIVENESS

(p. 39-40) Article, with 1 table ranking 6 consumer goods industries by shoppers' ratings on responsiveness to consumer needs, 1983, with comparisons to 1974 and 1979. Data are based on a 1983 survey of 1,940 households conducted by the Home Testing Institute for the National Housewares Manufacturers Assn, and on previous surveys.

IMPORTANCE OF PRICE SEEN LEVELING OFF

(p. 40-41) Article, with 1 chart and 1 table showing the following for 6 categories of housewares: sales share by type of outlet; and percent of all and single consumers citing price as most important factor in purchase decision; primarily 1979 and 1983. Data are from *Chain Store Age* and National Housewares Manufacturers Assn.

MARKETPOWER, ANNUAL FEATURE

(p. 41-86) Annual compilation of articles on space allocation and operating performance for store merchandise depts, 1983. Data are based on *Chain Store Age* research.

Includes the following data:

a. Top 20 merchandise depts ranked by sales, 1983, with comparison to 1982. 1 table.

b. Market share, sales per square foot, annual turnover, and gross margin, all by type of outlet, 1983, for the following depts: accessories; automotive; hardware; domestics; footwear; home computers; stationery; children's/infants', women's, and men's wear; cosmetics/health and beauty aids; sewing; hosiery; sporting goods; consumer electronics; toys; photo/camera; hobby/crafts; nonelectric and electric housewares; and lawn/garden. 1 chart and 1 table repeated for each dept.

C5150–7.510: Aug. 1984 (Vol. 60, No. 8)

CONSUMER BUYING INTENTIONS STUDY, ANNUAL FEATURE

(p. 17-94) Annual survey report on consumer buying practices. Covers 1984 purchases and 1985 buying intentions by detailed product category, with cross-tabulations by type of outlet, and selected comparisons to previous surveys.

Also includes data on shopping frequency and habits; outlet preferences by reason; prevalence of outlet and brand preference by product category; and price expectations and additional market analyses for individual product categories, including data by selected consumer sociodemographic characteristics.

Data by type of outlet also are shown for 4 individual major chains.

Data are from a 1984 survey of over 8,500 households conducted for *Chain Store Age* by Leo Shapiro and Associates, and a 1984 *Chain Store Age/Better Homes and Gardens* survey of 422 families.

Contains market overview, with 5 charts and 3 tables (p. 17-25); and reports on 13 product categories, with 14 charts and 37 tables (p. 29-94).

This is the 4th annual survey.

For description of previous article, for 1983, see C5150-7.502, above.

C5150–7.511: Sept. 1984 (Vol. 60, No. 9)

IS REAGAN GOOD FOR RETAILING?

(p. 23-25) Article reporting on retail executives' opinions of Reagan Administration economic policies. Data are from *Chain Store Age* interviews with retail/trade assn executives and survey responses of 75 chief executive officers (CEOs) of general merchandise chains.

Includes 2 charts showing retailer ratings for Reagan Administration's handling of selected economic issues; and views of CEOs on whether retail industry and own company are in better, worse, or same position compared to time of Reagan's election in 1980.

Data corrections appear in the Oct. 1984 issue (see C5150-7.512 below)

CANADIAN CONSUMERS GIVE RETAILERS THE COLD SHOULDER

(p. 30-37) Article, with 1 table showing top 10 retail chains in Canada ranked by sales (in Canadian dollars), 1982-83. Data are from Clayton Research Associates Ltd. and *Chain Store Age*.

CONSUMER IGNORANCE TRIMS TRUE TRADEUP

(p. 117-118) Article on consumer preferences regarding fabric content of bed linens. Data are based on responses to a *Chain Store Age*/Leo Shapiro and Associates survey. Includes 1 undated chart.

BINOCULAR SALES LOOKING UP: 9% BOOST EXPECTED

(p. 121) Article, with 1 undated chart showing consumer use of binoculars, distributed by purpose. Data are from *Chain Store Age* and Bushnell Co.

C5150–7.512: Oct. 1984 (Vol. 60, No. 10)

QUARTERLY TABLE

(p. 96) Retail chain earnings, 2nd quarter 1984.

CORRECTION

(p. 18) Corrections for data on retail executives' opinions of Reagan Administration economic policies, appearing in Sept. 1984 issue; for description, see C5150-7.511 above.

LOWER NICHE RETAILERS PRODUCE HIGH RETURNS

(p. 30-33) Article, with 1 undated table showing selected financial and operating ratios for 7 major discount store chains, with aggregated averages for 16 unnamed chains. Data are from First National Bank of Chicago.

DEPARTMENT STORES OUTPACE DISCOUNTERS

(p. 34) Article, with 1 table showing sales change from previous year for department vs. discount divisions of 4 major retail chains, Feb.-July 1984. Data are from Prudential-Bache Securities.

CLOCK/RADIO/PHONE SALES ARE GROWING

(p. 52) Article, with 1 chart showing consumer preferences concerning store vs. name brand clock/radio/phone sets, with detail for 7 most preferred name brands. Data are from 1984 *Chain Store Age*/Leo Shapiro and Associates Consumer Buying Intentions survey.

For description of complete survey results, see C5150-7.510 above.

MICROWAVE GROWTH GOES MACROSCALE

(p. 57-58) Article, with 1 table showing percent of shoppers buying a microwave oven in 1982, and planning purchase in 1984, by census division. Data are from a *Chain Store Age*/Leo Shapiro and Associates survey.

SLOW COOKING WITH PRIVATE LABELING

(p. 65) Article, with 1 table showing percent of shoppers choosing store brand, nationally advertised brand, or expressing no preference regarding purchases of 4 types of housewares, 1983-84. Data are from *Chain Store Age*/Leo Shapiro and Associates.

PLAYLAND PLANS ARE TO ENTER NEW TERRITORIES

(p. 66-69) Article, with 1 table showing sales and number of stores for 3 major toy store chains, as of Jan. 31, 1984. Data are from *Chain Store Age* research.

C5150–8   APPAREL MERCHANDISING
Monthly.   Approx. 50 p.
ISSN 0746-889X.
SRI/MF/not filmed.

Monthly trade journal of the retail clothing industry, including reports on marketing developments and trends, and consumer buying patterns. Most data are from industry sources and the journal's own research.

Issues contain news and feature articles, some with statistics, including recurring "Consumer Watch" features on consumer buying practices for specific types of clothing as reported through surveys conducted by the Gallup Organization.

Features with substantial statistical content are described, as they appear, under "Statistical Features." Each issue of the journal is reviewed, but an abstract is published in SRI monthly issues only when statistical features appear.

Prior to Jan. 1984, journal was published as a separate 2nd section of *Chain Store Age, General Merchandise Edition;* for description, see C5150-7 above.

Availability: Apparel Merchandising, Subscription Department, 99 Park Ave., New York NY 10157, retailers $18.00 per yr., others $30.00 per yr.; SRI/MF/not filmed.

Issues reviewed during 1984: Jan.-Oct. 1984 (P) (Vol. 3, Nos. 1-10) [Vol. 3, Nos. 1-4 incorrectly read Vol. 2, Nos. 10-13].

STATISTICAL FEATURES:

C5150–8.501: Jan. 1984 (Vol. 3, No. 1)
[Issue incorrectly reads Vol. 2, No. 10.]

CHILDREN'S WEAR: ARE THE HEIRS APPARENT?

(p. 18-19) Article, with 1 undated table showing distribution of total, women's, men's, and children's clothing purchases by retail outlet type. Data are from Management Horizons, Inc.

RETAIL WATCH: MEN'S ATHLETIC SOCKS

(p. 22-23) Article, with 1 table showing retailers' anticipated change in stocks (increase, same level, decrease) for branded, unbranded, and private label men's socks during next 2 years. Data are from a recent Lebhar-Friedman survey of 30 men's wear executives at 100 leading mass merchandise chains.

C5150–8.502: Feb. 1984 (Vol. 3, No. 2)
[Issue incorrectly reads Vol. 2, No. 11.]

CONSUMER WATCH: CHILDREN'S JEANS AND ATHLETIC SHOES

(p. 26-27) Article on consumer purchases of children's denim jeans and athletic shoes. Data are preliminary results from a Gallup survey of women with children aged 7-14.

Includes 3 undated tables showing distribution of most recent purchases of jeans and shoes by brand, and of jeans by retail outlet type, all by respondent's income and child's age group.

For description of final results from the survey, see C5150-8.504, below.

DEPARTMENT STORES SNAG PANTYHOSE SALES

(p. 31-32) Article, with 1 chart showing distribution of pantyhose sales, by retail outlet type, FY83. Data are from Market Research Corp. of America.

C5150–8.503: Mar. 1984 (Vol. 3, No. 3)
[Issue incorrectly reads Vol. 2, No. 12.]

CONSUMER WATCH: MEN'S SWEATERS

(p. 26-30) Article on men's purchases of sweaters. Data are from a Nov.-Dec. 1983 Gallup survey of men age 18/over.

Includes 1 chart and 5 tables showing response distribution concerning brand vs. private label preference; when most recent purchase was made, price paid, retail outlet shopped, and whether sale price paid, by income and/or age group; and preference for domestic or imported sweaters, by region.

MANUFACTURERS TAKE THE WRAP IN WOMEN'S ROBES

(p. 43-46) Article, with 1 chart showing sales volume for women's robes, 1977 and 1979-82. Data are from Market Research Corp. of America.

LARGE SIZES: EXPANDING IN NEW DIRECTIONS

(p. 49-53) Article on merchandising of large-size women's clothing. Data are based on a Russell Marketing Research, Inc. survey of store buyers for 28 department and specialty chains specializing in large sizes.

Includes 5 undated tables showing the following merchandising data for large-size blouses or tops, at department and specialty stores: ratio to sales of skirts/slacks, sales share by fabric type, percent of stores with name brand sales above and below 50%, and brands cited as top-sellers.

C5150–8.504: Apr. 1984 (Vol. 3, No. 4)
[Issue incorrectly reads Vol. 2, No. 13.]

MANUFACTURERS SIZE UP DRESS DEMAND

(p. 13-16) Article on merchandising of women's dresses. Data are from a Lebhar-Friedman survey of 30 department store executives.

Includes 8 charts and 1 table showing the following undated survey responses on dresses: expected change in space allocation, sales volume, and stocks by fabric type; distribution of stocks by label type (brand, no brand, or private label) and by place of manufacture (domestic, imported, or American made abroad); best-selling brands; sales share and expected change for career dresses; and share for promotion sales.

BUYERS SCOUT ALTERNATE IMPORT ROUTES

(p. 25-28) Article on retailer imports of private label clothing. Data are from a Lebhar-Friedman survey of executives at department, specialty, and mass merchandise stores.

Includes 11 charts and 2 tables showing survey response for the following, primarily 1983 or 1984: expected level of change in private label imports, and preferred countries or world areas of origin, with detail by clothing type; private label share of stock; buying methods for private label imports; and expected change in private label imports by place of origin.

CONSUMER WATCH: CHILDREN'S JEANS AND ATHLETIC SHOES

(p. 38-39) Article on consumer purchases of children's denim jeans and athletic shoes. Data are from a Gallup survey of women with children aged 7-14.

Includes 4 undated tables showing distribution of most recent jean and shoe purchases by brand and retail outlet type, by respondent's income and child's age group.

C5150–8.505: May 1984 (Vol. 3, No. 5)

CONSUMER WATCH: WOMEN'S SLIPS

(p. 18-19) Article on women's purchases of slips. Data are from a Gallup survey of women age 18/over.

Includes 4 undated tables showing survey response concerning preferred retail outlet type, and incidence of impulse buying, by age and income group; and slips owned and preferred type, frequency of purchase, expected price and whether bought on sale, and whether worn with similar lingerie, by age group.

MEN'S ACCESSORIES SHOW SLOW GAINS

(p. 49-52) Article, with 8 tables showing retail sales share for men's accessories, by outlet type; for ties, belts, and wallets, by outlet type and price range; and for ties by fabric type; 1982-83. Data are from NPD Group of Marketing and Research Services.

C5150–8.506: June 1984 (Vol. 3, No. 6)

SPECIALISTS GET ON FAST TRACK

(p. 11-14) Article, with 1 table showing top 25 clothing specialty store chains ranked by sales, with number of stores and detail for subsidiaries, 1983 with comparison to 1982. Data are from company reports filed with the SEC.

OFF-PRICERS STEP INTO NATIONAL ARENA

(p. 31-32) Article, with 1 table showing top 16 off-price clothing retailers ranked by sales, with number of stores, 1983 with comparison to 1982. Data are from *Apparel Merchandising.*

C5150–8.507: July 1984 (Vol. 3, No. 7)

OFF-PRICERS LAND 25% OF JEANS, RECURRING FEATURE

(p. 7) Recurring article, with 1 table showing sales volume share for men's/boys' jeans and slacks, by retail outlet type, 1983. Data are from a survey of 180,000 households conducted by National Family Opinion, Inc.

C5150–8.508: Aug. 1984 (Vol. 3, No. 8)

WORK CLOTHES' SALES BOOSTED BY HOME USE

(p. 40-42) Article, with 2 undated tables showing retail sales shares for work clothing, by clothing type and retail company or outlet type. Data are from the Red Kap division of Blue Bell, Inc.

C5150–8.509: Sept. 1984 (Vol. 3, No. 9)

GALLUP ON DRESS SHIRTS: A SELECTION SUITS SHOPPERS

(p. 34-40) Article on consumer purchases of men's dress shirts. Data are from a recent Gallup survey of consumers age 18/over.

Includes 2 charts and 6 tables showing response distribution concerning purchase frequency; purchase plans or preferences for specific styles, brands, fabrics, and patterns; retail outlet preferences; and prices paid; with selected detail by sex, age, and income.

C5150–8.510: Oct. 1984 (Vol. 3, No. 10)

CAN PENNEY AFFORD HALSTON?

(p. 10-12) Article, with 4 tables showing retail market shares for women's clothing, 1973 and 1983; and percent of women's blouses, slacks, and skirts sold on sale and at regular price, with average prices and market shares, 1st half 1983-84; all by major retailer or outlet type. Data are from *Apparel Merchandising*.

WOMEN SUIT UP SOFTLY FOR SPRING

(p. 14-16) Article, with 1 table showing sales volume and value for women's suits, 1979-83. Data are from Market Research Corp. of America.

DEPARTMENT STORES FEEL THE SLACK IN JEANS SALES, RECURRING FEATURE

(p. 20) Recurring article, with 1 table showing market share for men's/boys' jeans and slacks, by retail outlet type, Mar./Apr. 1983-84. Data are from a survey of 30,000 households conducted by National Family Opinion, Inc.

GALLUP ON CHILDREN'S WEAR: SCHOOL CLOTHES MAKE THE GRADE

(p. 44-48) Article on consumer purchases of children's clothing. Data are from a Gallup survey of women with children aged 6-12.

Includes 5 charts and 4 tables showing survey responses concerning retail outlet and brand preferences, composition of child's wardrobe, and importance of price in buying decision, generally shown separately for school, dress, and play clothing, with selected detail by respondents' income and child's sex (no dates).

C5175
Lippincott and Peto

C5175–1 RUBBER WORLD
Monthly. Approx. 60 p.
ISSN 0035-9572.
LC 54-54214.
SRI/MF/excerpts, shipped quarterly

Monthly trade journal of the rubber industry, reporting on technical developments, market activity, and related topics. Covers tire, hose, carbon black, and other major rubber and rubber chemical industry sectors.

Issues contain articles, primarily narrative or technical in nature, but occasionally including market statistics; regular news and editorial depts; and 2 monthly tables and 1 irregularly recurring table.

Monthly and irregularly recurring tables are listed below. Monthly tables appear in most issues. All additional features with substantial statistical content are described, as they appear, under "Statistical Features;" page location and latest period of coverage for irregularly recurring table are also noted. Nonstatistical features are not covered.

Availability: Rubber World, PO Box 5485, 1867 W. Market St., Akron OH 44313, $23.00 per yr., single copy $3.00; SRI/MF/excerpts for monthly tables and all portions covered under "Statistical Features;" shipped quarterly.

Issues reviewed during 1984: Nov. 1983-Oct. 1984 (P) (Vol. 189, Nos. 2-6; Vol. 190, Nos. 1-6; Vol. 191, No. 1).

RECURRING TABLES:

MONTHLY TABLES

[Tables generally show data cumulatively for current year through month 4-5 months prior to cover date, with comparisons to same period of previous year. Detail may vary.]

[1] Rubber Manufacturers Assn (RMA) industry rubber report [supply and demand data, usually including natural rubber imports, exports, and consumption; and synthetic rubber production, imports, exports, and consumption, by type of rubber].

[2] RMA monthly tire report [shipments (original equipment, replacement, and export) and production, for all and radial passenger car and truck/bus tires; often also includes manufacturers' inventory].

IRREGULARLY RECURRING TABLE

[1] Carbon black industry in the U.S. [production and shipments by product type, and total domestic shipments, generally for quarter ending 4-7 months prior to cover date and/or cumulative for year to date, with change from same period of previous year; data are from Columbian Chemicals Co. *Quarterly Consumption Report,* covered in SRI under B2320-1].

STATISTICAL FEATURES:

C5175–1.501: Dec. 1983 (Vol. 189, No. 3)

RECURRING TABLE

[1] Carbon black industry in the U.S. [with accompanying table showing SBR black rubber production, for 1st half 1983]. (p. 11)

C5175–1.502: Jan. 1984 (Vol. 189, No. 4)

TECH SERVICE: TOP PRIORITY TO MANUFACTURERS, ANNUAL FEATURE

(p. 18-20) Annual article, by Joseph Kuebler, reporting on technical service available to rubber product manufacturers from their suppliers and independent testing laboratories. Data are based on recent *Rubber World* surveys involving 210 manufacturers, 75 suppliers, and an unspecified number of testing laboratories.

Includes 6 charts showing distributions of manufacturers' principal products and markets; manufacturers' views on most beneficial services offered by suppliers, and desired services; and percent of suppliers and laboratories owning 23 types of equipment.

This is the 1st annual article.

C5175–1.503: Feb. 1984 (Vol. 189, No. 5)

MARKETS, NEWS: IISRP CONSUMPTION FORECAST FOR NORTH AMERICA AND WESTERN EUROPE, ANNUAL FEATURE

(p. 10-13) Annual article, with 2 tables showing consumption of new natural rubber and synthetic rubber by type for North America and Western Europe, and including tire rubber consumption for North America, various years 1982-88.

Data are from International Institute of Synthetic Rubber Producers.

CUSTOM MIXERS OPTIMISTIC ABOUT 1984

(p. 17-23) By David Given. Article reporting on activities of companies that custom mix rubber polymers. Data are based on a *Rubber World* survey of 39 companies. Includes 2 charts and 1 table showing respondents' expansion activity and plans; percent of companies involved in export business and offering calendering services; volume of polymers mixed, by type, 1983; and industry capacity and utilization, 1982-83.

Also includes directory of companies, with capacity data.

C5175–1.504: Mar. 1984 (Vol. 189, No. 6)

RECURRING TABLE

[1] Carbon black industry in the U.S. [1st 9 months 1983]. (p. 14)

C5175–1.505: Apr. 1984 (Vol. 190, No. 1)

1982 CENSUS OF MANUFACTURES

(p. 10) Table showing the following for tire/inner tube industry (SIC 3011) and miscellaneous fabricated rubber product industry (SIC 3069), for 1972, 1977, and 1982:

a. Companies; total establishments and establishments with 20/more employees; employment and payroll; production workers, hours, and wages; cost of materials, value-added, and shipments value; new capital expenditures; and end-of-year inventories.

b. Degree of specialization (primary product shipments/total product shipments ratio) and degree of coverage (ratio of primary products shipped by rubber industry establishments to total shipments of such products by all manufacturing establishments).

Data are from U.S. Censuses of Manufactures.

C5175–1.506: May 1984 (Vol. 190, No. 2)

RECURRING TABLE

[1] Carbon black industry in the U.S. [with accompanying table showing SBR black rubber production, 1983]. (p. 13)

MARKETS, NEWS: IISRP FORECAST, ANNUAL FEATURE

(p. 13) Annual article presenting rubber consumption projections of the International Institute of Synthetic Rubber Producers (IISRP). Includes 2 tables showing world consumption of synthetic and natural rubber by region, and of new rubber by type, various years 1982-88.

C5175–1.507: June 1984 (Vol. 190, No. 3)

MARKETS, NEWS

(p. 9-12) Article reporting on world rubber supply and demand. Data are from International Rubber Study Group. Includes 5 tables showing production and consumption of natural and synthetic rubber, by country or world area, 1982-83.

HISTORICAL STATISTICS FOR THE RECLAIMED RUBBER INDUSTRY

(p. 12) Table showing the following for reclaimed rubber industry (SIC 3031), for 1972, 1977, and 1982:

a. Companies; total establishments and establishments with 20/more employees; employment and payroll; production workers, hours, and wages; cost of materials, value-added, and shipments value; new capital expenditures; and end-of-year inventories.

b. Degree of specialization (primary product shipments/total product shipments ratio) and degree of coverage (ratio of primary products shipped by rubber industry establishments to total shipments of such products by all manufacturing establishments).

Data are from U.S. Censuses of Manufactures.

C5175–1.508: July 1984 (Vol. 190, No. 4)

MANUFACTURERS INCREASING MACHINERY PURCHASES

(p. 42-43) By Don R. Smith. Article, with 3 tables showing the following for rubber and chemical industries: percent change in sales and new plant/equipment expenditures, 1982-84; and capacity utilization rates, with comparison to preferred rates, quarterly June 1982-Dec. 1983. Data are from Commerce Dept.

C5175–1.509: Aug. 1984 (Vol. 190, No. 5)

RECURRING TABLE

[1] Carbon black industry in the U.S. [1st quarter 1984]. (p. 11)

EXCITING GROWTH AHEAD FOR THE ADHESIVE AND SEALANT INDUSTRY

(p. 14-15) By William R. Schmitz. Article, with 1 table showing adhesive/sealant industry shipments, total employment, production workers and average earnings, capital expenditures, PPI, exports, imports, and import/shipments and import/new supply ratios, selected years 1972-84. Data are from Census Bureau and Bureau of Industrial Economics.

C5175–1.510: Oct. 1984 (Vol. 191, No. 1)

BRIGHTER DAYS FOR CHEMICALS, MATERIALS

(p. 17-21) By Don R. Smith. Article, with 4 charts and 1 table showing rubber consump-

tion by type; production of rubber processing chemicals; and natural and synthetic rubber consumption, by world area; various periods 1970-88.

Data are from Rubber Manufacturers Assn, USITC, and International Institute of Synthetic Rubber Producers.

C5225
Maclean Hunter Media, Inc.

C5225–1   PROGRESSIVE GROCER
Monthly.   Approx. 150 p.
ISSN 0033-0787.   LC 80-858.
SRI/MF/not filmed.

Monthly trade journal of the supermarket/grocery store industry, covering food retailing, advertising and sales promotion, new products, merchandising trends, finance, technology, store design, product use and sales, and Federal Government regulation.

Data are from Federal Government, *Progressive Grocer* Data Center and surveys, private publishers, and research assns.

General contents:

a. "Seasonal Best Sellers" monthly table, showing index of supermarket items with high seasonal sales, for cover date or month 1-3 months subsequent, based on average sales for same month of 4-5 previous years; data are from Selling Areas Marketing, Inc.

b. Feature articles on current industry topics, occasionally with statistics; and editorial depts.

Annual statistical features include Nielsen review of retail grocery trends, a comprehensive report on the grocery industry, and a report on supermarket product movement and consumer use. An annual directory of equipment manufacturers is published in Dec.

"Best Sellers" table appears in most issues. All additional features with substantial statistical content are described, as they appear, under "Statistical Features." Nonstatistical contents are not covered.

Availability: Progressive Grocer, 1351 Washington Blvd., Stamford CT 06902, $42.00 per yr., single copy $5.00, Apr. Annual Report issue $20.00, July Sales Manual $15.00; SRI/MF/not filmed.

Issues reviewed during 1984: Nov. 1983-Oct. 1984 (P) (Vol. 62, Nos. 11-12; Vol. 63, Nos. 1-10).

STATISTICAL FEATURES:

C5225–1.501: Nov. 1983 (Vol. 62, No. 11)

FINANCIAL MEASURES OF THE FIRST HALF, RECURRING FEATURE

(p. 11) Recurring summary article, with 1 table showing percent annual change in sales and earnings 1st-2nd quarters 1983, and net income as percent of sales 1st-2nd quarters 1982-83, aggregated for 38 food chains and 16 wholesalers.

For description of last previous appearance, see SRI 1983 Annual, under C5225-1.407.

AMERICA'S GROWING FAVORITE

(p. 24-39) By Mary Johnson. Article, with 3 tables showing wine market shares by color

and type, and for imported, Californian, and other domestic wine, 1960, 1970, and 1982. Data are from Impact, Inc.

C5225–1.502: Dec. 1983 (Vol. 62, No. 12)

SIZING UP C-STORES

(p. 13) Article, with 1 undated table showing convenience store sales distribution and average profit margin for 9 product categories. Data are from *C-Store Business.*

1983 NIELSEN REVIEW OF RETAIL GROCERY STORE TRENDS, ANNUAL FEATURE

(p. 29-55) Annual report on trends in grocery store sales, space allocations, and new product development, 1970s-83. Data are primarily from A. C. Nielsen Co.

Data by geographic region are shown for New England, NYC, Middle Atlantic, East Central, Chicago, West Central, Southeast, Southwest, Los Angeles, and Pacific.

Contains 9 sections, with 23 charts and 9 tables showing the following:

a. Grocery sales, total 1980-83, and by region 1983, with distributions by chain and independent store sales size; CPI for selected components, June 1982-83; and per capita grocery sales, share of grocery income and population, and cumulative 5-year change in sales and population shares, by region, 1982. (p. 30-31)

b. Retail sales, with distribution by product or outlet type; and food-away-from-home sales, with share by establishment type; various periods 1978-83. (p. 32)

c. Product movement trends, including percent changes in tonnage and sales by packaged product type, and tonnage shares for controlled and generic brands; and new items and brands introduced, with new item detail by product category; various periods 1975-83. (p. 34-37)

d. Warehoused product average shelf space, annual inventory turns, and sales per month per storage foot, by product type, aggregated for chains with sales over $1 million; and store delivered products share of total grocery sales, with percent sales change by product type; various periods 1980-Apr./May 1983. (p. 38)

e. Health and beauty aids: sales, with share by product type; and percent change in sales volume; with detail by outlet type; various periods 1977-83. (p. 40-42)

f. Frozen and refrigerated foods average shelf space, total 1979-82, and by product type 1981-82, all by region, aggregated for chains with sales over $1 million. (p. 47-48)

g. Scanning equipped stores, various periods 1977-83; scanning sales as a percent of total by region, and top 10 chains ranked by number of scanning equipped stores, May 1983; and potential impact of scanning data on sales promotion effectiveness, by product category. (p. 50-52)

h. Salt/sodium in foods, including consumer awareness and perceptions, number of new low/no sodium products introduced, and grocery store sales volume of light salt/salt substitutes, various periods 1979-83. (p. 54-55)

This is the 1st annual report to appear in *Progressive Grocer.* Report previously appeared in *Chain Store Age, Supermarkets;* for description of report published in 1982, see SRI 1982 Annual, under C5150-1.311.

C5225–1.503: Jan. 1984 (Vol. 63, No. 1)

FROZENS BECOME FASHIONABLE

(p. 28-44) By Mary Ann Linsen. Article, with 1 table showing 4-week, 12-week, and 52-week percent change in retail grocery sales volume for 58 frozen food product categories, ranked by 52-week sales volume, all for periods ending Sept. 16, 1983. Data are from Selling Areas Marketing Inc.

C5225–1.504: Feb. 1984 (Vol. 63, No. 2)

FARE THEE WELL

(p. 19) Brief article on food retailing industry outlook, 1984. Data are from Census Bureau and other Federal agencies. Includes 2 tables showing retail food industry sales, employment, and average hourly earnings, 1972-83; and total retail sales distribution by type of establishment or product, 1973 and 1983.

CAR CARE SHIFTS INTO HIGH

(p. 51-58) By Glenn Snyder. Article on merchandising of auto care products in grocery stores. Data are based on *Progressive Grocer* surveys of nonfood executives and automotive buyers among chains, multi-unit independents, wholesalers, and service merchandisers.

Includes 1 table showing response distribution concerning current and future outlook for auto care sales, profits, and customer interest, 1981 and 1984.

MOTOR OIL: CAR CARE'S KINGPIN MAKING NEW MOVES

(p. 58, 80-82) Article on grocery store sales and marketing of motor oil. Data are from *Progressive Grocer* surveys (as described for preceding article) and Selling Areas Marketing, Inc. Includes 1 table and 1 chart showing respondent ratings of motor oil as a customer attraction, 1981 and 1984; and grocery store sales of motor oil, 1978-83.

FOODS AND SERVICES BEING FEATURED BY U.S. SUPERMARKET DELIS

(p. F6) Article, with 1 undated chart showing percent of supermarket delicatessens featuring selected foods or services. Data are from a *Progressive Grocer* survey.

CHANGING MEAT PREFERENCES: HEALTH OR PRICE DRIVEN?

(p. 99-107) By Mary Ann Linsen. Article on meat purchasing patterns of consumers. Data are based on a 1983 Leo J. Shapiro and Associates survey of 500 consumers. Includes 1 table and 4 charts showing response distribution concerning meat purchasing habits, with detail by type of meat, and frequency of meat purchases at fast-food outlets, and attitude toward meat consumption as related to health.

C5225–1.505: Mar. 1984 (Vol. 63, No. 3)

FOOD EXPENDITURES AS A PERCENT OF DISPOSABLE INCOME

(p. 13) Chart showing expenditures for food at home and food away from home, as a percent of disposable income, selected years 1960-83. Data are from the Dept of Commerce.

C5225–1.506: Apr. 1984 (Vol. 63, No. 4)

51st ANNUAL REPORT OF THE GROCERY INDUSTRY

(p. 35-120) First part of a 2-part annual report on all facets of the grocery industry, 1983. First part focuses on store finances and operations, and outlook for 1984.

Most data for the report are based on responses to *Progressive Grocer* surveys of chain and independent supermarket owners and managers, and chain and wholesaler executives.

Contains introduction (p. 35-37); 39 charts and 28 tables, described below, presented in 6 sections, with interspersed narrative (p. 41-120).

Part II of this report for 1983 appears in the May 1984 issue (for description see C5225-1.507, below). Part II of the report for 1982 was published separately (for description see C5225-2, below).

TABLES AND CHARTS:

[Data generally show survey responses or response distribution, for independent and chain stores, and/or chain and wholesale executives, on the topics described below. Most data are for 1983, occasionally with 1- or 2-year trends; other dates are noted below.

Selected outlook, competition, cost, and operating data are shown by some or all of the following store characteristics: region, sales volume, size (square footage and/or checkouts), and format (superstore, conventional, economy, and combination.)]

a. Overview: includes consumer spending for food, 1970s-83; food store growth outlook; sales and number of stores, for supermarkets by sales size, convenience stores, and other stores; chain store opening/closing summary by chain size, and expected openings in 1984; wholesaler firms, branches/divisions, and sales, by wholesaler type; and views on effects of inflation, Reagan Administration economic policies, and recession. 8 charts and 2 tables. (p. 41-50)

b. Outlook: expectations and plans for 1984, including problem areas; general economic conditions, price stability, grocery profits, and personal financial situation; and levels of sales, labor costs, competition, and other operating factors. 11 charts and 2 tables. (p. 55-70)

c. Competition: includes use of various competitive tactics and promotion techniques; media distribution of advertising budget and use; and perceived competition from and prospects for other grocery stores. 1 chart and 7 tables. (p. 77-82)

d. Costs and prices: includes change in marketing costs by item; CPI for food away from home, and food at home by commodity; average equipment expenditures, 1976-83; types of equipment purchased; store age, and remodeling and energy costs; unionization status and wage rates for clerks and meat cutters; wage expense ratios, and gross margin; change in wholesaler productivity and employee turnover; and wage increases for 1984. 7 charts and 8 tables. (p. 87-96)

e. Store operations: includes sales productivity measures; store selling area and inventory; checkouts, weekly transactions, and scanner use; employment; weekly coupon redemptions; store hours; special services and product lines offered; product availability measures, including out-of-stock rate; employee turnover; type of warehouse used; and food stamp percentage of sales. 8 charts and 6 tables. (p. 97-110)

f. Manufacturer relations: includes views on retailer/manufacturer relations, frequency of deal/allowance offers and sales visits, and use of manufacturer services and supplies including display material. 4 charts and 3 tables. (p. 115-120)

Other Feature

IT'S BACK ON TRACK FOR GM

(p. 145-158) By Glenn Snyder. Compilation of articles on marketing outlook for general merchandise (GM) in food stores, 1984. Data are from a *Progressive Grocer* survey and Food Marketing Institute.

Includes 5 charts and 5 tables showing GM sales change 1983-84, and merchandising plans for 1984 with detail by selected product category, for food store chains, wholesalers, and service merchandisers; and GM and health and beauty aid sales, shelf space, and gross profit, relative to all merchandise, by store format (no date).

C5225–1.507: May 1984 (Vol. 63, No. 5)

TELLING IT ON TV, ANNUAL FEATURE

(p. 14) Brief annual article, with 1 table showing TV advertising expenditures of top 10 food chain advertisers, 1983 with percent change from 1982. Data are from TV Bureau of Advertising, based on Broadcast Advertisers Reports.

51st ANNUAL REPORT OF THE GROCERY INDUSTRY

(p. 49-72) Second part of a 2-part annual report on all facets of the grocery industry, 1983. Part 2 focuses on consumer behavior and wholesaler and chain operations.

Most data are based on responses to a survey of 700 households conducted by Home Testing Institute, 126 responses to a *Progressive Grocer* survey of wholesalers, and 51 responses to a Cornell University survey of grocery chains.

Contains introduction (p. 49); and 3 charts and 9 tables, described below, presented in 2 sections, with interspersed narrative (p. 51-72).

Part I of this report for 1983 appears in the Apr. 1984 issue (for description see C5225-1.506, above). Part II of the report for 1982 was published separately (for description see C5225-2, below).

CHARTS AND TABLES:

[Consumer data generally show survey response distribution for the topics listed below. Unless otherwise noted, data are for 1983 and often include comparisons to 1982. Wholesaler types include voluntary, cooperative, and unaffiliated.]

a. Consumers: includes consumers' perceptions of price change by product category, supermarket profits, and economic situation; primary food shopper by sex, and shopping patterns by employment status and frequency by store type; use of cost-saving methods as seen by consumers and independent and chain managers; grocery shopping planning; and consumer ranking of 42 supermarket characteristics/services by importance. 3 charts and 6 tables. (p. 51-58)

b. Operating data: wholesaler employment, wages, distribution centers, annual stock turnover, sales productivity, profit, business share by retail store type, generics and brand label share of business, and selected other financial and operating ratios, by wholesaler type and sales size; sales and earnings of public chains and wholesalers by company; and composite chains' gross margin, expenses by item, earnings, stock turns, and selected other operating ratios, 1977/78-1982/83. 3 tables. (p. 65-72)

Other Features

INSIDE NON-FOODS

(p. 109) Article, with 1 undated chart on views of general merchandise (GM) executives concerning the effect of expanded supermarket food sections on GM space allotments. Data are from a *Progressive Grocer* survey of chain, wholesaler, and service merchandiser GM executives.

WHO'S BUYING WHAT?

(p. 173-175) Brief article on food store equipment purchases, 1983. Data are from a *Progressive Grocer* survey. Includes 3 charts and 1 table showing average equipment expenditure, years since last remodeling, and percent of stores purchasing equipment by type, by sales size, 1983; and distribution of stores by date of last remodeling, 1974/earlier-1983; for chains and/or independents.

C5225-1.508: June 1984 (Vol. 63, No. 6)

PROGRESSIVE GROCER'S 1984 SURVEY OF BUYERS AND MERCHANDISERS

(p. 22-32) First of 2 articles on professional and personal characteristics and perceptions of buyers/merchandisers at grocery retail chains and wholesale companies. Data are based on a 1984 *Progressive Grocer* survey, and are shown separately for chains and wholesalers.

Includes 13 charts and 1 table showing survey responses concerning profit outlook and major problems for the industry, average salary and hours, job functions, grocery industry experience, perceived quality of competition, existence of formal electronic data training, operational role of store manager, job satisfaction, and expected job position in next 5 years.

ANOTHER BANNER YEAR FOR HBA, ANNUAL FEATURE

(p. 77-86) Annual compilation of articles on health and beauty aid (HBA) sales and marketing in supermarkets, 1983 and trends. Data are from Dancer Fitzgerald Sample Advertising, Newspaper Advertising Bureau, and *Progressive Grocer* surveys.

Includes 6 charts and 1 table showing HBA sales and growth rates, new products introduced, and advertising expenditures, with comparison to total grocery industry, various years 1950-83; and buyer/merchandiser ratings of merchandising problem areas, and current and expected change in HBA profit margin as seen by chain, wholesaler, and service merchandisers, 1983.

C5225-1.509: July 1984 (Vol. 63, No. 7)

PROGRESSIVE GROCER'S 1984 SURVEY OF BUYERS AND MERCHANDISERS: PART II

(p. 21-30) Second of 2 articles on professional and personal characteristics and perceptions of buyers/merchandisers at grocery retail chains and wholesale companies. Data are based on a 1984 *Progressive Grocer* survey and a similar 1978 survey, and are shown separately for chains and wholesalers.

Includes 12 charts and 2 tables showing survey results concerning respondents' age and education; whether grocery field was 1st career choice; political ideology and party affiliation; leisure activities; primary social, personal, and professional concerns; and median salary and hours; 1984 with some comparisons to 1978.

1984 SUPERMARKET SALES MANUAL, ANNUAL FEATURE

(p. 41-210) Annual compilation of articles on supermarket industry sales and profits, by product category and detailed type, 1983. Data are from *Progressive Grocer.*

Includes 1 summary table (p. 42); and 34 product category profiles, each with 1-15 tables showing sales, profit, profit margin, and assortment, usually by detailed product type, 1983, with selected comparisons to 1982.

Some profiles also include data on weekly unit movement for a typical supermarket.

This is the 1st annual compilation to appear in *Progressive Grocer.* Data were previously included in an annual report published in *Chain Store Age, Supermarkets;* for description of 1982 data, see SRI 1983 Annual, under C5150-1.409.

C5225-1.510: Aug. 1984 (Vol. 63, No. 8)

A BETTER WAY TO DO BUSINESS

(p. 71-74) By Robert E. O'Neill. Article on development of the uniform communications standards (UCS) system for handling computerized communication among supermarket industry buyers, distributors, and suppliers. Data are based on a 1980 study by Arthur D. Little, Inc.

Includes 2 tables showing UCS system potential savings and costs, for chains/wholesalers, manufacturers, and brokers, by type and/or sales size; and estimated number of total communications, by type of transaction.

C5225-1.511: Sept. 1984 (Vol. 63, No. 9)

HEALTH CARE COSTS: A GROWING BURDEN FOR THE FOOD INDUSTRY

(p. 20-34) By Robert E. O'Neill. Article examining employer health care costs and policies, with focus on the food industry. Data are primarily from 602 responses to a Health Research Institute survey of 1,500 large companies and public employers; 292 responses to a Food Marketing Institute survey of member companies; and an A. S. Hansen, Inc., survey of corporate employees.

Includes 4 tables and 4 charts showing the following:

a. Health care expenditures, selected years 1960-2000; and corporate health care cost per employee, and as percent of sales, payroll, and earnings, 1981-82.

b. Food industry medical benefits, including cost changes, types of plans and services

provided, cost-saving services encouraged, prevalence of plans with deductibles and of deduction increases, and company policies concerning 2nd opinions (no dates).

c. Corporate employees' willingness to accept selected cost-saving health services (no date).

1984 GUIDE TO PRODUCT USAGE, ANNUAL FEATURE

(p. 47-148) Annual report on supermarket product movement, consumer use, and user characteristics, 1983. Data are primarily from Simmons Market Research Bureau survey of 19,248 consumers, and Selling Areas Marketing Inc. (SAMI) monitoring of withdrawals from food chain and wholesaler warehouses in 49 market areas.

Contents:

a. Introduction, explanation of data, and data sources. (p. 47-49)

b. "Winners and Losers." 1 table showing percent change in sales value and tonnage, by supermarket product category, year ended Mar. 2, 1984 vs. previous 12-month period. (p. 52)

c. "Usage of Supermarket Products." 1 table ranking detailed products within supermarket depts, by percent of surveyed consumers using, and also showing percent of consumers using daily and using 1 brand exclusively. (p. 53-55)

d. Index to product profiles (p. 56)

e. Profiles for 28 product categories, each with 4-9 tables showing most or all of the following by product type: percent change in sales value and tonnage, percent of consumers using and using heavily, heavy users' share of consumption, and demographic characteristics of heavy users compared to average. (p. 58-148)

Profiles for general merchandise and health/beauty aid products include an additional table (p. 131-133) presenting data as described above for "Usage of Supermarket Products."

1984 NIELSEN REVIEW OF RETAIL GROCERY STORE TRENDS, ANNUAL FEATURE

(p. 165-191) Annual report on trends in grocery store sales, space allocations, and new product development, various periods 1977-86. Data are primarily from A. C. Nielsen Co.

Data by geographic region are shown for New England, NYC, Middle Atlantic, East Central, Chicago, West Central, Southeast, Southwest, Los Angeles, and Pacific.

Contains 7 sections, with 21 charts and 15 tables showing the following:

a. Grocery sales, with detail by region and distributions by chain and independent store sales size; CPI for selected components; retail sales, with distribution by kind of business; food-away-from-home expenditures, with share by establishment type; and sales shares for branded, controlled, and generic products; various periods 1978-84. (p. 166-168)

b. Product movement trends, including percent changes in sales value and tonnage, tonnage, prices, and inventories, and average annual turns, all by packaged product type; and new items and brands introduced, with new brand detail by product category; various periods 1977-84. (p. 170-174)

c. Health and beauty aids: percent change in sales value and volume, and prices, by product category and outlet type; and sales shares by product, by outlet type; various years 1979-83. (p. 176-178)

d. Warehoused product average shelf space, annual inventory turns, and sales per month per storage foot, by product type; and average shelf space for fresh meat, and refrigerated and frozen foods by type, by region; all aggregated for chains with sales over $1 million; various periods 1979-83. (p. 182-185)

e. Coupons distributed and redeemed, for all products, with distribution detail by media; and grocery coupons distributed by face value, and redemption by media; various years 1979-83. (p. 186-188)

f. Scanning equipped stores, and scanning stores' share of all sales, total 1977-86, and by major market 1983; and analysis of sales promotion effectiveness. (p. 190-191)

This is the 2nd annual report. For description of previous report, for 1983, see C5225-1.502 above.

C5225–1.512: Oct. 1984 (Vol. 63, No. 10)

CHAINS WITH MUSCLE: 10 SUPERMARKET GIANTS

(p. 30-56) Article on sales and operations of the top 10 publicly owned supermarket chains, 1983. Data are from *Progressive Grocer*.

Includes 1 table ranking top 10 chains by total sales, and also showing earnings, 5-year sales growth, inventory turns, returns on equity and assets, and food store sales, stores, and square footage, 1983. Also includes company profiles, each with 1-2 charts showing trends in sales and number of food stores, 1979-84.

C5225–2 MID-YEAR EXECUTIVE REPORT, 1983: Progressive Grocer

Monograph. July 1983.
82 p.
SRI/MF/not filmed

Second part of a 2-part annual report on all facets of the grocery industry, 1982 and trends. Second part is directed to industry executives, and includes summaries of basic industry statistics and analyses of 53 metro markets.

Data are from a variety of Federal and private sources, including surveys of industry executives and supermarket managers/owners.

Contains introduction, contents listing, and introductory article (p. 4-7); and 7 sections, with feature articles and narrative summaries, interspersed with 91 charts and 35 tables, described below (p. 8-82).

First part of the report for 1982 was published in the Apr. 1983 issue of *Progressive Grocer* (for description see SRI 1983 Annual, under C5225-1.405). Previous year's report was presented in a single installment, in *Progressive Grocer*. First part of the report for 1983 was published in the Apr. 1984 issue of *Progressive Grocer* (for description see C5225-1.506, above).

Availability: Maclean Hunter Media, Inc., 1351 Washington Blvd., Stamford CT 06902, $30.00+$2.50 postage and handling; SRI/MF/not filmed.

TABLES AND CHARTS:
[Store formats generally include superstores (with 30 thousand/over square feet), conventional supermarkets, warehouse, combination, convenience, and limited assortment and/or other stores. Wholesaler types are voluntary, cooperative, and unaffiliated.]

a. Financial data: sales and earnings, 1982; growth in sales, income, earnings per share, and retail outlets, 1976-81 period; and stock price as of June 17, 1983; all for 41-46 supermarket chains and 8-50 wholesalers, with selected rankings and detail by wholesaler type. 4 tables. (p. 9-13)

b. Competitive activities: use of various promotional techniques, with detail for aggregate top 50 markets; and perceived competitiveness and prospects of store formats; as reported by managers and/or executives of independent, chain, and wholesale operations. 3 charts and 6 tables. (p. 14-18)

c. Advertising: top 200 product brands ranked by advertising expenditures; advertising space allocation, and private label advertising as percent of total, by product category; feature advertising by product category and region, and feature price index compared to CPI; top 12 grocery chains ranked by local TV advertising; and distribution of advertising for independent food stores, by media and region; various periods 1979-82. 8 charts and 12 tables. (p. 28-38)

d. Supermarket census: population; households; and supermarkets, sales, square footage, and number of employees and checkouts, with various store and labor productivity measures; for 53 metro markets with summary U.S. comparison; 1983. 1 summary table and 1 detailed table. (p. 44-50)

e. Market analysis: household distribution, number of supermarkets, and number of supermarkets with sales over $6 million, for 10 market types (based on sociodemographic characteristics) with index comparisons to total U.S., repeated for 53 metro markets (no date). 53 charts and 1 table. (p. 52-65)

f. Operations and prices: food stores and sales by format and supermarket sales size, distribution of independent and chain stores by type of warehouse supplier, food CPI, and changes in farm production value and food marketing cost, mostly 1982; BLS food price index, selected years 1920-82; wage rate and union membership for clerks and meat cutters at independent and chain stores, by sales size, region, and format, 1982; and independent store wage/sales ratio, 1981-82. 3 charts and 5 tables. (p. 70-72)

g. Wholesaler operations: firms, branches/divisions, and sales, by wholesaler type; distribution of wholesalers by backhaul volume rate; and employment, wages and unionization, distribution centers and size, annual turnover and selected other operating and financial ratios, and business shares by retail outlet and brand types, by wholesaler type and sales size; 1982 with comparisons to 1981. 4 charts and 2 tables. (p. 74-75)

h. Financial report for food chains, including gross margin, itemized expenses, net operating profit and earnings, and stock turns, FY77-82; and number of distribution centers by type, by chain size group (no date). 2 tables. (p. 76)

i. Outlook: executives' survey responses concerning overall economy, major industry concerns, planned operating changes, and retailer/wholesaler relations, variously shown for independent, chain, and wholesale executives. 19 charts and 2 tables. (p. 78-82)

C5250
Magazines for Industry, Inc.

C5250–1 BEVERAGE INDUSTRY, 1984 Annual Manual
Annual.

SRI now covers this publication under C4390-1.

C5250–2 BEVERAGE INDUSTRY
Monthly.

SRI now covers this publication under C4390-2.

C5250–3 PAPERBOARD PACKAGING
Monthly.

SRI now covers this publication under C4390-3.

C5680
MarketPlace Publications

C5680–1 PROFILE OF 960,000 OF AMERICA'S PROFESSIONALS. The 1984 Erdos and Morgan Comparable Profile Measurement of the MarketPlace Reader
Biennial. Aug. 1984.
4+131 p.
SRI/MF/complete

Biennial report, for 1984, on personal characteristics, income, and buying habits of professionals who subscribe to MarketPlace publications, including corporate presidents, dentists, physicians, lawyers, and certified public accountants.

Data are from 3,243 responses to 2 mail surveys of subscribers, conducted in spring/summer 1984 by Erdos and Morgan, Inc.

Contains contents listing (2 p.); survey results in 6 sections, each preceded by a table listing, with 68 tables described below (p. 1-119); and methodology, with 2 tables on survey sample, and questionnaire facsimiles (p. 123-131).

Previous report, for 1982, is described in SRI 1982 Annual, under this number.

Availability: MarketPlace Publications, PO Box 4515, 600 W. Putnam Ave., Greenwich CT 06830, †; SRI/MF/complete.

TABLES:

C5680–1.1: Survey Responses
[Tables show data for total respondents, and separately for each professional group.]

a. Personal and household demographic and income characteristics and leisure activities; type and tenure of residence; and ownership of other real estate, photographic equipment, audio and video equipment, and other consumer goods, with detail for personal computer ownership by type, cost, and use. 20 tables. (p. 2-27) *b.* Cars and special utility vehicles owned, leased, and company supplied (total, and for multi-vehicle households), with detail by domestic and import make and model, model years, and whether new or used. 16 tables. (p. 32-69)

c. U.S. travel, by transportation mode and purpose of trip; outside U.S. travel, by purpose and transportation mode, and places visited; and household members with valid passport. 16 tables. (p. 74-91)

d. Investments held by type and value, including stocks, bonds, mutual funds, and life insurance. 11 tables. (p. 96-106)

e. Respondent line of business and title or position; and MarketPlace publication reading habits. 5 tables. (p. 109-119)

C5800
McGraw-Hill

C5800-2   ENGINEERING NEWS-RECORD

Weekly. Approx. 100 p.
ISSN 0013-807X.
LC 1-16396.
SRI/MF/not filmed

Weekly publication (except final week of year) reporting developments and trends in the U.S. construction industry, including costs, materials prices, bidding, contracts, wages, and new construction plans; top design firms and executives; and U.S. participation in world markets.

Most data are derived from *Engineering News-Record* (ENR) surveys and field reports.

Issues contain articles and other items on management, labor, and recent industry developments and trends; and regular editorial features.

The following statistics are presented:

a. Weekly "Market Trends" section on costs, bidding, plans, capital, machinery sales, contract failures, wage rates, and materials prices; with 2-3 varying charts, and 4 weekly and 11 monthly tables.

b. Weekly "Unit Prices" section on contract bidding, with 1-2 tables.

c. Weekly "Materials Prices" section, with 12 monthly tables on prices in 22 selected cities for representative items in 28 materials categories, and on wage rates for key building construction trades.

d. 1-2 monthly tables on construction new plans and bidding volume.

e. Monthly "Stock Track" table tracing stock and financial performance of selected U.S. companies, and quarterly "International Stock Track" table showing corresponding data for selected companies worldwide.

f. Quarterly "Cost Roundup" compilation of statistical articles on cost trends in major construction sectors.

g. Quarterly table on construction labor shortages.

h. Annual statistical articles, including an industrywide report and forecast, and articles on performance of top construction and design firms and specialty contractors, foreign contract awards, top executive earnings, and other industry interests.

i. Occasional statistical articles.

Weekly and monthly tables are listed below. All additional features with substantial statistical content are described, as they appear, under "Statistical Features;" page locations and latest periods of coverage for weekly and monthly tables are also noted. Nonstatistical features are not covered.

Availability: Engineering News-Record, Fulfillment Manager, PO Box 2026, Mahopac NY 10541, qualified subscribers $35.00 per yr., single copy $2.00; SRI/MF/not filmed.

Issues reviewed during 1984: Nov. 3, 1983-Oct. 25, 1984 (P) (Vol. 211, Nos. 18-25; Vol. 212, Nos. 1-26; Vol. 213, Nos. 1-17)[Vol. 213, No. 11 incorrectly reads Vol. 212].

WEEKLY TABLES:

C5800-2.1: Market Trends, Weekly Tables

[Tables [2-4] show data for week prior to or week of publication, and for year to date with percent change from previous year to date. For description of article explaining ENR cost indexes, see C5800-2.521 below.]

[1] Cost indexes [for construction, building, common labor, skilled labor, and materials; for week prior to publication, with percent change from previous month and year, based on a sampling of 20 cities; 1913=base year].

[2] Bidding volume [value for heavy/highway, nonresidential building, and multi-unit housing construction].

[3] New plans [value for approximately 20 types of heavy and highway, nonresidential building, and multi-unit housing (excludes 1-2 family) construction].

[4] New construction capital [corporate securities and State/municipal totals, with subtotals for housing and for other building/heavy construction].

C5800-2.2: Unit Prices

Weekly feature consisting of 1-2 brief articles each on the bidding of a significant construction project. Each article includes 1 table showing total bids of top competitors, and unit prices of individual items included in the accepted bid.

MONTHLY TABLES:

[All tables appear at 4-5 week intervals, but week of publication may vary from month to month.]

C5800-2.3: Market Trends, Monthly Tables

[Most tables show data for most recent available month, generally month of publication or previous month. Most also show comparative data for previous month and/or same period of previous year.]

COSTS

[For description of article explaining ENR cost indexes, see C5800-2.521 below.]

[1] Wage rates, 20 cities' average [for common and skilled laborers, bricklayers, structural ironworkers, and carpenters].

[2] Material prices, 20 cities' average [for 16 selected materials].

[3] ENR index review [indexes for construction and building costs, and for skilled and

common labor wage rates (1913 and 1967=base years), for month of publication and previous 12 months].

[4] ENR cost indexes in 22 cities [construction and building costs, by city; 1913=base year].

[5] ENR wage, materials, and cost indexes, 20 cities [for common and skilled labor wages, materials prices, and construction and building costs, by city; 1967=base year].

CONSTRUCTION TRENDS

[6] New construction planning backlog [value of total private, State/municipal, and Federal backlogs; and of 7 types of public and 3 types of private backlog].

[7] New industrial plans and contracts [value, for approximately 15 types, including manufacturing plants for 9 industry groups].

[8] New orders and construction bidding volume indexes [construction bidding volume (actual and seasonally adjusted), and fabricated structural steel bookings, 1967=base year; prior to Oct. 25, 1984 issue, table included data on southern pine and douglas fir new orders].

[9] Construction machinery distributor sales indexes, reported by Associated Equipment Distributors [sales and inventories, surveys of 194-280 dealers; and inventory-sales ratio in months].

BOND SALES

[10] State/municipal bond sales for construction [for 3 types of buildings, 8 types of heavy and highway construction, and general improvement/unclassified].

CONTRACTOR FAILURES

[11] Contractor failures [and liabilities], reported by Dun & Bradstreet [for general building, other general, and special trade contractors, current to approximately 15 months prior to month of publication; liabilities data begin with the Oct. 25, 1984 issue].

C5800-2.4: Materials Prices Tables

[All tables except table [8] show monthly market quotations by ENR field reporters for representative items within the category indicated by the table title. All show data current as of cover date; and, except table [4], for 22 cities (all cities generally are not covered for all materials).]

[1] Cement, aggregate, ready mixed concrete: f.o.b. city.

[2] Asphalt, road oil: f.o.b. city.

[3] Iron and steel products: f.o.b. warehouse, per 100 lb., base price.

[4] Mill base price: carlot quantities [steel; for selected mill areas].

[5] Plumbing, heating, sewer pipe, and tubing: delivered carload lots.

[6] Lumber, timber, plywood, piles, ties.

[7] Window glass, explosives.

[8] Wage rates for key building construction trades: total of union base rate plus fringes [for 18 types of common and skilled building labor, equipment operators, and truck drivers].

[9] Building board, lath, and insulation: quoted in trucklots, delivered to job.

[10] Structural clay building tile, brick, and lime: quoted in carlots, delivered to job.

[11] Plaster, light weight aggregate and metal sheets: quoted in trucklots, delivered; building sheets are f.o.b. warehouse.

[12] Paint and roofing: quoted in carlots, delivered to job.

C5800–2.5: New Plans and Bidding Volume Tables

1-2 tables showing value of new plans and bidding for heavy construction (12 types), non-residential building (9 types), and multi-unit housing (total and apartments); for month prior to cover date and year to date, with percent change from previous month and year.

C5800–2.6: Stock Track Table

Table showing stock price, revenue, earnings, and profitability ratios, for approximately 40 publicly owned companies (grouped as design firms, general and specialty contractors, and conglomerates). Most data are shown for latest available 12 months (identified by company).

STATISTICAL FEATURES:

C5800–2.501: Nov. 3, 1983 (Vol. 211, No. 18)

WEEKLY TABLES

a. Market trends, for week ended Oct. 27, 1983. (p. 118)

b. Unit prices, for North Carolina bridge construction and highway reconstruction contracts. (p. 117)

MONTHLY TABLES

a. Market trends, tables [1-3] for Oct. or Nov. 1983. (p. 118)

b. Materials prices, tables [1-2] for Nov. 1, 1983. (p. 100-101)

C5800–2.502: Nov. 10, 1983 (Vol. 211, No. 19)

WEEKLY TABLES

a. Market trends, for week ended Nov. 3, 1983. (p. 57)

b. Unit prices, for Houston International Airport taxiway construction contract. (p. 46)

MONTHLY TABLES

a. Market trends, tables [4-5] for Nov. 1983. (p. 57)

b. Materials prices, tables [3-5] for Nov. 10, 1983. (p. 42-43)

c. New plans and bidding volume, for Oct. 1983. (p. 34)

INDUSTRY FAILURES DECLINING, RECURRING FEATURE

(p. 15) Recurring article, with 1 chart, showing construction contractor failures, 1976-82 and 1st 10 months 1983. Data are from Dun and Bradstreet, Inc.

WAGE HIKES AT NEW LOW

(p. 65) Article, with 1 table showing average wage rate increase for 1st year and total duration of contract, and workers involved, for all, manufacturing, nonmanufacturing, and construction industries' collective bargaining agreements, 1st 9 months 1983. Data are from BLS.

C5800–2.503: Nov. 17, 1983 (Vol. 211, No. 20)

WEEKLY TABLES

a. Market trends, for week ended Nov. 10. (p. 50)

b. Unit prices, for improvement of Midland Texas Regional Airport. (p. 49)

MONTHLY TABLES

a. Market trends, tables [6-7] for Oct. 1983. (p. 50)

b. Materials prices, tables [6-7] for Nov. 17, 1983. (p. 46-47)

c. Stock track, for various periods, identified by company. (p. 34)

BUILDERS' RECEIPTS CLIMB

(p. 20) Article, with 1 table showing general contractor receipts, for building construction by type, and nonbuilding and nonspecified construction, 1977 and 1982. Data are from Census Bureau.

WORKER INJURY RATES MODERATING

(p. 66) Article, with 1 table showing injuries and lost workdays per 100 employees, for private sector, construction industry, and 3 contractor types, 1981-82. Data are from BLS.

C5800–2.504: Nov. 24, 1983 (Vol. 211, No. 21)

WEEKLY TABLES

a. Market trends, for week ended Nov. 17, 1983. (p. 56)

b. Unit prices, for California highway undercrossing and Nevada sewer outfall contracts. (p. 55)

MONTHLY TABLES

a. Market trends, tables [8, 10] for Oct. 1983, [9] for June 1983, and [11] for July 1982. (p. 56)

b. Materials prices, tables [10-12] for Nov. 24, 1983. (p. 42)

C5800–2.505: Dec. 1, 1983 (Vol. 211, No. 22)

WEEKLY TABLES

a. Market trends, for week ended Nov. 24, 1983. (p. 133)

b. Unit prices, for West Virginia dam contract. (p. 129)

MONTHLY TABLES

a. Market trends, tables [1-3] for Nov. or Dec. 1983. (p. 133)

b. Materials prices, tables [8-9] for Dec. 1, 1983. (p. 96-97)

INTERNATIONAL STOCK TRACK: FOREIGN FIRMS FACE MIXED FUTURES, QUARTERLY FEATURE

(p. 51) Quarterly article on recent market performance of 43 publicly owned international construction companies. Includes 1 table showing stock price, revenue, earnings, and profitability ratios, for 43 companies based in UK, France, West Germany, Netherlands, Japan, and Canada. Data are for latest available 12 months or latest closing date.

Data sources are Datastream, London, England; Financial Post Investment Databank, Toronto, Canada; and WestLB (Boursys), Duesseldorf, West Germany.

C5800–2.506: Dec. 8, 1983 (Vol. 211, No. 23)

WEEKLY TABLES

a. Market trends, for week ended Dec. 1, 1983. (p. 63)

b. Unit prices, for construction contract for 3 Tennessee highway bridges. (p. 59)

MONTHLY TABLES

a. Market Trends, tables [4-5] for Dec. 1983. (p. 63)

b. Materials prices, tables [1-2] for Dec. 8, 1983. (p. 54-55)

c. New plans and bidding volume, for Nov. 1983. (p. 33)

A-E LIABILITY COSTS EASING

(p. 64) Article on construction design firm insurance liability and cost. Data are from responses of 1,527 firms to an American Consulting Engineers Council survey. Includes 1 table showing insurance premium cost as percent of gross billings, by company employment size, 1980-83.

C5800–2.507: Dec. 15, 1983 (Vol. 211, No. 24)

WEEKLY TABLES

a. Market trends, for week ended Dec. 8, 1983. (p. 57)

b. Unit prices, for Washington State highway construction contract. (p. 49)

MONTHLY TABLES

a. Market trends, tables [6-7] for Nov. 1983. (p. 57)

b. Materials prices, tables [3-5] for Dec. 15, 1983. (p. 40-41)

c. Stock track, for various periods, identified by company. (p. 24)

EPA WATER ENFORCEMENT SLAMMED

(p. 10) Article on General Accounting Office investigation into EPA enforcement of water pollution control standards in 6 States. Data are based on a weighted random sample of effluent discharges conducted during the 18-month period ending Mar. 31, 1982. Includes 1 table showing total municipal and industrial dischargers, and number violating and significantly violating EPA standards.

C5800–2.508: Dec. 22, 1983 (Vol. 211, No. 25)

WEEKLY TABLES

a. Market trends, for week ended Dec. 15, 1983. (p. 103)

b. Unit prices, for Texas dam rehabilitation and Missouri highway construction contract. (p. 79, 82)

MONTHLY TABLES

a. Market trends, tables [8, 10] for Nov. 1983, [9] for July 1983, and [11] for July 1982. (p. 103)

b. Materials prices, tables [6-7] for Dec. 22, 1983. (p. 64-65)

QUARTERLY COST ROUNDUP

(p. 53-87) Quarterly report, for 4th quarter 1983, on construction industry cost trends and outlook. Data sources include Federal and State agencies, private organizations, and ENR surveys, and are identified on most tables and charts.

Contains introduction and 12 articles. Statistical contents of individual articles are described below.

a. "Forecast: Surveying the Recovery." Includes 3 tables showing building and construction cost indexes (total and for 20 cities), common and skilled labor wage rates and indexes, materials price index, and prices for 3 primary products, Dec. 1983-84 and percent change from 1982. (p. 56-57)

b. "Forecast: DRI, Inflation Makes a Slow Comeback." Includes 1 table showing percent change in prices for 26 types of construction material and equipment, 1980/81 average and 1982-85. (p. 58)

c. "Wages: Labor Costs Respond to Recession." Includes 1 table showing construction wage indexes for common and skilled labor, electricians, equipment operators, and mechanical trades, for 20 cities, 1982-83. (p. 61)

d. "Materials Prices: Prices Split Between Recovery, Recession." Includes 2 tables showing price indexes for steel, lumber, and cement, total and by type, for 20 cities, Nov. or Dec. 1982-83. (p. 64-67)

e. "Utility Costs: Market Slump Slows Inflation." Includes 1 chart and 1 table showing value of electric utility construction awards; and construction cost indexes for steam, nuclear, and hydroelectric power plants, by region; various years 1975-83. (p. 68)

f. "Builders' Indexes: Indexes Show Inflation Slowing." Includes 1 table showing 19 indexes of builders' construction costs, 1980-82 and monthly Dec. 1982-Dec. 1983. (p. 72)

g. "Machinery: Machinery Cost Increases Curbed." Includes 1 table showing price indexes for 43 types of construction equipment, Apr., July, and Oct. 1983 and percent change from Oct. 1982. (p. 73)

h. "Water and Power: Water Project Costs Move Higher." Includes 1 table showing Bureau of Reclamation cost indexes for water and power related construction, including dams, pumping plants, hydroelectric power plants, and transmission lines, Oct. 1977-83. (p. 74)

i. "Treatment Plants: Urban Sewerage Costs Lead Upturn." Includes 3 tables showing cost indexes, total and by cost component, for 5 and 50 million gallons per day municipal wastewater treatment plants, and for complete urban sewer systems, for 25 cities, 3rd quarter 1983 and percent change from 3rd quarter 1982. (p. 75)

j. "Money: Fed Fine-Tunes Credit Cost Path." Includes 1 chart showing value of new State/municipal construction bond sales and distribution by type of construction, Jan.-Nov. 1983 period. (p. 76-77)

k. "World Costs: Overseas Costs Rise Moderately." Includes 1 table showing replacement cost indexes for industrial buildings and machinery, for 7 countries, Jan. and/or July 1981-84 and annually 1970-80. (p. 78)

l. "Highways: Robust Market Hikes Bid Prices." Includes 2 tables showing highway bid price indexes, for 20 States and for Federal-aid excavation, surfacing, and struc-

ture projects; 3rd quarter 1983 with quarterly trends from 1979 or 1981, and annual trends from 1974 (Federal projects only). (p. 86-87)

LABOR SUPPLY REMAINS STABLE, QUARTERLY FEATURE

(p. 119) Quarterly article on construction industry labor shortages, as of Dec. 1983, based on ENR survey of contractors in 93 cities.

Includes list of cities in which contractors reported no shortage; and 1 table showing the following for each city in which some shortage was reported: number of contractors surveyed, number reporting no shortage, and percent reporting shortages for 19 construction trades and welders.

C5800–2.509: Jan. 5, 1984 (Vol. 212, No. 1)

WEEKLY TABLES

a. Market trends, for week ended Dec. 29, 1983. (p. 51)

b. Unit prices, for Utah highway construction contract. (p. 57)

MONTHLY TABLES

a. Market trends, tables [1-3] for Dec. 1983 or Jan. 1984. (p. 51)

b. Materials prices, tables [1-2] for Jan. 5, 1984. (p. 48-49)

OPEN SHOP GRABS MECHANICAL WORK, ANNUAL FEATURE

(p. 74) Annual article, with 1 table, on nonunion share of mechanical construction market, by type of structure, 1982-83. Data are from responses of 295 member firms to a Mechanical Contractors Assn of America survey.

C5800–2.510: Jan. 12, 1984 (Vol. 212, No. 2)

WEEKLY TABLES

a. Market trends, for week ended Jan. 5, 1984. (p. 108)

b. Unit prices, for Texas highway construction contract. (p. 115)

MONTHLY TABLES

a. Market trends, tables [4-5] for Jan. 1984. (p. 108)

b. Materials prices, tables [3-5] for Jan. 12, 1984. (p. 104-105)

ENR OUTLOOK '84, ANNUAL FEATURE

(p. 62-97) Annual construction industry overview, with 6 articles analyzing trends and outlook for the industry as a whole and for its major subdivisions, 1982-85. Includes introductory article (p. 62-68), with 1 chart and 3 tables showing the following:

a. Value of contracts, by type (excluding homebuilding), 1982-85; and Federal spending for public works, by type of project and agency or program, FY82-84.

b. Value of new plans and contract bidding: by region, 1982-83; and for top 10 States in 9 types of heavy and nonresidential construction, 1983 with percent change from 1982.

Data are from ENR and Bureau of Industrial Economics.

C5800–2.511: Jan. 19, 1984 (Vol. 212, No. 3)

WEEKLY TABLES

a. Market trends, for week ended Jan. 12, 1984. (p. 65)

b. Unit prices, for Bureau of Reclamation dam project in Utah. (p. 48)

MONTHLY TABLES

a. Market trends, tables [6-7] for Dec. 1983. (p. 65)

b. Materials prices, tables [6-7] for Jan. 19, 1984. (p. 44-45)

c. New plans and bidding volume, for Dec. 1983. (p. 32)

d. Stock track, for various periods, identified by company. (p. 23)

DEMAND FOR NEW FACILITIES BOOSTS MEDICAL CONSTRUCTION

(p. 32) Article, with 1 chart showing percent change in construction bidding value for public and private medical facilities, 1979-83 period. Data are from ENR.

C5800–2.512: Jan. 26, 1984 (Vol. 212, No. 4)

WEEKLY TABLES

a. Market trends, for week ended Jan. 19, 1984. (p. 57)

b. Unit prices, for Colorado highway grading and Idaho highway bridge construction contracts. (p. 40)

MONTHLY TABLES

a. Market trends, tables [8, 10] for Dec. 1983, [9] for July 1983, and [11] for July 1982. (p. 57)

b. Materials prices, tables [10-12] for Jan. 26, 1984. (p. 36-37)

C5800–2.513: Feb. 2, 1984 (Vol. 212, No. 5)

WEEKLY TABLES

a. Market trends, for week ended Jan. 26, 1984. (p. 49)

b. Unit prices, for 4 West Virginia sewer construction contracts. (p. 40)

MONTHLY TABLES

a. Market trends, tables [1-3] for Jan. or Feb. 1984. (p. 49)

b. Materials prices, tables [8-9] for Feb. 2, 1984. (p. 36-37)

ENGINEERS' SALARIES GREW 2.8% IN '83, SAYS AAES

(p. 63) Article, with 1 table showing salaries of engineers in supervisory and nonsupervisory positions, by years since bachelor's degree, 1982-83. Data are based on an American Assn of Engineering Societies survey covering 130,-000 engineers and 800 employers in 11 industries.

Full survey reports are covered in SRI under A0685-3 and A0685-5.

C5800–2.514: Feb. 9, 1984 (Vol. 212, No. 6)

WEEKLY TABLES

a. Market trends, for week ended Feb. 2, 1984. (p. 103)

b. Unit prices, for Vermont highway improvement contract. (p. 101)

MONTHLY TABLES

a. Market trends, tables [4-5] for Feb. 1984. (p. 103)

b. Materials prices, tables [1-2] for Feb. 9, 1984. (p. 82-83)

C5800–2.515: Feb. 16, 1984 (Vol. 212, No. 7)

WEEKLY TABLES

a. Market trends, for week ended Feb. 9, 1984. (p. 45)

b. Unit prices, for North Carolina highway grading contract. (p. 37)

MONTHLY TABLES

a. Market trends, tables [6-7] for Jan. 1984. (p. 45)

b. Materials prices, tables [3-5] for Feb. 16, 1984. (p. 32-33)

c. New plans and bidding volume, for Jan. 1984. (p. 19)

PUBLIC BUILDINGS TOP COST LIST

(p. 14-15) Article presenting results of a University of Tennessee study of building construction costs. Data were derived by comparing cost of constructing a standard 1-floor manufacturing building in 1972 with costs of a random sampling of 180,260 building contracts compiled by McGraw-Hill's F. W. Dodge Division.

Includes 1 table showing construction cost per square foot above or below the cost of the standard building, by building type and framing material, and for selected States and regions.

MICHIGAN CONTRACTORS FACE SHIFT IN INDUSTRIAL WORK

(p. 19) Article, with 1 table showing value of Michigan construction market by structure type, 1983, with percent change from 1982 and from 1977-79 average. Data are from ENR Construction Economics Dept.

C5800–2.516: Feb. 23, 1984 (Vol. 212, No. 8)

WEEKLY TABLES

a. Market trends, for week ended Feb. 16, 1984. (p. 47)

b. Unit prices, for California highway construction contract. (p. 36)

MONTHLY TABLES

a. Market trends, tables [8, 10] for Jan. 1984, [9] for Aug. 1983, and [11] for July 1982. (p. 47)

b. Materials prices, tables [6-7] for Feb. 23, 1984. (p. 34-35)

c. Stock track, for various periods, identified by company. (p. 21)

ENGINEERS' SALARIES INCH UP

(p. 18) Article, with 1 table showing engineers' average base salary, by level of responsibility, 1982-83. Data are from a D. Dietrich Associates Inc. survey of 298 companies employing 129,550 engineers.

CONCRETE CONSTRUCTORS GAIN

(p. 19) Article, with 1 table showing concrete construction firms' receipts, by type of building and nonbuilding structure, 1977 and 1982. Data are from Census Bureau.

C5800–2.517: Mar. 1, 1984 (Vol. 212, No. 9)

WEEKLY TABLES

a. Market trends, for week ended Feb. 23, 1984. (p. 49)

b. Unit prices, for Utah highway section construction contract. (p. 45)

MONTHLY TABLES

a. Materials prices, tables [8-12] for Mar. 1, 1984. (p. 40-41)

INTERNATIONAL STOCK TRACK: MODEST RECOVERY STARTS OVERSEAS, QUARTERLY FEATURE

(p. 32) Quarterly article on recent financial performance of 43 publicly owned international construction companies. Includes 1 table showing stock price, revenue, earnings, and profitability ratios, for 43 companies based in UK, France, West Germany, Netherlands, Japan, and Canada. Data are for latest available 12 months or latest closing date.

Data sources are Datastream, London, England; Financial Post Investment Databank, Toronto, Canada; and WestLB (Boursys), Duesseldorf, West Germany.

ENR REGIONAL MARKETS: EARTHWORK AND WATERWAYS

(p. 49) Two charts showing value of new plans and bidding, for earthwork/waterway construction, by region, 1983 and percent change from 1982. Data are from ENR. Charts appear in "Market Trends" section.

C5800–2.518: Mar. 8, 1984 (Vol. 212, No. 10)

WEEKLY TABLES

a. Market trends, for week ended Mar. 1, 1984. (p. 45)

b. Unit prices, for New Jersey highway reconstruction contract. (p. 40)

MONTHLY TABLES

a. Market trends, tables [1-3] for Feb. or Mar. 1984. (p. 45)

b. Materials prices, tables [1-2] for Mar. 8, 1984. (p. 36-37)

INFRASTRUCTURE FUND-GAP MAPPED

(p. 12-13) Article, with 1 table showing top 10 States ranked by funding shortage for infrastructure construction, and including total infrastructure funding requirements, 1984-2000 period. Data are from a study commissioned by the Joint Economic Committee of Congress.

C5800–2.519: Mar. 15, 1984 (Vol. 212, No. 11)

WEEKLY TABLES

a. Market trends, for week ended Mar. 8, 1984. (p. 45)

b. Unit prices, for Colorado highway construction contract. (p. 38)

MONTHLY TABLES

a. Market trends, tables [4-5] for Mar. 1984. (p. 45)

b. Materials prices, tables [3-5] for Mar. 15, 1984. (p. 36-37)

c. New plans and bidding volume, for Feb. 1984. (p. 20)

d. Stock track, for various periods, identified by company. (p. 18)

CONTRACT ILLS TOP PRIORITY

(p. 11) Article on problems associated with the construction contracting process. Data are from 790 responses to an Arthur Andersen and Co. survey of 5,000 construction companies, contractors, and design firms. Includes 1 undated chart showing distribution of respondents by greatest contracting problem.

C5800–2.520: Mar. 22, 1984 (Vol. 212, No. 12)

WEEKLY TABLES

a. Market trends, for week ended Mar. 15, 1984. (p. 49)

b. Unit prices, for Nebraska canal construction contract. (p. 43)

MONTHLY TABLES

a. Market trends, tables [6-7] for Feb. 1984. (p. 49)

b. Materials prices, tables [6-7] for Mar. 22, 1984. (p. 30-31)

ELECTRICAL RECEIPTS CLIMB

(p. 20) Article, with 1 table showing receipts of electrical contractors, by type of building and nonbuilding structure, 1977 and 1982. Data are from Census of Construction Industries.

C5800–2.521: Mar. 29, 1984 (Vol. 212, No. 13)

WEEKLY TABLES

a. Market trends, for week ended Mar. 22, 1984. (p. 167)

b. Unit prices, for California, Vermont, and Utah bridge construction contracts. (p. 85)

MONTHLY TABLES

a. Market trends, tables [8, 10] for Feb. 1984, [9] for Sept. 1983, and [11] for July 1982. (p. 167)

b. Materials prices, tables [8-9] for Mar. 29, 1984. (p. 160-161)

TUNNEL JOBS FUEL RECEIPTS

(p. 42) Article, with 1 table showing receipts of heavy construction contractors, by type of building and nonbuilding structure, 1977 and 1982. Data are from Census of Construction Industries.

QUARTERLY COST ROUNDUP

(p. 67-107) Quarterly report, for 1st quarter 1984, on construction industry cost trends and outlook. Data sources include Federal and State agencies, private organizations, and ENR surveys, and are identified on most tables.

Contains introduction and 8 articles. Statistical contents of individual articles with substantial data are described below.

a. "Materials Prices: Price Levels Adjust to Recovery." Includes 1 table showing average prices for cement, ready-mix concrete, structural steel shapes, crushed stone, mortar, and brick, aggregated for 20 cities, quarterly 1977-1st quarter 1984. (p. 70-72)

b. "Water and Power: BuRec Costs Rise Moderately." Includes 1 table showing Bureau of Reclamation cost indexes for water and power related construction, including dams, pumping plants, hydroelectric power plants, and transmission lines, Jan. 1978-84. (p. 79)

c. "Machinery: Cost Increases Held to 1.6%." Includes 1 table showing price indexes for 41 types of construction equipment, July and Oct. 1983 and Jan. 1984. (p. 80)

d. "Wages: Earlier Pacts Keep Lid on Costs." Includes 1 table showing construction wage indexes for common and skilled labor, electricians, equipment operators, and mechanical trades, for 20 cities, 1983-84. (p. 83)

e. "Highways: Bid Prices Climb in Hot Market." Includes 2 tables showing highway bid price indexes for 20 States, quarterly 1979-83; and Federal-aid highway bid price indexes, overall and for excavation, surfacing, and structures, 1974-83, with quarterly detail for 1980-83. (p. 90-93)

f. "Builders' Indexes: Cost Trends Remain Moderate." Includes 1 table showing 19 indexes of builders' construction costs, annually 1981-83 and monthly Mar. 1983-84. (p. 97-99)

INDEX HISTORY: CONSTRUCTION COSTS TRACKED FOR U.S., ANNUAL FEATURE

(p. 100-107) Annual article explaining ENR indexes of construction-related costs, and presenting historical trends in the indexes. Includes 3 tables, based on a 20 city sampling, showing building and construction cost indexes (1913 base year) as follows: total U.S., annually 1906 or 1913 to 1983, and monthly 1965-Mar. 1984; and for 20 cities, annually 1958-73, and last month of each quarter Mar. 1974-Mar. 1984.

Also includes 2 charts showing index components. Feature appears in the "Quarterly Cost Roundup" section.

C5800-2.522: Apr. 5, 1984 (Vol. 212, No. 14)

WEEKLY TABLES

a. Market trends, for week ended Mar. 29, 1984. (p. 76)

b. Unit prices, for Connecticut highway reconstruction contract. (p. 66)

MONTHLY TABLES

a. Market trends, tables [1-3] for Mar. or Apr. 1984. (p. 76)

b. Materials prices, tables [1-2] for Apr. 5, 1984. (p. 60-61)

PRISON CONSTRUCTION BOOM CONTINUES

(p. 11) Article, with 1 table showing number of local and State correctional institutions proposed/under construction, for top 10 States, 1984. Data are from National Moratorium on Prison Construction.

C5800-2.523: Apr. 12, 1984 (Vol. 212, No. 15)

WEEKLY TABLES

a. Market trends, for week ended Apr. 5, 1984. (p. 61)

b. Unit prices, for Maine bridge contract. (p. 48)

MONTHLY TABLES

a. Market trends, tables [4-5] for Apr. 1984. (p. 61)

b. Materials prices, tables [3-5] for Apr. 12, 1984. (p. 42-43)

c. New plans and bidding volume, for Mar. 1984. (p. 19)

C5800-2.524: Apr. 19, 1984 (Vol. 212, No. 16)

WEEKLY TABLES

a. Market trends, for week ended Apr. 12, 1984. (p. 122)

b. Unit prices, for Kentucky dam construction and Montana highway repaving contracts. (p. 120)

MONTHLY TABLES

a. Market trends, tables [6-7] for Mar. 1984. (p. 122)

b. Materials prices, tables [6-7] for Apr. 19, 1984. (p. 116-117)

c. Stock track, for various periods, identified by company. (p. 52)

TOP 400 CONTRACTORS, ANNUAL FEATURE

(p. 64-99) Annual report, for 1983, on new construction contract awards, based on an ENR survey of 2,500 contractors. Report covers domestic and foreign contracts, and includes the following data, shown for 1983 with selected comparisons to 1982:

a. Firms reporting over $1 billion in contracts; value of total and foreign contracts, construction management contracts as percent of total, and specialty, for top 400 construction firms; and foreign contract value and number of firms, by world area and contract type (design/construction, design only, and construction management). 3 tables.

b. Total contract value, value of all domestic and design/construction contracts, number of firms, and profit and loss; and value of management contracts, with detail for management at risk and fee only contracts and firms; all for top 400 firms grouped in aggregates of 40. 2 tables.

c. Management contract value (total and foreign) for top 75 program/construction managers; value of domestic contracts for top 50 general building contractors; and domestic contract value and specialty for top 25 heavy contractors. 3 tables.

d. Design construction contract value, with detail for foreign, design only, and design/construction management contracts; and specialty; for top 50 design/construction firms. 1 chart and 1 table.

e. Location of foreign contracts, by country and firm. 1 map.

This is the 21st annual report.

C5800-2.525: Apr. 26, 1984 (Vol. 212, No. 17)

WEEKLY TABLES

a. Market trends, for week ended Apr. 19, 1984. (p. 60)

b. Unit prices, for Colorado canal construction contract. (p. 59)

MONTHLY TABLES

a. Market trends, tables [8, 10] for Mar. 1984, [9] for Oct. 1983, and [11] for July 1982. (p. 60)

b. Materials prices, tables [10-12] for Apr. 26, 1984. (p. 50-51)

OPEN SHOPPERS RELEASE WAGE DATA

(p. 10) Article, with 1 table showing employment, hourly wage, and benefits value, for nonunion workers by selected craft, 1983. Data are based on responses of 248 contractors to a late 1983 survey conducted by Personnel Administration Services, Inc.

MECHANICAL REVENUES JUMP

(p. 20) Article, with 1 table showing mechanical contractor revenues for building, nonbuilding, and unspecified construction work, with detail by type of structure, 1977 and 1982. Data are from Census Bureau.

C5800-2.526: May 3, 1984 (Vol. 212, No. 18)

WEEKLY TABLES

a. Market trends, for week ended Apr. 26, 1984. (p. 36)

b. Unit prices, for NYC subway rehabilitation and Mississippi bridge substructure contracts. (p. 35)

MONTHLY TABLES

a. Materials prices, tables [8-9] for May 3, 1984. (p. 30-31)

OPEN SHOP AND UNIONS TOE TO TOE, ANNUAL FEATURE

(p. 28) Annual article, with 1 table showing number of union and open shop companies on ENR's list of the top 400 construction contractors for 1983, and average contract value, 1982-83, for 10 ranked groups from top 400. Data are from an annual survey of 2,500 contractors.

For description of full survey report, see C5800-2.524 above.

ENR REGIONAL MARKETS: MANUFACTURING FACILITIES

(p. 36) Two charts showing value of new plans and bidding, for manufacturing facility construction, by region, 1984 with comparisons to 1983. Data are from ENR. Charts appear in "Market Trends" section.

NCA: AN OPEN SHOP DROP?

(p. 52) Article, with 1 table showing number and value of nonunion construction projects in 14 States, 1981 and 1983. Data are from the National Constructors Assn.

C5800-2.527: May 10, 1984 (Vol. 212, No. 19)

WEEKLY TABLES

a. Market trends, for week ended May 3, 1984. (p. 55)

b. Unit prices, for New Jersey dam construction and Nevada airport runway reconstruction contracts. (p. 53)

MONTHLY TABLES

a. Market trends, tables [1-3] for Apr. or May 1984. (p. 55)

b. Materials prices, tables [1-2] for May 10, 1984. (p. 46-47)

WAGE HIKES OFF IN EARLY BARGAINING

(p. 56) Article, with 1 chart showing average wage rate percent change in 1st-year settlements for construction industries' collective bargaining agreements, 1979-83 and 1st quarter 1984. Data are from BLS.

C5800–2.528: May 17, 1984 (Vol. 212, No. 20)

WEEKLY TABLES

a. Market trends, for week ended May 10, 1984. (p. 174)

b. Unit prices, for Texas highway construction contract. (p. 171)

MONTHLY TABLES

a. Market trends, tables [4-5] for May 1984. (p. 174)

b. Materials prices, tables [3-5] for May 17, 1984. (p. 162-163)

c. Stock track, for various periods, identified by company. (p. 153)

TOP 500 DESIGN FIRMS: DESIGN BILLINGS, ANNUAL FEATURE

(p. 40-60) Annual report on 1983 billings of architectural and engineering design firms, based on an ENR survey of 500 largest firms. Report covers domestic and foreign billings, and includes the following:

a. Overview, with 4 charts and 1 table showing billings distribution and billings per staff member, by firm type, 1983; and total billings, foreign billings, and construction management fees, 1980-83.

b. Ranked list of top 500 design firms in 1983 total billings, grouped by billings size, showing type of firm and services offered-;and notes showing constituent firms for top 500.

c. Construction management (CM) and foreign summary, with ranked list of top 50 CM firms, showing CM percent of total billings; 1 chart showing foreign billings by world region; and notes showing locations of foreign operations for top 500.

This is the 20th annual report.

PAY UP 2.8% FOR A-E EXECS

(p. 189) Article, with 1 table showing executive compensation at architectural/engineering design firms, by position, 1983-84. Data are from a Jan. 1984 survey conducted by *Professional Services Management Journal.*

C5800–2.529: May 24, 1984 (Vol. 212, No. 21)

WEEKLY TABLES

a. Market trends, for week ended May 17, 1984. (p. 42)

b. Unit prices, for Nevada viaduct and Alaska highway construction contracts. (p. 41)

MONTHLY TABLES

a. Market trends, tables [6-7] for Apr. 1984. (p. 42)

b. Materials prices, tables [6-7] for May 24, 1984. (p. 34-35)

c. New plans and bidding volume, for Apr. 1984. (p. 21)

C5800–2.530: May 31, 1984 (Vol. 212, No. 22)

WEEKLY TABLES

a. Market trends, for week ended May 24, 1984. (p. 93)

b. Unit prices, for California highway interchange reconstruction contract. (p. 87)

MONTHLY TABLES

a. Market trends, tables [8, 10] for Apr. 1984, [9] for Nov. 1983, and [11] for July 1982. (p. 93)

b. Materials prices, tables [8-12] for May 31, 1984. (p. 80-81)

POWER FUELS HEAVY WORK

(p. 36, 39) Article, with 1 table showing heavy construction contractor receipts for building, nonbuilding, and unspecified construction work, with detail by structure type, 1977 and 1982. Data are from Census Bureau.

C5800–2.531: June 7, 1984 (Vol. 212, No. 23)

WEEKLY TABLES

a. Market trends, for week ended May 31, 1984. (p. 51)

b. Unit prices, for Vermont highway bridge construction contract. (p. 43)

MONTHLY TABLES

a. Market trends, tables [1-3] for May or June 1984. (p. 51)

b. Materials prices, tables [1-2] for June 7, 1984. (p. 36-37)

INTERNATIONAL STOCK TRACK: FOREIGN FIRMS FACE PALE FUTURE, QUARTERLY FEATURE

(p. 31) Quarterly article on recent financial performance of 42 publicly owned international construction companies. Includes 1 table showing stock price, revenue, earnings, and profitability ratios, for 42 companies based in UK, France, West Germany, Netherlands, Japan, and Canada. Data are for latest available 12 months or latest closing date.

Data sources are Datastream, London, England; Financial Post Investment Databank, Toronto, Canada; and WestLB (Boursys), Duesseldorf, West Germany.

UNION WAGE SCALE SLIDING, RECURRING FEATURE

(p. 58-59) Recurring article, with 1 table showing construction industry collective-bargaining settlements, workers covered, and average 1st-year wage change, by region, 1st 5 months 1984. Data are from Construction Labor Research Council.

C5800–2.532: June 14, 1984 (Vol. 212, No. 24)

WEEKLY TABLES

a. Market trends, for week ended June 7, 1984. (p. 49)

b. Unit prices, for Montana highway construction contract. (p. 41)

MONTHLY TABLES

a. Market trends, tables [4-5] for June 1984. (p. 49)

b. Materials prices, tables [3-5] for June 14, 1984. (p. 34-35)

COSTA RICA BEATS U.S.

(p. 51) Article, with 1 chart showing construction spending as percent of GDP for 11 countries, 1982. Data are from Associated General Contractors and the Confederation of International Contractors' Associations.

C5800–2.533: June 21, 1984 (Vol. 212, No. 25)

WEEKLY TABLES

a. Market trends, for week ended June 14, 1984. (p. 157)

b. Unit prices, for Louisiana highway interchange construction contract, and California and North Carolina highway reconstruction contracts. (p. 77)

MONTHLY TABLES

a. Market trends, tables [6-7] for May 1984. (p. 157)

b. Materials prices, tables [6-7] for June 21, 1984. (p. 148-149)

QUARTERLY COST ROUNDUP

(p. 67-106) Quarterly report, for 2nd quarter 1984, on construction industry cost trends and outlook. Data sources include Federal and State agencies, private organizations, and ENR surveys, and are identified on most tables.

Contains introduction and 13 articles. Statistical contents of articles with substantial data are described below.

a. "Highways: Bid Prices Yield to Competition." Includes 6 tables showing highway contracting and bid price indexes, by State; and Federal-aid highway bid price indexes for excavation, surfacing, and structures; various periods 1975-1st quarter 1984. (p. 72-74)

b. "Machinery: Prices Begin To Tack Higher." Includes 1 table showing price indexes for 44 types of construction equipment, Apr. 1984, with comparison to selected prior periods. (p. 79)

c. "Treatment Plants: Treatment Plant Inflation Quickens." Includes 3 tables showing cost indexes, total and by cost component, for 5 and 50 million gallons per day municipal wastewater treatment plants, and for complete urban sewer systems, for 25 cities, 1st quarter 1984 and change from 1st quarter 1983. (p. 80)

d. "Electric Utility: Cost Rise Sets Slower Pace." Includes 1 table showing construction cost indexes for steam, nuclear, and hydroelectric power plants, by region, Jan. 1976-84. (p. 83)

e. "Water and Power: Cost Increases Slow to a Crawl." Includes 1 table showing Bureau of Reclamation cost indexes for water and power related construction, including dams, hydroelectric power plants, and transmission lines, Apr. 1978-84. (p. 86)

f. "Airport Costs: Airport Facilities Costs Climb in the Northeast." Includes 2 tables showing airport facility cost index, Mar. 1976-84; and index weights, by component. (p. 89)

g. "Water Utility: Water Utility Inflation Slows." Includes 1 table showing construction cost indexes for water utility equipment by type, by region, Jan. 1976-84. (p. 91)

h. "Builders' Indexes: Building Costs Stay Down." Includes 2 tables showing percent change in building construction costs for 20 cities in 5 midwestern States, 1982-84; and 19 indexes of builders' construction costs, 1981-83 and monthly June 1983-June 1984. (p. 92)

i. "Materials Prices: Price Hikes Pace Slow Recovery." Includes 1 table showing average prices for selected construction materials including pipe (3 types), asphalt paving, portland cement, ready-mix concrete, and crushed stone, aggregated for 20 cities, quarterly 1978-2nd quarter 1984. (p. 99-100)

j. "Money: Borrowing Cost Jitters Worsen." Includes 1 table showing value of multi-family housing starts by type (2-4 family, condominium, and nonsubsidized and HUD Section 8 rental), 1979-83. (p. 104-105)

k. "Wages: Concessions Pervade Wage Pacts." Includes 1 table showing construction wage indexes for common and skilled labor, electricians, equipment operators, and mechanical trades, for 20 cities, 1983-84. (p. 106)

PAY FREEZES FEW FOR UNION HEADS

(p. 162-163) Article, with 1 table showing president's salary, allowance, and compensated expenses, for AFL-CIO Building and Construction Trades Dept and 16 affiliated unions, 1983. Data are from ENR and Dept of Labor.

C5800–2.534: June 28, 1984 (Vol. 212, No. 26)

WEEKLY TABLES

a. Market trends, for week ended June 21, 1984. (p. 65)

b. Unit prices, for Florida highway construction contract. (p. 59)

MONTHLY TABLES

a. Market trends, tables [8, 10] for May 1984, [9] for Dec. 1983, and [11] for July 1982. (p. 65)

b. Materials prices, tables [8-12] for June 28, 1984. (p. 46-47)

c. New plans and bidding volume, for May 1984. (p. 23)

d. Stock track, for various periods, identified by company. (p. 32)

INDUSTRY NEEDS MOTIVATION LESSON

(p. 66) Article, with 1 undated table showing average time lost due to delays in equipment/materials/tools/information, for 10 construction trades. Data are from the University of Michigan Dept of Civil Engineering.

C5800–2.535: July 5, 1984 (Vol. 213, No. 1)

WEEKLY TABLES

a. Market trends, for week ended June 28, 1984. (p. 77)

b. Unit prices, for Utah highway construction contract. (p. 71)

MONTHLY TABLES

a. Market trends, tables [4-5] for July 1984. (p. 77)

b. Materials prices, tables [1-2] for July 5, 1984. (p. 58-59)

EXEC'S PAY UPPED 9% TO $343,000, ANNUAL FEATURE

(p. 40-44) Annual report on construction industry executive compensation for FY83, based on a survey covering 292 executives at 60 publicly owned design firms, general and specialty contractors, conglomerates, and builders and developers. Data were collected for ENR by Sibson and Co.

Includes 2 tables showing salary, securities/bonus/benefits value, position, and company, for 10 most highly paid executives, FY83; and net profit, and total pay and position for each surveyed executive, by company arranged by type of firm, FY83 with percent change from FY82.

C5800–2.536: July 12, 1984 (Vol. 213, No. 2)

WEEKLY TABLES

a. Market trends, for week ended July 5, 1984. (p. 52)

b. Unit prices, for Connecticut highway reconstruction contract. (p. 51)

MONTHLY TABLES

a. Market trends, tables [1-3] for June or July 1984. (p. 52)

b. Materials prices, tables [3-5] for July 12, 1984. (p. 44-45)

MILITARY MUSTERS CONSTRUCTION'S FORCES

(p. 24-34) Compilation of articles on military construction plans and expenditures. Data are from DOD and Data Resources, Inc.

Includes 1 chart and 2 tables showing distribution of military construction spending, by service branch and for all other defense agencies, FY85; and defense expenditures for new construction by type and for maintenance/repair, and construction supplier revenue from military projects by type of equipment/material, in constant 1972 dollars, biennially FY83-89.

C5800–2.537: July 19, 1984 (Vol. 213, No. 3)

WEEKLY TABLES

a. Market trends, for week ended July 12, 1984. (p. 101)

b. Unit prices, for Idaho highway reconstruction and Louisiana maintenance dredging contracts. (p. 95)

MONTHLY TABLES

a. Market trends, tables [6-7] for June 1984. (p. 101)

b. Materials prices, tables [6-7] for July 19, 1984. (p. 92-93)

c. New plans and bidding volume, for June 1984. (p. 44)

d. Stock track, for various periods, identified by company. (p. 43)

TOP INTERNATIONAL CONTRACTORS, ANNUAL FEATURE

(p. 54-81) Annual report on foreign contract awards to world's largest international construction contractors, 1983. Presents ENR industry survey data on 250 firms. Includes the following data, for 1983:

a. Foreign contract awards and number of firms (total and for projects in 4 developing world regions), by firms' country; and profit margin for foreign and domestic contracts, by total value of foreign and domestic contracts. 8 tables.

b. Top 250 firms ranked by foreign contract awards, with total contract awards and construction specialty; and top 50 firms ranked by design-construction/design-only foreign contract awards, with separate totals for both types. 2 tables.

c. List showing contract work locations by country and firm.

This is the 6th annual survey.

MANAGEMENT WAGES TO RISE

(p. 115) Article, with 1 table showing construction industry average base salary and total compensation for 14 management positions, as of Mar. 1984. Data are from Personnel Administration Services, Inc.

C5800–2.538: July 26, 1984 (Vol. 213, No. 4)

WEEKLY TABLES

a. Market trends, for week ended July 19, 1984. (p. 53)

b. Unit prices, for California highway interchange construction contract. (p. 50)

MONTHLY TABLES

a. Market trends, tables [8] for May 1984, [9] for Jan. 1984, [10] for June 1984, and [11] for July 1982. (p. 53)

b. Materials prices, tables [10-12] for July 26, 1984. (p. 46-47)

C5800–2.539: Aug. 2, 1984 (Vol. 213, No. 5)

WEEKLY TABLES

a. Market trends, for week ended July 26, 1984. (p. 67)

b. Unit prices, for Utah highway interchange construction contract. (p. 59)

MONTHLY TABLES

a. Materials prices, tables [8-9] for Aug. 2, 1984. (p. 56-57)

OVERSEAS FIRMS CLOSING IN ON U.S.

(p. 10-11) Article on role of foreign construction contractors and design firms in the U.S. market. Data are from ENR. Includes 1 table showing number of firms, value of U.S. contracts or billings, and share of business awarded to all foreign firms, for 9 countries with largest shares of U.S. contract and design business, 1983.

TOP INTERNATIONAL DESIGN FIRMS, ANNUAL FEATURE

(p. 36-47) Annual report on foreign contract billings of 200 largest international construction design firms, 1983. Data are based on an ENR survey and include the following, shown for 1983:

a. Foreign and total billings, and number of firms, with detail for projects in 4 developing world regions; and percent of firms planning to increase and reduce domestic and foreign staff; all by firms' country. 6 tables.

b. Ranking of 200 firms grouped by size of foreign billings, showing foreign billings as percent of total company billings, type of company, and design specialties. 1 table.

c. List of contract work locations by country and firm.

This is the 6th annual survey.

ENR REGIONAL MARKETS: COMMERCIAL BUILDINGS

(p. 67) Two charts showing value of new plans and bidding, for commercial building construction, by region, 1st half 1984 with comparison to 1st half 1983. Data are from ENR. Charts appear in "Market Trends" section.

LABOR COSTS IN MANY AREAS FALLING, RECURRING FEATURE

(p. 82) Recurring article, with 1 table showing construction industry collective-bargaining settlements, workers covered, and average 1st- and 2nd-year change in wages/benefits, by region, 1st half 1984. Data are from Construction Labor Research Council.

MORE CONSTRUCTION JOBS SEEN

(p. 84) Article, with 1 chart showing growth rate in construction employment, for 8 occupational groups, 1982-95 period. Data are from BLS.

C5800–2.540: Aug. 9, 1984 (Vol. 213, No. 6)

WEEKLY TABLES

a. Market trends, for week ended Aug. 2, 1984. (p. 49)

b. Unit prices, for Charlotte, N.C., street reconstruction and Massachusetts airport runway reconstruction contracts. (p. 41)

MONTHLY TABLES

a. Market trends, tables [1-3] for July or Aug. 1984. (p. 49)

b. Materials prices, tables [1-2] for Aug. 9, 1984. (p. 34-35)

PENSIONS PLANS ARE HEALTHIER

(p. 51) Article, with 2 charts showing distribution of construction industry pension plans by percent of vested benefits funded, 1983-84. Data are based on a survey of 273 multi-employer pension plans, conducted by Martin E. Segal Co.

For description of a similar article showing data by industry division, see SRI 1983 Annual, under C5800-2.438.

C5800–2.541: Aug. 16, 1984 (Vol. 213, No. 7)

WEEKLY TABLES

a. Market trends, for week ended Aug. 9, 1984. (p. 57)

b. Unit prices, for Washington State highway bridge construction and West Virginia highway resurfacing contracts. (p. 40)

MONTHLY TABLES

a. Market trends, tables [4-5] for Aug. 1984. (p. 57)

b. Materials prices, tables [3-5] for Aug. 16, 1984. (p. 36-37)

c. New plans and bidding volume, for July 1984. (p. 24)

d. Stock track, for various periods, identified by company. (p. 32)

REPORT DETAILS FALL INJURIES

(p. 18) Article, with 1 chart on construction workers injured in falls, showing distribution of injuries by type of activity. Data are derived from a BLS survey of 774 workers in all industries who were injured in falls during an unspecified 6-month period.

ARIZONA MARKETS GAIN 95% IN THE FIRST HALF OF 1984

(p. 24) Article, with 1 chart showing value of new construction contracts (excluding 1-2 family houses), for 7 western States, 1st half 1984 with percent change from 1st half 1983. Data are from ENR.

C5800–2.542: Aug. 23, 1984 (Vol. 213, No. 8)

WEEKLY TABLES

a. Market trends, for week ended Aug. 16, 1984. (p. 123)

b. Unit prices, for Alaska airport and Vermont highway construction contracts. (p. 121)

MONTHLY TABLES

a. Market trends, tables [6-7] for July 1984. (p. 123)

b. Materials prices, tables [6-7] for Aug. 23, 1984. (p. 114-115)

TOP SPECIALTY CONTRACTORS: SPECIALTY CONTRACTORS TAKE CAUTIOUS TURN TO RECOVERY, ANNUAL FEATURE

(p. 50-69) Annual article on revenues and new contracts for largest specialty construction contractors, with comparative data for all specialty contractors, 1983. Data are from an ENR industry survey covering 7 specialty areas. Includes the following data:

a. Revenues and value of new contracts, and revenue from renovation/repair, aggregated for largest mechanical and electrical contractors, various years 1979-83. 4 charts.

b. Rankings by total revenue, with revenue from foreign work and percent from renovation, value of new contracts, and types of specialties, for 100 largest mechanical and electrical contractors, and for 15-30 largest roofing/sheet metal, excavation/foundation, demolition/wrecking, steel erection, and glazing/curtain wall contractors, 1983. 7 tables.

c. Number of firms; and revenues, with distribution among building, nonbuilding, and other contracts; for all mechanical, electrical, roofing/sheet metal, excavation/foundation, and steel erection contractors, 1972, 1977, and 1982. 4 charts.

This is the 7th annual survey.

C5800–2.543: Aug. 30, 1984 (Vol. 213, No. 9)

WEEKLY TABLES

a. Market trends, for week ended Aug. 23, 1984. (p. 57)

b. Unit prices, for California light rail line construction contract. (p. 45)

MONTHLY TABLES

a. Market trends, tables [8, 10] for July 1984, [9] for Feb. 1984, and [11] for July 1982. (p. 57)

b. Materials prices, tables [8-12] for Aug. 30, 1984. (p. 34-35)

ABC RELEASES WAGE SURVEY

(p. 59) Article, with 1 table showing average hourly wage in 9 construction crafts, for nonunion journeymen and foremen working in Virginia. Data are from responses of 354 nonunion contractors to an early 1984 Virginia Polytechnic Institute survey sponsored by Associated Builders and Contractors.

C5800–2.544: Sept. 6, 1984 (Vol. 213, No. 10)

WEEKLY TABLES

a. Market trends, for week ended Aug. 30, 1984. (p. 59)

b. Unit prices, for North Carolina highway construction contract. (p. 41)

MONTHLY TABLES

a. Market trends, tables [1-3] for Aug. or Sept. 1984. (p. 59)

b. Materials prices, tables [1-2] for Sept. 6, 1984. (p. 38-39)

INTERNATIONAL STOCK TRACK: FOREIGN FIRMS FACE SLACK TIMES, QUARTERLY FEATURE

(p. 21) Quarterly article on recent financial performance of 43 publicly owned international construction companies. Includes 1 table showing stock price, revenue, earnings, and profitability ratios, for 43 companies based in UK, France, West Germany, Netherlands, Japan, and Canada. Data are for latest available 12 months or latest closing date.

Data sources are Datastream, London, England; Financial Post Investment Databank, Toronto, Canada; and WestLB (Boursys), Duesseldorf, West Germany.

CONSTRUCTION PAY STAGNATES

(p. 62) Article, with 1 table showing average annual wages in construction and all industry, for 16 States and total U.S., 1983 with percent change from 1982. Data are from BLS.

C5800–2.545: Sept. 13, 1984 (Vol. 213, No. 11)

[Issue incorrectly reads Vol. 212, No. 11.]

WEEKLY TABLES

a. Market trends, for week ended Sept. 6, 1984. (p. 47)

b. Unit prices, for California highway interchange reconstruction contract. (p. 41)

MONTHLY TABLES

a. Market trends, tables [4-5] for Sept. 1984. (p. 47)

b. Materials prices, tables [3-5] for Sept. 13, 1984. (p. 38-39)

C5800–2.546: Sept. 20, 1984 (Vol. 213, No. 12)

WEEKLY TABLES

a. Market trends, for week ended Sept. 13, 1984. (p. 173)

b. Unit prices, for California and Alaska highway resurfacing contracts, and Vermont highway reconstruction contract. (p. 95)

MONTHLY TABLES

a. Market trends, tables [6-7] for Aug. 1984. (p. 173)

b. Materials prices, tables [6-7] for Sept. 20, 1984. (p. 160-161)

QUARTERLY COST ROUNDUP

(p. 67-113) Quarterly report, for 3rd quarter 1984, on construction industry cost trends and outlook. Data sources include Federal and State agencies, private organizations, and ENR surveys, and are identified on most tables.

Contains introduction and 10 articles. Statistical contents of articles with substantial data are described below.

a. "Wages: Focus on Jobs Curbs Labor Costs." Includes 3 tables showing hourly construction wage by detailed trade in 34 cities (including 2 in Canada), Aug. 1, 1984, and for 5 trades in 78 cities, May 1984; and construction wage indexes for common and skilled labor, equipment operators, electricians, and mechanical trades, in 20 cities, Sept. 1983-84. (p. 73-85)

b. "Water and Power: BuRec Costs Move Slowly Upward." Includes 1 table showing Bureau of Reclamation cost indexes for water and power related construction, including dams, pumping plants, hydroelectric power plants, and transmission lines, July 1978-84. (p. 86)

c. "Builders' Indexes: Indexes Show Minor Cost Gains." Includes 1 table showing 18 indexes of builders' construction costs, 1981-83 and monthly Sept. 1983-Sept. 1984. (p. 92)

d. "Machinery: Equipment Prices Edge Higher." Includes 1 table showing price indexes for 35 types of construction equipment, Jan., Apr., and July, 1984 and percent change from July 1983. (p. 98)

e. "Canadian Costs: Competition Curbs Canadian Costs." Includes 1 table showing Canadian construction cost index, nationwide and in 10 cities, Jan. 1979-84 and July 1984 with percent change from July 1983. (p. 103)

f. "Insurance: Insurance Rates Show Few Signs of Change." Includes 1 table and 1 chart showing construction workers' compensation insurance rates, by detailed type of work by State, and averages for 10 States with highest overall rates, July 1984. (p. 104-105)

g. "Materials Prices: Price Hikes Bow to Competition." Includes 1 table showing average prices for selected construction materials including structural steel, building sheet and plate, and copper pipe, aggregated for 20 cities, 2nd quarter 1978-3rd quarter 1984. (p. 109-110)

h. "Highways: Fewer Bidders Fuel Higher Costs." Includes 2 tables showing highway bid price indexes, for 20 States and for Federal-aid excavation, surfacing, and structure projects, 2nd quarter 1984, with quarterly trends from 1980 or 1981, and annual trends from 1975 (Federal projects only). (p. 112-113)

WAGES MOVE UP SLIGHTLY, RECURRING FEATURE

(p. 175) Recurring article, with 1 table showing construction industry collective-bargaining settlements, workers covered, and average 1st-year wage change, total and for 10 crafts, 1st 8 months 1984. Data are from Construction Labor Research Council.

C5800-2.547: Sept. 27, 1984 (Vol. 213, No. 13)

WEEKLY TABLES

a. Market trends, for week ended Sept. 20, 1984. (p. 57)

b. Unit prices, for Maine bridge-deck reconstruction contract. (p. 55)

MONTHLY TABLES

a. Market trends, tables [8, 10] for Aug. 1984, [9] for Mar. 1984, and [11] for July 1982. (p. 57)

b. Materials prices, tables [8-12] for Sept. 27, 1984. (p. 46-47)

c. Stock track, for various periods, identified by company. (p. 32)

HIGHWAY SPENDING UP 23%, ANNUAL FEATURE

(p. 12-13) Annual article on State highway construction plans, 1984-85. Data were compiled by ENR Construction Economics Dept. Includes 1 table showing planned highway construction spending, by State, 1984-85, with change from 1983, and repair/rehabilitation/reconstruction share of 1984 spending.

C5800-2.548: Oct. 4, 1984 (Vol. 213, No. 14)

WEEKLY TABLES

a. Market trends, for week ended Sept. 27, 1984. (p. 101)

b. Unit prices, for Wyoming and California highway reconstruction contracts. (p. 95)

MONTHLY TABLES

a. Market trends, tables [1-3] for Sept. or Oct. 1984. (p. 101)

b. Materials prices, tables [1-2] for Oct. 4, 1984. (p. 82-83)

BIG HOLES IN HEALTH EFFECTS RESEARCH

(p. 20-21) Article, with 1 table ranking problems affecting potable water supply, currently and in 5-10 years. Data are from responses of 34 water experts to a 1983 survey conducted by Malcolm Pirnie, Inc.

C5800-2.549: Oct. 11, 1984 (Vol. 213, No. 15)

WEEKLY TABLES

a. Market trends, for week ended Oct. 4, 1984. (p. 57)

b. Unit prices, for Minnesota highway construction contract. (p. 51)

MONTHLY TABLES

a. Market trends, tables [4-5] for Oct. 1984. (p. 57)

b. Materials prices, tables [3-5] for Oct. 11, 1984. (p. 38-39)

c. New plans and bidding volume, for Sept. 1984. (p. 25)

C5800-2.550: Oct. 18, 1984 (Vol. 213, No. 16)

WEEKLY TABLES

a. Market trends, for week ended Oct. 11, 1984. (p. 87)

b. Unit prices, for Missouri highway reconstruction contract. (p. 75)

MONTHLY TABLES

a. Market trends, tables [6-7] for Sept. 1984. (p. 87)

b. Materials prices, tables [6-7] for Oct. 18, 1984. (p. 66-67)

c. Stock track, for various periods, identified by company. (p. 58)

CONSTRUCTION PACs EXPANDING

(p. 14) Article, with 1 table showing top 6 political action committees sponsored by the construction industry, ranked by receipts, 1981/82 and 1983/84. Data are from ENR.

INDUSTRY HEADED FOR A SLOWER PACE, ANNUAL FEATURE

(p. 53-57) Annual article on 1983-85 construction industry trends and outlook, based on ENR fall 1984 survey of 209 design firms.

Includes 1 table and 1 chart showing actual and forecast contract value for all construction (excluding homes), and for heavy, nonresidential building, and multi-unit residential construction, by type, 1983-85; and value of new plans and bidding volume, by region, 1st 9 months 1983-84.

C5800-2.551: Oct. 25, 1984 (Vol. 213, No. 17)

WEEKLY TABLES

a. Market trends, for week ended Oct. 18, 1984. (p. 65)

b. Unit prices, for Florida bridge construction contract. (p. 61)

MONTHLY TABLES

a. Market trends, tables [8, 10] for Sept. 1984, [9] for Apr. 1984, and [11] for 1981-82. (p. 65)

b. Materials prices, tables [10-12] for Oct. 25, 1984. (p. 46-47)

CONSTRUCTION SPURS ECONOMY

(p. 11) Article, with 1 table showing number of jobs created in contract construction and other industries, assuming a $10 billion per year increase in Federal construction spending, 1984-90. Data are from Data Resources, Inc.

DEMOLITION HOT IN UK, TOO

(p. 26-27) Article, with 2 undated charts showing distribution of costs for decommissioning a Japanese pressurized-water nuclear reactor through land and sea disposal of wastes. Data are from Gilbert/Commonwealth International, Inc.

MCAA FIRMS ON THE SKIDS

(p. 67) Article, with 1 chart showing aggregate pre-tax net income, for 90 member firms of the Mechanical Contractors Assn of America (MCAA), biennially 1975-83. Data are from MCAA.

C5800-3 MCGRAW-HILL ANNUAL SPRING AND FALL SURVEYS OF BUSINESS' PLANS FOR NEW PLANTS AND EQUIPMENT
Series. For individual publication data, see below.
SRI/MF/complete

Series of 2 annual reports on planned capital investment for plants and equipment in approximately 25 industry groups, 1982-87. Data are from annual spring and fall surveys conducted by McGraw-Hill Economics Dept. Companies surveyed account for approximately 28-33% of all U.S. capital spending.

Reports present previous year actual, current year planned or estimated, and future 2-3 years preliminary planned capital spending data, and also include data on expectations for sales, prices, and industry growth.

Reports generally contain narrative analysis, methodology, and 10-15 tables. Reports for fall 1983 and spring 1984 are described below.

An executive summary for each report is also published, but is not covered by SRI.

Availability: McGraw-Hill, Economics Department, 1221 Ave. of the Americas, New York NY 10020; SRI/MF/complete.

C5800-3.1: 30th Annual McGraw-Hill Fall Survey of Preliminary Plans for New Plants and Equipment, 1983-85

[Annual. Nov. 1983. 24 p. $45.00. SRI/MF/complete.]

Annual fall survey of approximately 530 business firms to determine preliminary capital spending plans, 1983-85, with some actual data for 1982. Also covers capital spending for energy conservation and automation, and assessments of sales and economic outlooks.

Includes narrative report, with 4 text tables showing real and inflation-adjusted plant/equipment spending, quarterly 1983-84; selected financial indicators of capital spending strength, various periods 1975-83; operating rate, and percent change in sales and in profits, by major manufacturing industry group, 1983; and indicators of economic health in selected nonmanufacturing industries, 1982-83 (p. 1-15). Also includes table listing (p. 16); and 8 tables showing data by major industry group, as follows:

a. Capital spending, actual 1982, estimated 1983, and planned 1984-85; and expectations for plant/equipment and product price changes, and sales and real sales amounts, 1983-84. 4 tables. (p. 17-20)

b. Percent of respondents anticipating recession, and slow, normal, and rapid growth in 1984, weighted by company size and unweighted; percent of capital spending for energy conservation, 1983-84, and for automation, 1982-84; and survey sample size. 4 tables. (p. 21-24)

C5800-3.2: 37th Annual McGraw-Hill Spring Survey of Business' Plans for New Plants and Equipment, 1984-87

[Annual. May 1984. 25 p. $50.00. SRI/MF/complete.]

Annual spring survey of 540 business firms to determine capital spending plans for 1984-87.

Contains narrative analysis, with 5 tables showing capital spending summary and selected economic indicators, various periods 1981-84 (p. 1-15); table listing (p. 16); and 9 detailed tables showing the following data by industry group:

a. Capital spending amounts, and percent for expansion, replacement/modernization, buildings, motor vehicles, and machinery/equipment, various periods 1983-87. Tables I-III. (p. 17-19)

b. Capacity expansion index, 1983-85; rates of operation, 1982-83; actual sales, 1983; and expected sales and inflation rate, and sample firms' percent of total industry capital spending, 1984. Tables IV-IX. (p. 20-25)

C5800-4   AVIATION WEEK AND SPACE TECHNOLOGY

Weekly. Approx. 100 p.
ISSN 0005-2175.
LC 18-14054.
SRI/MF/not filmed

Weekly trade journal reporting on developments in air transport, space technology, aeronautical and missile engineering, business flying, avionics, and military aviation.

Data are from individual airline reports, NASA, CAB, I. P. Sharp Associates, and other sources, and are current to 1-6 months prior to publication date.

Contents:

a. Articles and news items, occasionally containing substantial statistics.

b. 1 monthly and 3 quarterly tables on airline traffic, income, and expenses; and aircraft operating and cost data; by airline.

c. 1 monthly table on business and utility aircraft shipments.

d. Semiannual subject index to articles and features.

e. Annual features, including marketing directory to products and services in the aerospace industry (Dec.); aerospace industry forecast and inventory; civil aviation fuel supply-demand outlook; Federal aerospace budget proposals; and list of top 100 DOD contractors.

Monthly and quarterly tables are listed below. All additional features with substantial statistical content are described, as they appear, under "Statistical Features;" page locations and latest periods of coverage for monthly and quarterly tables are also noted. Nonstatistical features and issues are not covered.

Availability: Aviation Week and Space Technology, Fulfillment Manager, PO Box 1505, Neptune NJ 07753, qualified subscribers $48.00 per yr., selected others $60.00 per yr., single copy $4.00, special issues $8.00; SRI/MF/not filmed.

Issues reviewed during 1984: Nov. 7, 1983-Oct. 29, 1984 (P) (Vol. 119, Nos. 19-26; Vol. 120, Nos. 1-26; Vol. 121, Nos. 1-18) [Vol. 121, Nos. 15-17 incorrectly read Vol. 122].

MONTHLY TABLES:

[Tables may not appear every month.]

AIRLINE STATISTICS

[1] Airline traffic [number of revenue miles, enplaned passengers, revenue passenger miles, available seat miles, passenger load factor, and total and freight revenue ton-miles, for over 30 domestic, international, large regional, Alaskan, Hawaiian, and all cargo airlines, for month of coverage].

AIRCRAFT SHIPMENTS STATISTICS

[2] Business and utility aircraft shipments [number of aircraft shipped by manufacturers, by model, for month of coverage and year to date; total factory billings, by manufacturer, for month of coverage; and total and export shipments and billings for all manufacturers during month of coverage, year to date, and same periods of previous year].

QUARTERLY TABLES:

[Data are shown for quarter of coverage.]

[1]   Operating and cost data, 747, 767, A300B, DC-10, and L-1011 [shows the following items for the 5 major wide-body aircraft models, by carrier:

a. Scheduled passenger service: revenue, revenue passenger, and available seat miles; average passenger load and seat capacity; and passenger load factor.

b. All services: selected operating data, including revenue, revenue ton, and available ton miles; average ton load and capacity, and

overall load factor; nonrevenue miles as percent of revenue; revenue and nonrevenue hours; average aircraft and utilization; departures; average flight length and duration; and fuel and oil use.

c. Operating expenses: for crew, fuel/oil/taxes, insurance, aircraft maintenance, and other operations; and write-off for rentals and flight depreciation].

[2]   Airline income and expenses [shows operating revenues from passengers, freight, and charters; total operating expense; and net profit/loss; for over 30 major domestic and international, national, large regional, Alaskan, and Hawaiian carriers. Prior to July 16, 1984 issue, table also showed subsidies for Alaska and local service carriers].

[3]   Narrow-body aircraft direct expenses [shows most of operating and cost data similar to that described in quarterly table [1] above, for 5 narrow-body models, by carrier; table begins with the Jan. 9, 1984 issue].

STATISTICAL FEATURES:

C5800-4.501: Nov. 14, 1983 (Vol. 119, No. 20)

INTERNATIONAL AIR TRANSPORT, ANNUAL FEATURE

Annual collection of features on international air transport operations and finances. Data are from International Air Transport Assn (IATA), CAB, and other sources. Features with substantial statistical content are individually described below.

ANNUAL TABLES

(p. 101, 129-138, passim) Four annual tables showing national domestic and regional airline industry operating revenues and expenses, and revenue and available ton-miles, quarterly 1977-2nd quarter 1983.

INDUSTRY EXPECTS STABILITY IN FUEL PRICES, AVAILABILITY, ANNUAL ARTICLE

(p. 109-110) Annual article, by Whitt Flora, on civil aviation fuel supply/demand and price outlook. Includes 1 table showing jet fuel and aviation gasoline consumption, for air carriers and general aviation, FY78-94.

FREIGHT GAINS LEAD TO GREATER CAPACITY IN LOWER DECK DESIGN

(p. 154-156) By Anne Randolph. Article on growth of air freight volume and carrier capacity. Includes 1 chart showing revenue ton-kilometer growth rates for containerized and palletized belly cargo, worldwide, various periods 1973-97.

WORLD ANNUAL COMMERCIAL AIRPLANE DELIVERIES

(p. 194) Chart showing value of commercial aircraft open orders, sales, and deliveries, for U.S. and foreign airlines, various periods 1950-95. Data are from Boeing Commercial Airplane Co.

C5800-4.502: Nov. 21, 1983 (Vol. 119, No. 21)

CARRIERS INTENSIFY LABOR COST DRIVE

(p. 27-30) By James Ott. Article on airline strategies to reduce labor costs. Data are from Air Transport Assn. Includes 1 chart and 2 tables showing percent change in employee compensation and output, fares, profit margin, and total productivity, compared to CPI and total industry profit margin, various periods 1972-82; and selected operating costs as percent of total, 1978 and 2nd quarter 1983.

C5800-4.503: Nov. 28, 1983 (Vol. 119, No. 22)

MONTHLY TABLE

[2] Business and utility aircraft shipments, for Oct. 1983. (p. 119)

GERMANY PLANS $10 BILLION U.S. DEFENSE BUY

(p. 21) Brief article, with text data on West German plans for weapons system procurement from U.S. industry, by manufacturer and model.

CAB URGED TO REDUCE BIAS IN RESERVATIONS SYSTEMS

(p. 34-35) Article on airline computer reservations systems. Data are from Justice Dept. Includes 1 table showing number of travel agencies and value of revenues generated, by computer reservations system and total for unautomated agencies, FY83.

EUROPEANS SEEK UNIFIED ARMS DEVELOPMENT, SALES

(p. 131-132) Article on EC proposal to limit European arms sales to developing countries. Data are from European Parliament. Includes 2 tables showing value of world arms exports to developing countries, by country or area of origin, 1970-79 period; and value of EC arms exports, total and as a percent of all national exports, by country, 1980.

C5800-4.504: Dec. 19, 1983 (Vol. 119, No. 25)

MONTHLY TABLE

[1] Airline traffic, for June 1983. (p. 37)

C5800-4.505: Jan. 2, 1984 (Vol. 120, No. 1)

MONTHLY TABLES

[1] Airline traffic, for July-Aug. 1983. (p. 32, 36)

[2] Business and utility aircraft shipments, for Nov. 1983. (p. 61)

C5800-4.506: Jan. 9, 1984 (Vol. 120, No. 2)

QUARTERLY TABLE

[3] Narrow-body aircraft direct expenses, 1st half 1983. (p. 40-41)

NATO COUNTRY DEFENSE EXPENDITURES, ANNUAL FEATURE

(p. 54) Annual article, with 2 tables showing NATO defense expenditures and expenditure share of GDP, by country, various years 1979-83.

C5800-4.507: Jan. 16, 1984 (Vol. 120, No. 3)

MILITARY SEEKING UPGRADED CAPABILITIES

(p. 84-89) Article, with 1 table showing Army helicopter fleet modernization plans, by model and application, decennially 1980-2010.

C5800-4.508: Jan. 30, 1984 (Vol. 120, No. 5)

MONTHLY TABLE

[2] Business and utility aircraft shipments, for Dec. 1983. (p. 50)

JAPAN SEEKS $12.5 BILLION DEFENSE BUDGET, ANNUAL FEATURE

(p. 21) Annual table showing aircraft and weapons requested and approved for procurement in Japan, for air, ground, and maritime self-defense forces, by manufacturer and model, FY84. Includes brief narrative.

U.S. AIRLINE TRAFFIC RISES BY ESTIMATED 8% IN 1983, RECURRING FEATURE

(p. 35-36) Recurring report, by Carole A. Shifrin, with 2 tables showing Dec. and full-year revenue passenger miles and available seat miles 1983, and load factor 1982-83, for 11 major and 13 other domestic airlines.

C5800-4.509: Feb. 6, 1984 (Vol. 120, No. 6)

SPECIAL REPORT: FISCAL 1985 AEROSPACE BUDGETS, ANNUAL FEATURE

Annual collection of articles analyzing FY85 aerospace budget proposals of DOD, NASA, and FAA. Articles with substantial statistical content are individually described below.

DEFENSE DEPT STRESSES RESEARCH, READINESS, UPGRADES, ANNUAL FEATURE

(p. 14-18) Annual article, by Clarence A. Robinson, Jr., analyzing DOD budget requests for FY85. Includes listings of FY85 funding requests for major weapons systems; and 1 table showing military R&D obligations and outlays, by program, 1983-85.

FISCAL 1985 MAJOR WEAPON SYSTEMS SPENDING DESCRIBED BY MILITARY SERVICE, ANNUAL FEATURE

(p. 16-17) Annual listing of Air Force, Navy, and Army funding requests for aircraft and missiles, showing manufacturer and model, budget request, and number to be procured or developed, FY85.

SPACE STATION FUNDING BID ADDS NEW NASA LINE ITEM, ANNUAL FEATURE

(p. 25-27) Annual article, by Craig Covault, on NASA proposed budget for FY85. Includes 1 table showing NASA budget requests, by program component, FY83-85.

Other Article

HELICOPTER COMPANIES EXPECTING UPTURN THIS YEAR

(p. 44-51) By Robert R. Ropelewski. Article, with 3 charts showing North American vs. foreign and civil vs. military helicopter deliveries, 1974-83 and 1984-93 periods; and high and low forecasts of total delivery volume and value, 1982-91 period. Data are from General Motors Corp. and Bell Helicopter Textron.

C5800-4.510: Feb. 13, 1984 (Vol. 120, No. 7)

TRAFFIC DROPS SLIGHTLY IN JAN., RECURRING FEATURE

(p. 28-29) Recurring report, by Carole A. Shifrin, on traffic of major and nonmajor airlines, Jan. 1984, with comparisons to same period of 1983.

Includes text data on 9 nonmajor carriers; and 1 table showing revenue passenger miles, available seat miles, and load factors, for 11 major carriers.

DEFICITS MAY FORCE 'BUY EUROPE' POLICY

(p. 135-140) By Michael Feazel. Article, with 2 tables showing EC/U.S. civil aircraft trade balance, by country; and market share of EC-built transport aircraft, by selected world area; various years 1977-82.

C5800-4.511: Feb. 27, 1984 (Vol. 120, No. 9)

USAF, NAVY ACCIDENT RATES CONTINUE TO IMPROVE

(p. 64-67) By David M. North. Article, with 2 tables showing Navy and Air Force flight hours, accidents, and accident rates, by aircraft model; with detail for Air Force Commands and summary for Marine Corps; 1983.

C5800-4.512: Mar. 12, 1984 (Vol. 120, No. 11)

AEROSPACE FORECAST AND INVENTORY, ANNUAL FEATURE

(p. 8-267) Annual feature forecasting aerospace industry sales growth, technology development, and air travel in 1980s. Includes detailed analyses of defense and space programs, by country; aircraft and spacecraft specifications; R&D; and commercial sector traffic and finances. Also includes some historical trends.

Contains numerous articles, summary and trend charts, and the following more substantial statistics:

a. Sales by aerospace industry sector, 1983-86; and U.S. and European defense and space budget procurement requests, by manufacturer and model (U.S. data based on FY85 budget requests). Text data and 1 chart. (p. 8-17)

b. Military: USSR strategic and tactical weapons production/inventory vs. U.S. FY85 budget requests, by weapons system; EC-designed aircraft as percent of military fleets, by world area, 1977 and 1981; sales of individual European aerospace companies, 1979-82; and aerospace industry revenues for U.S. and 6 European countries, 1978-81. Text data, 1 chart, and 3 tables. (p. 24-93)

c. Specifications: international aircraft, surface effect and launch vehicles, spacecraft, research rockets, missiles, and engines, by country, manufacturer, and model, with detail for U.S. and Soviet Union. 28 tabular lists. (p. 135-173)

d. Air transport: value of aircraft in service/on order, by manufacturer 1977-82, and for U.S. and by European country 1982. 2 tables. (p. 196-197)

e. Business flying: market shares of U.S. and EC business aircraft and helicopters in service, by European country, various years 1977-81. 2 tables. (p. 265-267)

C5800-4.513: Mar. 19, 1984 (Vol. 120, No. 12)

MONTHLY TABLE

[2] Business and utility aircraft shipments, for Jan. 1984. (p. 108)

FOURTH-QUARTER RISE FAILS TO YIELD 1983 NET PROFIT, RECURRING FEATURE

(p. 36-37) Recurring article, by Carole A. Shifrin, on finances of major domestic carriers in 4th quarter and full year 1983, with comparisons to 1982.

Includes 1 table showing revenues, expenses, and net profit or loss, for 11 major carriers, 1983, with percent change from 1982.

C5800–4.514: Mar. 26, 1984 (Vol. 120, No. 13)

TRAFFIC DROPS AGAIN IN FEB., RECURRING FEATURE

(p. 28-29) Recurring report, by Carole A. Shifrin, on traffic of major and nonmajor airlines, Feb. 1984, with comparisons to same period of 1983.

Includes 1 table showing revenue passenger miles, available seat miles, and load factors, for 11 major carriers and 16 nonmajor carriers.

SMOKING BAN WILL COVER COMMUTER-CLASS AIRCRAFT

(p. 31-32) By James Ott. Article, with 1 table showing passenger capacity of aircraft affected by 1984 tobacco smoking ban imposed on carriers with 30 or fewer seats, by manufacturer and model.

EARNINGS OF SMALLER CARRIERS IMPROVE, RECURRING FEATURE

(p. 37, 39) Recurring article, by Carole A. Shifrin, on finances of nonmajor domestic carriers in 4th quarter and full year 1983, with comparisons to 1982.

Includes 1 table showing revenues, expenses, and net profit or loss, for 14 nonmajor carriers, 1983, with percent change from 1982.

C5800–4.515: Apr. 2, 1984 (Vol. 120, No. 14)

QUARTERLY TABLE, ERRATA

[3] Narrow-body aircraft direct expenses, 1st half 1983, corrected data. Table originally was issued in Jan. 9, 1984 issue. (p. 34-35)

TRANSCONTINENTAL CAPACITY RISING

(p. 26-28) By James Ott. Article on U.S. transcontinental air traffic, 1st half 1983. Data are from Air Transport Assn and individual carriers. Includes 1 table showing revenue passengers, by carrier, for 6 transcontinental routes, 1st half 1983.

C5800–4.516: Apr. 9, 1984 (Vol. 120, No. 15)

JAPANESE FIRMS FORECAST AEROSPACE GROWTH

(p. 91) Brief article, with 1 table showing Japanese production, sales, and exports of aircraft, engines, parts/components, and equipment, FY83-84. Data are from Society of Japanese Aerospace Companies.

C5800–4.517: Apr. 16, 1984 (Vol. 120, No. 16)

MONTHLY TABLE

[1] Airline traffic, for Sept.-Oct. 1983. (p. 46-47)

QUARTERLY TABLES

[1] Operating and cost data [wide-body aircraft], for 1st half 1983. (p. 38-39)

[2] Airline income and expenses, 3rd quarter 1983. (p. 48)

C5800–4.518: Apr. 23, 1984 (Vol. 120, No. 17)

MONTHLY TABLE

[1] Airline traffic, for Nov. 1983. (p. 52)

JAPANESE DEFENSE CONTRACTS TOTAL $4.9 BILLION

(p. 61) Brief article, with 1 table showing top 10 Japanese defense contractors ranked by value of contract awards from Japan's Defense Agency, FY83 with comparison to FY82.

GENERAL DYNAMICS LEADS TOP 100 DEFENSE CONTRACTORS FOR FY83, ANNUAL FEATURE

(p. 166-173) Annual table showing top 100 defense contractors ranked by value of DOD contract awards, with detail by subsidiary, and including awards as percent of all DOD contract expenditures, FY83.

C5800–4.519: Apr. 30, 1984 (Vol. 120, No. 18)

MONTHLY TABLE

[2] Business and utility aircraft shipments, for Feb. 1984. (p. 54)

SAR PROGRAM ACQUISITION COST SUMMARY

(p. 60-61) Special table showing DOD selected acquisition report (SAR) cost estimates for weapons systems, by manufacturer and model, arranged by military branch, as of Dec. 31, 1983.

C5800–4.520: May 14, 1984 (Vol. 120, No. 20)

MONTHLY TABLE

[1] Airline traffic, for Dec. 1983. (p. 45)

FUTURE GROWTH IN CARGO FORECAST

(p. 27-30) By James Ott. Article, with 1 chart showing distribution of air freight revenue ton-miles, by type of carrier, 1973 and 1983. Data are from CAB.

MAJORS POST COMBINED OPERATING PROFIT, RECURRING FEATURE

(p. 31-33) Recurring article, by Carole A. Shifrin, on finances of major and other domestic carriers in 1st quarter 1984. Includes 1 table showing revenues, expenses, and net profit or loss, for 11 major and 15 other carriers, 1st quarter 1984 with comparisons to 1st quarter 1983.

C5800–4.521: May 21, 1984 (Vol. 120, No. 21)

MONTHLY TABLE

[2] Business and utility aircraft shipments, for Mar. 1984. (p. 165)

WARSAW PACT INCREASES ARMS DELIVERY

(p. 147-149) Article, with 2 tables showing Soviet arms exports to 6 developing countries, and Warsaw Pact military personnel based in developing countries by country or area of origin, 1981-82. Data are from NATO.

C5800–4.522: June 4, 1984 (Vol. 120, No. 23)

MONTHLY TABLES

[1] Airline traffic, for Jan. 1984. (p. 39)

[2] Business and utility aircraft shipments, for Apr. 1984. (p. 71)

C5800–4.523: June 11, 1984 (Vol. 120, No. 24)

MONTHLY TABLE

[1] Airline traffic, for Feb. 1984. (p. 40)

C5800–4.524: June 18, 1984 (Vol. 120, No. 25)

AIRLINE TRAFFIC IN MAY EXTENDS UPWARD SWING, RECURRING FEATURE

(p. 36) Recurring article, with 1 table showing revenue passenger miles and available seat miles May 1984, and load factor 1984-85, for 19 domestic airlines.

TOP 100 DEFENSE RDT&E CONTRACTORS LISTED

(p. 85) Table showing top 100 defense contractors ranked by value of DOD contract awards for research/development/test/evaluation, FY83.

C5800–4.525: July 9, 1984 (Vol. 121, No. 2)

MONTHLY TABLE

[2] Business and utility aircraft shipments, for May 1984. (p. 67)

C5800–4.526: July 16, 1984 (Vol. 121, No. 3)

MONTHLY TABLE

[1] Airline traffic, for Mar. 1984. (p. 40)

QUARTERLY TABLE

[2] Airline income and expenses, 4th quarter 1983. (p. 37)

U.S. MAJOR AIRLINES' TRAFFIC CONTINUES TO RISE IN JUNE, RECURRING FEATURE

(p. 30-31) Recurring article, with 1 table showing revenue passenger miles, available seat miles, and load factor, for 11 major airlines and 14 other carriers, June 1984 with comparison to June 1983.

C5800–4.527: July 23, 1984 (Vol. 121, No. 4)

AIRLINES WORLDWIDE EARNED PROFIT IN 1983, ANNUAL FEATURE

(p. 54, 59) Annual article, by Michael Feazel, on world airline operations and finances in 1983, with detail for International Air Transport Assn (IATA) members. Data are from IATA.

Includes 3 tables showing scheduled and nonscheduled air traffic; airline revenues, expenses, and profit; and aggregate IATA airline employment, passenger capacity, and aircraft; 1981-83.

C5800–4.528: July 30, 1984 (Vol. 121, No. 5)

MONTHLY TABLE

[1] Airline traffic, for Apr. 1984. (p. 45)

C5800–4.529: Aug. 6, 1984 (Vol. 121, No. 6)

QUARTERLY TABLES

[1] Operating and cost data [wide-body aircraft], for 2nd half 1983. (p. 38-39)

[2] Airline income and expenses, 1st quarter 1984. (p. 44)

C5800–4.530: Aug. 13, 1984 (Vol. 121, No. 7)

MONTHLY TABLE

[2] Business and utility aircraft shipments, for June 1984. (p. 153)

QUARTERLY TABLE

[3] Narrow-body aircraft direct expenses, 2nd half 1983. (p. 44-45)

MAJORS' OPERATING PROFIT SHOWS TENFOLD INCREASE, RECURRING FEATURE

(p. 34-35) Recurring article, by Carole A. Shifrin, on finances of major and other domestic carriers in 2nd quarter 1984. Includes 1 table showing revenues, expenses, and net profit or loss, for 11 major and 15 other carriers, 2nd quarter 1984 with comparisons to 2nd quarter 1983.

TRAFFIC RESULTS IN JULY CONTINUE UPWARD TREND AT REDUCED RATE, RECURRING FEATURE

(p. 36) Recurring article, with 1 table showing revenue passenger miles, available seat miles, and load factor, for 11 major airlines and 6 other carriers, July 1984 with comparison to July 1983.

C5800–4.531: Aug. 20, 1984 (Vol. 121, No. 8)

MONTHLY TABLE

[1] Airline traffic, for May 1984. (p. 39)

C5800–4.532: Aug. 27, 1984 (Vol. 121, No. 9)

QUARTERLY TABLE

[1] Operating and cost data [wide-body aircraft], for 1st quarter 1984. (p. 40-41)

C5800–4.533: Sept. 3, 1984 (Vol. 121, No. 10)

SMALL FIRMS COOPERATE FOR U.S. MARKET

(p. 87-92) Article, with 1 table showing aerospace industry revenue (in European Currency Units) with distribution by sector (airframes, engines, equipment, and space), for 6 European countries, 1981.

GOVERNMENTS' ATTITUDES ON EXPORTS VARY

(p. 113-115) Article, with 1 table showing aerospace equipment/component balance of trade (in European Currency Units) between 9 European countries and U.S., 1980-82. Data are from EC.

INCOME UNCERTAINTY SLOWS AIRLINE FLEET REPLACEMENT

(p. 168-171) Article on the market outlook for airline fleet replacement. Data are from CAB.

Includes 5 tables and 1 chart showing debt-equity ratio, operating cost per available seat mile, labor and fuel costs as percent of operating cost, and cash/short-term investments, for 12 airlines, 1st quarter 1983-1st quarter 1984; and value of aircraft equipment deliveries for 1979-1st quarter 1984 period, and of aircraft orders and options placed as of June 1, 1984.

CANADA TO CONTINUE INDUSTRY INVESTMENT

(p. 224-227) Article on Canadian Government support of the aerospace industry. Data were compiled by Commerce Dept from Canadian Government documents. Includes 2 tables showing value of selected R&D and other government support programs for aerospace, 1981-84.

C5800–4.534: Sept. 10, 1984 (Vol. 121, No. 11)

MONTHLY TABLE

[2] Business and utility aircraft shipments, for July 1984. (p. 135)

QUARTERLY TABLE

[3] Narrow-body aircraft direct expenses, 1st quarter 1984. (p. 62-63)

JAPAN REQUESTS 7% INCREASE IN DEFENSE

(p. 131) Brief article, with 1 table showing Japanese Defense Agency's aircraft and weapon purchases by type, actual FY84, and requested FY85.

C5800–4.535: Sept. 17, 1984 (Vol. 121, No. 12)

UNION PENSION CONCERN SPARKS WALKOUT

(p. 39-40) By James Ott. Article on airline expenses for employee pension plans. Data are from a Johnson and Higgins study of large corporate pension plans, compiled from annual reports covering Apr. 1, 1983-Mar. 31, 1984 period. Includes 1 table showing pension expense, pretax profits before pension expense, employees, and value of pension plan benefits and assets, for 12 airlines.

C5800–4.536: Oct. 1, 1984 (Vol. 121, No. 14)

MONTHLY TABLE

[2] Business and utility aircraft shipments, for Aug. 1984. (p. 98)

JAPANESE FORECAST $2.37 BILLION IN AEROSPACE SALES

(p. 29) Brief article, with 1 table showing Japan aerospace industry sales and new orders, for aircraft and engine production and overhaul, and parts and equipment production, 1983-84. Data were compiled by Society of Japanese Aerospace Companies from reports by 30 companies.

RISING VALUE OF U.S. DOLLAR HINDERS EUROPE OPERATIONS

(p. 59, 61) By Michael Feazel. Article, with 1 table showing twin-engine business aircraft fleet size for 10 European countries, 1978 and 1982.

C5800–4.537: Oct. 8, 1984 (Vol. 121, No. 15)

[Issue incorrectly reads Vol. 122.]

MONTHLY TABLE

[1] Airline traffic, for June-July 1984. (p. 39, 41)

ACT ACCELERATES, STRETCHES ARMS PROGRAMS

(p. 19) Brief article, with 1 table listing Army, Navy, and Air Force weapon systems for which Congress authorized lower FY85 production rates than were requested by the Administration. Table includes requested and authorized rate for each system.

C5800–4.538: Oct. 15, 1984 (Vol. 121, No. 16)

QUARTERLY TABLE

[3] Narrow-body aircraft direct expenses, 2nd quarter 1984. (p. 40-41)

AIRLINE TRAFFIC EXTENDS GAINS IN SEPT., RECURRING FEATURE

(p. 31-32) Recurring article, by James Ott, with 1 table showing revenue passenger miles, available seat miles, and load factor, for 11 major airlines, Sept. and 1st 9 months 1983-84.

C5800–4.539: Oct. 22, 1984 (Vol. 121, No. 17)

[Issue incorrectly reads Vol. 122.]

QUARTERLY TABLE

[1] Operating and cost data [wide-body aircraft], for 2nd quarter 1984. (p. 42-43)

U.S. TRANSPORT SALES IN MIDEAST HAMPERED BY EXPORT CONTROLS

(p. 111-112) By Paul Mann. Article, with 1 table showing value of Middle East imports of aircraft/parts from industrial countries, with detail for 6 importing countries, and aircraft share of total and machinery/equipment imports, 1978 and 1982. Data are from UN, OECD, and Data Resources, Inc.

C5800–5   COAL AGE

Monthly.   Approx. 250 p.
ISSN 0009-9910.
LC GS 12-841.
SRI/MF/not filmed

Monthly publication reporting on developments and trends in the U.S. coal industry, including production, processing, marketing, technology, employment, management, regulation, and finance. Data are from various Federal Government, private, and industry sources.

Contains news brief sections; feature articles, occasionally with statistics; and monthly "Economic Scene" section, with 1 table described below.

An annual article on industry outlook (Feb. issue), and an annual equipment and services buyers guide (Sept. issue) are also featured. An annual editorial index appears in the Dec. issue.

Monthly "Economic Scene" feature appears in all issues. All additional features with substantial statistical content are described, as they appear, under "Statistical Features." Nonstatistical features are not covered.

Prior to the Mar. 1984 issue, journal also includes "Port Watch" feature, with 1 table showing number of coal ships waiting in line and average wait, and coal shipment data, for Hampton Roads, Baltimore, Mobile, Philadelphia, and Long Beach.

Availability: Coal Age, Fulfillment Manager, PO Box 430, Hightstown NJ 08520, qualified subscribers †, others $20.00 per yr., single copy $4.00, Sept. Buyer's Guide $5.50; SRI/MF/not filmed.

Issues reviewed during 1984: Nov. 1983-Oct. 1984 (P) (Vol. 88, Nos. 11-12; Vol. 89, Nos. 1-10).

ECONOMIC SCENE TABLE:

Shows bituminous and anthracite coal production; bituminous consumption and inventories at utilities, and total exports; weekly railroad coal carloadings; coal operating rate, employment, production workers, and average hours and earnings; weekly electricity output and raw steel production; blast furnace/steel mill new orders; and No. 6 fuel oil price.

Data are shown for various dates ranging from 1 week to 4 months prior to cover date, previous week or month, and same period of previous year.

STATISTICAL FEATURES:

C5800–5.501: Dec. 1983 (Vol. 88, No. 12)

JAPANESE BUYERS SHOW NO YEN FOR U.S. COAL

(p. 11-12) Article, with 2 charts on Japan's steam coal imports, showing total imports and amount from U.S., 1981-82; and price for U.S. and 4 other countries of origin, 1983. Data sources include customs clearance data.

C5800–5.502: Feb. 1984 (Vol. 89, No. 2)

DATA RESOURCES SCALES DOWN EUROPEAN IMPORT FORECAST, RECURRING FEATURE

(p. 25) Recurring article, with 1 table forecasting coal imports of 12 European countries, selected years 1982-2000. Data are from Data Resources Inc., Europe, semiannual forecasts. For description of previous forecast, see SRI 1983 Annual, under C5800-5.409.

OUTLOOK 1984: THERE REALLY IS LIGHT AT THE END OF THE TUNNEL, ANNUAL FEATURE

(p. 50-58) Annual article, by Joseph F. Wilkinson, on coal industry national and regional review and outlook, 1983-84. Data are from State mining depts, DOE, Keystone, and other energy forecasters. Includes 2 tables showing 7 comparison forecasts for bituminous/lignite exports and domestic consumption, 1983-84; and bituminous/lignite production by State, and Pennsylvania anthracite production, for deep and strip mines, 1983.

C5800–5.503: Mar. 1984 (Vol. 89, No. 3)

REAGAN AGAIN ASKS LOW SPENDING ON FOSSIL ENERGY

(p. 16) Article, with 1 table showing budget authority and outlay for coal R&D, by DOE Fossil Energy Division program, FY83-84, and Reagan Administration request for FY85.

C5800–5.504: May 1984 (Vol. 89, No. 5)

TOP COAL PRODUCERS POST MIXED EARNINGS

(p. 11-13) Article, with 1 table showing top 15 coal producing companies ranked by production, and also showing revenue and earnings, 1983 with comparisons to 1982. Data are from individual companies and *Coal Age* estimates.

C5800–5.505: Aug. 1984 (Vol. 89, No. 8)

LONGWALLS REBOUND WITH ECONOMY

(p. 45-59) By Paul C. Merritt. Article discussing longwall operations in U.S. and Canadian coal mines, with summary comparisons to other countries. Data are from American Longwall Statistics, and a *Coal Age* census of longwall operations.

Includes 2 tables showing longwall average face length, for U.S., West Germany, and UK, selected years 1976-83; and capacity, year of initial installation, operational characteristics, seam name, and mine and location, for U.S. and Canadian operating longwall installations, arranged by company, as of June 1984.

Addendum appears in the Oct. 1984 issue; for description, see C5800-5.507, below.

LONGWALL PRODUCTIVITY SHOWS SOLID GROWTH

(p. 61) By Cecil V. Peake. Article, with 1 table showing the following for longwall installations in coal mines: average, high, and low cut-

ting height, panel size, output, shifts, and labor productivity, by height of installation, 1983. Data are from results reported by approximately 50% of all longwall operations.

C5800–5.506: Sept. 1984 (Vol. 89, No. 9)

DRI LOWERS COAL IMPORT PROJECTION FOR EUROPE IN 2000, RECURRING FEATURE

(p. 17) Recurring article, with 1 table forecasting coal imports of 11 European countries, selected years 1982-2000. Data are from Data Resources Inc., Europe, semiannual forecasts.

C5800–5.507: Oct. 1984 (Vol. 89, No. 10)

STEELMAKERS TAKE THEIR COAL TO MARKET

(p. 11-13) Article, with 1 table showing the following for 7 major steel companies: coal reserves, operating mines, production capacity, output, and consumption in steelmaking, 1984.

ADDITION TO CENSUS

(p. 38) Addendum for article discussing longwall coal mining operations, appearing in Aug. 1984 issue.

For description of article, see C5800-5.505, above.

C5800–6   AMERICAN MACHINIST

Monthly. Approx. 250 p.
ISSN 0002-9858.
LC 39-6898.
SRI/MF/not filmed

Monthly trade journal reporting on developments in the metalworking industry, including equipment, production, trade, and finance. Data are from McGraw-Hill Economics Dept, National Machine Tool Builders' Assn, Dept of Commerce, and other sources. Data are current to 3-6 months prior to cover date.

General format:

a. Monthly "Metalworking Trends" section containing news briefs and text statistics on industry outlook, labor, government regulation, equipment and materials, and plant operations; 3 monthly tables with corresponding charts; and 1 quarterly table on foreign trade.

b. Feature articles on machine tool technology, new products, processing, and R&D, occasionally with statistics.

c. Special reports section, usually covering an industrial process or technological development, some with statistics.

d. Narrative editorial depts.

Annual features include industry outlook, and world tool production and trade.

Monthly and quarterly tables are listed below. Monthly tables appear in all issues. All additional features with substantial statistical content are described, as they appear, under "Statistical Features;" page location and latest period of coverage for quarterly table are also noted. Nonstatistical features are not covered.

Availability: American Machinist, Fulfillment Manager, PO Box 430, Hightstown NJ 08520, industry subscribers †, others $40.00 per yr., single copy $6.00; SRI/MF/not filmed.

Issues reviewed during 1984: Nov. 1983-Oct. 1984 (P) (Vol. 127, Nos. 11-12; Vol. 128, Nos. 1-10).

MONTHLY TABLES:

[Tables appear in "Metalworking Trends" section. Month of data coverage is 3 months prior to cover date. Tables show data for month of coverage, previous month, and same month of preceding year.]

[1] Production and price indexes and operating rate [selected metalworking industry sectors].

[2] Machine tool orders and shipments [including net new and export orders, total and export shipments, backlogs, and cancellations; and new orders indexes for builders and distributors (1978-80 = 100)].

[3] Materials price index [total and for plastics and 7 metals categories].

QUARTERLY TABLE:

[1] U.S. trade in machine tools [export and import values, for 10 leading customer and supplier countries, cumulative for current year through quarter ended approximately 6 months prior to cover date].

STATISTICAL FEATURES:

C5800–6.501: Nov. 1983 (Vol. 127, No. 11)

13th AMERICAN MACHINIST INVENTORY OF METALWORKING EQUIPMENT, 1983

(p. 113-144) Report on *American Machinist* 13th survey of metalworking equipment, conducted 1978-83 period. Data are primarily from the survey, and are weighted for the entire industry based on a sample of 12,306 plants. Includes article on impact of numerically controlled (NC) machines on metalworking industry; and 29 tables showing the following, for the survey period unless otherwise noted:

a. Inventory summary, showing percent of plants owning metalworking machines, and number of machines by age, by detailed machine type, total and for 19 SIC 2- and 3-digit industries.

b. Metalcutting and metalforming machines: in use for metalworking and other industries, used for training, and in storage/surplus; owned by DOD, by age; in U.S. and 6 foreign countries, total and distribution by age, various years 1975-83; and percent change in number of machines since 12th inventory, by machine type.

c. Metalworking machines by general type (with distribution by age and percent of plants owning), metalcutting and metalforming NC machines, and metalworking employees, for 41 SIC 2- and 3-digit industries; and number of machines and distribution by age, by plant employment size and machine type.

d. By region: total and NC metalcutting and metalforming machines, with distribution of total by age; percent of plants owning NC machines, by application; and machine tools, metalworking employees, 1980 population, machines per 1,000 population for selected years 1968-83, and number of plants (total and with more than 20 employees).

Also includes 1 table on sample characteristics.

This is the 1st inventory report covered by SRI. The 12th report was published in 3 installments during 1976-78.

C5800–6.502: Dec. 1983 (Vol. 127, No. 12)

QUARTERLY TABLE

[1] U.S. trade in machine tools [by country], 1st half 1983. (p. 27)

C5800–6.503: Jan. 1984 (Vol. 128, No. 1)

JOB-RELATED INJURIES DROP MARKEDLY IN '82

(p. 25-27) Article, with 1 table showing job-related injury rates, including lost-workday cases and days lost, and nonfatal cases without lost workdays, for selected metalworking industries, 1981-82. Data are from BLS.

'84 OUTLOOK: A RATHER FRAGILE RECOVERY, ANNUAL FEATURE

(p. 85-92) Annual article forecasting 1984 metalworking industry production, shipments, and finances, with comparisons from 1970s. Data are from Federal agencies, National Machine Tool Builders' Assn, and McGraw-Hill Economics Dept. Includes several charts and 9 tables showing:

a. Shipment values, 1973-84; production and price indexes, monthly 1979-Oct. or Nov. 1983; and preferred operating rates (no date); for SIC 2- and 3-digit metalworking industries.

b. GNP by major sector, including net exports, 1979-84; and capital spending, for SIC 2- and 3-digit metalworking industries, other manufacturing, and nonmanufacturing, 1981-85.

c. Industrial goods production index and consumer durable goods production, by commodity, 1979-84; and nonelectrical machinery new orders, and cutting and forming machine tool shipments and net new orders, quarterly 1982-84.

C5800–6.504: Feb. 1984 (Vol. 128, No. 2)

QUARTERLY TABLE

[1] U.S. trade in machine tools [by country], 1st 9 months 1983. (p. 29)

MACHINE TOOLS POST A SLOW YEAR, ANNUAL FEATURE

(p. 74-78) Annual article, by Anderson Ashburn, on estimated world machine tool production and trade for 1983, with brief analyses for U.S. and selected other countries. Data are compiled by *American Machinist*.

Includes 2 tables showing value of cutting and forming tool production, and of total machine tool exports, imports, and consumption, all for 25-35 countries, 1982-83.

C5800–6.505: June 1984 (Vol. 128, No. 6)

QUARTERLY TABLE

[1] U.S. trade in machine tools [by country], full year 1983 [table incorrectly reads 1980]. (p. 31)

C5800–6.506: Sept. 1984 (Vol. 128, No. 9)

QUARTERLY TABLE

[1] U.S. trade in machine tools [by country], 1st quarter 1984. (p. 49)

C5800–6.507: Oct. 1984 (Vol. 128, No. 10)

MANUFACTURING SALARIES OUTPACE INFLATION

(p. 25) Brief article, with 1 undated table showing average manufacturing salaries for 14 managerial positions. Data are from Society of Manufacturing Engineers.

C5800–7   BUSINESS WEEK

Weekly.   Approx. 150 p.
ISSN 0007-7135.
LC 31-6225.
SRI/MF/not filmed

Weekly news journal (year-end combined issue) of current developments in domestic and foreign business and investments.

Issues generally contain news briefs; numerous articles, occasionally with substantial statistical content; and the following weekly statistical features:

a. "Business Week Index," with 2 charts showing aggregate production indicator trends.

b. "Figures of the Week," with 2 tables, further described below, presenting weekly and monthly data on prices, and production and economic indicators.

c. "Financial Figures of the Week," with 1 table showing selected money market rates; monetary indicators including M1 money supply, bank business loans and free reserves, and value of commercial paper issued by nonfinancial corporations; bond rates; stock index averages and NYSE volume; and prime interest rates and currency exchange rates, for 7 countries; generally for week 2 weeks prior to publication, and preceding week, month, and year, with averages for 1973 or 1974.

Prior to Nov. 14, 1983 issue, most "Financial Figures of the Week" data were presented in "Foreign Exchange Trader" and "Investment Figures of the Week" sections.

Additional statistical features include a monthly table on personal income; quarterly Corporate Scoreboard, also described below; recurring World Economic Outlook reports; recurring reports on *Business Week*-sponsored Louis Harris & Associates opinion surveys of general public and corporate executives; and annual features, many presenting financial data for individual companies.

Weekly features appear in all issues. All additional features with substantial statistical content are described, as they appear, under "Statistical Features;" page locations and latest period of coverage for quarterly Corporate Scoreboard are also noted. Nonstatistical features are not covered.

Availability: Business Week, PO Box 430, Hightstown NJ 08520, $39.95 per yr., single copy $2.00, special issues $2.50; SRI/MF/not filmed.

Issues reviewed during 1984: Nov. 7, 1983-Oct. 29, 1984 (P) (Nos. 2815-2866).

FIGURES OF THE WEEK TABLES:

[Tables include comparisons to previous week and/or month, same period of previous year and 1967 average.]

[1] Figures of the week [*Business Week* production index, and production in 9-10 major industry sectors; economic indicators including *Business Week* leading index, corporate bond yield, business failures, money supply (M2), real estate loans, unemployment insurance initial claims, and stock and industrial materials price indexes; and prices for 6-7 commodities; shown for week 2-4 weeks prior to cover date].

[2] Monthly figures [for 4-5 different economic indicators each week, including composite leading indicators, CPI, manufacturing operating rates, construction spending, employment, unemployment rate, inventories, weekly pay, exports and imports, personal income, housing starts, conventional 1st mortgage rate, PPI, retail sales, manufacturing earnings, air cargo, industrial production index, and durable goods orders; shown for month 1-3 months preceding cover date month].

QUARTERLY CORPORATE SCOREBOARD:

Quarterly feature reviewing financial performance of approximately 900 companies in 39 industries for quarter ending 6-10 weeks prior to issue date. Data are from Standard & Poor's Compustat Services, Inc. Generally includes:

a. Narrative analysis with 2 charts showing 3-4 year aggregate trends in profits and margins; and 3-4 tables usually ranking 10 best and worst industry groups in profit change and 10 leading companies in sales and earnings growth.

b. Listing of companies grouped by industry, showing the following for each: sales and profits for quarter of coverage and cumulative for year to date, with percent change from previous year; and return on equity, earnings per share, and price/earnings ratio for varying recent 12-month periods.

c. Index of companies.

Feature for 4th quarter covers 1,200 companies and also includes full-year data.

STATISTICAL FEATURES:

C5800–7.501: Nov. 7, 1983 (No. 2815)

FATTER LOAN RESERVES TRIM BANK PROFITS

(p. 45) Article, with 1 table showing bank loan loss reserves as a percent of total loans, for 7 major banks, as of Sept. 30, 1982-83.

Data are from Keefe, Bruyette, and Woods, Inc.

CHAINS TAKE OVER COMPUTER RETAILING

(p. 70-83) Article on computer retail marketing activity. Data are from Future Computing, Inc. Includes 1 chart showing total computer retail stores, and distribution by type (single location, Computerland and other multi-location, and Radio Shack and other manufacturer-owned), June 1982-83.

HOMEBUILDING'S NEW LOOK

(p. 92-99) Article, with 1 table showing the following for 10 major homebuilders: revenues from homebuilding, 1982-83; stock price as of Oct. 20, 1982-83; and latest 12-month price/earnings ratio.

Data are from Data Resources, Inc.

HOW AN LDC DEFAULT WOULD HIT THE U.S. ECONOMY

(p. 118-121) Article, with 1 table showing potential changes in selected U.S. economic indicators in event of foreign loan defaults by Argentina, Brazil, and all South America, 1984.

Data are from Data Resources, Inc.

HEAVY CRUDE HAS BACKFIRED ON THE REFINERS

(p. 126-130) Article analyzing factors affecting refineries that have retooled to use heavy-grade crude oil. Data are from Purvin and Gertz, Inc.

Includes 1 chart showing price difference between Mexican heavy and light crude oil, 1982-Oct. 1983.

C5800–7.502: Nov. 14, 1983 (No. 2816)

BUSINESS WEEK/HARRIS POLL: RESOUNDING SUPPORT FOR PRICE COMPETITION

(p. 24) Article on executives' views concerning retail price setting by manufacturers. Data are from a survey of 600 executives by Louis Harris and Associates for *Business Week.* Includes 1 chart.

BONN BEGINS TO GET OUT OF THE PRIVATE SECTOR

(p. 60-61) Article on West German Government plans to sell interests in private companies. Data are from *Business Week.*

Includes 1 table showing the following for 6 West German companies wholly or partly owned by the Government: main business activity, percent government ownership, and sales, 1982.

CORPORATE SCOREBOARD, QUARTERLY FEATURE

(p. 91-136) "Quarter's Profits Are Even Stronger Than Expected." Covers corporate financial performance of 890 companies, for 3rd quarter 1983. For data description, see C5800-7, above.

RESTRUCTURING BIG OIL

(p. 138-150) Article on oil industry corporate reorganization activities. Data are from *Business Week* and Donaldson, Lufkin and Jenrette Securities Corp.

Includes 2 charts showing stock price as of Oct. 20, 1983, and estimated liquidation asset value per share, for 4 major integrated (producing and marketing) oil companies and for 4 producing companies, and pretax percent return on assets for each integrated company, 1982.

C5800–7.503: Nov. 21, 1983 (No. 2817)

MARKETING: THE NEW PRIORITY

(p. 96-106) Article on corporate marketing trends. Data are from the Census Bureau, Donnelley Marketing Information Services, and Data Resources Inc.

Includes 1 chart showing population by age and households by size; 1970, 1980, and 1988.

WORLD ECONOMIC OUTLOOK: AS THE UPTURN SPREADS LDCs WILL GRADUALLY JOIN IN, RECURRING FEATURE

(p. 152-165) Recurring feature analyzing world commodity market, and growth trends and outlook for 5 less developed world areas, 1982-84. Series data are based on Project Link, an econometric model developed by Wharton Econometric Forecasting Associates, and papers submitted by Project Link members.

Analysis is accompanied by 38 charts illustrating selected trends, including GDP in industrial vs. developing countries, world trade, international debt in Brazil and Mexico, GNP and farm output in India, and GNP and inflation in selected African countries, 1982-84.

C5800–7.504: Nov. 28, 1983 (No. 2818)

QUANTUM LEAP FOR COMMUNICATIONS

(p. 92-96) Article on telephone industry operations after American Telephone and Telegraph Co. (AT&T) reorganization. Data are from AT&T and La Blanc Associates.

Includes 1 table showing average monthly charges for residential telephone services and equipment, 1983-84 and 1990.

PERSONAL INCOME FOR JULY

(p. 128) Monthly table showing personal income, by State and census division, July and year to date 1983, with comparisons to 1982.

TAKING THE TRUTH ABOUT TAXES OUT OF THE FINE PRINT

(p. 133-134) Article on proposed method of accounting for income tax liabilities in corporate annual reports. Data are from Standard & Poor's Compustat Services, Inc. and *Business Week.*

Includes 1 table showing the following for 8 major companies: pretax income, and tax reported and paid/due, FY82; and cumulative deferred tax, and deferred tax as percent of equity, as of Dec. 31, 1982.

C5800–7.505: Dec. 5, 1983 (No. 2819)

WHY VENEZUELA IS THE NEW SICK MAN OF LATIN AMERICA

(p. 98-101) Article reporting on Venezuela's economic situation. Data are from Petroleos de Venezuela and Venezuela Ministry of Energy and Mines. Includes 1 chart showing Venezuela oil export revenues, 1979-83.

C5800–7.506: Dec. 12, 1983 (No. 2820)

BUSINESS WEEK/HARRIS POLL: GOOD AND BAD NEWS FOR REAGAN ON ARMS

(p. 18) Article on public opinion concerning defense spending. Data are from a Nov. 1983 survey by Louis Harris and Associates for *Business Week,* and previous Harris surveys. Includes 1 table showing percent of respondents favoring increased, decreased, or current level of defense spending, selected months 1971-83.

C5800–7.507: Dec. 19, 1983 (No. 2821)

BUSINESS WEEK/HARRIS POLL: WATT'S DEPARTURE IS HELPING REAGAN

(p. 14) Article on public opinion concerning antipollution standards. Data are based on a Nov. 1983 Louis Harris and Associates survey for *Business Week,* and previous surveys. Includes 1 chart showing responses on how strict Clean Air Act and Clean Water Act provisions should be.

SMOKERS ARE STARTING TO CHOKE ON SOARING PRICES, ANNUAL FEATURE

(p. 62-63) Annual article reporting on cigarette sales, 1983. Includes 2 tables showing sales volume and market share by manufacturer and for top 20 brands, 1981-83.

TURNOVER AT THE TOP

(p. 104-106) Article discussing recent trends in executive turnover rate. Data are from Michigan State University. Includes 1 chart showing average annual executive resignations from top 2 positions, aggregated for 100 major corporations, selected periods 1960-83.

C5800–7.508: Dec. 26, 1983/Jan. 2, 1984 (No. 2822)

BUSINESS WILL KEEP LABOR IN LINE, ANNUAL FEATURE

(p. 20-21) Annual article reporting on issues in labor negotiations, 1984. Data are from the Labor Dept and *Business Week.* Includes 1 table showing union, expiration date, employer, and number of workers covered, for labor contracts expiring in 1984.

INVESTMENT OUTLOOK, 1984, ANNUAL FEATURE

(p. 47-167, passim) Annual feature on outlook for personal and institutional investment, 1984. Contains 5 sections, with narrative analyses; numerous charts, most showing trends and/or outlook for selected economic indicators and types of investment; and the following tables:

a. Economists' 1984 forecast: annual table showing forecasts by 27 economists and 13 econometric services of real GNP and price changes and unemployment rate, 1984. (p. 55)

b. Executives' investment plans: 1 table, based on Louis Harris and Associates 1983 survey of over 600 executives, showing percent of executives with current and/or planned personal investments, by investment type. (p. 65)

c. Pension funds: 1 undated chart showing distribution of pension fund investments, by type. (p. 75)

d. Stocks: 1 annual table showing industry sectors and companies with best and worst market performance, June 1-Nov. 1983 period. (p. 79)

e. Investment outlook scoreboard: annual listing of approximately 900 companies, showing each company's stock price, book value, price/earnings ratio, dividend rate, yield, shares outstanding, market value change, shares held by institutions, and stock turnover, 1983, and actual or estimated earnings per share, 1982-84; and 1 additional table showing industry sectors with best and worst earnings per share, 1983-84. (p. 112-141)

f. Mutual funds: 1 annual table showing best and worst performing mutual funds, for 11-month and 5-year periods ended Nov. 30, 1983. (p. 147)

Scoreboard data are primarily from Standard & Poor's Compustat Services, Inc. Other data are from SEI Funds Evaluation and Lipper Analytical Services, Inc.

C5800–7.509: Jan. 9, 1984 (No. 2823)

INDUSTRY OUTLOOKS 1984, ANNUAL FEATURE

(p. 51-83) Annual feature forecasting market conditions and business performance for 16 industries in 1984. Forecast is accompanied by 5 charts, repeated for each industry and for Standard & Poor's 400, illustrating selected trends including profits, and R&D spending and change in retained earnings as percent of income, 1979-83 period.

C5800–7.510: Jan. 16, 1984 (No. 2824)

PERSONAL INCOME FOR AUG.

(p. 76) Monthly table showing personal income, by State and census division, Aug. and year to date 1983, with comparisons to 1982.

PERSONAL BUSINESS: WEIGH THAT JOB OVERSEAS CAREFULLY, ANNUAL FEATURE

(p. 99-100) Annual article, with 1 table comparing cost of housing, transportation, taxes, and goods/services, in 12 foreign cities, 1984. Data are for a family of 4 renting overseas, with an annual salary of $40,000. Data are from Runzheimer and Co.

C5800–7.511: Jan. 23, 1984 (No. 2825)

BUSINESS WEEK/HARRIS POLL: THE ISSUES BEHIND OPPOSITION TO REAGAN

(p. 24) Article analyzing opposition to Reagan's reelection. Data are from a public opinion survey conducted by Louis Harris and Associates for *Business Week*. Includes 1 chart showing distribution of likely anti-Reagan voters, by primary social or political issue of concern.

C5800–7.512: Jan. 30, 1984 (No. 2826)

BUSINESS WEEK/HARRIS POLL: THE DEFICIT: CONCERN, BUT FEW ANSWERS

(p. 8) Article on public opinion concerning proposed solutions to Federal deficit problem. Data are from a Dec. 1983 survey by Louis Harris and Associates for *Business Week*. Includes 1 chart showing percent of respondents favoring and opposing various deficit reduction measures.

MELTDOWN FOR NUCLEAR POWER

(p. 18-19) Article on economic problems in the nuclear power industry. Data are from Salomon Brothers and *Business Week* estimates.

Includes 1 undated table showing the following for 8 nuclear power projects under construction: parent utility, projected cost, percent completed, and investment as percent of stockholders' equity. The projects shown are described as causing concern among investors.

WALL STREET WILL CAST THE DECISIVE VOTE

(p. 77-80) Article, with 1 table showing presidential incumbent and election winner, and percent change in Standard & Poor's 500 stock index, election years 1964-80. Data are from Standard & Poor's Corp.

C5800–7.513: Feb. 6, 1984 (No. 2827)

BATTLE OF WILLS OVER ARGENTINA'S DEBT

(p. 63-64) Article on Argentina's foreign debt. Data are from Keefe, Bruyette, and Woods, Inc., and *Business Week* estimates. Includes 1 undated chart showing Argentina's debt to 9 U.S. banks as percent of each bank's capital.

DISK-DRIVE BOOM HAS SUPPLIERS SPINNING

(p. 68-70) Article on computer disk-memory market. Data are from Dataquest, Inc. Includes 2 charts showing unit sales of floppy and rigid disk drives, with market shares for top 3 and all other manufacturers, 1983.

C5800–7.514: Feb. 13, 1984 (No. 2828)

WHY WALL STREET IS SO WARY

(p. 32-34) Article on business reaction to the Reagan Administration budget. Includes 1 table comparing projections of the Administra-

tion and Data Resources Inc. on percent increase in real GNP and CPI, and interest rates on 91-day Treasury bills, 1984-89.

WHY AT&T WILL LOSE MORE LONG-DISTANCE BUSINESS

(p. 102-110) Article, with 1 table showing revenues, profits or losses, and number of subscribers, for American Telephone and Telegraph Co. and 6 other long-distance carriers, 1983. Data are from Sanford C. Bernstein and Co.

WHY INFLATION ACCOUNTING MAY GO OFF THE BOOKS

(p. 120) Article on use of inflation-adjusted accounting procedures to report corporate earnings. Includes 1 table showing earnings per share, as reported vs. adjusted for inflation, for 10 major companies, FY83.

C5800–7.515: Feb. 20, 1984 (No. 2829)

BUSINESS WEEK/HARRIS POLL: COMPANIES FEEL UNDERRATED BY THE STREET

(p. 14) Article presenting business executives' views on whether market valuation of their company's stock accurately reflects real value. Data are from a Jan. 1984 survey of high-level executives by Louis Harris and Associates for *Business Week*. Includes 1 chart.

PLANT OUTLAYS WILL BOOST THE ECONOMY

(p. 45) Article on UK capital spending activities. Data are from DRI Europe, Inc. Includes 1 chart showing value of investment in UK manufacturing plant/equipment, 1980-84.

WORLD ECONOMIC OUTLOOK: THE REBOUND IS HERE, BUT IT LOOKS LOPSIDED, RECURRING FEATURE

(p. 108-118) Recurring feature analyzing economic growth trends and outlook in 15 industrialized countries, 1983-85. Series data are based on Project Link, an econometric model developed by Wharton Econometric Forecasting Associates, and papers submitted by Project Link members.

Includes:

a. General summary, with 1 trend chart, and 1 table showing "misery index" (unemployment rate plus inflation rate minus growth rate) by country, 1983-85.

b. 11 sections, most with text data and 2 charts generally showing percent change in real GDP or GNP, and unemployment rates, by country, 1983-85.

C5800–7.516: Feb. 27, 1984 (No. 2830)

DO FALLING TAX RATES MAKE REAGAN A SURE WINNER?

(p. 25) Brief article, with 1 table relating tax rate trends to presidential election outcomes, 1945-80. Table shows marginal tax rate at beginning and end of each incumbent's term of office, and party affiliation of incumbent and election winner. Also shows tax rates for 1984 incumbent's term of office.

Data are from *Business Week* estimates.

WHAT IS SENDING PROPERTY PRICES THROUGH THE ROOF

(p. 122-123) Article on real estate investment developments. Data are from National Council of Real Estate Investment Fiduciaries, Frank Russell Co., and *Business Week* estimates.

Includes 1 table showing average annual percent return on investment in real estate compared to Standard & Poor's 500 stock index and Salomon Brothers corporate bond index, 1980-83.

PERSONAL INCOME FOR SEPT.

(p. 144) Monthly table showing personal income, by State and census division, Sept. and year to date 1983, with comparisons to 1982.

CONSUMER RUSH IS ON FOR ANYTHING ELECTRONIC

(p. 148-150) Article, with 4 charts showing factory sales to dealers, for color TV sets, videocassette recorders, videodisc players, and home computers, 1980-84 or 1982-84. Data are from Electronic Industries Assn and *Business Week* estimates.

C5800–7.517: Mar. 5, 1984 (No. 2831)

FOR STEELMAKERS, NO MERGERS MAY MEAN MORE BANKRUPTCIES

(p. 76-77) Article on steel industry mergers and other restructuring strategies. Data are from the American Iron and Steel Institute. Includes 1 table showing steel consumption and import share, and aggregate profit/loss for 7 largest steelmakers, 1979-83.

C5800–7.518: Mar. 12, 1984 (No. 2832)

ALL-AMERICAN SMALL CAR IS FADING

(p. 88-95) Article, with 1 table showing 17 domestic and imported auto makes ranked by customer satisfaction index, 1983. Data are from J. D. Power and Associates.

BIG—AND BRUISING—BUSINESS OF SELLING TELEPHONES

(p. 103-106) Article, with 1 chart showing telephone retail sales for 5 types of instruments, 1982-84. Data are from AT&T.

NEW APPEAL OF MORTGAGE SECURITIES

(p. 136-138) Article, with 1 table showing financial features, and amounts outstanding as of Dec. 1983, for mortgage-backed securities issued by GNMA, Federal Home Loan Mortgage Corp., FNMA, and private issuers.

C5800–7.519: Mar. 19, 1984 (No. 2833)

BUSINESS WEEK/HARRIS POLL: A CAUTIOUS NOD TO 'INDUSTRIAL POLICY'

(p. 15) Article presenting executives' views on the outlook for basic ("smokestack") industries during the economic recovery. Data are based on surveys of 600 executives conducted in Mar. 1983 and Jan. 1984 by Louis Harris and Associates for *Business Week*. Includes 1 chart.

NEXT TRADE CRISIS MAY BE JUST AROUND THE CORNER

(p. 48-56) Article on outlook for services exports. Data are from Office of the U.S. Trade Representative. Includes 1 table showing percent increase in services exports, 1977-81 period; and percent of economy dependent on services exports (no date); for U.S. and 15 other countries.

PEN STROKE COULD SWELL SOFTWARE PROFITS

(p. 71-72) Article on computer software companies' practice of reporting product development costs as R&D (with immediate tax writeoff) or assets (with deferred writeoff).

Data are from Alex Brown and Sons. Includes 1 table showing earnings per share as reported and with deferred writeoff, for 8 companies, 1983.

C5800–7.520: Mar. 21, 1984 (No. 2834)

SCOREBOARD SPECIAL ISSUE

Special compilation of articles and statistics providing detailed information on the performance of corporations and industries in the U.S. and foreign countries.

Most of the statistical material has appeared in similar or identical form in previous issues of *Business Week,* primarily as annual features in the magazine's regular Corporate Scoreboard series. These features have already been described in SRI, and include the following:

a. Investment outlook, including 1984 GNP, price, and unemployment forecasts of 27 economists and 13 econometric services; and investment outlook scoreboard, with detailed stock performance data for 900 companies, various years 1982-84 (see C5800-7.508, above; and p. 6-10, 102-124 in Scoreboard Special Issue).

b. Corporate balance sheet scoreboard, including balance sheet data for 890 nonfinancial corporations (see SRI 1983 Annual, under C5800-7.437; and p. 68-98 in Scoreboard Issue).

c. Inflation scoreboard, including data showing impact of inflation on sales, profits, and dividends of 517 companies (see SRI 1983 Annual, under C5800-7.424; and p. 132-150 in Scoreboard Issue).

d. International corporate scoreboard, including sales, profit, and stock performance data for approximately 930 foreign corporations (see SRI 1983 Annual, under C5800-7.435; and p. 152-178 in Scoreboard Issue).

e. Bank scoreboard, including detailed financial data for 200 largest banks (see SRI 1983 Annual, under C5800-7.421; and p. 180-186 in Scoreboard Issue).

f. Executive compensation scoreboard, including compensation paid to top executives in 278 companies (see SRI 1983 Annual, under C5800-7.425; and p. 188-201 in Scoreboard Issue).

g. R&D scoreboard, including R&D expenditures of 776 companies (see SRI 1983 Annual, under C5800-7.431; and p. 202-224 in Scoreboard Issue).

h. Pension fund financial data, for 100 companies, 1982 and trends (see SRI 1983 Annual, under C5800-7.442; and p. 226-228 in Scoreboard Issue).

i. Cigarette industry sales and market share data, for 20 companies, 1981-83 (see C5800-7.507, above; and p. 230-231 in Scoreboard Issue).

j. Liquor industry sales, by brand, 1982 and trends (see SRI 1983 Annual, under C5800-7.424; and p. 231-232 in Scoreboard Issue).

k. 1984 outlook analysis for 16 industries, with selected summary financial trends for 1979-83 (see C5800-7.509, above; and p. 236-286 in Scoreboard Issue).

Most of the scoreboard features noted above present data for individual companies, grouped by industry, for calendar or fiscal year 1982, usually with comparisons to 1980 and/or 1981.

Scoreboard Issue features that have not appeared in previous issues, or that contain updated statistics, are described below.

ECONOMIC FORECASTING: FEW HITS, MANY ERRORS

(p. 12) Article evaluating the accuracy of 30 economists and 10 econometric services in forecasting GNP and price changes for 1983. Includes 1 table.

CORPORATE SCOREBOARD, QUARTERLY FEATURE

(p. 15-66) "How 1,200 Companies Performed in 1983." Corporate financial performance, 4th quarter and full year 1983. For description of data, see C5800-7, above. Also includes the following:

a. 15 leading companies in sales, earnings, and return on equity, 1983; and in earnings per share growth, 1979-83 period.

b. For each of the 1,200 companies: profit margins, quarterly 1983; share value, Feb. 29, 1983; dividend yield, and book value per share, 1983; and growth in earnings per share and common equity, 1979-83 period.

PERSONAL INCOME SCOREBOARD

(p. 128-129) Article presenting Jan. 1984 revisions for monthly data on personal income by State and census division. Includes 1 table showing revised data for Oct. 1982-Sept. 1983.

C5800–7.521: Mar. 26, 1984 (No. 2835)

INTEREST RATES BEGIN TO BITE

(p. 30-31) Article, with 1 undated table on oil industry acquisitions, showing participants, purchase price, and acquisition loans extended, for 4 acquisitions. Data are from Shearson/American Express Inc. and *Business Week.*

HOW TO CUT THE DEFICIT

(p. 50-54) Article, with 1 chart showing Federal Government revenues and expenditures, FY85. Data are from OMB and *Business Week.*

'FLAT' TAXES: THE WINNERS AND LOSERS

(p. 99) Brief article on personal income tax reform proposals. Data were compiled by Joseph A. Pechman and John K. Scholz. Includes 1 table showing average annual income tax under present law, and proposed 17% "flat rate" tax and Bradley-Gephardt plan, by income class (no date).

NOW ANYONE CAN BE A VENTURE CAPITALIST

(p. 114-115) Article, with 1 table showing portfolio value and cost, and recent stock prices, for 5 publicly held venture capital companies, as of Sept. 30, 1983. Data are from *Venture Capital Journal* and *Business Week.*

ARITHMETIC BEHIND A BLITZ OF STOCK BUYBACKS

(p. 115-116) Article, with 1 undated table on corporate stock repurchases by 5 companies, showing number and price of repurchased shares, and repurchased shares as percent of shares outstanding, for each company. Data are from *Business Week.*

C5800–7.522: Apr. 2, 1984 (No. 2836)

BUSINESS WEEK/HARRIS POLL: ARE THE NEW PHONE BILLS TOO HIGH?

(p. 16) Article on public opinion regarding telephone service and rates since AT&T reorganization. Data are based on a 1984 survey by Louis Harris and Associates for *Business Week.* Includes 2 charts showing percent of respondents willing to pay a supplemental flat rate of $2 for local service if long distance charges are reduced by an equal amount, and those favoring or opposing rate structure based on usage.

U.S. MEMORY MAKERS ARE REGAINING LOST GROUND

(p. 70-71) Article reporting on developments in the computer memory chip industry. Data are from Montgomery Securities. Includes 1 chart and 1 table showing price per million characters of storage, and sales value and volume (billions of bits), for largest available random access memory chip, selected years 1973-90.

C5800–7.523: Apr. 9, 1984 (No. 2837)

CHASE'S BATTLE TO CATCH UP

(p. 74-81) Article reporting on Chase Manhattan Bank activities. Data are from Keefe, Bruyette and Woods Inc., Federal Reserve Board, and company financial reports. Includes 1 table showing selected measures of capital position including assets, growth in earnings and capital, and various operating ratios, for the 5 largest banks ranked by assets, 1984, with selected comparisons to 1983.

BANK SCOREBOARD: SOLID LOOKING FIGURES TURN OUT TO BE A VENEER, ANNUAL FEATURE

(p. 83-97) Annual feature, for 1983, on the financial performance of the 200 largest banks. Data are from Standard & Poor's Compustat Services, Inc.

Includes narrative analysis, with 1 summary table showing 5 best and worst banks in growth in deposits, loans, and profits, and in return on assets; and ranked listing of 200 banks, showing the following for each bank:

a. Year-end assets and rank; year-end deposits, and percent time, demand, and foreign; and loans outstanding at year end, loan loss provision, and chargeoffs and Federal funds borrowed as percent of loans outstanding.

b. Net income, return on assets, leverage, return on equity, net interest income, and 5-year growth in earnings per share.

Data are shown for 1983, with selected changes from 1982.

This is the 12th annual *Bank Scoreboard.*

C5800–7.524: Apr. 16, 1984 (No. 2838)

BUSINESS WEEK/HARRIS POLL: STILL NO CONFIDENCE IN LABOR LEADERS

(p. 16) Article on public opinion regarding labor unions. Data are from a 1984 survey by Louis Harris and Associates for *Business Week.* Includes 1 chart showing respondent views on extent of union responsibility for problems in auto and steel industries.

AUDITING THE IRS

(p. 84-92) Article, with 1 chart and 1 table showing percent of income tax returns audited by IRS, by income class (no date); and income declared for tax purposes and estimated actual income, by type, 1981. Data are from IRS.

THE RUSH TO REPLACE MONEY BROKERS

(p. 149) Article, with 1 chart showing value of deposits obtained through brokers, for federally insured savings and loan assns, year end 1981-83. Data are from FHLBB.

PERSONAL INCOME FOR OCT. AND NOV.

(p. 165) Monthly table showing personal income, by State and census division, Oct.-Nov. and year to date 1983, with comparisons to 1982.

C5800–7.525: Apr. 23, 1984 (No. 2839)

OFFICE BUILDINGS ARE LOSING THEIR VACANCY SIGNS

(p. 27) Article, with 1 table showing office vacancy rate, occupancy increase, and space under construction, for 10 cities, 1983. Data are from Office Network Inc.

PUSH IS ON TO GET BABY-BOOMERS TO SAVE

(p. 94-95) Article reporting on efforts of financial institutions to attract clients from the "baby-boom" generation. Data are from Merrill Lynch and Co. Includes 1 table showing estimated percent increase in households earning $50,000/over, by age of household head, 1980-90 period.

C5800–7.526: Apr. 30, 1984 (No. 2840)

INFLATION SCOREBOARD: THE REAL NEWS IN PROFITS, ANNUAL FEATURE

(p. 74-92) Annual feature on the impact of inflation on sales, profits, and dividends of 510 industrial companies in 34 industries, 1983, with comparisons to 1982 and compound 4-year growth rates. Data are from Business Week computer analysis of company annual reports. Includes the following:

a. Two summary tables showing 11 best and worst industries, ranked by constant-dollar profits (after adjustment for CPI) and by current-dollar profits (after adjustment for specific price changes), both as percent of historical costs, 1983; and compound growth rates for profits, sales, and dividends, by industry, 1979-83 period.

b. Inflation scoreboard listing: historical-cost sales, 1983, and reported and inflation-indexed change from 1982; historical-cost, constant-dollar, and current-cost profits, 1983, with change from 1982; monetary gain/loss, 1983; and 4-year growth rates for reported and inflation-indexed sales and for reported, constant-dollar, and current-cost profits; all by company, grouped by industry.

c. Index of companies

This is the 4th annual Inflation Scoreboard.

C5800–7.527: May 7, 1984 (No. 2841)

CAN THE RAILS STAY LEAN AND PROFITABLE?

(p. 72-76) Article, with 1 chart showing railroad freight ton-miles, 1st quarter 1980-84. Data are from the Assn of American Railroads.

EXECUTIVE PAY: THE TOP EARNERS, ANNUAL FEATURE

(p. 88-116) Annual survey reporting on compensation paid to top executives of 269 major

companies in 36 industries, 1983 and trends. Also presents pay performance index, based on compensation compared to shareholder returns. Data are from Sibson and Co. and Standard & Poor's Compustat Services, Inc. Includes the following:

a. 2 summmary tables on 25 highest paid executives and 10 executives with best and worst pay performance index.

b. Executive scoreboard: salary, salary/bonus, and long-term compensation, 1983, with salary/bonus change from 1982; and compensation as percent of industry standard, and pay performance index, 1983 and 1981-83 period; generally shown for top 2 executives in each company, grouped by industry,

Executive scoreboard also shows each company's sales and return on equity, 1983; and return on equity and shareholder return, both as percents of industry standards, 1983 and 1981-83 period.

ANNUAL LIQUOR SURVEY: WHY CONSUMPTION IS DOWN, ANNUAL FEATURE

(p. 120-122) Annual article on liquor industry market trends. Data are from Business Week and Clark Gavin Associates, Inc. Includes 2 tables showing market shares by type of distilled spirit, and total liquor consumption, 1973 and 1982-83; and liquor brands ranked by retail sales volume, 1981-83.

MINEFIELD IN DEFENSE ELECTRONICS

(p. 137) By Gene G. Marcial. Article, with 1 table showing the following for 8 defense electronics companies: year-end 1983 stock price, with percent change from 1982, and recent price. Data are from Prescott, Ball and Turben, Inc. and Business Week.

LABOR'S VOICE ON CORPORATE BOARDS: GOOD OR BAD?

(p. 151-153) Article, with 1 table showing the following for 14 companies with employee representation on board of directors: principal union, employees and percent stock ownership, and names and affiliations of employee representatives on boards, 1984. Data are from Business Week.

C5800–7.528: May 14, 1984 (No. 2842)

BUSINESS WEEK/HARRIS POLL: A FEELING THAT PRICE STABILITY IS ENDING

(p. 20) Article presenting executives' views on 12-month outlook for various economic indicators. Data are based on surveys of more than 600 executives conducted in Mar. 1983 and Apr. 1984 by Louis Harris and Associates for Business Week. Includes text data and 1 chart.

OIL'S PROFIT RELIEF MAY BE SHORT-LIVED

(p. 41) Article, with 1 table showing 11 major oil companies ranked by change in earnings, 1983-84. Data are from Business Week.

CORPORATE SCOREBOARD, QUARTERLY FEATURE

(p. 85-121) "Great Leap Forward in 1st-Quarter Profits." Covers corporate financial performance of 900 companies, for 1st quarter 1984. For description of data, see C5800-7, above.

Also includes the following for each company: profit margins, 1st quarter 1983-84; return on invested capital for most recent 12 month period; 10-year growth in common equity and earnings per share; and market value of shares outstanding, as of Apr. 19, 1984.

C5800–7.529: May 21, 1984 (No. 2843)

BARGAINING BEHIND THE AGENT ORANGE DEAL

(p. 39-40) Article, with 1 undated table on sales of defoliant Agent Orange to Federal Government, showing shares of sales and of total dioxin content for 7 Agent Orange manufacturers. Data are from Dow Chemical Co.

C5800–7.530: May 28, 1984 (No. 2844)

BUSINESS WEEK/HARRIS POLL: A GET-TOUGH MOOD ON INSIDER TRADING

(p. 16) Article on executives' views concerning rules restricting stock trading by insiders (people with access to confidential information about companies). Data are from an Apr. 1984 survey of more than 600 executives by Louis Harris and Associates for Business Week.

Includes 1 chart showing percent of respondents identifying various corporate job categories as insider positions.

REAGAN TAX CUTS: WERE THE SUPPLY SIDERS RIGHT?

(p. 68-69) Article, with 1 chart showing percent change in gross income and average tax, for all taxpayers and those in top 5% and remaining 95% income groups, 1981-82. Data are from IRS and James Gwartney of Florida State University.

PERSONAL INCOME FOR DEC.

(p. 76) Monthly table showing personal income, by State and census division, Dec. and full year 1983, with comparisons to 1982.

INSURERS' BIG PUSH FOR HOME HEALTH CARE

(p. 128, 130) Article, with 1 undated table showing cost per month for care as hospital inpatient vs. at home, for 4 types of medical disorders, Data are from Aetna Life and Casualty Co.

C5800–7.531: June 4, 1984 (No. 2845)

HOW OVERSEAS INVESTORS ARE HELPING TO REINDUSTRIALIZE AMERICA

(p. 103-104) Article, with 1 table showing foreign investments in U.S. for 10 leading investing countries/world areas, 1973 and 1983. Data are from Commerce Dept and Business Week.

C5800–7.532: June 11, 1984 (No. 2846)

BUSINESS WEEK/HARRIS POLL: VOTERS KNOW WHAT THEY DON'T LIKE

(p. 19) Article on 1984 presidential voting intentions of the electorate. Data are based on a May 1984 survey by Louis Harris and Associates for Business Week.

Includes 2 charts showing percent of respondents likely to vote against each candidate, and voting intentions of those who dislike both candidates.

C5800–7.533: June 18, 1984 (No. 2847)

WAR OF NERVES OVER LATIN DEBT

(p. 20-21) Article, with 1 table showing the following for 10 major U.S. banks: value of outstanding loans to 4 Latin American countries, and loans as percent of total assets, as of Dec. 31, 1983. Data are from Keefe, Bruyette, and Woods, Inc.

WHERE IRAN GETS THE MUSCLE TO KEEP ON FIGHTING

(p. 23-24) Article, with 1 chart showing Iranian oil exports, 1981-84. Data are from Wharton Econometrics.

C5800–7.534: June 25, 1984 (No. 2848)

BUSINESS WEEK/HARRIS POLL: TOP EXECUTIVE PAY PEEVES THE PUBLIC

(p. 15) Article on public opinion regarding executives' compensation. Data are based on a 1984 survey by Louis Harris and Associates for *Business Week.*

Includes 1 chart showing respondent views on whether professional athletes, entertainers, executives, and elected officials are underpaid, overpaid, or paid what they are worth.

HIDDEN VULNERABILITY OF FOREIGN BANKS

(p. 53) Article on stability of foreign banks. Data are from IBCA Banking Analysis Ltd. Includes 1 undated table showing loans to Latin America as percent of equity for 4 U.S. banks and 4 British banks.

CORPORATE BALANCE SHEET SCOREBOARD: 1ST QUARTER 1984, ANNUAL FEATURE

(p. 68-102) Annual table showing selected balance sheet data for 900 nonfinancial corporations in 36 industries, as of most recent available fiscal period (1st quarter 1984 for most companies), with selected comparisons to 1983.

Table includes the following: assets; short-term and long-term debt; current ratio, fixed charge coverage ratio, and 5-year cash flow as percent of growth needs; common equity as percent of total investment capital; and stock price as percent of book value, and Standard & Poor quality rating, as of June 1984.

Data are from Standard & Poor's Compustat Services.

Also includes accompanying article and index of companies.

HOW IBM MADE 'JUNIOR' AN UNDERACHIEVER

(p. 106-107) Article describing marketing problems with IBM microcomputers. Data are from Future Computing Inc. and *Business Week.* Includes 2 charts showing shipment value, and market shares of 3-5 manufacturers and others, for home and office microcomputers, 1982 and 1984.

MOST UNION HONCHOS ESCAPED THE SQUEEZE THAT PINCHED THE RANK AND FILE, ANNUAL FEATURE

(p. 109, 112) Annual article on compensation of top labor union officials, 1983. Data are from Dept of Labor, *Business Week,* and Teamsters for a Democratic Union. Includes 1 table showing salary, allowance, expenses, and total compensation paid to top 1-3 officials in each of 37 unions, 1983.

For description of last previous article, see SRI 1982 Annual, under C5800-7.323.

C5800–7.535: July 2, 1984 (No. 2849)

DIVIDING THE BODY TO CONQUER THE MARKET

(p. 48) Article, with 2 charts showing sales growth for makeup and skin care preparations, 1979-83 period. Data are from *Product Marketing.*

BABY BOOMERS PUSH FOR POWER

(p. 52-62) Article, with 6 charts showing the following for the baby boom generation: population and labor force growth during 1970-83 period; percent with college degree (no date); 1982 voter registration and participation; self-perception as liberal, moderate, or conservative (no date); and 1984 presidential candidate perceived as best representing interests of baby boomers; most with comparison to older generation or total population.

Data are from Census Bureau, BLS, and Louis Harris and Associates.

BUSINESS WEEK/HARRIS POLL: YES, THEY ARE DIFFERENT

(p. 56-57) Article comparing views of baby boom and older generations. Data are based on a June 1984 survey by Louis Harris and Associates for *Business Week.* Includes 3 charts showing attitudes toward reductions in defense spending and Federal regulation of business; and perceived sources of economic growth (computers/high technology, revitalization of old industries, or trade protectionism); for respondents age 20-36 and 50-64.

IT CAN PAY OFF BIG TO TURN COMMON INTO PREFERRED

(p. 76) Article, with 1 chart comparing average percent price growth for common stock acquired by corporations via buyback vs. exchange for preferred stock, 1980-83 period. Data are from Mitchell and Co.

C5800–7.536: July 9, 1984 (No. 2850)

BUSINESS WEEK/HARRIS POLL: BUSINESS RAPS WASHINGTON ON TRADE

(p. 10) Article on executives' views regarding foreign trade situation. Data are from a June 1984 survey of 600 executives conducted by Louis Harris and Associates for *Business Week.* Includes 2 charts showing responses to questions on principal cause of trade deficit, and effectiveness of Federal Government in reducing foreign trade barriers.

R&D SCOREBOARD: A DEEPENING COMMITMENT TO R&D, ANNUAL FEATURE

(p. 64-78) Annual feature on R&D expenditures and financial performance of 800 companies in 32 industries, 1983. Data are compiled by Standard & Poor's Compustat Services, Inc., from SEC Form 10K filings.

Contents:

a. Narrative analysis, with 3 tables showing 15 leading companies in 3 measures of R&D spending, 1983; and glossary. (p. 64-65)

b. List of companies grouped by industry, showing the following for each: sales, profits, and R&D total and per employee expenditures, 1983, generally with change from 1979 and/or 1982; and average annual change in employment, 1979-83. (p. 64-77)

c. Index of companies. (p. 78)

MYTH OF THE VANISHING MIDDLE CLASS

(p. 83, 86) Article, with 1 chart showing wages for wholesale/retail trade, financial services, and other service industries, all as percents of manufacturing wages, 1969, 1979, and 1983. Data are from BLS and *Business Week.*

C5800–7.537: July 16, 1984 (No. 2851)

EUROPE'S COMPUTER MAKERS REALIZE THEY MUST BAND TOGETHER TO SURVIVE

(p. 92-98) Article, with 2 charts on computer equipment market, showing sales in Europe, Japan, and U.S. as percents of world total; and European, Japanese, and U.S. manufacturers' market shares in Europe, U.S., and Asia (no date). Data are from InfoCorp.

MIXED MARRIAGES WORRYING LONDON MARKETS

(p. 128) Article on mergers and acquisitions involving London financial institutions and stock brokerage firms. Data are from *Business Week.* Includes 1 table showing acquiring and acquired companies, and size and/or type of transaction, 1984.

PERSONAL INCOME FOR JAN. AND FEB.

(p. 148) Monthly table showing personal income, by State and census division, Jan.-Feb. and year to date 1984, with comparisons to 1983.

C5800–7.538: July 23, 1984 (No. 2852)

WORLD BANKING: HOW NEW YORK GOT TO THE TOP

(p. 104) Article, with 1 chart showing distribution of world bank foreign loans/other external assets by country/world area and for U.S. offshore branches, 1979 and 1983. Data are from Bank for International Settlements.

INTERNATIONAL CORPORATE SCOREBOARD: BEST PROFITS IN MORE THAN A DECADE, ANNUAL FEATURE

(p. 160-182) Annual feature on the sales, profits, equity, and earnings per share of approximately 1,025 foreign corporations in 63 countries, 1983. Data are compiled by Standard & Poor's Compustat Services, Inc.

Contains brief introduction, with 1 summary table showing net sales and profits of 20 largest foreign corporations, 1983; and International Scoreboard table, showing the following data by company, arranged by country and world region:

a. Sales and profits, 1983, with percent change from 1982; profit margins, 1982-83; and earnings per share, 1983.

b. Book value and rate of return, and market value of shares outstanding, 1983.

This is the 12th annual article.

C5800–7.539: July 30, 1984 (No. 2853)

NAILING DOWN THE ELECTORAL VOTE: THE NUMBERS LOOK DAUNTING

(p. 30-31) Article, with 1 table showing number of electoral votes needed to win 1984 presidential election, votes considered safe for each candidate, and number undecided, as of July 1984.

BUSINESS WEEK/HARRIS POLL: DISENCHANTMENT WITH THE DEMOCRATS

(p. 94-95) Article on public perceptions regarding the Republican and Democratic Parties. Data are from a July 1984 survey of 1,252 adults conducted by Louis Harris and Associates for *Business Week.* Includes 1 chart showing respondents' opinions on which party would best stimulate economic growth and preserve peace.

C5800–7.540: Aug. 6, 1984 (No. 2854)

BUSINESS WEEK/HARRIS POLL: PRESIDENT FAILS A CRITICAL TEST

(p. 8) Article on public opinion regarding President Reagan's foreign policy. Data are based on a July 1984 survey of 1,252 adults by Louis Harris and Associates for *Business Week*. Includes 1 chart showing responses to questions on world situation as a result of Administration policy, and outlook for hardline military policy in event of Reagan reelection.

VCR BOOM PUTS BLANK TAPES INTO FAST FORWARD

(p. 92-93) Article, with 1 chart showing market share for 6 manufacturers of blank videotapes, 1984. Data are from Yankee Group.

C5800–7.541: Aug. 13, 1984 (No. 2855)

WINNERS AND LOSERS FROM CHEAPER OIL

(p. 57) Article analyzing potential impact of oil price cuts on developing nations. Data are from American Express International Banking Corp. Includes 1 undated chart showing change in balance of payments (current account) for every $1 decline in oil prices, for 8 developing nations that are major borrowers in international financial markets.

C5800–7.542: Aug. 20, 1984 (No. 2856)

PERIL IN FINANCIAL SERVICES

(p. 52-57) Article, with 1 table showing the following for 18 major financial service companies acquired during 1980-84: acquiring company, name and type of acquired company, and acquisition date and price. Data are from *Business Week*.

SHRINKING MARKET HAS BEERMAKERS BRAWLING

(p. 59, 63) Article, with 1 chart showing beer market share for major breweries, 1978 and 1983. Data are from R. S. Weinberg and Associates.

CORPORATE SCOREBOARD, QUARTERLY FEATURE

(p. 65-100) "A First in 5 Years: Profits Across the Board." Covers corporate financial performance of 900 companies, for 2nd quarter 1984. For description of data, see C5800-7, above.

C5800–7.543: Aug. 27, 1984 (No. 2857)

BUSINESS WEEK/HARRIS POLL: AN OUTCRY AGAINST HOSTILE TAKEOVERS

(p. 16) Article on executives' views of "hostile takeovers" (acquisitions involving a company not in favor of the transaction). Data are based on an Aug. 1984 survey of approximately 600 executives by Louis Harris and Associates for *Business Week*. Includes 1 chart showing survey response on whether hostile takeovers are harmful or beneficial and whether bidding or target company holds the advantage.

LONDON'S MERGER FEVER: WILL AMERICAN INVESTORS CATCH THE BUG?

(p. 42) Article, with 1 table showing value and companies involved for 9 largest mergers in UK, 1st half 1984. Data are from *Business Week*.

MASS TRANSIT: THE EXPENSIVE DREAM

(p. 62-69) Article, with 1 table showing the following for 10 cities planning new rail mass transit systems and for 10 cities planning extension of existing systems: system or extension length, projected completion date, and estimated cost. Data are from American Public Transit Assn and *Business Week*.

DOES THE FREQUENT-FLIER GAME PAY OFF FOR AIRLINES?

(p. 74-75) Article, with 2 tables showing 4 major airlines ranked by membership of 'frequent flier' promotional programs, and including free travel share of total revenue passenger miles, with detail for Pan American airline, as of early 1984. Data are from *Business Week*.

HAVEN FOR CORPORATE CASH: ARP FUNDS

(p. 82-83) Article, with 1 table showing 8 major adjustable-rate preferred stock mutual funds, ranked by total asset value as of July 31, 1984. Data are from Fidelity Investments.

PAYING FOR COLLEGE: PLOT A COURSE NOW

(p. 98-99) Article, with 1 table showing amount of savings required to pay costs at a top private university and a State university, assuming 10% annual cost increase and 5% and 10% return on savings, yearly for 1-10 years prior to matriculation. Data are from Touche Ross and Co. and are based on 1984 costs.

C5800–7.544: Sept. 3, 1984 (No. 2858)

BUSINESS WEEK/HARRIS POLL: A VOTE OF CONFIDENCE FOR REAGANOMICS

(p. 78-79) Article on public opinion regarding fairness of Reagan Administration economic policies toward general public, the poor, and the rich. Data are based on an Aug. 1984 survey of 1,287 likely voters conducted by Louis Harris and Associates for *Business Week*. Includes 1 chart.

PERSONAL INCOME FOR MAR.

(p. 104) Monthly table showing personal income, by State and census division, Mar. and 1st quarter 1984, with comparisons to 1983.

C5800–7.545: Sept. 10, 1984 (No. 2859)

BUSINESS WEEK/HARRIS EXECUTIVE POLL: INFLATION FEARS ARE ON THE WANE

(p. 37) Article on executives' views regarding outlook for inflation in next 12 months. Data are from an Aug. 1984 survey of 602 executives conducted by Louis Harris and Associates for *Business Week*. Includes 1 chart.

SHOWDOWN IN DETROIT

(p. 102-110) Article, with 1 chart showing domestically produced autos; and imports, and autos produced abroad for U.S. manufacturers, by place of origin (variously including Japan, Europe, Korea, and Mexico), 1983 and 1987. Data are from United Auto Workers and *Business Week*.

C5800–7.546: Sept. 17, 1984 (No. 2860)

PENSION SCOREBOARD: A CONTROVERSIAL GLOW OF HEALTH, ANNUAL FEATURE

(p. 153-160) Annual article on the financial condition of corporate pension funds, 1983. Includes 1 table showing the following pension fund data for each of the 100 largest companies: total and vested benefits, assets, vested funding position, net worth, assumed rate of return, and expense, 1983, with selected comparisons to 1982.

Also includes 2 summary tables showing 10 corporate pension funds with largest assets, and 18 funds with largest unfunded liabilities.

C5800–7.547: Sept. 24, 1984 (No. 2861)

BUSINESS WEEK/HARRIS POLL: CHURCH-STATE SEPARATION IS STILL SACRED

(p. 24) Article on public opinion regarding religious involvement in politics. Data are based on responses of 1,211 adults to a Sept. 1984 survey conducted by Louis Harris and Associates for *Business Week*. Includes 1 chart showing public opinion on whether evangelical preachers should urge church members to vote on basis of candidates' positions on abortion, tax exemptions for segregated schools, school prayer, and Equal Rights Amendment.

NOW MERGER MAY BE THE THRIFTS' ONLY HOPE

(p. 124-127) Article on financial condition of thrift institutions since enactment of Garn-St. Germain Act of 1982 enabling such institutions to issue certificates of net worth to Federal regulators in exchange for promissory notes covering up to 70% of institutions' losses. Data are from FDIC, FSLIC, and the National Council of Savings Institutions.

Includes 1 undated table showing total assets and value of net worth certificates issued, for top 10 institutions ranked by certificates' value. The ranked institutions represent 71% of all certificates issued.

NEW FOOD GIANTS

(p. 132-138) Article, with 1 table showing the following for 14 major food companies that acquired other firms during 1982-84: companies acquired, and acquisition date and price. Data are from *Business Week*.

PERSONAL INCOME FOR APR. AND MAY

(p. 157) Monthly table showing personal income, by State and census division, Apr.-May and year to date 1984, with comparisons to 1983.

C5800–7.548: Oct. 8, 1984 (No. 2863)

BUSINESS WEEK/HARRIS POLL: REAGAN IS RUNNING FAR AHEAD OF THE REPUBLICANS

(p. 64) Article on trends in voter political preferences shortly before the 1984 presidential elections. Data are based on responses of 1,326 likely voters to a Sept. 1984 survey by Louis Harris and Associates for *Business Week*. Includes 1 chart showing respondents' views on desirability of a Republican-controlled Congress should President Reagan be reelected.

IMPORT INVASION: NO INDUSTRY HAS BEEN LEFT UNTOUCHED

(p. 172-174) Article, with 1 table showing top 16 non-oil companies in U.S. ranked by value of imports, 1983. Data are from *Business Week*.

C5800–7.549: Oct. 15, 1984 (No. 2864)

PERSONAL INCOME FOR JUNE

(p. 76) Monthly table showing personal income, by State and census division, June and 1st half 1984, with comparisons to 1983.

BUSINESS WEEK/HARRIS POLL: AMERICANS PRESCRIBE RADICAL SURGERY

(p. 148) Article on public opinion regarding health care costs. Data are from responses of 1,211 likely voters to a Sept. 1984 survey by

Louis Harris and Associates for *Business Week*. Includes 1 chart showing respondents' views on the acceptability of selected cost control measures.

CANADIAN BANK STOCKS HAVE A 'PERCEPTION PROBLEM'

(p. 164) Article, with 1 table showing earnings per share for 5 major Canadian banks, as reported by the banks and as calculated with method used by U.S. banks, 1983. Data are from Dominion Bond Rating Service Ltd.

C5800–7.550: Oct. 22, 1984 (No. 2865)

BUSINESS WEEK/HARRIS POLL: MONDALE'S NEW LEASE ON LIFE

(p. 34-35) Article on effects of the Oct. 7, 1984 presidential debate. Data are from responses of over 1,000 likely voters to an Oct. 1984 survey by Louis Harris and Associates for *Business Week,* and a similar survey conducted in Sept. 1984.

Includes 1 chart comparing pre- and postdebate survey findings on voters' perception of confidence inspired by Reagan vs. Mondale, with detail for selected voter groups.

ITT's BIG GAMBLE

(p. 114-122) Article, with 1 chart showing telephone PBX (private branch exchange) industry market shares, for 8 leading and all other manufacturers, 1983. Data are from Northern Business Information, Inc.

SMALL IS BEAUTIFUL NOW IN MANUFACTURING

(p. 152-156) Article, with 1 chart comparing average number of employees, for plants built before 1970 and still operating in 1979, opened during 1970s, and opening in 1980s, all aggregated for 410 major manufacturers.

Data are based on a study by Roger W. Schmenner of Duke University, and *Business Week* estimates.

C5800–7.551: Oct. 29, 1984 (No. 2866)

BEHIND THE BANKING TURMOIL

(p. 100-103) Article on impact of nonperforming loans on banking industry. Data sources include FDIC; corporate financial reports; and Keefe, Bruyette & Woods, Inc. Includes 1 chart and 2 tables showing the following:

a. FDIC-insured banks: number of failures, and number on FDIC's problem list, 1974-84.

b. Major banks: assets, operating loss, loan charge-offs, and sectors designated as problem borrowers, for 5 banks with significant losses from problem loans; and nonperforming assets and loan charge-offs as percents of total loans, for 16 of the 25 largest banks, with average for 25 largest; various periods 1983-84.

C5800–8   CHEMICAL ENGINEERING
Biweekly.   Approx. 100 p.
ISSN 0009-2460.
LC 11-12192.
SRI/MF/not filmed

Biweekly publication reporting developments and trends in chemical engineering and in basic chemicals and chemical process industries. Includes articles on plant and project management, process technology, R&D, government regulation and funding, problem solving theory, and

personnel training and management; and regularly appearing data on chemical plant and equipment costs and output.

Most data are from Federal Government sources, McGraw-Hill Economics Dept, or private research and consulting firms, and are compiled and analyzed by *Chemical Engineering*.

Issues generally contain:

a. Three monthly "Economic Indicators" tables, showing indexes of chemical plant and equipment costs, output, and operating rate, with 5 accompanying charts.

b. Articles, generally narrative or technical in nature, but occasionally including broad based industry statistics; and narrative editorial depts.

Additional recurring statistical features include a semiannual list of major chemical process industry construction projects; and an annual feature on salaries of chemical engineers. Annual subject and author indexes appear in the last issue in Dec.

Monthly tables are listed below and appear in every other issue. All additional features with substantial nontechnical statistical content are described, as they appear, under "Statistical Features." Nonstatistical features are not covered.

Availability: Chemical Engineering, Fulfillment Manager, PO Box 1482, Riverton NJ 08077, industry subscribers $24.50 per yr., single copy $5.00; SRI/MF/not filmed.

Issues reviewed during 1984: Nov. 14, 1983-Oct. 29, 1984 (P) (Vol. 90, Nos. 23-26; Vol. 91, Nos. 1-22).

MONTHLY TABLES:

[Tables usually appear on p. 7 of issue.]

[1] Plant cost index [total, for 7 types of chemical engineering equipment, machinery, and supports, and for construction labor, buildings, and engineering/supervision; for month 1-3 months prior to cover date, 2 previous months, and same month of previous year; and annual total index for 11 previous years].

[2] Equipment cost index [total and for 12 chemical process and related industries; for quarter 1-2 quarters prior to cover date, and 2 previous quarters; and annual total index for 11 previous years].

[3] Current business indicators [chemical process industry output index, value of output, and operating rate; and indexes of construction costs, industrial chemicals producer prices, industrial activity, and chemicals/allied products hourly earnings and productivity; variously for week, month, or quarter 1-5 months prior to cover date, previous 2 periods, and same period of previous year].

STATISTICAL FEATURES:

C5800–8.501: Jan. 9, 1984 (Vol. 91, No. 1)

ON-LINE INFORMATION

(p. 69-72) By Monica E. Baltatu. Article on online data bases of interest to chemical engineers. Includes 1 undated table showing total and online machine-readable data bases, by general application.

Also includes 2 tabular lists of online bibliographic and numerical data bases identifying subject covered, supplier, user fee, vendors, number of available materials, and/or period of coverage.

ESTIMATING OPERATING COSTS

(p. 97-100) By Gregory A. Vogel and Edward J. Martin. Article on operating costs for hazardous waste incineration. Includes technical illustrations, and 2 tables showing typical salary and salary/benefit value, by type of incinerator plant employee (undated); and preheating fuel costs and heat content, by fuel type, Mar. 1981.

C5800–8.502: Feb. 20, 1984 (Vol. 91, No. 4)

CRITICS CHIP AWAY AT BIGGER FEDERAL BUDGET

(p. 37-39) Article on FY85 Federal budget proposed by President Reagan, focusing on environmental and health appropriations. Data are from EPA. Includes 1 chart showing EPA appropriations, FY74-85, with detail for Superfund (designed to assist in dealing with hazardous wastes) for FY81-85.

C5800–8.503: Mar. 19, 1984 (Vol. 91, No. 6)

CE ALERT: NEW CONSTRUCTION, SEMIANNUAL FEATURE

(p. 161-169) Semiannual tabular list of major chemical process industry projects in the planning stage, under construction, or completed, in U.S., Canada, and Mexico, announced from late summer 1983 to early 1984.

List shows project product, location, plant capacity, and construction status, frequently with costs, by company for over 130 projects in 10 chemical process industries.

This is the 58th semiannual tabulation.

C5800–8.504: Apr. 2, 1984 (Vol. 91, No. 7)

CHEMICAL ENGINEERING SALARIES COME THROUGH ROUGH TIMES, ANNUAL FEATURE

(p. 93-95) Annual article, by Kenneth J. McNaughton, on salaries of chemical engineers. Data are from BLS, and surveys conducted by Executive Compensation Service, College Placement Council, and American Institute of Chemical Engineers.

Includes 4 tables presenting summary results from the surveys, including salary levels, new hires, and job and salary offers, by highest degree earned, 1983 with comparisons to 1982; and CPI and inflation rate, 1960-83.

C5800–8.505: Apr. 16, 1984 (Vol. 91, No. 8)

MANMADE-FIBERS COMEBACK

(p. 19-23) Article, with 1 chart showing share of man-made fiber production, for U.S., Western Europe, Japan, and all other world regions, 1983.

LET'S GET THE GOVERNMENT OFF THE TAXPAYER'S BACK

(p. 87-90) By J. Peter Grace. Article on Federal Government spending and taxation trends, with brief analysis of the current tax system. Includes 5 tables and 1 chart showing the following:

a. Taxes paid, tax rate, and after-tax income, by family gross income class (in 1983 dollars); and median family income, taxes, actual tax rate, and tax rate needed to balance Federal budget; various years 1948-83.

b. Federal spending trends from the 1940s with comparison to 1789; distribution of family spending by category including taxes, and defense and human resource expenditures as percent of all Federal spending and of GNP, various years 1962-82; and income and consumption taxes as percent of all taxes, and savings as percent of disposable income, for U.S. and 5 other countries (no date).

C5800–8.506: June 25, 1984 (Vol. 91, No. 13)

PROCESS TRIO SELECTIVELY PRODUCE OLEFINS FROM LPG

(p. 40-41) By Jay Chowdhury. Article, with 2 tables showing surplus/deficit of liquefied petroleum gas (LPG), by world region, 1985 and 1990; and typical investment and operating costs for propylene and butene catalytic production. Data are from Purvin and Gertz, Inc. and Air Products and Chemicals Co.

C5800–8.507: Aug. 20, 1984 (Vol. 91, No. 17)

SHOCKING IS THE WORD FOR CPI's ELECTRIC BILL

(p. 30-35) Article, with 2 tables showing U.S. chemical industry energy consumption, by energy type, 1972 and 1981; and chemical industry electricity prices at 3 load factors, for 6 European countries, as of Apr. 1984. Data are from DOE, Electricity Council (London), and *Chemical Engineering* estimates.

C5800–8.508: Sept. 3, 1984 (Vol. 91, No. 18)

SALES TO BIOTECH FIRMS ARE BOOMING

(p. 28-30) Article, with 1 table showing sales of laboratory and fermentation chemicals and equipment/instruments to biotechnology firms, 1983-85, 1990, and 1995. Data are from Business Communications Co.

READERS SAY 'THUMBS UP' TO PERFORMANCE APPRAISALS

(p. 52-64) By Jay Matley and Richard Greene. Article presenting survey findings on the conduct and value of job performance appraisals. Data are from responses of 2,951 *Chemical Engineering* readers to a Feb. 1984 survey.

Includes 16 charts and 3 tables showing survey responses on the following topics, with occasional detail for supervisors: value of appraisals to company and employee; workings of appraisal system, including fairness and accuracy, criteria that should be used, and how supervisors use appraisals; and whether employees should be able to appraise supervisors.

C5800–8.509: Oct. 15, 1984 (Vol. 91, No. 21)

CE ALERT: NEW CONSTRUCTION, SEMIANNUAL FEATURE

(p. 111-122) Semiannual tabular list of major chemical process industry projects in the planning stage, under construction, or completed, in U.S., Canada, and Mexico, announced from early 1984 to late summer.

List shows project product, location, plant capacity, and construction status, frequently with costs, by company for over 200 projects in 10 chemical process industries.

This is the 59th semiannual tabulation.

C5800–9   THIRTY-THREE: METAL PRODUCING

Monthly.   Approx. 100 p.
ISSN 0149-1210.
LC 77-641061.
SRI/MF/not filmed

Monthly trade journal reporting on operating, financial, and technological developments and outlook in the U.S. and world primary metal manufacturing industries (SIC major group 33): iron and steel, aluminum, copper, lead, zinc, and other nonferrous metals. Primary emphasis is on steel.

Includes data from McGraw-Hill surveys and publications, U.S. Government reports, and industry assns.

Issues generally contain:

a. Narrative articles, often with text statistics on individual companies; and regular editorial depts.

b. Monthly "Economic Notes" feature, with brief analyses of selected steel industry economic topics, and 3 tables described below.

An annual statistical steel and nonferrous metals industry outlook report is included in the Dec. issue. Aug. issue includes a nonstatistical new product buyer's guide.

Monthly tables are listed below and appear in all issues. All additional features with substantial statistical content are described, as they appear, under "Statistical Features." Nonstatistical features are not covered.

Availability: 33 Metal Producing, Fulfillment Manager, PO Box 695, Hightstown NJ 08520, industry subscribers †, nonindustry subscribers $35.00 per yr., single copy $3.00; SRI/MF/not filmed.

Issues reviewed during 1984: Nov. 1983-Oct. 1984 (P) (Vol. 21, Nos. 11-12; Vol. 22, Nos. 1-10).

ECONOMIC NOTES MONTHLY TABLES:

[Data are shown for month 2-3 months prior to cover date, with comparisons to previous month and year. Base year for indexes is 1967.]

[1] Steel performance trends [steel consumption index and indexes for 6 major consuming industries].

[2] Indicators of current [steel industry] operations [consumption and production indexes, operating rates, output per worker-hour, shipments, raw steel output, inventories, mill price index, and industry employment, earnings, and hours].

[3] Indicators of prospective steel industry trends [new and unfilled orders for blast furnace/steel mill products, electrical and nonelectrical machinery, and freight cars; new orders for automotive equipment; and contract awards and new plans for manufacturing/commercial/apartments construction].

STATISTICAL FEATURES:

C5800–9.501: Nov. 1983 (Vol. 21, No. 11)

US REBOUND ONLY BRIGHT SPOT IN WORLD STEEL OUTLOOK

(p. 58-61) By John J. Dwyer, Jr. Article on world steel consumption and production outlook. Data are from International Iron and Steel Institute. Includes 2 tables showing apparent steel consumption for Western and Communist world, and Western steel production capacity, by country or world region, various years 1974-90.

'TIME BOMB' IN STEEL'S BACKYARD

(p. 67) Article, with 1 table showing furnace coke supply/demand balance, by country or world region, 1985, 1990, and 2000. Data are from *World Coke Dynamics*.

C5800–9.502: Dec. 1983 (Vol. 21, No. 12)

1984 OUTLOOK: FULL STEAM AHEAD! ANNUAL FEATURE

(p. 35-43) Annual analysis of steel and nonferrous metals industry economic outlook for 1984, with trends from 1979. Includes several articles, and 8 tables showing the following for 1979-84:

a. Raw steel production, net shipments, foreign trade, and apparent consumption; steel and aluminum product shipments by end-use market; aluminum product exports; and steel and nonferrous metals capital investment by purpose, and spending for R&D, pollution control, and safety/health.

b. Sales, net profit, depreciation, and inventories, for steel and nonferrous metals industries; and indexes of industrial prices and manufacturing hourly earnings, and of steel mill prices, average hourly earnings, output per hour, and labor cost.

C5800–9.503: Mar. 1984 (Vol. 22, No. 3)

STEEL'S NEW PLUNGE INTO ELECTROGALVANIZING

(p. 56-58) By Walter P. Jacob. Article, with 2 tables showing shipments of galvanized steel sheet/strip, by type, 1978-82; and automotive industry consumption of zinc-coated steel, by type for 3 auto manufacturers, 1982-83. Data are from American Iron and Steel Institute and Zinc Institute.

C5800–9.504: Apr. 1984 (Vol. 22, No. 4)

WAITING FOR ANSWERS ON MERGERS

(p. 58-61) By Walter P. Jacob. Article examining Federal Government's involvement in corporate merger activity. Data are from Justice Dept. Includes 1 table showing corporate premerger notifications filed with Federal Government; and Justice Dept requests for additional information, and antitrust case filings based on premerger notifications and initiated in absence of notification; 1979-83.

SIZING UP HIGH-TECH'S TOLL ON STEEL INTENSITY: AN ECONOMETRICIAN LOOKS AHEAD

(p. 83) Article, with 2 tables showing steel consumption relative to GNP, for 10 countries; and apparent steel consumption, by world region; various periods 1970-95. Data are from Chase Econometrics Associates.

C5800–9.505: May 1984 (Vol. 22, No. 5)

COKEMAKING CAPACITY: A COOLER APPRAISAL

(p. 39-50) By Joseph J. Innace. Article, with 3 tables showing summary coke supply data; and steelmakers' and merchant producers' coke production capacity, by company and plant; as of May 1, 1984. Data are from a *33 Metal Producing* survey.

'A NOOSE AROUND OUR NECKS'

(p. 61) Brief article, with 1 table showing volume of steel imports from EC, Japan, and all other countries, Feb. 1983 and Jan.-Feb. 1984. Data are from Commerce Dept.

C5800–9.506: June 1984 (Vol. 22, No. 6)

ALUMINUM EXTRUSIONS NEAR RECORD LEVELS

(p. 16-17) Article, with 1 table showing shipments of aluminum extrusions to construction, transportation, and other industries, selected years 1966-84.

STEEL SCENE: CLOUDED PROSPECTS IN AN ERA OF CHANGE

(p. 38-42) Article on Canadian steel industry trends and outlook. Data are from Merrill Lynch Canada, Inc. Includes 1 table showing Canadian steel ingot production; operating rate; domestic shipments by end use; exports, total and to U.S.; imports; and apparent supply; 1977-83.

C5800–9.507: Sept. 1984 (Vol. 22, No. 9)

STEEL AND THE PRESIDENCY

(p. 39-44) By Walter P. Jacob and Joseph J. Innace. Article, with 1 table showing steel industry shipments, profits, average monthly employment, and productivity, during Reagan Administration and 5 previous administrations. Data are from American Iron and Steel Institute.

C5800–11   U.S. BUSINESS OUTLOOK, Short-Term
        Quarterly.   Approx. 15 p.
        SRI/MF/complete

Quarterly analysis of factors affecting the general business climate, and expected performance of the economy over the next 4-6 quarters. Includes consumer spending, capital investment, and fiscal and monetary policy. Data are compiled by the McGraw-Hill Economics Dept, and are current to quarter ended 2 months prior to publication.

Contains narrative analysis, with text statistics and usually trend tables and charts on various aspects of the economy; and 1 table showing the following, for quarter of coverage and forecast for following 4-6 quarters, with annual summary:

a. National Product Accounts, including GNP, consumer spending, fixed investment, inventory change, government purchases, and net exports.

b. Key economic indicators, including housing starts, auto sales, unemployment rate, CPI, industrial production index, 90-day Treasury bill rate, corporate bond yield, and personal income.

Most indicators are in all issues.

Availability: McGraw-Hill, Economics Department, 1221 Ave. of the Americas, New York NY 10020, $60.00 per yr.; SRI/MF/complete.
Issues reviewed during 1984: Nov. 1983-Aug. 1984 (P).

C5800–12   MODERN PLASTICS
        Monthly.   Approx. 180 p.
        ISSN 0026-8275.
        LC 42-3582.
        SRI/MF/not filmed

Monthly trade journal (2 issues in Oct.) reporting on developments and trends in plastics manufacturing, management, R&D, marketing, and consumption. Includes data on plastics production capacity, output, sales, and prices; and production in plastics-using industries. Data are from McGraw-Hill Economics Dept, petroleum and chemical companies, BLS, and other sources.

General format:

a. Monthly "Barometer" feature, with 1 table forecasting production trends in 9-10 major plastics end-use markets for the month of publication and following month, with comparison to previous year; and 2 charts summarizing price and production trends for plastics.

b. Regular editorial depts and feature articles, occasionally with substantial nontechnical statistics.

An annual *Modern Plastics Encyclopedia,* published as 2nd issue in Oct., contains material and process information, technical specifications, and a directory of suppliers.

Monthly "Barometer" feature appears in all issues except special encyclopedia issue. All additional features with substantial nontechnical statistical content are described, as they appear, under "Statistical Features." Nonstatistical contents are not covered.

Availability: Modern Plastics, Fulfillment Manager, PO Box 430, Hightstown NJ 08520, qualified subscribers $28.00 per yr., selected others $32.00 per yr., single copy $5.00, encyclopedia $36.95 (library edition); SRI/MF/not filmed.

Issues reviewed during 1984: Nov. 1983-Oct. 1984 (P) (Vol. 60, Nos. 11-12; Vol. 61, Nos. 1-10A).

STATISTICAL FEATURES:

C5800–12.501: Nov. 1983 (Vol. 60, No. 11)

THERE MAY BE MORE PROFITS IN LARGER-PARTS BLOW MOLDING

(p. 48-51) By George R. Smoluk. Article, with 2 undated tables showing capital investment requirements for blow molding equipment and molds, by type or application. Data are from Hoover Universal and Midland Ross Corp.

VINYL COMPOUNDING BUILDUP IS A BONANZA FOR USERS

(p. 52-55) By Robert Martino. Article, with 1 undated table showing production capacity, plant location, and specialty, for 38 U.S. and Canadian vinyl molding and extrusion compound suppliers. Data are from individual suppliers.

C5800–12.502: Dec. 1983 (Vol. 60, No. 12)

EXTRUDER ADD-ONS AND DESIGN VARIATIONS SQUEEZE OUT BIG PRODUCTIVITY BONUSES

(p. 36-38) By Joseph A. Sneller. Article on plastics extruding equipment technology, with 1 undated table showing gear pump component costs. Data are from Normag.

BIG NEW BOTTLE-BLOW MARKET: MULTI-LAYER CONTAINERS

(p. 44-46) By George R. Smoluk. Article, with 3 undated tables showing composite plastic bottle production costs and major uses.

C5800–12.503: Jan. 1984 (Vol. 61, No. 1)

AUTOMATION BRINGS HIGH RETURN ON INVESTMENT

(p. 26) Brief article, with 1 table showing injection molding machine automation cost savings and effect on cash flow over a 5-year period. Data are from Nelmor Co.

MATERIALS '84, ANNUAL FEATURE

(p. 45-67) Annual report, for 1984, on plastics industry technological and market developments, including data on sales, use, and prices, and U.S. and Canadian production capacity.

Contains introduction; 9 narrative articles on market outlook of industry sectors, with 2 tables (p. 47-48) showing linear low density polyethylene and polypropylene supply/demand; and industry statistics section (p. 57-67) presenting the following data compiled by *Modern Plastics* from industry contacts and from Society of the Plastics Industry reports:

a. Domestic sales, 1982-83, and quarterly prices, 3rd quarter 1980-4th quarter 1983, by resin type. 2 tables. (p. 57)

b. Sales: by type of market (including exports), manufacturing process, and end use, for individual resin types; and by resin type for major markets (including appliances, building materials, electrical/electronics, furniture, housewares, packaging, toys, and transportation), and including specific end use for some markets; 1982-83. 39 tables. (p. 58-65)

c. Production capacity in U.S. and Canada, by company, for selected resin types, as of Jan. 1, 1984, and planned additions through 1986; and Canadian domestic demand and foreign trade by resin, 1982-83. 7 tables. (p. 66-67)

C5800–12.504: Feb. 1984 (Vol. 61, No. 2)

BOOM TIME FOR PVC PIPE? OR JUST ANOTHER FIZZLE?

(p. 50-52) By Robert Martino. Article, with 1 table showing polyvinyl chloride (PVC) pipe manufacturing cost, wholesale price, and producer profit share, quarterly 1983. Data are from M&T Chemicals, Inc., and other industry sources.

FUTURE FOR METALLIZED PLASTICS

(p. 90-92) Article, with 1 table showing consumption of metal plated/coated plastics, by end use, selected years 1970-95. Data are from Margolis Marketing and Research Co.

C5800–12.505: Apr. 1984 (Vol. 61, No. 4)

ENGINEERING RESINS IN 1984 AND BEYOND

(p. 20) Brief article, with 1 undated table showing engineering thermoplastics sales volume worldwide, by resin. Data are from Celanese Engineering Resins.

UPDATE ON CONTROLS, ANNUAL FEATURE

(p. 33-112) Annual report on recent developments in plastics processing equipment, 1982-83. Data are from industry estimates, *Modern Plastics* studies, Commerce Dept, and Society of the Plastics Industry.

Includes introduction and 5 articles, with 3 tables (p. 34-35) showing machinery shipments and sales value by equipment type (shown variously for total, domestic, exports, and imports), 1982-83.

C5800–12.506: May 1984 (Vol. 61, No. 5)

ADDITIVES FOR HYBRIDS, LOW-SMOKE PHOSPHORUS; WHEREVER YOU LOOK THERE'S SOMETHING NEW IN FLAME RETARDANTS FOR URETHANE FOAMS

(p. 58-60) By A. Stuart Wood. Article on development of flame retardant polyurethane foam.

Data are from Fire Retardant Chemicals Assn and industry estimates. Includes 1 table showing combustion-modified polyurethane foam consumption, by end use market, 1983 and 1988.

LOOK TO LASERS FOR A PRACTICAL WAY TO DO THE TOUGH FABRICATING JOBS

(p. 61-63) By George R. Smoluk. Article on use of laser technology in production of plastic products. Data are from Laser Machining, Inc. Includes 1 undated table showing potential investment and operating costs.

C5800–12.507: June 1984 (Vol. 61, No. 6)

FLOOD OF SAUDI PE? MOBIL SAYS NO

(p. 12) Article, with 1 table showing owner, location, technology used, startup date, and nameplate capacity, for foreign polyethylene plants beginning operation or scheduled during 1980-88. Data are from Mobil Chemical.

CRISIS BREWING IN PHENOL SUPPLY

(p. 22) Article, with 1 undated table showing phenol capacity of 9 producers. Data are from producer reports.

TiO2 SUPPLY COULD BECOME TIGHT

(p. 25) Brief article, with 1 undated chart showing distribution of titanium dioxide market, by end use and world area.

RESINS AND COMPOUNDS: COST PRESSURES ARE DOWN; CHOICES ARE UP, RECURRING FEATURE

(p. 107) Recurring table showing market price for crude oil and 10 resins and feedstocks, quarterly 1981-1st quarter 1984 and Apr. 1984. Includes accompanying article (p. 106-107).

C5800–12.508: July 1984 (Vol. 61, No. 7)

FILLERS AND REINFORCEMENTS, ANNUAL FEATURE

(p. 51-58) Annual collection of 3 articles on fillers and reinforcements used in the plastics industry. Data sources include individual producers. Includes 2 tables showing consumption of glass, minerals, and other fillers and reinforcements, various years 1982-85.

C5800–12.509: Aug. 1984 (Vol. 61, No. 8)

HERE ARE NEW WAYS TO REAP PROFITS FROM EPS MOLDING

(p. 50-52) By George R. Smoluk. Article discussing costs and benefits of modifying expandable polystyrene (EPS) molding systems to use vacuum processing techniques. Data are from Michael J. Gehrig & Associates. Includes technical data, and 2 undated tables illustrating modification costs with detail for shape molding presses.

USE OF STANDARDS IN INTERNATIONAL TRADE

(p. 62-66) By Keith Gorton et al. Article discussing the use of various industrial standards in international trade. Data are from responses of 202 organizations in 4 European countries to a 1980-82 survey conducted by American Society for Testing and Materials.

Includes several charts and tables on sample characteristics; and 3 tables showing survey response concerning membership on selected standards committees, reasons for using foreign/international standards, and acceptability of selected standards.

C5800–12.510: Sept. 1984 (Vol. 61, No. 9)

ADDITIVES, ANNUAL FEATURE

(p. 61-86) Annual feature on chemicals and additives used in the plastics industry. Includes text statistics on 1984 price and expansion trends; and 12 tables showing consumption of flame retardants, lubricants, plasticizers, and 10 other product categories, by type and/or end use, primarily 1982-84.

WATCH FOR THE NEW POLYPROPYLENES: CLEANER, MORE UNIFORM, BETTER PROPERTY-BALANCED

(p. 94-95) Article, with 3 tables showing selling price, manufacturing cost, demand, and effective capacity, for polypropylene, various periods 1979-85, with operating detail for 1 manufacturer.

C5800–13   TEXTILE WORLD
Monthly. Approx. 140 p.
ISSN 0040-5213.
LC 8-32834.
SRI/MF/not filmed

Monthly trade journal reporting on trends and developments in the textile industry. Covers yarn manufacturing, fabric formation, chemical treatment and finishing, management, marketing, and other topics of interest to the textile industry. Month of data coverage is 1-3 months prior to cover date.

Issues generally contain feature articles, occasionally with statistics; and regular editorial depts, including the following monthly statistical features:

a. "Activity Indicators," with 1 trend chart, and 1 table showing index of textile manufacturing activity for month of coverage, with estimates for 2-3 subsequent months and comparisons to prior periods; and 1 "Figures of the Month" table, showing 22-24 textile industry indicator indexes or amounts, including employment, earnings, hours worked, PPI, sales, inventories, operating rate, and trade, and selected national economic indicators, for month of coverage, previous month, and same month of previous year.

b. "Market Outlook," with narrative analysis, 1 trend chart, and 1 table showing textile mill products price index for month of coverage, with estimates for subsequent month and comparisons to prior periods.

Other statistical features include a quarterly table on sales and earnings of selected textile companies; a quarterly feature on industry financial ratios; and annual reports on industry trends and outlook, plant closings, carpet manufacturers, and financial performance of leading firms. An annual buyer's guide appears in the July issue.

"Activity Indicators" and "Market Outlook" appear in all issues. All additional features with substantial statistical content are described, as they appear, under "Statistical Features." Non-statistical features are not covered.

Availability: Textile World, Circulation Department, PO Box 523, Hightstown, NJ 08520, qualified subscribers †, textile students $17.50 per yr., others $35.00 per yr., single copy $11.00, Buyers Guide $15.00; SRI/MF/not filmed.

Issues reviewed during 1984: Nov. 1983-Oct. 1984 (P) (Vol. 133, Nos. 11-12; Vol. 134, Nos. 1-10).

STATISTICAL FEATURES:

C5800–13.501: Nov. 1983 (Vol. 133, No. 11)

EMPLOYEE ASSISTANCE PLANS SAVE DOLLARS AND PEOPLE

(p. 71-72) Article reporting on a Russell Corp. (clothing and textile manufacturer) program for assisting employees with personal problems. Data are based on experiences of 502 program enrollees.

Includes 1 chart and 1 table showing enrollee distribution by type of problem, Sept. 1980-81 period; and performance evaluation for employees 1 year after referral to program by supervisor.

C5800–13.502: Dec. 1983 (Vol. 133, No. 12)

QUARTERLY TABLE

(p. 27) Sales and earnings for 14 textile companies, for various quarter-ending dates Aug. 28, 1983-Oct. 2, 1983.

C5800–13.503: Jan. 1984 (Vol. 134, No. 1)

TEXTILES HIT A CRUISING SPEED FOR CONTINUED GROWTH, ANNUAL FEATURE

(p. 34-42) Annual report on textile industry trends and outlook, 1979-84.

Covers mill fiber consumption, by fiber type; production indexes; employment, hours, and earnings, with selected detail by type of mill; expenditures for pollution control, employee health/safety, and R&D; foreign trade; mill inventory value, inventory/sales ratio, and operating rate; and WPI, by textile category.

Also includes apparel and nondurable goods retail sales, disposable income, housing starts, and new car sales.

Data are from a McGraw-Hill Dept of Economics/Data Resources Inc. survey, Federal sources, and American Textile Manufacturers Institute.

Contains narrative analysis, with 4 illustrative charts and 24 tables.

C5800–13.504: Feb. 1984 (Vol. 134, No. 2)

TEXTILES REGAINED LOST GROUND IN '83, ANNUAL FEATURE

(p. 23-27) Annual article, with 1 table showing the following for textile plant closings in North Carolina, South Carolina, and Georgia: company, location, and employees affected, 1983. Data are from North Carolina Commerce Dept, South Carolina Development Board, and Georgia Dept of Industry and Trade.

Data corrections appear in the Apr. 1984 issue (see C5800-13.506 below).

C5800–13.505: Mar. 1984 (Vol. 134, No. 3)

QUARTERLY TABLE

(p. 27) Sales and earnings for 14 textile companies, for various quarter-ending dates Nov. 3, 1983-Jan. 1, 1984.

IMPORTS: OUT OF CONTROL

(p. 63-74) Article discussing measures to regulate textile/apparel imports. Data are from Commerce Dept and BLS. Includes 2 charts showing the following for 3 Asian nations: textile exports to U.S., 1973 and 1983; and average hourly compensation in textile and apparel industries, with comparison to U.S. (no date).

C5800–13.506: Apr. 1984 (Vol. 134, No. 4)

CORRECTION

(p. 30) Corrected data for article on textile plant closings in southeastern States in 1983, appearing in Feb. 1984 issue; for description, see C5800-13.504 above.

C5800–13.507: May 1984 (Vol. 134, No. 5)

TEXTILES BUILDS LIQUIDITY AS RECOVERY MODERATES, QUARTERLY FEATURE

(p. 32) Quarterly article analyzing textile industry financial trends. Data are from Census Bureau. Includes 1 table showing textile industry selected financial ratios, 4th quarter 1982 and 3rd-4th quarter 1983.

This is the 1st quarterly article.

PREPARE YOUR CARPET FIRM FOR THE NEXT DOWNTURN, ANNUAL FEATURE

(p. 35-38) Annual article describing characteristics of successful carpet manufacturing firms, with outlook for 1984. Data are from Commerce Dept and International Management. Includes 1 table showing industry shipments by carpet type, 1979-84 with quarterly detail for 1983.

C5800–13.508: June 1984 (Vol. 134, No. 6)

INDUSTRY REBOUNDS AFTER 1982 SLUMP, ANNUAL FEATURE

(p. 23-27) Annual article on textile manufacturers' financial performance, 1983. Data are from Kurt Salmon Associates 13th annual performance profile of textile companies.

Includes 2 tables showing top 12 textile companies ranked by return on total equity and net aftertax income on sales, 1983, with 1983 sales and comparative 1982 rankings.

For description of Salmon Associates profile, see B8130-1.

C5800–13.509: July 1984 (Vol. 134, No. 7)

QUARTERLY TABLE

(p. 24) Sales and earnings for 18 textile companies, for various quarter-ending dates Feb. 29-May 27, 1984.

BALANCE SHEETS REFLECT MILL'S CONFIDENCE, QUARTERLY FEATURE

(p. 32) Quarterly article analyzing textile industry financial trends. Data are from Census Bureau. Includes 1 table showing textile industry selected financial ratios, 1st quarter 1983, and 4th quarter 1983-84.

C5800–13.510: Aug. 1984 (Vol. 134, No. 8)

DYEBATH REUSE TESTS VERIFY QUICK PAYBACK

(p. 107-110) Article on potential benefits of reusing dyebath solutions in textile mills. Includes 2 tables showing cost savings per cycle with reuse of dyebath, and percent reduction in discharge of various pollutants associated with dyeing process.

C5800–13.511: Sept. 1984 (Vol. 134, No. 9)

QUARTERLY TABLE

(p. 27) Sales and earnings for 15 textile companies, for various quarter-ending dates May 31-July 1, 1984.

THROWSTERS NEED TO CUT COSTS, AND THEY CAN

(p. 65-66) Article reporting on developments in the textured yarn industry. Data are from Rieter-Scragg Ltd. Includes 2 undated tables showing the following for 3 operations associated with textured yarn production: costs per year with selected production variables, and estimated savings with automation.

C5800–13.512: Oct. 1984 (Vol. 134, No. 10)

SLOWER SALES TRIGGER MOVES ON TEXTILE BALANCE SHEETS, QUARTERLY FEATURE

(p. 35) Quarterly article analyzing textile industry financial trends. Data are from Census Bureau. Includes 1 table showing textile industry selected financial ratios, 2nd quarter 1983-84, and 1st quarter 1984.

C5800–14   ELECTRONICS WEEK
Weekly.   Approx. 200 p.
ISSN 0748-3252.
LC 36-15816.
SRI/MF/not filmed

Weekly journal reporting trends and developments in the U.S. and international electronics industry. Covers R&D, technology, new products, marketing, and business activity. Includes data on general economy, and electronics shipments, employment, PPI, and trade. Data are from reports of Federal agencies, McGraw-Hill Economics Dept, and other private sources.

Issues generally contain numerous articles, occasionally with statistics; and regular editorial features, including a weekly business activity section, with 1 weekly table showing electronics industry composite index current to cover date, and 6 monthly tables presenting general economic and electronics industry data current to 2-3 months prior to cover date month. Weekly and monthly tables are listed below.

An annual forecast of worldwide electronics markets appears in a Jan. issue.

Weekly table appears in all issues beginning with July 23, 1984 issue. All monthly tables generally appear each month. All additional features with substantial statistical content are described, as they appear, under "Statistical Features." Nonstatistical features are not covered.

Prior to the July 23, 1984 issue, journal was published biweekly and was titled *Electronics*.

Availability: Electronics Week, Circulation Manager, CN 807, Martinsville NJ 08836, industry individuals $32.00 per yr., industry companies $40.00 per yr., single copy $3.00, nonindustry rates available on request; SRI/MF/ not filmed.

Issues reviewed during 1984: Nov. 3, 1983-July 12, 1984 (biweekly); July 23-Oct. 29, 1984 (weekly) (P) (Vol. 56, Nos. 22-25; Vol. 57, Nos. 1-29).

TABLES:

WEEKLY TABLE

[1] *Electronics Week* index [electronics industry composite index (1982=base year), generally for week of publication, previous week, and same week of preceding year; table begins with the July 23, 1984 issue].

MONTHLY TABLES

[Table format may vary. Data are shown for month of coverage, previous month, and same month of preceding year.]

[1] Industrial production index [for 5 electronics sectors].

[2] Electronics economic indicators [production workers and shipments, each for 4 sectors].

[3] General economic indicators [index of leading indicators, Federal budgeted outlays (total and DOD), industry operating rate and production index, and housing starts].

[4] Electronics imports and exports [for 8 product categories].

[5] Electronic components PPI [for 7 components].

[6] General economic indicators [prime rate, retail sales, and unemployment rate].

STATISTICAL FEATURES:

C5800–14.501: Nov. 3, 1983 (Vol. 56, No. 22)

ARTIFICIAL INTELLIGENCE: COMMERCIAL PRODUCTS BEGIN TO EMERGE FROM DECADES OF RESEARCH

(p. 127-129) By Tom Manuel and Stephen Evanczuk. Article, with 1 chart and 1 table showing artificial intelligence market shares, by end-use sector and for software, hardware, and services segments, 1983 and 1993; and market value by product type, 1983-90. Data are from International Resource Development, Inc., and DM Data, Inc.

C5800–14.502: Nov. 17, 1983 (Vol. 56, No. 23)

MICROCOMPUTERS: EE-PROM ADDS ON-CHIP FLEXIBILITY

(p. 99-100) By J. Robert Lineback. Article on technological advances and market outlook for alterable memory microcomputer chips. Data are from Motorola Semiconductor. Includes text data and 1 chart showing market value for 8-bit microcomputers, and market share by memory design type, 1987.

ROBOTICS

(p. 116-129) By Erik L. Keller. Article, with 2 tables showing value and/or number of installed industrial robots, by type and intelligence capability, for 12-18 countries, as of 1982. Data are from Robot Institute of America's *1982 Worldwide Robotics Survey*.

C5800–14.503: Dec. 1, 1983 (Vol. 56, No. 24)

WORLD PRODUCTION OF ELECTRONIC EQUIPMENT

(p. 36-37) Four tables showing worldwide electronic equipment production value, by end-use sector and world area, 1982-84 and 1987.

C5800–14.504: Dec. 15, 1983 (Vol. 56, No. 25)

NATA SHOW POINTS TO COMING SHAKEOUT

(p. 52-54) Article on market outlook for telephone instruments following divestiture of American Telephone and Telegraph. Data are from the North American Telecommunications Assn. Includes 1 table forecasting telephone and private branch exchange shipment volume and value, with volume detail for Western Electric and independent companies, 1984-87.

U.S. ATTACKS THE C3I PROBLEM

(p. 98-107) By Larry Waller. Article on market outlook for designers and suppliers of electronic gear for DOD's C3I (Communications, Command, Control, and Intelligence) program. Data are from DMS Inc. Includes 1 table showing C3I funding for nuclear and conventional force management, information/communication, electronic warfare, and intelligence, triennally 1984-93.

C5800–14.505: Jan. 12, 1984 (Vol. 57, No. 1)

JAPAN'S GIANTS GO ON SPENDING SPREE

(p. 112-114) By Michael Berger. Article comparing Japanese and U.S. semiconductor industry capital spending, FY82-83. Data are from the Japanese daily newspaper *Nihon Keizai Shimbun* and Dataquest.

Includes 2 tables showing capital expenditures, for top 6 Japanese semiconductor producers ranked by sales, and for 8 U.S. producers, FY82-83.

GLOWING YEAR FORESEEN AS STRONG GROWTH RESUMES, ANNUAL FEATURE

(p. 123-154) Compilation of 3 annual survey articles on electronics industry market conditions and outlook in U.S., Western Europe, and Japan, 1982-87. Data are based on an annual *Electronics* survey.

Includes 4 summary charts (p. 124-125); 1 table showing Federal electronics outlays by agency or purpose, 1982-84 and 1987 (p. 137); and 23 tables showing value of electronics consumption by detailed product type for the following categories:

a. U.S.: software; data processing, consumer, communications, industrial, semiconductor production, test/measurement, and medical equipment; and analytical instruments, semiconductors, and components; 1982-84 and 1987. (p. 126-141)

b. Western Europe and Japan: data processing, consumer, communications, test/measurement, industrial, medical, and (Japan only) automotive equipment; power supplies; and components; 1982-84. (p. 142-153)

Data corrections appear in the Jan. 26, 1984 issue (see C5800-14.506, below).

C5800–14.506: Jan. 26, 1984 (Vol. 57, No. 2)

1984 WORLD MARKETS FORECAST ERRATA

(p. 8) Correction of Jan. 12, 1984 "Glowing Year Foreseen as Strong Growth Resumes" article on world electronics markets. Includes 1 table showing corrected data for U.S. electronic component consumption table. For description of original table, see C5800-14.505, above.

C5800–14.507: Feb. 9, 1984 (Vol. 57, No. 3)

SURFACE MOUNTING ALTERS THE PC-BOARD SCENE

(p. 113-124) By Jerry Lyman. Article on technological impacts of surface mounting of electronic components on printed-circuit boards. Data are from Dan Rose Associates.

Includes 1 table showing the following for integrated circuits in U.S., Japan, and Europe, 1983: largest end-user industry, dominant reason for surface mounting, share of world consumption, number and percent surface mounted, and dominant surface-mounting approach.

C5800–14.508: Feb. 23, 1984 (Vol. 57, No. 4)

CONGRESS GIRDS FOR $305 BILLION DOD BLITZ

(p. 91-92) By Ray Connolly. Article, with 1 table showing DOD tactical air defense budget funding for Air Force and Navy modernization, electronic warfare, and target acquisition/surveillance/warning, all by weapons system, FY83-86. Data are from DOD.

FINALLY, SOFTWARE GETS ITS OWN CONFERENCE

(p. 95-96) By J. Robert Lineback. Article on growth of computer software suppliers not associated with hardware manufacturing. Data are from International Data Corp. and International Resource Development.

Includes 2 tables showing worldwide revenues of U.S. packaged software suppliers by type of software, for hardware-related and independent companies; and U.S. sales of personal computer software tailored to specific businesses; various years 1982-92.

C5800–14.509: Mar. 22, 1984 (Vol. 57, No. 6)

SPAIN TO BOLSTER ITS ELECTRONICS INDUSTRY

(p. 100-101) By Robert T. Gallagher. Article, with 1 table showing market value, in Spain, for electronics equipment and components by type, 1982-84. Data are from *Electronics*.

WHERE THE MARKET IS

(p. 122) Article on world market for flat-panel electronic displays. Data are from Arthur D. Little, Inc. Includes 1 table showing value of demand for large-area flat panels, for U.S., Western Europe, and Japan, and by display type, selected years 1982-92.

MULTIPROCESSING 32-BIT BUSES ARE STARTING TO BLOSSOM

(p. 124-125) By Robert Rosenberg and Erik L. Keller. Article, with 2 charts showing market share by manufacturer, for 2 leading 32-bit microcomputer buses, 1984; and world market value for 16/32-bit microcomputer boards, with distribution by type, 1982 and 1988.

C5800–14.510: May 3, 1984 (Vol. 57, No. 9)

CONFIDENCE GROWING, U.S. CHIP MAKERS RUSH TO BUILD CAPACITY

(p. 47-48) By J. Robert Lineback. Article, with 1 chart showing world sales of electronic semiconductors, 1982-84. Data are from Texas Instruments, Inc.

C5800–14.511: May 17, 1984 (Vol. 57, No. 10)

SPECIAL REPORT: WORK STATIONS, INTEGRATING THE ENGINEER'S ENVIRONMENT

(p. 121-130) By Stephen Evanczuk. Article, with 1 chart showing market share by vendor, for computer-aided engineering work stations, 1983. Data are from Strategic, Inc.

C5800–14.512: May 31, 1984 (Vol. 57, No. 11)

MEMORY MAKERS PONDER WORDWIDE MEGABIT CHIPS

(p. 43-44) By J. Robert Lineback. Article, with 1 chart showing share of computer memory market, for read-only and random-access memory systems, 1985 and 1990. Data are from Mostek Corp.

C5800–14.513: June 14, 1984 (Vol. 57, No. 12)

AGING SOFTWARE SWAMPS BUREAUCRACY

(p. 115-116) By Karen Berney. Article, with 1 table ranking top 10 Federal agencies by computer software budgets, FY85-89. Data are from OMB.

SEMICONDUCTORS RACE TO BEST YEAR EVER WORLDWIDE; MARKETS ZOOM ACROSS THE BOARD, ANNUAL FEATURE

(p. 125-137) Annual article, by Robert J. Kozma, on world semiconductor markets, 1980s. Data are from Integrated Circuit Engineering Corp., Semiconductor Industry Assn, and other sources.

Includes 6 tables showing the following data on semiconductors: value of U.S./European shipments, by product type; top 10 manufacturers in U.S., Europe, and Japan, ranked by production value; value of shipments from U.S., western Europe, Japan, and other countries; and top 9 Japanese manufacturers ranked by capital investment; various years 1982-86.

C5800–14.514: June 28, 1984 (Vol. 57, No. 13)

BOOM SQUEEZES CAPTIVE CHIP MAKERS

(p. 89-90) By Wesley R. Iversen. Article, with 1 table showing the following data for integrated circuit captive manufacturers (producers of circuits for internal company use): employment (no date) and production value 1983-84, for 6 major manufacturers and all others. Data are from Integrated Circuit Engineering Corp.

C5800–14.515: July 23, 1984 (Vol. 57, No. 15)

MANUFACTURERS IN THE U.S. AND ABROAD SCRAMBLE FOR BUSINESS AFTER THE BELL SYSTEM'S BREAKUP

(p. 46-48) Article, with 3 tables showing growth rate and value for telecommunications equipment shipments, exports, imports, and domestic consumption, by equipment type, various periods 1983-93. Data are from USITC.

DATA PROCESSING CONTINUES ITS STRONG GROWTH, WHILE IBM's DOMINATION OF THE INDUSTRY INCREASES

(p. 87-89) Article, with 1 table showing value of computer system shipments, by system size, 1983-85. Data are from International Data Corp.

DIVESTITURE AT AT&T PRODUCES FASTER-THAN-EXPECTED GROWTH FOR MAKERS OF TELECOMMUNICATIONS EQUIPMENT

(p. 92-93) Article, with 1 table showing factory and retail value of shipments, and number of lines, for private branch exchange systems, 1982-87. Data are from Venture Development Corp.

INCREASED CAPITAL SPENDING FOR PRODUCTIVITY IMPROVEMENTS PROVES A BOON FOR THE INDUSTRIAL EQUIPMENT MARKET

(p. 95-97) Article, with 1 table ranking top 10 robot vendors by estimated sales, 1984 with comparison to 1983. Data are from Prudential-Bache Securities Inc.

COMPUTER VENDORS SEE 10%-TO-20% GROWTH, EXPECTED TO LAST FOR THE NEXT SEVERAL YEARS

(p. 104-105) Article, with 1 table ranking top 9 Japanese computer firms by total sales, and also showing domestic and export sales, 1983. Data are from *Nihon Keizai Shimbun.*

C5800–14.516: July 30, 1984 (Vol. 57, No. 16)

GATE ARRAY MAKERS MUST SHRINK DIES TO EXPAND MARKETS IN THE FACE OF A STRONG CHALLENGE FROM STANDARD CELLS

(p. 19-21) Article, with 1 table showing world market value for nonstandard integrated circuits by type, 1981-1990, and compound annual growth rate. Data are from Integrated Circuit Engineering Corp.

C5800–14.517: Aug. 20, 1984 (Vol. 57, No. 19)

ADVENT OF OPTICAL DISK SYSTEMS A MIXED BLESSING FOR INTEGRATORS

(p. 19-23) Article, with 1 table showing sales volume for optical disk drive systems, by storage capacity, 1984, 1987, and 1990. Data are from Freeman Associates.

CALIFORNIA GROUP TO PUSH EXPORTS

(p. 41) Article, with 1 table showing value of U.S. imports and exports of electronic products, 1980-83. Data are from Electronics Assn of California.

C5800–14.518: Aug. 27, 1984 (Vol. 57, No. 20)

RCA SETTLING DOWN TO GATHER CMOS

(p. 61-62) Article, with 1 table showing top 10 integrated circuit manufacturers, ranked by sales, 1983 with 1984 forecast. Data are from Intergrated Circuit Engineering Corp.

DISTRIBUTORS POISED TO ENTER THE 'FOURTH ERA'

(p. 67-73). By George Leopold. Article, with 1 chart showing value of electronics distribution market, 1970, 1980, and 1990. Data are from Arthur D. Little Inc.

MILITARY ICs MAKE UP FOR LOST GROUND

(p. 75-78) By Wendy Engelberg. Article, with 1 table and 4 charts showing value of semiconductor shipments to the military, by application and product type, 1983-85 and 1988.

C5800–14.519: Sept. 24, 1984 (Vol. 57, No. 24)

JAPANESE FIRMS BOOST SPENDING FOR SHORT-, LONG-TERM PROJECTS

(p. 32-36) Article, with 1 table showing R&D expenditures for 16 major Japanese firms, FY84 with percent change from FY83. Data are from *Nihon Keizai Shimbun* and *Electronics Week.*

C5800–14.520: Oct. 1, 1984 (Vol. 57, No. 25)

ANALYSTS DIFFER ON HOW MUCH GOLD CAN BE PANNED FROM SERVICE CALLS

(p. 30-32) Article, with 1 table showing revenues for the electronics service industry, by product group, 1983 and 1990. Data are from a survey of 100 service company executives, conducted by Arthur Andersen and Co.

C5800–14.521: Oct. 8, 1984 (Vol. 57, No. 26)

ATE COSTS ARE SWELLING AS CHIPS SHRINK

(p. 71-74) By Jon Turino. Article, with 3 charts showing automatic test equipment (ATE) sales, including detail for chip and board testers, various years 1984-88.

C5800–14.522: Oct. 15, 1984 (Vol. 57, No. 27)

SURGE IN SHIPMENTS WILL CARRY 8-BIT MICROCONTROLLERS PAST THEIR 4-BIT PREDECESSORS, LONG-TIME MARKET LEADERS

(p. 16-17) Article, with 1 table showing worldwide shipments of single-chip microcomputers, by bit size, 1984-85 and 1989. Data are from Dataquest Inc.

WITH MARKET POSITION SECURE, ARROW FOCUSES ON PROFITABILITY

(p. 39-40) Article, with 1 table showing top 10 electronics product distributors ranked by market share, 1983 with comparison to 1982. Data are from Hambrecht and Quist Inc.

C5800–14.523: Oct. 29, 1984 (Vol. 57, No. 29)

VLSI TESTERS HELP GUARANTEE CHIP QUALITY

(p. 63-66) By Scott Kline. Article, with 2 charts showing the following for semiconductor automatic test equipment: market value, 1979-88; and market distribution among integrated circuit captive manufacturers, merchant manufacturers, and end users (no date). Data are from Prime Data, Inc.

C5800–15   ARCHITECTURAL RECORD
Monthly. Approx. 200 p.
Oversized.
ISSN 0003-858X.
LC 12-17303.
SRI/MF/not filmed

Monthly publication (semimonthly in Apr. and Sept.) reporting developments in the architectural field, including building design and technology, new projects, and finances.

Contains narrative editorial depts and articles, occasionally with statistics; and quarterly statistical features on Dodge/Sweet's construction outlook, and metro area building cost indexes, presenting data derived from McGraw-Hill Information Systems Co. reports.

All features with substantial statistical content are described, as they appear, under "Statistical Features." Each issue of the journal is reviewed, but an abstract is published in SRI monthly issues only when quarterly or other statistical features appear.

Availability: Architectural Record, Subscription Department, PO Box 2023, Mahopac NY 10541, $35.00 per yr., single copy $6.00; SRI/MF/not filmed.

Issues reviewed during 1984: Nov. 1983-Oct. 1984 (P) (Vol. 171, Nos. 13-14; Vol. 172, Nos. 1-12).

STATISTICAL FEATURES:

C5800–15.501: Nov. 1983 (Vol. 171, No. 13)

DODGE/SWEET'S CONSTRUCTION OUTLOOK: IS 1984 THE YEAR FOR NONRESIDENTIAL BUILDING? QUARTERLY FEATURE

(p. 39-49) Quarterly article on construction activity, primarily for 1983 with forecasts for 1984. Includes 6 tables showing the following:

a. Residential and nonresidential building construction contract value and floor area, new dwelling units, and nonbuilding contract value, all by construction type, with contract value detail by region; and total contract value index; 1983-84.

b. New dwelling units, new floor space for retail and manufacturing uses and for nonresidential buildings by type, manufacturing capacity utilization, and high rise share of all new office space, various years 1970-85.

C5800–15.502: Jan. 1984 (Vol. 172, No. 1)

COSTS: TO BE A USEFUL ESTIMATING TOOL, THESE COST INDEXES REQUIRE KNOWING HOW TO APPLY THEM, QUARTERLY FEATURE

(p. 37) Quarterly article on metro area building cost indexes, 1977-83. Includes 2 tables showing number of metro areas and percent increase in construction costs, by region, for 1977-Oct. 1983 period and 3- and 12-month periods ending Oct. 1983; and average nonresidential construction cost indexes for 21 SMSAs, 1977-80 and 2nd quarter 1981-3rd quarter 1983.

Article provides an explanation of methodology used to develop indexes.

C5800–15.503: Apr. 1984 (Vol. 172, No. 4)

CONSTRUCTION ECONOMY UPDATE: A STEADY COURSE WITH CHANGING EMPHASIS FOR 1984, QUARTERLY FEATURE

(p. (27-31) Quarterly article on construction activity, 1983, with forecasts for 1984. Includes 3 tables showing the following:

a. Residential and nonresidential building construction contract value and floor area, new dwelling units, and nonbuilding contract value, all by construction type, with contract value detail by region; and total contract value index; 1983-84, updated as of Mar. 1984.

b. Contract values for residential and nonresidential buildings, and nonbuilding construction, by type and quarter; 1983-84.

COSTS: DESPITE ALL FEARS, COSTS CONTINUE STABLE, QUARTERLY FEATURE

(p. 39) Quarterly article on metro area building cost indexes, 1977-83. Includes 3 tables showing number of metro areas and percent change in construction costs, by region and for metro New York-New Jersey, various periods 1977-Jan. 1984; and average nonresidential construction cost indexes for 21 SMSAs, 1977-80 and quarterly 3rd quarter 1981-4th quarter 1983.

An explanation of methodology used to develop indexes appears in the Jan. 1984 issue; for description, see C5800-15.502 above.

C5800–15.504: July 1984 (Vol. 172, No. 8)

COSTS: BALANCE IS THE KEY TO CONTINUING STABILITY, QUARTERLY FEATURE

(p. 33) Quarterly article on metro area building cost indexes, 1977-84. Includes 2 tables showing number of metro areas and percent increase in construction costs, by region, for 1977-Jan. 1984 period and 3- and 12-month periods ending Jan. 1984; and average nonresidential construction cost indexes for 21 SMSAs, 1977-81, and 1st quarter 1982-1st quarter 1984.

An explanation of methodology used to develop indexes appears in the Jan. 1984 issue; for description, see C5800-15.502 above.

C5800–15.505: Sept. 1984 (Vol. 172, No. 10)

CONSTRUCTION ECONOMY UPDATE: SHORT-TERM INCENTIVES COMBINE TO KEEP MOST BALLS ROLLING, QUARTERLY FEATURE

(p. 33-37) Quarterly article, by George A. Christie, on construction activity, 1983, with forecasts for 1984. Includes 2 tables showing residential and nonresidential building construction contract value and floor area, new dwelling units, and nonbuilding contract value, all by construction type, with contract value detail by region, and total contract value index; 1983-84, updated as of July 1984.

C5800–16   ENGINEERING AND MINING JOURNAL

Monthly.   Approx. 150 p.
ISSN 0095-8948.
LC 21-7292.
SRI/MF/not filmed

Monthly publication reporting on worldwide exploration, mining, milling, smelting, refining, and processing of metals and nonmetallic minerals, except coal, oil, and stone.

Contents:

a. Feature articles and news briefs, occasionally with statistics.

b. Regular editorial depts, including "Markets" monthly feature presenting price quotations for selected metals, ores, concentrates, ferroalloys, and nonmetallic minerals, for month prior to cover date, based on data from *Metals Week,* Handy & Harman, London Metal Exchange, and other sources.

Annual features include surveys of international mine and plant expansions, and mineral commodities outlook; and a nonstatistical buyers guide.

Monthly "Markets" feature appears in all issues. All additional features with substantial statistical content are described, as they appear, under "Statistical Features." Nonstatistical contents are not covered.

Availability: Engineering and Mining Journal, Fulfillment Manager, PO Box 1516, Neptune NJ 07753, industry subscribers $20.00 per yr., others $38.00, single copy $3.50, Sept. issue (Buyers Guide) $5.50; SRI/MF/not filmed.

Issues reviewed during 1984: Nov. 1983-Oct. 1984 (P) (Vol. 184, Nos. 11-12; Vol. 185, Nos. 1-10).

STATISTICAL FEATURES:

C5800–16.501: Nov. 1983 (Vol. 184, No. 11)

AUSTRALIAN MINING: INNOVATING TO STAY COMPETITIVE

(p. 38-43) By R. Lane White et al. Article, with 2 tables showing the following for Australia: stock prices for 10 largest mining companies, Dec. 31, 1982 and Sept. 30, 1983; and mine production by mineral (no date).

ALUMINUM PRODUCERS SEE POTENTIAL FOR SIGNIFICANT GROWTH IN BAUXITE, ALUMINA, AND ALUMINUM PRODUCTION

(p. 71-87) Article on prospects for development of aluminum resources in Australia. Includes 1 undated table showing annual capacity and managing company, for bauxite production by mine, and for alumina refining and aluminum smelting by plant.

C5800–16.502: Dec. 1983 (Vol. 184, No. 12)

1983 CENSUS OF WORLD-WIDE AUTOGENOUS AND SEMI-AUTOGENOUS GRINDING MILLS

(p. 36-41) Article, with 1 tabular list of world autogenous/semi-autogenous grinding mills, showing number and types of mills, motors and horsepower per mill, ore type milled, manufacturer, and date ordered, by mill size, as of 1983. Data are from a private researcher.

Data correction appears in the Jan. 1984 issue (see C5800-16.503, below).

C5800–16.503: Jan. 1984 (Vol. 185, No. 1)

CORRECTED SAG AND AUTOGENOUS MILL CENSUS FOR S.A.

(p. 17) Data correction for article on world autogenous/semi-autogenous grinding mills, appearing in Dec. 1983 issue (for description, see C5800-16.502 above). Shows corrected data for South Africa.

MINING INVESTMENT 1984, ANNUAL FEATURE

(p. 33-47) Annual E&MJ international survey of plans for new and expanded mines and plants through the early 1990s. Includes:

a. Table showing mineral industry capital investment plans (number of projects and amount of investment) for 6 metals by world area, and totals for 15 other metals and nonmetals. (p. 33)

b. Tabular list of projects arranged by metal or nonmetallic mineral and world area, showing the following data by company or operator: location, type of project, planned and/or current capacity, investment, starting year, stage of project development, and notes on special features. (p. 34-47)

C5800–16.504: Feb. 1984 (Vol. 185, No. 2)

KNOW THY LABORATORY

(p. 9) Article, with 1 table showing assay costs by type of analysis, for 18 elemental metals, metalloids, and fluorine, 1983. Data are from G. Jim Cardwell.

MINERAL SANDS

(p. 47-49) By R. Lane White. Article on Australian production of sand-extracted heavy minerals, 1982. Data are from Australia's Bureau of Mineral Resources, Geology, and Geophysics. Includes 1 table showing production of rutile, ilmenite, and zircon, for 4-5 Australian States, 1970, 1976, and 1982.

C5800–16.505: Mar. 1984 (Vol. 185, No. 3)

HOW STRONG IS GOVERNMENT INFLUENCE OVER METAL PRODUCTION?

(p. 17-19) Article, with 1 table showing production of 9 metals in non-Communist countries (total and state-controlled), and in Communist bloc countries, 1983. Data are from Shearson/American Express.

115th ANNUAL SURVEY AND OUTLOOK FOR WORLD MINERAL COMMODITIES

(p. 35-107) Annual survey, for 1983, of metals prices and U.S. and worldwide supply and demand situation and outlook for 43 metals and nonmetallic minerals. Data are derived from *Metals Week* price quotations, and Government and industry sources.

Contents:

a. Average annual prices of 16 major, minor, and precious metals, ferroalloys, and light metals, by trading exchange, 1982, and 1983 high and low; and average weekly prices for 5 major metals, silver, and mercury, 1983. 2 tables. (p. 35-37)

b. Average annual prices for 5 major metals, silver, and mercury, 1925-83. 1 table. (p. 39)

c. Market analyses, including short-term outlook for 43 metals and nonmetallic minerals, generally presenting the following for each: text statistics and 1-6 tables showing supply and demand, for U.S., and worldwide by country or area; and, for some commodities, prices and foreign trade; 1983, with selected forecasts and trends, 1976-92. (p. 41-107)

C5800–16.506: Apr. 1984 (Vol. 185, No. 4)

CHILE EYES A NEAR DOUBLING OF COPPER OUTPUT IN NEXT 10 YEARS AS CODELCO REFUTES U.S. CHARGES

(p. 17-19) By Joan C. Todd. Article, with 1 table showing Chilean copper production, by State-owned and private site, 1984-93. Data are from Comision Chilena del Cobre.

MEXICO MOVES QUICKLY TO EXPLOIT NEW GOLD FIND

(p. 25, 103) Article, with 1 undated table showing major Mexican mining projects currently under development or being investigated, and including proven or probable reserves of selected minerals, by project.

C5800–16.507: June 1984 (Vol. 185, No. 6)

URANIUM EXPLORATION IN CANADA: THE ASIAN CONNECTION

(p. 9, 11) By Stephen Salaff. Article, with 1 table showing the following for 3 Canadian uranium exploration projects in which Japanese and Korean firms bought equity during 1982-83: location, uranium discovery date and estimated reserves, and names and ownership shares of companies involved. Data are from industry sources.

SOUTH AFRICAN GOLD PRODUCERS PLAY A WAITING GAME ON GOLD PRICE

(p. 15, 17) By Joan C. Todd. Article, with 1 table showing South African gold ore milled, average grade, gold production, and milling costs, by site, for 5 companies, 4th quarter 1983 and 1st quarter 1984.

APCOM '84

(p. 55-58) By John R. Burger. Article summarizing proceedings of the 1984 Application of Computers and Mathematics in the Mineral Industries (APCOM) symposium. Data are from a paper by Alfred Weiss of Mineral Systems Inc., and are based in part on a worldwide survey by Weiss.

Includes 3 charts primarily showing distribution of mineral industry computing costs by category and resources by business function; and 1 table showing cost-benefit analysis of 9 computer applications deemed profitable for mining companies. No data dates are provided.

C5800–16.508: Aug. 1984 (Vol. 185, No. 8)

PERU'S RISING SILVER PROFILE

(p. 46-49) Article on Peru's silver mining industry, with summary comparisons to total world.

Includes 6 tables showing world silver production, by country or country group, 1982-83, with detail for Peru by mine, type of deposit, and company, 1983; Peru silver treatment capacity, by company, 1983; and share of ownership in individual Peruvian silver mining companies, for Peruvian government and private investors, and for foreign investors (no date).

C5800–16.509: Sept. 1984 (Vol. 185, No. 9)

U.S. COPPER CAN STAY COMPETITIVE: OSBORNE

(p. 21-25) Article, with 2 tables showing copper mine production 1983, and estimated production costs 1984, by country or world region, with production cost detail for Asarco Inc.

CHILE DETAILS NEW THREE-YEAR PLAN TO BOOST MINERAL OUTPUT

(p. 184-186) Article, with 1 table showing Chile's national production goals for 5 metals, 1983-86. Data are from the Chilean Government.

C5800–16.510: Oct. 1984 (Vol. 185, No. 10)

STUDY SAYS "PORPHYRY TIN" IS GOOD EXPLORATION TARGET

(p. 9-11) Article, with 1 table showing selected cost components for tin exploration in 5 developing countries, as of Jan. 1984. Data are from a study by Australian Mineral Economics Pty. Ltd.

JAPAN WORKS TO BOLSTER COPPER SEGMENT OF ITS RAW MATERIAL BASE

(p. 19-23) Article, with 2 undated tables showing distribution of Japan's imports of 6 minerals, by country of origin; and the following for 13 major projects providing minerals to Japan: mineral involved; investment amount and date; production, total and Japan's share; Japanese and foreign partner participants; and location.

NORTH AMERICAN HARDROCK GOLD DEPOSITS

(p. 50-57) By Hans W. Schreiber and Mark E. Emerson. Article analyzing gold discovery costs and earning potential in U.S. and Canada, 1961-83 period.

Presents cash flow analyses for gold mining operations under selected price and operational assumptions, lists of principal gold deposits and exploration companies, and exploration expenditures for gold and all minerals (in current and constant 1983 dollars) 1961-83, generally for U.S. and Canada; and gold discoveries, for U.S. by grade, and for Canada by region, 1961-83 period.

Data were compiled by the authors from a variety of governmental and private sources. Includes 1 map, 4 charts, and 21 tables and lists.

C5800–17   ELECTRICAL WHOLESALING

Monthly.   Approx. 80 p.
ISSN 0013-4430.
LC 22-6962.
SRI/MF/not filmed

Monthly trade journal reporting trends and developments in electrical equipment sales and marketing. Most data are compiled by McGraw-Hill Publications Research Dept.

Issues contain articles, occasionally with statistics; and regular editorial depts. Recurring statistical features include a biennial article presenting operating data for the largest wholesale distributors; an annual regional fact book (Nov. issue); and an annual industry outlook feature (Aug. issue).

Features with substantial statistical content are described, as they appear, under "Statistical Features." Each issue of the journal is reviewed, but an abstract is published in SRI monthly issues only when statistical features appear.

Availability: Electrical Wholesaling, Subscription Manager, PO Box 430, Hightstown NJ 08520, qualified subscribers $10.00 per yr., single copy $5.00; selected others $30.00 per yr., single copy $10.00; SRI/MF/not filmed.

Issues reviewed during 1984: Nov. 1983-Oct. 1984 (P) (Vol. 64, Nos. 11-12; Vol. 65, Nos. 1-10).

STATISTICAL FEATURES:

C5800–17.501: Nov. 1983 (Vol. 64, No. 11)

MAKINGS OF A TOP DISTRIBUTOR

(p. 45-51) By Andrea Herbert. Article on factors contributing to success of high-performance electrical wholesalers. Data are from a 1983 survey of wholesalers conducted by *Electrical World.* Includes 1 table showing employment, number of outlets, rank among 250 largest wholesalers, and headquarters location, for 13 leading electrical wholesalers, 1982.

REGIONAL FACTBOOK, ANNUAL FEATURE

(p. 61-74) Statistical section of 5th annual "Market Planning Guidebook," presenting electrical wholesaler market area characteristics. Data are from the *Electrical Wholesaling* Statistics Dept, BLS, and Census Bureau. Includes 3 national summary tables; and 4 basic tables on electrical wholesalers, repeated for each census division, showing:

a. Product and customer distribution, by type (no date).

b. Sales, by State and SMSA, 1979-83.

c. Employment, with comparative data for related industries and selected industry divisions, by State and SMSA, 1982-83.

C5800–17.502: Dec. 1983 (Vol. 64, No. 12)

NEW AREAS THAT YOUR CUSTOMERS ARE EXPLORING

(p. 10) By George Ganzenmuller. Article, with text statistics on types of new technology introduced for the electrical construction market. Data are based on 800 responses to a 1983 *Electrical Construction and Maintenance* reader survey.

WHAT MAKES A GOOD DISTRIBUTOR?

(p. 47-51) By William F. Jelin. Article on factors contributing to success of high-performance electrical wholesalers. Data are from surveys of wholesale distributors conducted by Bacon Stifel Nicolaus.

Includes 2 tables showing 9 leading publicly owned wholesalers ranked by sales, with electrical distribution sales as percent of total sales; and 20 high-performance wholesalers ranked by 5-year average net return on equity, with sales and income growth rates; generally FY83.

ASSN NEWS

(p. 74) Article, with 1 table showing anticipated percent change in value of electrical equipment shipments, by equipment type, 1983-84. Data are from a 1983 National Electrical Manufacturers Assn member survey.

C5800–17.503: Feb. 1984 (Vol. 65, No. 2)

TELECOMMUNICATIONS OPPORTUNITY IS NOW

(p. 71-76) By J. Michael Mills. Article on telecommunications market for electrical wholesalers. Data are from Commerce Dept. Includes 2 tables showing shipment value of telecommunications equipment, by type, 1981-82; and estimated equipment and investment needed by wholesalers to enter the telecommunications market.

C5800–17.504: Mar. 1984 (Vol. 65, No. 3)

HOW MUCH INFLATION?

(p. 10-11) Article, with 1 table showing percent change in CPI, PPI, and 5 other inflation indexes, various periods 1982-83. Data were compiled from various Federal and private sources.

C5800–17.505: Apr. 1984 (Vol. 65, No. 4)

INDUSTRY'S 250 BIGGEST DISTRIBUTORS, BIENNIAL FEATURE

(p. 71-81, 160) Biennial article presenting operating data for 250 largest electrical wholesaler distributors ranked by employment size, 1983. Data were compiled by *Electrical Wholesaling.*

Includes 1 table showing headquarters, sales, number of locations, office/warehouse footage, chief executive officer, and date founded, for each of 250 companies ranked by number of employees, 1983.

This is the 8th biennial report. For description of the 7th report, see SRI 1982 Annual, under C5800-17.304.

C5800–17.506: May 1984 (Vol. 65, No. 5)

REGIONAL ELECTRICAL RATES AND THEIR EFFECT ON SELLING ENERGY MANAGEMENT PRODUCTS

(p. 58) Article, with 1 table showing electric power prices for commercial and industrial customers in 25 major cities, 1982. Data are from DOE.

C5800–17.507: July 1984 (Vol. 65, No. 7)

FOCUS ON THE BIG CHAINS

(p. 43-55) Article on independent electrical wholesaling chains. Data are from a May-June 1984 survey conducted by *Electrical Wholesaling*.

Includes 1 table and map, repeated for each of 35 firms, showing headquarters location, and numbers of branches and employees.

C5800–17.508: Aug. 1984 (Vol. 65, No. 8)

1984 MID-YEAR OUTLOOK: TROUBLE AHEAD? ANNUAL FEATURE

(p. 56-61) Annual article on economic outlook for the electrical supply wholesaler industry, 1984-85. Data are from McGraw-Hill Economics Dept; Data Resources, Inc.; and an *Electrical Wholesaling* analysis of 301 companies. Includes the following:

a. Key economic indicators: GNP; housing starts; nonresidential construction value; total, electrical, and nonelectrical machinery industrial production indexes; new car sales; CPI percent increase; 90-day Treasury bill rate; and unemployment rate; 3rd quarter 1984-3rd quarter 1985, and annually 1983-85. 1 table.

b. Construction expenditures, by structure type, 1980-85; and electrical wholesalers' sales, by census division and for 24 SMSAs, 1982-84, with 1985 percent change for census divisions. 5 tables.

C5800–18   12th ANNUAL MCGRAW-HILL SURVEY OF INVESTMENT IN EMPLOYEE SAFETY AND HEALTH
Annual. June 1984. 9 p.
SRI/MF/complete

Annual survey report on capital spending for employee safety/health, actual 1972-83 and planned 1984-85. Data are shown for manufacturing and nonmanufacturing sectors and for selected industry groups, and include comparisons to total capital spending.

Data are national estimates based on responses of 540 companies, accounting for 28% of total capital spending, to a Mar./Apr. 1984 McGraw-Hill survey.

Contains narrative summary, with 2 charts; table listing; and 4 tables.

Availability: McGraw-Hill, Department of Economics, 1221 Ave. of the Americas, New York NY 10020, $20.00; SRI/MF/complete.

C5800–19   29th ANNUAL MCGRAW-HILL SURVEY OF BUSINESS' PLANS FOR RESEARCH AND DEVELOPMENT EXPENDITURES, 1984-87
Annual. May 1984. 26 p.
SRI/MF/complete

Annual report on survey of planned industrial R&D expenditures, 1984-87, with trends from 1953. Also covers new product sales expectations. Most data are national estimates based on responses of over 300 companies to a Mar./Apr. 1984 McGraw-Hill survey. Historical expenditure trends are from NSF.

Contains narrative analysis with 3 charts (p. 1-5); and table listing, and 10 detailed tables listed below (p. 6-26).

Availability: McGraw-Hill, Department of Economics, 1221 Ave. of the Americas, New York NY 10020, $45.00; SRI/MF/complete.

TABLES:

[Tables show data by manufacturing industry group. Some tables also show nonmanufacturing industry total.]

I. R&D expenditures [estimated 1982-83, and planned 1984 and 1987]. (p. 7)

II. New products sales (as a percent of total sales), 1987. (p. 8)

III. Percent of R&D expenditures going for new products, new processes, and improvement of existing products [actual 1983, and planned 1984-85]. (p. 9)

IV-V. R&D as a percent of sales and of capital spending [1983-84]. (p. 10-11)

VI-VIII. Historical R&D expenditures [1953-81], and as a percent of capital investment and of sales [1953-82]. (p. 12-20)

IX. New products as a percent of sales 4 years ahead, historical expectations [of 1957 and 1960-83]. (p. 21)

X. Percent of R&D going for new products, new processes, and improvement of existing products, historical [1974-82]. (p. 24)

C5800–20   17th ANNUAL MCGRAW-HILL SURVEY OF POLLUTION CONTROL EXPENDITURES, 1983-85
Annual. May 1984. 12+8 p.
SRI/MF/complete

Annual report on survey of planned industry expenditures for pollution control by type and industry group, 1983-85, with trends from 1967. Data are national estimates based on responses of 540 companies to a Mar./Apr. 1984 McGraw-Hill survey. Respondents account for 28% of total capital spending.

Contains narrative analysis, with 3 charts and 1 summary table (p. 1-6); and table listing, and 7 tables listed below (p. 7-12, 8 p.).

Availability: McGraw-Hill, Department of Economics, 1221 Ave. of the Americas, New York NY 10020, $45.00; SRI/MF/complete.

TABLES:

[All tables show data for manufacturing and nonmanufacturing, with detail for selected industry groups. Tables I-IV show actual 1983, and planned 1984-85, spending.]

I. Investment for pollution control. (p. 8)

II-III. Pollution control expenditure: air, water, and solid waste (percent of capital spending) [and dollar amount]. (p. 9-10)

IV. Pollution control as a percent of capital spending. (p. 11)

V. Total pollution control expenditures, historical [1967-82]. (p. 12)

VI. Historical pollution control expenditures, air and water [1970-82] and solid waste [1975-82]. (p. 14-18)

VII. [Data in table IV are repeated for 1967-82.] (p. 19)

C5800–24   26th ANNUAL MCGRAW-HILL SURVEY of Overseas Operations of U.S. Industrial Companies, 1984-86
Annual. Aug. 1984. 19 p.
SRI/MF/complete

Annual survey of planned overseas capital investment expenditures of foreign affiliates of U.S. industrial companies, 1984-86, with actual expenditures for 1983. Includes expenditures by major type, industry, and world region. Also includes export sales of all U.S. manufacturers, and foreign affiliate expected sales and profit margin levels.

Most data are based on a July-Aug. 1984 survey of 62 companies accounting for approximately 29% of all foreign spending in 1983. Dollar amounts for overseas capital expenditures are extrapolated to represent all companies.

Contains narrative report, with 1 trend chart (p. 1-6); and table listing, and 8 tables listed below (p. 7-19).

Availability: McGraw-Hill, Economics Department, 1221 Ave. of the Americas, New York NY 10020, $35.00; SRI/MF/complete

TABLES:

[Unless otherwise noted, tables show data for 6 manufacturing industries, petroleum, and all manufacturing and industry.]

I-III. Overseas capital expenditures [total; in Canada and 7 world regions; and for property, buildings, and machinery/equipment; 1983-86]. (p. 8-14)

IV. Export sales expectations of American manufacturers [for 5 manufacturing industries and all manufacturing, 1983-85]. (p. 15)

V-VI. Expected profit margins on sales [higher, lower, same]: overseas subsidiaries vs. U.S. [1984-85; and annual change, 1984-85]. (p. 16-17)

VII. Expected sales of foreign affiliates [annual change, 1984-85]. (p. 18)

VIII. Survey sample size [percent of total capital spending represented by surveyed firms]. (p. 19)

C5800–26   1984 DODGE/SWEET'S CONSTRUCTION OUTLOOK
Annual. 1983. 10 p.
SRI/MF/complete

Annual forecast of construction activity in nonresidential, residential, and nonbuilding sectors, 1984, with comparisons to 1983.

Contains narrative analysis, interspersed with 4 trend charts and 7 text tables, including manufacturing capacity utilization and industrial construction, various years 1970-85; and 2 detailed tables, listed below.

Data are updated in spring and summer following publication of *Dodge/Sweet's Construction Outlook*. Updates are covered by SRI, as they appear, under C5800-29.

Availability: McGraw-Hill Information Systems Co., F. W. Dodge Division/Sweet's Division, 1221 Ave. of the Americas, New York NY 10020, †; SRI/MF/complete.

TABLES:

[Tables show 1983 preliminary and 1984 forecast data.]

[1] National estimates [nonresidential and residential building construction contract values and floor area, number of residential units, and nonbuilding contract value, all by type; and all construction value and index]. (p. 3)

[2] Regional estimates [contract value for nonresidential, residential, and nonbuilding construction, by type and region]. (p. 7)

C5800–27   CAPITAL SPENDING CHECK-UP SURVEY
Annual. Mar. 1984. 25 p.
SRI/MF/complete

Annual survey report on capital spending intentions and business outlook of manufacturing and nonmanufacturing industries through 1985, including inflation expectations.

Most data are from a Jan.-Feb. 1984 McGraw-Hill survey of over 700 firms representing 29.5% of total capital expenditures. Dollar amounts are extrapolated to represent all companies.

Contains narrative analysis, with 8 trend charts and 1 summary table (p. 1-16); and table listing, and 8 tables listed below (p. 17-25).

Availability: McGraw-Hill, Economics Department, 1221 Ave. of the Americas, New York NY 10020, $40.00; SRI/MF/complete.

TABLES:

[All tables show data by major manufacturing group and for selected nonmanufacturing industries.]

I. Plans for capital spending [estimated 1983 and planned 1984-85]. (p. 18)

II. Inflation expectations [percent change expected in plant/equipment prices and real capital spending, 1983/84]. (p. 19)

III-VII. Capital spending on computers/other office equipment, manufacturing equipment, autos/trucks, and factory and office construction [1983-84]. (p. 20-24)

VIII. Survey sample size [percent of total capital spending represented by surveyed firms]. (p. 25)

C5800–28   ELECTRICAL WORLD
Monthly. Approx. 150 p.
ISSN 0013-4457.
LC 12-32507.
SRI/MF/not filmed

Monthly trade journal reporting on electric utility industry developments in technology and management; power generation, transmission, and distribution activities of public and private utilities; and financing, regulation, and rates.

Data are from *Electrical World* surveys of utilities, and reports of Federal Government agencies, the Edison Electric Institute, and other private research organizations.

Issues generally include articles and recurring editorial features, occasionally with statistics; and the following regularly appearing statistical features:

a. Monthly electric power generation feature, with 1 table showing electricity output, by region, for final week of month prior to publication date, calendar year to date, and 52 weeks to date, with percent change from same periods of previous year, and total output for 4 prior weeks; and 2 charts showing weekly output trends for current and previous years; all appearing in "News Beat" section.

b. Annual statistical report on U.S. and Canadian utility industry operations, and annual or biennial reports on capacity additions, transmission and distribution construction, facilities maintenance, steam station design and operations, peak loads, union negotiations, salaries for engineers, and industry outlook.

A nonstatistical directory of technical papers and a nonstatistical buyers' guide appear annually in the June issue.

Monthly table appears in all issues. All additional features with substantial nontechnical statistical content are described, as they appear, under "Statistical Features." Nonstatistical features are not covered.

Availability: Electrical World, Fulfillment Manager, PO Box 430, Hightstown NJ 08520, industry companies $6.00 per yr., industry individuals $12.00 per yr., selected others $38.00 per yr., single copy $5.00, special issues $10.00; SRI/MF/not filmed.

Issues reviewed during 1984: Nov. 1983-Oct. 1984 (P) (Vol. 197, Nos. 11-12; Vol. 198, Nos. 1-10).

STATISTICAL FEATURES:

C5800–28.501: Nov. 1983 (Vol. 197, No. 11)

23rd STEAM STATION COST SURVEY, BIENNIAL FEATURE

(p. 49-60) Biennial report, by Gordon D. Friedlander and Mary Clair Going, presenting detailed cost and operating data for steam-powered electric generating stations, 1982. Data are based on survey responses from 31 stations that either began service or added capacity during 1981/82.

Includes 10 charts and 1 table showing selected aggregate cost and operating data, with comparisons to previous surveys; 1 table on unit design features and station space use; and 1 detailed table showing the following for each (unnamed) station:

a. General information, including region; generating capacity; number of generators and boilers; plant site acreage; fuel storage by type (coal, oil, gas, nuclear); and employees by function.

b. Output; fuel consumption and costs, by type; operation and investment costs, by item; energy cost components, including taxes; and station performance indicators, including fuel- and employee-output ratios.

For description of 22nd biennial survey, see SRI 1982 Annual, under C5800-28.301.

C5800–28.502: Dec. 1983 (Vol. 197, No. 12)

CORRECTION

(p. 35) Data corrections for article on investor-owned utility finances. Article is described in SRI 1983 Annual under C5800-28.411.

MUNI CUTS PEAK WITH LOAD CONTROLLERS

(p. 65-67) By Eugene F. Gorzelnik. Article on the use of power demand controllers to reduce residential peak-period electricity use. Data are from an analysis of the Public Service Co. of Colorado. Includes 1 undated table showing summer and winter rates for residential heating energy use, and for kW demand with and without controllers.

COMMUNITY LOAD CONTROL YIELDS MIXED RESULTS

(p. 66-67) Article on experimental community programs to reduce residential peak-period electricity use. Data are from Pacific Gas and Electric Co. Includes 1 table showing energy use reduction attributed to programs in 5 California cities, 1980 and 1981.

C5800–28.503: Jan. 1984 (Vol. 198, No. 1)

EXECUTIVE PAY RISES 10%; BONUSES INCREASE

(p. 27-29) By H. A. Cavanaugh. Article presenting survey data on salaries and bonuses of corporate chief executives and other officers, for utilities and other industry divisions. Data are from a Conference Board analysis of 1982 compensation of executives in 1,155 companies, including 92 utilities. Includes 3 tables.

Complete Conference Board study is covered in SRI under R4105-19.

ENGINEERS PAY RISES 16%, 'NOT ENOUGH'

(p. 31-32) Article, with 2 tables showing salaries of electrical engineers, by industry and area of expertise, 1983. Includes median, 1st and 3rd quartile, and 1st and 9th decile salaries. Data are based on over 12,000 responses to a 1983 Institute of Electrical and Electronics Engineers member survey.

ANNUAL GENERATION CONSTRUCTION SURVEY

(p. 49-64) Annual report, by Gordon D. Friedlander and Mary Clair Going, on electric plants planned or under construction as of Dec. 31, 1983. Covers nuclear, fossil, hydroelectric, and combustion turbine powered plants. Data are from an *Electrical World* survey of utilities, and from the National Electric Reliability Council (NERC).

Includes the following, repeated for each NERC region within the above plant categories, as applicable:

a. List of plants planned or under construction, showing owner, capacity, equipment type and/or manufacturer, architect/engineer, builder, service date, and project status.

b. NERC and/or *Electrical World* forecasts of total summer generating capacity, 1983-90.

This is the 4th annual survey.

NEMA: SALES WILL OUTPACE GNP IN 1984

(p. 97) Article presenting results of a business outlook survey of National Electrical Manufacturers Assn members. Includes 1 table showing respondents' expected annual percent change in shipments, by industry group, 1983-84.

C5800–28.504: Feb. 1984 (Vol. 198, No. 2)

REGULATORY WAGE MEDDLING SUBSIDES, ANNUAL FEATURE

(p. 24-25) Annual article on contract negotiations between electric utilities and the International Brotherhood of Electrical Workers during 1983. Includes 2 tables showing number of contracts and average percent wage increase negotiated, by type of utility ownership; with detail for negotiated increase and lineman rate, by company; 1983, with selected comparisons to 1982.

HOW MUCH DO UTILITY EXECUTIVES TAKE HOME?

(p. 31-35) By H. A. Cavanaugh. Article presenting results of a Utilities Consulting Group survey of executive compensation practices at 133 investor-owned utilities. Includes 1 chart and 1 table showing executives in deferred compensation plans, with portion or type of compensation deferrable and interest rate used, by company; and mean compensation of principal officers of utilities, by position; 1982.

HOW MUCH DO UTILITIES PAY THEIR ENGINEERS? ANNUAL FEATURE

(p. 39-40) Annual article on salaries of electric utility engineers. Data are from a 1983 survey by the Engineering Manpower Commission of the American Assn of Engineering Societies.

Includes text statistics and 1 table showing engineers' median starting salaries, salaries after 10 years, and supervisor salaries, by industry including gas and electric utilities, 1983.

Full survey report is covered in SRI under A0685-3.

UTILITY FINANCINGS DROP 23% IN 1983

(p. 47) Article, with 1 table showing investor-owned electric utility security offerings by type and purpose, 1980-83. Data are from Ebasco Business Consulting Co., a division of Ebasco Services Inc.

COUNTER COAL-CONVERSION BOILER DERATING

(p. 61-64) By Gordon D. Friedlander. Article on electric utility generator capacity derating due to conversion from oil/gas to coal fuel, and measures to recover lost capacity. Includes 1 undated table showing electric capacity and cost of conversion to coal fuel, for 7 electric power plants.

C5800–28.505: Mar. 1984 (Vol. 198, No. 3)

ANNUAL-REPORT STUDY FINDS KEY FINANCE TRENDS

(p. 27-30) By H. A. Cavanaugh. Article on financial reporting and accounting practices of investor-owned utilities, based on a Price Waterhouse survey of 1982 annual reports from 65 electric/combination and 35 water/gas utilities. Includes 1 table ranking surveyed electric/combination utilities by revenues, net income, and assets.

JOLTS OF JANUARY

(p. 42-43) Article on financially troubled nuclear power plant projects. Data are from Thomson McKinnon Securities, Inc.

Includes 1 table comparing stock performance of 8 utilities with problems related to nuclear plant costs, and 11 utilities with no or partial nuclear-based generation. Table shows

the following for each utility: earnings per share 1982-84, and/or stock price, dividend, and yield (no date); and type of fuel used, and/or comments on financial condition.

C5800–28.506: Apr. 1984 (Vol. 198, No. 4)

HAVE THE COMMISSIONS TAKEN A TURN FOR THE WORSE?

(p. 27-29) By H. A. Cavanaugh. Article, with 1 undated table showing public utility commission membership by political party, and return on equity allowed and test period used, all by State. Data are from Salomon Bros.

1984 ANNUAL STATISTICAL REPORT

(p. 49-72) Annual report, by Mary C. Going, on electric utility industry finances, sales, capability, and capital projects, 1983-84 and trends. Data are from an *Electrical World* survey of U.S. and Canadian utilities, and from Edison Electric Institute, DOE, and various other industry and Federal sources.

Contains introduction, with 1 table showing size and composition of survey sample (p. 49); and 7 statistical sections, with narrative analyses and 28 tables listed below (p. 50-72).

This is the 80th annual survey.

TABLES:

[Data by region are generally shown for 9 NERC regions, 4 subregions, total contiguous U.S., and Alaska/Hawaii. Data "by ownership" are shown for investor-owned utilities, municipal/State/power district systems, cooperatives, and Federal agencies.

Expenditure types are generally generation, transmission, distribution, and miscellaneous. Types of prime mover include some or most of the following: fossil, combustion or gas turbine, nuclear, conventional hydro, steam, pumped storage, and internal combustion.]

CAPITAL EXPENDITURES

[1] Total electric power system capital expenditures [by type, for total industry and investor-owned utilities, 1973-84]. (p. 50)

[2] Electric power system spending, by ownership [and by expenditure and prime mover types, 1983-84]. (p. 51)

[3-5] 1983-84 electric utility capital spending [by region, ownership, and prime mover and expenditure types]. (p. 52-54)

TRANSMISSION AND DISTRIBUTION CONSTRUCTION

[6-9] 1983-84 new expenditures for lines and substations, and new lines and substations energized, [shown for overhead and underground transmission lines and primary distribution lines, and transmission and distribution substations, all by region and ownership]. (p. 56-59)

CAPABILITY

[10] Electric power industry capability [by prime mover, as of Dec. 31, 1983, and planned additions 1984/beyond]. (p. 60)

[11-12] Consumption and energy generated, by type of fuel [1973-83; and by month and region, 1983]. (p. 61)

[13] Future generating capability additions, by regions [and by prime mover, 1983-87/beyond]. (p. 62)

[14-15] Installed generating capacity, by type of ownership [1973-83]; and by States [and census division, cross-tabulated by prime mover, with number of plants] (Dec. 31, 1983). (p. 63-64)

SALES

[16-20] Electric customers, revenue, and energy sales, and average annual use and bill [all for residential, small and large light/power, and other, 1973-83]. (p. 65-66)

INVESTOR-OWNED UTILITY FINANCES

[21] Distribution of electric revenue [by expense category, 1979-83]. (p. 67)

[22-23] Electric rate increases [granted and pending at year end] and decreases [number of actions and amounts, 1973-83]. (p. 67)

[24] Offerings of securities by investor-owned electric utilities [value of long-term debt, common and preferred stock, and total financing by purpose and type, 1977-83]. (p. 68)

[25-26] Investor-owned electric utility income [and expenses] and combined balance sheets, [1979-83]. (p. 68-69)

CANADA

[27] Electric plant construction [spending, by prime mover and expenditure types]; and line and substation construction, and line and substations energized [similar detail to tables [6-9]; all by Province, 1983-84]. (p. 70-71)

COOPERATIVES

[28] Annual statistics of Rural Electrification Administration-financed systems [including loans by source and purpose; advances; active borrowers; and total and residential consumers served, energy sold, revenue, energy cost, and average annual use; 1981-83]. (p. 72)

C5800–28.507: May 1984 (Vol. 198, No. 5)

UTILITIES LEAD IN PENSION CONTRIBUTIONS, ANNUAL FEATURE

(p. 35-38) Annual article, by H. A. Cavanaugh, on corporate pension plan contributions. Data are from reports by Johnson and Higgins, and Council for Financial Aid to Education (CFAE).

Includes 4 tables showing pension cost, average cost per employee and company, unfunded vested benefits, net worth, net income, assets, and value of charitable contributions with detail for education, by industry group including utilities, 1981 and/or 1982.

Full Johnson and Higgins report is covered in SRI under B4790-2; full CFAE report is covered under A4325-1.

SECOND ANNUAL MAINTENANCE SURVEY, ANNUAL FEATURE

(p. 49-55) Annual article on actual and planned maintenance expenditures of U.S. and Canadian electric utilities, 1983-84. Data are from an *Electrical World* survey of utilities.

Includes 6 tables showing maintenance expenditures on labor and materials, for generation by prime mover, and for transmission and distribution; all for contiguous U.S. by North American Electric Reliability Council region and subregion (shown by type of ownership) and for Alaska/Hawaii, Puerto Rico, and each Canadian Province, 1983-84. Includes some detail for noncapitalized equipment upgrading.

Also includes 1 table on summary characteristics of survey sample relative to total U.S. utilities.

C5800–28.508: July 1984 (Vol. 198, No. 7)

CRITICISM OF NEW UTILITY RANKING SYSTEM BEGINS

(p. 19-20) By Louis Iwler. Article, with 1 table showing top 10 and bottom 10 electric utilities ranked by percent change in overall financial and operating performance, 1972-81 period. Data are from a private study based on reports filed with DOE.

C5800–28.509: Aug. 1984 (Vol. 198, No. 8)

HOW DO PRIVATE AND PUBLIC CEO SALARIES COMPARE?

(p. 27-29) By Herbert A. Cavanaugh. Article on compensation and characteristics of chief executive officers (CEOs) in the electric utility industry, 1983. Data are from responses of 408 electric utilities to a recent survey conducted by Towers, Perrin, Forster & Crosby.

Includes 5 charts and 2 tables showing number of CEOs and average base salary or total compensation, and average corporate revenues, by utility revenue size, with detail by utility type; prevalence of selected perquisites for CEOs; and distribution of CEOs, by age group, year of hire, and year of entry into position; 1983 with some trends from 1981.

19th ANNUAL T&D CONSTRUCTION SURVEY

(p. 49-56) Annual article presenting data on electric utility transmission and distribution (T&D) construction activity and outlook, 1977-90. Data are based on responses of 219 utilities to an *Electrical World* survey. Respondents represent 77.1% of total generating capacity and 73.2% of total customers.

Includes 10 tables showing number, mileage, and/or voltage capacity of actual and/or planned T&D equipment installations, including transformers, circuit breakers, capacitors, substation banks, and overhead and underground lines, various periods 1977-90; and construction activity and number of customers serviced, by North American Electric Reliability Council region, 1983.

C5800–28.510: Sept. 1984 (Vol. 198, No. 9)

ON RECRUITING

(p. 32-33) Article on employer preferences of engineering students. Most data are from responses of 2,684 students to a *Graduating Engineer* survey.

Includes 2 tables showing top 50 companies ranked by mechanical and electrical engineering students' preferences for employment, 1983 with comparative rank order for 1981; and factors influential in forming employer images, as cited by engineering students by field (no date).

ON FINANCE

(p. 33-34) Article, with 1 table and 1 chart showing value of securities offerings of investor-owned electric utilities, by type of security and financing, 1980-83 and 1st half 1984; and electric utility construction expenditures (total and internally financed), 1980-86. Data are from Ebasco Business Consulting Co. and Salomon Bros., Inc.

35th ANNUAL ELECTRIC UTILITY INDUSTRY FORECAST

Annual report on electric utility trends and forecasts, 1973-2000, including kWh sales, revenues, generating capacity, and capital expenditures. Also includes selected general economic indicators. Data are from reports of DOE, industry assns, *Electrical World,* and McGraw-Hill Economics Dept, and generally are shown for 1973-90, 1995, and 2000. Contains the following annual articles:

ECONOMIC RECOVERY DRIVES kWh SALES UP

(p. 49-52) Includes 5 tables showing the following:

a. Electric utility kWh sales by sector, including industrial, residential, commercial, street/highway lighting, other public authority, railroad, and interdepartmental; and GNP and GNP deflator.

b. Industrial sector: electricity used in manufacturing, in primary aluminum production, by DOE for uranium enrichment, and for all industrial purposes; electricity generated by industrial plants; industrial production index; and aluminum production.

c. Residential sector: mid-year customers; housing starts; and electricity use per customer, revenue (total and per kWh), average annual bill, and heating kWh sales.

NATIONAL PEAK IS UP 2%, BUT REGIONAL PEAKS VARY WIDELY

(p. 53-56) Includes 3 tables showing electric utility kWh sales and output; peak load, capability at peak, and peak margin; capacity additions, by type of generation; and capital expenditures for generation, transmission, distribution, and other.

C5800–28.511: Oct. 1984 (Vol. 198, No. 10)

BARGED STEAM-COAL COULD TAME WILD RAIL RATES

(p. 57-72) By Michael G. McGraw. Article analyzing interrelations between barge and railroad industries in coal transportation.

Includes 2 tables and 2 charts showing location, terminal points, water miles, and locks/dams, for 10 coal-hauling inland waterways; rail rate reductions to meet barge competition, for 5 rail routes; coal traffic volume for selected waterways, 1982; and distribution of domestic and foreign bulk-commodity waterway commerce, by type of commodity, 1980 or 1982.

C5800–29   1984 DODGE/SWEET'S CONSTRUCTION OUTLOOK, First Update

2 per year. Mar. 1984. 4 p. SRI/MF/complete

Periodic report, issued twice yearly, presenting updated forecasts, for 1984, of construction activity in nonresidential, residential, and non-building sectors, by region. Report updates *1984 Dodge/Sweet's Construction Outlook,* described under C5800-26.

Contains narrative analysis, and updated data for 1983 (actual) and 1984 (forecast), as follows:

a. Quarterly trends in building contract values, by sector and type of construction. 3 tables.

b. National and regional estimates of construction contract value for each sector, by detailed construction type; and national estimates of nonresidential and residential building floor area, number of residential units, and all construction contract value and Dodge index. 2 detailed tables.

Updates are issued in spring and summer following publication of *Dodge/Sweet's Construction Outlook.*

Availability: McGraw-Hill Information Systems Co., F. W. Dodge Division/Sweet's Division, 1221 Ave. of the Americas, New York NY 10020, †; SRI/MF/complete.

C6615
New Jersey Associates

C6615–1   NEW JERSEY MUNICIPAL DATA BOOK, 1984 Edition
Annual. 1984. xiii+595 p.
ISSN 0277-9218.
ISBN 0-911273-05-0.
LC 81-649215.
SRI/MF/complete

Annual compilation of general socioeconomic and governmental statistics for New Jersey municipalities and counties. Data are primarily from State and Federal reports and are shown for various years 1980-83, with population comparison to 1970.

Contains contents listing, introduction, and bibliography (p. iii-xiii); and 1 data page repeated for each municipality (p. 3-569) and county (p. 575-595), with listings of selected officials and the following statistics:

a. Demographic and land area: population, by age, sex, and race/ethnicity (including American Indian, Asian/Pacific Islander, and Hispanic); median age; high school graduates as percent of population; per capita income; population density; total area; and (for counties only) land and water area.

b. Public services and crime: police employees; total and violent crime rates; library holdings; and (for municipalities only) volunteer and paid fire fighters, and residential properties served by piped-in water and sanitary sewers.

c. Real property: housing units; number of property parcels and percent of total valuation, by property type; and total and single-family residential building permits.

d. Government finances: total and per capita debt; bond rating; general tax rate; taxable net valuation, and equalized value and ratios; revenues by major source, and expenditures by object; and tax levy per capita and (for municipalities only) percent collected.

e. School system: teachers; enrollment; revenues, expenditures, and per pupil cost; and (for municipalities) buildings owned and classrooms used, and (for counties) number of school districts.

Report also includes list of municipalities, by county (p. 572-574).

Availability: New Jersey Associates, Box 505, Montclair NJ 07042, $59.95+shipping and tax; SRI/MF/complete.

C6615–2   **NEW JERSEY ECONOMIC ALMANAC, 1984**

Annual. Nov. 1983.
xii + 374 p.
ISBN 0-911273-04-2.
SRI/MF/complete

Annual compilation, for 1984, of detailed social, governmental, and economic statistics for New Jersey. Data are shown primarily for 1970s-83, with selected trends from 1961 and population projections to 2000. Most data are from Federal and State agencies.

Report is designed to present a socioeconomic overview of the State. Extensive socioeconomic, demographic, and geographic breakdowns are shown, as applicable, for most topics. These breakdowns include data by city, county, SMSA, urban-rural status, commodity, income, industry, occupation, age, educational attainment, marital status, race, and sex. Comparisons to total U.S. are also often included.

Contains contents listing (p. v); introduction (p. ix-xii); 201 tables arranged in 20 sections, described below (p. 3-367); and index (p. 371-374).

This is the 2nd edition.

Availability: New Jersey Associates, Box 505, Montclair NJ 07042, $33.00; SRI/MF/complete.

TABLE SECTIONS:
[Data sources appear beneath each table.]

C6615–2.1: Profile

(p. 3) Contains 1 table. Includes summary data on land area, population characteristics, labor force and employment, personal and family income, business incorporations and failures, business telephone gains, farms and acreage, educational enrollment, and property value.

C6615–2.2: Population

(p. 7-28) Contains 19 tables. Includes population projected to 2000; households and families; housing units, occupancy, and structural and financial characteristics; total and per capita personal and disposable income; total, illegitimate, and plural births; deaths by cause; crimes by offense; and police employment.

C6615–2.3: Labor Force

(p. 31-53) Contains 27 tables. Includes labor force by employment status; part-time employment; hours worked; production worker hours and earnings; insured unemployment, and initial claims and exhaustions; characteristics of the unemployed; labor union and employee assn membership; and work stoppages, workers involved, and days idle.

C6615–2.4: Agriculture

(p. 57-95) Contains 25 tables. Includes State ranking in agricultural production and farm taxes and value; crop acreage, yield, production, prices, and value; livestock and poultry inventory, value, marketings, and production, by species; milk, dairy product, and egg marketings and/or production; and bee colonies, and honey and beeswax production and prices.

Also includes farm production costs, income, property value and taxes levied, and cash receipts from marketings; nurseries and acreage in stock; cut flower and mushroom production, area, sales, value, and prices; farms and acreage; fertilizer consumption; farms and acres sold; and agricultural service employment, payroll, and establishments.

C6615–2.5: Banking, Finance, and Insurance

(p. 99-126) Contains 20 tables. Includes finances and number of State-regulated and other financial institutions, including assets and liabilities; savings/building and loan assns, membership, and deposits; mortgage transactions; consumer complaints against financial institutions; operating and financial data for federally insured savings and loan assns, Federal credit unions, and life insurance companies; and banking and insurance employment, payroll, and establishments.

C6615–2.6: Communication

(p. 129-130) Contains 5 tables. Includes newspapers and circulation; radio and TV stations; and residential and business telephones and selected operating data.

C6615–2.7: Construction

(p. 133-146) Contains 10 tables. Includes construction establishments, proprietors/working partners, employment, receipts, and payroll; residential and nonresidential construction contracts awarded; and housing permits issued.

C6615–2.8: Education

(p. 149-165) Contains 16 tables. Includes elementary and secondary enrollment and schools, including vocational schools; dropouts; high school graduates and postgraduate activities; expenses per pupil; higher education enrollment by institution, and degrees conferred; and educational services employment, payroll, and establishments.

C6615–2.9: Energy

(p. 169-176) Contains 8 tables. Includes average retail prices for gasoline, diesel fuel, and fuel oil; natural gas and electricity sales volume and retail prices by utility, by consuming sector; fuel types used by electric utilities; and sales of gasoline, diesel fuel, gasohol, and liquefied petroleum gas.

C6615–2.10: Fishing and Forestry

(p. 179-185) Contains 5 tables. Includes commercial fish landings and value; fish processing and wholesale plants and employment, and fishery product plants; forest products harvest and value; and forestry and lumber and wood products employment, payroll, and establishments.

C6615–2.11: Government

(p. 189-199) Contains 7 tables. Includes total and per capita State and local government revenues by source, expenditures by function, indebtedness and cash/security holdings, and State/local revenues and expenditures per $1,000 of personal income.

C6615–2.12: Manufacturing

(p. 203-242) Contains 6 tables. Includes manufacturing establishments, employment, and payroll; production workers and hours and wages; and value added, materials cost, shipments value, capital expenditures, and end-of-year inventories.

C6615–2.13: Mining

(p. 245-251) Contains 7 tables. Includes nonfuel mineral production and value; sand/gravel and crushed stone quantity and value sold/used; number of sand/gravel producing companies; and mining employment, payroll, and establishments.

C6615–2.14: Real Estate

(p. 255-261) Contains 2 tables. Includes taxable property values; and real estate employment, payroll, and establishments.

C6615–2.15: Recreation

(p. 265-281) Contains 12 tables. Includes State forests, parks, recreation and natural areas, and historic sites, and attendance and/or acreage; fish hatcheries and game farms, and acreage and production; small game hunters, hunting man-days, and harvests by species.

Also includes thoroughbred and harness racing days, wagers, and attendance, by track; casino revenues, operating days, taxes, table games and slot machines, and employment, all by casino; and casino industry licensing activity, labor organizations registered, hotel rooms, and convention space.

C6615–2.16: Service Industries

(p. 285-302) Contains 3 tables. Includes service industry establishments, receipts, sole proprietorships, partnerships, payroll, and employment.

C6615–2.17: Taxation

(p. 305-321) Contains 9 tables. Includes State and local tax collections; local property tax revenues; State tax rates; sales and use tax collections, and receipts and deductions, including for exempt organizations; State and Federal income tax returns, exemptions, and collections, and taxable income by source; and State and local taxes per capita and as percent of personal income.

C6615–2.18: Transportation

(p. 325-338) Contains 12 tables. Includes aircraft facilities by ownership, and abandonments; pilots, flight instructors, and nonpilot aviation personnel; domestic and international aircraft departures, passengers, and revenue tonnage; general aviation aircraft and hours flown; and air transportation employment, payroll, and establishments.

Also includes railroad operating data; total and new car registrations, and average gasoline consumption; traffic volume and miles traveled on 2 major toll roads; highway fund receipts, disbursements, and bond obligations; road/street mileage and miles traveled; and traffic activity at Port Authority of New York-New Jersey bridges, tunnels, airports, and bus and marine terminals.

C6615–2.19: Wholesale and Retail Trade

(p. 341-367) Contains 7 tables. Includes wholesale and retail trade establishments, sales, payroll, and employment; wholesale trade inventories and operating expenses; and retail trade proprietorships and partnerships; and central business district retail stores, sales, payroll, and employment.

C6985
PennWell Publishing Co.

C6985–1   OIL AND GAS JOURNAL

Weekly. Approx. 200 p.
ISSN 0030-1388.
LC 79-3435.
SRI/MF/not filmed

Weekly publication reporting developments and trends in the U.S. petroleum and natural gas industries, including exploration, processing, production, distribution, and finance. Also covers U.S. and worldwide supply and demand, reserves, and construction.

Data are from the American Petroleum Institute (API), American Gas Assn, and other industry and Government sources.

Issues contain numerous articles and regular editorial features. The following statistics are presented:

a. Weekly industry scoreboard table on fuel supply and demand.

b. Weekly industry statistics section, on oil and gas production, stocks, prices, and imports; with 8 weekly and 6 monthly tables.

c. 4 monthly tables on well completions and on Nelson indexes for refinery operating and equipment costs.

d. Quarterly features on refinery cost indexes, oil industry profits, pipeline cost indexes, and drilling activity by technological level.

e. Annual and semiannual features, including world oil and gas industry outlook and review; refining operations, U.S. and Canada; offshore drilling; construction; gas processing; pipeline economics; drilling activity; financial data for top 400 oil and gas companies; and worldwide report on reserves, production, and refining capacity.

Weekly and monthly tables are described below. All additional features with substantial nontechnical statistical content are described, as they appear, under "Statistical Features;" page locations and latest periods of coverage for weekly and monthly tables are also noted. Nonstatistical features are not covered.

Availability: Oil and Gas Journal, Circulation Services Manager, PO Box 1260, Tulsa OK 74101, industry subscribers $34.00 per yr., nonindustry subscribers $82.00 per yr., single copy $3.00; SRI/MF/not filmed.

Issues reviewed during 1984: Nov. 7, 1983-Oct. 29, 1984 (P) (Vol. 81, Nos. 45-52; Vol. 82, Nos. 1-44) [Vol. 82, No. 1 incorrectly reads Vol. 81].

WEEKLY TABLES:

C6985–1.1: Industry Scoreboard Table

Table showing demand for gasoline, distillate, jet fuel, residual fuel oils, and other products; supply in terms of crude production and imports, product imports, and crude runs to stills; stocks of crude, motor gasoline, distillate, jet fuel, and residual fuel oils; and rotary rigs in operation.

Data are shown for approximately 1 week prior to publication, previous week, and same period of previous year.

C6985–1.2: Industry Statistics, Weekly Tables

[Tables [1-8] appear in most issues; most tables show data for previous week or month and same period of previous year. Data are from API, DOE, Smith International, Inc., and Hughes Tool Co. Table sequence may vary.]

PRODUCTION AND STOCKS

[1] O&GJ production report [crude oil/lease condensate by selected States].

[2] API refinery report [input, crude runs, and operable capacity and utilization; and average daily output by product; by PAD district and subarea].

[3] Hughes rig count [rotary rigs in operation, by State, selected State districts or regions including offshore, and land and offshore Canada].

[4] API crude and product stocks [by PAD district].

[5] Smith rig count [and percent of rigs under footage contracts, by proposed well depth interval; and total inland, land, and offshore rigs; table begins in Mar. 26, 1984 issue (an article introducing the table appears in the Mar. 19, 1984 issue)].

PRICES AND IMPORTS

[6] Refined product and world crude prices [New York and Rotterdam spot prices for gasoline, No. 2 heating oil, and No. 6 residual fuel oil; and world crude oil prices (total, OPEC, non-OPEC, and U.S. imports)].

[7] API imports of crude and products [Canadian and other foreign crude, and products by type, for total U.S. and PAD Districts 1-4 and 5].

[8] Gasoline prices [price excluding tax, and pump prices, for approximately 45 major cities, and by PAD district].

MONTHLY TABLES:

C6985–1.3: Industry Statistics, Monthly Tables

[1] Total U.S. land and marine seismic crews [generally for previous 2 months, and for corresponding previous month of prior year; data are from Society of Exploration Geophysicists].

[2] Worldwide crude oil and gas production [crude daily average and gas total, current and previous month, and current and/or previous year to date; for 60-75 countries and for Western Hemisphere, Western Europe, Middle East, Asia/Pacific, Africa, and Communist world areas; data are current to 2-3 months prior to date of publication].

[3] Selected U.S. and world crude prices [for 25-30 major producing U.S. regions and States, and countries; most prices are current to month of publication; data are from O&GJ, DOE, and Alaska Dept of Natural Resources].

[4] Active rigs abroad [in approximately 70 countries arranged by world region, land and offshore rigs, for month 1-2 months prior to cover date, and total rigs for same month of previous year; data are from Hughes Tool Co.].

[5-6] Smith rig count [and average proposed well depth], by State and [rig type (inland, land, and offshore); and land rig count and

average depth, by contract type (daywork or footage); for week ended 10 days prior to publication date, with comparisons to previous week and/or same period of previous year, and year-to-date totals; tables begin in Mar. 26, 1984 issue (an article introducing the tables appears in the Mar. 19, 1984 issue)].

C6985–1.4: U.S. Wells Drilled

Two monthly tables showing total and exploratory new oil, gas, dry, and service (total only) wells and footage drilled in U.S., by State, State area (including offshore), and Federal offshore region.

Data are from API, and are shown for month 1-2 months prior to cover date, with U.S. totals for same month of previous year and for current and previous years to date.

C6985–1.5: Nelson Cost Indexes

[Tables appear in the 1st issue of each month and show data for the most recent month available (approximately 5 months prior to date of publication), previous month, same month of previous year, and selected earlier years. Charts of the indexes are published each year in a late Jan. issue.]

[1] Refinery construction [cost indexes for pumps/compressors, electrical machinery, internal combustion engines, instruments, heat exchangers, miscellaneous equipment, materials component, and labor component; and refinery inflation index] (1946=base year).

[2] Refinery operating [cost indexes for fuel, labor, wages, productivity, investments/maintenance, and chemicals; and operating indexes for refinery and process units] (1956=base year).

STATISTICAL FEATURES:

C6985–1.501: Nov. 7, 1983 (Vol. 81, No. 45)

WEEKLY TABLES

a. Industry scoreboard, for Oct. 28, 1983. (p. 4)

b. Industry statistics, as of Oct. 28-Nov. 2, 1983 (table [5] is omitted). (p. 158-159)

MONTHLY TABLES

a. Nelson Cost Indexes, for June 1983. (p. 98)

b. Industry statistics: selected U.S. and world crude prices, for Nov. 1983; and worldwide crude oil and gas production, for Aug. 1983. (p. 159-160)

HARD TIMES SET BACKDROP FOR OCAW, OIL FIRM CONTRACT TALKS

(p. 61-64) By G. Alan Petzet. Article discussing labor contract negotiations between the oil refining industry and the Oil, Chemical, and Atomic Workers (OCAW) international union. Data are from BLS, OCAW, and National Petroleum Refiners Assn.

Includes 1 chart showing mid-1983 OCAW contract wage rates (actual and adjusted for taxes and inflation), and 3 tables showing the following:

a. Refinery shutdowns: date, company, location, crude capacity, and employees in bargaining unit, for OCAW represented refineries, 1981-Jan. 1984.

b. Total crude capacity and jobs in bargaining unit, by region, for refineries with OCAW contracts (no date); and average wages of workers in petroleum refining, all manufacturing, and 5 selected industries, June 1973 and June 1983.

ANALYSIS GIVES BLOWOUT CAUSES, TRENDS, COSTS

(p. 125-134) By A. L. Podio et al. Conclusion of 2-part series on oil well blowouts along the Gulf of Mexico coast. Data are from University of Texas at Austin.

Includes 3 charts and 1 table showing blowouts by type of activity underway and time elapsed before bridging (no date); casing and drilling depths at time of blowout, for 45 Texas wells, 1980-82 period; and total and average cost of well control, by cost range, aggregated for 82 Texas blowouts, 1978-82 period.

Part 1 is described in SRI 1983 Annual, under C6985-1.453.

C6985–1.502: Nov. 14, 1983 (Vol. 81, No. 46)

WEEKLY TABLES

a. Industry scoreboard, for Nov. 4, 1983. (p. 4)

b. Industry statistics, as of Oct. 28-Nov. 9, 1983. (p. 256-257)

MONTHLY TABLES

a. U.S. wells drilled, for Sept. 1983. (p. 240-242)

ESSO: UK NORTH SEA COULD YIELD 90 MORE FIELDS

(p. 90) Article, with 1 table showing forecast offshore oil/gas exploration/appraisal drilling, in rig-years, for 7 European countries, 1981-88. Data are from Wood, Mackenzie.

U.S. OUTLAYS FOR EOR SEEN GROWING 12%/YEAR

(p. 96) Article, with 1 chart showing actual and forecast enhanced oil recovery (EOR) expenditures, by displacement technique, 1982 and 1990. Data are from Frost and Sullivan, Inc.

IPAA: NOW IS THE TIME TO DRILL WELLS, SEMIANNUAL FEATURE

(p. 102-105) Semiannual article forecasting crude oil and petroleum products supply and demand, and presenting semiannual cost indexes for drilling and equipping oil/gas wells, semiannual energy consumption forecast, and annual data on tubular goods consumption and oil/gas well drilling activity. Data are from Independent Petroleum Assn of America. Includes 4 tables showing the following:

a. Drilling and equipping cost indexes for 21 components, 1978-82.

b. Tubular goods shipments, exports, and imports; active rigs; wells and footage drilled; and stacked and active rotary rigs; annually 1973-82, and July 1982 and Jan. 1983.

c. Domestic demand for 6 petroleum products; total exports; domestic production for crude oil and natural gas liquids; imports of crude oil and 6 products; other supply; closing stocks of 6 products, unfinished oils, natural gas liquids, and crude oil; and crude runs to stills; quarterly 1984.

d. Energy consumption, by energy source, 1982-84.

ANNUAL API ISSUE

Annual compilation of articles discussing world and U.S. petroleum and other energy industry developments and market outlook. Articles are individually described below.

OIL DEMAND: WHERE IT'S BEEN, WHERE IT'S GOING

(p. 109-113) By Bob Tippee and Bob Beck. Article, with 4 charts showing the following:

a. World energy consumption, by energy source, biennially 1972-82; and world refining capacity and crude runs, 1976-82.

b. Distribution of petroleum product consumption by type: for U.S./Canada, Western Europe/Japan, and rest of non-Communist world, 1982; and for total non-Communist world, selected years 1972-82.

Data are from DOE and British Petroleum.

MOTOR GASOLINE FORECASTING: AN EMBRYO SCIENCE

(p. 114-118) By Y. P. Tong and D. W. Houser. Article, with 1 table showing motor gasoline consumption by vehicle type, 1982. Data are from DOE and Standard Oil of California.

DISTILLATE: SMALL GAIN IN 1983, BIGGER ONE IN 1984

(p. 118-121) By Lowell S. Young. Article, with 2 tables showing sales of distillate fuel oil by end-use sector, with comparison to real GNP and industrial production index, various years 1962-84.

HERE'S A LOOK AT THE SHORT- AND LONG-TERM DEMAND PICTURE FOR U.S. RESIDUAL FUEL

(p. 122-130) By T. H. Gilbert. Article, with 9 tables showing the following:

a. Residual fuel oil demand, by sector, 1981-90; and electricity generated, by energy source, 1981-84; with selected detail by quarter and by PAD district.

b. Residual fuel oil domestic demand, exports, stock change, supply, imports, crude runs, and closing stocks, quarterly 1981-84; and natural gas demand by end use, and supply by type and location (contiguous U.S., Canada, and Mexico), 1982-85 and 1990.

ASSESSING SUPPLY/DEMAND FOR LPG

(p. 135-151) By W. R. Lund and D. N. McClanahan. Article, with 3 tables showing world propane and butane demand by end-use sector, and demand and supply by world area, for 1982, and for 1990 based on 1-3 price policy assumptions.

FOREIGN OIL DEMAND TO INCREASE 23% IN LDCs, HOLD LEVEL IN INDUSTRIAL COUNTRIES TO 1990

(p. 152-158) By Tor Meloe. Article, with 1 chart and 2 tables showing the following:

a. Energy demand by energy type, with detail for petroleum products, for industrial and developing countries in non-Communist world outside U.S., 1973, 1982, and 1990.

b. Western European percent change in oil and energy use per unit of output, for basic metals, electric generation, paper/pulp, and all industries, 1973-81 period.

REVIEW OF ENERGY CONSUMPTION, OIL DEMAND

(p. 159-163) By L. J. Deman. Article, with 1 chart showing energy consumption by energy type, 1970, 1980, and 1990.

C6985–1.503: Nov. 21, 1983 (Vol. 81, No. 47)

WEEKLY TABLES

a. Industry scoreboard, for Nov. 11, 1983. (p. 4)

b. Industry statistics, as of Nov. 4-16, 1983. (p. 92-93)

MONTHLY TABLE

a. Industry statistics: total U.S. land and marine seismic crews, for Oct. 1983. (p. 92)

RANK THEM HIGHER

(p. 12) Corrections to data for Petro-Lewis Corp. reported in *OGJ 400* appearing in Oct. 17, 1983 issue (for description, see SRI 1983 Annual under C6985-1.451).

FIRM'S ENVIRONMENTAL OUTLAY UP IN 1982

(p. 30) Brief article, with text data and 1 chart showing oil industry environmental R&D, administrative/operating/maintenance, and capital expenditures, 1973-82. Data are from American Petroleum Institute.

MORE EUROPEAN PETROCHEM JOLTS SEEN

(p. 42-43) Article, with 1 table showing petrochemical capacity closed by product type, for 6 Western European countries, 1981/82, actual and as percent of 1980 capacity. Data are from EniChemica SpA.

STOCKS SEEN HEADING OFF PRICE SPIRAL

(p. 48-49) Article discussing world oil market responses to threatened disruptions of oil supply, and use of emergency petroleum stocks to prevent spot price increases. Data are from Data and Decisions, London.

Includes 1 table showing risk of disruption and volume of oil threatened, size of surplus capacity, and change in stock levels, 4th quarter 1983-86.

UPDATE ON MAJOR INTERNATIONAL PIPELINE PROJECTS AROUND THE WORLD: 1985-2000

(p. 66-70) By Stephen T. Davenport. Article, with 8 charts and 8 tables showing world oil, gas, and coal demand and production, 1983 and 2000; and number of additional oil and gas pipelines and coal slurry pipeline/coal railroad systems needed to meet demand and production, 2000; all by world area.

C6985–1.504: Nov. 28, 1983 (Vol. 81, No. 48)

WEEKLY TABLES

a. Industry scoreboard, for Nov. 18, 1983. (p. 4)

b. Industry statistics, as of Nov. 11-21, 1983 (table [7] is omitted). (p. 150-151)

MONTHLY TABLE

a. Industry statistics: active rigs abroad, for Oct. 1983. (p. 151)

PIPELINE ECONOMICS, ANNUAL FEATURE

Annual feature, for 1983, on oil and natural gas pipeline system capital investment and construction costs. Most data are from FERC permit applications and cost reports filed by pipeline companies. Includes the following statistical features.

U.S. INTERSTATE PIPELINE SYSTEM GROWS, ANNUAL FEATURE

(p. 71-106) Annual article, by Earl Seaton, reviewing pipeline traffic and construction cost trends, 1982. Includes 8 summary charts and the following tabular data:

a. Interstate gas and liquids pipeline mileage, 1972-82; crude and product pipeline investments, by detailed expenditure category for 5 major unnamed companies, 1982; and onshore pipeline construction costs for right-of-way, materials, labor, and other expenditures, and cost range per mile, by pipe diameter, FY74-83. 3 tables. (p. 72-73)

b. Current pipeline costs, by pipe size and State; current compressor station costs, by State; costs for stations completed during 1981, by station type and State; and summary for gas pipeline/compressor construction, 1976-81. Current projects are those with construction permits filed June 1982-May 1983. Data are shown for on- and offshore projects, by expenditure category, with pipeline mileage and station horsepower. 4 tables. (p. 74-76)

c. Interstate gas transmission pipelines: operation and maintenance expenses, mileage, and value of sales, 1981. 1 table. (p. 84)

d. Project costs for 54 selected on- and offshore pipeline projects, compressor station units, and metering/dehydration/separation facilities, by cost item. 54 tables. (p. 87-100)

e. Liquids pipelines, showing mileage by line type, crude oil and products deliveries and trunk-line traffic, value of carrier property and annual change, operating revenue, and net income, all by company, 1982, with totals for 1981-82. 1 table. (p. 102-104)

f. Gas pipelines, showing mileage by line type, transmission and other compressor stations, total sales, value of gas plant and additions, operating revenues, and net income, all by company, 1982, with totals for 1981-82. 1 table. (p. 104-106)

OCJ-MORGAN OIL PIPELINE COST INDEX: PIPELINE BUILDING COSTS FOR FIRST QUARTER OF 1983 SHOW A MODEST INCREASE AS RECESSION LINGERS, QUARTERLY FEATURE

(p. 107-109) Quarterly article, by Joseph M. Morgan, presenting oil pipeline construction cost indexes for 1st quarter 1983 (1974=base year). Includes 1 table showing indexes for 18 cost components, 1978-82 and 1st quarter 1983.

Other Article

Sii-DAC DRILLING ACTIVITY: DRILLING-ACTIVITY SLIPPAGE CONTINUES IN THIRD QUARTER AS WELLS DROP 9%, FOOTAGE 5%, QUARTERLY FEATURE

(p. 123-125) Quarterly report, by Randy Hall and Joe McDonough, on oil and gas drilling activity for 3rd quarter 1983. Data are presented in terms of the Smith International, Inc. Drilling Activity Correlator, which distinguishes 3 types of drilling activity on the basis of technological sophistication.

Includes 3 tables showing wells and footage drilled by type, by quarter 1980-3rd quarter 1983, and by region 1st 9 months 1982-83.

C6985-1.505: Dec. 5, 1983 (Vol. 81, No. 49)

WEEKLY TABLES

a. Industry scoreboard, for Nov. 25, 1983. (p. 4)

b. Industry statistics, as of Nov. 25-30, 1983 (table [5] is omitted). (p. 164-165)

MONTHLY TABLES

a. Nelson Cost Indexes, for July 1983. (p. 142)

b. Industry statistics: selected U.S. and world crude prices, for Dec. 1983; and worldwide crude oil and gas production, for Sept. 1983. (p. 165-166)

COLD WEATHER, ECONOMIC GROWTH TO HIKE U.S. WINTER FUEL DEMAND, ANNUAL FEATURE

(p. 57-62) Annual article, by Robert J. Beck and Glenda E. Smith, on fuel oil and natural gas supply and demand outlook for winter 1983/84. Data are from DOE, API, and O&GJ.

Includes 3 tables showing the following:

a. Middle distillate and residual fuel demand (domestic and export), supply (refined, imports, from stocks, and direct crude), and end of season stocks; and natural gas demand, by sector; winter 1981/82-1983/84.

b. Distillate and residual fuel stocks as of Sept. 30, and winter daily average demand, 1974-83.

DEVELOPMENT OF UTAH TAR SAND EYED

(p. 64-66) Article, with 1 table showing production and operating data for 5 planned tar sand mining/processing projects in Utah, by company. Data are from Bureau of Land Management.

U.S. TAPS MOSTLY MEXICAN CRUDE FOR SPR FILL

(p. 66) Article, with 1 table showing volume of crude oil in U.S. Strategic Petroleum Reserve (SPR), by country of origin, as of Oct. 31, 1983. Data are from DOE.

U.S. DEMAND FOR JET FUEL FORECAST TO RISE THROUGH 1987

(p. 67) Article, with 1 chart forecasting domestic and international jet fuel consumption, based on 2 growth assumptions, 1983-87. Data are from Air Transport Assn of America survey of 82 airlines.

THIRD QUARTER BUOYS OGJ GROUP 9 MONTH PROFITS, QUARTERLY FEATURE

(p. 71-73) Quarterly article on U.S. oil industry profits, 1st 9 months 1983. Includes 2 tables showing net profits and revenues, ranked for 26 companies; and capital/exploration expenditures for 13 companies; 3rd quarter and/or 1st 9 months 1983, and percent change from 1982.

C6985-1.506: Dec. 12, 1983 (Vol. 81, No. 50)

WEEKLY TABLES

a. Industry scoreboard, for Dec. 2, 1983. (p. 4)

b. Industry statistics, as of Nov. 18-Dec. 7, 1983. (p. 163-164)

NUCLEAR FRAC COULD BE FEASIBLE FOR CARBONATE RESERVOIRS

(p. 84-92) By J. H. Howard and J. E. King. Article, with cost and technical data on use of nuclear explosions to stimulate oil field production. Presents analysis based on results of a 1965 experiment in Soviet Union. Includes text data, 7 charts, and 1 table.

C6985-1.507: Dec. 19, 1983 (Vol. 81, No. 51)

WEEKLY TABLES

a. Industry scoreboard, for Dec. 9, 1983. (p. 4)

b. Industry statistics, as of Nov. 25-Dec. 14, 1983. (p. 125-126)

USGS EYES OIL, GAS POTENTIAL IN WILDERNESS AREAS

(p. 64) Article summarizing findings of a U.S. Geological Survey report on potential petroleum resources of Federal wilderness areas in 11 western States. Includes 2 undated tables showing volume of undiscovered recoverable oil and gas, and acreage classified by petroleum potential rating, for each State.

STUDY OF EIA INDICATES DRILLING COSTS FOR 1983 CONTINUE SLOWED DECLINE TO 63% OF 1981 HIGHS

(p. 92-95) By Ted Anderson and Velton T. Funk. Part 1 of a 2-part series presenting Energy Information Administration estimates of oil and gas drilling costs, 1981-83. Includes 1 table showing oil/gas well drilling costs 1983, and cost indexes 1981-83 (1976=100), by well depth.

COST OF RESERVES BY DISCOVERY vs. ACQUISITION: IS IT CHEAPER TO BUY OIL THAN TO FIND IT?

(p. 96-104) By James C. Dyer. Article analyzing costs of purchasing vs. discovering oil/gas reserves. Includes 5 tables showing the following:

a. Stock performance for selected energy industries and for 13 companies with substantial reserves, various periods 1982-83; and buyer, seller, and price, for selected reserve acquisitions (no date).

b. Estimated discovery costs, 1981-83; and discovery-acquisition cost ratio, by time from discovery to sale, 1981 and 1983.

C6985-1.508: Dec. 26, 1983 (Vol. 81, No. 52)

WEEKLY TABLES

a. Industry scoreboard, for Dec. 16, 1983. (p. 4)

b. Industry statistics, as of Dec. 2-19, 1983 (table [7] is omitted). (p. 188-189)

MONTHLY TABLES

a. U.S. wells drilled, for Oct. 1983. (p. 177-178)

b. Industry statistics: total U.S. land and marine seismic crews, and active rigs abroad, for Nov. 1983; and worldwide crude oil and gas production, for Oct. 1983. (p. 188-190)

WORLDWIDE REPORT, ANNUAL FEATURE

(p. 77-139) Annual feature reporting results of O&GJ survey of world petroleum reserves, production, and refining capacity, 1983.

Contains narrative summary with text statistics, and the following 4 tables showing data by country:

[1] Worldwide oil and gas at a glance [estimated oil and gas proved reserves, Jan. 1, 1984; producing oil wells as of July 1, 1983; estimated daily oil production, 1983 and change from 1982; and refining capacity by process, Jan. 1, 1984; all data are also shown by world region]. (p. 80-81)

[2] Worldwide production [discovery date, depth, number of wells by type, and 1st half 1983 cumulative and average daily production, for specified producing fields, grouped by company]. (p. 87-109)

[3] Survey of operating refineries worldwide (capacities as of Jan. 1, 1984) [number of plants, average daily input of crude, and capacity by type of process and product]. (p. 110-111)

[4] Worldwide refining [same input and capacity data as in table [3], shown for specified refineries, grouped by company]. (p. 114-139)

COST TRENDS FROM EIA STUDY POINT OUT REGIONAL VARIANCE FOR 13 CONTIGUOUS U.S. AREAS

(p. 146-152) By Ted Anderson and Velton T. Funk. Conclusion of 2-part series presenting Energy Information Administration estimates of oil and gas drilling costs, 1981-83.

Includes 4 tables showing contiguous U.S. onshore oil and gas well drilling costs 1983, and cost indexes 1981-83 (1976=100), by well depth and region.

FIELD SIZE DISTRIBUTION RELATED TO BASIN CHARACTERISTICS

(p. 168-176) By H. D. Klemme. Article discussing relationship between field size and potential petroleum reserves, based on an analysis of 65 petroleum producing basins worldwide. Data are from scholarly articles.

Includes 2 tables showing average time required to find 75% and 100% of aggregate resources of the 5 largest fields within a basin, by basin type, various periods 1880-1980.

WORLD WELL COMPLETIONS, 1982 AAPG, API DATA; ANNUAL FEATURE

(p. 180-181) Annual table showing wells and footage or meters drilled, by country and world region, 1982. Includes varying detail by type of well (oil, gas, dry, and wildcat). Data are from American Assn of Petroleum Geologists and American Petroleum Institute.

C6985–1.509: Jan. 2, 1984 (Vol 82, No. 1)
[Issue incorrectly reads Vol. 81.]

WEEKLY TABLES

a. Industry scoreboard, for Dec. 23, 1983. (p. 4)

b. Industry statistics, as of Dec. 23-28, 1983 (table [5] is omitted). (p. 86-87)

MONTHLY TABLES

a. Nelson Cost Indexes, for Aug. 1983. (p. 62)

b. Industry statistics: selected U.S. and world crude prices, for Jan. 1984. (p. 87)

LINGERING U.S. GAS SURPLUS PREDICTED

(p. 32-33) Article, with 1 table showing natural gas productive capacity and volume shut in, by region, and by Natural Gas Policy Act classification, as of Oct. 1, 1983. Data are from responses of 63 natural gas producers to an O&GJ survey conducted late 1983.

OUTLAY FOR 1982 U.S. WELLS SETS RECORD, ANNUAL FEATURE

(p. 34-35) Annual article on energy drilling activity and costs, 1982. Data are from a joint survey by 3 industry assns. Includes 2 tables showing number, footage, and cost of wells drilled, for all wells by depth interval, and for oil and gas wells and dry holes, 1981-82.

Full *Joint Association Survey* is covered in SRI under A2575-9.

QUARTERLY COSTIMATING: HOW INDEXES HAVE CHANGED

(p. 58-59) Quarterly feature, by Gerald L. Farrar, on Nelson indexes of refinery operating, construction labor, and equipment and material costs. Includes 2 tables showing indexes for refinery construction and operating wages, and operating productivity, monthly 1981-82; and refining cost indexes by itemized component, and indexes of refinery inflation, operation, and process operation, selected years 1954-82 and Aug. 1983.

C6985–1.510: Jan. 9, 1984 (Vol 82, No. 2)

WEEKLY TABLES

a. Industry scoreboard, for Dec. 30, 1983. (p. 4)

b. Industry statistics, as of Dec. 16, 1983-Jan. 4, 1984 (p. 122-123).

MONTHLY TABLES

a. U.S. wells drilled, for Nov. 1983. (p. 116-117)

HOT SANTA MARIA BASIN PLAY MAY COOL SOON

(p. 55-63) Article, with 1 fold-out map and accompanying table, showing well status and depth, water depth, and operating company, for California's Santa Maria Basin tracts leased under Outer Continental Shelf sales 53, 48, and RS-2, by tract (undated).

C6985–1.511: Jan. 16, 1984 (Vol. 82, No. 3)

WEEKLY TABLES

a. Industry scoreboard, for Jan. 6, 1984. (p. 4)

b. Industry statistics, as of Dec. 16, 1983-Jan. 11, 1984. (p. 143-144)

MONTHLY TABLES

a. Industry statistics: total U.S. land and marine seismic crews, for Dec. 1983. (p. 143)

$500 MILLION EXPOSED FOR GULF TRACTS

(p. 56-58) Article reporting results of a Federal sale of Outer Continental Shelf oil and gas lease tracts in the Gulf of Mexico, held Jan. 5, 1984. Data are from Minerals Management Service of Dept of Interior.

Includes 1 table showing apparent high bidder and bid, for top 15 tracts.

PROJECTED FREE WORLD OIL FINDS THROUGH 2000

(p. 138-139) By L. F. Ivanhoe. Article, with 1 table showing projected volume of oil discoveries in U.S. and rest of non-Communist world, 1982-2000 period, with comparison to actual 1982 production. Data are author's estimates.

C6985–1.512: Jan. 23, 1984 (Vol. 82, No. 4)

WEEKLY TABLES

a. Industry scoreboard, for Jan. 13, 1984. (p. 4)

b. Industry statistics, as of Jan. 6-18, 1984. (p. 117-118)

NON-COMMUNIST INDUSTRY SETS SIGHTS ON 34,267 MILES OF NEW PIPELINES, ANNUAL FEATURE

(p. 25-30) Annual article, by Earl Seaton and Paul Hart, on pipeline construction planned or

underway in the non-Communist world, 1984 and beyond. Data are from O&GJ survey and industry projections.

Includes map, text statistics, and 2 tables showing mileage to be completed for gas, crude, and product pipelines in the U.S., Canada, and 5 world areas, by diameter of line.

U.S. DRILLING FUNDS REPORT SLUMP IN INVESTMENT RETURN

(p. 52) Article on performance of public oil/gas drilling funds. Data are from Robert A. Stanger and Co. Includes 1 table showing number of programs, investment, percent of investment returned in cash, and total expected return ratio, by fund drilling objective and program structure, 1970-81 period.

OGJ-MORGAN GAS PIPELINE COST INDEX: GAS PIPELINE BUILDING COSTS INCREASE SLIGHTLY, QUARTERLY FEATURE

(p. 60-62) Quarterly article, by Joseph M. Morgan, presenting gas pipeline construction cost indexes for 1st quarter 1983 (1976=base year).

Includes 4 tables showing indexes for 13 cost components and composite index, 1978-82 and 1st quarter 1983; number, length, and cost of gas pipeline projects, by pipe diameter, with detail for Gulf of Mexico projects, 1st quarter 1983; and onshore vs. offshore construction costs for 3 pipe diameters, 1st quarter 1983.

C6985–1.513: Jan. 30, 1984 (Vol. 82, No. 5)

WEEKLY TABLES

a. Industry scoreboard, for Jan. 20, 1984. (p. 4)

b. Industry statistics, as of Jan. 13-23, 1984 (table [7] is omitted). (p. 182-183)

MONTHLY TABLES

a. Industry statistics: active rigs abroad, for Dec. 1983. (p. 183)

REFINERS IN W. EUROPE BRACED FOR MOVE TO UNLEADED GASOLINE

(p. 65-68) By Roger Vielvoye. Article, with 3 tables showing the following for motor gasoline in Western Europe: lead limit and octane specifications for premium and regular grades, as of Jan. 1, 1984, with planned changes; consumption, 1976-82; and premium grade share of total, biennially 1976-82; all by country. Data are from Purvin & Gertz Inc.

PERU SEEKS TO HALT PRODUCTION DECLINE

(p. 80-81) Article discussing outlook for Peru oil industry. Data are from Petroleos del Peru (Petroperu). Includes 2 tables showing exploration/development spending in Peru, 1980-84; and number of development and wildcat wells located offshore, on northern coast, and in jungle areas, 1982-84; all by company.

FORECAST/REVIEW, ANNUAL FEATURE

(p. 95-136) Annual survey, for 1983-84, of oil and gas industry supply and demand, including exploration, production, employment, imports, and exports.

Includes 3 articles with text statistics and tables, and additional separate tables, some accompanied by charts. All tables are listed below.

TABLES:

SUPPLY AND DEMAND FORECASTS

[1] Journal forecast of supply and demand [domestic demand, by refined product; product exports; supply of crude oil/lease condensate and of natural gas liquids/other hydrocarbons; imports and stocks of crude oil and products; processing gains/losses; and crude runs to stills; most shown for PAD Districts 1-4 and 5; annually 1983-84, and quarterly 1984]. (p. 99)

[2] U.S. energy demand [for oil, natural gas, coal, hydroelectric/geothermal, and nuclear power, 1982-84]. (p. 100)

[3] U.S. natural gas demand [natural gas production in Texas, Louisiana, and all other States; imports from Canada and Mexico; liquefied natural gas imports from Algeria; supplemental gas; losses; exports; and stock change; 1981-84]. (p. 100)

[4] Crude and products prices fall; gas up [crude oil average U.S. wellhead and import prices, natural gas average wellhead price, and regular motor gasoline pump and No. 2 heating oil retail prices, 1971-83]. (p. 102)

[5] U.S. energy efficiency improves again [energy consumption compared to GNP, 1973-84]. (p. 102)

TRENDS

[Tables 6-16] show annual data for 1974-83.]

[6] U.S. production of crude oil/lease condensate [by PAD district and State or geographic area, with cumulative data for 1859-1983]. (p. 107)

[7] Supply and demand for crude in the U.S. [imports and production; refinery runs, direct use/loss, exports, and use for Strategic Petroleum Reserve (SPR); stock change; and primary and SPR stocks]. (p. 107)

[8] Rotary rig activity by States [and selected State regions including offshore, and for onshore and offshore Canada, with 1983 low and peak numbers]. (p. 110)

[9] Marketed production of natural gas [by State, and total imports and exports]. (p. 111)

[10] U.S. employment and earnings [all manufacturing, petroleum refining, and petroleum/natural gas production], and price indices [producer, crude oil, and refined products]. (p. 111)

[11] Refinery runs by [PAD] districts [and geographic subdivisions; and refinery capacity utilization for 1983]. (p. 112)

[12] Refined products [by type], natural gas liquids, and crude stocks. (p. 112)

[13] Production of natural gas liquids and liquefied refinery gases [by product]. (p. 117)

[14] Crude imports by country of origin. (p. 120)

[15-16] Imports of refined products, and exports of refined products and crude, [with detail by product type]. (p. 120)

WELL FORECAST

[17] The majors' score [total wells (1981-84) and wildcat wells (1983-84) drilled, by State and major producing State regions including offshore]. (p. 125)

[18] O&GJ well forecast for 1984 [total, wildcat, and/or field wells, and total footage drilled, 1983-84, by State and major producing State region including offshore, and for west Canada by Province, and offshore east coast Canada]. (p. 126)

[19] Quarter-century historical record of U.S. well completions [total wells, footage, and wildcat wells, 1959-1983]. (p. 128)

[20] Big independent operators' score [total and wildcat wells drilled in 1983 and planned for 1984, by State and major producing State region including offshore]. (p. 128)

MAJOR OIL FIELD PRODUCTION

[21] [Production, 1983; cumulative production, as of Jan. 1, 1984; and estimated reserves and wells; for major oil fields, arranged by State.] (p. 134-136)

C6985–1.514: Feb. 6, 1984 (Vol. 82, No. 6)

WEEKLY TABLES

a. Industry scoreboard, for Jan. 27, 1984. (p. 4)

b. Industry statistics, as of Jan. 27-Feb. 1, 1984 (table [5] is omitted). (p. 151-152)

MONTHLY TABLES

a. Nelson Cost Indexes, for Sept. 1983. (p. 117)

b. Industry statistics: selected U.S. and world crude prices, for Feb. 1984; and worldwide crude oil and gas production, for Nov. 1983. (p. 152-153)

INDUSTRY HITS IRS PLAN TO REVAMP SUPERFUND TAX

(p. 82-83) Article on tax collections under the Hazardous Substance Response Revenue Act of 1980 (Superfund act). Data are from National Petroleum Refiners Assn. Includes 3 charts showing portions collected from petroleum, inorganic chemicals, and petrochemicals, as of June 30, 1983, and projected under IRS proposed revisions.

Sii-DAC DRILLING ACTIVITY: SLUMP IN TYPE III BLUNTS YEAR-END DRILLING SURGE, QUARTERLY FEATURE

(p. 104-106) Quarterly report, by Randy Hall, on oil and gas drilling activity for 4th quarter 1983. Data are presented in terms of the Smith International, Inc. Drilling Activity Correlator, which distinguishes 3 types of drilling activity on the basis of technological sophistication.

Includes 1 chart and 3 tables showing wells and footage drilled by type, by quarter 1977-83, and by region, 1982-83.

ANALYSIS DICTATES H2 PURIFICATION PROCESS

(p. 111-117) By S. I. Wang et al. Article discussing off-gas hydrogen purification processes in refineries. Data are from Air Products and Chemicals, Inc. Includes 1 table comparing product results and costs, for 3 methods of purifying a catalytic reformer off-gas stream.

C6985–1.515: Feb. 13, 1984 (Vol. 82, No. 7)

WEEKLY TABLES

a. Industry scoreboard, for Feb. 3, 1984. (p. 4)

b. Industry statistics, as of Jan. 27-Feb. 8, 1984. (p. 139-140)

MONTHLY TABLES

a. U.S. wells drilled (total only), for Dec. 1983. (p. 133)

OIL SEEN LOSING MARKET SHARE TO OTHER FUELS

(p. 42) Article, with 1 chart projecting non-Communist world petroleum demand, by product category, 1990 and 2000, with actual data for 1982. Data are from Texaco, Inc.

STEADY GROWTH FORECAST FOR U.S. ADDITIVES DEMAND

(p. 51) Article, with 1 table showing demand for fuel, alcohol, and lubricant additives, by type, selected years 1982-92. Data are from Business Communications Co.

BOOMERANG EFFECT OF ROYALTY TRUSTS

(p. 107-109) By Edward Symonds. Article on development of royalty trusts in the petroleum industry. Data sources include Donaldson, Lufkin & Jenrette, and Energy Economics & Finance.

Contains 2 tables showing volume and value of natural gas and oil reserves in the U.S., 1982; and natural gas stock prices, as of Jan. 1, 1984 and Feb. 26, 1982; by company arranged by company type (international, U.S. integrated, natural gas pipelines, and royalty trusts).

RESULTS IN FOR TVA's AMMONIA-FROM-COAL PLANT

(p. 110-112) Article, with 1 table comparing estimated capital costs by item, for 3 types of ammonia-from-coal facilities. Data are based on costs for an experimental TVA project, and Brown and Root Development Inc. studies. Estimates are stated in 1983 dollars.

C6985–1.516: Feb. 20, 1984 (Vol. 82, No. 8)

WEEKLY TABLES

a. Industry scoreboard, for Feb. 10, 1984. (p. 4)

b. Industry statistics, as of Feb. 3-15, 1984. (p. 84-85)

MONTHLY TABLE

a. Industry statistics: total U.S. land and marine seismic crews, for Jan. 1984. (p. 84)

C6985–1.517: Feb. 27, 1984 (Vol. 82, No. 9)

WEEKLY TABLES

a. Industry scoreboard, for Feb. 17, 1984. (p. 4)

b. Industry statistics, as of Feb. 10-20, 1984 (table [7] is omitted). (p. 131-132)

MONTHLY TABLE

a. Industry statistics: active rigs abroad, for Jan. 1984. (p. 132)

U.S. CAPITAL, EXPLORATION BUDGETS DIP 3.9% IN 1984, ANNUAL FEATURE

(p. 43-46) Annual report on U.S. oil industry capital spending plans for 1984, including exploration/drilling, production, Outer Continental Shelf lease bonuses, refining, petrochemicals, marketing, and pipelines. Data are from an O&GJ survey.

Includes 2 tables showing planned or actual spending for domestic and foreign operations, by function, 1982-84.

CANADIAN INDUSTRY WILL TRIM 1984 SPENDING BY 4.1%, ANNUAL FEATURE

(p. 45) Annual report, for 1984, on Canadian oil industry capital spending plans. Includes 1 table showing planned or actual capital spending, by function (similar breakdowns as preceding article), 1982-84.

SALOMON BROS.: OPEC SLIP COULD CUT OIL PRICE

(p. 55) Article, with 1 table showing outlook for world oil supply-demand, including non-OPEC supply, OPEC crude oil and natural gas liquid sales, and inventory change, 1982-90. Data are from Salomon Bros.

OGJ-MORGAN OIL PIPELINE COST INDEX: SECOND-QUARTER OIL PIPELINE BUILDING COSTS REMAINED SLUGGISH, QUARTERLY FEATURE

(p. 94-96) Quarterly article, by Joseph M. Morgan, presenting oil pipeline construction cost indexes for 2nd quarter 1983 (1974=base year). Includes 1 table showing indexes for 18 cost components, 1978-82 and 1st-2nd quarter 1983.

INTERNATIONAL SEISMIC CREW COUNT, RECURRING FEATURE

(p. 131) Recurring table showing land and marine seismic crews, for U.S., Canada, Mexico, and 5 world areas, June and Sept. 1983. Data are from Society of Exploration Geophysicists.

Table appears in "Industry Statistics" section.

C6985–1.518: Mar. 5, 1984 (Vol. 82, No. 10)

WEEKLY TABLES

a. Industry scoreboard, for Feb. 24, 1984. (p. 4)

b. Industry statistics, as of Feb. 24-29, 1984 (table [5] is omitted). (p. 132-133)

MONTHLY TABLES

a. Nelson Cost Indexes, for Oct. 1983. (p. 79)

b. Industry statistics: selected U.S. and world crude prices, for Mar. 1984. (p. 133)

LONE STAR YEAREND TALLY SHOWS DECLINE IN OCTG INVENTORIES, SEMIANNUAL FEATURE

(p. 66) Semiannual article on oil country tubular goods (OCTG) supply and demand. Data are from Lone Star Steel Co. Includes 1 table showing OCTG inventories, by drilling region, June and Dec. 1983.

REPLACING OLDER GAS COMPRESSOR DRIVERS MAY PAY OUT FAST

(p. 71-76) By Richard P. Lang. Article, with 7 tables presenting 3 case studies analyzing economics of replacing existing gas compressor drivers in natural gas pipeline systems with new equipment. Data are author's estimates.

C6985–1.519: Mar. 12, 1984 (Vol. 82, No. 11)

WEEKLY TABLES

a. Industry scoreboard, for Mar. 2, 1984. (p. 4)

b. Industry statistics, as of Feb. 24-Mar. 7, 1984. (p. 126-127)

MONTHLY TABLES

a. U.S. wells drilled (exploratory only), for Dec. 1983. (p. 120)

b. Industry statistics: worldwide crude oil and gas production, for Dec. 1983. (p. 128)

DECLINE IN WORLD OIL PRODUCTION SEEN ENDING, ANNUAL FEATURE

(p. 25-28) Annual article reviewing world oil production, 1983. Includes 1 chart and 1 table showing oil production for U.S., for Canada, and by world area, and quarterly OPEC production by member country, 1983, with comparisons to 1982.

HODEL HINTS AT EARLY USE OF SPR DURING SHORTAGE

(p. 51) Article, with 2 charts showing days of supply available in crude and total oil stocks, 1977-83. Data are from Energy Information Administration.

ANNUAL PETROCHEMICAL REPORT

(p. 55-77) Annual compilation of articles, for 1984, discussing trends and outlook for petrochemical processes, equipment, feedstocks, and products. Articles containing nontechnical statistics are described below. In 1983, feature contained technical articles only.

OUTLOOK FOR CARBON PRODUCTS FEEDSTOCK IS GOOD

(p. 62-68) By Charles A. Stokes and Vincent J. Guercio. Article examining the industrial carbons market, with focus on the availability of feedstocks. Includes 9 tables presenting technical data, and the following nontechnical statistics:

a. Needle coke capacity, plant location and owner, feedstock used, and 1st year of operation, by plant, for U.S. and 4 other countries, 1983 or 1984.

b. Carbon black demand in U.S., Soviet Bloc/China, and rest of world; and world heavy aromatic oils (HAO) supply and demand, by type; 1983 and 1990.

c. U.S. carbon black feedstock exports to Canada and other world areas, 1982; and distribution of U.S. decant oil, by type of disposition (undated).

SYNTHESIS GAS: AN EXCITING FUTURE IS EXPECTED

(p. 68-73) By A. J. Moll and R. L. Dickenson. Article with 1 undated table showing typical operating and capital costs for synthesis gas produced from natural gas, petroleum residue and coke, and coal, with comparative costs for natural gas-based production in Saudi Arabia.

Other Article

ECONOMICS OF MARGINAL OFFSHORE OIL DISCOVERIES IN CHINA

(p. 79-84) By G. C. L. Jones et al. Article, with text data and 4 tables showing estimates of profitability for development of offshore oil fields on the Chinese Continental Shelf, under selected cost, production, investment, and government policy assumptions.

C6985–1.520: Mar. 19, 1984 (Vol. 82, No. 12)

WEEKLY TABLES

a. Industry scoreboard, for Mar. 9, 1984. (p. 4)

b. Industry statistics, as of Mar. 2-14, 1984. (p. 215-216)

MONTHLY TABLE

a. Industry statistics: total U.S. land and marine seismic crews, for Feb. 1984. (p. 215)

1983 PROFITS FOR JOURNAL GROUP SHOW SLIGHT GAIN TO $22.4 BILLION, QUARTERLY FEATURE

(p. 71-74) Quarterly article, by Robert J. Beck and Glenda E. Smith, on U.S. oil industry profits, 1983. Includes 3 tables showing net profits and revenues for 26 companies; net income and capital/exploration expenditures for 14 companies; and rates of return measures for 8 companies; 4th quarter and/or full year 1983, with comparisons to 1982.

Note that column headings for table on p. 72 incorrectly read 9 months and 3rd quarter. Correct headings are full year and 4th quarter.

NEW RIG REPORT TALLIES NUMBER OF ACTIVE RIGS BY DEPTH, TYPE OF CONTRACT, FOOTAGE vs. DAYWORK

(p. 138-146) By W. D. Moore III. Article introducing weekly and monthly tables on rig drilling activity, as compiled by Smith International, Inc.

Includes 3 tables showing rig count and average depth, by State and rig type (land, inland, and offshore); rig count and percent under footage contracts, by depth interval; and land rig count and average depth, by type of contract (daywork and footage); all for weeks ended Feb. 3 and 10, 1984 and Feb. 11, 1983, with year-to-date totals 1983-84.

C6985–1.521: Mar. 26, 1984 (Vol. 82, No. 13)

WEEKLY TABLES

a. Industry scoreboard, for Mar. 16, 1984. (p. 4)

b. Industry statistics, as of Mar. 9-21, 1984. (p. 162-164)

MONTHLY TABLES

a. U.S. wells drilled, for Jan. 1984. (p. 158-159)

b. Industry statistics: Smith rig count, for Mar. 16, 1984; and selected U.S. and world crude prices, for Mar. 1984. (p. 164)

ANNUAL REFINING REPORT

Annual report, for 1983-84, on U.S. and Canada oil refinery operations and outlook, presented in 7 articles. Articles with substantial nontechnical statistics are described below.

U.S., CANADIAN REFINERS STILL RETRENCHING, ANNUAL FEATURE

(p. 71-74) Annual article, by Leo R. Aalund, on developments in U.S. and Canadian oil refining capacities, based on an O&GJ industry survey. Data are for U.S. only.

Includes 4 tables showing refining capacity, Jan. 1, 1983-84, and scheduled for completion in 1984-85; 19 largest companies ranked by capacity, with number of refineries (no date); and number of refining companies, refineries, and capacity, by capacity size group, Jan. 1, 1983-84. Capacity data include varying detail for specific refining processes.

ANNUAL REFINING SURVEY

(p. 111-125) Annual report, by Ailleen Cantrell, on processing capacities at U.S. and Canadian oil refineries, based on an O&GJ industry survey. Includes 3 tables showing crude capacity, and charge and production capacities by process, for individual operating refineries grouped by company, State, and Canadian Province, Jan. 1, 1984. Also includes listing of inactive refineries, with capacity and location for each.

HOW VARIABLE SPEED AND CONSTANT-SPEED MOTORS COMPARE FOR PIPELINE PUMP DRIVERS

(p. 127-132) By Randall J. Hartman. Article, with 2 tables analyzing economic feasibility of using variable speed vs. constant-speed pump motors in pipeline systems, as represented by 3 case studies. Also includes several technical charts and tables.

C6985–1.522: Apr. 2, 1984 (Vol. 82, No. 14)

WEEKLY TABLES

a. Industry scoreboard, for Mar. 23, 1984. (p. 4)

b. Industry statistics, as of Mar. 16-26, 1984 (table [7] is omitted). (p. 169-170)

MONTHLY TABLES

a. Nelson Cost Indexes, for Nov. 1983. (p. 128)

b. Industry statistics: active rigs abroad, for Feb. 1984; and worldwide crude oil and gas production, for Jan. 1984. (p. 170-171)

CANADA'S 1983 COMPLETIONS SHOW 8.1% INCREASE

(p. 66) Article, with 1 table showing Canadian total and wildcat oil/gas wells and meters drilled, by Province, 1982-83. Data are from Canadian Petroleum Assn.

EOR SET TO MAKE SIGNIFICANT CONTRIBUTION, BIENNIAL FEATURE

(p. 83-105) Biennial article, by Jim Leonard, presenting review and outlook for world and U.S. enhanced oil recovery (EOR) projects, as of 1984. Data are from an O&GJ staff survey. Includes 12 tables showing the following:

a. Summary U.S. data: EOR production 1980, 1982, and 1984; and number of active projects, 1971 and biennially 1974-84; by recovery method.

b. Planned EOR projects: operator, project type, location, size, depth, technical data, and target date, for fields in U.S., Canada, Hungary, and Venezuela.

c. Active EOR projects: location, date started, size and depth, technical data, number of production and injection wells, total and enhanced daily oil production, and project and profitability evaluations, for fields arranged by operator, in Canada, Trinidad/Tobago, Venezuela, and 8 other countries, and in U.S. by detailed project type, as of 1984.

For description of 1982 report, see SRI 1982 Annual, under C6985-1.323.

QUARTERLY COSTIMATING: HOW NELSON INDEXES HAVE CHANGED

(p. 112-113) Quarterly feature, by Gerald L. Farrar, on Nelson indexes of refinery operating, construction labor, and equipment and material costs. Includes 2 tables showing cost indexes for 6 refining chemicals or chemical types, quarterly 1979-1982; and cost indexes by itemized component, and indexes of refinery inflation, operation, and process operation, selected years 1954-82 and Nov. 1983.

C6985–1.523: Apr. 9, 1984 (Vol. 82, No. 15)

WEEKLY TABLES

a. Industry scoreboard, for Mar. 30, 1984. (p. 4)

b. Industry statistics, as of Mar. 23-Apr. 4, 1984. (p. 145-146)

MONTHLY TABLES

a. U.S. wells drilled for full year 1983, and (total wells only) for Feb. 1984. (p. 139-141)

EPA FINDS COST BENEFITS IN 0.1 g/GAL LEAD LIMIT

(p. 65) Article, with 2 tables showing selected direct and indirect costs and benefits resulting from low-lead and unleaded motor fuel requirements, 1988; and demand for leaded and unleaded gasoline with and without misfueling (inappropriate use of leaded fuel), biennially 1982-90. Data are from EPA.

OGJ-MORGAN GAS PIPELINE COST INDEX: COMPETITION HELD DOWN GAS PIPELINE BUILDING COSTS FOR SECOND QUARTER OF 1983, QUARTERLY FEATURE

(p. 92-94) Quarterly article, by Joseph M. Morgan, presenting gas pipeline construction cost indexes for 2nd quarter 1983 (1976=base year).

Includes 2 tables showing indexes for 13 cost components, and composite index, 1978-82 and 1st-2nd quarters 1983; and horsepower, and costs by type (equipment/materials, installation, miscellaneous, and/or land), for gas compressor station onshore additions, new onshore installations, and offshore installations, 2nd quarter 1983.

C6985–1.524: Apr. 16, 1984 (Vol 82, No. 16)

WEEKLY TABLES

a. Industry scoreboard, for Apr. 6, 1984. (p. 4)

b. Industry statistics, as of Mar. 30-Apr. 11, 1984. (p. 97-98)

MONTHLY TABLES

a. U.S. wells drilled (exploratory only), for Feb. 1984. (p. 92)

b. Industry statistics: total U.S. land and marine seismic crews, for Mar. 1984. (p. 93)

STEADY WORK IN GULF COAST AREA HELPS PROP UP U.S. RIG COUNT

(p. 25-28) By Rick Hagar and Glenda E. Smith. Article, with 1 table showing drilling rig count, for total U.S., and for Gulf of Mexico region by State and State area, weekly Jan. 2-Apr. 2, 1984. Data are from Hughes Tool Co.

C6985–1.525: Apr. 23, 1984 (Vol. 82, No. 17)

WEEKLY TABLES

a. Industry scoreboard, for Apr. 13, 1984. (p. 4)

b. Industry statistics, as of Apr. 6-18, 1984 (Smith rig count table is omitted). (p. 147-148)

WORLDWIDE CONSTRUCTION, SEMIANNUAL FEATURE

(p. 97-128) Semiannual list, by Aileen Cantrell, of worldwide construction for refineries, petrochemicals, sulfur, gas processing, related fuels, and pipelining projects, showing the following data, where available, for each: capacity, contractor, estimated costs, and completion date. Listings are by company arranged by country, for each project type.

C6985–1.526: Apr. 30, 1984 (Vol. 82, No. 18)

WEEKLY TABLES

a. Industry scoreboard, for Apr. 20, 1984. (p. 4)

b. Industry statistics, as of Apr. 13-23, 1984 (table [7] is omitted). (p. 90-91)

MONTHLY TABLES

a. Industry statistics: Smith rig count, for Apr. 20, 1984; and selected U.S. and world crude prices, for Apr. 1984. (p. 92)

THAILAND ACTION SHIFTS TO DEVELOPMENT

(p. 24-26) Article on drilling activity in Thailand, with 1 map showing type and/or number of wells and line miles of seismic surveys planned, and incidence of banned/stalled development, by company, as of early 1984. Data are from Petroleum Authority of Thailand.

BIDDING REINED FOR NAVARIN ACREAGE

(p. 33-34) Article reporting results of a Federal sale of Outer Continental Shelf oil and gas lease tracts in the Navarin Basin off Alaska, held Apr. 17, 1984. Data are from Minerals Management Service of Dept of Interior. Includes 1 table showing apparent high bidder and bid, and bid per acre, for top 16 tracts.

GULF DEEPWATER TRACTS SPARK BIDDING

(p. 36-40) Article reporting results of a Federal sale of Outer Continental Shelf oil and gas lease tracts in the Gulf of Mexico, held Apr. 24, 1984. Data are from Minerals Management Service of Dept of Interior, and Electronic Rig Stats. Includes 1 table showing apparent high bidder and bonus bid, for top 20 tracts.

MBTE COULD COMPETE WITH ALKYLATE FOR ISOBUTYLENE

(p. 47-52) By T. A. Ring et al. Article examining the viability of diverting isobutylene from the manufacture of alkylate to the manufacture of methyl tertiary butyl ether (MTBE) during gasoline refining. Data are authors' estimates. Includes technical data; and 2 tables projecting costs, savings, and profitability, associated with the incorporation of an MTBE unit into existing refineries, 1986 and 1990.

INTERNATIONAL SEISMIC CREW COUNT, RECURRING FEATURE

(p. 78) Recurring table showing land and marine seismic crews, for U.S., Canada, Mexico, and 5 world areas, Sept. and Dec. 1983. Data are from Society of Exploration Geophysicists.

OIL, GAS POTENTIAL OF WEST U.S. WILDERNESS LANDS

(p. 79-83) By Betty M. Miller. Article discussing findings of a U.S. Geological Survey report on potential petroleum resources of Federal wilderness areas in 11 western States.

Includes 2 undated tables showing low, high, and mean estimates of undiscovered recoverable oil and gas, and acreage classified by petroleum potential rating, for areas in each State designated or proposed as wilderness lands as of July 1981.

C6985–1.527: May 7, 1984 (Vol. 82, No. 19)

WEEKLY TABLES

a. Industry scoreboard, for Apr. 27, 1984. (p. 4)

b. Industry statistics, as of Apr. 20-May 2, 1984. (p. 229-230)

MONTHLY TABLES

a. Nelson Cost Indexes, for Dec. 1983. (p. 185)

b. Industry statistics: worldwide crude oil and gas production, for Feb. 1984. (p. 231)

CLARIFICATION OF EUROPEAN ENERGY POLICIES URGED

(p. 83) Article, with 1 table showing energy consumption and import share of consumption, by type of energy, aggregated for European OECD members, 1983 and late 1990s. Data are from Royal/Dutch Shell Group.

OFFSHORE REPORT: OFFSHORE DRILLING INCREASES, ATTRITION, CUT MOBILE RIG SURPLUS, ANNUAL FEATURE

(p. 103-105) Annual article, by W. D. Moore III, summarizing world offshore drilling activity. Data are from O&GJ and Hughes Tool Co.

Includes 1 chart and 2 tables showing mobile rigs by type, and idle and working mobile rigs by world area, 1984; active rigs by world area, 1982-84; and rig utilization rate by type, and by world area, as of May 1979-84, with overall utilization rate, 1975-84.

PRODUCTION FLEXIBILITY FOR BTX CAN MAXIMIZE PROFITS

(p. 159-163) By S. J. Penny et al. Article discussing possible economic benefits, for refineries and petrochemical plants, of varying the product mix of benzene, toluene, and xylene (BTX) in response to market demand. Data sources include Predicasts, Inc. and authors' estimates.

Includes technical data; 1 table showing world demand for benzene, toluene, and xylene, selected years 1960-95; and 2 tables illustrating technical and economic results of 2 methods of producing benzene under specified conditions.

C6985–1.528: May 14, 1984 (Vol. 82, No. 20)

WEEKLY TABLES

a. Industry scoreboard, for May 4, 1984. (p. 4)

b. Industry statistics, as of Apr. 27-May 9, 1984. (p. 148-149)

UN AGENCIES TALLY HEAVY OIL, BITUMEN RESERVES

(p. 66-67) Article presenting UN survey estimates of world reserves of heavy/extra heavy oil and of oil in bitumen deposits. Includes 1 undated table showing the following for both types of oil: original oil in place, proved reserves, and cumulative and annual production, by country and world area, with detail by Canadian Province and U.S. State.

EIA: N. AFRICAN NATIONS MUST PRESS EXPLORATION

(p. 70-71) Article, with 1 table showing discovered recoverable oil and cumulative oil output, for Libya, Algeria, and Egypt, as of 1981. Data are from Energy Information Administration.

Sii-DAC DRILLING ACTIVITY: FIRST QUARTER DRILLING BUCKS TREND, QUARTERLY FEATURE

(p. 106, 111-114) Quarterly report, by Randy Hall, on oil and gas drilling activity for 1st quarter 1984. Data are presented in terms of the Smith International, Inc. Drilling Activity Correlator, which distinguishes 3 types of drilling activity on the basis of technological sophistication.

Includes 1 chart and 3 tables showing wells and footage drilled by type, quarterly 1980-1st quarter 1984, with detail by region for 1st quarter 1984.

FIRST QUARTER DRILLING IN CANADA

(p. 134) Table on Canadian drilling activity, showing oil, gas, and service wells, dry holes, and total and exploratory wells and footage drilled, by Province and for East Coast offshore, 1st quarter 1984. Data are from *Nickle's Daily Oil Bulletin.*

C6985–1.529: May 21, 1984 (Vol. 82, No. 21)

WEEKLY TABLES

a. Industry scoreboard, for May 11, 1984. (p. 4)

b. Industry statistics, as of May 4-16, 1984. (p. 195-196)

MONTHLY TABLES

a. Industry statistics: total U.S. land and marine seismic crews, for Apr. 1984. (p. 187)

b. U.S. wells drilled, for Mar. 1984. (p. 190-191)

U.S. PRODUCTS DEMAND SEEN RISING 2.9% IN 1984, SEMIANNUAL FEATURE

(p. 69-70) Semiannual article presenting Independent Petroleum Assn of America forecast for crude oil and petroleum products supply and demand situation through 4th quarter 1984.

Includes 1 table showing the following: domestic demand for 6 petroleum products; total exports; domestic production for crude oil and natural gas liquids; imports of crude oil and 6 products; other supply; closing stocks of 6 products, unfinished oils, natural gas liquids, and crude oil; and crude runs to stills; quarterly 1984.

DRILLING, EQUIPPING COSTS DOWN 17.9% IN 1983, SEMIANNUAL FEATURE

(p. 71-72) Semiannual article presenting cost indexes for drilling and equipping oil/gas wells, by component, 1978-83. Data are from Independent Petroleum Assn of America. Includes 1 table.

WHITE HOUSE WANTS TO SLASH SFC FUNDS

(p. 78) Article, with 1 undated table showing project type and location, amount of aid, status of commitment, and type of guarantee, for synfuel projects receiving U.S. Synthetic Fuels Corp. (SFC) assistance. Data are from SFC.

OIL FIRMS WITHDRAW BIDS ON 11 SANTA MARIA BASIN TRACTS

(p. 84) Article reporting on withdrawal of bids from Federal sale of Outer Continental Shelf oil and gas lease tracts in Santa Maria Basin off California, held in 1981. Data are from Minerals Management Service of Dept of Interior.

Includes 1 table showing lease status and amount of bonus bid, for original high bidders on 19 tracts.

ONLY DEEP DRILLING LAGS IN MIDCONTINENT

(p. 100-103) By G. Alan Petzet. Article, with 1 table showing oil and gas well completions for Oklahoma and Kansas, 1979-83.

C6985–1.530: May 28, 1984 (Vol. 82, No. 22)

WEEKLY TABLES

a. Industry scoreboard, for May 18, 1984. (p. 4)

b. Industry statistics, as of May 11-21, 1984 (table [7] is omitted). (p. 154-156)

MONTHLY TABLES

a. Industry statistics: active rigs abroad, for Apr. 1984; Smith rig count, for May 18, 1984; and selected U.S. and world crude prices, for May 1984. (p. 155-156)

NPC SEES 14.5 BILLION bbl FROM EOR

(p. 56-57) Article, with 1 chart showing ultimate additions to oil reserves from enhanced oil recovery (EOR), by EOR method. Data are estimates from National Petroleum Council.

UK OIL, GAS RESOURCE ESTIMATES INCREASE IN '83

(p. 57) Article, with 1 table showing UK proved, probable, and possible oil/gas resources, for fields under production/development and for discoveries not fully appraised, estimated as of 1982-83. Data are from UK Dept of Energy.

PINCH CONCEPT HELPS TO EVALUATE HEAT-RECOVERY NETWORKS FOR IMPROVED PETROCHEM OPERATION

(p. 113-118) Article discussing application of pinch techniques for improving energy efficiency of heat exchanger networks during chemical processing. Includes 1 undated table showing chemical process involved, whether new or modified project, energy cost reduction per year, capital cost, and investment payback period, for 9 Union Carbide Corp. projects using pinch technology.

OGJ-MORGAN OIL PIPELINE COST INDEX: LINGERING RECESSION TRIMS OIL-PIPELINE-BUILDING COSTS, QUARTERLY FEATURE

(p. 119-122) Quarterly article, by Joseph M. Morgan, presenting oil pipeline construction cost indexes for 3rd quarter 1983 (1974=base year). Includes 2 tables showing indexes for 18 cost components, 1950-82 and 1st-3rd quarter 1983.

C6985–1.531: June 4, 1984 (Vol. 82, No. 23)

WEEKLY TABLES

a. Industry scoreboard, for May 25, 1984. (p. 4)

b. Industry statistics, as of May 18-30, 1984. (p. 91-92)

MONTHLY TABLES

a. Nelson Cost Indexes, for Jan. 1984. (p. 79)

b. U.S. wells drilled (total only), for Apr. 1984. (p. 88)

c. Industry statistics: worldwide crude oil and gas production, for Mar. 1984. (p. 93)

SPR: A GROWING CUSHION AGAINST SHOCK OF LOST U.S. CRUDE IMPORTS

(p. 25-30) By Patrick Crow. Article on status of Strategic Petroleum Reserve (SPR). Data are from DOE.

Includes 2 tables showing the following for SPR: sweet and sour crude oil stored as of May 1984, planned vs. actual storage capacity as of Mar. 1984, and initial drawdown capability by phase (1984, 1986, and 1990), for 6 storage sites; and crude oil stored, by country or State of origin, as of Jan. 1, 1984.

PROFITS JUMP FOR OGJ GROUP OF FIRMS, QUARTERLY FEATURE

(p. 42-43) Quarterly article on U.S. oil industry profits, 1st quarter 1984. Includes 2 tables showing net profits and revenues for 25 companies; and net income and capital/exploration expenditures for 14 companies; 1st quarter 1984, with percent change from 1983.

EIA: OIL PRICES WON'T REBOUND QUICKLY

(p. 48-49) Article, with 1 table showing energy production by type of energy, quinquennially 1973-83, and under 3 world oil price assumptions, 1990 and 1995. Data are from Energy Information Administration.

CATALYTIC GAS-SWEETENING PROCESS SELECTIVELY CONVERTS HYDROGEN SULFIDE TO SULFUR, TREATS ACID GAS

(p. 60-62) By L. C. Hardison. Article evaluating equipment and operating cost for a catalytic gas sweetening process allowing the conversion of hydrogen sulfide to solid sulfur. Includes 2 tables.

N.E. CALIFORNIA AREA DRAWING INTEREST

(p. 83-87) By Mark H. Alldredge and Joe V. Meigs. Article discussing oil and gas exploration in northeastern California. Data are from county records and State Bureau of Land Management. Includes 4 tables showing Federal and fee acreage held, and beginning date for lease acquisition programs, by company or individual lease holder, for 4 counties, as of Feb. 15, 1984.

C6985–1.532: June 11, 1984 (Vol. 82, No. 24)

WEEKLY TABLES

a. Industry scoreboard, for June 1, 1984. (p. 4)

b. Industry statistics, as of May 25-June 6, 1984. (p. 161-162)

1983 RESULTS SET STAGE FOR YEAR OF RECOVERY BY OGJ GROUP, ANNUAL FEATURE

(p. 43-48) Annual article, by Robert J. Beck and Glenda E. Smith, on financial condition and operations of 26 major and 20 smaller oil firms, 1983. Includes 1 summary table, and 3 detailed tables showing assets ranking and the following data by company, 1983 with comparisons to 1982:

a. Major companies: net profits, revenues, working capital, funds from operations, capital/exploration expenditures, percent return on stockholders' equity, assets, liquids and natural gas net production and estimated reserves, net wells drilled, crude runs to stills, and refined product sales.

b. Smaller companies: net profits, revenue, percent return on stockholders' equity, and assets.

NORTH SEA OIL FLOW HITS ALL-TIME HIGH

(p. 73-76) Article, with 1 table showing active rigs by type, for offshore northern Europe, monthly 1983-Apr. 1984. Data are from Wood Mackenzie.

C6985–1.533: June 18, 1984 (Vol. 82, No. 25)

WEEKLY TABLES

a. Industry scoreboard, for June 8, 1984. (p. 4)

b. Industry statistics, as of June 1-13, 1984. (p. 175-176)

SLIDE MAY RESUME FOR U.S. DEEP DRILLING, NOW STABLE AT 1980 LEVEL

(p. 73-78) By G. Alan Petzet. Article, with 1 table showing deep well drilling costs by type,

in Anadarko basin, various periods 1979-83. Data are from Parker Drilling Co. and Society of Petroleum Engineers.

COLOMBIA SEEKS MORE FOREIGN FIRMS

(p. 90-92) Article, with 1 chart and 1 table showing distribution and growth rate of Colombia's energy demand, by type of energy, various periods 1976-90. Data are from Empresa Colombiana de Petroleos (Ecopetrol).

SEVERANCE TAX IMPACT OFTEN MISREPRESENTED

(p. 133-137) By John Lohrenz. Article presenting an econometric analysis of the impact of selected severance tax rates on tax collections and on oil/gas exploration and development. Data are from author's estimates and scholarly articles. Includes 5 tables illustrating results of the analysis for 3 types of fields.

C6985–1.534: June 25, 1984 (Vol. 82, No. 26)

WEEKLY TABLES

a. Industry scoreboard, for June 15, 1984. (p. 4)

b. Industry statistics, as of June 8-20, 1984. (p. 130-132)

MONTHLY TABLES

a. Industry statistics: total U.S. land and marine seismic crews, for May 1984; Smith rig count, for June 15, 1984; and selected U.S. and world crude prices, for June 1984. (p. 127, 132).

b. U.S. wells drilled (exploratory only), for Apr. 1984. (p. 128)

MARKER PRICE SYSTEM SET UP FOR GULF COAST GAS

(p. 30) Article discussing use of marker (weighted average) natural gas prices as a basis for contract price escalator clauses. Data are compiled by Energy Planning Inc., based on State severance tax records. Includes 1 table showing Texas Gulf Coast wellhead marker prices, monthly 1983.

C6985–1.535: July 2, 1984 (Vol. 82, No. 27)

WEEKLY TABLES

a. Industry scoreboard, for June 22, 1984. (p. 4)

b. Industry statistics, as of June 15-25, 1984 (table [7] is omitted). (p. 82-83)

MONTHLY TABLES

a. Nelson Cost Indexes, for Feb. 1984. (p. 54)

b. Industry statistics: active rigs abroad, for May 1984; and worldwide crude oil and gas production, for Apr. 1984. (p. 83-84)

SALOMON BROS. JUMPS ESTIMATE OF U.S. UPSTREAM EXPENDITURES

(p. 41) Article, with 1 table showing exploration/production capital expenditures of 25 oil companies, actual 1983, and planned 1984. Data are from Salomon Bros., Inc.

PROBLEMS HINDER FULL USE OF OXYGENATES IN FUEL

(p. 59-65) By George H. Unzelman. Article discussing factors affecting use of oxygenates as gasoline blending agents. Includes 12 tables presenting technical data, and the following:

a. Capacity, location, and owner, for methyl tertiary butyl ether (MTBE) and methanol

plants, with process used at MTBE plants; and ethyl alcohol capacity, process used, and end uses, by major producer; (no dates).

b. Ethyl alcohol and methanol prices, various periods 1960-84; and octane improvement costs by method, and economic values associated with selected blending agents and gasoline types (no date).

QUARTERLY COSTIMATING: HOW NELSON INDEXES HAVE RISEN

(p. 66-67) Quarterly feature, by Gerald L. Farrar, on Nelson indexes of refinery operating, construction labor, and equipment and material costs. Includes 2 tables showing cost indexes for 6 refining chemicals or chemical types, quarterly 1980-83; and cost indexes by itemized component, and indexes of refinery inflation, operation, and process operation, selected years 1954-83 and Feb. 1984.

C6985–1.536: July 9, 1984 (Vol. 82, No. 28)

WEEKLY TABLES

a. Industry scoreboard, for June 29, 1984. (p. 4)

b. Industry statistics, as of June 22-July 4, 1984. (p. 135-136)

C6985–1.537: July 16, 1984 (Vol. 82, No. 29)

WEEKLY TABLES

a. Industry scoreboard, for July 6, 1984. (p. 4)

b. Industry statistics, as of June 29-July 11, 1984. (p. 155-156)

'WINDFALL' TAX REVENUES LAG ESTIMATES, ANNUAL FEATURE

(p. 32-33) Annual article, with 2 tables showing Federal receipts from windfall profits tax, as estimated at time of enactment for calendar and fiscal years 1980-90, and actual FY80-83 with detail by component.

GAS PROCESSING REPORT ANNUAL FEATURE

Annual report on worldwide developments in the natural gas processing industry. Includes the annual statistical features described below.

GAS-PROCESSING VOLUMES FIGHT BACK FROM VESTIGES OF WORLDWIDE RECESSION SLUMP

(p. 55-60) Annual article, by Ted Wett, on trends in world natural gas and natural gas liquids (NGL) processing, 1970s-84. Includes 8 tables showing the following:

a. U.S. NGL production, by product; U.S., Canadian, and rest of world gas throughput and proved reserves, and NGL production; and U.S. gas processing plants, throughput, capacity, and NGL production, by State, and installations by process; various years 1980-83.

b. World gas processing plants under construction/planned 1983-84, gas production 1976-83, and gas reserves as of Jan. 1, 1984, all by country or world area; and top 20 countries ranked by gas production, 1983.

WORLDWIDE GAS PROCESSING

(p. 80-117) Annual tabular presentation, compiled by Aileen Cantrell, of world gas processing facilities as of Jan. 1984. Includes 2 summary tables; and 1 extended table showing gas capacity, throughput, process method, and average daily production by type of product, all by company and plant, arranged by U.S. State, Canadian Province, and 33 other countries.

Other Articles

OGJ-MORGAN GAS PIPELINE COST INDEX: THIRD QUARTER BROKE INFLATION IN GAS-LINE BUILDING COSTS, QUARTERLY FEATURE

(p. 123-125) Quarterly article, by Joseph M. Morgan, presenting gas pipeline construction cost indexes for 3rd quarter 1983 (1976=base year).

Includes 4 tables showing indexes for 13 cost components, and composite index, 1978-82 and 1st-3rd quarters 1983; and total and offshore gas pipeline projects, length, and cost, with land and offshore cost comparisons, by pipe size, 3rd quarter 1983.

TEXAS COMPTROLLER'S DRILLING INDEX NEARS PAR

(p. 129-133) Article, with 1 table showing oil/gas industry employment by function, and total employment, for Texas compared to U.S., Jan. 1983. Data are from Texas Employment Commission and BLS.

C6985-1.538: July 23, 1984 (Vol. 82, No. 30)

WEEKLY TABLES

a. Industry scoreboard, for July 13, 1984. (p. 4)

b. Industry statistics, as of July 6-18, 1984. (p. 84-85)

MONTHLY TABLE

a. U.S. wells drilled (total only), for May 1984. (p. 82)

MORE GULF DEEPWATER TRACTS DRAW BIDS

(p. 24-26) Article reporting results of a Federal sale of Outer Continental Shelf oil and gas lease tracts in the Gulf of Mexico, held mid-July 1984. Data are from Minerals Management Service of Dept of Interior. Includes 1 table showing high bidder and cash bonus bid, for top 20 tracts.

API: LEASE BANS DENY PRODUCTION, FEDERAL REVENUES

(p. 26) Article, with 1 undated table showing Federal bonuses and royalties lost due to congressional moratoriums on Outer Continental Shelf leasing, for 7 areas. Data are from American Petroleum Institute.

EPA MOVING TO CUT GASOLINE LEAD LEVEL

(p. 28-29) Article estimating costs and benefits of an EPA proposal to lower gasoline lead content standards beginning in 1986. Data are from EPA. Includes 1 table showing cost, and value of benefits by type, in constant 1983 dollars, 1986-88.

EIA: SOUTH CHINA SEA AREA OIL OUTPUT COULD RISE

(p. 29) Article, with 1 table showing oil production, proved and indicated reserves, and estimated undiscovered resources, for Indonesia, Malaysia, Brunei, and Thailand, as of Jan. 1, 1983. Data are from Energy Information Administration (EIA).

DOE TO DETAIL OIL MINING/DRAINAGE PROJECTS

(p. 33) Article discussing a DOE study on the application of various mining methods at oil mining/drainage projects in 3 fields. Data are from DOE. Includes 1 undated table estimating resources, recoveries, capital cost, and revenue, by method, for each field.

WRITEOFF, DOWNSTREAM LOSS TRIM CANADIAN NET

(p. 40) Article, with 1 table summarizing revenue, costs, and net income, for Canadian petroleum industry, 1982-83. Data are from Canada's Petroleum Monitoring Agency.

C6985-1.539: July 30, 1984 (Vol. 82, No. 31)

WEEKLY TABLES

a. Industry scoreboard, for July 20, 1984. (p. 4)

b. Industry statistics, as of July 13-23, 1984 (table [7] is omitted). (p. 225-227)

MONTHLY TABLES

a. Industry statistics: total U.S. land and marine seismic crews, and active rigs abroad, for June 1984; Smith rig count, for July 20, 1984; and selected U.S. and world crude prices, for July 1984. (p. 214, 226-227)

1984 MIDYEAR REVIEW AND FORECAST, ANNUAL FEATURE

Annual feature, for 1984, on oil and gas industry supply-demand situation, covering exploration, production, imports, exports, and prices. Most data are from journal surveys and DOE. Includes the following annual statistical articles:

RECOVERY FROM WORST U.S. DRILLING SLUMP ON TRACK

(p. 123-132) Annual article, by John C. McCaslin, forecasting oil and gas well drilling activity in U.S. and Canada, by State and Province, 1984, with trends from 1982. Includes 4 tables showing the following:

a. Top independent companies' aggregate field and wildcat wells completed 1983-1st half 1984, and planned 2nd half 1984; and top 20 companies' aggregate wildcat wells drilled 1983 and planned 1984, and total wells drilled 1982-1st half 1984 and planned 2nd half 1984; all by State.

b. Field and wildcat wells and total footage to be completed, by State and Canadian Province, 1st half and full year 1984; and rotary rig peak, low, and average activity, 1st half 1983-84, by State and for Canada.

Data by State and for Canada are also shown for selected geographic subdivisions, including offshore.

U.S. DEMAND, IMPORTS TO RISE; PRODUCTION OFF SLIGHTLY

(p. 133-172) Annual article, by Robert J. Beck, on U.S. and worldwide oil supply and demand situation and outlook, 1970s-84. Includes 12 tables showing the following:

a. U.S.: refinery crude runs, input to distillation units, capacity, and utilization rate, 1978-84; stocks of crude oil and 7 refined products, 1982-84; and refiner crude acquisition cost, and retail gasoline and residential heating oil prices, 1976-84.

b. U.S.: oil supply and demand forecast, including demand by type of product, exports, imports, and stock change, all for PAD Districts 1-4 combined and 5; and crude runs and total input to stills, and refinery capacity and utilization rate; 1st half and 3rd-4th quarters 1984.

c. U.S. daily crude oil and refined product imports, by country of origin, 3-month average 1982-84; OPEC oil production and ceiling, by country, 1st half 1983 and/or 1984; and U.S. crude/condensate production by PAD district and State, 1st half 1983-84.

d. U.S. exports of refined products by type and of crude oil, 3-month average 1982-84; U.S. energy demand, by type of energy, 1982-84; and world crude oil prices of 7 OPEC and 4 non-OPEC countries, and domestic U.S. oil prices, Jan. 1982-84 and summer 1984.

e. U.S. GNP compared to total and oil energy consumption, selected years 1929-84; and world crude production, by country, 1st half 1983-84.

C6985-1.540: Aug. 6, 1984 (Vol. 82, No. 32)

WEEKLY TABLES

a. Industry scoreboard, for July 27, 1984. (p. 4)

b. Industry statistics, as of July 20-Aug. 1, 1984. (p. 89-90)

MONTHLY TABLES

a. Nelson Cost Indexes, for Mar. 1984. (p. 62)

b. Industry statistics: worldwide crude oil and gas production, for May 1984. (p. 91)

URALS CRUDE PRICE CUT COULD TROUBLE SOVIET TRADE EARNINGS

(p. 26-27) Article, with 1 table showing value of Soviet oil and gas exports, by country of destination and for total non-Communist and Communist world areas, 1982-83. Data are from Soviet Ministry of Foreign Trade.

IEA REDUCES PREDICTION OF WORLD OIL DEMAND

(p. 43) Article, with 1 table showing oil demand of non-Communist world, by supplier group (OECD, OPEC, non-OPEC developing countries, Eastern bloc net exports, and other), 1983, and projected for 1990 and 2000. Data are from International Energy Agency.

C6985-1.541: Aug. 13, 1984 (Vol. 82, No. 33)

WEEKLY TABLES

a. Industry scoreboard, for Aug. 3, 1984. (p. 4)

b. Industry statistics, as of July 27-Aug. 8, 1984. (p. 152-153)

HUGHES PREDICTS 12.2% GAIN IN U.S. ACTIVE RIGS NEXT YEAR

(p. 65) Article, with 1 table forecasting oil/gas active rigs, wells, footage, and cost, 1984-85. Data are from Hughes Tool Co.

OGJ-MORGAN OIL PIPELINE COST INDEX: 1983 WAS A SLUGGISH YEAR FOR OIL PIPELINE BUILDING COSTS, ANNUAL FEATURE

(p. 89-94) Annual article, by Joseph M. Morgan, presenting oil pipeline component and construction cost summary for 1983, with cost index trends from 1978. Includes 4 tables showing the following:

a. Pipeline cost indexes for 18 cost components and total composite index, annually 1978-82, and quarterly 1983.

b. Steel line pipe inventory mileage and tonnage, purchased tonnage, mill price, and average cost, with comparison to 1974 average cost, by pipe diameter; pipeline construction projects, length, cost range, and total cost, by pipe diameter; and number of steel storage tanks erected, capacity, weight, and cost, by tank type; all for 1983.

Sii-DAC DRILLING ACTIVITY: TREND TOWARD DEEPER DRILLING CONTINUES, QUARTERLY FEATURE

(p. 129-131) Quarterly report, by Randy Hall, on oil and gas drilling activity for 2nd quarter 1984. Data are presented in terms of the Smith International, Inc. Drilling Activity Correlator, which distinguishes 3 types of drilling activity on the basis of technological sophistication.

Includes 1 chart and 3 tables showing wells and footage drilled by type, quarterly 1983-2nd quarter 1984, with detail by region for 1st half 1983-84.

MIDCONTINENT RIFT: A FRONTIER OIL PROVINCE

(p. 144-150) By Carol Kindle Lee and S. Duff Kerr. Article, with technical data, and 1 table showing sediment thickness and ultimate reserves of gas and/or oil, for 7 geological rift basins worldwide, estimated as of various dates 1970-84. Data are from scholarly sources.

C6985–1.542: Aug. 20 1984 (Vol. 82, No. 34)

WEEKLY TABLES

a. Industry scoreboard, for Aug. 10, 1984. (p. 4)

b. Industry statistics, as of Aug. 3-15, 1984. (p. 146-147)

MONTHLY TABLE

a. U.S. wells drilled (exploratory only), for May 1984. (p. 143)

C6985–1.543: Aug. 27, 1984 (Vol. 82, No. 35)

WEEKLY TABLES

a. Industry scoreboard, for Aug. 17, 1984. (p. 4)

b. Industry statistics, as of Aug. 10-20, 1984 (table [7] is omitted). (p. 122-124)

MONTHLY TABLES

a. Industry statistics: active rigs abroad, for July 1984; Smith rig count, for Aug. 17, 1984; and selected U.S. and world crude prices, for Aug. 1984. (p. 123-124)

ECONOMIC RECOVERY GIVES BOOST TO PROFITS FOR OGJ GROUP OF FIRMS, QUARTERLY FEATURE

(p. 25-28) Quarterly article, by Robert J. Beck and Glenda E. Smith, on U.S. oil industry profits, 1st half 1984. Includes 2 tables showing net profits and revenues for 24 companies, and net income and capital/exploration expenditures for 12 companies, 2nd quarter and/or 1st half 1984, with percent change from 1983.

EXXON LEADS SPENDING IN MOBILE BAY LEASE SALE

(p. 30-31) Article reporting results of an Alabama sale of Outer Continental Shelf oil and gas lease tracts in State waters, held Aug. 14, 1984. Data are from Alabama Dept of Conservation and Natural Resources, and Minerals Management Service of Dept of Interior.

Includes 1 table showing winning bidder and amount of bonus, by tract.

U.S. TUBULAR GOODS INVENTORIES DROP, SEMIANNUAL FEATURE

(p. 52) Semiannual feature on oil country tubular goods (OCTG) supply and demand. Data are from Lone Star Steel Co. Includes 1 table showing OCTG inventories, by drilling region, Dec. 1983 and June 1984.

AUSSIE DRILLING SURGE MAY BE SHORT-LIVED, ANNUAL FEATURE

(p. 69-72) Annual article, by Keith Orchison, on oil exploration and development activity in Australia. Data are from Australian Petroleum Exploration Assn. Includes 1 chart showing Australian oil/gas new field discoveries, 1970-83.

SOLVENT DEHYDRATION SYSTEM CUTS ENERGY USE, IMPROVES DEWAXED OIL YIELD

(p. 84-86) By John M. Scalise et al. Article discussing potential benefits of a dehydration system as opposed to conventional steam stripping methods for removing solvent from refined petroleum products. Includes 2 tables illustrating operating costs and expected savings by item, for a typical unit using dehydration system, as of Apr. 1983.

C6985–1.544: Sept. 3, 1984 (Vol. 82, No. 36)

WEEKLY TABLES

a. Industry scoreboard, for Aug. 24, 1984. (p. 4)

b. Industry statistics, as of Aug. 17-29, 1984. (p. 114-115)

MONTHLY TABLES

a. Nelson Cost Indexes, for Apr. 1984. (p. 94)

b. U.S. wells drilled (total only), for June 1984. (p. 108)

c. Industry statistics: worldwide crude oil and gas production, for June 1984. (p. 116)

FIRST HALF WORLD OIL PRODUCTION REBOUNDS FROM LONG DECLINE, ANNUAL FEATURE

(p. 25-28) Annual article, by Robert J. Beck et al., reviewing world crude oil production trends through 1st half 1984. Includes 2 charts and 1 table showing oil production by world area, including aggregate Communist countries, and detail for OPEC by country, 1st half 1984 with percent change from 1st half 1983.

E&D SLUMP CALLED 'CYCLIC' IN INDONESIA

(p. 29-30) Article summarizing Indonesian energy exploration and development (E&D), with 1 table showing energy investments by purpose, consumption and exports by selected type of energy, and seismic survey activities, various periods 1981-89. Data are from Indonesia's Pertamina.

ASHLAND: CRUDE PRICES TO STAY WEAK

(p. 36-38) Article discussing energy supply and demand in the non-Communist world through 1990. Data are from Ashland Oil Inc.

Includes 4 tables showing price of Arab light crude oil, non-Communist world demand for energy by energy type, crude oil supply and demand (including OPEC supply), and product demand by type, various years 1973-83, and projected under selected assumptions, various years 1984-90; and crude oil reserves by non-Communist world area, as of Dec. 1982.

CAPACITY DOWN, PRODUCTION UP: Rx FOR ETHYLENE'S '84 OUTLOOK, ANNUAL FEATURE

(p. 55-59) Annual article, by Ted Wett, on world ethylene production capacity, 1984 and trends. Includes 2 tables showing: ethylene and co-product capacity, types of feedstocks and co-products, and location, by plant grouped by company and country, midyear 1984; and world ethylene capacity, by country and world area, midyear 1982-84.

OPTIMIZING AN ENTIRE OLEFINS PLANT PAYS OFF

(p. 74-78) By G. L. Funk and C. C. Kania. Article discussing potential benefits of using a simulation model to optimize all operations of an olefins plant. Includes technical data, and 1 table illustrating output, operating costs, income, and profit, for a typical plant with and without entire plant optimization.

C6985–1.545: Sept. 10, 1984 (Vol. 82, No. 37)

WEEKLY TABLES

a. Industry scoreboard, for Aug. 31, 1984. (p. 4)

b. Industry statistics, as of Aug. 24-Sept. 5, 1984. (p. 235-236)

MONTHLY TABLE

a. Industry statistics: total U.S. land and marine seismic crews, for July 1984. (p. 211)

OGJ 400, ANNUAL FEATURE

(p. 103-137) Annual article presenting financial and operating data for top 400 oil and gas producing companies, with rankings. Data are for 1983 company fiscal year, and are compiled by O&GJ. Contains narrative report and the following:

a. Top 10 companies ranked by rates of return on assets, revenues, and stockholders equity. 3 charts. (p. 104)

b. Name changes from 1983 OGJ 400; and top 10 companies ranked by amount of new reserves, with percent increase in reserves from previous year. 1 list and 1 chart. (p. 105-106)

c. Top 20 companies ranked by each of the 14 categories listed below. 7 tables. (p. 106-110)

d. Top 400 companies ranked by assets, also showing revenue, net income, stockholders equity, capital/exploratory spending, worldwide and U.S. liquids and natural gas production and reserves, and U.S. net wells drilled, all with rankings. 1 table. (p. 112-135)

e. Alphabetical index of companies. (p. 136-137)

This is the 2nd annual feature.

WORLD PETROLEUM-DERIVED SULFUR PRODUCTION, ANNUAL FEATURE

(p. 160-169) Annual feature, by Ailleen Cantrell, on worldwide petroleum-based sulfur recovery plant production and capacity. Contains 1 extended table showing sulfur source material and daily production and capacity, by plant arranged by company and country, 1983.

INTERNATIONAL SEISMIC CREW COUNT, RECURRING FEATURE

(p. 211) Recurring table showing land and marine seismic crews, for U.S., Canada, Mexico, and 5 world areas, 4th quarter 1983-1st quarter 1984. Data are from Society of Exploration Geophysicists.

C6985–1.546: Sept. 17, 1984 (Vol. 82, No. 38)

WEEKLY TABLES

a. Industry scoreboard, for Sept. 7, 1984. (p. 4)

b. Industry statistics, as of Aug. 31-Sept. 12, 1984. (p. 162-163)

MONTHLY TABLES

a. U.S. wells drilled, for June (exploratory wells), and for July (total wells), 1984. (p. 152, 158)

ARCO: BIG 'SUPERFUND' TAX DANGEROUS

(p. 61-63) Article estimating medium-term effects (2-5 years) on polypropylene and styrene production and trade resulting from increases in Federal "superfund" crude oil/chemical feedstocks tax. Estimates are based on 1982 data and were developed by Management Analysis Center, Inc., for Atlantic Richfield Co. Includes 6 charts.

PERU PUSHING NEW EXPLORATION PACTS

(p. 72-74) Article, with 1 table showing Peru's crude oil exploration and exploration/development spending, reserves, and production, for Petroperu (the national petroleum agency) and contracted operations, with detail by contractor and region, various periods 1979-84. Data are from Petroperu.

C6985–1.547: Sept. 24, 1984 (Vol. 82, No. 39)

WEEKLY TABLES

a. Industry scoreboard, for Sept. 14, 1984. (p. 4)

b. Industry statistics, as of Sept. 7-19, 1984. (p. 123-125)

MONTHLY TABLES

a. U.S. wells drilled (exploratory only). for July 1984. (p. 120)

b. Industry statistics: selected U.S. and world crude prices, for Sept. 1984; and Smith rig count, for Sept. 14, 1984. (p. 125)

COGENERATION SEEN BOOSTING GAS DEMAND, AIDING PROFITS IN PROCESSING

(p. 25-28) By Rick Hagar and Bob Williams. Article, with 1 table showing owner, and ranking by capacity, for 16 largest electric power cogeneration plants certified by FERC during 1980-83 period. Data are from FERC.

EIA REVISIONS ACCOUNT FOR U.S. RESERVES STABILITY, ANNUAL FEATURE

(p. 34-35) Annual article on Energy Information Administration oil and gas reserve estimates through 1983. Includes 1 table showing proved reserves, reserve adjustments and additions including discoveries, and production, for crude oil, natural gas, and natural gas liquids, various periods 1976-83.

MEXICO AIMS TO PRODUCE MORE, USE LESS ENERGY

(p. 42-43) Article discussing Mexico's national energy program for 1984-88. Data are from *Petroleos Mexicanos.*

Includes 2 tables showing the following, for Mexico: production, domestic sales, exports, and imports, generally for crude oil, natural gas, refined products by type, and petrochemical products, 1st half 1983-84; and planned production of crude oil, refined products by type, and natural gas and natural gas liquids, 1983 and projected for 1984 and 1985-88 period.

WOOD MACKENZIE SEES $10 BILLION IN NORTH SEA OUTLAYS

(p. 44) Article, with 1 table showing operating company, and estimated reserves of oil and/or gas, start-up date, and capital cost, for 14 development projects in the North Sea off UK expected to begin operation by 1995. Data are from Wood Mackenzie.

C6985–1.548: Oct. 1, 1984 (Vol. 82, No. 40)

WEEKLY TABLES

a. Industry scoreboard, for Sept. 21, 1984. (p. 4)

b. Industry statistics, as of Sept. 14-24, 1984 (table [7] is omitted). (p. 210-211)

MONTHLY TABLES

a. Nelson Cost Indexes, for May 1984. (p. 161)

b. Industry statistics: total U.S. land and marine seismic crews, and active rigs abroad, for Aug. 1984; and worldwide crude oil and gas production, for July 1984. (p. 189, 211-212)

CHI SEES DOUBLING OF WORLD CATALYST MARKET

(p. 98) Article, with 2 tables showing value of catalyst sales worldwide, by consuming sector, 1984; and distribution of sales by world area, quinquennially 1975-90. Data are from Chemical Hitech Inc., Paris.

ANNUAL DRILLING ISSUE

Annual compilation of articles discussing oil/gas drilling activity. Statistical articles are described below.

Previous compilation included only 1 article with nontechnical statistics (for description see SRI 1983 Annual, under C6985-1.446).

DRILLING STABILIZES AT SUSTAINABLE LEVEL WITH BROAD IMPROVEMENT DUE IN 1985, ANNUAL FEATURE

(p. 103-107) By W. D. Moore III. Article, with 1 chart and 1 table showing rotary rig count trends, 1940-88; and rig count, and wells and footage drilled, 1971-86.

A brief related article, with text data showing alternative drilling rig count forecasts, appears on p. 69.

API TO REVISE MONTHLY DRILLING REPORTS FOR BETTER CORRELATION

(p. 128-130) Article discussing American Petroleum Institute (API) planned revisions of data on drilling activity, beginning in Jan. 1985. Includes 2 tables comparing actual well completions with completions reported, various periods 1970-83.

A related article appears in the Oct. 15, 1984 issue; for description, see C6985-1.550 below. API reports are covered in SRI under A2575.

DRILLING INDEX SHOWS CONFIDENCE ON THE REBOUND, DESPITE LOWER-THAN-AVERAGE PROSPECTS

(p. 140-141) By Dale Craymer. Article discussing trends in Texas comptroller's drilling confidence index, a measure of oil/gas companies' willingness to invest in well exploration. Data are from Texas comptroller of public accounts.

Includes 2 tables showing drilling confidence index, quarterly 1977-2nd quarter 1984; and drilling index compared to current oil price and oil price expected for 1983-85, for 4th quarter 1981 and 2nd quarter 1983.

Other Article

QUARTERLY COSTIMATING: HOW INDEXES HAVE RISEN

(p. 162-163) Quarterly feature, by Gerald L. Farrar, on Nelson indexes of refinery operating, construction labor, and equipment and material costs. Includes 2 tables showing cost indexes for overall refinery fuel and 6 fuel items, quarterly 1980-83; and cost indexes by itemized component, and indexes of refinery inflation, operation, and process operation, selected years 1954-83 and May 1984.

C6985–1.549: Oct. 8, 1984 (Vol. 82, No. 41)

WEEKLY TABLES

a. Industry scoreboard, for Sept. 28, 1984. (p. 4)

b. Industry statistics, as of Sept. 21-Oct. 3, 1984. (p. 115-116)

BIG POTENTIAL SEEN IN U.K. NORTH SEA

(p. 32-33) Article discussing potential oil and gas development in UK North Sea to 2000. Data are from UK Offshore Operators Assn.

Includes 2 tables showing capital and operating spending (in constant 1984 British pounds) required for new oil and gas field development, at selected development levels, cumulatively mid 1980s-2000; and aggregate future reserves and distribution of fields, by field size range (no date).

INTERFACIAL SPREADING AGENTS AID CYCLIC STEAM PRODUCTION

(p. 90-94) By Charles M. Blair, Jr., et al. Article comparing production and economic results of chemically treated vs. steam-only cyclic methods of enhanced oil recovery. Data are based on results from 44 wells. Includes 4 tables.

C6985–1.550: Oct. 15, 1984 (Vol. 82, No. 42)

WEEKLY TABLES

a. Industry scoreboard, for Oct. 5, 1984. (p. 4)

b. Industry statistics, as of Sept. 28-Oct. 10, 1984. (p. 163-164)

NEW PROCEDURE ELIMINATES LAG IN WELL-COMPLETION REPORTS

(p. 95-100) By William Trapmann et al. Article discussing effects of reporting lags on drilling activity data compiled by American Petroleum Institute (API). Presents a statistical model for adjusting data to account for lags. Data are from DOE, based on statistics from API and Hughes Tool Co.

Includes 3 tables showing rotary rigs in operation, wells drilled by type, and footage drilled, 1973-Feb. 1984, with monthly detail for 1982-84; and reporting lags and related statistical analysis.

A related article appears in the Oct. 1, 1984 issue; for description, see C6985-1.548 above.

SCRUBBING CARBON DIOXIDE FROM PLANT EXHAUSTS PROVIDES ECONOMIC SOURCES OF GAS FOR EOR PROJECTS

(p. 112-124) By R. T. Ellington et al. Article discussing economic and operational feasibility of recycling carbon dioxide from plant exhausts for use in enhanced oil recovery projects, 1980s-2000. Data are from DOE and University of Oklahoma. Includes 4 tables.

OGJ-MORGAN GAS PIPELINE COST INDEX: 1983 TURNED OUT TO BE A COMPETITIVE YEAR FOR NATURAL-GAS PIPELINE CONSTRUCTION COSTS, QUARTERLY FEATURE

(p. 128-134) Quarterly article, by Joseph M. Morgan, presenting gas pipeline construction cost indexes for 4th quarter 1983 (1976=base year).

Includes 5 tables showing indexes for 13 cost components, and composite index, 1979-82 and quarterly, 1983; steel pipe inventory and estimated cost in 1983, and average cost in 1976, by pipe size; and total and offshore gas pipeline projects, length, and cost, with cost comparison for land projects, by pipe size, 1983.

C6985–1.551: Oct. 22, 1984 (Vol. 82, No. 43)

WEEKLY TABLES

a. Industry scoreboard, for Oct. 12, 1984. (p. 4)

b. Industry statistics, as of Oct. 5-17, 1984. (p. 163-164)

SALE OFF CALIFORNIA DRAWS LITTLE INTEREST

(p. 64-65) Article reporting results of a Federal sale of Outer Continental Shelf oil and gas lease tracts off southern California, held Oct. 1984. Data are from Minerals Management Service of Dept of Interior. Includes 1 table showing high bidder, apparent high bonus bid, and bid per acre, by tract.

INDEPENDENT SECTOR SLOWLY RECOVERING, ANNUAL FEATURE

(p. 87-93) Annual article, by Jim West and Glenda E. Smith, on the financial condition and exploration activities of independent oil and gas drilling companies, with comparisons to major companies. Data sources include Census Bureau, company reports, and O&GJ. Includes 3 charts and 3 tables showing the following:

a. Net profits and revenues for 226 independent companies ranked by profits, 1st half 1984 with percent change from 1983.

b. Fixed field assets; crude oil/condensate and natural gas production and revenue; royalty/other production revenue; expenditures for exploration, development, and production; and wells and footage drilled, and expenditures, by well type; with detail by company size, including aggregate 8 largest, 9-32 largest, and all other companies, 1982.

c. Natural gas and crude oil price comparisons for 27 independent companies, 1983-84; and crude oil windfall profits tax for 17 independent companies, 1st half and 2nd quarter 1983-84.

C6985–1.552: Oct. 29, 1984 (Vol. 82, No. 44)

WEEKLY TABLES

a. Industry scoreboard, for Oct. 19, 1984. (p. 4)

b. Industry statistics, as of Oct. 12-22, 1984 (table [7] is omitted). (p. 137-139)

MONTHLY TABLES

a. Industry statistics: total U.S. land and marine seismic crews, for Sept. 1984; active rigs abroad, for Sept. 1984; Smith rig count, for Oct. 19, 1984; and selected U.S. and world crude prices, for Oct. 1984. (p. 128, 138-139)

SLIGHT GAIN SEEN FOR U.S. OIL DEMAND, SEMIANNUAL FEATURE

(p. 29-30) Semiannual article presenting Independent Petroleum Assn of America forecast for crude oil and petroleum product supply and demand situation through 4th quarter 1985. Includes 2 tables showing the following:

a. Domestic demand for 6 petroleum products; total exports; domestic production for crude oil and natural gas liquids; imports of crude oil and 6 products; other supply; closing stocks of 6 products, unfinished oils, natural gas liquids, and crude oil; and crude runs to stills; quarterly 1985.

b. Energy consumption, by type of energy, 1983-85.

INDEX PINPOINTS DRILLING/COMPLETION COST SLIDE, SEMIANNUAL FEATURE

(p. 30-31) Semiannual article presenting cost indexes for drilling and equipping oil/gas wells, and including annual data on tubular goods consumption and oil/gas well drilling activity. Data sources include Independent Petroleum Assn of America. Includes 2 tables showing the following:

a. Drilling and equipping cost indexes, by component, 1973-83.

b. Tubular goods shipments, exports, and imports; active rigs; wells and footage drilled; and stacked and active rotary rigs; annually 1973-83, and Jan. 1983 and July 1984.

STEADY RISE IN REAL GAS PRICES NECESSARY TO TRIGGER ENOUGH DRILLING TO MAINTAIN RESERVE LEVELS

(p. 64-66) By Edward Symonds. Article, with 3 tables showing average annual percent change in non-Communist world natural gas production, for U.S. and 5 world areas, 1984-90 and 1990-2000 periods; and domestic gas well completions and footage drilled, by State and for Outer Continental Shelf, 1979-84.

Data are from Chevron, American Petroleum Institute, and Energy Economics and Finance.

WORLDWIDE CONSTRUCTION, SEMIANNUAL FEATURE

(p. 87-118) Semiannual list, by Aileen Cantrell, of worldwide construction for refineries, petrochemicals, sulfur, gas processing, related fuels, and pipelining projects, showing the following data, where available, for each: capacity, contractor, estimated costs, and completion date. Listings are by company arranged by country, for each project type.

C6985–2   OFFSHORE

Monthly. Approx. 175 p.
ISSN 0030-0608.
LC 67-3959.
SRI/MF/not filmed

Monthly trade journal (semimonthly in July) reporting on offshore oil and gas exploration, production, transportation, and finance. Also includes trends in related scientific research, engineering and construction, and equipment manufacturing.

Data are from *Offshore* surveys of producers and operators, Electronic Rig Stats, and private and Federal sources.

Issues generally contain feature articles, often focusing on a single industry aspect or area, and occasionally including statistics; narrative editorial depts; and monthly offshore rig report, with the following statistics:

a. Number of mobile rigs working, idle, and en route, by country or world area; and rigs under construction, by type. 1 table.

b. Top 5 petroleum companies ranked by number of working rigs; and rigs in use by water depth. 2 charts.

Rig report data are current to month prior to cover date; table includes comparisons to previous year. Charts begin in the Sept. 1984 issue. Prior to July 1984, report also included 1 chart showing rig trends for 5-8 previous years.

Annual statistical features include tabulations of offshore platform construction projects, offshore drilling support vessels, deepwater drilling activity, and worldwide drilling and production trends.

Prior to Aug. 1984, journal also presented a monthly summary of mobile rig activity, including utilization rates. Prior to Nov. 1983, journal also presented a quarterly descriptive listing of rigs by country or area, and rigs on order by type.

Monthly offshore rig report appears in all issues. All additional features with substantial statistical content are described, as they appear, under "Statistical Features." Nonstatistical features are not covered.

Availability: Offshore, Circulation Department, PO Box 1260, Tulsa OK 74101, qualified subscribers †, selected others $45.00 per yr., single copy $3.00; SRI/MF/not filmed.

Issues reviewed during 1984: Nov. 1983-Oct. 1984 (P) (Vol. 43, Nos. 13-14; Vol. 44, Nos. 1-11).

STATISTICAL FEATURES:

C6985–2.501: Nov. 1983 (Vol. 43, No. 13)

PLATFORM ORDERS DROP; NORTH SEA INCREASES, ANNUAL FEATURE

(p. 59-72) Annual *Offshore* survey report on offshore oil and gas platform projects under construction, planned, and under study worldwide, 1983. Includes brief narrative, and 1 detailed list showing platform name, location, fabricator, type, design characteristics, status, and installed date, by operating company and world area.

C6985–2.502: Jan. 1984 (Vol. 44, No. 1)

NEW LEASES SPUR GULF RIG ACTIVITY

(p. 51-52) By Leonard A. LeBlanc. Article reporting on petroleum exploration activity in the Gulf of Mexico, 1983. Data are from Offshore Oil Scouts Assn. Includes text data, 1 map, and 1 table showing exploratory and development wells drilled by area, discoveries, platforms installed, and seismic crew-weeks, 1st half 1983.

STEEL TRIPOD PLATFORM FAVORED IN 300-METER PRODUCTION COMPARISON

(p. 54-58) Article, with 1 table comparing investment costs for 5 types of deepwater production systems, for a hypothetical deepwater oil discovery. Data are from a paper presented by the Italian company, AGIP, at the Deep Offshore Technology Conference, Oct. 1983.

PLATFORM RIG MARKET DUE RECOVERY, ANNUAL FEATURE

(p. 68-75) Annual *Offshore* survey report on the status of platform drilling rigs worldwide, as of Jan. 1984. Includes tabular list showing operator, location, drilling capacity, and work status, by drilling company and rig, grouped by country or world area; and list of rigs under construction.

C6985–2.503: Feb. 1984 (Vol. 44, No. 2)

AUSTRALIA BEGINS '84 ON BETTER NOTE

(p. 51-57) By Keith Orchison. Article, with 2 tables showing Australian total and offshore petroleum resources by type, with offshore resources by basin, as of Dec. 31, 1982; and offshore exploration and development wells and depth completed, and seismic activity, 1977-1st 9 months 1983. Data are from Australia Petroleum Exploration Assn.

C6985–2.504: Mar. 1984 (Vol. 44, No. 3)

NEAR TERM BRIGHTENS FOR BOAT MARKET

(p. 42-43) By Eldon R. Ball. Article, with 1 table showing number of offshore drilling support vessels worldwide, by type, 1984.

WORKBOAT NUMBERS DECLINE AS SLOWDOWN CONTINUES, ANNUAL FEATURE

(p. 52-73) Annual listing, for 1984, of offshore drilling support vessels in operation and under construction. Data are from an *Offshore* worldwide survey of 383 vessel-operating firms.

Covers tugboats, crew ships, and other types of workboats. Shows number of vessels, design specification, and (for vessels under construction only) shipyard location, delivery date, and estimated value (when available); all by vessel type and operating company.

C6985–2.505: Apr. 1984 (Vol. 44, No. 4)

MOBILE BAY HURT BY TAXES, REGULATIONS

(p. 33-38) By Jim Redden. Article on natural gas lease sales and drilling activity in State coastal waters of Alabama. Data are from Alabama Dept of Conservation and Natural Resources.

Includes 2 tables showing the following by tract and State lease number: currently leased tracts, with acreage, lessee, sale date, bonus, royalty percent, and annual rental per acre; and wells drilled, with operator, completion date, depth, and working status; as of 1984.

C6985–2.506: May 1984 (Vol. 44, No. 5)

MIDYEAR REPORT, ANNUAL FEATURE

(p. 81-142) Annual compilation of articles on operational developments in the offshore energy industry, as of mid-1984. Data sources include Federal, State, and foreign governments, and private companies and journals. Articles with substantial statistical content are described below. Data content of most annual articles in this feature varies from year to year.

U.S. OIL TO DECLINE, OPEC RISE, ANNUAL FEATURE

(p. 81-94) Annual article on outlook for U.S. and world oil supply, demand, and prices. Includes 5 tables showing the following:

a. U.S. energy demand by type of energy, 1973-90, and energy consumption vs. GNP, 1973-85; and world oil consumption and production by country or country group, including OPEC, 1979-84; shown for selected years within the ranges noted.

b. U.S. oil and gas reserves added, production, and costs, for 10 major and 10 independent companies, 1980-82 period; and production of oil/gas liquids and natural gas, aggregated for 10 largest and all other companies, 1978-83.

OFFSHORE DRILLING TO INCREASE IN 1984, ANNUAL FEATURE

(p. 96-108) Annual article forecasting world oil exploration for 1984. Includes 1 table showing completions of offshore exploratory/appraisal and development wells, by country and world region, 1983-84.

OFFSHORE PRODUCTION MAKES SIGNIFICANT GAINS

(p. 110-119) Article, with 3 tables showing world offshore oil production, by country and world region, 1983-84; Gulf of Mexico oil/condensate production in Federal, Louisiana, and Texas waters, various years 1954-83; and discovery date, production 1983, cumulative production as of Jan. 1984, and estimated reserves, for individual giant crude oil fields in Gulf of Mexico.

SUBSEA SYSTEMS PLAY ROLE IN PRODUCTION

(p. 122-125) Article, with 1 map and 1 table showing world offshore and total daily average crude oil production, 1979-84, with offshore detail by world area, 1983.

BRIGHT SPOTS, BUT OVERSUPPLY IS THE CONCERN, ANNUAL FEATURE

(p. 126-132) Annual article on demand for support craft for the offshore drilling industry. Includes 1 chart and 1 table showing index of support vessel charter rates, 1972-82; and top 15 offshore supply boat companies ranked by fleet size, and also including headquarters location, 1982.

MERGER ACTIVITY, DEEPWATER LEASING BRIGHTEN DIVING PICTURE

(p. 132-139) Article, with 1 undated table summarizing operating characteristics and cost ranges for typical manned diving methods, by type.

SEISMIC ACTIVITY RECOVERING SLOWLY; EQUIPMENT MAKERS STILL GLOOMY, ANNUAL FEATURE

(p. 141-142) Annual article on trends in marine seismic energy exploration activity. Includes 1 text table showing seismic vessels operated by contractors and oil firms in U.S. waters, as of Feb. 1978-84.

Other Article

NORWAY: TECHNOLOGY EXPORT ADDS MARKETS FOR INDUSTRY

(p. 231-232) Article, with 1 table showing oil industry share of GDP, export earnings, total taxes, and employment, for Norway, 1977-82.

C6985–2.507: June 1984 (Vol. 44, No. 6)

DEEPWATER DRILLING EXPECTED TO INCREASE, ANNUAL FEATURE

(p. 68-86) Annual article, by Roger Tanner, on world deepwater oil and gas drilling activity and outlook. Data are from *Offshore* and Electronic Rig Stats.

Includes 2 tables showing status, type, name, and other operating data for 18 rigs with rated water depths of 3,000 feet or more, as of May 1984; and deepwater drill barges, drillships, and semisubmersibles, by rated water depth (no date).

Also includes annual list of worldwide deepwater wells drilled or planned, 1982-86, and development wells drilled, 1982-83, with operator and rig name, well location, and depth.

C6985–2.508: July 1984 (Vol. 44, No. 7)

ALASKA FIELDS TO BE COSTLY

(p. 29-34) By Marvin Feldman and William Wade. Article, with 2 tables illustrating oil development possibilities for 5 Bering Sea basins, as follows: lease sale dates; oil resources; peak annual production; and capital investment requirements for offshore facilities, ships, and terminals, by type; for 1983-87 lease sales. Data are from Dames and Moore.

JAPAN'S BUILDERS STUDY PLATFORMS

(p. 36-37) By Robert G. Burke. Article, with 1 table showing offshore drilling rigs built in Japan by type, 1974-79 and 1979-83 periods.

C6985–2.509: July 20, 1984 (Vol. 44, No. 8)

DAY RATE ASSUMPTIONS

(p. 5) Table showing day rate ranges for offshore mobile rigs in moderate and severe environments, by rig type, 1980/81, 1984, and 1987, and also showing estimated replacement cost. Data are from Smith Barney, Harris Upham and Co. Table is accompanied by a brief narrative.

INDUSTRY TURNS TO OFFSHORE FOR GAINS IN PRODUCTION

(p. 11) Article, with 1 table showing offshore oil production for 9 major producing countries, with comparison to total offshore production and world demand, quinquennially 1970-85.

WORLDWIDE EXPLORATION, ANNUAL FEATURE

Annual compilation of articles on offshore oil and gas exploration, development, and production, for selected countries or world areas. Articles with substantial statistical content are described below.

GULF OF MEXICO: DRILLERS TARGET CENTRAL LOUISIANA TRACTS, ANNUAL FEATURE

(p. 45-51) Annual article, by Leonard A. LeBlanc, on Gulf of Mexico oil and gas leasing and exploration activity, 1983. Data are primarily from Offshore Oil Scouts Assn. Includes text data and 2 tables on Louisiana, Texas, and Florida oil and gas drilling activity, and depth of individual Texas and Louisiana discoveries, 1983; and 4 tables showing the following for total Gulf of Mexico, 1983:

a. Liquids and gas production, exploration and development wells, wildcat success ratio, discoveries, platforms installed and removed, seismic crew-weeks, and acreage leased.

b. Production and remaining reserves for 7 large crude oil fields; wildcat, field wildcat, and field deep wells; and location, operator, slots, and depth, for new platforms.

OFFSHORE CRUDE, GAS PRODUCTION INCREASE, ANNUAL FEATURE

(p. 52-58) Annual article, with 3 tables showing offshore gas and daily average oil production by world area and/or country, and world total offshore/onshore daily average oil production, 1979-83; and number of oil/gas wells by country, 1979-84.

NORTH SEA DUE DRILLING, FABRICATION GAINS

(p. 60-63) Article, with 1 table showing oil/gas exploration/appraisal wells drilled in the North Sea, by 5 countries, 1982-84.

EXPLORATION SLOWS OFFSHORE AFRICA

(p. 73) Article, with 1 table showing offshore oil wells drilled by 11 African countries, 1982-84.

BRAZIL PUSHES PRODUCTION UP AGAIN

(p. 78-81) Article, with 1 table showing oil/gas exploration and development wells and aggregate meters drilled, for offshore Brazil, 1979-83.

MEXICO REDUCES OPERATIONS TO MINIMUM

(p. 82) Article, with 1 text table showing offshore oil/gas exploratory, development, and service wells drilled, for Mexico, 1983.

JAPAN PROVIDES FUNDS, ENCOURAGES WORLDWIDE OIL SEARCH

(p. 90-94) Article, with 2 tables showing number of foreign exploration, development, and production wells in which Japan holds interest, by world region; and Japanese onshore and offshore wells and exploration investment (in yen); 1980-82.

C6985–2.510: Aug. 1984 (Vol. 44, No. 9)

INDUSTRY CHANGES

(p. 6) Brief article, with 1 table showing drilling rigs outside the U.S., for Canada, 5 world areas, and total onshore and offshore, 1983-85. Data are from Smith Barney, Harris Upham and Co.

NORTH SEA REPORT: MARGINAL FIELD IMPORTANCE GROWS

(p. 53-56) By Roger Tanner. Article, with 1 undated table showing estimated recoverable reserves, water depth, year on stream, and transport method, for 34 marginal oil/gas fields producing or under development in the North Sea.

C6985–2.511: Sept. 1984 (Vol. 44, No. 10)

ROV ROLE GROWS AS DEPTHS INCREASE

(p. 43-57) By Jim Redden. Article discussing use of remotely operated vehicles (ROV) in offshore oil/gas exploration. Includes worldwide directories for the following: ROV contractors, with number of ROVs in fleet and in use, and expansions planned, by model, for each contractor (no dates); and ROV manufacturers, with specifications by model.

OPERATORS SEE FUTURE IN GULF DEPTHS

(p. 80) Article on area-wide Outer Continental Shelf lease sales in the Gulf of Mexico, with 1 table showing bids submitted, rejected, and accepted; tracts receiving bids; tracts by depth; and value of high bids; by Gulf region and sale date, 1983-84. Data are from Minerals Management Service of Dept of Interior.

A related article (p. 9) includes 1 table presenting summary data and also showing aggregate tract acreage for each lease sale.

C6985–2.512: Oct. 1984 (Vol. 44, No. 11)

WORLD OFFSHORE: ALABAMA

(p. 13-14) Article on State sale of oil/gas leases for Outer Continental Shelf tracts in Mobile Bay off Alabama, Aug. 1984. Includes 1 table showing high bidder and bonus bid, for 19 blocks.

C6985–3   INTERNATIONAL PETROLEUM ENCYCLOPEDIA, 1984

Annual. 1984. 410 p.
ISBN 0-87814-256-8.
LC 77-76966.
SRI/MF/excerpts

Annual compilation, for 1984, of information on the world petroleum industry. Includes detailed data on oil exploration, production, refining, reserves, consumption, and industry finances. Also includes data on natural gas and pipelines.

Most data are shown by country, with selected detail for individual U.S. States, Canadian Provinces, companies, and fields. Data are shown primarily for 1970s-84, with selected historical trends, and projections to 1995.

Data are based primarily on reports of industry trade assns and major companies, and government agencies.

Contents:

a. Contents listing, index to maps, and subject index (p. 2-3); and special analysis on less developed countries' oil production and consumption, with 3 maps/charts and 4 tables. (p. 4-29).

b. Atlas section, detailing petroleum industry developments by world region and country, with narrative, text data, maps, 15 charts, and 6 tables. (p. 30-245)

c. Index to oil fields covered in atlas. (p. 247)

d. Articles on seismic technology, offshore California and other operations, OPEC, U.S. strategic petroleum reserve, pipelines, and tankers, interspersed with statistical sections on world oil production, oil rigs and wells, consumption, refining, and major company finances, with 12 charts and 44 tables. (p. 248-395)

e. Directory of foreign and U.S. oil agencies and trade assns, by country; statistical section on gas processing, with 2 tables; and conversion measures. (p. 396-408)

All tables, and charts presenting substantial data not covered in tables, are described below.

This is the 17th edition of the *Encyclopedia*.
Availability: PennWell Publishing Co., PO Box 1260, Tulsa OK 74101, $65.00; SRI/MF/excerpts for all tables and charts described below.

TABLES AND CHARTS:

C6985–3.1: Special Analysis and Atlas
SPECIAL ANALYSIS

a. Less developed countries: oil and gas production, consumption, and investments, for all and oil-importing developing countries; World Bank energy project loans, and number of financed projects, by energy type; and effect of $28 per barrel oil price on oil import value and volume, for 12 countries; various periods 1970-95. 4 tables. (p. 13-14, 27)

ATLAS

U.S.

b. Oil supply and demand; active rigs, and wells by depth, for oil and gas; and new field discoveries by size; various periods 1974-83. 1 chart and 2 tables. (p. 30-31)

c. Reserve additions from exploratory drilling, aggregated for 23 major companies and compared to total industry, 1980-82; refinery capacity, selected years 1978-84, and projected refinery needs, 1985 and 1990, both by process; and potential onshore and offshore gas supply, by region. 1 chart and 2 tables. (p. 39-40)

Canada and PRC

d. Canada: gas export volume requested and approved by the National Energy Board, by company, Jan. 1983. 1 table. (p. 76)

e. PRC: number of offshore drilling areas under contract, and active rigs, by location, 1983-85. 1 table. (p. 242)

C6985–3.2: Seismic Technology and Offshore California

a. Land and marine seismic crews operating, and crew months of geophysical exploration, by country or world area, various years 1956-83. 2 tables. (p. 250-252)

b. California offshore well operators, water and well depths, and well status, for tracts sold in 2 recent sales of offshore property in the Santa Maria basin (no date). 1 table. (p. 256)

C6985–3.3: Worldwide Production and Consumption

a. World oil and gas proved reserves, and crude oil refining capacity by process, Jan. 1, 1984; oil producing wells, July 1, 1983, and average daily production, 1983 and change from 1982; and number of refineries (no date); all by country and world region. 1 table. (p. 264-265)

b. Foreign fields: discovery date; depth; number of wells by type; and cumulative production through, and average daily production during, 1st half 1983; all by field, generally grouped by company within each foreign country. 1 table. (p. 266-285)

c. U.S. fields: discovery date; number of wells; production during, and cumulatively through, 1983; and estimated remaining reserves; by U.S. field grouped by State. 1 table. (p. 285-287)

d. Rigs active, 1976-83, with 1981-83 detail for land and offshore rigs; and well completions (total and wildcat oil, gas, and dry wells, and total footage), 1982; all by country and world region. 2 tables. (p. 288-291)

e. U.S. well drilling and producing depth records, including owner and location, various years 1930-83. 2 tables. (p. 292-295)

f. Gas production, by country and world region, 1983. 1 table. (p. 296)

C6985-3.4: OPEC and U.S. Strategic Petroleum Reserve

a. OPEC current account balances, by country, 1980-83; U.S. oil imports from OPEC and other sources, and share of total consumption, selected years 1973-82; OPEC production quotas 1983, and maximum sustainable and available capacities 1982, by country; and world consumption of OPEC and non-OPEC oil, and other energy resources by type, 1979 and 1981-83. 1 chart and 3 tables. (p. 310-314)

b. Strategic Petroleum Reserve (SPR) underground storage capacity available and filled, by storage site, as of Jan. 1, 1984; and SPR crude oil imports, by country of origin, as of Jan. 1, 1984. 4 tables. (p. 318-322)

C6985-3.5: Production Trends and Refining Capacity

PRODUCTION TRENDS

a. Average daily and annual oil production, selected years 1940-83, and consumption, 1980-82, by country and world region. 2 tables. (p. 323-327)

REFINING CAPACITY

b. Average daily and annual refining capacity, by country and world region, selected years 1940-84; crude oil, catalytic cracking, and catalytic reforming capacities by individual refinery, arranged by country and company, with summary data by country and detail for U.S. States and Canadian Provinces, as of Jan. 1, 1984. 5 tables. (p. 328-345)

c. Middle East export-oriented refinery capacity, by process, by country and company (no date). 1 table. (p. 349)

C6985-3.6: Pipelines and Tankers

a. Pipeline construction in non-Communist countries, for gas, crude, and product pipelines by size, by country or world area, 1984 and planned; U.S. interstate gas and liquids pipeline mileage, 1972-82; liquids pipeline investment by item, for 5 unnamed companies, 1982; and U.S. construction costs, by category, for onshore pipelines by size, FY74-83, and for onshore and offshore pipelines and compressor stations by location, 1982/83. 7 tables. (p. 369-378)

b. Tankers (very large crude carriers): world fleet and tonnage size, Oct. 1983; deliveries and number lost by reason, 1969-73; laid up by type of ownership, by duration (no date); conversions by type, with year built and tonnage, 1982-83; tonnage used for storage, quarterly 1981-2nd quarter 1983; and single point mooring facilities, with owner, maximum vessel size accommodated, water depth, and year built, arranged by country, 1983. 6 tables. (p. 383-392)

C6985-3.7: Major Companies, Gas Processing, and Reserves

MAJOR COMPANIES

a. Capital/exploration expenditures, natural gas and net crude oil/natural gas liquids production, refined product sales, crude runs to stills, and net income and gross operating revenue, for 25-29 individual companies, mostly 1975-82. 6 tables. (p. 393-395)

GAS PROCESSING AND RESERVES

b. Gas plants, capacity, and throughput, as of Jan. 1, 1983; average daily production by product type, 1982; and oil and gas reserves, selected years 1974-84; all by country, with detail for world regions, U.S. States, and Canadian Provinces. 2 tables. (p. 406-407)

C7000
Penton/IPC

C7000-1   PRECISION METAL: 1983 State of the Industry Report
Monthly (selected issue).
Nov. 1983. (p. 25-60).
Vol. 41, No. 11.
ISSN 0032-714X.
SRI/MF/excerpts

Annual survey report, by Michael Sheehan and Patricia Hochwarth, on 7 metalforming industries, covering shipments, equipment, and employment, mostly for 1983, with comparisons to 1982 and equipment plans for 1984. Industries covered are die casting, extrusion, forging, investment casting, powder metallurgy, roll forming, and stamping.

Presents various operating data for each industry, including average plant employment and shipments; shipment volume and trend, by metal; equipment census, age and condition, and purchase and rebuild plans; custom vs. captive business; origin or source of machinery and tooling (inhouse or other); and future expansion plans.

Also includes data on end-use markets for extrusion shipments; raw material consumption and sources, for roll forming and stamping industries; and selected general economic indicators relevant to metal forming industries, including metal products GNP, 1981 and 1985.

Most data are from *Precision Metal* annual industry survey.

Contains introduction, with 4 tables (p. 25-29); and 43 charts and 40 tables with accompanying narrative, arranged in 7 industry sections (p. 30-60).

Precision Metal is a monthly periodical reporting trends and developments in metalworking industries and does not normally contain substantial statistics. The annual industry survey is the only feature described by SRI.

Availability: Precision Metal, PO Box 95795, Cleveland OH 44114, qualified subscribers †, others $30.00 per yr., single copy $4.00; SRI/MF/excerpts covering annual survey article.

C7000-2   FOUNDRY MANAGEMENT AND TECHNOLOGY
Monthly. Approx. 100 p.
ISSN 0360-8999.
LC 75-642185.
SRI/MF/not filmed

Monthly trade journal reporting on trends and developments in foundry metalcasting industry, including production, management, and marketing. Data are based on studies by American Metal Market, Foundry Equipment Manufacturers Assn, BLS, and other sources. Month of data coverage is 4-6 months prior to cover date.

General format:

a. News briefs and other depts, including new products, upcoming events, environmental protection, and government regulation.

b. Feature articles on processing technology, materials, labor trends, occupational health and safety, and other subjects relating to foundries, including annual outlook articles.

c. Monthly statistical section, "Foundry Statistics," with 10 monthly tables.

d. 2 monthly and 2 quarterly price tables.

An annual buyer's guide appears in Sept. issue. Dec. issue is a nonstatistical catalog of suppliers.

Monthly and quarterly tables are listed below; monthly tables appear in all issues, except Dec. catalog issue. All additional features with substantial statistical content are described, as they appear, under "Statistical Features;" page locations and latest periods of coverage for quarterly tables are also noted. Nonstatistical features are not covered.

Availability: Foundry Management and Technology, Circulation Department, Penton Plaza, 1111 Chester Ave., Cleveland OH 44114, industry subscribers †, nonindustry subscribers $35.00 per yr., single copy $4.00; SRI/MF/not filmed.

Issues reviewed during 1984: Nov. 1983-Oct. 1984 (P) (Vol. 111, No. 11; Vol. 112, Nos. 1-10) [Dec. issue is unnumbered].

MONTHLY AND QUARTERLY TABLES:
[Tables [1-13] appear monthly; tables [14-15] appear quarterly.]

FOUNDRY STATISTICS

[1-8] [Shipments: total and/or for sale, and unfilled orders, for gray iron, steel, malleable iron, aluminum, and copper- and zinc-base castings, with shipment detail by casting type; and for magnesium castings and ductile iron; for month of coverage, previous 12 months, and 2-3 prior years.]

[9] Index of foundry equipment orders [monthly for 4 years through month of coverage].

[10] Production workers: estimated number [for ferrous and nonferrous industry workers], and average weekly hours and earnings [for gray iron, malleable iron, steel, and nonferrous industry workers; for month of coverage, previous month, and same month of previous year].

PRICES OF FOUNDRY METAL AND COKE

[Tables show data as of end of 1st or 2nd week of month prior to cover date month.]

[11-13] Foundry coke and pig iron [prices in approximately 5 cities; and price of silvery iron in Keokuk, Iowa].

[14-15] Nonferrous ingot, and iron and steel scrap [prices of 5 types of ingot, and of 7 types of scrap in 15 cities; tables appear quarterly].

STATISTICAL FEATURES:

C7000–2.501: Nov. 1983 (Vol. 111, No. 11)

WHY ADVERTISE CASTINGS?

(p. 28-30) By Robert C. Rodgers. Article, with 1 table showing average cost for closing an industrial sale, by number of sales calls made, 1981. Data are from responses of 605 companies to a 1982 McGraw-Hill survey. Survey sample covered a variety of industries.

C7000–2.502: Jan. 1984 (Vol. 112, No. 1)

QUARTERLY TABLES

[14-15] Nonferrous ingot, and iron and steel scrap [prices as of Dec. 9, 1983]. (p. 20)

CASTING SHIPMENTS WILL RECOVER 24.8% IN 1984, ANNUAL FEATURE

(p. 22-26) Annual journal survey article on expected foundry industry growth, 1982-88. Data are from a survey of 2,905 foundry managers, with a 30.4% response rate. Includes 1 chart and 12 tables showing:

a. Perceived major industry problems, 1983-84; casting shipments, 1982-1st half 1983; planned equipment purchases by type, total and for diecasters, 1984; average capacity utilization, 1983; and percent of companies with capital improvement plans for 1984 and long-term.

b. Expected changes (increase, same level, or decrease) in: casting shipments, casting production, capital expenditures, and capacity, various periods 1982-88.

Most data are shown by major metal and by plant employment size.

RECESSION AND RECOVERY WILL AFFECT LABOR BARGAINING, ANNUAL FEATURE

(p. 50-51) Annual article, by Charles T. Sheehan, on major foundry unions and labor negotiations. Includes 1 table showing foundry labor agreement average wage increases for all contracts and package costs for 3-year contracts, 1973-83; with detail on number of settlements, for contracts with and without cost-of-living adjustments, 1976-83.

C7000–2.503: Apr. 1984 (Vol. 112, No. 4)

QUARTERLY TABLES

[14-15] Nonferrous ingot, and iron and steel scrap [prices as of Mar. 12, 1984]. (p. 24)

NFA MEETING EMPHASIZES COMMUNICATIONS WITH LABOR

(p. 136-140) By Robert C. Rodgers. Article, with 1 table showing total labor contract settlements at foundries, and number preceded by strikes, 1976-83. Data are from National Foundry Association (NFA).

C7000–2.504: June 1984 (Vol. 112, No. 6)

LABOR SCENE

(p. 14) By Charles T. Sheehan. Article, with 1 table showing foundry industry employment, hours, and earnings, for iron/steel, gray and malleable iron, steel, nonferrous, and aluminum industries, 1981-83. Data are from BLS.

C7000–2.505: July 1984 (Vol. 112, No. 7)

QUARTERLY TABLES

[14-15] Nonferrous ingot, and iron and steel scrap [prices as of June 11, 1984]. (p. 16)

MIDYEAR SURVEY INDICATES CONTINUING CASTING RECOVERY

(p. 22-23) Article on expected foundry industry growth, 2nd half 1984. Data are from a summer 1984 survey of foundrymen conducted by *Foundry Management and Technology*.

Includes 5 tables showing average capacity utilization, expected trend (increase, same level, or decrease) in casting production and capital expenditures, and percent of companies with capital improvement plans, for total foundry industry and by major metal group and plant employment size, various periods 1983-84.

BUREAU OF THE CENSUS REVISES NONFERROUS CASTING STATISTICS

(p. 42-43) Article explaining Census Bureau revisions for calculation of nonferrous casting shipments. Includes 1 table showing revised data, by type of casting, 1962-82.

C7000–2.506: Aug. 1984 (Vol. 112, No. 8)

COST-EFFECTIVE FOUNDRY MELTING, PART I

(p. 22-25) By Jack C. Miske. Article, with 2 tables showing number of furnaces in U.S./Canadian foundries, by furnace type, selected years 1957-83; and number of U.S. and Canadian foundries using 9 furnace types, 1983.

C7000–2.507: Sept. 1984 (Vol. 112, No. 9)

COST-EFFECTIVE FOUNDRY MELTING, PART II

(p. 32-40) By Jack C. Miske. Article, with technical data, and 1 undated table showing foundry preheating fuel consumption and comparative costs, at selected temperatures.

C7000–2.508: Oct. 1984 (Vol. 112, No. 10)

QUARTERLY TABLES

[14-15] Nonferrous ingot, and iron and steel scrap [prices as of Sept. 13, 1984]. (p. 20)

C7000–3 INDUSTRY WEEK

Biweekly. Approx. 150 p.
ISSN 0039-0895.
LC 73-640505.
SRI/MF/not filmed

Biweekly journal (monthly in Dec.) of industrial management, reporting current business and economic news, corporate production and marketing strategies, labor-management practices, developments in major industries, and profiles of prominent executives. Includes detailed business and economic trends and forecasts.

Data are from journal analysis, trade assns, BLS, Federal Reserve System, and Commerce Dept.

Issues contain feature articles, occasionally with statistics; news briefs and editorial depts; and 2 statistical features, "Economic Trends" and "Business Trends," with narrative analysis, charts, and 13 recurring tables, listed below. Most data are current to 1-3 months prior to cover date.

Recurring tables appear as explained below. All additional features with substantial statistical content are described, as they appear, under "Statistical Features;" page location and latest periods of coverage for monthly table are also noted. Nonstatistical features are not covered.

Availability: Industry Week, Penton Plaza, 1111 Chester Ave., Cleveland OH 44114, qualified executives †, other professionals $25.00 per yr., others $50.00 per yr., single copy $2.00; SRI/MF/not filmed.

Issues reviewed during 1984: Oct. 31, 1983-Oct. 15, 1984 (P) (Vol. 219, Nos. 3-6; Vol. 220, Nos. 1-6; Vol. 221, Nos. 1-7; Vol. 222, Nos. 1-6; Vol. 223, Nos. 1-2).

BIWEEKLY TABLES:

[Tables [1-10] show data annually for selected years from mid-1970s to coming year, and quarterly for current and coming year. Actual data are current to 1-2 quarters preceding cover date; all other data are *Industry Week* forecasts. Tables appear in varying order; not all tables appear in every issue.

Tables [11-12] show data for latest available week, month, or quarter, identified for each item, with comparisons to previous periods. Data generally are current to 2-5 weeks or 1-3 months prior to cover date. Tables appear in every issue].

ECONOMIC TRENDS

[1-6] GNP [in current and 1972 dollars, occasionally with detail by component]; industrial production [index]; consumer and producer price indexes; capital spending; prime interest rate; and housing starts.

[7-10] Unemployment [rate]; profits; retail sales; and income and savings [rate].

[11] Mood of the economy [11 indicators including building permits issued, business failures, help-wanted index, industrial building cost index and vacancy rate, manufacturers' new orders, and weekly workhours].

[12] Business barometers [including aluminum, automobile, oil refinery, electric power, and raw steel output; prime interest rate; coal, lumber, and paperboard production; railroad revenue ton-miles; appliance and aircraft shipments; TV sales to dealers; housing starts; freight car, industrial supplies/machinery, and machine tool orders; manufacturers' inventories; and retail sales].

MONTHLY TABLE:

BUSINESS TRENDS

[1] Manufacturing shipments [value for 20 SIC 2-digit industries, including percent change from previous month and year, accompanied by chart showing summary data for year to date for current and previous years. Data are current to 2-3 months prior to cover date].

STATISTICAL FEATURES:

C7000–3.501: Oct. 31, 1983 (Vol. 219, No. 3)

MONTHLY TABLE

[1] Manufacturing shipments, for Aug. 1983. (p. 69)

ARE YOU READY FOR ELECTRONIC MAIL?

(p. 59-63) By Margaret Price. Article on trends and outlook for computer-based messaging system (CBMS) industry. Data are from International Data Corp. Includes 3 tables showing CBMS revenues and number of terminals, by type of vendor, 1982 and 1987; and CBMS revenues and market shares for 5 leading computer service bureaus, 1982.

MORE BUDGET WOES AHEAD

(p. 78) By Michael K. Evans. Article, with 1 table showing projected Federal outlays by program, tax receipts by source, and deficit, FY84-88. Data are from Evans Economics, Inc.

C7000–3.502: Nov. 28, 1983 (Vol. 219, No. 5)

MONTHLY TABLE

[1] Manufacturing shipments, for Sept. 1983. (p. 80)

CEOs FORECAST 1984, ANNUAL FEATURE

(p. 40-50) Annual survey article, by Dale W. Sommer, on chief executive officers' (CEOs) economic expectations for 1984. Data are based on a fall 1983 *Industry Week* survey of over 700 CEOs.

Includes 8 charts showing distribution of responses to questions on business conditions (better, worse, unchanged, or don't know) in past year and in next 6 and 12 months; and expected changes in company operating indicators, 1984.

This is the 12th annual survey.

PUMPING UP ECONOMY FOR THE ELECTIONS?

(p. 86) By Michael K. Evans. Article, with 1 table showing percent change in money supply, government expenditures, interest rates, and real GNP; and unemployment rate; for presidential election years and years preceding election, 1955-80. Data are from Evans Economics, Inc.

C7000–3.503: Jan. 9, 1984 (Vol. 220, No. 1)

MONTHLY TABLE

[1] Manufacturing shipments, for Oct. 1983. (p. 76)

C7000–3.504: Jan. 23, 1984 (Vol. 220, No. 2)

MONTHLY TABLE

[1] Manufacturing shipments, for Nov. 1983. (p. 63)

JAPANESE ON THE ATTACK!

(p. 63) Brief article, with 1 table showing Japanese import shares of U.S. electronic office equipment market, by equipment type, 1983 and 1987. Data are from Frost and Sullivan, Inc.

C7000–3.505: Feb. 6, 1984 (Vol. 220, No. 3)

COMMODORE TAKES OFF THE GLOVES

(p. 15-16) By James E. Braham. Article, with 1 chart showing home computer market shares, for 5 manufacturers and all others, 1982-83. Data are from Future Computing, Inc.

C7000–3.506: Feb. 20, 1984 (Vol. 220, No. 4)

MONTHLY TABLE

[1] Manufacturing shipments, for Dec. 1983. (p. 111)

BYE-BYE, BIG EIGHT

(p. 21-22) By Donald B. Thompson. Article, with 1 table showing the following for 8 steel manufacturers: share of domestic steel shipments, and percent of company shipments going to auto industry, 1982; and salaried employment reductions, various periods 1980-83. Data are from the American Iron and Steel Institute.

MILK-CONTAINER WARS

(p. 109-111) By Greg Johnson. Article, with 1 chart showing milk packaging market shares for plastic, glass, and paper containers, 1965 and 1982. Data are from Milk Industry Foundation.

C7000–3.507: Mar. 5, 1984 (Vol. 220, No. 5)

PC COMMUNICATIONS

(p. 88) Brief article, with 1 chart showing market shares for personal computer (PC) communications equipment, by type, 1987. Data are from Frost and Sullivan, Inc.

C7000–3.508: Mar. 19, 1984 (Vol. 220, No. 6)

NOT EYEBALL TO EYEBALL

(p. 15-16) Article comparing perceptions of corporate managers and chief executive officers concerning managers' career opportunities and likelihood of resigning within next 5 years. Data are from a Research and Forecasts Inc. survey conducted for *Industry Week*. Includes 4 charts.

1983 FINANCIAL ANALYSIS OF INDUSTRY AND A PREVIEW OF 1984, ANNUAL FEATURE

(p. 31-60) Annual article, by Dale W. Sommer, reporting on the financial condition of 308 companies in 23 industries, 1983.

Contains introduction, with 1 summary table; and analyses of 23 industries, each including 1 table showing revenues, net income or loss, and profit margin, by company and generally as industry average, 1983 with comparisons to 1982. Companies are ranked by revenues.

This is the 12th annual analysis.

HIGH COST OF HIGH TECH

(p. 79) Brief article, with 1 chart showing corporate expenditures for computers and related products/services, by cost component, 1982. Data are from International Data Corp.

C7000–3.509: Apr. 2, 1984 (Vol. 221, No. 1)

MONTHLY TABLE

[1] Manufacturing shipments, for Jan. 1984. (p. 73)

BOOM FOR CRT PHONES

(p. 66) Brief article, with 1 chart showing shipments of cathode-ray tube (CRT) phone terminals, 1982-84. Data are from Venture Development Corp.

C7000–3.510: Apr. 30, 1984 (Vol. 221, No. 3)

MONTHLY TABLE

[1] Manufacturing shipments, for Feb. 1984. (p. 95)

HOUSING LIFTS OFF

(p. 38-45) Article, with 1 table showing projected housing starts for 10 leading States, 1984-93 period. Data are from LSI Systems Inc.

C7000–3.511: May 14, 1984 (Vol. 221, No. 4)

ARE CEOs WORTH $1 MILLION? ANNUAL FEATURE

(p. 43-46) Annual article, by Bruce A. Jacobs, on compensation paid top corporate executives, 1983. Data are from statements filed with the SEC.

Includes 1 table showing the following for 50 highest paid executives: company, executive's name and title, and cash/cash equivalent compensation, 1983, with change from 1982.

C7000–3.512: May 28, 1984 (Vol. 221, No. 5)

MONTHLY TABLE

[1] Manufacturing shipments, for Mar. 1984. (p. 122)

C7000–3.513: June 11, 1984 (Vol. 221, No. 6)

SURVIVING THE MICRO ATTACK

(p. 39-46) By William P. Patterson. Article, with 2 charts showing distribution of personal computer use among clerical, managerial, and professional workers, aggregate for 1,300 largest U.S. corporations, 1983-84. Data are from Newton-Evans Research Co.

C7000–3.514: June 25, 1984 (Vol. 221, No. 7)

MONTHLY TABLE

[1] Manufacturing shipments, for Apr. 1984. (p. 89)

C7000–3.515: July 9, 1984 (Vol. 222, No. 1)

POWERS AT THE PUMP

(p. 52) Brief article, with 1 table showing 9 leading gasoline marketers ranked by gasoline market share, 1983. Data are from Lundberg Survey, Inc.

C7000–3.516: July 23, 1984 (Vol. 222, No. 2)

MONTHLY TABLE

[1] Manufacturing shipments, for May 1984. (p. 64)

C7000–3.517: Aug. 6, 1984 (Vol. 222, No. 3)

COMPUTER ARRIVES IN EXECUTIVE SUITE

(p. 15) By Perry Pascarella. Article on executives' computer use, based on an *Industry Week* survey. Includes 1 undated table showing distribution of respondents by frequency of computer/word processor use, and availability of and plans to acquire equipment.

DETROIT GETS HOT

(p. 15-16) By Greg Johnson. Article, with 1 chart showing retail sales volume and average price for new and used cars, selected years 1970-83. Data are from Hertz Corp.

Rx FOR PHARMACEUTICALS

(p. 32-36) By Greg Johnson. Article, with 1 table showing world sales for 10 major pharmaceutical firms, 1980 and 1983. Data sources include Merck and Co., Inc.

C7000–3.518: Aug. 20, 1984 (Vol. 222, No. 4)

MONTHLY TABLE

[1] Manufacturing shipments, for June 1984. (p. 28)

C7000–3.519: Sept. 3, 1984 (Vol. 222, No. 5)

COMING TO GRIPS WITH AMERICA'S TRADE SLIDE

(p. 62-68) By John S. McClenahen. Article, with 1 chart and 1 table showing value of exports by selected industry; and imports as a percent of apparent domestic consumption, by selected commodity; 1983. Data are from Commerce Dept.

C7000–3.520: Sept. 17, 1984 (Vol. 222, No. 6)

SAVING ON T&E

(p. 28) By Marilyn Much. Article, with 1 undated table showing average travel/entertainment (T&E) expenses per employee and per regular traveling employee, by company employment size. Data are from American Express Co.

C7000–3.521: Oct. 1, 1984 (Vol. 223, No. 1)

MONTHLY TABLE

[1] Manufacturing shipments, for July 1984. (p. 36)

C7000–4   AIR TRANSPORT WORLD
Monthly. Approx. 100 p.
ISSN 0002-2543.
LC 66-98382.
SRI/MF/not filmed

Monthly trade journal of U.S. and foreign commercial air transport industry, including statistics on passenger, cargo, and commuter traffic, financial and operating performance, and costs. Most statistics are compiled from CAB data and airline reports. Data are generally current to 3-4 months prior to cover date.

Issues generally contain a special report section, with articles on a single topic, often with data from surveys by *Air Transport World;* feature articles, often focusing on specific airlines; editorial depts; and the following regular statistical features:

a. "Facts and Figures," with 6 monthly tables and 2 irregularly recurring tables on traffic levels and cost and consumption of fuel, and 1 quarterly table on financial performance.

b. "Aircraft Operating Data," with 1 monthly table showing data for different aircraft each month, on a quarterly basis for some aircraft.

c. "Commuter/Regional Statistics," with 1 monthly table.

Annual statistical features include reports on maintenance/engineering expenditures, traffic and financial forecasts, U.S. and world airline operations, and travel agent commissions from airlines.

Monthly, irregularly recurring, and quarterly tables are described below. All additional features with substantial statistical content are described, as they appear, under "Statistical Features;" page locations and latest periods of coverage for "Aircraft Operating Data" and quarterly table are also noted, as are aircraft covered in "Aircraft Operating Data." Nonstatistical features are not covered.

Availability: Air Transport World, PO Box 95759, Cleveland OH 44101, qualified subscribers †, others $35.00 per yr., single copy $4.00; SRI/MF/not filmed.

Issues reviewed during 1984: Nov. 1983-Oct. 1984 (P) (Vol. 20, Nos. 11-12; Vol. 21, Nos. 1-10).

TABLES:

[Most tables include percent change from same period of previous year. Monthly tables [1-5], quarterly table, and commuter/regional statistics show data for individual airlines, usually indicating rank.]

The following abbreviations are used: RPK (revenue-passenger-kilometers), FTK (freight-ton-kilometers), RPM (revenue-passenger-miles), ASM (available-seat-miles).]

FACTS AND FIGURES
Monthly Tables

[1] World airline traffic [passengers, RPKs, and FTKs, for approximately 60 foreign airlines; year to date].

[2] Freight traffic (U.S. airlines) [transatlantic, transpacific, and Latin America FTKs for approximately 10 airlines; year to date and same period of previous year].

[3] U.S. airline system traffic [passengers, RPKs, and FTKs, for approximately 30 carriers; year to date].

[4-5] U.S. national and large regional carriers and major carriers scheduled domestic operations [passengers, RPMs, ASMs, load factors, and average trip length, for approximately 20 carriers; month of coverage].

[6] Fuel cost and consumption [aggregated for major, national, and regional carriers' scheduled and nonscheduled service, with totals for domestic and international flights; month of coverage; table may not appear in every issue].

Irregularly Recurring Tables

[1] North Atlantic traffic [east- and westbound passengers, freight and mail tonnage, passenger load factor, and passenger and cargo flights; for scheduled and charter services, year to date; table appeared in Nov. 1983, and Apr., June, July, and Oct. 1984 issues].

[2] Intra-European and inter-European passenger and freight air traffic [year to date; table appeared in Feb., Apr., May, June, and July 1984 issues].

Quarterly Table

[1] U.S. airlines financial performance [operating revenues, expense, and profit or loss; and net income or loss; for approximately 40 national, major, and regional carriers, quarter ending month of coverage; data are shown for 1 or more carrier types, in 1 or more tables, as space permits].

AIRCRAFT OPERATING DATA

Selected aircraft, 12- or 3-months' data [including fleet size, revenue miles and hours flown, fuel use, average speed and passengers per mile, and operating and maintenance expenses, for 1-6 aircraft models, year or quarter ending 2-5 months prior to month of coverage].

COMMUTER/REGIONAL STATISTICS

U.S. large regional, small regional/commuter, and cargo commuter carrier traffic [passengers, load factors, RPMs, and/or pounds of freight, for approximately 80 airlines, year to date].

STATISTICAL FEATURES:

C7000–4.501: Nov. 1983 (Vol. 20, No. 11)

AIRCRAFT OPERATING DATA

(p. 114) For Boeing 727-200 and 757-200, and McDonnell Douglas DC-9-80 aircraft, quarter ended June 30, 1983.

COMMUTER/REGIONAL AIRFRAMES AND ENGINES: TURBOPROP EVOLUTION SPARKS REVOLUTION

(p. 72-77) By Lou Davis. Article, with 1 chart showing world sales of commuter/regional airplanes, 1975-92. Data are from Fairchild Industries.

EQUIPMENT INVENTORY, ANNUAL FEATURE

(p. 78-99) Annual article describing airplanes, helicopters, and engines, suitable for commuter/regional operations. Descriptions are arranged alphabetically by manufacturer, and show some or all of the following for each model: development and FAA certification summary, specifications, price, delivery start date, and aircraft delivered, on order, and on option.

C7000–4.502: Dec. 1983 (Vol. 20, No. 12)

AIRCRAFT OPERATING DATA

(p. 104) For Boeing 727-200 and 767, McDonnell Douglas DC-8-71, and Airbus A300B2 and A300B4 aircraft, quarter ended June 30, 1983.

EARLY END SEEN TO GLUT IN USED AIRCRAFT MARKET

(p. 75-77, 134) By Henry Lefer. Article, with 1 table showing air traffic growth; and total aircraft retirements, and new aircraft requirements and deliveries; 1978-84. Data are from Avmark.

C7000–4.503: Jan. 1984 (Vol. 21, No. 1)

AIRCRAFT OPERATING DATA

(p. 96) For Boeing 737-200, and McDonnell Douglas DC-9-10, DC-9-30, DC-9-50, and DC-9-80 aircraft, quarter ended Sept. 30, 1983.

FACTS AND FIGURES QUARTERLY TABLE

[1] Financial performance, for major and national carriers, 3rd quarter and 9 months 1983. (p. 91-92)

1984 FORECAST: NOT A BOOM, BUT AT LEAST A POP, ANNUAL FEATURE

(p. 18-35) Annual outlook article, by Danna K. Henderson, on world airline traffic and financial performance in 1984. Data are based in part on 60 responses to an *Air Transport World* survey of U.S. and foreign carriers. Includes 5 tables showing the following:

a. World and U.S. passenger and freight traffic, and world revenues and expenses, 1975-84.

b. World traffic and financial forecasts, by airline, for 1984, with selected comparisons to estimates for 1982-83.

CHILDREN OF DEREGULATION HAVE BROUGHT OUT THE BEST AND WORST IN THEIR ELDERS

(p. 52-57) By Joan M. Feldman. Article, with 1 table showing revenue passenger miles and market share, for 19 airlines, 1st 10 months 1982-83. Data are from First Boston Corp.

C7000-4.504: Feb. 1984 (Vol. 21, No. 2)

AIRCRAFT OPERATING DATA

(p. 94) For Boeing 747-100, 747-200, and 747-200F, and McDonnell Douglas DC-8-50F, DC-8-63F, and DC-8-61 aircraft, quarter ended Sept. 30, 1983.

SPECIAL REPORT: AIR FREIGHT INDUSTRY EXPECTS HEALTHY GAINS IN 1984, ANNUAL FEATURE

(p. 26-33) Annual article, by Danna K. Henderson, on cargo operations of U.S. and foreign airlines in 1983 and outlook for 1984. Data are from responses of 55 airlines to an *Air Transport World* survey. Includes 4 tables showing the following, by airline:

a. Capital expenditure plans for containers, cargo handling equipment, and terminals.

b. Freight traffic and revenues for 1983, small package share, and forecast change for 1984; and percent of total revenues derived from freight, 1982-84.

c. Fleet inventory; and planned aircraft acquisition and disposal.

SPECIAL REPORT: COMMUTER/REGIONAL SAFETY

(p. 69-79) By Lou Davis and J. A. Donoghue. Article, with 4 tables showing commuter airline accidents, fatalities, accident rates, and aircraft operations, 1975-83 with comparisons to all scheduled airlines, 1983; and accident rates of commuter vs. major airlines (no date), and total accidents 1980-82, by aircraft size. Data are from Regional Airline Assn, CAB, and General Accounting Office.

C7000-4.505: Mar. 1984 (Vol. 21, No. 3)

AIRCRAFT OPERATING DATA

(p. 67, 92) For Boeing 767, 727-200, and 757-200, British Aerospace 146, Metro, Beech 99, F27, EMB-110, Shorts 330 and 360, DHC-6, DHC-7, and YS-11 aircraft, quarter ended Sept. 30, 1983.

SPECIAL REPORT: AIRFRAMES AND ENGINES

(p. 33-38) By Danna K. Henderson. Article on developments in airframe and engine technology. Data are from 58 responses to an *Air Transport World* survey of U.S. and foreign airlines. Includes 1 table showing new aircraft acquisitions and cost during the 1982-84 period, and planned aircraft investments beyond 1984, by airline.

WHERE HAS ALL THE MONEY GONE?

(p. 60-66) By Joan M. Feldman. Article, with 2 charts and 2 tables showing value of aircraft deliveries open for U.S. and foreign airlines to 1995; and airline industry long-term debt and stockholder equity, and debt as a percent of capital for selected airlines, various periods 1978-83. Data are from Merrill Lynch and Air Transport Assn.

C7000-4.506: Apr. 1984 (Vol. 21, No. 4)

AIRCRAFT OPERATING DATA

(p. 104) For Lockheed L-1011-100, Airbus A300B2 and A300B4, McDonnell Douglas DC-10-10 and DC-10-30, and Boeing 747 aircraft, quarter ended Sept. 30, 1983.

SPECIAL REPORT: AVIONICS, ANNUAL FEATURE

(p. 60-65) Annual article, by Danna K. Henderson, on world airline investment in avionic systems and test equipment, 1983. Data are based on responses from 52 airlines to an *Air Transport World* survey.

Includes 1 table showing 1983 spending on avionic equipment, planned spending in next 2 years, and types of purchases; percent of fleet with automated cockpit systems in use and planned; whether data link is planned; and long-range navigational system in use, and whether change is planned; all by airline.

C7000-4.507: May 1984 (Vol. 21, No. 5)

1983 MARKET DEVELOPMENT REPORT, ANNUAL FEATURE

(p. 62-159) Annual review, for 1983, of U.S. and foreign airline operations. Data are from CAB, International Air Transport Assn, International Civil Aviation Organization, and airline reports.

Includes 1983 data on passenger and cargo traffic, financial performance, fleet size, employment, fuel consumption, and operating ratios, shown primarily by airline, often with comparative data for 1982, and occasionally with data for prior years.

Contents:

a. "U.S. Majors Lead World Airline Traffic and Financial Turnaround." Includes 4 tables showing top 25 world airlines in passengers, RPKs, cargo, fleet size, employees, and operating revenues and profits; financial results for 58 non-U.S. carriers; U.S. carrier fuel consumption and per gallon cost, by type of service; and North Atlantic passenger and freight traffic. (p. 62-72)

b. "World Airline Statistics, 1983." Presents 1 extended table showing traffic, employees, and fleet size for approximately 300 U.S. and foreign carriers. (p. 76-81)

c. "Africa, Asia/Pacific, Canada, Europe, Latin American/Caribbean, and Middle East." Brief profiles of individual airlines in each world area. (p. 84-105)

d. "U.S. Majors." Brief profiles of 11 major airlines, with 5 tables showing the following, by airline: totals and rank for financial results, traffic (total system, domestic, and international), and load factors. (p. 106-113)

e. "Delta, Southwest Take the Lead Again in Receiving Fewest Passenger Complaints." Article reviewing record of airline passenger complaints filed with CAB in 1983. Includes 1 table showing rank and complaint rate per 100,000 passengers for 11-15 U.S. major and national carriers, 1981-83. (p. 114)

f. "U.S. Nationals, New Entrants, Cargo Carriers, Large Regionals, and Small Regionals/Commuters." Brief profiles of individual airlines, with 8 tables showing financial results and traffic for national and cargo carriers; load factors for national carriers; and financial results for new entrants, and large and small regional carriers. (p. 116-140)

g. "World Airline Fleets." Presents 2 tables showing number of jet, turboprop, piston, and helicopter aircraft in fleet and on order, by model; and number of aircraft in fleet/on order, by model and airline. (p. 146-159)

This is the 21st annual report.

Other Article

PROS AND CONS OF GOING PUBLIC

(p. 167-168, 196) By Joan M. Feldman. Article, with 1 table showing airline public stock offerings (number and value of shares), percent of company sold, and investment firm managing equity sale, for 30 airlines, various periods 1980-84. Data are from Blyth Eastman Paine Webber.

C7000-4.508: June 1984 (Vol. 21, No. 6)

AIRCRAFT OPERATING DATA

(p. 100) For Boeing 737-200, and McDonnell Douglas DC-9-10, DC-9-30, DC-9-50, and DC-9-80 aircraft, quarter ended Dec. 31, 1983.

LABOR WAGE STANDARDS ADRIFT UNDER DEREGULATION PRESSURES

(p. 16-19) By J. A. Donoghue. Article on world airline labor-management relations. Data are from an *Air Transport World* survey.

Includes 1 table showing the following for 47 U.S. and foreign carriers: total and part-time employees, and percent unionized; number of unions; hiring plans in next year; and average wages of pilots, flight attendants, mechanics, and station personnel; 1983 with selected comparisons to 1979.

FACTS AND FIGURES ANNUAL TABLE

(p. 98) Annual table showing U.S. airline advertising analysis including passengers, passenger revenue, advertising and sales promotion expendiutres, and selected ratios, for major carrier domestic and international operations, 1983.

C7000-4.509: July 1984 (Vol. 21, No. 7)

AIRCRAFT OPERATING DATA

(p. 104) For Boeing 747F, and McDonnell Douglas DC-8-63F, DC-8-61F, and DC-8-50F aircraft, quarter ended Dec. 31, 1983.

FACTS AND FIGURES QUARTERLY TABLE

[1] Financial performance, for major and national/large regional carriers, 1st quarter 1984. (p. 101, 103)

MAINTENANCE COSTS RISING, ATW SURVEY SHOWS, ANNUAL FEATURE

(p. 28-32) Annual article, by Danna K. Henderson, on maintenance and engineering (M&E) activities and expenditures of 50 U.S. and foreign airlines in 1983, based on an *Air Transport World* survey. Includes 4 tables showing the following, by airline:

a. M&E expenditures and employment, 1983 with change from 1982 and forecast for 1984; and M&E employment as percent of total, 1983.

b. M&E work distribution by type (in-house, contracted to others, and performed for others), and revenues from outside maintenance work, 1983; and planned M&E facility/equipment spending, 1984/85.

Not all data are shown for every airline.

C7000-4.510: Aug. 1984 (Vol. 21, No. 8)

AIRCRAFT OPERATING DATA

(p. 110) For Boeing 727-200, 757-200, and 767, and British Aerospace 146 aircraft, quarter ended Dec. 31, 1983.

AIR TRAFFIC DELAYS STAGING A COMEBACK

(p. 18-21) By J. A. Donoghue. Article, with 2 tables showing air traffic delays per 1,000 flights, at top 22 airports ranked by total traffic operations; and total delays of 15/more minutes, with distribution by cause and whether occurring during arrival, departure, or en route; June 1984, with delay comparisons to June 1983 and/or May 1984, and percent change in airport operations from 1981. Data are from FAA.

C7000–4.511: Sept. 1984 (Vol. 21, No. 9)

AIRCRAFT OPERATING DATA

(p. 121) For Lockheed L-1011-100, L-1011-500, Airbus A300B2, A300B4, and McDonnell Douglas DC-10-10, DC-10-30, DC-10-40 aircraft, quarter ended Mar. 31, 1984.

SPECIAL REPORT: PASSENGER HANDLING IN A COMPETITIVE ENVIRONMENT, ANNUAL FEATURE

(p. 49-57) Annual article, by Danna K. Henderson, on world airline passenger handling operations, 1983. Data are from CAB, and an *Air Transport World* survey of approximately 40 airlines. Includes 8 tables showing the following, 1983 with comparisons to 1982 or 1979:

a. Passenger handling personnel (number and as percent of total employment) and expenditures (total and per passenger), percent change in employment and boardings, and boardings per passenger handling employee; additional seating purchases; and inflight meals served, cost per meal, and revenue from beverage sales; for 20-35 world airlines.

b. Passenger service and food expenses, enplaned passengers, passengers denied boarding and receiving compensation, passengers voluntarily "bumped," and expenses resulting from boarding denials and "bumping," for 11 U.S. airlines; and use of inflight entertainment, and expenses associated with lost/mishandled baggage, delayed passengers, and boarding denials, for 20-35 world airlines.

Last previous report covered 1981; for description see SRI 1982 Annual, under C7000-4.311.

C7000–4.512: Oct. 1984 (Vol. 21, No. 10)

AIRCRAFT OPERATING DATA

(p. 130) For Boeing 737-200, McDonnell Douglas DC-9-10, DC-9-30, DC-9-50, DC-9-80 aircraft, quarter ended Mar. 31, 1984.

FACTS AND FIGURES QUARTERLY TABLE

[1] Financial performance, for major and national carriers, 2nd quarter and 6 months, 1983-84. (p. 126-128)

IATA MEMBERSHIP GROWING BUT PROBLEMS REMAIN FORMIDABLE, ANNUAL FEATURE

(p. 60-71) Annual article on International Air Transport Assn (IATA), presenting data on airline financial results for various periods, 1979-1st half 1984. Includes 2 summary charts, and 9 tables showing:

a. Traffic distribution by world region; and North Atlantic operations, including number of airlines, scheduled and charter flights, passengers by class of service, passenger load factor, and freight; 1979-83.

b. IATA traffic data for 65 airlines, Jan.-June 1984; and airline estimated traffic, fleet size, and operating revenues and expenses, 1979-83.

c. Top 10 IATA airlines in 1983 ranked by passengers, passenger load factor, freight, total and charter revenue-passenger-kilometers (RPKs), and charter percent of total RPKs, with percent change from 1982; top 20 nations in scheduled RPKs, 1983 with percent change from 1982; and top 21 nations in traffic growth, 1982-83 period.

d. IATA traffic data for 107 airlines, 1983, with percent change from 1982.

IATA AIRLINES REGISTER PRODUCTIVITY GAINS IN '83, ANNUAL FEATURE

(p. 72-80) Annual analysis of per-employee productivity for approximately 100 IATA member airlines, 1983. Includes 3 tables showing the following:

a. Employees, passenger and freight traffic, traffic per employee, and operating revenues, 1979-83.

b. Productivity measures for 107 airlines, including per-employee total ton-kilometers, passenger boardings, revenue-passenger-kilometers, and freight-ton-kilometers; and rankings of top 10 airlines for each measure; both by airline, 1983 with percent change from 1982.

SPECIAL REPORT: TRAVEL AGENT COMMISSION SURVEY SHOWS DISCOUNT PASSENGERS DECLINING

(p. 83-86) Annual article presenting data on travel agent commissions from airlines, 1st half 1984 and trends. Data are based on a survey by *Air Transport World*. Includes 3 tables showing:

a. Travel agent commission rates, including detail for domestic and international flights, percent of revenue generated by travel agents, percent of passengers using discount fares, commissions paid, commissions as percent of revenue, and average revenue per passenger; 1st half 1984, with comparison to 1983 and 1979; for 36-38 U.S. and foreign airlines.

b. Passenger revenue and commissions paid, for international and domestic services of 9-11 U.S. major carriers, and for 12 national carriers, 1982-83 and 1st half 1984.

C7000–5   LODGING HOSPITALITY: Lodging's 400 Top Performers

Monthly (selected issue).
Aug. 1984. (p. 34-61).
Vol. XL, No. 8.
ISSN 0148-0766.
LC 77-640897.
SRI/MF/excerpts

Annual article, for 1984, presenting financial and operating data for the 400 leading lodging facilities in 5 categories: center city, resort, suburban, highway, and airport. Data are from survey responses of *Lodging Hospitality* subscribers, and Laventhol and Horwath.

Contains narrative report, with 22 charts and 7 tables showing the following for 1984:

a. Affiliation, years in operation, facilities and services offered, automation, chain reservation system use, business booked through reservation systems, and growth plans: distribution for aggregate 400 leading performers.

b. Occupancy rate; sales and payroll expenses per room; employees per 100 rooms; sales per employee; and distribution of sales from guest rooms, food/beverage, and other: aggregates for 400 leading performers compared to total industry, with selected detail for each facility category.

c. Guest rooms/suites, total sales, room and food/beverage sales, other revenues, and average occupancy rate and employees, with selected rankings: by individual facility arranged by category.

d. For 25 leading lodging chains: U.S. facilities by type of management, and number of rooms; average daily room rate and percent occupancy; and U.S./foreign facilities and rooms.

Article is an annual feature of the monthly publication, *Lodging Hospitality*. Publication contains generally narrative articles. The annual article on lodging's top 400 performers is the only feature covered by SRI to date.

Availability: Lodging Hospitality, PO Box 95759, Cleveland OH 44101, $40.00 per yr., single copy $4.00; SRI/MF/excerpts for annual article described.

C7550
Pick Publishing Corp.

C7550–1   PICK WORLD CURRENCY REPORT

Monthly, discontinued.
Approx. 20 p.
ISSN 0048-4113.
LC 55-22942.
SRI/MF/not filmed

Monthly report on official and black market/free exchange rates for 96 foreign currencies vis-a-vis the U.S. dollar; and prices of precious metals, gems, and selected other metals, in the U.S. and prominent world markets. Also shows gold sales volume. Data are current through month preceding cover date.

Issues contain narrative analyses of commodity market and currency developments; occasional special or annual statistical features; 4 summary charts; and 8 tables showing the following data for month of coverage with selected comparisons for previous months and years:

a. London daily silver spot prices, and futures prices for 3-month, 6-month, and 1-year delivery; and principal trade unit rates for hand payments dollar in NYC, and Eurodollar and Eurosterling in London. 2 tables.

b. Exchange rates (official and free/black market) for 96 currencies per U.S. dollar. 1 table.

c. Gold 1-year delivery contract prices in NYC, London, Singapore, and Hong Kong; gold sales in international markets; prices per ounce and per kilogram for gold in 46 world markets, platinum in NYC, and silver in NYC and London; and daily closing trading ranges for gold in Zurich. 3 tables.

d. Free market quotations for 17 metals and forms of steel; and dealer prices for 4 carat size groups of commercial grade diamonds. 2 tables.

Monthly tables appear in all issues. Additional features with substantial statistical content are described, as they appear, under "Statistical Features." Nonstatistical features are not covered.

Report has been discontinued with the Feb. 17, 1984 issue.

Issues reviewed during 1984: Nov. 15, 1983-Feb. 17, 1984 (P) (Vol. 38, Nos. 11-12; Vol. 39, Nos. 1-2).

STATISTICAL FEATURES:

C7550–1.501: Nov. 15, 1983 (Vol. 38, No. 11)

PRIVATE GOLD HOARDS, 1983, ANNUAL FEATURE

(p. 1-3, 12) Annual article, with 1 chart and 2 tables showing the following for gold: volume and value of private holdings in France and 4 world areas, volume of official world reserves, and free market price, for year ended Oct. 1983 with trends from 1975.

C7550–1.502: Jan. 17, 1984 (Vol. 39, No. 1)

U.S. DOLLAR IN FREE FOREIGN EXCHANGE MARKETS, ANNUAL FEATURE

(p. 12) Annual table showing percent change in foreign exchange value of U.S. dollar in 133 countries, Dec. 1982-83.

1983 PERCENTAGE CHANGES OF FREE MARKET PRICES, ANNUAL FEATURE

(p. 14) Annual table ranking approximately 45 world markets by annual percent change in bar gold and gold coin prices, 1983.

C7600
Pit and Quarry
Publications

C7600–1   CONCRETE: 1983 Review, 1984 Outlook
Monthly (selected issue).
Jan. 1984. (p. 30, 37-47).
Vol. 47, No. 9.
ISSN 0279-4705.
LC 59-37674.
SRI/MF/excerpts

Annual compilation of articles reviewing concrete industry production and operating trends and expectations, by sector, 1982-84. Also summarizes construction industry trends.

Data sources include F. W. Dodge, Portland Cement Assn, Commerce Dept, *Concrete* annual survey of industry producers, and other Federal and private sources.

Contains introductory article summarizing survey findings (p. 30); and 6 statistical articles, described below (p. 37-47).

Concrete is a monthly periodical reporting trends and developments in the cement industry, and normally contains primarily narrative articles. The annual concrete industry review and outlook feature is the only feature of *Concrete* covered in SRI.

Availability: Concrete, Circulation Department, One E. First St., Duluth MN 55802, $12.00 per yr., single copy $3.00; SRI/MF/excerpts for features described.

STATISTICAL FEATURES:

VIEWS OF NATIONAL ASSN LEADERS, ANNUAL FEATURE

(p. 37-40) Annual review and outlook article on cement and 4 concrete product industries. Includes 1 table projecting portland cement shipments by region, 1983-88.

CONSTRUCTION ACTIVITY SPARKS READY-MIX PRODUCTION UPTURN, ANNUAL FEATURE

(p. 41-43) Annual article, by Sid Levine, on ready mixed concrete industry. Includes 1 chart, and 7 tables showing:

a. New housing starts, value of new construction, and ready mixed concrete consumption and value of shipments, generally 1977-83.

b. Ready mixed concrete industry survey: reported changes in production, prices, wages, and various operating costs, 1982-83, expected changes in volume of business, 1983-84, and sales dollar allotments for promotion expenditures, 1983, all by region; and capital expenditure plans for 1984; mostly shown as percent of respondents or averages.

MASONRY PRODUCTION HEADS UPWARD IN '83, ANNUAL FEATURE

(p. 43-44) Annual survey article, by Patricia Murphy, with 3 tables on concrete masonry, showing industry survey data similar to data described above for ready mixed concrete. Data also include changes in product mix and in costs by region.

PRECAST CONCRETE, PRESTRESSED CONCRETE, AND CONCRETE PIPE, ANNUAL FEATURE

(p. 45-47) Three annual articles, by Rick Tiller, with 3 tables on precast and prestressed concrete and concrete pipe, showing industry survey data similar to data described above for ready mixed concrete. Data omit promotion allotment and regional detail.

C7600–2   PIT AND QUARRY
Monthly.   Approx. 125 p.
ISSN 0032-0293.
LC 80-1511.
SRI/MF/excerpts, shipped quarterly

Monthly journal reporting U.S. and worldwide trends and developments in the stone products, cement, and other nonmetallic mineral industries. Covers exploration, production, technical developments, R&D, plants and equipment, working conditions, management, government regulation, and finance.

Journal includes feature articles, occasionally statistical; regular editorial depts; and a monthly table on construction contract values, described below.

Annual statistical features include industry review and outlook, and world cement report, both in the Jan. issue. An annual editorial index appears in the Dec. issue.

Monthly table appears in most issues. All additional features with substantial statistical content are described, as they appear, under "Statistical Features." Nonstatistical features are not covered.

Availability: Pit and Quarry Publications, Circulation Department, PO Box 6830, Duluth MN 55802-9914, $12.00 per yr., single copy $3.00; SRI/MF/excerpts for monthly table and all portions described under "Statistical Features;" shipped quarterly.

Issues reviewed during 1984: Nov. 1983-Oct. 1984 (P) (Vol. 76, Nos. 5-12; Vol. 77, Nos. 1-4).

MONTHLY TABLE:

COMPARISON OF CONSTRUCTION CONTRACT VALUES

Table showing contract values for nonresidential and residential building, and nonbuilding construction, for year to date and same period of previous year; and Dodge index, for 3 consecutive months; through month 3-4 months prior to cover date. Data are from F. W. Dodge Division of McGraw-Hill Information Systems Co.

STATISTICAL FEATURES:

C7600–2.501: Jan. 1984 (Vol. 76, No. 7)

1982 REVIEW AND 1983 OUTLOOK, ANNUAL FEATURE

Annual collection of articles reviewing U.S. cement, construction aggregate, and other nonmetals production and operating trends, and construction industry activity for 1983, with forecasts for 1984.

Data sources include Bureau of Mines, Portland Cement Assn, F. W. Dodge, and a *Pit and Quarry* annual aggregate industry survey. Statistical articles are described below.

VIEWS FROM NATIONAL ASSN LEADERS, ANNUAL FEATURE

(p. 48-56) Annual review and outlook article on cement, crushed stone, and other nonmetallic mineral industries. Includes 1 table projecting cement use by region, 1983-88.

PORTLAND CEMENT IN THE U.S.: PRODUCTION AND PROJECT SURVEY, ANNUAL FEATURE

(p. 58-64) Annual article, by Sid Levine, on portland cement industry developments in 1983. Includes text data on equipment and operations for 10 new and proposed plants and expansion projects, by company, 1982-85; and 14 tables showing the following:

a. Shipments of portland cement, imports of hydraulic cement/clinker, and housing starts and value of new construction in current and constant 1972 and 1977 dollars; 1977-83.

b. Hydraulic cement shipments; clinker capacity, active plants, and production; masonry cement production and shipments; Puerto Rico clinker production, plants, and capacity, and portland cement shipments; average mill value of portland and prepared masonry cement; distribution of portland cement consumption by region; and cement consumption by type; various years 1977-84.

c. Cement plant closings and transfers, 1982-83 period; finish grinding capacity of 15 largest cement companies; and foreign-owned plants and clinker capacity, 1983; all by company.

P&Q's ANNUAL AGGREGATES SURVEY, ANNUAL FEATURE

(p. 64-68) Annual survey article, by Sandy Herod, with 1 table showing the following, for sand/gravel, crushed stone, and lightweight aggregates:

a. Reported change in production, prices, wages, maintenance costs, fuel/energy costs, and productivity, 1983.

b. Anticipated change in production; and percent of respondents reporting plans for new plants, plant expansion, and new equipment; 1984.

This is the 28th annual survey.

OTHER MAJOR NONMETALS, ANNUAL FEATURE

(p. 68-70) Annual article, by Sid Levine, profiling other major nonmetal industries, including agstone/aglime, barite, feldspar, fluorspar, gypsum, lime, phosphate rock, potash, and talc/pyrophyllite. Profiles include text data on production value and/or volume, consumption distribution by end use, and occasionally imports, for 1982, with selected comparisons to 1980-81.

INTERNATIONAL CEMENT SCENE: PLANT AND PRODUCTION UPDATE, ANNUAL FEATURE

(p. 79-106) Annual report, by Sid Levine, on world cement production, 1980-82. Data are primarily from company annual reports.

Includes 1 chart and 1 table showing world cement production summary, and production of 20 leading countries, various years 1977-82; and country profiles, with text data on capacity and start-up dates for new and planned plants and plant expansions, and cement production, 1980-82, by country arranged by world area.

C7600–2.502: May 1984 (Vol. 76, No. 11)

CONSERVATION TILLAGE: A GROWING MARKET FOR AGLIME

(p. 55-57) By Bruce W. Remick. Article, with 1 table showing crop acreage under conventional tillage, and under conservation tillage by type, selected years 1973-83. Data are from USDA.

C7600–2.503: July 1984 (Vol. 77, No. 1)

U.S. CEMENT: RECOVERING AS A CHANGED INDUSTRY

(p. 83-88) By Roy A. Grancher. Article, with 1 table showing number of wet and dry cement plants, for 13 leading cement companies, 1979 and 1984.

C7600–2.504: Aug. 1984 (Vol. 77, No. 2)

SAFETY AWARDS FEATURE OF NSA OPERATOR'S MEETING

(p. 111) Article, with 1 text table showing number of slag processing plants receiving National Slag Assn awards for operating 1/more years without lost-time injury, by company, 1983.

C7715
Polk, R. L., and Co.

C7715–2   PASSENGER CAR AND TRUCK SCRAPPAGE AND GROWTH in the U.S.
Annual.   Mar. 12, 1984.   7 p.
SRI/MF/complete

Annual press release presenting number of motor vehicles in use as of 1st and last day of year, and new vehicles registered and vehicles scrapped during year, for autos and trucks, years ended June 30, 1947-83. Data are compiled from State records.

Contains narrative summary and 3 tables.

Availability: R. L. Polk and Co., Motor Statistical Division, 431 Howard St., Detroit MI 48231, †; SRI/MF/complete.

C7715–3   POCKET SUMMARY OF REGISTRATIONS: New Cars, New Trucks
Monthly.   Approx. 5 p.
SRI/MF/complete, shipped quarterly

Monthly report on new passenger car and truck registrations, by make and/or model, including imports, and registration totals for previous 10 years.

Data are compiled from State records. Reports are issued approximately 2 months after month of coverage.

Contains 8 tables, listed below.

Availability: R. L. Polk and Co., Motor Statistical Division, 431 Howard St., Detroit MI 48231, †; SRI/MF/complete, shipped quarterly.

Issues reviewed during 1984: Sept. 1983-Aug. 1984 (D).

TABLES:

[1-3] New passenger car registrations [by domestic make and model, and total imports]; and new truck registrations [by domestic and import make; all for month of coverage, year to date, and same periods of previous year].

[4] Trucks by weight groups, year to date [and total for previous year, by domestic and import make].

[5-7] New imported cars, and new imported and domestic light trucks, leading makes [year to date, current and previous year].

[8] New vehicle registrations, U.S., calendar year totals [cars and trucks, for previous 10 years].

C7800
Prentice-Hall, Inc.

C7800–1   ALMANAC OF BUSINESS AND INDUSTRIAL FINANCIAL RATIOS, 1984 Edition
Annual.   [1983.]
xxvii+371 p.
LC 72-181403.
SRI/MF/not filmed

Annual report, by Leo Troy, presenting composite operating and financial ratios for corporations in approximately 200 SIC 2- to 4-digit industries, for fiscal year ended June 30, 1980. Data are aggregated for all corporations within each industry, and for those operating at a profit.

Data are based on the latest IRS tax return statistics available and are presented for corporations in 12 asset size categories, from zero to $250 million/over.

Contains introduction, methodology, and definitions (p. vii-xvii); contents listing (p. xix-xxvii); and table I (for all corporations) and table II (for profitable corporations), repeated for each detailed industry, and showing: number of reporting establishments and total receipts; 12 operating factors as percent of net sales or of total receipts; and, as applicable, 6 financial ratios, and 4 financial factor percentages; all by corporation asset size, FY80 (p. 2-363).

Industries are presented as follows:

a. Agriculture, forestry, and fishing; mining, including oil/gas extraction; and construction. (p. 2-33)

b. Manufacturing. (p. 34-175)

c. Transportation; communication; electric, gas, and sanitary services; and wholesale and retail trade. (p. 176-267)

d. Banking; credit agencies other than banks; security and commodity brokers, and allied services; insurance; real estate; and holding and other investment companies. (p. 268-317)

e. Service industries, including medical, legal, and other services. (p. 318-363)

Also includes index. (p. 367-371)

Availability: Prentice-Hall, Inc., Mail Order Sales, Old Tappan NJ 07675, $35.00; SRI/MF/not filmed.

C7875
Production Publishing Co.

C7875-1   PRODUCTION

Monthly.   Approx. 150 p.
LC 48-13360.
SRI/MF/excerpts, shipped
quarterly

Monthly trade journal reporting on developments in metalworking industry operations, including production processes, new equipment and materials, and management methods. Publication is directed to engineers and managers responsible for improving manufacturing efficiency, costs, and quality.

Issues include feature articles, occasionally with statistics; regular narrative depts, including news briefs, production tips, and lists of new literature and equipment; and monthly "Manufacturing Outlook" feature, usually presenting brief summaries of economic developments in or affecting manufacturing industries, and also occasionally including statistics.

Features with substantial statistical content are described, as they appear, under "Statistical Features." Each issue of the journal is reviewed, but an abstract is published in SRI monthly issues only when statistical features appear.

Availability: Production, PO Box 101, Bloomfield Hills MI 48303-0101, qualified subscribers †, others $35.00 per yr., single copy $4.00, Planbook $7.50; SRI/MF/excerpts for all portions covered under "Statistical Features;" shipped quarterly.

Issues reviewed during 1984: Nov. 1983-Oct. 1984 (P) (Vol. 92, Nos. 5-6; Vol. 93, Nos. 1-6; Vol. 94, Nos. 1-4).

STATISTICAL FEATURES:

C7875-1.501: Jan. 1984 (Vol. 93, No. 1)

JUST-IN-TIME WORKS!

(p. 42-46) By Drew Winter. Article on "just-in-time" (JIT) inventory management concept. Includes 3 charts showing foreman's workday activity distribution under traditional and JIT inventory management; and problems in implementing JIT, as perceived by auto manufacturers and suppliers surveyed in summer 1983 by Arthur Andersen & Co.

1984 CAPITAL SPENDING UP 32%, ANNUAL FEATURE

(p. 50-51) Annual article, by Edward D. McCallum, Jr., on equipment capital spending forecasts for metalworking industries, 1984, presenting highlights from an annual survey of 2,525 plants.

Includes 2 charts and 2 text tables showing the following: distribution of equipment spending by type; typical expenditures by plant employment size; reasons for investment; and current and planned use of robots, by function; 1984, with selected 5-year averages.

For description of complete survey, see C7875-1.502, below.

C7875-1.502: Mar. 1984 (Vol. 93, No. 3)

Annual "Manufacturing Planbook" issue. Includes narrative articles and buyers guide; and 1 statistical feature, described below.

CAPITAL SPENDING, 1984, ANNUAL FEATURE

(p. 41-47) Annual article, by Edward D. McCallum Jr., on capital equipment spending forecasts for metalworking industries, 1984, based on responses of 2,525 plants to a fall 1983 survey. Responses are weighted to represent all 13,500 plants originally contacted for the survey.

Includes 2 charts and 12 tables showing the following:

a. Equipment spending amount; and distribution of equipment spending in selected SIC 3-digit industries; all by equipment type.

b. Percent of respondents planning to purchase computer numerical control equipment and electrical discharge machines, by type; and percent using and planning to use computerized data systems and robots, by production function; 1984-86 period.

For description of related article, see C7875-1.501, above.

C7875-1.503: Apr. 1984 (Vol. 93, No. 4)

CAD/CAM INDUSTRY STILL EXPANDING, ANNUAL FEATURE

(p. 11) Annual article, with 1 chart showing computer-aided design/computer-aided manufacturing system market shares, by vending company, 1983. Data are from Daratech, Inc.

C7875-1.504: May 1984 (Vol. 93, No. 5)

R&D EXPENDITURES RISE 9 PERCENT IN 1984

(p. 9) Brief article, with 2 charts showing distribution of R&D funding and performance among Federal Government, industry, universities, and other nonprofit institutions, 1984. Data are from Battelle Memorial Institute.

Full Battelle report is covered in SRI under R3300-1.

C7975
Providence Journal Co.

C7975-1   1984 JOURNAL-BULLETIN RHODE ISLAND ALMANAC, 98th Annual Edition

Annual.   [1984.]   292 p.
LC 51-24546.
SRI/MF/excerpts

Annual compilation, for 1984, of reference information and statistics for Rhode Island, including history, economy, government, and social composition. Data are primarily for various years 1980-83, with historical trends from as early as 1730. Most data are from State and Federal government reports.

Report is designed to present a comprehensive overview of the State. Various socioeconomic, demographic, and geographic breakdowns are shown, as applicable, for selected topics. These breakdowns include data by city, county, school district, age, race/ethnicity, urban-rural status, industry, and occupation. Comparisons to total U.S. are also often included.

Contains contents listing (1 p.); and the following:

a. Calendars; astronomical, climatological, and historical information; State and city/town organization, depts, officials, personnel, and finances including selected salaries; bridges and airports; elections; and miscellaneous information; interspersed with text data and 13 tables. (p. 1-156)

b. Education, including selected data for individual colleges and universities; libraries; population, housing, and employment characteristics; selected business data; health facilities and capacity; newspapers; civic and service organizations; villages; radio and TV stations; highways; disasters, including damages and lives lost; and sports information; interspersed with text data and 33 tables. (p. 157-279)

c. Subject index. (p. 280-292)

All tables are described below.

Availability: Providence Journal Co., Providence Journal-Bulletin Almanac, 75 Fountain St., Providence RI 02902, $3.75; SRI/MF/excerpts for text data and statistical portions described below.

TABLES:

C7975-1.1: Statistics

a. **Finances:** selected taxation, expenditure, and social indicators, with Rhode Island rank among the 50 States; State officials' salaries; State finances, including Federal grants by program; State debt; and assessed property value and taxes levied. 6 tables. (p. 27, 58-60, and 113)

b. **Elections:** 1980 U.S. presidential voting results by candidate and State; and 1982-83 State and municipal primary, general, and special election results, by office and candidate, and referenda approvals and rejections. 7 tables. (p. 122-142)

c. **Education:** superintendents and salaries, educational finances, including school transportation costs, average daily membership and attendance, enrollment, staff, minimum staff salary, and number of buildings. 5 tables. (p. 169-171)

d. **Market and population data:** population; manufacturing share of employment; retail sales; occupied housing units; U.S. population by State and for 100 largest cities; Rhode Island and Providence population, from 1730; newspaper circulation; and population and housing characteristics. 8 tables. (p. 175-181)

e. **Employment and earnings:** labor force, by employment status; unemployment insurance claims; wages; manufacturing employment, hours, and earnings; personal income by source; housing units; financial institutions operating data; business firms, employment, and payroll; residential building permits; and U.S. CPI by item. 14 tables. (p. 182-191)

f. **Highways and miscellaneous:** newspaper circulation; churches and membership, by denomination; highway distances from Providence for selected U.S. cities; and State highway mileage and fatalities. 6 tables. (p. 212-213, 225, 254-256)

C8075
Restaurant Business, Inc.

C8075-1   RESTAURANT BUSINESS
Monthly.
SRI now covers this publication under C1200-5.

C8111
Rodale Press

C8111-1   CORNUCOPIA PROJECT REPORTS
Series. For individual publication data, see below.
SRI/MF/complete

Continuing series of reports evaluating current U.S. food system and presenting recommendations for future development. Covers environmental concerns and aspects of production, marketing, and finance. Includes data on individual States' dependence on food imports from out of State, by commodity.

Data are collected for the Rodale Press Cornucopia Project from Federal and State agencies and various private sources.

Series presents reports on individual States and occasional special reports. Special reports are covered in SRI only when they include substantial statistical content.

State reports generally include detailed narrative analysis, and a food imports table showing the most recently available data for the following, by commodity: quantity and retail value of the State's production and consumption; value of shipments to and from the State; and amount of land required to meet total State consumption.

Reports reviewed during 1984 are listed below; additional data accompanying narrative analyses are noted.

Availability: Cornucopia Project, Publications Department, 33 E. Minor St., Emmaus PA 18049; SRI/MF/complete.

REPORTS:

C8111-1.19: Step Toward Regeneration: A Study of the Nebraska Food System
[Monograph. May 1984. 55 p. $4.00. SRI/MF/complete.]
By Paul S. Estenson. Report also includes 3 undated tables showing Nebraska consumption, production, and imports, and U.S. per capita consumption, for specific vegetable crops; and analysis of production costs for tomatoes, and for corn for grain, on a typical Nebraska farm.
Report also includes directory of Nebraska food organizations.

C8111-1.20: Texas Food System: Prospects for Sustainability
[Monograph. 1984. 62 p. $5.00. SRI/MF/complete.]
By C. Ronald Carroll et al. Report also includes directory of Texas food organizations.

C8111-1.21: Vermont Food System: Toward a Traditional Self Reliance
[Monograph. 1984. 61 p. $5.00. SRI/MF/complete.]

By Richard Tarlov. Report also includes 2 charts showing distribution of Vermont land area by use, 1977, and agricultural receipts by commodity group, 1980; 1 table showing Vermont population, farms, and farm acreage, selected years 1850-1981; and directories of Vermont agricultural organizations and "pick-it-yourself" growers.

C8115
Roscoe, John F.

C8115-1   1984: THIRTEENTH ANNUAL DOLLARS PER DAY SURVEY of the Small Food Store Industry
Annual. 1984. 177 p.
SRI/MF/complete
Annual survey report on financial condition and operations of the 12 largest publicly held convenience store chains in the small food store industry, for latest fiscal year (FY83 for most chains), with survey trends from the early 1970s. Data are presented for individual chains, often on a dollars per day per store basis, with selected rankings.

Covers number of stores; sales and profits, with comparison to CPI; stores purchased, opened, closed/sold, planned, and owned vs. leased; stock performance and holdings, including shares held by largest stockholders and by officers and directors; inventory valuation methods; salaries of top executives and directors; and detailed data on gasoline operations.

Also includes analysis of electricity costs in surveyed companies' headquarters cities; data on overall convenience store share of food store and gasoline sales; and selected data for chains not covered in current survey.

Report is based on an annual survey of company annual reports, proxy statements, and 10-K reports filed with the SEC. The surveyed companies represent approximately 33% of all convenience stores. The report is intended in part to permit convenience store operators to compare their operations with those of the surveyed companies.

Contains contents listing (1 p.); introduction, methodology, and 2 summary tables (p. 1-9); report, with 3 trend charts and 76 tables interspersed with survey correspondence, excerpts from company annual reports or prospectuses, directory of survey companies, and narrative analyses (p. 10-151); and editorial articles, comments, and excerpts from previous surveys (p. 152-177).

Availability: Dollars per Day Survey, PO Box 886, Benicia CA 94510, $60.00 1st copy, $20.00 each additional copy; SRI/MF/complete.

C8115-2   WHAT DO THE 25 LARGEST OIL COMPANIES HAVE TO SAY ABOUT GASOLINE MARKETING IN 1983?
Annual. 1983. 197 p.
SRI/MF/complete
Annual report on top 25 oil companies' gasoline marketing operations and finances, 1980-82, with selected trends from 1970s. Includes data on sales, earnings, employment, return on equity, domestic gasoline sales as percent of worldwide

sales, annual financial report characteristics, percent of stock owned by corporate officers/directors, number of service stations owned, gasoline product sales volume, and refinery capacity utilization rate, all by company.

Report also includes data for selected companies on refining/marketing revenues, capital expenditures, operating loss/profit, and income; refinery crude oil runs; and refined products produced.

Also includes data on U.S. motor vehicle registrations; motor fuel consumption and passenger car efficiency; vehicle mileage; top 40 refiners crude distillation capacity; and convenience store establishments and gasoline units, and gallons sold, gasoline operating margins, and gasoline share of total sales, all by chain for 10 chains, with convenience store share of gasoline market, and average gasoline retail price; various years 1950-83.

Data sources include oil company annual reports to shareholders, reports of DOE and DOT, and the 13th annual *Dollars per Day Survey of the Small Food Store Industry.*

Contents:

a. Contents listing and introduction. (2 p.)

b. Excerpts from company 1982 annual and 1983 quarterly reports, with 34 tables and text statistics. (p. 5-139)

c. Summary and related background information, with 20 tables. (p. 140-180)

d. Convenience store section, with text statistics and 14 tables. (p. 181-195)

This is the 3rd edition of the report.

Availability: Gasoline Marketing Survey, 1765 Park Rd., Benicia CA 94510, $50.00; SRI/MF/complete.

C8130
Schwartz Publications

C8130-1   DISCOUNT MERCHANDISER
Monthly. Approx. 100 p.
ISSN 0012-3579.
LC 66-93756.
SRI/MF/not filmed
Monthly trade journal reporting on general merchandise retail stores selling at low margins, with minimum annual revenue of $500,000 and minimum size of 10,000 sq. ft. Covers management, sales, space allocation, discount customers and their shopping habits, and major categories of merchandise.

Data are from studies by the National Mass Retailing Institute, reports from individual retail stores, *Discount Merchandiser* (DM) annual census of stores, and other sources.

Issues generally contain the following:

a. Monthly "Scoreboard" table, showing sales and net earnings after taxes of approximately 40 individual companies. Data are for various periods, identified for each company, and include percent change during specified period.

b. Editorial depts; and news and feature articles, occasionally with substantial statistics.

Annual statistical features include reports on discount chain store operations, with extensive statistics; and growth of combination stores in the supermarket and drug industries.

Monthly "Scoreboard" table appears in most issues, on a space available basis. All additional features with substantial statistical content are described, as they appear, under "Statistical Features." Nonstatistical features are not covered.

Issues subsequent to Feb. 1984 were not available for review.

Availability: Discount Merchandiser, Circulation Department, Two Park Ave., New York NY 10157, $30.00 per yr., single copy $3.50, special issues $20.00; SRI/MF/not filmed.

Issues reviewed during 1984: Nov. 1983-Feb. 1984 (P) (Vol. 23, Nos. 11-12; Vol. 24, Nos. 1-2).

STATISTICAL FEATURES:

C8130–1.501: Jan. 1984 (Vol. 24, No. 1)

DISCOUNTERS HOLD OWN IN RECORD AND TAPE SALES

(p. 18) Article, with 1 table showing distribution of record/tape sales, by type of music, 1981-82. Data are from Recording Industry Assn of America.

NAVIGATING THE CONSUMER ELECTRONICS COSMOS

(p. 43-63) Article, with 1 table showing estimated discount store sales of consumer electronics, by product type, 1983. Data are from *Discount Merchandiser.*

C8130–1.502: February 1984 (Vol. 24, No. 2)

COMBO STORES ARE UNSTOPPABLE, ANNUAL FEATURE

(p. 42-71) Annual report on growth of combination stores in the supermarket and drug industries. Consists of brief articles, interspersed with 1 chart and 2 tables showing the following for both industries:

a. Trends in number of combination stores and sales, 1977 and 1980-83. 1 chart. (p. 42)
b. By company: total and combination stores, 1983; number of combination stores planned for 1984/85; and typical size of new stores; for approximately 45 companies. 2 tables. (p. 68-70)

This is the 3rd annual report.

TOYS STAGE STRONG COMEBACK

(p. 102-120) Article, with 1 table (p. 108) showing discount store toy sales by type of toy, 1982. Data are from *Discount Merchandiser.*

C8400
Simmons-Boardman
Publishing Corp.

C8400–1   RAILWAY AGE
Monthly.   Approx. 80 p.
ISSN 0033-8834.
LC 52-38523.
SRI/MF/excerpts, shipped quarterly

Monthly trade journal reporting on trends and developments in railroads and rail rapid transit industry operations, finances, traffic, equipment, new technology, and regulation. Includes data from U.S. Railway Assn, Assn of American Railroads (AAR), ICC, Data Resources, Inc. (DRI), individual company reports, and other sources.

General format:

a. News briefs, editorial depts, and articles, occasionally with substantial statistical content, including annual outlook and review features.
b. Monthly "Market Outlook" and "Market Indicators" features, with 1 chart showing rail freight traffic trends; 5 monthly tables; and special or annual tables.
c. Quarterly table on rail company revenues and expenses, compiled by AAR from reports submitted to ICC.

Monthly and quarterly tables are listed below. Most monthly tables appear in all issues. All additional features with substantial statistical content are described, as they appear, under "Statistical Features;" page location and latest period of coverage for quarterly table are also noted. Nonstatistical features are not covered.

Prior to the Aug. 1984 issue, journal also includes monthly "DRI railroad industry monitor" table comparing selected economic indicators with Class I rail freight traffic by commodity.

AAR weekly and monthly reports, from which quarterly revenue and expense data are derived, are covered in SRI under A3275-2 and A3275-3, respectively.

Availability: Railway Age, Subscription Department, PO Box 530, Bristol CT 06010, qualified subscribers $12.00 per yr., others $30.00 per yr., single copy $3.00; SRI/MF/excerpts for monthly tables and all portions covered under "Statistical Features."

Issues reviewed during 1984: Nov. 1983-Oct. 1984 (P) (Vol. 184, Nos. 11-12; Vol. 185, Nos. 1-10) [Vol. 184, No. 12 incorrectly reads Vol. 185].

RECURRING STATISTICS:

MONTHLY TABLES

[1] Freight cars [ordered and delivered, and on order/undelivered as of 1st day of month, for month 1-3 months prior to cover date, previous month, and year to date, with comparisons to previous year].

[2] Locomotives (new/rebuilt) [delivered, and backlog as of 1st day of month, for month 1-3 months prior to cover date and previous month, with year-to-date deliveries and comparisons to previous year].

[3] Estimated ownership: all revenue freight cars [by type of car and rail revenue class, as of 1st day of month 1-2 months prior to cover date, and same date of previous year].

[4-5] Revenue freight carloadings [by commodity], and piggyback loadings; [for various weeks 3-7 weeks prior to cover date, with percent change from previous year, and year-to-date freight revenue ton-miles and piggyback loadings].

QUARTERLY TABLE

[1] Revenues and expenses of railways [shows operating revenues and expenses, operating ratio, income after fixed charges, net operating income, and net income, for approximately 30 railroad companies, for quarter and year to date, ending 3-4 months prior to cover date, and same periods of previous year].

STATISTICAL FEATURES:

C8400–1.501: Nov. 1983 (Vol. 184, No. 11)

ROADWAY TRAIN ACCIDENTS: DOWN, IRREGULARLY

(p. 60) Brief article, with 1 table showing number and reportable cost of railroad accidents caused by track and roadbed defects, 1979-82. Data are from Federal Railroad Administration and other sources.

C8400–1.502: Dec. 1983 (Vol. 184, No. 12)

[Issue incorrectly reads Vol. 185.]

1984 OUTLOOK: MOMENTUM AT WORK, ANNUAL FEATURE

(p. 32-36) Annual article, by Gus Welty, forecasting railroad traffic and equipment growth in 1984. Includes 1 table showing revenue piggyback carloadings, selected years 1957-83.

C8400–1.503: Jan. 1984 (Vol. 185, No. 1)

QUARTERLY TABLE

[1] Revenues and expenses of railways, 3rd quarter 1983. (p. 66-67)

MARKET INDICATORS SPECIAL TABLE

(p. 14) Table showing freight car order and delivery outlook, 1984. Data are from American Railway Car Institute survey of 27 carbuilders, component suppliers, and others.

PASSENGER-CAR MARKET AT A GLANCE, ANNUAL FEATURE

(p. 61) Annual feature on rail passenger industry outlook for 1984. Includes 2 charts and 4 tables showing passenger car delivery and backlog trends from 1976; passenger cars delivered and on order, by purchaser, type, and builder, 1983; and passenger car order outlook, by purchaser and type, 1984 and 1985-89 period.

C8400–1.504: Feb. 1984 (Vol. 185, No. 2)

18 RAILROADS POST POSITIVE RETURNS

(p. 20) Brief article, with 1 text table showing return on investment of 18 Class I railroads, 1983. Data are from railroad reports to ICC.

FREIGHT RAILROADING IN 1983: A STATISTICAL REVIEW, ANNUAL FEATURE

(p. 61-63) Annual compilation of data on railroad industry developments in 1983, with selected trends from 1972. Most data are from Federal and railroad assn sources.

Includes 8 summary charts, and 13 tables listed below. Most tables show data for Class I line-haul railroads. Data for Amtrak and

Auto-Train Corp. are incorporated only in table [10]. Unless otherwise noted, tables show data for 1972-83.

Traffic and Finances

[1] Freight traffic [revenue and piggyback carloadings, and revenue ton-miles]. (p. 61)

[2] Methods of shipping motor vehicles from factories [total shipments, and highway and rail distribution], 1972-82. (p. 61)

[3] Condensed income account, 1972 and 1982-83. (p. 61)

[4] Carloadings of major commodities [by type], 1982-83. (p. 62)

[5] Capital expenditures [for rolling stock and facilities] and retained funds. (p. 62)

[6] Operating revenues [freight, passenger, and other], 1972 and 1982-83. (p. 62)

[7] Railway current [assets, liabilities, and] ratio. (p. 62)

[8] Net railway operating income, rate of return on net investment, and net income. (p. 62)

Equipment and Indexes

[9] Spot price indices of fuel and materials/supplies (1977=100) [selected dates 1981-83]. (p. 63)

[10] New/rebuilt equipment installed [by vehicle type]. (p. 63)

[11] Prices and revenue averages [PPI for railroad equipment, railroad freight price index, and revenue ton-mile]. (p. 63)

[12] Rail revenue adequacy standard [ICC approved debt, equity, and return on investment rates], 1978-82. (p. 63)

[13] Railroad cost recovery index [labor, fuel, materials/supplies, other costs, and total] (1977=100). (p. 63)

C8400–1.505: Apr. 1984 (Vol. 185, No. 4)

QUARTERLY TABLE

[1] Revenues and expenses of railways, 4th quarter 1983. (p. 66-67)

C8400–1.506: May 1984 (Vol. 185, No. 5)

CHANGE IN THE '80s: THE INTERMODAL REVOLUTION

(p. 35-38) By Gus Welty. Article, with 1 chart showing rail piggyback carloadings, quinquennially 1958-83.

C8400–1.507: June 1984 (Vol. 185, No. 6)

TWELVE RAILROADS BEAT THE AVERAGE

(p. 27) Brief article, with 1 table ranking top 12 Class I railroads by percent return on investment, 1983. Data are from ICC.

C8400–1.508: July 1984 (Vol. 185, No. 7)

QUARTERLY TABLE

[1] Revenues and expenses of railways, 1st quarter 1984. (p. 96)

MIDYEAR REPORT: THE COMEBACK BLUES, ANNUAL FEATURE

(p. 37-39) Annual article, by Luther S. Miller, on railroad performance in 1st half 1984, based on Assn of American Railroads reports.

Includes 1 chart and 1 table showing carloadings, 1st half 1980-84; and railroad operating revenues and expenses, return on investment, and ordinary and net operating income, 1st quarter 1983-84.

FOR SUPPLIERS, A SLOW TURNAROUND

(p. 39) Brief article, with 1 table showing average, median, low, and high forecasts for railroad freight car orders and deliveries, 1985. Data are from responses of 24 carbuilders and others to a survey conducted by American Railway Car Institute.

DETECTORS GET SMARTER

(p. 78-83) By John Armstrong. Article, with 1 table and 1 chart showing railroad defective equipment detection devices in operation as of Dec. 1983, and planned for 1984 or 1984-89 period, by equipment type, for individual U.S. and Canadian railroads; and cost resulting from selected types of U.S. railroad accidents involving detectable defects, 1979-83.

Data are from a *Railway Age* survey, and Federal Railroad Administration.

C8400–1.509: Aug. 1984 (Vol. 185, No. 8)

MARKET INDICATORS SPECIAL TABLE

(p. 14) Table showing GNP, industrial production index, auto sales, housing starts, and corporate profit margin, 1983-85 and quarterly 1984-85. Data are from Goldman, Sachs and Co.

C8400–1.510: Sept. 1984 (Vol. 185, No. 9)

MARKET INDICATORS SPECIAL TABLE

(p. 15) Table showing coal production; consumption by utilities, steelmakers, and other users; exports; and synthetic fuel use; selected years 1974-95. Data are from National Coal Assn.

RAIL: THE POINT OF THE PYRAMID

(p. 57-68) By John Armstrong. Article examining methods of producing high quality steel rails. Data are from the American Iron and Steel Institute. Includes 1 table showing steel mill shipments for standard rails and total steel products, 1974-83.

C8400–1.511: Oct. 1984 (Vol. 185, No. 10)

QUARTERLY TABLE

[1] Revenues and expenses of railways, 2nd quarter 1984. (p. 72-73)

MARKET INDICATORS SPECIAL TABLE

(p. 14) Table ranking major commodities by share of total railroad freight tonnage and revenue, 1983. Data are from ICC.

C8400–2   PLANT LOCATION, 1984
Annual. 1984. 256 p.
SRI/MF/complete

Annual report compiling demographic, employment, and other data relevant to the selection of industrial plant sites, for U.S., Canada, and Puerto Rico. Data generally are current to 1982 or 1983. Includes some or all of the following for each State and Province and for Puerto Rico:

a. Financial assistance programs available to industries; tax rates; higher education and medical facilities; high school graduates; percent unionized workers; population, by SMSA or Canadian Census Metropolitan Area; and population and climate data, by major city.

b. Labor force and unemployment, by SMSA; manufacturing employment, hours, and earnings, by industry and SMSA; manufacturing

earnings, for selected occupations and SMSAs; railroad, airline, and utility services; nonfuel mineral production, by type; and listing of industry-related government agencies.

Data are from a variety of public and private sources, primarily U.S. Census Bureau, BLS, and Statistics Canada.

Contains contents listing (p. 5); 4 narrative articles on aspects of plant location (p. 6-24); directories of railroads, port authorities, and U.S. foreign trade zones (p. 25-33); data sources (p. 34); statistical section (p. 35-245); and directory of foreign development offices (p. 245-249).

Availability: Plant Location, 508 Birch St., Bristol CT 06010, $40.00 (prepaid); SRI/MF/complete.

C8450
Sosland Publishing Co.

C8450–2   MILLING AND BAKING NEWS: 1984 Grain Directory/Buyer's Guide
Annual. 1983. 110 p.
SRI/MF/excerpts

Annual *Milling and Baking News* directory and buyer's guide, for 1984, listing U.S. and Canadian grain and grain transportation companies, equipment, and services, including U.S. storage elevator and rail fleet capacity, by type and company. Data are compiled by *Milling and Baking News.*

Contents:

a. Contents listing. (p. 5)

b. Directory of U.S. multiple elevator companies, with capacity and number of elevators (p. 9-17); article on new units and expansions (p. 19-20); U.S. statistical section, with 5 tables listed below (p. 2l); and directories of U.S. grain exporting companies (p. 22), and terminal, subterminal, river, and port elevator companies, with capacity (p. 23-45).

c. Directories of Canadian multiple, terminal, and transfer elevator companies, with capacity and number of elevators or berths (p. 46-50); index to companies (p. 55-58); buyer's guide (p. 59-92); and index to executives (p. 95-102).

d. Directories of U.S. grain transporting railroads with track mileage and number of cars, barge companies with number of vessels, and motor freight companies with number of trailers and/or tractors (p. 103-104); and manufacturer and product guides (p. 105-107).

For description of 1983 directory, see SRI 1982 Annual, under C8450-4.

Milling and Baking News is a weekly journal reporting on marketing developments in the milling/baking industry. The only feature of the weekly journal covered to date in SRI is a special report on the 1977 Census of Manufactures, described in SRI 1980 Annual, under C8450-1.

Milling and Baking News publishes 2 other directories: *Milling Directory,* covered in SRI under C8450-3; and *Baking Directory,* which is nonstatistical.

Availability: Milling and Baking News, Board of Trade Bldg., 4800 Main St., Kansas City MO 64112, $20.00; SRI/MF/excerpts for all portions except buyer, manufacturer, and product guides.

TABLES:

[Data are derived from information gathered for the 1984 directories.]

[1-4] Port, terminal, subterminal, and river elevators [number, and upright and flat capacity, by State]. (p. 21)

[5] Top 20 U.S. grain storage companies [ranked by capacity, with number of elevators owned]. (p. 21)

C8650
Technical Publishing Co.

C8650-1 DATAMATION

Semimonthly. Approx. 200 p.
ISSN 0011-6963.
LC 58-24546.
SRI/MF/excerpts, shipped
quarterly

Semimonthly trade journal reporting developments and trends in the computer, data processing, and information management industries. Covers equipment, technology, costs, uses, and marketing. Data are generally based on *Datamation* surveys and other commercial sources.

Issues contain feature articles, occasionally with statistics; regular editorial depts; and news items.

Annual statistical features include minicomputer/microcomputer and computer mainframe market surveys; users' ratings of software packages; data processing (dp) salaries; and financial performance of the top 100 U.S. dp companies, and the top dp companies operating in Europe.

Features with substantial statistical content are described, as they appear, under "Statistical Features." Each issue of the journal is reviewed, but an abstact is published in SRI monthly issues only when statistical features appear.

Prior to the Apr. 1, 1984 issue, journal was published monthly.

Availability: Datamation, Subscription Department, 875 Third Ave., New York NY 10022, qualified subscribers †, others $50.00 per yr., qualified students and public and school libraries $38.00 per yr., single copy $3.00; SRI/MF/excerpts for all portions described under "Statistical Features;" shipped quarterly.

Issues reviewed during 1984: Nov. 1983-Mar. 1984 (monthly); Apr. 1-Oct. 15, 1984 (semimonthly) (P) (Vol. 29, Nos. 11-12; Vol. 30, Nos. 1-17) [Vol. 30, No. 17 incorrectly reads Vol. 30, No. 16].

STATISTICAL FEATURES:

C8650-1.501: Nov. 1983 (Vol. 29, No. 11)
MINIS LOSE OUT TO PCs, ANNUAL FEATURE

(p. 44-52) Annual article, by John W. Verity, on mini/microcomputer use by business/other organizations. Data are based on responses of 7,012 users to a 1983 survey by *Datamation* and Cowen and Co., and cover recent and planned equipment purchases.

Includes the following survey response data, generally shown by equipment supplier, with comparison to previous surveys:

a. Top 10 minicomputer systems, based on number of respondents acquiring systems and number of units acquired, with estimated value; personal computer supplier choice for new users; and correlation between mainframe and personal computer supplier. 1 table and 2 charts.

b. Personal computer supplier choice for software and hardware; and minicomputer current and planned supplier with detail for communication industry. 4 charts.

c. Non-phone local network current and planned installations; 32-bit system purchases; and whether substantial price concession received with last minicomputer purchase. 3 charts.

MICROS AT BIG FIRMS: A SURVEY

(p. 161-174) Article on personal computer (PC) use in large business/institutional settings. Data are based on 1,001 responses to an Apr.-June 1983 random survey covering installations that have purchased/leased equipment with equivalent monthly rental fees exceeding $50,000. Survey was designed by Data Decisions Inc. and conducted by Beta Research Corp.

Includes 8 tables showing survey response on personal computers as follows:

a. Current, anticipated, and "ideal" role of data processing (DP) dept in purchase decision, and in providing selected user services; factors affecting PC selection; role of various individuals or depts in non-DP dept equipment choice; and depts using PCs and average number in use.

b. Organizational level using, current and anticipated uses, and vendor choice, for DP and other depts.

EXCESS OF MONEY

(p. 195-198) By Larry Marion. Article on computer companies making initial public stock offering during year ended Sept. 1983. Data are from Securities Data Corp.

Includes 2 tables showing date and value of initial offering, price/earnings ratio, and net income, for 10 companies with largest offering (also shows revenue for latest 12 months, stock premium over book value, and type of product or service), and for 10 companies with highest price/earnings ratio (also shows price per share).

C8650-1.502: Dec. 1983 (Vol. 29, No. 12)
SYSTEMS SOFTWARE SURVEY, ANNUAL FEATURE

(p. 105-150) Annual report presenting users' ratings of 106 systems-oriented software packages. Data are based on 5,681 responses to a July 1983 Data Decisions, Inc. survey of data processing dept managers.

Includes tabular list of mean ratings; and 1 chart, repeated for all packages, 6 package types, and each individual package, showing ratings on overall satisfaction with product and support services, performance, vendor support, and operations.

DP CAREER PATHS

(p. 178-188) By Kate M. Kaiser. Article on data processing careers, based on 1979 and 1983 surveys of 27-35 large private companies. The surveys covered 59 data processing system and user staff members involved in major development projects.

Includes respondent characteristics, and 1 table showing position title, 1979 and 1983; number of title changes, 1979-83 period; and desired job title, 1988.

HOLD THE PHONE

(p. 246.3-246.6) By Paul Tate. Article reporting on West European private branch exchange (PBX) industry. Data are from Pactel. Includes 1 table showing market value for PBX systems over and under 100 lines installed and shipped, for 5 West European countries or areas, 1982 and 1986.

1984 MARKET FORECAST

(p. 247.3-247.6) By John W. Verity. Article reporting on market outlook for original equipment manufacturers (OEMs) and systems houses, organizations that develop customized computer systems for resale using components from various manufacturers. Data are from responses of approximately 7,700 OEMs and systems houses to a summer 1983 Cowen and Co. and *Datamation* survey.

Includes 2 charts showing percent of OEMs and systems houses purchasing micro-based personal computers and components in 1983, and planning to buy minicomputers and personal computers in 1984.

C8650-1.503: Jan. 1984 (Vol. 30, No. 1)
GOING GLOBAL WITH WORLDWIDE NETWORKS

(p. 200.3-200.5) By Paul Tate. Article reporting on trends and developments in international communications networks. Data are from UK Dept of Trade and Industry. Includes 1 table showing number of communications cable channels linking 8 major world routes (no date).

C8650-1.504: Feb. 1984 (Vol. 30, No. 2)
WORKSTATION MARKET GAMBLE

(p. 199.5-199.8) By Alexander Stein. Article, with 2 charts showing computer workstation use by application (undated); and worldwide expenditures for microcomputers, 1982-87. Data are from Dataquest, Inc.; workstation data are from a survey of 900 users.

C8650-1.505: Mar. 1984 (Vol. 30, No. 3)
APPLICATIONS SOFTWARE SURVEY, ANNUAL FEATURE

(p. 198-224) Annual article presenting users' ratings of 82 applications-oriented software packages. Data are based on 3,376 responses to a Sept.-Oct. 1983 survey designed by Data Decisions, Inc.

Includes tabular list of mean ratings; and 1 chart repeated for all packages, 7 package types, and each individual package, showing ratings on overall satisfaction, performance, vendor support, operations, and input/output.

Survey supplements July 1983 survey of user ratings of systems-oriented software packages, which was reported in Dec. 1983 issue. For description, see C8650-1.502 above.

SOFTWARE/SERVICES SCENE

(p. 224.11-224.16) By John Lamb. Article on the Western European computer software/services industry. Data are from Quantum Science MAPTEK Europe, OECD, and other sources.

Includes 2 tables and 1 chart showing top 20 computer service companies ranked by European revenues, with country of majority shareholding, owner, services offered, and employees; user expenditures for computing services, inflation and industry growth rates, and GDP, by country; and user expenditures by computing service category; mostly 1982.

C8650-1.506: Apr. 1, 1984 (Vol. 30, No. 4)

MIDAS TOUCH IN MANUFACTURING

(p. 166.3-166.6) By Paul Tate. Article on European market outlook for computer-aided-design/computer-aided-manufacturing (CAD-/CAM) systems. Data are from Creative Strategies International.

Includes 1 table and 1 chart showing the following for the European CAD/CAM market: volume and value of new equipment installed, and total number of new installations, 1984-87; and market distribution by country or area, 1987.

C8650-1.507: Apr. 15, 1984 (Vol. 30, No. 5)

DP BUDGET SURVEY: PCs MAKE WAVES

(p. 82-89) By Larry Marion. Article on corporate spending for personal computers. Data are from responses of 1,083 data processing (dp) managers to a 1983 *Datamation* survey.

Includes 2 charts and 3 tables showing dp budget percent change, budget as percent of total revenue, and budget distribution by component, by selected industry; and mean and median dp spending outside of dp budget, by category; 1984 and/or 1983.

SELLING OF SOFTWARE

(p. 125-128) By Efrem Sigel. Article examining marketing developments among computer software publishers. Data are primarily from Communications Trends Inc.

Includes 3 tables and 1 chart showing top 5 software programs ranked by sales volume, as of 1983; value of customer purchases and publisher receipts for business/professional software, 1981-84; revenues, selling/general/administrative cost as percent of revenue, and pretax profit margin, for 4 publishers, various periods 1983; and distribution of sales dollar for business/professional software, by profit/cost component (no date).

C8650-1.508: May 1, 1984 (Vol. 30, No. 6)

MAINFRAME BUSINESS GRAPHICS

(p. 89-95) By Maxine D. Brown. Article, with 4 charts showing computer graphics market share by application and product type, various years 1981-87; and impact of graphics use on business meeting length and success, 1982. Data are from Frost and Sullivan, and a 1982 Wharton School Applied Research Center study.

EUROPEAN MICRO MOVES

(p. 144.3-144.9) By Paul Tate. Article, with 1 table showing volume and value of business microcomputer shipments in Europe, with volume detail by country or area, 1984-89. Data are from Logica.

C8650-1.509: May 15, 1984 (Vol. 30, No. 7)

SURVEYING THE MAINFRAME LANDSCAPE, ANNUAL FEATURE

(p. 89-99) Annual survey report, by John W. Verity, on computer mainframe user equipment use and expansion plans, with detail for major vendors' products. Data are based on responses of 4,993 users to a Feb. 1984 survey by Cowen & Co. and *Datamation*.

Includes 8 charts showing 1984 survey responses to questions in the following areas, with selected comparisons to previous surveys:

a. Planned and installed IBM-compatible central processing units; personal computer (PC) purchases from IBM by model; plans for PC connections to mainframe system; and word processing/office system purchases, by vendor.

b. Network choice for future local site data communications; choice of supplier for local area network and of database management software for use on IBM mainframes; and percent of data processing budget used for software packages.

C8650-1.510: June 1, 1984 (Vol. 30, No. 8)

DATAMATION 100: FATHOMING THE INDUSTRY, ANNUAL FEATURE

(p. 53-144) Annual report, by Pamela Archbold, analyzing financial performance of the top 100 data processing (dp) companies, as ranked by dp revenues in 1983.

Contents:

a. Narrative summary, with 8 tables showing revenues of top 9-15 companies in 4 industry segments; employment for 10 companies with greatest increase and decrease; and revenues for 10 best and 10 worst performing companies; 1983 with comparisons to 1982. (p. 53-57)

b. Ranked listing of the top 100, showing the following for each company: total and dp revenues, employment, R&D expenditures, net income, return on assets, and dp revenues from foreign sources as percent of total dp revenues, all for 1983, with rank and selected other comparisons to 1982. (p. 60-63)

c. Profiles of developments in each company, with 1 chart repeated for each of the top 50 companies showing dp revenues by product segment, 1983. (p. 66-144)

EUROPE WARMS TO THE RISING SUN

(p. 144.9-144.12) By Fred Lamond. Article, with 3 tables showing value and volume of Japanese computer equipment exports to Western Europe, by equipment category and country or region of destination, 1982-83. Data are from John Aczel.

C8650-1.511: June 15, 1984 (Vol. 30, No. 9)

IS THE OEM MARKET MATURING? ANNUAL FEATURE

(p. 210.11-210.20) Annual article on 1983 market performance of original equipment manufacturers (OEMs)/systems houses, organizations that develop customized computer systems for resale using components from various manufacturers. Data are from a Sentry Database Publishing survey of 2,007 OEMs and systems houses.

Includes 10 tables showing respondents' unit sales of minicomputers, personal computers, and various peripheral products, with selected market share detail by company; and shipments and percent change in sales by systems application; various years 1979-83.

C8650-1.512: July 15, 1984 (Vol. 30, No. 11)

EVOLUTION OF THE INFORMATION CENTER

(p. 127-130) By Tor Guimaraes. Article, with 1 table presenting summary characteristics for corporate personal computer systems, including presence of formal training programs and other user aids, 1982 and 1984. Data are from an early 1982 survey of 96 Ohio business organizations and a 1984 follow-up survey.

C8650-1.513: Aug. 1, 1984 (Vol. 30, No. 12)

CROWNING EUROPE'S DP ROYALTY, ANNUAL FEATURE

(p. 136.5-136.24) Annual article on top 25 data processing (dp) companies ranked by European dp revenues, 1983. Data are from a survey conducted by Logica.

Includes 3 summary tables, and 1 table showing the following for each company: headquarters country; European, world, and parent company domestic dp revenues; European and world total revenues; European and world employees and net income or loss; CY83 or FY83, with selected comparisons to 1982.

Also includes company profiles, with summary charts for the top 10.

C8650-1.514: Sept. 1, 1984 (Vol. 30, No. 14)

BANKING ON PCs

(p. 26-38) By Edith Myers. Article on home banking through personal computers. Data are from Arlen Communications, Inc. Includes 1 undated table showing geographic area of operations, number of users, and software package, for 21 banks providing home banking service.

WANTED: RENAISSANCE PEOPLE

(p. 134-144) By Andrew Friedman and Joan Greenbaum. Article on personnel and management developments for corporate data processing (dp) depts. Data are from responses of 95 managers of dp depts, to a summer 1983 survey conducted by International Computer Occupations Network.

Includes 4 charts showing survey response concerning organizational structure for development staff; extent of user involvement in new application design; and specification, design, and coding standards used. Also includes 1 chart showing survey sample characteristics.

C8650-1.515: Sept. 15, 1984 (Vol. 30, No. 15)

BIG WALLET ERA, ANNUAL FEATURE

(p. 76-88) Annual article, by Larry Marion, on data processing (dp) salaries in business, education, and government. Data are based on 715 responses, primarily from dp managers, to a June 1984 *Datamation* subscriber survey.

Includes 5 tables showing 1984 dp salary increase and turnover rate; and average salary for each of 26-27 dp positions; by industry sector and for 13-14 metro areas. Average salary is also shown for installations with value over and under $1 million.

Complete survey report is available from the issuing agency for $100.00.

CHALLENGE OF USERS AND UNIONS

(p. 93-100) By Andrew Friedman et al. Article on personnel and management developments for European corporate data processing (dp) depts. Data are from responses of 199 dp managers in Norway, Sweden, and UK, to a survey conducted by International Computer Occupations Network.

Includes 3 undated charts showing survey response concerning trade union participation rates, total and for public sector, computer services, and private sector; expected educational background for programmers and programmer analysts; and level of user involvement in project development; all for U.S. and Europe.

For description of a similar report covering the U.S. only, see C8650-1.514 above.

VIDEOTEX: INTO THE CRUEL WORLD

(p. 133-144) By Efrem Sigel. Article on market outlook for the videotex industry. Data are from Communications Trends Inc.

Includes 4 tables showing number of principal suppliers and retail outlets, and advertising/promotion expenditures, for videotex and personal computer markets, 1984; subscribers to electronic home banking services, total and for selected services, June and Dec. 1984; and characteristics of selected videotex suppliers and services.

C8650–2   PURCHASING WORLD
Monthly.

SRI now covers this publication under C4670-1.

C8650–3   RESEARCH AND DEVELOPMENT
Monthly. Approx. 200 p.
ISSN 0746-9176.
LC 84-642292.
SRI/MF/excerpts, shipped quarterly

Monthly publication (semimonthly in Feb.) reporting trends and developments in industrial design and quality assurance. Covers R&D funding, management, and new product developments and applications.

Issues contain regular editorial depts, including a recurring "Opinion Poll" reader survey feature; news articles on scientific and technological developments; and feature articles, occasionally statistical.

Annual features include an R&D funding forecast; surveys of R&D professionals' salaries, and the use and planned purchase of analytical instruments; and subject and author indexes. Second Feb. issue is an annual industry telephone directory.

Prior to Jan. 1984 issue, journal title was *Industrial Research and Development*.

Features with substantial statistical content are described, as they appear, under "Statistical Features." Each issue of the journal is reviewed, but an abstract is published in SRI monthly issues only when statistical articles appear, or when "Opinion Poll" data are on topics pertaining to the R&D sector.

Availability: Research and Development, Circulation Department, PO Box 5365, New York NY 10150, qualified subscribers †, others $36.00 per yr.; SRI/MF/excerpts for all portions described under "Statistical Features;" shipped quarterly.

Issues reviewed during 1984: Nov. 1983-Oct. 1984 (P) (Vol. 25, Nos. 11-12; Vol. 26, Nos. 1-10).

STATISTICAL FEATURES:

C8650–3.501: Nov. 1983 (Vol. 25, No. 11)
USE OF ELECTRICAL AND ELECTRONIC INSTRUMENTS, ANNUAL FEATURE

(p. 118-121) Annual article, by C. J. Mosbacher, with 1 table showing use of and plans to acquire electrical and electronic instruments and equipment, by type, for engineers, life/medical scientists, and physical scientists. Data are from responses of 1,057 subscribers to a summer 1983 *Industrial Research and Development* survey.

C8650–3.502: Jan. 1984 (Vol. 26, No. 1)
FUNDS FOR R&D WILL REACH ALMOST $98 BILLION IN 1984, ANNUAL FEATURE

(p. 77-78) Annual article, by C. J. Mosbacher, forecasting R&D funding and expenditures. Data are from NSF. Includes 1 chart showing amount of R&D money to be provided and spent by the Federal Government, industry, and other sectors, 1984.

C8650–3.503: Feb. 1984 (Vol. 26, No. 2)
USES OF ANALYTICAL INSTRUMENTS AND EQUIPMENT, 1984, ANNUAL FEATURE

(p. 156-159) Annual article, by C. J. Mosbacher, with 2 tables showing 33 analytical instruments ranked by growth in current or planned use, 1983-84; and use of and plans to acquire analytical instruments and equipment, by type, for engineers, physical scientists, and life/medical scientists. Data are from responses of 1,730 subscribers to a fall 1983 *Research and Development* survey.

OPINION POLL RESULTS: SURVEY SHOWS HIGH R&D INVOLVEMENT IN QUALITY ASSURANCE

(p. 169-170) Article reporting results of recent *Research and Development* reader survey on involvement of R&D personnel in quality assurance activities. Includes text data showing distribution of responses from approximately 900 readers.

C8650–3.504: Mar. 1984 (Vol. 26, No. 3)
SALARIES FOR WORKERS IN R&D HOLD UP FOR MOST, BUT JUST BARELY, ANNUAL FEATURE

(p. 97-100) Annual article, by Robert R. Jones, analyzing trends in salaries of R&D professionals, by discipline. Data are from over 4,200 responses to an annual *Research and Development* reader survey, 1984; and earlier surveys.

Includes 25 summary charts, and 14 tables showing the following:

a. Median salary, with rankings, 1983-84 surveys; and medians and ranges for salary, years with present employer, age, and years of experience, 1984 survey; all by scientific discipline.

b. Respondent distribution by range of salary percent increase, 1980-84 survey.

This is the 1st of 2 articles reporting the salary survey findings. For description of 2nd article, see C8650-3.506, below.

C8650–3.505: Apr. 1984 (Vol. 26, No. 4)
OPINION POLL RESULTS: R&D WORKERS CONTINUE LOVE AFFAIR WITH PERSONAL COMPUTER

(p. 184-185) Brief article reporting results of recent *Research and Development* reader survey on use of personal computers and peripherals, and adequacy of software, by respondent's professional specialty. Includes 1 table showing distribution of responses from approximately 2,400 readers.

C8650–3.506: May 1984 (Vol. 26, No. 5)
INDUSTRY PULLS AHEAD OF GOVERNMENT IN R&D MEDIAN SALARIES, ANNUAL FEATURE

(p. 112-115) Annual article, by Robert R. Jones, examining relationship of professional R&D salary levels to sex, experience, education, and type of employer. Data are from over 4,200 responses to an annual *Research and Development* reader survey, 1984, and earlier surveys.

Includes 5 tables showing median salary by degree level, and by sex by type of employer; and respondent distribution by salary level, past year's salary increase (with detail by sex), years with present employer, age, years of experience, highest degree, profession, type of employer, and sex; 1984 survey, with selected comparisons to surveys from 1980.

This is the 2nd of 2 articles reporting the salary survey findings. For description of 1st article, see C8650-3.504, above.

OPINION POLL RESULTS: TECHNOLOGY SHOULD ASSIST, NOT REPLACE, OLDER INDUSTRY

(p. 181) Article reporting results of recent *Research and Development* reader survey on role of high technology in modernization of heavy industries. Includes text data showing distribution of responses from approximately 2,000 readers.

C8650–3.507: Sept. 1984 (Vol. 26, No. 9)
OPINION POLL RESULTS: SHUTTLE, SPACELAB HOLD IMPORTANT POTENTIAL FOR R&D

(p. 187) Brief article reporting results of recent *Research and Development* reader survey on R&D potential of space shuttle and proposed space station. Includes text data showing distribution of responses from approximately 1,-900 readers.

C8650–4   ELECTRIC LIGHT AND POWER
Monthly. Approx. 80 p.
Oversized.
ISSN 0013-4120.
LC 27-16630.
SRI/MF/excerpts, shipped quarterly

Monthly trade journal covering developments in electric utility management, technology, regulation, and operations. Data are from journal surveys, and reports of private firms and DOE.

Issues generally contain numerous news and feature articles, occasionally with statistics, and regular editorial depts. Annual statistical features include rankings of top 100 electric utilities in financial and operating performance.

Features with substantial statistical content are described, as they appear, under "Statistical Features." Each issue of the journal is reviewed, but an abstract is published in SRI monthly issues only when statistical features appear.

Availability: Electric Light and Power, Circulation Department, PO Box 1030, Barrington IL

60010, qualified subscribers †, others $38.00 per yr., single copy $4.00; SRI/MF/excerpts for all portions covered under "Statistical Features;" shipped quarterly.

Issues reviewed during 1984: Nov. 1983-Oct. 1984 (P) (Vol. 61, Nos. 11-12; Vol. 62, Nos. 1-10) [Vol. 62, No. 1 incorrectly reads Vol. 63].

STATISTICAL FEATURES:

C8650–4.501: Nov. 1983 (Vol. 61, No. 11)

CENSUS BUREAU DOCUMENTS GAINS IN HOME HEATING BY ELECTRICITY

(p. 19) Article, with 1 table showing distribution of households by type of heating fuel used, decennially 1940-80. Data are from Census Bureau.

C8650–4.502: Dec. 1983 (Vol. 61, No. 12)

SUMMER HEAT BOOSTS 3rd QUARTER UTILITY REVENUES

(p. 1, 51) Article, with 1 table showing earnings per share and operating revenue, for 34 electric utilities, 3rd quarter 1983 and change from 3rd quarter 1982. Data are from an EL&P survey.

1984 TO BE YEAR OF FINANCIAL REBUILDING, REDUCED CONSTRUCTION SPENDING FOR UTILITIES

(p. 15-16) By Robert A. Lincicome. Article, with 2 tables showing electric utilities' capital spending plans for generation, substations, transmission, distribution, and other purposes, 1984; and generation capacity, 1983 and planned 1984; all by North American Electric Reliability Council (NERC) region. Data are from an EL&P survey of electric utility organizations and NERC projections.

TVA QUALIFIES VALUE OF BURNING PHYSICALLY CLEANED COAL FOR PLANT OPERATING, MAINTENANCE, FGD COSTS

(p. 19) Article on a TVA study into use of washed coal to reduce electric plant operating and maintenance costs. Data are from a study of boiler performance and coal quality at 60 TVA generating units, conducted by Battelle-Columbus and Hoffman-Holt during 1962-80.

Includes 3 tables showing the following for a typical plant: maintenance cost and hours of generation outage, by level of sulfur and ash content in coal, with outage detail by boiler age; and selected generation efficiency and cost factors, for 2 levels of sulfur/ash content in coal.

C8650–4.503: Jan. 1984 (Vol. 62, No. 1)
[Issue incorrectly reads Vol. 63.]

ACID RAIN REGS WILL BE FALLING ON UTILITIES IN '84, BUT NOT TOO HARD

(p. 8-10) By Robert Smock. Article on impacts of EPA regulation of electric utility sulfur dioxide emissions. Data are from EPA, Ontario Ministry of Environment, and National Acid Precipitation Assessment Program. Includes 3 tables showing the following:

a. Ranking of 50 coal-fired power plants in eastern North America with highest sulfur dioxide emissions, 1979; and characteristics of 5 retrofit emission control techniques, including capital cost per kWh and emission reduction effectiveness (no date).

b. EPA emission regulation impacts: eastern States' utility and industrial sulfur dioxide

emissions, utility cost increases, coal production by region, western coal shipments, percent change in electric rates, and flue-gas scrubber capacity, under 4 regulatory options, 1995, with comparison to 1980.

C8650–4.504: Feb. 1984 (Vol. 62, No. 2)

COAL INDUSTRY SEES MODEST GAINS IN '84; FEELS UTILITIES WON'T BUILD UP INVENTORIES AS STRIKE HEDGE

(p. 17) Article, with 1 table showing coal domestic consumption by sector; exports to Canada and overseas; imports; consumer and production/distribution stock changes; and production by region (East and West); 1982-83 and forecast 1984. Data are from National Coal Assn.

C8650–4.505: Mar. 1984 (Vol. 62, No. 3)

CAN THE UTILITY INDUSTRY FIND A FOUNTAIN OF YOUTH FOR ITS AGING GENERATING CAPACITY?

(p. 14-17) By Robert Smock. Article, with 3 tables showing percent of electrical generating capacity that is 10 years old/less and more than 30 years old, decennially 1970-2000; megawatts of new capacity by type of generating unit, 5-year periods 1900-95; and generating units, total capacity, and average age, by type of unit (no date).

Data are from Westinghouse and DOE.

OPERATING UNIT HEAT RATES CAN BE CUT, SAYS EPRI; NEW UNITS CAN BE 10% MORE EFFICIENT

(p. 24) By Robert Smock. Article, with 2 undated tables showing 20 most efficient electric generating units operated by 100 largest investor-owned utilities, ranked by unit heat rate, with capacity and utility name; and generator specifications of advanced heat-efficient plants designed by General Electric and Westinghouse.

Rankings data are from Electrical Power Research Institute.

C8650–4.506: Apr. 1984 (Vol. 62, No. 4)

ELECTRIC UTILITIES FARE WELL IN '83; WEATHER PLAYS BIG ROLE

(p. 3) By Don Minner. Article, with 2 tables showing total revenues and earnings per share; for 40 investor-owned electric utilities, 1983 with percent change from 1982; and for aggregate top 100 utilities, 1978-82. Data are from EL&P surveys.

C8650–4.507: May 1984 (Vol. 62, No. 5)

HIGH VOLTAGE D-C TRANSMISSION PLANS ARE RE-ENERGIZED; HARMONICS ISSUES EMERGE

(p. 35-37) By Dan Utroska. Article, with 1 table showing capacity of high voltage direct-current projects completed/being built/planned, for U.S. and Canada by project, and for 13 other countries or world areas, as of early 1984.

C8650–4.508: June 1984 (Vol. 62, No. 6)

19th ANNUAL TOP 100 ELECTRIC UTILITIES REPORT: MOST MAJOR UTILITIES' 1983 PERFORMANCES IMPROVED; FINANCIAL POSITIONS STRENGTHENED

(p. 19-22) Annual article, by Robert A. Lincicome, presenting operating and financial performance rankings for 100 largest investor-owned electric utilities, 1983.

Includes 3 summary tables; and 4 detailed tables showing earnings per share, kWh sales and distribution by customer type, long-term debt percent change and ratio to net plant value, net income, revenue, interest coverage ratio, high and low share prices, electric and gas customers and revenues, and after-tax income, all by company with rankings for most items, 1983 and/or percent change from 1982.

Also includes average annual sales growth, 1978-83 period.

C8650–4.509: July 1984 (Vol. 62, No. 7)

CANADIAN POWER IMPORTS TO RISE IN NEXT 10 YEARS

(p. 15) Article, with 1 table showing buyer and seller group, and contract capacity, sales volume, and dates, for 11 contracts covering Canadian electric power sales to New York/New England. Contract beginning dates range from 1982 to 1987; expiration dates range from 1984 to 2002. Data are from a recent study by Energy Ventures Analysis, Inc.

C8650–4.510: Aug. 1984 (Vol. 62, No. 8)

ACID RAIN JEOPARDIZES U.S. RESOURCES, SAYS OTA

(p. 2) Article, with 1 undated table estimating cost of emission controls to reduce acid rain, for Eastern utilities using wet scrubbers and most cost-effective control method, at selected emission reduction levels. Data are from Office of Technology Assessment.

NARUC's UTILITY PERFORMANCE STUDY SCRUTINIZED FOR USEFULNESS

(p. 3) By Don Minner. Article, with 1 table showing top and bottom 5 electric utilities ranked by overall financial performance ratio, 1972-81 period. Data are from a study of 130 major electric companies, conducted by National Assn of Regulatory Commissioners.

TOP 100 ELECTRIC UTILITIES' 1983 OPERATING PERFORMANCE, ANNUAL FEATURE

(p. 7-11) Annual article, by Robert Smock, presenting operating data for 100 leading investor-owned electric utilities, 1983 with selected comparisons to 1982. Data are based on Uniform Statistical Reports filed by the utilities.

Includes 3 summary tables; 2 tables showing top 20 generating units ranked by heat rate (Btu/kWh) and including capacity and utility owner, and top 10 utilities using only fossil-fueled boilers ranked by heat rate; and 4 detailed tables presenting the following data for each utility:

a. Heat rate and ranking; consumption of coal, oil, and gas; peak demand; total system and owned capacity and reserve rate; and load factor.

b. Electricity production, by type of generating power; and transmission and distribution line mileage and additions, with detail for underground and overhead distribution lines.

Corrected data appear in the Oct. 1984 issue; for description, see C8650-4.512 below.

UTILITIES AIM AT TURNING AROUND THE DECLINE IN NUCLEAR PLANT PERFORMANCE

(p. 25-26) By Robert Smock. Article on U.S. nuclear plant performance as compared to other countries, cumulatively through 1983. Most data are from papers delivered at an Atomic Industrial Forum conference held in May 1984.

Includes 2 tables and 1 chart showing nuclear reactor average capacity utilization rate and total electricity generated, for 19 countries; world's top 20 nuclear reactors ranked by average capacity utilization rate, and including capacity and location; and number of nuclear reactors and average capacity, for U.S. and Japan; all as of 1983.

Corrected data appear in the Sept. 1984 issue; for description, see C8650-4.511 below.

SUMMER PEAK DEMAND TO GROW AT 2.5% RATE

(p. 34) Article, with 1 table showing summer peak demand for electric power, by North American Electric Reliability Council (NERC) region, selected years 1983-93. Data are from an annual NERC report.

Full NERC report is covered in SRI under A8630-2.

C8650–4.511: Sept. 1984 (Vol. 62, No. 9)

INTERCONNECTIONS PROVIDE NEW OPERATING ECONOMIES, AS WELL AS BACKUP DURING EMERGENCY, PEAK PERIODS

(p. 15, 23) By Robert A. Lincicome. Article on energy transmission ties among regional members of the North American Electric Reliability Council (NERC). Includes 1 table and 1 map showing number of member and associate systems, by NERC region; and interregional bulk power capability available for transfer under emergency conditions; (no dates).

CORRECTION

(p. 43) Corrected chart for article on U.S. nuclear plant performance as compared to other countries.

For description of article, see C8650-4.510, above.

NUCLEAR PACs CARRY CLOUT, SAYS CRITICAL MASS

(p. 55) Brief article on campaign contributions from political action committees (PACs) sponsored by the nuclear industry. Data are from the Public Citizen's Critical Mass Energy Project.

Includes 3 tables showing top 20 nuclear utilities ranked by PAC contributions, 1981/82 and 1983/84; and top 10 House and Senate members ranked by money received from nuclear PACs, with percent of votes against the nuclear industry (no date).

C8650–4.512: Oct. 1984 (Vol. 62, No. 10)

CORRECTION

(p. 4) Corrected data for 2 companies covered in annual article on 100 leading investor-owned electric utilities.

For description of article, see C8650-4.510, above.

C8650–5   DUN'S BUSINESS MONTH
Monthly.   Approx. 150 p.
ISSN 0279-3040.
LC 81-646138.
SRI/MF/excerpts, shipped
quarterly

Monthly magazine reporting developments of interest to corporate executives. Covers government policy and legislation, the economy, finance, specific companies and industries, labor relations, management, marketing, technological innovations, news media, and world affairs.

Data are from Dun & Bradstreet surveys, FHLBB, and private sources.

Issues generally contain news briefs; numerous articles, occasionally with statistics; and editorial depts, including brief summaries of recent surveys and studies. The following statistical features are presented:

a. "Investment Update" monthly table, appearing in "Personal Finance" section, showing recent price or yield, and value and percent change, for $10,000 invested 1 month and 1 year earlier for 6 types of investment (unnamed common stock index fund, 30-year Treasury bond paying 11¾%, unnamed money market fund, gold Krugerrands, and existing and new houses).

b. Annual features on the executive job market, corporations with consistent dividend growth, and corporate vehicle fleets.

c. Series of business trend articles based on surveys of the Dun & Bradstreet 5000, a representative sample drawn from a data base covering over 5 million companies.

"Investment Update" table appears in all issues. All additional features with substantial statistical content are described, as they appear, under "Statistical Features." Nonstatistical features are not covered.

Availability: Dun's Business Month, Circulation Department, 875 Third Ave., New York NY 10022, qualified subscribers †, others $30.00 per yr., single copy $3.00; SRI/MF/excerpts for "Investment Update" and all portions described under "Statistical Features;" shipped quarterly.

Issues reviewed during 1984: Nov. 1983-Oct. 1984 (P) (Vol. 122, Nos. 5-6; Vol. 123, Nos. 1-6; Vol. 124, Nos. 1-4) [Vol. 122, No. 5 incorrectly reads Vol. 123].

STATISTICAL FEATURES:

C8650–5.501: Nov. 1983 (Vol. 122, No. 5)
[Issue incorrectly reads Vol. 123.]

WALL STREET BETS ON NEW BELLS

(p. 46-51) Article on the investment outlook for 7 regional telephone companies created by the AT&T divestiture. Data are from Sanford C. Bernstein and Co.

Includes 1 table showing estimated assets, and book value per share, 1984; yield and price range; and growth rate, 1984-90 period; by company.

WHY COMPANIES DON'T EXPORT

(p. 53) Article, with 2 undated tables showing total and exporting companies, by industry division; and obstacles to exporting cited by nonexporting and formerly exporting companies. Data by industry cover all companies and are from Dun's Marketing Services. Data on obstacles are from a recent Dun & Bradstreet survey of 100 manufacturers/wholesalers with sales of $5-100 million.

FIRM REBOUND IN EXECUTIVE JOBS, ANNUAL FEATURE

(p. 90-115) Annual survey report on the executive job market as of Nov. 1983, based on job openings listed by 20 leading executive recruiters.

Includes tabular list of current openings in 13 functional areas, showing position title, industry, region, and salary. Also includes list of participating recruiters.

Survey has been conducted since 1974.

C8650–5.502: Dec. 1983 (Vol. 122, No. 6)

DIVIDEND ACHIEVERS SUFFER FIRST SETBACK, ANNUAL FEATURE

(p. 121-133) Annual listing of 414 U.S. and Canadian corporations that have consistently increased dividend payments over the last 10 years. Data were compiled by Moody's Investors Service.

Includes introduction and 1 extended table showing the following for each company: current indicated and 1973 dividends, and 10-year growth rate and rank; recent stock price, current yield, latest earnings per share, and 1982 payout; and annual sales, net income, return on sales, stockholders' equity, and return on equity.

This is the 5th annual listing.

C8650–5.503: Jan. 1984 (Vol. 123, No. 1)

PENSION PLANS: PROBLEMS OF PLENTY

(p. 39-43) Article on corporate pension plan terminations as a means of recapturing excess assets. Includes 1 undated table showing value of recaptured assets, for 23 companies that terminated or plan to terminate pension plans.

DUN'S 5000: NEW YEAR LOOKS GOOD

(p. 73) Survey article on corporate executives' expectations for their own companies' 1984 sales, profits, employment, and prices. Includes 1 table.

Article is part of a series based on surveys of the Dun & Bradstreet 5000. Current survey had an 85% response rate.

C8650–5.504: Feb. 1984 (Vol. 123, No. 2)

INFLATION: WILL THE MONSTER REAPPEAR IN 1984?

(p. 33-34) Article, with 1 table showing 1984 price increases for selected consumer and industrial goods and services, as forecast by Wharton Econometric Forecasting Associates.

BUSINESS FAILURES: IS THE RISE OVER?

(p. 37) Article, with 2 tables showing number of business failures, with distribution by industry division and by unmet liability of over or under $100,000; and Dun & Bradstreet business failure index; all quarterly 1983.

C8650–5.505: Mar. 1984 (Vol. 123, No. 3)

CRUNCH HASN'T COME—YET

(p. 41) Article, with 1 table showing total private/public borrowing; and borrowing by Federal Government from public, for guaranteed loans, and other; 1979-83. Data are from the Budget of the U.S.

HAS JUSTICE KILLED STEEL COMEBACK?

(p. 48-55) Article on steel industry conditions and outlook. Data are from International Iron and Steel Institute and other sources. Includes 3 charts and 1 table showing the following:

a. World steel production capacity and consumption, for North America, Western Europe, Japan, developing countries, and other, 1980 and 1990.

b. U.S. domestic shipments and imports for 1983, names of manufacturers, and extent of minimill involvement, all by type of steel product; and shipments of minimills vs. major producers, 1976-80 period, 1990, and 2000.

Data correction appears in the May 1984 issue; for description, see C8650-5.507 below.

C8650–5.506: Apr. 1984 (Vol. 123, No. 4)
LONG HAUL TO THE TOP

(p. 52-71, passim) Article profiling career and personal characteristics of corporate chief executive officers (CEOs). Data are based on a *Dun's Business Month* analysis of CEOs at 237 of the largest corporations.

Includes 1 table showing distribution of CEOs by age, degree level with some detail by field, years with present company, number of other employers, and career background including employment overseas.

C8650–5.507: May 1984 (Vol. 123, No. 5)
CORRECTION

(p. 8) Corrected data for article on steel industry condition and outlook, appearing in the Mar. 1984 issue; for description of article, see C8650-5.505 above.

DUN'S 5000: BUILDING IS UNEVEN—AND SO IS THE RECOVERY

(p. 55) Article, with 1 table showing percent change in building permit value by region, and top 10 cities ranked by value of permits issued, 1982-83. Data are from a *Dun's Business Month* survey covering 200 cities.

BEHIND THE DECLINE IN PENSION COSTS

(p. 62-66) Article on corporate pension plans, with 1 chart showing value of employer contributions to fixed-benefit pension plans, 1982-83; percent of pension liabilities funded, 1979-83; distribution of pension, profit-sharing, and thrift plan investments by type of instrument (no date); and percent of companies with individual retirement account (IRA) and 401(K) salary reduction plans, and percent of plans with $1 billion in assets (no date).

Data are from a 1983 survey of 1,639 companies conducted by Greenwich Research Associates.

C8650–5.508: June 1984 (Vol. 123, No. 6)
DUN'S 5000: MID-SIZED FIRMS TAKE OFF THE WRAPS

(p. 59) Survey article on corporate expectations for plant/structure and capital equipment spending in 1984 (more, less, or same, compared to 1983), by company employment size. Includes text data and 2 charts.

Article is part of a series based on surveys of the Dun & Bradstreet 5000.

C8650–5.509: July 1984 (Vol. 124, No. 1)
1985: A WATERSHED YEAR FOR THE BUDGET?

(p. 40) Article on accuracy of 5-year Federal budget projections by Administrations and Congress. Includes 1 table comparing actual and Administration-projected budget deficits for FY76-83.

CASH FLOW: THE TOP 200

(p. 47-58) Article, with 1 table ranking top 200 nonfinancial corporations by cash flow, and also showing net income, discretionary cash flow, revenues, return on equity, and debt/equity and cash flow/revenue ratios, 1983, with selected comparisons to 1982.

Also includes a related article (p. 45-46). Corrected data appear in Oct. 1984 issue; for description, see C8650-5.12 below.

C8650–5.510: Aug. 1984 (Vol. 124, No. 2)
SPREADING WAVE OF STOCK BUYBACKS

(p. 40-46) Article, with 1 table showing the following for 49 companies that announced stock repurchase programs of at least $500 million during 1st half 1984: number and value of shares involved in repurchase, and shares involved as percent of total shares outstanding. Data are from Securities Data Corp.

DUN'S 5000: MORE EVIDENCE OF ECONOMIC STRENGTH

(p. 65) Survey article on corporate executives' expectations for their own companies' sales, profits, employment, prices, and inventory, for 3rd quarter 1984, with comparisons to previous periods. Includes text data and 1 chart.

Article is part of a series based on surveys of the Dun & Bradstreet 5000. Current survey was conducted in May 1984.

C8650–5.511: Sept. 1984 (Vol. 124, No. 3)
DUN'S 5000: ROSY OUTLOOK FOR SALES

(p. 53) Survey article on corporate executive expectations for their own companies' sales in 1984. Includes text statistics and 1 chart.

Article is part of a series based on surveys of the Dun & Bradstreet 5000.

C8650–5.512: Oct. 1984 (Vol. 124, No. 4)
CASH FLOW, CORRECTION

(p. 8) Corrected data for "Cash Flow: The Top 200," appearing in the July 1984 issue. Data are for Wickes Companies, Inc.

For description of article, see C8650-5.509 above.

FLEET MANAGEMENT: UPDATE '85, ANNUAL FEATURE

(p. 19-44) Annual compilation of articles on developments in auto and light truck/van fleet management and operations. Data are from Runzheimer and Co.

Includes 1 table (p. 34) showing ownership and operating costs, and specifications, for ten 1985 auto makes/models.

C8650–6   INDUSTRIAL DISTRIBUTION

Monthly. Approx. 60 p.
ISSN 0019-8153.
LC 13-8201.
SRI/MF/excerpts, shipped quarterly

Monthly trade journal reporting on management, marketing, and operating strategies for distributors of general and special line industrial supplies.

General format:

a. "Industry News" briefs, including a monthly "Indicators" section with business activity index data.

b. "Regional Report" statistical feature, with 1 chart, and 2 tables on industrial supplies sales and receivables outstanding, by census division.

c. Feature articles, occasionally with statistics, including a recurring survey of purchasing managers' assessments of business conditions, and an annual survey of distributors' operations; and narrative editorial depts.

d. Quarterly inflation index feature, with 2 tables.

Monthly and quarterly statistical features are described below. Monthly statistics appear in all issues. All additional features with substantial statistical content are described, as they appear, under "Statistical Features;" page locations and latest periods of coverage for quarterly feature are also noted. Nonstatistical features are not covered.

Both the 1983 and 1984 issues of *Industrial Distribution* are numbered Vol. 73 to correct an earlier error in volume numbering.

Prior to the Aug. 1983 issue, journal was published by Morgan-Grampian Publishing Co. and was described in SRI under C6185-2.

Availability: Industrial Distribution, Circulation Department, PO Box 1063, Barrington IL 60010, qualified subscribers †, others $50.00 per yr., single copy $6.00; SRI/MF/excerpts for all monthly statistics and for portions described under "Statistical Features;" shipped quarterly.

Issues reviewed during 1984: Nov. 1983-Oct. 1984 (P) (Vol. 73 (1983), Nos. 11-12; Vol. 73 (1984), Nos. 1-10) [Vol. 73 (1984), Nos. 1 and 3 incorrectly read Vol. 74].

MONTHLY STATISTICS:
[Month of coverage is 3 months prior to cover date, for most data.]

INDUSTRY NEWS

"Indicators" section, with text statistics on approximately 10 manufacturer and distributor assn business activity indexes; for month of coverage, with selected comparisons to previous month or year.

REGIONAL REPORT

[Data are shown for general and special line industrial supplies, for U.S. and by census division.]

[1] Receivables [average days outstanding, for month of coverage and same month of previous year].

[2] Sales by regions (percent change) [usually for month of coverage vs. selected previous periods; also includes detail for selected States, groups of States, and metropolitan areas].

QUARTERLY INFLATION INDEX:

Quarterly feature, usually with narrative analysis and 2 tables showing *Industrial Distribution* inflation index (1967=100) for approximately 35 product categories, for quarter ending 3-4 months preceding cover date and year to date, with comparisons to selected previous periods, and summary comparisons to 7-8 other inflation indexes. Data are prepared by Alan Silver and Associates from BLS statistics.

STATISTICAL FEATURES:

C8650–6.501: Nov. 1983 (Vol. 73, No. 11)
STATE OF THE INDUSTRY: SPECIALTY TOOLS AND FASTENERS

(p. 59-63) Article, with 1 chart showing annual percent change in specialty tool and fastener industry sales, by region and for Canada, 1st-2nd quarter 1983. Data are from Specialty Tools and Fasteners Distributors Assn.

A LOOK AT CONSTRUCTION

(p. 61) Brief article, with 1 table showing office vacancy rates inside and outside business district and overall, for 20 cities. Data are from a Sept. 1983 Office Network, Inc. survey.

C8650–6.502: Dec. 1983 (Vol. 73, No. 12)

SMALL DISTRIBUTORS SUFFER AS PUBLIC COMPANIES GAIN MARKET SHARE

(p. 7) Article, with 1 undated table showing sales and assets for 11 industrial distributors, for most recent fiscal year, with percent change from previous year. Data are from Bacon Stifel Nicolaus.

C8650–6.503: Jan. 1984 (Vol. 73, No. 1)

[Issue incorrectly reads Vol. 74.]

QUARTERLY INFLATION INDEX

(p. 149-151) For 3rd quarter 1983. For data description, see C8650-6, above.

EXPECTED GROWTH FOR THE INDUSTRIAL ROBOTS MARKET TO EXCEED 20% A YEAR

(p. 7, 13) Article, with 1 chart showing sales of industrial robots (pick/place and intelligent), and related services, parts, and accessories, 1982 and 1992. Data are from Frost and Sullivan, Inc.

PEOPLE, PLACES, MARKETS

(p. 45-51) Article on regional variations in industrial siting. Data are from Commerce Dept. Includes 3 charts showing percent change in employment in high technology and heavy ("smokestack") industries, by census division and industry group, various periods 1979-87.

C8650–6.504: Feb. 1984 (Vol. 73, No. 2)

CONFERENCE BOARD AND NAPM PREDICT A HEALTHY 1984

(p. 12-17) Article, with 1 table showing GNP, CPI, PPI, industrial production index, and corporate profits, 1982-84. Data are from the Conference Board.

C8650–6.505: Mar. 1984 (Vol. 73, No. 3)

[Issue incorrectly reads Vol. 74.]

QUARTERLY INFLATION INDEX

(p. 58-59) For 4th quarter 1983. For data description, see C8650-6, above.

CONSTRUCTION EQUIPMENT DISTRIBUTORS PREDICT EXPANDING BUSINESS FOR 1984

(p. 7) Brief article, with 1 table showing expected percent change in construction equipment rentals, and in sales of parts, service, supplies, and new and used equipment, by U.S. region and for Canada, 1st half 1984 vs. 1st half 1983. Data are from an Associated Equipment Distributor survey of approximately 300 distributor members.

1984 NTMA SALES FORECAST TO INCREASE 18% OVER 1983

(p. 18) Brief article, with 1 chart forecasting percent change in shipments for machine tool industry and selected specialties, 1984. Data are from National Tooling and Machining Assn.

C8650–6.506: Apr. 1984 (Vol. 73, No. 4)

FASTENERS: THE MARKET, NO LIMITS

(p. F9-F11) Article, with 1 table showing shipment value of industrial fasteners by type, by end-use industry, 1982. Data are from *Industrial Fasteners Market in the U.S.*

PURCHASING MANAGERS SEE SLOWDOWN BUT EXPECT THE RECOVERY TO CONTINUE, RECURRING FEATURE

(p. 93) Recurring article on corporate purchasing managers' assessment of recent business conditions. Data are from 1984 National Assn of Purchasing Management surveys.

Includes 1 table showing response distribution by number of days ahead of need, for purchases of production materials, maintenance/repair/operating supplies, and capital equipment, monthly Nov. 1983-Jan. 1984.

C8650–6.507: May 1984 (Vol. 73, No. 5)

INDUSTRIAL DISTRIBUTION: 1990...

(p. 77-86) Article, with 2 tables showing manufacturing employment distribution, and earnings, by region, various years 1955-2000. Data are from McGraw-Hill and Bureau of Economic Analysis.

VIEWPOINT

(p. 119-121) By Dickey Dyer. Article, with 1 chart showing GNP, and real growth projections for distribution/wholesaling industry, 1981-90. Data are from Commerce Dept and Congressional Budget Office.

NEED SHORT TERM HELP? THINK 'TEMPORARIES'

(p. 217-226) Article, with 1 undated table showing typical hourly billing rates for temporary employees, by occupation and region.

C8650–6.508: June 1984 (Vol. 73, No. 6)

NTMA SEES SALES GROWING BY 22% IN REVISED FORECAST

(p. 11) Brief article, with 1 chart forecasting percent change in sales of machine tools by type, 1984. Data are from National Tooling and Machining Assn (NTMA).

C8650–6.509: July 1984 (Vol. 73, No. 7)

QUARTERLY INFLATION INDEX

(p. 67-70) For 1st quarter 1984. For data description, see C8650-6, above.

DISTRIBUTORS ARE BUILDING INVENTORY AS REAL GROWTH HEADS FOR A DECLINE

(p. 7, 13) Article, with 1 table showing percent change in real GNP, and inventory investment value, selected quarters 1973-81. Data are from Evans Economics, Inc.

38th ANNUAL SURVEY OF DISTRIBUTOR OPERATIONS: '83 SALES SHORT OF RECOVERY GOAL

(p. 43-51) Annual survey report on industrial distributor sales, profits, and operations, 1983. Most data are based on journal's annual survey of distributors throughout the U.S.

Includes 2 maps, 26 charts, and 1 table showing the following, with selected detail by region and for general line and specialist distributors:

a. Sales compared to Index of Industrial Production, 1973-83; and sales and price change forecasts for 1984.

b. Financial and operating data for various years, 1982-84, including sales and profits, total and per employee; selected operating ratios; insurance and data processing costs; inventory value and valuation method; year-end receivables value and collections days outstanding; stocking and branch locations; invoices per year; total and sales employees; payroll; warehouse square footage; and computer use.

Most data are shown as response medians or distributions.

Data corrections appear in Sept. 1984 issue (see C8650-6.510, below).

C8650–6.510: Sept. 1984 (Vol. 73, No. 9)

COST OF INDUSTRIAL SALES CALL TOPS $200

(p. 13-14) Article on costs of closing industrial sales. Data are from McGraw-Hill surveys. Includes 1 table showing average closing cost for an industrial sale and number of companies responding, by selling method, 1981 and 1983.

CORRECTION

(p. 14) Correction to annual article on industrial distributor sales, profits, and operations. Includes corrected data on regional profits as a percent of sales.

For description of original article, see C8650-6.509, above.

MECHANIC'S HAND TOOLS: THE MARKET, PROFIT AND POTENTIAL

(p. HT11-HT13) Article, with 2 tables showing hand tool consumption value, number of plants, and employment, by industry (no date); and hand tool production, exports, imports, and apparent consumption, 1978-82. Data are from Commerce Dept and industry sources.

C8650–6.511: Oct. 1984 (Vol. 73, No. 10)

QUARTERLY INFLATION INDEX

(p. 119-120) For 2nd quarter 1984. For data description, see C8650-6 above.

ASMMA SURVEY GIVES DISTRIBUTOR SALES DEMOGRAPHICS

(p. 16) Brief article, with 1 table showing top 25 metropolitan areas ranked by share of total U.S. industrial distributor sales, 1983 with comparisons to 1981-82. Data are from American Supply and Machinery Manufacturers' Assn.

C8700
Telephony Publishing Corp.

C8700–1   TELEPHONY
Weekly.   Approx. 150 p.
ISSN 0040-2656.
LC 12-20223.
SRI/MF/excerpts, shipped quarterly

Weekly trade journal (except 2 issues in 2nd week of Aug. and only 3 issues in Dec.) of the telephone industry. Covers developments and trends in international telecommunications, including digital technology, communication satellites, management, government regulation, and operating costs.

Publication is primarily narrative and is intended to serve telephone engineering and management personnel. Data are from *Telephony* surveys, American Telephone and Telegraph Co. (AT&T), and other sources.

Issues contain feature articles, occasionally with statistics; and regular editorial depts. Annual statistical features include industry review and forecast (Jan.); and world telecommunications construction forecast (Feb.).

Features with substantial nontechnical statistical content are described, as they appear, under "Statistical Features." Each issue of the journal is reviewed, but an abstract is published in SRI monthly issues only when statistical features appear.

C8700–1 Telephony Publishing Corp.

Availability: Telephony, Circulation Department, 55 E. Jackson Blvd., Chicago IL 60604, qualified subscribers $33.00 per yr., others $39.00 per yr., single copy $3.00; SRI/MF/excerpts for all portions described under "Statistical Features;" shipped quarterly.

Issues reviewed during 1984: Nov. 7, 1983-Oct. 29, 1984 (Vol. 205, Nos. 20-26; Vol. 206, Nos. 1-26; Vol. 207, Nos. 1-19) [Vol. 206, Nos. 8-9 incorrectly read Nos. 7-8, respectively; title page of Oct. 29, 1984 issue, Vol. 207, No. 19 incorrectly reads Aug. 15, 1983, Vol. 203, No. 8; Vol. 207, No. 15 is published in 2 parts].

STATISTICAL FEATURES:

C8700–1.501: Jan. 16, 1984 (Vol. 206, No. 3)

COMPOSITE TELECOM INDUSTRY POISED TO SPEND $31 BILLION IN 1984, ANNUAL FEATURE

(p. 34-50) Annual state-of-the-industry feature, by Del Myers and Czatdana Inan, with data on independent telecommunication company and AT&T Communications construction spending, plant investment, employment, and operations, various years 1976-85. Also includes activities of specialized common carriers (SCCs), which provide microwave transmission service; and business premises equipment.

Data are from AT&T, FCC, and *Telephony* surveys of independent companies and business users of telecommunication services.

Includes 13 tables showing the following:

a. Construction expenditures of independent telephone companies, regional Bell companies, AT&T Communications, SCCs, and business customer premises equipment, 1978-84.

b. Major independent and regional Bell company construction expenditures, total revenues and expenses, long distance revenues, plant investment, equipment by type, and employees, by company, various years 1981-84, and summary trends from 1976.

c. Regional Bell company access lines and telephones by company, by State or region, various years 1979-83.

d. Characteristics of large business users of telecommunication equipment/services, including responsibilities of voice and data communication managers, and telecommunication expenditures, 1984/85.

C8700–1.502: Feb. 27, 1984 (Vol. 206, No. 9)

[Issue incorrectly reads No. 8.]

WORLD TELECOM 1984 SPENDING TO LEVEL OUT AT $78.8 BILLION, ANNUAL FEATURE

(p. 42-49, 96) Annual article, by Del Myers and Czatdana Inan, forecasting world telecommunication developments, 1984. Data are from *Telephony* surveys and world telecommunication authorities.

Includes 4 tables showing summary capital spending plans, 1979-84; Western European business communications equipment by country (no date); access lines, equipment, and plant investment, by country, as of Jan. 1, 1982 or most recent available date, with detail by company for selected countries; and Africa's telephones and investment, by country, 1983 and projected to 2000.

WORLD TELECOMMUNICATIONS TARIFFS VARY WIDELY, UK FIRM REPORTS

(p. 58) By R. J. Raggett. Article, with 1 table showing telephone and telex charges (in UK pounds) for local, long distance, and/or international service, for U.S., Canada, and 5 Western European countries, 1983-84. Data are from National Utility Services, Ltd.

C8700–1.503: Mar. 5, 1984 (Vol. 206, No. 10)

EXCHANGE COST STUDIES: AN ESSENTIAL INGREDIENT FOR TELEPHONE COMPANIES

(p. 40-47) By Stuart G. McDaniel and William Wohlhagen. Article on the effect of competition on telephone rate structure. Includes 1 undated table showing cost per residential access line, and present and proposed monthly residential rate, for telephone exchanges in rural, suburban, and urban areas.

ROUTINE SUBSCRIBER LOOP MEASUREMENTS PAY DIVIDENDS

(p. 58-64) By Doug Kulm. Article on potential for use of computer technology to monitor telephone transmission quality on subscriber circuits. Data are from experience reported by 1 telephone exchange. Includes technical data; and 1 table comparing transmission quality measures and repair costs before and after implementation of computerized monitoring, 1980 and 1982.

C8700–1.504: Apr. 23, 1984 (Vol. 206, No. 17)

VIEWDATA IS MATURING RAPIDLY IN EUROPE

(p. 32-35) By Julian Hewett. Article on development of European public viewdata (videotex) systems since 1979. Data are from Logica's Telematica Service and other sources.

Includes 1 chart showing distribution of UK viewdata terminals by application, 1983; and 1 undated table showing viewdata terminals in use, equipment suppliers, and actual or planned startup date, by system, for 9 European countries.

C8700–1.505: May 14, 1984 (Vol. 206, No. 20)

JAPAN'S TELECOM INDUSTRY RUSHES INTO THE INFORMATION AGE

(p. 138-150) By Gene Gregory. Article on Japan's telecommunication industry, with 2 tables showing average monthly optical fiber production capacity for top 6 Japanese cable manufacturers; and telecommunication material exports from selected Japanese producers to major U.S. and European telecommunication equipment manufacturers, by company; 1982.

C8700–1.506: May 21, 1984 (Vol. 206, No. 21)

IS THERE A SATELLITE IN KOREA'S FUTURE?

(p. 35-48) By Eitel M. Rizzoni and Donald K. Dement. Article on a feasibility study for a South Korean satellite system to be integrated with the national telecommunications system. Data are from Teleconsult, Inc.

Includes 2 tables showing potential investment and operating costs over a 7 year period.

C8700–1.507: May 28, 1984 (Vol. 206, No. 22)

TELECOMMUNICATIONS IN RURAL FINLAND

(p. 53) Brief article, with 1 table showing Finland's population density, telephones per 100 population, and telephone mean order delivery and repair time, for urban and rural areas, 1982. Data are from Finnish National Telecommunication Administration (PTT).

C8700–1.508: July 9, 1984 (Vol. 207, No. 2)

PROGRESS REPORT: NORTH AMERICAN INSTALLATIONS OF TIME DIVISION DIGITAL SWITCHES, ANNUAL FEATURE

(p. 55-57) Annual article, by Amos E. Joel, Jr., with 6 tables showing North American telecommunication time division digital switching equipment in service or on order, by system, with selected detail for largest offices/installations within each system, 1981-83.

IEEE: THE PIVOT OF STANDARDS WORK IN THE U.S.

(p. 100-105) By J. L. Koepfinger. Article on the role of Institute of Electrical and Electronics Engineers (IEEE) in developing technical standards. Includes 1 undated table showing number of communications industry standards developed, by IEEE component group.

C8700–1.509: July 23, 1984 (Vol. 207, No. 4)

NORDIC MOBILE TELEPHONE SYSTEM SETS THE STAGE FOR FUTURE MOBILE SYSTEMS

(p. 54-56) By Arthur Cornwell. Article, with 1 table showing mobile telephone sales volume in 4 Scandinavian countries, by brand, 1983. Data are from *Mobira News.*

C8700–1.510: Sept. 3, 1984 (Vol. 207, No. 11)

BIG SPENDERS ARE SPENDING MORE

(p. 50-51) By Norman H. Sefton and Mark V. Morawiec. Article on business expenditures for telecommunications services. Data are based on 254 responses from companies, universities, hospitals, and government agencies, to a 1984 survey conducted by International Communications Assn, and a similar 1981 survey.

Includes 2 tables showing 17-22 industries ranked by telecommunications expenditures as a percent of sales and as a percent of operating expenses, 1980 and 1983.

C8700–2 TELEPHONY'S DIRECTORY AND BUYERS' GUIDE, 1983

Annual. 1983. 740 p.
ISSN 0196-139X.
LC 79-644663.
SRI/MF/excerpts

Annual directory, for 1983, of U.S. and Canadian telephone equipment distributors, assns and organizations, regulatory and other government agencies, and companies. Also includes listings of international telephone operations, and selected telephone industry statistics. Data are compiled from FCC, BLS, and telephone company reports.

Contents:

a. Contents listing; and directories of products and services, and manufacturers and suppliers. (p. 5-383)

b. Independent telephone companies in U.S., with 1 table (p. 386) showing number of companies in 13 size categories by State and Canadian Province; 1 table for each State showing population, business and residence telephones, independent network access lines, and total Bell system telephones; and directory entries for individual companies arranged by city and State, most with selected operating data. (p. 385-587)

c. Directory of interconnect companies (firms that sell or lease terminal equipment for interconnection to telephone company lines), with text data on branch offices and employment. (p. 589-636)

d. AT&T and associated Bell system company directory and cities served, with 1 map, and 1 table (p. 640) showing number of central office codes, telephones by type, employment by sex, and equipment, for 25 Bell affiliated companies, as of Dec. 31, 1982. (p. 637-658)

e. Directory of special carriers. (p. 659-660)

f. Statistical section, with article on world telephone capital investment and equipment, and 2 charts and 19 tables, described below. (p. 661-683)

g. Directories of independent telephone investment and holding companies, U.S. and Canadian telephone assns, and U.S. regulatory and other government agencies. (p. 685-707)

h. Directories of international telephone operations organizations; international record carriers; and telephone administrations in foreign countries, most with selected operating data. (p. 709-727)

i. Canadian telephone information, including directory entries for individual telephone companies arranged by city and Province, most with selected operating data; and Bell system operating data. (p. 728-735)

j. Directory of domestic and international schools and universities offering telecommunications training programs. (p. 735-737)

Operating data variously include number of telephones by type, other equipment, and cable mileage and other plant statistics; and financial data, including plant investment, operating revenues, and construction budget, various years 1980-83, with some 1984 construction budgets.

Data for foreign countries also include cost of basic telephone service. Bell Canada data also include employment.

This is the 88th annual edition. For description of previous report, for 1982, see SRI 1982 Annual under this number.

Availability: Telephony Publishing Corp., 55 E. Jackson Blvd., Chicago IL 60604, industry $18.00, others $50.00; SRI/MF/excerpts for statistical portions and Bell system city directory.

TABLES AND CHARTS:

C8700-2.1: U.S. Data

a. Residence and business telephones, and Bell system companies, by State, as of Jan. 1, 1983; independent companies' composite income statement, and composite summary of equipment, plant investment, and capitalization, as of Dec. 31, 1977-81; and selected composite financial, equipment, local and toll call, employment, and compensation data for telephone carriers reporting to FCC, 1956-81. 4 tables. (p. 662-664)

b. Bell-owned and connecting telephones, and Bell-owned plant investment, telephones in use, and sources of revenue, 1958-82; and estimated total U.S. telephones, 1887-1982. 4 tables. (p. 665-666)

c. AT&T principal subsidiaries, telephones, and connecting access lines, 1981; and Rural Electrification Administration and Rural Telephone Bank loans and financing approved, with selected data by purpose and class of borrower, various periods 1949-82. 2 tables. (p. 666-667)

C8700-2.2: International Data

a. World population and telephone growth since 1921; and telephones by continental area, and countries with 1 million or more telephone/15 per 100 population, including city reporting most telephones per 100, all as of Jan. 1, 1981. 2 charts and 1 table. (p. 668)

b. "World Telecom Spending To Reach $78.5 Billion Level This Year," by Del Myers et al. Article on world telecommunication capital investment. Includes 4 tables showing total and public telephones, and telephone equipment by type, by country arranged by world area, as of Jan. 1, 1982. Data are based primarily on a *Telephony* annual survey. (p. 669-678)

c. World telephones, total and per 100 population, number in private and government operation, and percent automatic, by country; and telephones and population of principal world cities; as of Jan. 1, 1981. 2 tables. (p. 679-682)

C8700-2.3: Independent Companies and Summary

a. Top 25 independent companies, ranked by number of access lines, with market share and operating revenues; and summary of independent and Bell telephone companies, access lines, exchanges, finances, employees, and shareholders; as of Dec. 31, 1982. 2 tables. (p. 683)

C8850
Textile Economics Bureau

C8850-1   **TEXTILE ORGANON**
Monthly. Approx. 15 p. per issue; cumulative pagination throughout year.
ISSN 0040-5132.
LC 32-5553.
SRI/MF/complete, shipped quarterly

Monthly report providing current data on man-made fibers and manufactures, and on raw and manufactured cotton and wool, with some data on silk. Covers U.S. domestic production and shipments, consumption, stocks, and imports and exports. Also includes data on international textile industry.

Data are drawn primarily from Dept of Agriculture and Census Bureau sources, and are shown in detail by fiber and manufactured fabric.

Report includes a monthly review of fiber shipment and/or production levels during the previous month, usually with 1-2 summary tables;

notes on developments of interest to the industry; 3 monthly and 5 quarterly tables, listed below; and special, annual, or other recurring features, usually containing statistics.

Annual statistical features include U.S. textile fiber end-use survey; world natural fiber review; overview of the textile industry; U.S. fiber consumption, and import-export review; world man-made fiber survey, with directory of producers; and hosiery production.

Issues also include a semiannual report on U.S. man-made fiber industry production and capacity. An annual index is published in the Dec. issue.

Beginning with the May 1984 issue, tables are numbered consecutively within each issue. The table numbers assigned below do not correspond to numbers appearing in the reports.

Monthly tables appear in all issues. All additional features with substantial statistical content are described, as they appear, under "Statistical Features;" page locations and periods of coverage for quarterly tables are also noted. Nonstatistical features are not described.

Availability: Textile Economics Bureau, Textile Organon, 101 Eisenhower Pkwy., Roseland NJ 07068, $125.00 per yr., schools and nonprofit institutions $25.00 per yr., single copy $15.00; June, Sept., and Nov. issues $20.00; SRI/MF/complete, shipped quarterly.

Issues reviewed during 1984: Sept./Oct. 1983-Sept. 1984 (P) (Vol. 54, Nos. 9-11; Vol. 55, Nos. 1-8) [Sept./Oct. 1983 and Mar./Apr. 1984 are combined issues].

MONTHLY TABLES:
[Data are usually shown monthly for year to date, current to 1-2 months prior to cover date, and cumulatively for current and previous year to date. Sequence of tables varies from issue to issue.]

[1] U.S. man-made fiber imports for consumption [by cellulosic and noncellulosic fiber type, and for other fiber tops, yarn, and thread].

[2] Selected U.S. man-made fiber imports for consumption by country of origin [for cellulosic and noncellulosic yarn/monofil/strips and staple+tow].

[3] Selected U.S. monthy textile fiber data [man-made fiber shipments and end-of-month stocks for yarn+monofilaments and staple+-tow+fiberfill, by type of fiber; and wool and cotton consumption].

QUARTERLY TABLES:
[Tables show data quarterly, for 5-12 quarters ending 1-2 quarters preceding publication.]

TRADE

[1] U.S. exports of man-made fibers [cellulosic and noncellulosic fibers by type, and textile glass fiber].

[2] U.S. imports, exports, and balance of man-made fiber [yarn+monofilaments, staple+-tow, and waste products of cellulosic and noncellulosic fibers] and [10 man-made fiber] manufactures, cotton manufactures, and wool manufactures.

QUARTERLY MAN-MADE FIBER REVIEW

[3] Quarterly man-made fiber data [shows production, domestic and export shipments, ending stock, and imports for 4 types of yarns+monofilaments and 5 types of staple+-tow, and for textile glass fiber].

[4-5] Filament yarn and staple and tow domestic shipments [by end product type (hosiery and other knits, carpets, tires, cordage, and others); and by product group (apparel, home furnishings, and industrial); also includes annual data for 4 previous years].

STATISTICAL FEATURES:

C8850–1.501: Sept./Oct. 1983 (Vol. 54, No. 9)

QUARTERLY TABLES

[4-5] Filament yarn and staple + tow domestic shipments [annually 1979-82 and quarterly 1982-2nd quarter 1983]. (p. 154-155)

TEXTILE FIBER END USE SURVEY, ANNUAL FEATURE

(p. 137-153) Annual survey report on U.S. textile fiber consumption by end use, 1976-82. Includes 1 summary chart, and 10 tables as follows:

Tables:

[All tables show data for 1976-82. All tables except [1], [5], and [10] show data for man-made fibers (usually by type), cotton, and wool.]

[1] End use summary changes [for total and man-made fiber]. (p. 137)

[2] U.S. end use summary. (p. 140)

[3] Mill consumption + semimanufactured imports. (p. 141)

[4] End use vs. available supply. (p. 141)

[5] Imports for consumption [raw, semimanufactured, and finished silk, linen, jute, and sisal/other fibers]. (p. 141)

[6-8] Apparel, home furnishings, and industrial/other consumer-type products [consumption of fibers by type of product]. (p. 142-147)

[9] Exports of domestic products [by type of product]. (p. 148)

[10] Summary of man-made fiber and semimanufactured imports. (p. 149)

C8850–1.502: Nov. 1983 (Vol. 54, No. 10)

QUARTERLY TABLES

[1] U.S. exports of man-made fibers [quarterly 1982-3rd quarter 1983]. (p. 171)

[2] U.S. imports, exports, and balance of man-made fiber and manufactures, cotton manufactures, and wool manufactures [quarterly 1982-2nd quarter 1983]. (p. 170)

U.S. MAN-MADE FIBER PRODUCERS, ANNUAL FEATURE

(p. 162-168) Annual directory of U.S. man-made fiber producers, updating listings appearing in the Sept. 1982 and June 1983 issues. Also includes 1 undated table showing number of producing plants, by fiber type, State, and region.

REVIEW OF U.S. IMPORT/EXPORT BALANCE OF MAN-MADE MANUFACTURES

(p. 168-169) Brief article, with 2 tables showing imports and exports of aggregate man-made fiber manufactures including and excluding apparel, 1973-82.

U.S. EXPORTS AND IMPORTS OF MAN-MADE FIBERS

(p. 172-173) Two tables showing export and import volume and value for man-made fibers by type, 1979-1st half 1983.

C8850–1.503: Dec. 1983 (Vol. 54, No. 11)

QUARTERLY TABLES

[3] Quarterly man-made fiber data [quarterly 1982-3rd quarter 1983]. (p. 186-187)

[4-5] Filament yarn and staple + tow domestic shipments [annually 1979-82 and quarterly 1982-3rd quarter 1983]. (p. 188-189)

U.S. MAN-MADE FIBER PRODUCING CAPACITY, SEMIANNUAL FEATURE

(p. 178-179) Report on semiannual survey of U.S. man-made fiber production and capacity, Nov. 1983, with trends from 1970 and projections to 1985. Includes 2 tables showing the following:

a. Actual production of cellulosic and noncellulosic yarn + monofilaments and staple + tow, and textile glass fibers, 1970-82.

b. Actual and projected capacity for production of same fibers, with additional detail for noncellulosic fibers, generally Nov. 1970-85 and May 1984-85.

WORLD NATURAL FIBER REVIEW, ANNUAL FEATURE

(p. 180-184) Annual report on world raw cotton and wool industry, with 7 tables as follows:

[1] World [U.S. and foreign] production, consumption, exports, and carryover of raw cotton [5-year averages 1950-79, and annually 1970-83]. (p. 180)

[2] World raw cotton production [by world region and for 10 countries, same periods as Table [1]]. (p. 181)

[3] Supply and distribution of domestic and foreign raw cotton in the U.S. for the seasons beginning Aug. 1st [1972-83]. (p. 182)

[4] U.S. calendar year imports and exports of raw cotton and cotton products [1967-82]. (p. 182)

[5] U.S. cotton acreage, [production], and yield [1964-83]. (p. 183)

[6] World raw wool production by the principal producing countries [and Eastern Europe/PRC and all others, 5-year averages 1935-79 and annually 1965-83]. (p. 183)

[7] Disappearance of wool in the U.S. [includes mill consumption, imports, and exports, by type of product, 1969-82]. (p. 184)

SIX MONTH U.S. EXPORTS OF MAN-MADE FIBERS BY COUNTRY

(p. 190-191) Table showing exports of cellulosic yarn/monofil/strips; noncellulosic textile yarn and industrial yarn/monofil/strips; and cellulosic and noncellulosic staple + tow; all by country of destination, 1981-82 and 1st half 1983.

C8850–1.504: Jan. 1984 (Vol. 55, No. 1)

QUARTERLY TABLE

[2] U.S. imports, exports, and balance of man-made fiber and manufactures, cotton manufactures, and wool manufactures [quarterly 2nd quarter 1982-3rd quarter 1983]. (p. 9)

CAPACITY UTILIZATION REVIEW, ANNUAL FEATURE

(p. 3-8) Annual report on man-made fiber industry, with 8 tables showing production, capacity, and capacity utilization rates for cellulosic and noncellulosic yarn + monofilaments and staple + tow, and textile glass fibers, 1970-83.

INTERNATIONAL TRADE SUPPLEMENT

(p. 10-13) Special report on world man-made fiber trade, with 3 tables as follows:

[1] 1982 man-made fiber production, import, export, and net available supply [of cellulosic and noncellulosic yarn and staple + tow] by country (except olefin and textile glass). (p. 11)

[2] Selected exports of man-made fiber to Eastern Europe and PRC [by 16 exporting and 9 importing countries, 1979-82]. (p. 12)

[3] Exports of man-made fibers to certain nonproducing countries [and 4 world regions, 1981-82]. (p. 13)

Special report includes data usually found in annual reviews of world man-made fiber trade, and of imports, exports, and trade balance.

C8850–1.505: Feb. 1984 (Vol. 55, No. 2)

QUARTERLY TABLES

[1] U.S. exports of man-made fibers [quarterly 1982-83]. (p. 30)

[3] Quarterly man-made fiber data [quarterly 1982-83]. (p. 26-27)

IMPACT OF IMPORTS, AN EXAMINATION OF THE GROWTH OF APPAREL IMPORTS

(p. 19-23) Special report on apparel imports, with summary charts and text data, and 1 table showing the following: imports of apparel yarn and fabric, imports and exports of garments, and supply available for domestic consumption, for cotton, wool, and man-made fibers; cotton and wool fabric from U.S. mills; and man-made fiber domestic shipments for apparel, and exports of semimanufactured products; 1973-83.

1983 PRODUCTION, SHIPMENT, AND INVENTORY ANALYSIS, ANNUAL FEATURE

(p. 24-25) Annual article, with 1 table generally repeating data from quarterly table [3], annually 1980-83.

C8850–1.506: Mar./Apr. 1984 (Vol. 55, No. 3)

QUARTERLY TABLES

[2] U.S. imports, exports, and balance of man-made fiber and manufactures, cotton manufactures, and wool manufactures [quarterly 3rd quarter 1982-4th quarter 1983; table is included in 1983 review of textile industry, described below]. (p. 40)

[4-5] Filament yarn and staple + tow domestic shipments [annually 1980-83 and quarterly 1982-83]. (p. 56-57)

1983: A YEAR IN PERSPECTIVE, ANNUAL FEATURE

(p. 35-43) Annual article on textile industry fiber production, trade, and consumption, 1983 and trends. Includes 13 tables, as follows:

Tables:

[Tables show data for 1960s-83 or 1970s-83. Data on man-made fiber usually include detail by fiber type.]

[1] Mill consumption by fiber. (p. 35)

[2] U.S. mill consumption of [total] man-made fiber, cotton, and wool. (p. 35)

[3-4] Man-made fiber production; and noncellulosic fiber production detail. (p. 36)

[5] Man-made fiber distribution [domestic and export shipments, imports, and domestic consumption]. (p. 37)

[6] U.S. mill consumption of fiber and domestic consumption of fiber/products [man-made, cotton, wool, and silk, with detail for imports and exports]. (p. 38)

[7-8] Raw fiber equivalent of imports and exports; and U.S. imports, exports, and balance; of man-made fiber, cotton and wool manufactures [by type of product]. (p. 39, 41)

[9] U.S. imports, exports, and balance of man-made fibers. (p. 42)

[10-11] Raw cotton consumption and raw silk deliveries [monthly]. (p. 42)

[12] Filament yarn domestic shipments by denier [acetate, polyester and nylon textile, and nylon carpet]. (p. 43)

[13] Producers' waste shipments [of rayon and noncellulosic fiber]. (p. 43)

1983 IMPORT/EXPORT REVIEW, ANNUAL FEATURE

(p. 44-51) Annual report, for 1983, on U.S. exports and imports of man-made fibers and products, with trends from 1977. Includes 7 tables, as follows:

[1] U.S. imports of selected man-made fiber manufactures [amount and value for various types of knit fabric in the piece, and broad woven fabrics, 1979-83]. (p. 44)

[2] U.S. general imports of man-made fiber apparel [by country of origin, 1977-83]. (p. 45)

[3] Selected U.S. man-made fiber imports by country of origin [noncellulosic staple+tow and yarn-singles, cellulosic and noncellulosic waste and spun yarns, and textile glass, 1982-83]. (p. 46)

[4] Selected U.S. man-made fiber and manufactures imports for consumption, by country of origin [broad woven fabrics, knit fabric in the piece, and fibers, 1979-83]. (p. 47)

[5] Selected U.S. exports by country of destination [amount and value for cellulosic yarn, monofil/strips; noncellulosic textile yarn; noncellulosic industrial yarn, monofil/strips; and cellulosic and noncellulosic staple+tow; 1982-83]. (p. 48-49)

[6] U.S. exports of man-made fibers [amount and value for various types of cellulosic and noncellulosic fibers, and textile glass fiber, 1979-83]. (p. 50)

[7] U.S. imports of man-made fibers [amount and value for various types of cellulosic and noncellulosic fibers, and other man-made fiber tops, yarn, and thread, 1979-83]. (p. 51)

MEASURING PRODUCTIVITY: INDEXES OF OUTPUT FOR THE U.S. MAN-MADE FIBER INDUSTRY

(p. 52-55) Article, with 2 tables showing indexes of output, employment, and hours, for production and nonproduction workers in the synthetic fiber industries (SIC 2823, 2824), 1957-82. Data are from the Textile Economics Bureau, Census Bureau, and BLS.

SELECTED U.S. MONTHLY TEXTILE FIBER DATA (REVISED)

(p. 60) Table presenting revised data for monthly table [3] on textile fiber shipments and stocks, 1982 and monthly 1983.

C8850–1.507: May 1984 (Vol. 55, No. 4)

QUARTERLY TABLES

[1] U.S. exports of man-made fibers [quarterly 1983-1st quarter 1984]. (p. 75)

[3] Quarterly man-made fiber data [quarterly 1982-1st quarter 1984]. (p. 76-77)

1983 PER CAPITA CONSUMPTION REVIEW, ANNUAL FEATURE

(p. 67-71) Annual article, with 8 tables as follows:

Tables:
[Unless otherwise noted, tables show data for 1970-83.]

1. U.S. population, GNP (goods produced), and per capita GNP. (p. 68)

2A-2B. U.S. average annual [man-made, cotton, and wool] fiber available for consumption [per capita], including textile/nontextile glass fiber and excluding nontextile glass fiber [and also showing population, various periods 1920-83]. (p. 68)

3. Domestic consumption of [man-made, cotton, and wool] fiber/products. (p. 68)

4. Mill consumption by [type of man-made] fiber [and for cotton and wool]. (p. 70)

5. Percent analysis of population, per capita GNP (goods produced), and per capita consumption of man-made fiber, cotton and wool. (p. 70)

6-7. Raw fiber equivalent of imports of man-made fiber, cotton, and wool manufactures; and per capita consumption of imports of man-made fiber, cotton, and wool manufactures as compared to per capita consumption of [all] man-made fiber, cotton, and wool; [1978-83]. (p. 71)

MAY 1984 CAPACITY SURVEY ANALYSIS, SEMIANNUAL FEATURE

(p. 72-74) Report on semiannual survey of U.S. man-made fiber production and capacity, May 1984, with trends from 1970 and projections to 1986. Includes 2 tables showing the following:

a. Actual production of cellulosic and noncellulosic yarn+monofilaments and staple+tow, and textile glass fibers, 1970-83.

b. Actual and projected capacity for production of same fibers, with additional detail for noncellulosic fibers, Nov. 1970-85 and May 1984-86.

C8850–1.508: June 1984 (Vol. 55, No. 5)

QUARTERLY TABLES

[4-5] Filament yarn and staple+tow domestic shipments [annually 1980-83 and quarterly 1983-1st quarter 1984]. (p. 116-117)

WORLD MAN-MADE FIBER SURVEY, ANNUAL FEATURE

(p. 81-115) Annual report on world man-made fiber production, planned capacity, and plants, by country and world region, 1970s-85. Data are in metric tons, and will be repeated in millions of pounds in the July 1984 issue.

Includes 10 tables, listed below (p. 81-93, 115); directory of world man-made fiber producers by country, with plant sites and type of fiber produced (p. 94-113); and list of producer affiliations, with headquarters country, owning company, company owned, and percent of capital ownership (p. 113-115).

Tables:
[Tables generally show production data for 1977-83, and capacity data for 1984-85. Tables [2-10] show data by country or world region.]

1. World production of certain textile fibers [total cellulosic fibers, noncellulosic fibers except olefin, and cotton, wool, and silk]. (p. 81)

2. World noncellulosic fiber production [and capacity, for yarn+monofilaments and staple+tow+fiberfill] by fiber except olefin [acrylic+modacrylic, nylon+aramid, polyester, and other fibers]. (p. 83)

3a-4b. World noncellulosic fiber (except olefin) and cellulosic fiber production [and capacity]. (p. 84-91)

5. Rayon vs. acetate filament yarn production [and capacity, for high and regular+intermediate tenacity viscose rayon yarn, cuprammonium rayon yarn, and acetate+triacetate yarn]. (p. 92)

6. World glass fiber production and producing capacity. (p. 93)

7. Estimated world cigarette tow production. (p. 93)

8. World acetate staple production and capacity. (p. 93)

9. World olefin fiber production. (p. 93)

10. Number of man-made fiber producing plants (except olefin) [cellulosic, noncellulosic, and textile glass; no date]. (p. 115)

C8850–1.509: July 1984 (Vol. 55, No. 6)

QUARTERLY TABLE

[2] U.S. imports, exports, and balance of man-made fiber and manufactures, cotton manufactures, and wool manufactures [quarterly 4th quarter 1982-1st quarter 1984]. (p. 137)

WORLD MAN-MADE FIBER SURVEY, ANNUAL FEATURE

(p. 124-135) Annual report repeating in millions of pounds most of the data presented in metric tons in the 1983 world man-made fiber survey article appearing in the June 1984 issue.

For description of June 1984 article, see C8850-1.508 above.

U.S. PRODUCTION OF HOSIERY, ANNUAL FEATURE

(p. 136) Annual table showing production of women's, men's, and children's hosiery, by type, 1970-83. Data are from National Assn of Hosiery Manufacturers.

C8850–1.510: Aug. 1984 (Vol. 55, No. 7)

QUARTERLY TABLE

[3] Quarterly man-made fiber data [quarterly 1982-2nd quarter 1984]. (p. 150)

IMPORT UPDATE, QUARTERLY FEATURE

(p. 144-149) Quarterly report on apparel imports, with summary charts and text data, and 1 table showing the following: imports of apparel yarn and fabric, imports and exports of garments, and supply available for domestic consumption, for cotton, wool, and man-made fibers; cotton and wool fabric from U.S. mills; and man-made fiber domestic shipments for apparel, and exports of semimanufactured products; 1973-83 and 1st-2nd quarter 1984.

This is the 1st quarterly update of a special report published in the Feb. 1984 issue; for description see C8850-1.505, above.

C8850–1.511: Sept. 1984 (Vol. 55, No. 8)

QUARTERLY TABLES

[4-5] Filament yarn and staple+tow domestic shipments [annually 1980-83 and quarterly 1983-2nd quarter 1984]. (p. 172-173)

TEXTILE FIBER END USE SURVEY, ANNUAL FEATURE

(p. 155, 158-171) Annual survey report on U.S. textile fiber consumption by end use, 1977-83. Includes 9 tables as follows:

Tables:

[All tables show data for 1977-83. All tables except 1 and 5 show data for man-made fibers (usually by type), cotton, and wool.]

1. End use summary changes [for total and man-made fiber]. (p. 155)

2. U.S. end use summary. (p. 159)

3. Mill consumption+semimanufactured imports. (p. 160)

4. End use vs. available supply. (p. 160)

5. Summary of man-made fiber and semimanufactured imports [by type]. (p. 161)

6-8. Apparel, home furnishings, and industrial/other consumer-type products [consumption of fibers by type of product]. (p. 162-167)

9. Exports of domestic products [by type of product]. (p. 168)

For description of previous report, for 1976-82, see C8850-1.501 above.

C8900
Time, Inc.

C8900–1   **FORTUNE**

Biweekly. Approx. 150 p.
ISSN 0015-8259.
LC 31-7716.
SRI/MF/excerpts, shipped quarterly

Biweekly magazine on business and industry, presenting the annual *Fortune* 500 directory of the 500 largest industrial corporations, other major annual directories, and feature articles on corporate developments and outlook, domestic and foreign economic conditions, investment prospects, Government regulation, taxes, and financial markets.

General format:

a. Feature articles, often with a few summary charts or "Investors Snapshot" profiles of selected companies, and sometimes with more extensive statistics.

b. Regular editorial depts, including "Fortune Forecast" on outlook for selected economic indicators, and "Personal Investing," each usually including 1-3 supporting charts or tables.

c. Annual statistical directory features presenting financial and employment data for the 500 largest industrial companies; 500 largest nonindustrial companies; 50 leading exporters; 50 largest industrial companies worldwide; and 500 largest industrial and 100 largest commercial banking companies outside the U.S.

Features with substantial statistical content are described, as they appear, under "Statistical Features." Each issue of the magazine is reviewed, but an abstract is published in SRI monthly issues only when statistical features appear.

Availability: Fortune, Circulation Department, Time-Life Bldg., 541 N. Fairbanks Ct., Chicago IL 60611, $39.00 per yr., single copy $3.00, Fortune 500 issue $3.50; SRI/MF/excerpts for all portions described under "Statistical Features;" shipped quarterly.

Issues reviewed during 1984: Nov. 28, 1983-Oct. 29, 1984 (P) (Vol. 108, Nos. 11-13; Vol. 109, Nos. 1-13; Vol. 110, Nos. 1-9).

STATISTICAL FEATURES:

C8900–1.501: Dec. 26, 1983 (Vol. 108, No. 13)

TAPPING THE RICHES IN COMPANY PENSION PLANS

(p. 129-134) By Arthur M. Louis. Article discussing the use of overfunded company pension plans as a source of corporate financing. Includes 1 table showing amount drawn from pension plans by 11 companies drawing at least $10 million, as of fall 1983.

C8900–1.502: Jan. 9, 1984 (Vol. 109, No. 1)

AMERICA'S MOST ADMIRED CORPORATIONS, ANNUAL FEATURE

(p. 50-62) Annual article, by Nancy J. Perry, on business community's ratings of 250 companies in 25 industries. Data are from responses of approximately 3,500 corporate executives/outside directors/financial analysts to a 1983 *Fortune* survey.

Includes 3 tables showing ratings for 3-10 most and least admired companies overall, in 8 performance categories, and in 25 industries.

PAY CUTS BEFORE THE JOB EVEN STARTS

(p. 75-77) By Steven Flax. Article discussing growth in 2-tier union wage contracts, which allow companies to hire future employees at lower wage rates than current employees. Includes 1 undated table showing the following for 8 major companies with 2-tier contracts: number of workers covered by contract and principal union involved, and entry-level wage under old and new contracts.

C8900–1.503: Jan. 23, 1984 (Vol. 109, No. 2)

DEALS OF THE YEAR, ANNUAL FEATURE

(p. 54-58) Annual list, with narrative analysis, by Daniel P. Wiener, of the 50 largest U.S. corporate financial transactions, 1983, ranked by value of transaction, and showing value (actual and as percent of book value), date, and type of transaction; companies involved and type of industry; and financial intermediary and fee charged.

List covers mergers, acquisitions, and debt and equity offerings.

HOW THE CHAMPS DO LEVERAGED BUYOUTS

(p. 70-78) By Irwin Ross. Article on leveraged buyouts of company stock by management. Includes 1 table showing acquisition price, company and investment banker involved, and date, for 10 largest leveraged buyouts, 1980-82 and pending.

C8900–1.504: Feb. 6, 1984 (Vol. 109, No. 3)

RECOVERY SKIPS MIDDLE MANAGERS

(p. 112-120) By Jeremy Main. Article, with 1 table showing percent of companies cutting middle management jobs, Aug. 1982-83, by industry division, type of economic problem facing company, and company profit and growth status. Data are from an Aug. 1983 survey of large corporations conducted for Harvard Business School by LdG Associates.

C8900–1.505: Feb. 20 (Vol. 109, No. 4)

EUROPE BRACES FOR FREE-MARKET TV

(p. 74-82) By Andrew C. Brown. Article, with 1 undated chart showing total and TV advertising expenditures in 4 European countries.

C8900–1.506: Mar. 5, 1984 (Vol. 109, No. 5)

INFLATION HEDGES FOR THE '80s

(p. 30-33) By Ford S. Worthy. Article, with 1 table ranking 9 types of personal investments by compounded annual rates of return, with comparisons to CPI, for inflationary period June 1976-81 compared to disinflationary period June 1982-83. Data are from Salomon Brothers.

U.S. STEEL AND LTV FIND HIDDEN CHARMS IN LOSERS

(p. 118-132) By Carol J. Loomis. Article, with 1 table showing the following for 4 steel companies involved in mergers: sales and steel share of sales, losses, production, capacity utilization, and employment, 1983, with date and amount of peak employment during past 10 years.

C8900–1.507: Mar. 19, 1984 (Vol. 109, No. 6)

ARE YOU UNDERPAID?

(p. 20-25) By Lisa Miller Mesdag. Article, with 1 table showing pre-tax and after-tax cash compensation for corporate middle and upper middle managers, 1979, 1981, and 1983; and per capita GNP, 1981; for U.S. and 11 other countries. Data are from The Hay Group, Population Reference Bureau, and other sources.

Data corrections appear in the Apr. 16, 1984 issue; for description, see C8900-1.508 below.

C8900–1.508: Apr. 16, 1984 (Vol. 109, No. 8)

WORLDWIDE COMPENSATION

(p. 29) Letter to the editor, with editor's response correcting data in article on management compensation in U.S. and 11 other countries. For description of article, see C8900-1.507 above.

TRUE FACE OF BANK EARNINGS

(p. 82-86) By Gary Hector. Article, with 1 table on profit impacts of U.S. bank loans to financially troubled foreign countries. Table shows the following for 10 largest bank holding companies: projected earnings per share in 1984; and reduction per share, if bank regulators call for a 1% reserve against losses on loans from Argentina, Brazil, Mexico, and Venezuela, and if these countries force a 2% drop in interest rates on their loans. Data are from Keefe, Bruyette, and Woods, Inc.

C8900–1.509: Apr. 30, 1984 (Vol. 109, No. 9)

MILITARY BOOST TO INDUSTRY

(p. 42-48) By Bruce Steinberg. Article, with 1 table showing FY83 DOD contract value and total 1983 sales, for 10 leading defense contractors, with Fortune 500 rank.

WHEN PAYING OFF A RAIDER BENEFITS THE SHAREHOLDERS

(p. 152-158) By Richard I. Kirkland, Jr. Article on corporate practice of repurchasing a major shareholder's stock at a high price, in order to avoid a takeover by the shareholder. Includes 1 table on 7 such repurchases between Nov. 1983 and Apr. 1984, showing date, company, seller, seller's gross profit from transaction, and per-share premium over market price paid.

FRANCE FLIRTS WITH THIRD WORLD DEBTOR STATUS

(p. 166) Article, with 1 undated table showing external debt, and debt as percent of GDP, for France compared to 6 other countries. Data are estimates by U.S. banks.

TEN YEARS THAT SHOOK THE FORTUNE 500

Compilation of articles, most with statistics, reviewing selected aspects of the economic performance of the 500 largest U.S. industrial corporations over the last decade. Feature also includes the annual *Fortune* 500 directory. Statistical articles are described below.

CORPORATE STARS THAT BRIGHTENED A DARK DECADE

(p. 224-232) By Carol J. Loomis. Article, with 1 table ranking 13 top *Fortune* 500 companies by average return on equity, 1974-83 period.

INVESTMENT LESSONS FROM THE DECADE

(p. 239-247) By Edward C. Baig. Article, with 1 chart showing aggregate annual rates of return on shareholders' equity and sales, total rate of return to shareholders, and earnings per share growth, 1973-83 period, for 25 companies with best and worst performance in each measure during 1963-73 period.

PRINCES OF PRODUCTIVITY

(p. 253-256) By Peter Nulty. Article, with 1 chart showing percent change in sales per employee, by selected industry group, 1973-83 period.

DECADE'S WORST MERGERS

(p. 262-270) By Anne B. Fisher. Article on 7 worst acquisitions during 1973-83, from perspective of acquiring companies' shareholders. Based on a *Fortune* survey of over 30 merger specialists and security analysts.

Includes 1 table showing the following for each acquisition: date; acquiring and acquired company, and lines of business; purchase price and payment method; acquirer's 1983 after-tax profits, and acquired company's contribution; and acquirer's 1983 earnings per share, actual and if acquisition hadn't occurred.

FORTUNE DIRECTORY OF THE LARGEST U.S. INDUSTRIAL CORPORATIONS, ANNUAL FEATURE

(p. 274-322) Annual directory presenting sales, income, other financial data, and employment, for the 500 largest U.S. industrial corporations ranked by total sales in 1983.

Contents:

a. Narrative summary, with 1 table showing selected aggregate performance measures for the *Fortune* 500, 1982-83. (p. 274-275)

b. Ranked listing of the *Fortune* 500, showing sales, assets, net income, stockholders' equity, employees, and net income as percents of sales and equity, 1983; earnings

per share, 1973 and 1982-83; and return to investors, 1983 and annual average 1973-83 period; rankings for most items; and major industry group. (p. 276-295)

c. Eleven analytical tables showing the best and/or worst performing companies, and industry medians, for selected financial performance and productivity measures; companies with operating losses ranked by amount; and arrivals to and departures from the *Fortune* 500 list. (p. 296-299)

d. Summary rankings among *Fortune* 500 for 14 measures, by company arranged by industry group. (p. 300-318)

e. Alphabetical index to corporations, and notes. (p. 320-322)

This is the 30th annual directory.

Narrative correction appears in the Aug. 6, 1984 issue; for description, see C8900-1.515 below.

C8900–1.510: May 14, 1984 (Vol. 109, No. 10)

MORE POWER TO THE PC CHAINS

(p. 83-88) By Joel Dreyfuss. Article, with 1 table showing number of company-owned and franchised stores, and principal brands sold, for top 10 personal computer retail chains, as of Mar. 1984.

HOSPITAL STOCKS: THE VITAL SIGNS ARE GOOD

(p. 200) Article, with 1 table showing recent revenues, net income, and price/earnings ratio, and stock price range over last 12-month period, for 6 major hospital companies. Data are from Lynch, Jones, and Ryan's Institutional Brokers Estimate System.

C8900–1.511: May 28, 1984 (Vol. 109, No. 11)

CONGLOMERATES ARE DOING BETTER THAN YOU THINK

(p. 50-60) By Royal Little. Article, with 1 table showing 1983 sales, and median, low, and high return on stockholder's equity for 1978-83 period, for top 39 conglomerates among *Fortune* 500 industrial companies, ranked by median return.

C8900–1.512: June 11, 1984 (Vol. 109, No. 12)

SPECIAL REPORT: THE FORTUNE SERVICE 500

Compilation of articles, some with statistics, reviewing selected aspects of the economic performance of the 500 largest U.S. nonindustrial corporations over the last decade. Feature also includes the annual *Fortune* 500 service directory. Statistical articles are described below.

HOW THE SERVICE STARS MANAGED TO SPARKLE

(p. 158-166) By Carol J. Loomis. Article, with 1 table ranking 12 top *Fortune* 500 service companies by average return on equity, 1974-83 period, and also showing return for best and worst year.

FORTUNE DIRECTORY OF THE LARGEST U.S. NON-INDUSTRIAL CORPORATIONS, ANNUAL FEATURE

(p. 170-194) Annual directory presenting financial and employment data for the 100 larg-

est companies in diversified service, commercial banking, and diversified financial services; and for the 50 largest companies in life insurance, retailing, transportation, and utilities; 1983.

Contents:

a. Narrative review of 1983 financial performance in the 7 industries covered, with 1 table ranking top 10 utility companies by estimated assets for 1984. (p. 170-171)

b. Ranked listings of the 100 or 50 largest companies in each industry, generally showing assets, net income, stockholders' equity, employment, earnings per share, return to investors, and, as applicable, sales, deposits, loans, revenues, and insurance in force, 1983, with selected comparisons to 1973 and/or 1982, and rankings for most items. (p. 172-191)

c. Alphabetical index to corporations, and notes. (p. 192-194)

Other Article

GOLDEN PROFITS IN DANGEROUS DROSS

(p. 220) Article, with 1 table showing the following for 5 major hazardous waste management companies: revenues, net income, recent price/earnings ratio, stock price range over last 12-month period, and fiscal year end date.

C8900–1.513: June 25, 1984 (Vol. 109, No. 13)

TOP LIFE INSURERS WEIGH GOING PUBLIC

(p. 96) Article, with 1 table ranking top 10 mutual life insurance companies by assets, and also showing surplus, as of Dec. 31, 1983. The ranked companies are considering conversion from policyholder to stock ownership.

C8900–1.514: July 9, 1984 (Vol. 110, No. 1)

PROFITS FROM STOCK BUY-BACKS

(p. 197-198) Article, with 1 table showing the following for 10 major corporations repurchasing their own common stock during 1st half 1984: number of shares outstanding, as of Dec. 31, 1983; dates, method, and number of shares involved in buyback; stock price range since mid-1980; and recent stock price/earnings ratio.

DEFENSE STOCKS AFTER THE BIG RETREAT

(p. 199) Article, with 1 table showing revenues and net income, 1983, stock price range over last 12-month period, and recent price/earnings ratio, for 8 leading defense contractors.

C8900–1.515: Aug. 6, 1984 (Vol. 110, No. 3)

CORRECTIONS

(p. 12) Correction to narrative of *Fortune* 500 directory of the largest U.S. industrial corporations, appearing in the Apr. 30, 1984 issue.

For description of directory, see C8900-1.509, above.

50 LEADING EXPORTERS, ANNUAL FEATURE

(p. 64-65) Annual listing, with accompanying article, ranking 50 leading companies by export sales, 1983. Also shows rank for 1982, total sales and rank for 1983, major products, and exports as percent of sales.

MOBILE PHONES: HOT NEW INDUSTRY

(p. 108-113) By Colin Leinster. Article, with 1 table showing cellular mobile telephone system revenues and markets served, for 8 companies, 1990.

C8900–1.516: Aug. 20, 1984 (Vol. 110, No. 4)

EARLY REPORTS FROM THE WAR OF THE PAINKILLERS

(p. 101) Article, with 1 chart showing nonprescription analgesic sales, and market shares by major company, 1984. Data are from Oppenheimer & Co.

FORTUNE INTERNATIONAL 500, ANNUAL FEATURE

Annual compilation of articles on world economic trends, with directories of 500 largest industrial corporations and 100 largest commercial banks outside the U.S., and 50 largest industrial corporations in the world. Statistical articles and directories are described below.

RECOVERY COMES ON STRONG, ANNUAL FEATURE

(p. 176-181) Annual article analyzing world economic trends. Data are from OECD, IMF, BLS, and Morgan Guaranty Trust Co.

Includes 4 charts and 1 table showing percent change in GDP and consumer prices, and unemployment rate, for OECD and 5 member countries, various periods 1971-85; and external debt of 10 developing countries, 1984.

FORTUNE DIRECTORY OF THE LARGEST INDUSTRIAL CORPORATIONS OUTSIDE THE U.S., ANNUAL FEATURE

(p. 200-215) Annual directory, presenting financial and employment data for the 500 largest industrial corporations outside the U.S., 1983. Includes narrative analysis and the following:

a. Ranked listing of companies, showing for each: sales rank, 1982-83; country; type of industry; and sales, assets, net income, stockholders' equity, and employees, 1983.

b. 5 analytical tables showing the following: annual changes in sales and profits, for 10 best- and 10 worst-performing companies, and industry medians; companies added/returned to and deleted from the foreign 500 list; money losers; and distribution of companies by country; 1983.

c. Alphabetical index.

Also includes brief insert article presenting annual ranking of 50 largest industrial companies worldwide, by sales, 1983, also showing rank for 1982, net income for 1983, and headquarters.

Data corrections appear in the Sept. 17, 1984 and Oct. 15, 1984 issues; for description, see C8900-1.518 and C8900-1.520, below.

100 LARGEST COMMERCIAL BANKING COMPANIES OUTSIDE THE U.S., ANNUAL FEATURE

(p. 216-219) Annual listing, with accompanying article, ranking the 100 largest commercial banks outside the U.S., by assets, 1983. Also shows asset comparison to 1982; deposits and rank, loans, net income, stockholders' equity, offices, and employees, 1983; and country.

C8900–1.517: Sept. 3, 1984 (Vol. 110, No. 5)

JAPAN'S LATEST ASSAULT ON CHIPMAKING

(p. 76-81) By Bro Uttal. Article, with 1 chart showing world market shares held by U.S., Japanese, and all other manufacturers, for 3 advanced types of semiconductor manufacturing equipment, 1979 and 1983. Data are from VLSI Research, Inc.

C8900–1.518: Sept. 17, 1984 (Vol. 110, No. 6)

CORRECTIONS

(p. 24) Data corrections to *Fortune* 500 directory of largest industrial corporations outside of U.S., appearing in the Aug. 20, 1984 issue.

For description of directory, see C8900-1.516, above.

C8900–1.519: Oct. 1, 1984 (Vol. 110, No. 7)

HOW GOOD ARE WALL STREET'S SECURITY ANALYSTS?

(p. 130-136) By Anne B. Fisher. Article, with 1 chart showing percent average error in securities analysts' estimates for corporate earnings in 12 industry groups, FY84. Data are from Zacks Investment Research.

MA BELL'S OFFSPRING ARE RINGING UP PROFITS

(p. 172) Article, with 1 table showing the following for 7 regional telephone holding companies created by the breakup of AT&T: revenues, income, and stock price range and recent price, 1st half 1984. Data are from Lynch, Jones, and Ryan's Institutional Brokers Estimate System.

C8900–1.520: Oct. 15, 1984 (Vol. 110, No. 8)

CORRECTIONS

(p. 24) Includes data corrections to the *Fortune* directory of the 500 largest industrial corporations outside the U.S., appearing in Aug. 20, 1984 issue.

For description of directory, see C8900-1.516, above.

THRIFT INDUSTRY IS UNDER SIEGE AGAIN

(p. 175-185) By Gary Hector. Article, with 1 table showing the following for top 10 savings and loan assns ranked by assets: value of assets, net worth as defined by thrift regulators and as reported to the SEC, and tangible net worth (excludes goodwill from acquisitions), as of Mar. 31, 1984. Data are from Lyons, Zomback & Ostrowski, and FHLBB.

NEW ISSUES: WHO UNDERWROTE THE LEMONS

(p. 189) Article, with 1 table showing number of new issues underwritten in 1983, and median percent change in price as of Sept. 1984, for 5 most and 5 least successful securities underwriters. Data are from Interactive Data.

C8910
Times Journal Co.

C8910–1   MILITARY MARKET
Monthly. Approx. 70 p.
ISSN 0026-4067.
LC SN 79-2666.
SRI/MF/excerpts, shipped
quarterly

Monthly trade journal on retail grocery and department store operations of the military commissary and post exchange systems in the U.S. and overseas. Includes features on merchandising trends, advertising and sales promotion techniques, and new products.

Data are from official military and civilian supermarket industry sources.

General format:

a. Articles, occasionally with statistics on sales of single departments or products; and regular news and editorial depts.

b. "Military Market Index," monthly table showing commissary and exchange systems sales, by service branch, domestic and overseas, for month 3-4 months preceding cover date, year to date, and same periods of previous year.

c. "Military Market Survey," monthly feature reporting on a survey of 20-30 military commissary and exchange managers concerning purchasing and marketing issues, with text data on survey response.

Annual features include an almanac and directory issue (July), with statistics on military personnel and compensation, and commissary and exchange sales; and a nonstatistical buyer's guide (Jan.).

Monthly "Military Market Index" appears in all issues. All additional features with substantial statistical content are described, as they appear, under "Statistical Features"; "Military Market Survey" topics are also noted. Nonstatistical contents are not covered.

Prior to Nov. 1983 issue, journal was described in SRI under C0500-1. Issuing agency name has changed from Army Times Publishing Co.

Availability: Military Market Magazine, Subscription Department, Springfield VA 22159-0210, qualified subscribers †, others $20.00 per yr., single copy $2.00, Jan. and July issues $5.00; SRI/MF/excerpts for monthly market index feature and all portions described under "Statistical Features;" shipped quarterly.

Issues reviewed during 1984: Nov. 1983-Oct. 1984 (P) (Vol. 34, Nos. 11-12; Vol. 35, Nos. 1-10).

STATISTICAL FEATURES:

C8910–1.501: Nov. 1983 (Vol. 34, No. 11)
MILITARY MARKET SURVEY: AUTO ACCESSORIES ENJOY STEADY GROWTH, MONTHLY FEATURE

(p. 6) Covers survey responses on the automotive products market.

C8910–1.502: Dec. 1983 (Vol. 34, No. 12)
MILITARY MARKET SURVEY: VENDOR ACCESS, MONTHLY FEATURE

(p. 14) Covers survey responses on vendor access to post exchanges.

GOING TO THE CATS

(p. 34-40) By David B. Cooley. Article on sales of pet food and pet supplies. Data are from *Pet Food* and *Petfood Industry*. Includes 2 charts showing pet food and supplies sales, by type, 1982.

C8910–1.503: Jan. 1984 (Vol. 35, No. 1)

MILITARY MARKET SURVEY: GENERICS IN THE COMMISSARY, MONTHLY FEATURE

(p. 16) Covers survey responses on marketing of generic products in military commissaries.

C8910–1.504: Feb. 1984 (Vol. 35, No. 2)

MILITARY MARKET SURVEY: GOOD HOLIDAY FOR EXCHANGES, MONTHLY FEATURE

(p. 6) Covers survey responses on Christmas 1983 sales performance of post exchanges.

CANNED MEAT AND FISH: FUTURE PRICES LOOK BRIGHT

(p. 20-21) By David B. Cooley. Article, with 1 table showing volume and value of canned seafood produced, by type, 1982. Data are from U.S. Commerce Dept.

RESALE WARMS UP TO FROZENS

(p. 22-28) By Guy Lamolinara. Article, with 1 chart showing annual change in sales volume of frozen foods, by type, for year ending Oct. 1983. Data are from Selling Areas Marketing Inc.

C8910–1.505: Mar. 1984 (Vol. 35, No. 3)

MILITARY MARKET SURVEY: WHAT DO MILREPS THINK? MONTHLY FEATURE

(p. 12) Covers survey responses on vendor registration programs, as perceived by vendor sales representatives.

WHITE PAPER, GRACE COMMISSION: WILL IT BRING DOWN THE COMMISSARIES?

(p. 18-24) Article discussing final report of the President's Private Sector Survey on Cost Control (Grace Commission) as it pertains to military commissary operations. Data are from the report, DOD, and private sources. Includes 2 charts and 2 tables showing the following:

a. Grace Commission's estimates of savings through commissary reorganization; commissary direct appropriations, FY82 and requested FY84; and estimated military pay increase necessary if commissaries abolished, FY82.

b. Items carried, hours of operation, selling area, average order size, surcharge/gross margin, and selected productivity measures, for commissaries by service branch, and for supermarkets and warehouse stores, various periods 1983.

C8910–1.506: Apr. 1984 (Vol. 35, No. 4)

MILITARY MARKET SURVEY: HIGH TECH IN THE COMSTORES, MONTHLY FEATURE

(p. 12) Covers survey responses on use of computerized ordering methods in military commissaries.

GET JOHNNY A GUN?

(p. 21) Article on violence in TV programs for children, with 1 table showing number of violent occurrences per hour for 8 cartoon programs, 1983. Data are from National Coalition on TV Violence.

SALTY FOODS SHOW A GOLDEN GLOW

(p. 25-30) By David B. Cooley. Article, with 1 chart showing salted snack food sales by type of snack, 1982. Data are from International Potato Chip/Snack Food Assn.

UNIFORM COMMUNICATIONS SYSTEM: NO NEED FOR ANXIETY

(p. 53-55) By Guy Lamolinara. Article on grocery industry use of the Uniform Communications System (UCS), a computerized system for direct ordering. Data are from Arthur D. Little, Inc. Includes 1 undated table showing UCS operating cost and potential savings, for distributors, brokers, and manufacturers.

MILREPS: SOME SURPRISING DEMOGRAPHICS

(p. 55) Brief article, with 1 table on business characteristics of military representatives (milreps), brokers/distributors who deal with military resale agencies. Table includes military organizational level dealt with, length of time in milrep business, and previous experience with a resale agency. Data are from responses of 70 milrep companies to a *Military Market* survey.

C8910–1.507: May 1984 (Vol. 35, No. 5)

MILITARY MARKET SURVEY: SHOPPERS SNAP UP CAMERAS, MONTHLY FEATURE

(p. 6) Covers survey response on marketing of camera products in military exchanges.

SLUGGING IT OUT IN BEVERAGES

(p. 32-37) By David B. Cooley. Article, with 3 tables showing military personnel, and beer sales in military clubs/package stores and exchanges, for U.S. and overseas, 1979-82; and total U.S. beer and soft drink retail sales, for top 10 brands and all others, 1983. Data are from the Army Times Research Dept, *Beverage World,* and *Beverage Digest.*

MANUFACTURERS LOOK TO THE FUTURE

(p. 44-48) By David B. Cooley. Article, with 2 tables showing number of supermarkets and/or total nonphoto outlets selling photo supplies, 1960 and 1984; and sales volume for lower-priced cameras, by type, FY83. Data sources include Haking Industries.

C8910–1.508: June 1984 (Vol. 35, No. 6)

MILITARY MARKET SURVEY: PX/BX SCANNING, A SUCCESS, MONTHLY FEATURE

(p. 6) Covers survey responses on conversion to electronic checkout scanners in military post exchanges.

HEAT IS ON: THAWING THE FROZENS MARKET

(p. 24-27) By David B. Cooley. Article, with 1 table showing orange juice sales volume in military commissaries, 1978-83. Data are from the Florida Dept of Citrus.

REACHING THE YOUNG, MINORITY FASHION SHOPPER: ARE THE RESALES DOING ENOUGH?

(p. 28-31) By Jay Blucher. Article, with 5 tables showing the following:

a. Average waist and chest size, height, and weight, for black and white men by age group (no date).

b. Minority percent of population, and of DOD officers and enlisted personnel, by minority group (black, Hispanic, American Indian, Asian/Pacific, other), 1980 or 1983.

Data are from HHS, DOD, and Census Bureau.

C8910–1.509: July 1984 (Vol. 35, No. 7)

MILITARY MARKET SURVEY: COUPONING REDEMPTIONS UP, MONTHLY FEATURE

(p. 6) Covers survey responses on the use of coupons in military commissaries.

25th ANNUAL STATISTICAL REVIEW OF THE MILITARY RESALE MARKET

(p. 17-26) Annual review of commissary/exchange system developments during 1983, with data on sales and military population characteristics. Includes the following tables and charts:

Military Community

[1] Reserve forces in paid status [officers and enlisted personnel, by service branch, as of Sept. 30, 1983]. (p. 18)

[2] Population of the military community [reserve, retired, and active duty personnel and dependents, as of Mar. 1984]. (p. 18)

[3] Age breakdown of active duty military [as of Sept. 30, 1983]. (p. 18)

[4-5] Age distribution of dependent children and wives of active duty military personnel [as of Mar. 31, 1984]. [charts] (p. 19)

[6] Race breakdown of active duty military [including Hispanic, as of Sept. 1983]. [chart] (p. 19)

[7] Active duty military personnel by sex [as of Sept. 30, 1979-83]. (p. 19)

[8] Active duty military personnel by rank, sex, and service [as of Sept. 30, 1983]. (p. 20)

[9] Income of the military community [for active duty, retired, and reserve personnel, by income source], FY84. (p. 21)

[10-11] FY84 active duty military average compensation [by component, and total FY77-84]. (p. 21)

Military Sales

[12-19] [Overseas and domestic sales, by product and system type, and total world-wide sales, 1977-83; for exchanges and commissaries.] [4 tables and 4 charts] (p. 22-25)

[20-21] Largest [10] supermarket and [9] department/variety store chains [including domestic and worldwide commissaries and exchanges, ranked by sales, 1983 with comparison to 1982]. (p. 26)

[22-23] Combined commissary and exchange sales [1977-83], and [separate] commissary and exchange sales [1983]. (p. 26)

C8910–1.510: Aug. 1984 (Vol. 35, No. 8)

MILITARY MARKET SURVEY: OUT-OF-STOCKS, MONTHLY FEATURE

(p. 3) Covers survey responses on shelf stock maintenance in military exchanges.

AUDIO/VIDEO MARRIAGE IS AT HAND

(p. 22-26) By Jay Blucher. Article, with 1 text table showing unit sales to dealers and factory sales value, for videocassette recorders, 1980-85. Data are from Electronics Industries Assn.

C8910–1.511: Sept. 1984 (Vol. 35, No. 9)

MILITARY MARKET SURVEY: COMMISSARY DISTRIBUTORS, MONTHLY FEATURE

(p. 6) Covers survey responses on performance of merchandise distributors serving commissaries.

C8910–1.512: Oct. 1984 (Vol. 35, No. 10)

MILITARY MARKET SURVEY: COMMISSARY COUPONS, 'JUST AS GOOD AS MONEY,' MONTHLY FEATURE

(p. 6) Covers survey responses on the use of coupons in commissaries.

TOBACCO: MARKETERS SCURRY AS BRAND LOYALTY DIMINISHES

(p. 18-24) By Jay Blucher. Article, with 2 tables showing cigarette sales in military exchanges, commissaries, and clubs, 1973-83; and market share rankings of cigarette brands, overall and on military bases, 1984. Data are from Army Times Research Dept, *Maxwell Report,* and Army and Air Force Exchange Service.

COUPONS: A FLURRY OF MERCHANDISING ACTIVITY

(p. 34-42) By Guy Lamolinara. Article, with 2 charts showing number of coupons distributed and redeemed, 1979-83. Data are from A. C. Nielsen Co.

H&BA: NEW AND IMPROVED VARIETIES FUEL OTC SALES

(p. 44-48) By Jay Blucher. Article, with 1 undated table showing Army and Air Force Exchange Service (AAFES) data on sales volume for AAFES-brand health/beauty aids, by product, with product source and price.

C8920
Titsch Communications, Inc.

C8920–1   CABLEFILE/84
Annual.   For individual
publication data, see below.
ISSN 0363-1915.
LC 76-645575.
SRI/MF/excerpts

Annual directory, for 1984, of cable TV system operators, programming services, equipment distributors, and satellites and ground terminals. Also presents FCC regulations; and selected cable industry statistics, including subscription and financial trends, and operating profiles of individual systems. Data are compiled from FCC reports and original research.

Directory is issued in 2 volumes, individually described below. This is the 9th annual directory.

Availability: International Thomson Communications, Inc., PO Box 5208-TA, Denver CO 80217-5208, $119.95 (prepaid), $124.95 (if billed), for 2 volume set; SRI/MF/excerpts for market lists, directories containing statistics, and all tables, tabular lists, and profiles.

C8920–1.1: Volume 1
[Annual. 1984. 1020 p. SRI/MF/excerpts.]
Contains foreword, contents listing, and the following:

a. FCC, congressional committee, public utility commission, cable assn, and related directories; and FCC regulations pertaining to cable TV, with lists of top 100 TV markets and their communities, and all TV markets and their geographic coordinates. (p. 15-86)

b. Cable programming services, including directories of basic and pay cable, and other service companies, with satellite and transponder, start-up date, number of subscribers and affiliated stations, programming hours, and subscription price for each company, as of Apr. or May 1983, with selected trends from 1978; satellite directory, listing satellites and transponder users by system; program producer directory; and 1 table showing TV households, and basic and pay cable subscribers, 1970-90. (p. 89-130)

c. Advertising agency directory, and glossary. (p. 133-148)

d. Financial information for the cable industry, including 12 tables showing FCC reporting entities, communities served, and subscribers and rates; aggregate income and balance sheet statements and financial ratios; loans outstanding to the industry and forecast loan activity, by type of lending institution; leading institutions lending to the industry, ranked by loans outstanding; top 50 cable companies, ranked by total revenues, with net and operating income, cable revenues, assets, and stock prices; and new and replacement miles of cable, and construction expenditures by item; various years 1975-83. (p. 151-182)

e. Consultant, attorney, and financial analyst directories; and index to related periodicals. (p. 185-410)

f. Catalogs of suppliers, services, and equipment; and directory of executives of cable and related companies ("callbook"). (p. 413-1019)

C8920–1.2: Volume 2
[Annual. 1984. 1118 p. SRI/MF/excerpts.]
Contains foreword, contents listing, and the following:

a. Cable multiple system operator (MSO) information, including 1 tabular list showing top 100 MSOs ranked by subscribers; and directory, including number of operating systems, basic and pay subscribers, and homes passed for most MSOs; as of most recent available month, generally Apr.-Sept. 1983. (p. 15-86)

b. Industry statistics, including 5 tables showing top 250 cable systems ranked by subscribers and homes passed, as of various months 1982-83; number of systems and subscribers, by channel capacity and by number of pay services carried (no date); and systems, number of communities served, basic and pay subscribers, and homes passed, by State and for aggregate U.S. territories (no date). (p. 89-104)

c. Profiles of all operating systems, arranged alphabetically by community served, by State and for U.S. territories, each generally including MSO, franchise expiration dates, turn-on date, population, homes passed, miles of cable, channel capacity, basic and/or pay rates, programming tiers and services available, and pay and basic subscribers; as of most recent available month, generally Apr.-Sept. 1983. (p. 107-1084)

d. Profiles of subscription TV stations, with community served and population, subscri-

bers, and subscription fees, as of July 1983; and directory of multipoint distribution service systems. (p. 1087-1109)

C8920–2   CABLEVISION
Weekly.   Approx. 100 p.
ISSN 0361-8374.
LC 76-642520.
SRI/MF/excerpts, shipped quarterly

Weekly trade journal of the cable TV industry, covering developments in cable systems, programming services, satellites, equipment, and government regulation. Includes subscriber data for individual cable systems and programming services, current to 1-3 months prior to publication. Also presents data on cable franchising and construction activity, and finances.

Data sources include FCC, A. C. Nielsen Co., Arbitron Co., International Communications Research, and the journal's own research.

Issues generally contain several news and feature articles, occasionally statistical; numerous editorial depts, including 1 weekly table showing current stock performance of cable TV operating, service/finance, and manufacturing/distributing companies; and "Cable Stats" feature, with occasional special tables, and the following recurring tables and lists:

a. 6 semimonthly and monthly tables, listed below.

b. Recurring lists, most appearing monthly, showing films carried on cable TV, including film title, distributor, and carrying network; national advertisers' contract status; satellites, including announced recent or planned launchings, and member cable networks listed by transponder number for existing satellites; and franchising status of core cities in top 20-50 markets, and of selected communities.

Annual statistical features include data on cable construction, franchise awards, and finances of top 50 cable TV companies.

Each issue contains a supplemental section, *CableVision Plus,* with 3-5 articles covering a selected topic.

Features with substantial statistical content are described, as they appear, under "Statistical Features;" page locations and latest periods of coverage for monthly and semimonthly "Cable Stats" tables are also noted. Nonstatistical features are not covered.

Availability: CableVision, PO Box 5208-TA, Denver CO 80217-5208, $64.00 per yr., single copy $3.00; SRI/MF/excerpts for "Cable Stats" feature and all portions covered under "Statistical Features;" shipped quarterly.

Issues reviewed during 1984: Nov. 7, 1983-Oct. 29, 1984 (P) (Vol. 9, Nos. 10-52; Vol. 10, Nos. 1-9).

CABLE STATS:

[Tables are included on a space-available basis. Tables [3-5] show data available as of 1-3 months prior to publication date.]

SEMIMONTHLY TABLES

[1] Cable industry growth chart [TV households, homes passed, and basic and pay subscribers, 1975-90; prior to Apr. 30, 1984 issue, table is titled "Pay/basic cable growth" and shows basic and pay subscribers, and percent of TV households].

[2] Cable barometer [TV households, homes passed by cable, and basic and pay subscribers, most current available data].

[3-4] Top MSOs and systems [20-100 multiple system operators and cable system companies ranked by number of basic subscribers].

MONTHLY TABLES

[5] Cable services subscriber count [number of affiliates and subscribers, by service, and percent change in subscribers from previous month; table title may vary].

[6] Franchising calendar [status of franchises, including homes passed, by city for selected States, most current available data].

STATISTICAL FEATURES:

C8920–2.501: Nov. 7, 1983 (Vol. 9, No. 10)

CABLE STATS

Semimonthly Tables

[3-4] Top 20 MSOs and systems [various months Dec. 1982-Sept. 1983]. (p. 84)

RANKS ARE SWELLING

(p. 30) Brief article reporting Arbitron's estimate of cable TV penetration, for 15 largest Areas of Dominant Influence (ADIs) and 4 ADIs with greatest and least penetration, based on surveys conducted Nov. 1982-fall 1983. Includes 1 table.

C8920–2.502: Nov. 14, 1983 (Vol. 9, No. 11)

CABLE STATS

Special Table

[A] Top 30 markets: cable operational status [cable company, homes passed, and basic subscribers, with detail by sub-market area (undated)]. (p. 86, 88)

C8920–2.503: Nov. 21, 1983 (Vol. 9, No. 12)

CABLE STATS

Monthly Table

[6] Franchising calendar [primarily for May-Dec. 1983]. (p. 78, 80)

C8920–2.504: Nov. 28, 1983 (Vol. 9, No. 13)

CABLE STATS

Semimonthly Tables

[1] Pay/basic cable growth [1976-90]. (p. 62)
[2] Cable barometer [as of Aug. 31, 1983]. (p. 62)
[3-4] Top 100 MSOs and systems [various months Dec. 1981-Nov. 1983]. (p. 64)

C8920–2.505: Dec. 5, 1983 (Vol. 9, No. 14)

CABLE STATS

Semimonthly Tables

[1] Pay/basic cable growth [1976-90]. (p. 134)
[2] Cable barometer [as of Aug. 31, 1983]. (p. 134)

Monthly Table

[5] Subscriber counts [mostly as of Oct. 31, 1983]. (p. 134)

DRESSING A SYSTEM FOR SUCCESS

(p. 62-69) By Sally Russell. Article on financial and technological aspects of upgrading and re-building cable TV systems. Includes 1 table showing distribution of systems planning to rebuild over next 10 years, by number of basic subscribers and for systems in top 50 and 2nd 50 largest markets and others.

C8920–2.506: Dec. 12, 1983 (Vol. 9, No. 15)

CABLE STATS

Semimonthly Tables

[3-4] Top 20 MSOs and systems [various months June-Nov. 1983]. (p. 72)

C8920–2.507: Dec. 19, 1983 (Vol. 9, No. 16)

CABLE STATS

Semimonthly Tables

[1] Pay/basic cable growth [1976-90]. (p. 195)
[2] Cable barometer [as of Aug. 31, 1983]. (p. 195)

Special Tables

[A] Cable program services [ranked by number of subscribers, also showing start up date and number of affiliates (undated)]. (p. 195)
[B] Top 10 MSO overview [number of operating systems, basic and pay subscribers, and homes passed, various months June-Oct. 1983]. (p. 196)
[C] Municipally owned cable systems [basic subscription rate and subscribers, channel capacity, plant miles, and homes passed, for 32 cities, various months Dec. 1982-Nov. 1983]. (p. 204)

LOCAL AD DOLLARS TO RISE

(p. 25) Brief article, with 1 table showing estimated local advertising revenues for broadcast and cable TV, 1980-84. Data are from Broadcast Marketing Company's *Major Local Media/Trends and Projections.*

C8920–2.508: Dec. 26, 1983 (Vol. 9, No. 17)

CABLE STATS

Monthly Table

[6] Franchising calendar [primarily for Aug. 1983-Jan. 1984]. (p. 70)

C8920–2.509: Jan. 2, 1984 (Vol. 9, No. 18)

CABLE STATS

Semimonthly Tables

[1] Pay/basic cable growth [1976-90]. (p. 57)
[2] Cable barometer [as of Aug. 31, 1983]. (p. 57)

Special Table

[A] STV [Subscription TV] operators [including location, parent company, initial broadcast date, basic subscribers (mostly June-Dec. 1983), installation and subscription rates, additional tiers and costs, and population, for 15 systems; table continued in Jan. 9 issue]. (p. 57-58)

C8920–2.510: Jan. 9, 1984 (Vol. 9, No. 19)

CABLE STATS

Semimonthly Tables

[1] Pay/basic cable growth [1976-90]. (p. 86)
[2] Cable barometer [as of Aug. 31, 1983]. (p. 86)
[3-4] Top 20 MSOs and systems [various months June-Dec. 1983]. (p. 88)

Special Table

[A] STV [Subscription TV] operators [including location, parent company, initial broadcast date, basic subscribers (mostly July-Dec. 1983), installation and subscription rates, additional tiers and costs, and population, for 10 systems; table continued from Jan. 2 issue]. (p. 86, 88)

LOOKING TO THE FUTURE

(p. 38-50) By Brian Bremner. Article on government policies and other factors affecting Canadian cable TV. Data are from Matthews CATV. Includes 1 undated list of top 5 Canadian multiple system operators showing headquarters location, and number of systems and actual and potential subscribers.

CONSTRUCTION FORECAST: BUILDING FOR THE FUTURE, ANNUAL FEATURE

(p. 59-64) Annual article on cable TV construction activity and expenditures. Data are based on a *CableVision* survey of cable system operators and manufacturers.

Includes 2 tables showing new and replacement aerial and underground construction miles; new and replacement costs by type of equipment; and major established and expected franchise awards, with city, company, homes passed, and award date, 1983-84.

This is the 9th annual survey.

CANADIANS PUSH PAY

(p. 67-68) Brief article reporting results of a 1983 Canadian Cable TV Assn survey on marketing activities of cable TV operators. Includes 1 table showing average marketing expenditures, total and per subscriber, by number of subscribers, year ended Apr. 30, 1983.

C8920–2.511: Jan. 16, 1984 (Vol. 9, No. 20)

CABLE STATS

Monthly Table

[5] Subscriber counts [mostly as of Nov. 30, 1983]. (p. 47)

CRT INTEREST RATES

(p. 12) Article on cable TV interest payments on copyright debts. Data are from U.S. Copyright Office. Includes 1 table showing copyright fees collected from the cable TV industry, with and without imposed interest payments, 1980-82 and 1st 6 months 1983.

Table headings are incorrect; corrected table appears in the Jan. 23, 1984 issue (for description see C8920-2.512, below).

C8920–2.512: Jan. 23, 1984 (Vol. 9, No. 21)

CABLE STATS

Special Table

[A] Major franchise awards [with company, city, homes passed, and award date] 1983 [and expected awards, Jan.-Feb. 1984]. (p. 104)

COPYRIGHT FEES COLLECTED FROM THE CABLE INDUSTRY SINCE 1980, CORRECTION

(p. 78) Table showing corrected format for copyright table in Jan. 16, 1984 issue; for description of original table, see C8920-2.511, above.

C8920–2.513: Jan. 30, 1984 (Vol. 9, No. 22)

CABLE STATS

Semimonthly Tables

[1] Pay/basic cable growth [1976-90]. (p. 62)

[2] Cable barometer [as of Aug. 31, 1983]. (p. 62)

Monthly Table

[6] Franchising calendar [primarily for June 1983-Jan. 1984]. (p. 62)

C8920–2.514: Feb. 6, 1984 (Vol. 9, No. 23)

CABLE STATS

Semimonthly Tables

[1] Pay/basic cable growth [1976-90]. (p. 54)

[2] Cable barometer [as of Dec. 31, 1983]. (p. 54)

[3-4] Top 100 MSOs and systems [various months Dec. 1981-Jan. 1984]. (p. 56)

C8920–2.515: Feb. 13, 1984 (Vol. 9, No. 24)

CABLE STATS

Monthly Table

[5] Subscriber counts [mostly as of Dec. 31, 1983]. (p. 70)

CABLE GAINS IN RATINGS

(p. 22) Brief article, with 1 table on cable TV programming services with viewer gains in 1983. Table shows the following for 3 superstations and 5 networks: number of markets in which qualified for Arbitron TV ratings reports, Nov. 1982-83.

C8920–2.516: Feb. 20, 1984 (Vol. 9, No. 25)

CABLE STATS

Semimonthly Tables

[3-4] Top 20 MSOs and systems [various months Sept. 1983-Jan. 1984]. (p. 64)

C8920–2.517: Feb. 27, 1984 (Vol. 9, No. 26)

CABLE STATS

Semimonthly Tables

[1] Pay/basic cable growth [1976-90]. (p. 86)

[2] Cable barometer [as of Dec. 31, 1983]. (p. 86)

Monthly Table

[6] Franchising calendar [primarily for Jan. 1984]. (p. 86)

C8920–2.518: Mar. 5, 1984 (Vol. 9, No. 27)

CABLE STATS

Semimonthly Tables

[1] Pay/basic cable growth [1976-90]. (p. 62)

[2] Cable barometer [as of Dec. 31, 1983]. (p. 62)

[4] Top 100 MSOs and systems [various months Dec. 1981-Jan. 1984]. (p. 64)

UK CABLE RISKS

(p. 29-31) By Eric Taub. Article, with 1 undated list of UK new cable franchises, including homes passed, structure, number of basic channels, subscriber cost per month, and total set-up cost.

C8920–2.519: Mar. 12, 1984 (Vol. 9, No. 28)

CABLE STATS

Monthly Table

[5] Subscriber counts [mostly as of Jan. 31, 1984]. (p. 90)

C8920–2.520: Mar. 19, 1984 (Vol. 9, No. 29)

1983 CABLE TV FRANCHISE AWARDS, ANNUAL FEATURE

(p. 62-64) Annual table showing cable TV franchise awards, 1983, including company, community, homes in franchise area, and month awarded, arranged by State.

C8920–2.521: Mar. 26, 1984 (Vol. 9, No. 30)

CABLE STATS

Semimonthly Table

[3] Top 20 MSOs and systems [various months Oct. 1983-Jan. 1984]. (p. 64)

C8920–2.522: Apr. 2, 1984 (Vol. 9, No. 31)

CABLE STATS

Semimonthly Tables

[1] Pay/basic cable growth [1976-90]. (p. 62)

[2] Cable barometer [as of Dec. 31, 1983]. (p. 62)

Monthly Table

[6] Franchising calendar [primarily for Aug. 1983-Apr. 1984]. (p. 62, 64)

C8920–2.523: Apr. 9, 1984 (Vol. 9, No. 32)

CABLE STATS

Semimonthly Tables

[1] Pay/basic cable growth [1976-90]. (p. 126)

[2] Cable barometer [as of Mar. 30, 1984]. (p. 126)

[3-4] Top 100 MSOs and systems [various months Dec. 1981-Feb. 1984]. (p. 128)

C8920–2.524: Apr. 16, 1984 (Vol. 9, No. 33)

CABLE STATS

Monthly Table

[5] Subscriber counts [mostly as of Feb. 29, 1984]. (p. 62)

C8920–2.525: Apr. 23, 1984 (Vol. 9, No. 34)

CABLE STATS

Semimonthly Tables

[3-4] Top 20 MSOs and systems [various months Dec. 1983-Feb. 1984]. (p. 64)

C8920–2.526: Apr. 30, 1984 (Vol. 9, No. 35)

CABLE STATS

Semimonthly Tables

[1] Cable industry growth chart [1975-90]. (p. 62)

[2] Cable barometer [as of Mar. 30, 1984]. (p. 62)

Monthly Table

[6] Franchising calendar [primarily for Aug. 1983-May 1984]. (p. 62, 64)

C8920–2.527: May 7, 1984 (Vol. 9, No. 36)

CABLE STATS

Semimonthly Tables

[1] Cable industry growth chart [1975-90]. (p. 82)

[2] Cable barometer [as of Mar. 30, 1984]. (p. 82)

[3-4] Top 100 MSOs and systems [various months Apr. 1983-Mar. 1984]. (p. 84)

STUDY CLAIMS MMDS NO THREAT

(p. 25-30) Article on development of subscription multichannel monitor distribution services (MMDS) and competition with the cable TV industry. Data are from LINK Resources Corp. and Browne, Bortz and Coddington.

Includes 2 undated tables showing estimated average MMDS programmer capital costs, and operating costs and revenues by item; and range of MMDS potential subscribers in top 50 market groups.

C8920–2.528: May 14, 1984 (Vol. 9, No. 37)

CABLE STATS

Monthly Table

[5] Subscriber counts [mostly as of Mar. 31, 1984]. (p. 56)

C8920–2.529: May 21, 1984 (Vol. 9, No. 38)

CABLE STATS

Semimonthly Tables

[3-4] Top 20 MSOs and systems [various months Dec. 1983-Mar. 1984]. (p. 57)

C8920–2.530: May 28, 1984 (Vol. 9, No. 39)

CABLE STATS

Semimonthly Tables

[1] Cable industry growth chart [1975-90]. (p. 136)

[2] Cable barometer [as of Mar. 30, 1984]. (p. 136)

Monthly Table

[6] Franchising calendar [primarily for Aug. 1983-Apr. 1984]. (p. 136, 138)

C8920–2.531: June 4, 1984 (Vol. 9, No. 40)

CABLE STATS

Semimonthly Tables

[1] Cable industry growth chart [1975-90]. (p. 56)

[2] Cable barometer [as of Mar. 30, 1984]. (p. 56)

[3-4] Top 100 MSOs and systems [various months Apr. 1983-Apr. 1984]. (p. 57)

ICR SCALES BACK GROWTH PROJECTIONS

(p. 16) Article, with 1 table showing basic and pay cable subscribers, and percent of TV households, projected for 1984-90 as of Dec. 31, 1983 and Mar. 30, 1984. Data are from International Communications Research.

C8920–2.532: June 11, 1984 (Vol. 9, No. 41)

CABLE STATS

Special Tables

[A-B] Top 100 Cable MSOs and systems [includes basic and pay subscribers, and homes passed, as of various months Apr. 1983-Apr. 1984]. (p. 222-224)

TOP 50 COMPANIES IN CABLE, ANNUAL FEATURE

(p. 52-188, passim) Annual article profiling top 50 companies with cable interests. Contains brief summary; company profiles; and financial overview table (p. 54-57), showing each company's total and cable revenues, total net income and assets, cable operating income and identifiable assets, and high and low stock prices, 1982-83.

C8920–2.533: June 18, 1984 (Vol. 9, No. 42)

CABLE STATS

Monthly Table

[5] Subscriber counts [mostly as of Apr. 1984]. (p. 94, 96)

CABLE TURNS ON SUBSCRIBERS

(p. 35) Article, with 1 undated chart showing former and current cable TV subscribers' reasons for cancelling their service. Data are based on 1,501 responses to a telephone survey conducted by International Communications Research.

C8920–2.534: June 25, 1984 (Vol. 9, No. 43)

CABLE STATS

Semimonthly Tables

[3-4] Top 20 MSOs and systems [various months Dec. 1983-Apr. 1984]. (p. 56)

WILL VCRs KO PAY CABLE?

(p. 27-33) By Sally Russell. Article, with 4 tables showing value of factory sales and/or volume of sales to dealer, for videocassette recorders and for blank and pre-recorded videocassette tapes; and number of pay cable and videocassette recorder households; various years 1980-85. Data are from Electronics Industries Assn, Link Resources, and the Yankee Group.

C8920–2.535: July 2, 1984 (Vol. 9, No. 44)

CABLE STATS

Semimonthly Tables

[1] Cable industry growth chart [1975-90]. (p. 88)

[2] Cable barometer [as of Mar. 30, 1984]. (p. 88)

Monthly Table

[6] Franchising calendar [primarily for Aug. 1983-May 1984]. (p. 88, 90)

C8920–2.536: July 9, 1984 (Vol. 9, No. 45)

CABLE STATS

Semimonthly Tables

[1] Cable industry growth chart [1975-90]. (p. 54)

[2] Cable barometer [as of Mar. 30, 1984]. (p. 54)

[3-4] Top 100 MSOs and systems [various months Apr. 1983-May 1984]. (p. 56)

ELRA FINDS SUBS HAPPY WITH CABLE

(p. 22) Article, with 1 chart showing distribution of cable TV subscriber cancellations, by reason. Data are from a Jan./Feb. 1984 survey of 2,000 households, conducted by ELRA Group.

C8920–2.537: July 16, 1984 (Vol. 9, No. 46)

CABLE STATS

Monthly Table

[5] Subscriber counts [mostly as of May 31, 1984; table incorrectly reads Mar. 31]. (p. 62)

C8920–2.538: July 23, 1984 (Vol. 9, No. 47)

CABLE STATS

Semimonthly Tables

[3-4] Top 20 MSOs and systems [various months Dec. 1983-May 1984]. (p. 72)

BUILDING A CABLE EMPIRE

(p. 34-37) By Victoria Gits. Article, with 1 table showing subscribers and acquisition date, for cable TV systems acquired during 1981-84 by 3 recently developed small-system corporations.

C8920–2.539: July 30, 1984 (Vol. 9, No. 48)

CABLE STATS

Semimonthly Tables

[1] Cable industry growth chart [1975-90]. (p. 54)

[2] Cable barometer [as of Mar. 30, 1984]. (p. 54)

Monthly Table

[6] Franchising calendar [primarily for Aug. 1983-July 1984]. (p. 54, 56)

C8920–2.540: Aug. 6, 1984 (Vol. 9, No. 49)

CABLE STATS

Semimonthly Tables

[1] Cable industry growth chart [1975-90]. (p. 54)

[2] Cable barometer [as of Mar. 30, 1984]. (p. 54)

[3-4] Top 100 MSOs and systems [various months Apr. 1983-June 1984]. (p. 56)

MARKETING REGIONAL SPORTS NETWORKS

(p. 24-28) By Simon Applebaum. Article, with 1 table showing number of systems, subscribers, and States covered, for 5 pay TV sports services premiering Apr. 1984, with selected projections through Apr. 1985.

C8920–2.541: Aug. 13, 1984 (Vol. 9, No. 50)

CABLE STATS

Monthly Table

[5] Subscriber counts [mostly as of June 30, 1984]. (p. 46)

MAKING RADIO WAVES

(p. 29-33) By Victoria Gits. Article on communications companies entering radio paging and mobile telephone businesses. Includes 1 undated table showing annual sales and/or subscribers and employees, for radio common carrier (RCC) or cellular branches of 3 communications companies; and RCC or cellular permit applications of 3 companies.

C8920–2.542: Aug. 20, 1984 (Vol. 9, No. 51)

CABLE STATS

Semimonthly Tables

[3-4] Top 20 MSOs and systems [various months Dec. 1983-June 1984]. (p. 72)

NIELSEN STUDY: CABLE UP B'CAST DOWN IN VIEWING

(p. 23) Article, with 1 table showing audience shares and weekly minutes viewed per household, for cable, pay, network, independent, and public TV, in cable and pay TV households, 1st half 1983-84. Data are from A. C. Nielsen Co.

C8920–2.543: Aug. 27, 1984 (Vol. 9, No. 52)

CABLE STATS

Semimonthly Tables

[1] Cable industry growth chart [1975-90]. (p. 54)

[2] Cable barometer [as of Mar. 30, 1984]. (p. 54)

Monthly Table

[6] Franchising calendar [primarily for Aug. 1983-Aug. 1984]. (p. 54, 56)

C8920–2.544: Sept. 3, 1984 (Vol. 10, No. 1)

CABLE STATS

Semimonthly Tables

[1] Cable industry growth chart [1975-90]. (p. 94)

[2] Cable barometer [as of Mar. 30, 1984]. (p. 94)

[3-4] Top 100 MSOs and systems [various months June 1983-July 1984]. (p. 96)

AT THE CROSSROADS: CABLE AND TELCOS

(p. 41-69) Article on developments in business partnerships between cable TV and telephone companies. Data are from a study by International Communications Research and Coopers & Lybrand.

Includes 1 table showing number of cable systems, homes passed, and asset valuation and replacement cost, for 4 types of cable systems that could benefit from a partnership with a telephone company, 1984.

C8920–2.545: Sept. 10, 1984 (Vol. 10, No. 2)

CABLE STATS

Monthly Table

[5] Subscriber counts [mostly as of July 31, 1984]. (p. 98)

Special Table

[A] Economics of basic cable networking [profit/loss, advertising revenue, and fee income], 1983-85, [and startup and breakeven dates, all for 12 cable TV networks]. (p. 100)

VIEWING OF CABLE UP, RIVALS BROADCAST TOTALS

(p. 38) Article, with 1 table showing audience shares and weekly minutes viewed per household, for cable, pay, network, independent, and public TV, in cable TV households, July 1983-84. Data are from A. C. Nielsen Co.

C8920–2.546: Sept. 17, 1984 (Vol. 10, No. 3)

CABLE STATS

Semimonthly Tables

[3-4] Top 20 MSOs and systems [various months Dec. 1983-July 1984]. (p. 49)

C8920–2.547: Sept. 24, 1984 (Vol. 10, No. 4)

CABLE STATS

Monthly Table

[6] Franchising calendar [primarily for Jan.-Sept. 1984]. (p. 62, 64)

Special Tables

[A-B] Percent of systems [and subscribers] by channel capacity, and percent of systems by subscriber size, [as of May 31, 1983-84]. (p. 62)

C8920–2.548: Oct. 1, 1984 (Vol. 10, No. 5)

CABLE STATS

Semimonthly Tables

[1] Cable industry growth chart [1975-90]. (p. 46)

[2] Cable barometer [as of Aug. 31, 1984]. (p. 46)

[3-4] Top 100 MSOs and systems [various months June 1983-July 1984]. (p. 48)

C8920–2.549: Oct. 8, 1984 (Vol. 10, No. 6)

CABLE STATS

Monthly Table

[5] Subscriber counts [mostly as of July 31, 1984]. (p. 54)

C8920–2.550: Oct. 15, 1984 (Vol. 10, No. 7)

CABLE STATS

Semimonthly Tables

[3-4] Top 20 MSOs and systems [various months Dec. 1983-July 1984]. (p. 49)

C8920–2.551: Oct. 22, 1984 (Vol. 10, No. 8)

CABLE STATS

Monthly Table

[6] Franchising calendar [primarily for Jan.-Sept. 1984]. (p. 62, 64)

Special Tables

[A-B] Percent of systems [and subscribers] by channel capacity, and percent of systems by subscriber size, [as of May 31, 1983-84]. (p. 62)

C8920–2.552: Oct. 29, 1984 (Vol. 10, No. 9)

CABLE STATS

Semimonthly Tables

[1] Cable industry growth chart [1975-90]. (p. 58)

[2] Cable barometer [as of Aug. 31, 1984]. (p. 58)

[3-4] Top 100 MSOs and systems [various months June 1983-July 1984]. (p. 60)

C8950
TL Enterprises

C8950–2   RV BUSINESS
Monthly.   Approx. 110 p.
ISSN 0744-9569.
SRI/MF/excerpts, shipped quarterly

Monthly trade journal on the recreational vehicle (RV) industry, covering production, marketing, servicing, and management trends and developments for dealers in vehicles, parts, and accessories, and for campgrounds.

Data are from Recreation Vehicle Industry Assn (RVIA), publisher surveys of dealers and manufacturers, and other sources. Month of data coverage is 2-3 months prior to cover date.

Issues contain:

a. Special articles and regular features, occasionally with statistics.

b. Monthly "Perspective" section, with 2 tables on RV sales by a sample of Dealer Advisory Board member dealers.

c. Monthly "Shipments" section, with 1 monthly table on total RV shipments, and quarterly survey data on performance of RV/mobile home distributors.

Prior to Dec. 1983 issue, "Shipments" section also includes monthly table on aftermarket sales by item for a sample of dealers.

An annual directory and buyers guide is also included in subscription.

Monthly tables are listed below and appear in all issues. All additional features with substantial statistical content, including quarterly distributor survey, are described, as they appear, under "Statistical Features." Nonstatistical features are not covered.

Availability: RV Business, Circulation Department, 29901 Agoura Rd., Agoura CA 91301, qualified subscribers †, others $24.00 per yr., single copy $2.00, Directory and Buyer's Guide $9.95; SRI/MF/excerpts for monthly tables and portions described under "Statistical Features;" shipped quarterly.

Issues reviewed during 1984: Nov. 1983-Oct. 1984 (P) (Vol. 34, Nos. 8-12; Vol. 35, Nos. 1-7).

MONTHLY TABLES:

[All tables show data for month of coverage, year to date, and same periods of previous year; prior to Apr. 1984 issue, data from tables [1-2] are shown in 9 tables.]

PERSPECTIVE

[1-2] [Unit sales of new and used RVs, total and for motorhomes, travel trailers, fifth-wheels, truck campers, and camping trailers; and total sales value.]

SHIPMENTS

[3] RVIA [shipments of travel and folding camping trailers, fifth-wheels, truck campers, multi-use vehicles, motorhomes, van campers, and mini-motorhomes].

STATISTICAL FEATURES:

C8950–2.501: Jan. 1984 (Vol. 34, No. 10)

WDA QUARTERLY SALES FIGURES

(p. 18) Two quarterly tables showing percent change in sales volume for members of Ware-house Distributors Assn for Leisure and Mobile Products, by region, 3rd quarter and 1st 9 months 1982-83. Data are from an assn survey.

VAN MARKET

(p. 47-62) By Don Wright. Article on market for vans modified for leisure and recreational use. Data are from Motor Vehicle Manufacturers Assn and Data Resources Inc. Includes 1 chart showing number of vans sold, 1974-85.

C8950–2.502: Apr. 1984 (Vol. 35, No. 1)

WDA QUARTERLY SALES FIGURES

(p. 28) Two quarterly tables showing percent change in sales volume for members of Warehouse Distributors Assn for Leisure and Mobile Products, by region, 4th quarter 1983. Data are from an assn survey.

C8950–2.503: July 1984 (Vol. 35, No. 4)

BAROMETER: CENSUS TALK

(p. 33-35) Article, with 3 tables showing the following for recreational/utility trailer dealers: number of establishments, sales, payroll, and paid employees, by State; and sales distribution by line of merchandise; 1982, with quinquennial trends from 1967. Data are based on preliminary findings from the 1982 Census of Retail Trade.

WDA QUARTERLY SALES FIGURES

(p. 38) Quarterly table showing percent change in sales volume for members of Warehouse Distributors Assn for Leisure and Mobile Products, by region, 1st quarter 1984. Data are from an assn survey.

C8950–2.504: Oct. 1984 (Vol. 35, No. 7)

WDA QUARTERLY SALES FIGURES

(p. 34) Quarterly table showing percent change in sales volume for members of Warehouse Distributors Assn for Leisure and Mobile Products, by region, 2nd quarter 1984. Data are from an assn survey.

C9380
Variety, Inc.

C9380–1   VARIETY
Weekly.   Approx. 100 p.
Oversized.
ISSN 0042-2738.
SRI/MF/not filmed

Weekly trade journal of the entertainment industry, covering developments in film, TV, radio, music, and stage. Includes reporting on production activity, finances, marketing, attendance, and related topics; and data on film and stage boxoffice receipts, and entertainment industry stock quotations.

Data are primarily from *Variety* and other industry sources.

Issues contain numerous newspaper-style news and feature articles; occasional statistical articles and special tables; recurring lists of current top U.S. recordings and radio songs, and occasionally of top British and Australian recordings; and the weekly and monthly data described below.

Most weekly data appear in all issues. Statistical articles and special tables are described, as they appear, under "Statistical Features;" page locations and latest periods of coverage for monthly data are also noted. Nonstatistical features are not covered.

Availability: Variety, Inc., 154 W. 46th St., New York NY 10036, $75.00 per yr., single copy $1.50, special issues $2.50; SRI/MF/not filmed.

Issues reviewed during 1984: Oct. 26, 1983-Oct. 31, 1984 (P) (Vol. 312, No. 13; Vol. 313, Nos. 1-13; Vol. 314, Nos. 1-13; Vol. 315, Nos. 1-13; Vol. 316, Nos. 1-13; Vol. 317, No. 1).

WEEKLY DATA:

FILM

["U.S. Boxoffice Report" presents *Variety* national estimates and "50 Top-Grossing Films" presents actual sample data. Both features are based on data compiled by Standard Data Corp. from a sampling of approximately 2,000 theaters in 20 markets, representing approximately 11% of U.S. theaters.]

a. "U.S. Boxoffice Report" table showing receipts for week ended approximately 1 week prior to publication, year to date, and same periods of previous 2 years.

b. "Weekend Film Boxoffice Reports" table showing national receipts and number of screens for individual films grossing over $1 million during weekend prior to publication, with previous weekend comparison, total days in release, and cumulative receipts.

c. "50 Top-Grossing Films" table showing individual film receipts and rank, number of cities playing, and 1st run and showcase screens, for week ended 1 week prior to publication date, with receipts and rank for previous week, total weeks in top 50, and cumulative receipts; and including selected totals for all other films currently in release.

d. "Film Production" or "Production Pulse" feature showing major film production starts announced during current year through cover date, with comparisons to previous year, by company (prior to Aug. 1984 issues, feature was published on an irregularly recurring basis and is described under "Statistical Features").

e. Articles with text data on recent boxoffice receipts for specific films and theaters in key U.S. cities, and for selected films in London, Paris, Australia, and, occasionally, other foreign locations.

STOCK MARKET

f. "Amusement Stock Quotations," showing NYSE, AMEX, and over-the-counter stock trading data for selected entertainment corporations, for week prior to publication.

STAGE

g. "Season Boxoffice Totals" table showing number of shows, value of receipts, and total playing weeks, aggregated for shows on Broadway and on the road, with Broadway attendance and new shows; all for week prior to publication date and/or theater season to date, for current season, and seasons 1, 10, and 20 years previous.

h. Articles with text data on recent boxoffice receipts of specific plays and theaters, for Broadway shows in New York and on the road, and for regional theaters. Occasionally includes similar text data for other types of stage productions on tour.

MONTHLY DATA:

i. "Variety Boxoffice Index" table presenting seasonally adjusted index of film receipts (1980=100) for month prior to publication, previous month, and same month of previous year; data are national estimates, as in "U.S. Boxoffice Reports."

STATISTICAL FEATURES:

C9380–1.501: Oct. 26, 1983 (Vol. 312, No. 13)

FILM PRODUCTION, RECURRING FEATURE

(p. 173) Recurring list of 1983 film production starts as of Oct. 26, with comparisons to 1982, by company.

JAPANESE FOREIGN FILM IMPORTS

(p. 276) Table showing film imports for Japan, by country of production, 1978-82.

RENTALS OF U.S. MAJORS IN JAPAN, ANNUAL FEATURE

(p. 277) Annual table showing 5 major U.S. film distributors ranked by rental income in Japan, and including number of films released, 1st half 1983, with rental comparison to 1st half 1982.

TOP 10 LOCAL PICS IN HONG KONG, RECURRING FEATURE

(p. 294) Recurring table showing Hong Kong's top 10 domestic films ranked by boxoffice gross, and also showing film distributor, 1st 8 months 1983.

ALL-TIME TOP FILMS, JAPAN

(p. 295) Table showing all-time top 37 films in Japan ranked by rental income, as of Sept. 1983, and including year released and film distributor.

RENTALS OF JAPANESE MAJORS, ANNUAL FEATURE

(p. 295) Annual table showing 4 Japanese film companies ranked by rental income, 1st half 1982-83.

ALL-TIME TOP GROSSERS IN SPAIN

(p. 343) Table showing all-time top 25 films in Spain ranked by boxoffice gross, as of Mar. 1983, and including film release date.

TOP FILMS IN BRAZIL

(p. 358) Four tables showing top domestic and foreign films in Brazil ranked by attendance, as follows: top 10 for 1st half 1983; and top 35 for 1970-1st half 1983 period (also shows release dates).

C9380–1.502: Nov. 2, 1983 (Vol. 313, No. 1)

AVERAGE PIC COST UP 15% TO $11.3 MIL

(p. 3, 37) By Lawrence Cohn. Article, with 1 table showing average production budget and number of films for 9 major film distributors, for 1981-83 releases, and for 1984 scheduled releases as of Oct. 1983.

C9380–1.503: Nov. 9, 1983 (Vol. 313, No. 2)

MONTHLY DATA

(p. 3) *Variety* Boxoffice Index, for Oct. 1983.

DECADE-HIGH RATINGS TALLY FOR PICS FROM THE MAJORS; INDIE PICKUPS CUE INCREASE

(p. 7, 34-35) Article, with 1 table showing number of films released, by Motion Picture Assn of America ratings for type of audience, for aggregate 13 major/minor production companies, and all independents, years ended Oct. 1969-83.

C9380–1.504: Nov. 23, 1983 (Vol. 313, No. 4)

FILM PRODUCTION, RECURRING FEATURE

(p. 24) Recurring list of 1983 film production starts as of Nov. 23, with comparisons to 1982, by company.

13th ANNUAL CANADIAN FILM AND ENTERTAINMENT REVIEW

Annual compilation of articles on the Canadian entertainment industry. Articles with substantial statistical content are described below.

COPRODS: 'LET'S MAKE A DEAL'

(p. C2-C3, C30) Article, with 1 table showing the following for individual films produced through combined Canada/other country ventures: year of production, Canada and other country participation shares, Canadian producer, director, and budget (in Canadian dollars), 1964-83.

MULTILINGUAL TV AND WORLDVIEW AIR ETHNIC SERVICES FOR 8,000,000

(p. C26, C52) By Susan Devins. Article, with 1 table showing Canadian population by primary language spoken. Data are from Statistics Canada 1981 census.

CANADIAN RECORD BIZ REBOUNDS FROM RECESSION; CASSETTES EXPLODE

(p. C35, C45) By Ken Terry. Article, with 1 table showing Canadian record and prerecorded tape sales by Canadian region, 1st 8 months 1983, with percent change from 1982. Data are from Statistics Canada.

C9380–1.505: Nov. 30, 1983 (Vol. 313, No. 5)

FILM PRODUCTION, RECURRING FEATURE

(p. 34) Recurring list of 1983 film production starts as of Nov. 30, with comparisons to 1982, by company.

CHI ARTS SPENDING PER CAPITA

(p. IL4) Article, with 1 undated table showing 5 U.S. cities with population over 1 million ranked by per capita arts expenditures, and including population and total arts expenditures, with summary comparisons to 5 smaller cities. Data are from a 1982 report *City Arts Support: Status and Issues.*

Article appears in a special section dealing with the entertainment industry in Illinois.

C9380–1.506: Dec. 7, 1983 (Vol. 313, No. 6)

MONTHLY DATA

(p. 3) *Variety* Boxoffice Index, for Nov. 1983.

HOLLYWOOD MORE ORIGINAL THAN SUPPOSED

(p. 5, 30) By Lawrence Cohn. Article, with 1 table showing major film company aggregate releases, by film type (sequels/series, remakes, other adaptations, and originals), 1981-83 and scheduled for 1984 as of Dec. 1983.

TRACKING THE EUROPEAN SATELLITES

(p. 60) Table showing operating company or country, purpose and/or launching date, and number of channels, for European telecommunications/broadcast satellites (no date).

C9380–1.507: Jan. 11, 1984 (Vol. 313, No. 11)

[Special issue price is $2.50.]

78th SHOW BUSINESS ANNUAL

MONTHLY DATA

(p. 7) *Variety* Boxoffice Index, for Dec. 1983.

BIG PIX NOW 25% OF MAJORS' SKED, ANNUAL FEATURE

(p. 1, 87) Annual article, by Lawrence Cohn, on films with budgets of $14 million or more scheduled for 1984 release. Includes 1 table showing 1984 big-budget films ranked by estimated budget, and also showing producer and distributor for each film.

'83 A BOOM YEAR FOR H'WOOD PRODUCTION, ANNUAL FEATURE

(p. 9, 82) Annual article, by Todd McCarthy, on U.S. film industry output, with comparison of domestic and foreign-based productions, 1983. Data are from *Variety*. Includes 2 tables showing 17 companies ranked by film production, 1983 with comparison to 1982; and U.S. and foreign-based productions, aggregated for major/minor companies and independents, 1973-83.

MEGABUCK PIX INCREASED RATIOS OF RENTAL TO BUDGET IN '82-83; FIGURES PARITY CAN SPELL PROFIT; ANNUAL FEATURE

(p. 10, 50, 82) Annual article, by Lawrence Cohn, on production of films with budgets of $14 million or more. Includes 1 table showing estimated budget, domestic rentals to date, producer, distributor, and month of release, for big-budget movies released 1980-83.

BIG RENTAL FILMS OF 1983, ANNUAL FEATURE

(p. 13, 80) Annual table showing value of U.S./Canadian rentals; name of director, producer, and distributor; and month of release; for films with rentals of $1 million or more during 1983, in rank order. Data are from *Variety*. Includes accompanying article.

ALL-TIME FILM RENTAL CHAMPS, ANNUAL FEATURE

(p. 16-78, passim) Annual table showing value of U.S./Canadian rentals; name of director, producer, and distributor; and year of release; for all films with all-time rentals of $4 million or more, in rank order. Data are from *Variety*.

U.S. THEATER CIRCUITS RANKED BY SIZE

(p. 36, 38) Table showing 68 motion picture theater companies ranked by total number of screens as of Dec. 1983, and also showing headquarters, total theater locations, drive-in screens, States of theater locations, year company was founded, and number of screens added in 1981-84.

FILM PRODUCTION, RECURRING FEATURE

(p. 48) Recurring list of 1984 major film production starts announced as of Jan. 1, with comparisons to 1983, by company.

STATISTICS ON UK TV SETS

(p. 92) Table showing sets in use and annual individual license fee for color and monochrome TV sets in the UK, and license fee income to British Broadcasting Corp. public service broadcaster, various periods 1982-83.

UK CABLE PROJECTIONS

(p. 100) Table showing the following for UK cable TV: total and upgraded subscribers, mile-age added, homes per cable mile, new homes passed, penetration growth, and subscribers added, 1984-88. Data are from the Financial Times Business Information Service.

ESTIMATES OF UK CABLE DEVELOPMENT

(p. 102) Table showing UK cable TV subscribers as projected by 8 advertising industry organizations, various years 1986-95.

ITV PROGRAM MAKEUP

(p. 102) Table showing UK average TV viewing hours per week and distribution of weekly programming schedule, all by type of program, for independent stations, 1982/83.

UK HOMEVIDEO FACTS

(p. 103) Table showing the following for UK: number of videocassette recorders (VCR), percent of color TV homes with VCR, blank and prerecorded cassette sales volume, VCR market share by format, and distribution of home videocassette sales and rentals by program type, various periods 1981-83.

Includes related article (p. 103, 112).

TOP BRITISH FILMS IN THE UK 1982-83, ANNUAL FEATURE

(p. 116) Annual table showing earnings from UK rentals and Eady fund payments (government distribution of boxoffice tax), for year ended Sept. 1983; cumulative earnings since release; production company; and registration date; for top British films ranked by 1982/83 earnings. Data are shown in UK pounds, with cumulative earnings also shown in U.S. dollars.

Data are from Assn of Independent Producers. Includes accompanying article.

BBC-TV PROGRAMMING

(p. 117) Table showing British Broadcasting Corp. TV broadcast hours, by type of program, for year ended Mar. 1983.

1983 RIAA HOMEVID AWARDS

(p. 138-139) List of videocassettes and videodisks receiving gold and platinum awards for high sales, 1983. Shows title, producer/rights owner, and date of award. Data are from Recording Industry Assn of America.

1983-84 NETWORK 'SECOND SEASON' NEW SHOWS AT A GLANCE

(p. 158) Table showing day and hour of appearance, episode length, supplier, production principals, cast, and estimated production fee per episode, for all "second season" prime time TV series from 3 major networks, 1983/84 season.

50 TOP SELLING LPs/TAPES AND BEST SELLING POP SINGLES OF '83, ANNUAL FEATURE

(p. 222, 224) Two annual tables showing weeks on best selling list, highest position reached, production label, artist, and record title, for 50 best selling LPs/tapes and singles, 1983. Data are from *Variety* sampling of retail sales in top 25 markets.

GOLD AND PLATINUM RECORDS OF 1983, ANNUAL FEATURE

(p. 225, 227) Annual list of records receiving platinum and gold awards for high sales, 1983. Shows record title, label, and artist, and date of award. Data are from Recording Industry Assn of America.

20 YEARS OF B'WAY PRODUCTIONS, BY ORIGIN

(p. 262) Table showing number of Broadway shows by type of production, 1963/64-1982/83.

BROADWAY LONG RUNS

(p. 273) Table showing all stage shows playing over 1,000 performances on Broadway ranked by number of performances as of Jan. 8, 1984, and also including type of show and dates of run for each.

C9380–1.508: Jan. 18, 1984 (Vol. 313, No. 12)

FOX WAS DOMESTIC MARKET CHAMP IN '83

(p. 5, 40) By A. D. Murphy. Article, with 1 table showing value of U.S./Canadian film rentals as percent of total market, for 6 major U.S. distributors, 1977-83. Data are from *Variety*.

C9380–1.509: Jan. 25, 1984 (Vol. 313, No. 13)

HORRID YEAR FOR HORROR PIX AT THE B.O.

(p. 3, 36) By Lawrence Cohn. Article, with 2 tables showing U.S. and foreign horror film productions; and horror and science fiction U.S. rental value and aggregate share of film market; 1970-83. Data are from *Variety*.

C9380–1.510: Feb. 8, 1984 (Vol. 314, No. 2)

MONTHLY DATA

(p. 5) *Variety* Boxoffice Index, for Jan. 1984.

DOMESTIC BOXOFFICE, RECURRING FEATURE

(p. 5) Recurring table showing 8 major film distributors ranked by market share, January 4-31, 1984. Includes accompanying article.

OFF-NETWORK FUTURES, RECURRING FEATURE

(p. 64, 90) Recurring table showing distributor, episode length, and number of episodes, for TV network shows available for syndication, 1984-87. Table is accompanied by a list of made-for-syndication TV shows arranged by program type.

C9380–1.511: Feb. 15, 1984 (Vol. 314, No. 3)

SWEDEN'S TOP 10 PICS, RECURRING FEATURE

(p. 69) Recurring table showing top 10 films in Sweden ranked by boxoffice gross, and also showing film distributor, number of tickets sold, and release date, 1982/83. Data are from Swedish Film Institute. Includes accompanying article.

C9380–1.512: Mar. 7, 1984 (Vol. 314, No. 6)

[Special issue price is $2.50.]

FOURTH AMERICAN FILM MARKET EDITION

MONTHLY DATA

(p. 5) *Variety* Boxoffice Index, for Feb. 1984.

ALL TIME FOREIGN GROSSERS IN JAPAN

(p. 89) Table showing all-time top 30 foreign films in Japan ranked by rental income (in yen), as of Jan. 1984, and including release date and distributor for each.

FILM PRODUCTION, RECURRING FEATURE

(p. 160) Recurring list of 1984 major film production starts announced as of Mar. 7, with comparisons to 1983, by company.

GERMAN-SPEAKING MARKET AT A GLANCE, ANNUAL FEATURE

(p. 336, 350, 352) Annual compilation of socioeconomic and film industry data for West Germany and Austria. Data, shown for various years 1979-83, were compiled by *Variety* from unspecified sources. Includes some or all of the following for each country:

a. Socioeconomic: population, labor force and unemployment, households, income, inflation rate, GNP, TV sets, newspapers and magazines, home video equipment, and leisure time and expenditures.

b. Film: top grossing films; all-time top films in rental income; theaters, ticket sales and prices, and foreign and domestic releases; film production and marketing; distribution receipts; market share, by nation and distributor; and feature films shown on TV.

c. Audience: film admissions by sex, age, income, and population size.

Also includes summary socioeconomic data and number of film theaters for Switzerland.

BLUE-COLLAR CROWD LOVES VIDEO; PRICE CUTS STRENGTHEN DEALERS

(p. 355, 372) Article on West German market for videocassettes and related equipment. Data sources include German Video Institute. Includes text data on videocassette recorder sales volume, and cassette distributors and releases, primarily 1983; and number of pre-recorded cassettes released to dealers, 1980-83.

FILMS NEWLY RELEASED IN U.S.

(p. 414) Table showing motion picture releases by type of distributor or film, 1982-84.

C9380–1.513: Mar. 21, 1984 (Vol. 314, No. 8)

BOLIVIA'S TOP FILMS

(p. 48) Table showing top 5 films in Bolivia ranked by rental income, 1983. Data are shown in Bolivian pesos.

VENEZUELA'S '83 TOP GROSSERS

(p. 49) Table showing top 15 films in Venezuela ranked by boxoffice gross receipts (in bolivares), and also showing release date, 1983.

MAJORS' BRAZIL BILLINGS

(p. 49) Table showing film billings in Brazil, for 8 U.S. distributors, 1983. Data are shown in cruzeiros, and are accompanied by an exchange rate table and a related article (p. 50).

BRAZILIAN MKT. SHARE

(p. 50) Table showing distribution of film billings in Brazil, by city or marketing area, 1983.

U.S. HISPANO POPULATION

(p. 52) Article, with 1 table showing Hispanic population (total and as a percent of full population), for 30 U.S. cities, 1980. Data are from the Census Bureau.

COLOMBIA'S TOP GROSSERS

(p. 52) Table showing top 12 films in Colombia ranked by net billings, and also showing film distributor, 1st 10 months 1983.

TOP FOREIGN PICS IN BRAZIL, '83

(p. 56) Table showing top 15 foreign films in Brazil ranked by admissions, 1983.

PERU'S TOP GROSSERS

(p. 58) Table showing top 7 films in Peru ranked by boxoffice gross, for an unspecified period ended Mar. 20, 1984.

DISTRIB GROSSES IN VENEZUELA

(p. 58) Table showing motion picture gross receipts in Venezuela, by major film distributor, 1981-83. Data are shown in Venezuelan bolivares.

U.S. RELEASES IN BRAZIL

(p. 58) Table showing number of films released in Brazil, for 8 U.S. distributors (no date).

MEXICO'S TOP '83 GROSSERS

(p. 58) Table showing top 30 films in Mexico ranked by boxoffice gross receipts and also showing country of origin, 1983. Data are from Compania Operadora de Teatros, S.A.

C9380–1.514: Mar. 28, 1984 (Vol. 314, No. 9)

MONTHLY DATA

(p. 3) *Variety* Boxoffice Index, for Mar. 1984.

C9380–1.515: Apr. 4, 1984 (Vol. 314, No. 10)

INDIES PACE SOARING FILM RELEASES

(p. 1, 39) By Lawrence Cohn. Article, with 1 table showing motion picture releases by type of distributor or film, 1st quarter 1982-84.

C9380–1.516: Apr. 11, 1984 (Vol. 314, No. 11)

DOMESTIC BOXOFFICE, RECURRING FEATURE

(p. 3) Recurring table showing 8 major film distributors ranked by market share, 1st quarter 1984.

ACAD COMES TO 'TERMS' WITH FIVE OSCARS

(p. 5, 25) By Jim Harwood. Article, with 2 tables showing number of "Academy Awards" won by 7 major films and 5 leading distributors, 1984 (covering films released in 1983). Table is accompanied by a listing of 1984 award winners (p. 4, 29).

SYNDIE RUNDOWN

(p. 68) Article, with 2 tables showing syndicated TV programs ranked by Nielsen rating, and including audience share and number of markets broadcasting, for programs receiving 3.0/ higher rating among all viewers and women aged 25-54, Feb. 1984. Data are from A. C. Nielsen Co.

C9380–1.517: Apr. 18, 1984 (Vol. 314, No. 12)

PRODUCTION PULSE, RECURRING FEATURE

(p. 8) Recurring feature on 1984 major film production starts announced as of early 1984, with comparisons to 1983, by company.

CANADA TV FUND AN UNEXPECTED SUCCESS

(p. 49, 110) By Sid Adilman. Article on operations of Canada's Broadcast Fund, a government-sponsored funding source for TV productions administered by Telefilm Canada. Includes 1 table showing number of funded projects, total budget, and Telefilm investment, for contracted, accepted, and pending French- and English-language projects, by program type, July 1983-Feb. 1984 period.

EUROPEAN SATELLITE PRIMER

(p. 57) Table showing operating company or country, purpose and/or launching date, sponsor country, orbital location, and number of transponders, for European telecommunications/broadcast satellites (no date).

ARAB TV: WHO, WHAT & WHERE

(p. 154, 156) Directory of state-owned TV broadcasting authorities in 16 Arab countries, with summary data on population, number of TV sets and broadcasting channels, and TV advertising price (no date).

Also includes directory information for 6 joint broadcasting agencies; and a brief related article (p. 151).

PIRATES' BIG PIECE

(p. 156) Brief article, with 1 table showing the following for 9 Arab countries: population, and number of TV sets, videocassette recorders, and video software outlets, primarily as of Jan. 1984. Data are from United Video International.

Also includes aggregate text data on imports of blank videocassettes.

C9380–1.518: Apr. 25, 1984 (Vol. 314, No. 13)

FILM PRODUCTION, RECURRING FEATURE

(p. 36) Recurring list of 1984 major film production starts announced as of Apr. 25, with comparisons to 1983, by company.

1983-84 REGULAR SERIES RATINGS, ANNUAL FEATURE

(p. 76, 80) Annual table ranking TV series by rating, and also showing audience share, 1983/ 84 season.

C9380–1.519: May 2, 1984 (Vol. 315, No. 1)

MONTHLY DATA

(p. 3) *Variety* Boxoffice Index, for Apr. 1984.

DOMESTIC B.O., RECURRING FEATURE

(p. 3, 38) Recurring table showing 8 major film distributors ranked by market share, 1st 4 months 1984.

FILM PRODUCTION, RECURRING FEATURE

(p. 32) Recurring feature on 1984 major film production starts announced as of May 2, with comparisons to 1983, by company.

AUSTRALIAN FACTS

(p. 47) Table showing the following for Australia: population; inflation and unemployment rates; number of film theaters; and top film admission price, and average weekly wage (in Australian dollars). No data dates are given.

ALL-TIME AUSSIE RENTAL CHAMPS, ANNUAL FEATURE

(p. 50, 52) Annual table showing release date, distributor, and rental value, for all films with total Australian rentals of more than $500,000 (Australian dollars), in rank order as of Jan. 1, 1984.

Includes accompanying brief article.

TOP 10 NATIONAL TV PROGRAMS, ANNUAL FEATURE

(p. 86) Annual table showing top 10 TV programs in Australia ranked by audience size, and also showing network. No data dates are given. Data are from McNair Anderson Associates.

AUSSIE TV VIEWING PATTERNS, ANNUAL FEATURE

(p. 86) Annual table showing Australian TV households; families viewing TV; and average viewing time, with detail by sex and age group aggregated for 6 capital cities. No data dates are given.

N.Z. ALL-TIME RENTAL CHAMPS

(p. 114) Table showing all-time top 20 films in New Zealand ranked by rental value (New Zealand dollars). No data date is given.

C9380–1.520: May 9, 1984 (Vol. 315, No. 2)

[Special issue price is $2.50.]

27th INTERNATIONAL FILM ANNUAL

WEEKEND B.O. HIGHS REDEFINE BUSINESS

(p. 5, 522) By A. D. Murphy. Article, with 1 table showing top 33 domestic films ranked by highest weekend boxoffice gross, and also showing number of screens for each, 1978-early 1984 period. Data are from individual distributors.

Table showing films with highest weekend boxoffice gross, for 1st 5 months 1984, is described below under C9380-1.523

ALL-TIME FILM RENTAL CHAMPS, ANNUAL FEATURE

(p. 116-226, passim) Annual table showing value of U.S./Canadian rentals; name of director, producer, and distributor; and year of release; for films with all-time rentals of $4 million or more as of Dec. 31, 1983, arranged in alphabetical order. Data are from *Variety*.

FILM PRODUCTION, RECURRING FEATURE

(p. 211) Recurring feature on 1984 major film production starts announced as of May 9, with comparisons to 1983, by company.

ITALIAN PRODUCTION, 1979-83, ANNUAL FEATURE

(p. 303) Annual table showing films produced through Italian and combined Italian/other country ventures, 1979-83. An accompanying table shows investment value and number of films financed through Banca Nazionale del Lavoro (p. 304).

IMPORTS OF FILMS FOR TV AND TV PROGRAMS

(p. 303) Table showing the following for Italy: number and value of imported films for TV and TV program episodes, by country of origin, 1983 with comparison to 1982.

SPAIN'S ALL-TIME TOP GROSSERS

(p. 398) Table showing all-time top 25 films in Spain ranked by boxoffice gross (no date), and including film release dates.

TOP 10 SPANISH PICS

(p. 408) Table showing top 10 domestic films in Spain ranked by boxoffice gross, 1983.

'83 AUSSIE RELEASES

(p. 415) Table showing number of film releases in Australia, by distributor, 1983.

EXHIBITION DOWN UNDER

(p. 415) Table showing number of motion picture theater screens in Australia, for top 3 theater circuits (no date).

TOP 10 FILMS IN AUSTRALIA, 1983

(p. 416) Table showing top 10 films in Australia ranked by rental income (Australian dollars), and including film distributor, 1983.

HONG KONG ALL-TIME TOP 10 FILMS, RECURRING FEATURE

(p. 432) Recurring table showing all-time top 10 films in Hong Kong ranked by boxoffice gross (in Hong Kong dollars), and also showing release date and film producer, as of early 1984.

JAPAN'S TOP 25 ALL-TIME GROSSERS

(p. 432) Table showing all-time top 25 films in Japan ranked by rental income, and also showing release date and film distributor, as of Dec. 1983.

JAPAN vs. U.S.

(p. 433) Table showing the following for Japan and the U.S.: film boxoffice gross, attendance, average ticket price, and number of screens and releases; and population and TV households; primarily 1983 with comparisons to 1982. Data are from Eiren and Motion Picture Assn of America.

Includes accompanying article (p. 433, 450).

UIP, COL-FOX, WB DOMINATE DANISH MARKET: 65% SHARE

(p. 462, 468) Article, with 1 table showing film distributors ranked by share of Danish market, 1983.

SWEDEN'S TOP 20 PICS, RECURRING FEATURE

(p. 468) Recurring table showing top 20 films in Sweden ranked by boxoffice gross (in Swedish kronor), and also showing producer/distributor and attendance (no date).

BRAZIL PIC OUTPUT

(p. 482) Table showing Brazilian film production, 1975-83.

PROPORTIONS OF GERMAN RENTALS

(p. 494) Table showing number of prerecorded videocassette titles available on the West German market, by film type, 1983. Data are from the German Video Institute.

AUSSIE HOMEVIDEO FACTS

(p. 496) Table showing the following for Australia: number and percent of TV homes with videocassette recorders, with market share for VHS and Beta equipment; value of video software turnover, with share for rentals and sales; and number of video equipment retailers, and average rental fee and royalty paid to producers. No data dates are given.

C9380–1.521: May 16, 1984 (Vol. 315, No. 3)

PRODUCTION PULSE, RECURRING FEATURE

(p. 6) Recurring feature on 1984 major film production starts announced as of May 16, with comparisons to 1983, by company.

C9380–1.522: May 23, 1984 (Vol. 315, No. 4)

FILM PRODUCTION, RECURRING FEATURE

(p. 44) Recurring feature on 1984 major film production starts announced as of May 23, with comparisons to 1983, by company.

C9380–1.523: May 30, 1984 (Vol. 315, No. 5)

DOMESTIC B.O., RECURRING FEATURE

(p. 3, 125) Recurring table showing 8 major film distributors ranked by market share, 1st 5 months 1984.

11 PICS HIT $5-MIL AT WEEKEND B.O. SO FAR THIS YEAR

(p. 3, 29) By A. D. Murphy. Article, with 1 table showing top 28 domestic films ranked by highest weekend boxoffice gross, and also showing number of screens for each, 1st 5 months 1984.

Table showing films with highest weekend boxoffice gross, for 1978-early 1984 period, is described under C9380-1.520, above.

PRODUCTION PULSE, RECURRING FEATURE

(p. 6, 123) Recurring feature on 1984 major film production starts announced as of May 30, with comparisons to 1983, by company.

C9380–1.524: June 6, 1984 (Vol. 315, No. 6)

MONTHLY DATA

(p. 3) *Variety* Boxoffice Index, for May 1984.

LEGIT HAD AN IMPRESSIVE SEASON, ANNUAL FEATURE

(p. 1, 80-81, 89) Annual article, by Hobe Morrison, reviewing characteristics of the 1983/84 theater season for Broadway and road performances.

Includes 4 tables showing Broadway attendance and average ticket price, 1975/76-1983/84; Broadway and road total playing weeks and boxoffice receipts, and shows playing and receipts for biggest week, 1948/49-1983/84; and playing weeks, shows played, and boxoffice receipts, for cities with receipts over $1 million, 1982/83-1983/84.

FILM PRODUCTION, RECURRING FEATURE

(p. 30, 32) Recurring feature on 1984 major film production starts announced as of June 6, with comparisons to 1983, by company.

WARNER HOME VIDEO TOPS GERMAN MARKET

(p. 34) Table showing top 21 video distributors in West Germany ranked by total sales, and also showing market share, 1983.

1983-84 BROADWAY PRODUCTIONS

(p. 80) List of Broadway productions by success, failure, or other status, 1983/84 season.

B'WAY PRODUCTION RECORD, 1899-1984, ANNUAL FEATURE

(p. 80) Annual table showing the following for Broadway: new plays and musicals, and revivals, 1899/1900-1983/84; and return shows and pre-opening flops, 1972/73-1983/84.

BROADWAY THEATER MANAGEMENTS, BOOKINGS, RECEIPTS

(p. 84) Table showing managing company, number of weeks lighted, list of shows played, and total boxoffice receipts, for individual Broadway theaters, 1983/84 season. Includes related article.

C9380–1.525: June 13, 1984 (Vol. 315, No. 7)

MAJORS STEP ON IN-HOUSE PROD'N PEDAL

(p. 5, 32) By Lawrence Cohn. Article on film production and distribution activity of major distributors, 1984. Includes 1 table showing number of new film releases produced in-house and through independent/affiliated companies, classic films re-released, and films shelved, for 9 major distributors, 1980-84.

PRODUCTION PULSE, RECURRING FEATURE

(p. 6, 24) Recurring feature on 1984 major film production starts announced as of June 13, with comparisons to 1983, by company.

C9380–1.526: June 20, 1984 (Vol. 315, No. 8)

FILM PRODUCTION, RECURRING FEATURE

(p. 32-33) Recurring feature on 1984 major film production starts announced as of June 20, with comparisons to 1983, by company.

C9380–1.527: June 27, 1984 (Vol. 315, No. 9)

HOT PICS CLOG RELEASE SCHEDULES

(p. 1, 32) By Lawrence Cohn. Article, with 1 table showing releases of major distributors' new and classic films, and of independents' subtitled import and other films, 2nd quarter and 1st half 1982-84.

DOMESTIC B.O., RECURRING FEATURE

(p. 3) Recurring table showing 8 major film distributors ranked by market share, 1st half 1984.

FILM PRODUCTION, RECURRING FEATURE

(p. 36) Recurring feature on 1984 major film production starts announced as of June 27, with comparisons to 1983, by company.

C9380–1.528: July 4, 1984 (Vol. 315, No. 10)

PRODUCTION PULSE, RECURRING FEATURE

(p. 6, 36) Recurring feature on 1984 major film production starts announced as of July 4, with comparisons to 1983, by company.

C9380–1.529: July 11, 1984 (Vol. 315, No. 11)

MONTHLY DATA

(p. 31) *Variety* Boxoffice Index, for June 1984.

FILM PRODUCTION, RECURRING FEATURE

(p. 30, 34) Recurring feature on 1984 major film production starts announced as of July 11, with comparisons to 1983, by company.

SYNDIE SCORECARD FOR MAY

(p. 38, 62) Brief article, with 1 table ranking syndicated TV programs broadcast in 30/more markets by rating, and including number of markets, market share, percent of U.S. covered, and rating among women in 18-49 age group, May 1984. Data are from A. C. Nielsen Co.

C9380–1.530: July 18, 1984 (Vol. 315, No. 12)

DOMESTIC BOXOFFICE, RECURRING FEATURE

(p. 4) Recurring table showing 9 major film distributors ranked by market share, cumulative Jan. 1-July 8, 1984.

PRODUCTION PULSE, RECURRING FEATURE

(p. 6, 22) Recurring feature on 1984 major film production starts announced as of July 18, with comparisons to 1983, by company.

C9380–1.531: July 25, 1984 (Vol. 315, No. 13)

PRODUCTION PULSE, RECURRING FEATURE

(p. 6, 27) Recurring feature on 1984 major film production starts announced as of July 25, with comparisons to 1983, by company.

C9380–1.532: Aug. 1, 1984 (Vol. 316, No. 1)

DOMESTIC RENTALS SOAR OVER PROD. COSTS

(p. 3, 24, 28-29) By Lawrence Cohn. Article, with 5 charts and 1 table showing aggregate major companies' film production cost and domestic rental value, and number of films produced and released by production budget range, selected periods 1981-84; and typical expenses and revenues for low-, average-, and big-budget films (no date).

C9380–1.533: Aug. 8, 1984 (Vol. 316, No. 2)

EXHIBITION REVENUES TILTING WESTWARD

(p. 3, 30) By A. D. Murphy. Article, with 1 table showing distribution of film rental values, by film exchange region, selected periods 1930s-80s. Data are from industry records.

DOMESTIC BOXOFFICE, RECURRING FEATURE

(p. 4) Recurring table showing 9 major film distributors ranked by market share, 1st 7 months 1984.

MAJORS CLOSING SOME BRAZILIAN OFFICES; IMPORT VOLUME REDUCED

(p. 6, 24) Article, with 2 tables showing Brazil's population, and film imports, theaters, and attendance, 1975-83.

C9380–1.534: Aug. 15, 1984 (Vol. 316, No. 3)

MONTHLY DATA

(p. 28) *Variety* Boxoffice Index, for July 1984.

C9380–1.535: Aug. 22, 1984 (Vol. 316, No. 4)

DISTRIBS' SHARE OF B.O. DIPS BELOW 40%

(p. 3, 138) By A. D. Murphy. Article, with 1 table showing film distributors' share of domestic boxoffice receipts, 1977-83.

C9380–1.536: Aug. 29, 1984 (Vol. 316, No. 5)

GLOBAL PRICES FOR TV, RECURRING FEATURE

(p. 76) Recurring table showing price range for TV half-hour episodes and feature films exported from U.S., by purchasing country (no date).

C9380–1.537: Sept. 5, 1984 (Vol. 316, No. 6)

LABOR DAY KIND TO CURRENT B.O. HITS

(p. 3, 30) By James Greenberg. Article, with 1 table showing top 9 films ranked by boxoffice gross, May 25-Sept. 3, 1984 period.

C9380–1.538: Sept. 12, 1984 (Vol. 316, No. 7)

MONTHLY DATA

(p. 3) *Variety* Boxoffice Index, for Aug. 1984.

DOMESTIC BOXOFFICE, RECURRING FEATURE

(p. 34) Recurring table showing 9 major film distributors ranked by market share, 1st 8 months and summer 1984. Includes accompanying article (p. 1, 34).

C9380–1.539: Sept. 19, 1984 (Vol. 316, No. 8)

HISPANIC VOTING POTENTIALS

(p. 49) Table showing Hispanic total and voting age population, persons eligible to vote, and actual or projected voter registration and turnout, 1976, 1980, and 1984. Data are from Census Bureau.

Includes accompanying article (p. 51, 86).

NEW PRODUCT OPENNESS

(p. 63) Table showing percent of total and Hispanic population seeking selected new products and services, including TV programs, foods, retail outlets, and consumer items, 1981 and 1984. Data are from Yankelovich, Skelly, and White, Inc.

C9380–1.540: Sept. 26, 1984 (Vol. 316, No. 9)

1984-85 NETWORK PRIMETIME SEASON AT A GLANCE, ANNUAL FEATURE

(p. 44-45, 81, 104) Annual table showing day and hour of appearance, episode length, supplier, production principals, cast, and estimated production fee per episode, for all prime time TV series from 3 major networks, 1984/85 season.

SYNDICATION AT A GLANCE, RECURRING FEATURE

(p. 54, 58, 62) Recurring table showing distributor and number of episodes available, for syndicated TV programs arranged by type, 1984-87. Data are from Katz Programming.

THEATRICAL MOVIE RANKINGS FOR 1983-84, ANNUAL FEATURE

(p. 55) Annual table showing made-for-theater movies broadcast on TV ranked by rating, and including network, date of appearance, and audience share, Sept. 1, 1983-Aug. 31, 1984 period.

PROGRAM TRACK RECORD: AT START OF 1984-85 SEASON, ANNUAL FEATURE

(p. 59) Annual tabular list showing prime time TV series ranked by number of years on the air, by network, for series returning for the 1984-85 season.

1982-83 SEASON MINISERIES RATINGS, ANNUAL FEATURE

(p. 59) Annual table showing TV miniseries ranked by average rating, and also showing average audience share, Sept. 1, 1983-Aug. 31, 1984 period.

UK INDIE TV STATION COSTS

(p. 67) Table showing the following for 14 UK independent TV companies: transmitter rental payments, and required payments to Government treasury and for funding of Government TV station (channel 4), various 12-month periods ended Apr. 1983-Mar. 1984. Data are shown in UK pounds and U.S. dollars.

HOMEVID RENTAL SHARES

(p. 68) Table showing UK market shares for home video software, by company, based on Feb. 13-Aug. 17, 1984 rentals. Data are from Gallup Organization. Includes accompanying article (p. 68, 76).

CABLE SYSTEMS ON INTERIM FRANCHISE ROLL

(p. 68) Table showing areas and number of homes served by 11 UK cable TV operators granted interim franchises by the Government in 1983.

C9380–1.540   Variety, Inc.

MADE-FOR-TV MOVIE RANKINGS FOR 1983-84, ANNUAL FEATURE

(p. 84, 86, 88) Annual table showing made-for-TV movies ranked by rating, and including network, date of appearance, supplier, and audience share, Sept. 1, 1983-Aug. 31, 1984 period.

C9380–1.541: Oct. 3, 1984 (Vol. 316, No. 10)

PIC RELEASES CONTINUE ON THE UPSWING

(p. 5, 41) By Lawrence Cohn. Article, with 1 table showing motion picture releases by type of distributor or film, 1st 9 months and 3rd quarter 1982-84.

1983-84 PRIMETIME SPECIALS RATINGS, ANNUAL FEATURE

(p. 66-68, 72) Annual table showing prime time TV specials ranked by audience rating, and including network, date of appearance, and audience share, Sept. 1, 1983-Aug. 31, 1984 period.

C9380–1.542: Oct. 10, 1984 (Vol. 316, No. 11)

[Special issue price is $2.50.]

FIFTH HOME VIDEO ANNUAL

MONTHLY DATA

(p. 5) *Variety* Boxoffice Index, for Sept. 1984.

JAPAN VIDEO AT A GLANCE

(p. 37) Table showing the following for Japan: percent of TV households owning, and total production, for videotape and videodisk players; and sales volume and value for videotape and videodisk software, with aggregate rental market share; 1984 and 1986. Data are from Nippon Broadcasting Systems.

WHERE VID SOFTWARE IS SOLD IN JAPAN

(p. 38) Table showing distribution of home video software retail sales in Japan, by outlet type, 1982-83. Data are from Nippon Broadcasting Systems.

TOP 10 GROSSERS IN SWEDEN, RECURRING FEATURE

(p. 89) Recurring table showing top 10 films in Sweden ranked by boxoffice gross, and also showing film distributor and release date, for year ended June 1984. Data are from Swedish Film Institute.

SCANDINAVIA AT A GLANCE

(p. 89) Table showing the following for 5 Scandinavian countries: film admissions and value of rentals 1983, and boxoffice gross 1983-84; and population, TV households, number of cinemas and screens and videocassette recorders, video retailer and distributor revenues, and video titles on market (no dates).

C9380–1.543: Oct. 17, 1984 (Vol. 316, No. 12)

HOLLAND: FIGURES ON DUTCH FEATURES; SMALL HALLS LOOM LARGE; MARKET SHARES; THEATRICAL ADMISSIONS; STUDIO'S ALL-TIMERS; AND CINEMA STRUCTURE; ANNUAL FEATURES

(p. 50-53, 58) Annual compilation of 1 chart and 6 tables on the motion picture industry in the Netherlands. Includes the following data for various years 1974-83:

a. Number of films in release, and distribution of movie screen time and boxoffice re-

ceipts, for domestic films and for foreign films by country of origin; and number of theaters and total seats, and distribution of admissions, by theater seating capacity.

b. Film admissions in 9 individual cities and aggregate for 53 cities; all-time top 10 domestic films ranked by total admissions, and showing year of release; Dutch films as a percent of total films released in the Netherlands; and number of theater screens and seats.

Includes accompanying articles (p. 51-72).

BELGIAN HOMEVIDEO SCORES GAINS AND IS BEATING BACK THE PIRATES

(p. 62) Article, with 1 table showing the following for Belgium: videocassette recorders in use and used for playing rented cassettes; and prerecorded cassette rentals, average rental fees and taxes, and rental income; 1983.

GLOBAL PRICES FOR TV, RECURRING FEATURE

(p. 122) Recurring table showing price range for TV half-hour episodes and feature films exported from U.S., by purchasing country (no date).

C9380–1.544: Oct. 24, 1984 (Vol. 316, No. 13)

[Special issue price is $2.50.]

TENTH MIFED FILM MARKET REVIEW

RENTALS OF AMERICAN MAJORS IN JAPAN; AND RENTALS OF JAPANESE MAJORS; ANNUAL FEATURES

(p. 294-295) Two annual tables showing 4 major U.S. film distributors ranked by rental income in Japan; and 4 Japanese film companies ranked by rental income, and including number of films released; 1st 8 months 1984, with comparisons to 1983. Includes accompanying articles (p. 294-295, 389).

For description of previous tables, see C9380-1.501 above.

RENTALS OF JAPANESE FILM IMPORTERS

(p. 296) Table showing 3 Japanese film importing companies ranked by rental income, 1st half 1984.

TOP 10 HONG KONG GROSSERS, RECURRING FEATURE

(p. 296) Recurring table showing Hong Kong's top 10 domestic films ranked by boxoffice gross, and also showing release date and film distributor (no date).

ISRAEL: TOP GROSSING FILMS; THEATERS AND ATTENDANCES; TOP 10 DOMESTIC FILMS; AND PIX DISTRIBBED BY COUNTRY

(p. 331, 333-334) Four tables showing the following for Israel: top 10 foreign and domestic films ranked by admissions; number of theaters (with number opening and closing), admissions, and average ticket price; and number of films in release, by country of origin; various periods 1974-84.

Includes accompanying articles (p. 331-344).

WEST GERMANY: U.S. DISTRIBS GROSS; FEATURE PICS; WEST GERMANS HIKE CINEMA-GOING; AND U.S. TOPS WEST GERMAN FILM TAKE

(p. 346, 352) Four tables showing the following for West Germany: distribution of film boxoffice gross 1979-83, and number of films in release and aggregate distributors' earnings (in German marks) 1983, by country of origin; and number of tickets sold, 1974-83.

Includes accompanying articles.

C9380–1.545: Oct. 31, 1984 (Vol. 317, No. 1)

1984 SUMMER SERIES RATING AVERAGES, ANNUAL FEATURE

(p. 65) Annual table showing prime time TV series ranked by average rating, Apr. 16-Sept. 23, 1984 period.

C9470
Vending Times, Inc.

C9470–1   VENDING TIMES: Census of the Industry, 1984
Monthly (selected issue).
July 1984. 74 p.
Vol. 23, No. 7-A.
ISSN 0042-3327.
LC SC 76-332.
SRI/MF/not filmed

Annual *Vending Times* report, for 1984, on the vending industry. Includes sales of vended products and number of machines, by product type; and operating ratios; various years 1973-83. Also includes data on coffee service, music, and game equipment. Data are from a survey of operating companies and manufacturers.

Contents:

a. Contents listing, introduction, analysis, and 1 summary table. (p. 6-12)

b. Vended product sales and delivery, with 16 tables listed below. (p. 17-50)

c. Operating patterns, with 1 table showing total operating companies, and distribution by number of full-time employees, 1982-83. (p. 51)

d. Coffee service, music and games, and bulk vending, including text data and 1 chart (p. 63) on coin-operated phonographs; and 11 tables also listed below. (p. 52-68)

e. Operating ratio study, with 4 tables showing National Automatic Merchandising Assn members' composite average operating ratios, and profit and sales analysis by product, 1981-83. (p. 70-71)

This is the 38th annual report. *Vending Times* is a monthly journal reporting on vending industry trends and developments, and normally does not contain statistics. The annual industry census is the only feature covered by SRI.

Availability: Vending Times, Inc., 545 Eighth Ave., New York NY 10018, $20.00 per yr., census issue $10.00, single copy $2.00; SRI/MF/not filmed.

TABLES:

C9470–1.1: Vending Sales and Delivery

[Tables [1-11] and [13] are for vended products, and generally show total dollar and unit sales, weekly unit sales, and number of machines on location, 1973 and 1981-83; and sales distribution by vended price and/or product categories, 1981-83 or 1983.

Manual sales data are for vending machine operators who also serve food manually.]

[1-4] Hot drinks; and bottle, cup, and can cold drinks. (p. 17, 27-30)

[5-6] Confections/snacks and pastries. (p. 32-34)

[7-8] Cigarettes and cigars [price/product category data omitted for cigars]. (p. 36)

[9-10] Milk and ice cream. (p. 40-41)

[11] Hot canned foods. (p. 42)

[12] Vending and manual locations [number of sites, 1982-83, and sales value, 1983, by type of location]. (p. 44)

[13] All-purpose food vendors [includes data on canned juice, 1981-83]. (p. 47)

[14] Vended food service/commissary operations [including percent of food service operators with own commissary and with outside food sources; percent using microwave ovens; and sales distribution of commissary-prepared foods by product and of vended foods by type of location, 1983]. (p. 48)

[15] Manual food service [distribution of manual food sales by type of location and product, 1981-83; and of operator expansion into manual foods, by period service started]. (p. 49)

[16] Truck and van use [1981-83]. (p. 50)

C9470–1.2: Coffee Service, Amusement Equipment, and Bulk Vending

COFFEE SERVICE

[Tables [1-2] show data for 1980-83.]

[1] Coffee service, equipment [average accounts and purchases, and percent of firms using approximately 15 types of coffee brewing and noncoffee equipment]. (p. 52)

[2] Coffee service, product [average purchase for 3 types of coffee and 7 related products, average sales dollar volume, cup purchases, and distribution of firms by sales volume range]. (p. 53)

AMUSEMENT EQUIPMENT AND BULK VENDING

[Tables [3-9] show data for 1979 and 1981-83. Tables [4-9] show annual and weekly average dollar volume, and number of units on location.]

[3] Amusement equipment dollar volume [for 8 types of games and rides]. (p. 56)

[4-7] Video games, flipper [pinball] games, pool tables, and shuffle alleys. (p. 58-60)

[8-9] Soccer tables, and arcade games (specialized). (p. 64)

[10] 1983 review and outlook [selected data primarily on amusement equipment operations, including average commission rate, earnings life, and units operated, by game type; reported and anticipated income percent change, by equipment type; and types of locations served]. (p. 66)

[11] Bulk vending [machines on location, and dollar sales, by product type, 1983; and sales distribution by vended price, 1981-83]. (p. 68)

C9700
Ziff-Davis Publishing Co.

C9700–3 WEEKLY OF BUSINESS AVIATION

Weekly. Approx. 10 p. cumulative pagination throughout volume. SRI/MF/excerpts, shipped quarterly

Weekly publication reporting on developments in general aviation, commuter airlines, and aviation-related Federal regulation. Includes monthly statistics on business/personal aircraft shipments.

Issues contain numerous brief news articles; recent Federal airworthiness directives and regulatory exemption activities; 1 monthly table and 2 other recurring tables, listed below; and occasional special tables and articles with statistics. A quarterly subject index is published separately.

Monthly table usually appears in 2nd or 3rd issue of the month. All additional features with substantial statistical content are described, as they appear, under "Statistical Features;" page locations and latest periods of coverage for other recurring tables are also noted. Nonstatistical features and issues are not covered.

Availability: Ziff-Davis Publishing Co., Business Publications Division, 1156 15th St., NW, Washington DC 20005, $210.00 per yr., $125.00 per 6 months; SRI/MF/excerpts for monthly table and all portions covered under "Statistical Features;" shipped quarterly.

Issues reviewed during 1984: Nov. 7, 1983-Oct. 29, 1984 (P) (Vol. 37, Nos. 19-26; Vol. 38, Nos. 1-26; Vol. 39, Nos. 1-18).

RECURRING TABLES:

MONTHLY TABLE

[1] Business/personal aircraft industry unit shipments [by model, for each of approximately 20 manufacturers, for month prior to cover date and current calendar and fiscal years to date, with 3-year trends by manufacturer, and some manufacturers' exports and/or net billings for current month].

OTHER RECURRING TABLES

[Month of coverage is 2-3 months prior to cover date.]

[1] Regional commuter carriers traffic [passengers, load factor, revenue passenger miles, and available seat miles, by commuter airline, for month of coverage].

[2] Airport and Airway Trust Fund status [balance, receipts by source, expenditures by function, assets, liabilities, and equity, for month of coverage and fiscal year to date; data are from U.S. Treasury Dept].

STATISTICAL FEATURES:

C9700–3.501: Jan. 2, 1984 (Vol. 38, No. 1)
RECURRING TABLE

[2] Airport and Airway Trust Fund status, Oct. 31, 1983. (p. 7a)

C9700–3.502: Jan. 23, 1984 (Vol. 38, No. 4)

ACCIDENTS, FATALITIES, AND RATES OF U.S. GENERAL AVIATION AND COMMUTER AIR CARRIERS

(p. 29a, 30a) Two tables presenting the following National Transportation Safety Board statistics: total and fatal accidents and fatalities, and hours flown, with total and fatal accident rates, for general aviation and commuter carriers; and aircraft miles and number of departures for commuter carriers; 1974-83 or 1975-83.

C9700–3.503: Jan. 30, 1984 (Vol. 38, No. 5)

HELICOPTER SALES TO INCREASE 18% BY 1983

(p. 36, 38a, 39a) Article, with 2 charts showing total helicopter deliveries to free world; and distribution by foreign vs. North American destination, military vs. civilian use, and engine type; various periods 1974-93. Data are from Allison Gas Turbine Operations.

C9700–3.504: Feb. 6, 1984 (Vol. 38, No. 6)

FAA BUDGET PROPOSAL SEEKS SHARPLY INCREASED SPENDING AUTHORITY

(p. 41, 42a) Article, with 1 table showing FAA budget allocations, by program and function, actual FY83, and estimated FY84-85.

C9700–3.505: Feb. 13, 1984 (Vol. 38, No. 7)

RECURRING TABLE

[1] Regional commuter carriers traffic, Dec. 1983. (p. 55a)

C9700–3.506: Feb. 27, 1984 (Vol. 38, No. 9)

FORECAST OF INCREASED GA ACTIVITY MAY SET STAGE FOR NEW CONSTRAINTS

(p. 65, 66a, 67a) Article, with 2 charts showing distribution of traffic at airports with FAA traffic control service and of instrument-flight-rated traffic handled by FAA air route traffic control centers, all by type of aircraft (air carrier, commuter/air taxi, and general aviation), 1983 and 1995.

C9700–3.507: Apr. 9, 1984 (Vol. 38, No. 15)

TAKEOFF, LANDING PHASE ACCIDENTS INCREASED IN 1983

(p. 114a-119a, passim) Article, with 2 charts and 3 tables showing accidents (total and fatal) and fatalities for turbojet and turboprop aircraft operated by corporations and others, and number of single-pilot turboprop operators, 1979-83; corporate and commercial aircraft accident distribution by flight phase, with comparison to corporate flight time distribution by phase, various periods 1970-83; and aircraft accident rate trends. Data are from Robert E. Breiling of SimuFlite Training International, Inc.

C9700–3.508: Apr. 16, 1984 (Vol. 38, No. 16)

RAA REPORTS SHARP RISE IN PASSENGERS, RPMs BY COMMUTERS IN 1983, ANNUAL FEATURE

(p. 123-127a, passim) Annual article on regional airline fleet characteristics and utilization, 1983. Data are from Regional Airline Assn.

Includes 4 tables showing regional/commuter passenger and cargo carriers, total aircraft and hours in use, cargo carried, and passenger data including revenue-passenger miles, airports, and average trip length; regional passenger service aircraft, hours in use, and percent of total seating capacity, by aircraft model; regional passenger aircraft, by type and manufacturer; and top 100 regional airlines ranked by number of passengers; 1983, with selected comparisons to 1982.

Previous table on top regional airlines, for 1982, appeared as a separate feature; for description see SRI 1983 Annual, under C9700-3.416.

C9700–3.509: June 4, 1984 (Vol. 38, No. 23)

RECURRING TABLE

[2] Airport and Airway Trust Fund status, Mar. 31, 1984. (p. 181a, 182a)

C9700–3.510: July 30, 1984 (Vol. 39, No. 5)

RECURRING TABLE

[2] Airport and Airway Trust Fund status, May 31, 1984. (p. 39a).

C9700–3.511: Sept. 3, 1984 (Vol. 39, No. 10)

RECURRING TABLE

[2] Airport and Airway Trust Fund status, June 30, 1984. (p. 79a)

Independent Research Organizations

R1960
American College Testing Program

R1960–1 COLLEGIATE ENROLLMENTS IN THE U.S.
Annual, discontinued.

Annual report on enrollment and teaching staff at 2- and 4-year colleges and universities, discontinued with the report for 1980/81 (for description, see SRI 1982 Annual, under this number).

R2110
American Enterprise Institute for Public Policy Research

R2110–1 PUBLIC OPINION
Bimonthly. Approx. 60 p.
ISSN 0149-9157.
LC 78-642154.
SRI/MF/excerpts

Bimonthly journal reporting results of recent public opinion surveys conducted by major polling organizations on U.S. and foreign attitudes toward current social, political, and economic issues.

Issues generally contain original articles, occasionally with substantial statistics; and an "Opinion Roundup" section with current opinion data from the Roper Organization, Gallup Organization, and other polling organizations.

Bimonthly Opinion Roundup and all additional features containing substantial, specifically identified survey or other data are described, as they appear, under "Statistical Features." Nonstatistical features are not covered.

Availability: American Enterprise Institute for Public Policy Research, Public Opinion, Circulation Department, 1150 17th St., NW, Washington DC 20036-9964, $26.00 per yr., single copy $5.00; SRI/MF/excerpts for all portions described under "Statistical Features."

Issues reviewed during 1984: Oct./Nov. 1983-Aug./Sept. 1984 (P) (Vol. 6, Nos. 5-6; Vol. 7, Nos. 1-4).

STATISTICAL FEATURES:

R2110–1.501: Oct./Nov. 1983 (Vol. 6, No. 5)

BLACK VOTING, BLOC VOTING, AND THE DEMOCRATS

(p. 12-15, 59) By I. A. Lewis and William Schneider. Article examining black voting trends and political and social attitudes. Data are from a *Los Angeles Times* nationwide survey of 599 blacks and 1,054 whites/others, conducted Sept. 17-22, 1983.

Includes 2 tables showing distribution of response to questions on presidential voting preferences, personal and national economic condition, political ideology, racial discrimination, and Reagan presidential performance; all shown by economic class and/or race.

PARTY PRIMER

(p. 20, 41, 58) By Everett Carll Ladd. Article examining differences between Democratic and Republican Parties, based on data from National Opinion Research Center and ABC News/*Washington Post* surveys.

Includes 2 tables showing distribution of political party affiliation, by age; and belief that hard work results in success, by party affiliation and educational level.

OPINION ROUNDUP

(p. 21-40) Compilation of 76 charts and 13 tables presenting results of recent public opinion surveys by major polling organizations. Opinion data often include comparisons to earlier surveys, usually for 1970s and 1980s. Topics include the following:

a. Political issues: whether presidential campaigns begin too early; Republican, Democratic, and independent voters' socioeconomic characteristics, ideology, and attitudes on selected issues; and presidential preferences.

b. Quality of life: perceptions of living in a "rat race" and whether lifestyle has changed.

PRESIDENTIAL POPULARITY: DO PEOPLE LIKE THE ACTOR OR HIS ACTIONS?

(p. 42-44) By Burns Roper. Article, with 1 table showing presidential popularity and performance ratings for Carter and Reagan, various periods 1977-83. Data are from Gallup Poll and Roper Organization.

MISSILE GAP: THE GERMAN PRESS AND PUBLIC OPINION

(p. 45-49) By Elisabeth Noelle-Neumann. Article on media influence on West German public attitudes toward the U.S. Data are from Allensbach Institute and other sources.

Includes 5 tables showing distribution of German response to questions on support for Western defense alliance or neutrality; whether U.S. should withdraw troops from Europe; Soviet commitment to peace; and preference for closer ties with U.S. or Soviet Union; various periods 1956-83.

TABLES TURNED: IF EAST EUROPEANS COULD VOTE

(p. 53-57) By Henry O. Hart. Article on Eastern European attitudes toward Radio Free Europe, and political attitudes. Data are from surveys of 8,000-12,000 Eastern European travelers in Western Europe, from each of 5 countries. Surveys were conducted by Radio Free Europe.

Includes 8 tables showing distribution of response to questions on role of Radio Free Europe, and political party preferences if free elections were held; various periods 1968-81.

R2110–1.502: Dec. 1983/Jan. 1984 (Vol. 6, No. 6)

WHAT ARE MOVIEMAKERS MADE OF?

(p. 14-18) By Stanley Rothman and S. Robert Lichter. Article on characteristics of leading professionals in the motion picture industry. Data are from a 1982 survey of 149 writers, directors, and producers of top 50 films, 1965-82.

Includes 6 tables showing respondent socioeconomic characteristics; presidential voting patterns, 1968-80; attitudes on economic, political, social, and foreign policy issues; and views on influence of various leadership groups, reliability of selected information sources, and quality and role of TV entertainment.

OPINION ROUNDUP

(p. 21-40) Compilation of 67 charts and 7 tables summarizing results of recent public opinion surveys by major polling organizations, with selected trends from 1970s or earlier. Topics include the following:

a. Generational change in public opinion since 1970s, including views on Communism, capital punishment, free speech, high income, extramarital sex, abortion, marijuana, pornography, quality of life, women's employment, political ideology, suicide, church attendance, interracial marriage, and minority president, with selected detail for high school seniors.

b. Sociodemographic indicator trends, including marital status of population, median age at first marriage, unmarried couple households, married women in labor force, and illegitimate births, various years 1930-83.

c. Generational change in public opinion since 1970s, including confidence in big business and military; views on quality of life and world situation; smoking, drinking, and reading habits; and views on violence, child behavior, ideal family size, and defense spending.

d. West German attitudes on balance of power between West and Soviet Union; U.S. missile deployment in West Germany; disarmament; and NATO membership.

e. Ethics: public opinion on ethics/honesty level in society; and personal involvement in driving while intoxicated, personal use of company telephones or supplies, overstating tax deductions, marijuana or cocaine use, and sick leave misuse, for business executives vs. general public.

INTERNATIONAL CRISES: A RALLYING POINT FOR THE PRESIDENT?

(p. 41-43, 60) By Richard Brody. Article examining presidential popularity following international incidents, 1947-83. Data are from Gallup and other major polling organizations. Includes 1 chart and 1 table showing change in public approval following selected incidents, for Reagan and 7 preceding Presidents.

SHATTERED IMAGES: POLITICAL PARTIES IN THE 1984 ELECTION

(p. 44-48) By John Kenneth White and Dwight Morris. Article examining public perceptions of ideological differences between Republican and Democratic parties. Data are from various major opinion polling firms.

Includes 1 chart and 4 tables showing distribution of response to questions on party best able to handle selected national problems, various periods 1980-83.

VOTER TURNOUT: AN INTERNATIONAL COMPARISON

(p. 49-55) By David Glass et al. Article on voter turnout in U.S. compared to 24 foreign countries. Data are from *International Almanac of Electoral History,* University of Michigan Center for Political Studies, and other sources.

Includes 5 tables showing voter turnout by country, as of 1981; U.S. voter turnout in 5 States with election-day registration, 1980; and U.S. registration and voter turnout, by age group, educational level, and stated interest in politics, 1980.

ISRAELI REFLECTIONS ON THE HOLOCAUST

(p. 58-60) By Hanoch Smith. Article on Israeli public opinion on the Holocaust and anti-Semitism. Data are from a May 1983 survey of 1,018 Israeli residents, conducted by the Smith Research Center.

Includes 8 text tables showing distribution of response to questions on influence of the Holocaust on personal life; role of Western leaders during Holocaust; mistrust of non-Jews as consequence of Holocaust; perceived anti-Semitism of Moslems and Christians; Holocaust as factor in establishment of Israel; and potential for recurrence of Holocaust.

R2110–1.503: Feb./Mar. 1984 (Vol. 7, No. 1)

PUBLIC CONFIDENCE, POPULAR CONSENT: A COMPARISON OF BRITAIN AND THE U.S.

(p. 9-11, 60) By Richard Rose. Article comparing U.S. and UK public confidence in government and major institutions of society. Data are from Gallup Poll, British Gallup Poll, and European Values Systems Study Group.

Includes 2 tables showing popularity level of Presidents and Prime Ministers, 1945-83; and confidence ratings of selected societal institutions in U.S. and 4 European countries, 1981.

UPS AND DOWNS AND INS AND OUTS OF IDEOLOGY

(p. 12-15) By John Robinson. Article on differences between conservative and liberal ideological identification. Data are from surveys of 5 major polling organizations. Includes 2 tables showing ideological distribution of population, 1970-83; and correlation between ideology and position on selected issues.

STRAIGHT STORY ON HOMOSEXUALITY AND GAY RIGHTS

(p. 16-20, 59) By William Schneider and I. A. Lewis. Article on public attitudes toward homosexuality and gay rights. Data are from 3,542 responses to national and California surveys conducted by *Los Angeles Times,* Sept.-Oct. 1983.

Includes 3 tables showing survey response regarding attitudes toward homosexuality and gay rights issues; and personal acquaintance

with homosexuals, and perceived reason for homosexual orientation, by selected respondent socioeconomic characteristics.

OPINION ROUNDUP

(p. 21-40) Compilation of 75 charts and 18 tables summarizing results of recent U.S. and foreign public opinion surveys by major polling organizations. Opinion data often include comparisons to earlier surveys, usually for 1970s and 1980s. Topics include the following:

a. Quality of life, including national and personal condition and outlook, with detail by sex and race and comparisons to selected foreign countries; national economic condition and outlook; belief in rewards of hard work; national pride and patriotism; and confidence in government; with selected trends from 1939.

b. Political issues, including party identification; popularity of Reagan and 7 preceding Presidents; voter preferences among presidential candidates; and perceived success of Reagan's economic policy, and treatment of selected groups.

c. Equal employment opportunity for both sexes in 14 occupations.

FEAR OF LIVING DANGEROUSLY: PUBLIC ATTITUDES TOWARD NUCLEAR POWER

(p. 41-44) By Ronald Inglehart. Article on U.S. and European public perceptions of the safety of nuclear power. Data are from responses to surveys conducted by University of Michigan Research Center, Cambridge Reports, Inc., and Commission of the European Community, various years 1979-83.

Includes 2 tables showing distribution of responses to surveys in U.S. and 9 European countries on likelihood of explosions occurring at nuclear power plants, and support for nuclear energy development.

DEATH OF POLITICS IN NEW HAMPSHIRE

(p. 56-57) By David Moore. Article, with 1 table showing New Hampshire voters' preferences among four 1984 Democratic presidential candidates, as of various dates Dec. 1983-Feb. 1984. Data are from surveys conducted by 5 polling organizations.

R2110–1.504: Apr./May 1984 (Vol. 7, No. 2)

MEDIA COVERAGE OF CAMPAIGN '84: A PRELIMINARY REPORT

(p. 9-13) By William C. Adams. Article comparing 1984 Democratic presidential candidate popularity to extent of news media coverage. Data are from Gallup polls, and major TV and newspaper reports.

Includes 2 tables showing candidate popularity and news coverage rankings; and voter exit poll response on when voting decision was made, for primary elections in 3 States; by candidate, various periods 1982-84.

TEFLON POLITICS

(p. 14-18) By Michael Jay Robinson and Maura Clancey. Article, with 2 tables showing distribution of survey responses to questions concerning most memorable news events of previous year, and ethical standards of President Reagan and members of his administration. Data are from responses of 366 adults to an Apr. 1984 survey conducted by the authors.

OPINION ROUNDUP

(p. 21-40) Compilation of 77 charts and 10 tables presenting results of recent public opinion surveys by major polling organizations. Data generally are from surveys conducted during 1980s. Topics include the following:

a. Independent voter preferences and characteristics compared to Democrats and Republicans, including preferred presidential candidates, political party perceived most capable of solving national problems, opinions on selected social issues, ideological outlook and voting patterns, and demographic characteristics, with trends from 1948.

b. Foreign policy, including approval of Reagan Administration policies in general, and with regard to handling of Korean airline tragedy and Lebanese situations, and relations with Soviet Union; perceived national security and risk of nuclear war; opinions on Communism; support for U.S. military intervention under specified circumstances; and perceptions of military activities in Latin America.

c. Performance ratings of national leaders in U.S., UK, France, and Spain.

IS ELECTION '84 REALLY A CLASS STRUGGLE?

(p. 41-46, 51) By Everett Carll Ladd. Article, with 3 tables showing presidential popularity and voting intentions, by region, political party, and demographic characteristics, various years 1952-84. Data are from Gallup Organization, Roper Organization, and *Los Angeles Times.*

WHO'S THE FAIREST OF THEM ALL?

(p. 47-51) By Karlyn H. Keene. Article on perceived fairness of Reagan Administration toward selected population groups. Data are from survey results of major polling organizations.

Includes 4 tables showing respondent distribution concerning perceptions of government responsibility for improving poor people's standard of living, solving national problems, helping pay medical bills, and providing special aid to blacks because of past discrimination, all by respondent income class, 1975 and 1983.

AND TYLER, TOO

(p. 52-54) By Martin P. Wattenberg. Article, with 2 tables showing presidential and vice-presidential candidate preferences, and net advantage represented by vice-presidential candidates on winning tickets, election years 1952-80. Data are from Survey Research Center, Center for Political Studies, University of Michigan.

PUBLIC AND THE TEACHER UNIONS: OUT OF STEP ON THE BASICS?

(p. 55-58) By Terry Hartle. Article, with 1 table showing distribution of survey responses concerning most important problems facing public schools, 1977 and 1983. Data are from Gallup Organization.

R2110–1.505: June/July 1984 (Vol. 7, No. 3)

AS THE DUST SETTLES: CENTRISM AT WORK IN THE PARTICIPATORY STATE

(p. 2-6) By Ben J. Wattenberg. Article, with 1 table showing percent of public believing that government spends too little on defense, inflation is most important issue, and "big government" is biggest threat to Nation, selected years 1959-81. Data are from Gallup Organization.

OPINION ROUNDUP

(p. 19-42) Compilation of 73 charts and 28 tables presenting election results and public opinion surveys, mostly 1968-84, with trends from 1952. Topics include the following:

a. Electoral college votes, and winning party in last 8 Presidential elections, by State.

b. Census division profiles: voting patterns in last 4 Presidential and last 2 House elections, by party and State; population distribution, by party and ideology, union status, religion, and race/ethnicity; and political parties of gubernatorial, State legislative, and congressional officeholders, and per capita personal income, unemployment rate, and population distribution by race, by State; repeated for 9 census divisions.

c. Presidential voting patterns in last 4 elections, by race, region, party and ideology, education, age, religion, race/ethnicity, sex, occupation, and union status.

CONGRESSIONAL ELECTIONS: WHAT'S AHEAD

(p. 43-46) By Thomas E. Mann and Norman J. Ornstein. Article, with 1 table showing support for Democratic vs. Republican Members of Congress in elections or polls conducted July 1946-Apr. 1984. Data are from Gallup Organization and Census Bureau.

R2110–1.506: Aug./Sept. 1984 (Vol. 7, No. 4)

OPINION ROUNDUP

(p. 21-40, 48) Compilation of 59 charts and 2 tables presenting results of recent public opinion surveys by major polling organizations. Data generally are from surveys conducted during 1980s, and include detail by respondent sociodemographic characteristics. Topics include the following:

a. Personal aspirations, habits, and preferences, including most frequent daydreams; dieting habits; perception of appearance; views on male-female relationships; trust in family and others; importance of possessions; leisure activities; use of TV, newspaper, and selected periodicals; airline travel; food, sports, and music preferences; knowledge of selected public figures; and most enjoyable time of life.

b. Quality of life, including satisfaction with life and family situations; health condition; own and childrens' finances; personal fears; knowledge of someone who uses drugs; use of alcohol; experience of a gun threat or physical violence; male and female roles, responsibilities, job priorities, and work relationships; and reasons for working.

c. Political preferences for 1984 presidential candidates, and party affiliation.

DELEGATE POLLS: 1944 TO 1984

(p. 43-45) By Barbara G. Farah. Article, with 1 table showing distribution of delegates to the Democratic and Republican national conventions by sex, education, occupation, and political ideology, various years 1944-84. Also includes average age of delegates.

Data are from surveys conducted by CBS News and other major polling organizations.

1984 NATIONAL PRIMARY

(p. 52-53) By Adam Clymer. Article, with 1 table showing persons voting in the 1984 Democratic primary elections, by sex, race, age, income, education, and political ideology; with detail for voters supporting 3 leading candidates. Data are from exit polls in 24 State primaries, conducted by *New York Times* and major news networks.

WHAT THE ISRAELI ELECTION PORTENDS

(p. 54-56) By Asher Arian. Article on Israeli voters' foreign policy attitudes, and preferences in the July 1984 election. Data are based on a July 1984 survey of 1,259 Israeli adults, conducted by DAHAF Research Institute.

Includes 2 tables showing distribution of votes cast by political party, by ethnic identification, continent of father's and/or own birth, and educational attainment; and responses to questions concerning the future of Israeli territories and territory residents, by party affiliation.

EUROPEAN PARLIAMENTARY ELECTION 1984

(p. 57-58) By Richard Rose. Article, with 1 table showing the following by country, for the 1984 European Parliament election: voter turnout, and distribution of votes cast by political party. Data are from European Parliament Office.

R2800
American Productivity Center

R2800–1 MULTIPLE INPUT PRODUCTIVITY INDEXES
Quarterly. Approx. 30 p.
ISSN 0741-6490.
SRI/MF/complete

Quarterly report, tracking quarterly and annual productivity changes for major sectors of the private economy and for industry groups. Data are current to 2 quarters or 1-2 years prior to cover date, and include trends from 1948.

Report focuses on the multiple input productivity index, which relates weighted labor and capital inputs to price adjusted value-added output.

Indexes are computed from BLS and Bureau of Economic Affairs data, and are updated according to latest benchmark revisions. Indexes are based on 1977 reference year.

Issues generally contain a summary of recent productivity developments; and all or some of the following recurring data, which are continuously revised and updated:

a. Productivity change rates: average annual rate of change in indexes and index components, by economic sector, sometimes with detail by industry, selected periods 1948-current year.

b. Productivity indexes: total factor, labor, capital, and capital/labor ratio indexes, by economic sector; shown for current quarter and 4-7 prior quarters.

c. Productivity levels: labor productivity (real output per hour) in 1972 constant dollars, by economic sector, selected years 1948-current year.

Data by economic sector usually are shown for private business economy, goods producing and service producing sectors, farming, manufacturing and nonmanufacturing industry, and nonfinancial corporate business. Data by industry are shown by industry division and manufacturing industry group.

Presentation of recurring data varies from issue to issue. The 1st issue of the volume year is a base issue, and includes productivity index trends from earlier years, plus detail by industry for productivity change rates and indexes.

Report occasionally presents special analyses for selected industries, some updated annually; and other statistical analyses. These analyses are described, as they appear, under "Statistical Features."

Availability: American Productivity Center, 123 N. Post Oak Lane, Houston TX 77024, $50.00 per yr., 1st issue of volume year $25.00; SRI/MF/complete.

Issues reviewed during 1984: Jan.- Aug. 1984 (P) (Vol. 4, Nos. 3-4; Vol. 5, No. 1).

STATISTICAL FEATURES:

R2800–1.501: Aug. 1984 (Vol. 5, No. 1)

SERVICE PRODUCERS PROVE TO BE DRAG ON ECONOMY DURING 1983

(p. 1-2) Article, with 1 chart and 2 tables showing percent change in output, labor input, and output/labor ratio, for goods producing sector, and for service producing sector with detail by major industry, 1980-83 period.

FIRST QUARTER 1984 REGISTERS STRONG LABOR, TOTAL PRODUCTIVITY GROWTH

(p. 3-4) Article, with 2 tables showing total factor and labor productivity indexes; for the business economy, and goods and service producing sectors, 1st quarter 1984; and for business economy during the 5th recovery quarter of 6 economic cycles since 1954.

SPECIAL ANALYSES, ANNUAL FEATURE

(p. 61-66) Annual compilation of 11 tables showing selected input, output, and productivity ratio indexes, including labor, capital, value added, materials, energy, and/or total factor, for the following industries: blast furnace/basic steel products (SIC 331); cereal breakfast foods, pet foods, roasted coffee, and food preparations not elsewhere classified (SIC 2043, 2047, 2095, and 2099, respectively); and miscellaneous plastic products (SIC 3079); various years 1958-83.

R2800–2 PRODUCTIVITY PERSPECTIVES, 1983 Edition
Annual. Dec. 1983. 19 p.
ISSN 0741-6458.
SRI/MF/complete

Annual report, for 1983, analyzing productivity trends and outlook for U.S. and other industrial countries. Presents data on productivity levels and changes, and productivity-related economic indicators. Data are shown primarily for various periods 1970s-83, but also include some trends from 1940s and 1960s as noted below.

U.S. data include labor, capital, and "total factor" productivity, by economic sector and manufacturing industry group, with selected comparisons to Japan; and productivity changes during business cycle phases since 1949.

Other U.S. data include capital stock distribution by industry, and distribution of R&D activity by sector and spending by category, various years 1960-82; Federal Government and private borrowing as percent of GNP; and inflation rate for major commodities and services.

Data shown for U.S. and 5-15 foreign countries include labor and manufacturing productivity; balance of trade; GNP growth; inflation; unemployment; R&D as percent of GNP, selected periods 1961-80; savings as percent of disposable personal income; and capital formation as percent of GNP.

Data are from American Productivity Center, BLS, U.S. Dept of Commerce, and other government and private sources.

Contains listings of contents, charts, and tables (p. 1-2); introduction (p. 3-4); narrative analysis in 3 sections, interspersed with 19 charts and 10 tables (p. 3-17); and statistical appendix, with 4 tables (p. 18-20).

This is the 3rd edition of the report.

Availability: American Productivity Center, 123 N. Post Oak Lane, Houston TX 77024, $25.00; SRI/MF/complete.

R3300
Battelle Memorial Institute

R3300–1 **PROBABLE LEVELS OF R&D EXPENDITURES IN 1984: Forecast and Analysis**
Annual. Dec. 1983. 20 p.
SRI/MF/complete

Annual report analyzing R&D funding and expenditure outlook for 1984, with trends from 1960. Data are shown by funding and performing sector, including Federal Government, industry, colleges/universities, and other nonprofit institutions, with selected detail by Federal agency and function and by manufacturing industry group.

Also includes cost index for performing R&D per scientist/engineer, by sector.

Data are from NSF, McGraw-Hill surveys, and Battelle Memorial Institute estimates.

Contains summary (p. 1-2); analysis and forecast, with text statistics, 4 charts, and 6 tables (p. 2-18); and appendix, with definitions and information on Battelle's Columbus Division (p. 19-20).

Availability: Battelle Memorial Institute, Columbus Division, Publications, 505 King Ave., Columbus OH 43201-2693, †; SRI/MF/complete.

R3840
Children's Defense Fund

R3840–2 **CHILDREN'S DEFENSE BUDGET: An Analysis of the President's FY85 Budget and Children**
Annual. 1984. ix+280 p.
ISSN 0736-6701.
ISBN 0-938008-30-7.
SRI/MF/complete

Annual report analyzing the impact of Reagan Administration budget proposals on low-income families. Includes actual and proposed funding levels for Federal programs affecting children and families, FY81-85; change in net household income resulting from changes in taxes and benefits, by income group, 1984; and children in poverty and with unemployed parents, by race-ethnicity and family type, various periods 1978-83.

Also includes comparison between DOD cost and market price for 14 spare parts (no date); per capita expenditures on defense vs. programs for low-income families/children, FY81-89; defense budget, FY69 and FY81-89; illustrative FY85 budget increases proposed as part of Children's Survival Bill; and children in poverty compared to number receiving Medicaid and AFDC, and program payments per recipient with detail by State, various years 1972-83.

Also includes welfare provisions for pregnant women; effect of budget cuts on 29 cities' welfare payments, by race-ethnicity; participants in Title I of Elementary and Secondary Education Act; and Title XX child care expenditures; all by State, various periods 1980-83.

Data are compiled by Children's Defense Fund (CDF) from Budget of the U.S., other Federal sources, and National Governors' Assn.

Contains contents listing (p. v-ix); introduction, with 1 table (p. 1-14); 15 chapters, with narrative, text statistics, 9 charts, and 10 tables (p. 15-220); and 3 appendices, with 4 charts, 12 tables, congressional committee rosters and budget-related timetables, and lists of data sources and CDF publications (p. 222-280).

This is the 3rd annual report.

Availability: Children's Defense Fund, 122 C St., NW, Suite 400, Washington DC 20001, $14.95; SRI/MF/complete.

R3850
Commission on Professional and Hospital Activities

R3850–1 **LENGTH OF STAY, BY DIAGNOSIS AND OPERATION, 1982**
Annual series. For individual publication data, see below.
LC 73-173193.
SRI/MF/complete, delayed

Annual series of 14 reports presenting detailed data on short-term hospital admissions and length of stay, by diagnosis and type of operation, for all patients in the U.S., each census region, and Canada, and for geriatric and pediatric patients in the U.S., 1982.

Data are primarily from records submitted by approximately 1,430 U.S. and 220 Canadian nonfederal hospitals participating in the Professional Activity Study (PAS) of the Commission on Professional and Hospital Activities.

Each report contains the following:

a. Contents listing; and data explanation, with 1 table showing hospitals and beds, by hospital capacity and census division or Province, for all short-term non-Federal hospitals and for PAS participants, 1982.

b. Length of stay data, with 1-2 summary tables; and 1 detailed table, repeated for 398 diagnosis and/or 264 operation categories in International Classification of Diseases (ICD) order, showing number of patients, average length of stay, and length of stay by percentile, all shown by patient age, single and multiple diagnosis status, and (for diagnosis only) whether surgically treated, 1982.

c. Appendix of ICD codes, and index.

Reports covering all patients present diagnosis and operation data separately in 2 volumes for each geographic area. Reports covering geriatric and pediatric patients combine diagnosis and operation data in single volumes.

Series began in 1963. Reports for 1982 are listed below. Data are also available from issuing agency on computer-readable magnetic tape.

Availability: Commission on Professional and Hospital Activities, 1968 Green Rd., PO Box 1809, Ann Arbor MI 48106, $40.00 per volume, $70.00 per region; SRI/MF/complete, delayed shipment in Dec. 1984.

REPORTS:

R3850–1.1: By Diagnosis: U.S., 1982
[Annual. Oct. 1983. v+258 p. SRI/MF/complete, delayed.]

R3850–1.2: By Operation: U.S., 1982
[Annual. Oct. 1983. v+116 p. SRI/MF/complete, delayed.]

R3850–1.3: By Diagnosis: U.S., North Central Region, 1982
[Annual. Oct. 1983. v+258 p. SRI/MF/complete, delayed.]

R3850–1.4: By Operation: U.S., North Central Region, 1982
[Annual. Oct. 1983. v+116 p. SRI/MF/complete, delayed.]

R3850–1.5: By Diagnosis: U.S., Northeastern Region, 1982
[Annual. Oct. 1983. v+258 p. SRI/MF/complete, delayed.]

R3850–1.6: By Operation: U.S., Northeastern Region, 1982
[Annual. Oct. 1983. v+116 p. SRI/MF/complete, delayed.]

R3850–1.7: By Diagnosis: U.S., Southern Region, 1982
[Annual. Oct. 1983. v+258 p. SRI/MF/complete, delayed.]

R3850–1.8: By Operation: U.S., Southern Region, 1982
[Annual. Oct. 1983. v+116 p. SRI/MF/complete, delayed.]

R3850-1.9: By Diagnosis: U.S., Western Region, 1982
[Annual. Oct. 1983. v+258 p. SRI/MF/complete, delayed.]

R3850-1.10: By Operation: U.S., Western Region, 1982
[Annual. Oct. 1983. v+116 p. SRI/MF/complete, delayed.]

R3850-1.11: By Diagnosis: Canada, 1982
[Annual. Oct. 1983. v+258 p. SRI/MF/complete, delayed.]

R3850-1.12: By Operation: Canada, 1982
[Annual. Oct. 1983. v+116 p. SRI/MF/complete, delayed.]

R3850-1.13: Geriatric Length of Stay by Diagnosis and Operation, U.S., 1982
[Annual. Oct. 1983. v+355 p. SRI/MF/complete, delayed.]

R3850-1.14: Pediatric Length of Stay by Diagnosis and Operation, U.S., 1982
[Annual. Oct. 1983. v+355 p. SRI/MF/complete, delayed.]

R4105
Conference Board

R4105-3 STATISTICAL BULLETIN
Monthly. Approx. 15 p.
ISSN 0010-5554.
LC 73-644166.
SRI/MF/complete, shipped quarterly

Monthly report on selected U.S. business, consumer, industrial, and government economic performance indicators.

Most data are from Conference Board analyses of Dept of Commerce, BLS, and other Federal or industry source reports, and are current to 1-2 months or 1-2 quarters preceding cover date.

Contains contents listing; narrative analysis, with 1-2 summary charts; and 10 tables, described below, interspersed with 21 charts illustrating selected economic trends.

Availability: Conference Board, 845 Third Ave., New York NY 10022, associates only, price on request; SRI/MF/complete, shipped quarterly.

Issues reviewed during 1984: Oct. 1983-Sept. 1984 (P) (Vol. 16, Nos. 10-12; Vol. 17, Nos. 1-9).

MONTHLY TABLES:

a. Status (rising, level, or declining) of approximately 20 leading economic indicators, including capital investment commitments, housing permits, inventory investment and purchasing, selected financial flows, profitability, and average workweek, and unemployment claims; for the latest available month, with percent change over latest 3 months and from same month of previous year. 1 table.

b. Conference Board diffusion indexes: 12 indexes for latest available month, 3 previous months, and same month of previous year. 1 table.

c. Business executives' expectations: appraisal of current economic conditions compared

with 6 months ago, and expectations for the economy and for own industry 6 months ahead; for selected months of current and previous 2-3 years. 1 table.

d. Conference Board estimates of capital appropriations and expenditures, by 1,000 largest manufacturers and by investor-owned utilities, for quarter of coverage and previous 6 quarters. 1 table.

e. Economic forecasts by 8 leading forecasting institutions, for level and percent change of GNP (current and constant dollars), GNP deflator index, and unemployment rate; mostly as of month preceding cover date, with actual data for quarter preceding cover date and forecast data for 8-9 following quarters. 1 table.

f. Perspective on the Federal budget: amounts for current services, President's proposal, and congressional estimate or resolution, for receipts by source, outlays by function, and deficit; for current and previous or following fiscal years. 1 table.

g. Conference Board help-wanted advertising indexes for 51 newspapers, by city arranged by census division, with advertising rate comparisons to unemployment rates; for month 2 months prior to cover date, previous 2 months, and same month of previous year. 1 table.

h. Conference Board indexes of consumer confidence and buying plans, monthly for 2 previous years and current year to date. 1 table.

i. Conference Board estimates of discretionary purchasing power, saving, and spending, quarterly for current year to date and preceding 3-4 years. 1 table.

j. Conference Board estimates of new auto sales, by 10-day periods, for previous 3-4 years to latest available period. 1 table.

R4105-4 CONSUMER ATTITUDES AND BUYING PLANS
Monthly. Approx. 2 p.
ISSN 0547-7204.
LC SC 79-4258.
SRI/MF/complete, shipped quarterly

Monthly report, by Fabian Linden, on consumer expectations of business conditions, and intended durable goods purchases and travel during the next 6 months. Data are current to month prior to cover date, and are based on monthly surveys conducted by NFO Research, Inc.

Contains brief narrative analysis with 2 trend charts, and 1 table showing survey responses for current month (preliminary data), and 12 previous months, as follows:

a. Composite index series: consumer confidence (present situation and expectations) and buying plans.

b. Appraisal of present situation: business conditions (good, bad, or normal); and employment (plentiful, not so plentiful, or hard to get).

c. Expectations for next 6 months: business conditions (better, worse, or same); employment (more or fewer jobs, or same); and personal income (increase, decrease, or same).

d. Plans to buy within 6 months: auto (yes, and new, used, or uncertain); home (yes, and new, lived in, or uncertain); major appliances (total plans and for 8 appliances); and carpet.

e. Vacation intended within 6 months (in home State, other States, or foreign country); and travel mode (auto, airplane, or other); for every other month.

Availability: Conference Board, 845 Third Ave., New York NY 10022, associates only, price on request; SRI/MF/complete, shipped quarterly.

Issues reviewed during 1984: Oct. 1983-Sept. 1984 (P).

R4105-5 ECONOMIC ROAD MAPS
Series. For individual publication data, see below.
LC 82-20303.
SRI/MF/complete

Continuing series of brief reports presenting summary data, primarily charts, on business and economic trends, developments, and issues. Series includes recurring reports on taxation, corporate profits, and capital investment; and a subject index, published annually in the spring.

Data are compiled by the Conference Board's Business Conditions Analysis Dept from Federal Government and private sources.

Approximately 12 reports are issued annually, each focusing on a specific topic. Reports reviewed during 1984 are described below.

Availability: Conference Board, 845 Third Ave., New York NY 10022, price on request; SRI/MF/complete.

R4105-5.62: International Debt and Financing
[Monograph. Oct. 1983. 4 p. Nos. 1960-1961. SRI/MF/complete.]

Report on international debt trends, 1973-83, with 1982 detail including non-oil developing countries' short- and long-term foreign debt, long-term debt by type of creditor, and debt service payment.

Contains analysis and 20 charts.

R4105-5.63: Help-Wanted Advertising in the Business Cycle
[Monograph. Nov. 1983. 4 p. Nos. 1962-1963. SRI/MF/complete.]

Report analyzing help-wanted advertising activity during business cycles. Includes unemployment rates during Oct. 1979-Aug. 1983 business cycle, and distribution of national labor force, all by census division.

Contains analysis and 38 charts.

R4105-5.64: Health Care Expenditures: Past, Present, and Future
[Monograph. Dec. 1983. 4 p. Nos. 1964-1965. SRI/MF/complete.]

Report on health care expenditure trends and projections, 1950-90. Covers expenditures by type, including percent for medical research and facilities construction; hospital room charges; and distribution of public and private expenditures by type, with detail for Federal and State/local spending for Medicare, Medicaid, Workmen's Compensation, and other programs.

Contains analysis and 21 charts.

R4105-5.65: Government Employment and Pay: An International Survey
[Monograph. Jan. 1984. 4 p. Nos. 1966-1967. SRI/MF/complete.]

Report on impact of government employment on a nation's economy, 1960-82. Includes employment distribution, and employment as percent of population and of total nonagricultural employment, all by level of government including nonfinancial public enterprises; and public sector wages as percent of total wages and GDP; for industrial and developing nations, with selected detail by world area or country.

Data sources include an IMF survey of 64 developing countries and 21 OECD members. Contains analysis and 11 charts.

R4105–5.66: Population Growth and Migration

[Monograph. Mar. 1984. 4 p. Nos. 1968-1969. SRI/MF/complete.]

Report presenting population trends and projections, 1940-2000. Includes population density, by State, 2000. Contains analysis, map, and 7 charts.

R4105–5.67: Economic Road Maps 1983 Index

[Annual. [1984.] 2 p. SRI/MF/complete.]

Index to 1983 *Economic Road Maps* reports, arranged by subject and report numbers.

R4105–5.68: Two-Way Squeeze, 1984

[Annual. Apr. 1984. 2 p. No. 1970. SRI/MF/complete.]

Annual report on inflation, income, and tax trends, including pretax income needed to equal 1970 after-tax purchasing power, with Federal income and social security taxes, and amount to cover inflation, for 5 income levels, selected years 1975-84. Contains brief analysis, 6 charts, and 1 table.

R4105–5.69: Income and Taxes

[Monograph. Apr. 1984. 2 p. No. 1971. SRI/MF/complete.]

Report on Federal, Social Security, and State/local tax trends, including tax rates and burden among income groups, 1960-83. Contains analysis and 5 charts.

R4105–5.70: Employment and Unemployment in Industrial Countries

[Monograph. May 1984. 4 p. Nos. 1972-1973. SRI/MF/complete.]

Report on employment conditions in industrial nations, 1960-85. Includes labor force and employment change in agriculture, industry, and other sectors, for U.S., Japan, and aggregate 4 major European countries, 1975-82 period; and long-term unemployment as percent of total employment, by duration of unemployment, for 5 countries, 1980 and 1982.

Contains analysis and 14 charts.

R4105–5.71: Profit Trends, 1984

[Annual. June 1984. 4 p. Nos. 1974-1975. SRI/MF/complete.]

Annual report analyzing corporate profit trends, various years 1960-83. Includes "illusory profits" resulting from undercosting of inventories used in production and underdepreciation of fixed capital, 1980 and 1982-83. Contains brief analysis, 15 charts, and 1 text table.

R4105–5.72: Women: A Progress Report

[Monograph. July 1984. 4 p. Nos. 1976-1977. SRI/MF/complete.]

Report on labor force status and earnings of women, with comparisons to men, various periods 1965-83. Includes female labor force by marital status, women not in labor force by reason, full- and part-time employment by sex, lifetime earnings by education and sex, percent of businesses and receipts owned by women, and earnings of husbands vs. wives.

Also includes female divorce rate by race; female and total holders of selected public offices; and female householders, and children and other family members in household, with percent below poverty level.

Contains analysis and 17 charts.

R4105–5.73: Perspective on the Economic Expansion

[Monograph. Aug. 1984. 4 p. Nos. 1978-1979. SRI/MF/complete.]

Report on trends in selected economic indicators during the 1982-84 business cycle expansion, with comparison to previous business cycles. Includes brief analysis and 21 charts.

R4105–6   INTERNATIONAL ECONOMIC SCOREBOARD
Monthly.   Approx. 4 p.
ISSN 0270-045X.   LC 80-429.
SRI/MF/complete, shipped quarterly

Monthly report presenting comparable economic indexes for the U.S., Canada, UK, West Germany, France, Italy, Japan, and (beginning in the Aug. 1984 issue) Australia.

Data are prepared by the Center for International Business Cycle Research at Columbia University, from composites of approximately 65 economic indicators, and are generally current to 2-3 months prior to cover date.

Contains narrative analysis, with 1 summary table and occasional special tables and charts; feature articles, sometimes with substantial statistics; and 1 detailed table showing composite economic performance index and leading business cycle index for each country (and various countries combined), monthly for year to date and selected previous months, with percent changes from same months of preceding year, and with 10-year annual growth rate for period ending approximately 7 years prior to year of coverage.

Monthly data appear in all issues. All additional features with substantial statistical content are described, as they appear, under "Statistical Features." Nonstatistical features are not covered.

A more detailed report, presenting economic time series data, is described by SRI under U1245-1.

Availability: Conference Board, 845 Third Ave., New York NY 10022, price on request; SRI/MF/complete, shipped quarterly.

Issues reviewed during 1984: Oct. 1983-Sept. 1984 (P).

STATISTICAL FEATURES:

R4105–6.501: Oct. 1983

JAPAN'S GROWTH RATE NOT AS HIGH AS IT SEEMS

(2 p.) By Geoffrey H. Moore. Article, with 1 table showing Japan's GNP, export and import values, and net export surplus, in current and 1975 prices, 1978 and 1982. Data are from Japan's Economic Planning Agency, and the Columbia University Business School.

R4105–6.502: Feb. 1984

RECORD OF THE LEADING INDICATORS

(2 p.) Article, with 1 undated table showing median lead or lag time at business cycle turning points, for selected economic indicators in 7 countries. The indicators shown are the basis of the composite leading index presented each month for the same 7 countries.

R4105–6.503: Aug. 1984

NEW INDEXES FOR AUSTRALIA

(2 p.) Article, with 3 tables showing Australia composite economic performance and leading business cycle indexes, monthly 1982-May 1984, with percent change over 1969-79 period; and median lead or lag time at business cycle turning points, for selected economic indicators which form the basis of the composite performance index, for Australia, U.S., Japan, and UK (no dates).

Data are from Center for International Business Cycle Research at Columbia University.

R4105–7   CORPORATE DIRECTORSHIP PRACTICES: Compensation 1983
Biennial.   1983.   ix+35+1 p.
Rpt. No. 843.
ISBN 0-8237-0284-7.
SRI/MF/complete

Biennial report, by Jeremy Bacon, on compensation of corporate directors, 1983, covering forms and amounts of payments to outside and employee directors for regular board service and for service on committees.

Includes data by industry category (manufacturing, nonmanufacturing, and financial); major manufacturing industry group; sales size; and individual company (identified by number only).

Also covers related compensation practices, including insurance benefits and liability coverage available to board members.

Data are based on responses of 1,000 companies to a 1983 survey.

Contains contents and table listings, foreword, and methodology (p. iii-ix); 4 chapters, with narrative analysis and 30 tables (p. 1-15); 3 detailed tables (p. 16-35); and list of related publications (inside back cover).

Previous report, for 1981, is described in SRI 1982 Annual, under this number.

Availability: Conference Board, 845 Third Ave., New York NY 10022, price on request; SRI/MF/complete.

R4105–8   ANNUAL SURVEY OF CORPORATE CONTRIBUTIONS, 1984 EDITION (An Analysis of Survey Data for the Calendar Year 1982)
Annual.   1984.   iv+43 p.
Rpt. No. 848.
ISBN 0-8237-0289-8.
LC 76-24946.
SRI/MF/complete

Annual report, by Kathryn Troy, on corporate philanthropic gifts to charitable and public interest organizations and activities, 1982, with comparisons to the 1970s and trends from 1936. Covers charitable tax-deductible contributions, and corporate assistance (financial and other donations not deductible for tax purposes).

Includes value of charitable contributions and corporate assistance, by type; total and per employee contributions, and pre-tax income, by major industry group; contributions to company foundations; contributions relative to pre-tax income, by size of contributions, income, assets, and employment; and contributions by major industry group, by detailed recipient category within health/human services, education, culture/art, civic/community activities, and other areas.

Also includes top 75 unnamed companies ranked by charitable contributions and social expenditures, with pre-tax income for each; trends in contributions and in income before and after taxes, 1936-82; forecast of contributions relative to pre-tax income through 1987; and survey sample characteristics.

Data are based on Apr. 1983 survey responses of 534 corporations, accounting for approximately 45% of all U.S. giving during 1982.

Contains listings of contents, tables, and charts, and introduction (p. ii-iv); narrative report, with 7 charts and 4 text tables (p. 1-16); 27 detailed tables (p. 17-40); and appendix, with methodology and 5 tables (p. 41-43).

This is the 17th edition of the report.

Availability: Conference Board, 845 Third Ave., New York NY 10022, price on request; SRI/MF/complete.

R4105–9   FINANCIAL INDICATORS AND CORPORATE FINANCING PLANS: A Semiannual Survey
Semiannual.   Apr. 1984.   3 p.
SRI/MF/complete, Apr. 1983, Oct. 1983, & Apr. 1984 reports

Semiannual report on corporate financial executives' general economic expectations and past and planned sources for corporate financing. Data are based on responses of 38 corporate financial executives to a semiannual survey conducted Apr. 1984.

Contains narrative review of results, and 4 tables showing survey responses regarding the following:

a. Inflation outlook to 1989; and new Aaa industrial bond and prime interest rates, Dow Jones Industrial Average, and real GNP and GNP deflator rates of change, 2nd-3rd quarters 1984, and annually 1984-85.

b. Corporate finance: percent raised from bond issues, private placements, net new equity, bank term and short-term loans, commercial paper, and other external sources, and from internal funds; for past 12 months, with expected change in coming 12 months.

c. Foreign exchange rate changes for 4 currencies against U.S. dollar, and change in price of gold, June 30, 1984 and Sept. 30, 1984 (based on responses from companies with international operations).

This is the 16th semiannual survey.

The following reports have also been received, and are also available on SRI microfiche under this number:

Apr. 1983 [Semiannual. Apr. 1983. 3 p. price on request].

Oct. 1983 [Semiannual. Oct. 1983. 3 p. price on request].

Availability: Conference Board, 845 Third Ave., New York NY 10022, price on request; SRI/MF/complete.

R4105–11   UTILITY INVESTMENT STATISTICS: Utility Appropriations
Quarterly.   Approx. 3 p.
ISSN 0360-523X.
LC 75-648802.
SRI/MF/complete

Quarterly report on investor-owned electric and gas utility company capital appropriations and expenditures.

Data are compiled from surveys of electric companies accounting for approximately 95% of all investor-owned companies' plant investment and sales; and from gas companies accounting for approximately 50% of revenues of all investor-owned gas utilities. Usually includes preliminary data for quarter of coverage, and revised data for previous quarters.

Reports are generally published 3-4 months after end of quarter covered.

Contains 3 trend charts, narrative summary, and 1 table showing unadjusted and seasonally adjusted amounts for opening and closing backlogs, appropriations, canceled appropriations, and capital expenditures, for all, electric, and gas utilities, for quarter of coverage and previous 8-9 quarters.

Data in this report are available on-line through Conference Board Data Base.

Availability: Conference Board, 845 Third Ave., New York NY 10022, price on request; SRI/MF/complete.

Issues reviewed during 1984: 2nd Qtr. 1983-1st Qtr. 1984 (D).

R4105–12   CAPITAL APPROPRIATIONS and Capital Investment and Supply Conditions
Quarterly.   Approx. 10 p.
SRI/MF/complete

Quarterly report on manufacturing industry capital appropriations and expenditures, and on manufacturers' assessments of capital investment levels, need for external capital funds, and external supply shortages.

Data are from Conference Board quarterly surveys of 1,000 large manufacturers. Surveys are conducted the month following each quarter. Report is issued approximately 3 months after quarter of coverage.

Contains 1 trend chart, occasional summary tables, and 2 sections with narrative analysis and 10 quarterly tables listed below.

Availability: Conference Board, 845 Third Ave., New York NY 10022, price on request; SRI/MF/complete.

Issues reviewed during 1984: 3rd Qtr. 1983-2nd Qtr. 1984 (D).

QUARTERLY TABLES:

APPROPRIATIONS AND EXPENDITURES
[Most tables show data for all manufacturing and by durable and nondurable goods industry sectors, with selected totals for all manufactur-

ing excluding petroleum. Tables 1-2 show data in seasonally adjusted current and constant dollars.]

1. Percent changes in capital appropriations and expenditures [quarterly for current and 2 previous quarters, and current quarter compared to same quarter of previous year].

2. Capital appropriations and expenditures [including appropriation backlogs, new approvals, and cancellations; for current and 3 previous quarters].

3. Proportion of appropriations for plant [percent for current and 8-9 previous quarters].

4. Percent change in capital appropriations and expenditures [for all manufacturing, all manufacturing except petroleum, durable and nondurable goods, and petroleum and other nondurable goods; actual for previous 1-2 years, expected for coming year, and/or estimated for current year].

5. Capital appropriations and expenditures, annual totals [for previous 3-4 years].

CAPITAL INVESTMENT AND SUPPLY CONDITIONS
[Tables show percent distribution of responses for all manufacturing and for durable and nondurable goods. Most tables show responses for current and 9 previous survey months.]

1. Adequacy of capital facilities [inadequate, sufficient, or more than adequate].

2. Change in capital facilities expected from current spending programs [expansion, no change, or reduction].

3. External supply shortages [raw materials, processed goods, or both].

4. Anticipated sources of funds for capital expenditures [internal and external sources, for 9-10 half-year periods, through 1st or 2nd half of coming year].

5. Availability of external capital funds compared with 3 months earlier [easier, same, or tighter].

R4105–14   ANNOUNCEMENTS OF FOREIGN INVESTMENT IN U.S. MANUFACTURING INDUSTRIES
Quarterly.   Approx. 4 p.
SRI/MF/complete

Final issues of quarterly tabular listing of recent foreign capital investments in U.S. manufacturing firms, by industry group. Shows name and country of investing firm; nature of investment; and, as available, amount invested and employment.

Data are compiled from selected business and financial reports, and *Sales Prospector.*

Publication of the report was discontinued after the issue for 4th quarter 1983.

Availability: Conference Board, Investment Data Department, 845 Third Ave., New York NY 10022, associates $40.00 per yr., others $60.00 per yr.; SRI/MF/complete.

Issues reviewed during 1984: 1st-4th Qtrs. 1983 (D).

R4105–17   WORLDBUSINESS PERSPECTIVES

Series. For individual publication data, see below.
ISSN 0084-1455. LC 77-252.
SRI/MF/complete

Series of bimonthly and occasional special reports discussing issues and developments in world business, trade, and financial markets. Data are compiled by the Conference Board from original surveys and research, private financial publications, and Federal agency reports.

Each report focuses on a specific subject, including semiannual (June and Dec.) reports on U.S. manufacturers' foreign capital investment intentions; and recurring reports on implications of U.S. balance of trade position and activities of U.S. multinational corporations.

Reports reviewed during 1984 are described below.

Availability: Conference Board, 845 Third Ave., New York NY 10022, price on request; SRI/MF/complete.

R4105–17.25: International Trade in Services: A Growing Force in the World Economy

[Monograph. Oct. 1983. 4 p. No. 75. SRI/MF/complete.]

Report on international trade in services, including investment income, travel and transportation, fees and royalties, military transfers, and other services. Data are from Commerce Dept.

Includes 1 chart showing receipts and payments for U.S. service transactions, 1972 and 1982.

R4105–17.26: Bankers View Export Trading Companies

[Monograph. Nov. 1983. 4 p. No. 76. SRI/MF/complete.]

Special report, with some text data, on bank participation in export trading as permitted under provisions of the Export Trading Company Act of 1982.

Report is based on 160 responses to a Bank Administration Institute/Conference Board survey conducted Aug. 1983.

R4105–17.27: Foreign Capital Expenditures by U.S. Companies: Upturn in 1984

[Semiannual. Dec. 1983. 2 p. No. 77. SRI/MF/complete.]

Semiannual report on a survey of U.S. manufacturing company capital spending plans for foreign affiliates in 1984, as of Oct. 1983. Data are based on responses of 241 companies to an Oct. 1983 Conference Board survey, and include comparisons to previous surveys. Includes 3 charts showing respondents anticipating more, less, or same level of spending.

R4105–17.28: Foreign Investment in the U.S.: A Tentative Upswing

[Annual. Feb. 1984. 4 p. No. 78. SRI/MF/complete.]

Annual report on direct investment in U.S. by foreign manufacturers. Includes text data and 4 charts showing investment trends, including number of foreign investments in U.S. manufacturing industries, 1983.

R4105–17.29: U.S. Foreign Trade in 1983: Spilling Red Ink

[Annual. Apr. 1984. 4 p. No. 79. SRI/MF/complete.]

Annual report analyzing selected measures of U.S. trade balance. Includes 2 tables showing trade balance expressed as f.a.s. (value of imports at port of exportation) and as c.i.f. (value of imports including all expenses incurred during delivery), 1974-83; and U.S. foreign trade value, and 10 leading trading partners ranked by share of total U.S. imports and exports, 1983.

R4105–17.30: Foreign Capital Expenditures by U.S. Companies: Reaching for a New Peak

[Semiannual. June 1984. 2 p. No. 80. SRI/MF/complete.]

Semiannual report on a survey of U.S. manufacturing company capital spending plans for foreign affiliates in 1984, as of Apr. 1984. Data are based on responses of 247 companies to an Apr. 1984 Conference Board survey, and include comparisons to previous surveys. Includes 3 charts showing respondents anticipating more, less, or same level of spending.

R4105–17.31: Productivity in Manufacturing: A New Country Alignment?

[Monograph. Aug. 1984. 4 p. No. 81. SRI/MF/complete.]

Report analyzing manufacturing productivity trends in industrial countries. Includes 2 tables showing trends in output per employee hour for 7 countries, various periods 1950-83.

R4105–19   TOP EXECUTIVE COMPENSATION, 1983 Edition

Annual. 1983. vi+66 p.
Rpt. No. 840.
ISBN 0-8237-0280-4.
LC 73-151220.
SRI/MF/complete

Annual report, by Harland Fox, on compensation of top executive positions in manufacturing, retail trade, gas/electric utilities, commercial banking, insurance, and construction, 1982, with trends from 1973. Covers total compensation, base salary, and bonus awards, shown generally as median and/or as middle 50% range, often with regression analyses relating sales volume or comparable business measures to compensation levels.

Data are shown for each of 5 highest paid positions in each industry division. Manufacturing industry data include further detail by major industry group.

Also presents data on use of various incentives, including restricted stock, long-term performance, and stock option plans.

Data are from a 1982 survey of 1,155 companies.

Contains contents listing (p. ii-iii); highlights and report rationale (p. iv-vi); and survey report in 8 chapters, with narrative analysis, 37 charts, and 105 tables (p. 1-66).

This is the 21st survey report; previous surveys were conducted biennially.

Availability: Conference Board, 845 Third Ave., New York NY 10022, associates $25.00, others $125.00; SRI/MF/complete.

R4105–29   RESEARCH BULLETIN

Series. For individual publication data, see below.
SRI/MF/complete

Continuing series of reports on topics relevant to corporate management, including aspects of domestic and international economic development. Each report covers one topic.

Reports generally summarize Conference Board surveys and forums. SRI describes only those reports containing substantial statistics.

Reports reviewed during 1984 are described below.

Availability: Conference Board, 845 Third Ave., New York NY 10022, price on request; SRI/MF/complete.

R4105–29.29: Corporate Social Programs: Nontraditional Assistance

[Monograph. 1983. 11 p. No. 146. SRI/MF/complete.]

By Anne Klepper. Report on corporate nontraditional social assistance (financial and other donations not deductible for tax purposes). Data are based on survey responses of 62 companies with 1981 tax-deductible charitable contributions totalling approximately $450 million (about one-third of all corporate contributions), and nontraditional assistance valued at $136 million.

Includes 3 tables ranking individual unnamed companies' tax-deductible contribution budgets, and tax-deductible contributions and nontraditional assistance as percents of pretax net income; and showing total value of nontraditional assistance, by type; 1981.

R4105–29.30: Repurchasing Common Stock

[Monograph. 1983. 15 p. No. 147. SRI/MF/complete.]

By Francis A. Lees. Report on stock repurchase practices among NYSE-listed companies. Covers companies' repurchase of their own common stock for purposes other than converting the company to private ownership. Includes both direct repurchases, and indirect repurchases through employee benefit plans.

Presents survey data on repurchase strategy, objectives, and success in meeting objectives; trend in shares repurchased, 1978-82; method of acquiring shares; and types of employee plans involved in repurchases.

Also includes data on total NYSE companies reporting repurchases for any reason, number purchasing 100,000/more and 1 million/more shares, total shares acquired, and identity and purchase size for largest repurchaser, 1973 and 1980-82; and distribution of companies by percent of own capital stock held in company treasury, 1981.

Data are from NYSE; and from survey responses of 134 companies with direct repurchases of 100,000/more shares in 1981, or with indirect repurchases.

Includes text data and 5 tables.

R4105–29.31: International Outlook, 1984

[Annual. 1983. 12 p. No. 149. SRI/MF/complete.]

Annual report, by John Hein, on 1984 world economic outlook as forecast by 12 corporate analysts responding to a 1983 Conference Board survey. Data are primarily from OECD and the surveyed analysts.

Includes 2 tables showing real GNP and GNP deflator change rates forecast by OECD for member countries; and panelists' forecasts for changes in real GNP and consumer prices for 12 small industrial and major developing countries; various periods 1983-84.

This is the 8th annual report.

R4105-29.32: Labor Outlook, 1984
[Annual. 1983. 15 p. No. 150. SRI/MF/complete.]

Annual report, by Audrey Freedman et al., on employment and wage/benefit outlook for 1984, presenting opinions of participants in the Conference Board Labor Outlook Panel, convened Nov. 3, 1983. The 9 panel members are primarily corporate employee-relations executives and labor union leaders.

Includes 1 table showing panelists' forecasts (median and range) of quarterly unemployment rate, and of percent increase in CPI, wage/benefits during 1st year of major labor settlements, average hourly earnings, and manufacturing labor costs per output unit, 1984.

Also includes list of selected major union contract expirations, identifying company, union, and industry, Jan.-Oct. 1984; and brief insert article with 1 table showing survey findings of 5 consulting firms on corporate percent salary increase in 1983 and planned for 1984.

R4105-29.33: Economic Outlook, 1984
[Annual. 1983. 21 p. No. 151. SRI/MF/complete.]

Annual compilation of articles examining U.S. economic trends and outlook. Articles were prepared by participants in the Conference Board Economic Forum, convened Nov. 10, 1983. Includes 4 trend charts, and 3 tables showing the following:

a. General economic indicators: GNP; implicit price and industrial production indexes; CPI; PPI; unemploymnet rate; personal consumption expenditures and private domestic investment, by category; net exports; personal income and corporate profits, by component; physical output value; and general price index; 1982-84.

b. National budget outlay distribution for defense, interest payments, social security/railroad retirement, Medicare, and other purposes; and off-budget outlays; selected years 1972-88.

R4105-29.34: Business Leaders' Views on Protectionism in Western Europe
[Monograph. 1984. 13 p. No. 145. SRI/MF/complete.]

By Josef Adamek. Report on European business opinions concerning outlook for protectionist trade policies. Data are from responses of 90 companies (most based in EC and European Free Trade Assn countries) to a Conference Board survey.

Includes 4 tables showing opinion on circumstances justifying protectionism, and appropriate time limits for protective measures in each circumstance; preferred protective measures, and measures to counter protectionism; protective measures with greatest effect on own company; and desirability and likelihood of free trade worldwide and in selected regions.

R4105-29.35: Measuring Business Performance
[Monograph. 1984. 15 p. No. 153. SRI/MF/complete.]

By Francis J. Walsh, Jr. Report on executives' use of company financial indicators in formulating policy. Data are from responses of 101 high-level executives of major companies to a Conference Board survey.

Includes text data and 4 tables, primarily showing types of decision-making situations in which various financial ratios and other indicators are used; perceived importance of each indicator; indicators for which inflation adjustments are made; external sources of financial information; and views on whether use of financial indicators fosters short-term thinking. Most data are shown separately for chief executive officers and other executives.

R4105-29.36: U.S. Regional Economies: An Updated View of 1983-84
[Annual. 1984. 13 p. No. 154. SRI/MF/complete.]

Annual compilation of articles updating regional economic trends and outlook as originally presented in *U.S. Regional Outlook, 1983-84*. Articles were prepared by participants in the Conference Board Regional Economic Forum, held in Feb. 1983. Includes 5 tables presenting selected economic indicators for each region, various periods 1979-83.

For description of *U.S. Regional Outlook, 1983-84*, see SRI 1983 Annual, under R4105-29.25.

R4105-29.37: Hiring Teens for Summer Work
[Monograph. 1984. 7 p. No. 152. SRI/MF/complete.]

By Nathan Weber. Report on private sector involvement in summer youth employment programs, 1983. Data are from BLS, and a Conference Board review of programs coordinated by the private sector in 14 cities.

Includes 1 table showing the following for each city: youth unemployment, 1981-82; and job goals, placements in private and public sector, and number of corporate participants, for private summer youth employment programs, 1982-83.

For description of a similar report for 1982, see SRI 1983 Annual, under R4105-29.26.

R4105-29.38: Pay and Performance: The Interaction of Compensation and Performance Appraisal
[Monograph. 1984. 23 p. No. 155. SRI/MF/complete.]

By Charles Peck. Report on corporate practices and policies regarding performance-based compensation programs for exempt salaried employees. Data are from responses of 557 corporate compensation executives to a Conference Board survey of manufacturing, banking, insurance, and diversified financial companies.

Includes 26 tables showing survey sample characteristics; and survey response for the following, often shown separately for each surveyed industry:

a. Compensation program objectives; success of performance-based programs; use of formal salary structures and of separate struc-

tures for exempt and non-exempt employees; and job evaluation systems used.

b. Prevalence of merit, general, and cost-of-living salary policies for exempt employees, with detail for merit policies; use of bonuses and other nonsalary compensation; types and objectives of performance appraisal methods; and problems encountered in administering performance based programs.

R4105-29.39: Dollar and U.S. Exports: Some Qs and As
[Monograph. 1984. 13 p. No. 158. SRI/MF/complete.]

By John Hein. Report analyzing U.S. trade situation and factors affecting exports. Data are from Dept of Commerce, the Conference Board, and other private and governmental sources.

Includes 4 tables showing U.S. trade balance, GNP, and net exports; share of industrial country total and manufacturing exports for 5 countries, and U.S. share of industrial country GNP; U.S. exports to Latin America by commodity and for 4 major importing countries; and OPEC total imports and imports from the U.S.; various periods 1970-83.

R4105-29.40: U.S. Regional Outlook, 1984-85
[Annual. 1984. 21 p. No. 161. SRI/MF/complete.]

Annual compilation of articles examining regional economic trends and outlook. Articles were prepared by participants in the Conference Board Regional Economic Forum, held in Feb. 1984.

Includes 8 tables showing selected economic indicators for individual regions, with some comparison to total U.S., various periods 1970-84.

For description of previous report, see SRI 1983 Annual, under R4105-29.25.

R4105-29.41: Restricted Stock for Executives
[Monograph. 1984. 9 p. No. 159. SRI/MF/complete.]

By Harland Fox. Report on use of restricted stock awards in incentive programs for top executives and middle management. Restricted stock cannot be sold or transferred, and must be surrendered if employment is terminated, during a specified restriction period. Data are based on May 1983 survey responses of 91 companies with restricted stock programs.

Includes text data and 6 tables showing the following:

a. Total companies, and number with restricted stock award plans, by industry division.

b. Top executives: restricted stock award plans, by number of participants, salary range of lowest paid recipient, and size of award as percent of salary for highest, average, and lowest paid recipient, with median and middle range salaries and awards; and award plans and partial vesting schedules, by length of restriction period.

c. Middle management: awards, number of persons eligible, salary of lowest and highest paid eligible person, award median and range as percent of salary, years for full vesting, and partial vesting schedules, for 9-14 unnamed companies with middle management award plans.

R4105–29.42: Disclosure of Business Data: Technological and Regulatory Trends

[Monograph. 1984. 21 p. No. 164. SRI/MF/ complete.]

By Nathan Weber. Report examining effect of computer technology and government deregulation on access to business information.

Data are based on survey responses of 403 investor relations executives in companies with $50 million/over in sales, 116 registered representatives of brokerage houses, and 75 security analysts.

Includes 1 chart and 6 tables showing security analysts' use of computers for various purposes, and views on relative importance of various types of company-released information; trends in establishment of corporate investor-relations programs, purposes of such programs, and personnel responsible; company vs. personal ownership of computer equipment used in business; and corporate reasons for wanting to know shareholders' identities.

R4105–29.43: Managing Capital Investments

[Monograph. 1984. 31 p. No. 165. SRI/MF/ complete.]

By Patrick J. Davey. Report on corporate planning and management of capital expenditures. Data are based on responses of 95 manufacturing and 30 nonmanufacturing companies to a 1984 Conference Board survey.

Includes 5 tables primarily showing survey response on financial analysis techniques used in planning capital expenditures.

Also includes a tabular summary of capital expenditure authority structures at responding companies, grouped by industry and capital budget size. Companies are identified by letter code only.

R4105–33   OPERATING FOREIGN SUBSIDIARIES: How Independent Can They Be?

Monograph. 1983. ix+38 p.
Rpt. No. 836.
ISBN 0-8237-0276-6.
SRI/MF/complete

By Ronald E. Berenbeim. Survey report on corporate management of foreign subsidiaries, 1983. Covers local managers' decisionmaking authority, by type of activity; types of demands made by governments and other interests in host countries, company response to host country demands, and countries in which demands are most frequent; and local managers' autonomy, by country.

Data are based on 109 responses to a 1983 survey of U.S., Canadian, and European corporations with at least 20% foreign sales and 1 foreign subsidiary.

Contains contents and table listings, and highlights (p. iii-ix); narrative report in 5 chapters, interspersed with 2 charts and 13 tables (p. 1-33); and appendix, with narrative and 2 tables (p. 36-38).

Availability: Conference Board, 845 Third Ave., New York NY 10022, price on request; SRI/MF/complete.

R4105–35   ORGANIZING CORPORATE MARKETING

Monograph. 1984. ix+53 p.
Rpt. No. 845.
ISBN 0-8237-0286-3.
SRI/MF/complete

By David S. Hopkins and Earl L. Bailey. Survey report on the structure of marketing functions in multibusiness manufacturing companies. Covers presence and role of chief marketing executive, with detail by selected company characteristics; organizational level at which specific marketing activities are carried out; and organization and role of marketing research unit.

Also includes data on degree and nature of relatedness among company businesses; and sources of company strength, by degree of business relatedness.

Data are based on responses of 294 executives to a Conference Board survey.

Contains listings of contents, tables, and charts, and narrative highlights and foreword (p. iii-ix); report in 5 chapters, with 2 charts and 22 tables (p. 1-47); and 3 appendices, including 6 tables (p. 48-53).

Availability: Conference Board, 845 Third Ave., New York NY 10022, price on request; SRI/MF/complete.

R4105–36   MANAGING BUSINESS-STATE GOVERNMENT RELATIONS

Monograph. 1983. ix+59 p.
Rpt. No. 838.
ISBN 0-8237-0278-2.
SRI/MF/complete

By Seymour Lusterman. Survey report on corporate policies and practices regarding relations with State governments. Includes data on extent of State-relations involvement (direct activity, reliance on trade assns/other organizations, no activity); needed improvements in State-relations programs; key issues addressed by programs in 1981/82; perceived effectiveness of general business organizations and trade assns; use of State relations specialists; and time spent on State relations.

Also includes ranking of States by concentration of corporate State-relations activity, 1981/ 82; and proportion of Political Action Committee contributions going to State office candidates, 1980.

Selected data are shown by industry division, with detail for aggregate top 200-250 and top 50 companies.

Data sources include 253 responses to a Conference Board survey of large companies, interviews with trade assn/business organization officials, company materials, and published articles/reports.

Contains listings of contents, tables, and charts (p. iii-v); highlights, with 1 table (p. vii-ix); 6 chapters, with narrative analysis, 5 charts, and 11 tables (p. 1-52); and appendix presenting sample job descriptions of State relations specialists (p. 53-59).

Availability: Conference Board, 845 Third Ave., New York NY 10022, price on request; SRI/MF/complete.

R4105–37   BUSINESS EXECUTIVES' EXPECTATIONS

Quarterly. Approx. 2 p.
SRI/MF/complete

Quarterly report on chief executive officers' expectations concerning the general economy and conditions in their own industries. Data are based on Conference Board surveys conducted in the 2nd month of each quarter. Report is issued in month following quarter of coverage.

Contents:

a. Narrative summary and 4 trend charts.

b. Quarterly table showing executives' assessment of current conditions compared with 6 months ago, and expectations 6 months ahead, for the general economy and for their own industries (by industry division and major manufacturing group); and overall measure of business confidence; all for current and 5-13 previous quarters.

c. 1-4 other tables covering a different survey topic each quarter, with updates appearing annually.

Quarterly table appears in all issues. Other tables are described, as they appear, under "Statistical Features."

Report has been published since 1977. SRI coverage begins with 3rd quarter 1983 issue.

Availability: Conference Board, 845 Third Ave., New York NY 10022, price on request; SRI/MF/complete.

Issues reviewed during 1984: 3rd Qtr. 1983-3rd Qtr. 1984 (D).

STATISTICAL FEATURES:

R4105–37.501: 3rd Qtr. 1983

SELLING PRICE EXPECTATIONS, ANNUAL FEATURE

Two annual tables showing chief executives' expectations for selling prices (drop, no change, or rise faster, slower, or at same rate) during coming year, by industry division, as of 3rd quarter 1982-83. Data are from Conference Board surveys.

R4105–37.502: 4th Qtr. 1983

PROFIT EXPECTATIONS, ANNUAL FEATURE

Annual table showing chief executives' expectations for profits (substantially better or worse, moderately better, or same) during coming year, as of 4th quarter 1976-83. Data are from Conference Board surveys.

R4105–37.503: 1st Qtr. 1984

EMPLOYMENT EXPECTATIONS, ANNUAL FEATURE

Two annual tables showing chief executives' expectations for employment in their own industries during current year, as of 1st quarter 1978-84. Tables show expected trend in employment (no change, and up or down 1-3% or 3%/more); and expected difficulty finding qualified employees, for all industries and in manufacturing. Data are from Conference Board surveys.

R4105–37.504: 2nd Qtr. 1984

CAPITAL INVESTMENT PROGRAMS, ANNUAL FEATURE

Two annual tables showing distribution of companies by level of change in capital investment programs since Jan. 1 (no change, and increase or decrease of more or less than 10%), for all industries, and for manufacturing, mining/construction/transport/utilities, and other nonmanufacturing industries, as of 2nd quarter 1982-84. Data are from Conference Board surveys.

R4105–37.505: 3rd Qtr. 1984
SELLING PRICE EXPECTATIONS, ANNUAL FEATURE

Four annual tables showing chief executives' expectations for selling prices (drop, no change, or rise faster, slower, or at same rate) during coming year, by industry division, as of 3rd quarter 1983-84. Data are from Conference Board surveys.

For description of tables for 3rd quarter 1982-83, see R4105-37 above.

R4105–38   CENTRALLY PLANNED ECONOMIES: Economic Overview, 1983
Annual. June 1983. 63 p.
Rpt. No. 841.
SRI/MF/complete

Annual report, by Josef Adamek, presenting an overview of economic development in centrally planned economies (CPEs), by country, generally for 1982, with some trends from 1975.

Covers population, land area, total and per capita GNP, military expenditures, and military share of GDP, by CPE country.

Also includes foreign trade and balance of payments data, national income growth rate, level and productivity of investment, and free market vs. official exchange rates, for selected CPEs; aggregate CPE foreign trade and GDP; value of arms deliveries from Soviet Union and Eastern Europe; and Soviet Union natural gas exports to OECD, by destination country.

Some data include comparisons by continent, and with other economic systems or country groups.

Data are from various intergovernmental organizations, U.S. Federal agencies, and private sources.

Contains contents listing, foreword, and list of abbreviations (p. 3-6); 5 chapters, with narrative sections and text data on each country, and 19 interspersed tables (p. 7-57); and 4 appendices, with definitions and listings of tables, sources, and official country names (p. 59-63).

This is the 1st annual edition of the report.
Availability: Conference Board, 845 Third Ave., New York NY 10022, price on request; SRI/MF/complete.

R4105–39   ECONOMIC OVERVIEW 1984: Medium Term Corporate Forecasts
Annual. 1984. 46 p.
Rpt. No. 846.
SRI/MF/complete

Annual report, by Frank Wittendal, presenting forecasts of comparable economic indicators for U.S., Canada, Mexico, Japan, and 14 Western European countries, 1980s.

For some indicators, data are forecasts based on a Conference Board survey of 350 corporate economists, and are shown for 1982-87. For other indicators, data are 1984 forecasts by 2 or more banks or other forecasting organizations,

with comparisons to 1982 actual values and 1983 estimates. For a few indicators, both survey-based and organizational forecasts are presented. Most forecasts are as of year end 1983.

Covers all or most of the following indicators for each country: GDP/GNP; public and private fixed investment; investment in machinery/equipment and construction or housing; public and private consumption; imports and exports; CPI; balance of payments on current account (amount and as percent of GNP); currency exchange rate vs. U.S. dollar; industrial production; productivity; total wage bill per employee; and unemployment rate.

Forecasts are expressed as actual values for balance of payments, exchange rate, and unemployment rate, and as percent change from previous year for other indicators.

Also includes comparison of year end 1983 and year end 1982 survey-based forecasts, for GNP/GDP and inflation rates.

Contains contents listing, summary table, and introduction (p. 2-7); country overviews, each with narrative analysis and 2 tables (p. 8-43); and list of forecasting organizations and contributors (p. 44-46).

This is the 7th edition of the report; SRI coverage begins with this edition.
Availability: Conference Board, 845 Third Ave., New York NY 10022, price on request; SRI/MF/complete.

R4105–40   ADAPTING PRODUCTS FOR EXPORT
Monograph. 1983. vii+40 p.
Rpt. No. 835.
ISBN 0-8237-0275-8.
SRI/MF/complete

By Virginia M. Yorio. Report on factors affecting corporate decisions to adapt products for export, with analysis of organizational structures involved in adaptation decisions.

Includes data on prevalence of centralization for export and other international activities in companies with overall divisional organization; position or group responsible for decision to adapt products for export; and involvement of functional executives when adaptation decision rests with a committee.

Data are from responses of over 200 companies to a Conference Board survey. Survey period is not specified.

Contains listings of contents, tables, and charts (p. iii-iv); highlights, methodology, and preface (p. v-vii); and narrative report, interspersed with several charts and evaluation form facsimiles, and 3 tables (p. 1-40).
Availability: Conference Board, 845 Third Ave., New York NY 10022, price on request; SRI/MF/complete.

R4500
East-West Center: East-West Population Institute

R4500–1   PAPERS OF THE EAST-WEST POPULATION INSTITUTE
Series. For individual publication data, see below.
ISSN 0732-0531.
SRI/MF/complete

Continuing series of reports on economic, social, psychological, and environmental aspects of population in Asian and Pacific countries and the U.S.

Reports are based on original field studies sponsored by the Institute, the UN, individual countries, and U.S. agencies and universities.

Most reports include contents listing, summary, narrative analysis, and bibliography.

Reports are usually statistical but occasionally consist of narrative analyses only. All reports are described in SRI. Reports reviewed during 1984 are described below.
Availability: East-West Center: East-West Population Institute, Publications Office, 1777 East-West Rd., Honolulu HI 96848, $12.00 per yr., single copies † to those engaged in demographic research or programs, single copies for others vary in price according to length; SRI/MF/complete.

R4500–1.28: Influences on Childbearing Intentions Across the Fertility Career: Demographic and Socioeconomic Factors and the Value of Children
[Monograph. June 1983. ix+153 p. No. 60-F. $3.00. ISBN 0-86638-043-4. LC 83-11639. SRI/MF/complete.]

By Rodolfo A. Bulatao and James T. Fawcett. Sixth in a continuing subseries of papers on the Value of Children project analyzing determinants of childbearing intentions. Data are from 1975-76 surveys of 1,000-3,000 married women of childbearing age and 250-750 of their husbands in the U.S., Philippines, Turkey, Indonesia, South Korea, Taiwan, and Singapore.

Includes 16 tables showing results of regression analyses correlating men's and women's childbearing intentions with approximately 40 factors, including sociodemographic characteristics, actual and ideal family size and gender composition, and views on advantages and disadvantages of having children.

Data are shown by country.

R4500–1.29: Effects of Induced Abortion on Subsequent Reproductive Function and Pregnancy Outcome: Hawaii
[Monograph. June 1983. xi+144 p. No. 86. $3.00. ISBN 0-86638-046-9. LC 83-11536. SRI/MF/complete.]

By Chin Sik Chung et al. Report comparing pregnancy outcomes for women with and without history of induced abortion. Data are from a 1971-78 study of Hawaii vital statistics records covering subsequent pregnancy outcomes for 3,910 women who had undergone induced abortion during 1970-74, and outcomes for 98,046 women with no abortion history.

Includes 99 tables showing sociodemographic characteristics of the 2 groups; and study results presented as actual incidence and/or multivariate, regression, and risk analyses, for the following outcomes: premature birth, selected pregnancy and labor complications including ectopic pregnancy, spontaneous fetal loss by gestational period, low birth weight, congenital malformations, and infant death.

Data are shown variously by race (white, Hawaiian, Filipino, Oriental, and other), age, marital status, number of previous births and/or abortions, and method and complications of previous abortion.

Also includes data on abortions by month, and elective and therapeutic abortions, 1970-74.

R4500–1.30: Population Mobility and Wealth Transfers in Indonesia and Other Third World Societies

[Monograph. July 1983. v+50 p. No. 87. $2.00. ISBN 0-86638-045-0. LC 83-14008. SRI/MF/complete.]

By Graeme J. Hugo. Report on the flow of wealth between urban workers and their rural families in developing countries. Data are primarily from a survey of 1,067 West Javanese (Indonesian) households, conducted July 1972-June 1973.

Includes 2 tables showing annual rural household income (mean and range), including value of goods/money from urban workers, for households supported by commuters, permanent migrants, and migrants who return to rural households, with comparison to households without urban workers.

R4500–1.31: Structural Change and Prospects for Urbanization in Asian Countries

[Monograph. Aug. 1983. v+46 p.+erratum. No. 88. $1.75. ISBN 0-86638-047-7. LC 83-16373. SRI/MF/complete.]

By Gavin W. Jones. Report on impact of rural and industrial employment patterns on urbanization trends in Asia, with comparisons to other world areas, various years 1901-81. Data sources include UN, independent researchers, and national censuses. Includes 6 tables showing the following:

a. Urban population as percent of total population, various years 1901-81; and total urban population, 1980 or 1981; for 11 Asian countries.

b. Labor force in industry and agriculture compared to population in urban areas; and distribution of urban and rural labor force, by occupational category; all by world area or for selected Asian countries, various years 1946-80.

R4500–1.32: Urban Growth and Local Taxes in Less Developed Countries

[Monograph. Sept. 1983. v+33 p. No. 89. $1.25. ISBN 0-86638-050-7. LC 83-16427. SRI/MF/complete.]

By Roy Bahl et al. Report analyzing the potential impact of rapid urbanization on tax revenues of developing countries. Data are from World Bank and independent researchers.

Includes 2 tables showing population and auto registration growth rates, 1960-70 period; and revenues from automotive taxes as percent

of urban road expenditures, various unspecified periods 1970-73; all for 8-16 cities in developing countries.

R4500–1.33: False Fertility Transition: The Case of American Blacks

[Monograph. Feb. 1984. vii+81 p. No. 90. $2.50. ISBN 0-86638-054-X. LC 84-1666. SRI/MF/complete.]

By Paul Wright and Peter Pirie. Report examining the impact of venereal disease on fertility trends for U.S. blacks. Data are from the Federal Government and various private studies, and are shown for various periods 1905-1957.

Includes 6 tables showing the following:

a. Age-specific fertility rates for blacks in rural Mississippi and in Malaya; venereal disease rates among World War I servicemen, and blacks as percent of population, for 6 southern States; and admission rates for venereal disease treatment for World War I servicemen stationed in U.S. and Europe, by race. (p. 13, 27-28)

b. Fertility rates, child-to-woman ratios, and age-specific birth rates, by syphilis incidence rate group, for blacks in a 6-State southern region; and average number of children born, and percent with no children, for wives of farm operators and laborers by race, in 2 selected age groups. (p. 48-49, 67)

R4500–1.34: Old-Age Economic Security Value of Children in the Philippines and Taiwan

[Monograph. Mar. 1984. vii+72 p. No. 60-G. $3.00. ISBN 0-86638-056-6. LC 84-6081. SRI/MF/complete.]

By Susan De Vos. Seventh in a continuing subseries of papers on the Value of Children project analyzing determinants of childbearing intentions. Data are from 1975-76 surveys of over 3,000 married women in the Philippines and Taiwan, and a subset of their husbands and mothers-in-law.

Includes 19 tables showing percent of respondents mentioning old-age support as an advantage of having children, and support expectations by selected sociodemographic characteristics and family attitudes, including desired family size and child gender preference.

Tables also show regression analyses interrelating variables described above, and estimating the effect of a hypothetical government pension on the relationship between support expectations and gender preference.

R4800
Editorial
Projects in Education

R4800–2   EDUCATION WEEK
Weekly. Approx. 25 p.
Oversized.
ISSN 0277-4232.
LC SN 81-1539.
SRI/MF/excerpts, shipped quarterly

Weekly journal (issued 42 times per year) reporting on developments in elementary/secondary education. Covers public and private schools; regular, special, vocational, and adult education programs; and, in less detail, higher education.

Data are primarily from NCES, other Federal agencies, and professional assns.

Issues generally contain numerous news and feature articles, occasionally with substantial statistics; and regular departmental features, including "Databank" statistical section usually with several tables and/or charts on such topics as educational enrollment, finance, and staffing.

Features with substantial statistical content are described, as they appear, under "Statistical Features." Each issue of the journal is reviewed, but an abstract is published in SRI monthly issues only when statistical features appear.

Journal suspends publication during 1st week in Jan., last week in June through 2nd week in Aug., and last 2 weeks of Dec.

Availability: Education Week, PO Box 1939, Marion OH 43305, $39.94 per yr., back issues $2.00; SRI/MF/excerpts for all portions covered under "Statistical Features;" shipped quarterly.

Issues reviewed during 1984: Nov. 2, 1983-Oct. 31, 1984 (P) (Vol. III, Nos. 9-41/42; Vol. IV, Nos. 1-9).

STATISTICAL FEATURES:

R4800–2.501: Nov. 2, 1983 (Vol. III, No. 9)

DATABANK: U.S. EDUCATION BUDGET

(p. 14-15) Table showing Federal education appropriations by purpose, final FY83-84, and Administration, House, and Senate recommendations FY84.

Includes related article (p. 1, 14).

R4800–2.502: Nov. 23, 1983 (Vol. III, No. 12)

NIE ISSUES SCHOOL PRICE INDEX TO MEASURE EFFECTS OF INFLATION

(p. 14) By Thomas Toch. Article describing a school price index developed by National Institute of Education to measure inflation's impact on school budgets.

Includes 2 tables showing the following for public elementary/secondary schools: average daily attendance, and expenditures in current and constant 1975 dollars, 1975-81; and school price index and selected component indexes, 1975-82.

R4800–2.503: Dec. 14, 1983 (Vol. III, No. 14)

DATABANK: DROPOUT RATES OF HIGH SCHOOL STUDENTS

(p. 15) Brief article with text statistics and 2 tables showing 1980 high school sophomore dropout rates, with distribution by reason and most recent job, all by sex. Data are from an NCES 1980 survey and a 1982 follow-up survey.

R4800–2.504: Dec. 21, 1983 (Vol. III, No. 15)

GROWTH SEEN IN STATES' EDUCATION FUNDS

(p. 9) Article, with 1 table showing State education appropriations (total, per student, per capita, per $1,000 personal income, and as a percent of all expenditures), by State, academic year 1982/83 with percent change from 1977/78. Data are from *State Support for Education 1982-83* by Augenblick, Van de Water and Associates.

R4800–2.505: Jan. 11, 1984 (Vol. III, No. 16)

FEDERAL EDUCATION FUNDS FOR STATES STABLE, STUDY FINDS

(p. 12) By Cindy Currence. Article, with 1 table showing value of Federal grants-in-aid to State/local governments, for education, 11 other functions, and general purpose fiscal assistance, FY82-84. Data are from National Conference of State Legislatures, and National Governors' Assn Federal Funds Information for States System.

R4800–2.506: Jan. 18, 1984 (Vol. III, No. 17)

DATABANK: STATE EDUCATION STATISTICS

(p. 12-13) Table presenting the following education-related data by State, with State rankings, generally for 1972 and 1982:

a. Performance outcomes: American College Test or Scholastic Aptitude Test scores, with percent of high school seniors taking test; and high school graduation rate.

b. Resource inputs: pupil/teacher ratio, average teacher salary, Federal funds as percent of school revenues, and education expenditure per pupil and as percent of per capita income.

c. Population characteristics: per capita income, percent of 5-17 year olds in poverty, median educational attainment, and minority and handicapped students' percents of enrollment.

Data were compiled by Dept of Education and are from NCES, other Federal agencies, State education depts, and Educational Testing Service. Includes accompanying notes (p. 10-11)

R4800–2.507: Jan. 25, 1984 (Vol. III, No. 18)

EDUCATORS QUESTION JTPA STRATEGY

(p. 10, 15) By Susan G. Foster. Article on Job Training Partnership Act (JTPA) funding and project requirements. Data are from Dept of Labor.

Includes 1 table showing the following data by State and outlying territory: unemployment rate; JTPA Title II-A, II-B, and III allotments for training programs, summer jobs, and dislocated workers; and required matching funds; July 1984-June 1985.

R4800–2.508: Feb. 1, 1984 (Vol. III. No. 19)

SURVEY FINDS SIGNIFICANT CORPORATE INTEREST IN DONATIONS TO SCHOOLS

(p. 5) By Sheppard Ranbom. Article, with 1 table showing value of corporate support for precollege education institutions, by type of support (cash, equipment, and matching gifts) and type of institution (public and private elementary and secondary schools, and other organizations), 1982. Data are from a survey of 193 companies, conducted by the Council for Financial Aid to Education.

DATABANK: PROPOSED 1985 BUDGET FOR EDUCATION

(p. 12-13) Table showing Federal appropriations, FY83-84; and President's FY85 budget request; all by education function and program.

Table is accompanied by a related article (p. 1, 12).

R4800–2.509: Feb. 8, 1984 (Vol. III, No. 20)

APPROPRIATIONS FOR THE FEDERAL BILINGUAL EDUCATION PROGRAM

(p. 16) Chart showing Federal budget appropriations for bilingual education, FY69-84. Data are from Dept of Education.

Chart is accompanied by a related article (p. 1, 12-16).

DATABANK: AMERICAN COLLEGE FRESHMAN, FALL 1983, ANNUAL FEATURE

(p. 21-22) Annual compilation of 2 tables presenting data on college freshman characteristics, activities, and attitudes, based on a fall 1983 survey of over 254,000 freshmen at 489 2- and 4-year colleges. Data are from *American Freshman: National Norms for Fall 1983* (for description of full report, see U6215-1, below).

Tables show response distributions for questions on students' socioeconomic background; academic and career plans; methods of financing education; and work- and recreation-related activities, political views, attitudes on a variety of current issues, and personal objectives, with detail by sex and by type of school including Catholic, Protestant, and predominantly black colleges.

Includes accompanying article (p. 8).

R4800–2.510: Feb. 15, 1984 (Vol. III, No. 21)

DECLINE IN MARIJUANA USE REPORTED AMONG SENIORS

(p. 9) By Cindy Currence. Article, with 1 table showing high school seniors' use (ever and during last year) of illicit drugs by type, alcohol, and cigarettes, 1975-83. Data are from *Drugs and American High School Students, 1975-83,* based on annual surveys administered by the National Institute on Drug Abuse. The 1983 survey covered 16,000 seniors in 130 public and private schools.

SURVEY SHOWS 30 STATES HAVE ADOPTED TEACHER-COMPETENCY TESTS

(p. 12) By Charlie Euchner. Article, with 2 tables listing States with mandatory teacher competency testing programs enacted or planned/under discussion, as of 1983. Tables show program characteristics, and year of mandate, implementation, and/or initial planning. Data were compiled by J.T. Sandefur.

R4800–2.511: Feb. 22. 1984 (Vol. III, No. 22)

DATABANK: TEACHER SUPPLY/DEMAND BY FIELD AND REGION, ANNUAL FEATURE

(p. 10-11) Annual compilation of 3 tables presenting indexes of elementary/secondary teacher shortage/surplus, by instructional field, 1976 and 1979-84; and average salaries for beginning elementary/secondary and special education teachers with bachelor's and master's degrees, 1981/82-1983/84; most shown by region and for Alaska and Hawaii.

Data are from surveys of university teacher-placement officials conducted by Assn for School, College, and University Staffing. Current data are based on responses of 60 officials.

Tables are accompanied by a related article (p. 11, 17).

INCREASE FOUND IN HANDICAPPED PUPILS ENROLLED IN SPECIAL-EDUCATION CLASSES, ANNUAL FEATURE

(p. 13, 15) Annual article, by Susan G. Foster, on implementation of the Education for All Handicapped Children Act. Data are from an Education Dept report to Congress.

Includes 1 chart and 1 table showing enrollment of persons aged 3-21 in special education programs, by type of handicap by State (including outlying territories and Bureau of Indian Affairs); 1982/83, with summary comparison to 1976/77.

R4800–2.512: Feb. 29, 1984 (Vol. III, No. 23)

MAGNET SCHOOLS: THE NEW HOPE FOR VOLUNTARY DESEGREGATION

(p. 1, 15-16) By Peggy Caldwell. Article on the growth of urban high schools with district-wide open enrollment and theme-oriented curricula (magnet schools). Data are from James H. Lowry and Associates. Includes 1 chart showing number of school districts applying for and receiving Federal magnet school grants, under Emergency School Assistance Act and other programs, 1976/77-1981/82.

NUMBER OF U.S. PUBLIC SCHOOL SYSTEMS: 1939/40-1982/83

(p. 3) Chart showing number of public school systems, decennially 1939/40-1979/80 and 1982/83. Data are from NCES.

DATABANK: EDUCATION AND POLITICS: A SAMPLING OF PUBLIC OPINION

(p. 11) Compilation of 8 tables on public opinion regarding education and other national issues, and their importance for the 1984 elections. Data were compiled by Roper Center for Public Opinion Research from a variety of surveys primarily conducted during Dec. 1983.

Includes survey responses on perceived importance of education, school prayer, and other socioeconomic issues, and their impact on candidate selection; political party most able to handle major issues; level of confidence in selected social and economic institutions, including public schools; and whether progress has been made in solving public education problems.

R4800–2.513: Mar. 21, 1984 (Vol. III, No. 26)

DATABANK: PROJECTED HIGH-SCHOOL GRADUATES BY STATE

(p. 11) Table showing graduates from public or public/private high schools, by State, actual 1980/81, and projected for selected years 1983/84-1999/2000. Data are from a report of the Western Interstate Commission for Higher Education (WICHE).

Full WICHE report is covered in SRI under A9385-4.

R4800–2.514: Apr. 4, 1984 (Vol. III, No. 28)

STUDENTS' INTEREST IN EDUCATION, CAREERS FOUND TO BE INCREASING

(p. 8) By Alex Heard. Article on students' opinions and attitudes concerning various aspects of their own lives and of society in general. Data are from a 1983 survey of 1,500 students in grades 7-12, sponsored by National Assn of Secondary School Principals (NASSP).

Includes 7 tables showing survey response regarding most important world and national problems, reasons for liking school, participation in co-curricular activities, worst influences on young people, importance of selected courses, and career and life goals, with some detail by sex.

Full NASSP report, *Mood of American Youth,* is described under A7085-1, above.

R4800–2.515: Apr. 11, 1984 (Vol. III, No. 29)

DATABANK: ENROLLMENT IN PRIVATE SCHOOLS, 1970-82

(p. 15) Brief article on private education, with 4 tables showing the following:

a. Private elementary/secondary school enrollment and mean tuition, for all and church-related schools, by race and Spanish origin, family income, education of household head, and census region, 1982.

b. Percent of elementary/secondary students enrolled in private schools, by State and for 75 most populous cities; and private schools, students, and teachers, by academic level and whether religious affiliated, with detail for Catholic schools; various years 1970-80.

R4800–2.516: Apr. 18, 1984 (Vol. III, No. 30)

NUMBER OF COMPUTERS IN SCHOOLS DOUBLES

(p. 1, 14) By Thomas Toch. Article on computer use in elementary and secondary schools. Data are from Market Data Retrieval.

Includes 2 charts and 2 tables showing States ranked by percent of public schools using microcomputers, with number of students per computer by academic level of school; students per computer, by student poverty and urban-rural status and school size; and number of computers in schools, and school buildings with computers, by major brand, fall 1983.

R4800–2.517: Apr. 25, 1984 (Vol. III, No. 31)

SURVEY OF CATHOLIC SCHOOLS

(p. 11) Compilation of data profiling Catholic secondary education. Data are based on a Search Institute survey of 910 Catholic high school principals.

Includes text statistics on characteristics of school administration; teachers and students; academic, co-curricular, and religious education programs; computer use; operations, policies, and finances; parental involvement; and goals and perceived achievements.

CHAPTER 2 ALLOCATIONS FOR 1984/85

(p. 14) Table showing funding under Chapter 2 of the Educational Consolidation and Improvement Act of 1981, by State and territory, 1984/85. Data are from Dept of Education.

R4800–2.518: May 2, 1984 (Vol. III, No. 32)

CATHOLIC SCHOOLS ASKED TO 'INFUSE' STUDY OF PEACE INTO CURRICULUM

(p. 1, 17) By Cindy Currence. Article, with 4 undated tables showing the following for Catholic high schools: distribution of principals, administrators, and teachers by sex and religious vs. lay status; average graduation requirements, by discipline; prevalence of selected admissions policies; and course offerings and student participation, by subject.

Data are from National Catholic Educational Assn.

DATABANK: SCHOOLS 1983—STATISTICS FROM THE N.E.A.

(p. 11) Four tables showing elementary and secondary school teachers and average salary; and school revenues and expenditures per pupil; 1973/74-1983/84. Data are from National Education Assn (NEA) report, *Estimates of School Statistics, 1983/84.*

Full NEA report is covered in SRI under A7640-1.

R4800–2.519: May 9, 1984 (Vol. III, No. 33)

WIDE VARIATION FOUND IN TUITION RATES OF PUBLIC COLLEGES

(p. 10) By Sheppard Ranbom. Article, with 1 table showing public college appropriations and tuition per student, by State, 1983/84. Data are from National Institute of Education.

R4800–2.520: May 16, 1984 (Vol. III, No. 34)

SERVICE AREAS TO EXCEED HIGH-TECH IN JOB GROWTH

(p. 11) Article, with 3 tables showing employment 1982 and increase for 1982-95 period, average education 1980, and relative earnings 1979, for occupations with most job openings and with greatest increase in openings during 1982-95 period; and employment by industry division and occupational group, selected years 1900-95. Data are from Federal Government sources.

DATABANK: STUDENT AND STAFF PATTERNS IN 44 URBAN DISTRICTS

(p. 12) Table showing the following for elementary/secondary school systems in 44 large cities: population; instructional and administrative staff; enrollment, with distribution by race/ethnicity (including Asian/Pacific Islander, Hispanic, and Native American); and handicapped, vocational education, and bilingual pupils; 1980/81 or 1981/82. Data are from National School Board Assn.

Table title incorrectly reads "43 urban districts."

R4800–2.521: Aug. 22, 1984 (Vol. III, No. 39/40)

HOW TEACHER SALARIES COMPARE TO THOSE IN PRIVATE INDUSTRY OVER 10 YEARS

(p. 4) Chart showing average starting salary of teachers vs. 10 other occupations, 1974 and 1984. Data are from National Education Assn and U.S. Dept of Labor and Office of Personnel Management.

MOST TEACHERS SUPPORT SCHOOL REFORMS, SURVEY FINDS

(p. 14, 27) By Linda Chion-Kenney. Article examining teachers' opinions and attitudes concerning various aspects of their profession. Data are based on responses of 1,981 public elementary/secondary school teachers to a June 1984 Metropolitan Life Insurance Co. survey.

Includes 2 tables showing survey response concerning effects of proposed changes in educational system on quality of teaching and education, including changes in teacher certification and salaries, and in school curricula, discipline, graduation, and competency requirements.

PROBLEMS IN MATH, SCIENCE EDUCATION SPUR VARIED POLICY INITIATIVES

(p. 15) By Thomas Toch. Article, with 1 table showing average years of science and mathematics education taken by high school students who graduated in 1982, by students' sex, race-ethnicity (including Hispanic, American Indian, and Asian American), type of high school program, socioeconomic status, school type, educational aspirations, and census division. Data are from NCES.

R4800–2.522: Aug. 29, 1984 (Vol. III, No. 41/42)

SCHOOLING TO COST $240 BILLION IN 1984/85

(p. 1, 12) By James Hertling. Article, with 1 chart showing expenditures on public and private elementary/secondary and higher education, 1984/85. Data are from NCES.

SOURCES OF REVENUE FOR PUBLIC SCHOOL SUPPORT

(p. 3) Table showing public elementary/secondary school revenues from Federal, State, and local government, selected years 1919/20-1981/82. Data are from NCES.

R4800–2.523: Sept. 5, 1984 (Vol. IV, No. 1)

CRACKING THE CODE: LANGUAGE, SCHOOLING, LITERACY

Special report on issues and developments affecting instruction in reading, writing, and comprehension skills. Report is a separately paginated insert and contains numerous articles, including interviews with educators, and a bibliography. Features with substantial statistical content are described below.

AMERICA'S QUEST FOR UNIVERSAL LITERACY

(p. L3-L5) By Thomas Toch. Article, with 3 tables showing percent of population designated as book and other readers, and as nonreaders, 1978 and 1983; and recent book readers by educational level, and book and other readers by most important reason for reading, (no date). Data are from Book Industry Study Group, Inc.

READING DEMANDS ON THE JOB

(p. L11) Table on job-related reading tasks, including types of reading materials used, frequency and importance of reading tasks, readability of materials, and time spent reading. Data are from a survey of 107 workers in 100 occupations reported in the Dec. 1980 issue of *Journal of Reading.*

IT ALL STARTS IN ELEMENTARY SCHOOL

(p. L18-L19, L57-L58) By Linda Chion-Kenney. Article, with 2 tables showing public/private elementary and secondary day school enrollment, and supply and demand for new elementary/secondary teachers, 1984-90. Data are from NCES.

GRADE-SCHOOL TRAINING UNCHANGED IN 50 YEARS

(p. L23, L70) Article, with 1 undated table showing average weekly hours of instruction, by subject, for early and upper elementary schools. Data are based on teachers' reports, and are from Institute for the Development of Educational Activities, Inc.

FORTY OCCUPATIONS WITH LARGEST JOB GROWTH

(p. L28) Table showing increase in employment for occupations with greatest increase in openings during 1982-95 period. Data are from BLS.

TOTAL ENROLLMENT AND EXPENDITURES FOR VOCATIONAL EDUCATION

(p. L32) Two charts showing total enrollment and expenditures for vocational education programs, FY72, FY75, and FY79. Data are from HHS and Dept of Education.

'ENORMOUS' POTENTIAL REMAINS UNREALIZED

(p. L45-L47) Article on computer use in elementary and secondary schools. Data are from Market Data Retrieval. Includes 3 tables showing number of public schools using microcomputers, number of computers in schools, and school buildings with computers, by school level with detail for major computer brands, various years 1981-83.

R4800–2.524: Sept. 19, 1984 (Vol. IV, No. 3)

NUMBER OF TEACHER STRIKES, 1973-83

(p. 4) Table showing number of teacher strikes sponsored by American Federation of Teachers (AFT) and National Education Assn (NEA), 1973/74-1983/84. Data are from AFT and NEA.

MANY HISPANICS NURTURE IDENTITY, SURVEY SHOWS

(p. 8) Article on language skills and educational attainment among Hispanics. Data are from interviews with 775 Hispanics conducted in 1983-84 by Yankelovich, Skelly, and White, Inc., for the Spanish International TV Network. Includes 2 tables showing respondent distribution by English- and Spanish-speaking ability and proficiency goals, and by educational attainment (with comparison to total U.S.), 1981 and 1984.

R4800–2.525: Oct. 10, 1984 (Vol. IV, No. 6)

DATABANK: CHANGES IN STATE FISCAL CONDITIONS AND APPROPRIATIONS FOR EDUCATION

(p. 11) Two tables showing year-end general fund balance as a percent of general fund spending, FY84-85; and percent change in appropriations for elementary/secondary education, FY85 vs. FY84; by State. Data are from National Conference of State Legislatures.

DATABANK: PRIVATE SCHOOLS WITH HIGHEST 1982/83 SUPPORT

(p. 15) Table showing the following for 81 private elementary/secondary schools with greatest amount of voluntary support: enrollment; amount of voluntary support for current operations and capital purposes; voluntary support by source; total alumni, alumni soliciting and making donations, and amount of support; expenditures; and market value of school endowment; 1982/83. Data are from Council for Financial Aid to Education (CFAE). Includes accompanying article (p. 14).

Full CFAE report, *Voluntary Support of Education,* is covered in SRI under A4325-2.

R4800–2.526: Oct. 17, 1984 (Vol. IV, No. 7)

DATABANK: DISTRIBUTION OF COURSE GRADES BY SUBJECT, SELECTED STUDENT CHARACTERISTICS, AND GRADE LEVEL: 1980 SOPHOMORES WHO GRADUATED BY FALL 1982

(p. 12) Table showing distribution of high school students who graduated in 1982 by grades received in 12 subject areas, by race-ethnicity (white, black, and other) and type of high school (public, Catholic, and other private). Data are from NCES.

R5025
Group of Thirty

R5025–1 STUDY GROUP REPORTS
Series. For individual publication data, see below. SRI/MF/complete

Continuing series of reports analyzing developments in the international economic system, with emphases on the international monetary system and on policy analysis.

Reports are prepared or commissioned by the Consultative Group on International Economic and Monetary Affairs, Inc. (the Group of Thirty), generally under the direction of special study groups.

Reports usually include statistics but occasionally consist of narrative analyses only; all reports are described in SRI. The series begins with the reports described below.

Availability: Group of Thirty, 725 Park Ave., New York NY 10021, $15.00 each; SRI/MF/complete.

R5025–1.1: Towards a Less Unstable International Monetary System
[Monograph. Feb. 1980. 19 p. SRI/MF/complete.]

Report discussing stability of single- vs. multicurrency reserve asset arrangements in the international monetary system, with analysis of policy alternatives including the Special Drawing Rights substitution account in the IMF.

Contains introductory statement (p. 1-2); and narrative report (p. 3-19).

R5025–1.2: Foreign Exchange Markets Under Floating Rates
[Monograph. 1980. 49 p. SRI/MF/complete.]

Report on foreign exchange market functioning since the advent of floating exchange rates. Data sources include central bank estimates, and responses from approximately 35 U.S. and foreign commercial/merchant banks and 20 multinational corporations to surveys conducted summer/fall 1979.

Contains contents listing (1 p.); introduction and summaries (p. 1-8); and narrative presentation of responses, with 4 tables showing central bank estimates of average range and interbank share of foreign exchange turnover and dollar share of total foreign exchange transactions, and survey response on reasons for loss of efficiency in exchange markets, mostly 1979 (p. 9-49).

Data are shown for London, Frankfurt, Paris, and/or Zurich markets.

R5025–1.3: Balance-of-Payments Problems of Developing Countries
[Monograph. 1981. 36 p. SRI/MF/complete.]

Report discussing imbalance in international payments of non-oil developing countries, and international monetary system responses, 1980 and trends.

Contains contents listing (1 p.); and narrative report, with 1 table (p. 18) showing IMF Special Drawing Rights committed to industrial and developing countries for new loans and other uses, and trust fund loans disbursed to developing countries, 1973-80 (p. 1-36).

R5025–1.4: Outlook for International Bank Lending
[Monograph. Aug. 1981. 51 p. SRI/MF/complete.]

Report presenting bankers' opinions on the outlook for international lending, including effects of OPEC monetary surpluses and debt situation of non-oil developing countries, 1980s.

Also includes data on ratio of international to total assets for European banks; non-OPEC deficits, reserves, and market financing; average capital/assets ratio for major banks in U.S., UK, and Germany; current payments balance for OECD, OPEC, non-oil developing countries, and others; and OPEC and non-OPEC developing country international bond market and Eurocredit borrowings; various years 1970-82.

Data sources include survey responses of 52 international banks worldwide, IMF, OECD, and Morgan Guaranty Trust Co.

Contains contents listing (1 p.); preface, introduction, and list of survey questions (p. 1-9); discussion of survey results, with text statistics and 16 tables (p. 11-44); and appendix, with 5 tables (p. 47-51).

R5025–1.5: Reserve Currencies in Transition
[Monograph. 1982. 73 p. LC 82-987. SRI/MF/complete.]

Compilation of articles discussing growth of multiple reserve currency system in international finance. Data sources include IMF, Bank for International Settlements, and individual country central banks.

Contains contents listing (1 p.); 5 articles, some with statistics, discussing the multiple reserve currency experience for the international financial system as a whole, and for the currencies of 4 countries (p. 1-49); and 2 appendices, with 14 tables (p. 50-73).

Statistical articles and appendices are described below.

STATISTICS:

YEN: A NEWLY-EMERGING RESERVE CURRENCY

(p. 24-31) By Michiya Matsukawa. Article, with 5 tables showing balance of payments for Japan, value of yen bond issues floated in Japan and in Euro-market, and Japan's overseas claims and liabilities outstanding, 1975-80; nonresidents' outstanding claims in yen deposits, Japanese securities, and Euro-Yen, 1970-80; and distribution of Japan's export contracts by currency, by type of commodity, Apr. 1981.

UK's EXPERIENCE IN WINDING DOWN THE RESERVE ROLE OF STERLING

(p. 42-49) By Christopher W. McMahon. Article, with 1 table showing sterling balances outside UK, by type of organization holding the balance, 1962-June 1981.

FUNCTIONING OF THE ECU

(p. 50-55) By Wolfgang Rieke. Appendix article, with 1 table showing composition of the European Currency Unit (ECU), by currency, as of selected dates 1974-81.

DEUTSCHEMARK AS A RESERVE AND INVESTMENT CURRENCY

(p. 56-73) Appendix, with table listing, and 13 tables showing composition of foreign exchange reserves by country groups, and international bank claims, all by currency; composition of official and private portfolios in Deutschemarks, by type of holder, with selected detail by type and/or location of claim; newly arisen German export claims and import payments, by currency; and major items of Germany's balance of payments; various periods 1967-81.

R5025–1.6: How Central Banks Manage Their Reserves

[Monograph. Apr. 1982. 32 p. SRI/MF/complete.]

Report on currency diversification of foreign exchange reserves. Includes data on reserve policies and practices, based on survey responses of 22 central banks and 12 international commercial/investment banks worldwide.

Also includes data on currency composition of foreign exchange reserves in industrial and nonindustrial countries, and effective U.S. dollar exchange rates, 1970-1st quarter 1981, with 1980 detail for 4 country groups.

Contains contents listing (1 p.); analysis of survey findings, with text data (p. 1-27); and appendix with 3 tables (p. 29-32).

R5025–1.7: How Bankers See the World Financial Market

[Monograph. May 1982. 60 p. SRI/MF/complete.]

Report presenting bankers' opinions on world financial market, including international lending practices and the role of supervisory agencies. Data are based on late 1981/early 1982 survey responses from 111 international banks in 30 countries (primarily in North America and Europe), and also including 9 consortium banks.

Contains contents listing (1 p.); preface, introduction, and summary of findings (p. 1-6); discussion of survey responses, with text data and 12 summary tables (p. 7-23); and statistical analysis section (p. 24-60) with preface, and 51 tables showing survey response to detailed questions in the following areas:

a. International lending activity, profitability, risk trends and outlook, and serious threats to individual banks and to system as a whole.

b. Effects of variation in national bank regulation among countries, and assessment of selected regulatory issues.

c. Determinants of spreads and profits; national response to problems; safeguards for the financial system; and development and uses of country risk analyses.

d. Debt rescheduling arrangements; and bank management and interbank deposit practices.

Survey responses are shown for all banks, and often for banks grouped by size and/or world region, with occasional detail for consortium banks.

R5025–1.8: Risks in International Bank Lending

[Monograph. May 1982. 76 p. SRI/MF/complete.]

Report analyzing risks associated with increased international bank lending during the 1970s, and presenting risk management recommendations and data on the Eurocurrency credit market.

Contains contents listing (2 p.); introduction and narrative report (p. 1-35); and appendices A-D, with 3 narrative articles, and 1 statistical article described below (p. 36-76).

STATISTICAL ARTICLE:

TRENDS IN EUROCURRENCY CREDIT PARTICIPATION, 1972-1980

(p. 57-70) By Diane Page and Walter D. Rogers. Article, with 4 charts and 6 tables showing Eurocurrency loan value; and loan volume and number of financial and parent institutions participating in Eurocurrency credit markets, by country or world area; various years 1972-80. Data sources include World Bank.

R5025–1.9: Bank Supervision Around the World

[Monograph. 1982. 70 p. LC 82-11877. SRI/MF/complete.]

By Richard Dale. Report describing bank regulatory practices in major financial center countries, 1982.

Contains contents listing (1 p.); preface and summary (p. 1-4); and narrative report in 3 chapters, including profiles of regulations in 13 countries (p. 4-70).

R5025–1.10: International Monetary Fund and the Private Markets

[Monograph. Mar. 1983. 41 p. SRI/MF/complete.]

Report analyzing options for supplementing IMF resources through borrowing from private financial markets. Data are primarily from IMF.

Contains contents listing and preface (2 p.); narrative report, with 1 table showing value of IMF Special Drawing Rights and dollar assist-

ance, and complementary commercial bank financing, for 5 Latin American countries, mid-1982 to Feb. 1983 period (p. 1-11); and 2 appendices on IMF operations, with text data and 5 IMF financial statements, various periods 1978-82 (p. 13-41).

R5025–1.11: Future of the International Oil Market

[Monograph. 1983. 54 p. SRI/MF/complete.]

By Edwin A. Deagle, Jr. Report on trends and outlook for the world oil market, with analysis of the oil market's effect on the world economy. Data sources include OECD, OPEC, and private organizations.

Contains contents listing (1 p.); introduction (p. 1-3); report, with 7 tables described below (p. 4-35); and 3 separately authored appendix articles, also described below, with 3 trend charts and 4 tables (p. 36-54).

REPORT TABLES AND APPENDICES:

REPORT TABLES

a. OECD energy and oil consumption trends relative to GDP, selected periods 1960-81; and OPEC oil production by country, and aggregate current account balances, 1980-82. Tables 1-3. (p. 7-11)

b. Energy consumption of non-Communist world by energy type, 1980, 1990, and 2000; and non-Communist world oil supply and demand, including U.S. and foreign demand, OPEC and non-OPEC supply, and total inventory, various periods 1977-1st quarter 1983. Tables 4-5. (p. 14-17)

c. Oil demand for industrialized and developing non-Communist countries, non-OPEC production, and OPEC supply required to balance demand, as forecast by 3 organizations; and low and high production estimates for 5 OPEC countries; 1990. Tables 6-7. (p. 19-21)

APPENDICES

d. "Effect of Exchange Rates on Oil Prices," by Edwin A Deagle, Jr. Includes 1 table showing OPEC oil price, and real cost in constant 1980 dollars for 6 countries, selected months 1980-82. (p. 36)

e. "Note on Availability of Non-Oil Energy Supplies," by Bijan Mossavar-Rahmani. Includes 2 tables showing non-Communist world energy consumption, by energy type, selected years 1970-2000. (p. 37-40)

f. "Oil Stockpile Management and the Stability of the World Oil Market in the 1980s," by Edward N. Krapels. Includes 1 table showing industry crude oil inventories in U.S., Japan, France, and West Germany, selected months 1979-82. (p. 41-54)

R5025–1.12: Commercial Banks and the Restructuring of Cross-Border Debt

[Monograph. 1983. 36 p. SRI/MF/complete.]

By M. S. Mendelsohn. Report analyzing renegotiations of country external debt, 1982/83 and trends.

Includes amount of public and private sector debt being renegotiated with commercial banks, and gross and net liabilities to international banks, 1982/83; and amount of debt restructured with commercial banks, 1978-82; all by debtor country.

Data sources include Bank for International Settlements and International Bank for Reconstruction and Development.

Contains contents and table listings (1 p.); and report, including 2 tables, and case histories of Mexican and Brazilian debt restructuring, 1982-83 (p. 3-36).

R5025–1.13: Foreign Direct Investment, 1973-87

[Monograph. 1984. 42 p. SRI/MF/complete.]

Report presenting review and outlook for foreign direct investment, mostly for 1970s-80s. Data are from UN and other international organizations, and responses of 52 major international corporations to a 1983 Group of Thirty survey. Respondent corporations account for almost half of foreign direct investment worldwide.

Contains contents listing (1 p.); and report in 4 sections (p. 1-42), with 22 tables presenting estimates and survey responses for the following, generally by world economic or geographic group:

a. Value of gross and net foreign direct investment flows, various years 1960-82.

b. Developing countries' current account deficits, net capital flows by type, use of reserves/other capital, official and private debt outstanding, debt service as percent of exports, and debt service and other financial measures as percent of GNP; and US GDP deflator for industrialized countries; 1982 and 1995, with trend from 1970.

c. Actual and expected trends in foreign direct investment flows; share of corporate sales attributable to foreign subsidiaries; and geographic distribution of assets and pre- and post-tax profits; various periods 1970s-87.

d. Reasons for foreign direct investment, and target payback periods by industry division, 1970 and 1983; perceived trend in climate for foreign direct investment; whether company monitors political risk; and percent of seriously studied investments actually made.

e. Changes in type of investment (plant vs. management/technology); form of investment (new ventures, full acquisition and portfolio control of businesses abroad, and joint ventures); and investment financing method; mostly 1970s-87.

R5025–1.14: Economic Cooperation from the Inside

[Monograph. 1984. 3+46 p. SRI/MF/complete.]

Report discussing views of international economic/monetary negotiators regarding trends in international economic and monetary cooperation and the effectiveness of international monetary institutions. Report is based on interviews conducted Jan.-Sept. 1983.

Contains list of interview participants (2 p.); contents listing (1 p.); narrative report (p. 1-28); and 2 appendices (p. 29-46).

R5025–2   ROLE OF THE DOLLAR AS AN INTERNATIONAL CURRENCY

Monograph. 1983. 33 p.
Occasional Paper No. 13.
LC 83-14174.
SRI/MF/complete

By Peter B. Kenen. Report on trends in prevalence of the dollar and other currencies in international trade, foreign exchange markets, and international financial markets, 1970s-81.

Includes data on the comparative position of U.S. dollar vs. various other major currencies in official foreign exchange holdings and foreign trade transactions, by selected country or world area; and dollar and other foreign currency claims on nonresidents reported by European banks.

Also includes value of Eurobond issues, by type of issuer and currency; and distribution of developing countries by method of setting exchange rates.

Data sources include Bank for International Settlements, IMF, and scholarly articles.

Contains contents listing (1 p.); narrative report (p. 3-15); statistical section, with 13 tables (p. 16-30); and list of references (p. 31).

Availability: Group of Thirty, 725 Park Ave., New York NY 10021, $10.00; SRI/MF/complete.

R5580
Institute of International Education

R5580–1   OPEN DOORS: 1982/83 Report on International Educational Exchange

Annual. 1984. vii+183 p.
ISSN 0078-5172.
ISBN 87206-125-6.
LC 55-4594.
SRI/MF/not filmed

Annual report on foreign students' personal and academic characteristics, and enrollment by State, institution, and country of origin, 1982/83, with trends from 1954/55. Also includes data on U.S. college-sponsored study-abroad programs and students.

Data are based primarily on responses from 2,795 institutions to the 29th annual IIE census of foreign students in the U.S., 1982/83; and UNESCO and NCES reports.

Contents:

Highlights, introduction, contents listing, and definitions. (p. i-vii)

Part I. Annual Census. Includes 42 summary charts, and 79 tables described below. (p. 1-76)

Part II. Expenditures for Living Costs. Includes 1 chart and 2 tables showing number of reporting institutions and foreign students reported, 1982/83, and estimated expenditures, 1983/84, by State and SMSA. (p. 77-79)

Part III. Intensive English Language Programs (IELP). Includes 2 charts and 8 tables showing IELP programs and foreign student enrollments, with enrollment detail for leading institutions and countries of origin, and by

State, world region of origin, visa type, and sex, various years 1978/79-1982/83. (p. 80-83)

Part IV. U.S. College-Sponsored Study-Abroad Programs. Includes 2 charts and 14 tables showing U.S. study-abroad programs and/or students studying abroad, by world region, leading country, sex, sponsoring institution, and field of study, with various cross-tabulations, various years 1977/78-1981/82. (p. 84-93)

App. 1-2. Includes 2 tables showing foreign student enrollment by institution and State, and by country and world region of origin, 1981/82-1982/83. (p. 94-147)

App. 3-7. Listings of fields of study, countries, States, and territories; data collection methodology; and facsimile questionnaires. (p. 148-167)

App. 8-9. 2 tables showing foreign student IELP enrollment, by institution and State, 1981/82-1982/83; and U.S. study-abroad programs by field of study, and students by sex, both cross-tabulated by country and world region, 1981/82. (p. 168-177)

App. 10-11. 2 tables showing foreign students in U.S. and other leading host countries; and foreign students in U.S., total population, GNP, personal income category, educational expenditure per capita, and literacy rate, by country and world region of origin; various years 1977-1982/83. (p. 178-181)

App. 12. Definitions and data sources. (p. 182-183)

Data by State generally include selected U.S. territories.

Availability: Institute of International Education, 809 United Nations Plaza, New York NY 10017, $22.95; SRI/MF/not filmed.

PART I TABLES:

R5580–1.1: Annual Census of Foreign Students in the U.S.

[Most data are for 1982/83, and generally include trends from as early as 1954/55. All data refer to foreign students in the U.S., unless otherwise noted.]

PERSONAL AND ACADEMIC CHARACTERISTICS

a. U.S. overview and world summary: number of U.S. institutions with foreign students; and foreign students by world region and country of origin, and total domestic/foreign enrollment, for U.S. and other leading host countries. 11 tables. (p. 1-11)

b. Nationality: origin of foreign students by continent, continental subregion, and leading country, and for OPEC and non-OPEC; foreign students, by characteristics of country of origin, including personal income category and literacy rate; and selected characteristics of individual leading countries of origin, including population, GNP, educational expenditure per capita, and literacy rate. 17 tables. (p. 12-31)

c. Academic characteristics: foreign students by field of study, academic level, and full- and part-time status, generally by institution type and control. 9 tables. (p. 32-39)

d. Personal characteristics: foreign students by sex, marital status, primary source of funds, and visa type, generally by institution type and control. 8 tables. (p. 40-45)

DISTRIBUTION

e. Geographic location: foreign students by region and State of study, with selected cross-tabulations by world region and leading country of origin. 9 tables. (p. 46-56)

f. Foreign students in 2- and 4-year institutions: by State, from 5 leading countries of origin within each world region, by OPEC country, and for 10 States and 10 institutions with largest foreign enrollment. 10 tables. (p. 57-64)

g. Foreign students in public and private institutions: by State, from 5 leading countries of origin within each world region, by OPEC country, and for 10 States and 10 institutions with largest foreign enrollment. 10 tables. (p. 65-71)

h. Institutional rankings: foreign and total enrollment in institutions with 1,000 or more foreign students, and in 20 institutions with highest percent of foreign students, 1982/83; 10 institutions with highest foreign enrollment, selected years 1954/55-1982/83; and foreign students and nationalities represented in institutions with students from 100 or more nations, 1982/83. 5 tables. (p. 72-76)

R5580–2   PROFILES: The Foreign Student in the U.S.
Recurring (irreg.)   1983.
iv + 179 p.
ISBN 87206-118-3.
SRI/MF/not filmed

Recurring report presenting foreign student enrollment in U.S. higher education institutions, variously cross-tabulated by world region and country of origin, field of study, academic level, and sex, academic year 1981/82 with trends from 1949/50. Also includes foreign enrollment by institution, grouped by U.S. State and territory, 1980/81-1981/82.

Data are from responses of 1,845 institutions representing 197,089 foreign students, to a 1981/82 survey conducted in conjunction with IIE's Annual Census of Foreign Students in the U.S.

Contains contents listings, definitions, and acknowledgements (p. iii-iv); introduction and 6 report sections, with 15 charts and 33 tables (p. 1-46); and 7 appendices, with 5 extended tables, lists of field-of-study and foreign area codes, questionnaire facsimile, and 1 summary table (p. 48-179).

For description of previous report, presenting data for 1979/80 school year, see SRI 1982 Annual under this number.

Report is intended to complement *Open Doors,* an annual report also published by IIE and covered in SRI under R5580-1.

Availability: Institute of International Education, Communications Division, 809 United Nations Plaza, New York NY 10017, $22.95; SRI/MF/not filmed.

R5650
Japan Economic Institute

R5650–2   JEI REPORT
Weekly, in 2 parts.
Approx. 20 p. var. paging.
ISSN 0744-6489.
LC SN 82-20877.
SRI/MF/excerpts, shipped quarterly

Weekly report, published in 2 sections, on Japanese economic and political issues and developments, and relations with U.S. Data are generally from Japanese Government and private sources and U.S. Government agencies.

General Format:

Section A. Analysis of a selected topic, frequently including statistics.

Section B. Several brief news and feature articles, occasionally containing statistics, including reports on U.S.-Japanese competition in specific industries; statistical supplement, with 2 monthly tables; and 1 quarterly table.

Report also includes semiannual or quarterly subject indexes.

Annual statistical features include articles on Japanese economic growth outlook, Japanese investment in U.S. industry, and U.S.-Japanese trade.

Monthly and quarterly tables are listed below. Monthly tables usually appear in 3rd or 4th issue of month. All additional features with substantial statistical content are described, as they appear, under "Statistical Features;" page locations and latest period of coverage for quarterly table are also noted. Nonstatistical features are not covered.

Prior to Feb. 1984 issues, report included a monthly "Section C" presenting narrative review of U.S. Government actions affecting international trade.

Availability: Japan Economic Institute, 1000 Connecticut Ave., NW, Washington DC 20036, $40.00 per yr.; SRI/MF/excerpts for monthly tables, and all portions covered under "Statistical Features;" shipped quarterly.

Issues reviewed during 1984: Nov. 4, 1983-Oct. 26, 1984 (P) (1983 Nos. 42-47; 1984 Nos. 1-41) [No issues were published for Nov. 25, Dec. 23, and Dec. 30, 1983, and Sept. 7, 1984; no section A was published for Jan. 27, 1984 issue].

TABLES:

MONTHLY TABLES

[Data are shown for month 2-3 months prior to cover date, 2 previous months, current and previous years to date, and 2 previous full years.]

[1] Trade and payments data [Japanese balance of payments detail, and trade balance including detail for automobile and steel exports and crude oil imports; yen-dollar exchange rate; and U.S.-Japan trade balance for industrial supplies, capital and consumer goods, food/feed, and automotive products; most shown in dollars].

[2] Japanese economic indicators [job openings/applications ratio, and percent change from previous year for 12 indicators].

QUARTERLY TABLE

[1] Japan's real GNP at constant prices (1975 prices) [personal consumption spending, private residential construction and fixed non-residential investment, change in business and government inventories, government current expenditures and fixed investment, and exports and imports; data are shown in yen, for quarter ending 3-5 months prior to cover date, 3 previous quarters, and usually 2 previous fiscal years].

STATISTICAL FEATURES:

R5650–2.501: Dec. 9, 1983 (No. 46A)
ROLE OF INTERNATIONAL TRADE IN THE JAPANESE ECONOMY

(10 p.) Article, with 4 tables showing the following as percent of GNP: exports and imports for Japan and U.S., 1965 and 1970-82, and for 6 other industrial countries, 1982; and Japanese Government deficit, and current account surplus/deficit, 1973-82.

Data are from U.S. Commerce Dept, IMF, and private Japanese sources.

R5650–2.502: Dec. 9, 1983 (No. 46B)
LDP FACTIONAL MANEUVERS KEY TO GENERAL ELECTION

(p. 1-4) Article discussing Japanese elections for the Diet's Lower House, Dec. 18, 1983. Includes 1 table showing number of candidates, 1980 and 1983 elections, and total seats held prior to 1983 elections, by political party.

R5650–2.503: Jan. 6, 1984 (No. 1A)
YEAR-END REVIEW OF FOREIGN ECONOMIC LEGISLATION

(9 p.) Article reporting on activities of U.S. Congress during 1983 regarding foreign economic matters, and analyzing outlook for 1984.

Includes 1 table showing days in session, bills enacted and vetoed, number of measures by legislative stage, quorum calls, and votes, all by house for the 98th Congress, 1st session (1983).

Also includes list of selected legislation with international implications.

R5650–2.504: Jan. 6, 1984 (No. 1B)
QUARTERLY TABLE

[1] Japan's GNP [3rd quarter 1983]. (p. 7)

ELECTIONS FORCE POLITICAL CHANGES IN JAPAN

(p. 1-4) Article reporting on results of Japanese elections for the Diet's Lower House, Dec. 18, 1983. Includes 1 table showing number of candidates and seats and percent of vote won, by political party, 1980 and 1983 elections; and lists of Prime Minister Nakasone's second cabinet members and Liberal Democratic Party leaders, showing age, position, and faction.

R5650–2.505: Jan. 13, 1984 (No. 2A)
U.S.-JAPAN RELATIONS: BEFORE AND AFTER THE ELECTIONS

(10 p.) Article analyzing results of Japanese elections for the Diet's Lower House, Dec. 18, 1983.

Includes 4 tables showing composition of lower house before and after election and after formation of coalition government, and share of popular vote won, by party; voter turnout; and Liberal Democratic Party factional balance in upper and lower houses and in cabinet and party administration, with pre-election comparisons; various years 1976-83.

R5650–2.506: Jan. 20, 1984 (No. 3A)

JAPAN-EC RELATIONS 1983: THE WINDING ROAD

(11 p.) Article, with 5 tables showing Japan's export and import trade with EC, with detail for selected products covered under voluntary export restraint agreement; manufactured goods as percent of total imports for Japan and EC; total exports and imports of Japan, EC, and U.S., with trilateral trade detail; and changes in exchange rate for yen and major European currencies; various periods 1955-83.

Data are from Japanese and U.S. Government agencies, and private sources.

R5650–2.507: Jan. 20, 1984 (No. 3B)

EPA SEES 4.1 PERCENT GNP GROWTH IN FY84, ANNUAL FEATURE

(p. 5-7) Annual article, with 1 table on economic growth outlook for Japan, showing forecasts of Japanese Economic Planning Agency and 14 private research organizations for selected economic indicators, FY84.

R5650–2.508: Jan. 27, 1984 (No. 4B)

FY84 CAR EXPORT QUOTA ALLOCATED

(p. 5-6) Article, with 1 table showing the following by Japanese automobile manufacturer: quota for exports to U.S., FY83-84; and U.S. retail sales volume, 1982-83. Data are from *Nihon Keizai Shimbun*.

JAPAN RUNS RECORD TRADE SURPLUS IN 1983

(p. 9-11) Article, with 1 text table showing U.S. GNP percent change, and Japanese trade balance, 4th quarter 1982-4th quarter 1983.

R5650–2.509: Feb. 10, 1984 (No. 6A)

JAPAN'S DEFENSE: PERCEPTIONS AND REALITIES

(17 p.) Article, with 6 tables showing total and per capita defense expenditures (in yen), with comparisons to total budget and GNP, for Japan and 20 other countries; Japanese defense spending distribution by purpose, and general account and defense budget outlays; and Japanese military weapons inventory with detail for up-to-date equipment and obsolete equipment, by service branch and type of weapon; various years 1955-83.

Data are from Japan Defense Agency and *Armed Forces Journal*.

R5650–2.510: Feb. 10, 1984 (No. 6B)

JAPAN'S 1983 BALANCE OF PAYMENTS

(p. 9-10) Article, with 1 table showing Japan's balance of payments, by component, 1979-83.

R5650–2.511: Feb. 17, 1984 (No. 7A)

JAPAN'S BUDGET: LEADERSHIP AND CONTROL

(10 p.) Article, with 3 tables showing the following for Japan: government revenues and expenditures by category, FY84 and percent change from FY83; deficit financing as percent of budget, with comparison to 4 other industri-

al nations, 1965-84; and annual percent change in total and defense budgets and in defense budget share of total budget, general expenditures, and GNP, FY62-84.

Data are from Japan Ministry of Finance.

R5650–2.512: Mar. 2, 1984 (No. 9A)

U.S.-JAPAN COMPETITION IN ROBOTS: AN UPDATE

(p. 1-12) Article, with 2 tables showing value and volume for U.S. industrial robot production, consumption, exports, and imports, 1979-83; and for Japan's production by type of robot, 1979-82. Data are from USITC and Japan Industrial Robot Assn.

R5650–2.513: Mar. 16, 1984 (No. 11A)

JAPAN'S SATELLITE DEVELOPMENT PROGRAM

(13 p.) Article, with 2 tables listing Japan's satellites, and showing mission objective, launch date, status, and selected other information for each. Data are from Japanese agencies.

R5650–2.514: Mar. 23, 1984 (No. 12B)

AUSTERE BUDGET PASSES LOWER HOUSE AS PRIVATE SECTOR PICKS UP STEAM

(p. 3-4) Article, with 1 table showing selected Japanese economic indicators, including unemployment rate and percent change in shipments, Jan. 1984 compared to Jan. and Dec. 1983.

R5650–2.515: Mar. 30, 1984 (No. 13A)

SECOND NAKASONE CABINET

(p. 1-10) Article, with list of Prime Minister Nakasone's second cabinet members, showing age, position, district, faction, number of times elected, previously held posts, former career, and value (in yen) of real property, credit/securities, and debt.

R5650–2.516: Mar. 30, 1984 (No. 13B)

QUARTERLY TABLE

[1] Japan's GNP [4th quarter 1983]. (p. 12)

CHINA AWAITS JAPAN'S PRIME MINISTER

(p. 1-4) Article, with 1 table showing value of trade between Japan and PRC, by selected major industry group or commodity, 1979-83 and Jan.-Feb. 1984. Data are from Japan's Ministry of Finance.

R5650–2.517: Apr. 6, 1984 (No. 14A)

WORLD ECONOMY IN 1983

(p. 1-14) Article, with 5 tables showing GDP and consumer price percent changes, interest rates, and value of imports and exports, by country arranged by world area or classification (industrial countries, and oil-exporting and non-oil-exporting developing countries); and wholesale price indexes for selected commodities; 1979-83, with selected quarterly detail for 1983.

Data sources include IMF and U.S. Commerce Dept.

R5650–2.518: Apr. 13, 1984 (No. 15A)

JAPAN'S EXPANDING U.S. MANUFACTURING PRESENCE: 1983 UPDATE, ANNUAL FEATURE

(24 p.) Annual article on Japanese investment in U.S. industry, 1983. Data are from a survey

by Japan Economic Institute. Includes alphabetical list of Japanese owned or affiliated manufacturing companies in U.S., in operation or under construction as of Dec. 31, 1983, showing the following for each: plant locations and year opened/acquired, parent company and ownership share, whether new or acquired, SIC 4-digit industry, and number of employees.

Also includes list of companies arranged alphabetically by State; list of companies arranged by SIC 4-digit industry; and list of sales, mergers, closings, and other changes since 1980-82 surveys.

R5650–2.519: Apr. 20, 1984 (No. 16B)

JAPAN'S ANNUAL WAGE NEGOTIATIONS UNDER WAY

(p. 11-13) Article, with 2 tables showing 1984 wage increase demands by labor unions and offers by industries in Japan, with comparison to 1983 settlements. Tables show demands for 13 union groups, and offers for 4 industrial sectors (with selected detail for individual companies), and include amount and percent of wage increase.

R5650–2.520: Apr. 27, 1984 (No. 17A)

MINISTRY OF FINANCE: AN UNWELCOME EXPOSURE TO INTERNATIONAL ISSUES

(p. 1-8) Article, with 1 undated table showing number of former Japanese government officials in the lower house of the Diet, by former agency.

R5650–2.521: May 4, 1984 (No. 18A)

JAPAN'S FISCAL POLICY

(14 p.) Article, with 4 tables showing Japan and U.S. current deficit, debt service outlays, and accumulated debt, expressed as actual levels and as percent of budget and/or GNP; and total revenues and expenditures, with detail for Japan general account expenditures by major category and by ministry; various years FY46-84.

Data are from the Japanese Ministry of Finance and U.S. Council of Economic Advisers, and are shown in yen for Japan.

R5650–2.522: May 11, 1984 (No. 19A)

U.S. EXPORTS TO JAPAN: A REVIEW OF 1983 SALES, ANNUAL FEATURE

(10 p.) Annual article, with 1 table showing volume and/or value of U.S. exports to Japan, 1982-83; and Japan's share of all U.S. exports, 1983; by detailed commodity. Data are from U.S. Commerce Dept.

R5650–2.523: May 18, 1984 (No. 20A)

JAPANESE ECONOMY IN 1983, ANNUAL FEATURE

(9 p.) Annual article, with 1 table showing Japanese GNP and components, 1982-83 and quarterly 1983. Table repeats data shown in quarterly table. Data are from Japanese Economic Planning Agency.

R5650–2.524: June 8, 1984 (No. 22A)

BEEF AND CITRUS ISSUE: A FRAGILE SHOCK ABSORBER

(p. 1-7) Article, with 2 tables showing Japanese beef and orange import quotas, and actual imports with selected detail by country of origin, 1979-83. Data are from the Japanese Ministry of Finance.

R5650–2.525: June 8, 1984 (No. 22B)

ENERGY SITUATION IN JAPAN

(p. 6-8) Article, with 1 table showing Japan's imports of crude oil by country or world area of origin, 1980-83 and Jan.-Apr. 1984. Data sources include Petroleum Assn of Japan, and Japanese Ministry of Finance.

R5650–2.526: June 15, 1984 (No. 23A)

RECENT TRENDS IN U.S. DIRECT INVESTMENT IN JAPAN

(p. 1-12) Article, with 2 tables presenting number and value of major direct foreign investments in Japan by type (new firm, existing firm, and expanded holdings), shown by investing country or world area and for investments from individuals and subsidiaries, 1982-83. Data are from Japanese Ministry of Finance.

R5650–2.527: June 15, 1984 (No. 23B)

JAPAN'S PROGRESS ON ODA GOALS

(p. 9-10) Article, with 1 table showing Japanese net official development assistance (ODA) disbursements, by type of assistance, 1982-83. Data are from Japanese Ministry of Foreign Affairs.

R5650–2.528: June 22, 1984 (No. 24A)

U.S. IMPORTS FROM JAPAN: A REVIEW OF 1983 SALES, ANNUAL FEATURE

(11 p.) Annual article, with 1 table on U.S. imports from Japan, showing volume and value, 1982-83; and percent of all U.S. imports, 1983; by detailed commodity. Data are from U.S. Commerce Dept.

R5650–2.529: June 22, 1984 (No. 24B)

JAPANESE UNIONS SIGN WAGE SETTLEMENTS FOR 1984

(p. 10-11) Article on results of wage contract negotiations in Japan, with 1 table showing amount and percent of average monthly increase 1983-84, and new monthly standard wage 1984, for 17 major industry groups. Data are from *Nihon Keizai Shimbun*.

R5650–2.530: June 29, 1984 (No. 25B)

QUARTERLY TABLE

[1] Japan's GNP [1st quarter 1984]. (p. 2)

R5650–2.531: July 6, 1984 (No. 26B)

JAPAN'S STEEL MILLS FACE NO-WIN SITUATION ON COAL IMPORTS

(p. 4-6) Article, with 1 table showing Japan's imports of coking coal from U.S., Australia, and Canada, 1973-83. Data are from Japan Tariff Assn.

R5650–2.532: July 13, 1984 (No. 27A)

EQUAL OPPORTUNITY LEGISLATION IN JAPAN

(p. 1-10) Article, with 3 tables showing the following, for Japan: women's employment and percent of total employment, by industry division; percent of married women employed, by income class; and percent of employed women working part-time; 1982, with selected trends from 1960. Data are from the Japan Prime Minister's Office.

Also includes appendix (p. 7), with chronology of equal employment legislation enacted in Japan.

R5650–2.533: July 13, 1984 (No. 27B)

U.S. CORPORATE R&D SPENDING CONTINUES TO OUTSTRIP JAPANESE FUNDING

(p. 3-5) Article, with 1 table showing top 10 Japanese and top 10 American companies ranked by R&D spending, with comparison to sales, fiscal or calendar years 1979 and 1983. Data are from *Business Week* and *Nihon Keizai Shimbun*.

R5650–2.534: July 20, 1984 (No. 28A)

JAPAN'S PROGRESS IN ALTERNATIVE ENERGY DEVELOPMENT, ANNUAL FEATURE

(16 p.) Annual article on Japan's energy industry. Data sources include Petroleum Assn of Japan, and Japan's Ministries of Finance and of International Trade and Industry. Includes 9 tables showing the following for Japan:

a. Crude oil production, throughput, operating rate, and inventories; imported crude oil volume and value; wholesale price index for gasoline, naphtha, and fuel oil; consumer price index and retail price for gasoline and propane; energy imports and household energy consumption, by type of energy; and electric utility output, by type of fuel; annually 1979-82 and monthly 1983-early 1984.

b. Consumption of energy, by industry sector and type of energy, quarterly 1983-1st quarter 1984; energy supply by type, and demand by consuming sector, various years FY82-2000; and New Energy Development Organization expenditures, by type of project, FY82-83.

R5650–2.535: July 20, 1984 (No. 28B)

JAPANESE ECONOMY GATHERING MOMENTUM

(p. 4-7) Article, with 2 tables showing change in corporate profits for FY83-84, and in selected economic indicators for FY84, for Japan, as forecast by 4-8 Japanese organizations.

R5650–2.536: July 27, 1984 (No. 29B)

JAPANESE FOREIGN INVESTMENT REMAINS ON UPSWING IN FY83

(p. 10-14) Article, with 2 tables showing Japan's direct foreign investment, by country or world area, and by industry sector, FY79-83 and as of Mar. 31, 1984.

R5650–2.537: Aug. 3, 1984 (No. 30A)

U.S. AGRICULTURAL EXPORTS TO JAPAN: A REVIEW OF 1983 SALES, ANNUAL FEATURE

(13 p.) Annual article, with 7 tables on U.S. agricultural exports, showing value by importing country, 1979-83; and volume and value, by detailed commodity for exports to Japan, and by importing country for selected commodities, 1981-83. Data are from USDA.

R5650–2.538: Aug. 10, 1984 (No. 31B)

FINANCE MINISTRY ADOPTS 7 PERCENT DEFENSE BUDGET CEILING

(p. 3-4) Article, with 1 table showing Japan's actual defense budget and amount proposed by Ministry of Finance, by funded group, FY84 with percent change from FY83. Data are from Japanese Ministry of Finance.

BILATERAL TRADE DEFICIT LIKELY TO TOP $30 BILLION IN 1984

(p. 8-11) Article, with 1 table showing value of U.S. exports to Japan, and U.S. imports from Japan, by detailed commodity, 1st half 1983-84.

R5650–2.539: Aug. 24, 1984 (No. 33B)

BILATERAL ECONOMIC DISCUSSIONS TO RESUME

(p. 5-8) Article, with 2 text tables showing Japan's quotas on orange juice and fresh orange imports from the U.S. for FY84-87, as of Aug. 14, 1984.

R5650–2.540: Aug. 31, 1984 (No. 34A)

JAPAN'S SOGO SHOSHA: FAST MOVERS IN FAST-CHANGING MARKETS

(p. 1-12) Article discussing market trends and outlook for the 16 general trading companies of Japan, known collectively as "sogo shosha." Data sources include Japan Foreign Trade Council, Inc., and company annual reports. Includes 5 tables showing the following:

a. Sogo shosha trade distribution, by type (export, import, offshore, and domestic), and by commodity group, with detail for 4 companies; and value of Japanese exports and imports, and amount handled by sogo shosha, various years FY78-83.

b. Sogo shosha offices and personnel in Japan and by world area, as of Jan. 1984; and top 10 companies ranked by sales (in yen), FY83 with percent change from FY82.

R5650–2.541: Aug. 31, 1984 (No. 34B)

AGING CAPITAL STOCK WORRIES JAPAN

(p. 4-6) Article, with 1 table comparing average age of industrial plants/equipment in Japan and U.S., by selected major industry group, fiscal or calendar years 1974 and 1983. Data are from Nikkei Economic Electronic Databank System, and Standard & Poor's Corp.

R5650–2.542: Sept. 14, 1984 (No. 35A)

JAPAN'S FOREIGN AID POLICY: AN ANNUAL UPDATE

(p. 1-10) Annual article, with 6 tables showing Japan's total outflow of capital to developing countries/multilateral agencies, by type of transaction; Japan's aid grants relative to all bilateral loans and official development assistance (ODA); Japan's ODA by world area and purpose; and ODA of individual OECD Development Assistance Committee countries, total and as percent of GNP; various years 1979-83.

Data are from Japanese Ministry of Foreign Affairs.

R5650–2.543: Sept. 21, 1984 (No. 36A)

U.S.-JAPAN COMPETITION IN MACHINE TOOLS: AN UPDATE

(p. 1-22) Article, with 13 tables showing dollar values for the following, 1979-83 unless otherwise noted:

a. U.S. machine tools: new orders, shipments, and backlog, 1972-83, and apparent consumption; and shipments, and foreign trade (total and with Japan), by detailed tool type.

b. Japanese machine tools: apparent consumption; and production, and foreign trade (total and with U.S.), by detailed tool type.

Data are from U.S. Census Bureau and National Tool Builder's Assn; and Japanese Ministries of International Trade and Industry, and Finance.

R5650–2.544: Sept. 21, 1984 (No. 36B)
PARTY FUNDS HIT NEW RECORD IN 1983

(p. 9-10) Article, with 2 tables showing aggregate major donations (in yen and dollars) to Japan's political parties, by party, 1983 with percent change from 1982; and donations (in yen) to 5 major factions of the Liberal Democratic Party, 1982-83. Data are from Japan's Ministry of Home Affairs.

R5650–2.545: Sept. 28, 1984 (No. 37A)
REGIONAL INVESTMENT PROMOTION: THE KYUSHU EXPERIENCE

(p. 1-10) Article, with 2 tables showing population and land area for Japan's Kyushu Island, by prefecture (no date); and distribution of industrial shipment value, by commodity category, for Japan and Kyushu, 1980.

R5650–2.546: Oct. 5, 1984 (No. 38B)
QUARTERLY TABLE

[1] Japan's GNP [2nd quarter 1984; table is included in article described below]. (p. 3)

FY84 GROWTH FORECAST RAISED AFTER SOLID SECOND QUARTER

(p. 1-4) Article revising economic growth outlook for Japan, FY84. Data are from Japanese Economic Planning Agency. Includes quarterly table, and 1 text table showing revised vs. previous forecasts for selected economic indicators, FY84.

Previous forecast is described under R5650-2.507, above.

R5650–2.547: Oct. 12, 1984 (No. 39A)
VENTURE CAPITAL IN JAPAN

(p. 1-18) Article discussing venture capital market in Japan, with comparisons to U.S. Data are from Japanese Ministry of International Trade and Industry, Venture Business Research Group, *Venture,* and *Nikkei Sangyo Shimbun.* Includes 6 tables showing the following:

a. Capital (in yen), date established, number of stockholders and major stockholder, and selected financial measures, for Japanese venture capital companies arranged by type of affiliation (securities company, banks, and other), FY83; and selected measures of value (in dollars) for U.S. venture capital companies ranked by total value, 1983.

b. Japan's venture businesses and small/medium businesses aggregated by size of capital (in yen) and employment, with distribution of firms by sales, profit, age, market share, major industry group, R&D personnel and share of sales, and sources of finance (no dates).

c. Venture capital funds of local governments: capital (in yen), interest rate, term, use, and date established, by Japanese prefecture and selected city (no dates).

d. Top 19 Japanese venture businesses FY85, and top 20 U.S. venture businesses 1983, ranked by sales growth rate; both with type of business and actual sales, various periods FY79-85.

R5650–2.548: Oct. 12, 1984 (No. 39B)
FOREIGN DIRECT INVESTMENT IN JAPAN CONTINUES UPSWING

(p. 4-7) Article, with 2 tables showing foreign-affiliated firms in Japan, by major industry group, headquarters country or world area, and extent of foreign ownership, FY82; and overseas capital, sales, and employment, for Japanese companies' foreign affiliates in developed and developing countries, with detail for manufacturing, FY80-82.

Data are from survey responses of 1,052 firms in Japan with over 50% of investment controlled by foreign companies, and responses of 1,469 overseas firms controlled by Japanese companies. Surveys were conducted by Japanese Ministry of International Trade and Industry.

R5650–3 JAPAN'S INDUSTRIAL POLICIES
Monograph. Apr. 1984.
56 p.
SRI/MF/complete

Report analyzing the role of Japan's Government in the development and support of industry, with comparisons to U.S. industrial policies, various periods 1953-83.

Includes data on sources and distribution of Japanese Government loan funds; loans of government-related financial institutions by recipient industry, with detail by major company, comparisons to other investment sources, and effect on industry profit ratios; government-approved industrial cooperation activity including number of cartels organized under various special industry laws, with production and marketing detail for computer leasing; and extent of government aid to foreign trade.

Also includes data on implications of public works policies, including trends in residential plumbing facilities and telephone service, and public vs. private housing investment; GNP forecast and actual growth under various long-term economic plans; comparisons to U.S., including government spending as percent of GNP, and composition of personal financial assets; and U.S. Government revenue losses from business-related tax incentives.

Most data are from Japanese and U.S. Government sources.

Contains contents listing (2 p.); summary and introduction (p. 1-6); and narrative report interspersed with 21 tables (p. 7-56).

Availability: Japan Economic Institute, 1000 Connecticut Ave., NW, Washington DC 20036, †; SRI/MF/complete.

R5685
Joint Center for Political Studies

R5685–1 BLACK ELECTED OFFICIALS: A National Roster, 1984
Annual. May 1984.
x+428 p.
ISBN 0-89059-033-8.
LC 84-051421.
SRI/MF/complete

Annual report, for 1984, on black elected officials, presenting statistical summary and roster of officials by State. Covers Federal, State, regional, county, municipal, judicial/law enforcement, and educational offices.

Data are from surveys of officials included in the Joint Center's data base, telephone inquiries, a newspaper clipping service, Census Bureau, and Council of State Governments.

Contents:

a. Listings of contents, tables, and charts; preface; overview; and explanatory notes. (p. v-x, 1-7)

b. Statistical summary, with 1 chart and 9 tables showing total and female black elected officials, by detailed office and State, and by office category and census division; and racial composition of congressional districts represented by blacks, of State legislatures, and of cities with black mayors; mostly as of Jan. 1984, with summary trends in number of black officials from 1970. (p. 8-20)

c. References. (p. 21)

d. State rosters, each including the following: overview, with description of governmental organization and data on total and black population, voting age population, and registered voters; and list of black elected officials, grouped by office, showing title, jurisdiction, address, and term expiration date. (p. 23-391)

e. Alphabetical index to officials. (p. 393-428)

Data by State and rosters also include D.C. and Virgin Islands.

This is the 13th edition of the report. The 12th edition presented data from 1982 surveys (for description, see SRI 1983 Annual, under this number). No 1983 edition was published; however, data from the Joint Center's 1983 surveys of black officials appeared in the Feb. 1984 issue of *Focus* (for description, see R5685-4.503, below).

Beginning with the 13th edition, this report is published and distributed for the Joint Center by UNIPUB, a division of R. R. Bowker Co.

Availability: UNIPUB, PO Box 1222, Ann Arbor MI 48106, $27.50+$1.50 postage and handling; SRI/MF/complete.

R5685–4 FOCUS
Monthly.
Approx. 7 p.
ISSN 0740-0195.
LC 73-643826.
SRI/MF/complete, shipped quarterly

Monthly newsletter (combined Nov./Dec. issue) focusing on topics of concern to blacks, including black political participation, and economic and social issues. Data are from Federal and private sources and the Center's own research.

Issues contain feature articles, some with statistics; and narrative depts. Recurring features include summary data from the Center's annual survey of black elected officials. An annual index is published in the Nov./Dec. or Jan. issue.

Articles with substantial statistics are described, as they appear, under "Statistical Features." Each issue of the publication is reviewed, but an abstract is published in SRI monthly issues only when statistical features appear.

Availability: Focus, 1301 Pennsylvania Ave., NW, Suite 400, Washington DC 20004, $12.00 per yr., single copy $1.25; SRI/MF/complete, shipped quarterly.

Issues reviewed during 1984: Nov./Dec. 1983-Oct. 1984 (P) (Vol. 11, Nos. 11/12; Vol. 12, Nos. 1-10).

STATISTICAL FEATURES:

R5685–4.501: Nov./Dec. 1983 (Vol. 11, Nos. 11-12)

FOREIGN TRADE POLICY AND UNEMPLOYMENT

(p. 5-6) By Kevin D. Armstrong. Article, with 2 tables showing women and minorities as percent of all workers, in 10 U.S. industries with most business lost to imports, and in 10 industries with most business gained from exports, 1980. Data are from Labor Dept.

R5685–4.502: Jan. 1984 (Vol. 12, No. 1)

BLACK FLIERS

(p. 3a-4a) By Wade S. Gatling. Article, with 3 tables showing blacks as percent of military flight personnel, Oct./Nov. 1983; and number of student pilots and attrition rates, by race, various periods Oct. 1979-May 1983; all by service branch.

Data are from the Army, Navy, and Air Force.

LARGEST INCREASE IN BEOs SINCE 1976

(p. 8) Article, with 1 table showing number of black elected officials by office category (Federal, State, substate/regional, county, municipal, judicial/law enforcement, and education), 1970-83. Data are from Joint Center for Political Studies.

R5685–4.503: Feb. 1984 (Vol. 12, No. 2)

NATIONAL PROFILE OF BLACK ELECTED OFFICIALS

(p. 3-6) By Milton D. Morris. Article, with 4 tables showing total and female black elected officials, by detailed office and State; mayor, term expiration date, and total population and percent black, for cities (50,000/more population) with black mayors; and congressman, principal city, and racial composition, for districts represented by blacks; all as of July 1983.

Data are from the Joint Center for Political Studies.

R5685–4.504: May 1984 (Vol. 12, No. 5)

BLACKS ON THE MOVE

(p. 7) By William P. O'Hare. Article, with 1 table showing net migration by race and census region, 1975-80, 1980/81, and 1981/82 periods. Data are from Census Bureau.

R5685–4.505: June 1984 (Vol. 12, No. 6)

SOUTHERN VOTER REGISTRATION

(p. 9) Table showing voter registration by race, for 11 southern States, 1980 and 1984. Data are from *American Political Report* and the Voter Education Project.

R5685–4.506: July 1984 (Vol. 12, No. 7)

PAY EQUITY

(p. 4-5) By Cynthia C. Dittmar. Article, with 1 undated chart showing average monthly salary for 6 predominantly male occupations compared with 6 predominantly female occupations judged to be of comparable worth, for selected locations. Data are from *The New York Times,* and are based on a study of government jobs.

R5685–4.507: Oct. 1984 (Vol. 12, No. 10)

EMPLOYMENT RECOVERY BYPASSES BLACKS

(p. 7) Article, with 1 table showing unemployment rate for total labor force and for whites, blacks, Hispanics, and total and black teenagers, July 1981 and Aug. 1984. Data are from BLS and the Full Employment Action Council.

R5685–5   BLACK ELECTED OFFICIALS and Their Constituencies

Monograph. 1983. v+38 p.
ISBN 0-941410-28-5.
SRI/MF/complete

By Thomas E. Cavanagh and Denise Stockton. Report examining trends in the number of blacks serving in elective offices, 1970s-82. Includes number of black elected officials, by level of government (with detail for selected offices), and by census region and State; and distribution of black elected officials, by political party, and size of jurisdiction's total and black population.

Data are from Joint Center for Political Studies and other private sources, including 1,523 responses to a 1980 survey of black elected officials.

Contains listings of contents, tables, and charts, and foreword (p. iii-v); narrative report, interspersed with 2 charts and 7 tables (p. 1-25); and bibliography and questionnaire facsimile (p. 26-35).

Availability: Joint Center for Political Studies, 1301 Pennsylvania Ave., NW, Suite 400, Washington DC 20004, $4.95; SRI/MF/complete.

R5685–6   WEALTH AND ECONOMIC STATUS: A Perspective on Racial Inequity

Monograph. 1983. vii+36 p.
ISBN 0-941410-35-8.
LC 83-22171.
SRI/MF/complete

By William P. O'Hare. Report comparing characteristics of personal wealth, by race, 1979, with summary comparisons to 1967. Presents data on total and/or average value of holdings, and percent of households with holdings, for the following types of assets: equity in home, vehicles, rental property, own business, and farm; financial assets by type; and household goods/other assets; all by race.

Also includes black/white median income ratios by age and family status, 1981; and distribution of black families by income group, selected years 1960-82.

Most data are from the 1979 Income Survey Development Program, conducted by the Census Bureau for HHS. The survey covered a representative sample of approximately 7,000 households.

Contains listings of contents, tables, and charts, and foreword (p. v-vii); narrative analysis interspersed with 2 charts and 7 tables (p. 1-28); discussion of data limitations (p. 29-30); and bibliography (p. 31-33).

Availability: Joint Center for Political Studies, 1301 Pennsylvania Ave., NW, Suite 400, Washington DC 20004, $4.95; SRI/MF/complete.

R5685–7   CHANGING PATTERNS OF BLACK FAMILY INCOME, 1960-82

Monograph. Jan. 1984.
xiii+66 p.+errata sheet.
ISBN 0-941410-43-9.
LC 84-5654.
SRI/MF/complete

By Henry E. Felder. Report examining trends in the economic status of blacks relative to that of whites, 1960s-80s. Includes data on the following, generally shown by race:

a. Median family income, by metro status and region; income sources; distribution of families by income level; and poverty rates; with selected detail by family composition.

b. Family composition, including detail for black female householders by marital status and presence of children; and children living with both parents.

c. Labor force nonparticipation rates, by age group; unemployment rates for adults and teenagers; youth labor force status indicators; earnings, by educational attainment; and earnings and workers, by occupational category; most by sex.

Data are from Census Bureau and Dept of Labor.

Contains listings of contents, tables, and charts (p. v-viii); foreword and summary (p. ix-xiii); narrative analysis in 7 chapters, interspersed with 5 charts and 18 tables (p. 1-57); and bibliography (p. 58-62).

Availability: Joint Center for Political Studies, 1301 Pennsylvania Ave., NW, Suite 400, Washington DC 20004, $4.95; SRI/MF/complete.

R5685–8   PUBLIC SCHOOL DESEGREGATION in the U.S., 1968-80

Monograph. Apr. 1983.
xii+64 p.
ISBN 0-941410-29-3.
LC 83-187197.
SRI/MF/complete

By Gary Orfield. Report on trends in public elementary/secondary school desegregation, by region, State, city school district, and metro area, 1960s-80. Includes data on black and Hispanic students' enrollment in predominantly minority vs. predominantly white schools; white students' share of total enrollment in schools attended by a "typical" black and Hispanic student; enrollment composition, usually shown for blacks, whites, and Hispanics, but occasionally also including American Indians and Asians; and related measures of desegregation.

Data are shown variously for 5 regions; 50 States and DC; over 100 large city school districts; and selected metro areas.

Report was prepared by JCPS for the House of Representatives Subcommittee on Civil and Constitutional Rights, and is based on data from DBS Corp. and the Dept of Education.

Contains contents and table listings (p. v-viii); foreword and preface (p. ix-xii); 4 chapters with narrative analysis and 27 tables (p. 1-49); appendices with 2 tables and technical notes (p. 51-58); and notes, references, and lists of JCPS officials and publications (p. 59-64).

Availability: Joint Center for Political Studies, 1301 Pennsylvania Ave., NW, Suite 400, Washington DC 20004, $4.95; SRI/MF/complete.

R5685-9   JCPS CONGRESSIONAL DISTRICT FACT BOOK
Biennial. 1984. 32 p.
ISBN 0-941410-34-X.
LC 83-25159.
SRI/MF/complete

Biennial report, for 1984, presenting statistics on socioeconomic and political characteristics of individual congressional districts and States. Includes the following:

a. Black and Hispanic percents of voting-age population, rural and college-educated percents of total population, blue collar percent of total employment, and owner-occupied percent of total housing (all undated); population percent change, 1970-80 period; per capita income index, 1979; and unemployment rate (States only), 1979.

b. Name and political party of incumbent U.S. Representatives and Senators; percent of vote received by incumbents in 1982 or most recent election, and next year incumbent Senators face reelection; percent of incumbents' 1982 roll call votes approved by organizations associated with liberal, conservative, minority, labor, and business interests; and campaign spending by 1982 Democratic and Republican candidates for U.S. Representative.

c. Electoral votes (States only); and 1980 presidential election voter turnout, and percent of votes for Carter, Reagan, and Anderson.

Also includes rankings of top and/or bottom 10 districts for many of the characteristics noted above, and for the following: population shares of selected ethnic and ancestry groups, working women, persons in poverty, elderly persons, college students, government workers, Armed Forces members, mass transit commuters, and farm residents; and population density.

Data are from the Census Bureau, BLS, and various publications.

Contains contents listing and foreword (p. 3-4); introduction, with methodology and analysis (p. 5-7); 1 table for districts (p. 8-21); 1 table for States (p. 22-25); and 40 ranking tables (p. 26-32).

This is the 1st edition of the report.

Availability: Joint Center for Political Studies, 1301 Pennsylvania Ave., NW, Washington DC 20004, $5.95; SRI/MF/complete, delayed shipment in Jan. 1985.

R5685-10   BLACK EMPLOYMENT IN CITY GOVERNMENT, 1973-80
Monograph. Dec. 1983.
viii+56 p.
ISBN 0-941410-32-3.
LC 83-24847.
SRI/MF/complete

By Peter K. Eisinger. Report examining trends in employment of blacks in municipal government jobs, for 40 cities, 1973-80. Includes data on blacks' actual share of municipal work force compared to a "fair-share" index (based on black share of city population), by city. Data are shown for all, administrative, and professional jobs, 1980, with change from 1973.

Also includes statistical analyses correlating municipal employment of blacks with trends in city population (total and black), municipal work force, and Federal and State aid, and with presence of a black mayor; and ratios comparing percents of black vs. white municipal employees earning over $16,000 and $25,000, by presence of black mayor.

Data are based on 40 responses to a survey of personnel depts in cities with at least 50,000 total population and at least 10% blacks. The survey excluded part-time and provisional workers, public school personnel, CETA workers, and employees appointed by chief executives.

Contains listings of contents, tables, and chart, and foreword (p. v-vii); 7 chapters, with narrative analysis, 1 chart, and 10 tables (p. 1-50); 2 appendices, with methodology and 1 table on sample characteristics (p. 51-52); and references (p. 53-56).

Availability: Joint Center for Political Studies, 1301 Pennsylvania Ave., NW, Suite 400, Washington DC 20004, $4.95; SRI/MF/complete.

R6000
National Academy of Sciences:
National Research Council

R6000-7   SUMMARY REPORT, 1983: Doctorate Recipients from U.S. Universities
Annual. [1984.] 1+53 p.
LC SN 84-10316.
SRI/MF/complete

Annual summary report on doctorate degree recipients during period July 1, 1982 to June 30, 1983, with trends from 1959. Includes data on recipient race/ethnic group, sex, citizenship, field of study, sources of support, State location of doctoral institution, and postdoctoral study and employment plans.

Data are from the National Research Council annual Survey of Earned Doctorates, and represent all 31,190 doctorate recipients during the survey period. Data are based on questionnaire responses from 29,794 recipients, and on commencement bulletin information for others. The survey covers research and applied research doctorates and excludes professional degrees.

Contents:

a. Highlights (inside front cover); foreword (p. 3); and narrative summary, with 7 charts and 6 trend tables (p. 4-21).

b. Explanation, and 6 basic tables listed below (p. 22-39); technical appendix, with 2 tables on conversion of survey findings to new classification of specialties (p. 40-49); and sample questionnaire, specialties list, codes, and abbreviations (p. 50-52 and inside back cover).

This is the 17th annual report.

Availability: National Academy of Sciences: National Research Council, Doctorate Records Project, Office of Scientific and Engineering Personnel, 2101 Constitution Ave., NW, Washington DC 20418, †; SRI/MF/complete.

BASIC TABLES:
[Data by race/ethnic group are shown for American Indian, Asian, black, white, Puerto Rican, Mexican/American, and other Hispanic. Data by citizenship generally are shown for U.S. citizens, and for noncitizens with permanent and temporary visas. All data are for 1982/83.]

1. Number of doctorate recipients, by sex and subfield. (p. 24)

1A. Number of doctorate recipients, by citizenship, racial/ethnic group, and subfield. (p. 26)

2. Statistical profile of doctorate recipients [including marital and citizenship status, median age, percent with bachelor's and doctorate degrees in same field, percent with master's degree, median time from bachelor's to doctorate degree, postdoctoral study and employment plans, and location of postdoctoral employment (census division or foreign), all by sex], by field of doctorate. (p. 30-35)

3. [Detailed] sources of support in graduate school of doctorate recipients, by sex and summary field. (p. 36)

4. State [including Puerto Rico], of doctoral institution of doctorate recipients by sex, and summary field. (p. 37)

5. Statistical profile of doctorate recipients, by racial/ethnic group and U.S. citizenship status. (p. 38)

R6400
National Center for Higher Education Management Systems

R6400-1   HIGHER EDUCATION FINANCING IN THE FIFTY STATES: Interstate Comparisons, FY81
Annual. Mar. 1984.
xvi+546 p.
LC 78-21570.
SRI/MF/current report delayed, previous report complete

Annual report, by Marilyn McCoy and Kent Halstead, on higher education finances for each State, by institution control and type, FY81. Also includes data on student enrollment, State expenditures and tax collections by type, and faculty salaries.

Data are from NCES, Census Bureau, and other government and private sources.

Contents:

Content and table listings, foreword, preface, and user guide. (p. v-xvi)

Chapter 1. Introduction. (p. 1-10)

Chapter 2. General Trends Among the States. Includes narrative summary with text tables; and 46 detailed tables showing State rankings and indexes based on U.S. averages, for most of the data items covered in Chapter 3. (p. 11-67)

Chapter 3. State by State Report. Includes narrative summary, and 11 charts and 15 tables described below, repeated for U.S. average and each State. (p. 69-485)

Appendix A-B. Includes listing of institutions by State arranged by type, data sources and definitions. (p. 487-546)

This is the 3rd edition of the report (previous editions were published on an irregular schedule). The 2nd edition, for FY79, has also been reviewed by SRI, and is also available on SRI microfiche, under this number [Recurring. Dec. 1982. xiii+515 p.+errata sheet. $29.95+$0.50 shipping and handling]. SRI coverage begins with these editions.

The 1st edition was issued by the National Institute of Education and is described in *American Statistics Index*, a companion Congressional Information Service publication. For description, see ASI 1980 Annual under 4914-1.

Availability: National Center for Higher Education Management Systems, Publications Office, PO Drawer P, Boulder CO 80302, $29.95+$0.50 shipping and handling; SRI/MF/ current report complete, delayed shipment in Mar. 1985; previous report complete.

TABLES AND CHARTS:

R6400–1.1: State by State Reports

[Tables and charts for U.S. and each State cover the data topics described below. Data generally are shown for 1981 or FY81, with selected trends from FY77. Most data are shown separately for public and independent institutions, with selected detail for all and research universities with and without medical programs, and for comprehensive, baccalaureate, 2-year, and professional/specialized institutions.]

a. State/local expenditures per capita and distribution by function, with detail for higher education including student aid; population and FTE enrollment; in-State and out-of-State enrollment, and high school graduates and number entering higher education, per 1,000 population; and State/local potential and collected revenues by tax type.

b. Institutional revenues, including State/local appropriations, tuition, private gifts/grants, and government grants/contracts; and expenditures for instruction, academic support, research, and public service; generally shown per student or faculty member.

c. Faculty size, and average salary by academic rank; number and mean size of institutions; and enrollment distribution by class level, including graduate students.

R8490
Northeast-Midwest Institute

R8490–5 **STATE OF THE REGION, 1983: A Preview**
Biennial. Jan. 1983. 106 p.
SRI/MF/complete

Biennial report, for 1983, analyzing economic trends for the Northeast and Midwest regions and States, and presenting selected economic data for all regions and States, 1980-81 and trends.

Data are primarily from Federal Government sources, noted with each table.

Contains 4 parts: narrative analyses for Northeast and Midwest regions (7 p.) and for 19 Northeastern and Midwestern States (38 p.); 7 trend charts (7 p.); and 27 tables, listed below (54 p.).

This is the 3rd edition of the report. For description of previous edition, for 1981, see SRI 1981 Annual, under this number.

Availability: Northeast-Midwest Institute, Publications Office, PO Box 37209, Washington DC 20013, price on request; SRI/MF/complete.

TABLES:

[All tables show data by State and for 5 regions. Data are for 1980 or 1981, generally with comparisons to 1970 and/or 1976, unless otherwise noted.]

R8490–5.1: Economic Trends by State and Region

POPULATION AND INCOME

1-3. Total, and urban and rural population change. (6 p.)

4-6. Personal and disposable income; and percent of population with income below 125% of poverty, 1969, 1975, 1979. (6 p.)

EMPLOYMENT, UNEMPLOYMENT, AND EDUCATIONAL ATTAINMENT

7-11. Labor force; and nonagricultural, manufacturing sector, service sector, and chemical, steel, and motor vehicle manufacturing employment. (10 p.)

12-14. Unemployment and unemployment rates; and long-term (over 15 weeks) and youth unemployment [including youth labor force]. (6 p.)

15. Educational levels (percent of population over 25 years old) [completing at least 4 years of high school and 4 years of college]. (2 p.)

CONSTRUCTION AND AGRICULTURAL RECEIPTS

16. Investment in nonresidential construction. (2 p.)

17. Agricultural cash receipts. (2 p.)

ENERGY

18. Industrial energy prices [by fuel type]. (2 p.)

19-20. State energy consumption and expenditures; and average household energy costs [for home energy and motor gasoline]. (4 p.)

21-22. State energy production as a percent of total U.S. production [by energy type]; and energy self-sufficiency index. (4 p.)

GOVERNMENT FINANCES

23. Tax capacity of the States, 1975, 1979, 1980. (2 p.)

24. Maximum monthly AFDC and food stamp potential benefits [for 1-parent family of 3 persons]. (2 p.)

25-26. Federal balance of payments [and spending and taxes per person]; and Federal civilian employment. (4 p.)

27. Urban development action grants, [private investment, and jobs created and retained], cumulative FY78-82. (2 p.)

R8750
Population Reference Bureau

R8750–1 **POPULATION TODAY**
Monthly. Appprox. 12 p.
LC SC 84-7804.
SRI/MF/complete, shipped quarterly

Monthly review of current topics related to international population size and growth, including birth rates and fertility, migration trends, contraception and family planning, food supplies, and health conditions.

Data are from foreign government agencies and statistical yearbooks; NCHS; books, journal articles, and research papers; and the bureau's own research.

Issues contain narrative articles, some with statistics; book reviews; and regular departmental features, including the following:

a. "Speaking Graphically" feature on population trends or projections for selected countries, generally presenting summary charts only, but occasionally including more substantial data.

b. "Demographer's Page" article, usually including 1 or more tables.

c. "Population Update" monthly data showing U.S. vital statistics for 12-month period ending approximately 5 months prior to cover date, with 3-4 year trends; U.S. population estimates for month 4-5 months prior to cover date, and same month of previous year; and world population and annual growth estimates, as of cover date month.

d. "Spotlight" profile of a country or country subarea, showing population, land area, and other summary vital statistics and economic data.

"Population Update" monthly data appear in all issues. All additional features with substantial statistical content are described, as they appear, under "Statistical Features;" page locations and areas and dates of coverage for "Spotlight" profiles are also noted. Nonstatistical features are not covered.

Prior to the Jan. 1984 issue, publication was titled *Intercom* and was published bimonthly. *Intercom* general format, and content and title of "Population Update" feature, varied slightly from this description.

Availability: Population Reference Bureau, 2213 M St., NW, Washington DC 20037, members †, back issues $2.00; SRI/MF/complete, shipped quarterly.

Issues reviewed during 1984: Sept./Oct.-Nov./Dec. 1983 (bimonthly); Jan.-Oct. 1984 (monthly) (P) (Vol. 11, Nos. 9/10-11/12; Vol. 12, Nos. 1-10).

STATISTICAL FEATURES:

R8750–1.501: Sept./Oct. 1983 (Vol. 11, No. 9/10)

DEMOGRAPHER'S PAGE: A 'NUMBERS' APPROACH TO THE 1983 DATA SHEET

(p. 8-10) By Leon F. Bouvier. Article, with 1 table showing projected births, deaths, infant deaths, and population growth, 1983-2000 period, and mid-1983 population, for world by development level, by world area, and for 10 most populous countries. Data are based on unpublished computer printouts used in preparing *1983 World Population Data Sheet*.

Data correction appears in the Jan. 1984 issue; for description, see R8750-1.502 below.

STATE POPULATIONS OF THE FUTURE PROJECTED

(p. 12-13) Article, with 1 table showing population projections by census division and State, 1990 and 2000, with actual data for 1980. Data are from Census Bureau.

R8750–1.502: Jan. 1984 (Vol. 12, No. 1)

SPOTLIGHT: EGYPT

(p. 12) Profile of Egypt, as of various years 1981-83.

DEMOGRAPHER'S PAGE: SUN BELT GROWTH: NOT WHAT IT SEEMS?

(p. 6-7) By Carl Haub. Article, with 2 tables showing States ranked by migration rate and also showing actual migration, and States ranked by ratio of births per 100 deaths, 1980-82 period. Data are from Census Bureau.

CORRECTION

(p. 10) Data correction to "Demographer's Page" article on population projections appearing in Sept./Oct. 1983 issue; for description, see R8750-1.501 above.

R8750–1.503: Feb. 1984 (Vol. 12, No. 2)

SPOTLIGHT: VIETNAM

(p. 12) Profile of Vietnam, as of 1982 or 1983.

1980 STATE FERTILITY RATES

(p. 8) Article, with 1 table showing States ranked by fertility rate, and also including U.S. average, 1980. Data are from NCHS.

R8750–1.504: Mar. 1984 (Vol. 12, No. 3)

SPOTLIGHT: BARBADOS

(p. 12) Profile of Barbados, as of various years 1979-83.

ASIAN BIRTH DATA IN U.S. RELEASED

(p. 5) Article, with 1 table showing U.S. births, by race, and for Chinese, Japanese, Hawaiian, Filipino, and other Asian ethnic groups, 1980. Data are from NCHS.

DEMOGRAPHER'S PAGE: SWEDEN'S POPULATION GROWS, SWEDISH POPULATION DOESN'T

(p. 6-7) By Murray Gendell. Article, with 3 tables showing the following for Sweden: mean population; birth, death, immigration, and emigration rates; and citizens' and aliens' natural population increase, with some detail for birth and death rates; various years 1970-81. Data are from Sweden's National Central Bureau of Statistics.

R8750–1.505: Apr. 1984 (Vol. 12, No. 4)

SPOTLIGHT: WASHINGTON, D.C.

(p. 12) Profile of Washington, D.C., as of various periods 1970-82.

CENSUS CLUES TO IRANIANS IN U.S.

(p. 8) Article, with 1 table showing top 10 States ranked by size of population with Iranian ancestry, 1980. Data are from Census Bureau.

R8750–1.506: May 1984 (Vol. 12, No. 5)

SPOTLIGHT: CANADA

(p. 12) Profile of Canada, as of various years 1981-84.

SPEAKING GRAPHICALLY

(p. 5) Includes 2 charts showing distribution of U.S. population, and of persons voting in Federal election, by age, 1982. Data are from Census Bureau.

DEMOGRAPHER'S PAGE: THE CASE OF THE ELUSIVE INFANT MORTALITY RATE

(p. 6-7) By Robert B. Hartford. Article, with 1 table showing U.S. and 30 other countries ranked by infant mortality rate, 1980 with comparative data for 1981-82.

TAKE A NUMBER: SUN BELT CITIES

(p. 10) Brief article, with 1 table showing top 10 U.S. cities ranked by population, as of July 1, 1982 with comparison to Apr. 1, 1980. Data are from Census Bureau.

R8750–1.507: July/Aug. 1984 (Vol. 12, No. 7/8)

SPOTLIGHT: LIBYA

(p. 12) Profile of Libya, as of various years 1980-84.

LATEST UN ASSESSMENTS PROJECT POPULATION TO COME

(p. 5) Article, with 1 table showing world population growth rate, and crude birth and death rates, 1980-84 period; and population forecast for Africa, Latin America, China, and total world, 1985; all with high, medium, and low projections for 2025 or 2020-25 period. Data are from the UN.

R8750–1.508: Sept. 1984 (Vol. 12, No. 9)

SPOTLIGHT: MEXICO

(p. 12) Profile of Mexico, as of various years 1982-84.

CHINA'S BIRTH DATA SHOW ANOMALY IN SEX RATIOS

(p. 3) Article, with 1 table showing sex ratios for China's urban and rural births, by birth order, 1981. Data are based on China's 1982 census.

R8750–1.509: Oct. 1984 (Vol. 12, No. 10)

SPOTLIGHT: ALASKA

(p. 16) Profile of Alaska, as of various years 1980-83.

SPEAKING GRAPHICALLY

(p. 5) Includes 2 charts showing distribution of world population between developing and industrialized countries, 1980 and projected for 2100. Data are from the UN.

DEMOGRAPHER'S PAGE: A DEMOGRAPHER LOOKS AT THE 1984 OLYMPIC GAMES

(p. 6-7) By Leon F. Bouvier. Article, with 3 tables showing population, and participants and medals won in the 1984 Summer Olympic Games, for 10 countries winning the most medals.

R8750–2 **POPULATION BULLETIN**
Series. For individual publication data, see below.
ISSN 0032-468X.
LC 52-19281.
SRI/MF/complete

Continuing series of reports examining selected aspects of world and U.S. demography, including population growth in developed and developing countries, fertility, child development, and family planning.

Each issue focuses on a specific topic or country, and contains approximately 40 pages of narrative analysis with interspersed charts and tables.

Reports are issued 3-4 times yearly, in varying months. Reports reviewed during 1984 are described below.

Availability: Population Reference Bureau, Circulation Department, 2213 M St., NW, Washington DC 20037, distributed to all PRB members (varying membership rates), or single copy $4.00; SRI/MF/complete.

R8750–2.25: Changing American Family
[Monograph. Oct. 1983. 44 p. Vol. 38, No. 4. SRI/MF/complete.]

By Arland Thornton and Deborah Freedman. Report examining changes in American family structure, 1950s-82, with historical trends. Data are from Census Bureau and other specified sources. Includes 7 charts, and 5 tables showing:

a. Premarital sexual activity, pregnancies, and abortions among urban women aged 15-19, 1971, 1976, and 1979; child care arrangements of working women, 1958 and 1977; and household size distribution, and average persons per household, 1790, 1900, and decennially 1930-80.

b. Living arrangements of persons aged 65/ over, by marital status, 1900, 1962, and 1975; and of never-married persons aged 25-34, by sex, selected years 1950-82.

R8750–2.26: Planet Earth 1984-2034: A Demographic Vision
[Monograph. Feb. 1984. 41 p. Vol. 39, No. 1. SRI/MF/complete.]

By Leon F. Bouvier. Report on world demographic trends and projections, various years 1884-2034. Data are from UN, author's estimates, and other specified sources.

Includes 6 tables showing fertility rates in 19 developed countries, selected years 1970-82; world population, selected years 1884-1984; world's top 10 metro areas 1984, and top 10 metro areas and countries 2034, ranked by population size; and median age, and percent of population under age 15 and over age 65, for 10 countries with highest and lowest median age, 1985.

R8750–2.27: Israel's Population: The Challenge of Pluralism
[Monograph. Apr. 1984. 41 p. Vol. 39, No. 2. SRI/MF/complete.]

By Dov Friedlander and Calvin Goldscheider. Report reviewing demographic developments in Israel, 1942-82, with population projections to 2015. Data are from Israeli Central Bureau of Statistics and authors' estimates. Includes 1 chart and 7 tables showing the following for Israel, unless otherwise noted:

a. Employed men, with distribution by occupational group, selected years 1965-82; and population, by religion, ethnic origin, and place of birth, selected years 1948-82.

b. Median age at 1st marriage, by sex; fertility rate; life expectancy; percent of employed males in white-collar jobs; percent of women aged 25-34 in labor force; annual rate of natural population increase; and net immigration; for Jews by birthplace and/or ethnic origin, and for Moslem and Christian Arabs, various periods 1948-82.

c. Distribution of immigrants to Israel by country or world region of origin, various periods 1942-82; and population projections, for Israel/occupied areas, with detail for Arabs and for Jews by age, 1985, 2000, and 2015.

Also includes 1 table on population projection methodology.

R8750–5   1984 WORLD POPULATION DATA SHEET
Annual.   Apr. 1984.
1 p. Foldout.
SRI/MF/complete

Annual data sheet, for 1984, on population size and characteristics, and GNP per capita, shown for approximately 170 countries arranged by world region, with aggregate data for developing countries. Data are most recent available as of mid-1984, and are from UN, World Bank, Census Bureau, and official country publications. Data dates and sources are specified in table footnotes.

Contains 1 table showing the following:

a. Population: estimated mid-1984, projected to 2000 and 2020, annual percent natural increase, "doubling time" at current rate, percent under age 15 and over age 64, and percent urban.

b. Birth, death, infant mortality, and fertility rates; Government perception of fertility level (high, satisfactory, and low); life expectancy at birth; and per capita GNP, 1982.

This is the 22nd data sheet.

Availability: Population Reference Bureau, PO Box 35012, Washington DC 20013, $2.00; SRI/MF/complete.

R8750–9   U.S. POPULATION DATA SHEET
Annual.   Sept. 1984.
1 p. Oversized.
SRI/MF/complete, current & previous year reports

Annual data sheet, compiled by Carl Haub, on population size and selected demographic and socioeconomic characteristics, 1980s with trends from 1960. Data are from the Census Bureau, NCHS, and other Federal agencies.

Contains 1 table showing the following data for total U.S., and by census region and division, and State:

a. Population size: resident population as of July 1983, and Apr. 1970 and 1980; rank, 1960 and 1983; and projections, 1990.

b. Vital and demographic data: birth, death, and infant mortality rates, 1981; fertility rate, population born in State, and black and Hispanic population, 1980; births per 100 deaths, 1980-83; and population age 65/over, and below age 18, 1983.

c. Socioeconomic data: per capita personal income, 1983; and unemployment rate, Apr. 1984.

d. Miscellaneous: land area, and rank; population density, and rank, 1983; net migration, Apr. 1980-July 1983; and electoral votes, and estimates of voting-age population, 1984.

This is the 4th annual data sheet.

Previous report was also reviewed in 1984 and is also available on SRI microfiche, under this number [Annual. Sept. 1983. 1 p. Oversized. $2.00].

Previous report is similar in format and content, but also includes median age, voter participation in 1980 presidential election, population completing high school, crime rate, and seats in the House of Representatives; and omits fertility rate, population under age 18, births per 100 deaths, population born in State, electoral votes, and estimates of voting-age population.

Availability: Population Reference Bureau, 2213 M St., NW, Washington DC 20037, $2.00; SRI/MF/complete.

R8750–13   PRB OCCASIONAL SERIES: The Caribbean
Series.   For individual publication data, see below.
SRI/MF/complete

By Leon F. Bouvier. Series of 8 reports, each focusing on a single country in the Caribbean area, presenting population trends and projections 1840s-2030, and labor force projections 1980s-2030.

Data are primarily based on individual country and British Commonwealth censuses, U.S. Government reports, and a private study on Caribbean population.

Each report contains listing of contents/tables/charts; and analysis and appendix, with 5 charts, and 7-10 tables showing some or all of the following:

a. Population, crude birth and death rates, and percent natural population increase, various years 1843-1982; and native-born emigrants to the U.S., various periods 1955-80.

b. Population by age group, and labor force, under various fertility/migration rate assumptions, decennially 1980-2030.

Some reports include additional population data. Reports are listed below; data omissions and additional data are noted.

Availability: Population Reference Bureau, 2213 M St., NW, Washington DC 20037, $2.00 each; SRI/MF/complete.

REPORTS:

R8750–13.1: Barbados: Yesterday, Today and Tomorrow
[Monograph. Dec. 1983. 16 p. SRI/MF/complete.]

Report also includes Barbados population by sex, selected years 1844-1980; and infant mortality and life expectancy rates, by sex, selected periods 1920-71. Report omits crude birth and death rates, and percent natural population increase.

R8750–13.2: Saint Lucia: Yesterday, Today and Tomorrow
[Monograph. Jan. 1984. 17 p. SRI/MF/complete.]

Report also includes St. Lucia births, deaths, and net migration, selected periods 1946-60.

R8750–13.3: St. Kitts/Nevis: Yesterday, Today and Tomorrow
[Monograph. Feb. 1984. 16 p. SRI/MF/complete.]

Report also includes Anguilla population, selected years 1844-1946. Report omits St. Kitts/Nevis crude birth and death rates, and percent natural population increase.

R8750–13.4: Antigua and Barbuda: Yesterday, Today and Tomorrow
[Monograph. Feb. 1984. 16 p. SRI/MF/complete.]

Population trends are shown separately for the 2 islands.

R8750–13.5: Dominica: Yesterday, Today and Tomorrow
[Monograph. Mar. 1984. 17 p. SRI/MF/complete.]

R8750–13.6: St. Vincent and the Grenadines: Yesterday, Today and Tomorrow
[Monograph. Mar. 1984. 16 p. SRI/MF/complete.]

R8750–13.7: Grenada: Yesterday, Today and Tomorrow
[Monograph. Apr. 1984. 16 p. SRI/MF/complete.]

R8750–13.8: Belize: Yesterday, Today and Tomorrow
[Monograph. Apr. 1984. 16 p. SRI/MF/complete.]

Report also includes Belize population distribution by race/ethnicity [American Indian, white, black (Creole), Asian, Carib, and mixed], 1946 and 1980.

R8765
Potential Gas Committee

R8765-1   POTENTIAL SUPPLY OF NATURAL GAS IN THE U.S. as of Dec. 31, 1982
Biennial.   June 1983.
iv+74 p.+maps.
SRI/MF/complete

Biennial report presenting estimates of potential natural gas reserves, by region, as of 1982, with trends from 1966. Also includes data on drilling trends. Data are based on Potential Gas Committee estimates, government and industry assn reports, and individual studies.

Contents:

  Part I. Report of the Potential Gas Committee. Includes narrative summary; definitions and estimation procedures; and 21 tables showing estimated U.S. potential natural gas supply (probable, possible, and speculative, onshore and offshore), by region (including Alaska) and depth, as of Dec. 31, 1982, with comparative biennial estimates from 1966. (p. 1-40)

  Part II. Report of the Potential Gas Agency. Includes review of ultimately recoverable gas volume in U.S., with 6 tables showing cumulative production, proved reserves, and estimated potential supply, biennially 1966-82, with selected detail by region; and drilling trends, 1972-82. (p. 41-49)

  Part III. Policy Guidelines and Membership of the Potential Gas Agency and Potential Gas Committee. (p. 51-74)

  Maps of natural gas reserves in the continental U.S. and Alaska. (back cover pocket)

Parts I-III include tables of contents.
  Previous report, for 1980, is described in SRI 1982 Annual, under this number.

Availability: Potential Gas Agency, Colorado School of Mines, Golden CO 80401, $20.00; SRI/MF/complete.

R8780
Princeton
Religion Research Center

R8780-1   EMERGING TRENDS
Monthly.
Approx. 6 p. no paging.
LC 82-20489.
SRI/MF/complete, shipped quarterly

Monthly report (except July and Aug.) presenting results of surveys conducted by Gallup International on varied religious and social issues, including prevalence of religious beliefs and practices, and perceptions of organized religion in society and personal life.

  Each issue contains articles on several topics; some topics recur annually or several times per year. Articles include text statistics characterizing poll results, and usually tables and/or charts showing response distribution for specific survey questions, sometimes shown by respondent characteristics.

  Tables and charts are described, as they appear, under "Statistical Features."
Availability: Princeton Religion Research Center, Publications Department, 53 Bank St., PO Box 310, Princeton NJ 08542, $30.00 per yr.; SRI/MF/complete, shipped quarterly.
Issues reviewed during 1984: Nov. 1983-Sept. 1984 (P) (Vol. 5, Nos. 9-10; Vol. 6, Nos. 1-7).

STATISTICAL FEATURES:
[Unless otherwise noted, data are from recent surveys; and data by religion are shown for Protestants and Catholics.]

R8780-1.501: Nov. 1983 (Vol. 5, No. 9)
Contains distribution of responses to questions in the following areas:

  a. Participation in 10 types of religious activities; beliefs regarding Bible origin, with trends from 1965; and frequency of Bible reading. 3 tables.

  b. Teenagers' views on importance of religion in own vs. parents' life, by sex, age, above and below average academic performance, region, religion, and regularity of church attendance. 3 tables.

  c. Satisfaction with personal life and general U.S. outlook, by race, with trends from 1979; and church contribution as a percent of income, by religion, with detail for 4 Protestant denominations. 3 tables.

R8780-1.502: Dec. 1983 (Vol. 5, No. 10)
Contains distribution of responses to questions in the following areas:

  a. Church/synagogue membership, and comparison of persons who do and do not belong to/attend church, variously by sex, age, religion (including Jews and Eastern Orthodox), race, educational attainment, and region, with summary membership trends from 1937. 3 tables.

  b. EC youth and adult perceptions of own religiousness, with family/household status of religious youth, 1982 survey. 2 tables.

  c. Ethics: opinions on level of ethics in society, business, and politics; reported unethical or illegal activities; and perceptions of various activities as wrong; compared for general public and business executives, and for persons who do and do not belong to/attend church. 4 tables.

  d. Willingness to vote for atheist presidential candidate, selected years 1958-83. 1 table.

R8780-1.503: Jan. 1984 (Vol. 6, No. 1)
Contains distribution of responses to questions concerning influence of religion on American life, including perceptions of change, and perceived importance in own life, by sex, age, and religion, with selected detail for Protestant denominations, and trends from 1952. 9 tables.

R8780-1.504: Feb. 1984 (Vol. 6, No. 2)
Contains distribution of responses to questions in the following areas:

  a. Church/synagogue attendance, and church attendance by religion, with trends from 1958. 2 tables.

  b. Teenagers: preferences regarding religious discussion with parents, by race, sex and age, religion, and regularity of church at-

tendance; and marijuana use and views on decriminalization, by sex, age, race, academic performance, white or blue collar background, region, and urban or rural location, with trends from 1978. 2 tables.

  c. Pope John Paul II, public opinion with comparisons to 2 previous Popes, by religion, selected dates 1960-Jan. 1984. 2 tables.

  d. Alcoholism and drug abuse, public opinion on seriousness in U.S. and 11-12 foreign countries. 2 tables.

R8780-1.505: Mar. 1984 (Vol. 6, No. 3)
Contains distribution of responses to questions in the following areas:

  a. Religious preference (Protestant, Catholic, Jewish, other, and none), 1974-83, and quinquennially 1947-72. 1 table.

  b. Public belief in second coming of Christ, by religion and age; and participation in charismatic movement; 1983, with trends from 1976. 4 tables.

  c. Iowa residents' ratings of 15 activities as sins, by age group. 2 tables.

  d. Public approval for establishing diplomatic relations with the Vatican, by religion and selected denomination. 1 table.

  e. Reported hunger and deprivation, including inability to purchase food, clothing, and health care, and pay bills, by race, 1974 and 1984. 5 tables.

R8780-1.506: Apr. 1984 (Vol. 6, No. 4)
Contains distribution of responses concerning support for prayer in public schools and constitutional amendment permitting prayer, 1984 and selected trends from 1982. 3 tables.

R8780-1.507: May 1984 (Vol. 6, No. 5)
Contains distribution of responses to questions in the following areas:

  a. College students' sexual experience and characteristics of premarital sexual relationships, attitudes toward marital fidelity and premarital sex, and perceived difference between men and women regarding sex drive, thought processes, general intelligence, and assertiveness in classroom settings, all by sex. 12 tables.

  b. Most admired 10 men, for adults and teenagers. 2 tables

  c. Importance of religion in own life at present and ever; and persons who have never been very religious, by selected demographic characteristics, region, religion, and belief in God. 3 tables.

  d. Teenagers' opinions on ease of obtaining divorce, and whether people try hard enough to avoid divorce; and belief in selected supernatural phenomena; with various detail by sex, age, and religion, and comparisons to 1978. 4 tables.

  e. Political party affiliation and ratings of Reagan's job performance, for 5-6 Protestant denominations. 2 tables.

R8780-1.508: June 1984 (Vol. 6, No. 6)
Contains distribution of responses in the following areas:

  a. Daily religious observances and spiritual activities. 1 table.

b. Teenagers: receiving religious training and considering religion as a vocation, by sex, age, race, academic performance, religion, and regularity of church attendance; and ratings of ethical standards of persons in 10 professional groups. 3 tables.

c. UK: preferred and expected topics to be addressed during an upcoming visit by evangelist Billy Graham; and attitudes toward ordination of women as priests. 4 tables.

Issue also includes 1 table showing value of charitable contributions to religious organizations/causes, 1970-83. Data are from *Giving USA,* covered in SRI under A0700-1.

R8780–1.509: Sept. 1984 (Vol. 6, No. 7)

Contains 2 tables showing distribution of Canadian's responses concerning the relevance of organized religion in their own lives, by region, sex, and age, 1978 and 1984; and church/synagogue attendance, with detail by religion, selected years 1957-84.

Issue also includes 2 tables showing churches/synagogues and membership for major religions, with membership detail for Christian denominations, 1981 and/or 1982. Data are primarily from *Yearbook of American and Canadian Churches,* covered in SRI under C0105-1.

R8780–2   RELIGION IN AMERICA, 1984
Annual.   Mar. 1984.   97 p.
Gallup Rpt. No. 222.
SRI/MF/complete

Annual report, for 1984, presenting Gallup Poll findings pertaining to religion in America. Covers religious denomination preferences, church/synagogue membership and attendance, and member sociodemographic profiles; opinion data on influence of religion on American life, confidence in organized religion and other institutions, and importance of religion in own life; and contributions to religious organizations.

Also includes data on popularity of Pope John Paul II; and teenager opinions and religious practices including frequency of Bible reading and prayer, religious training, and views on reincarnation, sexual freedom, marijuana use, school prayer, most important problem, and other social issues.

Most data are based on Gallup Polls conducted in 1983-84, with trends from as early as 1937, and include detail by respondent sociodemographic characteristics.

Contents:

a. Contents listing (1 p.); and commentary and notes (p. 1-21).

b. General survey findings in 4 parts, with text data, 4 charts, and 40 tables (p. 23-59); and survey findings on teenagers, with text data and 20 tables (p. 60-77).

c. Discussion of ways to strengthen the church, with 2 tables (p. 78-91); and technical appendix on methodology, Gallup election poll accuracy record, and church seasonal attendance trends, with 1 chart and 5 tables (p. 91-96 and inside back cover).

This is the 6th annual report. Report is also usually published as an issue in the monthly *Gallup Report,* covered in SRI under C4040-1.

Availability: Princeton Religion Research Center, PO Box 628, Princeton NJ 08540, $25.00; SRI/MF/complete.

R9050
Tax Foundation

R9050–1   FACTS AND FIGURES ON GOVERNMENT FINANCE: 22nd Biennial Edition, 1983
Biennial.   1983.   364 p.
ISBN 0-9606762-3-6.
LC 44-7109.
SRI/MF/complete

Biennial compilation of statistics on government finance, including revenues, expenditures, taxation, assets, and debt of Federal, State, and local governments. Also includes data on selected economic indicators, and financial data for the 46 largest cities and for 40 selected SMSAs.

Data are primarily for FY81, with selected trends from 1900s and earlier, and projections to 2000. Data are mainly compiled from reports of Federal agencies, including Treasury Dept, Bureau of Economic Analysis, and Census Bureau.

Contains foreword, introduction, and contents listing (p. 5-9); 283 tables, listed below, arranged in 6 sections, each preceded by a table listing (p. 11-334); and glossary and index (p. 336-364).

Previous report, issued in 1981, is described in SRI 1981 Annual, under this number.

Availability: Tax Foundation, One Thomas Circle, NW, Suite 500, Washington DC 20005, $20.00; SRI/MF/complete.

TABLES:

R9050–1.1: Section I: Federal, State, and Local Governments

GOVERNMENT AND THE ECONOMY

1. Government and the changing economy [annual percent changes for selected Federal, State, and local financial indicators, and 7 national economic indicators], selected periods FY40-81. (p. 13)

2. Number of governmental units in the U.S. [total units by level, selected years 1942-82; and by State, 1982]. (p. 14)

FISCAL OPERATIONS OF ALL GOVERNMENTS

3. Summary of total government revenue, expenditures, and debt, selected years FY27-81. (p. 15)

4-5. Government receipts and expenditures in the national income accounts [by component], selected years 1929-81; and surpluses/deficits by level of government [for social insurance and other funds], 1940-82. (p. 16-17)

6-8. Expenditures of all governments by function and level of government, FY81; and expenditures and distribution by function, selected years FY60-81. (p. 18-20)

9-10. Federal, State, and local expenditures: [total] and per capita and percentage distribution, selected years FY02-82. (p. 21-22)

11. Revenue of all governments by source and level of government [overlapping in intergovernmental sources], FY81. (p. 23)

12-13. Tax and nontax revenue of all governments [actual and] percentage distribution by source, selected years FY60-81. (p. 24-25)

14-15. Federal, State, and local tax receipts: [total] and per capita and percentage distribution, selected years FY02-82. (p. 26-27).

16. Tax index and tax receipts by type of tax, 1965-82. (p. 28)

17. "Tax freedom day" [day average person finishes paying taxes if all earnings since Jan. 1 were used to fulfill tax obligations], and "tax bite in the 8-hour day" [time spent earning money to pay tax obligations], 1929-82. (p. 29)

18-19. Gross debt of Federal, State, and local governments, and per capita and percentage distribution, end of selected years FY02-82. (p. 30-31)

20-22. Government employees, wages/salaries, and average annual earnings, by level of government and major category, selected years 1929-81. (p. 32-34)

23-24. Civilian employment and payrolls of governments, Oct., selected years 1940-81; and civilian employment of governments by State, Oct. 1981. (p. 35-36)

25-26. Payments under social insurance and related programs, by risk and program, selected years 1940-80; and by State [and program], 1980. (p. 37-39)

27. Employer and employee contributions for social insurance by program, selected years 1929-81. (p. 40)

28. Government transfer payments to persons by level of government and major program, selected years 1939-81. (p. 41)

29. Social welfare expenditures under public programs, by source of funds and type, selected years FY29-80. (p. 42)

30. National health expenditures by source of funds and type, selected years 1965-81. (p. 43)

GOVERNMENT AND SIZE OF THE ECONOMY

31-32. Government expenditures and GNP, and net national product and tax receipts, 1929-82. (p. 44-45)

33-34. Tax revenues in relation to GDP [taxes as share of GDP, selected years 1960-80, and per capita taxes, 1980]; and percentage distribution of tax revenues, by source, FY80; [all for 23] selected countries. (p. 46-47)

R9050–1.2: Section II: Selected Economic Series

POPULATION AND EMPLOYMENT

35. Total and resident population of the U.S., July 1, selected years 1901-82. (p. 51)

36. Number of households and average population per household, Mar., selected years 1900-81. (p. 51)

37. Resident population and number of households by State, selected [dates and] years 1960-82. (p. 52)

38. Estimates and projections of the population by age groups, July 1, selected years 1960-2000. (p. 53)

39-40. Labor force by employment status, annual averages for selected years 1929-82; and estimates and projections of the civilian labor force by sex and age, annual averages in selected years 1975-90. (p. 54-55)

NATIONAL OUTPUT, INCOME, AND PRICES

41. GNP by purchaser [personal consumption, private domestic investment, exports, and government purchases] and type of product, selected years, 1929-81. (p. 56)

R9050–3 TAX FEATURES

Monthly. Approx. 4 p.
ISSN 0047-8040. LC 76-229.
SRI/MF/complete, shipped
quarterly

Monthly publication, with several combined issues each year, presenting news and analytical articles on taxation and government spending at the Federal, State, and local level. Data are compiled by Tax Foundation, Inc., from government sources.

Issues contain an editorial column; and articles and occasional insert supplements, often with statistics. Recurring statistical features include articles on Tax Foundation, Inc. tax index trends; and trends in State/local general tax revenues, Federal tax dollar allocations, Federal aid costs to States, taxpayer purchasing power, and government spending.

All articles with substantial statistics are described, as they appear, under "Statistical Features." Each issue of the publication is reviewed, but an abstract is published in SRI monthly issues only when statistical features appear.

Prior to Aug./Sept. 1984 issue, publication was titled *Monthly Tax Features.*

Availability: Tax Foundation, Suite 500, One Thomas Circle, NW, Washington DC 20005, members, educators, and libraries †; SRI/MF/complete, shipped quarterly.

Issues reviewed during 1984: Oct. 1983-Aug./Sept. 1984 (P) (Vol. 27, No. 8; Vol. 28, Nos. 1-7) [No issues were published for Nov.-Dec. 1983; June/July and Aug./Sept. 1984 are combined issues].

STATISTICAL FEATURES:

R9050–3.501: Oct. 1983 (Vol. 27, No. 8)

TOP U.S. EARNERS PAY NEARLY HALF OF TAXES ON INDIVIDUAL INCOME

(p. 1) Article, with 1 table showing income level, and Federal income tax revenue share and average tax payment, for highest and lowest 10, 25, and 50% taxpayer income categories, 1976 and 1981. Data are from Dept of Treasury.

CORPORATE PROFITS BOOST TAX INDEX, RECURRING FEATURE

(p. 2) Recurring article analyzing tax index trends through 2nd quarter 1983. Includes 1 table showing tax index by level of government compared to GNP (current and constant prices) and implicit price deflator indexes, quarterly 1980-2nd quarter 1983, and selected years from 1970.

SOCIAL SECURITY BENEFITS TAXED FOR FIRST TIME UNDER NEW 1983 LAW

(p. 4) Article on taxation of Social Security benefits under Social Security Amendments of 1983. Includes 1 table comparing 1983 benefit amount and tax situation of retirees at 2 pre-retirement income levels, according to income source distribution (earned, taxable investment, nontaxable interest).

R9050–3.502: Feb. 1984 (Vol. 28, No. 2)

STATE/LOCAL TAX TAKE RISES DESPITE CONTRACTION OF U.S. ECONOMY, ANNUAL FEATURE

(p. 1-2, 4) Annual article, with 1 map and 1 table showing State/local tax collections per capita and per $1,000 of personal income, by State, FY72 and FY82, with State rankings for FY82.

RECORD NONTAX REVENUES REACH $102.9 BILLION IN STATES AND LOCALITIES

(p. 1, 6) Article, with 1 table showing State and local nontax revenue from charges and miscellaneous sources, with State/local aggregate data by detailed source, FY75 and FY80-82.

R9050–3.503: Mar. 1984 (Vol. 28, No. 3)

TAX INDEX REACHES RECORD LEVELS AS 4Q83 TAXES RISE BY $79.4 BILLION, RECURRING FEATURE

(p. 1-2, 4) Recurring article analyzing tax index trends through 4th quarter 1983. Includes 1 table showing tax index by level of government, compared to GNP (current and constant prices) and implicit price deflator indexes, quarterly 1981-83, and selected years from 1970.

STATES' BIGGEST HAUL FROM SALES TAXES—$50.3 BILLION FOR '82

(p. 1-2) Article on State revenue sources, with 1 table showing major tax types and rates in use, by State, as of Jan. 1984.

CORPORATE TAXES ALIVE AND WELL

(p. 3-4) Article, with 1 table showing Federal revenue from individual and corporate income taxes, social insurance taxes/contributions, and other taxes, selected years 1975-87.

R9050–3.504: Apr. 1984 (Vol. 28, No. 4)

TAX FREEDOM DAY—MAY 1! ANNUAL FEATURE

(p. 1, 4) Annual article, with 3 tables showing allocation of average workday by time spent earning money to pay taxes and other living expenses, 1979-84; and daily worktime required for tax payments, and date average worker finishes working to pay for taxes (Tax Freedom Day), selected years 1930-84.

CA, NY, TX TOP LIST FOR TOTAL TAX BURDEN OF U.S. GOVERNMENT, ANNUAL FEATURE

(p. 1-2) Annual article comparing States' Federal tax burdens, FY82-84. Includes 1 table showing total and per capita Federal tax collections, by State, FY83-85, with rankings for FY84.

HOW U.S. SPENDS WORKER'S DOLLARS, ANNUAL FEATURE

(p. 3-4) Annual article, with 1 table allocating Federal tax dollar expenditures by function, total and for an average worker (sole supporter of a 4-person family, $26,000 annual income), FY84.

R9050–3.505: May 1984 (Vol. 28, No. 5)

AID TO STATES UP 4% IN FY83; NY, CA, IL, TX LEAD THE FIELD, ANNUAL FEATURE

(p. 1-2) Annual article comparing States' tax payments for and receipts from Federal grant-in-aid programs, FY83. Includes 1 table showing payments and receipts, and rankings by tax burden per dollar of aid, all by State.

CONGRESS TO SPEND 16% MORE ON ITSELF IN FISCAL 1984; $1.7 BILLION TOTAL BUDGET, ANNUAL FEATURE

(p. 1, 4) Annual article on Federal legislative expenditure growth, FY70-84. Data are from OMB. Includes 1 table showing legislative branch budget outlays by unit, including both Houses of Congress and 8 legislative agencies, and deductions for offsetting receipts, selected years FY70-84. Data are from OMB.

LOCALITIES BECOMING MORE SELF SUPPORTING, ANNUAL FEATURE

(p. 3-4) Annual article, with 1 table showing local government general revenues, by source, selected years FY02-82. Data are from Census Bureau.

R9050–3.506: June/July 1984 (Vol. 28, No. 6)

ERTA's TAX RELIEF NO PANACEA FOR TOP EARNERS

(p. 1-2) Article, with 1 table showing income level, and Federal income tax revenue share and average tax payment, for highest 5% and highest and lowest 10, 25, and 50% taxpayer adjusted gross income categories, 1981-82.

FAMILY'S BUYING POWER CUT 7.3% FROM 1974 TO 1984 BY INFLATION AND U.S. TAXES, ANNUAL FEATURE

(p. 1-2) Annual article estimating the impact of inflation and Federal tax increases on family purchasing power, 1974-84. Includes 1 table showing median family income, Federal income and social security tax payments, and after-tax income in current and 1974 dollars, 1974-84.

GOVERNMENTS NOW SPENDING $16,652 PER U.S. FAMILY, ANNUAL FEATURE

(p. 4) Annual article on trends in government spending, with 1 table showing per household and per capita expenditures aggregated for all government levels, and Federal and State/local government total expenditures, selected years FY50-84.

R9050–3.507: Aug./Sept. 1984 (Vol. 28, No. 7)

TF's TAX INDEX JUMPS 17.2%, OUTPACING ECONOMIC GROWTH RATE, RECURRING FEATURE

(p. 1-2) Recurring article analyzing tax index trends through 1st quarter 1984. Includes 1 table showing tax index by level of government, compared to GNP (current and constant prices) and implicit price deflator indexes, quarterly 1981-1st quarter 1984, and selected years from 1970.

U.S. DEFICIT ESTIMATES LOWERED BUT INTEREST COSTS CLIMB, RECURRING FEATURE

(p. 1-2, 4) Recurring article on Federal debt trends. Includes 1 table showing Federal receipts, outlays, and debt outstanding and interest, FY74-85.

SOCIAL WELFARE CLAIMS 34 CENTS PER SPENDING $, ANNUAL FEATURE

(p. 3) Annual article, with 1 table allocating Federal/State/local tax dollar expenditures by function, selected years FY60-82.

INDIVIDUAL INCOME TAX BIGGEST REVENUE RAISER, ANNUAL FEATURE

(p. 4) Annual article, with 1 table allocating Federal/State/local revenue dollar by tax and nontax source, selected years FY60-82.

R9200
TRAFFIC (U.S.A.)

R9200–10   CITES APPENDIX I SPECIES IN CAPTIVITY, 1977-81
Monograph.   1983.
vi+29+App 42 p.
SRI/MF/complete

By Lynn Gray-Schofield. Report on the maintenance and breeding in captivity of endangered animal species. Data are shown for mammals, birds, reptiles, and amphibians listed on Appendix I of the Convention on International Trade in Endangered Species of Wild Fauna and Flora (CITES). Includes animals held and bred in captivity, by detailed species, various years 1977-81.

Data are from *International Zoo Yearbook*, the International Species Inventory System (I-SIS), and *Inventory of Live Reptiles and Amphibians in North American Collections*.

Contains listings of contents, tables, and charts (p. iv-vi); introduction, 3 report chapters with 7 charts and 5 tables, and list of references (p. 1-29); and 4 appendices with 4 tables (p. vii-xlvii).

Availability: TRAFFIC (U.S.A.), World Wildlife Fund, 1601 Connecticut Ave., NW, Washington DC 20009, $7.50; SRI/MF/complete.

R9372
U.S. Committee for Refugees

R9372–1   WORLD REFUGEE SURVEY, 1983
Annual. 1983. 77 p.
ISSN 0197-5439.
ISBN 0-936548-04-5.
LC 80-644592.
SRI/MF/complete

Annual report reviewing developments in world refugee movement, resettlement, and aid contributions, by country of origin and/or asylum, 1983, with selected trends from 1975.

Contains contents listing (p. 1); 13 articles on international refugee problems and policies, some with statistics (p. 2-59); world refugee statistical section (p. 60-63); summary reports on refugee situation in selected countries and world areas (p. 64-72); and directory of international and U.S. refugee assistance agencies, and data sources (p. 73-77).

All sections with substantial statistical content are described below.

Availability: U.S. Committee for Refugees, 20 W. 40th St., New York NY 10018, $6.00+$1.00 postage and handling; SRI/MF/complete.

STATISTICAL SECTIONS:

PALESTINIAN REFUGEES: DEFINING THE HUMANITARIAN PROBLEM

(p. 20-27) By Howard Adelman. Article tracing the population, migration, and settlement patterns of Palestinian refugees since 1947. Data sources include the UN Relief and Works Agency for Palestinian Refugees, and various scholarly journals. Includes 6 tables showing Arab Palestinian population and migration, by country or area of settlement, and citizenship status, selected periods 1947-82; with comparative summary for non-Jewish non-Arab Palestinians, 1948.

ECONOMIC ADJUSTMENT OF SOUTHEAST ASIAN REFUGEES IN THE U.S.

(p. 51-55) By Robert L. Bach et al. Article on the economic condition of Southeast Asian refugees living in the U.S. Most data are from a 1982 HHS survey of 1,182 households containing 6,767 Southeast Asian refugees.

Includes 3 tables showing the following for Southeast Asian refugees: labor force participation and unemployment rates, fall 1982, and refugee distribution by period of entry into U.S., 1975-82, by occupational category in country of origin; and selected household composition and employment characteristics for households receiving and not receiving public cash assistance, fall 1982.

1983 WORLD REFUGEE STATISTICS

(p. 60-63) Compilation of data on worldwide refugee populations. Most data are from UN High Commissioner for Refugees, and U.S. State Dept. Includes 1 chart and 8 tables showing the following, primarily for 1982:

a. Refugees in need and refugees settled/resettled/not requiring international aid, by country and world region of asylum, with detail by country of origin for refugees in need; top 7 countries of origin ranked by number of refugees; and total population, refugees in need and resettled, and GNP, for leading countries of asylum and resettlement ranked by ratio of refugees to total population.

b. Refugees voluntarily repatriated by selected country of origin, with some detail by country of asylum, various periods 1975-82; and internally displaced persons by selected country or world area.

c. International refugee assistance: total contributions to 3 major agencies; top 20 countries ranked by total and per capita contributions, with population and per capita GNP; and total EC contributions.

R9375
U.S. Travel Data Center

R9375-1   TRAVEL PRINTOUT
Monthly. Approx. 4 p.
ISSN 0744-6233.
LC SN 82-2592.
SRI/MF/complete, shipped quarterly

Monthly newsletter on travel and tourism, including frequency, duration, mode, and purpose of travel; trends in economic factors influencing tourist travel; attendance at national parks; and travel volume. Data, current to 2-3 months preceding publication, are from the National Park Service, other Federal Government agencies, private assns, and the center's own research.

Contains narrative review of travel-related developments usually with 1-2 charts; and 3 monthly tables, listed below.

Beginning with Feb. 1984 issue, table [2] on regional national park visits has been temporarily suspended.

Availability: U.S. Travel Data Center, 1899 L St., NW, Suite 610, Washington DC 20036, $45.00 per yr.; SRI/MF/complete, shipped quarterly.

Issues reviewed during 1984: Nov. 1983-Sept. 1984 (P) (Vol. 12, Nos. 11-12; Vol. 13, Nos. 1-9).

TABLES:
[Tables [2-3] show data for month of coverage, percent change from previous month and same month of previous year, and percent annual change for year to date.]

[1] Monthly and annual rates of change in the travel price index and components [and CPI; for month of coverage].

[2] Visitor volume at national parks [for 9 tourist regions].

[3] Current travel indicators [receipts/sales for eating/drinking places, hotels/motels, and gas stations; commercial lodging demand and/or hotel occupancy rate; highway traffic volume; air, rail, and bus passenger traffic; travel price index; total and vacation person-trips; visits and overnight stays in national parks; foreign arrivals from and U.S. citizen departures to overseas and Canada; and motor gasoline demand per day].

R9375-2   SURVEY OF STATE TRAVEL OFFICES, 1983-84
Annual. Apr. 1984. i+92 p.
ISSN 0361-8307.
LC 74-191723.
SRI/MF/complete

Annual report on administration, promotional activities, budgets, and research of State travel development agencies, FY82-84. Data are from a June 1983-Jan. 1984 survey of agencies in the 50 States and selected U.S. territories.

Contains contents listing (1 p.); preface (p. i); summary and analysis, with 3 summary tables (p. 1-10); and 7 extended tables showing the following data, by State and outlying area, for individual travel development agencies:

a. General administration: travel agency directory; name and length of service of director and assistant; full- and part-time staff size; and organization characteristics. 1 table. (p. 11-20)

b. Advertising: characterization of staff and organization, advertising agency, and advertising objectives; and handling of inquiries, including number received in 1982. 1 table. (p. 21-32)

c. Budget: FY83-84 budget totals and State rank, and funding sources other than State general revenue; FY83-84 general budget allocations by function, and advertising budget by medium; and FY84 promotion budget allocations by function, number of travel shows in which participated, foreign advertising budget allocations by medium and country, and foreign promotion and press/public relations budget by country. 1 table. (p. 33-58)

d. General promotion, press/public relations, and research: characteristics of current programs; press/travel writer tours in 1982 and planned for 1983; and research activity costs for university faculty member and private research group employment. 3 tables. (p. 59-83)

e. Welcome centers, including number, employees, and 1982 visitors. 1 table. (p. 85-88)

This is the 11th annual report.

Availability: U.S. Travel Data Center, 1899 L St., NW, Suite 610, Washington DC 20036, $50.00; SRI/MF/complete.

R9375-3   NATIONAL TRAVEL SURVEY
Quarterly. Approx. 100 p.
ISSN 0737-2620.
SRI/MF/complete

Quarterly report on the number, region, purpose, and transportation mode of trips by U.S. adults. Data are from monthly telephone interviews of a national probability sample of approximately 1,-400 persons, conducted by RL Associates.

Contains contents listing, introduction, and narrative summary with text tables; and appendices, with approximately 60 tables listed below, glossary, and methodology.

Report is issued 3-6 months after quarter of coverage. Travel Data Center also publishes an annual report supplementing the quarterly data, described under R9375-5.

Availability: U.S. Travel Data Center, 1899 L St., NW, Suite 610, Washington DC 20036, $65.00 per issue; SRI/MF/complete.

Issues reviewed during 1984: 1st Qtr. 1983-1st Qtr. 1984 (D).

TABLES:
[Destination and residence areas are large and small SMSAs, and non-SMSA; destination area also includes outside U.S.]

TOTAL TRAVEL
[Tables 1A-1J show data for quarter of coverage and same period of previous year.]

1A. Monthly average number and percent of U.S. adults taking trips, by major trip characteristics.

1B. Number of trips and person-trips for major trip characteristics.

1C-1J. Percent distribution of total trips [and/or] person-trips by round trip distance and mode of transport, duration of trip and type of lodging, purpose and type of trip, travel party size and structure, family income and age, destination region, region of trip origin, and area of destination and residence.

BY MODE AND PURPOSE
2A-7H. [Tables 1C-1J are repeated for air, auto/truck/recreational vehicle, business/convention, pleasure, vacation, and weekend trips, for current quarter only.]

YEAR TO DATE
8A-8B. [Repeats tables 1A-1B, showing data quarterly for year to date. Not included in 1st quarter report.]

R9375-5   1983 NATIONAL TRAVEL SURVEY, Full Year Report
Annual. 1984.
119 p. var. paging.
ISSN 0737-2620.
LC 83-641929.
SRI/MF/complete

Annual report, for 1983, summarizing results of the monthly National Travel Survey on the number, region, purpose, and transportation mode of trips by U.S. adults. Data are from monthly telephone interviews of a national probability sample of approximately 1,400 persons, conducted by RL Associates.

Contents:

a. Executive summary; contents listing; introduction; report guide; and brief narrative on travel factors, with 1 table showing selected economic indicators for 1982-83. (2 p., p. 1-7) *b.* Narrative overview, with 3 tables correlating travel by regions of origin and destination; and 2 tables and usually 1 chart showing average persons, miles, and nights per trip, and selected sociodemographic characteristics (including credit card ownership), repeated for all, air, auto/truck/RV, business/convention, pleasure, vacation, and weekend travel, 1982 and/or 1983. (p. 9-33)

c. Appendix A, with 65 tables listed below. (p. A1-A65)

d. Appendices B-F, with glossary, survey methodology, questionnaire facsimile, and notes on sampling error. (p. B1-F3)

Availability: U.S. Travel Data Center, 1899 L St., NW, Suite 610, Washington DC 20036, $90.00; SRI/MF/complete.

TABLES:

[Tables 1A-1K show data for 1982-83; all other tables show 1983 data only. Destination and residence areas are large and small SMSAs and non-SMSA; destination areas also include outside U.S.]

TOTAL TRAVEL

1A. Monthly average number and percent of U.S. adults taking trips, by major trip characteristics. (p. A1)

1B. Number of trips and person-trips for major trip characteristics. (p. A2)

1C-1K. Percent distribution of total trips and person-trips by: round-trip distance and mode of transport; duration of trip and type of lodging; purpose and type of trip [vacation, weekend, and other]; travel-related services; travel party size and structure; family income and [individual traveler] age; destination region; region of origin; and area of destination and residence. (p. A3-A11)

BY MODE AND PURPOSE

2A-7I. [Tables 1C-1K are repeated, with applicable data, for air, auto/truck/RV, business/convention, pleasure, vacation, and weekend travel.] (p. A12-A65)

R9375–7   IMPACT OF TRAVEL ON STATE ECONOMIES, 1982
Annual. July 1984.
57 p. var. paging.
ISSN 0730-9813.
LC 81-644365.
SRI/MF/complete

Annual report estimating the economic impact of domestic travel on each State and on selected industries, 1982. Includes estimates of travel-related expenditures, business receipts, payroll, employment, and tax revenues.

Estimates are based on economic model analysis of data from the U.S. Census Bureau and numerous other sources.

Contains summary and contents listing (2 p.); introduction, and 5 sections with 12 tables, listed below (p. 1-41); and 4 appendices, presenting description of the model, glossary, list of States showing SIC 2-digit industries providing more jobs than travel-related industries, and data sources (p. A1-D2).

Availability: U.S. Travel Data Center, 1899 L St., NW, Suite 610, Washington DC 20036, $45.00; SRI/MF/complete.

TABLES:

[Tables show data for 1982. Most data are shown by State, and (except for tax revenues, and expenditure and employment rank) by selected U.S. industry category including public and automobile transportation, lodging, food, entertainment/recreation, incidental purchases, general retail trade, and travel arrangement; with totals for U.S. territories and foreign visitor spending.]

1-3. Travel expenditures in the U.S.; and domestic travel expenditures for all trips, with State ranking, share [of U.S. total travel], and percent change [from 1981]. (p. 3-11)

4-7. Travel-generated business receipts and payroll. (p. 13-25)

8-10. Travel-generated employment; and share of total employment and rank among private [sector] industries. (p. 27-36)

11-12. Travel-generated tax receipts and revenues [by level of government]. (p. 37-41)

R9375–10   U.S. MARKET FOR PACKAGE TOURS
Monograph. 1984.
78 p. var. paging.
SRI/MF/complete

Report on the package tour market, including traveler and trip characteristics for U.S. residents taking domestic and foreign package tours, 1981/82.

Covers traveler household and personal characteristics, including household composition, housing tenure, income, region of residence, marital status, educational attainment, race, sex, age, and occupational group; and trip characteristics, including purpose, duration, mode of transport, travel agent use, type of lodging, metro-nonmetro origin, and region visited.

Data are shown for total domestic and foreign package tours; domestic package tours by air and bus; and escorted and unescorted foreign package tours; with selected detail by region of origin.

Package tours are defined as prepaid tours in which 2 or more elements were purchased together. Also includes data for nonpackage tour trips of 5 nights/longer.

Data were compiled from 1981-82 monthly National Travel Survey telephone interviews with 1,400 adults.

Contains preface, summary, and contents listing (3 p.); narrative report in 5 chapters, interspersed with 3 charts and 18 tables (p. 1-32); references (p. 33); and 3 appendices, with 7 detailed tables, methodology, and glossary (p. A1-C5).

Availability: U.S. Travel Data Center, 1899 L St., NW, Washington DC 20036, $60.00; SRI/MF/complete.

**R9385
West Virginia
Research League**

R9385–1   WEST VIRGINIA RESEARCH LEAGUE 1983 STATISTICAL HANDBOOK
Annual. [1983.] 76 p.
ISSN 0091-6102.
LC 73-643039.
SRI/MF/complete

Annual compilation, for 1983, of social, governmental, and economic statistics for West Virginia. Data, mostly for calendar or fiscal years 1973-82, are primarily from Federal and State agency reports.

Contains contents and table listing (p. 3-6); and 60 tables, described below. Some tables include comparisons to total U.S.

Availability: West Virginia Research League, 1107 Charleston National Plaza, Charleston WV 25301, $5.63; SRI/MF/complete.

TABLES:

[Data source is given at the bottom of each table.]

R9385–1.1: Economic Summary

(p. 7) Contains 1 table. Includes total population; total and per capita personal income; civilian labor force and number unemployed; employment by industry division; and average weekly earnings in manufacturing, bituminous coal mining, construction, and gas/electric/water utilities.

R9385–1.2: State Government Finances, Welfare Caseloads, and Work Accidents

(p. 8-28) Contains 18 tables. Includes major State tax rates and fees; State government receipts and disbursements, by fund; net revenues by major fund and source; expenditures by function; and bonds outstanding.

Also includes operating data for general revenue, State road, welfare, and workmen's compensation funds; motor vehicle registrations by vehicle class; welfare caseloads by program; and workmen's compensation accidents reported (fatal and nonfatal) by county.

R9385–1.3: Unemployment Insurance

(p. 29-31) Contains 3 tables. Includes unemployment compensation claims, payments, and weeks compensated; and covered employment, by industry division.

R9385–1.4: Education

(p. 32-42) Contains 11 tables. Includes general school fund balances, receipts by fund and source, and expenditures by fund and function; and public school buildings, enrollment, average daily attendance, per capita cost, teachers, and pupil/teacher ratio.

Also includes higher education operating revenue and expenditures of State-supported institutions; and enrollment and degrees conferred, by public and private institutions.

R9385–1.5: Property Taxes

(p. 43-49) Contains 6 tables. Includes assessed valuation and taxes levied, by property type; and property tax rates by county.

R9385-1.6: Federal Data, Personal Income, and Banking

(p. 50-60) Contains 10 tables. Includes Federal aid payments and taxes collected by type; Federal individual income tax returns filed by adjusted gross income bracket, and taxable income and tax liability; personal income by type and industry division; transfer payments by source; total and per capita personal income by county; per capita transfer income by county; population; and State and national banks, deposits, and loans.

R9385-1.7: Local Government Finances

(p. 61-67) Contains 7 tables. Includes State/ local revenues and expenditures per capita and per $1,000 personal income, including expenditures for education, highways, and welfare; and local government revenue by source, expenditures by function, and indebtedness.

R9385-1.8: Natural Resources

(p. 68-74) Contains 4 tables. Includes State park and forest attendance, by area; underground and surface mine coal production by county; and crude petroleum and natural gas production.

I. Military and social trends [military expenditures, arms trade, foreign economic aid, per capita and total GNP, population, armed forces, physicians, and teachers]: world, developed, and developing countries, 1960-81. (p. 32)

II. Comparative resources [total and urban population; total and arable land; GNP; public expenditures for military, international peacekeeping, education, health, and foreign economic aid; and armed forces, physicians, and teachers]. (p. 33-35)

III. Ranking of countries, military and social indicators [military expenditures per capita, per soldier, and per land area; economic/social ranking; per capita GNP; per capita education expenditures, percent of school age population in school and number per teacher, women as percent of university enrollment, and literacy rate; per capita health expenditures, population per physician and hospital bed, infant mortality rate, and life expectancy; calorie and protein supply per capita; and percent of population with safe drinking water]. (p. 36-41)

R9447
World Priorities

R9447-1   WORLD MILITARY AND SOCIAL EXPENDITURES, 1983

Annual. Aug. 1983.
46 p.+errata sheet.
ISSN 0363-4795.
LC 75-300012.
SRI/MF/not filmed

Annual report, by Ruth Leger Sivard, comparing 142 nations' military expenditures to their socioeconomic resources and nonmilitary public expenditures, various years 1960-83. Data are from UN agencies and other international organizations, the Federal Government, and foreign government statistical services.

Contents:

a. Contents listing. (p. 4)

b. Review of world military and social trends, with selected data on military growth including foreign bases and personnel; Third World countries under military control, and use of violence against citizenry; nuclear weapons proliferation, testing, and arms control agreements; nuclear power industry growth; and casualties of war, refugees, arms trade, and other developments. 20 charts and 11 tables. (p. 4-31)

c. Statistical annex, with 3 detailed tables described below; and data notes, methodology, and sources. (p. 32-46)

This is the 9th annual edition.

Availability: World Priorities, PO Box 25140, Washington DC 20007, $4.00; SRI/MF/not filmed.

DETAILED TABLES:

[Tables II-III show data for 142 countries, 9 world regions, NATO and Warsaw Pact members, total developed and developing countries, and worldwide, 1980.]

State Governments

S0090   ALABAMA
Department of
Agriculture and Industries

**S0090-1   ALABAMA AGRICULTURAL
STATISTICS, 1981 Revised,
1982 Preliminary**
Annual.   Sept. 1983.   47 p.
Bull. 25.
LC 54-63111.
SRI/MF/complete

Annual report on Alabama agricultural production, marketing, and income, 1981 and preliminary 1982, with selected trends from the 1970s. Data are generally shown by commodity and/or county and district.

Report covers production, prices, and sales and/or value, and, as applicable, acreage, yield, or inventory, for field crop, potato, fruit and nut, livestock, dairy, and poultry sectors.

Report also includes data on number and acreage of farms; farm income by source, and prices paid for selected feed items; and cash receipts from farm forest products, nonfarm commercial timber, and greenhouse/nursery products.

Data are from surveys of farmers and agricultural businesses conducted by Alabama Crop and Livestock Reporting Service, and reports by Alabama Cooperative Extension Service and USDA.

Contains contents listing and foreword, with 2 tables (p. 2-4); and report, with 1 chart, 11 maps, and 41 tables, interspersed with narrative highlights (p. 5-47).

This is the 25th edition of the report.

Previous report, presenting data through 1981, is described in SRI 1982 Annual, under this number.

Availability: Alabama Crop and Livestock Reporting Service, PO Box 1071, Montgomery AL 36192, †; SRI/MF/complete.

S0110   ALABAMA
Department of
Banking

**S0110-1   ANNUAL REPORT OF
SUPERINTENDENT OF
BANKS of the State of
Alabama, for the Fiscal Year
Ending Sept. 30, 1983**
Annual.   Jan. 17, 1984.
34 p.
SRI/MF/complete

Annual report, for FY83, on financial condition of Alabama State-chartered financial institutions, presenting consolidated balance sheet data and/or income and expenses for commercial banks, small loan and consumer credit agencies, and credit unions, as of Dec. 31, 1982, or Sept. 30, 1983, with selected comparisons to the previous year.

Also includes assets of individual banks, savings and loan assns, and credit unions, arranged by city or rank; deposits of individual banks; small loan and consumer credit agencies' loan operations and delinquent account legal actions; and credit union membership, loan operations, and earnings distribution.

Contains lists of Banking Dept officials (p. 1-5); and report sectors, with narrative summaries, lists of bank status changes and banks affiliated with holding companies, and 19 tables (p. 6-34).

Availability: Alabama Department of Banking, 651 Administrative Bldg., 64 N. Union St., Montgomery AL 36130, †; SRI/MF/complete.

S0115   ALABAMA
Department of
Corrections

**S0115-1   DEPARTMENT OF
CORRECTIONS ANNUAL
REPORT for Fiscal Year Oct.
1, 1982-Sept. 30, 1983,
Alabama**
Annual.   [1984.]   2+40 p.
LC 83-640467.
SRI/MF/complete

Annual report on corrections in Alabama, presenting data on prison population, including inmate admissions, releases, sentence length, commitment offense, and demographic characteristics, FY83. Some data are shown by State institution and selected other locations, including Alabama inmates in other States.

Also includes data on Corrections Dept finances and personnel; prison industry and agriculture operations; escapes; community-based facilities; and work release program participation and finances.

Contains contents listing, and directories of institutions and personnel (p. 1-12); and 31 tables (p. 13-40).

Availability: Alabama Department of Corrections, Research, Monitoring, and Evaluation Unit, 101 S. Union St., Montgomery AL 36130-1301, †; SRI/MF/complete.

S0118   ALABAMA
Administrative
Office of the
Courts

**S0118-1   ALABAMA JUDICIAL
SYSTEM ANNUAL REPORT,
FY83**
Annual.   [1984.]   95 p.
LC 82-645231.
SRI/MF/complete, current &
previous year reports

Annual report on Alabama judicial system, including trial and appellate court caseloads and case dispositions, FY83, with trends from FY79. Covers supreme, appeals, circuit, and district courts. Includes trial court data by case type, judicial district, and county.

Case types shown are civil, criminal, traffic, small claims, domestic relations, juvenile, and municipal cases.

Also includes data on number and cost of jury trials; and on judicial dept finances.

Contains contents listing (p. 1); narrative report with 3 charts and 10 tables (p. 2-20); lists of judicial assignments (p. 21-32); and 3 appendices with 27 tables (p. 33-95).

Prior to the FY83 edition, reports generally were issued in 2 volumes: a primarily narrative report and a statistical supplement. Previous report, for FY82, was also reviewed in 1984 and is also available on SRI microfiche under this number [Annual. [1983.] 23 p.; Annual. [1983.] 15 p.; †].

Prior to the report for FY82, SRI covered only the statistical supplement. No supplement was published for FY81. For description of report for FY80, see SRI 1982 Annual under this number.

Availability: Alabama Administrative Office of the Courts, 817 S. Court St., Montgomery AL 36130-0101, †; SRI/MF/complete.

S0119   ALABAMA
Criminal Justice
Information Center

S0119-1   1983 CRIME IN ALABAMA
Annual.   [1984.]   i+169 p.
LC 84-644818.
SRI/MF/complete

Annual report presenting data on Alabama crimes and clearances, by Index offense and locale, 1983 and trends. Also includes data on Index and non-Index offense arrests, with selected demographic detail; value of stolen property; law enforcement employment; and assaults on police.

Data are from reports of law enforcement agencies, submitted under the Uniform Crime Reporting system.

Contains contents listing (1 p.); preface (p. i); introduction, explanation of data collection, and glossary (p. 1-13); 38 charts and 69 tables, accompanied by brief narrative summaries with text data (p. 14-134); and 4 appendix tables (p. 136-169).

All tables and charts are described below.

This is the 8th annual report.

Availability: Alabama Criminal Justice Information Center, Statistics Analysis Center, 858 S. Court St., Montgomery AL 36130-5201, ‡; SRI/ MF/complete.

TABLES AND CHARTS:

[Data are for 1983, unless otherwise noted. Index offenses include homicide, rape, robbery, assault, burglary, larceny, and motor vehicle theft. Arson also is classified as an Index offense, but data are reported separately and usually are not included in tables showing data by Index offense.]

S0119-1.1: Index Offenses and Non-Index Arrests

INDEX OFFENSES, STATE DATA

[Summary and sections on individual offenses include data on offenses and clearances, adult and juvenile arrests, and arrests by race and/or sex, 1979-83; and the additional data described below.]

a. Summary: also including offenses by month 1983, crime rate trends from 1979, and arrests by age, all by offense; value of stolen/damaged property, by detailed offense classification; and value of stolen and recovered property, by property type. 9 charts and 14 tables. (p. 15-31)

b. Homicide: also including offenses by victim and offender race, sex, and relationship, and by type of weapon and circumstance. 5 charts and 6 tables. (p. 33-36)

c. Rape: also including offenses by victim and offender race and relationship, and by type of weapon and location. 5 charts and 7 tables. (p. 38-41)

d. Robbery: also including offenses by type of weapon and premises. 4 charts and 4 table. (p. 43-45)

e. Assault: also including offenses by type of weapon. 3 charts and 3 table. (p. 47-49)

f. Burglary, larceny, and motor vehicle theft: also including burglaries by type of entry; residential and nonresidential burglaries by time of day; larceny offenses and value stolen, by type of theft and property value; and motor vehicle thefts by type of vehicle, and stolen and recovered locally or in other jurisdictions. 10 charts and 13 tables. (p. 51-61)

g. Arson: also including reported and unfounded offenses, total clearances, clearances involving juveniles, offenses involving uninhabited/abandoned structures, and value of property damage, all by property classification. 2 charts and 2 tables. (p. 63-65)

INDEX OFFENSES BY LOCATION

h. Index crimes, 1982-83, and clearances, 1983, by city arranged by population size group, and by county; and offenses and rate per 100,000 population, by MSA, 1979-83; all by offense, with selected summaries. 7 tables. (p. 66-116)

NON-INDEX OFFENSE ARRESTS

i. Arrests, by age and non-Index offense; and adult and juvenile drug violation arrests for sale and possession, by substance, sex, and race. 3 tables. (p. 120-121)

S0119-1.2: Police Employment and Assaults

a. Full-time sworn and civilian employees by sex, for sheriffs' offices and by city population size group, MSA, university campus, and agency. 5 tables. (p. 122-130)

b. Assaults on police: by injury status, weapon, type of assignment and activity, and time of day; and clearances, by type of activity. 5 tables. (p. 132-134)

S0119-1.3: Appendix

(p. 136-169) 4 tables showing Index crimes by offense, and population, by law enforcement agency and county.

S0121   ALABAMA
Department of
Economic and
Community Affairs

S0121-2   ALABAMA COUNTY DATA BOOK, 1983
Annual.   Dec. 1983.   92 p.
Unique Rpt. No.
ALA-ADECA-EDA-TA-01.
LC 83-622267.
SRI/MF/complete

Annual data book presenting general economic, social, and governmental statistics for Alabama counties, and including summary data for municipalities. Data are from specified Federal, State, and private sources, and are shown primarily for 1980 or 1981-82, with selected trends from 1960s and population projections to 2000.

Report is designed to present an overview of the State. Municipal data are shown by city; all other data are shown by county. Socioeconomic and demographic breakdowns are shown, as applicable, for selected topics. These breakdowns include industry division, age, and urban-rural status.

Contains contents listing (p. 1); 52 tables and 20 maps arranged in 13 sections (p. 2-89); and index and notes (p. 90-92).

All tables and selected maps are described below.

This is the 8th annual report. Previous reports were issued by Office of State Planning and Federal Programs before it became a part of the Dept of Economic and Community Affairs, and were covered in SRI under S0173-1.

Availability: Alabama Department of Economic and Community Affairs, State Planning and Federal Programs Office, State Capitol, Montgomery AL 36130, $4.00; SRI/MF/complete.

DATA SECTIONS:

a. General government: voter registration and participation in general elections; property value, tax rate, and debt limit; local government revenues from local, State, and Federal sources and from property, sales, and all taxes; and revenue sharing program receipts. 6 tables. (p. 2-13)

b. Education: population age 25/over, and percent high school and college graduates, and enrolled in private schools; and public elementary/secondary school expenditures, enrollment, and teachers. 3 tables. (p. 14-17)

c. Transportation, communications, and utilities: highway mileage; licensed airports and runway lengths; radio and TV stations; daily and weekly newspapers; and circulation and location of largest newspapers. 4 tables. (p. 18-28)

d. Natural resources, recreation, and culture: land area and use; farms and acreage; farm cash receipts; timber production; oil, gas, and coal production; nonfuel mineral production value; recreational areas and attractions; alcoholic beverage restrictions; and public library appropriations and book stocks. 6 tables and 1 map. (p. 29-43)

e. Public safety: violent and property crimes; juvenile delinquency and dependency court cases; traffic accidents, injuries, and fatalities; and motor vehicle registrations. 4 tables. (p. 44-47)

f. Health and social services: births; total and infant death rates; physicians, dentists, and registered nurses; hospital and nursing home beds and bed/population ratio; public assistance expenditures by program; and Federal outlays by agency. 6 tables. (p. 48-53)

g. Economics: retail sales; manufacturing establishments and value added; covered employment and wages; commuting patterns; and labor force and unemployment. 8 tables. (p. 54-66)

h. Housing and population: housing units, and selected occupancy and condition characteristics; housing median value; population projected to 2000; land area; nonwhite population; and net migration. 9 tables. (p. 67-75)

i. Income and banking: median family income and percent of families in poverty; farm and nonfarm earnings; personal income by source; per capita income; and commercial bank assets, and time and demand deposits. 5 tables. (p. 77-81)

j. Municipal data: total and black population; median family income; and high school graduates and persons in poverty as percent of population. 1 table. (p. 84-89)

S0121-3   ANNUAL POPULATION ESTIMATES BY AGE, RACE, AND SEX FOR ALABAMA COUNTIES, 1980-90
Monograph.   June 1983.
142 p. no paging+errata sheets.
SRI/MF/complete

Report presenting population projections for Alabama, by sex, age, and race, by county, 1980-90. Data are Alabama State Data Center estimates based on 1970 and 1980 census data.

Contains introduction and methodology, with 1 text table comparing Alabama population projections of 4 organizations, 2000 and/or 1990 (p. 1-6); and 4 detailed tables repeated for each county and total State (136 p.).

Availability: Alabama Department of Economic and Community Affairs, State Planning and Federal Programs Office, State Capitol, Montgomery AL 36130, $6.50; SRI/MF/complete.

S0121–4   1980 ALABAMA CENSUS OF POPULATION AND HOUSING COUNTY PROFILES
Monograph.   Aug. 1982.
136 p. var. paging.
SRI/MF/complete

Report presenting 1980 U.S. Census of Population and Housing detailed findings for Alabama, by county. Covers population, household, and housing unit characteristics.

Data are from 1980 U.S. Census Summary Tape File 1.

Data topics are the same as those described in the sample table listing for Summary Tape File 1 reports (see S9990-1).

Contains 52 tables, repeated for State and each county (136 p.).

Availability: Alabama Department of Economic and Community Affairs, State Planning and Federal Programs Office, State Capitol, Montgomery AL 36130, $6.00; SRI/MF/complete.

S0124   ALABAMA
Department of Education

S0124–1   STATE OF ALABAMA DEPARTMENT OF EDUCATION ANNUAL REPORT, 1982: Statistical and Financial Data for 1981/82
Annual.   [1984.]   105 p.
Bull. 1982—No. 2.
SRI/MF/complete

Annual report, for 1981/82, on Alabama public schools, covering enrollment, staff, finances, and transportation, by school system. Includes data on services for crippled children and vocational rehabilitation, with trends from FY78, and some data for FY83.

Data are compiled by the Division of Administrative and Financial Services.

Contains listings of contents and school systems (p. 4-6); and 4 sections, with 27 tables listed below (p. 8-105).

Previous report, for 1980/81, is described in SRI 1983 Annual, under S0120-1.

Availability: Alabama Department of Education, State Office Bldg., 501 Dexter Ave., Montgomery AL 36130, †; SRI/MF/complete.

TABLES:
[Most financial data are for FY82; other data are for the school year ended June 30, 1982, unless otherwise noted.]

S0124–1.1: Sections I-II: Summary, and Pupils and Teachers

SUMMARY
[Tables [1-9] generally show data for total State and for total counties and cities.]

[1] School census [by sex], enrollment, average daily attendance (ADA), number of teaching positions, and transportation [also includes dropouts by level, and high school graduates; most shown by race]. (p. 8-9)

[2-5] Finance receipts [by source] and payments [by object], handled and not handled by custodians of school funds. (p. 10-14)

[6-8] Finance miscellaneous: amount and percent of revenue receipts derived from various sources, percent of current expense devoted to each function, and percent of total expenditures, [all for finances] handled by custodians of school funds. (p. 15)

[9-10] Finance: analysis of expenditures; and vocational education [State and Federal] funds available [and expenditures by type]. (p. 16-17)

[11-12] Source and disposition of [State, Federal, and trust] funds handled by the State Dept of Education [including dispositions to higher education], and distribution of departmental expenditures. (p. 18-25)

[13] Selected information from 1982/83 annual school budgets: budgeted salary and travel for superintendent, [and] teacher salary schedules [by school system]. (p. 26-27)

PUPILS AND TEACHERS
[Data are shown by school system, and are generally for kindergarten, elementary, junior high, and senior high.]

[14-15] Enrollment of pupils, by grade [and race]. (p. 30-33)

[16] Aggregate attendance and ADA of all pupils. (p. 34)

[17] Number of transported pupils, number of days transportation, and attendance of transported pupils. (p. 36)

[18-19] Number of teaching positions [by sex and race]. (p. 38-41)

S0124–1.2: Sections III-IV: School Finance, Crippled Children Services, and Vocational Rehabilitation

SCHOOL FINANCE
[Data are shown by school system.]

[1] Beginning unappropriated surplus/reserves [by fund]. (p. 44-49)

[2] Revenues and receipts: State, Federal, county, district, and other revenues; nonrevenue receipts; and revenue from and payments to other school systems; [by detailed program or source]. (p. 50-89)

[3] Expenditures, all funds [by object]. (p. 90-95)

[4-5] Local funds reported by principals: receipts, expenditures, and balances; and budgetary breakdown of expenditures [by object]. (p. 96-101)

CRIPPLED CHILDREN AND VOCATIONAL REHABILITATION
[Tables show caseload data and Federal and State/local funding, FY78-82.]

[6] Crippled children service. (p. 104)

[7-8] Vocational rehabilitation. (p. 105)

S0129   ALABAMA
Department of Finance

S0129–1   STATE OF ALABAMA ANNUAL REPORT, Fiscal Year Ending Sept. 30, 1983
Annual.   Sept. 30, 1983.
4+281 p. Foldouts.
LC 40-28377.
SRI/MF/complete

Annual report on financial condition of Alabama State government, for FY83, presenting receipts by source, disbursements by function and object, and fund balances, by detailed fund, dept, and agency.

Also includes State bank deposits by institution; assessed property valuation and tax revenue, by county; property inventory and value, by State agency; detail on composition of investments and State bonded debt; and bank and insurance company securities on deposit.

Contains contents listing (1 p.); State Comptroller's report, with 6 charts and 10 exhibits (p. 1-100); State auditor's report, with 28 schedules (p. 102-200); State treasurer's report, with 10 tables (p. 203-228); and report of bonded indebtedness, with 83 schedules (p. 230-281).

Previous reports are described in SRI under S0125-1.

Availability: Alabama Department of Finance, State Comptroller, 119 State Capitol Bldg., Montgomery AL 36130, †; SRI/MF/complete.

S0160   ALABAMA
Department of Insurance

S0160–1   1983 ALABAMA INSURANCE REPORT: Business of 1982, Company Directory
Annual.   Feb. 21, 1984.
111 p.
LC 63-63468.
SRI/MF/complete

Annual report on Alabama insurance industry financial condition and underwriting activity, by company and type of insurance, 1982. Covers assets, liabilities, premiums written and/or earned, capital/surplus, losses incurred, and life insurance premium/annuity considerations and insurance in force.

Data are shown, as applicable, for fire/casualty, life, title, and fraternal insurance companies; and mutual aid assns.

Data for selected types of insurance include breakdowns by detailed line of coverage, including homeowner, medical malpractice, accident/health, workers compensation, automobile, and surety.

Also includes number of licensed companies; and Insurance Dept receipts by source and disbursements.

Data are from annual statements filed by individual companies.

Contains contents listing (p. 2); Insurance Dept report, with 1 table, and lists of company admissions and status changes (p. 7-19); 13 company financial tables (p. 20-108); and Fire Marshal's Office annual report, with text statistics (p. 109-111).

Availability: Alabama Department of Insurance, 135 S. Union St., Montgomery AL 36130-3401, †; SRI/MF/complete.

S0170   ALABAMA
Department of
Pensions and Security

S0170–1   STATISTICS, Alabama Department of Pensions and Security
Monthly.   Approx. 40 p.
SRI/MF/complete, shipped quarterly

Monthly report on Alabama public welfare cases, recipients, and payments, by county and program. Includes data on old age pensions, Aid to Blind, Aid to Permanently and Totally Disabled, aid to dependent children, aid to refugees, social services including foster and day care, food stamps, and child support.

Contains contents listing, and 22 tables listed below.

Only reports for the last month in each quarter are distributed to the agency's mailing list. However, the report is available in agency offices, and on SRI microfiche, on a monthly basis. Report is issued approximately 3 months after month of data coverage.

An annual report, presenting fiscal year totals for each monthly table, and additional data on public welfare funding and expenditures, is available from the public information office of the issuing agency. Annual report is not covered in SRI.

Availability: Alabama Department of Pensions and Security, Data Analysis and Reporting Division, 64 N. Union St., Montgomery AL 36130-1801, †; SRI/MF/complete, shipped quarterly.

Issues reviewed during 1984: Aug. 1983-Aug. 1984 (D).

TABLES:
[Tables show data by county for month of coverage, unless otherwise noted. Tables 1-8 show number of cases or recipients, and average or total payment.]

STATE SUMMARY

1. Cases under care: Pensions and Security [State totals, by program, for month of coverage, previous month, and same month of previous year].

FINANCIAL ASSISTANCE

2. Number of cases receiving financial assistance and average amount of payments to these cases.

3-5. State supplementation: old age pensions, Aid to Blind, and Aid to Permanently and Totally Disabled.

6. Family assistance: aid to dependent children.

7-8. Special assistance: individual and family grants [in presidentially declared disasters, as they occur, State total]; and aid to refugees.

9-11. Cases receiving financial assistance through county depts of pensions and security;

cases approved as categorically related and eligible for Title XIX, but receiving no money payment; and applications which were in process of investigation by county depts; [all for programs covered in tables 3-6].

SOCIAL SERVICES

12. Number of open primary clients.

13. Aid to children receiving day care [children and payments, for day care centers and homes, and in-home care].

14-15. Adult day care and foster care [recipients and payments, by eligibility category, with State totals for emergency shelter care].

16-17. Foster care maintenance payments, and aid to children in foster care [children and average payment].

18. Number of children in the legal custody of the State Dept of Pensions and Security [State totals].

19. Number of individuals certified as currently eligible for medical assistance under Title XIX by the Dept of Pensions and Security to Alabama Medicaid Agency [State totals, by eligibility category].

CHILD CARE FACILITIES

20. Children under care of public and private facilities [and number of facilities, by facility type; State totals].

FOOD STAMPS AND CHILD SUPPORT

21. Food stamp program [households, recipients by public assistance status, and value of stamps issued].

22. Child support cases [by AFDC status] and collections [for most recent full quarter].

S0175   ALABAMA
Department of
Public Health

S0175–2   ALABAMA'S VITAL EVENTS for 1982
Annual.   [1983.]   vii+259 p.
ISSN 0095-3431.
LC 74-648227.
SRI/MF/complete

Annual report, for 1982, on Alabama vital statistics, covering population, births, deaths by cause, marriages, and divorces. Includes data by county and Public Health Area (PHA), selected U.S. comparisons, and trends from 1940. Also includes data on Vital Statistics Bureau operations.

Data are primarily from records filed with the State registrar of vital statistics. Population data are from U.S. Census Bureau and estimates by University of Alabama Center for Business and Economic Research.

Contains listings of contents, charts, and tables (p. iii+vii); introduction (p. 3-6); 6 statistical sections, with brief text, illustrative charts, and 110 tables listed below (p. 7-252); and technical appendix, with data sources, notes, and definitions (p. 254-259).

Previous report, for 1981, is described in SRI 1982 Annual, under this number. A quarterly vital statistics report is also available from issuing agency but is not covered in SRI.

Availability: Alabama Department of Public Health, Vital Statistics Bureau, Special Services Administration, State Office Bldg., Montgomery AL 36130, $10.00; SRI/MF/complete.

TABLES:
[Tables show data for Alabama, 1982, unless otherwise noted. Data by attendant usually are shown for physician, midwife, other, and none.]

S0175–2.1: Summary Data and Population

VITAL EVENTS

2.1. Vital events [summary], 1972 and 1981-82. (p. 9)

BUREAU OF VITAL STATISTICS OPERATIONS

2.2-2.3. Pieces of mail and fees received [by month], 1979-82. (p. 10-13)

2.4-2.5. Expenditures from all funds FY79-82, and by source of funds FY82, by purpose of expenditure. (p. 14)

2-6-2.7. Certified copies issued and sold at service counter [by month], 1979-82. (p. 16-17)

2.8-2.9. Birth amendments and delayed [birth] certificates filed, 1972-82. (p. 18-19)

2.10-2.11. Reports of adoption [of persons born in and out of Alabama]; and legitimations; 1972-82. (p. 20-21)

POPULATION

3.1. Live births, deaths, and natural increase, selected years 1940-82. (p. 25)

3.2. Population by county, PHA, and race, midyear 1982. (p. 29)

3.3-3.4. 1980 census: population of [40] selected cities [by race]; and population by age groups [by sex]. (p. 30-31)

S0175–2.2: Natality
[Most tables show data by race.]

LIVE AND RESIDENT BIRTHS

4.1-4.2. Live births and live birth rates, and age-sex-adjusted birth rates, Alabama and U.S., selected years 1940-82. (p. 35-37)

4.3. Resident births with birth rates, by county and PHA. (p. 39)

4.4-4.6. Live births: by month of occurrence; and by sex and area of residence, by age of mother. (p. 41-42)

4.7-4.8. Live births: by live birth order and age of mother; and by plurality and sex [by PHA]. (p. 43-44)

4.9-4.10. Live births by birth weight: by age of mother and period of gestation. (p. 45-46)

4.11-4.13. Live births by Apgar score: by sex; at 1 and 5 minutes; and at 1 minute by age of mother. (p. 47-48)

4.14-4.16. Live births: by legitimacy, total birth order, and month of pregnancy prenatal care began; all by education of mother. (p. 49-51)

4.17. Live births, by age of mother and number of prenatal visits. (p. 52)

4.18. Live births by attendant [in and not in hospital] and PHA. (p. 53)

IMMATURE BIRTHS

4.19-4.21. Immature births and immaturity ratios: [total] 1960-82; and by county, PHA, and age of mother, 1982. (p. 54-58)

ILLEGITIMACY

4.22-4.23. Illegitimate births and illegitimacy ratios: selected years 1940-82; and by county and PHA, 1982. (p. 60-63)

4.24. Live births, illegitimate births, and illegitimacy ratios, [all by age of mother]. (p. 64)

4.25. Illegitimacy ratios, by age of mother, 1980-82. (p. 64)

FERTILITY

4.26. Fertility rates [and age-specific birth rates; not by race], selected years 1940-82. (p. 66)

4.27-4.28. Fertility rates [and age-specific birth rates] for white females and all other females, 1966-82. (p. 67)

OTHER

4.29. Live births, by county, PHA, and age of mother. (p. 68-72)

4.30. Resident births in [32] selected cities, by age of mother. (p. 73)

4.31. Live births by county and PHA by number of prenatal visits. (p. 76-80)

4.32. Live births, by [county and] hospital of occurrence, and sex. (p. 81-85)

4.33. Births, [total and] by selected characteristics [under 3 prenatal visits, birth malformations, low weight births, maternal age under 20, midwives out of hospital, and illegitimate, by county and PHA]. (p. 86-91)

S0175-2.3: Mortality

[Causes of death are coded in accord with *International Classification of Diseases, 9th Revision, Adapted.* Many tables show both number of deaths and rates, by race.]

SUMMARY DATA

5.1-5.2. Mortality rates, and age-adjusted mortality rates, Alabama and U.S., selected years 1940-82. (p. 95-97)

5.3. Resident deaths and death rates, by county and PHA. (p. 99)

CAUSES OF DEATH

5.4. Important causes of death. (p. 101)

5.5-5.6. Leading causes of death: [total] and by age group. (p. 103-105)

5.7. Major causes of death by age group. (p. 106)

5.8-5.9. Resident deaths: by month of occurrence, 1980-82; and by sex and attendant, 1982. (p. 108)

5.10. Mortality and age-specific mortality rates, 1980-82. (p. 109)

5.11-5.12. Resident deaths, by age group and by selected cities. (p. 109-110)

5.13. Heart disease mortality by age [and sex]. (p. 112)

5.14. Malignant neoplasms mortality [by sex and primary site of neoplasm]. (p. 113)

ACCIDENTAL DEATHS

5.15. Comparative accidental death rates, Alabama and U.S., selected years 1940-82. (p. 116)

5.16. Accidental mortality, by age. (p. 117)

5.17-5.18. Accidental deaths: by type of accident; and by type and age group, occurrence data [including work accidents by industry division]. (p. 118-119)

INFANT MORTALITY

5.19-5.20. Infant mortality rates: Alabama and U.S., selected years 1940-82; and by county and PHA, 1982. (p. 123-126)

5.21. Infant mortality by cause. (p. 127)

5.22-5.23. Neonatal mortality, by county, PHA, and cause. (p. 128-130)

5.24-5.25. Infant mortality, by age, county, and PHA. (p. 132-134)

5.26. Perinatal deaths, by county and PHA. (p. 135-136)

FETAL DEATHS

5.27-5.36. Fetal deaths: Alabama and U.S., selected years 1945-82; and by county, PHA, cause, age of mother, sex, number of previous deliveries, weight and gestational age of fetus, and attendant [with selected cross-tabulations], 1982. (p. 138-146)

MATERNAL DEATHS

5.37-5.40. Maternal mortality: Alabama and U.S., selected years 1940-82; and by county, age group, and cause, 1982. (p. 148-151)

BY CAUSE AND LOCATION

5.41-5.42. Selected causes of death [by county and PHA]. (p. 152-224)

S0175-2.4: Marriage and Divorce

MARRIAGES

6.1-6.2. Marriages [and/or] marriage rates: Alabama [by race] and U.S., selected years 1940-82; and by county and PHA, [by race] 1982. (p. 227-230)

6.3. Marriages and marriage rates by month of occurrence. (p. 231)

6.4-6.6. Marriages: by previous marital status; by official performing ceremony; and by age and race of bride and groom. (p. 232-233)

6.7-6.8. Previous marriages by age of bride and groom. (p. 234-235)

6.9-6.11. Marriages: by age and previous marital status [of bride and groom]; by age of bride [by age of] groom; and by State of residence of bride and groom. (p. 236-239)

DIVORCES

7.1. Comparative [divorces and/or] rates, Alabama and U.S., selected years 1940-82. (p. 243)

7.2. Divorces and annulments, by county and PHA. (p. 245)

7.3-7.5. Divorces and annulments, by duration of marriage and number of minor children. (p. 247-249)

7.6. Divorces and [annulments, and total] rates, by month. (p. 250)

7.7-7.9. Divorces and annulments: by party to whom granted; by number of this marriage [for husband and wife]; and by legal grounds for decree. (p. 251-252)

S0175-4   ALABAMA'S POPULATION, 1930-80
Monograph.   July 1983.
80 p.
LC 83-622742.
SRI/MF/complete

Report presenting Alabama population trends, decennially 1930-80. Includes population by county, sex, race, age, urban and rural location, marital status, and educational attainment, and for selected cities; with various cross-tabulations.

Also includes data on fertility and birth rates, migration by race and county, employment by industry division, per capita personal income, and life expectancy.

Most data are from Census Bureau.

Contains listing of contents, charts, and tables (2 p.); introduction (p. 1); and 5 sections with narrative analysis, 1 map, 30 charts, and 23 tables (p. 4-80).

Availability: Alabama Department of Public Health, Vital Statistics Bureau, Special Services Administration, State Office Bldg., Montgomery AL 36130, †; SRI/MF/complete.

S0175-5   1970 AND 1980 CENSUS POPULATION OF ALABAMA COUNTIES by Race, Sex, and Age
Monograph.   [1984.]
1+201 p.
LC 84-622385.
SRI/MF/complete

Report presenting population data for Alabama counties, 1970 and 1980. Includes population by race and sex, cross-tabulated by age group, for each county. Data are from Census Bureau.

Contains introduction (1 p.); and 2 charts and 2 tables, repeated for each county (p. 1-201).

Availability: Alabama Department of Public Health, Vital Statistics Bureau, Special Services Administration, State Office Bldg., Montgomery AL 36130, †; SRI/MF/complete.

S0180   ALABAMA
Public Library Service

S0180-1   ALABAMA PUBLIC LIBRARY SERVICE Annual Report, 1982
Annual.   [1983.]   38 p.
LC 78-645263.
SRI/MF/complete

Annual report on Alabama public libraries, including finances, resources, circulation, staff, and population served, by county or State region and library, for FY82.

Contains contents listing (p. 1); narrative report with 2 charts (p. 3-9); 3 tables listed below, and 1 summary table showing total system services and resources (p. 10-19); 1983 directories by city and region (p. 21-34); and index, list of staff, organizational chart, and map of library districts (p. 35-38).

Availability: Alabama Public Library Service, 6030 Monticello Dr., Montgomery AL 36130, †; SRI/MF/complete.

TABLES:

[All data are shown for FY82. Unless otherwise noted, tables show the following data, by library and location: population, weekly hours open, FTE staff, book stock, nonbook resources, newspaper/periodicals, book and nonbook circulation, receipts by source, and expenditures by function.]

[1] Public libraries statistical reports. (p. 10-17)

[2] Multicounty regional libraries: headquarters report. (p. 18-19)

[3] Regional libraries: totals for member libraries and regional library services [omits hours, and includes total number of titles held]. (p. 18-19)

S0185   ALABAMA
Department of Public Safety

S0185-1   SUMMARY OF MOTOR VEHICLE TRAFFIC ACCIDENTS, 1983, Alabama
Annual.   For individual publication data, see below.
SRI/MF/complete

Annual report on Alabama traffic accidents, injuries, and fatalities, by vehicle and accident type, location, time, and other circumstances; and driver and victim characteristics; 1983. Also includes data on alcohol involvement and use of safety equipment.

Report is issued in 2 volumes, each described below.

A summary of rural traffic accidents is also available from the issuing agency, but is not covered by SRI.

Availability: Alabama Department of Public Safety, Highway Patrol Division, PO Box 1511, Montgomery AL 36192, †; SRI/MF/complete.

S0185-1.1: Summary of Motor Vehicle Traffic Accidents for the Period Jan. 1, 1983-Mar. 31, 1983
[Annual. [1984.] 30 p. no paging. SRI/MF/complete.]

Presents Alabama traffic accident data as described above, for 1st quarter 1983. Includes data by driver occupation and by involvement of special use vehicles.

Contains 30 tables.

S0185-1.2: Alabama Accident Summary: Statewide Accidents, Apr.-Dec. 1983
[Annual. [1984.] 33 p. no paging. SRI/MF/complete.]

Presents Alabama traffic accident data as described above, for 9-month period ended Dec. 31, 1983. Includes data on hazardous cargo, oversized loads, and vehicle attachments by type.

Contains contents listing (1 p.), and 31 tables.

S0275   ALASKA
Department of Administration

S0275-1   ANNUAL FINANCIAL REPORT for the Fiscal Year July 1, 1982-June 30, 1983, State of Alaska
Annual.   Nov. 10, 1983.
ix+227 p.
ISSN 0098-9916.
LC 75-646776.
SRI/MF/complete

Annual report on financial condition of Alaska State government, for FY83, presenting assets, liabilities, reserves, and fund equities; revenues by source; and expenditures by function; for all, general, special revenue, debt service, capital projects, enterprise, intragovernmental service, and trust and agency funds. Most data are shown by specific State agency, institution, program, or project.

Also includes actual vs. budgeted revenues and expenditures; bonded indebtedness; and selected general data, including property valuation, voters, State employees, fire depts and personnel, correctional institution inmates, educational enrollments and teachers, highway and ferry mileages, air carrier traffic, public recreation areas, population by age, and personal income, mostly for 1970s-83.

Data were compiled by the Director of Finance.

Contains contents listing (5 p.); introduction, including summary text tables (p. i-ix); 72 financial statements and schedules (p. 1-189); statistical data section, with 16 tables (p. 191-216); and index (p. 217-227).

Availability: Alaska Department of Administration, Finance Division, Pouch C, Juneau AK 99811, †; SRI/MF/complete.

S0280   ALASKA
Department of Commerce and Economic Development

S0280-2   COMPARATIVE STATEMENT OF ASSETS, LIABILITIES, AND CAPITAL ACCOUNTS of Alaska Banks
Quarterly.   Approx. 2 p.
SRI/MF/complete

Quarterly report on the financial condition of Alaska State-chartered commercial and mutual savings banks, and national banks, by institution and type. Report, compiled by the Division of Banking, Securities, Small Loans, and Corporations, is issued 3-9 months after end of quarter covered.

Contains 2 tables showing:

a. Comparative statement of assets, liabilities (including deposits by type), and equity capital, by central institution, as of end of quarter covered.

b. Comparative consolidated statement of condition (assets, liabilities, and equity capital), by bank type as of end of quarter covered, with totals for same date of previous year.

Availability: Alaska Department of Commerce and Economic Development, Banking, Securities, Small Loans, and Corporations Division, State Office Bldg., Pouch D, Juneau AK 99811-0800, $10.00 per yr.; SRI/MF/complete.

Issues reviewed during 1984: June 30, 1983-June 30, 1984 (D).

S0280-3   INSURANCE REPORT, 1983: 45th Annual Report to the Governor of Alaska and Legislature
Annual.   [1984.]   iv+167 p.
ISSN 0149-4864.
LC 60-62888.
SRI/MF/complete

Annual report on Alaska insurance industry underwriting activity, and investments, by company and type of insurance, 1982. Covers investments by type; premiums written and earned; benefits paid or losses incurred; and insurance in force, issued, and terminated; for companies headquartered in Alaska and elsewhere.

Data are shown, as applicable, for life, fire/casualty, and surplus line insurance companies, with underwriting detail by line of coverage, including accident/health, medical malpractice, auto, surety, and workers compensation; and for title insurance companies, fraternal benefit societies, and health care service organizations.

Title insurance company data also include assets, liabilities, capital, net income, and surplus.

Also includes data on Insurance Division fees and taxes collected, expenditures, and licensing activity, for FY83; trends in Division finances and company underwriting activity, from as early as 1937; and finances of insolvent companies.

Contains contents listing (p. iii-iv); Insurance Division report, with 8 tables (p. 1-30); and 21 company financial tables (p. 31-167).

Availability: Alaska Department of Commerce and Economic Development, Insurance Division, Pouch D, Juneau AK 99811, $10.00; SRI/MF/complete.

S0280-4   ALASKA PUBLIC UTILITIES COMMISSION FOURTEENTH ANNUAL REPORT to the Alaska Legislature for the Year Ending Dec. 31, 1983
Annual.   Aug. 15, 1984.
2+73 p.
SRI/MF/complete

Annual report presenting Alaska public utility regulatory, financial, and operating data, by company and/or utility type, 1983, with selected trends from 1980. Utility types covered in detail are electric, gas, refuse collection, sewer, telecommunications, and water.

Regulatory data include certifications, rate increases, complaints, and hearings and proceedings of the Alaska Public Utilities Commission (APUC). Financial and operating data include revenues, net income, plant value, users, and rates by community.

Also includes data on APUC finances, FY80-83; regulatory data for cable TV utilities and oil pipeline carriers; oil pipeline property value, revenues, and throughput, by company; electric utility sales to residential and commercial/other sectors; and telephone facilities.

Data are from APUC records and company reports.

Contains contents listing (1 p.); introductory material (p. 1-4); 2 sections on APUC activities, with narrative, 7 charts, and 6 tables (p. 5-28); utility statistics, with 15 tables and interspersed lists of companies (p. 29-62); and appendix, with miscellaneous narrative and 2 tables (p. 63-73).

Availability: Alaska Department of Commerce and Economic Development, Public Utilities Commission, 420 L St., Suite 100, Anchorage AK 99501, $5.00+postage; SRI/MF/complete.

S0285 ALASKA
Department of Community and Regional Affairs

S0285-1   ALASKA TAXABLE, 1983

Annual. Jan. 1984.
3+123 p. Vol. XXIII.
ISSN 0147-2348.
LC 75-649634.
SRI/MF/complete

Annual report, for 1983, on Alaska State and locally determined property values and taxes, public debt, and tax exemption provisions, with trends from 1970s.

Contents:

a. Contents and table listing. (2 p.)

b. 4 report chapters, with description of property tax regulations; overview of valuation, population, and bonded debt, with 6 summary tables; explanation of assessment ratios; and 14 numbered tables, listed below, usually preceded by explanatory notes. (p. 2-64)

c. Appendices A-G, including background legislative texts; 7 tables, also listed below; and directory of oil/gas property tax jurisdictions. (p. 67-122)

This is the 21st annual report.

Availability: Alaska Department of Community and Regional Affairs, Municipal and Regional Assistance Division, State Assessor's Office, Pouch BH, Juneau AK 99811, †; SRI/MF/complete.

TABLES:
[Most tables show data for assessed municipalities by borough and/or city.]

S0285-1.1: Values, Taxes, and Public Debt

I. Valuation, population, and G.O. [general obligation] bonded debt [summary, 1973-83; and by municipality, 1983]. (p. 9-11)

II. Local assessment policy [type of assessment and exemption status, for 6 property categories]. (p. 18)

III.A-III.B. 1983 statistical evaluation table, real property only [assessment/sales ratios and number of sales]; and cross-correlation of cost per parcel vs. coefficient of dispersion vs. weighted mean ratio and assessment cycle. (p. 20-21)

IV. Local assessments vs. full value [for real and personal property]. (p. 23-24)

V-VI.B. Full value determinations [locally and State assessed]: Jan. 1, 1983; comparison, 1979-83; and summary, 1873-83. (p. 26-31)

VII-VIII. Real property staff statistics [number of appraisers and real parcels, jurisdiction area, assessment budget, and assessment cycle]; and contract revaluation costs [by contract]; 1983. (p. 33-34)

IX-X. Municipal property and sales tax rates [by detailed local area and type of service including administration, schools, police, fire, and others, as applicable, 1981-83]. (p. 37-61)

XI.A-XI.B. Estimated 1983 property [by type] and sales tax revenue recap: assessed values and revenues. (p. 63-64)

S0285-1.2: Appendix Tables

[Tables generally show program summary data as indicated, by municipality for FY83, and statewide for various periods, from as early as FY75.]

DEFERRED FARM TAXES

[B1] Farm use land assessment [applicants, acres, value, and deferred tax]. (p. 70)

SENIOR CITIZEN EXEMPTIONS

[C1-C2] Senior citizen homeowner exemption [applications approved, assessed value exempt, total revenue reimbursement, and average value and tax per application]. (p. 75-76)

[C3] Senior citizen renter payment program summary [applications approved, and annual rent and payment, FY83 only]. (p. 81)

[D1] Senior citizen sewer/water assessment deferment, 5-year performance summary [applications approved, reimbursement, accounts with liens, and revenue collections]. (p. 87)

[E1-E2] Senior citizen motor vehicle registration tax program [affidavits and reimbursement]. (p. 92-93)

S0290 ALASKA
Court System

S0290-1   ALASKA COURT SYSTEM 1983 Annual Report

Annual. [1983.]
179 p. var. paging.
LC 78-645480.
SRI/MF/complete

Annual report, for FY83, on Alaska judicial system, including trial and appellate court caseloads and case dispositions. Covers supreme, appeals, superior, and district courts. Includes trial court data by case type and court location, and trends from 1976.

Case types shown are criminal and civil for most courts, with some additional detail for probate cases, including adoption, estate, guardianship, and sanity hearings; and domestic relations, juvenile, small claims, administrative review, and traffic cases. Criminal cases are occasionally shown by offense.

Report also includes data on appellate case processing time; State court system finances and personnel, including employees by race (Caucasian, Alaskan Native, black, Asian/Pacific Islander, and other); and police, lawyers, and judges compared with population, by city and judicial district.

Data are from reports submitted to the State by judicial officers and court clerks.

Contains introduction and table of contents (p. i-iii); report with 27 summary charts and tables (p. 1-93); and statistical supplement, with foreword and table listing (p. S.i-S.iv), and 66 tables (p. S.3-S.76).

Availability: Alaska Court System, 303 K St., Anchorage AK 99501, †; SRI/MF/complete.

S0295 ALASKA
Department of Education

S0295-1   EDUCATION IN ALASKA: A Report to the People, 1982/83

Annual. [1984.] 40 p.
LC 79-643587.
SRI/MF/complete

Annual report on public elementary/secondary education in Alaska, for school year 1982/83 or FY82. Covers enrollment, attendance, staff, and finances, by school district, for Regional Education Attendance Area (REAA) and city/borough schools.

Contains contents/table listing (1 p.); narrative report (p. 1-15); and 19 tables, listed below (p. 16-40).

Availability: Alaska Department of Education, Pouch F, Juneau AK 99811, †; SRI/MF/complete.

TABLES:
[Tables show data by school district, grouped for city/borough and REAA schools, for 1982/83 or FY82, unless otherwise noted.]

S0295-1.1: Enrollment, Attendance, and Staff

[Tables include totals for centralized correspondence schools.]

[1-2] Final enrollment by grade. (p. 16-19)

[3-4] Final average daily attendance and membership, [high school] graduates, and [professional and classified] personnel. (p. 20-21)

S0295-1.2: Staff, Finances, and Summary

STAFF

[1-2] Professional personnel [by position and sex]. (p. 22-23)

[3-4] Professional personnel salaries [1981/82-1982/83, and salary range 1982/83]. (p. 24-25)

FINANCES

[5-8] Audited district revenues [by source]; and food service, pupil activity, and special revenue funds [revenues and expenditures]. (p. 26-31)

[9-10] State aid for retirement of school construction debt [entitlements paid]; and cigarette tax distribution; [all by city/borough district only]. (p. 32-33)

[11-12] Audited district expenditures [by function, including vocational and special education, plant operation/maintenance, and pupil transport]. (p. 34-37)

[13-14] District fund balances. (p. 38-39)

SUMMARY

[15] Statistical summary, all schools [student and staff data aggregated for public schools by type; and enrollment and high school graduates, for private, military base, and selected other nonpublic school categories]. (p. 40)

S0310   ALASKA
Office of the Governor

S0310–3   ALASKA ECONOMIC INFORMATION AND REPORTING SYSTEM
Quarterly Report
Quarterly, discontinued.

Quarterly report on Alaska economic trends and forecast, discontinued with Nov. 1982 report (for description, see SRI 1983 Annual, under this number).

Publication has been discontinued due to organizational changes in issuing agency. Data will be available in *Alaska Economic Review and Outlook,* a new annual report scheduled for publication in the near future.

S0320   ALASKA
Department of Labor

S0320–1   ALASKA ECONOMIC TRENDS
Monthly.   Approx. 25 p.
ISSN 0160-3345.
LC 78-640712.
SRI/MF/complete, shipped quarterly

Monthly report presenting estimates of Alaska nonagricultural employment, labor force, and average hours and earnings, by industry and/or locale. Month of data coverage is 2-3 months preceding cover date.

Issues contain narrative summaries of labor market conditions, interspersed with employment trend charts and 9 monthly tables; and usually 1 or more feature articles, frequently containing statistics.

Issues also often contain additional tables showing trends and/or geographic detail for data topics covered in the monthly tables.

Monthly tables are listed below and appear in all issues. All additional features with substantial statistics on topics not covered in monthly tables are described, as they appear, under "Statistical Features." Nonstatistical features are not covered.

Availability: Alaska Economic Trends, PO Box 1149, Juneau AK 99802, †; SRI/MF/complete, shipped quarterly.

Issues reviewed during 1984: Nov. 1983-Oct. 1984 (P) (Vol. 3, Nos. 11-12; Vol. 4, Nos. 1-10).

MONTHLY TABLES:
[Data are shown for month of coverage and previous month, with comparison to preceding year.]

[1-7] Nonagricultural wage/salary employment by place of work [industry division and selected major group] for Alaska, Anchorage, Anchorage-Matsu, Fairbanks, interior, gulf coast, and southeast Alaska, [and often for 1-3 additional subareas].

[8] Labor force [by employment status] by region and census division [of Alaska].

[9] Alaska hours and earnings [by industry division and selected group].

STATISTICAL FEATURES:

S0320–1.501: Nov. 1983 (Vol. 3, No. 11)
ENGINEER SHORTAGE: MYTH vs. REALITY

(p. 1-9) By Betsy Jensvold. Article on engineer supply and demand in Alaska and total U.S. Data are from BLS, University of Alaska, and Alaska Dept of Labor. Includes 4 tables and 3 charts showing the following:

a. U.S.: average salary for beginning and experienced engineers relative to averages for 5 combined other professions and male college graduates; and engineers' unemployment rate; 1963-82.

b. Alaska: University of Alaska engineering degrees awarded, by level, field, and campus, 1973/74-1982/83; and engineering employment distribution, by specialty, region, and selected industry group, 1983.

CPI AND ANCHORAGE'S TAX INCREASE LIMITATION

(p. 13, 15) Article, with 1 table showing CPI for Anchorage and the U.S., 1979-82 and bimonthly Jan.-July 1983.

S0320–1.502: Jan. 1984 (Vol. 4, No. 1)
JUNEAU 1972-82: GROWTH AMID UNCERTAINTY

(p. 1-4) By John Boucher. Article, with 1 table showing Juneau nonagricultural employment by industry division and selected group, 1972 and 1982, with comparison to statewide percent change for the 10-year period.

S0320–1.503: Feb. 1984 (Vol. 4, No. 2)
ALASKA DURING STATEHOOD: DEMOGRAPHICS OF THE FIRST 25 YEARS

(p. 1-4) By Jo Van Patten. Article on Alaska demographic changes, 1960-80. Includes 2 tables showing fertility rates by mothers' age group, 1960 and 1980; and distribution of government employment by level, 1970 and 1980.

ALASKA SHELLFISH AND GROUNDFISH CATCH

(p. 10) Table showing Alaska's shellfish catch by type, and total groundfish catch, 1980/81-1983/84 fishing seasons. Data are from Alaska Dept of Fish and Game.

Table is accompanied by a related article (p. 8, 10).

S0320–1.504: Mar. 1984 (Vol. 4, No. 3)
FORESTRY

(p. 10, 12) Brief article, with 1 table showing Alaska timber industry average annual employment, by sector including pulp/paper, 1978-83.

S0320–1.505: Apr. 1984 (Vol. 4, No. 4)
ALASKA WAGE RATES

(p. 1-11) By John Van Houten. Article, with 3 tables showing job openings and mean hourly wage by occupation, for Alaska jobs with 25 or more openings listed with the State Job Service, and for Anchorage and Fairbanks jobs with 15 or more listings, 1983. Data are from Alaska Job Service.

Also includes directory of Job Service offices.

ANCHORAGE CONSUMER PRICE INDEX

(p. 17-18) Brief article, with 1 table showing Anchorage CPI by major expenditure category, 1983 with percent change from 1982.

S0320–1.506: May 1984 (Vol. 4, No. 5)
ALASKA OCCUPATIONAL EMPLOYMENT

(p. 1-13) By John Van Houten. Article presenting Alaska Dept of Labor recent estimates of occupational employment.

Includes 22 charts showing employment distribution by industry division and occupational group, for Alaska and 8 State areas, with selected U.S. comparison, 1983 or 1984; and distribution of Alaska employment by region 1983, and of employment and job openings by occupational group for various periods 1979-88.

ALASKA

(p. 16-20) By Ed Eboch. Article discussing outlook for oil and gas industry in Alaska and worldwide. Data are from Alaska Dept of Labor and *Petroleum Economist.*

Includes 1 chart and 1 table showing Alaska oil/gas industry employment, quarterly 1980-1st quarter 1984; and world oil production, with detail for 11 countries, OPEC, and Persian Gulf area, 1979-83, with year and amount of peak production since 1973.

MUNICIPAL BUILDING ACTIVITY

(p. 24) Table showing number and value of building permits, by type of construction, for Anchorage/Matsu region, 1st quarter 1983-84. Data are from municipal building activity report.

FAIRBANKS AND KENAI PENINSULA'S UNEMPLOYMENT INSURANCE CLAIMANTS, 1983

(p. 26, 30) Two tables showing unemployment insurance claimants, by occupational group, industry division, and age, for Fairbanks and Kenai Peninsula, 1983. Tables are accompanied by 2 related articles (p. 25-31).

S0320–1.507: June 1984 (Vol. 4, No. 6)
REGIONAL NATIVE CORPORATIONS

(p. 1-6) By Ed Eboch. Article on operations of Alaska's Regional Native Corporations established under the Alaska Native Claims Settlement Act. Data are from Dept of Labor and questionnaire responses from the corporations. Includes 2 tables showing Regional Native Corporation employment, by industry division and State region, 1980-83.

ANCHORAGE NONRESIDENT JOB SEEKERS

(p. 10-12, 14-16) By Greg Huff. Part 1 of a 2-part article on characteristics of Anchorage job seekers whose last employment was outside the Anchorage area. Part 1 focuses on job seekers from outside Alaska. Data are based on a Feb.-May 1984 study of 250 applications filed with the Anchorage Job Service.

Includes 4 tables showing distribution of applicants by geographic origin (U.S. region and State and aggregate foreign countries), occupational group, reason for leaving last job, race (including American Indian/Native, Hispanic, and Pacific Asian), age, family size, and educational attainment.

PROFILE OF KODIAK'S UNEMPLOYED

(p. 19-21) Article, with 3 tables showing unemployment insurance claimants, by industry division, occupational group, and age, for Kodiak Island, 1983. Data are from unemployment insurance claims filed with the State.

S0320–1.508: July 1984 (Vol. 4, No. 7)

ALASKA OCCUPATIONAL EMPLOYMENT OUTLOOK

(p. 1-13) By John Van Houten. Article, with 1 table showing Alaska estimated employment, 1983, and change during 1983-88 period, for 39 occupations projected to have the most job openings during this period. Data are from Alaska Dept of Labor Occupational Employment Statistics industry surveys.

PROFILE OF THE ANCHORAGE NONRESIDENT JOBSEEKER

(p. 18-22) By Greg Huff. Part 2 of a 2-part article on characteristics of Anchorage job seekers whose last employment was outside the Anchorage area. Part 2 focuses on jobseekers from elsewhere in Alaska. Data are based on a Feb.-May 1984 study of applications filed with the Anchorage Job Service.

Includes 3 tables showing distribution of applicants by geographic origin (State region), occupational group, reason for leaving last job, race (white and American Indian/Native), age, family size, and educational attainment.

FAIRBANKS' INCOME PICTURE

(p. 23, 25-26) By Neal Fried. Article, with 2 tables showing per capita annual income in current and 1970 constant dollars, for Fairbanks, State of Alaska, and U.S., 1970-82.

S0320–1.509: Aug. 1984 (Vol. 4, No. 8)

ALASKA'S VISITOR SURVEY

(p. 1-10) By Jeff Hadland. Article on economic impact and characteristics of visitors to Alaska. Data are based on surveys of visitors leaving Alaska during Oct. 1982-Sept. 1983, and of visitor-affected businesses in spring 1983.

Includes 8 charts and 5 tables showing the following for Alaska, various periods 1982-83:

a. Employment by industry division; and employment, compensation, employment share by occupational group, and sales, for various visitor-related industries, with detail for business associated with nonresident and resident visitors.

b. Nonresident visitors: departures by month and transport mode; and distribution by place of residence (Canada, other foreign countries, and selected States), age, income, education, and marital status.

KENAI PENINSULA BOROUGH'S INCOME PICTURE

(p. 21-23) By Neal Fried. Article, with 2 tables showing per capita income in current and constant 1970 dollars, for U.S., Alaska, Kenai-Cook Inlet, and Seward, 1970-82. Data are from U.S. Commerce Dept.

S0320–1.510: Sept. 1984 (Vol. 4, No. 9)

MILITARY ROLE IN ALASKA'S ECONOMY

(p. 1-8) By Neal Fried and Greg Huff. Article, with 1 table and 1 chart showing military personnel and civilian employees/dependents in Alaska, by State area, 1983 with aggregate personnel trends from 1945. Data are from State and Federal sources.

ALASKA: SHIFT/SHARE ANALYSIS

(p. 9-13) Article, with 2 tables showing U.S. and Alaska employment, and change in Alaska employment due to national growth and industry mix and to local factors, all by industry division, various periods 1978-83.

S0320–1.511: Oct. 1984 (Vol. 4, No. 10)

ANCHORAGE RETAIL TRADE

(p. 10-12, 14) By Greg Huff. Article, with 2 tables showing Anchorage retail firms, sales, payroll, and employment, by kind of business, 1977 and/or 1982. Data are from the Census Bureau.

FAIRBANKS' SERVICE SECTOR

(p. 15, 17) By Neal Fried. Article, with 1 table showing Fairbanks services industry employment, by industry group, 1973 and 1983.

S0320–4   ALASKA POPULATION OVERVIEW, 1983
Annual.   1984.   66 p.
LC 83-623053.
SRI/MF/complete

Annual report presenting Alaska population data by locale, sex, and age, 1983, with trends from 1945. Also includes data on population change components, education, and income.

Population data are compiled by Alaska Dept of Labor in accordance with Census Bureau guidelines, and are based primarily on 1980 decennial census.

Contains contents listing (1 p.); preface (p. 1); and the following:

Sections I-II. Population Data. 5 maps and 10 tables, including population for various years 1960-83, with selected detail for military and civilian sectors and by age and sex, shown variously by Alaska census area, borough, city, and incorporated place; and statewide population, births, deaths, and migration, 1945/46-1982/83. (p. 6-52)

Section III. Special Reports. 3 articles on Alaskan demography, including the 2 statistical articles described below. (p. 55-66)

Availability: Alaska Department of Labor, Research and Analysis Section, PO Box 1149, Juneau AK 99802, †; SRI/MF/complete.

STATISTICAL ARTICLES:

S0320–4.1: Alaskan Demographics, Education, and Income

ALASKA DURING STATEHOOD: DEMOGRAPHICS OF THE FIRST 25 YEARS

(p. 57-58) By Jo Van Patten. Article, with 2 tables showing Alaska births per 1,000 women by age group, 1960 and 1980; and Federal, State, and local shares of government employment, 1970 and 1980.

EDUCATION AND INCOME IN ALASKA

(p. 61-66) By Greg Williams. Article, with 3 tables showing population age 25/older, and percent with high school and college degrees; number of households, families, and persons; and median household and family income, and percent of persons below the poverty line; all for U.S., Alaska, and individual Alaska census areas, with detail for whites and Indians/Eskimos/Aleuts, 1980.

S0320–5   ALASKA PLANNING INFORMATION
Annual.   Jan. 1984.   4+84 p.
SRI/MF/complete

Annual planning report, for 1983, analyzing Alaska labor supply and demand. Includes data on population, labor force, employment, cost of living, income, and characteristics of unemployment insurance claimants, with selected detail by industry, occupation, and census location, and comparisons to U.S. Data generally are current to 1983, and include selected trends from the 1930s and forecasts to 1985.

Data are from Alaska Dept of Labor, BLS, and the Census Bureau.

Contains listing of contents, tables, and charts (3 p.); 7 chapters with narrative analyses, interspersed with 2 charts and 41 tables (p. 1-56); glossary (p. 57-61); and appendix, with 15 tables (p. 62-84).

All tables are listed below.

Availability: Alaska Department of Labor, Research and Analysis Section, PO Box 1149, Juneau AK 99802, †; SRI/MF/complete.

TABLES:

[Data and census classifications are for Alaska, unless otherwise noted. Data by industry are generally shown by nonagricultural industry division, often with additional detail for selected major industry groups.]

S0320–5.1: Area and Population

I.1-I.2. Conversion of 1980 census areas to corresponding 1970 census divisions, and of 1970 census divisions to 1980 census areas. [tabular lists] (p. 4-6)

I.3. Total land area and population, by census area, 1980. (p. 7)

II.1-II.2. Population by 1970 census division [1970 and 1980] and by 1980 census area [1970, 1980, and 1982; all with rankings]. (p. 8-9)

II.3-II.4. Population by age and sex, 1970, 1980, and July 1982. (p. 10-11)

S0320–5.2: Labor Force, Employment, and Unemployment Insurance Claimants

LABOR FORCE

III.1. Current Population Survey: labor force participation and unemployment rates, 1982 annual average [and population, all by sex, race, and marital status, with selected detail for youth]. (p. 14)

III.2. Alaska and U.S.: labor force characteristics, 1980 Census of Population [including total and female labor force, by employment status, with selected detail for women by age group of children, for duration of employment and unemployment, 1979 and/or 1980; employment by class of worker, occupation, and industry, 1980; and families by number of workers, 1979]. (p. 15)

III.3. Annual average unemployment rate (not seasonally adjusted) [Alaska and U.S., 1976-82]. (p. 17)

III.4. Labor force data [U.S.] by State [and census region and division], annual average 1982. (p. 18)

III.5. 1982 annual average [U.S.] unemployment [rate] ranked by State. (p. 19)

III.6. Civilian labor force, employment, unemployment, and unemployment rate, statewide [by month] Jan. 1976-Sept. 1983. (p. 20-21)

III.7. Labor force, [employment status, and unemployment rate] by [State] region and census division [1977-82]. (p. 23)

NONAGRICULTURAL EMPLOYMENT

IV.1. Types of employment [tabular description of 3 measures]. (p. 25)

IV.2.-IV.8. Nonagricultural wage/salary employment by [industry and] place of work for State, Anchorage/MatSu, Anchorage, Interior, Fairbanks, Gulf Coast, and Southeast, 1982. (p. 27-30)

IV.9.-IV.11. Industry employment forecast: monthly average employment by quarter [1983-2nd quarter 1985]; and annual average monthly employment, and annual change, [various periods 1981-85]. (p. 33-34)

UNEMPLOYMENT INSURANCE CLAIMANTS

[Table titles begin "All claimants, or Alaska unemployment insurance claimants, benefit year beginning calendar year 1982..."]

V.1. Percent distribution of local office within industry, and of industry within local office. (p. 37)

V.2. Occupational categories containing over 100 claimants. (p. 38)

V.3. Percent distribution of local office within occupational category, and of occupational categories within local office. (p. 39)

S0320–5.3: Cost of Living and Income Measures

COST OF LIVING

VI.1. Anchorage CPI [for wage/clerical workers and all urban consumers, selected months 1969-83]. (p. 43)

VI.2. Yearly CPI and percentage change, wage/clerical workers only [for U.S., Seattle, Anchorage, and Fairbanks; various months and years, 1967-82]. (p. 44)

VI.3. Cost of select items [food at home, electricity, heating oil, gasoline, and lumber] in select Alaskan communities, Mar. and June 1983. (p. 44)

INCOME MEASURES

VII.1. Income measures [tabular description of 4 measures.] (p. 46)

VII.2. Average earnings, unemployment insurance (UI) covered employment by [selected] industry, 1982. (p. 48)

VII.3. Number of workers, employment, and income levels in UI covered employment [by industry division], 1982. (p. 48)

VII.4. Hours and earnings for selected industries, 1982 annual average. (p. 49)

VII.5. OMB poverty guidelines for Alaska, effective date May 1983, and aggregate for all States except Alaska/Hawaii, 1983; [all by family size]. (p. 49)

VII.6. Personal income [total and per capita, U.S. and by Alaska] census division, 1981. (p. 52)

VII.7. Total and per capita personal income, Alaska and U.S., 1970-82. (p. 53)

VII.8. 1982 per capita [U.S.] personal income, ranked by State. (p. 53)

VII.9. Estimated 1981 median income of 4-person families [with State rankings]. (p. 54)

VII.10. Alaska and U.S. income and poverty status in 1979: 1980 census [results, including number of households, families, and unrelated individuals, by income level; per capita income; and selected detail by income type, number of workers in family, presence and age

of children, and for female householders and older persons, total and/or below poverty level]. (p. 55-56)

S0320–5.4: Appendix Tables

A.1-A.6. [Table III.6 is repeated for Anchorage/Matanuska/Susitna, Gulf Coast, interior, northern, southeast, and southwest regions.] (p. 62-67)

A.7.-A.13. [Tables IV.2-IV.8 are repeated for 1978-81.] (p. 68-79)

A.14. Insured employment by major industry division, 1938- 62. (p. 80)

A.15. Nonagricultural wage/salary employment [statewide, by industry division, monthly 1963-77, with annual averages]. (p. 81-84)

S0350 ALASKA
Department of Public Safety

S0350–1 1983 CRIME IN ALASKA
Annual. [1984.] 100 p.
LC 79-641000.
SRI/MF/complete

Annual report on Alaska crimes, arrests, and clearances, by offense and jurisdiction, 1983. Also includes data on demographic characteristics of arrestees, law enforcement employment, assaults on officers, stolen property value, and drug enforcement activity.

Data are compiled from local law enforcement agency reports, under the State Uniform Crime Reporting (UCR) Program.

Contains listings of contents, tables, and charts (2 p.); UCR program description, crime clocks, Part I offense summary with 3 charts and 2 tables, and law enforcement personnel section with 3 tables (p. 3-14); 5 detailed tables repeated for each reporting agency, with State totals (p. 15-89); drug enforcement report, with 1 chart and 3 tables (p. 90-96); and definitions (p. 97-100).

All tables are described below.

Availability: Alaska Department of Public Safety, Uniform Crime Reporting and Statistical Analysis Center, Pouch N, Juneau AK 99811, †; SRI/MF/complete.

TABLES:

[Data are for Alaska, 1983, unless otherwise noted.

Part I offenses are criminal homicide, forcible rape, robbery, aggravated assault, burglary, larceny/theft, and motor vehicle theft. Part II offenses include 21 other categories.]

S0350–1.1: Part I Offense Summary, and Law Enforcement Personnel

a. Part I crimes, by offense; and population; 1980-83. 2 tables. (p. 6)

b. Law enforcement officers killed and assaulted, by local agency and for State troopers; officers assaulted, by type of activity and assignment, weapon, and injury status; and assaults cleared. 2 tables. (p. 12-13)

c. Law enforcement sworn and civilian employees, by city and for Public Safety Dept; and total employees, by sex. 1 table. (p. 14)

S0350–1.2: Data by Reporting Agency

[Most data described below are repeated for: Alaska State troopers (p. 15-17), each local law enforcement agency (p. 18-86), and State total (p. 87-89).]

a. Part I reported, unfounded, and actual offenses; total clearances; and clearances involving juveniles; shown for criminal homicides by subclassification, forcible rapes and rape attempts, robberies and assaults by type of weapon, burglaries by entry classification, larcenies/thefts, and motor vehicle thefts by vehicle type. 1 table.

b. Stolen property offenses and value, by Part I offense, with additional detail by robbery, burglary, and larceny circumstances, and for vehicles stolen and recovered locally vs. elsewhere. 1 table.

c. Value of property stolen and recovered, by property type. 1 table.

d. Adult and juvenile arrests by Part I and Part II offense, by age, sex, and race-ethnicity (including Indian, Asian, and Eskimo); with disposition summary for juveniles. 2 tables.

S0350–1.3: Drug Enforcement Activities

a. Narcotics enforcement personnel and budget; arrests of adults and juveniles for sale and possession of drugs/narcotics, by substance; amount and value of narcotics seized, by substance; and total drug charges; various years 1980-83. 3 tables. (p. 87-88)

S0450 ARIZONA
Department of Administration

S0450–1 STATE OF ARIZONA ANNUAL FINANCIAL REPORT, 1982-83
Annual. Dec. 1, 1983.
3+55 p.
ISSN 0098-9924.
LC 75-646570.
SRI/MF/complete

Annual report on financial condition of Arizona State government, for FY83, presenting assets, liabilities, and fund balances; revenues by source; expenditures variously by agency, function, or object; and appropriations; for general, special revenue, trust and agency, enterprise, internal service, and debt service funds; with selected comparisons from FY82.

Also includes property taxes receivable, by year of levy and county.

Data are compiled from records of the Finance Division.

Contains contents listing (1 p.); and 14 financial statements (p. 1-55).

A detailed list of revenue recipients is presented in *Office of the State Treasurer of Arizona Annual Report,* available from that office. Report is not covered in SRI.

Availability: Arizona Department of Administration, Finance Division, State Capitol, Rm. 809, 1700 W. Washington, Phoenix AZ 85007, †; SRI/MF/complete.

S0460   ARIZONA
Banking Department

S0460-1   CONDENSED STATEMENT OF REPORTS OF STATE AND FEDERAL SAVINGS AND LOAN ASSOCIATIONS, Arizona
Quarterly.
Approx. 1 p. Oversized.
SRI/MF/complete

Quarterly report on assets, liabilities, and equity capital of Arizona State and Federal savings and loan assns. Data are based on reports by assns to the Superintendent of Banks. Report is issued 2-3 months after quarter of coverage.

Contains 1 table showing assets, liabilities, and equity capital, by item; and number of branch offices; by institution, as of end of quarter covered.

Availability: Arizona Banking Department, Commerce Bldg., Rm. 101, 1601 W. Jefferson, Phoenix AZ 85007, †; SRI/MF/complete.

Issues reviewed during 1984: Sept. 30, 1983-June 30, 1984 (D).

S0460-2   CONDENSED STATEMENT OF REPORTS OF STATE AND NATIONAL BANKS of Arizona
Quarterly. Approx. 10 p. no paging.
SRI/MF/complete

Quarterly report on assets, liabilities, and equity capital of Arizona State and national banks. Data are based on reports by banks to the Superintendent of Banks. Report is issued 2-3 months after quarter of coverage.

Contains 1 table showing assets, liabilities, and equity capital, by item; and number of branch offices; by institution, as of end of quarter covered.

Availability: Arizona Banking Department, Commerce Bldg., Rm. 101, 1601 W. Jefferson, Phoenix AZ 85007, †; SRI/MF/complete.

Issues reviewed during 1984: Sept. 30, 1983-June 30, 1984 (D).

S0460-3   ANNUAL REPORT OF THE CONSUMER FINANCE COMPANIES, 1982-83, Arizona
Annual. [1984.] 13 p.
LC 71-618077.
SRI/MF/complete

Annual report, for FY83, on the financial condition of consumer finance companies licensed to operate in Arizona. Presents composite balance sheet; income and expenses; and analysis of small loan activity, delinquent accounts, recovery suits, wage assignments, and chattel activity. Also includes small loan trends from FY73.

Contains listings of licensees by city and type of license, and new and surrendered licenses (p. 1-5); and 8 financial schedules and 1 table (p. 7-13).

Availability: Arizona Banking Department, Commerce Bldg., Rm. 101, 1601 W. Jefferson, Phoenix AZ 85007, †; SRI/MF/complete.

S0465   ARIZONA
Department of
Economic Security

S0465-1   ARIZONA LABOR MARKET NEWSLETTER
Monthly.   Approx. 15 p.
SRI/MF/complete, shipped quarterly

Monthly report on Arizona labor market trends, including employment by county and industry, unemployment insurance activities, and production worker hours and earnings. Data are compiled by the Arizona Dept of Economic Security from various sources. Month of coverage is 2-3 months prior to cover date.

Issues generally contain articles, often with statistics; summary data on Arizona unemployment rates and Phoenix CPI, with comparisons to U.S., and U.S. PPI; and 5 monthly tables, with accompanying analysis.

Monthly tables are listed below; most appear in all issues. All additional features with substantial statistics on Arizona are described, as they appear, under "Statistical Features." Nonstatistical features, and articles which contain only widely available U.S. statistics, are not described.

Availability: Arizona Department of Economic Security, Labor Market Information Publications, Site Code 733A, PO Box 6123, Phoenix AZ 85005, †; SRI/MF/complete, shipped quarterly.

Issues reviewed during 1984: Nov. 1983-Oct. 1984 (P) (Vol. VII, Nos. 11-12; Vol. VIII, Nos. 1-10) [Vol. VIII, No. 10 incorrectly reads Vol. VII].

MONTHLY TABLES:
[All data are shown for Arizona, for month of coverage. Tables [1] and [4-5] also show data for previous month and same month of previous year. Table order may vary from month to month.]

[1] Labor force and employment; and nonagricultural wage/salary employment, by [industry division and selected major group; all for State and Maricopa and Pima Counties].

[2] Nonmetro counties labor force and employment [by industry division, by county].

[3] Labor force and employment, for [consideration in] economic assistance programs [by county].

[4] Estimated hours and earnings of production workers in selected industries.

[5] Unemployment insurance activities [claimants served, benefits paid, average number of weeks unemployed, and unemployment trust fund balance].

STATISTICAL FEATURES:

S0465-1.501: Nov. 1983 (Vol. VII, No. 11)
U.S. JOB GROWTH 28 MILLION BY 2000
(p. 7) Brief article, with 1 table showing average annual employment growth rate, overall and by industry division, for U.S. and 9 western States, 1980-2000 period. Data are from the National Planning Assn.

S0465-1.502: Dec. 1983 (Vol. VII, No. 12)
JTPA: ARIZONA IMPLEMENTS ITS PROGRAM
(p. 4-5) Article, with 1 chart showing Arizona Job Training Partnership funding allocation by function, 1984.

S0465-1.503: Jan. 1984 (Vol. VIII, No. 1)
COMMUTING IN ARIZONA
(p. 5-6) Article, with 1 table showing commuting destinations of Arizona workers, by county of residence, 1980. Data are from 1980 U.S. Census.

ARIZONA RECEIVES FINAL JTPA ALLOCATION
(p. 7) Article, with text statistics and 1 table showing Arizona Job Training Partnership Act funding, by category and local service delivery area, Jan.-Sept. 1984. Data are from U.S. Labor Dept.

S0465-1.504: Feb. 1984 (Vol. VIII, No. 2)
BLACKS IN THE ARIZONA LABOR FORCE
(p. 4-6) Article, with 1 chart and 1 table showing Arizona black labor force participation, by occupation and sex, 1970 and 1980. Data are from Census of Population and Housing Equal Employment Opportunity Special Tape File.

RECESSIONS AND THE ARIZONA ECONOMY: A COMPARISON OF 1974/75 AND 1981/82
(p. 12-13) Article, with 2 tables showing Arizona and U.S. annual growth rates for employment and total and per capita personal income, with selected detail by industry division, various years 1974/75-1981/82. Data are from Commerce Dept.

S0465-1.505: Mar. 1984 (Vol. VIII, No. 3)
WHAT IS THE MODEL?
(p. 17-19) Article describing econometric model used to develop Arizona economic forecasts published annually in the Mar. *Newsletter*. Includes 1 table showing employment by industry division, for Maricopa and Pima Counties and balance-of-State, 1983 forecast and 1983 pre- and post-benchmark levels.

S0465-1.506: Apr. 1984 (Vol. VIII, No. 4)
JTPA 1984-85 FINAL ALLOCATIONS
(p. 5) Article, with 1 table showing Job Training Partnership Act funding in Arizona, statewide, by county, and for all Indian reservations, FY84-85. Data are from Arizona Dept of Labor.

WHERE WE LIVE, WHERE WE WORK AND WHAT WE EARN
(p. 6-7) Article, with 1 table showing business establishments, employment, population, and median family income, for Phoenix and 8 other cities within Maricopa County, 1983. Data are from Arizona Dept of Economic Security.

S0465-1.507: May 1984 (Vol. VIII, No. 5)
DECLINING AGRICULTURE?
(p. 1-6) Article, with text data and 1 table showing Arizona farm sales by price range, farms and acreage by use, farm product market value, and hired and contract labor cost and employment, by county, 1978 and 1982, with employment summary from 1976. Data are from Census Bureau and Arizona Crop and Livestock Reporting Service.

ECONOMIC RECOVERY IN ARIZONA: HOW LONG AND HOW STRONG?

(p. 7-9) Article, with 2 tables showing Arizona nonagricultural employment by industry division and total unemployment rate, with comparison to selected U.S. economic indicators, as forecast under 3 growth assumptions, 1983-86. Data are from Dept of Economic Security.

BOATING IN ARIZONA

(p. 15-16) Article, with 2 text tables showing ratio of persons to boats 1980, and per capita boating expenditure 1982, for Arizona and 3-8 other States. Data sources include National Marine Manufacturers Assn.

S0465-1.508: June 1984 (Vol. VIII, No. 6)

TEACHING SALARIES IN ARIZONA

(p. 4-5) Article, with 2 tables showing U.S. average starting salary for bachelor's degree graduates, by selected field of study (no date); and average Arizona teaching salary in current and constant 1974/75 dollars, 1974/75-1983/84.

Data sources include *U.S. News and World Report.*

PROPRIETARY SCHOOLS EDUCATE FOR JOBS

(p. 12-13) Article on the role of Arizona proprietary (for-profit) vocational schools. Data are from State agencies. Includes 2 tables showing Arizona top 20 occupations ranked by employment, 1983; and graduates of proprietary schools, by school type, 1979/80-1982/83.

ARIZONA'S POSTSECONDARY STUDENTS: THEIR CHARACTERISTICS, INCOME AND EXPENDITURES

(p. 14-15) Article, with 1 table showing Arizona postsecondary education student expenses, by type of expense and type of institution, 1983. Data are from a spring 1983 survey of students in 36 Arizona postsecondary schools.

ARIZONA EDUCATION: A STATISTICAL OVERVIEW

(p. 21-23) Compilation of 12 tables showing the following for Arizona, various years 1980-84:

a. Median education, and population distribution by educational status, by county; national rankings based on higher education appropriations; public and private schools and enrollment; public school teachers, expenditures, and revenues; and public university tuition and fees.

b. State appropriations; funds received from State trust lands; enrollment; and faculty and average salaries, by sex and academic rank; all for higher education, by institution and/or institution type.

Most data are from State agencies.

S0465-1.509: July 1984 (Vol. VIII, No. 7)

GAMING IN ARIZONA?

(p. 1-6) Article discussing potential impact of casino gambling on Arizona economy, and analyzing Nevada gaming industry trends.

Includes 5 tables showing Nevada firms, employment, and wages, by industry division, 1982; job openings, by major occupational category, 1976-85 period; and hotel/gaming/recreation industry 1984 employment and 1979 wage ranges, and culinary union 1979 wage rates, all by detailed occupation; with selected detail by location including Las Vegas and Reno SMSAs.

S0465-1.510: Aug. 1984 (Vol. VIII, No. 8)

ARIZONA'S CHANGING INDUSTRIAL COMPOSITION

(p. 1-4) Article, with 2 tables showing distribution of employment by industry division, for U.S., Arizona, and Maricopa, Pima, and aggregate nonmetro Arizona counties, 1971 and 1983.

ARE ANNUAL SAVINGS UP TO $767 PER EMPLOYEE POSSIBLE FROM UI TAXES ALONE?

(p. 7-8) Article on Arizona's unemployment insurance (UI) tax rate structure. Includes 1 table showing Arizona UI tax rate, taxable wage base, cost per insured employee, and trust fund balance, with Arizona's rank, and high and low data, among the States, 1983.

S0465-1.511: Sept. 1984 (Vol. VIII, No. 9)

1982 MINING EMPLOYEES: WHERE ARE THEY NOW?

(p. 1-5) Article on employment changes in Arizona copper mining industry, 1982-83. Data are from Arizona Dept of Economic Security.

Includes 2 charts and 2 tables showing the following as of 4th quarter 1983, for persons who were employed in copper mining in 1st quarter 1982: number working in same and different mine, different industry, and outside Arizona; number in same and different mine, and different industry, by range of wage increase; and distribution of persons working in different industry, by industry group.

S0465-1.512: Oct. 1984 (Vol. VIII, No. 10)

[Issue incorrectly reads Vol. VII.]

EMPLOYMENT IN ARIZONA: FORECAST UPDATE, ANNUAL FEATURE

(p. 1-6) Annual article, with 4 tables showing labor force by employment status, and employment by industry division, for Arizona, Maricopa and Pima Counties, and aggregate nonmetro counties, 1983-86.

CHANGES IN THE MARICOPA COUNTY LABOR FORCE, 1970-80

(p. 12-13) Article, with 2 tables showing percent male and female employment in selected occupations dominated by the opposite sex, for Maricopa County, Ariz., 1980. Data are from the U.S. census.

S0465-4   STATISTICAL BULLETIN, Arizona Department of Economic Security

Monthly.   Approx. 15 p. no paging.
SRI/MF/complete, shipped quarterly

Monthly report on Arizona public assistance cases, recipients, and payments, by program, county, and district. Covers AFDC, general and emergency assistance, tuberculosis control, supplemental payments, and food stamp programs. Report is issued 1-2 months after month of coverage.

Contains narrative summary, approximately 20 trend charts, and 6 monthly tables listed below.

Monthly tables are included in all issues; Aug. 1984 issue also includes an additional table with revised monthly data for number of food stamp recipients, 1983-1st half 1984.

Availability: Arizona Department of Economic Security, Family Assistance Administration, Site Code 960A, PO Box 6123, Phoenix AZ 85005, †; SRI/MF/complete, shipped quarterly.

Issues reviewed during 1984: Sept. 1983-Aug. 1984 (D).

TABLES:

[Unless otherwise noted, data are shown by State district and county, for month of coverage, with change from previous month and same month of previous year. Tables 1-2 and 4-5 show cases and/or recipients and payments.]

1. AFDC [for adult and child recipients; also includes (in footnotes) State totals for cases, recipients, and payments to Navajo/Hopi Indians, children in foster homes, and refugee resettlement program].

2. General assistance [including (in footnotes) refugee resettlement program].

3. Emergency assistance [number and value of payments].

4-5. Tuberculosis control; and supplemental payments program.

6. Food stamp program [households, persons, and coupon issuance value].

S0465-5   ANNUAL PLANNING INFORMATION: A Planning Guide for Employment and Training, FY86, Arizona

Annual.   Nov. 1984.
v+219 p.
LC 82-640185.
SRI/MF/complete, current & previous year reports

Annual planning report, for FY86, identifying Arizona population groups most in need of employment services, and presenting data on occupational supply and demand through 1990. Includes data on population, labor force, economically disadvantaged, public assistance, correctional institution population, and unemployment insurance, mostly by county, with selected sociodemographic characteristics, various periods 1959-86.

Selected data are shown for individual Job Training Partnership Act (JTPA) service delivery areas, including 9 counties and county consortiums, Phoenix, and Indian reservation consortium.

Contains preface and contents listing (p. iii-v); analyses of State and JTPA areas, with narrative summaries and 96 tables (p. 1-151); 14 appendices, with 20 tables, and lists of growing and declining industries and related occupations by county (p. 153-211); and glossary, methodology for population estimates, and acknowledgements (p. 213-219).

All tables are described below.

Previous report, for FY85, was also reviewed in 1984 and is also available on SRI microfiche under this number [Annual. Jan. 1984. v+198 p. †]. Previous report is substantially similar in format and content, but includes additional racial/ethnic data for public assistance recipients, and omits data on wages, population with less than 12 years of school, correctional institution population, probation, work incentive program, and unemployment insurance.

Availability: Arizona Department of Economic Security, Labor Market Information Publications, Site Code 733A, PO Box 6123, Phoenix AZ 85005, †; SRI/MF/complete.

TABLES:

[Data by race/ethnicity generally include white, black, American Indian/Eskimo/Aleut, Asian/Pacific Islander, and Spanish origin.]

a. Labor force by employment status, population, persons below poverty level, and persons with work disability by labor force status, 1986, and public assistance recipients by program, FY84, with detail by age, sex, and race/ethnicity, for Arizona and by JTPA area with detail for Tucson; high school graduates, and nongraduates by employment status, by race/ethnicity, 1986; and Indian reservation population, by county, 1983-86. 96 tables. (p. 3-151)

b. Economically disadvantaged youth and adults eligible for JTPA services, by county (no date); poverty level guidelines, 1984; and average weekly wages by industry division, by county, 4th quarter 1983. 4 tables. (p. 155-159)

c. Education: population with less than 12 years of school, by age, sex, and county, 1986; high school graduates, and nongraduates by employment status, by county and for Phoenix and Tucson, 1986; General Educational Development (GED) tests administered and certificates issued, 1959-83; and population age 5/over by English speaking ability, by county and for Phoenix, Tucson, and Indian reservations, 1986. 4 tables. (p. 160-163)

d. Births by mother's age group and county of residence, 1978-83; veterans by county, Mar. 31, 1984, and number receiving compensation or pension, Sept. 1983; average daily correctional institution population, by adult and juvenile institution, FY83; adults and juveniles on probation, by county, June 1984; and work incentive demonstration program registrants and employment activity, 2nd quarter 1984. 7 tables. (p. 164-168)

e. Unemployment insurance recipients by age and sex, and persons unemployed 13 weeks/more receiving and having exhausted benefits, July 31, 1984; and unskilled workers by employment status and as percent of total employment, 1986; all by county, with detail for Phoenix. 4 tables. (p. 169-171)

f. Occupational projections: employment and job openings, by county and detailed occupation, various periods 1985-90. 1 table. (p. 197-211)

S0470   ARIZONA
Department of Education

S0470-1   ANNUAL REPORT OF THE SUPERINTENDENT OF PUBLIC INSTRUCTION, Statistical Section, for FY83, Arizona
Annual. Nov. 1983. 543 p.
ISSN 0095-5310.
LC 74-647146.
SRI/MF/complete

Annual report on Arizona public school enrollment characteristics, administration, facilities, and finances, by school district and county, with comparative enrollment data for private schools, 1982/83 or FY83. Data are from reports submitted to the State by school officials.

Contains contents listing (p. 5); 10 tables, listed below (p. 9-533); appendices, with data variances and adjustments (p. 535-539); and index (p. 541-543).

Availability: Arizona Department of Education, 1535 W. Jefferson, Phoenix AZ 85007, $9.56+$2.50 postage and handling; SRI/MF/complete.

TABLES:

[Data are for 1982/83 or FY83, and are shown for public schools, unless otherwise noted. Data by grade include special education.]

[1] Statistics in education [public and private schools and enrollments; public school average daily membership (ADM), and number of superintendents, principals, and teachers; and total and operating school districts]. (p. 9)

[2] District expenditures [by function] and percentage of total expenditures [and revenues by source]. (p. 9-10)

[3] State summary, by grade of pupil enrollment [enrollment by race and ethnic group including Hispanic, American Indian/Alaskan Native, and Asian/Pacific Islander; dropouts; and graduates]. (p. 13)

[4] State summary of number and type of schools [and school districts, by county]. (p. 14)

[5] Private schools statistics [enrollment by grade; and schools and enrollment by county]. (p. 15)

[6] Food service programs statistics [meals served, value of donated commodities, and expenditures, by county and school district]. (p. 16-21)

[7-8] Business and financial services, State-appropriated funds and Federal grants-in-aid: statement of revenues or grants, and expenditures. (p. 24-29)

[9] Summary: annual financial report of the county school superintendent [expenditures, special county school reserve fund operations, and disbursements, by county]. (p. 32-35)

[10] Arizona school district, county, and State summary [ADM 1980/81-1982/83; enrollment, pupils promoted and retained, high school graduates, dropouts, and teachers by sex; schools; assessed valuation; and detailed revenues by source and expenditures by function, including finances for teacher salaries, retirement, school projects, special education

programs by type, and pupil transportation; repeated for each school district and county, and for the State]. (p. 42-533)

S0480   ARIZONA
Department of Health Services

S0480-1   1982 ARIZONA VITAL HEALTH STATISTICS
Annual. [1983.] 45 p.
ISSN 0160-9610.
LC 78-642237.
SRI/MF/complete

Annual report on Arizona vital statistics, by county, 1982. Covers births, deaths, marriages, divorces/annulments, and abortions. Includes data by sex, race/ethnicity, age, and education, with trends from 1950 or earlier, and comparisons with U.S. Data are from documents filed in Vital Records Section prior to Mar. 15, 1983.

Contains introduction and table listing (3 p.); methodology and definitions (p. 1); and 44 tables, described below (p. 2-45).

Availability: Arizona Department of Health Services, Vital Records and Information Services Bureau, Research and Statistical Analysis Section, 1740 W. Adams St., Phoenix AZ 85007, †; SRI/MF/complete.

TABLES:

[Data are shown for Arizona, 1982, unless otherwise noted. Trends from 1950 generally are shown quinquennially 1950-70 and annually 1971-82. Most data are shown by county of residence and/or occurrence. Data are shown as numbers and/or rates. Data by race usually include American Indian and Asian.]

POPULATION AND BIRTHS

a. Population, decennially 1930-80 and 1981-82. Table 1.1. (p. 2)

b. Low birth weight births: 1970-82; and by child's race and sex, and mother's age group, 1982. Tables 2.1-2.4. (p. 3-6)

c. Births: to unwed mothers and total, by mother's age group, race, and education; birth trends from 1950; births by month, selected years 1970-82, and by child's race (including Hispanics) and sex, 1982; and births with congenital anomalies, by type of anomaly and child's race and sex, 1982. Tables 2.5-2.17. (p. 7-19)

DEATHS

d. Deaths: trends from 1950; by month, selected years 1970-82; and by race and sex, 1982. Tables 3.1-3.5. (p. 20-24)

e. Fetal deaths: trends from 1950; and by child's race and sex, 1982. Tables 3.6-3.8. (p. 25-27)

f. Infant mortality: by child's age and selected cause, child's race and sex, and whether neonatal or postneonatal; and total and neonatal trends from 1950. Tables 3.9-3.15. (p. 28-34)

g. Deaths, by selected cause and age group. Tables 3.16-3.18. (p. 35-37)

MARRIAGES, DISSOLUTIONS, AND ABORTIONS

h. Marriages and dissolutions, monthly 1982, and annually 1955-82. Tables 4.1-4.6. (p. 38-43) *i.* Abortions, 1978-82, with detail for total State by in-State vs. out-of-State residence, women's age group, marital status, race, education, previous live births and abortions, type of facility and procedure; and weeks of gestation, existence of complications, and reasons for termination. Tables 5.1-5.2. (p. 44-45)

S0483   ARIZONA
Department of Insurance

S0483–1   70th ANNUAL REPORT OF THE DEPARTMENT OF INSURANCE, State of Arizona
Annual.   Sept. 30, 1983.
351 p.
LC 17-14279.
SRI/MF/complete

Annual report on Arizona insurance industry financial condition and underwriting activity, by company and/or type of insurance, 1982. Covers assets, liabilities, capital, surplus, and Arizona premium income, for companies with headquarters in Arizona and elsewhere.

Data are shown for life/disability, property/casualty, mortgage guaranty, and title insurance companies, and for various types of health services organizations.

Also includes Insurance Dept finances for FY83; and insurance company receiverships, and other status changes.

Contains contents listing (1 p.); Insurance Dept report, including activity summary, 5 tables on dept finances, and lists of status changes (p. 2-23); company directory and financial profiles (p. 24-344); selected lists, including companies in receivership (p. 345-347); and 5 summary tables (p. 348-351).

Availability: Arizona Department of Insurance, Administrative Division, 1601 W. Jefferson, Phoenix AZ 85007, $10.00; SRI/MF/complete.

S0495   ARIZONA
Department of Library, Archives and Public Records

S0495–1   ARIZONA LIBRARIES, 1982/83: Statistical Report and Directory
Annual.   [1984.]   1+44 p.
LC 84-622072.
SRI/MF/complete

Annual report, for FY83, on Arizona public and State institution libraries, including finances, holdings, staff, and population served, by county and institution.

Contents:

a. Directories of libraries. (p. 1-26)

b. Public and State institutional library statistical and financial reports, showing the following data by county and library, and by State agency and institution, FY83: population served; staff; volunteers; weekly hours; col-

lections and circulation, with selected comparisons to FY82; and funding by source and expenditures by object. 3 tables. (p. 27-43)

c. List of public libraries by county. (p. 44)

Availability: Arizona Department of Library, Archives and Public Records, Library Extension Service, Capitol Bldg., 3rd Floor, 1700 W. Washington, Phoenix AZ 85007, †; SRI/MF/complete.

S0497   ARIZONA
Department of Mineral Resources

S0497–1   PRIMARY COPPER INDUSTRY OF ARIZONA in 1982
Annual.   Jan. 1984.   55 p.
Special Rpt. No. 6.
SRI/MF/complete

Annual report, by Clifford J. Hicks, on Arizona copper industry, including production, reserves, employment, and earnings, for 1982, with trends from 1948. Also includes data on Arizona production of molybdenum, gold, silver, lead, zinc, and other minerals; U.S. copper production, stocks, and prices; and world copper stocks.

Data are derived primarily from reports of the Arizona Depts of Mineral Resources and Economic Security, U.S. Bureau of Mines and BLS, and company annual reports.

Contains contents and table listing (2 p.); introduction, summary, highlights of individual copper company operations, and tax descriptions (p. 1-17); and 20 tables listed below (p. 18-55).

Availability: Arizona Department of Mineral Resources, Mineral Resources Bldg., Fairgrounds, Phoenix AZ 85007, $2.00+$0.63 postage; SRI/MF/complete.

TABLES:
[Tables show data for Arizona, unless otherwise noted.]

S0497–1.1: Production and Industry Indicators
[Tables I-IV, VII-IX, and XIII show data by company and/or mine.]

I-II. Copper and molybdenum production of large copper mines, 1982; and leach copper production [1973-82]. (p. 18-23)

III-IV. Rank of copper companies and mines by production of copper and molybdenum, 1982. (p. 24-25)

V. Mine production of recoverable copper in short tons [monthly 1979-lst 7 months 1983]. (p. 26)

VI. Indicators of mining growth [taxable sales, employment, payrolls, and per capita wages], 1970-82. (p. 27)

VII-VIII. Average copper content of ore produced and percent contained copper recovered at copper mines [by major mineral type, 1972-82]. (p. 28-32)

IX. Stripping ratios at open-pit copper mines [1972-82]. (p. 33)

X. Production and value of copper, molybdenum, gold, and silver recovered from copper ore [1970-82]. (p. 35)

XI. Mine production (recoverable) of gold, silver, copper, lead, and zinc [and number of mines, and total materials sold/treated] in 1982, by class of ore or other source material. (p. 37)

XII. Nonfuel mineral production [quantity and value, for 13 mineral categories, 1981-82]. (p. 39)

XIII. Copper mine capacity [current estimate]. (p. 40)

XIV. Mine production of recoverable copper in the U.S. [by State, with rank, 1981-82]. (p. 41)

S0497–1.2: Employment, Inventories, Prices, and Reserves

EMPLOYMENT

XV. Covered employment and wages in copper mining/smelting [average number of covered employees, total wages, average annual and weekly wage, and tons of ore produced, 1948-82]. (p. 42)

XVI. Industries covered by social security [average number of employees, total wages, and average annual and weekly wage, for copper mining and processing and 8 other industry groups], 1982. (p. 44)

XVII. Employment, earnings, and hours in copper mining in the U.S. and Arizona [including average earnings per man per year, aggregate man-hours, and ore mined per man-hour, 1970-82]. (p. 45)

INVENTORIES AND PRICES

XVIII. Refined copper inventories at month end [U.S. stock, stock outside U.S., and world stock, monthly 1979-82]. (p. 48)

XIX. Average quoted price of electrolytic copper wirebar, domestic, delivered [monthly 1973-Jan. 1983]. (p. 49)

RESERVES

XX. Copper reserves [name of deposit, major mineral type, millions of tons, average copper content, selected comments on characteristics, and data source; by company, as of Dec. 31, 1982, or most recent estimate]. (p. 50-55)

S0500   ARIZONA
Oil and Gas Conservation Commission

S0500–1   OIL, GAS, AND HELIUM PRODUCTION, State of Arizona
Monthly.
Approx. 4 p. Oversized.
SRI/MF/complete, shipped quarterly

Monthly report on Arizona oil, natural gas, and water production from 4-5 fields in Apache County accounting for total State oil and gas production. Report also includes total helium production to date; there is no current production. Report is compiled by the Arizona Oil and Gas Conservation Commission and is issued approximately 2 months following month of coverage.

Contains 1 table showing production by field, operator, and well, for month of coverage, year to date, and all-time cumulative production. Also shows gas distribution (flared/vented, used on lease, sold, and lost), for month of coverage.

Availability: Arizona Oil and Gas Conservation Commission, 1645 W. Jefferson, Suite 420, Phoenix AZ 85007, †; SRI/MF/complete, shipped quarterly.

Issues reviewed during 1984: Sept. 1983-Aug. 1984 (D).

S0505   ARIZONA
Department of
Public Safety

S0505–1   CRIME IN ARIZONA, 1983
Annual.   Apr. 1984.
xv+80 p.
LC 79-642700.
SRI/MF/complete

Annual report, for 1983, on Arizona crimes and arrests, by type of offense, with selected trends 1975-85. Also includes data on clearances, value of property stolen and recovered, local law enforcement employment, assaults on police, and selected data by county.

Data are compiled from local law enforcement agency reports, under the State Uniform Crime Reporting Program.

Contains listings of contents, tables, and charts (v-viii); foreword and general information including crime clock (p. ix-xv); narrative report in 5 sections, interspersed with 34 tables and 41 charts described below (p. 1-60); and appendices, with glossary, references, and 14 tables also described below (p. 63-80).

Availability: Arizona Department of Public Safety, Operational and Management Analysis Section, 2310 N. 20th Ave., PO Box 6638, Phoenix AZ 85005, †; SRI/MF/complete.

TABLES AND CHARTS:

[Data are for 1983, unless otherwise noted. Data by race are shown for white, black, Indian, and Asian; data by ethnic origin are shown for Hispanic and non-Hispanic.

Index (Part I) crimes are murder, rape, robbery, aggravated assault, burglary, larceny, motor vehicle theft, and arson. Part II crimes are approximately 25 other offenses.]

S0505–1.1: Summary and Index Offenses

STATE CRIME SUMMARY

a. Population, violent and property Index crimes, and value of property stolen and recovered, with some detail by offense and county, various periods 1975-83 and selected forecasts for 1984-85. 12 tables and 6 charts. (p. 1-13)

PART I INDEX CRIMES

[In addition to the data described below, each Index crime section includes 1 chart showing offenses and clearances, 1979-83.]

b. Murder: victims by relationship with offender, age, sex, race, and ethnic origin; and offenses by type of weapon. 1 table and 4 charts. (p. 16-18)

c. Forcible rape and attempted rape. 3 charts. (p. 20-21)

d. Robbery: offenses by month and type of weapon, and offenses and value stolen by location. 2 tables and 2 charts. (p. 23-24)

e. Assault by type of weapon. 1 table and 2 charts. (p. 25-26)

f. Burglary: by month and means of entry; and value stolen for day and night residence and nonresidence occurrences. 2 tables and 3 charts. (p. 28-30)

g. Larceny-theft: offenses by month, and value stolen, both by value range and type of theft. 3 tables and 2 charts. (p. 32-34)

h. Motor vehicle theft: recoveries, 1979-83; stolen vehicles by type; and recovery summary by month. 2 tables and 2 charts. (p. 36-38)

i. Arson: offenses by month, clearances, and damaged property value, by property type. 2 tables and 2 charts. (p. 40-41)

S0505–1.2: Arrests, Police Data, and Appendix

ARREST DATA

a. Arrests for aggregate Part I and Part II offenses; percent of crimes resulting in arrest, and total clearances, by Part I offense; and arrests and/or arrest distribution, by sex, race, ethnic origin, and whether adult or juvenile; various years 1975-83. 7 tables and 7 charts. (p. 43-51)

LOCAL POLICE DATA

b. Jurisdiction population; employees per 1,000 population; and sworn and civilian employees, by sex; all by law enforcement agency as of Oct. 31, 1983, with summary trends from 1975. 1 table and 3 charts. (p. 53-56)

c. Officers assaulted by type of weapon and assignment, and assaults cleared, by circumstance; assaults with and without injury, by type of weapon; various years 1975-83. 1 table and 5 charts. (p. 56-59)

APPENDIX

d. Crimes and stolen property value by county, and stolen property value by month, by Part I offense, with varying detail by type of weapon, property, and circumstance; and arrests by age, sex, race, and ethnic origin, by Part I and Part II offense; with some data on arrest rates and summary trends from 1975. 14 tables. (p. 67-80)

S0515   ARIZONA
Department of
Revenue

S0515–1   ARIZONA DEPARTMENT OF
REVENUE 1982-83 Annual
Report
Annual.   [1984.]   2+46 p.
ISSN 0362-9627.
LC 76-644453.
SRI/MF/complete

Annual report, for FY83, on Arizona State tax revenues, by source. Covers tax rates, assessments, and collections, and distribution of funds to local governments.

Contains transmittal letter and contents listing (2 p.); dept activities and highlights, with organizational chart and 2 tables (p. 1-10); 6 statistical sections, with 26 tables and brief accompanying narrative (p. 11-36); and tax legislation review for 1983 and recommendations for 1984 (p. 37-46).

All tables are listed below.

Availability: Arizona Department of Revenue, State Capitol, 1700 W. Washington St., Phoenix AZ 85007, †; SRI/MF/complete.

TABLES:

[Data are for Arizona, FY79-83, unless otherwise noted.]

REVENUE SUMMARY, INCOME TAXES, AND REVENUE SHARING

1. Major 1983 legislation affecting the Dept of Revenue [tabular listing]. (p. 3)

2. Collections of audit assessments and delinquent tax, FY82-83. (p. 4)

3-4. Gross revenue collected, and net revenue [deposited] to State general fund [both by tax source]. (p. 11-12)

5. Income tax collections [from wage withholding, individual/fiduciary, and corporation sources]. (p. 14)

6. Exemptions, deductions, and credits indexed to inflation [1977-82 tax years]. (p. 15)

7. Selected individual income tax credits [credits and claimants for solar energy, residential insulation, property tax, and renters]. (p. 16)

8-9. Distribution of income tax as urban revenue sharing to municipalities, FY83; and urban revenue sharing [total amount distributed], FY75-83. (p. 17)

SALES, SEVERANCE, AND LUXURY TAXES

10-11. Gross sales, use, and severance tax collections [by source]; and distribution of sales tax collections [by recipient government level], FY83. (p. 20)

12. Sales and severance tax rates [by type of taxable activity or industry classification], FY83. (p. 21)

13. Net taxable sales, by sales tax [industry] classification. (p. 22)

14-15. State sales tax distribution to counties and municipalities [for transaction privilege tax and food tax reimbursement], FY83. (p. 23-24)

16-17. Municipal sales tax collection program: collections [and tax rates] by city, FY83; and [total collections and number of cities in program], FY75-83. (p. 25)

[A]-18. Luxury tax rates [no date] and collections [FY79-83, both by type of tobacco and alcoholic beverage product]. (p. 26-27)

ESTATE AND PROPERTY TAXES

19-20. Estate tax collections [by source]; and distribution of estate tax collections [by fund], FY83. (p. 29)

[B] [Assessment ratios (percent of value used as tax base) by property class, 1983.] (p. 30)

21. Dept of Revenue property tax collections [flight and private rail car property taxes, and nuclear plan assessment, FY75-83]. (p. 31)

22. Net assessed valuation by county [1981-83]. (p. 32)

23. Property assessment responsibility [by county], 1983. (p. 33)

24. Average property tax rates [by taxing entity (school district, county, State city, community college, or special district), 1980-83]. (p. 34)

25-26. Summary of primary and secondary tax levies [by taxing entity, by county], 1983-84. (p. 35-36)

S0525   ARIZONA
Supreme Court

S0525-1   ARIZONA COURTS: 1983 Caseload, Financial, and Personnel Report
Annual. [1984.] 231 p.
SRI/MF/complete

Annual report, for 1983, on Arizona judicial system, including trial and appellate court caseloads, case dispositions, personnel, and finances, with selected trends from 1974. Covers supreme, appeals, superior, justice of the peace, and municipal courts. Includes data by case type, county, and municipality.

Case types shown are criminal and civil, for most courts, with some additional detail for habeas corpus, unemployment insurance, juvenile, domestic relations, probate, adoption, small claims, and traffic case types.

Report also includes data on age of pending cases; probation activity, including offender characteristics, restitution, and public service work hours; judicial system appropriations for FY83-84; petitions for domestic violence protection orders; and mental health hearings.

Data are from reports submitted to the supreme court by individual lower courts, a survey of superior and justice court finances, and budget statements compiled by the Arizona League of Cities and Towns.

Contains contents listing, judicial organization, and introduction (p. 1-5); and report in 5 sections, with 1 map, 15 charts, and 360 tables (p. 6-231).

A companion volume, *1983 Annual Judicial Report,* presenting narrative analysis with summary data, is also available from the Arizona Supreme Court but is not covered by SRI.

Availability: Arizona Supreme Court, Administrative Office of the Courts, State Capitol, 211 W. Wing, Phoenix AZ 85007, †; SRI/MF/complete.

S0530   ARIZONA
Department of Transportation

S0530-1   ARIZONA TRAFFIC ACCIDENT SUMMARY, 1983
Annual. [1984.] 56 p.
LC 78-640943.
SRI/MF/complete

Annual report on Arizona traffic accidents, injuries, and fatalities, by accident and vehicle type, location, time, and other circumstances; and driver and victim characteristics; 1983, with trends from as early as 1930.

Also includes vehicle registrations and mileage, 1930-83; economic loss from accidents; licensed drivers by age and sex; and detailed data on school busing, and pedestrian, bicycle, motorcycle, and alcohol-related accidents.

Data are based on reports submitted to the State Dept of Transportation.

Contains contents listing and transmittal letter (p. 1-2); and 8 sections, with 3 maps, 23 charts, and 32 tables (p. 3-56).

Availability: Arizona Department of Transportation, Safety Projects Services, 205 S. 17th Ave., Rm. 222, Phoenix AZ 85007, †; SRI/MF/complete.

S0632   ARKANSAS
Bank Department

S0632-1   SIXTY-NINTH REPORT OF THE BANK COMMISSIONER of the State of Arkansas, for the Year Ended June 30, 1983
Annual. Aug. 23, 1983.
221 p.
ISSN 0149-6107.
LC 77-645167.
SRI/MF/complete

Annual report on financial condition of Arkansas State-chartered banks, trust companies, and industrial loan institutions, presenting assets, liabilities, and equity capital, as of June 30, 1983. Data are shown by institution, with aggregate trends from FY49.

Also includes State Bank Dept receipts and disbursements, FY83; number of State and national banks and branches by county; and capital as percent of assets, by bank.

Data are compiled from call reports filed with the State Bank Dept.

Contains lists of banking officials and facilities interspersed with 7 summary tables (p. 1-26); and 1 balance sheet table repeated for each financial institution, arranged by institution type, alphabetically by city (p. 28-221).

Previous reports are covered by SRI under S0635-1. Issuing agency has changed from Arkansas Dept of Commerce.

Availability: Arkansas Bank Department, One Capitol Mall, 6D-305, Little Rock AR 72201-1093, †; SRI/MF/complete.

S0635   ARKANSAS
Department of Commerce

S0635-1   REPORT OF THE BANK COMMISSIONER of the State of Arkansas
Annual.
SRI now covers this publication under S0632-1.

S0635-2   ARKANSAS OIL AND GAS Statistical Bulletin
Monthly.
SRI now covers this publication under S0737-1.

S0635-3   ARKANSAS PUBLIC SERVICE COMMISSION Annual Report.
Annual.
SRI now covers this publication under S0757-1.

S0635-4   ANNUAL REPORT, STATE OF ARKANSAS INSURANCE DEPARTMENT
Annual.
SRI now covers this publication under S0712-1.

S0652   ARKANSAS
Crime Information Center

S0652-1   CRIME IN ARKANSAS, 1983
Annual. May 1984. 101 p.
LC 82-642805.
SRI/MF/complete

Annual report, for 1983, on Arkansas crimes and arrests, by type of offense and county, with selected comparisons from 1975. Includes data on offender and victim characteristics, clearances, value of property stolen and recovered, law enforcement personnel, and assaults on officers.

Data are compiled by the Arkansas Crime Information Center from reports of law enforcement agencies participating in the Uniform Crime Reporting (UCR) Program.

Contains contents listing (1 p.); description of UCR program (p. 1-8); and 7 statistical sections, with 9 charts and 62 tables described below (p. 9-101).

Availability: Arkansas Crime Information Center, Research and Statistics Division, One Capitol Mall, Little Rock AR 72201, †; SRI/MF/complete.

CHARTS AND TABLES:
[Data are shown for 1983, with selected comparisons to 1982, unless otherwise noted. Index crimes are murder, rape, robbery, aggravated assault, burglary, theft, motor vehicle theft, and arson.]

CRIME SUMMARY
[Index crimes are shown by offense.]

a. Trends in UCR, 1975-83; Index crimes, and number of reporting and contributing agencies, by month; and population of 5 largest metro law enforcement jurisdictions and aggregate Index crimes vs. State totals. 7 tables. (p. 10-14)

STATE TOTALS
[In addition to the data described below, each individual offense section includes 3 tables and 1 chart showing offenses by month, clearances, and clearance rates.]

b. Murder offenses by weapon type, circumstance, and victim/offender relationship; and number of victims by age, sex, and race. 1 chart and 7 tables. (p. 18-21)

c. Rape/attempted rape; robbery offenses by weapon type, and offenses and value stolen by site; and aggravated assaults by weapon type. 3 charts and 13 tables. (p. 24-33)

d. Burglary offenses and value stolen by classification (day and night, residence and nonresidence), and offenses by type of entry; theft by type and value stolen; motor vehicle theft by vehicle type, and recovery by jurisdiction; and arson offenses, clearances, and damaged property value, by property type. 4 charts and 18 tables. (p. 35-50)

BY REPORTING AGENCY

e. Index crimes by offense, total crime rates, and percent cleared, by county and reporting agency. 1 table. (p. 52-57)

STOLEN PROPERTY VALUES

f. Value of property stolen and recovered, by month, property type, county, and reporting agency; and value of property stolen by Index offense, excluding assault and arson, and including robbery by site, burglary by classification, and theft by type. 4 tables. (p. 60-67)

ARRESTS

g. Arrests for Index offenses and 23 other crimes, by offense: by age, race, and sex of persons arrested; and by county and reporting agency. 4 tables. (p. 72-87)

PERSONNEL

h. Sworn and civilian employees by sex, by county and reporting agency. 1 table. (p. 90-95)

i. Officers assaulted, by type of activity, assignment, time of assault, injury status, and weapon used; and clearances. 1 chart and 7 tables. (p. 98-101)

S0660   ARKANSAS
Department of
Education

S0660-1   STATISTICAL SUMMARY FOR THE PUBLIC SCHOOLS of Arkansas, 1981-83

Annual. Apr. 1984. 96 p.
LC 42-39578.
SRI/MF/complete

Annual report on Arkansas public school enrollment, graduates, staff, and finances, 1982/83, with trends from FY03, and selected projections to 1987/88. Also includes data on transportation and food service.

Contains listing of tables and maps (p. 3-4); 1 map, and 39 tables listed below (p. 5-36); and 1 extended table showing pupil enrollment by grade and for special education, and number of teachers, all by school and school district, arranged by county, Oct. 1, 1983 (p. 37-96).

Availability: Arkansas Department of Education, School Statistics and Fiscal Services Office, Administrative Services Division, Education Bldg., Rm. 204-A, Little Rock AR 72201, †; SRI/MF/complete.

TABLES:

[Tables show Arkansas data for 1981/82-1982/83, unless otherwise noted.]

S0660-1.1: County and Student Data

[Tables [2], [4-5], [7], and [11] include data for special education.]

[1] Selected information pertaining to schools, by county: [enrollment; average daily attendance (ADA); high school graduates; per child assessed valuation, revenue, and expenditures; and average teacher and administrator salaries]; 1982/83. (p. 5)

[2-3] Public and nonpublic school enrollment data [by grade and county; graduates by county; and nonpublic schools and teachers by grade level (State totals)]; 1982/83. (p. 6-7)

[4-5] Average number belonging and ADA [transported and nontransported, by grade]. (p. 9)

[6] Pupil enrollment trends [by grade, and graduates], 1973/74-1987/88. (p. 10)

[7-8] Enrollment, average number belonging, and ADA; by type of school. (p. 11)

[9] Fall enrollment [by grade and race], 1982-83. (p. 12)

[10-11] High school graduates, and enrollment by grades, [by sex]. (p. 13)

S0660-1.2: Administrative and Transportation Data

[1] Length of school term in days. (p. 13)

[2-3] Number of professional (certificated) positions and average salaries in school districts [by sex]; and nonteaching (noncertificated) positions and average salaries; [regular and Federal, by position]. (p. 14-16)

[4] Value of school property [and insurance coverage]. (p. 17)

[5] School losses [buildings destroyed/damaged by cause, estimated loss, and insurance coverage]. (p. 17)

[6] School bus accidents [including injuries, deaths, and property damage]. (p. 18)

[7] Selected statistics on transportation [school districts providing busing; buses; pupils transported; expenditures; transportation personnel average salary; and amount of aid from transportation fund]. (p. 19)

[8-12] Number of school districts: based on area; by number of certificated personnel; by ADA and type of program operated; by type of organization; and according to status of professional administration. (p. 20-22)

[13] Office staff of county board of education [by position]. (p. 22)

S0660-1.3: Finances and Historical Trends

[1] County school administration [receipts and expenditures]. (p. 23)

[2-3] Free textbook fund [receipts and expenditures, by grade level]. (p. 24-25)

[4] School food service program [receipts and expenditures]. (p. 26)

[5] Building fund [receipts and expenditures] of local school districts. (p. 27)

[6] Net receipts of local school districts [by detailed local, State, Federal, and nonrevenue sources, with balances by fund]. (p. 28)

[7] Expenditures of local school districts [by fund, function, and object]. (p. 29)

[8] Expenditures for elementary/secondary education [by source of funds, 1957/58-1983/84]. (p. 30)

[9-10] Permanent school revolving loan fund and revolving loan certificate proceeds account [balance sheets]. (p. 31)

[11] Public school indebtedness [by type, as of June 30, 1982-83]. (p. 32)

[12-13] Public school grants and aid account and Dept of Education operations account: statements of receipts and disbursements, FY83. (p. 33-34)

[14-15] Summary of pertinent school information: [receipts by source, total and per child expenditures, average teacher salaries, per capita apportionment, and number of school districts, FY15-83; and assessed valuation, enumeration by race, enrollment, ADA, length of school term, and teaching positions, generally, FY03-83]. (p. 35-36)

S0685   ARKANSAS
Department of
Health

S0685-1   ARKANSAS VITAL STATISTICS, 1982

Annual. [1984.] iii+77 p.
ISSN 0364-0728.
LC 76-647425.
SRI/MF/complete

Annual report, for 1982, on Arkansas vital statistics, including population, births, deaths by cause, abortions, marriages, and divorces. Includes data by age, sex, race, county, and health systems area. Also includes trends from 1914.

Contains contents and table listing (1 p.); introduction, definitions, and rate formulas (p. i-iii); and 7 statistical sections with summary, 53 tables listed below, and 9 interspersed maps showing vital statistics rates by county (p. 1-77).

Availability: Arkansas Department of Health, Health Statistics and Epidemiology Division, 4815 W. Markham St., Little Rock AR 72201, †; SRI/MF/complete.

TABLES:

[Tables show data for 1982, unless otherwise noted. Tables frequently include data on rates.]

S0685-1.1: Vital Statistics Trends

[1] Comparison of rates for Arkansas and U.S. [birth, infant and maternal mortality, death, marriage, and divorce rates, 1970 and 1975-82]. (p. 2)

[2] Vital statistics summary [includes births and deaths of Arkansas residents occurring in and out of State, and of nonresidents occurring in Arkansas]. (p. 3-4)

[3] Vital statistics summmary, earliest recorded year to present [births, 1914-82; population by race, 1920-82; marriages and divorces, 1936-82; deaths by race, 1933-82; and deaths from 4 leading causes, 1939-82]. (p. 5-6)

S0685-1.2: Marriages and Divorces

[Tables show data by county of occurrence.]

[1] Marriages and divorces/annulments. (p. 7)

[2] Marriages, 1975-82. (p. 8)

[3] Divorces/annulments, 1975-82. (p. 10)

S0685-1.3: Births, Abortions, and Fetal Mortality

BIRTHS AND ABORTIONS

[1] Births, stillbirths, and abortions, [and illegitimate births; all] by age of female. (p. 12)

[2] Teenage fertility data [total and illegitimate births, induced and spontaneous abortions, and fetal deaths, by age]. (p. 13)

[3] Birth defects reported on birth certificates, ICD [*International Classification of Diseases*] codes 740-759. (p. 14)

[4] Births by county of residence, race, and sex. (p. 15)

[5-10] Births and illegitimate births by county of residence, by age of mother [and race]. (p. 17-22)

[11] Births [by race] by county of residence, attendant [doctor and midwife/other], and locale of delivery [hospital and other]. (p. 23)

S0700   ARKANSAS
Department of Human Services

S0700–1   SOCIAL SERVICES DIVISION OF DEPARTMENT OF HUMAN SERVICES Annual Report, July 1, 1982-June 30, 1983, Arkansas
Annual. [1984.] 5+115 p.
LC 73-646186.
SRI/MF/complete.

Annual report on Arkansas public assistance program case activity, services, recipient characteristics, and payments, by program, FY83, with selected data by county and trends from 1937. Includes data on AFDC, medical and social services, and food programs.

Contains organizational charts and contents listing (4 p.); expenditure and cost summaries, with 3 charts and 4 tables (p. 1-4); and program narrative summaries, with 11 charts and 54 tables (p. 5-115).

All tables, and charts presenting data not covered in tables, are listed below.

Availability: Arkansas Department of Human Services, Social Services Division, Research and Statistics, Seventh and Main Sts., PO Box 1437, Little Rock AR 72203, †; SRI/MF/complete.

CHARTS AND TABLES:
[Data are for Arkansas, FY83 or as of June 30, 1983, unless otherwise noted. Data by county usually include totals for 5 State areas. Several tables show separate data for child and adult recipients.

Recipient categories include Aid to the Aged, Blind, and Disabled; AFDC; foster care children; and persons under age 18.]

COMMODITY DISTRIBUTION AND CHILD NUTRITION PROGRAMS

[4-5] Commodity distribution: school and institution participation [amount and dollar value by commodity, with total schools, school districts, and institutions served, and participants]. (p. 79-80)

[6-7] Child nutrition programs: [State administrative expenses and program funds, institutions and facilities involved, and meals provided, by program]. (p. 81)

SOCIAL SERVICES SUMMARY

[8-9] Purchased services: [recipients and cost, total and for selected recipient categories, medical and income eligibles, and without regard to income, all by service type]. (p. 83-85)

[10-11] Direct services [recipients, total and for persons not identified as active service cases, selected recipient categories, Medicaid and income eligibles, child welfare service, and without regard to income, all by service type]. (p. 86-88)

SUBSTITUTE CARE SERVICES FOR CHILDREN

[12] Characteristics of children in foster care [race (including American Indian, Spanish American, and other/unknown); length of time in foster care; age; legal status; location; reason for entry; and sex]. (p. 89)

[13] Number of children for whom board payments were made, by source of funds [State and AFDC, monthly]. (p. 90)

[14] [Reasons for discharge from foster care, 1981-83.] (p. 90)

INTERSTATE COMPACT ACTIVITIES

[15] Report [on Interstate Compact on Juveniles activities involving runaways and juvenile offenders]. (p. 91)

[16] [Interstate Compact on Placement of Children: activities, including placements in- and out-of-State]. (p. 92)

SUPPORTIVE SERVICES

[17-18] [Recipients of supportive services to children in their own homes and services to youth in need.] (p. 93-94)

[19] [Comprehensive maternity care services for unmarried parents, including infants released for adoption]. (p. 95)

CHILD DEVELOPMENT UNIT

[20] [Child Care Licensing Unit/Child Care Facility Review Board licensing activities]. (p. 100)

HOME ENERGY ASSISTANCE PROGRAM

[21] [Households served and benefit expenditures, by season]. (p. 102)

[22-23] Home energy assistance summer and winter programs [denials, approvals, and persons served, by county]. (p. 103-106)

MISCELLANEOUS

[24] Categorical assistance cases [by selected recipient category], Jan. 1937-83. (p. 108)

[25] Total State population [by county, 1980]. (p. 109)

[26] Percentages by race of recipient population [by county and selected recipient category]. (p. 110-115)

S0712   ARKANSAS
Insurance Department

S0712–1   102nd ANNUAL REPORT, 1982, State of Arkansas Insurance Department
Annual. [1983.] 248 p.
SRI/MF/complete

Annual report on Arkansas insurance industry financial condition and underwriting activity, by company and type of insurance, 1982. Covers assets, liabilities, capital, and surplus; investment income; premiums written, earned, and/or received; insurance in force; losses incurred or claims paid; loss- and expense-premium ratios; and operating and underwriting profit/loss; for companies based in Arkansas and elsewhere.

Data are shown, as applicable, for stock and mutual fire/casualty insurance companies; farmers mutual aid assns; Lloyds underwriters; title insurance, stock life insurance, stipulated premium plan, prepaid legal insurance, and mutual assessment companies; nonprofit hospital/medical service corporations; fraternal benefit societies; and life/accident/health and property/liability insurance companies.

Data on property/liability insurance include additional breakdowns by detailed line of coverage, including medical malpractice, workers compensation, automobile, and surety.

Also includes data on public employee workers' compensation claims; and companies licensed, Insurance Dept receipts and disbursements, and firemen and police officer relief/pension fund tax premiums and payments by city.

Contains contents listing (p. 3); Insurance Dept activities, with 5 tables (p. 4-43); and 17 company financial tables including 2 with directories (p. 45-248).

Previous reports are covered in SRI under S0635-4. Issuing agency has changed from Arkansas Dept of Commerce.

Availability: Arkansas Insurance Department, 400 University Tower Bldg., Little Rock AR 72204, †; SRI/MF/complete.

S0715   ARKANSAS
Judicial Department

S0715–1   SIX MONTH TRANSITION REPORT from Calendar Year to Fiscal Year Annual Reporting, Jan. 1-June 30, 1983
Annual. [1984.] 97 p.
SRI/MF/complete, Jan. 1-June 30, 1983 and CY83 reports

Annual report on Arkansas judicial system, including trial and appellate court caseloads and case dispositions. Presents data for 1st half 1983, to implement planned transition from calendar to fiscal year reporting.

Covers supreme, appeals, circuit, chancery, probate, juvenile, municipal, and city courts. Includes trial court data by case type and court location. Case types shown are criminal and civil, for most courts, with some additional detail for domestic relations, guardianship, adoption, commitment, estate probate, small claims, and traffic case types.

Also includes data on case processing time, and on costs assessed and fines collected in local courts.

Data are from dept records.

Contains contents listing and transmittal letter (p. 1-2); and 19 tables (p. 3-97).

Beginning in 1984, report will be presented on a fiscal year basis. First report for this period will cover July 1, 1983-June 30, 1984, and will be issued in the latter part of calendar year 1984.

Report for calendar year 1983, consisting of caseload statistics for circuit, chancery, and probate courts, has also been received, and is also available on SRI microfiche, under this number [Annual. [1984.] 82 p. †].

Availability: Arkansas Judicial Department, Justice Bldg., Little Rock AR 72201, †; SRI/MF/complete.

S0720   ARKANSAS
Department of Labor

S0720–1   ARKANSAS LABOR FORCE STATISTICS: Annual Averages, State and Areas, 1975-83
Annual. July 1984.
vi+43 p.
LC 83-620563.
SRI/MF/complete

Annual report on Arkansas civilian labor force, by employment status and locale, 1975-83. Includes total employment and unemployment; agricultural employment; domestic service/self-employed/unpaid family workers; and nonagricultural manufacturing and nonmanufacturing wage/salary employment, by SMSA, county, and labor area. Data were compiled by the Arkansas Labor Dept.

Contains introduction, contents listing, and definitions (p. ii-vi); 1 map and 6 summary charts (p. 1-7); and 1 table repeated for State and each locale (p. 8-43).

Availability: Arkansas Department of Labor, Employment Security Division, Research and Analysis Section, PO Box 2981, Little Rock AR 72203, †; SRI/MF/complete.

S0720–3   ANNUAL PLANNING INFORMATION, State of Arkansas, FY84
Annual. Feb. 1984.
xxv+234 p.
LC 80-643449.
SRI/MF/complete

Annual planning report, for FY84, identifying Arkansas population groups most in need of employment services. Includes data on population and labor force characteristics, part-time workers, unemployment, personal income, and economically disadvantaged; by Service Delivery Area (SDA), SMSA, and county, various years 1970s-84. Also includes data on unemployment insurance claimants and exhaustees, and veteran population and employment.

Data are from State Employment Security Division, Lawrence Berkeley Laboratory, and Dept of Commerce.

Contains listings of contents, tables, and maps (p. iii-xxv); highlights and conclusions (p. 1);

State report, with 19 tables (p. 2-23); SDA reports, with 132 tables (p. 26-168); SMSA reports, with 28 tables (p. 172-204); and appendix, with 15 tables (p. 208-234). All tables are listed below.

For description of previous report, for FY83, see SRI 1982 Annual, under this number.

Availability: Arkansas Department of Labor, Employment Security Division, Research and Analysis Section, PO Box 2981, Little Rock AR 72203, †; SRI/MF/complete.

TABLES:

[Data are shown for Arkansas, FY84, unless otherwise noted.]

S0720–3.1: State Data

INCOME, POPULATION, AND LABOR FORCE

1. Per capita and total personal income, U.S. and Arkansas, 1980-82 and projected 1984. (p. 4)

2-3. Civilian population by race, sex, and age groups, 1980 and projected 1984. (p. 5)

4-5. Civilian labor force and projections [including total labor force; unemployment; and total, agriculture, and domestic service/self-employed/unpaid family worker employment; various years] FY79-84. (p. 7)

6-7. Characteristics of civilian labor force [and unemployment, by race, sex, and age group], 1970 and projected FY84. (p. 8)

BY INDUSTRY AND OCCUPATION

8-9. Nonagricultural wage/salary employment and projections [by industry division and major manufacturing group, various years], FY79-84. (p. 11-13)

10. Employment [actual 1978 and projected 1983], and [estimated] labor demands [1984 and total period] 1983-88, by [broad] occupational category. (p. 14)

UNEMPLOYMENT ESTIMATES

11. Workers employed part-time for economic reasons, [long-term unemployed, and unemployed age 16/over, all by sex and race]. (p. 16)

12-13. Projected veteran population and unemployment, and number in need of manpower services [includes selected detail for Vietnam-era and disabled veterans]. (p. 17)

ECONOMICALLY DISADVANTAGED

14. Poverty guidelines, continental U.S. (p. 18)

15. Characteristics of job service applicants active any time during [FY83, total and economically disadvantaged applicants by age, race, sex, and education], as of Sept. 30, 1983. (p. 19)

16. Estimated economically disadvantaged 16 years of age/over [by race]. (p. 20)

JOB TRAINING PARTNERSHIP ACT (JTPA) ELIGIBILITY

17. Population potentially eligible for JTPA programs by age group, race, and sex, 1984. (p. 21)

18-19. Total and economically disadvantaged populations by age, race [including Native American, Asian, and Hispanic], and sex; and by target groups [including veterans, ex-offenders, welfare recipients, school dropouts, unemployment insurance claimants, handicapped, and single head of household with dependent children]; 1984. (p. 22-23)

S0720–3.2: SDAs and SMSAs

SDAs

[Tables 20-31 show data for Little Rock SDA.]

20-28. [Data in tables 1-3, 6-7, 11, and 17-19, described above, are repeated.] (p. 29-36)

29. Poverty status by race [population below poverty level, including American Indian, Asian, and Spanish origin], 1979. (p. 37)

30. Poverty status of families [total and female head of household with children]; and population of handicapped persons and dislocated workers; 1980. (p. 38)

31. Unemployment insurance exhaustees, 1982. (p. 40)

32-44. [Tables 20-31 are repeated for Central SDA, with selected additional detail by county.] (p. 43-54)

45-46. Secondary school vocational labor supply by county, and labor supply post secondary vocational education programs [both showing current enrollment and completions, by program], Central SDA (includes Little Rock SDA), 1983 (p. 55-56)

47-151. [Tables 32-46 are repeated for 7 additional SDAs.] (p. 59-168)

SMSAs

152-179. [Data in tables 1-3, 6-7, 11, and 16 are repeated for 4 SMSAs, with selected detail by county.] (p. 176-204)

S0720–3.3: Appendix Tables

[Tables 1-8 show data by county; tables 9-14 show data by SDA. Data by race include Indian, Asian, and Spanish origin.]

1-4. Per capita and total personal income, 1981 and 1984; population, 1980, and 1984; and estimated economically disadvantaged 16 years of age/over, FY84. (p. 208-214)

5-6. Projected veteran population and unemployment, and number in need of manpower services [includes selected detail for Vietnam-era and disabled veterans]. (p. 215-218)

7-8. Estimated number of school dropouts, FY84; and individuals receiving AFDC, Sept. 1983. (p. 219-220)

9. Unemployment insurance exhaustees, 1982. (p. 221)

10-11. General characteristics of the population [age, sex, and race]; and educational [attainment] by race and age group; 1980. (p. 222-226)

12-13. Persons below poverty status [by race], 1979; and labor force status by race and sex, 1980. (p. 228-230)

14. Educational characteristics of unemployed youth ([age] 16 to 19; years of school completed; and labor force status), 1980. (p. 232)

15. Job openings and active applicants by occupational category, [by] employment security division local offices, Sept. 1983. (p. 233)

S0737   ARKANSAS
Oil and Gas Commission

S0737–1   ARKANSAS OIL AND GAS
Statistical Bulletin
Monthly. Approx. 10 p.
LC 52-35586.
SRI/MF/complete, shipped quarterly

Monthly report on Arkansas crude oil and natural gas production and disposition, and in-State refining stocks, receipts, products manufactured, and residue disposition. Data are compiled by the Arkansas Oil and Gas Commission from monthly field reports.

Contains narrative summary, and 8 monthly tables listed below.

Due to production problems, this report was suspended from Nov. 1981-June 1982. Report had been issued approximately 10 months after month of coverage. Issuing agency is publishing on an irregular basis until that schedule is reestablished.

Prior to July 1982 issue, report is covered in SRI under S0635-2. Issuing agency has changed from Arkansas Dept of Commerce.

Availability: Arkansas Oil and Gas Commission, 314 E. Oak St., El Dorado AR 71730, †; SRI/MF/complete, shipped quarterly.

Issues reviewed during 1984: July 1982-Nov. 1983 (D) (Vol. 43, Nos. 7-12; Vol. 44, Nos. 1-11).

MONTHLY TABLES:

[Unless otherwise noted, data are shown for month of coverage.]

[1] Consolidated review [crude oil/condensate production, pipeline runs, natural gas reported, gas pipeline and gasoline plant intake, and products manufactured; average daily totals for month of coverage and same month of preceding year].

[2] South Arkansas oil and gas report [production by field].

[3] Oil pipeline report [receipts, stocks, imports, and deliveries].

[4] Disposition of gas [lease use, pipelines, vented, injected, and gasoline plants].

[5] Refinery report [including stocks, receipts, and dispositions].

[6] Gasoline plant report [gas received by source, products manufactured, and disposition of residue].

[7-8] North Arkansas gas report [production by field]; and disposition of gas [pipelines and drilling purposes].

S0757   ARKANSAS
Public Service Commission

**S0757–1   ARKANSAS PUBLIC
SERVICE COMMISSION
Forty-Ninth Annual Report,
Year Ending Dec. 31, 1983**
Annual.   Jan. 31, 1984.
2+37 p.
LC 52-26080.
SRI/MF/complete

Annual report presenting Arkansas public utility regulatory data for 1983, and financial and operating data for 1982, by utility type and company. Utility types are electric, gas, water/sewer, and telephone.

Includes data on Arkansas Public Service Commission Utilities Division staff, complaints received, finances, and regulatory orders issued; and utility revenues, plant investment, and customers and sales by consuming sector.

Data are from commission records and company reports.

Contains contents listing (1 p.); introduction, and commission activities report, with text statistics and 3 tables (p. 1-18); and utility company statistics, with 8 tables (p. 19-37).

Previous reports are described in SRI under S0635-3. Public Service Commission is no longer part of the Arkansas Dept of Commerce.

Availability: Arkansas Public Service Commission, Utilities Division, 1000 Center Bldg., PO Box C-400, Little Rock AR 72203, ‡; SRI/MF/complete.

S0775   ARKANSAS
Office of the
Secretary of
State

**S0775–1   1982 ARKANSAS
ELECTIONS: A Compilation
of Primary, Run-Off, and
General Election Results for
State and District Offices**
Biennial.   May 1983.
97 p. Oversized.
LC 84-622866.
SRI/MF/complete

Biennial report presenting results of Arkansas primary elections held May 25, 1982, and general elections held Nov. 2, 1982. Shows voting for U.S. and State senators and representatives; Governor, attorney general, and land commissioner; circuit and chancery judges; prosecuting attorneys; 3 State constitutional amendments; and 1 State referendum.

Also includes voter registration and turnout. Data are shown by district and county.

Contains introduction, contents listing, and election laws (p. 1-6); and maps and tabular lists (p. 7-97).

Previous report, covering 1980 elections, is described in SRI 1982 Annual, under this number.

Availability: Arkansas Office of the Secretary of State, State Capitol, Rm. 256, Little Rock AR 72201, † first copy, $5.00 for each additional copy; SRI/MF/complete.

S0810   CALIFORNIA
Banking Department

**S0810–1   SEVENTY-FOURTH ANNUAL
REPORT: Superintendent of
Banks, State of California,
1983**
Annual.   Oct. 30, 1983.
83+A985 p.
LC 11-12664.
SRI/MF/complete

Annual report on financial condition of all banks and trust companies operating in California during FY83. Presents assets, liabilities, income, and expenses, for State and national banks, foreign banking organizations with representation in California, and trust companies. Data are shown by institution, with selected aggregate trends from the 1970s.

Also includes data on bank applications, openings and closings, mergers, and licenses and other regulatory activities; top 25 banks ranked by deposits; and compensation of Banking Dept personnel.

Data are compiled from annual call reports.

Contains contents and table listing (p. 3-5); narrative report, interspersed with 25 tables (p. 9-44); appendices I-V, including directories, lists, and 5 tables (p. 47-68); and appendix VI, with index (p. 71-83), and financial statements consisting of 1-3 tables for each institution (p. A1-A985).

Availability: California Banking Department, 235 Montgomery St., Suite 750, San Francisco CA 94104-2980, †; SRI/MF/complete.

S0815   CALIFORNIA
Office of the
Controller

**S0815–1   ANNUAL REPORT OF THE
STATE OF CALIFORNIA for
the Fiscal Year Ended June
30, 1983**
Annual.   June 1984.
A29+483 p.
LC 10-11500.
SRI/MF/complete

Annual report on financial condition of California State government, presenting assets, liabilities, reserves, and fund balances; revenues by source; and expenditures; for general, governmental cost, working capital and revolving, public service enterprise, bond, retirement, and trust and agency funds; FY83 with selected trends from FY74.

Detailed appropriations and expenditures are shown by agency and function for general and all other governmental cost funds.

Also includes data on State investments by type; bonded debt; bank and/or savings and loan assn account balances outside of State treasury system; and receipts from Federal Government, by State agency.

Contains contents listing and transmittal letter (p. A2-A5); notes, 4 summary statements, and 4 trend charts and tables (p. A8-A29); 5 sections, with 33 financial statements (p. 2-476); and index (p. 478-483).

Availability: California Office of the Controller, Accounting Division, PO Box 1019, Sacramento CA 95805, †; SRI/MF/complete.

S0825   CALIFORNIA
Department of
Education

**S0825–4   CENSUS AND THE
SCHOOLS: Selected
Statistics (1980)**
Monograph.   1983.   iii+25 p.
LC 84-621280.
SRI/MF/complete

Report presenting selected education-related statistics for California, from the 1980 U.S. Census of Population and Housing. Also includes some data from the State Education Dept.

Contains contents and table listing (p. iii); introduction and narrative report interspersed with 10 tables described below (p. 1-19); and appendices, with glossary and data sources (p. 21-25).

Availability: California Department of Education, Publications Sales, PO Box 271, Sacramento CA 95802, †; SRI/MF/complete.

TABLES:
[Data are for California, and are shown for 1980, unless otherwise noted.]

a. Population by age and educational attainment, labor force, and public school enrollment and staff, all by race and ethnicity (including American Indian/Alaskan Native, Asian/Pacific Islander, Filipino, and Hispanic); and persons age 5-17 of limited English proficiency, by language spoken at home, with detail for public school students, 1980 and/or 1983. Tables 1-3. (p. 3-7)

b. Population, by urban-rural status; families with children, by poverty status; school-age population compared to public/private school enrollment; median housing value, rent, and family income; and distribution of housing units by value or rent; all by county. Tables 4-5. (p. 9-12)

c. Persons age 16-19, by whether in school, military, or labor force (including employed and unemployed); distribution of children by type of living arrangement; and labor force status of persons 16/older, by sex. Tables 6-8. (p. 13-15)

d. Labor force, by industry division; and distribution of labor force, and of secondary education students in vocational education courses (1980/81-1982/83), by occupational group. Tables 9-10. (p. 17-19)

S0827   CALIFORNIA
Postsecondary
Education Commission

S0827-1   INFORMATION DIGEST: Postsecondary Education in California
Annual, discontinued.

Annual report on California postsecondary education, discontinued with Oct. 1982 report (for description, see SRI 1982 Annual, under this number). Report has been discontinued due to lack of funds.

Data may be obtained upon request from California Postsecondary Education Commmission, 1020 12th St., Sacramento CA 95814.

S0830   CALIFORNIA
Employment
Development Department

S0830-1   CALIFORNIA LABOR MARKET BULLETIN
Monthly.   Approx. 5 p.
SRI/MF/complete, shipped quarterly

Monthly report on California employment and unemployment, earnings, and hours. Data, compiled by the State in cooperation with the U.S. Labor Dept, are shown variously by age group, race, sex, industry, and county. Report is issued 2-6 months after month of coverage.

Contains narrative summary; and 5 monthly tables, listed below.

Availability: California Employment Development Department, Employment Data and Research Division, Estimates and Economic Research Group, 800 Capitol Mall, Sacramento CA 95814, †; SRI/MF/complete, shipped quarterly.

Issues reviewed during 1984: Sept. 1983-Aug. 1984 (D).

MONTHLY TABLES:
[Most tables show data for month of coverage, previous 1-2 months, and same month of previous year. Table 5 shows data for month of coverage only.]

1. Employment and unemployment [and civilian labor force; seasonally adjusted and unadjusted].

2. Employment status of the working age population [by age group (16-19 and 20/over), sex, and race].

3. Earnings and hours of production/related workers in manufacturing.

4. Monthly wage/salary employment analysis [by industry group].

5. Monthly labor force data [by employment status] for counties.

S0830-2   ANNUAL PLANNING INFORMATION, California, 1984-85
Annual.   Apr. 1984.
ix+98 p.
LC 79-643631.
SRI/MF/complete

Annual planning report, for 1984-85, identifying California population groups most in need of employment services, and presenting data on employment by industry and occupation. Also includes data on income levels. Data generally are shown for various years 1980-83, with some trends from 1970s or earlier.

Data are compiled from Census Bureau and other Federal and State sources.

Contains listings of contents, tables, charts, and maps (p. ii-ix); report, with narrative analyses, 2 maps, 21 charts, and 30 tables (p. 1-62); 2 appendices, with methodology and 13 tables (p. 65-92); and glossary (p. 93-98). All tables are listed below.

Availability: California Employment Development Department, Employment Data and Research Division, Estimates and Economic Research Group, 800 Capitol Mall, Sacramento CA 95814, †; SRI/MF/complete.

TABLES:
[Data are for California, unless otherwise noted. Most data by race are shown for white, black, American Indian/Alaskan Native, Asian/Pacific Islander, and other. Most data by ethnic origin are for Hispanic and other.]

S0830-2.1: Text Tables
[Data are for 1980, unless otherwise noted.]

POPULATION AND LABOR FORCE

A. Total population of counties [1980 census and July 1981-83], with annual percent change. (p. 4)

B. Labor force, employment, unemployment: [quarterly] 1983-85, seasonally adjusted. (p. 17)

C. Nonagricultural wage/salary employment forecast [by industry division, 1983-85]. (p. 18)

1-1E. Total population by age, sex, race [including Native American by type (American Indian, Eskimo, and Aleut) and Asian/Pacific Islander by country of ancestry], and ethnic origin [including Hispanic by country of ancestry; with various cross-tabulations]. (p. 32-37)

2A-2B. Labor force [and employment] status [including armed forces personnel] by race, sex, and ethnic origin, for persons 16 years old/over. (p. 38-39)

2C. Labor force status of persons with work disabilities. (p. 40)

2D. School and labor force [and employment] status [including persons in armed forces] of youth 16-19 years old, [with detail by whether high school graduate]. (p. 41)

PUBLIC ASSISTANCE

3A. Public assistance recipients by program [food stamps, general relief, refugee cash assistance, and adults and children receiving AFDC], June 1981-83. (p. 42)

3B. AFDC, characteristics of recipients 16 years old/over [by sex, age, race, and ethnic origin], June 1981-83. (p. 43)

3C. SSI recipients by program [aged, and blind/disabled including children], Dec. 1980-82. (p. 44)

POVERTY STATUS AND FAMILIES AND HOUSEHOLDS

4A. Poverty status by race and ethnic origin. (p. 45)

4B. [Number of persons, by] ratio of personal income to poverty. (p. 46)

4C. Families [total and headed by single females] by presence [and age] of children [by] poverty status. (p. 47)

5A-5B. Households and families [by income level]; and family income, by race and ethnic origin. (p. 48-49)

5C. [Households by] household type and presence of children, by race and ethnic origin. (p. 50)

EDUCATION AND LANGUAGE

6. Years of school completed by race and ethnic origin [for] persons age 25 years/over. (p. 51)

7. Primary language spoken at home [English, Spanish, and other] and ability to speak English [for persons age 5-17 and 18/older]. (p. 52)

VETERANS AND OFFENDERS

8. Veterans by sex and all periods of active duty. (p. 53)

9A-9B. Felons newly received from superior court and paroled to California supervision, by sex, 1980-82. (p. 54)

10. Population of [adults and juveniles] under jurisdiction of local criminal justice agencies [by type of facility and for probationers], 1980-82. (p. 55)

11. Veterans by periods of active duty, Mar. 1983. (p. 56)

LABOR MARKET INFORMATION

12. Labor market information reports [tabular list of labor market areas that have submitted labor reports, 1984]. (p. 60-62)

S0830-2.2: Appendix Tables

LABOR FORCE TRENDS

13-16. U.S. civilian and California labor [force by employment status, monthly] 1970-83, seasonally adjusted and not seasonally adjusted. (p. 66-73)

EMPLOYMENT BY INDUSTRY AND OCCUPATION

17-18. Estimated number of wage/salary workers in nonagricultural establishments, by [selected SIC 2- to 3-digit] industry; and agricultural wage/salary employment [for products and services]; 1972-83, and [by month] 1983. (p. 74-81)

19. Nonagricultural wage/salary employment by industry [division], 1939-83. (p. 83)

20-22. 1980 census data for civilian labor force 16 years/over by race [and ethnic origin, by detailed] occupation [and sex]. (p. 84-89)

POPULATION AND LABOR FORCE DETAIL

23. Population by sex and detailed race/ethnic group, 1980. (p. 90)

24-25. Labor force status by weeks worked, disability status, and sex, [by race and ethnic origin, primarily] 1979. (p. 91-92)

S0835   CALIFORNIA
Board of
Equalization

S0835-1   ANNUAL REPORT, 1982-83: California State Board of Equalization

Annual   Dec. 31, 1983.
127 p. var. paging.
ISSN 0068-5801.
LC SC 79-3387.
SRI/MF/complete

Annual report, for FY83, on operations of the California Board of Equalization, established to equalize property assessments among counties. Covers board revenue by source and expenditures by function, sales/use tax by kind of business and county, other tax revenues, and revenue distributions to counties and cities. Also covers assessed property values and tax exemptions for FY84. Selected data are also shown by company.

Data are compiled from State Board of Equalization records.

Contents:

a. Contents listing. (inside front cover)

b. Narrative analysis of board organization and functions, property tax structure, economic trends, business and sales taxes, and tax litigation, with 11 interspersed summary tables, including 2 tables (p. 52) showing business tax field audits, costs, and amounts recovered, by type of tax, FY83 and trends. (p. 5-80)

c. Statistical appendix, with 37 detailed tables listed below. (p. A1-A42)

Availability: California Board of Equalization, PO Box 1799, Sacramento CA 95808, †; SRI/MF/complete.

DETAILED TABLES:

S0835-1.1: Administrative Data
[Tables 1-3A begin "Summary of..."]

1. Expenditures of the board [by function, FY82-83]. (p. A1)

2. Revenues from taxes administered by the board, [selected years] FY73-83. (p. A2)

3A. Total costs of performing board functions [by program], FY82-83. (p. A3)

3B. Revenues and ratios of board expenditures and total costs to revenues from assessments made by the board [by tax type], FY82-83. (p. A3)

S0835-1.2: Property Taxes
[Tables show data for FY84, unless otherwise noted. Tables 5-10 and 14-15 show data by county.]

4. Summary of assessed values of property subject to local general property taxes, assessment ratios, and average tax rates [by assessment agency and type of property], FY74-84. (p. A4)

5-7. Assessed value of State- and county-assessed property subject to general property taxes, inclusive of homeowners' exemption, by class of property. (p. A5-A7)

8. Number of veterans' exemptions and exempt value of veterans', college, church, religious, and welfare exemptions. (p. A8)

9. Gross assessed value of State- and county-assessed property, number of homeowners' exemptions, exempt value by type of exemption, and net assessed value subject to general property taxes. (p. A10)

10. Net State- and county-assessed value of property subject to general property taxes on the secured and unsecured rolls. (p. A11)

11. Assessed value of State- and county-assessed property subject to general property taxes, inclusive of homeowners' exemption, by incorporated cities. (p. A12)

12A-12B. Assessed value of property assessed by the State Board of Equalization; and subject to local taxation, by company. (p. A15-A17)

13. [Temporarily suspended.]

14. FY83 general property tax levies as compiled for computation of the average tax rate. (p. A19)

15. FY83 general property tax dollar [distribution among city, county, school, and other districts]. (p. A20)

16. [Discontinued.]

17A. Assessed value of private cars [rolling stock of companies that are not railroads], assessed by the State Board of Equalization and subject to exclusive State taxation, by company. (p. A21)

17B. Private car tax assessments, tax rates, and tax levies, [and average number of cars, selected periods] FY38-84. (p. A22)

S0835-1.3: Sales/Use Taxes
[Tables 19-21B show data for FY83.]

18. State sales/use tax collections and number of permits, [selected periods] FY33-83. (p. A23)

19-20. State sales/use tax statistics [taxable transactions, State sales tax, and number of permits], by type of business; and [taxable sales of retail stores, and all outlets, State tax, and number of permits], by county. (p. A24-A25)

21A. Revenues distributed to cities and counties from local sales/use taxes and the State cigarette tax [by county and city]. (p. A26)

21B. Revenues distributed to counties from county transportation tax [by county]. (p. A29)

21C. Local sales/use tax rates imposed by California cities on July 1, 1983 [by county and city]. (p. A29)

22. Local sales taxes, distributions, and administrative charges to cities and counties, FY57-83. (p. A30)

S0835-1.4: Highway Taxes

23. Gasoline and jet fuel tax statistics [taxable distributions, revenue, and, for gasoline only, refunds and tax-paying distributors, selected periods] FY23-83. (p. A31)

24. Taxable distributions of gasoline and tax assessments, by distributor, FY82-83. (p. A32)

25. Diesel fuel and liquefied petroleum gases statistics [taxable distributions, total tax, self-assessed taxes, active permits, and tax paid at reduced rate by transit districts, selected periods] FY37-83. (p. A33)

26. [Discontinued.]

S0835-1.5: Alcoholic Beverage and Cigarette Taxes

27. Beer, wine, and distilled spirits excise tax collections, [selected periods] FY32-83. (p. A34)

28-29. Apparent and per capita consumption of beer, wines, and distilled spirits, [various periods] FY35-83. (p. A35-A36)

30A. Cigarette tax revenue [including amount set aside for cities/counties], FY60-83. (p. A37)

30B. Cigarette distributions and per capita consumption, FY60-83. (p. A37)

S0835-1.6: Insurance Taxes and Total Tax Collections

INSURANCE TAXES

31. 1982 taxable insurance premiums and total taxes assessed in 1983, by company. (p. A38)

32. Summary of insurance taxes assessed in 1982-83 against companies authorized to do business in California, by type of insurer. (p. A40)

33. Insurance tax assessments against licensed insurers, tax rate, taxes on premiums, local property tax credits allowed, taxes on ocean marine business, and total taxes assessed, [selected periods] 1911-83. (p. A41)

TOTAL TAXES

34. Federal, State, and local tax collections, FY51-83. (p. A42)

S0840   CALIFORNIA
Department of
Finance

S0840-1   CALIFORNIA ECONOMIC INDICATORS

Bimonthly.   Approx. 30 p.
ISSN 0364-2895.
LC 76-646945.
SRI/MF/complete

Bimonthly report on California economic indicators and developments. Most data are current to 1-2 months preceding cover date, and are from reports of State and Federal agencies, professional assns, and financial institutions.

Issues generally contain:

a. Narrative review of recent economic developments, with text data and 1 economic indicators table.

b. 18 economic indicator charts, and 1 table presenting basic data for charts, on leading, coincident, and other indicator series.

c. Chronology of significant economic events, 1969 to month of publication; and list of data sources.

An annual article on economic outlook for California usually appears in the Jan. issue.

Bimonthly indicator tables are listed below and appear in all issues. Issues also occasionally include additional special charts or text tables showing revised data for indicators; these data are not described. Annual economic outlook article is described, as it appears, under "Statistical Feature." Nonstatistical features are not covered.

Availability: California Department of Finance, Financial Research Unit, PO Box 151, Sacramento CA 95801, $5.00 per yr.; SRI/MF/ complete.

Issues reviewed during 1984: Nov. 1983-Sept. 1984 (P).

TABLES:

[Table [1] shows data monthly for 4 consecutive months ending 1-2 months prior to cover date, and for 2 latest months in same period of previous year. Table [2] generally shows data monthly for 4 years ending 1-2 months prior to cover date.]

[1] Current California economic data [including employment by industry division and unemployment; manufacturing hours and earnings; retail sales and new car registrations; new incorporations; CPI for State and 3 largest cities; petroleum, cement, steel, and redwood mill production; and authorized residential construction, and nonresidential construction value].

[2] Basic data for California economic series [approximately 20 indicators, including help-wanted advertisements in Los Angeles area; manufacturing hours, overtime, and employment; housing units authorized; insured unemployment initial claims and average duration; personal income; wages/salaries for mining/manufacturing/construction; taxable sales; DOD prime contract value; CPI for 2 largest cities; net new savings and loan assn savings; and electricity production].

STATISTICAL FEATURE:

S0840–1.501: Jan. 1984

ECONOMIC OUTLOOK FOR 1984-85, ANNUAL FEATURE

(p. 3-4) Annual article on U.S. and California economic outlook through 1985. Data were prepared for Governor's FY85 budget. Includes 1 table showing the following data for 1984-85:

a. U.S. real GNP and major components (personal consumption expenditures, gross private domestic investment, net exports, and government purchases of goods and services); current dollar GNP; GNP deflator; and CPI.

b. California and U.S. personal income, pre-tax corporate profits, wage/salary employment and unemployment rate, housing starts or units authorized, and new car sales or registrations; and California labor force by employment status, and total taxable sales.

S0840–2 CALIFORNIA STATISTICAL ABSTRACT, 1983
Annual. [1984.] viii+230 p.
LC 58-63807.
SRI/MF/complete

Annual compilation of detailed social, governmental, and economic statistics for California. Data are for various years 1970s-82, with selected historical trends from 1940. Data are from reports of State and Federal governments, public utilities, and financial institutions.

Report is designed to present a comprehensive overview of the State. Extensive socioeconomic, demographic, and geographic breakdowns are shown, as applicable, for most topics. These breakdowns include data by city, county, SMSA and other State areas, urban-rural status, industry, income, occupation, sex, race/ethnicity, age, marital status, commodity, and government agency. Comparisons to total U.S. are also included.

Contains contents listing, introduction, and list of SMSAs (p. v-viii); 165 tables arranged in 15 sections, described below (p. 1-221); and appendix, with list of data sources, and index (p. 223-230). Each section begins with a summary description of data sources.

This is the 24th edition of the *Abstract.*

Availability: California Department of Finance, Financial, Economic, and Demographic Research Unit, 1025 P St., Rm. 83, Sacramento CA 95814-5790, $5.00; SRI/MF/complete.

TABLE SECTIONS:

S0840–2.1: Section A: Area, Geography, and Climate

(p. 1-10) Contains 6 tables. Includes land and water areas; acreages of Federal Government real property, and national and State parks and other recreation areas; and elevations and climatological data, by weather station.

S0840–2.2: Section B: Population

(p. 11-20) Contains 4 tables. Includes births, deaths, and migration; and population since 1940.

S0840–2.3: Section C: Labor Force and Employment

(p. 21-52) Contains 21 tables. Includes labor force by employment status; nonfarm employment, with detail for women; manufacturing, covered, State government, and farm employment; production workers average and overtime hours and earnings; and workers compensation underwriting data including covered disabling work injuries/illnesses.

Also includes employment service applicants; registered apprentices; union membership; work injury/illness incidence; and work stoppages, workers involved, and days idle.

S0840–2.4: Section D: Income and Cost-of-Living

(p. 53-62) Contains 9 tables. Includes personal and corporate income tax returns filed, taxes assessed, and taxable income; personal income by source; and CPI by item.

S0840–2.5: Section E: Health and Welfare

(p. 63-88) Contains 25 tables. Includes live births, marriages, and dissolutions; deaths by cause and notifiable disease cases; licensed health facilities and bed capacity; rehabilitated clients, and rehabilitation benefits and costs, by disability; institutionalized narcotic addict population received and released, offenses, and outpatient status; and State mental hospital admissions, population, deaths, and discharges, by hospital.

Also includes general home relief, AFDC, foster care, and food stamp program participants and expenditures; adoptions; disability and unemployment insurance activity; covered employment, establishments, and wages; unemployment fund transactions and balance; and Medi-Cal program and SSI caseloads and payments.

S0840–2.6: Section F: Education

(p. 89-95) Contains 6 tables. Includes higher education enrollment and degrees; public school apportionments and revenues by source; public and private schools, enrollment, personnel, and graduates; and libraries, expenses, staff, books, and operations.

S0840–2.7: Section G: Resource Industries

(p. 97-145) Contains 30 tables. Includes irrigated acreage and reservoir storage capacity; major dams and reservoirs, and specifications; municipal water supply; State Water Project water deliveries and power plant characteristics; agricultural prices received, cash receipts, and production; farms and farmland, harvested acreage, value, and yield; value of leading farm exports; and livestock and poultry inventories.

Also includes timber production; sawtimber volume; forest land ownership and acreage managed by U.S. Forest Service; fishing and hunting licenses; commercial fish landings; mineral production and value; mineral industry establishments, employees, value added, and capital expenditures; and oil and gas wells, and oil, gas, and water production.

S0840–2.8: Section H: Manufacturing

(p. 147-156) Contains 8 tables. Includes manufacturing firms, employment, payroll, value added, capital expenditures, and production workers, hours, and wages; aerospace industry employment; DOD prime contracts to California firms; and energy purchased by manufacturers.

S0840–2.9: Section I: Construction

(p. 157-162) Contains 6 tables. Includes new housing units authorized and value; nonresidential valuation; housing units by value or rent; and general housing occupancy characteristics.

S0840–2.10: Section J: Transportation and Public Utilities

(p. 163-174) Contains 13 tables. Includes State highway and public road mileage; taxable motor, jet, and diesel fuel gallonage; motor vehicle registrations; licensed drivers and accident involvement; traffic accidents, injuries, and fatalities; total and airborne export and import values; electric power production; and telephones, and average monthly gas, electric, and telephone bills.

S0840–2.11: Section K: Trade and Services

(p. 175-183) Contains 7 tables. Includes taxable retail sales; alcoholic beverage consumption; wholesale and retail trade establishments, sales, and payrolls; retail trade employment; and licensed professional and vocational personnel.

S0840–2.12: Section L: Banking and Finance

(p. 185-188) Contains 3 tables. Includes commercial banks and savings and loan assns, and, as applicable, assets, loans, deposits, branches, savings, and net worth; and business failures and liabilities.

S0840–2.13: Section M: Public Finance

(p. 189-207) Contains 18 tables. Includes Federal aid payments, revenues, expenditures, and tax collections; State bonds outstanding, revenues by source, and expenditures by function; and receipts, payments, and bonded indebtedness, by type of local jurisdiction.

Also includes assessed property value, and property tax allocations, levies, average rate, and distribution by type of local jurisdiction; and senior citizen property tax and rental assistance.

S0840–2.14: Section N: Law Enforcement

(p. 209-213) Contains 5 tables. Includes felons received, by offense; and prison population and juvenile wards received and released, and parole status.

S0840–2.15: Section O: Elections

(p. 215-221) Contains 4 tables. Includes voter registration by party; and votes cast, by office and candidate.

S0840–3   ECONOMIC REPORT OF THE GOVERNOR, 1984, California

Annual. 1984.
8+59+App 48 p.
SRI/MF/complete

Annual report on the economic condition of California, 1983 with selected trends from the 1960s. Covers population, employment and earnings, income, government finances, and business activity. Data are compiled from reports of Census Bureau, State agencies, and private sources.

Contains contents listing (1 p.); narrative report in 10 sections, with text data, 21 charts, and 36 tables, described below (p. 1-59); and statistical appendix, with table listing, and 38 tables listed below (p. A3-A48).

Availability: California Department of Finance, Financial, Economic, and Demographic Research Unit, 1025 P St., Rm. 325, Sacramento CA 95814, †; SRI/MF/complete.

TABLES, CHARTS, AND TEXT DATA:

[Data are shown for California, unless otherwise noted.]

S0840–3.1: Narrative Report

[In addition to the data described below, charts and tables also include summaries of data presented in appendix tables.]

a. Employment: service industry employment by kind of business, 1982-83; unemployment rates for 7-8 highest and lowest counties, and by sex, age, and race/ethnicity (including Hispanic), various periods 1982-83; labor force participation rates for women, by county, 1980; and major wage negotiations, with industries and workers involved, 1984. Text data, 6 charts, and 9 tables. (p. 2-15)

b. Inflation, income, and trade: CPI changes, by item, and monthly changes, for 3 California SMSAs compared to State and/or U.S., 1983; and retail sales, by type of business, and for 4 SMSAs, 1982-83. 5 charts and 5 tables. (p. 17-26)

c. Construction activity: residential construction permits authorized, for 10 highest volume counties, 1983; subdivision application monthly filings, 1982-83; median home value, contract rent, and household income, for State and U.S., 1979; existing home median sales prices by State region, and sales distribution by price range, Dec. 1982 and/or 1983; office space trends for selected cities, 1980-83; and State highway capital outlays and projects, 1979-84. 3 charts and 9 tables. (p. 28-35)

d. Finance: value of U.S. home mortgages outstanding, by type of lender, 1982; and California State-chartered and national banks, assets, and deposits, as of Dec. 31, 1982-83. 5 charts and 2 tables. (p. 36-41)

e. Resources: agricultural production value by leading commodity, 1981-82; commercial forest acreage, timber harvest from public and private lands, sawmills and shift capacity, and number of veneer and plywood plants, various years 1952-2000; and natural gas price and change in electricity sales, by consuming sector, various periods 1960-84. 1 chart and 5 tables. (p. 43-50)

f. Tourism and foreign trade: travel-related expenditures, payroll, employment, and tax receipts, with detail by county, various years 1978-82; employment generated, by travel industry category, 1980; tickets distributed, and economic impact summary, for Los Angeles 1984 Olympics; and foreign trade value, selected years 1960-83. Text data, 1 chart and 6 tables. (p. 54-59)

S0840–3.2: Statistical Appendix

POPULATION AND LABOR FORCE

1-2. Population of U.S. and California, and components of change in California's civilian population [natural increase, net migration, and gains from military], 1960-83. (p. A5-A6)

3. Total population of counties, Jan. 1, 1983. (p. A7)

4. Civilian labor force [by employment status, annually 1967-83, and monthly 1982-83]. (p. A8)

EMPLOYMENT, EARNINGS, AND HOURS

5-6. Wage/salary workers in nonagricultural establishments [annually 1972-83, and monthly 1982-83; and in 16 SMSAs], 1982-83; [all] by major industry division. (p. A9-A11)

7. Wage/salary workers in manufacturing [by industry group], 1978-83. (p. A12)

8. Aerospace employment [by industry group, annually] 1960-83 [and monthly 1983]. (p. A15)

9-10. Average weekly and hourly earnings and average hours worked per week, production and related workers in manufacturing, California and U.S., 1960-83; and in selected nonmanufacturing industries, California, 1983. (p. A16-A17)

PERSONAL INCOME, TAXES, AND CPI

11-12. Personal income, total and per capita; [and total] by major sources; 1960-83. (p. A18-A19)

13. Disposable personal income [total and per capita], 1960-82. (p. A20)

14. Industrial sources of earnings, California and U.S., 1980-82. (p. A21)

15. Number of personal income tax returns, adjusted gross income, taxable income, and tax assessed, 1960-81. (p. A22)

16. Personal income tax statistics [adjusted gross income, total and joint returns and median income, and tax assessed], by county, 1981 income year. (p. A23)

17. CPI, [for] U.S., California, Los Angeles, San Francisco, and San Diego, 1960-83. (p. A25)

AGRICULTURE

18. Cash farm receipts, production expenses, and income, 1960-82. (p. A26)

19-20. Cash farm receipts: all crops, livestock/poultry, miscellaneous, and government payments; and from crops [all, fruit/nut, vegetable, and field]; 1960-82. (p. A27-A28)

21. Agricultural employment [in production and services, annually] 1972-83 [and monthly 1983]. (p. A29)

BUSINESS AND COMMERCE

22. Corporate profits from operations [number of corporations with net income and net loss, and with no income/loss; and total net income and losses], 1960-81. (p. A30)

23. Bank and corporation franchise tax returns reporting net income subject to State taxation [number and amounts], by industry [group, 1980-81]. (p. A31)

CONSTRUCTION AND TRADE

24. Building permit activity: nonresidential valuation by selected types of construction [commercial, industrial, other, and additions/alterations], 1963-83. (p. A33)

25. Private residential housing units authorized by permits [number of single and multiple units, and additions/alterations, and total value authorized], 1963-83. (p. A34)

26. Taxable transactions [all outlets and retail stores], and outstanding sales tax permits by type of outlet [retail, personal service, and other], 1960-83. (p. A35)

27. Taxable transactions by type of business, 1977-82. (p. A36)

FINANCE

28-29. Demand and time deposits; and gross loans by major categories [real estate, commercial/industrial, agricultural, personal, and other]; all insured commercial banks, 1960-82. (p. A37-A38)

30. [Mortgage loans closed and net new savings during year, and year-end mortgages outstanding and savings capital], savings and loan assns, 1960-83. (p. A39)

31-32. Selected data on federally- and State-chartered credit unions [including number of institutions, membership, assets, shares, and loans outstanding], 1960-82. (p. A40-A41)

33-34. Selected data on finance companies [number and amount of consumer/commercial loans]; and on industrial loan companies [total assets, investment certificates, and number and amount of consumer, commercial, and premium finance agency loans]; 1971-82. (p. A42-A43)

35. Summary of State tax collections [general and special funds collected and taxes per capita and per $100 of personal income, FY61-85]. (p. A44)

36. Comparative yield of State taxes [including sales/use, personal income, inheritance/gift, horse racing, fuel, and selected excise taxes, and motor vehicle fees], FY61-85. (p. A45)

37. Assessed value of tangible property, tangible property tax levies, and average tax rate [FY61-84]. (p. A46)

38. Allocations of general property tax levies [by type of jurisdiction including school districts] as compiled for computation of the average tax rate, by county, FY83. (p. A47)

S0840-4   PROJECTED TOTAL POPULATION OF CALIFORNIA COUNTIES

Monograph. Oct. 1983.
75 p. no paging. Rpt. 83-P-3.
SRI/MF/complete

Report presenting California population projections by age, and projected median age, by sex and county, quinquennially 1985-2000 and for 2020, with actual data for 1980.

Projections are prepared by Dept of Finance and are based on the 1980 census.

Contains narrative summary with 5 charts, and projection methodology (15 p.); and 1 basic table repeated for each county (59 p.).

Availability: California Department of Finance, Population Research Unit, 1025 P St., Sacramento CA 95814-4998, †; SRI/MF/complete.

S0850   CALIFORNIA
Department of Food and Agriculture

S0850-1   CALIFORNIA AGRICULTURAL STATISTICS, 1983

Annual series. For individual publication data, see below.
SRI/MF/complete

Series of annual reports presenting California agricultural statistics for 1983, with selected trends from 1970s or earlier, including data by county or reporting district for most commodities, and selected comparisons to U.S. and other States.

Series includes an overview; individual reports on major commodity groups; and a 2-volume report on exports.

Data sources include California Crop and Livestock Reporting Service, USDA, State and local agencies, grower assns, shippers, and processors.

Reports for 1983 reviewed during 1984 are described below. Reports for 1982 are covered in SRI under S0850-2.

Issuing agency also publishes the following related reports, not covered in SRI: *Grape Acreage Bulletin, Grape Crush Bulletin,* and *Fruit and Nut Acreage Bulletin.*

Availability: California Crop and Livestock Reporting Service, PO Box 1258, Sacramento CA 95806; SRI/MF/complete.

S0850-1.1: California Fruit and Nut Statistics, 1982-83

[Annual. Feb. 1984. ii+10 p. $2.00. SRI/MF/complete.]

Annual report on California fruit and nut production, marketing, and income, 1982 and preliminary 1983, with trends from 1974. Data are shown by commodity and/or variety.

Report covers acreage, production, value, utilization, average grower returns, and price, for grapes, tree nuts, citrus fruits, and deciduous and semitropical tree fruit.

Contains foreword and contents listing (p. i-ii); and user notes and 14 tables (p. 1-10).

S0850-1.2: California Livestock Statistics, 1983

[Annual. June 1984. 3+25 p. $2.00. ISSN 0361-9095. LC 75-64945. SRI/MF/complete.]

Annual report on California livestock production, finances, and marketing, mostly for 1974-83, with some data for 1984, and trends from the 1920s. Data are shown by species.

Report covers production, income, prices, value, inventory by county, slaughter, and shipments into California by State of origin, for cattle, sheep, and hogs.

Also includes comparisons to U.S.; California income from poultry products and honey/beeswax, rangeland condition, milk cow inventory and production, number of farms by type, sheep shorn and wool production, and inshipments of hogs by State of origin; and U.S. livestock on farms, by species and State.

Contains foreword and table listing (3 p.); and 42 tables (p. 1-25).

S0850-1.3: California Agriculture, 1983

[Annual. July 1984. 17 p. $2.00. SRI/MF/complete.]

Annual summary report presenting data on California agricultural production, marketing, and finance, 1983, with some data for 1984 and selected trends from 1950. Data are generally shown by commodity; selected data are shown by district and county.

Report covers production, value, national rank, and, as applicable, acreage; for field crop, vegetable, berry, fruit and nut, nursery, livestock, poultry, apiary, and dairy sectors. Price data and value of exports are included for selected commodities.

Report also includes data on land value by irrigation status and use type, number of farms and acreage, and rainfall by weather station; and top 20 States ranked by agricultural cash receipts.

Contains contents listing and narrative summary (p. 1-3); 12 tables (p. 4-15); and listings of State agriculture officials (p. 16-17).

S0850-1.4: Exports of Agricultural Commodities Produced in California, 1983

[Annual. [1984.] 1+18 p. $2.00. SRI/MF/complete.]

Annual report on California agricultural export volume and value, by detailed commodity, 1983, with selected trends from 1979. Also includes comparisons to U.S.; and data on total California agricultural production, and acreage required to produce exports.

Contains listings of contents and tables, and data limitations and sources (p. 1-3); 5 tables, interspersed with highlight summaries (p. 4-18); and contents description of Statistical Appendix volume described below (inside back cover).

S0850-1.5: Exports of Agricultural Commodities Produced in California, 1983, Statistical Appendix

[Annual. [1984.] p. 19-113. $4.00. SRI/MF/complete.]

Annual report on volume and value of agricultural exports through California ports, and total U.S. agricultural exports to 25 countries by transport mode, all by detailed commodity and country of destination, 1983.

Contains listings of contents and tables, introduction, notes, and abbreviations (p. 19-23); and 3 tables (p. 24-113).

S0850-1.6: California Vegetable Crops, 1982-83

[Annual. [1984.] iv+8 p. $2.00. SRI/MF/complete.]

Annual report on California vegetable production and marketing, 1982-83, with summary trends from 1974. Data are shown by commodity and/or variety, use category, and county.

Report covers production, acreage, yield, value, prices, and sales for vegetables, berries, and melons.

Contains foreword, contents and table listings, and 1 chart (p. i-iii); and brief narrative summary and 8 tables (p. iv, 1-8).

S0850-2   CALIFORNIA AGRICULTURAL STATISTICS, 1982

Annual series. For individual publication data, see below.
SRI/MF/complete

Series of annual reports presenting California agricultural statistics for 1982, with selected trends from 1970s or earlier, including data by county or reporting district for most commodities, and selected comparisons to U.S. and other States.

Series includes an overview; individual reports on major commodity groups; and a 2-volume report on exports.

Data sources include California Crop and Livestock Reporting Service, USDA, State and local agencies, grower assns, shippers, and processors.

Reports for 1982 are described below, and in SRI 1983 Annual under this number. Reports for 1981 are described in SRI 1982 and 1983 Annuals, under S0850-1. Reports for 1983 are also covered in SRI under S0850-1; those reviewed during 1984 are described above.

Issuing agency also publishes the following related reports, not covered in SRI: *Grape Acreage Bulletin, Grape Crush Bulletin,* and *Fruit and Nut Acreage Bulletin.*

Availability: California Crop and Livestock Reporting Service, PO Box 1258, Sacramento CA 95806; SRI/MF/complete.

S0850-2.4: California Fruit and Nut Statistics, 1981-82

[Annual. Feb. 1983. ii+12 p. $2.00. SRI/MF/complete.]

Annual report on California fruit and nut production, marketing, and income, 1981 and preliminary 1982, with trends from 1973. Data are shown by commodity and/or variety.

Report covers production, acreage, price, value, utilization, and average grower returns, for grapes, tree nuts, citrus fruits, and deciduous and semitropical tree fruit.

Contains foreword and contents listing (p. i-ii); and user notes and 14 tables (p. 1-12).

Previous report, for 1980/81, is described in SRI 1982 Annual under S0850-1.1.

S0850–2.5: California Dairy Industry Statistics, 1982

[Annual. [1983.] 63 p. $3.00. SRI/MF/complete.]

Annual report on California dairy production and marketing, 1982, with selected trends from 1962. Data are shown by product, and by county, district, and/or marketing area. Covers production; farm cash receipts; average and minimum producer prices; utilization; and sales volume, with detail for milk by type of trade and container size and type.

Also includes comparisons to U.S. and other States; and data on California dairy cattle inventories and productivity, per capita consumption of selected products, and number of plants reporting milk sales by county.

Contains contents listing and foreword (p. 2-5); and 68 tables, interspersed with brief narrative summaries (p. 6-63).

S0850–2.6: California Agriculture, 1982

[Annual. July 1983. 17 p. $1.50. SRI/MF/complete.]

Annual summary report presenting data on California agricultural production, marketing, and finance, 1982, with some data for 1983 and selected trends from 1950. Data are generally shown by commodity; selected data are shown by district and county.

Report covers production, value, national rank, and, as applicable, acreage, for field crop, vegetable, berry, fruit and nut, nursery, livestock, and poultry sectors. Price data and value of exports are included for selected commodities.

Report also includes data on land value by irrigation status and use type, number of farms and acreage, and rainfall by weather station; and top 20 States ranked by agricultural cash receipts.

Contains contents listing and narrative summary (p. 1-3); 13 tables (p. 4-15); and listings of State agriculture officials (p. 16-17).

S0850–2.7: Exports of Agricultural Commodities Produced in California, 1982

[Annual. July 1983. 18 p. $2.00. SRI/MF/complete.]

Annual report on California agricultural export volume and value, by detailed commodity, 1982, with selected trends from 1978. Also includes comparisons to U.S.; and data on total California agricultural production, and acreage required to produce exports.

Contains listings of contents and tables, and data limitations and sources (p. 1-3); 5 tables, interspersed with highlight summaries (p. 4-16); and abbreviations, and contents description of Statistical Appendix volume described below (p. 17-18).

S0850–2.8: Exports of Agricultural Commodities Produced in California, 1982, Statistical Appendix

[Annual. July 1983. p. 19-111 $3.00. SRI/MF/complete.]

Annual report on volume and value of agricultural exports through California ports, and total U.S. agricultural exports to 25 countries by mode, all by detailed commodity and country of destination, 1982.

Contains listings of contents and tables, introduction, notes, and country abbreviations (p. 19-22); and 3 tables (p. 23-111).

S0855   CALIFORNIA Franchise Tax Board

S0855–1   STATE OF CALIFORNIA FRANCHISE TAX BOARD Annual Report, 1982

Annual.   [1983.]   102 p.
LC 51-62397.
SRI/MF/complete

Annual report on California individual and corporate income tax returns, for 1981 tax year. Includes data on filings and assessments; individual income by source, and tax credits and deductions; and bank/corporate franchise income, by major industry group. Selected data are shown by adjusted gross income (AGI) class and county.

Also includes summary trends from 1935; and data on property tax assistance for aged and blind/disabled homeowners and renters, 1982.

Contents:

a. Listing of contents, tables, and charts. (p. 2-3)

b. 5 narrative sections, with 16 charts and 15 tables, mostly summary but including 1 table (p. 4) on general fund collections by source 1981-82, and 2 tables (p. 14, 20) on solar and energy conservation personal and corporate tax credits claimed. (p. 4-32)

c. Statistical appendices, with 5 tables showing major tax law changes affecting rates, exemptions, and deductions since 1929, and 30 detailed tables listed below. (p. 33-102)

Availability: California Franchise Tax Board, Attention: Research and Statistics, Sacramento CA 95867, †; SRI/MF/complete.

TABLES:

[In addition to data noted below, all tables show number of returns, except tables for homeowner and renter assistance programs, which show number of claimants.]

S0855–1.1: Personal Income Taxes

[Unless otherwise noted, data are for 1981. Table titles begin "Personal income tax statistics..."]

1-3. Comparison by income years, 1935-81; by AGI class, 1978-81; and by AGI class, percentages cumulated, 1981; [generally showing AGI, taxable income, and tax assessed]. (p. 38-40)

[4A-4F] Comparison by AGI class: State totals [for income types, credits, and deductions]; and single returns, separate returns, joint returns, head of household returns, and surviving spouse returns [all for AGI, deductions, taxable income, computed tax, and tax credits, for taxable and nontaxable returns]. (p. 41-60)

5. Comparison by major industry [business/profession and partnership net profit and loss, by industry division]. (p. 61)

6. Comparison by county [all returns AGI, all and joint returns median average income and rank, total tax assessed, and population]. (p. 62)

7. County data by AGI class [all, joint, renters credit, and taxable returns; and dependents, AGI, and tax assessed]. (p. 63-78)

8. Fiduciary returns by gross income class [gross and taxable income, distribution to beneficiaries, other deductions, total credits, and tax assessed, for taxable and nontaxable returns]. (p. 79)

9. Taxes paid by high income individuals [total and taxable returns, total tax liability, and number of returns by size of tax liability and average tax rate, all for 4 income size groups within 4 income concept classes]. (p. 80-81)

S0855–1.2: Bank/Corporation Taxes

[Table titles 1-4 begin "Bank/corporation franchise tax statistics..."]

1-2. Comparison by income years [income reported for Federal and State taxation], 1936-81; and comparison by State net income class [net income less net loss, 1981; both including tax assessed]. (p. 84-85)

3-4. Comparison by [major industry group], 1980-81; and by accounting period [including tax assessed, 1981; both showing corporations reporting net income subject to State taxation and amount, and all reporting corporations' net income less net loss]. (p.86-87)

5. Corporation income tax statistics, comparison by net income class [income reported for Federal and State taxation, and tax assessed, 1981; with summary totals for returns reporting net income, 1961-81]. (p. 88)

S0855–1.3: Homeowner and Renter Assistance, for Blind, Disabled and Senior Citizens

[Unless otherwise noted, data are for 1982.]

HOMEOWNER ASSISTANCE

[Table titles 1-6 begin "Homeowners property tax assistance statistics..." Tables 1-4 show number of claimants paid, household income, property tax paid, and amount of assistance.]

1. Comparison by calendar years 1969-82 [includes homeowner's property tax exemption]. (p. 92)

2-4. Comparison by county, size of household income, and [claimant's] year of birth. (p. 93-95)

5. [Number of claimants, by] household income by amount of property taxes paid. (p. 96)

6. Major sources of household income [including social security, interest/dividends, pensions/annuities, public assistance, and net rental and business income, by household income class]. (p. 97)

RENTER ASSISTANCE

[Table titles 7-10 begin "Renters' property tax assistance statistics..."]

7-9. [Tables 2-4 are repeated for renters' assistance.] (p. 98-100)

10. [Table 6 is repeated for renters' assistance.] (p. 101)

CLAIMANTS

11. Homeowners' [and] renters' property tax assistance statistics: types of claimants [senior citizens and blind/disabled], by size of household income. (p. 102)

S0865   CALIFORNIA
Department of Health Services

S0865-1   VITAL STATISTICS OF CALIFORNIA, 1981
Annual. Nov. 1983.
ix + 198 p. + 2 microfiche sheets.
ISSN 0094-0356.
LC 74-636455.
SRI/MF/complete

Annual report, for 1981, presenting California vital statistics, including population, births, deaths by detailed cause, and marriages and dissolutions. Includes data by county and demographic characteristics, trends from 1940, and selected U.S. comparisons.

Data are primarily from documents registered with the Dept of Health Services.

Contains contents listing and highlights (p. iv-ix); 17 charts and 61 tables arranged in 7 sections, each preceded by a listing of charts and tables (p. 1-166); data sources, definitions, and limitations (p. 167-181); appendix, with report form facsimiles (p. 183-198); and 2 microfiche with extended table (64 p.) on deaths by detailed cause, by age group and sex.

All tables are listed below.

Hard copies of the microfiched table are available from the issuing agency for $10.00.

Availability: California Department of Health Services, Center for Health Statistics, Health Demographics Unit, 714 P St., Rm. 1476, Sacramento CA 95814, †; SRI/MF/complete.

TABLES:
[Data are for California, 1981, unless otherwise noted. Most tables specify data as place of residence or place of occurrence. Data by race often include some or all of the following ethnic groups: Mexican American, Indian, Chinese, Japanese, Filipino, and other.]

S0885   CALIFORNIA
Department of
Highway Patrol

S0885-1   1983 ANNUAL REPORT OF FATAL AND INJURY MOTOR VEHICLE TRAFFIC ACCIDENTS, California
Annual.   [1984.]   x+95 p.
LC 67-66062.
SRI/MF/complete

Annual report on California traffic accidents, fatalities, and injuries, by detailed accident and vehicle type, location, time, and other circumstances; and driver and victim characteristics; 1983, with trends from 1933.

Also includes data on motor vehicle registrations and licensed drivers, miles traveled, population, and roadway mileage.

Data are from reports submitted by local police and sheriff offices and State Highway Patrol offices to the Statewide Integrated Traffic Records System.

Contains 1 summary table, preface, contents and table listings, and highlights (p. i-x); 10 charts and 63 tables arranged in 8 sections (p. 1-88); and definitions and dept staff (p. 89-95).
Availability: California Department of Highway Patrol, Staff Services Section, PO Box 898, Sacramento CA 95804, $3.50; SRI/MF/complete.

S0900   CALIFORNIA
Department of
Insurance

S0900-1   ONE HUNDRED AND FIFTEENTH ANNUAL REPORT OF THE INSURANCE COMMISSIONER of the State of California, for the Year Ended Dec. 31, 1982
Annual.   Aug. 1, 1983.
175 p.
LC 45-33033.
SRI/MF/complete

Annual report on California insurance industry financial condition and underwriting activity, by company and type of insurance, 1982. Covers assets, liabilities, capital/surplus, underwriting and investment gain or loss, dividends, premiums collected or earned, and losses or benefits paid and/or incurred, for companies with headquarters in California and elsewhere.

Data are shown for life/disability, fire/marine/casualty/miscellaneous, and real estate title insurers.

Also includes data on Insurance Dept receipts and disbursements, employees, securities on deposit, licensing activity, and consumer complaints; and finances of companies in conservation or liquidation.

Data are compiled from unaudited statements filed by all licensed insurers, and dept internal records.

Contains contents listing (p. 3); dept report, with 17 tables (p. 7-52); liquidation and conservation report, with 1 table repeated for each company (p. 53-145); and 3 company financial tables (p. 149-175).

Availability: California Department of Insurance, 100 Van Ness Ave., San Francisco CA 94102, †; SRI/MF/complete.

S0905   CALIFORNIA
Judicial Council

S0905-1   1984 ANNUAL REPORT, JUDICIAL COUNCIL OF CALIFORNIA
Annual.   Jan. 1, 1984.
xiv+277 p.+insert.
LC 67-65214.
SRI/MF/complete

Annual report on the California judicial system, including trial and appellate court caseloads and case dispositions, mostly for FY82-83. Covers supreme, appeals, superior, and lower courts. Includes trial court data by case type, county, municipality, and judicial district; with some data for FY84 and selected trends from FY74.

Case types shown are criminal and civil, for all courts, with some additional detail for probate/guardianship, eminent domain, family, juvenile, mental health, habeas corpus, traffic, and small claims case types.

Report also includes data on judicial personnel, including judge-substitute commissioners and referees; number of judicial districts and courts; attorney disciplinary proceedings; juries; case processing time; and court finances.

Contains contents listing and introduction (p. iii-xiv); Judicial Council report in 7 chapters, with text statistics, 1 chart, and 24 tables (p. 1-63); Administrative Office report in 2 chapters, with 22 charts and 56 tables (p. 65-179); 50 appendix tables (p. 181-274); and glossary (p. 275-277).
Availability: California Judicial Council, Administrative Office of the Courts, 3154 State Bldg., 350 McAllister St., San Francisco CA 94102, †; SRI/MF/complete.

S0910   CALIFORNIA
Department of
Justice

S0910-2   CRIMINAL JUSTICE PROFILE, 1982, Statewide, California
Annual.   Oct. 1983.
iii+121 p.
LC 80-649518.
SRI/MF/complete

Annual statistical profile of the California criminal justice system, presenting data on offenses and arrests, probation, court dispositions, correctional actions, personnel, and expenditures, 1982, with trends from 1973. Data are from State records, and are shown variously by county and by offender age, race, and sex.

Contains contents and table listing (p. i-iii); introduction (p. 1); report, with 49 tables, listed below (p. 3-105); and methodology and glossary (p. 106-121).

Previous report, for 1981, is described in SRI 1982 Annual, under this number.

Report is part of a series of criminal justice profiles, covering the State and each county. It is designed to supplement the annual Bureau of Criminal Statistics publication, *Crime and Delinquency in California,* which contains similar data, but with greater focus on offenses and arrests. Only the statewide *Profile* is covered by SRI.

Availability: California Department of Justice, Criminal Statistics and Special Services Bureau, 4949 Broadway, PO Box 13427, Sacramento CA 95813, †; SRI/MF/complete.

TABLES:
[Data for "7 major offenses" are for homicide, rape, robbery, aggravated assault, burglary, theft, and motor vehicle theft. Data by offense include these and several other categories.]

S0910-2.1: State Summary Trends
[Tables show data for 1973-82, unless otherwise noted.]

[1] 7 major offenses and clearances reported by law enforcement agencies. (p. 5)

[2-4] Adult felony and misdemeanor and juvenile arrest offenses reported by law enforcement agencies [by offense]. (p. 6-8)

[5-6] Adult and juvenile probation [caseload data]. (p. 9-10)

[7-8] Dispositions and percents of adult felony arrests [1975-82]. (p. 11-12)

[9] Criminal justice expenditures [by dept, FY73-82]. (p. 13)

[10] Authorized full-time personnel [by dept and function]. (p. 14)

[11] Persons [adults and juveniles] under local supervision [by facility type]. (p. 15)

S0910-2.2: Detailed Tables, 1982
[All tables show data for 1982. Data by race/ethnic group are for white non-Hispanic, Hispanic, black, and other, unless otherwise noted.]

ARRESTS

[1] FBI Crime Index and 7 major offenses, offense by county. (p. 19)

[2-3] Arson offenses: type of property by county; and offenses reported and cleared [with property damage value, by property type], statewide. (p. 21-23)

[4-5] Adult felony and misdemeanor arrests reported, offense by county and sex. (p. 24-37)

[6] Adult arrests reported, age by specific offense, statewide. (p. 38)

[7-8] Juvenile arrests reported, offense by county and sex; and age by specific offense, statewide. (p. 40-48)

[9] Adult and juvenile arrests reported, level of arrest and law enforcement disposition by county and sex. (p. 49-56)

[10-11] Adult and juvenile arrests reported, sex and law enforcement disposition, and race/ethnic group, by specific offense, statewide. (p. 57-60)

DISPOSITIONS

[12-14] Dispositions of adult felony arrests, type of disposition: by county, by arrest offense, and by percent distribution of arrest offense. (p. 61-74)

[15-16] Adult felony arrestees convicted and sentenced, type of sentence: by convicted offense and by percent distribution of convicted offense. (p. 75-76)

[17-22] Dispositions of adult felony arrests: type of disposition and percent distribution of race/ethnic group, sex, and age. (p. 77-82)

PROBATION

[Data for ethnic groups generally include American Indian, Chinese, Japanese, and Filipino.]

[23-26] Adult probation active caseload on Dec. 31, 1982, and adults placed on probation, type of court; and adults removed from superior and lower court probation, type of removal; by county. (p. 83-90)

[27-29] Referrals of juveniles to probation depts for delinquent acts: new referrals showing probation dept disposition by county, referral offense, sex, age, race/ethnic group, detention, referral source, and prosecutor action. (p. 91-94)

[30] Dispositions of juveniles referral to probation depts for delinquent acts: new referrals showing sex and race/ethnic group by type of disposition. (p. 95)

[31] Referrals of juveniles to probation depts for delinquent acts: referral type and probation dept disposition by referral offense. (p. 96)

[32-35] Juvenile court dispositions resulting from petitions for delinquent acts: new referrals showing court disposition by county, offense, sex, age, race/ethnic group, and defense representation; and petition type and court disposition by offense. (p. 97-101)

[36] Removals and changes of status of juveniles on probation for delinquent acts, sex and race/ethnic group by reason for change. (p. 102)

[37-38] Current status of juveniles on probation for delinquent acts on Dec. 31, 1982: current status by county, and percent by sex, age, and race/ethnic group. (p. 103-105)

S0980   COLORADO
Department of Administration

S0980–1   COMPREHENSIVE ANNUAL FINANCIAL REPORT for the Year Ended June 30, 1983, State of Colorado
Annual.   Oct. 26, 1983.
15+72 p.
LC 80-648197.
SRI/MF/complete

Annual report on financial condition of Colorado State government, for FY83, presenting assets, liabilities, and fund equity and balances; revenues by source; and expenditures by function, object, and/or agency; for all, general, current restricted, special revenue, debt service, capital project, enterprise, internal service, trust, loan, and agency funds. Includes selected trends from FY74.

Also includes budgeted vs. actual revenues and expenditures; data on State government employment; appropriations and expenditures by institution; bonded debt; and socioeconomic trends, including population, personal income, sales, assessed property values, labor force and employment by industry division, and unemployment, with selected comparisons to the U.S.

Financial data are from the State Controller's unaudited records.

Contains contents listing and introduction, with 2 text tables and 13 charts (15 p.); financial section, with 31 financial statements and accompanying notes (p. 1-61); and statistical section, with 11 tables (p. 63-72).

Availability: Colorado Department of Administration, Accounts and Control Division, 1525 Sherman St., Rm. 706, Denver CO 80203, †; SRI/MF/complete.

S0985   COLORADO
Department of Agriculture

S0985–1   1984 COLORADO AGRICULTURAL STATISTICS
Annual.   July 1984.   94 p.
Bull. 1-84.
LC 52-62059.
SRI/MF/complete

Annual report on Colorado agricultural production, marketing, and finances, 1970s-83, with some data for 1984 and selected trends from as early as 1940. Data are generally shown by commodity and/or district and county, with some comparisons to other States and total U.S.

Report covers production, prices, disposition, value, and, as applicable, acreage, yield, or inventory, for field crop, fruit, vegetable, livestock, dairy, and poultry sectors.

Also includes data on number of farms and acreage; irrigation use; fertilizer consumption; precipitation; farm income and production expenses; pasture/range feed condition; cattle and sheep shipments into Colorado from selected States and foreign countries; and U.S. per capita consumption of major food and beverage products.

Data are compiled by the Colorado Crop and Livestock Reporting Service in cooperation with USDA.

Contains contents listing (p. 1); 14 maps, 4 charts, and 117 tables grouped into 4 sections, each including brief narrative (p. 2-90); and index (p. 91-94).

Availability: Colorado Crop and Livestock Reporting Service, PO Box 17066, Denver CO 80217, †; SRI/MF/complete.

S0995   COLORADO
Department of Corrections

S0995–1   COLORADO DEPARTMENT OF CORRECTIONS Annual Statistical Report, FY83
Annual.   Jan. 5, 1984.   63 p.
LC 82-643356.
SRI/MF/complete

Annual report, for FY83, on corrections in Colorado, presenting data on prison population, including inmate admissions, commitment offense, sentence length, age, ethnicity/race, criminal background, and releases, with selected detail for female offenders and trends from 1970s. Some data are shown by institution.

Also includes data on offenders in community corrections programs, institutional cost per offender, commitments and parolees by county and/or State region, and correctional facility capacity.

Report was compiled by Office of Research and Reporting.

Contains contents listing (2 p.), and 5 sections, with 18 charts and 38 tables (p. 1-63).

Note that publication date on document incorrectly reads Jan. 5, 1983.

Availability: Colorado Department of Corrections, Research and Reporting Office, 2860 S. Circle Dr., Suite 2200, North Bldg., Colorado Springs CO 80906, †; SRI/MF/complete.

S1000   COLORADO
Department of Education

S1000–2   STATISTICAL SERIES: Colorado Department of Education
Annual series.   For individual publication data, see below.
SRI/MF/complete

Series of 3 annual reports on Colorado public elementary and secondary education. Reports cover certificated personnel and salaries; enrollment and graduates; and revenues and expenditures; generally by county and/or school district.

Most data are compiled from reports filed by school districts with the State Dept of Education.

Reports reviewed during 1984 are described below.

Availability: Colorado Department of Education, Administrative Support and Technical Services Unit, 303 W. Colfax Ave., 6th Floor, Denver CO 80204, $4.00 each; SRI/MF/complete.

S1000–2.1: Pupil Membership and Related Information, Fall 1983
[Annual.   Mar. 1984.   iv+62 p.   LC 75-648933. SRI/MF/complete.]

Contains contents listing and definitions (p. iii-iv); and the following tables showing data by school district and county unless otherwise noted:

1-3. Comparison of pupil membership by size of district, fall 1982-83; and fall pupil membership in each grade [including special education] and by ethnic group [American Indian, Asian/Pacific Islander, black, white, and Hispanic], 1983. (p. 1-23)

4. Fall, closing day, and average daily membership, and average daily attendance entitlement [1974/75-1983/84]. (p. 24-46)

5. Public high school graduates [by sex, 1978/79-1982/83]. (p. 47-59)

6-7. Past and [high, medium, and low] predicted enrollment 1978-88, by grade; and relationship between enrollments and [live births, various periods 1945-88; State only]. (p. 61-62)

S1000–2.2: Certificated Personnel Salaries and Related Information, Fall 1983

[Annual. Mar. 1984. vi+35 p. SRI/MF/complete.]

Contains contents listing, definitions, and listing of school districts (p. iii-vi); and the following tables showing data for Colorado, fall 1983, unless otherwise noted:

[A] Comparison of Colorado and national classroom teachers' average salaries [and number of teachers, 1974/75-1983/84; with accompanying chart]. (p. 1)

1. Certificated personnel summary by position [by sex, including average age and experience, and personnel and average salary by highest degree]. (p. 2-6)

2-3. College preparation of certificated [instructional and other] personnel, and types of certificates held by certificated personnel, fall 1978 and 1982-83. (p. 7-8)

4-5. Classroom teachers and professional staff FTE average salary, average experience, and percent [with] masters or higher degree, [by school district grouped by urban-rural status and average daily attendance]. (p. 10-23)

6-7. Average salaries [and number] of classroom teachers, total certificated personnel, superintendents, principals, and assistant principals, by [district urban-rural status and average attendance], fall 1982-83. (p. 24-25)

8. Certificated personnel by ethnic group [American Indian, black, Asian American, Spanish surnamed, and other], by school district. (p. 26-35)

S1000–2.3: Revenues and Expenditures, Calendar Year 1983

[Annual. June 1984. 87 p. SRI/MF/complete.]

Contains contents listing and explanations of data categories (p. 1-3); and the following tables, showing data by school district grouped by county, with totals for boards of cooperative services, 1983:

a. Revenues by local, State, and Federal source, for all funds except building fund; and building fund bond receipts. Table I. (p. 4-31)

b. Revenues and expenses, for building, capital reserve, bond redemption, and all other funds; and total current expense, including and excluding transportation. Table II. (p. 32-59)

c. Expenditures, by detailed category, including salaries, benefits, transportation, and food services. Table III. (p. 60-87)

Includes total amounts, and amounts per Oct. 1982 average daily attendance entitlement.

S1010   COLORADO
Department of
Health

S1010–1   ANNUAL REPORT OF VITAL STATISTICS, Colorado, 1981

Annual. [1983.]
90 p. var. paging.
ISSN 0588-456X.
LC 75-646408.
SRI/MF/complete

Annual report on Colorado vital statistics, covering population growth, births, deaths by cause, marriages, and divorces, for the State and by county, health service area (HSA), and planning region, 1981, with historical trends from 1860. Also includes data on adoptions.

Data are from certificates of vital events registered in the Dept of Health prior to Apr. 15, 1982.

Contains preface, with 1 summary table (p. i-iii); listing of contents, tables, and charts (4 p.); narrative report in 9 sections, interspersed with 5 charts and 41 tables (p. 1-41); and appendices, with 3 maps and 14 tables, and disease classification list, definitions, available tabulation reports, and sample certificates (43 p.).

All tables are listed below. Previous report, for 1980, is described in SRI 1982 Annual, under this number.

Availability: Colorado Department of Health, Health Policy, Planning and Statistics Division, Health Statistics Section, 4210 E. 11th Ave., Denver CO 80220, $2.00; SRI/MF/complete.

TABLES:
[Unless otherwise noted, data are for Colorado, 1981. Data by race are usually shown for Anglo and Spanish surname white; black, Indian, and other nonwhite; and Spanish and non-Spanish origin.]

S1010–1.1: Population and Summary Data

1. Vital statistics [summary]: State residents [by occurrence in and out of State] and occurrence [to residents and nonresidents]. (p. i)

2. Population by age and sex, 1970 and 1980. (p. 4)

3. Population, population growth, natural increase and net in-migration, with median age, [decennially] 1860-1980. (p. 5)

4-5. Population, births, and illegitimate births; and [total], infant, neonatal, and maternal deaths; Colorado residents [number and rates] and U.S. rates, [decennially 1910-50 and annually 1950-81]. (p. 6-7)

6. [Population 1980, and] total births and deaths [1975-81], for selected incorporated cities (1980 population [above] 2,500), by city of residence [and for balance of State]. (p. 9)

7. Summary vital statistics by month of occurrence, Colorado residents and occurrence [includes resident deaths by cause]. (p. 10)

8. Population; live births [by sex], low birth weight births, and illegitimate births; deaths and infant deaths [by sex]; and neonatal, fetal, and perinatal deaths; [all] by race, Colorado residents. (p. 11)

9-10. Total pregnancies, live births, induced abortions, and spontaneous fetal deaths, for all

women and women under 20 years of age: Colorado occurrence, 1970-81; and by legitimacy, Colorado residents and occurrence, 1981. (p. 12)

S1010–1.2: Births, Deaths, Adoptions, and Marriages

BIRTHS
[Tables 12-18 show data for Colorado residents.]

11. Birth and fertility rates, Colorado residents and U.S. rates [and Colorado population and women aged 15-44], selected years 1940-81. (p. 13)

12. Age-specific [births, women, and] fertility rates, 1970 and 1980. (p. 14)

13. Selected birth statistics, 1970-81. (p. 14)

14. Live births by education of mother, other living children, and month in which prenatal care began. (p. 15)

15-16. Live births by race of child, birth weight, prenatal visits, and age of mother. (p. 16)

17. Live births, low birth weight births, and illegitimate births by single year age of mother. (p. 17)

18. Congenital anomalies reported on birth certificate. (p. 18)

DEATHS
[Tables 19-23 show data for Colorado occurrences; tables 24-36 show data for Colorado residents.]

19. Fetal deaths by age of mother, length of gestation, and race of fetus. (p. 20)

20-21. Induced abortions by age and race of patient, and by type of procedure and length of gestation. (p. 21)

22-23. Infant deaths by trimester in which prenatal care began and age of mother at birth, and by birth weight. (p. 22)

24-25. Infant, [neonatal, hebdomadal, and 1st day] deaths: from leading causes by age, and by race and sex. (p. 23)

26-27. Leading causes of death: and death rates for Colorado residents and U.S.; and by underlying cause by total mentions. (p. 24-25)

28-29. Total number of causes of death, and leading causes of death by sex, by age. (p. 25-26)

30. Deaths and death rates from leading causes [and rank order of top 10 causes], selected years 1940-81. (p. 28)

31. Age-specific mortality rates [and deaths and persons], 1970 and 1980. (p. 30)

32-33. Deaths from leading causes by age, sex, and race. (p. 31-32)

34. Deaths by race, [sex], and age. (p. 33)

35. Violent deaths by age and sex, [and cause]. (p. 34)

36. Reported cases and deaths from selected notifiable diseases, selected years 1940-81. (p. 36)

ADOPTIONS, MARRIAGES AND DISSOLUTIONS, AND CERTIFICATES

37. Adoptions processed, 1979-81, by year of decree [selected periods 1970-81]. (p. 38)

38-39. Type of adoption [both parents, step and single parent, legitimation, relative, and adjudication], and sex and age of child, for all processed adoptions. (p. 39)

40. Marriages and marriage dissolutions (divorces/annulments), Colorado occurrence [and rates] and U.S. rates, 1970-81. (p. 40)

41. Certified copies of birth/death certificates [FY41 and FY51-82]. (p. 41)

S1010–1.3: Appendix Tables
[All data are shown by county, planning region, and HSA.]

POPULATION

A1. Estimated population, population growth [from 1980], and population density, with ranks. (2 p.)

A2. Population and median age by sex; percent population by race; and number of families, households, and persons in group quarters; 1980. (2 p.)

A3. Population by age group, 1980. (2 p.)

BIRTHS AND DEATHS
[Tables A7-A13] show data for Colorado residents.]

A4-A6. Live, low birth weight, and illegitimate births; and total, infant, neonatal, fetal, and perinatal deaths, with rates; Colorado residents 1981 and 1977-81 period, and Colorado occurrence 1981. (6 p.)

A7. Birth, fertility, and pregnancy rates, with selected birth statistics [including induced abortions, and percent of women giving live birth with 12/more years education]. (2 p.)

A8-A9. Live births: by age group of mother; and by race and sex of child. (6 p.)

A10. Total deaths and death rates by sex, and percent of deaths by sex and selected age group. (2 p.)

A11-A12. Deaths: by age group at death; and by race and sex. (6 p.)

A13. Deaths and death rates for 10 leading causes. (2 p.)

MARRIAGES AND DISSOLUTIONS

A14. Marriages, marriage dissolutions, and separate maintenance, Colorado occurrence. (2 p.)

S1010–2   DEMOGRAPHIC PROFILES, Colorado
Recurring (irreg.) Feb. 1983. xvii+58 p. no paging. No. 1. SRI/MF/complete

Recurring report on Colorado demographic and socioeconomic characteristics, and vital statistics, including births, deaths by cause, and marriages and dissolutions, primarily 1980-81 with some data shown for the 1970s.

Data are from the 1980 Census of Population and Housing Summary Tape Files 1A and 3, and various State agencies.

Contains introduction, contents and table listing, 2 maps, and index (p. i-vii); technical notes and documentation (p. viii-xvii); and 29 tables, described (58 p.)

This is the 1st edition of the report.

Availability: Colorado Department of Health, Health Statistics and Vital Records Division, 4210 E. 11th Ave., Denver CO 80220, †; SRI/MF/complete.

TABLES:
[Data are for Colorado, and are shown by county, planning region, and health service area. Data by race include white, black, Indian and Asian/Pacific Islander.]

POPULATION, HOUSING, AND MISCELLANEOUS
[Data are for 1980, unless otherwise noted.]

a. Population, 1970-81; land area; urban and rural population and housing units; median and mean persons per housing unit; households; and families. Tables 1-3.

b. Population and median age by sex; population distribution by race and for Spanish origin; median age, and population by age group, 1980-81, with detail by sex, 1980; single person households by sex of householder; 2 or more person households by household type; population by household type and relationship to others in household; and population age 15/over by sex, by marital status. Tables 4-8.

c. Year round housing units; occupied housing units by tenure, and median value or rent; year round, occupied, and renter occupied housing units without plumbing facilities for exclusive use; and persons in housing units without plumbing and with 1.01/more persons per room. Table 9.

d. Labor force and employment, with percent employed in agriculture, 1981; personal income, 1979; assessed valuation, with percent for industrial, agricultural, and mining/natural resource sectors, 1981; and retail sales. Table 10.

e. AFDC, Aid to Needy and Disabled, and Old Age Pension caseloads, and persons on welfare and eligible for Medicaid, FY81; women needing family planning services; and reported Index crimes and crime rate. Table 11.

EDUCATION

f. Public schools and school districts; primary and secondary school enrollment; immunized students as percent of new enrollments; number of institutions and enrollment for 2- and 4-year public colleges/universities, and all private colleges; and percent of population with high school education; various periods 1978-81. Table 12.

HEALTH AND VITAL STATISTICS

g. Number and rate of live births, marriages, marriage dissolutions, and deaths (total, infant, neonatal, fetal, and perinatal); number of women age 15-44; fertility rate; first born births as percent of total; and low birth weight and illegitimate births; 1980-81. Tables 13-14a.

h. Number and rate of deaths by 10 leading causes, 1980; and rates and/or reported cases for 9 reportable diseases, number of ambulance services and vehicles, emergency medical personnel by level of training, and number of 1st response/nontransport services, 1981. Tables 15-17.

i. Physicians and nurses by type, dentists, and other health professionals by field, various years 1978-80; and hospitals and beds by type, emergency outpatient visits and occupancy rate for general acute care hospitals, nursing homes and beds by type, and nursing home residents, 1979. Tables 18-21.

FAMILY INCOME

j. Median family income; families by income group; and families below poverty level, total and with female householder; 1979. Table 22.

S1035   COLORADO
Judicial Department

S1035–1   ANNUAL REPORT OF THE COLORADO JUDICIARY, July 1, 1982-June 30, 1983
Annual. For individual publication data, see below. ISSN 0094-7504. LC 74-646050. SRI/MF/complete

Annual report, for FY83, on Colorado judicial system, including trial and appellate court caseloads and case dispositions. Covers supreme, appeals, district, and county courts. Includes trial court data by case type, judicial district, and county; and trends from FY65.

Case types include civil and criminal for most courts, with additional detail for domestic relations, probate, juvenile, mental health, small claims, traffic, and other case types.

Data are from reports filed with the Office of the State Court Administrator.

Report is presented in 2 volumes, individually described below.

Availability: Colorado Judicial Department, State Court Administrator's Office, Two E. 14th Ave., Denver CO 80203, $6.00; SRI/MF/complete.

S1035–1.1: Main Report
[Annual. Sept. 22, 1983. iii+119 p. SRI/MF/complete.]

Report on Colorado court organization and activities, FY83. Includes data on trial court caseloads by court type, district, and county, with summary trends from FY80; and supreme and appellate court caseloads by case type, with trends from 1960s or 1970s.

Also includes data on Judicial Dept finances, judicial workloads, water court cases, probation activities, restitution paid to crime victims, and community correction programs.

Contains table of contents (1 p.); table listing (p. i-iii); introductory materials (p. 1-4); and 10 report sections, with narrative, 16 charts, and 39 tables (p. 5-119).

S1035–1.2: Statistical Appendix
[Annual. Aug. 22, 1983. 39 p. SRI/MF/complete.]

Statistical appendix on Colorado court caseloads, FY83. Includes trial court data on filings, terminations, court and jury trials, and civil filings by money amount, all shown by detailed case type, district, and county.

Also includes caseload trends for supreme court and court of appeals.

Contains list of tables (p. i-ii); and 23 tables (p. 3-39).

S1040   COLORADO
Department of Labor and Employment

S1040–3   ANNUAL PLANNING INFORMATION REPORT, FY85, Colorado
Annual.   Apr. 1984.
9+ii+335 p.
SRI/MF/complete

Annual planning report, for FY85, identifying Colorado population groups most in need of employment services. Includes data on population, labor force, and personal income, by county and job service area; and employment by industry and occupation; various periods 1976-86.

Data are primarily from U.S. Dept of Labor and State Division of Employment and Training.

Contents:

a. Contents and table listing (9 p.); and preface and map (p. i-ii).

b. National and State narrative sections, with text data, 2 charts, and 8 tables showing industry and occupational employment outlook for the 1980s, with some projections to 1995; and employment in high-technology industries, by industry group, 1982. (p. 1-29)

c. Statistical sections, with 108 tables, listed below. (p. 33-321)

d. Appendices, with methodology, labor surplus areas eligible for Federal contract preference, poverty guidelines, job service center locations, and glossary. (p. 325-335)

Availability: Colorado Department of Labor and Employment, Employment and Training Division, Research and Development Section, 251 E. 12th Ave., Denver CO 80203, †; SRI/MF/complete.

TABLES:
[Data are shown for Colorado, unless otherwise noted. Data by race or race/ethnicity generally include Hispanics and often Indians, Indians/Eskimos, or Asian/Pacific Islanders.]

S1040–3.1: Population, Labor Force, and Income

[1-2] Estimated labor market data summary [including population]; and individuals requiring employability services [total and long-term unemployed, and persons in poverty, by race]; FY83-86. (p. 33-34)

[3] FY84 annual average estimated [labor force by] employment status, by race and sex. (p. 35)

[4] Population by age, sex, and race/ethnicity, Apr. 1980 and FY85-86. (p. 36)

[5] Labor force estimates [by employment status], by county, annual average 1983. (p. 37)

[6] Unemployment rate ranking, annual average 1983, by county. (p. 38)

[7] Population estimates for counties for Dec. 1983-85 [with Apr. 1980 census population]. (p. 40)

[8-9] Estimate of youth population and labor force [by employment status, with detail for disadvantaged youth]; and estimated youth labor force, by race and Spanish origin [by all or selected counties and selected metro areas], FY84 annual average. (p. 42-51)

[10] Veteran [and Vietnam era veteran] population [and total civilian population age 16/over], by county, 1980 census. (p. 52)

[11-12] Per capita personal income, by county and by JTPA (Job Training Partnership Act) service delivery area, 1976-81. (p. 54-56)

S1040–3.2: Employment and Wages by Industry, and CPI

[1] Estimated industry employment by place of work [industry division, 1984 and 1989, with annual average growth rates and openings due to growth]. (p. 57)

[2] Major industry group forecasts [of employment], FY84-86. (p. 58)

[3] Average weekly wage, by [SIC] 2-digit industry, private sector, 2nd quarter 1983. (p. 62)

[4] Estimated total new hires [due to growth and turnover] by selected major industry groups, FY85-86. (p. 64)

[5] CPI, all items, all urban consumers, U.S. and Denver-Boulder area, [monthly or bimonthly] 1978-83. (p. 68)

S1040–3.3: Employment Services and Local Area Data

STATE DATA

[1] Over-the-year change analysis of services to individuals [types of services performed for all, female, youth, veterans (total and Vietnam era), minority, and migrant/seasonal farmworker applicants], FY82-83. (p. 69)

[2] Colorado Employment and Training Division job service [total and female] applicants by occupation, [by age group, veterans and handicapped status, and educational attainment, by race/ethnicity], FY 83. (p. 70-75)

[3] Operating report data [caseloads and services performed] for FY83 vs. FY82, E.S. [Employment Services] programs, [by job service center], Sept. 1983. (p. 76-80)

[4] Characteristics of the insured unemployed [including sex, race/ethnicity, occupation, industry division and selected SIC 2-digit industry, unemployment duration, age, selected metro area, and county, and data for interstate claimants, with selected cross-tabulations], annual average 1983. (p. 81-95)

DENVER/BOULDER LABOR MARKET AREA

[5] Major industry division forecasts [of employment], FY84-86, [and actual employment, FY83]. (p. 99)

[6-9] [Tables [1-4] listed above under S1040-3.1 are repeated for Denver/Boulder labor market area.] (p. 100-103)

[10] Estimated annual number of new hires due to turnover, by selected [SIC 2-digit industries], FY85. (p. 104)

[11] [Table [2] listed above under S1040-3.3 is repeated for Denver/Boulder labor market area.] (p. 106-111)

SERVICE DELIVERY AREAS

[12-91] [Repeats the following for each of 10 JTPA service delivery areas: tables [5-11] as described for Denver/Boulder labor market area; and 1 table showing average monthly number of dislocated workers provided services by type of service, by age, sex, educational attainment, race/ethnicity, and for veterans, handicapped, welfare recipients, migrant and

seasonal workers, and economically disadvantaged, FY84 (through Feb. 29).] (p. 113-321)

S1040–4   COLORADO LABOR FORCE REVIEW
Monthly, with annual supplement.   Approx. 25 p.
SRI/MF/complete, shipped quarterly

Monthly report (not published for Dec.), with annual supplement, on Colorado employment and unemployment, earnings, hours, and economic indicators comprising the Colorado Business Composite (CBC). Includes selected data by industry and locale, and comparisons to neighboring States and U.S. Also includes Denver CPI.

Data are from State, Federal, and private sources. Report is issued 2 months after month of data coverage.

Contains contents listing; Colorado and Denver/Boulder narrative reviews; occasional special articles, sometimes containing statistics; CBC feature, with trend charts, 2 monthly tables, and quarterly employment summary; statistical section, with 7 monthly tables; and quarterly feature on insured unemployment, with 2 tables.

Annual statistical features on Colorado labor market developments and outlook appear in the Jan. Data Supplement and Oct. issue, respectively.

Monthly and quarterly tables are listed below. Monthly tables appear in all issues. All additional features with substantial statistical content are described, as they appear, under "Statistical Features;" page locations and latest periods of coverage for quarterly tables are also noted. Nonstatistical features are not covered.

Availability: Colorado Department of Labor and Employment, Employment and Training Division, Labor Market Information Section, 251 E. 12th Ave., Denver CO 80203, †; SRI/MF/complete, shipped quarterly.

Issues reviewed during 1984: Aug. 1983-Aug. 1984 (D) (Vol. XX, Nos. 8-11; Vol. XXI, Nos. 1-8); and Jan. 1984 Data Supplement (P).

TABLES:

MONTHLY TABLES
[Tables [3-8] show data for month of coverage, usually with comparison to previous 1-2 months and same month of previous year.]

[1-2] CBC, and data series for leading indicators comprising CBC [including State stock market index, bank deposits, housing permits, and business formation index, monthly for current year to date and approximately 10 previous years].

[3] Seasonally adjusted labor force data [total employment, unemployment, and nonagricultural wage/salary jobs by industry division, for State and Denver/Boulder labor market area (LMA)].

[4] Denver area CPI by component [in alternate months presents data for all items and for food at home].

[5] State and Denver/Boulder LMA [unemployment, agricultural and nonagricultural employment, wage/salary employment by major industry group, and labor disputants].

[6] Colorado labor force estimates [employment and unemployment, by county and SMSA and for Denver/Boulder LMA].

[7] Hours and earnings for selected industries [State and Denver/Boulder LMA].

[8] Selected monthly activities, Division of Employment [unemployment insurance claims and benefits, and employment service applications and placements; State and Denver area].

[9] Area labor force comparisons [unemployment and employment, for U.S., Colorado, and 6 neighboring States; previous month].

QUARTERLY TABLES

[1-2] Characteristics of the insured unemployed [industry, occupation, age, weeks unemployed, and sex, usually for quarter ending 1 month after month of coverage, previous quarter, and same quarter of previous year; with detail for current quarter, including data by race, for Hispanics, and for major LMAs].

[3] Colorado quarterly [employment] summary [average employment for current and previous 4 quarters].

STATISTICAL FEATURES:

S1040–4.501: Sept. 1983 (Vol. XX, No. 9)

QUARTERLY TABLE

[3] Colorado quarterly employment summary, for 3rd quarter 1983. (p. 5)

INDUSTRIAL COMPOSITION OF THE LABOR FORCE

(p. 10-13) Article, with 2 tables showing Colorado and U.S. nonagricultural employment percent change and distribution, by industry division and for total goods and services industries, with selected detail for 4 Colorado areas, various periods 1950-82.

S1040–4.502: Oct. 1983 (Vol. XX, No. 10)

QUARTERLY TABLES

[1-2] Characteristics of the insured unemployed, for 3rd quarter 1983. (p. 11-15)

COLORADO LABOR MARKET OUTLOOK, ANNUAL FEATURE

(p. 9-10) Annual article on labor market outlook, based on projections by over 60 business and government leaders attending the 19th annual Business-Economic Outlook Forum, held Dec. 1983. Includes 1 table showing unemployment and rate, employment by type, and wage/salary employment by industry division, 1982-84.

S1040–4.503: Nov. 1983 (Vol. XX, No. 11)

QUARTERLY TABLES

[1-2] Characteristics of the insured unemployed, for 4th quarter 1983. (p. 8-11)

S1040–4.504: Jan. 1984 Data Supplement

1983 LABOR MARKET DEVELOPMENTS, ANNUAL FEATURE

(p. 2-3) Annual article, with 1 table showing average annual growth or loss in employment, including changes in poorest and best years, by industry division, various periods 1973-83.

REVISED STATISTICS, ANNUAL FEATURE

(p. 4-27) Annual data revisions, with 21 tables showing trends or revisions for selected topics covered in monthly tables, various years 1976-83.

S1040–4.505: Feb. 1984 (Vol. XXI, No. 2)

QUARTERLY TABLES

[1-2] Characteristics of the insured unemployed, for 1st quarter 1984. (p. 8-11)

S1040–4.506: Mar. 1984 (Vol. XXI, No. 3)

QUARTERLY TABLE

[3] Colorado quarterly employment summary, for 1st quarter 1984. (p. 5)

WOMEN IN COLORADO'S LABOR FORCE

(p. 10-11) Article, with 2 tables showing 10 Colorado counties with highest and lowest labor force participation rate and median income for women, 1979 or 1980. Data are from Census Bureau.

S1040–4.507: Apr. 1984 (Vol. XXI, No. 4)

MILITARY IS TOP INCOME GAINER DURING 1982, ANNUAL FEATURE

(p. 7-9) Annual article, with 2 tables showing Colorado total and per capita personal income, by industry division and for Federal military, by county, 1982, with summary income growth from 1977 compared to U.S. Data are from Commerce Dept.

S1040–4.508: May 1984 (Vol. XXI, No. 5)

QUARTERLY TABLES

[1-2] Characteristics of the insured unemployed, for 2nd quarter 1984. (p. 9-12)

COLORADO ANNUAL PLANNING INFORMATION

(p. 13-18) By Kenneth McNulty. Article, with 1 table showing Colorado employment by industry division, actual FY83 and forecasts for FY84-86.

S1040–4.509: June 1984 (Vol. XXI, No. 6)

QUARTERLY TABLE

[3] Colorado quarterly employment summary, for 2nd quarter 1984. (p. 6)

S1040–4.510: Aug. 1984 (Vol. XXI, No. 8)

QUARTERLY TABLES

[1-2] Characteristics of the insured unemployed, for 3rd quarter 1984. (p. 10-14)

S1055   COLORADO
Department of Local Affairs

S1055–1   CRIME IN COLORADO: Uniform Crime Report, 1983
Annual. [1984.] 2+81 p.
SRI/MF/complete

Annual report, for 1983, on Colorado crimes and arrests, by type of offense, county, and local law enforcement agency. Also includes data on clearances, assaults on police, and offender characteristics; and selected comparisons to 1982.

Data are from reports from sheriff depts and municipal and other local law enforcement agencies, submitted under the Uniform Crime Reporting Program to State Bureau of Investigation.

Contains contents listing and introduction (p. 1-2); definitions and 3 summary tables (p. 3-5); and 24 detailed tables, described below (p. 7-81).

Availability: Colorado Department of Local Affairs, Investigation Bureau, 2002 S. Colorado Blvd., Denver CO 80222, †; SRI/MF/complete.

TABLES:

[Data are for 1983, unless otherwise noted. Index crimes covered are: criminal homicide, forcible rape, robbery, assault, burglary, larceny-theft, and motor vehicle theft. Arson is classified as an Index offense, but data are reported separately and are not included in the Crime Index totals. Non-Index crimes include 19 other categories.]

a. Index offenses reported by type and circumstances of crime, including robbery and assault weapon, cross-tabulated by county and local law enforcement agency, with population by county, and total clearances for each agency. 2 tables. (p. 9-17)

b. Value of property stolen and recovered, by property type; value of property stolen, by Index offense; and number of stolen/recovered vehicles. 3 tables, repeated for State and each county. (p. 21-53)

c. Arson incidents, total and juvenile clearances, and dollar loss, by type of structure or vehicle. 1 table. (p. 54)

d. Arrest trends, including statewide data for juvenile and adult arrests, by sex and offense, 1982-83; and adult and juvenile arrests, by Index and non-Index offense, by county and local law enforcement agency. 4 tables. (p. 56-75)

e. Assaults on law enforcement officers, by type of activity, assignment, weapon, injury status, and time of day; and assaults cleared. 6 tables. (p. 76-77)

f. Criminal homicide: victims and offenders, by age, sex, and race/ethnicity (including Indian and Asian); and persons killed or offenses, by type of weapon, month, and victim/offender relationship; 1982-83. 8 tables. (p. 79-81)

S1055–3   STATE OF COLORADO, 1983: Thirteenth Annual Report, Division of Property Taxation
Annual. May 3, 1984.
2+207 p.
SRI/MF/complete

Annual report on Colorado assessed property valuations, tax levies, and tax revenues, including data by property class, county, and local improvement and service district, mostly 1982-83. Property classes include residential, commercial, industrial, agricultural, pollution control, natural resource, and public utility properties.

Contents:

Section I-II. Table of contents, lists of dept officials and county assessors, and administrative information. (2 p., p. 1-5)

Section III. Assessed valuation: total, 1870-1983; and by property class and type, 1982-83. 3 tables. (p. 8-10)

Section IV. Property tax revenue, by jurisdiction type, selected years 1930-83. 1 chart and 2 tables. (p. 12-13)

Section V. Public utility assessed valuation, by county, utility type, and company, 1982-83. 4 tables. (p. 16-27)

Section VI-VIII. Property and improvement assessed valuation, and number of taxable units, by detailed property class; exempt property and improvement valuation, by type (including government, religious, private school, and charities); and assessment summary; all by county, mostly 1982-83. 96 tables. (p. 31-94)

Section IX. Listing of municipal governments, and local districts. (p. 96-104)

Section X. Property tax levy and revenues for bond redemption and other funds, and assessed valuation, by purpose, city/town, and/or local district, by county, as of Jan. 1, 1984. 3 tables repeated for each county. (p. 106-201)

Section XI. Revenue and levy summary, 1982-83; and disposition of property tax petitions, 1981-83; by county. 4 tables. (p. 204-207)

Availability: Colorado Department of Local Affairs, Property Taxation Division, 1313 Sherman St., 623 State Centennial Bldg., Denver CO 80203, ‡; SRI/MF/complete.

S1060   COLORADO
Department of
Natural Resources

S1060-1   COLORADO SMALL GAME, FURBEARER, AND VARMINT HARVEST
Annual, discontinued coverage.

Annual report described in SRI 1983 Annual, under this number. SRI selection criteria now exclude State reports on wildlife, hunting, and fishing. Coverage of this report will not be continued.

S1070   COLORADO
Department of
Regulatory Agencies

S1070-1   COLORADO INSURANCE INDUSTRY Statistical Report, 1982
Annual. 1984. xx+172 p.
ISSN 0361-6568.
LC 81-642980.
SRI/MF/complete

Annual report on Colorado insurance industry financial condition and underwriting activity, by company and type of insurance, 1982. Covers assets, liabilities, capital, surplus, operating gain/loss, investment/other income, dividends, premiums earned, losses incurred or claims paid, loss ratios, and insurance written and in force; for companies based in Colorado and elsewhere.

Data are shown, as applicable, for multiple line, fire, casualty, and life insurance companies, with underwriting detail by line of coverage, including accident/health, workers compensation, medical malpractice, automobile, and fidelity/surety.

Data are also shown for fraternal benefit assns, county mutual protective assns, reciprocal or interinsurance exchanges, title insurance companies, nonprofit health service corporations, HMOs, and captive insurance companies.

Also includes data on Insurance Division finances and operations, including consumer com-

plaints received and resolved, and fee and tax receipts, FY83; underwriting trends from as early as 1900; trust funds and/or contracts in force, for sellers of cemetery space and funeral contracts; and licensed motor clubs.

Contains contents listing (p. i); Insurance Division summary, with text statistics, 4 charts, and 5 tables (p. ii-xx); and report, with directories and 29 financial tables (p. 1-172).

Availability: Colorado Department of Regulatory Agencies, Insurance Division, 303 W. Colfax Ave., Suite 500, Denver CO 80204, $5.00; SRI/MF/complete.

S1070-2   SEVENTY-FOURTH ANNUAL REPORT OF STATE BANK COMMISSIONER of the State of Colorado, 1983
Annual. Dec. 31, 1983.
371 p.
SRI/MF/complete

Annual report on financial condition of Colorado State-chartered financial institutions, 1983, presenting assets, liabilities, and equity capital, aggregate and by institution, for commercial and industrial banks, and for trust companies. Aggregate data include comparison to 1982.

Also includes aggregate assets, liabilities/capital, loans, and income and expenses of credit unions.

Data are compiled from annual reports submitted to the Division of Banking by all institutions.

Contains lists of State banking personnel and officials (p. 2-3); commercial bank section, prefaced with data on new bank charters and capital stock changes (p. 4-206); trust company section (p. 207-213); and industrial bank section (p. 214-371). Each section generally includes regulatory amendments, alphabetical index, 1 summary table, and 1 table repeated for each institution.

Availability: Colorado Department of Regulatory Agencies, Banking Division, 303 W. Colfax Ave., Suite 700, Denver CO 80204, $15.00; SRI/MF/complete.

S1070-3   FINANCIAL REPORT ON COLORADO STATE CHARTERED SAVINGS AND LOAN ASSOCIATIONS, 1983
Annual. May 1984. 3+24 p.
SRI/MF/complete

Annual report on financial condition of Colorado State-chartered savings and loan assns, presenting assets, liabilities, and net worth, by institution, 1983; and composite financial and operating data, 1980-83.

Data are compiled from reports filed with Division of Savings and Loan.

Contains table of contents (1 p.); summary, and directory of savings and loan assns and officers (p. 1-13); and 3 financial tables (p. 14-24).

Availability: Colorado Department of Regulatory Agencies, Savings and Loan Division, 1525 Sherman St., Rm. 110, Denver CO 80203, $2.00; SRI/MF/complete.

S1075   COLORADO
Department of
Revenue

S1075-1   ANNUAL REPORT, 1983, Colorado Department of Revenue
Annual. Dec. 23, 1983.
152 p.
LC 43-52674.
SRI/MF/complete

Annual report on Colorado tax revenues, by type of tax, FY83, with trends from FY50. Includes sales tax by county, municipality, and industry. Also includes data on motor vehicle registrations and accidents, driver's licenses, and State lottery revenues.

Contains contents listing (p. 1-2); 1 table showing Colorado population by county, 1970, 1980, and 1982 (p. 3); narrative report on Revenue Dept organization and State tax legislation (p. 7-37); and 10 statistical sections, with statutory references, tax rates or fees, facsimile tax reporting forms, 1 chart, and 56 tables listed below (p. 41-152).

This is the 42nd annual report.

Availability: Colorado Department of Revenue, State Capitol Annex Bldg., 1375 Sherman St., Rm. 486, Denver CO 80261, †; SRI/MF/complete.

S1075-1.1: Collections, Refunds, and Administrative Costs
[Data are shown for FY83, unless otherwise noted.]

[1] Total collections and cost of administration, FY50-83. (p. 41)

[2-3] Collections [FY82-83]; and refunds and net collections, FY83; by source. (p. 42-44)

[4] Gross collections and cost of administration, by fund and tax source. (p. 45)

[5] Administrative expenditures, by purpose. (p. 47)

[6] Number of audits, assessments, and refunds [by tax section]. (p. 48)

S1075-1.2: Alcoholic Beverage and Cigarette Taxes

ALCOHOLIC BEVERAGE TAXES

[1] Comparison of [liquor tax] receipts and refunds, FY81-83. (p. 53)

[2] Liquor tax statistical summary [receipts from license fees by type, and from excise tax], FY83. (p. 54)

[3] Taxable gallons of beer, wine, and spirituous liquors, FY72-83. (p. 55)

[4-5] Liquor licenses in force [by type, FY83]; and total number of State liquor licenses issued, by county [1978-82]. (p. 56-57)

[6-7] Violations of the liquor code and 3.2% Beer Act [hearings, revocations, suspensions, denials, court cases, and local hearings]; and activities of field men; FY81-83. (p. 58)

CIGARETTE TAX

[8-9] Cigarette tax [gross amount, wholesaler's discount, refunds, and gross and net collections]; and distribution of net collections [city/county and State shares]; FY74-83. (p. 62)

S1075–1.3: Estate and Income Taxes and Lottery Revenues

ESTATE TAX

[1] Estate, inheritance, and gift tax activity, [returns/documents reviewed, and statements/certificates/receipts and refunds issued, FY82-83]. (p. 67)

[2] Estate, inheritance, and gift tax net collections, FY71-83. (p. 68)

INCOME TAX

[Tables [3-4] and [7-10] show data by type of return: individual, corporation, and fiduciary.]

[3] Number of taxable and nontaxable returns [also includes partnership returns], FY83. (p. 74)

[4] Tax liability [FY73-83]. (p. 75)

[5] Surtax liability [for individual returns, FY74-83]. (p. 75)

[6] Number of individual returns and adjusted gross income, FY71-83. (p. 76)

[7] Tax liability, credits, payments, and overpayments, FY83. (p. 77)

[8-10] Refunds issued [FY77-83]. (p. 78)

[11] Returns filed for old age property tax/heat credits [and refund/credit amount, FY72-83]. (p. 79)

LOTTERY REVENUES

[12] Lottery sales [and days in game, by game], FY83. (p. 85)

[13] 1983 lottery distributions by fund. (p. 86)

S1075–1.4: Mileage/Fuel and Motor Vehicle Taxes, and Other Motor Vehicle Data

MILEAGE/FUEL TAXES

[1] Motor fuel: gross gallons, gallons exempted, and net gallons taxed, FY82-83. (p. 91)

[2] Motor and special fuel tax refund, by use, FY82-83. (p. 92)

[3] Motor fuel: gross gasoline gallonage [by month, FY79-83]. (p. 93)

[4] Special fuel tax gallonage and collections, FY75-83. (p. 94)

[5] Motor fuel, diesel fuel, LPG [liquefied petroleum gas], and other taxable fuel collections [including gasohol], FY82-83. (p. 94)

[6] Gross ton-mile tax [collections and refunds], FY74-83. (p. 95)

[7-8] Port of entry truck activities [includes special fuel permits, agricultural licenses and inspection certificates, and health/brand inspections, FY81-83]; and trucks cleared and weighed, by port, FY83. (p. 96-97)

MOTOR VEHICLE DATA

[9] License fees and ownership tax collected [by county], 1982. (p. 105)

[10] Number of registrations, by type of license, by county, 1982. (p. 106)

[11] Motor vehicle emissions program [licensing activity, certificates sold, and collections], FY83. (p. 109)

[12] Standard summary of motor vehicle traffic accidents, [injuries and fatalities; includes detailed data by accident and vehicle type; location; age and sex of driver and victim, including data for pedestrians and bicyclists; mileage traveled; contributing circumstances; and helmet and eye protection use; 1982, with summary comparisons to 1981]. (p. 110)

[13] Driver's license activity [types of licenses and permits issued, endorsements, and examinations, at total State and county offices], 1982. (p. 112)

[14] Driver improvement [license suspensions, revocations, denials, and cancellations, by type; reinstatements; and financial responsibility reports received; 1981-82]. (p. 113)

S1075–1.5: Sales and Use Taxes, and Severance Tax

SALES AND USE TAXES

[Data are shown for FY83, unless otherwise noted. Data by business class are shown by industry division, with additional detail for hotels/lodging and types of retail trade.]

[1-2] Sales tax collections; and [consumer and retailer] use tax; FY74-83. (p. 119-120)

[3-4] Number of returns, gross sales, deductions, and net taxable sales; and retail sales, by county; by business class. (p. 121-123)

[5-6] Retail trade sales and retail sales; by county, 1973-82. (p. 124-125)

[7] Number of returns, sales by type of sales, and sales tax, by county. (p. 126)

[8] Number of returns, retail sales, and net tax collected, by business class. (p. 128)

[9] Gross sales, retail sales, and net tax collected, for selected cities [and] by county. (p. 131-140)

[10] Summary of local sales tax rates: number of tax jurisdictions, by tax rate. (p. 141)

[11-13] County and city sales tax rates collected by the State; and city sales [tax rates] not collected by the State. (p. 142-145)

SEVERANCE TAX

[14] Severance tax collections [for oil/gas, coal, and metallic minerals/molybdenum, FY78-83]. (p. 152)

S1085 COLORADO
Department of
Social Services

S1085–1 COLORADO STATE DEPARTMENT OF SOCIAL SERVICES Annual Report, FY82

Annual. [1983.] 52 p.
SRI/MF/complete

Annual report on Colorado public assistance program cases, recipients, and payments, by program and county, FY82 and trends. Covers food stamp, AFDC, Medicaid, veteran assistance, aging, pension, child welfare, energy assistance, and other programs. Also includes data on reported child abuse cases.

Contains contents listing (1 p.); statutory authority and transmittal letter (p. 1-2); program data with brief narratives, and 3 charts and 27 tables listed below (p. 3-49); and membership listings for State social service commissions (p. 50-52).

For description of previous report, for FY81, see SRI 1982 Annual, under this number.

Availability: Colorado Department of Social Services, 1575 Sherman St., Rm. 619, Denver CO 80203, †; SRI/MF/complete.

CHARTS AND TABLES:

[Data are for Colorado, FY82, unless otherwise noted.]

SUMMARY AND MEDICAL ASSISTANCE

[1] Dept of Social Services expenditures [of State and Federal funds, by function or program including vocational rehabilitation]. (p. 3-4)

[2] Estimated Medicaid and OAP [old age pension] health and medical fund [payments] by type of recipient. [chart] (p. 10)

[3] [Social Services Dept] appropriations/expenditures [by program]. [chart] (p. 11)

[4] Medicaid payments by category of services. [chart] (p. 12)

CHILD WELFARE AND VETERAN SERVICES

[5] [Child abuse cases reported, 1970-81.] (p. 15)

[6] Interstate compact on the placement of children [in- and out-of-State placements by type, and case disposition, July 1980-June 1981]. (p. 18)

[7] Services summary [including adoptions, daycare, and homemaker and family planning services; recipients by program and county, FY81]. (p. 19-20)

[8] Veterans affairs program [caseload distribution]. (p. 21)

[9] [Veterans' nursing homes: capacity, occupancy, and cost per day, by facility, FY81-82]. (p. 22)

[10] Veterans affairs [awards and monetary recoveries FY81-82; and awards and payments, by type of benefit, FY82]. (p. 23)

ENERGY ASSISTANCE, AFDC, AND CHILD SUPPORT

[11] Low income energy assistance program [cases and expenditures by program, FY81-82]. (p. 25)

[12-13] AFDC [net expenditures, FY78-82; and average monthly caseloads and recipients, FY67-82]. (p. 26)

[14] Average monthly data, AFDC [cases and expenditures], by county. (p. 27-28)

[15-16] Child support enforcement program [collections, expenditures, and cases], FY81-82; and caseload and collections, by county, FY82. (p. 30-32)

REFUGEE SERVICES, PENSIONS, AND MEDICAL ASSISTANCE

[17] Refugee services program [cases and expenditures, FY78-82]. (p. 33)

[18-23] OAP, aid to the needy disabled, and aid to blind/blind treatment [expenditures, and cases or recipients, FY78-82, and by county, FY82]. (p. 34-42)

[24] Average monthly Medicaid eligibles [cases by county]. (p. 44)

FOOD ASSISTANCE PROGRAMS

[25] Average monthly number of household participation [in food stamp program, for public assistance recipients and others, FY71-82]. (p. 45)

[26] Food stamp program [value of coupons issued, estimated economic impact, public assistance and other households participating, and recipients, by county and district]. (p. 46-47)

[27] [Donated foods] dollar value and net weight of food issued [by program, including school lunch and breakfast]. (p. 48)

S1155   CONNECTICUT
Department of Agriculture

S1155–1   CONNECTICUT AGRICULTURAL STATISTICS, 1982
Annual. Nov. 1983. 62 p.
ISSN 0573-6269.
LC 82-641380.
SRI/MF/complete

Annual report on Connecticut agricultural production, marketing, and finances, 1982, with some data for 1983 and trends from 1971. Data are generally shown by commodity.

Report covers production, prices, cash receipts, value, and, as applicable, acreage, yield, inventory, and/or disposition, for field crop, vegetable, fruit, livestock, dairy, and poultry sectors.

Also includes data on number of farms and acreage; farm assets, debt, and production expenses; weather; value of agricultural exports; dairy farm inspections; milk pasteurizing plants; farmland preservation program; shellfish harvest and licenses; Northeast or New England region comparisons, including production expenses; and U.S. per capita consumption of major food commodities.

Data are primarily from Connecticut Dept of Agriculture and USDA.

Contains contents listing (1 p.); highlights, and statistical section with 8 charts and 55 tables (p. 1-35); and State Dept of Agriculture activities, with 10 text tables (p. 40-62).

Availability: Connecticut Department of Agriculture, Marketing Division, State Office Bldg., Hartford CT 06106, †; SRI/MF/complete.

S1160   CONNECTICUT
Department of Banking

S1160–1   ANNUAL REPORT OF THE BANKING COMMISSIONER of the State of Connecticut, for the Year Ended Dec. 31, 1983
Annual. 1983. vi+232 p.
LC 6-3169.
SRI/MF/complete

Annual report on financial condition of Connecticut State-chartered financial institutions, presenting assets, liabilities, income, and expenses by institution, and composite securities and/or operating data, generally for State banks and trust companies, savings banks, savings and loan assns, credit unions, and small loan licensees; 1983 with comparative trends from 1944.

Also includes data on Banking Dept receipts and expenditures; bank trust dept accounts and funds; savings bank life insurance issued; Connecticut Development Credit Corp. balance sheet; assets of bank holding companies, national banks, and Federal savings and loan assns; small loan company credit life insurance; and Securities Division data, including enforcement activities, and broker-dealer and investment adviser registrants by main-office State.

Contains contents and table listings (p. iv-vi); and report, with text data, 1 chart, and 57 tables, interspersed with directories, including branch offices by city (p. 1-232).

Availability: Connecticut Department of Banking, Banking Commissioner's Office, State Office Bldg., 165 Capitol Ave., Hartford CT 06106, $15.00; SRI/MF/complete.

S1170   CONNECTICUT
Office of the Comptroller

S1170–1   REPORT OF THE STATE COMPTROLLER TO THE GOVERNOR for the Fiscal Year Ended June 30, 1983, Connecticut
Annual. Aug. 31, 1983.
106 p.
Public Document No. 1.
LC 83-645088.
SRI/MF/complete

Annual report on financial condition of Connecticut State government, FY83, presenting assets and liabilities, reserves, fund balances, and surplus; receipts by source; and disbursements by function; for all, general, special revenue, debt service, capital project, internal service, enterprise, and fiduciary funds.

Also includes data on general fund budgeted vs. realized revenues by source, and appropriations vs. expenditures by detailed agency and program; bonded debt; current expenses by type, fixed charges, capital outlays, and property valuation, by agency; and inventory trends from FY79.

Data are from the records of the comptroller's office.

Contains contents listing and certificate of audit (p. 2-4); and 25 exhibits and schedules (p. 5-106).

Availability: Connecticut Office of the Comptroller, Central Accounting Division, 30 Trinity St., Hartford CT 06106, †; SRI/MF/complete.

S1185   CONNECTICUT
Department of Education

S1185–1   CONNECTICUT PUBLIC SCHOOLS: Condition of Education, 1981/82
Annual. For individual publication data, see below.
SRI/MF/complete

Annual report, for 1981/82, on Connecticut public schools, covering finances, programs, personnel, and students. Data are compiled from school district reports, State Dept of Education studies, and other sources.

Report is issued in 2 volumes as follows:

  Vol. 1: Annual report of programs and evaluations of Connecticut State Board of Education.

  Vol. 2: Town and school district profiles.

Volumes are individually described below. Previous report, for 1980/81, included a 3rd volume, presenting extensive statistics on Connecticut education trends. Issuing agency does not plan to publish Volume 3 for 1981/82.

Availability: Connecticut Department of Education, Research, Planning, and Evaluation Bureau, PO Box 2219, Hartford CT 06115, †; SRI/MF/complete.

S1185–1.1: Volume 1: Annual Report of Elementary and Secondary Programs and Evaluations
[Annual. 1983. 238 p. SRI/MF/complete.]

Compilation of narrative reports on State Dept of Education division activities, with interspersed data, including summary financial and staff data for most divisions and bureaus.

Also includes data on Board of Education expenditures and authorized personnel, Dept programs and grants administered, teacher certificates awarded and certification fees collected, and General Educational Development applications processed and diplomas issued, generally 1980/81-1981/82.

Contains contents listing (1 p.); preface, and overview, with organizational chart and 2 tables (p. 1-12); and division reports, with text tables (p. 13-238).

S1185–1.2: Volume 2: Town and School District Profiles
[Annual. Oct. 1983. vi+374 p. BRPE Pub. No. 83-10. LC 81-640868. SRI/MF/complete.]

Contains contents listing and preface (p. v-vi); statistical profiles, each generally including tabular listing of program offerings, and 3-10 tables as indicated below (p. 1-355); and definitions and sources, and index (p. 357-374).

TABLES:

STATEWIDE

[1] Community data [including population; per capita income; equalized property value; percent students enrolled in public schools and population age 25/over completing high school and college; percent children in single-parent families; median family income; percent families below poverty level; and median value of housing units; various years 1979-80]. (p. 2)

[2] District students [including minority, special education, non-English home language, economically disadvantaged, and nonresident students; students in vocational/technical schools and vocational/agriculture centers; and high school graduates, with distribution by postgraduate activity], 1981/82. (p. 2)

[3] EERA [Education Evaluation and Remedial Assistance] 9th grade proficiency test results [by subject], fall 1981. (p. 2)

[4] Staff data [number of total professional staff, teachers, support staff, and administrators; per pupil ratios; mean age, experience, and salary; percent with Master's/higher degree; and staff cost per pupil], 1981/82. (p. 3)

[5-7] Revenue data and selected State and Federal grants, 1981/82. (p. 3)

[8] Educational equalization data [per capita property value, equalized school tax rate, and student need]; 1980/81. (p. 3)

[9] Aid and expenditure data [per pupil equalization aid and minimum expenditure requirement; and percent for special education, transportation, and school construction]; 1982/83. (p. 3)

[10] Expenditure data [total and per pupil, and State median per pupil, by function], 1981/82. (p. 3)

TOWNS THAT OPERATE SCHOOL DISTRICTS

Tables [1-10] are generally repeated for each town operating a school district. Table [8] includes State rankings; table 10 includes expenditure comparisons to State median; and table [3] is omitted for some towns. (p. 6-303).

TOWNS THAT DO NOT OPERATE SCHOOL DISTRICTS

Tables [1] and [8-9] are generally repeated for each town not operating a school district. Table [8] includes State rankings; and table [9] omits detailed distribution. (p. 306-315)

REGIONAL DISTRICTS

Tables [2-10] are generally repeated for each regional school district. Table [10] includes expenditure comparisons to State median. (p. 318-349)

MISCELLANEOUS SCHOOLS

Tables [2-4] are repeated for 3 endowed/incorporated academies and E. O. Smith School. (p. 352-355)

S1222   CONNECTICUT
Insurance Department

S1222–1   STATE OF CONNECTICUT One-Hundred Seventeenth Annual Report of the Insurance Commissioner, 1983
Annual.   Oct. 11, 1983.
3+109 p.
SRI/MF/complete

Annual report on Connecticut insurance industry financial condition and underwriting activity, by company and type of insurance, 1982. Covers assets, liabilities, capital/guaranty fund, surplus, and premiums written; for life, fire/casualty, and title companies.

Premium data are generally shown by line of coverage, including accident/health, medical malpractice, workmen's compensation, automobile, and surety.

Data are compiled from annual statements submitted by individual insurers.

Contains contents listing (1 p.); 9 tables (p. 1-106); and table addenda (p. 107-109).

Availability: Connecticut Insurance Department, 165 Capitol Ave., Hartford CT 06106, $28.25; SRI/MF/complete.

S1235   CONNECTICUT
Labor Department

S1235–1   CONNECTICUT LABOR SITUATION
Monthly.   Approx. 10 p.
SRI/MF/complete, shipped quarterly

Monthly report on Connecticut nonagricultural employment, earnings, hours, and selected other economic indicators. Data are from State labor records, and are shown by industry group and labor market area. Month of coverage is 1 month prior to cover date.

Contains narrative summary with text statistics; 8 monthly tables, listed below; an annual article on labor force demographic composition; and occasional special articles or summary tables, including data from BLS annual area wage surveys.

Monthly tables appear in all issues; Dec. 1983 issue also includes 1 additional table showing summary wages and employment, by industry group and kind of business, 1982. Additional features with substantial nonsummary statistical content are described, as they appear, under "Statistical Features." Nonstatistical features are not covered.

The Employment Security Division also issues a biweekly press release on unemployment claims; and monthly or quarterly reviews of conditions in each of the States' 16 labor market areas. These reports are not covered by SRI.

Availability: Connecticut Labor Department, Employment Security Division, Research and Information Office, 200 Folly Brook Blvd., Wethersfield CT 06109, †; SRI/MF/complete, shipped quarterly.

Issues reviewed during 1984: Nov. 1983-Oct. 1984 (P).

MONTHLY TABLES:

[Tables [1-6] show data for month of coverage, previous month, and same month of previous year. Table 8 begins in the Feb. 1984 issue.]

[1] Nonagricultural employment (excluding domestics/self-employed) [by industry division and major group].

[2] Earnings and hours, manufacturing production/related workers [by major industry group] and on-site construction workers.

[3] Unemployment, by [labor market] area.

[4] U.S. CPI, all urban consumers.

[5] Area nonagricultural wage/salary employment, by place of work [manufacturing and nonmanufacturing, by labor market area].

[6] Earnings and hours by labor market area, manufacturing/production/maintenance/related workers.

[7] Connecticut economic indicators [employment, average weekly initial unemployment benefit claims, unemployment rate, personal income, new auto registrations, average workweek hours, and manufacturing output index; monthly for year to date and previous year].

[8] Unemployment insurance benefit financial data [insured unemployed, benefits paid, and employer contributions, monthly for year to date and previous year, with trends from the 1970s; Federal loans and direct repayments,

and repayments via employer tax credit reduction, annually from the 1970s; and loans outstanding and State Unemployment Compensation Fund balance, as of 2 months prior to cover date].

STATISTICAL FEATURE:

S1235–1.501: Sept. 1984
PROFILE OF THE LABOR FORCE IN CONNECTICUT, 1983, ANNUAL FEATURE
(p. 10-11) Annual article, with 2 tables showing Connecticut population, labor force by employment status, and employment distribution by occupation, all by race and sex, with detail for youth, 1982-83. Data are from BLS.

S1242   CONNECTICUT
State
Library

S1242–1   PUBLIC LIBRARY STATISTICAL REPORT, 1983, Connecticut
Annual.   May 1983.   2+19 p.
SRI/MF/complete

Annual report on Connecticut public library holdings, circulation, finances, and staff, FY82. Data are from public library annual reports.

Contents:

Map, and list of Connecticut State library personnel (2 p.); and introduction, contents listing, and explanations of data categories (p. 1-3).

Section 1-2. Statewide statistics, with 1 highlights table; and 7 summary tables showing mean, median, and percentile values for selected per capita operating and financial data, by population size group. (p. 4-5)

Section 3-4. 2 extended tables showing Cooperating Library Service Unit membership; weekly hours; branches; FTE staff and union membership; book, nonbook, and periodical holdings; circulation; income from local taxes, State, and other sources; and expenditures including wages/salaries; all by library, arranged by town and population size group, FY82, with population served and rank for each town, 1980. (p. 6-19)

Previous report, for FY81, is described in SRI 1982 Annual under this number.

Availability: Connecticut State Library, 231 Capitol Ave., Hartford CT 06106, †; SRI/MF/complete.

S1255   CONNECTICUT
Office of
Policy and Management

S1255-5   CONNECTICUT OCCUPATIONAL STATISTICS OF THE CIVILIAN LABOR FORCE for Equal Employment Opportunity and Affirmative Action Planning: 1980 Census of Population and Housing, EEO Special File
Monograph.   For individual publication data, see below.
LC 84-621075.
SRI/MF/complete

Report presenting 1980 census data, for Connecticut, on civilian labor force by detailed occupation, cross-tabulated by sex and race-ethnicity (black, white, Hispanic, American Indian/Eskimo, Asian/Pacific Islander, and other). Data are shown by county, SMSA, and for cities with population 50,000/over.

Also includes summary data on employment and unemployment by major occupational category.

Data are from the Equal Employment Opportunity Special File, which is based on the long-form questionnaire distributed to a sample of households in the 1980 Census of Population and Housing. The EEO file includes the entire civilian labor force in its universe, whereas much of the other census data on occupations (e.g., Summary Tape File 3) covers only employed civilians. The EEO file was produced to help meet the needs of government and private industry in planning for EEO/Affirmative Action.

Report is presented in 3 volumes, listed below. Each volume covers a specific State area, and includes the following: contents listing (1 p.); introduction and methodology, with 2 tables (p. i-xii); 1 detailed table, repeated for the entire State and for each location within the State area covered (285- 337 p.); and a glossary (p. G1-G7).

Availability: Connecticut Office of Policy and Management, Comprehensive Planning Division, Connecticut Census Data Center, 80 Washington St., Hartford CT 06106-4459, $10.00 per volume + $2.00 shipping and handling per order; SRI/MF/complete.

REPORT VOLUMES:

S1255-5.1: Volume 1: Western Connecticut
[Monograph. Nov. 1983. 335 p. var. paging. SRI/MF/complete.]

S1255-5.2: Volume 2: South-Central Connecticut
[Monograph. Nov. 1983. 309 p. var. paging. SRI/MF/complete.]

S1255-5.3: Volume 3: Northcentral and Eastern Connecticut
[Monograph. Nov. 1983. 361 p. var. paging. SRI/MF/complete.]

S1256   CONNECTICUT
Department of
Public Safety

S1256-1   CRIME IN CONNECTICUT, 1982
Annual.   [1983.]   iii + 236 p.
LC 83-645941.
SRI/MF/complete

Annual report, for 1982, on Connecticut crimes and arrests, by type of offense. Also covers value of stolen property, clearances, assaults on police, and law enforcement employment. Includes offense and arrest data by law enforcement jurisdiction, and arrests by age, sex, and race.

Data are from reports by State and local law enforcement agencies, submitted under the Uniform Crime Reporting (UCR) Program.

Contains highlights, crime clock, and contents listing (p. i-iii); UCR Program description (p. 1-3); and 7 statistical sections, with 16 charts and 226 tables, described below (p. 5-236).

This is the 5th annual report. For description of the 4th annual report, see SRI 1982 Annual, under this number. A *Quarterly Crime Index* is also issued, but is not covered by SRI.

Availability: Connecticut Department of Public Safety, State Police Division, Uniform Crime Reporting Program, 294 Colony St., Meriden CT 06450-2098, †; SRI/MF/complete.

CHARTS AND TABLES:
[Data are for 1982, unless otherwise noted. Data by race are for white, black, Indian, and Asian. Index offenses covered in detail are murder, rape, robbery, burglary, larceny, aggravated assault, and motor vehicle theft. Arson is classified as an Index offense, but data are reported separately and are not included in the Crime Index totals.]

S1256-1.1: State Index Offense Summary, and Stolen Property Value
[In addition to the data described below, sections on Index offenses also include 1 chart showing monthly trends.]

INDEX OFFENSES, GENERAL
a.   Offenses and clearance rates, 1981-82; and offenses, clearances, and value of property loss, by offense (including arson) and subcategory, 1982. 1 chart and 2 tables. (p. 5-6)

SPECIFIC INDEX OFFENSES
[Data for each specific offense also include 1 table showing total offenses, and crime and clearance rates, 1981-82.]
b.   Murder: victims and offenders, by age, sex, and race, and for Hispanic and non-Hispanic; and offenses, by victim/offender relationship and type of weapon. 2 charts and 3 tables. (p. 7-9)
c.   Rape: percent forcible and attempted. 2 charts and 1 table. (p. 10)
d.   Robbery: offenses and value of property stolen, by place of occurrence; and distribution of offenses by weapon type. 2 charts and 2 tables. (p. 11-12)
e.   Aggravated assault: offenses, by weapon used; and percent simple and aggravated. 3 charts and 1 table. (p. 13-14)

f.   Burglary: offenses and value of property stolen, for day and night residential and nonresidential offenses; and distribution of offenses by type of entry. 2 charts and 2 tables. (p. 15-16)
g.   Larceny: offenses and value of property stolen, by type and amount of theft (including shoplifting). 1 chart and 2 tables. (p. 17-18)
h.   Motor vehicle theft: offenses, by vehicle type; and locally stolen vehicles recovered, and value of all locally stolen and all recovered vehicles. 1 chart and 3 tables. (p. 19-20)

ARSON
i.   Arson: offenses, and crime and clearance rates, 1981-82; and offenses, average value of damage, and percent cleared, by property type. 2 tables. (p. 21)

STOLEN PROPERTY VALUE
j.   Value of property stolen and recovered, monthly, and by property type. 1 chart and 2 tables. (p. 23-24)

S1256-1.2: State Arrest Summary, and Data by Jurisdiction
[Detailed data on arrests are shown by age, sex, and race, for 28 Index and non-Index offenses, with summary totals for Hispanic and non-Hispanic arrests. Data by jurisdiction are repeated for 99 city, university, and State police depts.]
a.   Arrests 1981-82; and arrest detail for 1982; State totals. 2 tables. (p. 26-28)
b.   Offenses, clearances, and value of property stolen, by Index offense (including arson) and subcategory, arranged by jurisdiction, and usually showing population. 99 tables. (p. 30-128)
c.   Arrest detail by jurisdiction. 99 tables. (p. 130-228)

S1256-1.3: Assaults on Police, and Law Enforcement Employment
a.   Police officers killed and injured, 1981-82; officers assaulted and clearance rates, by type of activity at time of assault; and number assaulted by type of assignment, time of assault, and weapon used. 1 chart and 5 tables. (p. 230-231)
b.   Full-time sworn and civilian law enforcement employees by sex, and, generally, population served, for city and university agencies grouped by county, and for State police. 1 table. (p. 234-236)

S1256-2   CONNECTICUT STATE POLICE Highway Safety Report
Annual, discontinued coverage.

Annual report on Connecticut highway traffic accidents. SRI coverage of this report is discontinued with the 1980 edition (for description see SRI 1981 Annual, under this number).

SRI coverage is discontinued in favor of a more comprehensive report *Statewide Accidents;* for description, see S1275-1 below.

S1275   CONNECTICUT
Department of
Transportation

**S1275–1   1982 STATEWIDE
ACCIDENTS: Connecticut
DART Univariate Distribution**
Annual.   [1984.]
35 p.+2 attachments.
SRI/MF/complete, current &
previous year reports

Annual report on Connecticut traffic accidents by accident and vehicle type, location, time, and other detailed circumstances; and driver and pedestrian victim characteristics, including alcohol and drug use, 1982. Also includes data on fatalities and injuries, State of vehicle registration and driver residence, number of vehicles requiring towing, local residence of Connecticut drivers, and safety device usage.

Data are based on reports submitted to the Connecticut Motor Vehicle Dept.

Report contains contents listing (1 p.); and 34 pages of statistical tabulations.

Previous report, for 1981, has also been reviewed and is also available on SRI microfiche under this number [Annual. [1983.] 35+5 p. †]. SRI coverage begins with these editions.

A less detailed report, *Connecticut State Police, Highway Safety Report,* was previously covered by SRI. For description of the 1979-80 reports, see SRI 1981 Annual, under S1256-2.

Availability: Connecticut Department of Transportation, Planning and Research Bureau, Planning Inventory and Data, PO Drawer A, Wethersfield CT 06109-0801, †; SRI/MF/complete.

S1330   DELAWARE
Department of
Administrative Services

**S1330–1   SIXTY-FOURTH ANNUAL
REPORT OF THE STATE
BANK COMMISSIONER OF
DELAWARE for the Fiscal
Year Ended June 30, 1983**
Annual.   Oct. 31, 1983.
98 p.
Doc. No. 20-15/83/11/02.
LC 21-27231.
SRI/MF/complete

Annual report on financial condition of Delaware financial institutions, FY83, presenting assets, liabilities, and equity or total capital, aggregate and by institution, for State-chartered commercial banks, nondeposit trust companies, mutual savings banks, national banks, and State and federally chartered savings and loan assns. Aggregate data include comparison to FY82.

Also includes data on Bank Commissioner Office finances; and small loan company aggregate personal and retail loan activity, FY65-83.

Data are compiled from bank call reports and other reports filed with State.

Contains contents listing (p. 4); 10 tables (p. 5-15); statements of individual institutions, arranged by type (p. 17-92); and lists of registered small loan companies and 7 other types of licensed financial companies (p. 94-98).

Availability: Delaware Department of Administrative Services, State Bank Commissioner's Office, 540 S. DuPont Hwy., Third Floor, Thomas Collins Bldg., PO Box 1401, Dover DE 19903, †; SRI/MF/complete.

S1345   DELAWARE
Department of
Community Affairs

**S1345–2   QUARTERLY REVIEW OF
HOUSING PRODUCTION in
Delaware**
Quarterly.   Approx. 50 p. var.
paging.
SRI/MF/complete

Quarterly report on single- and multi-family residential housing production and construction costs in Delaware counties and major cities. Includes data on new housing, mobile home sales, rehabilitation housing, and demolitions; and on new unit heating fuels used, square footage, and number of bedrooms.

Data are from building permit local records. Report is issued approximately 2-4 months after quarter of coverage.

Contains foreword, contents listing, introduction, and highlights with summary charts and/or text tables; occasional feature articles, some with statistics; 8 quarterly tables, listed below; and 8 trend charts. Issue for 4th quarter includes an annual summary, with 1 table showing housing production trends from the 1970s.

Quarterly tables appear in all issues. All additional features with substantial statistical content are described, as they appear, under "Statistical Features." Nonstatistical features are not covered.

Availability: Delaware Department of Community Affairs, Housing and Community Development Division, 18 The Green, PO Box 1401, Dover DE 19903, †; SRI/MF/complete.

Issues reviewed during 1984: 3rd Qtr. 1983-2nd Qtr. 1984 (D) (Vol. XI, No. 4; Vol. XII, Nos. 1-3).

TABLES:
[Data are shown by county and major city, unless otherwise noted. Tables 1A-3C show data for quarter of coverage and 4 previous quarters. Tables 4A/B-8 show data for quarter of coverage, same quarter of previous year, and current and previous years to date.]

1A-1C. On-site [single- and multi-family housing] permits issued, and mobile home sales.

2A-3C. Total and average cost of on-site [single- and multi-family] construction.

4A-4B. Number of bedrooms in new [single- and multi-family] housing units.

5. Number of new units by square foot per unit.

6. Heating fuel [oil, gas, electric, and other] in new housing units.

7. Rehabilitation housing (units and cost).

8. Residential demolitions.

STATISTICAL FEATURE:

S1345–2.501: 4th Qtr. 1983 (Vol. XII, No. 1)

MORTGAGE REVENUE BONDS IN DELAWARE: A SUCCESSFUL PAST, AN UNCERTAIN FUTURE (p. 7-15) By David C. Sorber. Article on mortgages made available through mortgage revenue bond (MRB) programs administered by State and local governments in Delaware, 1970s-84.

Includes 9 tables showing value of MRBs sold, mortgage money raised, and interest rate charged, by issuer; total mortgage demand, and amount financed through MRB programs; number of MRB program loans, by issuer and county; and distribution of Delaware State Housing Authority MRB program borrowers, by income, age, family size, and home price and down payment; various periods 1975-84.

**S1345–3   1983 REPORTS OF THE
DELAWARE PUBLIC
LIBRARIES**
Annual.   [1983.]   48 p.
No. 50-10-84-01-03.
SRI/MF/complete

Annual report on Delaware public library services, holdings, circulation, and finances, for FY83. Data are from reports by individual libraries, and Division of Libraries records.

Contents:

a.   Contents listing (1 p.); public library directory, map, trustees and advisory council members, standards, and hours of operation (p. 1-20); local public library statistics, with 7 tables, listed below (p. 21-27); and multitype library network members and officers (p. 28-31).

b.   State library agency statistics, with 3 text tables showing funds by source and expenditures by category and program (p. 37), and 9 other tables, also listed below (p. 32-48).

Availability: Delaware Department of Community Affairs, Libraries Division, PO Box 639, Dover DE 19903, †; SRI/MF/complete.

TABLES:
[Data are for FY83.]

LOCAL LIBRARIES
[Tables [1-6] show data by library arranged by county.]

[1-3] Financial report [expenditures by category; and income by source, including government levels]. (p. 21-23)

[4-6] Output measures [population served, book holdings, circulation, library visits, programs sponsored and attendance, and registered borrowers]. (p. 24-26)

[7] Summary of public libraries data [population, materials owned and loaned, and total expenditures, by county and per capita]. (p. 27)

STATE LIBRARY AGENCIES

[8] Interlibrary loan statistics [requests filled and unfilled, by network]. (p. 32)

[9] Statistical summary [of Library Division programs, FY82-83]. (p. 41)

[10] Books-by-mail statistics [by community]. (p. 42)

[11] Delaware films cooperative: circulation, by library. (p. 43)

[12] PDQ library line-toll free telephone reference [questions received]. (p. 44)

[13] Library services to the blind/physically handicapped [including user registrations, and circulation by type of material]. (p. 45)

[14] Kent [County] bookmobile circulation statistics [monthly]. (p. 46)

[15] Division of Libraries collections and circulation [by type of material]. (p. 47)

[16] Institutional library services [expenditures, population served, weekly library hours, available materials, and circulation, by institution]. (p. 48)

S1360   DELAWARE
Administrative Office of the Courts

S1360-1   1983 ANNUAL REPORT OF THE DELAWARE JUDICIARY
Annual.   Nov. 30, 1983.
188 p.
ISSN 0098-0927.
LC 75-641321.
SRI/MF/complete

Annual report, for FY83, on Delaware judicial system, including trial and appellate court caseloads and case dispositions. Covers supreme, chancery, public guardian, superior, family, common pleas, municipal, justice of the peace, and alderman's courts. Includes trial court data by case type and city and/or county, with selected trends from FY74 or earlier and projections to FY88.

Case types shown are criminal and civil, for most courts, with some additional detail for juvenile, domestic relations, adoption, traffic, and landlord/tenant cases.

Also includes data on court finances and case processing time.

Data are from court records.

Contains contents listing (p. 3-4); and report, with 21 charts and 65 tables, interspersed with law library and court directories (p. 6-188).

Availability: Delaware Administrative Office of the Courts, Carvel Delaware State Bldg., 11th Floor, 820 N. French St., Wilmington DE 19801, †; SRI/MF/complete.

S1375   DELAWARE
Executive Office of the Governor

S1375-2   DIMENSIONS ON DELAWARE: A Statistical Abstract
Biennial, discontinued.

Biennial compilation of detailed social, demographic, governmental, and economic statistics for Delaware, discontinued with 1979 edition (for description, see SRI 1981 Annual, under this number).

S1375-4   DELAWARE DATA BOOK
Annual.   Mar. 1984.
124 p. var. paging, looseleaf.
Doc. No. 1003-84-02-03.
SRI/MF/complete

Annual looseleaf compilation of economic and social statistics for Delaware, 1984. Data are shown for various periods 1964-84, and are compiled from State and Federal agencies, and private firms.

Report is designed to present an overview of the State. Socioeconomic, demographic, and geographic breakdowns are shown, as applicable, for selected topics. These breakdowns include data by city, county, income, industry, age, and sex. Comparisons to total U.S., neighboring States, and cities in nearby States are also often included.

Contains transmittal letters and State description, with 1 map (4 p.); and 12 maps, 8 charts, and 57 tables, arranged in 10 sections, described below (114 p.).

This is the 3rd edition of the *Data Book,* which is intended primarily to promote economic development.

Availability: Delaware Development Office, 99 Kings Hwy., PO Box 1401, Dover DE 19903, $25.00; SRI/MF/complete.

SECTIONS:
[Each section generally begins with a 1-page contents listing and narrative highlights. Data sources are noted beneath each table.]

a. **Economic Overview:** includes unemployment rates; listing of major employers; and State government expenditures, with cumulative cash balance, budgetary dollar sources and uses, bond and short-term debt issues value, and debt service share of general fund receipts. 6 charts. (p. I.2-I.10)

b. **Taxes:** includes State tax rates for banks and corporations; license fees and taxes; excise and miscellaneous taxes and fees; typical industrial, commercial, and homeowner property tax rates; income tax rates and liabilities; unemployment insurance and workers compensation tax rates, premiums, and/or benefits. 17 tables. (p. II.1-II.16)

c. **Financing:** includes summary of business financing programs; and branches and assets of commercial and mutual savings banks, and savings and loan assns. 3 tables. (p. III.1-III.13)

d. **Labor:** includes labor force; employment; total and production workers average earnings; salary differentials for comparable standard of living in selected areas; labor productivity

and value added; union membership and union election results; work stoppages, workers involved, and days idle; and average duration of unemployment claims. 1 chart and 10 tables. (p. IV.1-IV.9)

e. **Education/Training:** includes vocational training enrollment, by curriculum; school districts and enrollment; and listing of postsecondary institutions. 2 maps and 1 table. (p. V.1-V.13)

f. **Markets/Transportation:** includes automobile transportation cost index and average insurance premiums; and airports and services. 5 maps and 2 tables. (p. VI.1-VI.12)

g. **Utilities/Resources:** includes residential and industrial electric average monthly bills and industrial rates; and gas utility prices by service class. 2 maps and 4 tables. (p. VII.1-VII.8)

h. **Site Selection:** includes average annual commercial casualty/liability insurance premiums; and narrative review of State and local zoning regulations and business permits. 1 table and 1 map. (p. VIII.1-VIII.10)

i. **Construction Costs:** includes comparisons of industrial site acquisition and residential and commercial construction costs; building operating costs; building trades union wage indexes; office space rental rates; and construction costs and specifications for 4 commercial buildings. 10 tables. (p. IX.1-IX.10)

j. **Quality of Life:** includes cost-of-living indexes; average home market value and insurance premiums; residential lot costs; listing of towns/cities and recreation facilities, including State parks and cultural attractions; average temperatures; crime rates for violent crimes; and health care facilities, medical personnel, and average hospital costs. 2 maps, 1 chart, and 9 tables. (p. X.1-X.19)

S1385   DELAWARE
Department of Health and Social Services

S1385-1   PUBLIC ASSISTANCE GRANTS STATISTICAL REPORT, Delaware
Quarterly.   Approx. 6 p.
SRI/MF/complete

Quarterly report on Delaware public assistance payments, cases, and recipients, by program. Includes caseload data by county. Covers AFDC, general and emergency assistance, food stamps, and SSI. Report is issued 2-3 months after month of coverage.

Contains 4 tables, listed below.

Availability: Delaware Department of Health and Social Services, Planning, Research, and Evaluation Division, Human Services Planning Bureau, Delaware State Hospital, New Castle DE 19720, †; SRI/MF/complete.

Issues reviewed during 1984: Sept. 1983-June 1984 (D).

TABLES:
[Data are shown by program. Tables [2-4] include detail for AFDC program categories and for SSI State supplementation and Federal pay-

ments. Tables [2-3] also include detail for AFDC and general assistance recipients under age 18.]

[1] Financial statement, State funds [amounts available for year and disbursed, for all programs except food stamps, cumulative for fiscal year through month of coverage].

[2-3] Public assistance monthly and cumulative statistics [payments, cases, and/or recipients, for fiscal year through month of coverage, with comparison to same cumulative period of previous fiscal year].

[4] Comparative caseloads by county [cases and/or recipients, for month of coverage].

S1405   DELAWARE
Department of
Labor

S1405–2   DELAWARE AND WILMINGTON SMSA LABOR MARKET TRENDS
Quarterly. Approx. 12 p.
SRI/MF/complete

Quarterly report on Delaware employment, unemployment, earnings, hours, and unemployment insurance (UI), with selected detail for Wilmington SMSA and other State areas. Also includes Philadelphia CPI. Some data are shown by major industry group. Report is issued approximately 2 months after quarter of coverage.

Contains highlights; 6 quarterly tables listed below, interspersed with narrative analyses, text data on unfilled job openings and job seeker characteristics, and brief special articles; and contents and table listing.

Availability: Delaware Department of Labor, Occupational and Labor Market Information Office, PO Box 9029, Newark DE 19714-9029, †; SRI/MF/complete.

Issues reviewed during 1984: 3rd Qtr. 1983-2nd Qtr. 1984 (D) (Vol. 28, Nos. 3-4; Vol. 29, Nos. 1-2).

TABLES:
[Data are shown monthly for quarter of coverage; all tables except table 4 include comparisons to same months of previous year.]

1. Civilian labor force, employment, and unemployment, by place of residence [Delaware, Wilmington SMSA, 4 neighboring States, and total U.S.].

2-3. Nonagricultural wage/salary employment, by [industry division and selected major manufacturing group, and total persons involved in work stoppages]; and average hourly and weekly earnings and hours worked by production workers in selected [major] manufacturing industry groups; [all for Delaware and Wilmington SMSA].

4. Number and amount of unemployment compensation payments for UI regular and extended benefits programs, by [county and] local office.

5. Delaware UI regular continued claim counts [auto industry and other; includes data for 1 week of each month in quarter of coverage, and same weeks of previous year].

6. CPI [by category] and percent changes for all urban consumers, Philadelphia area [with comparisons to U.S.].

S1430   DELAWARE
Department of
Public Instruction

S1430–1   STATE OF DELAWARE REPORT OF EDUCATIONAL STATISTICS, 1982/83
Annual. Oct. 1983.
viii + 162 p. Document No.
95-01/83/09/05.
ISSN 0362-8787.
LC 76-641222.
SRI/MF/complete

Annual report, for the 1982/83 school year, on students, staff, finances, and facilities of Delaware elementary and secondary public schools. Also includes data for nonpublic schools and historical trends from 1960. Data are compiled from reports of local school districts, by the Delaware Dept of Public Instruction.

Contains foreword, chart and table listings, and definitions (p. i-viii); and 12 charts, and 88 tables listed below (p. 3-162).

Two less comprehensive reports, *September Enrollments* and *Nonpublic Schools in Delaware,* are also available from the issuing agency, but are not covered in SRI.

Availability: Delaware Department of Public Instruction, Planning, Research, and Evaluation Division, Townsend Bldg., PO Box 1402, Dover DE 19903, †; SRI/MF/complete.

TABLES:
[Tables show public school data for academic year 1982/83, or as of Sept. 30, 1982, unless otherwise noted. Data by racial/ethnic group include American Indian, Asian or Asian/Pacific Islander, and Hispanic.]

S1430–1.1: Statistical Summaries
[Tables show data for 1978/79-1982/83.]

1. Summary of statistics: pupils [enrollment, attendance, and high school graduates], personnel [administrative, instructional, and other], and schools. (p. 3)

2. Summary statistics: public school expenditures [total by function, and per pupil]. (p. 4)

S1430–1.2: Pupils
[All tables except tables 7, 9, and 11-12 show data by county and district.]

ATTENDANCE AND ENROLLMENT

3. Average daily membership (ADM) and average daily attendance (ADA) of pupils [by grade level]. (p. 15)

4-5. Enrollments by grades in all school districts (FTE); and for regular, part-time special, and full-time special students. (p. 16-21)

6. Pupil enrollment by racial/ethnic group in all school districts. (p. 22)

7. Comparison of Sept. 30 enrollments [by grade level], 1960-82. (p. 23)

SCHOOLS AND TEST SCORES

8. Unit allotments based on enrollments reported by local school districts [by grade level and type including regular, vocational, and special]. (p. 24-35)

9. Educational assessment program, average normal curve equivalent scores [by content area, for selected grades 1-11], 1980/81-1982/83. (p. 36)

GRADUATES AND DROPOUTS

10. Secondary school graduates [by sex], July 1, 1982-June 30, 1983. (p. 38)

11-12. Number and percent of dropouts: of total enrollment, by county and [for] State; and by race and sex, statewide. (p. 39)

S1430–1.3: Staff
[Most tables show data by position.]

PERSONNEL AND SALARIES

13-14. Dept of Public Instruction professional personnel, and educational personnel profile [total and by sex, race, and educational attainment; and average age and experience]. (p. 43-44)

15-16. Number FTE employees and instructional personnel, by [county and] district. (p. 45-46)

17-18. Salary level: [distribution of State] FTE educational personnel; and average annual salary for full-time professional personnel, all sources of funding, county and statewide. (p. 47-48)

TEACHER SUPPLY AND DEMAND

19. Demand data: source of full-time educational personnel [total, new, and returning]. (p. 49)

20. State of bachelor degree: full-time educational personnel. (p. 51)

21. [Type and number of] renewals and new certificates issued. (p. 52)

22-23. Demand trend data: professional educational personnel (FTE), by assignment classification; and source of full-time classroom teachers [new and returning; various years 1972/73-1982/83]. (p. 54-55)

24. Supply trend data: occupations of education graduates, University of Delaware/Delaware State College [total and employed in public and nonpublic schools, 1979/80-1981/82]. (p. 56)

25. Graduates from Delaware State College/University of Delaware, showing the number, by subject area; trained and teaching in Delaware [public and nonpublic schools, 1979/80-1982/83]. (p. 57)

26. Full-time professional personnel [by sex, 1960/61-1982/83]. (p. 58)

S1430–1.4: Finance
[All tables except tables 51-53 and 57-58 show data by county and district.]

SUMMARY DATA

27. Income, expense, and balances. (p. 61)

INCOME

28. Income sources. (p. 63)

29-31. Revenue receipts: State appropriations, Federal sources, and local sources. (p. 64-69)

32-33. District revenue receipts per pupil, based on ADA and enrollment. (p. 70-71)

34. Nonrevenue receipts [State and local bonds; other State; and local property sale, insurance adjustments, and other]. (p. 72)

EXPENSES

35-36. Total and current expenses, summary. (p. 73-74)

37-43. Current expenses: administration, instruction, [attendance/health services, transportation], maintenance and operation of plant, fixed charges, and food and community services. (p. 76-84)

44. Summary of expenditures per pupil. (p. 85)

45-46. Capital outlay and debt service; and school construction funds. (p. 86-87)

47. Bonds outstanding, assessed value of real estate, and estimated value of school facilities, June 30, 1983. (p. 88)

TAXES

48. District assessment, number of capitations, and authorized tax rates for debt service, current expense, tuition, minor capital improvement, and total levies. (p. 89)

49. Combined tax rates on assessed valuation of real estate (rates per $100 of assessed value). (p. 90)

50. Equalized assessment per pupil and relative ability of districts (based on Sept. 30, 1982 enrollments and full value of real estate). (p. 91)

VOCATIONAL PROGRAMS

51. Vocational-technical expenditures [State and Federal funds statewide]. (p. 92)

STATE FUNDING, AND FINANCING REFERENDA

52. Public school State funding: Division II and Division III [1971/72-1982/83]. (p. 93)

53. Referenda by local school districts [votes cast and outcome]. (p. 93)

OTHER PROGRAM COSTS

54. Pupil transportation [buses, pupils, and costs]. (p. 94)

55. Revenue and expenditures: national school lunch/school breakfast/special milk child nutrition programs. (p. 95)

56. National school lunch and school breakfast programs [attendance and participation]. (p. 96)

57. Year-round child care food program, non-school feeding, for day care/Headstart/family day care homes/after school hour programs, [by county only]. (p. 97)

58. Summer food service program for children, P.L. 94-105 [by sponsor, statewide]. (p. 97)

S1430–1.5: Federal Programs

[Tables generally show grant awards by project, and, where applicable, enrollment and employees, by county and district or specific agency or institution.]

59. Federal grants [by program, statewide]. (p. 101)

60-61. Programs for educationally deprived and delinquent children: P.L. 97-35; and P.L. 89-10, Migrant; ECIA [Education Consolidation and Improvement Act], Chapter I. (p. 102-105)

62-63. Federal programs for the handicapped, funding source: ECIA-Chapter I (H), and P.L. 94-142 EHA(B) [Education of the Handicapped]. (p. 106-112)

64. Federal vocational education programs under amendments of 1976, funded under P.L. 94-482. (p. 113-123)

65. Adult Basic Education Reading, Writing, Computation, and Consumer Living Skills: P.L. 91-230 as amended. (p. 124-125)

S1430–1.6: Services

[Tables show data by county, district, or institution.]

66. Immunization levels: percent adequately immunized, by vaccine type. (p. 129)

67. Summary of health services provided by school nurses. (p. 129)

68. James H. Groves Adult High School: pregnant students, State grant programs [funding, enrollments, and FTE employees]. (p. 130)

69-70. Adult driver education program; and driver education/traffic safety, public and nonpublic schools; [pupil enrollment and status]. (p. 131-133)

S1430–1.7: Facilities

[Data are shown by county, district, project, or institution, generally for FY83 unless otherwise noted.]

71-75. Senate Bill No. 677 and House Bill No. 448 minor capital improvement program and school building maintenance program [total allocations and expenditures], and House Bill No. 448 minor capital improvement program contingency allocation, [various years FY81-83]. (p. 137-141)

76-78. Status of funded capital improvement projects, certificates of necessity approved by State Board of Education, and school construction programs [with] State Board final approval. (p. 142-143)

79-81. House Bill No. 809, 1983 minor capital improvement program contingency allocation [expenditures], and 1983 minor capital improvement and school building maintenance programs [total allocations and expenditures]. (p. 143-145)

S1430–1.8: Nonpublic Schools

[Data are for nonpublic schools. School types are Catholic, other religious affiliation, and independent.]

82. Pupils and staff [enrollment by ethnic/racial group, June 1982 graduates, instructional personnel, and number of schools, all by school type]. (p. 149)

83. Enrollment, by grade [by school type and institution]. (p. 150)

84. Enrollment by district of residence, by grade or program, and by type of school. (p. 153)

85. Trend data: enrollment, 1960-82. (p. 154)

86-87. Instructional staff (FTE) [by position], and ADM and ADA of pupils, [by school type and institution]. (p. 155-160)

88. Pupil transportation cost, nonpublic/nonprofit schools. (p. 161-162))

S1435   DELAWARE
Department of
Public Safety

S1435–1   1983 ANNUAL REPORT AND STATISTICAL ANALYSIS, Delaware State Police Traffic Section
Annual.   Apr. 30, 1984.
4+77 p.
SRI/MF/complete

Annual report on Delaware traffic accidents, injuries, and fatalities, by accident and vehicle type, location, time, and other circumstances; and by driver and victim characteristics; 1983, with selected comparisons to 1982, and trends from as early as 1927.

Also includes data on seatbelt and motorcycle helmet use; vehicle registrations, travel mileage, and licensed drivers; motor fuel taxes; State police law enforcement activity; and detailed data on traffic arrests and alcohol-related accidents including results of blood alcohol content tests and dispositions of driving while intoxicated cases.

Data are from reports by State and local police and other State agencies.

Contains contents listing (p. i); introduction, highlights, 11 charts, and 50 tables (p. 1-63); and appendix, with National Safety Council summary table repeated for total accidents and 6 accident types (p. 64-77).

Availability: Delaware Department of Public Safety, State Police Traffic Section, PO Box 430, Dover DE 19903, †; SRI/MF/complete.

S1435–2   CRIME IN DELAWARE, 1983: An Analysis of Uniform Crime Report Data
Annual.   May 1984.   4+61 p.
No. 10-10/84/05/03.
SRI/MF/complete

Annual report, for 1983, on Delaware crimes and arrests, by type of offense, with trends from 1977. Includes data on stolen property value, assaults on law enforcement officers, and data by county and local agency.

Data are from reports of State and local law enforcement agencies, submitted under the Uniform Crime Reporting Program.

Contains introduction and listing of contents, charts, and tables (4 p.); definitions and narrative summary (p. 1-3); 19 charts and 25 tables, interspersed with narrative analyses (p. 3-32); and appendix, with 3 tables (p. 33-61).

All tables, and selected charts with substantial statistics not included in tables, are described below.

Availability: Delaware Statistical Analysis Center, 60 The Plaza, Dover DE 19901, †; SRI/MF/complete.

TABLES AND CHARTS:

[Data are for 1983, unless otherwise noted. Index (Part I) offenses covered in detail are homicide, rape, robbery, aggravated assault, burglary, larceny, and motor vehicle theft. Arson is classified as an Index offense, but data are reported separately and generally are not included in the Crime Index totals. Part II and III offenses are less serious crimes.]

S1435–2.1: Crime Summary

STATE SUMMARY

a. Crimes by offense, arrests, and incarceration rate, 1982-83; and total crime and population by county, offenders incarcerated, and Part I offense crime clocks, 1983. 3 charts and 1 table. (p. 3-6)

PART I OFFENSES

b. Arrests of adults and juveniles by Part I offense; and Part I offenses by type and county, with detail for forcible and attempted rape, robbery and aggravated assault crimes and arrests by weapon, burglary by type of entry, and motor vehicle theft by type of vehicle; various years 1977-83. 3 charts and 18 tables. (p. 11-18)

c. Stolen property value and number of offenses, by type of offense, with detail for robberies by setting, day and night residential and nonresidential burglaries, and larcenies by type; and value of stolen and recovered property, by property type. 7 tables. (p. 19-23)

S1435–2.2: Appendix

a. Arson offenses, total and juvenile clearances, offenses involving abandoned structures, and damaged property value, all by property classification; and law enforcement officers assaulted, by type of activity and assignment, weapon used, injury status, and time of day, with total clearances. 2 tables. (p. 33-34)

b. Complaints received and clearances, for each Part I offense, including arson, and for total Part II, Part III, and narcotic drug law offenses; all for total State and by county and local agency. 1 table. (p. 35-61)

S1507
DISTRICT OF COLUMBIA
Office of the
Controller

S1507–1   DISTRICT OF COLUMBIA COMPREHENSIVE ANNUAL FINANCIAL REPORT, Year Ended Sept. 30, 1983
Annual.   Jan. 27, 1984.
72 p.
SRI/MF/complete

Annual report on financial condition of District of Columbia government, for FY83, presenting assets, liabilities, revenues by source, expenditures by object and/or function, and fund balances, for general, capital projects, university, enterprise, internal service, and fiduciary funds, with comparisons to FY82.

Includes data on D.C. actual vs. budgeted revenues and expenditures; estimated capital expenditures for Washington metro area transit authority through FY88; long-term debt requirements; Federal payments to D.C., FY74-83; and lottery sales.

Also includes data on delinquent property taxes; population, median age, and per capita income; property valuations, including market value of top 10 commercial, residential, and tax-exempt properties; construction; bank deposits; and income taxpayers and distribution of payments, by income level.

Also includes various other financial, social, and economic indicators, including land use, public service facilities, government employment by function, and school enrollments; and selected trends from the 1970s.

Data are from records of the controller's office.

Contains listing of contents, fund statements, and tables (p. 1-2); transmittal letter, with summary text data (p. 3-11); financial section, with 22 fund statements (p. 16-62); and statistical section, with 17 tables (p. 63-72).

Availability: District of Columbia Office of the Controller, 415 12th St., NW, Rm. 412, Washington DC 20004, †; SRI/MF/complete.

S1515
DISTRICT OF COLUMBIA
Courts

S1515–1   1983 ANNUAL REPORT, District of Columbia Courts
Annual.   [1984.]   vii+99 p.
LC 79-642641.
SRI/MF/complete

Annual report, for 1983, on District of Columbia court caseloads and case dispositions, for appeals and superior courts, by case type, with selected trends from 1975.

Case types include criminal and civil, with additional detail for landlord/tenant, small claims, juvenile, domestic relations, mental health and retardation, probate, tax, social service, and traffic cases.

Also includes judicial system revenues and expenditures; bar applications, admissions, disbarments, and other disciplinary actions; juror utilization; and marriage bureau activity.

Contains listing of contents, tables, and charts (p. iii-v); and report, with 16 charts and 42 tables (p. 1-99).

Availability: District of Columbia Courts, Executive Office, 500 Indiana Ave., NW, Suite 1500, Washington DC 20001, †; SRI/MF/complete.

S1527
DISTRICT OF COLUMBIA
Department of
Employment Services

S1527–3   METROPOLITAN WASHINGTON, D.C., AREA LABOR SUMMARY
Monthly.   Approx. 10 p.
SRI/MF/complete, shipped quarterly

Monthly report on labor force conditions in District of Columbia and Washington, D.C. SMSA. Includes employment, earnings, and hours, by industry. Also includes selected unemployment insurance data. Report is issued approximately 2 months after month of data coverage.

Contains narrative summary interspersed with 5 monthly tables, listed below. Also occasionally includes a table showing employment estimates before and after latest benchmark revisions; and other statistical features, including a recurring table on D.C. CPI.

Most monthly tables appear in all issues. All additional features with substantial D.C. statistics not covered in monthly tables are described below, under "Statistical Features." Nonstatistical features are not covered.

Availability: District of Columbia Department of Employment Services, Labor Market Information, Research, and Analysis Division, 500 C St., NW, Suite 201, Washington DC 20001, †; SRI/MF/complete, shipped quarterly.

Issues reviewed during 1984: Sept. 1983-Aug. 1984 (D).

MONTHLY TABLES:

[Tables show data for D.C. and Washington, D.C. SMSA, for month of coverage, previous month, and 1-2 comparable months of previous year, unless otherwise noted. Table sequence and titles may vary from issue to issue.]

[1] Labor force data by place of residence [employment, and unemployment, for District, SMSA, and suburban ring].

[2] Wage/salary employment by [major] industry [group] and place of work.

[3] Unemployment in selected cities [shows unemployment rate in D.C. and 23 other central cities, for month prior to month of coverage and same month of previous year; table begins in the Nov. 1983 issue].

[4] Selected unemployment insurance benefit statistics [initial claims, weeks claimed, benefits paid, recipients, and average weeks of duration, for State, Federal, and ex-serviceperson's programs; D.C. only].

[5] Earnings [and average hours] of production workers in manufacturing [industry groups], Washington SMSA.

STATISTICAL FEATURES:

S1527–3.501: Dec. 1983

DISTRICT OF COLUMBIA CPI (ALL URBAN CONSUMERS), RECURRING FEATURE

(1 p.) Recurring table showing D.C. CPI for all items and by sector, Nov. 1983, with comparison to previous periods. Data are from BLS.

S1527–3.502: Jan. 1984

DISTRICT OF COLUMBIA CPI (ALL URBAN CONSUMERS), RECURRING FEATURE

(1 p.) Recurring table showing D.C. CPI for all items and by sector, Jan. 1984, with comparison to previous periods. Data are from BLS.

S1527–3.503: Mar. 1984

CHARACTERISTICS OF THE DISTRICT'S UNEMPLOYED

(2 p.) Article, with 1 table showing D.C. unemployment, by city ward, 1983. Data are from D.C. Dept of Employment Services.

DISTRICT OF COLUMBIA CPI (ALL URBAN CONSUMERS), RECURRING FEATURE

(1 p.) Recurring table showing D.C. CPI for all items and by sector, Mar. 1984, with comparison to previous periods. Data are from BLS.

S1527–3.504: Apr. 1984

DISTRICT COLLECTIVE BARGAINING CALENDAR, 1984

(1 p.) Brief article, with 1 table showing number of collective bargaining agreements expiring in D.C., and workers affected, 1981-84.

S1527–3.505: May 1984

DISTRICT OF COLUMBIA CPI (ALL URBAN CONSUMERS), RECURRING FEATURE

(1 p.) Recurring table showing D.C. CPI for all items and by sector, Mar. 1984, with comparison to previous periods. Data are from BLS.

S1527–3.506: June 1984

PROFILE OF ASIANS, PACIFIC ISLANDERS AND THE FOREIGN BORN FROM THE 1980 CENSUS

(p. 12-13) Brief article, with 3 text tables showing D.C. Asian/Pacific Islander population by ethnicity, and distribution by occupation; and total population below poverty level, by race-ethnicity, 1980. Data are from 1980 census.

S1527–3.507: July 1984

DISTRICT OF COLUMBIA CPI (ALL URBAN CONSUMERS), RECURRING FEATURE

(1 p.) Recurring table showing D.C. CPI for all items and by sector, July 1984, with comparison to previous periods. Data are from BLS.

S1535
DISTRICT OF COLUMBIA
Executive Office of the Mayor

S1535–2   1982 CRIME AND ARREST PROFILE STATISTICAL UPDATE, Crime in the District of Columbia
Annual.   Oct. 7, 1983.
34 p. no paging.
SRI/MF/complete

Annual report, for 1982, on District of Columbia crimes and arrests by offense and location, with trends from 1972. Also includes comparisons to suburban areas and selected cities, and data on offender characteristics, value of property stolen and recovered, and assaults on police.

Data are from law enforcement agency reports submitted under the Uniform Crime Reporting Program, unpublished data of the D.C. Metropolitan Police Dept, and Census Bureau.

Contains table listing (2 p.); and 30 tables, described below (31 p.).

Availability: District of Columbia Executive Office of the Mayor, Statistical Analysis Center, Criminal Justice Plans and Analysis Office, 421 Eighth St., NW, Washington DC 20004, †; SRI/MF/complete.

TABLES:

[Unless otherwise noted, data are for D.C., 1982. Index crime data generally are shown by offense and include totals for violent and property crimes. Index offenses covered are murder/non-negligent manslaughter, forcible rape, robbery, aggravated assault, burglary, larceny/theft, motor vehicle theft, and arson. Part II offenses include 17 other categories.]

a. Population by age; population, and Index crimes and rates, 1972-82; Index crimes, by month, day of week, and police district; and population, and Index crimes and rates, by D.C. metro area suburban jurisdiction, and for D.C. and 9 other cities. Tables 1-8. (8 p.)

b. Robberies, burglaries, and larcenies/thefts, by type of location and property; value of property stolen and recovered, by Index offense; and violent Index offenses, and assaults on police, by type of weapon. Tables 9-13. (6 p.)

c. Arrests of adults and juveniles, by Index and Part II offense, with Index offense detail by age, race, sex, and police district, and selected trends from 1972; Part II crimes, by offense; and Part II crimes involving weapons, by weapon type. Tables 14-30. (17 p.)

S1535–3   INDICES: A Statistical Index to District of Columbia Services
Annual.   June 1984.
vi+109 p.
SRI/MF/complete

Annual report, for 1984, presenting detailed social, governmental, and economic statistics for the District of Columbia. Data are shown primarily for various years 1970s-84, with development projections to 2000. Data are from D.C. and Federal sources.

Report is designed to present a comprehensive overview of D.C. Extensive socioeconomic, demographic, and geographic breakdowns are shown, as applicable, for most topics. These breakdowns include data by city ward, income, industry, age, educational attainment, race, and sex. Comparisons to total U.S. and other jurisdictions in the D.C. metro area are also included.

Contains contents listing and preamble (p. ii-v); and 6 data sections, described below, containing 30 charts and maps, and 128 tables (p. 1-109).

This is the 1st annual report.

Availability: District of Columbia Executive Office of the Mayor, Office of Policy and Program Evaluation, District Bldg., Rm. 412, 1350 Pennsylvania Ave., NW, Washington DC 20004, $5.00; SRI/MF/complete.

DATA SECTIONS:

[Each section is preceded by a contents listing. Data sources appear beneath each table.]

S1535–3.1: Washington, the Government, and the People

(p. 1-26) Contains 5 charts/maps and 29 tables. Includes visits to popular tourist sites; Commission on the Arts and Humanities expenditures; directory of elected officials; population; per capita and median family income; household characteristics; and land area and assessed valuation, with distribution by use and detail for D.C. government property.

Also includes D.C. government expenditures by program and revenues by source, with detail for Federal payments; tax revenues lost due to Federal exemptions; government employees; capital improvement projects and expenditures, and loans from U.S. Treasury; D.C. government buildings by agency, and lease and energy costs; energy conservation cost savings; and low income energy assistance program caseloads and payments.

S1535–3.2: Economic Development

(p. 27-48) Contains 6 maps/charts and 27 tables. Includes downtown D.C. development goals; Redevelopment Land Agency urban renewal projects; building permits and valuation; licensed businesses and professionals;

D.C. loans to business, and jobs created/retained; and private services firms and employment.

Also includes minority firms and contracts with D.C. government, employment, D.C. residents by place of work, unemployment benefits and characteristics of the unemployed, and youth training expenditures.

Also includes housing sales, average price, and assessment/sales price ratio; condominium conversions and new projects; housing units and occupancy rates by tenure; median rent, and value of owner-occupied units; housing affordability; HUD Section 8 and D.C. low-income rental assistance projects and goals; and public housing funding and capital spending.

S1535–3.3: Public Education and Recreation

(p. 49-58) Contains 2 maps and 11 tables. Includes public school and special education program enrollment; student-teacher ratios; school building occupancy rates; student performance on basic skills tests and Scholastic Aptitude Test (SAT); and per pupil expenditures.

Also includes University of the District of Columbia enrollment and degrees awarded; public library circulation, holdings, and per capita book expenditures; Recreation Dept facilities, including swimming pools; D.C. and National Park Service park acreage; and D.C. owned water acreage.

S1535–3.4: Human Services

(p. 59-80) Contains 12 charts/maps and 32 tables. Includes population in poverty; AFDC, income support, and SSI cases and payments; in-home care recipients; Office on Aging expenditures and service recipients; and nutrition program recipients.

Also includes child day care facilities and capacity; abused and neglected children; foster care caseload; total and subsidized adoptions; men's, women's, and family emergency shelter use; new cases of tuberculosis and venereal disease reported; infant mortality rate; and death rates by cause.

Also includes hospital beds and resident discharge rates, by facility; hospital expenditures, employment, and distribution of discharges by payment source; D.C. General Hospital operating and expense data; clinic visits by type of service; community mental health center caseloads; alcohol and drug abuse center admissions, discharges, and caseloads; nursing home beds, and operating summary for 3 facilities; and Medicaid recipients, payments, and expenditures.

S1535–3.5: Public Works

(p. 81-92) Contains 1 chart and 15 tables. Includes miles of streets, sidewalks, and alleys, and number of bridges, street lights, and signal intersections; means of travel to work; miles of road resurfaced; traffic accidents and fatalities; and parking meters and revenues collected.

Also includes Washington Metropolitan Area Transit Authority rail and bus operations and finances; water/sewer billings and collections; water customers and meters installed/replaced; average daily wastewater treatment and sludge generated; and solid waste collection and disposal.

S1535–3.6: Public Safety

(p. 93-109) Contains 4 charts/maps and 14 tables. Includes fire and fire loss data, and ambulance services; crimes reported, and adult and juvenile arrests, by major offense; activities of Pretrial Services Agency and Public Defender Service; disposition of cases presented to U.S. Attorney; and court case filings and outcomes.

Also includes juvenile detentions and commitments; probation cases and officers; appeals court case filings and dispositions; detainees and prisoners by facility or facility type; and parole population, removals, and revocations.

S1565
DISTRICT OF COLUMBIA
Department of
Human Services

**S1565–1   SOCIAL SERVICES
MONTHLY STATISTICAL
REPORT, District of
Columbia**
Monthly.   Approx. 15 p. no paging.
SRI/MF/complete, shipped quarterly

Monthly report on District of Columbia public welfare programs, covering AFDC, general assistance (GA), food stamps, emergency family shelter, and institutions for children. Includes cases, payments, and/or recipients by program, and selected detail for individual service centers and institutions. Also includes quarterly data on emergency assistance, and food stamp race/ethnic group participation. Report is issued 3-8 months after month of coverage.

Contains contents listing, and 9 monthly and 7 quarterly tables, listed below. Monthly tables appear in all issues. Quarterly tables appear in Mar., June, Sept., and Dec. issues.

Availability: District of Columbia Department of Human Services, Policy and Planning Office, Research and Statistics Division, 425 I St., NW, Rm. 3001, Washington DC 20001, †; SRI/MF/ complete, shipped quarterly.

Issues reviewed during 1984: June 1983-Mar. 1984 (D).

TABLES:

MONTHLY TABLES
[Tables generally show data for month of coverage, with selected comparisons to prior periods. Table numbers vary when issues include quarterly tables.]

1. Public assistance cases, [persons], and payments [by category]: Income Maintenance Administration.

2-3. AFDC and GA applications [and disposition], and cases, by service center: Income Maintenance Administration.

4. Food stamp program cases and persons participating [and value of coupons redeemed and average bonus per family] by type of household [public assistance and other]: Income Maintenance Administration.

5-6. Temporary emergency family shelter, case activity and cumulative admissions and discharges [by shelter]: Family Services Administration.

7-9. Institutions for children: population statistics and cumulative admissions and discharges, and comparison of average population [by specific facility or type of facility]: Youth Services Administration.

QUARTERLY TABLES
[Most data are shown for quarter ending with month of coverage. Tables [D] and [F] begin with the Dec. 1983 issue.]

[A-B] Reason for denials of AFDC applications, and AFDC discontinuances by reason for discontinuance: Income Maintenance Administration.

[C] Average distribution of public assistance [cases, and Medicaid and food stamp families not receiving public assistance], by ward: Income Maintenance Administration.

[D] Emergency assistance [total families and recipients, and] amount of payment approved for each type of emergency: Income Maintenance Administration [for each month of quarter].

[E] Food stamp program average monthly racial/ethnic group participation [white, black, Oriental, Native American, Spanish American, Vietnamese, Cambodian, and other]: Income Maintenance Administration.

[F] Blair/Pierce temporary shelters for men [total sheltered, 1st time users, and number of nights of shelter]: Family Services Administration [for each month of quarter].

[G] Child protection register, number of child abuse and neglect reports, and ward distribution [all for families and children]: Family Services Administration.

**S1565–2   VITAL STATISTICS
SUMMARY, 1981, District
of Columbia**
Recurring (irreg.)   [1984.]
97 p.
ISSN 0419-4381.
LC 74-642073.
SRI/MF/complete, current & previous year reports

Recurring report on District of Columbia vital statistics, 1981, with trends from the 1960s. Covers births, deaths by cause, and population. Includes data by race, age, sex, and ward or census tract.

Data are compiled from District records.

Contains listings of symbols, contents, tables, and charts (p. 2-6); introduction and definitions (p. 7-10); narrative report, interspersed with 1 map, and 13 tables listed below (p. 12-26); and statistical section, with 28 tables, also listed below (p. 28-97).

Previous report, for 1980, has also been reviewed and is also available on SRI microfiche under this number [Recurring (irreg.) [1984.] 108 p. †].

Availability: District of Columbia Department of Human Services, Policy and Planning Office, Research and Statistics Division, 425 I St., NW, Rm. 3107, Washington DC 20001, †; SRI/MF/ complete.

TABLES:
[Data are for the District of Columbia, 1981, unless otherwise noted.]

S1565–2.1: Narrative Section Tables
[Tables A-L show data for D.C. residents, 1970-81, unless otherwise noted.]

[1] [Births by birth weight and infant mortality rate, with comparisons to U.S.] (p. 12)

A. Live births and birth rates, by race and sex. (p. 14)

B-C. Deaths [total], and infant and neonatal deaths, and death rates, by race. (p. 15-16)

D. Three-year moving average of infant mortality rate, by age at death, 1961/63-1979/81. (p. 17)

E-F. Fetal and perinatal deaths and death rates, by race. (p. 18-19)

G. Out-of-wedlock births, by race. (p. 20)

H. Incidence of low birth weight, by race. (p. 21)

I. Number and percent distribution of live births by birth weight and wedlock status [1981]. (p. 22)

J-K. Births to adolescent mothers [under age 20 and under age 18], and maternal mortality, by race. (p. 23-24)

L. Recorded events, and resident events in other States [showing births and deaths in D.C. and resident births and deaths outside D.C.]. (p. 25)

S1565–2.2: Statistical Section Tables
POPULATION AND TRENDS

1. Estimated population by age, race, and sex. (p. 28)

2-4. Number of total, black, and white resident live births and deaths, [and] number and rates of infant, neonatal, and fetal deaths, 1975-81 and averages [for selected periods] 1945-79. (p. 29-31)

BIRTHS

5. Out-of-wedlock ratios [births per 1,000 live births] by age of mother and race, 1975-81. (p. 32)

6. Number and percent distribution of resident live births by live-birth order and race, 1978-81 and averages [for selected periods] 1965-79. (p. 33)

7-12. Live births: by live birth order, age of mother, and plurality, all races; and by live birth order and age of mother, and by ward and age of mother, [by race]. (p. 34-41)

13. Number and percent distribution of resident live births, and births with selected characteristics (out-of-wedlock, premature, immature, and with inadequate prenatal care), by race and ward. (p. 42)

DEATHS
[Note that table 19 precedes table 18.]

14-15. Resident deaths and crude death rates, for 20 leading causes, by race and sex. (p. 45-46)

16. Principal causes of death of residents, by age group and sex, with rates. (p. 47)

17. Number of resident deaths and crude and age-adjusted death rates by age, race, and sex. (p. 50)

19. Resident deaths for 20 leading causes, by ward. (p. 51)

18. Deaths from 72 selected causes, by age, race, and sex. (p. 52-78)

FETAL AND INFANT DEATHS

20. Infant deaths and death rates by age and race, and fetal deaths by race, 1975-81 and averages [for selected periods] 1950-79. (p. 79)

21. Resident infant deaths and death rates by age, 1960-81. (p. 80)

22. Infant death rates by ward and age, 1980-81. (p. 81)

23. Resident infant deaths by cause and age. (p. 82)

24. Three-year moving average of infant mortality rate, by age at death, 1961/63-1979/81. (p. 85)

MISCELLANEOUS

25. Live births, out-of-wedlock births, infant deaths, fetal deaths, [and] total deaths, by place of occurrence [D.C. and elsewhere, for events involving D.C. residents], and residence [D.C., Maryland, Virginia, or elsewhere, for events occurring in D.C.]. (p. 86)

26. Recorded number of live births and deaths: number and rates of infant, neonatal, and fetal deaths, by race, 1975-81 and averages [for selected periods] 1940-79. (p. 87)

27. Resident live births, out-of-wedlock births, births with no prenatal care, immature births, total deaths, and infant deaths, by census tract. (p. 90-96)

28. Recorded deaths from accidental causes by age and type of accident. (p. 97)

S1590
DISTRICT OF COLUMBIA
Metropolitan
Police Department

**S1590-1   DISTRICT OF COLUMBIA
ANNUAL TRAFFIC REPORT,
1982**
Annual. [1984.]
100 p. var. paging.
LC 83-646104.
SRI/MF/complete

Annual report on District of Columbia traffic accidents, injuries, and fatalities, by detailed accident and vehicle type, street location, police district, time, and other circumstances; and driver and victim characteristics; 1982, with trends from 1951.

Also includes data on costs of accidents, bicycle registrations, highways and streets, seat belt usage, alcohol arrests and other traffic enforcement activity, and selected comparisons to other cities.

Data are compiled by the D.C. Metropolitan Police Dept.

Contains contents listing (p. iii-iv); and 5 sections, with 3 charts and 59 tables (p. 1-84, and addendum 12 p.).

Availability: District of Columbia Metropolitan Police Department, Special Operations Division, Traffic Enforcement Branch, Traffic Analysis Unit, 501 New York Ave., NW, Washington DC 20001, ‡; SRI/MF/complete.

S1605
DISTRICT OF COLUMBIA
Public Schools

**S1605-1   DISTRICT OF COLUMBIA
PUBLIC SCHOOLS DATA
RESOURCE BOOK, School
Year 1983/84**
Annual.   Feb. 1984.
iii+30 p.
SRI/MF/complete

Annual report, for academic year 1983/84, on District of Columbia public and private school enrollment, graduates, standardized test results, finances, and staffing. Data are from D.C. Education Dept reports.

Contains contents listing (p. iii); lists of school board, administration, and regional officials, with 1 map (p. 1-6); and narrative description, interspersed with 15 tables listed below (p. 7-30).

This is the 12th annual data resource book.

Availability: District of Columbia Public Schools, Quality Assurance Division, 415 12th St., NW, Rm. 1013, Washington DC 20004, †; SRI/MF/complete.

TABLES:
[Tables show data for 1983/84, unless otherwise noted.]

STUDENTS
[Tables A-C generally show enrollment data for elementary, junior high, senior high, career development, and special education schools, including some individual institutions or programs; and tuition grant students and regular and special preschool students; as of Oct. 13, 1983.]

A. Membership [with comparisons to Oct. 1982]. (p. 7)

B-C. Student membership: by race [and ethnic group, including American Indian, Asian/Pacific Islander, and Hispanic]; and by region. (p. 9-11)

D. Adult/continuing education [membership by sex and level, as of Dec. 31, 1983]. (p. 12)

E. Graduates [from senior high schools, STAY school, Street Academy, career development centers, and Ellington School of the Arts, 1979/80-1982/83]. (p. 12)

F. Nonpublic [parochial, private, and other, by type] and public school enrollment [all by race]. (p. 13)

G. Special education [students served, by local and State program type, 1982/83]. (p. 15)

H. Student assessment [standardized test results: reading and mathematics median grade equivalents for grades 3, 6, 8, 9, and 11, May 1979-83]. (p. 17)

I. Food services [number of meals served, 1982/83, and prices, 1983/84, by level of education]. (p. 18)

J. School calendar [and day school advisory periods]. (p. 19-20)

ADMINISTRATION

K. Budget [appropriations for capital outlay, and regular and Federal operating expenses and per pupil expenditure, FY82-84]. (p. 22)

L. Federal grants [by source and program, FY84]. (p. 23)

M. Staffing [by position, and professional employees by degree level, FY84]. (p. 25)

N-O. Number of schools and instructional programs [by level or program, all by region]; and alphabetical listing and regional designation of the public schools. (p. 26-30)

S1685   FLORIDA
Department of
Agriculture and
Consumer Services

**S1685-1   FLORIDA AGRICULTURAL
STATISTICS**
Annual series.   For individual publication data, see below.
SRI/MF/complete

Series of 6 annual reports on Florida agricultural production, finances, and marketing, for citrus, vegetable, poultry, livestock, field crop, and dairy sectors. Data generally are shown by commodity and/or county, with selected comparisons to other States and total U.S.

Data are from USDA; State and local government agencies; growers assns; and agricultural, transportation, and food industry firms.

Reports reviewed during 1984 are described below.

Related, less comprehensive publications available from the issuing agency, but not covered in SRI, include 2 biennial citrus reports, *Acres and Tree Inventory* and *Maturity Summary*.

Availability: Florida Crop and Livestock Reporting Service, 1222 Woodward St., Orlando FL 32803, series of 6 reports $12.00, single report $2.50; SRI/MF/complete.

**S1685-1.1: Florida Agricultural Statistics,
Citrus Summary, 1983**
[Annual. Jan. 1984. 46 p. LC 74-644777. SRI/MF/complete.]

Annual report on Florida citrus fruit production, acreage, yield, utilization, prices, value, shipments, and trade, by fruit type. Data are shown for various crop years 1960s-1982/83, with selected trends from 1886.

Includes selected comparisons to Arizona, California, and Texas; production and acreage by county; and U.S. and Florida citrus exports, by country of destination.

Also includes citrus shipments in U.S. and Canada, including cartons received in approximately 25 cities, by transport mode and source (State, Mexico, and other); U.S. per capita citrus consumption; and comparative citrus fruit production of selected foreign countries.

Contains contents listing (1 p.); narrative summary, with 3 tables (p. 1-3); 3 charts and 34 detailed tables (p. 4-45); and data sources (p. 46).

**S1685-1.2: Florida Agricultural Statistics,
Vegetable Summary, 1983**
[Annual. Mar. 1984. iv+69 p. LC A63-7731. SRI/MF/complete.]

Annual report on Florida vegetable, melon, and strawberry production, acreage, yield, prices, shipments, and trade, by commodity, with selected data by county or State area. Most data are shown for 1968/69-1982/83 crop years.

Also includes Florida monthly shipments to other States/Canada and exports, and shipments received in 24 U.S. and Canadian cities by source (Florida and other States), both by transport mode and commodity; and monthly imports of Mexican tomatoes; various periods 1979/80-1982/83.

Contains production calendar and contents listing (p. iii-iv); narrative summary, with 1 table (p. 1-11); and 137 detailed tables (p. 12-69).

S1685-1.3: Florida Agricultural Statistics, Livestock Summary, 1983

[Annual. May 1984. 21 p. LC A64-7767. SRI/MF/complete.]

Annual report on Florida livestock production, value, inventories, shipments, dispositions, marketing, income, slaughter, and prices, by species, mostly 1974-83, with some data for 1984, and some comparisons to other States and total U.S.

Also includes data on feeder calf outshipments, by State of destination; apiary sector production, value, inventory, and prices; U.S. livestock inventories, by State; and U.S. per capita consumption of meat, fish, poultry, and eggs, 1942-83.

Contains contents listing (1 p.); narrative summary and methodology, with 1 table (p. 1); 28 detailed tables (p. 2-20); and a directory of cattle/hog auctions (p. 21).

S1685-1.4: Florida Agricultural Statistics, Poultry Summary, 1983

[Annual. July 1984. 33 p. LC A64-7653. SRI/MF/complete.]

Annual report on Florida poultry and egg production, income, and prices, and poultry inventories, mostly 1974-83, with selected trends from 1969, and some comparisons to other States and total U.S.

Contains contents listing (1 p.); narrative summary, with glossary (p. 1); and 2 charts, 3 maps, and 23 tables (p. 2-33).

S1685-1.5: Florida Agricultural Statistics, Dairy Summary, 1983

[Annual. Aug. 1984. 2+24 p. LC 75-646842. SRI/MF/complete.]

Annual report on Florida dairy production, value, utilization, income, and prices, by county and/or product, 1983, with selected trends from 1974, and some comparisons to other States and total U.S.

Also includes data on Florida cattle inventories, raw milk inshipments, and cattle inshipments by State of origin; and U.S. per capita dairy product consumption, 1960-83.

Contains contents listing (1 p.); and brief narrative summary, 2 charts, and 22 tables (p. 1-24).

S1685-1.6: Florida Agricultural Statistics, Field Crops Summary, 1983

[Annual. Aug. 1984. 2+18 p. SRI/MF/complete.]

Annual report on Florida field crop and nut acreage, yield, production, prices, and value, by commodity and/or district and county, 1982-83, with trends from 1973.

Contains contents listing (1 p.); narrative summary (p. 1-2); and 17 tables (p. 3-18).

S1717   FLORIDA
Office of the Comptroller

S1717-1   ANNUAL REPORT OF THE COMPTROLLER for the Fiscal Year Ended June 30, 1983, State of Florida

Annual. Dec. 15, 1983.
233 p.+Attachment 28 p.
LC 10-11492.
SRI/MF/complete

Annual report on financial condition of Florida State government for FY83, presenting receipts by source and month; expenditures, by function, object, dept, and institution; and fund balances; for specific general revenue, trust, working capital, and Federal revenue sharing funds, with selected comparisons from FY74 and earlier.

Also includes data on appropriations compared to disbursements; tax collections and allocations, educational program disbursements, and welfare program assistance, by county; revenue distribution to municipalities; investment holdings; State retirement systems; pari-mutuel wagering receipts and disbursements; and assets and liabilities of various fund types and long-term debt account.

Data are from records of the comptroller's office and various State agencies.

Contains foreword and table listing (p. 5-6); 2 charts and 24 tables (p. 8-230); agency index (p. 231-233); and 6 tables and notes on financial statements (28 p., attached to back cover).

Availability: Florida Office of the Comptroller, Banking and Finance Department, Capitol Bldg., Tallahassee FL 32301, †; SRI/MF/complete.

S1717-2   ANNUAL REPORT OF THE DIVISION OF BANKING, 1982, Florida

Annual. [1983.]   175 p.
LC 76-643004.
SRI/MF/complete

Annual report on financial condition of Florida State-chartered financial institutions, presenting assets, liabilities, capital, and operating income and expenses for commercial banks, industrial savings banks, nondeposit trust companies, savings and loan assns, and credit unions, as of Dec. 31, 1982, with selected comparisons to 1981.

Includes data for State-located national banks and international bank agencies. State and national commercial bank data are shown by institution and county; generally, only assets are shown individually for other institution types.

Also includes selected summary trends from 1895; bank operating ratios; top 10 State and national banks ranked by assets; total bank employment; and financial data for multi- and 1-bank holding companies, and independent banks, by county.

Contains contents listing (p. 1-2); dept personnel lists (p. 4-9); 5 charts and 40 tables, interspersed with status changes and other lists (p. 10-118); and dept regulatory information (p. 119-175).

Availability: Florida Department of Banking and Finance, Banking Division, Capitol Bldg., Suite 1301, Tallahassee FL 32301, ‡; SRI/MF/complete.

S1720   FLORIDA
Department of Corrections

S1720-1   ANNUAL REPORT, FY83, Florida Department of Corrections

Annual. Dec. 1, 1983.   96 p.
LC 80-648829.
SRI/MF/complete

Annual report, for FY83, on corrections in Florida, presenting data on the prison and parole/probation population, including admissions, releases, demographic and socioeconomic characteristics, criminal background, primary offense, and sentence length or supervision period. Includes selected data by institution and county of commitment and post-release supervision, with trends from 1973, and projected prison and parole/probation populations to 1985 or 1986.

Also includes crime trend comparisons to southern States and U.S.; interstate transfers of parolees and probationers; prison escapes; population under pretrial supervision; prison industry trust fund financial statements; inmates' IQ, and alcohol and narcotic use; corrections dept finances; prison operating costs; and status of capital projects.

Contains contents listing (p. 1); introduction and narrative summary, with 11 charts and 2 tables (p. 2-40); 2 statistical sections, with 5 charts and 50 tables (p. 41-90); directory of correctional institutions and parole/probation service offices (p. 91-94); and index (p. 95-96).

Availability: Florida Department of Corrections, 1311 Winewood Blvd., Tallahassee FL 32301, †; SRI/MF/complete.

S1725   FLORIDA
Department of Education

S1725-1   FACT BOOK, 1982/83, State University System of Florida

Annual. Feb. 1, 1984.
xi+194 p.   BOR 84-4.
ISSN 0093-9617.
LC 74-642941.
SRI/MF/complete

Annual report, for 1982/83 academic year, on Florida State-supported universities. Covers enrollment, finances, degree programs, contracts and grants, and staff, for 9 universities in the State University System (SUS). Includes enrollment and appropriation trends from 1970s.

Report is based on individual university surveys, State agency studies, and Higher Education General Information Survey (HEGIS) reports.

Contains listing of contents, tables, and charts (p. v-xi); introductory material (p. 1-11); 11 charts and 59 tables (p. 12-177); and functional directory, glossary, and index (p. 181-194).

All tables, and charts presenting substantial data not covered in tables, are described below.

Availability: Florida Department of Education, Board of Regents, State University System of Florida, 107 W. Gaines St., Tallahassee FL 32301, ‡; SRI/MF/complete.

TABLES AND CHARTS:

[Most data are shown for total SUS and by individual institution. Data by race also include Hispanic and, occasionally, Asian/Pacific Islander and American Indian/Alaskan Native.]

a. **Institutional characteristics:** including locale, campus size and housing units, enrollment and financial summaries, number of National Merit Scholars, and endowed faculty chairs, various years 1979-83. Table 1. (p. 12-19)

b. **Admissions:** applicants, admissions, and enrollment, by student category; admissions, by entrance examination scores and high school grade point average; 1st-time student enrollment, by county of residence; and community college transfers to SUS; fall 1982. Tables 2-8. (p. 25-37)

c. **Enrollment:** FTE enrollment and average credit hour load, by academic level; headcount enrollment, by county and State of residence, nation of citizenship, full- and part-time status, sex, and race; noncredit programs and participants; continuing education units awarded; FTE enrollment, by on- and off-campus site; and median student age; fall 1982 or 1982/83, with enrollment trends from 1973/74. Tables 9-23. (p. 41-73)

d. **Degree programs:** programs offered; headcount enrollment by discipline, cross-tabulated by level, race (also nonresident aliens), and sex; undergraduate and graduate course work distribution, by discipline of student and course; degrees granted, by level, discipline, race, and sex; and participation in exchange programs with other institutions; fall 1982 or 1982/83. Tables 24-37. (p. 77-119)

e. **Student and institution finances:** tuition and required fees, with detail for medical programs, 1983/84; room and board charges, and out-of-State tuition/fee waivers, 1982/83; financial aid, by type and race, 1982/83; appropriations to SUS, by type including libraries, various years 1974/75-1983/84; instructional expenditures, by HEGIS category, 1982/83; SUS data processing costs, by type, FY82; and summary revenues by source and expenditures by function, FY83. Charts 3-4 and tables 38-50. (p. 123-152)

f. **Contracts and grants:** copyrights and patents granted; research/service contract/grant funds by source and expenditures by discipline; contract/grant indirect costs recovered and amounts transferred to trust fund; and Federal contract/grant awards, by sponsoring agency; FY83. Tables 51-56. (p. 155-164)

g. **Personnel:** "Manyear" distribution, by budget classification and function; total personnel, by function, race, and sex; and faculty, by tenure status, race, sex, academic rank, and age; 1982/83. Charts 5-11 and tables 57-59. (p. 167-177)

S1725–2   PROFILES OF FLORIDA SCHOOL DISTRICTS, 1982/83
Annual. [1984.] ii+204 p.
Profile XIII, Vol. II.
SRI/MF/complete

Annual report, for 1982/83, on Florida public schools, with comparative data for 1981/82 and trends from 1901. Includes statistics on enroll-

ment, finances, graduates, and staff, all by school district. Also includes selected data for nonpublic schools.

Contains contents listing (p. i); introduction and list of school districts and regions (p. 1-2); historical data, with 3 charts and 4 tables (p. 3-6); State and school district profiles (p. 8-153); appendix, with 3 detailed tables, and notes (p. 156-203); and 1 data map showing population by congressional district, 1980 (inside back cover).

All profiles and tables are described below.

Report is Volume II of the Commissioner of Education's annual report on Florida public schools. Volume I is a narrative description of programs and is not covered by SRI.

Availability: Florida Department of Education, Public Schools Division, Education Information Services/MIS, 275 Knott Bldg., Tallahassee FL 32301, †; SRI/MF/complete.

PROFILES AND TABLES:

[Data by race are generally for white, black, Hispanic, Asian/Pacific Islander, and American Indian/Alaskan Native.]

S1725–2.1: State Historical Data

a. Total population, population aged 5-17, enrollment, high school graduates, teachers, average teacher salary, schools, assessed valuation of property, and total and per pupil expenses, 1901/02-1982/83. 1 table. (p. 3)

b. Percent of class survival, 1st grade through college entrance, for classes beginning 1961-71; revenue receipts, total and from Federal, State, and local sources, 1959/60-1982/83; and enrollment, teachers, and administrative staff, 1978/79-1982/83. 3 tables. (p. 4-6)

S1725–2.2: School District Profiles

Profiles for the State (p. 8-9) and 5 school regions and 67 school districts (p. 10-153) present data described below. Most data in items b-e are shown for 1981/82-1982/83 school years.

a. Community: population by race and sex, by age, 1982; and urban and rural population, adults by race and educational attainment, and median family income, 1980.

b. Students: FTE count for elementary/secondary, adult, vocational, and exceptional students; fall membership by race; total graduates and percent entering college and technical school; SSAT (State student assessment test) performance by subject area and grade; number of public schools; and number of nonpublic schools and students.

c. Staff: number of personnel by position and race; personnel distribution and ratios by position, and percent of professional personnel resigning; FTE students per FTE teacher by grade level; and salary range by certification status.

d. Finance: revenues, including receipts by source (Federal, State, and local), categorical/special allocations by program, operating tax millage and yield, assessed property value, required local effort, and bonded indebtedness; and expenditures, including capital outlay, debt service, and expenditures for elementary and secondary education by grade level, and for exceptional, vocational, and adult education by type of program; with per pupil amounts for selected items.

e. Transportation: cost per pupil, and expenditures of State and district funds.

S1725–2.3: Appendix

[Tables show data by school district, fall 1982 or 1982/83.]

I. Student data [nonpublic students and graduates; public graduates and dropouts; SSAT results by subject and grade; public student membership by race; and final unweighted FTE count for vocational (high school and adult) and exceptional student programs, by program or handicap, and for basic education by level, including adult basic/high school and educational alternatives]. (p. 156-166)

II. Staff data [full-time and support staff by position; and full-time professional and support staff by sex and race]. (p. 167-168)

III. Fiscal data [revenues by source (Federal, State, and local), and detail by fund; expenditures by fund and detailed object; and long-term debt]. (p. 169-193)

S1745   FLORIDA
Department of Health and Rehabilitative Services

S1745–3   FLORIDA VITAL STATISTICS, 1982
Annual. Oct. 1983.
vi+126 p.
LC 83-643734.
SRI/MF/complete

Annual report, for 1982, on Florida vital statistics, including population, births, deaths by cause, marriages, and marriage dissolutions. Includes data by location, race, age, and sex, and trends from 1959. Data are derived primarily from records filed with the Office of Vital Statistics; population data are from University of Florida Bureau of Economic and Business Research.

Contents:

a. Listing of Florida counties, with Health and Rehabilitative Services (HRS) district or subdistrict and Health Service Agency district shown for each. (p. iii)

b. Contents and table listings. (p. v-vi)

c. Introduction; and 6 sections with 43 detailed tables listed below, and 36 interspersed summary/trend tables including data on population by age group and sex, fertility, life expectancy, underwater diving deaths, and accidental deaths by detailed type and victim characteristics. (p. 1-126)

More detailed data are also available from the issuing agency.

Availability: Florida Department of Health and Rehabilitative Services, Publications, Public Health Statistics Section, PO Box 210, Jacksonville FL 32231, †; SRI/MF/complete.

TABLES:

[Tables show data for Florida, by race, 1982, unless otherwise noted.]

S1745–3.1: Population and Live Births

[Tables show data by county, unless otherwise noted.]

POPULATION

1. Midyear population estimates, 1980 and 1982. (p. 6)

LIVE BIRTHS

2-3. Recorded and resident live births and birth rates per 1,000 population, 1982 and annual averages 1979-81. (p. 10-11)

4. Live births, by place of occurrence and residence, for 101 incorporated cities of 10,000 or more population. (p. 12)

5. Percent of resident live births attended by physicians [in and out of hospital], midwives, and others. (p. 13)

6-7. Resident live births: by sex, by weight at birth; and by age of mother. (p. 14-19)

8-10. Resident live births to unwed mothers [with] rates per 100 total live births, 1982 and annual average 1979-81; and by age of mother, and by birth order, 1982. (p. 20-24)

S1745–3.2: Mortality and Marriages and Dissolutions

[Data are shown by county, unless otherwise noted. Causes of death are shown according to the 9th Revision of the International Classification of Diseases. Tables on mortality often include rates.]

MORTALITY

11-16. Resident fetal, recorded and resident neonatal, resident perinatal, and recorded and resident infant deaths [1982 and annual average 1979-81]. (p. 27-32)

17-18. Resident neonatal and infant deaths from selected causes, by age. (p. 33-38)

19-20. Recorded and resident deaths, 1982 and annual average 1979-81. (p. 49-50)

21. Deaths, by place of occurrence and by place of residence, for 101 incorporated cities of 10,000 or more population. (p. 51)

22. Resident death rates per 10,000 population, 40 important cause groups. (p. 52-61)

23. Resident deaths, by age groups [by sex]. (p. 62)

24. Resident deaths for 360 cause groups, by age [not by county]. (p. 67)

25. Resident deaths from selected causes, by sex. (p. 72-105)

MARRIAGES AND DISSOLUTIONS

[Data are not shown by race.]

26. [Total] marriages performed, by month. (p. 109)

27. [Total] dissolutions of marriage by month granted, and annulments. (p. 110)

S1745–3.3: HRS Districts

[Tables show data by HRS district and subdistrict. Tables often include rates.]

28-29. Live births, and live births to unwed mothers [resident and recorded]. (p. 112)

30-31. Resident live births to teenage mothers and percent of live births; and resident live births to unwed teenage mothers and percent of live births to unwed mothers; [by age group]. (p. 113)

32-33. Resident first order and low weight live births [total and] to unwed mothers. (p. 114)

34-35. Resident live births in hospital, and nonhospital, by attendant, and percent of live births. (p. 115-116)

36-39. Fetal deaths 20 or more weeks gestation, and neonatal, perinatal, and infant deaths [recorded and resident]. (p. 117-118)

40-41. [Recorded and] resident deaths, and resident deaths for leading causes. (p. 119-122)

42. [Total] accidental deaths by ranked external cause [not by race]. (p. 123)

43. Marriages and [total] dissolutions of marriage. (p. 126)

S1745–4   ANNUAL STATISTICAL REPORT, FY82-83, Florida Department of Health and Rehabilitative Services
Annual.   Jan. 1984.   33 p.
LC 79-644487.
SRI/MF/complete

Annual report, for FY83, on Florida public welfare programs, including cases, recipients, and payments, by program and county. Covers AFDC, SSI, food stamps, low-income home energy assistance, and medical assistance. Includes demographic characteristics of medical assistance recipients, and types of medical services financed.

Data are compiled by the Office of Revenue Management.

Contains contents listing (1 p.); and 21 tables, listed below. Some tables are accompanied by charts, generally showing trends from the 1970s. This is the 17th annual report.

Availability: Florida Department of Health and Rehabilitative Services, Revenue Management Office, 1317 Winewood Blvd., Bldg. 3, Rm. 315, Tallahassee FL 32301, †; SRI/MF/complete.

TABLES:

[Data are shown for FY83, unless otherwise noted. Data by county are also shown by district.]

S1745–4.1: Direct Assistance Programs

SUMMARY

1. Direct assistance payments by county [and program, including SSI, AFDC, and Cuban/Haitian and Indo-Chinese refugee assistance]. (p. 1-6)

AFDC

2. Applications approved [families and persons, for financial/medical and medical only], denied/otherwise disposed of, and pending [by county]. (p. 7)

3-4. Recipients [families, children, and persons] and direct assistance [by county and month]. (p. 9-11)

5. Children in foster care [and payments, by month]. (p. 12)

REPATRIATED AMERICANS AND SSI

6. Assistance to repatriated Americans, Federal funds [maintenance/transportation, medical assistance, and repayments, by month]. (p. 13)

7. Optional State supplementation [average monthly cases and direct assistance, by county]. (p. 14)

8. SSI payments [average monthly cases and direct assistance, by county, for Old Age Assistance, Aid to the Blind, and Aid to the Disabled]. (p. 15)

9-11. Total [monthly cases and] payments to SSI recipients: aged, blind, and disabled in-

dividuals [from Federal funds, and from optional State supplementation funds]. (p. 17-19)

S1745–4.2: Food Stamps and Medical Assistance

FOOD STAMPS

12. Households, persons, and value of food stamps issued, by participating counties [includes participants by public assistance status]. (p. 21-22)

ENERGY ASSISTANCE

13. Low-income Home Energy Assistance Program [households, persons, and payments, by county]. (p. 23)

MEDICAL ASSISTANCE

[Tables 14-21 show data by type of medical facility and service, for year ended Sept. 30, 1983.]

14-19. Recipients of medical care, and medical vendor payments: by age in years; by race/ethnicity [including American Indian/Alaskan Native, Asian/Pacific Islander, and Hispanic]; and by sex. (p. 26-28)

20. Use and cost: [health care costs and recipients, for aged, blind, disabled, and AFDC child and adult categories]. (p. 29)

21. Medical payments by month. (p. 32)

S1750   FLORIDA
Department of Highway Safety and Motor Vehicles

S1750–2   TRAFFIC ACCIDENT FACTS, 1982, Florida
Annual.   [1984.]   18+4 p.
LC 74-645046.
SRI/MF/complete

Annual report on Florida traffic accidents, injuries, and fatalities, by accident and vehicle type, location, time, and other circumstances; and driver and victim characteristics; 1982, with trends from the 1960s.

Also includes data on economic cost of accidents, motor vehicle registrations, licensed drivers, miles traveled, and use of seat belts.

Data are compiled by the Florida Dept of Highway Safety and Motor Vehicles.

Contains contents listing (1 p.); highlights (p. 1); 14 charts and 4 tables (p. 2-18); and standard summary section, with 3 detailed tables (4 p.).

Availability: Florida Department of Highway Safety and Motor Vehicles, Administrative Services Division, Traffic Accident Records and Forms Management, Neil Kirkman Bldg., 2900 Apalachee Pkwy., Tallahassee FL 32301-8209, †; SRI/MF/complete.

S1760   FLORIDA
Department of
Insurance

S1760–1   REPORT OF THE DEPARTMENT OF INSURANCE, State of Florida, for the Fiscal Year Ending June 30, 1983
Annual. July 1, 1983.
399 p.+errata sheets.
SRI/MF/complete

Annual report on Florida insurance industry financial condition and underwriting activity, by company and line of coverage, 1982, with summary comparisons from 1980. Covers assets, liabilities, capital, surplus, premiums written and earned, losses incurred and/or paid, operating and underwriting gain/loss, dividends paid, and selected operating ratios.

Data are shown, as applicable, for fire and marine/casualty/surety/inter-insurance, title, and life insurance companies; fraternal benefit societies; and accident and health insurance business of life insurance companies.

Data by line of coverage include detail for automobile, worker compensation, and medical malpractice.

Also includes data on fire marshal activities, FY83; firefighter and police pension fund tax allocations, by city, 1982; insurance company bail bond business, 1st half 1983; and insurance industry employment, investments, market shares of top companies by insurance line, and consumer complaints, 1982.

Data are from annual insurer statements filed with the Insurance Dept, and from dept records.

Contains index to contents, transmittal letter, and lists of companies and status changes (p. 3-10); dept report, with text tables (p. 11-23); and 38 insurance tables (p. 24-399).

For description of previous report, for 1981, see SRI 1982 Annual, under this number.

Availability: Florida Department of Insurance, Insurance Commissioner, The Capitol, Tallahassee FL 32301, †; SRI/MF/complete.

S1765   FLORIDA
Department of
Labor and
Employment Security

S1765–3   FLORIDA EMPLOYMENT STATISTICS
Monthly. Approx. 10 p.
ISSN 0364-8311.
LC 76-648230.
SRI/MF/complete, shipped quarterly

Monthly report on Florida employment, unemployment, hours, earnings, and unemployment insurance claims. Month of coverage is approximately 2 months prior to cover date.

Contains brief narrative analysis; and 5 monthly tables, listed below.

Prior to the Mar. 1984 issue, report was published quarterly, and also included a table on labor market indicators.

Similar reports for individual MSAs are also available from the issuing agency, but are not covered by SRI.

Availability: Florida Department of Labor and Employment Security, Employment Security Division, Caldwell Bldg., Tallahassee FL 32301, †; SRI/MF/complete, shipped quarterly.

Issues reviewed during 1984: Nov. 1983-Feb. 1984 (quarterly); Mar.-Aug. 1984 (monthly) (P) (Nos. 411-418).

MONTHLY TABLES:
[Unless otherwise noted, data are shown for month of coverage, previous month, and same month of previous year. Table sequence may vary.]

[1] Labor force summary [by employment status].

[2] Estimated employment in nonagricultural establishments [by major industry group].

[3] Average hours and earnings in manufacturing [and selected nonmanufacturing] industries.

[4] Seasonally adjusted nonagricultural employment [by industry division].

[5] Unemployment compensation activity [initial claims, weeks claimed, and total payments].

S1770   FLORIDA
Department of
Law Enforcement

S1770–1   UNIFORM CRIME REPORTS, State of Florida: 1983 Annual Report
Annual. Mar. 29, 1984.
v+258 p.+errata sheet.
ISSN 0363-9231.
LC 78-643781.
SRI/MF/complete

Annual report, for 1983, presenting detailed data on Florida crimes and arrests, by type of offense and locale. Also includes data on stolen property value, offender and victim characteristics, drug seizures, law enforcement personnel, and assaults on police.

Data are from reports of State and local law enforcement agencies, submitted under the Uniform Crime Reporting (UCR) program.

Contains contents and table/chart listings (p. iv-v); introduction, with crime clocks and explanation of State UCR program (p. 1-12); 5 statistical sections, each preceded by a narrative summary, with 21 charts and 72 tables described below (p. 13-246); and glossary and index (p. 247-258).

This is the 13th annual report.

Availability: Florida Department of Law Enforcement, PO Box 1489, Tallahassee FL 32302, †; SRI/MF/complete.

CHARTS AND TABLES:
[Index crimes are murder, forcible rape, robbery, aggravated assault, burglary, larceny, and motor vehicle theft. Data by community type are shown by population size group within several urban, suburban, and rural classifications.
Data are for 1983 and often include comparisons to 1982 and/or trends from 1979 or earlier.]

S1770–1.1: Index Offenses and Arson

a. Crime rate by county, and arrest rate, based on population and on population plus tourists; and crimes, rate, and percent cleared, by Index offense. 10 charts and 4 tables. (p. 16-21)

b. Murder and rape: murders, by weapon, day of week, and circumstances; murder victims, by age, sex, and race; forcible and attempted rapes; and rape arrests, by age. 2 charts and 5 tables. (p. 24-27)

c. Robbery, assault, and larceny: robberies by weapon, and stolen property value, both by type of location; aggravated assaults, by weapon; assault arrests, by age; residence and nonresidence burglaries and stolen property value for day and night offenses; and larcenies and stolen property value, by type of theft. 6 tables. (p. 28-31)

d. Motor vehicle theft and arson: motor vehicle thefts and clearances, and value of stolen and recovered vehicles by type; arsons, total and juvenile clearances, arsons of uninhabited structures, and property damage, by property type. 3 tables. (p. 32-33)

e. Index crime summary, including motor vehicle thefts by vehicle type, and quarterly trends; and crimes, rate, and percent cleared, by community type; all by Index offense. 2 charts and 3 tables. (p. 34-39)

f. Value of stolen property by Index offense, and of stolen and recovered property by property type; percent of clearances involving adults and juveniles, by Index offense; and Index crime projection summary. 1 chart and 3 tables. (p. 40-49)

g. Local data: value of stolen and recovered property, by property type and county; and Index crimes by offense and aggregate crime rate and clearances, by judicial circuit, county, community and community type, university, airport, and Indian reservation. 4 tables. (p. 52-90)

S1770–1.2: Arrests, Drug Seizures, Agricultural Crimes, and Victims
[Arrests by offense are shown for 7 Index offenses and 23 other offenses.]

a. Arrest rate; arrests, by age, sex, and race (including American Indian and Oriental); and percent nonresident arrests; all by offense. 1 chart and 11 tables. (p. 94-105)

b. Adult and juvenile arrests by quarter; and adult and juvenile arrests, total arrest rate, percent nonresident, and arrests by offense, all by judicial circuit, county, community and community type, university, airport, and Indian reservation. 5 tables. (p. 106-161)

c. Narcotics arrests for sale and possession of paraphernalia and specified substances, and gambling arrests by offense, by sex, race (including American Indian and Oriental), age, judicial circuit, county, and community type. 8 tables. (p. 164-189)

d. Drug seizures and arrests, by substance; and drug seizures, by type of location. 1 table. (p. 192)

e. Agricultural crimes: offenses, by type of incident and location; resident and nonresident arrests; and value of stolen and recovered property, by offense and property type. 1 table. (p. 193) *f.* Rape and assault victims, by sex, race, age, and relationship to offender. 3 charts and 3 tables. (p. 196-198)

S1770–1.3: Law Enforcement Personnel

a. Officers killed, offenses cleared, offenders and arrests, and offender disposition; assault clearances, by circumstance; assaults, by circumstance, whether injury incurred, type of weapon and assignment, and time of day; and assault and law enforcement employment summary, by community type. 2 charts and 12 tables. (p. 204-217)

b. Injury and noninjury assaults, and law enforcement personnel by sex and whether civilian or sworn, by judicial district, county, community and community type, State agency, university, airport, and Indian reservation. 3 tables. (p. 220-246)

S1790   FLORIDA
Public Service Commission

S1790–1   FLORIDA PUBLIC SERVICE COMMISSION 1983-84 Report
Annual. [1984.] 68 p.
SRI/MF/complete

Annual report presenting Florida public utility regulatory, financial, and operating data, primarily by utility type and company, 1983, with selected trends from 1960. Utility types covered are telephone, gas, and electric, with regulatory data only for railroads and water/sewer systems.

Includes data on Public Service Commission finances and regulatory activities, including consumer complaints; utility plant value, revenue, customers, and return on equity; telephone facilities and call completion rates; average residential electricity consumption, and electricity and gas bills; electric utility fuel costs and conservation practices, and planned vs. actual generating performance; nuclear power plants; and natural gas accidents, injuries, and fatalities.

Also includes data on average U.S. residential electricity use, bill, and revenues, by census division; and electric rates in selected U.S. cities, including 25 with highest and lowest rates.

Data are from FPSC records and company reports.

Contains contents listing (1 p.); report, with regulatory text tables (p. 1-27); table listing (p. 29); and statistical section, with 33 tables (p. 33-68).

Availability: Florida Public Service Commission, Consumer Affairs Department, 101 E. Gaines St., Tallahassee FL 32301, †; SRI/MF/complete.

S1800   FLORIDA
Department of State

S1800–2   1983 FLORIDA LIBRARY DIRECTORY with Statistics
Annual. Aug. 1983. 186 p.
LC 52-62285.
SRI/MF/complete

Annual report on Florida public, academic, and institution libraries, with data for FY82. Includes finances, holdings, staff, capacity, and population served, by library system, county, and institution. Data are compiled from reports of participating libraries.

Contents:

a. Preface and contents listing (p. 3-5); and directories of library assns, libraries, and school media personnel (p. 7-113).

b. Statistical sections, with 2 maps and 16 tables listed below (p. 116-170); and personnel index (p. 173-186).

Previous report, for FY81, is described in SRI 1982 Annual, under this number.

Availability: Florida Department of State, State Library, Library Services Division, R. A. Gray Bldg., Tallahassee FL 32301-8021, $12.50; SRI/MF/complete.

TABLES:

PUBLIC LIBRARIES
[Data are for FY82, and are shown for regional systems, and by county and library.]

1. Volumes of books and periodicals, titles of selected [microform, audiovisual, and current periodical] materials, [population served, and volumes per capita]. (p. 118-123)

2. Use of library [registered borrowers; total circulation; interlibrary loans; book turnover rate; and per capita circulation, reference transactions, program attendance, and interlibrary materials use]. (p. 124-128)

3. Service delivery [number of public service outlets, library capacity, and hours per week]. (p. 129-133)

4. Personnel in FTE, [and annual salaries for library director and new librarians]. (p. 134-138)

5-7. Financial information: receipts by source [including State and Federal aid and nonresident fees]; financial information ranked by population [operating expenditures with percent by category, capital outlay, and per capita expenditures; and rank order of libraries and systems] by expenditures. (p. 139-149)

ACADEMIC LIBRARIES
[Data are shown by institution.]

1. Volumes of books and bound periodicals, [government documents, and microforms], fall 1982. (p. 153)

2. Loan transactions by type, 1981/82, and FTE personnel, fall 1982. (p. 155)

3. Financial information: library operating expenditures [by category], 1981/82. (p. 157)

INSTITUTION LIBRARIES
[Data are shown by State agency and institution, FY82.]

1. Number of residents, books and periodicals, and other materials. (p. 161)

2. Library capacity, hours, and staff [with head librarian salary]. (p. 163)

3. Financial information: income by source, and operating expenditures by category. (p. 165)

STATE LIBRARY

[A] [Budget expenditures by object and fund, circulation, and collections by type, 1981/82.] (p. 168)

GENERAL DATA

[B] State library information network [number of borrowing libraries, books supplied by source, subject and title requests received, and percentage supplied], 1981/82. [table and map] (p. 168-169)

[C] Status of library development, 1983 [number of counties, aggregate 1981 population, and percent of State population served and unserved, all by 5 library service categories (regional and countywide systems, and substandard, limited, and no public service); and State and unincorporated population 1970 and 1981]. [table and map] (p. 170)

S1805   FLORIDA
Supreme Court

S1805–1   REPORT OF THE FLORIDA STATE COURTS SYSTEM, 1982-83
Biennial. For individual publication data, see below.
SRI/MF/complete

Biennial report on Florida judicial system, including trial and appellate court caseloads and case dispositions, 1982-83. Covers supreme, appeals, circuit, and county courts, by case type and court location.

Trial court case types are criminal and civil, with additional detail for jury trials and for drug, contract, marriage dissolution, condemnation, probate (including mental health and guardianship), juvenile, traffic, and reopened cases.

Data are from reports filed by clerks of the courts.

Report is issued in 3 sections, further described below.

Previous report, for 1980-81, is described in SRI 1983 Annual, under this number.

Availability: Florida Supreme Court, State Courts Administrator's Office, Supreme Court Bldg., Tallahassee FL 32301; SRI/MF/complete.

S1805–1.1: Main Report
[Biennial. [1984.] 3+85+App 9 p. †. SRI/MF/complete.]

Presents caseload and case disposition data for supreme, appeals, circuit, and county courts, 1982-83, with selected comparisons to 1978 and 1981.

Also includes number of judges for each court, appeals court cases by processing time, and population and attorneys by circuit and county, 1983 with some data for 1982.

Contains listings of contents, tables, and charts (3 p.); narrative report, interspersed with 1 map, 33 charts, and 64 tables (p. 1-85); and appendices, with 14 tables and facsimile reporting system forms (p. A.1-A.4, B.1-B.5).

S1805–1.2: Florida Trial Courts Summary Data Report, 1982

[Biennial. [1984.] 176 p. ‡. SRI/MF/complete.]

Presents detailed caseload and case disposition data for circuit and county courts, 1982. Contains 7 tables repeated for each circuit and for each county arranged by circuit.

S1805–1.3: Florida Trial Courts Summary Data Report, 1983

[Biennial. [1984.] 176 p. ‡. SRI/MF/complete.]

Presents detailed caseload and case disposition data for circuit and county courts, 1983. Contains 7 tables repeated for each circuit and for each county arranged by circuit.

S1855   GEORGIA
Department of Agriculture

S1855–1   GEORGIA AGRICULTURAL FACTS, 1983

Annual. [1983.] 84 p.

SRI/MF/complete

Annual report on Georgia agricultural production, marketing, and finances, 1982, with trends mostly from the 1970s. Data are generally shown by commodity and/or county or district.

Report covers production, prices, sales, value, and, as applicable, acreage, yield, disposition, stocks, and/or inventory, for field crop, vegetable, fruit and nut, poultry, apiary, livestock, and dairy sectors.

Report also includes data on number of farms, by type; grain storage facilities and capacity; farm income, expenses, assets, and liabilities; prices paid by farmers for selected items; weather; export value of selected commodities; farm acreage and value; fertilizer consumption; farm labor and wages; and U.S. per capita consumption of selected foods.

Data are compiled by the Georgia Crop Reporting Service in cooperation with USDA.

Contains contents listing (1 p.); foreword (p. 1); and report, with 19 maps, 17 charts, and 86 tables (p. 2-84).

Availability: Crop Reporting Board Publications, South Bldg., Rm. 5829, U.S. Department of Agriculture, Washington DC 20250, $5.00; SRI/MF/complete.

S1860   GEORGIA
Department of Audits

S1860–1   REPORT OF THE STATE AUDITOR OF GEORGIA, Year Ended June 30, 1983

Annual. Dec. 30, 1983.

x+359 p.

LC 81-649640.

SRI/MF/complete

Annual report on financial condition of Georgia State government and university system for FY83, covering assets, liabilities and fund equity, fund balances, revenues by source, and expenditures by function and object. Most data are shown by fund type, with selected detail for individual State agencies and higher education institutions, and summary comparisons to FY82.

Governmental and fiduciary funds and account groups covered include general, budget, State revenue collections, debt service, capital projects, public and private trust and agency, and general fixed assets and long-term debt. University system fund types covered include current, loan, endowment, plant, and agency.

Also includes data on bonded debt, and comparisons of budgeted to actual financial activity.

Data are compiled from audit reports submitted by all State agencies and higher education institutions.

Contains transmittal letter and contents listing (p. v-x); and auditor's reports on all funds (p. 3-11), State agencies (p. 13-227), and university system (p. 229-359), with text statistics and 36 tables.

Three supplemental volumes, showing detailed salary, travel, and/or other reimbursed expenses, or professional fees or expenses paid, by recipient, are also available from Georgia Dept of Audits, but are not covered in SRI.

Availability: Georgia Department of Audits, Trinity-Washington Bldg., Rm. 214, 270 Washington St., SW, Atlanta GA 30334, †; SRI/MF/complete.

S1865   GEORGIA
Department of Banking and Finance

S1865–1   DEPARTMENT OF BANKING AND FINANCE, State of Georgia: Sixty-Fourth Annual Report, Year Ending Dec. 31, 1983

Annual. [1984.] xvi+64 p.

ISSN 0095-4039.

LC 74-648638.

SRI/MF/complete

Annual report on financial condition of Georgia financial institutions, presenting assets for individual State and national banks, State-chartered credit unions, and savings and loan assns, all arranged by city, and for international bank agencies; and composite assets, liabilities, capital, income, and expenses, for banks by asset size, and for credit unions and savings and loan assns; as of Dec. 31, 1983, usually with comparative data for 1982.

Also includes dept revenues and disbursements, FY83; real estate loan interest rate ceilings, Jan.-Mar. 1983; organizational activities of financial institutions including bank holding companies; unpaid claims and unliquidated assets of State banks and credit unions in liquidation; firms and agents licensed under Georgia Sale of Checks Act; and Georgia Credit Union Deposit Insurance Corp. financial statement.

Data are from institution annual reports and dept records.

Contains contents listing (1 p.); dept overview with 1 map and 2 tables (p. i-xvi); and 15 financial tables, with accompanying lists of activities (p. 1-64).

Availability: Georgia Department of Banking and Finance, 2990 Brandywine Rd., Suite 200, Atlanta GA 30341, †; SRI/MF/complete.

S1880   GEORGIA
Criminal Justice Coordinating Council

S1880–1   GEORGIA CRIMINAL JUSTICE DATA, 1983

Annual. Aug. 1984.

vi+143 p.

SRI/MF/complete

Annual report presenting detailed data on Georgia criminal justice system, mostly 1979-83, with trends from 1972. Includes data on crimes and arrests, law enforcement personnel, assaults on officers, traffic fatalities, court caseloads, correctional institution population, probation, and parole board activity.

Data are from State agency reports.

Contains listings of contents, tables, and charts (p. ii-vi); introduction and 4 sections with narrative analyses, 56 charts, and 77 tables (p. 1-130); and statements from senior officials, and appendix with data analysis techniques (p. 133-143).

All tables, and charts presenting data not covered in tables, are described below.

Previous reports were titled *Crime in Georgia* and presented crime and arrest data only. Last previous report covered 1981 (for description, see SRI 1983 Annual, under this number). No report was issued covering 1982 exclusively.

Availability: Georgia Crime Information Center, PO Box 370748, Decatur GA 30037-0748, †; SRI/MF/complete.

TABLES AND CHARTS:

[Unless otherwise noted, data are for Georgia and are shown for 1983 with selected trends from 1979.]

S1880–1.1: Law Enforcement

[Part I Index crimes are murder/non-negligent manslaughter, forcible rape, robbery, aggravated assault, burglary, larceny, motor vehicle theft, and arson; Part II crimes are 20 other offenses.]

CRIMES

a. Crimes and arrests, aggregated for Part I and Part II offenses; and crimes and crime rate, and offense characteristics, including victim-offender relationship, type of weapon used, place of occurrence, months of highest occurrence, value of property stolen, arrest/crime ratio, and persons arrested by age, sex, and race, all by Part I offense. Tables 1-12. (p. 9-29)

b. Population, and Part I crimes by offense, by MSA and component county, and for total nonmetro areas; with data on crime rates and comparisons to total and southern U.S. Tables 13-19. (p. 31-38)

c. Part II crimes; and crimes against children, and arrests by sex; all by offense. Tables 20-22B. (p. 39-41)

ARRESTS AND COUNTY PROFILES

d. Arrests, and arrest rates, by Part I and Part II offense, with detail by age, sex, and race; drug arrests by substance; and clearances and clearance rates, by Part I and Part II offense; various years 1972-83. Tables 23-38. (p. 43-57)

e. Part I crimes by offense, and aggregate crime rate; full-time law enforcement sworn and civilian employees, by sex; and law enforcement employees per 100,000 population; all by county, with selected rankings. Tables 39-43. (p. 59-75)

OFFICERS ASSAULTED AND TRAFFIC ENFORCEMENT

f. Officers killed; and officers assaulted, by type of activity and weapon, injury status, type of assignment, and time of day, with total clearances. Table 44. (p. 76)

g. Driving under the influence (DUI) arrests by county, with ranking by arrest rate; and DUI arrests by age. Tables 45-47. (p. 78-83)

h. Traffic deaths and miles traveled, 1973-83; fatal accidents and fatalities (total, DUI, and other alcohol-related); traffic fatalities by urban-rural location and type (pedestrian, motorcycle, and other vehicle); and accidents, injuries, and fatalities, by holiday. Charts 25-27 and tables 48-53. (p. 85-87)

S1880–1.2: Courts and Corrections

COURTS

a. Case dispositions and/or caseloads by type: for superior, State, probate, and juvenile courts, by circuit or county, FY83 with aggregate trends from FY79; and for supreme and appeals courts, 1983 and/or 1982. Charts 29-32 and tables 54-59. (p. 93-109)

CORRECTIONS

b. Correctional institution population, by type of facility, individual institution, age, sex, race, length of sentence, number of prior arrests, most serious type of crime, and offense, with various cross-tabulations. Tables 60-69. (p. 114-121)

c. Probation population by race, sex, age, most serious type of crime, offense, and first offender status, with various cross-tabulations; and parole board case dispositions and other actions. Tables 70-77. (p. 122-130)

S1885   GEORGIA
Department of Education

S1885–2   1983 GEORGIA PUBLIC LIBRARY STATISTICS
Annual.   1984.   64 p.
LC 65-65192.
SRI/MF/complete

Annual report on Georgia public library holdings, services, construction, and finances, including State agency services and special programs, for FY83.

Contains contents listing and introduction (p. 1-3); 6 tables, listed below (p. 4-22); and library directories (p. 23-64).

Availability: Georgia Department of Education, Public Library Services Division, 156 Trinity Ave., SW, Annex Bldg., Atlanta GA 30303, †; SRI/MF/complete.

TABLES:
[All data are for FY83.]

[1] Statistics for library systems [population, number of counties and branches, staff, circulation, holdings, funds by source, and expenditures by object, by library system]. (p. 4-9)

[2] Audiovisual materials [by type, by library system]. (p. 10)

[3] Analysis of Federal funds received (libraries receiving other than LSCA [Library Services and Construction Act], Title I) [amount and funding source, by library]. (p. 13)

[4] Construction [project status, size, and funding by source, by library and location]. (p. 14)

[5] State agency services [large group loans; State film collection holdings, circulation, and audience; technical services, including microforms; and reader services]. (p. 16-21)

[6] LSCA, Title I, special programs directed to national/regional priorities [including disadvantaged, institutionalized, and limited English-speaking; and library for the blind/physically handicapped (holdings and circulation, by medium)]. (p. 22)

S1895   GEORGIA
Department of Human Resources

S1895–1   VITAL STATISTICS DATA BOOK, 1982, Georgia
Annual.   June 1984.
331 p. no paging.
LC 76-646236.
SRI/MF/complete

Annual report, for 1982, on Georgia vital statistics, covering births, abortions, deaths by cause, marriages, divorces, and population, by demographic characteristics and location. Data are primarily from records received by DHR prior to Mar. 31, 1983.

Contains introduction, technical notes, and glossary (8 p.); and 2 tables, described below, repeated for various geographic breakdowns (323 p.).

This is the 36th annual report.

Availability: Georgia Department of Human Resources, Public Health Division, 47 Trinity Ave., SW, Atlanta GA 30334, †; SRI/MF/complete.

TABLES:

a. Vital statistics, 1982: total births, births to unwed mothers, and spontaneous and induced abortions, by age of mother or abortion recipient and birth weight; out of hospital births; marriages and divorces; and deaths by age and cause; all with number and rate by race, repeated for State (2 p.), DHR health districts (20 p.), health service areas (8 p.), SMSAs and total non-SMSA (10 p.), counties (160 p.), and cities and total outside cities (excludes rates) (74 p.).

b. Population, by age, race, and sex, 1982, repeated for counties and State (40 p.), DHR health districts (5 p.), health service areas (2 p.), and SMSAs and total non-SMSA (2 p.).

S1903   GEORGIA
Judicial Council

S1903–1   TENTH ANNUAL REPORT ON THE WORK OF THE GEORGIA COURTS, July 1, 1982-June 30, 1983
Annual.   Feb. 1984.   1+36 p.
No. J-0284-A-01.
ISSN 0363-9320.
LC 76-644657.
SRI/MF/complete

Annual report, for FY83, on Georgia judicial system, including trial and appellate court caseloads and case dispositions, with trends from FY79. Covers supreme, appeals, superior, State, probate, and juvenile courts. Includes trial court data by case type, circuit, and county.

Case types shown are generally civil and criminal, with additional detail for domestic relations, deprived and delinquent children, guardianship, commitment, habeas corpus, and various other cases.

Also includes data on judicial finances, manpower, and seminar attendance and certification; and sentence review panel caseloads.

Contains contents listing (inside front cover); foreword and report, with 1 map, 4 charts, and 12 tables (p. 1-32); and appendices on judicial personnel and agencies, with 1 table (p. 33-36).

Availability: Georgia Judicial Council, Administrative Office of the Courts, Suite 550, 244 Washington St., SW, Atlanta GA 30334, †; SRI/MF/complete.

S1905   GEORGIA
Department of Labor

S1905–1   GEORGIA LABOR MARKET TRENDS

Monthly.   Approx. 20 p.
LC 77-640865.
SRI/MF/complete, shipped quarterly

Monthly report on Georgia employment and unemployment, by industry and SMSA. Also includes data on hours and earnings by manufacturing industry.

Report is issued 1 month after month of coverage.

Contains narrative articles and selected news briefs on economic developments, occasionally with substantial statistics; 2-3 summary charts with trends; and 18 monthly tables, listed below, with interspersed analysis.

Monthly tables appear in all issues; additional features with substantial statistics are described below.

Availability: Georgia Department of Labor, Employment Security Agency, Labor Information Systems, 254 Washington St., SW, Atlanta GA 30334, †; SRI/MF/complete, shipped quarterly.

Issues reviewed during 1984: Sept. 1983-Aug. 1984 (D) (Vol. X, Nos. 1-8) [volume/issue numbering begins with Jan. 1984 issue].

MONTHLY TABLES:

[All data are shown for month of coverage, previous month, and same month of preceding year.]

ESTABLISHMENT DATA

[Data on employment are shown by industry division and major group; other data are shown by major manufacturing industry group.]

[1] Nonagricultural employment.

[2] Production workers.

[3] Hours and earnings.

[4-6] [Tables [1-3] are repeated for Atlanta.]

[7-11] [Table [1] is repeated for Albany, Athens, Augusta, Columbus, and Macon.]

[12-14] [Tables [1-3] are repeated for Savannah.]

RESIDENCE DATA

[15-18] U.S. and Georgia labor force estimates; and civilian labor force [for Georgia and 7 SMSAs, for neighboring State residents in Augusta and Columbus SMSAs, and for metro and nonmetro residents; all by employment status], by place of residence.

STATISTICAL FEATURES:

S1905–1.501: Apr. 1984 (Vol. X, No. 4)

GEORGIA RECORDS THIRD LARGEST INCREASE IN PER CAPITA INCOME

(p. 1-2) Article, with 2 tables showing per capita personal income for Georgia and 11 other southeastern States, 1983, with comparisons to U.S., and Georgia comparisons to 1982. Data are from Commerce Dept.

S1905–1.502: July 1984 (Vol. X, No. 7)

SUMMER YOUTH PROGRAM CREATES JOBS

(p. 1-2) Article, with 2 tables showing Georgia population, and labor force by employment status, for youth aged 16-19, 1983; and youth unemployment rates in poverty and nonpoverty areas for total U.S. and for metro and nonmetro areas, 1st quarter 1984; all by sex and race. Data are from BLS.

S1915   GEORGIA
Department of Offender Rehabilitation

S1915–1   GEORGIA DEPARTMENT OF OFFENDER REHABILITATION Biennial Report, 1982-83

Biennial.   [1984.]   38 p.
ISSN 0093-7096.
LC 80-640501.
SRI/MF/complete

Biennial report, for FY82-83, on corrections in Georgia, presenting data on prison admissions and releases; escapes and apprehensions; and inmate population by detailed demographic and other characteristics, including IQ, family background, commitment offense, security status, and number of sentences.

Also includes data on prison farm production and costs, by commodity; community-based transition facility residents and finances; inmate health care activities and costs; prison inmate population and costs, by institution; and DOR finances.

Contains contents listing (1 p.); and narrative report, interspersed with 7 charts and 19 tables (p. 1-38).

Prior to FY82-83 edition, report was published annually.

Availability: Georgia Department of Offender Rehabilitation, Information and Legislative Services Division, Two Martin Luther King Jr. Dr., SE, Floyd Bldg., East Tower, Rm. 856, Atlanta GA 30334, †; SRI/MF/complete.

S1920   GEORGIA
Office of Planning and Budget

S1920–3   GEORGIA DESCRIPTIONS IN DATA, 1984

Annual.   [1984.]   191 p.
SRI/MF/complete

Annual compilation, for 1984, of detailed social and economic statistics for Georgia. Data are primarily for 1970s-83, with selected population trends from 1940s. Data are from State and Federal agencies.

Report is designed to present an overview of the State. Extensive socioeconomic, demographic, and geographic breakdowns are shown, as applicable, for most topics. These breakdowns include data by city, county, MSA, urban-rural status, industry, occupation, age, marital status, race, and sex. Comparisons to total U.S. and other southeastern States are also occasionally included.

Contents:

a. Contents and table listing (p. 4-6); and 1 summary profile table, and 34 detailed tables in 11 sections, described below (p. 9-164).

b. Explanatory notes (p. 167-170); 6 appendices with directories of State agencies and 3 maps (p. 171-180); and index to current and previous editions (p. 183-191).

This is the 3rd annual edition.

Availability: Georgia Office of Planning and Budget, State Data Center, Trinity-Washington Bldg., 270 Washington St., SW, Atlanta GA 30334, $7.50; $12.50 for 1982-84 issues purchased together; 1982-83 issues available separately for $5.00 each; SRI/MF/complete.

SUMMARY PROFILE AND TABLE SECTIONS:

S1920–3.1: Profile

(p. 9-16) Contains 1 table. Includes summary data on population characteristics, housing, income, State revenues, business and industry, agriculture, labor force and employment, education, transportation, health, environment, veterans, and worker disability.

S1920–3.2: Section I-II: Population and Housing

a. **Population:** State rankings of population characteristics and other general data; and Georgia local area characteristics, including housing units by tenure, per capita personal income, persons and families in poverty, high school and college graduates, employment and unemployment, public use airports, highway mileage, public libraries, State parks, colleges, arts organizations, and crime rate. Tables 1-5. (p. 17-34)

b. **Housing:** median value and contract rent; and housing units and occupancy. Tables 6-7. (p. 35-50)

S1920–3.3: Section III-IV: Income and Economic Data, and Education

a. **Income and economic data:** per capita personal income; median family income; persons and families in poverty; sales/use tax receipts; personal income reported and tax liability; taxable sales; motor vehicle registrations; property assessed valuation, millage rates, and mills levied; and school revenues and average daily attendance. Tables 8-13. (p. 51-81)

b. **Education:** years of school completed; public and private school enrollment; higher education enrollment, and degrees awarded by institution; and high school graduates. Tables 14-18a. (p. 82-110)

S1920–3.4: Section V-VII: Employment, Business and Industry, and Commuting

a. **Employment:** nonagricultural employment, labor force by employment status, wages, and unemployment compensation. Tables 19-22. (p. 111-118)

b. **Business and industry:** new/expanded domestic and foreign plants, jobs created, and investment; and business establishments, employment, and payroll. Tables 23-24. (p. 119-122)

c. **Commuting:** work force by place of work and mean travel time, and workers commuting outside county of residence. Tables 25-26. (p. 123-141)

S1920–3.5: Section VIII-XI: Health, Public Safety, Transportation, and Agriculture

a. **Health:** hospital and nursing home beds, active physicians and dentists, birth rate, and death rate by cause. Tables 27-29. (p. 142-157)

b. **Public safety:** Index crimes committed, by offense; and traffic accidents, injuries, and fatalities. Tables 30-31. (p. 158-159)

c. **Transportation:** interstate highway vehicle traffic; and public transit ridership. Tables 32-33. (p. 160)

d. **Agriculture:** farms and acreage; farm property value; and value of agricultural products sold. Table 34. (p. 161-164)

S1925   GEORGIA
Department of Public Safety

S1925–1   GEORGIA DEPARTMENT OF PUBLIC SAFETY, 1982
Annual Report
Annual. [1983.]   48 p.
SRI/MF/complete

Annual report on Georgia traffic accidents, fatalities, and injuries, by accident and vehicle type, location, and other circumstances; and driver and victim characteristics; 1982, with selected trends from 1973.

Also includes data on miles of travel, traffic law enforcement, drivers licenses, handicapped parking permits, driver school licensing and inspection activity, State police duties and hours, and public safety dept budget.

Contains contents listing (inside front cover); 3 trend charts, highlights, and departmental organization (p. 1-8); and statistical summary, with 1 map and 26 tables (p. 12-48).

Availability: Georgia Department of Public Safety, 959 E. Confederate Ave., SE, PO Box 1456, Atlanta GA 30371-2303, †; SRI/MF/complete.

S1950   GEORGIA
Department of Revenue

S1950–1   STATISTICAL REPORT FOR 1983, Georgia Department of Revenue
Annual.   Nov. 30, 1983.
vi+42 p.
LC 41-52330.
SRI/MF/complete

Annual report, for FY83, on Georgia Dept of Revenue activities, including tax collections, by type and county; State revenue trends from 1900; and tax valuations of general property, public utilities, and intangibles.

Contains foreword and contents listing (p. ii-vi); report in 4 sections, with narrative highlights, 9 charts, and 23 tables listed below (p. 1-41); and index (p. 42).

Availability: Georgia Department of Revenue, Trinity-Washington Bldg., Rm. 401, 270 Washington St., SW, Atlanta GA 30334, †; SRI/MF/complete.

TABLES:

S1950–1.1: State Revenue Collections and Trends

H1. Net revenue collections, FY39-83. (p. 6)

[H1.A] Monthly revenue collections [FY80-Oct. FY84]. (p. 6)

H2. Net revenue collections by [detailed] kind of tax, FY81-83. (p. 8)

H3. Trend in total State tax revenues by major source, FY73-83. (p. 10)

H4. Comparative trends in personal income and State income tax receipts, FY68-83. (p. 10)

S1950–1.2: Tax Data by Type and/or County

DATA BY TYPE OF TAX

1-2. Sales/use tax revenues, FY83; and adjusted gross sales and use tax receipts, 1982 with index of change [1980-82]; by business group. (p. 15-16)

3. Growth trend of personal income tax [number of returns, adjusted gross and taxable income reported, and tax liability, 1969-81]. (p. 17)

4. Motor fuels and motor carriers: detailed revenue data for FY83. (p.18)

5. Personal income tax, returns by income class [number of returns, net taxable income, tax, number of dependents, and additional selected statistics], 1981 income. (p. 19)

6. Details of revenue from selective excise taxes and business license fees [for alcoholic beverages, cigars/cigarettes, and motor fuels], FY83. (p. 20)

7-8. Summary of revenues from motor vehicle tags, titles, and related items, FY81-83; and number of motor vehicle tags sold by major category, and number of titles sold, 1980-82. (p. 21)

9. Taxable values and tax rates for general property and public utilities, selected years 1900-82. (p. 22)

10. Summary of net property tax collections, by category, FY83. (p. 22)

11. Taxable values of general property, public utilities, and intangibles, by class of property, 1981-82. (p. 23)

DATA BY COUNTY
[Tables show data by county.]

12. 1981 personal income tax data: 1981 earnings [number of returns, adjusted gross income less deficit, net taxable income, and amount of tax liability; also shows 1980 population]. (p. 24)

13. Selected tax statistics and estimates [including sales and use tax receipts, general property and public utility assessed value, and motor vehicle tags sold by vehicle type], 1982. (p. 27)

14. Four economic indicators, with ranking and per capita amounts [taxable sales, auto registrations, and net property/utility digest, 1982; and adjusted gross income reported, 1981]. (p. 32-37)

CORPORATE TAX RETURNS

15. [Domestic and foreign] corporation income tax returns [and net taxable income] by taxable income class, 1981 tax year returns. (p. 38)

MILLAGE RATES AND INTANGIBLE ASSESSMENTS

16-17. 1982 millage rates by county, alphabetically and numerically listed. (p. 39-40)

18. Gross intangible tax assessments, by county, 1982. (p. 41)

S2030   HAWAII
Department of Agriculture

S2030–1   STATISTICS OF HAWAIIAN AGRICULTURE, 1982
Annual.   July 1983.
4+100 p.
SRI/MF/complete

Annual report on Hawaii agricultural production and marketing, mostly 1978-82, with selected trends from 1972. Data are generally shown by commodity, with selected detail by island.

Report generally covers production, sales, prices, value, and, as applicable, number of farms, acreage, yield, utilization, and inventory, for field and specialty crops, including flowers and nursery products, coffee, and sugar, with detail for molasses; and for fruit and nut, vegetable and melon, livestock, dairy, apiary, and poultry sectors.

Report also includes data on farm income from government payments; precipitation; market supply of commodities by source (Hawaii and inshipments); outshipments of selected commodities, including detail for anthuriums by country of destination; prices paid by farmers for feed and other production items; fertilizer consumption; and agricultural employment and wage rates.

Data are compiled by Hawaii Agricultural Reporting Service in cooperation with USDA.

Contains contents listing (p. 1); 25 charts and 136 tables, interspersed with narrative analyses (p. 2-96); and definitions, methodology, and list of additional reports available from issuing agency (p. 97-100).

For description of previous report, for 1981, see SRI 1982 Annual, under this number.

Availability: Crop Reporting Board Publications, South Bldg., Rm. 5829, U.S. Department of Agriculture, Washington DC 20250, $5.00; SRI/MF/complete.

S2035   HAWAII
Department of the
Attorney General

S2035–1   CRIME IN HAWAII, 1983: A
Review of Uniform Crime
Reports
Annual. Apr. 1984. ii+89 p.
SRI/MF/complete

Annual report on Hawaii crimes and arrests, by
offense and county, 1983. Also includes arrests
by offender age, race, and sex; and selected comparisons to 1982.

Data are from State and local agency reports
submitted under the Uniform Crime Reporting
Program.

Contains contents and table listings (p. ii), introduction (p. 1-4), and the following:

a. Crime summary with 29 charts and 16 tables
generally showing summary data, including
distribution of selected offenses by weapon
and type of property involved; percent of
murder victims by race, age, and relationship
to offender; and percent changes in Index offense occurrences from 1979; and crime
clocks. (p. 5-40)

b. State comparisons, with 1 table showing
States ranked by total, violent, and nonviolent crime rates, 1982. (p. 41-42)

c. 2 statistical sections on offenses and arrests,
with 4 charts, and 31 detailed tables listed
below; and definitions. (p. 43-86)

This is the 9th annual report.

Availability: Hawaii Department of the Attor-
ney General, Criminal Justice Data Center,
Kekuanao'a Bldg., 1st Floor, 465 S. King St.,
Honolulu HI 96813, †; SRI/MF/complete.

DETAILED TABLES:

[Crime Index offenses are murder, forcible rape,
robbery, aggravated assault, burglary, larceny/
theft, and motor vehicle theft. Arson is classified
as an Index offense, but data are reported separately, and are not included in the Crime Index
tables. Data are for Hawaii, 1983, unless otherwise noted.]

S2035–1.1: Offense Statistics

[All tables except tables 5-6 show number of
Index offenses by type. Tables 1-2 also show
rates per 100,000 population.]

[A] Percent [and number] of offenses cleared
[by offense and county.] (p. 43)

1. Crime Index. (p. 44)

2. Index of crime: U.S. and Hawaii, 1982. (p.
45)

3-4. Crime Index offenses known to police, by
county; and offenses reported, by month. (p.
46-47)

5-6. Value of property stolen and recovered
by county; and for total State [by type of prop-
erty]. (p. 48-49)

7-9. Value of property stolen: by [5] types of
offense; [by type of] larceny/theft; and by
county by [6] types of offense. (p. 50-52)

S2035–1.2: Arrest Statistics

[Data by race or ethnic stock are for Caucasian, black, American Indian, Chinese, Japanese, Filipino, Samoan, Korean,
Hawaiian/part Hawaiian, and other.]

SUMMARY AND DRUG ARRESTS

10-11. Population and arrests [by] ethnic
stock and age. (p. 54-55)

12-13. Drug abuse arrests by age and race of
persons arrested [for sale/manufacturing and
possession, by substance]. (p. 56-57)

ADULT ARRESTS

14. Age and sex of adults arrested, by month
for Part I and Part II [Index and non-Index]
offenses. (p. 58)

15. Crime Index arrests of adults, by [offense
and] county [1982-83]. (p. 59)

16-20. Age and sex of adults arrested: by [27]
offenses; and by Crime Index offense, by county. (p. 61-72)

21. Race of adults arrested, by offense. (p. 73)

JUVENILE ARRESTS

[B] Police disposition of juveniles [arrested].
(p. 75)

22. Age and sex of juveniles arrested, by
month, for Part I and Part II offenses. (p. 76)

23. Crime Index arrests of juveniles, by [of-
fense and] county [1982-83]. (p. 77)

24-28. Age and sex of juveniles arrested: by
[29] offenses; and by Crime Index offense, by
county. (p. 79-84)

29. Race of juveniles arrested, by offense. (p.
85-86)

S2065   HAWAII
Department of
Health

S2065–1   STATISTICAL
SUPPLEMENT,
DEPARTMENT OF HEALTH,
State of Hawaii, 1982
Annual. Oct. 1983. 244 p.
LC 61-63740.
SRI/MF/complete

Annual report, for 1982, on Hawaii vital statistics; Dept of Health programs and services; incidence and treatment of chronic, communicable,
and mental health diseases; types of hospital and
nursing care; and environmental and health protection services.

Data primarily are from Hawaii government
agencies.

Selected data are shown by demographic characteristics and by county, major city, and/or
island.

Contains contents listing; and 10 statistical
sections, with text statistics, 6 charts, and 250
tables listed below, arranged by health agency
and division or branch reporting.

This report is the statistical supplement to a
descriptive report issued separately by the Dept
of Health. The descriptive report is not covered
in SRI.

For description of previous report, for 1981,
see SRI 1982 Annual, under this number.

Availability: Hawaii Department of Health,
Research and Statistics Office, PO Box 3378,
Honolulu HI 96801, †; SRI/MF/complete.

TABLES:

[Data are for State of Hawaii, 1982, unless otherwise noted. Data by residence or geographic area
are generally shown for counties, cities, and/or
islands.

Data by race are generally shown for Caucasian, Hawaiian, part-Hawaiian, Chinese, Filipino, Japanese, Puerto Rican, Korean, Samoan,
Negro, Portuguese, Vietnamese, other, and unknown.]

S2065–1.1: Vital Statistics

POPULATION

1. Estimated population by residence and
military status, 1970, 1980, and 1982. (p. 7)

BIRTHS

2-3. Live births by place of occurrence reallocated to place of residence and race of child
and mother. (p. 9)

4-7. Live births: by race of mother and [12]
types of congenital malformation; by place and
month of occurrence; by race of child and
[type of] attendant at birth; and by race of
father and of mother. (p. 10-11)

8-10. Live births, by race of mother: and
month of first prenatal visit, number of children born to mother, and number of children
born alive to mother. (p. 12-13)

11-12. Live births by age of mother: and number of children born, and number of children
born alive. (p. 13-14)

13-14. Single live births by weight at birth and
race of child and mother. (p. 14-15)

15-16. Single male and female live births by
weight and gestation period. (p. 15-16)

17-19. Live births: by race, sex, plurality of
birth, and low birth weight; by race and age of
mother; and by age of father and mother. (p.
16-17)

20-22. Illegitimate live births: by place of occurrence reallocated to place of residence and
race of mother; by weight at birth and race of
child; and by race and age of mother. (p. 18-
19)

23. Resident births occurring outside State by
age of mother, and race and sex of child. (p.
19)

DEATHS

24. Total deaths by place of occurrence reallocated to usual residence, by race. (p. 20)

25-27. Resident deaths: by place and month of
occurrence; by place of occurrence, age, and
sex; and by age and race. (p. 20-21)

28. Total recorded deaths, by age, race, and
sex. (p. 22)

29. Total resident deaths recorded by age
groups [and median age at death] for selected
years 1962-82. (p. 22)

30. Resident deaths by age, sex, and marital
status. (p. 23)

31. Leading causes of death for 1982 and
comparative data for selected years 1962-82.
(p. 23)

32-32E. Resident deaths by age group by sex
and by [detailed] selected causes of death [for
State and 4 counties]. (p. 24-34)

33. Total recorded deaths from malignant
neoplasm by major and [detailed] selected
sites, sex, and age [groups]. (p. 35)

34. Resident deaths occurring outside the
State by race, age [group], and sex. (p. 37)

35. Total recorded deaths by island of occurrence, by method of disposition and autopsy
performed. (p. 37)

INFANT DEATHS

[Data by age of infants are shown for under 1 day, 1-6 days, 7-27 days, and 28 days to 11 months.]

36. Infant deaths by place of occurrence reallocated to usual residence by race of child. (p. 39)

37-38. Resident infant deaths: by age and race of mother; and by race of mother and month of first prenatal visit. (p. 39-40)

39. Resident infant mortality by race of child: [by] age, [and for] low birth weight infant deaths. (p. 40)

40. Resident infant mortality by selected causes: by birth weight, sex, and age; [and for] neonatal deaths. (p. 41)

FETAL DEATHS

[Standard fetal deaths are deaths due to spontaneous or unknown causes, and exclusive of elective abortion.]

41-42. Standard fetal deaths by place of occurrence reallocated to usual residence of mother and gestation period and by race [of fetus]. (p. 41-42)

43-45. Standard fetal deaths: by cause and gestation period; by age of mother and gestation period; and by race and age of mother. (p. 42-43)

ELECTIVE ABORTIONS

46-49. Elective abortions: by race and age of mother; by age of mother and length of gestation period; and by legitimacy status and race and age of mother. (p. 44-45)

50-51. Elective abortions: by type of procedure and gestation period; and by county of residence and county of occurrence. (p. 45-46)

MARRIAGE

52-54. Marriages: by place and month of occurrence; by age of groom and bride; and by previous marital status of groom and bride by age. (p. 47-48)

55-59. Marriages: by occupation and previous marital status of groom and bride; by number of times groom and bride previously married; and by race and age of groom and bride. (p. 48-50)

60-61. Marriages by residence and race of groom and bride. (p. 50-51)

DIVORCE AND ANNULMENT

62-66. Divorces and annulments: by place and month of occurrence, number of children reported under 18 years, and by race and age of husband and wife. (p. 51-53)

67-70. Divorces and annulments: by legal grounds and duration of marriage; and by education, residence, and age of husband and wife. (p. 53-55)

S2065–1.2: Hawaii Tumor Registry

[Data are shown by sex.]

1-2. Most common cancers reported by site and race for residents, 1981. (p. 57)

3-4. Tumor registrations: [by] race and age, 1981. (p. 58)

5-6. Tumor registrations, recent years [of diagnosis, 1978-81]; vital status. (p. 59)

7-8. Tumor status in living patients, recent years [of diagnosis, 1978-81]. (p. 60)

S2065–1.3: Health Surveillance Program, and Health Planning and Development Agency

PREVALENCE OF CHRONIC AND ACUTE DISEASE

[Data are from a 1982 annual survey of 16,309 persons in 6,822 households.]

1-14. Prevalence of selected chronic conditions, and number per 1,000 persons per year, by geographic area and age [by sex], and [by race]. (p. 62-75)

15. Number of [selected] chronic conditions per 1,000 persons per year (1977-82). (p. 76)

16-18. Distribution [and number] of persons by activity limitation status due to chronic conditions according to sex and family income, [by] age. (p. 77-79)

19-28. Incidence of [selected] acute conditions, and number per 100 persons per year, by geographic area, age, [sex] by age, and race. (p. 80-89)

29. Number of [selected] acute conditions per 100 persons per year (1977-82). (p. 90)

30-35. [Total and] average number per person per year of restricted and bed days, and of work days lost for persons 17 years of age and older, by geographic area and age. (p. 91-96)

36. Total number and average school days lost per person 6-16 years of age, by geographic area. (p. 97)

HEALTH PLANNING AND DEVELOPMENT AGENCY

1-3. SHPDA [State Health Planning and Development Agency] recognized acute, long-term, and specialty care bed capacity [by specialty or facility type, by individual institution]. (p. 101-102)

4-7. Average length of stay, occupancy rates, average daily [patient] census, and number of admissions, [all] by county [for long-term, total acute, medical/surgical, critical, obstetric, pediatric, and psychiatric care, with selected data for mentally retarded and other care types, 1977-82]. (p. 102-105)

S2065–1.4: Family Health Services Division

MATERNAL AND CHILD HEALTH BRANCH

1. Women receiving family planning services in publicly subsidized clinics, FY82. (p. 112)

2. Number of women and infants receiving services at the maternity and infant care project by type of service [including prenatal care, deliveries, and family planning admissions]. (p. 112)

3. Waimanalo children and youth project activities [by service type]. (p. 113)

4. Infants and children provided public health nursing services in child health conferences [by county, FY82]. (p. 113)

CRIPPLED CHILDREN'S BRANCH

5. Distribution of children receiving services by status [new and old cases] and age, FY82. (p. 113)

6. Staff services provided by branch, by type of service, FY82. (p. 113)

7. Distribution of primary medical conditions among children receiving services by diagnostic group and age of child, FY82. (p. 114)

DEVELOPMENTALLY DISABLED BRANCH

8. Infant and child development services provided by number of children served and geographic area covered [by selected service providers], FY82. (p. 115)

9. Number of mentally retarded in case management services, FY82. (p. 115)

10. Statistical movement of residents from Waimano Training School and Hospital [for the retarded], FY82. (p. 115)

11. Leave population, Waimano, June 30, by measured intelligence, FY82. (p. 115)

SCHOOL HEALTH SERVICES BRANCH

12-13. Activity and respite care programs, numbers served and geographic areas covered, FY82. (p. 116)

14. Total numbers of health room visits, reasons for visit and disposition, by school year 1977/78-1981/82. (p. 116)

15. Requests for administration of medication by [type of] condition and medication, 1981/82. (p. 117)

16. Health problem summary list [selected health conditions, by district], 1981/82. (p. 118)

17. Number of cases referred to school nurses [by island and school level], 1981/82. (p. 118)

18-19. Vision and hearing statistics [includes screenings, referrals, completed referrals, and deficit findings; by screening source], 1981/82. (p. 119)

20-21. Number of students receiving occupational and physical therapists' services, by category and district, FY82. (p. 120)

22. Number of students receiving occupational therapy assistant services, by category and district, FY82. (p. 121)

23-25. Age and sex distribution, referral source, [and school type, by] follow-up recommendations of children evaluated for learning disability. (p. 122-123)

S2065–1.5: Communicable Disease Division

EPIDEMIOLOGY BRANCH

1. Number of cases and deaths from communicable diseases, 1978-82. (p. 127)

2. Selected communicable disease rates per 100,000 population, 1978-82. (p. 128)

3. Communicable disease report by geographic areas. (p. 128)

4. Venereal disease cases reported to the Dept of Health by diagnosis and source of report. (p. 129)

5-6. Total primary and secondary syphilis and total gonorrhea cases by age, 1977-82. (p. 129)

7. Number and rate per 100,000 population of total reported gonorrhea cases [by age group], 1969-82. (p. 129)

8. Gonorrhea morbidity: case rate per 100,000 population, and by sex and resistance to penicillin (1973-82). (p. 130)

9. Infectious syphilis morbidity trend, by [stage of syphilis] and sex (1973-82). (p. 130)

HANSEN'S DISEASE PROGRAM

1. Total leprosy patients registered by register status, 1976-82. (p. 132)

2-3. Leprosy patients [by] Kalaupapa registry status, and total cases of leprosy registered by type and location, 1977-82. (p. 132-133)

4-6. New cases of leprosy by age group, island of residence, and place of birth, 1977-82. (p. 133-134)

7-9. [Cases and rate per 100,000] of leprosy, by island of residence and [age group], and for Hawaii-born vs. foreign-born. (p. 134-135)

10. New cases of leprosy by place of residence at onset of symptoms. (p. 135)

11. Sex-specific incidence [cases and rate per 100,000] of Hansen's disease. (p. 135)

TUBERCULOSIS (TB) BRANCH

1. X-ray survey activities for TB by county. (p. 137)

2. TB cases reported by geographic area of residence, [1981-82]. (p. 137)

3. TB cases by place of birth and length of residence, and number of persons admitted to Hawaii with permanent visas, [1981-82]. (p. 138)

4-7. TB cases: by location of disease, source of report, and reason for examination, by county of residence; and by age, race, and sex. (p. 138-140)

8-9. Reactivations reported: by bacteriology and number of reactivations, by county; and by age, sex, and county. (p. 140-141)

10. Number of TB deaths, and new cases reported by year, [decennially] 1930-80 and 1981-82. (p. 141)

S2065–1.6: Dental Health Division
[Data are for FY82, unless otherwise noted.]

1. Summary of dental health services [prevention and detection, and treatment]. (p. 145)

2. Distribution of dental hygiene services by counties [schools and children served]. (p. 145)

3. Dental treatment status of children in 178 schools [aggregate] by areas, 1981/82 [with totals for 1980/81]. (p. 146)

4. Treatment data: hospital dentistry and community services branch [number of patients and selected procedures]. (p. 146)

S2065–1.7: Environmental Protection and Health Services Division

POLLUTION INVESTIGATION AND ENFORCEMENT BRANCH

1. Summary of air quality data (24-hour sampling) [of suspended particulates and sulfur dioxide at 11 sampling stations]. (p. 148)

2. Water quality on [39] public beaches [includes number of samples and fecal coliform density], 1981. (p. 150-151)

CONSTRUCTION GRANTS PROGRAM

1. [Federal grants awarded for individual public wastewater treatment construction projects, amount and status of completion.] (p. 152)

2. [Projects completed.] (p. 152)

ENVIRONMENTAL PERMITS BRANCH

1. [National pollutant discharge elimination system] permits issued or renewed. (p. 153)

2. [Air pollution control and solid waste management permits issued.] (p. 153)

FOOD AND DRUG BRANCH

1. Summary of samples examined. (p. 155)

2. Samples and analyses of various products for heptachlor epoxide [by county]. (p. 156)

3-4. Samples and analyses of milk, milk products, and frozen desserts, by county. (p. 157-158)

5. Foods and drugs [weight and retail value] condemned/destroyed, by county. (p. 158)

6. Selected activities [including poison permits issued by county]. (p. 158)

SANITATION BRANCH
[Data are for 3 islands and Maui county, unless otherwise noted.]

1. Average daily production of pasteurized milk. (p. 160)

2. Dairies and milk plants as of Dec. 31, 1982, by type. (p. 160)

3. Distribution of sanitary inspections by type. (p. 161)

4-5. Summary of activities by sanitarians, and daily summary of food service and food establishment [inspection, investigation, enforcement, education, and technical review/consultation provided]. (p. 162-166)

6. Public water systems [by island]. (p. 167)

VECTOR CONTROL BRANCH

1. Principal activities of the vector control branch on [selected] islands [including surveillance, inspections, breeding sources abated, and fish stocked for mosquito control]. (p. 169)

2. Total small mammal retrievals by [selected] island, activity, and species. (p. 170)

3. Summary of zoonosis laboratory activities and findings by [geographic] area. (p. 171)

LITTER CONTROL PROGRAM

1. Litter campaign [participants and activities], Apr. 1982. (p. 174)

2. State recycling campaign [participants, amount of paper and aluminum collected, and total earnings], Feb. 1982. (p. 174)

3-4. Litter bags provided for public use; and educational and promotional litter control materials distributed. (p. 175)

S2065–1.8: Medical Health Services Division

CHRONIC DISEASE BRANCH

I-III. Diabetes screening survey by age, sex, race, and island, FY82. (p. 179-181)

IV. Uterine cervical cancer screening [1972-82]. (p. 182)

V. Blood pressure screening, FY82. (p. 182)

HOSPITALS AND MEDICAL FACILITIES BRANCH

1-2. Number and type of facility, and bed count in facilities, by island. (p. 184-185)

3. Licensed beds by type of facility [1978-82]. (p. 185)

LABORATORIES BRANCH
[Tables 2-8 show data from Central Laboratory on Oahu, FY82.]

1. Number of samples submitted to various units of the laboratories branch and number of bacteriological, parasitological, serological, and chemical examinations performed upon them by type of specimen and island, FY82. (p. 187)

2-3. Incidence of salmonella by type: [by] age [of individuals affected], and from nonhuman sources. (p. 188-189)

4-6. Incidence of: parasites from humans [by type], gram negative diplococcus from gonorrhea cultures submitted, and mycobacteria from human sources. (p. 190-191)

7. Viral isolations [type and number of specimens]. (p. 192)

8. Viral serologies [type and number]. (p. 193)

PUBLIC HEALTH NURSING BRANCH
[Data are for FY82.]

1. Cases admitted to public health nursing service and visits made, by county [by type of service]. (p. 195)

2. Clinics conducted by public health nursing service by type of clinic, number of sessions and attendance by county. (p. 196)

3-6. Public health nursing service to schools and day care centers by county and type of clinic, and to care homes by county. (p. 198)

NUTRITION BRANCH

1. Nutrition branch services [number by type, including nutrition education sessions, consultations and inspections, and special supplemental food program for women, infants, and children]. (p. 200)

S2065–1.9: Mental Health Division
[All data are for State mental health facilities. Mental diagnoses include alcoholism, drug addiction, and mental retardation.]

1-1B. Patients active Dec. 31, 1982, by most recent problems, by age [and sex]. (p. 204-209)

2-3B. Patients [in- and out-care] active Dec. 31, 1982: by comprehensive centers or special services, and most recent problems and age. (p. 210-214)

4-6. Admissions, by age and problems on admission; by [race] and catchment area; and by referral source and community mental health center or service. (p. 215-218)

7-7B. Unduplicated admissions, [by sex, race, and] problems on admission, and mean age on admission. (p. 219-230)

8-10. Terminations, by age and problems on termination, and by community mental health center or service and disposition; and unduplicated count of patients served, by problems and age. (p. 231-235)

S2065–1.10: Refugee Screening Project and Waimano Training School and Hospital Division

REFUGEES

1. Demographic breakdown of refugees entering Hawaii (primary arrivals) [by age and sex for 3 Southeast Asian countries and Afghanistan/Ethiopia], Oct. 1981-Sept. 1982 [period]. (p. 239)

WAIMANO

1. Waimano Training School and Hospital [for the retarded] statistical movement of patients [FY75-82]. (p. 243)

2. Resident population, Waimano, June 30 distribution by measured intelligence [FY75-82]. (p. 243)

S2070   HAWAII
Department of Labor and Industrial Relations

S2070–2   LABOR MARKET REVIEW, HAWAII
Annual, discontinued.

Annual planning report identifying Hawaii population groups most in need of employment services, and presenting data on labor force and occupational supply and demand. Due to budgetary constraints, report has been discontinued with Aug. 1983 edition (for description, see SRI 1983 Annual, under this number).

Similar data are available in *Occupational Outlook*, issued by Hawaii Department of Labor and Industrial Relations, PO Box 3680, Honolulu HI 96811. *Occupational Outlook* is not currently covered by SRI.

Selected data on labor force and related topics are available in *State of Hawaii Data Book* and *Quarterly Statistical and Economic Report, State of Hawaii*, covered in SRI under S2090–1 and S2090–2, respectively.

S2090   HAWAII
Department of Planning and Economic Development

S2090–1   STATE OF HAWAII DATA BOOK, 1983: A Statistical Abstract
Annual. Dec. 1983.
663 p. + errata sheet.
ISSN 0073-1080.
LC 68-66724.
SRI/MF/complete

Annual compilation, for 1983, of detailed demographic, social, governmental, and economic statistics for Hawaii. Data are shown primarily for 1970s-82, with trends from as early as 1826. Data are primarily from State and Federal sources.

Report is designed to present a comprehensive overview of the State. Extensive socioeconomic, demographic, and geographic breakdowns are shown, as applicable, for most topics. These breakdowns include data by city, county and other State region (including island), urban-rural status, commodity, industry, occupation, age, educational attainment, marital status, race, and sex.

Contents:

a. Contents listing, map of Hawaii counties and districts, introduction, guide to tabular presentation, and weights and measures table. (p. 3-10)

b. 3 population maps and 620 tables arranged in 24 sections, described below. Tables in each section are preceded by a 1-2 page narrative on methodology, primary statistical sources, and definition of terms. (p. 11-635)

c. Bibliography, with 1 table on printing history of the statistical abstract, and detailed subject index. (p. 636-663)

This is the 17th edition of the *Data Book*, which was first published in 1962.

Availability: Hawaii Department of Planning and Economic Development, Information Office, PO Box 2359, Honolulu HI 96804, Hawaii residents $5.00, others $10.00; SRI/MF/complete.

TABLE SECTIONS:
[Data sources appear beneath each table.]

S2090–1.1: Section 1: Population

(p. 11-64) Contains 3 maps and 41 tables. Includes population from 1831; resident, military, and visitor population; land area; households; centenarian population, social security beneficiaries, and deaths; farm population; resident ancestry; and birthplace by military status.

Also includes citizenship status, by residence length; resident comprehension of English, and language spoken at home; aliens by nationality; persons in group quarters; voting age persons by congressional district; family characteristics; and churches, clergy, and members, by religion and denomination.

Also includes population change components, by military status; and immigration and naturalization, by selected country of origin.

S2090–1.2: Section 2: Vital Statistics and Health

(p. 65-102) Contains 42 tables. Includes births, deaths, and fertility rates, by military status; illegitimate births; infant and fetal deaths; most common names and surnames; catastrophic deaths; deaths by cause, and corpse disposition method; life expectancy; selected health conditions and resulting mobility limitations; communicable disease cases and deaths; leprosy patients; and survey of use of coffee, cigarettes, alcohol, and legal and illegal drugs.

Also includes hospitals and health care facilities, utilization, beds, and finances; mental health and retardation facility admissions, patients, and beds; physicians, dentists, nurses, and pharmacists; drugstores, sales, and prescriptions filled; health care expenditures; dental condition and services received; marriages and dissolutions; average body measurements; average student nutrition; and average daily food intake and nutritive value.

S2090–1.3: Section 3: Education

(p. 103-120) Contains 20 tables. Includes public, private, and parochial schools, teachers, enrollment, and high school graduates; public school expenditures for operations, capital outlays, and teacher salaries; military dependent and other federally connected pupils in public schools; and elementary student achievement test results.

Also includes enrollment and degrees awarded at University of Hawaii and at private colleges, by institution; Federal aid to selected colleges and universities; educational attainment; State library system outlets, personnel, and hours; and State and university library system collections and circulation.

S2090–1.4: Section 4: Law Enforcement, Courts, and Corrections

(p. 121-143) Contains 24 tables. Includes criminal justice expenditures, employment, and payroll; offenses reported and clearances; value of stolen and recovered property; white-collar crime losses; marijuana confiscated; disposition of adult and juvenile arrests; and child abuse and neglect cases.

Also includes legal service establishments, employment, and finances; judges and lawyers; court cases, by court and type of action; State correctional facility inmates; parole activity; and executions since 1826.

S2090–1.5: Section 5: Geography and Environment

(p. 144-183) Contains 36 tables. Includes selected distances from Honolulu, Hilo, and Kure Atoll; channel widths and depths; shorelines, and land and water areas; topographic features including summits, streams, waterfalls, and lakes; and volcanic eruptions, earthquakes, tsunamis, hurricanes, and cyclones, and resulting deaths and property damage.

Also includes dams; water services and consumption; public beach water quality; air pollutant source emissions; Oahu noise levels; climatic data by station; bird counts, by species; trees along streets and in parks; and endangered flora.

S2090–1.6: Section 6: Land Use and Ownership

(p. 184-197) Contains 15 tables. Includes land use and area; Oahu improved acreage uses, structure age, and housing inventory; land parcels; public and private land ownership; leased and unleased private lands; acreage owned by 6 major landowners; and native Hawaiian homestead acreage, lessees, and applicants.

S2090–1.7: Section 7: Recreation and Tourism

(p. 198-243) Contains 49 tables. Includes visitor demographic and travel characteristics, including accommodations and country or world area of residence; meetings/conventions and attendance; visitor expenditures; jobs and income generated by visitor expenditures; Hawaii Visitors Bureau finances; out-of-State travel by Hawaii residents; and passports issued, by destination.

Also includes Honolulu symphony orchestra personnel, performances, attendance, and expenses; Oahu performing arts productions, performances, and attendance, by organization; attendance at museums and other cultural attractions; nonprofit cultural organizations, finances, and volunteer hours; and zoo animals and visitors, by zoo.

Also includes recreational facilities and participation; national, State, and county parks, visits, and/or acres; Honolulu beach visits and water safety/emergency activities; fishing, hunting, and camping permits issued and participation; public hunting areas and wildlife refuges; sandy shoreline miles; professional baseball, and selected academic and amateur sports events, results, and attendance; and dog licenses issued.

S2090–1.8: Section 8: Government Finances and Employment

(p. 244-271) Contains 28 tables. Includes tax receipts by level of government and source; tax burden for Oahu family of 4; State and local revenues by source and expenditures by function; excise and use tax collections; and property tax valuations and tax rates.

Also includes Federal and State individual income tax returns and adjusted gross income; Federal outlays in Hawaii; State and county bonded debt; government employment by level; and State civil service employment and salary schedules.

S2090–1.9: Section 9: Social Insurance and Welfare Services

(p. 272-288) Contains 17 tables. Includes social welfare expenditures; public assistance payments and recipients; food stamp participation; social security recipients and benefits; OASDI beneficiaries and benefits; and Medicare enrollment and reimbursement.

Also includes covered employment and wages, and unemployment insurance recipients, benefits, average benefit duration, and exhaustion rate; State retirement system pensioners, assets, and benefits; child adoptions; nonprofit foundations and finances; United Way revenues and outlays; social services organizations, employment, payroll, and services provided; and Quality of Life Index rankings.

S2090–1.10: Section 10: National Defense

[Most data are shown by service branch.]

(p. 289-300) Contains 14 tables. Includes residents on active military duty; military personnel, dependents, and families; Army and Air National Guard strength; military housing units; civilian employment; DOD military and civilian personnel, by installation; defense expenditures; military prime contract awards; veterans by period of service; and military retirees and pay.

S2090–1.11: Section 11: Labor Force, Employment, and Earnings

(p. 301-336) Contains 32 tables. Includes labor force by employment status; characteristics of insured unemployed; job counts; public and private sector employment and wages; covered employers; manufacturing labor turnover rates; hours and earnings; minimum wage rates since 1942; and jobseeker migration to and from mainland.

Also includes work and transportation disability status of population; industrial accidents, deaths, and insurance payments; occupational injuries and illnesses, and lost workdays; labor union and employee assn membership; State and county employees in collective bargaining units; and work stoppages, workers involved, and days lost.

S2090–1.12: Section 12: Income, Expenditures, and Wealth

(p. 337-359) Contains 17 tables. Includes direct income from 4 major export industries; total and per capita GSP, and expenditure account components; personal income by source and disposition by object; household and family income; families and unrelated individuals below poverty level; poverty income guidelines; Oahu family income and expenses; and aggregate characteristics of top wealthholders.

S2090–1.13: Section 13: Prices

(p. 360-377) Contains 11 tables. Includes Honolulu CPI and retail food prices; annual family budgets for 4-person family and retired couple at 3 budget levels, for Honolulu and Oahu; and Federal employee Hawaii cost-of-living pay adjustment compared to Washington, D.C.

S2090–1.14: Section 14: Elections

(p. 378-399) Contains 22 tables. Includes election districts and precincts, and number of elected positions by level of government; voting age population; registered voters; votes cast by type of election, political party, and major candidate and office; campaign expenditures by office and party; Oahu neighborhood board election results; and votes cast for Office of Hawaiian Affairs Board of Trustees.

Also includes party affiliation of county councils; and State legislature party affiliation, demographic composition, and bill and resolution dispositions.

S2090–1.15: Section 15: Banking, Insurance, and Business Enterprise

(p. 400-424) Contains 27 tables. Includes firms, branches, and assets of banks, savings and loan assns, industrial loan licensees, and trust companies; bank and savings and loan assn deposits; small loan licensees and assets; bank clearings; consumer credit outstanding at banks; credit unions, assets, and shares; and total resident shareholders, and shareholders in 9 major Hawaii companies.

Also includes insurance companies; insurance premiums and claims/benefits paid, by class; State-based, other U.S., and foreign insurance companies and operating data; health insurance coverage, payments, and premiums, with hospital average stay and costs; and prepaid health plan membership and dues.

Also includes Honolulu fire alarms, deaths, and losses; total and small business establishments, employment, and payroll; corporations and partnerships formed, dissolved/merged, and on record; taxable and nontaxable corporations, partnerships, and proprietorships, and receipts; revenues and net income of 24 major Hawaii corporations; women-owned business firms, employment, payroll, and receipts; and business failures and liabilities.

S2090–1.16: Section 16: Communications

(p. 425-438) Contains 17 tables. Includes post offices, postal receipts, and mail handled; telegraph messages; telephone service; TV and radio stations; cable TV companies, subscribers, and revenues; TV households and viewers; newspaper circulation; periodicals published; Hawaii University Press books and scholarly journals published, sales, and revenues; and Honolulu postage, telephone, and telegraph rates, and newspaper prices.

S2090–1.17: Section 17: Energy and Science

(p. 439-463) Contains 27 tables. Includes energy consumption, by energy source and sector; electric and natural gas utilities customers, capacity and/or sales, average use and rates, and revenues; liquid fuel consumption, by type; fuel oil deliveries, by end use; Oahu gasoline prices since 1909; and gasoline service stations and sales.

Also includes Honolulu customs district fuel and diesel bunker oil laden on U.S. and foreign vessels; boilers and pressure vessels; sugar fac-

tory energy generation, consumption, and sales; manufacturing energy use and expenditures; and housing units with solar heaters.

Also includes Federal R&D obligations; R&D expenditures at postsecondary institutions; and patents issued to residents.

S2090–1.18: Section 18: Transportation

(p. 464-508) Contains 50 tables. Includes street/highway mileage, bridges, tunnels, traffic signal intersections, and metered parking spaces; motor vehicle registrations; households by number of vehicles available; taxicabs and registered bicycles; drivers licenses in force; vehicle fuel consumption and mileage; highway speed monitoring data; traffic accidents, injuries, and deaths; Oahu bus service, ridership, and revenues; and commuters by mode.

Also includes railroad track mileage and passengers; airports and heliports; civil aircraft, traffic, and operations by field; Pacific region pilots and flight personnel; inter-island and transpacific air travel; local airline operating data; airline passenger origins and destinations; and air fares.

Also includes commercial harbor specifications, vessel arrivals, and freight and passenger traffic, by harbor; documented and undocumented vessels and characteristics; boating accidents, injuries, fatalities, and property damage; and overseas and inter-island shipping.

S2090–1.19: Section 19: Agriculture

(p. 509-527) Contains 20 tables. Includes farms, acreage, and operating characteristics; crop and livestock marketings; livestock inventory; flower production and value; market supply of specified foods; farm productivity rating and soil loss; land use; fertilizer consumption; and aquaculture production and value, including freshwater prawn operations.

S2090–1.20: Section 20: Forests, Fisheries, and Mining

(p. 528-541) Contains 13 tables. Includes forest acreage; commercial timberland ownership, timber volume, and growing stock; forest fires and acres burned; forest products harvested, price, and value; commercial fishermen, vessels, fisheries, and landings; and fish inventory at specified sampling sites.

Also includes mineral industry operations; and nonfuel mineral production and value.

S2090–1.21: Section 21: Construction and Housing

(p. 542-581) Contains 41 tables. Includes residential and nonresidential building permits and value; government construction contract awards by level; residential construction and demolition; condominium projects and conversions; Honolulu construction cost indexes; construction industry establishments, employment, and receipts; and contracting and rental excise tax base.

Also includes housing units, occupancy, and structural and financial characteristics; Hawaii Housing Authority units and resident population, assets, revenues, and average rent; Oahu housing vacancies; and migration by military status.

Also includes Oahu housing prices and multiple listing service listings and sales; Honolulu office building occupancy rates, available space, and average rent; deeds filed, and value of land conveyed or transferred; real estate licensees; mortgages recorded, foreclosures, and sale agreements; mortgage loans outstanding, by type of financial institution; and FHA-insured housing characteristics and home purchaser profile.

Also includes elevators and escalators; height of tallest structures; and seating capacities of selected Oahu stadiums, theaters, and churches.

S2090–1.22: Section 22: Manufactures

(p. 582-592) Contains 12 tables. Includes manufacturing employment and payroll, production workers and hours and wages, establishments, value added, shipments, production costs, capital investments, and inventories; and industrial parks and acreage.

Also includes excise tax base for sugar processing, pineapple canning, and manufacturing; pineapple and sugar companies and plants; processed pineapple, sugar, and molasses production; sugar industry strikes, cane acreage, average price, and government payments; and pineapple and sugar industries employment, earnings, and sales.

S2090–1.23: Section 23: Domestic Trade and Services

(p. 593-623) Contains 32 tables. Includes retail and wholesale trade and service industry establishments, sales or revenues, excise tax base, and other operations; available retail space; department stores and sales; eating and drinking places, including franchise holders, and sales; major shopping center characteristics; and retail stores, employment, and sales for 10 major companies.

Also includes armed forces retail facilities and sales; membership organizations, expenses, and employment; operating data for tourist-oriented businesses, hotels, and motels; condominium properties and units; hotel units under construction/planned; motion picture and TV production data; Oahu liquor licenses and sales; liquor and tobacco tax bases; and alcoholic beverage consumption and tax revenues, by beverage type.

S2090–1.24: Section 24: Foreign and Interstate Commerce

(p. 624-635) Contains 13 tables. Includes Hawaii-mainland trade; foreign trade through Honolulu customs district, by mode and country of origin and destination; fireworks imports; foreign trade zone users, user employment, merchandise value, and revenues and expenditures; foreign-owned farmland and business operations, and direct investment by country; export-related employment; and Hawaii balance of payments.

S2090–2   QUARTERLY STATISTICAL AND ECONOMIC REPORT, State of Hawaii

Quarterly. Approx. 50 p.
SRI/MF/complete

Quarterly report on Hawaii business and economic conditions, with data on income, employment, State taxes, tourism, construction activities, and population. Includes selected 10-year trends, 1- and 2-year forecasts, U.S. comparisons, and data by county. Data generally are current to 1-2 quarters preceding cover date.

Data are compiled by Dept of Planning and Economic Development (DPED) from Federal and State government and private sources.

Report contains listings of contents, tables, and charts; and usually 5-8 sections, with narrative summaries and approximately 30 tables, occasionally accompanied by charts. The number, sequence, and content of tables vary considerably from issue to issue.

Recurring table topics are described below.

Issuing agency also publishes *The Economy of Hawaii: Annual Economic Report and Outlook,* which includes summary data for many of the topics covered in the quarterly report. The annual report is not covered in SRI.

Availability: Hawaii Department of Planning and Economic Development, Research and Economic Analysis Division, PO Box 2359, Honolulu HI 96804, ‡; SRI/MF/complete.
Issues reviewed during 1984: 4th Qtr. 1983-3rd Qtr. 1984 (P).

RECURRING TABLE TOPICS:

[Tables present most recent available data, with comparisons to prior periods. Many tables show data for quarter prior to cover date, with quarterly trends for current and previous year, and annual data for selected earlier years, from 1970.

Economic forecasts are for current and 1-2 future years. Labor force, tourist, construction, and population data usually include detail by county (island).]

a. Economic outlook, income, and prices: forecasts for selected economic indicators; total and disposable personal income; and Honolulu CPI.

b. Employment, business activity, and tax revenues: jobs by industry (including self-employed and workers involved in labor disputes), and labor force by employment status; value of business transactions subject to State excise/use tax for selected industries; and collections of major State taxes, and distribution to State general fund.

c. Visitor industry, construction, and housing: data on visitors to Hawaii; hotel rooms, occupancy, and rates; value of completed and authorized construction, by type; government construction contracts; and construction employment, hours, earnings, and cost index.

d. Major sources of income, and population: visitor and defense expenditures; sugar and pineapple production value and/or sales; and population.

S2090–3   POPULATION TRENDS BY DISTRICTS AND CENSUS TRACTS, 1920-80, Hawaii

Monograph. Dec. 15, 1983.
12 p. no paging.
Rpt. No. CTC-55.
SRI/MF/complete

Report presenting Hawaii population by island and district, with detail for Honolulu and rest-of-Oahu by census tract, decennially 1920-80. Data are from U.S. and State census counts and other specified private and governmental sources.

Contains narrative summary (1 p.); and 3 maps and 3 tables (11 p.).

Availability: Hawaii Department of Planning and Economic Development, State Census Statistical Areas Committee, PO Box 2359, Honolulu HI 96804, †; SRI/MF/complete.

S2090–4   POPULATION AND ECONOMIC PROJECTIONS for the State of Hawaii, 1980-2005

Monograph. July 17, 1984.
22 p.
LC 84-622934.
SRI/MF/complete

Report presenting projections of Hawaii population, jobs, income, and visitors, by county, quinquennially 1980-2005, with selected trends from 1970.

Includes resident and de facto population, jobs by industry division and selected group (including armed forces and self-employed), personal income, and visitors, all by county.

Also includes statewide population by age and sex, and exclusive of armed forces/dependents; labor force and employment; GSP and disposable personal income; Japanese vs. other visitor arrivals; and comparison of population projections from selected organizations, with some data through 2030 and detail for Oahu.

Most projections are from Hawaii Dept of Planning and Economic Development.

Contains explanatory note, and contents and table listings (p. 3-4); introduction and narrative summary (p. 5-9); and 8 tables (p. 10-22).

Availability: Hawaii Department of Planning and Economic Development, Research and Economic Analysis Division, PO Box 2359, Honolulu HI 96804, †; SRI/MF/complete.

S2120   HAWAII
Department of
Taxation

S2120–1   DEPARTMENT OF TAXATION ANNUAL REPORT, 1982-83, Hawaii

Annual. Oct. 4, 1983.
26 p. + App 6 p.
ISSN 0360-2931.
LC 75-647948.
SRI/MF/complete

Annual report of the Hawaii Dept of Taxation, presenting data on tax collections and allocation, FY83, with comparisons to FY82, and selected trends from FY78.

Contains contents listing (p. 1); narrative report, with 7 summary charts and 14 tables (p. 2-26); and appendix, including contents listing, 5 tables, and outline of Hawaii's tax system (p. A1-A6).

All tables are listed below.

Previous report, for FY82, is described in SRI 1982 Annual, under this number.

Availability: Hawaii Department of Taxation, Tax Research and Planning Office, PO Box 259, Honolulu HI 96809, †; SRI/MF/complete.

TABLES:

[Unless otherwise noted, tables show data for FY82-83, often with average annual percent change, FY78-83 and FY82-83.]

S2120–1.1: Text Tables

[1-2] Compliance Division [delinquent tax collection program activities]. (p. 3)

[3] Staffing pattern (number of authorized permanent positions) [by function]. (p. 4)

[4] Tax litigation [appeals cases, shown for review boards by county, and for supreme and tax appeal courts by case type and court, FY83]. (p. 11)

[5-6] [Income] taxes paid by individuals and corporations [including amount withheld from wages, and refunds]. (p. 13-15)

[7] General excise and use tax base and taxes [by source]. (p. 16)

[8-9] Inheritance and estate taxes, and public service company tax. (p. 17)

[10] Gallons of fuel consumed [by fuel type and use, including boating and aviation]. (p. 18)

[11] Allocation of fuel taxes [by fund, including detail by fuel type and county]. (p. 19)

[12] Miscellaneous taxes [collected]. (p. 20)

[13-14] Distribution of collections [by fund; and] tax collections [by county]. (p. 20-21)

S2120–1.2: Appendix Tables

[1-2] Tax collections [by source of revenue] and distribution [to State funds by fund, and total county by source]. (p. A1-A2)

[3] State general fund [revenue by source]. (p. A2)

[4] Fuel tax rates per gallon [State and county rates, by county, FY83]. (p. A2)

[5] Dept of Taxation training programs [employees and training hours], FY83. (p. A3)

S2205   IDAHO
Department of
Agriculture

S2205–1   IDAHO AGRICULTURAL STATISTICS, 1984
Annual. [1984.] 72 p.
ISSN 0094-1271.
LC 74-642213.
SRI/MF/complete

Annual report on Idaho agricultural production, finances, and marketing, 1970s-83, with selected trends from 1920. Data are generally shown by commodity, with selected data by county, and some comparisons to other States and regions and to U.S.

Report generally covers production, prices, disposition, value, and, as applicable, acreage, yield, or inventory, for field crop, vegetable, fruit, livestock, dairy, and poultry sectors.

Also includes data on farms and acreage; temperature and precipitation; cash receipts by commodity; farm income, production expenses, workers, and wage rates; range/pasture condition; sheep and lamb losses by cause; mink bred and pelts produced; potatoes in cold storage; and fertilizer consumption; and potatoes in cold storage, by U.S. region.

Data are compiled by the Idaho Crop and Livestock Reporting Service in cooperation with the USDA Statistical Reporting Service.

Contains contents listing (p. 3); 1 map, and 100 tables, interspersed with brief narrative summaries (p. 5-71); and list of other reports available (p. 72).

This is the 13th edition.

Availability: Idaho Crop and Livestock Reporting Service, PO Box 1699, Boise ID 83701, $5.00; SRI/MF/complete.

S2215   IDAHO
Office of the
Auditor

S2215–1   ANNUAL REPORT OF THE STATE AUDITOR, State of Idaho, July 1, 1982-June 30, 1983
Annual. [1984.]
70 p. var. paging. Foldouts.
SRI/MF/complete

Annual report on financial condition of Idaho State government, for FY83, presenting assets and liabilities, reserves, balances, and fund transfers; receipts by source; and disbursements by functions; by account type, with selected detail by specific agency account.

Also includes data on appropriations vs. expenditures, by function and agency; liquor account distributions to local areas; bond sales, redemptions, and indebtedness; and summary tax levies and collections, 1980-82.

Data are from the records of the auditor's office.

Contains transmittal letter, foreword and contents description, and 4 charts (7 p.); and 15 exhibits and schedules (63 p.).

This is the 10th annual report.

Availability: Idaho Office of the Auditor, 700 W. State St., Boise ID 83720, †; SRI/MF/complete.

S2222   IDAHO
Administrative
Office of the
Courts

S2222–1   IDAHO COURTS 1983 Annual Report
Annual. For individual publication data, see below.
SRI/MF/complete

Annual report, for 1983, on Idaho judicial system, including trial and appellate court caseloads and case dispositions. Covers supreme, appeals, district, and magistrate courts. Includes trial court data by case type, judicial district, and county.

Case types shown are criminal and civil, with additional detail for domestic relations, small claims, traffic, Youth Rehabilitation Act, Child Protective Act, adoption, guardianship, probate, and habeas corpus case types.

Data are from dept records.

Report is presented in 2 volumes, individually described below.

Availability: Idaho Administrative Office of the Courts, Supreme Court Bldg., 451 W. State St., Boise ID 83720; SRI/MF/complete.

S2222–1.1: Idaho Courts Annual Report, 1983 Edition
[Annual. [1984.] 8 p. †. SRI/MF/complete.]

Narrative report with several newspaper-style articles on Idaho court operations and caseloads, interspersed with 11 charts and 2 tables showing caseload trends from 1976, and appeals and trial court case processing times, 1982-83.

S2222–1.2: Idaho Courts 1983 Annual Report: Appendix
[Annual. [1984.] 2+107 p. ‡. SRI/MF/complete.]

Statistical appendix volume, showing detailed caseload data by Idaho court, judicial district, and county.

Contains contents listing and introduction (2 p.); 4 appellate court tables (p. 1-3); and 2 district and magistrate court tables, repeated for State and each district and county (p. 4-107).

S2225   IDAHO
Department of
Education

S2225–1   1983/84 FALL ENROLLMENT REPORT, Idaho
Annual. Oct. 1, 1983.
7 p. Oversized.
SRI/MF/complete

Annual report containing 1 table showing Idaho public and nonpublic elementary and secondary school enrollment, by grade K-12 and for secondary ungraded, by school district and/or county, Oct. 1983, with change from 1982 totals.

Availability: Idaho Department of Education, Finance Division, Research and Statistics Unit, Len B. Jordan Bldg., 650 W. State St., Boise ID 83720, †; SRI/MF/complete.

S2225–2   FINANCIAL SUMMARIES, IDAHO SCHOOL DISTRICTS, July 1, 1982-June 30, 1983
Annual. [1984.] iv+153 p.
LC 60-63291.
SRI/MF/complete

Annual report, for FY83, on Idaho public school district revenues by source and expenditures by object, for approximately 20 funds, with statewide comparisons to FY81-82. Also includes data on attendance, market valuation, bonded debt, Foundation Program receipts, and transportation.

Data are compiled from annual reports submitted by school districts to the State Dept of Education.

Contains introduction, table listing, and list of school districts (p. i-iv); 3 tables showing summary statistics for the State, FY83, with selected comparisons to FY81-82 (p. 1-3); and 12 tables described below, generally showing data by school district (p. 4-153).

Availability: Idaho Department of Education, Finance Division, Research and Statistics Unit, Len B. Jordan Bldg., 650 W. State St., Boise ID 83720, †; SRI/MF/complete.

TABLES:
[Tables show data for FY83.]

a. Attendance and enrollment; market valuation and bonded debt; expenditures per average daily attendance (ADA); maintenance/operation expenditures, including costs for social security, retirement, and administration; Foundation Program State allowance receipts; and transportation data, including number transported, expenditures, and average daily bus miles; all by school district arranged by county. 7 tables. (p. 4-31)

b. District rankings, by ADA, and by general fund expenditures and market value per ADA; and monies requested in successful supplemental maintenance/operation levy elections; by district. 4 tables. (p. 32-37)

c. Finances: revenues by source and expenditures by object, all by fund, including general, school plant facility, bond interest/redemption, bond building, adult and driver education, school lunch, insurance adjustment, Federal forest, Elementary and Secondary Education Act by title, Indian education funds, and other special funds. 1 table, repeated for State and each school district. (p. 38-153)

S2225-3   1983/84 STATISTICAL REPORT: Public School Certified Personnel and Employees in Noncertified Positions
Annual. [1984.] iv+21 p.
SRI/MF/complete

Annual report on Idaho public school certified and noncertified personnel characteristics and salaries, by position, 1983/84 school year. Data are from reports submitted by school districts to State Dept of Education in fall 1983.

Contains contents listing (1 p.); introduction (p. i-iv); 1 table showing school districts ranked by enrollment and including number of teachers (p. 1-5); and 14 tables, described below (p. 6-21).

Availability: Idaho Department of Education, Len B. Jordan Bldg., 650 W. State St., Boise ID 83720, †; SRI/MF/complete.

TABLES:
[Most data are shown by position, with selected comparisons by enrollment size.]

a. Certified staff: FTE, actual number, and average base salary and extra pay, by sex; average salary expenditure per child; years of experience in education, age group, highest degree earned, and source of education (Idaho institutions and other); and turnover rates, by sex and reason. 11 tables. (p. 6-16)

b. Noncertified staff: FTE and actual number; and average annual and hourly salary; by sex. 3 tables. (p. 17-21)

S2230   IDAHO
Department of Employment

S2230-3   ANNUAL PLANNING REPORT, FY85, Idaho
Annual. Feb. 1984. ii+67 p.
LC 79-640461.
SRI/MF/complete

Annual planning report, for FY85, identifying Idaho population groups most in need of employment services. Includes data on population and labor force, employment, income, public assistance recipients, and characteristics of unemployment insurance claimants and job service applicants; and data by industry, occupation, county, and planning area; various years 1976-FY85.

Data are generally from Census Bureau and State agencies, including Employment Service Automated Reporting System.

Contains contents/table listing (p. i-ii); introduction and highlights (p. 1-4); and 48 tables described below, arranged in 7 sections, each preceded by brief narrative (p. 5-67).

Availability: Idaho Department of Employment, Research and Analysis Bureau, Box 35, Boise ID 83735, †; SRI/MF/complete.

TABLES:
[Data by race often also include the following ethnic groups: Native American or American Indian, Asian/Pacific Islander, and Hispanic.]

S2230-3.1: Population, Labor Force, Unemployment Insurance Claimants, and Employment

a. Population: by sex and race, by county; and by sex and age by planning area; FY85. Tables 1-4. (p. 6-9)

b. Labor force and unemployment, by sex, age, and race, by planning area and/or county, FY85; and monthly unemployment rate trends, 1976-83. Tables 5-17. (p. 11-19)

c. Unemployment insurance claimants by race, educational atttainment, sex, industry division, age, and occupational group, with cross-tabulations by duration of unemployment; all by planning area, 1983; and unemployment, with distribution by reason, 1977-82. Tables 18-25. (p. 22-30)

d. Employment: by industry division and selected group, class of worker, and occupational group, all by county; by occupational group by planning area; and by race and sex, by occupation; 1980 or 1982. Tables 26-30. (p. 32-37)

S2230-3.2: Socioeconomic Characteristics

a. Income for households, families, and unrelated individuals over age 15, by county, 1979; personal income by type and industry division, 1980-82; per capita personal income by county, 1976-81; average annual wages by industry division and selected group, by county, 1982; and hourly salaries, by detailed occupation (no date). Tables 31-35. (p. 40-48)

b. Economically disadvantaged population by age group, by county and planning area, FY85; poverty guidelines; and persons in poverty by race and county, 1980. Tables 36-39. (p. 49-51)

c. Public assistance recipients by program, FY83 with detail by age and sex for Feb. 1984; and food stamp recipients, FY83; generally by planning area. Tables 40-42. (p. 52-53)

d. Veterans by period of service, and female veterans, by county, 1980; and job service applicants and characteristics, including data for handicapped, veterans, unemployment insurance claimants, migrants, and farm workers, and by age group, sex, education, urban or rural residence, race, and family income, FY83. Tables 43-45D. (p. 54-67)

S2235   IDAHO
Department of Finance

S2235-1   STATE OF IDAHO DEPARTMENT OF FINANCE Sixty-Fifth Report
Annual. [1984.] 50 p.
LC 6-16846.
SRI/MF/complete

Annual report on financial condition of Idaho State-regulated financial institutions, mostly as of Dec. 31, 1982 or June 30, 1983, presenting assets, liabilities, and generally equity capital or net worth, for State-chartered banks, savings and loan assns, and credit unions. Data are generally shown by institution.

Also includes composite balance sheet data for State-located national banks; composite financial and loan activity of regulated lenders; credit union and regulated lender loan delinquencies; bank consumer loans by purpose; and dept staffing and finances.

Contains contents listing and foreword (p. 5-6); and report, with 32 tables and lists of selected institutions (p. 7-50).

Availability: Idaho Department of Finance, Statehouse, Boise ID 83720, 1st copy †, additional copies $2.00; SRI/MF/complete.

S2245   IDAHO
Office of the Governor

S2245-2   IDAHO ECONOMIC FORECAST
Quarterly. Approx. 65 p.
SRI/MF/complete

Quarterly report (combined Winter/Spring issue) on Idaho and U.S. economic trends and forecasts. Includes data on population and change components; housing starts and stock; personal income and components; employment, by industry division and major manufacturing group; Federal transfer payments to State/local governments; and, for U.S. only, GNP and selected price deflators, interest rates, and production indexes.

Historical data are compiled from State and Federal sources. Forecasts are from Data Resources, Inc. Macroeconomic Model and the Idaho Economic Model, and are usually generated in 2nd month of cover date period.

General format:

a. Contents listing and introduction; 2 summary forecast tables; narrative summary; and alternative forecasts of selected indicators based on varying assumptions about the national economy, with 1-2 tables.

b. Feature article, frequently with statistics.

c. Detailed table, showing actual and forecast data for the indicators noted above, annually for 17-18 years beginning 13-14 years prior to cover date, and quarterly for 18 quarters beginning with 3rd quarter of year 1-2 years prior to cover date.

d. Appendix, with descriptions of forecast models.

Summary and detailed tables and alternative forecast appear in all issues. Additional features with substantial statistical content are described, as they appear, under "Statistical Features." Nonstatistical features are not covered.

Availability: Idaho Economic Forecast, Financial Management Division, Statehouse, Rm. 122, Boise ID 83720, Idaho residents $7.50 per yr., others $15.00 per yr.; SRI/MF/complete.

Issues reviewed during 1984: Autumn 1983-Summer 1984 (P) (Vol. V, No. 3; Vol. VI, Nos. 1-2).

STATISTICAL FEATURES:

S2245-2.501: Autumn 1983 (Vol. V, No. 3)
IDAHO IN TRANSITION, 1970-2000

(p. 19-27) By Richard A. Slaughter. Article, with 1 table showing Idaho new jobs in manufacturing/mining/construction, service, and government, selected periods 1950-95.

S2245-2.502: Winter/Spring 1984 (Vol. VI, No. 1)
SUMMARY OF THE REPORT OF THE GOVERNOR'S ECONOMIC RESEARCH COUNCIL ON THE IDAHO ECONOMY

(p. 19-26) Article, with 1 table showing change in Idaho State/local tax revenue, including reductions due to legislative and supreme court actions and increases by tax type, 1977-FY84 period.

S2250   IDAHO
Department of
Health and Welfare

S2250-1   QUARTERLY WELFARE STATISTICAL BULLETIN, Idaho

Quarterly. Approx. 20 p.
ISSN 0364-1104.
LC 75-645543.
SRI/MF/complete

Quarterly report on Idaho public welfare program caseloads, recipients, and expenditures, with some data by county and State region. Report is issued 3-6 months after quarter of coverage.

Contains 1 map; chart and table listing; 7 trend charts; and 2 charts and 9 tables, listed below.

Availability: Idaho Department of Health and Welfare, Welfare Division, Research and Statistics Section, Statehouse, Boise ID 83720, †; SRI/MF/complete.

Issues reviewed during 1984: July/Sept. 1983-Apr./June 1984 (D) (Vol. 28, Nos. 3-4; Vol. 29, Nos. 1-2).

QUARTERLY TABLES AND CHARTS:
[Data are for quarter of coverage, or middle month of quarter, unless otherwise noted. Data indicated as monthly are shown for each month of quarter.]

1. Summary of [monthly] obligations incurred, cases, and average payment, by program [including Old Age Assistance (OAA), Aid to the Blind, Aid to the Permanently and Totally Disabled (APTD), Aid to Dependent Children, and medical assistance].

[A] Sources, and uses [by program], of funds. [chart]

2. Medical assistance expenditures [recipients, days/services, and amount paid, by type of service; and expenditures and recipients, by welfare program].

3. Reasons for approving AFDC cases [monthly].

[B] Selected characteristics of AFDC caseload, percent of cases by $50 grant increments and by length of time since most recent case opening, [for Feb. or Mar. in 1st-2nd quarter issues, and Aug. or Sept. in 3rd-4th quarter issues]. [chart]

4. Reasons for closing OAA, AB, APTD, and AFDC [cases].

5. Percent of population receiving assistance by county and region [with detail for population under 18].

6. Summary of adoption activity [monthly adoptions, by child's age group, and for Indian, Negro, and Mexican children].

7. Foster care statistics [children in and number of foster homes and institutions, and amount paid, by program and region].

8. Food stamp activity [assistance and nonassistance recipients, and value of coupons issued, by county and region].

9. Recovery of child support payments [average amount collected per month, by quarter for current year and annually for previous 9-11 years].

S2250-2   1982 ANNUAL SUMMARY OF VITAL STATISTICS, Idaho

Annual. [1983.] vi+112 p.
ISSN 0362-9279.
LC 76-644913.
SRI/MF/complete

Annual report, for 1982, on Idaho vital statistics, covering population, births, deaths by cause, marriages, and divorces, all by county and health district, with trends from the 1970s and comparison with U.S. Data are compiled from State records and Census Bureau reports.

Contains contents listing and definitions (p. ii-v); 6 statistical sections, with 1 map, 24 charts, and 68 tables (p. 1-85); and appendices, with 4 tables (p. 87-112).

All tables, and selected charts showing data not included in tables, are listed below.

Availability: Idaho Department of Health and Welfare, Health Division, Vital Statistics, Standards and Local Health Services Bureau, 450 W. State St., Boise ID 83720, †; SRI/MF/complete.

TABLES AND CHARTS:
[Unless otherwise noted, tables and charts show data for Idaho, 1982. Most data by race also include American Indian, Japanese, other, and Spanish surname or origin.]

S2250-2.1: Population and Trends
POPULATION

[1-5] Apr. 1, 1980 census of population: U.S. regions and States; Idaho districts and counties [by race]; Idaho cities; Idaho districts and counties, by age and sex; and Idaho, age by sex; [with selected comparisons to 1980 and estimates for 1981-82]. (p. 2-12)

TRENDS AND SUMMARY
[Tables [6-8] show numbers and rates.]

[6] Vital statistics [live births and deaths by sex, out-of-wedlock and immature live births, and stillbirths, infant and maternal deaths, marriages, and divorces], 1973-82. (p. 15)

[7-8] Summary of vital statistics: births, deaths, marriages, and divorces; and infant, fetal, and perinatal mortality; [by district and county]. (p. 17-18)

S2250-2.2: Natality
ALL BIRTHS

[1-4] Resident live births and rates, 1978-82; and resident live births, by sex of child and race of mother, by age of mother, and by attendant at and place of birth, 1982; [all by district and county of residence]. (p. 21-24)

[5] Idaho live birth [rate, 1982], and fertility rates [1981-82], by district and county of residence. (p. 25)

[6] Resident live births, [by] live birth order by age of mother. (p. 26)

[7] 1982 age-specific fertility rates [compared to 1980 U.S. rate]. (p. 26)

[8-13] Resident live births: trimester of pregnancy when prenatal care began (percent), and educational attainment of mother, [by district and county of residence]; complications and malformations, [total] and by prenatal care; and Apgar scores, 1 minute [by] 5 minutes. (p. 28-31)

IMMATURE BIRTHS
[All tables, except table [17], begin "Immature live births..." Tables [14-15] and [18] show data by district and county of residence.]

[14-15] By race and age of mother. (p. 32-33)

[16] By live birth order by age of mother. (p. 34)

[17] Age-specific immaturity rates. (p. 34)

[18] By weight at birth. (p. 35)

OUT-OF-WEDLOCK BIRTHS

[19-20] [Out-of-wedlock births: U.S. 1980, and Idaho 1982; and] Idaho nonwhite ratio [1978-82; all by race]. (p. 36)

[21-23] Out-of-wedlock live births: by race and age of mother [by district and county of residence]; and live birth order by age of mother. (p. 37-39)

[24] Age-specific out-of-wedlock live birth ratios. (p. 39)

S2250-2.3: Mortality and Morbidity
DEATH RATES AND CAUSES

[1-3] Resident deaths and rates, 1978-82; and resident deaths, by sex and race, and age at death, 1982; [all by district and county of residence]. (p. 43-45)

[4-6] 10 leading causes of death [by sex]; leading causes by age group [charts]; and malignant neoplasm deaths by primary site [by sex]. (p. 46-51)

[7] Resident deaths from selected causes, by district and county of residence. (p. 52-53)

[8] Age/sex adjusted death rates by selected causes, 1970-81. (p. 54)

[9] Accidental deaths occurring in Idaho, by category and age group, 1981-82. (p. 57)

[10-11] Reported morbidity: from selected diseases, 1978-82; and by district and county of residence, 1982. (p. 59-61)

INFANT MORTALITY

[12-14] Resident infant deaths and rates, 1978-82; and resident infant deaths by sex and race of child, and neonatal and postneonatal, 1982; [all by district and county of residence]. (p. 64-66)

[15-17] Causes of infant deaths: by neonatal and postneonatal periods, and by district of residence, and totals for U.S. and Idaho. (p. 67-68)

[18-19] Resident stillbirths and perinatal deaths and ratios, by district and county of residence, 1978-82. (p. 69-70)

ABORTIONS

[20] [Induced abortions, ratio per live births and females, for U.S., 1980, and Idaho, 1982.] (p. 71)

[21] Induced abortions reported: [total and for residents, by district and county], 1981-82. (p. 72)

[22-27] Induced abortions reported: age of patient by marital status, previous induced abortions and number of living children, termination procedure by length of gestation, reported complications by termination procedure, and age and race of patient by district and county of residence. (p. 73-76)

S2250–2.4: Marriages and Divorces

MARRIAGES

[1-5] Marriages occurring in Idaho: by district and county of occurrence, 1973-82; and by age and race of bride by age and race of groom, and age of bride and groom by previous marital status, 1982. (p. 78-81)

DIVORCES

[6-9] Divorces granted in Idaho: by district and county of occurrence, 1973-82; number of children affected, 1982; and divorces and annulments granted, by legal grounds, 1982; and duration of marriage, 1980-82. (p. 82-85)

S2250–2.5: Appendices

A-B. Vital statistics profile [summary] by district and county; and detailed causes of death by age. (p. 87-109)

1-2. Comparable category numbers and estimated comparability ratios for 72 selected causes of death, and for 10 selected causes of infant deaths, according to the 9th and 8th revisions [of the International Classification of Diseases]. (p. 110-112)

S2260   IDAHO
Department of Insurance

S2260–1   EIGHTY-SECOND ANNUAL REPORT: STATE OF IDAHO, DEPARTMENT OF INSURANCE, for the Year Ended June 30, 1983
Annual.   [1983.]   iii+48 p.
LC 60-45313.
SRI/MF/complete

Annual report on Idaho insurance industry financial condition and underwriting activity, by company and type of insurance, 1982. Covers assets and liabilities, capital, surplus, net income or loss, and premiums written in Idaho.

Data are shown for life, disability, property, marine/transportation, casualty, surety, title, and mortgage guaranty companies; and, in slightly different detail, for fraternal benefit societies, motor clubs, hospital/professional service corporations, hospital liability trusts, and county mutual/fraternal fire companies.

Also covers Insurance Dept receipts, expenditures, regulatory and licensing activity, and consumer services, FY83, with revenue trends from FY78; and 1982 business summary, including premiums, claims paid, and/or premium/loss ratios, by type of company and by line of business including medical malpractice, workmen's compensation, and automobile insurance.

Contains contents listing (p. i); Insurance Dept report and summary, with 12 tables (p. 1-15); and 7 company financial tables (p. 16-48).

Availability: Idaho Department of Insurance, 700 W. State St., Boise ID 83720, †; SRI/MF/complete.

S2275   IDAHO
Department of Law Enforcement

S2275–2   IDAHO UNIFORM CRIME REPORTING PROGRAM: 1983 Annual Report
Annual.   [1984.]   vii+282 p.
LC 80-645204.
SRI/MF/complete

Annual report, for 1983, on Idaho crimes and arrests, clearances, value of property involved, assaults on police, and law enforcement personnel. Includes data by offense, victim and offender characteristics, reporting enforcement agency, and county; and selected trends from 1973.

Data are from reports by State and local law enforcement agencies, submitted under the Uniform Crime Reporting Program.

Contains contents listing (p. v-vii); introduction (p. 1-5); and statistical sections, with 31 charts and 62 tables described below, interspersed with narrative summaries (p. 7-282).

Availability: Idaho Department of Law Enforcement, Police Services Division, Technical Services Unit, PO Box 55, Boise ID 83707, †; SRI/MF/complete.

CHARTS AND TABLES:

[Data are for 1983, unless otherwise noted. Index (Part I) offenses are murder, forcible rape, robbery, aggravated assault, burglary, larceny, motor vehicle theft, and arson.

Data by race include black, white, American Indian/Alaskan Native, Asian/Pacific Islander, Hispanic, and non-Hispanic.]

S2275–2.1: Offenses, Arrests, and Law Enforcement Personnel

INDEX OFFENSE SUMMARY

a. Crime clocks; Index offenses and rates, 1979-83; total violent and nonviolent crimes by month; and Index offenses by population size group and State region. 2 charts and 6 tables. (p. 7-15)

b. Crimes cleared by arrest; Index crime and population trends, 1973-83; and value of stolen and recovered property, by type of property. 4 charts and 4 tables. (p. 16-19)

INDEX OFFENSES AND VANDALISM

[Data shown for each offense include number and rate, 1982-83; number by month; and most frequent month of occurrence and other characteristics. Trend data, various years 1973-83, are shown for all offenses except vandalism. Each offense section also includes narrative summary with text statistics. Additional data are described below.]

c. Murder by age group of assailant, by victim age, sex, and race, and by type of weapon; and forcible and attempted rapes. 7 charts and 7 tables. (p. 23-34)

d. Robbery and stolen property value by place of occurrence, and offenses by weapon; aggravated assault by weapon; burglary and stolen property value, by day and night residence and nonresidence occurrence; and larceny and stolen property value, by type of larceny. 11 charts and 15 tables. (p. 37-60)

e. Motor vehicle theft by type of vehicle; arson and value of property damage by type of property; and vandalism damage value by month, with offenses, rate, and damage value, by reporting agency and county. 5 charts and 11 tables. (p. 63-80)

ARREST DATA

[Data by offense are shown for Part I offenses and 22 Part II offenses.]

f. Arrests and rate by offense; police disposition of juveniles; and arrests by offense, by age, sex, and race. 6 tables. (p. 85-92)

g. Drug arrests by substance: by race; for juveniles and adults by sex, and for sale/manufacturing and possession, by age group. 1 chart and 4 tables. (p. 93-96)

h. Adult and juvenile arrests by offense, and total rate, by reporting agency and county. 1 table. (p. 97-123)

LAW ENFORCEMENT PERSONNEL

i. Officers assaulted, by type of activity, assignment, weapon, time of day, and reporting agency and county. 1 chart and 4 tables. (p. 128-132)

j. Police officer and civilian employees, by sex, and rate per 1,000 population, all by agency and county, as of Oct. 31, 1983. 1 table. (p. 136-142)

S2275–2.2: Offenses and Clearances by Agency and County

a. Part I total offense rate by county, with ranked lists, various years 1979-83. 2 tables. (p. 143-144)

b. Offenses and clearances, with rates, for Part I offenses, by reporting agency and county, 1979-83. 1 table. (p. 145-282)

S2295   IDAHO
Department of Revenue and Taxation

S2295–1 THIRTY-NINTH ANNUAL REPORT OF STATE TAX COMMISSION, State of Idaho

Annual. Dec. 1, 1983.
iv + 112 p. var. paging.
LC 47-32622.
SRI/MF/complete

Annual report on Idaho tax collections by type, and property valuations, for fiscal or calendar year 1983, as applicable. Includes selected detail by county and for regulated industries by company, and trends from as early as FY63.

Report also includes a separately paginated supplement to the annual report for 1982.

Data are compiled from dept records.

Contents:

a. Transmittal letter, foreword, and contents listing. (p. i-iv)

b. Narrative report, with lists of major tax legislation changes enacted in 1983; and summary text data on tax rates and revenues, and dept activities. (p. 1-25)

c. Statistical section, with 49 tables listed below, some with accompanying charts and narrative. (p. 26-100)

d. Supplement to 1982 report, with contents listing, and 8 tables also listed below. (p. i, 1-11)

Availability: Idaho Department of Revenue and Taxation, State Tax Commission, Property Tax Section, 700 W. State St., PO Box 36, Boise ID 83722, †; SRI/MF/complete.

TABLES:

S2295–1.1: Tax Collections and Allocations

[1-2] Comparative statement of cash receipts by source [gross collections and/or distributions by tax type and fund], and by account, FY82-83. (p. 26-32)

[3] Comparative statement of tax collections and cost of administration, FY69-83. (p. 33)

[4] Expense by program for the State Tax Commission, FY83. (p. 33)

[5] Summary of audit and collections recoveries on current and delinquent returns [with amounts recovered by tax type], FY71-83. (p. 34)

[6] Comparative statement of gross tax collections [by type], FY79-83. (p. 34)

[7] Summary of income tax collections [by type, including delinquent taxes], by taxable years [1982 and/or FY83, as applicable]. (p. 35)

[8] Summary of tax refunds [number and amount, by tax type], FY83. (p. 36)

[9-10] Individual and corporation income tax returns processed: comparative table of growth [number of returns and tax liability, FY63-83]. (p. 37-38)

[11] KWh tax [and kWh generated, not sold, and used for industry and irrigation], by months, FY83. (p. 39)

[12] KWh tax: gross collections (distributed to general fund) [FY70-83]. (p. 39)

[13] Comparative statement of [gross] sales tax collections [and taxable sales], by county, FY82-83. (p. 40)

[14-16] Distribution of income tax collections, allocation of sales tax funds, and comparative statement of miscellaneous tax collections, FY79-83. (p. 41)

[17-18] Total, [exempt, and use] taxable sales, and tax paid, by county and industry [type of business], FY83. (p. 42-46)

S2295–1.2: Property Valuation and Taxation

[Data are preliminary estimates for 1983, unless otherwise noted. All tables except [23], [25-28], and [30-31] show estimated total and/or taxable market value, and additional data as noted.]

REAL AND PERSONAL PROPERTY

[All tables except table [6] show data by county.]

[1-2] Class 1 real property: lands [includes acreage and speculative tax-exempt value]; and improvements on land and lots; [all by type of property]. (p. 51-64)

[3] Class 2 personal property [by type of property]. (p. 65)

[4-5] Summary of assessed valuation: Class 1 and 2 property [by major category]. (p. 69-70)

[6] Market value Class 1 and 2 [summary by major category; 1970 and 1982]. (p. 71)

OPERATING PROPERTY

[Data are shown for Class 3 operating properties. Tables [8], [12], and [14] include value of microwave and leased equipment.]

[7] Operating property [by type: assessed value 1970, and estimated market value 1983]. (p. 72)

[8-9] Railroad companies [by company and line, including mileage; and by county]. (p. 73-75)

[10-11] Railroad car companies under and over $500,000 assessed valuation [by county and/or company]. (p. 76-81)

[12] Electric power companies [by company and county, including mileage and allocation per mile for transmission and distribution lines]. (p. 82)

[13-14] Telephone and telegraph companies by counties; [and mileage; by company]. (p. 84-85)

[15] Mobile radio telephone services [by company and county]. (p. 86)

[16-18] Pipeline and water companies [including mileage]; and water transportation companies; [all by company]. (p. 87-88)

[19] Pipeline, gas distribution, and water companies by county [and company]. (p. 89)

[20] Summary of utilities [by type and county]. (p. 90)

[21] Operating property [by county, 1982-83]. (p. 92)

SPECIAL TAXES, EXEMPTIONS, AND OTHER DATA

[22] Estimated market value, percentage and amount of exemption allowed electric power and natural gas distribution companies for generating and delivering energy for pumping water for irrigation/drainage purposes on land [by company]. (p. 93)

[23] Special taxes: rural electrical assns [amount of 1982 tax due in 1983, and consumer rebate for pumping irrigation water, by company and county]. (p. 93)

[24] Estimated market value recapitulation [value of 1982 subsequent and 1983 real/personal property assessment rolls; and 1983 utility company market value; all by county]. (p. 95)

[25] 1973 water pollution control refunding bond sinking fund taxes [collected in 1983, by county]. (p. 96)

[26] Special State tax charges made by State Tax Commission [taxes collected and average levy, for water pollution control sinking bond fund and private railroad car companies, 1973-83]. (p. 96)

[27-28] Analysis of property tax levied, 1978-82; and per dollar distribution, 1982; [by type of tax district]. (p. 97)

[29] Total calendar year property tax charges for all taxing units using market value [1970-82]. (p. 98)

[30] Property taxing districts [number by type, 1979-83]. (p. 99)

[31] Amount of money paid from sales tax fund to county treasurers as reimbursement for exemption of business inventory [by county, selected periods 1982-83]. (p. 100)

S2295–1.3: 1982 Supplement

[Data are shown by county and for 1982, unless otherwise noted.]

[1] 1981 individual income tax returns statistics [including salaries; business, farm, and asset sales gains and losses reported; total and taxable income; taxes withheld and paid with return; Keogh and private retirement payments, and education and political contributions reported; and number of returns and exemptions]. (p. 1)

[2-3] Summary of estimated market value: [Class 1 and Class 2 property by major category]. (p. 4-5)

[4] Estimated market value [of Class 1 and Class 2 property, by major category]. (p. 6)

[5] Recapitulation of estimated market value of real/personal property assessment rolls, subsequent personal property assessment rolls, and utilities. (p. 7)

[6-7] Property tax charges: by major functions, Class 3 operating property [for total county, all cities, and school and other districts; and by type of utility]. (p. 8-10)

[8] Statement showing gross tax, amount of [consumer] rebate, and net tax for electric current and natural gas utility companies generating and delivering energy for pumping water for irrigation/drainage purposes on land [by company only]. (p. 11)

S2315   IDAHO
Department of Transportation

S2315-1   STATE OF IDAHO MOTOR VEHICLE TRAFFIC ACCIDENTS, Statewide Summary, from Jan. 1, 1983-Dec. 31, 1983
Annual. July 21, 1984. 4 p.
SRI/MF/complete

Annual report, for 1983, on Idaho traffic accidents, injuries, and fatalities, by accident and vehicle type, location, time of day, and other circumstances, including ambulance response time; and by driver and victim characteristics.

Also includes data on motor vehicle travel mileage and safety device usage.

Contains 32 tables (4 p.).

Availability: Idaho Department of Transportation, Traffic Section, 3311 W. State St., PO Box 7129, Boise ID 83707, †; SRI/MF/complete.

S2390   ILLINOIS
Department of Agriculture

S2390-1   ILLINOIS AGRICULTURAL STATISTICS, Annual Summary, 1983
Annual. Oct. 1983.
6+127 p. Bull. 83-1.
LC 51-62568.
SRI/MF/complete

Annual report on Illinois agricultural production, marketing, and finances, 1982, with some data for 1983 and trends from as early as 1910. Data generally are shown by commodity and/or district or county.

Report covers production, prices, value, and, as applicable, acreage, yield, or inventory, for field crop, fruit, vegetable, livestock, poultry, and dairy sectors.

Also includes data on number of farms; farm acreage, income, expenses, labor, and wages; total and farm population; weather; mink pelt production; grain storage facilities and capacity; fertilizer use; and Illinois share of U.S. agricultural exports.

Data are compiled by the Illinois Cooperative Crop Reporting Service.

Contains contents listing (3 p.); and 9 sections, with 12 maps, 8 charts, and 145 tables (p. 1-126).

Availability: Illinois Cooperative Crop Reporting Service, PO Box 429, Springfield IL 62705, Illinois residents †, others $5.00; SRI/MF/complete.

S2395   ILLINOIS
Commissioner of Banks and Trust Companies

S2395-1   1982 ANNUAL REPORT, COMMISSIONER OF BANKS AND TRUST COMPANIES, State of Illinois
Annual. June 1983. 75 p.
SRI/MF/complete

Annual report on financial condition of Illinois State-chartered banks and trust companies, 1982, presenting assets, liabilities, capital/surplus, and profits/reserves for individual bank and trust companies, arranged by city.

Also includes Commissioner's Office finances; assets of licensed foreign banks by institution, and aggregate resources and liabilities of institutions with trust powers; bank income and expenses, total and as percents of earnings, by asset size group; and number of banks and assets, by State district.

Contains contents listing and personnel rosters (p. 2-5); 5 financial tables (p. 6-64); and lists of bank status changes, with 4 tables (p. 65-75).

Availability: Illinois Commissioner of Banks and Trust Companies, Reisch Bldg., Rm. 400, 119 S. Fifth St., Springfield IL 62701-1296, †; SRI/MF/complete.

S2405   ILLINOIS
Department of Commerce and Community Affairs

S2405-2   ILLINOIS MONTHLY ECONOMIC DATA SHEETS
Monthly. Approx. 25 p.
SRI/MF/complete, shipped quarterly

Monthly statistical compilation of economic, business, and industrial activity indicators for Illinois. Includes historical trends, and comparisons to total U.S.

Data are compiled from State and Federal agency sources, Dun and Bradstreet, Coldwell Banker, and other private sources. Most forecasts are by Chase Eeonometrics Associates and Data Resources, Inc. Month of coverage for most data is 1-4 months prior to cover date.

Contains narrative highlights and table listing; and 28 indicator tables, listed below, most accompanied by 2 illustrative charts. Most tables appear in all issues.

Prior to July 1984 issue, report also included data on number and liabilities of business failures.

Quarterly updates of the GSP are available from the Office of Research of the Dept of Commerce and Community Affairs, but are not covered by SRI.

Availability: Illinois Department of Commerce and Community Affairs, Research Office, 620 E. Adams St., Springfield IL 62701, †; SRI/MF/complete, shipped quarterly.

Issues reviewed during 1984: Nov. 1983-Sept. 1984 (P) [No issues were published for Dec. 1983, and Jan., Mar., June, and Aug. 1984; Apr./May is a combined issue].

INDICATOR TABLES:
[Most tables show trends for previous 3-13 years, and monthly data for current year through month of coverage. Data are for Illinois, unless otherwise noted. Many tables include percent comparisons to U.S.]

[1-2] GSP, and total [and per capita] personal income [annually and by quarter].

[3-5] Cash receipts from farm marketings, bituminous coal production [surface and underground], and contracts for future construction [by type].

[6-11] Labor force, employed [and unemployed [and insured unemployed]; total nonagricultural employment; employment by industry [division, for State and 9 SMSAs]; manufacturing employment; and hours and earnings of production workers in manufacturing.

[12-14] Unemployment rate [including historical data by race, and data by SMSA and county].

[15] Help-wanted advertising indexes [for U.S., East North Central region, Chicago, and St. Louis; monthly for year to date and previous year].

[16-17] New business incorporations [including data by census division]; and [business and nonbusiness] bankruptcy filings [by State district and selected city, current year data are cumulative; data begin with the July 1984 issue].

[18-19] Manufacturing production and productivity [including inventories and capacity utilization rate]; and new capital expenditures and gross book value of depreciable assets.

[20] Interest rates [national averages, for approximately 20 types of instrument].

[21-23] Population [including data for blacks, change components, and projections to 2010, annual data only]; State exports [including agricultural value for 6-8 products, and manufacturing value by major industry group, and related employment]; and U.S. and Chicago [area] CPI.

[24] Industrial and office vacancy rates [for Chicago and 4-6 other U.S. cities or areas, quarterly for current year through most recent available quarter and previous 3 years].

[25] Sales of all retail stores [including data for Chicago city and SMSA].

[26] [Chicago] purchasing managers survey [business activity composite index, and indexes for production, new orders, order backlog, inventories, employment, vendor deliveries, and prices paid; monthly for current year only].

[27-28] State transactions, general funds [revenues and expenditures]; and State employment and payroll [for education and all other agencies; both monthly, for current year only].

S2410   ILLINOIS
Commerce Commission

S2410–1   ILLINOIS UTILITIES STATISTICS

Annual series. For individual publication data, see below.
SRI/MF/complete

Series of 2 annual reports presenting Illinois electric and gas utility financial and operating data, by company and class of service, 1982-83. Data are from annual reports filed with the State Commerce Commission by 12 electric and 17 gas utilities.

Each report contains contents and table listing, introduction, and 13 tables showing the following data, by company, for 1982-83: sales revenue, sales volume (kWh or therm), and average number of customers, all by ultimate consumer class of service, and for sales for resale and interdepartmental sales; and other operating revenues.

Ultimate consumer classes of service covered in each report are described below.

Availability: Illinois Commerce Commission, Chief Clerk, 527 E. Capitol Ave., Springfield IL 62706, $2.00 each; SRI/MF/complete.

S2410–1.1: Illinois Gas Utilities: A Comparative Study of Gas Sales Statistics for Calendar Years 1983 and 1982

[Annual. May 1984. ii+34 p. Research Bull. No. 110. SRI/MF/complete.]

Ultimate consumer classes of service covered are: residential and commercial/industrial, with and without space heating; interruptible commercial/industrial; and all other.

S2410–1.2: Illinois Electric Utilities: A Comparative Study of Electric Sales Statistics for Calendar Years 1983 and 1982

[Annual. May 1984. ii+17 p. Research Bull. No. 111. SRI/MF/complete.]

Ultimate consumer classes of service covered are: residential, large industrial, small commercial, public street/highway lighting, other public authorities, and railroad/railways.

S2410–2   OPERATING STATISTICS OF TELEPHONE COMPANIES IN ILLINOIS for Calendar Year 1983

Annual. May 1984.
iii+55 p. Rpt. No. 214.
LC 81-644032.
SRI/MF/complete

Annual report presenting Illinois Class A and B and cooperative telephone company financial and operating data, by company, 1983. Includes number of facilities, value of plant in service and under construction, capitalization, revenues, expenses, and income.

Contains company index (p. i-iii); and 55 tables (p. 1-55).

Availability: Illinois Commerce Commission, Chief Clerk, 527 E. Capitol Ave., Springfield IL 62706, $2.00; SRI/MF/complete.

S2415   ILLINOIS
Office of the
Comptroller

S2415–1   ILLINOIS ANNUAL REPORT, 1983

Annual. Feb. 1984. 399 p.
ISSN 0360-8719.
LC 80-644544.
SRI/MF/complete

Annual report on financial condition of Illinois State government, for fiscal year ended June 30, 1983, and "lapse period" July 1-Sept. 30, 1983. Presents revenues by source; expenditures of individual agencies, by object and function; and fund balances; for general, highway, university/college income, special State, bond financed, debt service, Federal and State trust, and revolving funds. Includes selected comparisons to FY82.

Also includes Capital Development Board funding for individual projects; and comparison of budgeted vs. actual expenditures.

Data are from the records of the comptroller's office.

Contains contents and table listing (p. 3-4); and 9 tables (p. 7-399).

An annual summary report on Illinois financial condition is also available from the Office of the Comptroller, but is not covered by SRI.

Availability: Illinois Office of the Comptroller, Statehouse, Rm. 201, Springfield IL 62706, †; SRI/MF/complete.

S2430   ILLINOIS
Administrative
Office of the
Courts

S2430–1   ADMINISTRATIVE OFFICE OF THE ILLINOIS COURTS 1982 Annual Report to the Supreme Court of Illinois

Annual. [1984.] 246 p.
ISSN 0536-3713.
LC 74-640509.
SRI/MF/complete

Annual report, for 1982, on Illinois judicial system, including trial and appellate court caseloads and case dispositions. Covers supreme, appellate, and circuit courts. Includes trial court data by case type, judicial district, and county; with extensive detail for Cook County by jurisdiction and type of criminal offense.

Case types shown for most courts are civil and criminal, with additional detail for chancery, eminent domain, tax, municipal corporations, mental health, divorce, family relations, juvenile, felony, misdemeanor, small claims, probate, ordinance, traffic, and conservation cases.

Also includes data on State judicial elections and budget, medical experts' court-related activities, legal internship program, judges and workloads, law jury cases and processing time, sentences imposed in felony cases, circuit court revenues and expenditures, and probation dept and juvenile detention home personnel and caseloads.

Contains contents listing (p. 3-6); narrative report, with 20 summary charts and tables (p. 7-86); statistical section, with 3 charts and 112 tables (p. 88-241); and appendices (p. 242-246).

Availability: Illinois Administrative Office of the Courts, Supreme Court Bldg., Springfield IL 62706, †; SRI/MF/complete.

S2457   ILLINOIS
Department of
Financial Institutions

S2457–1   ILLINOIS CHARTERED CREDIT UNIONS 1983 Annual Report

Annual. Apr. 10, 1984.
2+26 p.
SRI/MF/complete

Annual report on financial condition of Illinois State-chartered credit unions, presenting assets, shares, members, and loans, by institution, as of Dec. 31, 1983.

Also includes data on real estate lending, and mergers and liquidations; consolidated operating ratios, balance sheet, and statement of income and expense; selected data by credit union type and county; and selected comparisons to 1982, with trends from 1929.

Contains contents listing (p. 1); and report, with text data, 2 charts, and 15 tables (p. 2-26).

Availability: Illinois Department of Financial Institutions, Credit Union Division, 421 E. Capitol Ave., Springfield IL 62706, †; SRI/MF/complete.

S2465   ILLINOIS
Executive
Office of the
Governor

S2465–2   ILLINOIS POPULATION TRENDS from 1970-2025, 1984 Edition

Biennial. July 1984.
5+237 p.
LC 83-621576.
SRI/MF/complete

Biennial report presenting Illinois population trends and projections by age, for total State and each county, quinquennially 1970-2025. State data are also cross-tabulated by race and sex. Also includes historical population trends, from 1820 for the State, and from 1870 for each county.

Data are based on the 1980 Census of Population final count, and prior censuses.

Contains contents listing (3 p.); introduction, census procedures, and analysis interspersed with 12 charts and 4 summary tables (p. 1-16); State data, with 2 tables (p. 17-27); county data, with 2 basic tables and 1 illustrative chart repeated for each county (p. 28-231); and methodology (p. 233-237).

This is the 8th edition of the report.

Availability: Illinois Bureau of the Budget, Planning and Financial Analysis Division, 605 Stratton Bldg., Springfield IL 62706, †; SRI/MF/complete.

S2470   ILLINOIS
Department of Public Health

S2470–1   VITAL STATISTICS, Illinois, 1981
Annual.   Mar. 1984.
178 p. var. paging.
LC A60-9072.
SRI/MF/complete, current & previous year reports

Annual report, for 1981, on Illinois vital statistics, covering population, births, deaths by detailed cause, marriages, divorces, and annulments, by demographic characteristics, city, county, and health service area (HSA). Includes selected trends from 1918. Data are from vital statistics certificates filed with the Dept of Health as of Feb. 15, 1982.

Contents:

a. Contents and table listing. (5 p.)

b. Introduction, and general summary, with 7 text tables, and 23 lettered tables. (p. I.01-I.30)

c. 1 detailed table repeated for State, HSAs, Chicago, and counties, with index (p. II.001-II.115); and 5 tables showing data by city (p. III.01-III.07)

d. Methodology, facsimile of vital statistics certificates, definitions, and list of causes of death based on 9th Revision, International Classification of Diseases. (p. IV.01-IV.19)

All tables are listed below.

Previous report, for 1980, was also reviewed in 1984 and is also available on SRI microfiche under this number [Annual. Nov. 1983. 178 p. var. paging. †]. Previous report is substantially similar in format and content, but also includes data on population natural increase and migration for nonmetro areas and by SMSA, and omits life expectancy data.

Availability: Illinois Department of Public Health, Health Information and Evaluation Division, 525 W. Jefferson St., Springfield IL 62761, †; SRI/MF/complete.

TABLES:
[Unless otherwise noted, data are for Illinois, 1981. Data on births and deaths are usually for Illinois residents. Data on marriages, divorces, annulments, and abortions are for events occurring in Illinois.]

S2470–1.1: Text Tables
1. Resident live birth rates by age of mother and race of child, 1970 and 1980-81. (p. I.02)

2. Resident live births occurring outside of hospitals, by attendant, 1976-81. (p. I.02)

3. Percent of resident live births with low birth weight by age of mother and race of child, 1980-81. (p. I.04)

4. Induced abortions and abortion rates by age group, 1981. (p. I.05)

5. Motor vehicle accident death rates by type of accident, 1978-81. (p. I.06)

6-7. Life [expectancy] tables for males and females, 1979-81. (p. I.07-I.08)

S2470–1.2: Births, Deaths, Marriages, and Divorces
[Data by color are for white and nonwhite.]

TRENDS
A. Live births, deaths, infant deaths, neonatal deaths, and maternal deaths, with rates for each, and fetal deaths, with ratios, 1918-81. (p. I.11)

BIRTHS
B-C. Live births: by birth weight, sex, and color; and by race, classified by sex, legitimacy status, place of birth [hospital and nonhospital], attendant [physician, midwife, and other], and age of mother; [all for] Illinois, Chicago, and downstate. (p. I.12-I.13)

D. Live births and births to unmarried women, with ratios, 1950-81. (p. I.14)

DEATHS
E. Causes of fetal death among infants born to Illinois mothers, by weight at birth. (p. I.14)

F. Perinatal losses and mortality ratio by race and sex, Illinois, Chicago, and downstate. (p. I.15)

G-H. [10] leading causes: of infant [neonatal, and post neonatal] deaths, by age; and of deaths among white and nonwhite races. (p. I.15-I.16)

I-K. Components of heart disease deaths; cancer deaths by site; and deaths due to cerebrovascular disease [by lesion type; all by age]. (p. I.16-I.17)

L. Accidental deaths [and rates] by type of accident and age of decedent. (p. I.18)

M. Accidental deaths occurring in Illinois by type of accident and place where accident occurred [metro and nonmetro counties and Chicago], by population class. (p. I.19)

N. Deaths and death rates from the principal diseases affecting the respiratory system, [selected years] 1950-81. (p. I.20)

O-P. 12 leading causes of death and death rates by age and color, among residents of Illinois, Chicago, and downstate. (p. I.21-I.26)

Q. Leading causes of death by selected age groups. (p. I.27)

MARRIAGES, DIVORCES, AND ANNULMENTS
R. Marriages, divorces, and annulments, 1958-81. (p. I.28)

S. Marriages classified by sex and age. (p. I.28)

T. Number of previous marriages of bride and groom. (p. I.29)

U. Marital status of bride and groom at time of marriage. (p. I.29)

V-W. Divorces classified by sex and age; and divorces and annulments classified by the duration of marriage. (p. I.30)

S2470–1.3: Local Area Data
STATE, HSAs, AND COUNTIES
[Table [A] is repeated for total State; 11 HSAs, including city of Chicago; and HSA component counties.]

[A] Selected vital statistics among residents [includes population (total, and age 65/over by sex); live births by sex; total and illegitimate live births and fetal deaths (to all mothers and mothers under age 20); premature live births and fetal deaths; neonatal and infant deaths; perinatal loss, by sex; and nonfetal deaths, to-

tal and by 21 causes, with selected data by sex and for age 65/over; all by race, for 1981, with rates for 1976-80 period and 1981]. (p. II.001-II.114)

CITIES
[Data are shown for residents of 66 cities.]
1-2. Live births, infant deaths, neonatal deaths, fetal deaths, and rates, by race. (p. III.01-III.02)

3. Live births with percentage rates for premature births and hospital births, infant deaths by age with rates, and maternal deaths. (p. III.03)

4-5. Deaths and death rates from important causes. (p. III.04-III.07)

S2475   ILLINOIS
Board of Higher Education

S2475–1   DATA BOOK ON ILLINOIS HIGHER EDUCATION, 1984
Annual.   1984.   ix+256 p.
ISSN 0098-5279.
LC 75-643784.
SRI/MF/complete

Annual report, for academic year 1983, on Illinois higher education. Covers enrollment, degrees, staff, and finances, for private and public colleges and universities and for community colleges. Most data are shown by individual institution. Includes trends from as early as 1951.

Data are from institution surveys conducted or coordinated by Board of Higher Education staff.

Contains contents and table listings (p. iii-ix); introduction (p. 1-4); and 82 tables listed below, grouped into 10 sections, each preceded by descriptions of tables, definitions, and data sources (p. 5-256).

This is the 11th annual report.

Availability: Illinois Board of Higher Education, Four W. Old Capitol Square, 500 Reisch Bldg., Springfield IL 62701, †; SRI/MF/complete.

TABLES:
[Tables show data for Illinois, by individual institution, unless otherwise noted.]

S2475–1.1: Enrollment and Degrees
[Instructional locations are on-campus, off-campus, and home study. Attendance status is full- or part-time. Data are for fall 1983, unless otherwise noted.]

CURRENT ENROLLMENT
I.1. General characteristics of enrollment [summary by institution type]. (p. 13)

I.2-I.4. Characteristics of degree credit enrollment at public universities, public community colleges, and private colleges and universities, by location of instruction, level or type of instruction, and attendance status. (p. 14-20)

I.5. FTE degree credit enrollment at public universities, by level of instruction and location of instruction. (p. 21)

I.6-I.11. Degree credit headcount enrollment and FTE degree credit enrollment: at public universities; at public community colleges by instructional program; and at private institutions; [all] by class level. (p. 22-35)

STUDENT CHARACTERISTICS

[Tables II.1-II.13 generally show data for degree credit students.]

II.1. [Headcount, by] sex, by level of instruction. (p. 41-46)

II.2. Course load, by level [of instruction and attendance status]. (p. 47-52)

II.3-II.7. Age distribution: by level of instruction, type of institution, and sex; and of 1st-time freshmen, undergraduate students, and graduate students, by attendance status, and type of institution. (p. 53-57)

II.8. Average age, by sex and level of instruction. (p. 58-63)

II.9-II.10. Race or national origin [white, black, American Indian/Alaskan Native, Asian/Pacific Islander, Hispanic, and nonresident alien]. (p. 64-70)

II.11-II.13. Home State of 1st-time freshmen students; and home county of in-State 1st-time freshmen [by attendance status]; by type of institution. (p. 71-78)

ENROLLMENT TRENDS

III.1. Fall degree credit headcount enrollments [U.S. total, and Illinois by institution type], 1951-83. (p. 81)

III.2-III.3. Fall FTE degree credit enrollment; and fall off-campus and home study headcount enrollment; [both by level of instruction and type of institution], 1965-83. (p. 82-83)

III.4. Fall degree/certificate credit enrollments [selected years 1965-83]. (p. 84-105)

III.5-III.6. Fall term on-campus degree credit headcount enrollment, by class level; and degree credit enrollments, by location of instruction and attendance status; [by type of institution], 1974-83. (p. 106-107)

ACADEMIC PROGRAM ENROLLMENT

IV.1-IV.4. Headcount majors in public universities, by discipline [and instructional level]. (p. 111-114)

ADMISSIONS AND TRANSFERS

V.1-V.2. Applications, acceptances, and enrollments of 1st-time freshmen, transfer students, and entering professional and graduate students. (p. 117-124)

V.3. Institutional origin of undergraduate transfer students. (p. 125-156)

DEGREES

VI.1-VI.2. Number of bachelor, masters, doctorate, and 1st professional degrees conferred; and number of associate degree and certificate awards conferred; 1980/81-1982/83. (p. 159-164)

VI.3-VI.8. Bachelor's, master's, doctoral, and professional degrees conferred, and associate degrees and certificates conferred, by discipline [aggregate for all schools, selected years] 1970/71-1982/83. (p. 165-170)

VI.9-VI.11. Number and percent of degrees conferred, by field of study and level: by type of institution; sex; and racial and ethnic category [American Indian/Alaskan Native, Asian/Pacific Islander, Hispanic, and nonresident alien; aggregate data,] 1982/83. (p. 171-194)

STAFF AND SALARIES

[Tables VII.1-VII.3 and VII.5-VII.9 present data for public universities.]

VII.1-VII.2. State appropriated staff earnings; and budgeted staffing levels in staff years, by staff classification and fund source [appropriated or nonappropriated; both for administrative, faculty, civil service, and student employees], FY84. (p. 201-202)

VII.3-VII.4. Number and sex of full-time faculty in public universities and private colleges and universities, by rank, fall 1983. (p. 203-205)

VII.5-VII.7. Average salary, (9- and 12-month contracts), 1983/84; and percent tenured, fall 1983 (all contracts); of full-time faculty, by rank and sex. (p. 206-208)

VII.8. Staff-year faculty assignment, by instructional activity and level of instruction, 1982/83. (p. 209)

VII.9. Statewide student credit hours per staff year faculty (direct instruction) by discipline and level [aggregate], 1982/83. (p. 212)

STUDENT COSTS

VIII.1-VIII.5. Annual tuition and fees of full-time undergraduates, graduates, and [health, law, and theology] professional students; detailed undergraduate fee charges in public universities; public community college charges [by district only]; and annual charges for room and board; 1983/84. (p. 215-223)

STUDENT FINANCIAL AID

[Data are shown by type of institution.]

IX.1. Student financial assistance by source [including Federal, State, and institutional], FY79-83. (p. 227)

IX.2. Number of [undergraduate and graduate] financial aid recipients, FY80-83. (p. 228)

IX.3-IX.5. Undergraduate grants, scholarships, and tuition waivers [number and value, by type of award and source], FY83; and value of undergraduate and graduate level financial assistance, by type, FY79-83. (p. 229-231)

FINANCIAL TRENDS

[Table titles for X.1-X.7 begin "Historical record of..." Only data for public universities are shown by institution.]

X.1. State higher education operating appropriations [summary, including data for public universities], FY79-84. (p. 238)

X.2-X.5. State appropriations: to public community colleges and State scholarship commission for operations and grants; for health education grants to private institutions; and for State universities retirement system; FY79-84. (p. 239-242)

X.6. State appropriations to public universities, by source of funds, FY82-84. (p. 243)

X.7. Total audited revenues [by source] for public community colleges, FY80-83. (p. 244)

CURRENT REVENUES AND EXPENDITURES

X.8-X.9. Current fund revenues by source at nonpublic institutions, FY82; and current funds expenditures at public universities by function (all funds), FY83. (p. 245-247)

X.10. Audited expenditures [aggregate] for public community colleges, by functional classification, FY80-83. (p. 248)

X.11-X.12. Current fund expenditures, by function, at public community colleges and nonpublic institutions, FY82. (p. 249-253)

INSTRUCTIONAL COSTS AND CAPITAL APPROPRIATIONS

X.13. Instructional costs per credit hour, by student level, at public universities, FY83. (p. 254)

X.14. Total instructional costs per credit hour, [aggregate for] public universities, by discipline and level, FY83. (p. 255)

X.15. Appropriations [new and reappropriated] for capital projects, FY82-84. (p. 256)

S2487   ILLINOIS
Commission on
Intergovernmental
Cooperation

S2487–1   SOCIO-ECONOMIC PROFILE OF ILLINOIS, 1970-80
Monograph. Sept. 1983.
ii + 35 p.
Research Memorandum No. 73.
LC 84-620510.
SRI/MF/complete

Report presenting Illinois socioeconomic data, by county, 1980, with comparison to 1970. Includes population, unemployment rate, percent adult population finishing high school and college, median family income, percent persons below the poverty level, percent housing units with 1.01/over persons per room and with deficient plumbing, assessed property valuation, public aid expenditures, and percent population receiving public aid.

Data are from various State and Federal sources.

Contains preface (1 p.); contents/table listing (p. i-ii); introduction (p. 1); and 5 maps and 19 tables, arranged in 9 sections, each prefaced by a brief narrative (p. 3-35).

Availability: Illinois Commission on Intergovernmental Cooperation, 707 Stratton Office Bldg., Springfield IL 62706, †; SRI/MF/complete.

S2490   ILLINOIS
Department of
Labor

S2490–4   ANNUAL PLANNING INFORMATION REPORT, State of Illinois
Annual, discontinued.

Annual planning report, identifying Illinois population groups most in need of employment services, and presenting data on employment, job vacancies, and population and labor force characteristics. Due to funding reductions and change from CETA to Job Training Partnership Act program, report has been discontinued with the FY83 edition (for description, see SRI 1983 Annual, under this number).

Data for individual labor market areas are available on request from Illinois Department of Labor, Employment Security Bureau, Research and Analysis Division, 910 S. Michigan Ave., Chicago IL 60605.

S2490–7   COMMUTING PATTERNS IN ILLINOIS
Monograph.   [1984.]
1+34 p.
SRI/MF/complete

Report presenting 1980 census data on commuting patterns in Illinois, covering points of origin and destination for Illinois residents and for non-residents employed in the State. Data are cross-tabulated among Illinois counties and neighboring States.

Data are based on unpublished tabulations from Summary Tape File 4 of the 1980 Census of Population and Housing.

Contains summary data map (1 p.); introduction and brief analysis (p. 1, 34); and 1 extended table (p. 2-33).

Availability: Illinois Department of Labor, Employment Security Bureau, Research and Analysis Division, 910 S. Michigan Ave., Chicago IL 60605, †; SRI/MF/complete.

S2497   ILLINOIS
Department of
Law Enforcement

S2497–1   CRIME IN ILLINOIS, 1982
Annual.   [1983.]   199 p.
LC 81-641713.
SRI/MF/complete

Annual report, for 1982, on Illinois crimes and arrests, by type of offense. Also includes data on crime trends, stolen property, clearances, assaults on police, and law enforcement employment. Offenses are shown by location, and arrests by offender race, age, and sex.

Data are from State and local law enforcement agency reports, submitted under the Uniform Crime Reporting (UCR) Program.

Contents:

Contents listing, and introduction, including UCR Program description and offense classification. (3 p., p. 1-4)

Section I. Crime trends, with 15 charts and 48 tables. (p. 6-74)

Section II-V. Crime Index, SMSAs, offense and clearance data, Chicago detail, and law enforcement agency information, with 9 charts and 39 tables. (p. 77-199)

All charts and tables are described below.

This is the 11th annual report. The 10th annual report is described in SRI 1982 Annual, under this number.

Availability: Illinois Department of Law Enforcement, Support Services Division, Identification Bureau, 726 S. College, Springfield IL 62704, †; SRI/MF/complete.

CHARTS AND TABLES:

[Unless otherwise noted, data by race are shown for white, black, Mexican, Puerto Rican, American Indian/Alaskan, Asian/Pacific Islander, and other Hispanic. Data by age are shown for adult and juvenile.

Index offenses are murder/voluntary manslaughter, forcible rape, aggravated assault, robbery, burglary, theft, motor vehicle theft, and arson.]

S2497–1.1: Crime Trends

[Summary data for total violent and property crimes, and data on individual Index offenses, include 1 chart, and 2 tables showing population; crime volume and rate; and arrests by age, sex, and race; 1981-82. Additional data are described below.]

CRIME INDEX SUMMARY

a. Index offenses and rates 1980-82, and arrest distribution 1982, by offense; and arrests by age, sex, and race, 1981-82. 1 chart and 2 tables. (p. 6-7)

VIOLENT CRIMES

b. Summary, with arrest distribution by offense, 1982. 2 charts and 2 tables. (p. 8-9)

c. Murder/voluntary manslaughter: offenses by month, 1981-82; offenses by victim-offender relationship, victim's sex and race (white, black and other), situation (multiple or single victims and offenders), and weapon type, 1981 and monthly 1982; and number of victims, by reporting agency, 1982. 1 chart and 8 tables. (p. 10-14)

d. Forcible rape. 1 chart and 2 tables. (p. 15-16)

e. Robbery: offenses by weapon type; and day and night offenses, and value of property stolen, recovered, and destroyed, by type of setting and property; 1982. 2 charts and 4 tables. (p. 17-22)

f. Aggravated assault, battery, and attempted murder: offenses by weapon type, 1982. 1 chart and 3 tables. (p. 23-25)

CRIMES AGAINST PROPERTY

[Summary and individual property crime data include some or all of the following: day and night offenses and items stolen, and value of property stolen, recovered, and destroyed, by type of setting and property, 1982.]

g. Summary, with some detail by offense. 2 charts and 5 tables. (p. 26-34)

h. Burglary, theft, burglary from motor vehicles, and motor vehicle theft. 3 charts and 14 tables. (p. 35-61)

i. Arson and vandalism. 2 charts and 8 tables. (p. 62-74)

S2497–1.2: Crime Index and SMSAs, Offense and Clearance Data, Chicago Detail, and Law Enforcement Agency Information

a. Index offenses: by local reporting agency and county, with State totals for sheriff offices, police depts, and universities; by reporting unit for railroad police, State police, park districts, hospitals, and other agencies; and totals for all SMSAs, SMSA core city, SMSA suburban, rural areas, and other cities; 1981-82. 12 tables. (p. 78-134)

b. Offense and clearance summary: offenses known to police, actually occurred, and total clearances; and adult and juvenile arrests; all by detailed Index and non-Index offense, 1981-82. 2 tables. (p. 138-147)

c. Chicago Police Dept: most of the data described above under S2497-1.1 and S2497-1.2 are shown for Chicago, various periods 1980-82. 16 tables. (p. 152-165)

d. Audit research reports: estimated verified incidents, for selected Index crimes, 1982. 9 charts and 1 table. (p. 168-179)

e. Law enforcement officers killed or assaulted, by type of activity, weapon, and assignment, and clearances, 1982; and full- and part-time law enforcement officers and full-time civilian employees, arranged by city/town population size and by agency grouped by type; as of Oct. 31, 1982. 8 tables. (p. 186-199)

S2505   ILLINOIS
Department of
Mental Health and
Developmental Disabilities

S2505–1   ILLINOIS MENTAL HEALTH STATISTICS, FY83
Annual.   Feb. 1984.
4+108 p.
LC 79-644938.
SRI/MF/complete

Annual statistical report on the patient population of mental health facilities in Illinois, FY83. Presents data on admissions, discharges, length of stay, and patient census for Dept of Mental Health and Developmental Disabilities (DMHDD) inpatient facilities, State operated outpatient and grant-in-aid facilities, general hospitals, and private sanitaria. Also includes specific data for Chicago area.

Contains definitions and contents listing (4 p.); and 2 maps, 1 chart, and 61 tables listed below (p. 1-108).

A monthly report with similar but less complete data is also published by DMHDD, but is not covered by SRI.

Availability: Illinois Department of Mental Health and Developmental Disabilities, 401 S. Spring St., Springfield IL 62706, †; SRI/MF/complete.

TABLES:

[Unless otherwise noted, data are for FY83 or as of June 30, 1983. Data by facility include data by region.]

S2505–1.1: Outpatient Data by Age, Treatment, and Facility

[Tables [2-5] show data by individual facility.]

[1] Summary of patient data, by age group, treatment category, and facility type [case openings/admissions, closings/separations, active cases/residents plus home visits, and patients served/client contacts]. (p. 2)

[2] Case movements and number of client contacts/patients served: State operated outpatient, grant-in-aid facilities, and private/general hospitals. (p. 4-14)

[3] Unduplicated count of patients served by treatment category: State operated outpatient and grant-in-aid facilities. (p. 15-23)

[4] Patients served by treatment category: private/general hospitals. (p. 24)

[5] Count of client contacts by treatment category: State operated outpatient and grant-in-aid facilities. (p. 26-34)

[6] Unduplicated clients served/duplicated client contacts by treatment category and region of facility [State operated outpatient and grant-in-aid facilities]. (p. 36)

[7] Case closings and separations by number of days open, and by treatment category within type of facility [State operated outpatient and grant-in-aid facilities, and private/general hospitals]. (p. 37)

S2505–1.2: DMHDD Inpatient Census, Admissions, and Separations

[All tables show data for DMHDD inpatient facilities.]

CENSUS

[1] Changes in inpatient population: residents plus home visits [by facility, various periods FY81-83]. (p. 38)

[2-4] Residents plus home visits by age group; temporary absence data by type of absence; and average daily populations by sex; [all] by facility. (p. 39-41)

[5-6] Residents plus home visits: by age group and diagnosis; and by treatment category [and facility]. (p. 42-43)

[7] Resident plus home visit days for recipients by treatment category [and facility]. (p. 44)

[8-12] Residents plus home visits: by treatment category; by age group, total and diagnostic category of mentally ill and developmentally disabled; and by facility; all by time in residence. (p. 45-49)

ADMISSIONS AND SEPARATIONS

[13] Net additions and patients served [by facility]. (p. 50)

[14-17] Admissions by mental health code legal status [voluntary and involuntary]; total admissions by age group and sex and by treatment category [by facility]; and admissions by age group, sex, and average age within diagnosis. (p. 51-54)

[18-21] First and readmissions by age group and facility, and by age and diagnosis; and readmissions by type of termination of previous episode, by facility and by days stay in community. (p. 55-58)

[22-24] Live discharges: by age group and facility; by age group and diagnosis; and by treatment category [and facility]. (p. 59-61)

[25-28] Live discharges: by treatment category; by age group, total and diagnostic category of developmentally disabled; and by facility; by length of stay. (p. 62-66)

[29-32] Total deaths by age group and length of stay, total and diagnostic category of mentally ill and developmentally disabled. (p. 67-69)

[33] Terminations of on-books population, by type of termination [by facility]. (p. 70)

S2505–1.3: Region, Subregion, and County Data, and Employment

[All tables showing data by county and most showing data by region include separate figures for suburban Cook County and Chicago.]

REGIONAL AND COUNTY DATA

[1] Transfers to DMHDD inpatient facilities [by receiving facility] according to region of facility from which transferred. (p. 71)

[2-6] Residents plus home visits: at inpatient facilities, by treatment category and county of residence; at DMHDD inpatient facilities, by region of legal residence [and facility]; by treatment category and recipients region of

residence; and at DMHDD inpatient facilities, by age group and by time in residence, by region of residence. (p. 72-78)

[7] Admissions and case openings by type of service and treatment category within region of residence. (p. 79)

[8] Population movements at DMHDD inpatient facilities, by treatment category and region of residence. (p. 81)

[9-11] Case openings and admissions by type of facility and county of residence; and admission, discharge, and census data [including rates], by county and region of residence. (p. 82-90)

[12-13] Readmissions: time in residence for previous episodes, and time (in community) since last discharge, by treatment category and region of residence. (p. 91-92)

[14-16] Live discharges from DMHDD inpatient facilities: by treatment category and county to which discharged; by age group and region of residence; and by length of stay and region to which discharged. (p. 93-97)

[17] Absolute discharges to community placement program by region of placement, DMHDD inpatient facilities. (p. 98)

FACILITY EMPLOYMENT DATA

[18] Changes in employment, filled positions (general revenue/federally funded) [by pay facility, various periods June 30, 1981-83]. (p. 99-100)

S2505–1.4: Health Service Area (HSA) Data

[1] Residents plus home visits and admissions by patient's HSA, number and rate per 100,000 general population. (p. 102)

[2-3] Residents plus home visits at DMHDD inpatient facilities, and admissions to DMHDD inpatient facilities; by treatment category and HSA. (p. 102-108)

S2535   ILLINOIS
Office of the
Secretary of
State

S2535–1   ILLINOIS LIBRARIES: Public Library Statistics, 1982-83
Monthly (selected issue).
Nov. 1983.
p. 533-646 (cumulative pagination throughout year).
Vol. 65, No. 9.
ISSN 0019-2104.
LC 29-23175.
SRI/MF/complete

Annual statistical issue of *Illinois Libraries*, presenting public library statistics for FY83. Includes data on library holdings, staff, and finances.

Data are from reports of public libraries, 1980 census, and State agencies. Data were prepared by the Library Research Center, University of Illinois Graduate School of Library and Information Science.

Contents:

a. Contents listing, and definitions. (2 p.)

b. 1 detailed table showing population served, nonresident fee, weekly hours, transactions, FTE staff, volumes added and held, films and recordings held, periodicals received, municipal tax valuation and rate, local government and total receipts, and salary and materials expenditures, all by library, mostly for FY83. (p. 535-557)

c. 1 summary table showing number of district, county, township, city, town, and village libraries. (p. 558)

d. Directories and index of public libraries and librarians. (p. 559-646)

Statistical issue is published each Nov., and is the only issue of *Illinois Libraries* described by SRI.

Availability: Illinois Office of the Secretary of State, State Library, Centennial Bldg., Springfield IL 62756, †; SRI/MF/complete.

S2540   ILLINOIS
Department of
Transportation

S2540–1   1983 ACCIDENT FACTS, ILLINOIS
Annual. [1984.]   24 p.
LC 80-620689.
SRI/MF/complete

Annual report on Illinois traffic accidents, fatalities, and injuries, by accident and vehicle type, location, time, and other circumstances; and driver and victim characteristics; 1983 with trends from 1974.

Also includes data on economic cost of accidents, blood alcohol content of driver fatalities by age group, motor vehicle registrations, travel mileage, and drivers licenses; and detailed data on pedestrian, motorcycle, and school bus accidents.

Contains contents listing (inside front cover); and highlights, 2 data maps, 6 charts, and 13 tables (p. 1-24).

A booklet containing additional motorcycle accident data is also available from the issuing agency, but is not covered by SRI.

Availability: Illinois Department of Transportation, Traffic Safety Division, 2300 S. Dirksen Pkwy., Rm. 319, Springfield IL 62764, †; SRI/MF/complete.

S2570   INDIANA
Office of the Auditor

S2570-1   ANNUAL REPORT OF THE AUDITOR OF STATE of the State of Indiana for the Fiscal Year Ending June 30, 1983
Annual. Dec. 1, 1983.
xiii+369 p.
LC 10-13355.
SRI/MF/complete

Annual auditor's report on financial condition of Indiana State government for FY83, covering assets, liabilities and fund equity, revenues by detailed source, appropriations and expenditures by function and object, and fund balances, for general, special revenue, capital projects, enterprise, internal service, and pension and other trust funds, with selected detail by individual account.

Also includes data on State motor vehicle highway fund receipts, administrative expenses, and distributions; property tax levies, assessed values, and collections and distributions, and other tax levies, by county and type; and selected trends from 1973.

Contains introductory material, including 6 summary charts, and contents listing (p. iii-xiii); general purpose, and combining and individual fund financial statements and schedules, with 29 tables (p. 1-71); and statistical section, with 13 tables (p. 73-369).

Availability: Indiana Office of the Auditor, State House, Rm. 240, Indianapolis IN 46204, †; SRI/MF/complete.

S2608   INDIANA
Department of Education

S2608-1   1982/83 REPORT OF STATISTICAL INFORMATION for Indiana School Corporations
Annual. [1984.] v+170 p.
SRI/MF/complete

Annual report, for 1982/83 school year, on Indiana public schools, covering enrollment, staff, finances, and transportation, by school corporation or county. Also includes selected data for nonpublic schools, and State trends from 1975/76.

Data are compiled from reports by local school corporations to the State Dept of Education.

Contains table listing (p. v); 11 tables with data by county and school corporation (p. 3-164); and 7 tables with State trends from 1975/76 (p. 167-170). Tables are listed below.

Previous report, for 1981/82, is described in SRI 1983 Annual under S2680-1. Issuing agency name has changed from Indiana Dept of Public Instruction.

Availability: Indiana Department of Education, Publications Division, State House, Rm. 224, Indianapolis IN 46204, $5.00; SRI/MF/complete.

TABLES:

S2608-1.1: Local Data
[Data are shown by county and/or school corporation, for 1982/83 school year, unless otherwise noted.]

ENROLLMENT

A-B. Number of pupils enrolled in public and nonpublic schools [by grade 1-12, and for nursery school, kindergarten, ungraded and special education grade ranges 1-6 and 7-12, and postgraduate], fall 1982. (p. 3-29)

PERSONNEL AND TRANSPORTATION

C. Public fall enrollment, certified personnel, [and] pupil/teacher ratio [for kindergarten, and grade ranges 1-6 and 7-12; and including special education personnel and enrollment]. (p. 33-42)

D. Public school noncertificated personnel [by position]. (p. 45-52)

E. Transportation [cost, depreciation, State reimbursement; number of drivers by sex, trips, miles, and buses by type of ownership; private, parochial, and public kindergarten and grade 1-12 pupils transported; and ratios]. (p. 55-70)

FINANCES

F. Summary of receipts [by fund and by source, including Federal, State, and local]. (p. 73-88)

G. Revenue from State sources [by program, including special and vocational education, FY83]. (p. 91-98)

H. Summary of expenditures by program, and per pupil costs, FY83. (p. 101-116)

I. School corporation wealth ratio [adjusted assessed valuation per average daily attendance (ADA)], 1982/83; assessments and tax rates payable for 1983. (p. 119-132)

J. Summary of indebtedness: principal outstanding [for 5 loan categories, school and civil aid bonds, and public/private holding], FY83. (p. 135-145)

K. Summary of expenditures by object [including salaries, employee benefits, and capital outlay], and percent of total expenditures, FY83. (p. 149-164)

S2608-1.2: State Trends
[Data are State totals. Tables I-III show data for 1975/76-1982/83 school years.]

I. [Public and parochial school] enrollment and [public school] ADA. (p. 167)

II. Select statistics [cost per ADA, pupil/teacher ratio, mobility/withdrawal rate for grade level 7-12, high school graduates, and number of public and nonpublic schools]. (p. 167)

III. Transportation [private/parochial, kindergarten, and public pupils transported; cost; daily mileage; and number of buses]. (p. 167)

IV-V. Sources of revenue, and expenditures [by program, FY76-83]. (p. 168)

VI. Assessed valuation and per pupil wealth, [calendar years] 1976-83. (p. 168)

VII. Full-time certificated personnel and average salaries [by position, 1977/78-1982/83]. (p. 169-170)

S2620   INDIANA
Employment Security Division

S2620-3   INDIANA LABOR MARKET TRENDS
Quarterly. Approx. 50 p. no paging.
SRI/MF/complete

Quarterly report on Indiana labor market trends, including employment, earnings, and unemployment insurance data, by industry and local area. Most data are from Indiana Employment Security Division. Report is issued 4-6 months after quarter of coverage.

Issues contain contents and table listing; brief narrative analysis, with 1 quarterly table showing summary employment data; articles on aspects of Indiana economy, often with statistics; 11 other quarterly tables, listed below; and directory of State employment service offices.

Issue for 1st quarter includes list of articles and special features appearing in previous year, and additional summary employment data.

Quarterly tables appear in all issues. All additional features with substantial statistical content are described, as they appear, under "Statistical Features." Nonstatistical features are not covered.

Monthly reports for each labor market area are also available from the issuing agency, but are not covered by SRI.

Availability: Indiana Employment Security Division, Labor Market Information and Statistical Services, Ten N. Senate Ave., Indianapolis IN 46204, †; SRI/MF/complete.

Issues reviewed during 1984: 3rd/4th Qtrs. 1983-1st Qtr. 1984 (D) [3rd/4th Qtrs. 1984 is a combined issue].

QUARTERLY TABLES:
[Unless otherwise noted, data are for Indiana and are shown annually for 6-11 previous years and monthly for current year through quarter of coverage. Data by industry are shown by industry division and major manufacturing industry group.]

I. CPI [U.S., for all urban wage earners/clerical workers and consumers, by item and for 5 major cities, for final month of quarter of coverage, with change from previous month and year, and 5-year monthly trends].

II. Annual average unemployment rates, U.S. and Indiana [11-year trend, through previous year].

III. Indiana labor force summary [by employment status] with U.S. unemployment rates.

IV. Nonagricultural wage/salary employment, by industry.

V. Average weekly earnings for production workers, by industry.

VI. Labor force status summary for major labor market areas.

VII. Nonagricultural wage/salaried employment in establishments in major labor market areas, by industry.

VIII. Summary of unemployment insurance activities [including new and continuing claims; claims exhausted and from other States; payments; and claims and payments for Federal and extended benefit programs; usually for quarter of coverage and/or previous quarter, same quarter of prior year, and cumulative year to date].

IX-X. Unemployment insurance payments [number and amount] by local office and by industry [monthly for quarter of coverage and/ or previous quarter, with cumulative comparisons to same quarter of previous year].

[XI] Covered employment and payrolls, [and average weekly earnings for all and manufacturing workers, by county, for most recent available quarter or quarters, with monthly employment detail].

STATISTICAL FEATURES:

S2620–3.501: 3rd/4th Qtrs. 1983

INDIANA RANKS 48th IN 1982 PAY INCREASE

(3 p.) Article, with 2 tables showing average annual pay of workers covered by State/Federal unemployment insurance programs, for Indiana and U.S. by industry division, with summary comparisons for 4 neighboring States; 1981-82. Data are from BLS.

INITIAL CLAIMS AND INSURED UNEMPLOYMENT BY WEEKS, ANNUAL FEATURE

(2 p.) Annual table showing Indiana insured unemployment and initial claims by program type, and claims for extended benefits and Federal supplemental compensation, weekly 1983. Data are from Indiana Employment Security Division.

S2620–3.502: 1st Qtr. 1984

1980 CENSUS COMMUTING PATTERNS OF INDIANA COUNTIES

(2 p.) Table showing Indiana population working in county of residence and in other counties, with number not reporting commuting practices, all by county, 1980. Data are from the 1980 U.S. census.

S2625   INDIANA
Department of
Financial Institutions

S2625–1   **DEPARTMENT OF FINANCIAL INSTITUTIONS, State of Indiana, July 1, 1982-June 30, 1983**
Annual. [1984.] 74 p.
LC 35-27683.
SRI/MF/complete

Annual report on financial condition of Indiana State-chartered financial institutions, for FY83, presenting composite assets, liabilities, income, and expenses, for banks, industrial loan and investment companies, building and loan assns, pawnbrokers, and credit unions, as of June 30, 1983 or Dec. 31, 1982, with selected comparisons from Dec. 31, 1981.

Includes assets by type, and total deposits; building and loan assn total assets; and credit union total assets, loans, and shares; by individual institution and location.

Also includes dept receipts and expenditures, FY81-83; bank balance sheet ratios; and consumer loan licensees and pawnbroker loan activities.

Data are compiled from call reports submitted by individual institutions.

Contains contents listing (p. 3); dept summary, with 1 table (p. 5-9); and division reports, with 19 tables (p. 12-74).

Availability: Indiana Department of Financial Institutions, 1024 Indiana State Office Bldg., Indianapolis IN 46204, †; SRI/MF/complete.

S2635   INDIANA
Commission for
Higher Education

S2635–1   **ANNUAL REPORT OF THE COMMISSION FOR HIGHER EDUCATION, 1983, Indiana**
Annual. Mar. 1984.
106 p. var. paging.
SRI/MF/complete

Annual report, for 1983, on Indiana higher education, covering enrollment, degrees awarded, and finances, by institution, for public and independent schools. Also includes comparisons to other States, and Scholastic Aptitude Test (SAT) scores for high school seniors.

Contains contents listing (1 p.); Indiana higher education statistical trends, with 13 summary tables (p. I.1-I.18); activities of Commission for Higher Education, including 1 table showing start-up funding for selected programs (p. II.1-II.10); and 10 charts, and 23 tables listed below (p. III.1-III.70).

Availability: Indiana Commission for Higher Education, 400 Harrison Bldg., 143 W. Market St., Indianapolis IN 46204-2892, †; SRI/MF/ complete.

TABLES:
[Unless otherwise noted, data are for 1982/83.]

S2635–1.1: Enrollment, Degrees, SAT Scores, and Finances

ENROLLMENTS AND DEGREES
[Data are shown for public and private institutions, unless otherwise noted. Student characteristics include percent male, State resident, foreign, on-campus, black, other minority, full-time, and over age 25.]

A1. Statewide fall enrollments [full- and part-time, 1973-83]. (p. III.1)

A2. Fall headcount enrollment by campus [1975-83]. (p. III.3)

A3. 1981/82-1982/83 annual enrollment statistics by campus [full- and part-time, semester credit hours, and FTE]. (p. III.7)

A4. Selected student characteristics for annual enrollment by campus. (p. III.11)

A5-A6. Annual enrollment headcount by student level and campus; and annual enrollment by degree type and program area. (p. III.15-III.21)

A7-A8. Annual enrollment by student [characteristics] and program; and by origin of student [including top 5 State and 5 foreign countries]. (p. III.24-III.29)

A9. Student characteristics by [Indiana] county of origin [for all institutions]. (p. III.30)

A10-A11. Degrees awarded by campus and degree type; and by program area and degree type. (p. III.34-III.38)

SAT SCORES
A12-A13. SAT scores for seniors in the 1982/83 school year [by sex and type of institution to which applying]; and Indiana and nationwide averages [1971//72-1982/83]. (p. III.39-III.40)

FINANCES
[Tables A16-A18 show data for public institutions only, by campus.]

A14. Tuition/regularly assessed fees for colleges and universities [by campus, 1976/77-1983/84]. (p. III.42)

A15. Student aid funds for Indiana [by Federal and State grant program, 1976/77-1983/84]. (p. III.46)

A16. Funding for higher education institutions, selected general fund data [institutional general operating appropriation, student fees, and fee replacement, 1975/76-1984/85]. (p. III.49-III.52)

A17. State appropriations and bond authorizations for capital expenditure, by expenditure class [biennially 1973/75-1983/85]. (p. III.54)

A18. Average annual rates of increase for salaries of continuing employees [by occupational category, 1975/76-1983/84]. (p. III.56)

DEGREE PROGRAMS
A19. Degree programs by level and academic area aggregated by type of institution. (p. III.58-III.63)

S2635–1.2: Comparisons to Other States

B1. Comparison of tuition and fee levels [for in-State and out-of-State students at selected institutions, for Indiana and 6 neighboring States]. (p. III.64)

B2. How Indiana ranks among 50 States according to the 1980 census [shows rank for approximately 30 demographic, socioeconomic, and educational items]. (p. III.65)

B3. Comparative State appropriation increases to higher education [for Indiana and 12 other States, 1981/82-1983/84]. (p. III.66)

B4. National rankings of 1983/84 State appropriations [per capita and per $1,000 of personal income, and 2- and 10- year change] for higher education, Indiana and [16] other selected States. (p. III.67)

S2675   INDIANA
State
Police Department

S2675–1   **SUMMARY OF MOTOR VEHICLE TRAFFIC ACCIDENTS in Indiana, 1983**
Annual. Feb. 16, 1984. 2 p.
SRI/MF/complete

Annual report on Indiana traffic accidents, injuries, and fatalities, by vehicle and accident type, location, and other circumstances; and by driver and victim characteristics; 1983, with selected comparisons to 1982.

Data are from dept records, based on reports available as of Feb. 16, 1984.

Report contains 19 tables.

Similar reports showing detail for truck, motorcycle, train, interstate, urban, and rural accidents are also available from the issuing agency, but are not covered by SRI.

Availability: Indiana State Police Department, 301 State Office Bldg., 100 N. Senate Ave., Indianapolis IN 46204, †; SRI/MF/complete.

Indiana S2685–1.6

S2685
Department of
Public Welfare

INDIANA

S2685–1 GRAPHIC OVERVIEW: INDIANA'S PUBLIC WELFARE PROGRAMS for FY84
Annual. [1984.]
194 p. var. paging.
LC 82-642200.
SRI/MF/complete

Annual report, for FY84, on Indiana public welfare caseloads, recipients, and expenditures, by program, source of funds, county, and selected recipient demographic characteristics, with trends from FY72. Includes detailed data on child abuse and neglect. Also includes comparisons to U.S., by State and territory.

Contains contents listing, and directories of welfare officials (p. i-ix); 2 summary charts (p. xi-xiii); and 7 sections with 53 charts and 42 tables (p. A1-G11). All tables, and charts with substantial statistics not covered in tables, are listed below.

Issuing agency publishes similar data in a semiannual statistical report, not covered in SRI.

Availability: Indiana Department of Public Welfare, State Office Bldg., Rm. 701, 100 N. Senate Ave., Indianapolis IN 46204, †; SRI/MF/complete.

TABLES AND CHARTS:
[Unless otherwise noted, data are for Indiana, FY84. Tables showing data by State often include data for various U.S. territories. Data by race generally include Hispanics, and occasionally, American Indians/Alaskan Natives and Orientals.]

S2685–1.1: Expenditures and Sources of Funds
[1] Expenditures for welfare, FY72-84. [chart] (p. xi)

[2] Expenditures for welfare [by program; assistance repayments; and funding from Federal, State, and county sources]. [chart] (p. xiii)

S2685–1.2: Public Assistance
AFDC SUMMARY
[1] Total expenditures [and average monthly recipients], FY73-84. [chart] (p. A1)

[2] Comparative data [money cases, money and nonmoney grant adult and child recipients, and money payments], for June or full year FY83-84. (p. A3)

[3] Average monthly money payment per family [U.S. and Indiana], Nov. 1983. (p. A7)

[4-6] Percentage of population receiving AFDC assistance [by county], and comparison of AFDC distribution with population [in 5 largest counties], June 1984; and percentage of population receiving AFDC [for U.S., by State], Nov. 1983. [charts] (p. A11-A15)

AFDC QUALITY CONTROL DATA
[7] Comparison of current activities with initial base period [Apr.-Sept. 1973 and Oct. 1983-Mar. 1984 periods]. [chart] (p. A17)

[8] Payment error rates [Oct. 1981-Mar. 1982 period, and target FY82], by State. (p. A19)

AFDC CHARACTERISTICS
[9-10] AFDC [family distribution by] race [Oct. 1983-Mar. 1984 period, and case distribution by] number of children in case [June 1984]. [charts] (p. A21)

[11] Need standards and payment amounts [by State], as of Jan. 1984. (p. A23)

[12] Average payment per family, excluding medical care, by State, Nov. 1983. [chart] (p. A25)

OTHER ASSISTANCE PROGRAMS
[13] Fair hearings, number of appeals requested, by program [monthly]. (p. A26)

[14] Medical review team: number of cases approved and denied for permanent and total disability [FY76-84]. [chart] (p. A27)

[15-16] Assistance to residents in county homes [monthly recipients and room/board, personal needs, and medical payments], FY84; [and cases and payments for aged and disabled, by county], June 1984. (p. A29-A30)

[17] Room/board assistance program [monthly recipients and payments]. (p. A31)

[18] Eye treatment [monthly caseload and expenditures], FY83-84. (p. A32)

[19] Welfare recipient fraud [suspected cases, and action reported]. (p. A33)

[20-21] Total welfare savings generated by State welfare Work Incentive Program (WIN) [FY75-84, chart]; and WIN summary of total welfare savings and number of persons removed from AFDC [by county], FY84. (p. A35-A37)

S2685–1.3: Child Support
[Data are for the child support program (Title IV-D).]

[1-2] Disbursement of child support collected [by source, and AFDC and non-AFDC recipients], various years FY79-84. [charts] (p. B1-B3)

[3] Child support collections by intercept program [State revenue dept and employment security division, and IRS], FY83-84. [chart] (p. B5)

[4] Child support amount collected and how distributed [by county and general fund function]. (p. B7-B10)

S2685–1.4: Medicaid
EXPENDITURES
[1] Total Medicaid expenditures, and monthly average number of recipients who received Medicaid, FY74-84. [chart] (p. C1)

PARTICIPATING POPULATION
[2] Number of persons enrolled, as compared to persons who actually received Medicaid (monthly average) [FY74-84]. [chart] (p. C3)

[3] Percentage of population enrolled in Medicaid program [by county], as of June 1984. [chart] (p. C5)

EXPENDITURES BY TYPE OF PROVIDER OR SERVICE
[Data for providers and services include nursing homes, pharmacies, dentists, other facilities/agencies/practitioners/suppliers, transportation, physicians, optometric, hospitals, and mental hospitals.]

[4] Medicaid program expenditures by counties, selected categories of service. (p. C7)

[5] Total Medicaid payments by type of provider, percentage of total [FY83-84]. [chart] (p. C9)

[6] Medical services payments by category [AFDC, aged, disabled, blind, and intermediate care facilities for the mentally retarded/inpatient psychiatric hospitals, FY83-84]. [chart] (p. C11)

[7] Number of Medicaid claims processed by provider category [and claims denied and paid]. [chart] (p. C13)

[8-9] Medicaid program: total expenditures for ancillary services and medical supplies (in descending order by cost), FY83-84 [table]; and number of hospitals and nursing homes participating [by county], as of June 1984 [chart]. (p. C15-C17)

[10] Medicaid quality control payment error rates, by State [FY81-82]. (p. C19)

[11] Medical assistance [caseloads by program and total expenditures] for patients in Medicaid certified mental health facilities and intermediate care facilities for the mentally retarded, FY83-84. (p. C21)

[12] Certified mental health facilities and intermediate care facilities for the mentally retarded, location and number of beds. (p. C22)

S2685–1.5: Food Stamps
PARTICIPATION BY COUNTY OR STATE
[1] Total value of ["free" and purchased] food stamps issued [FY76-84]. [chart] (p. D1)

[2-3] Food stamp participation [general public and AFDC households and persons], by month, FY84; and total stamps issued by county, FY83-84. (p. D3-D5)

[4] Average monthly value of food stamps received per person [Indiana, Oct. 1983 and June 1984; and U.S., Oct. 1983]. (p. D7)

[5] Number of persons and households certified to receive food stamps (monthly average) [FY77-84]. [chart] (p. D9)

[6-7] Percentage of population certified in food stamp program, June 1984 [chart]; and persons certified for food stamps, June 1983-84; [both by county]. (p. D13-D16)

[8] U.S. percentage of population participating in food stamp program [by State], Oct. 1983. [chart] (p. D17)

[9] Food stamp quality control data: comparison of current activities with initial base period [July-Dec. 1973 and Oct. 1983-Mar. 1984 periods]. [chart] (p. D21)

[10] Percent of food stamp dollars in error, by State, Oct. 1981-Mar. 1982 [period]. (p. D23)

[11] Food stamp participation by race [by county], Apr. 1984. (p. D25)

S2685–1.6: Child Welfare
SUMMARY DATA
[1] Child welfare expenditures, FY74-84. [chart] (p. E1)

[2] Number of child welfare institutions [foster homes, day care homes and centers, child placing agencies, and child caring institutions] licensed by State welfare, FY76-84. [chart] (p. E3)

CHILD PROTECTION SERVICE PROGRAM
[3-4] Child abuse and neglect [total cases FY80-84, chart]; and number of children [in-

volved in substantiated, indicated, and unsubstantiated cases, by county], FY84. (p. E5-E8)

[5-6] Child abuse and neglect substantiated/indicated cases, action taken, [FY83-84]. [charts] (p. E9-E11)

[7-8] [Children involved, by] type of abuse and neglect by age group, for substantiated/indicated [cases; and total deaths]. (p. E13-E14)

[9-10] Number of children reported as victims of sexual abuse, and fatalities due to abuse [and] neglect, (substantiated/indicated cases) [FY80-84]. [charts] (p. E15)

[11] Source of initial child abuse and neglect reports. [chart] (p. E17)

[12-13] Abuse and neglect, race and sex [distribution] of all children. [charts] (p. E19)

[14-15] Relationship of perpetrator to child abuse and neglect victims (for substantiated/indicated children). [charts] (p. E21)

[16] Age group of perpetrators for substantiated/indicated [physical and sexual abuse and total neglect] cases. (p. E23)

[17] Child abuse in sexual abuse reports, only substantiated/indicated cases [demographic characteristics and relationship of child and perpetrator]. (p. E24)

[18] Number of abuse/neglect children per 1,-000 population under the age of 18 [by county]. [chart] (p. E25)

[19-20] Institutional [physical and sexual] abuse and [total] neglect reports [FY82-84; chart]; and by type of facility [for substantiated, indicated, and unsubstantiated investigations, FY84]. (p. E27-E29)

[21-24] [Children involved, by] type of institutional abuse and neglect by age group, race, and sex (for substantiated/indicated children). (p. E30-E31)

[25] Child abuse and neglect fatalities [by selected sociodemographic characteristics of child and perpetrator]. (p. E32)

CHILD CARE FACILITIES AND ADOPTION

[26] Number of county welfare dept juvenile wards, [total and] per 1,000 population [by county, June 1984]. (p. E33)

[27] Case activity for children in substitute care, July 1983-June 1984 period [including children entering and leaving care during period, children leaving care by reason and race, and type of placement for children at end of period by race.] (p. E34)

[28-29] Children free for adoption by age and race, and type of placement; and [number of] adoptions finalized by type of adoptive home. (p. E35)

[30-31] Children in adoptive placement by length of time free for adoption prior to adoptive placement by age and race; and children in substitute care [by] age, race, and [other] special needs with regard to placement. (p. E36-E37)

[32-33] Number of child caring residential facilities, full-time foster homes, intermediate foster homes, and day care homes and centers licensed by State welfare as of June 30, 1984, by county. [charts] (p. E39-E41)

[34] Total number of children adopted during 1973-83. [chart] (p. E43)

S2685–1.7: Crippled Children

[1] Crippled children program total expenditures, Federal vs. State [and] county disbursement of funds [FY74-84]. [chart] (p. F1)

[2-3] Number of children receiving services [FY74-84, chart]; [and by county] FY84. (p. F3-F5)

[4] Diagnostic and treatment centers: location and services available [and number of children assigned]. (p. F6)

S2685–1.8: Miscellaneous

[1] Federal dollars that State treasury receives via welfare programs [by program], and percent to total by type of revenue. [chart] (p. G1)

[2] Summarized expenditure report [disbursing agency and source of funds, by program]. (p. G3)

[3] Caseload information by program [and by type of service and county] for the month of June 1984. (p. G6-G11)

S2703   INDIANA
Supreme Court

**S2703–1   1983 INDIANA JUDICIAL
            REPORT**
Annual. [1984.]
iii+352 p. Oversized.
SRI/MF/complete

Annual report on Indiana judicial system, covering trial and appellate court caseloads and case dispositions, 1983, with selected trends from 1978. Covers supreme, appeals, circuit and superior, county, Marion County municipal and small claims, and city and town courts. Includes data by case type, and by jurisdiction for trial courts.

Case types shown are criminal and civil for all courts, with some additional detail for juvenile, marital dissolution, probate/adoption, traffic, guardianship, and small claims cases.

Report also includes data on judicial system finances and personnel, by county and/or city; and trial judges and population, by county.

Data are from reports filed with the Court Administration Division, and from the annual State auditor's report.

Contains contents listing (p. i-iii); introduction and narrative summary, with organizational chart (p. 1-8); and report, with 93 tables, and judicial roster (p. 9-352).

Availability: Indiana Supreme Court, State Court Administration Division, State House, Rm. 323, Indianapolis IN 46204, †; SRI/MF/complete.

S2735   IOWA
Department of
Agriculture

**S2735–1   IOWA AGRICULTURAL
            STATISTICS, 1984**
Annual. June 1984.
4+106 p.
LC 76-646749.
SRI/MF/complete

Annual report on Iowa agricultural production, marketing, and finances, 1982-83, with trends from the 1950s. Data are generally shown by commodity and/or county or district, with some comparisons to other States and total U.S.

Report generally covers production, prices, sales, value, and, as applicable, acreage, yield, or inventory, for field crops, livestock, dairy, and poultry sectors.

Also includes number of farms and acreage; temperature and precipitation; farm income, production expenses, fertilizer use, land value, rental rates, real estate debt outstanding, and labor and wages; Corn Belt livestock profit margins; and U.S. agricultural foreign trade (with detail by commodity and country), and food consumption.

Data are compiled by the Iowa Crop and Livestock Reporting Service in cooperation with the USDA.

Contains contents listing (1 p.); and report in 4 sections, with 25 maps, 17 charts, and 123 tables, interspersed with narrative (p. 1-106).

Availability: Iowa Crop and Livestock Reporting Service, Federal Bldg., Rm. 833, 210 Walnut St., Des Moines IA 50309, $3.00; SRI/MF/complete.

S2745   IOWA
Department of
Banking

**S2745–1   ANNUAL REPORT OF THE
            SUPERINTENDENT OF
            BANKING of the State of
            Iowa, for the Year Ending
            June 30, 1983**
Annual. Aug. 31, 1983.
63 p.
LC 46-37477.
SRI/MF/complete

Annual report on financial condition of Iowa State-chartered bank and trust companies, presenting assets, liabilities, and equity capital, by institution arranged by city, as of June 30, 1983; and composite income, expenses, and financial ratios, 1980-82; with selected summary trends from 1891.

Also includes data on dept receipts and disbursements; consumer loans by type of collateral; small loan licensee composite finances, loan activity, and delinquent account legal action; and loan insurance activity.

Data are compiled from reports filed by the institutions with the Banking Dept.

Contains contents listing (p. 5); lists of State banking officials and banks, 1 trend table, and status changes (p. 6-27); bank financial section, with 5 tables (p. 28-51); small loan licensee statistical section, with 8 tables (p. 54-58); and list of small loan, debt management, and money order companies (p. 59-63).

Availability: Iowa Department of Banking, 530 Liberty Bldg., 418 Sixth Ave., Des Moines IA 50309, †; SRI/MF/complete.

S2755   IOWA
College Aid Commission

S2755–1   DATA DIGEST ON IOWA POSTSECONDARY INSTITUTIONS, 1982/83
Annual. [1984.] 175 p.
LC 80-640449.
SRI/MF/complete

Annual report on Iowa higher education, covering enrollment, student expenses and financial aid, degrees conferred, faculty salary and tenure, and finances, by individual institution, 1982/83, with trends from 1975, and student expense data for 1983/84. Most data are from Higher Education General Information Survey.

Contains preface and contents listing (p. 1-6); directory of colleges, universities, and specialized schools (p. 7-19); and 1 chart and 25 tables described below, arranged in 6 sections, each preceded by a brief narrative (p. 21-175).

This is the 8th annual report.

Availability: Iowa College Aid Commission, 201 Jewett Bldg., Des Moines IA 50309, Iowa State agencies and postsecondary institutions †, others $10.00; SRI/MF/complete.

TABLES:
[Data by individual institution are arranged by institution type and generally are accompanied by summary tables. Institution types include regents universities, independent 4- and 2-year institutions, and area, Bible/theological, business, nursing, and professional schools.]

a. Enrollment: undergraduate and graduate students, 1975-82; and full- and part-time undergraduate and graduate/professional students, by sex and residency status, by individual institution, fall 1982; all by institution type. 3 tables. (p. 23-30)

b. Student budget expenses and/or tuition/fees: for 2- and 4-year public and private institutions, Iowa and U.S. averages; by resident status; and by individual institution; 1977/78 and 1981/82-1983/84. 2 tables. (p. 33-38)

c. Degrees and other awards conferred: by level and sex, by discipline and individual institution, 1981/82. 5 tables. (p. 41-76)

d. Faculty salaries and tenure: average faculty salaries, by institution type and faculty rank and sex, 1975 and 1982, with comparisons to U.S., 1982/83; and total and tenured employment and mean salary for full-time instructional faculty, by academic rank, sex, length of contract, and individual institution, 1982/83. 3 tables. (p. 79-91)

e. Finances: revenues by source, expenditures by function, net physical plant assets, and endowment, by individual institution, FY82. 5 tables. (p. 97-156)

f. Student financial aid by source (including Federal, State, institutional, and other); summary by institution type, and Independent College Assistance Center aid by individual institution, both by program, 1982/83; student aid distribution, by institution type, 1981/82; nonrepayable student aid, loans, and employment, by program and institution type, 1981/82; and total aid value by type, students assisted, and full- and part-time fall enrollment, by individual institution, 1981/82. 1 chart and 7 tables. (p. 159-175)

S2780   IOWA
Development Commission

S2780–1   IOWA, A PLACE TO GROW: 1984 Statistical Profile of Iowa
Annual. 1984. ix+118 p.
LC 75-650016.
SRI/MF/complete

Annual statistical profile, for 1984, presenting detailed social, economic, and governmental data on Iowa. Data are primarily for various years 1960-82, with population trends from 1840 and projections to 2000. Most data are from State and Federal sources.

Report is designed to present a comprehensive overview of the State. Extensive socioeconomic, demographic, and geographic breakdowns are shown, as applicable, for most topics. These breakdowns include data by city, county and other State region, SMSA, urban-rural status, commodity, income, industry, occupation, age, educational attainment, race, and sex. Comparisons to other North Central States and U.S. are also often included.

Contains contents listing, glossary, map of State program planning areas, and metric conversion formulas (p. vi-ix); and 13 maps, 19 charts, and 152 tables arranged in 22 sections, described below (p. 1-118).

Availability: Iowa Development Commission, Research and Development Group, 600 E. Court Ave., Suite A, Des Moines IA 50309, †; SRI/MF/complete.

TABLE SECTIONS:
[Data sources appear beneath each table.]

S2780–1.1: Agriculture and Industry

(p. 1-21) Contains 2 maps, 2 charts, and 27 tables. Includes farm operators, income by source, cash receipts, workers, and wage rates; type of farm ownership; Federal farm payments by program; farm machinery inventory and retail sales; and selected indicators of agricultural efficiency for U.S. and 10 foreign countries.

Also includes farms, and average size and value; corn and soybean yield and production; and livestock and poultry marketings, by species.

Also includes new and expanded industrial development, capital investment, and jobs created; industrial, pollution control, and health facility revenue bonds issued; *Fortune* 500 firms with Iowa plants; production value per worker and value added per payroll dollar; and manufacturing firms, employment, payroll, wages, hours, and operating data.

S2780–1.2: International, Travel, and Transportation

(p. 22-41) Contains 1 chart and 30 tables. Includes value of farm exports, total and by importing country; value and volume of manufactured product exports, and related employment; and Iowa export share of U.S. balance of payments.

Also includes fishing and hunting licenses issued; recreation areas and acreage; hunters and game harvested, by major species; State park total and camping attendance, by park; travel-generated expenditures, payroll, employment, and State and local tax receipts; and trip and traveler characteristics.

Also includes rail and road mileages; airports and runways; railroad, truck, and river freight; transportation industry establishments, employees, and payroll; public transit miles serviced and passengers; road construction contracts; traffic fatalities; registered aircraft; and motor vehicle registrations.

S2780–1.3: Workforce and Employment

(p. 42-48) Contains 3 maps and 9 tables. Includes union membership; work stoppages, workers involved, and days idle; labor force by employment status; unemployment insurance contribution rates, by State; value added per production worker and hour; manufacturing employment, earnings, and hours; nonfarm employment and union membership; manufacturing and construction wages; and unemployment rates.

S2780–1.4: Economy and Energy

(p. 49-56) Contains 12 charts and 10 tables. Includes personal income by source; CPI; GSP; total and farm energy consumption, by fuel type; industrial electricity kWh prices, by State; industrial energy use and cost; average residential electric bills; and gas and electric utilities sales and revenues, by consuming sector.

S2780–1.5: Income and Taxes

(p. 57-75) Contains 2 maps, 2 charts, and 18 tables. Includes total and per capita personal income; personal income and earnings, by type; and business establishments, employment, and payroll.

Also includes per capita public debt, by State; total and per capita expenditures, by function; revenues by source and expenditures by function per $1,000 of personal income; general fund receipts, and tax revenues and rates, by type; and property valuation and tax levies, by property class.

S2780–1.6: Wholesale and Retail Trade, and Communication Industry

(p. 75-79) Contains 6 tables. Includes retail and wholesale trade establishments, employees, and payrolls; taxable retail sales by type of business; telephones in use; newspapers and circulation; radio and TV stations; and cable TV systems and subscription.

S2780–1.7: Construction, Education, and Libraries

(p. 80-88) Contains 19 tables. Includes housing units, occupancy, and median value or rent; building permits issued and value; new residential construction and value; and construction industry establishments, employment, and payroll.

Also includes public and nonpublic school enrollment and graduates; special education enrollment; high school retention rates; higher education enrollment and degrees conferred; community college enrollment by institution and program; teacher salaries; educational attainment of population; and educational finance.

Also includes public libraries; and library finances, holdings and circulation, other operations, and staff.

S2780–1.8: Finance, Insurance, Real Estate, and Housing

(p. 89-93) Contains 10 tables. Includes bank deposits and loans; insurance companies, and financial and underwriting data, by type of coverage; bank, savings and loan assn, small loan company, and State-chartered credit union establishments and financial data; and housing units, occupancy, and value or rent.

S2780–1.9: Medical Care and Service Industries

(p. 94-96) Contains 2 maps and 4 tables. Includes physicians; hospitals; hospital discharge rates by disease; beds, admissions, occupancy rates, average length of stay, and average daily cost; licensed health professionals; and service industries establishments, employment, and payroll.

S2780–1.10: Climate, Crime, and Mining

(p. 97-103) Contains 3 maps, 2 charts, and 10 tables. Includes monthly climatological data; crime rates; violent and property crimes reported, by offense; mineral production and value; and coal production, mine price, and value.

S2780–1.11: Population

(p. 104-118) Contains 1 map and 9 tables. Includes population from 1840; families, households, and persons in group quarters; land area; housing units; and population projected to the year 2000.

S2780–2   IOWA DEVELOPMENT COMMISSION DIGEST
Monthly.   Approx. 15 p.
ISSN 0193-8460.
LC SC 79-3388.
SRI/MF/complete, shipped quarterly

Monthly report (combined Nov./Dec. issue), on Iowa business and economic activity, including employment, construction, and agricultural prices. Data are from Iowa Development Commission; Iowa Dept of Job Service; Robert C. Westlund, Piper, Jaffray, & Hopwood, Inc.; and other sources.

General format:

a. Several news briefs, editorial depts, and feature articles, usually nonstatistical.

b. Monthly "Iowa Ag & Business Indicators" feature, with 10 monthly and 2 bimonthly tables, listed below.

c. Bimonthly "Available Buildings" feature, listing square footage, community location, and former use of selected commercial buildings for sale.

d. Quarterly "Iowa Economic Indicators" feature, with 2 tables and accompanying charts showing Iowa GSP, personal income, industrial production index (total and for selected industries), and labor/proprietor/corporate income by industry division and selected ma-

jor manufacturing group; and selected U.S. indexes; for month or quarter ended 3-8 months prior to cover month, with comparisons to preceding comparable period and 2 previous years.

e. Quarterly "Labor Market Information" feature, with 2 tables and 1 chart showing State labor force by employment status, with comparisons to U.S.; and nonagricultural wage/salary employment by industry division; for month 3-4 months prior to cover date, with comparisons to various previous periods.

Monthly tables appear in all issues; bimonthly tables generally appear in alternate issues. All additional features with substantial statistical content are described, as they appear, under "Statistical Features;" page locations and latest dates of coverage for quarterly features are also noted. Nonstatistical features are not covered.

Availability: Iowa Development Commission, Communications Group, 600 E. Court Ave., Suite A, Des Moines IA 50309, †; SRI/MF/complete, shipped quarterly.

Issues reviewed during 1984: Nov./Dec. 1983-Oct. 1984 (P) (Vol. XII, No. 12; Vol. XIII, Nos. 1-9).

TABLES:

[Tables show data for various periods, generally current to 2-6 months prior to cover date, with comparisons to specified prior periods.]

MONTHLY TABLES

[1] Labor demand and supply [State Job Service placements and new applicants/renewals, by service area].

[2-3] U.S. CPI, and composite construction cost index.

[4] Business data [new car registrations, savings and loan assn loans closed and savings, and labor force by employment status].

[5] Value of new dwellings [by major city].

[6] Personal income.

[7] Stock index [Iowa and Dow Jones Industrial].

[8-10] Average prices received and paid by farmers, and commodity feed price ratios, [by commodity].

BIMONTHLY TABLES

[1] Farm retail price spreads [for 4 commodities].

[2] Leading States for farm marketing [value, including livestock/products and crops; for U.S. and top 9 States].

STATISTICAL FEATURES:

S2780–2.501: Jan. 1984 (Vol. XIII, No. 1)

QUARTERLY FEATURES

[For full description, see S2780-2 above.]

a. Iowa economic indicators, for 2nd quarter or Sept. 1983. (Also includes unemployment insurance initial claims index.) (p. 7-9)

b. Labor market information, for Sept. 1983. (Omits wage/salary employment by industry division, and includes earnings and hours by industry division and major manufacturing group.) (p. 10)

S2780–2.502: Apr. 1984 (Vol. XIII, No. 4)

QUARTERLY FEATURES

[For full description, see S2780-2 above.]

a. Iowa economic indicators, for 3rd quarter or Jan. 1984. (p. 9-11)

b. Labor market information, for Jan. 1984. (p. 12)

S2780–2.503: Oct. 1984 (Vol. XIII, No. 9)

WORKFORCE AND BUSINESS ESTABLISHMENT CHANGES

(p. 10) Table showing Iowa business establishments and employment, by employment size class, 1980 and 1982. Data are from Census Bureau.

S2795   IOWA
Department of Health

S2795–1   VITAL STATISTICS OF IOWA, 1982
Annual.   [1984.]   4+91 p.
LC 79-644698.
SRI/MF/complete

Annual compilation of Iowa vital statistics, covering population, births, deaths by cause, marriages, and divorces, by demographic characteristics and location. Data are for 1982, with selected trends from 1915, and were compiled from State records and Census Bureau population reports.

Contains chart and table listings (3 p.); narrative analysis with 20 summary charts (p. 2-23); 42 tables listed below (p. 27-88); and definitions (p. 90-91).

Vital Statistics Pocket Guide is also issued by the Iowa Dept of Health, but is not covered in SRI.

Availability: Iowa Department of Health, Statistical Services Unit, Management and Budget Office, Lucas Office Bldg., Des Moines IA 50319, ‡; SRI/MF/complete.

TABLES:

[Tables are for Iowa, 1982, unless otherwise noted. Data by color are for white and nonwhite. Most data show percent or rate and/or number.]

S2795–1.1: Summary Tables

[Unless otherwise noted, tables show resident data. Marriages and dissolutions are shown as occurrences only.]

1. Summary of vital statistics by event [live births by sex and color, and out-of-wedlock live births; deaths by sex, color, and marital status; and marriages and dissolutions]; by month, resident data. (p. 27)

2-3. Population, live births (total and out-of-wedlock), deaths (total, infant, neonatal, fetal, and maternal), marriages, and dissolutions; and rates; [includes some occurrence data for births and deaths]; 1915-82. (p. 28-29)

4-6. Summary of selected vital events [including live births with congenital malformations, perinatal deaths, and deaths by 67 selected causes] for the State [occurrence and resident data], and by county and city. (p. 33-58)

S2795–1.2: Natality

[All tables show resident data.]

7. Live births by color and sex of child, live birth order, birth weight, and plural births; by age of mother. (p. 59)

8-10. Live births by live birth order, and 1st and 2nd live birth orders by age of mother, 1978-82. (p. 60-61)

11. In-wedlock and out-of-wedlock live births, by age and color of mother. (p. 62)

12. Out-of-wedlock live births by year, by age of mother, 1950-82. (p. 63)

13-15. In-wedlock and out-of-wedlock live births, by age of mother; and live births by teenage mothers; 1978-82. (p. 63-64)

16. Premature live births, as percents of total live births, within each age group of mother, in-wedlock and out-of-wedlock. (p. 65)

S2795–1.3: Mortality

[All tables except table 26 show resident data.]

CAUSE OF DEATH

17. Selected causes of death, 1972-82. (p. 65)

18. Deaths by color and age, by sex. (p. 66)

19. Leading causes of death, by selected age groups. (p. 67)

20. 15 leading causes of death, by number and percent of total deaths, by male and female. (p. 68)

21-23. Heart disease, malignant neoplasms, and cerebrovascular disease deaths, by age, by sex. (p. 69-70)

24-25. Suicide deaths by age, by sex; and by age, by method, by sex. (p. 70-71)

26. Accidental deaths by type of accident [including work-related deaths by industry division], by age, occurrence data. (p. 72)

INFANT MORTALITY

27. Fetal deaths by age of mother, by in-wedlock and out-of-wedlock. (p. 73)

28-29. Fetal and infant deaths by cause, by color. (p. 74-75)

30-31. Infant deaths by cause, sex, and color, 1982; and infant deaths by year, 1960-82; [both] by subdivision of the 1st year of life. (p. 76-77)

S2795–1.4: Marriages and Divorces

[Tables show occurrence data.]

32-35. Marriages: by month performed, and by age of groom and bride, 1978-82; and by age of groom by age of bride, 1982. (p. 78-81)

36-37. Dissolutions: by age, by color of husband and wife; and by age by primary marriage and remainder, by husband and wife. (p. 82-83)

38-39. Dissolutions, by age of husband and wife, and by duration of marriage, 1978-82. (p. 84-85)

40-41. Dissolutions by duration of marriage, and involving children under 18 years of age, [both] by color. (p. 86-87)

42. Dissolutions by month performed, 1978-82. (p. 88)

S2802   IOWA
Department of Human Services

S2802–1   MONTHLY PUBLIC ASSISTANCE STATISTICAL REPORT, Iowa
Monthly. Approx. 25 p.
Rpt. Series A-1.
SRI/MF/complete, shipped quarterly

Monthly report on Iowa public welfare and social service program caseloads, recipients, and payments, by program and county. Covers aid to dependent children (ADC) and SSI programs. Report is issued 1-2 months after month of coverage.

Contains 2 charts, and 4 tables listed below.

Availability: Iowa Department of Human Services, Management Information Bureau, Management and Budget Division, Research and Statistics Section, Hoover State Office Bldg., 1305 E. Walnut St., Des Moines IA 50319, ‡; SRI/MF/complete, shipped quarterly.

Issues reviewed during 1984: Oct. 1983-Sept. 1984 (D).

MONTHLY TABLES:

ADC

[1] ADC program [regular and unemployed parent ADC cases, total and child recipients, payments, and average costs; and child support recoveries; for month of coverage, previous month, and same month of previous year].

[2] [ADC total and net costs, child support recoveries, and Federal and State funding, for current fiscal year to date and same period of previous year.]

[3] Public assistance programs [ADC, ADC-unemployed parent, and subsidized adoption cases, recipients, grant value, and cases opened and closed, by county, for month of coverage].

SSI

[4] SSI program [SSI and Federal and State supplementation cases and payments, for aged, blind, and disabled, by county, for month of coverage].

S2805   IOWA
Insurance Department

S2805–1   1984 REPORT OF THE INSURANCE DEPARTMENT of Iowa
Annual. July 1984. 184 p.
LC 46-43626.
SRI/MF/complete

Annual report on Iowa insurance industry financial condition and underwriting activity, by company and type of insurance, 1983. Covers assets; liabilities; capital stock; surplus; premiums in force, written, or collected; dividends; taxes; underwriting and investment income and expenses; losses incurred or paid; benefits paid; and other financial data; for companies with headquarters in Iowa and elsewhere.

Data are shown, as applicable, for fire/casualty/multiple line companies, mortgage guaranty insurers, reciprocal exchanges, State and county mutual insurance assns, hospital/medical service corporations, life insurance companies, and fraternal beneficiary societies.

Data for fire/casualty/multiple line companies and reciprocal exchanges include additional breakdowns for 22 lines of coverage, including medical malpractice, workers compensation, fidelity/surety, accident/health, and automobile.

Also includes lists of company admissions, withdrawals, mergers, and name changes, 1983; data on value of securities on deposit, by company, Dec. 1983; and State Insurance Dept appropriations, receipts, and disbursements, for FY83.

Most data are compiled from annual statements filed by individual insurers.

Contains Insurance Dept summary, with 2 tables (p. 3-14); 32 company financial schedules and tables (p. 17-181); and index (p. 182-184).

This is the 115th annual report.

Availability: Iowa Insurance Department, Lucas State Office Bldg., Des Moines IA 50319, †; SRI/MF/complete.

S2810   IOWA
Department of Job Service

S2810–2   LABOR MARKET INFORMATION FOR IOWA Job Training Partnership Act
Annual. Mar. 1984.
4+100 p.
SRI/MF/complete

Annual planning report on Iowa labor market conditions, 1983, and outlook to 1986. Presents data on population, labor force, employment by industry and occupation, and characteristics of job service applicants and insured unemployed, with selected trends from the 1970s.

Data are from Iowa Dept of Job Service, Census Bureau, and other State sources.

Contains preface and listings of contents, tables, and charts (5 p.); narrative report, with 14 charts, and 12 text tables (p. 3-40); and appendices with 13 tables, and list of labor market information sources (p. 41-100).

All tables are listed below.

Availability: Iowa Department of Job Service, Audit and Analysis Department, Labor Market Information Unit, 1000 E. Grand Ave., Des Moines IA 50319, †; SRI/MF/complete.

TABLES:
[Data are for Iowa, unless otherwise noted.]

S2810–2.1: Text Tables

EMPLOYMENT AND POPULATION SUMMARY

[1] Nonagricultural wage/salary employment [by industry division], U.S. and Iowa (in percent), Dec. 1983. (p. 10)

2. Total resident population of the U.S. and Iowa, [decennially 1940-80]. (p. 13)

3. Population by age and sex, 1980 census. (p. 15)

LABOR SUPPLY AND DEMAND

4. Labor force participation rates [by sex, age, and race], 1980 and 1985. (p. 16)

5. Labor force summary [and employment status], by age, race, and sex, FY85 (projected). (p. 18)

6. Top [40] occupations [ranked by total job openings and showing growth-related job openings: undated]. (p. 23)

7. Occupational employment trends [by broad occupational group, selected years 1983-86]. (p. 24)

8. Fastest growing occupations [employment in 42 positions, 1983]. (p. 27)

9-10. Labor supply and demand [job service applicants and openings] by occupational group; and job openings by [SIC 2-digit] industry; Oct. -Dec. 1982 and/or 1983 [period]. (p. 29-32)

JOB SERVICE CLIENTS

[11] Characteristics of job service applicants [welfare recipients and others, by age, sex, educational attainment, race and ethnic group (including Hispanic, American Indian, and Asian/Pacific Islander); and whether unemployment insurance claimant, veteran, handicapped, or food stamp recipient], Oct.-Dec. 1983 [period]. (p. 36)

12. Characteristics of the insured unemployed, by sex, [monthly] Oct.-Dec. 1983. (p. 38)

S2810–2.2: Appendix Tables

POPULATION

[1] Population of [8] metro areas and their component counties [and total metro and nonmetro population, Apr. 1,] 1970 and 1980. (p. 43)

[2] Nonwhite population, 1980: U.S., Iowa, and [6] selected counties. (p. 44)

[3] Population [and change components] of counties, Apr. 1, 1970 and 1980. (p. 45)

[4] Nonwhite population [white, black, American Indian, Eskimo, Aleut, Asian/Pacific Islander by country of ancestry, and other], 1980, Iowa and selected counties. (p. 48)

[5] Civilian population by age, race, and sex, 1980 and 1985. (p. 51-52)

EMPLOYMENT, HOURS, AND EARNINGS

[6-7] Nonagricultural wage/salary employment [by industry group], 1970-83. (p. 55-56)

[8] Report on hours and earnings [by industry division and major manufacturing industry group, monthly] 1983. (p. 59-61)

JOB OPENINGS AND APPLICANTS

[9] Job openings and applicants by [detailed] occupation, Oct. 1-Dec. 31, 1983 [period]. (p. 65-79)

[10] Labor supply and demand for [16 employment] service delivery areas [by occupational group], Oct.-Dec. 1983 [period]. (p. 83-88)

UNEMPLOYMENT COMPENSATION

[11-13] Regular/veterans/Federal civilian employees, extended benefits, and Federal supplemental compensation: number of weeks compensated and amount of benefits paid, under State and Federal unemployment insurance programs, by county [and total out of State], 1983. (p. 91-96)

S2815   IOWA
Judicial Department

S2815–1   1983 ANNUAL STATISTICAL REPORT: Report to the Supreme Court of Iowa by the Court Administrator of the Judicial Department
Annual.   Apr. 9, 1984.
vii+86 p.
LC 78-640215.
SRI/MF/complete

Annual report on the Iowa judicial system, including trial and appellate court caseloads, case dispositions, and processing time, 1983, with trends from 1956. Covers supreme, appeals, and district courts. Includes trial court data by case type and district.

Case types shown are criminal and civil, for all courts, with some additional detail for lawyer disciplinary, domestic relations, probate, juvenile, hospitalization, small claims, and ordinance cases.

Also includes data on judicial dept personnel; search warrant applications and seized property hearings; and traffic violations handled by court clerks, by county.

Data are from dept records.

Contains contents listing and highlights (p. ii-vii); report, with text statistics, 1 map, 2 charts, and 30 tables (p. 1-78); and 8 appendices, with 2 maps and 6 tables (p. 79-86).

Availability: Iowa Judicial Department, Capitol Bldg., 10th and Grand, Des Moines IA 50319, †; SRI/MF/complete.

S2825   IOWA
Library Commission

S2825–1   IOWA PUBLIC LIBRARY STATISTICS, 1982-83
Annual.   1984.   iv+175 p.
LC 81-643203.
SRI/MF/complete

Annual report, for FY83, on Iowa public library finances, holdings, circulation, and staff. Data are shown for individual libraries, grouped by size of population served, operating income, and county. Data are from Library Commission annual survey of city and county libraries, and from Census Bureau.

Contents:

Contents listing (1 p.); introduction and explanatory notes (p. i); and 6 summary tables, including data on acquisitions by type (p. ii-iv).

Section I-III. 3 basic tables, listed below, presenting data for individual libraries. (p. 1-114)

Section IV-VI. Statistical analyses: 3 tables showing average and percentile values for selected operating and financial data and ratios, by population and budget size group; and county summaries, each including city and rural population, municipal income, and municipal library circulation, unit cost, and holdings by city. (p. 115-168)

Survey explanatory notes. (p. 169-175)

Availability: Iowa Library Commission, Library Development Office, Historical Bldg., E. 12th St. and Grand Ave., Des Moines IA 50319, †; SRI/MF/complete.

BASIC TABLES:
[All tables show data for city libraries arranged by population size group, and for county libraries, FY83. Each entry includes location, State region, and population. Types of material include books, periodicals, audiovisual, and microform.]

I. Financial information [income from municipal, county, Federal, and miscellaneous sources; and expenditures for wages/salaries, plant operation, capital outlays, equipment, and materials by type]. (p. 2-45)

II. Materials holdings and circulation [by type]. (p. 48-91)

III. Personnel, hours open, and salary ranges [includes professional staff, by highest degree held; technical/clerical and plant staff; director's salary; and salary ranges for professional, support/technical, and clerical/secretarial staff]. (p. 93-114)

S2840   IOWA
Office for
Planning and Programming

S2840–1   IOWA POPULATION PROJECTIONS: 1980-2000
Monograph.   July 1984.
118 p. no paging.
SRI/MF/complete

Report presenting Iowa population projections by age and sex, by county and State program planning region, quinquennially 1985-2000, with actual data for 1980.

Projections are prepared by Office for Planning and Programming and are based on the 1980 census.

Contains notes on projection methodology (1 p.); 1 summary table (1 p.); and 1 basic table repeated for each county and program planning region (116 p.).

Availability: Iowa Office for Planning and Programming, State Demographer's Office, 523 E. 12th St., Des Moines IA 50319, †; SRI/MF/complete.

S2850   IOWA
Department of
Public Safety

S2850–1   IOWA UNIFORM CRIME
REPORTS, 1981-82
Annual. Spring 1984.
2+v+378 p.
LC 80-645121.
SRI/MF/complete

Annual report, for 1982, on Iowa crimes and arrests, by type of offense. Includes data on clearances, value of stolen property, law enforcement employment, and assaults on police. Data are shown for State and counties, suburban and nonsuburban cities, rural areas, and geographic districts; and by age, race, and sex of offender.

Data are from State and local law enforcement agency reports, submitted under the Uniform Crime Reporting Program.

Contents:

Listings of contents, tables, and charts. (p. i-v)

Introduction and methodology. Includes 1 table showing number of reporting agencies by type, 1982. (p. 1-9)

Part I. State level analysis of reported crimes. Includes 65 charts described below. (p. 11-54)

Part II. Statistical data, in computer printout format, from local reporting jurisdictions; with 69 tables, listed below. (p. 57-378)

This is the 6th annual report. Previous report, for 1980, is described in SRI 1981 Annual under S2850-2. No report was issued for 1981. Summary 1981 data are included in the 1982 report; detailed 1981 data are available on request from the issuing agency.

Availability: Iowa Department of Public Safety, Research and Development Bureau, Wallace State Office Bldg., Des Moines IA 50319, †; SRI/MF/complete.

CHARTS AND TABLES:

[Most data are shown by specific offense. Index (Part I) crimes covered in detail are homicide, rape, robbery, aggravated assault, burglary, larceny, and motor vehicle theft. Non-Index (Part II) crimes are less serious offenses. Although arson is classified as an Index offense, most data are reported separately and are not included in the Crime Index tables.

Data by race often also include Native American/Indians.]

S2850–1.1: Part I: State Level Analysis of Reported Crimes

[Data for Index offenses and rates are shown for 1977-82. All other data are for 1981-82, unless otherwise noted.]

a. Total index offenses and rates; violent and property index offenses and rates; and stolen property value by type of property, including farm-related theft. Charts 1-12. (p. 13-20)

b. Murder: offenses and rates; victims and offenders by age, sex, and race; and distance by relationship of victims and offenders, whether multiple or single victim and offender, location, weapon, and circumstance. Charts 13-36. (p. 22-34)

c. Offenses and rates for rape, robbery, and aggravated assault; robberies by weapon and location; and aggravated assaults by weapon. Charts 37-48. (p. 36-42)

d. Offenses and rates for burglary, larceny, and motor vehicle theft; burglaries by day and night residence and nonresidence occurrence and by type of entry; larcenies by type; and motor vehicle thefts by type of vehicle; and arson offenses 1980-82, with distribution by type of structure. Charts 49-65. (p. 44-54)

S2850–1.2: Part II: Statistical Data from Local Reporting Jurisdictions

[Data for individual jurisdictions are arranged by population categories, generally including city population size groups (with totals for suburban and nonsuburban city size groups), suburban and rural areas, suburban sheriffs, and universities. All data are for 1982.]

GENERAL STATISTICS

[Tables 1-6 show data for Index offenses by type.]

1. Index of crime [by reporting agency in each county, and by district, with population and crime rate]. (p. 57-80)

2. Monthly trend of offenses. (p. 81)

3. Offenses known, crime rates, and percent cleared by arrest, by [individual jurisdictions]. (p. 82-88)

4-5. Offenses cleared by arrest of juveniles by [individual jurisdictions], percent of total clearances; and percent of offenses cleared by arrest and percent of total clearances attributed to juveniles, by geographic district and county. (p. 89-102)

6. Offense breakdowns [for rape, robbery, aggravated and non-aggravated assault, burglary, and motor vehicle theft, by type]. (p. 103)

7-8. Value of property stolen, by offense [robbery and burglary by type, theft by value and type, and murder, rape, and motor vehicle theft]; and type and value of property stolen and recovered. (p. 104-105)

9. Farm theft [incidents and value of property stolen and recovered] by population category.] (p. 106)

10. Arson statewide [offenses reported, total and juvenile clearances, vacant structure, and damage value, by property classification; and total by time of day]. (p. 109)

PART I AND PART II ARRESTS

11-13. Number of Part I arrests and arrest rates: by reporting agencies [in each county arranged by district]; monthly trend; and by population categories. (p. 110-134)

14-25. Total, city, suburban, and rural Part I arrests by age and sex, and by race and sex, and total adult Part I arrests by race and sex. (p. 135-150)

26-28. Number of Part II arrests and arrest rates, by reporting agencies [in each county arranged by district]; monthly trend; and by population categories. (p. 151-200)

29-40. Total, city, suburban, and rural Part II arrests [by categories described in tables 14-25]. (p. 201-232)

41-42. Adult controlled substance arrests [for] sale or manufacture, and possession, [by] substance involved; by [individual jurisdiction]. (p. 233-244)

JUVENILE PART I AND PART II ARRESTS

43-44. Number of juvenile Part I arrests and arrest rates by reporting agencies [and districts], and by population categories. (p. 245-270)

45-52. Total, city, suburban, and rural juvenile Part I arrests by age and sex, and by race and sex. (p. 271-278)

53-62. Number of juvenile Part II arrests [repeated for categories described in tables 43-52]. (p. 279-346)

63-64. Juvenile controlled substance arrests [repeated for categories described in tables 41-42]. (p. 347-358)

65. Law enforcement disposition of juveniles by [individual jurisdiction; handled within dept and released, juvenile court/probation dept, welfare agency, other police agency, and adult/criminal court]. (p. 359-364)

LAW ENFORCEMENT EMPLOYEES

66. Law enforcement management data [full-time officer and civilian employees, by individual jurisdiction; including employee ratio per population; Index crimes per employee; and Part I and Part II arrests per officer]. (p. 365-370)

67-69. Total assaults on law enforcement officers: [by types of weapon, assignment, and activity, and by time of day, with clearances by activity type]; by [individual jurisdiction, with and without injury, and officers killed]; and by population categories, [and] weapons used [with and without injury]. (p. 371-378)

S2860   IOWA
Department of
Revenue

S2860–1   IOWA RETAIL SALES AND
USE TAX REPORT
Quarterly, with annual
summary. Approx. 140 p.
LC 75-648610.
SRI/MF/complete

Quarterly report, with annual fiscal year summary, presenting data on Iowa retail sales and use taxes, by county, town, selected cities, size of computed tax due and gross sales, and kind of business. Types of use tax are motor vehicle/ trailer, retailers, hotel/motel, and consumer use.

Data are from business tax returns filed with Iowa Dept of Revenue. Report is issued approximately 7-14 months after period of coverage.

Contains contents listing, foreword, and glossary; and narrative review, with 16 quarterly tables listed below.

Availability: Iowa Department of Revenue, Research and Management Services Division, Hoover State Office Bldg., 1305 E. Walnut St., Des Moines IA 50319, †; SRI/MF/complete.

Issues reviewed during 1984: 1st-2nd Qtrs. 1983 (D); and annual summary for FY83.

QUARTERLY TABLES:

[Unless otherwise noted, data are shown for quarter of coverage.]

SUMMARY TABLES

[Tables [1], [4-5], and [8] also show number of businesses.]

[1] Taxable sales, by business group [for current quarter and same quarter of preceding year].

[2] Number of returns filed, taxable retail sales, and computed tax, by county.

[3] Computed tax, by population [size] group [of cities and towns, and for rural areas].

[4] Retail sales tax collection, by [size of] computed tax due.

[5] Gross sales and computed tax, by size of gross sales.

[6] Retailers use tax, by business group [number of returns and computed tax].

[7] Comparison of use taxes [number of returns and computed tax value for retailers, motor vehicle registrations, and consumers, for current quarter and same quarter of preceding year].

[8] Retailers use tax collection report, by [size of] computed tax due.

[9] Local option hotel/motel tax [collected and rate, by jurisdiction].

RETAIL SALES AND USE TAXES

[All tables show computed tax. Tables [10-12] and [14] also show number of businesses.]

[10] Retail sales tax [and taxable sales], by county and town.

[11] Retail sales tax by county and selected cities, by business class.

[12] Retail [taxable] sales, by [SIC 3-digit] business classification.

[13] Use tax report on motor vehicles/trailers [number of units], by counties.

[14] Retailers use tax [and taxable sales], by business classification.

[15-16] Consumer use tax [and number of returns], by [major] business classification and by county.

S2880   IOWA
Department of
Transportation

S2880–1   1982 IOWA ACCIDENT FACTS
Annual.   Aug. 1983.
iv+59 p.
LC 82-647424.
SRI/MF/complete

Annual report on Iowa traffic accidents, fatalities, and injuries, by accident and vehicle type, location, time, and other circumstances; and driver and vehicle characteristics; 1982, with selected trends from 1962.

Also includes data on vehicle miles of travel; licensed drivers and vehicle registrations; and accident drug and alcohol involvement for drivers and pedestrians, and seat belt and motorcycle helmet use.

Data were compiled by the Iowa Office of Safety Programs from accident report forms.

Contains foreword, contents listing, and glossary (p. i-iv); and 4 charts and 207 tables (p. 1-59).

Availability: Iowa Department of Transportation, Motor Vehicle Division, Driver Services Office, Lucas State Office Bldg., Des Moines IA 50319, †; SRI/MF/complete.

S2885   IOWA
Treasurer

S2885–1   REPORT OF THE TREASURER OF STATE, IOWA for the Fiscal Year July 1, 1982-June 30, 1983
Annual.   [1984.]   55 p.
LC 80-642423.
SRI/MF/complete

Annual financial report of the Iowa State treasurer, for FY83, presenting receipts/credits, disbursements, and balances, for revenue, trust, and special funds, by detailed fund and account, FY83.

Also includes data on revenues by source, FY79-83; appropriations by government function, FY82-84; and public employees' retirement loan program receipts and expenditures, FY83.

Contains transmittal letter (p. 1); and 7 financial schedules and statements (p. 3-55).

Report is issued as Part I of 2 parts comprising the State Treasurer's biennial report for the biennium ending June 30, 1984.

Availability: Iowa Treasurer, State Capitol Bldg., 10th and Grand, Des Moines IA 50319, †; SRI/MF/complete.

S2900   KANSAS
Department of
Administration

S2900–1   STATE OF KANSAS DEPARTMENT OF ADMINISTRATION FINANCIAL REPORT for Period July 1, 1982-June 30, 1983
Annual.   For individual publication data, see below.
LC 78-642377.
SRI/MF/complete

Annual report on financial condition of Kansas State government, FY83, with comparisons to FY82. Presents financial data for the following funds: general; Federal revenue sharing; special revenue; highway; capital projects; enterprise; intragovernmental service; trust and agency; clearing, refund, and suspense; and payroll clearing.

Also includes data on bonded indebtedness, tax balances by type and county, property valuations, and legislative appropriation limitations.

Data are based on State records.

Report is published in 2 volumes, individually described below. This is the 30th annual report.

Availability: Kansas Department of Administration, Accounts and Reports Division, State Office Bldg., Topeka KS 66612-1574, †; SRI/MF/complete.

S2900–1.1: Volume I
[Annual. Nov. 10, 1983. xxiv+117 p. SRI/MF/complete.]

Presents assets and liabilities, balances, revenues by source, and expenditures by object, for combined funds and by fund type.

Also includes data on revenues by tax type; State and Federal assistance to local areas, and Federal grants, by purpose; employment security fund revenues and expenditures; and revenue bond indebtedness.

Contains contents listing (p. iii); highlights, with 6 charts and 13 tables (p. iv-xxiv); 13 sections with 43 exhibits and schedules, and accompanying notes (p. 1-113); and directory to Volume II (p. 117).

S2900–1.2: Volume II
[Annual. Nov. 10, 1983. p. 119-282+4 p. SRI/MF/complete.]

Presents detailed appropriation accounts for 3 funds, fund balances for 8 funds, and revenue statements for all funds, by governmental function, agency, and appropriation or fund title.

Also includes tax account balances for 3 capital project building funds; property and motor vehicle tax balances, property valuations and tax levies, and estimated motor vehicle tax revenues for 2 building funds, all by county; legislative appropriation limitation compared to expenditures, by agency and fund title; and receipts from fees and licenses by type, fines/forfeitures/penalties, interest on idle funds, and sales tax, by county.

Contains contents listing (p. 119); 11 schedules and statements (p. 120-282); and cross-reference index (4 p.).

S2925   KANSAS
Office of the
Attorney General

S2925–1   CRIME IN KANSAS, 1983: Uniform Crime Report
Annual.   May 21, 1984.
xviii+155 p.
SRI/MF/complete

Annual report, for 1983, on Kansas crimes and arrests, by type of offense. Also includes data on crime trends, clearances, offender and victim characteristics, value of stolen property, assaults on police, and law enforcement employment. Selected data are shown by city, county, and individual reporting agency.

Data are from reports of State and local law enforcement agencies, submitted under the Uniform Crime Reporting Program. Report also includes data on fires, with focus on arson, based on reports to the State Fire Marshal's Office.

Contains summary, and listings of contents, tables, and charts (p. iii-xviii); introduction (p. 3-4); 4 sections, with narrative summaries, and 17 charts and 54 tables described below (p. 7-147); and glossary and statutory requirements (p. 151-155).

Availability: Kansas Office of the Attorney General, Investigation Bureau, Statistical Analysis Center, 1620 Tyler, Topeka KS 66612, †; SRI/MF/complete.

TABLES AND CHARTS:

[Data are for 1983, unless otherwise noted. Data by city are shown for cities with over 10,000 population and balance of State.

Data by race generally also include breakdowns for American Indians and Asians; data by ethnicity are shown for Hispanics and non-Hispanics.

Index offenses covered in detail are murder/non-negligent manslaughter, rape, robbery, and aggravated assault (violent crimes); and burglary, larceny/theft, and motor vehicle theft (property crimes). Arson is classified as an Index offense, but data are reported separately and are generally not included in the Crime Index tables.]

S2925-1.1: Index Offenses, Arson and Fires, and Arrests

INDEX OFFENSES

[A chart showing crime trends and projections, 1974-84, is repeated for total crimes, violent crimes, and each individual offense. Crime clocks, showing offense frequency, are presented for total crimes and selected offense categories. Other data are described below.]

a. Offenses and value of stolen and recovered property, by offense and/or property type, city, and reporting agency; offenses and clearances, by offense, 1973-83; clearances, by city and offense; Crime Index and violent and property crime rates, by reporting agency; and violent crime summary. Charts 1-5, tables 1-11. (p. 8-53)

b. Murder/non-negligent manslaughter: offenses by month; type of weapon used; victim and offender age, sex, race, and ethnicity; victim-offender relationship; and offense circumstance. Chart 6, tables 12-17. (p. 57-61)

c. Rapes, by month, time of day, victim and offender age and race, victim-offender relationship, type of weapon, and location; robberies and value of stolen property, by type of location, by city; aggravated assaults; and property crimes. Charts 7-11, tables 18-26. (p. 64-77)

d. Burglary residence and nonresidence offenses and stolen property value, by day or night occurrence; larceny offenses and stolen property value, by larceny type; and motor vehicles recovered, by where stolen and recovered; all by city. Charts 12-14, tables 27-31. (p. 80-89)

ARSON AND FIRES

e. Arson comparisons to 1982; and offenses by month and city, clearances, and loss value by city, all by property type, including uninhabited/abandoned structures. Chart 15, tables 32-34. (p. 92-94)

f. Total fires, incendiary and suspicious fires by month, day of week, and time of day, and loss value for incendiary/suspicious fires, all by property type; and firefighter and citizen injuries and fatalities due to all and incendiary/suspicious fires. Tables 35-40. (p. 95-98)

ARRESTS

g. Crime Index arrests, 1974-84, with detail by offense, 1973-83; juvenile and adult arrests by offense, for Index and 31 other offenses, all by age, sex, race, and ethnicity; arrests by Index and other offenses, by county and reporting agency; and juvenile dispositions, by type. Chart 16, tables 41-48. (p. 102-128)

S2925-1.2: Police Assaults and Employment

ASSAULTS

a. Assaults on officers, by injury status, weapon, circumstance, and type of assignment, variously cross-tabulated; and by time of day. Chart 17, tables 49-52. (p. 132-134)

EMPLOYMENT

b. Aggregate police dept and sheriff's office sworn officers and civilian personnel, by sex, race, ethnicity, education, and length of service (total and with agency), and average age; and sworn and civilian personnel by sex, by reporting agency arranged by county. Tables 53-54. (p. 138-147)

S2940   KANSAS
Department of Corrections

S2940-1   STATISTICAL PROFILE: FY83 OFFENDER POPULATION of the Kansas Department of Corrections
Annual.   Jan. 31, 1984.
vii+56 p.
SRI/MF/complete

Annual report on corrections in Kansas, presenting data on prison and parolee population, including inmate admissions, releases, escapes, and sentence length; and inmate and parolee demographic characteristics, previous criminal experience, and commitment offense category; FY83, with trends from FY74. Some data are shown by institution and county.

Also includes data on work release programs and interstate compact probationers or parolees serving in and sent from Kansas, by State.

Contains contents and table listing, and preface with 1 chart (p. ii-vii); and narrative report, interspersed with 2 maps, 7 charts, and 18 tables (p. 1-56).

SRI coverage of *Statistical Profile* begins with this edition. Data in the profile are comparable to the statistical component of Dept of Corrections' *Annual Report,* previously covered by SRI under this number.

Availability: Kansas Department of Corrections, Planning, Research, Evaluation and Accreditation Unit, Jayhawk Towers, 700 Jackson, Topeka KS 66603, †; SRI/MF/complete.

S2945   KANSAS
Department of Education

S2945-1   ANNUAL STATISTICAL REPORT, 1982/83, Kansas State Department of Education
Annual.   [1984.]   429 p.
LC 80-640571.
SRI/MF/complete

Annual report, for 1982/83, on Kansas public schools, covering finances, students, personnel, facilities, and transportation services. Presents enrollment and financial data by school district and county. Also includes enrollment and operating data for nonpublic schools. Data are compiled from school district annual reports.

Contains the following 2 sections, each beginning with a contents listing:

Part 1. Statistical tables and charts for the State. 4 charts, generally showing trends from 1970/71; and 29 tables listed below. (p. 1-46)

Part 2. Detailed listings. 2 extended tables showing: nonpublic school teachers, enrollment (as of Sept. 1982), and average daily attendance (ADA) by school level, all by school; and public school enrollment, graduates, dropouts by sex, summer school enrollment and staff by school level, expenditures by object and revenues by source for funds covered in Part 1, and pupil transportation service, all by school district arranged by county, 1982/83. (p. 47-429)

Availability: Kansas Department of Education, Kansas State Education Bldg., 120 E. Tenth St., Topeka KS 66612, †; SRI/MF/complete.

STATE TABLES:

[Tables show data for 1982/83, unless otherwise noted.]

S2945-1.1: Part 1: Statistical Tables and Charts

SCHOOLS AND STUDENTS

1. Number of accredited public schools [by type], 1978/79-1982/83. (p. 3)

2. Fall enrollment, ADA, and average daily membership [all by school type]. (p. 3)

3. High school graduates and dropouts [by sex]. (p. 3)

SUMMARY FINANCES

[Expenditure objects are classified as series 100-1400.]

4. Financial statement—general fund [revenue from local, county, State, and Federal sources; total expenditures; and balances]. (p. 4)

5. General fund expenditures by category [series], 1973/74-1982/83. (p. 6)

6. Estimated cost of vandalism. (p. 8)

7-8. Estimated operational costs and cost per pupil in ADA, 100-800 series; and total expenditures 100-1400 series (excluding 1100 and 1300 series); year ending June 30, 1983. (p. 8)

9. General fund expenditures, each series expressed as a percent of year's total, 100-1400 series (excluding 1300 series), 1977/78-1982/83. (p. 10)

10. General fund salaries for administration and instruction, 1979/80-1982/83. (p. 10)

SPECIAL FUNDS

11-21. Special assessment, capital outlay, vocational education, transportation, special education, co-op special education, driver training, food service, adult education, adult supplementary education, and teacher retirement funds [showing for each, opening and closing balances, receipts, and expenditures]. (p. 12-16)

PERSONNEL AND OPERATING DATA

22. Personnel data [certified and noncertified, by position]. (p. 17)

23-24. Pupil transportation services and costs. (p. 19-21)

25. School facilities [schools and classrooms in use and abandoned]. (p. 22)

26. Summer school [enrollment, ADA, staff, and expenditures], 1983. (p. 22)

27. Nonpublic schools [teachers and ADA, by school level; graduates and dropouts by sex; and enrollment by grade]. (p. 23)

SCHOOL DISTRICTS

[28-29] [State equalization and transportation aid payments; and enrollment (Sept. 1982), income tax rebates, and rebate per pupil; by school district arranged by county.] (p. 25-46)

S2975   KANSAS
Department of
Health and Environment

S2975–1   ANNUAL SUMMARY OF VITAL STATISTICS, Kansas, 1982
Annual. Nov. 1983.
vii+123 p.
ISSN 0364-2372.
LC 76-647679.
SRI/MF/complete

Annual report on Kansas vital statistics, covering births, deaths by cause, population growth and density, abortions, marriages, and divorces and annulments, 1982, with trends from 1952. Includes data by Health Service Area (HSA), county, city, age, race, and sex. Most data are from State vital statistics and health records.

Contents:

a. Listings of contents, tables, and charts; and highlights with 1 chart, introduction, methodology, and definitions. (p. iii-vii, 1-12)

b. Report narrative and appendix, with 35 interspersed numbered tables, listed below; and additional illustrative charts, maps, and text data, including population density by county (p. 24), births by mother's race and child's sex and by birth order (p. 29), abortion trends (p. 37), and fetal deaths by mother's age (p. 39). (p. 14-119)

c. Index of tables and charts. (p. 122-123)

Monthly updated data on births, deaths, diseases, and changes in marital status are provided in *Monthly Summary of Vital Statistics,* not covered by SRI. Copies are available from the Division of Health Resources of the Bureau of Registration and Health Statistics.

Availability: Kansas Department of Health and Environment, Registration and Health Statistics Bureau, Forbes Field, Topeka KS 66620, †; SRI/MF/complete.

TABLES:

[Unless otherwise noted, tables show 1982 data for Kansas.]

S2975–1.1: General Data

SUMMARY

1-2. Vital events, [number] and percent change, 1972 and 1980-81, and by number, rate, and ratio, 1972-82. (p. 14-16)

3. Population, natural increase, and net migration, 1953-82. (p. 22)

INFANT BIRTHS AND DEATHS

4. Live births by age group of mother, by selected characteristics [birth weight, prematurity, and illegitimacy]. (p. 32)

5. Perinatal period III mortality [fetal and hebdomadal deaths], selected years 1952-82. (p. 42)

6. Infant deaths by cause of death and age group of infant. (p. 45)

DEATHS

7. Deaths by race [including American Indians] and sex, by age group and average age at death. (p. 53)

8. Selected causes of death, by age group and average age at death. (p. 54)

9. 10 leading causes of death by sex, by number, rate, and average age at death. (p. 56)

10. Selected leading causes of death by number and rate, Kansas and U.S. (p. 57)

11. Heart disease deaths by age group and sex. (p. 61)

12. Malignant neoplasm deaths by site of lesion, age group, and sex. (p. 63)

13-15. Cerebrovascular disease, selected chronic disease, and accidental deaths, by [type], age group, and sex. (p. 64- 67)

16. 10 leading causes of death: underlying cause by nonunderlying cause. (p. 71)

MARRIAGES, DIVORCES, AND ANNULMENTS

17-18. Marriages by age group and premarital status of bride and groom. (p. 77-78)

19. Divorces and annulments by duration of marriage in years. (p. 83)

20. Divorces and annulments by number and percent by number of minor children. (p. 84)

S2975–1.2: Appendix: Geographical Divisions

HSA DATA

21-22. Vital statistics [summary], and selected causes of death, by HSA. (p. 88-89)

COUNTY DATA

[Unless otherwise noted, data are shown by county of residence.]

23-24. Population, and live births by number and rate, 1978-82. (p. 90-93)

25-26. Live and out-of-wedlock births, by age group of mother. (p. 94-97)

27. Induced abortions by age group of patient. (p. 98)

28. Perinatal period III deaths. (p. 100)

29. Infant deaths by component [and infant age]. (p. 103)

30. Deaths by number and rate, 1978-82. (p. 105)

31. Deaths by age group and average age at death. (p. 107)

32. 20 leading causes of death. (p. 110)

33. Marriages by number and rate, by county of marriage, 1978-82. (p. 114)

34. Divorces/annulments by number and rate, by county of action, 1978-82. (p. 116)

CITY DATA

35. Population, live births, and total deaths by city of residence, 1981-82. (p. 118)

S2985   KANSAS
Department of
Human Resources

S2985–1   KANSAS ANNUAL PLANNING INFORMATION, 1984
Annual. Mar. 1984.
3+60 p. Rpt. Series No. 17.
SRI/MF/complete

Annual planning report, for 1984, identifying Kansas population groups most in need of employment services, and presenting data on general population, employment and labor force, income, and business closures, by county and service delivery area, various periods 1980-85.

Most data are from Kansas Dept of Human Resources and U.S. Census Bureau.

Contains contents and table listings (2 p.); highlights, and 2 report sections with 13 tables (p. 1-40); appendix with 6 tables (p. 41-57); and glossary (p. 58-60).

All tables are described below.

Availability: Kansas Department of Human Resources, Employment and Training Division, Research and Analysis Section, 401 Topeka Ave., Topeka KS 66603, †; SRI/MF/complete.

TABLES:

[Data are shown by Kansas county and service delivery area (SDA), unless otherwise noted.]

a. Population and income: population by sex, age, and race/ethnicity (including Hispanic, American Indian, and Hawaiian/Pacific Islander), and for high school dropouts, handicapped, veterans, and economically disadvantaged persons aged 16-21 and 22/older, 1980; per capita income, 1977-81; U.S. urban CPI by major item, 1982 and monthly 1983; and employment and wages, FY83. 8 tables. (p. 5-24)

b. Employment and labor force: employment by industry division, and unemployment, State total only, FY82-85; labor force, by employment status 1983, and with participation rate 1980; unfilled job openings by occupational group, by duration and industry division, State total only, Feb. 1984; and active job applicants by occupational group, Jan. 1984. 5 tables. (p. 26-40)

c. Business closures and population groups: closings of establishments with 10/more employees, and employment at peak and at closing, with SDA detail by SIC 2-digit industry group, 1st 10 months 1983; and persons unemployed 15/more weeks, persons with limited English ability, parolees, divorced/widowed persons, unemployment insurance exhaustees, and recipients of AFDC and general and refugee assistance, various periods 1980-83. 6 tables. (p. 41-57)

S2990   KANSAS
Department of
Insurance

S2990–1   ONE HUNDRED FOURTEENTH ANNUAL REPORT OF THE KANSAS INSURANCE DEPARTMENT, for Year Ending Dec. 31, 1983
Annual. [1984.] 3+127 p.
SRI/MF/complete

Annual report on Kansas insurance industry financial condition and underwriting activity, by company and type of insurance, 1983. Covers assets, liabilities, surplus/capital, income, disbursements, net gain, dividends, insurance written and in force, premiums earned or written, claims/benefits or losses paid, losses incurred, loss ratios, and other operating ratios, for companies with headquarters in Kansas and elsewhere.

Data are shown, as applicable, for fraternal and other life insurance companies (with detail for accident/health insurance); hospital and medical service corporations (including Blue Cross and Blue Shield); HMOs; and fire/casualty companies.

Also includes data on Insurance Dept receipts, company admissions, agent/broker certifications, consumer complaints and assistance, and rate review; insurance company security deposits; underwriting activities of workers compensation assigned risk and State automobile insurance plans; and firemen's relief fund collections and distributions.

Data are compiled from Insurance Dept internal records and annual statements filed by individual insurers.

Contains contents listing (1 p.); and report, with narrative and 37 tables (p. 1-127).

Availability: Kansas Department of Insurance, 420 S.W. Ninth St., Topeka KS 66612, Kansas residents †, others $2.75; SRI/MF/complete.

S3000   KANSAS
State
Library

S3000–1   KANSAS PUBLIC LIBRARY STATISTICS, 1983
Annual. [1984.] iii+139 p.
LC 75-613256.
SRI/MF/complete

Annual report, for 1983, on Kansas public library and library system holdings, population served, staff, and finances, by library and by regional library system. Data are from 312 responses to questionnaires mailed to all 315 public libraries in the State.

Contains contents listing (2 p.); introduction, with summary text data (p. i-iii); directories of public libraries, regional systems of cooperating libraries, State Library personnel, and advisory commission members (p. 1-19); and 14 tables, listed below (p. 21-139).

Availability: Kansas State Library, State Capitol, 3rd Floor, Topeka KS 66612, $12.00; SRI/MF/complete.

TABLES:
[All data are for 1983. Tables [1-6] show data by library, grouped within 7 regional library systems; tables [7-14] show data by library system only. Tables [1-6] and [9] include data on population served.]

INDIVIDUAL LIBRARIES
[1] Support [from local taxes, Federal revenue sharing, library system grants, State aid, and other]. (p. 21-35)
[2] Expenditures [on books, periodicals, nonbook materials, salaries, and other operations; and total budget for next year]. (p. 36-51)
[3-4] Resources [weekly hours and volumes owned and added; periodical subscriptions; record, reference, art print, and film holdings; number of regular borrowers; and interlibrary loan requests received]. (p. 52-82)
[5] Circulation [adult, juvenile, and other circulation, and interlibrary loans sent]. (p. 83-97)
[6] Personnel [positions at each library, hourly wage, salary range, weekly hours, and educational attainment]. (p. 98-127)

LIBRARY SYSTEMS
[7] Support [funds from system tax, State/Federal aid, and other]. (p. 128)
[8] Expenditures [by object]. (p. 129)
[9] Types and number of member libraries [public libraries in counties levying system tax; contracting, club, school, and college/university libraries; service outlets; and nonparticipating libraries]. (p. 131)
[10] Resources [total and added volumes; and reference, large-print, periodical, sound recording, art print, film, and slide holdings]. (p. 132)
[11] Circulation [by program; and total circulation and reference questions received]. (p. 133)
[12] Interlibrary loan [transactions]. (p. 134)
[13] Miscellaneous [Mail-a-Book and rotating book services, workshops, and beginning librarian salary]. (p. 135)
[14] Personnel [position titles, salaries, weekly hours, and educational requirements]. (p. 136-139)

S3035   KANSAS
Supreme Court

S3035–1   ANNUAL REPORT ON THE COURTS of Kansas, FY83
Annual. Nov. 15, 1983.
3+140 p.
LC 79-644946.
SRI/MF/complete

Annual report, for FY83, on Kansas judicial system, including trial and appellate court caseloads and case dispositions. Covers district, supreme, and appeals courts. Includes trial court data by case type, judicial district, and county.

Trial court case types shown are criminal and civil, with some additional detail for domestic relations, traffic, juvenile, probate, fish/game violations, small claims, adoption, mental illness treatment, and alcoholism treatment cases.

Also includes roster of judges; and data on case processing time.

Contains contents listing and preface (2 p.); index of district court tables (1 p.); and report, with 17 tables (p. 12-140).

This is the 6th annual report.

Availability: Kansas Supreme Court, Judicial Center, Judicial Administration Office, 301 W. Tenth St., Topeka KS 66612, ‡; SRI/MF/complete.

S3040   KANSAS
Department of
Transportation

S3040–1   KANSAS MOTOR VEHICLE TRAFFIC ACCIDENTS, 1982
Annual. [1983.]
26 p. var. paging.
SRI/MF/complete

Annual report on Kansas traffic accidents, injuries, and fatalities, by vehicle and accident type, location, time, and other circumstances; and driver and victim age; 1982.

Also includes data on vehicle mileage, alcohol involvement including blood alcohol levels, citations issued, and use of safety devices.

Report is a computer printout consisting of 13 tables. Issuing agency also publishes an annual summary of traffic accidents, including selected trends from 1979. Summary is also available on SRI microfiche under this number.

SRI coverage of the report begins with the 1982 edition.

An annual *Highway Safety Plan* report, including some accident statistics, is also published by the issuing agency, but is not covered in SRI.

Availability: Kansas Department of Transportation, Rural and Urban Development Bureau, Traffic Safety Section, State Office Bldg., 10th and Topeka Ave., Topeka KS 66612, †; SRI/MF/complete.

S3085   KENTUCKY
Department of
Agriculture

S3085–1   KENTUCKY AGRICULTURAL STATISTICS, 1983-84
Annual. Sept. 1984. 120 p.
LC 50-63276.
SRI/MF/complete

Annual report on Kentucky agricultural production, marketing, and finances, 1982-83, with selected trends from 1970s or earlier. Data generally are shown by commodity and/or county and district, with some comparisons to other States and total U.S.

Report covers production, value, prices, and, as applicable, acreage, stocks, inventory, and disposition, for field crop, fruit, livestock, poultry, mink, and dairy sectors.

Also includes data on weather; wool production; off-farm grain storage capacity; farm income and production expenses; prices paid by farmers; fertilizer use and sales; farms and acreage; agricultural exports; production rankings and farm value and rents, by State; and Census of Agriculture summary findings.

Report is prepared by the Kentucky Crop and Livestock Reporting Service.

Contains contents listing, and foreword with 2 charts (p. 2-4); 7 sections, with narrative summaries, 19 maps, 5 charts, and 86 tables (p. 6-119); and list of reports available from Crop and Livestock Reporting Service (p. 120).

Availability: Kentucky Crop and Livestock Reporting Service, PO Box 1120, Louisville KY 40201, †; SRI/MF/complete.

S3095   KENTUCKY
Department of
Banking and Securities

S3095–1   ANNUAL REPORT OF THE COMMISSIONER OF BANKING AND SECURITIES, Division of Banking of the Commonwealth of Kentucky
Annual.   June 30, 1983.
73 p.
LC 74-649680.
SRI/MF/complete

Annual compilation of 5 reports on financial condition of Kentucky State-chartered banks and trust companies, credit unions, savings and loan assns, and industrial loan companies, and State-licensed consumer loan companies, as of June 30, 1983, or Dec. 31, 1982. Presents aggregate balance sheets for each type of institution, and assets by institution and city for most types.

Also includes Banking Division expenditures for FY83; summary asset trends from as early as 1912; bank, savings and loan, and credit union status changes; and directories of industrial and consumer loan companies.

Contains 5 reports, with 13 tables (p. 1-73).

This is the 71st annual bank report, the 49th annual credit union report, the 38th annual industrial loan report, and the 65th annual savings and loan report.

Availability: Kentucky Department of Banking and Securities, Banking Division, 911 Leawood Dr., Frankfort KY 40601-3392, †; SRI/MF/complete.

S3103   KENTUCKY
Council of
Economic Advisors

S3103–2   KENTUCKY ECONOMY: Review and Perspective
Quarterly.   Approx. 15 p.
ISSN 0270-1421.
LC SN 80-12933.
SRI/MF/complete

Quarterly report on Kentucky business activity and economic performance indicators and trends, with selected U.S. comparisons. Data are current to quarter preceding cover date month.

Report is prepared by the Kentucky Council of Economic Advisors (KCEA) research staff from reports of various Federal, State, and private agencies.

General format:

a. Newsbriefs; and feature articles, often with statistics.

b. "Selected Indicators of Economic Activity" section, with 2 quarterly tables described below.

Quarterly tables appear in all issues. All additional features with substantial statistical content are described, as they appear, under "Statistical Features." Nonstatistical features are not covered.

Availability: University of Kentucky: Center for Business and Economic Research, College of Business and Economics, 301 Mathews Bldg., Lexington KY 40506-0047, †; SRI/MF/complete.

Issues reviewed during 1984: Sept.-Dec. 1983; Spring-Summer 1984 (P) (Vol. 7, Nos. 3-4; Vol. 8, Nos. 1-2).

QUARTERLY INDICATORS TABLES:
[Data are shown for quarter ending 3 months preceding date of publication, total and by month, with percent change from previous quarter and same quarter of previous year.]

[1] U.S. data [including CPI and PPI, by major item, with detail for energy sector; labor force and employment; personal income; GNP; index of industrial production; residential building permits; and outstanding installment credit].

[2] Kentucky data [including labor force; employment by industry division; manufacturing hours and earnings; coal mining output, hours, earnings, and severance tax receipts; residential construction permits and value; life insurance sales; loans by savings and loan assns; car registrations; and State government sales, income, and other tax receipts].

STATISTICAL FEATURES:

S3103–2.501: Sept. 1983 (Vol. 7, No. 3)
KCEA REVIEW AND FORECAST

(p. 1, 6) By Charles W. Hultman. Article, with 1 table showing Kentucky seasonally adjusted employment by industry division, manufacturing hours, and authorized housing units, Aug. 1982-July 1983. Data are from Kentucky Information System.

ATTITUDES ON MAJOR ECONOMIC ISSUES IN KENTUCKY

(p. 7) By Richard S. Snyder. Article presenting rankings of major economic issues facing Kentucky. Data are based on 64 responses to an Apr. 1983 survey of 207 Kentucky Economic Assn members. Includes 1 table.

REVISED OUTLOOK FOR KENTUCKY REVENUES FOR FY84, ANNUAL FEATURE

(p. 10-12) Annual article presenting Kentucky Revenue Cabinet forecasts of FY84 State tax receipts. Includes 1 table showing actual FY83 and forecast FY84 general and transportation fund tax receipts by type.

KENTUCKY REVENUES IN 1982-83 AND THE OUTLOOK FOR 1983-84, ANNUAL FEATURE

(p. 13-15) Annual article, by Lawrence K. Lynch, presenting actual and forecast tax receipts for Kentucky general and transportation funds by tax source, FY82-84. Forecasts are the author's. Includes 2 tables.

RELATIVE GROWTH IN PERSONAL INCOME, POPULATION, AND PER CAPITA PERSONAL INCOME, 1979-82

(back cover) Table showing total and per capita personal income, and population as of July 1, by US region and for 12 southeastern States, 1979 and 1982.

S3103–2.502: Dec. 1983 (Vol. 7, No. 4)
KCEA REVIEW AND FORECAST

(p. 1, 10) By Charles W. Hultman. Article, with 1 table showing new jobs created in total U.S., by industry division, 1982-95 period. Data are from BLS.

KENTUCKY EDUCATIONAL FINANCE: METHODS AND PROBLEMS

(p. 3-5, 8-9) By Don M. Soule. Article, with 1 chart showing Kentucky real property tax rate per $100, 1976-83. Data are from the Kentucky Economic Information System.

INCOME IMPLICATIONS OF INTERINDUSTRY EMPLOYMENT CHANGES

(p. 11) Brief article, with 2 charts showing percent change in employment for lower and higher wage industries, by industry division, for Kentucky and total U.S., 1980-83 period.

S3103–2.503: Spring 1984 (Vol. 8, No. 1)
KENTUCKY'S PUBLIC INFRASTRUCTURE NEEDS: A PRELIMINARY ASSESSMENT

(p. 3-5, 11) By Phillip W. Roeder and Dennis B. Murphy. Article, with 2 tables showing funding requirements for public works construction/maintenance (in constant 1982 dollars), by type of project (including transportation and water supply and treatment systems, dams, flood control facilities, and river ports), for Kentucky FY89 and FY2000, with selected comparisons to U.S. for 1983-2000 period.

Data are from University of Kentucky Bureau of Policy Research and a study commissioned by the Joint Economic Committee of Congress.

UPDATE ON KENTUCKY EMPLOYMENT

(p. 8-10) Article, with 5 tables showing Kentucky employment index (1970=base year), by industry division and major manufacturing group; and Kentucky and U.S. nonagricultural employment, with distribution for goods- and service-producing industries; various years 1963-83. Data are from Kentucky Economic Information System.

KENTUCKY PERSONAL INCOME: SUMMARY, BY QUARTERS, ANNUAL FEATURE

(back cover) Annual table showing Kentucky personal income by source and earnings by industry division, and contributions to social insurance, 4th quarter 1982-4th quarter 1983. Data are from U.S. Bureau of Economic Analysis.

S3103–2.504: Summer 1984 (Vol. 8, No. 2)
1984-86 KENTUCKY STATE BUDGET

(p. 3-7, 17) By Ronald J. Carson. Article presenting summary trends and forecasts of Kentucky State budget revenues and expenditures, with detail for actual vs. budgeted funds by agency, various periods FY74-86.

PRELIMINARY LOOK AT DEVELOPMENTAL PROGRESS IN RURAL KENTUCKY, 1960-80

(p. 8-9, 12-16) By Cynthia L. Duncan. Article on socioeconomic conditions in rural Kentucky counties. Data are from Kentucky Economic Information System, Census Bureau, and other specified sources. Includes 4 tables showing the following for various years 1959-80:

a. Distribution of labor/proprietors' income, by industry division and for coal mining, for total State and rural areas.

b. Social indicators for U.S., State, nonmetro counties, and counties with economies based on farm, coal, manufacturing, and government/mixed sectors, generally including data on the following for each: per capita and median family income (in constant and 1972 dollars), low income families, educational attainment, housing units with complete plumbing, net migration, and mobile homes.

SELECTED ECONOMIC AND SOCIAL INDICATORS: KENTUCKY AND THE U.S.

(p. 18-19) Table showing selected demographic and socioeconomic data for Kentucky and U.S., with State ranking for Kentucky. Data are shown for most recent available year, primarily late 1970s-82.

Includes approximately 70 items within the following categories: population characteristics, land area, vital statistics, health care, housing, crime, education, employment, income and poverty, government finances, voter participation, motor vehicle use, traffic fatalities, energy consumption, weather, farms, mineral production, construction, manufacturing shipments, and retail sales.

Data were compiled by U.S. Census Bureau.

KENTUCKY COUNTIES IN RANK ORDER, 1982 PER CAPITA PERSONAL INCOME, BY PLACE OF RESIDENCE

(back cover) Table showing Kentucky counties ranked by per capita personal income, 1982. Data are from U.S. Commerce Dept.

S3103–4   COUNCIL OF ECONOMIC ADVISORS ANNUAL REPORT, 1983, Kentucky
Annual. [1984.] vii+45 p.
ISSN 0270-238X.
LC 80-647821.
SRI/MF/complete

Annual report, for 1983, comparing Kentucky and U.S. economy, generally 1970-82. Includes data on unemployment rates and State/local government revenues; and indexed values for personal income, earnings by industry division and manufacturing group, farm income, and coal mining and construction activity.

Data are primarily from U.S. Commerce Dept, and Kentucky Economic Information System.

Contains contents listing and preface (p. iv-vii); and introduction, and narrative report in 13 chapters, with 21 charts, and 18 tables described below (p. 1-45).

This is the 12th annual report.

Availability: University of Kentucky: Center for Business and Economic Research, College of Business and Economics, 301 Mathews Bldg., Lexington KY 40506-0047, public and nonprofit institutions †, others $10.00; SRI/MF/complete.

TABLES:
[Data are shown for Kentucky and U.S., 1970-82, unless otherwise noted. Most data are expressed as index values with 1970 as base year.]

a. Per capita personal income as percent of U.S. average, for Kentucky and aggregate Southeastern States, selected years 1940-82; distribution of personal income by major source; per capita personal income, and level relative to State average, by Kentucky area development district, and for 10 highest and lowest counties, 1970-81. Tables 1-3D. (p. 3-13)

b. Nonfarm wage/salary income, by industry division and major manufacturing group; and total and insured unemployment rates. Tables 4-8. (p. 17-26)

c. State/local government general revenue distribution from Federal aid and State/local tax and nontax source; and tax revenue per capita and as percent of personal income; 1970-81. Tables 9-10. (p. 29-32)

d. Coal production, with detail for major Kentucky and U.S. regions, selected years 1960-82; coal employment and wage/salary income; farm income by source, 1970-81, with cash receipts detail for 1982; and contract construction wage/salary income, and value of contracts awarded for total building/nonbuilding and for residential/nonresidential building. Tables 11A-13. (p. 36-44)

S3104   KENTUCKY
Department of Economic Development

S3104–1   1984 KENTUCKY ECONOMIC STATISTICS
Annual. 1984. 123 p.
SRI/MF/complete

Annual compilation of detailed socioeconomic statistics for Kentucky. Data are shown primarily for 1980-82, with selected population trends from 1930 and projections to 2020. Most data are from specified State and Federal sources.

Report is designed to present a socioeconomic overview of the State by geographic area, including area development district, county, SMSA, and city. Various socioeconomic breakdowns are shown, as applicable, for most topics. These breakdowns include income, industry, commodity, race, urban-rural status, age, and sex.

Contains contents/table listing (2 p.); 4 maps and 48 tables, arranged in 5 sections, described below (p. 1-118); and definitions and index (p. 119-123).

This is the 20th edition.

Availability: Kentucky Department of Economic Development, Research and Planning Division, Capital Plaza Tower, Frankfort KY 40601, $4.00+$1.00 postage and handling; SRI/MF/complete.

TABLE SECTIONS:
[Some tables include comparisons to total U.S.]

S3104–1.1: State Data

(p. 3-11) Contains 14 tables. Includes population from 1930; housing construction; nonresidential construction value; U.S. CPI; unemployment rate; households and families; persons and families below poverty level; total and per capita personal income; nonfarm employment; manufacturing hours, earnings, production, value added, and shipment value; farm income; and mineral production and value.

S3104–1.2: Area Development District Data

(p. 15-19) Contains 5 tables. Includes land area; net migration; population projected to 2020; labor force, farm and nonfarm employment, and unemployment; and total and per capita personal income.

S3104–1.3: County Data

(p. 23-94) Contains 21 tables. Includes land area and county seat; net migration; percent individuals and families below poverty level; households, and average household size; persons in group quarters; population projected to 2020; labor force, farm and nonfarm employment, and unemployment; and covered wages and manufacturing employment.

Also includes total and per capita personal income; median family income for nonmetro counties; banks and deposits; motor vehicle registrations; and individual income tax and sales tax receipts, and property assessments.

S3104–1.4: SMSA and City Data

(p. 97-118) Contains 8 tables. Includes population by SMSA and component county; banks and deposits, median family income, and total and per capita personal income, all by SMSA; and population, households, average household size, and persons in group quarters, by city.

S3105   KENTUCKY
Administrative Office of the Courts

S3105–1   KENTUCKY COURT OF JUSTICE 1982-83 Annual Report
Annual. [1983.] 69 p.
SRI/MF/complete, current & previous year reports

Annual report, for FY83, on Kentucky judicial system, including trial and appellate court cases and dispositions. Covers supreme, appeals, circuit, and district courts. Includes data on trial court cases by type and court location, and selected trends from FY77.

Case types shown include criminal, civil, domestic relations, probate, adoption/termination, mental health, workers compensation, traffic, small claims, juvenile, and other.

Also includes data on judicial dept personnel, revenues, and expenditures; State law library reader services and staff attorney activities; pretrial services, including diversion, mediation, and interviewing activities; economical litigation project caseloads and impact on due process; judicial caseloads; and Judicial Retirement and Removal Commission cases and dispositions.

Contains narrative report, interspersed with 9 charts and 20 tables (p. 1-69).

Previous report, covering FY81-82, has also been received and is also available on SRI microfiche, under this number [Annual. [1983.] 59 p. †].

For description of report covering 1979-June 1980, see SRI 1981 Annual, under this number.

Availability: Kentucky Administrative Office of the Courts, 403 Wapping St., Frankfort KY 40601, †; SRI/MF/complete.

S3110   KENTUCKY
Department of
Education

S3110–1   PROFILES OF KENTUCKY PUBLIC SCHOOLS, FY83
Annual.   [1984.]   vii+140 p.
LC 70-649005.
SRI/MF/complete

Annual report presenting data for 17 indicators of public education quality in Kentucky, by school district and educational development region, 1982/83, with State averages, 1971/72-1982/83.

Contents:

a. Foreword and contents listing. (p. v-vii)

b. Introduction and methodology. (p. 1-5)

c. 17 indicators, listed below, repeated as follows: State averages and trends, 1971/72-1982/83, with 17 charts and 1 table (p. 7-26); and by educational development region and school district, including deviations from State averages, 1982/83, with 1 map and 18 tables (p. 29-140).

This is the 16th edition of the report. Profiles of individual school districts, as well as annual reports on detailed public school finances, are also available from the issuing agency but are not covered by SRI.

Availability: Kentucky Department of Education, Administrative Services Office, Capital Plaza Tower, Frankfort KY 40601, †; SRI/MF/complete.

INDICATORS:

[1] Annual current expenses per pupil in ADA [average daily attendance].

[2-3] Average annual salaries for classroom teachers; and percent supplement for instructional salaries.

[4] Percent of instructional staff with rank II or higher [standard certificate and master's degree or equivalent].

[5] Percent of 9th graders completing high school.

[6] Percent of attendance.

[7] Local financial index [ratio of local revenue per pupil to assessed value per pupil].

[8-9] Cost per pupil for educational materials and for instruction.

[10] Percent of instructional staff with less than rank III [not fully qualified].

[11] Pupil/teacher ratio.

[12] Percent of high school graduates entering college.

[13] Cost per pupil for administration.

[14-16] Percent of revenue from local, State, and Federal sources.

[17] Percent of economically deprived children.

S3110–2   SUPERINTENDENT OF PUBLIC INSTRUCTION BIENNIAL REPORT, 1981-83, Kentucky
Biennial.   For individual publication data, see below.
Vol. LI.
SRI/MF/complete

Biennial report, for academic years 1981/82-1982/83, on Kentucky public education, covering finances, enrollment, graduates, and personnel. Also includes data on special programs and services, and nonpublic schools.

Report is published in 2 volumes, a primarily narrative report and a statistical report, individually described below.

For description of report for 1979/80-1980/81 (Vol. XLIX), see SRI 1982 Annual, under this number. No Volume L was issued.

Availability: Kentucky Department of Education, Capital Plaza Tower, Frankfort KY 40601, †; SRI/MF/complete.

S3110–2.1: Part I. Narrative
[Biennial. [1984.] v+3+86 p. SRI/MF/complete.]

Contains State rankings table (inside front cover); contents listing (3 p.); and narrative report, in 7 chapters, interspersed with 11 charts and 34 tables showing the following:

a. Enrollment, school census, and average daily attendance; percent of 9th graders completing high school; States ranked by average SAT (Scholastic Aptitude Test) verbal and math scores; basic skills test scores for selected grades; dropout rate for grades 7-12; and holding power of public and nonpublic schools; various years 1969/70-1982/83. 5 charts and 4 tables. (p. 3-21)

b. Adult literacy rates for U.S., southern region, and 12 southern States, selected years 1900-80; adult education enrollment and performance, including citizenships received; and high school diplomas and GED (General Educational Development) certificates issued, various years 1973-83. 3 tables. (p. 22-23)

c. Classes taught by teachers out of their specialty fields vs. total classes (grades 7-8 and high school); math/science teacher education scholarship loan applicants, loans, and recipients by major field; college grads completing teacher education in science and math; and percent of school districts with computers for instructional use, by field; various periods 1971/72-1983/84. 2 charts and 2 tables. (p. 36-44)

d. Rehabilitation services clients served, costs per case, and client earnings; special education classrooms, by program and type of handicap; special education teacher traineeships awarded; and enrollment and cost per student at State schools for blind and deaf; various periods 1955/56-1982/83. 5 tables. (p. 46-51)

e. Vocational education funds by source, including Federal and State sources, FY81-83; membership in vocational education student organizations, June 30, 1983; and financial and operating summary, 1973/74-1982/83. 3 tables. (p. 52-58)

f. Personnel by position, by sex and race; average salaries and percent increases, by position; and teacher wages vs. wages in selected other occupations; various years 1973/74-1982/83. 2 charts and 2 tables. (p. 59-61)

g. Finances for local districts, including revenues by source, and expenditures by function and program; and education

appropriations, by school level; various years 1971/72-1982/83. 2 charts and 5 tables. (p. 63-67)

h. Schools and enrollment, public and nonpublic, by type of grade organization and enrollment size group; Education Dept buildings, by function; teachers, size, and costs for new/expanded educational facilities; school revenue bonds issued by district; national school lunch program participation, funding, and cost per pupil; surplus property acquisition costs; and health and life insurance costs; various periods 1973/74-1984. 10 tables. (p. 68-76)

S3110–2.2: Part II. Numbers
[Biennial. [1984.] 204 p. SRI/MF/complete.]

Contains table listing (1 p.); and 21 tables, listed below (p. 1-204).

FINANCES, STAFF, AND STUDENT SUMMARY

1. Summary of receipts and disbursements, FY82-83. (p. 1)

2-3. Summary of finance and pupil attendance and accounting reports, and district reports [income by source, expenditures by object, and building fund and Foundation Program capital outlay fund activity; pupil census, enrollment, promotions and retentions, year-end membership by sex, average daily attendance and membership, days taught, and number completing 8th and 12th grades; and certified and noncertified personnel, by position; shown for State and by school district], 1981/82-1982/83. (p. 2-182)

DETAILED STUDENT DATA

[Tables 4-11 and 13-20 show data aggregated for county and independent districts and total State.]

4-6. Number of children in the May 1, 1982 school census, by age, race, and sex. (p. 183-185)

7. Number of children from 6 to 17, inclusive, not in membership in any school [by] cause of nonmembership, [by race], May 1, 1982. (p. 186)

8. Enrollment by grades [and for exceptional children], for school year 1981/82. (p. 187)

9-10. Membership at close of school year, 1981/82, showing number promoted and retained [and membership by sex; both by grade]. (p. 188-189)

11. Number of high school graduates by sex and age, for school year 1981/82. (p. 190)

12. Nonpublic school attendance data [enrollment, membership at year end, average daily attendance and membership, and graduates of 8th and 12th grades, by public school districts], 1981/82. (p. 191)

13-21. [Tables 4-12 are repeated for 1982/83.]

S3130   KENTUCKY
Council on
Higher Education

S3130-1   FACTS ABOUT KENTUCKY PUBLIC HIGHER EDUCATION, 1982/83
Annual. [1983.] 29 p.
SRI/MF/complete

Annual report on Kentucky postsecondary education, covering enrollment, finances, degree programs, graduates, and staff, for public universities and community colleges, various years 1981-83.

Contains contents listing (1 p.); institution and education agency directories (p. 1-2); 15 tables, listed below (p. 3-16); and rosters of education officials, and institution descriptions (p. 17-29).

Availability: Kentucky Council on Higher Education, W. Frankfort Office Complex, U.S. 127 S., Frankfort KY 40601, †; SRI/MF/complete.

TABLES:
[All tables show data by university and community college system; tables on enrollment, degrees, and land holdings also show data by individual community college.]

[1-3] Headcount [full- and part-time], FTE [graduate and undergraduate], and resident and nonresident enrollment, fall 1982. (p. 3-7)

[4-5] Degrees and other formal awards conferred [by level], summer 1981-spring 1982; and numbers of degree programs, fall 1983. (p. 7-9)

[6] Faculty and staff [full- and part-time], fall 1982. (p. 10)

[7-8] Operating expenditures, and State operating budget support, FY82. (p. 11-12)

[9-10] State educational/general appropriations per FTE student, and capital construction expenditures, FY82. (p. 12)

[11-12] Education/general debt service, and auxiliary enterprise debt service (principal/interest), FY82. (p. 12-13)

[13] Operating budgets, FY83. (p. 13)

[14] Land holdings, fall 1983. (p. 13)

[15] Tuition/fees [resident and nonresident], 1982/83. (p. 15)

S3140   KENTUCKY
Cabinet for
Human Resources

S3140-1   1982 VITAL STATISTICS REPORT, Kentucky
Annual. [1984.]
vii+187 p.+addendum.
LC 51-61842.
SRI/MF/complete

Annual report on Kentucky vital statistics, covering 1981 population; and births, deaths by major cause, and marriages and divorces, with data by age, sex, race, and county, 1982 with trends from as early as 1940. Data are primarily from certificates filed with the State registrar of vital statistics.

Contains introduction, district map, and contents/table listing (p. i-vii); 4 sections, each preceded by narrative summary, with 11 summary charts, 1 chart showing percent of deaths from 5 leading causes for 1940 and 1982 (p. 105), and 36 tables listed below (p. 1-175); and appendix with definitions and 3 maps (p. 177-187).

Availability: Kentucky Cabinet for Human Resources, State Center for Health Statistics, Health Services Department, 275 E. Main St., Frankfort KY 40621, $15.00; SRI/MF/complete.

TABLES:
[Unless otherwise noted, data are for 1982 and are shown by district and county.]

POPULATION AND NATALITY
[Tables B1-B11 begin "Resident live births..."]

A1-A2. Population by race, sex, and age, 1981. (p. 3-10)

B1. By age of mother, number and rate, 1975 and 1980-82 [State only]. (p. 17)

B2-B5. By age of mother: by sex and race, trimester prenatal care began, legitimacy and race (with rate), and birthweight [all for State only]. (p. 21-29)

B6. By legitimacy and race, number and rate. (p. 31)

B7. By race and sex. (p. 37)

B8. By age of mother, number and rate. (p. 41-48)

B9. To teenage mothers by race and legitimacy. (p. 49-53)

B10. And stillbirths by trimester prenatal care began. (p. 55-59)

B11. By place of delivery and attendant at birth. (p. 61)

B12. Resident premature live births by age of mother. (p. 65)

B13. Selected resident birth data: [1st and 4th/over births, illegitimacy and fertility rates, and number and rate of births with congenital anomalies]. (p. 69-73)

B14-B15. Resident stillbirths and occurrence live births, by legitimacy and race, number and rate. (p. 75-82)

MORTALITY
[Tables show number and rate.]

C1. Resident live births; and deaths: fetal, infant, neonatal, and maternal; [State only], 1950-82. (p. 87)

C2. Resident deaths by age group, [State only], selected years 1950-82]. (p. 91)

C3-C6. Resident deaths from malignant neoplasms, heart disease, accidents, and suicide, [State only], 1950-82. (p. 95-101)

C7. Leading causes of resident deaths by age group [State only]. (p. 103)

C8. Leading causes of resident deaths by sex and race [State only]. (p. 107)

C9-C10. Resident deaths by race, sex, and age group. (p. 109-120)

C11. Resident birth-related and infant deaths. (p. 121)

C12. Leading causes of resident deaths. (p. 125-142)

C13-C16. Resident deaths from: accidents and suicide by age group, accidents by type, and malignant neoplasms by category. (p. 143-162)

C17. Occurrence deaths by race. (p. 163-166)

MARRIAGE AND DIVORCE
[Tables show number and rate.]

D1. Marriages and divorces [State only], 1965-82. (p. 169)

D2. Marriages and divorces by race. (p. 171-175)

S3140-2   PUBLIC ASSISTANCE IN KENTUCKY
Monthly, with annual summary. Approx. 150 p.
PA-264 Rpt. Series.
LC 73-648644.
SRI/MF/complete

Monthly report on Kentucky public assistance program recipients and payments, by program, type of service, and county. Programs covered include AFDC, Medicaid, and State supplementation to aged, blind, and disabled.

Report is issued 2-5 months after month of coverage.

Contains narrative summary and history of programs, contents and table listing, and 24 monthly tables listed below.

Publication of this report was suspended following the Nov. 1983 issue, due to computer problems. Back data will be issued when publication resumes.

Availability: Kentucky Cabinet for Human Resources, Social Insurance Department, Management and Development Division, 275 E. Main St., Frankfort KY 40621, †; SRI/MF/complete.

Issues reviewed during 1984: July-Nov. 1983 (D).

MONTHLY TABLES:
[All data are for month of coverage and appear in all issues. Most tables show data by program or service, by county, and include State guardianship cases.]

PART A: SUMMARY

1. Grand total public assistance payments: money payments and vendor medical payments.

2. Grand total eligible recipients, by eligibility factor: categorically needy and medically needy.

PART B: AFDC

[1] Recipients and payments: money payment cases.

PART C: STATE SUPPLEMENTATION TO AGED, BLIND, AND DISABLED

[1] Recipients and payments, by eligibility factor and type of need: money payment cases: State funds only.

PART D: TITLE XIX, MEDICAID

[All tables except table 2 show data by type of medical service, including hospital, nursing home, physician, drugs, dental, screening, clinic, mental health facilities, lab/X-ray, home health, family planning, and ambulance. Tables 5-12.5 begin "Medicaid payments to..."]

1-1A. State total utilizers (recipients) and utilization rates; and Medicaid payments and average payments per utilizer: categorically needy and medically needy.

2. Utilizers (recipients), by eligibility factor: categorically needy and medically needy.

3. Utilizers (recipients): categorically needy/medically needy.

4. Summary of Title XIX, Medicaid payments: categorically needy/medically needy.

5-7. Aged, blind, and disabled, categorically needy cases: receives Title XVI/SSI/State supplementation.

8-8.2. Families with dependent children, categorically needy cases: receives Title IV AFDC (basic/foster care, death/absence/incapacity, and foster care).

9-11. Aged, blind, and disabled: medically needy cases.

12-12.2. Families with children [aggregate]; basic [medical assistance] families with children (death/absence/incapacity of parent); and families with unemployed parents (Federal definition of unemployment): medically needy cases.

12.3-12.5. Children in foster care (non-AFDC), from AFDC families, and in medical institutions: medically needy cases.

S3150   KENTUCKY
Department of
Justice

S3150–1   1983 UNIFORM CRIME REPORTS, Commonwealth of Kentucky
Annual. [1984.] 7+117 p.
SRI/MF/complete

Annual report, for 1983, presenting detailed data on Kentucky crimes and arrests, by type of offense. Includes data on crime trends, clearances, victim and offender characteristics, value of stolen property, law enforcement employment, and assaults on police. Selected data are shown by location and by victim and offender age, sex, and race.

Data are from reports of State and local law enforcement agencies, submitted to the State police under the Uniform Crime Reporting Program.

Contains crime clock (1 p.); contents listing (2 p.); introduction and methodology, with 1 table showing Kentucky population by area development district, 1980 and 1983 (p. 1-11); and report in 3 sections, with narrative summaries, and 9 charts and 41 tables described below (p. 14-115).

This is the 14th annual report.

Availability: Kentucky Department of Justice, State Police Bureau, Information Systems Section, 1250 Louisville Rd., Frankfort KY 40601, †; SRI/MF/complete.

CHARTS AND TABLES:
[Data are for 1983, with selected trends from 1974. Index (Part I) crimes are murder, rape, robbery, aggravated assault, burglary, larceny, and auto theft. Part II crimes include approximately 20 other categories.

Data by district are shown for 15 area development districts. Data by ethnic origin are for Hispanics and non-Hispanics.]

S3150–1.1: Index Offenses

STATE SUMMARY
a. Part I crimes: offenses by district, and rates and percent cleared, by offense; and total offenses. 4 tables. (p. 14-17)

BY LOCATION
b. Index offenses by detailed type, with summary crime and/or clearance rates, by county and city. 2 tables. (p. 18-39)

INDIVIDUAL OFFENSES
[Data for each type of offense include 2 tables showing offenses and rate; and arrestees, by age, sex, race, and ethnic origin; all by district. Additional data are noted below.]

c. Murder: offenders by relationship to victim and whether known or suspected felony involved; victims by age, cross-tabulated by type of weapon, sex, race (including American Indian/Alaskan Native and Asian/Pacific Islander), and ethnic origin. 5 tables. (p. 41-45)

d. Rape. 2 tables. (p. 47-49)

e. Robbery: offenses and value of property stolen, by place of occurrence. 3 tables. (p. 51-53)

f. Aggravated assault: distribution of offenses by type of weapon; and assaults on police, by time of day, and type of activity and weapon. 5 charts and 2 tables. (p. 55-60)

g. Burglary: offenses and value of property stolen, by day and night residential and nonresidential occurrence. 3 tables. (p. 61-63)

h. Larceny: value of property stolen and recovered, by type of property; and offenses and value of property stolen, by type of theft. 4 tables. (p. 64-67)

i. Auto theft. 2 tables. (p. 69-71)

S3150–1.2: Arrests

a. Distribution of gambling arrests, by type; arrests by Part I and Part II offense, by age, sex, race (including American Indian/Alaskan Native and Asian/Pacific Islander), and ethnic origin; and drug arrests, by county and substance. 2 charts and 9 tables. (p. 75-88)

b. Arrests by county, by Part I and Part II offense; and Part I clearance rates by offense, clearances by district, and percent juvenile and adult clearances by district and offense. 1 chart and 3 tables. (p. 90-103)

S3150–1.3: Law Enforcement Employment and Identification Activity

a. Municipal police, sheriff dept, and State and county police officers and civilian employees, by jurisdiction. 3 tables. (p. 106-114)

b. Kentucky State Police Information Systems Section latent fingerprint cases received and identifications made. 1 chart. (p. 115)

S3150–2   KENTUCKY TRAFFIC ACCIDENT FACTS, 1983
Annual. [1984.] 3+28 p.
SRI/MF/complete

Annual report on Kentucky traffic accident fatalities and injuries, by detailed accident and vehicle type, location, time, and other circumstances; and driver and victim characteristics; 1983, with trends from 1948.

Also includes data on licensed drivers, miles traveled, safety equipment use, and alcohol involvement in fatal accidents.

Report is compiled from law enforcement agency accident reports to the State Police.

Contains contents listing (1 p.); 24 charts and 15 tables, with interspersed narrative and text data (p. 1-27); and definitions (p. 28).

Availability: Kentucky Department of Justice, State Police Bureau, Information Systems Section, 1250 Louisville Rd., Frankfort KY 40601, †; SRI/MF/complete.

S3165   KENTUCKY
Department for
Libraries and Archives

S3165–1   STATISTICAL REPORT OF KENTUCKY PUBLIC LIBRARIES, FY83
Annual. Feb. 1984. 32 p.
SRI/MF/complete

Annual report on Kentucky public library finances and operations, for FY83. Data are from public library annual reports.

Contains contents listing (1 p.); and the following data:

a. State summary library data, FY80-83; library grants by type and congressional district, and county rankings by selected library indicators, FY83; and population, by county, 1980. 7 tables. (p. 1, 3-8)

b. By county and State region: library income by source, salaries of director and bookmobile librarian, expenditures by object, employees, volunteers, hours, branches, bookmobiles, interlibrary loan activity, complaints about materials, removal of materials from shelf as result of complaints, book holdings, registered borrowers, circulation of books and audiovisual materials, and programs and participants; and tax rates; FY83. 1 extended table. (p. 9-31)

Also includes definitions (p. 2); and county index (p. 32).

Availability: Kentucky Department for Libraries and Archives, Field Services Division, PO Box 537, Frankfort KY 40602-0537, †; SRI/MF/complete.

S3175   KENTUCKY
Department of
Mines and Minerals

S3175–1   ANNUAL REPORT OF THE DEPARTMENT OF MINES AND MINERALS, Commonwealth of Kentucky, for the Year Ending Dec. 31, 1983
Annual. [1984.] 6+180 p.
LC GS 15-945.
SRI/MF/complete, current & previous year reports

Annual report, by Willard Stanley, on Kentucky Dept of Mines and Minerals programs and activities, 1983. Includes data on coal mine production, employment, and safety, by mine and county, with selected historical trends. Also includes data on clay mines, and oil and gas wells and drilling permits.

Data were compiled from mine reports and other industry sources.

Contains introduction with 1 summary table on coal production, contents listing, and directories of mining-related assns and agencies (6 p.); and 7 report sections, including text statistics and 29 tables, as follows:

COAL MINE SECTION

a. Coal mine statistics, with 10 tables on inspection and licensing activities, production, employment, number of active and abandoned mines, fatalities by cause, and tons mined per fatality; shown variously by mine type, county, and inspection district, mostly for 1983, with selected trends from as early as 1890. (p. 2-12)

b. Coal mine inspection districts, with 2 tables repeated for each of 6 districts showing selected summary data for the district and each county, and the following for individual mines: company, location, mine type, production, employment, days worked, seam and height, and fatal and nonfatal accidents, 1983. (p. 17-125)

OTHER DEPT SECTIONS

c. Clay mining section, including 2 tables showing total production, 1982-83; production by county, 1983; and location, company, and employment, for individual mines, 1983. (p. 126-128)

d. Safety and casualty section, including directory of mine rescue stations, text data on mine fires and explosions, and list of rescue simulation contest winners. (p. 129-135)

e. Miner training, education, and certification section, with 1 table showing number of 1983 certificates issued, by type; and lists of certificate recipients. (p. 137-160)

f. Mine safety analysis and explosives and blasting sections, with 1 table showing number of blasters by county, 1983. (p. 163-172)

g. Oil and gas conservation section, with 3 tables showing number and status of oil and gas wells, and drilling permits issued by county, 1983. (p. 175-180)

This is the 104th edition of the report.

Previous report, for 1982, was also reviewed in 1984 and is also available on SRI microfiche under this number [Annual. [1983.] 6+185 p. $15.00].

Availability: Kentucky Department of Mines and Minerals, PO Box 680, Lexington KY 40586, $15.00; SRI/MF/complete.

S3195   KENTUCKY
Public Service Commission

S3195-1   TWENTY-FIFTH BIENNIAL REPORT OF THE PUBLIC SERVICE COMMISSION of Kentucky, July 1, 1981-June 30, 1983
Biennial.   June 1984.
2+37 p.
LC 38-28710.
SRI/MF/complete

Biennial report presenting Kentucky public utility financial and operating summaries for 1981-82, and regulatory data for FY82-83 biennium, by type of utility. Covers customers by sector, revenue/income by source, and operating expenses by item; number of utilities; and regulatory orders by case type, with value for orders involving securities, rates, and construction.

Utility types include investor-owned electric and water companies, rural electric cooperative generators and distributors, gas companies/districts, radio-telephone, telephone companies/rural telephone cooperatives, water districts/assns, and sewer companies/districts.

Data were compiled by the Commission.

Contains introduction (p. 1-7); and narrative report, interspersed with 9 charts and 12 tables (p. 8-37).

For description of the 24th biennial report, see SRI 1982 Annual, under this number.

Availability: Kentucky Public Service Commission, 730 Schenkel Lane, PO Box 615, Frankfort KY 40602, †; SRI/MF/complete.

S3265   LOUISIANA
Department of Commerce

S3265-1   REPORTS OF THE STATE BANKS, SAVINGS AND LOAN ASSOCIATIONS, CREDIT UNIONS, CONSUMER CREDIT, AND SALE OF CHECKS in the State of Louisiana
Annual.   [1984.]   448 p.
LC 81-643716.
SRI/MF/complete

Annual report on financial condition of Louisiana State-chartered banks, savings and loan assns, and credit unions, presenting assets, liabilities, and equity or net worth, by institution arranged by city, as of Dec. 31, 1983.

Also includes regulatory activities; number of banks with Federal Reserve System and FDIC membership; branch facilities and capital stock increases for selected institutions; composite bank operating ratios, income and expenses, and loans outstanding by type; consumer credit supervised lenders' composite assets, liabilities, income, and expenses; and Sale of Checks Act licensees and branches.

Contains bank section, with 7 tables (p. 5-244); savings and loan assn and credit union sections, with 2 tables (p. 246-408); and consumer credit division and Sale of Checks Act sections, including supervised lenders directory, and 2 tables (p. 410-448).

Availability: Louisiana Department of Commerce, Financial Institutions Office, PO Box 44095, Capitol Station, Baton Rouge LA 70804, $10.00; SRI/MF/complete.

S3275   LOUISIANA
Department of Culture, Recreation, and Tourism

S3275-1   PUBLIC LIBRARIES IN LOUISIANA, Statistical Report, 1983
Annual.   [1984.]   36 p.
LC 57-36645.
SRI/MF/complete

Annual report on Louisiana public library personnel, operations, holdings, circulation, and finances, by library, 1983.

Contains contents listing, and list of parishes (p. 2-3); 9 tables, listed below (p. 4-33); and glossary (p. 34-36).

Availability: Louisiana Department of Culture, Recreation, and Tourism, State Library Office, PO Box 131, Baton Rouge LA 70821, ‡; SRI/MF/complete.

TABLES:

[Data are for 1983. Tables 1-7 show data by parish and for 3 municipalities.]

1. Library profile [includes population and land area served, branches, deposit stations, bookmobiles, and holdings by type of material]. (p. 4-11)

2. Additions to resources (gross) [by type of material]. (p. 12)

3. Library use: loan transactions [by type of distribution and material, and interlibrary loans]. (p. 14)

4. Operating receipts, by source [includes local and Federal funds by type, gifts, and State aid]. (p. 18)

5. Operating expenditures, by purpose [salaries and related costs, materials by type, and other]. (p. 22)

6. Capital project fund [expenditures, by object]. (p. 26)

7. Personnel [work week; head librarian salary; FTE librarians and library associates, and lowest and highest salaries paid; and total FTE staff]. (p. 28)

8-9. Library systems: services [including requests received and filled, borrowers' cards issued, and books loaned]; and operating expenditures, by purpose; [all by library system]. (p. 32-33)

S3280
Department of
Education

LOUISIANA

S3280–1   LOUISIANA DEPARTMENT OF EDUCATION One Hundred Thirty-Fourth Annual Report, Session 1982/83
Annual. [1983.] ix+311 p.
Bull. 1472.
LC E11-207.
SRI/MF/complete

Annual report, for 1982/83 school year, on Louisiana public and nonpublic schools, with enrollment projections through 1986/87, and selected U.S. comparisons and trends from mid-1970s or earlier. Includes enrollment, dropouts, graduates, personnel, facilities, transportation, food services, finances, and special programs, shown for the State and by parish/city school district. Most data on students and personnel are shown by race.

Data are compiled from reports by parish and city school systems and by divisions of the State Dept of Education, and from National Education Assn, NCES publications, and other sources.

Contains listings of contents, tables, charts, and school district profiles (p. iii-ix); narrative State summary and comparisons to the U.S., with illustrative charts/tables, and 57 summary tables listed below (p. 1-101); State and 66 parish/city district profiles, each with 19 tables, also listed below (p. 103-306); and index (p. 307-311).

Availability: Louisiana Department of Education, Research and Development Office, Research Bureau, PO Box 44064, Baton Rouge LA 70804, †; SRI/MF/complete.

TABLES:

S3280–1.1: Students, Personnel, and Programs

POPULATION CHARACTERISTICS

I.1. Population of parishes, 1970 and final 1980. (p. 10)

I.2. Percent [of] families in poverty [by parish, 1969 and 1979]. (p. 11)

I.3-I.4. Birth rates per 1,000 population, and estimated school-age (5-17) population as percent of total population; [U.S. and Louisiana, various years 1960-82]. (p. 12)

I.5. Comparison of Louisiana and the U.S.: population characteristics [school-age children per 100 adults, 1982; migration rate, 1970-79 period; population changes, 1972-82 period; percent of population with high school diplomas, with college education, and lacking 5th grade education, 1980; and median school years completed, 1976]. (p. 13)

STUDENT CHARACTERISTICS

I.6. Student registration [by race], with percent increase or decrease over previous year, public and nonpublic, 1973/74-1982/83. (p. 14)

I.7-I.8. Public/nonpublic student registration in elementary, secondary, kindergarten, and special education; and registration by grade level, [various years] 1973/74-1986/87. (p. 15-16)

I.9. Trends in average daily membership (ADM), average daily attendance (ADA), and percent attendance, for public schools, 1973/74-1982/83. (p. 17)

I.10-I.11. Enrollment [secondary and adult] in vocational education programs, 1973/74-1982/83; and adult basic education and Act 43 adult education programs [including student average age, enrollment by sex and race, achievement, and dropouts], 1974/75-1982/83. (p. 18-19)

I.12. Comparison of Louisiana and the U.S.: enrollment and attendance [1981-1982/83]. (p. 20)

RETENTION, DROPOUTS, AND GRADUATES

II.1. Comparison of Louisiana and the U.S.: estimated U.S. and actual Louisiana retention rates, 5th grade through high school graduation, in public/nonpublic schools, selected years [fall 1968-72]. (p. 25)

II.2-II.4. Trends in public school dropouts [number by race, 1973/74-1982/83]; and comparison of white and nonwhite dropouts by age and grade level, and on selected dimensions [parent's education, student's scholastic rating and extracurricular activities, and school's evaluation of reasons for dropouts], 1982/83. (p. 26-27)

II.5-II.7. Comparison of white and nonwhite suspension and expulsions, public schools [includes registration, students suspended and expelled, students suspended 2 and 3/more times, days suspended, and total suspensions]; and most frequent reasons for suspension/expulsion, white and nonwhite students; 1982/83. (p. 28-29)

II.8. Number of high school graduates [by race], with percent increase or decrease over previous year, public and nonpublic, 1973/74-1982/83. (p. 30)

ACHIEVEMENT TESTS

II.9-II.10. Comparisons of Louisiana and national ACT [American College Test] scores for freshmen, 1972/73-1982/83; and comparison of Louisiana and national students' satisfaction with various aspects of local high schools, 1983 ACT data. (p. 31-32)

II.11. Comparisons of Louisiana and national SAT [Scholastic Aptitude Test] scores for freshmen, 1973/74-1982/83. (p. 33)

PERSONNEL

III.1-III.2. Professional and nonprofessional personnel in the public school systems, 1973/74-1982/83; [and by position and sex], 1982/83. (p. 39)

III.3. Sex and race of public school principals and classroom teachers, 1974/75-1982/83. (p. 40)

III.4-III.5. Professional training of public school instructional staff [number of teachers/principals, by years of college completed or degree held], 1974/75-1982/83; and total experience of principals/teachers in public school systems, 1973/74-1982/83. (p. 41-42)

III.6. Average annual salaries of public school teachers and principals [by race], 1973/74-1982/83. (p. 43)

III.7-III.8. Student/teacher ratios for public schools, accompanied by student registration and number of teachers [by grade level, and for special education], 1982/83; and comparison of Louisiana and the U.S.: pupils enrolled per teacher in public elementary/secondary schools, [biennially] fall 1972-82. (p. 44-45)

III.9. Staff characteristics [including instructional and noninstructional FTE staff, 1981; pupil/teacher ratios, 1982; and percent male teachers and average teacher salary, 1982/83]. (p. 46)

S3280–1.2: Facilities and Finances

FACILITIES

IV.1-IV.3. Number of public and nonpublic schools; inventory of public school property [number and cost of buildings and sites, and cost of equipment]; and public school libraries [number of libraries, full- and part-time librarians, and books, value of books/equipment, and total expenses; all] 1973/74-1982/83. (p. 50-51)

IV.4-IV.6. Percentage distribution of class size, and mean class size, by classroom type [regular, ungraded, special and compensatory education, vocational education, and other], elementary and secondary grade levels, 1982/83. (p. 52-53)

FINANCES

V.1-V.2B. Revenue from local, State, and Federal sources for education, 1977/78-1982/83; and revenue from ESEA [Elementary and Secondary Education Act] Title I funds, 1973/74-1982/83. and ECIA [Education Consolidation and Improvement Act] funds, 1982/83. (p. 59-60)

V.3. Minimum Foundation Program [including costs and local support], 1973/74-1982/83. (p. 61)

V.4-V.7. Expenditure of all State revenues (State revenues/Federal grants), and of State revenues, by function of State government, 1972/73-1982/83; education expenditure, by function, 1978/79-1982/83; and expenditures per pupil, 1973/74-1982/83. (p. 62-65)

V.8-V.9. State and Federal expenditures for special education and vocational education programs, 1973/74-1982/83. (p. 66-67)

V.10-V.11. State totals for bonded and other debt, 1980/81-1982/83; and total ending balances for cash, petty cash, and investments [as of June 30, 1982-83]; for parish/city school systems. (p. 68)

V.12. Revenues and expenditures [by function and detailed object] for the Dept of Education, FY83. (p. 69-76)

V.13. Comparison of Louisiana and U.S.: general financial resources and government revenue [including per capita personal income, and personal income per school-aged child, 1981; and per capita State/local government general and property tax revenues, 1980/81]. (p. 77)

V.14. Comparison of Louisiana and the U.S.: school revenues [per pupil; and distribution by local, State, and Federal source]; based on 2 independent national reports [1982/83]. (p. 78)

V.15. Comparison of Louisiana and national direct expenditures for all government functions and for education, by per capita amount and percent of per capita income, 1973-81. (p. 79)

V.16. Comparison of Louisiana and the U.S.: current expenditure per pupil in ADA and ADM [1981/82-1982/83]. (p. 80)

V.17. Louisiana and national percentage distribution of school districts, by core current expenditure per pupil, school year ending 1980. (p. 80)

V.18. Summary of Louisiana and national expenditure, by specific purpose, for public elementary/secondary education, as percentage of total expenditure, 1979/80. (p. 81)

S3280-1.3: Parish/City School District Profiles

[Tables are repeated for total State and each parish/city school district. District profiles also include names of superintendent and school board chairperson, number of school board members, square mile area, and number of school days. Data are for 1982/83, unless otherwise noted.

Data by ethnicity are for American Indian, Asian, black, Hispanic, and white.]

1. Student registration [by] ethnicity and sex [for public and nonpublic schools].

2-3. Public and nonpublic student registration [by grade and for special education, and graduates, actual 1982/83 and (except for special education) projected 1983/84-1986/87].

4. Membership at end of session, ADM, and ADA [public and nonpublic, by grade level].

5. Number of high school graduates [public and nonpublic, by ethnicity and sex].

6. Dropouts from public schools [by ethnicity, by grade and for special education and kindergarten].

7. Number and type of public schools in terms of pupil registration [by grade level].

8. Public staff information [by ethnicity, sex, and position].

9. Number and type of nonpublic schools.

10. Experience of public teachers [number of elementary and secondary teachers in each category of experience].

11. Pupils in membership being served by exceptional children program [by grade level, by type of handicap, and for gifted children].

12. Basic skills and State assessment results [reading, math, and writing; grades 2,3, 7, and 10].

13-16. Sources of revenue, expenditures [by function], and school system bonded status and taxation.

17. School food services [meals served, Federal reimbursements, and State/local support, all for public and nonpublic schools].

18. School transportation [buses, public and nonpublic pupils transported, miles driven, and cost].

19. [Other data and] rankings [amounts and, for parishes, rank among parishes, for expenditure per pupil; public school pupil/teacher ratios, percent of graduates continuing education, mean salary of teachers, and teacher/administrator ratio; assessed property valuation per student; and 1980 and 1981 per capita income; 1981/82-1982/83].

S3285   LOUISIANA
Office of the Governor

S3285-2   STATE OF LOUISIANA ANNUAL FINANCIAL REPORT, June 30, 1983
Annual.   Mar. 5, 1984.
13+110+3 p.
SRI/MF/complete

Annual report on financial condition of Louisiana State government, presenting assets and liabilities, reserves, and fund balances; revenues by source; and expenditures by function; for general, special purpose, capital projects, debt service, enterprise, trust, and agency funds; FY83 with summary trends from FY74.

Also includes data on bonded indebtedness, with selected detail by State-supported postsecondary institution.

Contains contents listing and summary, with text data (16 p.); 3 statistical sections, with 4 charts and 44 financial statements (p. 1-110); and index (3 p.).

Availability: Louisiana Office of the Governor, Administration Division, State Accounting Office, State Capitol Bldg., PO Box 44095, Baton Rouge LA 70804, ‡; SRI/MF/complete.

S3285-4   LOUISIANA: TRENDS, 1983 Edition
Monograph.   May 1983.
5+70 p.
LC 83-622407.
SRI/MF/complete

Compilation of demographic, economic, and governmental statistics for Louisiana. Data are primarily for 1977-82, with selected trends from the 1960s. Most data are from Federal and State government sources.

Contains preface and contents and table listing (5 p.); and 29 illustrative charts, and 75 tables arranged in 9 sections described below (p. 1-70).

Availability: Louisiana Office of the Governor, State Planning Office, PO Box 44426, Baton Rouge LA 70804, †; SRI/MF/complete.

TABLES:
[Tables show data for Louisiana, with occasional comparisons to total U.S.. Tables are often accompanied by illustrative charts. Data sources appear beneath each table.]

SOCIAL AND ECONOMIC DATA

a. **Socioeconomics:** population, per capita personal income, unemployment rate, labor force, median weekly earnings, and nonagricultural employment by industry division. Tables I.1-I.8. (p. 1-8)

b. **Commerce:** tax exempt and bonded industrial investment; investment under State inducement programs, by selected SIC 2-digit industry; oil and gas industry employment by sector; and manufacturing and nonmanufacturing employment, and distribution by industry division. Tables II.1-II.5. (p. 9-14)

c. **Transportation:** foreign and domestic waterborne trade, by port and commodity, with foreign trade value for New Orleans; aircraft landing facilities; passenger enplanements for 7 major airports; traffic accidents, injuries, fatalities, and citations/arrests; and truck

weighing activity, and oversize and overweight permits issued. Tables III.1-III.8. (p. 15-20)

d. **Natural Resources and Energy:** surface and groundwater use by purpose; oil, gas, and dry wells completed, and permits issued; oil and gas production; severance tax revenues from selected resources; revenues from mineral production on State property; energy consumption by sector; commercial fish harvest by species; and trapping activity and licenses issued. Tables IV.1-IV.12. (p. 21-32)

GOVERNMENT, VITAL STATISTICS, AND EDUCATION

e. **Government:** Includes State government revenues by source, and expenditures by agency and function; tax collections by type; bond sales, capital outlays, debt service costs, and debt outstanding; Federal aid by function; unemployment insurance claimants, exhaustees, and payments; registered voters by race and party; and State legislators by party. Tables VI.1-VI.10. (p. 33-42)

f. **Vital Statistics, Human Services, and Housing:** births; deaths by leading cause; infant mortality rates; reportable disease cases; marriages and divorces; hospitals and beds, by type of control; health care admissions by facility type; and new housing units for 7 major cities. Tables VI.1-VI.9. (p. 43-50)

g. **Education:** private and public enrollment by level; high school graduates; dropouts by race; per pupil expenditures; college entrance test scores; teachers/principals by years of experience, and average salaries; education revenues by government level; special, vocational, and postsecondary enrollment; and postsecondary degrees conferred. Tables VII.1-VII.14. (p. 51-61)

CRIMINAL JUSTICE AND RECREATION

h. **Crimes and Courts:** Index crimes and rates; and court cases filed in State supreme, district, and family/juvenile courts. Tables VIII.1-VIII.5. (p. 62-66)

i. **Tourism and Recreation:** visitors to State tourist information centers by site; travel generated expenditures, payroll, employment, and State and local tax receipts; fishing, hunting, and trapping licenses sold; and motorboat registrations. Tables IX.1-IX.4. (p. 67-70)

S3295   LOUISIANA
Department of Health and Human Resources

S3295-1   1980 VITAL STATISTICS of Louisiana
Annual.   [1984.]
xviii+107 p.
ISSN 0460-1009.
LC 74-646004.
SRI/MF/complete

Annual report, for 1980, on Louisiana vital statistics, covering population, births, deaths by cause, morbidity, marriages, and divorces. Data are shown by age group, race, sex, parish, city, State planning district, and health service area. Most data are from State records.

Contains contents and table listings, and 1 map (2 p.); and the following:

a. Narrative introduction with definitions, and 4 tables showing U.S. deaths and infant deaths according to the International Classification of Diseases, 8th and 9th Revisions, 1976; and Louisiana population by race, by planning district and parish, 1970 and 1980, with data for total State by age and sex, 1980. (p. i-ix)

b. Summary, with 4 charts, and 5 tables showing the following, generally for U.S. and Louisiana, 1980: percent of low weight births, by age and race of mother; illegitimate birth rates and reported abortions, by age of mother; death rates for 9 leading causes; and infant mortality rates, by selected cause. (p. x-xviii)

c. 36 tables, listed below, arranged in 5 sections. (p. 1-107)

Previous report, for 1979, is described in SRI 1982 Annual, under this number.

A semiannual report presenting provisional data on births, deaths by cause, and morbidity, by parish and/or city, is also available from the issuing agency, but is not covered by SRI.

Availability: Louisiana Department of Health and Human Resources, Public Health Statistics, PO Box 60630, New Orleans LA 70160, †; SRI/MF/complete.

TABLES:

[All data are for 1980. "A" and "B" versions of tables show data by parish, State planning district, and health service area. Data by major city are for cities with over 10,000 population.]

S3295–1.1: Natality

I.A-I.B. Live births by place of occurrence, reallocated to mother's usual residence and shown by age of mother, and by sex and race of child. (p. 1-6)

II. Live births by place of occurrence [parish and major city], reallocated to mother's usual residence and shown by sex of child, race, and attendant [physician, midwife, and other]. (p. 7)

III. Live births showing hospital in which birth occurred, by sex and race. (p. 8)

IV. Congenital anomalies specified on birth certificates, shown by type of anomaly and age of mother. (p. 12)

V. Immature births [by race, sex, and weight group], showing hospital in which birth occurred. (p. 13-17)

VI. Live births by birth order by weight of child. (p. 18)

VII. Live births by weight of child, shown by sex and race. (p. 18)

VIII. Live births by birth weight, age of mother, and race of child. (p. 19)

IX. Live births by birth order, shown by age of mother and race of child. (p. 20)

X.A-X.B. Illegitimate births by place of occurrence, reallocated to mother's usual residence and shown by age of mother and race of child. (p. 21-25)

S3295–1.2: Mortality and Morbidity

FETAL MORTALITY

XI.A-XI.B. Stillbirths by place of occurrence, reallocated to mother's usual residence and shown by age of mother, by race. (p. 27-31)

XII. Stillbirths shown by selected causes, age of mother, and race of child. (p. 32)

XIII-XIX. Reported induced terminations of pregnancy occurring in Louisiana: by parish of residence and occurrence; by woman's State of residence; by weeks of gestation, [by] woman's age and race, and type of procedure; and by woman's age and marital status, [by] race. (p. 28-37)

OTHER MORTALITY

XX.A-XX.B. Deaths (exclusive of stillbirths) by place of occurrence, reallocated to usual residence of the deceased and shown by sex, race, and age [includes data by major city]. (p. 39-46)

XXI. Deaths showing hospital in which death occurred, by age. (p. 47-51)

XXII. Principal causes of death, by parish. (p. 52)

XXIII. Deaths (exclusive of stillbirths) shown by selected causes, sex, race, and age. (p. 54-79)

XXIV. Accidental deaths by type of accident [motor vehicle, home, occupational, other public, and not stated], shown by geographic location where accident occurred [parish and major city]. (p. 80)

XXV.A-XXV.B. Infant deaths (exclusive of stillbirths) by place of occurrence, reallocated to mother's usual residence and shown by sex, race, and age [includes data by major city]. (p. 81-88)

XXVI. Infant mortality rates by place of residence, shown by age at death and race, by State planning district and health service areas. (p. 89)

XXVII. Infant deaths (exclusive of stillbirths) shown by selected causes, sex, race, and age. (p. 90-94)

XXVIII. Maternal deaths by place of occurrence [parish], reallocated to usual residence of deceased and shown by race and age. (p. 95)

XXIX. Maternal deaths by cause, shown by race and age. (p. 96)

MORBIDITY

XXX-XXXI. Reportable diseases by parish [and major city], and by race and age. (p. 97-104)

S3295–1.3: Marriage and Divorce

XXXII. Marriages, final divorces, and annulments granted [by parish]. (p. 105)

XXXIII-XXXV. Marriages, by month of occurrence; and by race [including American Indian, Chinese, Japanese, and other] and previous marital status of bride and groom. (p. 106)

XXXVI. All marriages by age of bride, by age of groom. (p. 107)

S3320   LOUISIANA
Department of Labor

S3320–1   ANNUAL PLANNING REPORT for Louisiana
Annual. Sept. 1984. 88 p.
SRI/MF/complete

Annual planning report identifying Louisiana population groups most in need of employment services, primarily 1982-83, with some data for 1st half 1984 and trends from 1965. Also includes data on labor force, personal income, employment by industry, insured unemployed, State job service activity, and employment projections.

Data are from Employment Security Automated Reporting System and other sources.

Contains contents listing (1 p.); State description (p. 2-3); population summary, with 1 map and 1 table (p. 6-9); and 11 sections, with 33 tables, sources of labor market information, and definitions (p. 12-88). All tables are listed below.

Availability: Louisiana Department of Labor, Employment Security Office, Research and Statistics Unit, Rm. 220, PO Box 44094, Baton Rouge LA 70804-9094, †; SRI/MF/complete.

TABLES:

[Data are shown for Louisiana, unless otherwise noted.]

S3320–1.1: Population and Labor Force Characteristics

[1] [Parishes with over 100,000 population and their largest cities, and total State population, 1983.] (p. 9)

[2] Unemployment rates [for State and U.S., with State ranking, 1971-83]. (p. 12)

[3] Unemployment rates (not seasonally adjusted), statewide and national [1982 and monthly 1983]. (p. 13)

[4] Total personal and per capita income [1965-83]. (p. 14)

[5] CPI [for all urban consumers and urban wage/clerical workers, total U.S., 1967-83 and monthly Dec. 1982-Aug. 1984]. (p. 15)

[6-7] 1983 population estimates [by race, sex, minority status, parish, and Labor Market Area (LMA)]. (p. 18-19)

[8] Occupational breakout of civilian labor force by sex and [minority status], 1983. (p. 20)

[9] Labor force summary [showing labor force by employment status, monthly] 1970-83. (p. 22)

[10-11] Nonagricultural wage/salary employment [by selected industry division and group, monthly 1982-83]. (p. 24-27)

[12-14] Average earnings and hours of production workers in manufacturing [groups] and mining, and nonsupervisory workers in other selected industries [monthly 1983]. (p. 28-30)

S3320–1.2: Insured Unemployed, Job Service Applicants and Openings, Local Labor Force, and Employment Projections

1-6. Insured unemployed: by age, industry [division], and occupation [cross-tabulated by race and sex; and by industry division [cross-tabulated by] duration of unemployment and weekly benefit amount; 2nd quarter 1984. (p. 32-37)

[7] Insured unemployed by industry [division, race], and occupation group for the week including the 19th of Aug. 1983. (p. 38)

[8-9] Characteristics of active file applicants placed [showing total, minority, female, and veteran applicants]; and total agricultural and nonagricultural job openings received, filled, and unfilled; by major occupational groups, Oct. 1983-Mar. 1984 period. (p. 40-41)

[10] [Federal poverty guidelines, Mar. 1984.] (p. 44)

[11-14] SDA [service delivery area] information for JTPA [Job Training Partnership Act] administration [includes labor force by employment status, high school dropouts, AFDC and food stamp recipients, private and government employment, and total and economically disadvantaged population by age groups, all by parish and/or city, various years 1980-84]. (p. 55-70)

[15-16] Applicants and nonagricultural job openings by occupation [tables show data by occupational code only, 1st half 1984]. (13 p.)

[17-18] Employment projections by major occupational and industrial category [1980 and 1990]. (p. 86-87)

[19] Most rapidly growing occupations, 1980-90 [period]. (p. 88)

S3320–2   LOUISIANA LABOR MARKET INFORMATION
Monthly.   Approx. 15 p. no paging.
SRI/MF/complete, shipped quarterly

Monthly report on Louisiana employment, hours, and earnings, by industry and SMSA. Also includes employment data by parish. Report is issued 1 month after month of coverage.

Contains narrative analysis, and 4 monthly tables and 1 quarterly table, listed below.

Monthly tables appear in all issues; quarterly table appears in Oct. 1983 and Apr. 1984 issues.

Availability: Louisiana Department of Labor, Employment Security Office, Research and Statistics Unit, Rm. 220, PO Box 44094, Baton Rouge LA 70804-9094, †; SRI/MF/complete, shipped quarterly.

Issues reviewed during 1984: Sept. 1983-Aug. 1984 (D).

TABLES:

MONTHLY TABLES
[Data are shown for month of coverage, previous month, and same month of previous year. Table [2] is repeated for State, Alexandria labor market area, and each SMSA. Table [3] is repeated for State and 3 SMSAs, with SMSA data shown for manufacturing industries only.]

[1] Civilian labor force summary [by employment status, for Alexandria labor market area and by SMSA].

[2] Nonagricultural wage/salary employment [by industry division and major industry group].

[3] Average hours and earnings in manufacturing [major industry groups] and selected nonmanufacturing industry [divisions].

[4] Employment situation by labor market area [data in table [1] are repeated by parish].

QUARTERLY TABLE

[5] Insured unemployed by industry [division] and occupation group for the week including the 19th of [month 1-2 months prior to month of coverage, by race and SMSA].

S3345   LOUISIANA
Department of Public Safety

S3345–1   STATE OF LOUISIANA SUMMARY OF MOTOR VEHICLE TRAFFIC ACCIDENTS, 1983
Annual.   1984.
15 p. var. paging.
ISSN 0741-4358.
SRI/MF/complete

Annual report on Louisiana traffic accidents, fatalities, and injuries, by vehicle and accident type, location, time, and other circumstances; and by driver and victim characteristics; 1983, with selected comparisons to 1982.

Also includes data on safety device use and vehicle miles traveled.

Report contains 15 tables.

Availability: Louisiana Department of Public Safety, State Police Office, Traffic Records Section, PO Box 66614, Baton Rouge LA 70896, †; SRI/MF/complete.

S3365   LOUISIANA
Department of Revenue and Taxation

S3365–1   40th REPORT, FY82-83, Louisiana Department of Revenue and Taxation
Annual.   [1984.]   39 p.
SRI/MF/complete

Annual report on Louisiana State tax revenue collections, by tax type, FY83 with selected trends from FY74. Includes individual income tax returns and payments by income bracket, and sales and severance taxes by parish and commodity group.

Contains contents listing and highlights, with summary chart and table showing total dept collections, various years FY76-83 (p. 1-3); summary of dept operations, with 1 table showing operating expenditures by object, FY83 (p. 4-7); and 22 tables described below, interspersed with explanatory notes and 17 summary charts (p. 10-38).

Prior to the 40th edition, report was issued biennially.

Availability: Louisiana Department of Revenue and Taxation, Public Relations Section, PO Box 201, Capitol Station, Baton Rouge LA 70821, †; SRI/MF/complete.

TABLES:
[Data on taxes show value of revenue collections.]

a. Total taxes, and revenue collections by detailed source, various years FY77-83. 2 tables. (p. 10-12)

b. Beverage taxes, corporation franchise and income taxes, and individual income taxes, FY78-83; individual income tax returns by filing status, and total returns and payments by State and Federal tax bracket and State zip code area, tax year 1982. 8 tables. (p. 14-19)

c. Severance taxes by resource and parish; petroleum product taxes and inspection fees; motor fuel consumption and taxable gallonage, by fuel type; sales tax collections, by parish and commodity group; tobacco product tax; and miscellaneous taxes and fees, by type; FY82-83 with selected trends from FY74. 12 tables. (p. 20-38)

S3375   LOUISIANA
Supreme Court

S3375–1   ANNUAL REPORT 1983: The Judicial Council of the Supreme Court of Louisiana
Annual.   Feb. 21, 1984.
26 p.
LC 73-641954.
SRI/MF/complete

Annual report on Louisiana trial and appellate court caseloads and case dispositions, 1983, with selected trends from 1981. Covers supreme, appeals, district, family and juvenile, and city and parish courts. Includes trial court data by case type and jurisdiction.

Case types shown include civil, criminal, traffic, and trials.

Data are from court reports to Judicial Administrator's Office.

Contains contents listing, letter of transmittal, and roster of supreme court judges (p. 1-3); narrative report, with rosters of judges and clerks (p. 4-17); and statistical appendix with 2 charts and 6 tables (p. 18-26).

This is the 28th annual report.

Availability: Louisiana Supreme Court, Judicial Administrator's Office, Supreme Court Bldg., Rm. 109, 301 Loyola Ave., New Orleans LA 70112, $15.00; SRI/MF/complete.

S3429   MAINE
Department of Business, Occupational and Professional Regulation

S3429–1   ANNUAL STATISTICAL REPORT OF THE BUREAU OF BANKING, Maine
Annual.   June 15, 1984.
17 p. no paging.
SRI/MF/complete

Annual report presenting aggregate financial data for Maine financial institutions, by institution type, county, and State economic area, 1976-83, with selected trends from 1950.

Includes assets, deposits or shares, loans, and number of institutions and branches, for commercial bank/trust companies, national banks, savings and industrial banks, and State and Federal savings and loan assns and credit unions.

Also includes loans by type, demand and savings/time deposits, and negotiable orders of withdrawal, all by county; and total and per capita deposits, total loans, per capita installment and real estate debt, and number of offices reporting by institution type, all by State economic area.

Data are compiled by the Banking Bureau from reports filed by individual institutions.

Contains 3 tables, and list of economic areas.

Prior to 1984, report was covered by SRI under S3430-1; issuing agency name has changed from Maine Dept of Business Regulation.

Availability: Maine Department of Business, Occupational, and Professional Regulation, Bank Superintendent's Office, Banking Bureau, State House Station 36, Augusta ME 04333, †; SRI/MF/complete.

S3435   MAINE
Department of
Educational and
Cultural Services

S3435–1   MAINE EDUCATIONAL FACTS, 1982/83
Annual. [1984.] ii+27 p.
LC 76-626298.
SRI/MF/complete

Annual report on elementary/secondary education in Maine, 1982/83. Covers public and private school enrollment, graduates, postsecondary education, and dropouts. Also includes data on public school units and districts, special education, schooling of Indian children, and growth trends in staffing and expenditures from 1960s. Selected data are shown by county.

Data are from reports submitted by local school administrators.

Contains contents listing (p. ii); brief narrative summary (p. 1); and 24 tables, listed below (p. 2-27).

Availability: Maine Department of Educational and Cultural Services, Management Information Division, Education Bldg., Station 23, Augusta ME 04333, †; SRI/MF/complete.

TABLES:
[Data are for 1982/83, unless otherwise noted.]

S3435–1.1: Public Schools
[1] Distribution of municipalities [and school systems] in Maine [by type of school supervision district]. (p. 2)

[2] Units that do not operate schools. [list] (p. 3)

[3] Universe of public school districts [number of local units, nonoperating local units, schools, and average daily membership (ADM)], by county [and for schooling of Indian children and children in unorganized territories]. (p. 4)

[4] One-room schools in Maine [enrollment, by school], fall 1982. (p. 5)

[5] Units that do not have kindergarten. [list] (p. 6)

S3435–1.2: Enrollment
[Data by grade include special education and postgraduates. Public school data generally include separate totals for Indian children and children in unorganized territories.]

[1] Net [public school] enrollment, State totals by grade [and high school graduates, total population, and births; 1933-83]. (p. 7)

[2-6] Fall enrollment for public and private schools, by grade and county, 1983/84. (p. 9-13)

[7-10] Oct. 1, 1982 and Apr. 1, 1983 resident enrollment, by county and grade. (p. 14-17)

[11] Enrollment comparisons by year [and school level, Oct. 1, 1972-82]. (p. 18)

S3435–1.3: Summary Year-End Data, Dropouts, and Postsecondary Enrollment
[1] Year-end data, as reported in the "Report of the Public School System, 1982/83" [enrollment, and dropouts, by grade; average daily attendance and ADM; number of public, private, and discontinued schools; and public and private school pupils conveyed on municipal and private buses]. (p. 19)

[2] Dropout [numbers and] rates, by county. (p. 21)

[3-4] Rate [and number] of 1982 and 1983 graduates [going] on to college, by county. (p. 22-23)

[5-6] 1982 and 1983 [public and private] school students enrolled in postsecondary education or training [postgraduate high school course, junior college, college/university, vocational/commercial/technical, and other continuing education, inside and outside Maine]. (p. 24-25)

S3435–1.4: Finances and Growth Trends
[1] Local school expenditures and source of revenues [local, State, and Federal, including Elementary and Secondary Education Act and school lunch funds, 1967/68-1982/83]. (p. 26)

[2] Growth of public education in Maine [teachers, average salary, expenditures, and resident pupils, 1961/62-1982/83]. (p. 27)

S3435–2   LIBRARIES IN MAINE: Directory and Statistics, 1982
Annual. [1984.] 46 p.
LC 73-646640.
SRI/MF/complete

Annual report, for 1982, on Maine libraries, presenting directory of public, institutional, and special libraries and personnel; and data on holdings, circulation, and finances of individual public libraries, by city. Data are from annual reports submitted by public libraries to the State library.

Contents:
a. Contents listing (1 p.); introduction (p. 1); and directories of library officials and libraries (p. 2-38).

b. Public library statistics: 1 table showing summary data for State, 1981-82 (p. 39); and 1 extended table showing hours, holdings, circulation, expenditures for books and salaries, municipal appropriations, and total operating expenditures, 1982, and population, 1980, for individual public libraries, by town (p. 40-46).

Availability: Maine Department of Educational and Cultural Services, Maine State Library, Library Development Services, State House Station 64, Augusta ME 04333, †; SRI/MF/complete.

S3450   MAINE
Department of
Finance and Administration

S3450–1   STATE OF MAINE FINANCIAL REPORT for Period July I, 1982-June 30, 1983
Annual. 1983. 3+138 p.
LC 45-27740.
SRI/MF/complete

Annual report on financial condition of Maine State government for FY83, with comparisons to FY82, presenting assets, liabilities and reserves, and fund balances; revenues by source; and expenditures by object and agency; for general, highway, special revenue, bond proceed, debt and internal service, enterprise, and trust/agency funds.

Also includes data on budgeted vs. actual revenues and expenditures; State bonded debt and fixed assets; and summary trends from FY79.

Contains contents listing (2 p.); and 58 financial exhibits (p. 1-138).

Availability: Maine Department of Finance and Administration, Accounts and Control Bureau, State Office Bldg., Rm. 300, Station No. 14, Augusta ME 04333, †; SRI/MF/complete.

S3450–2   MAINE STATE GOVERNMENT ANNUAL REPORT, 1982-83
Annual. 1983. xxiii+743 p.
LC 76-643347.
SRI/MF/complete

Annual compilation of reports, for FY83, of approximately 450 Maine State depts and agencies. Each report generally includes information on agency's purpose, organization, employees, activities, licenses/permits and/or publications issued; and usually 1 table showing expenditures by object and fund, FY83. Some reports also include additional tables, described below, on regulatory activities and related data.

Data are compiled by the State Bureau of Budget.

Contains foreword, contents listing, and lists of organizational changes (p. vii-xxiii); agency annual reports, arranged alphabetically by function (p. 1-726); and index (p. 727-743).

Availability: Maine Department of Finance and Administration, Purchases Bureau, Reprographics Division, State House Station 91, Augusta ME 04333, $6.24 payable to Maine Treasurer of State; SRI/MF/complete.

ADDITIONAL TABLES:
[Unless otherwise noted, data are shown for FY83.]

a. Baxter State Park Authority: visitor use, revenues, and expenditures, 1978-82. 1 table. (p. 68)

b. Consumer Credit Protection Bureau: lending institutions requesting/receiving licenses, by type of institution, FY83. 1 table. (p. 91)

c. Real Estate Commission: consumer complaint/dispute cases and dispositions. 1 table. (p. 115)

d. Corrections Dept: Parole Board case activity; and supervised probationers and parolees. 2 tables. (p. 159,163)

e. Civil Emergency Preparedness Bureau: Federal assistance grants, by program. 1 table. (p. 177)

f. Historic Preservation Commission: Federal grant awards, by project category. 1 table. (p. 213)

g. School Management Bureau: school nutrition program meals served, Dec. and summer 1982. 2 tables. (p. 233-234)

h. Environmental Protection Dept: air, land, and water quality monitoring and enforcement activity; and oil pollution control program activity. 6 tables. (p. 263-272)

i. Insurance Advisory Board: premiums and claims paid by major lines of State administered insurance. 1 table. (p. 326-328)

j. Taxation Bureau: elderly householder tax/rent refunds, FY82-83; assessments of individual and corporate nonfilers of State tax returns; sales/income/fuel and property tax revenues. 4 tables. (p. 336-338)

k. Guarantee Authority: industrial and recreational loan guarantees, by company; loan commitments; municipal securities approvals, by city; and fund finances. 4 tables. (p. 342-347)

l. Health Planning and Development Bureau: number of consumer and provider members on health coordinating council; and capital expenditure savings, for health care projects reduced or disapproved by project review program, 1982. 2 tables. (p. 392-393)

m. Nursing Board: examination results and licensure activity for registered and practical nurses. 4 tables. (p. 413)

n. Inland Fisheries and Wildlife Dept: fish stocked from State hatcheries/rearing stations; guide licenses passed and denied, by type; and game warden hours by enforcement activity; generally 1982. 3 tables. (p. 447-456)

o. Judicial Dept: law bar examination results, 1980-83. 1 table. (p. 474)

p. Labor Dept: apprenticeship program activity; boiler, elevator, and tramway inspections and certifications; industrial safety activities; minimum wage regulatory activity; and Bureau of Employment Security detailed finances. 6 tables. (p. 483-514)

q. Maritime Academy: revenues and expenditures, by item. 1 table. (p. 569)

r. State Police Bureau: crime laboratory, gambling, and other enforcement and licensing activities, 1982 or FY83. 3 tables. (p. 636-638)

s. State Retirement System: detailed finances, including assets and trust fund reserves, with selected comparisons to FY82; and payments, contributions, and recipients, FY78-83; for State and local employees, and teachers. 9 tables. (p. 649-656)

t. School Building Authority: construction financed since 1951; and bond activities and debt. 2 tables. (p. 662)

u. Transportation Dept: Construction Bureau contracts. 1 table. (p. 684-685)

v. University of Maine: full-time employees, by category and funding source, Oct. 1982; and revenues and expenditures by item. 2 tables. (p. 709-710)

w. Workers' Compensation Commission: premiums written, taxes paid to general fund, and losses, 1964 and 1974-82. 1 table. (p. 726)

S3460   MAINE
Department of Human Services

S3460-2   MAINE VITAL STATISTICS, 1982
Annual. 1984. vii+95 p.
ISSN 0160-7421.
LC 78-642135.
SRI/MF/complete

Annual report, for 1982, on Maine vital statistics, covering population, births, deaths by cause, marriages, and divorces. Includes data by demographic characteristics and location, and selected trends from 1900. Data are from State records.

Contains table listing, introduction, and additional data availability (p. iii-vii); technical notes, and definitions (p. 1-7); and 20 tables listed below, arranged in 4 sections, each preceded by narrative summary (p. 9-95).

Availability: Maine Department of Human Services, Data and Research Division, Health Planning and Development Bureau, State House Station 11, Augusta ME 04333, 1st copy †, additional copies $6.00; SRI/MF/complete.

TABLES:
[Unless otherwise noted, data are for 1982.]

S3460-2.1: Population, Births, and Deaths
POPULATION AND HISTORICAL DATA

1. Population estimates by age group, July 1, 1982; [and population on Apr. 1, 1980, natural increase, and net migration; all by county]. (p. 11)

2. Population, live births, deaths, marriages, and divorces, [and] rates for births, deaths, infant deaths, neonatal deaths, termination of pregnancy, and maternal deaths, [selected years, 1900-82]. (p. 12)

NATALITY

3. Terminations of pregnancy by type and gestation. (p. 15)

4. Summary of natality statistics by county [number and/or rate, for total live births, live births by sex, and hospital, illegitimate, immature, and nonwhite births]. (p. 17)

5. Resident live births by selected characteristics [sex, illegitimacy, 1st-born, under 2,500 grams, plural birth, congenital anomalies, mother under age 20, no prenatal care, born in hospital, and race (nonwhite, Negro, and American Indian), all by county and town]. (p. 18-30)

6. Selected characteristics of resident induced abortions [in hospital, pregnancy complication, previous abortion, and surgical procedure; patient under age 20, unwed, nonwhite, and with high school/less education; and by gestational period; all by county]. (p. 31)

MORTALITY

7. Summary of mortality statistics by county [deaths by sex; infant, neonatal, and maternal deaths; and selected rates]. (p. 37)

8. Leading causes of death, rate per 100,000 population, life lost per 1,000 population, percent of total deaths and percent of total life lost. (p. 38)

9. Leading causes of death [and rate], by sex. (p. 39)

10. 72 causes of resident deaths: number of deaths, and the ratio of multiple to underlying causes. (p. 40)

11. Deaths from accidents [by] county of occurrence by place of accident. (p. 42)

12. Percent of county occurrence deaths by place of death and percent of selected causes of death occuring in hospital [by county]. (p. 43)

13. Infant deaths, total deaths by sex, and deaths from 72 causes, by county and selected minor civil division. (p. 44)

14-15. Resident deaths from 282 selected causes, and resident infant deaths from 65 selected causes, by age and sex. (p. 48-78)

S3460-2.2: Marriages and Divorces

16. Marriages, divorces, and annulments, by county of occurrence. (p. 82)

17-19. Divorces and annulments: by legal grounds for decree, plaintiff, number of children reported under 18 years of age, and by duration of marriage in years. (p. 82-83)

20. Selected characteristics of resident marriages [Maine born, under age 20, 1st marriage, high school/less education, and Maine resident, for bride and groom; and total marriages, civil ceremonies, and mixed marriages; all by county and town]. (p. 88-95)

S3460-3   POPULATION PROJECTIONS by Minor Civil Divisions, Sex, Age Group, and County, Maine
Annual. June 1984.
iv+68 p.
LC 84-645712.
SRI/MF/complete, current & previous year reports

Annual report presenting Maine population projections for each minor civil division (primarily towns), and for each county by age and sex, 1982-92. Data are based on State government estimates.

Contains contents listing and acknowledgments (p. iii-iv); introduction and methodology (p. 1-4); and 2 extended tables (p. 7-68).

This is the 2nd annual edition. The 1st annual edition was also reviewed by SRI in 1984, and is also available on SRI microfiche, under this number [Annual. Sept. 1983. iv+68 p. $5.00]. SRI coverage of this report begins with the 1st annual edition; previous editions were published on an irregular basis.

Population projections by town by age are also available from the issuing agency, but are not covered by SRI.

Availability: Maine Department of Human Services, Data and Research Division, Health Planning and Development Bureau, State House Station 11, Augusta ME 04333, 1st copy †, additional copies $4.00; SRI/MF/complete.

S3460-4   INTERCENSAL POPULATION ESTIMATES FOR MINOR CIVIL DIVISIONS BY AGE GROUP AND COUNTY, Maine, 1971-79

Monograph.   Dec. 1983.
iv + 165 p.
LC 84-621675.
SRI/MF/complete

Report presenting Maine intercensal population estimates, July 1971-79, with comparison to Apr. 1970 and Apr. 1980 census counts, by age, for each county and each minor civil division. The intercensal estimates supersede all previous estimates of Maine's population for 1971-79.

Contains contents listing and acknowledgements (p. iii-iv); introduction and methology (p. 1-4); and 2 extended tables (p. 7-165).

Availability: Maine Department of Human Services, Data and Research Division, Health Planning and Development Bureau, State House Station 11, Augusta ME 04333, $7.00; SRI/MF/complete.

S3463   MAINE
Judicial Department

S3463-1   STATE OF MAINE JUDICIAL DEPARTMENT 1983 Annual Report with Statistical Supplement

Annual.   Apr. 12, 1984.
iii + 172 p.
SRI/MF/complete

Annual report, for 1983, on Maine judicial system, including trial and appellate court caseloads, case dispositions, and processing time. Covers supreme law court, and superior, district, and administrative courts. Includes administrative court cases by agency; trial court data by case type, district, county, and city; and trends from 1976.

Case types shown are civil and criminal for all courts, with some detail for workers compensation, damages, personal injury, contract, Uniform Reciprocal Enforcement of Support Act (interstate child support agreement), divorce, habeas corpus, bail review, family abuse, small claims, juvenile, mental health, and traffic cases.

Also in includes data on jury selection process, and judicial dept personnel and finances.

Data are from reports submitted to the Administrative Office.

Contains listing of contents, tables, and charts (p. i-iii); narrative report with 8 charts and 8 tables (p. 1-37); and 5 statistical appendices, with 9 charts and 50 tables (p. 39-172).

This is the 8th annual report. Report is accompanied by an executive summary, not covered in SRI.

Availability: Maine Judicial Department, Administrative Office of the Courts, 66 Pearl St., PO Box 4820 D.T.S., Portland ME 04112, †; SRI/MF/complete.

S3465   MAINE
Department of Labor

S3465-1   MAINE OCCUPATIONAL STAFFING PATTERNS

Series.   For individual publication data, see below.
SRI/MF/complete

Continuing series of reports, published in a 3-year cycle, each covering Maine employment in a group of selected industries, by detailed occupation.

Data are from Occupational Employment Statistics (OES) surveys, conducted over a 3-year period and updated triennially, on the following industries: nonmanufacturing; manufacturing; wholesale and retail trade, and regulated industries; Federal, State, and local government; hospitals; and education.

General format of each report:

a.   Contents listing; and introduction, sometimes with charts or tables showing trends, summary data, and/or survey sample characteristics.

b.   1 table, repeated for each SIC 2- or 3-digit industry covered, showing estimated employment by detailed occupational group, including percent of surveyed establishments/units reporting each occupation.

c.   Methodology.

Report reviewed in 1984 is described below. For description of last previous report, see SRI 1982 Annual, under this number.

Availability: Maine Department of Labor, Employment Security Bureau, Economic Analysis and Research Division, 20 Union St., Augusta ME 04330, †; SRI/MF/complete.

S3465-1.7: Maine Occupational Staffing Patterns for Selected Nonmanufacturing Industries, Second Quarter 1981

[Triennial. Feb. 1983. vi + 50 p. Pub. No. OES-19. SRI/MF/complete.]

Covers construction; banks and other credit agencies; insurance and real estate; hotels and other lodging places; personal, business, legal, and social services; automotive repair and services; motion pictures; amusement and recreation services; health services (except hospitals); membership organizations; miscellaneous services; and selected SIC 3-digit industries.

Data are based on industry mail surveys conducted 2nd quarter 1981.

Previous report, for 2nd quarter 1978, is described in SRI 1980 Annual, under S3465-1.1.

S3465-2   MAINE LABOR MARKET DIGEST

Monthly.   Approx. 6 p.
SRI/MF/complete, shipped quarterly

Monthly report on Maine employment trends, earnings, and unemployment insurance claimants, prepared from reports to the Maine Dept of Labor. Report is issued 4-8 weeks after month of coverage.

Contains narrative article, occasionally with accompanying tables and/or charts, usually on employment in specific industry sectors; 6 trend charts; and 6 monthly tables and 1 irregularly appearing table, listed below.

Monthly tables appear in all issues. Irregularly recurring table appears in Feb.-May and July-Aug. 1984 issues. Other tables presenting substantial statistics not covered in monthly tables are described, as they appear, under "Statistical Features."

Availability: Maine Department of Labor, Employment Security Bureau, Economic Analysis and Research Division, 20 Union St., Augusta ME 04330, †; SRI/MF/complete, shipped quarterly.

Issues reviewed during 1984: Sept. 1983-Aug. 1984 (D).

TABLES:

[Tables generally show data for month of coverage, previous month, and same month of previous year. Data are for Maine, unless otherwise noted. Data for 2 SMSAs are for Portland and Lewiston-Auburn SMSAs.]

MONTHLY TABLES

[1] Nonfarm wage/salary employment by place of work [industry division and major manufacturing group, and total involved in labor-management disputes, for State and 2 SMSAs].

[2] Earnings and workweek of production workers in manufacturing industries [for State by manufacturing group, and totals for 2 SMSAs; also shows average hourly earnings for 3 preceding years].

[3] Female labor force [total, unemployed, and resident employed].

[4] U.S. CPI.

[5] Labor force, employment, and unemployment [for Maine labor markets, 2 SMSAs, 5 other New England States, and total U.S.].

[6] Midmonth insured unemployment (less partials) [continued-week claimants and insured unemployment rate, for State and 2 SMSAs].

IRREGULARLY RECURRING TABLE

[7] Selected characteristics of unemployment insurance claimants [distribution by occupation and age].

STATISTICAL FEATURE:

S3465-2.501: June 1984

PRIVATE PAYROLL EARNINGS RISE IN MAINE

(p. 2, 6) Article, with 1 table showing Maine private nonfarm payroll, by industry division, and for durable and nondurable goods manufacturing, 1st quarter 1983-84. Data are from U.S. Commerce Dept.

S3465-3   ANNUAL PLANNING INFORMATION, Maine Statewide, Planning Year 1984

Annual.   Aug. 1984.
ix + 104 p.
Pub. Series No. SAPI-5.
SRI/MF/complete

Annual planning report, for 1984, identifying Maine population groups most in need of employment services, and presenting data on employment by industry and occupation through 1983. Also includes employment projections by occupation through 1990; and data on population, labor force, and income, by county, 1980s and trends.

Data are from Census Bureau, Maine Labor Dept, and other sources.

Contains listings of contents, tables, and charts (p. v-ix); introduction and narrative report, with 6 charts, and 34 tables listed below (p. 3-88); glossary (p. 91-100); and information sources (p. 103-104).

This is the 5th annual report. For description of the 4th annual report, see SRI 1982 Annual, under this number.

Availability: Maine Department of Labor, Employment Security Bureau, Economic Analysis and Research Division, 20 Union St., Augusta ME 04330, $4.00; SRI/MF/complete.

TABLES:

[Data are shown for Maine, unless otherwise noted. Data by ethnic group include American Indian/Eskimo/Aleut, Asian/Pacific Islander, and Hispanic.]

S3465–3.1: Population Characteristics

POPULATION

1-2. Resident population of the U.S. and [6] New England States, 1970, 1980, and 1983. (p. 8)

3. Population of Maine and Maine counties, 1970 and 1980. (p. 9)

4. Population, by age and sex, 1970 and 1980. (p. 12)

5. Percent distribution of population, by age and county, 1980. (p. 13)

6. Minority population [blacks and by ethnic group] of Maine and Maine counties, 1980. (p. 14)

7-9. Total population and economically disadvantaged population; age distribution of the economically disadvantaged population; and economically disadvantaged persons 16/over, females and high school dropouts: Maine and Maine counties, 1980. (p. 16-19)

LABOR FORCE

10. Civilian labor force, unemployment, and resident employment, annual average, 1976-83. (p. 22)

11. Population, labor force, labor force participation rate, unemployment, and unemployment rate, by age and sex, 1970 and 1980. (p. 23)

12. Civilian labor force, unemployment, and resident employment, by county, annual average, 1983. (p. 24)

SCHOOL ENROLLMENT

13. School enrollment [public], by county and grade, [and total private school enrollment], 1983/84 school year. (p. 28)

14. Public secondary school enrollment, dropouts, and dropout rates, by county, 1979-83 (p. 29)

15. 1983 [public and private] high school graduates enrolled in post-high school education programs [by type of program within and outside Maine]. (p. 30)

INCOME

[Tables 17-18 and 21-22 show data for the State and by county.]

16. Per capita personal income for the U.S., New England, Maine, and Maine counties, 1970 and 1982. (p. 34)

17-18. Median household effective buying income, 1975 and 1982; and percent distribution of households by effective buying income, 1982. (p. 35-36)

19-20. Average weekly wages paid in covered employment, by industry [division] and by county, 1970 and 1982. (p. 37-38)

21. Income in counties as a percent of State-wide income for selected income measures [per capita, average weekly wages in covered employment, and median household buying income], 1982. (p. 39)

22. Income assistance programs [AFDC, food stamps, and general assistance cases and recipients], 1982 averages. (p. 40)

23. Selected components of personal income [total and per capita wage/salary disbursements and government transfer payments], 1970 and 1983. (p. 41)

JOB SERVICE APPLICANTS

24. Percent distribution of selected characteristics of active applicants [includes sex, age, education, race, and ethnic group; and veteran, handicapped, and unemployment insurance claimant status], Mar. 1984. (p. 44)

25. Percent distribution of the characteristics of the unemployed [sex, education, veteran status, unemployment reason, family responsibility, occupation, and industry division of separation], Mar. 1984. (p. 45)

S3465–3.2: Current and Projected Employment

[Most data by industry are shown by industry division and major manufacturing and/or non-manufacturing industry group.]

26-27. Nonfarm wage/salary employment in Maine and the U.S., by industry, 1947 and 1983. (p. 52-53)

28-30. Nonfarm wage/salary employment, by industry: 1975, 1979, and 1983; 1st quarter 1983 and 1st quarter 1984; and by month and annual average, 1983. (p. 56-64)

31. Annual average workweek and hourly and weekly earnings of production workers employed in manufacturing industries [by industry group], 1978-83. (p. 66)

32. Characteristics of nonfarm industries [employment, number of firms, and average weekly wages, by industry], 1983. (p. 67)

33. Industry-indicator matrix [average employment, 1980 and 1983; and number of firms, unemployment insurance claimants as percent of employment, average weekly wages, and composite index, 1983; by SIC 2-digit industry]. (p. 79)

34. Occupation-indicator matrix [including employment, 1978 and 1983; average hourly wages, 1982/83; job service applicants (no date); and projected employment change, 1980-90 period; all by detailed occupation]. (p. 86-88)

S3475
Department of
Public Safety

MAINE

S3475–1   CRIME IN MAINE, 1983
Annual. [1984.]
2+v+127 p.
LC 77-643188.
SRI/MF/complete

Annual report on Maine crimes and arrests by type of offense, 1983, with selected comparisons to 1982. Includes data on value of stolen property, police employment, and officers assaulted. Selected data are shown by county and law enforcement agency.

Data are compiled from local law enforcement agency reports, under the State Uniform Crime Reporting (UCR) Program.

Contains listings of contents, tables, and charts (p. i-v); 26 charts and 28 tables, interspersed with narrative (p. 1-96); and discussion of UCR methodology and uses, and sample Penobscot County profile with 5 tables (p. 97-127).

All tables, except sample county profile tables, are described below. Charts presenting data not covered in tables are also described below.

This is the 9th annual report.

Availability: Maine Department of Public Safety, Uniform Crime Reporting Division, 36 Hospital St., Augusta ME 04333, †; SRI/MF/complete.

TABLES AND CHARTS:

[Index crimes are murder, rape, robbery, aggravated assault, burglary, larceny/theft, motor vehicle theft, and arson. Most tables show data for 1983, often with comparisons to 1982.]

S3475–1.1: Index Crimes

[Data for each Index offense include a monthly trend chart, in addition to the data described below.]

a. Index crimes: individual offenses, total rates, percent of total crimes cleared by arrest, and aggregate monthly crimes, by county; and clearances and rates, by offense; with selected comparisons to U.S. and New England. 1 chart and 5 tables. (p. 8-11)

b. Violent and property Index crimes, by offense. 4 charts and 2 tables. (p. 14-17)

c. Murder: by weapon, motive, age and sex of victim and offender, and relationship of victim to offender. 3 charts and 2 tables. (p. 20-22)

d. Forcible rape. 1 chart. (p. 24)

e. Robbery: by type of weapon; and offenses and value of property stolen, by place of occurrence. 4 charts and 1 table. (p. 26-28)

f. Assault: domestic assaults by county, type of weapon, and situation/relationship. 1 chart and 2 tables. (p. 30-32)

g. Burglary: by type; and residential and non-residential offenses and value of property stolen, by time of day. 3 charts and 2 tables. (p. 34-36)

h. Larceny/theft: offenses and value of property stolen, by type of larceny. 3 charts and 1 table. (p. 38-40)

i. Motor vehicle theft: by vehicle type and whether recovered locally. 3 charts. (p. 42-43) *j.* Arson: offenses and value of property loss, by type of property and county. 1 chart and 2 tables. (p. 46-47)

k. Value of property stolen and recovered, by type of property and county. 3 tables. (p. 49-53)

l. Index offense clearances, and percent involving juveniles and adults, all by crime. 1 chart and 1 table. (p. 55)

S3475-1.2: Arrests, Police, and Local Data

a. Arrests: by age and sex, for individual Index and non-Index offenses, with disposition of arrested juveniles and detail for drug and alcohol offenses. 4 tables. (p. 59-67)

b. Police: full-time sworn municipal and sheriff dept officers (total and per 1,000 population), by county; total State police; and assaults on officers, by county and time of day. 1 chart and 2 tables. (p. 71-75)

c. Local data: population, Index crimes by offense, and clearance and crime rates, all by county, law enforcement agency, and urban and rural area. 1 table repeated for each county and for State. (p. 80-96)

S3593   MARYLAND
Department of Agriculture

S3593-1   MARYLAND AGRICULTURAL STATISTICS, 1983
Annual. Sept. 1984   56 p.
MDA 113-84.
LC 64-64330.
SRI/MF/complete

Annual report on Maryland agricultural production, marketing, and finances, 1983, with some data for 1984 and selected trends from as early as 1960. Data are generally shown by commodity and/or county, with some comparisons to neighboring States and total U.S.

Report covers production, prices, sales, value, and, as applicable, acreage, yield, disposition, and inventory, for field crop, fruit, vegetable, poultry, dairy, and livestock sectors.

Report also includes data on farms; farm acreage, value, rents, income and production expenses; weather; fertilizer sales; and field crop production in Delmarva counties.

Data are compiled by the Maryland Crop Reporting Service in cooperation with USDA.

Contains contents listing and foreword (p. 2-4); and report, with 3 maps, 3 charts, and 60 tables (p. 5-56).

Availability: Maryland Crop Reporting Service, 50 Harry S. Truman Pkwy., Rm. 202, Annapolis MD 21401, †; SRI/MF/complete.

S3605   MARYLAND
Department of Economic and Community Development

S3605-1   MARYLAND STATISTICAL ABSTRACT, 1984-85
Biennial.   Dec. 15, 1983.
xvii+264 p.
ISSN 0580-9029.
LC 80-644045.
SRI/MF/complete

Biennial compilation, for 1984-85, presenting detailed social, governmental, and economic statistics for Maryland. Data are primarily for selected years 1970-82, with population trends from 1790 and projections to 1990. Most data are from reports of State and Federal government, and University of Maryland.

Report is designed to present a comprehensive overview of the State. Various socioeconomic, demographic, and geographical breakdowns are shown, as applicable, for most topics. These breakdowns include data by city, county, State region, Baltimore and Washington SMSAs, commodity, race, sex, age, and educational attainment. Comparisons to total U.S. and neighboring States are occasionally included.

Contents:

a. Contents and table listings. (p. i-xvii)

b. Introductory section, with 1 map, and 4 summary tables showing Maryland regions, and topographical and socioeconomic highlights. (p. 1-24)

c. 216 tables arranged in 16 sections, described below. (p. 25-264)

Previous edition of the *Abstract,* for 1980, was intended to be the 1st annual edition, but publication has resumed biennial periodicity. For description of 1980 edition, see SRI 1981 Annual, under this number.

Availability: Maryland Department of Economic and Community Development, Public Affairs Division, 45 Calvert St., Annapolis MD 21401, $20.00; SRI/MF/complete.

TABLE SECTIONS:
[Data sources are given beneath each table.]

S3605-1.1: Population and Vital Statistics

(p. 25-46) Contains 21 tables. Includes population from 1790 and projected to 1990; migration to and from Maryland, by State and census division; land area; population by nativity; births and deaths; marriages, annulments, and divorces; total, infant, and neonatal death rates; and deaths for 10 leading causes.

S3605-1.2: Education and Health

(p. 47-73) Contains 25 tables. Includes educational attainment of population; elementary and secondary schools; public and nonpublic school enrollment; public school attendance, teacher-pupil ratio, teachers/principals, cost and State aid per pupil, and teacher salaries; high school holding power, graduates, and continuing education plans; and public school finances.

Also includes higher education enrollment and degrees conferred; public postsecondary faculty, tenure status, and average salaries; and Federal higher education outlays by type of activity and dept/agency; all by institution.

Also includes hospital and licensed institution beds, physicians, and general surgeons; health professionals; and State psychiatric facility inpatient population, treatments, admissions, and net releases.

S3605-1.3: Climate and Natural Resources

(p. 74-101) Contains 21 tables. Includes weather station location, elevation, and climatological data, by site; forests, by type and land ownership; growing stock and sawtimber; forest products harvested; and forest fires and acreage burned, by cause.

Also includes commercial fishermen and gear; fish landings and value; processed seafood value, establishments, and employment; hunting and fishing licenses sold; and mineral production and value.

S3605-1.4: Labor Force and Employment, and Manufacturing

(p. 102-133) Contains 30 tables. Includes labor force, employment, and unemployment; percent of labor force working outside county of residence; commuting patterns; youth unemployment rates; Employment and Training Dept program activities and finances; Maryland State and Federal employees; civilian Federal employment by State; military and civilian DOD personnel, by service branch; and work stoppages, workers involved, and workdays idle.

Also includes manufacturing establishments, total employment and production workers, average earnings, payroll, and value added; and labor/proprietors income from manufacturing and nonmanufacturing.

S3605-1.5: Travel and Trade

(p. 134-147) Contains 12 tables. Includes travel expenditures, and travel- generated employment and payroll; and retail and wholesale trade, and selected service industries establishments, sales or receipts, payroll, and employment.

S3605-1.6: Personal Income and Spending

(p. 148-166) Contains 18 tables. Includes GSP; personal income by source; transfer payments by State; median income; total families and number below poverty level; spendable income; retail sales, by kind of business, and per household by State; income maintenance expenditures, funding, and caseloads, by program; food stamps sold and household participation; urban 4-person family budgets in 16 U.S. cities; CPI; and earnings indexes in 29 SMSAs.

S3605-1.7: State Finances

(p. 167-177) Contains 9 tables. Includes Maryland State revenues by source and expenditures by function; sales tax receipts; local distributions of government revenues by source and expenditures by function; and Federal revenue sharing.

S3605-1.8: Financial Institutions/Media

(p. 178-193) Contains 15 tables. Includes establishments, assets, and liabilities of national banks, Maryland-chartered bank and trust companies, mutual savings banks, credit unions, consumer loan companies, and savings and loan assns; branches, assets, liabilities, and deposits of 8 largest banks; commercial bank offices and deposits; life insurance policies in force and value; and ordinary life insurance purchases.

Also includes TV stations; cable TV subscribers; and newspaper circulation by paper.

S3605–1.9: Courts and Law Enforcement

(p. 194-205) Contains 13 tables. Includes judges and civil and criminal caseload per judge; court case activity and processing time; Index crime rates by offense; offenders institutionalized by offense and sentence length; juvenile court case dispositions; and juvenile and adult institutional population and capacity, and institutionalization cost per capita, by institution.

S3605–1.10: Energy/Transportation

(p. 206-231) Contains 29 tables. Includes Baltimore SMSA fuel CPI; natural gas customers, revenues, and consumption; electric utility capacity and production, by fuel source and ownership; electric sales to commercial and industrial customers; and electric utility residential kWh sales, customers, revenues, rate, and average customer consumption and bill, by utility.

Also includes coal production by State; gasoline consumption and prices; and telephones in use, and industry employment, payroll, capital expenditures, and long distance revenues.

Also includes Port of Baltimore foreign trade volume and value, by country; principal U.S. seaports ranked by foreign trade; Baltimore Harbor freight and passenger traffic; waterborne commerce by waterway; Baltimore-Washington International Airport air traffic and operations; commercial airports and heliports; motor vehicles registration; tollway traffic by facility; and highway and vehicle mileage.

S3605–1.11: Agriculture

(p. 232-237) Contains 5 tables. Includes farm cash receipts; farm price indexes for crops and livestock; farms and farmland; and livestock and poultry inventory and value.

S3605–1.12: Housing and Real Estate

(p. 238-242) Contains 5 tables. Includes housing units, and structural and occupancy characteristics; building permits; real properties, assessed value, and assessment level ratios; and federally owned and leased property and value.

S3605–1.13: Federal Outlays, Elections, and Recreation Areas

(p. 243-264) Contains 13 tables. Includes Federal outlays by agency and function; and Federal expenditures by function in Appalachian portion of State.

Also includes registered voters by political party; and general election results by candidate and congressional district.

Also includes total, year-round, and vacant/seasonal/migratory recreation homes; and open space land percentage, and number of camping facilities in forests and parks.

S3610   MARYLAND
Department of Education

S3610–1   FACTS ABOUT MARYLAND PUBLIC EDUCATION, 1983/84: A Statistical Handbook
Annual. [1984.]
44 p. Pocket size.
LC 73-646032.
SRI/MF/complete

Annual statistical summary, for 1983/84, on Maryland elementary and secondary education, covering public and nonpublic school enrollment and facilities, and public school staff, finances, and programs. Includes selected data by county and for Baltimore City, and trends from 1978.

Contains contents list (p. 1), and 6 charts and 23 tables showing the following:

a. Summary: population, 1983; number of public and nonpublic schools, and public school professional staff, pupils transported, local education budget, cost per pupil, teacher average salary, adult and total enrollment, and percent of students passing reading and math competency tests, 1983/84; teaching certificates issued, 1982/83; and Maryland's rank among the States in selected education-related areas, various periods 1980/81-1982/83. 2 tables. (p. 2-3)

b. Enrollment for public and nonpublic schools by level, and for State institution educational programs, and public schools by county, fall 1978 and 1982-83; and for public schools by level, by county, Sept. 1983. 3 tables. (p. 4-6)

c. Nonpublic schools, and public schools by level, by county, 1983/84. 1 table. (p. 7)

d. General Educational Development (GED) test results, by test center, July 1982-June 1983 period; and 7th-12th grade pupil withdrawals by cause, 1982/83. 2 tables. (p. 8-10)

e. Employment and salaries: minimum and maximum salary for teachers with bachelor's degree; and staff employment, by function; all by county, 1983/84. 2 tables. (p. 11-13)

f. Finances: disbursements by government source and function, and per pupil costs, State aid, and local wealth, by county, 1982/83; and State aid by expenditure category 1983/84. 4 charts and 1 table. (p. 14-21)

g. Food service programs, including Federal and State revenue, and meals served, by county, 1982/83. 2 tables. (p. 22-25)

h. Federal aid to disadvantaged children, and children eligible and participating, by county; and correctional institution education program enrollment and staff, with number completing 8th grade, high school, and vocational programs, by institution; 1982/83. 2 tables. (p. 26-27)

i. Library media centers, materials, expenditures, and employment, by county, 1981/82; public library income, staff, and book circulation, by county, 1982/83; and distribution of instructional TV broadcast hours, by curriculum area and school level, 1983/84. 1 chart and 2 tables. (p. 28-32)

j. Vocational and adult educational and testing programs: extended elementary education enrollment, schools, and staff, 1983/84; enrollment in vocational/technical and industrial arts, adult, vocational adult and apprentice, and community education programs, by program, including school volunteers, 1983/84; and students receiving special education and related services, by handicap or type of program, 1982/83; all by county. 5 tables. (p. 33-41)

k. Vocational rehabilitation program caseloads and rehabilitations by county, and rehabilitations by nature of disability, 1983. 1 chart and 1 table. (p. 42-44)

Availability: Maryland Department of Education, 200 W. Baltimore St., Baltimore MD 21201-2595, †; SRI/MF/complete.

S3610–3   MARYLAND PUBLIC SCHOOLS, 1984
Annual series. For individual publication data, see below.
SRI/MF/complete

Series of annual reports, issued in 1984, on Maryland elementary and secondary schools, covering enrollment, staff, salaries, finances, and transportation. Data are shown by county and for Baltimore City. Some reports include nonpublic school data.

Reports issued and reviewed in 1984 are described below. Reports issued in 1983 are covered in SRI under S3610-2. Issuing agency also publishes a detailed, less current annual report, not covered in SRI, compiling data covered in the series.

Availability: Maryland Department of Education, Management Information Systems Office, 200 W. Baltimore St., Baltimore MD 21201-2595, †; SRI/MF/complete.

S3610–3.1: Salary Schedules of Professional Personnel, Maryland Public Schools, 1983/84
[Annual. Dec. 1983. 13 p. var. paging. Rpt. No. MSDE-ADM 04100(R)250. SRI/MF/complete.]

Contains 5 tables showing public school salary schedules for teachers and 7 administrative positions, by degree level and county, 1983/84. Includes minimum and maximum amounts, and amount by salary schedule step; with longevity provisions and salary components, by county.

S3610–3.2: Public School Enrollment, State of Maryland, Sept. 30, 1983
[Annual. Jan. 1984. 10 p. no paging. Rpt. No. MSDE-OMIS 04100(R)001. SRI/MF/complete.]

Contains 6 tables showing public school enrollment, by grade (including special education) and sex, by county, Sept. 30, 1983.

S3610–3.3: Number of Maryland Public Schools by Organization and Enrollment, Sept. 30, 1983
[Annual. Jan. 1984. 11 p. no paging. Rpt. No. MSDE-OMIS 04100(R)005. SRI/MF/complete.]

Contains 6 tables showing number of public schools, by grade organization and pupil membership, by county, Sept. 1983.

Also includes lists of middle schools, vocational/technical schools, and schools with special education programs only.

S3610–3.4: Statistics on Enrollment and Number of Schools, Public and Nonpublic: Sept. 30, 1983, Maryland

[Annual. Feb. 1984. 20 p. no paging. Rpt. No. MSDE-OMIS 04100(R)003. LC 84-622980. SRI/MF/complete.]

Contains 14 tables showing public and non-public school enrollment trends, by county, 1978 and 1982-83; enrollment and number of schools by grade level, number of FTE teachers, and enrollment by specific grade (including special education), for public, Catholic, and other nonpublic schools, by county; and State institution educational program enrollment, by institution and grade level; Sept. 30, 1983.

S3610–3.5: Staff Employed at School and Central Office Levels, Maryland Public Schools, 1983/84

[Annual. Mar. 1984. 10 p. no paging. Rpt. No. MSDE-ADM 04100(R)100. SRI/MF/complete.]

Contains 8 tables showing staff employment by detailed function and county, 1983/84, with summary per-pupil ratios and comparisons to 1982/83.

S3610–3.6: Selected Financial Data, Part 1: Maryland Public Schools, 1982/83

[Annual. May 1984. 24 p. no paging+errata sheets. Rpt. No. OMIS 04100(R)200. SRI/MF/complete.]

Contains contents and table listing, introduction, definitions, and 13 tables showing the following, by county, for 1982/83:

a. Revenue by source (State, Federal, and local government) and purpose (current expenses, school construction, debt service, and food service); and State and Federal revenues by detailed category.

b. Basic State aid compared to local wealth; assessed property valuation; and local school appropriations compared to total local revenue, assessed valuation, and net taxable income.

S3610–3.7: Selected Financial Data, Part 2: Maryland Public Schools, 1982/83

[Annual. May 1984. 19 p. no paging. Rpt. No. MSDE-OMIS 04100(R)201. SRI/MF/complete.]

Contains table listing and 13 tables showing disbursements by detailed function and object, by county, 1982/83.

S3610–3.8: Selected Financial Data, Part 3: Maryland Public Schools, 1982/83

[Annual. May 1984. 12 p. no paging+errata sheets. Rpt. No. OMIS 04100(R)202. SRI/MF/complete.]

Contains table listing and 11 tables showing: costs per pupil belonging and attending, by expenditure function, with selected county rankings; local appropriations and per pupil costs for tuition; per pupil costs for textbooks, library books, and materials; school property value per pupil; and average salary per teacher and principal; all by county, 1982/83, with trends from 1972/73.

S3610–3.9: Selected Financial Data, Part 4: Maryland Public Schools, 1982/83

[Annual. July 1984. 15 p. no paging. Rpt. No. OMIS 04100(R)203. SRI/MF/complete.]

Contains table listing and 14 tables showing summary time series data by county, 1973/74-1982/83, for selected items covered in Parts 1-3, above.

S3610–3.10: Summary of Pupil Transportation, Maryland Public Schools, 1982/83

[Annual. Aug. 1984 (incorrectly reads Aug. 1983). 14 p. no paging. Rpt. No. OMIS 04100(300). SRI/MF/complete.]

Contains table listing, and 13 tables showing the following: public school pupils transported, by grade level; transportation vehicles, by capacity; contract and public vehicle mileage, and driver and aide hours; public and nonpublic school handicapped pupils transported, by means; total disbursements and State aid for transportation; and cost per pupil transported; all by county, 1982/83, with selected trends from 1973.

S3610–3.11: Federal Program Expenditures for Maryland Public Schools, 1982/83

[Annual. Aug. 1984. 18 p. no paging. Rpt. No. OMIS 04100(210). SRI/MF/complete.]

Contains table listing; preface; 2 charts; and 10 tables showing expenditures of Federal funds for public schools, by program and function, by county, 1982/83.

S3610–5 MARYLAND PUBLIC LIBRARY STATISTICS, FY82

Annual. [1983.]
5 p. no paging.
SRI/MF/complete

Annual report, for FY82, on Maryland public libraries. Covers finances, staff, holdings, and circulation. Consists of 5 tables showing population, and the following for public libraries, by county, FY82:

a. State operating/capital aid; operating income by source, including Federal and State aid, and local appropriations; and operating expenditures by type, including salaries, materials, and equipment.

b. Professional librarians, library associates, support staff, and CETA employees; minimum salaries for professional librarians; library holdings by type; book and film circulation; and registered borrowers.

SRI coverage of this report begins with the FY82 edition.

Availability: Maryland Department of Education, Library Development and Services Division, 200 W. Baltimore St., Baltimore MD 21201-2595, †; SRI/MF/complete.

S3616 MARYLAND
Department of Employment and Training

S3616–1 LABOR MARKET DIMENSIONS, Maryland

Monthly. Approx. 15 p.
SRI/MF/complete, shipped quarterly

Monthly report on Maryland employment and unemployment, hourly and weekly earnings, and unemployment insurance claims. Most employment data are shown by major industry group; separate data are generally shown for Baltimore metro area.

Data are compiled by the Dept of Employment and Training, and are issued approximately 2-3 months after month of coverage.

Contains narrative review of reported data; 6 monthly tables and 2 quarterly tables, listed below; and 1 additional table (Dec. issue) showing 1983 annual averages for monthly table [1].

Monthly tables appear in all issues. Page locations and latest period of coverage for quarterly tables are noted, as the tables appear, under "Statistical Features."

Prior to the Aug. 1983 issue, report was published by Maryland Department of Human Resources, and was described in SRI under S3645-1.

Availability: Maryland Department of Employment and Training, Research and Analysis Division, 1100 N. Eutaw St., Baltimore MD 21201, †; SRI/MF/complete, shipped quarterly.
Issues reviewed during 1984: Aug. 1983-Aug. 1984 (D).

RECURRING TABLES:

[Unless otherwise noted, data are shown for current and previous month, and for same month of previous year. Data in tables [2-4] are shown separately for Maryland and Baltimore metro area.]

MONTHLY TABLES

[1] Civilian labor force, employment, and unemployment, by place of residence [by State region and county; for current and previous month].

[2] Nonagricultural payroll employment by industry [group], by place of employment.

[3] Gross average hourly and weekly earnings and hours worked by production workers in selected [major] manufacturing industry groups.

[4] State regular unemployment insurance compensation program [claims and payments].

[5] Maryland Federal programs [unemployment compensation initial and continued claims].

[6] Estimated nonagricultural payroll employment by industry, by place of employment: Maryland [aggregate] counties in the Washington, D.C. metro area; Baltimore City; western Maryland; and balance of State.

QUARTERLY TABLES

[7] Females and production workers: estimated nonagricultural payroll employment by industry, by place of employment [employed in Maryland; by month for quarter ended 1 month prior to cover date].

[8] Characteristics of the active applicants [at the State job service, including data by age, sex, and race, and for Hispanics, veterans, handicapped, and welfare recipients], active applicants by occupation, and nonagricultural job openings by occupation [all usually for current month, same month of previous year, and last month of previous quarter].

STATISTICAL FEATURES:

S3616-1.501: Sept. 1983
QUARTERLY TABLE

[8] Job service applicant characteristics, and applicants and openings by occupation, Sept. 1983. (p. 13)

S3616-1.502: Oct. 1983
QUARTERLY TABLE

[7] Females and production workers nonagricultural employment, July-Sept. 1983. (p. 15)

S3616-1.503: Dec. 1983
QUARTERLY TABLE

[8] Job service applicant characteristics, and applicants and openings by occupation, Dec. 1983. (p. 13)

S3616-1.504: Jan. 1984
QUARTERLY TABLE

[7] Females and production workers nonagricultural employment, Oct.-Dec. 1983. (p. 15)

S3616-1.505: May 1984
QUARTERLY TABLES

[7] Females and production workers nonagricultural employment, Jan.-Mar. 1984. (p. 20)

[8] Job service applicant characteristics, and applicants and openings by occupation, Mar. 1984. (p. 15)

S3616-1.506: June 1984
QUARTERLY TABLE

[8] Job service applicant characteristics, and applicants and openings by occupation, June 1984. (p. 14)

S3616-1.507: July 1984
QUARTERLY TABLE

[7] Females and production workers nonagricultural employment, Apr.-June 1984. (p. 17)

S3618   MARYLAND
Department of
Fiscal Services

S3618-1   LOCAL GOVERNMENT FINANCES IN MARYLAND for the Fiscal Year Ended June 30, 1983
Annual.   Mar. 20, 1984.
451 p.
LC 79-615811.
SRI/MF/complete

Annual report presenting data on the financial condition of Maryland counties, incorporated municipalities, and other local taxing jurisdictions, FY83. Also includes status of local pension plans. Data are compiled from State agency and local government reports.

Contents:

Section I. Transmittal letter, and contents and table listing (p. 1-3).

Section II-III. Report, with 14 detailed financial tables, listed below, showing data for counties and special districts (p. 7-215) and for cities, towns, villages, and special taxing areas (p. 217-420).

Section IV. Appendices, with 13 tables, described below, including data on local tax rates and bond issues. (p. 421-443)

Section V-VI. Notes and index. (p. 445-451)

This is the 35th annual report.

Availability: Maryland Department of Fiscal Services, Fiscal Research Division, Legislative Services Bldg., Rm. 200, 90 State Circle, Annapolis MD 21401-1991, †; SRI/MF/complete.

TABLES:
[Data by county are also shown for Baltimore City.]

S3618-1.1: Detailed Financial Tables
[Data are for FY83, unless otherwise noted.]
BY COUNTY
[Tables show data by county. Data in tables I-II are shown by applicable jurisdictional unit, variously including library, education, community college, social services, and health boards; State highway administration account; sanitary districts; transit authorities; relevant commissions; and others.

Revenues are generally shown by source, including local property and income taxes, licenses/permits, revenue sharing, and Federal and State grants. Expenditures are generally shown by function.]

I. Financial summaries [property valuation, public debt detail, and aggregate revenues and expenditures]. (p. 7-38)

II. Statements of revenue and expenditure [including data for governmental (operating and capital) and enterprise operations]. (p. 39-90)

III. Five-year summary: statements of revenue and expenditure, FY79-83. (p. 91-117)

IV. Statements of revenue and expenditure, percent of total. (p. 119-125)

V. Statements of per capita revenue and expenditure. (p. 127-133)

VI. Analyses of county accounts with State highway administration, boards of education, boards of trustees for community colleges, and library boards. (p. 135-183)

VII. Five-year summary: statements of public debt [general obligation, State loans, enterprise, and special assessment], FY79-83. (p. 185-191)

VIII. Pension plan disclosures [local pension plan descriptions, groups covered, accounting and funding policies, costs, and funding status (assets compared to nonvested and/or vested benefits), all by individual plan], as of the 2 most recent plan valuation dates. (p. 193-215)

BY MUNICIPAL AREA
[All data arranged by county. Municipal areas are cities, towns, villages, and special taxing areas.]

I-II. [Tables I-II, listed above, are repeated for individual municipal areas; data are not shown by jurisdictional unit, except data in table II are shown by operations fund type.] (p. 219-333)

III. [Table III, listed above, is repeated for aggregate municipal areas.] (p. 335-356)

IV-VI. [Tables IV-V and VIII, listed above, are repeated for individual municipal areas.] (p. 357-420)

S3618-1.2: Appendix Tables
a. Population and land area, by county and municipality or special taxing district, 1983; and municipal and/or county tax rates for property, admissions/amusement, income, property transfer, recordation, sales/service, and trailer parks, mostly for FY83. App. I-VIII. (p. 421-434)

b. County and municipal bond issues, FY83; local issuances of industrial revenue bonds, 1983; county bond ratings, 1983; local public housing authority income and expenses, various years FY78-82; and State aid received compared to taxes paid, by county, FY77-83. App. IX-XIII. (p. 435-443)

S3635   MARYLAND
Department of
Health and
Mental Hygiene

S3635-1   ANNUAL VITAL STATISTICS REPORT, Maryland, 1981
Annual.   [1984.]   xxiii+85 p.
SRI/MF/complete

Annual compilation, for 1981, of Maryland vital statistics, including population, births, deaths by cause, marriages, and divorces, by region and county, with selected demographic characteristics, trends from 1940, and comparisons to U.S. Data are compiled from State records.

Contains contents and table listing, highlights with 8 summary tables, and definitions (p. iii-xxiii); and 8 statistical sections with 61 tables, listed below (p. 1-85).

Availability: Maryland Department of Health and Mental Hygiene, Health Statistics Center, 201 W. Preston St., Baltimore MD 21201, †; SRI/MF/complete.

TABLES:
[Data are for Maryland, 1981, unless otherwise noted. Political subdivisions are Maryland counties and Baltimore City.]

S3635–1.1: Population and Trends

POPULATION

[Tables 1-4 show data by State region and political subdivision.]

1-5. Estimated population by race, age group, and sex, July 1, 1981. (p. 3-9)

TRENDS

[Tables show data decennially 1940-70 and annually 1971-81.]

6-11. Births, deaths, and rates; and infant, neonatal, postneonatal, and fetal deaths and rates; by race. (p. 13-15)

12. Marriages by resident status and type of ceremony. (p. 16)

13. Absolute divorces and annulments by legal grounds for decree. (p. 16)

S3635–1.2: Births

14-15. Births and birth rates; and births, births of low birth weight, and percent of births of low birth weight; by race, region, and political subdivision. (p. 19-20)

16. Single and plural births, by birth weight and race. (p. 21)

17. Births, by month of birth, race, and sex. (p. 21)

18A-18F. Births and birth rates, by age of mother and race; and general fertility rates; by region and political subdivision. (p. 22-27)

19. Births, by birth order, age of mother, and race. (p. 28)

20-21. Births by live birth order; and births to unmarried women by race; by region and political subdivision. (p. 29-30)

22-23. Births to unmarried women, by age of mother and birth order, by race. (p. 31)

24. Births, by hospitalization, type of hospital [military, civilian, and not in hospital], and attendant; by region and political subdivision. (p. 32)

25-26. Births by plurality, by age of mother and length of pregnancy, by race. (p. 33-34)

27. Births, by birth weight, onset of prenatal care, and race. (p. 35)

28. Births, by place of residence and occurrence, race, region, and political subdivision. (p. 36)

29. Births to residents of Maryland, and births occurring in Maryland, by area of residence and area of occurrence. (p. 37)

S3635–1.3: Deaths

30. Deaths and death rates, by race, region, and political subdivision. (p. 41)

31-32. Deaths by month of death; and deaths and death rates by age and sex; by race. (p. 42)

33. Deaths and death rates for 12 leading causes, by sex and race. (p. 43)

34-35. 8 leading causes of male and female deaths in specified age groups. (p. 44-45)

36. Deaths from 72 selected causes, by age. (p. 46-50)

37-38. Deaths from 34 selected causes, and death rates for 7 leading causes, by region and political subdivision. (p. 51-55)

39. Accidental deaths by type of accident, by sex and [age]. (p. 56)

40-41. Deaths occurring in institutions [hospitals and nursing homes]; and deaths by place of residence and occurrence; by race, region, and political subdivision. (p. 57-58)

42. Deaths to residents of Maryland, and deaths occurring in Maryland, by area of residence and occurrence. (p. 59)

S3635–1.4: Fetal and Infant Deaths

[Tables show data by race, region, and political subdivision.]

43-44. Fetal and infant deaths and death and infant mortality rates. (p. 63-64)

45. Neonatal deaths, neonatal mortality rates, and perinatal death rates. (p. 65)

S3635–1.5: Marriages and Divorces

MARRIAGES

[Types of ceremony are civil and religious. Table titles begin "Marriages..."]

46. By resident status and type of ceremony, by region and political subdivision of occurrence. (p. 69)

47-48. By age of bride and groom, by previous marital status. (p. 70)

49. By age of bride, by age of groom. (p. 71)

50-51. By previous marital status and residence of bride and groom. (p. 73)

52. By previous marital status of bride and groom, by type of ceremony. (p. 74)

53. By State of residence of bride and groom. (p. 74)

DIVORCES

[Table titles begin "Absolute divorces and annulments..."]

54. By legal grounds for decree, region, and political subdivision of occurrence. (p. 77)

55-56. By party to whom decree was granted, and by place where marriage was performed, 3 Maryland areas of occurrence. (p. 78)

57-59. By age of husband and wife at time of decree; by number of children reported under 18 years of age and duration of marriage; and by number of marriages of husband and wife. (p. 79-80)

S3635–1.6: Comparative Vital Statistics

[Tables show data by race for Maryland and U.S., 1971-81.]

60. Selected natality data [birth and fertility rates; and percent of births of low birth weight, to unmarried women, of 4th order/higher, and with late/no prenatal care]. (p. 83)

61. Selected mortality data [death rates; and infant and neonatal mortality rates per 1,000 live births]. (p. 85)

S3635–3   MARYLAND MEDICAL CARE PROGRAMS: The Year in Review, FY83

Annual.   Feb. 1984.
iii+89 p.+errata sheet.
SRI/MF/complete

Annual report, for FY83, on Maryland health care services for low-income residents. Covers payments and number of enrollees, recipients, and/or services, by eligibility category; by detailed type of health service; by county and Baltimore City; by enrollee and recipient age, race, and sex; and by individual health care facility.

Eligibility categories are 14 federally matched and nonmatched indigent and medically indigent programs. Types of service include hospital inpatient and outpatient, nursing home, physician, pharmacy, dental, home/community health, and special services.

Also includes data on population compared to program enrollment by county and for Baltimore City, fraud investigations and recoveries, program trends from FY79, and summary enrollment from FY71.

Most data are compiled by the State Center for Health Statistics.

Contains contents and table listing (p. i-iii); narrative report, with 4 charts and 10 tables (p. 1-27); 34 detailed tables (p. 30-84); and glossary and technical note, with 1 table (p. 85-88).

Availability: Maryland Department of Health and Mental Hygiene, Medical Care Programs, Program Review and Planning Division, 300 W. Preston St., 2nd Floor, Baltimore MD 21201, †; SRI/MF/complete.

S3645   MARYLAND
Department of
Human Resources

S3645–1   LABOR MARKET DIMENSIONS, Maryland

Monthly.

Beginning with the Aug. 1983 issue, this report is issued by Maryland Department of Employment and Training and is covered by SRI under S3616-1.

S3645–2   INCOME MAINTENANCE ADMINISTRATION Statistical Report, Maryland

Monthly, with annual supplement.   Approx. 25 p. SRI/MF/complete, shipped quarterly

Monthly report, with annual supplement, on Maryland public welfare program applicants, recipients, and expenditures, by program and by county. Also includes data on current welfare fraud investigations. Report is issued approximately 3 months after month of coverage.

Generally contains data revisions or additions for previous reports, 1-6 summary charts, and 19 monthly tables listed below. Most tables appear in all issues.

An annual supplement is also issued, summarizing caseload data by program and county for the previous fiscal year. Publication of the supplement begins with the edition covering FY83, which also includes trends from FY79.

Availability: Maryland Department of Human Resources, Income Maintenance Administration, Research and Analysis Division, 300 W. Preston St., Rm. 511, Baltimore MD 21201, †; SRI/MF/complete, shipped quarterly.

Issues reviewed during 1984: Aug. 1983-July 1984; and FY83 annual supplement (D) [Nov. 1983 title page incorrectly reads Nov. 1984].

TABLES:

[Unless otherwise noted, data are for month of coverage, and are shown by county and for Baltimore City.]

SUMMARY TABLES AND AFDC

1-2. Public assistance payments, cases, and recipients [by program, State only; includes selected comparisons of budgeted and actual amounts, year-to-date totals, and previous month data].

3-5. AFDC total and [with and without unemployed parents (AFDC-UP): applications, cases, dispositions, child and adult recipients, and payments].

EMERGENCY, GENERAL PUBLIC, AND MEDICAL ASSISTANCE

6. Emergency assistance (EA) payments: EAFC [emergency assistance to families with dependent children] and EA [paid cases and expenditures].

7-8. General public assistance (GPA) and general public assistance to employables (GPA-E) [applications, cases, dispositions, recipients, and payments].

9-10. Medical assistance [applications received and disposition, for nonpublic assistance (NPA) and SSI].

CHANGES AND RECONSIDERATIONS

11A-11B. Reconsiderations and interim changes completed [by program].

FOOD STAMP PROGRAM

12. Food stamp program, NPA [applications received, and dispositions].

13. Food stamp program [certified households, and participating households and individuals, for public assistance and NPA; and total dollar value of coupons].

CHILD SUPPORT COLLECTIONS

14-15. Child support collections [net, gross, and intra-State incentives]; and case data; [AFDC and non-AFDC].

EMERGENCY ASSISTANCE, AND INVESTIGATIONS

16-18. Emergency assistance (EA and EAFC) [applications approved, by program, State only]; emergency requests, number received and number approved; and emergency payment [by program, State only]; [all by type of emergency, for month 1-3 months prior to month of coverage; tables may not appear in every issue].

19. Investigations of recipient fraud [referrals made to investigative units, investigations completed (indicating fraud or nonfraud), and total cases under investigation; for public assistance, medical assistance-NPA, and food stamp-NPA].

S3655   MARYLAND
Department of Licensing and Regulation

S3655–1   ONE HUNDRED TWELFTH ANNUAL REPORT OF THE INSURANCE COMMISSIONER of the State of Maryland
Annual. Jan. 10, 1984.
ii+87 p.
LC 32-16079.
SRI/MF/complete

Annual report on Maryland insurance industry financial condition and underwriting activity, by company and type of insurance, 1982. Covers assets, liabilities, capital/surplus, premium income, losses or claims incurred and/or paid, insurance in force, and gain from underwriting and investments, for insurers based in Maryland and elsewhere.

Data are shown, as applicable, for property/casualty and title insurance companies, nonprofit hospital service and medical indemnity corporations, HMOs, life insurance companies, and fraternal beneficiary assns.

Also includes data on company admission applications processed, regulatory filings, broker and agent licensing, and Insurance Division receipts.

Data are compiled mostly from unaudited annual insurer statements filed with the Insurance Division.

Contains contents listing (p. ii); Insurance Division report, with 4 text tables (p. 1-15); 18 corporate financial tables (p. 17-84); and statement of Insurance Division receipts, with 1 chart and 1 table (p. 86-87).

Availability: Maryland Department of Licensing and Regulation, Insurance Division, 501 St. Paul Pl., Baltimore MD 21202-2272, †; SRI/MF/complete.

S3655–2   SEVENTY-THIRD ANNUAL REPORT OF THE BANK COMMISSIONER of the State of Maryland, June 30, 1983
Annual. [1984.] 56 p.
LC 12-33233.
SRI/MF/complete

Annual report on financial condition of Maryland State-chartered banks and other financial institutions for FY83, presenting assets, liabilities, equity capital, income, and expenses, for commercial banks, trust companies, mutual savings institutions, credit unions, and secondary loan mortgage companies, generally as of June 30, 1983 or Dec. 31, 1982. Data on assets and liabilities are usually shown by institution, with composite trends from 1960.

Also includes data on dept fee receipts and disbursements; banks and assets, by county; and credit union financial ratios.

Contains contents listing (1 p.); dept report, with 2 text tables and regulatory activities (p. 1-14); and 14 financial tables, interspersed with lists of financial institutions and licensees (p. 15-56).

Availability: Maryland Department of Licensing and Regulation, State Bank Commissioner, 2005 Blaustein Bldg., One N. Charles St., Baltimore MD 21201, †; SRI/MF/complete.

S3660   MARYLAND
Department of State Planning

S3660–6   FINAL POPULATION PROJECTIONS, Maryland
Triennial Series.
For individual publication data, see below.
SRI/MF/complete

Triennial series of 7 reports presenting projections of Maryland population to 2000, with census data for 1980. Data generally are shown by sex, race, and age, for Maryland, each county, and Baltimore city.

Each report contains 1 table repeated by location. Most reports are issued in 3 parts providing separate coverage for total, white, and nonwhite population.

Reports are further described below.

Availability: Maryland Department of State Planning, Planning Data Office, Research and State Data Center, 301 W. Preston St., Baltimore MD 21201-2365, complete set of reports $35.00, individual report prices vary; SRI/MF/complete.

S3660–6.1: Final Population Projections by Age, Race, and Sex, 1980-2000 (Total, White, Non-White)
[Triennial. Oct. 1983. 3 parts, 50 p. each, no paging. $2.00 each. SRI/MF/complete.]

Presents Maryland population projections quinquennially 1985-2000, with census data for 1980. Report is issued in 3 parts.

S3660–6.2: Final Population Projections: Selected Age Cohorts, 1980-2000 (Total, White, Non-White)
[Triennial. Oct. 1983. 3 parts, 25 p. each, no paging. $1.50 each. SRI/MF/complete.]

Presents Maryland population projections 1981-90, 1995, and 2000, with census data for 1980. Data by age are shown for school, labor force, and other age cohorts. Report is issued in 3 parts.

S3660–6.3: Final Population Projections: Births by Race and Sex, 1980-2000
[Triennial. Oct. 1983. 24 p. no paging. $1.50. SRI/MF/complete.]

Presents projections of Maryland births, 1980-2000. Data are not shown by age. Data for total State are omitted.

S3660–6.4: Final Population Projections: Summary Report, 1980-2000
[Triennial. Oct. 1983. 32 p. no paging. $2.00. SRI/MF/complete.]

Presents Maryland projected population in households and group quarters, quinquennially 1985-2000, with census data for 1980; and projected births, deaths, and net household migration, 5-year periods 1980-2000. Also includes data by planning region. Data are not shown by age.

S3660–6.5: Final Population Projections: Individual Years, 1980-90 (Total, White, Non-White)

S3660–6.5　Maryland

[Triennial. Oct. 1983. 3 parts, 100 p. each, no paging. $4.00 each. SRI/MF/complete.]

Presents Maryland population projections 1981-90, with census data for 1980. Report is issued in 3 parts.

S3660–6.6: Final Population Projections: Household Population, 1980-2000 (Total, White, Non-White)

[Triennial. Oct. 1983. 3 parts, 50 p. each, no paging. $2.00 each. SRI/MF/complete.]

Presents Maryland projected population in households, quinquennially 1985-2000, with census data for 1980. Report is issued in 3 parts.

S3660–6.7: Final Population Projections: Group Quarter Population, 1980-2000 (Total, White, Non-White)

[Triennial. Oct. 1983. 3 parts, 50 p. each, no paging. $2.00 each. SRI/MF/complete.]

Presents Maryland projected population in group quarters, quinquennially 1985-2000, with census data for 1980. Report is issued in 3 parts.

S3660–7　1980 CENSUS LABOR FORCE OCCUPATIONAL CHARACTERISTICS, Maryland

Monograph.　Aug. 1983.
xliv+416 p.　Pub. No. 83-11.
SRI/MF/complete

Report presenting 1980 census data, for Maryland, on civilian labor force by detailed occupation, cross-tabulated by sex and race-ethnicity (white, black, American Indian/Eskimo/Aleut, Asian/Pacific Islander, Hispanic, and other). Data by major occupational category are shown for State, 7 planning regions, individual counties, and Baltimore City. Data by detailed occupation are shown for State and 5 regions.

Also includes unemployed labor force (no work experience since 1975) for each demographic group and locale; and labor force participation rates by race, sex, and region, with comparisons to 1970.

Data are from the Equal Employment Opportunity Special Tape File of the 1980 Census of Population and Housing. The EEO file, based on a 20% sample of the census questionnaire, includes the entire civilian labor force in its universe, whereas much of the other census data on occupations (e.g., Summary Tape File 3) covers only employed civilians. The EEO file was produced to help meet the needs of government and private industry in planning for EEO/Affirmative Action.

Contents:

Contents listing and foreword. (p. i-v)

Summary of findings, with 4 charts and 16 tables; report organization; and source data characteristics. (p. vii-xliv)

Section 1-2: data by major occupational category, for State and planning regions (p. 1-81) and for counties and Baltimore City (p. 83-193); with 1 table repeated for each geographic entity, and accompanying summary charts for State and regions.

Section 3: data by detailed occupation, with 1 table repeated for State and each of 5 regions. (p. 195-412)

Appendix: comparable 1970 definitions for 1980 major census occupation groups. (p. 413-416)

Availability: Maryland Department of State Planning, Planning Data Office, Research and State Data Center, 301 W. Preston St., Baltimore MD 21201-2365, $10.00; SRI/MF/complete.

S3665　MARYLAND
Department of Public Safety and Correctional Services

S3665–1　1983 STATE OF MARYLAND UNIFORM CRIME REPORTS

Annual.　For individual publication data, see below.
SRI/MF/complete

Annual report, for 1983, on Maryland crimes and arrests, by type of offense, with trends from 1979. Includes data on value of property stolen and recovered, clearances, assaults on police, and law enforcement employment. Selected data are shown by State region, county, municipality, and law enforcement agency.

Data are from reports of State and local law enforcement agencies, including park police, submitted under the Uniform Crime Reporting Program.

Report is published in 2 volumes, described below. This is the 9th annual report. For description of 8th annual report, for 1982, see SRI 1983 Annual, under S3665-2.

Availability: Maryland Department of Public Safety and Correctional Services, Uniform Crime Reporting Section, Criminal Records-Central Repository, Maryland State Police, Pikesville MD 21208-3899, †; SRI/MF/complete.

S3665–1.1: 1983 Crime in Maryland

[Annual. Aug. 17, 1984. viii+172 p. SRI/MF/complete.]

Contains listings of contents, tables, and charts (p. vi-viii); introduction, with 2 summary tables (p. 1-9); crime classifications and methodology (p. 11-23); and 26 charts, and 29 tables described below, interspersed with narrative analyses (p. 27-172).

TABLES:

[Index crimes are murder, rape, robbery, aggravated assault, breaking/entering, larceny, and motor vehicle theft. Although arson is classified as an Index crime, data are reported separately, and generally are not included in Crime Index tables. Data by region are shown for 6 State regions.]

INDEX OFFENSES AND ARSON

a. Offenses, clearances, and clearance rates, for total, violent, and property Index crimes, and by Index offense, 1982-83; and value of property stolen and recovered, by type, 1983, and total 1979-83. 3 tables. (p. 33-35)

b. Murders, by circumstance 1983, and by type of weapon used 1979-83. 2 tables. (p. 41-42)

c. Rapes (forcible and attempted), 1979-83. 1 table. (p. 47)

d. Robberies and value of property stolen, by type of location, 1983; and robberies by type of weapon, 1979-83. 2 tables. (p. 53-54)

e. Aggravated assaults, by type of weapon, 1979-83. 1 table. (p. 59)

f. Breaking/entering offenses and value of property stolen, by classification (residential and nonresidential day and night), 1983; and forced, nonforced, and attempted offenses, 1979-83. 2 tables. (p. 65-66)

g. Larcenies and value of property stolen, by larceny type, 1983. 1 table. (p. 71)

h. Motor vehicles (autos, trucks, and other) stolen, and value of vehicles stolen and recovered; 1979-83. 2 tables. (p. 77-78)

i. Arson offenses, loss value, and clearance rate, by type of property, 1983. 1 table. (p. 83)

LOCAL OFFENSE AND ARREST DATA

j. Index offenses: crime rate and/or offenses by type, all by region, county, law enforcement agency, and municipality, including arson data for municipalities and selected other jurisdictions, and also including population, clearances, and clearance rates for jurisdictions except municipalities; 1982-83. 2 tables. (p. 88-128)

k. Arrests of juveniles and adults, and for drug abuse violations by substance and gambling violations by type, and arrest rates by Index offense, 1979-83; and arrests by detailed Index and non-Index offense, by sex, race (white, black, American Indian, and Asian), and age, 1983. 6 tables. (p. 136-143)

LAW ENFORCEMENT EMPLOYEES

l. Assaults on police officers, by type of weapon, activity, and injury status, 1979-83; and assaults by type of weapon, injuries, and clearances, by region, county, and law enforcement agency, 1983. 4 tables. (p. 150-163)

m. Employment in law enforcement, and rate per 1,000 population, by region and county; and sworn officers, civilian employees, and total employees by sex, by region, county, and law enforcement agency; 1983. 2 tables. (p. 166-172)

S3665–1.2: Maryland Arrest Data: Supplement to 1983 Crime in Maryland

[Annual. Aug. 1984. 64 p. no paging. SRI/MF/complete.]

(64 p.) Contains 1 extended table showing adult and juvenile arrests, and arrests by detailed Index and non-Index offense, by region, county, and law enforcement agency, 1982-83.

S3665–3　CRIMINAL JUSTICE AGENCY PROCESSING STATISTICS, MARYLAND

Annual Series.　For individual publication data, see below.
SRI/MF/complete

Series of 2 annual reports on corrections in Maryland, including Division of Correction (DOC) inmate population, and related data on crimes and parole activities, FY and CY 1983, with comparisons to 1982 and inmate population summary from 1977. Some data are shown by month.

Covers DOC sentenced inmates and number in local jails, escapes, and prison admissions and releases by reason; inmates and average sentence length, and life and death sentences, by committing jurisdiction; inmates by sex, race/ethnicity (including Indian), age, sentence length, and commitment offense, by facility; and selected detail for Patuxent Institution.

Also includes data on crimes by major offense; adult and juvenile arrests; local jail admissions, departures, and average population by reason for incarceration; Division of Probation and Parole cases added, closed, under active supervision, and being administered, by type of case; and disposition of Parole Commission hearings, for DOC-related cases.

Data are from reports filed with various State agencies.

Series consists of 1 fiscal year and 1 calendar year report. Both reports contain contents listing (p. 1); and 6 statistical sections, with narrative summaries, and 36 charts and 31-32 tables (p. 2-68). Reports reviewed in 1984 are listed below. SRI coverage begins with the 1983 reports.

Availability: Maryland Department of Public Safety and Correctional Services, Research and Statistics Office, One Investment Pl., Suite 500, Towson MD 21204, †; SRI/MF/complete.

REPORTS:

S3665–3.1: Criminal Justice Agency Processing Statistics, FY83 vs. FY82
[Annual [1983.] 68 p. Oversized. SRI/MF/complete.]

S3665–3.2: Criminal Justice Agency Processing Statistics, CY83 vs. CY82
[Annual Feb. 1984. 68 p. Oversized. LC 84-621704. SRI/MF/complete.]

S3685   MARYLAND
Comptroller of the Treasury

S3685–1   1982 SUMMARY REPORT, Maryland Income Tax Division
Annual. [1983.] 54 p.
LC 79-643507.
SRI/MF/complete

Annual report on Maryland 1982 individual income tax returns, with data on filings, income, and tax liability, generally shown by State adjusted gross income (AGI) class, county, and city or town.

Data are from a complete tabulation of all resident and nonresident individual income tax returns filed in 1983 with the comptroller of the treasury.

Contains contents listing (1 p.); introduction with text tables (p. 1-4); and 13 detailed tables, listed below (p. 6-54).

This is the 15th edition of the report.

Availability: Maryland Comptroller of the Treasury, Income Tax Division, State Income Tax Bldg., Annapolis MD 21401, †; SRI/MF/complete.

DETAILED TABLES:

[Unless otherwise noted, data are for 1982. All tables include number of returns filed, usually shown for taxable and nontaxable returns. Tables [1-3] and [6-10] show data by county and for Baltimore City and nonresidents.]

[1-3] Maryland gross income [and Federal AGI and modifications], net taxable income [and deductions and number and amount of exemptions]; and net State tax, [local tax and tax rate, and total State/local tax]. (p. 6-8)

[4-5] AGI classes [Maryland AGI, total deductions, exemptions, and net taxable income]; and net State and local tax; by AGI classes. (p. 9-10)

[6] Nontaxable returns, with selected data [Federal AGI, modifications, and Maryland gross income]. (p. 11)

[7] Numbers of returns filed, and net taxable income. (p. 12)

[8] Summary of refunds [number and total amount]. (p. 13)

[9] Selected tax credits [gross State and out-of-State income tax, personal property tax, and net State income tax]. (p. 14)

[10] Resident tax returns filed, 1976-82. (p. 15)

[11] Nonresident return statistics [net taxable income and net and average State tax, by State AGI class]. (p. 16)

[12] [Net taxable income, net State tax, and local tax, for nontaxable returns and by Maryland AGI class; repeated for each county and Baltimore City.] (p. 18-41)

[13] [Total tax, by city and town, and for rural/unincorporated areas, arranged by county.] (p. 44-54)

S3685–2   STATE OF MARYLAND COMPREHENSIVE ANNUAL FINANCIAL REPORT for the Year Ended June 30, 1983
Annual. Dec. 1, 1983. 78 p.
SRI/MF/complete

Annual report on financial condition of Maryland State government, for FY83, presenting assets and liabilities, revenues by source, and expenditures by function, for general, special revenue, debt service, capital projects, enterprise, trust and agency, and higher education/university hospital funds.

Also includes data on budgeted revenues and appropriations, by function and fund, FY84; long-term bonded indebtedness; retirement fund finances; State aid, and property valuations and levies, by county; and property tax delinquencies, and valuations by property type.

Also includes socioeconomic data, including population, per capita income, school enrollment, unemployment rate, and bank deposits; State highway mileage; land area; police facilities; higher education campuses, educators, and students; recreation facilities, including State parks and forests; number of State employees; and selected trends from FY74.

Data were compiled by the Office of the Comptroller of the Treasury.

Contains contents listing (p. 3-4); introductory section, with text data (p. 7-16); 24 financial statements and schedules, with accompanying notes including text statistics (p. 19-70); and statistical section, with 11 tables (p. 73-78).

Availability: Maryland Comptroller of the Treasury, General Accounting Division, Financial Reporting Section, PO Box 466, Annapolis MD 21404-0466, †; SRI/MF/complete.

S3777   MASSACHUSETTS
Executive Office for Administration and Finance

S3777–1   COMMONWEALTH OF MASSACHUSETTS FINANCIAL REPORT for the Fiscal Year Ended June 30, 1983
Annual. [1983.] xiv+101 p.
House No. 500.
LC 82-641564.
SRI/MF/complete

Annual report on financial condition of Massachusetts State government, for FY83, presenting assets, liabilities, and fund balances; revenues by source; and expenditures by agency, object, and agency account; generally by specific fund.

Funds covered are general, special revenue, capital projects, proprietary, and trust and agency.

Also includes data on State bonded debt, budgeted vs. actual revenues and expenditures, and selected trends from FY74.

Contains transmittal letter with 2 text tables, contents listing, and 2 summary exhibits with accompanying charts and tables (p. iii-xiii); auditor's report, with 6 financial statements (p. 1-26); individual fund sections, with 20 statements (p. 27-67); debt service section, with 6 schedules (p. 69-81); statement of appropriations by fund (p. 83-85); and statistical section, with 9 schedules (p. 87-101).

Availability: Massachusetts Executive Office for Administration and Finance, Comptroller's Division, John W. McCormack Bldg., One Ashburton Pl., Boston MA 02108, †; SRI/MF/complete.

S3805   MASSACHUSETTS
Department of Correction

S3805–1   STATISTICAL DESCRIPTION OF RESIDENTS OF THE MASSACHUSETTS CORRECTIONAL INSTITUTIONS on Jan. 1, 1984
Annual. July 1984. 122 p.
Pub. No. 13721.
LC 77-644275.
SRI/MF/complete

Annual report on Massachusetts correctional institutions, with data on the inmate population, including demographic and socioeconomic characteristics, criminal background, commitment offense, and sentence length, as of Jan. 1, 1984. Data are shown by institution.

Also includes data on community-based correctional programs, escapes, inmate prior drug use, and paroles and furloughs.

Data are from the Correction and Parole Management Information System.

Contains contents and table listing (p. 1-8); introduction and summary (p. 9-13); 2 statistical sections, with 52 tables repeated for correctional institutions (p. 14-119); and glossary (p. 120-122).

Availability: Massachusetts Department of Correction, Leverett Saltonstall State Office Bldg., 100 Cambridge St., Boston MA 02202, †; SRI/MF/complete.

S3807 MASSACHUSETTS Office of the Chief Administrative Justice of the Trial Court

S3807–1 ANNUAL REPORT OF THE MASSACHUSETTS TRIAL COURT, 1983
Annual. Mar. 5, 1984.
3+175 p.
LC 80-644980.
SRI/MF/complete

Annual report on Massachusetts trial court caseloads and case dispositions, FY83. Covers municipal court of Boston; and district, housing, juvenile, land, probate/family, and superior courts. Includes data by case type and court location, with selected trends from FY79.

Case types shown are criminal and civil, for most courts, with some additional detail for traffic, domestic relations, mental health commitment, violent crime victim claims, spouse abuse, small claims, juvenile, adoption, and other case types. District court data also include appeals.

Also includes detail for Boston municipal court, and data on probation dept activities and expenditures, child support collections, drunk driving cases, age of active trial caseloads, and probate/family court investigations.

Contains contents listing (1 p.); and 3 sections, with narrative summaries, 9 charts, and 75 tables (p. 1-175).

Availability: Massachusetts Office of the Chief Administrative Justice of the Trial Court, Trial Court, 300 New Court House, Boston MA 02108, †; SRI/MF/complete.

S3808 MASSACHUSETTS Executive Office of Economic Affairs

S3808–1 MASSACHUSETTS EMPLOYMENT REVIEW
Monthly. Approx. 10 p.
SRI/MF/complete, shipped quarterly

Monthly report on Massachusetts labor force, employment, and unemployment, including unemployment insurance claims, all by local area, with selected detail by industry. Also includes job service applicants and openings.

Data are from State and Federal sources; report is issued approximately 3 months after month of coverage.

Contains narrative overview of labor market conditions, occasionally with summary text tables or charts; 1 summary table; 9 detailed tables, listed below; and glossary.

Prior to Sept. 1983 issue, report was covered in SRI under S3860-3.

Availability: Employment Review, Massachusetts Employment Security Division, Research and Policy Department, Charles F. Hurley Bldg., Government Center, Boston MA 02114, †; SRI/MF/complete, shipped quarterly.

Issues reviewed during 1984: Sept. 1983-July 1984 (D) (Vol. 10, Nos. 9-11; Vol. 11, Nos. 1-7) [No Dec. 1983 issue was published].

MONTHLY TABLES:
[Unless otherwise noted, data are for month of coverage, previous month, and same month of previous year. Data for labor areas are shown by SMSA and labor market area (LMA).]

[1] Labor force, employment, and unemployment: Massachusetts and the labor areas.

[2] Job matching service data [available applicants and unfilled openings, for State].

[3-7] Nonagricultural wage/salary employment: Massachusetts, Boston SMSA, Springfield/Chicopee/Holyoke and Worcester LMAs, and by [selected other labor] area [by major manufacturing group and industry division, including Federal, State, and local employees].

[8] Preliminary estimates [labor force by employment status, by city and town, month of coverage only].

[9] Unemployment insurance claims [initial and continued, for State and labor areas].

S3808–2 OCCUPATIONAL PROFILES: MASSACHUSETTS
Series. For individual publication data, see below.
SRI/MF/complete

Series of reports, published in a 3-year cycle, each providing data on Massachusetts nonagricultural employment in an industry division, by detailed occupation.

Data are from a series of Occupational Employment Statistics surveys, conducted over a 3-year period and updated triennially, covering the following industry sectors: nonmanufacturing; manufacturing; Federal Government; State and local governments; education; hospitals; wholesale and retail trade, and regulated industries; services, finance, insurance, real estate, and construction; and possibly others.

General format of each report:

a. Summary, contents listing, introduction, list of industries covered in survey, and summary charts and/or tables including employment trends.

b. 1 table, repeated for each SIC 2- or 3-digit industry covered, showing employment by detailed occupation for survey period; usually accompanied by narrative summary and an additional table ranking major occupations within the industry.

c. Methodology and description of occupational categories covered.

Report reviewed during 1984 is described below. Prior to 1984, series was covered in SRI under S3860-1.

Availability: Massachusetts Employment Security Division, Job Market Research Publications, Charles F. Hurley Bldg., Government Center, Boston MA 02114, †; SRI/MF/complete.

S3808–2.1: Occupations in Trade, Transportation, Communications, and Utilities, 1982
[Triennial. Aug. 1983. vi+124 p. Rpt. No. 18. SRI/MF/complete.]

Covers occupational employment in transportation; electric and gas utilities and sanitary services; wholesale trade; building materials, hardware, garden supply and mobile home dealers; general merchandise stores; food stores; automotive dealers and gasoline service stations; furniture and home furnishings and equipment stores; and miscellaneous retail establishments; with detail by SIC 3-digit industry, including public warehousing and clothing stores.

Data are based on responses of 3,277 establishments to a 1982 mail and telephone survey. Establishments were randomly selected from businesses included in 2nd quarter 1982 report on employment and wages covered by the Massachusetts Employment Security Law.

For description of previous report, for 1979, see SRI 1981 Annual, under S3860-1.6.

S3840 MASSACHUSETTS Department of Food and Agriculture

S3840–1 MASSACHUSETTS AGRICULTURE, 1983
Annual. [1984.] 4+74+5 p.
ISSN 0092-9794.
LC 74-640739.
SRI/MF/complete

Annual report on Massachusetts agricultural production, marketing, and finances, by commodity, 1970s-83, with selected comparisons to other regions and U.S.

Report covers production, prices, income, value, and, as applicable, acreage, yield, inventory, and disposition, for livestock, apiary, dairy, poultry, mink, field crop, maple syrup, and fruit and vegetable sectors; and farm income and production expenses.

Also includes data on fertilizer consumption; farms and acreage, including State agricultural preservation program lands and expenditures; government inspections of seeds, fruit and vegetables, feed and fertilizers, nurseries, and apiary colonies by county; and U.S. food consumption.

Report also presents selected preliminary findings from the 1982 Census of Agriculture, including data on farms and farmland by use; type of farm ownership; farm operator characteristics, including tenure, age group, and race, whether farming is primary occupation, and female operators; value of farm equipment; and production and marketing by commodity; with comparisons to 1978.

Data are compiled by the New England Crop and Livestock Reporting Service.

Contains table of contents (2 p.); 2 sections, with narrative summaries, and 5 charts and 67 tables (p. 1-74); and Census of Agriculture data, with 6 tables (p. 75-79).

Availability: Massachusetts Department of Food and Agriculture, Leverett Saltonstall Bldg., 100 Cambridge St., Government Center, Boston MA 02202, †; SRI/MF/complete.

S3850   MASSACHUSETTS Department of Public Health

S3850-1   ANNUAL REPORT, VITAL STATISTICS OF MASSACHUSETTS, 1981
Annual. Nov. 1983.
2+142 p. Pub. Doc. No. 1.
LC 79-3383.
SRI/MF/complete

Annual report on Massachusetts vital statistics for 1981, with trends from as early as 1900. Covers births, deaths by cause, abortions, marriages, divorces, and population. Includes data by city/ town, county, health service area (HSA), age, sex, and race.

Data are from the State Registry of Vital Records and Statistics and Census Bureau.

Contains listing of contents, tables, and charts (p. 1-3); 3 summary and trend charts, and 39 tables listed below, interspersed with narrative summaries (p. 5-123); and appendix, with methodology, facsimiles of vital statistics certificates, definitions, and maps (p. 126-142).

This is the 140th annual report.

Availability: Massachusetts Department of Public Health, Health Statistics and Research Division, Vital Records and Statistics Registry, 150 Tremont St., Rm. B-3, Boston MA 02111, †; SRI/MF/complete.

TABLES:

[Data are for Massachusetts, 1981, unless otherwise noted.]

S3850-1.1: Summary and Natality

SUMMARY

A1. Summary of 1981 [and 1980] vital events. (p. 6)

A2. Vital events, by month. (p. 8)

A3-A4. Crude rates of vital events, Massachusetts and U.S.; and State resident births and deaths and resultant natural increase; [various years] 1900-81. (p. 9-10)

A5. Births and deaths, by town, county, and HSA of occurrence and residence [includes resident mature and immature births, total deaths, and infant and neonatal deaths, by sex], with natural increase. (p. 12-27)

NATALITY

B1. Resident births, by sex and race. (p. 31)

B2. Resident live births, by age, race, and marital status of mother. (p. 32)

B3. Resident live births to teenage mothers [by age], 1970-81. (p. 33)

B4. Births: parity, by age of mother. (p. 34)

B5. Age-specific birth rates among women, 1980-81. (p. 35)

B6. Resident live births, by age [and marital status] of mother and weight of infant. (p. 36)

B7. Births, by hospital of occurrence [and by HSA], 1970, 1975, and 1980-81. (p. 37)

S3850-1.2: Mortality, Abortions, Marriages and Divorces, and Population

MORTALITY

C1. Resident deaths, by age, sex, and race. (p. 43)

C2-C3. Leading causes of death: Massachusetts and U.S., 1980-81; and by HSA [1981]. (p. 44-45)

C4. Leading causes of death, by age group and sex. (p. 46)

C5. Selected causes and rates per 100,000 of resident deaths, by sex and age. (p. 48)

C6a-C6c. 10 selected causes of death, by city/ town, county, and HSA of residence. (p. 52-62)

C7-C8. Deaths by selected underlying causes and mentioned conditions; and atherosclerosis, hypertensive disease, and diabetes mellitus underlying cause and mentioned conditions, by age group and sex. (p. 63-64)

C9-C10. Medical examiner certified deaths: by county of occurrence and cause; and by cause, sex, race, and age. (p. 65-67)

C11. Resident deaths, by [detailed] cause, sex, and race. (p. 68-99)

INFANT AND NEONATAL MORTALITY

D1. Resident infant and neonatal deaths, 1970-81. (p. 102)

D2-D3. Infant and neonatal deaths: by age, sex, and race; and by cause, age, and sex. (p. 103-105)

D4. Neonatal mortality by birth weight [1970-81]. (p. 106)

ABORTIONS

E1. Age of patient (abortions) in comparison to age of mother (births). (p. 109)

MARRIAGES AND DIVORCES

F1. Marriages and divorces, and rates per 1,- 000 population, [selected years] 1900-81. (p. 112)

F2-F3. Marriages and divorces, by county; and marriages by age and marital status [of bride and groom]. (p. 113-114)

POPULATION

G1. 1980 population, by sex and age. (p. 116)

G2-G4. Population: by counties, [quinquennially 1955-80; and by] cities/towns and HSAs, 1970 and 1980. (p. 117-123)

S3855   MASSACHUSETTS Board of Regents of Higher Education

S3855-1   HIGHER EDUCATION GENERAL INFORMATION SURVEY: Summary Report, 1982, Massachusetts
Annual. [1983.] 4+43 p.
No. 13367-53-400-9-83-CR.
SRI/MF/complete, current & previous year reports

Annual report, for 1982, on Massachusetts postsecondary education. Covers enrollment, by degree level, full- or part-time status, and race/ethnic group, fall 1982; degrees awarded, by degree level and field of study, July 1, 1981- June 30, 1982; and faculty, by tenure status, 1982.

Includes data by sex, by type of institution, and for individual public institutions. Enrollment also is shown for individual public and independent institutions in Boston area.

Institution types are public and independent universities, 4-year colleges, and 2-year colleges. Data by race/ethnic group include totals for nonresident alien, white, black, American Indian/ Alaskan Native, Asian/Pacific Islander, and Hispanic.

Also includes summary trend data on degrees awarded, 1970s.

Data are from NCES reports and responses of 120 institutions to the NCES Higher Education General Information Survey (HEGIS).

Contains foreword and table of contents (2 p.); 2 sections, with 8 charts and 37 tables (p. 1-37); and 4 appendices including 2 tables (p. 38-43).

Previous report, for 1981, has also been reviewed and is also available on SRI microfiche, under this number [Annual. [1983.] 3+51 p. †]. Previous report is similar in format and content, but also includes data on degrees awarded by race/ethnic group, and excludes data on enrollment by race/ethnic group, and degree trends.

Report for 1980 is described in SRI 1982 Annual, under this number.

Availability: Massachusetts Board of Regents of Higher Education, McCormack Bldg., Rm. 619, One Ashburton Pl., Boston MA 02108- 1530, †; SRI/MF/complete.

S3860   MASSACHUSETTS Department of Labor and Industries

S3860-3   MASSACHUSETTS EMPLOYMENT REVIEW
Monthly, with annual supplement.

SRI now covers this publication under S3808-1.

S3870   MASSACHUSETTS
Board of
Library Commissioners

S3870-1   DATA FOR
MASSACHUSETTS, FY83:
Comparative Public Library
Report
Annual.   Dec. 1983.
63 p.+addendum.
LC 79-641407.
SRI/MF/complete

Annual report, for FY83, on Massachusetts public library holdings, circulation, finances, and
staff, by municipality. Data are based on reports
by approximately 320 of the State's 347
municipalities with libraries.

Contains contents listing (1 p.), and the following:

Introduction, with 1 table showing selected library trends for FY81-83; and user guide. (p.
1-11)

Section 1. 9 summary tables showing mean,
median, and percentile data for selected library indicators, aggregated for municipalities in 6 population size groups, FY83. (p.
13-17)

Section 2. 7 municipal tables showing library
per capita income, municipal appropriations, operating expenditures by object,
holdings, and circulation; hours open; FTE
employees; and average workweek; all by
municipality, arranged in 7 population size
groups, FY83, with rankings by 1980 population. (p. 19-43)

Section 3. Facsimile report forms, with definitions. (p. 46-56)

Index to municipal population groups, and addendum. (p. 58-63, 1 p.)

Availability: Massachusetts Board of Library
Commissioners, Development of Library Services Office, Planning and Research Unit, 648
Beacon St., Boston MA 02215, ‡; SRI/MF/com-
plete.

S3900   MASSACHUSETTS
Department of
Public Safety

S3900-1   CRIME IN
MASSACHUSETTS, 1983
Annual.   [1984.] ii+90 p.
Pub. No. 13612-90-1,
250-6-84-P.S.
LC 79-641148.
SRI/MF/complete

Annual report on Massachusetts crimes reported, by offense and local agency, 1983, with
trends from 1978. Also includes data on clearances, assaults on police, property loss from arson, and law enforcement employment. Data are
from State and local law enforcement agency reports, submitted under the Uniform Crime Reporting (UCR) Program, and include selected
comparisons to U.S.

Contains contents listing (2 p.); list of participating agencies (p. 1-3); and the following
sections:

Section 1. UCR Program, with overview and
definitions. (p. 4-13)

Section 2. Officers Assaulted and Killed. Includes 3 charts and 1 table showing assaults
on police, by type of weapon, assignment,
and activity; clearances by type of activity;
and assaults by injury status and time of day;
1983. (p. 14-17)

Section 3-4. Crime Index and Reported Index
Offenses by Agency. Includes 11 summary
charts, and 23 tables described below. (p.
18-72)

Section 5. Law Enforcement Employees. 1 table showing population, sworn officers by
sex, and total civilian employees, by city,
State agency, and campus police dept, 1983.
(p. 73-89)

Issuing agency also publishes *Massachusetts Uniform Crime Report,* a semiannual report on Index crimes by city, not covered by SRI.

Availability: Massachusetts Department of
Public Safety, Crime Reporting Unit, 1010 Com-
monwealth Ave., Boston MA 02215, †; SRI/
MF/complete.

TABLES:
[Data are for Massachusetts, 1983, unless otherwise noted. Data on Index crimes generally are
shown by offense, for murder, forcible rape, robbery, aggravated assault, burglary, larceny, and
motor vehicle theft.]

a. Index crimes, total and daily average, 1982-
83; aggregate Index crimes by major city;
crime clock; and number and rate of Index
crimes, with comparison to U.S. and trends
from 1978. 14 tables. (p. 19-32)

b. Arson offenses reported, unfounded reports,
actual offenses, total and juvenile clearances,
offenses involving abandoned buildings, and
value of property damage, all by type of structure. 1 table. (p. 34)

c. Murder offenses and rates, 1979-83; and
murders by month, circumstance, victim-offender relationship, weapon used, victim's
age, and victim and offender sex and race or
ethnic group (including American Indian/
Alaskan Native and Asian/Pacific Islander
victims). 7 tables. (p. 36-41)

d. Index crimes, and total crime and clearance
rates, all by city arranged by population size,
State agency by county, and college/universi-
ty campus. 1 table. (p. 43-72)

S3917   MASSACHUSETTS
Department of
Revenue

S3917-1   ANNUAL REPORT, 1982-83:
Commonwealth of
Massachusetts, Department
of Revenue
Annual.   [1984.] vi+42 p.
SRI/MF/complete

Annual report, for FY83, of the Massachusetts
Dept of Revenue. Includes data on tax collections and revenues by fund and/or source, tax
bills paid, State aid to municipalities and school
districts, and assessments/charges to towns/cit-
ies, FY79-83.

Contains transmittal letter, contents listing,
and highlights (p. iii-vi); narrative report interspersed with 12 charts, and 7 tables listed below (p.
1-40); and tabular list of tax specifications (p.
41-42).

Availability: Massachusetts Department of
Revenue, Leverett Saltonstall Bldg., 100 Cambridge St., Boston MA 02204, †; SRI/MF/com-
plete

TABLES:
[All tables show data for Massachusetts, FY79-
83. Revenue sources include selected types of
property, income, sales, excise, and use taxes.]

[1] Net State tax collections [by source]. (p.
12)

[2] Net State tax collections by fund [general,
local aid, highway, and other]. (p. 14)

[3] State revenue collections [in current and
1967 constant dollars]. (p. 16)

[4] State/local tax revenue [by detailed
source]. (p. 18)

[5] Selected bill payment information [a-
mount and number of bills paid, by tax type].
(p. 20)

[6] Local aid receipts for cities/towns and regional school districts [reimbursements and
distributions, by type of aid]. (p. 22)

[7] Assessments/charges [to cities/towns, by
type]. (p. 24)

S3919   MASSACHUSETTS
Department of
Social Services

S3919-2   POPULATION CHANGE IN
MASSACHUSETTS,
1970-80. Part II: The
Spanish Language
Background Population
Monograph.   Dec. 1983.
47 p.
SRI/MF/complete

Report on Massachusetts Spanish-language
population, 1970s-80. Presents data on Spanish-
language population, by place of origin, city/
town over 50,000 total population, and Dept of
Social Services region and area, with some comparisons to whites and blacks, primarily 1970 and
1980.

Also includes Spanish-language population
over age 18, and illiteracy rate, by selected city/
town, 1972.

Data are from 1970 and 1980 Censuses of Population and Housing and other Census Bureau data.

Contains contents listing, summary, and introduction (p. 2-4); methodology and narrative report interspersed with 1 chart and 14 tables (p. 5-43); and footnotes and table index (p. 44-47).

A related report, covering Massachusetts total population, is described in SRI 1983 Annual, under S3919-1.

Availability: Massachusetts Department of Social Services, Research, Evaluation, and Planning Unit, Professional Services Office, 150 Causeway St., Boston MA 02114, †; SRI/MF/complete.

S3950   MICHIGAN
Department of
Agriculture

S3950–1   MICHIGAN AGRICULTURAL STATISTICS, 1984
Annual.   July 1984.   88 p.
LC 54-23119.
SRI/MF/complete

Annual report on Michigan agricultural production, marketing, and finances, mostly for 1979-83, with some data for 1984, and trends from as early as 1866. Data generally are shown by commodity and/or county and district, with some comparisons to other States and total U.S.

Covers production, prices, sales, value, and, as applicable, acreage, yield, utilization, disposition, and inventory, for field crop, fruit, vegetable, livestock, poultry, and dairy sectors.

Also includes data on Michigan farms and farm acreage; gasohol sales; farm fertilizer use, income, prices paid for selected items, labor, and wages; mink production; USDA soil conservation and Payment-in-Kind program participation; and Census of Agriculture summary findings, including irrigated farm acreage.

Also includes U.S. farm population and real estate value, by State and region; U.S. urban-rural population distribution by census division; and farm production expenditures for upper Midwest region.

Data are compiled by the Michigan Agricultural Reporting Service in cooperation with USDA.

Contains contents listing (p. 3); and report, with 50 charts and maps, and 118 tables, interspersed with narrative summaries (p. 4-88).

Availability: Michigan Agricultural Reporting Service, PO Box 20008, 201 Federal Bldg., Lansing MI 48901, $3.00; SRI/MF/complete.

S3956   MICHIGAN
Department of
Civil Rights

S3956–1   MICHIGAN COMMUNITY PROFILES from the 1980 Census
Monograph.   For individual publication data, see below.
Research Rpt. 83-4.
SRI/MF/complete

Report presenting 1980 U.S. Census of Population and Housing selected findings for Michigan, by race/ethnic group, by county and city. Includes data on population and housing characteristics, households, employment, education, income, and poverty.

Data are from 1980 U.S. Census Summary Tape File 3A.

Report is issued in 2 consecutively paginated volumes. Volume I presents data for the State and each county; Volume II presents data for cities. Each volume includes 9 basic tables, described below, repeated for each geographic entity. Volume formats are further described below.

Availability: Michigan Department of Civil Rights, Research and Planning Bureau, 1200 Sixth St., Detroit MI 48226, ◆; SRI/MF/complete.

BASIC TABLES:
[Tables show data for whites, blacks, Hispanics, Indians, and Asians.]

a.   Population by age group and sex; households by composition including presence of children; school enrollment by level; and persons age 25/over by educational attainment. 4 tables.

b.   Labor force status for persons age 16/over by sex and employment status; family income and poverty level status; occupied housing units, by tenure status and selected characteristics including absence of vehicle and lack of central heating; and monthly rent or mortgage payments. 5 tables.

VOLUMES:

S3956–1.1: Volume I: State and Counties
[Monograph. June 1983. vii+700 p. SRI/MF/complete.]
Contents:

a.   Preface and contents listing for both volumes (p. i-vii); and 16 illustrative maps and charts (p. 1-16).

b.   For Michigan: 3 summary minority population tables with detail for Asian/Pacific Islanders by country of origin and for Hispanics by country of descent and race (p. 17); and 9 basic tables (p. 18-25).

c.   For each county: 1 table showing population by race (p. 26-36); and 9 basic tables (p. 37-700).

S3956–1.2: Volume II: Cities
[Monograph. June 1983. p. 701-1375. SRI/MF/complete.]

Contains 1 table on minority population, repeated for cities with 400/over minority residents, and for cities with 10% and less than 400 minority residents (p. 701-715); and 9 basic tables repeated for 95 cities (p. 716-1375).

S3957   MICHIGAN
Department of
Commerce

S3957–1   ANNUAL REPORT, Financial Institutions Bureau, Calendar Year 1983, Michigan
Annual.   [1984.]   iii+163 p.
ISSN 0145-4021.
LC 76-649778.
SRI/MF/complete

Annual report, for 1983, on financial condition of Michigan State and federally chartered banks and savings and loan assns, State chartered safe/collateral deposit companies and credit unions, and State regulated loan companies.

For most types of institutions, report presents consolidated assets, liabilities, income, and expenses, 1982-83; assets and various other financial data for individual institutions, 1983; and various trends, including operating ratios and lending activity, generally from 1970s. Only consolidated and trend data are presented for loan companies.

Also includes data on Financial Institutions Bureau revenues, expenditures, and regulatory activity; bank holding companies and subsidiary deposits; consumer inquiries and complaints; loan company delinquent accounts, credit life insurance, and secondary mortgages; and results of surveys on automated teller machines owned/leased by depository institutions.

Most data are compiled from internal records and reports filed by individual institutions.

Contains contents listing (p. i-iii); summary of Bureau activities and regulatory developments, with 1 chart and 3 tables (p. 1-49); remarks by Financial Institutions Bureau Commissioner (p. 50-57); division reports, with text statistics, 4 charts, and 61 statements and tables (p. 59-161); and directory of Bureau personnel (p. 162-163).

Availability: Michigan Department of Commerce, Financial Institutions Bureau, Reporting and Publications Division, PO Box 30224, Lansing MI 48909, †; SRI/MF/complete.

S3960   MICHIGAN
Department of
Corrections

S3960–1   MICHIGAN DEPARTMENT OF CORRECTIONS 1982 Statistical Presentation
Annual.   Fall 1983.   5+88 p.
LC 76-646695.
SRI/MF/complete

Annual report, for 1982, on correctional activities in Michigan, presenting data on prison population, including inmate admissions, commitment offenses, criminal background, sentence length, demographic characteristics, and releases. Some data are shown by institution, with selected trends from 1974.

Also includes data on State court cases and dispositions, by district and detailed offense; prison incidents, capacity, and work and education programs; paroles and community programs; and prison finances and personnel.

Data are primarily from the State Bureau of Administrative Services.

Contains contents listing (3 p.); 8 report sections, with narrative and 24 tables, 36 charts, 2 maps, and directory (p. 2-88).

Availability: Michigan Department of Corrections, Public Information Office, Stevens T. Mason Bldg., Lansing MI 48909, †; SRI/MF/complete.

S3962   MICHIGAN
Court Administrative Office

S3962–1   REPORT OF STATE COURT ADMINISTRATOR, Michigan
Annual series. For individual publication data, see below.
SRI/MF/complete

Annual series of 4 reports, for FY82, on Michigan judicial system. Series consists of base report and 3 supplements, described below. Prior to FY82, probate court data were presented in the base report rather than in a separate supplement.

Availability: Michigan Court Administrative Office, PO Box 30048, Lansing MI 48909, ‡; SRI/MF/complete.

S3962–1.1: 1981-82 Report of State Court Administrator, Michigan
[Annual. [1984.] 3+45 p. SRI/MF/complete.]

Annual report, for FY82, on Michigan judicial system, including trial and appellate court caseloads and case dispositions. Covers supreme, appeals, circuit, Detroit recorder's, probate, district, municipal, and claims courts. Includes trial court data by case type, with probate court detail by county, and municipal court detail for 2 cities.

Case types shown are criminal and civil for most courts, with some additional detail for family relations, labor relations, mental illness, guardianship, adoption, juvenile, child abuse and neglect, traffic, and small claims case types.

Report also includes data on supreme and appeals court caseload trends, assignment of judges, disciplinary actions and/or grievances against judges and lawyers, and public defender caseloads.

Contains contents listing (1 p.); system overview (p. 1); and 10 sections, with narrative summaries and 23 tables (p. 2-45).

S3962–1.2: Circuit Court Supplement to the 1981-82 Annual Report of the State Court Administrator, Michigan
[Annual. [1984.] 3+106 p. SRI/MF/complete.]

Annual supplement, for FY82, presenting data on Michigan circuit court caseloads and case dispositions, by case type and county. Case types shown are criminal and civil appeals; and criminal, personal injury, family relations, product liability, and labor relations.

Contains contents listing (3 p.); and 1 table repeated for total State, 5 regions, and each county (p. 1-106).

S3962–1.3: District Court Supplement to the 1981-82 Annual Report of the State Court Administrator, Michigan
[Annual. [1984.] 5+189 p. SRI/MF/complete.]

Annual supplement, for FY82, presenting data on Michigan district court caseloads and case dispositions, by case type and district. Case types shown are criminal and civil, including detail for traffic and small claims cases.

Contains contents listing (5 p.); and 1 table repeated for total State, 5 regions, and each district and division (p. 1-189).

S3962–1.4: Probate Court Supplement to the 1981-82 Annual Report of the State Court Administrator, Michigan
[Annual. [1984.] 4+173 p. SRI/MF/complete.]

Annual supplement, for FY82, presenting data on Michigan probate court caseloads and case dispositions, by case type and county. Case types include estates and trusts, mental illness, guardians, adoption, and marriages.

Also includes filing fees and inheritance taxes collected, and detail for juvenile division, including delinquency caseload by type of offense, and child abuse and neglect cases, all by county.

Contains contents listing (4 p.); 1 table, repeated for each half of FY82, for total State and each county (p. 1-166); and juvenile division report, with 3 tables (p. 167-173).

S3965   MICHIGAN
Board of Education

S3965–3   1982/83 MICHIGAN K-12 PUBLIC SCHOOL DISTRICTS Ranked by Selected Financial Data
Annual. [1984.] 37 p.
Bull. 1014.
SRI/MF/complete

Annual report on Michigan public school finances, by district, 1982/83. Includes school enrollments, per pupil costs, and average teacher salary. Data are from reports by 529 elementary and secondary school districts.

Contains foreword and glossary (p. 1-5); 1 summary table (p. 7) showing selected data for total school districts grouped by active membership size; and 1 detailed table (p. 8-37) showing the following data for individual school districts arranged by county, 1982/83:

a. Per pupil general fund revenues by source, and expenditures by purpose including salaries.

b. Average salary per teacher; State aid members (pupils), and State equalized valuation per member; and millage rates for operations, building site, and debt retirement.

School district rankings are also shown for most of the items noted above.

Issuing agency also publishes an annual report with similar data, *Analysis of Michigan Public School Revenues and Expenditures,* not covered by SRI.

Availability: Michigan Department of Education, Public Affairs Office, PO Box 30008, Lansing MI 48909, ‡; SRI/MF/complete.

S3980   MICHIGAN
Department of Labor

S3980–1   ANNUAL PLANNING INFORMATION, FY85, Michigan
Annual. [1984.]
81 p. var. paging.
LC 79-640079.
SRI/MF/complete

Annual planning report, for FY85, identifying Michigan population groups most in need of employment services. Also includes data on labor force and job service applicants.

Data are from Michigan Employment Security Commission, U.S. Census Bureau, and BLS.

Contains preface, and contents and table listings (p. iii-vii); report, with 18 tables interspersed with narrative summaries (p. 1-34); and 3 appendices, with glossary, and 4 tables (p. 35-43, 34 p.). All tables are listed below.

Similar reports for individual Job Training Partnership Act (JTPA) service delivery areas are also available from the issuing agency, but are not covered by SRI.

Availability: Michigan Employment Security Commission, Labor Market Analysis Unit, 7310 Woodward Ave., Detroit MI 48202, †; SRI/MF/complete.

TABLES:
[All data are shown for Michigan. Data by race/ethnicity generally include white, black, American Indian/Alaskan Native, Asian/Pacific Islander, Hispanic, and others.

Tables 1-3 and 6-9 show data for total and economically disadvantaged persons].

TARGETED POPULATIONS

1. Title II [of JTPA] eligible population [by sex, age, and race/ethnicity, with detail for labor force attached/economically disadvantaged persons], 1982. (p. 4)

2-3. Teenage parents, and [persons with] limited English proficiency, by service delivery area, [1980]. (p. 5-6)

4. Alcoholics and [drug] addicts [admitted to treatment programs, by county and service delivery area], FY82. (p. 7)

5. Offenders, [paroles and correction center inmates, by service delivery area, 1983]. (p. 11)

6. Handicapped population [in labor force, and not in labor force but able to work, by sex, age, and race/ethnicity, 1980]. (p. 12)

7. High school dropouts [and total population, by age, sex, and race/ethnicity, 1980]. (p. 13)

8-9. Veterans [population and labor force], and displaced homemakers, by service delivery area, [1980]. (p. 14-15)

LABOR FORCE DATA

10. Civilian government [and private] wage/salary employment, by service delivery area, [1982]. (p. 16)

11. Ratio of private employment to population, by service delivery area, [with comparison to U.S.]. (p. 17)

12-13. ADC-WIN [Aid to Dependent Children/Work Incentive program] registrants [total and] economically disadvantaged; and welfare recipients [by sex, age, and race/ethnicity]; Dec. 1, 1983. (p. 18)

14. Labor force [by employment status], and wage/salary employment [in manufacturing, nonmanufacturing, and government, FY83-85]. (p. 26)

15. Civilian labor force [by employment status], by age, sex, and race, FY85. (p. 27)

16. Favorable employment industries. (p. 30)

17. Private industry employment analysis, [by major industry group, 1st quarter 1982-83]. (p. 31-32)

18. Occupations with favorable outlook. (p. 34)

APPENDIX TABLES

[A] Unemployment insurance [regular and Federal supplemental] claimants by service delivery area, Oct. 1983. (p. 42)

[B] Occupational employment projections, 1980 and 1990 [and average annual openings, by detailed occupation]. (25 p.)

[C-D] Job service applicants by veteran status, and by [occupation, both by sex and race/ethnicity], FY83. (9 p.)

S3980-2   MICHIGAN LABOR MARKET REVIEW
Monthly.
Approx. 4 p. no paging.
SRI/MF/complete, shipped quarterly

Monthly report on Michigan labor force, including employment, unemployment, hours, earnings, and unemployment insurance claims. Data sources include BLS and Current Employment Statistics program. Selected data are shown by industry and labor market area. Month of coverage is 1 month prior to cover date.

Contains narrative summary, 4 monthly tables, and list of labor surplus areas eligible for Federal procurement preference.

Monthly tables are listed below and appear in all issues.

The issuing agency also publishes monthly reports on labor conditions in each of the State's 13 labor market areas. These reports are not covered by SRI.

Availability: Michigan Employment Security Commission, Research and Statistics Bureau, 7310 Woodward Ave., Detroit MI 48202, †; SRI/MF/complete, shipped quarterly.

Issues reviewed during 1984: Oct. 1983-June 1984 (P) (Vol. XXXIX, Nos. 10-12; Vol. XXXX, Nos. 1-6) [Vol. XXXIX, No. 10 incorrectly reads Vol. XXXIV; Vol. XXXX, No. 6 incorrectly reads No. 5].

MONTHLY TABLES:

[1-2] Civilian labor force, employment and unemployment estimates [by labor market area, for month of coverage; and for total State, including employment by industry division and major manufacturing group, and workers involved in labor disputes, for month of coverage, 1-2 previous months, and same month of previous year].

[3] Weekly [initial and continued] claims for unemployment insurance [regular and Federal supplemental programs; weekly for month of coverage].

[4] [Average hours and earnings of manufacturing production workers, with detail for selected major industry groups; for month of coverage, previous month, and same month of previous year.]

S3982   MICHIGAN
Library

S3982-1   1983 MICHIGAN LIBRARY STATISTICS
Annual.   [1983.]   98 p.
SRI/MF/complete

Annual report, for 1982, on Michigan public libraries and library cooperatives. Covers income, operating expenses, resources, services, and audiovisual materials. Includes data by individual library and cooperative.

Data are compiled from applications filed with the State library by Feb. 1, 1983, and cover the last completed 12-month operating year.

Contents:

a. Public libraries, with 5 detailed tables, listed below; and 2 summary tables showing data for 6 population size groups. (p. 1-57)

b. Library cooperatives, with 1 table showing income by source and expenditures by major item (p. 60-61); and library directories and profiles, including population served and libraries serving the blind and physically handicapped (p. 62-97).

Report for 1981 was published by Michigan Board of Education; for description, see SRI 1983 Annual, under S3965-2.

Availability: Library of Michigan, PO Box 30007, Lansing MI 48909, †; SRI/MF/complete.

PUBLIC LIBRARY TABLES:
[All data are shown by public library in each population size group, 1982.]

[1] Income [general revenue sharing, penal fine receipts, other local income, contractual fees, State aid, and nonresident fee rate]. (p. 2-10)

[2] Operating expenditures [salaries/wages, books, periodicals/newspapers, audiovisual materials, other, and per capita expenditures]. (p. 12-20)

[3] Resources [collection volumes added and available in central library and branches; total items available; and volumes and total items per capita]. (p. 22-30)

[4] Resources and services [collection of periodicals/newspapers and audiovisual materials; circulation for central library and branch stations/bookmobiles, and per capita; and certified and total employees]. (p. 32-40)

[5] Audiovisual resources [by type]. (p. 42-50)

S3983   MICHIGAN
Department of
Licensing and Regulation

S3983-1   STATE OF MICHIGAN INSURANCE BUREAU 1983 Annual Statistical Report
Annual.   Sept. 17, 1984.
1+112 p.
LC 78-643284.
SRI/MF/complete

Annual report on Michigan insurance industry financial condition and underwriting activity, by company and type of insurance, 1983. Covers assets, liabilities, capital/surplus, premiums written and/or earned, losses incurred and/or paid, net worth, income, benefits paid, and gain from operations, for companies with headquarters in Michigan, other States, and foreign countries.

Data are shown, as applicable, for property/liability and life insurance companies, HMOs (including enrollment data), farm mutual insurance companies, and fraternal benefit societies.

Data are also shown for the top 20 companies ranked by Michigan market share of property/liability, accident/health, and life/annuity insurance.

Also includes data on Insurance Bureau licensing activities, revenues, and expenditures, including financial status of malpractice arbitration and State accident funds; and claims and financial data for companies in receivership.

Contains contents listing (p. 1); list of Insurance Bureau officials, and organizational chart (p. 2-4); Insurance Bureau activities, with list of company status changes and 12 tables (p. 6-17); 10 company financial tables and 1 summary table (p. 18-41); and directory of admitted companies (p. 43-112).

Availability: Michigan Department of Licensing and Regulation, Insurance Bureau, PO Box 30220, Lansing MI 48909, †; SRI/MF/complete.

S3985   MICHIGAN
Department of
Management and Budget

S3985-1   ECONOMIC REPORT OF THE GOVERNOR, 1984, State of Michigan
Annual.   Aug. 1984.
ix+162 p.
SRI/MF/complete

Annual compilation of data on Michigan economic developments, for 1983, with 1984 estimates. Covers employment and unemployment, personal income, prices, consumer spending, population, motor vehicle industry, energy, finance, construction, agriculture, mineral supplies and mining, transportation, tourism, and international trade.

Also includes some interstate and regional comparisons.

Data are derived from Federal and State government, commercial, private assn, university, and other sources.

Contains listings of contents, tables, and charts (p. vii-ix); and 17 mostly narrative sections, with interspersed data, and appendices, as follows:

a. Summaries of 1983 economic events, 1984 economic forecast, and national economic developments and outlook. (p. 3-10)

b. Employment and unemployment (including number of unemployment insurance beneficiaries), personal income, and prices, various years 1970-84. 1 chart and 11 tables. (p. 11-31)

c. Consumer installment credit, retail sales tax collections, State or regional comparisons of personal income and employment, and population, various years 1970-83. 2 charts and 8 tables. (p. 32-51)

d. Motor vehicle industry, including motor vehicle production and U.S. sales, by vehicle type; various years 1975-84. 3 charts and 2 tables. (p. 55-62)

e. Energy and finance, including electric and gas company sales, service capacity, net plant investment, customers, and revenues by sector; U.S. financial indicators; and State savings deposits by type of institution; various years 1977-83. 2 charts and 5 tables. (p. 63-77)

f. Construction, agriculture, and mineral supplies and mining, including building permits for single- and multi-family units, construction contract awards by sector, and mineral production and value by mineral, various years 1966-83. 1 chart and 6 tables. (p. 78-89)

g. Transportation, tourism, and international trade, including camping at State parks, travel center visitors, Mackinac bridge crossings, and lodging sales/use tax collections; manufactured goods exports; U.S. trade in cars, trucks, and parts with Canada; and State agricultural export values, by commodity; various periods 1972-83. 5 tables. (p. 90-102)

h. Appendices A-B: 1983 Michigan Public Acts; and table listing, and 44 tables listed below, generally presenting additional detail for narrative section topics. (p. 103-162)

This is the 16th annual report.

Availability: Michigan Department of Management and Budget, Revenue and Tax Analysis Office, Lewis Cass Bldg., Lansing MI 48913, †; SRI/MF/complete.

APPENDIX TABLES:

[Data are for Michigan, unless otherwise noted.]

S3985–1.1: Michigan Economy

EMPLOYMENT AND UNEMPLOYMENT

[Tables B1, B3-B6, and B8 include monthly data for 1982-83.]

B1. Labor force and employment estimates [including workers involved in labor-management disputes], 1970-83. (p. 113)

B2. Labor force, employment, and unemployment, quarterly averages, 1975-83. (p. 114)

B3. Manufacturing and durable goods employment [by major industry group], 1972-83. (p. 115)

B4-B5. Manufacturing and nondurable goods employment [by major industry group]; and nonmanufacturing employment [by industry division]; 1974-83. (p. 116-117)

B6. [Federal, State, and local] government employment, 1970-83. (p. 118)

B7. SMSA and county employment and unemployment rates, 1982-83. (p. 119)

B8. U.S. and Michigan manufacturing industries average weekly and hourly earnings, 1973-83. (p. 121)

B9-B10. Manufacturing industries average weekly earnings and hours [by major industry group], 1971-83. (p. 122-123)

INCOME

[Major income sources include labor and proprietors' income by type and industry division.]

B11-B12. Personal income by major sources, 1974-83, and quarterly 1977-82. (p. 124-126)

B13. U.S. and [12] major industrial States: personal income and real per capita personal income, 1979-82. (p. 127)

PRICES

B14-B17. U.S. and Detroit CPIs: [for approximately 30 items]; all urban consumers [monthly] 1983 and annual averages 1970-83; and inflation rates, 1953-83. (p. 128-132)

S3985–1.2: Sector Analysis

FINANCE AND CONSTRUCTION

B18. New incorporations [profit, nonprofit, and out-of-State], 1955-83. (p. 133)

B19. Liquid assets [demand and time deposits, savings/loan shares, and credit union shares/deposits], 1970-83. (p. 134)

B20. U.S. interest rates (percent per annum) [Treasury bills, commercial paper, and municipal and corporate bonds], 1961-83. (p. 135)

B21. New private housing units authorized in SMSAs [by SMSA], 1977-83. (p. 136)

TRANSPORTATION

B22. Motor vehicle registrations [State autos and trucks/buses, U.S. total motor vehicles, and State to U.S. ratio], 1962-83. (p. 137)

B23. New passenger car sales, 1967-83. (p. 138)

B24. State share of passenger car assemblies, 1971-83 model years [for 19 States]. (p. 139)

B25. U.S. motor vehicle production [passenger cars and trucks/buses, 1976-83, and monthly 1982-83]. (p. 140)

B26-B27. U.S. auto sales, truck sales, inventories, and stock [including domestic and foreign import sales]; and U.S. and Michigan motor vehicle industry employment, earnings, and hours; 1957-83. (p. 141-142)

B28. U.S. auto price indices, personal consumption expenditures, and installment credit, 1958-83. (p. 143)

B29. U.S. motor vehicle production and auto sales [auto and truck/bus production, and domestic and import auto sales], quarterly 1978-83. (p. 144)

PUBLIC UTILITIES

B30. Rate changes granted to regulated utilities in 1983 [telephone, electric, and gas companies, by company]. (p. 145)

AGRICULTURE

B31. Prices received by farmers [by commodity], 1972-83. (p. 146)

B32. Farm income components [cash receipts, government payments, nonmoney income, farm production expenses, net changes in inventories, and net and other farm income], 1967-83. (p. 147)

B33. Number of farms, average size, and land in farms, 1955-83. (p. 148)

POPULATION AND SCHOOL ENROLLMENTS

B34. U.S. and Michigan resident population, July 1, 1951-83. (p. 149)

B35. Population by county [including births, deaths, and net migration, selected periods] 1980-83. (p. 150)

B36. U.S. population ranked by State, 1980. (p. 153)

B37. School enrollment grades K-12 [public and nonpublic, by grade level, 1974/75-1987/88]. (p. 154)

B38. Elementary, secondary, and higher education student enrollments [for public and private schools, generally 1972/73-1983/84]. (p. 156)

TAX LEVIES AND VALUATIONS

B39. Real/personal property values, taxes, and tax rates [with county and State equalized valuations], 1953-83. (p. 157)

B40. Real and personal property values by class [agriculture, commercial, industrial, residential, and timber cut over or utility], 1969-83. (p. 158)

B41. General property taxes by local unit of government [school, city, county, township, and village], 1960-82. (p. 159)

B42. School property taxes [amount and millage rate for operating and debt/building/site expenditures], 1960-82. (p. 160)

CURRENT AND REAL PERSONAL INCOME

B43-B44. U.S. and Michigan [current] personal and per capita income, 1960-83; and real personal and per capita income, 1965-83. (p. 161-162)

S3985–2   ANNUAL FINANCIAL REPORT OF THE STATE OF MICHIGAN, Fiscal Year Ended Sept. 30, 1983

Annual. Apr. 10, 1984.
x+171 p.
ISSN 0095-1463.
LC 74-647935.
SRI/MF/complete

Annual report on financial condition of Michigan State government, for FY83, presenting assets, liabilities, and fund balances; revenues by source; and expenditures by function and/or object; for general, special revenue, debt service, capital projects, State authorities, enterprise, internal service, trust, and agency funds.

Also includes bonded debt, and financial and socioeconomic trends from 1973.

Data are compiled by the Dept of Management and Budget.

Contains contents listing, and transmittal letter with State organizational chart and list of principal officials (p. ii-ix); financial section, with auditors reports and 49 statements and schedules, interspersed with explanatory notes and text statistics (p. 2-154); and statistical section with 10 trend tables (p. 158-171).

Availability: Michigan Department of Management and Budget, Accounting Division, PO Box 30026, Lansing MI 48909, †; SRI/MF/complete.

S3997   MICHIGAN
Department of State Police

S3997–1   1982 UNIFORM CRIME REPORT FOR THE STATE OF MICHIGAN
Annual. [1983.] 103 p.
ISSN 0360-9146.
LC 75-648835.
SRI/MF/complete

Annual report, for 1982, on Michigan crimes and arrests, by type of offense, with trends from 1977. Includes data on crime trends, clearances, victim and offender characteristics, value of stolen property, and assaults on police. Selected data are shown by county and jurisdiction.

Data are from reports of State and local law enforcement agencies, submitted to State police under the Uniform Crime Reporting (UCR) Program.

Contains foreword and contents listing (2 p.); description of UCR Program, definitions, and summary, with 1 table showing number of participating agencies, 1982 (p. 1-7); and statistical section, with 20 charts, and 47 tables listed below (p. 9-103).

This is the 24th annual report. For description of previous report, for 1981, see SRI 1982 Annual, under this number.

Availability: Michigan Department of State Police, 714 S. Harrison Rd., East Lansing MI 48823, ‡; SRI/MF/complete.

TABLES:
[Index crimes covered in detail are murder, rape, robbery, aggravated assault, burglary, larceny, motor vehicle theft, and arson. Data by race/ethnicity include white, black, American Indian/Alaskan Native, Asian/Pacific Islander, and Hispanic.]

S3997–1.1: Index and Total Crime
[The following tables are repeated for each topic listed in a-j below:

[1-3] Offenses and offenses cleared [including crime rate and offenses cleared by juvenile arrest]; and persons arrested [including percent age 17/under and median age; 1977 and 1981-82].

Additional tables, described below, generally present data for 1982, with percent change from 1977 and 1981.]

a. Murder, with 1 additional table showing murders reported, by victim age, sex, and race/ethnicity, and by weapon used and circumstance. (p. 12)

b. Rape. (p. 14)

c. Robbery, with 2 additional tables showing offenses by weapon type, and offenses and value of stolen property, by robbery setting. (p. 16)

d. Aggravated assault, with 1 additional table showing assaults by weapon type. (p. 18)

e. Burglary, with 1 additional table showing offenses and value of stolen property, for day and night residential and nonresidential burglaries. (p. 20)

f. Larceny, with 2 additional tables showing offenses and value of stolen property by type of offense and value range. (p. 22)

g. Motor vehicle theft, with 2 additional tables showing offenses by vehicle type and recoveries for vehicles stolen locally and elsewhere. (p. 24)

h. Arson. (p. 26)

i. Total Index offenses, with 1 additional table showing value of stolen and recovered property, by type. (p. 28)

j. Total Index/non-Index crime. (p. 30)

S3997–1.2: Data by Age and County, and Assaults on Police

[1] 1982 State total arrests [by age, by race/ethnicity and sex, for 42 offenses]. (p. 36-50)

[2-3] Total actual offenses and total arrests by county [for individual Index and selected non-Index crimes, by reporting agency, with data by population size, urban and rural area, and adult and juvenile arrests by county and agency], 1982. (p. 52-85)

[4] Other summaries by county [including crime rates and clearances, motor vehicle recovery, disposition of juveniles, stolen and recovered property value, arson offenses and property damaged, and police officers killed and assaulted; all by reporting agency, with data by population size and urban and rural area], 1982. (p. 86-102)

[5-6] Michigan law enforcement officers killed [1973-82]; or assaulted [by weapon and assignment, and clearances, all by type of activity; with injury status by weapon, and totals by time], 1982. (p. 103)

[7] [Total officers, rate per 1,000 population, and percent involved in assaults, 1980-82.] (p. 103)

S3997–2   MICHIGAN TRAFFIC ACCIDENT FACTS, 1982
Annual. [1983.] 56 p.
LC 54-63117.
SRI/MF/complete

Annual report on Michigan traffic accidents, fatalities, and injuries, by detailed accident and vehicle type, location, time, and other circumstances; and driver and victim characteristics; 1982 with comparisons from 1970s and trends from as early as 1933.

Also includes data on motor vehicle registrations and revenue, licensed drivers, vehicle miles traveled, economic cost of accidents, vehicle safety restraint use, driver and pedestrian alcohol use, and intoxicated drivers arrested.

Data are compiled by the State Police Dept from State and local police and sheriff reports, and from other State depts.

Contains preface, contents listing, highlights, and trends, with 7 charts and 2 tables (p. 1-8); and report, with 1 map, 1 chart, and 32 tables (p. 9-56).

Availability: Michigan Department of State Police, Attention: Analysis Section, Traffic Services Division, 7150 Harris Dr., Lansing MI 48913, †; SRI/MF/complete.

S4010   MICHIGAN
Department of Social Services

S4010–1   ASSISTANCE PAYMENTS STATISTICS, Michigan
Monthly. Approx. 150 p. no paging. Pub. No. 67.
SRI/MF/complete

Monthly report on Michigan public assistance programs, including number of cases, recipients, and payments, by program and county. Programs covered are Aid to Dependent Children (ADC), general assistance, State and federally funded emergency assistance, medical assistance, food stamps, and SSI.

Data are compiled by the Dept of Social Services. Report is issued approximately 9 weeks after month of coverage.

Contains 27 monthly tables, listed below; most tables appear in all issues. Issues also frequently contain additional charts and tables; those presenting substantial statistics not covered in monthly tables are described, as they appear, under "Statistical Features."

Availability: Michigan Department of Social Services, 300 S. Capitol Ave., PO Box 30037, Lansing MI 48909, †; SRI/MF/complete.

Issues reviewed during 1984: Sept. 1983-Aug. 1984 (D).

MONTHLY TABLES:
[Data are for month of coverage only, unless otherwise noted. All tables except 1 and 22 show data by county; some tables also include data by district.]

SUMMARY

1. Summary of public assistance cases, recipients, and expenditures [by program; month of coverage, previous month, and same month of previous year].

2. Total number of recipients and expenditures under ADC, emergency needs program, general assistance, energy assistance, and food stamps [month of coverage, and percent change from previous month and same month of previous year].

AID TO DEPENDENT CHILDREN PROGRAM

3-5. ADC: families and money payments to families: [total, and] regular and unemployed-parent segments [for month of coverage, previous month, and same month of previous year].

6. ADC: number of child and adult recipients, by program segment.

GENERAL ASSISTANCE

7-9. General assistance: number of cases and amount of gross payments [all cases, and] regular and State funded emergency needs cases [for month of coverage, previous month, and same month of previous year].

10. General assistance: number of cases and amount of gross payments by type of case [with and without children], by program segment.

11. General assistance: number of child and adult recipients by type of case and program segment.

EMERGENCY AND MEDICAL ASSISTANCE, FOOD STAMPS, AND SSI

12. State funded emergency needs program, burials: number of cases and amount of gross payments.

13-14. Federal and State funded emergency needs: number of cases and recipients, and amount of gross payments, by basis of eligibility.

15. Food stamps: households, persons, and value of food stamps issued, by type of case [total, ADC, general assistance, and other].

16. Medical assistance: number of cases and persons eligible for medical assistance only (medically needy), by type of case [age 65/over, blind, disabled, families with dependent children, and other children under 21].

17. SSI: number of cases eligible for SSI by basis of eligibility [age 65/over, blind, and disabled].

ASSISTANCE APPLICATIONS

18. Number of applications received for assistance, by program [AFDC, general and medical assistance, food stamps and recertifications, emergency needs, county hospitalization, and other].

19-20. Pending applications for assistance, by program [AFDC, general and medical assistance, food stamps, emergency needs, county hospitalization, and other]; and for food stamp recertifications [public and nonpublic assistance; all] by length of time pending.

ALLOCATIONS, RECIPIENTS, AND PAYMENTS

21. SSI: recipients and money payments to aged/blind/disabled persons [Federal payments and State supplements].

22. Medical assistance: recipients and expenditures, by basis of eligibility, type of case, and type of service.

23-24. Medical assistance (Medicaid): amount of vendor payments and number of recipients, by type of service [inpatient general and mental hospitals, skilled nursing, mentally retarded and other intermediate care facilities, physicians, dental, and 8 other categories].

25-26. General assistance, medical: amount of vendor payments and number of recipients by type of service.

27. LIHEAP (ENP/HEAT and GA/HAP) [low-income home energy assistance emergency needs program] unduplicated number of cases and recipients, and amount of gross payments.

STATISTICAL FEATURES:
[Fiscal year data are for year ending Sept. 30.]

S4010-1.501: Sept. 1983
QUARTERLY AND ANNUAL TABLES
Six quarterly and 6 annual tables showing ADC and general assistance applications approved and denied, and cases closed, by reason and county, 4th quarter and full year FY83. Includes approvals due to exhaustion of unemployment benefits, layoff/discharge, and strike or strike-related layoff.

S4010-1.502: Oct. 1983
SEMIANNUAL TABLES
Two semiannual tables showing food stamp households, by race and ethnic group (includes Hispanic, American Indian/Alaskan Native, and Asian/Pacific Islander), by county, Oct. 1983.

S4010-1.503: Dec. 1983
SPECIAL CHART
Chart showing distribution of emergency needs program payments by type of service, FY83.

SEMIANNUAL TABLES
Four tables showing ADC and general assistance cases by race/ethnicity (including American Indian and Mexican), by county, Dec. 1983.

RECURRING TABLE
Table showing the following for hospitalization assistance: persons hospitalized, length of stay, central office payments for doctors/surgeons and inpatient care, and total local office payments, by county, FY83.

For description of table covering FY81, see SRI 1982 Annual, under S4010-1.305.

S4010-1.504: Jan. 1984
[Tables show data by county.]
QUARTERLY TABLES
Six quarterly tables showing ADC and general assistance applications approved and denied, and cases closed, by reason, for quarter ended Dec. 1983. Includes approvals due to exhaustion of unemployment benefits, layoff/discharge, and strike or strike-related layoff.

SEMIANNUAL TABLES
Two semiannual tables showing ADC children by age, Jan. 1984.

SPECIAL TABLE
Table showing refugee/Cuban/Haitian assistance average monthly recipients and payments for regular relief and medical assistance, FY83.

S4010-1.505: Mar. 1984
QUARTERLY TABLES
Six quarterly tables showing ADC and general assistance applications approved and denied, and cases closed, by reason and county, with selected detail by district, for quarter ended Mar. 1984. Includes approvals due to exhaustion of unemployment benefits, layoff/discharge, and strike or strike-related layoff.

S4010-1.506: May 1984
SEMIANNUAL TABLES
Two semiannual tables showing food stamp households, by race and ethnic group (includes Hispanic, American Indian/Alaskan Native, and Asian/Pacific Islander), by county, Apr. 1984.

S4010-1.507: June 1984
[All tables show data by county, with selected detail by district.]
SEMIANNUAL TABLES
Five tables showing ADC and general assistance cases by race/ethnicity (including American Indian and Mexican), and distribution of ADC children by age, June 1984.

QUARTERLY TABLES
Six quarterly tables showing ADC and general assistance applications approved and denied, and cases closed, by reason, for quarter ended June 1984. Includes approvals due to exhaustion of unemployment benefits, layoff/discharge, and strike or strike-related layoff.

S4010-1.508: July 1984
ANNUAL TABLE
Annual table showing Michigan public assistance recipients and rates, by program (ADC, general assistance, and public assistance and nonpublic assistance food stamps), June 1984; and population as of July 1, 1983; all by county.

S4130   MINNESOTA
Department of Agriculture

S4130-1   MINNESOTA AGRICULTURAL STATISTICS, 1984
Annual. July 1984. 79 p.
SRI/MF/complete

Annual report on Minnesota agricultural production, marketing, and finances, 1983, with trends primarily from 1979 and some data for 1984. Data are generally shown by commodity and/or county and district, with some comparisons to other States and total U.S.

Covers production, prices, value, and, as applicable, acreage, yield, stocks, and inventory, for field crop, vegetable, fruit, livestock, poultry, and dairy sectors.

Also includes data on number of farms and acreage; farm income and production expenses; agricultural export values; weather; pesticide use; prices paid by farmers for selected feed and energy commodities; custom farming rates; and U.S. food industry employment by State, and farm value share of retail price of 12 food items.

Data are compiled by the Minnesota Dept of Agriculture in cooperation with USDA.

Contains contents listing (1 p.); 8 maps, 23 charts, and 61 tables, interspersed with narrative summaries (p. 1-78); and index (p. 79).

Availability: Minnesota State Documents Center, 117 University Ave., St. Paul MN 55155, $4.70; SRI/MF/complete.

S4160   MINNESOTA
Department of Economic Security

S4160-1   MINNESOTA LABOR MARKET INFORMATION
Summary for 1985
Annual. Apr. 1984.
iii+107 p.
SRI/MF/complete

Annual report, for 1985, on Minnesota labor market conditions, identifying population groups most in need of employment services. Includes data on labor force characteristics, the insured unemployed, and job applicants, with selected data by industry and occupation, various years 1970-85. Also includes population projections through 1990.

Data are from Minnesota Depts of Economic Security, Education, and Public Welfare; and Census Bureau, BLS, and other Federal sources.

Contains contents and table listings, and introduction (p. i-iii); and 4 narrative sections interspersed with 4 charts and 23 tables (p. 1-107). All tables are listed below.

Similar reports for individual SMSAs are also available from issuing agency, but are not covered by SRI.

Availability: Minnesota Department of Economic Security, Research and Statistical Services Office, 390 N. Robert St., St. Paul MN 55101, †; SRI/MF/complete.

TABLES:
[Tables show data for Minnesota, unless otherwise noted. Data by ethnicity generally are shown for Spanish, American Indian, and Asian/Pacific Islander.]

S4160–1.1: Population and Labor Force

1. Distribution of population by age group, 1970, 1980, and projected 1990. (p. 2)

2-3. Population [by age group and race-ethnicity, 1980, and by race-ethnicity, 1980 and projected 1985]. (p. 4-5)

4. Counties with the largest 1970 to 1980 percentage population changes, and projections to 1985. (p. 6)

5-6. Public secondary school enrollments and dropouts, 1975/76-1980/81; and [persons age 25/over, by] years of school completed, 1970 and 1980. (p. 7-8)

7. [Population age 15/over by] marital status, 1970 and 1980. (p. 9)

8. Employment by industry [division and major group, and total agricultural employment], 1976-83. (p. 14)

9. Official labor force data [by employment status, monthly 1980-Feb. 1984]. (p. 17)

10. 1983 county [and selected SMSA] labor force estimates [by employment status]. (p. 18)

11. Average weekly insured unemployment [by sex], 1970-83. (p. 20)

12-13. Monthly distribution of insured unemployment by age, sex, and occupation, 1983. (p. 21-22)

14-15. Characteristics of insured unemployed [including females, minorities, and by age, educational attainment, and duration of unemployment]: by industry attachment and by occupational category [for Minnesota and by service delivery area], 1983. (p. 23-48)

16. Labor force [by employment status, 1978-85]. (p. 49)

17. Population, labor force, and participation rates, 1978-85. (p. 49)

18. Projected 1985 population, labor force, participation rate, and unemployment rate, by age group and sex. (p. 50)

S4160–1.2: Labor Supply and Demand, and Job Training Partnership Act (JTPA)

19-20. Department of Economic Security: characteristics of applicants (total and female) [shows experienced and entry level job applicants by age and race/ethnicity, and for handicapped and veterans, by occupational group, all for Minnesota and by service delivery area], FY83. (p. 53-78)

21. Characteristics of applicants (total) [including age, educational attainment, veteran status, disabled, handicapped, race/ethnicity, welfare recipients, and work incentive program participants, with selected detail for females, all for Minnesota and by service delivery area], FY83. (p. 79-91)

22. 1985 JTPA population groups and JTPA eligible [by sex, age group, and race/ethnicity]. (p. 95)

23. Estimate JTPA eligible population [by sex, race/ethnicity, and age group, all by service delivery area], FY85 (revised). (p. 96-107)

S4160–3   REVIEW OF LABOR AND ECONOMIC CONDITIONS, Minnesota
Quarterly, with monthly supplements.
Approx. 40 p. var. paging or 4 p.
SRI/MF/complete

Quarterly report, with monthly supplements, on Minnesota labor and economic conditions, presenting data on employment and unemployment, earnings, hours, characteristics of insured unemployed, and selected economic indicators. Includes data by industry and locale, historical trends, and comparisons to total U.S.

Quarterly issues are published 2 months after quarter of coverage, and generally contain contents listing, editorial comment, and the following:

a. "Research Summaries" article; "Job Market" feature, usually including review of employment conditions in a selected Minnesota industry, and supply/demand summary for specific occupations in Minnesota regions; and a feature article; all often including statistics.

b. Narrative review of U.S. and Minnesota economic conditions; and 23 trend charts and 10 quarterly tables.

Monthly supplement, entitled *Current Minnesota Labor Market Conditions,* is published in the 8 months for which no quarterly report is published. Supplement presents selected data also covered in quarterly report. Data are shown for month prior to month of publication, generally with comparisons to previous periods. Monthly supplements are filmed and shipped with the subsequent quarterly issue.

Quarterly tables are listed below and appear in all quarterly issues. All additional features with substantial statistical content are described, as they appear, under "Statistical Features." Non-statistical features are not covered.

Availability: Minnesota Department of Economic Security, Research and Statistical Services Office, 390 N. Robert St., St. Paul MN 55101, †; SRI/MF/complete.

Issues reviewed during 1984: Quarterly Review: 3rd Qtr. 1983-2nd Qtr. 1984 (D) (Vol. 10, Nos. 3-4; Vol. 11, Nos. 1-2).

Issues reviewed during 1984: Monthly Supplements: Sept. 1983-July 1984 (P) [Sept. 1983 supplement incorrectly reads July 1983].

QUARTERLY TABLES:
[Unless otherwise noted, data are for Minnesota and U.S. Tables 1, [3], and [5-10] show data for quarter of coverage and/or subsequent month, generally with comparison to prior periods. Data in tables 1, [3], and [6-8] are also included in monthly supplement.]

JOB SERVICE APPLICANTS AND OPENINGS

1. Experienced supply [of job service applicants, and] job openings demand [by occupation, for Minnesota only; table begins regular

appearance with the 1st quarter 1984 issue, but is also included in Sept.-Nov. 1983 monthly supplements].

LABOR FORCE

[2] Forecasts of GNP, and Minnesota payroll employment [by industry division, for quarter of coverage and 8 subsequent quarters].

[3] Labor force estimates [by employment status].

[4] Historical labor force series [by employment status, for previous 12-14 years].

[5] Labor force and establishment data [including agricultural employment; labor utilization rates; and nonagricultural employment, and average hours and wages, by industry division].

[6] Persons claiming benefits [for unemployment insurance, by age, sex, industry division, occupation, and duration of unemployment; for Minnesota only].

[7] Minnesota nonagricultural wage/salary employment [and production worker] hours and earnings, [by industry division and selected industry groups].

[8] Labor force [and unemployment] data: State, SMSAs, and counties.

ECONOMIC INDICATORS

[9] Income and purchasing power [including total and per capita personal income, real median family income, production workers' earnings, poverty level income, CPI for 4 items, and purchasing power of dollar].

[10] Output, expenditure, money, and credit conditions [including retail sales, private housing permits, interest rates, and selected other indicators].

STATISTICAL FEATURES:

S4160–3.501: 3rd Qtr. 1983 (Vol. 10, No. 3)

RESEARCH SUMMARIES: THE OCCUPATIONAL DISTRIBUTION OF MINNESOTA'S LABOR FORCE, 1960-80

(p. 3-4) By B. Steuernagel. Article, with 2 tables showing Minnesota labor force by sex, by occupation, decennially 1960-80. Data are from U.S. Census Bureau.

JOB MARKET: THE PRINTING AND PUBLISHING INDUSTRY

(p. 5-6) By B. Jones. Includes 1 table showing Minnesota printing/publishing industry employment distribution by occupational group, 1970, 1978, and 1985.

S4160–3.502: 4th Qtr. 1983 (Vol. 10, No. 4)

RESEARCH SUMMARIES: COMPARING WAGE LEVELS BETWEEN METROPOLITAN AREAS

(p. 3-4) By B. Steuernagel. Article, with 2 tables showing labor force, average annual pay, and hourly or weekly earnings by occupation, for 12 SMSAs, with comparison to aggregate 314 SMSAs, various periods 1982-83. Data are from BLS.

JOB MARKET: THE PROFESSIONAL AND SCIENTIFIC INSTRUMENTS MANUFACTURING INDUSTRY

(p. 5-6) By B. Jones. Includes 1 table showing Minnesota employment distribution by occupational group, for professional/scientific instruments manufacturing industry, 1970, 1978, and 1985.

1984 ECONOMIC OUTLOOK, ANNUAL FEATURE

(p. 9-16) Annual article, by R. Pinola, analyzing economic outlook for Minnesota and U.S. in 1984. Includes 3 tables showing percent change in GNP and components, 1984; and U.S. and Minnesota labor force by employment status, 1983-84.

S4160–3.503: 1st Qtr. 1984 (Vol. 11, No. 1)

RESEARCH SUMMARIES: TRENDS IN EMPLOYEE BENEFITS

(p. 3-4) By B. Steuernagel. Article, with 2 tables showing employee benefit payment distribution, and benefit payment as percent of wages/salaries, all by benefit type; and total value of wages/salaries and benefits; decennially 1951-81. Data are from Chamber of Commerce of the U.S.

JOB MARKET: EATING AND DRINKING ESTABLISHMENTS

(p. 5-6) By B. Jones. Includes 1 table showing Minnesota eating/drinking establishment employment distribution by occupational group, 1970, 1978, and 1985.

CONTINUED TRENDS IN WAGES AND SALARIES IN MINNESOTA 1981 THROUGH 1983

(p. 9-16, 30) By Ron Pederson. Article, with 3 tables showing Minnesota median monthly wage and median wage index, by occupational group with some detail by State region; and St. Paul/Minneapolis CPI; selected years 1970-83. Data are primarily from Minnesota Dept of Economic Security.

S4160–3.504: 2nd Qtr. 1984 (Vol. 11, No. 2)

RESEARCH SUMMARIES: A COMPARISON OF REGIONAL TRENDS IN EMPLOYMENT AND UNEMPLOYMENT IN MINNESOTA, 1978-84

(p. 3-4) By B. Steuernagel. Article, with 2 tables showing distribution of employment by industry division; and percent change in covered employment for goods- and service-producing industries, and in unemployment rate; all for Minnesota and 8 State regions, various periods 1979-84. Data are from Census Bureau.

JOB MARKET: THE HOTELS, MOTELS, AND OTHER LODGING PLACES INDUSTRY

(p. 5-6) By B. Jones. Includes 1 table showing Minnesota employment distribution by occupational group, for hotel/motel/lodging industry, 1970, 1978, and 1985.

CHANGES IN THE U.S. POPULATION AND LABOR FORCE, 1970-80

(p. 9-16) By S. Hamper and W. Graner. Article, with 3 tables showing U.S. population age 16/over, labor force, and employment and unemployment, by sex and region, and by State, 1970 and 1980. Data are from Census Bureau.

S4165 MINNESOTA
Department of Education

S4165–1 SCHOOL DISTRICT PROFILES, 1982/83, Minnesota
Annual. Aug. 1984. 46 p.
LC 81-643881.
SRI/MF/complete

Annual report, for 1982/83 school year, on Minnesota public school districts, with trends from 1972/73. Includes data on enrollment, finances, and staff, by school district, county, and development region.

Contents:

a. Contents listing, and introduction including data notes and sources. (p. 1-3)

b. Trend analysis, with 3 charts and 4 tables showing selected summary data, various years 1972/73-1982/83. (p. 4-9)

c. Definitions, list of school districts, and map showing counties and development regions. (p. 10-14)

d. 1 detailed table, described below, presenting data for 1982/83 as follows: by school district (p. 15-36); by county and development region (p. 37-42); by Education Cooperative Service Unit region (p. 41-42); for 5 elementary-only and nonoperating districts, and by enrollment size group (p. 43-44); and State summary, with high, low, and selected percentile values (p. 45-46).

Availability: Minnesota State Documents Center, 117 University Ave., St. Paul MN 55155, $0.50+$1.50 handling; SRI/MF/complete.

DETAILED TABLE:

Table shows average daily membership, by grade level (including prekindergarten handicapped); percent minority students; attendance rate; percent students transported; FTE professional staff, and pupil/staff ratio; tax rates; pupil units; Federal, State, and local/other revenues; and expenditures by function, operating funds balance, funds balance change, State/local operating costs, long-term debt, and 1982 assessed valuation, all per pupil unit.

S4165–2 MINNESOTA LIBRARIES: Minnesota Public Library Statistics, 1982
Quarterly (selected issue).
Spring 1983. (p. 123-156).
Vol. XXVII, No. 5.
ISSN 0026-5551.
LC 10-33240.
SRI/MF/complete

Annual *Minnesota Libraries* statistical issue, for 1982, on public library holdings, staff, services, circulation, and finances. Data are shown by facility and system for consolidated and federated regional library systems, and for unaffiliated libraries.
Data are from reports of each library.

Contents:

a. Introduction, and 2 charts and 1 table showing summary statistics, including area served for each library system; and library administrative units and branches. (p. 123-127)

b. Individual library statistics, with 1 detailed table showing the following for each system and facility (including bookmobiles), as appropriate: population served, professional and total FTE staff, weekly hours, stations, whether union affiliated and open on Sundays, holdings by type, circulation, loan period, program attendance, local and State/Federal receipts, indirect receipts/expenditures, and personnel and materials expenditures. (p. 128-145)

c. Directory of public libraries. (p. 146-156)

All data are for 1982. *Minnesota Libraries* is a quarterly publication which is primarily narrative; the annual library statistical issue is the only issue described and filmed by SRI.

Availability: Minnesota Department of Education, Library Development and Services Office, 440 Capitol Square Bldg., 550 Cedar St., St. Paul MN 55101, †; SRI/MF/complete.

S4180 MINNESOTA
Department of Finance

S4180–1 STATE OF MINNESOTA COMPREHENSIVE ANNUAL FINANCIAL REPORT, for the Year Ended June 30, 1983
Annual. Dec. 15, 1983.
126 p.
LC 77-646853.
SRI/MF/complete

Annual report on financial condition of Minnesota State government, for FY83, presenting assets and liabilities, revenues by source, expenditures by major function or object, and changes in fund balances; for all, general, special revenue, capital projects, debt service, enterprise, internal service, and fiduciary funds.

Also includes budgeted vs. actual revenues and expenditures; detail on retirement fund finances and investments; and debt service obligations to 2003.

Contains contents listing and financial highlights (p. 3-10); and report, with 34 financial statements and accompanying notes (p. 11-125).

This is the 5th annual edition; prior to FY79, report was published biennially.

Availability: Minnesota Department of Finance, 309 State Administration Bldg., St. Paul MN 55155, †; SRI/MF/complete.

S4190   MINNESOTA
Department of Health

S4190–1   REPORTED INDUCED ABORTIONS, Minnesota, 1982

Annual. Dec. 1983.
vii + 37 p. Rpt. No. 8.
LC 80-646615.
SRI/MF/complete

Annual report, for 1982, on number of induced abortions performed in Minnesota, by patient demographic and other characteristics. Data are from reports submitted by 25 facilities enrolled in the State Abortion Surveillance system.

Contains listings of contents, tables, and charts (p. iii-vi); introduction and narrative summary, with 1 chart showing trends from 1973 (p. 1-8); 1 map, 5 illustrative charts, and 20 tables listed below (p. 9-34); and definitions and survey form facsimile (p. 35-37).

This is the 8th annual report.

Availability: Minnesota Department of Health, Health Statistics Center, 717 Delaware St., SE, PO Box 9441, Minneapolis MN 55440, †; SRI/MF/complete.

TABLES:

[Tables show data for 1982, unless otherwise noted. Tables 1-19 begin "Reported induced abortions." Tables by residence are shown for total and Minnesota resident abortions, and generally include resident/total ratios.]

1. Selected surveillance results and comparisons, 1978-82. (p. 9)

2-5. By age group, individual age for teenage patients, selected age group, race/ethnic group [including American Indians and Hispanics], and marital status; [all] by residence. (p. 11-14)

6. By age group and marital status, State residents. (p. 15)

7. By gestation and residence. (p. 17)

8. By age group by weeks of gestation, State residents. (p. 18)

9-10. By number of prior abortions; and patients reporting prior abortions, by age group; [both] by residence. (p. 19-21)

11-12. By number of prior live births; and patients reporting prior live births, by age group; [both] by residence. (p. 22-23)

13-14. By method: by weeks of gestation, State residents, and by complications and residence. (p. 24-25)

15-17. By age group and marital status, by reported contraceptive use; and by age group by type of contraception at conception; [all for] State residents. (p. 27-29)

18. By quarter and residence. (p. 31)

19. Occurring in Minnesota to non-Minnesota residents, by State or country of residence. (p. 33)

20. Number of abortions occurring in [8] other States to Minnesota resident women. (p. 34)

S4190–2   MINNESOTA HEALTH STATISTICS, 1981

Annual. Mar. 1984.
5 + 106 p.
LC 74-645678.
SRI/MF/complete

Annual report, for 1981, on Minnesota vital statistics, by county and city, covering population, births, deaths by cause, marriages, and divorces. Also includes data on occupational injuries and illnesses. Most data were compiled from records submitted to the Dept of Health prior to Aug. 1, 1982. Population data are from U.S. Census Bureau.

Contains foreword and listings of contents, tables, and charts (5 p.); technical notes (p. 1-5); 7 statistical sections, with 2 charts, 29 tables, and interspersed narrative analysis (p. 9-94); and definitions, errata sheets, list of related publications, sample certificates, and map (p. 95-106).

All tables are listed below.

This is the 31st annual report.

Availability: Minnesota Department of Health, Health Statistics Center, 717 Delaware St., SE, PO Box 9441, Minneapolis MN 55440, †; SRI/MF/complete.

TABLES:

[Unless otherwise noted, data are for Minnesota. Data by race include Indian.]

S4190–2.1: 1981 Vital Statistics

[Data generally are for Minnesota residents, 1981, unless otherwise noted.]

OVERVIEW

1. Percent changes between 1980 and 1981 selected health statistics. (p. 9)

2. Births, deaths, infant deaths, fetal deaths, marriages, and divorces/annulments, by month, Minnesota occurrences. (p. 10)

3. Live births, fetal deaths, deaths, infant deaths, and neonatal deaths, by urban area of residence. (p. 11-15)

LIVE BIRTHS

4. Live births by county of occurrence distributed according to residence [in-county, other Minnesota, or out-of-State], and resident live births distributed according to place of birth [in-State or out-of-State, by county of residence]. (p. 20)

5. Selected resident natality statistics [including birth and fertility rates, births by selected characteristics (sex, race, legitimacy, birth order, plurality, prematurity, mother's age and education, prenatal care history, presence of congenital anomalies and other significant conditions, and risk status), infant, neonatal, and fetal deaths by race, and maternal deaths], by county and cities over 90,000. (p. 22-31)

6. Live birth weight by live birth order and sex. (p. 32)

7. Live births by age of mother and live birth order. (p. 33)

8. Prenatal care and race by age of mother and by legitimacy status [and fetal deaths by legitimacy, race, and mother's age]. (p. 34)

INFANT MORTALITY AND FETAL DEATHS

9. Infant, neonatal, and postneonatal deaths by cause. (p. 37)

10. Fetal deaths of 20 weeks and over by cause and weight of fetus. (p. 38)

GENERAL MORTALITY

11. Deaths by county of occurrence distributed according to residence, [and] resident deaths distributed according to place of death [same detail as table 4]. (p. 42)

12. Deaths from selected causes [arranged by International Classification of Diseases, 9th Revision], by age group and sex. (p. 44-48)

13. Deaths due to selected causes, by race. (p. 49)

14. 15 leading causes of death, death rates per 100,000 population, and percent of total deaths. (p. 50)

15. Leading causes of death by selected age groups. (p. 51)

16. Deaths occurring in Minnesota by cause and autopsy status. (p. 52)

17. Selected resident mortality statistics [including rates by age and numbers by sex, race, and selected causes] by county and cities over 90,000. (p. 53-61)

MARRIAGE AND DIVORCE

18. Marriages, divorces, and annulments, by county of occurrence. (p. 65)

19-20. Marriages occurring in Minnesota by race and age of bride and groom [also includes data for Chinese, Japanese, other Asian]. (p. 66-67)

21. Marriages reported in Minnesota by State of residence [of bride and groom]. (p. 68)

22. Divorces and annulments by age of husband and wife. (p. 69)

S4190–2.2: Occupational Illness/Injury, and Population

OCCUPATIONAL ILLNESS AND INJURY

[Tables 23-28 show data for 1980-81.]

23. Estimated number of injuries and illnesses by major industrial category. (p. 73)

24. Annual average employment, percent of total employment, and rate of occupational injuries/illnesses per 1,000 workers, by industrial category. (p. 74)

25. Estimated number of injuries/illnesses by major occupational category. (p. 75)

26-28. Estimated number of occupational injuries/illnesses, by type of accident, nature of injury, and part of body injured. (p. 76-79)

POPULATION

29. Population estimates by region, county, cities over 90,000, and sex [all cross-tabulated by age], 1981. (p. 84-94)

S4230   MINNESOTA
Department of Public Safety

S4230–1   MINNESOTA CRIME INFORMATION, 1982
Annual. July 1, 1983.
xi+119 p.
LC 74-641518.
SRI/MF/complete

Annual report on Minnesota crimes, arrests, and clearances, by type of offense, 1982. Includes data by location and by offender and victim characteristics. Also includes data on stolen property; police employment, casualties, and firearms use; and summary crime trends from 1936.

Data are from reports by county and municipal law enforcement agencies, submitted under the Uniform Crime Reporting Program to the Bureau of Criminal Apprehension.

Contains preface, and listings of contents, charts, and tables (p. v-xi); introduction and explanation of offense classifications (p. 1-7); narrative analyses with some text data, interspersed with 33 charts and 31 tables, described below (p. 8-118); and glossary (p. 119).

Previous report, for 1981, is described in SRI 1982 Annual, under this number.

Availability: Minnesota Department of Public Safety, Criminal Apprehension Bureau, Criminal Justice Information Systems Section, 1246 University Ave., St. Paul MN 55104, †; SRI/MF/complete.

CHARTS AND TABLES:

[Data are for Minnesota, 1982, unless otherwise noted. Index or Part I offenses are homicide, rape, assault, robbery, burglary, larceny, motor vehicle theft, and arson. Part II offenses are less serious crimes.]

S4230–1.1: Offenses

SUMMARY

a. Number of contributing agencies, and population represented, by urban and rural population size group; and violent and property crimes committed, by offense, 1977-82. Charts 1-3 and table 1. (p. 8-12)

VIOLENT CRIMES

b. Homicides by victim/offender relationship and weapon used; murder victims and offenders by age, sex, and race (including Indians); and homicides by situation (multiple or single victims and offenders) and circumstance. Charts 4-5 and tables 2-3. (p. 15-18)

c. Rape, including percent of reported cases unfounded, cleared by arrest, and attempted, 1977-82; number of robberies, and average and total stolen property value, by place of occurrence; and aggravated assault by weapon. Charts 6-10. (p. 20-24)

PROPERTY CRIMES

d. Burglaries, attempted and by forced and unlawful entry; residence and nonresidence burglaries by time of day, and value of property stolen, various years 1976-82; and larceny thefts by value categories and by type, with average and total stolen property values. Charts 11-17. (p. 26-32)

e. Motor vehicle theft by vehicle type, total stolen and recovered value, and percent of vehicles recovered in own and other jurisdiction, 1978-82. Charts 18-19. (p. 34-35)

f. Arson, including unfounded and actual offenses, total and juvenile clearances, and estimated property damage, all by detailed property type; and arson offenses by type of structure not in use. Table 4. (p. 37)

INDEX CRIMES AND PROPERTY LOSS

g. Index crimes reported, and percent cleared, for sheriff's depts and municipal police depts in 6-7 population size groups; value of property stolen and recovered in own and other jurisdiction, by property type; average loss per property offense, 1981-82; and distribution of dollar loss to serious crimes, by offense. Charts 20-21 and tables 5-8. (p. 38-43)

h. Statewide known/reported and actual offenses, unfounded complaints, crime rate, and total and juvenile clearances by arrest, all by Part I and Part II offense; property offenses and value stolen and recovered, by type of property or crime; total Part I and Part II crimes reported and percent cleared, by reporting agency area, including population; and Index crimes reported, by offense, 1936-82. Tables 9-12. (p. 45-52)

S4230–1.2: Arrests and Regional Analysis

ARRESTS

[Data by race are shown for white, Negro, Indian or Indian/Alaskan, Asian or Asian/Pacific Islander, Hispanic, and unknown.]

a. Total arrests by age, offense, and sex; total and juvenile arrests by race and offense; narcotics arrests, 1974-82; narcotics arrests by substance by age, and by sex and race; narcotics arrests for sale and possession, by substance, 1981-82; and narcotics arrests by substance and sex, by county, and/or city. Charts 22-25 and tables 13-17. (p. 54-68)

URBAN, RURAL, AND REGIONAL AREAS

b. Urban and rural known/reported and actual offenses, unfounded complaints, crime rate, and total and juvenile clearances by arrest, all by Part I and Part II offense; and urban and rural property offenses and value stolen and recovered, by type of property or crime. Tables 18-21. (p. 70-73)

c. Urban and rural comparison of offenses by sex and by Part I and Part II offense; and State planning region summary, including number of Part I and Part II offenses reported and cleared, and rates and arrests, by region. Chart 26 and tables 22-24. (p. 74-79)

S4230–1.3: Police Employment and Casualties, and County Offense Summary

a. Police urban and rural employees (sworn and civilian) as of Oct. 31, 1982, by city and county, arranged by population size group; municipal police, sheriff, and State patrol employees; and rate of police employees per 1,000 inhabitants. Tables 25-28. (p. 82-86)

b. Assaults on law enforcement officers: by type of weapon used, type of officer activity, type of assignment, and time of day. Charts 27-30. (p. 88-91)

c. Firearms discharge summary, including type of assignment, weapon used, purpose, and result, by type of activity; time of occurrence; whether felony or misdemeanor; and number of firearm discharges by size of community served. Charts 31-33 and tables 29-30. (p. 92-96)

d. Summary of Part I and Part II offenses and clearances, by offense, by county and municipality reporting agencies. Table 31. (p. 98-118)

S4230–2   MINNESOTA MOTOR VEHICLE CRASH FACTS, 1983
Annual. [1984.] x+96 p.
LC 79-643000.
SRI/MF/complete

Annual report on Minnesota traffic accidents, fatalities, and injuries, by detailed accident and vehicle type, location, time, and other circumstances, and driver and victim characteristics, 1983, with trends from the 1970s.

Also includes data on economic cost of accidents; motor vehicle registrations and licensed drivers; road and travel mileage; seatbelt, child restraint, and motorcycle helmet use; blood alcohol content of driver and pedestrian fatalities; alcohol-related arrests and license revocations; and selected detail for teenage drivers.

Data are compiled by Minnesota Office of Traffic Safety from accident reports submitted by citizens and law enforcement agencies.

Contains listing of contents, charts, and tables (p. iii-viii); introduction (p. ix-x); and 11 parts, with narrative summaries, 1 map, 17 charts, and 93 tables (p. 1-96).

Issuing agency also publishes *Minnesota 1983 Motor Vehicle Crash Facts Summary,* not covered by SRI.

Availability: Minnesota Department of Public Safety, Public Information Office, 318 Transportation Bldg., St. Paul MN 55155, †; SRI/MF/complete.

S4240   MINNESOTA
Department of Public Welfare

S4240–1   SUMMARY OF MINNESOTA PUBLIC ASSISTANCE TRENDS
Monthly. Approx. 30 p.
SRI/MF/complete, shipped quarterly

Monthly report on Minnesota public welfare programs, covering general, medical, and supplemental assistance, and AFDC. Includes cases, recipients, and expenditures, by county and program.

Data are compiled by the Operations Review Division of the Dept of Public Welfare. Report is issued approximately 6 months after month of coverage.

Issues generally include narrative summary, with 1 summary table and scattered text data; 23 detailed monthly tables; and technical notes and glossary.

Detailed monthly tables are listed below; most appear in all issues. Text tables and charts generally show trends for topics covered in monthly tables, often by State subarea; these trends are not described in SRI. All other additional features with substantial statistical content are described, as they appear, under "Statistical Features." Nonstatistical contents are not covered.

Availability: Minnesota Department of Public Welfare, Operations Review Division, Reports and Statistics Office, Space Center Bldg., 2nd Floor, 444 Lafayette Rd., St. Paul MN 55101, †; SRI/MF/complete, shipped quarterly.

Issues reviewed during 1984: Apr. 1983-Mar. 1984 (D).

TABLES:

PROGRAM TRENDS

[Tables show data for current month and 12 previous months, unless otherwise noted. Tables [1-9] and [12-14] show number of recipients and/or cases, expenditures or payments, and additional data as indicated below.]

[1] Public assistance programs (excluding food stamps).

[2] Food stamps.

[3] AFDC [including current month detail by program category and for special supplements].

[4] Emergency assistance program [including current month detail by program category and for defined emergencies].

[5] SSI.

[6] Minnesota supplemental aid (MSA) [including current month detail for aged, blind, and disabled].

[7-8] General assistance, and general assistance medical care [including current month detail by case type].

[9] General assistance by [Minnesota Emergency Employment Development and/or job service] exemption/referral status of responsible person [for current month and 2-5 previous months; table begins in the Dec. 1983 issue].

[10] General assistance subprogram payment trends [including shelter for battered women].

[11] General assistance medical care expenditures by category of service [for current month and fiscal year to date].

[12] Medical assistance program [including eligible persons, recipients, and expenditures, by basis of eligibility, for current month].

[13] Medical assistance by category of service [for current month, with expenditures also shown for fiscal year to date].

[14] Nursing home care by basis of eligibility [and level of care, current month only].

[15] Public assistance programs: applications and cases [by program, with detail for medical assistance by basis of eligibility; for current month, preceding month, and same month of preceding year].

DATA BY COUNTY

[Tables show cases and/or persons, and payments, and additional data as indicated below. Data are shown by county for current month. Several tables also include summary data by type of county (urban, suburban, and/or rural), and change from previous month.]

I. AFDC [including caretakers and children].

II. SSI and MSA.

III. General assistance [including detail for single cases, and families with children and with adults only].

IV-V. General assistance medical care: cases concurrently receiving general assistance, and medical care only cases.

VI-VII. Medical assistance: recipients [including adult and caretaker/child] concurrently receiving SSI, MSA, or AFDC, and receiving medical assistance only, [with detail for Indochinese cases.]

PRELIMINARY DATA

[16] Preliminary report on income maintenance programs [cases, persons, and payments, by program and category for 3 coming months, and selected month of previous year].

S4250   MINNESOTA
Department of Revenue

S4250–1   1981 MINNESOTA STATE INDIVIDUAL INCOME TAX
Annual. Aug. 1983.
81 p. var. paging.
Bull. No. 58.
ISSN 0093-1578.
LC 80-643649.
SRI/MF/complete

Annual report on Minnesota individual income tax returns, 1981 tax year. Covers filers, gross and taxable income, Federal tax deductions, and tax liability. Presents State totals by income group and filing status; and data by county and city, combined for all categories of filers.

State totals include selected additional data, including filers claiming low-income credits and political contribution credits, and amount claimed.

Report also includes trends in tax rates, filing requirements, personal credits, filers, and income, various years 1933-82.

Current data are from returns filed in 1982.

Contains contents and table listing (1 p.); introduction, summary, and family income section, with text data and 13 tables (p. 1-21); statistical appendix of 2 charts and 12 tables (p. 23-49); and income tax form facsimile (32 p.).

Availability: Minnesota Department of Revenue, Research Office 113, PO Box 64446, St. Paul MN 55164, †; SRI/MF/complete.

S4250–2   MINNESOTA CORPORATION INCOME TAX: Returns Filed During 1981
Annual. Nov. 1983.
3+31+5 p.   Bull. No. 57.
LC 79-649271.
SRI/MF/complete

Annual summary report on income taxes paid by corporations and banks in Minnesota, based on returns filed in 1981, with selected trends from 1977. Includes data by industry and income size.

Contains foreword, and contents listing (3 p.); summary of filing requirements, definitions, and tax rate trends (p. 1-4); summary analysis of re-

turns filed, with 7 text tables showing returns for State and multi-State corporations, by industry division, sales size, and selected ratios (p. 5-10); statistical appendix, with 35 tables, listed below (p. 13-31); and tax form facsimile (5 p.).

For description of previous report, for 1980, see SRI 1982 Annual, under this number.

Availability: Minnesota Department of Revenue, Research Office, B-95 Centennial Office Bldg., 658 Cedar St., St. Paul MN 55145, †; SRI/MF/complete.

TABLES:

[Unless otherwise noted, data are for 1981. Tables 1-21 show number of returns, gross sales, cost of goods sold, total and net income, State net and taxable income, and tax liability. All tables begin "Minnesota corporation income tax returns..."]

BY CORPORATION TYPE

[Tables show data for all, regular, minimum, multi-State, and 100% Minnesota corporations.]

1-5. By size of gross sales. (p. 13-15)

6-15. By size of total net income; and by size of State taxable income. (p. 15-20)

16-20. By major industry group [industry division]. (p. 20-22)

ALL CORPORATIONS

21. By industry classification. (p. 23)

TRENDS

[Tables show number of returns, total net and State taxable income, and tax liability, 1977-81.]

22-29. By size of total net income; and by size of State taxable income. (p. 25-28)

30-33. By major industry group [industry division]. (p. 29-30)

BANK CORPORATIONS

[Tables show number of returns, total and net income, State net and taxable income, and tax liability.]

34-35. By size of State taxable income; and by size of total net income. (p. 31)

S4310   MISSISSIPPI
Department of Agriculture and Commerce

S4310–1   MISSISSIPPI AGRICULTURAL STATISTICS, 1981-82
Annual. Nov. 1983. 62 p.
Supplement No. 17.
SRI/MF/complete

Annual report on Mississippi agricultural production and marketing, by commodity and/or county and district; and farm prices and operations; 1981-82, with some data for 1983.

Covers production, value and/or price, and, as applicable, acreage, yield, stocks, inventory, and disposition, for field crop, fruit and nut, livestock, dairy, apiary, and poultry sectors.

Also includes data on number and acreage of farms; value of exports; cash receipts by commodity; cotton ginning; off-farm grain storage facilities; catfish operations; feed prices paid by farmers; and agricultural employment, hours, and wage rates.

Data are compiled by the Mississippi Crop and Livestock Reporting Service in cooperation with the USDA.

Contains contents listing (3 p.); and 12 maps and 71 tables (p. 1-62).

Availability: Mississippi Crop and Livestock Reporting Service, Agricultural Statistician, PO Box 980, Jackson MS 39205, †; SRI/MF/complete.

S4325   MISSISSIPPI
Department of Banking and Consumer Finance

S4325–1   ANNUAL REPORT OF THE DEPARTMENT OF BANKING AND CONSUMER FINANCE, State of Mississippi, Jan. 1, 1983-Dec. 31, 1983
Annual. [1984.] 100 p.
LC 71-648929.
SRI/MF/complete

Annual report on financial condition of Mississippi financial institutions as of Dec. 1983. Covers composite assets, liabilities, equity capital, income, and expenses, for State-chartered commercial banks, credit unions, and small loan lenders; composite assets, liabilities, and equity capital, for nationally chartered banks; and assets of individual banks and credit unions.

Also includes regulatory activity and departmental finances; and lists of banks, branches, and other financial institutions, by location.

Contains contents listing (p. 4-5); and 15 tables, interspersed with rosters, directories, and lists (p. 5-100).

Availability: Mississippi Department of Banking and Consumer Finance, 1206 Woolfolk State Office Bldg., PO Drawer 731, Jackson MS 39205-0731, †; SRI/MF/complete.

S4340   MISSISSIPPI
Department of Education

S4340–1   ANNUAL REPORT OF THE STATE SUPERINTENDENT OF PUBLIC EDUCATION TO THE LEGISLATURE OF MISSISSIPPI: Statistical Reports 1982/83, Volume II
Annual. [1984.] 143 p.
LC 78-646492.
SRI/MF/complete

Annual report, for 1982/83, on Mississippi public elementary and secondary school enrollment, staff and salaries, and finances, by school district. Also includes data on public and private colleges and selected trends from 1950s.

Contains 7 statistical sections, with 2 charts and 74 tables described below (p. 1-140); and index (p. 141-143).

Volume I of report contains recommendations and summaries of dept activities, and is not covered in SRI.

Availability: Mississippi Department of Education, Administrative and Finance Division, PO Box 771, Jackson MS 39205-0771, †; SRI/MF/complete.

CHARTS AND TABLES:
[Data are for Mississippi, 1982/83, unless otherwise noted. Data by grade usually include prekindergarten, kindergarten, and special and ungraded elementary and secondary sections. Data by type of position for instructional personnel are generally for principals and assistant principals, supervisors, guidance counselors, librarians, and teachers.]

S4340–1.1: Schools, Enrollment, Staff, and Finances
[Data by district type are generally shown for some or all of the following: county, consolidated, municipal separate, special municipal separate, and intermediate. Data by size are shown by number in average daily attendance (ADA).]

a. School districts and schools: school districts by type and size; agricultural high schools and junior colleges; school board members by district type; number of schools by education level and size; number of elementary and secondary schools, 1971/72-1982/83; and accredited public and private secondary and elementary schools. 9 tables. (p. 1-6)

b. Students: cumulative and fall enrollment, ADA, average daily membership, promotions and nonpromotions, and dropouts, all by grade level; high school graduates, by sex; grade 1-12 enrollment, for children born in 1965; and retention rate between 5th grade and college; various years 1956/57-1982/83. 9 tables. (p. 7-15)

c. Staff: total staff, by position; characteristics of administrative and instructional personnel, variously including age, sex, salary, training level, and experience, with selected detail by position and district type; teacher salary and training trends, various years 1952/53-1982/83; and instructional personnel, salaries, and expense per pupil, for U.S. and 12 southeastern States. 13 tables. (p. 16-25)

d. Finances: Total expenditures and expenditures per pupil, by function and object, with detail by district type, and comparisons to total U.S. and southeastern States; receipts by source; general fund appropriations and receipts, including detailed appropriations for public education and higher education, FY82-83 or FY83; value of capital facilities and equipment; and school and nonschool food program participation and finances. 2 charts and 10 tables. (p. 26-35)

S4340–1.2: Higher Education, Transportation, and Vocational Education and Rehabilitation
a. Higher education: public junior college finances, administrative districts and campuses, and transportation and housing services; enrollment in public and nonpublic junior colleges, 4-year Bible colleges and theological schools, and colleges and universities, by program and/or class level, all by institution; and public/nonpublic college enrollment by class level, 1966/67-1982/83. 7 tables. (p. 36-42)

b. Transportation: privately and publicly owned vehicles in use and purchased, mileage traveled, and pupils transported; and school bus accidents, injuries, and property damage. 1 table. (p. 43)

c. Vocational/technical education and vocational rehabilitation finances; vocational enrollment by program and level, including disadvantaged and handicapped students; and vocational rehabilitation division activities, including cases by race and major disabling condition, recipients by type of service rendered, and average weekly earnings at acceptance and closure; FY83. 5 tables. (p. 44-47)

S4340–1.3: School Districts
[All tables show data by school district.]
a. Fall enrollment and ADA by grade level; and instructional personnel and average salaries, by type of position. 3 tables. (p. 48-69)

b. Financial report, including expenditures by function; revenue receipts by detailed local, State, and Federal source, including taxes by type; income from nonrevenue transactions; tax levies by type and 1982 assessments, for county, consolidated, and municipal separate districts. 12 tables. (p. 70-120)

c. Classroom teachers, pupil/teacher ratios, average salaries, fall enrollment, ADA, expenditures per pupil, revenues, and wealth and ad valorem tax collections per pupil unit; with rankings for each district. 5 tables. (p. 121-140)

S4345   MISSISSIPPI
Employment Security Commission

S4345–1   ANNUAL PLANNING INFORMATION, State of Mississippi, PY84
Annual. July 1984. 111 p.
SRI/MF/complete

Annual planning report, for planning year 1984, identifying Mississippi population groups most in need of employment services, and presenting data on employment by industry and occupation, with selected trends from 1960. Includes data on population and labor force, job openings, unemployment insurance, and veterans. Most data are shown for the State, with selected data shown by county.

Planning year 1984 (PY84) is the year ended June 30, 1985. Data are compiled by the Employment Security Commission.

Contains contents listing (2 p.); highlights and conclusions, and State geographical description (p. 3-11); 9 narrative sections, interspersed with 5 maps and 34 tables, listed below (p. 15-103); and appendix, with glossary and list of additional reports published by issuing agency (p. 107-111).

Availability: Mississippi Employment Security Commission, Labor Market Information Department, PO Box 1699, Jackson MS 39205-1699, †; SRI/MF/complete.

TABLES:

S4345–1.1: Population, Labor Force, and Unemployment Characteristics

[Tables [1-11] show data for PY84 and by race, sex, and age group, unless otherwise noted.]

POPULATION AND LABOR FORCE

[1] Population [1960, 1970, 1980, and 1985]. (p. 16)

[2-3] Labor force; and participation rate, 1960, 1970, 1980, and 1985. (p. 18-19)

[4] Veteran status: population 16/over [by period served and race]. (p. 20)

[5] Vietnam era veterans and labor force status, by age and race. (p. 21)

UNEMPLOYMENT

[6-9] Number unemployed and unemployment rate, number of different individuals unemployed, and long-termed unemployed (15 weeks or more). (p. 26-28)

[10-11] Experienced unemployed by occupation and service [by race and sex]; and weeks worked. (p. 29-31)

[12] Civilian labor force, total employment, total unemployment, and unemployment rates, [monthly] 1977-83. (p. 36-39)

S4345–1.2: Insured Unemployed and Employment Characteristics

INSURED UNEMPLOYED

[Data are shown quarterly for 1983.]

[1-2] UI [unemployment insurance] claimants, by age, occupation, race, and sex. (p. 44-45)

[3-4] UI claimants by duration of unemployment [by sex and race], and by industry of attachment. (p. 46-47)

EMPLOYMENT BY INDUSTRY AND OCCUPATION

[5] [Residence-based civilian labor force, by employment status; establishment-based employment, by industry division and major manufacturing group; persons involved in labor-management disputes; and insured unemployed]; PY77-84. (p. 52)

[6] Nonagricultural wage/salary average annual openings [by detailed occupation], 1980-90 [period]. (p. 57-66)

S4345–1.3: Employment Services and Characteristics of Economically Disadvantaged

EMPLOYMENT SERVICES

[Data are shown quarterly for 1983, by occupational category.]

[1] Unfilled job openings [total and unfilled 30 days or more]. (p. 71)

[2-3] Job openings received and filled. (p. 72-73)

[4-5] Occupations of job applicants, and experienced applicants available at end of quarter, by sex and minority status. (p. 74-75)

ECONOMICALLY DISADVANTAGED

[Data are by race, for PY84. Tables [7] and [10-14] also show data by sex.]

[6] Economically disadvantaged individuals [total and under age 18] in families with income below poverty level, [and] unrelated individuals [total and over age 65] with income below poverty level. (p. 80)

[7] Civilian family heads: labor force [and/or] poverty status. (p. 81)

[8] Related children under 18 years of age, by type of family [male and female heads], poverty status, and age [group]. (p. 82)

[9] Older individuals [65/over], by poverty status. (p. 83)

[10] Poverty level by age. (p. 84)

[11] Persons 14/above by type of income [wage/salary, nonfarm and farm self-employment, social security/railroad retirement, welfare, and other]. (p. 85)

[12-13] Youth enrolled in school (3-24 years of age), and youth 14-24 not in school, [total and below] poverty level, by age. (p. 86)

[14] Employed part-time for economic reasons [and total employed]. (p. 87)

S4345–1.4: Socioeconomic Characteristics

POPULATION AND HOUSING

[Data are shown by county.]

[1-2] Population: percent change 1970-83 [period]; and percent minority, 1980. [maps] (p. 92-93)

[3-4] Housing units, percent change 1970-80 [period]; and persons per housing unit, 1970 and 1980. [maps] (p. 94-95)

INCOME

[5] Per capita income as percent of national [by county and SMSA], 1981. [map] (p. 96)

[6] Total income [distribution by source (interest/dividends/rent, transfer payments, and earnings by industry division) by county], 1982. (p. 97-102)

[7] Average weekly wages, by industry [division and major manufacturing group, 1977-85]. (p. 103)

S4348   MISSISSIPPI
Office of the Governor

S4348–1   UNIFORM CRIME REPORT, State of Mississippi Annual Report, Jan.-Dec. 1982
Annual. [1983.]
108 p. var. paging.
SRI/MF/complete

Annual report on Mississippi crimes by type of offense and locale, 1982. Also includes data on arrests by age and sex, value of stolen property, murder victim characteristics, and law enforcement personnel.

Data are compiled from monthly reports of State and local law enforcement agencies, submitted under the Uniform Crime Reporting Program.

Contains foreword, contents and table/chart listings, and introduction (p. i-vii); report, with brief narrative summaries, 22 charts, and 22 tables (p. 1-58); and 5 appended tables (43 p.).

Charts and tables are described below.

This is the 2nd edition of the report.

Availability: Mississippi Office of the Governor, Criminal Justice Planning, Uniform Crime Reporting Division, 510 George St., Suite 246, Jackson MS 39202, †; SRI/MF/complete.

CHARTS AND TABLES:

[All data are shown for 1982. Reporting agencies include sheriffs' offices, police depts, and universities. Index offenses are murder, rape, robbery, aggravated assault, burglary, larceny, and motor vehicle theft. Non-Index offenses include numerous less serious crimes.

In addition to the topics described below, Index offense data include illustrative and trend charts, and 1 table (repeated for each offense) showing number of offenses by month and reporting agency. Note that table on murders by month and agency mistakenly repeats rape data for sheriffs' offices.]

a. Index offense summary, including arson; and value of stolen and recovered property, by type. 6 charts and 2 tables. (p. 6-13)

b. Murder: distribution of offenses by type of weapon used; victim's age, sex, race (including Indian), and relationship to offender; and circumstances. 2 charts and 7 tables. (p. 15-20)

c. Rape. 2 charts and 1 table. (p. 22-25)

d. Other Index offenses: robberies and assaults, by type of weapon; robberies by type of location; burglaries by type of entry and classification (day and night, residence and nonresidence); larcenies by classification; and motor vehicle thefts by type of vehicle, and number stolen and recovered locally and elsewhere; also including value of property stolen within each offense category. 12 charts and 12 tables. (p. 27-58)

e. By reporting agency and county: population, Index offenses by type (including arson), and crime rate. 1 table. (p. A1-A27)

f. Arrests: juvenile and adult, by age and sex, by Index and non-Index offense. (p. B1-B2, C1-C2)

g. Months in which agencies reported; and full-time sworn officers and civilian employees, by sex; all by agency. 2 tables. (p. D1-D8, E1-E5)

S4360   MISSISSIPPI
Board of Trustees
of State Institutions
of Higher Learning

S4360–1   STATISTICAL REPORT OF INFORMATION REGARDING THE ENROLLMENT, STUDENT CREDIT HOURS, DEGREES CONFERRED, AND FINANCES of the State-Supported Universities in Mississippi for the Summer of 1982 and the 1982/83 Regular Session
Annual. Nov. 1983.
4+vi+144 p.
SRI/MF/complete

Annual report on Mississippi public university operations, covering enrollments, degrees conferred, credit hours, and finances, all by institution, summer 1982 and/or academic year 1982/83, with selected trends from 1978/79. Includes detail by student level and field of study.

Contains preface (2 p.); contents and table listing (p. i-vi); and 6 statistical sections, with 1 chart and 54 tables described below (p. 1-144).

Availability: Mississippi Board of Trustees of State Institutions of Higher Learning, 3825 Ridgewood Rd., PO Box 2336, Jackson MS 39205, †; SRI/MF/complete.

TABLES:
[All data are shown by institution, often including on-campus study, off-campus degree granting and resident centers, and extension classes. Data are generally for 1982/83 summer session.]

a. Enrollments: FTE and/or headcount enrollments, by term, resident status, class level, sex, and subject area, including medical center, with selected trends from 1978/79; full- and part-time on-campus enrollments; and summary comparison of total enrollments at all Mississippi institutions of higher learning, including private and junior colleges. 1 chart and 31 tables. (p. 1-38)

b. Degrees conferred and credit hours produced, by level and field of study. 10 tables. (p. 39-123)

c. Finances: restricted and unrestricted revenues by source, including Federal and State appropriations, and expenditures by function, including scholarships/fellowships; and unrestricted on-campus student credit hour cost for instruction/related academic support, by level and field of study. 13 tables. (p. 125-144)

S4370   MISSISSIPPI
Library Commission

S4370–1   STATISTICS FOR PUBLIC LIBRARIES: Annual Report of Mississippi Public Libraries, FY83
Annual. [1984.] ii+27 p.
LC 81-623578.
SRI/MF/complete

Annual report on Mississippi public libraries, FY83. Covers library personnel, operations, holdings, circulation, income, and expenditures.

Contains contents listing (p. ii); narrative summary with 3 charts (p. 1-4); 3 tables listed below (p. 6-19); and directories of library administrative units and library commission (p. 21-27).

Availability: Mississippi Library Commission, PO Box 10700, Jackson MS 39209-0700, †; SRI/MF/complete.

TABLES:
[Tables show data by library, for FY83, unless otherwise noted.]

[1] Administrative units [director, organizational structure, and hours and days open; population served, 1980; and stationary and mobile service units, personnel, items owned, and circulation, FY82-83]. (p. 6-11)

[2] Income [operating and capital outlay, by funding source]. (p. 12-15)

[3] Expenditures [by object, including salaries/benefits and construction]. (p. 16-19)

S4395   MISSISSIPPI
Department of
Public Accounts

S4395–1   STATE OF MISSISSIPPI ANNUAL REPORT OF THE STATE AUDITOR OF PUBLIC ACCOUNTS for the Fiscal Year Ended June 30, 1983
Annual.   Sept. 1, 1983.
iii+307 p.
SRI/MF/complete

Annual report on financial condition of Mississippi State government, for FY83, presenting revenues by source, expenditures by function and object, and fund balances; for all, general, and special funds, with selected comparisons to FY82 and summary trends from FY70. Most data are also shown by detailed dept and agency.

Also includes data on appropriations to individual counties, cities, and school districts by fund; and to junior colleges, selected universities, and hospital facilities by institution.

Data are from the records of the State auditor of public accounts.

Contains contents listing (1 p.); introduction (p. i-iii); 4 trend tables (p. 3-50); 18 statements (p. 53-303); and roster of State auditors (p. 307).

Availability: Mississippi Department of Public Accounts, State Auditor, PO Box 1060, Jackson MS 39205, †; SRI/MF/complete.

S4400   MISSISSIPPI
Department of
Public Safety

S4400–1   ANNUAL SUMMARY OF TRAFFIC ACCIDENT AND ENFORCEMENT ACTIVITIES of the Mississippi Department of Public Safety, 1982
Annual.   [1983.]   v+104 p.
LC 57-35954.
SRI/MF/complete

Annual report on Mississippi traffic accidents, fatalities, and injuries, by accident and vehicle type, location, and other circumstances; and driver and victim characteristics; 1982, with trends from as early as 1938.

Also includes data on travel and highway miles; motor vehicle registrations, licensed drivers, and license testing; value of property damage; highway patrol enforcement personnel and activities including arrests; drunken driving and related medical tests; license revocations and other administrative procedures; and Driver Services Bureau vehicle use and revenues.

Data are compiled by the Dept of Public Safety.

Contains contents listing and highlights (p. iii-v, 1); 2 maps, 35 charts and 42 tables (p. 2-93); and glossary and index (p. 94-104).

Availability: Mississippi Department of Public Safety, Driver Services Bureau, Statistics Division, PO Box 958, Jackson MS 39205, †; SRI/MF/complete.

S4410   MISSISSIPPI
Department of
Public Welfare

S4410–1   MISSISSIPPI STATE DEPARTMENT OF PUBLIC WELFARE ANNUAL REPORT, FY83
Annual.   Oct. 24, 1983.
4+43 p.
ISSN 0098-5120.
LC 75-644224.
SRI/MF/complete

Annual report on Mississippi public welfare cases, recipients, and payments, by program and county, FY83, with trends from FY78. Covers Aid to Dependent Children (ADC), food stamps, adoption, foster care, child support, and general relief. Includes data on suspected fraud cases.

Contains listings of contents, tables, and charts (2 p.); narrative report arranged by division, with 12 maps and charts and 15 tables (p. 1-39); and information on employee attendance at conferences and related expense (p. 40-43).

All tables, and maps and charts with substantial statistical content not covered in tables, are listed below.

Availability: Mississippi Department of Public Welfare, PO Box 352, 515 E. Amite St., Jackson MS 39205, †; SRI/MF/complete.

MAPS, CHARTS, and TABLES:
[Data are for Mississippi, FY83 or as of June 1983, unless otherwise noted.]

STATE SUMMARY AND TRENDS

[1-3] Statement of expenditures by program [by object and funding source; and expenditures for assistance payments, by county [with summary trends from FY78]. [table, map, and chart] (p. 1-2, 4, 7)

[4] Child support activities [parents located, legal actions filed, and orders received, FY80-83]. (p. 8)

[5-6] Participation in the food stamp program by households, persons, and coupon value; and value by county. [table and map] (p. 9, 11)

[7-8] Adoption unit placements, and total number of certified special needs children receiving adoption assistance payments [by age, and by foster and nonfoster parent race]. (p. 13)

FRAUD CASES, HEARINGS, AND REVIEWS

[9] Court survey [suspected food stamp and public assistance fraud cases and dispositions; and fraud/refund investigation referrals and completions, by program, FY82-83]. (p. 19)

[10-12] Fair hearings and reviews [by program, and] administrative disqualification hearings [and dispositions]. (p. 23)

BY COUNTY
[Data are by county, unless otherwise noted.]

[13-15] [ADC:] applications handled, individuals eligible for assistance, and number of money payments, recipients, amount of assistance, and minimum and maximum grants. (p. 26-30)

[16] Child support: cases and collections [ADC and non-ADC]. (p. 31-32)

[17] Percentage of population participating in food stamp program [national average and by State], Oct. 1982. [map] (p. 35)

[18] Social service cases under care: primary and secondary service recipients. (p. 36)

[19] Foster home care payments. [map] (p. 38)

[20] General relief [cases and payments]. (p. 39)

S4415   MISSISSIPPI
Research and Development Center

S4415–1   HANDBOOK OF SELECTED DATA for Mississippi
Recurring (irreg.)   Oct. 1983.
ix + 106 p.
SRI/MF/complete

Handbook on Mississippi population, education, employment, business, income, and resources, various years 1960-83. Most data are shown by county on a series of State maps. Data are from Federal and State agencies.

Contains 64 maps, most with statistics, 2 charts, and 11 tables, grouped in 10 sections described below. Data source accompanies each map, chart, or table.

Previous report, issued in 1981, is described in SRI 1982 Annual, under this number.

Availability: Mississippi Research and Development Center, Information Services Division, 3825 Ridgewood Rd., Jackson MS 39211-6453, † + $2.00 postage and handling; SRI/MF/complete.

SECTIONS:

a. **Population:** total and voting age population, persons age 65 and older, and net migration, by county and race; population density and percent urban, by county; and population for cities over 10,000, and by SMSA. 12 maps and 2 tables. (p. 3-17)

b. **Education:** public school enrollment, graduates, and dropouts, by district; nonpublic, State-supported, and vocational school enrollment, by county; location and enrollment of postsecondary institutions, and vocational programs offered; percent of persons 25 years/over with 4 years of high school, by county; and per pupil expenditure for elementary and secondary education, by State. 7 maps, 1 chart, and 4 tables. (p. 21-37)

c. **Employment:** total and manufacturing employment, and unemployment, by county; net change in manufacturing employment and establishments, by major city; employment within and outside county of residence; and average unemployment rate, by State. 9 maps, 1 chart, and 1 table. (p. 41-51)

d. **Business:** gross and retail sales, and retail sales per capita, by county and major city; and business births and deaths, by county. 4 maps and 3 tables. (p. 55-61)

e. **Income:** major sources of personal income, per capita and median family income, and percent of families below poverty level, by county; per capita income by State; and Federal outlays by agency, by county. 5 maps and 1 table. (p. 65-70)

f. **Natural resources:** location of national forests, national and State parks, and reservoirs; percent of land in commercial forests; and mineral products and production value; by county. 8 maps. (p. 73-80)

g. **Utilities:** electric and gas facilities, and counties served; and water assns and companies. 4 maps. (p. 83-87)

h. **Multicounty districts and organizations:** congressional, supreme court, Highway Commission, Public Service Commission, Army Corps of Engineers, and water, planning, and industrial development districts. 6 maps. (p. 91-94)

i. **Transportation:** motor carrier terminals; railroad systems; major ports and channels; and airports. 5 maps. (p. 97-100)

j. **Miscellaneous:** national historic landmarks; number of doctors, dentists, registered nurses, and licensed practical nurses, by county; and number of farms and farm product value, by county. 4 maps. (p. 103-106)

S4435   MISSISSIPPI
Tax Commission

S4435–1   SERVICE BULLETIN, FYE June 30, 1983, Mississippi State Tax Commission
Annual.   Dec. 31, 1983.
139 p.
SRI/MF/complete

Annual report presenting detailed data on Mississippi tax collections by type of tax, and disbursements by locality and function, FY83. Includes data by industry, county, and city.

Also includes data on property value assessments, reimbursements, motor vehicle fuel consumption and registrations, and Alcoholic Beverage Control (ABC) Division sales and profits.

Data were compiled by the Tax Commission in cooperation with the State auditor.

Contains contents listing (1 p.); and 8 statistical sections, with 7 charts, and 52 tables listed below (p. 7-139).

Availability: Mississippi Tax Commission, PO Box 960, Jackson MS 39205, †; SRI/MF/complete.

TABLES:
[Unless otherwise noted, data are for FY83.]

S4435–1.1: Statistical Sections
SUMMARY
[1-4] General and special fund total receipts [by source] and expenditures [by function]. (p. 11-17)

AD VALOREM TAX, HOMESTEAD EXEMPTION
[5] Assessment [summary of property and utilities by class, and including real property acreage] 1982. (p. 21)

[6] Total assessments of each county, [1974-82]. (p. 22)

[7-8] Assessment of personal property and real estate, by classes [and county], 1982. (p. 23-24)

[9] Ad valorem assessments [by type and county], 1982. (p. 25)

[10] Comparative statement of assessments: public utilities [by company], 1976-82. (p. 26)

[11] Assessment of public utilities by classes [and county], 1982. (p. 27)

[12-13] County and separate school district applications classified according to value [by county and district], 1982. (p. 28-29)

[14-15] Counties, municipalities, and municipal separate school districts: reimbursements for elderly/disabled [with some detail for regular reimbursements, all by county or district] 1981-82. (p. 30-31)

[16] Adjustments in homestead exemption tax loss claims, counties/municipal separate school districts/municipalities combined [regular and elderly/disabled reimbursements 1981-82, and total adjustments 1981/82, by county]. (p. 32)

[17-18] Exempt assessed valuation [for individual] counties and municipal separate school districts, [biennially 1974-82]. (p. 33-34)

ABC FINANCES
[Tables 19-23 begin "ABC Division..."]

[19-20] Collections and distributions of revenue [by major source or recipient], and revolving fund statement of operations, FY82-83. (p. 37-38)

[21] Wet [and] dry counties [list]. (p. 40)

[22] Seventeen-year comparison of revenue collections [by source, 1967-83]. (p. 41)

[23] Schedule of local governing authorities permit licenses fees [collected]. (p. 42-45)

INCOME AND FRANCHISE TAXES
[24-25] Selected corporate income and franchise tax information [number of taxpayers, income revenue, taxable income, franchise tax, and annual fee, by industry division and county, and for out of State]. (p. 49-51)

[26] Selected personal income tax information [number of taxpayers, gross income tax, and net taxable income, by county and for out of State]. (p. 52-53)

SEVERANCE AND PETROLEUM TAXES
[27] Payments to counties: oil, gas, and timber severance taxes. (p. 57-58)

[28-37] Tax collected on gasoline; interstate fuel tax; fuel tax collected at scales; tax collected on other motor fuel and on liquefied compressed gas for highway use; collections on permits and decals; distributors compressed tax; and tax collected on jet fuel, and on oils; [generally showing monthly taxable gallons and amount collected, with detail by type of fuel or oil]. (p. 61-70)

[38] [Monthly] seawall tax collections [and taxable gallons for 3 counties]. (p. 71)

[39] Petroleum tax distribution to counties [municipal and county share, and surplus]. (p. 72)

[40-41] Petroleum Tax Division receipts [by source] and disbursements [by category]. (p. 74-75)

MOTOR VEHICLE REGISTRATIONS, FEES, AND TAXES
[42] Regular registration/tag fees [and taxes collected, and decals/plates issued, by vehicle type and other classification]. (p. 79)

[43] Motor vehicle license tag plates: number issued by tax collectors [by county], for tag year 1982. (p. 80)

[44-45] Prorate registrations fees and taxes, FY83; and passenger coach [revenue] distribution for 1983 [for 6 cities]. (p. 82)

[46] Privilege tax distribution to counties. (p. 83)

[47-48] Privilege Tax Division and Title Division [receipts and disbursements]. (p. 85-86)

SALES TAX

[49] Basic classification of sales [number of businesses and gross tax and sales, by kind of business]. (p. 89)

[50] Sales tax payments to individual municipalities and amounts diverted for repayment of air/water pollution control grants. (p. 93-99)

[51-52] Sales and tax [and number of taxpayers, by selected] industry group, [by county and city, and for total noncity]. (p. 100-139)

S4480   MISSOURI
Department of Agriculture

S4480–1   MISSOURI FARM FACTS, 1984
Annual.   May 1984.   4+56 p.
ISSN 0544-5507.
LC 77-648377.
SRI/MF/complete

Annual report on Missouri agricultural production, marketing, and finances, mostly 1979-83, with some data for 1984, and selected historical trends. Data generally are shown by commodity and/or county, with some comparisons to total U.S.

Report covers production, prices, sales, value, and, as applicable, acreage, yield, or inventory, for field crop, fruit, livestock, dairy, and poultry sectors.

Report also includes data on population; weather; grain storage facilities; commercial fertilizer consumption; farm income, production expenses, telephone and electricity use and costs, and balance sheet; number of farms, acreage, and average rent; farm real estate value, taxes, and debt; and foreign-owned agricultural land.

Data are compiled by the Missouri Crop and Livestock Reporting Service in conjunction with USDA.

Contains contents listing (1 p.); and 4 report sections, with 9 maps and charts, 83 tables, and interspersed narrative (p. 1-55).

Availability: Missouri Crop and Livestock Reporting Service, PO Box L, Columbia MO 65205, †; SRI/MF/complete.

S4500   MISSOURI
Department of Consumer Affairs, Regulation and Licensing

S4500–1   ANNUAL REPORT AND STATISTICAL DATA, Missouri, 1983
Annual.   1983.   158 p.
LC 74-647069.
SRI/MF/complete

Annual report on Missouri insurance industry financial condition and underwriting activity, by company and type of insurance, 1982. Covers assets, liabilities, capital stock, surplus, net gain/loss and/or net income, premiums written, securities on deposit, and premium tax payments, for life and property/casualty insurance companies.

Also includes data on Insurance Division licensing activities and revenues; and workers compensation premium taxes and 2nd injury fund assessment for self-insured companies and assns and property/casualty companies.

Data are from annual statements filed by individual companies.

Contains contents listing (p. 3); Insurance Division report, with 8 tables and list of company status changes (p. 9-46); and company directory and financial profiles (p. 47-158).

This is the 114th edition.

Availability: Missouri Department of Consumer Affairs, Regulation and Licensing, Insurance Division, PO Box 690, Jefferson City MO 65102-0690, $5.00; SRI/MF/complete.

S4505   MISSOURI
Department of Elementary and Secondary Education

S4505–1   134th REPORT OF THE PUBLIC SCHOOLS OF MISSOURI for the School Year Ending June 30, 1983
Annual.   Jan. 1, 1984.
149 p.
ISSN 0145-2975.
LC 80-643870.
SRI/MF/complete

Annual report, for 1982/83 school year, on Missouri public schools, with selected trends from the 1970s. Covers education program activities, finances, enrollment, attendance, graduates, and staff, shown for the State and by school district and county. Also includes State data on vocational, adult, and special education.

Report is prepared by Missouri Board of Education.

Contains contents listing (p. 3), and the following sections:

Part I. Narrative report on 1982/83 activities and priorities, with 1 summary table. (p. 8-15)

Part II. "Nation at Risk." Reprint of the complete text of the 1983 report of the National Commission on Excellence in Education. (p. 18-25)

Part III. Statewide data, with 2 summary charts, and 43 tables listed below. (p. 28-67)

Part IV. Local data, by county and school district, with 4 extended tables, also listed below. (p. 70-149)

Availability: Missouri Department of Elementary and Secondary Education, PO Box 480, Jefferson City MO 65102, ‡; SRI/MF/complete.

PART III-IV TABLES:
[Tables show data for 1982/83 school year, unless otherwise noted.]

S4505–1.1: Statewide Data
[Several table titles begin "Summary of..." Data by types of district are for districts maintaining elementary schools only and for those also maintaining high schools, often with detail by accreditation classification.]

FINANCES

1a-1b. Receipts by sources available for use for current expenditures; and revenue and nonrevenue receipts [by source] in public schools. (p. 28)

2a-2c. Receipts, expenditures, and levies of public school districts [by fund]; and detailed analysis of receipts [by source and fund] and of expenditures [by function and object]. (p. 29-30)

2d. Expenditures [total and per average daily attendance (ADA), 1970-83]. (p. 30)

3-4. Expenditures [by function and] object, by fund. (p. 31-32)

5-6. Tax levies for districts maintaining high school and 6-director elementary schools; and valuation, levies, value of school property, and indebtedness. (p. 32)

7-8b. Average tax levy per hundred dollars valuation, and bonds outstanding and issued [1975/76-1982/83]; and short-term borrowing, 1982/83. (p. 33)

9a-9b. Foundation program apportionments and payments [1975/76-1982/83]; and payment record, 1982/83. (p. 33)

10. Expenditure factors [eligible pupils and current expenditures, 1976/77-1982/83]. (p. 33)

TRANSPORTATION

11-12a. Average daily number of pupils transported [1975/76-1982/83]; and transportation of public school pupils [including vehicles, mileage, and costs], 1982/83. (p. 34)

12b. State maximum cost factor 106%. (p. 34)

ENROLLMENT, ATTENDANCE, AND GRADUATES

13. Live births in Missouri [1974-83]. (p. 34)

14-16. Accumulated enrollment [elementary and high school, 1976/77-1982/83]; and number of districts by fall enrollment range, grades 9-12 [1976-83], and grades K-12, 1982/83. (p. 34)

17. Fall enrollment by grade in public elementary and secondary schools [1978/79-1983/84]. (p. 35)

18. Fall enrollment by grades. (p. 36)

19-20b. Accumulated enrollment [by grade level and sex]; and eligible pupil data [including resident ADA and membership; by type of district, various periods 1977/78-1982/83]. (p. 36)

21-22. ADA [for residents and nonresidents by grade level including preschool special education, and summer schools, by type of district, 1982/83; and for high school and State districts, 1976/77-1982/83]. (p. 37-38)

23-24. Graduates [by sex]; and follow-up data on graduates [number entering college, special schools, jobs, and military; various years 1975/76-1983/84]. (p. 38)

25a-25b. Number in graduating classes in high school districts [1977/78-1982/83]; and persistence to graduation in public high schools [by class level], 1955-83. (p. 38-39)

TEACHERS, SCHOOL DISTRICTS, AND CURRICULUM
[Tables 26-31 show data for teachers and other professional personnel, by position and type of district, and, except for tables 29-30, by school level.]

26-27. Numbers of teachers and average annual teachers salaries [by sex]. (p. 40-41)

28. Breakdown of teachers by degree. (p. 42)

29-30. Tenure and experience. (p. 43-44)

31. Teachers turnovers from 1982 to 1983 [total and 1st-year teachers]. (p. 45)

32-33. [Teachers'] certificates issued [by type, 1982/83; and total, 1978/79-1982/83]. (p. 46)

34. Number of school districts [by type, 1976-83]. (p. 46)

35A-35B. Classification data: school district classification; and high schools holding membership in the North Central Assn [including elementary and nonpublic high schools; all by district or school type, including State institutional schools]. (p. 46)

36-37. Courses offered in subject matter fields [number of districts offering courses and enrollment, by course title, 1982/83; and summary trends 1971/72-1982/83; all by subject]. (p. 47-52)

VOCATIONAL, ADULT, AND SPECIAL EDUCATION

38A-38B. Vocational education: financial and statistical data summary [including Federal and State allotments and expenditures; expenditures by function and program; and number of districts, teachers, and students for secondary, postsecondary, and adult programs, by subject], FY83. (p. 53)

39a-39f. Adult education: special fields non-reimbursed public school adult education [enrollments by subject]; manpower training section (CETA) and adult basic education [school districts or schools, teachers, and enrollments]; veterans education [approved schools and business establishments, and trainees]; high school equivalence [applications and certificates issued]; and community education program [schools, personnel by type, facilities, and funding by source; various years 1977/78-1982/83]. (p. 54-55)

40A-40C. Special education: financial and statistical data summary, programs data, and school trust funds [selected data on special education programs and State schools for blind, deaf, and severely handicapped, including State and Federal funding, expenditures by object, number of children served, number of teachers, and trust fund balance sheets], FY83. (p. 55-59)

41A-41D. Vocational rehabilitation [selected program data, including number of clients, costs, and client occupations and earnings], year ending Sept. 30, 1983. (p. 60)

TESTS

42A-42K. Testing and assessment program data [including performance on 8th grade basic essential skills test and subtests, and on various statewide tests for selected other grades; and Scholastic Aptitude and American College Test scores as compared to national norms; various years 1971/72-1982/83]. (p. 61-66)

FOOD SERVICE

43a-43g. School food services program [including participation and Federal and State funding]. (p. 67)

S4505–1.2: Local Data
[Tables 1-4 show data by county and school district.]

1. Apportionment and payment of State school and textbook monies. (p. 70-92)

2. Summary of financial data [including resident ADA and membership, eligible pupils, expenditure per pupil, assessed valuation, total levy, and operating tax levy]. (p. 93-114)

3. Classification and organization [including accreditation category, grade span, units of approved credit in high schools, enrollment, and total staff members]. (p. 115-132)

4. Receipts by source [local/county, State, and Federal] available for use for current expenditures. (p. 133-149)

S4520   MISSOURI
Coordinating Board for
Higher Education

S4520–1   1983 ANNUAL REPORT, Coordinating Board for Higher Education, Missouri
Annual. Dec. 1983.
4+17 p.
ISSN 0361-1191.
LC 75-649670.
SRI/MF/complete

Annual report, for 1983, of Missouri Coordinating Board for Higher Education (CBHE). Includes data on enrollment 1982-83, program development FY83, and financial summaries FY83-85.

Data are from State records and reports by institutions.

Contains contents and table listings (2 p.); and narrative report, interspersed with 11 tables, listed below (p. 1-17).

Availability: Missouri Coordinating Board for Higher Education, Higher Education Department, 101 Adams St., Jefferson City MO 65101, $1.75; SRI/MF/complete.

TABLES:

S4520–1.1: Academic Enrollment, Programs, and Financial Planning

ENROLLMENT SUMMARY
[Data are shown by type of institution: State and independent 2- and 4-year colleges, independent universities, University of Missouri, and technical/professional schools.]

1. Summary of on-campus, on-schedule head-count enrollment with percent change, fall 1982 and fall 1983. (p. 2)

2-3. Summary of on-campus, on-schedule enrollment by full- and part-time headcount, with percent change, fall 1982 and fall 1983. (p. 3-4)

4. Summary of on-campus, on-schedule, FTE enrollment, fall 1982 and fall 1983. (p. 5)

ACADEMIC PROGRAMS
[Tables 5-7 show data for FY83. Institutional types are public and private.]

5-6. New program action [CBHE approvals] by degree level, [by] institutional type and [individual] institution. (p. 6-7)

7. Distribution of new degree programs approved [by the CBHE], by broad disciplinary area and institutional type. (p. 7)

8. Number of out-of-district courses approved and offered, with enrollment, in 1982.

CBHE FINANCIAL PLANNING
[All recommendations are made by CBHE.]

9. General revenue summary [by institution or program, FY84-85]. (p. 13)

10. Summary of recommendations [for] capital improvements [by type including energy conservation and handicapped accessibility, by institution], FY84. (p. 14)

11. Community/junior college State aid [by institution], FY83-85. (p. 15)

S4520–2   DIRECTORY OF MISSOURI LIBRARIES: Public, Special, College and University, FY83
Annual. [1984.] x+68 p.
ISSN 0092-4067.
LC 73-645566.
SRI/MF/complete

Annual directory, for FY83, of Missouri public, special, and academic libraries, with data on finances, holdings, circulation, staff, and services.

Contents:

a. Map; lists of higher education board members, State library staff, and library organizations; 3 State summary tables on public library expenditures, income, volumes, and staff, Federal fund expenditures by object, and interlibrary loan activity; and foreword and abbreviations key. (p. ii-x)

b. Library directory by city, including some or all of the following for each library: address; hours open; assessed valuation; tax rate; income by source, including State and Federal grants, and gifts; population served; staff and total payroll; expenditures by object; volumes; total and juvenile circulation; bookmobile service; branches; and cooperative and Federal program participation. (p. 1-43)

c. Library directory by county, including total county assessed valuation and tax levy rate, and generally operating income, volumes available, and State aid. (p. 44-55)

d. Index. (p. 56-68)

Availability: Missouri Coordinating Board for Higher Education, Missouri State Library, PO Box 387, Jefferson City MO 65102, †; SRI/MF/complete.

S4530   MISSOURI
Department of
Labor and
Industrial Relations

**S4530–2   ANNUAL REPORT, Missouri
            Department of Labor and
            Industrial Relations, 1983**
Annual.   Dec. 15, 1983.
41 p.
LC 57-63397.
SRI/MF/complete

Annual report, for FY83, on Missouri Dept of Labor and Industrial Relations activities and programs, with data on Missouri employment, earnings, unemployment insurance, work injuries and deaths, and mining production.

Contains contents listing, introduction, and organizational chart (2 p.); and 7 departmental reports, interspersed with 2 maps, 2 charts, and 42 tables (p. 1-41). Maps and tables are listed below.

This is the 9th annual report.

Availability: Missouri Department of Labor and Industrial Relations, PO Box 59, Jefferson City MO 65104, †; SRI/MF/complete.

TABLES AND MAPS:

S4530–2.1: Labor and Industrial Relations Commission

[1-2] Appeals to the Labor and Industrial Relations Commission: employment security appeals and workers' compensation cases [by type and disposition, 1982-83]. (p. 1)

S4530–2.2: Division of Workers' Compensation

WORK REVIEW REPORT

1. Reports of injuries by years reported, 1926-82. (p. 2)

2. Statement of expenses [for personal service, and expense/equipment, monthly] 1982. (p. 4)

STATISTICS ON 1982 CASES

1. Incidence frequency by age. (p. 4)

2-7. Cost by type of disability for all incidences, 1982 and 1977-81 (revised to July 1, 1983) [for number of incidences, compensation, and medical payments]. (p. 5-6)

WORK INJURY ANALYSIS

[Tables show data for 1982. Data by severity are for fatalities, disabling cases, medical treatment/1st aid cases, and other. Data by type of accident are for 8 causes of injuries. Data by source of injury are for 9 objects or substances causing injury. Most data by type of disability are for temporary total, permanent partial, fatalities, and others.

Tables 1-5 and 12 show data by industry division.]

1-5. Accidents and diseases by severity, type, source and nature [of injury], and affected [body] part. (p. 7-8)

6A-6D. Cost data by injury category: [accident type, source and type of injury, and affected body part; includes number of cases, compensation, and medical payments]. (p. 8-9)

7-10. Type, source and nature of injury, and part of body affected, by type [of disability]. (p. 10)

11. Cost by type of disability, by county. (p. 11)

12. Cost [compensation and medical payments] by industry [division] and type of disability. (p. 12)

S4530–2.3: Division of Labor Standards

[1] [Labor inspections and investigations by type, including child labor violations, FY83.] (p. 18)

[2] Mineral production [by commodity, FY82-83]. (p. 18)

[3-8] Clay, coal, iron, lead, zinc, copper, silica sand, and shale, [production and fatal accidents, by operator, and, for coal only, by county, FY83; and total production, 1974-83] . (p. 19-20)

[9] Granite [production and fatal accidents, by operator, FY83]. (p. 20)

[10] Fatal accidents in mines [and miners killed, 1982]. (p. 20)

[11] [Prevailing Wage Law enforcement activities, including inspections, violations, and wage/penalties collected, FY82-83.] (p. 22)

[A] Prevailing Wage Section, number of wage determinations [by county (no date)]. [map] (p. 22)

S4530–2.4: Division of Employment Security

[1] [Civilian labor force by employment status, and manufacturing and nonmanufacturing employment, FY80-83.] (p. 26)

[B] Unemployment rates [for counties, SMSAs, and labor market areas], 1982 annual averages. [map] (p. 26)

[2] Labor force summary [by employment status, annual averages 1981-82]. (p. 33)

[3] Employment, [weekly and hourly] earnings, [and weekly hours, all by major manufacturing group and industry division], 1982 annual averages. (p. 34)

[4] Job service activities [job openings, applications, referrals, and placements, by local State employment office], FY83. (p. 35)

[5] Unemployment insurance programs [covered workers and employers; wages of covered workers; employer contributions and contribution rates; unemployment insurance fund balance and interest earned on fund; and amount and duration of unemployment insurance payments, various years FY38-65, and annually FY70-83]. (p. 37)

[6] Unemployment compensation fund [balances at beginning and end of year, and receipts and disbursements by type], FY83. (p. 38)

[7] Unemployment insurance contributions and benefits, by county of residence: all programs [employer contributions, initial claims, weeks claimed and paid, and amount of State and Federal benefits paid], FY83. (p. 39-40)

**S4530–3   MISSOURI AREA LABOR
            TRENDS**
Monthly.   Approx. 15 p.
ISSN 0148-4214.
SRI/MF/complete, shipped
quarterly

Monthly report on Missouri labor market conditions, including employment, hours, and earn-

ings, by industry, for State and selected SMSAs. Also includes data on employment by county; unemployment insurance claims and benefits; and persons involved in labor-management disputes, employment service activities, and characteristics of the insured unemployed, for selected SMSAs. Report is issued approximately 2 months after month of coverage.

Contains 1 trend chart, and narrative review of labor conditions statewide and in Kansas City, St. Louis, and Springfield SMSAs, interspersed with the following data shown for month of coverage, previous month, and same month of previous year, unless otherwise noted:

a. Labor force by employment status, by SMSA, labor market area, and county. 1 table.

b. Total nonagricultural wage/salary employment, and production worker average hours and earnings, by industry division and selected manufacturing industry group; and total employees involved in labor disputes. 1-2 tables, repeated for State (excludes labor dispute data) and for each of the 3 SMSAs noted above.

c. Summary labor force data; average weekly insured unemployment; and unemployment insurance average weekly initial claims, exhaustions, and benefits paid. 1 table.

d. Employment and unemployment data for Missouri, and Kansas City and St. Louis SMSAs, including demographic and other characteristics of job applicants and persons placed; demographic characteristics, industry attachment, and occupational distribution of insured unemployed; and, for St. Louis, occupational distribution of job openings and placements; for current month, with selected comparisons to previous months and/or years. 1 table and text data.

Availability: Missouri Department of Labor and Industrial Relations, Employment Security Division, PO Box 59, Jefferson City MO 65104, †; SRI/MF/complete, shipped quarterly.

Issues reviewed during 1984: Sept. 1983-Aug. 1984 (D).

S4560   MISSOURI
Department of
Public Safety

**S4560–1   MISSOURI TRAFFIC
            CRASHES, 1984 Edition**
Annual.   [1984.]   21 p.
LC 65-64878.
SRI/MF/complete

Annual report on Missouri traffic accidents, injuries, and fatalities, by accident and vehicle types, location, time, and other circumstances; and driver and victim characteristics; 1983, with trends from 1952. Also includes data on total economic loss, motor vehicle registrations, miles traveled, and licensed drivers.

Data are compiled by the State Highway Patrol.

Contains introduction and index (p. 1-2); and 3 maps, 4 charts, and 24 tables (p. 3-21).

Availability: Missouri Department of Public Safety, State Highway Patrol, 301 W. High St., PO Box 749, Jefferson City MO 65102-0749, †; SRI/MF/complete.

S4570   MISSOURI
Department of Revenue

S4570–1   ANNUAL COMBINED FINANCIAL REPORT: Missouri Department of Revenue and Office of the State Treasurer, FY83
Annual. [1984.] 74 p.
LC 74-643144.
SRI/MF/complete

Annual financial report on the operations of the Missouri Dept of Revenue and the State Treasurer's Office, FY83. Includes data on Revenue Dept tax collections and distributions, and State fund balance investments held by banks.

Contains contents and table listing (1 p.); Dept of Revenue report, with narrative summary and 20 tables listed below (p. 7-55); and State Treasurer's report, with letter of transmittal, 2 text tables, and 9 other tables also listed below (p. 56-74).

The Dept of Revenue also publishes a monthly brochure on collections, which is not covered by SRI.

Availability: Missouri Department of Revenue, Management, Planning, and Policy Office, PO Box 629, Jefferson City MO 65105, $11.20; SRI/MF/complete.

TABLES:
[Tables show data for FY83 or June 30, 1983, unless otherwise noted.]

S4570–1.1: Dept of Revenue Report
[Tables show data for the Dept of Revenue, unless otherwise noted.]

GENERAL

1-2. Administrative costs [salaries, equipment, and operations], and 5-year summary [FY79-83]. (p. 8)

3. Review of legislation [bill number and subject of legislation]. (p. 10-12)

COLLECTIONS

4. Major taxes administered [description, tax rate, collections, and disposition, by tax]. (p. 12-15)

5. Individual income tax rates. (p. 16)

6. Five-year tax history [amounts collected, by tax, 1979-83]. (p. 17)

7-7A. Major fees and licenses administered [rates, collections, and disposition, by type]; and license plate categories, rates and fees [by type of carrier]. (p. 19-20)

8. Summary of activities, Division of Motor Vehicle and Licensing [drivers licenses, and motor vehicle and marine registrations and titles issued]; and Division of Taxation [income tax returns filed, and number and amount of refunds, with detail for senior citizens tax credits]. (p. 21)

9. State revenue, tax and nontax, by funds [general revenue, and Federal, highway, and other]. (p. 22-27)

10. General revenue fund receipts, FY83, and original estimate, FY84 [by source]. (p. 28)

11. Nonrecorded revenue, by funds [general revenue, agency/program, and State Highway Dept]. (p. 29)

DISTRIBUTIONS

12. Distribution summary [of] financial institution taxes [bank, credit institution, farmers cooperative, and total taxes collected, and refunds, distribution, and interest to county treasurer, by county], 1982. (p. 30)

13-14. Gasoline tax allocation [to counties], and to cities [all by locality]. (p. 31-40)

15-16. City and St. Louis County sales tax distribution [all by city], 1982. (p. 41-46)

17. County sales tax distribution [by county], 1982. (p. 46)

BALANCE SHEETS

18-19. Highway Reciprocity Commission cash report [revenues from motor vehicle and prorate fees, and permits; and license plates issued; and] administrative costs. (p. 47)

20. Nonappropriated funds: sources and application [receipts, expenditures, assets, and beginning and ending balances; for State agencies and funds administered by each dept, including universities, mental health centers and hospitals, and correctional institutions]. (p. 48-55)

S4570–1.2: State Treasurer Report

21. Analysis of average daily balances of State funds [by month]. (p. 59)

22-23. Time deposits: general and water pollution bond/interest reports of the transactions of the State treasury, for the month ending June 30th, showing the balances in the [individual] banks. (p. 59-69).

24. List of balances in several funds [current and previous balance, receipts, and disbursements]. (p. 70)

25-25A. State indebtedness: water pollution control and 3rd State building bonds [including number, denomination, interest rate, and amount retired and outstanding]. (p. 72-73)

26-28. Treasury funds invested in U.S. securities; and State seminary and public school fund investments. (p. 73)

29. Report of the transactions of the State treasury for the month ending June 30, 1983, showing [aggregate] balances in the various banks [by type of account or investment]. (p. 74)

S4575   MISSOURI
Department of Social Services

S4575–1   MISSOURI VITAL STATISTICS, 1982
Annual. July 1983.
viii+116 p. Pub. No. 4.27.
ISSN 0098-1974.
LC 75-643234.
SRI/MF/complete

Annual report, for 1982, on Missouri vital statistics, covering population, births, abortions, deaths by cause, marriages, and divorces, with selected trends from 1911. Includes data by county, city, age, sex, and race. Data are compiled from State records and Census Bureau reports.

Contains table and chart listing, and map of regional planning commission areas (p. v-vii); 7

charts and 57 tables, listed below (p. 1-110); and appendix, with methodology and definitions (p. 111-116).

Availability: Missouri Department of Social Services, Health Division, Center for Health Statistics, Broadway State Office Bldg., PO Box 570, Jefferson City MO 65102, †; SRI/MF/complete.

CHARTS AND TABLES:
[Data are for Missouri, 1982, unless otherwise noted. Most tables with historical trends show data quinquennially prior to 1970 and annually for 1970-82.]

S4575–1.1: Population Trends, and Births
TRENDS

A. Live birth and death rates per 1,000 population, 1911-81. [chart] (p. 1)

1-2. Population, recorded births and deaths with rates per 1,000 population, and natural increase, 1911-82; and resident births and deaths, 1945-82. (p. 2-3)

B. Total fertility rates, 1911-82. [chart and table] (p. 4)

3. Fertility rates per 1,000 females by age of mother, [selected years] 1911-82. (p. 5)

C. Crude and age-adjusted death rates per 1,000 population, 1911-82. [chart and table] (p. 6)

4. Age-specific death rates per 1,000 population, [selected years] 1911-82. (p. 7)

BIRTHS

5. Resident live births by selected characteristics [including sex, attendant (physician, midwife, and other), place and month of birth, mother's smoking habits during pregnancy, and complications], by race of child. (p. 8)

6-7. Resident live births and teenage resident live births, by age of mother, by live birth order, by legitimacy, by race of child. (p. 9-10)

8. Percent low birth weight and resident live births, by birth weight, by age of mother, by race of child. (p. 11)

9. Resident live births, by legitimacy, by race, with percentages by county and cities with 25,000 or more population. (p. 12)

10A-10C. Resident live births by selected characteristics [including birth weight, type of delivery (including cesarean), whether mother smoked during pregnancy, age and size of mother, and birth order], by race, regional planning commission, county, and cities with 25,000 or more population. (p. 16-43)

S4575–1.2: Abortions

11. Resident teenage pregnancies and abortions by selected ages by county of residence. (p. 44)

D. Resident abortion ratios per 1,000 live births [and number of abortions], 1971-82. [chart and table] (p. 46)

12. Resident abortions by race, age of woman, type of procedure, and complications, by weeks of gestation. (p. 47)

13. Resident abortions by age, marital status, and education, by race. (p. 48)

14A-14B. Resident abortions and ratios per 1,000 live births by county of residence and regional planning commission. (p. 49-50)

15-16. Resident abortions, by age and marital status of woman, and by number of living children and number of previous abortions. (p. 50)

S4575-1.3: Population Natural Increase, and Deaths

POPULATION NATURAL INCREASE

17. Resident and recorded live births, deaths, and natural increase, with rates, by counties [also shows population] and cities with 25,000 or more population. (p. 51)

18. Resident and recorded live births and deaths, by cities with 2,500-24,999 population. (p. 55)

DEATHS

19. 12 leading causes of death by race, with percentages, and with rates per 100,000 for all races, resident data. (p. 58)

20. 5 leading causes of death for selected age groups, with percentages, resident data. (p. 59)

21. Resident deaths, age groups by race by sex, with age-specific rates per 1,000 by sex. (p. 60)

22A-22C. Resident deaths [total, male, and female], age groups by selected causes of death. (p. 61-66)

E. Infant death rates per 1,000 live births [and infant deaths], 1911-44 (recorded) and 1945-82 (resident). [chart and table] (p. 67)

23A-23B. Resident perinatal, infant, fetal, neonatal, postneonatal, and maternal deaths: by county and cities with 25,000 or more population; and by regional planning commission, with rates per 1,000 live births. (p. 68-70)

24. Resident infant deaths by age, cause, and race, with rates per 1,000 live births by cause and race. (p. 71)

25-26. Resident infant deaths and rates per 1,000 live births, by age of mother by birth order, and by birth weight by race. (p. 72)

27A-27C. Resident deaths by selected causes of death: for State total by race, with rates per 100,000 for all races; and by regional planning commission, county, and cities with 25,000 or more population. (p. 73-93)

28. Recorded deaths by type of accident, age, and sex. (p. 94)

LIFE EXPECTANCY

29. Abridged life table for total population, and by sex. (p. 95)

S4575-1.4: Marriages and Dissolutions

MARRIAGES

F. Marriage rates per 1,000 population [and number of marriages], 1949-82. [chart and table] (p. 98)

30. Reported marriages by age of groom, by age of bride. (p. 99)

31-33. Reported marriages: by age and previous marital status of bride and groom; by previous marital status of bride and groom; and by race of bride by race of groom. (p. 101-102)

34A-34B. Reported marriages by county and regional planning commission of recording, with rates per 1,000 population. (p. 103-104)

DISSOLUTIONS

G. Dissolution rates per 1,000 population [and number of dissolutions], 1949-82. [chart and table] (p. 105)

35. Reported dissolutions of marriage, by type of decree. (p. 106)

36-42. Reported dissolutions/invalidities: by number of previous marriages for husband and wife; by duration of marriage; by number of children affected; by petitioner by disposition of children; by type of maintenance and settlement; and by age and race, wife by husband. (p. 106-108)

43A-43B. Reported dissolutions/invalidities, by county and regional planning commission of recording, with rates per 1,000 population. (p. 109-110)

S4575-2   EIGHTH ANNUAL REPORT, FY82, Missouri Division of Family Services

Annual.   Nov. 9, 1983.
115 p.
ISSN 0148-5474.
LC 77-640889.
SRI/MF/complete

Annual report, for FY82, on activities of the Missouri Division of Family Services, including number of recipients and expenditures for public welfare, medical, and other assistance programs, by program and county.

Contents:

Contents listing. (p. 3-5)

Part I. Review of the year, with 4 tables showing average monthly public assistance recipients and payments, and total expenditures, by program, FY38-82; and Division of Family Services employees, replacements, and separations, quarterly FY82 (table 1). (p. 7-13)

Part II. Legislative developments, with 1 table showing division State and Federal appropriations by type of service and program, FY83. (p. 14-16)

Part III-VII. Summary review of public assistance, medical and social services, services to the blind, and child support enforcement; with text statistics, 3 charts, and detailed tables 2-50 described below. (p. 17-90)

Part VIII. Summary of expenditures and sources of funds; with 2 charts, and tables 51-52 described below. (p. 91-95)

App. A-B, with contents and appendix table listing, chronology of activities affecting programs, and supplementary statistical tables I-VI, listed below. (p. 96-115)

Availability: Missouri Department of Social Services, Family Services Division, Broadway State Office Bldg., PO Box 88, Jefferson City MO 65103, $3.80; SRI/MF/complete.

TABLES:
[Tables show data for FY82, unless otherwise noted.]

S4575-2.1: Parts III-VIII: Public Assistance, Medical, and Other Services

PUBLIC ASSISTANCE
[Most tables show data by month.]

a. AFDC program: number of recipients and amount of payments; applications received and disposition; cases opened and closed, and applications rejected, by reason; and recipients and payments for dependent children families with foster care status. Tables 2-7. (p. 18-23)

b. General relief, blind pension, supplemental nursing care, and supplemental aid to the blind programs: number of recipients and amount of payments; and caseloads, usually including applications received and disposition, and cases opened and closed, often with detail by reason. Tables 8-23. (p. 24-38)

c. Adult supplementary programs funded by SSI and State supplement aid (includes Aid to Blind, Aid to Permanently and Totally Disabled, and Old Age Assistance): number of recipients by program and amount of payments. Tables 24-25. (p. 39-40)

d. Appeals/fair hearings caseload analysis; and food stamp and USDA-donated food distribution program participation and distribution amounts. 1 text table and tables 26-27. (p. 41-41-43)

MEDICAL, CHILD, AND BLIND SERVICES

e. Medical services: expenditures by service and program, with selected comparisons to FY81; expenditures, recipients, and Medicaid eligibles, by month; number of recipients and cost of payments for physician, inpatient hospital, prescription drug, dental, skilled nursing home, intermediate care facility, outpatient, and clinic services, all by program; medical assistance applications received and disposition, by month; and cases opened and closed, and applications rejected, by reason. Text data and tables 28-40. (p. 46-66)

f. Foster care cases active and opened and average age of child, subsidized adoption cases and payments, protective service cases, and reports of child abuse/neglect, all by month; children receiving interstate compact placement services, by type; and number and capacity of licensed day care facilities, by type, as of June 1982. Tables 41-46. (p. 71-81)

g. Services for the blind: rehabilitation teaching cases and turnover; vocational rehabilitation caseloads, and expenditures by funding source and object; and expenditures for prevention of blindness by service. Tables 47-50. (p. 84-86)

h. Child support enforcement program: cases and/or money collected, by month and district, for AFDC and non-AFDC. 2 text tables. (p. 89)

EXPENDITURES SUMMARY

i. Expenditures charged against all funds for assistance and administration, by program and fund source (Federal, State, and donated/local); and administrative costs by specific item. Tables 51-52. (p. 92-95)

S4575-2.2: Appendix B, Supplementary Statistics

[All tables show data for programs administered by the Division of Family Services. Tables I-II and VI show data by county. Tables III-V show data by month.]

I-II. Average monthly number of recipients, and cash payments extended to recipients, by program. (p. 100-107)

III-IV. Number of recipients, and amount of cash expenditures (exclusive of vendor medical care), [by program], FY81-82. (p. 108-111)

V. Amount of medical assistance expended, by type of service. (p. 112)

VI. Average monthly number of households and persons, and total dollar value of stamps, for food stamp program. (p. 114)

S4585   MISSOURI
Supreme Court

S4585–1   MISSOURI JUDICIAL REPORT, FY83
Annual. [1984.] viii + 108 p.
ISSN 0099-0558.
LC 82-640897.
SRI/MF/complete

Annual report, for FY83, on Missouri judicial system, including trial and appellate court caseloads and case dispositions. Covers supreme, appeals, and circuit courts. Includes data by case type, by district (for appeals courts), and by circuit and county (for circuit courts).

Case types shown are civil and criminal for all courts. Circuit court data include detail for felony, misdemeanor, juvenile, traffic, small claims, probate (including mental health), domestic relations, child abuse/neglect, adoption, tort, contract, eminent domain, and other case types.

Also includes State judicial appropriations, and distribution by function; writs of habeas corpus; number of judges and workload analysis; and selected trends from FY74.

Contains listings of contents, charts, and tables (p. iv-viii); narrative analysis, with 19 charts and 22 tables (p. 1-31); statistical section, with 45 tables (p. 33-101); and appendices, with Missouri court profile (p. 103-108).

Availability: Missouri Supreme Court, State Courts Administrator's Office, 1105 Rear Southwest Blvd., Jefferson City MO 65101, $3.15 + $0.75 postage and handling; SRI/MF/complete.

S4653   MONTANA
Department of Administration

S4653–1   MONTANA COMPREHENSIVE ANNUAL FINANCIAL REPORT for the Fiscal Year Ended June 30, 1983
Annual. Dec. 27, 1983.
126 p.
ISSN 0090-6042.
LC 73-644597.
SRI/MF/complete

Annual report on Montana State government financial condition, for FY83, presenting assets and liabilities, fund balances, revenues by source, and expenditures by function, for individual funds grouped by category.

Fund categories covered are governmental (general, special revenue, debt service, and capital projects); proprietary (enterprise and internal service); fiduciary (expendable and nonexpendable trust, pension trust, and agency); account groups; and higher education.

Also includes data on budgeted vs. actual revenues and expenditures, long-term bonded indebtedness, leases, and finances of the State housing authority and liquor division.

Also presents miscellaneous data including land area; highway mileage; parks; State employees; personal income; labor force by employment status; property values; construction permits and value; bank deposits; public education enrollment, for elementary/secondary and by postsecondary institution; tax rates and collections; and State indebtedness; various years 1973-83.

Report is compiled by Montana Dept of Administration.

Contains contents listing (3 p.); introduction with organizational chart (p. 1-6); 24 financial statements, interspersed with explanatory notes and summary statistics (p. 10-109); and statistical section with 14 tables (p. 113-126).

Previous report, for FY82, is described in SRI 1982 Annual, under this number.

Availability: Montana Department of Administration, Accounting Division, Mitchell Bldg., Rm. 255, Helena MT 59620, †; SRI/MF/ complete.

S4655   MONTANA
Department of Agriculture

S4655–1   MONTANA AGRICULTURAL STATISTICS, 1983
Annual. Sept. 1983.
81 p. + errata sheet. Vol. XX.
LC 48-13383.
SRI/MF/complete

Annual report on Montana agricultural production, marketing, prices, and stocks, 1982, with selected trends from 1910, and some data for 1983. Data generally are shown by commodity and/or county and district.

Covers production, prices, value, and, as applicable, acreage, yield, and stock or inventory, for field crop, livestock, dairy, poultry, and apiary sectors, and sweet cherries.

Also includes data on number and acreage of farms; land area by ownership and use; farm income by source; irrigation; fertilizer use; weather; wheat detail, including seeded acreage by variety, and out-of-State shipments by transport mode and region of destination; and value of U.S. and Montana agricultural exports.

Data are compiled by Montana Crop and Livestock Reporting Service.

Contains introduction and contents listing (p. 4-7); 11 maps, 14 charts, and 81 tables (p. 8-80); and list of additional reports available (p. 81).

Previous reports were incorrectly identified as biennial.

Availability: Montana Department of Agriculture, Crop and Livestock Reporting Service, PO Box 4369, Helena MT 59604, †; SRI/MF/complete.

S4690   MONTANA
Department of Health and Environmental Sciences

S4690–1   MONTANA VITAL STATISTICS, 1982
Annual. Dec. 1983. 88 p.
ISSN 0077-1198.
LC 73-641210.
SRI/MF/complete

Annual report on Montana vital statistics, covering population, births, deaths by cause, abortions, reportable diseases, marriages, and divorces, 1982, with selected trends from 1910. Includes data by age, sex, race, and county. Data are compiled from records of the Dept of Health and Environmental Sciences.

Contains contents listing (1 p.); introduction, definitions, and 1 chart (p. 1-6); 8 sections, with narrative summaries, text statistics, summary tables, 1 map, 14 charts, and 31 detailed tables listed below (p. 8-87); and note on data availability (p. 88).

Report has been published annually since 1954.

Availability: Montana Department of Health and Environmental Sciences, Records and Statistics Bureau, Cogswell Bldg., Helena MT 59620, †; SRI/MF/complete.

TABLES:

[Unless otherwise noted, data are for Montana, 1982, and are residence-based for births and deaths and occurrence-based for marriages and divorces.]

S4690–1.1: General Data, Births, and Deaths
[Data prior to 1946 are based on place of occurrence.]

GENERAL

1. [Population], deaths, live births, and fetal, infant, and maternal deaths [quinquennially 1910-25 and annually 1930-82]. (p. 9)

2. Populations [by county], 1980 and 1982. (p. 10)

3. Deaths, live births, [and] fetal, infant, and maternal deaths, by [county] of occurrence and residence. (p. 11)

4. Deaths, live births, and fetal deaths, by race [white, Indian, and other; by county]. (p. 12)

BIRTHS

5. Summary of live births [sex, legitimacy status, multiple births, and previous living children], 1981-82. (p. 17)

6. Number and percentage distribution of live births, by attendant [born on arrival/in hospital, and physician and other not in hospital], by [county] of occurrence. (p. 18)

7. Live births, by birth weight group [premature and mature, by county]. (p. 19)

8. Number and percent of live-born infants, by years of education of mother and number of children born alive. (p. 20)

DEATHS

[Causes of death are shown according to the International Classification of Diseases Adapted, 9th Revision.]

9. Deaths, by [detailed] cause, sex, and color. (p. 25-35)

10. Leading causes of death, by age group. (p. 36)

11. Deaths from selected accidents, by age, by place of occurrence. (p. 37)

12. Deaths from selected causes, by county. (p. 38)

13. Infant mortality by race and age group, and 5-year [1978-82 period] infant mortality rates [all by county]. (p. 39)

14. Infant mortality from selected causes, by age group [and race]. (p. 40)

15-16. Communicable disease historical mortality statistics [10 diseases], and selected cause-specific death rates, [quinquennially 1910-25 and annually 1930-82]. (p. 41-44)

S4690–1.2: Abortions, Marriages and Divorces, County Summaries, Pregnancy, and Morbidity

ABORTIONS

17-19. Induced abortions, by woman's total number of previous pregnancies; by 5-year age groups; and by type of procedure and completed week of gestation. (p. 49-50)

MARRIAGES AND DIVORCES

20. Marriages, marital dissolutions, and invalid marriages [by county]. (p. 55)

21. Marriages and [divorces/annulments, number and rate], 1944-82. (p. 56)

22-23. Marriages, by month of occurrence, and by age and previous marital status of bride and groom. (p. 56-57)

24-25. First marriages by age of bride by age of groom; and marriages by race [and ethnic group] of bride and groom. (p. 58)

26-28. Marital terminations: by legal grounds for decree; by age of husband and by age of wife; and by number of children [under 18 years of age] by age of mother. (p. 59-60)

COUNTY SUMMARIES

29. Selected vital statistics [includes population; residence-based live births and deaths by sex, infant and fetal deaths, and 10 leading causes of death; and occurrence-based live births, total and accidental deaths, marriages, and marital terminations; all by county]. (p. 63-70)

PREGNANCY

30. Total reported pregnancies by type of outcome [live births, fetal deaths, and induced abortions], by county of residence and age with percent distribution. (p. 73-84)

MORBIDITY

31. Reported cases of reportable diseases, by [county] of residence. (p. 86)

S4690–2   MONTANA HEALTH DATA BOOK and Medical Facilities Inventory, 1983
Annual. [1984.]   106 p.
LC 82-623390.
SRI/MF/complete

Annual report on Montana health care facilities, 1978-82, and personnel, 1983. Covers private hospital and long-term care facility capacity, utilization, and finances, by individual institution, region, and bed-size category; and number of physicians and dentists, by county. Also includes patient residence data.

Data are primarily from State Dept of Health and Environmental Sciences (DHRS) annual surveys, and from the Montana Hospital Assn.

Contains contents listing (1 p.); and 5 statistical sections with 19 tables, listed below (p. 3-106).

This is the 4th edition of the report.

Availability: Montana Department of Health and Environmental Sciences, Cogswell Bldg., Helena MT 59620, Montana residents †, others $4.00; SRI/MF/complete.

TABLES:
[Tables show data for 1982, unless otherwise noted.]

S4690–2.1: Hospitals and Patient Residence
[Tables show data for individual hospitals, usually grouped by region.]

1982 SURVEY DATA

[1-4] Selected service load and service capacity measures by bed size category and by region, using licensed beds to calculate parameters. (p. 4-15)

[5] Medicare days and admissions [number and] as percent of total [also shows total days and admissions], 1980-82. (p. 16-21)

HISTORICAL DATA
[Tables [6-8] show data for 1978-82.]

[6] Total paid expenses. (p. 25)

[7-8] Adjusted expenses per inpatient day, and per admission. (p. 27-36)

PATIENT RESIDENCE

[9] Hospital patient origin summary [patients discharged, by county of residence and for out-of-State patients]. (p. 38-65)

S4690–2.2: Long-Term Care Facilities
[Tables [1-4] show data for individual long-term care facilities, grouped by region.]

[1] Skilled beds, intermediate beds, staffed beds, patient days, admissions, and discharges as reported from 1982 survey. (p. 68)

[2] Estimated operating revenue sources: percent of total revenue [from Medicare, Medicaid, private, and other sources]. (p. 71)

[3] Number of patients by sex, in age groups. (p. 74)

[4] Patient origin data: admissions from same county as facility, adjacent counties, and other areas. (p. 77)

[5-8] Repeats data in tables [1-4], grouped by bed size category. (p. 80-91)

S4690–2.3: Personnel

[1] Counts of physician specialties by county [as of Sept. 8, 1983]. (p. 93-104)

[2] Number of dental practices [including full- and part- time], by county and region, 1983. (p. 105)

S4705   MONTANA
Department of Justice

S4705–1   CRIME IN MONTANA, 1983
Annual Report
Annual.   July 1984.   v+31 p.
ISSN 0160-7103.
LC 77-643354.
SRI/MF/complete

Annual report on Montana crimes and clearances, 1983, with selected trends from 1973. Includes data by offense, county, and law enforcement agency. Data are compiled from law enforcement agency reports, submitted under the Uniform Crime Reporting Program.

Contains foreword and contents listing (p. iii-v); introduction, program description, and definitions (p. 1-6); and 2 maps, 1 illustrative chart, and 8 charts and 9 tables described below, interspersed with brief narrative (p. 7-31).

Availability: Montana Department of Justice, Crime Control Board, Criminal Justice Data Center, 303 N. Roberts St., Helena MT 59620, †; SRI/MF/complete.

CHARTS AND TABLES:
[Index crimes are homicide, rape, robbery, aggravated assault, burglary, larceny/theft, and motor vehicle theft. Non-Index offenses are less serious crimes, reported in 14 categories.

Crime rates are calculated using Index offenses. Data are for 1983, unless otherwise noted.]

a. State data: Index and non-Index offenses, with number of actual and unfounded offenses, total and juvenile clearances by arrest, detail on motor vehicle theft by vehicle type and narcotics offenses by substance, offense comparisons to 1982, and Index crime clocks and rates, all by offense; and percent change in Crime Index, crime rate, and population, 1973-83. 4 charts and 3 tables. (p. 8-14)

b. By locality: ranking of counties by crime rate; and population, crime rate, and Index crimes by offense, all by county and reporting agency, including Indian tribes and Glacier National Park. 2 tables. (p. 16-22)

c. Youth court: referrals by type of violation, sex, and age; top ten violations ranked by referrals; referrals detained by reason and sex, and total not detained; and detainees and total hours detained, by length of detention. 4 charts and 4 tables. (p. 27-31)

S4705–2   ANNUAL REPORT, 1983,
Montana Highway Patrol
Annual.   [1984.]
103 p. no paging.
SRI/MF/complete

Annual report on Montana traffic accidents, injuries, and fatalities, by accident and vehicle type, location, time, and other circumstances; and driver and victim characteristics including alcohol consumption; 1983, with fatalities by county from 1935.

Also includes economic loss; accidents by type of traffic control; detailed data on safety device use; and vehicles involved by place of registration (U.S. States and territories, and Canadian Provinces).

Data are from Montana Highway Patrol records.

Contains contents listing, highlights, and analysis, with 1 chart and 3 tables (6 p.); and report in 4 sections, with 2 maps, 9 charts, and 10 tables (96 p.).

Availability: Montana Department of Justice, Highway Patrol, Accident Records Bureau, 303 N. Roberts St., Helena MT 59620, †; SRI/MF/ complete.

S4710   MONTANA
Department of
Labor and Industry

S4710–1   MONTANA EMPLOYMENT AND LABOR FORCE
Quarterly. Approx. 20 p.
SRI/MF/complete

Quarterly report on Montana employment and unemployment, hours and earnings, new business firms, and unemployment insurance claims. Employment data are shown by State area and industry division and group. Data are from BLS and State sources.

Contents:

a. Glossary; and narrative analysis of economic highlights and employment outlook for the State and 14 local areas, with 1 labor force summary table, and 1 table showing U.S. monthly CPI for current year to date and 2 previous years.

b. 13 detailed quarterly tables, listed below; and occasional trend data.

Quarterly tables appear in all issues. All additional features with substantial trend data are described, as they appear, under "Additional Data."

Availability: Montana Department of Labor and Industry, Research and Analysis Bureau, PO Box 1728, Helena MT 59624, †; SRI/MF/complete.

Issues reviewed during 1984: 3rd Qtr. 1983-2nd Qtr. 1984 (D) (Vol. 13, Nos. 3-4; Vol. 14, Nos. 1-2) [Vol. 13, No. 3 incorrectly reads Vol. 1, No. 3].

QUARTERLY TABLES:
[Unless otherwise noted, data are for Montana and are shown by month for quarter of coverage. Labor force data include employment and unemployment.]

I. Civilian labor force, not seasonally adjusted [includes persons involved in labor/management disputes, and unemployment comparisons to U.S.; monthly for current year to date and 2 previous years].

II. Employment, by industry [division; includes change from last month of same quarter of previous year].

III. Labor market areas, civilian labor force [by area and for Great Falls and Billings SMSAs].

IV.A-IV.C. Monthly labor force, by county.

V. Female employment, by industry [division].

[A] Real spendable [and] average weekly earnings of private nonagricultural production workers [monthly for current year to date and 2 previous years].

VI. Hours and earnings for private nonagricultural industries [by industry division and selected major group].

VII. New business firms [by labor market area, county, and SMSA, and for foreign corporations/multicounty businesses; includes year-to-date totals for current and previous years].

[B] Selected unemployment insurance activities [claims, payments, and trust fund balance; includes selected year-to-date totals for current and previous years, and change from last month of same quarter of previous year].

VIII-IX. Distribution of unemployment insurance [claims and payments, by county and for interstate; includes cumulative data for year to date].

ADDITIONAL DATA:

S4710–1.501: 1st Qtr. 1984 (Vol. 14, No. 1)

ANNUAL TABLES

(p. 22-27) Six annual tables showing summary data on subjects covered in selected quarterly tables, 1981-83.

S4710–2   ANNUAL REPORT, FY83, DIVISION OF WORKERS' COMPENSATION, Montana
Annual. [1984.] 39 p.
LC 66-64329.
SRI/MF/complete

Annual report on Montana work injuries, workers' compensation and medical benefit payments, and Division of Workers' Compensation fund balances, revenues, and expenditures, FY83, with selected trends from FY72. Also covers status of crime victim compensation fund.

Work injury data are from injury reports, and from responses of 700 employers to a 1982 survey.

Contains contents listing and preface (p. 1-2); and 6 sections, with 1 chart showing survey response rates and 25 tables described below (p. 3-39).

This is the 69th annual report.

Availability: Montana Department of Labor and Industry, Workers' Compensation Division, Five S. Last Chance Gulch, Helena MT 59601, †; SRI/MF/complete.

TABLES:

a. Financial reports: assets, liabilities, revenues by source, expenditures by program or object, changes in balances, and investments by instrument, shown for various programs and/or funds related to injured worker and crime victim compensation, FY83, with selected comparisons to FY82. 9 tables. (p. 8-22)

b. Insurance coverage plans: employers, annual payroll or premium, number of work injuries and occupational diseases reported, claims filed, compensation and medical/burial benefits paid, and uninsured employers assessments, all for employers using self-insurance, private carriers, and State fund compensation plans, FY81-83. 1 table. (p. 23)

c. State compensation insurance fund: assets and liabilities; reserves, balances, and changes; and income and expenses; FY83. 3 tables. (p. 25-27)

d. Uninsured employers' fund: compensation claims paid, investigations, audits, employers fined, number and amount of collections, revenues by source, and program costs, FY82-83. 1 table. (p. 29)

e. Crime victims' compensation: claims received, by source, disposition, type of crime, victim characteristics, and crime location; and fund revenue sources and program costs; FY82-83. 2 tables. (p. 31-32)

f. Work injury reports: injuries by degree of disability; fatalities by cause, by industry division and compensation insurance plan type; injuries and accidents, by type, including injuries by body part, source, industry division, and victim age and sex; and injury/illness incidence and lost workday rates by industry division; various years FY72-83. 9 tables. (p. 34-39)

S4710–3   ANNUAL PLANNING INFORMATION, CY85, State of Montana
Annual. June 1984. 103 p.
LC 79-642770.
SRI/MF/complete

Annual planning report, for 1985, identifying Montana population groups most in need of employment services. Includes data on labor force; employment and job openings by industry and/ or occupation; and data by labor market area (LMA), service delivery area (SDA), and county. Also includes 1980 census data on labor force by occupation.

Data are shown for various years 1970-85, with selected earlier trends and projections to 1990. Data are from State and Federal sources, including Census Bureau; and Lawrence Berkeley Laboratory projections.

Contains contents listing (1 p.), and the following:

a. Glossary and introduction, with 1 table showing Montana's rank among the States in population, land area, and selected demographic and socioeconomic characteristics. (p. 1-3)

b. Narrative report, interspersed with 2 charts, and 1 map and 23 tables listed below. (p. 4-42)

c. Equal employment opportunity census report, with 1 table repeated for State and each county, showing experienced labor force by occupation and long-term unemployed (total and for women), by race/ethnicity (including American Indian/Eskimo/Aleut, Asian/ Pacific Islander, and Hispanic), 1980. (p. 43-103)

Previous report covered FY83 (for description, see SRI 1983 Annual, under this number). No report covering the period between FY83 and 1985 was published.

Availability: Montana Department of Labor and Industry, Employment Security Division, Research and Analysis Bureau, PO Box 1728, Helena MT 59624, †; SRI/MF/complete.

MAP AND TABLES:
[Data are for Montana, unless otherwise noted.]

LABOR FORCE AND POPULATION DATA

[1] Labor force composition projections [by employment status, by age and sex, 1980 and 1985]. (p. 13)

[2-4] Population and labor force composition projections [by age, sex, and race, repeated for State and by SDA], 1985. (p. 14-19)

[5] Employment status of civilian noninstitutional population 16 years/over [with comparison to U.S., 1970-85]. (p. 20)

[6] 1983 average unemployment rates by LMA. [map] (p. 21)

INDUSTRY AND OCCUPATION DATA

[7] Major industries [employment, 1980 and 1990; and annual average wage, 1983; all by industry division]. (p. 23)

[8] Industry employment estimates: industries with employment growth of over 500, 1980 and 1990. (p. 24)

[9] Distribution of employment by major occupational group, 1980 and 1990. (p. 26)

[10] Annual average job openings [due to growth and separations, for] occupations with 50/more openings per year, 1980-90 [period]. (p. 27)

[11] Annual average nonagricultural employment [by industry division and major group, selected years 1950-83]. (p. 29)

[12-14] Annual labor force report [labor force by employment status, and employment by industry division and major group, monthly] 1981-83. (p. 30-32)

[15-16] Hours and earnings series [by] month: average hours and earnings in private, nonagricultural industries [by division and major group], 1982-83. (p. 33-34)

[17] Female employment by industry [division, monthly] 1982-83]. (p. 35)

[18-20] Current population survey data [labor force by employment status, by county], 1981-83. (p. 36-38)

[21-22] New corporations and businesses by industry [division, monthly] 1983. (p. 39)

ECONOMICALLY DISADVANTAGED POPULATION DATA

[23] Economically disadvantaged [by sex, race/ethnicity (including Native American, Asian/Pacific Islander, and Spanish origin), and age group, for State and by SDA], 1980. (p. 40)

[24] Economically disadvantaged [by age/income] categories [and total population, by county], 1980. (p. 41-42)

S4725   MONTANA
Library Commission

**S4725-1   MONTANA LIBRARY
DIRECTORY, 1983, with
Statistics of Montana Public
Libraries, July 1, 1981-June
30, 1982**
Annual. [1983.] 92 p.
ISSN 0094-873X.
LC 74-646588.
SRI/MF/complete

Annual directory, for FY82, of Montana public, institutional, and special libraries and personnel, with selected circulation, holdings, employment, and financial data for public libraries.

Contents:

a. Lists of members and officials of Montana library organizations (p. 1-15); and directory of public, academic, special, institutional, and school libraries (p. 17-76).

b. Individual public library data with 2 tables showing titles added during year; total titles and volumes; local and bookmobile circulation; periodicals received; hours; staff; nonresident borrowers fee; 1980 population; taxable valuation; income by source, including taxes and revenue sharing; total and per capita expenditures; spending for personnel, materials, and federation contract; and potential tax receipts and spending per capita; all by library and county. (p. 78-92)

Previous report, for FY81, is described in SRI 1982 Annual, under this number.

Availability: Montana Library Commission, 1515 E. Sixth Ave., Helena MT 59620, †; SRI/MF/complete.

S4740   MONTANA
Office of
Public Instruction

**S4740-1   MONTANA PUBLIC
SCHOOL ENROLLMENT
DATA, Fall 1983**
Annual. [1984.] 41 p.
Rpt. No. FA17784.
SRI/MF/complete

Annual report on Montana public school fall enrollment, 1983. Presents data by school, county, and level, including special education.

Contains contents listing (1 p.), and 6 tables as follows:

a. Prekindergarten through 8th grade and special education elementary enrollment, by grade, county, and school, Oct. 1, 1983. 1 table. (p. 1-17)

b. Junior high and high school (grades 7-12) and special education enrollment by grade, and high school graduates, by county and school, cross-tabulated by sex, Oct. 1, 1983; and total enrollment, all levels, by grade, by county, 1983/84. 5 tables. (p. 18-41)

Availability: Montana Office of Public Instruction, Financial Aid and Transportation Division, State Capitol, Helena MT 59620, †; SRI/MF/complete.

S4755   MONTANA
Department of
Social and
Rehabilitation Services

**S4755-1   STATISTICAL REPORT,
Montana**
Monthly, with annual
summary. Approx. 30 p.
ISSN 0091-1143.
LC 73-643173.
SRI/MF/complete, shipped
quarterly

Monthly statistical report, with fiscal year summary, on Montana public assistance programs, including number of cases, recipients, and payments, by program and county. Programs covered include AFDC, general and medical assistance, food stamps, and energy assistance.

Data are compiled by the Management Information Office. Report is issued approximately 3 months after month of coverage.

Contains contents listing, 3 charts, and 10 monthly and 9 quarterly tables, listed below; and occasionally revised data for previous issues.

Most monthly tables appear in all issues; latest period of coverage for quarterly tables is noted under "Statistical Features."

Fiscal year summary, issued with the Aug. 1983 report, presents totals for most data covered in the monthly reports.

Prior to May 1984, issues also included 2 tables on public assistance applications and dispositions.

Availability: Montana Department of Social and Rehabilitation Services, Management Information Office, Centralized Services Division, PO Box 4210, Helena MT 59604, †; SRI/MF/complete, shipped quarterly.

Issues reviewed during 1984: Aug. 1983-July 1984 (D); and FY83 annual summary.

TABLES:
[Data are for month of coverage, unless otherwise noted. Tables 2-10 show data by county.]

MONTHLY TABLES

1. Summary of public assistance and medical care [obligations incurred, recipients, and average payments, by program, State totals, for month of coverage, previous month, and same month of previous year].

2. Total expenditures for public assistance and medical care [aid to dependent children, medical assistance, and general assistance/county medical].

3-4. AFDC [cases, recipients, and amount], and medical assistance [cases and amount], compared with the same month last year and 5 years ago.

5. Medical assistance: number of recipients and amount of payments by type of service [hospital inpatient and outpatient, physicians, drugs/supplies, nursing home, other practitioners, lab/X-ray/radiology, dental, and miscellaneous].

6. Medical assistance: number of recipients and amount of payments by basis of eligibility [aged, AFDC adult and child, blind, and disabled].

7. Analysis of general assistance by family and 1-person cases [cases and payments].

8. Expenditures for general assistance, county medical, burials, and transient relief.

9. Number of households [public assistance and other, and individuals] receiving food stamps, and value of food stamps.

10. Low income energy assistance [including handicapped and senior citizen cases, and payments, cumulatively from Oct. through month of coverage].

QUARTERLY TABLES

[Most data are shown by county for quarter ending in month of coverage, or most recently completed quarter.]

1. Disposition of social services cases.

2. Social services, number of cases receiving each service [including adoption, day care, foster care, homemaker services, and investigative and protective services].

3-4. Activity of WIN [work incentive program] cases, welfare savings resulting from the WIN program; and WIN services provided [by type of service; all by local office].

5-9. Rehabilitation/visual caseload by type of disability and severity of the disability; status of open rehabilitation and visual cases [for month of coverage]; and rehabilitation and visual applications closed and cases closed [including cost per case].

STATISTICAL FEATURES:

S4755–1.501: Aug. 1983

QUARTERLY TABLES

1-2. Title XX social cases, disposition, and services provided, for quarters ended Mar. and June 1983.

S4755–1.502: Sept. 1983

QUARTERLY TABLES

3-9. WIN, rehabilitation, and visual service data, for quarter ended Sept. 1983.

S4755–1.503: Oct. 1983

QUARTERLY TABLES

1-2. Disposition of social service cases, and number of cases receiving each service, for quarter ended Sept. 1983.

S4755–1.504: Dec. 1983

QUARTERLY TABLES

3-9. WIN, rehabilitation, and visual service data, for quarter ended Dec. 1983.

S4755–1.505: Jan. 1984

QUARTERLY TABLES

1-2. Disposition of social service cases, and number of cases receiving each service, for quarter ended Dec. 1983.

S4755–1.506: Mar. 1984

QUARTERLY TABLES

3-9. WIN, rehabilitation, and visual service data, for quarter ended Mar. 1983.

S4755–1.507: Apr. 1984

QUARTERLY TABLES

1-2. Disposition of social service cases, and number of cases receiving each service, for quarter ended Mar. 1984.

S4755–1.508: June 1984

QUARTERLY TABLES

3-9. WIN, rehabilitation, and visual service data, for quarter ended June 1983.

S4825   NEBRASKA
Department of Administrative Services

S4825–1   STATE OF NEBRASKA ANNUAL FISCAL REPORT, Year Ending June 30, 1983
Annual. Dec. 7, 1983. 74 p.
SRI/MF/complete.

Annual report on financial condition of Nebraska State government for FY83, presenting revenues by source; expenditures by function, object, and agency; and fund balances; for general, cash, capital construction, Federal, and revolving funds, with selected comparisons from FY79.

Also includes comparison of appropriations vs. expenditures, by fund and agency; and data on State investment holdings and trust funds.

Data are compiled by the Accounting Division.

Contains contents listing (1 p.); introduction and definitions (p. 1-9); and 6 charts and 10 tables (p. 13-74).

Availability: Nebraska Department of Administrative Services, Accounting Division, State Capitol Bldg., Rm. 1210, Lincoln NE 68509, †; SRI/MF/complete.

S4845   NEBRASKA
Department of Banking and Finance

S4845–1   REPORT OF THE DEPARTMENT OF BANKING AND FINANCE, State of Nebraska, July 1, 1982-June 30, 1983
Annual. Aug. 1, 1983.
vi + 37 p.
LC 79-644411.
SRI/MF/complete

Annual report, for FY83, presenting composite assets and liabilities for Nebraska State-chartered commercial banks, savings and loan and cooperative credit assns, credit unions, and trust, industrial loan and investment, and installment loan companies, as of Dec. 31, 1982, or June 30, 1983, with comparisons to previous year and selected trends from 1897.

Also includes data on Banking and Finance Dept receipts, disbursements, and regulatory activities; bank paid-in capital stock and capital debentures issued, by institution; and bank operating expenses and earnings as percent of gross earnings, and balance sheet detail as percent of total assets, by asset size.

Also includes installment loan companies finances, loan and insurance activities, and legal actions; securities broker/dealer applications, registrations, and issues; and Consumer Finance Division and Bureau of Securities financial transactions.

Contains contents listing (p. iv); and report, with lists of financial institutions and 24 tables (p. 1-37).

Availability: Nebraska Department of Banking and Finance, 301 Centennial Mall, S., Lincoln NE 68509, †; SRI/MF/complete.

S4855   NEBRASKA
Department of Economic Development

S4855–1   NEBRASKA STATISTICAL HANDBOOK, 1984-85
Biennial. [1984.] xi + 307 p.
ISSN 0097-9325.
LC 73-622040.
SRI/MF/complete

Biennial compilation, for 1984-85, of detailed demographic, social, governmental, and economic statistics for Nebraska. Data are primarily for 1970s-83, with selected trends from as early as 1860 and population projections to 2020. Data are primarily from State and Federal sources.

Report is designed to present a comprehensive overview of the State. Extensive socioeconomic, demographic, and geographic breakdowns are shown, as applicable, for most topics. These breakdowns include data by city, county and other State region, SMSA, urban-rural status, commodity, industry, age, race, and sex. Comparisons to U.S. are also occasionally included.

Contains listings of contents, tables, and charts (p. v-xi); 21 maps/charts and 160 tables arranged in 14 sections, described below (p. 3-300); and appendix, with data sources (p. 303-307). Tables in each section are preceded by a brief introduction.

For description of 1982-83 report, see SRI 1982 Annual, under this number.

Availability: Nebraska Department of Economic Development, Research Division, PO Box 94666, 301 Centennial Mall, S., Lincoln NE 68509, $5.00; SRI/MF/complete.

TABLE SECTIONS:
[Data sources appear beneath each table.]

S4855–1.1: Section A: Area and Climate

(p. 3-12) Contains 2 maps/charts and 5 tables. Includes land area and monthly precipitation and temperatures.

S4855–1.2: Section B: Population

(p. 15-44) Contains 3 maps/charts and 13 tables. Includes population from 1900 and projected to 2020; net migration; population density; and births, deaths, and marriages and divorces.

S4855–1.3: Section C: Labor Force and Employment

(p. 47-57) Contains 1 chart and 7 tables. Includes labor force by employment status; agricultural and nonagricultural employment; manufacturing production worker hours and earnings; and CPI.

S4855-1.4: Section D: Personal Income and State Product

(p. 61-79) Contains 3 charts and 8 tables. Includes personal income by source; per capita personal income; and GSP.

S4855-1.5: Section E: Agriculture

(p. 83-115) Contains 5 maps/charts and 21 tables. Includes farms and acreage, and farm property value, since 1860; farm labor and operator tenure; farmland use; crop value, production, and yield; livestock inventory; milk production; agricultural production index and farm prices; farm income, production costs, and sales; irrigation wells and acreage; and fertilizer use.

S4855-1.6: Section F: Manufacturing, Mining, and Business

(p. 119-150) Contains 1 chart and 21 tables. Includes manufacturing establishments, employment, and payroll since 1899; production workers, hours, and wages; value added; capital expenditures; and exports.

Also includes mineral production and value; oil and gas wells and production; retail and wholesale trade and service establishments, and sales or receipts; domestic, foreign, and nonprofit corporations; and business failures and liabilities.

S4855-1.7: Section G: Finance and Insurance

(p. 153-163) Contains 9 tables. Includes commercial banks and savings and loan assns, and finances; life and property/liability insurance companies, and underwriting data; fraternal beneficiary society life insurance issued and in force; and assessment companies, receipts, and payments.

S4855-1.8: Section H: Transportation and Communications

(p. 167-195) Contains 21 tables. Includes motor vehicle registrations; traffic accidents by circumstance, and injuries and fatalities; miles traveled; highway construction and mileage; railroad track mileage by company, and freight tonnage and revenues; aircraft, pilots, airports, and air traffic; telephones; newspapers and circulation; TV and radio stations; and cable TV companies and subscribers.

S4855-1.9: Section I: Construction and Housing

(p. 199-214) Contains 1 chart and 10 tables. Includes construction contract value; new housing authorized and value; savings and loan assn mortgages; housing units, occupancy, structural characteristics, and median value or rent; and principal home heating fuels.

S4855-1.10: Section J: Education

(p. 217-232) Contains 1 chart and 12 tables. Includes public and nonpublic school enrollment and teachers; public school revenues and expenses; high school graduates; higher education enrollment and degrees awarded, by curriculum and/or institution; and vocational education enrollment and expenditures.

S4855-1.11: Section K: Health and Welfare

(p. 235-247) Contains 6 tables. Includes hospitals and beds; physicians and dentists; 10 leading causes of death; welfare expenditures; and public assistance payments and income maintenance cases, by program.

S4855-1.12: Section L: Government

(p. 251-267) Contains 1 map and 9 tables. Includes State and local government revenues by source and expenditures by function; property and State individual income tax revenues; voter registration by party; and votes cast in presidential elections, and for gubernatorial candidates since 1880.

S4855-1.13: Section M: Recreation and Tourism

(p. 271-282) Contains 3 charts and 5 tables. Includes State park and recreation area income and attendance; attendance at museums and other cultural attractions; outdoor recreation activity participation; and visitor origins and destinations.

S4855-1.14: Section N: Energy

(p. 285-300) Contains 13 tables. Includes energy consumption by fuel type and sector; natural gas utilities sales, revenues, and pipeline mileage; industrial, commercial, and residential typical electric bills; electric utilities generating capacity, sales, customers, and revenues; and coal shipments.

S4865   NEBRASKA
Department of
Education

S4865-1   STATISTICS AND FACTS ABOUT NEBRASKA SCHOOLS, 1983/84
Annual. [1984.]   iv+122 p.
ISSN 0561-9440.
LC 76-646956.
SRI/MF/complete

Annual report on Nebraska public and nonpublic school enrollments by county and district, school districts, high school graduates, and personnel, for school year 1983/84. Includes trends from 1969/70 and projections to 1993.

Contains table listing and explanation of school district classes (p. i-iii); and 4 charts, and 23 tables listed below (p. 1-122).

Availability: Nebraska Department of Education, Management Information Services, 301 Centennial Mall, S., PO Box 94987, Lincoln NE 68509, †; SRI/MF/complete.

TABLES:
[Data are for school year 1983/84, unless otherwise noted.]

DISTRICTS, SCHOOLS, AND ENROLLMENTS
[Tables [1-3] and [5] show data for public schools by class of district, and for total State-operated and nonpublic schools.]

1. State total: number of districts, enrollment, and FTE of certified staff. (p. 1)

2. [Number of] operating school districts, and number of schools [by type, including special education]. (p. 2)

3. Enrollment by grade. (p. 3)

4. Enrollment by grade, reported by type of school (public schools only). (p. 4)

5. 3-year comparison of the number of districts and enrollment [1981/82-1983/84]. (p. 5)

ENROLLMENT TRENDS AND PROJECTIONS

6. County enrollments by school system, all schools [individual data for each public, State-operated, and nonpublic school district, arranged by county, with totals, all by grade]. (p. 6-51)

7. Percent of change in county enrollment [by county, 1973/74 and 1982/83-1983/84]. (p. 52)

8a-8c. 15-year history of enrollment by grade [and for special education], State total, public/ State-operated, and nonpublic schools [1969/ 70-1983/84]. (p. 53-55)

9. Public/nonpublic schools estimated enrollment [by grade], 1984-93. (p. 58)

10a-10e. District ranking by enrollment: [public school district] classes I, II-V, and VI; State-operated; and nonpublic systems; [includes enrollment by grade level, and elementary and secondary FTE teachers and pupil/teacher ratio]. (p. 59-85)

11. Enrollment report by race [Asian/Pacific Islander, Hispanic, American Indian/Alaskan Native, black, and white], and sex [by district and county for public and nonpublic schools]. (p. 86-113)

BIRTHS AND SCHOOL CENSUS

12. Nebraska birth rate, [estimated population, and number of births], 1956-82. (p. 114)

13. School census: number of males and females [under 20 years old] by age within county, as of June 1983. (p. 116-117)

GRADUATES

14. Comparison of high school graduates to [9th and 12th grade] fall enrollment [by graduation year 1971/72-1986/87]. (p. 119)

STAFF

15a-15c. FTE of certified personnel by position assignment [and sex], State total, nonpublic, and State-operated schools [no dates]. (p. 120-122)

S4885   NEBRASKA
Department of
Health

S4885-1   NEBRASKA BUREAU OF VITAL STATISTICS 1983
Annual Statistical Report
Annual. [1984.]   5+111 p.
LC 75-640799.
SRI/MF/complete

Annual report, for 1983, on Nebraska vital statistics, covering births, deaths by cause, marriages, divorces, and population, with selected trends from 1925. Includes data by age, race, sex, and location. Data are compiled primarily from State records.

Contains foreword and listing of contents, charts, and tables (5 p.); introduction, with 2 tables showing selected vital statistics, 1925-83 and monthly 1983 (p. 1-4); 4 sections, with narrative summaries, text statistics, list of health planning regions, 3 maps, 7 charts, and 62 tables listed below (p. 5-110); and definitions (p. 111).

Availability: Nebraska Department of Health, Health Data and Statistical Research Division, Vital Statistics Bureau, 301 Centennial Mall, S., PO Box 95007, Lincoln NE 68509, †; SRI/MF/complete.

TABLES:

[Unless otherwise noted, data are for Nebraska, 1983. Data by race are for white, black, Indian, Mexican, and other. Data by place of residence and/or occurrence are usually shown by county and selected city.]

S4885–1.1: Births

[1-2] Births: by place of occurrence and by usual residence of mother, for health planning regions [and for counties and selected cities, 1981-83]. (p. 10-16)

[3] Births: sex, race, and plurality, by place of residence. (p. 17)

[4] Birth order by age of mother. (p. 21)

[5-6] Births, prenatal care: gravidity and prenatal visits, by trimester in which prenatal care started (percent). (p. 22)

[7-8] Births: by education of father and mother, and by weight. (p. 23-24)

[9-11] Out-of-wedlock births: by place of residence, 1983; by age and race of mother [generally 1979-83]; and by age of mother and birth order, 1983. (p. 25-28)

[12-14] Births, congenital anomalies: by county of residence, [month of birth, age of mother, birth weight, sex, race, and type of defect]. (p. 29-31)

[15] Births: selected defects by number and rate [per 1,000 live births]. (p. 32)

[16] [Births and deaths for Nebraska residents by State of occurrence, and births and deaths occurring in Nebraska for nonresidents by resident State.] (p. 33)

S4885–1.2: Deaths

[Tables [1-22] begin "Nebraska deaths..."]

DEATHS BY LOCATION AND CAUSE

[1-2] By place of occurrence and by usual residence of deceased, for health planning regions [and for counties and selected cities, 1981-83]. (p. 38-42)

[3] Sex and race, by place of residence. (p. 43-46)

[4-6] Six leading causes by age group and sex; and age- specific rates. (p. 49-50)

[7] Rates for 6 leading causes, by place of residence. (p. 51)

[8] Principal and other causes, by place of residence [with totals by sex]. (p. 55-59)

[9] Blacks, by leading cause and sex [and deaths in hospital and not in hospital, and infant deaths and rate]. (p. 60)

[10-11] Principal and other causes and rates per 100,000 population [1979-83]. (p. 61-62)

[12-13] Cancer by site and sex, and rates by site [1979-83]. (p. 63-64)

ACCIDENTAL DEATHS

[14-15] Accidents: by principal and other causes, by place of residence; and for [detailed types of] accidents by occurrence [including at work by industry division, all by age group]. (p. 65-69)

[16] Accidents by cause [and total by sex, and rate per 100,000 estimated population, 1979-83]. (p. 70)

[17-19] Drownings by site; and farm fatalities and suicides, by type; all by sex and age group. (p. 71-72)

DEATHS OCCURRING IN HOSPITALS AND ELSEWHERE

[20] Hospital and nonhospital, by [place of] occurrence and residence. (p. 73)

INFANT AND FETAL DEATHS

[21] Under 1 year of age by cause [and race, by sex; and by birth weight]. (p. 78)

[22] Infant, neonatal, perinatal, and fetal, by place of residence. (p. 79)

[23-24] Fetal deaths by cause of death, and by month, age group of mother, sex, race, and place of delivery. (p. 83-84)

S4885–1.3: Marriages, Divorces, and Population

MARRIAGES

[Most tables begin "Nebraska marriages..."]

[1] Number and rate, by county [1980-83]. (p. 87)

[2] Number of county residents married per 1,000 population [by county]. (p. 89)

[3-7] By education, race, number of marriages, residence status, and previous marital status of bride and groom. (p. 90-92)

[8] Nonresident brides and grooms [by resident State]. (p. 93)

[9-11] Number of marriages, by age of bride and [by age of] groom; [and total] marriages, and 1st marriages, by age of bride and groom. (p. 94-96)

[12] By occupation of bride and groom. (p. 97)

DIVORCES

[Tables begin "Nebraska divorces..."]

[13] Number and rate by county [1980-83]. (p. 99)

[14] By age of husband and wife. (p. 101)

[15] By duration of marriage [1981-83]. (p. 102)

[16-17] By race of husband and wife; and number of children affected. (p. 103)

[18-19] Number of marriage [of] husband and wife; and settlements made [by type]. (p. 104)

[20-21] By education and occupation of husband and wife. (p. 105-106)

POPULATION

[22] Nebraska population by county, U.S. census [decennially 1930-80]. (p. 109)

S4890   NEBRASKA
Department of
Insurance

S4890–1 SUMMARY OF INSURANCE BUSINESS IN NEBRASKA for the Year 1983
Annual. [1984.] 416 p.
LC 10-8606.
SRI/MF/complete

Annual report on Nebraska insurance industry financial condition and underwriting activity, by company and type of insurance, 1983. Covers assets, liabilities, capital, surplus, premiums received or written and earned, losses incurred, claims or benefits paid, insurance issued and in force, and membership fees and/or size, for companies with headquarters in Nebraska and elsewhere.

Data are shown, as applicable, for property/liability and life insurance companies, fraternal benefit societies, assessment companies, county and hospital/physician mutual assns, HMOs, legal service insurance and dental service corporations, service contract organizations, and motor clubs.

Property/liability insurance data include additional breakdowns for automobile, accident/health, medical malpractice, surety, workers' compensation, and other detailed lines of coverage.

Also includes data on Insurance Dept consumer complaints, agent licensing and examination results, and revenues; number of companies by type of insurance; finances of insurers in liquidation; securities on deposit by company; and State guaranty assn financial condition.

Contains contents listing (p. 2); Insurance Dept report, including assorted lists and directories, and 24 tables (p. 3-72); and 13 extended financial tables (p. 73-416).

Availability: Nebraska Department of Insurance, 301 Centennial Mall, S., PO Box 94699, Lincoln NE 68509-4699, $7.00; SRI/MF/complete.

S4895   NEBRASKA
Department of
Labor

S4895–1 NEBRASKA WORK TRENDS
Monthly. Approx. 30 p.
SRI/MF/complete, shipped quarterly

Monthly report on Nebraska labor force, including employment and unemployment by county and MSA, and employment by industry. Also includes data on unemployment insurance claims.

Reports are issued approximately 3 months after month of coverage, and generally contain contents listing, 2 illustrative charts, and 9 monthly tables listed below.

Monthly tables appear in all issues; Aug. 1984 issue also includes 2 tables showing Nebraska labor force by employment status, by State region and district, Aug. 1983 and July-Aug. 1984.

Availability: Nebraska Department of Labor, Employment Division, Research and Statistics

Section, PO Box 94600, State House Station, 550 S. 16th St., Lincoln NE 68509, †; SRI/MF/complete, shipped quarterly.

Issues reviewed during 1984: Aug. 1983-Aug. 1984 (D).

MONTHLY TABLES:

[Data are for Nebraska, unless otherwise noted. Table format may vary slightly from issue to issue.]

[1-2] Estimates: of labor force data [by employment status, for State and Omaha and Lincoln MSAs]; and of nonfarm employment data [by industry group; preliminary for month of coverage, and revised for preceding month and same month of preceding year].

[3] Monthly report on labor force, [employment], and unemployment [by county, MSA, and selected metro area, as of selected date during 1-2 months following month of coverage.]

[4-5] Summary of initial and continued claims [for unemployment insurance, monthly for current year to date and previous year].

[6] Estimates of hours and earnings in manufacturing [by selected major group, for State and Omaha and Lincoln MSAs, for month of coverage, previous month, and same month of previous year; table begins with the Dec. 1983 issue].

[7-8] [Table [2] is repeated for Omaha and Lincoln MSAs.]

[9] CPI, all urban consumers [by item, usually for U.S., Kansas City, Denver, and St. Louis, for month of coverage and trends].

S4900   NEBRASKA
Commission on
Law Enforcement
and Criminal Justice

S4900–1   UNIFORM CRIME REPORTS, 1983, Nebraska
Annual. [1984.] iv+61 p.
NE Pub. Clearinghouse No. L2500S001.
ISSN 0090-3221.
LC 75-647156.
SRI/MF/complete, current & previous year reports

Annual report, for 1983, on Nebraska crimes and arrests, by type of offense, county, and local police agency, with comparisons to 1982. Includes data on property loss values, assaults on police, and law enforcement employment.

Data are from reports of State and local law enforcement agencies, submitted under the Uniform Crime Reporting (UCR) Program.

Contains summary, and listing of contents, tables, and charts (p. ii-iv); description of UCR Program (p. 1-4); and report, with brief narratives interspersed with 12 charts and 40 tables (p. 5-61).

All tables, and selected charts with data not included in tables, are described below.

Previous report, for 1982, was also reviewed in 1984 and is also available on SRI microfiche under this number [Annual. [1983.] 58 p. ‡].

Availability: Nebraska Commission on Law Enforcement and Criminal Justice, Uniform

Crime Reporting Section, 301 Centennial Mall South, PO Box 94946, Lincoln NE 68509, ‡; SRI/MF/complete.

CHARTS AND TABLES:

[Data are for Nebraska, 1983, unless otherwise noted. Part I (Index) crimes are murder/manslaughter, rape, robbery, felony assault, burglary, larceny/theft, motor vehicle theft, and arson. Part II crimes are all other offenses.]

S4900–1.1: Offenses and Arrests

[Tables with data by race usually include white, black, Indian, and Asian.]

INDEX OFFENSES

a. Summary: number of offenses, rate, and percent cleared, by Index offense; and value of stolen and recovered property, by type. Tables 1-3. (p. 5-6)

b. Murder victims and offenders, by age, sex, and race; and murder/manslaughter, by circumstance, type of weapon, victim/offender relationship, and value of stolen and recovered property. Chart 2, tables 4-8. (p. 7-10)

c. Rapes, by type (forcible and attempted), age of victim, place of occurrence, victim/offender relationship, and value of stolen and recovered property. Chart 4, tables 9-12. (p. 12-13)

d. Robberies, by place of occurrence; robberies and felony assaults, by type of weapon; burglaries, by place and time of occurrence; larceny/theft offenses, by type; and arson offenses, by type of property; also including data on value of property recovered and damaged, or lost. Charts 6 and 7, tables 13-20. (p. 14-26)

ARRESTS

e. Arrest rates per 100,000 population, and adult and juvenile arrests, total 1982-83, and by age, sex, and race, 1983, all by Part I and Part II offense; and drug abuse arrests by substance, total 1982-83, and by sex and race, 1983. Tables 21-31. (p. 28-38)

S4900–1.2: Police Assaulted, Law Enforcement Employees, and County Data

a. Officers assaulted: by time of day and type of activity, 1982-83; and by type of weapon and assignment, 1983. Tables 32-35. (p. 39-41)

b. Law enforcement sworn and civilian employees by sex, officers per 1,000 population, and officers assaulted, by agency, for county sheriff depts, and for cities over and under 5,000 population. Tables 36-38. (p. 42-45)

c. County data: Index offenses by type and total clearances, population, crime rate, adult and juvenile arrests, and arrests by Part I and Part II offenses, all by county and local police agency. 2 tables. (p. 47-61)

S4950   NEBRASKA
Department of
Revenue

S4950–1   NEBRASKA DEPARTMENT OF REVENUE 1982 ANNUAL REPORT
Annual. [1984.] 91 p.
ISSN 0092-9220.
LC 73-647511.
SRI/MF/complete

Annual report, on Nebraska State tax revenues, by tax type and county, 1982 with selected trends from 1867. Also includes individual tax returns by income bracket, and sales tax by municipality and detailed industry. Data are from State and Federal sources.

Contains contents and table listing (1 p.), and the following sections:

a. General information, with summary of State Revenue Dept organization and activities, and overview of revenue sources; 2 trend charts; 1 chart showing U.S. per capita tax revenues by State, 1982; and 3 tables showing Nebraska per capita and/or total personal income by county 1980-81, allocation of funds to local governments by type of aid FY82, and chronology of income and sales tax rates as of various dates 1967-83. (p. 1-12)

b. 4 statistical sections, with narrative summaries, 5 charts, and 42 tables (including 2 maps designated as 1 table) listed below. (p. 13-89)

c. Index. (p. 91)

Availability: Nebraska Department of Revenue, Research Division, PO Box 94818, Lincoln NE 68509, †; SRI/MF/complete.

TABLES:
[All tables show data for Nebraska.]

S4950–1.1: Income Taxes

[Data are for tax year 1981, unless otherwise noted.]

1-2. Individual income tax statistics [including exemptions, food tax credit, Federal adjusted gross income (AGI), and Federal and calculated State taxes]; and liability [total returns, returns with tax liability, and calculated liability, by Federal AGI bracket]; by county. (p. 17-22)

3. Average individual income tax liability per return and per capita [by county]. [maps] (p. 23)

4. Analysis of individual income tax liability [returns with and without liability, and calculated liability, by Federal AGI bracket]. (p. 24)

5-8. General fund individual, fiduciary, and corporate income tax cash receipts; and withholding tax cash revenues; [by month, 1981-82]. (p. 24-26)

9. Analysis of corporate income tax returns [number of corporations, State taxable income, and calculated tax, by State income classification]. (p. 26)

S4950–1.2: Sales Tax

[Data are shown for 1982, unless otherwise noted. Tables 1-4 show net taxable sales and sales tax.]

1. Total net taxable sales and State sales tax [by county and municipality]. (p. 30-34)

2. Sales tax on motor vehicles [by county]. (p. 35)

3-4. Sales tax statistics by [detailed] business classification; and business classification sales by county [by industry division]. (p. 36-50)

5. City sales tax returned to [11] municipalities [1981-82]. (p. 51)

6-7. General fund sales tax cash revenues and receipts [by month, 1981-82]. (p. 52)

S4950-1.3: Miscellaneous Tax

1. General fund miscellaneous tax cash receipts [by source, 1981-82]. (p. 55)

2. Alcoholic beverage gallonage and revenue [beer, alcohol/spirits, and wine, by month 1982, with totals annually 1970-82, and tax rates from 1935]. (p. 56)

3. Cigarette tax receipts [and number of packages taxed, 1964-82]. (p. 57)

4. Comparative pari-mutuel report [amounts wagered and taxable, and tax paid, by 5 organizations, 1981-82; and tax rates, 1959-82]. (p. 58)

5-8. Importing dealers, special fuels, interstate motor carriers, and aviation fuels: net taxable gallons and calculated net tax due [monthly 1982]. (p. 59-60)

9-10. Gasohol net taxable gallons and litter fee receipts [monthly 1981-82]. (p. 61)

11. Lodging tax returned to [19] counties, 1981-82; [and] chronology of lodging tax. (p. 62)

S4950-1.4: Property Tax

[Data are shown for 1982, unless otherwise noted. Tables 3 and 5-15 show data by county.]

1. History of assessed valuation and total property tax [and total mill levy, various years 1867-1982]. (p. 67)

2. Tangible property taxes levied [general levies for local governments, and special assessments, 1972-82]. (p. 68)

3. Actual valuation, property taxes levied, rate, and distributions of State aid [to counties and homestead exemption]. (p. 69)

4. Cities and villages valuations and levies. (p. 70-74)

5. Distribution of payments in lieu of taxes by public power districts [by recipient: State, counties, cities/villages, and school and miscellaneous districts]. (p. 75)

6. Selected property taxes levied [by tax type: county, city/village, township, and rural fire district; miscellaneous; education taxes for city/village and rural schools, county/rural high schools, and special education; and payments in lieu of taxes by public power districts]. (p. 76)

7. Actual value as set by State Board of Equalization [for tangible property (from assessment abstract), public utilities (from franchise assessment), and railroads]. (p. 78)

8. Valuation of all personal property, [special schedules, and property assessed by State Board]. (p. 79)

9. Valuation of all [urban and rural] real estate, and oil/mineral interest. (p. 80)

10-11. Actual value of personal property [including mobile homes]; and of miscellaneous schedules [utilities and motor vehicles; by property type]. (p. 81-82)

12. Number of [regular and special] property tax schedules returned. (p. 83)

13-15. Actual value of rural, agricultural, and urban real estate [by property type]. (p. 84-89)

S5010   NEVADA
Department of Agriculture

S5010-1   1983 NEVADA AGRICULTURAL STATISTICS
Annual.   Sept. 1984.
2+37 p.
SRI/MF/complete

Annual report on Nevada agricultural production, marketing, and finances, 1983, with some data for 1984, and selected trends from 1970s or earlier. Data generally are shown by county and commodity, with some comparisons to total U.S.

Report generally covers production, value, prices, and, as applicable, acreage, disposition, yield, or inventory, for field crop, livestock, dairy, apiary, and poultry sectors.

Also includes data on number of farms, farm acreage, weather, pesticide use, pasture/rangeland condition, fertilizer consumption, and agricultural production costs and income.

Data are compiled jointly by USDA, University of Nevada, and Nevada Dept of Agriculture.

Contains foreword and contents listing (1 p.); and 49 tables, accompanied by brief narrative summaries (p. 1-36).

Availability: Nevada Department of Agriculture, Statistical Reporting Service, PO Box 8880, Reno NV 89507, †; SRI/MF/complete.

S5025   NEVADA
Office of the Controller

S5025-1   STATE OF NEVADA COMPREHENSIVE ANNUAL FINANCIAL REPORT for the Fiscal Year Ended June 30, 1983
Annual.   May 25, 1984.
iii+154 p.
LC 10-33042.
SRI/MF/complete

Annual report on financial condition of Nevada State government, for FY83, presenting balance sheets; and statements of revenue by source, expenditures by function, and fund balances; for all, general, special revenue, debt service, capital projects, enterprise, internal service, trust, and agency funds.

Also includes data on general fixed assets by type and function; spending authority compared to actual expenditures, by dept; tax collections by county; cash holdings analysis; finances of State-assisted postsecondary and correctional institutions; debt service obligations to 2009; socioeco-

nomic indicators, including per capita income comparisons to total U.S. and California, population by county, average annual employment, and commercial bank deposits; and selected trends from 1960.

Data are from records of the controller's office, and other State and Federal sources.

Contains listing of contents, exhibits, and tables (p. i-iii); introduction (p. 1-6); auditors report and 36 financial statements and schedules, with accompanying notes (p. 78-138); and statistical section on financial and socioeconomic trends, with 12 tables (p. 141-154).

Availability: Nevada Office of the Controller, State Capitol Bldg., Carson City NV 89710, †; SRI/MF/complete.

S5040   NEVADA
Employment Security Department

S5040-1   ECONOMIC UPDATE, Nevada
Quarterly.   Approx. 10 p. no paging.
SRI/MF/complete

Quarterly report on Nevada labor market and related economic trends, including employment by industry, average hours and earnings, gaming revenues, and taxable sales, with detail for Las Vegas and Reno. Data are from employer reports and Federal sources. Report is issued approximately 6 weeks after quarter of coverage.

Contains narrative summary of economic changes during quarter of coverage; 1 or more feature articles, occasionally with statistics; and 9 quarterly tables.

Quarterly tables are listed below and appear in all issues. All additional features with substantial statistical content are described, as they appear, under "Statistical Features." Nonstatistical features are not covered.

A monthly summary and additional reports covering various State labor market areas are also published by issuing agency, but are not covered by SRI.

Availability: Nevada Employment Security Department, Employment Security Research Section, 500 E. Third St., Carson City NV 89713-0001, †; SRI/MF/complete.

Issues reviewed during 1984: 3rd Qtr. 1983- 2nd Qtr. 1984 (D).

QUARTERLY TABLES:
[Most data are shown for Nevada, Las Vegas, and, except for tables [8-9], Reno. Tables show data for quarter of coverage, generally by month; tables [1-7] also include comparisons to same periods of previous year.]

[1] Economic indicators [unemployment rate, gross gaming revenues, and taxable sales; also includes U.S. unemployment rate and all-urban CPI].

[2-7] Labor force summary [by employment status, and persons involved in work stoppages]; and establishment-based industrial employment [by major industry group].

[8-9] Average hours and earnings in selected industries.

STATISTICAL FEATURES:

S5040–1.501: 3rd Qtr. 1983

GAMING REVENUE ANALYSIS

(p. 5-6) By Ted Zuend. Article, with 1 table showing Nevada seasonally adjusted gross gaming revenues (in current and constant 1982 dollars), and unemployment rate, by quarter, 1977-2nd quarter 1983. Data are from Gaming Control Board.

RESIDENTIAL HOUSING

(p. 9-10) By Gary Lungstrum. Article, with 1 table showing percent change in single- and multi-family housing permits issued for Las Vegas and Reno SMSAs, 1979-82 and 1st-3rd quarters 1983.

NEVADA INDUSTRY EMPLOYMENT SHARES: TRENDS AND OUTLOOK

(p. 11-12) By Ted Zuend. Article, with 1 table showing Nevada employment distribution by industry division, selected years 1970-82.

S5040–1.502: 4th Qtr. 1983

1983 NEVADA WAGE SURVEY

(p. 4-5) By George Anastassatos. Brief article announcing publication of *1983 Nevada Wage Survey,* available from Employment Security Dept. Includes 1 table showing Nevada average wage ranges, employees, and employing firms, for 7 occupations, by State area, 1983.

NEVADA'S HIGH TECH PROFILE

(p. 5-9) By Fred Couzens. Article, with 1 table showing number of high technology companies located in Nevada, by SIC 3-digit industry and location, as of end of 2nd quarter 1983. Data are from reports by State Employment Security Dept.

ROLE OF THE MINING INDUSTRY IN NEVADA COUNTIES

(p. 10-11) By Kimberly Spielman. Article, with 1 table showing Nevada mining industry share of employment, payrolls, and property tax collections; and value of nonfuel production; all by county, various years 1970-82.

NEVADA, LAS VEGAS, RENO INDUSTRIAL SIZE AND WAGES

(p. 11-12, 17) By Robert Murdock. Article, with 1 table showing average number of business firms and average wage, by industry division, for State and 2 largest SMSAs, 1981-82. Data are from Employment Security Research

S5040–1.503: 1st Qtr. 1984

DATA REVISIONS

(p. 4-7) By Daniel Culbert. Article, with 4 tables presenting revised estimates of nonagricultural employment by industry division, 1981-83; and labor force by employment status, 1982-83; for Nevada, Reno, and Las Vegas. Data are from Employment Security Dept.

WAGES IN THE LAS VEGAS HOTEL/MOTEL INDUSTRY

(p. 7-8) By Robert Murdock. Article, with 2 tables showing Las Vegas hotel/motel employment and average hourly wages, for 14 tipped and nontipped occupations, with selected detail by sex, Sept. 1983. Data are from responses of 35 employers, representing 35,542 workers, to a Sept. 1983 BLS survey.

NEVADA UNEMPLOYMENT RATES

(p. 9-10) By Kenneth Sceirine. Article, with 1 chart and 1 table showing Nevada unemployment rate by county, with summary comparison to U.S. and 7 other western States, 1982-83 and Mar. 1983-84. Data are from BLS.

ECONOMIC RECOVERY: ANOTHER BAROMETER

(p. 11-12) By Gary Lungstrum. Article, with 2 tables showing Nevada per capita disposable personal income (with comparisons to U.S. and California), taxable sales, and gross gaming revenues, all adjusted for inflation, mostly 1980-83.

NEW BUSINESS GROWTH IN NEVADA

(p. 13-15) By Kimberly Spielman. Article, with 1 table showing number of new business firms in Nevada, with detail for service and trade firms and firms with over 20 employees, by county, year ended June 1983.

S5040–1.504: 2nd Qtr. 1984

PER CAPITA PERSONAL INCOME, ANNUAL FEATURE

(p. 7-8) Annual article, by George Anastassatos, with 1 table showing per capita personal income for total U.S., Far West region, and 4 western States, and by Nevada county, 1980-82. Data are from U.S. Commerce Dept.

1982 PRELIMINARY REPORT OF THE CENSUS OF AGRICULTURE

(p. 9-12) By George Anastassatos. Article, with 2 tables showing Nevada farms by size, product sales range, and type of ownership; acreage of farms, harvested cropland, and irrigated land; crop and livestock/poultry/product sales; farm operators by race; and number and acreage of farms operated by women; all for 1978 and 1982. Data are from U.S. Census of Agriculture.

MANUFACTURING FIRM GROWTH AND DEVELOPMENT IN NEVADA

(p. 11-13) By Kimberly Spielman. Article, with 1 table showing Nevada new (operating less than 1 year) and established manufacturing firms and employment, for companies with under and over 20 employees, by selected SIC 2-digit industry, with detail for established firms in Clark and Washoe Counties, primarily as of June 1983. Data were compiled by Nevada Employment Security Dept.

EMPLOYMENT AND PAYROLLS, 1983

(p. 14) By Daniel Culbert. Article, with 2 tables showing insured employment and payroll, for 9 western States, with Nevada detail by industry division, 1983.

S5062   NEVADA
Gaming Control Board

S5062–1   NEVADA GAMING ABSTRACT, 1983
Annual. Apr. 1984.
84 p. var. paging.
LC 78-641572.
SRI/MF/complete

Annual report on Nevada casino revenues, expenses, and employment, by location and gaming revenue range, FY83. Also includes average win per unit, by type of game or device. Data are compiled by the Nevada State Gaming Control Board from casino financial reports.

Contains introduction, terminology, and contents listing (4 p.); and 4 separately paginated statistical sections, with table listing for each, and 75 tables listed below (80 p.).

Monthly Gross Gaming Revenue Report is also available from the issuing agency, but is not covered by SRI.

Availability: Nevada Gaming Control Board, Publications, 1150 E. William St., Carson City NV 89710, $10.00; SRI/MF/complete.

TABLES:
[Tables show data for FY83, unless otherwise noted.]

HOTEL/CASINO COMPLEXES AND PUBLICLY OWNED CASINOS

[Tables show data for complexes with gaming revenues of $2 million or over by revenue range, and for all publicly owned casinos with revenues of $10 million or more.]

[1] Condensed income statement [including total, average, median, and quartile revenue amounts]. (p. 1.1)

[2-6] Casino, rooms, food, beverage, and other dept income statements [including bad debt, payroll, and payroll tax/benefits expenses]. (p. 1.2-1.6)

[7] Schedule of general and administrative expenses [including advertising/promotion, complimentaries, and music/entertainment]. (p. 1.7)

[8] Condensed balance sheet [including average, median, and quartile assets], at June 30, 1983. (p. 1.8)

[9] Financial statement ratios. (p. 1.9)

[10-14] Schedule of employment [number of employees and amount paid, by dept, quarterly and FY83]. (p. 1.10-1.14)

[15] Rate of room occupancy [available rooms and percent occupied, by month; and average revenues and sales by type, rooms dept payroll, and room rate, all per room per day]. (p. 1.15)

[16-20] Average win per unit [median and quartiles, by type of game and device, quarterly and FY83]. (p. 1.16-1.20)

[21] Percent of revenue produced by games and devices [and number of locations and units, by type of game and device; and number of casinos, average area, and gaming revenue per square foot, for pit, slot, keno, and poker areas]. (p. 1.21-1.23)

CASINOS BY REVENUE RANGE AND GEOGRAPHICAL AREA

[22-44] [Tables 1-14 and 16-21 are repeated for Las Vegas Strip, downtown Las Vegas, and

Reno/Sparks casinos with gaming revenues of $1 million and over, by revenue range.] (p. 2.1-2.23)

CASINOS GROSSING MORE THAN $1 MILLION

[45-67] [Tables 1-14 and 16-21 are repeated for casinos with gaming revenues of $1 million and over for Las Vegas Strip, downtown Las Vegas, Laughlin, Reno/Sparks, Douglas and Elko Counties, and balance of State.] (p. 3.1-3.23)

CASINOS GROSSING LESS THAN $1 MILLION

[68-75] Condensed income statement of casinos with gaming revenues of less than $1 million [revenues by source, cost of sales, expenses by item, and net operating income]; and average annual win per unit [and number of units, by game or device; all by gaming revenue range, for State, Clark County, Washoe County, and balance of State]. (p. 4.1-4.8)

S5065 NEVADA
Office of the
Governor

S5065–2 NEVADA PROFILES
Series. For individual publication data, see below. LC 83-621739. SRI/MF/complete

Series of 18 profiles presenting detailed demographic, socioeconomic, and governmental statistics for Nevada, 16 counties, and Carson City. Data generally are shown for various calendar or fiscal years 1980-82, with some trends from 1970s or earlier, and population projections to 2000. Data topics include the following:

a. **Population characteristics:** population, by census designated area, age and sex, urban-rural status, marital status, and race-ethnicity (including Indian and Hispanic); births, deaths, marriages, and divorces; families, with detail for number of parents and sex of single parents; and households.

b. **Housing characteristics:** housing units, by occupancy status and urban-rural location; seasonal/2nd homes; housing median value and cash rent; and housing units receiving government assistance for construction/operation and for purchase or rental payment.

c. **Economic activity:** median and per capita income; average earnings; unemployment rate; public and private wage rates for selected occupations; firms or agencies, employment, and payroll, by industry division and government level; production and related data for selected agricultural commodities; Federal oil/gas and geothermal leases and leased acreage; gaming revenues; and residential and nonresidential construction value.

d. **Transportation, communications, and utilities:** registered vehicles; road/street mileage; transportation facilities and services, including airports, air traffic, railroads, bus and truck lines, and elderly/handicapped transportation services; and newspapers and circulation, radio stations, electrical and gas/propane/heating oil services, waste disposal and water services and population served, and telephone services, all by city or other service area.

e. **Land use, physical environment, and water resources:** including exempt land acreage, by ownership; county and total acreage on tax rolls; listings of major mineral and wildlife resources; climatic data; water resources, by detailed type and location; water use, by community; and water quality monitoring frequency.

f. **Local government, taxes, and public services:** including number of county and city employees; local government budgets; tax revenue collections, by tax type; assessed valuation of property and mines; senior citizen property tax rebate program participants and rebates; fire protection and law enforcement personnel; library volumes; recreational facilities; churches; and community organizations.

g. **Education:** including enrollment in elementary/middle and secondary public and private schools; special education enrollment; public school personnel and expenditures; and number of schools and colleges.

h. **Human services:** including income maintenance and employment program participants, by program; hospital, long-term care, and mental health facilities, beds, admissions or discharges, average length of stay, occupancy rate, and revenues or expenditures, by facility; public health program participants, by program; and meal, energy assistance, and weatherization program activity.

i. **Indian tribes:** including tribal population, by sex and age; labor force by employment status, sex, and earnings level; HUD-constructed housing units; cigarette sales; school enrollment; acreage, by ownership; and irrigated acreage; all by reservation.

Most data are from State agencies and the Census Bureau.

State profile covers selected additional topics, including detailed data on Federal expenditures in Nevada, and is further described below.

Profiles for Carson City and each county are listed below. Each contains contents listing; maps; 15 sections, with approximately 80 tables covering the data topics described above, as applicable; and data sources.

SRI also covers the biennial *Nevada Statistical Abstract,* last described in SRI 1982 Annual, under S5065-1.

Availability: Nevada Office of the Governor, Capitol Complex, 401 N. Carson, Carson City NV 89710; SRI/MF/complete.

PROFILES:

S5065–2.1: Nevada Statewide Profile, 1982-83
[Monograph. 1982. 3+101 p. ‡. SRI/MF/complete.]

Presents State summary data, occasionally with detail by county, for most of the data topics described above. Additional data topics include the following:

a. Migration into and out of Nevada, by region of origin or destination.

b. Households, by income; persons in poverty, by race-ethnicity (including Indian, Asian/Pacific Islander, and Spanish origin) and age; and population, by poverty status; all by county.

c. Employment and payroll detail by major industry group; number and acreage of farms/ranches; financial institutions, assets, loans, and deposits, by type of institution; gaming licenses in force, by type of game; licensed slot machines; and gaming revenue detail for games/tables and slot machines.

d. Licensed drivers, by sex; electricity and natural gas sales, by consuming sector; electricity generated, purchased, and sold to out-of-State customers; and telephones in use.

e. Federally administered public land acreage, by agency; courts and justices of the peace; State revenues by type of tax, fee, and fine; Federal revenues from and payments to Nevada for public lands; unemployment and worker compensation benefit payments and/or revenues; vocational education enrollment; Federal expenditures in Nevada, by detailed type and Federal agency; and Nevada State government expenditures, by function.

Contains introduction and contents listing (2 p.); 19 sections, with 142 tables (p. 1-97); and data sources (p. 98-101).

S5065–2.2: Carson City Profile, Nevada
[Monograph. 1982. iii+41 p. ◆. SRI/MF/complete.]

S5065–2.3: Churchill County Profile, Nevada
[Monograph. 1982. iii+42 p. ‡. SRI/MF/complete.]

S5065–2.4: Clark County Profile, Nevada
[Monograph. 1982. v+48 p.+errata sheets. ◆. SRI/MF/complete.]

S5065–2.5: Douglas County Profile, Nevada
[Monograph. 1982. ii+43 p. ◆. SRI/MF/complete.]

S5065–2.6: Elko County Profile, Nevada
[Monograph. 1982. iii+46 p. ‡. SRI/MF/complete.]

S5065–2.7: Esmeralda County Profile, Nevada
[Monograph. 1982. ii+32 p.+errata sheet. ‡. SRI/MF/complete.]

S5065–2.8: Eureka County Profile, Nevada
[Monograph. 1982. ii+37 p. ‡. SRI/MF/complete.]

S5065–2.9: Humboldt County Profile, Nevada
[Monograph. 1982. ii+43 p. ‡. SRI/MF/complete.]

S5065–2.10: Lander County Profile, Nevada
[Monograph. 1982. ii+41 p. ‡. SRI/MF/complete.]

S5065–2.11: Lincoln County Profile, Nevada
[Monograph. 1982. iii+39 p. ‡. SRI/MF/complete.]

S5065–2.12: Lyon County Profile, Nevada
[Monograph. 1982. iv+42 p. ‡. SRI/MF/complete.]

S5065–2.13: Mineral County Profile, Nevada
[Monograph. 1982. ii+40 p. ‡. SRI/MF/complete.]

S5065–2.14: Nye County Profile, Nevada
[Monograph. 1982. ii+42 p. ‡. SRI/MF/complete.]

S5065–2.15: Pershing County Profile, Nevada
[Monograph. 1982. iii+40 p. ‡. SRI/MF/complete.]

S5065–2.16: Storey County Profile, Nevada
[Monograph. 1982. ii+31 p.+errata sheet. ‡. SRI/MF/complete.]

S5065–2.17: Washoe County Profile, Nevada
[Monograph. 1982. v+47 p. ◆. SRI/MF/complete.]

S5065–2.18: White Pine County Profile, Nevada
[Monograph. 1982. ii+42 p. ‡. SRI/MF/complete.]

S5075   NEVADA
Department of
Human Resources

**S5075–1   NEVADA 1982 VITAL
STATISTICS REPORT**
Annual. Apr. 1984. 5+55 p.
ISSN 0147-9444.
LC 77-641051.
SRI/MF/complete

Annual report on Nevada vital statistics, covering population, births, deaths by cause, abortions, marriages, and divorces, 1982 and trends. Most data are shown by county, and include selected detail by race, age, and sex.

Data are from records filed with the State Vital Statistics Section.

Contents:

a. Contents listing and foreword. (4 p.)
b. Summary section, with 1 chart and 3 tables showing population, and births, deaths, marriages, and divorces, by county, 1982, with annual trends from 1973. (p. 1-4)
c. 7 detailed sections, with 41 tables listed below. (p. 5-48)
d. Growth section, with 16 charts and 12 tables showing population, births and deaths by sex, marriages, divorces, abortions, and suicides by age group; generally for 1978-82, with selected comparisons to U.S., and trends from 1971. (p. 49-55)

Availability: Nevada Department of Human Resources, Health Division, Vital Statistics Section, 505 E. King St., Rm. 102, Carson City NV 89710, †; SRI/MF/complete.

TABLES:
[Tables show data for Nevada, 1982, unless otherwise noted. Data by county include breakdowns for Carson City. Racial categories are white, black, Indian, and other.]

S5075–1.1: Births, Deaths, and Abortions

BIRTHS
[Tables [1-11] show births as indicated. Immature births are under 2,500 grams.]

[1-3] By county of residence: [totals]; and by sex, race of mother, age of mother, attendant at birth, and place of birth. (p. 5-7)

[4] [Immature] births, by birth order and [mother's] age. (p. 8)

[5] [Immature births and percent of total births], by age of mother. (p. 9)

[6] [Births with complications of pregnancy/delivery and with congenital malformations, by trimester prenatal care began.] (p. 10)

[7-8] [Immature] births by county of residence, by race and [mother's] age. (p. 11-12)

[9] By birth order and [mother's] age. (p. 13)

[10-11] By county of residence and trimester prenatal care began, and rate per 1,000 population. (p. 14-15)

[12] Outcome of pregnancy [live births, fetal deaths, and induced abortions], by county of residence and age of mother. (p. 16-19)

PERINATAL AND INFANT DEATHS
[13-15] Perinatal deaths, stillbirths, and infant deaths, [and rates] per 1,000 live births; by county of residence. (p. 20-22)

[16] Infant deaths, by county of residence, sex, and race. (p. 23)

ABORTIONS
[Table titles [17-21] begin "Induced terminations of pregnancy..."]

[17] By age and race. (p. 24)

[18-19] By type of procedure and period of gestation; and by number of previous terminations and race. (p. 25-26)

[20-21] By county of residence: by county of occurrence, and by marital status. (p. 27-28)

DEATHS BY DEMOGRAPHIC CHARACTERISTICS
[22-24] Deaths by county of residence: by age, sex, and race; and by rate per 1,000 population. (p. 29-31)

DEATHS BY CAUSE
[25-26] [Accidental] deaths by county of residence and occurrence, by type of accident. (p. 32-33)

[27-29] Twelve leading causes of death: by age; by county of occurrence; and rate per 100,000, by sex. (p. 34-36)

SUICIDES
[Table titles [30-41] begin "Suicides..."]

[30-31] By county of residence: by county of occurrence, and by age. (p. 37-38)

[32-33] By day of occurrence; and by place of occurrence, by age and sex. (p. 39-40)

[34-35] By county of residence and method; and by month and day of week. (p. 41-42)

[36] By occupation, marital status, and sex. (p. 43)

[37] By method and age. (p. 44)

[38] By occupation, age, and sex. (p. 45)

[39] By age, sex, and marital status. (p. 46)

[40-41] By county of occurrence, age, and sex; and by method, race, and sex. (p. 47-48)

S5095   NEVADA
State
Library

**S5095–1   NEVADA LIBRARY
DIRECTORY and Statistics,
1984**
Annual. 1984. 106 p.
LC 77-644335.
SRI/MF/complete

Annual directory of public, academic, and special libraries in Nevada, with statistics on holdings, circulation, finances, and operations, FY83 and trends. Data are from reports of individual libraries to the State Library.

Contains user guide and contents listing (p. 1-3); directories of libraries and personnel (p. 4-72); statistical summary, with 9 tables, listed below (p. 73-86); and list of school library personnel (p. 87-106).

Availability: Nevada State Library, Library Development Division, Capitol Complex, Carson City NV 89710, $3.00; SRI/MF/complete.

TABLES:
[Data are for Nevada, FY83, unless noted otherwise. Tables [4-5] show data by county and/or library.]

[1] [Circulation per volume and expenditures per circulation, FY79-83.] (p. 73)

[2] State library statistics [income, staff, holdings by type, and circulation; reference, archival, and other activities; and blind/handicapped talking book circulation and patrons]. (p. 75)

[3] State library general fund appropriation [FY61-84]. (p. 76)

[4] Public library resources and support [population served, staff, holdings, circulation, income by source, expenditures by object, interlibrary loan activity, and hours open, for libraries serving populations over 3,000]. (p. 77-81)

[5] Bookmobile circulation. (p. 82)

[6] Public libraries comparative statistical summary [FY82-83]. (p. 83)

[7] Federal Library Services and Construction Act (LSCA) funds granted to Nevada libraries [FY58-83]. (p. 84)

[8] Tax-supported college and university libraries [enrollment, and library staff, expenditures, holdings, and interlibrary loan transactions, by institution]. (p. 85)

[9] Public school library resources and support [enrollment, schools, staff, and book and media holdings, by school district]. (p. 86)

S5175　NEW HAMPSHIRE Department of Administration and Control

S5175–1　NEW HAMPSHIRE DEPARTMENT OF ADMINISTRATION AND CONTROL, Fifty-Second Annual Report, Fiscal Year Ended June 30, 1983
Annual.　Nov. 11, 1983.
6+247 p.
SRI/MF/complete

Annual report on financial condition of New Hampshire State government, FY83, presenting assets and liabilities; revenues by source (including detailed Federal grants); appropriations and expenditures by agency or function; expenditures by object; and fund balances; all by fund, with comparisons to FY82 and earlier.

Funds covered include general, special revenue, highway, fish/game, debt service, capital projects, enterprise, and trust/agency.

Also includes data on bonded indebtedness, and Liquor, Sweepstakes, Horse Racing Commission and Greyhound Racing Commission operations.

Data are from the records of the comptroller's office.

Contains contents listing (6 p.); introduction with 2 charts (p. 1-10); and 89 financial statements arranged in 8 sections (p. 12-247).

Availability: New Hampshire Department of Administration and Control, Accounts Division, State House Annex, Rm. 310, Concord NH 03301, †; SRI/MF/complete.

S5185　NEW HAMPSHIRE Banking Department

S5185–1　HUNDRED THIRTY-NINTH ANNUAL REPORT OF THE BANK COMMISSIONER of the State of New Hampshire, for the Year Ending Dec. 31, 1983
Annual.　1983.　225 p.
LC 6-3171.
SRI/MF/complete

Annual report, for 1983, on financial condition of New Hampshire State-chartered financial institutions. Presents assets, liabilities, income, expenses, and other operating data, by institution arranged by city, for trust companies, mutual/guaranty savings banks, cooperative banks, credit unions, and the New Hampshire Business Development Corp., with composite data for 2nd mortgage and small loan licensees.

Also includes data on number of retail sellers and finance companies offering motor vehicle installment loans, and small loan licensee loan activities including legal actions.

Contains contents listing and index of institutions (p. 5-9); foreword, with 1 table (p. 10-16); and 10 sections, with regulatory and legislative information, directories, 3-7 tables repeated for each type of institution, and 3 charts (p. 17-225).

Availability: New Hampshire Banking Department, 97 N. Main St., Concord NH 03301, †; SRI/MF/complete.

S5200　NEW HAMPSHIRE Department of Education

S5200–1　EDUCATIONAL STATISTICS for New Hampshire, 1982/83
Annual series.　For individual publication data, see below.
SRI/MF/complete

Series of annual reports, for 1982/83 school year, each presenting data on an aspect of New Hampshire elementary and secondary education. Topics include public school and academy enrollment, finance, administration and staff, facilities, and programs. Some nonpublic school data are also included.

Data are compiled from individual school and school district reports to the New Hampshire Dept of Education, and other State and local agencies.

Reports for 1982/83 reviewed during 1984 are described below. Reports for 1981/82 and 1983/84 are covered under S5200-2 and S5200-3, respectively.

Availability: New Hampshire Department of Education, Computer and Statistical Services, 101 Pleasant St., Concord NH 03301-3860, †; SRI/MF/complete.

S5200–1.9: Valuations, Property Tax Assessments, and School Tax Rates of School Districts, 1982/83
[Annual. Jan. 9, 1984. 6 p. SRI/MF/complete.]

Annual table showing net assessed and equalized valuations, property tax assessments for schools and total, and school tax and property tax rates, by school district, 1982/83 school year.

Report for 1981/82 is described in SRI 1982 Annual, under S5200-2.8.

S5200–1.10: Preliminary Expenditures of School Districts, 1982/83, New Hampshire
[Annual. Feb. 29, 1984. 1 p. SRI/MF/complete.]

Annual table presenting preliminary data on school district expenditures, for 1982/83 school year. Includes total and per-pupil expenditures, by function, and average daily membership, with selected detail for elementary, middle/junior high, and high schools.

S5200–1.11: Total Net Revenue and Expenditures of School Districts, 1982/83, New Hampshire
[Annual. Mar. 1, 1984. 5 p. SRI/MF/complete.]

Two annual tables showing revenues, by detailed source, including Federal, State, and local governments; and expenditures, by function, for elementary, middle/junior high, and high school, and general expenses; 1982/83 school year.

S5200–1.12: Average Expenditures per Pupil for All Grades, 1982/83, New Hampshire
[Annual. Apr. 18, 1984. 3 p. SRI/MF/complete.]

Annual table showing average expenditures per pupil, by function, for elementary, middle/junior high, and high school, and general expenses, 1982/83 school year.

S5200–1.13: 1983 Equalized Valuation per Pupil, 1982/83, of New Hampshire School Districts
[Annual. June 8, 1984. 7 p. SRI/MF/complete.]

Two annual tables showing 1983 equalized valuation by school district, based on 1982/83 enrollment, for districts organized for grades K-12 or 1-12 (table 1), and for districts with grade spans less than 1-12 (table 2).

Includes total and per pupil equalized valuation, and average daily membership. Proportional equalized valuation is shown for table 2.

S5200–1.14: Fact Sheets: Approved Elementary, Middle, Junior High, and High Schools (by District for School Year 1982/83), New Hampshire
[Annual. June 20, 1984. 9 p. SRI/MF/complete.]

Four annual tables showing summary enrollment and financial data, by school district, for elementary, middle, junior high, and high schools, 1982/83 school year. Covers fall enrollment, per pupil cost and assessed property value, property tax levy rates, and district ranks.

S5200–1.15: 1982/83 Average Daily Memberships Based upon Attendance and Residence, New Hampshire
[Annual. Apr. 17, 1984. 9 p. SRI/MF/complete.]

Annual table showing average daily membership in attendance and residence, by school district, for elementary, middle/junior high, and high school, 1982/83 school year.

Previous report, for 1981/82, is described under S5200-2.16, below.

S5200–2　EDUCATIONAL STATISTICS for New Hampshire, 1981/82
Annual series.　For individual publication data, see below.
SRI/MF/complete

Series of annual reports for 1981/82 school year, each presenting data on an aspect of New Hampshire elementary and secondary education. Topics include public school and academy enrollment, finance, administration and staff, facilities, and programs. Some nonpublic school data are also included.

Data are compiled from individual school and school district reports to the New Hampshire Dept of Education, and other State and local agencies.

Report for 1981/82 reviewed during 1984 is described below. Reports for 1982/83 and 1983/84 are described under S5200-1 and S5200-3, respectively.

Availability: New Hampshire Department of Education, Computer and Statistical Services, 101 Pleasant St., Concord NH 03301-3860, †; SRI/MF/complete.

S5200–2.16: 1981/82 Average Daily Memberships Based upon Attendance and Residence, New Hampshire

[Annual. May 25, 1983. 9 p. SRI/MF/complete.]

Annual table showing average daily membership in attendance and residence, by school district, for elementary, middle/junior high, and high school, 1981/82 school year.

Previous report, for 1980/81, is described in SRI 1982 Annual under S5200–1.3.

S5200–3 EDUCATIONAL STATISTICS for New Hampshire, 1983/84

Annual series. For individual publication data, see below.
SRI/MF/complete

Series of annual reports, for 1983/84 school year, each presenting data on an aspect of New Hampshire elementary and secondary education. Topics include public school and academy enrollment, finance, administration and staff, facilities, and programs. Some nonpublic school data are also included.

Data are compiled from individual school and school district reports to the New Hampshire Dept of Education, and other State and local agencies.

Reports for 1983/84 reviewed during 1984 are described below. Reports for 1981/82 and 1982/83 are described under S5200–2 and S5200–1, respectively.

Availability: New Hampshire Department of Education, Computer and Statistical Services, 101 Pleasant St., Concord NH 03301, †; SRI/MF/complete.

S5200–3.3: Enrollments in Grades 9-12 in New Hampshire Approved Public Secondary Schools and Approved Public Academies, Sept. 1983

[Annual. Jan. 11, 1984. 2 p. SRI/MF/complete.]

Annual table showing Sept. 1983 secondary school enrollment by individual school, arranged by size. Includes high school, separate grade 9, and total State enrollments.

S5200–3.4: Fall Enrollments, 1983/84, by School Administrative Unit

[Annual. Jan. 19, 1984. 6 p. SRI/MF/complete.]

Annual table showing fall 1983 enrollments by school administrative unit, for elementary, middle/junior high, and high schools, with State totals.

S5200–3.5: Fall Enrollments in New Hampshire Public Schools and Approved Public Academies, Sept. 1983

[Annual. Jan. 19, 1984. 4 p. SRI/MF/complete.]

Annual table showing fall 1983 enrollment by school district for elementary, middle/junior high, and high schools, with district and State totals.

S5200–3.6: Estimated Expenditures of School Districts, 1983/84, New Hampshire

[Annual. Feb. 29, 1984. 1 p. SRI/MF/complete.]

Annual table estimating school district expenditures, for 1983/84 school year. Includes total and per-pupil expenditures, by purpose, and average daily membership, with selected detail for elementary, middle/junior high, and high schools.

S5200–3.7: Preliminary Costs per Pupil for Purposes of Tuition, 1983/84, New Hampshire

[Annual. May 28, 1984. 5 p. SRI/MF/complete.]

Annual preliminary report on average cost per pupil for New Hampshire public school operations, 1983/84 school year. Costs are estimates based on previous year's spending, and exclude transportation, capital outlay, and debt obligations.

Includes 1 table showing average per pupil costs by school district, for elementary, middle/junior high, and high schools.

S5200–3.8: Teacher Salary Schedules 1983/84: New Hampshire School Districts

[Annual. Nov. 17, 1983. 4 p. SRI/MF/complete.]

Annual table showing teacher salary rates by school district for the 1983/84 school year. Includes minimum and maximum rates, and number of salary steps between each, for teachers with bachelor's degrees, master's degrees, and additional credit hours.

S5205 NEW HAMPSHIRE Department of Employment Security

S5205–1 ECONOMIC CONDITIONS IN NEW HAMPSHIRE

Monthly. Approx. 15 p.
SRI/MF/complete, shipped quarterly

Monthly report on employment developments in New Hampshire, including unemployment rates, placements, unemployment insurance claims, and hours and earnings. Data are from local State employment offices, and cooperating employers. Report is issued 3-4 months after cover date.

Contains narrative analysis, 2 summary charts, and 8 monthly tables listed below; and occasional additional tables, usually showing summary, trend, or revised data for topics covered in monthly tables.

Most monthly tables appear in all issues. All other tables with substantial statistics for New Hampshire on topics not covered in monthly tables are described, as they appear, under "Statistical Features." Nonstatistical features are not covered.

Reports for local labor market areas are also available from the issuing agency, but are not covered by SRI.

Availability: New Hampshire Department of Employment Security, Economic Analysis and Reports Section, 32 S. Main St., Concord NH 03301-4857, †; SRI/MF/complete, shipped quarterly.

Issues reviewed during 1984: Aug. 1983-July 1984 (D) (1983 Nos. 8-12; 1984 Nos. 1-7).

MONTHLY TABLES:

[Tables show data for month of coverage, usually with comparison to preceding month and same month of previous year. Tables [1] and [6-7] show data for New Hampshire, and Manchester and Nashua labor market areas. Table order may vary.]

[1] Labor force, total employment and unemployment [and persons involved in labor disputes], and nonagricultural wage/salary employment [by industry division and major manufacturing group], as of the middle of the month.

[2] Total unemployment and labor force by labor market area and county.

[3] U.S. CPI.

[4] Weekly [unemployment insurance initial and continuing] claims filed during [month of coverage], classified by local office.

[5] Unemployment compensation fund balance [at] end of month [and contributions received, benefits paid, and interest].

[6] Average earnings and hours of production workers in manufacturing industries [by major industry group].

[7] Number of [State employment service total] active file applicants and female applicants, by major occupational category.

[8] Employment service activity [applications, openings received, and placements].

STATISTICAL FEATURES:

S5205–1.501: Sept. 1983 (No. 9)

STAFFING PATTERNS, TRADE INDUSTRIES

(p. 5) Table showing New Hampshire wholesale and retail trade employment, with distribution by occupational category, by SIC 2- and 3-digit industry, June 1982. Data are from State *Occupational Employment Statistics Survey,* 1982 report.

S5205–1.502: Feb. 1984 (No. 2)

FIRMS BY SIZE: UNIT, EMPLOYEES, AND WAGES, AUG. 1983, ANNUAL FEATURE

(p. 5) Annual table showing number of industrial firms and employment, Aug. 1983; and wages, 3rd quarter 1983; all by employment size group. Data are based on State unemployment compensation coverage.

S5205–1.503: May 1984 (No. 5)

POPULATION ESTIMATES FOR YOUTH BY SEX AND COUNTY

(p. 5) Table showing New Hampshire population age 14-21, by age group and sex, by county, 1985. Data are from Lawrence-Berkeley Laboratory.

S5205–2 PEOPLE AT WORK: Occupational Employment Statistics

Series. For individual publication data, see below.
SRI/MF/complete

Continuing series of reports on New Hampshire nonagricultural employment, by occupation. Each report covers 1 or more industry sectors, presenting data by detailed managerial, professional, technical, service, production, clerical, and sales occupational categories, within SIC 2- and 3-digit industry groups.

Most data are from mail surveys conducted for the Occupational Employment Statistics Program, and cover industry sectors on a 3-year cycle.

General format of each report:

a. Contents listing, preface, introduction, and summary.

b. Statistical section, with 2-5 tables repeated for each SIC 2- and 3-digit industry covered, usually including employment for 5-15 occupations with largest number of workers and most frequently reported occupations, and estimated employment by detailed occupation, for survey period, with comparisons to previous surveys.

c. Methodology and appendix, with description of occupational categories covered.

Reports reviewed during 1984 are described below.

Availability: New Hampshire Department of Employment Security, Economic Analysis and Reports Section, 32 S. Main St., Concord NH 03301-4857, †; SRI/MF/complete.

S5205–2.7: New Hampshire Staffing Patterns in Federal Government, 1980; State Government, 1982; Local Government, 1982

[Triennial. Oct. 1983. i+26 p. SRI/MF/complete.]

Covers occupational employment in Federal, State, and local governments. Also includes summary comparisons to U.S., 1972-82; and State and local government employment by county.

Federal employment data are from BLS, as of Oct. 1980; State data are from State Dept of Personnel, as of May 1982; and local data are based on responses from 55 local government units to a mail survey covering payroll period including May 12, 1982.

For description of previous report, presenting data for 1977 or 1979, see SRI 1981 Annual, under S5205-2.3.

S5205–2.8: New Hampshire Staffing Patterns in Wholesale and Retail Trade Industries, 1982

[Triennial. Oct. 1983. i+65 p. SRI/MF/complete.]

Covers occupational employment in the following:

a. Wholesale trade, including durable and nondurable goods.

b. Retail trade, including building materials/hardware/garden supply/mobile home dealers; general merchandise stores; food stores; automotive dealers/gasoline service stations; apparel/accessory stores; furniture/home furnishings/equipment stores; eating/drinking places; and miscellaneous.

Data are based on responses of 1,340 establishments with 250 or more employees to mail surveys conducted June-Dec. 1982.

For description of previous report, for 1979, see SRI 1981 Annual, under S5205-2.5.

S5205–3   ANNUAL PLANNING INFORMATION, New Hampshire, FY85

Annual. June 1984.
4+146 p.
LC 78-646549.
SRI/MF/complete

Annual planning report, for FY85, identifying New Hampshire population groups most in need of employment services, and presenting data on employment by industry and occupation through 1991. Also includes data on population and labor force by county, selected years 1980-85. Data are compiled from various State and Federal sources.

Contains 2 maps and contents listing (3 p.); narrative analysis, with 11 summary tables (p. 1-14); glossary (p. 15-19); and appendix, with table listing, and 29 detailed tables listed below (p. 20-146).

Separate county reports are also available from issuing agency, but are not covered in SRI.

Availability: New Hampshire Department of Employment Security, Economic Analysis and Reports Section, 32 S. Main St., Concord NH 03301, †; SRI/MF/complete.

APPENDIX TABLES:

[Unless otherwise noted, data are for New Hampshire, 1985 or FY85, and are shown by county. Data by industry are generally shown by manufacturing major industry group, non-manufacturing industry division, and government by level.]

S5205–3.1: Population, Labor Force, Employment, Unemployment, and Personal Income

POPULATION

1. Population by sex and minority status [including black, American Indian, Asian, and Hispanic], July 1985. (p. 22)

2. Population estimates for youth [by age group, by sex], with percent distribution. (p. 23)

3-4. Population characteristics by age, sex, and racial status, 1980 and 1985; and population estimated by age, July 1985. (p. 24-36)

LABOR FORCE

5. Population, labor force, and labor force participation rate, by age and sex, 1980 and 1985. (p. 37-47)

UNEMPLOYMENT, EMPLOYMENT, AND WAGES

6. Total unemployment and labor force and percent of labor force unemployed, by sex. (p. 49)

7. Total number of different individuals unemployed during [the year] and the average number of long-term unemployed, by sex. (p. 50)

8. Nonagricultural wage/salary average annual employment (percentage distribution) by industrial division, New Hampshire and U.S. [only, 1980-83]. (p. 51)

9. Estimated nonagricultural employment in New Hampshire, and Manchester and Nashua labor market areas [only], 1983 preliminary revised (excluding the self-employed, domestic service workers, and persons on strike)[by industry, by month]. (p. 52)

10. Number of units, average employment, total wages, and percent changes (workers covered by unemployment compensation in private industry)[by industry], 1980-82. (p. 55-67)

11. Average employment, and total and average weekly wages, classified by industry, 3rd quarter 1983. (p. 68-92)

12-13. Employment changes and average weekly wages [also includes 2 labor market areas and New Hampshire portion of Lawrence-Haverhill SMSA], 3rd quarter 1983 and percent change from 1982. (p. 93-94)

DISADVANTAGED, VETERANS, AND JOB SERVICES

14. Number of persons employed part-time for economic reasons [by sex]. (p. 95)

15. Estimated all poor persons, those 18 years old/over, [those 65 years/older], black, and Hispanic [no date]. (p. 96)

16-17. Persons receiving welfare assistance [AFDC, foster care children, persons age 65/older, and disabled/blind], 1983, and Jan. 1984. (p. 97-98)

18. Estimated civilian labor force status of [total and Vietnam era] veterans. (p. 99)

19. Placements as a percent of applicants available by selected applicant characteristics [female, eligible claimants, handicapped, minority, total and Vietnam era veterans, and age group], Oct. 1, 1983- Apr. 30, 1984. (p. 100)

20. Active applicants [by sex and age group, and for veterans, minority, poor, and handicapped, all by occupational classification], as of Mar. 31, 1984. (p. 101-112)

INSURED UNEMPLOYED

21-22. Exhaustees: by weekly benefit amount [and totals, by sex], 1st quarter 1984. (p. 113-125)

23-25. [Insured unemployed, by selected industry division, occupation, weeks of current unemployment, sex, and age, shown for State, Hillsborough County, and balance of State only], Apr. 1984. (p. 126-128)

PERSONAL INCOME

26. Total and per capita personal income for the U.S. and [6] States in New England, 1980-82. (p. 129)

27. Percent change of personal income by major industrial division in the U.S. and [6] New England States, 1981-82. (p. 130)

PROJECTED EMPLOYMENT

28. Occupations projected to 1991 [employment 1981, 1985, and 1991; and average annual job openings due to growth and replacement needs, and annual growth rate, 1981-91 period; all by detailed occupation, State only]. (p. 131-145)

29. Occupations with the largest number of employees, 1991, and with the largest percentage employment increase, 1981-91 [State only]. (p. 146)

S5215   NEW HAMPSHIRE
Department of
Health and Welfare

**S5215-1   VITAL STATISTICS REPORT
for the State of New
Hampshire, 1983**
Annual.   July 1984.   34 p.
ISSN 0270-3378.
LC SN 80-8221.
SRI/MF/complete

Annual report on New Hampshire vital statistics, covering population, births, deaths by cause, and marriages and divorces, 1983, with selected trends from 1950. Data are shown variously by age, sex, county, and town, and are from Census Bureau and State records.

Contains contents listing (1 p.); introduction (p. 1); report in 4 sections, with narrative summaries, 4 maps, 3 charts, and 33 tables listed below (p. 2-31); appendix, with definitions and rate formulas (p. 32-33); and index (inside back cover).

Availability: New Hampshire Department of Health and Welfare, Vital Records/Health Statistics Bureau, Public Health Services Division, Health and Welfare Bldg., Hazen Dr., Concord NH 03301, †; SRI/MF/complete.

TABLES:
[Unless otherwise noted, data are for New Hampshire, 1983.]

S5215-1.1: Summary, Population, and Natality

SUMMARY

1. Summary vital statistics [occurrence- and residence-based numbers and rates]. (p. 2)

2. 14-year vital events summary: numbers and rate, 1970-83. (p. 3)

POPULATION

3. Population change [natural increase and in-migration, selected periods] 1950-83. (p. 4)

4. Population, percent change and density, by county, [decennially] 1960-80 and 1983. (p. 5)

5-6. Number and percent distribution of the population by age, 1980 and 1983; and projections of the resident population by age and sex, 1990 and 2000. (p. 6)

7. Population, [resident] births and deaths [by sex], and marriages, by county and town; and divorces by county. (p. 7-10)

NATALITY

[Tables 8-15 present resident data only.]

8. Number of [live births] and number per 1,000 births according to age of mother, 1979-83. (p. 11)

9-11. Number and percent: live births with no or late prenatal care, low birth weight births, and out-of-wedlock births, by county, 1979-83. (p. 12-13)

12. Number and percent, teen-mother births according to marital status, by county. (p. 13)

13. Number and percent, home births and hospital births, 1979-83. (p. 13)

14. Live births according to selected characteristics [sex, 1st born, plural birth, under 2,500 grams, complication of pregnancy/labor/birth, mother under age 20, no prenatal care, and born in hospital], by county and town of mother's residence. (p. 14)

15. Live births according to county of mother's residence, by hospital and other places of birth. (p. 18)

16. Occurrences of live births; and fetal, neonatal, and infant deaths; by hospital and other places of occurrence. (p. 18)

S5215-1.2: Mortality, Marriages, and Divorces

MORTALITY

[Tables 17-28 present resident data only.]

17. Death rates for the 10 leading causes of death and percent change, 1982-83 [with comparison to U.S., 1983]. (p. 20)

18. Leading cause of death in age group, by sex. (p. 20)

19-21. Death rates for heart and cerebrovascular disease, and cancer, by county, 1979-83. (p. 21-22)

22. Deaths due to cancer according to selected sites of malignancy, by sex. (p. 22)

23. Type of accidental deaths, by sex. (p. 23)

24. Death rates for motor vehicle and all other accidents, by county, 1979-83. (p. 23)

25. Number of deaths for 25 selected causes of death with ICD9 [International Classification of Diseases, 9th Revision] code number, by county and selected locations. (p. 24)

26. Fetal, early neonatal, perinatal, neonatal, and infant deaths [and] rates, by county. (p. 27)

27. Number of infant deaths, by sex; and number according to age: by county. (p. 28)

28. Causes of infant deaths, by sex according to age. (p. 28)

MARRIAGE AND DIVORCE

29. Age of bride by age of groom, marriage occurrences. (p. 30)

30. Education of bride by education of groom, marriage occurrences. (p. 30)

31. Number of marriage for bride by number of marriage for groom, marriage occurrences. (p. 31)

32. Number of divorces and number involving minor children, with number of minors, by county. (p. 31)

33. Award of physical custody of minor children in uncontested and contested cases of physical custody awards, divorce occurrences. (p. 31)

S5227   NEW HAMPSHIRE
State Library

**S5227-1   NEW HAMPSHIRE LIBRARY
STATISTICS, Jan.-Dec. 1982**
Annual.   [1983.]
24 p. no paging.
LC 64-63685.
SRI/MF/complete

Annual report, for 1982, on New Hampshire public, college, and State libraries, including finances and holdings, by city and institution.

Contents:

a. Summary statistics, with 3 tables showing public, college, and State library holdings, circulation, and expenditures, 1981-82. (2 p.)

b. Public library statistics, with 1 detailed table showing the following, by city and library, arranged by population size group: population served; circulation, by type of material; books borrowed by bookmobiles and central library from State library; weekly hours open; total volumes, and adult and juvenile volumes added; city appropriations and total receipts; and expenditures including detail for salaries and books; 1982. (18 p.)

c. College and State library statistics, with 1 table showing the following: total operating expenditures, salaries/wages, and expenditures for books/binding; and volumes added, periodicals received, and total volumes; by college (also shows enrollment), fall 1982, and for State library, FY83. (2 p.)

d. List of towns with no/inactive public library, and population. (1 p.)

Availability: New Hampshire State Library, 20 Park St., Concord NH 03301, $2.00; SRI/MF/complete.

S5250   NEW HAMPSHIRE
Department of
Safety

**S5250-2   CRIME IN NEW
HAMPSHIRE, 1983**
Annual.   July 31, 1984.
2+43 p.
ISSN 0731-745X.
LC 82-641382.
SRI/MF/complete

Annual report on New Hampshire crimes, arrests, and clearances, by type of offense, 1983, with trends from 1978. Also covers assaults on police officers, domestic violence, and value of property stolen and recovered. Includes offenses by county and reporting agency, and arrests by offender age, race, and sex.

Data were compiled from local law enforcement agency reports under the State Uniform Crime Reporting Program.

Contains index (1 p.); and 22 charts and 35 tables, described below (p. 1-43).

This is the 7th annual report.

Availability: New Hampshire Department of Safety, State Police Division, Concord NH 03301, †; SRI/MF/complete.

CHARTS AND TABLES:
[Unless otherwise noted, data are shown for 1983, often with comparisons to 1982. Index crimes are murder, rape, robbery, aggravated assault, burglary, larceny, motor vehicle theft, and arson.]

S5250–2.1: State Data

INDEX CRIMES

[In addition to the data described below, each Index crime section includes 1 monthly trend chart, and 2 tables showing offenses and clearances, and offenders by age.]

a. Summary: total Index offenses, 1978-83; number and rate of offenses, and percent cleared, by Index crime; and crime clocks. 4 charts and 2 tables. (p. 1-4)

b. Murder: offenses by circumstance, weapon used, victim-offender relationship, and age and sex of victim; and offenders by sex. 3 charts and 4 tables. (p. 5-6)

c. Rape: forcible and attempted rapes. 1 chart and 3 tables. (p. 7)

d. Robbery: value of property stolen, by type of setting; and offenses, by type of weapon. 3 charts and 2 tables. (p. 8-9)

e. Aggravated assault: offenses, by type of weapon. 1 chart and 3 tables. (p. 10)

f. Burglary: offenses, by type of entry; and value of property stolen, for day and night residence and nonresidence occurrences. 3 charts and 2 tables. (p. 11-12)

g. Larceny: offenses and value of property stolen, by type of larceny. 1 chart and 3 tables. (p. 13-14)

h. Motor vehicle theft: offenses, by type of vehicle; value of vehicles stolen and recovered; and vehicles stolen and recovered locally and elsewhere. 3 charts and 3 tables. (p. 15-16)

i. Arson: offenses and property value, by property type. 1 chart and 3 tables. (p. 17-18)

OFFICERS ASSAULTED, DOMESTIC VIOLENCE, AND STOLEN PROPERTY

j. Law enforcement officers assaulted, and clearance rate, by type of activity; assaults by assignment and time of day; and assaults and injuries by weapon. 2 charts and 4 tables. (p. 19-21)

k. Domestic assaults: by type of weapon and victim-offender relationship. 1 table. (p. 22)

l. Stolen property: value of property stolen and recovered, by property type. 1 table. (p. 23)

S5250–2.2: Local Data, and Arrests

a. Index crimes by offense, by county and reporting agency, including municipal and State police depts and sheriffs' offices. 2 tables. (p. 24-35)

b. Juvenile and adult arrests, by age, type of jurisdiction (local, county, and State), and race (white, Negro, Indian, Chinese, Japanese, and other), all shown by sex for Index and non-Index offenses (including detailed breakdown of drug offenses); and disposition of juvenile arrests. 2 tables. (p. 36-43)

S5350   NEW JERSEY
Department of Agriculture

S5350–1   NEW JERSEY AGRICULTURE, 1983
Annual. Oct. 1983. v+68 p.
Circular 503.
LC 58-63411.
SRI/MF/complete

Annual report on New Jersey agricultural production, finances, and marketing, mostly 1977-82, with some data for 1983 and selected trends from 1965. Data are generally shown by commodity and/or county, with comparisons to selected States and U.S.

Report covers production, prices, sales, value, and, as applicable, acreage and yield or inventory, for field crop, vegetable, fruit and berry, livestock, dairy, poultry, and apiary sectors.

Also includes data on precipitation and average temperature; pasture condition; farm income and production expenses; farms, farm acreage, and value; fertilizer consumption; U.S. potato production and consumption per capita; and agricultural productivity indexes for northeast U.S.

Data are primarily from New Jersey Dept of Agriculture and USDA.

Contains contents listing (p. iv-v); 7 statistical sections, with 10 maps, 9 charts, and 64 tables (p. 1-53); list of issuing agency reports (p. 54); and narrative *Highlights of the Annual Report* (p. 55-68).

This 1983 edition incorporates 2 previous annual reports: *New Jersey Agricultural Statistics,* previously covered in SRI under this number, and *Highlights of the Annual Report, New Jersey Department of Agriculture,* not previously covered in SRI.

Availability: New Jersey Crop Reporting Service, Health and Agriculture Bldg., Rm. 204, CN 330, Trenton NJ 08625-0330, $5.00; SRI/MF/complete.

S5355   NEW JERSEY
Department of Banking

S5355–1   STATE OF NEW JERSEY, COMMISSIONER OF BANKING, Annual Report, 1983
Annual. July 12, 1984.
xiii+200 p.
ISSN 0098-8073.
LC 76-644048.
SRI/MF/complete

Annual report on assets and liabilities of New Jersey State-chartered commercial and savings banks, credit unions, insurance premium finance companies, pawnbrokers, secondary mortgage and small loan companies, and savings and loan assns, by institution, as of Dec. 31, 1983.

Also includes data on national bank assets and liabilities; other licensed financial institutions by type; savings and loan assn aggregate membership, deposits, and loan closings by type, by county; asset and deposit rankings for savings and loan assns; consumer complaints by nature and type of institution; State cemetery board trust fund balances, and licensed cemeteries by county; and selected summary trends from 1900.

Contains contents listing and Banking Dept activities, including organizational chart (p. iv-xiii); division reports, with text statistics and 40 tables (p. 1-195); and amendments to State financial statutes (p. 198-200).

Availability: New Jersey Department of Banking, Savings and Loan Associations Division, CN 040, Trenton NJ 08625, $10.00; SRI/MF/complete.

S5375   NEW JERSEY
Administrative Office of the Courts

S5375–1   1983 ANNUAL REPORT, NEW JERSEY JUDICIARY, Sept. 1, 1982-Aug. 31, 1983
Annual. Mar. 16, 1984.
102 p.
LC 81-643674.
SRI/MF/complete, current & previous year reports

Annual report, for court year ended Aug. 31, 1983, on New Jersey judicial system, including trial and appellate court caseloads and case dispositions. Covers supreme, superior, juvenile and domestic relations, county district, tax, and municipal courts. Includes trial court data by case type and county, with comparisons to 1982 and selected trends from 1973.

Case types shown are criminal and civil for all courts, with some additional detail for traffic and small claims cases.

Also includes data on judges and probation dept activities.

Contains contents listing (1 p.); and report, with 45 charts and 70 tables (p. 3-102).

Previous report, for court year ended Aug. 31, 1982, was also reviewed in 1984 and is also available on SRI microfiche, under this number [Annual. 1983. 4+97 p. †].

Prior to report for court year ended Aug. 31, 1982, report consisted of a narrative analysis and a statistical supplement; only the statistical supplements were described in SRI.

Availability: New Jersey Administrative Office of the Courts, State House Annex, CN 037, Trenton NJ 08625, †; SRI/MF/complete.

S5385   NEW JERSEY
Department of
Education

S5385-1   VITAL EDUCATIONAL
STATISTICS, 1982/83, New
Jersey
Annual. For individual
publication data, see below.
LC 79-644249.
SRI/MF/complete

Annual report on New Jersey elementary and
secondary education for the 1982/83 school
year, with summary trends from 1978/79. Covers public school students, staff, and facilities, by
county. Data are compiled from reports of individual school districts.

Report is published in 2 volumes. Vol. I, covering students and facilities, is described in SRI
1983 Annual, under S5385-1.1. Vol. II, covering
staff, is described below.

This is the 9th edition of the report. Issuing
agency also publishes an additional annual report
with detailed breakdowns on enrollments and
dropouts by race/ethnicity, sex, county, and district; report is not covered by SRI.

Availability: New Jersey Department of Education, Information Services and Support Office,
225 W. State St., CN 500, Trenton NJ 08625, †;
SRI/MF/complete.

VOLUME:

[Most tables show data for public schools by
county, as of Sept. 30, 1982. Data by racial/
ethnic origin are usually for black, white, Hispanic, American Indian/Alaskan Native, and
Asian/Pacific Islander.]

S5385-1.2: Volume II

[Annual. July 1983. vi+39 p. PTM No.
300.79. SRI/MF/complete.]

Contains contents and table listing (p. v-vi);
introduction with 2 tables showing trends in
staff characteristics, 1978/79-1982/83 (p. 1-
2); 2 sections with summary analysis and comparisons to 1977/78, and 23 tables listed below
(p. 3-33); and glossary and appendix with sample data collection forms (p. 34-39).

Previous report, for 1981/82, is described in
SRI 1982 Annual, under this number.

TABLES:

CERTIFICATED STAFF

[Data by major assignment category are for
administrators/supervisors, classroom teachers, and educational support services.]

I. Full-time and part-time staff employed by
major assignment category. (p. 9)

II-IV. Full-time and part-time certificated
staff assigned to elementary school, secondary
school, and system-wide positions, by type of
position; and to elementary and secondary
schools, by major position assignment category. (p. 10-12)

V-VII. Sex, highest degree held, and certificate held by administrators/supervisors, classroom teachers, and educational support
services personnel employed. (p. 13-15)

VIII-X. Racial/ethnic distribution of full-time
administrators/supervisors, classroom teachers, and educational support services personnel employed in school districts. (p. 16-18)

XI-XVI. Age distribution and total educational experience of administrators/supervisors,
classroom teachers, and educational support
services personnel in school districts. (p. 19-
24)

XVII. Certificated personnel entering and
leaving, by [major assignment category] during
the period Oct. 1, 1981-Sept. 30, 1982. (p. 25)

XVIII-XX. Number of full-time classroom
teachers employed, beginning and reentering,
and separations, by position (subject). (p. 26-
28)

NONCERTIFICATED STAFF

XXI. FTE assignments of full-time noncertificated personnel employed, by support service program areas. (p. 31)

XXII. Racial/ethnic distribution and sex of
full-time noncertificated support services personnel. (p. 32)

XXIII. FTE assignments of all noncertificated
personnel employed, by support service program areas. (p. 33)

S5385-2   NEW JERSEY PUBLIC
LIBRARY STATISTICS for
1982
Annual. Nov. 1983.
41 p.+errata sheet.
SRI/MF/complete

Annual report on New Jersey public library operations, 1982. Covers population served, finances,
holdings, staff, and circulation, by county and
library. Data are from annual library reports.

Contains contents listing (1 p.); introduction
and definitions (p. 1-4); 8 tables, described below
(p. 5-39); and staff directories (p. 40 and inside
back cover).

Availability: New Jersey Department of Education, State Library Division, 185 W. State St.,
CN 520, Trenton NJ 08625-0520, †; SRI/MF/
complete.

TABLES:

a. Per capita library expenditures, by county,
1982, with county rankings from 1977; and
selected State summary data. 6 tables. (p. 5-
11)

b. By county and institution: population served;
equalized property valuation; income (total,
and from local taxes and State aid); expenditures (total, and for salary/wage and materials); staff; volumes owned and added;
circulation; periodical subscriptions; and
weekly hours open; 1982. 2 tables. (p. 13-39)

S5410   NEW JERSEY
Department of
Higher Education

S5410-1   DATA BRIEF SERIES
Series. For individual
publication data, see below.
SRI/MF/complete

Continuing series of reports, each presenting
data on a selected aspect of New Jersey higher
education. Topics include enrollment, tuition
and fees, degrees, and student characteristics;
most topics are covered annually. Data generally
are shown by institution, including public colleges and universities, community colleges, and
independent colleges.

Data are compiled from Higher Education
General Information Survey reports.

Reports reviewed during 1984 are described
below.

Availability: New Jersey Department of Higher Education, Research and Manpower Office,
225 W. State St., CN 542, Trenton NJ 08625, ‡;
SRI/MF/complete.

S5410-1.3: Tuition and Required Fees,
New Jersey Colleges and Universities,
1977/78-1983/84

[Annual. Dec. 1983. ii+20+App 16 p.
ORM Vol. 4, Brief No. 1. SRI/MF/com-
plete.]

Annual report on New Jersey higher education
tuition/fees by student category, by institution
and institution type, academic years 1977/78-
1983/84. Student categories include graduate
and undergraduate, full- and part-time, and
resident and nonresident.

Also includes data on tuition as percent of
educational costs, and maximum allowable tuition aid grants.

Contains listings of contents, charts, and tables (2 p.); introduction and summary (p. 1-3);
narrative analysis, with 3 charts and 9 tables
(p. 3-20); and statistical appendix, with 16 tables (16 p.).

S5410-1.4: Enrollment in New Jersey Col-
leges and Universities, Fall 1983 Compared to Fall 1982

[Annual. Feb. 1, 1984. 8 p. no paging. SRI/
MF/complete.]

Annual tables on New Jersey higher education
enrollment by student category, by institution
and institution type, fall 1982-83. Student
categories are full- and part-time undergraduate and graduate/professional.

Includes 6 tables.

SRI coverage of this report begins with this
edition.

S5415   NEW JERSEY
Department of
Human Services

S5415-1   PUBLIC WELFARE STATISTICS, New Jersey
Monthly, with annual summary. Approx. 20 p. var. paging.
SRI/MF/complete, shipped quarterly

Monthly report, with annual summary, on New Jersey public welfare programs, including cases, recipients, payments, and case processing, by program and county or municipality. Covers AFDC, general assistance, State medical assistance for the aged, food stamps, emergency assistance, and child support and paternity programs.

Report is issued 6-10 months after cover date.

Issues generally contain contents listing; 18 monthly tables; and brief narrative with text statistics on State medical assistance for the aged.

Monthly tables are listed below and generally appear in all issues; occasionally selected data are unavailable at time of publication, and affected tables are issued as addenda at a later date. Annual summary is described, as it appears, under "Statistical Features."

Availability: New Jersey Department of Human Services, Public Welfare Division, Six Quakerbridge Plaza, CN 716, Trenton NJ 08625, †; SRI/MF/complete, shipped quarterly.

Issues reviewed during 1984: May-Nov. 1983 (D); and annual summaries for FY82-83.

MONTHLY TABLES:
[Tables [1-3] show data for month of coverage, previous month, and same month of previous year; all other tables show data for month of coverage only. All tables except tables [1-3] and II.D-II.G show data by county.]

SUMMARY
[1-3] Public assistance, AFDC, and general assistance programs [including applications processed, cases closed, recipient cases and persons, and expenditures].

AFDC
[Tables show total cases; adults, children, and total persons; and payments.]

I.A-I.D. AFDC program, statistical summary: all segments [also includes applications processed and cases closed]; and C, F, and N segments.

ASSISTANCE AND FOOD STAMP PROGRAMS
II.A-II.F. Statistical summary for general assistance program, [total and] employable and unemployable segments: [by county and] for 21 municipalities; [variously showing applications processed; cases approved, closed, and aided; and persons aided and assistance commitments, with detail for maintenance and hospital assistance].

II.G. Statistical summary for general assistance employment program (GAEP), for 21 municipalities [employable and unemployable recipients; and employable recipient referrals and case dispositions, including terminations by reason; not included in every issue].

III.A-III.B. Food stamp program: participating households; and persons participating, coupons issued, and average per person participating.

IV. Statistical summary for emergency assistance program [federally and nonfederally matchable and total cases, persons, and expenditures].

CHILD SUPPORT
V. Child support and paternity account [collections and distribution].

STATISTICAL FEATURES:

S5415-1.501: May 1983
ANNUAL REPORT, FY82
(10 p.) Annual report, for FY82, summarizing New Jersey welfare program finances and caseloads, with comparative data for FY80-81.

Report for FY82 is similar to report for FY83 described under S5415-1.502 below, but also includes data on Indo-Chinese refugee program. Report for FY81 is described in SRI 1982 Annual, under S5415-1.301.

S5415-1.502: Sept. 1983
ANNUAL REPORT, FY83
(10 p.) Annual report, for FY83, summarizing New Jersey welfare program finances and caseloads, with comparative data for FY81-82. Includes 5 exhibits showing the following:

1. Selected statistics, public assistance programs [gross expenditures; and average monthly cases, recipients, and grants per case and recipient; for assistance to SSI recipients, emergency assistance, 3 AFDC program segments, public and nonpublic assistance food stamps, general assistance, Cuban/Haitian entrant program, refugee resettlement, and home energy assistance], FY81-83.

2. Statistical summary: "Medicaid only" assistance to aged, blind, and disabled; AFDC; "Medicaid only" institutional program; and [State] medical assistance for the aged; [application and caseload activity], FY83.

3. Summary of financial transactions [Federal, State, and county share of net assistance, social services, and administrative expenditures, and of reimbursements, for most programs listed in exhibit 1], FY83.

4. General assistance program statistical and financial summary [caseload activity, average monthly grants, and municipal and State shares of assistance and administrative expenditures], FY83.

5. Child support and paternity program, AFDC: comparison of collections, distribution, and administrative expenditures, FY81-83.

S5420   NEW JERSEY
Department of
Insurance

S5420-1   STATE OF NEW JERSEY, ANNUAL REPORT OF THE COMMISSIONER OF INSURANCE for the Year Ending Dec. 31, 1982
Annual. Mar. 1, 1983.
195 p.
LC 73-640312.
SRI/MF/complete

Annual report on New Jersey insurance industry financial condition and underwriting activity, by company and type of insurance, 1982, with summary comparisons to 1981. Covers premiums written, received, or earned; losses incurred; assets and liabilities; capital and/or surplus; gain from underwriting and investments; loss and underwriting expense ratios; insurance in force; income and disbursements; and claims or benefits paid, and claims outstanding; for New Jersey-based, other U.S., and non-U.S. companies.

Data are shown, as applicable, for fire/casualty and life insurance companies; fraternal benefit societies; hospital, medical, and dental service corporations; title insurance and mortgage guaranty companies; and 1 investment assn.

Data on fire/casualty insurance include additional detail by line of coverage, including medical malpractice, workers compensation, automobile, credit, and surety; and policyholders' surplus for surplus lines insurers.

Data are compiled from annual statements submitted by individual insurers.

Contains contents and table listing (p. 3-6); Insurance Dept summary, with lists of company status changes, and 1 summary table (p. 7-24); and 16 financial tables, interspersed with company directories (p. 26-195).

Availability: New Jersey Department of Insurance, Financial Examination Division, 201 E. State St., CN-325, Trenton NJ 08625, †; SRI/MF/complete.

S5425   NEW JERSEY
Department of
Labor

S5425-1   NEW JERSEY ECONOMIC INDICATORS
Monthly. Approx. 40 p.
ISSN 0098-227X.
LC 75-640647.
SRI/MF/complete, shipped quarterly

Monthly report reviewing selected New Jersey economic indicators, including employment, earnings, business and construction activity, retail sales, and unemployment claims.

Data are from the State Dept of Labor, BLS, and other Federal or private sector sources. Month of coverage is 1-4 months prior to month of publication.

Contents:

a. Article reviewing economic situation in U.S. and in New Jersey for the month of coverage, with 1 table and generally 12 charts.

b. Articles on aspects of New Jersey economy, often with statistics, including annual features on economic trends, employment, and personal income.

c. Statistical section with 13 tables showing 4-year data for 39 indicator series by month, with accompanying charts showing trends from 1960s; and 11 tables showing employment and earnings data by detailed industry sector, and summary indicators.

Monthly statistical section tables are listed below; most appear in all issues. All additional features with substantial statistics pertaining to New Jersey are described, as they appear, under "Statistical Features." Nonstatistical contents, and Federal data not pertaining specifically to New Jersey, are not covered.

Availability: New Jersey Department of Labor, Planning and Research Division, Publications Office, CN 056, Trenton NJ 08625-0056, †; SRI/MF/complete, shipped quarterly.

Issues reviewed during 1984: Nov. 4, 1983-Oct. 26, 1984 (P) (Nos. 232-243).

MONTHLY TABLES:

LONG-TERM INDICATORS, BY MONTH
[Tables I-II show seasonally adjusted official BLS data and "unofficial" data prepared by State analysts from a combination of sources. Most other tables show seasonally adjusted and unadjusted data.

Data are shown monthly, usually for current year through month of coverage, and for preceding 3 years.]

I-II. Resident labor force indicators [labor force and participation rate; employment and ratio to population; and unemployment and rate].

III-IV. Establishment employment indicators [nonfarm, private and public sectors, manufacturing, construction, and service employment].

V. Production workers indicators [manufacturing employment, and weekly hours and manhours].

VI. Earnings and price indicators [weekly earnings of production workers, urban CPI for U.S. and NYC and Philadelphia metro areas, and net spendable earnings of manufacturing workers].

VII. General business indicators [new business incorporations and business failures; failures shown through July 1982 only].

VIII-IX. Construction contracts and residential building permits indicators, [by type].

X. Trade indicators [retail sales and passenger car registrations].

XI. Labor market indicators [nonfarm job openings and placements, and unemployment insurance average weeks claimed].

XII-XIII. Unemployment insurance claimants indicators [insured unemployment rate, initial claims weekly average, insurance exhaustions; and unemployment in manufacturing, construction, and service industries].

EMPLOYMENT AND EARNINGS, BY INDUSTRY
[Tables [1] and [3-5] show data monthly for month of coverage and 12 preceding months, by SIC 2- and 3-digit industries in New Jersey.]

[1] Nonfarm payroll employment.

[2] Nonfarm payroll workers by major industries [annually for approximately 25 years].

[3-4] Average weekly gross dollar earnings and hours of production workers.

[5] Average hourly gross dollar earnings of production workers.

SUMMARY TABLES
[Tables [6-8] show data for month of coverage, previous month, and same month of previous year.]

[6] Labor force data [by employment status].

[7] Unemployment insurance claims [by program].

[8] Characteristics of insured unemployed [sex, race and ethnic group, industry of previous employment, age, and duration of unemployment].

[9] Residential construction authorized by building permits [units and value; month of coverage, previous month, and current and previous year to date].

[10] Official BLS sample estimates, standard errors, and coefficients of variation [for resident employment, unemployment, and unemployment rate, monthly for current year through month of coverage, and for preceding 1-3 years].

[11] Comparative U.S. and New Jersey civilian labor force trends [by employment status, annually for previous 5-6 years, and monthly for current year through month of coverage and for preceding 2 years].

STATISTICAL FEATURES:

S5425–1.501: Nov. 4, 1983 (No. 232)

TAX WITHHOLDING REDUCTION CHANGES SPENDABLE EARNINGS FORMULA

(p. 6-7) By C. Ronald Parker. Article on New Jersey Dept of Labor calculations for determining spendable earnings of manufacturing production workers (as reported in monthly table VI).

Includes 1 table showing average gross weekly earnings, and unadjusted and CPI-adjusted net earnings for workers with no dependents and with 3 dependents, Jan. 1981-July 1983, with net earnings shown before and after adjustment for tax cut of July 1983.

COMMUTING TO WORK: 1980

(p. 8-12) By Connie O. Hughes. Article on commuting patterns of New Jersey workers. Data are from 1970 Census of Population and 1980 Census of Population Summary Tape File 4.

Includes 3 tables showing New Jersey workers by residence county, and by workplace county, SMSA, or neighboring State, 1980 with summary comparisons to 1970.

S5425–1.502: Dec. 9, 1983 (No. 233)

POPULATION ESTIMATES FOR NEW JERSEY COUNTIES AND MUNICIPALITIES, JULY 1, 1982, ANNUAL FEATURE

(p. 6-10) Annual article, by Alfred Toizer and Scott Campbell Brown, analyzing New Jersey population trends. Includes 5 tables showing New Jersey population by county and municipality; and population change due to natural increment and migration, and population aged 65 and over, by county; generally for 1970, 1980, and 1982.

Data for 1982 are New Jersey Labor Dept estimates. Other data are census counts.

COVERED EMPLOYMENT WAGES IN 1982, ANNUAL FEATURE

(p. 11-13) Annual article, by Robert Vaden, with 2 tables showing average wage of New Jersey employees covered by unemployment insurance, by industry division, and by county for employees working in the private sector, 1981-82.

Data are from reports submitted by employers covered by State and Federal unemployment insurance programs.

S5425–1.503: Jan. 6, 1984 (No. 234)

ANNUAL STATEMENT OF THE ECONOMIC POLICY COUNCIL, ANNUAL FEATURE

(p. 6-15) Annual article analyzing economic conditions and outlook for New Jersey and U.S., 1981-84.

Includes 9 tables showing selected U.S. and New Jersey indicators, including total labor force and employment; nonagricultural employment by industry division; unemployment rate by sex, race, and age group; personal income; and retail sales and car registrations (State only); various periods 1981-84.

S5425–1.504: Feb. 10, 1984 (No. 235)

HOUSEHOLD FORMATION IN NEW JERSEY: 1970 TO 1980

(p. 7-11) By Connie O. Hughes. Article, with 4 tables showing New Jersey households by size and composition; population 15 years and over, by sex by marital status; and families by composition including presence of children; 1970 and 1980.

Data are from the Census Bureau.

S5425–1.505: Mar. 9, 1984 (No. 236)

BUSINESS 'BIRTHS' LONG-RUN EMPLOYMENT IMPACT

(p. 4-9) By Robert Vaden. Article on New Jersey new business establishments' survival and employment. Data are from employer reports filed with the New Jersey Dept of Labor.

Includes 4 tables showing the following for businesses established in 1975-76: employment and number of units, annually through 1982; average employment per unit, with comparison to all firms, 1982; and number of new units, and number still operating in 1982; all by industry division.

N.J.'s UNEMPLOYMENT RATE RANKS 37th IN U.S.

(p. 10) Brief article, with 1 table showing unemployment rate for New Jersey and total U.S., and New Jersey's rank among the States, 1979-83.

S5425–1.506: Apr. 6, 1984 (No. 237)

EDUCATIONAL ATTAINMENT IN NEW JERSEY, 1970-80

(p. 4-9) By Connie O. Hughes. Article, with 6 tables showing New Jersey population and years of school completed, by sex and race, 1970 and 1980; population and number of high school and college graduates by county, and percent of population graduating from high school and college by age by sex, 1980; and summary comparisons to U.S. and 2 adjacent States, various years 1940-80.

Data are from Census Bureau.

NONAGRICULTURAL EMPLOYMENT ESTIMATES REVISED TO A 1983 BENCHMARK, ANNUAL FEATURE

(p. 10-13) Annual article, by Waldemar Falk, presenting revised 1983 New Jersey monthly employment and labor force benchmarks. Includes 3 tables showing original and revised monthly nonfarm employment, 1982-83; and estimated and benchmark employment, by State labor area and by industry division and manufacturing industry group, Mar. 1983.

S5425-1.507: May 23, 1984 (No. 238)

N.J. RANKS THIRD IN PER CAPITA INCOME, ANNUAL FEATURE

(p. 7) Annual article, with 1 table showing per capita personal income, for U.S., mideastern region, and New Jersey and 5 neighboring States, with national ranking for most locations, 1983 with percent change from 1982. Data are from Commerce Dept.

S5425-1.508: June 20, 1984 (No. 239)

1982 PERSONAL INCOME FOR NEW JERSEY AND COUNTIES, ANNUAL FEATURE

(p. 6-7) Annual article, by Roger Linder, with 1 table showing New Jersey total and per capita personal income, by county, with comparison to total U.S., 1981-82. Data are from Commerce Dept.

S5425-1.509: July 27, 1984 (No. 240)

ESTIMATES OF NEW JERSEY'S POPULATION, BY AGE: JULY 1, 1983, ANNUAL FEATURE

(p. 6) Annual article, by Frederick W. Hollmann, with 1 table showing New Jersey population by age group, Apr. 1, 1980 and July 1, 1982-83, with comparisons to U.S. population. Data are from Census Bureau.

S5425-1.510: Sept. 28, 1984 (No. 242)

POPULATION ESTIMATES FOR NEW JERSEY COUNTIES AND MUNICIPALITIES, JULY 1, 1983, ANNUAL FEATURE

(p. 6-11) Annual article, by Alfred Toizer, analyzing New Jersey population trends. Includes 5 tables showing population by county and municipality; and population change due to natural increment and migration, and population aged 65/over, by county; generally for 1970, 1980, and 1983.

Data for 1983 are New Jersey Labor Dept estimates. Other data are census counts.

For description of previous article, for 1982, see S5425-1.502, above.

ECONOMIC BRIEF: 1983 STATE PER CAPITA PERSONAL INCOME

(p. 12-13) Article, with 1 table showing per capita personal income by region and State, 1983, with rankings and change from 1979. Data are from the U.S. Commerce Dept.

S5425-1.511: Oct. 26, 1984 (No. 243)

COVERED EMPLOYMENT WAGES IN 1983, ANNUAL FEATURE

(p. 6-7) Annual article, by William Saley, with 3 tables showing average wage of New Jersey employees covered by unemployment insurance, by industry division and by county, for employees working in the private sector, with selected comparisons to U.S., 1982-83.

Most data are from reports submitted by employers covered by State and Federal unemployment insurance programs.

For description of previous article, for 1982, see S5425-1.502 above.

S5425-3   NEW JERSEY RESIDENTIAL BUILDING PERMITS, 1983 Summary
Annual. Aug. 1984. 38 p.
SRI/MF/complete

Annual report on construction and demolition of residential units authorized by New Jersey building permits, including estimated costs for new construction and additions/alterations, by county and municipality, 1983 with selected trends from 1960.

Data are based on monthly reports submitted by local agencies.

Contains contents listing (1 p.); narrative analysis with text statistics, and 8 tables listed below (p. 1-35); and technical notes (p. 37-38).

Monthly report on permits and construction costs is also available from issuing agency, but is not covered by SRI.

Availability: New Jersey Department of Labor, Planning and Research Division, Demographic and Economic Analysis Office, CN 388, Trenton NJ 08625-0388, †; SRI/MF/complete.

TABLES:
[Most data are shown for units authorized by building permits and by dwelling unit size. Tables I-II and VI include public housing units and estimated residential construction costs (total, new, and additions/alterations).]

I-II. Residential construction [total], 1960-83; and by county, 1983. (p. 2-4)

III. Counties ranked by number of dwelling units authorized [1982-83]. (p. 6)

IV-V. Average construction costs of dwelling units, 1973-83; and housing units authorized for demolition, 1982-83. (p. 7)

VI. Residential construction, by month, 1983. (p. 8)

[A] Conversions [dwelling unit gain or loss due to conversions, by municipality, 1983]. (p. 9-10)

VII. Dwelling units [1983; and number of residential demolitions, 1982-83; by county and municipality]. (p. 13-35)

S5425-4   ANNUAL LABOR MARKET REVIEW, State of New Jersey
Annual, discontinued.

Annual manpower planning report presenting data on New Jersey population, income, labor force, and industry, discontinued with the Apr. 1983 edition (for description, see SRI 1983 Annual, under this number). Report has been discontinued due to lack of funds.

Data for individual State labor market areas are available from New Jersey Department of Labor, Planning and Research Division, CN 056, Trenton NJ 08625-0056.

S5425-7   HOTEL-CASINO EMPLOYEE MIGRATION to the Atlantic City Region
Monograph. Mar. 1982.
iii+22 p.+errata sheet.
SRI/MF/complete

Report on migration of hotel-casino employees to the Atlantic City region. Includes the following data for employees as of Apr. 1981: current county of residence, residence 1 year prior to license application; birthplace; and age, sex, race, type of license held, and year of license application, by migration status.

Prior residence and birthplace data variously include New Jersey counties, U.S. regions and/or States, foreign, and Puerto Rico.

Data are from Casino Control Commission records, and are based on a sample of 2,060 of 25,243 employees.

Contains contents and table listings (p. ii-iii); introduction, highlights, methodology, and analysis (p. 1-6); 13 tables (p. 8-20); and facsimile of data collection form (p. 22).

Availability: New Jersey Department of Labor, Planning and Research Division, Demographic and Economic Analysis Office, CN 388, Trenton NJ 08625-0388, †; SRI/MF/complete.

S5430   NEW JERSEY
Department of
Law and Public Safety

S5430-1   UNIFORM CRIME REPORTS, State of New Jersey, 1983
Annual. [1984.] viii+193 p.
ISSN 0548-5851.
LC 82-643666.
SRI/MF/complete

Annual report on New Jersey crimes and arrests by type of offense, 1983, with trends from 1974. Also includes data on clearances, value of stolen property, law enforcement employment, assaults on police, and domestic violence. Selected data are shown by county, municipality, and college and university campus, and by age, race, and sex.

Data are from reports by State and local law enforcement agencies, submitted under the Uniform Crime Reporting Program to the State Police.

Contains listings of contents, tables, and charts (p. v-viii); explanation of program (p. 2-8); report in 9 sections interspersed with narrative summaries and text statistics, and 20 charts and 54 tables described below (p. 9-190); and glossary and calculations (p. 191-193).

Availability: New Jersey Division of State Police, Uniform Crime Reporting Unit, PO Box 7068, West Trenton NJ 08625, †; SRI/MF/complete.

CHARTS AND TABLES:
[Data are for 1983, with selected comparisons to 1982, unless otherwise noted. Data by race are for white, black, American Indian/Alaskan Native, and Asian/Pacific Islander.

Index (Part I) offenses are murder, rape, robbery, aggravated assault, burglary, larceny-theft, and motor vehicle theft; Part II offenses are less serious crimes. Arson is classified as an Index offense, but data are reported separately and are generally not included in the Crime Index tables.]

S5430–1.1: Index Offenses

SUMMARY

a. Index offense frequency; number of offenses, rate, and clearances, by weapon, method, and other detail; and adult and juvenile clearances; all by offense. 3 charts and 2 tables. (p. 10-14)

b. Value of property stolen and recovered, by property type. 1 table. (p. 15)

c. Trend in number of index offenses, 1979-83; and percent change in offenses for New Jersey, U.S., and northeastern States; all by offense. 2 tables. (p. 16-20)

INDEX OFFENSES

d. Murder: offenses by day of week; by age, sex, and race of victims; and by type of weapon, victim/offender relationship, and circumstance. 4 charts and 1 table. (p. 22-25)

e. Robbery, assault, and burglary: robberies and value of stolen property, by place of occurrence; weapons used in robberies and assaults; and residential and nonresidential burglaries and value of stolen property, by day or night entry. 2 charts and 2 tables. (p. 28-32)

f. Larceny-theft, motor vehicle theft, and arson: type and value of larceny-thefts; motor vehicle thefts by vehicle type, and vehicles stolen and recovered and value; and arson offenses, value of damage, and total and juvenile clearances, by type of property. 2 charts and 4 tables. (p. 34-38)

S5430–1.2: State and County Arrests, and County Offenses

ARRESTS

a. Arrests by Part I and II offenses: total arrests, by age; total and juvenile arrests by sex; and total, adult, and juvenile arrests by race. 7 tables. (p. 40-48)

b. Arrests by county: total, adult, and juvenile arrests by Part I and II offenses, and rates; adult and juvenile arrests by sex and race; and police disposition of juveniles taken into custody. 9 tables. (p. 49-61)

c. Drug abuse arrests, by type of substance. 3 charts. (p. 66-67)

OFFENSES BY COUNTY

[All data are shown by county.]

d. Index offenses by type, total violent and nonviolent crimes, and rates; robberies by place of occurrence; residential and non-residential burglaries, by day or night entry; and larceny offenses, by type. 3 tables. (p. 72-79)

e. Value of property stolen and recovered, by type. 1 table. (p. 80-81)

S5430–1.3: Urban, Rural, University, and Municipal Data

a. Index offenses by university and college institution and campus, and by 7 municipal population size groupings. 2 tables. (p. 94-95)

b. Index offenses and total violent and nonviolent crimes 1979 and 1983, and rates 1982-83, for urban, suburban, and rural areas. 4 tables. (p. 96-99)

c. Index offenses for State and 2 urban population size categories, by type of offense,

1974 and 1983 and total period; and 6 street crimes, aggregate for 15 urban municipalities, 1974-83. 3 tables. (p. 102-106)

d. Municipal profiles: Index offenses (including arson); population, land area, and population density; whether urban, suburban, or rural; and number of police officers by sex, and civilian police employees; all by municipality and county. 1 table. (p. 108-163)

S5430–1.4: Police Employee and Domestic Violence Data

a. Police employment: number of police officers by sex, and civilian employees, for municipal, county, and State, and other police, and by State agency, university and college campus, and county and dept. 1 chart and 5 tables. (p. 166-171)

b. Police assaults: police officers killed 1974-83; police assaulted, by type of weapon, activity, and time of day; and municipal police employed and assaulted, by county. 2 charts and 3 tables. (p. 176-180)

c. Domestic violence: offenses, by county, victim/offender relationship, type of weapon, extent of injury, day of week, time of day, and month; and arrests; with selected detail by type of offense. 3 charts and 4 tables. (p. 184-190)

S5430–2   FATAL MOTOR VEHICLE ACCIDENT Comparative Data Report, 1982, New Jersey State Police

Annual. [1983.] 1+47 p.
LC 75-642363.
SRI/MF/complete

Annual report on New Jersey fatal traffic accidents and fatalities, by accident and vehicle type; accident location and other circumstances; and driver and victim characteristics, including alcohol and drug use; 1982, with trends from 1970s. Includes detailed chronology of fatal accidents for each county.

Also includes summary trends for total and injury accidents, and data on interstate highway mileage.

Data are compiled by the Fatal Accident Unit of the New Jersey State Police.

Contains contents listing (1 p.); and report with 1 chart, 31 tables, and 1 map (p. 1-47).

Previous report, for 1981, is described in SRI 1982 Annual, under this number.

Availability: New Jersey Department of Law and Public Safety, State Police Division, PO Box 7068, West Trenton NJ 08625, †; SRI/MF/complete.

S5455   NEW JERSEY
Department of the Treasury

S5455–1   STATE OF NEW JERSEY ANNUAL FINANCIAL REPORT for the Year Ended June 30, 1983

Annual. Dec. 28, 1983.
194 p.
LC 82-621084.
SRI/MF/complete

Annual report on financial condition of New Jersey State government, presenting assets, liabilities, and fund balances; revenues by source; and expenditures by function; for all, general, special revenue, debt service, capital projects, and trust and agency funds, FY83, with comparisons to FY82 and summary trends from FY74.

Also includes data on long-term debt, projected to 2008; property tax relief, gubernatorial election, and casino control and revenue funds; and appropriations compared to expenditures.

Also presents socioeconomic indicators, including property valuation, population, personal income, labor force by employment status, employment and earnings by industry, employment of top 50 employers, retail sales, new housing value, farm cash receipts, and school enrollments with detail for higher education by selected institution, various years 1972-83.

Data are compiled by the Dept of the Treasury from State, Federal, and private sources.

Contains contents listing (2 p.); introduction with 2 text tables and organizational chart (p. 1-4); financial section, with 32 financial statements, and accompanying notes with 20 text tables (p. 5-168); and statistical and economic data section with narrative and 15 tables (p. 169-194).

Issuing agency also publishes an interim financial report with data for the 1st half of the fiscal year. SRI does not cover the interim report.

Availability: New Jersey Department of the Treasury, Budget and Accounting Division, PO Box 2447, State House, Trenton NJ 08625, †; SRI/MF/complete.

S5455–2   STATE OF NEW JERSEY ANNUAL REPORT OF THE DIVISION OF TAXATION in the Department of the Treasury, for FY83

Annual. [1984.]
xii+444 p.+errata sheet.
LC 51-30726.
SRI/MF/complete

Annual report, for FY83, on sources of New Jersey State revenue, with detailed data on tax rates, assessments, collections, and apportionment to local governments, by type and county. Includes summaries of new tax legislation and history of each current tax, tax court decisions, comparative data on other States' taxes, and revenue trends from as early as 1960.

Contents:

Transmittal letter; and listings of contents, tables, and charts. (p. v-xii)

Chapters I-V. Taxation Division history and summary; processing and administration activities, with text tables; local property and public utility assessment and taxes; audit report, with text data showing financial results of the audits; and report of special procedures and investigations branch, with text data summarizing branch collections, by type of activity. Includes 1 chart and 8 numbered tables. (p. 1-38)

Chapters VI-VII. Sources of revenue administered by the Division, with description, history, and disposition for each current tax, including text data on collection trends, rates, and/or licensing activity; State revenue sharing distribution; and recent tax legislation, court decisions, and attorney general opinions. Includes 13 numbered tables. (p. 39-200)

App. I-IV. Miscellaneous statistics; tax calendars; directories of county boards of taxation and county tax assessors and collectors; and description of distributions to local governments. Includes 16 numbered tables. (p. 201-437)

Index. (p. 439-444)

All numbered tables, chart, and selected text tables with substantial statistical content not described above or covered in the numbered tables, are listed below.

Availability: New Jersey Department of the Treasury, Taxation Division, W. State and Barrack Sts., Trenton NJ 08646, †; SRI/MF/complete.

TABLES AND CHART:
[Data are for FY83, unless otherwise noted.]

S5455–2.1: Text Tables

SUMMARY TRENDS

1. Major State tax collections (net) [by source], FY81-83. (p. 4-5)

2. State and local tax structure [taxes collected by the Division and by the State outside the Division, and administered by counties and municipalities]. (p. 6)

LOCAL PROPERTY AND PUBLIC UTILITY TAXES

Figure 2. Tax dollar [municipal property tax revenues, by type of property taxed and use, 1983]. [chart] (p. 14)

3. Local property tax growth by years [1974-83]. (p. 15)

4. 1982 summary of farm assessment: regular farm (3a) and qualified farm (3b) [by county]. (p. 19)

5. Public utilities gross receipts and franchise taxes collected by the State for distribution to municipalities [for electric, gas, water, sewer, telephone/telegraph, and municipal electric companies, 1983]. (p. 24)

6-7. Summary of exempt property values reported in county abstract of ratables; and summary of local property taxes [by tax type; 1982-83]. (p. 25)

8. Summary of local property: net valuations taxable [by county, 1982-83]. (p. 26)

SOURCES OF REVENUE

[Most of the tables showing tax rates include comparisons to 5-7 other States and selected additional cities.]

9-10. Alcoholic beverage tax rates [for beer, liquor, and wines]; and tax collections and gallonage, FY81-83. (p. 41-42)

11. Cigarette tax rates. (p. 47)

[A] [Cigarette] license fees [licenses issued, and amount, by type of licensee]. (p. 47)

12. New Jersey comparative sales, packs of cigarettes [FY74-83]. (p. 48)

13. Corporation business tax: [rate and basis of tax]. (p. 55)

[B] [State motor fuel tax exempt gallonage and refunds, by use.] (p. 69)

14. Motor fuels tax [rates per gallon of gasoline and diesel]. (p. 71)

15. Motor fuels distributors, jobbers, and dealers license fees [and licenses issued]. (p. 71)

16. Realty transfer fee tax rates. (p. 83)

17. Sales and use tax rates. (p. 88)

18. Sales and use tax exemptions [on 9 items]. (p. 88)

19. State taxes on banks and financial institutions [rate and basis of tax]. (p. 91)

20. Transfer inheritance and estate tax [rates]. (p. 99)

STATE REVENUE SHARING

21. State revenue sharing distribution [municipalities' share, property tax and veteran deductions, and homestead rebate, including number of claims; by county and municipality]. (p. 102-125)

S5455–2.2: Appendix Tables

COMPARATIVE DATA

22. Major State tax rates [by State, for sales, motor fuels, cigarette, and corporate and personal income taxes]. (p. 202)

23. Sales and use tax cash collections, by type of business, 1980-82 (p. 204)

24. Sales tax base and sales and use tax cash collections, by type of business, 1982. (p. 204)

25. State tax collections and property taxes, adjusted for changes in population and in the purchasing power of the dollar [1960-82]. (p. 205)

26. State and local taxes [total, and] as a percentage of personal income, and per capita, by State [with selected rankings], FY81. (p. 206)

27. State and local taxes [total and property taxes, by State], FY81. (p. 208)

CORPORATE TAX RETURNS, TIME LIMITS, AND TAX HISTORY

28-30. Corporation tax returns, [payments, and credit]: by total, net income, and net worth tax liability, 1981. (p. 209-211)

31. Statute of limitations and other time limits. [list] (p. 214-221)

32. Calendar of tax events due dates [by type of tax]. [list] (p. 222)

33. Summary history of taxes [beginning tax rates and changes]. [list] (p. 224-225)

MUNICIPALITY TAX RATES AND ASSESSMENT APPEALS

34. Effective property tax rates by municipality [arranged by county], 1981-83. (p 240-245)

35. Summary of county tax board appeals [number of appeals by property class and filing fee category; dispositions; and value of original assessments, and assessment reductions and increases]; 1982. (p. 250-251)

STATE TAXES FOR COUNTIES AND MUNICIPALITIES

36. Taxes collected by the State for distribution to municipalities [by tax type and municipality, with totals by county], 1983. (p. 276-302)

LOCAL PROPERTY TAX RATES AND EXEMPTIONS

[C] Abstract of ratables and exemptions in the State [by county and municipality, generally including for each: taxable value of land and improvements thereon, partial exemptions, taxable value of machinery/equipment of telephone/telegraph/messenger system companies, general tax rate, true value of Class II railroad property, equalization, apportionment of taxes by general function, miscellaneous revenues for local municipal budget, and deductions allowed for senior citizens and veterans]. (p. 304-407)

37. State equalization table [assessed value of personal and real property, percent by which assessed value of real property should be increased, and true value of real property, by county], 1982. (p. 408)

[D] Compilation of equalized valuation in the State as of Oct. 1, 1983 [aggregate real property assessed valuation and true value, assessed valuation of Class II railroad and all personal property, and equalized valuation; by county and municipality]. (p. 410-437)

S5530   NEW MEXICO
Department of Agriculture

S5530–1   **NEW MEXICO AGRICULTURAL STATISTICS, 1983**
Annual.   June 1984.   72 p.
Bull. No. 23.
LC 63-54681.
SRI/MF/complete

Annual report on New Mexico agricultural production, finances, and marketing, 1983, with selected trends from 1940 and some data for 1984. Data are generally shown by county and/or commodity.

Report covers production, prices, value, and, as applicable, acreage, yield, disposition, and inventory, for field crop, vegetable, fruit and nut, livestock, dairy, and poultry sectors.

Report also includes data on weather; irrigated acreage; fertilizer inshipments; number of farms; farm acreage; range/pasture condition; cattle feedlots; cattle in- and out-shipments by State of origin and destination, and for Mexico and/or Canada; and farm assets and debts, and income including government payments.

Data are compiled by the New Mexico Crop and Livestock Reporting Service in conjunction with USDA.

Contains contents listing and transmittal letters (p. 1-3); and 8 maps, 4 charts, and 88 tables, interspersed with narrative (p. 4-72).

This is the 23rd annual report.

Availability: New Mexico Crop and Livestock Reporting Service, PO Box 1809, Las Cruces NM 88004, †; SRI/MF/complete.

S5575   NEW MEXICO
Department of Education

S5575–2   NEW MEXICO SCHOOL DISTRICT PROFILE, 1982/83 School Year
Annual. [1984.] i+191 p.
LC 80-642386.
SRI/MF/complete

Annual statistical report on New Mexico public elementary/secondary school pupils, teachers, and finances, by school district, 1982/83 school year.

Contains introduction (p. i); narrative overview, and 6 summary text tables with trends from as early as 1973/74 (p. 1-7); 1 detailed table (p. 8-13); and 8 charts, repeated for each district (p. 14-191). Detailed table shows the following, by district, 1982/83:

a. Average daily membership, and percent change from 1977/78; percent kindergarten, bilingual, special education, and Title I students; pupil/teacher ratio; teachers' average salary and experience, and percent with master's/higher degree; percent Anglo, Hispanic, and Indian teachers and students; and student primary grade repeaters, high school dropouts, and mobility rate.

b. Expenditure per pupil, with comparison to 1981/82; percent income from local, State, and Federal sources; students taking American College Test, and mean score; high school graduates, and percent planning to attend college; percent passing high school proficiency exams, and mean score; and composite score on comprehensive test of basic skills, by grade.

This is the 13th edition of the report.

Availability: New Mexico Department of Education, Evaluation, Testing, and Data Management Unit, Education Bldg., Santa Fe NM 87501-2786, †; SRI/MF/complete.

S5578   NEW MEXICO
Employment Security Department

S5578–1   JOB TRAINING PARTNERSHIP ACT: Labor Market Information
Annual. Mar. 1984. 92 p.
LC 78-642503.
SRI/MF/complete

Annual planning report identifying New Mexico population groups most in need of employment services, 1970s-83. Includes data on employment by industry division, population, job openings by occupation, income, and poverty, with selected projections to 2000, and detail by location and demographic characteristics.

Data are from 1980 census, New Mexico Employment Security Dept, University of New Mexico, and other State sources.

Contains contents listing (1 p.); introduction, and summaries of information available from Employment Security Dept (p. 1-4); report, with narrative summaries, 2 maps, 19 charts, and 52 tables (p. 5-85); and technical notes and definitions (p. 86-92).

All tables, and 1 chart presenting data not shown in tables, are described below.

Availability: New Mexico Employment Security Department, Economic Research and Analysis, PO Box 1928, Albuquerque NM 87103, †; SRI/MF/complete.

TABLES AND CHART:
[Data are for New Mexico, unless otherwise noted. Some data include U.S. comparisons. Data by race are shown for white, black, Indian, Asian/Pacific Islander, and Spanish origin.]

POPULATION AND LABOR FORCE

a. Population: by planning district; by county and race; by age and sex, with age detail for Bernalillo County; and by city; various years 1970-82, with projections by county and planning district to 2000. 6 tables. (p. 9-15)

b. Labor force by employment status, by county and for Albuquerque area and Las Cruces MSA, and by race and sex; nonagricultural employment by industry division and major group, with detail for Albuquerque area and Las Cruces MSA; and agricultural employment by county; various periods 1970-83. 17 tables. (p. 16-45)

c. Projected employment by industry division and major group, 1981 and 1990; job openings in high demand occupations with detail for Albuquerque, and openings by occupational group, annual averages 1981-90 period; and employment and/or new hires, by industry division and selected major group, various periods FY82. 1 chart and 5 tables. (p. 48-59)

d. Per capita personal income, compared to Western States and regions 1981-82, and by county 1981; persons below poverty level by race, and total and female-headed families below poverty level, by county and planning district, 1979; and distribution of households by income size and source, and of persons below poverty level by race, for State, Albuquerque area, and Las Cruces MSA, 1980. 6 tables. (p. 60-65)

JOB TRAINING PARTNERSHIP ACT TARGET GROUP DATA

e. Labor force by employment status; youth unemployment and rate by sex, and youth population, by county; labor force by employment status for all youths and high school dropouts, for State and Bernalillo County; and unemployment and labor force participation rates for high school graduates and dropouts; all by age group, various years 1980-83. 6 tables. (p. 68-73)

f. Economically disadvantaged by age and county, and by race and education for State and Bernalillo County; veterans by age, period of service, race, and labor force and employment status, with period of service detail by county, and disability status for State and Bernalillo County; and total unemployment and rate by county; 1980 or 1983. 6 Tables. (p. 74-79)

g. Single heads of households with dependent children; persons unemployed 15/more weeks; disabled persons, by labor force status; persons with limited English proficiency; by county, 1979 or 1980. 4 tables. (p. 80-83)

h. Persons registered with State employment service, by age, sex, education, race, and veteran and welfare status, and for handicapped and seasonal farmworkers, for State and Ber-

nalillo County; and recipients of AFDC and medical and food assistance, by planning district and county; as of various dates 1983. 2 tables. (p. 84-85)

S5578–2   NEW MEXICO LABOR MARKET REVIEW
Monthly. Approx. 10 p.
SRI/MF/complete, shipped quarterly

Monthly report on New Mexico employment, unemployment, hours, and earnings, by industry and local area. Data are compiled by the Employment Security Dept in cooperation with the U.S. Labor Dept. Reports are issued approximately 1 month after month of coverage.

Contains narrative summary interspersed with 8 monthly tables listed below. Jan. issue also includes 4-5 annual tables showing revised estimates for New Mexico labor force and employment, for current and/or previous year.

Availability: New Mexico Employment Security Department, Economic Research and Analysis, PO Box 1928, Albuquerque NM 87103, †; SRI/MF/complete, shipped quarterly.

Issues reviewed during 1984: Sept. 1983-Aug. 1984 (D) (Vol. 12, Nos. 9-12; Vol. 13, Nos. 1-8).

MONTHLY TABLES:
[Data are shown for New Mexico, for month of coverage, previous month, and same month of previous year, unless otherwise noted.]

[1] Summary [civilian labor force by employment status].

[2] Estimated nonagricultural wage/salary employment [by industry division and major group].

[3] [Table [1] is repeated for Albuquerque SMSA.]

[4-5] [Table [2] is repeated for Albuquerque and Las Cruces SMSAs.]

[6] Average hours and earnings estimates [of production, construction/nonsupervisory employees, for State by selected industry division, and for Albuquerque manufacturing employees].

[7] U.S. CPI [month of coverage only].

[8] Official labor force estimates [by employment status, for State and by SMSA and county].

S5585   NEW MEXICO
Department of Finance and Administration

S5585–1   ANNUAL FINANCIAL REPORT, 71st Fiscal Year, State of New Mexico
Annual. [1984.] 398 p.
LC 76-615237.
SRI/MF/complete

Annual report on financial condition of New Mexico State government, for FY83, presenting revenues by source, disbursements by function, and fund balances, for combined, general, special revenue, bond, working capital, and trust and agency funds.

Also includes assets and liabilities for combined funds and selected fund categories; State bonded indebtedness; detailed cash transactions, and appropriations and actual expenditures, by agency and function; and selected comparisons for FY82 and estimates for FY84.

Data are from Financial Control Division internal records.

Contains contents listing, and general comments (p. 3-8); 8 sections with contents listings, 3 charts, and 32 statements and exhibits (p. 9-379); and index (p. 380-398).

This is the 21st annual report.

Availability: New Mexico Department of Finance and Administration, Financial Control Division, Bataan Memorial Bldg., Rm 166, Santa Fe NM 87501, †; SRI/MF/complete.

S5585–2   STATISTICS: OFFICE OF EDUCATION, State of New Mexico
Annual.   Dec. 1983.
268 p. var. paging.
LC 59-63589.
SRI/MF/complete

Annual report of the New Mexico Dept of Finance and Administration, on public school finances, 1982/83 and projected 1983/84, with selected trends from 1970s. Also includes data on pupil membership, personnel, salaries, and vocational schools. Most data are shown for individual school districts grouped by county.

Contains contents listing (1 p.); lists of school districts and superintendents (p. A1-A2); and 3 charts, and 42 tables listed below (p. B1-G9).

This is the 20th edition of the report. Additional data on New Mexico public school pupils, teachers, and finances are available in *New Mexico School District Profile,* covered in SRI under S5575-2.

Availability: New Mexico Department of Finance and Administration, Public School Finance Division, 515 Don Gaspar Ave., Santa Fe NM 87501-4498, $20.00; SRI/MF/complete.

TABLES:
[Tables show data by school district for 1982/83, unless otherwise noted.]

S5585–2.1: School Districts and Membership
[1] Number of school districts in State, Sept. 1 [decennially 1950-80, by county]. (p. A3)

[2] Average daily membership [ADM, aggregate for] grades 1-12, special education C & D [more and less severely handicapped students], nonprofit (private special education), and early childhood education FTE (State funded only). (p. B1)

[3-4] Statewide membership: by grade by funding period, [and for various] reporting periods, 1973/74-1982/83. (p. B5-B6)

S5585–2.2: Income, Expenditures, and Cash Balances
INCOME
[Tables [3-5], [10], and [12] show State totals only.]

[1-2] Actual income by fund; and actual revenue [by detailed source], operational fund. (p. C1-C17)

[3] Total appropriations and distributions [by fund]. (p. C18)

[4] State appropriations to public schools [by function], 10-year comparison, 1973/74-1983/84. (p. C19)

[5] Analysis of receipts [by source]. (p. C22)

[6] Special education ADM served in private D nonprofit training centers, and program cost generated by ADM. (p. C23)

EXPENDITURES AND CASH BALANCES
[7] Expenditures by line item. (p. C24-C98)

[8-9] Supporting information, actual expenditures: 11. series special projects (operational); and 17. series Federal projects (non-operational). (p. C99-C103)

[10] Expenditure comparison by budget category, 1979/80-1982/83 inclusive. (p. C104)

[11] Operational expenditures per pupil, by school size. (p. C105)

[12] Net operational expenditures per pupil, 10-year study, 1973/74-1982/83. (p. C108)

[13] Cash balances as of June 30, 1983, all funds [by fund]. (p. C109-C112)

S5585–2.3: Income Projections and Budgets
[Tables show projected data for 1983/84.]

[1-2] Appropriations [State total], and projected income; by fund. (p. D1-D6)

[3] Estimated revenue [by detailed source], operational fund. (p. D7-D19)

[4] Final approved budget [by function and object]. (p. D20-D94)

[5-6] Supporting information, final approved budgets: 11. series special projects (operational); and 17. series Federal projects (non-operational). (p. D95-D99)

[7] Reconciliation of estimated revenue and budget [by fund; State total]. (p. D100)

S5585–2.4: Assessed Valuations and Bonded Indebtedness
[1] Comparison of actual assessed valuations: local, corporate, and oil/gas, actual 1981-82. (p. E1)

[2] District tax rates and statewide average tax rates, 1983/84. (p. E5)

[3] Bonded debt of school districts, as of June 30, 1983. (p. E10-E13)

S5585–2.5: Personnel and Salaries
[1] Average teacher salary, 10-year study [State total, 1973/74-1983/84]. (p. F1)

[2] School district ranking by average salaries of full-time classroom teachers, and related information [including number of teachers, pupil/teacher ratio, beginning and highest salary on schedule, average years of experience, and percent of teachers with master's/higher degree]. (p. F2)

[3-4] Certified and noncertified personnel average annual salaries, by [position and] school size (paid from operational budgets). (p. F5-F22)

[5] Total number of Federal employees, by Federal project employed [and position; State total]. (p. F23)

S5585–2.6: Vocational Schools
[Data are shown for 3 technical and/or vocational institutions: Albuquerque vocational-technical institute, Luna area vocational-technical school, and Tucumcari area vocational school.]

[1-2] FTE and operational fund distributions summary; and capital outlay appropriations summary; [various periods 1978/79-1982/83]. (p. G1-G2)

[3-4] Degree and nondegree personnel average annual salaries (paid from operational budget) [by position]. (p. G3)

[5-10] Budget report [and/or] final revenue and expenditure report, 1982/83; and finalized budget, 1983/84. (p. G4-G9)

S5620   NEW MEXICO
Department of Human Services

S5620–1   INCOME SUPPORT DIVISION Monthly Statistical Report, New Mexico
Monthly, discontinued.

Monthly report on New Mexico public welfare programs, discontinued with report for Sept. 1982 (for description, see SRI 1983 Annual or 1983 Issue 1/2, under this number). Report has been discontinued because the issuing agency has been disbanded.

S5627   NEW MEXICO
State Library

S5627–1   NEW MEXICO STATE LIBRARY ANNUAL REPORT: Library Statistics, FY83
Annual.   Jan. 1984.   23 p.
LC 81-649870.
SRI/MF/complete

Annual report, for FY83, on New Mexico public library holdings, circulation, finances, services, and staff. Data are from reports of libraries, and the 1980 census.

Contains introduction and library directories (p. 1-7); and 7 tables, listed below (p. 8-23).

Availability: New Mexico State Library, 325 Don Gaspar Ave., Santa Fe NM 87503, †; SRI/MF/complete.

TABLES:
[Data are shown for FY83, generally by location and/or library. Tables show data for some or all of the following: hours open; FTE staff; circulation; holdings (including volumes, titles, periodical subscriptions, technical reports, microforms, and audiovisual); interlibrary loans; municipal, county, State, and/or other income; population, communities, and/or borrowers served; and salary, materials, and other operating expenditures. Additional data are noted below.]

[1-3] Public, community, and academic libraries. (p. 8-17)

[4] Special libraries [also includes library subject specialty]. (p. 18)

[5] State institutions [residents' libraries in correctional, health/environment, and vocational rehabilitation/educational institutions, including State schools for the deaf and visually handicapped; income sources are institution, Library Services and Construction Act funds, and other Federal funds]. (p. 20)

[6] State library program statistics [shows selected data for books-by-mail, library for the blind/physically handicapped, large-print

book circuit, information services, OCLC network services; and expenditures by object]. (p. 22)

[7] State library regional bookmobile service [also includes data on stops, mileage, film programs, and deposit collections and locations]. (p. 23)

S5645   NEW MEXICO
Public Service Commission

S5645-1   THIRTY-NINTH ANNUAL
REPORT, 71st Fiscal Year,
July 1, 1982-June 30, 1983:
New Mexico Public Service
Commission
Annual. Oct. 31, 1983.
82 p.
LC 43-52821.
SRI/MF/complete

Annual report presenting New Mexico public utility regulatory data for FY83; and financial and operating data, mostly for 1981-82; by type of utility. Utility types covered are electric, gas, and water.

Covers operating summary, including plant investment, operating revenue and expenses, stockholders' equity, and bonded and long-term debt; selected financial and operating ratios; and customers, sales volume, gross revenues, average customer use and bill, and monthly rates by community and company, all by customer class; for all utility types.

Also includes security issuances, by company; and Commission receipts, disbursements, and regulatory caseloads, including rate cases and consumer complaints.

Data are compiled from Commission records and utility company reports.

Contains contents and table listing, introduction, and Commission authority and finance summary (p. 4-10); and utility data and regulatory summaries, with 13 tables, and a list of regulated companies (p. 11-82).

Availability: New Mexico Public Service Commission, Bataan Memorial Bldg., Santa Fe NM 87503, †; SRI/MF/complete.

S5652   NEW MEXICO
Regulation and
Licensing Department

S5652-1   69TH ANNUAL REPORT,
New Mexico Financial
Institutions Division, 1983
Annual. [1983.] 134 p.
LC 79-644636.
SRI/MF/complete

Annual report on the financial condition of New Mexico State- and/or federally-chartered financial institutions for 1983, presenting assets and liabilities for commercial banks, savings and loan assns, and credit unions, all by institution. Includes equity capital, net worth, or reserves, and number of branches, as appropriate; and consolidated statements of income and expenses for each type of State-chartered institution.

Also includes Financial Institutions Division activities, workloads, revenues, and expenditures; State bank loans outstanding by type; Consumer Credit Bureau composite financial, insurance, loan, and legal data for small loan licensees; State Securities Bureau registration activity, including receipts by type; and selected trends from 1920.

Contains contents listing (p. 5); and report, with directories and 29 tables (p. 6-134).

Prior to 1983 edition, report was issued by the New Mexico Commerce and Industry Dept, and was described in SRI under S5545-1.

Availability: New Mexico Regulation and Licensing Department, Financial Institutions Division, Lew Wallace Bldg., Santa Fe NM 87503, ‡; SRI/MF/complete.

S5665   NEW MEXICO
Transportation Department

S5665-1   NEW MEXICO TRAFFIC
ACCIDENT DATA, 1983
Annual. Apr. 1984. v+27 p.
SRI/MF/complete

Annual report on New Mexico traffic accidents, injuries, and fatalities, by accident and vehicle types, location, time, and other circumstances; and driver and victim characteristics; 1983, with trends from 1974.

Also includes data on accidents in pueblos and reservations, motor vehicle registrations, miles traveled, licensed drivers, and safety device use.

Data are from accident reports submitted to State agencies and compiled by the University of New Mexico Institute for Applied Research Services.

Contains contents listing, introduction, and definitions (p. ii-v); and highlights, 3 maps, 23 charts, and 32 tables (p. 1-27).

Availability: New Mexico Transportation Department, Planning and Development Division, Traffic Safety Bureau, PO Box 1028, Santa Fe NM 87503-1028, †; SRI/MF/complete.

S5700   NEW YORK STATE
Department of
Agriculture and Markets

S5700-1   NEW YORK AGRICULTURAL
STATISTICS, 1983
Annual. June 1984. 75 p.
LC 79-648711.
SRI/MF/complete

Annual report on New York State agricultural production, marketing, and finances, mostly 1974-83, with some data for 1984. Data generally are shown by commodity, with some detail by county and area, and selected comparisons to other States and total U.S.

Covers production, cash receipts, value, prices, and, as applicable, acreage, yield, inventory, and disposition, for field crop, vegetable, fruit, livestock, dairy, poultry, and apiary sectors.

Also includes data on farm finances, utility use, pasture condition, labor and wages, acreage, and value; apple holdings in cold storage; maple syrup and mink industries; weather; fertilizer consumption; and U.S. food consumption.

Data are compiled by the New York State Crop Reporting Service and USDA in cooperation with the State Dept of Agriculture and Markets.

Contains contents listing (p. 5); 2 maps, 6 charts, and 108 tables, with interspersed narrative summaries (p. 6-74); and list of State agriculture reports available (p. 75).

Availability: New York State Crop Reporting Service, State Campus, Bldg. 8, Rm. 800, Albany NY 12235, †; SRI/MF/complete.

S5710   NEW YORK STATE
Department of
Audit and Control

S5710-1   STATE OF NEW YORK 1983
ANNUAL REPORT OF THE
COMPTROLLER
Annual. [1984.] 105 p.
ISSN 0098-6372.
LC 75-644665.
SRI/MF/complete

Annual report on financial condition of New York State, FY83, presenting fund assets, liabilities, and equity; revenues by source; disbursements by function, program, or debt; and fund balances; with selected comparisons to FY82.

Covers government and fiduciary funds, and public benefit corporations. Funds include general, special revenue, debt service, capital projects, trust and agency, and State administered retirement systems funds. Public benefit corporations include power, transportation, and dormitory authorities, housing finance agency, urban development corporation, and State insurance fund.

Also includes data on long-term bonded debt, by purpose and issue; pension trust investments by type, and retirement system participation; State and Federal assistance to counties and NYC; monthly investment yields and balances; and Port Authority of New York/New Jersey 1982 finances.

Data are based primarily on records maintained by the comptroller's office.

Contains overview and contents listing (p. 1-15); and 44 financial statements and schedules, with explanatory notes (p. 17-105).

An annual financial report on municipal affairs is also available from the comptroller's office, but is not covered by SRI.

Availability: New York State Department of Audit and Control, Comptroller's Press Office, Alfred E. Smith State Office Bldg., Albany NY 12236, †; SRI/MF/complete.

S5720   NEW YORK STATE Department of Commerce

S5720–1   PROFILE OF PEOPLE, JOBS, AND HOUSING, 1980, New York
Monograph.   [1984.]
34 p. no paging.
SRI/MF/complete

Report presenting selected 1980 U.S. Census of Population and Housing findings for New York State, each New York county, and NYC. Covers the following:

a. Population and households: population, by urban-rural status, race-ethnicity (black, white, Spanish origin), age, and whether in household or group quarters (with detail for inmates of institutions); and number of households.

b. Employment and income: labor force, and percent women; employment, by class of worker (including self-employed, government, and unpaid family workers), industry division, and occupational group; median family income; and distribution of families by income group.

c. Education and commuting: educational attainment status of persons age 25/older; educational enrollment status of persons age 16-19; and distribution of employed persons by proximity of workplace to residence (same or different county), means of transportation to work, and travel time to work.

d. Housing units and characteristics: number of units, by occupancy status, year built, year occupant moved in, number of units at address, rent or value, type of heating fuel used, presence of air conditioning, and presence of public sewer and water systems; mobile homes as percent of total housing units; and median rent and value.

Contains contents listing and notes (2 p.), and 16 tables (32 p.).

Also available from the issuing agency, but not covered in SRI, are similar profiles for individual counties, with data for municipalities and census-designated places within the county.

Availability: New York State Department of Commerce, Economic Research and Statistics Division, One Commerce Plaza, Rm. 905, Albany NY 12245, †; SRI/MF/complete.

S5745   NEW YORK STATE Education Department

S5745–1   ANNUAL EDUCATIONAL SUMMARY, 1981/82: Statistical and Financial Summary of Education in New York State for the Year Ending June 30, 1982
Annual.   [1983.]   x+198 p.
ISSN 0085-4077.
LC 74-644306.
SRI/MF/complete

Annual report, for academic year 1981/82, on enrollment, finances, and staffing for New York State elementary and secondary schools and institutions of higher education. Includes data for NYC, Boards of Cooperative Educational Services (BOCES) programs, and public libraries, with trends from 1960/61.

Most data are from the State Education Dept's Information Center on Education.

Contains listings of contents, tables, and charts (p. v-x); 7 chapters, interspersed with 2 charts and 53 tables (p. 1-58); and appendix, with 14 tables (p. 59-198). All tables are listed below.

Availability: New York State Education Department, Information Center on Education, Publications Distribution Desk, State Education Bldg., Albany NY 12234, †; SRI/MF/complete.

TABLES:
[Types of school districts are: NYC, other cities, independent superintendencies, and supervisory districts. Data by location are generally for 5 major cities and rest of State.]

S5745–1.1: Statistical Highlights of 1981/82; and Public Elementary and Secondary Schools, Classrooms, and Staff

1. Education summary [for elementary/secondary schools, colleges/universities, and libraries], 1979/80-1981/82. (p. 2)

2-4. Number of public school districts by [enrollment] size and type of organization; and number of public schools by level; [various years] 1960/61-1981/82. (p. 5-7)

5. Professional positions in public day schools [and BOCES positions, various years] 1960/61-1981/82. (p. 8)

6-7. Pupil/staff ratios in public school districts, by type of district; and major pupil personnel services [medical, psychologists, guidance counselors, attendance, and social work] in public schools; 1979/80-1981/82. (p. 9-10)

S5745–1.2: Public Elementary and Secondary School Students
ENROLLMENT
[Tables 9-12 show data for 1960/61-1981/82.]

8. Fall enrollment in public schools by grade [including ungraded handicapped and BOCES], 1979/80-1981/82. (p. 12)

9-10. Fall enrollment in public schools by [grade] level and by type of district [and BOCES]. (p. 13-14)

11. Percentage of pupils enrolled in public school districts, by type of school district and [urban and nonurban] location. (p. 15)

12. Fall enrollment and average daily attendance (ADA) in public schools [in NYC and rest of State]. (p. 16)

SPECIAL PROGRAMS
13. Resident handicapped children [by type of handicap], by agency where services are received [in home district and by type of service], fall 1981. (p. 17)

14. Enrollment in occupational education programs by type of agency, [level of program], and major program area, 1981/82. (p. 18)

HIGH SCHOOL GRADUATES ENTERING COLLEGE
15-16. Percent of public high school graduates entering institutions of higher education, [by type] within and outside New York State, [various periods 1969/70-fall 1982]. (p. 19)

MINORITY STUDENTS
17-18. Percent distribution of public school students by racial/ethnic origin [black, Hispanic, and other]; and distribution of black and Hispanic students; [by location, various years] 1977/78-1981/82. (p. 20-21)

SUMMER SCHOOL
19. Public summer high schools [number and enrollment], 1980-82. (p. 21)

S5745–1.3: Finances of Public Elementary and Secondary Schools

20-22. Public school general, debt service, and Federal aid fund: revenues by major source and expenditures [by type; with selected detail by district type, various years] 1960/61-1981/82. (p. 23-25)

23-24. Public school general and debt service fund expenditures: per pupil in weighted average daily attendance (WADA) [by type of expense]; and percent distribution by major object of expense; [by district type, various years] 1979/80-1981/82. (p. 26-27)

25. Trends in public school expenditures [by type of fund], 1960/61-1981/82. (p. 28)

26. Public school capital funds [receipts and disbursements], 1979/80-1981/82. (p. 29)

S5745–1.4: Nonpublic Schools, Enrollment, and Staff

27. Fall enrollment in nonpublic schools by grade [including ungraded handicapped], 1979/80-1981/82. (p. 31)

28-29. Number of nonpublic schools and enrollment by religious [and other group] affiliation [and grade level]; and distribution of enrollment by location and racial/ethnic origin [including American Indian/Alaskan Native, Asian/Pacific Islander, and Hispanic]; 1981/82. (p. 32-34)

30-31. Number of nonpublic high school graduates, 1963/64-1981/82; and percent entering institutions of higher education [by type], fall 1965-82. (p. 35-36)

32. Professional positions in nonpublic schools [by position], 1979/80-1981/82. (p. 37)

33. Nonpublic summer high schools [number and enrollment]; 1980-82. (p. 37)

S5745–1.5: Colleges and Universities

[All tables show data for institutions of higher education. Data by type of institution are generally for 2- and 4-year or more public, independent, and proprietary institutions. Data by institutional classification are basically for same categories, with additional detail by type of SUNY (State University of New York), CUNY (City University of New York), and independent institution.]

INSTITUTIONS AND APPLICATIONS

34. Number of degree-granting institutions [by type], 1977/78-1981/82. (p. 39)

35-36. Undergraduate applications received, accepted, and full-time students actually enrolled in class, fall 1981; and graduate and 1st-professional applications received and accepted for full- and part-time study, July 1, 1980-June 30, 1981; by institutional classification. (p. 40-41)

ENROLLMENT AND DEGREES CONFERRED

37. Degree-credit enrollment [by type of institution], fall 1977-81. (p. 42)

38. Degree-credit [full- and part-time] and noncredit enrollment by level of program and institutional classification, fall 1981. (p. 43)

39. Degree trends by type of institution, level of degree, and year, 1977/78-1981/82. (p. 44)

40. Degrees conferred by level of degree [by sex] and institutional classification, 1981/82. (p. 45)

FACULTY AND STAFF

41-42. Number, tenure status, and mean salary of full-time instructional faculty by length of contract; and number of full- and part-time employees by occupational activity; [both by] institutional classification, 1981/82. (p. 46-47)

S5745–1.6: Special Services of the State Education Dept

CONTINUING EDUCATION, LIBRARIES, AND REGENTS EXAMINATIONS

43. Continuing education in public school districts by field of study [number of districts, classes, and registrations], 1981/82. (p. 49)

44. Public/free assn libraries [number and population served, holdings, circulation, staff, and expenditures], 1979-81. (p. 50)

45. Number of State Regents examination papers written in secondary schools, by subject area, 1960/61-1981/82. (p. 51)

STUDENT AID

46-47. Number and cost of State scholarships, fellowships, and tuition assistance program awards, by year and type, 1980/81-1981/82. (p. 52)

48. Student loan program administered by the New York State Higher Education Services Corp. [recipients, loans guaranteed and refused, and amounts], 1979/80-1981/82. (p. 53)

49. State-funded programs of postsecondary opportunity [student characteristics, number of graduates, funds per student, and freshmen scholastic and income background; for SUNY, CUNY, and independent institution programs], 1981/82. (p. 54)

PROFESSIONAL CERTIFICATES

50. Teaching and administrative certificates issued [permanent and provisional, by type of position], 1979-81. (p. 55)

51. Professional certificates and licenses, other than educational, issued FY80-82. (p. 56)

52. Professional registration [by occupation], FY82. (p. 57)

HIGH SCHOOL EQUIVALENCY GRADUATES

53. High school equivalency diplomas issued, 1960/61-1981/82. (p. 58)

S5745–1.7: Appendix Tables: District, County, and Region Data

[All data are shown by region, county, and school district. Tables 56-67 show data for 1981/82.]

54-55. Public school enrollment by grade [and ungraded handicapped; includes data for BOCES], fall 1981. (p. 60-83)

56-57. Unadjusted ADA [by grade level] and WADA. (p. 84-96)

58-61. General fund, debt service fund, and Federal aid fund revenues [by source] and expenditures [by type]. (p. 98-151)

62-63. Expenditures per pupil in WADA [by fund and expenditure type]. (p. 152-177)

64-67. Real property valuation and tax levy [total, and] per pupil in resident WADA. (p. 178-198)

S5745–2   PUBLIC AND ASSOCIATION LIBRARIES STATISTICS, 1982, New York State
Annual. Aug. 19, 1983.
vi+184 p.
ISSN 0077-9326.
LC 76-646730.
SRI/MF/complete

Annual report on New York State public and assn libraries for 1982. Presents data on population and area served, holdings, circulation, staff, and finances, by library. Data are based on reports from individual libraries.

Contains contents listing, introduction, and reference notes (p. iv-vi); 10 tables, listed below (p. 1-89); and 6 appendices, with report forms and instructions, abbreviations, and indexes (p. 91-184).

This agency also issues *Institution Libraries Statistics* and *Directory of College and University Libraries in New York State,* not covered by SRI.

Availability: New York State Education Department, Library Development, Cultural Education Center, Rm. 10B41, Empire State Plaza, Albany NY 12230, †; SRI/MF/complete.

TABLES:
[Tables II-V show data for 1982.]

I. Comparative study [population and counties served by system and nonsystem libraries, number of systems and libraries, holdings and circulation, staff, and finances, 1957 and 1980-82]. (p. 1)

II-IIA. System summary [population, land area, and number of counties served; book stock; circulation; operating fund disbursements for salaries/benefits and library materials; total operating/capital fund disbursements; and operating fund receipts, by source]; and public outlets [including bookmobiles; all by library system]. (p. 2-3)

IIIA. System statistics—general [book and nonbook holdings, professional and nonprofessional staff, book and audiovisual additions,

circulation, and interlibrary loan use, by library, arranged by system and county]. (p. 4-23)

IIIB-IIIC. System statistics—financial disbursements [by object] and receipts [by source; by library, arranged by system and county]. (p. 24-65)

IVA-IVC. [Tables IIIA-IIIC are repeated for nonsystem libraries.] (p. 66-71)

V. System and nonsystem statistics, by [library, ranked by size of] population served [books added, book holdings, circulation, hours open per week, staff, and finances]. (p. 72-89)

S5760   NEW YORK STATE Executive Department

S5760-3   NEW YORK STATE CRIME AND JUSTICE Annual Report, 1982
Annual. [1983.] vii+295 p.
ISSN 0095-4047.
LC 74-648505.
SRI/MF/complete

Annual report, for 1982, presenting detailed data on New York State crimes and arrests, by type of offense, and summary data on law enforcement personnel, court operations, probation and parole, corrections, and crime victim compensation. Data include trends from FY67, and generally are shown for the State, NYC, and by county or State region.

Data are from reports by State and local law enforcement agencies submitted under the Uniform Crime Reporting (UCR) Program, and from the Division of Criminal Justice Services and other State agencies. Population data are based on 1980 census findings.

Contains contents, table, and chart listing (4 p.); introduction, with description of UCR Program and county map (p. i-vii); and report in 2 sections, with 64 charts and 148 tables, interspersed with narrative summaries (p. 1-294).

All tables, and selected charts with substantial statistics not covered in tables, are described below.

This is the 8th annual report.

Availability: New York State Executive Department, Criminal Justice Services Division, Policy Analysis Office, Research and Statistical Services, Executive Park Tower, 10th Floor, Stuyvesant Plaza, Albany NY 12203-3764, $5.00; SRI/MF/complete.

CHARTS AND TABLES:

[Part I offenses are murder and manslaughter, rape, robbery, assault, burglary, larceny, and motor vehicle theft. Part II offenses are other crimes.]

S5760-3.1: Offenses
PART I OFFENSES

a. State summary: offenses by type and month, and rates, 1981-82 with selected trends from 1978; and crime clock, 1982. 11 charts and 3 tables. (p. 5-14)

b. Offense analysis: murder and negligent manslaughter; forcible and attempted rapes, by type of weapon used; robberies and assaults, by setting and type of weapon; residential and nonresidential, day and night burglaries, by type of entry; larceny/ theft, by value of property stolen and type of property or setting; motor vehicle theft, by type and location of vehicle; and total and juvenile clearances for each offense type; shown for State, NYC, and upstate, 1982. 3 tables. (p. 15-17)

c. Local and miscellaneous data: population, offenses by type, and crime rate, shown by county, 1981-82; and distribution of selected occurrence characteristics for robbery, burglary, assault, and larceny, for State, and/or NYC, other metro planning area (MPA) counties, and counties with populations over and under 100,000, 1982. 7 charts and 1 table. (p. 18-27)

d. Property loss: value of property stolen, by offense type; value of property stolen and recovered, by type of property; and number of motor vehicles stolen/recovered; 1981-82. 2 charts and 1 table. (p. 28-30)

e. Agency data: offenses by type, and crime rate, shown by reporting jurisdiction (sheriffs' offices, police depts, and other law enforcement agencies, grouped by county), 1981-82. 1 extended table. (p. 31-72)

PART II OFFENSES

f. Number of offenses and clearances for 51 offense classifications, including commercial and residential arson, and drug offenses by type and substance; shown for State, NYC, and upstate area, 1981-82. 3 tables. (p. 73-75)

HANDGUNS

g. Percent of murders, rapes, robberies, assaults, and dangerous weapons offenses involving handguns, 1982. 1 chart. (p. 76)

HOMICIDE ANALYSIS

h. Includes location, circumstance, type of weapon, and month; and victim and offender relationship, age, sex, and race (white, black, Hispanic, and other); 1982, with selected trends from 1978. 3 charts and 19 tables. (p. 83-102)

ARSON AND DOMESTIC VIOLENCE

i. Arson incidents, incidents involving abandoned buildings, total and juvenile clearances, and rates, by type of property and month, shown for State, NYC, other MPAs, and rest of State, 1982. 1 chart and 10 tables. (p. 106-115)

j. Domestic violence offenses by type and offender/victim relationship, for NYC, suburban NYC counties, and upstate counties, 1982. 1 table. (p. 117)

S5760–3.2: Arrests and Dispositions
[Most data are shown for 1981-82.]

ARRESTS
[Data by county are also shown for NYC.]

a. By Part I and II offenses: adults and juveniles, by offense, age, and sex; and totals by county. 1 chart and 4 tables. (p. 124-139)

b. For all offenses: adults and juveniles, by age and sex, shown by county. 4 tables. (p. 140-151)

c. For drug sales/manufacture and use/ possession by substance, gambling, prosti-

tution, and driving while intoxicated: by county. 1 chart and 2 tables. (p. 152-158)

d. By Part I and Part II offense: total arrests by race (white, black, Indian, and Asian) and ethnic origin (Hispanic and non-Hispanic). 1 table. (p. 159-160)

e. Felony arrests: drug and nondrug, for State, NYC, suburban NYC, and upstate, and by county. 1 table. (p. 161-170)

FELONY INDICTMENTS AND DISPOSITIONS

f. Indictments for drug and nondrug felonies by judicial dept, and for State, NYC, suburban NYC, and upstate; and total indictments, dispositions, and convictions, by county, special agency, and for nursing homes. 3 tables. (p. 176-179)

g. Defendant processing flow, including dispositions by outcome (dismissed, acquitted, convicted, and other), convictions by circumstances (guilty plea, jury trial, and nonjury trial) and sentence, and median processing time from indictment to disposition; shown for total and drug charges, for State, NYC, suburban NYC, and upstate; and for total charges by judicial dept. 52 tables with accompanying flowcharts. (p. 181-207)

SENTENCES AND OFFENSE COMPARISON

h. Felony sentences by selected offense, by sentence type and by duration of State imprisonment and probation. 3 tables. (p. 210-215)

i. Arrests, indictments, and disposition, shown for homicide and robbery; and total and drug felony charges, 1978-82. 4 charts. (p. 217-220)

S5760–3.3: Law Enforcement Employees, and Court Operations

LAW ENFORCEMENT EMPLOYEES

a. Deaths and assaults: officers killed; and officers assaulted, by time of day, and by type of activity, assignment, and weapon; 1982. 4 charts. (p. 223)

b. Employment and vehicles: full- and part-time uniformed employees by sex, and civilian employees; and vehicles; shown by agency for municipal police depts grouped by county, NYC agencies, sheriffs' offices, and multi-jurisdiction agencies; 1982. 3 tables. (p. 224-237)

COURT OPERATIONS

c. Selected caseload and caseflow data, by type of court and/or jurisdiction, mostly for 1982. 5 tables. (p. 240-244)

S5760–3.4: Probation, Corrections, Parole, and Victim Compensation

PROBATION

a. Probation case-processing data: intake, investigations, supervision, and fines and restitutions collected; shown statewide and for NYC, upstate, MPAs, and NYC boroughs, 1982. 3 tables. (p. 246-248)

b. Historical trends: probation supervision caseflow and investigations completed, various years 1970-82. 2 tables. (p. 249-250)

c. Recent trends: cases on probation at year end, and predisposition cases received, for State, upstate, and NYC; and family and criminal probationers received; 1979-82. 3 charts. (p. 251-253)

CORRECTIONS

d. Trends: State prison admissions and releases, by classification, and inmates under custody, various years 1971-82. 3 charts and 1 table. (p. 256-259)

e. New commitments for violent and 2nd felonies, by offense, 1982. 1 table. (p. 260)

f. Inmate population characteristics: commitment offense, geographic area of commitment, prior criminal record, minimum and maximum sentence, race/ethnicity (black, white, Puerto Rican, other), age group, and prior education, as of Dec. 31, 1982. 8 tables with accompanying charts. (p. 261-268)

g. Youth: admissions to youth facilities by offense, placement level, adjudication status, sex, and race/ethnicity (black, white, Puerto Rican, Asian, American Indian, and other Hispanic); and by level of placement by type of admission; 1982. 6 tables. (p. 281-284)

PAROLE

h. Parole board release interviews and outcome, institutional parole activity, and community parole supervision caseload data; FY81-82. 4 tables. (p. 285-289)

VICTIM COMPENSATION

i. Crime Victims Board claims, payments, and awards, FY67-82; award amounts by type, FY82; monthly claims accepted by age and sex, Apr. 1982-Mar. 1983; and claims processed for the elderly, FY80-83. 2 charts and 3 tables. (p. 292-294)

S5765   NEW YORK STATE Department of Health

S5765–1   VITAL STATISTICS of New York State, 1982
Annual. [1984.]
169 p. var. paging.
ISSN 0097-9449.
LC 75-642675.
SRI/MF/complete

Annual compilation, for 1982, of vital statistics for New York State, including births, deaths by cause, marriages, and divorces for the State, NYC, all counties, and cities over 10,000 population, 1980-82, with birth and death trends from 1900.

Report is compiled from the automated vital and health statistics information system of the Bureau of Health Statistics. Major data sources are certificates of birth, death, marriage, and dissolution of marriage; Census Bureau; and related Federal and State information systems.

Contains listings of contents, charts, maps, and tables (3 p.); narrative report, with 6 charts, 14 maps, and 4 summary tables (p. 9-61); 36 tables, listed below (101 p.); and technical notes. (5 p.).

Bureau of Health Statistics also produces a quarterly report, *Vital Statistics Review,* that contains provisional summary data and special studies, but is not covered by SRI. A list of articles in the quarterly and annual reports, 1970-82, appears on the final 6 pages of this annual report.

This is the 103rd annual report.

Availability: New York State Department of Health, Health Statistics Bureau, Rm. 321, ESP Tower Bldg., Albany NY 12237, †; SRI/MF/ complete.

TABLES:

[Upstate New York is the State exclusive of NYC.]

S5765–1.1: Trends, 1962-82

[Tables 1-6 show data for State, NYC, and upstate New York. Tables 2-6 show data for 1962-82.]

1. Estimated population by sex and age, July 1, 1982. (1 p.)

2. Live births, live birth rates, and general fertility rates. (1 p.)

3. Spontaneous fetal deaths 20+ weeks gestation and fetal mortality rates. (1 p.)

4. Deaths, crude death rates, and age-sex-adjusted death rates. (1 p.)

5. Infant deaths (deaths under 1 year of age) and infant mortality rates. (1 p.)

6. Neonatal deaths (deaths under 28 days of age) and neonatal mortality rates. (1 p.)

S5765–1.2: State Data

[All tables show data for 1982. Tables show data for State and upstate New York, unless otherwise noted. Data by color are shown for white and nonwhite.]

LIVE BIRTHS

7-8. Live births by birth weight and color, month in which prenatal care began and color, by age of mother. (2 p.)

9-10. Live births by sex and color, live birth order and color, by age of mother. (2 p.)

DEATHS

11. Deaths and death rates by age and sex. (1 p.)

12-14. Deaths and death rates from selected causes [includes data for NYC]. (3 p.)

15-16. Deaths from 5 leading causes, by age and color. (2 p.)

17-20. Infant deaths (under 1 year of age) from selected causes, [total and] among non-whites, by age and sex. (4 p.)

S5765–1.3: County Data

[Tables show data by resident county and mother's age, 1982.]

21. Live births. (1 p.)

22. Induced abortions. (1 p.)

23. Fetal deaths (gestation 20 weeks and over) excluding induced abortions. (1 p.)

24. Live births, induced abortions, and spontaneous fetal deaths, gestation 20 weeks and over. (1 p.)

25. Out-of-wedlock live births. (1 p.)

26. Live births with live birth order 4 or higher. (1 p.)

S5765–1.4: Marriages and Dissolutions of Marriage

27. Marriages occurring in upstate New York by ages of bride and groom, 1982. (1 p.)

28. Dissolutions of marriage by duration of marriage and type of dissolution: certificates of dissolution of marriage filed in New York State, 1982. (1 p.)

S5765–1.5: Detail by Community, and Reportable Diseases

29.01-29.60. Basic New York State vital statistics by county and by cities and villages with 10,000 or more population: 1980-82 [including estimated population, live births, fetal deaths, deaths by age and 5 causes, nonwhite deaths, marriages, and dissolutions of marriage by type of decree]. (60 p.)

30. Reportable diseases, cases, and deaths: New York State, NYC, and upstate New York, 1981-82. (1 p.)

S5765–1.6: Trends, 1900-82

[Tables show data for State, NYC, and upstate New York, 1900-82.]

31-33. Live births, deaths, fetal deaths, infant deaths, neonatal deaths, and rates. (6 p.)

34-36. Deaths and death rates from [5] selected causes. (6 p.)

S5775   NEW YORK STATE Department of Labor

S5775–1   EMPLOYMENT REVIEW, New York State
Monthly.   Approx. 50 p.
ISSN 0013-6883.
LC 75-645033.
SRI/MF/complete

Monthly report on employment, earnings, and hours, for workers in New York State, NYC, and selected areas of upstate New York. Also covers women's employment. Data are shown by SIC 1- to 3-digit industries.

Data are from Federal and State government records. Report is issued approximately 4 months after month of coverage.

Contents:

a. Contents listing and narrative review of labor situation.

b. 4 monthly summary tables showing labor force status of State and NYC population, for current month, 12 previous months, and annually from 1970s; and employment, unemployment, and unemployment rate, by county and major labor area, for month of coverage, previous month, and same month of previous year.

c. 23 detailed monthly tables on employment, earnings, hours, and women's employment, by industry.

d. 20 quarterly tables on insured employment and payrolls.

e. Special features, usually with tables.

f. Data explanations and publications list.

Detailed monthly and quarterly tables are listed below. Monthly tables appear in all issues. All additional features with substantial statistical content are described, as they appear, under "Statistical Features;" page locations and latest periods of coverage for quarterly tables are also noted. Nonstatistical features are not covered.

Availability: New York State Department of Labor, Research and Statistics Division, Publications Office, State Campus, Bldg. No. 12, Albany NY 12240, †; SRI/MF/complete.

Issues reviewed during 1984: Aug. 1983-July 1984 (D) (Vol. 36, Nos. 8-12; Vol. 37, Nos. 1-7).

DETAILED MONTHLY TABLES:

[Monthly tables A3-D3 generally show data for month of coverage, with comparisons to previous month and/or same month of previous year.]

NEW YORK STATE EMPLOYMENT, EARNINGS, AND HOURS

A1. Employees in nonagricultural establishments, by industry division [annually from 1939 and monthly for 13 or more consecutive months through month of coverage].

A2. Earnings and hours of production workers in manufacturing establishments [annually from 1947 and monthly for 13 or more consecutive months through month of coverage].

A3. Employees, earnings, and hours in nonagricultural establishments, by [SIC 2- and 3-digit] industry.

A4. Average weekly hours and average overtime hours of production workers in selected [SIC 2-digit] manufacturing industries.

NEW YORK COMBINED AREA AND UPSTATE AREA EMPLOYMENT, EARNINGS, AND HOURS

B1-B5. [Data in table A3 are repeated for New York combined area, NYC, Westchester County, Rockland County, and Nassau-Suffolk area.]

C1-C11. [Data in table A3 are repeated for 9-11 upstate counties or areas.]

WOMEN'S EMPLOYMENT

D1-D3. Women as percent of all employees in manufacturing industries [geographic detail similar to tables B1-B5 and C1-C11].

QUARTERLY TABLES:

[All quarterly tables begin "Reporting units, employment, and payrolls covered by unemployment insurance..." Tables show employment for each month of the quarter ending 5-8 months prior to month of coverage, and payroll for the total quarter.]

1-10. In New York State, NYC, and 8 State areas, by industry [division and major group].

11. [By county and industry division.]

C1-C9. [In 9 selected counties with employment of 100,000 or more], by industry division and major group.

STATISTICAL FEATURES:

S5775–1.501: Aug. 1983 (Vol. 36, No. 8)

QUARTERLY TABLES

1-11 and C1-C9. Reporting units, employment, and payrolls covered by unemployment insurance, by industry, labor market area, and county, 4th quarter 1982, with average employment and total payroll 1982. (p. 34-63, 75-83)

AVERAGE WEEKLY EARNINGS IN INSURED EMPLOYMENT, 1978-82, ANNUAL FEATURE

(p. 64-73) Annual feature presenting 5 tables showing the following:

a. Average weekly earnings of employees covered by New York State unemployment insurance law: by industry division and major group, for New York State and NYC; by industry division for 8 major labor market areas; and by county; 1978-82.

b. Reporting units, average monthly employment, and average weekly earnings of Federal and State/local government employees covered by unemployment insurance, New York State, 1982.

S5775-1.502: Oct. 1983 (Vol. 36, No. 10)

QUARTERLY TABLES

1-11 and C1-C9. Reporting units, employment, and payrolls covered by unemployment insurance, by industry, labor market area, and county, 1st quarter 1983. (p. 31-73)

S5775-1.503: Dec. 1983 (Vol. 36, No. 12)

QUARTERLY TABLES

1-11 and C1-C9. Reporting units, employment, and payrolls covered by unemployment insurance, by industry, labor market area, and county, 2nd quarter 1983. (p. 32-73)

S5775-1.504: Jan. 1984 (Vol. 37, No. 1)

ANNUAL REVISIONS OF NONFARM EMPLOYMENT ESTIMATES, NEW YORK STATE, NEW YORK COMBINED AREA, NYC, AND UPSTATE AREAS BY INDUSTRY, 1982-83, ANNUAL FEATURE

(p. 4-47) Annual table, repeated for New York State, New York combined area, NYC, and 14 upstate counties or areas, presenting revisions of monthly employment estimates by industry, based on the 1983 benchmark. Revisions supersede estimates previously published for 1982-83 in the Jan.-Dec. 1983 issues of *Employment Review*.

EARNINGS AND HOURS IN NONAGRICULTURAL ESTABLISHMENTS, ANNUAL AVERAGES, 1983, ANNUAL FEATURE

(p. 48-58) Annual table, repeated for New York State, New York combined area (including NYC and neighboring counties), and 11 upstate counties or areas, showing manufacturing hours and earnings, generally by industry group, 1983.

S5775-1.505: Feb. 1984 (Vol. 37, No. 2)

1983 IN REVIEW, ANNUAL FEATURE

(p. 6-10) Annual article, by Vincent F. DeSantis et al., with 4 tables showing New York State population and labor force by employment status, by sex and race and for Hispanics, with selected detail for youth aged 16-19; wage/salary employment by industry division, and change from 1977; and employment and unemployment, by State labor area; 1982-83.
    Data are from Current Population Survey of Households.

S5775-1.506: Apr. 1984 (Vol. 37, No. 4)

QUARTERLY TABLES

1-11 and C1-C9. Reporting units, employment, and payrolls covered by unemployment insurance, by industry, labor market area, and county, 3rd quarter 1983. (p. 35-77)

S5775-1.507: May 1984 (Vol. 37, No. 5)

UNEMPLOYMENT INSURANCE TAX RATES, 1983, ANNUAL FEATURE

(p. 6-25) Annual article, by Elias D. Loizides, on New York State unemployment insurance taxes, with 10 tables showing tax data, including number of employer accounts and average tax rates for 1983, tax contributions and bene-

fit charges for 1982, and total and taxable payrolls for year ending Sept. 30, 1982, all by SIC 1- and 2-digit industry and size of firm.

S5800   NEW YORK STATE
Department of
Social Services

S5800-2   STATISTICAL SUPPLEMENT, 1982 ANNUAL REPORT, New York State Department of Social Services
Annual. [1984.]   4+57 p.
SRI/MF/complete.

Annual report, for 1982, on New York State public welfare caseloads, recipients, expenditures, and payments. Data are shown by month, source of funds, program, and county or welfare district.
    Contains table and chart listings (4 p.); and 6 sections with 15 charts, and 40 tables listed below (p. 1-57).
    Report is the statistical supplement to *Department of Social Services Annual Report*, which is largely narrative. Narrative report is published 6-8 months prior to supplement and is not covered in SRI.
    A monthly report with similar but less detailed data on New York State welfare is also issued, but is not covered in SRI.
Availability: New York State Department of Social Services, Ten Eyck Bldg., 40 N. Pearl St., Albany NY 12243, †; SRI/MF/complete.

TABLES:
[Tables show data for New York State, NYC, and rest of State, 1982, unless otherwise noted. Sources of funds are local and/or Federal and State aid.]

S5800-2.1: Public Assistance and Services Programs

1. Expenditures in the State-aided public assistance and services programs [by source of funds, program, and object of expense]. (p. 1)
2. Cost of local administration of State-aided public assistance and medical assistance programs, by source of funds [and program]. (p. 2)
3. Expenditures in State-aided [and federally-aided] programs, by public assistance program and welfare district. (p. 3)

S5800-2.2: Public Assistance
[Tables 8-9 and 11-18 show data for 1972-82. Reasons for opening and closing cases include health, family, financial, and legal.]

SUMMARY AND TRENDS

4. Cases and persons receiving aid in the public assistance program, by program and month. (p. 4)
5. Expenditures for public assistance, by program and month [and source of funds]. (p. 5)
6-7. Monthly average number of cases and persons, and monthly average payment per case and per person, in the public assistance programs, by program and welfare district. (p. 6-7)
8-9. Monthly average number of cases and persons receiving assistance; and amount of assistance by source of funds. (p. 8-9)

10. Annual payments by source of funds, and monthly average cases, persons and payments in the public assistance program. (p. 12)

AID TO DEPENDENT CHILDREN

11. Monthly average number of families and persons receiving assistance, amount of assistance, and monthly average payment. (p. 14)
12-13. Reasons for opening and closing cases [State totals only]. (p. 17-18)

HOME RELIEF

14-16. Monthly average number of cases and persons receiving assistance, amount of assistance, and monthly average payment. (p. 19-21)
17-18. Reasons for opening and closing cases [State totals only]. (p. 25-26)

S5800-2.3: Medical Assistance
[All tables except tables 24-26 show data by welfare district.]

19. Monthly average number of medical assistance eligible persons by category of eligibility. (p. 27)
20-22. Medical assistance expenditures by source of funds and major types of care; and percentage distribution of medical assistance by major type of care (parts I and II). (p. 29-33)
23. Estimated monthly average number of medical assistance beneficiaries. (p. 35)
24-26. Monthly average number of beneficiaries receiving care, amount of expenditures by source of funds, and yearly average payment, 1972-82. (p. 36-39)

S5800-2.4: Children's Services, Food Stamps, and Other Programs
[Tables 27-28, 33, 36, and 38-39 show data by welfare district.]

SERVICES SUMMARY

27-28. Cases and expenditures for services by type [including day and foster care, adult/children preventive and protective, adoption, adult care, administrative, and other]; and expenditures, by local district claiming schedule. (p. 40-41)

FOSTER CARE AND OTHER CHILDREN'S SERVICES
[Data by type of foster care are shown for some or all of the following: institutions; group, foster family, and boarding homes; and other.]

29. Children in foster care, by type of care, and county of residence, Dec. 31, 1982. (p. 42)
30. Children in foster care, by type of care, end of year 1971-82. (p. 44)
31. Expenditures for foster care and adoption subsidies, New York State (only), 1972-82. (p. 46)
32. Adoptions completed [by sex, age, race including Hispanic, and subsidy status]. (p. 47)
33. Day care: monthly average number of children [including cash grant, family/in-home, and group care recipients]. (p. 48)
34. Trends in abuse and neglect reports registered, 1973-82. (p. 49)

FOOD STAMPS
[Tables show data for public assistance recipients and others.]

35. Food stamp program participants and total coupon values, by month. (p. 50)

36. Monthly average number of households and persons participating in the food stamp program, and total coupon values. (p. 51)

37. Annual coupon values, monthly average number of households and persons participating in the food stamp program, 1975-82. (p. 52)

CHILD SUPPORT AND SSI

38. Child support collections from [absent Aid to Dependent Children (ADC) and non-ADC parents]. (p. 55)

39. SSI: recipients, total program expenditures, Federal expenditures, and State supplement. (p. 56)

40a-40b. Monthly average number of SSI recipients by living arrangement and location and category of assistance. (p. 57)

S5885   NORTH CAROLINA Department of Agriculture

S5885–1   NORTH CAROLINA AGRICULTURAL STATISTICS, 1983
Annual. [1983.] 72 p.
No. 151.
SRI/MF/complete

Annual report on North Carolina agricultural production, marketing, and finances, mostly 1981-82, with some data for 1983 and selected trends from the 1970s. Data generally are shown by commodity and/or county and district, and include selected comparisons to other States.

Report generally covers production, prices, sales, value, and, as applicable, acreage, yield, and stocks or inventory, for field crop, fruit and nut, livestock, poultry, dairy, and apiary sectors.

Report also includes data on number, acreage, and value of farms; pasture condition; farm income, expenses, and labor; agricultural exports; fertilizer shipments; and weather.

Data are compiled by the North Carolina Crop and Livestock Reporting Service from reports of the North Carolina and U.S. Agriculture Depts.

Contains contents listing (1 p.); report, with narrative summaries, 20 maps, 3 charts, and 107 tables, grouped in 5 sections (p. 4-71); and lists of additional reports available from State Crop Reporting Service, and counties by crop reporting districts (p. 72-73).

For description of previous report, for 1980-81, see SRI 1982 Annual, under this number.

Availability: North Carolina Crop and Livestock Reporting Service, Agricultural Statistician, PO Box 27767, One W. Edenton St., Raleigh NC 27611, †; SRI/MF/complete.

S5900   NORTH CAROLINA Department of Correction

S5900–1   NORTH CAROLINA DEPARTMENT OF CORRECTION Statistical Abstract
Quarterly.   Approx. 65 p.
SRI/MF/complete

Quarterly report on North Carolina correctional institution population, admissions, and separations, by county, offense, and inmate demographic characteristics. Includes data on inmates who are on work and conditional releases, parole, and temporary leave, and data on reasons for terminations of releases and paroles.

Data are from a central inmate master file, updated daily by correctional institutions. Reports are issued approximately 6 weeks after quarter of coverage.

Contains contents listing, introduction, and 36 tables listed below.

The 4th quarter issue shows cumulative data for current year (except average prison population, which is for 4th quarter).

Availability: North Carolina Department of Correction, Research and Evaluation, 831 W. Morgan St., Raleigh NC 27603, †; SRI/MF/complete.

Issues reviewed during 1984: July/Sept. 1983-Apr./June 1984 (D).

QUARTERLY TABLES:
[Unless otherwise noted, tables show data for misdemeanants and felons, for quarter of coverage. Data by location are shown by State and youth institution, and by county arranged by region.

Data by type of offense are shown for 22 offenses.]

S5900–1.1: Inmate Admissions, Separations, and Population

ADMISSIONS

[Tables [1-9] show data by type of admission: new admission, probation and parole revoked, capture, and conditional release revoked.]

[1-4] Admissions by total sentence length, current offense, [type of] sentencing court, and county of conviction.

[5-8] Admissions by race [including Indian and Oriental], sex, age, education, and marital status.

[9] Admissions by admitting location.

SEPARATIONS

[Tables [10-18] show data by type of separation: discharge, court, parole, conditional release, death, escape, and pardon.]

[10-17] Tables [1-8] are repeated for separations.

[18] Separations by separation location.

INMATE POPULATION

[19-25] [Tables [2-8] are repeated for end of period stock population; all data are cross-tabulated by total sentence length.]

[26] Average population [by] present location [data are not shown by misdemeanant and felon status].

S5900–1.2: Paroles/Probations, Releases, and Violations

PAROLES AND TERMINATIONS

[1] End of period parole population, by race, sex, and county of supervision.

[2] Parole terminations, by time under supervision and type of termination [completion, violation by type, and arrests by type of offense].

CONDITIONAL RELEASES AND TERMINATIONS

[3] End of period conditional release population, by race, sex, and county of supervision.

[4] End of period conditional release terminations, by time under supervision and type of termination [same breakdowns as table [2]].

RULE VIOLATIONS

[5] Rule violations by type of violation and location.

WORK RELEASES AND TERMINATIONS

[6] On work release, by how placed [parole and court] and location.

[7] Off work release, by why removed [discharge, parole, escape, infraction, administrative, health, job, and other] and location.

[8] End of period work release population, by time on program and location.

TEMPORARY LEAVES

[9] Temporary leaves, by type of visit [job, medical, training, funeral, illness, and other] and location.

[10] Temporary leaves [terminations] by number of visits, and type of violation.

S5910   NORTH CAROLINA Department of Cultural Resources

S5910–1   STATISTICS AND DIRECTORY OF NORTH CAROLINA PUBLIC LIBRARIES, July 1, 1982-June 30, 1983
Annual.   Jan. 1984.   34 p.
ISSN 0164-0844.
LC 78-647664.
SRI/MF/complete

Annual report, for FY83, on North Carolina public library finances, holdings, circulation, and personnel, by library system. Also includes directory of public libraries and directors.

Contains contents listing (p. 4); statistical summary table (p. 5); 6 tables, listed below (p. 6-23); and directory (p. 25-34).

State library also publishes *Statistics of North Carolina Special Libraries* and *Statistics of North Carolina University and College Libraries,* not covered by SRI.

Availability: North Carolina Department of Cultural Resources, State Library Division, 109 E. Jones St., Raleigh NC 27611, ‡; SRI/MF/complete.

TABLES:
[All tables show data by regional, county, municipal, and Indian reservation library systems, FY83. Tables I and III-IV also show estimated 1981 population.]

I. Finance [operating receipts, by source; and operating expenditures for personnel, books, periodicals, audiovisuals, microforms, binding, and processing; and capital outlay]. (p. 6)

II. Sources of local receipts [county, municipality, other, and balance brought forward]. (p. 10)

III. Public library collections [total, adult, and juvenile books; volumes and titles added, and volumes withdrawn; and periodicals, recordings, slides, microform titles, films, and filmstrips]. (p. 12)

IV. Use of books [circulation by type of book; circulation for main library, branches, mobile units, mail, and in-house; reference questions answered; and interlibrary loans]. (p. 16)

V. Use of nonbook materials [and audience for library-sponsored and nonlibrary-sponsored progams]. (p. 20)

VI. Miscellaneous [professional and non-professional FTE personnel; and vehicles operated, by type]. (p. 22-23)

S5915   NORTH CAROLINA Department of Public Education

S5915-1   STATISTICAL PROFILE, North Carolina Public Schools, 1984
Annual. 1984.
389 p. var. paging.
ISSN 0148-2742.
LC 75-622263.
SRI/MF/complete, current & previous year reports

Annual report on North Carolina elementary and secondary public school pupils, personnel, and finances, 1982/83 academic year, with trends from 1972/73, some data for 1983/84, and enrollment projections through 1993. Includes data by local education agency (LEA) and regional education center.

Data are compiled by the Public Education Dept.

Contents:

Introduction, and contents and table listings. (p. iii-x)

Part I. State Summary. Includes 1 map; and 1 chart and 32 tables, listed below, with interspersed narrative. (p. I.1-I.83)

Part II. Local Education Agencies. Includes definitions; and 4 tables, also listed below, repeated for each LEA and 8 regional education centers. (p. II.1-II.305)

This is the 10th annual report.

Previous report, for 1983, was also reviewed in 1984 and is also available on SRI microfiche under this number [Annual. May 1983. 379 p. var. paging. $12.00+postage].

Availability: North Carolina Department of Public Education, Information and Publications, Education Bldg., Rm. 352, Raleigh NC 27611, $12.00; SRI/MF/complete.

CHART AND TABLES:

S5915-1.1: State Summary

GRADE ENROLLMENT, ATTENDANCE, AND PROMOTIONS

[Tables 1-7 show data by grade, for 12 grades and kindergarten, and usually for elementary and high school exceptional children classes. Tables 1-6 show data for 1973/74-1982/83 school years; tables 1-3 also show data for 1st month, 1983/84 school year.]

1. Final enrollment. (p. I.3)

2-3. Final average daily membership and attendance. (p. I.4-I.5)

4. Membership last day. (p. I.6)

5-6. Promotions and nonpromotions. (p. I.7-I.8)

7. Nonpromotion rate, 1978/79-1982/83. (p. I.9)

ENROLLMENT PROJECTIONS AND CHARACTERISTICS

[Tables 8-10 show data by LEA.]

[A] Projected final average daily membership, by grade, 1983/84-1987/88. (p. I.10)

8. Projected final average daily membership, 1984/85-1988/89. (p. I.11)

9. Pupils in membership being served by exceptional children programs [by type of handicap, and for gifted students and pregnant students, as of Dec. 1, 1983]. (p. I.14)

10. Pupils in membership by race [and ethnic origin, including American Indian, Asian, and Hispanic], and sex, 1983/84. (p. I.17)

11. Pupil membership by race/ethnic origin [including American Indian/Alaskan Native, Asian/Pacific Islander, and Hispanic, 1972/73-1983/84]. (p. I.20)

HIGH SCHOOL GRADUATES AND DROPOUTS

[Intentions include postsecondary enrollment by institution type, in- and out-of-State; military enlistment; and seeking employment.]

12. 1983 high school graduates intentions including 1982 summer school [by sex, by race and for American Indian and other ethnic groups]. (p. I.21)

13. Intentions of high school graduates: a 5-year history [1979-83]. (p. I.22)

14. Estimated annual high school dropout rate [for regular and extended day program, 1982/83; and estimated retention rate (1982/83 graduates as percent of 1979/80 ninth grade enrollment); all by LEA]. (p. I.24-I.26)

15. Projection of public high school graduates [by LEA], 1984-93. (p. I.28-I.30)

PUBLIC SCHOOL PERSONNEL

[Tables 16-20 show data for 1983/84.]

16. Public school full-time personnel [by position, by source of funds (government level and vocational funding), and by sex and race]. (p. I.32)

17. [Employment] experience status of instructional personnel [by LEA]. (p. I.33)

18. Highest degree held by professional personnel [by LEA]. (p. I.36)

19. Teacher profile by subject area (grades 7-12) [and sex]. (p. I.39)

20. Selected characteristics of public school staff [percent of teachers with graduate degree and with no prior experience, and percent of professional staff paid entirely from local funds, with rankings, by LEA]. (p. I.41-I.43.)

FINANCES AND PERSONAL INCOME

[Unless otherwise noted, data are for 1982/83. Sources of funds are Federal, State, and local.]

21. Current expense expenditures by source of funds [and object, total and per pupil]. (p. I.46)

22. Distribution of the dollar for public education. [chart] (p. I.47)

23. Comparison of per pupil expenditures, current expense expenditures only [by source of funds, 1973/74-1982/83]. (p. I.48)

24-25. Per pupil expenditure ranking [and amount by source of funds, by LEA]. (p. I.49-I.54)

26. Revenue [current expense and capital outlay, by detailed item]. (p. I.55)

27. Current expense expenditures by [detailed program including special, adult, and vocational education, and support services; by object and source of funds]. (p. I.56-I.63)

28. Capital outlay expenditures by source of funds [for 3 project categories and other]. (p. I.64)

29. Local revenue and expenditure for public education [total and per pupil, by county], 1981/82. (p. I.66)

30. 1981 per capita personal income by counties [with ranking]. (p. I.68)

TRANSPORTATION AND COURSE MEMBERSHIP

31. Student transportation on public school buses [number of buses and miles, and cost, by LEA], 1982/83. (p. I.70-I.72)

32. Course membership summary [number of classes and students, by course, aggregate for grades 7-12], 1983/84. (p. I.73-I.82)

S5915-1.2: Local Education Agencies

[The 4 tables listed below are repeated for each LEA and regional education center. Data for LEAs also include number of elementary and secondary schools.]

[1] Pupil accounting [enrollment, average daily membership, and average daily attendance, 1982/83 and 1st month 1983/84; and membership last day, promotions, and nonpromotions, 1982/83; all by grade and for exceptional children classes].

[2] 1982/83 high school graduate intentions [same breakdowns as in State summary table 12].

[3] 1983/84 public school personnel summary [same breakdowns as in State summary table 16].

[4] 1982/83 current expense expenditures by source of funds [same breakdowns as in State summary table 21].

S5925 NORTH CAROLINA Employment Security Commission

S5925–2 NORTH CAROLINA LABOR FORCE ESTIMATES, 1984, by County, Defined Multi-County Labor Areas, State, Multi-County Planning Regions
Annual. Oct. 1984. 272 p.
ISSN 0093-6588.
LC 77-648711.
SRI/MF/complete, current & previous year reports

Annual report estimating North Carolina civilian labor force, unemployment, and employment, by industry division and SIC 2-digit manufacturing group, all by location, monthly 1983, and annual average estimates, 1974-83.

Contents:

a. Preface, contents listing, and 1 summary table. (p. 1-11)

b. 1 basic table repeated by county (p. 15-214), by multi-county labor area (including 7 SMSAs) (p. 217-242), for total State (p. 244-246), and by multi-county planning region (annual averages only) (p. 249-266).

c. Appendices, with explanatory notes, definitions, data sources, and SIC 2-digit code titles. (p. 269-272)

This is the 23rd report in the series.

Previous report, for 1982, was also reviewed in 1984 and is also available on SRI microfiche, under this number [Annual. Dec. 1983. 272 p. †].

Availability: North Carolina Employment Security Commission, Labor Market Information Division, PO Box 25903, Raleigh NC 27611, †; SRI/MF/complete.

S5925–5 STATE LABOR SUMMARY, North Carolina
Monthly. Approx. 12 p.
SRI/MF/complete, shipped quarterly

Monthly report on North Carolina nonagricultural employment, hours, and earnings, by industry division and group. Also includes demographic characteristics of registered job applicants, and number of job openings by occupation.

Report, compiled by the Employment Security Commission, is issued approximately 2 months after month of coverage.

Contains narrative summary; and 7 monthly tables, listed below.

Additional monthly and bimonthly reports showing labor force data by SMSA are also available from issuing agency, but are not covered in SRI.

Availability: North Carolina Employment Security Commission, Labor Market Information Division, PO Box 25903, Raleigh NC 27611, ‡; SRI/MF/complete, shipped quarterly.

Issues reviewed during 1984: Aug. 1983-Aug. 1984 (D).

MONTHLY TABLES:
[Unless otherwise noted, tables show data for North Carolina for month of coverage, preceding month, and same month of previous year. Order of tables may vary from issue to issue. Tables [2-3] may not appear in every issue.]

[1] Civilian labor force [by employment status].

[2] Statewide active applicant file [by age group, sex, race, and ethnic group (Hispanic, American Indian/Alaskan Native, and other); and whether eligible claimant, veteran, handicapped, and seasonal farmworker; for last day of month of coverage only].

[3] Statewide job openings data [number received and filled, for month of coverage and fiscal year to date; and number unfilled as of last day of month of coverage, total and for 30 days or more; all by occupational group].

[4-5] Estimated wage/salary employment in nonagricultural industries [unadjusted and seasonally adjusted, by industry division and group].

[6] Estimated number of production workers in selected manufacturing industries.

[7] Estimated average weekly earnings, average weekly hours, and average hourly earnings of production workers in selected manufacturing industries and nonsupervisory employees in selected nonmanufacturing industries.

S5925–6 OCCUPATIONAL EMPLOYMENT REPORTS, North Carolina
Series. For individual publication data, see below.
SRI/MF/complete

Continuing series of reports covering employment in selected groups of North Carolina industries, by detailed occupation.

Data are from Occupational Employment Statistics (OES) surveys of employers in the various industry groups, conducted over a 3-year cycle and covering the following sectors: manufacturing, hospitals, trade, transportation and communication, public utilities, nonmanufacturing, government, and education.

General format of each report:

a. Contents listing; introduction, with 3-5 summary and trend charts; and methodology.

b. 1 table, repeated for each SIC 2- or 3-digit industry covered, showing estimated employment by detailed occupation, at survey date.

Report reviewed during 1984 is described below.

Availability: North Carolina Employment Security Commission, Labor Market Information Division, PO Box 25903, Raleigh NC 27611, †; SRI/MF/complete.

S5925–6.6: Occupational Employment in Trade, Transportation, Communication, Public Utilities, State and Local Government, North Carolina, 1982
[Triennial. Nov. 1983. iv+40 p. SRI/MF/complete.]

Covers occupational employment in 17 SIC 2- or 3-digit industry groups in transportation, communications, public utilities, wholesale trade, and retail trade; and in State and local government. Tables also show relative error measures for most estimates.

Data are based on responses of 4,300 establishments to a survey conducted July 1982-Mar. 1983.

This is the 2nd report on transportation, communication, public utilities, and trade, and the 3rd report on State and local government. For description of previous reports, see SRI 1982 Annual, under S5925-6.2 and S5925-6.3, respectively.

S5925–7 ANNUAL PLANNING INFORMATION, North Carolina
Annual, discontinued.

Annual planning report for North Carolina, discontinued with the FY84 edition (for description, see SRI 1983 Annual, under this number.) Report identified population groups in need of employment services, and presented data on employment by industry and occupation, population, and labor force.

Report has been discontinued due to lack of funding. Issuing agency publishes several related reports, including *North Carolina Labor Force Estimates, State Labor Summary,* and *Occupational Employment Reports,* covered in SRI under S5925-2, S5925-5, and S5925-6, respectively.

S5930 NORTH CAROLINA Office of the Governor

S5930–2 SUMMARY STATISTICS FOR SELECTED AREAS: 1980 Census of Population and Housing, North Carolina
Monograph. Aug. 1983.
62 p. Technical Rpt. No. 3.
LC 83-623339.
SRI/MF/complete

Report presenting 1980 U.S. Census of Population and Housing selected findings for North Carolina SMSAs, planning regions, and counties, and for U.S. census regions and States. Includes data on population and housing characteristics, households, employment, commuting, education, income, and poverty.

Data are from 1980 U.S. Census Summary Tape File 3 (STF 3).

Contains contents listing (1 p.); introduction and highlights (p. 1-7); 3 tables presenting rankings of States and North Carolina locales for selected census items (p. 8-15); 4 detailed tables described below (p. 16-55); and footnotes and glossary (p. 56-62).

Availability: North Carolina Office of the Governor, State Budget and Management Office, Research and Planning Services, 116 W. Jones St., Raleigh NC 27611, $2.00; SRI/MF/complete.

TABLES:
[Tables present data on the topics described below. Data are shown for each of the geographic entities mentioned above, and for total U.S., and North Carolina total metro and nonmetro areas.]

a. Population by urban-rural and farm status; family, household, and individual income, and family income by householder's race; families by composition and presence of children; poverty status of families and individuals, with detail by race and for children and persons 65/over.

b. Labor force status, with detail by sex, for women by presence of children, and for persons with work disability; workers by place of work (in or out of residence county) and by method of travel to work, with average travel time.

c. Education, including years of school completed for persons 25/over; and school enrollment by level, with detail for private schools.

d. Housing, including monthly owner costs by mortgage status; gross rent; household income level by tenure; occupied units without telephone; and number of units (including mobile homes) at address.

S5930–3   EQUAL EMPLOYMENT OPPORTUNITY SPECIAL FILE: 1980 North Carolina Census of Population
Monograph. Sept. 1983.
32 p. Technical Rpt. No. 4.
LC 84-620672.
SRI/MF/complete

Report presenting 1980 census data, for North Carolina, on civilian labor force by detailed occupation and by educational attainment, crosstabulated by sex and race-ethnicity. Educational data include further detail by age group. Ethnic groups include American Indians (for occupational data) and Indian/Eskimo/Aleut and Asian/Pacific Islander (for educational data).

Data are from the Equal Employment Opportunity (EEO) Special File, which is based on the long-form questionnaire distributed to a sample of households in the 1980 Census of Population and Housing. The EEO file includes the entire civilian labor force in its universe, whereas much of the other census data on occupations (e.g. Summary Tape File 3) covers only employed civilians. The EEO file was produced to help meet the needs of government and private industry in planning for EEO/Affirmative Action.

Contains contents listing (1 p.); introduction and user notes (p. 1-5); 2 tables (p. 7-21); definition of occupational categories and terms (p. 22-31); and facsimile of census questionnaire on occupations (p. 32).

Availability: North Carolina Office of the Governor, State Budget and Management Office , Research and Planning Services, 116 W. Jones St., Raleigh NC 27611, $2.00; SRI/MF/complete.

S5930–4   NORTH CAROLINA STATE GOVERNMENT STATISTICAL ABSTRACT, Fifth Edition, 1984
Biennial. 1984. xl+575 p.
LC 84-623001.
SRI/MF/complete

Biennial compilation, for 1984, of detailed demographic, social, governmental, and economic statistics for North Carolina. Data are shown primarily for 1970s-82, with trends from as early as 1900. Data are primarily from State and Federal sources.

Report is designed to present a comprehensive overview of the State. Extensive socioeconomic, demographic, and geographic breakdowns are shown, as applicable, for most topics. These breakdowns include data by city, county and other State region, SMSA, urban-rural status, commodity, government agency, income, industry, occupation, age, educational attainment, marital status, race, and sex. Comparisons to other States and total U.S. are also occasionally included.

Contents:

a. Preface; contents and table listings; and introduction containing the following: 2 maps of North Carolina MSAs and State planning regions, 1 chart showing county composition of 1983 MSAs vs. 1980 SMSAs, 3 tables showing summary data for each SMSA from the 1980 Census of Population and Housing, and 1 table showing comparative State rankings in 21 selected socioeconomic areas. (p. iii-xl)

b. 12 data sections, described below, containing 72 charts and maps, and 378 tables. Each section also includes a glossary. (p. 1-568)

c. Index. (p. 571-575)

Report for 1979 is described in SRI 1980 Annual under S5880-1. Name of issuing agency has changed from North Carolina Dept of Administration. The report for 1984 is the 1st published since 1979; issuing agency plans to return to a biennial publication schedule.

North Carolina Statistical Register, providing an inventory of statistical information available from State government agencies, is also available from the issuing agency, but is not currently covered by SRI.

Availability: Librarian, State Budget and Management Office, Research and Planning Services, 116 W. Jones St., Raleigh NC 27611, $15.00; SRI/MF/complete.

DATA SECTIONS:
[Data sources appear beneath each table.]

S5930–4.1: Section 1: Population and Housing

(p. 1-50) Contains 4 charts/maps and 28 tables. Includes population from 1910; median age; rural farm and nonfarm population; residence in 1975, including different county, specific U.S. regions, and abroad; population change components, including births, deaths, and migration by region and State; land area; and resident ancestry and birthplace.

Also includes households and housing occupancy, including persons in group quarters; housing units and structural and financial characteristics; and new public housing authorized.

S5930–4.2: Section 2: Vital Statistics and Health

(p. 51-103) Contains 7 charts/maps and 40 tables. Includes births, deaths by cause, infant and fetal deaths, abortions, morbidity rates for selected communicable diseases, marriages and divorces, life expectancy, fertility rates, percent of adults reporting chronic and neurological diseases, occupational injuries/illnesses and workdays lost, and percent of children in 1st grade meeting minimum immunization requirements.

Also includes exercise and smoking habits, main source of medical care and travel time required, and health insurance coverage, all based on surveys; physicians, dentists, nurses, and other health professionals; hospitals, nursing homes, mental health facilities, group homes, and beds or residents; medical costs; and local health dept funds by source.

Also includes mental health facility population movement, employees, and expenditures, with detail for mental health hospitals and clinics, and centers for alcoholic rehabilitation and mentally retarded; and blind and visually impaired persons.

S5930–4.3: Section 3: Social and Human Services

(p. 105-149) Contains 6 charts/maps and 26 tables. Includes AFDC, SSI, Medicaid, and social security recipients and payments; AFDC grant reductions due to work incentive programs; State/county special assistance aged and disabled recipients and payments; food stamp recipients and value of coupons; Medicare enrollment; and veterans by period of service and VA expenditures.

Also includes State and local government retirement system summary; persons with work disabilities, by labor force status; vocational rehabilitation client characteristics and dispositions; child day care facilities, enrollment, employees, and sponsors; neglected and abused children; and child support enforcement activity.

S5930–4.4: Section 4: Education

(p. 151-206) Contains 6 charts/maps and 43 tables. Includes educational attainment of population; enrollment for public and private nursery, elementary, and secondary schools since 1939/40; public school professional personnel; and nonpublic schools.

Also includes high school graduates and postgraduate plans; dropouts; public school expenditures by source of funds; special education enrollment, by type of handicap, and for gifted and pregnant students; textbook inventory and expenditures; school bus services and cost; and school lunch and breakfast program participation, income, and cost.

Also includes persons speaking foreign language in home; postsecondary enrollment since 1900, with detail by institution, program, discipline, and type of student housing; degrees conferred, by institution and discipline; and faculty by institution and academic rank.

S5930–4.5: Section 5: Law Enforcement, Courts, and Corrections

(p. 207-248) Contains 3 charts/maps and 33 tables. Includes serious crimes reported, clearances, and offense and/or victim characteristics; arrests; local law enforcement budget, personnel, salaries and benefits, and operations; stolen and recovered property value; narcotics arrests; and traffic violations and dispositions.

Also includes civil and criminal cases filed; case processing times; juvenile cases; legal aid cases and expenditures; youth services school admissions, and average daily population by institution; State prison population, admissions, and separations; parole and probation; recidivism rates; and State residents in Federal prisons.

S5930–4.6: Section 6: Environment, Recreation, and Resources

(p. 249-285) Contains 7 charts/maps and 28 tables. Includes monthly climatological data; air pollution levels; hazardous waste generated, and treatment facilities and methods; water sources and population served; and land area and use summary.

Also includes outdoor recreation areas and acreage; national and State park attendance; fishing license sales; bicycle accidents and characteristics; State zoo attendance and visitor characteristics; museum and historic site attendance; art museum collection acquisitions and value, and events and attendance; symphony concerts and attendance; and public library holdings and circulation, by regional library.

S5930–4.7: Section 7: Energy and Utilities

(p. 287-323) Contains 8 charts/maps and 23 tables. Includes energy consumption by type of fuel and sector; electric, telephone, and gas utility operating and financial data, by class and utility, with detail for electricity generation by prime mover; assessed value of public service corporation property; and average electric power prices and monthly bills.

Also includes occupied housing units with telephones; rural telephone and electric service; year-round housing units by type of heating equipment and fuel, source of water, and method of sewage disposal; and household characteristics by main type of heating fuel.

S5930–4.8: Section 8: State and Local Government Finances and Elections

(p. 325-392) Contains 7 charts/maps and 44 tables. Includes State budget by source of funds; State expenditures by fund source and dept; State and local revenues by source, revenue sharing receipts, indebtedness, cash/security holdings, and tax collections; local expenditures by function; property assessed valuations and tax rates; and alcoholic beverage control store sales.

Also includes voting age population; registered voters by political party; precincts; votes cast in presidential and gubernatorial elections; U.S. and State legislature composition; and characteristics of congressional districts.

S5930–4.9: Section 9: Employment and Income

(p. 393-462) Contains 9 charts/maps and 40 tables. Includes labor force by employment status; average travel time to work; nonagricultural employment; covered employment and wages; unemployment claimants and benefits; and youth employment certificates issued.

Also includes military personnel; persons not in labor force; working women with children; State and local employees and earnings; Federal employees; teacher salaries; law enforcement and corrections employment and expenditures; unionization elections, by union; union membership, total and as percent of nonagricultural employment, by State; and employee benefit program characteristics.

Also includes total and per capita personal income; unrelated individual, household, and family income; poverty guidelines and persons below poverty level; cost of living for 4-person family; consumer attitudes on economic conditions and personal financial situation; and inflation trends.

S5930–4.10: Section 10: Business and Industry

(p. 463-508) Contains 3 charts/maps and 35 tables. Includes banks, deposits, and financial data; savings and loan assns and finances since 1910; credit unions, finances, and membership; insurance company financial and underwriting activity; daily newspaper circulation; and alcoholic beverage control board sales.

Also includes women- and black-owned businesses, employment, payroll, and receipts; business incorporations; traveler expenditures; retail and wholesale sales, establishments, payroll, and employees; and wholesale inventories.

Also includes manufacturing firms, capital investments, payroll, employees, production

worker hours and wages, value added, cost of materials, and shipment values including exports.

Also includes mineral production and value; construction establishments, employees, payroll, and finances; residential, nonresidential, and alteration/addition construction and cost; and commercial fisheries' landings and value.

S5930–4.11: Section 11: Agriculture

(p. 509-538) Contains 6 charts/maps and 20 tables. Includes State ranking in agricultural production; farms and acreage; livestock and poultry inventory; farm employment and wage rates; farm property value; and characteristics of farm operators.

Also includes crop production, value, and acreage; milk and egg production and marketings; flower and nursery plant sales; crop and livestock cash receipts, and government payments; farm production expenses; timber stocks; net farm income; and value of agricultural exports.

S5930–4.12: Section 12: Transportation

(p. 539-568) Contains 5 charts and 18 tables. Includes trip and traveler characteristics; manufacturing shipments, by transport mode and distance; truck inventory and use; truck, bus, and railroad operations and finances; airlines and enplanements, by airport; and vessels, domestic and foreign trade, and revenues passing through State ports.

Also includes commuting data; households by number of vehicles available; motor vehicle registrations; traffic accidents, injuries, and fatalities, and driver characteristics; and highway and street mileage and maintenance expenditures.

S5930–5   NORTH CAROLINA POPULATION PROJECTIONS, 1984 Edition

Monograph.   Apr. 1984.
iv+211 p.+errata sheets.
SRI/MF/complete

Report presenting North Carolina actual and projected population, by age, sex, and race, for the State and by MSA and county, various years 1980-2000, with selected trends from as early as 1950.

Also includes birth, death, and migration trends; and fertility and survival rate trends and projections.

Contains contents listing (p. iii-iv); introduction (p. 1); and report in 6 sections, with brief summary, methodology and assumptions, 1 map, 3 charts, and 17 tables (p. 5-211).

Availability: Librarian, State Budget and Management Office, Research and Planning Services, 116 W. Jones St., Raleigh NC 27611, $5.00; SRI/MF/complete.

S5940   NORTH CAROLINA Department of Human Resources

S5940–1   NORTH CAROLINA VITAL STATISTICS, 1982

Annual. For individual publication data, see below.
LC 79-644285.
SRI/MF/complete

Annual report presenting North Carolina vital statistics, by county, region, and selected city, 1982, with trends from 1978. Covers population, births, deaths by cause, marriages, and divorces. Includes data by race.

Report is issued in 2 volumes, described below. This is the 67th annual vital statistics report. Every 3 years Vol. 2 is expanded to include sociodemographic detail and analyses. Vol. 2 for 1981 is the most recent expanded edition.

Other reports available from the issuing agency, but not covered in SRI, include *Detailed Mortality Statistics,* showing deaths by cause, by age, race, and sex; and *North Carolina Vital Statistics: Annual Provisional Report,* presenting provisional data on births, deaths, marriages, and divorces/annulments, by county and major city.

Availability: North Carolina Department of Human Resources, Health Services Division, State Center for Health Statistics, PO Box 2091, Raleigh NC 27602, †; SRI/MF/complete.

S5940–1.1: Volume 1: Births, Deaths, Population, Marriages, Divorces

[Annual. Sept. 1983. 208 p. var. paging. SRI/MF/complete.]

Contains contents listing (1 p.); introduction, trend analysis, methodology, definitions, and formulas, with illustrative charts and tables (p. 1.1-1.42); and 1 detailed table, described below, repeated for the State (p. 2.1), and by DHR region (p. 3.1-3.4), health service area (p. 4.1-4.6), perinatal care region (p. 5.1-5.6), county (p. 6.1-6.100), and city (p. 7.1-7.43).

Counties and cities are arranged in alphabetical order.

TABLE:

[Births and deaths are shown in detail for residents, with totals for all occurrences regardless of residency. Marriages and divorces are shown by place of occurrence only.

Table shows numbers for 1982, and rates for 1982 and the period 1978-82. Data are shown for whites and nonwhites, unless otherwise noted.]

a. Population, by sex, and natural increase; live births, by sex, and by type of attendant; premature and out-of-wedlock births; and total live birth occurrences.

b. Perinatal deaths, fetal deaths by type of attendant, and out-of-wedlock fetal deaths; neonatal, postneonatal, and infant deaths; and deaths (excluding fetal deaths), by sex, age group, and location (hospital, other institution, home/noninstitution), and total occurrences.

c. Marriages, and divorces/annulments [data are not shown by race].

Tables for cities omit data on population by sex, marriages, and divorces/annulments.

S5940–1.2: Volume 2: Leading Causes of Mortality

[Annual. Dec. 1983. 125 p. var. paging. SRI/MF/complete.]

Contains contents listing and preface (p. iii, vii); and the following sections:

Sections I-IV. Technical Notes, and Mortality Highlights. Includes 2 tables showing North Carolina death rates 1982 and 1979-82 period, and deaths by cause, 1982, with age/race/sex adjusted rates for selected counties. (p. 1.1-4.3)

Section V. Mortality Statistics. Includes 47 maps, and basic table showing deaths and death rates for State, and by DHR region, health service area, and county, 1982 and 1979-82 period. Table is repeated for each of 26 death causes. (p. 5.3-5.149)

Section VI. Multiple Conditions Present at Death. Includes 6 maps, and 2 tables showing underlying causes of death related to primary cause, 1982. (p. 6.3-6.17)

S5955   NORTH CAROLINA Department of Justice

S5955–1   STATE OF NORTH CAROLINA UNIFORM CRIME REPORT, 1983

Annual. [1984.] x+214 p.
ISSN 0096-3208.
LC 75-641275.
SRI/MF/complete

Annual report, for 1983, on North Carolina crimes and arrests, by type of offense, county, and reporting agency. Includes crime analyses by age, sex, and race; data on police employment and assaults on police; and selected trends and forecasts, 1979-84.

Data are compiled by the State Police Information Network from reports of State and local law enforcement agencies, as part of the Uniform Crime Reporting Program.

Contains contents listing (p. ix-x); reporting methodology and definitions, with 1 summary chart and table (p. 1-19); 5 statistical sections with 3 maps and 49 charts, and 70 tables described below, interspersed with narrative (p. 21-203); tabular history of contributing agency participation (p. 205-209); and glossary (p. 211-214).

Maps and charts with substantial data not included in tables are also described below.

Availability: North Carolina Department of Justice, Police Information Network, PO Box 27047, Raleigh NC 27601, $15.00; SRI/MF/complete.

MAPS, CHARTS, AND TABLES:

[Data are shown for North Carolina, 1983 or 1982-83, unless otherwise noted. Index offenses are murder, forcible rape, robbery, aggravated assault, burglary, larceny, and motor vehicle theft. Arson is classified as an Index offense, but data are reported separately and usually are not included in the Crime Index tables.

Data by race are generally shown for white, black, Indian, and Asian; data by ethnicity are for non-Hispanic and Hispanic.]

S5955–1.1: Crime Index

BY INDEX OFFENSE

[With the exception of arson, data for each individual Index offense, and for total, violent, and property Index offenses, include 2 charts and 2 tables showing offenses by month 1982-83; and total offenses, rate per 100,000 population, and percent cleared, annually 1979-83. All additional data are described below.]

a. Total Index crime and violent crime distribution by offense; and crime clocks. 1 map, 9 charts, and 4 tables. (p. 22-31)

b. Murders: by day of week; by age, sex, race, and ethnicity of victim and offender; by victim/offender relationship, weapon type, circumstance, and county; and by occurrence in conjunction with other types of felonies. 1 map, 4 charts, and 7 tables. (p. 34-39)

c. Forcible rapes: by whether actual or attempted and intraracial or interracial; by place, time, and day of week of occurrence; alcohol/drug influence on victim and offender; by victim race, age group, injury status, and relationship to offender; by offender race and age; number of offenders involved per offense; and by weapon used. 4 charts and 14 tables. (p. 42-47)

d. Robberies by type of weapon, and offenses and value stolen by type of premise; bank robberies by institution type and time of day, and value of property stolen and recovered; and aggravated assaults by weapon type. 5 charts and 7 tables. (p. 50-55)

e. Property crime distribution by offense; burglaries by type of entry, and offenses and value stolen by residence and nonresidence day and night occurrence; larceny offenses by type and value stolen; and motor vehicle thefts by vehicle type, with total value stolen and recovered. 10 charts and 12 tables. (p. 58-71)

f. Arson: offenses, rate per 100,000 population, and percent cleared, 1980-83; and offenses by property type, with total value of property damage. 1 chart and 2 tables. (p. 74)

PROJECTIONS

g. Projected and actual Index crimes by offense, 1979-84. 10 charts and 1 table. (p. 76-81)

BY COUNTY AND REPORTING AGENCY

h. Total, violent, and nonviolent crime rates, by county; and Index crimes by offense, and community type and population, employed officers by sex, and civilian employees, by county and reporting agency. 2 tables. (p. 88-145)

STOLEN PROPERTY VALUES

i. Value of property stolen and recovered by month and property type; value stolen, by selected Index offense and offense classification; and value stolen and recovered, by county. 1 chart and 5 tables. (p. 148-158)

S5955–1.2: Arrests, Officers Assaulted, and Summary Data

ARRESTS

a. Arrests for Index offenses and 19 other (Part II) crimes, by age, sex, race, ethnicity, and county. 5 tables. (p. 160-190)

b. Adult and juvenile drug arrests for sale and possession by substance, by sex. 1 table. (p. 192)

OFFICERS ASSAULTED

c. Officers killed, by circumstance, 1974-83 period, and offenders by prior arrest record, annually 1974-83; and assaults by month, type of circumstance and assignment, time of day, weapon, and injury status; and assault clearances. 4 charts and 5 tables. (p. 194-197)

SUMMARY

d. Index offenses, clearances and arrests with rates, and value of stolen property, all by offense; value of recovered property; offense trends by type, 1979-83; and U.S. Index crimes and rates by State, with population, 1982. 1 chart and 5 tables. (p. 200-203)

S5990   NORTH CAROLINA Department of Transportation

S5990–1   NORTH CAROLINA TRAFFIC ACCIDENT FACTS, 1983

Annual. [1984.] 25 p.
SRI/MF/complete, current & previous year reports

Annual report on North Carolina traffic accidents, fatalities, and injuries, by accident type, location, time, and other circumstances, and driver's age, 1983, with trends from as early as 1930.

Also includes data on motor vehicle registrations and mileage; detail for bicycle, moped, motorcycle, and school bus accidents; and licensed drivers and seatbelt usage.

Contains contents listing (1 p.); accident summary (p. 1-2); 8 charts and 16 tables (p. 3-24); and definitions (p. 25).

Previous report, for 1982, was also reviewed in SRI during 1984, and is also available on SRI microfiche, under this number [Annual. [1983.] 3+26 p. †].

SRI coverage begins with the report for 1982.

Availability: North Carolina Department of Transportation, Motor Vehicles Division, 1100 New Bern Ave., Raleigh NC 27697, †; SRI/MF/complete.

S6020   NORTH CAROLINA Utilities Commission

S6020–1   NORTH CAROLINA
UTILITIES COMMISSION:
1984 Report
Annual.   May 1, 1984.
vi+156 p.   Vol. XV.
LC 37-27878.
SRI/MF/complete

Annual report presenting North Carolina public utility financial, operating, and regulatory data, by utility type and/or company, 1981-82 with selected trends from 1960. Utility types are electric, gas, telephone, water/sewer, motor freight and passenger carriers, and railroads.

Includes revenues, expenses, assets, liabilities, rates, customers, employment, salaries/wages, and security issuances, for most utility types; electricity capacity by type of generation; telephones and exchanges; water/sewer systems and customers by county; motor passenger carrier fleet and mileage; and railroad track mileage, freight tons by commodity, highway grade crossings, and grade crossing accident injuries and fatalities.

Also includes number of utilities regulated; Commission finances, regulatory caseload, and motor carrier inspections; electricity demand through 1997; economic impact of utilities on employment, compensation, and selected taxes and fees; and comparative residential electric bills in 9 States and U.S.

Data are from reports filed with the Commission, and Federal and State agency and industry assn published reports.

Contains listings of contents, tables, and charts (p. iii-vi); and 12 chapters, with 35 maps and charts and 69 tables (p. 3-156).

This is the 15th annual report. For description of 14th annual report, see SRI 1982 Annual, under this number.

Availability: North Carolina Utilities Commission, Finance, Statistics, Budget, and Planning Division, PO Box 991, Raleigh NC 27602, $6.00; SRI/MF/complete.

S6070   NORTH DAKOTA Department of Banking and Financial Institutions

S6070–1   STATE OF NORTH DAKOTA
REPORT TO THE STATE
BANKING BOARD, STATE
CREDIT UNION BOARD,
AND TO THE GOVERNOR
for the Biennial Period July
1, 1981-June 30, 1983
Biennial.   [1983.]   1+77 p.
ISSN 0363-3756.
LC 76-645467.
SRI/MF/complete

Biennial report on financial condition of North Dakota State-chartered financial institutions for FY82-83 or 1981-82. Covers banks, trust companies, savings and loan assns, credit unions, and small loan/consumer finance companies.

Includes aggregate assets, liabilities, income, and expenses for most institution types. Also includes bank and trust company equity capital; selected trends for savings and loan assns and credit unions, including financial ratios, 1978-82; and detail on small loan/consumer finance company loan activity and legal action, with summary trends from 1976.

Contains State Banking Board overview, with 5 tables (p. 1-12); and 36 financial tables, interspersed with directories and licensing information (p. 13-77).

Previous biennial report, for FY80-81, was described in SRI 1982 Annual, under this number.

Availability: North Dakota Department of Banking and Financial Institutions, 1301 State Capitol, Bismarck ND 58505-0139, †; SRI/MF/complete.

S6110   NORTH DAKOTA Board of Higher Education

S6110–1   FALL 1983 ENROLLMENTS,
NORTH DAKOTA
INSTITUTIONS OF HIGHER
EDUCATION
Annual.   Dec. 1983.
vi+36 p.
ISSN 0147-5037.
LC 74-622476.
SRI/MF/complete

Annual report on enrollment in 13 North Dakota higher education institutions, fall 1983. Presents data on headcount enrollment by institution, county, and selected student characteristics.

Contains definitions, abbreviations, and contents and table listings (p. iii-vi); and 14 maps and 12 tables, listed below (p. 1-36).

Availability: North Dakota Board of Higher Education, Postsecondary Education Commission, State Capitol, 10th Floor, Bismarck ND 58505-0154, †; SRI/MF/complete.

TABLES:
[Most data are shown by institution, fall 1983. Tables 1-6 and 12 show number of students in 4 undergraduate levels, special and unclassified status, and graduate and professional degree programs.]

1-2. Headcount and full-time enrollments. (p. 1-2)

3-4. Total student credit hours and FTE enrollments of part-time students. (p. 3-4)

5. Total of full-time and FTE of part-time enrollment. (p. 5)

[6] FTE enrollments based on total student credit hours (p. 6)

7-8. Nonresident headcount undergraduate and graduate/professional enrollments, by State [and from Canada and other foreign countries] (p. 7-11)

9. Headcount enrollments by county of residence for North Dakota students. (p. 12)

[9A-9B] Total in-State enrollment [and for each institution], by county of origin [1978-83]. 14 maps. (p. 15-28)

10-11. Headcount enrollments at North Dakota colleges by race [American Indian, Afro-American, Oriental American, Spanish

surname American, American white, and other]; and by citizenship, veteran status, sex, marital status, and transfer status. (p. 29-30)

12. Total student credit hours produced by course level. (p. 31-36)

S6115   NORTH DAKOTA Highway Department

S6115–1   NORTH DAKOTA HIGHWAY
STATISTICS, 1983
Annual.   Jan. 1984.   20 p.
LC 77-625853.
SRI/MF/complete

Annual report on North Dakota highway and street use and finances, and vehicle registrations, 1983. Most data are shown for calendar or fiscal years 1974-83, with some data for 1973.

Covers road and travel mileage, by type of road or vehicle; Federal-aid highway fund disbursements; motor fuel consumption and tax receipts; private and public motor vehicle registrations by type of vehicle; revenues from registration and road user fees; and State Highway Dept receipts by source, and disbursements by function.

Data are compiled by the State Highway Dept from reports and records of State, local, and Federal agencies.

Contains contents listing (1 p.); preface (p. 1); and report, with narrative summaries, 1 chart, and 13 tables (p. 2-20).

Previous report, issued in Nov. 1982, also included selected data by county, including receipts and disbursements for streets/roads, taxable valuations, and property tax levies.

Availability: North Dakota Highway Department, Planning Division, 600 E. Boulevard Ave., Bismarck ND 58505-0178, †; SRI/MF/complete.

S6115–2   1983 NORTH DAKOTA
VEHICULAR ACCIDENT
FACTS
Annual.   July 1984.   27 p.
ISSN 0362-9171.
LC 76-644562.
SRI/MF/complete

Annual report on North Dakota traffic accidents, fatalities, and injuries, by accident and vehicle type, location, time, and other circumstances; and driver and victim characteristics; 1983, with trends from 1974.

Also includes data on economic cost of accidents, blood alcohol content of traffic fatalities, licensed drivers, traffic violations/convictions, use of safety devices, and traffic accidents due to vehicle defects.

Data are compiled primarily from State law enforcement reports.

Contains contents listing (1 p.); introduction and highlights (p. 1-2); and 1 map, 3 charts, and 28 tables (p. 3-27).

Availability: North Dakota Highway Department, Planning Division, 600 E. Boulevard Ave., Bismarck ND 58505-0178, †; SRI/MF/complete.

S6130   NORTH DAKOTA
Office of Director of Institutions

S6130–1   STATE OF NORTH DAKOTA DIRECTOR OF INSTITUTIONS Seventh Biennial Report to the Governor, FY82-83
Biennial. Nov. 30, 1983.
249 p.
SRI/MF/complete

Biennial compilation of reports on selected North Dakota institutions, FY82-83. Covers facilities for the mentally retarded, blind, and deaf; adult and juvenile correctional institutions; radio communications dept; and the State library. Data are from reports submitted to North Dakota Director of Institutions.

Also includes data on Director of Institutions office expenditures by object.

Contains biennial reports of Director of Institutions office (p. 2-5); Grafton State School and San Haven (p. 6- 21); State School for the Deaf (p. 22-40); State School for the Blind (p. 42-66); North Dakota Industrial School (p. 67- 96); State Penitentiary and Farm, and Rough Riders Industries (p. 97-169); radio communications dept (p. 170-210); and State library (p. 211-249).

Reports are individually described below.

For description of previous report, for FY80-81, see SRI 1983 Annual under this number.

Availability: North Dakota Office of Director of Institutions, State Capitol Bldg., Bismarck ND 58505, ‡; SRI/MF/complete.

S6130–1.1: Grafton State School, San Haven, and State Schools for the Deaf and Blind

(p. 6-66) Biennial reports, for FY82-83, on North Dakota Grafton State School and San Haven facilities for the mentally retarded, and State schools for the deaf and blind. Includes data on revenues by source, and/or expenditures by program or object, for each facility.

Also includes data on Grafton State School daily per resident cost of care, employee turnover trends from FY77, and resident population movement by sex for FY83; and San Haven resident census by month and ambulatory status.

Contains narrative reports, interspersed with 8 tables.

S6130–1.2: State Industrial School

(p. 67-96) Biennial report, for FY82-83, on North Dakota Industrial School (NDIS) for juvenile offenders, including student admissions, releases, commitments by age and by agency, previous institutionalizations by facility, and sociodemographic characteristics including county of residence, all by sex; and NDIS financial statements, including expenditures by program and object, and revenues by source.

Includes 1 organizational chart and 9 tables.

S6130–1.3: State Penitentiary and Farm, and Prison Industries

(p. 97-169) Biennial reports, for FY82-83, on North Dakota State Penitentiary and Farm, presenting data on the prison population, including inmate admissions, releases, commit-

ment offense (including drug and alcohol involvement), sentence length, demographic and socioeconomic characteristics and criminal background. Includes data by county of commitment, and by State or country of birth and residence; and selected trends from 1964.

Also includes data on inmate services, including counseling program caseloads, educational activities with funding sources, and infirmary activities; interstate and Federal prisoner transfers; penitentiary and prison industry finances; and detail on prison industry operations, including inmate employment, and financial results by industry.

Contains narrative reports, with 64 tables.

S6130–1.4: Radio Communications Department

(p. 170-210) Biennial report, for FY82-83, on North Dakota radio communications dept activities, including 2-way radio, teletype, and highway emergency and dept telephone use, 1981-1st half 1983; incidents by type and agencies handling emergency dispatches; system maintenance by site; and dept staff, hours, and finances.

Also includes data on hours worked by staff; and National Crime Information Center computer system inquiries and entries, by subject area.

Includes 14 tables.

S6130–1.5: State Library Report

(p. 211-249) Biennial report, for FY82-83, on North Dakota State Library, including staff, holdings, circulation, services, and finances. Includes data on number of interlibrary loan requests received and filled, by requesting library or library type.

Includes 19 tables.

S6140   NORTH DAKOTA
Job Service

S6140–2   ANNUAL PLANNING REPORT, FY85, North Dakota
Annual. Aug. 1984.
1+99 p.
LC 82-644178.
SRI/MF/complete

Annual planning report, for FY85, presenting data on North Dakota employment and income by industry, occupational employment, and population and labor force demographic characteristics, with comparisons to U.S.

Most data are current to 1982 or 1983, with trends from the 1970s. Selected data are shown by county.

Data are primarily from Census Bureau and other Federal agencies.

Contents:

a. Contents and table listing, and map. (3 p.)

b. 8 narrative sections, with interspersed summary and text statistics, including 1 table (p. 54) showing unemployment insurance claimants residing out of State, 1981-2nd quarter 1984; and bibliography. (p. 1-58)

c. 5 appendices, with 23 tables, listed below (p. 59-99); and directory of local job service offices (inside back cover).

Availability: North Dakota Job Service, Research and Statistics Section, 1000 E. Divide Ave., PO Box 1537, Bismarck ND 58502, †; SRI/MF/complete.

TABLES:

[Data are for North Dakota, unless otherwise noted. Data by county are arranged by State planning regions. Data by industry generally are shown by industry division.

Data for urban and rural counties include detail for rural counties with significant employment in synthetic natural gas plant construction industry.]

S6140–2.1: Appendices

POPULATION

1-2. Population projections to 1983 and 1985, by age; and population by age, sex, and county, 1980. (p. 61-64)

3-4. Enrollment in grades 7-12, by county; and percent change in the number of junior and senior high school students for urban and rural [counties, by grade]; 1982/83-1983/84 school years. (p. 65-66)

LABOR FORCE, CENSUS OF AGRICULTURE, AND OCCUPATIONS

5-6. Civilian population, and labor force [by employment status], estimates by sex and age, 1982-83. (p. 69-70)

7. Summary data from the 1982 Census of Agriculture [number of farms, by size; farm operators by age, by principal occupation (farming and nonfarming) by residence (on and off farm), and by days of off-farm work; and selected production expenditures; 1978 and 1982]. (p. 71)

8. Occupations of employed persons, by age and sex (census week April 1, 1980). (p. 72-74)

EMPLOYMENT

9. Nonagricultural wage/salary employment by major industry, history and projections [various periods 1970-85]. (p. 77)

10. Employment change, [selected periods] 1970-83; and average [monthly] covered earnings, 1982; by industry. (p. 78)

11. Average growth during 1979-82 [period] in covered employment by industry for urban and rural [counties, and multicounty] portions. (p. 79)

12. Numeric change and average growth in nonagricultural wage/salary employment by county and industry [1979/80-1981/82]. (p. 80)

13-15. Nonagricultural job insurance covered wage/salary employment by industry and county, 1980-82 annual averages. (p. 83-85)

POVERTY

16-17. Households and persons receiving food stamps, by county, quarterly average, 1st quarter 1983-84. (p. 89-90)

18. Characteristics of AFDC caretaker families [number of eligible children and adults, and families with eligible children], by county, quarterly average, 1st quarter 1983. (p. 91)

EARNINGS AND INCOME

19-21. Covered employment and average monthly earnings per job, by industry [including Federal, State, and local government], for the U.S. and North Dakota, 1979-81. (p. 95-97)

22-23. Job insurance covered employment, average monthly earnings per job, and total earnings, by quarter, 1978-83; and average monthly earnings per job, by industry, 1980-83. (p. 98-99)

S6140–4   NORTH DAKOTA LABOR MARKET ADVISOR
Monthly.   2 p.
SRI/MF/complete, shipped quarterly

Monthly report on North Dakota employment, hours, and earnings, by industry division and/or location. Report is published approximately 2 months after month of coverage.

Contains 7 monthly tables, listed below. Feb. issue also includes 4 annual tables showing previous year totals for most data covered in monthly tables [4-7].

SRI coverage of this report begins with the June 1983 issue.

Similar quarterly data were published in *Prairie Employer Review,* discontinued by issuing agency in May 1983. For description, see SRI 1983 Annual, under S6140-1.

Availability: North Dakota Job Service, Research and Statistics Section, 1000 E. Divide Ave., PO Box 1537, Bismarck ND 58502, †; SRI/MF/complete, shipped quarterly.

Issues reviewed during 1984: June 1983-Sept. 1984 (D) (Vol. 2, Nos. 6-12; Vol. 3, Nos. 1-9) [Vol. 2, No. 7 incorrectly reads No. 6].

MONTHLY TABLES:
[Data are for North Dakota, unless otherwise noted. Most data are shown for month of coverage, preceding month, and same month of previous year.]

[1-2] U.S. CPI, all urban consumers; and PPI, U.S. average.

[3] Manufacturing hours and earnings [for U.S., North Dakota, and Fargo-Moorhead MSA].

[4] Labor force [by employment status, for U.S., North Dakota, and 3 MSAs].

[5] Employment by industry [division and selected major group].

[6] Labor force, by county by region [by employment status, with 1980 population].

[7] Nonagricultural wage/salary employment [by industry division, for 3 MSAs].

S6160   NORTH DAKOTA
Library Commission

S6160–1   NORTH DAKOTA LIBRARY STATISTICS, July 1980-June 1981
Annual.   Nov. 1983.
vii+49 p.
SRI/MF/complete, current & previous year reports

Annual report, for FY81, on North Dakota public, academic, and health science libraries. Includes finances, holdings, operations, and staff, by library.

Most data are from reports submitted by individual libraries.

Contains contents listing, preface, and definitions (p. iii-vii); and 14 tables listed below (p. 1-49).

Previous report, for July 1979-June 1980, was also reviewed in 1984, and is available on SRI microfiche, under this number [Annual. Dec. 1982. vii+50 p. †]. SRI coverage begins with the report for July 1979-June 1980.

Availability: North Dakota Library Commission, Liberty Memorial Bldg., Capitol Grounds, Bismarck ND 58505, †; SRI/MF/complete.

TABLES:
[All data are for FY81. All tables show the following data, as applicable, for the library groupings noted below: population served; income by source; expenditures by function and object; fixed assets and holdings, both by type; circulation and interlibrary loan activity; service hours, staff, square footage, seats, and bookmobiles; and assessed valuation.]

DATA BY INSTITUTION
[1-4] City, city-county, county, and multi-county libraries. (p. 1-23)

[5] School-public libraries. (p. 24-26)

[6-9] State college, State university, and community college libraries; and private college libraries. (p. 27-36)

[10-12] State, Federal, and health science libraries. (p. 37-45)

SUMMARIES
[13-14] Regional and State totals. (p. 46-49)

S6185   NORTH DAKOTA
Public Service Commission

S6185–1   STATE OF NORTH DAKOTA, PUBLIC SERVICE COMMISSION, NINETY-SECOND AND NINETY-THIRD ANNUAL REPORT to the Governor and Office of Management and Budget for the Biennial Period Ending June 30, 1983
Biennial.   [1984.]   106 p.
LC 9-14661.
SRI/MF/complete

Biennial report on finances and operations of regulated utility and transportation industries in North Dakota, 1981-82, with regulatory data for FY82-83. Industries are electric, gas, and telephone utilities; and motor carriers and railroads. Data are shown by company (except for motor carriers).

Covers regulatory cases and dispositions; and industry revenue, expenses, customers, and sales, as applicable; electric generation; freight carried, by commodity; and railroad assets, liabilities, and accidents by type.

Also includes number of licensed grain elevators; coal production by mine, and permit acreage by county; tests of measuring devices, by type; electric distribution cooperatives and operations; and Public Service Commission (PSC) finances.

Data are from PSC records and company reports.

Contains contents listing and PSC activities, with 11 tables (p. 1-59); regulated industry operations, with 29 tables (p. 60-99); and PSC finances, with 6 tables (p. 100-106).

For description of previous report, for biennial period ended June 30, 1981, see SRI 1982 Annual under this number.

Availability: North Dakota Public Service Commission, Secretary of Public Service Commission, Capitol Bldg., Bismarck ND 58505, †; SRI/MF/complete.

S6210   NORTH DAKOTA
Supreme Court

S6210–1   ANNUAL REPORT OF THE NORTH DAKOTA JUDICIAL SYSTEM, 1983
Annual.   [1984.]   38 p.
LC 78-646491.
SRI/MF/complete

Annual report on North Dakota judicial system, including trial and appellate court caseloads and case dispositions, 1982-83 with selected trends from 1976. Covers supreme, district, county, and municipal courts. Includes trial court data by case type and court location.

Case types shown are civil and criminal, for all courts, with extensive detail for juvenile cases; and some detail for traffic, small claims, probate, mental health commitment, and guardianship cases.

Also includes data on supreme court case processing time; State judicial budget; lawyer and judge disciplinary complaints and dispositions; and State bar applications and certifications, 1983.

Contains contents listing (p. 3); report, with text statistics, 11 charts, and 22 tables (p. 4-37); and judicial council directory (p. 38).

Availability: North Dakota Supreme Court, Court Administrator's Office, State Capitol, Bismarck ND 58505, †; SRI/MF/complete.

S6215   NORTH DAKOTA Tax Department

S6215–1   THIRTY-SIXTH BIENNIAL REPORT from the Office of State Tax Commissioner to the Governor and the Office of Management and Budget, State of North Dakota
Biennial.   Dec. 1, 1983.
2+38 p.
LC 13-33356.
SRI/MF/complete

Biennial report on North Dakota State tax collections by tax type, selected disbursements and estate tax assessments by county, and sales and use tax by business classification, FY82- 83, with selected trends from 1970. Data are compiled by North Dakota Tax Dept.

Contains contents listing (1 p.): narrative summary of dept functions and activities (p. 1-18); 8 charts and 17 tables, listed below, interspersed with narrative summaries on tax types (p. 19-37); and list of publications available from Tax Dept (p. 38).

Previous report, for FY80-81, is described in SRI 1982 Annual, under this number.

Availability: North Dakota Tax Department, State Capitol Bldg., 9th Floor, Bismarck ND 58505, †; SRI/MF/complete.

TABLES AND CHARTS:
[Unless otherwise noted, data are shown for FY82-83. Most table and chart titles begin "North Dakota State Tax Dept..."]

COLLECTION SUMMARY
[1-2] Gross monthly collections by tax commissioner; and comparative statement of changes in collection data [gross and net collections, and refunds; all by tax type]. (p. 19-20)

[3] Trends in gross collections, FY73-83. [illustrative chart] (p. 21)

SALES/USE AND INCOME TAXES
[4-6] Sales/use tax gross general fund collections during FY74-83; sales/use tax statistics by business classification [1982]; and gross income tax [corporate, individual, and withholding] and surtax collections during FY74-83. [charts] (p. 22-24)

ENERGY PRODUCTION AND TAXES
[7-8] Annual crude oil production and [average] domestic oil price per barrel, 1972-82; and oil/gas gross production and oil extraction tax gross collections, FY73-83. [charts] (p. 25)

[9] Net oil/gas gross production tax revenue distributions [to State and county, by county]. (p. 26)

[10-11] Coal conversion facilities tax and coal severance tax [quarterly kWh or tonnages, collections, and distribution of collections, by county]. (p. 27-28)

MISCELLANEOUS TAXES
[12] Transmission line tax collections [FY80-83]. (p. 29)

[13] Taxes certified to counties for collection [from rural electric cooperatives and mutual/cooperative telephone companies, 1979-82]. (p. 29)

[14] Special fuels tax and motor vehicle fuel tax collections, gallonage, and disbursements [by purpose]. (p. 30)

[15] Taxes certified to counties for collection [from banks and building/loan assns, 1977-81]. (p. 31)

[16-17] Business/corporation privilege tax, and cigarette and tobacco products tax collections [FY80-83]. (p. 31)

[18] Taxes certified to State treasurer [from airlines and car lines, 1979-82]. (p. 31)

[19] Estate taxes assessed [by type and county]. (p. 32)

PROPERTY TAX
[20-21] Where general ad valorem property taxes, special property taxes, and special assessments come from and go (levied in 1982 and payable in 1983). [table and chart] (p. 33-34)

[22] Property tax information: senior citizens/disabled persons property tax refunds and credits [number of persons receiving renter refunds and homeowner credits, and value of homeowner property exempted, 1970-82]. (p. 35)

[23-24] General fund revenues and expenditures [for total biennium, by function]. [charts] (p. 36)

TAX DEPT EXPENDITURES
[25] Statement of expenditures [by Tax Dept division, by object]. (p. 37)

S6260   OHIO
Department of Development

S6260–1   OHIO ECONOMIC INDICATORS QUARTERLY
Quarterly.   Approx. 10 p.
SRI/MF/complete

Quarterly report presenting economic activity indicators for Ohio and the U.S. Most data are from Federal sources. Quarter of coverage is quarter ending 4 months prior to cover date.

Contains narrative highlights; 9 tables, listed below, with accompanying illustrative and trend charts; and an additional chart showing composite business activity index for 8 Ohio metro areas, 1978-quarter of coverage.

Quarterly tables and charts appear in all issues.

Availability: Ohio Department of Development, Data Users Center, PO Box 1001, Columbus   OH   43216, $7.50   per   yr.; SRI/MF/complete.

Issues reviewed during 1984: July 1983-July 1984 (P) (Vol. 3, Nos. 3-4; Vol. 4, Nos. 1-3).

QUARTERLY TABLES:
[Unless otherwise noted, tables show data for Ohio and U.S., for quarter of coverage, previous quarter (Ohio only), and same quarters of preceding year.]

1. Personal income [by type, including farm, nonfarm by industry division, unemployment insurance benefits, and transfer payments].

2. Labor force [by employment status, and employment by industry division].

3. CPI [all items and 7 major components for U.S. and Cleveland and Cincinnati SMSAs, for quarter of coverage, previous quarter, and same quarters of preceding year].

4. Retail sales [durable and nondurable goods].

5. Commercial banking indicators [loans and deposits, by type].

6. Permit authorized private construction [units and value, by detailed type].

7. Electric energy sales, by type of consumer.

8. Collection of selected State taxes [general sales/gross receipts, motor fuel, tobacco product and alcoholic beverage sales, individual and corporate income, and other].

[9] Ohio index of leading indicators (1973=100) [for quarter ending 1 month prior to cover date, with quarterly trends from mid-1970s].

S6260–2   1984 OHIO COUNTY PROFILES
Annual.   Mar. 1984.
368 p. no paging.
ODUC 84-02.
SRI/MF/complete

Annual compilation, for 1984, of basic economic and social statistics and Census of Population and Housing selected findings for each of Ohio's 88 counties. Data are shown for various years 1970-83, with quinquennial population projections to 2005.

Data are primarily compiled from reports of State and Federal agencies, and 1980 U.S. Census Summary Tape Files 1A and 3A.

Contains introduction and list of counties (2 p.); 4 pages of statistics, described below, generally repeated for the State and each county (356 p.); and appendices, with census definitions and methodology, and data sources (10 p.).

Previous report, published in 1983, was entitled *1982 Ohio County Profiles.* No report entitled *1983 Ohio County Profiles* was published. Previous report contained detailed findings from 1980 U.S. Census Summary Tape File 1A; for description, see SRI 1983 Annual, under this number.

A summary report, presenting census data described in paragraph b below for the State and each county, is also available from the issuing agency [Report No. 80-32, *Area Demographic Summary* ($20.00)]. Similar summaries are available on request for individual counties, townships, cities, and zip codes. The summaries are not covered in SRI.

Availability: Ohio Department of Development, Data Users Center, PO Box 1001, Columbus OH 43216, $35.00; SRI/MF/complete.

STATISTICS:
a. Population projected quinquennially to 2005. (1 p.)

b. Census of Population and Housing findings: population by race/ethnicity; occupied housing units by tenure, and median value or rent; households and persons per household; families; population by age; educational attainment of persons 25/over; labor force and employment status by race/ethnicity; households and families by income level; per capita income; and households and persons below poverty level. (1 p.)

c. Land area and use; schools and enrollment, by type; public libraries and operations; hospitals and beds, and physicians; State parks/recreation facilities and acreage; radio and TV stations, and newspapers and circulation; population; personal income; highway and railroad mileage; nearest airport and characteristics; construction activity and value; and value of Federal contracts. (1 p.)

d. Farm average size, farm value and income, and principal products; banks and savings and loan assns, and deposits; employment by industry division; labor force by employment status; and manufacturing, wholesale and retail trade, and service industry employment, establishments, and, as applicable, shipments, sales, and receipts. (1 p.)

S6260–5   1983 OHIO ENERGY STATUS REPORT
Annual.   Mar. 1, 1984.
89 p. var. paging.
SRI/MF/complete, current & previous year reports

Annual report, for 1983, on Ohio energy supply and demand situation, presenting consumption, production, reserve, and price trends, by energy type, mostly 1970s-82; and electric generating capacity and energy consumption projections to 1993. Includes selected data by consuming sector and utility.

Also includes coal and gas supply by source; coal prices by producing State; oil refining capacity and retail market shares of top companies; renewable energy production by fuel source; energy consumption in U.S. and Ohio, and relation to GNP and GSP; oil consumption by refined product; gasoline prices in Cincinnati and Cleveland; electric power generation and disposition by utility; and Ohio well completions.

Data are from dept records, DOE, and other State, Federal, and private sources.

Contains summary (p. i-iii); listings of contents, tables, and charts (2 p.); introduction (p. 1-3); 3 narrative sections, interspersed with 23 tables (p. 4-40a); statistical section, with 10 charts and 25 tables (p. 41-80); and glossary (p. 81-83).

Previous report, for 1982, was also reviewed in SRI during 1984, and is also available on SRI microfiche, under this number [Annual. Oct. 1, 1982. ii+48 p. †].

Availability: Ohio Department of Development, Energy Division, 65 E. State St., Suite 206, Columbus OH 43215, †; SRI/MF/complete.

S6260–6   ASSESSMENT OF THE SUPPLIES OF NATURAL GAS AND FUELS FOR GENERATING ELECTRICITY IN OHIO, July 1983-June 1984
Semiannual.   Aug. 15, 1983.
v+101 p.
SRI/MF/complete

Semiannual report forecasting Ohio electricity and natural gas supply and demand, by utility system, monthly July 1983-June 1984, with selected trends from 1981 or earlier. Includes data on fuel supplies, by type and source; and energy demand, by consuming sector. Also includes degree-day and natural gas price trends.

Data are from individual utility reports.

Contains listings of contents, tables, and charts (p. i-v); introduction, with 1 chart and 1 table (p. 1-7); electricity report, with 9 charts and 8 tables (p. 8-33); natural gas report, with 14 charts and 16 tables (p. 34-71); and 2 appendices, with 21 tables (p. 72-101).

Report generally is issued in Dec. of each year for the Nov.-Oct. forecast, and in Aug. for the July-June forecast. Report previously was issued by the Ohio Dept of Energy, now a division of the Ohio Dept of Development, and was described in SRI under S6275-1.

Availability: Ohio Department of Development, Energy Division, 65 E. State St., Suite 206, Columbus OH 43215, †; SRI/MF/complete.

S6260–7   EEO DETAILED OCCUPATION REPORT: 1980 Census of Population, Ohio
Monograph.   Jan. 1983.
11+36 p. var. paging.
SRI/MF/complete

Report presenting 1980 census data, for Ohio, on total and female civilian labor force by detailed occupation, cross-tabulated by race-ethnicity (black, white, American Indian/Eskimo/Aleut, Asian/Pacific Islander, Hispanic, and other). Also includes unemployed labor force (no work experience since 1975) for each demographic group.

Data are from the Equal Employment Opportunity Special Tape File of the 1980 Census of Population and Housing. The EEO file, based on a 20% sample of the census questionnaire, includes the entire civilian labor force in its universe, whereas much of the other census data on occupations (e.g., Summary Tape File 3) covers only employed civilians. The EEO file was produced to help meet the needs of government and private industry in planning for EEO/Affirmative Action.

Report is issued in 2 parts, as follows:

Documentation, including methodology, definitions, and occupational codes. (11 p.)

Data, with 1 extended table, repeated to show data as numbers and percents. (36 p.)

The following reports are also available from the Data Users Center, but are not covered in SRI: *EEO Aggregated Occupation Report* [No. 80-25, $1.00]; and *EEO Educational Attainment Report* [No. 80-24, $1.00]. Additional tabulations from the EEO file, including data by geographic location, are available from the Center on request.

Availability: Ohio Department of Development, Data Users Center, PO Box 1001, Columbus OH 43216, $10.00; SRI/MF/complete.

S6265   OHIO
Department of Education

S6265–1   ANNUAL FINANCIAL AND STATISTICAL REPORT, School Year 1982/83, Division of Special Education, Ohio
Annual.   Mar. 1984.   56 p.
LC 60-64038.
SRI/MF/complete

Annual report on Ohio special education expenditures, services, and enrollments, by type of handicap and by school district and county, 1982/83, with summary trends from 1978/79. Data are from Division of Special Education.

Contains contents listing (2 p.); and 15 tables, listed below (p. 1-56).

Availability: Ohio Department of Education, Special Education Division, 933 High St., Worthington OH 43085, †; SRI/MF/complete.

TABLES:

[Tables by county and school district show data for 1982/83; other tables show data for 1978/79-1982-83.]

SUMMARY

[1] Comparison of the number of pupils and approved costs paid for all special education services [including transportation, teacher training, and total costs certified for payment]. (p. 1)

INDIVIDUAL INSTRUCTIONAL SERVICES

[Tables show number of pupils, hours instructed, and amount paid, for total State, and by county and school district.]

[2-4] Individual instructional services: home instruction [total and for] orthopedically/other health impaired and severe behavioral handicaps. (p. 4-27)

[5-6] Individual instructional services: [for specific learning disabled, and hearing and visually handicapped]. (p. 28-46)

INDIVIDUAL SUPPLEMENTAL SERVICES

[Tables show number of pupils and amount paid, for total State and by county and school district, unless otherwise noted.]

[7] Individual supplemental services [aggregate, State only]. (p. 47)

[8-12] Interpreter services; and reader and guide services, for visually handicapped children. (p. 48-52)

[13-14] Attendant services for crippled children. (p. 53-55)

ADMINISTRATION

[15] Administration monies [from general revenue and enabling legislation, FY80-83]. (p. 56)

S6265–2   STATE BOARD OF EDUCATION OF OHIO ANNUAL REPORT, 1983: Investing in Education
Annual.   Feb. 1984.   33 p.
LC 59-62559.
SRI/MF/complete

Annual report on public education in Ohio, covering enrollment, test scores, staff, finances, special and vocational education, and Federal assistance, 1982/83, with trends from 1977/78.

Contains contents listing (1 p.); narrative report, with 1 table showing educational expenditures for FY82-83, and appropriations for FY84, by program (p. 1-14); and statistical section, with 6 charts and 25 tables (p. 25-33).

All statistical section tables, and charts containing data not covered in tables, are listed below.

Additional detailed reports on costs per pupil and salaries of educational personnel are also available from the issuing agency but are not covered by SRI.

Availability: Ohio Department of Education, Educational Media Center, Rm. 808, 65 S. Front St., Columbus OH 43215, †; SRI/MF/complete.

TABLES AND CHARTS:
[Data are for Ohio, 1978/79-1982/83 or 1979-83, unless otherwise noted.]

S6265-2.1: Student, Staff, and Financial Data

ENROLLMENT
[1-2] Total public school enrollment and public high school graduates. (p. 25)

[3] Enrollment by grades, 1982/83. (p. 25)

STAFF
[4] Pupil/teacher ratio [with number of full-time teachers, and total enrollment]. (p. 25)

[5] Degree status [of teachers] in Ohio [distribution for nondegree, bachelor, 5-year, and master], 1983. [chart] (p. 25)

TEST SCORES
[6-7] American College Test Composite and Scholastic Aptitude Test math and verbal [test scores, Ohio and total U.S., FY78-83]. [charts] (p. 26)

SCHOOL DISTRICTS
[8] Number of public school districts [city, exempted village, local, and total, 1979-84]. (p. 26)

DISADVANTAGED PUPIL EXPENDITURES
[9] Disadvantaged pupil program funds (DPPF) [expenditures and number of programs]. (p. 26)

FINANCE
[10-11] Revenue by source [local, State, and Federal, FY82-83]; and average expenditure per pupil [city, exempted village, local, and State, 1977/78-1981/82]. (p. 27)

[12] Ohio school districts total property valuation, valuation per pupil, State average millage, and local revenue generated, [FY79-83]. (p. 27)

[13] SF-12 [School Foundation] calculation. (p. 27)

S6265-2.2: Special Educational Services and Federal Assistance

SPECIAL EDUCATION
[1] Handicapped children receiving full services [by type of handicap, program placement, and age group], as of Dec. 1982. (p. 28)

[2] Special education foundation units [and districts, by program type], 1982/83. (p. 29)

VOCATIONAL EDUCATION
[3-5] Vocational education: secondary and adult enrollment [in agriculture, business/office, distributive, home economics, and trade/industrial]; and total enrollment [secondary, adult, and career education, with State expenditures for secondary vocational education]. (p. 29-30)

[6] Students served in DPPF programs [by type of program, 1982/83]. (p. 31)

FEDERAL ASSISTANCE
[7-8] Chapter 1 programs for disadvantaged pupils: percent of participants by grades, and district participation and funds available. (p. 32)

[9-10] Chapter 1 programs for migrant children and for neglected/delinquent children in State-operated schools [participants and funds]. (p. 32)

[11] Adult basic education programs [funded, enrollment, and Federal, State, and local funding]. (p. 32)

[12] Grants through public laws 81-874 and 81-815 [for maintenance/operation, construction, and major natural disasters]. (p. 33)

[13] Funds administered by the Division of Federal Assistance [by program], 1982/83. (p. 33)

TRANSPORTATION
[14-15] Pupil transportation statistics [pupils transported, annual miles, and average cost per pupil and per mile]; and driver education [pupils served and subsidy]. (p. 33)

S6270   OHIO
Bureau of
Employment Services

S6270-1   EMPLOYMENT, HOURS, AND EARNINGS in Ohio
Monthly.   Approx. 32 p.
SRI/MF/complete, shipped quarterly

Monthly report on Ohio employment, hours, and earnings, by MSA and industry. Data are compiled by the State in cooperation with the U.S. Dept of Labor. Report is issued approximately 1 month after month of coverage.

Contains summary, 11 monthly tables listed below, and definitions.

Bureau of Employment Services also issues an annual edition of the monthly report. Annual report is not covered by SRI.

Availability: Ohio Bureau of Employment Services, Labor Market Information Division, 145 S. Front St., PO Box 1618, Columbus OH 43216, †; SRI/MF/complete, shipped quarterly.

Issues reviewed during 1984: Oct. 1983-Sept. 1984 (D).

MONTHLY TABLES:
[Unless otherwise noted, tables show data for month of coverage or previous month, with comparison to preceding 12 months and 11 years. Tables [1-4] show data for 8 MSAs, tables [5-9] for the entire State.]

[1] Employment [nonagricultural wage/salary, and manufacturing].

[2] Manufacturing production workers and average weekly hours.

[3] Earnings [average hourly and weekly].

[4] Civilian labor force estimates [by employment status].

[5] Civilian labor force estimates [by employment status, with U.S. unemployment rate].

[6-7] Nonagricultural wage/salary employment [manufacturing and nonmanufacturing]; and nonmanufacturing wage/salary employment [by industry division].

[8] Employment, hours, and earnings in [durable and nondurable] manufacturing.

[9] Employment and average weekly earnings in selected major manufacturing industries.

[10-11] Nonagricultural wage/salary employment, and hours and gross earnings of production/nonsupervisory workers [by SIC 2- and 3-digit industry, for month of coverage, previous month, and same month of previous year; repeated for State and each MSA].

S6285   OHIO
Department of
Health

S6285-1   REPORT OF VITAL STATISTICS for Ohio, 1982
Annual.   Feb. 1984.
6+166 p.
LC 77-646834.
SRI/MF/complete

Annual report on Ohio vital statistics, covering births, deaths by cause, marriages, and divorces, by county and selected demographic characteristics, 1982. Also includes trends from 1940 and data on abortions and population. Most data are from Division of Vital Statistics records as of Mar. 20, 1983.

Contains contents and table listings, and summary charts (6 p.); methodology and definitions (p. 1-4); and 64 tables, listed below (p. 5-166).

Availability: Ohio Department of Health, Statistical Analysis Unit, Data Services Division, 246 N. High St., 7th Floor, Columbus OH 43215, †; SRI/MF/complete.

TABLES:
[Tables show data for Ohio, 1982, unless otherwise noted.]

S6285-1.1: Summary Data and Births

VITAL STATISTICS SUMMARY
[A] Vital statistics summary [by race, including births by sex, type of delivery (single, twin, and triplets/more), and whether born in hospital, premature, and involving congenital anomaly; median age of mother; fertility ratio; illegitimate births; and deaths (maternal, infant, neonatal, fetal, and perinatal)]; 1981-82. (p. 5)

BIRTHS
[Tables 9-18 show data by county.]

1. Total live, premature, and illegitimate births, classified by color: number and rate, by county, city, and balance of county. (p. 7-18)

2. Live births, by month: number and percentage distribution, by sex and color. (p. 19)

3. Number of live births and premature births, by age of mother and color, and by birth weight. (p. 20)

4. Live births, classified by maturity status, color, and length of pregnancy in weeks: number and percent. (p. 21)

5. Number of live births, by live birth order and color, and by age of mother. (p. 22)

6. Live births, classified by age and selected completed levels of education of mother. (p. 23)

7-8. Live births, classified by color and time of 1st prenatal visit, [cross-tabulated by] age of mother and number of prenatal visits. (p. 24-25)

9. Number of live births by age of mother. (p. 26)

10. Resident live births to mothers under 20 years of age, classified by single years of age. (p. 29)

11. Number of live births by live birth order. (p. 32)

12. Number of births, classified by month of birth. (p. 35)

13. Resident live births, classified by place of birth [hospital, clinic, home, and other]. (p. 38)

14. Live births with malformations/anomalies indicated on birth certificate, number and rate per 1,000 live births. (p. 40)

15. Resident and recorded live births. (p. 41)

16. Live births by trimester prenatal care began, [and no prenatal care]. (p. 42)

17. Live births with birth weights 2,500 grams/under (premature), by weight group. (p. 44)

18. Number of resident illegitimate births by age of mother. (p. 46)

S6285–1.2: Deaths

[Most tables include rates.]

19. Classification of leading causes of death according to 9th Revision of the International Classification of Diseases [list of code numbers for 37 causes]. (p. 49)

20-23. Resident deaths: total all causes, fetal, neonatal, infant, and maternal; and from [15] leading causes; by county, city, and balance of county. (p. 50-97)

24. Resident and recorded deaths, classified by county. (p. 98)

25-26. 10 leading causes of death, classified by sex and by color, with percent of all deaths. (p. 99-100)

27. 5 leading causes of death, classified by sex and age group. (p. 101-105)

28. Deaths: all causes and [detailed] selected causes, classified by sex and color and by age group. (p. 106-114)

29. Total deaths: by age group, color, and sex. (p. 115)

30. Resident and recorded fetal deaths, classified by county. (p. 116)

31-32. Fetal deaths, classified by maturity status, color, and length of pregnancy in weeks; and by color, time of 1st prenatal visit, and age of mother. (p. 117-118)

33. Resident fetal deaths, by selected cause of death and color. (p. 119)

34. Resident and recorded infant deaths, classified by county. (p. 120)

35-36. 10 leading causes of infant and neonatal deaths, classified by color, with percent of all infant and neonatal deaths. (p. 121-122)

37. Perinatal deaths, classified by county. (p. 123)

38. Number of maternal deaths, classified by selected cause [including abortion], color, and age. (p. 124)

S6285–1.3: Marriage and Divorce

39-41. Marriages: by age and number of present marriage of bride and groom; and by month of occurrence, [by] marriage order of bride and groom. (p. 126-128)

42-44. Number of marriages with rates per 1,-000 population, classified by month and by age of bride and groom, [all] by county where license was issued. (p. 129-137)

45. Number of divorces/annulments/dissolutions, with rates per 1,000 population, classified by county where decree was issued and by month of final decree. (p. 138)

46. Divorces and annulments, by legal grounds for decree. (p. 141)

47-48. Divorces, annulments, and dissolutions, by number of children reported under 18 years of age, and by duration of marriage. (p. 142-143)

S6285–1.4: Trends, Population, and Abortions

TRENDS

49. Live births by color: number and rate per 1,000 population, and percent occurring in hospitals, 1940-82. (p. 144)

50. Resident live births, classified by color and age of mother, 1957-82. (p. 145)

51. Number of illegitimate births, classified by color, with rate per 1,000 live births, 1949-82. (p. 148)

52. Fertility rates, classified by color and age of mother, 1972-82. (p. 149)

53. Deaths, by color: number and rate per 1,-000 population, 1940-82. (p. 150)

54-57. Infant, fetal, maternal, and neonatal deaths: number and rate per 1,000 or 10,000 live births, classified by color, 1940-82. (p. 151-154)

58. Deaths, classified by age group, 1949-82. (p. 155)

59. Leading causes of death, with rates per 100,000 population, 1973-82. (p. 156)

60. Marriages and divorces/annulments: number and rate per 1,000 population, 1950-82. (p. 157)

POPULATION

[Tables 61-62 show data as of Apr. 1, 1980.]

61-62. Enumerated population, by county, city, and balance of county; and by age, sex, and color. (p. 158-164)

ABORTION

63. Number of induced abortions, by ethnic group [white, black, all others, and not reported], age group, and marital status. (p. 165)

S6310   OHIO
Department of
Insurance

S6310–1   116th ANNUAL REPORT OF THE DIRECTOR OF INSURANCE, Ohio
Annual. Mar. 1984.
v+273 p.
ISSN 0360-4799.
LC 41-21841.
SRI/MF/complete

Annual report on Ohio insurance industry financial condition and underwriting activity, by company and line of coverage, 1982. Covers assets, liabilities, capital, surplus, premium and total income, losses and/or claims paid, disbursements, underwriting gain/loss, and types of policies and risks written and in force; and Ohio direct premiums written and losses and/or dividends paid; for companies headquartered in Ohio and elsewhere.

Data are shown, as applicable, for fire/casualty companies and reciprocals, title and title guaranty/trust companies, mutual protective assns, life insurance companies, fraternal benefit societies, nonprofit hospital service and health/dental care assns, and HMOs.

Ohio underwriting data for fire/casualty companies include breakdowns for specific lines of coverage, including automobile, accident/health, medical malpractice, surety, and workers' compensation.

Also includes number of companies by type of insurance; and underwriting tax, fee, and expenditure trends from 1973.

Contains contents listing (p. iii-v); introduction, with regulatory summary and 4 tables (p. 1-14); and 2 statistical sections, with 57 tables (p. 16-273).

Availability: Ohio Department of Insurance, Examination Division, 2100 Stella Ct., Columbus OH 43215, ◆; SRI/MF/complete.

S6320   OHIO
State
Library

S6320–1   1984 STATISTICS OF OHIO LIBRARIES
Annual. July 1984. 100 p.
SRI/MF/complete

Annual report on Ohio public, academic, special, institution, and school libraries, 1983, with some data for 1983/84 and trends from 1969. Includes finances, holdings, circulation, and staff, by library and location. Also includes intangible property tax distribution trends. Most data are compiled from reports of individual libraries.

Contains introduction and contents listing (p. 2-3); and 22 tables, listed below (p. 4-100).

Availability: State Library of Ohio, 65 S. Front St., Columbus OH 43215, $8.00; SRI/MF/complete.

TABLES:

[Unless otherwise noted, data are for 1983, or 1982/83 academic year. Tables [1], [7], and [15-22] generally include staff size, total volumes,

volumes added during year, holdings of various other types of materials, and operating expenses including salaries and materials; additional data are noted below.]

SUMMARY AND TRENDS

[1] Summary of library statistics [by type of library; also shows number of libraries]. (p. 4)

[2] Statewide summary of public library statistics [libraries, volumes, circulation, State intangible property tax collections and distribution to libraries; and library income and expenditures], 1979-83. (p. 5)

LIBRARY INCOME

[3] Distribution of intangible personal property taxes [to libraries and local governments], 1969-83. (p. 5)

[4] Intangibles tax collection and distribution, county summary [including 1980 population, number of libraries, and total library income]. (p. 6)

[5-6] Counties ranked by percentage of intangible tax distributed to libraries and by per capita income of libraries. (p. 8-9)

PUBLIC LIBRARIES

[7] Public library statistics [by county and library; also shows population served, weekly hours open, circulation, loan period, total and tax income, and total expenditures]. (p. 12-21)

[8-11] Public libraries ranked by circulation, total volumes, total operating expenses, and number of staff. (p. 22-45)

[12-13] Extension services: bookmobiles and branches [number, circulation, and bookmobile stops, all by library; also includes State library bookmobile data]. (p. 46-48)

[14] Audio-visual materials [holdings and circulation by type of material, and attendance at film presentations, all by library]. (p. 49-53)

ACADEMIC, SPECIAL, AND INSTITUTION LIBRARIES

[15] Academic library statistics [by institution; also shows enrollment and hours of student assistance]. (p. 56)

[16-19] Academic libraries ranked by enrollment, total volumes, total expenditures for books/library materials, and total operating expenses. (p. 60-75)

[20-21] Special library statistics and institution library statistics [by library; also shows population served and circulation for institution libraries]. (p. 78-85)

SCHOOL LIBRARIES

[22] School library media center statistics [by school district; also shows enrollment, buildings, certified librarians, and librarians with masters' degrees, 1983/84]. (p. 88-100)

S6405   OKLAHOMA
Department of Agriculture

S6405–1   OKLAHOMA AGRICULTURAL STATISTICS, 1983
Annual. [1984.] v+106 p.
LC 80-643362.
SRI/MF/complete

Annual report on Oklahoma agricultural production, finances, and marketing, 1983, with trends from 1960 and some data for 1984. Data generally are shown by commodity and/or county and district, and include some comparisons to neighboring States and U.S.

Covers production, prices, disposition, value, and, as applicable, stocks, inventories, and total and irrigated acreage and yield, for crop, fruit and nut, livestock, dairy, and poultry sectors.

Also includes data on farms, acreage, value, tax rates, and rent; weather; pasture condition; and farm income and production expenses.

Also includes selected preliminary findings from the 1982 Census of Agriculture, including data on farm operators by ownership status and age.

Data are compiled by the State Crop and Livestock Reporting Service, and are based primarily on sample surveys of farmers and ranchers.

Contains contents listing and methodology (p. iii-v); overview, with 10 tables (p. 1-5); 7 sections, most with narrative reviews, and 15 maps, 14 charts, and 63 tables (p. 6-102); and list of other reports available (p. 106).

Availability: Oklahoma Crop and Livestock Reporting Service, PO Box 1095, Oklahoma City OK 73101, $5.00; SRI/MF/complete.

S6415   OKLAHOMA
Banking Department

S6415–1   REPORT OF THE BANK COMMISSIONER of the State of Oklahoma, 1983
Annual. [1984.] 26 p.
LC A66-7772.
SRI/MF/complete

Annual report, for FY83, on financial condition of Oklahoma State-chartered banks, trust companies, savings and loan assns, and credit unions, presenting composite assets and liabilities, by type of institution, as of June 30, 1983 or Dec. 31, 1982, with summary trends from 1974.

Also includes consolidated bank operating ratios; money order agencies by company; number and location of perpetual care cemeteries; and Banking Dept receipts and disbursements, FY79-83.

Contains Banking Dept overview, with 3 tables (p. 1-7); and 9 financial tables with accompanying lists, and regulatory activities (p. 8-26).

Availability: Oklahoma Banking Department, 4100 N. Lincoln Blvd., Oklahoma City OK 73105, †; SRI/MF/complete.

S6423   OKLAHOMA
Department of Education

S6423–1   1982/83 ANNUAL REPORT OF THE OKLAHOMA STATE DEPARTMENT OF EDUCATION
Annual. [1984.]
2+274 p.+foldout+errata sheets. Oversized.
LC 76-646002.
SRI/MF/complete

Annual report on Oklahoma public schools, covering finances, programs, personnel, and students, 1982/83. Presents valuations and Federal, State, and local funding data by school district and county. Also includes data on teacher education and salaries, special education, Indian education, and pupil transportation.

Contains contents listing, organizational chart, and 47 tables listed below; and detached foldout table showing summary educational revenues, by source and county, FY83.

Availability: Oklahoma Department of Education, Communications Section, Administration Division, Oliver Hodges Memorial Education Bldg., 2500 N. Lincoln Blvd., Oklahoma City OK 73105, ‡ ($1.00 postage); SRI/MF/complete.

TABLES:
[Tables show data by county for 1982/83 school year or FY83, unless otherwise noted.]

S6423–1.1: Teachers and Allocation of State and Federal Funds

[1] State Dept of Education fiscal services [State total expenditures by function and object, with total Federal funds]. (p. 2)

[2] Statistical information on teachers [State total teachers by years of experience, and average salaries, by degree level; and number of FTE personnel and total and average salaries for 35 positions]. (p. 3)

[3] Textbook allocations [and enrollment]. (p. 5)

[4-5] State programs [amount received under career education and library media improvement programs, by school district]. (p. 6-8)

[6-7] School lunch division [disbursements by program, with totals for Federal and State funds]; and school lunch [State and Federal] funds distributed to districts. (p. 9-12)

[8] Driver and safety education, reimbursements to public schools [by object, and number of pupils]. (p. 13)

[9] Federal funds paid to school districts and certain other agencies under [9] major Federal education assistance acts. (p. 16)

[10] Federal programs [amount received, by county and school district or agency, for Chapter 1 (compensatory education)]. (p. 19-25)

[11] Johnson-O'Malley funds distributed by Indian Education Section [for special programs and educational support, by county and school]. (p. 26)

[12-17] Federal programs [amount received by county and school district or agency, for Title I, ESEA-89-313 (special education); transition program for refugee children; Chap-

ter 2 Federal financial assistance programs; Title IV-C (innovative programs); Title XIII, educational amendments 1978, P.L. 95-561 (adult education); and Title EHA-B (special education)]. (p. 29-43)

[18-19] P.L. 874 [school plant services receipts, with detail for disaster payments, by county and school district], July 1, 1983. (p. 44-48)

[20-21] Federal programs [amount received by county and school district or agency, for Title IV-A (Indian education) and Career Education Incentive Act]. (p. 49-53)

S6423-1.2: Teacher Education, Schools, and Students

TEACHER EDUCATION

[Tables [1-3] show State totals only. Tables [1-2] show data by sex and teaching level, including special education.]

[1] Report of the new supply of instructional personnel [students completing preparation for teaching certificates]. (p. 55)

[2] Occupation [employment status] on Nov. 1, 1982, of graduates completing preparation in 1981/82 with qualifications for standard teaching certificates in Oklahoma. (p. 56)

[3] Approved teacher education programs in Oklahoma [tabular listing of program subjects, grade levels, and degrees, repeated for 20 institutions]. (p. 57-74)

SCHOOLS, STUDENTS, SUPERINTENDENT SALARIES, AND DISTRICT DATA

[4] Instruction division, number of high school districts, high schools, mid-high schools, junior high schools, and elementary schools [and middle, dependent elementary, vocational/technical, and north central schools], for school year 1981/82 and 1982/83. (p. 75)

[5] Attendance, membership, and transportation [State totals from superintendents' and auditing section reports]. (p. 78)

[6] Scholastic population [as of Apr. 1983], and high school graduates [by sex]. (p. 79)

[7] Original entries, kindergarten through 12th grade [by specific grade and for ungraded special education]. (p. 80)

[8] Enrollment [for all grades and for 11th and 12th grades, and high school graduates, State totals, 1960/61-1982/83]. (p. 83)

[9] County superintendents' salaries, showing amount paid by the State, number of dependent districts, and number of teachers employed. (p. 84)

[10] Annexations and consolidations, State school districts [mandatory and elective, since 1946]. (p. 85)

[11-12] Original entries and total average daily attendance (ADA), 20-year comparison [State totals, 1963/64-1982/83]; and Finance Division original entries and total ADA [by county, 1982/83; all by school level]. (p. 86-89)

S6423-1.3: Revenues, Expenditures, and Valuations, and Pupil Transportation

[1] Comparable data concerning the public schools of Oklahoma, beginning with 1924/25 [State totals for ADA, number of teachers, average salary, State aid, total and per capita expenditures, and net valuation]. (p. 90)

[2] Finance Division, comparative data, 20-year period [State totals for number of districts and teachers, average salary, and revenues by source, 1963/64-1982/83]. (p. 92)

[3-6] State totals: [detailed] sources of revenue and amount collected from each source, FY83; school district net valuations, 1983/84; revenue received by school districts [total, per capita, and by source], 1982/83; and classification of general fund expenditures as shown by the financial reports for FY83. (p. 94-95)

[7-8] State aid claims filed [statewide, by claim number]; and State aid paid [by county; both by purpose]. (p. 96-107)

[9-10] School district net valuations [including value of real and personal property and public services, total and per capita valuation, levies by fund, and July 1983 general fund surplus], 1983/84; and total revenue received by school district [total, per capita, and by local/county, State, and Federal source, 1982/83; all by school district, repeated for each county]. (p. 108-261)

[11] Per capita revenues by source, and percentage of total revenue. (p. 262)

[12] Pupil transportation [number of buses, miles traveled, average daily pupils transported, and State aid and total expenditures]. (p. 264)

[13] Classification of general fund expenditures. (p. 266-273)

[14] County valuations per ADA. (p. 274)

S6430 OKLAHOMA Employment Security Commission

S6430-2 OKLAHOMA LABOR MARKET
Monthly. Approx. 10 p.
ISSN 0030-1744.
LC 52-44621.
SRI/MF/complete, shipped quarterly

Monthly report on Oklahoma labor force, covering employment and unemployment, hours and earnings, and characteristics of the insured unemployed. Includes data by industry, MSA, and county.

Data are from Federal and State agencies. Month of coverage is 1-2 months prior to cover date.

Contains narrative summary; and 5 monthly and 3 quarterly tables, listed below.

Monthly tables appear in all issues; quarterly tables appear in Jan., Apr., and July 1984 issues.

Availability: Oklahoma Employment Security Commission, Research and Planning Division, 310 Will Rogers Memorial Office Bldg., Oklahoma City OK 73105, †; SRI/MF/complete, shipped quarterly.

Issues reviewed during 1984: Oct. 15, 1983-July 1984 (P).

TABLES:

[Data are for Oklahoma, unless otherwise noted. Tables [1] and [3] show data for month of coverage, previous month, and same month of previous year. Prior to 1984, table format varies slightly from this description. Quarterly tables begin with Jan. 1984 issue.]

MONTHLY TABLES

[1] Labor force summary [by employment status, agricultural and domestic service/self-employed/unpaid family workers, and workers idled by labor disputes; and nonfarm wage/salary employment, by major industry group].

[2] Labor force data, total employment and unemployment [and unemployment rate, by MSA and county for month of coverage, with unemployment rate also for previous month and same month of previous year].

[3] Hours and earnings in selected industries [by major industry group].

[4] [U.S. urban] CPI [for all consumers and wage earners/clerical workers, for month of coverage and previous month, with trends from selected previous months and years].

[5] Comparisons of unemployment rates, U.S. and Oklahoma [unadjusted and seasonally adjusted, monthly current year to date and 3 previous years].

QUARTERLY TABLES

[I-III] Characteristics of the insured unemployed: industry [division and group], major occupational group, age, sex, duration [of unemployment], and race [variously cross-tabulated, for a selected week of month of coverage].

S6445 OKLAHOMA Department of Health

S6445-1 OKLAHOMA HEALTH STATISTICS, 1983
Annual. [1984.] 8+230 p.
ISSN 0098-5651.
SRI/MF/complete

Annual report, for 1983, on Oklahoma vital statistics, covering population, births, deaths by cause, marriages, and divorces. Includes data by location, race, and age, and selected trends from 1920.

Data were compiled from birth and death certificates filed with the State Dept of Health prior to Apr. 15, 1984; and from reports by county court clerks on marriages and divorces.

Contains prefatory material, and contents and table listing (8 p.); methodology and directory of county health depts (p. 1-9); 21 tables, listed below (p. 11-223); and technical appendix, with definitions and sample birth and death certificates (p. 224-230).

A less detailed monthly vital statistics report is also published by the issuing agency, but is not covered by SRI.

Availability: Oklahoma Department of Health, Public Health Statistics Section, Data Management Division, 1000 NE Tenth St., PO Box 53551, Oklahoma City OK 73152, †; SRI/MF/complete.

TABLES:

[Tables present data for Oklahoma, 1983, unless otherwise noted. Data by race are shown for white, black, and Indian.

Tables I-II, V-VII, and X-XI show live and stillbirths by attendant (physician in and out of hospital, and midwife/other/unknown). Tables I-II, V-VII, and XIX also show population.]

BIRTH AND MORTALITY TRENDS

I-II. Resident births; fetal deaths (stillbirths); [total, infant, and neonatal] deaths; and deaths by 34 selected causes: number and rate, 1930-83; and by race, 1983. (p. 11-30)

III. Births and deaths, number and rate, 1920-83. (p. 31)

BIRTH WEIGHTS

IV. Resident live births by age of mother, race, and number and percent of low-weight births. (p. 32)

BIRTHS AND DEATHS BY LOCALITY

V-VII. Resident births, fetal deaths (stillbirths), [total, infant, and neonatal deaths], and deaths by 34 selected causes: number and rate, by race, by county, MSA, and cities of 2,500/or more. (p. 33-134)

VIII-IX. Resident births and deaths by county, race, and sex. (p. 135-136)

DEATHS BY CAUSE AND AGE

X-XI. Resident births; fetal deaths (stillbirths); [total, infant, and neonatal deaths]; and deaths by 34 selected causes: by month, and by age, race, and sex. (p. 137-186)

XII-XIII. 10 leading causes of deaths, number and rank: by race and sex, and by age. (p. 187-188)

XIV. Resident deaths by 3-digit ICDA [International Classification of Diseases Adapted] codes, number and rate, and race. (p. 189-213)

XV. Fetal deaths by ICDA, by race. (p. 214)

BIRTHS AND DEATHS BY PLACE OF OCCURRENCE AND RESIDENCE

XVI. Births and deaths of Oklahoma residents by State of occurrence; and births and deaths of out-of-State residents occurring in Oklahoma, by State of residence. (p. 215)

XVII. Births, fetal deaths (stillbirths), [total] deaths, and infant and neonatal deaths, by county of residence and occurrence. (p. 216)

MARRIAGES, DIVORCES, AND ACCIDENTAL DEATHS

XVIII. Marriages, divorces, [and annulments], number and rate, by county. (p. 217)

XIX. Deaths resulting from accidents occurring in Oklahoma: by type of accident, by race. (p. 218)

LIFE EXPECTANCY

XX. Life expectancy [by age group, with calculation]. (p. 221)

XXI. Estimated average life expectancy, by county and age. (p. 222-223)

S6450   OKLAHOMA
Regents for
Higher Education

S6450-1   TWENTY-SECOND BIENNIAL REPORT, PART I, Oklahoma State Regents for Higher Education, Fiscal Year Ending June 30, 1983
Biennial. [1984.] 4+203 p.
LC 43-52673.
SRI/MF/complete, current and previous year reports

Biennial report on Oklahoma higher education programs and activities for 2- and 4-year accredited colleges and universities, with data on State supported institution enrollment, finances, and operations, for FY83.

Report is published in 2 parts, presenting separate data for each fiscal year of the biennium. Part I is published in even-numbered years; Part II is published in odd-numbered years. Current Part I presents data for FY83, with selected trends from as early as FY09.

Data are from Oklahoma State System of Higher Education and other sources.

Contents:

Part II of the 21st biennial report was also reviewed in SRI during 1984, and is also available on SRI microfiche, under this number [Biennial. [Feb. 1983.] iv+199 p. †]. Part I of the 21st report is described in SRI 1982 Annual under this number.

Availability: Oklahoma Regents for Higher Education, 500 Education Bldg., State Capitol Complex, Oklahoma City OK 73105, †; SRI/MF/complete.

TABLES:
[Unless otherwise indicated, all data are for Oklahoma State System of Higher Education.]

S6450-1.1: Enrollment and Degrees
[Tables [3] and [5-7] show data by institution.]
ENROLLMENT

[1] Oklahoma high school graduates, by county [and sex], 1983. (p. 83)

[2] Geographic origin of students enrolled in public institutions in 1982/83, by county, State, and country. (p. 84)

[3] Comparison of main and branch campus fall semester enrollments, 1972-82. (p. 87)

[4] Veteran enrollment [by institution type, for State and other institutions], as of Oct. 1, 1983. (p. 88)

[5] Summary of fall off-campus enrollments, 1881/82-1982/83. (p. 88)

[6] Enrollment by county, 1st semester 1982/83. (p. 89)

DEGREES

[7] Summary of degrees granted [by level and subject area], 1982/83. (p. 93)

S6450-1.2: Finances
STUDENT AID

[1] State scholarships granted [students helped, and funds used and authorized, by institution], 1982/83. (p. 99)

[2-3] Guaranteed student loan program "in-school" loans, as of June 30, 1983; and tuition aid grant and SSIG [State student incentive grants] program, FY83; [recipients and value, by institution, for State and other institutions]. (p. 101-105)

EXPENDITURES AND BUDGETS
[Tables [6-7] and [10-12] show data by institution.]

[4] Regents' office expenditures [by object] and [summary of budgeted] State and Federal funds, 1982/83. (p. 127)

[5] Summary of appropriation acts [and amounts], 39th Oklahoma Legislature, FY83. (p. 128)

[6-7] Educational and general operating budget: Part I summary [State and other funds available], FY83; and Part II, allocations for sponsored research and other sponsored programs [FY82-83]. (p. 129-131)

[8] State Regents' No. 220 loan fund [status, as of June 30, 1983]. (p. 138)

[9] Expenditures for State purposes since statehood: budget office totals [FY09-83]. (p. 139)

[10] Current operating income [by source] and expenditures [by function], 1982/83. (p. 140)

[11] Bonded indebtedness, as of June 30, 1983. (p. 144-148)

[12] Section 13 and new college funds [available and expended], 1982/83. (p. 151)

S6450-2   COLLEGE AND UNIVERSITY SALARIES IN TEN MID-WESTERN STATES, 1982/83 Academic Year
Annual. Nov. 1983. 12 p.
SRI/MF/complete

Annual report, for academic year 1982/83, on public college and university faculty salaries in Oklahoma and 9 midwestern States, by institution and faculty academic rank. Also includes data on student/faculty ratios, staff benefits, and selected administrative salaries.

Data are based on a questionnaire survey of 178 midwestern State institutions.

Contains table listing (1 p.); list of participating institutions, and highlights (p. 1-2); and 10 tables (p. 3-12).

Availability: Oklahoma Regents for Higher Education, 500 Education Bldg., State Capitol Complex, Oklahoma City OK 73105, †; SRI/MF/complete.

S6455   OKLAHOMA
Department of
Human Services

S6455–1   OKLAHOMA DEPARTMENT OF HUMAN SERVICES
Annual Report, FY83
Annual. For individual
publication data, see below.
SRI/MF/complete

Annual report on Oklahoma public welfare programs, cases, clients, services, and finances, FY83, with selected historical trends from FY37. Data are from Dept of Human Services (DHS) records and other State sources.

Report is issued in 2 volumes: narrative report and a statistical report. Volumes are individually described below. Prior to FY83, report was issued in 1 volume.

A quarterly *"Statistical Bulletin"* is also available from the issuing agency, but is not covered by SRI.

Availability: Oklahoma Department of Human Services, Research and Statistics Division, Editorial Office, PO Box 25352, Oklahoma City OK 73125, †; SRI/MF/complete.

S6455–1.1: Main Report
[Annual. Nov. 1, 1983. 27 p. DHS Pub. No. 83-53. SRI/MF/complete.]

Contains transmittal letter and introduction (p. 2-3); narrative report interspersed with 26 charts and 3 tables showing summary data also included in the statistical report (p. 4-27); and contents listing (back cover).

S6455–1.2: Statistical Report
[Annual. [1983]. 48 p. DHS Pub. No. 83-58. SRI/MF/complete.]

Contains 3 trend charts and 1 summary table (p. 1-2); contents/table listing (p. 3); 44 charts, and 35 tables listed below (p. 4-48); and listing of committee members (p. 47).

TABLES:
[Data are for FY83, unless otherwise noted. Data by category generally cover State supplemental payments for aged, blind, and disabled; AFDC; and, sometimes, payments for medically needy, food stamps, general assistance, and AFDC emergency. Data by race include white, black, Indian, Hispanic, and Asian.]

SUMMARY EXPENDITURES, EMPLOYEES, AND COLLECTIONS

1. Expenditures [by program/activity area], FY82-83. (p. 4)

[A] DHS [FTE] employees, by program, 1983. (p. 4)

2. DHS program expenditures: by [State and Federal] source of funds FY37-83. (p. 5)

3. Sales tax dollar: collections, expenditures, and amounts returned, by county. (p. 6)

PUBLIC ASSISTANCE

4-7. Public assistance payments, monthly average payment, and average monthly cases and persons, [all] by category FY37-83; and payments by category and county FY83. (p. 8-12)

8-9. Application and case movement, and appeals and dispositions; by category. (p. 12-13)

10-11. Public assistance cases opened and closed, by reason: cases and percent. (p. 13-14)

FOOD STAMP ASSISTANCE AND DONATED FOOD

12. Food stamp program: cases, persons, and value, by category [AFDC and non-AFDC] and county. (p. 15)

13. Donated food commodities: average retail value, by issue [schools, institutions, elderly nutrition, child care, summer camps, and needy Indian and other families], by county. (p. 17)

STATE SUPPLEMENTAL AND AFDC RECIPIENTS

14. Recipients of State supplemental payments [to the aged, blind, and disabled], by race, sex, and county. (p. 19-23)

15. AFDC recipients [families and children] by race and county. (p. 24)

16-18. Recipients of State supplemental payments to the aged, blind, and disabled by age, race, and sex. (p. 26)

19. Children in AFDC by age and sex. (p. 27)

MEDICAL ASSISTANCE

20. Medical payments by category [combined adult, AFDC, medically needy by age group, vocational rehabilitation, and crippled children], and type of service. (p. 28)

21-22. Medicaid payments and recipients by type of service and county. (p. 29-32)

23. Vocational rehabilitation medical services cases and payments by type of service [including hospital, physician, and other services] and by county. (p. 33)

24. Hospitalization: persons, days, and payments, by hospital. (p. 35)

ELDERLY AND CHILD SERVICES, AND TEACHING HOSPITALS

25. Nutrition programs for the elderly: meals served by type [congregate and at-home] and by county. (p. 39)

26. Child abuse and neglect [cases alleged and confirmed], by county. (p. 40)

27-28. Adoptive homes, applications and completed studies; and adoptive homes placements, case movement and ages. (p. 41)

29. Children's services, caseload by type of placement, FY82-83. (p. 41)

30. Foster homes applications and approvals. (p. 41)

31. Children receiving services from court related and community services, by county. (p. 42)

32. Homes and schools: population movement by facility. (p. 44)

33. Oklahoma teaching hospitals [inpatient beds, admissions, discharges, average occupancy, and outpatient clinic visits, by hospital], [FY81-83]. (p. 45)

34. Child support enforcement: collections and absent parent cases, by category [AFDC and non-AFDC] and activity, FY82-83. (p. 46)

S6465   OKLAHOMA
Bureau of
Investigation

S6465–1   STATE OF OKLAHOMA UNIFORM CRIME REPORT, Jan.-Dec. 1983
Annual. [1984.] ix + 125 p.
LC 78-648358.
SRI/MF/complete

Annual report on Oklahoma crimes and arrests, by type of offense, 1983, with comparisons to 1981-82. Includes crimes by locale, and arrests by age, race, and sex. Also includes data on value of property stolen and recovered, disposition of juvenile cases, assaults on police, and police employment.

Data are from reports of local sheriffs' offices and police depts, submitted under the Uniform Crime Reporting (UCR) Program.

Contents:

a. Listings of contents, tables, and charts; and introduction. (p. vi-ix)

b. Summary, with 1 table; and UCR program description, with offense definitions. (p. 1-11)

c. 6 statistical sections, with 26 charts and 52 tables described below, and interspersed narrative. (p. 13-117)

d. Statement of policy for release of UCR information; appendix, with 1 table showing law enforcement officers and civilian employees, by sex, 1983; and glossary. (p. 119-125)

This is the 10th annual report. A quarterly report with summary data is also available from the issuing agency, but is not covered by SRI.

Availability: Oklahoma Bureau of Investigation, Uniform Crime Reporting Division, Cimarron Station, PO Box 11497, Oklahoma City OK 73136, †; SRI/MF/complete.

CHARTS AND TABLES:
[Data are shown for 1981-83, unless otherwise noted. Index offenses are murder, rape, robbery, felonious assault, burglary, larceny/theft, and motor vehicle theft. Arson is also classified as an Index offense, but data are reported separately and are not included with data shown by Index offense.]

S6465–1.1: Index Offenses, Stolen Property, and Arrests
[Data by race/ethnic group generally are shown for white, black, Indian, Hispanic, non-Hispanic, and other, including Asian.]

INDEX OFFENSES
[For most individual Index offenses, tables and charts include number of offenses by month for 1981-83 and by season for 1983, in addition to the data described below.]

a. Total, violent, and nonviolent offenses, by month; and frequency of occurrence, by offense. 7 charts and 3 tables. (p. 14-19)

b. Murder: offenses by day of week, and victims by age, sex, and race/ethnic group, 1981-83; and offenses by circumstance, victim-offender relationship, and weapon, 1983. 2 charts and 6 tables. (p. 21-23)

c. Rape: forcible and attempted rapes. 2 charts and 3 tables. (p. 25)

d. Robbery and felonious assault: robberies and value of property stolen, by place of occurrence; and robberies and aggravated assaults, by weapon. 4 charts and 7 tables. (p. 26-29)

e. Burglary, larceny, and motor vehicle theft: burglary offenses, by type of entry; residence and nonresidence burglary offenses and value of property stolen, by day or night occurrence; larceny offenses by value of property stolen, and offenses and value by type of theft; and motor vehicle thefts, by type of vehicle. 8 charts and 15 tables. (p. 31-38)

f. Arson: offenses and value of property damage, by type of property. 1 table. (p. 40)

STOLEN PROPERTY

g. Value of property stolen and recovered, by month, 1981-83, with selected 1983 detail by type of property and offense. 1 chart and 5 tables. (p. 43-46)

ARRESTS AND CLEARANCES

h. Clearances (total, number involving adults and juveniles, and rates), by Index offense, 1983, with rate trends from 1981; juvenile and adult arrests, by sex, age, and race/ethnic group, for 36-38 types of offense, including drug sale/manufacturing and possession by substance, 1983; and juvenile dispositions (releases and referrals), 1981-83. 2 charts and 4 tables. (p. 49-56)

S6465–1.2: Police Assaulted, Offenses by Locale, and UCR Participation

a. Assaults on officers, by type of assignment, circumstance, weapon, injury status, and time of day. 5 tables. (p. 58-61)

b. Population, Index crime rate, and Index offenses by type, by county and law enforcement agency. 1 table. (p. 65-106)

c. UCR participation, by agency, 1983, with totals for police depts and sheriffs offices, 1981-83, all by month. 2 tables. (p. 110-117)

S6470   OKLAHOMA
Department of Libraries

S6470–1   ANNUAL REPORT AND DIRECTORY OF OKLAHOMA LIBRARIES, 1983
Annual. [1984.] 111 p.
SRI/MF/complete, current & previous year reports

Annual report, for FY83, on Oklahoma public, academic, institutional, school, and special library holdings, finances, and personnel, by library. Data are from State library annual reports and the Census Bureau.

Contains contents listing (1 p.); summary analysis, and 16 tables described below (p. 1-67); and directories of public and institutional libraries, library boards, and librarians (p. 69-111).

Previous report, for FY82, was also reviewed in 1984 and is also available on SRI microfiche under this number [Annual. [1983.] 114 p. †].

Availability: Oklahoma Department of Libraries, 200 N.E. 18th St., Oklahoma City OK 73105, ‡; SRI/MF/complete.

TABLES:
[Most data are for FY83, by individual library. Sections generally include data on expenditures by object, circulation, total and added volumes, periodical subscriptions, audiovisual materials, total staff, staff with master of library science degrees, hours open, and seating capacity. Additional data are noted below.]

a. Public libraries: also shows 1980 population; income by source; registered borrowers; and availability of selected services and programs. 4 tables. (p. 4-33)

b. Academic libraries. 2 tables. (p. 35-41)

c. Institutional libraries: also shows population served; income by source; and availability of selected services and programs. 6 tables. (p. 43-51)

d. School libraries: also shows student population. 2 tables. (p. 53-62)

e. Special libraries. 2 tables. (p. 64-67)

S6482   OKLAHOMA
Department of Public Safety

S6482–1   1982 OKLAHOMA TRAFFIC ACCIDENT FACTS
Annual. [1983.] 35 p.
LC 80-646638.
SRI/MF/complete

Annual report on Oklahoma traffic accidents, fatalities, and injuries, by accident type, location, time, and other circumstances; and driver and victim characteristics; 1982, with selected trends from as early as 1937.

Also includes data on highway mileage, vehicle miles traveled, number of licensed drivers and registered vehicles, economic cost of accidents, blood alcohol test results, and motorcycle helmet use; and details for school bus accidents.

Contains contents listing (1 p.); statistical highlights (p. 1-2); and 21 charts and 14 tables (p. 3-35 and back cover).

Availability: Oklahoma Department of Public Safety, Services and Records Division, PO Box 11415, Oklahoma City OK 73136, †; SRI/MF/complete.

S6493   OKLAHOMA
Supreme Court and Court of Criminal Appeals

S6493–1   ANNUAL REPORT ON THE OKLAHOMA JUDICIARY, 1982-83
Annual. Jan. 2, 1984.
182 p. var. paging.
LC 79-641067.
SRI/MF/complete

Annual report on Oklahoma judicial system, including trial and appellate court caseloads and case dispositions, for FY83, with selected trends from 1978. Covers supreme, appeals, and district courts. Includes trial court data by case type and county.

Trial court case types shown are civil, domestic relations, probate, small claims, criminal misdemeanor and felony, and traffic (including driving under influence cases).

Also includes data on special jurisdiction courts and councils, including tax review and judicial complaints activity; and local court fund collections and disbursements by fund or purpose, by county; and district court bond forfeitures, by case type and county.

Contains contents listing (p. i-iv); introduction and narrative review (p. 1-7); report, with 2 charts and 29 tables (p. 10-166) and appendices, with 6 charts, 4 maps, and 6 tables (A1-A26).

Availability: Oklahoma Supreme Court, Court Services Division, 5005 N. Lincoln, Suite 225, Oklahoma City OK 73105, †; SRI/MF/complete.

S6495   OKLAHOMA
Tax Commission

S6495–1   ANNUAL REPORT OF THE OKLAHOMA TAX COMMISSION, Fiscal Year Ended June 30, 1983
Annual. [1984.] ii+22 p.
LC 32-27747.
SRI/MF/complete

Annual report presenting detailed data on Oklahoma tax revenues by source, and apportionment to local governments and State agencies and funds, FY83, with trends from FY46.

Data are compiled by the Oklahoma Tax Commission.

Contains 1 chart, and 5 detailed tables listed below.

Availability: Oklahoma Tax Commission, McConnors Bldg., 2501 Lincoln Blvd., Oklahoma City OK 73194-0001, †; SRI/MF/complete.

TABLES:
[Major tax sources are alcoholic beverage, beverage, cigarette, corporation franchise, gasoline/fuels excise, gross production, income, estate, motor vehicle excise, sales, tobacco, and vehicle taxes and/or license fees.

Breakdowns for revenue apportionment are for counties by function, cities/towns, and individual State agencies and funds.]

[1] Review of 1982/83 taxes and collections [tax rate, definitions, and amounts, by type of tax]. (p. 1-5)

[2] Comparative statement of all tax collections [by type, FY82-83]. (p. 6)

[3] Apportionment of statutory revenues [FY82-83]. (p. 10)

[4] State revenue [by source] and apportionment. (p. 12-17)

[5] Revenue growth from major tax sources [by type], FY46-83. (p. 18-21)

S6575   OREGON
Department of Agriculture

S6575–1   OREGON AGRICULTURAL STATISTICS, 1982-83
Annual. Nov. 8, 1983.   56 p.
SRI/MF/complete

Annual report on Oregon agricultural production, marketing, and finances, 1982, with trends from as early as 1870. Data are shown by commodity and/or county or district.

Report covers production, value, prices, and, as applicable, acreage, yield, stocks or inventory, and disposition, for field crop, fruit, nut, berry, vegetable, livestock, dairy, and poultry sectors.

Also includes number of farms and acreage; farm income and expenses; precipitation; fertilizer consumption; cold storage holdings of selected fruits and vegetables; manufactured dairy products production; mink breeding and pelt production; and U.S. potato consumption, and production and stocks by State.

Data are compiled by the Oregon Crop and Livestock Reporting Service in cooperation with USDA.

Contains foreword and contents listing (p. 3-4); and 7 charts and 72 tables, interspersed with brief narrative summaries (p. 5-56).

This is the 2nd annual report.

Availability: Oregon Department of Agriculture, 635 Capitol St., NE, Salem OR 97310-0110, †; SRI/MF/complete.

S6580   OREGON
Department of Commerce

S6580–1   SEVENTY-SIXTH ANNUAL REPORT OF THE SUPERINTENDENT OF BANKS, 1983, Oregon
Annual. [1984.] 79 p.
SRI/MF/complete

Annual report on financial condition of Oregon State-chartered financial institutions, presenting assets, liabilities, revenues, expenses, and profits, for banks/trust companies, credit unions, and consumer finance licensees, all as of Dec. 31, 1983, with selected trends from 1979. Includes data for State-located national banks. Most data on assets and liabilities are shown by institution.

Also includes data on State Banking Fund receipts and disbursements; capital stock changes; aggregate trust balance sheet; number of banks and resources from 1909; bank deposits and loans, by institution and location; and pawnbroker and consumer finance loan analyses.

Contains contents listing (p. 3); and 17 tables interspersed with lists of status changes and directories (p. 5-79).

Availability: Oregon Department of Commerce, Banking Division, 280 Court St., NE, Salem OR 97310, †; SRI/MF/complete.

S6580–3   FIFTY-FOURTH ANNUAL REPORT OF THE SAVINGS AND LOAN SUPERVISOR for the Calendar Year Ended Dec. 31, 1983, Oregon
Annual. Apr. 13, 1984.
28 p.
LC 80-649545.
SRI/MF/complete

Annual report on financial condition of Oregon State-chartered savings and loan assns, presenting assets, liabilities, income, expenses, and operating ratios, by institution, as of Dec. 31, 1983, with selected composite trends from 1973. Also includes summary data on employment, and new loans by purpose.

Contains contents listing (p. 1); brief narrative report, 1 map, 5 charts, and 11 tables (p. 5-21); and directory of assns, with individual balance sheets and list of branches (p. 22-28).

Availability: Oregon Department of Commerce, Savings and Loan Section, Commerce Bldg., 158 12th St., NE, Salem OR 97310, †; SRI/MF/complete.

S6590   OREGON
Department of Education

S6590–1   OREGON EDUCATIONAL STATISTICS, 1983/84
Annual series. For individual publication data, see below.
SRI/MF/complete

Series of annual reports, for academic year 1983/84, each presenting data on an aspect of Oregon elementary and secondary education. Topics include public school enrollment, finance, and staff. A report on nonpublic schools is also included.

Reports for 1983/84 reviewed during 1984 are described below. Reports for 1981/82 and 1982/83 are covered under S6590-2 and S6590-3, respectively.

Two nonstatistical reports in the series, listing 1-teacher and middle schools, are not covered in SRI.

Availability: Oregon Department of Education, School District Services Office, School Finance and Data Information Services, 700 Pringle Pkwy., SE, Salem OR 97310, †; SRI/MF/complete.

S6590–1.1: Number of Public Schools, 1983/84, Oregon
[Annual. Dec. 1983. 1 p. SRI/MF/complete.]

Annual table showing number of elementary, secondary, and special public schools, by educational service district/county and type of school, as of Oct. 1, 1983.

S6590–1.2: Approved Secondary Schools in Oregon, Fall of 1983
[Annual. Nov. 1983. 14 p. SRI/MF/complete.]

Annual table showing estimated enrollment in public junior high schools and high schools, grouped by county and school district, fall 1983.

S6590–1.3: Estimated Full-Time Equivalency of Public School District Personnel, as of Oct. 1, 1983, Oregon
[Annual. Dec. 1983. 1 p. SRI/MF/complete.]

Annual table showing number of FTE official/administrative, professional/educational, and nonprofessional public school personnel, by position, sex, and race/ethnicity (including Hispanic, Asian/Pacific Islander, and American Indian/Alaskan Native), as of Oct. 1, 1983.

S6590–1.4: Estimated 1983/84 per Student Current Expenditures, Oregon
[Annual. [1984.] 19 p. SRI/MF/complete.]

Two annual tables estimating public school expenditures per resident average daily membership (ADM), assessed value per ADM, and total school tax rate, by school district and county, and by school district arranged by type and size, 1983/84.

S6590–1.5: 1983/84 Summary of Valuations and Taxes Levied, Oregon
[Annual. Mar. 1984. 25 p. SRI/MF/complete.]

Three annual tables showing assessed value, local extended levy, county school fund levy, and ESD (educational service district) levy amounts, by ESD, county, and school district; and tax rates, by school district; 1983/84.

S6590–2   OREGON EDUCATIONAL STATISTICS, 1981/82
Annual series. For individual publication data, see below.
SRI/MF/complete

Series of annual reports, for academic year 1981/82, each presenting data on an aspect of Oregon elementary and secondary education. Topics include public school enrollment, finance, and staff. A report on nonpublic schools is also included.

Reports for 1981/82 reviewed during 1984 are described below. Reports for 1982/83 and 1983/84 are covered in SRI under S6590-3 and S6590-1, respectively.

Two nonstatistical reports in the series, listing 1-teacher schools and middle schools, are not covered in SRI.

Availability: Oregon Department of Education, School District Services Office, School Finance and Data Information Services, 700 Pringle Pkwy., SE, Salem OR 97310, †; SRI/MF/complete.

S6590–2.20: Audited Current Expenditures for Resident Students, 1981/82
[Annual. May 1983. 10 p. SRI/MF/complete.]

Two annual tables showing public school expenditures per average resident daily membership, and expenditures by function, all by school district and educational service district/county, 1981/82.

S6590–2.21: School District Audit Summary, 1981/82
[Annual. [1983.] 12 p. Oversized. SRI/MF/complete.]

Annual table showing public school revenues by source by fund; and expenditures by fund, function, and object; for the total State, 1981/82.

S6590-2.22: Summary of 1981/82 Audited Resources of Oregon School Districts and ESDs

[Annual. July 26, 1983. 15 p. Oversized. SRI/MF/complete.]

Annual table showing public school resources by source, by school district and educational service district/county, 1981/82.

S6590-3   OREGON EDUCATIONAL STATISTICS, 1982/83

Annual series. For individual publication data, see below.
SRI/MF/complete

Series of annual reports, for academic year 1982/83, each presenting data on an aspect of Oregon elementary and secondary education. Topics include public school enrollment, finance, and staff. A report on nonpublic schools is also included.

Reports for 1982/83 reviewed during 1984 are described below. Reports for 1981/82 and 1983/84 are covered in SRI under S6590-2 and S6590-1, respectively.

Two nonstatistical reports in the series, listing 1-teacher and middle schools, are not covered in SRI.

Availability: Oregon Department of Education, School District Services Office, School Finance and Data Information Services, 700 Pringle Pkwy., SE, Salem OR 97310, †; SRI/MF/complete.

S6590-3.8: Oregon School District Census (Between Ages 4 and 20 Years) by ESD Lines

[Annual. May 1983. 4 p. SRI/MF/complete.]

Annual table showing Oregon population aged 4-20 years, by school district and county, Oct. 1982.

S6590-3.9: Summary of 1982/83 Oregon Private and Parochial Schools

[Annual. Aug. 4, 1983. 24 p. SRI/MF/complete.]

Two annual tables showing the following for private and parochial schools in Oregon:

a. School address, district, denomination, grades taught, enrollment, average daily membership (ADM), and high school graduates by sex, for individual schools, arranged by county, 1982/83.

b. Enrollment by grade for grades P-12 and unclassified elementary and secondary; and ADM for grade ranges P-8, 9-12, and P-12; all by county, June 30, 1983.

S6590-3.10: 1983 Oregon Public High School Graduates

[Annual. Aug. 16, 1983. 8 p. SRI/MF/complete.]

Annual table showing number of 1983 Oregon high school graduates, by sex, by school, arranged by county and school district.

S6590-3.11: Oregon School Districts, June 30, 1983

[Annual. [1983.] 15 p. SRI/MF/complete.]

Annual report listing Oregon school districts alphabetically and by county. Includes each district's average daily pupil membership as of June 30, 1983.

S6590-3.12: Actual and Projected Public School Average Daily Membership and Enrollment, Oregon

[Annual. Sept. 1983. 2 p. SRI/MF/complete.]

Two annual tables showing public school average daily membership and enrollment, by grade for grades K-12, and for unclassified elementary and secondary, 1979/80-1984/85.

Prior to 1982/83, table on enrollment was issued separately.

S6590-3.13: Oregon Public and Private High School Graduates, Actual and Projected

[Annual. Mar. 1984. 1 p. SRI/MF/complete.]

Annual table showing number of public and private high school graduates, 1964/65-1984/85.

S6590-3.14: Net Enrollment Summary and Average Daily Membership Attending, Year Ending June 30, 1983, Oregon

[Annual. [1983.] 2 p. SRI/MF/complete.]

Two annual tables showing net enrollment and average daily membership of public schools, by grade K-12, and for unclassified elementary and secondary, all by educational service district/county, year ending June 30, 1983.

Prior to 1982/83, table on net enrollment was issued separately.

S6590-3.15: Status of School District Tax Bases, 1982/83, Oregon

[Annual. [1984.] 8 p. SRI/MF/complete.]

Annual table showing tax base and date established, for Oregon school districts grouped by county, 1982/83.

Previous report, for 1981/82, is described in SRI 1982 Annual under S6590-2.1.

**S6603   OREGON
Executive Department**

S6603-2   ANNUAL FINANCIAL REPORT for the Year Ended June 30, 1983, State of Oregon
Annual. Oct. 31, 1983.
100 p.
LC 80-647882.
SRI/MF/complete

Annual report on financial condition of Oregon State government, FY83, presenting assets and liabilities, reserves, and fund balances; revenues by source; and expenditures by object and program area; for all, general, special revenue, debt service, capital project, enterprise, internal service, and trust and agency funds, with selected comparisons from FY79.

Also includes data on budgeted vs. actual revenues and expenditures; State retirement system membersip and finances; State penitentiary industry finances; fixed assets; long-term debt; analyses of cash holdings, investments by type of instrument, and indebtedness; economic trends and employment projections; and energy consumption by type.

Data are compiled from reports of State and Federal agencies.

Contains contents listing (1 p.); and report in 14 sections, with introduction (p. 1-6), and 3 charts and 67 tables, interspersed with narrative analyses (p. 7-100).

Availability: Oregon Executive Department, Accounting Division, 155 Cottage St., NE, Salem OR 97310, †; SRI/MF/complete.

**S6615   OREGON
Department of
Human Resources**

S6615-2   OREGON LABOR TRENDS
Monthly. Approx. 10 p.
LC SN 82-21132.
SRI/MF/complete, shipped quarterly

Monthly report on Oregon labor force, employment, and average hours and earnings. Data are compiled from employers' reports and readership surveys, and generally are current to 1-2 months prior to publication date.

Contains features on economic and employment conditions, occasionally statistical, including recurring labor force data by county and SMSA; 1-3 charts; and 4 monthly tables listed below.

Some issues include additional tables presenting recent trends for data covered in monthly tables.

Monthly tables appear in all issues. All additional features presenting Oregon data not covered in monthly tables are described, as they appear, under "Statistical Features." Nonstatistical features are not covered.

Dept of Human Resources also issues a monthly table entitled *Resident Oregon Labor Force and Unemployment by Area;* and 16 monthly reports on employment in local areas, each under the title *Labor Force Trends.* These publications are not covered in SRI. The latter may be requested as a group or for individual counties or regions.

Availability: Oregon Department of Human Resources, Employment Division, Attention: R&S-LMI, 875 Union St., NE, Salem OR 97311, †; SRI/MF/complete, shipped quarterly.

Issues reviewed during 1984: Oct. 1983-Sept. 1984 (P).

MONTHLY TABLES:

[Tables [2-4] show data for most recent month available, preceding month, and same month of previous year.]

[1] [Month] indicators [including CPI for Portland SMSA, and selected summary comparisons to U.S. and to various prior months].

[2] Resident Oregon labor force [by employment status, and seasonally adjusted unemployment rate].

[3] Nonagricultural wage/salary employment [by industry division and major group; and workers involved in labor-management disputes, and Oregon diffusion index].

[4] Average hours and earnings of industrial production workers [by industry division and manufacturing group].

STATISTICAL FEATURES:

S6615–2.501: Oct. 1983

RESIDENT OREGON LABOR FORCE AND UNEMPLOYMENT BY AREA, RECURRING FEATURE

(p. 8) Recurring table showing Oregon labor force by employment status, by SMSA and county, Sept. 1983.

S6615–2.502: Nov. 1983

HIGH TECH vs. OREGON'S FUTURE JOBS

(p. 5-6) Article, with 2 tables showing Oregon employment in 10 industries with greatest employment growth, 1990; and in 18 occupations with greatest demand, 1981 and 1990; ranked by number of jobs created, 1981-90 period.

S6615–2.503: Feb. 1984

RESIDENT OREGON LABOR FORCE AND UNEMPLOYMENT BY AREA, RECURRING FEATURE

(p. 5) Recurring table showing Oregon labor force by employment status, by SMSA and county, Jan. 1984.

S6615–2.504: June 1984

OREGON LABOR AREA UNEMPLOYMENT RATES

(p. 7-8) By Graham Slater. Article, with 1 table ranking Oregon counties and MSAs by unemployment rate, 1983, with comparisons to 1982.

S6615–2.505: July 1984

LABOR SURPLUS AREAS

(p. 7) By Graham Slater. Article, with 1 table showing average unemployment rate for 34 Oregon jurisdictions classified as labor surplus areas by the U.S. Dept of Labor, 1982/83.

EMPLOYERS CORNER

(p. 8) By Dorothy Monnier. Article, with 2 text tables showing Oregon Employment Division staff reductions as of July 13, 1984; and job openings and placement transactions, FY83-84.

S6615–2.506: Sept. 1984

EASTERN OREGON ECONOMY LAGS

(p. 7-8) By William Street. Article, with 1 table showing unemployment rate and rank within the State, for 10 counties in eastern Oregon, Mar. and June 1984.

S6615–3   ADULT AND FAMILY SERVICES in Oregon
Monthly. Approx. 15 p.
SRI/MF/complete, shipped quarterly

Monthly report on Oregon public welfare caseloads, recipients, and expenditures, by program or type of medical service received, city, and State region. Report is issued approximately 2 months after month of coverage.

Contains contents listing, 4 maps, list of counties and cities in each State region, and 3 monthly tables listed below.

Availability: Oregon Department of Human Resources, Adult and Family Services Division, 400 Public Service Bldg., Salem OR 97310-0380, $15.00 per yr.; SRI/MF/complete, shipped quarterly.

Issues reviewed during 1984: Sept. 1983-July 1984 (D) (Vol. 48, Nos. 9-12; Vol. 49, Nos. 1-7).

MONTHLY TABLES:
[All tables show data for month of coverage by city branch office and State region.]

A. [Persons and/or] cases receiving nonmedical payments [and total and average payments, for general assistance, Old-Age Assistance, Aid to Blind, aid to disabled, aid to dependent children, and 2- and 1-parent emergency assistance].

B. Persons and payments for medical services [for physicians, hospitals, drugs, and dental and visual services].

C. Food stamp activity [bonus value of coupons, and number of public assistance and nonassistance persons and households participating].

S6615–5   OREGON PUBLIC HEALTH STATISTICS REPORT for Calendar Years 1981-82
Annual. [1984.] 207 p.
LC 73-640513.
SRI/MF/complete

Annual report on Oregon vital statistics, 1981-82. Covers population, births, deaths by cause, reportable diseases, and marriages and dissolutions. Includes data by county, age, sex, and race; and trends from as early as 1908.

Data are primarily from reports filed with the Oregon State Health Division.

Contents:

a. Listings of contents, charts, and tables. (6 p.)

b. Introduction, with 10 charts and 8 tables primarily showing summary data, but also including poverty and urban-rural status of population, with urban detail by county, and years of lost life by major cause of death and accident type, with selected U.S. comparisons. (p. 3-29)

c. 7 statistical sections, with 6 maps, 12 charts, and 66 tables listed below. (p. 32-201)

d. Appendix, with definitions and sources. (p. 205-207)

For description of previous report, for 1980, see SRI 1982 Annual, under this number. No separate report was issued for 1981.

Availability: Oregon Department of Human Resources, Health Division, Center for Health Statistics, State Office Bldg., PO Box 116, Portland OR 97207, †; SRI/MF/complete.

TABLES:
[Data by race are generally shown for white, black, Indian, Chinese, Japanese, other Asian/Pacific Islander, Filipino, and other nonwhite. Data are for Oregon, 1981-82, unless otherwise noted.]

S6615–5.1: Summary

1-2. Population; live births; births to unwed mothers; deaths; maternal, infant, neonatal, and fetal deaths; and marriages and dissolution of marriages; [for] U.S. 1945-82, and Oregon 1908-82. (p. 33-35)

3. Population; live births; births to unwed mothers; deaths; and infant, neonatal, and fetal deaths; by county of residence, and marriages and dissolutions of marriages, by county of occurrence. (p. 36)

4. Population, births, and deaths, by city of residence. (p. 38-39)

S6615–5.2: Population and Natality

POPULATION

5. Population distribution by age and sex, 1950, 1960, 1970, 1975-82. (p. 43)

NATALITY

[Tables 7-13 begin "Resident births..."]

6. Age specific birth rates, fertility rates, and total fertility rates, [decennially] 1940-70 [and annually] 1975-82. (p. 47)

7. By age group of mother, 1955-82. (p. 50)

8. By race of child, 1955-82. (p. 51)

9-12. [To all and] to unwed mothers, by age of mother and birth weight. (p. 52-53)

13. By age of mother and live birth order. (p. 54)

14. Total pregnancies by type of outcome [including induced abortions] and age groups [of mother]. (p. 55)

15-16. Births [to all and] to unwed mothers, by county of residence and age groups of mother. (p. 56-59)

17. Births by county of residence, by sex and race [and Hispanic ethnicity] of child. (p. 60)

18. Low birth weight infants by county of residence. (p. 62)

19. Congenital malformations by site reported on birth certificate by county of residence. (p. 64)

20. Maternal risk factors [late or no prenatal care; 4/higher birth order; plural birth; and selected maternal characteristics (age 17/younger or 35/older, nonwhite, unwed, and less than 12 years education)], by county of residence. (p. 66)

21. Births by county of occurrence by type of institution [in or not in hospital], and by delivery attendant [including midwives]. (p. 70-73)

S6615–5.3: Mortality

LEADING CAUSES OF DEATH

22. Age specific death rates by sex, [decennially] 1940-70 [and annually] 1975-82. (p. 77)

23. Selected leading causes of deaths with rates, Oregon residents, 1965-82. (p. 79)

24. Five principal causes of death, by age groups [and sex]. (p. 80)

25. Leading causes of death, by rank order for males and females. (p. 84)

26. Age specific death rates, by sex, for the leading causes of death. (p. 86)

27. Deaths by marital status, sex, and age groups. (p. 88)

28. Resident deaths for selected causes, by age and sex. (p. 90-109)

HOMICIDE, SUICIDE, AND ACCIDENTAL DEATHS

29. Resident deaths due to or mentioning external factors [by cause]. (p. 110)

30. Resident deaths from suicide, homicide, [and] external causes undetermined whether accidentally or purposely inflicted, by age, sex, and method. (p. 114)

31. Resident accidental deaths, by type or source of injury, age groups, and sex. (p. 116)

32. Deaths occurring in Oregon, by type of accident and age groups. (p. 118)

INFANT DEATHS

33. Infant, neonatal, and post-neonatal deaths, 1978-82, by maternal risk factors and infant characteristics, for residents at birth. (p. 121)

34-35. Resident infant deaths by cause and county of residence [by] age at time of death. (p. 122-125)

DEATHS BY LOCATION

[Data are shown by county of residence, unless otherwise noted.]

36. Deaths, by age groups and sex. (p. 126)

37. Leading causes of death. (p. 130)

38. Deaths, by sex and race [including Hispanic Americans]. (p. 134)

39. Accidental deaths, by principal classes and county of accident. (p. 136)

40. All deaths and medical examiner's cases, by county of occurrence and autopsy. (p. 138)

41. Deaths occurring in Oregon by disposal of remains. (p. 140)

42-43. Deaths, by selected causes with rates, for Oregon, [3] selected cities, and by county of residence. (p. 142-161)

S6615–5.4: Marriage and Divorce

MARRIAGE

44. Marriages, by month of occurrence. (p. 165)

45-48. Marriages, by age groups and previous marital status of groom and bride. (p. 166-167)

49. All marriages and 1st marriages for both bride and groom, by age groups. (p. 168)

50-51. Marriage, by county of occurrence, by age groups of bride and groom. (p. 170-173)

DIVORCE

[Tables 53-56 and 59 begin "Dissolution of marriages and annulments..."]

52. Dissolution of marriages (including annulments), by month of occurrence. (p. 177)

53-54. By age of husband and wife, [by] duration and order of marriage. (p. 178-181)

55. By duration of marriage and order of marriage for husband and wife. (p. 182)

56. By State or region where marriage occurred [census division, Mountain and Pacific division State, Virgin Islands, and foreign country] by duration of marriage. (p. 184)

57-58. Dissolution of marriages by county of occurrence, by age groups of wife and husband. (p. 186-189)

59. By number of minor children affected. (p. 190)

S6615–5.5: Morbidity

60. Reported cases [and occurrence rates] of gonorrhea, by sex and age groups, 1978-82. (p. 193)

61. Reported cases [and occurrence rates] of syphilis, by age groups and year, 1977-82. (p. 193)

62. Reported tuberculosis cases and deaths, with rates, 1945-82. (p. 194)

63. Reported cases with rates of syphilis and gonorrhea, by year, 1945-82. (p. 195)

64-65. Cases of reportable diseases [by type], by month of report, and by county of residence. (p. 196-199)

66. Reported cases [and occurrence rates] of syphilis and gonorrhea, by county of residence and type of infection. (p. 200-201)

S6615–7   ANNUAL ECONOMIC REPORT, State of Oregon
Annual, discontinued.

Annual report presenting Oregon labor force trends and projections, discontinued with July 1983 report (for description, see SRI 1983 Annual, under this number). Report has been discontinued due to lack of funding.

Individual labor force reports for SMSAs and counties are available from Oregon Department of Human Resources, Employment Division, Research and Statistics-LMI, 875 Union St., NE, Salem OR 97311. These reports are not covered in SRI.

S6620   OREGON
Department of Justice

S6620–1   ANALYSIS OF CRIME in Oregon, Jan.-Dec. 1982
Annual. [1983.]
viii + 117 + App 4 p.
ISSN 0145-6903.
LC 77-644178.
SRI/MF/complete

Annual report, for 1982, on Oregon crimes and arrests, by type of offense, county, and law enforcement agency, with selected comparisons to 1981, and trends from 1977. Includes data on clearances, assaults on police, property loss value, and victim and offender characteristics.

Report is based on data submitted by State and local law enforcement agencies under the Uniform Crime Reporting (UCR) Program.

Contents:

a. Listings of contents, tables, and charts; summary, with 1 table; and text data on State population, land area, and income. (p. i-viii)

b. Overview of crime reporting system. (p. 1-3)

c. 3 sections, with narrative analyses, and 27 charts and 31 tables described below. (p. 5-117).

d. Appendices with offense definitions and methodology. (p. A1-B1)

This is the 9th annual report. Previous report was issued by the Oregon Executive Dept and is described in SRI 1982 Annual under S6603-3.

Availability: Oregon Department of Justice, Crime Analysis Center, Criminal Justice Division, Justice Bldg., Salem OR 97310, $5.00; SRI/MF/complete.

CHARTS AND TABLES:

[Unless otherwise noted, data are for 1982, occasionally with comparisons to 1981. Index (Part I) crimes are murder, rape, robbery, aggravated assault, burglary, larceny-theft, motor vehicle theft, and arson. Part II offenses are less serious crimes.]

S6620–1.1: Statewide Data

SUMMARY, AND PROPERTY LOSS

a. Index and Part II offenses, 1981-82, and Index arrests and clearances, 1977-82, all by offense, with selected rates; and value of property stolen and recovered by property type, and value of property stolen/damaged/destroyed by offense, 1982. Charts 1-3, tables 1-5. (p. 5-13)

ARRESTS

b. Arrests for Index and Part II offenses, by age and sex, with summary trends from 1978. Chart 4, tables 6-10. (p. 15-22)

INDEX OFFENSES

[Data for each Index offense include rate trends from 1977, in addition to the data described below.]

c. Murder offenses by type of weapon, by victim's age, sex, and race (white, Negro, Indian, and Asian), and by circumstances; forcible and attempted rape offenses, clearances, and rates; and rape offenses by type of weapon. Charts 5-8, tables 11-13. (p. 23-28)

d. Robbery offenses and value of property stolen, by type of location; and robbery offenses, and aggravated assaults, both by type of weapon. Charts 9-10, tables 14-16. (p. 29-32)

e. Burglary offenses, by type of entry, and residential and nonresidential by time of day; and larceny offenses by type; all with value of property stolen. Charts 11-17, tables 17-18. (p. 33-41)

f. Motor vehicle thefts, by type of vehicle; and arson offenses and property loss value, by type of property. Charts 18-19, tables 19-20. (p. 42-45)

PART II OFFENSES

g. Forgery/counterfeiting, fraud, embezzlement, vandalism, and family offenses, by type; value of property loss for fraud and embezzlement; arrests for drug abuse by type of substance, and for drunk driving by blood alcohol level, with detail by sex and for adults and juveniles; and number of other Part II offenses; with selected offense rate trends from 1977. Charts 20-27, tables 21-28. (p. 46-59)

S6620–1.2: Local Data

a. Counties ranked by Index, violent, and property crime rates, 1982. Table 29 (incorrectly reads table 27). (p. 60)

b. Offenses, clearances, and arrests, by Index and Part II offense including drug abuse by substance, and number of police officers assaulted, all by county and law enforcement agency arranged by district; and arrests by Part I and Part II offense by age group, by county. 2 unnumbered tables. (p. 62-117)

S6655   OREGON
Public Utility Commissioner

**S6655-2   1983 OREGON UTILITY
STATISTICS**
Annual. [1984.] 3+106 p.
ISSN 0091-0546.
LC 73-642994.
SRI/MF/complete, current &
previous year reports

Annual report presenting Oregon public utility
financial and operating data, by type of utility
and company, 1983. Utility types covered are
electric, gas, steam heat, telephone, and water.
Data are grouped by type of ownership or revenue class within each utility type.

Includes assets, liabilities, revenues, and expenses, by detailed item; and sales and/or customers, by sector; for most utility types. Also
includes income and balance sheet data for joint
utilities; selected electric and gas utility trends
from 1974, and conservation activities; electricity output and capacity, by type of generation; gas
production; and telephone access lines.

Data are from unaudited company reports
filed with the Commissioner.

Contains contents listing (2 p.); and 12 charts
and 23 tables grouped in 6 sections, each preceded by foreword and company index (p. 1-106).

Previous report, for 1982, was also reviewed
during 1984, and is also available on SRI microfiche under this number [Annual. [1983.] 99
p. $7.50 (prepaid)].

Availability: Oregon Public Utility Commis-
sioner, Research Division, Labor and Industries
Bldg., Salem OR 97310, $7.50 (prepaid); SRI/
MF/complete.

S6680   OREGON
Department of
Transportation

**S6680-1   OREGON TRAFFIC
ACCIDENTS, 1983:
Summary**
Annual. June 1984.
141 p. no paging.
ISSN 0093-1934.
LC 82-641440.
SRI/MF/complete

Annual report on Oregon traffic accidents, fatalities, and injuries, by accident and vehicle type,
location, and other circumstances; and driver
and victim characteristics; 1983, with summary
trends from 1979.

Data are compiled by the Motor Vehicles
Division.

Contains 14 tables, repeated for State, rural
and urban areas, and each city and county; interspersed with 5 summary tables.

Traffic accident reports for trucks, pedestrians,
motorcycles, and bicycles are also available from
the issuing agency, along with reports on accidents involving alcohol, and on licensed drivers,
accident involvement, and violation convictions.
These reports are not covered in SRI.

Availability: Oregon Department of Transportation, Motor Vehicles Division, 1905 Lana
Ave., NE, Salem OR 97314, †; SRI/MF/com-
plete.

S6760   PENNSYLVANIA
Department of
Agriculture

**S6760-1   1983 CROP AND
LIVESTOCK Annual
Summary, Pennsylvania**
Annual. [1984.] ii+86 p.
Order No. 995.
ISSN 0079-046X.
LC A55-9126.
SRI/MF/complete

Annual report on Pennsylvania agricultural production, marketing, and finances, 1983, with
trends from 1940. Data generally are shown by
commodity and county, with selected comparisons to other States.

Covers production, value, prices, and, as applicable, acreage, yield, inventory, and disposition,
for livestock, poultry, dairy, mink, field crop,
vegetable, fruit, and nursery sectors.

Also includes data on weather; prices paid for
selected production items; farm income and expenses; custom work rates; fertilizer consumption; number, acreage, and value of farms; U.S.
food consumption; and cropland rental fees and
farm property value, by State.

Data are compiled by the Pennsylvania Crop
Reporting Service in cooperation with USDA.

Contains contents listing (p. ii); 3 maps, 2
charts, and 107 tables, interspersed with narrative summaries (p. 1-83); and facsimile of data
reporting form, list of State agriculture reports
available, and map of crop reporting districts (p.
84-85).

Availability: Crop Reporting Board Publications, South Bldg., Rm. 5829, U.S. Department
of Agriculture, Washington DC 20250, Pennsylvania farmers †, others $5.00; SRI/MF/com-
plete.

S6775   PENNSYLVANIA
Department of
Commerce

**S6775-1   1984 PENNSYLVANIA
STATISTICAL ABSTRACT**
Annual. 1984. viii+248 p.
ISSN 0476-1103.
ISBN 0-8182-0048-0.
LC A59-9073.
SRI/MF/complete

Annual compilation, for 1984, of detailed social,
demographic, governmental, and economic statistics for Pennsylvania. Data are primarily for
1970s-83, with historical trends from 1790 and
population projections to 2030.

Data are primarily from reports of State and
Federal agencies.

Report is designed to present a comprehensive
overview of the State. Extensive socioeconomic,
demographic, and geographical breakdowns are
shown, as applicable, for most topics. These
breakdowns include data by city, county and other State region, SMSA, urban-rural status, commodity, income, industry, occupation, age,
educational attainment, marital status, race, and
sex. Comparisons to total U.S. are also occasionally included.

Contains listings of contents, tables, charts/
maps, and Pennsylvania SMSAs (p. iv-viii); 19
charts/maps and 230 tables arranged in 9 sections, described below (p. 1-240); and subject index (p. 241-248). Tables in each section are
preceded by a listing of data sources and definitions. Data sources appear beneath each table.
This is the 26th edition.

Availability: State Book Store, Management
Services Bureau, PO Box 1365, Harrisburg PA
17125, $11.00; SRI/MF/complete.

TABLE SECTIONS:

**S6775-1.1: Section 1: Population, Births,
Deaths, Marriages, and Divorces**

a. **Population:** projections to 2030 and
trends from 1790; household, family, and
fertility characteristics; land area; educational attainment, labor force, and income
characteristics; elderly household characteristics; and veterans by period of service.
Tables 1-15. (p. 4-19)

b. **Vital statistics:** births; deaths by leading
cause; accidental deaths by cause; suicides
and homicides; and marriages and divorces. Tables 16-23. (p. 20-25)

**S6775-1.2: Section 2: Commerce, Manu-
facturing, and Banking**

a. **Economic development:** State industrial
development loans, and planned employment and payroll; revenue bond and mortgage program projects, cost, and
employment; Federal coastal energy impact and small community planning allocations; and State grants for housing,
development, and small communities. Tables 24-29. (p. 27-30)

b. **Finance:** financial institutions (including
pawnshops), and balance sheet data, by institution type; and savings and loan assn
and credit union membership and assets.
Tables 30-35. (p. 31-37)

c. **Business, trade, and construction:** State
liquor stores and sales; insurance companies and underwriting data by type of company; and nonresidential construction
value and housing units constructed. Tables 36-40. (p. 38-41)

d. **Housing units:** housing tenure and occupancy; median number of rooms and rent
or value; vacancy rate; housing units by
fuel type; monthly housing costs; and housing demolition and building permits. Tables
41-44. (p. 42-44)

e. **Foreign trade at ports of Philadelphia:**
cargo traffic; quantity and value of imports
and exports by country of origin and destination; and U.S. customs receipts. Tables
45-47. (p. 45-48)

f. **Industry:** establishments, employment,
and payroll; and travel generated expenditures, payroll, employment, and State and
local tax receipts. Tables 48-49. (p. 49-51)

g. **Commerce:** State funding and project
summaries for partnership, community
facilities, site development, and Appalachian region programs; State capital loan fund
activity; and minority business development projects, loans, and jobs created or
preserved. Tables 50-55. (p. 52-53)

S6775-1.3: Section 3: Employment and Income

a. **Employment:** labor force by employment status; youth employment; covered employment and wages/salaries; job service activities; unemployment compensation; and hours and earnings. Tables 56-69. (p. 56-77)

b. **Income:** household, family, and unrelated individual income; median family income; families and persons below poverty level; total and per capita personal income; and GSP. Tables 70-76. (p. 78-85)

c. **Industrial injuries:** fatal and nonfatal injuries. Table 77. (p. 86)

S6775-1.4: Section 4: Education

a. **Elementary and secondary education:** public and private school enrollment; and public school buildings and classrooms, and buildings deactivated. Tables 78-82. (p. 87-90)

b. **Vocational education:** enrollment, graduates, and employment/activity status, by level and program. Tables 83-85. (p. 90-91)

c. **Educational personnel and finance:** personnel, education, salary, and years of service; State and Federal expenditures by function or program; per pupil expenditures; revenues by source; school districts; and tax collections. Tables 86-94. (p. 92-101)

d. **Higher education:** enrollment; expenditures and average tuition/fees; faculty and average salaries; State financial assistance applicants and grants; State funding, by institution; Federal funding for scientific education and R&D; and degrees conferred, by field and level. Tables 95-105. (p. 102-115)

e. **Libraries:** public libraries, holdings, staff, population served, operations, finances, and Federal and State aid, with detail by selected library. Tables 106-107. (p. 116-118)

S6775-1.5: Section 5: Social Services

a. **Health care:** occupational disease compensation cases and payments; hospitals, admissions, and beds; State supported residents in private mental retardation facilities; State mental retardation center residents by facility, and applicants awaiting admission; vocational rehabilitation caseload and expenditures; and VA expenditures. Tables 108-113. (p. 119-123)

b. **Public welfare:** public assistance and medical assistance recipients and/or expenditures; child welfare recipients; blind caseload; and food service facilities. Tables 114-123. (p. 124-132)

S6775-1.6: Section 6: State and Local Government and Taxes

a. **Elections:** characteristics of congressional and State legislative districts; voter registration by political party; and votes cast for President, Governor, and other Federal and State offices. Tables 124-133. (p. 134-156)

b. **Local government:** county seats and municipalities; municipal employment, payroll, and financial condition; property

valuations and tax rates; municipal authorities; and bond issues, projects, and debt. Tables 134-144. (p. 157-167)

c. **State government:** State expenditures by object and revenues by source and fund; bonded indebtedness; lottery income and expenses; State employment by dept or agency and employment status; and State Human Relations Commission complaints and disposition. Tables 145-153. (p. 168-175)

d. **Taxes:** individual income tax returns and taxable income; municipal tax levies; and sales/use tax collections. Tables 154-159. (p. 176-180)

S6775-1.7: Section 7: Law Enforcement, Crime, and Correction

a. **Corrections and sentencing:** correctional population, by institution; correctional admissions and releases; and State Board of Probation and Parole operations, caseload, and parolees and parole agents. Tables 160-171. (p. 181-189)

b. **Courts:** common pleas court cases, dispositions, and inventory. Table 172. (p. 190)

c. **Crime and law enforcement:** State police traffic arrests by violation; offenses and clearances, by type of offense; and Crime Index offenses. Tables 173-175. (p. 191-193)

S6775-1.8: Section 8: Agriculture, Natural Resources, and Conservation

a. **Agriculture:** farm operating summary; crop acreage and production; livestock, dairy, and poultry farms and production; milk prices; and cash receipts. Tables 176-184. (p. 194-203)

b. **Climate:** temperature and precipitation extremes and/or averages. Tables 185-186. (p. 204-205)

c. **Resources:** coal production, employment, productivity, fatalities, and exports; mineral and cement production value; petroleum shipments and connected wells; and watershed projects and costs. Tables 187-191. (p. 206-210)

d. **Conservation and environment:** conservation program acreage and landowner participation; forest fires, area burned, and control costs; pollution abatement and capital expenditures; State Bureau of Air Quality Control expenditures and caseload; and river basins showing water quality change. Tables 192-200. (p. 211-216)

e. **Recreation:** attendance at State and national parks, historical sites, and museums, by site; hunting and fishing licenses issued; game released and sport fish stocked, by species; and motorboat registrations. Tables 201-207. (p. 216-223)

S6775-1.9: Section 9: Communications, Utilities, Energy, and Transportation

a. **Communications and utilities:** public TV viewership, by station; finances and operations of electric, natural gas, telephone, and water utilities, and sewer authorities; regulated transportation and other utilities, and revenues; energy production; and energy consumption by fuel type and sector. Tables 208-220. (p. 224-231)

b. **Accidents:** traffic accident circumstances; traffic accidents, fatalities, and injuries; and vehicle traffic and average speeds. Tables 221-224. (p. 232-234)

c. **Transportation:** State Motor License Fund financial statement; transportation program expenditures; urban mass transit total and senior citizen patronage and fleet characteristics, by agency; Pennsylvania Turnpike vehicle flow; highway mileage; and motor vehicle registrations. Tables 225-230. (p. 234-240)

S6790   PENNSYLVANIA
Department of Education

S6790-2   1982 PENNSYLVANIA PUBLIC LIBRARY STATISTICS
Annual. 1984. i+110 p.
LC A60-9149.
SRI/MF/complete

Annual report on Pennsylvania public libraries, covering personnel, holdings, circulation, and finances, 1982 or FY83, with selected comparisons from 1975. Report is compiled from public library annual reports.

Contains contents listing, map of district library centers, and introduction (3 p.); and 9 report sections, with 4 charts, 15 tables described below, and list of reporting libraries (p. 1-110).

Availability: Pennsylvania Department of Education, State Library, PO Box 1601, Harrisburg PA 17108, †; SRI/MF/complete

TABLES:

a. Services and finances, including population served; hours; new and total registrations; volunteer and salaried staff; book and periodical holdings; circulation; interlibrary loans; income by source, including State and Federal aid; capital expenditures; and operating expenditures by object and source of funds; shown for public libraries arranged by county, and district library centers, 1982. 8 tables. (p. 1-60)

b. Rankings of libraries by total operating expenditures, population served, holdings, and circulation, 1982. 5 tables (p. 63-97)

c. State library operating hours, professional and clerical staff, holdings, interlibrary loans, and services, FY82-83; and summary of public library operations, 1981-82 with percent change from 1975 and 1980. 2 tables (p. 109-110)

S6790-5   STATISTICAL REPORTS
Series. For individual publication data, see below.
SRI/MF/complete

Series of annual statistical reports, each presenting data on a selected aspect of Pennsylvania elementary and secondary education, higher education, and vocational education.

Reports reviewed during 1984 are described below.

Data on public schools and higher education also are included in the annual *Status Report on Education in Pennsylvania,* not covered in SRI.

Availability: Pennsylvania Department of Education, Education Statistics Division, Data Services, 333 Market St., Harrisburg PA 17126-0333, †; SRI/MF/complete.

S6790–5.1: Degrees and Other Formal Awards Conferred, 1982/83, Pennsylvania

[Annual. Apr. 1984. 3+28 p. SRI/MF/complete.]

Annual report on Pennsylvania higher education degrees conferred, by degree level, institution type, sex, detailed field of study, and race/ethnicity (including nonresident alien, American Indian/Alaskan Native, Asian/Pacific Islander, and Hispanic), academic year 1982/83, with trends from 1973/74.

Contains listing of contents, tables, and charts (1 p.); introduction, 4 charts, and 9 tables (p. 1-27); and glossary (p. 28).

S6790–5.2: Higher Education Summer and Fall Enrollments, 1983, Pennsylvania

[Annual. May 1984. 3+23 p. SRI/MF/complete.]

Annual report on Pennsylvania higher education enrollments, by sex, full- or part-time status, and degree level, all by institution, summer and/or fall 1983, with trends from 1974.

Covers State and private colleges and universities, State-related commonwealth universities, private State-aided institutions, community colleges, theological seminaries, private junior colleges, specialized degree-granting institutions, and State school of technology.

Contains listings of contents, tables, and charts (1 p.); introduction, 3 charts, and 7 tables (p. 1-21); and glossary (p. 23).

S6790–5.3: Preparation and Occupational Pursuits of Teachers, 1982/83, Pennsylvania

[Annual. June 1984. 2+15 p. LC 84-623256. SRI/MF/complete.]

Annual report on newly certified teachers prepared by Pennsylvania higher education institutions, by type of certification, field of preparation, occupational status, and institution type, 1973/74-1982/83, with selected detail by institution for 1982/83.

Certification types are elementary, secondary, combined, and special education. Occupational status categories are teaching in and out of State, otherwise employed, continuing study, seeking teaching and nonteaching position, and other.

Contains highlights, and listing of contents, tables, and charts (2 p.); introduction, 3 charts, and 7 tables (p. 1-13); and glossary (p. 15).

S6790–5.4: Public School Professional Personnel, 1983/84, Pennsylvania

[Annual. July 1984. 2+46 p. LC 84-641002. SRI/MF/complete.]

Annual report on Pennsylvania public school professional employees, 1983/84. Presents number of employees by sex, educational attainment, years of service, salary range, and age; and average educational attainment, years of service, and salary, by sex; for 46 positions in 3 occupational categories (administrative/supervisory, classroom teachers, and coordinate services), and/or by certified assignment category.

Also includes withdrawals by reason, by certified assignment category; number of personnel by sex, total and average salary, and average years of service and educational attainment, with selected rankings, all by administrative unit; and summary trends from 1974/75.

Contains highlights, and listing of contents, tables, and charts (2 p.); and introduction, 4 charts, and 10 tables (p. 1-46).

S6790–5.5: Higher Education Financial Statistics, 1982/83, Pennsylvania

[Annual. July 1984. 3+20 p. LC 84-644822. SRI/MF/complete.]

Annual report on Pennsylvania higher education finances, FY83 with summary trends from FY74. Presents data on revenues by source; expenditures by function; physical plant assets and indebtedness; and endowment and other fund balances; all by institutional type.

Revenue sources include tuitions/fees, government funds by level, private gifts, and endowments. Expenditure functions include instruction, research, and scholarships/fellowships.

Contains highlights, and listing of contents, tables, and charts (3 p.); introduction, and 5 charts and 12 tables (p. 1-18); and appendices (p. 19-20).

S6790–5.6: Higher Education Faculty and Staff, 1983/84, Pennsylvania

[Annual. June 1984. 2+10 p. LC 84-622484. SRI/MF/complete.]

Annual report on Pennsylvania higher education faculty employment and compensation at public and private institutions, 1983/84, with trends from 1974/75. Presents the following data for instructional faculty with 9- and 12-month contracts: number and mean salary by rank, sex, and institution category; and number of faculty covered by and expenditures for fringe benefits by type of benefit.

Contains highlights, and listing of contents, tables, and charts (2 p.); and introduction, 2 charts, and 7 tables (p. 1-10).

S6790–5.7: Public and Nonpublic School Enrollments, 1983/84, Pennsylvania

[Annual. Aug. 1984. 3+39 p. LC 84-623502. SRI/MF/complete.]

Annual report on Pennsylvania elementary and secondary public and nonpublic schools and enrollment, 1983/84, with trends from 1974/75.

Includes enrollment detail by grade and county; public school enrollment by race/ethnicity (including American Indian/Alaskan Native, Asian/Pacific Islander, and Hispanic), school district, type of secondary school (including technical/vocational and special education institutions), and selected secondary school academic subjects; and private school enrollment by religious affiliation of institution.

Also includes data on number of public and nonpublic schools in operation, by level; and public high school graduates, by sex and post-graduate educational enrollment.

Contains highlights, and listing of contents, tables, and charts (3 p.); introduction, 5 charts, and 15 tables (p. 1-37); and glossary (p. 39).

S6790–5.8: Public and Nonpublic High School Graduates, 1983, Pennsylvania

[Annual. Sept. 1984. 3+19 p. SRI/MF/complete.]

Annual report on Pennsylvania public and nonpublic high school graduates by county, sex, and race/ethnicity (including American Indian/Alaskan Native, Asian/Pacific Islander, and Hispanic); and by type of post-high school activity, including continuing education by type of institution, enlistment in armed forces, employment in selected occupations, and unemployment, with selected detail by race/ethnicity; 1983, with selected trends from 1974.

Contains highlights, and listing of contents, tables, and charts (3 p.); introduction, 5 charts, and 9 tables (p. 1-17); and glossary (p. 19).

S6810   PENNSYLVANIA
Office of
the Governor

S6810–3   PENNSYLVANIA ENERGY PROFILE, 1960-81

Biennial.   Jan. 1984.
vi+94 p.
SRI/MF/complete

Biennial compilation of statistics on Pennsylvania energy supply-demand trends, various years 1960-82. Includes energy production, and consumption and prices by sector, all by fuel type; and electricity generating facilities, capacity, and fuel costs. Some data include U.S. comparisons.

Also includes data on electricity purchases, by SIC 2-digit manufacturing industry; nonenergy petroleum product consumption; energy indicators, including housing units by type of heating fuel used; heating and cooling degree days by city; OPEC oil production, prices, and reserves, by country; and U.S. petroleum imports, by country of origin.

Data are from Federal and State agencies, and industry sources.

Contains contents listing, foreword, introduction, and highlights (p. iii-vi); 5 sections, with narrative summaries, 1 map, 33 charts, and 26 tables (p. 1-69); and appendices, with table listing, and 1 map, 1 chart, 9 tables, glossary, and conversion factors (p. 71-93 and inside back cover).

This is the 2nd edition. For description of the 1st edition, see SRI 1982 Annual, under this number. Periodicity of the 1st edition was designated as annual.

Availability: Pennsylvania Office of the Governor, Energy Council, Energy Policy and Planning Bureau, PO Box 8010, Harrisburg PA 17105, †; SRI/MF/complete.

S6820   PENNSYLVANIA
Department of Health

S6820–1   PENNSYLVANIA VITAL STATISTICS Annual Report, 1982
Annual.   Feb. 1, 1984.
xi+168 p.
SRI/MF/complete

Annual report on Pennsylvania vital statistics, covering population, births, and deaths by cause, 1982, with selected trends from 1930. Data, shown by age, sex, race, and locality, are from State records.

Contains listings of contents, tables, and charts (p. iii-xi); preface (p. 1-2); 4 sections, with narrative summaries, 26 maps and charts, and 71 tables listed below (p. 5-155); and technical notes and methodology (p. 159-168).

Prior to 1982 edition, report included data on marriages and divorces. These data now are presented in a separate publication, which will be covered in SRI when it is received.

Availability: Pennsylvania Department of Health, State Health Data Center, PO Box 90, Harrisburg PA 17108, †; SRI/MF/complete.

TABLES:
[Unless otherwise noted, tables show data for Pennsylvania, 1982. Many tables include rate per 1,000 population.]

S6820–1.1: Population and Natality
POPULATION
A1-A4. Population: by age and sex, county, selected municipality, and health service area (HSA), 1980 and 1982. (p. 8-13)

NATALITY
[All tables titles begin "Resident live births..."]

B1-B2. By age of mother [quinquennially 1965-80 and 1982]; and by age of mother, [by] sex and race of child, 1982. (p. 22-23)

B3-B4. By age of mother and trimester of 1st prenatal visit; and by birth weight, [by] sex and race of child. (p. 23-24)

B5-B11. By age of mother: by birth weight, number of previous pregnancies and live births, marital status and education of mother, place of delivery and attendant at birth, type of medical condition, and method of delivery. (p. 24-28)

B12a-B12b. By Apgar score at 1 and 5 minutes, by race and sex. (p. 29)

B13-B20. By age of mother, sex and race, number of previous pregnancies and live births, month [of birth], birth weight, and education and marital status of mother; all by HSA. (p. 30-34)

B21-B31. By age of mother, sex and race, birth weight, number of previous pregnancies and live births, education and marital status of mother, month [of birth], trimester of 1st prenatal visit, place of delivery and attendant at birth, and type of medical condition; all by county. (p. 35-57)

B32-B35. By age of mother, sex and race, birth weight, and marital status of mother; all by selected municipality. (p. 58-61)

S6820–1.2: Mortality
C1. Resident deaths; live births; and fetal, infant, neonatal, and maternal deaths; 1940-82. (p. 72)

C2. Leading causes of death [decennially 1930-80 and 1982]. (p. 73)

C3. Resident deaths by age group [decennially 1940-80 and 1982]. (p. 76)

C4a-C4e. Leading causes of death by age group [by sex and race]. (p. 79-83)

C5-C7. Resident deaths, resident infant deaths by age at death, and fetal deaths, all by cause. (p. 84-97)

C8a-C8b. Heart disease deaths, 1930-82; and resident deaths by type [of heart disease] and age, 1982. (p. 98)

C9a-C9b. Malignant neoplasm deaths, 1930-82; and resident deaths by [site of malignant neoplasm] and age, 1982. (p. 101)

C10a-C10b. Accidental deaths, 1930-82; and resident deaths by type of [accident] and age, 1982. (p. 104)

C11-C13. Pneumonia/influenza, suicide, and homicide deaths, 1930-82. (p. 107-109)

C14-C22. Resident deaths, live births, and fetal, infant, and neonatal deaths; resident deaths by age group; and leading causes of death; all by HSA, county, and selected municipality. (p. 110-145)

D1. Resident deaths by underlying cause and selected conditions mentioned on death certificate. (p. 151-155)

S6820–2   HEALTH PROFILES FOR PENNSYLVANIA COUNTIES, 1984
Biennial.   June 1984.
68 rpts., 4 p. each.
H200.201P-H200.268P.
SRI/MF/complete

Set of 68 biennial Pennsylvania State and county profiles on vital statistics, health facilities and services, and licensed health personnel, 1981-84. Data are from Pennsylvania Dept of Health and other State agencies.

Each profile contains the following data, shown for latest available year 1981-84:

a. Population characteristics: population by age and sex, per square mile, and change from 1980; per capita income, percent population receiving cash and medical assistance, and unemployment rate; marriages, births, infant and total deaths, and deaths from 5 leading causes by age group; and incidence of 12 notifiable diseases.

b. Health services and facilities: hospitals by type, special services/facilities offered including neonatal care, and number of beds and admissions; average hospital room rates; long-term care facilities, total beds and number per 1,000 population aged 65/over, and median room rate, all by facility type; State-supported drug/alcohol treatment facilities by type, admissions, discharges, and average caseload; emergency health personnel and vehicles; agencies/facilities serving disabled, by type of disability; and primary health care centers and licensed boarding homes.

c. Licensed health personnel: medical doctors, osteopathic physicians, and registered nurses, by specialty; and health personnel shortage areas for physicians and dental and psychiatric care.

This is the 5th set of State and county profiles. For description of 1982 profiles, see SRI 1982 Annual, under this number.

Availability: Pennsylvania Department of Health, State Health Data Center, PO Box 90, Harrisburg PA 17108, †; SRI/MF/complete.

S6835   PENNSYLVANIA
Insurance Department

S6835–1   REPORT OF THE INSURANCE COMMISSIONER OF THE COMMONWEALTH OF PENNSYLVANIA for the Period July 1, 1982-June 30, 1983
Annual.   Dec. 15, 1983.
4+230 p.
LC 10-33069.
SRI/MF/complete

Annual report on Pennsylvania insurance industry financial condition and underwriting activity, by company and type of insurance, 1982. Covers assets; surplus or surplus/assets ratio; net underwriting gain/loss; return; total return/net worth, operating income/premium earnings, and loss ratios; premiums written and/or earned; dividends or benefits paid; insurance and certificates in force; and losses incurred; for companies with headquarters in Pennsylvania and elsewhere.

Data are shown, as applicable, for fire/casualty insurance companies; fraternal benefit societies; title and life insurance companies; nonprofit hospital and medical service corporations; and HMOs.

Data are also shown for companies ranked by Pennsylvania market share in each line of coverage, including workmen's compensation, automobile, surety, medical malpractice, and accident/health.

Also includes data on Insurance Dept licensing activities and finances, including premium tax revenues by type of insurance, FY83; and National Assn of Insurance Commissioners May 1983 ranking of companies/groups by total U.S. premiums written, with headquarters State, life and casualty premium value, and market share.

Most data are compiled from annual statements filed by individual companies with the Insurance Dept.

Contains contents listing (2 p.); Insurance Dept data, with 5 tables (p. 1-9); and 41 company financial tables (p. 10-230).

Availability: Pennsylvania Insurance Department, Companies Division, Strawberry Sq., Rm. 1311, Harrisburg PA 17120, $14.50; SRI/MF/complete.

S6840   PENNSYLVANIA
Department of Justice

S6840-1   PENNSYLVANIA BUREAU OF CORRECTION 1983 Annual Statistical Report
Annual.   May 1984.
iii + 56 p.
LC 80-647886.
SRI/MF/complete

Annual report, for 1983, on corrections in Pennsylvania, presenting data on prison population, including inmate admissions, demographic characteristics, commitment offense, sentence length, releases, and average time served. Includes data by institution and committing county; with selected trends from 1954 and some data for 1st quarter 1984.

Also includes data on capacity, operating costs, and staff positions, by institution; interstate compact prisoner transfers; offenders in community service centers and group homes; Probation and Parole Board activities; inmate assaults and escapes; and inmates with death sentences.

Contains contents listing (1 p.); introduction, definitions, and summary (p. 1-5); and 5 charts and 46 tables (p. 6-56).

Availability: Pennsylvania Department of Justice, Correction Bureau, PO Box 598, Camp Hill PA 17011, †; SRI/MF/complete.

S6845   PENNSYLVANIA
Department of Labor and Industry

S6845-1   PENNSYLVANIA EMPLOYMENT AND EARNINGS
Quarterly, with interim monthly supplements.
Approx. 10 p. or 2 p.
SRI/MF/complete, shipped quarterly

Quarterly report, with interim monthly supplements, on Pennsylvania labor force, employment, unemployment, hours, and earnings, by industry, with summary data by labor market area (LMA). Report is issued 1 month after month of coverage.

Each issue contains narrative summary, and 1 chart showing unemployment rate trends; quarterly issues include occasional articles, and 7 tables listed below; and monthly supplements include 2 tables, also listed below.

Quarterly reports are the Sept. and Dec. 1983 and Mar. and June 1984 issues.

Reports for individual LMAs are also available from the issuing agency, but are not covered by SRI.

Availability: Pennsylvania Department of Labor and Industry, Employment Security Office, Research and Statistics Division, Labor and Industry Bldg., Rm. 1200, Seventh and Forster Sts., Harrisburg PA 17121, †; SRI/MF/complete, shipped quarterly.

Issues reviewed during 1984: Aug. 1983-July 1984 (D) (Vol. XXVIII, Nos. 9-13; Vol. XXIX, Nos. 1-7).

TABLES:

QUARTERLY ISSUES
[Data are shown for month of coverage, previous 3 months, and same month of previous year, unless otherwise noted. Table numbers may vary.]

[A] Quarterly average adjusted unemployment by LMAs: number and rate [for quarter ending in month of coverage, previous quarter, and same quarter of previous year; a similar table, presenting Oct.-Nov. 1983 employment data, appears in the Nov. 1983 monthly supplement].

1. Resident employment, unemployment, and unemployed rate [Pennsylvania and U.S., for month of coverage, several previous months and quarters, and 14-18 previous years].

2. Nonagricultural wage/salary employment [by industry group and division; and total workers involved in labor disputes].

3. Selected employment indices [for selected industry groups and divisions; includes annual averages for 3 previous years].

4. Actual and real gross earnings of manufacturing production workers [for previous 11 years].

5. Employment, payrolls, and manhours of manufacturing production workers.

6. Hours and earnings for manufacturing and selected nonmanufacturing industry [groups].

MONTHLY SUPPLEMENTS
[Data are for month of coverage, previous month, and same month of previous year.]

[A] Total civilian labor force, employment, and unemployment.

[B] Manufacturing and selected nonmanufacturing industry detail [employment, and production worker average hours and earnings, by industry division and major group; and total workers involved in labor disputes].

S6845-3   ANNUAL PLANNING INFORMATION REPORT for Pennsylvania, FY85
Annual.   Oct. 1984.
iv + 87 p.
LC 82-644175.
SRI/MF/complete, current & previous year reports

Annual planning report, for FY85, identifying Pennsylvania population groups most in need of employment services, and presenting data on employment by industry and occupation. Also includes data on population, income, labor force, job openings, school enrollment, and the economically disadvantaged. Data generally are current to 1983 or 1984, and include selected trends, projections to 1990, detail by location, and comparisons to U.S.

Data sources include State Office of Employment Security, other State agencies, and U.S. Depts of Labor and Commerce.

Contains preface, and listings of contents and tables/charts (p. i-iv); narrative analysis in 5 sections, with 2 charts, and 32 tables listed below (p. 1-82); and appendix, with definitions and sources (p. 83-87).

Annual planning reports for individual SMSAs are also issued by the Dept, but are not covered by SRI.

Report for FY84 has also been reviewed in 1984, and is also available on SRI microfiche,

under this number [Annual. Oct. 1983. v + 108 p. †]. FY84 report is substantially similar in format and content, but also includes data on disabled/handicapped persons, school dropouts, veteran population, teenage pregnancy, impact of recessions on jobs, and U.S. job openings and pay ranges, and does not include projections for Pennsylvania job openings.

Report for FY83 is described in SRI 1982 Annual, under this number.

Availability: Pennsylvania Department of Labor and Industry, Employment Security Office, Research and Statistics Division, Labor and Industry Bldg., Rm. 1200, Seventh and Forster Sts., Harrisburg PA 17121, †; SRI/MF/complete.

TABLES:
[Tables show data for Pennsylvania, unless otherwise noted.]

S6845-3.1: Population and Labor Force
[Data by race/ethnicity generally are shown for white, black, Hispanic, and other.]

POPULATION

1. Population of counties, 1980 and 1970. (p. 10)

2. Comparison of population totals [by SMSA] and age group, 1980 and 1984. (p. 11)

3. Population characteristics [population under 16 and 16/over, by sex and race/ethnicity (including American Indian/Eskimo/Aleutian and Asian/Pacific Islander)], 1980. (p. 12)

LABOR FORCE
[Tables show data for 1983.]

4. Pennsylvania and U.S. civilian labor force profile [distribution by sex, age group, race/ethnicity, employment status, industry division and selected manufacturing group, and occupational group]. (p. 14)

5. Labor force characteristics: employment and unemployment by sex, age [group for youth, and race/ethnicity, and for Vietnam era veterans]. (p. 15)

6-9. Civilian labor force [by employment status]: for white and nonwhite persons; by sex; for 16-19 and 20-21 year olds; and for Vietnam era veterans; [all] by county of residence. (p. 18-22)

S6845-3.2: Employment, Income, and Wages

EMPLOYMENT

10. Nonagricultural wage/salary employment [by industry division and major manufacturing group, with total persons involved in labor-management disputes, selected periods] 1973-84. (p. 27)

11. [Pennsylvania and U.S.] ratios of private sector employment to population and of civilian government employment to private sector employment [includes State population age 16/over and employment totals, 1981-85]. (p. 29)

INCOME

12. Per capita personal income by county: 1982. (p. 30)

13. States ranked on per capita income, 1983 [with percent change from 1980]. (p. 31)

WAGES

14. 1982 average annual wages [by SMSA and county]. (p. 32)

15-16. Job openings filled and related wage data for selected occupations and industries, [Oct. 1983-June 1984 period]. (p. 33-34)

17. Employment, [employers], total wages, and average wages paid, in selected industries, 4th quarter 1983. (p. 35)

18. Rank [by average weekly earnings for] selected [major] manufacturing industries [1983 with comparison to 1973]. (p. 36)

19. Actual and adjusted gross [weekly] earnings of manufacturing production workers, [and U.S. CPI], 1967-83, [and Jan.-June] 1984. (p. 37)

20. Average gross earnings and manhours of manufacturing production workers in major labor market areas [2nd quarter 1983-2nd quarter 1984]. (p. 38)

S6845–3.3: Education, Unemployment, Job Openings, and Economically Disadvantaged

VOCATIONAL EDUCATION AND ENROLLMENT

21. Vocational education curriculum completers [secondary, adult, and postsecondary, by curriculum], 1981/82 school year. (p. 43-54)

22. [Public and nonpublic elementary and secondary] school enrollment [1971/72-1982/83]. (p. 56)

OCCUPATIONS AND JOB OPENINGS

23. Staffing structure: occupational patterns [distribution by industry group (no date)]. (p. 57)

24. Projected occupational growth: average annual openings, 1980-90 [period]. (p. 58)

25. Registered applicants, [active applicants by sex], and nonagricultural job openings [received and filled], by primary occupational categories and for selected occupations, [Oct. 1983-June 1984 period]. (p. 60-68)

UNEMPLOYMENT

26. Characteristics of the insured unemployed [distribution by sex, age, industry division, and major occupational group, quarterly 1983]. (p. 73)

27. Rank and recent unemployment trends in labor market areas, 1982-83. (p. 74)

28. Labor supply classification [shortage or surplus, and unemployment and unemployment rate], by county, 2nd quarter 1984. (p. 75)

29-30. [Lists of] labor surplus areas eligible for Federal procurement preference, Oct. 1, 1984-Sept. 30, 1985 [period]; and civil jurisdictions with high unemployment eligible for assistance under P.L. 98-8. (p. 76-77)

ECONOMICALLY DISADVANTAGED

31. Economically disadvantaged on public assistance, by selected categories [AFDC, work incentive program, and general assistance; and estimated number employable]; by county, Mar. 1984. (p. 80)

32. U.S. OMB annual income poverty level criteria for continental U.S. [effective Apr. 1982-84], and Employment and Training Administration 1984 lower living standard income level [for Philadelphia and Pittsburgh SMSAs and for Pennsylvania metro and nonmetro areas, all by family size]. (p. 82)

S6860   PENNSYLVANIA
State
Police

S6860–1   UNIFORM CRIME REPORT: Commonwealth of Pennsylvania, Annual Report, 1983
Annual. [1984.]
234 p. var. paging.
ISSN 0095-5752.
LC 75-640313.
SRI/MF/complete

Annual report, for 1983, on Pennsylvania crimes and arrests by type of offense, with trends from 1979. Includes Part I and Part II offenses by county and jurisdiction, police employment, and value of stolen property. Selected data are shown for Philadelphia and Pittsburgh.

Part I offenses are murder, rape, aggravated assault, robbery, burglary, larceny/theft, motor vehicle theft, and arson. Part II offenses include 20 other categories.

Data are compiled from local law enforcement agency reports, under the State Uniform Crime Reporting Program.

Contents:

a. Listings of contents, tables, and charts. (3 p.)

b. Introduction, with 3 summary tables on 1983 reported offenses, clearances, and arrests. (p. 1-13)

c. Part I offenses: narrative summary interspersed with 34 charts and 54 summary tables, including data on trends for each offense, 1979-83; and crime frequency, stolen property value, murders by victim/offender relationship and circumstances, burglaries by type of entry and time occurred, motor vehicle theft by vehicle type, arson by property classification, and weapons used in offenses, mostly for 1983. (p. 14-66)

d. Part II offenses: narrative with 14 charts and 21 summary tables showing offenses, arrests, and clearances, including detail for selected categories 1983, with trends from 1979. (p. 67-92)

e. Law enforcement employees, with 2 charts and 6 tables on employment trends, 1979-83; and police depts by size, 15 largest local police agencies ranked by employment, and assaults on law enforcement officers by month, 1983. (p. 93-101)

f. Appendix A, with 25 detailed tables, listed below. (p. A1-A20)

g. Appendix B-C, with computer tabulations of Part I and Part II offenses and clearances, by offense, county, and jurisdiction, with jurisdiction populations, 1983. (p. B1-B42, C1-C60)

Availability: Pennsylvania State Police, Research and Development Bureau, 1800 Elmerton Ave., Harrisburg PA 17109, †; SRI/MF/complete.

APPENDIX A TABLES:
[Tables show data for Pennsylvania, 1983.]

S6860–1.1: Appendix A
[Data by county are also shown by State region.]

OFFENSES AND CLEARANCES

1. Offenses reported [and cleared, by Part I and Part II offense]. (p. A1)

2-3. Part I offenses and clearances reported [by offense], by county. (p. A2-A3)

4. Offenses by MSA [totals for Part I and Part II offenses]. (p. A4)

5-6. Murder victims and offenders, by age, sex, and race. (p. A5)

7-8. Part II offenses and clearances reported [by offense], by county. (p. A6-A7)

9-10. Part I and Part II arrests reported [by offense], by county. (p. A8-A9)

11. Persons arrested by age, sex, and race [includes Indian and Asian; and by offense charged]. (p. A10)

12-14. Arrests by major age grouping, sex, and race [by detailed offense, including drug possession and sales by substance]. (p. A12-A14)

15. Persons charged and disposition of persons charged by police [by offense]. (p. A15)

LAW ENFORCEMENT EMPLOYEES AND OFFICERS ASSAULTED
[Tables 17-25 begin "Assaults on Pennsylvania law enforcement officers..." Data "by population group" are shown for Philadelphia, Pittsburgh, 5 municipality size groups, State police, and sheriffs/other county police.]

16. Law enforcement employees [officers and civilians by sex], by county. (p. A16)

17-19. Injury rates and clearances, percent distribution of weapons used, and number of assaults and percent with injury; [all] by population group. (p. A17)

20. Type of weapon and type of police activity. (p. A18)

21. Percent cleared by type of police activity and population group. (p. A18)

22-24. Police activity by type of weapon; and type of assignment by police activity. (p. A19-A20)

25. Time of assaults by population group. (p. A20)

S6900   PENNSYLVANIA
Supreme Court

S6900–1   1982 ANNUAL REPORT, Administrative Office of Pennsylvania Courts
Annual. [1983.] 90 p.
ISSN 0148-9925.
LC 77-647649.
SRI/MF/complete

Annual report, for 1982, on Pennsylvania judicial system, including trial and appellate court caseloads and case dispositions. Covers supreme, superior, commonwealth, common pleas, district justice, Philadelphia traffic and municipal, and Pittsburgh magistrate courts. Includes trial court data by case type and county, and comparisons from 1978.

Case types shown are criminal and civil for most courts, with some additional detail for traffic, small claims, landlord/tenant, probate (orphans' court), divorce, domestic relations, and juvenile cases, and for cases involving fugitives.

Report also includes data on disciplinary actions against judges and lawyers; civil cases handled through arbitration; crime victim compensation costs; and judicial dept finances and personnel.

Data are from dept records.

Contains listings of contents, tables, and charts (p. 3); report, with 3 charts and 25 tables (p. 5-69); and judicial directory, and glossary (p. 70-90).

Availability: Pennsylvania Supreme Court, Administrative Office of the Courts, Three Penn Center Plaza, Rm. 1414, Philadelphia PA 19102, †; SRI/MF/complete.

S6905   PENNSYLVANIA Department of Transportation

S6905–2   1983 REPORT OF REGISTRATION by Type Vehicle by County, Pennsylvania
Annual. [1984.] 2+34 p.
LC 75-647301.
SRI/MF/complete

Annual report on Pennsylvania motor vehicles registered, by detailed vehicle type and county, as of Dec. 31, 1983. Contains introduction (1 p.); and 1 table, repeated for total State, for each county, and for out-of-State vehicles (p. A, 1-34).

Availability: Pennsylvania Department of Transportation, Motor Vehicles and Licensing Bureau, Transportation and Safety Bldg., G 132, Harrisburg PA 17122, †; SRI/MF/complete.

S6930   RHODE ISLAND Department of Administration

S6930–1   ANNUAL FINANCIAL REPORT OF THE STATE OF RHODE ISLAND AND PROVIDENCE PLANTATIONS for the Fiscal Year Ended June 30, 1983
Annual. Feb. 17, 1984.
6+286 p.
LC 42-13379.
SRI/MF/complete

Annual report on financial condition of Rhode Island State government, FY83, presenting assets and liabilities, revenues by source, expenditures by function or agency, and fund balances, for all, general, special revenue, university and college, debt service, capital projects, enterprise, internal service, and trust and agency funds, with selected comparisons to FY82 and earlier.

Also includes data on expenditures vs. appropriations by agency and program, bonded indebtedness, State retirement system finances and employee benefit costs, State aid to individual cities and towns, and investments by fund.

Data are from the records of the controller's office.

Contains contents listing (6 p.); introduction, with 3 charts and 6 summary tables (p. 1-10); and 3 sections, with 118 exhibits and schedules (p. 12-286).

A condensed version of the annual report is available from the Office of the State Controller, but is not covered by SRI.

Availability: Rhode Island Department of Administration, State Controllers's Office, Accounts and Control Division, 544 Elmwood Ave., Providence RI 02907, †; SRI/MF/complete.

S6930–2   1980 CENSUS OF POPULATION CHARACTERISTICS BY RACE AND TRACT, Rhode Island
Monograph.   Dec. 1983
27 p. var. paging.
Technical Paper No. 109.
SRI/MF/complete

Report presenting Rhode Island population by race, by county, city/town, and census tract, 1980. Data are shown for white, black, American Indian/Eskimo/Aleut, Asian/Pacific Islander, Hispanic, and other.

Also includes white, black, and other population for Rhode Island and selected cities, 1970.

Data are primarily from the 1980 Census of Population and Housing.

Contains preface, contents and table listings, and introduction (p. i-iii, 1-3); 4 tables (p. 4-16); and appendices, with glossaries (p. Al-B4).

Availability: Rhode Island Department of Administration, Statewide Planning Program, 265 Melrose St., Providence RI 02907, †; SRI/MF/complete.

S6945   RHODE ISLAND Department of Business Regulation

S6945–1   SEVENTY-SIXTH ANNUAL REPORT OF THE BANKING DIVISION to the General Assembly, 1984, Rhode Island
Annual. [1984.] x+56 p.
LC 9-6541.
SRI/MF/complete

Annual report on assets and liabilities of Rhode Island State-chartered savings banks, commercial banks and trust companies, loan and investment companies, building-loan assns, and credit unions, by institution, as of Dec. 31, 1982, with selected summary comparisons to 1981 and trends from 1974.

Also includes banking taxes assessed/paid and fees collected; number of accounts, interest credited, and dividend rates, for savings banks; composite balance sheet for finance companies; and assets of individual State-located national banks and Federal savings and loan assns.

Contains table and contents listings, and Banking Division report with 3 text tables (p. iii-x); and 42 financial statements and tables (p. 2-56).

Availability: Rhode Island Department of Business Regulation, Banking Division, 100 N. Main St., Providence RI 02903, $8.00; SRI/MF/complete.

S6945–2   ONE HUNDRED TWENTIETH ANNUAL REPORT OF THE INSURANCE DIVISION Made to the General Assembly, 1982, Rhode Island
Annual. July 1, 1982.
211 p.
LC 45-27257.
SRI/MF/complete

Annual report on Rhode Island insurance industry financial condition and underwriting activity, by company and type of insurance, 1981. Covers assets, liabilities, capital, surplus, direct premiums, losses or claims/benefits paid, and annuities; and insurance in force, issued, and terminated; for companies based in Rhode Island and elsewhere.

Data are shown, as applicable, for stock and mutual fire/casualty and life insurance companies, fraternal organizations, hospital/physician/dental service corporations, and reciprocals.

Data on fire/casualty insurance include additional breakdowns by detailed line of coverage, including medical malpractice, accident/health, worker compensation, automobile, and surety.

Also includes data on licenses issued and fees collected, FY82.

Data are compiled from annual statements filed by individual insurers.

Contains contents listing (p. 2); Insurance Division regulatory summary, and directory of companies (p. 4-30); 33 company financial statements (p. 32-64); and 2 statistical sections, with 14 tables (p. 66-211).

Previous report, for 1980, is described in SRI 1982 Annual under this number.

Availability: Rhode Island Department of Business Regulation, Insurance Division, 100 N. Main St., Providence RI 02903, $15.00; SRI/MF/complete.

S6970   RHODE ISLAND Department of Education

S6970–1   1982/83 STATISTICAL TABLES, Rhode Island Department of Education
Annual. Jan. 1984.
xii+43 p.
LC 50-63458.
SRI/MF/complete

Annual report on Rhode Island educational enrollment, graduates, personnel, and finances, by school district, community, and institution, for academic year 1982/83. Data are from records of State Depts of Education and Community Affairs.

Contains foreword, statistical overview, and contents and table listings (p. i-xii); 29 tables, listed below (p. 2-42); and glossary (p. 43).

Availability: Rhode Island Department of Education, Research and Evaluation Bureau, Educational Statistics, Roger Williams Bldg., 22 Hayes St., Providence RI 02908, †; SRI/MF/complete.

TABLES:

[Tables show data for Rhode Island, 1982/83, unless otherwise noted.]

S6970-1.1: Students

[Tables S1, S4-S5, and S9-S10 show data for fall 1982-83.]

DISTRICT SCHOOLS

[Tables show data by Local Education Agency (LEA) school district. Data for "others" are shown for prekindergarten, ungraded/unclassified, and postgraduate students.]

S1. Pupil summary [membership, attendance, and enrollment]. (p. 2)

S2-S3. Summary of daily membership by grade grouping, and "others" in daily membership. (p. 3-4)

S4-S4A. Enrollment by grades, and "others" in fall enrollment. (p. 5-10)

S5. Enrollment by grade grouping. (p. 11)

S6. Enrollment by race/ethnic origin [including American Indian/Alaskan Native, Asian/Pacific Islander, and Hispanic], and sex, fall 1983. (p. 11-12)

OTHER SCHOOLS

S7-S8. Enrollment by grade grouping and place of residence, for Catholic diocesan and independent schools, fall 1983. (p. 13-16)

S9-S10. Enrollment by grade grouping, by place of residence and school, for State-operated schools. (p. 17-18)

S6970-1.2: Graduates and Personnel

GRADUATES

D1-D3. Graduates of LEA and nonpublic high schools and State-operated schools, by sex [by school or State institution.] (p. 20-22)

D4. Summary of Rhode Island high school graduates [for regular and GED (general education development) diploma, by sex, by type of school]. (p. 23)

PERSONNEL

[Tables show data for personnel paid with funds from all sources, by LEA and sex.]

P1. Classroom teachers: number of FTE positions, by level [including special education]. (p. 25)

P2. Professional instructional personnel, by position. (p. 26)

S6970-1.3: Finances

[Tables FO1-FO6 and FC1 show data by LEA.]

OPERATIONS

FO1. Total operating expenditures [by function, including adult basic and continuing education, and transportation]. (p. 29)

FO2. Net resident expenditures, by source of funds [including tuition]. (p. 30)

FO3. Federal aid paid [by program]. (p. 31)

FO4. Per pupil costs based on average daily membership and total current operating expenditures for day schools and debt service expenditures. (p. 32)

FO5. State support for school operations [including programs for disadvantaged children, and vocational and bilingual education]. (p. 33)

FO6. State entitlements for school operations, 1982/83-1983/84. (p. 34)

FO7. State funds expended for education: Rhode Island Board of Regents for elementary and secondary education [by area of expenditure, including special populations], 1982/83-1983/84. (p. 35)

CAPITAL EXPENDITURES

FC1. Expenditures for debt service commitments for school construction. (p. 37)

S6970-1.4: Taxation

[All tables show data by community.]

T1. Assessed, full, and equalized weighted assessed property valuations, 1980. (p. 39)

T2. Rank of communities by effective tax rates on full property values for operation and construction of schools. (p. 40)

T3. Municipal tax rates per $1,000 assessed property value, 1982-83. (p. 41)

T4. Full property value per pupil in RADM [resident average daily membership]. (p. 42)

S6977 RHODE ISLAND Board of Elections

S6977-1 STATE OF RHODE ISLAND AND PROVIDENCE PLANTATIONS OFFICIAL COUNT OF THE BALLOTS CAST at the Election Tuesday, Nov. 2, 1982
Biennial. 1982. 407 p.
SRI/MF/complete

Biennial report presenting results of Rhode Island primary elections held Sept. 14, 1982, and May 24, 1983; general elections held Nov. 2, 1982; and special elections held June 21, 1983.

Shows voting for U.S. Senator and Representatives; State senators and representatives; State Governor, Lieutenant Governor, secretary of state, attorney general, and general treasurer; and 10 State questions, including referendum on nuclear weapon freeze.

Also includes data on voter participation; and voting in general elections of 1978 and 1980.

Data generally are shown by city or town and/or district, and candidate's party affiliation.

Contains index (p. 3); and tabular presentation of election results, interspersed with lists of candidates (p. 5-407).

For description of previous report, covering elections held in 1980, see SRI 1982 Annual under this number.

Availability: Rhode Island Board of Elections, 50 Branch Ave., Providence RI 02904, $16.60; SRI/MF/complete.

S6980 RHODE ISLAND Department of Employment Security

S6980-1 RHODE ISLAND EMPLOYMENT BULLETIN
Monthly. Approx. 4 p.
SRI/MF/complete, shipped quarterly

Monthly bulletin on employment and unemployment in Rhode Island, including unemployment insurance and job service activities, and data by industry and labor area. Data are current to 1-2 months preceding publication date.

Contains narrative highlights, and 6 monthly tables and 1 quarterly table, listed below.

Monthly tables appear in all issues; quarterly table appears in Sept., Dec., Mar., and June issues.

Availability: Rhode Island Department of Employment Security, Research and Statistics Unit, 24 Mason St., Providence RI 02903-1082, †; SRI/MF/complete, shipped quarterly.

Issues reviewed during 1984: Sept. 1983-Sept. 1984 (P) (Vol. 29, Nos. 9-12; Vol. 30, Nos. 1-9) [Vol. 30, No. 7 incorrectly reads Vol. 31].

RECURRING TABLES:

[Most data are shown for month of coverage, same month of previous year, and previous month.]

MONTHLY TABLES

[1] Employment service activities [placements, applications, and openings received].

[2] Employment security activities [claims, payments, and exhaustions].

[3] Federal supplemental compensation [claims and payments].

[4] Labor force and unemployment estimates, for State and Providence/Warwick/Pawtucket, Newport, and Westerly labor areas.

[5-6] Total establishment employment [by industry division]; and employment, earnings, and hours in manufacturing industries [by major industry group].

QUARTERLY TABLE

[7] Characteristics of the insured unemployed [number and percent by sex, age (under and over 45), industry division, and occupation; selected week of month of coverage only].

S6980-3 ANNUAL PLANNING INFORMATION for State of Rhode Island
Annual. May 1984.
iv+42 p.
SRI/MF/complete

Annual planning report, for FY85, identifying Rhode Island population most in need of employment services, and projecting job openings by occupation through 1985. Also includes data on population, labor force, and employment by industry.

Data are from Federal and State agencies.

Contains listings of contents, maps, and tables, and preface (p. ii-iv); narrative report in 5 sections, with 1 map, and 11 tables listed below (p. 1-35); appendix, with data sources and explanatory notes (p. 36-42).

Two additional tables show Providence-War-wick-Pawtucket labor force, unemployment, employment by industry division and manufacturing industry group, self-employed/ farm/other workers, and workers involved in labor disputes, monthly 1983. Tables previously were included in the annual planning report but now must be requested separately. Tables are also available on SRI microfiche under this number.

Availability: Rhode Island Department of Employment Security, Labor Market Information Section, 24 Mason St., Providence RI 02903-1082, †; SRI/MF/complete.

TABLES:
[Data are for Rhode Island, unless otherwise noted.]

[1] Population change, 1970 and 1980, in the U.S. and Rhode Island. (p. 3)

[2-3] Establishment employment [by industry division and major manufacturing group, and persons in labor disputes, monthly] 1982-83. (p. 6-7)

[4] Occupations with job openings unfilled for 30 days or more during 1983: range and monthly average number of openings unfilled. (p. 12-13)

[5] Occupations with 10 or more job openings unfilled for 30 days or more at the end of Mar. 1984. (p. 16-17)

[6] Average annual number of job openings, by occupation, during 1976-85 period. (p. 20-27)

[7] Occupations with 100 or more active applicants at the end of Feb. 1984. (p. 29)

[8-9] Labor force and unemployment, [monthly] 1982-83. (p. 31-32)

[10-11] Characteristics of the insured unemployed [by sex, age, industry division, and occupation], 1982-83. (p. 34-35)

S6995   RHODE ISLAND Department of Health

S6995–1   VITAL STATISTICS, 1982, Rhode Island
Annual.   Mar. 1984.
v + 144 p.
LC 63-63572.
SRI/MF/complete

Annual report on Rhode Island vital statistics, covering population, births, deaths by cause, marriages, and divorces, 1982, with selected trends from 1953. Includes data by age, sex, race, and locality. Data are from State records.

Contains chart and table listing (p. i-v); introduction, with narrative summary, 1 map, 17 charts, and 7 tables presenting selected summary data and trends (p. 1-36); and 48 detailed tables, listed below (p. 37-144).

Availability: Rhode Island Department of Health, Vital Statistics Division, Cannon Bldg., Rm. 101, 75 Davis St., Providence RI 02908, †; SRI/MF/complete.

TABLES:
[Tables show data for Rhode Island, 1982, unless otherwise noted. Tables showing births and deaths are generally for State residents. Marriages and divorces are shown for occurrences in State.]

S6995–1.1: Population and Summary

1. U.S. census population of Rhode Island, by race and age, by sex, 1970 and 1980. (p. 37)

2. Population of cities and towns, by county, census of 1970 and 1980, and 1982 estimate. (p. 38)

3. Number of live births, deaths, and marriages, with rates, by city and town. (p. 39)

4. Population, live births, deaths, marriages, and divorces, with rates per 1,000 population, 1953-82. (p. 40)

S6995–1.2: Births and Deaths

DEATHS

5. Number of infant, neonatal, perinatal, [and maternal] deaths, with rates, 1953-82. (p. 41)

6. Deaths, by city or town of residence, by age, race, and sex. (p. 42-47)

7. Deaths and death rates for [20] leading causes in 1982, with comparability ratios and for comparable causes in 1973-81. (p. 48)

LOCAL DATA

8. Selected health characteristics [population, 1980; and total and infant deaths, and total live, out-of-wedlock, and low-weight births], by neighborhood and city or town, 5-year totals with average rates, 1978-82. (p. 49)

BIRTHS

9. Number of births out of wedlock, with ratio per 1,000 live births, 1959-82. (p. 52)

10. Births out of wedlock, with ratio per 1,000 total births in specified age group, 1973-82. (p. 52)

11-12. Live births and births out of wedlock, by sex and race of child, age of mother, and live birth order. (p. 53-60)

13-15. Live births: [total], plural, and out of wedlock, by age of mother, race, and birth weight. (p. 61-69)

16. Births, by city or town, by selected characteristics [total, in-hospital, out-of-wedlock, and low-weight births, by race]. (p. 70)

17. Live births, by city or town, by month. (p. 71)

18. Selected natality data [total, out-of-wedlock, and low-weight births; births with malformation; and births by month prenatal care began]; by city or town, by census tract. (p. 72-79)

18A. Births and births out of wedlock, all ages and teen ages, by city or town of residence. (p. 80)

FETAL DEATHS
[Tables show data for occurrences in Rhode Island. Modes of delivery are spontaneous and induced.]

19A-19B. Fetal deaths, by race of fetus and weeks of uterogestation, by mode of delivery; and by month of delivery, by weeks of uterogestation. (p. 81)

20. Resident fetal deaths occurring in Rhode Island, by mode of delivery, by city or town and census tract of mother's residence, by marital status of mother. (p. 82-89)

21. Induced fetal deaths, by age and marital status of mother, and by number and nature of previous deliveries to mother. (p. 90)

22A-22B. Spontaneous fetal deaths of 20 weeks or more uterogestation and [total] spontaneous fetal deaths, by number of child in total birth order, number of previous fetal deaths, and age of mother. (p. 94-95)

23. Spontaneous fetal deaths of 20 weeks or more uterogestation, by weight of fetus and age of mother. (p. 96)

24. Fetal deaths, by selected cause of death and weeks of uterogestation. (p. 97)

DEATHS BY CAUSE AND LOCALITY

25. Deaths from 72 selected causes, by race, age, and sex. (p. 98-110)

26. Deaths, by city or town, by month. (p. 111)

27. Infant deaths from 61 selected causes, by age. (p. 112)

28. Accidental deaths, with non-motor vehicle accidents shown by New England Standard Locations [type or place of accident], by sex and age. (p. 114)

29A-29B. Selected mortality data [deaths by cause], by city or town, by census tract. (p. 116-131)

30. Accident deaths, by type and age. (p. 132)

31. 10 leading causes of death, by sex, with rates. (p. 133)

32. 5 leading causes of death in specified age groups. (p. 134)

S6995–1.3: Marriages and Divorces

MARRIAGES

33. Number of marriages and persons married, by city and town of residence of bride and groom. (p. 136)

34-35. Marriages, by age of bride by age of groom; and by age at marriage by previous marital status of bride and groom. (p. 137-138)

36. Number of times married for brides, by number of times married for grooms. (p. 139)

37-38. Marriages, by previous marital status of bride and groom; and according to last grade of school completed by bride and groom. (p. 139-140)

DIVORCES

39-40. Divorces, by age of wife by age of husband; and by number of times married before this divorce, by sex. (p. 141)

41. Divorces, by marital status and age of husband and wife. (p. 142)

42. Number of divorces of remarried persons, by previous marital history. (p. 142)

43. Number of divorces by county, with number of children under 18 known to be affected. (p. 143)

44. Divorces according to last grade of school completed, by sex. (p. 144)

S6995–2   RHODE ISLAND'S HEALTH
Annual.   Mar. 1984.
viii + 51 p.
LC 77-640048.
SRI/MF/complete

Annual report on Rhode Island health status indicators, and health care expenditures and utilization, 1981, with trends from 1974. Also includes data on cigarette smoking, and selected comparisons to U.S. Data are from Federal, State, and other sources.

Contains introductory matter, highlights, and listings of contents, tables, and charts (p. i-viii); 24 charts and 14 tables, each with accompanying narrative (p. 1-47); and list of data sources (p. 49-51). All tables are listed below.

For description of previous report, for 1980, see SRI 1982 Annual, under this number.

This is the 7th annual edition.

Availability: Rhode Island Department of Health, Health Planning and Resource Development Division, Data Evaluation Office, 409 Cannon Bldg., 75 Davis St., Providence RI 02908, †; SRI/MF/complete.

TABLES:
[Unless otherwise noted, data are for Rhode Island.]

HEALTH STATUS INDICATORS

I.1-I.3. Number of deaths and years of life lost before age 65, by cause of death and type of injury; and number of deaths by type of injury by age group; 1979-81 [period]. (p. 2-6)

II.1-II.2. Infant and neonatal deaths with associated rates; and live births, average birth weight, low birth weight births, low birth weight rate, and average prenatal care visits; 1974-81. (p. 14-16)

HEALTH CARE EXPENDITURES AND UTILIZATION

III.1-III.3. Annual [total and] per capita health expenditures, 1975-80; and per capita health expenditures by type, 1980; Rhode Island and U.S. (p. 20, 26-27)

IV.1.-IV.2. Geographic variation in per capita hospital costs, 1980-81; and in hospital and surgical days per 1,000 population, 1981; [by city]. (p. 33-35)

CIGARETTE SMOKING

V.1. Smoking rates among females age 20 and older by age, Rhode Island and U.S., 1980. (p. 40)

V.2. Five year change in percentage of population age 16 years and older currently smoking, by [age group and] sex, 1975-80. (p. 42)

V.3-V.4. Smoking status and quit rates, 1980; and five year percent change in smoking status, 1975-80; by family economic status. (p. 46)

S6995–3   FACTOR AND CLUSTER ANALYSIS OF THE 1980 CENSUS for Rhode Island
Monograph. May 1984.
iv + 107 p.
SRI/MF/complete

By Alan B. Humphrey et al. Report classifying Rhode Island census tracts by selected measures of socioeconomic status, based on statistical analysis of 1980 Census of Population and Housing data. Presents results of factor and cluster analyses grouping tracts by measures of wealth, suburban status, predominance of group quarters residents, and educational status. Also includes population and land area data for each tract.

Base data are from Summary Tape Files 1 and 3 of the 1980 census.

Contains listings of contents, tables, charts, and maps (p. i-iv); introduction, detailed methodology, summary, and references (p. 1-27); reference listing (p. 28); 10 tables (p. 31-74); and 32 charts and maps (p. 76-107).

Availability: Rhode Island Department of Health, Health Planning and Resource Development Division, Data Evaluation Office, 409 Cannon Bldg., 75 Davis St., Providence RI 02908, †; SRI/MF/complete.

S7015   RHODE ISLAND Department of Social and Rehabilitative Services

S7015–1   STATISTICS ON ASSISTANCE CASELOADS AND PAYMENTS, by City and Town, State of Rhode Island
Quarterly, with fiscal year summary. Approx. 10 p.
LC 80-643749.
SRI/MF/complete

Quarterly report, with fiscal year summary, on Rhode Island public assistance programs, including caseloads, recipients, and payments, by program and city. Covers AFDC, general public assistance (GPA), Medicaid, food stamps, and SSI.

Report is issued 2-6 months after month of coverage. Issuing agency compiles data on a monthly basis, but publishes data only for the last month of each quarter.

Contains contents listing, narrative comments, and 8 tables, listed below. Annual summary is issued with the June report and is similar in content to quarterly report.

Availability: Rhode Island Department of Social and Rehabilitative Services, Research and Statistics Office, Aime J. Forand Bldg., 600 New London Ave., Cranston RI 02920, †; SRI/MF/complete.

Issues reviewed during 1984: June 1983-June 1984 (D); and annual summary for FY83.

TABLES:
[All tables show data by city, with State totals, for month of coverage, unless otherwise noted.]

AFDC
[Data are shown for regular and unemployed segments.]

I. AFDC cases, current, last month, and last year.

II. AFDC children, parents, and total persons.

GPA
[Tables show family cases and persons, and individuals; payments for families and individuals; and total cases, persons, and payments.]

I-II. All GPA [combined] maintenance/medical and medical [only] caseloads and payments.

III. Medical caseloads and payments for closed cases and medically only needy (do not receive maintenance payments).

MISCELLANEOUS

I. Medicaid: [family] cases and persons eligible for medical assistance only [includes aged, blind, and disabled; and totals for recipients in State institutions].

II. Food stamps: [AFDC, GPA, and SSI/other] cases and persons authorized as of 1st of month.

III. SSI: persons receiving [aged, blind, and disabled, for adults and children].

S7125   SOUTH CAROLINA Budget and Control Board

S7125–1   SOUTH CAROLINA STATISTICAL ABSTRACT, 1983
Annual. [1984.] 360 p.
LC 72-611159.
SRI/MF/complete

Annual compilation, for 1983, of detailed social, economic, and governmental statistics for South Carolina. Most data are from reports of State and Federal agencies, and are shown for various years 1970-83 with decennial population trends from 1790 and projections to 2000.

Report is designed to present a comprehensive overview of the State. Extensive socioeconomic, demographic, and geographical breakdowns are shown, as applicable, for most topics. These breakdowns include data by city, county, SMSA, urban-rural status, commodity, income, industry, occupation, age, educational attainment, marital status, race, and sex. Comparisons to other southeastern States and total U.S. are occasionally included.

Contents:

a. Preface and contents listing; and 4 summary tables showing State rankings for selected socioeconomic and demographic characteristics, with glossary. (p. 3-12)

b. 19 sections with 34 maps, 28 charts, and 247 tables, described below. (p. 13-339)

c. Appendix, with source directory, index, and 2 tables showing State rankings of various indicators and 1980 census corrections. (p. 341-360)

Availability: South Carolina Budget and Control Board, Research and Statistical Services Division, Rembert C. Dennis Bldg., Rm. 337, 1000 Assembly St., Columbia SC 29201, $14.00; SRI/MF/complete.

TABLE SECTIONS:
[Data sources are listed beneath each table. Most sections begin with a contents listing and glossary.]

S7125–1.1: Sections 1-2: Agriculture and Seafood Production; and Area, Geography, and Climate

a. Agricultural acreage, yield, production, and value; cash receipts and government payments; farm population; farms and average size; and commercial fish and shellfish landings and value. 9 tables. (p. 15-22)

b. Land and water area; population; and temperature and precipitation. 7 maps and 4 tables. (p. 25-34)

S7125–1.2: Sections 3-4: Banking, Finance, and Insurance; and Capital Investment and Industry

a. Savings and loan assn and State bank balance sheets; consumer finance licensees, assets, and loans; credit unions, members, and finances; banks and deposits by type; State debt and trust fund holdings; and insurance premiums and claims, and life insurance in force. 9 tables. (p. 37-42)

b. Manufacturing and nonmanufacturing firms and employment; textile firms, mills, investment, production value, employment, and wages; manufacturing investments, wages, and production value; new and expanded plants, employment, and capital investments; and foreign manufacturing employment, and investments by country. 1 map, 3 charts, and 13 tables. (p. 45-52)

S7125–1.3: Section 5: Education

a. Public and private schools and enrollment; vocational and adult education enrollment; handicapped children receiving public school services; and high school graduates and postsecondary plans. 2 charts and 6 tables. (p. 56-61)

b. Educational receipts and expenditures; average teacher salaries; educational attainment; postsecondary enrollment by institution, including technical colleges; and degrees conferred. 2 maps, 5 charts, and 19 tables. (p. 62-82)

S7125–1.4: Sections 6-8: Employment, Energy Resources, and Government and Politics

a. Labor force by employment status; nonfarm, manufacturing, and textile employment; State and local government employment by function; average covered employment; and union membership, by union. 3 charts and 18 tables. (p. 85-116)

b. Electric utilities financial and operating data, by privately-owned company; electric and natural gas utility customers and sales or consumption, by sector; electricity generation by fuel source; and gasohol, gasoline, and diesel fuel consumption. 2 charts and 12 tables. (p. 119-123)

c. Local government jurisdictions, including school and special districts; and population and social characteristics of congressional districts. 4 maps and 3 tables. (p. 127-138)

S7125–1.5: Sections 9-10: Health and Housing

a. Nursing school graduates, and licensed and active nurses; active dentists and physicians, by specialty; and nonfederal health professionals. 5 tables. (p. 141-147)

b. Mental retardation patients; vocational rehabilitants, by disability; health care facilities, beds, admissions/discharges, and patient days; State mental hospital admissions, population, and patient movement; and alcohol/drug abuse clients treated. 4 maps and 7 tables. (p. 148-154)

c. Housing units and occupancy; persons, families, and households; median housing value and rent; median household income and percent below poverty level; and value of residential and nonresidential construction permits. 3 maps and 13 tables. (p. 157-182)

S7125–1.6: Section 11: Income and Selected Economic Indicators

a. Personal income by source; median family and household income; persons below poverty level; adjusted gross income, tax collections, and number of returns;

manufacturing and nonmanufacturing payroll, with detail for textile industry; and manufacturing hours and earnings. 1 map, 4 charts, and 20 tables. (p. 185-212)

b. Economic indicators, including net taxable and gross sales; auto registrations; vehicle mileage; construction permits; retail sales; and farm income, expenses, inventory changes, and marketing receipts. 1 map, 3 charts, and 5 tables. (p. 213-218)

S7125–1.7: Section 12: Law Enforcement, Courts, Crime, and Corrections

a. Crime Index rates, offenses, and clearances, by offense; homicide circumstances and victim characteristics; arrests by offense; police assaults by weapon and activity; and stolen and recovered property value. 8 tables. (p. 221-225)

b. Court caseload and disposition; correctional institution inmate admissions, by offense and sentence length; parole and probation cases, by offense; and defendants processed and receiving probation. 10 tables. (p. 226-234)

S7125–1.8: Sections 13-15: Natural Resources, Population, and Public Welfare

a. Forest and nonforest land; forest fires and acreage damaged by cause, and protected acreage; forest product volume and value; forest industry firms, capital investment, employment, and payroll; and mineral production value. 1 map and 6 tables. (p. 237-243)

b. Population trends from 1790 and projections to 2000; population change components; churches and membership, by denomination; elderly population characteristics, including employment, income, household size, and home ownership trends; persons with selected European ancestry; and unmarried and farm population. 5 maps, 2 charts, and 29 tables. (p. 247-282)

c. Medicare enrollment and payments; AFDC and SSI cases and payments; food stamp participants and benefits; and unemployment insurance initial claims and benefits. 1 chart and 6 tables. (p. 285-290)

S7125–1.9: Sections 16-17: Recreation and Tourism; and Revenues and Expenditures

a. State park attendance, by use and park; travel expenditures, and travel-generated payroll, employment, and tax revenues; boat registrations; hunting and fishing license sales, and fines collected; and land contributed to game management area programs, by landowner. 2 maps and 10 tables. (p. 293-300)

b. State tax allocations and tax rate changes, and Federal tax collections and refunds, by tax type; State revenues by source and expenditures by function; and population and county government finances, for counties with populations over 100,000. 11 tables. (p. 303-312)

S7125–1.10: Sections 18-19: Transportation and Vital Statistics

a. Seaport foreign trade volume and value; customs receipts; railroad track mileage operated and State taxes paid, by railroad; motor vehicle registrations; highway and vehicle mileage; traffic accidents, fatalities, injuries, and property loss; airports, Airport Development Aid Program funding, and general aviation aircraft; gasoline consumption; and labor force, by place of work and transport mode. 2 maps, 1 chart, and 14 tables. (p. 315-326)

b. Vital statistics, including population, net migration, births, total and infant deaths, deaths by leading cause, marriages, divorces/annulments, and marital status of population. 1 map, 2 charts, and 10 tables. (p. 329-339)

S7125–3   ECONOMIC REPORT, the State of South Carolina, 1984

Annual.   June 1984.   177 p.
ISSN 0145-3637.
LC 76-649684.
SRI/MF/complete

Annual report analyzing developments in the South Carolina economy, including data on employment, income, agriculture, financial institutions, manufacturing, transportation, and State government finances, primarily 1983, with selected trends and forecasts 1960s-85. Also includes comparisons to other southeastern States and U.S.

Data are from Federal and State agencies, private firms, and trade assns.

Contains contents listing (1 p.); narrative analyses interspersed with 2 maps, 17 charts, and 46 tables (p. 11-110); statistical appendix, with table listing and 52 tables (p. 113-168); and list of data sources (p. 171-177).

All tables, and charts presenting substantial data not covered in tables, are described or listed below.

This is the 11th annual report.

Availability: Editor, *South Carolina Economic Report*, Research and Statistical Services Division, Rembert C. Dennis Bldg., Rm. 337, 1000 Assembly St., Columbia SC 29201, $10.50; SRI/MF/complete.

CHARTS AND TABLES:

[Data are for South Carolina, unless otherwise noted.]

S7125–3.1: Economic Analysis

a. U.S. economy: GNP, various periods 1949-83; and summaries of selected consumption, investment, foreign trade, government finance, and other economic indicators, various years 1981-85. 3 charts and 8 tables. (p. 11-21)

b. South Carolina economy: summary economic indicators, various quarters 1982-83; nonagricultural employment by industry division and selected major group, and total and per capita personal income, with comparisons to U.S. and southeast region, 1970s-83; and forecasts of personal income, nonagricultural employment by major sector, and unemployment rate, 1984-85 with comparison to 1983. 1 chart and 9 tables. (p. 25-42)

S7125–3.2: Economic Activity

a. Agriculture: distribution of farm marketing receipts by commodity group, 1982; and U.S. and South Carolina farm income by source and expenditures by item, 1977-82. 2 charts and 2 tables. (p. 48-52)

b. Finance: number of institutions, assets, mortgage or total loans, and savings, for savings and loan assns (with comparison to other southeastern States) and credit unions; credit union membership; and selected short- and long-term interest rates; various periods 1981-83. 3 tables. (p. 56-58)

c. U.S. manufacturing growth rates by major group; and manufacturing hours and earnings, and employment by major group, with comparisons to U.S. and other southeastern States; primarily 1982-83 with some trends from 1970s. 5 charts and 12 tables. (p. 61-75)

d. Tourism and transportation: welcome center visitors, by center; travel-related spending, and travel-generated payroll and employment, by travel industry sector; travel-generated tax revenue, by level of government; and aircraft operations, by type of carrier; various periods 1982-83. 2 maps, 3 charts, and 6 tables. (p. 79-96)

S7125–3.3: General Fund Revenues

Includes general fund revenues by source FY82-85, and expenditures by function FY83; and individual income tax returns, adjusted gross income, and gross calculated tax, by income class, 1972 and 1982. 3 charts and 6 tables. (p. 101-110)

S7125–3.4: Statistical Appendix

AGRICULTURE

A1. Number of farms, land in farms, and average farm size, U.S. and South Carolina, 1969-83. (p. 117)

A2-A3. Cash receipts from farm marketings [livestock/livestock products and crops], 1969-82; and realized gross and net income from farming [and farm production expenses], 1970-82. (p. 118-119)

FINANCE

A4. Number of licensees, resources, and analysis of loans by consumer finance institutions [including loans receivable, number and amount of loans made, and year's average balance], 1970-83. (p. 120)

A5. Market interest rates [for mortgages and 6 financial instruments], 1975-83. (p. 121)

GENERAL FUND REVENUES

A6. General fund revenue [total], FY72-85. (p. 122)

A7-A8. General fund revenue by major categories [including sales tax, corporate and individual income taxes, and revenue sharing, FY78-85]. (p. 123-124)

A9. Estimated net taxable sales, personal income, and ratio of sales to personal income, FY72-85. (p. 125)

A10. Adjusted gross income reported on individual income tax returns, [and] relationship to personal income and individual income tax, 1972-84. (p. 126)

A11. Corporation income taxes, estimated net income, and relationships to U.S. corporate profits before tax, FY74-85. (p. 127)

A12. General fund expenditures by functional categories, FY78-83. (p. 128)

A13. Sales tax monitor [amount by industry division and selected kinds of business], July-May [periods ended 1983-84]. (p. 129)

HOUSING AND INSURANCE

A14. Value of [residential and nonresidential] construction permits, 1969-83. (p. 130)

A15. Insurer Licensing and Taxation Division activity growth [number of companies licensed/supervised, agents/brokers/adjusters/appraisers licensed, and premiums paid], FY71 and FY83. (p. 131)

A16-A18. Life insurance business [in force, premiums received, and claims paid]; accident/health insurance business [premium/contract fees received, and losses/claims paid]; and insurance property/casualty/allied lines of business [premiums written and claims paid]; 1970-82. (p. 132-134)

LABOR FORCE AND EMPLOYMENT

A19-A20. Civilian labor force, total employment, and total unemployment, 1970-83; and wage/salary workers in nonagricultural establishments by major industry division, 1976-83. (p. 135-136)

A21-A24. Wage/salary employment, 1977-83; and average weekly earnings and hours, and average hourly earnings, 1981-83; [all] in selected durable and nondurable goods manufacturing industries [by major group]. (p. 137-140)

MANUFACTURING

A25. Value of foreign investments [and] total industrial investments, 1968-83. (p. 141)

A26. Total industrial growth from new/expanded plants, by [selected major industry group], 1968-83. (p. 142)

A27. Capital investment and employment from new and expanded plants [and number of plants, by selected major industry group], 1983. (p. 143)

A28. New and expanded plants [and jobs created, and capital invested], 1968-83. (p. 144)

PERSONAL INCOME AND PRICES

A29-A30. Total and per capita personal income in the U.S., Southeast, and South Carolina, 1970-83. (p. 145-146)

A31-A32. Personal income and per capita personal income in constant [1972] dollars, and rates of change, 1970-83. (p. 147-148)

A33. Personal income by major sources [income type and industry division], 1977 and 1982-83. (p. 149)

A34. Disposable personal income in the U.S., Southeast, and South Carolina, 1970-82. (p. 150)

A35-A36. CPI [all items and 5] major components, U.S., 1967-83; and U.S. PPI by group of commodities, 1979-83. (p. 151-152)

ELECTRICITY

A37-A38. Electricity sales to ultimate customers [by customer type]; and electrical generation [by fuel type]; 1978-83. (p. 153-154)

SOUTHEASTERN STATES

[Tables A39-A41 show data for U.S., Southeast region, and 12 southeastern States.]

A39-A40. Southeast total and real personal income, 1981-83. (p. 155-156)

A41. Southeast per capita income [with national rank for the individual States], 1983 [and percent change from 1982]. (p. 157)

A42. Estimates of the resident population, U.S. and 12 southeastern States, 1980-83. (p. 158)

TRANSPORTATION

A43. Selected transportation indicators [new car and total car/bus registrations, and gasoline consumption and retail price], 1970-82. (p. 159)

A44. State Ports Authority activity in ocean commerce [volume of imports and exports, FY75-83]. (p. 160)

A45. State customs district dollar volume of [import and export] cargo [and of customs receipts], 1968-82. (p. 161)

U.S. ECONOMY

[Tables A46-A52 show data for U.S., 1970-83, unless otherwise noted.]

A46-A47. GNP [current and constant dollars]; and personal consumption expenditures [for durable and nondurable goods, and services]. (p. 162-163)

A48-A49. Gross private domestic investment; and government purchases of goods/services [current and constant dollars]. (p. 164-165)

A50. Employment: nonagricultural payrolls [by industry division], 1975-83. (p. 166)

A51. Disposition of personal income [including percent savings]. (p. 167)

A52. Civilian labor force, total civilian employment, and total unemployment. (p. 168)

S7127   SOUTH CAROLINA
Office of the
Comptroller General

S7127–1   STATE OF SOUTH CAROLINA, 1982 ANNUAL REPORT OF THE COMPTROLLER
Annual. For individual publication data, see below.
LC 8-13085.
SRI/MF/complete

Annual report on financial condition of South Carolina State and county governments, for FY82. Report is issued in 2 parts. County detailed report is described below. State summary report is described in SRI 1983 Annual under S7127-1.1.

Availability: South Carolina Office of the Comptroller General, Wade Hampton State Office Bldg., PO Box 11228, Columbia SC 29211, †; SRI/MF/complete.

S7127–1.2: Local Government Report
[Annual. June 1, 1983. 153 p.+foldouts. SRI/MF/complete.]

Presents the following data for each county: disbursements by source of funds, including homestead tax reimbursements and State shared revenues; county and school receipts and disbursements, for tax assessments, treasurer's cash account, delinquent tax account, and notes and bonds; property assessed value and number of units assessed, by property type; and total property tax for county, school, and special service district purposes. Data are for FY82 or tax year commencing Dec. 31, 1981.

Also includes 1981 gross receipts and 1982 Public Service Commission assessments, by utility.

Contains contents listing (p. 4); and report, in 3 parts, with 5 tables and brief narratives (p. 5-153 and foldouts).

For description of report for FY81, see SRI 1982 Annual, under this number.

S7127–2   STATE OF SOUTH CAROLINA, 1983 ANNUAL REPORT OF THE COMPTROLLER
Annual. For individual publication data, see below.
LC 8-13085.
SRI/MF/complete

Annual report on financial condition of South Carolina State and county governments, for FY83. Report is issued in 2 parts. State summary report is described below. Detailed county report has not yet been issued; for description of FY82 county report, see S7127-1.2 above.

Availability: South Carolina Office of the Comptroller General, Wade Hampton State Office Bldg., PO Box 11228, Columbia SC 29211, †; SRI/MF/complete.

S7127–2.1: State Summary
[Annual. [1983.] iv+48 p. SRI/MF/complete.]

Presents assets, liabilities, and fund equity; revenues by source; and expenditures by function, object, and/or agency; for general, special revenue, capital projects, debt service, enterprise, internal service, and trust and agency funds, FY83.

Includes detail on budgeted vs. actual financial activity; appropriations; State public education finances; State shared revenues, by type by county; homestead exemptions and value by county; bonded debt; and selected trends from 1978.

Also includes population; labor force and employment status; State and local government employment by government level; public and private college enrollment; and total, per capita, and disposable personal income, for State, U.S., and southeast region; mostly 1970s-82, with population trends from 1790 and labor force trends from 1940.

Contains transmittal message (p. i-ii); and 5 report sections, including listings of contents, tables, and charts, and 4 charts and 24 tables (p. iii-iv, 1-48).

S7135   SOUTH CAROLINA Department of Corrections

S7135–1   ANNUAL REPORT OF THE BOARD OF CORRECTIONS and the Commissioner of the South Carolina Department of Corrections for the Period July 1, 1982-June 30, 1983
Annual. [1984.] 131 p.
LC 77-648588.
SRI/MF/complete

Annual report, for FY83, on corrections in South Carolina, presenting data on prison population, including inmate admissions, releases, selected demographic characteristics, commitment offense, and sentence length, time served, and time remaining. Some data are shown by committing county and State district, with selected trends from 1960.

Also includes data on prison capacity and personnel, by institution; corrections expenditures; work credit, parole, and community programs; and juvenile corrections population.

Data are compiled by Division of Resource and Information Management.

Contains listings of contents, tables, and charts (p. 2-7); directories and organizational chart (p. 8-11); report sections, with 3 maps, 24 charts, and 32 tables (p. 12-120); and narrative appendices (p. 121-131).

Availability: South Carolina Department of Corrections, Statistics and Analysis, PO Box 21787, Columbia SC 29221, †; SRI/MF/complete.

S7145   SOUTH CAROLINA Department of Education

S7145–1   RANKINGS OF THE COUNTIES AND SCHOOL DISTRICTS of South Carolina, 1982/83
Annual. Mar. 1984.
xiv+320 p.
ISSN 0093-5115.
LC 74-642137.
SRI/MF/complete

Annual report ranking South Carolina counties and school districts by educational and socioeconomic characteristics, 1982/83. Covers pupils, staff, and finances, with selected comparisons to 1972/73. Data are from State Dept of Education, county and district superintendents of education, other State agencies, and Census Bureau.

Contents:

a. Foreword, contents and table listings, and explanatory notes (iii-xiv); and 107 tables, listed below (p. 1-306).

b. Footnotes with data sources for each table, and appendices A-C, including lists of area vocational centers for which revenues or expenditures were prorated among 2 or more school districts; multidistrict counties, with distribution of monies and average daily membership (ADM); and revenue and expenditure accounts used in compiling data for financial tables; 1982/83. (p. 307-320)

This is the 14th annual report.

Educational Trends in South Carolina, an annual report presenting comparative summaries of data for 4-5 years, is also available from the Dept of Education, but is not covered in SRI.

Availability: South Carolina Department of Education, Management Information Section, Rutledge Bldg., Rm. 605, 1429 Senate St., Columbia SC 29201, $5.50; SRI/MF/complete.

TABLES:

[Unless otherwise noted, tables 1-34 show data for 1982 by county, and tables 35-107 show data for 1982/83 by school district. Counties and school districts are arranged both alphabetically and by rank.

Tables which show percent also show data from which percentages were derived.]

S7145–1.1: Population

1-2. Total population as of Apr. 1, 1980; and percent change from Apr. 1, 1970. (p. 1-4)

3-4. Percent of population classified as nonwhite and as under 18 years of age, 1980. (p. 5-8)

5-6. Estimated population and percent classified as nonwhite, as of July 1, 1982. (p. 9-12)

7-8. Percent change in white and nonwhite population, Apr. 1, 1980-July 1, 1982. (p. 13-16)

9. Percent of population in public/nonpublic school membership (K-12), 1982/83. (p. 17)

10. Median age of population as of Apr. 1, 1980. (p. 19)

11. Median school years completed by population 25 years old or over, 1980. (p. 20)

12-14. Percent of population 25 years old or over with 4 or more years of college, with high school diploma, and with less than 5 years of elementary school, 1980. (p. 21-23)

15-16. Percent of population classified as urban, 1980, with percent change, 1970-80. (p. 24-27)

17. Percent of 1980 population below poverty level in 1979. (p. 28)

S7145–1.2: Economic Data

18-19. Per capita value of farm products and net taxable sales. (p. 29-32)

20-26. Percent of nonagricultural wage/salary employment in manufacturing, contract construction, transportation/public utilities, wholesale/retail trade, finance/insurance/real estate, services/mining, and government. (p. 33-46)

27. Percent of total civilian labor force unemployed. (p. 47)

28. Average weekly salary of workers covered in employment. (p. 49)

29-30. Per capita personal income, 1981; and percent increase, 1980 and 1981. (p. 50-53)

31-34. Percent of income tax returns with adjusted gross income of [4 income groups]. (p. 54-57)

S7145–1.3: Pupil Data

35-36. ADM (K-12), by school district and by county. (p. 58-60)

37. Percent of total school membership in private/special/denominational schools, by county [only]. (p. 61)

38. 35-day enrollment (K-12). (p. 63)

39. Percent change in enrollment (grades 1-12) [1972/73 and 1982/83]. (p. 65)

40. Percent of enrollment classified as nonwhite. (p. 69)

41-42. Percent change in white and nonwhite enrollment [1972/73 and 1982/83]. (p. 73-80)

43-44. Percent change in enrollment from 1st grade 1971/72 and from 9th grade 1979/80 to 12th grade 1982/83. (p. 81-88)

45. Percent of ADM in average daily attendance. (p. 89)

46-48. Percent of 1982 graduates entering junior/senior colleges, other postsecondary schools, and employment/other activities. (p. 93-104)

49. Enrollment in basic and high school adult education programs, by county [only]. (p. 105)

50. Percent of pupils eligible for free/reduced-price lunches, Oct. 1982. (p. 107)

51-57. Membership weighted according to the Education Finance Act [for] kindergarten, primary, elementary, high school, handicapped/homebound, vocational, and all classifications. (p. 111-136)

58. Dropouts as percent of enrollment for grades 9-12. (p. 137)

S7145-1.4: Professional Staff

59-61. Percent of professional staff with bachelor's degrees, master's degrees, and 6-year certificates/doctorates. (p. 141-152)

62-66. Average number of years of total education experience of the administrative, supervisory, kindergarten/elementary/secondary teaching, special education teaching, and library/guidance staffs. (p. 153-162)

67-70. Ratio of school membership to the administrative, supervisory, kindergarten/elementary/secondary teaching, and library/guidance staffs. (p. 163-178)

71. Percent of teachers who are men. (p. 179)

72. Percent of teachers teaching out of certification at least 50% of the time. (p. 183)

73. Teacher turnover rate, 1981/82-1982/83. (p. 187)

S7145-1.5: Financial Data, and Miscellaneous

TEACHERS' SALARIES

74-77. Salary schedules for teachers: with bachelor's and master's degrees and zero years experience; with bachelor's degree plus 18 hours and 10 years experience; and with master's degree and 17 years experience. (p. 189-196)

78. Average total annual salary for classroom teachers. (p. 197)

TAX ASSESSMENTS AND REVENUES

79-80. Total tax per capita assessed against real/personal property for county and school purposes, 1982, by county [only]. (p. 199-202)

81. Per capita total expenditures for public schools, by county [only]. (p. 203)

82-85. Amount of revenue for operating funds received per pupil in ADM from local, State, and Federal sources, and from [all] sources [combined]. (p. 205-220)

86-88. Percent change in revenue for operating funds received from local taxes, State sources, and local/State/Federal sources, 1980/81-1982/83. (p. 221-232)

89. Increase in revenue received per pupil for operating purposes, 1972/73 and 1982/83. (p. 233)

90. Revenue received per pupil in ADM for capital outlay and debt retirement purposes. (p. 237)

91-92. Assessed valuation per pupil in ADM, 1982/83; and change from 1972/73. (p. 241-248)

93. Wealth (fiscal capacity) per pupil [in ADM]. (p. 249)

94-95. Total tax levy in mills, 1982/83; and change from 1972/73. (p. 253-260)

96. Local tax effort [including ability index, equalized and actual tax revenues, and tax effort]. (p. 261)

EXPENDITURES

97. Current operating expenditures per pupil in ADM. (p. 265)

98. Increase in expenditures per pupil, 1972/73 and 1982/83. (p. 269)

99-102. Current operating expenditures per pupil in ADM for general administration, instructional services, plant operations/maintenance, and auxiliary services. (p. 273-288)

103-104. Expenditures per pupil in ADM for capital outlay and debt retirement. (p. 289-296)

MISCELLANEOUS

105. Average number of pupils in membership per school plant. (p. 297)

106. Percent of school plants on sites of 11 or more acres. (p. 301)

107. Area in square miles. (p. 305-306)

S7150   SOUTH CAROLINA Election Commission

S7150-1   REPORT OF THE SOUTH CAROLINA STATE ELECTION COMMISSION for the Period Ending June 30, 1983
Annual.   June 1983.   502 p.
SRI/MF/complete

Annual report presenting results of South Carolina primary election held June 8, 1982; run-off election held June 22, 1982; general election held Nov. 2, 1982, including absentee voting; and special election held Dec. 7, 1982. Shows voting for U.S. and State representatives; Governor and various State, district, and county officials; and State constitutional amendments.

Also shows voter turnout by sex and race, and registration and turnout by age, 1982; voters deleted from registration rolls, 1968-83 period; active and inactive voters and voting age population, by race, 1982 (includes narrative analysis); and voter registration, biennially 1956-66, and by race 1968-83.

Data are shown by precinct, legislative district, and/or county.

Report consists of contents listing and list of election commission members and staff (p. 1-5); and tabulations of election results and voter data (p. 8-502).

Report presenting 1980 election results is described in SRI 1982 Annual, under this number. Reports are issued annually but are covered in SRI only when major election results are included.

Availability: South Carolina Election Commission, 2221 Devine St., PO Box 5987, Columbia SC 29205, $15.00; SRI/MF/complete.

S7155   SOUTH CAROLINA Employment Security Commission

S7155-2   SOUTH CAROLINA EMPLOYMENT TRENDS
Monthly.   Approx. 20 p.
SRI/MF/complete, shipped quarterly

Monthly report on South Carolina employment, earnings, hours, and production workers, by industry group. Includes employment data for women, and by county and MSA. Data are compiled by the Employment Security Division, and are issued approximately 2 months after month of coverage.

Report generally contains brief articles on economic and employment conditions; summary features on employment service activities and plant openings/expansions; and 14 monthly tables, listed below.

Monthly tables appear in all issues. All additional features with substantial statistical content on topics not covered in monthly tables are described, as they appear, under "Statistical Features." Nonstatistical features are not covered.

Also described under "Statistical Features" are 2 quarterly tables on wages and employment, discontinued with the Oct. 1983 issue.

Availability: South Carolina Employment Security Commission, Labor Market Information Division, 1550 Gadsden St., PO Box 995, Columbia SC 29202, †; SRI/MF/complete, shipped quarterly.

Issues reviewed during 1984: Sept. 1983-Aug. 1984 (D).

TABLES:

MONTHLY TABLES
[Data are shown for current month, preceding month, and same month of preceding year. Tables 3 and 7 begin with the Jan. 1984 issue.]

1. Civilian labor force summary [by employment status, for State and 3 MSAs].

2. Summary of monthly earnings of manufacturing workers [for State and 3 MSAs].

3. Summary of monthly overtime hours of [durable and nondurable goods] manufacturing workers.

4. Productivity index [for production workers, durable and nondurable goods, textiles, and apparel].

5. Nonfarm wage/salary employment by major industry division and selected industry group.

6. Wage/salary manufacturing employment [by selected industry group].

7. Seasonally adjusted nonfarm wage/salary employment by industry [division and selected group].

8-10. [Data in table 5 are repeated for 6 MSAs and for female employment.]

11. Estimated number of production workers and average earnings and hours in manufacturing [by industry group].

12. Average earnings and hours in manufacturing industries in [3] major MSAs.

13. Nonfarm wage/salary [manufacturing and nonmanufacturing] employment for counties.

14. Labor force and unemployment by county.

STATISTICAL FEATURES:

S7155–2.501: Oct. 1983

QUARTERLY TABLES

(p. 22-23) Two tables showing wages and employment covered by South Carolina Employment Security Law, by county and industry division, 2nd quarter 1983.

Tables are discontinued with this issue; data are available from the issuing agency in *Employment Wages in South Carolina*.

S7155–2.502: Feb. 1984

SPECIAL TABLE

(p. 10) Table showing South Carolina average monthly employment covered by unemployment insurance, total wages, and number of firms by employment size class, for all industry, manufacturing, and 4 textile-related industries, 1982. Data are from *Covered Employment and Wages in South Carolina*.

S7155–2.503: Mar. 1984

SOUTH CAROLINA EMPLOYMENT PROJECTIONS TO 1990

(p. 7, 23) Article, with 1 table showing projected nonagricultural employment in South Carolina, by industry division and selected industry group, 1990. Data are from South Carolina Employment Security Commission.

S7155–2.504: July 1984

PER CAPITA INCOME IN SOUTH CAROLINA LABOR MARKET AREAS

(p. 11) Article, with 1 table showing South Carolina per capita income by labor market area, 1981-82, with percent change from 1980.

S7155–3   SOUTH CAROLINA LABOR MARKET REVIEW, 1984
Annual.   June 1984.
178 p. var. paging.
SRI/MF/complete

Annual planning report, for 1984, on South Carolina labor market conditions. Presents data on unemployment by industry and occupation, and population and labor force characteristics. Also includes data on State economic outlook, labor turnover, job service activities and applicants, the insured unemployed, and selected data by county and MSA; and trends and projections, various years 1950-95.

Data are primarily from State agencies, Census Bureau, and BLS.

Contents:

a. Contents listing and introduction (3 p.); geography and area statistics summary, with 2 tables showing climatic characteristics by State division and selected MSA (p. I.1-I.5).

b. Economic developments and outlook, with 6 tables showing economic indicator changes in recessionary periods, 1973-75 and 1981-82; trends in industry wages and employment, various periods 1972-82; and number of plants, new employment, and investment for new and expanded plants, 1960-83. (p. II.1-II.13)

c. Labor and population data, in 8 sections, with narrative summaries, 4 maps, 46 charts, and 90 tables; tables, and selected charts with substantial data not shown in tables, are described below. (p. III.1-X.20)

d. Summary section on population groups in need of employment training services, with 5 text tables. (p. XI.1-XI.3)

e. Appendix, with glossary, and organization and agency directories. (p. A1-A13)

Report formerly was titled *Annual Planning Information, South Carolina*.

Availability: South Carolina Employment Security Commission, Labor Market Information Division, 1550 Gadsden St., PO Box 995, Columbia SC 29202, †; SRI/MF/complete.

TABLES AND CHARTS:
[Data are for South Carolina, unless otherwise noted.]

S7155–3.1: Tourism, Employment, and Population

TOURISM, AND INDUSTRY EMPLOYMENT TRENDS

a. Travel expenditures by type; travel industry payroll and employment by industry category; and travel-generated tax revenues by level of government; with detail by county; 1982. 5 tables. (p. III.4-III.5)

b. Manufacturing and nonmanufacturing labor turnover (new hires, separations, and recalls), quarterly 1979-3rd quarter 1983; and nonfarm wage/salary employment by industry division and major manufacturing group, for U.S., South Carolina, and 3 MSAs, 1983. 6 tables. (p. III.9-III.19)

POPULATION

c. Population, by age, sex, race, MSA, and county, various periods 1950-90; and population age 65/over employment, median income, poverty status, living alone, and home ownership, by county, 1980. 12 tables. (p. IV.2-IV.14)

S7155–3.2: Labor Force, Insured Unemployment, and Job Service Activities

LABOR FORCE

a. Labor force by employment status; unemployment by duration and reason; employment and unemployment, by occupation, full- and part-time status, and county; and monthly unemployment rates; generally by race and sex, with selected data by age group and comparisons to total U.S., including unemployment rates by State; various years 1960-85. 23 tables. (p. V.1-V.27)

EMPLOYMENT

b. Nonfarm total and female employment, and manufacturing average earnings and hours, generally by major industry group, 1982-83, with some projections for 1990; and employment covered by employment security law, by industry division, 3rd quarter 1982-83. 5 tables. (p. VI.2-VI.7)

c. U.S. occupational employment distribution, 1982 and 1995; rankings of occupations with highest projected change in employment, fastest growth, and greatest employment decrease, 1982-95 period; and States ranked by employment and average weekly wages, 12-month period ended June 1983. 5 tables. (p. VI.9-VI.14)

INSURED UNEMPLOYMENT

d. Insured unemployment average volume and rate, by MSA and county of residence, 1982-83; and insured unemployment, by industry division, occupation, duration of unemployment, sex, and age, 1983. 6 tables (p. VII.2-VII.5)

e. Unemployment insurance initial claimant, beneficiary, and exhaustee distribution by sex, race, age, industry of previous employment, reason for separation from prior job, and education, with detail for textile industry; and long-term unemployment distribution, and percent of unemployment insurance claimants experiencing long-term unemployment, by county; 1983. 3 tables. (p. VII.7-VII.11)

JOB SERVICE

f. Job service applicants by service provided and occupational category, and work incentive program registrants, all by applicant characteristics, including age, sex, race, educational attainment, and veteran, handicapped, and migrant status; nonagricultural job openings and applicants by occupational category and detailed job title; and Targeted Jobs Tax Credit program eligibility determinations and certifications; various periods, FY83. 7 tables. (p. VIII.2-VIII.15)

g. Labor force groups especially in need of job services: distribution by age, race, sex, occupation, and other characteristics for economically disadvantaged, veterans, minorities, youth, women, and handicapped, FY82 or FY83. 34 charts. (p. IX.3-IX.13)

S7155–3.3: Income and Education

a. Income: total and/or per capita personal income, by county, MSA, and source (including earnings by industry division, transfer payments, and dividends/interest/rent), with selected comparisons to 11 southeastern States and total U.S.; median household and family income, by county; and persons below poverty level, by age, race, and county; various years 1969-83. 10 tables. (p. X.2-X.11)

b. Education: public and private/special/denominational schools and enrollment, public school vocational and adult education enrollment, public high school graduates and percent entering higher education and employment, and population age 25/over by educational attainment, all by county; and public and private higher education enrollment, by institutional category; various years 1960/61-1981/82. 8 tables. (p. X.13-X.20)

S7155–5   COMMUTING PATTERNS, SOUTH CAROLINA, 1980
Census Data
Monograph. Jan. 1984.
56 p. no paging.
SRI/MF/complete

Report presenting 1980 census data on commuting patterns in South Carolina, covering points of origin and destination for South Carolina residents and for nonresidents employed in the State. Data are cross-tabulated among counties and SMSAs of South Carolina and neighboring States.

Data are based on unpublished tabulations from Summary Tape File 4 of the 1980 Census of Population and Housing.

Contains foreword and highlights (2 p.); summary data with 2 maps and 2 tables (4 p.); and 1 table repeated for the State and each SMSA and county (48 p).

Availability: South Carolina Employment Security Commission, Labor Market Information Division, 1550 Gadsden St., PO Box 995, Columbia SC 29202, †; SRI/MF/complete.

S7165   SOUTH CAROLINA
Board of
Financial Institutions

**S7165–1   SEVENTY-SEVENTH
ANNUAL REPORT OF THE
STATE BOARD OF
FINANCIAL INSTITUTIONS
of the State of South
Carolina, 1983**
Annual.   Sept. 7, 1983.   70 p.
LC 79-615897.
SRI/MF/complete

Annual report on financial condition of South Carolina State-chartered financial institutions, FY83, presenting assets and liabilities, by institution, for banks, trust companies, and savings and loan assns; and restricted and supervised consumer finance company finances and loan activity, 1982.

Also includes data on Board of Financial Institutions revenues, expenditures, and licensing activity; aggregate bank income and expense analysis by deposit size; credit unions and funeral homes, by city; and consumer finance company delinquent account legal actions.

Contains contents listing (p. 2); and reports of Commissioner of Banking and Director of Consumer Finance Division, with lists of financial institution branches, offices, and status changes, and 25 tables (p. 4-70).

Availability: South Carolina Board of Financial Institutions, Commissioner of Banking, 1026 Sumter St., Rm. 217, Columbia SC 29201, †; SRI/MF/complete.

S7175   SOUTH CAROLINA
Department of
Health and
Environmental Control

**S7175–1   SOUTH CAROLINA VITAL
AND MORBIDITY
STATISTICS, 1982, Volume
I**
Annual.   June 1984.
9+vii+144 p.
ISSN 0094-6338.
LC 78-645478.
SRI/MF/complete, current &
previous year reports

Annual report on South Carolina vital statistics, covering population, births, deaths by cause, marriages and divorces, and communicable diseases, 1982, with selected trends from 1950. Includes data by sex, race, age, county, and city. Data are from State records.

Contains preface, and listings of contents, tables, and charts (8 p.); and the following:

a.   Introduction, methodology, and definitions, with 3 tables showing: 1981 births and deaths filed after Apr. 1, 1982; births and deaths allocated by residence and occurrence, by race, 1982; and resident live births, by race (including Indian, Chinese, Japanese, and other) of mother and father, 1982. (p. i-vii)

b.   9 summary and trend charts, and 1 chart and 78 tables listed below, arranged in 6 sections. (p. 1-136)

c.   Appendix, with facsimiles of vital statistics certificates, and list of codes and comparability ratios for 72 causes of death, and 10 causes of infant death, according to the International Classification of Diseases, 8th and 9th Revisions. (p. 137-144)

Companion Vol. II, *Detailed Mortality Statistics,* is covered in SRI under S7175-2.

Previous report, for 1981, was also reviewed in 1984 and is also available on SRI microfiche, under this number [Annual. Aug. 1983. vii+136 p. ‡]. Most recently issued Vol. II, for 1982, is described below.

Availability: South Carolina Department of Health and Environmental Control, Biostatistics Division, Vital Records and Public Health Statistics Office, 2600 Bull St., Columbia SC 29201, ‡; SRI/MF/complete.

TABLES:
[All tables show data for South Carolina.]

S7175–1.1: Vital Statistics and Population Summary
[Unless otherwise noted, data are for 1963-82. All tables, except table 5, show residence data. Most tables also show rates.]

1. Population, live births, deaths, marriages, and divorces, by race. (p. 1)

2. Out-of-wedlock, low weight births, fetal deaths, deaths under 1 year and under 28 days, and maternal deaths, by race. (p. 2)

3. Mortality from selected causes of death, by race, 1973-82. (p. 3)

[A] [Population by age group, 1970 and 1980.] (p. 5)

4. Population, live births, deaths, and natural increase. (p. 6)

5. Estimates of population, by race by county, July 1982. (p. 8)

S7175–1.2: Births
[Unless otherwise noted, data are for 1982. Most tables show residence data. Data by attendant are shown for physician, midwife (generally with breakdowns for in and out of hospital), other, and self-attended.]

STATE TOTALS
[Tables 6, 8, and 11-15 show data by race.]

6. Live births and birth rate, 1950-82. (p. 10)

7. Live births by attendant by place of delivery [hospital/clinic, doctor's office, en route, and residence]. (p. 11)

8. Percentages of births occurring in hospitals, 1973-82. (p. 11)

9-10. Percentage distribution of out-of-wedlock and [total] live births, by age of mother, 1978-82. (p. 12)

11. Live births by birth weight, with percentages of births in weight group. (p. 13)

12. Percent of births less than 2,500 grams, by age of mother. (p. 13)

13-14. Fertility rates and population of females age 15-44, 1950, 1960, and 1970-82. (p. 15)

15. Sex ratio of males per 100 females, 1978-82. (p. 16)

BIRTHS BY COUNTY
[Tables 16-30 generally show data by race and/or county.]

16-17. Live births and birth rates: each county and places of 2,500 or more population (residence and occurrence data). (p. 17-24)

18-19. Live births by sex (residence and occurrence data). (p. 25-26)

20. Total births by number of prenatal care visits. (p. 27)

21-23A. Live births by month prenatal care began and by attendant (residence and occurrence data). (p. 28-36)

24. Live births and percent of live births, by marital status, by age of mother. (p. 37)

25. Live births by age of mother. (p. 38)

26. Live births to mothers less than 20 years old. (p. 39)

27. Live births by birth weight and age of mother. (p. 40)

28-29. Low weight live births, and percent of low weight live births; and low weight live births by age of mother. (p. 41-42)

30. Live births by birth weight. (p. 43-47)

31. Out-of-wedlock live births and percent of live births out-of-wedlock. (p. 48)

32. Out-of-wedlock live births by age of mother. (p. 49)

CONGENITAL ANOMALIES

33. Live births with reported congenital malformations [and rates], 1980-82. (p. 50)

34. Live births with reported congenital malformations, by type [State total only], 1980-82. (p. 51)

S7175–1.3: Deaths
[Tables show residence data, 1982, unless otherwise noted. Many tables show data by race.]

STATE TOTALS

35. Total deaths and death rate, 1950-82. (p. 53)

36. Percentage distribution of deaths, by age, 1963 and 1982. (p. 54)

37. Leading causes of infant death, by age at death. (p. 55)

38. Maternal deaths by cause and age. (p. 56)

39. Violent deaths with rates, by type, 1978-82. (p. 57)

40. Types of accidental deaths, by sex. (p. 57)

41-42. Methods of suicidal and homicidal deaths, by sex. (p. 58)

43. Distribution of malignant neoplasms, by site. (p. 59)

44. Deaths from major cardiovascular diseases. (p. 60)

45. Mortality from 10 leading causes of death. (p. 61)

[B] Percentage distribution of the 10 leading causes of death and deaths from all causes, by sex. [chart] (p. 61)

46. Mortality from 5 leading causes of death in specified age groups. (p. 62)

DEATHS BY COUNTY
[Tables 47-64 show data by race and county, unless otherwise noted.]

47-48. Deaths and death rates: each county and places of 2,500 or more population (residence and occurrence data). (p. 63-70)

49-50. Deaths by sex (residence and occurrence data). (p. 71-72)

TL 51-51A. Deaths and death rates from selected causes, by sex [rates shown for State total only]. (p. 73-96)

52. Deaths from selected causes, by age and sex [State total only]. (p. 97-106)

53-54. Deaths by burial disposition (occurrence data). (p. 107-108)

55-56. Major causes of accidental death (residence and occurrence data) [not by race]. (p. 109-110)

57-58. Deaths from suicides by method and from homicides by type (occurrence data) [not by race]. (p. 111-112)

59-64. Infant, neonatal, postneonatal, fetal, and perinatal deaths and mortality rates. (p. 113-121)

65-66. Maternal deaths and maternal mortality rate (residence and occurrence data). (p. 122)

S7175–1.4: Marriages, Divorces, and Annulments
[All data are for 1982. Data by residential status are for resident and nonresident.]

67. Marriages by race [white, black, Indian, Chinese, Japanese, and other] of bride and groom. (p. 124)

68. Marriages by county in which license was issued, by residential status [of bride and groom]. (p. 125)

69. Marriages by residential status [of bride and groom], by county of marriage. (p. 126)

70-71. Marriages by race, by residential status, by age groups of brides and grooms. (p. 127-128)

72. Marriages by age of bride, by age of groom. (p. 129)

73. Divorces/annulments [and] number of children involved, by race: each county. (p. 130)

74. Divorces by plaintiff [and] legal grounds for decree; [and annulments]: each county. (p. 131)

75. Divorces by age groups, by race [of husband and of wife]. (p. 132)

76. Divorces by duration of marriage, by plaintiff, by legal grounds for decree; [and annulments]. (p. 133)

S7175–1.5: Morbidity
[Data are shown by county of occurrence, 1982, with 1981 totals.]

77. Reported cases of selected communicable diseases. (p. 134)

78. Reported cases of venereal disease [by type]. (p. 136)

S7175–2   DETAILED MORTALITY STATISTICS, SOUTH CAROLINA, 1982, Volume II
Annual. Jan. 1984.
4+141 p.
SRI/MF/complete

Annual report on South Carolina deaths, by cause, age, sex, and race, 1982, compiled by the Office of Vital Records and Public Health Statistics.

Contains data interpretation, and contents and code guides (4 p.); and 1 extended table showing resident deaths, by detailed cause, cross-tabulated by age, sex, and race (141 p.). Data are arranged according to the 9th revision of *International Classification of Diseases.*

Companion Vol. I, *Vital and Morbidity Statistics,* is covered in SRI under S7175-1. Most recently issued Vol. I, for 1981, is described above.

Availability: South Carolina Department of Health and Environmental Control, Biostatistics Division, Vital Records and Public Health Statistics Office, 2600 Bull St., Columbia SC 29201, ‡; SRI/MF/complete.

S7185   SOUTH CAROLINA Commission on Higher Education

S7185–2   STATE OF SOUTH CAROLINA HIGHER EDUCATION STATISTICAL ABSTRACT, Sixth Edition
Annual. Apr. 1984.
iii+69 p.
LC 72-624835.
SRI/MF/complete

Annual report on South Carolina higher education enrollment, faculty, degrees awarded, and finances, 1983, with trends from fall 1974. Most data are shown by public and/or private institution.

Contains table index (p. iii); and 1 chart, and 20 tables described below.

Availability: South Carolina Commission on Higher Education, 1429 Senate St., Rm. 1104, Columbia SC 29201, †; SRI/MF/complete.

TABLES:
[Unless otherwise noted, data by institution are shown for public senior colleges and universities.]

a. Enrollment trends: head count and FTE, by degree level and institution, fall 1974-83. 4 tables. (p. 1-4)

b. Fall 1983 enrollment, FTE and/or head count: by degree level and for entering freshmen, with summary percent change from 1981-82; by race for undergraduates and graduate students; and by sex for all students and nonresident aliens; all by public and private institution, including technical and junior colleges. 6 tables. (p. 7-16)

c. Faculty/student data: selected student characteristics, including percent from South Carolina; FTE faculty, by academic rank; faculty credit hour production and teaching hours; student/faculty ratio; and average students per class; all by institution, fall 1982-83. 2 tables. (p. 17-35)

d. Degrees awarded: aggregate by sex, race, and academic discipline; and by public and private institution; all by degree level, for the period July 1, 1982-June 30, 1983. 3 tables. (p. 36-42)

e. Finances: revenues by source and expenditures by function, by institution, 1982/83; State appropriations by institution, and aggregate for technical education, tuition aid grants to private colleges, elementary/secondary education, and education dept appropriations, with comparisons to total State revenues, 1974/75-1983/84. 4 tables. (p. 43-65)

f. FTE employees, by function and institution, fall 1983. 1 table. (p. 67-68)

S7190   SOUTH CAROLINA Department of Highways and Public Transportation

S7190–1   ANNUAL REPORT OF THE SOUTH CAROLINA DEPARTMENT OF HIGHWAYS AND PUBLIC TRANSPORTATION to the General Assembly, for Period July 1, 1981-June 30, 1982
Annual. [1983.]
126 p.+foldout.
LC 78-646535.
SRI/MF/complete

Annual report of the South Carolina Dept of Highways and Public Transportation, FY82, with trends from FY30. Covers revenues and expenditures, highway construction and maintenance, motor vehicle registrations, driver's licenses, and support services. Also includes summary traffic arrest and accident data, and dept employment and payroll.

Contains contents listing, personnel lists, and introduction with 1 summary financial chart and table (p. 3-14); and narrative report, with 51 tables, as follows:

a. Highway construction costs by type of material, compared to Federal Highway Administration construction cost index and Atlanta CPI, 1967-81; fuel consumption, selected years 1940-81; average speed and motorists exceeding limits, by highway type, FY80-81; and highway mileage by road width and traffic volume, road surveys, bridge and railroad crossing projects and finances, and expenditures for right of way, FY82, with selected trends. 10 tables. (p. 19-32)

b. Other State highway programs and activities, including maintenance program costs, FY81-82; and equipment purchases, radio and other electronic equipment in use, and highway patrol arrests for traffic and truck weight violations, FY82. 6 tables. (p. 35-40)

c. Motor vehicle division and highway safety program, including vehicle registrations and receipts, with trends from 1945; driver exam and licensing activities, FY81-82; vehicle titles issued, 1958-FY82; number of traffic accidents and fatalities 1980-81; and economic loss from accidents by county, 1979-81. 12 tables. (p. 41-56) *d.* Damage claims/suits and State damage recoveries, various years FY73-82; workmen's compensation payments by type, and Interagency Council on Public Transportation activities, FY82; and summary of State highway needs, as of Dec. 1980. 6 tables. (p. 56-68)

e. Statistical section, with 17 detailed tables listed below, and dept organizational chart. (p. 74-126, and foldout)

Previous report, for FY81, is described in SRI 1982 Annual, under this number.

Availability: South Carolina Department of Highways and Public Transportation, PO Box 191, Columbia SC 29202, ‡; SRI/MF/complete.

DETAILED TABLES:

S7190-1.1: Highway Dept Finances and Employment, and Vehicle Registrations and Driver's Licenses

FINANCIAL STATEMENTS, NET EXPENDITURES, AND CONSTRUCTION FUNDS
[Most tables show data for FY81-82.]

1-2. Comparative balance sheet; and comparative statement of general fund revenues [and] other receipts [by source], and expenditures [by agency and object]. (p. 74-82)

3A-5B. Statement of changes in invested capital, reserves, and fund balances; and of receipts and disbursements, [for] trust funds, and special deposits fund [by category of deposit]. (p. 83-93)

6. Net expenditures by objective classification. (p. 94-98)

7. Status of allocated highway construction funds [Federal and State, as of] June 30, 1982. (p. 99)

FUNDED DEBT, DEPT PAYROLL, AND HIGHWAY MILES
[Tables show data as of June 30, 1982.]

8. Funded debt, digest of obligations [by year due], and comparison with debt limitation. (p. 103)

9. Payroll statistics report [employment by category, and total employment and payroll compared to June 1981, all by organizational unit]. (p. 104-111)

10. Mileage summary record by counties [and road type]. (p. 112)

VEHICLE REGISTRATION AND DRIVER'S LICENSES

11-13. Net motor vehicle registrations and receipts, by classification and counties, 1980 and/or 1981. (p. 114-121)

14-15. Truck and passenger vehicle registrations by counties, 1975-81. (p. 122-123)

16. Driver's licenses issued and withdrawn [FY30-82]. (p. 124)

17. Summary by counties of driving privileges withdrawn [by cause and age group], FY82. (p. 126)

S7190-2   1983 SOUTH CAROLINA TRAFFIC ACCIDENTS
Annual. [1984.] 66 p.
LC 41-52472.
SRI/MF/complete

Annual report on South Carolina traffic accidents, injuries, and fatalities, by accident and vehicle type, location, time, and other circumstances; and by driver, victim, and vehicle characteristics; 1983, with trends from 1954.

Also includes data on property loss value; licensed drivers, motor vehicle registrations, and miles of travel; driver and pedestrian alcohol use, including blood alcohol content level of fatalities; safety belt use; and detail for motorcycle, school bus, urban and rural, and military vehicle accidents.

Report contains highlights and contents listing (p. 2-9); and 22 charts and 24 tables (p. 10-65).

Availability: South Carolina Department of Highways and Public Transportation, PO Box 191, Columbia SC 29202, †; SRI/MF/complete.

S7195   SOUTH CAROLINA Department of Insurance

S7195-1   SEVENTY-SIXTH ANNUAL REPORT OF THE DEPARTMENT OF INSURANCE of South Carolina
Annual. [1983.] 246 p.
LC 9-7968.
SRI/MF/complete

Annual report on South Carolina insurance industry financial condition and underwriting activity, by company, 1982. Covers total assets, liabilities, capital, surplus, and South Carolina premiums written, for property/casualty/allied line and life/accident/health insurance companies, with detailed balance sheet and income/expense data for South Carolina-based companies.

Also includes underwriting trends from 1950; and Insurance Dept revenues by source, expenditures by object, allocation to counties of additional premium tax and fire dept fund tax, and regulatory and consumer assistance caseloads, 1982 or FY83.

Company data are from annual statements filed by individual insurers.

Contains contents listing and legislative recommendations (p. 1-9); Insurance Dept report, with 13 tables (p. 12-43); financial tables, arranged alphabetically by company (p. 45-164); and detailed data for South Carolina-based companies (p. 166-246).

Availability: South Carolina Department of Insurance, PO Box 4067, Columbia SC 29240, ‡; SRI/MF/complete.

S7197   SOUTH CAROLINA Judicial Department

S7197-1   ANNUAL REPORT, 1982, Judicial Department of South Carolina
Annual. [1984.] 122 p.
SRI/MF/complete

Annual report, for 1982, on South Carolina judicial system, including caseloads and case dispositions for supreme, general sessions, common pleas, family, magistrate, and municipal courts.

Includes trial court data by court location, with magistrate and municipal court detail for driving under the influence and other traffic cases, jury and nonjury trials, and arrest and search warrant issuances.

Also includes data on age of pending cases; bail proceedings; judicial dept appropriations; expenditures for the defense of indigents, by county; grievances and disciplinary actions against judges; bar examinations and results; and selected trends from the 1970s.

Contains contents listing (p. 5-6); sections I-III, including narrative overview, 1 chart, and 7 tables (p. 7-25); and statistical section IV, with 5 charts and 36 tables (p. 26-122).

This is the 4th annual report.

Availability: South Carolina Judicial Department, Court Administrator's Office, PO Box 50447, Columbia SC 29250, †; SRI/MF/complete.

S7205   SOUTH CAROLINA Law Enforcement Division

S7205-1   CRIME IN SOUTH CAROLINA, 1983
Annual. Apr. 2, 1984.
2+62 p.
LC 78-620956.
SRI/MF/complete

Annual report on South Carolina crimes reported under the Uniform Crime Reporting (UCR) Program, 1983. Includes data on major Crime Index offenses and other crimes, arrests by offense, and assaults on police officers; and data by county and police agency.

Data are based on reports by law enforcement agencies under the State UCR Program.

Contains contents listing (1 p.); description of UCR Program (p. 1-3); and crime statistics, with 13 charts, 41 tables, and list of participating agencies (p. 4-62).

All tables, and charts presenting data not covered in tables, are listed below.

Availability: South Carolina Law Enforcement Division, Uniform Crime Report Section, PO Box 21398, Columbia SC 29221-9990, †; SRI/MF/complete.

TABLES AND CHARTS:
[Data are for South Carolina, and are shown for 1983 unless otherwise noted. Index offenses are murder, rape, robbery, aggravated assault, breaking/entering, larceny, and motor vehicle theft. Arson is classified as an Index offense, but data are reported separately and are generally not included in the Crime Index tables.]

S7205–1.1: Index Offenses and Officers Assaulted

INDEX CRIME SUMMARY

[Tables and charts [1-5] show data by Index offense.]

[1] Crime clock. [chart] (p. 4)

[2-3] Index crime trends, and crime rate per 10,000 population, 1981-83. (p. 5)

[4] Index crimes by month. (p. 6)

[5] Clearance trends [number of offenses, and total and juvenile clearances], 1981-83. (p. 7)

[6] Stolen and recovered property trends [value of property, by type], 1981-83. (p. 8)

INDEX CRIME DETAIL

[7-8] Murder victims by age, sex, and race; and murder distribution by circumstance and weapon. (p. 10-11)

[9-12] Murder by relationship [of victim to offender], murder circumstance and weapon trends, and murder distribution by day of week, 1981-83. (p. 12-14)

[13] Murder by premise. (p. 14)

[14-17] Relationship of rape victims to offenders [chart], and rape by premise [type], 1983; forcible and attempted rape trends, 1981-83; and rape distribution by day of week, 1983. (p. 16)

[18-19] Rape victims by age and race; and weapons used in rapes. (p. 17)

[20-21] Robbery: [offenses and stolen property value by premise, and offenses] by weapon type, 1981-83. (p. 19)

[22-23] Robbery by premise and time of day, and distribution by day of week. (p. 20)

[24] Aggravated assault by weapon type, 1981-83. (p. 21)

[25-26] Breaking/entering: [offenses by type of entry, and offenses and stolen property value by premise and time], 1981-83. (p. 23-24)

[27-28] Larceny trends [offenses and stolen property value, by type of larceny and] value group, 1981-83. (p. 26)

[29] Motor vehicle theft trends [by vehicle type; and total value]; 1981-83. (p. 27)

[30] Arson offenses reported, [total and juvenile clearances, offenses involving uninhabited structures, and estimated property value, by property classification 1983, with totals 1981-83]. (p. 28)

OFFICERS ASSAULTED

[31-34] Officers assaulted by type of assignment, by activity and weapon type, and by time of assault; and injuries to officers by weapon type; 1981-83. (p. 29-31)

[35] Police officers killed, by activity and weapon type, [cumulative] 1968-83. (p. 32)

S7205–1.2: Arrests

[Tables [1-3] and [6] show data for approximately 30 offense categories.]

[1] Arrests and rates per 10,000 population, 1981-83. (p. 34)

[2-3] Total arrests by race and sex, and by age. (p. 35-38)

[4-5] Drug law arrests, under age 17 and 17/over [by sex and race, for sale/manufacturing and possession by substance]. (p. 39)

[6] Arrest data by county. (p. 40-44)

[7-8] County crime rates per 10,000 population; and Index totals by county and agency; [both by Index offense, including arson]. (p. 45-62)

S7210   SOUTH CAROLINA State Library

S7210–1   FOURTEENTH ANNUAL REPORT: THE SOUTH CAROLINA STATE LIBRARY, July 1, 1982-June 30, 1983
Annual.   [1983.]
41 p.+foldouts.
LC 78-648699.
SRI/MF/complete

Annual report on South Carolina public and institutional library finances, services, holdings, and staff, FY83.

Contains contents listing (p. 2); narrative report, with text statistics, on South Carolina libraries' history, services, and activities (p. 3-25); and 9 tables, listed below, interspersed with directories (p. 26-41 and 3 foldouts).

Availability: South Carolina State Library, PO Box 11469, Columbia SC 29211, ‡; SRI/MF/complete.

TABLES:

[Tables show data for FY83, unless otherwise noted.]

[1] State library collections [summary of holdings by detailed type, as of June 30, 1982-83, with additions and withdrawals during year]. (p. 26-27)

[2] Interlibrary loan requests [including total and reference requests received, books loaned, and photocopies sent, by individual public library, and for interlibrary loans]. (p. 28-29)

[3] State library, State expenditures [includes salaries/wages and 27 other expense items]. (p. 30)

[4] State library, Federal expenditures [by title and project, FY81-83 funds]. (p. 31-32)

[5] Public library [per capita] bookstock, circulation, and [total and local] support, by county. (p. 40)

[6] Public library statistics [libraries and librarians; bookstock, circulation, and population; and library income; FY44, FY56, and FY83]. (p. 41)

[7] Public libraries, annual library statistics [1980 population of area taxed for support; operating income by source and expenditures by object; capital outlay; holdings; total and juvenile users and book circulation; interlibrary loans and borrowings; average weekly reference transactions; and number of branches/stations and bookmobiles; all by library]. (1 foldout)

[8] State supported institutions library statistics [residents, operating expenses by object, and funding; and summary data on holdings and professional and nonprofessional personnel; all by institution]. (1 foldout)

[9] Colleges and universities annual library statistics [operating expenses by object, holdings, and professional and nonprofessional FTE personnel; hours of student assistance; and total enrollment; all by institution]. (1 foldout)

S7252   SOUTH CAROLINA Department of Social Services

S7252–1   STATISTICAL REPORT, South Carolina Department of Social Services
Monthly.   Approx. 25 p.
SRI/MF/complete, shipped quarterly

Monthly report on South Carolina public welfare programs, including cases, recipients, and payments, by program and county. Covers AFDC, general disability assistance (GDA), medical assistance, food stamps, and work incentive (WIN) activities. Report is issued approximately 4 months after month of coverage.

Contains table and chart listings; 5-8 charts primarily illustrating recent trends, but also showing percent of population participating in food stamp program and receiving AFDC; and 17 monthly tables, listed below. Monthly tables appear in all issues.

Prior to the July 1984 issue, report includes an additional monthly table showing medical payments to vendors by type of service.

A slightly less detailed annual report on this subject is also available from the Office of Public Information of the issuing agency, but is not covered in SRI.

Availability: South Carolina Department of Social Services, Research and Statistics, PO Box 1520, Columbia SC 29202-9988, †; SRI/MF/complete, shipped quarterly.

Issues reviewed during 1984: Sept. 1983-Aug. 1984 (D) (Vol. 47, Nos. 3-12; Vol. 48, Nos. 1-2); and Aug. 1983 errata sheet.

MONTHLY TABLES:

[Data are for month of coverage, unless otherwise noted. Tables 4-17 show data by county. Table order may vary.]

APPLICATIONS

1-3. Cases approved, applications denied/otherwise terminated, and cases closed, for public assistance money payments, by category [AFDC and GDA], by reason.

4-5. AFDC and GDA money payment applications [pending, received, approved, and not approved].

ASSISTANCE PAYMENTS AND SERVICES

6. AFDC money payments, [cases, total recipients, and children].

7. GDA and SSI optional supplement gross money payments [and cases, and GDA persons].

8. CWS [child welfare service] foster care recipients and gross payments [total, State and local funds, and adoption supplement].

9. AFDC foster care and IV-E adoption supplement recipients and payments.

FOOD STAMPS

10-11. Food stamp participation [month of coverage and for fiscal year] to date [households, persons, and benefit value for coupon issuance and SSI/elderly cash out].

12-13. Food stamp monthly activity report [applications and disposition]; and Project Fair food stamp recipient claim collections, by type [intentional program violation/fraud and nonfraud client and agency error; tables begin with the Dec. 1983 issue].

WIN ACTIVITIES

14. WIN activities [initial certifications, and amounts of AFDC grant reductions].

SERVICES, VOLUNTEERS, AND LOCAL FUNDS

15. Title XX services authorization summary [including adoption, homemaker, and adult and child protective services].

16. Volunteer services report [hours worked, volunteers, and cash and in-kind contributions, month of coverage and fiscal year to date].

17. Disbursement of local funds [cases, persons, and payments, for medical and other payments].

S7255   SOUTH CAROLINA
Tax Commission

S7255–1   SIXTY-NINTH ANNUAL REPORT OF THE SOUTH CAROLINA TAX COMMISSION, 1983
Annual. Sept. 1, 1983.
159 p.
LC 16-27141.
SRI/MF/complete

Annual report, for FY83, on South Carolina tax revenues and collections by type, allocations to localities, and property assessments by county and company, with selected comparisons to FY81-82. Also includes data on corporate income tax returns by business classification, and personal income tax returns by tax liability bracket.

Data are compiled by the State Tax Commission.

Contains contents listing (p. 6-7); summary Tax Commission information, including 2 summary charts, and 2 tables listed below (p. 8-15); 5 division reports, with 51 tables, also listed below (p. 16-153); and narrative report of attorney general on tax litigation, and subject index (p. 154-159).

Availability: South Carolina Tax Commission, Box 125, Columbia SC 29202, †; SRI/MF/complete.

TABLES:
[Data are shown for South Carolina, FY83, unless otherwise noted.]

S7255–1.1: Commission Finances, and Income Taxes

COMMISSION SUMMARY FINANCES

1-2. Tax Commission comparative revenue statement (net) [collections by type, FY82-83; and appropriations and] expenses [by division and object], FY83. (p. 14-15)

INCOME TAXES

3. Statement showing amount of [individual and corporate] income tax revenue, and cash collected [from bank, savings and loan assn, corporation license, income, and insurance taxes, and unclaimed property]. (p. 16)

4. Distribution of 7½% income tax to counties. (p. 17)

5-6. Analysis of 1981-82 corporation returns by [SIC 4-digit] business classification [number of returns and amount of tax]. (p. 18-19)

7-10. Analysis of 1981-82 corporation and individual income tax returns [number of returns and amount of tax, by tax liability bracket]. (p. 20-22)

11-12. Number of returns, adjusted gross income, taxable income, income tax liability, total exemptions and deductions, and total tax, by adjusted gross income classes, 1982. (p. 23-24)

13. Additional tax collected by individual and corporate income tax [including number of delinquent returns and amount collected], FY82-83. (p. 25)

14. Bank tax distributions [to cities arranged by county]. (p. 26-30)

S7255–1.2: License, Gasoline, and Beverage Taxes

SUMMARY

15. License Tax Division: total collections [for 18 tax types]. (p. 31)

LICENSES

16-18. Business license, coin operated devices, and documentary stamp tax total net collections. (p. 32-33)

GASOLINE

19-20. Gasoline tax collected [by month]; and distribution to counties. (p. 34-35)

21. Gasoline tax refunded on gasoline purchased and used solely for agricultural purposes [number of claims and amount by county]. (p. 36)

22. Distribution of watercraft gasoline tax to counties [boats registered and amount distributed]. (p.38)

23. Refund on tax paid on motor fuels purchased by carriers in excess of that used on South Carolina highways [by month]. (p. 39)

BEVERAGES

24. Soft/bottled drinks tax total net collections [by type]. (p. 40)

25-26. Alcoholic liquors tax collections [from retail, wholesale, and additional case taxes; excise tax; surtax; and penalties; all by month]. (p. 41-42)

27-28. Alcoholic liquors tax distributions [to counties and selected cities arranged by county], and mini bottles [by county]. (p. 43-50)

29-30. Beer and wine tax net collections; and beer/wine tax distributions [to counties and selected cities arranged by county]. (p. 50-57)

S7255–1.3: Estate and Gift Taxes

31-32. Recapitulation of collections [by month] and of probate judges' commissions paid [by county] on account of inheritance/estate taxes. (p. 58-59)

33. Analysis of estate tax [number and amount by tax liability bracket], FY82-83. (p. 59)

34. Recapitulation of collections on account of gift tax [by month]. (p. 60)

S7255–1.4: Sales and Use Taxes

35. Statement showing amount of tax collected by the Sales and Use Tax Division. (p. 60)

36. Collections of sales/use tax by [SIC 4-digit] business classification [FY81-83]. (p. 61)

37. Collections from the retail license tax [number of returns and amount paid, by license fee amount]. (p. 63)

38. Analysis of sales/use tax returns [number of returns and amount of tax, by tax liability size]. (p. 64)

39. Summary: additional tax collected [number of audits and amount collected]. (p. 64)

40. Sales and use tax total active accounts. (p. 65)

S7255–1.5: Property Taxes

[Tables 42-53 show assessments for 1983.]

41. Statement showing amount of tax collected by the Property Tax Division from private car line tax and flight equipment. (p. 65)

42. Business personal property assessments [number of returns, inventory value, consigned merchandise, equipment depreciation value, and total and assessed values, by county]. (p. 66)

43. Manufacturing property: property tax assessments [by company and county]. (p. 67-138)

44. Pipeline companies: property tax assessments [for 11 companies, by county]. (p. 139)

45. Water companies: property tax assessments [by company and location]. (p. 140)

46-47. Assessed value of all railroad property [and miles of track] used in daily operation of [all] railroads and of the Seaboard Coastline Railroad System [by county]. (p. 142-143)

48-49. Assessed value of all property [and miles of track] used in the daily operation of the Southern Railway System and of the local railroads [by railroad]. (p. 144)

50-52. Light, heat, and power companies; electric cooperatives; and local telephone companies: property tax assessments [assessed value, by company and county]. (p. 145-152)

53. Major communications companies [AT&T, Southern Bell, and Western Union]: property tax assessments [by county]. (p. 153)

S7300   SOUTH DAKOTA
Department of Commerce and Regulation

S7300–2   COMPARATIVE STATEMENT OF INSURANCE BUSINESS in South Dakota During the Years 1981-82
Annual. May 1, 1983. 46 p.
LC 75-19531.
SRI/MF/complete

Annual report on South Dakota insurance industry underwriting activity, by company and type of insurance, 1981-82. Covers premiums written or collected, assets or policyholder surplus, and losses paid, for insurers based in South Dakota and elsewhere.

Data are shown, as applicable, for fire/casualty insurers; hospital/medical/dental services companies; HMOs; farm mutual assns; fraternal benefit societies; and life insurers (including amount of policies issued, and detail for accident/health insurance).

Contains 11 tables.

Previous report, for 1980-81, is described in SRI 1982 Annual, under this number.

Availability: South Dakota Department of Commerce, Insurance Division, Insurance Bldg., 320 N. Nicollet St., Pierre SD 57501-2297, †; SRI/MF/complete.

S7300–3   1983 SOUTH DAKOTA MOTOR VEHICLE TRAFFIC ACCIDENT SUMMARY
Annual. [1984.] 59 p.
ISSN 0147-0760.
LC 84-623404.
SRI/MF/complete

Annual report on South Dakota traffic accidents, injuries, and fatalities, by vehicle and accident type, time, location, and other circumstances; and by driver and victim characteristics; 1983, with trends from 1960.

Also includes data on alcohol involvement in accidents, arrests for driving while intoxicated, blood alcohol content test results for drivers involved in fatal accidents, travel mileage, motor vehicle registrations, fatality rate comparison with U.S. and 6 other western States, licensed drivers and motorcyclists, and safety device use.

Data are from accident reports submitted to State Dept of Commerce and Regulation.

Contains listings of contents, tables, and charts (3 p.); highlights, 15 charts, and 24 tables, with narrative analyses, and glossary (p. 1-41); and 3 appendices, with 16 tables and legislative summary (p. 43-59).

This is the 11th annual report. Report previously was issued by the South Dakota Dept of Public Safety, now a division of the South Dakota Dept of Commerce and Regulation, and was described in SRI under S7370-1.

Availability: South Dakota Department of Commerce and Regulation, Accident Records Program, 118 W. Capitol Ave., Pierre SD 57501-2080, †; SRI/MF/complete.

S7302   SOUTH DAKOTA Department of State Development

S7302–1   SOUTH DAKOTA AGRICULTURE, 1983/84
Annual. May 1984. 61 p.
SRI/MF/complete

Annual report on South Dakota agricultural production, marketing, and income, 1983, with selected trends from 1955. Data are generally shown by commodity, with crop data also by county and district, and some comparisons to other States and total U.S.

Report covers production, disposition, prices, sales, value, and, as applicable, acreage, yield, and inventory, for field crop, livestock, poultry, and dairy sectors.

Also includes data on number of farms and acreage; fertilizer consumption; farm income, production expenses, real estate value and taxes, title transfers, and cash rents; and State land area and use.

The 1983/84 edition of the report also presents selected preliminary findings from the 1982 Census of Agriculture, including total and irrigated farms and acreage; marketing; and hay and livestock production; all by county and district.

Data are compiled by the South Dakota Crop and Livestock Reporting Service in cooperation with USDA.

Contains contents listing (p. 1); 13 maps, 13 charts, and 68 tables, interspersed with narrative summaries (p. 2-53); Census of Agriculture data, with 7 tables (p. 54-60); and list of additional reports (p. 61).

Availability: South Dakota Crop and Livestock Reporting Service, 3528 S. Western Ave., PO Drawer V, Sioux Falls SD 57117, †; SRI/MF/complete.

S7315   SOUTH DAKOTA Department of Education and Cultural Affairs

S7315–1   1982/83 SOUTH DAKOTA EDUCATIONAL STATISTICS DIGEST
Annual. [1984.]
63+App 98 p.+addendum.
Research Bull. 3.4-12.
ISSN 0360-4772.
LC 75-646389.
SRI/MF/complete

Annual report on South Dakota elementary and secondary schools and school districts, covering students, staff, finances, and transportation, 1982/83, with selected trends from 1968/69. Also includes data on tax valuations and levies, and nonpublic schools.

Data are compiled by the Office of Support Services.

Contents:

a. Index (1 p.); and 1 table and accompanying map showing number of schools by educational level, 1- and 2-teacher schools, and school districts by county (p. 1).

b. 19 State summary and 6 detailed district tables, listed below. (p. 2-62)

c. Appendix with school district profiles, arranged alphabetically by district, including data on 1982 mill levies by fund, taxable valuation of property, school calendar, staff, school board members by sex, average daily attendance (ADA), average daily membership (ADM), revenues by government level of source, expenditures by function and fund, and number of bus routes and pupils transported. (p. App. 1-98)

Less comprehensive annual reports not covered in SRI but also available from the issuing agency are: *Public School Districts Fall Enrollment, Nonpublic Schools Fall Enrollment,* and *South Dakota Elementary and Secondary Educational Comparisons.*

Availability: South Dakota Department of Education and Cultural Affairs, Elementary and Secondary Education Division, Support Services Office, Kneip Bldg., 700 N. Illinois St., Pierre SD 57501-2281, †; SRI/MF/complete.

TABLES:
[Data are for 1982/83, unless otherwise noted.]

S7315–1.1: State Summary
OVERVIEW
[1] A look at enrollments and costs [1968/69-1984/85]. (p. 2)

[2-3] General information [cumulative enrollment, and ADM and ADA by grade level, with distribution by educational level 1978/79-1982/83; public and nonpublic 1983 high school graduates, by sex and postgraduation status (attending college or other educational institution, employed, and military service); and number of school districts, by enrollment size, fall 1982]. (p. 3-4)

REVENUES AND EXPENDITURES
[Funds shown include general, capital outlay, special education, pension, bond redemption, and sometimes trust/agency funds.]

[4] Statement of changes in fund balances [by fund, July 1982-June 1983]. (p. 5)

[5] General fixed assets [by type]. (p. 5)

[6] Receipts by funds [and by government source]. (p. 6)

[7-8] [General and special education funds] educational expenditures by functions and by objects. (p. 7-8)

[9] Capital outlay fund expenditures. (p. 9)

[10] Bond redemption fund disbursements. (p. 9)

[11] Costs of special programs [kindergarten and summer programs]. (p. 9)

[12] Per pupil costs [for general and capital outlay funds]. (p. 9)

ENROLLMENT, STAFF, AND MISCELLANEOUS DATA

[13] 1983 fall data [public and nonpublic school enrollment and FTE teachers]. (p. 10)

[14] 1983 fall enrollment: public and nonpublic [by grade and sex]. (p. 10)

[15] Miscellaneous data [including number of districts, and taxable valuation of agricultural and nonagricultural property, by nonagricultural mill levy range; and districts with levies above and below certain levels]. (p. 11)

[16] Staff information [certified and noncertified personnel by position, by sex]. (p. 12)

[17] Selected data [summary data, including State aid entitlements for 1983/84, and average classroom units (CRU) per district, cost per CRU, tax raised per resident child, ADM, and cost per pupil ADM]. (p. 12)

[18] Transportation data [number of districts reporting bus service, number of buses, pupils transported, mileage, and costs, for public and private ownership]. (p. 13)

NONPUBLIC SCHOOLS

[19] Summary of South Dakota nonpublic schools [schools and enrollment; teaching positions by sex, enrollment, ADM, and ADA, all by educational level; and special enrollment, by program]. (p. 14)

S7315–1.2: School District Summaries
[Tables show data for individual school districts.]

[1] Selected school data [ADM, expenditures, CRUs, tax raised per resident child, agricultural and nonagricultural property value and levies, special education levy, and transportation State aid entitlement]. (p. 15-20)

[2] General information: enrollment [by grade]; and instructional staff [and ADM, by educational level, and ADM in 1- and 2-teacher schools]. (p. 21-28)

[3] Financial information receipts [by government level; and from general, capital outlay, special education, and bond redemption funds]. (p. 29-41)

[4] Sale of securities [general fund and capital outlay, for selected districts]. (p. 41)

[5] Financial information expenditures [for instruction, support services, community services, nonprogrammed, debt service, co-curricular, special education, capital outlay, and bond redemption]. (p. 42-54)

[6] School bus transportation [cost, ADM, and mileage]. (p. 55-62)

S7345   SOUTH DAKOTA
Department of Health

S7345–1   SOUTH DAKOTA VITAL STATISTICS ANNUAL REPORT, 1982
Annual.   July 15, 1983.
viii+138 p.
ISSN 0095-4802.
LC 74-648589.
SRI/MF/complete

Annual report on South Dakota vital statistics, covering population, births, deaths by cause, marriages, divorces, abortions, and communicable disease, 1982, with trends from 1906. Includes data by age, sex, race, and county. Most data are from State Dept of Health records as of May 15, 1983.

Contains listings of contents, tables, and charts (p. i-viii); preface, and 6 statistical sections with narrative summaries, 28 charts, and 46 detailed tables (p. 1-120); notes and definitions (p. 123-126); and appendix, with 1 chart and 5 tables, and facsimiles of reporting forms (p. 129-138).

All tables, and selected charts with substantial statistics not covered in tables, are listed below.

Availability: South Dakota Department of Health, Vital Records Program, 523 E. Capitol Ave., Pierre SD 57501-9975, $3.00; SRI/MF/complete.

TABLES AND CHARTS:
[Unless otherwise noted, data are for South Dakota, 1982. Tables showing data by race generally include data for American Indians.]

S7345–1.1: Population, Summary, and Births

POPULATION AND SUMMARY

1. South Dakota and U.S. ratios [dependent/productive, aged dependent/productive, old/young, and male/female for total U.S. and for South Dakota total, white, and Indian population, 1970 and/or 1980]. (p. 6)

[A-C] [Total], white, and Indian population distribution [number and percent, by age and sex], 1980. [charts] (p. 7-9)

2. Population by race, by county, 1970 [and] 1980. (p. 10)

3-4. Vital statistics: [by event, selected years] 1906-82; and summary by county (birth, death, abortion, and fetal deaths by county of residence, marriage and divorce by county of occurrence), 1982; [both with number and rate]. (p. 12, 18)

BIRTHS

5-7. Births by county of mother's residence: by race and sex; by race of mother; and by mother's age. (p. 24-27)

8. Births by county of occurrence, by attendant at birth [physician, midwife, and other medical and nonmedical]. (p. 29)

9. Births with reported congenital anomalies by [type, mother's] race and [baby's] sex. (p. 31)

10. Out-of-wedlock births by county of mother's residence [and mother's race]. (p. 33)

11. Resident births by age, race, and marital status of mother. (p. 34)

12. Births by county of mother's residence by birth weight. (p. 35)

13. Percent of births receiving first trimester prenatal care by race and age of mother. (p. 37)

14. Single live births by age of mother, race of mother, and month prenatal care began. (p. 38)

15. [Resident] births by State of occurrence, and [births in South Dakota by] State of mother's residence, [by mother's race]. (p. 39)

S7345–1.2: Deaths

16. Leading causes of death [by race]. (p. 45)

17. Deaths by county of residence and occurrence, by race. (p. 48)

18-19. Resident deaths: by cause, by age group; and [from] 72 selected causes [by race and sex]. (p. 49-60, 65-66)

20. Deaths by county of residence by race [number and rate]. (p. 67)

21. Deaths by county of occurrence by place of death [hospital, other institution, and other]. (p. 68)

22. [Resident] deaths by State of occurrence, and [deaths in South Dakota by] State of residence, [by race]. (p. 69)

23. Deaths from malignant neoplasms, by county of residence. (p. 70)

24. Suicides [by sex, and rate per 100,000 population], 1960-82. (p. 75)

[E] Resident suicides [distribution by age group, sex, and race]. [charts] (p. 76)

25. External cause of death by location [setting] of injury and employment [by industry group]. (p. 77)

26-27. Deaths due to external causes by county of injury; and from selected external causes by race and sex. (p. 79-80)

28. Infant deaths by age and cause. (p. 84)

29. Five leading causes of infant deaths [percent of total infant deaths by cause, 1972-76 and 1977-81 periods and 1982]. (p. 85)

30. Fetal death rates by race, 1975-82. (p. 87)

31. Resident infant and fetal deaths [by race], 1960-82. (p. 88)

32. Infant and neonatal deaths by county of residence, by race. (p. 89)

33-34. Fetal death by mother's county of residence, race, and age; and resident fetal deaths by cause, by weeks of gestation. (p. 90-91)

S7345–1.3: Marriage, Divorce, Abortion, Communicable Disease, and Miscellaneous Trends

MARRIAGE AND DIVORCE

[F] Crude marriage and divorce rates [1957-82]. [chart](p. 96)

35. Marriages by county of occurrence, by residence status of bride and groom. (p. 97)

36. County of marriage and number of licenses issued. (p. 98)

37-38. Marital terminations by county of residence of party to whom granted; and by number of children and age of mother. (p. 99-100)

ABORTION

39. Females obtaining induced abortions by age and race (percent). (p. 104)

40-44. Induced abortions: by State and South Dakota county of residence; and by race, and number of living children and previous abortions; all by age of patient. (p. 105-107)

COMMUNICABLE DISEASE

45. Reported cases of specified notifiable diseases, 1973-82. (p. 118)

46. Reported cases of selected notifiable diseases by month of report. (p. 119)

TRENDS

A1. Elderly population [age 60/over] by race, age group, and sex, 1960, 1970, and 1980. (p. 129)

A2. U.S. marriage and divorce rates, selected years 1950-81. (p. 131)

[A-B] Causes of infant deaths: Indian and white [by age]. (p. 132-133)

A3. Infant deaths by age, race, and cause without adjustment for underlying cause of premature birth. (p. 134)

S7355   SOUTH DAKOTA
Department of Labor

S7355–1   SOUTH DAKOTA LABOR BULLETIN
Monthly.   Approx. 10 p.
LC 72-17677.
SRI/MF/complete, shipped quarterly

Monthly report on South Dakota labor force, covering employment, unemployment, hours and earnings, characteristics of the insured unemployed, and unemployment insurance claims and payments. Includes State and local data, shown by industry.

Data are based on State records, and are published approximately 1 month after month of coverage.

Issues generally contain narrative summary and feature articles, occasionally with statistics; and 6 monthly tables, listed below.

Monthly tables appear in all issues. Additional tables are sometimes included showing summary or trend data for topics covered in monthly tables; these tables are not described. All other additional features with substantial statistical content are described, as they appear, under "Statistical Features." Nonstatistical features are not covered.

Availability: South Dakota Department of Labor, Labor Market Information Center, 607 N. Fourth St., Box 1730, Aberdeen SD 57401, †; SRI/MF/complete, shipped quarterly.

Issues reviewed during 1984: Sept. 1983-Aug. 1984 (D).

MONTHLY TABLES:

[Tables generally show data for month of coverage, previous month, and same month of previous year. Table sequence may vary.]

1. Labor force, employment, and unemployment [for U.S., State, Sioux Falls MSA, and by county].

2. South Dakota and Sioux Falls MSA (Minnehaha County) nonagricultural wage/salary employment [by industry division, with detail by major group for the State].

3. Hours and earnings of [manufacturing] production workers [for the State and Sioux Falls MSA].

4. CPI: all urban consumers [by major item, for total U.S.].

5. Characteristics of the insured unemployed–statewide [sex, race, age group, industry and occupational attachment, and duration of unemployment].

6. Selected Labor Dept activities–statewide [unemployment insurance initial claims, weeks claimed, benefit payments, and fund balance; and Job Service applicants, placements, and job openings].

STATISTICAL FEATURES:

S7355–1.501: Feb. 1984

COMMUTING PATTERNS OF SOUTH DAKOTA WORKERS

(p. 1-2) Article, with 2 charts and 1 table showing distribution of South Dakota commuters by commuting time and means of transportation, 1980; and employment in and outside State and county of residence (no date). Data are from U.S. Census Bureau.

S7355–1.502: May 1984

SOUTH DAKOTA OCCUPATIONAL TRENDS: 1970 TO 1980

(p. 1-2) Article, with 1 table showing employment increase for women in South Dakota, by selected occupation, 1970-80 period. Data are from Census Bureau.

DID YOU KNOW IN SOUTH DAKOTA

(p. 10) Brief article, with 1 table showing number of veterans in South Dakota, by period of service, 1980. Data are from Census Bureau.

S7355–1.503: June 1984

GROWTH IN TOURISM-RELATED EMPLOYMENT

(p. 1) Article, with 1 table showing South Dakota employment in 6 tourism-related industries, selected months 1976 and 1983.

S7380   SOUTH DAKOTA
Department of
Revenue

S7380–1   SOUTH DAKOTA DEPARTMENT OF REVENUE ANNUAL STATISTICAL REPORT, FY83
Annual. Nov. 30, 1983.
ii+199 p.
LC 76-649355.
SRI/MF/complete

Annual report, for FY83, on South Dakota Revenue Dept activities, including data on State tax revenues by source, and distribution to local governments, Indian tribes, and State funds or agencies. Also includes data on 1982-83 property valuations and taxes payable in 1983. Most data are shown by type of tax and local area.

Contains listings of contents, tables, and charts (p. i-ii); and 7 report sections, with descriptions of dept and division functions, and 1 chart and 15 tables listed below (p. 1-199).

Availability: South Dakota Department of Revenue, Kneip Bldg., 700 N. Illinois St., Pierre SD 57501-2276, ‡; SRI/MF/complete.

CHART AND TABLES:

S7380–1.1: Revenue and Distribution

I.1-I.2. Taxes [rate-base and description], and disposition of revenues generated by taxes administered by the Dept of Revenue. [tabular lists] (p. 3-10)

I.3. Dept of Revenue statement of receipts [for 29 types of taxes and fees], FY80-83. (p. 11)

IV.1. Sales/use tax collections remitted to municipalities and Indian tribes [by city and tribe, FY82-83]. (p. 16-17)

V.1. Motor fuel tax fund distribution by county highway/bridge funds, FY83. (p. 20)

VI.1. Sales/property tax refunds [and claims] for the elderly and disabled: [singles and households (chart); and] by county; FY83. (p. 22-23)

S7380–1.2: Property Valuations and Taxes

VII.1-VII.2. Summarization of valuations and amount of taxes for principal classifications of property, and local government ad valorem tax dollar distribution, [both for] taxes payable in 1983. (p. 26)

VII.3. Property taxes collected from all sources [for counties, schools, townships, and cities/towns, by county], 1981 taxes collected in 1982. (p. 27)

VII.4. 1982 amount of taxable valuation levies and taxes [by type], for municipalities payable in 1983 [and population, all by city]. (p. 29-45)

VII.5. 1983 valuations [for full/true real estate, and taxable railroad, utility, telephone, and telegraph assessments, by county]. (p. 46)

[VII.6] [Full/true value of real estate and utilities, by classification, 1982-83; taxable values, mill levies, and taxes for schools, cities, townships, and county purposes, 1982; and number, valuation, and taxes paid on mobile homes, 1982; table is repeated for each county, arranged in alphabetical order, and total State.] (p. 48-181)

VII.7. Unaudited financial report [shows current, fixed, and other assets; current and long-term liabilities; equity; revenue; and expenditures; by county with detail for selected cities and schools], 1982. (p. 182-192)

VII.8. County warrants and encumbrances [by function and county], 1982. (p. 193-198)

VII.9. Property tax replacement distribution [by county, 1st and 2nd half FY83]. (p. 199)

S7385   SOUTH DAKOTA
Department of
Social Services

S7385–1   SOUTH DAKOTA DEPARTMENT OF SOCIAL SERVICES Annual Statistical Report, FY83
Annual. [1983.]   iv+71 p.
ISSN 0147-6467.
LC 77-641772.
SRI/MF/complete

Annual report on South Dakota public welfare recipients and payments, by county, for FY83. Covers aid to dependent children (ADC); SSI for the aged, blind, and disabled; and medical assistance. Also includes data on mental health services, food stamps, low income energy assistance, assistance to Asian refugees, and Work Incentive Program (WIN) grant reductions.

Contains listing of contents, tables, and charts (p. i-iv); 27 tables, interspersed with 1 map and 12 trend charts, showing statewide data (p. 1-44); and 15 tables showing district and county data (p. 46-71). All tables are listed below.

Statistical Analysis Report, a monthly publication presenting similar but less detailed data, is also issued, but is not covered by SRI.

Availability: South Dakota Department of Social Services, Statistical Analysis and Reports, Management Information Office, Kneip Bldg., 700 N. Illinois St., Pierre SD 57501-2291, †; SRI/MF/complete.

TABLES:
[Unless otherwise noted, data are for FY83.]

S7385–1.1: Statewide Data

[Tables 5-26 usually include average monthly recipients and/or cost.]

ADULT SERVICES AND AGING

[Tables 1-2 include data for economically and socially needy and by race/ethnic group, including Indians, Asians, and Hispanics.]

1. Elderly nutrition projects [including total meals and/or average monthly persons served congregate and home delivered meals]. (p. 2)

2. Social services for the elderly [number of persons served by type of service]. (p. 3)

DEVELOPMENTAL DISABILITIES SERVICES

3. Office of developmental disabilities [recipients and payments, by type of service]. (p. 5)

4. Number of clients in adjustment training centers, community residential facilities, community habilitation facilities, and follow-along, by funding source, as of June 30, 1983; and admissions and terminations, FY83. (p. 6)

ASSISTANCE PAYMENTS AND FOOD STAMP PROGRAM

5. Total ADC and Asian refugee payments [to families, adults, and children]; and recipients and payments of optional supplements. (p. 8)

6-7. Reasons for closing cases on money payment status; [and] denials and other dispositions of applications, by reason; ADC program, FY82-83. (p. 12-13)

8-9. Grant reductions [and closures] for WIN, [monthly] FY83; and WIN ADC reductions [including cases closed, grants reduced, and dollars saved], FY79-83. (p. 14-15)

10. Recipients and payments of SSI and the mandatory supplement [for aged, blind, and disabled.] (p. 17)

11. Food stamp program participation [public and nonpublic assistance households and persons participating, and value of coupons]. (p. 19)

MEDICAL SERVICES

12-14. Total recipients eligible for medical utilization, by basis of eligibility; and ADC [adult and children] recipients and Asian refugees eligible for medical utilization; [all by whether receiving money or nonmoney payment, monthly]. (p. 21- 23)

15-16. Average number of recipients per month receiving medical care, and [amount of] medical care payments, by type of service [including Indian health service] and basis of eligibility. (p. 24-25)

17-18. Supplemental medical insurance premiums, by basis of eligibility, FY83; medical assistance payments from Title XIX funds for Office of Children, Youth, and Family Services foster care, FY82-83. (p. 30-31)

19-21. Medical assistance payments for families with dependent children recipients, FY82-83; and for Asian refugees and renal disease services, FY83. (p. 32-33)

22. Total number of recipients and payments of skilled nursing homes, intermediate care facilities, and crippled children's hospital, [by type of care and physical and/or mental health status]. (p. 34)

23-24. Medical assistance payments for aged, blind, and disabled recipients; and total number of recipients and payments of supplemental long-term care (SB-201); [both by type of care and physical and/or mental health status]. (p. 38-40)

25. Supplemental payments for long-term care of aged, blind, and disabled (SB-201) [aggregate persons, by type of care and mental health status]. (p. 41)

26. Medical assistance payments from Title XIX funds for Indian health services, [for aged, blind, disabled, ADC, and foster care cases]. (p. 42)

CHILD SUPPORT ENFORCEMENT

27. Child support enforcement collections [and average number of paying cases, by region]. (p. 44)

S7385–1.2: County and District Data
[Data are shown by county and/or office location, grouped by State district, with district totals. All tables, except tables 29-30 and 38-39, show number of recipients and amount of payments.]

CHILDREN, YOUTH, FAMILIES, AND ADULT AND AGING SERVICES

28. Purchased services [including adoption] provided by Office of Children, Youth, and Family Services. (p. 46)

29-30. Children/youth/family services, and adult services and aging: number of persons receiving direct services [by type]. (p. 47-48)

31. Homemaker service (purchased). (p. 49)

MENTAL HEALTH SERVICES, ADC, SSI, AND FOOD STAMPS

32. Developmentally disabled services provided to persons under Title XX [by type of service]. (p. 50)

33-37. ADC maintenance; and mandatory [supplement for SSI recipients] and SSI [for aged, blind, and disabled]; and optional supplement. (p. 54-61)

38. Food stamp program participation [number of households and persons participating by public assistance status, and value of coupons]. (p. 62)

MEDICAL AND ENERGY ASSISTANCE

39. Average number of [aged, blind, disabled, and ADC] recipients per month eligible for medical utilization. (p. 64)

40. Supplemental long-term care [for aged, blind, and disabled, by type of care]. (p. 66)

41. Medical [assistance] by type of service. (p. 68)

42. Low income energy assistance. (p. 70-71)

S7395   SOUTH DAKOTA
Supreme Court

S7395–1   BENCHMARK 1983: Annual Report of the South Dakota Unified Judicial System
Annual. Jan. 1984. 4+40 p.
LC 79-642739.
SRI/MF/complete

Annual report on South Dakota judicial system, including supreme and circuit court caseloads and case dispositions, for FY83. Circuit court data are shown by case type, county, and circuit.

Case types shown are criminal and civil, with detail for divorce, small claims, probate, adoption, mental illness, guardianship, juvenile, and driving while intoxicated case types.

Also includes data on judicial system finances, personnel, and services; and selected trends from FY79.

Data are from reports of clerks of court and court services officers.

Contains contents listing (2 p.); and report, including narrative, 18 charts, and 12 tables (p. 1-40).

Availability: South Dakota Supreme Court, State Court Administrator's Office, 500 E. Capitol Ave., Pierre SD 57501, †; SRI/MF/complete.

S7460   TENNESSEE
Department of Agriculture

S7460–1   TENNESSEE AGRICULTURAL STATISTICS, 1983 Annual Bulletin
Annual. Oct. 1983.
4+104 p. Bull. T-20.
LC 64-64265.
SRI/MF/complete

Annual report on Tennessee agricultural production and marketing, by commodity and/or county and district, 1970s-82, with some data for 1983 and trends from as early as 1945. Covers production, value, prices, and, as applicable, acreage, yield, stocks, inventory, and disposition, for field crop, fruit, vegetable, livestock, poultry, and dairy sectors.

Also includes data on farm income by source, and production expenses, and prices paid for production items, with selected comparison to Appalachian region; number, acreage, and value of farms; fertilizer consumption; and value of U.S. and Tennessee agricultural exports.

Data are compiled by the Tennessee Crop Reporting Service.

Contains contents listing (2 p.); 10 sections, with narrative summaries, 13 maps, 14 charts, and 96 tables (p. 1-102); and list of reports available from State Crop Reporting Service (p. 103-104).

Availability: Crop Reporting Board Publications, South Bldg., Rm. 5829, U.S. Department of Agriculture, Washington DC 20250, †; SRI/MF/complete.

S7480   TENNESSEE
Department of Correction

S7480–1   STATE OF TENNESSEE DEPARTMENT OF CORRECTION Annual Report, FY82-83
Annual. Mar. 8, 1984.
iv+58 p.
LC 59-31964.
SRI/MF/complete

Annual report, for FY83, on corrections in Tennessee. Presents data on prison inmate admissions by committing county, releases, sociodemographic characteristics, commitment offense, sentence length, intelligence quotient (IQ), military service, and job classifications; and caseloads and/or operations of community rehabilitation centers, adult and juvenile probation services, and juvenile institutions, group homes, and foster care.

Also includes data on funding and expenditures by corrections dept, including prison industries and farms; and interstate compact transactions.

Selected data are shown for individual facilities.

Contains contents listing (1 p.); policy statement, introduction, and highlights (p. i-iv, 1-10); 4 charts and 36 tables organized in 3 sections (p. 12-51); and staff directory (p. 52-58).

Availability: Tennessee Department of Correction, Planning and Research Section, State Office Bldg., 4th Floor, Nashville TN 37219, †; SRI/MF/complete.

S7490   TENNESSEE
Department of
Education

S7490–2   ANNUAL STATISTICAL REPORT of the Department of Education for the Scholastic Year Ending June 30, 1983, State of Tennessee
Annual. Jan. 1984. 171 p.
LC 58-27757.
SRI/MF/complete

Annual report, for 1982/83, on Tennessee public schools, presenting data on students, staff, finances, operations, and special programs, shown for the State and by county, city, and special school district.

Contents:

a. Contents and table listing, and lists of public school officers. (p. 7-20)

b. State special schools: 3-4 tables showing enrollment by county or by sex and level, graduates by sex, staff, allotment, and expenditures by object, for State agricultural institute, preparatory school, and schools for blind and deaf. (p. 21-27)

c. Vocational-technical education: 2 tables showing enrollment by delivery system and instructional area. (p. 28-29)

d. State data: 18 summary tables presenting data for grades K-12 and special schools. (p. 32-38)

e. County and school district data: 39 detailed tables, listed below. (p. 40-171)

Availability: Tennessee Department of Education, Research and Development Division, 100 Cordell Hull Bldg., Nashville TN 37219, †; SRI/MF/complete.

COUNTY AND SCHOOL DISTRICT TABLES:
[Tables show data by county, city, and special school district, for 1982/83 school year, unless otherwise noted.]

S7490–2.1: Schools and Staff

I. Number of schools [by grade span, and for vocational and special education]. (p. 40)

II. Training of teachers [highest level of education attained, and number of years at college, by sex]. (p. 43)

III-IV. Assignment of teachers, administrators, and members of boards of education; and other employees of boards of education; [by position, mostly by elementary and secondary level]. (p. 46-54)

V. Average annual salary of instructional personnel. (p. 56)

S7490–2.2: Graduates, Attendance, and Enrollment

VI. Number of 12th grade graduates [regular and equivalency diplomas, by sex]. (p. 58)

VII. Average daily membership [and] average daily attendance [in kindergarten, grades 1-12, and special education], and length of school term in days. (p. 61)

VIII. Net enrollment [by grade, and for special education, by sex]. (p. 64-75)

IX. Record of pupil progress [number enrolled, dropped from rolls, re-entered, promoted, and failing]. (p. 76)

S7490–2.3: Special Programs, Transportation, and Buildings

X. Programs of education other than K-12 run by local boards of education [Head Start, summer school, adult education, and other pupils]. (p. 79)

XI. Number of handicapped children receiving special education services [by type of handicap, and for intellectually gifted students]. (p. 82)

XII. Pupil transportation [including mileage, vehicles, pupils transported, drivers by sex and salaries, and accidents by resulting injury, fatality, and damage]. (p. 85)

XIII-XIV. Complete new buildings and additions to existing buildings contracted for between July 1, 1982 and June 30, 1983 [including type of building and addition, and costs]. (p. 88-90)

XV-XVI. Maintenance of buildings/grounds [including number of schools receiving repairs and funding, acreage and costs of new and existing sites, classrooms available, and school property value]. (p. 91-96)

S7490–2.4: Finances

XVII. Distribution of school funds [including State, Federal, and vocational funds, by object and program]. (p. 97-105)

XVIII-XXIV. Receipts [State revenue, Federal funds received through the State and received directly, county and city or special district revenue receipts, other revenue receipts, and nonrevenue receipts, all by detailed source]. (p. 106-126)

XXV. Summary of receipts. (p. 127)

XXVI-XXXVII. Expenditures [for administration, instruction, education for handicapped, vocational education, pupil transportation, operation and maintenance of plant, food service, fixed charges, other services, capital outlay, and debt service, all by detailed object]. (p. 130-165)

XXXVIII. Current expenditures [by object, and total per pupil in average daily attendance]. (p. 166-168)

XXXIX. Financial statement summary as of June 30, 1983 [assets, liabilities, reserves, and fund balance for general purpose, Federal projects, and capital projects]. (p. 169-71)

S7495   TENNESSEE
Department of
Employment Security

S7495–1   TENNESSEE COVERED EMPLOYMENT AND WAGES BY INDUSTRY, Statewide and by County, 1982
Annual. Jan. 1984.
3+205 p.
ISSN 0094-4734.
LC 74-645399.
SRI/MF/complete

Annual report, for 1982, on Tennessee employment and wages, by county and industry, for firms covered by unemployment insurance. Also includes number of firms reporting, unemployment insurance contributions, and average tax rates.

Data are compiled from contribution and wage reports submitted by employers to the Tennessee Dept of Employment Security.

Contains contents listing and introduction (3 p.); and 5 tables, listed below (p. 1-205).

Availability: Tennessee Department of Employment Security, Research and Statistics Division, 519 Cordell Hull Bldg., Nashville TN 37219, †; SRI/MF/complete.

TABLES:
[All data are for Tennessee, 1982.]

[1-3] Covered employment and wages, by industry [group, showing reporting units and employment, total and taxable wages, and unemployment insurance premiums due and tax rates], statewide, by county, [and for firms not reporting in any particular county]. (p. 1-203)

[4-5] County ranking by average weekly wage; and by annual average employment. (p. 204-205)

S7495–2   LABOR MARKET REPORT, Tennessee
Monthly. Approx. 10 p.
SRI/MF/complete, shipped quarterly

Monthly report on Tennessee labor force, employment, hours, and earnings, and employment service activities, by SMSA. Data on employment, hours, and earnings are shown by industry group. Reports are issued 2-4 months after month of coverage.

Contains narrative summary, and narrative analysis usually with 8 trend charts, and 5 monthly tables listed below.

Most monthly tables appear in all issues.

Availability: Tennessee Department of Employment Security, Research and Statistics Division, 519 Cordell Hull Bldg., Nashville TN 37219, †; SRI/MF/complete, shipped quarterly.

Issues reviewed during 1984: Sept. 1983-Aug. 1984 (D).

MONTHLY TABLES:
[Data are mostly for current month, preceding month, and same month of preceding year. Tables [2-4] are repeated for State and 4-5 SMSAs. Selected data for Tri-Cities SMSA are shown separately for Tennessee and Virginia portions.]

[1] Civilian labor force summary [by employment status, for State and SMSAs].

[2] Estimated nonagricultural employment [by major industry group].

[3] Employment security activities [new applications, testing, enrolled in training, nonagricultural placements, and counseling; totals, and for nonwhite, veteran, and female; for current and previous month; table may not appear in every issue].

[4] Hours and earnings of production workers [by major industry group; not shown for Tri-Cities SMSA].

[5] CPI for all urban consumers.

S7495–4   ANNUAL PLANNING INFORMATION, FY85, Tennessee
Annual. June 1984. 372 p.
SRI/MF/complete

Annual planning report, for FY85, identifying Tennessee population groups most in need of employment services. Includes data on population and labor force, employment by occupation and industry, and characteristics of unemployment insurance recipients and the work disabled; by service delivery area (SDA). Also includes employment and wage data by county. Most data are for 1984, with selected projections for 1990.

Data are from U.S. Census Bureau and Dept of Labor, Lawrence Berkeley Laboratory, and Tennessee Dept of Employment Security.

Contains contents listing (1 p.); introduction, and table listing (p. 1-2); narrative summary, 1 map, 2 charts, and 17 tables listed below, repeated for each of 14 SDAs (p. 3-356); and appendix, with notes, references, and directories of SDA offices and field analysts (p. 358-372).

For description of previous report, for FY83, see SRI 1982 Annual, under this number. No report for FY84 was published.

Availability: Tennessee Department of Employment Security, Research and Statistics Division, 519 Cordell Hull Bldg., Nashville TN 37219, †; SRI/MF/complete.

TABLES:

[Data by race often also include Hispanics.]

I-IV. Total population [1980 and 1984]; and population summary and male and female population [by race], 1984; [all by age].

V-IX. Total and civilian labor force [by age, employment status, race, and sex, 1984 with comparisons to 1980]; and civilian labor force [age] 16-21 [by employment status, and whether enrolled in school and high school graduate, all by race, 1980].

X. Nonagricultural wage/salary employment by industry [division and major manufacturing group, 1982-83].

XI. Projected employment by broad occupational category, [1984 and 1990].

XII-XIII. Unemployment insurance claimant characteristics and occupations [number of claimants, with distribution by sex, educational attainment, age, and race, and for veterans, welfare recipients, and handicapped; summary and by detailed occupation, various periods 1983-84].

XIV-XV. Education [attainment] by race; and poverty status by age [by race; 1980].

XVI. Work disabled [by sex, with detail for single head of household, 1980].

XVII. Average annual wage [and employment, and total wages, by county, for total and service industries, 1982].

S7505   TENNESSEE
Department of Finance and Administration

S7505–1   TENNESSEE COMPREHENSIVE ANNUAL FINANCIAL REPORT for the Year Ended June 30, 1983
Annual. Dec. 21, 1983.
3+viii+87 p.
SRI/MF/complete

Annual report on financial condition of Tennessee State government, for FY83, presenting assets and liabilities, revenue by source, expenditures by function and/or object, and fund balances; for all, general, special revenues, debt service, capital projects, enterprise, internal service, trust/agency, and college/university funds.

Also includes data on general fund expenditures by dept; budgeted vs. actual revenues and expenditures; selected debt ratios; bond repayment schedules; and 1970s trends in State finances and selected economic indicators.

Economic indicators include GSP, earnings, manufacturing gross product, and employment, all by industry; personal and farm income; industrial expansions and capital investments; top 50 industrial employers, with number of plants; population; bank deposits; IRS collections; retail sales; building permit and property values; and educational enrollments, by level and post-secondary institution.

Data are compiled by the Finance and Administration Dept primarily from internal records and reports of other State agencies.

Contains contents listing (3 p.); introduction, with text data and 7 charts (p. i-viii); 52 financial statements (p. 1-72); and statistical and economic data sections, with 26 tables (p. 73-87).

The annual *Report of the Treasurer of the State of Tennessee,* presenting less comprehensive data on State treasury finances and retirement funds, is also available from the Treasury Department, State Capitol, Nashville TN 37219. Report is not covered by SRI.

Availability: Tennessee Department of Finance and Administration, Rm. 314, Andrew Jackson State Office Bldg., Nashville TN 37219, †; SRI/MF/complete.

S7507   TENNESSEE
Department of Financial Institutions

S7507–1   1983 TENTH ANNUAL REPORT, State of Tennessee Department of Financial Institutions
Annual. Apr. 11, 1984.
iv+113 p.
LC 78-642408.
SRI/MF/complete

Annual report on financial condition of Tennessee State-chartered banks, credit unions, and savings and loan assns, presenting assets, liabilities, income, and expenses, as of Dec. 31, 1983, with selected trends from 1960. Data on assets and liabilities are generally shown by institution, with selected rankings.

Also includes data on bank operating ratios; bank holding company assets and deposits; bank deposits and population data per office and bank, by county and SMSA; and credit union membership trends, including average loan amounts.

Most data are from required year-end call reports submitted by individual institutions.

Contains contents listing and organizational chart (p. iii-iv); narrative overview with list of bank status changes, including changes in bank capital stock (p. 1-17); bank profiles, with 11 tables (p. 18-74); list of credit union status changes and profiles, with 5 tables (p. 77-100); list of savings and loan status changes and profiles, with 3 tables (p. 102-108); and 4 charts (p. 110-113).

Prior to 1983 edition, report was issued by Tennessee Dept of Banking and was described in SRI under S7465-1.

Availability: Tennessee Department of Financial Institutions, James K. Polk State Office Bldg., 505 Deaderick St., 2nd Floor, Nashville TN 37219, †; SRI/MF/complete.

S7520   TENNESSEE
Department of Health and Environment

S7520–1   TENNESSEE MORBIDITY STATISTICS, 1982, Including Summary Tables for 1973-82
Annual. June 1984. v+23 p.
ISSN 0361-5324.
LC 74-647396.
SRI/MF/complete, current & previous year reports

Annual report on the occurrence in Tennessee of 36 diseases requiring notification of State health authorities, 1982, with trends from 1973. Includes number and/or rate of cases, by disease, age, race, and county. Data are based on reports to the Tennessee Health and Environment Dept.

Contains listings of contents, tables, charts, and diseases (p. iii-v); introduction and narrative, with 1 map, 4 charts, and 2 summary tables (p. 1-11); and 4 detailed tables (p. 12-23).

This is the 53rd annual report.

Previous report, for 1981, was also reviewed in 1984 and is also available on SRI microfiche under this number [Annual. May 1983. vii+47 p. †]. Report for 1981 is substantially similar in content, but also includes data by sex and State health region.

Report for 1980 is described in SRI 1982 Annual under S7563-1. Issuing agency name has changed from Tennessee Dept of Public Health.

Availability: Tennessee Department of Health and Environment, Information and Referral Unit, State Center for Health Statistics, C1-136 Cordell Hull Bldg., Nashville TN 37219-2505, †; SRI/MF/complete.

S7535   TENNESSEE Department of Human Services

S7535–1   TENNESSEE DEPARTMENT OF HUMAN SERVICES STATISTICS

Monthly. Approx. 30 p.
ISSN 0361-896X.
LC 76-641878.
SRI/MF/complete, shipped quarterly

Monthly report on Tennessee public welfare program caseloads, recipients, services, and payments, covering AFDC, food stamps, medical assistance, and social services. Most data are shown by county.

Report is compiled by Research and Statistics Division of State Dept of Human Services, and is issued 3-5 months after month of coverage.

Issues contain listings of contents, tables, and charts; narrative review; 14 monthly tables, listed below; and 3 trend charts.

A less detailed annual report, based on the monthly report and containing additional data on public assistance funding and expenditures, is also available from the issuing agency, but is not covered by SRI.

Monthly tables appear in all issues.

Availability: Tennessee Department of Human Services, Research and Statistics Section, 1720 West End Ave., Rm. 501, Nashville TN 37203, †; SRI/MF/complete, shipped quarterly.

Issues reviewed during 1984: Aug. 1983-June 1984 (D).

MONTHLY TABLES:
[Data are shown for month of coverage, generally by county.]

1. AFDC: applications on hand [number received, and disposition].

2-3. AFDC: reason for need (approvals) and reason for rejection [State only].

4. AFDC: applications pending, by length of time.

5-8. AFDC: approvals and closings; cases reviewed [total and per worker]; cases receiving money payments [families, total individuals, and children]; and amount of money payments.

9. AFDC: reason for closing [State only].

10. Food stamps [household and individual] certifications and participants, and value of coupons.

11-12. Medical assistance applications [received, disposed of, and pending]; and medical assistance approvals and caseload [shown vari-

ously for Medicaid-only, and medically and/ or categorically needy aged, blind, disabled, and women and/or children].

13. Social service work load report [recipients by type of service, for general and protective services, foster care, adoption, and information/referral, by county and State region].

14. Nursing home care (SSI) activity [income certification requests completed and cases terminated, and total cases active during month].

S7560   TENNESSEE Planning Office

S7560–1   ECONOMIC REPORT TO THE GOVERNOR OF THE STATE OF TENNESSEE on the State's Economic Outlook

Annual. For individual publication data, see below.
SRI/MF/complete

Annual report on Tennessee economic indicators, 1973-92, including employment and earnings by major industry group, energy consumption and prices, GSP by sector, agricultural cash receipts, and other measures of economic performance, with selected U.S. comparisons.

Prepared by Center for Business and Economic Research, University of Tennessee. Data are primarily from Tennessee Econometric Model.

Report is issued in 2 parts, described below. Part I is primarily a narrative analysis. Part II is a companion volume presenting detailed statistics under the title *Economic Forecasts for Tennessee.*

Availability: Part I: Tennessee Planning Office, 1800 James K. Polk State Office Bldg., 505 Deaderick St., Nashville TN 37219; part II: University of Tennessee, Center for Business and Economic Research, Knoxville TN 37996-4170, †; SRI/MF/complete.

S7560–1.1: Part I: Narrative Summary

[Annual. Nov. 1983. xi+50 p. SRI/MF/ complete.]

Contains foreword, and listings of contents, tables, and charts (p. v-xi); executive summary (p. 1-5); and narrative outlook, with 11 charts and 4 tables primarily summarizing statistics covered in Part II, but also including data on Federal deficits and interest rates, and Tennessee and U.S. nonfarm employment distribution by industry division, various periods 1981-92 (p. 7-50).

S7560–1.2: Part II: Detailed Statistics

[Annual. Nov. 1983. xiii+119 p. SRI/MF/ complete.]

Contains table listing (p. v-vii), executive summary (p. ix-xiii), and forecast and historical data grouped in 4 sections, each preceded by a table listing, with a total of 112 tables listed below. (p. 1-117)

TABLES:
[Data are for Tennessee, unless otherwise noted.]

QUARTERLY ECONOMETRIC MODEL FORECAST
[Data are shown for 1982-84 and quarterly 1983-3rd quarter 1985. Tables 10-29 show data by durable and nondurable goods major manufacturing industry group.]

1. Selected economic indicators [U.S. GNP and personal consumption deflator index; and Tennessee and U.S. personal income, nonagricultural and manufacturing jobs, manufacturing weekly hours, and unemployment rate]. (p. 2)

2. Comparative manufacturing indicators [Tennessee and U.S. durable and nondurable manufacturing jobs and weekly hours]. (p. 3)

3. Personal income [includes wage/salaries, proprietor income, transfer payments, and social insurance contributions]. (p. 4)

4-9. Nonagricultural employment [by industry division, and durable and nondurable goods major manufacturing industry group]. (p. 5-10)

10-15. Average hourly earnings, production workers [shown in constant 1972 seasonally adjusted and unadjusted dollars, and in current dollars.] (p. 11-16)

16-23. Person-hours per week and average weekly hours [seasonally adjusted and unadjusted.] (p. 17-24)

24-29. Average weekly earnings [shown in constant 1972 seasonally adjusted and unadjusted dollars, and in current dollars.] (p. 25-30)

30-32. Average annual wage/salary rate [by industry division, shown in 1972 seasonally adjusted and unadjusted dollars, and in current dollars.] (p. 31-33)

33-34. Civilian labor force [by employment status, and labor force participation rate, seasonally adjusted and unadjusted.] (p. 34-35)

ANNUAL ECONOMETRIC MODEL FORECAST
[Data are for 1983-92.]

1. Selected indicators [includes Tennessee population; and Tennessee and U.S. GSP or GNP, personal income, employment, unemployment rate, and manufacturing output per employee]. (p. 38)

2-16. GSP (current and 1972 dollars), [nonfarm] employment, and average annual wage/ salary (current and 1972 dollars), [all by industry division, and durable and nondurable goods major manufacturing industry group]. (p. 39-53)

17. Personal income by components [including wages/salaries, proprietor and property income, transfer payments, social insurance contributions, and IRS tax collections]. (p. 54)

18. Retail sales [automotive and nonautomotive in current and 1972 dollars; and motor vehicle registrations]. (p. 55)

19. Energy consumption [for coal, gasoline, and fuel oil, and by consuming sector for electricity and natural gas]. (p. 56)

20. Energy prices [for coal, and by consuming sector for electricity and natural gas]. (p. 57)

21. Commercial banks and savings and loans assets and liabilities. (p. 58)

22. Agricultural output [value in current and 1972 dollars; cash receipts from crops, meat animals, dairy products, and poultry/eggs; expenses; and farm employment]. (p. 59)

QUARTERLY ECONOMETRIC MODEL HISTORICAL DATA

1-34. [Quarterly forecast tables 1-34 (listed above, p. 1-35) are repeated for 1980-82 and 2nd quarter 1980-4th quarter 1982.] (p. 62-95)

ANNUAL ECONOMETRIC MODEL HISTORICAL DATA

1-22. [Annual forecast tables 1-22 (listed above, p. 38-59) are repeated for 1973-82.] (p. 98-119)

S7560–3   CHANGES IN TENNESSEE: What the 1980 Census Data Show
Monograph.   Apr. 1984.
x+131 p.
LC 84-622350.
SRI/MF/complete

By Patricia D. Postma et al. Report analyzing Tennessee population and socioeconomic changes, based primarily on data from 1970 and 1980 U.S. Censuses of Population and Housing. Includes population and housing characteristics, labor force, income and poverty, mortality, marriage, and fertility, with selected detail by locale.

Contains preface and listing of contents, tables, and charts (p. iii-x); and 5 chapters arranged in 2 sections, with narrative analysis, 6 charts, and 42 tables described below (1-131).

Availability: University of Tennessee: Center for Business and Economic Research, Glocker Building, Suite 100, Knoxville TN 37996-4170, $7.50; SRI/MF/complete.

TABLES:
[Data are for Tennessee, with occasional comparisons to U.S. Data generally are shown for 1970 and 1980, or for 1980 with change from 1970, with a few earlier trends.]

POPULATION AND DEMOGRAPHIC CHANGE

a. Population: by urban-rural status; by size of place; for MSAs, by component county and city; by county; by place of residence compared to 5 years earlier; and for in- and out-migrants, by State of former residence or destination. 8 tables. (p. 5-22)

b. Socioeconomic characteristics: households, by composition; population, including percent black, under age 18, and age 65/older; median age; families; total and single-person households; educational attainment; labor force participation, including detail for women and trends by occupational group; workers employed outside county; per capita and median family income; and poverty status, for all and female-headed families, all individuals, and blacks; mostly by county, with some data by MSA. 16 tables. (p. 26-61)

c. Housing characteristics: number of units, by occupancy status, tenure, age (including detail for selected cities on housing built since 1970), and number of units in structure; units with no phone, no automobile, 1.01/more persons per room, and no/limited bathroom facilities; and median housing value, owner monthly cost (with and without mortgage), and rent; with selected detail by county. 9 tables. (p. 63-84)

MORTALITY, MARRIAGE, AND FERTILITY TRENDS

d. Life expectancy at birth; infant mortality rates; and marriage, divorce, widowhood, and remarriage patterns; all by sex. 6 tables. (p. 86-93)

e. Fertility rates, by age group, development district, and county. 3 tables. (p. 107-125)

**S7563   TENNESSEE
Department of
Public Health**

S7563–2   ANNUAL BULLETIN OF VITAL STATISTICS for the Year 1979, Tennessee
Annual.   [1983.]   78 p.
LC 34-6645.
SRI/MF/complete

Annual report on Tennessee vital statistics, covering population, births, deaths by cause, marriages, divorces, and abortions, 1979. Includes data by race, sex, age, city, county, and health dept region, and selected trends from 1950. Data are primarily from reports filed with the Division of Vital Records as of Mar. 31, 1980.

Contains listings of contents, tables, and charts (p. 3-6); narrative analysis, including definitions and description of reporting criteria, 1 map, 10 charts, and 37 text tables (p. 7-26); and 12 detailed tables (p. 27-78). All tables are listed below.

This is the 53rd report. Previous report, for 1978, is described in SRI 1982 Annual, under this number.

Availability: Tennessee Department of Public Health, Cordell Hull Bldg., Nashville TN 37219-2505, †; SRI/MF/complete.

TABLES:
[Tables show resident data for Tennessee, 1979, unless otherwise noted. Rates are expressed as per 100,000 population, unless otherwise noted.
Causes of death are shown according to the *9th Revision, International Classification of Diseases.*]

S7563–2.1: Text Tables
[Data by type of county are for metro, intermediate, and rural.]

INTRODUCTORY DATA

1. Cities of 10,000 or more population for counties, 1970. [list] (p. 10)

2. Birth and death rates and rate of natural increase per 1,000 population, by race. (p. 12)

BIRTHS

3-4. Number of births, by month with average per day; and number and percentage of births according to attendant [physician, nurse/midwife, midwife, and other], by race. (p. 12-13)

5-6. Percentage of births occurring in hospitals: by race, 1960-79; and by type of county, by race, 1979. (p. 13)

7-8. Number and percentage of births: according to weight group, by race, and according to age of mother, by race of child. (p. 13-14)

9. Live births by number of prenatal visits, by month of pregnancy prenatal care began, by race of child. (p. 14)

10. Percentage of live births reported to be illegitimate, by race, 1950-79. (p. 14)

DEATHS

11-12. Number and percentage of fetal deaths, according to weight group and cause, by race. (p. 15)

13-14. Number of induced abortions: according to race of woman, with ratios per 1,000 recorded live births, 1974-79; and number and percent distribution according to age and race of woman, 1979. (p. 16)

15. Age-adjusted death rates per 1,000 population, by race, 1960-79. (p. 16)

16-17. Death rates per 1,000 population: by race, sex, and age; and by type of county, by race. (p. 17)

18. Number of deaths by month with average per day. (p. 17)

19. Infant mortality rates per 1,000 live births, by type of county, by race. (p. 18)

20-21. Number of infant deaths, by cause and by age at death, with rates per 1,000 live births, [all] by race. (p. 18)

22-24. Principal causes of death with rates: [total], by sex, and for 5 age groups. (p. 19-21)

25. Number of deaths from malignant neoplasms according to primary site with rates, by race. (p. 21)

26-28. Death rates for malignant neoplasms, for diseases of heart, and for accidents; by race, sex and age. (p. 22-23)

29-30. Number of deaths from accidents and adverse effects: according to type of accident, with rates; and by class of accident with percentages. (p. 23)

31. Death rates for accidents and adverse effects according to class of accident, by age. (p. 24)

32-33. Number of deaths: from home accidents according to type of accident, with rates, by race; and from motor vehicle accidents by type of accident, with percentages. (p. 24-25)

MARRIAGES AND DIVORCES

34-36. Number of marriages recorded: and persons married, with rates, 1970-79; by month with average per day, 1979; and according to previous marital status of bride and groom; 1979. (p. 25-26)

37. Number of divorces recorded and persons divorced, with rates per 1,000 population, 1970-79. (p. 26)

S7563–2.2: Detailed Tables
[Tables I-VIII and XI show data by race. Data by city are for cities of 10,000 or more population.]

I. Population; births and deaths with rates per 1,000 population; and fetal, infant, and neonatal deaths, with rates per 1,000 live births; recorded and resident data, 1960-79. (p. 27)

II-III. Deaths from important causes, and from selected causes by sex, with rates, 1960-79. (p. 28-33)

IV. Deaths according to cause, by sex and age. (p. 34)

V. Deaths according to 211 selected causes, with rates. (p. 37)

VI-VIII. Births, infant deaths, fetal deaths, induced terminations of pregnancy, and deaths by cause with rates, for the State and for counties, for cities, and for health dept regions. (p. 39-73)

IX. Births and deaths in hospitals with percentages, for cities, and for counties inclusive of cities, resident and recorded data. (p. 74)

X. Selected recorded data regarding [live] births [and] fetal deaths [in hospital, and out of hospital attended by physician, midwife, or other], and [total, neonatal, and infant] deaths, for cities, and for counties inclusive of cities. (p. 75)

XI. Number of induced terminations of pregnancy, by county, resident and recorded data. (p. 77)

XII. Selected data on marriages and divorces by recorded county, and on persons married by [race and] resident county. (p. 78)

S7565   TENNESSEE
Public
Service Commission

S7565–1   ANNUAL REPORT, TENNESSEE PUBLIC SERVICE COMMISSION, for the Year 1983
Annual. Dec. 31, 1983.
1+94 p.
LC 9-14680.
SRI/MF/complete

Annual report, for 1983, on regulatory activities of the Tennessee Public Service Commission, with property valuation, and financial and operating data for industries within the commission's jurisdiction. Industries covered include electric and telephone companies and cooperatives; and gas, pipeline, water/sewerage, bus, truck, railroad, railroad car, airline, barge, mobile phone, and other types of companies.

Includes assessed property values, by industry, individual company, county, and city, 1983, with summary trends from 1877; and plant value, revenues, expenses, and customers, shown for gas, water, telephone, and radio common carrier (mobile phone) industries, 1978-82.

Also includes commission disbursements and revenues; number of companies regulated; and rate reviews, consumer complaints, and other types of regulatory activities.

Data are from commission records.

Contains contents listing (1 p.); commission information and report, interspersed with text data and 10 tables (p. 1-45); and 4 tables on property valuation (p. 46-94).

Availability: Tennessee Public Service Commission, Cordell Hull Bldg., Nashville TN 37219, †; SRI/MF/complete.

S7580   TENNESSEE
Office of the
Secretary of
State

S7580–2   TENNESSEE PUBLIC LIBRARY STATISTICS, July 1, 1982-June 30, 1983
Annual. [1984.] ii+43 p.
LC 58-62849.
SRI/MF/complete

Annual report, for FY83, on Tennessee public library collections, finances, services, and staff, for metro and local libraries, regional centers, and Tennessee Regional Library for the Blind and Physically Handicapped. Data are compiled from individual library reports.

Contains contents listing (i-ii); 4 summary tables (p. 1-2); and 6 sections with 30 detailed tables, described below (p. 3-43).

Availability: Tennessee State Library and Archives, Development and Extension Services Section, 403 Seventh Ave., N., Nashville TN 37219, †; SRI/MF/complete.

TABLES:

[Data for libraries serving the general public cover population and area served, number of libraries/branches, book and nonbook holdings and circulation, bookmobiles, professional and nonprofessional staff, income by source, expenditures by object, and other topics as noted below.]

a. Metro and city libraries, by library; also including area resource center expenditures and services. 10 tables. (p. 3-12)

b. Regional centers and local libraries, by region and county; also including bookmobile operating data; books withdrawn, lost, and paid; and reference and loan services. 17 tables. (p. 13-38)

c. Tennessee Regional Library for the Blind and Physically Handicapped, including patrons served by service type, region, and county; and materials circulation. 3 tables. (p. 40-43)

S7585   TENNESSEE
Supreme Court

S7585–1   1983 ANNUAL REPORT: Office of the Executive Secretary, Tennessee State Supreme Court
Annual. [1984.] 150 p.
LC 73-640219.
SRI/MF/complete

Annual report, for 1983, on Tennessee judicial system, including trial and appellate court caseloads and case dispositions. Covers supreme, appeals, circuit, chancery, administrative hearing appeal, law/equity, and general sessions courts. Includes trial court data by case type and county, and selected trends from 1964.

Case types shown are criminal and civil, for most courts, with additional detail for domestic relations (including adoption), damages/torts, workers compensation, probate, administrative hearing appeal, contempt proceeding, mental health, tax, trust, and other case types.

Contains contents listing (1 p.); 9 report sections, with narrative summaries, and 2-4 tables repeated for each court type and jurisdiction (p. 1-134); and glossary, 2 tables, and listings of court officials and courts (p. 135-150).

Availability: Tennessee Supreme Court, Executive Secretary's Office, Judicial Information System, Rm. 415, Supreme Court Bldg., Nashville TN 37219, †; SRI/MF/complete.

S7630   TEXAS
Department of
Agriculture

S7630–1   1982 TEXAS COUNTY STATISTICS
Annual. Aug. 1983.
3+273 p. Bull. No. 214.
LC 72-622638.
SRI/MF/complete

Annual report on Texas agricultural production, marketing, and income, 1981-82. Most data are shown by crop reporting district and county.

Report covers production and, as applicable, acreage, yield, marketings, and inventory, for field crop, vegetable, fruit and nut, livestock, dairy, and poultry sectors, by commodity.

Also includes income from marketing and government payments; detail for irrigated crops; farm/ranch and pasture/rangeland acreage; and selected agricultural rankings for Texas and other leading States.

Data are compiled by Texas Crop and Livestock Reporting Service.

Contains map, foreword, and contents listing (3 p.); State agricultural rankings (p. 2-3); and 5 basic tables, repeated for the State and each district and county (p. 4-273).

Availability: Commissioner, Texas Department of Agriculture, PO Box 12847, Austin TX 78711; or Agricultural Statistician, Texas Crop and Livestock Reporting Service, PO Box 70, Austin TX 78767, †; SRI/MF/complete.

S7655   TEXAS
Comptroller of
Public Accounts

S7655–2   STATE OF TEXAS 1983 ANNUAL FINANCIAL REPORT, Fiscal Year Ended Aug. 31, 1983
Annual. For individual publication data, see below.
LC 76-648987.
SRI/MF/complete

Annual report on financial condition of Texas State government, for FY83. Report is issued in 2 volumes, described below.

A much less detailed report, *Summary of the Annual Financial Report,* is also available from the comptroller, but is not covered in SRI.

Availability: Texas Comptroller of Public Accounts, Planning and Research Office, 111 E. 17th St., Rm. 806, Austin TX 78774, †; SRI/MF/complete.

S7655-2.1: Financial Summary Report

[Annual. Nov. 7, 1983. vii+164 p. SRI/MF/complete.]

Annual report presenting summary overview of Texas State government financial transactions, including revenues by source, expenditures by object and agency, and cash balances by fund. Covers specific operating/disbursing, constitutional, trust, Federal, tax clearance, petty cash, and suspense funds.

Also includes data on State government and total nonagricultural employment; bonded debt; investment accounts; Foundation School Program budget and expenditures; population and personal income; oil and natural gas production and prices; and gross sales; with selected data by SMSA and trends from 1970.

Contains listings of contents, tables and charts, and introduction (p. iii-vii); brief economic overview, with 8 tables (p. 1-8); and report, with 12 charts and 54 financial tables (p. 9-164).

S7655-2.2: Detailed Report

[Annual. [1984.] ix+468 p. SRI/MF/complete.]

Annual report presenting revenues by source, expenditures by object, and cash balances, for over 300 Texas State government fund accounts, FY83.

Contains contents listing and introduction (p. i-ix); and cash condition summary and 1 extended table (p. 1-468).

S7657   TEXAS
Coordinating Board,
Texas College and
University System

S7657-1   STATISTICAL SUPPLEMENT, FY83, Coordinating Board, Texas College and University System
Annual.   Jan. 1984.
vi+147 p.
LC 74-648444.
SRI/MF/complete

Annual statistical supplement, for 1983, on Texas higher education, presenting data on individual public and private universities, colleges, and junior colleges. Includes statistics on enrollment, faculty, curricula, funding for education, and student aid, mostly 1982-83, with selected data for FY84-85, and trends from 1953.

Contains foreword, and contents listing (p. iii-vi); lists of institutions (p. 1-3); and 54 tables, listed below (p. 7-147).

Separate reports with data on research expenditures, funding formulas, degrees awarded, and degree program requests are also available from the issuing agency but are not covered by SRI.

Availability: Texas Coordinating Board, Texas College and University System, Publications Office, PO Box 12788, Austin TX 78711, †; SRI/MF/complete.

TABLES:

S7657-1.1: Student Enrollments and Faculty Data

[Tables [1-17] show data for fall semester. Tables [2-12] and [15-21] show data by institution. Data by ethnic origin are shown by race and for Hispanics, Asians, Indians, and aliens.]

STUDENTS

[Tables [1-14] show data for independent and/or public senior colleges/universities and junior colleges. Tables [1-10] include data for other professional, health-related, and/or medical and dental schools.]

[1] Summary of headcount enrollment [by type of institution, including public technical institutes], 1978-82. (p. 7)

[2-4] Headcount enrollment, 1978-82. (p. 8-14)

[5-10] Headcount enrollment by [academic] classification, ethnic origin, and sex, 1982. (p. 15-54)

[11-12] Resident and nonresident [and foreign] students, 1982. (p. 55-57)

[13-14] Texas resident students by county of origin; and out-of-State enrollments [by State/territory of origin]; 1982. (p. 58-61)

FACULTY

[Tables [18-20] show data for public senior colleges/universities.]

[15-17] Faculty headcount: [total] and tenured, by [academic] rank, public senior colleges/universities; [and totals for] public community junior colleges; [all] by ethnic origin and sex, 1982. (p. 65-80)

[18] Faculty salaries [averages], all [academic] ranks, 1978/79-1982/83. (p. 81)

[19] Faculty salaries [and ranges], by [academic] rank, (9 months) 1982/83. (p. 82)

[20] Student-faculty ratios, 1978/79-1982/83. (p. 85)

[21] Faculty salaries [and ranges], public junior colleges, (9 months) 1982/83. (p. 86)

S7657-1.2: Credit Hours and Physical Plant

[Tables [1-9] and [11-17] show data by institution.]

CREDIT HOURS

[1-8] Semester credit hours by [degree] level; undergraduate, master's, doctoral, and special professional semester credit hours, by program; and fall, spring, and summer semester credit hours [by degree level; all for] public senior colleges/universities, FY83. (p. 89-102)

[9] Semester credit hour enrollments, by curriculum area, public community junior colleges, fall 1982. (p. 103-108)

PHYSICAL FACILITIES

[Tables [10-12] show data for public senior colleges/universities and junior colleges. Tables [10-13] also show data for Texas A&M University System agricultural and engineering services, health-related units, and other agencies. Table [12] includes data for independent senior and junior institutions.]

[10] Investment in physical plant [by type of institution], FY82. (p. 111)

[11-13] Investment in physical plant [and value of land, buildings, other improvements, construction in progress, and equipment], FY82. (p. 112-114)

[14-17] Net assignable facilities space, by function in square feet, as of Oct. 31, 1983. (p. 115-119)

S7657-1.3: Financial Data

LEGISLATIVE APPROPRIATIONS

[1-2] Legislative appropriations, all funds and general revenue, agencies of higher education [by agency, FY84-85]. (p. 123-129)

[3] Legislative appropriations for educational and general purposes, by function, public senior colleges/universities [FY84-85]. (p. 130)

[4-5] Biennial legislative appropriations per FTE student, all funds and general revenue, public senior colleges/universities [1953/55-1983/85]. (p. 131-132)

STUDENT AID

[Tables [6-16] show data for or through FY83.]

[6-7] Hinson-Hazlewood College Student Loan Act: summary of loan transactions [by type of public and independent institution], and statement of collections [by status of account]. (p. 135-137)

[8-13] Hinson-Hazelwood College Student Loan Act: institutional status of accounts with payments seriously past due [by type of institution, and by individual institution, for public and independent senior colleges/universities and junior colleges, and other agencies of higher education]. (p. 138-144)

[14-16] Tuition equalization grants, State student incentive grants, and Texas public educational/State student incentive grants programs: [summaries of grants administered]. (p. 145-147)

S7660   TEXAS
Department of
Corrections

S7660-1   TEXAS DEPARTMENT OF CORRECTIONS 1983 Fiscal Year Statistical Report
Annual.   [1984.]   x+146 p.
SRI/MF/complete

Annual report, for FY83, on corrections in Texas, presenting data on the prison population, including inmate admissions, releases, demographic characteristics, criminal background, commitment offense, and sentence length. Includes summary data by institution and by SMSA of conviction and residence.

Also includes data on corrections dept finances; inmate educational and vocational enrollments; intelligence quotient (IQ) of inmate population; detail for inmates paroled and discharged under mandatory supervision, including average time served; and selected trends from 1967.

Contains preface, and contents and table listing (p. ii-x); introduction (p. 2-6); and 10 statistical sections, with 3 charts and 126 tables (p. 8-146).

This is the 7th annual report.

Availability: Texas Department of Corrections, Management Services, Box 99, Huntsville TX 77340, †; SRI/MF/complete.

S7670   TEXAS
Education Agency

S7670–1   STATISTICAL BRIEF, Texas, 1983/84
Annual series. For individual publication data, see below.
SRI/MF/complete

Annual series of reports, each presenting data on 1 aspect of Texas elementary and secondary education. Topics include enrollment and attendance, revenues and expenditures, professional personnel and salaries, and Foundation School Program (FSP) providing State aid to needy school districts.

Data are compiled by the Texas Education Agency (TEA).

Each report contains contents and table listings, and introduction; summary discussion, with charts and text tables; 5 detailed tables, listed below; and addenda, including definitions, technical notes, and samples of data collection forms.

There are gaps in time series coverage for some reports, due to publication delays.

Report for 1983/84 reviewed during 1984 is described below. Reports for 1981/82 and 1982/83 are covered in SRI under S7670-2 and S7670-3, respectively.

Availability: Texas Education Agency, Publications Distribution Office, 201 E. 11th St., Austin TX 78701; SRI/MF/complete.

DETAILED TABLES:

1. TEA ANALYZE report categories [data shown by district average daily attendance (ADA) grouping; urban, suburban, and rural classification; average market property value; and tax rate; for regular FSP districts only].

2. Education Service Center (ESC) regions [data shown by 20 regions, for all public school districts].

3. Regular FSP districts [data shown by district, for all public school districts eligible for State funding through the FSP, with estimates for county totals].

4. Special and State schools [data shown by district, for public school districts created by special legislative act (including schools associated with military bases and Masonic Home) or administered by a State agency (Mental Health and Retardation/Youth Council/Board of Education/Dept of Corrections)].

5. Historical State totals [trends for all school districts].

REPORT:

S7670–1.1: Fall Survey of Students in Texas Public Elementary and Secondary School Districts, 1983/84
[Annual.   Apr. 1984.   vi+59 p.   Series SB84FSY. $2.00. SRI/MF/complete.]

Detailed tables show enrollment by race/ethnic group (white, Hispanic, black, Asian, and American Indian), 1983/84, with trends from 1970/71.

Text tables show selected summary and analytical data based on the detailed tables; and enrollment by sex and race/ethnic group, both by grade level, 1983/84.

For description of report for 1982/83, see SRI 1983 Annual under S7670-3.1.

S7670–2   STATISTICAL BRIEF, Texas, 1980/81-1981/82
Annual series. For individual publication data, see below.
SRI/MF/complete

Annual series of reports, each presenting data on 1 aspect of Texas elementary and secondary education. Topics include enrollment and attendance, revenues and expenditures, professional personnel and salaries, and Foundation School Program (FSP) providing State aid to needy school districts. Other topics may be added in the future.

Data are compiled by the Texas Education Agency (TEA).

Each report contains contents listing and introduction; summary discussion, with charts and text tables; table listing and 5 detailed tables, listed below; and addenda, including definitions, technical notes, and samples of data collection forms.

There are gaps in time series coverage for some reports, due to publication delays. Report for 1981/82, reviewed during 1984, is described below. Reports for 1982/83 and 1983/84 are covered in SRI under S7670-3 and S7670-1, respectively.

Availability: Texas Education Agency, Publications Distribution Office, 201 E. 11th St., Austin TX 78701; SRI/MF/complete.

DETAILED TABLES:

1. TEA ANALYZE Report Categories [data shown by district average daily attendance (ADA) groupings; urban, suburban, and rural classification; average market property value; and tax rate; for regular FSP districts only].

2. Education Service Center (ESC) Regions [data shown by 20 regions, for all active school districts].

3. Regular FSP Districts [data shown by district, for all public school districts eligible for State funding through the FSP, with estimates for county totals].

4. Special statutory and State-administered schools [data shown by district, for public school districts created by special legislative act (schools associated with military bases and Masonic Home) or administered by a State agency (Mental Health and Retardation/Youth Council/Board of Education/Dept of Corrections)].

5. Historical State totals [trends for all active districts].

REPORT:

S7670–2.8: Superintendent's Annual Report for Public Elementary and Secondary Schools in Texas, 1981/82
[Annual.   Mar. 1984.   vii+71 p.   Series SB82SAR. $2.00. SRI/MF/complete.]

Detailed tables show original entries, average daily membership (ADM), ADA, and graduates and percent planning on college, all for 1981/82, with trends from 1971/72. One additional table shows original entries by age, reentries, withdrawals, eligible handicapped and migrant students, and attendance analysis, all by grade.

Text tables show selected summary and analytical data based on detailed tables; and trends in original entries by age, including comparison of 6-year-olds to births 6 years prior.

For description of report for 1980/81, see SRI 1982 Annual under S7670-2.1.

S7675   TEXAS
Employment Commission

S7675–1   TEXAS OCCUPATIONAL EMPLOYMENT STATISTICS
Series. For individual publication data, see below.
SRI/MF/complete

Continuing series of 6 reports, published in a 3-year cycle, each covering employment in a selected Texas industry sector, by detailed occupation. Sectors covered are manufacturing, nonmanufacturing, State and local government, trade and regulated industries, educational services, and hospitals.

Data are from Occupational Employment Statistics Program surveys of employers in the various sectors, conducted over the 3-year cycle and updated triennially.

General format of each report:
a. Contents listing, introduction, and methodology.
b. 1 table, repeated for each SIC 2- or 3-digit industry covered, usually showing estimated employment and relative standard error, by occupation.
c. Glossary and/or bibliography.

Report reviewed during 1984 is described below.

Availability: Texas Employment Commission, Economic Research and Analysis Department, TEC Bldg., 15th and Congress, Austin TX 78778, †; SRI/MF/complete.

S7675–1.10: Industry Staffing Patterns for Selected Trade and Regulated Industries
[Recurring (irreg.) Nov. 1983. viii+86 p. SRI/MF/complete.]

Covers occupational employment in selected SIC 2- and 3-digit transportation, public utility (including communications), and wholesale and retail trade industries.

Data are based on mail surveys conducted Apr.-June 1982.

Previous report, covering 1979 survey, is described in SRI 1981 Annual, under S7675-1.4.

S7675–2   ANNUAL PLANNING INFORMATION, State of Texas
Annual. [1984.]   35 p.
LC 78-642138.
SRI/MF/complete

Annual planning report, for FY84, identifying Texas population groups most in need of employment services. Presents data on population, labor force, employment, and the economically disadvantaged, generally for service delivery areas (SDAs) established under the Job Training Partnership Act, 1970s-84, with trends from 1960 and forecasts for 1985.

Data are derived from Texas Employment Commission records, U.S. Labor and Commerce Depts, and Lawrence Berkeley Laboratories.

Contains 37 tables described below, interspersed with brief narrative summaries.

Availability: Texas Employment Commission, Economic Research and Analysis Department, 15th and Congress Ave., Austin TX 78778, †; SRI/MF/complete.

TABLES:

[Data are for Texas. Data by race/ethnicity are generally shown for white, black, and Hispanic.]

POPULATION AND LABOR FORCE

[Most data are for 1980 and generally include forecasts for 1985 and selected trends from 1960.]

a. Population by age, sex, race/ethnicity, and SDA; and SDAs ranked by percent of population under 16 and 65/older, total population and growth, net migration, births, and deaths. 12 tables. (p. 1-12)

b. Labor force by employment status, and labor force participation rates, by sex, race/ethnicity, and age; SDAs ranked by labor force and growth, and by participation rates by sex and for women with and without children; and labor force status of women by presence of children in home. 13 tables. (p. 13-23)

EMPLOYMENT AND THE ECONOMICALLY DISADVANTAGED

[Data are for various periods 1979-84.]

c. Employment covered by unemployment insurance, by industry division and major manufacturing group; and employment, by occupational category with distribution by sex and race/ethnicity, and by class of worker (including government by level and self-employed). 4 tables. (p. 24-27)

d. SDAs ranked by percent of families receiving public assistance, percent of female householders in poverty by employment status (full- and part-time work, and no employment), and percent of persons with work disability (total, in labor force, and prevented from working), with selected totals for the State. 5 tables. (p. 28-31)

e. Insured unemployed by age, duration of unemployment, industry division, and occupational category, and for minorities and women; SDAs ranked by minority share of population and of unemployment insurance claimants; and AFDC families, children, recipients, and payments. 3 tables. (p. 32-35)

S7675-3   TEXAS LABOR MARKET REVIEWS

Monthly. Approx. 8 p.
SRI/MF/complete, shipped quarterly

Monthly report on Texas labor force, covering employment, hours, and earnings, by MSA and industry group; and unemployment insurance claims and benefits. Data are from the Texas Employment Commission.

Report contains narrative summary; and 7 monthly tables and 1 quarterly table, described below.

Monthly tables appear in all issues; quarterly table appears in Nov. 1983, Mar.-May 1984, and Sept. 1984 issues.

Availability: Texas Employment Commission, Economic Research and Analysis Department, 15th and Congress Ave., Austin TX 78778, †; SRI/MF/complete, shipped quarterly.

Issues reviewed during 1984: Oct. 1983-Sept. 1984 (P).

RECURRING TABLES:

[Unless otherwise noted, tables show data for Texas, for month prior to cover date, preceding month, and same month of preceding year].

MONTHLY TABLES

a. U.S. and Texas labor force, actual and seasonally adjusted, by employment status. 1 table.

b. Nonagricultural wage/salary employment: by MSA and industry division, and statewide by industry group. 2 tables.

c. Labor force, by employment status and MSA. 1 table.

d. Hours and earnings: statewide by industry division and selected group; and for durable and nondurable goods manufacturing in 3 largest MSAs. 2 tables.

e. Texas Employment Commission activities, including placements, and unemployment insurance claims and benefits, for month prior to cover date and same month of preceding year. 1 table.

QUARTERLY TABLE

f. Unemployment insurance benefits paid, by MSA, for quarter ending 2 months prior to issue date. 1 table.

S7680   TEXAS
Office of the Governor

S7680-3   CENSUS 1980: Population by Age, Sex, Race and Ethnicity for Texas

Monograph. Oct. 1982.
768 p. No. 1, Series 1982.
SRI/MF/complete

Report presenting 1980 census findings on Texas population, for the State and each county. Shows population by detailed age, cross-tabulated by sex and race-ethnicity (black, white, other race, and Spanish origin). Data are from Census Summary Tape File 2.

Contains 1 table, repeated for each county. Counties are arranged alphabetically in 2 volumes, listed below. Volume I also includes an introduction, and summary data for the State.

Availability: Texas Advisory Commission on Intergovernmental Relations, Data Management Program, PO Box 13206, Austin TX 78711, ◆; SRI/MF/complete.

REPORT VOLUMES:

S7680-3.1: Vol. I. Anderson-Jim Wells Counties

[SRI/MF/complete.]

S7680-3.2: Vol. II. Johnson-Zapata Counties

[SRI/MF/complete.]

S7685   TEXAS
Department of Health

S7685-1   TEXAS VITAL STATISTICS, 1983

Annual. [1984.] vi+99 p.
ISSN 0495-257X.
LC 76-641131.
SRI/MF/complete

Annual report, for 1983, on Texas vital statistics, covering births, deaths by cause, marriages, and divorces, by location and selected demographic characteristics, with trends from 1949. Data are compiled from State records and Census Bureau reports.

Contains listings of contents, tables, and charts (p. iii-vi); and 1 map, 7 charts, and 30 tables listed below, arranged in 4 sections (p. 1-99).

Availability: Texas Department of Health, Vital Statistics Bureau, Statistical Services Division, 1100 W. 49th St., Austin TX 78756, †; SRI/MF/complete.

TABLES:

[Data are for 1983, unless otherwise noted.]

TRENDS

[Tables I-VI show data for 1949-83.]

I. Births and deaths, and rates per 1,000 population. (p. 2)

II-III. Births, by attendant [physician and midwife/other] and place of delivery [hospital and home/other], and by race and sex. (p. 3-4)

IV. Deaths by race and sex. (p. 5)

V. Infant, maternal, and fetal deaths, and rates [or] ratios per 1,000 births. (p. 6)

VI. Infant deaths by age, and rates per 1,000 births. (p. 8)

VII. [Ten] leading causes of death in selected years and rates per 100,000 population based on census as of Apr. 1 each year [decennially 1950-80]. (p. 9)

VIII. Mortality from selected causes and rates per 100,000 estimated population, 1979-83. (p. 10)

BIRTHS AND DEATHS

IX-X. Births, by age of mother and birth weight, by race and sex. (p. 11)

XI. Births, deaths, and fetal deaths [number and rate] by month. (p. 12)

XII. [Ten] leading causes of death and rate per 100,000 estimated population. (p. 13)

XIII. Five leading causes of death by sex and age. (p. 14)

XIV. Deaths from selected causes, by race, sex, and age. (p. 15-26)

XV. Deaths from selected types of accidents, by race, sex, and age. (p. 28)

XVI-XVII. Deaths under 1 year and under 28 days from selected causes, by race and sex [with] rates per 1,000 births. (p. 30-33)

XVIII-XIX. Deaths under 1 year, and under 28 days, by age, race, and sex [with] rates per 1,000 births. (p. 34)

XX. Births and deaths [by sex and race] by public health region, county [including rural areas], and city of residence: cities over 2,500 population. (p. 36-47)

XXI.A.-XXI.B. Deaths from selected causes, by public health region and county of residence; and by city of residence [for] cities over 10,000 population. (p. 48-69)

XXII. Births; [and] infant, neonatal, maternal, and fetal deaths [with] rates [or] ratios per 1,-000 births; by public health region, county [including rural areas], and city of residence. (p. 70-76)

MARRIAGES AND DIVORCES

XXIII. Marriages by age of bride and age of groom. (p. 77)

XXIV. Marriages by county, sex, and age. (p. 78-87)

XXV-XXVI. Divorces by age of wife and age of husband; and by number of children [with total children affected]. (p. 88)

XXVII-XXVIII. Divorces by age of wife and age of husband [by] duration of marriage. (p. 89)

XXIX. Divorces by county, sex, and age. (p. 90-99)

S7695   TEXAS
Department of
Human Resources

S7695-1   TEXAS DEPARTMENT OF HUMAN RESOURCES 1983 Annual Report
Annual. [1983.] 2+69 p.
SRI/MF/complete

Annual report, for FY83, on Texas Dept of Human Resources (DHR) social, medical, and financial services, expenditures, and administration. Includes data by DHR region and by county.

Contains contents listing (1 p.); introduction, with 2 charts (p. 3-5); 3 narrative sections, with 5 charts (p. 9-36); and statistical summary, with 1 chart and 6 tables described below (p. 39-69).

Availability: Texas Department of Human Resources, Information Services Office, PO Box 2960, Austin TX 78769, †; SRI/MF/complete.

CHART AND TABLES:
[Tables show data for FY83.]

a. Estimated expenditures for agency administration, health care services, and services to families/children and aged/disabled adults, with percent from Federal, State, and other sources, all by function; and expenditures for AFDC payments, food stamps, families/children, and aged/disabled adults, by DHR region. 1 table and 1 chart. (p. 40-41)

b. Food stamp and AFDC monthly average participants and total value or payments, and aggregate fraud case dispositions, all by county; and AFDC and other child support collections, by DHR region. 2 tables. (p. 42-48)

c. Families and children benefits: payments for prescribed medicines and hospital/other services, and average monthly active Medicaid eligibles, number of clients served by protective services for children, children in day care purchased by DHR, and licensed day care and 24-hour child care facilities; all by county. 1 table. (p. 49-55)

d. Aged/disabled benefits: nursing home/mentally retarded/intermediate care facility clients and payments; payments for prescribed medicines and hospital/other services; average monthly active Medicaid eligibles; and clients served by community care services; all by county. 1 table. (p. 56-62)

e. DHR employees, medical assistance payments, food stamp value, and AFDC payments, all by county. 1 table. (p. 63-69)

S7703   TEXAS
Judicial Council

S7703-1   TEXAS JUDICIAL SYSTEM ANNUAL REPORT of Statistical and Other Data for Calendar Year 1983
Annual. May 1984. 672 p.
LC 75-648526.
SRI/MF/complete, current & previous year reports

Annual report, for 1983, on Texas judicial system, including trial and appellate court caseloads and case dispositions. Covers supreme, appeals, district, county, justice of the peace, and municipal courts. Includes trial court data by case type and location; and selected trends from 1972.

Case types shown are criminal (by type of offense) and civil, for most courts, with some additional detail for juvenile, workers compensation, probate, divorce, traffic, small claims, and commitment case types.

Report also includes data on judicial system appropriations; assignments and compensation of judges; characteristics of judges, including age, education, and experience; judicial misconduct complaints and dispositions; and sentences imposed and revenue collections for selected courts.

Data are from dept records.

Contains contents listing (p. 4-5); narrative report on judicial branch, with 10 maps, 3 charts, and 7 tables (p. 7-86); court activity analysis, with 1 map, 19 charts and 23 tables (p. 87-195); detailed statistics for district courts (p. 197-453) and county courts (p. 455-521), with 2 tables repeated for each county; and directories (p. 523-672).

This is the 55th annual report. Previous report, for 1982, was also reviewed in 1984 and is also available on SRI microfiche under this number [Annual. July 1983. 731 p. $5.85 (prepaid)].

Availability: Texas Judicial Council, Court Administration Office, Attention: Annual Report Purchase, PO Box 12066, Austin TX 78711, $5.94 (prepaid); SRI/MF/complete.

S7710   TEXAS
State Library

S7710-1   TEXAS PUBLIC LIBRARY STATISTICS for 1982
Annual. 1983. 225 p. var. paging+addendum.
ISSN 0082-3120.
LC 75-646379.
SRI/MF/complete

Annual report, for FY82, on Texas public libraries, presenting data on collections, services, finances, and personnel, for individual libraries. Also includes library directories.

Data are from reports submitted by 420 libraries.

Contains foreword and contents listing (p. i-iii); and 4 sections, each individually paginated, as follows:

Section I. General information, including directories of library officials, interlibrary loan centers, and historical resource and State document depositories. (p. 1-11)

Section II. Directory of public libraries and branches. (p. 1-69)

Section III. Statistical information with narrative introduction (2 p.); and 3 tables, listed below. (p. A1-C11)

Section IV. Index to directory section. (p. 1-31)

Issuing agency also publishes *Texas Academic Library Statistics,* not covered by SRI.

Availability: Texas State Library, Library Development Division, PO Box 12927, Capitol Station, Austin TX 78711, †; SRI/MF/complete.

TABLES:
[Data on library personnel are for Jan. 1983; total population data in table C are from 1980 census counts. All other data are for local FY82.]

[A] Statistics by library [arranged alphabetically by library system, and including location; population served; holdings by type; collections turnover rate; in-library usage; interlibrary loan items received; program attendance; library visits; reference transactions; expenditures by object including salaries and utilities, and by funding source; per capita tax support; budgeted FTE staff; and librarians with master's degrees in library science]. (p. A1-A84)

[B] Summary statistics [repeats most data in Table [A], by regional library system and for State; also includes State total bookmobiles]. (p. B1-B12)

[C] Statistics by county [total population, population served, maximum property tax allocation to libraries, and total library expenditures]. (p. C1-C11)

S7735   TEXAS
Department of Public Safety

S7735-2   TEXAS CRIME REPORT, 1983
Annual. [1984.] iv+67 p.
SRI/MF/complete

Annual report, for 1983, on Texas crimes and arrests, by type of offense. Includes offenses by county and reporting law enforcement agency; and arrests by age, sex, and race. Also covers stolen property value, clearances, murder victim characteristics, child sexual abuse, assaults on law enforcement officers, and law enforcement employees.

Report is compiled primarily from data submitted by local law enforcement agencies under the Texas Uniform Crime Reporting (UCR) Program. Child sexual abuse data are based on a sample survey of 25 agencies.

Contains contents listing (p. iii-iv); UCR Program description and offense classification (p. 3-7); 16 charts and 43 tables, with interspersed narrative and text data (p. 9-64); and glossary (p. 67). All tables, and selected text data and charts presenting data not covered in tables, are described below.

Availability: Texas Department of Public Safety, Uniform Crime Reporting Bureau, PO Box 4143, Austin TX 78765, †; SRI/MF/complete.

DATA:
[Unless otherwise noted, data are for 1983. Index offenses are murder, rape, robbery, aggravated assault, burglary, larceny-theft, and motor vehicle theft. Arson is classified as an Index offense, but data are reported separately and are not included in the Crime Index tables.]

S7735-2.1: Offenses

INDEX OFFENSES
[In addition to the tables described below, 1 table showing arrests by age, sex, and race is repeated for each Index offense except arson.]

a. Summary: stolen property value and percent recovered, by property type and/or offense; clearance rates, by offense; and percent property and violent crime. 4 charts and 1 table. (p. 11-13)

b. Murder: offense distribution by weapon, victim-offender relationship, circumstances, and victim age, sex, and race. 1 chart and 4 tables. (p. 14-15)

c. Rape: offense distribution by classification (forcible and attempted forcible). 1 chart and 1 table. (p. 16)

d. Robbery: offenses and stolen property value, by setting; and offense distribution by weapon. 2 charts and 2 tables. (p. 17)

e. Aggravated assault: offense distribution by weapon. 1 chart and 1 table. (p. 18)

f. Burglary: offense distribution by entry method and circumstances (residence or nonresidence, night or day). 2 charts and 1 table. (p. 19)

g. Larceny-theft: offenses and stolen property value, by type and size of theft. 1 chart and 2 tables. (p. 20)

h. Motor vehicle theft: offense distribution by vehicle type; and vehicles recovered in and outside jurisdiction where stolen. 1 chart and 2 tables. (p. 21)

i. Arson offenses, clearances, clearances involving juveniles, offenses involving uninhabited structures, and property damage value, by property classification. 1 table. (p. 22)

j. Crime frequency, 1983; population, offenses, and crime rate, 1973-83; and offenses, by urban-rural location, by area population size, and on college/university campuses, 1983; all by offense. 1 chart and 15 tables. (p. 23-27)

CHILD SEXUAL ABUSE, AND LOCAL OFFENSE DATA

k. Child sexual abuse analysis, including distribution by victim age and offense type. Text data and 1 chart. (p. 28)

l. Contributing agencies (sheriffs' offices, police depts, and colleges/universities); and Index offenses by type, by contributing agency, grouped by county. 2 tables. (p. 31-49)

S7735-2.2: Arrests and Law Enforcement Employee Data

ARRESTS

a. Juvenile and adult arrests, by sex and age, for 40 Index and non-Index offense classifications, including detailed breakdown for drug offenses. 4 tables. (p. 53-58)

LAW ENFORCEMENT EMPLOYEES

b. Law enforcement officers killed, 1974-83; and officers assaulted, by type of assignment, activity, weapon, whether injury resulted, and time of day, 1983. 1 chart and 5 tables. (p. 63-64)

c. Sworn and civilian law enforcement employees, by sex; and survey forms returned; by dept type. 2 tables. (p. 64)

S7735-3   MOTOR VEHICLE TRAFFIC ACCIDENTS, 1983, Texas
Annual. [1984.] 48 p.
LC 54-28420.
SRI/MF/complete

Annual report on Texas traffic accidents, fatalities, and injuries, by vehicle and accident type, location, time, and other circumstances; and driver and victim characteristics; 1983, with trends from as early as 1937.

Also includes data on accident economic loss, vehicle registrations and mileage, licensed drivers, use of safety devices, breath alcohol test results, and incidence of driving while intoxicated.

Contains contents listing and highlights (p. 1-3); and 5 charts and 34 tables (p. 4-48).

Availability: Texas Department of Public Safety, Statistical Services, PO Box 4087, Austin TX 78773, †; SRI/MF/complete.

S7745   TEXAS
Railroad Commission

S7745-1   GAS UTILITIES DIVISION ANNUAL REPORT, 1983, Railroad Commission of Texas
Annual. Nov. 1983.
158 p.+errata sheet.
SRI/MF/complete

Annual report on finances and operations of Texas regulated natural gas utilities, 1982, with regulatory and tax data for FY83 and selected trends from 1970.

Includes data by company on customers, consumption, average price, and revenue, for residential and small and large commercial/industrial service; gas purchased and unaccounted for, and average purchase and sale price; value of plant in service by type; revenues and expenses; and pipeline miles; with some detail by city.

Also includes Gas Utilities Division finances and regulatory activities; gross receipt taxes paid, by company; average annual residential bill for 25 largest Texas cities and 8 companies; degree days (deviation from normal temperature) for 25 largest cities; and selected comparisons to U.S., including average prices for residential gas by census division.

Data are from Division records and company reports.

Contains contents listing and transmittal letter (p. 1-7); regulatory and industry summary, with 10 charts and 10 tables (p. 9-31); detailed company operations, with 9 tables (p. 32-137); and list of companies filing annual reports, and directories of systems and Division offices (p. 138-158).

Availability: Texas Railroad Commission, Gas Utilities Division, Reports and Statistics Section, PO Drawer 12967, Capitol Station, Austin TX 78711, $3.00; SRI/MF/complete.

S7800   UTAH
Department of Agriculture

S7800-1   UTAH AGRICULTURAL STATISTICS, 1984
Annual. [1984.] 96 p.
LC 72-623245.
SRI/MF/complete

Annual report on Utah agricultural production, finances, and marketing, 1983, with selected data for 1984 and trends from as early as 1850. Data are generally shown by commodity and/or county, with some comparisons to total U.S.

Report generally covers production, prices, disposition, value, and, as applicable, acreage, yield, or inventory, for field crop, fruit, vegetable, livestock, dairy, and poultry sectors.

Also includes data on urban and rural population by county, and farm population; number of farms and acreage; land ownership and use; irrigation; farm income, including cash receipts by commodity; farm production expenses, labor, and wages; mink operations; and weather.

Data are primarily from Utah Dept of Agriculture and USDA.

Contains list of other publications available from issuing agency (1 p.); introduction and contents listing (p. 4-5); 13 charts and 88 tables, interspersed with narrative summaries (p. 6-90); and an article on model enterprise budgets, with 6 tables (p. 91-96).

Availability: Utah Department of Agriculture, Crop and Livestock Reporting Service, PO Box 25007, Salt Lake City UT 84125, †; SRI/MF/complete.

S7808   UTAH
Department of Community and Economic Development

S7808–1   UTAH PUBLIC LIBRARIES
Annual Report, 1983
Annual.   June 1984.   30 p.
SRI/MF/complete

Annual report, for 1983, on Utah public library finances and services, including data by library and county. Data are prepared by the Utah State Library.

Contains contents listing and highlights (p. 1-2); public library statistics, with 1 chart and 3 tables, listed below (p. 3-14); library and trustee directories (p. 15-20); and State library statistics, with 1 table showing State library revenues and expenditures for FY83, and 13 tables on division programs, also listed below (p. 21-30).

Availability: Utah Department of Community and Economic Development, State Library Division, 2150 South 300 West, Suite 16, Salt Lake City UT 84115, †; SRI/MF/complete.

TABLES:
[Data are for 1983 or FY83, unless otherwise noted.]

S7808–1.1: Public Libraries

[1] Public library statistics [staff, collections, services, income, and expenditures, by library and bookmobile in each county, and including circulation, 1980 population, tax income, salaries, and capital outlay]. (p. 4-11)

[2] Public library spending per capita [ranked by county and library]. (p. 12)

[3] Earning and spending profile [by major item]. [chart] (p. 13)

[4] Service potential, Utah public libraries [estimated 1980 population, and assessed valuation, potential receipts, total receipts and spending, expenditure outside capital outlay, present and potential spending per capita, and percent of capability]; by county. (p. 14)

S7808–1.2: Division Program Data

SPECIAL SERVICES PROGRAM
[Data by format include braille, cassette, and recorded disk.]

A. Special services collection [net holdings as of July 1, 1982-83, acquisitions, and withdrawals, all by format]. (p. 24)

B-C. Patrons [by selected State and format], and volunteers. (p. 24)

D. Materials [produced and duplicated locally, and multi-State center duplication, by format]. (p. 25)

E. Circulation [by selected State or institution and by format]. (p. 25)

BOOKMOBILE SERVICES PROGRAM
[A] Bookmobile services program [showing counties and population served, contractual cost, and total and per capita circulation, by bookmobile number]. (p. 27)

REFERENCE SERVICES PROGRAM
A-B. Information and reference requests, and interlibrary loan statistics, [requests and dispositions by source]. (p. 28)

C. Audiovisual statistics [circulation and attendance, FY81-83]. (p. 28)

D. Circulation [of Federal and State documents, and general and sample collections, for public and school libraries, State agencies/institutions, colleges/universities, and bookmobiles]. (p. 29)

E. Materials collections [reference services and audiovisual, including net holdings, July 1982-83, and acquisitions and withdrawals]. (p. 29)

F. State depository libraries (not L.S.C.A. funded) [publications received and mailed]. (p. 30)

TECHNICAL SERVICES PROGRAM
[G] Materials ordered and processed or cataloged [for State, public, and school libraries; institutions/colleges; and State agencies]. (p. 30)

S7815   UTAH
Office of Education

S7815–1   ANNUAL STATISTICAL REPORT OF SCHOOL DISTRICTS, 1982/83, Utah
Annual.   Dec. 1983.
ii + 276 p.
SRI/MF/complete

Annual report, for school year 1982/83, on Utah public school enrollment, attendance, and personnel, by school district and type of program. Also includes data on school dropouts, special and adult education, and pupil transportation.

Contains table listing (p. i-ii); and 42 tables, listed below (p. 1-276).

This is the most comprehensive report published by the Utah Dept of Education, which also issues 3 other annual reports not covered in SRI: *Salary Schedule Information on Utah School Districts, Status of Teacher Personnel in Utah,* and *Annual Report of the State Superintendent.*

Availability: Utah Office of Education, Administrative Services Division, 250 East Fifth South, Salt Lake City UT 84111, †; SRI/MF/complete.

TABLES:
[Tables show data by school district, 1982/83, unless otherwise noted. Data by racial breakdown also include the following ethnic groups: American Indian/Alaskan Native, Hispanic, and Asian/Pacific Islander.]

S7815–1.1: Enrollment, Dropouts, and Attendance

[Tables [3], [5], and [7-9] show data for elementary, middle, and secondary schools, by grade and for 13 types of special classes.]

[1] Number of public day schools in school district, by type of organized unit. (p. 1)

[2] Total year-end enrollment, ranked from highest to lowest [school district]. (p. 2)

[3] Year-end enrollment. (p. 3-12)

[4] Dropouts, by racial breakdown, grade, and sex. (p. 13-30)

[5] Aggregate days attendance. (p. 31-40)

[6] Comparison of pupils in average daily attendance [ADA], 1981/82-1982/83. (p. 41)

[7] ADA. (p. 42-51)

[8] Aggregate days membership. (p. 52-61)

[9] Average daily membership [ADM]. (p. 62-71)

[10] Percentage aggregate daily attendance is of aggregate daily membership [for kindergarten, elementary, middle, and secondary grade levels]. (p. 72)

S7815–1.2: School Personnel
[All tables show data by sex.]

[1] FTE classified personnel [by function and type of position]. (p. 73-126)

[2] Number of classified personnel, by racial breakdown (FTE). (p. 127)

[3] FTE classified personnel, nonregular day school [by type of position]. (p. 129)

[4] Number of classified personnel, by racial breakdown, nonregular day school. (p. 133)

[5] FTE certificated nonteaching personnel [by function and type of position]. (p. 135-170)

[6] FTE certificated teaching personnel [kindergarten and regular teachers grades 1-12; and] resource programs [by specialty], self-contained handicapped [by type of handicap], teacher interns, and subtotal regular and handicapped teachers [all by school level]. (p. 171-219)

[7] Grand total FTE all certificated professional personnel [by school level]. (p. 220)

[8] Certificated professional personnel by racial breakdown. (p. 223)

[9-10] FTE of extended year summer school [elementary and secondary] teachers who teach; and of summer vocational home economics and vocational agriculture, and extended year summer school teachers who teach. (p. 225-226)

[11] FTE certificated personnel [by function and position], nonregular day school. (p. 227-234)

[12] Certificated professional personnel, by racial breakdown, nonregular day school. (p. 235)

S7815–1.3: Special Programs and Pupil Data

SPECIAL PROGRAMS
[1-2] Handicapped resource program, and handicapped in self-contained classes: total elementary/secondary by student count and ADM [by type of handicap]. (p. 237-245)

[3] Special needs students [total and number homebound/hospitalized]. (p. 246)

[4] Driver education program for private school pupils, classroom instruction only [by grade, ADA and ADM]. (p. 247)

[5] Behind-the-wheel driver education, number of students [full-time and private school students, and adults] completing program. (p. 248)

[6] Extended year/summer/day program (summer 1983) [direct teacher instruction enrollments and teacher training participant hours]. (p. 249)

HIGH SCHOOL GRADUATES

[7] High school graduates by racial breakdown [and sex]. (p. 251)

ADULT EDUCATION

[8-9] Adult basic education/adult high school enrollees, by age and sex, and by sex, race, and selected ethnic groups. (p. 253-255)

[10-11] Adult basic education/adult high school programs: [graduates and transfers from regular day school, by sex]; and personnel (head count only, not FTE) [by type of position]. (p. 256-257)

[12] Adult basic education/adult high school impact data [including level of education achieved; public assistance discontinued; and job, citizenship, voter registration, and drivers license obtained]. (p. 258)

[13] Adult high school impact data: number of units of adult high school completion credit awarded from all sources, by [source]. (p. 260)

[14] Adult basic education/adult high school reasons for separation. (p. 262)

TRANSPORTATION

[15] Transportation: total annual bus mileage [by type]. (p. 264)

[16] Transportation: number of regular bus drivers by male/female (not FTE); [and number of pupils transported by district buses, contracted services, and parents, and number receiving subsistence in lieu of transportation, all by eligibility category]. (p. 266)

[17] Number of school buses purchased during FY83. (p. 270)

[18-19] Number of [regular, spare], and contracted school buses in use in pupil transportation program, by seating capacity. (p. 271-274)

[20] School bus accidents data [mileage, accidents, and accident rates, 1980-81]. (p. 275-276)

S7820 UTAH
Department of Employment Security

S7820–1   UTAH EMPLOYMENT, WAGES, AND REPORTING UNITS by Firm Size, 1983
Annual. Oct. 1983. 49 p.
SRI/MF/complete

Annual report, for 1983, presenting data on Utah nonagricultural employment, wages, and reporting business units, by firm employment size. Data are shown by SIC 2-digit industry and by county and planning district for 1st quarter 1983, with summary trends from 1970.

Data are compiled from employers' reports to the Dept of Employment Security.

Contains contents listing (1 p.); introduction (p. 1); brief narrative summary with text statistics (p. 3); and 3 detailed tables (p. 7-49).

Availability: Utah Department of Employment Security, Labor Market Information Services Section, 174 Social Hall Ave., PO Box 11249, Salt Lake City UT 84147, †; SRI/MF/complete.

S7820–2   ANNUAL PLANNING INFORMATION, Utah
Annual, discontinued.

Annual planning report, identifying Utah population groups most in need of job services, and presenting population, labor force, and employment data. Due to lack of funding, report has been discontinued with the FY83 edition (for description, see SRI 1982 Annual, under this number).

Data for individual labor market areas may be obtained directly from Utah Department of Employment Security, Research and Analysis Section, 174 Social Hall Ave., PO Box 11249, Salt Lake City UT 84147.

S7820–3   UTAH LABOR MARKET REPORT
Monthly. Approx. 10 p.
SRI/MF/complete, shipped quarterly

Monthly report on Utah nonagricultural employment, hours, and earnings, by industry, with selected data by locale. Also includes employment security activities.

Data are from reports of State and Federal agencies, and the American Chamber of Commerce Research Assn (ACCRA). Report is issued 1 month after month of coverage.

Contains brief narrative analysis, with 1-2 summary employment trend charts; recurring summary data on trends in Utah composite index of leading economic indicators and U.S. CPI; and 10 monthly tables.

Issues also occasionally contain additional statistical features, including quarterly cost-of-living data for selected western cities. Revised monthly employment estimates for the previous year appear in the Jan. issue.

Monthly tables are listed below and appear in all issues. All additional features with substantial statistical content are described, as they appear, under "Statistical Features." Nonstatistical features are not covered.

Prior to July 1984 issue, report included 1 additional monthly table on characteristics of the unemployed.

Quarterly reports for each planning district are also available from the issuing agency, but are not covered by SRI.

Availability: Utah Department of Employment Security, Research and Analysis Section, 174 Social Hall Ave., PO Box 11249, Salt Lake City UT 84147, †; SRI/MF/complete, shipped quarterly.

Issues reviewed during 1984: Oct. 1983-Sept. 1984 (D).

MONTHLY TABLES:
[Tables generally show data for month of coverage, with comparisons to varying prior periods. Some data are current only to 1-3 months prior to month of coverage. Data are for Utah, unless otherwise noted.]

1. Civilian labor force [by employment status].

2. Employees on nonagricultural payrolls, by industry [division and major group, and total involved in labor disputes].

3. Employment status of Utah's population, and nonagricultural jobs by industry [division] (seasonally adjusted).

4. Distribution of nonagricultural employment by sex, and production workers, by industry [division].

5. Labor force [by employment status] and employment [by industry division] in metro labor market areas [Salt Lake/Ogden and Provo/Orem].

6. Civilian labor force and components [unemployment rate and nonagricultural wage/salary jobs] by planning district and county.

7-8. Hours and earnings of production workers in Salt Lake-Ogden labor area and in Utah [by industry division and selected major group].

9. Employment security activities [including job openings, applicants, placements, and unemployment insurance claims and benefits].

[A] Current price indexes, U.S. [including CPI for all urban consumers by item, and PPI by commodity category].

STATISTICAL FEATURES:

S7820–3.501: Nov. 1983

UTAH LABOR MARKET REVIEW FOR 1983 AND OUTLOOK FOR 1984, ANNUAL FEATURE

(p. A-F) Annual articles presenting Utah employment review and outlook. Data are from Utah Dept of Employment Security. Includes 1 table showing civilian labor force by employment status, and employment by industry division, 1980-82 and forecast 1983-84.

S7820–3.502: Jan. 1984

NONFARM JOB ESTIMATES REVISED

(p. A-D) Article, with 2 tables showing Utah nonagricultural jobs, by month, 1983, with July-Sept. detail by industry division. Includes comparisons of actual data, previous estimates, and revised estimates.

ACCRA COMPOSITE COST-OF-LIVING COMPARISONS FOR SELECTED METRO AREAS, QUARTERLY FEATURE

(p. F) Quarterly table showing cost-of-living index for U.S., selected western cities, and cities with highest and lowest index, by item, 3rd quarter 1983.

Data are from American Chamber of Commerce Researchers Assn.

S7820–3.503: Apr. 1984

ACCRA COMPOSITE COST-OF-LIVING COMPARISONS FOR SELECTED METRO AREAS, QUARTERLY FEATURE

(p. B) Quarterly table showing cost-of-living index for U.S., selected western cities, and cities with highest and lowest index, by item, 4th quarter 1983.

Data are from American Chamber of Commerce Researchers Assn.

S7820–3.504: May 1984

SUMMARY OF KEY LABOR MARKET INFORMATION FOR UTAH, ANNUAL FEATURE

(p. A-K) Eleven annual tables showing Utah population, labor force by employment status, nonagricultural payroll employment and wages, establishments reporting in 1st quarter, and total and per capita personal income, all by planning district and county, 1970 and 1975-83.

S7820–3.505: June 1984

ACCRA COMPOSITE COST-OF-LIVING COMPARISONS FOR SELECTED METRO AREAS, QUARTERLY FEATURE

(1 p.) Quarterly table showing cost-of-living index for U.S., selected western cities, and cities with highest and lowest index, by item, 1st quarter 1984.

Data are from American Chamber of Commerce Researchers Assn.

S7820–3.506: Sept. 1984

ACCRA COMPOSITE COST-OF-LIVING COMPARISONS FOR SELECTED METRO AREAS, QUARTERLY FEATURE

(1 p.) Quarterly table showing cost-of-living index for U.S., selected western cities, and cities with highest and lowest index, by item, 2nd quarter 1984.

Data are from American Chamber of Commerce Researchers Assn.

S7830   UTAH
Department of
Financial Institutions

S7830–1   THIRD ANNUAL AND THIRTY-SEVENTH REPORT OF THE COMMISSIONER OF FINANCIAL INSTITUTIONS, State of Utah, for the Period July 1, 1982-June 30, 1983
Annual. [1983.] 103 p.
SRI/MF/complete

Annual report on financial condition of Utah State-chartered banks and other financial institutions, FY83, presenting assets, liabilities, and generally income and expenses, for commercial banks and trust companies, savings/building and loan assns, industrial loan corporations, credit unions, and supervised lenders. Asset and liability data are generally shown by institution.

Also includes data on dept appropriations, fee receipts, and expenditures; selected balance sheet data for State-located national banks and federally chartered savings/building and loan assns; and selected trends from 1978.

Contains contents listing (p. 2); dept report, with 3 text tables (p. 4-10); and 34 financial tables, interspersed with directories and status change listings (p. 12-103).

Availability: Utah Department of Financial Institutions, 160 East 300 South, PO Box 89, Salt Lake City UT 84110, †; SRI/MF/complete.

S7845   UTAH
Insurance Department

S7845–1   1983 SEVENTY-FOURTH ANNUAL REPORT OF THE INSURANCE DEPARTMENT, Business of 1982, Utah
Annual. Aug. 9, 1984.
257 p.
SRI/MF/complete

Annual report on Utah insurance industry financial condition and underwriting activity, by company and type of insurance, 1982. Covers assets, capital/surplus, policyholder dividends, premiums written and/or earned, claims/benefits paid or losses incurred and paid, and insurance in force.

Data are shown, as applicable, for life, accident/health, fire/casualty, fraternal, and title insurance companies; HMOs and nonprofit service organizations; and motor clubs. Data on fire/casualty insurers include additional breakdowns for property, automobile, medical malpractice, workers compensation, surety, and other lines of coverage.

Also includes data on Insurance Dept expenditures, taxes and other collections, and security deposits by company.

Data are compiled from reports submitted by individual insurers.

Contains index, Insurance Dept report with 4 tables, list of company status changes, and directory (p. 3-45); and 7 company financial tables (p. 47-257).

Availability: Utah Insurance Department, PO Box 5803, Salt Lake City UT 84110-5803, $5.00+$2.00 postage; SRI/MF/complete.

S7850   UTAH
Judicial Council

S7850–1   ANNUAL REPORT, UTAH COURTS, FY83
Annual. [1983.] 87 p.
ISSN 0098-9045.
LC 75-644191.
SRI/MF/complete

Annual report, for FY83, on Utah judicial system, including trial and appellate court caseloads and case dispositions. Covers supreme, district, circuit, and justice of the peace courts. Includes trial court data by case type and county and/or jurisdiction, and selected comparisons to FY82 and forecasts for FY84.

Case types shown are criminal and civil, by detailed case type, including specific criminal offenses; and domestic relations, child support, probate, adoption, guardianship, mental hearings, contract, property rights, habeas corpus, foreclosure, administrative agency, small claims, and traffic cases.

Also includes data on case processing time; and judicial dept finances, including trial court revenues by source and expenditures by object.

Data are from court clerk's reports filed under the State Judicial Information System.

Contains contents listing (1 p.); report in 3 sections, with text statistics, 7 charts, and 14 tables (p. 3-57); and appendix, with 16 detailed tables (p. 58-87).

This is the 10th annual report.

Availability: Utah Judicial Council, State Court Administrator's Office, 255 South Third East, Salt Lake City UT 84111, †; SRI/MF/complete.

S7890   UTAH
Department of
Public Safety

S7890–2   UTAH TRAFFIC ACCIDENT SUMMARY, 1983
Annual. July 1, 1984. 32 p.
SRI/MF/complete

Annual report on Utah traffic accidents and fatalities by accident and vehicle types, location, time, and other circumstances; injuries; and driver and victim sex, age, and other characteristics; 1983, with selected trends from as early as 1948.

Also includes data on miles traveled; detail for pedestrian and motorcycle accidents; alcohol involvement in accidents; use of safety devices; and blood alcohol content of drivers involved in fatal accidents.

Data are primarily from Utah Highway Safety Office records.

Contains contents listing (1 p.); introduction (p. 1-2); and 27 charts and 31 tables (p. 3-32).

Availability: Utah Department of Public Safety, Highway Safety Division, 4501 South 2700 West, Salt Lake City UT 84119, †; SRI/MF/complete.

S7890–3   CRIME IN UTAH, 1983
Annual. [1984.] 2+35 p.
Archives No. P840057.
LC 81-649761.
SRI/MF/complete

Annual report on Utah crimes, by type of offense, and by county and local jurisdiction, 1983, with trends from 1978. Also includes data on law enforcement officer employment, assaults on officers, and adult and juvenile arrests.

Data are compiled from local law enforcement agency reports under the State Uniform Crime Reporting Program.

Contains contents listing (1 p.); introduction, reporting procedures, and definitions, with 1 table and 1 chart showing Part I crime trends and State population, 1978-83, and frequency of major crimes, 1983 (p. 2-8); and 14 charts and 25 tables, described below (p. 11-35).

This is the 6th annual report. A less detailed semiannual report on crimes and arrests is also available from the issuing agency, but is not covered by SRI.

Availability: Utah Department of Public Safety, Uniform Crime Reporting Section, Criminal Identification Bureau, 4501 South 2700 West, Salt Lake City UT 84119, †; SRI/MF/complete.

CHARTS AND TABLES:

[Index (Part I) crimes are murder, rape, robbery, aggravated assault, burglary, larceny, motor vehicle theft, and arson. Part II crimes are less serious offenses.]

PART I CRIME SUMMARY

[In addition to tables and charts described below, data for each offense include 1 table showing number of offenses and clearances, and rate. Data are for 1983, with selected comparisons to 1982.]

a. Murder victims and offenders by age group; murders by type of weapon, day of week, and victim/offender relationship; rape offenses and attempts; robbery offenses and value of property stolen, by type of establishment; and aggravated assaults by type of weapon. 8 charts and 6 tables. (p. 11-15)

b. Burglary offenses and value of property stolen, by day or night occurrence, and whether residential or nonresidential; larceny/theft offenses and value of property stolen, by theft type; value of motor vehicles stolen and recovered; arson offenses, clearances, and property value and type; value of all property lost, by offense type; and value of property stolen and recovered, by property type. 5 charts and 8 tables. (p. 16-19)

OFFICER AND COUNTY DATA

c. Law enforcement officer assaults by time of day, circumstance, weapon, and whether injured; full-time officers, including sheriffs and municipal officers, and Index crimes reported by offense, all by county, reporting agency, and college and university campus, with county and reporting jurisdiction population data, 1983; and total Index offenses and crime rates by county, 1982-83. 1 chart and 6 tables. (p. 21-30)

ARRESTS

d. Juvenile and adult arrests: by offense, 1983; for liquor violations, drug sale/manufacture and possession, and for all Part I/Part II crimes, 1981-83; and by county, reporting agency, and college and university campus, 1983. 5 tables. (p. 32-35)

S7895   UTAH
Board of Regents/Office of the Commissioner of Higher Education

S7895-1   **FOURTEENTH ANNUAL REPORT TO THE GOVERNOR AND THE LEGISLATURE, Utah State Board of Regents, 1982/83**
Annual. Jan. 1984.
xvi+127 p.
ISSN 0360-8123.
LC 75-649010.
SRI/MF/complete

Annual report on Utah postsecondary education for the 1982/83 school year, with trends from 1967/68 and projections to 1994/95. Covers State-supported institution degree programs, enrollment, and finances; private institution degree programs and enrollment; and selected student characteristics.

Data are from Higher Education General Information Survey, Utah State Office of Education, and other sources.

Contents:

Availability: Utah Board of Regents/Office of the Commissioner of Higher Education, 807 E. South Temple, Suite 204, Salt Lake City UT 84102, †; SRI/MF/complete.

S7905   UTAH
Tax Commission

S7905-1   **TWENTY-SEVENTH BIENNIAL REPORT OF THE UTAH STATE TAX COMMISSION, Volume I**
Biennial. Mar. 15, 1984.
v+146 p.
LC 33-27803.
SRI/MF/complete

Biennial report volume, for FY83, on Utah State revenue collections by source, and distribution of revenues to local areas and State government funds. Also includes data on taxable retail purchases by industry, property valuations, Federal tax returns of Utah residents, and tax commission activities.

Report is published in 2 volumes, presenting separate data for each fiscal year of the biennium. Volume I is published in even-numbered years; Volume II is published in odd-numbered years. Current Volume I presents data for FY83; for description of Volume II for FY82, see SRI 1983 Annual under this number.

Contains contents listing (p. iii-v); 2 sections on commission activities and tax trends, with 2 charts and 8 tables (p. 5-23); and 20 sections on specific tax types, with facsimile tax reporting forms, descriptions of taxes, statutory references, tax rates or fees, 14 charts, and 24 tables (p. 27-145).

All tables are described below.

Availability: Utah Tax Commission, State Office Bldg., Rm. 202, Salt Lake City UT 84134, †; SRI/MF/complete.

TABLES:

[All tables show data for Utah.]

COMMISSION ACTIVITIES AND TAX TRENDS

a. Tax commission net State/local collections, administrative costs, total and audit FTE employees, and State population, FY73-83; and commission expenditures by division and item, FY82-83. 4 tables. (p. 10-12)

b. Net tax collections by type, FY74-83; gross collections and refunds/adjustments by source and fund, FY82-83; property taxes levied, 1973-82, and excise tax net collections, FY74-83; and State population by county, 1970 and 1980. 4 tables. (p. 16-23)

SPECIFIED TAXES

c. Sales/use tax collections FY64-83; and gross taxable retail purchases, by industry division and major group, 1980-82. 3 tables. (p. 29-37)

d. State individual income tax collections, FY64-83; and Federal tax returns filed, adjusted gross income, tax rate and taxes paid, and number of net exemptions, by income category and/or county, with average income, taxes, and exemptions for counties ranked by income, 1981, with comparisons to 1980. 4 tables. (p. 41-49)

e. Property assessed value and taxes, by class of property, 1981-82; tax collections for motor fuel tax and for local option sales/use tax, FY64-83; and sales/use tax distribution by locality, FY82-83. 4 tables. (59-79)

f. Collections for corporate franchise, insurance premium, mine occupation (oil/gas and metalliferous ore), local transit authority, special fuel, cigarette/tobacco, inheritance, transient room, beer, and oil gas/conservation taxes; with local transit authority and transient room tax distributions to participating counties; various years FY64-83. 13 tables. (p. 83-129)

S7995   VERMONT
Department of
Banking and Insurance

S7995–2   ANNUAL REPORT OF THE
BANK COMMISSIONER of
the State of Vermont for the
Year Ended Dec. 31, 1983
Annual. June 1, 1984. 63 p.
LC 76-626902.
SRI/MF/complete

Annual report on financial condition of Vermont State-chartered financial institutions, presenting assets and liabilities by institution, and composite income and expense data, for savings and commercial banks/trust companies, savings and loan assns, credit unions, and licensed lenders, 1983, with selected trends from 1855. Includes data for national banks and Federal credit unions.

Also includes data on banking division receipts and disbursements; populations for bank locations; rankings of banks by assets; trends in number of banks and value of deposits, from 1855; bank trust dept balance sheet; family financial counseling service clients and trust account value; and number of credit unions and members.

Other data include development credit corporation balance sheets; and Vermont Home Mortgage Guarantee Board loan guarantees, and trust fund balance sheet, FY83.

Contains contents listing (p. 3-4); preface, lists of financial institutions and status changes, and banking division finances, with 2 tables (p. 7-22); and 23 financial tables, interspersed with directories (p. 23-63).

Availability: Vermont Department of Banking and Insurance, Banking Division, State Office Bldg., 120 State St., Montpelier VT 05602-9974, †; SRI/MF/complete.

S8020   VERMONT
Department of
Education

S8020–2   VERMONT EDUCATION
STATISTICS, 1981/82
Annual series. For individual
publication data, see below.
SRI/MF/complete

Series of 4 annual reports, each presenting data on an aspect of Vermont elementary and secondary education, 1981/82. Topics covered are enrollment, facilities, administration and staff, and finances. Some reports include nonpublic school data.

Data are compiled by the Dept of Education from reports by individual school districts.

Report for 1981/82 reviewed during 1984 is described below. Other reports for 1981/82 are described in SRI 1982 Annual under this number. Reports for 1980/81 and 1982/83 are covered under S8020-1 and S8020-3, respectively.

Availability: Vermont Department of Education, Statistics and Information Office, State Office Bldg., 120 State St., Montpelier VT 05602, †; SRI/MF/complete.

S8020–2.4: 1981/82 Financial Statistics,
Vermont School Systems
[Annual. [1984.] 197 p. Rpt. No. 052. SRI/MF/complete.]

Contains contents listing (1 p.); and 7 extended tables showing the following data, by county, town, supervisory unit, and/or school district:

a. State aid analysis, including total aid, FY83; resident pupil average daily membership, FY82; and current expenses, FY81. (p. 2-15)

b. Measures of local effort and capacity, including median adjusted gross income, 1980; equalized school tax rate, FY81; and wealth indexes, FY82 or FY83. (p. 16-30)

c. Transportation costs, and number of students transported, 1981/82. (p. 32-63)

d. Revenues, by source; operating and other expenditures, by function; and cost per pupil; 1981/82. (p. 65-197)

S8020–3   VERMONT EDUCATION
STATISTICS, 1982/83
Annual series. For individual
publication data, see below.
SRI/MF/complete

Series of 4 annual reports, each presenting data on an aspect of Vermont elementary and secondary education, 1982/83. Topics covered are enrollment, facilities, administration and staff, and finances. Some reports include nonpublic school data.

Data are compiled by the Dept of Education from reports by individual school districts.

Report for 1982/83 reviewed during 1984 is described below. Other reports for 1982/83 are described in SRI 1983 Annual under this number. Reports for 1980/81 and 1981/82 are covered in SRI under S8020-1 and S8020-2, respectively.

Availability: Vermont Department of Education, Statistics and Information Office, State Office Bldg., 120 State St., Montpelier VT 05602, †; SRI/MF/complete.

S8020–3.3: 1982/83 Financial Statistics,
Vermont School Systems
[Annual. [1984.] 199 p. Rpt. No. 052. SRI/MF/complete.]

Contains contents listing (1 p.); and 7 extended tables showing the following data, by county, town, supervisory unit, and/or school district:

a. State aid distributed, including total aid, FY84; resident pupil long-term average daily attendance FY83; wealth indexes, FY84; and current expenses, FY82. (p. 2-15)

b. Measures of local effort and capacity, including median adjusted gross income, 1981; equalized school tax rate, FY82; and wealth and income indexes, various years FY81-84. (p. 17-32)

c. Transportation costs, number of students transported, and average cost per student as a percent of operating expenditures, 1982/83. (p. 34-65)

d. Revenues, by source; operating and other expenditures, by function; and cost per pupil; 1982/83. (p. 67-199)

For description of 1981/82 annual report, see S8020-2.4 above.

S8025   VERMONT
Department of
Employment and Training

S8025–1   WOMEN: LABOR FORCE,
EMPLOYMENT,
UNEMPLOYMENT, WAGES,
1982, Vermont
Annual. [1984.] 26 p.
SRI/MF/complete

Annual report on Vermont women's labor force by employment status, 1982, with comparisons to men and selected trends from the 1960s. Includes data by age, occupation, industry division and selected major group, county, and unemployment reason and duration.

Also includes data on population by sex; average earnings by industry division, sex, occupation, age, and educational attainment; and U.S. median earnings by sex and occupation, various years 1955-81.

Data are from Census Bureau, BLS, and quarterly reports of employees subject to Vermont's Unemployment Compensation Law.

Contains listing of contents, tables, and charts (1 p.); report, with summary, 5 charts, and 18 tables (p. 1-24); and glossary (p. 25-26).

Availability: Vermont Department of Employment and Training, Research and Statistics Section, PO Box 488, Green Mountain Dr., Montpelier VT 05602-0488, $5.00; SRI/MF/complete.

S8025–2   VERMONT ANNUAL
PLANNING INFORMATION,
1984
Annual. Aug. 1984. 35 p.
SRI/MF/complete

Annual report, for 1984, identifying Vermont population groups most in need of employment services. Includes data on population by county; employment by industry; labor force, by county and labor market area; and socioeconomic characteristics of job applicants; various years 1970-83 with employment projections for 1990.

Data are compiled from reports by various Federal and State agencies.

Contents:

a. Listings of contents, tables, and charts. (2 p.)

b. Foreword and highlights; and narrative report, interspersed with 2 maps showing Vermont counties and labor market areas, 3 charts, and 19 tables listed below. (p. 1-32)

c. Additional sources of information, glossary, and description of labor market areas. (p. 33-35)

Availability: Vermont Department of Employment and Training, Research and Statistics Section, PO Box 488, Green Mountain Dr., Montpelier VT 05602-0488, †; SRI/MF/complete.

TABLES:
[Data are for the State of Vermont, unless otherwise noted.]

S8025–2.1: Employment, Population, and Income
[Population data are shown for 1970, 1980, and estimated 1982.]

CITIES AND EMPLOYMENT

1. Population of major cities and towns. (p. 6)

2. Major employment centers, by county. [list] (p. 7)

3. Top 10 industries, estimated nonagricultural wage and salary employment, 1983. (p. 7)

POPULATION

4. Population by age group and sex. (p. 8)

5-6. Population of counties and labor market areas. (p. 9-10)

INCOME

7. Per capita income, annual average wages in covered employment, average hourly earnings, and the CPI, [for U.S. and Vermont], 1970-83. (p. 11)

8. Annual average wages and per capita income, by county, 1982. (p. 12)

S8025–2.2: Employment, Turnover, Labor Force, Unemployment, and Job Services

EMPLOYMENT BY INDUSTRY

9. Average estimated nonagricultural wage/ salary employment [by industry division, major manufacturing group, and government level], 1980 and 1982-83. (p. 14)

10. Employment by industry [and for government by level], 1980 and 1990. (p. 16)

LABOR FORCE

[Labor force tables also show employment. Tables 11A and 12-16A show current population survey estimates; tables 11B and 16B show "Handbook" estimates developed by the State.]

11A-11B. Labor force estimates, annual averages, [various years] 1970-83. (p. 19-21)

12. Labor force by age group [and for] white and nonwhite, 1983. (p. 23)

13. Labor force by sex and race, 1980 and 1983. (p. 24)

14. Comparison of unemployment rates: annual averages, U.S., New England, and Vermont, 1976-83. (p. 25)

15-16B. Labor force estimates: counties and labor market areas, annual averages, 1983. (p. 26-28)

CHARACTERISTICS OF UNEMPLOYED AND JOB APPLICANTS

17. Characteristics of the insured unemployed [receiving] regular benefits [sex, age, industry, occupation, and duration of unemployment], 1983 annual averages. (p. 29)

18. Characteristics of fully registered active applicants [sex, occupation, age, and educational attainment, and number of total and Vietnam era veterans and handicapped persons], Vermont job service, FY82-83. (p. 31)

JOB OPENINGS

19. Job openings received [by occupational category and duration of job], Vermont job service, FY82-83. (p. 32)

S8035   VERMONT
Department of Finance and Information Support

S8035–1   **ANNUAL REPORT OF THE COMMISSIONER OF FINANCE AND INFORMATION SUPPORT, State of Vermont, for the Fiscal Year Ended June 30, 1983**
Annual.   Dec. 31, 1983.
162 p.
ISSN 0093-2965.
LC 74-641290.
SRI/MF/complete

Annual report on financial condition of Vermont State government for FY83, presenting assets, liabilities, and fund balance; revenues by source; and expenditures by function, object, and/or agency; for general, transportation, fish/game, special, Federal revenue, bond, enterprise, internal service, and agency funds.

Also includes data on appropriations compared to actual expenditures; long-term bonded debt; and finances of State lottery.

Contains contents listing (p. 2-3); and report, with 52 financial exhibits and schedules (p. 4-162).

An annual summary report on financial condition, *Vermont, a Fiscal Summary of 1983,* is also published by the Finance and Information Support Dept but is not covered by SRI.

Availability: Vermont Department of Finance and Information Support, 133 State St., Montpelier VT 05602, †; SRI/MF/complete.

S8050   VERMONT
Office of the Governor

S8050–1   **COMMUNITY PROFILES, VERMONT**
Monograph.   May 1983.
752 p. var. paging.
SRI/MF/complete

Set of profiles for 246 Vermont communities, presenting demographic and socioeconomic data primarily for 1980, with comparisons to 1970, and population trends from 1960. Profiles cover the following:

a. Population, by sex, race, age group, marital status, educational attainment, and residence 5 years ago (including different Vermont county, specific U.S. region, and abroad); and median age.

b. Households and average size; men and women living alone; households with 6/more persons; percent of housing units with more than 1 person per room; mobile homes as percent of total housing units; households with 1/ more persons age 65/older (living alone, family, nonfamily, and institutionalized); and families by composition.

c. Employment and unemployment, by sex; percent employed in agriculture and manufacturing; labor force status of females with

children under age 6 and age 6/older, and of persons with work disability; and number of persons with public transportation disability.

d. Income distribution, and median income, for households and families; per capita income; poverty status of families and individuals, with detail for families with children, female-headed families, and persons age 65/older; and percent of population receiving Aid to Needy Families with Children, food stamps, and SSI.

Public assistance data are from the Vermont Dept of Social Welfare. All other data are from the Census Bureau.

Contains a 3-page profile, with 8 tables, for each community. Profiles are arranged by county.

Individual profiles may be requested from the issuing agency.

Availability: Vermont Office of the Governor, Policy Research Staff, Pavilion Office Bldg., 109 State St., Montpelier VT 05602, ◆; SRI/MF/complete.

S8050–2   **STF 3 PROFILES: 10 Largest Towns, Vermont**
Monograph.   [1983.]   122 p.
SRI/MF/complete

Compilation of profiles for the 10 largest towns in Vermont, presenting 1980 U.S. Census of Population and Housing detailed findings. Includes data on population and housing characteristics, households, employment, commuting, education, income, and poverty.

Data are from U.S. Census Summary Tape File 3.

Data topics conform to those noted in the basic data topic description for Summary Tape File 3 reports (see S9990-2).

Contains a 12-page profile, with tabular data, for each town.

Availability: Vermont Office of the Governor, Policy Research Staff, Pavilion Office Bldg., 109 State St., Montpelier VT 05602, $6.00; SRI/MF/complete.

S8054   VERMONT
Department of Health

S8054–1   **1982 ANNUAL REPORT OF VITAL STATISTICS in Vermont**
Annual.   Dec. 1983.
ix+146 p.
LC 77-641747.
SRI/MF/complete

Annual report, presenting Vermont vital statistics, including population estimates, births, deaths by detailed cause, marriages, and divorces, 1982, with trends from 1857. Data are shown by county of residence and/or occurrence and selected demographic characteristics. Data are from State health dept records.

Contains listings of contents, tables, and charts (p. iii-ix); introduction, with 3 charts and definitions (p. 2-8); report in 5 sections, with narrative summaries, and 12 trend charts and 78 tables (p. 10-140); and 4 appendices, with listings of State hospitals, death and injury classifications, and Public Health Statistics Division staff (p. 142-146).

All tables are listed below. Report is the 98th in a series begun in 1857.

Availability: Vermont Department of Health, Public Health Statistics Division, 60 Main St., PO Box 70, Burlington VT 05402, †; SRI/MF/ complete.

TABLES:

[Tables show data for Vermont, 1982, unless otherwise noted. Data by State of residence include Canada.]

S8054–1.1: Vital Events Summary

[A] Summary of vital events. (p. 10)

1. Vital statistics [historical] summary [includes midyear population; live and illegitimate births; infant, neonatal, fetal, maternal, and total deaths; marriages; and divorces; selected years] 1857-1982. (p. 13)

2. Estimated population by sex, age, and county. (p. 14)

3. Selected statistics [population, births, deaths, marriages, and divorces], by town of event [and/or] residence [includes births at home and with low birth weight; and infant deaths]. (p. 16-22)

S8054–1.2: Resident Births

[Table titles 5-21 begin "Vermont resident births..." Tables 12-21 show number of events and row or cumulative row percents.]

[B] Births [by 10 boys' and girls'] names most frequently given. (p. 24)

4. Geographic distribution of births [occurring in Vermont, by State of residence; and Vermont resident births, by State of occurrence]. (p. 27)

5-7. Sex, by month of birth, number of births and row percents; and selected characteristics [sex, legitimacy, plurality, and birth order] by age of mother and by county of residence. (p. 27-28)

8-9. Race of child [including American Indian], by age of mother and county of residence. (p. 29)

10-11. Age of mother by county of residence: number of events and row percents, and age specific fertility rates and crude birth rates. (p. 30-31)

12-15. Month of birth, education of mother, number of prenatal visits, and month prenatal care began, [all] by county of residence. (p. 32)

16-18. Birth weight in grams: by county of residence, weeks gestation, and age of mother and sex of child. (p. 36-40)

19-21. Month prenatal care began, by education of mother, number of prenatal visits, and age of mother. (p. 41-43)

22. [Vermont births by] county of residence, by place of birth. (p. 44)

23. [Births occurring in Vermont, by] attendant [doctor, midwife, nurse, family member, and other], by place of birth [including at home, individual hospitals, and physician's office]. (p. 45)

S8054–1.3: Resident Deaths

[Table titles 27-40 begin "Vermont resident deaths...," and generally show number of deaths.]

LEADING CAUSES

24. 10 leading causes of death, by sex, Vermont residents, 1982, with trends [for selected periods 1952-81, and] rates per 100,000 population. (p. 51)

25. Leading causes of death by age groups and sex, rates per 100,000 population. (p. 52)

DEMOGRAPHIC CHARACTERISTICS

26. Geographic distribution of deaths [occurring in Vermont, by State of residence; and Vermont resident deaths, by State of occurrence]. (p. 55)

27-28. Age at death, and age specific and crude death rates per 100,000 population, by county of residence. (p. 56)

29. Age at death by marital status and sex. (p. 57)

30-31. Month of death by county of residence and disposition of body [including burial, cremation, and medical study]. (p. 58)

32. Race by county of residence. (p. 59)

CERTIFICATION OF DEATH

33. Autopsy by certifier to death [doctor, medical examiner, and pathologist]. (p. 59)

SELECTED CAUSES OF DEATH

34-39. Sex, county of residence, age at death, and month of death; and assignment of selected causes as the underlying cause of death or as a multiple cause of death, and the ratio of multiple to underlying causes; [all] by 72 selected causes. (p. 60-71)

ACCIDENTAL DEATHS

[Place of accident includes home, farm, mine/ quarry, industrial, recreational, street/sidewalk, public building, resident institution, lake/river, others, and unknown.]

40. Number of deaths with mention of an external cause of death, by nature of injury; number of events and row percents. (p. 72)

41-42. Resident accidental deaths, [by] weekday of death by place of accident; and age at death by place of accident and sex. (p. 73-74)

PLACE OF DEATH

43. Vermont deaths [by] county of residence by place of death. (p. 70)

DETAILED CAUSE

44. Residents: [detailed] cause of death, by age at death and sex. (p. 76-107)

S8054–1.4: Infant and Fetal Deaths, and Abortions

INFANT AND FETAL DEATHS

45-51. Resident fetal, perinatal, neonatal, and infant deaths and rates, by age of mother, county of residence, weeks of gestation, and birth weight. (p. 112-116)

52. Resident fetal deaths: birth weight in grams by cause of death. (p. 117)

53. Resident infant deaths: [detailed] cause of death by age at death, and sex. (p. 118-120)

ABORTION

[Tables show data for abortions performed in Vermont. Data by county of residence include totals for out-of-State residents.]

54-61. Abortions, by age and race of patient, by State of residence; month of procedure by type of facility; age of patient by county of residence; county of residence by county of abortion; patient's education by county of resi-

dence; patient's marital status by number of living children; and weeks of gestation by abortion procedure. (p. 123-127)

S8054–1.5: Marriages and Divorces

MARRIAGES

62-68. Marriages, by State of residence of groom and bride; county of residence of bride by county of residence of groom; education of bride by education of groom; age of bride by age of groom; month of marriage by county of marriage; marriage number of bride by marriage number of groom; and race of bride and groom by respective residence. (p.132-135)

DIVORCES

[Table titles 69-78 begin "Vermont divorces..."]

69-73. Plaintiff and legal grounds for decree, month of divorce, length of separation, number of years married, and number of children under 18, [all] by county of decree. (p. 136-138)

74-78. Education of wife by education of husband; age of wife by age of husband at time of divorce; marriage number of wife by marriage number of husband; and length of marriage by husband's and wife's age at marriage. (p. 138-140)

S8054–2   VERMONT POPULATION PROJECTIONS, 1985-2000

Monograph.   Oct. 1983.
3+39 p.+addenda.
LC 84-620636.
SRI/MF/complete

Report presenting projections of Vermont population and population components. Includes births, deaths, net migration, and population by age and sex, by county; and population by town; quinquennially or 5-year periods 1980-2000.

Projections are shown for high and low migration assumptions, and are based on Census Bureau data.

Contains preface, and listings of contents, tables, and charts (3 p.); introduction with 4 charts and 3 tables (p. 1-9); summary methodology, and 2 extended tables (p. 10-33); appendix with detailed methodology, and references (p. 34-39); and addenda with 2 summary tables (2 p.).

Availability: Vermont Department of Health, Public Health Statistics Division, 60 Main St., PO Box 70, Burlington VT 05402, †; SRI/MF/ complete.

S8095   VERMONT
Department of
Public Safety

S8095–1   VERMONT DEPARTMENT OF PUBLIC SAFETY ANNUAL REPORT, FY83
Annual. Dec. 1, 1983.
iii+65 p.+errata sheet.
LC 49-45379.
SRI/MF/complete

Annual report, for FY83, of the Vermont Dept of Public Safety, reporting primarily on State Police enforcement activities. Includes data on fires, crimes by offense, traffic enforcement, and other dept activities.

Contains contents listing (p. i); and foreword and 5 division reports, as follows, with data shown for FY83 unless otherwise noted:

Foreword. Includes 2 tables showing dept personnel and vacancies, by division; and dept appropriations and expenditures, by division and source of funds. (p. ii-iii)

Section 1. Administration. Includes text data, 3 charts, and 2 tables showing explosives license fees collected; snowmobile and motorboat registrations and receipts; and snowfall accumulation, FY79-83. (p. 2-5)

Section 2. Civil Defense Division. Includes text data on number of assistance calls related to hazardous materials incidents and other problems. (p. 7-9)

Section 3. Criminal Division. Includes 2 charts and 9 tables showing cases and rates for 7 major crimes, FY68-83, with rate comparisons to U.S.; incidence of 26 minor crimes, FY82-83; population, 1960-85; polygraph exams, by purpose, agency, location, and results; fires by county, month, and day; fire damage value by county; and fire trends, including arsons, juvenile involvement, arrests, and deaths, FY77-83. (p. 11-25)

Section 4. Field Force Division. Includes text data, 2 charts, and 1 table showing fatal traffic accidents and deaths, 1979-82; 55 mph speed limit violations and enforcement hours; motor vehicle arrests, trucks weighed, and accident investigations, FY79-83; truck weighing, hazardous material transportation, marine safety, and canine program activities; dept vehicle maintenance activities and cost savings; and snowmobile accidents, FY79-83. (p. 27-45)

Section 5. Support Services Division. Includes text data on crime laboratory, training unit, community relations, and crime history unit activities. (p. 47-65)

Availability: Vermont Department of Libraries, c/o State Office Bldg. Post Office, Montpelier VT 05602, †; SRI/MF/complete.

S8125   VERMONT
Department of
Taxes

S8125–1   1982 VERMONT TAX STATISTICS
Annual. Nov. 1983. 89 p.
ISSN 0149-1385.
LC 77-623630.
SRI/MF/complete

Annual report on 1982 Vermont individual income tax returns. Includes data on income, filings, refunds, exemptions, tax credits, and Federal and State taxes, all by income class, county, and town. Also includes property and sales tax refunds, by income class and county.

Data are from 1982 individual income tax returns filed in 1983 with the Dept of Taxes.

Contains table listing (1 p.); and 18 tables, listed below (p. 1-89).

A biennial report with detail on other major State taxes is also issued by Vermont Dept of Taxes, but is not covered in SRI.

Availability: Vermont Department of Taxes, Pavillion Office Bldg., 109 State St., Montpelier VT 05602, †; SRI/MF/complete.

TABLES:

S8125–1.1: Personal Income Tax Returns
[Most table titles begin "1982 Vermont personal income tax returns..."]

STATE SUMMARY BY INCOME CLASS
[Tables [1-7] show data by adjusted gross income class. Tables [1-3] and [5-6] include returns for out-of-State and unclassified residence.]

[1] Number of returns filed, by marital status and type of tax credits [also shows number of exemptions, returns with refunds and no tax owed, taxes withheld and estimated, and adjusted tax]. (p. 1)

[2-3] Amount of [adjusted and taxable] income, [Federal and State] tax, and tax-offsets (credits). (p. 2-3)

[4] [Number of returns, by Vermont State taxable income]. (p. 4)

[5] Distribution of 1982 income tax refunds by refund range. (p. 5)

[6] Filed by aged 65/over individuals [including number by marital status, number of exemptions, number and amount of $7,000 credits, number with refunds, and amounts of Vermont income and Federal and State tax]. (p. 6)

[7] 1982 Vermont energy schedule statistics [including number of claims by energy system type]. (p. 7)

COUNTY AND TOWN DATA
[Tables [10], [12], and [15] include number of exemptions and/or returns with no tax owed, and amounts of income and State tax.]

[8-9] [Data similar to tables [1-2], repeated by county.] (p. 8-9)

[10] County distribution by income class. (p. 10)

[11] [Data similar to table [6], repeated by county.] (p. 13)

[12] Age 65, county distribution by income class. (p. 14)

[13-14] Distribution of numbers [data similar to table [1]; and of dollars [adjusted gross income, Federal and State tax, and credits by type]; by town. (p. 17-36)

[15] Town distribution by income class. (p. 37-73)

S8125–1.2: Property and Sales Tax Refunds
[Data are shown by county.]

[1-2] 1982 Vermont homeowner or renter [under and over age 65] rebates distribution [by household] income class. (p. 74-88)

[3] 1982 individual income tax system: sales tax refund statistics [number of claims and exemptions, and amount of refund, by income category], as of Oct. 29, 1983. (p. 89)

S8170   VIRGINIA
Office of the
Comptroller

S8170–1   ANNUAL REPORT OF THE COMPTROLLER TO THE GOVERNOR OF VIRGINIA for the Fiscal Year Ended June 30, 1983
Annual. Jan. 6, 1984. 92 p.
LC 30-27263.
SRI/MF/complete

Annual report on financial condition of Virginia State government, FY83, presenting assets and liabilities, revenues by source, expenditures by object and major function, and fund balances, for general, special revenue, debt service, capital projects, enterprise, internal service, public benefit corporations, trust and agency, and higher education funds, with comparisons to FY82 and selected trends from 1974.

Also includes general fund budget and anticipated revenues for FY84; bonded debt obligations through 2009; State aid to localities by program; and nonagricultural wage/salary employment by industry division, 1978 and 1982.

Contains listings of contents and charts (3 p.); transmittal letter and summary sections, with 21 summary charts and tables (p. 2-11); 2 financial sections, with 36 fund statements, accompanying footnotes, 16 text tables, and 9 charts (p. 13-83); and statistical section, with 7 tables (p. 85-92).

Availability: Virginia Office of the Comptroller, PO Box 6-N, Richmond VA 23215, †; SRI/MF/complete.

S8180   VIRGINIA
Corporation Commission

S8180–1   1983 INSURANCE COMPANY STATISTICAL REPORT, Virginia
Annual. [1984.]
738 p. var. paging.
SRI/MF/complete

Annual report on Virginia insurance industry financial condition and underwriting activity, by company and type of insurance, 1983.

Covers assets; liabilities; capital, reserves, and/or surplus; premiums written, earned, in force, terminated, and/or paid; dividends, losses incurred and paid, or claims paid; operating, investment, and/or underwriting gains or losses; taxes; and other income and expense data; as applicable for insurers based in Virginia and elsewhere.

Data are shown for property/casualty, mutual assessment fire, life/accident/sickness, and title insurers; workmen's compensation group self insurance assns; fraternal benefit and burial societies; prepaid health plans; and HMOs. Data on property/casualty insurers include detail for medical malpractice, fidelity/surety, automobile, and credit insurance policies.

Data are compiled from required reports submitted by individual insurers.

Contains index (1 p.); and 11 detailed tables (737 p.).

Previous report, for 1982, was titled *Report on Insurers Transacting Business in Virginia*, and was issued in 2 volumes.

Availability: Virginia Corporation Commission, Insurance Bureau, PO Box 1157, Richmond VA 23209, †; SRI/MF/complete.

S8180–2   1983 ANNUAL REPORT OF THE BUREAU OF FINANCIAL INSTITUTIONS, State Corporation Commission, Commonwealth of Virginia
Annual. [1984.]   141 p.
LC 80-642269.
SRI/MF/complete

Annual report presenting assets and liabilities for Virginia State-chartered banks, mutual and stock savings and loan assns, industrial loan assns, and credit unions, as of Dec. 31, 1983. Includes data for individual banks and savings and loan assns, arranged by city.

Also includes bank and credit union consolidated income and expenses; aggregate financial and operating ratios for banks by asset size; Virginia Credit Union Share Insurance Corp. assets and liabilities/equity; and summary comparisons to 1982.

Data are from reports filed with the State Bureau of Financial Institutions.

Contains contents listing (p. 2); and report, with institution status changes and directories, 2 charts, and 12 tables (p. 3-141).

Availability: Virginia Corporation Commission, Financial Institutions Bureau, PO Box 2AE, Richmond VA 23205, †; SRI/MF/complete.

S8190   VIRGINIA
Department of Education

S8190–2   FACING UP—18: Statistical Data on Virginia's Public Schools, 1982/83 School Year
Annual. May 1984.   61 p.
LC 70-626338.
SRI/MF/complete

Annual report on public education in Virginia, for school year 1982/83, covering enrollment, staff, salaries, finances, graduates, and test scores, by county and municipality.

Contains contents and table listing, and introduction with 1 summary table (p. 1-2); and 12 tables, listed below (p. 3-61).

Availability: Virginia Department of Education, Management Information Services Division, PO Box 6Q, Richmond VA 23216, †; SRI/MF/complete.

TABLES:
[Tables show data for Virginia, by county and municipality, 1982/83, unless otherwise noted.]

ENROLLMENT, CLASS SIZE, TEACHERS, AND SALARIES

1. Student membership, Sept. 30 [and] end-of-year membership [1980/81-1982/83]. (p. 3-7)

2-3. Ratio of [elementary and secondary] pupils to classroom teaching positions, regular day school; ratio of pupils to instructional personnel K-6; average salaries of classroom teaching positions; instructional personnel positions per 1,000 students in ADM [average daily membership; and] average salaries based on instructional positions; 1982/83 [and 1981/82 salaries]. (p. 8-17)

STUDENT PROMOTIONS AND TEST SCORES

4. Students promoted, 3-year period [1980/81-1982/83]. (p. 18-22)

5. National percentile equivalents of selected average scores, Virginia State Assessment Program [reading, language arts, and math; grades 4, 8, and 11]. (p. 23-27)

GRADUATES, POSTGRADUATE ACTIVITIES, AND DROPOUTS

6. Graduates [number and] as percent of 9th grade membership 4 years earlier [1980/81-1982/83]. (p. 28-32)

7. Graduates continuing education [including number attending 2- and 4-year colleges], job-entry skills [number not continuing education, and percent with marketable skills], and dropouts grades 8-12. (p. 33-37)

FINANCES

8. 1982-84 composite index of local ability-to-pay costs of standards of quality [true property value; personal income; taxable retail sales; ADM on Mar. 31, 1980; and total population]. (p. 38-42)

9. Total local expenditures for operations, and sources of financial support for expenditures. (p. 43-47)

10. State basic aid and categorical aid to localities for operations [by purpose, including special and vocational education, and pupil transportation; with per pupil totals]. (p. 48)

11. Per pupil expenditure for operations from local, State, and Federal funds. (p. 52-56)

12. Expenditures for capital outlay [buildings/sites, buses/other vehicles, furniture/equipment, and other] and debt service. (p. 57-61)

S8195   VIRGINIA
Board of Elections

S8195–1   COMMONWEALTH OF VIRGINIA OFFICIAL ELECTION RESULTS, 1983
Annual. [1984.]   51 p.
SRI/MF/complete

Annual report presenting results of the Virginia primary and general elections, held June 14-Nov. 8, 1983. Shows voting for State senators and delegates. Also includes general election voter registration and turnout.

Data are shown by county, city, and/or district. Also shows party affiliation of candidates.

Contains table of contents (p. 2); 1 summary table and index of counties and cities (p. 2-3); and 6 tables (p. 4-51).

Availability: Virginia Board of Elections, 101 Ninth St. Office Bldg., Richmond VA 23219-3497, †; SRI/MF/complete.

S8205   VIRGINIA
Employment Commission

S8205–5   EMPLOYMENT, HOURS, AND EARNINGS in Virginia and Its Metropolitan Areas
Monthly.   Approx. 20 p.
SRI/MF/complete, shipped quarterly

Monthly report on Virginia labor force, employment, hours, and earnings, shown by industry group, SMSA, and selected labor market areas. Includes data on female employment.

Most data are collected by the State Employment Commission in cooperation with BLS, and are based on payroll records of a sample of approximately 7,000 establishments. Month of coverage is 1 month preceding cover date.

Contains contents and table listing; highlights, occasionally with summary data; 28 monthly tables, listed below; and explanatory notes.

Prior to Mar. 1984 issue, report title was *Virginia Employment, Hours, and Earnings,* and report was described in SRI under S8270-2. Issuing agency has changed from Virginia Dept of Labor and Industry.

Availability: Virginia Employment Commission, Research and Analysis Division, 703 E. Main St., PO Box 1358, Richmond VA 23211-1358, †; SRI/MF/complete, shipped quarterly.

Issues reviewed during 1984: Mar.-Sept. 1984 (P) (Vol. 34, Nos. 3-9) [Mar. 1984 volume and issue numbers are omitted.]

MONTHLY TABLES:
[Most data are shown for month of coverage, preceding month, and same month of preceding year. Tables are listed in order of appearance.

Prior to May 1984 issue, report also includes 1 table on labor force estimates for SMSAs and labor market areas.]

A1. Estimated employment in nonagricultural industries [by industry group].

A2. Employees in nonagricultural establishments, by industry divisions, annual averages [for 10 previous years, and monthly for current year to date and 4 preceding years].

A3. Estimated female employment in nonagricultural industries [by industry group].

A4. Estimated number of production workers in manufacturing industries [by industry group].

A5-A14. Estimated employment in nonagricultural industries [by industry division and major manufacturing group, by SMSA and labor market area].

C1-C10. Hours and gross earnings of production workers in manufacturing industries [by industry group, by SMSA and labor market area].

E1. CPI for all urban consumers, U.S. city average [monthly for current year to date and 13-14 preceding years].

D1. Seasonally adjusted employment in nonagricultural industries [by industry group].

D2. Employees in nonagricultural establishments, seasonally adjusted, by industry divisions, annual averages [for 10 preceding years, and monthly for current year to date and 4 preceding years].

D3. Seasonally adjusted weekly hours of manufacturing production workers [by industry group].

S8225   VIRGINIA
Department of Health

S8225–1   1982 VITAL STATISTICS ANNUAL REPORT, Virginia
Annual. [1983.] v+168 p.
LC 56-32221.
SRI/MF/complete

Annual compilation, for 1982, of Virginia vital statistics, including population, births, deaths by cause, marriages, and divorces, by demographic characteristics and location. Also includes trends from 1963, and data on communicable diseases. Data are from State records, and are often shown by county and independent city.

Contents:

a. Listing of contents, charts, and tables. (p. i-v)

b. Introduction, definitions, and narrative analysis, with 7 charts and 59 text tables including data on births, deaths, and marriages involving residents of Virginia and bordering States, suicides and homicides by method, marriages and divorces by educational attainment of husband and wife, and cremations by place of occurrence and month. (p. 1-44)

c. 55 detailed tables, listed below. (p. 46-155)

d. Communicable disease analysis, with 6 tables, also listed below. (p. 158-168)

This is the 70th annual report.

Availability: Virginia Department of Health, Health Statistics Center, PO Box 1000, Richmond VA 23208-1000, $5.00; SRI/MF/complete.

TABLES:
[Data by location, place of residence, or place of occurrence are shown for individual counties, independent cities, and 22 health planning districts. Data by location generally refer to place of residence. Data are for 1982, unless otherwise noted.]

S8225–1.1: Summary, Population, Births, and Deaths

SUMMARY AND POPULATION

1. Vital events with rates [by location]. (p. 46)

2. Projected population for July 1, 1982, by race [by locality]. (p. 48)

TRENDS

[Tables 3-5 show data by race, 1963-82, with rates.]

3. Estimated population, births, deaths, marriages, and divorces. (p. 49)

4. Resident illegitimate births and immature births with percent of total births, and deaths under 1 year and under 28 days. (p. 50)

5. Resident total pregnancy terminations, live births, all fetal deaths, induced abortions, and natural fetal deaths. (p. 51)

BIRTHS AND FETAL DEATHS

6. Live births by place of occurrence and place of residence, with resident rate per 1,000 population, by race. (p. 52)

7-9. Live births by place of delivery [hospital, and nonhospital physician and midwife/other]; illegitimate live births, immature births, and congenital anomalies, with percent of total births; and resident live births by age of mother; [by location, generally by race]. (p. 54-64)

10-11. Resident live births, by birth order by birth weight, and by birth weight by race and age of mother. (p. 64-65)

12-13. Resident live births and percent distribution, by live birth order, by age and race of mother. (p. 66)

14-15. Resident live births by education of mother, by birth order and trimester care began. (p. 67)

16-17. Resident live births by birth order and age of mother, by trimester care began. (p. 67)

18-19. Resident births with Apgar score, by age of mother, race, and sex. (p. 68)

20-21. Complications of pregnancy and congenital anomalies reported for resident live births, by trimester care began. (p. 69)

22. Resident live births and natural fetal deaths by race and sex, by month of delivery and number of individuals delivered per confinement. (p. 70)

23. Resident live births by sex, and sex ratio, by race, 1973-82. (p. 70)

24. Resident pregnancy terminations (live births/induced abortions/natural fetal deaths) by race and legitimacy status, with percent illegitimate, by age of mother. (p. 70)

25-27. Resident live births, natural fetus deaths, and induced abortions, by race and legitimacy status, with percent illegitimate, by age of mother. (p. 71)

28. Teenage total pregnancy terminations, live births, induced abortions, and natural fetal deaths, [by age group and location]. (p. 72)

29-32. Natural fetal deaths by length of gestation, by race; resident natural fetal deaths by

age of mother; induced abortions by race and legitimacy status, with percent illegitimate; and resident induced abortions by age of mother; [all by location]. (p. 74-81)

33. Resident natural fetal deaths: length of gestation by race, by cause of death. (p. 82)

INFANT DEATHS

[Tables 34-36 show data by race, by location.]

34. Neonatal deaths with rates per 1,000 live births. (p. 83)

35. Infant deaths by place of occurrence and place of residence; with resident rate per 1,000 live births. (p. 84)

36. Perinatal mortality rate with infant deaths under 1 week and fetal deaths 28 weeks and over gestation. (p. 86)

37-38. Resident infant deaths: by race and sex, by cause of death, with rates per 100,000 live births; and by age and cause of death. (p. 88-91)

ALL DEATHS

39. Deaths by place of occurrence and place of residence, with resident rate per 1,000 population, by race. (p. 92)

40. Resident deaths from important causes, with rates per 100,000 population, by race, 1973-82. (p. 94)

41. Resident deaths by age, by cause, sex, and race. (p. 96-102)

42. Five leading causes of death in specified age groups, by race. (p. 103)

43-44. Resident accidental and home accident deaths, by age, by type of accident. (p. 104-105)

45. Deaths by place of occurrence and place of residence, by race, by cause. (p. 106)

46. Deaths by race, by cause [and location]. (p. 107-146)

S8225–1.2: Marriages, Divorces, and Communicable Diseases

MARRIAGES

47-48. Marriages: by type of ceremony, by month; and by previous marital status of bride [and] groom, according to race of groom. (p. 147)

49-50. Marriages: by place of [occurrence], residence of bride, and residence of groom, by race; and by age of bride by age of groom. (p. 148-150)

DIVORCES

51. Divorces (including annulments) and annulments only, by race, by month of decree. (p. 151)

52-53. Divorces (including annulments) by race of husband: by place of marriage [Virginia or elsewhere] and number of minor children in family; and by cause of divorce by [location] where granted. (p. 151-153)

54-55. Divorces (including annulments): by duration of marriage and person granted divorce, by plaintiff and cause of divorce; and by age of wife by age of husband. (p. 154-155)

COMMUNICABLE DISEASES

[A-B] New, active tuberculosis cases: by race; and [physiological] location of disease by bacteriologic status. (p. 161)

56. Reported cases of certain communicable diseases [by locality]. (p. 163)

57. Reported cases and deaths from certain communicable diseases, with case rates per 100,000 estimated population, 1973-82. (p. 165)

58. Reported cases of venereal disease [by type and location]. (p. 166)

59. Tuberculosis cases under supervision; and newly reported cases, with rates per 100,000 population; by race; [by location]. (p. 168)

S8270   VIRGINIA
Department of
Labor and Industry

S8270–1   1982-83 BIENNIAL REPORT, Department of Labor and Industry, Virginia
Biennial.   June 30, 1984.
111 p.
LC 9-219.   SRI/MF/complete

Biennial report of the Virginia Dept of Labor and Industry, with data on labor law enforcement; apprenticeship programs; occupational health and safety; employment; food prices; and natural gas, oil, coal, and other mineral production and related data; 1982-83.

Contains contents listing (p. 5); and 10 narrative sections (p. 7-111), with the following interspersed charts and tables, presenting data for 1982-83 unless otherwise noted:

a. Boiler/pressure vessel safety division activities, including registrations, inspections, inspectors, and inspector examination results; and number of reported violations, injuries, and fatalities. 1 table. (p. 11)

b. Labor law court cases, dispositions, and complaint investigations; employment certificates issued to minors, 1974-83; wages collected under State minimum wage/garnishment statutes, 1979-83; and value of child labor civil money penalties, with children involved and violations by type. 2 charts and 4 tables. (p. 13-18)

c. Apprenticeship programs and participants, by type of system, bargaining agency (labor union), area, occupation group, and company size (number of employees), with selected trends from 1940; and field staff activities, by area. 12 tables. (p. 20-32)

d. Inspections and other activities of the industrial safety, construction safety, and voluntary safety compliance and training divisions; and contract construction industry employment, by metro area, 1980-83. 4 tables. (p. 34-39)

e. Workers' compensation case distribution by type of accident and by body parts affected, with accident type detail by industry division and occupation, 1982; and occupational injury/illness incidence rates and lost workdays, by SIC 2- and 3-digit industry, 1981-82, with summary data for 1980 and comparisons to 1982 employment. 1 chart and 3 tables. (p. 42-47)

f. Employment (total and female) by industry group; and employment, hours, and earnings of production workers in selected manufacturing industries; generally shown for State and 7-8 metro areas, 1980-83. 18 tables. (p. 48-63)

g. Retail food price comparison for 3 metro areas, by detailed commodity, Jan. and Dec. 1982-83. 2 tables. (p. 65-66)

h. Manufacturers annual survey, showing employment and salaries/wages for all employees and production workers, value added by manufacturers, capital expenditures, and anticipated capital expenditures, by industry group, for State and 7 metro areas, 1981-82; and capital expenditures (State only), 1977-82. 1 chart and 16 tables. (p. 67-84)

i. Mine health and safety enforcement inspections, by type; miner education and training activities; and certificates and cards/permits issued. 4 tables. (p. 86-87)

j. Natural gas and/or crude oil wells, production, acreage under lease, and drilling activity; and natural gas reserves and deliveries to pipelines; by county and/or company. 13 tables. (p. 88-99)

k. Coal mine production and fatality trends, 1953-83; coal mines, production, employment, wages, days worked, injuries, and fatalities, by county; coal reserves, by bed name and county, 1951 and 1983-84; characteristics of fatal coal mining accidents and victims; and selected data for other minerals, including production, employment, salaries/wages, hours worked, capital expenditures, injuries, and fatalities. 9 tables. (p. 100-111)

For description of report presenting data for 1981, see SRI 1982 Annual, under this number. Report usually is issued annually; report for 1982-83 is the only biennial edition.

Availability: Virginia Department of Labor and Industry, PO Box 12064, Richmond VA 23241, †; SRI/MF/complete.

S8270–2   VIRGINIA EMPLOYMENT, HOURS, AND EARNINGS
Monthly.   Approx. 20 p.
SRI/MF/complete, shipped quarterly

Monthly report on Virginia labor force, employment, hours, and earnings, by industry group, SMSA, and selected labor market areas. Beginning with the Mar. 1984 issue, report is issued by the Virginia Employment Commission and is described in SRI under S8205-5.

Issues reviewed during 1984: Nov. 1983-Feb. 1984 (P) (Vol. 33, Nos. 11-12; Vol. 34, Nos. 1-2).

S8275   VIRGINIA
State
Library

S8275–1   STATISTICS OF VIRGINIA PUBLIC LIBRARIES AND INSTITUTIONAL LIBRARIES, 1981-82
Annual.   1983.   40 p.
LC 43-44579.
SRI/MF/complete

Annual report, for FY82, on Virginia public and institutional library services and holdings, finances, personnel, and related data, by library.

Contains table of contents (p. 1); 11 tables, listed below (inside front cover, p. 2-32); and directory of Virginia public libraries (p. 33-39).

Availability: Virginia State Library, Library Development Branch, 12th and Capitol Sts., Richmond VA 23219, †; SRI/MF/complete.

TABLES:

[Tables I-IV are repeated for Virginia regional and city libraries, and county and town libraries. Funding sources are generally local, State, and Federal aid, and other. Data are for FY82, unless otherwise noted.]

[A] Public library statistical summary [circulation, total volumes, and operating expenditures by source of income, for regional, county, city, and town public libraries; Federal and State-funded operating expenditures for library development programs, by program; number of public libraries by type; and Virginia population, total, and with and without library service]. (inside front cover)

I. Analysis of income and expenditures [population and square miles served, distribution of income by source and operating expenditures by object, local and total operating expenditures per capita, and unexpended income by source]. (p. 2-3, 10-11)

II. Analysis of circulation [books by type; nonbook materials; outlets by type, including branches and bookmobiles; and headquarters hours per week]. (p. 4-5, 12-13)

III. Analysis of collections [books by type; volumes and titles added and volumes withdrawn; and nonbook materials, including filmstrips, recordings, microforms, and number of periodical and newspaper titles]. (p. 6-7, 14-15)

IV. Additional statistics [full- and part-time personnel; outlets, including branches and bookmobiles; bookmobile hours open; interlibrary loan transactions; computer services; and registered borrowers]. (p. 8-9, 16-17)

[B] Local income sources [county, city/town, revenue sharing, common governmental fund, and other, by library; with summary]. (p. 18)

[C] Institutional libraries [under Rehabilitative School Authority, Dept of Mental Health/Mental Retardation, and Dept of Rehabilitative Services: residents, hours, operating expenditures, and collections, by library]. (p. 22)

[D] Comparative summary of public library statistics [population, counties, and cities served; book stock; circulation and operating expenditures by type; and number of libraries, bookmobiles, branches, and librarians], FY78-82. (p. 24)

[E] Virginia State library service data [volumes added and withdrawn, newspaper and periodical titles, government documents received and distributed, interlibrary and film loans, and reference inquiries]. (p. 24)

[F] College and university libraries [number of volumes and students, computer services, and lending restrictions]. (p. 25)

[G] Special libraries [list, showing name, librarian, subject specialty, computer services, and lending restrictions]. (p. 27-32)

S8293   VIRGINIA
Department of
Social Services

S8293-1   COMMONWEALTH OF VIRGINIA, DEPARTMENT OF WELFARE, Biennial Report, July 1, 1980-June 30, 1982
Biennial. [1984.]
58 p. no paging. Foldouts.
SRI/MF/complete

Biennial report on Virginia public welfare programs, including operations, cases, and recipients, by program; and expenditures by program, county, and city; FY81-82.

Contains narrative description, with organizational chart and personnel listings (6 p.); and 8 tables, listed below (52 p.).

Previous report, for FY80, is described in SRI 1981 Annual under S8320-1. Virginia Dept of Welfare became Virginia Dept of Social Services in July 1982.

Availability: Virginia Department of Social Services, Research and Reporting Bureau, 8007 Discovery Dr., Richmond VA 23288, †; SRI/ MF/complete.

TABLES:
[Data are for FY81-82, unless otherwise noted.]

I. Virginia Dept of Welfare statement of operations [including Federal and special balance, as of June 30, 1980-82; State appropriation; State, Federal, and special revenue, transfers/ adjustments, and expenditures; and total credits and debits; by program]. (12 p.)

II. Expenditures for public assistance and hospitalization of the indigent according to counties and cities [by program and source of funds]. (24 p.)

III. Public assistance cases receiving financial assistance and amount of assistance by program and month [with totals from FY77]. (6 p.)

IV. Food stamp program participation data by month [number of households and persons also receiving and not receiving public assistance; and total coupon value]. (2 p.)

V. Hospitalization under the State and local program for the indigent [including inpatient admissions, days paid for, and patients by race and sex; outpatient visits and expenditures; and fund sources]. (2 p.)

VI. Social services cases under care, by category and month. (2 p.)

VII. Persons receiving social services under title XX [by service and program]. (2 p.)

VIII. Actions on Aid to Dependent Children cases involving questions of fraud. (2 p.)

S8293-2   PUBLIC WELFARE STATISTICS, Virginia
Quarterly. Approx. 60 p.
SRI/MF/complete

Quarterly report on Virginia public welfare programs, including caseloads, recipients, and expenditures, by program, county, and city. Covers Aid to Dependent Children (ADC), emergency assistance to needy families, general relief including aid to refugees, foster care, adoptions, food stamps, day care, and child support collections.

Issuing agency collects data on a monthly basis, but presents most data only for last month of each quarter. Report is issued approximately 6 months after month of coverage.

Report contains table listing, and 21 quarterly tables listed below.

Report has been published since 1939. SRI coverage begins with Sept. 1983 issue. A biennial report with similar data is also published, and is covered in SRI under S8293-1.

Availability: Virginia Department of Social Services, Research and Reporting Bureau, 8007 Discovery Dr., Richmond VA 23288, †; SRI/ MF/complete.

Issues reviewed during 1984: Sept. 1983-Mar. 1984 (D) (Vol. XLV, Nos. 1-3).

QUARTERLY TABLES:
[Data are shown for month of coverage, unless otherwise noted. Table numbering varies.]

STATE SUMMARY
I-II. Cases receiving assistance and amount of assistance; and cases under care; [with comparisons to same month of previous year].

III. Application and case information [approvals, other dispositions, and payment discontinuations, for general relief, and for ADC and Medicaid cases (occasionally with detail by race), for quarter ending in month of coverage].

BY LOCALITY
[Tables generally show cases and/or recipients, and expenditures, by county and city, unless otherwise noted.]

IV. Auxiliary grant payments for the aged and disabled.

V-VI. ADC [regular]; and ADC foster care [entrusted and nonentrusted].

VII. Emergency assistance to needy families with children [by ADC status].

VIII. General relief [medical, burial/transient, and maintenance].

IX. General relief for refugees and Cuban/ Haitians.

X-XII. Foster care and subsidized and special needs adoptions.

XIII-XV. Food stamp program: monthly participation record [by public assistance status]; State participation [summary, compared with previous month and same month of previous year]; and percent of population participating.

XVI. Report of collections on food stamp overissuance claims [showing number and value of collections, by type of error, for quarter ending in month of coverage; table begins in the Mar. 1984 issue].

XVII. Service cases under care [by recipient category, including SSI/auxiliary grants for aged/blind/disabled, and Medicaid cases; expenditure data are omitted].

XVIII-XIX. Employment services program (ESP) day care and other purchased services; and day care other than ESP.

XX. Aid to refugees/Cuban/Haitians: ADC eligible/other.

XXI. Support enforcement collection summary for ADC and non-ADC cases, by region [amount collected during quarter of coverage, with comparison to same period of previous year].

S8295   VIRGINIA
Department of
State Police

S8295-1   VIRGINIA TRAFFIC CRASH FACTS, 1983
Annual. Apr. 1984. 114 p.
LC A44-5266.
SRI/MF/complete

Annual report on Virginia traffic accidents, fatalities, and injuries, including data by detailed accident and vehicle type, location, time, and other circumstances; and driver and victim characteristics; 1983 with comparisons to 1982 and trends from as early as 1952.

Also includes data on driver and pedestrian alcohol use, vehicle mileage and registrations, insurance coverage of vehicles in accidents, motor fuel consumption, and safety device use by accident victims.

Contains 2 charts, foreword, contents listing, and highlights (inside front cover and p. 1-5); report, with 13 charts and 26 tables (p. 6-41); and computer printouts of total State and rural accident detailed data, with 28 tables (p. 43-114).

Availability: Virginia Department of State Police, Safety Division, PO Box 27472, Richmond VA 23261-7472, †; SRI/MF/complete.

S8295-2   CRIME IN VIRGINIA, 1983
Annual. [1984.] vii+169 p.
ISSN 0146-5759.
LC 77-648613.
SRI/MF/complete

Annual report, for 1983, on Virginia crimes and arrests, by type of offense, and planning district. Also includes offense data by county and local police agency, value of stolen property, and assaults on police officers.

Data are from reports of State and local law enforcement agencies, submitted under the Uniform Crime Reporting (UCR) Program.

Contents:

Foreword, highlights, and contents listing. (p. iii-vii)

Section I. UCR Program description, with 1 summary table on Index offenses, rates, and clearances, 1982-83. (p. 1-4)

Section II-VI. Index offenses by offense and local jurisdiction, reporting agencies and employment, Index offense summary, and value of property stolen and recovered; with 29 charts and 44 tables, described below. (p. 5-81)

Section VII-IX. Arrests, law enforcement officers killed and assaulted, and planning district data; with 3 charts and 105 tables, described below. (p. 83-169)

Availability: Virginia Department of State Police, Uniform Crime Reporting Section, PO Box 27472, Richmond VA 23261-7472, †; SRI/MF/complete.

TABLES AND CHARTS:

[All tables and charts present data for 1983; many include comparative data for 1982. Index (Part I) offenses covered in detail are murder/non-negligent manslaughter, forcible rape, robbery, aggravated assault, burglary, larceny, and motor vehicle theft. Arson is classified as an Index offense, but data are generally reported separately and are not included in the Crime Index tables.

Data by ethnic group generally include American Indian/Alaskan Native, Asian/Pacific Islander, and Hispanic.]

S8295–2.1: Sections II-VI

HIGHLIGHTS

a. Monthly summary for Index offenses, including arson, negligent manslaughter, and simple assaults; and crime clocks, showing frequency of Index offenses. 1 chart and 3 tables. (p. 6-8)

BY OFFENSE

[Sections on individual offenses are prefaced with 1 summary table; all sections except arson include 1 trend chart showing monthly offenses. Additional data are described below.]

b. Murder/non-negligent manslaughter: victims and offenders, by age, sex, race, and ethnic group; and offenses, by victim-offender relationship, circumstances of murder, and type of weapon and situation (single or multiple victims/offenders). 3 charts and 5 tables. (p. 9-14)

c. Forcible rape: arrests, by age. 3 charts and 2 tables. (p. 15-17)

d. Robbery: offenses and value of property stolen, by place of occurrence; and offenses, by type of weapon. 3 charts and 4 tables. (p. 18-21)

e. Aggravated assault: distribution of offenses by type of weapon, with distribution of all assaults by whether simple or aggravated. 3 charts and 2 tables. (p. 22-24)

f. Burglary: day and night, residence and nonresidence offenses, and value of stolen property; offenses, by type of entry; and arrests, by age. 3 charts and 5 tables. (p. 25-28)

g. Larceny: offenses and value of property stolen, by type and amount of theft. 1 chart and 4 tables. (p. 29-32)

h. Motor vehicle theft: distribution of offenses by vehicle type; vehicles stolen and recovered locally and elsewhere; and arrests, by age. 3 charts and 4 tables. (p. 33-35)

i. Arson: offenses and value of property damage, by property type. 2 tables. (p. 36-37)

CRIME AND POLICE, BY LOCAL JURISDICTION

j. Population, crime and clearance rates, and Index offenses by offense, by reporting jurisdiction in each county and independent city; and clearance rates and offenses, by college and university and other agency. 1 table. (p. 40-56)

k. Law enforcement employment, including sworn officers by sex, and civilians, all by reporting agency in each county, city, and other jurisdiction. 1 table. (p. 58-61)

SUMMARY AND STOLEN PROPERTY

l. Total Index, violent, and property crime and clearance summary, by offense, with offenses by month and quarter, and juvenile and adult clearance rates. 7 charts and 5 tables. (p. 64-72)

m. Value of stolen property, by property type and offense; and value of recovered property, by type; including detail by month. 2 charts and 6 tables. (p. 74-81)

S8295–2.2: Sections VII-IX

[Arrest data by offense are shown for 27-29 Index and non-Index offenses.]

ARRESTS AND POLICE ASSAULTS

a. Monthly arrests; arrests by age, race, ethnic group, and sex, total and by offense; drug arrests, with detail for sale/manufacture and possession by substance, by age; arrest rates, by offense; and juvenile arrest dispositions. 1 chart and 13 tables. (p. 84-96)

b. Officers killed by felonious act and accidentally; officers assaulted, by type of activity, weapon, injury status, assignment, and time of day; and percent of officer assaults cleared, by type of activity. 2 charts and 4 tables. (p. 98-100)

DATA BY PLANNING DISTRICT

[The following tables are repeated for each of 22 planning districts.]

c. Index offenses and clearance rates; value of property stolen by robbery, burglary, larceny, and motor vehicle theft; and total value of property stolen and recovered, by type of property. 2 tables. (p. 103-124)

d. Arrest totals for adults and juveniles, by age and offense. 2 tables. (p. 126-169)

S8300   VIRGINIA
Supreme Court

S8300–1   1983 STATE OF THE JUDICIARY REPORT, Virginia

Annual. [1984.] 424 p.
LC 79-644178.
SRI/MF/complete

Annual report, for 1983, on Virginia judicial system, including trial and appellate court caseloads and case dispositions. Covers supreme, circuit, and district courts. Includes trial court data by case type and locality, and selected comparisons from as early as 1960.

Case types shown are civil and criminal, for all courts, with some additional detail for habeas corpus, traffic, juvenile, and domestic relations case types.

Report also includes data on case processing time; medical malpractice claims; indigent defense and involuntary commitment costs by district; judicial personnel and salaries; magistrates' activities; detailed court finances; and judges and workloads.

Data are from dept records.

Contains contents listing (p. 3-6); report, with 23 charts, 194 tables, and directories of judges (p. 8-422); and list of related publications (p. 424). This is the 9th annual report.

Availability: Virginia Supreme Court, Executive Secretary's Office, Supreme Court Bldg., 100 N. Ninth St., 3rd Floor, Richmond VA 23219, †; SRI/MF/complete.

S8305   VIRGINIA
Department of Taxation

S8305–1   DEPARTMENT OF TAXATION ANNUAL REPORT, 1982-83, Commonwealth of Virginia

Annual. [1984.] vii + 38 p.
LC 30-27254.
SRI/MF/complete

Annual report, for FY83, on Virginia tax revenues, by tax type, county, and independent city. Includes individual and corporate tax returns by income bracket, and taxable retail sales by major industry group. Also includes trends from 1972.

Contains contents listing and tax dept organizational summary (p. iii-vii); and the following:

a. Introduction and narrative sections, with 2 charts and 2 tables showing general and special fund revenue collections by source, FY82-83; and tax dept expenditures by budget program, FY83. (p. 1-8)

b. Appendix, with table listing, and 37 tables listed below. (p. 9-38)

State Taxation Dept also issues several related publications, including a quarterly taxable retail sales report, an annual real estate assessment/sales ratio study, and a summary of tax facts. These reports are not covered by SRI.

Availability: Virginia Department of Taxation, 2220 W. Broad St., PO Box 6-L, Richmond VA 23282, †; SRI/MF/complete.

APPENDIX TABLES:

[Data by locality are shown by county and independent city.]

S8305–1.1: Income Taxes

INDIVIDUAL INCOME TAX

[Data are shown for 1981 taxable year, unless otherwise noted.]

1.1. Adjusted gross income (AGI), total exemptions, total deductions, total taxable income, and total tax, by AGI classes. (p. 10)

1.2-1.4. Number and type of returns and exemptions, total AGI, total tax, and effective tax rate, by AGI classes. (p. 10-11)

1.5-1.7. Total AGI and total exemptions, total deductions, number of returns, total net taxable income, total amount taxed and income tax paid at each tax rate, and total income tax paid, all by locality. (p. 12-17)

1.8. Statewide individual income taxes, 1972-81. (p. 18)

CORPORATE INCOME TAX

2.1-2.2. Number of corporate returns, taxable income, and tax assessed, [by tax bracket], FY73-83. (p. 18-19)

S8305–1.2: Sales and Other Taxes

RETAIL SALES AND USE TAX

3.1. Retail sales/use tax business classification code. [list] (p. 20)

3.2. Annual sales by business classification made during FY83, as reflected by deposits of sales tax revenues made during the period Aug. 1, 1982-July 31, 1983. (p. 22)

3.3-3.4. State and local retail sales/use tax, FY74-83. (p. 23)

3.5. Aircraft sales/use tax, FY75-83. (p. 23)

3.6. Sales tax distribution [by locality], FY83. (p. 24)

OTHER STATE TAXES

4.1-4.3. Inheritance and gift taxes, FY74-83; and estate taxes [replacing inheritance/gift taxes], FY81-83. (p. 25)

4.4. State recordation taxes, FY74-83. (p. 26)

4.5. Taxes on capital not otherwise taxed, tax years 1973-82. (p. 26)

4.6. Assessed value of capital not otherwise taxed for the tax year 1982, and the State tax thereon at 30 cents per $100 valuation [by locality]. (p. 27)

4.7-4.8. State business, occupational, and professional license taxes, by [license] classification and locality, FY83. (p. 28-29)

4.9. State license taxes/penalties/fees, FY74-83. (p. 30)

4.10. Statement showing [county and city] assessment for the tax year beginning Jan. 1, 1983, of the net taxable capital of banks/trust companies. (p. 30)

4.11. [State and local] franchise tax on net capital of bank/trust companies, FY74-83. (p. 30)

4.12-4.14. Malt beverage, tobacco products, and miscellaneous excise taxes, FY74-83. (p. 31)

S8305–1.3: Local Property Taxes

[Tables 5.4-5.7 show data by locality, tax year 1982.]

5.1-5.3. Assessed values, levies assessed, and average nominal tax rates [by property type], tax years 1973-82. (p. 33)

5.4. Real estate: [land] area, fair market values, taxable values, and local levies on land books. (p. 34)

5.5-5.6. Tangible personal property, machinery/tools, and merchants' capital: local values and levies assessed on property books. (p. 36-37)

5.7. Public service corporations: assessed values and local levies. (p. 38)

S8310   VIRGINIA
Department of the Treasury

S8310–1   ANNUAL REPORT OF THE TREASURER to the Governor of Virginia for the Fiscal Year Ended June 30, 1983
Annual. [1984.] 51 p.
LC 10-17712.
SRI/MF/complete

Annual financial report of the Virginia Dept of the Treasury, presenting data for FY83, with comparisons to FY82, and trends from FY76. Includes financial statements, variously showing receipts, disbursements, fund balances, assets, liabilities, and long-term debt detail, for the following funds: public debt, construction, Richmond-Petersburg Turnpike, literary, special capital improvement, and public school authority.

Also includes data on State investment portfolio performance; revenues from unclaimed property; Treasury checks issued; constitutional debt limit; and bond activity of Virginia Public School Authority by locality and of individual higher education institutions.

Contains contents listing (p. 2-3); letter of transmittal, highlights, and summary (p. 4-7); description of dept operations with 13 charts (p. 9-17); and 18 financial statements (p. 21-51).

Annual Report of the Comptroller to the Governor of Virginia, presenting data on the State's general financial condition, is covered in SRI under S8170-1.

Availability: Virginia Department of the Treasury, PO Box 6-H, Richmond VA 23215, †; SRI/MF/complete.

S8340
WASHINGTON STATE Employment Security Department

S8340–2   ANNUAL PLANNING REPORT, Washington State
Annual, discontinued.

Annual planning report identifying Washington State population groups most in need of employment services, and presenting data on employment by industry and occupation, labor force, and related topics. Due to budgetary constraints, report has been discontinued with the July 1982 issue (for description, see SRI 1982 Annual, under this number).

Data for individual labor market areas are available from Washington State Employment Security Department, Research and Analysis Branch, 212 Maple Park, Olympia WA 98504.

Selected data on labor force and related topics are available in the monthly *Washington Labor Market,* covered in SRI under S8340-3.

S8340–3   WASHINGTON LABOR MARKET
Monthly. Approx. 10 p.
SRI/MF/complete, shipped quarterly

Monthly report on Washington State labor force, employment, unemployment, earnings, and hours. Data are shown by industry group and labor market area. Month of coverage is 1-2 months prior to cover date.

Issues generally contain narrative summary, with 1 text table; 1-5 summary charts; and 5 monthly and 2 annual tables, listed below.

Most monthly tables appear in all issues; annual tables appear in Feb. issue (Mar. 1984 issue includes revisions for annual table [7]).

Similar reports for selected SMSAs are available from the issuing agency on a quarterly basis, but are not covered in SRI.

Availability: Washington State Employment Security Department, Research and Analysis Branch, KG-11, Olympia WA 98504-5311, †; SRI/MF/complete, shipped quarterly.

Issues reviewed during 1984: Oct. 1983-Sept. 1984 (P) (Vol. 7, Nos. 10-12; Vol. 8, Nos. 1-9) [Vol. 7, Nos. 11-12 incorrectly read Vol. 8; Vol. 8, No. 9 incorrectly reads Vol. 9, No. 8].

TABLES:

MONTHLY TABLES

[Data are shown for month of coverage and selected prior periods. Table sequence may vary.]

[1] Nonagricultural wage/salary workers, place of work [by industry division and major manufacturing industry group; and total workers involved in labor-management disputes].

[2] CPI [urban consumers, for U.S. city average and Seattle-Everett SMSA; table begins in the Aug. 1984 issue].

[3-4] Resident labor force and employment; and estimates for Federal program purposes, in Washington State and labor market areas [including 7 SMSAs].

[5] Estimated average hours and earnings of production workers in manufacturing and of nonsupervisory workers in nonmanufacturing activities [by major manufacturing industry group and for selected nonmanufacturing industries; table may not appear in every issue].

ANNUAL TABLES

[6-7] [Monthly tables [1] and [3] are repeated, showing monthly data for previous year, with trends from the 1970s.]

S8345
WASHINGTON STATE
Office of
Financial Management

**S8345–2   WASHINGTON STATE
DATA BOOK, 1983**
Biennial.   Feb. 1984.
viii+289 p.
ISSN 0191-3018.
LC 79-642656.
SRI/MF/complete, current &
previous reports

Biennial report, for 1983, presenting detailed social, governmental, and economic statistics for Washington State. Data are primarily for various years 1960-83, with population trends from 1880. Data are from State and Federal sources.

Report is designed to present a comprehensive overview of the State. Extensive socioeconomic, demographic, and geographic breakdowns are shown, as applicable, for most topics. These breakdowns include data by city, county, SMSA, commodity, industry, age, race, and sex. Comparisons to total U.S. are also occasionally included.

Contains preface and contents listing (p. v-viii); State information, with 1 map, 10 charts, and 140 tables arranged in 10 sections, described below (p. 1-181); county and city information, with 1 map, 1 summary population table, and 12 tables also described below (p. 183-280); and directory of contributing agencies, and index (p. 281-289).

Previous report, for 1981, has also been reviewed and is also available on SRI microfiche, under this number [Biennial. Dec. 1981. v+280 p. ‡]. Report for 1981 is substantially similar in content, with the following exceptions: also includes data on refugees, boat registrations and accidents, search and rescue missions, and imported oil sources; and omits data on housing permits, bank deposits, and nursing homes, as well as selected foreign trade, transportation, and county profile data.

Report for 1979 is described in SRI 1980 Annual, under this number.

Availability: Washington State Office of Financial Management, Policy Analysis and Forecasting Division, Insurance Bldg., M.S. AQ-44, Olympia WA 98504, ‡; SRI/MF/complete.

TABLE SECTIONS:
[Tables in each section are preceded by a contents listing. Data sources appear beneath each table.]

S8345–2.1: Population and Economy

(p. 2-24) Contains 1 map and 24 tables. Includes population from 1880, land area, net migration, births and deaths, fertility rate, abortions, and marriages and divorces/dissolutions.

Also includes total and per capita personal income, components of personal income, implicit price deflator, U.S. and Seattle CPI, non-farm employment, labor force by employment status, interest rates on 3-month Treasury bills and mortgages, housing permits issued, bank deposits, foreign trade value and 12 leading trade partners, and value of waterborne trade by port.

S8345–2.2: State Government Organization and Finance

(p. 26-41) Contains 1 chart and 16 tables. Includes State revenues by source, and expenditures by function, fund source, and selected agency, including funding for State universities/colleges and community colleges; State expenditures as percent of total personal income; State FTE employees; and bonded debt.

S8345–2.3: Human Services

(p. 44-65) Contains 1 chart and 18 tables. Includes income assistance program grants and caseloads; community social service caseloads; developmental disability program expenditures and recipients; and medical assistance, public health, and mental health recipients, facilities, and/or expenditures.

Also includes communicable diseases reported, and deaths by 5 leading causes; licensed health professionals; general and psychiatric health care facilities, beds, daily population, admissions, average length of stay, and hospitalization cost; and nursing homes, beds, occupancy, and expenditures.

Also includes unemployment insurance and workers' compensation recipients and benefits; State employment service applications, placements, and job openings; State Industrial Safety and Health Agency covered employees, inspection activity, and expenditures; State Human Rights Commission expenditures, and discrimination complaints and caseload; vocational rehabilitation program expenditures and services; and veterans' services and expenditures.

S8345–2.4: Criminal Justice and Education

(p. 68-113) Contains 4 charts and 36 tables. Includes State criminal justice system operations summary; crimes and arrests by offense; State court commitments and/or caseloads; adult and juvenile correctional institution population, admissions, and releases; prison capacity; and daily local jail population by offense.

Also includes public school operating revenues by source, expenditures by program, funds from special levy referenda, and employees; public and private school enrollment; higher education institutions; university and community college operating costs by program, enrollment by institution, tuition and fees, and degrees awarded; vocational education expenditures, and enrollment by program and institution; and high school diplomas and equivalency certificates obtained.

S8345–2.5: Natural Resources

(p. 116-139) Contains 1 chart and 19 tables. Includes timber harvest and reforestation; forest products consumption and production value; production of wood and bark residue by end use; forest fires and acres burned; State income from public lands, and disbursements; farm production value; farms and acreage; and State ranking in agricultural production.

Also includes food fish production, salmon hatchery operations; fishing boats licensed, by vessel size; and mineral production value.

S8345–2.6: Environment

(p. 142-152) Contains 10 tables. Includes recreational vehicle registrations; State park acreage and visits; national site visits; deer and elk licensed hunters, harvest, and population estimates; small game harvest by species; and licensed sport fishermen, fish plantings, and harvest.

Also includes air and water pollution penalties, and total complaints; oil spills and penalties assessed; fish kills resulting from pollution, and resource damage assessments; and construction grants for municipal sewage treatment facilities.

S8345–2.7: Energy and Transportation

(p. 154-181) Contains 3 charts and 17 tables. Includes energy consumption by sector and type of fuel; petroleum consumption and prices by type of product; electricity consumption and average prices, and natural gas consumption and prices, all by sector; and energy expenditures, total, per capita, and as percent of personal income.

Also includes motor vehicle registrations; licensed drivers; road and vehicle mileage, and traffic accidents and fatalities; traffic citations issued; pilots; Seattle-Tacoma International Airport traffic; State ferry system traffic and finances; public transit system finances; and State motor vehicle fund revenues and disbursements.

S8345–2.8: County and City Profiles
COUNTY DATA

a. Population and components of change; land area; assessed property value; personal income; State revenues distributed to county; county revenues and expenditures; employment and earnings; public assistance grants and recipients; public school districts, employees, enrollment, and finances; and licensed drivers and vehicles. State map, summary population table, and 10 tables repeated for each county. (p. 184-264)

CITY AND TOWN DATA

b. Population from 1890, year of incorporation, and total and per capita State revenues distributed to city or town. 2 tables. (p. 266-280)

**S8345–3   STATE OF WASHINGTON
1983 ANNUAL FINANCIAL
REPORT, Fiscal Year Ended
June 30, 1983**
Annual.   Dec. 30, 1983.
iii+68 p.
SRI/MF/complete

Annual report on financial condition of Washington State government, FY83 and/or biennium ended June 1983. Presents assets, liabilities, and fund equity and balances; revenues by source; and expenditures by object and major function; for general, special revenue, debt service, capital projects, trust, enterprise, and internal service funds.

Also includes data on bonded debt by agency, institution, and purpose; and trends in fiscal and economic indicators, with selected comparisons to U.S.

Indicators covered include selected State financial and debt ratios; State government staff funding; educational enrollments; population size and change components; labor force; employment, wages, and business income, by industry; personal income; bank deposits; agricultural production value by commodity; international trade; and property valuations and tax rates; various years 1973-83.

Contains contents listing (p. iii); transmittal letter with 1 text table, listing of elected officials, and 4 charts and 3 summary tables (p. 1-8); auditor's report, and 4 combined financial statements with accompanying notes and text data (p. 10-40); and statistical section with 7 schedules and 22 indicator tables (p. 41-68).

Availability: Washington State Office of Financial Management, Accounting and Fiscal Services Division, Insurance Bldg. M.S. AQ-44, Olympia WA 98504, †; SRI/MF/complete.

S8345-4   1984 POPULATION TRENDS for Washington State
Annual. Oct. 1984. x+99 p.
SRI/MF/complete

Annual report on Washington State population trends, including data by county and city, various years 1910-1984. Also includes some data on households and housing units. Data are from Census Bureau and various State sources.

Contains contents listing, preface, highlights, and listings of tables and charts (p. i-x); 2 trend charts, and 1 other chart and 13 tables described below (p. 3-31); and 5 special report sections with 17 tables on population survey methodology and sampling error estimates, and 18 other tables described below (p. 35-99).

Availability: Washington State Office of Financial Management, Policy Analysis and Forecasting Division, M.S. AQ-44, Olympia WA 98504-0201, †; SRI/MF/complete.

TABLES AND CHART:
[Data by city are shown for cities and towns, and usually also include totals for unincorporated places. Data by ethnic group variously include Hispanic, Indian, and/or Asian.]

a. Population and housing units, 1980-84, with 1984 housing units by structure type, by city and county; population age 65/over and institutional population, by county, 1970-84; and population by age and race-ethnic group, various years 1980-84, with race-ethnic group detail by county and comparisons to 1970. 1 chart and 7 tables. (p. 3-16)

b. Population change components (births, deaths, and migration), selected years 1910-84, and by county for 1980-84 period; fertility rates, marriages, and divorces/dissolutions, various years 1930-84; city and town annexations (parcels, land area, dwelling units, and residents), by county and city, selected periods 1980-84; and population by city and town, Apr. 1984. 6 tables. (p. 19-31)

c. Spanish origin population: by county, 1970, 1980, and 1983, with 1980 detail by race-ethnic group; by age group, 1980; and selected socioeconomic characteristics, including median income, poverty and unemployment status, educational attainment, and urban vs. rural residence, 1980; with some comparisons to total population. 4 tables. (p. 53-56)

d. Military personnel by sex and age, 1970-80; military personnel and persons residing with them by age, sex, and labor force status (all by race-ethnic group), and by educational attainment, with educational enrollment for military dependents, 1980; and military housing, including type of living quarters occupied, and number of units in structure, 1980. 14 tables. (p. 64-77)

S8375
WASHINGTON STATE
Library

S8375-1   ANNUAL STATISTICAL BULLETIN: Public Library Statistics, 1983, Washington State Library
Annual. Oct. 1983. 46 p.
SRI/MF/complete

Annual report on Washington State public library operations, including finances, holdings, circulation, staff, and population served, shown by library or library system, primarily for 1982.

Contents:

a. Contents listing. (1 p.)

b. Library directory, and 1 summary table, including population without library service and number of municipalities and counties unserved. (p. 1-5)

c. List of libraries by county; and 1 table showing population served, professional and nonprofessional staff, hours of operation, circulation, and holdings by type, by library. (p. 7-18)

d. Assessed valuation, tax revenue and other income, expenditures by item, population served, circulation by outlet, holdings by type, hours of operation, professional and nonprofessional staff, and outlets and facilities served by type, 1982; and salaries by position, 1983; by municipal, county, and regional library system, arranged by size group of population served. 10 tables. (p. 19-46)

Availability: Washington State Library, Documents Distribution Center, Olympia WA 98504, †; SRI/MF/complete.

S8405
WASHINGTON STATE
Office of the Superintendent of Public Instruction

S8405-1   MINORITY ENROLLMENTS IN PUBLIC AND PRIVATE SCHOOLS, State of Washington, Oct. 1983
Annual. [1984.]
1+63+20 p.
SRI/MF/complete

Annual report on minority enrollment in Washington State public and private schools for 1983/84 school year. Contains 2 detailed tables showing enrollment for black, Asian/Pacific Islander, American Indian/Alaskan Native, Hispanic, and white pupils, by county, district, and school, for public schools (p. 1-63) and private schools (p. 1-20).

Availability: Washington State Office of the Superintendent of Public Instruction, Information Services, Old Capitol Bldg., FG-11. Olympia WA 98504, †; SRI/MF/complete.

S8415
WASHINGTON STATE
Department of Revenue

S8415-1   STATE OF WASHINGTON, 1983 TAX STATISTICS
Annual. [1983.] 83 p.
ISSN 0094-6885.
LC 64-6271.
SRI/MF/complete

Annual report, for FY83, on Washington State tax collections; actual and assessed real and personal property values; and valuation of operating property of intercounty public service companies, including transportation, communication, and energy providers.

Data are from State Revenue Dept and Office of Financial Management records.

Contains contents listing (p. 1); and 4 statistical sections, each preceded by table listing, with 41 tables listed below (p. 3-83).

Availability: Washington State Department of Revenue, Research and Information Division, General Administration Bldg., MS-AX-02, Olympia WA 98504, ‡; SRI/MF/complete.

TABLES:

S8415-1.1: Excise Taxes

1. Net Washington State tax collections [by source, including general and selective sales taxes, gross receipts, property and in-lieu excises, other State taxes, and licenses], selected years FY27-83. (p. 4-9)

2. Washington State general fund revenues [by source, including Federal revenue], FY83. (p. 10)

3. Department of Revenue collections [including State taxes by type, and administrative and local tax collections], FY82-83. (p. 11)

4. County/city sales/use tax distributions [by jurisdiction], FY79-83. (p. 12)

5. Public transportation systems: local sales/use tax distributions [by transit district], FY81-83. (p. 13)

6. Timber excise tax distributions by county, 1983. (p. 14)

7. Local leasehold excise tax distributions [by county], FY81-83 [with amounts for cities, FY83]. (p. 15)

8. Public utility district (PUD) excise tax, distributions [by county] in FY79-83. (p. 16)

9. Retail sales/use tax distributions for local stadium/convention center facilities [for total cities and total counties], FY77-83. (p. 17)

10. Real estate excise tax statistics [number and taxable value of sales, and tax revenue], FY74-83. (p. 17)

11. Number of State excise taxpayers, registered accounts by county [and for out of State] and reporting frequency, beginning of FY83-84. (p. 18)

S8415–1.2: Property Tax Levies and Collections

[Taxing districts by type include State, counties, cities/towns, school, fire, water, cemetery, hospital, and various others. Tables 12-15 show data for year due.]

12-13. Property tax levies, by [type of] major taxing district, 1980-83; and by county, 1982-83. (p. 20-22)

14. Property tax levies by county, countywide average rates per $1,000 assessed value, 1979-83. (p. 23)

15. Property tax [county, and State assessed] valuations, [total tax] levies, and average tax rates, [quinquennially 1910-50 and annually 1951-84]. (p. 24)

16. Number of taxing districts by type, 1978-83). (p. 25)

17-18. Property tax collections and year-end delinquency: amounts by county for 1982; and statewide totals [quinquenially 1935-70 and annually 1971-82]. (p. 26-29)

S8415–1.3: Property Valuations and Assessment Ratios

[Tables show data for 1983, unless otherwise noted. All tables except table 26 show data by county.]

19-20. Indicated property tax ratios: by assessment years 1978-83; and real, personal, and combined indicated ratios, assessment years 1982-83. (p. 32-33)

21. Assessed valuation of lands/improvements: locally assessed property [platted and unplatted lands in unincorporated areas, cities/towns, and total taxable value]. (p. 34)

22. Valuation of current use land: agricultural/timber/open space lands approved for current use assessment. (p. 35)

23. Valuation of forest land: privately owned classified and designated forest land, [acres and value]. (p. 36)

24. Other property valuation statistics: timber roll, valuation of reforestation lands, and senior citizens exempt property. (p. 36)

25-26. Assessed valuation of personal property by county; and comparison of 1982-83 values; [all] by category [includes livestock and other agricultural products; farm, logging/mining, and other machinery; merchandise held for sale; mobile homes not permanently attached to land; watercraft; and other property types]. (p. 38-40)

27. Assessed and actual value of taxable real and personal property, and computation of State property tax levy. (p. 41-43)

S8415–1.4: State-Assessed Utility Valuations

[Data are for 1983, unless otherwise noted. Tables 29-41 show actual and equalized assessed value of real and personal property, by company and county.]

28. Summary of public service company values, 1982-83, by type of utility [number of firms, and actual and equalized values, for 7 transportation types, 2 communication types, and 2 energy types]. (p. 46)

29-40. Air transportation, electric light/power, gas, [motor vehicle] freight and passenger transportation [property other than motor vehicles], pipeline, private car, railroad, telegraph, telephone, water transportation, and domestic water companies. (p. 47-71)

41. Recapitulation [of public utility companies] by county. (p. 72-83)

S8428
WASHINGTON STATE
Traffic Safety Commission

S8428–1   REVIEW OF TRAFFIC COLLISIONS in Washington, 1982
Annual. [1983.] 28 p.
SRI/MF/complete

Annual report on Washington State traffic accidents, fatalities, and injuries, by vehicle and accident type, location, time, and other circumstances; and driver and victim characteristics; 1982, with selected comparisons to 1981 and trends from 1969.

Also includes data on economic loss from accidents, vehicle registration and mileage, licensed drivers, accident-related arrests, alcohol involvement and toxicological test results, use of safety devices and characteristics of users, and detail for motorcycles.

Contains contents listing (1 p.); and 1 map, 9 charts, and 32 tables (p. 1-28).

SRI coverage begins with the 1982 review.

Availability: Washington State Traffic Safety Commission, 1000 S. Cherry St., Olympia WA 98504, †; SRI/MF/complete.

S8440
WASHINGTON STATE
Uniform Crime Reporting

S8440–1   CRIME IN WASHINGTON STATE, 1983
Annual. [1984.] vii+137 p.
SRI/MF/complete

Annual report on Washington State crimes, arrests, clearances, and law enforcement personnel, 1983, with selected comparisons to 1982. Includes data by county and law enforcement agency. Data are compiled from law enforcement agency reports, submitted under the Uniform Crime Reporting (UCR) Program.

Contains summary, and listings of contents, tables, and charts (p. i-vii); introduction and explanation of UCR program (p. 1-10); 16 charts and 23 tables, described below (p. 11-133); and glossary (p. 134-137).

This is the 4th annual crime report issued by the Washington Assn of Sheriffs and Police Chiefs.

Availability: Washington Association of Sheriffs and Police Chiefs, PO Box 826, Olympia WA 98507, ‡; SRI/MF/complete.

TABLES AND CHARTS:
[Data are for 1983 with selected comparisons to 1982. Data on offenses and arrests are shown by offense. Part I offenses are murder, rape, robbery, aggravated assault, burglary, larceny/theft, and motor vehicle theft. Arson also is classified as a Part I offense, but arson data are reported separately from data on other Part I offenses. Part II offenses are less serious crimes.

Data by race/ethnicity include American Indian, Asian, Hispanic, and non-Hispanic.]

a. Part I violent crime analysis: types of weapons used, by selected offense; murder victims and offenders, by age, sex, and race/ethnicity; murders, by city and county population size, month, victim/offender relationship, and circumstance; attempted and forcible rapes; and robbery value, by type of location. 8 charts and tables 1-5. (p. 11-23)

b. Part I property crime and arson analysis: burglaries, by type of entry; burglary value, for residence and nonresidence, day and night; larceny value and offenses, by offense type; motor vehicle thefts, by vehicle type; and arson offenses (total and abandoned structures), property loss value, and clearances, by type of property. 6 charts and table 6. (p. 24-31)

c. Arrest analysis and stolen property value: adult and juvenile arrests, by age, sex, and race/ethnicity, for Part I and II offenses; and value of property stolen and recovered, by Part I offense and/or property type. Tables 7-9. (p. 33-40)

d. Assaults on officers, by weapon, injury status, time, and type of assignment and circumstance; and clearances by circumstance. 2 charts and tables 10-14. (p. 43-48)

e. Local data: Part I offenses, and total and juvenile clearances, by agency and county; and offenses, by city and county population size group; with lists of reporting places. Tables 15-19. (p. 49-102)

f. Law enforcement personnel: commissioned and civilian law enforcement employees by sex, by agency, county, and agency type; and total and commissioned employees, by population size group, city, and county; with population for each agency and location. Tables 20-23. (p. 103-133)

S8450
WASHINGTON STATE
Utilities and Transportation Commission

S8450–1   STATISTICS OF UTILITY COMPANIES, 1982, Washington State
Annual series. For individual publication data, see below.
SRI/MF/complete

Series of 4 annual reports, for 1982, on the financial and operating conditions of utilities regulated by the Washington State Utilities and Transportation Commission. Covers electric, gas, telephone, and water companies. Data are compiled from annual reports filed by the companies with the commission.

Reports generally include individual company balance sheets and other financial data, and selected operating statistics.

Reports for 1982 reviewed during 1984 are described below. Reports for 1981 are covered in SRI under S8450-2.

Availability: Washington State Utilities and Transportation Commission, Finance and Accounts Division, Highways-Licenses Bldg., Olympia WA 98504-0087, †; SRI/MF/complete.

S8450-1.2: Statistics of Electric Companies, 1982, Washington State

[Annual. [1983.] 21 p. Oversized. SRI/MF/complete.]

Annual report presenting Washington State Class A electric utility financial and operating data, by company 1982, and aggregate 1981-82, with selected trends from 1978.

Includes balance sheet, income statement, operating ratios, fuel sources, sales and customers by customer class, generating capacity by fuel type, plant value, and equipment in use.

Also includes typical residential bill.

Contains contents listing and company index (p. 1-2); brief narrative with text tables (p. 3-4); 3 charts and 8 tables generally showing aggregate data (p. 5-15); and 6 tables showing company data (p. 16-21).

S8450-1.3: Statistics of Telephone Companies, 1982, Washington State

[Annual. [1983.] i+31 p. Oversized. SRI/MF/complete.]

Annual report presenting Washington State Class A-B telephone company financial and operating data, by company 1982, and aggregate 1981-82. Includes balance sheet, income statement, plant value, equipment in use, and operating ratios.

Contains contents listing (1 p.); company index (p. i); brief narrative, and 2 charts and 3 tables showing aggregate data (p. 1-7); and 9 tables showing company data (p. 8-31).

Previous report, for 1981, is described in SRI 1982 Annual, under S8450-2.2.

S8450-3   QUARTERLY STATISTICS OF CLASS I AND CLASS II MOTOR CARRIERS OF PROPERTY
Quarterly (selected issue).
Mar. 1984. 33 p. Oversized.
SRI/MF/complete

Annual compilation of statistics on the financial condition of Washington State Class I and II motor carriers of property, 1983, with comparisons to 1982 and detail for 4th quarter. Includes revenues, expenditures, and operating ratios, by company, with itemized detail by carrier type group.

Data are compiled from company reports filed with the Washington State Utilities and Transportation Commission.

Carrier groups are: local/statewide and large interstate scheduled line-haul general freight and household goods carriers; and nonscheduled general freight, Greater Puget Sound area, bulk commodity, agricultural/allied products, heavy machinery/building materials/forest products, refrigerated products, and miscellaneous commodity carriers.

Contains table of contents (1 p.); brief narrative (p. 1-2); and 2 basic tables, repeated for each carrier group (p. 3-33).

Annual data are published each year in the 4th quarter issue of *Quarterly Statistics of Class I and Class II Motor Carriers of Property;* 4th quarter issue is the only issue covered by SRI.

Commission also issues a series of annual reports on Washington State utility financial and operating statistics. Series is covered in SRI under S8450-1.

Availability: Washington State Utilities and Transportation Commission, Accounting Section, Highways and Licenses Bldg., Olympia WA 98504-0087, †; SRI/MF/complete.

S8455
WASHINGTON STATE Office of the Treasurer

S8455-1   WASHINGTON STATE TREASURER, 1983 Annual Financial Report
Annual. [1984.] v+77 p.
LC 80-644385.
SRI/MF/complete

Annual financial report of the Washington State treasurer, for FY83, with trends from FY74. Covers revenues by source; receipts, disbursements, and balances, by fund and account; disbursements to localities; State certificate of deposit investments, by financial institution; investment statement, by fund; and bonded debt, by fund and agency.

Fund types covered are general, restricted account, special revenue, debt and internal service, enterprise, trust, and agency.

Contains summary and contents/table listing (p. iv-v); narrative summary, with text statistics, 4 charts, and 5 tables (p. 1-18); 15 financial statements (p. 20-76); and definitions (p. 77).

State of Washington Annual Financial Report, issued by Office of Financial Management, is covered by SRI under S8345-3.

Availability: Washington State Office of the Treasurer, Legislative Office Bldg., Olympia WA 98504, †; SRI/MF/complete.

S8510   WEST VIRGINIA
Department of Agriculture

S8510-1   WEST VIRGINIA AGRICULTURAL STATISTICS, 1983
Annual. Nov. 1983.
3+88 p. C.R. Bull. No. 14.
LC 44-41812.
SRI/MF/complete

Annual report on West Virginia agricultural production, marketing, and finances, 1982, with some estimates for 1983, trends from 1970s, and selected historical statistics from 1867. Data are generally shown by commodity and/or county.

Report covers production, prices, sales, value, and, as applicable, acreage, yield, and inventory; for field crop, fruit, livestock, poultry, and apiary sectors.

Also includes data on West Virginia precipitation, pasture condition, feed and fertilizer sales, prices paid by farmers for selected production items, and farm income; Appalachian region farm production expenditures; and number of farms and acreage, by State.

Data are compiled by the West Virginia Crop Reporting Service in cooperation with USDA.

Contains 7 charts, 11 maps, and 66 tables, interspersed with narrative summaries (p. 1-88).

Availability: West Virginia Department of Agriculture, Crop Reporting Service, Charleston WV 25305, contributors to publication †, others $5.00; SRI/MF/complete.

S8540   WEST VIRGINIA
Department of Education

S8540-1   SEVENTIETH REPORT (TWENTY-NINTH ANNUAL REPORT) OF THE STATE SUPERINTENDENT OF SCHOOLS, West Virginia
Annual. For individual publication data, see below.
LC 72-621530.
SRI/MF/complete

Annual report, for 1982/83, on West Virginia public elementary and secondary education, with selected data for private schools. Report is published in 3 volumes as follows:

Vol. 1. Narrative report, describing Dept of Education activities, with selected facility and funding statistics.

Vol. 2. Statistical summary, presenting data on educational personnel, pupils, transportation, and facilities for public schools, and selected data for nonpublic schools.

Vol. 3. Financial report.

Volumes 1 and 2 are described below. Volume 3 has not yet been received. For description of volume 3 for 1981/82, see SRI 1983 Annual, under this number.

Availability: West Virginia Department of Education, Public Information Office, Capitol Complex, Bldg. 6, Rm. B-215, Charleston WV 25305, †; SRI/MF/complete.

S8540-1.1: Volume 1 (Narrative Report)
[Annual. Nov. 1, 1983. vi+27 p. SRI/MF/complete.]

Contains contents listing (p. v); introduction and organization chart (p. 1-2); and narrative report interspersed with 5 tables, listed below (p. 3-27).

TABLES:

BETTER SCHOOL BUILDING PROGRAM
[Tables I-IV show data by county.]

I-III. Comprehensive educational facilities [budget] plans and school construction projects approved by the State board of education; and school facilities projects completed/inspected to date; [including project costs, all by funding source (State, Federal/State, and local bond issue and levies/other, as of July 28, 1983]. (p. 21-23)

IV. Bond elections attempted since inception of Better School Building Program [including value of bond issues proposed, and value and percent of voter approval of approved and defeated issues, selected years 1971-82]. (p. 24)

EDUCATIONAL FUNDS

[A] Board of education funds processed [by expenditure category, and function or program, 1982/83]. (p. 26-27)

S8540-1.2: Volume 2 (Statistical Summary)
[Annual. [1983.] 2+94 p. SRI/MF/complete.]

Contains contents listing and foreword (2 p.); and 41 tables, listed below (p. 2-94).

20-22. Children entering, leaving, and in foster care [includes children by age, custodial program, and living arrangement; and case closures by reason].

23. Social services provided to adults [by type].

24-25. Living arrangements of aged/blind/disabled social service recipients; and social services provided [by type] to aged/blind/disabled adults.

26. Providers of social services [includes chore services, day care, emergency shelter, foster care for children, personal care, adult family care, and adoptive homes].

27-28. Day care expenditures: numbers and source of funds [Title XX AFDC and income eligible, and work incentive program], and type of care [in home, day care center, and family care home].

29-31. Foster care expenditures: numbers and type of care [foster family, institutions, and relatives], and source of funds [State funds, AFDC foster care (AFDC-FC), and Title XX emergency shelter]; and children in foster care, expenditures and average amounts [State funds, and AFDC-FC, for foster homes/relatives, and institutions/group homes].

32. Services to adults expenditures [by type of service].

33. Child protective services report [suspected child abuse and neglect referrals, clearances, and worker/caseload information].

34. Division of Special Projects: Medicaid waiver [by type of service and area; table begins in Feb. 1984 issue].

S8575   WEST VIRGINIA Department of Insurance

S8575–1   SEVENTY-FOURTH ANNUAL REPORT OF THE INSURANCE COMMISSIONER of the State of West Virginia, Year Ending Dec. 31, 1982
Annual. Nov. 14, 1983.
iii + 353 p.
LC 74-18892.
SRI/MF/complete

Annual report on West Virginia insurance industry financial condition and underwriting activity, by company and type of insurance, 1982. Covers assets, liabilities, and capital/surplus or net worth; premiums collected, or written and earned; losses incurred and paid; expenses or claims/benefits paid; and dividends; for insurers based in West Virginia and elsewhere.

Data are shown, as applicable, for HMOs (also includes enrollment); title insurance companies; fraternal benefit societies; fire/casualty, life, and accident/health insurance companies; and Blue Cross and Blue Shield organizations.

Includes detail for life, accident/health, and fire/casualty companies by line of coverage, including workmen's compensation, automobile, surety, and medical malpractice.

Also includes data on Insurance Dept receipts and expenditures; rate changes; excess line brokers, policy premiums, number of policies,

and taxes paid; consumer complaints filed; agent licensing examination activity; taxes paid by top 20 life and fire/casualty insurers; number of companies by type; and lists of company status changes; various calendar or fiscal years 1978-83.

Data are compiled from statements filed by insurers with the Insurance Commissioner.

Contains contents listing (p. ii-iii); narrative report on dept activities, with text data and 5 tables (p. 1-37); and approximately 35 tables and statistical directories (p. 38-353).

Availability: West Virginia Department of Insurance, Insurance Commissioner's Office, 2100 Washington St., E., Charleston WV 25305, $10.00; SRI/MF/complete.

S8590   WEST VIRGINIA Library Commission

S8590–1   1983 WEST VIRGINIA LIBRARY COMMISSION Statistical Report
Annual. 1983. 19 p.
ISSN 0094-6486.
LC 74-645697.
SRI/MF/complete

Annual report, for 1983, on West Virginia public, academic, and special libraries. Includes holdings, finances, staff, and services provided.

Contains contents listing (1 p.), and the following:

a. Statistical summary with 6 tables showing statewide data on number of libraries, services, finances, and population served; and directory of public libraries. (p. 1-4)

b. By library: population served, volumes added and total volumes, periodicals, recordings, book and nonprint circulation, staff, hours open weekly, income by source including revenue sharing, and expenditures by object, shown for each public library arranged by library service area, and for direct service area libraries arranged by county. 4 tables. (p. 5-10)

c. By county: local library population served; total and per capita volumes, circulation, and local receipts; and number of libraries, branches, and bookmobiles. 1 table. (p. 11)

d. Film service activity, including number of films shown and viewers by library, and for State institutions, government depts, parks, and Southern Community College. 5 tables. (p. 12-13)

e. College and university enrollment, library volumes held, interlibrary loans, microforms, audiovisual materials, periodicals, hours open weekly, staff, and total expenditures; and special library book and periodical holdings, by municipality; all by institution. 2 tables. (p. 14-18)

A narrative annual report on State library construction and services, with summary statistics, is also available from the issuing agency, but is not covered by SRI.

Availability: West Virginia Library Commission, Science and Cultural Center, Charleston WV 25305, †; SRI/MF/complete.

S8610   WEST VIRGINIA Department of Public Safety

S8610–1   CRIME IN WEST VIRGINIA, 1983
Annual. Aug. 1, 1984.
iii + 227 p.
ISSN 0095-1641.
LC 74-648125.
SRI/MF/complete

Annual report on West Virginia crimes and arrests, by type of offense, 1983 with comparisons to 1982. Also includes data on clearances, law enforcement employment, assaults on police, and value of stolen property; and detail by county and municipality.

Data are from reports of State and local law enforcement agencies, submitted under the State Uniform Crime Reporting Program.

Contains listings of contents, tables, and charts (2 p.); introduction, offense classifications, methodology, and statistical synopsis (p. 1-17); 8 statistical sections, interspersed with narrative summaries, and 11 charts and 57 tables described below (p. 19-217); and list of contributing agencies, and glossary (p. 218-227).

This is the 12th annual report.

Availability: West Virginia Department of Public Safety, Uniform Crime Reporting Section, Communications Office, 725 Jefferson Rd., South Charleston WV 25309, †; SRI/MF/complete.

CHARTS and TABLES:

[Data are for West Virginia. Data are shown for 1983 unless otherwise noted, and usually include comparisons to 1982. Data by race/ethnicity are generally for white, black, American Indian/Alaskan Native, Asian/Pacific Islander, Hispanic, and non-Hispanic. Data by agency type are generally shown for county sheriff's offices, and rural, State, and municipal police.

Part I Index offenses covered in detail are murder, rape, robbery, and felonious assault (violent crimes); and breaking/entering, larceny/theft, and motor vehicle theft (property crimes). Arson is classified as an Index offense, but data are reported separately and are not included in the Crime Index tables. Part II offenses are all other crimes.]

S8610–1.1: Index Offenses and Arrests, Law Enforcement Employment, and Assaults on Police

STATE INDEX OFFENSES

[One table, with illustrative chart, showing offenses by month, annual offense rate, and adult and juvenile clearances, is repeated for total, violent, and property crime, and for each individual Index offense. Additional data are described below.]

a. Stolen property value for 4 Index offenses, including motor vehicle theft; Index crime offenses and rates, by offense, 1979-83; murder by type of weapon and circumstance; and murder victims, by age, sex, and race/ethnicity. 5 charts and 8 tables. (p. 20-30)

b. Robbery offenses by weapon, and offenses and value stolen by place of occurrence; felonious assault by weapon; breaking/entering offenses by type of entry, and offenses and value stolen for day and night residential and nonresidential occurrences; larceny/theft offenses and value stolen, by type of theft; and motor vehicle theft by vehicle type. 5 charts and 12 tables. (p. 31-43)

STATE ARRESTS

c. Arrests by month, crime rate, and adult and juvenile arrests, for aggregate Part I and Part II offenses; crime rate, and arrests by race/ethnicity, sex, and age, for individual Part I and Part II offenses; and narcotic arrests by substance and age. 1 chart and 8 tables. (p. 48-53)

LAW ENFORCEMENT EMPLOYEE DATA

d. Sworn and civilian law enforcement employees, by sex and agency type (including Natural Resources Dept); officers assaulted, by type of weapon, time of day, and injury status, and clearances and population, all by agency type; officers killed; and assaults by type of assignment and circumstance. 3 tables. (p. 56-58)

S8610–1.2: Data by Agency and County, and Arson and Domestic Violence

DATA BY AGENCY AND COUNTY

a. Population, Index offenses by type, and total Index clearances; and Part I and Part II arrests by offense type, and total adult and juvenile arrests; all by county, agency type, and municipal agency. 3 tables. (p. 62-191)

b. Dept of Natural Resources: juvenile and adult arrests, by age, race/ethnicity, and Part I and Part II offense, including narcotics violations by substance, for 6 districts. 12 tables. (p. 194-205)

ARSON AND DOMESTIC VIOLENCE

c. Arson actual and unfounded offenses, total and juvenile clearances, offenses involving uninhabited structures, and property damage value, all by property classification. 1 table. (p. 208)

d. Domestic violence: victims, offenders, and complainants, by sex; repeat complainants; complaints by weapon used, extent of abuse, police action taken, victim-offender relationship, day of week, and month; child abuse/neglect caseloads, by month; and protection order violations; with some data by agency. 10 tables. (p. 210-215)

S8620 WEST VIRGINIA Board of Regents

S8620–4   STATISTICAL PROFILE OF HIGHER EDUCATION in West Virginia, 1983
Annual. Mar. 1984.
xiii + 148 p.
SRI/MF/complete

Annual report on West Virginia higher education, 1983. Covers enrollment, degrees conferred, and programs offered, for public and private institutions; and faculty characteristics and finances, for public institutions. Most data are shown by institution. Also includes selected trends from 1971.

Contains listings of contents, tables, and charts, and introduction (p. v-xiii); and 4 chapters, with narrative summaries and several charts, and 71 tables listed below (p. 1-148).

This is the 2nd annual report.

Availability: West Virginia Board of Regents, 950 Kanawha Blvd., E., Charleston WV 25301, †; SRI/MF/complete.

TABLES:
[Data are shown by institution, as of fall 1983 or academic year 1982/83, unless otherwise noted.]

S8620–4.1: Enrollment and Degrees
[Data are shown for public and private institutions, unless otherwise noted.]

ENROLLMENT
[Data by attendance status show full- and part-time, and data by residence show in- and out-of-State.]

[A-D] [Trends in] credit headcount enrollment, and FTE enrollment [for public institutions only, various years 1971-83]. (p. 5-7, 11)

[E] Age distribution of students enrolled in public institutions. (p. 15)

1.1. Credit headcount enrollment [aggregated for public and private institutions] by level of institution, [by] sex, attendance status, residence, [and level] of student, together with total noncredit headcount enrollment. (p. 16)

1.2-1.8. Credit headcount enrollment by residence, sex, attendance status, and level of student [with various cross-tabulations]. (p. 18-37)

1.9. In-State credit headcount enrollment, by county of residence. (p. 38)

1.10. Out-of-State credit headcount enrollment, by State of residence. (p. 42)

1.11-1.12. FTE enrollment in public institutions, by Regents' budget enrollment categories, and by course level. (p. 46-47)

DEGREES CONFERRED
[F] Total degrees conferred by public institutions [1973/74-1982/83]. (p. 51)

2.1-2.3. Total degrees conferred [aggregated for public and private institutions], by sex of student, level of degree, level of institution, and academic area of study [with various cross-tabulations]. (p. 55-59)

2.4-2.7. Total degrees conferred, by level of degree and sex of student; and number of different degree programs offered and total degrees conferred, by academic area of study and by level of degree. (p. 60-71)

S8620–4.2: Faculty and Finances
[Data are for public institutions only.]

FACULTY CHARACTERISTICS
[Tables 3.1-3.8 include aggregate trends for 1979-83.]

3.1-3.5. Academic rank of full-time faculty; highest earned academic degree of full- and part-time faculty; and full-time faculty members' years of experience at institution of present employment and in higher education. (p. 78-82)

3.6-3.8. Age and sex of full- and part-time faculty. (p. 83-85)

3.9. Tenure analysis of full-time faculty [exclusively in teaching and in teaching/other activity]. (p. 86)

3.10-3.13. Average 9-month salary of full-time faculty engaged exclusively in teaching, and engaged in teaching and some other function, by academic rank and highest degree held (medical colleges excluded) [with aggregate trends for 1974-83]. (p. 87-90)

3.14. Number of FTE resident teaching faculty, total resident teaching salary cost, and average 9-10 months instructional salary cost per FTE resident faculty. (p. 91)

3.15-3.30. Number of faculty, average 9-month salary, average years of experience at institution of present employment, average total years of higher education experience, and average age of full-time faculty members engaged exclusively in resident instruction, by academic rank, highest degree held, and by sex. (p. 92-123)

FISCAL DATA
[Data are for FY83, unless otherwise noted. Fund types are educational/general, auxiliary enterprises, medical schools/medical center, and student aid.]

4.1-4.2. Total operating revenue and expenditures [by fund type]. (p. 130-131)

4.3-4.4. Total operating revenue and expenditures [aggregate data, by fund type], FY79-83. (p. 132)

4.5-4.7. Educational/general revenue [from 6 sources, with] percentage distribution, and [amount] per FTE student. (p. 135-137)

4.8-4.9. Comparison of educational/general revenue and State general fund revenue [total and per FTE student], FY79-83. (p. 138-139)

4.10-4.12. Educational/general expenditures [for 7 functions, with] percentage distribution, and [amount] per FTE student. (p. 141-143)

4.13. Comparison of educational/general expenditures [total and per FTE student], FY79-83. (p. 144)

4.14-4.15. Auxiliary enterprise revenue [by source] and expenditures [by function]. (p. 146-147)

4.16. Total operating revenue [by source] and expenditures [by function], medical schools and medical center. (p. 148)

S8675   WISCONSIN
Department of
Administration

**S8675–2   WISCONSIN ANNUAL
FISCAL REPORT for the
Year Ending June 30, 1983**
Annual.   For individual
publication data, see below.
LC 75-642705.
SRI/MF/complete

Annual report on financial condition of Wisconsin State government, for FY83, presenting financial data for general, conservation, transportation, higher education, unemployment reserve, retirement, building trust, and capital improvement funds. Report is issued in 2 volumes, individually described below.

Availability: Wisconsin Department of Administration, Financial Operations Bureau, PO Box 7864, Madison WI 53707, †; SRI/MF/complete.

S8675–2.1: Main Report
[Annual. Oct. 7, 1983. 4+57 p. SRI/MF/complete.]

Presents assets, liabilities, receipts by source, disbursements by function and object, and fund balances, by fund, FY83, with comparisons from FY81.

Also includes comparison of appropriations and actual expenditures; population; State payments to localities for property tax relief and shared revenues, by county; State and Federal local assistance payments and aid to individuals and organizations, by agency and program; State bonded indebtedness; and property valuation.

Contains contents listing (1 p.); highlights, with 3 charts (p. 1-7); general purpose financial statements, with 4 exhibits (p. 8-17); financial section, with 2 charts and 12 exhibits (p. 20-40); and statistical section, with 1 chart and 9 exhibits (p. 42-57).

S8675–2.2: Appendix
[Annual. 1983. 48 p. SRI/MF/complete.]

Presents detailed statements of appropriations by source (general purpose or program); expenditures for State operations, aid, and local assistance; and balances; shown by function, agency, program, and fund, FY82-83.

Contains 1 summary exhibit and 8 detailed schedules.

S8680   WISCONSIN
Department of
Agriculture, Trade
and Consumer Protection

**S8680–1   1984 WISCONSIN
AGRICULTURAL
STATISTICS**
Annual.   June 1984.
ii+95 p.
ISSN 0512-1329.
LC 66-63464.
SRI/MF/complete

Annual report on Wisconsin agricultural production, marketing, and finances, 1970s-83, with some data for 1984 and selected trends from 1960. Data are generally shown by commodity and/or county and district, with some comparisons to other States and total U.S.

Report generally covers production, prices, disposition, value, and, as applicable, acreage, yield, and inventory, for field crop, vegetable, fruit, livestock, poultry, apiary, and dairy sectors.

Report also includes data on Wisconsin farm income and production expenses, farm real estate value and taxes, number of farms and acreage, farmland sales and prices, weather, hog and cattle shipments by destination, and mink operations; and prices paid by U.S. farmers for production commodities.

Report also presents Wisconsin findings from the Census of Agriculture, including data on number of farms, acres harvested or planted, and production, all by type of crop, with number of trees for fruit crops, 1974, 1978, and 1982; and farms, and acres irrigated, by county, 1982.

Data are compiled by the Wisconsin Agriculture Reporting Service .

Contains contents listing (p. ii); foreword, and 5 sections with narrative summaries, 25 maps, 26 charts, and 107 tables (p. 2-81); and a special supplement on specialty crops with 3 maps and 28 tables (p. 82-94 and inside back cover).

This is the 20th annual report.

Availability: Wisconsin Agriculture Reporting Service, PO Box 9160, Madison WI 53715, $3.00; SRI/MF/complete.

S8690   WISCONSIN
Department of
Development

**S8690–1   WISCONSIN ECONOMIC
PROFILE**
Recurring (irreg.)   [1983.]
6 p.+2 p. supplement.
SRI/MF/complete

Recurring report presenting data on Wisconsin population, income, employment, natural resources, business activity, government finances, housing and construction, and recreation, various periods, primarily 1970s-81.

Data are from Census Bureau and other Federal and State agencies.

Contains 11 tables, described below, and brief narrative summary of State economy (5 p.).

Report is accompanied by a 2-page supplement presenting a State summary of selected 1980 Census findings. Supplement data are the same as the county data presented in *State of Wisconsin Socio-Economic Characteristics,* described under S8690-2.

For description of previous edition of *Wisconsin Economic Profile,* published in 1980, see SRI 1980 Annual, under this number. Previous edition included county profiles as well as State data.

Availability: Wisconsin Department of Development, 123 W. Washington Ave., PO Box 7970, Madison WI 53707, †; SRI/MF/complete.

TABLES:
[Unless otherwise noted, tables show data for Wisconsin, with selected comparisons to the U.S.]

a. Population: size and density, net migration, and population by sex and age group; median family, total, and per capita personal income; income from top 3 industries; and employment, average weekly earnings, and number of business establishments, by industry division. 3 tables.

b. Resources: number of farms, farmland acreage and value per acre, and cash receipts by commodity group; forest acreage; growing stock, sawlogs harvested, and timber removed, by tree species; and nonfuel minerals production value and industry employment. 1 table.

c. Retail trade: establishments and sales by kind of business; and lodging, amusement/recreation, and total service industries and receipts. 1 table.

d. Manufacturing: establishments, employment, payroll, average earnings, value added, capital expenditures, and shipments value; manufacturing establishments by employment size and industry group; and location, product or business, and employees of 10 largest manufacturing and 5 largest nonmanufacturing employers. 1 table.

e. Government finance: property tax levies and assessments; State shared tax revenue; State funding for education, health/social services, and transportation; corporate and personal income, and sales tax collections; and population of 20 cities. 2 tables.

f. Housing: building permits issued and median value of owner occupied units; single family home average purchase price in North Central U.S.; and construction plans approved and square footage, by type of building. 2 tables.

g. Recreation: total acreage and Great Lakes/Mississippi River shoreline length; lakes and acreage; public recreation land acreage; canoe trails/pick-up services; swimming and skiing areas, golf courses, and campsites; hiking, bicycling, and snowmobiling trail mileage; and hunting acreage. 1 table.

**S8690–2   STATE OF WISCONSIN
SOCIO-ECONOMIC
CHARACTERISTICS**
Monograph.   [1983.]
144 p. no paging.
SRI/MF/complete

Report presenting 1980 U.S. Census of Population and Housing findings for Wisconsin by county. Includes data on population and household characteristics, housing units, income, commuting, poverty, and employment.

Data are from 1980 U.S. Census Summary Tape Files 1 and 3.

Contains 21 tables, described below, repeated for each county.

Similar reports for Wisconsin's minor civil divisions are also available from the issuing agency, but are not covered by SRI. A State summary version of *State of Wisconsin Socio-Economic Characteristics* is included as a 2-page supplement to *Wisconsin Economic Profile,* described under S8690-1.

Availability: Wisconsin Department of Development, 123 W. Washington Ave., PO Box 7970, Madison WI 53707, †; SRI/MF/complete.

TABLES:

a. Population, by age and sex; total and vacant year-round housing units; rural population and housing units; families by composition, and average size; and condominium and non-condominium units and value, and rental units and rent, by occupancy status. 9 tables.

b. Households by size and with persons age 60/over, persons per occupied unit, and household income, by tenure; households with persons under age 18, and with female heads; and families and households, by income level and poverty status. 8 tables.

c. Employed persons age 16/over, by place of work (within and outside State and county of residence), travel time to work, occupation, and class of worker. 4 tables.

S8700   WISCONSIN
Council on Criminal Justice

S8700–1   WISCONSIN CRIME AND ARRESTS, 1983
Annual. [1984.]   iii+111 p.
SRI/MF/complete

Annual report presenting detailed data on Wisconsin crimes and arrests, by type of offense, by county and law enforcement agency, 1983, with aggregate trends from 1973.

Data are from reports of law enforcement agencies submitted under the Uniform Crime Reporting Program.

Contains contents listing (p. iii); introduction and overview, with 3 summary tables (p. 1-7); crime clock, and 74 tables described below, with accompanying narrative summaries (p. 8-109); and glossary (p. 110-111).

Availability: Wisconsin Council on Criminal Justice, Statistical Analysis Center, 30 W. Mifflin St., Suite 1000, Madison WI 53702, $1.50+postage; SRI/MF/complete.

TABLES:
[Data are for 1983 with selected comparisons to 1982, unless otherwise noted. Index crimes are murder, forcible rape, robbery, aggravated assault, burglary, theft, motor vehicle theft, and arson.

Offense summary and sections on individual offenses each include 5 tables showing offenses and rates by population size group and for total suburban and rural sheriffs' offices; adult and juvenile arrests by sex and race (including American Indian); and clearance rates. Additional data are noted below.]

a. Summary: for total, violent, and property Index offenses. 15 tables. (p. 9-17)

b. Murder. 5 tables. (p. 18-20)

c. Forcible rape: also includes attempted rape offenses. 6 tables. (p. 21-23)

d. Robbery and aggravated assault: also include offenses by type of weapon. 12 tables. (p. 24-29)

e. Burglary: also includes offenses by type of entry. 6 tables. (p. 30-32)

f. Theft. 5 tables. (p. 33-35)

g. Motor vehicle theft: also includes offenses by vehicle type. 6 tables. (p. 36-38)

h. Arson. 5 tables. (p. 39-41)

i. Trends: offenses and rates, clearance rates, and ratio of arrest/offenses, for total, violent, property, and individual Index crimes, 1973-83. 4 tables. (p. 44-47)

j. By county and agency: offenses and rates, clearance rates, and juvenile clearances as percent of all clearances, for total, violent, property, and individual Index crimes; and adult and juvenile arrests, by Index crime, and for total and 10-13 non-Index offenses; all by county and local law enforcement agency. 8 tables. (p. 51-105)

k. Statewide adult and juvenile arrests, by sex, age, and race/ethnicity (including American Indian, Asian, and Hispanic), for individual Index and non-Index offenses. 2 tables. (p. 107-109)

S8715   WISCONSIN
Department of Health and Social Services

S8715–2   DIVISION OF CORRECTIONS STATISTICAL BULLETINS, 1983, Wisconsin
Annual series. For individual publication data, see below.
SRI/MF/complete

Series of annual and semiannual reports on corrections in Wisconsin, covering prisons, juvenile correctional facilities, community residential centers, and probation and parole programs. Includes data on admissions, releases, and offender characteristics.

Most data are shown by sex. Some data are shown by individual institution. Data by race/ethnic group generally include white, black, American Indian or Native American, and Asian, with selected data for Hispanics and non-Hispanics.

Reports received during 1984 are described below.

Issuing agency also publishes a monthly report on prison population movements, not covered in SRI.

Availability: Wisconsin Department of Health and Social Services, Corrections Division, Information Management and Operations Office, PO Box 7925, Madison WI 53707, †; SRI/MF/complete.

S8715–2.1: Residents in Wisconsin Adult Correctional Facilities on June 30, 1983, with Five-Year Trends for 1979-83
[Semiannual. Dec. 1983. 28 p. Statistical Bull. C-57. SRI/MF/complete.]

Semiannual report covering adult correctional institution inmates, by admission status, race/ethnic group, offense, length of sentence, county of commitment, age, county or State of birth, length of stay, and conviction for new offense after admission, all by institution, as of June 30, 1983, with selected trends from 1979.

Contains contents listing (1 p.); narrative highlights with 2 summary trend tables (p. 1-3); and 10 detailed tables (p. 4-28).

S8715–2.2: Fiscal Year Summary Report of Population Movement, 1983
[Annual. Jan. 1984. 20 p. Statistical Bull. C-60A. SRI/MF/complete.]

Annual report covering inmate population, admissions, transfers, releases, rereleases, deaths, and absences, for adult and juvenile correctional facilities, by institution; juvenile institutional and billable absence days, by facility type; and probation and parole adult and juvenile population, admissions, terminations, and absconders; FY83, with selected trends from FY79.

Contains highlights, with 9 summary trend tables (p. 1-8); footnotes (p. 9-10); and 5 detailed tables (p. 11-20).

S8715–2.3: Residents in Wisconsin Adult Correctional Facilities on Dec. 31, 1983, with Five-Year Trends for 1979-83
[Semiannual. July 1984. 37 p. Statistical Bull. C-57. SRI/MF/complete.]

Semiannual report covering adult correctional institution inmates, by admission status, race/ethnic group, offense, length of sentence, county of commitment, age, county or State of birth, disability status, military service, education, tested grade level and intelligence, length of stay, and conviction for new offense after admission, all by institution, as of Dec. 31, 1983, with selected trends from 1979.

Contains narrative highlights, with 2 charts and 2 summary trend tables (p. 1-5); and 15 detailed tables (p. 6-37).

S8750   WISCONSIN
Department of Industry, Labor and Human Relations

S8750–1   WISCONSIN EMPLOYMENT AND ECONOMIC INDICATORS
Monthly. Approx. 15 p.
ISSN 0147-6106.
LC 77-646943.
SRI/MF/complete, shipped quarterly

Monthly report on Wisconsin employment and economic conditions, including data on 27 economic indicators; and employment, hours, and earnings, by industry group and locality. Data sources include State and Federal agencies, and *Business Week.* Month of data coverage is 1-2 months prior to cover date.

S8750-1   Wisconsin

Contains list of data sources; narrative analysis of employment and economic developments during the month of coverage; 5 monthly tables; 1 feature article, often with statistics, including a quarterly economic outlook feature; and usually several economic trend charts.

Monthly tables are listed below and appear in all issues. All additional features with substantial statistical content, are described, as they appear, under "Statistical Features." Nonstatistical features are not covered.

Availability: Wisconsin Department of Industry, Labor and Human Relations, Job Service Division, Labor Market Information, 201 E. Washington Ave., PO Box 7944, Madison WI 53707, †; SRI/MF/complete, shipped quarterly.

Issues reviewed during 1984: Oct. 1983-Sept. 1984 (P).

MONTHLY TABLES:

[All tables show data for month of coverage or latest available month, preceding month, and same month of previous year. Tables [1-2] show both seasonally adjusted and unadjusted data. Tables [3-5] show unadjusted data.]

[1] Economic indicators [27 leading, coincident, and other indicators, including average manufacturing workweek and overtime hours, average weekly new unemployment compensation claims, job openings, new incorporations, net gain in business and residential phone access lines, and building plans examined; Milwaukee help-wanted index and CPI, natural gas and electric power sales, auto registrations, securities registrations, personal income, and cash receipts from farm marketing; birth, death, and marriage registrations; and population gain, prices received by farmers, and workers involved in labor disputes].

[2] Labor force estimates [civilian employment and unemployment for Wisconsin and U.S., and Wisconsin nonfarm wage/salary employment by industry division].

[3] Manufacturing employment [by industry group].

[4] Earnings and hours data [by manufacturing industry group].

[5] Summary of recent data [production workers' average hours and earnings, and manufacturing employment; for U.S., Wisconsin, 3 SMSAs, and 12 counties and cities].

STATISTICAL FEATURES:

S8750-1.501: Nov. 1983

WISCONSIN'S ECONOMIC OUTLOOK, QUARTERLY FEATURE

(p. 9-14) Quarterly article, by David H. Peterson, analyzing the economic outlook for Wisconsin through 1985.

Includes 3 tables showing Wisconsin total and per capita personal income; and employment by industry division, with quarterly detail by manufacturing industry group; 1982-85.

S8750-1.502: Jan. 1984

ECONOMIC RECOVERY: HOW SURE ARE WE

(p. 9-11) By Joseph Tumpach, Jr. Article, with 4 tables showing Wisconsin employment, unemployment, labor force, and unemployment rate, monthly 1982-83.

S8750-1.503: Feb. 1984

WISCONSIN ECONOMIC FORECAST, QUARTERLY FEATURE

(p. 10-11) Quarterly feature, with 3 tables showing Wisconsin total and per capita personal income; and employment by industry division, with quarterly detail by manufacturing industry group; 1982-85.

S8750-1.504: May 1984

WISCONSIN'S ECONOMIC OUTLOOK, QUARTERLY FEATURE

(p. 9-13) Quarterly article, by David H. Peterson, analyzing the economic outlook for Wisconsin through 1985. Includes 2 tables showing Wisconsin employment by industry division, with quarterly detail by manufacturing industry group, 1982-85.

S8750-1.505: Aug. 1984

WISCONSIN'S ECONOMIC OUTLOOK, QUARTERLY FEATURE

(p. 9-12) Quarterly article, by David H. Peterson and Gene Schubert, analyzing the economic outlook for Wisconsin through 1985. Includes 2 tables showing Wisconsin employment by industry division, with quarterly detail by manufacturing industry group, various periods 1982-85.

S8750-4   ECONOMIC PLANNING INFORMATION for the State of Wisconsin, 1984
Annual. [1984.]   40 p.
SRI/MF/complete

Annual report, for 1984, identifying Wisconsin population groups most in need of employment services, and presenting data on population, labor force, employment and unemployment, and job service applicants and openings. Most data are shown for 1982 and/or 1983. Includes population projections through 2010 and employment projections through mid-1986.

Data are compiled from State and Federal sources.

Contains contents listing (1 p.); and narrative analysis, interspersed with illustrative charts, maps, and 23 tables described below (p. 1-40).

Availability: Wisconsin Department of Industry, Labor and Human Relations, Job Service Division, Labor Market Information Section, 201 E. Washington Ave., PO Box 7944, Madison WI 53707, †; SRI/MF/complete.

TABLES:

[Data are for Wisconsin, unless otherwise noted. Data by ethnicity include Hispanic, American Indian/Eskimo, and Asian.]

a. Population by age and sex, births, deaths, and migration, quinquennially 1980-2010. 1 table. (p. 3)

b. Labor force by employment status, and employment by industry division, 1982 through mid-1986; and persons eligible for Job Training Partnership Act (JTPA) assistance, by sex, age, and race-ethnicity, and for selected groups including handicapped, displaced homemakers, school dropouts, teenage parents, dislocated workers, offenders/ex-offenders, veterans, and refugees (no date). 3 tables. (p. 12-13)

c. Selected U.S. and Wisconsin labor force trends, various periods 1982-84; and Wisconsin labor force participants and nonparticipants, by race and marital status, with selected detail by sex and for youths, 1982. 6 tables. (p. 15-20)

d. Employment by industry division, Dec. 1983, with change from 1979 and 1982; employment rate and wage/salary index compared to U.S., 1977-83; and job service applicants and openings, by occupational group, 4th quarter 1982-83, with ranking of hard-to-fill occupations, 4th quarter 1984. 8 tables. (p. 21-28)

e. Unemployment rates by age and sex, with comparison to U.S.; unemployment rate by county; and characteristics of unemployment compensation claimants, including sex, age, veteran status, education, race-ethnicity, average wage, reason for separation, potential duration of unemployment, and industry and occupational attachment; various periods 1982-83. 5 tables. (p. 30-39)

S8750-5   WISCONSIN'S COMMUTING PATTERNS
Monograph.   Jan. 1984.
145 p.+errata sheet.
SRI/MF/complete

Report presenting 1980 census data on commuting patterns in Wisconsin, covering points of origin and destination for Wisconsin residents and for nonresidents employed in the State. Data are cross-tabulated among Wisconsin counties and neighboring States.

Data are based on unpublished tabulations from Summary Tape File 4 of the 1980 Census of Population and Housing.

Contains 2 data maps repeated for each county (p. 2-145).

Availability: Wisconsin Department of Industry, Labor and Human Relations, Job Service Division, Labor Market Information Section, 201 E. Washington Ave., PO Box 7944, Madison WI 53707, †; SRI/MF/complete.

S8755   WISCONSIN
Office of the Commissioner of Insurance

S8755-1   WISCONSIN INSURANCE REPORT, Business of 1983
Annual.   [1984.]   iii+174 p.
LC 80-644240.
SRI/MF/complete

Annual report on Wisconsin insurance industry financial condition and underwriting activity, by company and type of insurance, 1983. Covers assets, capital/surplus, premiums/annuity considerations, losses and benefits incurred, gain from operations, benefits paid, net income, premiums written and/or earned, and loss and expense ratios; for companies based in Wisconsin and elsewhere.

Data are shown, as applicable, for property/liability and life/health insurers, including accident/health assns; fraternal societies; and mutual, stock, and reciprocal insurance companies.

Selected data are also shown for companies ranked by Wisconsin market share within specific lines of coverage, including medical malpractice, workers compensation, automobile, and surety.

Also includes data on finances of Insurance Commissioner's Office and 4 State-administered insurance funds, mostly for FY83; regulatory activities; finances of companies in liquidation; and consumer complaint caseloads.

Contains contents listing (1 p.); narrative report, with 16 tables (p. i-ii, 1-58); statistical section, with 7 tables (p. 61-111); and directory of licensed insurers (p. 115-174).

This is the 115th edition of the report.

Availability: Wisconsin Office of the Commissioner of Insurance, PO Box 7873, Madison WI 53707-7873, $2.00; SRI/MF/complete.

S8780   WISCONSIN
Legislative Reference Bureau

**S8780–1   STATE OF WISCONSIN
1983-84 BLUE BOOK**
Biennial.   June 1983.
x+983 p.
SRI/MF/complete

Biennial compilation, for 1983-84, of reference information and statistics on the economy, government, and population of Wisconsin. Data are primarily for various years 1970-82, with some trends from as early as 1836. Most data are from State and Federal government reports.

Report is designed to present a comprehensive overview of the State. Extensive socioeconomic, demographic, and geographical breakdowns are shown, as applicable, for most topics. These breakdowns include data by city, county, urban-rural status, commodity, industry, age, educational attainment, marital status, race, and sex. Data for total U.S. and by State are also included for comparative purposes.

Contents:

a. Contents listing and introduction (p. iv-x); and biographies of Wisconsin elected officials, and legislative district maps (p. 1-98).

b. Feature article on the history of Wisconsin's government and State capitol building, with 1 table (p. 108) showing population and number of legislative members, by county, 1836; and list of articles in prior editions. (p. 99-170)

c. Wisconsin constitution, with 2 tables (p. 211-218) showing constitutional amendment and referenda election results, 1846-1983. (p. 171-218)

d. Narrative summary of the State legislative, executive, and judicial branches, including lists of State officials and judges, text data on agency employment and budgets, and 7 tables described below. (p. 219-586)

e. Statistical section, with 5 charts, and 148 tables described below. (p. 587-812)

f. Political parties and 1982 party platforms; and 1982-83 State election results, with 25 tables described below. (p. 813-944)

g. Wisconsin symbols, addenda, and index. (p. 945-983)

Previous report, for 1981/82, is described in SRI 1982 Annual, under this number.

Availability: Wisconsin Department of Administration, Document Sales and Distribution, 202 S. Thornton Ave., Madison WI 53702, $2.00; SRI/MF/complete.

TABLES:

S8780–1.1:   Legislative and Executive Branches

a. Legislator demographic characteristics, biennially 1973-83; legislature political composition, biennially 1885-1983; legislative session length, measures introduced, vetoes and overrides, and laws enacted, 1848-1982; and population, by legislative district, 1980. 5 tables. (p. 235-254)

b. Current salaries of elected and appointed officials, 1983. 2 tables. (p. 310, 350-363)

S8780–1.2: Statistical Section
[Data are for Wisconsin, unless otherwise noted.]

AGRICULTURE

a. Farms: income, with detail for cash receipts; number, acreage, and value; operators by ownership status; land sales (including land diverted to nonagricultural uses); employment, and wage rates; and production, with State ranking. 11 tables. (p. 589-598)

COMMERCE AND INDUSTRY

b. Manufacturing value added; domestic articles of incorporation filed, foreign corporations licensed, and related fees, selected years 1905-82; energy consumption, by resource; petroleum consumption, by sector; and savings and loan assn and bank establishments, and financial activity. 10 tables. (p. 617-624)

CONSERVATION AND RECREATION

c. Recreational facilities, licenses and permits, fish and game taken, and restocking activity; wild fur harvest value; State park, forest, and trail acreage and attendance, by site; Outdoor Recreation Act Program expenditures, by program; natural resources land acquisitions and costs; and water and air pollution control and solid waste program expenditures. 9 tables. (p. 625-632)

EDUCATION

d. Enrollment in private colleges and universities by institution, in University of Wisconsin by campus and school, in vocational/adult education by institution, and in public and private elementary/secondary schools by grade level; school districts since 1848; and public school teachers and administrative staff, by educational background. 13 tables. (p. 634-641)

e. Public school teacher salary ranges, and median and average salary; public education expenditures; per capita expenditures compared to personal income; and number of high school diplomas and higher education degrees. 6 tables. (p. 641-646)

EMPLOYMENT AND INCOME

f. Income (total, per capita, and earned); personal income; manufacturing establishments, by type of product and number of employees; civilian labor force, by employment status; unemployment insurance claimants and weekly benefits; and work stoppages. 13 tables. (p. 648-660)

GEOGRAPHY AND HISTORY

g. Lakes and acreage; elevation of geographic high points; average monthly temperature and precipitation; and land and water area. 5 tables. (p. 661-667)

h. Historic site attendance, and State vote in presidential and gubernatorial elections. 3 tables. (p. 679, 686-689)

LOCAL GOVERNMENT

i. Population, land area, and number of county board supervisors. 6 tables. (p. 712-725)

j. State and local government employees, payroll, and earnings; minority, handicapped, and veteran State employees; and local government units. 7 tables. (p. 730-735)

MILITARY AND VETERAN AFFAIRS

k. Veterans Home membership, including dependents, by war, selected years 1888-1982; State benefits to war veterans and number of recipients; and number serving and killed in military, by war. 3 tables. (p. 736-739)

POPULATION AND VITAL STATISTICS

l. Population since 1840; and Indian population by tribe and reservation, and reservation land status. 8 tables. (p. 755-760)

m. Vital statistics trends, including infant and maternal deaths; live births and deaths; and marriages and divorces. 4 tables. (p. 761-764)

REVENUE

n. Revenues by source and expenditures by function, with detail for transportation fund; tax revenues; budget allocations by revenue source; State payments to localities for property tax relief and shared revenue; and State aid and shared taxes. 13 tables. (p. 773-785)

o. General property assessment and taxes levied, with trends from 1900 and selected data by type of property and governmental unit; public indebtedness; Federal aid; and Federal tax receipts. 14 tables. (p. 786-795)

SOCIAL SERVICES

p. Welfare expenditures, with detail by revenue source, public assistance grants and recipients, and type of medical assistance provider; State correctional and mental institution population, by institution; and correctional expenditures. 6 tables. (p. 797-802)

TRANSPORTATION

q. Bus and urban transit system use; urban transit revenues; selected motor vehicle accident trends, including motorcycle accidents and alcohol use; road mileage; motor vehicle registrations; railroad mileage, use, and revenue; airport system use; and waterborne freight, by port. 17 tables. (p. 804-812)

S8780–1.3: Election Data

Presents results of general election held Nov. 2, 1982, and of primaries and other elections held Apr. 1982-May 1983. Includes voting for U.S. and State legislators, Governor, judges, other State offices, State constitutional amendments, and referenda. (p. 861-943)

S8795   WISCONSIN
Department of
Public Instruction

S8795–1   WISCONSIN LIBRARY
SERVICE RECORD, 1982
Annual. [1984.] 80 p.
Bull. No. 3189.
LC 76-640787.
SRI/MF/complete

Annual report, for 1982, on Wisconsin libraries, presenting directories of academic, special, and public libraries; and data on staff, finances, and holdings of individual public libraries, and holdings of special libraries.

Contents:

Chapter 1-2. Academic and special library directories, with book and periodical holdings for most special libraries. (p. 1-27)

Chapter 3. Public library section, with narrative and 7 summary text tables; directories of libraries and library systems, including FTE staff of individual libraries; and 2 detailed tables, described below. (p. 29-80)

Availability: Wisconsin Department of Public Instruction, Library Services Division, 125 S. Webster St., PO Box 7841, Madison WI 53707, †; SRI/MF/complete.

DETAILED TABLES:
[Tables show holdings of books, periodicals, and audiovisual materials; operating income by source and expenditures by object; and the additional data described below.]

a. State summary, also including population served, number of libraries and professional librarians, direct loans, and capital expenditures, 1980-82. 1 table. (p. 29)

b. Individual library data arranged by county and library system, also including community population and direct and interlibrary loans, 1982. 1 table. (p. 34-61)

S8795–2   BASIC FACTS About
Wisconsin's Elementary and
Secondary Schools,
1983/84
Annual. [1984.] 118 p. var.
paging+errata sheet.
Bull. No. 4343.
SRI/MF/complete

Annual report on Wisconsin elementary and secondary school enrollment, staff, costs, and State aid distribution, by school district, 1983/84 with comparisons from 1979/80. Also includes pupil and staff data by ethnic category. Data are from State Depts of Public Instruction and Revenue, and reports of local school districts and private schools.

Contents:

Listings of contents and alternate school district and union high school (UHS) names. (2 p.)

Section A. Statewide summary, with 2 maps, and 9 tables listed below. (p. A1-A10)

Section B-C. 2 detailed tables, listed below. (p. B1-B12, C1-C12)

Section D-E. Narrative on State aid, with text data on guaranteed tax valuations by type of district, and State transportation aid rates per pupil; and 2 detailed tables, also listed below. (p. D1-D17, E1-E52)

Section F. Glossary. (p. F1-F7)

Availability: Wisconsin Department of Public Instruction, Publications Section, 125 S. Webster St., PO Box 7841, Madison WI 53707, $3.50; SRI/MF/complete.

TABLES:
[Most data by ethnic category include American Indian/Alaska Native, Asian/Pacific Islander, black, white, and Hispanic. Data by scope are for grades prekindergarten-8, prekindergarten-12, and 9-12 or UHS.]

STATEWIDE
[Tables 1-6 show data for 1982/83-1983/84.]

1. School summary information [number and enrollment of public and private schools, and professional staff of public schools]. (p. A1)

2. School district analysis summary [districts by scope and type; and total and high school districts by enrollment size]. (p. A2)

3. Student enrollments [for public and private schools, by grade, including prekindergarten and ungraded]. (p. A3)

4-5. Ethnic category enrollments and [professional and nonprofessional] staff. (p. A4)

6. Pupil/teacher [by scope] and pupil/total staff ratios. (p. A5)

7. Complete annual school cost per member [and cost less transportation, and Federal, State, and local shares, by scope and for total State, 1980/81-1982/83]. (p. A6)

8. Distribution of State aid dollars [including amounts paid to districts and counties, by program] for 1982/83. (p. A7)

9. General school aid eligibility [costs, aid, and valuation, total and per member, and levy rate, by scope and for total State] for 1983/84 [table incorrectly reads 1982/83]. (p. A8)

BY DISTRICT
[Tables [10-13] show data by district.]

[10] Student and staff data [public and private enrollments, for grades prekindergarten-8 and 9-12; public minority enrollments, by ethnic category; public high school graduates; public school FTE teachers and total professional staff; and school census; as of fall 1983]. (p. B2-B12)

[11] Complete annual school cost per member [and cost less transportation, and Federal, State, and local shares, 1980/81-1982/83]. (p. C1-C12)

[12] Distribution of State aid dollars [by program, including equalization, integration, transportation, tuition, common school fund, driver and handicapped children education, bilingual/bicultural, alcohol/drug abuse, school lunch, and elderly food service] 1982/83. (p. D6-D17)

[13] Estimated general school aid eligibility for 1983/84 [costs, State aid, and property valuation, total and per member, and levy rate]. (p. E3-E52)

S8800   WISCONSIN
Public Service Commission

S8800–1   STATISTICS OF
WISCONSIN PUBLIC
UTILITIES, 1982-1981-1980
Annual. Nov. 1983.
3+70 p. Bull. No. 8.
ISSN 0093-5689.
LC 74-641937.
SRI/MF/complete

Annual report presenting Wisconsin public utility financial and operating data, by utility type 1980-82, with selected data by company for 1982, and some trends from 1973. Utility types covered are electric, gas, telephone, water, and steam/water heating. Most data are shown separately for private and municipal utilities.

Covers value of plant in service; revenues and expenses, including depreciation, and corporate income and other taxes; and number of customers or telephone access lines. Also includes data on electric power consumption and/or sales by sector, generating capacity, and fuel use; and natural gas consumption by sector.

Data are from company reports.

Contains listings of contents, tables, and charts (3 p.); financial summary with text statistics, 9 charts, and 3 tables (p. 1-19); and 5 sections, with text tables, 8 charts, and 19 detailed tables (p. 20-70).

Availability: Wisconsin Public Service Commission, Accounts and Finance Division, 4802 Sheboygan Ave., PO Box 7854, Madison WI 53707, †; SRI/MF/complete.

S8815   WISCONSIN
Department of
Transportation

S8815–1   WISCONSIN ACCIDENT
FACTS, 1983
Annual. 1984. 32 p.
LC 44-31829.
SRI/MF/complete

Annual report on Wisconsin traffic accidents, injuries, and fatalities, by accident and vehicle types, location, time, and other circumstances; and driver and victim characteristics; 1983, with selected trends from 1973.

Also includes data on economic loss; vehicle registrations and travel miles; licensed drivers by age; driver fatality blood alcohol level, by age and sex; alcohol involvement in accidents, by county and age; and helmet use in motorcycle accidents.

Data are compiled from law enforcement accident reports.

Contains contents listing (inside front cover); and highlights, 4 charts, and 32 tables (p. 1-32).

Availability: Wisconsin Department of Transportation, Traffic Accident Data Section, Motor Vehicles Division, Rm. 694, PO Box 7917, Madison WI 53707, †; SRI/MF/complete.

S8855
**Department of
Administration
and Fiscal Control**

WYOMING

S8855–1   WYOMING TAX REVENUE REPORT, 9th Edition, 1984
Annual. 1984. 2+74+vi p.
LC 78-643743.
SRI/MF/complete

Annual report presenting detailed data on Wyoming sales tax revenues, by county and industry division, with detail for retail sector, primarily for FY73-84. Also includes data on State fund assets, and revenues from non-tax sources.

Data are compiled by Division of Research and Statistics. Data sources are State Auditor and Dept of Revenue and Taxation.

Contains preface and table of contents (2 p.); introduction (p. 1-4); and 5 report sections, as follows:

> Section I. Receipts and Revenues: 4 tables showing total assets by fund, FY79-83; general fund revenue by source (including 7 tax categories, licenses/permits/regulatory, fines/forfeitures/penalties, charges for sales/services, and Federal aid/grants), annually FY80-84 and monthly FY84; and selected tax revenues by source, including unemployment and workers' compensation, FY78-84. (p. 6-9)

> Section II. Sales Tax Collections Summary: tabular lists of tax rate adoption dates by county, and of taxable events and exemptions; 1 illustrative chart; and 4 tables showing tax collections and/or increases, annually by county, and monthly for total State, various periods FY70-84. (p. 11-18)

> Section III. Sales Tax Collections, by County, by Major Industrial Group: 1 trend chart; and 1 table, repeated for State and each county, showing collections by industry division, FY73-84. (p. 20-46)

> Section IV. Retail Sales Tax Collections, by County, by Sub-Group Level: 1 trend chart; and 1 table, repeated for State and each county, showing collections by kind of business, FY73-84. (p. 48-74)

> Glossary and bibliography. (p. i-v)

Data for counties generally also include totals for out of State.

The 9th edition is a combined report for 1983-84.

Availability: Wyoming Department of Administration and Fiscal Control, Research and Statistics Division, Emerson Bldg., Rm. 302, Cheyenne WY 82002, †; SRI/MF/complete.

S8855–2   WYOMING DATA HANDBOOK, 1983
Biennial. Dec. 8, 1983.
4+206 p.
LC 74-645995.
SRI/MF/complete

Biennial compilation, for 1983, of detailed social, economic, and governmental statistics for Wyoming. Data are primarily for various years 1960-83, with population trends from 1870 and projections to 1992. Data are from State and Federal sources.

Report is designed to present a comprehensive overview of the State. Extensive socioeconomic, demographic, and geographic breakdowns are shown, as applicable, for most topics. These breakdowns include data by city, county and other State region, urban-rural status, commodity, industry, occupation, age, race, and sex. Comparisons to U.S. are also occasionally included.

Contains contents listing and introduction (2 p.); State information, with 13 maps, 15 charts, and 131 tables arranged in 12 sections, described below (p. 1-100); county information, with 1 map, and 1 chart and 6 tables repeated for each of 24 counties, also described below (p. 103-194); and index (p. 195-206).

This is the 6th edition of the *Handbook.* Previous edition, issued in 1981, is described in SRI 1982 Annual under this number.

Availability: Wyoming Department of Administration and Fiscal Control, Research and Statistics Division, Rm. 302, Emerson Bldg., Cheyenne WY 82002, †; SRI/MF/complete.

TABLE SECTIONS:
[Data sources appear beneath each table.]

S8855–2.1: Demography
(p. 1-10) Contains 1 chart and 15 tables. Includes population from 1870 and projected to 1992; households, persons per household and in group quarters, and housing occupancy; births; deaths; marriages and divorces; employment; and total and per capita personal income.

S8855–2.2: Business and Industry
(p. 11-17) Contains 1 map, 3 charts, and 10 tables. Includes U.S. CPI; State cost-of-living index; employment, personal income, and covered wages; unemployment rate; occupational illness/injury rates; active domestic and foreign corporations; new corporate charters; and corporate tax schedule.

S8855–2.3: Agriculture
(p. 18-22) Contains 1 chart and 8 tables. Includes State ranking in agricultural production; farms and acreage; livestock inventory by species, bee colonies, and honey and beeswax production; field crop production and acreage; farm cash receipts and production costs; farm income from marketings and government payments; and farm employment.

S8855–2.4: Mining
(p. 23-38) Contains 5 maps, 4 charts, and 20 tables. Includes mining employment and personal income; mineral production and value; State ranking in mineral production; coal resources and production; active coal mines; and coal production and taxable value, by producer.

Also includes oil and natural gas reserves, production, and top 10 producers; pipeline taxable value by company; trona and uranium production by company; severance tax rates by mineral and proceeds distribution by State fund; and State revenues derived from mining.

S8855–2.5: Manufacturing and Construction
(p. 39-45) Contains 1 chart and 7 tables. Includes manufacturing and construction personal income and employment; manufacturing

firms, value added, cost of materials, shipments, capital expenditures, and production workers, hours, and wages; building and machinery/equipment gross book value; and receipts for new construction and maintenance/repair.

S8855–2.6: Transportation, Communications, and Public Utilities
(p. 47-58) Contains 4 maps and 17 tables. Includes transportation/communications/utility personal income and employment; highway traffic, and mileage; vehicle registrations; traffic accidents, deaths, and injuries; fatal accident circumstances; intercity bus companies and routes; and railroad track mileage and taxable value, by railroad.

Also includes newspapers, and TV and radio stations; taxable values of telephone/telegraph companies, privately owned utilities, and nonprofit rural electrification cooperatives, all by company; taxable value of municipal public utilities; and hydroelectric and thermopowered electric generating facilities, installed capacity, and transmission lines.

S8855–2.7: Finance, Services, and Trade
(p. 59-69) Contains 1 chart and 13 tables. Includes finance/insurance/real estate personal income and employment; and bank deposits, by national and State-chartered institution.

Also includes personal income, employment, establishments, and sales or receipts of service industries and retail and wholesale trade.

S8855–2.8: Government
(p. 70-84) Contains 1 map, 2 charts, and 23 tables. Includes State tax revenues; Federal revenue sharing program entitlements; State receipts and disbursements, by fund; bonded debt; and State employment (total and executive branch), earnings, and personal income.

Also includes public school revenues, expenditures, and assessed property value; public school average daily membership and cost; public school teachers, staff, and student enrollment; and enrollment at University of Wyoming and 7 community colleges.

Also includes health facilities' bed capacity, admissions, births, and occupancy rates, by institution; and public assistance/social services expenditures by program.

Also includes votes cast for President and Governor since 1890, and State legislature composition since 1930, all by party; and legislative reapportionment.

S8855–2.9: Resources
(p. 85-93) Contains 1 map, 1 chart, and 11 tables. Includes land area, use, and ownership; river basin outflow and drainage acres; water availability and consumption; taxable lands acreage and assessed value; fish and game harvest and big game inventory; and fish hatchery production, costs, and plantings, by station.

S8855–2.10: Outdoor Activities
(p. 94-100) Contains 1 map, 1 chart, and 7 tables. Includes national site visits; national forest acreage; State park visits; ski area characteristics; game and fish license sales; and sportsman recreation days.

S8855–2.11: County Information

(p. 102-194) Contains 1 map, 24 charts, and 144 tables. Includes 1 chart and 6 tables, repeated alphabetically by county, showing the following:

a. General information: land area, use, and ownership; climatological data; population; county seat elevation; assessed property value, taxes, and bank deposits, with selected detail for county seat; and cultural/recreational events and attractions.

b. Employment and earnings.

c. Agricultural summary: farms and acreage; farm production costs; value of products sold; and livestock inventory.

d. Revenue sharing fund entitlements.

e. Public schools, districts, enrollment and attendance, high school graduates, classrooms, certificated and support staff, students transported, and finances.

S8860   WYOMING
Department of
Agriculture

S8860–1   WYOMING AGRICULTURAL STATISTICS, 1983
Annual. [1984.] 92 p.
ISSN 0363-9339.
LC 76-646923.
SRI/MF/complete

Annual report on Wyoming agricultural production, marketing, and finances, mostly 1970s-82, with some data for 1983. Data are generally shown by commodity, with crop detail by county and some comparisons to total U.S.

Covers production, sales, prices, and cash receipts, and, as applicable, acreage, yield, inventory, and disposition, for livestock, poultry, apiary, field crop, and vegetable sectors.

Also includes data on farm income, production expenses, and employment; number of farms, acreage, value, and taxes; climatological conditions; sheep and lamb losses to weather and predatory animals; and detail for irrigated crops.

Data are compiled by the Wyoming Crop and Livestock Reporting Service.

Contains contents listing (p. 2); preface and list of reports published by issuing agency (p. 3-4); 1 map, 13 charts, and 80 tables (p. 7-88); and directory of USDA field offices (p. 91-92).

Availability: Wyoming Crop and Livestock Reporting Service, Agricultural Statistician, Box 1148, Cheyenne WY 82003, †; SRI/MF/complete.

S8867   WYOMING
Office of the
Attorney General

S8867–3   CRIME IN WYOMING, Jan.-Dec. 1983
Annual. [1984.] xiii+134 p.
LC 83-648086.
SRI/MF/complete

Annual report, for 1983, presenting detailed data on Wyoming crimes and arrests, by type of offense. Also includes data on law enforcement personnel, and value of stolen property. Data are shown for the State, and by county and reporting agency.

Data are from reports of police depts and sheriffs' offices submitted under the Uniform Crime Reporting Program.

Contains listings of contents, tables, and charts (p. v-xi); introduction (p. 1-4); 62 charts and 40 tables, described below, with accompanying narrative summaries (p. 5-123); 1 table showing selected data revisions for 1979-82 (p. 126-129); and offense definitions (p. 131-134).

Availability: Wyoming Office of the Attorney General, Criminal Identification Division, Uniform Crime Reporting Program Section, Boyd Bldg., 4th Floor, Cheyenne WY 82002, ‡; SRI/MF/complete.

CHARTS AND TABLES:

[Index (Part I) offenses are murder/non-negligent manslaughter, rape, robbery, assault, burglary, larceny/theft, motor vehicle theft, and arson. Non-Index (Part II) offenses include 21 other categories of crime. Data by jurisdiction are shown for police depts, sheriffs' offices, and campus police agencies, with county totals.

Data are for 1983, unless otherwise noted.]

S8867–3.1: Index Offenses, Assaults on Police, and Stolen Property

OFFENSE SUMMARY

a. Index offenses and rates, offenses compared to population, and monthly violent and property crimes, 1979-83; offenses and total and juvenile clearances by circumstance of offense, and offenses and clearances by month, 1983; generally by type of offense. 14 charts and 5 tables. (p. 6-26)

INDIVIDUAL OFFENSES, AND ASSAULTS ON POLICE

[In addition to the charts and tables described below, each section also includes 1 chart and/or table showing number of offenses, by month, 1979-83. Each index offense section also includes 1 table showing arrests by age, 1983.]

b. Murder/non-negligent manslaughter: offenses, by situation, circumstance, victim/offender relationship, and weapon; and by age, sex, and race of victims and offenders. 2 charts and 7 tables. (p. 28-31)

c. Forcible rape: offenses compared to total population, for all females and those aged 14-64; and rapes and attempted rapes. 4 charts and 2 tables. (p. 34-37)

d. Robbery: offenses and value of property stolen, by type of setting; and offenses, by type of weapon. 5 charts and 2 tables. (p. 40-43)

e. Aggravated and simple assaults: aggravated assaults, by type of weapon; and number of aggravated and simple assaults. 8 charts and 2 tables. (p. 46-53)

f. Law enforcement officers assaulted: assaults, by time of day, type of weapon, injury status, and type of activity cross-tabulated by type of weapon and assignment; and clearances by type of activity. 6 charts and 2 tables. (p. 56-61)

g. Burglary: offenses, by type of entry; and offenses and value of property stolen, for day and night, residential and nonresidential burglaries. 7 charts and 2 tables. (p. 64-68)

h. Larceny/theft: offenses and value of property stolen, by amount of theft; and offenses by month, and value of property stolen, both by type of theft. 4 charts and 4 tables. (p. 70-74)

i. Motor vehicle theft: offenses, compared to population and registered vehicles, and by vehicle type; and clearances and recoveries. 6 charts and 2 tables. (p. 76-80)

j. Arson: total offenses and clearances, offenses involving uninhabited/abandoned buildings, and estimated value of property damage, all by property type. 5 charts and 2 tables. (p. 82-85)

OFFENSES AND STOLEN PROPERTY, BY JURISDICTION
[Excludes arson.]

k. Index offenses by type, and population coverage, 1983; and total Index offenses, 1982; by jurisdiction. 1 table. (p. 88-93)

l. Value of stolen and recovered property, by type of property and jurisdiction; and offenses and value of stolen property, by detailed type of Index offense (excluding assault). 1 chart and 2 tables. (p. 95-100)

S8867–3.2: Arrests and Law Enforcement Personnel

a. Arrests by age, for Index offenses by type, and for total Index/non-Index offenses, 1983; and adult and juvenile arrests, by sex and offense, for 31 types of Index and non-Index crimes, for State 1982-83, and by jurisdiction arranged by county 1983. 4 tables. (p. 102-120)

b. Law enforcement employees: male and female officers and civilians, and officer/population and Index crime/officer ratios, by jurisdiction arranged by county, and aggregated by jurisdiction size for police depts and sheriffs' offices. 3 tables. (p. 121-123)

S8875
Office of the Auditor
WYOMING

S8875–1 STATE OF WYOMING, 1983 Annual Report of the State Auditor
Annual. Sept. 15, 1983.
iii+133 p.
LC 78-643833.
SRI/MF/complete

Annual report, for FY83, on financial condition of Wyoming State government, presenting revenues by source and expenditures by function for agency accounts; and assets, liabilities, reserves, and fund balances; all by individual fund.

Funds covered are general, earmarked revenue, Federal, trust and agency, debt service, highway, game and fish, permanent land, permanent land income, permanent Wyoming mineral trust, University of Wyoming, intragovernment, and enterprise.

Also includes data on appropriations vs. expenditures for selected funds; State bonded debt; division activities including audits conducted, and employee salaries and turnover; and summary comparisons from FY53.

Contains listings of contents and financial schedules (p. i-iii); introduction and summary report, interspersed with text tables and 4 charts (p. 1-25); and 1 chart and 66 financial schedules (p. 26-133).

Previous report, for FY82, is described in SRI 1982 Annual, under this number.

Availability: Wyoming Office of the Auditor, State Capitol Bldg., Rm. 114, Cheyenne WY 82002, †; SRI/MF/complete.

S8885
Department of Economic Planning and Development
WYOMING

S8885–1 1983 WYOMING MINERAL YEARBOOK
Annual. Dec. 1983. 125 p.
ISSN 0096-9842.
LC 75-641349.
SRI/MF/complete

Annual report, by John T. Goodier and Dale S. Hoffman, on Wyoming taxable mineral production, assessed valuation, and tax income, for various years 1969-83, with selected trends from 1865.

Data are compiled from reports of the Wyoming Dept of Revenue and Taxation, State Geological Survey, and Oil and Gas Conservation Commission, and from mineral company estimates of production.

Contents:

a. Contents listing (1 p.); and introduction with text tables and 4 summary charts (p. 1-4).

b. 10 mineral industry tax tables, listed below. (p. 5-15)

c. Review of mineral production, with 11 summary charts, and 7 tables showing production of bentonite, coal, iron ore, natural gas, petroleum, trona, and uranium, various years 1865-1982. (p. 17-62)

d. Narrative county profiles of mineral production and valuation, with text statistics for 23 counties, and 2 charts repeated for 16 counties, showing property valuation with distribution by mineral and for all other property, 1978 and 1983. (p. 64-102)

e. Production 1978-82, assessed valuation (total and per standard unit of measurement) 1979-83, and production projections 1983-87, for 8 major minerals (above types, plus gypsum), by county, with 20 tables; and list of references. (p. 104-125)

Availability: Wyoming Department of Economic Planning and Development, Mineral Division, Herschler Bldg., 3rd Floor, Cheyenne WY 82002, †; SRI/MF/complete.

MINERAL TAX TABLES:
[Tables I-VI show data for oil, gas, coal, uranium, trona, and usually other, for 1969-83 unless otherwise noted.]

I-II. Assessed valuation and ad valorem tax paid on production. (p. 6-7)

III. Assessed valuation per unit of production. (p. 8)

IV-V. Severance tax collections and tax rates. (p. 9-10)

VI. Severance tax distribution [by State fund or account], 1983. (p. 11)

VII. Sales/use tax [for oil/natural gas, coal, metal mining, and other mining, FY71-83]. (p. 12)

VIII. Government royalty (mineral royalty returns to State) [1970-83; and distribution of returns, by recipient]. (p. 13)

IX. Summary table [assessed valuation per unit, severance tax, average tax levy (mills), tax as percent of valuation, and average tax paid per unit, all by mineral, 1969 and 1983]. (p. 14)

X. Mineral income to the State of Wyoming [by type of tax, rent, and royalty], 1971-83. (p. 15)

S8890
Department of Education
WYOMING

S8890–1 STATISTICAL REPORT SERIES, Wyoming
Annual Series. For individual publication data, see below.
ISSN 0093-5530.
LC 74-642288.
SRI/MF/complete

Series of 3 annual reports on Wyoming public schools, enrollments, and staff as of fall 1983, and finances for FY83 or 1983 tax year. Includes data on property valuations, tax levies, bonded debt, and revenues and expenditures.

Data are from school district reports submitted to the State Dept of Education. Most data are shown by county and district.

Reports reviewed during 1984 are described below.

Availability: Wyoming Department of Education, Planning Unit, Planning and Vocational Services Division, Hathaway Bldg., Cheyenne WY 82002, †; SRI/MF/complete.

S8890–1.1: 1983 School District Property Valuations, Mill Levies, and Bonded Debt
[Annual. Oct. 1983. 2+11 p. Oversized. Rpt. No. 1. ISSN 0146-7948. SRI/MF/complete.]

Annual report, for tax year 1983, on Wyoming public school district property valuations, tax levies, and bonded debt, by county and district. Includes preface, contents listing, and 4 tables showing the following:

a. Property valuation 1982-83, and average daily membership 1982/83, by county arranged by district; and valuation by county for detailed types of real property, mineral production, utilities, and personal property, 1983. (p. 1-5)

b. Tax levies, by type (State school, mandatory county, operating, bond/interest, and other school), 1983; and bonded debt as of June 1982 and 1983, election amount approved, bonds issued, refunds, principal and interest paid, and percent of bonding capacity obligated; all by county arranged by district. (p. 6-11)

S8890–1.2: 1983 School Districts Fall Report of Staff, Teachers/Pupils/Schools, Enrollments, Special Education Student Count
[Annual. Feb. 1984. 2+120 p. Oversized. Rpt. No. 2. ISSN 0146-7972. LC 77-648346. SRI/MF/complete.]

Annual report, for fall 1983, on Wyoming public schools, staff, and enrollments. Includes preface, contents listing, and 4 tables showing the following, generally as of fall 1983:

a. FTE and other staff, by position and sex; and teachers, enrollment, and schools by level, with 1982/83 average daily membership; all by district arranged by county. 2 tables. (p. 1-53)

b. Enrollment by grade, including ungraded and special education; and special education students by disability; all by county, district, and school. 2 tables. (p. 54-120)

S8890–1.3: Wyoming Public Schools Fund Accounting and Reporting, 1982/83
[Annual. Apr. 1984. 3+64 p. Oversized. Rpt. No. 3. ISSN 0146-793X. SRI/MF/complete.]

Annual report, for FY83, on Wyoming public school revenues and expenditures, by school district. Includes preface, contents listing, and the following data for FY83:

a. General fund revenues, by specific local, county, State, and Federal source; and expenditures, by program and object. 3 charts and 2 tables. (p. 1-3)

b. Average daily membership (ADM) by grade, including exceptional students; classroom units by type; general fund revenues per ADM, by source; general fund expenditures, by program and object; and general fund expenditures per pupil and classroom unit; all by district, generally arranged by county. 6 tables. (p. 4-14)

c. Profiles for individual districts and the State, including revenues by source, expenditures by program, and cash balances, all by fund; costs per ADM and per classroom unit; and schools, fall enrollment, graduates by sex, dropout rate, average daily attendance, ADM, classroom units and value, staff, assessed valuation, bonded debt, students transported daily, annual bus miles, and district-owned buses. 3 tables repeated for each profile. (p. 15-64)

S8895   WYOMING Employment Security Commission

S8895–1   WYOMING LABOR FORCE TRENDS

Monthly.   Approx. 10 p.
ISSN 0512-4409.
LC SC 79-4113.
SRI/MF/complete, shipped quarterly

Monthly report on Wyoming employment and unemployment, unemployment insurance claims and payments, and job openings and placements. Also includes data on mining industry hours and earnings. Report is based on employer reports to the Employment Security Commission, and is issued approximately 2 months after month of coverage.

Contains narrative analyses with 1 summary trend chart; 5 monthly tables, listed below; and occasional articles and additional tables, some with substantial statistics, but most presenting summaries or recent trends for data covered in monthly tables.

Most monthly tables appear in all issues. Additional features presenting substantial Wyoming data not covered in monthly tables are described, as they appear, under "Statistical Features." Nonstatistical features and U.S. data reprinted from Federal sources are not covered.

Prior to the Feb. 1984 issue, report was published quarterly. Prior to the Mar. 1984 issue, report included an additional table showing hours and earnings of manufacturing production workers.

Availability: Wyoming Employment Security Commission, Research and Analysis Section, PO Box 2760, Casper WY 82602, †; SRI/MF/complete.

Issues reviewed during 1984: 3rd-4th Qtrs. 1983 (quarterly); Feb.-Aug. 1984 (monthly) (D) (Vol. 20, Nos. 3-4; Vol. 21, Nos. 1-7) [No Jan. 1984 issue was published; Vol. 21, No. 2 incorrectly reads No. 1].

MONTHLY TABLES:

[Most data are shown for month of coverage, previous month, and same month of previous year. Table format may vary from issue to issue.]

[A] Trend setters [shows summary data, for month of coverage and previous month; table begins with the May 1984 issue].

[B] [U.S.] CPI [by item, for month of coverage; occasionally includes trends from 1960s and data for Denver].

1. Selected economic indicators [including labor force and employment; total and insured unemployment rates; average hours and earnings for mining production workers; unemployment insurance claims filed, weeks compensated, and payments; employment service applications, openings, and placements; with selected U.S. comparisons].

2. Civilian labor force and unemployment, by county.

3. Nonfarm wage/salary employment [by industry division and selected major group, for Wyoming, Casper, and Cheyenne].

STATISTICAL FEATURES:

S8895–1.501: June 1984 (Vol. 21, No. 5)
WYOMING'S HOSPITALS

(p. 3, 8) Article, with 1 undated table showing Wyoming general hospital beds, adults admitted, births, and occupancy rates, by hospital and city. Data are from Wyoming Dept of Health and Social Services.

S8895–1.502: July 1984 (Vol. 21, No. 6)
WYOMING PER CAPITA INCOME RANKING DROPS TO 18th IN 1983

(p. 3) Article, with 1 table showing Wyoming and U.S. per capita personal income, with State ranking for Wyoming, 1975-83. Data are from the Commerce Dept.

S8895–2   WYOMING ANNUAL PLANNING REPORT, FY84

Annual.   Sept. 1983.
vii + 107 p.
LC 78-645546.
SRI/MF/complete

Annual planning report, for FY84, identifying Wyoming population groups most in need of employment services and projecting employment by industry and occupation through 1990. Includes data on population and labor force by county, earnings, job openings and applicants, and union membership. Most data are for 1982, with selected trends from 1970s and earlier, projections to 2000, and comparisons to other States and total U.S.

Data are from Wyoming Employment Security Commission, BLS, Commerce Dept, and other State, Federal, and private sources.

Contents:

a. Listings of contents, charts, and tables, and introduction (p. iii-vii); and narrative report in 11 sections, interspersed with 6 charts and 28 tables (p. 1-52).

b. Appendix, with 19 charts including rankings of 50 States and D.C. by population, employment, and unemployment insurance benefits, various periods 1981 or 1983; and 30 tables. (p. 53-102)

c. Glossary. (p. 103-107)

All tables, and selected charts providing Wyoming data not shown in tables, are listed below.

Availability: Wyoming Employment Security Commission, Research and Analysis Section, PO Box 2760, Casper WY 82602, †; SRI/MF/complete.

TABLES AND CHARTS:

[Data are for Wyoming, unless otherwise noted.]

S8895–2.1: Report Tables
POPULATION AND LABOR FORCE

1-3. Total population [decennially 1870-1970 and annually 1971-82]; population, by county [including per square mile] for selected years [1970-82]; and 1982 population, by age. (p. 3-4)

4. 1982 labor force [and employment status, by month]. (p. 6)

5. Summary table of economic assumptions [shows labor force and insured unemployment data, 1976-84]. (p. 7)

6. Projected 1984 civilian population [by age, sex, and race]. (p. 8)

UNEMPLOYMENT AND INFLATION TRENDS

7. Total unadjusted unemployment rates [compared to U.S., monthly] 1976-Apr. 1983. (p. 10)

8. U.S. CPI, all urban, all items [monthly 1967-Apr. 1983]. (p. 14)

9. Comparative cost-of-living index prices [for 23 cities and Lakewood County] as of Apr. 6/7/8, 1983. (p. 16)

10. Annual inflation rates by [State] region and by [expenditure] category, [unweighted] and weighted by population (1st quarter 1982-83). (p. 17)

INCOME AND EMPLOYMENT

11. Major sources of personal income [wage/salary disbursements, by industry division], summary level seasonally adjusted at annual rates [quarterly 1977-82]. (p. 18)

12. Annual average nonagricultural employment [by industry division and selected major group, 1976-82]. (p. 19)

[A] Severance tax rate changes [by mineral type, 1970 and 1980-81]. (p. 21)

[B] Total State assessed valuation [with distribution by mineral type and for all other property], 1972, 1977, and 1982. [chart] (p. 22)

13. Mining and manufacturing industries hours and earnings, U.S. and Wyoming [Dec. 1982 and Mar. 1983]. (p. 30)

14. Per capita income [by State], 1982 [and change from 1981]. (p. 31)

15-16. Average weekly wage in covered employment by industry [division], 4th quarter 1982; and per capita personal income [1976-81]; for Wyoming and counties. (p. 32-33)

JOB OPENINGS

17-18. Job openings [by occupational title] with ESARS [Employment Service Automated Reporting System] record showing no action taken for 30 days or more, periods ending Dec. 31, 1982 and Mar. 31, 1983. (p. 35-36)

19-20. Quarterly summary report of job openings [by occupation group] at job service centers, quarters ending Dec. 31, 1982 and Mar. 31, 1983. (p. 37-38)

MINORITIES AND ECONOMICALLY DISADVANTAGED

21-23. Population, and annual average labor force and unemployment, [all] by sex and race/ethnic group [white, black, Indian, Asian, Hispanic, and other, by county], for 1981 or 1982. (p. 43-45)

24. Estimated total population of economically disadvantaged [by sex, race, and for Hispanics], for 1980 and 1983. (p. 46)

JOB APPLICANTS AND EMPLOYMENT OUTLOOK

25. Number of applicants [total, female, veteran, minority, age 22-30, and age 45/over] in active file by occupation [group], period ending July 31, 1983. (p. 49)

26-27. Total employment by industry [division and selected major group], and by occupation, major occupational categories; 1981 actual and 1990 projections. (p. 50-51)

S8895–2.2: Appendix Tables

MINERAL RESOURCES AND PRODUCTION

[A] Estimated undiscovered resources and giant oil fields [oil and natural gas reserves; undated chart]. (p. 70)

[B] Energy and mineral production [coal, oil, and natural gas production, State and U.S., 2nd quarter 1980-1st quarter 1983]. (p. 70)

COUNTY EMPLOYMENT TRENDS AND PROJECTIONS

[Tables 2-13, 18-19, 23, and 26 show data by county.]

1. Total unemployment rate (not seasonally adjusted) [monthly 1960-Apr. 1983]. (p. 73)

2-9. Labor force, employment, unemployment, and unemployment rate [monthly 1982, and annual average 1970-82]. (p. 74-81)

10. Employment for standard industrial classification, [SIC industry divisions], 1984-85. (p. 82)

11. Age distribution [of the population, by sex], 1982-85. (p. 83)

12-13. Forecasts: final population and employment matrices [1980-93]. (p. 85-86)

14. Agriculture information: value of farm land/buildings, 1970-82; and number of farms and land in farms, [selected years 1920-82]. (p. 87)

15. Coal production, 1912-82; [and employment, 1918-82]. (p. 88)

16-17. Number and percent of employers [and employees] by industry [division] and [employment] size of firm, Sept. 1982. (p. 89-90)

18-19. 1982 annual average covered employment and weekly wages of covered employment [by industry division, also including data for Yellowstone Park]. (p. 91-92)

20. Total wages, and annual averages [for] UI [unemployment insurance] covered employment by industry [division], 1955-81. (p. 93)

21. Relationship of average weekly wages in covered employment to average weekly benefit payments, 1938-82. (p. 94)

22. Poverty status distribution rates estimated [as percent of population, by race, with detail for children and elderly (no date)]. (p. 95)

23. Union membership by industry [division] of employment, 1982. (p. 96)

24-25. Distribution of union membership [by sex] across industry [divisions]; and by skill level and sex within the industry [division] of employment; 1982. (p. 97-98)

26. 1980 civilian veteran population 16 years of age/over [by sex] and by job service center [with selected detail for Vietnam veterans]. (p. 99)

STATE COMPARISONS

[Tables 27-29 show data by State and for D.C.]

27. 1981 personal property taxes per person [and as percent of personal income]. (p. 100)

28. Annual average unemployment rates, 1980-82 [and percent change in unemployed, 1980-82 period]. (p. 101)

29. Projected population for the year 2000 [and comparison to 1980]. (p. 102)

S8907
Office of
State Examiner

WYOMING

S8907–1   STATE OF WYOMING 1983 ANNUAL REPORT OF THE STATE EXAMINER, Division of Banks
Annual.   Apr. 1984.   84 p.
LC 53-62930.
SRI/MF/complete

Annual report on financial condition of Wyoming State-chartered banks and savings and loan assns, presenting assets and liabilities, by institution, for 1981-83.

Also includes the following for banks: aggregate operating earnings and expenses, 1980-83; loans and capital accounts as percents of deposits, by institution, 1981-83; and number of banks, and aggregate deposits, loans/discounts, and loan/deposit ratio, 1926-83.

Contains lists of Bank Division personnel and banks supervised (p. 4-7); 7 financial tables (p. 8-80); and summary of 1984 State banking legislation (p. 81-84).

Availability: Wyoming Office of State Examiner, Banks Division, Herschler Bldg., 4th Floor, Cheyenne WY 82002, $5.00; SRI/MF/complete.

S8910
Game and Fish Department

WYOMING

S8910–1   ANNUAL REPORT, WYOMING GAME AND FISH DEPARTMENT
Annual, discontinued coverage.

Annual report described in SRI 1983 Annual under this number. SRI selection criteria now exclude State reports on wildlife, hunting, and fishing. Coverage of this report will not be continued.

S8920
Department of
Health and Social Services

WYOMING

S8920–2   SUMMARY OF WYOMING VITAL STATISTICS, 1982
Annual.   Apr. 1984.   ii+58 p.
LC 59-62576.
SRI/MF/complete

Annual report on Wyoming vital statistics, 1982, with selected trends from as early as 1922, and comparisons to U.S. Covers population, births, deaths by cause, marriages, and divorces, by demographic characteristics and/or county. Most data are from documents filed with the State as of Apr. 15, 1983.

Contains contents and table listings (p. i-ii); introduction, definitions, and summary report, interspersed with 5 charts and 7 text tables, generally showing trends and summary data (p. 1-24); and statistical section, with 33 detailed tables, listed below (p. 27-58).

Availability: Wyoming Department of Health and Social Services, Health and Medical Services Division, Vital Records Services, Hathaway Bldg., Cheyenne WY 82002, †; SRI/MF/complete.

STATISTICAL SECTION TABLES:

[Data are for 1982, unless otherwise noted. Data by race also include Indians. Data by county generally include Yellowstone National Park.]

S8920–2.1: Population, Births, and Deaths

POPULATION AND HISTORICAL DATA

1. Population by county, 1980-82. (p. 27)

2. Births, deaths, infant deaths, stillbirths, maternal deaths, [and population], 1922-82. (p. 28)

BIRTHS

[Tables 3-9 and 12 show data by county of residence.]

3. Births and rates, 1978-82. (p. 29)

4-5. Births by sex, race, and age of mother. (p. 30-31)

6. Births to unmarried mothers, by age of mother and race. (p. 32)

7. Low weight births, 1978-82. (p. 33)

8-9. Births by weight at birth and by live birth order. (p. 34-35)

10-11. Births by age of mother: by live birth order, and by trimester prenatal care began. (p. 36)

12. Births by trimester prenatal care began. (p. 37)

13. Births by county of occurrence, attendant, and place of delivery. (p. 38)

DEATHS

[Tables 14-16, 22-23, and 25 show data by county of residence.]

14. Deaths and rates, 1978-82. (p. 39)

15-16. Deaths by sex, race, age, and selected cause. (p. 40-41)

17. Leading cause of death by age group. (p. 42)

18-20. [Total], male, and female resident deaths by selected cause and age. (p. 43-45)

21. Accidental deaths occurring in State by age and sex [by type of accident]. (p. 46)

22. Infant deaths by age. (p. 47)

23. Infant and neonatal deaths [with 5-year rates], 1978-82. (p. 48)

24. Resident infant deaths by selected cause and age at death. (p. 49)

25. Stillbirths, 1978-82. (p. 50)

BIRTHS AND DEATHS

26. Births and deaths, by county of occurrence, 1978-82. (p. 51)

S8920–2.2: Marriages and Divorces

[All tables except tables 29-30 show data by county of occurrence.]

27. Marriages and rates, 1978-82. (p. 52)

28. Marriages by month. (p. 53)

29-30. Marriages by age and previous marital status of bride and groom. (p. 54-55)

31. Divorces/annulments with rates, 1978-82. (p. 56)

32-33. Divorces/annulments by duration of marriage, and by number of children affected. (p. 57-58)

S8925   WYOMING
Highway Department

S8925–1   WYOMING'S COMPREHENSIVE REPORT ON TRAFFIC ACCIDENTS, 1982
Annual. [1983.] 10+244 p.
LC 63-62626.
SRI/MF/complete

Annual report on Wyoming traffic accidents, injuries, and fatalities, by vehicle type and make; accident type, location, time, and other circumstances; and driver and victim characteristics; 1982, with trends from 1973.

Also includes data on vehicle registrations and travel miles; accident costs; alcohol involvement in accidents, and blood alcohol content test results; safety device use; and accidents involving youthful drivers.

Data are compiled from dept reports and National Safety Council records.

Contains contents listing, introduction, and definitions (9 p.); and 9 statistical sections, with 1 map, 48 charts, and 243 tables (p. 1-244).

Report consolidates data previously covered in 3 separate reports: *Wyoming Traffic Accident Facts, Wyoming Fatal Accident Facts,* and *Wyoming Truck Accident Facts.*

For description of *Wyoming Traffic Accident Facts, 1981,* see SRI 1982 Annual, under this number. Reports on fatal accidents and truck accidents were not covered in SRI.

Availability: Wyoming Highway Department, Highway Safety Branch, Safety Analysis Section, PO Box 1708, Cheyenne WY 82002-9019, 1st copy †, additional copies $5.00; SRI/MF/complete.

S8990   WYOMING
Department of
Revenue and Taxation

S8990–1   ANNUAL REPORT OF THE STATE BOARD OF EQUALIZATION, 1983, State of Wyoming
Annual. [1983.] 17+212 p.
LC 74-642856.
SRI/MF/complete

Annual report on Wyoming assessed property valuations and tax levies, including data by property type, tax purpose, county, city, and company, 1983, with summary trends from 1944.

Contains narrative summary with 2 text tables, and index (14 p.); 16 tables, described below (p. 1-211); and a list of county assessors and treasurers (p. 212).

Availability: Wyoming Department of Revenue and Taxation, Ad Valorem Tax Division, 122 W. 25th St., Cheyenne WY 82002-0110, †; SRI/MF/complete.

TABLES:
[Unless otherwise noted, tables show data for 1983.]

a. Detailed valuations, by property type and county, including land acreage where applicable. Table I. (p. 1-19)

b. Mineral, energy resource, and utility taxable production (1982) and/or valuation, by company: for coal, gas and oil (including detail by field), sand/gravel, trona, uranium, and other minerals, with ad valorem and collectible severance taxes by mineral type; and for municipally and privately owned utilities, pipeline companies, rural electricity cooperatives, railroads (including main track miles), and telephone and telegraph companies. Table II. (p. 20-187)

c. Taxes levied, by type, purpose (including school taxes), and county; municipal property valuation and taxes levied, by city or town; private railroad car valuation and taxes levied, by county; county tax summary; and special taxes on animals, by county. Tables III-VII. (p. 188-201)

d. Miscellaneous tax information, including average tax levies; distribution of valuation and taxes by property type and/or county; and homestead and veterans exemption valuations and tax benefits, by county. Tables VIII-XII. (p. 202-207)

e. State mill levies and taxable valuation, 1944-83; ad valorem taxes levied, by type, 1950-83; property tax expenditure distribution; and county valuation summary. 4 tables. (p. 208-211)

S9990   CENSUS
Summary Tape File Reports

A NOTE ABOUT STATE REPORTS BASED ON 1980 CENSUS OF POPULATION AND HOUSING

Beginning in 1983, SRI has expanded its coverage of State publications to include selected reports based on data from the 1980 Census of Population and Housing. Most of these reports are issued by State Data Centers. Some are issued by other State agencies, or by universities. Individual reports are described and filmed under the accession number of the issuing agency.

Many reports covered present data from Census Summary Tape Files 1 and 3 (STF1 and STF3). STF1 provides data based on questions asked of all respondents and covers population, household, and housing unit characteristics. STF3 is based on the long form of the census questionnaire, which was distributed to a 20% national sample. In addition to population and household characteristics, STF3 also covers education, employment, income, and more detailed housing characteristics.

STF1 and STF3 reports vary from State to State in level of geographic detail. Data may be shown for counties, minor civil divisions, congressional districts, SMSAs, and other geographic entities. STF3 reports also vary in range of topics covered.

Tables included in most STF1 reports are listed below, under S9990-1. Data topics available on the STF3 tape are described below, under S9990-2. Abstracts of most individual State reports indicate variations from these general descriptions, together with report organization and geographic entities covered. In some instances, individual reports are described in full.

SRI also covers selected other census-based State reports, including population projections

based on the 1980 census count; historical population trends from earlier censuses through 1980; detailed occupational data by sex and race, based on the Equal Employment Opportunity Special Tape File of the 1980 census; and data on commuting patterns, based on Summary Tape File 4. These reports are described in full, as they are received.

Data from summary tape files for Census geographic areas are available on request from all State Data Centers, regardless of whether the State has issued printed reports.

S9990–1   1980 CENSUS OF POPULATION AND HOUSING: SUMMARY TAPE FILE 1

Tables generally included in State reports based on STF 1 from the 1980 Census of Population and Housing are listed below. Table sequence varies from report to report. Data by ethnic group generally include American Indian, Eskimo, Aleut, and Asian/Pacific Islander.

BASIC TABLES:

SUMMARY DATA

1-3. Persons by urban and rural residence; families; and households.

4-5. Housing units (including vacant seasonal/migratory units), by urban and rural location; and year-round housing units by occupancy status.

PERSONS

6-9. Persons by sex, race and ethnic group (including Asian and Pacific Islander by place of ancestry), and Spanish origin (Mexican, Puerto Rican, Cuban, and other); and persons of Spanish origin by race and ethnic group.

10-13. Persons by sex, by age; median age of persons by sex; persons by age group, by race and ethnic group; and persons of Spanish origin by age group, by race.

14. Persons 15 years/over by sex, by marital status.

HOUSEHOLDS

15/20. Persons by age (total and 65/older), by household type and relationship to others in household.

16-17. Households by persons in household, and persons under 18 years by relationship to others in household, all by household type.

18. Related children by age (under 5 and 5-17).

19. Households with 1/more persons under 18 years, by household type.

21-22. Households with 1/more persons 60 and 65 years/over, by persons in household and household type.

23. Occupied housing units with 1/more persons 65 years/over, by tenure, by age of householder (under 65 and 65/older).

24. Households with 1/more nonrelative present.

HOUSING UNITS

25. Vacant housing units by vacancy status (including units for occasional use).

26-28. Occupied housing units by tenure: total; by race of householder; and with householder of Spanish origin, by race.

29. Condominium housing units, by tenure and vacancy status.

30-32. Year-round housing units, by rooms; and mean rooms in year-round housing units, by tenure and vacancy status.

33-37. Occupied housing units by tenure, by persons in unit; mean persons per unit; persons in occupied housing units by tenure; and occupied housing units by tenure, by persons per room.

38-42. Specified owner-occupied noncondominium housing units, by value; and specified owner-occupied and vacant-for-sale-only housing units by occupancy status, and mean value or price asked, by condominium status.

43-44. Specified renter-occupied housing units by contract rent; and median contract rent for specified renter-occupied housing units paying cash rent.

45/46. Specified renter-occupied units paying cash rent, and vacant-for-rent housing units, by occupancy status; and mean contract rent.

47. Year-round housing units by tenure and occupancy status, by plumbing facilities.

48-51. Occupied housing units with 1.01/ more persons per room by tenure, and total persons in occupied housing units, lacking complete plumbing facilities for exclusive use; and persons in occupied housing units with 1.01/more persons per room, by tenure and by plumbing facilities.

52-54. Vacant housing units which are boarded up; vacant-for-rent housing units which have been vacant for 2/more months; and vacant-for-sale-only housing units which have been vacant 6/more months.

UNITS PER ADDRESS

55. Year-round housing units, by number of units at address (and for mobile homes/trailers).

SUBSTITUTION AND ALLOCATION DATA

56-59. Persons and year-round housing units substituted, and not substituted with 1/more items allocated (substitutions and allocations are used by Census Bureau to account for missing data and to adjust conflicting data).

S9990-2 1980 CENSUS OF POPULATION AND HOUSING: SUMMARY TAPE FILE 3

Data topics covered in Summary Tape File 3 from the 1980 Census of Population and Housing are described below. Data by ethnic group generally include American Indian, Eskimo, Aleut, Asian/Pacific Islander, and Spanish origin. Data are for 1980 unless otherwise noted.

BASIC DATA TOPICS:

POPULATION AND HOUSEHOLDS

a. **Demographics:** urban-rural and farm status, race, detailed ethnic group (including Asian/ Pacific and Hispanic country or island), age, sex, and marital status; with selected cross-tabulations.

b. **Background:** ancestry; place of birth (foreign-born, and natives born in State of residence, different State, and elsewhere); and residence in 1975 relative to residence in 1980, including same or different house, county, SMSA, and State (with detail by region for persons residing in another State), and abroad; and veteran status, by sex and by period served.

c. **Language:** English speaking ability, and language spoken at home.

d. **Education:** school enrollment by level, with detail for private schools; enrollment, graduation, armed forces, and labor force status of persons 16-19; and years of school completed for persons 18/over and/or 25/over; with selected detail by race and ethnic group.

e. **Living arrangements:** household characteristics, including composition, size, and presence of own children, with selected detail by race and ethnic group; and residents of group quarters, by type of quarters (mental hospital, home for aged, military barracks, college dormitory, and other).

f. **Workplace and transportation:** proximity of workplace to residence, including same or different county, city, and SMSA; means of transportation to work, with detail for number of occupants in private vehicles; travel time to work; availability of vehicle at housing unit; and public transportation disability status, by age group.

LABOR FORCE AND INCOME

g. **Labor force:** status, including detail by sex, race and ethnic group, and for women by presence and age of children; employment by industry division, occupational group, and class of worker (including self-employed, government level and unpaid family worker); and work disability status.

Also includes 1979 employment and unemployment experience, covering weeks employed and unemployed, and usual weekly hours worked, with selected detail by sex and by race and ethnic group.

h. **Income in 1979:** family, household, and individual income; family income by householder's race and ethnic group; household income by type (including earnings, interest/dividend/rent, social security, and public assistance) and by housing tenure; family income by number of workers; and per capita income.

i. **Poverty in 1979:** poverty status of families, with detail by presence and age of children, by age of householder, and for female householders with no husband present; poverty status of individuals, with detail by age group and/or by race and ethnic group; and income as percent of poverty level.

HOUSING UNITS

j. **General characteristics:** urban or rural location; occupancy status, including vacant held for occasional use; and current householder's tenure, race and ethnic group, and year moved in.

k. **Physical characteristics:** number of units (including mobile homes) at address; number of stories in structure, and presence of elevator; year built; source of water; type of sewage disposal, heating equipment, and heating and cooking fuel; presence of complete kitchen, telephone (with detail for persons 60/over), and air-conditioning; and number of bedrooms and bathrooms.

Also includes presence of complete plumbing facilities, with detail by persons per room, structure age, and householder's race and ethnic group.

l. **Costs:** gross rent; inclusion of utilities in rent; mortgage status; monthly owner costs; and ratios of rent and owner costs to income, by income level; with selected detail by race and ethnic group.

U0280
Arizona State University: Bureau of Business and Economic Research

U0280-1 ARIZONA BUSINESS
Quarterly. Approx. 40 p.
ISSN 0093-0717.
LC 74-640105.
SRI/MF/complete

Quarterly report on Arizona business and economic trends and conditions, including detailed data on construction activity. Data are from Arizona State University survey studies, and various State, Federal, and commercial sources.

General format:

a. Feature articles, some with statistics, including quarterly "Arizona Business Scene," focusing on a specific State industry or economic sector.

b. 8 quarterly tables, generally accompanied by narrative analyses; with occasional supplementary charts or tables.

Quarterly tables are listed below; most appear in all issues. All additional features with substantial statistical content are described, as they appear, under "Statistical Features." Nonstatistical features are not covered.

Availability: Arizona State University: Bureau of Business and Economic Research, College of Business, Tempe AZ 85287, †; SRI/MF/complete.

Issues reviewed during 1984: 4th Qtr. 1983-2nd Qtr. 1984 (P) (Vol. 30, No. 4; Vol. 31, Nos. 1-2).

QUARTERLY TABLES:
[Data are generally current to quarter prior to cover date, with selected comparisons to prior periods. Tables [6-7] show data by county and local area.]

[1] Purchasing survey [percent of surveyed members of Arizona Purchasing Management Assn indicating higher, lower, or same levels for commodity prices, vendor delivery time, inventory levels, new orders, production, and employment, usually repeated for several survey months].

[2] Sales of electrical power [monthly for 2-7 months].

[3-4] CPI [by item, for Phoenix, U.S., and 2 cities outside Arizona.]

[5] Construction activity [number and value of building permits issued for single family units, apartments, office buildings, retail stores, and industrial, for Maricopa County, Pima County, and rest of State].

[6] Building permits [number and value of residential, commercial, industrial, and other permits].

[7] New housing starts [residential building permits by unit size (1 family, duplex, 3-4 family, and 5 or more) and mobile home permits].

[8] Metro Phoenix real estate sales [volume and median price for new and resale single family and townhouse/condominium units].

STATISTICAL FEATURES:

U0280-1.501: 4th Qtr. 1983 (Vol. 30, No. 4)

NATIONAL FORECAST: MINI-BOOM FOR 1984
(p. 5-6) By Robert J. Eggert. Article on economic outlook for 1984, based on forecasts of Eggert Economic Enterprises, Inc. Includes 1 table predicting the 14 best investments for 1984, and showing their 1983 rank and rate of return.

ARIZONA ECONOMY: A GOOD YEAR IN 1984, ANNUAL FEATURE
(p. 7-10) Annual article, by Richard D. Winkelman, examining Arizona economic outlook for 1984. Includes 1 table showing personal income, population, unemployment rate, Phoenix CPI, nonfarm employment, and GSP, 1981-84.

ARIZONA BUSINESS SCENE: INFLATION SLOWS
(p. 19-20) Article, with 1 table showing annual percent change in CPI, for selected major cities arranged by census division, as of Dec. 1982 and Sept. 1983. Data are from Labor Dept and Arizona State University.

U0280-1.502: 1st Qtr. 1984 (Vol. 31, No. 1)

PHOENIX INFLATION SLOWS TO RECORD LOW IN 1983, ANNUAL FEATURE
(p. 3-8) Annual article, by Timothy D. Hogan and Tom R. Rex, with 2 tables showing annual data for quarterly tables [3-4] on Phoenix CPI by item, 1982-83.

AIRLINE DEREGULATION AND SERVICE TO SMALL COMMUNITIES
(p. 15-24) By Martin T. Farris and Kenneth G. Bruno. Article on the impact of deregulation on major airline service to small communities, and quantity and quality of replacement service provided by commuter carriers. Data are from National Transportation Safety Board, Regional Airline Assn, and other sources.

Includes 1 chart and 4 tables showing air carriers serving selected Arizona communities, seat capacity, and annual subsidy, as of Dec. 1983; essential air service departures and seat capacity per week, by State, Dec. 1978 and Dec. 1983; airline accident rates by type of carrier, 1975-79; and subsidy payments, 1976-83.

ARIZONA CONSTRUCTION ACTIVITY: BEYOND EXPECTATIONS IN 1983, ANNUAL FEATURE
(p. 25-31) Annual article, by Jay Q. Butler, on Arizona construction activity and housing financing in 1983. Includes 1 chart and 3 tables showing:

a. Building permit activity: annual data for quarterly table [5], 1982-83; and Maricopa County single-family home permits and value, quarterly 1983.

b. Expectations of Maricopa County homebuilders, bankers, real estate brokers, and other groups, for conventional and FHA mortgage, prime and commercial interest, inflation, Treasury bill, unemployment, and apartment vacancy rates, 1984.

SURVEY OF ARIZONA BUSINESS CONDITIONS, ANNUAL FEATURE
(p. 37) Annual table accompanying quarterly purchasing survey, showing anticipated expenditure levels for new plant/equipment, compared with previous year, 1975-84. Data are from Purchasing Management Assns of Arizona and Southern Arizona.

SMALL TOWN, ARIZONA
(p. 41-42) By Tom R. Rex. Article, with 3 tables showing distribution of population in 4 small Arizona communities and statewide, by age, birthplace, residence in 1975, and occupation; 1980. Data are from 1980 U.S. Census Summary Tape Files 1A and 3A.

U0280-1.503: 2nd Qtr. 1984 (Vol. 31, No. 2)

ARIZONA'S GROSS STATE PRODUCT OUTPACES GNP
(p. 3-12) By Lee R. McPheters and Tom R. Rex. Article, with 4 charts and 3 tables showing the following for Arizona: GSP and quarterly percent change, by industry division, 1970-83; and output per employee, and industry share of total product, with comparison to U.S., 1982. Data are from Arizona State University Bureau of Business and Economic Research, and U.S. Commerce Dept.

ARIZONA FOOD COOPERATIVES AND THEIR PATRONS
(p. 20-26) By David R. Gourley et al. Article, with 17 tables on food cooperative patrons in Phoenix and Tucson, Ariz., 1982. Tables show demographic characteristics of patrons compared with the general population in the 2 cities; and patron profiles and opinions, including distance from co-op, leisure activities, reasons for shopping at co-op and conventional grocery stores, length of co-op membership and frequency of patronage, percent of food bill spent at co-op, and store preference for selected items.

Data are based primarily on responses of 565 shoppers at 3 Phoenix and Tucson area food cooperatives to a spring 1982 survey, conducted by the authors.

1983 CONSTRUCTION ACTIVITY STATEWIDE
(p. 38-41) By Tom R. Rex. Article, with 4 tables showing Arizona building permit volume and value, by type, 1977-83; with detail by county, 1983. Data are from Arizona State University Bureau of Business and Economic Research.

U1075
Clemson University: South Carolina Agricultural Experiment Station

U1075–1   SOUTH CAROLINA LIVESTOCK AND POULTRY STATISTICS, Inventory Numbers 1983-84; Production and Value of Livestock and Poultry Products, 1982-83
Annual.   July 1984.   4+41 p.
Rpt. No. AE432.
LC 81-640886.
SRI/MF/complete

Annual report on South Carolina livestock and poultry inventories, value, and disposition; and production, value, and sometimes prices, for dairy and poultry products; 1983, with some data for 1984, and trends from as early as 1867. Data are generally shown by commodity and/or county or district, with some comparisons to other States and total U.S.

Data are compiled by the South Carolina Crop and Livestock Reporting Service in cooperation with Clemson University and USDA.

Contains contents and table listing (2 p.); and report, with 5 maps and 44 tables, interspersed with narrative (p. 1-41).

Availability: South Carolina Crop and Livestock Reporting Service, PO Box 1911, Columbia SC 29202, †; SRI/MF/complete.

U1075–2   SOUTH CAROLINA CROP STATISTICS, 1982-83
Annual.   June 1984.   3+38 p.
Rpt. No. AE431.
LC 81-640880.
SRI/MF/complete

Annual report on South Carolina acreage, yield, production, value, and selected prices, for field crops, vegetables, and fruit, by commodity and county, 1983, with trends from as early as 1866 and some comparisons to total U.S.

Also includes data on farms and acreage, grain stocks, and fertilizer consumption.

Data are compiled by South Carolina Crop and Livestock Reporting Service.

Contains table of contents (1 p.); narrative summary (p. 1-4); and 10 maps and 34 tables (p. 5-38).

Availability: South Carolina Crop and Livestock Reporting Service, PO Box 1911, Columbia SC 29202, †; SRI/MF/complete.

U1120
College of William and Mary: Bureau of Business Research

U1120–1   VIRGINIA BUSINESS REPORT
Monthly.   Approx. 4 p.
SRI/MF/complete, shipped quarterly

Monthly report on Virginia business and economic conditions. Report is issued 1 month after month of coverage.

Presents all or most of the following indexes (base period=1977) for the State and each of 17 cities or SMSAs: bank debits, building permits, electricity and water consumption, newspaper advertising linage, new auto registrations, nonagricultural employment, retail sales, and postal receipts. Also includes a composite index for each city and SMSA.

Most indexes are shown for month of coverage, with percent change from same month and same year-to-date period of previous year. Occasionally comparisons to other previous periods are also included.

Issues generally contain narrative summary and feature article, with text statistics; summary charts; and 2-5 tables.

Monthly index data appear in all issues. All additional features with substantial statistical content are described, as they appear, under "Statistical Features." Nonstatistical features are not covered.

Availability: College of William and Mary: Bureau of Business Research, School of Business Administration, Williamsburg VA 23185, †; SRI/MF/complete, shipped quarterly.

Issues reviewed during 1984: Oct. 1983-Sept. 1984 (D) (Nos. 282-293).

STATISTICAL FEATURE:

U1120–1.501: June 1984 (No. 290)
GROWTH IN VIRGINIA AND ITS SMSAs

(2 p.) Article, with 3 tables showing Virginia nonagricultural employment by industry division, statewide and for 10 SMSAs, May 1984, with percent change from May 1983. Data are from the Joint Economic Committee, State Employment Commission, and Bureau of Business Research.

U1245
Columbia University: Center for International Business Cycle Research

U1245–1   INTERNATIONAL ECONOMIC INDICATORS
Monthly.   Approx. 70 p.
SRI/MF/complete, delayed

Monthly report presenting detailed economic time series data for U.S., Canada, UK, West Germany, France, Italy, Japan, and Australia. Presents 11-18 individual leading and coincident indicators for each country, and multicountry composite leading and coincident indicators aggregated for all countries, 7 countries excluding U.S., and 4 European countries. Data for Australia begin with the Aug. 1984 issue.

Data are shown by month, generally for current year to date and 3 previous years, with summary trends from the 1970s. Most data are current to 2-3 months prior to cover date.

June and Dec. issues also include appendices showing economic growth cycle trends for 10-13 countries, including dates of peaks and troughs since 1948, and median lead or lag of selected economic indicators at peaks and troughs.

Data are prepared by Columbia University Center for International Business Cycle Research.

Contains contents listing; notes on changes for current issue; and 3 statistical sections, with 2 summary tables, 32-35 charts, and detailed tabulations of country and composite indicators. June and Dec. appendices include growth cycle analysis with 4 tables, and user instructions.

Historical data for the indicators covered in this report are available from the issuing agency.

Availability: Center for International Business Cycle Research, Graduate School of Business, 808 Uris Hall, Columbia University, New York NY 10027, university or public libraries $250.00 per yr., corporations $450.00 per yr.; SRI/MF/complete, delayed shipment 4 months from cover date.

Issues reviewed during 1984: Nov. 1983-Oct. 1984 (P) (Vol. 6, Nos. 11-12; Vol. 7, Nos. 1-10).

U1245–2   RECESSION-RECOVERY WATCH
Bimonthly.   Approx. 20 p.
SRI/MF/complete

Bimonthly report analyzing U.S. business cycles as measured by changes in approximately 50 economic indicators. Data are primarily from Columbia University Center for International Business Cycle Research, and are generally current to 1-3 months preceding cover date.

Contains narrative analysis, with 1 or more summary tables and/or charts; list of indicator charts and user instructions; and 3 detailed tables, with accompanying illustrative indicator charts, showing actual levels and change from preceding business cycle peak or trough for approximately 50 indicators, for current cycle as of most recent month or quarter available, and for 7-8 comparable recessionary or expansionary periods, 1940s-82. Indicators are as follows:

a. Composite leading, coincident, and lagging indexes, including employment index and 6-7 country leading index.

b. Output, income, and sales, including real GNP, personal income, consumer expenditures, and retail sales; and industrial production index.

c. Employment and unemployment, including employment diffusion index, nonfarm employee hours, part-time employment ratio, manufacturing average workweek and overtime hours, layoff rate, and unemployment insurance initial claims.

d. Investment and inventory, including housing starts and permits, contracts/orders for plant/equipment, inventory/sales ratio, and capital appropriations.

e. Productivity and profitability, including output per hour, hourly compensation, unit labor costs, selling price index, price/labor cost ratio, corporate profit margin, business failures, industrial materials price index, CPI, and leading index of inflation.

f. Financial, including money supply; total, business/consumer, and Federal debt; and Treasury bill rate, corporate bond yield, and stock price index.

A special supplement, presenting detailed trend data for the indicators covered in this report, has also been received, and is also available on SRI microfiche, under this number [Monograph. [1984]. 3+93 p. $100.00]. Supplement is not included in the bimonthly report subscription, and must be ordered separately.

Availability: Center for International Business Cycle Research, Graduate School of Business, 808 Uris Hall, Columbia University, New York NY 10027, $75.00 per yr.; SRI/MF/complete.

Issues reviewed during 1984: Dec. 1983-Oct. 1984 (P) (Vol. 5, No. 6; Vol. 6, Nos. 1-5); and 1984 Supplement.

U1380
Cornell University:
New York
State College of
Agriculture and Life Sciences

U1380-1   OPERATING RESULTS OF SELF-SERVICE DISCOUNT DEPARTMENT STORES and the Mass Retailers' Merchandising Report, 1982-83
Annual.   Oct. 1983.
xiii+141 p.
ISSN 0474-2656.
LC 77-640100.
SRI/MF/complete

Annual report, by Gene A. German and Gerard F. Hawkes, providing detailed data on sales, expenses, earnings, and operating ratios of self-service discount department stores, by size of firm. Also includes "Mass Retailers' Merchandising Report" showing operating data by sales department. Data are shown for FY83, with selected trends from FY78.

Data are based on survey responses of 28 firms operating 3,426 stores with aggregate sales of $15.1 billion, and are shown separately for all firms and for 26 identical firms with 2 or more years of consecutive responses to the annual survey. Report is sponsored by the National Mass Retailing Institute.

Report is intended to permit individual stores to compare their performance with industry averages. This is the 19th annual report. For description of 18th report, see SRI 1982 Annual, under this number.

Contents:

Foreword and contents listing. (p. ii-viii)

Introduction and highlights. Includes 1 table showing percent change in 16 economic indicators, 1978-82. (p. ix-xiii)

Section 1, Part I. Six-year trends for all firms and identical firms. Includes 30 charts and 30 tables showing trends in 30 financial and operating indicators, including average sales per store and square foot, average sales and occupancy cost per selling area, and cumulative markup and stockturns for owned depts, mostly FY78-83. (p. 1-30)

Section 1, Part II-III. Identical and all firm analysis. Includes 1 highlights table, and 4 detailed tables listed below, repeated for identical firms (p. 32-70) and all firms (p. 72-113).

Section 2, Part I-II. Mass Retailers' Merchandising Report. Includes 7 tables showing net sales by payment type, and the following by dept: sales as percent of store total, stockturns, markup as percent of original retail, stock shortage and markdown as percent of owned dept sales, and gross margin as percent of owned dept sales; repeated for identical firms (p. 117-123) and all firms (p. 125-131).

Appendix. Includes survey methodology and questionnaire facsimile. (p. 133-141)

Availability: National Mass Retailing Institute, 570 Seventh Ave., New York NY 10018, members $60.00, nonmembers $75.00, educational institutions $32.00; SRI/MF/complete.

DETAILED TABLES:

[Data are shown as combined dollar averages FY82-83, and for middle range of firms FY83. Tables [1-3] are shown by sales, gross margin, expense, and payroll levels.]

[1] Gross margin, expense[s], and earnings [as] percent of sales [including expenses for payroll, advertising, taxes/licenses, utilities, and 13 other items].

[2] Assets [as] percent of total assets [for components of current and other assets and of property/equipment, and for total intangible assets].

[3] Liabilities and net worth [as] percent of total [for components of current liabilities, long-term debt, and net worth].

[4] Responsibility centers [expenses as percent of sales for 12 expenses categories, including advertising/promotion, accounting, data processing, employee benefits, warehousing, and transportation].

U1880
Georgia State University:
Economic Forecasting
Project

U1880-1   GEORGIA STATE UNIVERSITY FORECAST: The Nation
Quarterly.   Approx. 15 p. var. paging.
SRI/MF/complete

Quarterly report presenting 8-quarter forecasts of U.S. expenditures, income components of the GNP, derivation of personal income, Federal Government activity, export/import balance, and approximately 30 other indicators of the U.S. economy.

Data are from Economic Forecasting Project econometric model, and are current to quarter preceding publication date.

Contains narrative analysis, forecast assumptions, and brief summary; and 9 quarterly tables, listed below.

Availability: Georgia State University: Economic Forecasting Project, University Plaza, Atlanta GA 30303, $25.00 per yr.; SRI/MF/complete.

Issues reviewed during 1984: Nov. 10, 1983-Aug. 9, 1984 (P).

TABLES:

[Data are shown quarterly for 10 quarters beginning 2 quarters prior to cover date, and annually for 3 years, unless otherwise noted.]

1-2. Expenditures and real expenditures [by component].

3. Income related GNP components [including employee compensation by industry sector, proprietors' and rental income, and national income].

4. Derivation of personal income [including government transfer payments by type, disposable personal income, and personal savings rate].

5. Federal Government activity [including receipts and expenditures by line item, and Federal debt held by individuals].

6. Selected economic variables of the economy [approximately 30 indicators, including percent change in wages and productivity; and CPI, PPI, corporate profits, checkable deposits, money supply, prime rate, Treasury bill and Aaa corporate bond interest rates, conventional mortgage rates, housing starts, auto sales, and industrial production index].

7. Foreign trade accounts [exports and imports of merchandise by type, and balance of payments; annually only].

8. Implicit price deflators for personal consumption expenditures [by component].

9. Implicit price deflators with annual percentage changes [in approximately 15 indicators, including personal consumption, private domestic investment, foreign trade, and Federal and State/local government purchases and value added].

U1880–2 GEORGIA STATE UNIVERSITY FORECAST: Georgia and Atlanta

Quarterly. Approx. 15 p. var. paging.
SRI/MF/complete

Quarterly report presenting 2-year forecasts of employment and personal income levels in Georgia and the Atlanta MSA. Data are from Economic Forecasting Project econometric model, and are current to quarter preceding publication date.

Contains narrative analysis and summary; and statistical section, with 6 quarterly tables, listed below.

Feb. and Aug. issues include 2 additional tables showing 5-year employment and income forecasts for Georgia (Feb.) and Atlanta (Aug.).

Availability: Georgia State University: Economic Forecasting Project, University Plaza, Atlanta GA 30303, $25.00 per yr.; SRI/MF/complete.

Issues reviewed during 1984: Nov. 10, 1983-Aug. 9, 1984 (P).

QUARTERLY TABLES:

[Tables 1-4 and 6 present data for current, 1-2 previous, and 1-2 future years, revised each quarter. Income data are shown by industry division and source; employment data are shown by industry division and major manufacturing industry group.]

1-2. Georgia wage/salary employment, and personal income.

3-4. [Tables 1-2 are repeated for Atlanta MSA.]

5. Seasonally adjusted nonagricultural employment [for Georgia and Atlanta MSA, quarterly for 4-5 quarters ending quarter preceding publication, and for final month of most recent quarter].

6. Metro Atlanta [single- and multi-] housing permits [by county].

U1880–3 GSU ECONOMIC FORECASTING PROJECT NEWSLETTER: Monthly Projections

Monthly. Approx. 15 p. var. paging.
SRI/MF/complete, shipped quarterly

Monthly report presenting forecasts of economic indicators in the consumer, industrial, construction, and financial sectors, for approximately 18 months. Data are from Economic Forecasting Project econometric model, and are revised each month. Report is issued approximately 2 months after each forecast revision.

Contents:

a. Narrative analysis of current business conditions and economic factors affecting forecast assumption, usually with 1 table showing quarterly deflators for real, price, and nominal GNP.

b. 9 monthly indicator tables, described below.

Availability: Georgia State University: Economic Forecasting Project, University Plaza, Atlanta GA 30303, $50.00 per yr.; SRI/MF/complete, shipped quarterly.

Issues reviewed during 1984: Aug. 1983-Sept. 1984 (D).

INDICATOR TABLES:

[Data usually are shown for approximately 18 consecutive months beginning 5-7 months prior to month of current forecast revision, and include comparison to previous month's forecast. Table order may vary slightly from issue to issue.]

a. Employment, and personal income: including payroll and household employment, unemployment rate, indexes of hours worked and hourly earnings; and wage/salary income, disposable income, and personal savings and expenditures. 2 tables.

b. Consumption, and retail sales: including consumption and/or sales of durables, non-auto durables, autos, nondurables, and services; total real and personal consumption; and total retail sales. 2 tables.

c. Business activity, and construction: including business inventories, durable and nondefense capital goods orders, defense and nondefense shipments, and industrial production and capacity utilization indexes; and housing starts and permits, construction expenditures, and private nonresidential, residential, and public construction. 2 tables.

d. Prices, and miscellaneous: including CPI, PPI, merchandise trade balance, index of leading indicators, corporate inventory valuation adjustment (IVA) rate, and estimated GNP. 2 tables.

e. Financial markets: including money supply; and interest rates for Federal funds, 6-month Treasury bills, Aaa corporate and municipal bonds, commercial paper, 90-day certificates of deposit, and prime rate. 1 table.

U2030
Harvard University: Russian Research Center

U2030–1 RRC NEWSLETTER

Monthly. Approx. 4 p.
SRI/MF/complete, shipped quarterly

Monthly report on Soviet Union economy, including industrial production, currency exchange rates, and balance of trade. Data are from published Soviet sources.

Issues typically contain narrative briefs on recent events affecting U.S.-Soviet Union economic relations, and on upcoming conferences; and 3 monthly tables. Report also includes 1 irregularly recurring table, 2 quarterly tables, and 1 annual table.

Recurring tables are listed below. Most monthly tables appear in all issues; irregularly recurring table appears in Jan., July, and Sept. 1984 issues. Page locations and latest periods of coverage for quarterly and annual tables are noted, as they appear, under "Statistical Features." Nonstatistical features are not covered.

Availability: Harvard University: Russian Research Center, Prof. Marshall I. Goldman, 1737 Cambridge St., Cambridge MA 02138, subscriptions †, single copy ‡; SRI/MF/complete, shipped quarterly.

Issues reviewed during 1984: Nov. 5, 1983-Oct. 11, 1984 (P) (Vol. VIII, Nos. 3-12; Vol. IX, Nos. 1-2).

RECURRING TABLES:

[Data for tables [3-4] are current to approximately 4 months prior to cover date, and are shown for year to date, same period of previous year, and 3-5 previous full years.]

MONTHLY TABLES

[1] Industrial production figures [for approximately 20 varying products, including electricity, petroleum, natural gas, coal, steel, fertilizer, metal cutting tools, industrial robots, computer technology, tractors, paper, cement, meat, margarine, watches, radios, TV sets, and automobiles; for month 2 months prior to cover date and/or year to date, with comparisons to previous year].

[2] Currency figures [rates of exchange for rubles and 8-9 foreign currencies, including U.S. dollar; for month prior to cover date, previous 1-2 months, and same month of previous year].

[3] [Value of U.S. exports to and imports from USSR, by principal commodity group; table begins with the Jan. 7, 1984 issue.]

IRREGULARLY RECURRING TABLE

[4] [Value of U.S. exports to and imports from Eastern Europe, by principal commodity group, occasionally with detail by country.]

QUARTERLY TABLES

[5] Balance of trade [value of exports from and imports to Soviet Union, for U.S. and approximately 20 other non-Communist countries, for year to date through quarter ending 3-5 months prior to cover date, and same period of previous 1-6 years].

[6] Soviet balance of trade with Eastern Europe [value of exports from and imports to Soviet Union, for 6 countries, usually for year to date through quarter ending 3-6 months prior to cover date, and same period of previous 1-3 years].

ANNUAL TABLE

[7] Increase in sales of goods at state and cooperative stores [for 25-30 consumer items, previous year compared to 2 years ago].

STATISTICAL FEATURES:

U2030–1.501: Nov. 5, 1983 (Vol. VIII, No. 3)

QUARTERLY TABLE

[5] Balance of trade [USSR with U.S. and 19 other non-Communist countries], 1st half 1983. (p. 5)

U2030–1.502: Dec. 5, 1983 (Vol. VIII, No. 4)

QUARTERLY TABLES

[5] Balance of trade [USSR with U.S. and 19 other non-Communist countries], 1st 9 months 1983. (p. 4)

[6] Soviet balance of trade with Eastern Europe, 2nd half 1983. (p. 3)

U2030–1.503: Jan. 7, 1984 (Vol. VIII, No. 5)

QUARTERLY TABLE

[6] Soviet balance of trade with Eastern Europe, 3rd quarter 1983. (p. 3)

U2030–1.504: Mar. 8, 1984 (Vol. VIII, No. 7)

ANNUAL TABLE

[7] Increase in sale of goods at state/cooperative stores [30 consumer items], 1983 over 1982. (p. 1)

U2030–1.505: Apr. 12, 1984 (Vol. VIII, No. 8)

QUARTERLY TABLE

[5] Balance of trade [USSR with U.S. and 20 other non-Communist countries, and total Soviet balance of trade], 1983. (p. 4)

U2030–1.506: May 11, 1984 (Vol. VIII, No. 9)

QUARTERLY TABLE

[6] Soviet balance of trade with Eastern Europe, 1983. (p. 4)

U2030–1.507: Aug. 5, 1984 (Vol. VIII, No.12)

QUARTERLY TABLE

[5] Balance of trade [USSR with U.S. and 19 other non-Communist countries, and total Soviet balance of trade], 1st quarter 1984. (p. 6)

U2030–1.508: Sept. 2, 1984 (Vol. IX, No. 1)

QUARTERLY TABLE

[6] Soviet balance of trade with Eastern Europe, 1st quarter 1984. (p. 6)

U2160
Indiana University: Graduate School of Business

U2160–1   INDIANA BUSINESS REVIEW

Bimonthly. Approx. 5 p.
ISSN 0019-6541.
LC SN 78-4481.
SRI/MF/complete

Bimonthly report on Indiana business activities and economic trends. Data are from Federal and State agencies, R. L. Polk & Co., American Iron and Steel Institute, and McGraw-Hill Information Systems.

Issues generally contain feature articles, occasionally statistical, on a specific aspect of the Indiana economy; and 3 recurring tables. Report also includes a semiannual business conditions review and outlook analysis.

Recurring tables are listed below. All additional features with substantial statistical content are described, as they appear, under "Statistical Features;" page locations and latest periods of coverage for recurring tables are also noted. Nonstatistical features are not covered.

Prior to Jan./Feb. 1984 issue, report was published monthly.

Availability: Indiana University: Graduate School of Business, Division of Research, 10th and Fee Lane, Bloomington IN 47405, Indiana residents †, others ‡; SRI/MF/complete.

Issues reviewed during 1984: July/Aug. 1983-Nov./Dec. 1984 (monthly); Jan./Feb.-May./June 1984 (bimonthly) (P) (Vol. 58-59).

RECURRING TABLES:

[Data are shown for latest available month and selected prior periods. Most data are seasonally adjusted.]

[1] Indiana industrial electricity sales [by city].

[2] U.S. and Indiana business indicators [including indexes of employment and construction activity; weekly hours and earnings in manufacturing; unemployment rate; production indexes for bituminous coal, industrial electricity, manufacturing, and raw steel; personal income; and auto sales and registrations].

[3] U.S. and Indiana man-hours in industrial production [by manufacturing group].

STATISTICAL FEATURES:

U2160–1.501: July/Aug. 1983 (Vol. 58)

INDIANA POPULATION PROJECTIONS TO THE YEAR 2020

(p. 2-12) Article, with 7 tables showing Indiana population change, decennially 1910-2020; population by age group, 2020 with change from 1980; population and distribution by age group, by county, 1980 and 2020; and births, deaths, and net migration, by county, 1980-2020 period.

More detailed data are presented in *Indiana County Population Projections, 1985-2020,* described in 1983 SRI Annual under S2630-1.

U2160–1.502: Sept./Oct. 1983 (Vol. 58)

RECURRING TABLES

(p. 8-12) Most data are current to Sept. 1983. For data descriptions, see U2160-1 above.

INDIANA PROFILE: WHERE THE STATE STANDS

(p. 2-4) By Joel C. Webster. Article, with 1 table showing selected demographic and socioeconomic data for Indiana and U.S., with State ranking for Indiana. Data are shown for most recent available year, primarily late 1970s-82, with some trends.

Includes approximately 70 items within the following categories: population characteristics, land area, vital statistics, health care, housing, crime, education, employment, income and poverty, government finances, voter participation, motor vehicle use, traffic fatalities, energy consumption, weather, farms, minerals, construction, manufacturing, and retail sales.

Data were compiled by the Census Bureau.

SHIFTS IN PERSONAL INCOME

(p. 6-7) By Morton J. Marcus. Article, with 3 tables showing the following for Indiana and 4 neighboring States: personal income amount, percent change, and share of U.S. total, various periods 2nd quarter 1977-83.

Data are from Bureau of Economic Analysis.

U2160–1.503: Nov./Dec. 1983 (Vol. 59)

FORECAST OF THE ECONOMY, SEMIANNUAL FEATURE

Semiannual economic review and forecast issue, presenting analyses for U.S., Indiana, and 11 Indiana urban areas. Data are generally from State agency and university research center reports. Includes the following analyses with statistics:

INDIANA ECONOMY IN 1984

(p. 3-5) By Morton J. Marcus. Includes 2 tables showing personal income, 1976-84; and employment change by industry division and major manufacturing group, 1983-84 period.

INDIANAPOLIS

(p. 5-6) By Robert J. Kirk. Includes 3 tables showing multiplier measures of selected industries' importance to the Indianapolis economy (no date); employment indexes for U.S., Indianapolis, and 6 other metro areas, 1974-82 period; and population retention/attraction ratios for persons age 25-29 in 1970, by sex, for Indianapolis and 8 other metro areas, 1970-80 period.

EVANSVILLE

(p. 7) By Maurice Tsai. Includes 1 table showing Evansville area business index for industrial production, 4 industry divisions, and employment, monthly Jan.-Sept. 1983, and annually 1981-84.

SOUTH BEND AND ELKHART

(p. 8-9) By John E. Peck. Includes 2 tables showing employment by major sector, unemployment rate, help-wanted index, industrial electricity and natural gas sales, new car and truck sales, and number and value of housing permits; for South Bend and/or Elkhart, selected periods 1978-Aug. 1983.

MUNCIE-ANDERSON

(p. 10-12) By Robert R. Jost. Includes 1 table showing establishment employment for non-manufacturing and manufacturing durable and nondurable goods sectors; for Indiana and for Muncie and Anderson SMSAs, selected years 1973-83.

LAFAYETTE

(p. 15-16) By William C. Dunkelberg. Includes 1 table showing establishment employment, by industry division, for Lafayette-West Lafayette SMSA, selected periods 1979-Oct. 1983.

GARY-HAMMOND-EAST CHICAGO (CALUMET AREA)

(p. 17-18) By Leslie P. Singer. Includes 3 tables showing Calumet area employment by major sector, various periods 1978-85; and income, payroll, primary metals industry average wage, production workers, and selected business ratios, selected years 1964-85.

JEFFERSONVILLE-NEW ALBANY (LOUISVILLE AREA)

(p. 19-20) By Fay Ross Greckel. Includes 2 tables showing business activity indexes for 3 industry sectors, for Louisville metro area; and nonfarm and manufacturing employment, and total unemployment rate, for Louisville area and Clark/Floyd counties; various periods 1979-3rd quarter 1983.

U2160–1.504: Jan./Feb. 1984 (Vol. 59)

CITIZEN'S PERCEPTIONS OF BANKING SERVICES IN INDIANA

(p. 7-14) Article, with 10 tables showing Indiana residents' understanding of cross-county banking concept (banks with branches in more than 1 county), approval of or opposition to legislation permitting such expansion, and perceptions of benefit or harm; and consumer use of banking services; all by size of resident county.

Data are from 1,005 responses to a Nov. 1982 Indiana University telephone survey of registered voters.

BANKING STRUCTURE IN INDIANA AND NEIGHBORING STATES

(p. 15-25) By Hugh S. McLaughlin. Article analyzing State banking policies regarding branch offices and effect on distribution of deposits, for Indiana and 10 economically similar States, 1981, with selected comparisons to 1961 and 1971.

Includes the following for each State grouped by type of restriction regarding activities of branch offices: selected socioeconomic indicator trends including number of banks and total and per capita IPC (individual/partnership/corporation) bank deposits; number of independent banking organizations and distribution by size of IPC deposits; and share of deposits in largest banks, bank holding companies, and counties.

Also includes detail for Indiana by type of financial institution, including distribution of counties by number of financial institutions, and banking concentration in largest institutions and counties.

Data are presented in 12 tables.

BRANCHING REGULATION AND THE SMALL BUSINESS LOAN MARKET

(p. 26-32) By William C. Dunkelberg and Jeffrey A. Shapiro. Article examining adequacy of banking services to small businesses in States with various regulations regarding bank branch offices. Data are based on responses of 709 firms to an Apr. 1982 survey of small businesses in Indiana and 10 economically similar States.

Includes 12 tables showing the following by type of State banking law classification (bank holding companies permitted or not permitted, and unit, limited, or statewide branching regulation): survey sample size; and survey response on average loan size, interest rate and loans by length of maturity, loan repayment methods and collateral requirements, ratings of bank performance, whether credit needs were adequately met, incidence of loan refusal, and perceived change in competition among banks during past 5 years.

U2160-1.505; Mar./Apr. 1984 (Vol. 59)

INDIANA BANKING PROFILE

(p. 8-22) By William L. Sartoris and John A. Boquist. Article comparing banking structure and operations of Indiana and U.S. Data are from *FDIC Bank Operating Statistics,* and *Sheshunoff Banks of Indiana, 1982.* Includes 14 undated tables showing the following:

a. Indiana and U.S.: number of banks, bank/population ratio, deposits per capita, 5-year growth rate for deposits, percent of deposits over $100,000, loans by type and securities holdings relative to deposits and to assets or total loans, Federal funds market activity, level of correspondent activity between banks, and profitability ratios, all by deposit size category, with summary comparisons to 14-15 States with various types of bank branching or holding company regulations.

b. Indiana aggregate counties: maximum, mean, minimum, and upper and lower quartiles for deposits per capita, percent of deposits over $100,000, number of banks, bank/population ratio, and loan and profitability measures.

COUNTY LEVEL PERSONAL INCOME DURING THE GREAT RECESSION

(p. 22-24) By Morton J. Marcus. Article analyzing Indiana personal income trends, 1979-82. Data are from U.S. Commerce Dept. Includes 4 tables showing total and per capita personal income, for U.S., and for Indiana by county with selected rankings, 1979 and 1982, and average annual change for 1959-82 period.

U2160-1.506: May/June 1984 (Vol. 59)

MIDYEAR REVIEW OF THE INDIANA ECONOMY, SEMIANNUAL FEATURE

Semiannual economic review and forecast issue, presenting analyses for U.S., Indiana, and 11 Indiana urban areas. Data are generally from State agency and university research center reports. Includes the following analyses with statistics:

MID-YEAR REVIEW OF THE INDIANA ECONOMY IN 1984

(p. 3-5) By Richard L. Pfister. Includes 1 table showing econometric model quarterly data for personal income, employment, and unemployment rate, 4th quarter 1983-4th quarter 1984.

INDIANAPOLIS

(p. 5-6) By Robert J. Kirk. Includes 1 table showing Mar. 1984 employment comparisons to 1979-82 business cycle trough and peak months, by industry sector.

SOUTH BEND AND ELKHART

(p. 11-12) By Paul A. Jorey. Includes 2 tables showing manufacturing and nonmanufacturing employment, help-wanted index, unemployment rate, sales of industrial electricity and commercial and industrial gas, new car and truck sales, and number and value of housing permits, for South Bend and/or Elkhart, 1978, 1983, and Mar. 1983-84.

JEFFERSONVILLE-NEW ALBANY (LOUISVILLE AREA)

(p. 12-14) By Fay Ross Greckel. Includes 2 tables showing business activity indexes for industrial production and 3 industry sectors, for Louisville metro area; and manufacturing and nonmanufacturing employment, and total unemployment rate, for Louisville area and Clark/Floyd counties; various periods 1979-1st quarter 1984.

EVANSVILLE

(p. 15-16) By Maurice Tsai. Includes 1 table showing Evansville area business index for industrial production, 4 industry divisions, and employment, Aug. 1983-Mar. 1984.

GARY-HAMMOND-EAST CHICAGO (CALUMET AREA)

(p. 16-17) By Leslie P. Singer. Includes 2 tables showing Northwest Indiana employment by major sector; personal income; payroll for export, steel, and private sectors; and business activity index; selected periods 1984-85.

U2410
Iowa State University: North Central Regional Center for Rural Development

U2410-1   COUNTY GOVERNMENT COMPUTER UTILIZATION AND APPLICATION in Four North Central States
Monograph. Jan. 1983.
v+50 p.
SRI/MF/complete

By Curtis Braschler. Report examining county government computer use, equipment suppliers, and programming sources, in Iowa, Kansas, Michigan, and Missouri, 1982. Presents the following data for county governments in each State:

a. Computer use by brand, with detail by model; cooperative use with other local government entities; and use of private computer services, and of data storage systems by type.

b. Use of in-house developed vs. privately supplied software, with detail for 3 computer brands; primary computer applications and offices using computers; computer use relative to county assessed valuation and population size; computer language used; and computer purchasing plans or reasons for not purchasing.

Data are from responses of 400 counties to a spring 1982 survey conducted by the author.

Contains contents and table listings (p. i-iii); summary, conclusions, recommendations, and introduction (p. 1-14); narrative report interspersed with 28 tables (p. 15-49); and list of references (p. 50).

Computer Service Industry Serving County Government in Four North Central States During 1982, a narrative report with some supporting statistics, is also available from the issuing agency but is not covered in SRI.

Availability: Iowa State University: North Central Regional Center for Rural Development, Publications Office, 578 Heady Hall, Ames IA 50011, †; SRI/MF/complete.

U2480
Iowa State University: World Food Institute

U2480-1   WORLD FOOD TRADE AND U.S. AGRICULTURE, 1960-82
Annual. Aug. 1983.
v+73 p.
SRI/MF/complete

Annual report on U.S. and world agricultural production and trade, with selected data by country and commodity, various years 1960/61-1983/84. Includes data on value of U.S. agricultural imports and exports, including Government food assistance programs, by commodity. Most data are from USDA and UN Food and Agriculture Organization.

Contains listings of contents, tables, and charts (p. i-v); narrative analysis, interspersed with 23 charts mostly showing trends, and 44 tables (p.

1-51); bibliography and notes (p. 52-54); and 5 appendices, with country economic classifications, maps, 17 trend charts, and 2 tables (p. 55-73).

All tables, and selected charts showing data not included in tables, are described below.

This is the 3rd annual report.

Availability: Iowa State University: World Food Institute, 102 E. O. Bldg., Ames IA 50011, †; SRI/MF/complete.

TABLES AND CHARTS:

a. World grain production, utilization, exports, ending stocks, yields, and harvested area, for wheat, coarse grains, and rice; oilseed product production; oilseed and soybean yields and harvested area; and cassava, pulses, pork, poultry, and beef/veal production; with selected detail by major producing or exporting country and world area, various years 1960/61-1983/84. Tables 1-18. (p. 4-19)

b. Prices for Chicago cash corn and soybeans in dollars and selected foreign currencies, quarterly 1977-2nd quarter 1983; and outstanding foreign debt of selected countries, 1982. Tables 19-20. (p. 20-21)

c. U.S.: agricultural cash receipts by commodity group; agricultural export value; acreage planted by type of crop; fertilizer/primary plant nutrient use; off-farm grain storage facilities, and capacity by region; number and capacity of rail grain cars; and farmer reserve loan rates and average prices paid to farmers, for wheat and corn; various years 1970-1983/84. Tables 21-28. (p. 22-27)

d. Export volume shares of major exporting countries and world areas, for wheat, coarse grains, soybeans, soybean meal and oil, beef/veal, and pork; various years 1970-1983. Tables 29-35. (p. 28-31)

e. USSR: change in grain production, imports, and trade; imports of wheat, feed grain, soybeans, and soybean meal, from U.S. and non-U.S. sources; grain exports to USSR by country or area of origin; and grain used in feeding, with comparisons to U.S. and selected other countries; various years 1970/71-1982/83. Tables 36-39. (p. 32-34)

f. PRC: grain imports by country or world area of origin, 1972/73-1982/83; and purchases of U.S. soybeans, and share of total U.S. soybean and soybean oil exports, 1977/78-1981/82. Tables 40-41. (p. 35-36)

g. U.S. agricultural trade, including export and import value by commodity, with selected export detail by destination and top exporting State; concessional (Government-financed) exports by commodity and aid category; and corn, wheat, and soybean exports by port area of departure; various periods 1971-82. Charts 11-14, tables 42-44, and 2 appendix tables. (p. 39-43, 64, 72-73)

U2520
Johns Hopkins University: Population Information Program

U2520-1   POPULATION REPORTS
Series. For individual publication data, see below. Cumulative pagination throughout individual series. ISSN 0275-8792. LC 82-5055. SRI/MF/complete

Continuing series of reports on world family planning and fertility trends, covering aspects of health and reproduction, population growth and government policy, fertility research, and contraceptive practices in developing countries.

Most data are from research studies, UN agencies, foreign government reports, World Fertility Surveys, and U.S. Agency for International Development (USAID).

Each report focuses on a selected topic. Reports are presented in 13 subject series; each series is paginated consecutively.

General format:

a. Summary, and discussion of research findings, with illustrative charts, and tables presenting results of selected studies and/or more broad-based statistics.

b. Tabular description of studies, and research bibliography.

Only reports with substantial, broad-based statistics are described in SRI. Reports presenting only clinical data or narrowly focused research results are not covered.

Reports reviewed during 1984 are described below.

Availability: Johns Hopkins University: Population Information Program, Hampton House, 624 N. Broadway, Baltimore MD 21205, health personnel in developing countries †, individual copies for others $0.50 each; SRI/MF/complete.

U2520-1.26: Vasectomy—Safe and Simple
[Monograph. Nov./Dec. 1983. p. D61-D100. Vol. XI, No. 5 (Series D, Male Sterilization, No. 4). SRI/MF/complete.]

Report on worldwide vasectomy use and reversals. Data are from a variety of specified studies, and are shown for various developed and developing countries or world areas.

Includes 5 tables showing pregnancy rates following vasectomy reversals, by reversal method; couples relying on vasectomy as contraceptive method; vasectomies performed; and percent of married women using any contraceptive method, and knowing of and relying on vasectomies and female sterilization; various years 1967-83.

U2520-1.27: New Developments in Vaginal Contraception
[Monograph. Jan.-Feb. 1984. p. H157-H191. Vol. XII, No. 1 (Series H, Barrier Methods, No. 7). SRI/MF/complete.]

Report on worldwide vaginal contraceptive use. Data are from a variety of specified studies and other sources, and are shown for various developed and developing countries.

Includes 2 charts, and 7 tables showing percent of currently married women using vaginal contraception or any other method; percent of ever-married women who have heard of modern vaginal contraception or any other methods; and pregnancy rate, unit deliveries of vaginal contraceptives by major donor agency, and estimated couple-years of protection, all by type of vaginal contraceptive; various years 1970-83.

U2520-1.28: Healthier Mothers and Children Through Family Planning
[Monograph. May/June 1984. p. J657-J696. Vol. XII, No. 3 (Series J, Family Planning Programs, No. 27). SRI/MF/complete.]

Report on importance of family planning to maternal, infant, and child health, with focus on developing countries. Data are from UN, World Bank, and various specified studies. Includes 2 charts and 8 tables showing the following, for various periods 1951-82:

a. Developed vs. developing countries: population distribution by age group, and by sex for adults aged 15-49; percent of total population and of total deaths, for children under age 5; and female death rate from childbearing and from side effects of various contraceptives.

b. Maternal, infant, and child (age 1-4) death rates; and distribution of currently married women by child bearing plans, and percent using contraceptive methods; by developing country, with death rate comparisons to developed countries.

c. Pregnancy rate by type of contraceptive method used, including lowest reported rate, and rates from U.S. and Philippine surveys.

U2635
Kent State University: Kent Economic and Development Institute

U2635-1   KEDI ECONOMIC SURVEY
Monthly.

SRI now covers this publication under B4950-1.

U2730
Louisiana State University: Center for Energy Studies

U2730-1   LOUISIANA ENERGY INDICATORS
Quarterly. Approx. 6 p. Foldout. SRI/MF/complete

Quarterly report on Louisiana energy industry trends and developments, including production, consumption, employment, prices, and related State revenues.

Data are compiled from reports of State and Federal agencies, and energy publications. Quarter of data coverage is 2 quarters prior to quarter of publication.

Issues generally contain brief feature article, occasionally with statistics; quarterly historical presentation, with 1 or more tables and/or charts; and 3 quarterly tables accompanied by illustrative charts.

Quarterly tables are listed below and appear in all issues. All other features with substantial statistics are described, as they appear, under "Statistical Features."

Report begins publication with the Spring 1983 issue.

Availability: Louisiana State University: Center for Energy Studies, E. Fraternity Circle, Baton Rouge LA 70803-0301, †; SRI/MF/complete.

Issues reviewed during 1984: Spring 1983-Fall 1984 (P).

QUARTERLY TABLES:

[Tables show data monthly for quarter of coverage, quarterly for 3 preceding quarters, annually for 5 previous years, and cumulative year to date for current and previous year. Table format and content may vary from issue to issue.]

[1] Drilling [oil and gas wells completed, dry holes drilled, total and wildcat active rigs, running rigs, and crude oil allowable production, for north and south regions of State, and offshore; and total drilling permits].

[2] Production and consumption [oil and gas production for north and south regions of State, and offshore; refinery runs; crude oil stock; electricity production by type of fuel; gasoline consumption in State and total U.S.; electricity consumption by sector; and heating and cooling degree days].

[3] Prices, employment, and revenues [electricity prices by utility and user sector; interstate and intrastate natural gas prices; wellhead oil prices; retail gasoline prices in New Orleans and total U.S.; employment, wages, and establishments, by energy-related SIC 2-digit industry; and energy-related State revenues by source, compared to total State revenues].

STATISTICAL FEATURES:

U2730–1.501: Spring 1983

HISTORICAL PRESENTATION: NATURAL GAS

(1 p.) Includes 1 table showing Louisiana natural gas production and well completions, by State region and offshore; and interstate and intrastate natural gas prices; quarterly 1977-82.

U2730–1.502: Summer 1983

HISTORICAL PRESENTATION: REVENUES

(1 p.) Includes 1 table showing Louisiana State revenues from energy-related sources, including taxes, bonuses, rentals, and royalties; and energy percent of total State revenues; quarterly 1977-1st quarter 1983.

U2730–1.503: Fall 1983

HISTORICAL PRESENTATION: ELECTRICITY, ANNUAL FEATURE

(1 p.) Annual table showing Louisiana electricity production by type of fuel, consumption by sector, and New Orleans retail residential prices, quarterly 1977-2nd quarter 1983.

U2730–1.504: Winter 1983

LOUISIANA: THE OIL REFINING STATE

(2 p.) By Michael T. French. Article, with 2 tables showing Louisiana and total U.S. oil refinery operating rates as percent of refining capacity, and foreign oil percent of total input to refineries; and operable and idle capacity of individual Louisiana refineries, with type of process used; Jan. 1983. Data are from DOE.

HISTORICAL PRESENTATION: CRUDE OIL

(1 p.) Includes Louisiana oil wells completed and production, by State region and offshore; and wellhead price; 4th quarter 1977- 3rd quarter 1983.

U2730–1.505: Spring 1984

HISTORICAL PRESENTATION: REVENUES

(1 p.) Includes 1 table showing Louisiana State revenues from energy-related sources, including taxes, bonuses, rentals, and royalties; and energy percent of total State revenues; quarterly 1978-83.

U2730–1.506: Summer 1984

HISTORICAL PRESENTATION: PERMITTING AND PRODUCTION

(1 p.) Includes 1 table showing gas and oil production for north, south, and offshore Louisiana; and exploratory and developmental drilling permits issued statewide; quarterly 2nd quarter 1978-1st quarter 1984.

U2730–1.507: Fall 1984

HISTORICAL PRESENTATION: ELECTRICITY, ANNUAL FEATURE

(1 p.) Annual table showing Louisiana electricity consumption by sector, production by type of fuel, and New Orleans retail residential prices, 3rd quarter 1978-2nd quarter 1984.

U2735
Louisiana State University: College of Business Administration

U2735–1   LOUISIANA BUSINESS REVIEW

Quarterly. Approx. 25 p.
ISSN 0024-6751.
LC 40-35372.
SRI/MF/complete

Quarterly review of Louisiana business and economic developments, presenting articles on recent commercial activity, finance, foreign investments in the State, labor-management relations, projected socioeconomic conditions, and other topics.

Issues generally contain narrative editorial depts and feature articles, some with statistics.

Features with substantial statistical content are described, as they appear, under "Statistical Features."

Availability: Louisiana State University: College of Business Administration, Division of Research, Baton Rouge LA 70803, †; SRI/MF/complete.

Issues reviewed during 1984: Summer 1983-Summer 1984 (P) (Vol. 47, Nos. 2-3; Vol 48, Nos. 1-2) [No issue was published for Winter 1983].

STATISTICAL FEATURES:

U2735–1.501: Summer 1983 (Vol. 47, No. 2)

RESIDENTIAL SHELTER IN LOUISIANA

(p. 6-13) By John Duffy Jr. et al. Article, with 1 table showing residential building permit value, for Louisiana and 7 MSAs, 1st 7 months 1983, with change from 1982. Data are from U.S. Dept of Commerce.

HOUSING FORECASTS FOR THE 1980s

(p. 26-29) By James D. Shilling and D. Scott Laverty. Article on U.S. housing market conditions. Data are from Federal agencies. Includes 3 tables showing average home sales price and monthly mortgage payment, mortgage payment ratio to income, and rate of return on housing investment, selected periods 1962-83; and conventional mortgage interest rates vs. yield on 10-year Government securities, 1979-82.

HIGHER EDUCATION IN LOUISIANA, A RANKING AMONG SOUTHERN STATES

(p. 30-33) By Stephen Farber. Article, with 5 tables comparing selected measures of higher education quality in public doctorate-granting institutions, for Louisiana and 10 other southern States. Measures include science doctorates awarded, NSF obligations, State financing, faculty salaries, and library volumes, various periods 1977-83.

Data are from Southern Regional Education Board, NCES, American Assn of University Professors, and Assn of Research Libraries.

U2735–1.502: Fall 1983 (Vol. 47, No. 3)

IMPROVEMENT STRATEGY? LOUISIANA'S 1984 ECONOMIC FORECAST, ANNUAL FEATURE

(p. 6-15) Annual article, by James A. Richardson et al., presenting Louisiana Econometric Model forecasts of selected economic indicators through 1985.

Includes 14 tables, primarily showing Louisiana employment and earnings by industry division, personal income by type, population, bank and savings and loan assn financial activity, and energy production and consumption by sector, 1981-85, with comparison of actual vs. forecast data for 1982.

U2735–1.503: Spring 1984 (Vol. 48, No. 1)

ECONOMIES OF LOUISIANA AND ITS NEIGHBORS

(p. 25-34) By A. M. M. Jamal and David J. Molina. Article comparing demographic and economic trends for Louisiana, neighboring States, and U.S., 1960s-80s. Data are from Census Bureau, BLS, American Gas Assn, and other sources.

Includes 20 tables showing the following for Louisiana, Texas, Arkansas, Mississippi, Alabama, and total U.S., unless otherwise noted, various periods 1962-83:

a. Growth rates for population, personal income (total and per capita), labor force, employment, State revenues from Federal and State sources, and State expenditures per capita; and distribution of population by age, income by source (industry divisions and transfer payments), and State revenue and taxes by source.

b. Employment and unemployment; union/association members as percent of total labor force; State revenue and education expenditures per capita; and natural gas and electricity prices by type of user.

c. Cargo volume and value for 6 major southern ports, selected years 1962-82.

U2735–1.504: Summer 1984 (Vol. 48, No. 2)

ECONOMIC IMPACT OF A REGIONAL AIRPORT UPON THE LOCAL AREA

(p. 8, 16) By John E. Setnicky. Article, with 1 table estimating impact of Lafayette Regional Airport on the economy of Lafayette, La., city/parish, 1980-81. Data are from a joint University of Southwestern Louisiana/Louisiana Dept of Transportation and Development study.

WORLD'S FAIR: STAYING ALIVE

(p. 9-16) By William T. Moody and Joseph H. Wagner. Article on economic impact of the 1984 World's Fair at New Orleans, La. Data sources include Louisiana World Expo, Inc., and Harrison Price Co.

Includes 3 tables showing capital and operating expenditures of fair operators, and visitor expenditures at the fair and elsewhere; earnings and employment created by the fair, by industry division; and tax revenue generated, by source.

CONSPICUOUS CONSUMPTION: WATER IN LOUISIANA

(p. 17-24) By David J. Molina. Article on water supply-demand in Louisiana. Data sources include U.S. Interior Dept. Includes 6 tables showing total and/or per capita water use, for Louisiana, 3 neighboring States, and U.S., 1980; and percent increase in water use, for Louisiana, 1960-80 and 1980-2020 periods; all by user category.

GETTING COMPETITIVE: PORT DEVELOPMENT IN LOUISIANA

(p. 25-32) By Michael M. Liffmann. Article discussing port facility development in Louisiana. Data are from U.S. Army Corps of Engineers and other sources. Includes 2 charts and 5 tables showing the following, for Louisiana:

a. Freight traffic at 3 ports, 1972, 1975, and 1981, with 1981 detail by commodity and for foreign trade.

b. Federal funding for navigation improvements/port terminal projects, by agency and type of waterway; State funding for port terminal projects, by port; and requested vs. authorized capital spending on ports; FY77-82.

EXPORT TRADING COMPANY ACT

(p. 35-37) By Hsin-Min Tong and Timothy J. Watters. Article, with 1 table showing world trade shares for U.S. and 4 other industrialized countries, selected years 1970-83. Data are from U.S. Commerce Dept.

U2735–2   LOUISIANA ECONOMIC INDICATORS

Monthly.   Approx. 20 p.
ISSN 0279-6392.
LC SC 82-1131.
SRI/MF/complete, shipped quarterly

Monthly report on Louisiana State and local business and economic activity. Data are from State agencies, the Federal Government, and private or commercial sources. Data are current to month of publication or 1-3 months prior.

Issues generally contain brief narrative with summary charts and text tables, and 19 monthly economic indicator tables.

Beginning with June 1984 issue, report has undergone substantial revision; prior issues omit some monthly indicators.

Monthly indicator tables are listed below and appear in most issues. All additional features with substantial statistical content are described, as they appear, under "Statistical Features." Nonstatistical features are not covered.

Additional data may be found in the semiannual *Louisiana Business Survey,* available from the University of New Orleans, Division of Business and Economic Research, New Orleans LA 70148. *Business Survey* is not covered by SRI.

Availability: Louisiana State University: College of Business Administration, Division of Research, Louisiana Economic Indicators, Baton Rouge LA 70803, †; SRI/MF/complete, shipped quarterly.

Issues reviewed during 1984: Oct. 1983-June 1984 (P) (Vol. 3, Nos. 7-8; Vol. 4, Nos. 1-6) [No Dec. 1983 issue was published; Vol. 4, No. 4 incorrectly reads Vol. 4, No. 3].

MONTHLY TABLES:

[Unless otherwise noted, tables show data for month of coverage and 4-5 preceding months, with selected comparisons to previous periods. Data for parishes and other local areas generally include population.]

[1] Monthly summary [of State and U.S. indicators, for month of coverage only].

[2] Unemployment rate and leading indicators [index, for State and U.S., monthly for current year through month of coverage and 1-2 preceding years].

[3] Economic indicators: Louisiana [including employment by industry division; unemployment; unemployment insurance claims, payments, and exhaustions; manufacturing hours and earnings; tax revenues; construction contracts and value; beer sales; coal exports; corporate filings; telephone lines; mortgage loans; petroleum production by company; welfare recipients and payments; consumption of motor fuel by type; births and deaths; and car and truck sales by make].

[4-5] Louisiana State sales tax collections, by commodity [and kind of business], and by parishes.

[6] Louisiana State severance tax collections by parishes.

[7-9] Local sales tax collections, [by] parish school boards, police juries, and cities and towns, [including tax rates].

[10-17] Economic indicators: New Orleans, Baton Rouge, Lafayette, Lake Charles, Shreveport, Alexandria, Monroe, and Houma/Thibodaux metro areas, [generally including employment and unemployment, manufacturing earnings and hours; unemployment insurance claims and benefits; construction contracts and value; welfare recipients and payments; beer sales; convention attendance (New Orleans only); advertising linage; telephone lines; mortgage loans; port activity, with detail for exports and imports; airline cargo and passengers; births and deaths; sales and severance tax collections; and car and truck sales by make].

[18] Economic indicators: U.S. [including PPI, CPI, industrial production indexes, housing starts, bond yields, money supply, bank debits, financial institution deposits, employment, life insurance data, and energy production, consumption, and trade].

[19] Louisiana tourist traffic data: visitors to selected tourist attractions and information stations].

STATISTICAL FEATURES:

U2735–2.501: Feb. 1984 (Vol. 4, No. 2)

SPECIAL TABLE

[A] Louisiana commercial banks consolidated report of condition [including assets, liabilities, equity capital, operating income and expenses, and loan activity, 1978-82]. (p. 4-5)

U2735–2.502: May 1984 (Vol. 4, No. 5)

SPECIAL TABLE

[A] 60 largest commercial banks in Louisiana [ranked] by total assets [and including net income and loans, total deposits, bad debt expenses, return on assets and equity, earnings and dividends per share, and employment, as of] Dec. 31, 1983. (p. 21)

U2735–2.503: June 1984 (Vol. 4, No. 6)

SPECIAL TABLES

[A] Louisiana individual income tax [and general sales tax collections, and population, 1982-83; and per capita income, 1982; all by parish and MSA]. (p. 5)

[B] Minimum royalty payment [received] by parishes [1976-83]. (p. 6)

U2740
Louisiana State University: Department of Agricultural Economics and Agribusiness

U2740–1   AGRICULTURAL STATISTICS AND PRICES for Louisiana, 1978-83

Annual.   Aug. 1984.
39 p. no paging.
D.A.E. Research Rpt. No. 631.
LC 84-622963.
SRI/MF/complete

Annual report, by Lonnie L. Fielder, Jr., and Bergen A. Nelson, on Louisiana agricultural production, marketing, and finances, mostly 1978-83, with some data for 1984. Data are generally shown by commodity and/or parish and farming area, with some comparisons to total U.S.

Report covers production, prices, disposition, value, and, as applicable, acreage, yield, or inventory, for field crop, vegetable, fruit, nut, livestock, dairy, poultry, and apiary sectors.

Also includes data on farm income and production costs; number of farms and acreage; farmland use, ownership, and value; irrigated acreage; and feed/price ratios.

Data are compiled by the Dept of Agricultural Economics and Agribusiness of Louisiana State University, in cooperation with USDA.

Contains index (p. iii-v); and report, with 73 tables (34 p.).

Availability: Louisiana State University: Department of Agricultural Economics and Agribusiness, Baton Rouge LA 70803, †; SRI/MF/complete.

U2755
Louisiana State University: Middleton Library

U2755–1 STATISTICS OF SOUTHERN COLLEGE AND UNIVERSITY LIBRARIES, 1981/82
Annual. 1982. 3 p.
SRI/MF/complete

Annual report, compiled by Cecilia M. Landry, presenting library holdings, staff, and expenditures for 51 southern university libraries, 1981/82. Also includes data on 1981 fall enrollments.

Contains 1 table showing library volumes as of June 30, 1982; current periodicals, and microform titles and units held; expenditures for materials, salaries, and student help; total expenditures, expenditures from unrestricted (State-appropriated/self-generated) funds only, and ratios of library expenditures to total university expenditures; professional and other staff positions; and graduate and resident undergraduate enrollment; all by institution.

Availability: Louisiana State University: Middleton Library, Baton Rouge LA 70803-3300, †; SRI/MF/complete.

U3040
Memphis State University: Bureau of Business and Economic Research

U3040–1 MID-SOUTH BUSINESS JOURNAL
Quarterly. Approx. 15 p.
Pub. 885720.
LC 79-617891.
SRI/MF/complete

Quarterly report on economic, financial, and labor conditions in the U.S. and 5 Midsouth States (Alabama, Arkansas, Louisiana, Mississippi, and Tennessee). Data are from Federal, State, and private assn publications. Report is issued 1-2 months after quarter of coverage.

Each issue contains feature articles, often with statistics; and a statistical supplement insert, with 3 charts on economic indicator trends, and 4 tables listed below. Issues occasionally also include 1 table showing U.S. monthly CPI, 1970s-current quarter. An annual analysis of changes in the Midsouth economy appears in the 1st quarter issue.

Quarterly supplement statistics appear in all issues. All additional features with substantial statistical content are described, as they appear, under "Statistical Features." Nonstatistical features are not covered.

Availability: Memphis State University: Bureau of Business and Economic Research, Fogelman College of Business and Economics, Memphis TN 38152, †; SRI/MF/complete.

Issues reviewed during 1984: 3rd Qtr. 1983-2nd Qtr. 1984 (D) (Vol. III, No. 4; Vol. IV, Nos. 1-3).

QUARTERLY SUPPLEMENT TABLES:
[Most data are shown for 1 month of current quarter, with percent change from same month of previous year and/or during year to date. Data shown as percent change only are noted below. Data are shown by Midsouth State, with selected comparisons to U.S. and total Midsouth.]

[1] Labor [labor force, unemployment, manufacturing and nonmanufacturing employment, and average hours and earnings of manufacturing production workers].

[2] Construction [percent change in residential and nonresidential construction value, and dwelling unit permits issued].

[3] Finance [percent change in demand, time, and savings deposits].

[4] Savings and loan activity [mortgage loans made; and net savings flow].

STATISTICAL FEATURES:

U3040–1.501: 3rd Qtr. 1983 (Vol. III, No. 4)

MANUFACTURING GROWTH IN THE TENNESSEE VALLEY: TRENDS AND PROSPECTS

(p. 3-8) By Allan G. Pulsipher et al. Article on manufacturing growth in the TVA power service area, 1959-2000. Data are from government sources and scholarly reports. Includes 6 tables showing the following, for various periods within the ranges noted:

a. Manufacturing employment and production growth rates for TVA area, 1960-2000; and TVA and Bonneville Power Administration electric rates for large industrial customers, 1970-81; with comparisons to U.S.

b. Manufacturing jobs created in TVA area, by selected industry category, 1960-79; TVA area wage/salary per employee relative to U.S., for manufacturing and all sectors, 1959-79; and U.S. research-intensive and nonresearch-intensive manufacturing trade balances as percent of GDP, 1972-79.

EFFECT OF DISC ON SMALL EXPORTERS IN MANUFACTURING INDUSTRIES

(p. 15-19) By Clyde Posey and Joseph Szendi. Article on effectiveness of Domestic International Sales Corp. (DISC) legislation as a tax incentive for increasing exports of small manufacturers. Data are from a survey of 100 firms with sales of $50-100 million.

Includes 7 undated tables showing survey response concerning benefits and use of DISC.

U3040–1.502: 4th Qtr. 1983 (Vol. IV, No. 1)

ECONOMIC CHALLENGES AND OPPORTUNITIES FOR PROGRESS IN 1984

(p. 9-10) By John E. Gnuschke. Article, with 3 tables showing the following, generally for Oct. 1982-83: unemployment rate for U.S., Tennessee, and Memphis, with comparison to 1983 peak month; and Memphis SMSA retail sales in current and constant dollars, nonagricultural and manufacturing employment with comparison to lowest month in 1983, and coincident index of business activity.

ATTORNEYS AND EXPERT FINANCIAL WITNESSES

(p. 15-17, 20) By Linda M. Marquis and Virginia M. Moore. Article on attorneys' selection and use of expert financial witnesses. Data are from survey responses of 153 members of the Tennessee Trial Lawyers Assn and the Tennessee Defense Lawyers Assn.

Includes 4 tables showing survey response regarding professional characteristics of attorneys using and not using expert financial witnesses; types of cases in which expert financial witnesses are used; financial field or professional characteristics of expert witnesses chosen; and methods for locating financial experts.

U3040–1.503: 1st Qtr. 1984 (Vol. IV, No. 2)

POPULATION CHANGES IN TENNESSEE, 1970-80

(p. 3-9) By H. Ronald Moser and Kenneth W. Hollman. Article, with 3 tables showing population of 11 southern States; and Tennessee population by county, with county rank, and by city size category, with number of cities in each category; all for 1970 and 1980. Data are from the Census Bureau.

ANALYSIS OF ANNUAL CHANGES IN THE MID-SOUTH ECONOMY, ANNUAL FEATURE

(4 p.) Annual summary review of Midsouth economic indicator performance in 1983. Includes 1 chart and 6 tables cumulating data appearing in quarterly tables and also showing personal income for 1st 9 months and sales tax collections for full year 1983, with comparisons to 1982. Data generally are shown for 5 Midsouth States and U.S.

DEREGULATION OF PIGGYBACK: ITS IMPACT ON THE MEMPHIS RAILROAD INDUSTRY

(p. 19-22) By Thomas G. Ponzurick and R. Neil Southern. Article, with 1 table showing U.S. railroad piggyback (trailer on flat car) carloadings, 1961-83. Data are from *1982 Yearbook of Railroad Facts* and *Wall Street Journal.*

PRELIMINARY EVALUATION OF THE 1983 SOVIET SEED COTTON HARVEST

(p. 23-24) By Francis M. Stackenwalt. Article, with 2 tables showing Soviet Union seed cotton production targets, 1983-84, and actual production, 1983, by republic. Data are from *Cotton Outlook* and *Sovetskaia Kirgiziia.*

U3040–1.504: 2nd Quarter 1984 (Vol IV, No. 3)

ECONOMIC IMPACT OF THE MEDICAL COMMUNITY: A MEMPHIS CASE STUDY

(p. 3-8) By Howard P. Tuckman and Cyril F. Chang. Article analyzing impact of medical community on Memphis, Tenn., metro area economy. Data sources include Census Bureau, Tennessee Dept of Public Health, and University of Tennessee. Includes 4 tables showing the following, mostly for 1981:

a. FTE staff of individual hospitals and other health-related institutions or groups, with detail for short-term hospitals by occupation, training program, and hospital specialty.

b. Health service employment, and establishments by employment size, by establishment type (including drugstores and pharmaceutical companies); and expenditures of health care institutions and student groups, and health care expenditures of visitors, by institution or institution type.

CPE: DOES EXPERIENCE CHANGE ATTITUDES?

(p. 9-12) By Richard W. Jones et al. Article on accountants' opinions concerning State-mandated requirements for continuing professional education (CPE). Data are based on Jan. 1982 survey responses from 231 accountants in Florida (which requires CPE) and 213 accountants in Texas (no CPE as of survey date). Includes 7 tables.

IMPACT OF FEDERALLY-ASSISTED HOUSING ON SINGLE-FAMILY HOUSING SALES: 1970-1980

(p. 13-17) By Carol E. Babb et al. Article, with 4 tables comparing single-family home sale prices in areas with and without federally assisted housing, for selected Memphis, Tenn., neighborhoods, quadrennial periods 1968-79. Data sources include Census Bureau, Memphis Housing Authority, and Memphis Dept of Housing and Community Development.

U3130
Michigan State University:
Placement Services

U3130–1   RECRUITING TRENDS, 1983-84: A Study of 617 Businesses, Industries, Government Agencies, and Educational Institutions Employing New College Graduates
Annual. Nov. 28, 1983.
xi+69 p.
SRI/MF/complete

Annual report, by John D. Shingleton and L. Patrick Scheetz, on employer practices and plans with regard to hiring new college graduates, 1983/84 with selected comparisons to 1982/83.

Includes data on anticipated changes in new hires and starting salaries, by degree level, academic field, and employer type, and for women and minorities; employment offers vs. acceptances; use of on-campus interviews, reasons for changes, and percent of interviews resulting in hires; use of other recruiting methods; perception of new graduate quality; and factors affecting selection and rejection of applicants, including acceptable grade point averages, resume content, and interview questions.

Also includes data on total salaried employment; average starting salary by degree field and level; pre-employment cost per new hire; training programs, and incidence of underemployment among professional employees, by employer type; incidence of new hires resigning within 2 years, and reasons for resignation; types of corporate financial contributions to colleges/universities; and general employment outlook for new graduates by region.

Data are based on survey responses of 617 organizations employing new college graduates.

Contains summary (p. iii-xi); 45 tables, interspersed with brief narrative analyses (p. 1-63); and list of respondents (p. 64-69).

This is the 13th annual survey. SRI coverage begins with this edition.

Availability: Michigan State University: Placement Services, Student Services Bldg., East Lansing MI 48824-1113, $10.00; SRI/MF/complete.

U3255
Mississippi State University:
College of
Business and Industry

U3255–1   MISSISSIPPI EMPLOYMENT: 1976-81
Annual. Oct. 1983. v+97 p.
LC 84-621017.
SRI/MF/complete

Annual report providing data on farm and nonfarm employment in Mississippi counties, by industry division, 1976-81. Data are from ES-202 reports of the State Unemployment Insurance Programs and other Federal and private sources, and reflect employment location, rather than residence of employed persons.

Contents:

Preface; and listings of contents, tables, and chart. (p. ii-v)

Chapter I. Definitions and concepts. (p. 1)

Chapter II. Trends in employment in Mississippi. Includes narrative analysis, 1 map, and 3 summary tables showing distribution of farm and nonfarm employment in the U.S. and Mississippi, 1976-81; and employment growth rates for the U.S., Mississippi, and Mississippi SMSAs and counties, 1976-81 period. (p. 2-10)

Detailed area tables, with index, and 1 table repeated for the State and each SMSA and county, showing total employment; number of farm and nonfarm proprietors; farm employment; and nonfarm employment by industry division including government by level; 1976-81. (p. 11-97)

This is the 9th annual report.

Availability: Mississippi State University: College of Business and Industry, Research Division, PO Box 5288, Mississippi State MS 39762-5288, $7.75; SRI/MF/complete.

U3255–2   MISSISSIPPI BUSINESS REVIEW
Monthly. Approx. 20 p.
ISSN 0026-6167.
LC 54-40725.
SRI/MF/complete, shipped quarterly

Monthly report on Mississippi business activity, employment, industrial expansion, and other economic indicators. Also includes southeastern regional economic indicators, for 6 States and selected cities. Data are from Federal, State, and private sources. Month of data coverage is 2 months prior to cover date.

Each issue usually contains:

a. Feature articles, occasionally with statistics; and 11 monthly tables, listed below.

b. County indicators table, usually presenting annual data on an aspect of agricultural production, trade, employment, earnings, or tax revenues, for previous year or earlier.

Most monthly tables appear in all issues. Additional tables are sometimes included showing U.S. data reprinted from Federal sources; these tables are not described. All other additional features with substantial statistical content, including county indicator tables, are described, as they appear, under "Statistical Features." Nonstatistical features are not covered.

Availability: Mississippi Business Review, PO Box 5288, Mississippi State MS 39762-5288, $3.50 per yr.; SRI/MF/complete, shipped quarterly.

Issues reviewed during 1984: Oct. 1983-Sept. 1984 (P) (Vol. XLV, Nos. 4-12; Vol. XLVI, Nos. 1-3).

MONTHLY TABLES:

[Data are for Mississippi, unless otherwise noted. Most data are shown for month of coverage, preceding month, and same month of previous year. Table order may vary.]

[1] [Employment in] new and expanded industry [by location, firm, and product; no date; presents data available at time of publication].

[2] Indexes of selected economic indicators [retail and electric sales, gasoline consumption, and usually savings and loan assn loans].

[3] State economic indicators [employment by industry division, unemployment rate, average manufacturing earnings and hours, crude oil production, gasoline delivered to dealers, electricity sales, retail sales, agricultural receipts, and usually savings and loan assn and construction loans].

[4] Business activity by city [sales tax collections and building permits].

[5] SMSAs [employment data, and city sales tax collections, for Jackson and Biloxi-Gulfport].

[6] Sales indicated by sales tax collections, by county.

[7] Food stamp participation [payments and recipient households and persons], by county.

[8] Agriculture report [prices received and paid by farmers, by commodity].

[9] General fund collections [by source].

[10] Financial transactions, regional and U.S., from banks and S&L's [commercial bank, credit union, and savings and loan assn deposits, by type; and savings and loan assn mortgage commitments and mortgages outstanding; for U.S., Southeast region, and 6 southeastern States].

[11] Southeast regional economic indicators [including nonfarm employment, unemployment rate, plane passenger arrivals, value of nonresidential building permits, and number of residential single- and multi-family building permits, total and by selected city, for 6 southeastern States].

STATISTICAL FEATURES:

U3255–2.501: Oct. 1983 (Vol. XLV, No. 4)
COUNTY INDICATORS, ANNUAL TABLE

[A] Estimated effective buying income for designated counties, 1981-82. (back cover)

U3255–2.502: Nov. 1983 (Vol. XLV, No. 5)
COUNTY INDICATORS TABLE

[A] Estimates of population, by county, 1981-82. (back cover)

U3255–2.503: Dec. 1983 (Vol. XLV, No. 6)
EVALUATION OF THE DETERIORATING U.S. COMPETITIVE POSITION IN WORLD MARKETS

(p. 3-7) By Francis A. Sailer and B. R. Baliga. Article, with 2 tables showing share of U.S. market and share of world export market for 13 key U.S. industries, various years 1960-79. Data are from *Business Week.*

CASH RECEIPTS FROM FARM MARKETINGS, MISSISSIPPI, 1980-82

(p. 11) Table showing cash receipts from farm marketings by commodity, government payments to farmers, and value of products consumed on farms, 1980-82. Data are from the Mississippi Crop and Livestock Reporting Service.

U3255–2.504: Jan. 1984 (Volume XLV, No. 7)

COUNTY INDICATORS TABLE

[A] Sales indicated by sales tax collections by county, [and State total for wholesale and retail sales], FY83. (back cover).

U3255–2.505: Feb. 1984 (Vol. XLV, No. 8)

INFLATION HEDGES COMPOUND ANNUAL RATE OF RETURN

(p. 6) Table showing compound annual rate of return at 1, 5, and 10 years from investment, for real estate and various precious/rare commodities, with comparison to CPI (no date). Data are from *The Wall Street Journal*.

1983 ANNUAL CROP SUMMARY: ESTIMATED ACREAGE, YIELD AND PRODUCTION OF CROPS WITH 1982 COMPARISONS

(back cover) Table showing acres planted and harvested, yield, and production, by crop, for Mississippi and U.S., 1982-83. Data are from Federal and State agencies.

U3255–2.506: Mar. 1984 (Vol. XLV, No. 9)

AGRICULTURAL INDEXES, MISSISSIPPI AND U.S.

(p. 14) Table showing indexes of prices received by Mississippi farmers by commodity, with summary comparison to U.S. farm prices received and paid, Jan. 15, 1983-84 and Dec. 15, 1983. Data are from Mississippi Crop and Livestock Reporting Service.

MISSISSIPPI EMPLOYMENT SECURITY COMMISSION SALARY DATA: INDUSTRY OCCUPATIONS COMMON TO ALL INDUSTRIES

(back cover) Table showing employment and employers, average hours and starting salary, and salary range, for 33 occupations in Mississippi (no date). Data are from Mississippi Employment Security Commission.

U3255–2.507: Apr. 1984 (Vol. XLV, No. 10)

COUNTY INDICATORS, ANNUAL TABLE

[A] Annual wages of workers covered by Mississippi employment security law [by county], 1981-82. (back cover)

AGRICULTURAL REPORT, FEB. 1984

(p. 14) Table showing indexes of prices received by Mississippi farmers by commodity, with summary comparison to U.S. farm prices received and paid, Feb. 15, 1983-84 and Jan. 15, 1984. Data are from Mississippi Crop and Livestock Reporting Service.

U3255–2.508: May 1984 (Vol. XLV, No. 11)

COUNTY INDICATORS, ANNUAL TABLE

[A] Motor vehicle registration, by county, 1981-82. (back cover)

ANALYSIS OF RECENT SAVINGS AND LOAN ASSN MERGERS

(p. 3-10) By Theodor Kohers and W. Gary Simpson. Article identifying financial characteristics of savings and loan assns that are potential merger candidates, based on statistical analysis of financial ratios for matched samples of assns that did and did not merge during 1977-82. Data for sample assns were taken from reports filed with FHLBB.

Includes 5 tables presenting results of the statistical analysis.

U3255–2.509: June 1984 (Vol. XLV, No. 12)

COUNTY INDICATORS, ANNUAL TABLE

[A] Average monthly employment covered by the Employment Security Law, by county, 1981-82. (back cover)

U3255–2.510: July 1984 (Vol. XLVI, No. 1)

COUNTY INDICATORS, ANNUAL TABLE

[A] Timber severance tax collections by county, 1982-83 [with percent change from 1981]. (back cover)

CROP AND LIVESTOCK REPORTING SERVICE

(p. 13) Table showing indexes of prices received by Mississippi farmers by commodity, with summary comparison to U.S. farm prices received and paid, May 15, 1983-84 and Apr. 15, 1984. Data are from Mississippi Crop and Livestock Reporting Service.

U3255–2.511: Aug. 1984 (Vol. XLVI, No. 2)

COUNTY INDICATORS, ANNUAL TABLE

[A] Estimated effective buying income for designated counties, 1982-83. (back cover)

For description of previous table, for 1981-82, see U3255-2.501, above.

U3255–2.512: Sept. 1984 (Vol. XLVI, No. 3)

COUNTY INDICATORS, ANNUAL TABLE

[A] Indicated sales (retail/wholesale), by county [1982-83]. (back cover)

U3255–3 MISSISSIPPI PERSONAL INCOME: Selected Years 1976-81
Annual. Oct. 1983.
v+119 p.
LC 84-621016.
SRI/MF/complete

Annual report on personal income for Mississippi SMSAs and counties, by source, 1976-81. Data are from U.S. Commerce Dept Bureau of Economic Analysis.

Contents:

Preface; and listings of contents, tables, and charts. (p. ii-v)

Chapter I-II. Introduction, and definitions and concepts. (p. 1-6)

Chapter III. Trends in personal income in Mississippi. Includes narrative analysis, 1 chart, and 3 summary tables showing total and per capita annual personal income, Southeast and/or U.S. and Mississippi, 1963-82; and distribution of Mississippi earnings by source (farm, private nonfarm, and Federal and State/local government), selected years 1929-81. (p. 7-13)

Chapter IV. Mississippi county personal income. Includes 3 maps, and 4 tables showing total and per capita annual personal income for total State and by SMSA and county, 1976-81; county rankings in per capita income relative to State and U.S. in 1981; and State, SMSA, and county populations, 1976-81. (p. 14-32)

Detailed area tables, with index, and 1 table repeated for the State and each SMSA and county, showing labor and proprietor income by type and by industry division (including Federal civilian and military, and State/local government); data adjustments, including other sources of income, and conversion to residence basis; and per capita income; 1976-81. (p. 33-119)

This is the 12th annual report.

Availability: Mississippi State University: College of Business and Industry, Research Division, PO Box 5288, Mississippi State MS 39762-5288, $8.85; SRI/MF/complete.

U3255–4 MISSISSIPPI STATISTICAL ABSTRACT, 1983
Annual. Dec. 1983.
viii+812 p.
LC 75-629881.
SRI/MF/complete

Annual compilation, for 1983, of detailed demographic, social, governmental, and economic statistics for Mississippi. Data are mostly for 1980-82, with trends from the 1960s and selected historical data. Data are from Federal and State government, private industry, and research or trade assn sources.

Report is designed to present a comprehensive overview of the State. Extensive socioeconomic, demographic, and geographic breakdowns are shown, as applicable, for most topics. These breakdowns include data by city, county, SMSA, urban-rural status, school district, sex, age, race, marital status, industry, and commodity. Comparisons to U.S. and selected neighboring States are also often included.

Contains introduction and contents and chart listings (p. iii-viii); 26 maps, 24 charts, and 347 tables, arranged in 16 sections, described below (p. 1-802); and a subject index (p. 803-812).

This is the 15th annual edition of the *Abstract*.

Availability: Mississippi State University: College of Business and Industry, Research Division, PO Box 5288, Mississippi State MS 39762-5288, $23.00+$1.50 postage and handling; SRI/MF/complete.

TABLE SECTIONS:
[Tables in each section are preceded by a summary of principal data sources, and a table listing. Data sources are shown beneath each table.]

U3255–4.1: Section 1: Recreation, Geography, and Climate

(p. 1-78) Contains 3 maps and 15 tables. Includes land area; temperature and precipitation averages and extremes, by station; Federal lands; recreation areas, acreage, and attendance; parks, reservoirs, and national forest facilities; fish and wildlife area acreages; wild turkey and deer kills, by management area; lake acreage and fishermen, by lake; and certified boats.

U3255–4.2: Section 2: Population

(p. 79-106) Contains 2 maps, 2 charts, and 12 tables. Includes population and housing units; land area; and migration.

U3255–4.3: Section 3: Health and Vital Statistics

(p. 107-183) Contains 3 maps and 42 tables. Includes births; fertility rates; deaths by leading causes; infant and maternal deaths; marriages; and divorces, by cause, years of marriage, and number of minor children.

Also includes licensed nursing care institutions, capacity, admissions, patients, discharges, and deaths; hospitals, capacity, utilization, and staff; physicians by specialty; and dentists.

U3255–4.4: Section 4: Education

(p. 184-259) Contains 1 map, 3 charts, and 29 tables. Includes State finances; public and private schools; public school enrollment, attendance, finances, teachers and administrative staff and average salaries; high school graduates; and school dropouts, retention, and attrition.

Also includes junior college and college/university enrollment, by public and private institution; public junior college finances, facilities, and student transportation; education appropriations, by legislative bill and post-secondary institution; wealth and tax collections per pupil; and vocational/technical enrollment and finances.

U3255–4.5: Section 5: Labor Force, Employment, and Earnings

(p. 260-336) Contains 1 map and 19 tables. Includes nonfarm employment; selected industry hours and earnings; covered business establishments, employment, payroll, and wages; unemployment benefits paid, unemployment insurance tax rates, employer contributions, and trust fund balances; and labor force by employment status.

U3255–4.6: Section 6: Manufacturing and Trade

(p. 337-430) Contains 3 charts and 12 tables. Includes business establishments, employment, and wages; wholesale/retail activities, gross sales and taxes, and taxpayers; new and expanded industries, employment, and capital investment, by firm; and business births and deaths, active establishments, and ownership changes.

U3255–4.7: Section 7: Transportation

(p. 431-481) Contains 3 maps and 26 tables. Includes motor vehicle registrations; government vehicles; highway and motor use tax revenues; licensed motor carriers and revenues; railroad employment and taxes, and mileage operated by railroad; and ICC rail abandonment applications and status.

Also includes domestic and foreign freight traffic at 3 harbors; Mississippi River freight and passenger traffic at 8 ports; Yazoo River freight traffic; aircraft departures, by airport and type of aircraft; air passengers and cargo, including U.S. and foreign mail, by city; pilots and flight instructors; active and abandoned airports; and airport specifications.

U3255–4.8: Section 8: Communications and Public Utilities

(p. 482-506) Contains 2 maps and 17 tables. Includes newspapers; electricity revenues per kWh for all 50 States; radio and TV stations; post offices; electricity generation and capacity by type of fuel, and utility customers, revenues, and sales, by service class; public utility commission membership and employment; telephones in use and percent of households with telephone service; and natural gas utility prices, customers, sales, and revenues, by service class.

U3255–4.9: Section 9: Banking, Finance, and Insurance

(p. 507-541) Contains 1 chart and 27 tables. Includes assets, liabilities, income, and expenses, for credit unions, all lenders, and banks; failed banks, depositors, deposits, and FDIC disbursements; banks, branches, accounts, and deposits; bank assets by bank, arranged by city; and savings and loan assns and assets, and mortgage loan holdings.

Also includes life insurance policies and amount in force, purchases, and payments; health insurance benefit payments and hospitalization data; mortgages owned by life insurance companies; and loans by Veterans Farm and Home Board.

U3255–4.10: Section 10: Law Enforcement, Courts, and Crime

(p. 542-585) Contains 2 maps, 5 charts, and 23 tables. Includes State police employment and enforcement activities, including duty hours; traffic accidents, injuries, fatalities, and property damage; juvenile court cases, including place of detention; prisoners; and crimes and crime rate.

U3255–4.11: Section 11: Forest and Mineral Products

(p. 586-624) Contains 2 maps, 1 chart, and 27 tables. Includes forest land area, by ownership; forest fires and acreage burned; national forest acreage, timber sales and harvest, grazing use, visitors, reforestation and improvement needs, cooperative management activities, and road and bridge construction; State forestry commission finances; timber severance tax collections; and commercial timberland ownership, sawtimber, and growing stock.

Also includes mineral production and value; sand, gravel, and clay sales/use; principal producers of quarry products; natural gas marketed production; producing wells and oil, water, and gas production; petroleum refinery capacity, by refinery, and working storage capacity; liquefied petroleum gas and ethane sales; and energy consumption by type and using sector.

U3255–4.12: Section 12: Public Finance and Tax Revenue

(p. 625-654) Contains 6 charts and 10 tables. Includes State general and special fund receipts and expenditures; sales tax payments to cities, including amount to air/water pollution board; corporation taxpayers, revenue, taxable income, franchise tax collections, and annual fees; personal income taxpayers, taxable income, and gross tax; and oil, gas, and timber severance tax payments.

U3255–4.13: Section 13: Social Insurance and Welfare Services

(p. 655-679) Contains 4 maps and 11 tables. Includes welfare appeals hearings; welfare program finances, employees, caseloads, payments, and child support collections; foster home program board payments; individuals eligible for assistance under Aid to Dependent Children; and food stamp program coupon value.

U3255–4.14: Section 14: Government and Politics

(p. 680-732) Contains 2 maps, 1 chart, and 31 tables. Includes votes cast for President, presidential electors, and U.S. Representatives; voting age population; composition of U.S. Congress; and defense contract awards and payroll.

Also includes State/local government employment and payroll; Federal civilian employment; State/local government indebtedness and expenditures; veterans and veterans' benefits; and rosters of State elected and appointed officials, and court districts.

U3255–4.15: Section 15: Construction and Housing

(p. 733-753) Contains 1 chart and 12 tables. Includes housing units authorized and value; HUD disbursements; construction contract value; savings assn mortgage lending; FHA property improvement and mobile home loans and proceeds, mortgages insured, and defaults; savings and loan assn loans closed and savings activity; mortgage purchases, by type; FHA-insured mortgages and loans; and manufactured housing lenders and homes shipped to retailers.

U3255–4.16: Section 16: Agriculture

(p. 754-802) Contains 1 map, 1 chart, and 34 tables. Includes State rankings by farm cash receipts; farm income and production expenses; farm cash receipts, by commodity; Federal payments, by program; production, use, sales, and/or value, for selected field crops, sweet potatoes, pecans, and peaches; cotton production; calf crop; number of cattle/calves; and egg and broiler production.

U3350
New Mexico State University: Center for Business Research and Services

U3350–1   **1980 CENSUS FACT BOOK: STATE PLANNING AND DEVELOPMENT, New Mexico**
Series. For individual publication data, see below.
SRI/MF/complete

Report, published in 8 volumes, presenting 1980 U.S. Census of Population and Housing summary findings for New Mexico, with selected trends. Includes the following data, by county, for 1980 unless otherwise noted:

a. Population: trends, various years 1910-80; by urban-rural status, and by sex and age group,

1970 and 1980; age 15/older, by sex and marital status; by race-ethnicity (includes American Indian and Asian American), by age group; and Spanish origin, by race and age group.

b. Housing units: by tenure, by number of persons per unit; and owner occupied, by value.

c. Land area and population density, 1970 and 1980; and per capita personal income, 1970 and 1979.

Data are primarily from 1980 Census Summary Tape File 1.

Report consists of a State summary volume, with introduction, 7 charts repeated for the State and each planning district, and accompanying district analyses; and 1 volume for each planning district, with introduction, chart listing, and 8 charts. Each volume also includes 5 appendices, with demographic trend analysis, 4 tables, and Census information. Individual volumes are listed below.

Availability: New Mexico State University: Center for Business Research and Services, College of Business Administration and Economics, Box 3CR, Las Cruces NM 88003, $45.00; SRI/MF/complete.

VOLUMES:

U3350–1.1: State of New Mexico
[Monograph. [1983.] 95 p. no paging. SRI/MF/complete.]

U3350–1.2: District No. 1: McKinley and San Juan Counties, New Mexico
[Monograph. [1983.] 37 p. no paging. SRI/MF/complete.]

U3350–1.3: District No. 2: Colfax, Los Alamos, Mora, Rio Arriba, San Miguel, Santa Fe, and Taos Counties, New Mexico
[Monograph. [1983.] 65 p. no paging. SRI/MF/complete.]

U3350–1.4: District No. 3: Bernalillo, Sandoval, Torrance, and Valencia Counties, New Mexico
[Monograph. [1983.] 64 p. no paging. SRI/MF/complete.]

U3350–1.5: District No. 4: Curry, De Baca, Guadalupe, Harding, Quay, Roosevelt, and Union Counties, New Mexico
[Monograph. [1983.] 66 p. no paging. SRI/MF/complete.]

U3350–1.6: District No. 5: Catron, Grant, Hidalgo, and Luna Counties, New Mexico
[Monograph. [1983.] 49 p. no paging. SRI/MF/complete.]

U3350–1.7: District No. 6: Chaves, Eddy, Lea, Lincoln, and Otero Counties, New Mexico
[Monograph. [1983.] 55 p. no paging. SRI/MF/complete.]

U3350–1.8: District No. 7: Dona Ana, Sierra, and Socorro Counties, New Mexico
[Monograph. [1983.] 43 p. no paging. SRI/MF/complete.]

U3600
North Dakota State University: Agricultural Experiment Station

U3600–1   NORTH DAKOTA AGRICULTURAL STATISTICS, 1984
Annual.   June 1984.   96 p.
Ag. Statistics No. 53.
SRI/MF/complete

Annual report on North Dakota agricultural production and marketing, mostly 1982-83, with trends from the 1970s and some data for 1984. Data generally are shown by commodity, county, and/or district.

Report covers production, prices, sales, value, and, as applicable, acreage, yield, inventory, stocks, and/or storage, for crop, livestock, dairy, poultry, and apiary sectors.

Report also includes data on farm real estate and finances; weather; prices paid for selected items; farm labor, wages, and custom rates; fertilizer sales and use; share of U.S. exports; crop insurance; and grain shipments and storage capacity.

Data are compiled by North Dakota Crop and Livestock Reporting Service.

Contains contents listing (p. 2-3); 5 sections, with brief narrative summaries, 49 charts and maps, and 115 tables (p. 6-95); and guide to historical agricultural data series (inside back cover).

This is the 27th annual report.

Availability: North Dakota Crop and Livestock Reporting Service, 345 U.S. Post Office, Federal Bldg., PO Box 3166, Fargo ND 58108, $4.00; SRI/MF/complete.

U3730
Northwestern University: Placement Center

U3730–1   NORTHWESTERN ENDICOTT REPORT: Trends in the Employment of College and University Graduates in Business and Industry, 1984
Annual.   1983.
17 p. no paging.
ISSN 0097-6297.
LC 75-642040.
SRI/MF/complete

Annual survey report, by Victor R. Lindquist, on corporate plans for hiring 1984 college/university graduates. Includes number of bachelor's and master's degree recipients to be hired at various salary levels, by field, with comparison to 1983.

Also includes corporate outlook assessment; recruiting trends, and outlook to 1988; place of employee recruitment in company planning process; career planning advice for freshman students; and views on resumes, and on recruitment of persons with Master's in Business Administration (MBA) degrees, liberal arts graduates, teachers, and holders of PhD degrees in the humanities.

Data are based on responses of 262 companies in 26 States and D.C. to a Nov. 1983 survey. Most respondents are national large or medium-sized companies that have recruited college graduates for many years.

Contains introduction (1 p.); survey findings, with text statistics and 3 tables (15 p.); and summary (1 p.).

This is the 38th annual survey.

Availability: Northwestern University: Placement Center, Scott Hall, Evanston IL 60201, $5.00; SRI/MF/complete.

U3780
Ohio State University: Center for Human Resource Research

U3780–1   CENTER FOR HUMAN RESOURCE RESEARCH REPORTS
Series.   For individual publication data, see below.
SRI/MF/complete

Continuing series of reports by the Center for Human Resource Research on contemporary issues, with emphasis on labor market research and manpower planning.

Most reports are based on statistical analysis of data from the National Longitudinal Surveys (NLS) of Labor Market Experience, covering 20,000 older men, middle-aged women, and young men and women. The surveys have been conducted annually or biennially by the Census Bureau since 1966.

Beginning in 1979, the NLS project also includes an additional youth panel survey of approximately 13,000 young men and women, including military personnel. The youth panel is interviewed annually by National Opinion Research Center.

Only reports containing statistical material are covered in SRI. Reports reviewed during 1984 are described below. Previous reports in this series covered in SRI are described in SRI 1980 and 1981 Annuals, under this number.

Availability: Ohio State University: Center for Human Resource Research, College of Administrative Science, 650 Ackerman Rd., Suite A, Columbus OH 43202, $1.00 postage and handling; SRI/MF/complete.

U3780–1.16: Demographics of Alcohol Use Among Respondents of the 1982 National Longitudinal Survey of Labor Market Experience of Youth Panel
[Monograph. Jan. 1983. 10+12 p. SRI/MF/complete.]

By Joan E. Crowley. Paper discussing alcohol use patterns among youth, based on 1982 NLS youth panel survey. Includes 2 tables showing distribution of survey responses to questions about extent and type of alcohol use, by race/ethnicity (black, white, and Hispanic) and sex, and by age and sex, 1982.

U3780–1.17: Perceived Utility of Job Training Methods Among Young Men
[Monograph. Nov. 1983. 31 p. SRI/MF/complete.]

By Stephen M. Hills and Richard Santos. Paper discussing perceived usefulness of job training methods for young men, based on 1980 NLS survey of 3,370 men age 28-38.

Includes 13 tables primarily showing job training methods used and perceived as most helpful, with selected detail by race, educational attainment, occupation, and industry, 1980.

U3780–1.18: Welfare Incidence and Welfare Dependency Among American Women: A Longitudinal Examination

[Monograph. Feb. 1983. 58 p. var. paging. SRI/MF/complete.]

By Frank L. Mott. Paper analyzing patterns of welfare dependence among young women, by race, 1968-80. Examines relationship between welfare dependence and selected factors, including marital status, parenthood, employment, educational attainment, living in metro area, living in South, and parents' poverty and welfare status, with detail for AFDC and food stamp programs.

Data are based on responses of over 3,000 women age 14-24 in 1968, to 10 NLS reinterview surveys conducted during 1968-80.

Includes 15 tables showing response distributions and results of statistical analyses.

U3780–2 NATIONAL LONGITUDINAL SURVEYS HANDBOOK, 1983-84
Recurring (irreg.) 1983.
ii+152 p.
SRI/MF/complete

Recurring handbook for users of data from the National Longitudinal Surveys (NLS) of labor market experience, providing description of survey objectives, samples, and data organization.

NLS data are based on Census Bureau interviews of approximately 20,000 persons conducted annually or biennially since 1966. Beginning in 1979, an additional survey panel of 12,700 young men and women, including 1,300 military personnel, was added to the study, and is interviewed annually by National Opinion Research Center.

Contains preface and contents listing (p. i-ii); structure, development, and methodology of NLS project (p. 1-13); list of NLS data base variables, and description of computer file organization (p. 15-74); and bibliography, sample data pages, and order forms for survey data (p. 75-152).

Handbook was first issued in 1973 and is updated every 1½-3 years; for description of previous edition, for 1980, see SRI 1980 Annual, under this number.

A continuing series of research reports based on NLS data is covered by SRI under U3780-1.

Availability: Ohio State University: Center for Human Resource Research, College of Administrative Science, 650 Ackerman Rd., Suite A, Columbus OH 43202, †; SRI/MF/complete.

U3830
Ohio State University: Ohio Agricultural Research and Development Center

U3830–1 OHIO AGRICULTURAL STATISTICS, 1983
Annual. Aug. 1984. 57 p.
LC 58-40536.
SRI/MF/complete

Annual report on Ohio agricultural production, marketing, and finances, mostly 1982-83, with some data for 1984, and trends from 1961. Data generally are shown by commodity and county and/or district, with selected comparisons to other States and total U.S.

Generally covers production, prices, value, and, as applicable, acreage, yield, inventory, and disposition, for field crop, vegetable, fruit, livestock, poultry, and dairy sectors.

Also includes data on number and acreage of farms; commercial grain storage capacity; weather; exports; fertilizers; mink operations; prices paid by farmers for selected items; and farm value, rent, income, production costs, credit, and debt outstanding.

Data are compiled by the Ohio Crop Reporting Service.

Contains contents listing (p. 1); and 10 maps, 12 charts, and 89 tables, with interspersed narrative summaries (p. 2-56).

Availability: Ohio Crop Reporting Service, Rm. 608, Federal Bldg., 200 N. High St., Columbus OH 43215, ‡; SRI/MF/complete.

U4110
Pennsylvania State University: College of Business Administration

U4110–1 PENNSYLVANIA BUSINESS SURVEY
Monthly. Approx. 4 p.
ISSN 0031-4382.
LC A53-9621.
SRI/MF/complete, shipped quarterly

Monthly report on economic conditions in Pennsylvania. Includes data on industrial production, employment, and construction activity.

Contents:

a. Narrative analysis with approximately 5 trend charts, and occasional summary tables, including 1 table showing State leading and coincident indexes for month of publication and several previous months; and occasional special features with substantial statistical content.

b. Monthly table on Pennsylvania economic indicators, showing number and seasonally adjusted indexes for manufacturing and nonmanufacturing jobs, manufacturing hours and payroll, steel and coal mining production, industrial electric power sales, construction contracts awarded, labor force by employment status, CPI in 3 metro areas, and initial unemployment benefit claims, for month 2 months prior to cover date, previous month, and same month of previous year.

c. Quarterly personal income table, showing Pennsylvania and U.S. seasonally adjusted income, by type and industry division, for quarter ended approximately 6 months prior to cover date, with percent change from previous quarter and same quarter of previous year.

d. Quarterly employment table, showing Pennsylvania and U.S. employment percent change, employment, and unemployment and labor force participation rates, by sex and race and for youths, for quarter ended approximately 5 months prior to cover date and selected previous periods.

e. Quarterly "Around the State" feature, with trend charts and 1 table, repeated for each Pennsylvania SMSA and metro area, showing most of the economic indicators covered in the monthly State table, for quarter prior to cover date, previous quarter, and same quarter of previous year.

Quarterly features are accompanied by narrative summaries.

Monthly table appears in all issues. Special features with substantial statistical content are described, as they appear, under "Statistical Features;" latest periods of coverage for quarterly data are also noted. Nonstatistical features are not covered.

Availability: Pennsylvania State University: College of Business Administration, Center for Research, 103 Business Administration Bldg. II, University Park PA 16802, $6.00 per yr.; SRI/MF/complete, shipped quarterly.

Issues reviewed during 1984: Nov. 1983-Oct. 1984 (P) (Vol. 24, Nos. 11-12; Vol. 25, Nos. 1-10).

STATISTICAL FEATURES:

U4110–1.501: Nov. 1983 (Vol. 24, No. 11)
QUARTERLY DATA

"Around the State" local economic indicators, for 3rd quarter 1983.

U4110–1.502: Dec. 1983 (Vol. 24, No. 12)
QUARTERLY DATA

Personal income, for 2nd quarter 1983.

U4110–1.503: Jan. 1984 (Vol. 25, No. 1)
QUARTERLY DATA

Employment, for 3rd quarter 1983.

U4110–1.504: Feb. 1984 (Vol. 25, No. 2)
QUARTERLY DATA

"Around the State" local economic indicators, for 4th quarter 1983.

ANNUAL REVIEW OF MAJOR ECONOMIC INDICATORS, PENNSYLVANIA AND THE U.S.

Table presenting selected economic indicators for Pennsylvania and U.S., 1982-83. Indicators generally are the same as those presented in monthly table on Pennsylvania economic indicators, but also include wage/salary jobs by industry division.

U4110–1.505: Mar. 1984 (Vol. 25, No. 3)
QUARTERLY DATA

Personal income, for 3rd quarter 1983.

U4110–1.506: Apr. 1984 (Vol. 25, No. 4)

QUARTERLY DATA

Employment, for 4th quarter 1983.

U4110–1.507: May 1984 (Vol. 25, No. 5)

QUARTERLY DATA

"Around the State" local economic indicators, for 1st quarter 1984.

U4110–1.508: June 1984 (Vol. 25, No. 6)

PERSONAL INCOME GROWTH REMAINS MODERATE, ANNUAL FEATURE

(2 p.) Annual article, with 2 tables showing Pennsylvania total and per capita personal income, as follows: by SMSA, and for Beaver County and aggregate SMSA and non-SMSA counties, 1981-82; and for total State, 1983. Also includes each SMSA's per capita income ranking among U.S. SMSAs, 1982; and selected other comparisons to total U.S. Data are from U.S. Commerce Dept.

U4110–1.509: July 1984 (Vol. 25, No. 7)

QUARTERLY DATA

Employment, for 1st quarter 1984.

U4110–1.510: Aug. 1984 (Vol. 25, No. 8)

QUARTERLY DATA

"Around the State" local economic indicators, for 2nd quarter 1984.

U4110–1.511: Sept. 1984 (Vol. 25, No. 9)

QUARTERLY DATA

Personal income, for 1st quarter 1984.

SPATIAL VARIATIONS IN PENNSYLVANIA'S ECONOMY, 1962-81

(p. 4-5) By E. Willard Miller. Article, with 2 tables showing Pennsylvania average monthly employment in manufacturing and service-producing industries, for 16-17 leading counties arranged by State region, 1962 and 1981, with comparison to 1981 employment estimate based on statewide trend.

U4110–1.512: Oct. 1984 (Vol. 25, No. 10)

QUARTERLY DATA

Employment, for 2nd quarter 1984.

U4130
Pennsylvania State University: Pennsylvania State Data Center

U4130–3   PENNSYLVANIA COUNTIES: 1980 Census Data Atlas
Monograph. Sept. 1983.
91 p. Rpt. No. PSDC80-4-83.
SRI/MF/complete

Report presenting 1980 Census of Population and Housing selected findings for Pennsylvania counties. Includes population and household characteristics, income, poverty, employment, and housing.

Data are from Census Summary Tape File 3A (STF3A), and cover items most frequently requested from the Pennsylvania State Data Center.

Contains contents listing (1 p.); introduction, 1 summary table, and 16 maps preceded by index (p. 1-20); county profiles, with index, and 22 tables listed below, repeated for Pennsylvania and each county (p. 21-89); and appendix, with census definitions (p. 90-91).

A similar publication, presenting data for total U.S. and each census region, census division, and State, is also published by the issuing agency, but is not covered in SRI.

Availability: Pennsylvania State University: Pennsylvania State Data Center, Institute of State and Regional Affairs, Capitol Campus, Middletown PA 17057, $10.00; SRI/MF/complete.

TABLES:

[Tables show data for Pennsylvania and each county. Data are for 1980, unless otherwise noted.]

1-4. Total persons; population percent change, 1970-80 [period]; households; and families.

5-6. Persons by age and sex; and persons 15 years/over by marital status [and sex].

7. Households by [number of] persons in households.

8. Persons 25 years/over by years of school completed.

9-10. Employed persons 16 years/over by industry [division] and occupation [group].

11-12. Persons by household type; and persons in occupied housing by units in structure [and for mobile homes, with percent of units with telephone and owner occupied, and percent of persons 5 years/over in same residence since 1975].

13. Persons by race [and ethnic group including American Indians, Asian/Pacific Islanders, and Hispanics, by sex].

14. Persons 16/over with unemployment in 1979 [by race and Spanish origin, with mean weeks unemployed, all by sex; and total unemployment rate].

15. Poverty status by race and Spanish origin [and poverty rate].

16-17. Median income [of] households and families.

18. Median gross rent.

19. Families with workers in 1979 and [mean] family income [by number of workers].

20-22. Per capita income; median monthly homeowner costs; and 1970 population.

U4130–4   PENNSYLVANIA SCHOOL DISTRICTS: 1980 Census Data Summary
Monograph. Dec. 1983.
217 p.
Rpt. No. PSDC80-5-83.
SRI/MF/complete

Report presenting 1980 Census of Population and Housing selected findings for Pennsylvania school districts and counties. Includes data on population and household characteristics, including education, employment, income, and poverty status; and housing characteristics.

Data are from U.S. Census Summary Tape File 1F (STF1F) and Summary Tape File 3F (STF3F), and cover items most frequently requested from the Pennsylvania State Data Center, and items of special interest to school districts.

STF1F and STF3F were created by cross-referencing census data with school district boundary information collected by U.S. Dept of Education.

Contains contents and table listing (2 p.); introduction and census definitions (p. 1-3); and 15 extended tables, listed below (p. 4-217).

Availability: Pennsylvania State University: Pennsylvania State Data Center, Institute of State and Regional Affairs, Capitol Campus, Middletown PA 17057, $25.00; SRI/MF/complete.

TABLES:

[Tables show data for Pennsylvania by county and school district, 1980, unless otherwise noted.]

1. Summary of general population characteristics [total population and percent female, under 18, and 65/over; population by race and Spanish origin; and households, persons per household, and families]. (p. 4-18)

2. Total population by age [children 5/under and 6-18 and adults 19-64 and 65/over]. (p. 19-32)

3-5. Children by age [under 5 and 5-17] and by race; children under 18 by household type [living with own parents (married couple or single parent), not living with own parents, and in group quarters] and relationship [to others in household]; and children 5-17 by abililty to speak English [by whether only English, Spanish, or other language spoken at home]. (p. 33-75)

6. Summary of general housing characteristics [total and occupied units; owner-occupied units; occupied units lacking complete plumbing facilities, and with 1.01/more persons per room; and owner- and renter-occupied units by value or contract rent range, with median value and rent]. (p. 76-90)

7. Social and economic characteristics [including mean or median income per capita, and for families, households, and unrelated individuals; percent of persons and families below the poverty level; percent of persons graduated from high school and college, with work disability, and employed in service, retail/wholesale, and manufacturing sectors; and unemployment rate]. (p. 91-104)

8-9. Persons 3 years/over by school enrollment [by level including college, with detail for private schools]; and persons 16-19 by school enrollment, years of school completed, and labor force status [shows persons in school and in armed forces, and labor force status of high school graduates and nongraduates]. (p. 105-133)

10. Persons 25 years/over by years of school completed. (p. 134-147)

11-12. Persons 16 years/over: by labor force and employment status [and including persons in armed forces, and women in labor force with children present]; and employed persons by occupation [group]. (p. 148-175)

13-14. Family, household, and per capita income [with family income detail by householder's race]; and persons [below poverty level] by race and Spanish origin; 1979. (p. 176-203)

15. Families with children 0-17 years [and percent below poverty level] by family type [all families with children, and families headed by female]. (p. 204-217)

U5100–1.4: Section D: Employment and Personal Income

(p. 149-200) Contains 3 maps, 1 list, and 44 tables. Includes labor force by employment status; man-days idle as percent of working time; unemployment insurance benefits paid, beneficiaries, and exhaustees; 10 largest private employers; manufacturing, higher education, and government employees; licensed professionals; nonagricultural employment and income; production worker earnings and hours; and covered employment, earnings, and payroll.

Also includes union wage rates for selected trades; collective bargaining settlements and total and government work stoppages, with employees involved; total and per capita personal income; and labor and proprietors' income.

Also includes OASDHI payments; worker compensation accidents, employees covered, and benefits paid; CETA participants and expenditures; CPI; and older persons with income above and below poverty level.

U5100–1.5: Section E: Commerce and Industry

(p. 201-248) Contains 1 map and 36 tables. Includes selected economic and business activity indicators; business establishments, employment, and payroll; manufacturing capital expenditures, shipment value, and value added; service industry, retail, and wholesale receipts; and mining production and value added.

Also includes value of exports and imports, by custom district; alcoholic beverage licenses and brand labels issued and in effect; and alcoholic beverages sold.

Also includes construction sand/gravel sold/used; construction contract value by type of structure; cost of total and residential construction; number of new housing units and permits; and housing units demolished.

U5100–1.6: Section F: Banking and Insurance

(p. 249-262) Contains 17 tables. Includes savings in savings banks and savings and loan assns; NYSE listed stocks and sales; business loans outstanding in New York State Federal Reserve District; and financial institutions and assets in and outside NYC.

Also includes deposits of commercial banks/State-chartered savings banks; insurance industry assets, liabilities, firms, premiums, losses, and licensees, with selected detail for life insurance companies; and savings bank life insurance policies in force and number of issuing banks.

Also includes retirement system/pension fund assets and payments to annuitants/beneficiaries; property insurance policies issued; automobiles insured and underwriting activity; and assigned risk levels for automobile liability and collision insurance, by discount or surcharge category.

U5100–1.7: Section G: Energy and Utilities

(p. 263-291) Contains 6 charts and 27 tables. Includes energy production by type; oil and gas wells and reserves; gas stored underground; State revenues from oil and gas leasing/royalties; energy consumption, customer bills, and prices, by fuel type and sector; and

New York Power Authority revenues, energy production by prime mover, and sales by sector and other disposition.

Also includes private electric and gas utilities' generation by prime mover and/or sales by consuming sector; natural gas requirements and supply; electric and gas utility customers and finances, by company; utility assets, liabilities, revenues, and expenses, with detail by type of utility; and energy conversion factors.

U5100–1.8: Section H: Transportation

(p. 293-322) Contains 3 charts and 33 tables. Includes motor vehicle registrations; drivers licenses issued and in force; traffic accidents by severity and cause, and injuries and fatalities; and traffic violation convictions.

Also includes highway and vehicle mileage; highway construction contracts; operations and finances of New York State Thruway, Niagara Frontier Transportation Authority, and Metropolitan Transportation Authority; National Passenger Railroad Corp (Amtrak) and other public transit ridership; and estimated new car fuel efficiency.

Also includes rail freight traffic; waterborne freight traffic by canal and port; Port of Buffalo freight traffic and vessels; airfields; air passenger and freight traffic, and aircraft departures, by airport; and commuter airline passengers.

U5100–1.9: Section I: Agriculture

(p. 323-333) Contains 2 maps, 1 chart, 1 list, and 7 tables. Includes farms, acreage, and average farm value; receipts from livestock and crops; leading counties for selected agricultural products; livestock, dairy, and poultry inventory and/or production; and crop acreage harvested and production.

U5100–1.10: Section J: Natural Resources, Conservation, and Tourism

(p. 335-358) Contains 1 map and 23 tables. Includes State Environmental Conservation Dept lands; attendance at recreational, camping, park, and historic sites, by site, most with acreage; open space acreage; motorboat and snowmobile registrations; and fish distributed by State hatcheries.

Also includes forest fires and acres burned; seedlings distributed by State's Saratoga nursery; forest product sales by type including wood fuel; hunting, fishing, and trapping licenses; deer take; significant earthquakes since 1737; air pollution severity, sources, and sites exceeding State standards; municipal sewage treatment plants; and solid waste disposal sites.

U5100–1.11: Section K: Public Safety, Law Enforcement, and the Courts

(p. 359-397) Contains 2 charts and 44 tables. Includes local criminal justice expenditures; State criminal justice staffing by agency, and municipal police and sheriff dept employees; and State police computer information network inquiries, and laboratory submissions by crime.

Also includes pistol, firearm dealer, and gunsmith licenses; crimes, arrests, conviction rates, sentences, and prison inmate commitment offenses, all by crime; crime victim claims and compensation; court caseload activity; legal bar admissions and attorney disciplinary proceedings; and median criminal processing time.

Also includes county penitentiary and jail admissions; State Correctional Services Dept admissions and releases; parole board activity and parolee recidivism; reimbursements and allocations for deliquent youth and delinquency prevention services; and youth population.

U5100–1.12: Section L: Government Finance and Taxes

(p. 399-467) Contains 2 charts and 71 tables. Includes State/local government expenditures per capita; receipts and disbursements by fund; personal income; income tax returns and collections; and public debt.

Also includes public employee and teacher retirement systems' contributions, benefits, and common fund assets; State tax revenues; business firms, income, and taxes; mortgages recorded; horse racing revenues, and on- and off-track betting by track; lottery activity; license and record fee collections; corporation and commercial code filings; and notary public appointments and revenues.

Also includes Federal aid; State revenues from recreational facilities, Empire State Plaza Convention Center, and land transactions; local government entities and finances including State aid; and bonds issued and redeemed.

Also includes taxable property value, equalization rates, and/or acreage, for all, tax-exempt, and State-owned land (including forest preserves); and value of exempt real property by owner and use.

U5100–1.13: Section M: Government Employment and Operations

(p. 469-488) Contains 1 map, 1 chart, and 29 tables. Includes State civil service positions, examination activities, and health service examinations and nursing services; State employees by function; State University of New York physical plant size by campus, and rehabilitation program and repair appropriations; and dormitory authority capital project expenditures.

Also includes State office facilities, and rent paid; State and municipal capital projects; communications serving State agencies; computer center services, commodity contracts awarded to resident bidders and small businesses; Empire State Plaza Convention Center use; and disposition of State surplus personal property.

U5100–1.14: Section N: Elections

(p. 489-532) Contains 9 maps and 9 tables. Includes voter registration; and voting for President, U.S. and State senators and representatives, and selected State officials; by party and/or candidate.

U5680
University of Alabama: Center for Business and Economic Research

U5680-1   ALABAMA BUSINESS

Monthly.   Approx. 10 p.
ISSN 0002-4163.
LC 52-25749.
SRI/MF/complete, shipped
quarterly

Monthly report on Alabama business activity indicators, with data on industrial production and consumption, construction, finance, prices, employment, and trade. Data are current to 4 months preceding cover date.

Data are compiled by the Center for Business and Economic Research from reports of Federal and State agencies, and various private sources.

Each issue includes articles or brief commentaries, occasionally containing statistics; and 1 detailed table on general business indicators, including the following:

a. Industrial and construction activities, including production of selected energy commodities and pulp/paper/paperboard; consumption of cotton, industrial electricity, and cement; and value of building contracts awarded, by type.

b. Finance and prices: savings and loan assn savings; tax collections by tax type; and index of prices received by Alabama farmers.

c. Labor force: unemployment; employment by industry division and manufacturing industry group; State employment service job applicants and placements; unemployment compensation initial claims and payments; and labor force and unemployment rate, by county.

d. Trade: imports and exports through Port of Mobile; non-industrial electric energy consumption; gasoline sales volume; new car registrations; and retail sales, by kind of business, MSA, and county.

e. Building activity: value of residential and nonresidential building permits, for State and selected cities.

Table presents data for month of coverage and the preceding 12 months, and annually for the preceding 2 years.

Beginning with the Feb. 1984 issue, retail sales data for current months have been temporarily suspended; however, data for previous periods continue to appear.

Monthly table appears in all issues. All additional features with substantial statistical content are described, as they appear, under "Statistical Features." Nonstatistical features are not covered.

Publication of this report was suspended during 1982-83. Last previous issue was published Dec. 1981 (for description, see SRI 1982 Annual, under this number).

Availability: University of Alabama: Center for Business and Economic Research, PO Box AK, University AL 35486, †; SRI/MF/complete, shipped quarterly.

Issues reviewed during 1984: Jan.-Aug. 1984 (P) (Vol. 53, Nos. 1-8).

STATISTICAL FEATURES:

U5680-1.501: Mar. 1984 (Vol. 53, No. 3)
INTERSTATE MIGRATION AND ALABAMA

(p. 2) By E. P. Rutledge. Article, with 2 tables showing Alabama in- and out-migration, by origin or destination (specific region and State, and abroad), selected periods 1965-80. Data are from the Census Bureau.

U5680-1.502: Apr. 1984 (Vol. 53, No. 4)
UNDERSTANDING ALABAMA'S FOSSIL FUEL RESOURCES

(back cover) By Annette Jones Watters. Part 1 of a 2-part article on fossil fuel resources in Alabama and the U.S. Data are from State and Federal sources. Includes 1 undated table comparing average Btu rating and sulfur, moisture, and ash content of coal produced in 8 States.

U5680-1.503: May 1984 (Vol. 53, No. 5)
UNDERSTANDING ALABAMA'S FOSSIL FUEL RESOURCES--PART II

(p. 2) By Annette Jones Watters. Part 2 of a 2-part article on fossil fuel resources in Alabama and the U.S. Includes 1 table showing average yield of specific refined products from one barrel of crude oil, 1982.

1982 CENSUS OF AGRICULTURE FOR ALABAMA

(back cover) Article, with 1 table showing Alabama farms by size, farms and acreage by use (including irrigated land), and value of land/buildings, 1978 and 1982. Data are from Census of Agriculture.

U5680-1.504: July 1984 (Vol. 53, No. 7)
POVERTY AND AGE IN ALABAMA

(p. 2, 7) By E. P. Rutledge. Article, with 2 tables showing Federal poverty guidelines; and number of Alabama families and unrelated individuals in households with heads age 60/over, by poverty status, with detail for presence of social security income, 1979. Data are from Census Bureau.

U5680-2   ECONOMIC ABSTRACT OF ALABAMA, 1984

Recurring (irreg.)   [1984.]
xix+430 p.
Printed Series No. 49.
ISBN 0-943394-02-3.
LC 81-620979.
SRI/MF/complete

Recurring compilation, for 1984, of detailed economic and demographic statistics for Alabama. Data are shown primarily for 1970s-82, with population trends from 1900 and projections to 2030. Most data are from Federal and State government sources.

Report is designed to present a comprehensive overview of the State. Extensive socioeconomic, demographic, and geographic breakdowns are shown, as applicable, for most topics. These breakdowns include data by city, county, SMSA, urban-rural status, commodity, government agency, industry, occupation, age, race, and sex. Comparisons to neighboring States, Southeast region, and total U.S. are also included.

Contents:

a. Listings of contents, tables, and charts ; map of Alabama counties and MSAs; and foreword. (p. iii-xvii)

b. 12 maps/charts and 150 tables arranged in 14 sections, described below. Tables in each section are preceded by a 1-6 page narrative. (p. 1-424)

c. Subject index. (p. 425-430)

This is the 10th edition of the report. For description of previous edition, for 1982, see SRI 1983 Annual, under this number.

Availability: University of Alabama: Center for Business and Economic Research, PO Box AK, University AL 35486, libraries and government agencies $24.00, others $30.00, $3.00 postage and handling; SRI/MF/complete.

TABLE SECTIONS:
[Data sources appear beneath each table.]

U5680-2.1: Section 1: Agriculture

(p. 1-9) Contains 8 tables. Includes farm income and production expenses; cash receipts from marketings; acreage, yield, and production of 4 principal crops; farms, acreage, land use, and average property value; and value of farm products sold.

U5680-2.2: Section 2: Banking and Governmental Finance

(p. 11-20) Contains 9 tables. Includes State government revenues by source; sales, use, lodgings, and fuel tax collections; income tax liability; Federal grants in Alabama; life insurance sales; and commercial bank, savings and loan assn, and credit union deposits and related finances.

U5680-2.3: Section 3: Construction and Housing

(p. 21-33) Contains 2 charts and 12 tables. Includes construction industry establishments, proprietorships/partnerships, employment, receipts, payroll, expenditures, value added, capital investment, and depreciable assets.

Also includes portland cement consumption; value of building contracts awarded and residential and nonresidential building permits; and housing units, occupancy, structural characteristics, median value and rent, and vacancy rates.

U5680-2.4: Sections 4-5: Education and Employment

(p. 35-115) Contains 1 map and 22 tables. Includes public and private school enrollment; postsecondary enrollment by institution; labor force, employment, and unemployment; business establishments, employment, and payroll; and covered employment and wages.

U5680-2.5: Section 6: Energy

(p. 117-129) Contains 10 tables. Includes electricity consumption and production; total energy consumption by State, and by sector for Alabama; petroleum, gas, and coal consumption; oil, gas, and condensate production; and coal mining employment and production.

U5680-2.6: Section 7: Foreign Trade

(p. 131-145) Contains 5 tables. Includes value of imports and exports for Mobile customs district, by port, with detail by country of origin and destination for Port of Mobile.

U5680–2.7: Section 8: GSP/Economic Indicators

(p. 147-162) Contains 13 tables. Includes selected economic indicators, including GSP, employment, wage rates, personal income, labor productivity, retail sales, tax collections, and energy consumption.

U5680–2.8: Section 9: Income and Prices

(p. 163-255) Contains 1 map/chart and 9 tables. Includes per capita personal income by State; total and per capita personal income, population, employment, and labor/proprietors' income, all projected to 2030; earnings projected to 2000; personal income by source; dollar purchasing power since 1913; and CPI and PPI.

U5680–2.9: Section 10: Manufacturing

(p. 257-287) Contains 1 map and 9 tables. Includes the following data on manufacturing: establishments, employment, and payroll; production workers, hours, and wages; value added, materials cost, shipments value, capital expenditures, and operating ratios; and new and expanded plants, with capital investment and jobs created.

U5680–2.10: Section 11: Population

(p. 289-299) Contains 1 map and 8 tables. Includes population from 1900; land area; and population projections to 2000, by census division and State.

U5680–2.11: Section 12: Trade

(p. 301-374) Contains 6 charts and 18 tables. Includes retail, wholesale, and service industry sales or receipts, establishments, payroll, employment, and operating ratios; retail and service industry proprietorships and partnerships; and wholesale inventories and expenses.

U5680–2.12: Section 13: Transportation

(p. 375-412) Contains 16 tables. Includes resident birthplace and residence in 1975, including different State and county, specific U.S. regions, and abroad; workers by place of work in and outside area of residence; commuting data; trucking industry detailed vehicle and operational data; motor vehicle registrations; and gasoline sales.

Also includes waterborne passenger and/or freight traffic at Mobile Harbor and on major rivers; and Birmingham airport passenger arrivals and departures.

U5680–2.13: Section 14: Vital Statistics

(p. 413-424) Contains 11 tables. Includes births, deaths and mortality rates by cause, infant deaths, and marriages and divorces.

U5780
University of Alaska: Institute of Social and Economic Research

U5780–1   ALASKA REVIEW OF SOCIAL AND ECONOMIC CONDITIONS
Series. For individual publication data, see below.
ISSN 0162-5403.
LC 78-645273.
SRI/MF/complete

Continuing series of reports on Alaska socioeconomic developments, including industrial activity, employment, prices, income, energy resources and consumption, and State revenue, expenditures, programs, and services.

Each report covers a single topic and contains narrative analysis, often with tables and charts presenting data from Federal and State agencies, University of Alaska, and private sources and surveys. Only reports with statistical content are described in SRI.

Report reviewed during 1984 is described below.

Availability: University of Alaska: Institute of Social and Economic Research, 707 "A" St., Suite 206, Anchorage AK 99501, †; SRI/MF/complete.

U5780–1.9: Alaska's Economy Since Statehood: The ISER MAP Economic Data Base
[Monograph. Feb. 1984. 36 p. Vol. XXI, No. 1. SRI/MF/complete.]

By Scott Goldsmith et al. Report reviewing indicators of economic activity and population change in Alaska, 1960s-82. Most data are derived from information collected in conjunction with ISER's Man-in-the-Arctic economic modeling program (MAP).

Contains narrative summary (p. 1-3); and 17 tables showing the following for Alaska, with selected comparisons to the U.S., 1961-82:

a. Employment and total wages/salaries (nonfarm); and GSP, and nonfarm earnings per employee, in current and constant 1967 or 1972 dollars; all by industry division and major group. 6 tables. (p. 4-15)

b. Personal income by component, taxes deducted, and disposable personal income, with selected income adjustments and per capita detail in current and constant 1967 dollars; unemployment and rate; Anchorage CPI; special State indexes for prices, construction, and government operations; civilian and military population and migration; population natural increase; and public school average daily membership. 5 tables. (p. 16-21)

c. State and local finances, including revenues by source, and expenditures by function; State general and permanent fund balances, and general obligation debt; and local real/personal and petroleum property values. 5 tables. (p. 22-34)

d. Miscellaneous data, including gasoline consumption per vehicle, business licenses issued, business receipts, and tourist visitors. 1 table. (p. 35)

U5830
University of Arizona: Arizona Crop and Livestock Reporting Service

U5830–1   1983 ARIZONA AGRICULTURAL STATISTICS
Annual. June 1984.
iv+115 p. Bull. S-19.
SRI/MF/complete

Annual report on Arizona agricultural production, marketing, and finances, mostly 1979-83, with some data for 1978 and 1984. Data generally are shown by commodity and county.

Report covers production, prices, value, and, as applicable, acreage, yield, inventory, and disposition, for field crop, vegetable, fruit, livestock, dairy, wool, and poultry sectors.

Data are compiled by Arizona Crop and Livestock Reporting Service in conjunction with University of Arizona.

Contains contents listing (p. ii-iii); introduction, and 1 chart and 183 tables accompanied by brief narrative summaries (p. 1-115 and back cover).

This is the 19th edition of the report.

Availability: University of Arizona: Arizona Crop and Livestock Reporting Service, Agricultural Statistician, 201 E. Indianola, Suite 250, Phoenix AZ 85012, †; SRI/MF/complete.

U5930
University of Arkansas: Bureau of Business and Economic Research

U5930–1   ARKANSAS BUSINESS AND ECONOMIC REVIEW
Quarterly. Approx. 50 p.
ISSN 0004-1742. LC 78-510.
SRI/MF/complete

Quarterly report on business activity and management in Arkansas, Southeastern States, and the U.S. Data are mainly from Commerce Dept, BLS, and State agency reports.

Issues contain feature articles, usually statistical; and economic indicators section, with narrative review of quarter covered and 10 tables. The 4th quarter issue includes an annual index of articles.

Quarterly economic indicator tables are listed below and appear in all issues. All additional features with substantial statistical content are described, as they appear, under "Statistical Features;" page locations and quarter of coverage for quarterly tables are also noted. Nonstatistical features are not covered.

Availability: University of Arkansas: Bureau of Business and Economic Research, College of Business Administration, Fayetteville AR 72701, †; SRI/MF/complete.

Issues reviewed during 1984: Vol. 16, Nos. 2-4, 1983; Vol. 17, Nos. 1-2, 1984 (P).

QUARTERLY TABLES:

[Tables show data for Arkansas quarterly for current year through quarter of coverage, and annually or quarterly for 7 or more previous years, unless otherwise noted. Tables [1-8] are accompanied by text data showing percent change for 4 preceding quarters and from 1967 base year, some with comparisons to U.S.]

[1] Employment by major industry group in Arkansas [manufacturing and nonmanufacturing wage/salary, and agricultural]; and unemployment rate, Arkansas and U.S.

[2] Personal income.

[3] Value added by manufacture.

[4] Cash receipts from farm marketings.

[5] Economic activity of savings and loan assns [new loans and net new savings].

[6] Freight traffic, Arkansas River commerce [inbound, outbound, and internal tonnages].

[7-8] Residential and nonresidential construction contracts [value].

[9] Labor force estimates [total labor force, unemployment rate, and employment, for U.S., Arkansas, 4 SMSAs, and each county; generally as of 2nd or 3rd month following quarter of coverage].

[10] Consumer prices [U.S. CPI, by item, monthly for 13 months through quarter following quarter of coverage, and annually for 8 preceding years].

STATISTICAL FEATURES:

U5930–1.501: Vol. 16, No. 2, 1983

QUARTERLY TABLES

(p. 34-44) Quarter of coverage is 1st quarter 1983. For data descriptions, see U5930-1 above.

SOME FINANCIAL EFFECTS OF THE TERMINATION OF SOCIAL SECURITY COVERAGE

(p. 1-8) By William C. Letzkus. Article, with 2 tables showing potential impact of terminating social security coverage, for persons planning to retire at age 62 and age 65. Tables show value of benefits received and taxes paid, by wage level and age in 1983, under continuing coverage vs. coverage terminated as of Jan. 1983.

FISCAL INEQUITIES IN ARKANSAS SCHOOL DISTRICTS

(p. 12-22) By Ralph O. Gunderson. Article comparing relative tax efforts of Arkansas school districts. Data are from estimated 1981 property values.

Includes 5 tables showing per pupil revenue capacity of 20 highest and lowest districts; top 10 counties in forestland, cropland, and urban area, with tax effort index for each; and tax effort index and revenue capacity, by school district arranged by county.

ECONOMIC FORECAST FOR ARKANSAS THROUGH 1984, ANNUAL FEATURE

(p. 25-31) Annual article, by Harry French, presenting survey results on Arkansas economic outlook, and selected U.S. issues, 1983-84. Data are based on 83 responses to July/Aug. 1983 survey of Arkansas academicians, businessmen, and government officials, conducted by the issuing agency.

Includes 1 extended table showing respondents' expectations (increase, decrease, same level) for selected State economic indicators; and views on selected U.S. economic issues; 1983-84.

U5930–1.502: Vol. 16, No. 3, 1983

QUARTERLY TABLES

(p. 23-34) Quarter of coverage is 2nd quarter 1983. For data descriptions, see U5930-1 above.

U5930–1.503: Vol. 16, No. 4, 1983

QUARTERLY TABLES

(p. 22-34, passim) Quarter of coverage is 3rd quarter 1983. For data descriptions, see U5930-1 above.

MINERAL INDUSTRY OF ARKANSAS IN 1983, ANNUAL FEATURE

(p. 32-33) Annual article, with 1 table showing Arkansas nonfuel mineral production value and quantity, by commodity, 1982-83. Data are from U.S. Dept of Interior.

U5930–1.504: Vol. 17, No. 1, 1984

QUARTERLY TABLES

(p. 33-44) Quarter of coverage is 4th quarter 1983. For data descriptions, see U5930-1 above.

PRELIMINARY ANALYSIS OF THE BUS REGULATORY REFORM ACT OF 1982 ON ARKANSAS

(p. 1-10) By Grant M. Davis. Article, with 3 tables showing mileage, passengers, and finances, for 12 U.S. intercity bus companies, 1981-82; and population of Arkansas communities losing and gaining intercity bus service since Nov. 1982 deregulation. Data are primarily from Arkansas Transportation Commission.

DIVIDEND POLICIES AND PRACTICES OF CANADIAN CORPORATIONS: RESULTS OF A SURVEY

(p. 18-28) By Halim Bishara. Article on characteristics of stock dividend programs of Canadian corporations, including payment frequency and factors affecting dividend decisions, 1960s and 1970s. Data are based on 1971 and 1981 survey responses of approximately 150 Canadian corporations. Includes 13 tables.

CURRENT MERGER MOVEMENT: A CAUSE FOR CONCERN?

(p. 29-30) By Thomas B. McKinnon. Article, with 1 table showing 10 largest corporate mergers ranked by cost, 1981-84 period. Data are from W. T. Grimm and Co. and other sources.

U5930–1.505: Vol. 17, No. 2, 1984

QUARTERLY TABLES

(p. 22-32) Quarter of coverage is 1st quarter 1984. For data descriptions, see U5930-1 above.

HOME EQUITY CONVERSION: A POTENTIAL BENEFIT TO ELDERLY ARKANSANS

(p. 1-6) By Richard K. Ford et al. Article, with 2 tables showing Arkansas and U.S. population (total and age 65/older), decennially 1960-80; and Arkansas loan closings value by type of loan, number and value of homes owned by persons age 65/older, and estimated increase in loan activity under specified assumptions concerning older persons' participation in home equity conversion plans, 1980.

Data sources include Federal Reserve Bank, Little Rock.

USE OF COMPUTERS IN ARKANSAS UNIVERSITIES

(p. 7-9) By Ronald C. Kettering and Willard C. Kettering. Article, with 3 tables showing percent of U.S. and Arkansas business administration schools using mainframe and micro computers for selected administrative, instructional, and support tasks.

Data are based on 672 responses to a spring 1983 survey of members of the American Assembly of Collegiate Schools of Business.

U5945
University of Arkansas: Industrial Research and Extension Center

---

U5945–1 STATE AND COUNTY ECONOMIC DATA for Arkansas
Annual. Oct. 1983.
iii+19 p. Pub. L-2.
SRI/MF/complete

Annual compilation, by Frank H. Troutman and Neva Wayman, of Arkansas social and economic data, by SMSA and/or county, 1983. Data are compiled primarily from reports of State and Federal agencies.

Contains contents listing (p. iii); and 18 tables showing data for various periods 1959-82, by SMSA and/or county, as follows:

a. Population and components of change; labor force, employment, and unemployment rate; covered total and manufacturing employment, payrolls, and average weekly earnings; and total and per capita personal income. 9 tables. (p. 2-10)

b. Sales for retail, wholesale, and service establishments; bank deposits; manufacturing value added; value of agricultural products sold; motor vehicle registrations by type of vehicle; property assessments; and public school enrollment. 9 tables. (p. 11-19)

This is the 2nd annual edition.

Availability: University of Arkansas: Center for Information Services, Socio-Economic Data Services Division, 33rd and University Ave., Little Rock AR 72204, $1.00 for postage and handling; SRI/MF/complete.

U5960
University of Arkansas: Office of Institutional Research

U5960-1   **SEVENTEENTH ANNUAL RANK-ORDER DISTRIBUTION OF ADMINISTRATIVE SALARIES PAID, 1983/84**
Annual. Dec. 31, 1983.
iii+119 p.
SRI/MF/complete

Annual report, for 1983/84, on administrative salaries paid in doctorate-granting public universities. Data are based on a survey of 133 State-supported single campus universities in 45 States, and 33 multicampus university systems in 28 States.

Contains introduction and table of contents (p. i-iii); and tables I-III showing ranked and average salaries for the following: 70 administrative positions in single campus universities (p. 4-40); selected positions in 9 equal employment opportunity regions (p. 41-112); and 30 positions in multicampus university systems (p. 113-119).

Salaries are not specified by university; however a list of universities surveyed is presented at the beginning of each table.

Availability: University of Arkansas: Office of Institutional Research, 318 Administration Bldg., Fayetteville AR 72701, $7.00; SRI/MF/complete.

U6215
University of California at Los Angeles: Graduate School of Education

U6215-1   **AMERICAN FRESHMAN: National Norms for Fall 1983**
Annual. Dec. 1983. 176 p.
ISSN 0278-6990.
SRI/MF/complete

Annual survey, by Alexander W. Astin et al., of characteristics of full-time students entering college for the 1st time in fall 1983. Survey presents data on freshman biographic and demographic characteristics, career plans, educational aspirations, and financial arrangements.

Study is part of the Cooperative Institutional Research Program ongoing longitudinal study of U.S. higher education system, sponsored by the American Council on Education and currently administered by the University of California at Los Angeles Graduate School of Education.

Data for the 1983 survey are from a sample of approximately 254,000 freshmen entering 489 2- or 4-year colleges and universities. Data have been weighted to obtain summary data representative of all entering full-time students (national norms).

Contains contents listing (2 p.); introduction, and summary with 4 charts (p. 1-6); and 1 extended table presenting weighted national norms for 51 items, listed below and repeated for:

a. Freshman men (p. 9-24); freshman women (p. 25-40); and all freshmen (p. 41-56); all shown by type of institution (2-year public and private; 4-year public, private-nonsectarian, Protestant, and Catholic; public and private universities; and public and private predominantly black colleges).

b. Universities (public and private, of low, medium, and high selectivity), by sex (p. 57-72); and 4-year colleges (public, private-nonsectarian, other sectarian, and Catholic colleges, of low, medium, and high selectivity) (p. 73-88).

c. Geographic regions (East, Midwest, South, and West), by sex. (p. 89-104).

Also contains appendices A-F (p. 105-176), including research methodology, facsimile of student questionnaire form, list of participating institutions, and facsimile of report furnished to participating institutions.

This is the 18th annual report.

Availability: University of California at Los Angeles: Graduate School of Education, Cooperative Institutional Research Program, Los Angeles CA 90024, $8.25; SRI/MF/complete.

TABLE ITEMS:

U6215-1.1: Weighted Norms

Weighted national norms are presented for the following items:

BIOGRAPHIC DATA

[1] Year graduated from high school [1980-83 or earlier; high school equivalency, or never completed high school].

[2] Age by Dec. 31, 1983.

[3] Racial background [white/Caucasian, black/Negro/Afro- American, American Indian, Asian-American/Oriental, Mexican-American/Chicano, Puerto Rican-American, and other].

[4] Political orientation [far left, liberal, middle-of- the-road, conservative, and far right].

[5-6] [Average] grade and academic rank in high school.

[7] Estimated parental income.

[8-9] Persons currently dependent on parents for support; and number of other dependents currently attending college.

[10-12] Living with parents (for more than 5 consecutive weeks); listed as dependent on parental Federal income tax return; and receiving assistance worth $600 or more from parents.

[13] Marital status.

[14-15] Have met or exceeded recommended years of study in [English, math, foreign language, physical and biological sciences, civics, and social studies]; and type of high school attended [public or private].

[16-17] Racial composition of high school and neighborhood.

[18] Disabilities [by type].

CHOICE OF COLLEGE

[19] If no financial aid [were] received this year student would [attend same or different college, join military, or look for work].

[20-21] Reasons noted as very important in deciding to go to college; and as very important in selecting this college.

[22-23] Number of other colleges applied to for admission this year; and number of other college acceptances this year.

RELIGIOUS AND OTHER DATA

[24-26] Current religious preference; and father's and mother's religious preference.

[27-28] Highest degree planned here; and anywhere.

[29] U.S. citizen.

[30] Permission [granted] to use data.

ACADEMIC AND OTHER PLANS

[31] Probable major field of study: arts and humanities, biological science, business, education, engineering, physical science, professional, social science, technical, and other fields; [each field includes 6-11 subfields].

[32-36] Probable career occupation [by 44 categories]; and father's and mother's education and occupation.

[37] Activities engaged in by students during the past year [including attended religious service; smoked cigarettes frequently; took vitamins, tranquilizers, or sleeping pills; participated in demonstrations; attended recital/ concert; jogged frequently; drank beer; and worked in political campaign].

[38] Student rated self above average in [various abilities].

[39] This college is student's [1st, 2nd, 3rd, or less than 3rd choice].

[40] Twin status.

[41] Students estimate chances are very good [for 26 alternative possibilities including: obtaining a job to pay college expenses; joining fraternity/sorority; making at least a "B" average; getting a bachelor's degree; and finding a job in preferred field].

[42] Objectives considered to be essential or very important [including: be an authority in my field; raise a family; be very well off financially; and keep up with political affairs].

METHODS OF FINANCING EDUCATION

[43] Concern about financing college [no, some, or major concern].

[44-46] Sources for educational expenses: parental aid, grants, scholarships, and loans [including Pell Grants and Federal Guaranteed Student Loans].

[47] Work and savings [college work/study grant; part- or full-time employment; savings from summer work; other savings; spouse; own and parent's G.I. benefits; social security benefits; and other sources of support].

RESIDENCY PLANS AND POLITICAL/SOCIAL ATTITUDES

[48-50] Residence planned and preferred during fall term [with parents/relatives, other private home/apartment, college dormitory, fraternity/sorority house, and other campus housing]; and miles from home to college.

[51] Agree strongly or somewhat [on approximately 30 public policy, social, and academic issues including: government not protecting environment; inflation biggest domestic problem; abolish death penalty; abortion and marijuana should be legalized; legality of homosexual relationships; college officials' right to regulate student publications and ban speakers; women should get job equality; busing to achieve racial balance; and competency standards for college graduation].

U6395
University of Chicago: National Opinion Research Center

U6395-1   GENERAL SOCIAL SURVEYS, 1972-84: Cumulative Codebook
Annual. July 1984.
v+483 p.
Social Science Series No. 5.
ISSN 0161-3340.
ISBN 0-932132-30-8.
SRI/MF/complete

Annual report cumulating responses to General Social Survey interviews on selected values and socioeconomic attitudes of adult Americans. Results are shown for all respondents, 1972-82 period and 1983-84, and for an over-sample of black Americans, 1982. Covers questions pertaining to politics, government, religion, women's issues, racial issues, employment and economic situation, and other social and ethical matters. Also includes detailed data on respondents' background and family characteristics.

Data are from 11 national survey samples of approximately 1,500 persons each, conducted Feb.-Apr. 1972-78, 1980, and 1982-84, by the National Opinion Research Center, University of Chicago. General Social Surveys include 3 types of questions: permanent, occurring in each survey; rotating, occurring in 2 out of every 3 surveys; and 1-time questions.

Report is intended to be used in conjunction with a separately published machine-readable data file, not covered by SRI.

Contains contents listing and preface (p. iii-v); introduction, with index to data by mnemonic code and question number (p. 1-16); 303 survey questions, described below (p. 17-265); appendices A-Q, on survey methodology (p. 267-476); and subject index (p. 477-483).

Availability: Roper Center, University of Connecticut, Box U-164R, Storrs CT 06268; or University of Chicago: National Opinion Research Center, 6030 S. Ellis Ave., Chicago IL 60637 (single copies only), $12.00; SRI/MF/complete.

QUESTION AREAS:

RESPONDENT CHARACTERISTICS

a. Background of respondent, including employment, occupation, and industry; marital status; employment, occupation, and industry of spouse and father; number of siblings and children; age and education; parents' and spouse's education; and sex and race. Questions 1-21. (p. 17-37)

b. Home characteristics at 16 years of age; mother's work history; whether birthplace in or outside of U.S.; and country of ancestry; household size, composition, and income; vocabulary knowledge; military service; work hours for self and spouse; residence location; housing; and occupational relationship with data, people, and things, for self, spouse, and father. Questions 22-60. (p. 38-69)

POLITICAL PREFERENCE AND SELECTED ATTITUDES

c. Party affiliation, voting history, and political ideology; attitudes regarding government spending in selected areas, including space exploration, environment, and foreign aid; agreement with selected general opinions on government, business, and society; support for government reduction of income differences between rich and poor; and opinions on amount of Federal income tax paid. Questions 61-78. (p. 70-94)

d. Attitudes regarding censorship and civil liberties of persons with ideas considered bad or dangerous by others; attitudes regarding death penalty, gun control, courts, crime and law enforcement, wiretapping, legalization of marijuana, prospects of war, U.S. role in world affairs, continuation of U.S. in UN, and communism; and popularity rating of 8 countries. Questions 79-103. (p. 95-111)

RELIGIOUS PREFERENCE, SOCIAL ACTIVITIES, AND SELECTED ATTITUDES

e. Religious preferences, background, and beliefs, including view of life after death and image of God; spouse's religious preference and background; attitudes regarding prayer in public schools, and the Bible; and attitudes regarding selected race-related matters, including interracial marriage, personal race relations, community and school integration, busing, and equal employment opportunities for blacks, with some detail for black respondents only. Questions 104-151. (p. 111-147)

f. General attitudes toward life and society, including satisfaction with marriage and health; confidence in other people and in selected institutions; qualities desirable in children; social activities, and membership in 15 types of organizations; use of alcohol and tobacco; and attitudes toward money, and toward public officials. Questions 152-177. (p. 148-185)

JOB, FINANCIAL SITUATION, AND SELECTED ATTITUDES

g. Job security and satisfaction; importance ratings for selected job characteristics; social class; satisfaction with financial situation; family income category, and minimum income needed; job supervision; unemployment history and receipt of government aid; and labor union involvement. Questions 178-194. (p. 185-197)

h. Opinions about selected social issues, including women's rights and participation in politics and business, abortion, ideal family size, birth control, sex education, divorce, extramarital sex, homosexuality, pornography, euthanasia, and suicide. Questions 195-228. (p. 197-214)

ACTIVISM, VICTIMIZATION, MEDIA USE, AND SELECTED ATTITUDES

i. Participation in labor strike, and in civil rights, anti- or pro-war, and school-related demonstrations; history of being subject to physical violence; attitudes regarding justifiability of violence; crime victimization; perception of neighborhood safety; gun ownership; police record; and hunting participation. Questions 229-240. (p. 215-223)

j. Media use; and interview characteristics of respondent. Questions 241-248. (p. 223-225)

SOCIAL ISSUES AND MISCELLANEOUS

k. Opinions about women and race, including abortion, working mothers, Equal Rights Amendment, married women in business/industry, programs encouraging integration of suburbs, and racial differences. Questions 249-266. (p. 226-235)

l. Frequency with which interview topics are thought about; and family 5-year history of traumatic events including divorce, unemployment, hospitalization/disability, and death. Questions 267-278. (p. 236-245)

m. Opinions about level of defense spending, Federal Government efforts for minority groups, and Government services. Questions 279-281. (p. 245-248)

n. Value attached to various aspects of life, including family, work, leisure, friends, relatives, religion, and politics; concern about threats to privacy; interest in public affairs; personal time management; and perceptions of survey validity. Questions 282-287. (p. 248-252)

o. Attitudes on compulsory national service; armed service pay/benefits; women, Hispanics, and blacks in armed forces; draft vs. volunteer army; draft exemptions; Federal Government responsibility for poverty relief, medical assistance, and improvement of living standards for blacks; and sample frames/methods and weights. Questions 288-303. (p. 253-265)

U6430
University of Colorado: Business Research Division

U6430-1   COLORADO BUSINESS REVIEW
Monthly.   Approx. 8 p.
ISSN 0010-1524.
LC 59-33322.
SRI/MF/complete, shipped quarterly

Monthly report on selected Colorado State and city business indicators, including employment, energy production, construction, and farm prices. Data are from Colorado Dept of Labor and Employment, and Federal, other State, local, and private agencies. Month of data coverage is 4 months prior to cover date.

Contains 2 monthly tables on economic indicators; and occasional special articles.

Monthly tables are listed below and appear in all issues.

Availability: University of Colorado: Business Research Division, Graduate School of Business Administration, Campus Box 420, Boulder CO 80309, Colorado residents †, others $5.00 per yr.; SRI/MF/complete, shipped quarterly.

Issues reviewed during 1984: Oct. 1983-Sept. 1984 (P) (Vol. LVI, Nos. 10-12; Vol. LVII, Nos. 1-9) [Vol. LVII, No. 8 incorrectly reads No. 7].

MONTHLY TABLES:

[Tables show data for month of coverage, previous month, and same month of preceding year.]

[1] Colorado business indicators [including unemployment, agricultural employment, nonagricultural employment by industry division and selected major group; weekly hours and earnings in construction and manufacturing; bankruptcies; unemployment claims; State revenues and expenditures; energy production and consumption; construction permits; highway contractor payments; savings and loan assn new savings; national park visits; motor

vehicle title applications; Denver airport activity; and prices received by farmers for 6 agricultural commodities].

[2] Local business conditions [electric power use; banks and deposits; and residential and nonresidential construction value; for approximately 40 Colorado cities].

U6430–3   **ECONOMIC ANALYSIS OF NORTH AMERICAN SKI AREAS, 1982-83 Season**
Annual. 1983. xvii+137 p.
ISSN 0147-4243.
ISBN 0-89478-106-5.
LC 76-622253.
SRI/MF/complete

Annual report, by C. R. Goeldner et al., on the U.S. and Canadian ski industry, covering facility characteristics and finances for the 1982/83 ski season with selected trends from 1976/77. Most data are shown by geographic region, average area skier capacity and profitability, area type (day, weekend, or vacation), ski season length, and for areas with snowmaking and night operations.

Includes data on average acreage; assets; age; proximity to SMSA and competitive areas; days/nights of operation; skier visits; ski area and lodging capacity; site ownership; business characteristics, including involvement in land development by type; day vs. night use; ski lift and other ticket prices; other activities available; income; revenue and expenses; departmental margins; balance sheets and ratios; economic ratios; concession operations; and employment by dept.

Regions covered are New England/Quebec, Eastern States/Ontario, Midwest, Central and Northern Rockies, California/Nevada, and Pacific Northwest/British Columbia.

Report is based on a July 1983 survey of 118 National Ski Areas Assn members, and is intended to permit ski area managers to compare their operations with averages of other areas with similar characteristics.

Contains executive summary and preface, with 3 tables and 1 chart (p. ii-xi); contents and table listings (p. xii-xvii); 10 chapters with 91 tables (p. 1-121); and 4 appendices including directory of survey respondents, questionnaire facsimile, and glossary (p. 122-137).

This is the 15th annual report.

Availability: University of Colorado: Business Research Division, Graduate School of Business Administration, Campus Box 420, Boulder CO 80309, $45.00; SRI/MF/complete.

U6600
University of Delaware: Agricultural Experimental Station

U6600–1   **DELAWARE FARM INCOME: Crop and Livestock Production, 1982; Acreage of Crops and Livestock Numbers**
Annual. Feb. 1984. 15 p.
A. E. Pamphlet No. 79.
SRI/MF/complete

Annual report, by Raymond C. Smith, on Delaware agricultural production, marketing, and income, 1981-82, with some data for 1983 and selected trends from 1960. Data are shown by county and/or commodity.

Covers farm income, production, sales, prices, and, as applicable, acres harvested, yield, and inventory, for field crop, fruit, vegetable, livestock, poultry, and dairy sectors.

Also includes data on government subsidies; production expenses; number, acreage, and value of farms; irrigated acreage; and characteristics of farm operators.

Data are compiled from reports of USDA and Maryland-Delaware Crop Reporting Service.

Contains table listing (p. 1); and report, with narrative summary and 15 tables (p. 2-15).

Availability: University of Delaware: Agricultural Experimental Station, Agricultural Economics Department, Newark DE 19717-1303, †; SRI/MF/complete.

U6660
University of Florida: Bureau of Economic and Business Research

U6660–1   **1983 FLORIDA STATISTICAL ABSTRACT**
Annual. Aug. 1983.
8+700 p.
ISBN 0- 8130-0767-4 (cloth).
ISBN 0- 8130-0768-2 (pbk.).
LC A67-7393.
SRI/MF/complete

Annual compilation of social, governmental, and economic statistics for Florida. Data are primarily for 1978-82, with selected historical data from as early as 1830, and population projections to 2020. Most data are from Federal censuses, and other Federal and State sources.

Report is designed to present a comprehensive overview of the State. Extensive socioeconomic, demographic, and geographic breakdowns are shown, as applicable, for most topics. These breakdowns include data by city, county and other State district, SMSA and MSA, urban-rural status, commodity, government agency, income, industry, occupation, age, disease, educational attainment, marital status, race, and sex. Comparisons to Sun Belt States, other populous States, and U.S. are also often included.

Contains introduction, contents listing, and 3 maps (6 p.); 478 tables and 3 maps arranged in 25 sections, described below (p. 1-656); guide to statistical sources and index of census tables in previous *Abstract* editions (p. 657-672); and subject index (p. 673-700).

Report has been published annually since 1966. Tables are not generally repeated from previous *Abstract* if updated data are not available at time of printing. This applies to most census data.

Availability: University Presses of Florida, 15 N.W. 15th St., Gainesville FL 32603, $25.00 (cloth), $17.00 (pbk.), +$1.50 handling charge for 1st copy, $0.50 for each additional copy; SRI/MF/complete.

TABLE SECTIONS:
[Data source is given beneath each table.]

HUMAN RESOURCES

U6660–1.1: Section 1: Population

(p. 1-53) Contains 1 map and 30 tables. Includes population since 1830 and projected to 2020; U.S. population, by State; persons by language spoken at home; migration; nonpermanent residents; land area; institutional inmates/patients; veterans by period of service; Federal expenditures for veterans in Florida; and naturalized and resident aliens and immigrants admitted, by country of birth.

U6660–1.2: Section 2: Housing

(p. 54-86) Contains 15 tables. Includes housing units by occupancy status, tenure, and type of fuel used; households and household size; persons in group quarters; residential and nursing homes for aged, and capacity; mobile home sales and average price; public lodgings by type; and mobile home and recreational vehicle license sales.

U6660–1.3: Section 3: Vital Statistics and Health

(p. 87-101) Contains 15 tables. Includes live births, deaths, and rates; births by age of mother; abortions; infant deaths; deaths by cause; reportable diseases; marriages and annulments/dissolutions; and State mental hospital admissions and discharges, and resident patients by institution and type of disorder.

U6660–1.4: Section 4: Education

(p. 102-125) Contains 17 tables. Includes public schools and enrollment; graduates; dropouts; disciplinary measures; students referred to alternative programs and courts/juvenile authorities; teachers and average salaries; assessed property value; education expenditures; achievement test performance; bilingual education; nonpublic schools and enrollment; school lunch program participation and cost; educational attainment of population; postsecondary enrollment by institution; and public school transportation costs.

U6660–1.5: Section 5: Income and Wealth

(p. 126-188) Contains 32 tables. Includes income tax returns exemptions, deductions, credits, and taxes paid; personal income by source, including labor/proprietors income and transfer payments; median family income; and families and persons below poverty level.

Also includes U.S. cost-of-living budgets at 3 levels for a 4-person family and for a retired couple; and proprietorship and partnership establishments, receipts, payroll, and net income.

U6660–1.6: Section 6: Labor Force, Employment, and Earnings

(p. 189-224) Contains 17 tables. Includes employment and unemployment; civilian labor force; employment discrimination complaints received; covered employment and payroll; farm and nonfarm proprietors; earnings; employment and average job vacancies projected to 1990; unemployment insurance claimants and unemployment duration; top 50 employers and location of corporate headquarters; and average annual pay.

U6660–1.7: Section 7: Social Insurance and Welfare

(p. 225-245) Contains 1 map and 16 tables. Includes Medicare beneficiaries, participating health facilities, benefit payments, and hospital and nursing facility admissions; social security beneficiaries and payments; public assistance payments and caseload, by program; and medical assistance recipients.

Also includes food stamp value and participants; average weekly unemployment compensation; unemployment insurance contributions and disbursements, claims and benefits, and claimants exhausting benefits; and worker compensation payments.

PHYSICAL RESOURCES AND INDUSTRIES

U6660–1.8: Section 8: Geography and Climate

(p. 246-256) Contains 7 tables. Includes land and water area, and coastline; elevations; Federal and Indian lands; temperature and precipitation at National Weather Station offices; climate characteristics for Jacksonville, Miami, and 4 other U.S. cities; and air quality by specific sampling location.

U6660–1.9: Section 9: Agriculture

(p. 257-298) Contains 1 map and 46 tables. Includes farm population; veterinarians; farm proprietors and employees; seasonal agricultural employment by crop, and number migrant and foreign; fertilizer consumption; agricultural services and production establishments, employment, and payrolls; Federal payments by program; farm income and expenses; and cash receipts by commodity.

Also includes Agricultural Stabilization and Conservation Service payments; farm loans outstanding, including mortgage loans; farms, acreage, and product sales; foreign-owned farm acreage; and farm taxes.

Also includes citrus fruit production, acreage, value, and average price; orange juice sales; crop production data; livestock and poultry inventory, production, and marketing; and commercial dairy milk production.

U6660–1.10: Section 10: Forestry, Fisheries, and Minerals

(p. 299-313) Contains 17 tables. Includes hardwood and softwood net annual growth and harvest; national forest land acreage, by forest; commercial forest acreage, by ownership class; and tree farms and acreage, by State.

Also includes fisheries; fish and shellfish landings and value; and forestry, fishing/hunting, and mining establishments, employment, and payroll.

Also includes nonfuel mineral production and value; and phosphate rock production, use, trade, apparent consumption, and reserves.

U6660–1.11: Section 11: Construction

(p. 314-335) Contains 10 tables. Includes new housing units authorized; residential and non-residential construction value; mobile home shipments; U.S. construction cost indexes and PPI for construction materials; and construction establishments, employment, and payroll.

U6660–1.12: Section 12: Manufacturing

(p. 336-364) Contains 22 tables. Includes manufacturing establishments, employment, payroll, value added, value of shipments, and new capital expenditures; and employment and location of individual firms with 500 or more employees.

U6660–1.13: Section 13: Transportation

(p. 365-393) Contains 24 tables. Includes workers by means of transportation to work; road and vehicle mileage; highway receipts and expenditures, by government level; vehicle registrations, license tags sold and revenue, and drivers licenses issued.

Also includes transportation industry establishments, employment, and payroll; out-of-State vehicle registrations, by State of previous registration; traffic accidents, injuries, and fatalities; and accident circumstances.

Also includes waterborne and air foreign trade volume, by port; railroad mileage, taxes, employment, and earnings; assessed value of railroad property, by company; and civil and military aviation operations, and civil air passenger and cargo traffic, by airport.

U6660–1.14: Section 14: Communications

(p. 394-408) Contains 9 tables. Includes circulation of daily, weekly, university, black, and Spanish-language newspapers; post office zip codes and receipts; communications industry establishments, employment, and payroll; TV and radio broadcast stations; and telephone exchanges, access lines, finances, customers, and annual growth rate, by telephone company.

U6660–1.15: Section 15: Power and Energy

(p. 409-430) Contains 22 tables. Includes energy consumption by fuel type, sector, and end use; electricity sales and customers, by utility and rural cooperative; establishments, employment, and payrolls for electric, gas, and sanitary services; electrical generating capacity, by prime mover, type of ownership, and fuel, and average and seasonal peak electricity demand, projected to 1991.

Also includes fuel supply-demand for electrical generation, projected to 1990; finances, operations, customers, and typical residential electric bills, by electric utility; natural gas production, movement, and consumption; operations, finances, and typical residential gas bills, by company; motor fuel consumption; and gasoline, gasohol, and special motor fuel sales.

SERVICES

U6660–1.16: Section 16: Wholesale and Retail Trade

(p. 431-442) Contains 10 tables. Includes wholesale and retail establishments, sales, employment, and payroll; and gross and taxable sales, by type of business.

U6660–1.17: Section 17: Finance, Insurance, and Real Estate

(p. 443-465) Contains 25 tables. Includes commercial banks and trust companies, and financial and operating data; failed banks; banks, deposits, and loans, with detail for holding company affiliates; credit unions, membership, and finances; and foreign bank offices and assets, by country.

Also includes savings and loan assn assets and liabilities, offices, savings activity, and loans and mortgages; finance, insurance, and real estate establishments, employment, and payroll; licensed real estate brokers and salespersons; hospital insurance premiums written, and net losses paid and incurred; and insurance underwriting activity, by type.

U6660–1.18: Section 18: Personal and Business Services

(p. 466-474) Contains 10 tables. Includes selected service industries establishments, receipts, employment, and payroll; and licensed accountants and architects/engineers.

U6660–1.19: Section 19: Tourism and Recreation

(p. 475-494) Contains 18 tables. Includes visitors, expenditures, and average stay, by mode of travel; detailed trip and traveler characteristics; origin and destination of visitors; highway traffic; registered boats; outdoor recreation facilities and use; attendance at individual State and national parks and memorials; hotels, motels, and capacity; and eating places and seating capacity.

Also includes gross and taxable sales and tax collections, by type of business; and establishments, employment, and payroll for travel- and recreation-related businesses.

U6660–1.20: Section 20: Health, Education, and Cultural Services

(p. 495-533) Contains 29 tables. Includes establishments, employment, and payroll for health services and facilities, educational, cultural, and social services, and membership organizations; hospitals by type, and beds; VA hospitals, beds, and patients; nursing homes and capacity; health practitioners by type; and opticians and pharmacists.

Also includes public library expenditures and volumes, by library; public school teachers and staff; average teacher salaries; student-teacher ratios; public school finances, tax structure, and property assessed valuations; community college finances, by institution; State appropriations for arts agencies; and number and finances of foundations.

PUBLIC RESOURCES AND ADMINISTRATION

U6660–1.21: Section 21: Government and Elections

(p. 534-545) Contains 13 tables. Includes State and local government units, and school and special districts; voting-age population; apportionment in U.S. House of Representatives since 1840; registered voters by party; votes cast for President, U.S. Senator, and Governor; women and blacks holding public office; U.S. and State legislators, by party; and National Guard personnel and Federal funds obligated.

U6660–1.22: Section 22: Courts and Law Enforcement

(p. 546-564) Contains 16 tables. Includes Crime Index offenses, rates, and clearances; arrests; drug seizures and arrests; prisoners under death sentence; prisoners; parolees/probationers; criminal justice expenditures; legal service, justice, public order, and safety units, employment, and payroll; and lawyers by type of practice.

U6660–1.23: Section 23: Government Finance and Employment

(p. 565-626) Contains 37 tables. Includes Federal outlays in Florida, by programs; defense contracts and awards and payroll; State revenues, expenditures, indebtedness, and fund balances; sales tax collections by trade classification; and tax collections and fund distributions, by type.

Also includes gasoline sales; alcoholic beverage licenses issued; horse and dog racing and jai alai performances, days, attendance, and pari-mutuel wagering revenues and taxes; and State retirement benefits.

Also includes Federal, State, and local government units, employment, and payroll; local government revenues, expenditures, indebtedness, and intergovernmental transfers, special district revenues and expenditures; and real, personal, and railroad property valuations and tax rates.

ECONOMIC AND SOCIAL TRENDS

U6660–1.24: Section 24: Economic Indicators and Prices

(p. 627-642) Contains 15 tables. Includes State economic indicators, including unemployment rate, employment, and sales tax collections; housing units authorized by building permits; gross and taxable sales, and sales taxes paid; and commercial banks/trust companies, assets, capital accounts, loans/discounts, and deposits.

Also includes CPI and PPI; Miami energy prices; electricity prices; price level index, by major item; business failures; and State/local taxes paid by urban family of 4.

U6660–1.25: Section 25: Quality of Life

(p. 643-656) Contains 1 extended table. Includes quality-of-life data, covering population and housing characteristics; health care, educational, and economic conditions; climate; and other indicators.

U6660–2   BUSINESS AND ECONOMIC DIMENSIONS

Quarterly.   Approx. 30 p.
ISSN 0007-6457.
LC A65-7913.
SRI/MF/complete

Quarterly review of selected topics related to business and economic conditions in Florida. Data are from Federal and State government reports and private research studies.

Each issue contains feature articles, usually focusing on a single topic, and frequently containing statistics. Issue for 1st quarter includes an annual economic forecast.

Features with substantial statistical content are described, as they appear, under "Statistical Features." Each issue of the journal is reviewed, but an abstract is published in SRI monthly issues only when statistical features appear.

Availability: University of Florida: Bureau of Economic and Business Research, College of Business Administration, 221 Matherly Hall, Gainesville FL 32611, $15.00 per yr., single copy $5.00; SRI/MF/complete.

Issues reviewed during 1984: III 1983 (P) (Vol. 19, No. 3).

STATISTICAL FEATURES:

U6660–2.501: III 1983 (Vol. 19, No. 3)

MANAGING FLORIDA'S GROWTH, AN INTRODUCTION

(p. 2-7) By Hank Fishkind. Article, with 1 table showing Florida population, quinquennially 1970-2000. Data are from Bureau of Economic and Business Research.

FLORIDA'S INFRASTRUCTURE: PAST NEEDS AND FUTURE REQUIREMENTS

(p. 8-14) By Neil Sipe. Article analyzing spending requirements and resources for Florida's infrastructure, 1970s-2000. Data are from Bureau of Economic and Business Research and U.S. Dept of Commerce.

Includes 4 tables showing the following for Florida: Federal aid to State and local government, total and as percent of all revenue, selected years 1960-80; State/local government capital expenditures by category (total in current dollars and per capita in constant 1972 dollars), and population, 1975-81; and expenditure requirements and resources by infrastructure category, in 1982 dollars, various periods 1982-2000.

U6660–2.502: IV 1983 (Vol. 19, No. 4)

THE CASE FOR PROPOSITION NO. 1

(p. 10-14) By Hank Fishkind. Article on a proposed Florida constitutional amendment designed to limit State/local revenues. Data are from *Florida's Amendment 1—Facts, Fallacies and Philosophies.* Includes 2 tables showing CPI, 1979-82 and forecast 1983-85; and selected revenue and expenditure data for 1 Florida location, FY81-85.

U6660–3   POPULATION STUDIES BULLETIN

Series.   For individual publication data, see below.
ISSN 0071-6030.
LC 77-648516.
SRI/MF/complete

Continuing series of reports on Florida population and household composition. Reports generally contain a narrative analysis, with 1-3 accompanying tables showing data for the State and, often, by county and demographic characteristics.

Reports reviewed during 1984 are described below.

Availability: University of Florida: Bureau of Economic and Business Research, College of Business Administration, 221 Matherly Hall, Gainesville FL 32611, $20.00 per yr., single copy $6.00; SRI/MF/complete.

U6660–3.12: County Population Estimates by Age, Race, and Sex: Apr. 1, 1982

[Recurring (irreg.) Dec. 1983. 8 p. Bull. No. 66. SRI/MF/complete.]

Recurring report, by Marylou Mandell, with 1 table showing Florida population estimates by race and sex, by county and age group, as of Apr. 1, 1982. Data are based primarily on 1970 and 1980 census counts.

U6660–3.13: Number of Households and Average Household Size in Florida: Apr. 1, 1983

[Recurring (irreg.) Feb. 1984. 4 p. Bull. No. 67. SRI/MF/complete.]

Recurring report, by Stanley K. Smith and Faith Sincich, with 1 table showing Florida households and average household size, by county, as of Apr. 1, 1970 and 1980 (census), and 1983 (estimated). Data are from Census Bureau and estimates by the issuing agency.

For description of previous report, issued in 1983, see SRI 1983 Annual, under U6660-3.9.

U6660–3.14: Projections of Florida Population by County, 1985-2020

[Annual. Apr. 1984. 8 p. Bull. No. 68. SRI/MF/complete.]

Annual report, by Stanley K. Smith and Faith Sincich, estimating Florida population as of Apr. 1, 1983, and presenting high, low, and medium projections, selected years 1985-2020, all by county. Data primarily are based on Apr. 1, 1980 census counts. Includes 1 table.

U6660–3.15: Population Projections by Age and Sex: Florida Counties, 1985-2000

[Monograph. July 1984. 16 p. Bull. No. 69. LC 84-622932. SRI/MF/complete.]

By Stanley K. Smith and Faith Sincich. Report projecting Florida population by age group and sex, by county, quinquennially 1985-2000, with actual data for 1980. Data primarily are based on Apr. 1, 1980 census counts. Includes 1 table.

U6660–3.16: Projections of Black Population by Age and Sex: Florida Counties, 1985-2000

[Monograph. Aug. 1984. 16 p. Bull. No. 70. LC 84-622933. SRI/MF/complete.]

By Stanley K. Smith and Faith Sincich. Report projecting Florida's black population by age group and sex, by county, quinquennially 1985-2000, with actual data for 1980. Data primarily are based on Apr. 1, 1980 census counts. Includes 1 table.

U6660–4   FLORIDA ESTIMATES OF POPULATION, Apr. 1, 1983, State, Counties, and Municipalities

Annual.   Feb. 1984.   44 p.
LC 73-623497.
SRI/MF/complete

Annual report estimating Florida population by county, city, and MSA, as of Apr. 1, 1983. Estimates are used for State revenue-sharing distribution for FY84-85. Includes comparisons with decennial censuses from 1960.

Data are estimated from number of occupied housing units, based on residential building permits, electric utility customer records, and U.S. censuses.

Contains contents and table listing, analysis of population trends, and estimation methodology, with 1 text table showing U.S. average household size, selected years 1940-83 (p. 3-7); and 2 maps, and 9 tables listed below (p. 8-44).

Availability: University of Florida: Bureau of Economic and Business Research, College of Business Administration, 221 Matherly Hall, Gainesville FL 32611, $12.00; SRI/MF/complete.

TABLES:

[All population estimates are as of Apr. 1.]

1. Estimates of population [1980 and 1983; and inmates/patients in Federal/State-operated institutions, 1983]; by county and municipality [and unincorporated area]. (p. 8-27)

2-3. Components of population change [natural increase and net migration]; and resident live births and deaths, by race; by county, 1980-83 [period]. (p. 28-31)

4-6. Population change, by county, MSA, and planning district, [decennially 1960-80 and 1983]. (p. 32-37)

7. Rank in population and percentage change, 1970, 1980, and 1983, for [35] specified cities. (p. 38)

8-9. Rank of counties by population size, 1983; and population distribution, and population per square mile and rank according to density, 1970, 1980, and 1983; [all by county]. (p. 40-43)

U6660–5   BUILDING-PERMIT ACTIVITY in Florida

Monthly, with annual summary.   Approx. 10 p.
ISSN 0007- 3555 (monthly).
ISSN 0270-9317 (annual).
SRI/MF/complete, shipped quarterly

Monthly report, with annual summary, on the value of construction authorized by building permits in Florida, by county, city, and type of dwelling. Report is issued 1-2 months after month of coverage.

Contains 1 table showing value of private housekeeping and nonhousekeeping residential units, nonresidential units, and additions/alterations; number of housekeeping units in private 1-family houses and multi-family buildings; and value of public building permits; by county and city, with totals for county unincorporated areas; all for month of coverage.

Also includes a similar table showing late reports of building permit activity for previous months.

An annual summary issue (No. 13) is also published. Please note that ISSN in this annual summary incorrectly reads 0007-3555.

Availability: University of Florida: Bureau of Economic and Business Research, College of Business Administration, 221 Matherly Hall, Gainesville FL 32611, $15.00 per yr., annual summary $4.00, single copy $2.00; SRI/MF/complete, shipped quarterly.

Issues reviewed during 1984: Sept. 1983-Aug. 1984; and annual summary for 1983 (D) (Vol. XXIX, Nos. 9-13; Vol. XXX, Nos. 1-8).

U6730
University of Georgia: College of Business Administration

U6730–2   GEORGIA BUSINESS AND ECONOMIC CONDITIONS

Bimonthly.   Approx. 15 p.
ISSN 0279-3857.
LC 33-21288.
SRI/MF/complete

Bimonthly report on Georgia economic conditions and business indicators. Most data are from Federal and State sources, and are current to 2 months prior to cover date.

General format:

a. Feature articles, some with statistics; and occasional special tables.

b. Bimonthly table showing Georgia leading and coincident economic indicator indexes, employment, manufacturing employment and earnings, retail sales, building permits, construction value, agricultural price index, and personal income; Atlanta help-wanted advertising index; and CPI for southern U.S. and Atlanta; generally for month of coverage, previous 2 months, and same month of previous year.

Bimonthly table appears in all issues. All additional features with substantial statistical content are described, as they appear, under "Statistical Features." Nonstatistical features are not covered.

Availability: University of Georgia: College of Business Administration, Division of Research, Athens GA 30602, $12.00 per yr.; SRI/MF/complete.

Issues reviewed during 1984: Sept./Oct. 1983-Sept./Oct. 1984 (P) (Vol. 43, Nos. 5-6; Vol. 44, Nos. 1-5).

STATISTICAL FEATURES:

U6730–2.501: Sept./Oct. 1983 (Vol. 43, No. 5)

SERVICES INDUSTRIES IN GEORGIA: OUTLOOK FOR THE 1980s

(p. 1-5) By Phillip A. Cartwright. Article on employment and economic activity in Georgia's service industries. Data are from the U.S. Bureau of Economic Analysis.

Includes 7 tables showing Georgia employment, personal income distribution, average salary, and employment and income growth rates for various service industry groups; and average salary by industry division; primarily 1981, with trends from 1960 and comparisons to total U.S.

U6730–2.502: Nov./Dec. 1983 (Vol. 43, No. 6)

UNEMPLOYMENT PATTERNS IN GEORGIA: 1975, 1979, AND 1982; PART I

(p. 4-11) By Suzanne A. Lindsay. Part 1 of a 2-part article on Georgia unemployment patterns, with focus on relation to population and labor force size, 1970s-82. Data are from Census Bureau and Georgia Department of Labor.

Includes 3 data maps and 5 tables showing unemployment rate by county; and number of counties with low and very high unemployment rates, by total and urban population size, and by civilian labor force size; various periods 1970-82.

U6730–2.503: Jan./Feb. 1984 (Vol. 44, No. 1)

ECONOMIC OUTLOOK FOR SUPPORT FOR THE ARTS IN THE U.S. AND GEORGIA

(p. 1-6) By Phillip A. Cartwright and Richard S. Schneiderman. Article with 3 tables showing annual average growth rates for arts funding from Georgia State government, and from National Endowment for the Arts to Georgia and to total U.S., in current and constant 1967 dollars, various periods 1967-84. Data are from National Endowment for the Arts and Georgia Council for the Arts and Humanities.

UNEMPLOYMENT PATTERNS IN GEORGIA: 1975, 1979, 1982; PART II

(p. 7-13) By Suzanne A. Lindsay. Part 2 of a 2-part article on Georgia unemployment patterns, with focus on types of industry involved. Data are from the Dept of Commerce.

Includes 7 tables showing the following for groups of counties with low and very high unemployment rates: employment distribution in individual counties, and employment and earnings relative to State levels, all by industry division; percent of counties reporting employment in selected manufacturing industry groups; number of counties, by number of industry groups for which employment was reported; and personal income composition ranges (percent net earnings, transfer payments, and dividends/other); all for 1981.

U6730–2.504: Mar./Apr. 1984 (Vol. 44, No. 2)

SPECIAL TABLES

(p. 8-9) Two tables showing Georgia total and per capita personal income, by SMSA and county, 1970 and 1980-81; with per capita ranking and comparison to U.S., 1981.

ANNUAL DATA

(p. 10-13) Annual compilation of tables presenting selected economic indicators for Georgia, 1982-83. Data are from University of Georgia, Census Bureau, Georgia Dept of Labor, and R. L. Polk and Co. Contains the following tables showing data for 1982-83, unless otherwise noted:

[1] Taxable sales in Georgia, by [kind of business] and county, [1981-83].

[2-3] Residential and nonresidential construction authorized [number of units and total value], by selected cities and counties.

[4] Estimated unemployment rate, by county.

[5] New passenger car registrations, by SMSA and selected city-counties.

[6-7] Manufacturing average workweek and average hourly earnings, [by major industry group, for State and Atlanta].

[8] Nonagricultural employment, by industry [division] and SMSA.

U6730–2.505: May-June 1984 (Vol. 44, No. 3)

LOCAL SUPPORT FOR EDUCATION IN GEORGIA

(p. 1-10) By Suzanne A. Lindsay. Part 1 of a 2-part article analyzing funding of local school systems in Georgia, 1981/82 school year. Data are from the Georgia Dept of Education. Includes 9 tables showing:

a. Number of school systems, by the following: average attendance; dropout rate; cost per child; share of receipts from local, State, and Federal sources; local and total receipts per child; and required local funding effort (RLE, amount and as percent of local receipts for maintenance/operation).

b. For individual school systems: total and local receipts; RLE; and rankings in average attendance, RLE, local and total receipts per child, and cost per child.

1983 STATE UNEMPLOYMENT RATES

(p. 11-14) Article, 1 map and 4 tables showing unemployment rates for individual Georgia counties, 1983, with summary comparisons to 1982. Data are from Georgia Dept of Labor.

U6730–2.506: July/Aug. 1984 (Vol. 44, No. 4)

LOCAL SUPPORT FOR EDUCATION IN GEORGIA

(p. 1-5) By Suzanne A. Lindsay. Part 2 of a 2-part article analyzing funding of local school systems in Georgia, 1981/82 school year. Data are from Georgia Dept of Education, and Federal agencies. Includes 5 tables showing the following:

a. Number of school systems, by level of tax digest (value of taxable property) for maintenance/operation per student, and by maintenance/operation and bond levy range, 1981/82.

b. Personal income, school receipts as a percent of personal income, and rank order based on population and general economic condition, by county; and number of counties, by school receipts as a percent of personal income; various periods 1980-82.

GEORGIA'S BUDGETARY PROCESS

(p. 6-10) By John H. Baskin, III. Article, with 1 table showing Georgia initial and amended revenue estimates, and actual revenue, FY73-82. Data are from the State budget report.

U6730–2.507: Sept./Oct. 1984 (Vol. 44, No. 5)

ECONOMIC OUTLOOK: THIRD QUARTER 1984

(p. 1-2) By Phillip A. Cartwright. Article, with 1 table showing Georgia nonagricultural employment, by industry division, 1983-84.

MANUFACTURING EXPORTS FROM GEORGIA

(p. 3-4) By Cletus C. Coughlin. Article, with 2 tables showing export value and share of total shipments, by major manufacturing industry group, for Georgia and U.S.; and rankings within U.S. and Southeast region based on manufactured exports (total and per State employee), for 7 southeastern States; 1981. Data are from U.S. Commerce Dept.

PERSONAL INCOME IN GEORGIA: THE EARLY 1980s

(p. 5-15) By Suzanne A. Lindsay. Part 1 of a series of articles discussing trends in Georgia personal income. Data are from U.S. Commerce Dept.

Includes 2 maps and 6 tables showing nominal and real personal income and average annual growth rates, by MSA and county, with summary comparisons to U.S.; and number of counties, by level of personal income growth; various periods 1970-82, with summary data for 1983.

U6910
University of Illinois:
Bureau of Economic
and Business Research

U6910–1   ILLINOIS BUSINESS REVIEW
Bimonthly.   Approx. 12 p.
ISSN 0019-1922.
LC A44-1688.
SRI/MF/complete

Bimonthly review of Illinois economic conditions and business indicators, and selected U.S. and world economic developments. Data are compiled by the Bureau of Economic and Business Research from Federal and State government and private agency reports. Most data are current to approximately 3 months prior to cover date.

Issues generally include articles, often with statistics; and a bimonthly Illinois business index table showing the following:

a. Manufacturing employment and weekly hours and earnings, Chicago and St. Louis help-wanted advertising, retail sales, coal and petroleum production, vendor performance, building permits and value, and CPI; generally for month of coverage, 3 previous months, and selected months of preceding year.

b. Personal income, for 5-6 consecutive quarters through quarter ending 5-9 months prior to month of publication.

Bimonthly table appears in all issues. All additional features with substantial statistical content are described, as they appear, under "Statistical Features." Nonstatistical features are not covered.

Availability: University of Illinois: Bureau of Economic and Business Research, College of Commerce and Business Administration, 428 Commerce W., 1206 S. Sixth St., Champaign IL 61820, †; SRI/MF/complete.

Issues reviewed during 1984: Dec. 1983-Aug. 1984 (P) (Vol. 40, No. 6; Vol. 41, Nos. 1-4).

STATISTICAL FEATURES:

U6910–1.501: Dec. 1983 (Vol. 40, No. 6)

REAL ESTATE DEVELOPMENTS: SHARECROPPING AND ILLINOIS AGRICULTURE

(p. 6-8) By Salim Rashid et al. Article on the impact of sharecropping on efficiency of Illinois agricultural production. Data are based on business records of 8,230 farms, 1981.

Includes 4 tables showing per-acre corn and soybean yield by soil rating, labor cost, and investment in machinery, all by type of farm tenure, for north-central and southern Illinois, 1981.

U6910–1.502: Feb. 1984 (Vol. 41, No. 1)

REAL ESTATE DEVELOPMENTS: THE ELDERLY AS CONSUMERS OF SUBSIDIZED HOUSING—ANTICIPATED IMPACT OF THE RENT VOUCHER PROGRAM ON PRIVATE REAL ESTATE INVESTMENTS

(p. 6-9) By Leonard F. Heumann. Article on reactions of elderly residents of subsidized housing to proposed rent voucher program (rent subsidy issued directly to eligible recipients for use in private rental market). Data are from responses to a summer 1983 survey covering 117 subsidized housing facilities in Chicago and 9 other Illinois cities. Survey respondents were housing managers and other persons familiar with housing preferences and needs of the elderly.

Includes 2 tables showing percent of elderly residents in subsidized elderly housing and family housing projects who would move given various housing and/or subsidy choices, and reasons for staying or leaving, by race, with selected detail for Chicago and other locations.

U6910–1.503: Apr. 1984 (Vol. 41, No. 2)

ANNUAL FORECASTING MODEL FOR ILLINOIS TAXES

(p. 1-3) By Jane H. Leuthold. Article discussing Illinois tax structure. Data are from State agencies and University of Illinois. Includes 1 chart and 3 tables showing the following for Illinois: distribution of tax revenue by source, 1982; forecasts of tax revenue by type, based on various growth assumptions, FY84-85; and summary revenue and spending outlook, FY85.

REAL ESTATE DEVELOPMENTS: REAL ESTATE RETURNS, INFLATION, AND TAXES

(p. 6-8) By Roger G. Ibbotson and Laurence B. Siegel. Article analyzing effect of inflation on real estate investment return. Data sources include authors' estimates. Includes 2 tables showing inflation rate, and percent return on residential, farm, and business real estate investments; and regression analysis of inflation effect on real estate investments; generally 1947-82 and 1960-82 periods.

DEREGULATION: THE AIRLINE EXPERIENCE

(p. 8-11) By Carolyn Woj. Article, with 3 tables showing number of non-stop flights and seats per weekday to 13 Illinois metro areas; and regular and excursion air fares between 3 Illinois cities and 5 other U.S. cities; 1973 and 1983.

Data are from *Official Airline Guide* and travel agencies.

U6910–1.504: June 1984 (Vol. 41, No. 3)

EXPENDITURES FOR POLLUTION ABATEMENT IN ILLINOIS, 1980

(p. 5) Table showing Illinois expenditures for pollution abatement, by type and funding sector, 1980. Data are from U.S. Commerce Dept.

REAL ESTATE: THE LEGACY OF TAX ADVANTAGE

(p. 6-9) By J. Fred Giertz and A. James Heins. Article on real estate investment trends. Data are from Federal agencies. Includes 2 tables showing residential nonfarm real estate value and corporate debt and equity, 1965 and 1981; and price indexes for rental and owner-occupied housing, selected years 1965-82.

ILLINOIS TIMBER INDUSTRY

(p. 10-12) By Joseph Denig and Dwight R. McCurdy. Article, with 1 map and 4 tables showing Illinois timber purchased and logged, and number of sales and buyers by county; means by which buyers learned of sales, and purchase methods used; and percent of purchasers producing 6 types of timber products; 1976 and 1982.

Data are from a 1982 survey of all 365 licensed timber buyers (32% response), and a similar survey in 1976.

U6910–1.505: Aug. 1984 (Vol. 41, No. 4)

ILLINOIS FIREWOOD INDUSTRY

(p. 4-5, 11) By Dwight R. McCurdy et al. Article, with 8 tables showing selected operating characteristics of firewood dealers in northern and southern Illinois, 1982/83, with some comparisons to 1981/82. Data for 1982/83 are based on Southern Illinois University telephone surveys of 208 dealers.

REAL ESTATE DEVELOPMENTS: ILLINOIS EXPERIENCE WITH THE COMMUNITY REINVESTMENT ACT—USING A STEAM ROLLER TO CRUSH AN ANT

(p. 6-8) By Lewis Davids and Gola E. Waters. Article examining experience of Illinois banks in regard to the Community Reinvestment Act (CRA) of 1977, which encourages banks to meet the credit needs of the local community including low- and moderate-income neighborhoods. Data are based on responses of 281 banks to a University of Illinois survey.

Includes 2 tables showing trends in CRA-related complaints against Illinois banks, including data by county, 1977-83.

NONELECTRICAL MACHINERY IN ILLINOIS

(p. 8-10) By Carolyn Woj. Article, with 4 tables showing employment trends in Illinois nonelectrical machinery industry, including detail for selected metro areas and for export-related employment, and comparisons to all manufacturing and to U.S., various periods 1977-84.

U7095
University of Kansas: Institute for Economic and Business Research

U7095–1   KANSAS BUSINESS REVIEW
Quarterly.   Approx. 25 p.
LC 53-35519.
SRI/MF/complete

Quarterly report on Kansas business, employment, retail sales, farm prices, and financial activity.

Data are from State agencies, USDA, and commercial or private sources. Most data are current to 1-3 months prior to cover date.

General format:

a. Feature articles; and "Economic Conditions," quarterly feature containing 2 articles on U.S. and Kansas economies.

b. "Economic Indicators," 5 charts and 9 quarterly tables presenting national and State economic data.

Quarterly economic indicator tables are listed below and appear in all issues. All additional features with substantial statistical content are described, as they appear, under "Statistical Features." Nonstatistical features are not covered.

Availability: University of Kansas: Institute for Economic and Business Research, 218 Summerfield Hall, Lawrence KS 66045, †; SRI/MF/complete.

Issues reviewed during 1984: Fall 1983-Summer 1984 (P) (Vol. 7, Nos. 1-4).

QUARTERLY TABLES:
[Tables generally show data for latest date/period available, with percent change from previous period and/or year. Data are for Kansas, unless otherwise noted.

Prior to Summer 1984 issue, table format differed from this description.]

1. Economic indicators [personal income, employment, unemployment rate, retail sales, and Kansas City CPI, all with comparisons to U.S.].

2. National indicators [selected U.S. income, labor force, unemployment, general business, price, and banking and finance measures].

3. Employment [labor force, employment on farms and by industry division and major manufacturing group, unemployment insurance initial claims, and manufacturing average weekly hours].

4. Income [farm and nonfarm income, and earnings by industry division].

5. Retail sales subject to sales tax [by kind of business].

6. Employment [labor force and total and farm employment; and retail] sales; for [3] SMSAs, [Kansas portion of Kansas City SMSA], and [7] counties.

7. Agricultural indicators [crop and livestock prices received by commodity, and index of prices paid].

8-9. Banking activity [loans and/or deposits by type, for Federal Reserve members and all commercial banks; and savings and loan assn assets and net savings; all for State, Kansas City, Topeka, and Wichita].

STATISTICAL FEATURES:

U7095–1.501: Fall 1983 (Vol. 7, No. 1)

KANSAS HIGH-TECH LABOR FORCE: TRENDS AND PROJECTIONS

(p. 1-12) By Richard Sexton. Article on Kansas labor force characteristics, and projected high technology expansion to 1990. Data are from Census Bureau and other sources. Includes 2 charts and 12 tables showing the following for Kansas:

a. Labor force by occupational group, sex, and age; and high technology labor force, establishments, and employment, by occupation and/or industry group; with selected detail by SMSA and for Riley County, and comparisons to total U.S., various years 1969-90.

b. Population by age, 1980 and 1987; and postsecondary degrees awarded from Kansas institutions, by field, level, and selected institution, 1983-87.

FACTORS IN FIRMS' DECISIONS TO LOCATE OR EXPAND IN KANSAS

(p. 13-18) By Robert A. McLean et al. Article on industrial siting in Kansas, based on responses from 256 new and expanded Kansas establishments to a survey conducted by the Institute for Economic and Business Research.

Includes 7 tables showing characteristics of the sample; and ratings of factors influencing decisions to locate in Kansas.

FISCAL-RESTRAINT LEGISLATION: THE KANSAS EXPERIENCE

(p. 19-20) Article evaluating effectiveness of the Kansas legislature in limiting local government expenditures, based on data from Census Bureau and The Rand Corp.

Includes 2 tables showing revenues by source for Kansas, and Kansas City and Wichita SMSAs, 1976/77; and Kansas City and Wichita per capita expenditures, 1965-79 (shown in constant 1978 dollars).

CENSUS DATA PROFILES KANSAS YOUTH

(p. 20-22) Article, with 7 tables showing Kansas and U.S. population, median age, and percent of population by age group and in rural areas; and Kansas median years of school completed by urban-rural status, and school enrollment and labor force participation rates by age group; decennially 1960-80.

KANSAS ECONOMY

(p. 25-28) Includes 6 tables showing Kansas employment and unemployment, with detail for Wichita SMSA; U.S. civilian aircraft shipment value; Kansas and U.S. crop production and grain stocks; and prices received for Kansas farm products; various periods 1979-83.

U7095–1.502: Winter 1984 (Vol. 7, No. 2)

RESIDENTIAL MARKET VALUES, INCOME ELASTICITIES, AND PROPERTY TAXATION IN KANSAS

(p. 1-10) By Terri Sexton. Article on Kansas property tax structure and revenue forecasting methodology. Data are from Kansas Dept of Revenue.

Includes 3 tables showing urban and rural property tax, assessed and market value, and assessment/sales ratio, various years 1962-82; and residential property tax base income elasticities for estimating tax revenues, by county.

STATEWIDE REAPPRAISAL OF KANSAS PROPERTY

(p. 11-15) By Edwin G. Olson. Article, with 2 tables showing current and proposed Kansas property assessment ratios, by property classification, 1982. Data are from Kansas Dept of Revenue.

KANSAS ECONOMY

(p. 18-22) Includes 6 tables showing Kansas and U.S. nonfarm employment by selected industry group, 1979-83; and Kansas agricultural production and prices by commodity, and winter wheat acreage planted, with selected comparisons to other States and total U.S., various periods 1982-84.

U7095–1.503: Spring 1984 (Vol. 7, No. 3)

ECONOMIC ASPECTS OF OIL EXPLORATION IN KANSAS

(p. 1-7) By David Collins and Colleen Eck. Article, with 1 table showing U.S. average annual rotary drilling rig count, wellhead price of crude oil, and interest rate on 3-5 year constant maturity U.S. Treasury bills, 1949-83. Data are from various private and government sources.

ASSESSING THE IMPACTS OF INTERNATIONAL COMPETITION UPON THE KANSAS LABOR MARKET: AN EXPLORATORY ANALYSIS AND REVIEW OF THE AVAILABLE DATA

(p. 8-15) By Kenneth Walker. Article on labor market effects of international competition, with related trend data for Kansas and U.S. Data are from a previous *Kansas Business Review* study, Dept of Commerce, and Conference Board of Canada, Inc.

Includes 2 charts and 5 tables showing the following:

a. Wheat production value and wheat-related exports, for U.S.; and wheat acres sown and harvested, yield, production, price, and farm value, for Kansas; various years 1966-82.

b. Employment related to manufactured exports: by State; by economic sector, for Kansas and U.S.; and as a percent of total manufacturing employment, by State, for total U.S., and for Kansas by major industry group; various years 1972-80.

c. Value of export-related shipments as percent of total manufacturing output, for U.S., and for Kansas by major industry group; and value of imports as percent of total output, by selected industry, for U.S.; various years 1971-80.

ECONOMIC ANALYSIS OF A 'MAKE GOOD' PROGRAM: THE BLIND VENDING FACILITIES OPERATION IN KANSAS

(p. 16-19) By Robert Glass and Richard Sexton. Article analyzing the economic impact of a Kansas program offering blind persons opportunities to manage vending operations in public places. Data were compiled by the authors.

Includes 6 tables showing program impact, including effects on income, employment, and State and Federal tax revenues and government budgets, various years 1978-86.

RESEARCH NOTE: FEDERAL EXPENDITURES IN FY83

(p. 20-21) Article, with 4 tables comparing Federal fund expenditures for total U.S. and Kansas, by program, including direct payments to individuals, grants, agricultural subsidies, and Federal loans and insurance payments, FY83. Data are from Census Bureau.

ECONOMIC CONDITIONS: THE NATIONAL REVIEW

(p. 22-24) Article, with 1 table showing plant capacity utilization rates by major industry group, Mar. 1984. Data are from *Federal Reserve Bulletin*.

KANSAS ECONOMY

(p. 24-27) Includes 5 tables showing Kansas wage/salary employment by industry division, and unemployment rate, for selected counties, 1979 and 1983; U.S. and Kansas grain stocks and plantings, by grain type, 1983-84; and prices for Kansas grain by type, Mar. 1982-84.

U7095–1.504: Summer 1984 (Vol. 7, No. 4)

TRAVEL TO AND THROUGH URBAN CENTERS IN KANSAS: THE KANSAS CITY, KANSAS EXPERIENCE

(p. 1-9) By Richard Sexton and Robert Glass. Article on the economic impact of travel in Kansas and Kansas City SMSA. Data are from Census Bureau. Includes 10 tables showing the following, mostly for 1981/82:

a. Person-nights spent in Kansas City and Kansas by type of accommodation and purpose of trip; and travel mileage, cost per mile, and expenditures for transportation, by type of vehicle, for trips to Kansas City SMSA and overnight trips through Kansas.

b. Travel-related expenditures by sector, with detail for lodging and meals; and general economic impact of travel-related expenditures, by industry division and travel sector, with detail on employment and wages; for Kansas City or Wyandotte County.

DEMOGRAPHIC PROFILE OF KANSAS YOUTH

(p. 10-26) By Daniel L. Petree. Article, with 11 charts and 21 tables showing Kansas youth (age 14-17 and 18-24) population distribution and/or comparison with total population, by urban-rural status, sex, and race, with detail for 4 SMSAs and comparisons to U.S., 1960, 1970, and 1980. Data are from Census Bureau.

Also includes lists of counties with selected youth population shares higher or lower than statewide averages.

KANSAS ECONOMY

(p. 32-35) Includes 3 tables showing number of farms in Kansas by size and major commodity produced, 1978 and 1982; and market value of farm products sold, by commodity, 1982. Data are from Census Bureau.

U7175
University of Louisville: Urban Studies Center

U7175-2   KENTUCKY DEMOGRAPHICS
Series. For individual publication data, see below.
SRI/MF/complete

Continuing series of reports analyzing various aspects of Kentucky's population, labor force, housing characteristics, and income. Reports often contain data by demographic characteristics and location.

Data are primarily from the Census Bureau and are compiled by the University of Louisville, Urban Studies Center.

Only reports with substantial, broad-based statistics are described in SRI.

SRI coverage of this series begins with the reports described below.

Availability: University of Louisville: Urban Studies Center, College of Urban and Public Affairs, Attention: Publications, Gardencourt Campus, 1020 Alta Vista Rd., Louisville KY 40292; SRI/MF/complete.

U7175-2.1: Change in the Black Population of Kentucky: 1960-80
[Monograph. Aug. 1981. v+53 p. No. 5. $2.25. SRI/MF/complete.]

Report on changes in the size and location of Kentucky's black population, 1960s-80. Presents black population by Area Development District (ADD), SMSA, and county, and for 15 largest cities and total nonmetro areas, 1960, 1970, and 1980.

Also includes some comparisons to total and white population, and total U.S.; and summary population for 1900.

Contains listings of contents, tables, and maps (p. i-iv); introduction, and report with 5 maps and 25 tables (p. 1-43); and appendices, with 2 tables (p. 45-53).

U7175-2.2: Population, Housing, Income, and Labor Force in Kentucky: 1970-80
[Monograph. Aug. 1981. 4+12 p. No. 6. $1.25. SRI/MF/complete.]

Report on Kentucky population, housing, income, and labor force, by ADD and selected city. Presents the following by ADD, various years 1970-80:

a. Population by race, and housing units (also shown for 10 largest cities); population change by age; sex ratio; and square mileage.

b. Households; median family and average household income; families below poverty level; labor force; unemployment rate; adult population and percent in labor force, by sex; and marriage and divorce rates.

Contains contents and table listings (2 p.); and narrative summaries, with 3 maps and 13 tables (p. 1-12).

U7175-2.3: Social, Economic, and Housing Characteristics for Kentucky, 1970-80
[Monograph. June 1982. iv+30 p. No. 8. $3.00. SRI/MF/complete.]

Report presenting 1980 U.S. Census of Population and Housing findings for Kentucky, with comparisons to 1970. Includes data on housing characteristics, households, employment, commuting, education, income, and poverty.

Data are from U.S. Census Summary Tape File 3 (STF 3).

Data topics are similar to those noted in the basic data topic description for Summary Tape File 3 reports (see S9990-2), with the following omissions: ancestry, residence in 1975, residents of group quarters, workplace proximity and travel time, and presence of complete plumbing facilities. Data by ethnic group are shown only for Asian/Pacific Islander and Spanish origin.

Sequence of data topics differs from basic description.

Contains contents listing (p. iii); introduction (p. 1); report in 9 sections, each with narrative highlights and tabular data (p. 2-19); and appendix, with index and data topic explanations (p. 21-30).

U7175-2.4: Migration in Kentucky: Analysis and Net Migration Estimates, 1970-80
[Monograph. June 1983. iv+42 p. No. 9. $3.50. SRI/MF/complete.]

Report on migration patterns in Kentucky, primarily 1970-80 period with some trends from 1950. Presents net migration by State region and SMSA; net migration by age and race, and employment by industry division with correlation to migration rate, for metro and nonmetro areas; and net migration by age, sex, and race, by ADD and county.

Contains listings of contents, tables and maps (p. iii-iv); introduction, and report with 3 maps and 9 tables (p. 1-15); and appendix with brief summary, and 1 table repeated for Kentucky and each ADD and county (p. 17-42).

U7215
University of Maine: State Government Partnership Program

U7215-1   MAINE: Fifty Years of Change, 1940-90
Monograph.   Feb. 1983.
xviii + 194 p.
ISBN 0-89101-054-8.
LC 83-621988.
SRI/MF/complete

Report examining Maine social, governmental, and economic trends and outlook, with selected indicator data for various years 1940-90. Report documents proceedings of 2 conferences on Maine history and economic forecasting, held during 1982.

Data are from Federal and State agencies, and private and academic sources. Most projections are derived from the Maine Economic Policy Analysis Model.

Contains introductory matter and contents listing (p. iii-x); 7 primarily narrative chapters, interspersed with 23 charts, and 40 tables described below (p. 1-160); and appendices, including 1 table (p. 187) showing Maine employment, by industry, decennially 1970-90 (p. 161-194).

Availability: University of Maine at Orono, Bookstore, Orono ME 04469, $5.95; SRI/MF/ complete.

TABLES:
[Data are for Maine, unless otherwise noted.]

U7215-1.1: Economic Development and Population Trends
 a. GSP, employment, and labor/proprietors' income, by industry division and selected major industry group, various years 1940-90. 21 tables. (p. 10-40)
 b. Population distribution by age group, decennially 1940-80. 1 table. (p. 59)

U7215-1.2: Government Finances and Elections
 a. State/local total general revenue, general revenue from State sources, and taxes, all per $1,000 personal income, and per capita expenditures, with comparison to U.S., selected periods 1942-80; and projected State and local revenues and expenditures, 1990. 5 tables. (p. 91-96)
 b. Democratic percent of votes cast for selected State and national offices; votes and voter turnout in elections for Governor and President; voter registration by party; and State legislature membership by party; various years 1940-84. 4 tables. (p. 100-107)

U7215-1.3: Economic Projections
[The following data are shown primarily for 1990 compared to 1980, with selected comparisons to U.S.]
 a. Fuel use distribution by fuel type, for manufacturing and nonmanufacturing industry. 1 table. (p. 140)
 b. Growth in population, employment, and income (earnings and unearned); percent of new jobs with high and low earnings; population by age group; and employment by industry sector. 6 tables. (p. 142-146)

U7215-1.4: Population Characteristics, and Government Spending and Employment
[The following data are for 1980 and 1990.]
 a. School age children, population 65 years/ over, and population at or below 125% of poverty level. 1 table. (p. 157)
 b. State/local expenditures and employment for education, highways, health/welfare, and other functions. 1 table. (p. 158)

U7360
University of Massachusetts: Management Research Center

U7360-1   MASSACHUSETTS BUSINESS AND ECONOMIC REPORT
Quarterly.
Approx. 6 p. no paging.
SRI/MF/complete

Quarterly report presenting forecasts of selected Massachusetts business and economic indicators, and articles on topics affecting the Massachusetts economy. Forecasts are from a model developed by Data Resources, Inc.

Issues usually contain articles, occasionally with substantial statistics; and 1 quarterly table, "Control Forecast," occasionally with illustrative charts, including data on employment, wages, average weekly hours in manufacturing, rate of inflation, personal and disposable income, and business cost index.

Table usually presents data annually for current, prior, and coming years, and quarterly for 5 quarters beginning 1-2 quarters prior to date of issue.

Quarterly table appears in all issues. All additional features with substantial statistical content are described, as they appear, under "Statistical Features." Nonstatistical features are not covered.

Availability: University of Massachusetts: Management Research Center, Business Publications Services, School of Management, Amherst MA 01003, †; SRI/MF/complete.

Issues reviewed during 1984: Summer 1983-Summer 1984 (P) (Vol. 10, No. 4; Vol. 11, Nos. 1-3) [No Winter 1984 issue was published].

STATISTICAL FEATURE:

U7360-1.501: Spring 1984 (Vol. 11, No. 2)
MATURE INDUSTRIES IN MASSACHUSETTS
(3 p.) By Joseph Duffey. Article, with 2 tables showing Massachusetts employment and pay-

roll, for selected basic and high-technology industries, 1971 and 1981. Data are from Census Bureau.

U7455
University of Michigan: Graduate School of Business Administration

U7455-1   NEWLY PROMOTED EXECUTIVE: A Study in Corporate Leadership, 1983-84
Annual.   1984.   31 + App 4 p.
ISBN 0-87712-236-9.
SRI/MF/complete

Annual report, by Floyd A. Bond et al., examining characteristics and career advancement trends of business executives promoted during FY84. Data are from responses of 1,021 executives to a 1984 survey conducted by University of Michigan Graduate School of Business Administration.

Contains introduction (p. 1); 37 tables, described below, with accompanying narrative (p. 3-31); and appendix with questionnaire facsimile (4 p.).

This edition covers the 14th annual survey. SRI coverage begins with this edition.

Availability: University of Michigan: Graduate School of Business Administration, Division of Research, 904 Monroe St., Ann Arbor MI 48109-1234, $2.00; SRI/MF/complete.

TABLES:
[Data show survey response, generally for chairman of the board, president, and vice-president.]
 a. Position and perquisites after promotion; industry division and operating revenue of present employer; salary before and after promotion; years with present employer and in previous position; and method of promotion. 9 tables. (p. 3-8)
 b. Factors affecting decision to change position; number of employers prior to present employer; experience working abroad; major areas of responsibility at beginning of career and before and after promotion, and best areas for advancement; and corporate and nonprofit organization directorships held. 8 tables. (p. 9-15)
 c. Mean hours worked per week; importance of participation in external political activity and corporate development programs; educational attainment, major field of postsecondary study, and undergraduate and advanced degrees from 14 institutions; and most useful postsecondary curricula for future managers. 6 tables. (p. 16-21)
 d. Age; expected age at retirement; sex; place of birth (10 major States) and birth order in family; parental family income; occupation of mother and father; religious affiliation; race/ ethnicity, including Hispanic and Oriental; marital status; employment status and occupation of spouse, and importance of spouse to business success; and serious economic problems today and in 3 years. 14 tables. (p. 21-31)

U7475
University of Michigan: Institute for Social Research

U7475–1   SURVEYS OF CONSUMER ATTITUDES, Quarterly Report
Quarterly.
Summary approx. 15 p., tables approx. 70 p. no paging.
SRI/MF/complete

Quarterly report on survey measuring changes in consumer attitudes and expectations concerning personal finances and general business and market conditions. Questions cover attitudes affecting consumer decisions on discretionary purchases and savings, including perceptions of inflation and buying conditions for household goods, automobiles, and houses.

Survey is conducted by the University of Michigan Survey Research Center as part of a program monitoring economic change. Data are based on approximately 2,000 interviews conducted over several weeks and concluded in the final month of each quarter. Report is published 2-3 weeks after the end of quarter surveyed. A less comprehensive monthly report is also published (see U7475-2, below).

Survey report is presented in 2 parts:

a. Narrative summary of survey highlights, including changes during the quarter in consumer attitudes and outlook, usually with 1 or more charts and tables.

b. 34 tables (under separate cover), listed below, showing response percents by attitude and specific questions asked, most with 1-2 accompanying charts showing recent and historical trends; and explanatory charts and definitions.

Availability: University of Michigan: Institute for Social Research, Monitoring Economic Change Program, Survey Research Center, PO Box 1248, Ann Arbor MI 48106-1248, members $2000.00 per yr., sponsors $2500.00 per yr., non-profit groups $1200.00 per yr. (includes working papers series of same title); SRI/MF/complete.
Issues reviewed during 1984: Dec. 1983-Sept. 1984 (D).

TABLES:
[Tables 1-3 show quarterly data for current and preceding 7 years. Tables 4-34 show quarterly data for current and preceding 3 years, for all families, and families with incomes over $20,000.]

1. Index of consumer sentiment [for all families, and families with incomes over $20,000 and over $25,000].

2. Index of consumer sentiment within region and age subgroups [for all families].

3. Components of the index of consumer sentiment [for all families].

4-5. Current financial situation compared to a year ago, and selected reasons for opinions about personal financial situation.

6-7. Expected change in financial situation, and trend in personal financial situation.

8. Expected family income change during the next 12 months.

9-10. Past and expected changes in real family income.

11. Trend in family income and prices comparisons.

12-13. News heard and selected items of news heard of recent changes in business conditions.

14-16. Current business conditions compared to a year ago, expected change in a year, and reasons for opinions about [expected] changes.

17-19. Trend in past and expected changes in business conditions, and business conditions expected during the next 12 months and the next 5 years.

20-21. Expected change in unemployment and in interest rates.

22-23. Change in prices during the last 12 months and expected during the next 12 months.

24. Unemployment or inflation more serious economic hardship.

25. Opinions about the government's economic policy.

26-27. Buying conditions for large household goods, and selected reasons for opinions about buying conditions.

28-29. Buying conditions for houses, and selected reasons for opinions about buying conditions.

30-31. Buying conditions for cars, and selected reasons for opinions about buying conditions.

32-34. Plans to purchase an automobile during the next 12 months, and current and future vehicle purchase intentions.

U7475–2   SURVEYS OF CONSUMER ATTITUDES, Monthly Report
Monthly.
Summary approx. 10 p., tables approx. 60 p. no paging.
SRI/MF/complete

Monthly report on survey measuring changes in consumer attitudes and expectations concerning their personal financial situation and general business and market conditions. Questions cover attitudes affecting consumer decisions on discretionary purchases and savings, including perceptions of inflation and buying conditions for household goods, automobiles, and houses.

Data are based on approximately 700 interviews conducted over several weeks and concluded in the 3rd week of each month. Report is published 2-3 weeks after end of month of coverage.

Survey is presented in 2 parts:

a. Narrative summary of changes in consumer attitudes from preceding month, usually with 1 or more charts and text tables.

b. 34 tables (under separate cover), listed below, most with 1-2 accompanying charts showing recent and longer term trends; and contents listing, explanatory charts, and definitions.

Survey report is a companion to the more comprehensive quarterly survey, described by SRI under U7475-1. Quarterly survey includes additional detail by income group.

Availability: University of Michigan: Institute for Social Research, Monitoring Economic Change Program, Survey Research Center, PO Box 1248, Ann Arbor MI 48106-1248, members $3350.00 per yr., sponsors $3900.00 per yr., non-

profit groups $2100.00 per yr. (subscription includes quarterly report and working papers series of same title); SRI/MF/complete.
Issues reviewed during 1984: Oct. 1983-Sept. 1984 (D).

TABLES:
[Tables 1-3 show data for month of coverage and preceding 36 months. All other tables show data for month of coverage and preceding 12 months.]

1. Index of consumer sentiment [all families, and families with incomes over $20,000, and over $25,000].

2. Index of consumer sentiment within region and age subgroups.

3. Components of the index of consumer sentiment.

4-5. Current financial situation compared to a year ago, and selected reasons for opinions about personal financial situation.

6-7. Expected change in financial situation, and trend in personal financial situation.

8. Expected family income change during the next 12 months.

9-10. Past and expected changes in real family income.

11. Trend in family income and prices comparisons.

12-13. News heard and selected items of news heard of recent changes in business conditions.

14-16. Current business conditions compared to a year ago, expected change in a year, and reasons for opinions about [expected] changes.

17-19. Trend in past and expected changes in business conditions, and business conditions expected during the next 12 months and the next 5 years.

20-21. Expected change in unemployment and in interest rates.

22-23. Change in prices during the last 12 months, and expected during the next 12 months.

24. Unemployment or inflation more serious economic hardship.

25. Opinions about the government's economic policy.

26-27. Buying conditions for large household goods, and selected reasons for opinions about buying conditions.

28-29. Buying conditions for houses, and selected reasons for opinions about buying conditions.

30-31. Buying conditions for cars, and selected reasons for opinions about buying conditions.

32-34. Plans to purchase an automobile during the next 12 months, and current and future vehicle purchase intentions.

U7475–3   ECONOMIC OUTLOOK USA
Quarterly. Approx. 20 p.
cumulative pagination throughout year.
ISSN 0095-3830.
LC 74-648918.
SRI/MF/complete

Quarterly journal analyzing current economic conditions, and presenting selected measures of consumer economic expectations and buying attitudes.

Data are from the Commerce Dept, National Bureau of Economic Research, National Assn of Business Economists (NABE), and University of Michigan econometric forecast model and consumer surveys. Quarter of data coverage is 1 quarter prior to cover date.

Issues generally contain 2-6 "Economic Prospects" trend charts for selected economic indicators; quarterly and other articles, many with statistics; 2 quarterly economic indicator tables; and 12 quarterly trend charts on consumer attitudes and economic indicators.

Quarterly articles include a consumer survey feature, with 1 consumer sentiment index trend chart, and occasionally 1 or more tables; and NABE survey article, with data on business economists' opinions regarding economic issues and outlook.

An annual author index appears in autumn issue.

Quarterly economic indicator tables are described below. Most quarterly charts and tables appear in all issues. All additional features with substantial statistical content, including consumer survey tables, are described as they appear, under "Statistical Features." Nonstatistical features are not covered.

Availability: University of Michigan: Institute for Social Research, Survey Research Center, 426 Thompson St., PO Box 1248, Ann Arbor MI 48106, $27.00 per yr., academic subscribers $13.00 per yr.; SRI/MF/complete.

Issues reviewed during 1984: Autumn 1983-Summer 1984 (P) (Vol. 10, No. 4; Vol. 11, Nos. 1-3).

QUARTERLY TABLES:

a. Actual and projected data for 17 indicators, including industrial production index, corporate profits and bond yield, housing starts, Treasury bill rate, government purchases, and change in business inventories, shown quarterly for quarter of coverage and previous 6 and following 4 quarters, and annually for previous, current, and coming years; projections are from American Statistical Assn-National Bureau of Economic Research panel.

b. Current-dollar GNP accounts: 7 indicators including personal consumption expenditures, private domestic investment, government purchases, net exports, disposable personal income, and personal saving rate; quarterly for quarter of coverage and preceding 11 quarters, and annually for preceding 3 years.

STATISTICAL FEATURES:

U7475–3.501: Autumn 1983 (Vol. 10, No. 4)

CONSUMER OPTIMISM MAINTAINED AT RECORD LEVEL, QUARTERLY FEATURE

(p. 78-80) Quarterly consumer survey article, by Richard T. Curtin, with 1 table showing consumer willingness to finance major purchases by credit and by use of savings, 3rd quarter 1980-83.

RESULTS FROM THE AUG. NABE SURVEY, QUARTERLY FEATURE

(p. 81-82) Quarterly article, by Richard E. Barfield, on business economists' opinions on current economic issues and outlook. Data are from a survey of National Assn of Business Economists (NABE) members, conducted by University of Michigan Survey Research Center, Aug. 1983.

Includes 3 tables showing forecasts for selected economic indicators, generally through 4th quarter 1984; distribution of responses regarding satisfaction with fiscal and monetary policy, with trends from Nov. 1982; and distribution of responses on appropriate method for presidential administration to express disagreement with Federal Reserve policies, by respondent's professional affiliation.

SOME LESSONS FROM RESEARCH IN MACROECONOMIC FORECASTING

(p. 83-86) By Victor Zarnowitz. Article evaluating the accuracy of various methods for forecasting changes in 6 major economic indicators. Data are based on forecasts from participants in American Statistical Assn-National Bureau of Economic Research surveys conducted 4th quarter 1968-1st quarter 1980. Includes 2 tables.

EFFECTS OF CULTURAL ASSIMILATION AND EDUCATION ON MEXICAN AMERICAN WORKERS' EARNINGS

(p. 87-90) By Carlos H. Arce and David L. Torres. Article, with 1 table correlating assimilation measures, education, and salary, for Mexican Americans. Data are based on the "Chicano Survey" of 991 Mexican Americans, conducted by the Survey Research Center, 1979.

U7475–3.502: Winter 1984 (Vol. 11, No. 1)

U.S. ECONOMIC OUTLOOK FOR 1984, ANNUAL FEATURE

(p. 3-10) Annual article, by Saul H. Hymans et al., presenting Michigan Quarterly Econometric Model national economic forecasts through 1985. Forecasts are made by University of Michigan Research Seminar in Quantitative Economics (RSQE); actual data are from U.S. Depts of Commerce and Labor, and the Federal Reserve System.

Includes 1 summary chart covering 6 major indicators, 1983-85; and 3 tables showing the following:

a. Change in 19 economic indicators, actual 1981-82, and actual vs. forecast 1982-83; and Federal Government expenditures by type, and total receipts, FY83-85.

b. Forecasts for 27 economic indicators, including GNP and components, unemployment rate, corporate profits, 90-day Treasury bill rate, real disposable income, and personal saving rate, quarterly 4th quarter 1983-4th quarter 1985, and annually 1984-85, with actual data for 3rd quarter 1983.

RETURN OF SUSTAINED EXPANSION?

(p. 12-13) By Paul W. McCracken. Article, with 2 tables showing percent change in new plant/equipment expenditures for nonmanufacturing and durable and nondurable goods manufacturing, 1983-84; and manufacturing goods trade balance, and real effective exchange rate index, 1979-83. Data are from Commerce Dept and *World Financial Markets.*

RESULTS FROM THE NOV. NABE SURVEY, QUARTERLY FEATURE

(p. 17-19) Quarterly article, by Richard E. Barfield, on business economists' opinions on current economic issues and outlook. Data are from a survey of National Assn of Business

Economists (NABE) members, conducted by University of Michigan Survey Research Center, Nov. 1983.

Includes 4 tables showing company/industry summary operating trends for previous 3 months; forecasts for selected economic indicators, generally through 4th quarter 1984; distribution of responses regarding satisfaction with fiscal and monetary policy, with trends from Feb. 1983; and expected year for current business cycle peak, by respondent's professional affiliation.

U7475–3.503: Spring 1984 (Vol. 11, No. 2)

REIGN OF OPTIMISM, QUARTERLY FEATURE

(p. 31-34) Quarterly consumer survey article, by Richard T. Curtin, with 5 tables on views concerning the Federal budget deficit, Mar. 1984, with selected comparisons to earlier surveys.

Tables cover consumers' awareness of and concern about the deficit, expected changes in the deficit over the next 1-2 and 5-10 years, expected effect of deficit on business, and interest rate expectations and consumer sentiment index correlated with opinions about deficit.

BUSINESS ECONOMISTS FORESEE CONTINUED EXPANSION BUT URGE ACTION ON DEFICITS, QUARTERLY FEATURE

(p. 35-37) Quarterly article, by Richard E. Barfield, on business economists' opinions on current economic issues and outlook. Data are from a survey of National Assn of Business Economists (NABE) members, conducted by University of Michigan Survey Research Center, Feb. 1984.

Includes 4 tables showing company/industry summary operating trends for previous 3 months; forecasts for selected economic indicators, generally through 4th quarter 1984; distribution of responses regarding satisfaction with fiscal and monetary policy, with trends from May 1983; and expected year for current business cycle peak, by respondent's professional affiliation.

U7475–3.504: Summer 1984 (Vol. 11, No. 3)

CREDIT DEMAND, MONEY POLICY, AND THE OUTLOOK FOR THE ECONOMY

(p. 51-53) By Raymond J. Saulnier. Article discussing economic outlook for 1985. Data are from Federal Reserve Board, Federal Reserve Banks of St. Louis and New York, and *Business Conditions Digest.*

Includes 3 tables showing percent change in 3 measures of money supply, year ended July 9, 1984, with detail for 3 subperiods; and net borrowing of Federal Government and private and foreign sectors, various periods 1979-84.

BUSINESS ECONOMISTS PREDICT GOOD TIMES TO CONTINUE FOR A WHILE BUT EXPECT RECESSION NEXT YEAR, QUARTERLY FEATURE

(p. 61-63) Quarterly article, by Richard E. Barfield, on business economists' opinions on current economic issues and outlook. Data are from a survey of National Assn of Business Economists (NABE) members, conducted by University of Michigan Survey Research Center, May 1984.

Includes 4 tables showing company/industry summary operating trends for previous 3 months; forecasts for selected economic indicators, generally through 1985; distribution of responses regarding satisfaction with fiscal and monetary policy, with trends from Aug. 1983; and expected year for current business cycle peak, by respondent's professional affiliation.

TRACKING THE 1984 PRESIDENTIAL RACE

(p. 64-67) By Michael W. Traugott. Article, with 2 tables showing change in voter support associated with Democratic Party's selection of a female candidate for the vice-presidency, by sex and political party, June 1984; and level of support before and after political convention, for presidential party controlling and not controlling the presidency, election years 1964-84.

Data are from a June 1984 survey of Michigan residents, and national surveys conducted by Gallup Organization, Inc.

U7475–4   SURVEYS OF CONSUMER ATTITUDES: Working Paper Series

Series. For individual publication data, see below.
SRI/MF/complete

Series of special reports covering consumer and household financial transactions, credit and consumption patterns, durable goods ownership, and related topics. Includes data on consumer attitudes, and breakdowns by sociodemographic characteristics.

Data are primarily from monthly Surveys of Consumer Attitudes and other Institute for Social Research studies.

Reports usually contain analysis of survey findings, with text statistics, and 3 or more detailed tables showing response breakdowns.

Report reviewed during 1984 is described below.

Availability: University of Michigan: Institute for Social Research, Monitoring Economic Change Program, Survey Research Center, PO Box 1248, Ann Arbor MI 48106-1248, included in subscription to *Surveys of Consumer Attitudes,* available individually at $50.00 each; SRI/MF/complete.

U7475–4.16: Making of a Recovery: Consumers Strut the "Right Stuff"

[Monograph. Nov. 1983. 34 p. No. WP19. SRI/MF/complete.]

By Richard T. Curtin. Report on recent trends in consumer attitudes and expectations. Includes summary data on attitudes toward housing and auto markets (including influence of prices and interest rates), and toward use of credit and savings for major purchases, various quarters 1977-83; and selected household asset and liability ratios, quinquennially 1952-82.

Data are from Surveys of Consumer Attitudes and the Federal Reserve Board.

Contains narrative report (p. 1-14); 34 trend charts (17 p.); and 3 tables (2 p.).

U7475–5   MONITORING THE FUTURE: Questionnaire Responses from the Nation's High School Seniors, 1982

Annual. 1984. x+271 p.
ISR Code No. 4593.
ISSN 0190-9185.
ISBN 0-87944-291-3.
LC 79-640937.
SRI/MF/complete

Annual survey, for 1982, by Jerald G. Bachman et al., of the values, behavior, and lifestyle of U.S. high school seniors. Principal focus is on drug use and related attitudes, but study also includes responses on life satisfaction, leisure activities, personal relationships, changing roles of women, attitudes toward social institutions, conservation and ecology issues, and social and ethical attitudes.

Data are based on a national survey sample of 18,348 students in 116 public and 21 private high schools, conducted by the Survey Research Center of the University of Michigan in 1982.

The survey, 8th in a series begun in 1975, is designed to study trends in attitudes and behavior, and repeats a majority of the 1,500 questions asked each year. Questions are divided into 5 questionnaire forms answered by approximately 3,600 seniors for each form; approximately 100 questions appear on all 5 forms and are answered by the total sample.

Contents:

a. Contents listing; preface; and introduction, presenting study background and methodology, with 2 tables showing sample size and response rates, 1975-82, and list of 19 subject areas covered. (p. v-x, 1-11)

b. Descriptive results, with explanation of table format (p. 13-15); and responses to questions appearing on all survey forms (p. 16-33), and to questions on each form (p. 34-202).

c. Cross-time index of questionnaire items, 1975-83. (p. 203-242)

d. Appendices A-C, presenting sampling error estimates and methodology, with 2 charts and 5 tables; sample of questionnaire; and list of references. (p. 243-271)

Question topics are described below.

Previous report, for 1981, is described in SRI 1982 Annual under this number.

Availability: University of Michigan: Institute for Social Research, Publications Sales, PO Box 1248, Ann Arbor MI 48106, $40.00, $215.00 for 8 volume set; SRI/MF/complete.

QUESTION TOPICS:

[All responses are shown by sex, race, census region, 4-year college plans (yes or no), and lifetime illicit drug use (none, marijuana only, few pills, more pills, and any heroin).]

U7475–5.1: Questionnaire Forms 1-5

[Data show responses to approximately 100 questions appearing on all 5 questionnaire forms.]

a. Background data including ethnicity; marital status; household composition; parents' schooling; political beliefs; religious preferences; self-rating on ability and intelligence; and school grades and attendance record; questions C01-C20. (p. 16-20)

b. Activities including future plans; employment and recreation; traffic violations and accidents while drinking or using drugs; and expectations of military service; questions C21-C34. (p. 20-24)

c. Frequency and quantity of cigarette smoking; drinking of alcoholic beverages; and use of drugs, by type including marijuana, LSD, cocaine, heroin, and other narcotics and inhaled substances; questions B01-B17C. (p. 25-33)

U7475–5.2: Questionnaire Form 1

a. Views on personal happiness and relations with others, life satisfaction and goals, and the political system; questions A001-A011J. (p. 34-41)

b. Detailed questions on circumstances, frequency, and attitudes with respect to cigarette, alcohol, and drug use; questions B001-B104L. (p. 41-82)

c. Experiences in and attitudes toward school; experiences with school counselors; and health; questions D001-D018. (p. 83-89)

U7475–5.3: Questionnaire Form 2

a. Frequency of participation in leisure time activities including watching TV and reading; attitudes toward the economic system, social protest, marriage, and working couples sharing responsibilities; political attitudes and participation; U.S. foreign policies; frequency of delinquent behavior; and experiences of victimization; questions A01-A20G. (p. 90-104)

b. Drug availability; life satisfaction and self-ratings, and ratings of social institutions; assessment of the frequency with which friends engage in drug use by specific drug, and drink alcoholic beverages; and personal drug use, school grade in which first tried different drugs, and parents' knowledge of alcohol and drug use; questions A21-E06. (p. 104-113)

c. Reactions to anger; views on military service and draft; assessment of the influence of people in authority on the school system; experiences with school drug education; views on tests of basic academic skills; and eating, exercise, and sleep habits; questions E07-E20F. (p. 113-118)

U7475–5.4: Questionnaire Form 3

a. Attitudes toward equal employment of women; willingness to change behavior to conserve resources; importance of leisure and work; relations with other racial groups; plans for marriage and having children; and ratings of 12 types of public institutions; questions A01-A26. (p. 119-128)

b. Personal use of nonprescription drugs; attitudes toward and association with different types of drug users; frequency of selected physical symptoms; and attempts to stop using drugs and reasons; questions A27-D04. (p. 128-135)

c. Views on value of conservation and anti-pollution efforts and need for population and birth control; ratings of behaviors that give high status in high school; experiences of victimization; desire for material possessions; and school grade in which first tried different drugs; questions E01-E10M. (p. 136-145)

U7475–5.5: Questionnaire Form 4

a. Attitudes toward future, including controlling pollution and personal consumption; views on characteristics of a good job and job expect to have at age 30; attitudes toward premarital relationships and marriage; amount of TV watched daily, and reading habits; and influence various institutions should exert on society; questions A01-A19J. (p. 146-158)

b. Views on legalization of drugs; life and job satisfaction, and job experiences; world problems; frequency of use of alcoholic beverages; views on military life; similarity of student's, parents', and friends' attitudes on selected issues including drug use and drinking alcohol; and housing type and location preferences; questions A20-E09J. (p. 158-173)

U7475–5.6: Questionnaire Form 5

a. Concern with social problems; preparation for marriage and parenting; rating of work setting; experiences with other races; driving; consumer behavior; concern for others; and types of organizations likely to receive student's charitable contributions in the future; questions A01-A21. (p. 174-184)

b. Views on discrimination against women; risk of harmful effects from cigarettes, selected drugs, and alcohol; attitudes about self and others; financial and job security; and saving and spending habits; questions A22-D05E. (p. 184-194)

c. Personal attitudes and opinion on others' attitudes toward users of marijuana and other illegal drugs, and cigarette smoking; and consumption of caffeinated beverages; questions E01-E15. (p. 194-202)

U7860
University of Nebraska: Bureau of Business Research

U7860–1   BUSINESS IN NEBRASKA
Monthly.   Approx. 6 p.
ISSN 0149-4163.
SRI/MF/complete, shipped quarterly

Monthly review of business and economic activity in Nebraska. Data are from Federal and State agencies and private sources. Month of data coverage is 4 months prior to month of publication.

Each issue contains 1 feature article, usually with statistics; and 3 charts and 5 monthly tables, accompanied by narrative analysis.

Monthly tables are listed below and appear in all issues. All additional features with substantial statistical content are described, as they appear, under "Statistical Features." Nonstatistical features are not covered.

Availability: University of Nebraska: Bureau of Business Research, College of Business Administration, Rm. 200, Lincoln NE 68588-0406, †; SRI/MF/complete, shipped quarterly.

Issues reviewed during 1984: Nov. 1983-Sept. 1984 (P) (Nos. 470-480) [Dec. 1983, No. 471 incorrectly reads Nov. 1983, No. 470].

MONTHLY TABLES:
[Tables show data for month of coverage and/or current year to date, both as percent of same periods of previous year.]

1-2. Economic indicators: Nebraska and U.S. [indexes of physical output and dollar volume for agricultural, nonagricultural, construction, manufacturing, distributive, and government sectors; also shows change from 1967].

3. Net taxable retail sales of Nebraska regions and cities.

4. City business indicators [employment, building activity, and electric power/natural gas consumption, by city trading center].

5. Price indexes [consumer and wholesale for U.S., agricultural for Nebraska and U.S.].

STATISTICAL FEATURES:

U7860–1.501: Nov. 1983 (No. 470)

INFLATION: WHICH PRICES MATTER?

(p. 1-3, 6) Article describing CPI composition, with 1 chart and 1 table showing urban CPI percent increase attributable to top 5 and all other components, 1978-83; and weighted relative importance of old vs. 1983 revised urban CPI by item, Dec. 1982.

U7860–1.502: Dec. 1983 (No. 471)
[Issue incorrectly reads Nov. 1983 (No. 470).]

PERSONAL INCOME: NEBRASKA AND THE PLAINS STATES

(p. 1-3, 6) Article, with 3 tables showing total and per capita personal income for 7 Plains States and the U.S., 1969, 1979, and 1982; and personal income by source, and earnings by type and industry group, for Nebraska and highest and lowest Plains State, with comparison to U.S., 1982.

Data are from U.S. Bureau of Economic Analysis.

U7860–1.503: Jan. 1984 (No. 472)

ELEMENTARY AND SECONDARY EDUCATION FINANCING

(p. 1-3, 6) Article, with 1 detailed table showing Nebraska tax revenues for education (total and per student), by government level and county, 1981/82, with State aid comparison to 1971/72. Also includes 4 summary tables.

Data are from Nebraska Dept of Education.

U7860–1.504: Feb. 1984 (No. 473)

LOCAL EDUCATION TAXES

(p. 1-3) Article examining relationship between levels of personal income and property taxes for education, in Nebraska. Includes 3 tables showing property tax collections, personal income, and population, by county, FY81 and/or FY82.

U7860–1.505: Apr. 1984 (No. 475)

1981 AND 1982 NEBRASKA POPULATION ESTIMATES

(p. 1-3, 6) Article, with 1 table showing Nebraska population 1980-82, and net migration rate 1980-82 period, by county and MSA, and for total metro and nonmetro areas. Data are from University of Nebraska and Census Bureau.

U7860–1.506: May 1984 (No. 476)

U.S. WHEAT EXPORTS: PAST AND PROSPECTS

(p. 1-3) Article, with 2 tables showing the following for wheat flour/products: U.S. exports by country or world area of destination, world exports and production by country or world area, and U.S. and world consumption and ending stocks, primarily 1972-83. Data are from USDA.

U7860–1.507: June 1984 (No. 477)

NEBRASKA'S FARMLAND MARKET IN PERSPECTIVE

(p. 1-3, 6) Article, with 1 table showing Nebraska average farmland value by type of land, by crop reporting district, 1983-84. Data are from surveys conducted by University of Nebraska Dept of Agricultural Economics.

U7860–1.508: July 1984 (No. 478)

NEBRASKA RETAIL SALES, 1982-83, ANNUAL FEATURE

(p. 1-3) Annual article, with 2 tables showing Nebraska net taxable retail sales, by planning/development region, county, and selected trading center, 1982-83, with price-adjusted and unadjusted percent change.

U7860–1.509: Aug. 1984 (No. 479)

RETAIL SALES ATTRACTION OF NEBRASKA COUNTIES

(p. 1-3, 6) Article, with 2 tables on trends in the geographic distribution of retail sales in Nebraska, 1968-83. Tables present ratios comparing each county's share of sales to its share of population and income; and statewide ratios of geographic concentration, for sales, population, and income.

Data were compiled by the Bureau of Business Research, based on data from the Census Bureau, Nebraska Tax Commissioner, and others.

U7860–1.510: Sept. 1984 (No. 480)

COMPONENTS OF NEBRASKA'S PERSONAL INCOME

(p. 1-3, 6) Article, with 2 charts and 3 tables showing Nebraska and U.S. personal income by source, including wages/salaries by industry division, 1958-60 and 1980-82 periods, with selected 1982 detail for Nebraska.

Data are from U.S. Bureau of Economic Analysis.

U7870
University of Nebraska: Bureau of Sociological Research

U7870–1   NEBRASKA ANNUAL SOCIAL INDICATORS SURVEY
Series. For individual publication data, see below.
SRI/MF/complete

Continuing series of reports on Nebraska residents' attitudes toward selected economic and social issues relating to quality of life.

Series is based on Nebraska Annual Social Indicators Survey (NASIS) of approximately 1,900 persons, conducted by telephone by the Bureau of Sociological Research at the University of Nebraska-Lincoln. Series began in 1977, and a panel selected from 1977 respondents, supplemented by some new respondents, is reinterviewed each odd-numbered year. A new cross-sectional sample is interviewed each even-numbered year.

Each year, series includes 1 report documenting survey methodology; and 8-12 topical reports, each presenting narrative analysis and summary of survey findings pertaining to a selected issue, with a varying number of tables showing sample characteristics and detailed breakdowns of responses.

Reports reviewed during 1984 are described below, and are based on data from the 6th and 7th annual NASIS surveys, conducted in 1982 and 1983, respectively.

Availability: University of Nebraska: Bureau of Sociological Research, 732 Oldfather Hall, Lincoln NE 68588-0325; SRI/MF/complete.

1982 SERIES

U7870–1.37: Look at Nebraskan's Favorite Outdoor Recreational Activities
[Monograph. [1983.] 7+4 p. NASIS-82, No. 6. $0.75. SRI/MF/complete.]

By David R. Johnson and Laurie K. Scheuble. Report on Nebraskans' outdoor recreational activities. Includes 2 tables showing top 15 activities among respondents by sex, age, education, urban or rural location, and State region.

U7870–1.38: Social Security and Government Spending: The Elderly Speak Out
[Monograph. [1983.] 12 p. no paging. NASIS-82, No. 7. $0.75. SRI/MF/complete.]

By Jane C. Ollenburger. Report on attitudes of Nebraska's population age 65/over toward social security program and government spending. Includes 8 tables showing distribution of 376 elderly NASIS respondents, generally by sex, to questions concerning social security issues and future stability; support for reduced services vs. increased State taxes, with detail by tax type; and support for increased government spending by program area.

U7870–1.39: Support for Programs Related to Alcohol Problems
[Monograph. [1983.] 7+5 p. NASIS-82, No. 8. $0.75. SRI/MF/complete.]

By Helen A. Moore. Report on Nebraskans' opinions on specific programs and actions for reducing alcohol-related problems. Includes 2 tables showing responses regarding effectiveness of various programs; with detail for 5 programs rated very effective, by age, sex, education, and urban or rural residence, and for respondents who do and do not drink.

U7870–1.40: Nebraskans and Health Risks: Social Indicators of Health Status
[Monograph. [1983.] 7+6 p. NASIS-82, No. 9. $0.75. SRI/MF/complete.]

By Stephanie L. Shanks and Richard L. Meile. Report examining health risk factors among Nebraska's population. Includes 2 tables showing prevalence of selected risk factors, and frequency of limiting fat/cholesterol intake, by sex, marital and social status, age, and urban or rural residence.

U7870–1.41: Nebraskans' Views on Public Welfare Issues
[Monograph. [1983.] 9+2 p. NASIS-82, No. 10. $0.75. SRI/MF/complete.]

By Carol Moats Tomer and Mary Olsen. Report on Nebraskans' attitudes toward public welfare programs. Includes 4 text tables showing responses regarding private sector responsibility for program funding, government level

perceived best suited for program administration and funding, and support for continuation of selected programs.

U7870–1.42: New Religious Right: An Examination of the Value Dislocation Hypothesis
[Monograph. [1983.] 13+1 p. NASIS-82, No. 11. $1.00. SRI/MF/complete.]

By Helen A. Moore and Hugh P. Whitt. Report on Nebraskans' attitudes toward the Moral Majority organization. Includes 2 tables showing respondent awareness and approval of Moral Majority, and agreement with Moral Majority position on selected social issues, by sex, religion, place of residence, education, and age.

U7870–1.43: Risk Factors and Utilization of Physician and Hospital Services
[Monograph. [1983.] 11+7 p. NASIS-82, No. 12. $0.75. SRI/MF/complete.]

By Richard L. Meile and Stephanie L. Shanks. Report on Nebraskans' use of health care services. Includes 4 tables showing frequency of physician visits and hospitalization, by sex, age, urban or rural residence, marital and social status, presence of selected health risk factors, and limitation of fat/cholesterol intake.

1983 SERIES

U7870–1.44: Designs, Procedures, Instruments, and Forms for the 1983 NASIS
[Annual. [1984.] 167 p. var. paging. NASIS-83, No. 1. $7.50. SRI/MF/complete.]

Annual report, by Helen A. Moore, on methodology and respondent characteristics of NASIS, 1983.

Contents:

a. Narrative summary, with 7 tables showing sample data and survey costs. (p. 1-22)

b. Appendices, including study prospectus, questionnaire facsimile, interviewer manual, codes, and variables.

U7870–1.45: Effects of the Recession on Nebraskans
[Monograph. [1984.] 11 p. NASIS-83, No. 2. $1.00. SRI/MF/complete.]

By Alan Booth. Report on the effect of the recent economic recession on Nebraskans. Includes 5 tables showing affected households, by type of problem experienced; characteristics of persons reporting economic loss, including income, occupation, age, marital status, and community type or size; methods of coping with economic loss; types of help given to relatives; and impact of hardship on family relations.

U7870–1.46: Nebraskans Attitudes on Taxing and Spending: An Examination of the 'More for Less' Paradox
[Monograph. [1984.] 11 p. NASIS-83, No. 3. $1.00. SRI/MF/complete.]

By Susan Welch. Report on Nebraskans' opinions regarding increased spending for government services. Includes 2 tables showing support for increased spending on energy, crime, farm problems, poor/unemployed, elderly, water resources, health, and education;

and preferred funding method (including tax increase, other revenue increase, and reallocation); all by level of government.

U7920
University of Nevada: Bureau of Business and Economic Research

U7920–1   NEVADA REVIEW OF BUSINESS AND ECONOMICS
Quarterly.   Approx. 30 p.
ISSN 0148-5881.
LC 77-643077.
SRI/MF/complete

Quarterly report on Nevada business and economic activity indicators, including employment data by industry division, SMSA, and county. Quarter of data coverage is 2 quarters prior to cover date.

Data are from Federal, State, and local government reports, and from F. W. Dodge Co. and other private sources.

Contains feature articles, some with statistics; and "Nevada Economic Indicators" section, with 5 quarterly tables.

Quarterly tables are described below and appear in most issues. All additional features with substantial statistical content are described, as they appear, under "Statistical Features." Non-statistical features are not covered.

Availability: University of Nevada: Bureau of Business and Economic Research, College of Business Administration, Nevada Review of Business and Economics, Reno NV 89557-0016, †; SRI/MF/complete.

Issues reviewed during 1984: Fall 1983-Summer 1984 (P) (Vol. VII, Nos. 3-4; Vol. VIII, Nos. 1-2) [Vol. VII, No. 4 incorrectly reads No. 3].

QUARTERLY TABLES:
[All tables show total and monthly data for quarter of coverage, with percent change from previous quarter and same quarter of preceding year. Prior to summer 1984 issue, table [1] also included bank loans, investments, and deposits.]

[1] Statewide statistical data [including all or most of the following: labor force by employment status; employment by industry division and selected group; average earnings and hours in 5 industry divisions; construction value by type, and number of new dwellings; liquor, cigarette, and fuel tax collections; taxable sales; gaming revenues; and highway traffic flow].

[2-3] Las Vegas and Reno SMSAs [including labor force by employment status, employment by industry division and selected major group, construction value by type, number of new dwellings or permits, taxable sales, gaming revenues, air passenger and cargo traffic, highway traffic flow, and room tax collections, with selected detail for SMSA component areas; and electricity sales and customers (Las Vegas only)].

[4] Nevada statistical data by county [including all or most of the following: labor force by employment status; construction value by type, and number of new dwellings; taxable sales; and gaming revenues].

[5] Selected U.S. economic indicators [CPI and PPI by major item or commodity grouping, and labor force by employment status].

STATISTICAL FEATURES:

U7920–1.501: Fall 1983 (Vol. VII, No. 3)
COMMERCIAL STRUCTURE OF NEVADA'S ECONOMY AND PROSPECTS FOR DEVELOPMENT

(p. 2-7) By John L. Dobra and Thomas R. Harris. Article on Nevada's economic growth and diversification outlook through 2000, based on econometric research and recent surveys.

Includes 6 tables showing: employment and payroll multipliers, by county, 1969-81 period; sales and consumer purchasing patterns in Elko and Nye Counties (no date); and projected population and employment [total, gaming, and nongaming], decennially 1970-2000.

Employment and payroll multipliers indicate the extent of a local economy's dependence on expenditures by nonresidents.

U7920–1.502: Winter 1983/84 (Vol. VII, No. 4)
[Issue incorrectly reads No. 3.]

NEVADA ECONOMY: RECOVERY AND EXPANSION

(p. 2-7) By Thomas F. Cargill. Article, with 4 tables showing Nevada and U.S. nonfarm employment by industry division, unemployment rate, and percent change in nominal and real personal income; and Nevada mining industry share of nonagricultural payroll, by county; various periods 1969-84. Data are from Federal and State sources.

NEVADA BARITE INDUSTRY

(p. 8-11) By Keith G. Papke. Article, with 1 table and 1 chart showing U.S. barite consumption for all purposes and for oil/gas drilling, decennially 1940-80; and distribution of oil/gas drilling by region, 1982.

U7920–1.503: Spring 1984 (Vol. VIII, No. 1)
NEVADA POPULATION PROJECTIONS: 1983-2000

(p. 2-5) By John L. Dobra. Article, with 4 tables showing Nevada population projections, statewide under alternate employment and economic growth assumptions, and by county, 1983-2000.

Projections are based on econometric analysis of data from Census Bureau, Nevada Dept of Employment Security, and Federal Reserve Bank of San Francisco.

U7920–1.504: Summer 1984 (Vol. VIII, No. 2)
MANAGING ACCOUNTS RECEIVABLE

(p. 14-16) By Frederick C. Scherr. Article on corporate credit-granting considerations and techniques. Data are based on 245 responses to a 1981 survey of credit managers at Fortune 500 industrial firms.

Includes 6 tables showing responses on methods used to decide terms of sale, level of credit extended, and accounts receivable interest rate; and credit decision deemed most difficult, and information gathered for decision.

U7980
University of New Mexico: Bureau of Business and Economic Research

U7980–1   NEW MEXICO BUSINESS
Current Economic Report
Monthly.   Approx. 10 p.
LC 65-79758.
SRI/MF/complete, shipped quarterly

Monthly report (Jan./Feb. combined) reviewing economic, demographic, and other developments affecting business activity in New Mexico, the Southwest, and the U.S. Data are from Federal and State agencies, and private or commercial sources. Month of coverage for most data is 2 months prior to cover date.

Issues generally contain a narrative summary of recent State economic developments; 7 monthly economic indicator tables; and "1980 Census Facts," a feature presenting various data from the 1980 Census of Population and Housing for New Mexico. Jan./Feb. issue also includes an annual State economic profile.

Monthly tables are listed below and appear in all issues. All other features with substantial statistical content are described, as they appear, under "Statistical Features." Nonstatistical features are not covered.

Availability: University of New Mexico: Bureau of Business and Economic Research, Institute for Applied Research Services, Albuquerque NM 87131, $15.00 per yr., single copy $1.85; SRI/MF/complete, shipped quarterly.

Issues reviewed during 1984: Oct. 1983-Sept. 1984 (P) (Vol. 4, Nos. 9-11; Vol. 5, Nos. 1-8).

MONTHLY TABLES:

[Table [1] shows quarterly averages for most recent available quarter and 3 preceding quarters, and monthly averages for month of coverage and 2 preceding months, with percent change from same periods of previous year. Unless otherwise noted, all other tables show data for month of coverage, preceding month, and same month of previous year.]

[1] Economic indicators [including unemployment insurance claims, new business incorporations, business failure liabilities, agricultural receipts, mineral production, construction permits and contracts, manufacturing hours worked, bank loans and deposits, savings and loan assn deposits and savings, national park visits, and others].

[2] CPI and indexes of selected categories, U.S. city average.

[3] Hours and earnings of production/construction/nonsupervisory employees [for 6 industry divisions, and durable and nondurable goods manufacturing].

[4] Estimated civilian labor force and employment [by industry division, for State, and Albuquerque and Las Cruces SMSAs].

[5] Albuquerque banking data [net bank loans, and time and demand and savings/loan deposits, for most recent available quarter and previous quarter].

[6-7] Number and value of [residential and nonresidential] building permits, [18 selected cities and remainder of State; for month of coverage, current year to date, and same periods of previous year].

STATISTICAL FEATURES:

U7980–1.501: Oct. 1983 (Vol. 4, No. 9)
SPECIAL CHART

(p. 8) Map of U.S. showing number of persons moving from New Mexico to each State, 1975-80 period. Data are from University of New Mexico, Division of Government Research.

U7980–1.502: Nov. 1983 (Vol. 4, No. 10)
1980 CENSUS FACTS

(p. 8) Includes 1 table showing the following for 5 Indian reservations in New Mexico, 1980: total and Indian population, median age and family income, and percent of persons with high school degree, below poverty level, and unemployed.

U7980–1.503: Jan./Feb. 1984 (Vol. 5, No. 1)
NEW MEXICO ECONOMY 1983, ANNUAL FEATURE

(p. 1-21) Annual article reviewing the performance of the New Mexico economy in 1983, with analysis of employment and economic trends in 8 industry sectors, selected years 1973-83. Data are from Federal agencies, New Mexico Employment Security Dept, and other sources.

Includes 20 trend charts; and the following tables, showing data for New Mexico unless otherwise noted, generally for 1973 and 1977-83:

a. Per capita income in selected western States and SMSAs; and U.S. PPI, CPI, and construction cost index. 3 tables. (p. 1-3)

b. Civilian employment: labor force by employment status; and employment and current and constant dollar hourly earnings, by industry division. 3 tables. (p. 4-6)

c. Agriculture and mining: livestock prices and cash marketings of farm products; and mining production volume and value by mineral, employment by sector, and hours and earnings. 4 tables. (p. 7-10)

d. Construction and manufacturing: construction employment, and value of residential, nonresidential, and nonbuilding contracts awarded; and manufacturing employment by sector, and hours and earnings. 2 tables. (p. 11, 14)

e. Transportation, communications, utilities, and wholesale and retail trade: employment by sector, and wholesale/retail trade hours and earnings. 2 tables. (p. 15-16)

f. Finance, insurance, and real estate: employment by sector; bank assets, deposits, and loans; savings and loan assn deposits and new savings; life insurance sales; and new business incorporations. 2 tables. (p. 17-18)

g. Services, recreation, and tourism: employment in lodging establishments, eating/drinking places, and various other service businesses; and visits to State and national parks/monuments. 2 tables. (p. 19-20)

h. Government: civilian employment in Federal, State, and local government. 1 table. (p. 21)

1982 COUNTY POPULATION ESTIMATES FOR NEW MEXICO, ANNUAL FEATURE

(p. 22-23) Annual article, with 1 table showing New Mexico population estimates, by county, as of July 1, 1982 compared to Apr. 1, 1980. Data are from Census Bureau.

U7980-1.504: Mar. 1984 (Vol. 5, No. 2)
STATE POPULATION GROWTH, 1980-83

(p. 8) Brief article, with 1 table showing population of U.S., New Mexico, and 7 other mountain division States, 1980-83. Data are from Census Bureau.

U7980-1.505: June 1984 (Vol. 5, No. 5)
CITY POPULATION CHANGES: 1980-82

(p. 8) Brief article, with 1 table showing population of 18 New Mexico cities with 10,000/over population, Apr. 1, 1980 and July 1, 1982. Data are from Census Bureau.

U7980-2　NEW MEXICO STATISTICAL ABSTRACT, 1984 Edition
Biennial.　June 1984.
5+131 p.
LC 81-644287
SRI/MF/complete

Biennial compilation, for 1984, of detailed demographic, social, governmental, and economic statistics for New Mexico. Data are primarily for 1970s-1982, with population trends from 1910 and projections to 2000. Data are from State and Federal sources.

Report is designed to present a comprehensive overview of the State. Extensive socioeconomic, demographic, and geographic breakdowns are shown, as applicable, for most topics. These breakdowns include data by city, county, SMSA, urban-rural status, commodity, government agency, industry, age, educational attainment, race, and sex. Comparisons to other Southwest and Rocky Mountain States and U.S. are also occasionally included.

Contains listing of contents, tables, maps, and charts (4 p.); introduction (1 p.); and 79 maps/charts, and 129 tables arranged in 21 sections, described below (p. 1-131).

Last previous edition was issued in Dec. 1979; for description, see SRI 1980 Annual, under this number. No reports were issued during 1980-83 due to lack of funds.

Availability: University of New Mexico: Bureau of Business and Economic Research, Institute for Applied Research Services, Albuquerque NM 87131, $15.00+$3.00 postage and handling; SRI/MF/complete.

TABLE SECTIONS:
[Data sources generally appear beneath each table.]

U7980-2.1: Agriculture, Communications, and Construction

(p. 1-11) Contains 1 chart and 10 tables. Includes farms, acreage, and value; cash receipts from livestock and crops; livestock inventory and value, by species; market value of agricultural products sold; business and residential telephones, by independent company; newspapers and circulation; construction employment and value of contracts awarded; and building permits and value.

U7980-2.2: Education

(p. 13-17) Contains 9 tables. Includes public and nonpublic schools and average daily membership; public school student and teacher characteristics, expenditures per pupil, and income sources; educational attainment of population; and higher education institutions, enrollment, and degrees awarded.

U7980-2.3: Employment, Finance, and Housing

(p. 19-31) Contains 3 maps/charts and 16 tables. Includes labor force by employment status; nonagricultural employment, and hours and earnings; and military and civilian employment at selected military installations.

Also includes bank and savings and loan assn assets and deposits, and bank loans; business failures and liabilities; new business incorporations; housing units (including mobile homes), occupancy, and structural and financial characteristics; and water sources and sewage disposal methods.

U7980-2.4: Income, Land and Climate, and Law Enforcement

(p. 33-46) Contains 3 maps/charts and 13 tables. Includes total and per capita personal income; components of personal income; median family income; families below poverty level and with income above $25,000; elevation and climatic data by weather station; land and water area; Federal, State, private/other, and Indian land ownership; and crimes by offense, and law enforcement officers.

U7980-2.5: Manufacturing and Mining

(p. 47-52) Contains 6 tables. Includes manufacturing employment and establishments; value of nonfuel mineral production; production and value of selected minerals, crude oil, and natural gas; and natural gas utility customers and consumption.

U7980-2.6: Population

(p. 53-70) Contains 2 maps/charts and 13 tables. Includes population from 1910 and projected to 2000; births, deaths, and net migration; land area; Spanish-heritage population; and Indian population on reservations and reservation land area, by tribe.

U7980-2.7: Recreation, and Roads and Traffic

(p. 71-75) Contains 1 map/chart and 6 tables. Includes State park and national site visits; vehicle miles traveled; motor vehicle accidents, injuries, and fatalities; State and local road mileage; and motor vehicle registrations.

U7980-2.8: Taxes and Revenue, and Trade and Services

(p. 77-84) Contains 2 maps/charts and 8 tables. Includes State government revenues by source and expenditures by function; industry gross taxable receipts; total and per capita Federal expenditures in New Mexico; retail and wholesale trade and service industry establishments; and retail trade gross receipts.

U7980-2.9: Vital Statistics

(p. 85-90) Contains 8 tables. Includes population, births, deaths by cause, infant mortality rates, hospitals and physicians, communicable disease cases, and marriages and dissolutions.

U7980-2.10: Voter Statistics and Welfare

(p. 91-96) Contains 6 tables. Includes votes cast for presidential and gubernatorial candidates; voter registration by party; food stamp recipients and average benefits; and financial assistance cases, and payments by program.

U7980-2.11: County Data

(p. 97-131) Contains 67 maps and 34 tables. Includes 1 table, repeated for State and each county, showing the following:

a. Land area; population; births, deaths, and net migration; public school enrollment and median school years completed; per capita and median family income; families below poverty level; and financial assistance and food stamp recipients.

b. Employment and unemployment rate; value of nonfuel mineral production; average farm size and market value of agricultural products sold; bank and savings and loan assn assets; net taxable property value; and retail sales.

U8010
University of New Orleans: Division of Business and Economic Research

U8010-2　POPULATION PROJECTIONS TO THE YEAR 2000 for Louisiana and for Louisiana Planning Districts, Metropolitan Areas, and Parishes by Race, Sex, and Age: Series II Report, Special Limited Edition
Monograph.　Dec. 1983.
ii+357 p.
SRI/MF/complete

By Vincent Maruggi and Raul A. Fletes. Report presenting data on Louisiana population, by age, sex, and race, by planning district, MSA, and parish, actual 1980, and projected under 3 migration assumptions quinquennially 1985-2000. Data are based on 1980 U.S. census.

Contains contents listing, foreword, and preface (p. i-ii, 1-4); and 3 statistical sections, each covering 1 migration assumption and presenting 1 table repeated for each location (p. 6-357).

Two other reports, presenting projection summaries and methodology, are also available from the issuing agency but are not covered in SRI. Each of these reports costs $15.00+$1.00 postage and handling. In addition, customized projections may be requested from the issuing agency.

Availability: University of New Orleans: Division of Business and Economic Research, New Orleans LA 70148, $40.00+$2.00 postage and handling; SRI/MF/complete.

U8013
University of North Carolina

U8013-1   STATISTICAL ABSTRACT OF HIGHER EDUCATION in North Carolina, 1983/84
Annual.   Apr. 1984.
xii+178 p.
Research Rpt. 1-84.
LC 79-647373.
SRI/MF/complete

Annual report, for academic year 1983/84, on North Carolina higher education. Covers enrollment, degrees, faculty, and library resources; and student costs, financial aid, and housing; for public and private colleges and universities. Also includes selected trends from as early as 1900. Most data are shown by individual institution.

Data are compiled from information supplied by individual institutions.

Contains listings of contents, tables, and charts (p. ii-x); introduction and map (p. xi-xii); 11 statistical sections, with 14 charts, and 83 tables listed below (p. 1-169); and appendices, with data sources and definitions (p. 171-178).

This is the 17th annual report.

Availability: University of North Carolina, General Administration, Planning Division, PO Box 2688, 910 Raleigh Rd., Chapel Hill NC 27514, †; SRI/MF/complete.

TABLES:
[Unless otherwise noted, tables show data for North Carolina colleges and universities, by individual institution, usually including Bible colleges and theological seminaries.]

U8013-1.1: Enrollment
[Unless otherwise noted, enrollment data are shown for headcount enrollment.]

CURRENT ENROLLMENT
[Tables 1-25 and 27-29 show data for fall 1983.]

1. General characteristics of enrollment [aggregates for public and private institutions]. (p. 8)

2-4. Enrollment by residence status, full-time and part-time status, and sex; by class and level of instruction; and by level of instruction and residence status. (p. 9-17)

5. FTE enrollment by level of instruction and residence status. (p. 18)

6. Enrollment in community colleges and technical institutes/colleges [by type of curriculum]. (p. 21)

7-10. Percentage of enrollment by age distribution [by sex, full- and part-time status, and level of instruction; for] University of North Carolina [and total] private colleges/universities; for transfer enrollment at [total] community colleges; and for vocational/technical enrollment at [total] community colleges/technical institutes/technical colleges. (p. 22-23)

11-16. Average age of enrollment [by sex, full- and part-time status, and level of instruction, for individual institutions grouped by type, and including data for community college transfer students]. (p. 24-26)

17-20. Home county of in-State undergraduate enrollment and home State of out-of-State undergraduate enrollment, [aggregated] by type of institution, and for University of North Carolina [by campus]. (p. 27-32)

21-22. Home county and home State of total enrollment in [aggregate] community colleges/technical institutes/technical colleges [by type of curriculum]. (p. 33-35)

23. Geographic origin of undergraduate enrollment [same county as institution, adjacent counties, other in-State counties, and out-of-State]. (p. 36)

24. Graduate and 1st professional enrollment [by residence status and sex]. (p. 39)

25. Upper-division undergraduate and post-baccalaureate enrollment in the University of North Carolina by field of study. (p. 40)

26. Summer school unduplicated enrollment and credit hours registered [by level of instruction and residence status], 1983. (p. 41)

27. Foreign students enrolled by level of instruction [and sex]. (p. 43)

28. Racial composition of enrollment. (p. 45)

29. Extension credit enrollment in the University of North Carolina [by residence status and level of instruction]. (p. 48)

ENROLLMENT TRENDS
[Tables show data for fall 1973-83, unless otherwise noted.]

30. Enrollment trends [aggregate] in public and private colleges/universities, [selected years] fall 1900-83. (p. 51)

31. Enrollment. (p. 52)

32. Enrollment by residence status [aggregates for public and private institutions]. (p. 55)

33. Percentages of out-of-State enrollment in public colleges and universities, fall 1978-83 [by University of North Carolina campus, and aggregates for military centers and community colleges; all for entering freshmen, undergraduate, and total enrollment]. (p. 56)

34. Enrollment trends by level of instruction [aggregates for public and private institutions]. (p. 57)

35-36. Trend in county origin of in-State undergraduate enrollment and State origin of out-of-State undergraduate enrollment [aggregate for all institutions]. (p. 58-62)

UNDERGRADUATE TRANSFERS

37. Undergraduate transfers to colleges and universities [aggregates by type of institution transferred to and from], fall 1973-83. (p. 65)

38-42. Undergraduate transfer students: [aggregate] by type of institution and sex; and by institutions [transferred to and from]; fall 1983. (p. 66-72)

43. Undergraduate transfer students from out-of-State colleges/universities to North Carolina colleges/universities [aggregates by State by type of institution transferred to], fall 1983. (p. 73)

44. Transfers into non-college parallel programs at community colleges and technical institutes/colleges from other colleges and universities [by type of institution transferred from and the specific institution transferred to], fall 1983. (p. 74)

U8013-1.2: Degrees, Faculty, and Library Resources
[Data are for 1982/83, unless otherwise noted.]

DEGREES CONFERRED

45. Number of degrees conferred [by level], 1979/80-1982/83. (p. 80)

46. Number and percent of degrees conferred by field of study, type of institution [public and private], and level of degree. (p. 81)

47. Degrees conferred by field of study, level of degree, race [black, American Indian/Alaskan Native, Asian/Pacific Islander, Hispanic, and white, and for nonresident aliens] and sex [aggregated for all institutions]. (p. 84)

48-51. Number of bachelor's, 1st professional, masters, and doctorate degrees conferred, by sex and field of study. (p. 86-93)

52. Degrees and awards based on less than 4 years work beyond high school [by type and field of study]. (p. 94)

FACULTY

53. Academic rank and sex of full-time faculty, fall 1983. (p. 99)

54. Highest earned degree held by full-time faculty by academic rank, fall 1983. (p. 102-110)

LIBRARY RESOURCES

55. Library resources [by type]. (p. 112)

56. Library operating expenditures [by type, including salaries]. (p. 115-117)

U8013-1.3: Student Costs, Admissions, Financial Aid, and Housing

TUITION AND FEES
[Tables 58-61 show data for 1983/84.]

57. Undergraduate tuition/required fees combined [by residence status], 1978/79-1983/84. (p. 120)

58. Costs [tuition by residence status, fees, dormitory rooms, and board] to undergraduate students. (p. 123)

59. Detailed listing of required fees charged to regular undergraduate students. (p. 125)

60-61. Costs [tuition/academic fee by residence status, and fees] to students in 1st professional degree programs by type of program, and to graduate students. (p. 127)

ADMISSIONS
[Tables 63-72 show data for fall 1983.]

62. Average SAT [Scholastic Aptitude Test] scores of entering freshmen in the University of North Carolina [by campus], fall 1973-83. (p. 132)

63-64. Distribution of SAT scores of entering freshmen in the University of North Carolina [by campus]; and average SAT scores of entering freshmen in private colleges/universities [by residence status]. (p. 133-134)

65-66. High school class rank of entering freshmen. (p. 135-136)

67-70. Number of freshman and undergraduate transfer applications, acceptances, and enrollees [by residence status and sex]. (p. 137-144)

71-72. Number of graduate and 1st professional applications, acceptances, and enrollees in the University of North Carolina [by campus, by residence status and sex]. (p. 145)

FINANCIAL AID
[Data show number of students and amounts received, 1982/83.]

73. Employment [college work/study and other] of undergraduate students. (p. 148)

74. Scholarships, grants, and awards [by type] for undergraduate students. (p. 150)

75. Pell Grants (BEOG). (p. 153)

76. Loans [by type] provided to undergraduate students. (p. 156)

77-78. Financial aid [by type] for 1st professional and graduate students. (p. 159-160)

STUDENT HOUSING

79. Capacity and utilization of dormitories in the University of North Carolina, fall 1973-83. (p. 163)

80-81. Enrollment by type of housing, fall 1983. (p. 164-165)

STATE AID TO STUDENTS IN PRIVATE INSTITUTIONS

82. Fall 1983 undergraduate FTE enrollment and total allocations made to private colleges and universities in 1983/84. (p. 168)

83. North Carolina legislative tuition grants (NCLTG) [students and amounts], 1983/84. (p. 169)

U8080
University of North Dakota: Bureau of Governmental Affairs

U8080-5   VOTER TURNOUT IN NORTH DAKOTA, 1952-82
Monograph. Apr. 1983.
35 p. S.R. No. 73.
SRI/MF/complete

By Harlan Fuglesten. Report on North Dakota voter turnout, by county, 1952-82. Includes data for primary and general elections during presidential and nonpresidential election years.

Contains narrative analysis and 5 tables. Tables are on p. 13-21.

Availability: University of North Dakota: Bureau of Governmental Affairs, Grand Forks ND 58202, †; SRI/MF/complete.

U8130
University of Oklahoma: Center for Economic and Management Research

U8130-1   OKLAHOMA BUSINESS BULLETIN
Monthly. Approx. 5 p.
ISSN 0030-1671.
LC 40-25254.
SRI/MF/complete, shipped quarterly

Monthly report on Oklahoma economic indicators, including employment, retail trade, construction, and banking, shown variously by metro area or city. Data are based on Federal, State, and commercial sources, and are current to 3 months prior to cover date.

Issues usually contain 7 monthly tables, listed below. Mar., June, Sept., and Dec. issues also include "Business Highlights" narrative feature and additional quarterly data as noted below.

Mar. 1984 issue includes an additional table, described below under "Statistical Feature."

Availability: University of Oklahoma: Center for Economic and Management Research, 307 W. Brooks St., Rm. 4, Norman OK 73019, $4.00 per yr., single copy $0.50; SRI/MF/complete, shipped quarterly.

Issues reviewed during 1984: Oct. 1983-Sept. 1984 (P) (Vol. 51, Nos. 10-12; Vol. 52, Nos. 1-9).

MONTHLY TABLES
[Data are generally for month of coverage, and year to date for current and previous year, with percent changes from previous month and previous year. Not all data appear in all issues.]

[1] Summary of indicators [includes personal income (monthly average), crude oil production, industrial power sales, demand and savings bank deposits, savings and loan assn assets and new mortgages, and usually labor force, employment, and unemployment rate].

[2-3] Retail trade in [approximately 45] selected cities; and in metro areas and State [by kind of business].

[4] Retail trade and construction [value of durable and nondurable goods by kind of business, and permit-authorized construction units and value by type; table is titled "Selected Economic Indicators" every 3rd issue, and includes employment trends by industry division, and average weekly hours and earnings].

[5-7] [Employment, permit-authorized construction, and retail trade sales by kind of business, for 4 MSAs and Muskogee area, with additional detail for Oklahoma City and Tulsa MSAs on mortgage loans and bank deposits; every 3rd issue, data are presented in 4 tables, and also include industrial power sales, and, for Oklahoma City and Tulsa only, average weekly earnings and water and/or air transportation.]

STATISTICAL FEATURE:

U8130-1.501: Mar. 1984 (Vol. 52, No. 3)
BUSINESS HIGHLIGHTS

(p. 1-2) By Neil J. Dikeman, Jr. Includes 2 tables showing prices received by Oklahoma farmers for selected commodities, in current and constant 1974 dollars; and Oklahoma farm personal income (amount and as a percent of all personal income); 1974-75 and 1981-83. Data are from USDA and Commerce Dept.

U8570
University of South Carolina: College of Business Administration

U8570-1   BUSINESS AND ECONOMIC REVIEW
Quarterly. Approx. 40 p.
ISSN 0007-6503.
SRI/MF/complete

Quarterly journal on economic, financial, and management developments in South Carolina, other southeastern States, and the U.S. Issues contain editorial dept and feature articles, occasionally with statistics.

Features with substantial statistical content are described, as they appear, under "Statistical Features."

Prior to the Oct. 1983 issue, journal was published 6 times a year and contained recurring business indicator tables. Due to the reduction in statistical content, SRI coverage of this journal is discontinued with the Oct. 1984 issue.

Availability: University of South Carolina: College of Business Administration, Division of Research, Columbia SC 29208, †; SRI/MF/complete.

Issues reviewed during 1984: Oct. 1983-Oct. 1984 (P) (Vol. XXX, Nos. 1-4; Vol. 31, No. 1).

STATISTICAL FEATURES:

U8570-1.501: Jan. 1984 (Vol. XXX, No. 2)
NEW ECONOMIC STRATEGY: THE STATE

(p. 3-4) By Richard B. Robinson, Jr. Article, with 1 chart showing distribution of venture capital investment by State, 1981. Data are from SBA.

MAN-MADE FIBERS INDUSTRY: WHAT KIND OF FUTURE?

(p. 18-24) By David A. Ricks et al. Article, with 1 table showing U.S. mill consumption of man-made fibers, cotton, wool, and raw silk, selected years 1940-81. Data are from Man-Made Fiber Producers Assn, Inc.

U8570-1.502: Oct. 1984 (Vol. 31, No. 1)
EQUAL PAY

(p. 11-13) By Irvin B. Tucker, III, and Louis Amato. Article, with 1 table comparing average hourly wages of women and men, by marital and union membership status, education, occupational category, and whether resident of SMSA, 1980. Data are from University of Michigan *1980 Panel Study of Income Dynamics.*

WOMEN-OWNED BUSINESSES

(p. 14) Article, with 1 map showing States ranked according to female-operated share of sole proprietorships, 1981. Data are from Federal Government sources.

U8595
University of South Dakota: Business Research Bureau

U8595–1   SOUTH DAKOTA BUSINESS REVIEW
Quarterly. Approx. 12 p.
ISSN 0038-3260.
LC 58-24864.
SRI/MF/complete

Quarterly report on business trends and economic conditions in South Dakota. Includes new car and truck sales, employment, retail and services sales by city, and crop production and prices.

Data are from Dept of Commerce, BLS, State agencies, and private business, and are usually current to 1-2 months prior to cover date for data shown by month, or to quarter ending 2-5 months prior to cover date for data shown by quarter.

Issues generally contain:

a. Special articles, occasionally statistical, including a semiannual labor market forecast feature, and annual features on personal income, economic outlook, and crop plantings.

b. Business trends analysis, including 1 table showing quarterly State unemployment rate; and indexes for real personal and farm proprietor incomes, nonagricultural and construction employment, and new car and truck sales; for quarter of coverage, and preceding 5-7 quarters.

c. 7 quarterly economic indicator tables.

d. Semiannual table on retail sales by county.

Quarterly tables are listed below; most appear in all issues. Semiannual table and all additional features with substantial statistical content are described, as they appear, under "Statistical Features." Nonstatistical features are not covered.

Beginning in Mar. 1984, a bimonthly report showing taxable sales data is issued as a supplement to this report. For description, see U8595-2 below.

Availability: University of South Dakota: Business Research Bureau, School of Business, Vermillion SD 57069, †; SRI/MF/complete.

Issues reviewed during 1984: Nov. 1983-June 1984 (P) (Vol. XLII, Nos. 2-4).

QUARTERLY TABLES:
[Unless otherwise noted, tables show data for South Dakota, for current and preceding years. Table order may vary from issue to issue.]

[1] General indicators [South Dakota and U.S. personal and farm proprietor incomes, nonagricultural employment, unemployment rate, and total employment, for quarter of coverage, current year only].

[2] Total personal income, U.S., Plains Region, and [7] States [for quarter of coverage and preceding 4-6 quarters].

[3] Nonagricultural wage/salary employment [by industry division and selected industry group, and average manufacturing hours and earnings for month of coverage].

[4] Crop production summary [by crop, cumulative through month of coverage].

[5] Prices received by farmers for commodities [for month of coverage, and compared to 1910-14 base price].

[6] Local conditions indicators [taxable total, retail, and services sales; and percent change from previous year for telephone services, housing starts, postal sales, and employment; by selected city, generally for month or quarter of coverage].

[7] CPI, U.S. [by major item, monthly through month of coverage, current year only].

STATISTICAL FEATURES:

U8595–1.501: Nov. 1983 (Vol. XLII, No. 2)
PERSONAL INCOME 1982, ANNUAL FEATURE

(p. 1-2, 4-6) Annual article, by Claus Brueckner, analyzing trends in South Dakota total and per capita personal income, by type, industry source, and county, with comparisons to other Plains Region States, and growth in current and constant 1967 dollars, various years 1973-82. Data are from U.S. Dept of Commerce. Includes 12 tables.

S.D. LABOR MARKET MODEL FORECAST HIGHLIGHTS, SEMIANNUAL FEATURE

(p. 9) Semiannual article, by Ralph J. Brown, with 1 table showing South Dakota total and nonfarm personal, wage/salary, and farm income, in current and constant 1972 dollars; total, nonagricultural, and manufacturing employment; and unemployment rate; quarterly 2nd quarter 1983-4th quarter 1984 and annually 1983-84.

U8595–1.502: Mar. 1984 (Vol. XLII, No. 3)
PERSPECTIVE 1983, OUTLOOK 1984, ANNUAL FEATURE

(p. 1-6) Annual article on U.S. and South Dakota economic trends, and outlook through 1984. U.S. data are from *Business Conditions Digest;* State data are based on University of South Dakota's South Dakota Labor Market Model.

Contains narrative analysis, and 7 tables showing the following:

a. U.S.: percent change in real GNP by component, and other economic indexes, quarterly 1982-83; and change in real GNP and prices, and average unemployment rate, as forecast by 5 econometric firms, 4th quarter 1984 vs. 1983.

b. South Dakota: personal income, by source; employment, by industry division and selected major industry group; manufacturing average weekly hours; labor force, by employment status; and selected other economic indicators; most shown annually 1981-84 and quarterly 1982-84.

POSSIBILITY OF DUAL ECONOMIES IN SOUTH DAKOTA

(p. 7-8, 12) Article comparing economic conditions in urban and rural areas of South Dakota, 1970s-81. Includes 6 tables showing top 10 cities ranked by 1980 population, with comparison to 1970; and farm and nonfarm personal income and total taxable retail sales for urban and rural areas, and total personal income by source, various years 1976-81.

GROSS SALES AND USE TAX, SEMIANNUAL FEATURE

(p. 9) Semiannual table showing South Dakota retail sales, by region, county, and selected city, 1982-83.

Prior to the Nov. 1983 issue, data appeared quarterly.

U8595–1.503: June 1984 (Vol. XLII, No. 4)
SOUTH DAKOTA LABOR MARKET MODEL FORECAST HIGHLIGHTS, SEMIANNUAL FEATURE

(p. 9) Semiannual article, by Ralph J. Brown, with 1 table showing South Dakota total and nonfarm personal, wage/salary, and farm income, in current and constant 1972 dollars; total, nonagricultural, and manufacturing employment; unemployment rate; and selected U.S. economic indicators; quarterly 4th quarter 1982-3rd quarter 1984 and annually 1982-84.

PROSPECTIVE PLANTINGS, ANNUAL FEATURE

(p. 11) Annual table showing South Dakota acreage planted for 10 field crops, actual 1982-83 and intended 1984.

U8595–2   SOUTH DAKOTA DATA SUPPLEMENT
Bimonthly. 4 p.
SRI/MF/complete

Bimonthly report on South Dakota gross sales/use tax purchases and taxable retail sales, by region, county, and selected city. Occasionally includes rankings for cities or other areas, and summary U.S. comparisons.

Data are from State and Federal sources, and are shown for 2-month period ending approximately 3 months prior to cover date, with comparison to same period of previous year, and recent summary trends.

Contains brief narrative; 4 trend charts; and 2-4 bimonthly tables.

Bimonthly report, which begins with the Mar. 1984 issue, supplements the quarterly *South Dakota Busines Review,* covered in SRI under U8595-1.

Availability: University of South Dakota: Business Research Bureau, School of Business, 414 E. Clark St., Vermillion SD 57069, $3.00 per yr.; SRI/MF/complete.

Issues reviewed during 1984: Mar.-Sept. 1984 (P) (Vol. 1, Nos. 1-4).

U8710
University of Tennessee: Center for Business and Economic Research

U8710–1   SURVEY OF BUSINESS
Quarterly. Approx. 30 p.
ISSN 0099-0973.
LC 75-646621.
SRI/MF/complete

Quarterly journal on business trends and economic conditions in Tennessee and occasionally the U.S. Most data are from the Federal Government, the Business Center Tennessee Econometric Model, and private research firms.

Issues usually contain analytical articles focusing on a single topic, often with statistics. Winter issue features an annual economic outlook forecast.

Features with substantial statistical content are described, as they appear, under "Statistical Features."

Availability: University of Tennessee: Center for Business and Economic Research, College of Business Administration, Glocker Bldg., Suite 100, Knoxville TN 37996-4170, †, back issues $1.25; SRI/MF/complete.

Issues reviewed during 1984: Winter-Summer 1984 (P) (Vol. 19, Nos. 2-3; Vol. 20, No. 1) [No issue for Fall 1983 was published].

STATISTICAL FEATURES:

U8710–1.501: Winter 1984 (Vol. 19, No. 2)

ECONOMIC OUTLOOK 1984, ANNUAL FEATURE

Annual analysis of the economic outlook for Tennessee. Includes 2 statistical articles, described below. This is the 15th annual analysis.

1984 BUSINESS AND ECONOMIC PERSPECTIVES, ANNUAL FEATURE

(p. 7-21) Annual survey article, by David A. Hake and Donald R. Ploch, on the economic expectations of 145 Tennessee executives for 1984. Includes 10 charts and 1 table showing survey response for the following, often by State region and industry sector:

a. Expected level of change in overall economy and "most critical" economic indicators; and rating of public school system quality, programs perceived as most needed for school improvement, effect of school quality on economic development, and whether increased financial support is essential to school quality.

b. Support for increased State taxes, and preferred source for additional State revenue; whether Federal expenditures are appropriate to national needs; appropriate response to Federal deficit; support for Reagan Administration; and Federal budget reduction and expansion priorities.

Also includes 1 table showing Federal budget receipts and expenditures, by major category, FY82 and estimated FY84.

ECONOMIC OUTLOOK FOR TENNESSEE AND THE U.S., ANNUAL FEATURE

(p. 22-29) Annual article, by William F. Fox and Richard A. Hofler, on Tennessee and U.S. economic outlook through 1985. Data are from the Tennessee econometric model.

Includes 1 chart and 1 table showing U.S. GNP, and U.S. and Tennessee personal income, nonagricultural and manufacturing jobs, unemployment rates, and manufacturing average weekly hours, 2nd quarter 1983-4th quarter 1985 and annually 1983-85; and distribution of U.S. and Tennessee nonagricultural jobs, by industry division, 1981.

U8960
University of Utah:
Bureau of Economic
and Business Research

U8960–2   UTAH ECONOMIC AND BUSINESS REVIEW

Monthly.   Approx. 12 p.
ISSN 0042-1405.
LC 55-38145.
SRI/MF/complete, shipped quarterly

Monthly report (with 3-4 combined issues each year) on Utah business and economic activity. Data are from Federal and State agencies and private sources. Month of data coverage is 2 months prior to cover date.

Each issue contains 1 feature article, usually with statistics; a list of data sources; and 3 monthly tables, listed below.

Annual statistical features include population estimates and selected business statistics.

Monthly tables appear in all issues; combined issues include separate tables for each month covered. All additional features with substantial statistical content are described, as they appear, under "Statistical Features." Nonstatistical features are not covered.

Prior to the Dec. 1983 issue, monthly table [2] showed data for 7 multicounty planning districts and 3 major cities.

Availability: University of Utah: Bureau of Economic and Business Research, Graduate School of Business, Kendall D. Garff Bldg., Rm. 401, Salt Lake City UT 84112, †; SRI/MF/complete, shipped quarterly.

Issues reviewed during 1984: July/Aug. 1983-July/Aug. 1984 (P) (Vol. 43, Nos. 7/8-12; Vol. 44, Nos. 1-7/8) [Reports for July/Aug. and Sept./Oct. 1983 and Apr./May and July/Aug. 1984 are combined issues].

MONTHLY TABLES:

[Most data are shown for month of coverage and previous month, with comparisons to previous year.]

[1] Utah data [total personal income; new corporations; and detailed breakdowns under each of 7 categories: agriculture, construction, employment, finance, production (fuels by type, and copper), tourism/travel, and utilities (customers and telephone lines)].

[2] [County data: including nonagricultural employment, unemployment rate, value of authorized construction, new dwelling units, postal receipts, natural gas and electric customers, and telephone lines in service, all for 4 counties].

[3] National data [selected economic indicators for U.S.; table begins in Dec. 1983 issue].

STATISTICAL FEATURES:

U8960–2.501: July/Aug. 1983 (Vol. 43, Nos. 7/8)

PERSONAL INCOME IN UTAH COUNTIES, 1981, ANNUAL FEATURE

(p. 1-15) Annual article, by Boyd L. Fjeldsted, reviewing Utah personal income, by type, industry source, SMSA, and county, 1981. Data are from the Regional Economics Information

System of the U.S. Dept of Commerce. Includes 4 tables showing the following for Utah:

a. Per capita personal income, percent of U.S. average, and State rank, 1958-82.

b. By county: personal income by type; earnings by industry division, including government by level; and per capita income; 1981 and percent change from 1976.

c. Personal income, total and per capita, by SMSA and county, 1976-81.

For description of previous article, see SRI 1982 Annual, under U8960-2.308.

U8960–2.502: Sept./Oct. 1983 (Vol. 43, No. 9/10)

GREAT SALT LAKE: MAJOR ECONOMIC IMPACTS OF HIGH LAKE LEVELS

(p. 1-7) By Constance C. Steffen. Article on economic impact of rising water levels in the Great Salt Lake, Utah. Data are from a recent study conducted by the Bureau of Economic and Business Research, University of Utah. Includes 4 tables estimating private industry capital damages, industry and State/local government revenue losses, and reductions in household income, attributable to effects of rising water levels.

U8960–2.503: Nov. 1983 (Vol. 43, No. 11)

DEVELOPMENT POTENTIAL: MEDICAL SUPPLY AND BIOMEDICAL RESEARCH INDUSTRIES IN UTAH

(p. 1-8) By Constance C. Steffen. Article, with 3 tables showing U.S. health care expenditures as a percent of GNP, selected years 1955-81; and the following for 3 SIC 4-digit medical equipment industries: shipments, employment, production workers, establishments, and percent of industry shipments from aggregate 4 largest companies and individual 6 leading States, various years 1972-83. Data are from Commerce Dept.

U8960–2.504: Dec. 1983 (Vol. 43, No. 12)

1983 POPULATION ESTIMATES FOR UTAH, ANNUAL FEATURE

(p. 1-8) Annual article, by Brad T. Barber et al., presenting population estimates for Utah as of July 1, 1983, based on various estimating methods. Data are from Utah Population Estimates Committee.

Includes 1 map and 5 tables showing land area, population (total and enrolled in grades 1-8 or 2-9), net student and total migration, and natural population increase, all by county, 1982-83; population, by State planning district, July 1, 1970-83; and births and deaths, 1960-82.

U8960–2.505: Jan. 1984 (Vol. 44, No. 1)

UTAH ECONOMIC RECOVERY OF 1983-84

(p. 1-9) By Douglas A. Macdonald. Article examining recent Utah economic trends and activity. Data are from State agencies and private sources. Includes 4 tables showing selected U.S. economic indicators, and the following Utah data shown for various periods 1980-84:

a. Nonagricultural employment by industry division and wages/salaries, personal income by source, and State tax collections by type of tax.

b. Coal and oil production, crude oil and gasoline prices, dwelling units and construction value, population and vital statistics, and taxable sales; and top 40 employers ranked by employment size range.

U8960-2.506: Feb. 1984 (Vol. 44, No. 2)

SKIING IN UTAH: ITS CONTRIBUTION TO THE ECONOMY

(p. 1-5) By Constance C. Steffen. Article, with 2 tables showing expenditures of resident and nonresident skiers on ski trips in Utah, total and per visit, by item, 1982/83 ski season.

U8960-2.507: Mar. 1984 (Vol. 44, No. 3)

SELECTED BUSINESS STATISTICS, UTAH COUNTIES, ANNUAL FEATURE

(p. 1-13) Annual report, by Ronda Brinkerhoff, analyzing economic trends in Utah counties for 1983.

Includes 2 summary charts, 2 summary tables, and 1 table, repeated for each county and total State, showing: population; labor force and employment; monthly wage, annual payroll, and total and per capita personal income; property valuation and taxes, gross taxable sales, and sales tax collections; construction activity; car/truck registrations; and Federal payments in lieu of property tax under P.L. 94-565; 1980-83.

U8960-2.508: Apr./May 1984 (Vol. 44, Nos. 4/5)

UTAH STANDARD NEEDS BUDGET AND PUBLIC ASSISTANCE IN UTAH

(p. 1-7) By Boyd L. Fjeldsted and Constance C. Steffen. Article examining procedure used to determine minimum basic needs of low income families in Utah, with focus on AFDC. Data are from University of Utah and Utah Dept of Social Services.

Includes 3 tables showing Utah family budget needed to maintain a minimum standard of living (standard needs budget), by item and family size, fall 1983, with summary comparison to U.S.; and Utah AFDC households, by family income share of standard needs budget, Apr. 1984.

U8960-2.509: June 1984 (Vol. 44, No. 6)

SALT LAKE COUNTY APARTMENT CONSTRUCTION ACTIVITY

(p. 1-5) By James A. Wood. Article on Salt Lake County, Utah apartment construction activity and rents by project, with other residential building permits by type and apartment vacancy rates (with comparisons to U.S.), various years 1974-84. Data are from University of Utah and Census Bureau. Includes text statistics and 6 tables.

U8960-2.510: July/Aug. 1984 (Vol. 44, No. 7/8)

PERSONAL INCOME IN UTAH COUNTIES, 1982, ANNUAL FEATURE

(p. 1-15) Annual article, by Boyd L. Fjeldsted, reviewing Utah personal income, by type, industry source, and county, 1982. Data are from the Regional Economics Information System of the U.S. Dept of Commerce. Includes 4 tables showing the following for Utah:

a. Per capita personal income, percent of U.S. average, and State rank, 1962-83.

b. By county: personal income by type; earnings by industry division, including government by level; and per capita income; 1982 and percent change from 1977.

c. Personal income, total and per capita, by county, 1977-83.

For description of previous article, see U8960-2.501 above.

U9080
University of Virginia:
Tayloe Murphy Institute

U9080-1 DISTRIBUTION OF VIRGINIA ADJUSTED GROSS INCOME by Income Class and Locality, 1982
Annual. [1984.] 30 p.
ISSN 0148-6772.
LC 77-641301.
SRI/MF/complete

Annual report, by John L. Knapp and Beverly H. Capone, on income distribution among Virginia MSAs, cities, counties, and planning districts, as shown by adjusted gross income (AGI) on individual and married couple income tax returns, 1982. Data are based on State tax records.

Contains narrative analysis, with 2 charts and 1 table (p. 1-9); lists of MSAs and planning districts (p. 10-11); and 5 detailed tables, listed below (p. 12-30).

This is the 11th annual report.

Availability: University of Virginia: Tayloe Murphy Institute, Dynamics Bldg., 4th Floor, 2015 Ivy Rd., Charlottesville VA 22903-1780, †; SRI/MF/complete.

DETAILED TABLES:

[All tables show data for 1982, by county, city, MSA, and planning district.
Tables A1-A3 show number of returns, total AGI, median AGI per return, and distribution of returns by AGI size class.]

A1. AGI on all returns. (p. 12-16)

A2. AGI on married couple returns. (p. 17-21)

A3. AGI on individual returns. (p. 22-26)

A4. AGI per exemption [amount and index relative to State average]. (p. 27)

A5. Index of income concentration. (p. 29-30)

U9080-4 CONSUMER PRICE INDICATORS for Virginia Metropolitan Areas, 1984
Annual. Oct. 1984. v+65 p.
LC 81-641176.
SRI/MF/complete

Annual report, by Eleanor G. May, on consumer price indexes for 8 Virginia metro areas, 1975-84. Also includes data on population, personal income, and retail sales, for each area, and selected comparisons to U.S.

Data are primarily based on surveys of retail prices during the summer of 1984, conducted by the Tayloe Murphy Institute. Prices were surveyed for consumer items in the following major categories: food and beverages; housing (includ-

ing rent, fuel, and furnishings); apparel; transportation (including gasoline and automobile costs); and other goods and services (including medical care and entertainment).

Metro areas covered are Charlottesville, Lynchburg, and Roanoke MSAs, Newport News-Hampton, Norfolk-Virginia Beach-Portsmouth, Northern Virginia (Virginia portion of Washington, D.C. MSA), Petersburg-Colonial Heights-Hopewell, and Richmond.

Contains preface, and listings of contents, tables, and charts (p. iii-v); introduction and narrative analysis, with 2 charts and 15 tables (p. 1-29); and 18 appendix tables, including methodological data (p. 32-65).

This is the 10th annual report.

Availability: University of Virginia: Tayloe Murphy Institute, Dynamics Bldg., 4th Floor, 2015 Ivy Rd., Charlottesville VA 22903-1780, $10.00; SRI/MF/complete.

U9080-6 VIRGINIA ANNUAL GROSS STATE PRODUCT, 1958-82
Annual. Dec. 1983. 8 p.
SRI/MF/complete

Annual report, by John L. Knapp and Beverly H. Capone, estimating Virginia GSP in current and constant (1972) dollars, 1958-82, by industry division and per capita, with comparisons to U.S. GNP. Most estimates of data prior to 1982 are revisions which supersede figures published in previous Institute reports. Data are based on Commerce Dept and USDA publications.

Contains narrative summary, with 3 charts and 1 text table (p. 1-4); and 4 tables (p. 5-8).

A similar quarterly report is also available from the issuing agency, but is not covered in SRI.

Availability: University of Virginia: Tayloe Murphy Institute, Dynamics Bldg., 4th Floor, 2015 Ivy Rd., Charlottesville VA 22903-1780, †; SRI/MF/complete.

U9080-8 RETAIL SALES IN VIRGINIA, 1983
Annual. May 1984.
vi+40 p.
SRI/MF/complete

Annual report, by Eleanor G. May, on 1983 Virginia retail sales levels, for planning districts, counties, MSAs, and cities. Covers total taxable and GAF (general merchandise/apparel/furniture/appliances) retail sales.

Data sources are Census Bureau *Retail Sales* series, Virginia Dept of Taxation, Tayloe Murphy Institute, and other sources.

Contents:

a. Preface and contents listing. (p. iii-v)

b. Sales profiles for the State and each planning district and area, each with narrative summary and 1 table showing total and per capita taxable and GAF sales, and per capita personal income, 1983; and 3 interspersed tables showing U.S. census and/or State Dept of Taxation retail sales changes, for State, 10 metro areas, and U.S., with U.S. detail by GAF store type, quarterly 1983 compared to 1982. (p. 1-25)

c. Local data, with 2 tables showing taxable and GAF store sales, 1982-83, and sales index, 1979-83, by Virginia city and county arranged by planning district. (p. 26-38) *d.* Appendix, with methodolgy. (p. 39-40)

This is the 12th annual report.

Availability: University of Virginia: Tayloe Murphy Institute, Dynamics Bldg., 4th Floor, 2015 Ivy Rd., Charlottesville VA 22903-1780, $5.00; SRI/MF/complete.

U9080–9   ESTIMATES OF THE POPULATION OF VIRGINIA COUNTIES AND CITIES: July 1, 1981 (Final), July 1, 1982 (Provisional)

Annual. Dec. 1983. 21 p.
SRI/MF/complete

Annual report, by Julia H. Martin and Michael A. Spar, presenting 3 tables showing estimates of Virginia population and net migration, by county, city, planning district, and MSA, and for metro and nonmetro areas, various periods 1980-82, with summary comparison to 8 South Atlantic States.

Estimates are prepared by Tayloe Murphy Institute in cooperation with Census Bureau.

Contains narrative analysis (p. 1-4); 1 map and 3 tables (p. 5-17); and appendices with MSA list and methodology (p. 18-21).

Previous report, issued in 1982, is described in SRI 1982 Annual under this number.

Availability: University of Virginia: Tayloe Murphy Institute, Dynamics Bldg., 4th Floor, 2015 Ivy Rd., Charlottesville VA 22903-1780, †; SRI/MF/complete.

U9080–10   HOUSING UNITS AUTHORIZED IN VIRGINIA'S PLANNING DISTRICTS, COUNTIES, AND CITIES

Quarterly. Approx. 15 p.
SRI/MF/complete

Quarterly report (combined 1st/2nd quarter issue), by Michael A. Spar and Julia H. Martin, on Virginia local housing unit building permits issued and estimated construction costs, by construction type and location. Also includes annual data for nonresidential buildings. Data are from reports of local building officials to the U.S. Census Bureau.

Reports are issued 4-12 months after quarter of coverage.

Issues generally include narrative introduction and summary of trends, with 3 illustrative charts; and the following quarterly tables:

A. Aggregate construction costs [in constant (1972 and 1977) and current dollars; and Census Bureau construction cost index; 1970 to most recent full year].

1. Housing units authorized [and costs where available] by planning district, county, and city [for mobile, private, single family, duplex, and 3-4 and 5/more units; and number of private and public units demolished; for quarter or quarters of coverage].

B. Index of planning district membership of counties and cities.

Order of tables may vary.

Annual data appear in 4th quarter issue, and are described as they appear.

Availability: University of Virginia: Tayloe Murphy Institute, Dynamics Bldg., 4th Floor, 2015 Ivy Rd., Charlottesville VA 22903-1780, †; SRI/MF/complete.

Issues reviewed during 1984: 1st/2nd-3rd Qtrs. 1983 (D).

U9080–14   OCCUPATIONS IN VIRGINIA: Data from the 1980 Census

Monograph. May 1983.
xiii+431 p.+errata sheet.
SRI/MF/complete

Report presenting 1980 census data, for Virginia, on civilian labor force by detailed Standard Occupational Classification. Data are shown for State, SMSAs, counties, and independent cities.

Data are from the Equal Employment Opportunity Special Tape File, which is based on the long-form questionnaire distributed to a 20% sample of households in the 1980 Census of Population and Housing. The EEO file includes the entire civilian labor force in its universe, whereas much of the other census data on occupations (e.g., Summary Tape File 3) covers only employed civilians.

Contents:

a. Contents and table listings, and introduction and methodology. (p. iii-xiii)

b. 1 table repeated to cover State and each SMSA, county, and independent city. (p. 1-407)

c. Appendices with county and city composition of selected State administrative units; and index and census code cross-reference for occupational titles covered. (p. 409-431)

Additional occupational data cross-tabulated by sex and race/ethnic group are included in the EEO Special File. For availability contact issuing agency.

Availability: University of Virginia: Tayloe Murphy Institute, Dynamics Bldg., 4th Floor, 2015 Ivy Rd., Charlottesville VA 22903-1780, †; SRI/MF/complete.

U9080–15   VIRGINIA ISSUES: Reforming the Individual Income Tax

Monograph. Dec. 1983.
xx+125 p.
Virginia Issues No. 6.
LC 83-51544.
SRI/MF/complete

By John L. Knapp et al. Report on Virginia's individual income tax system, covering the system's history and current features, comparisons to systems in other States, and reform options. Includes the following data:

a. History: Virginia income tax revenues, and changes in tax rates/exemptions, various years 1844-1929; and individual income tax revenue compared to total tax revenue, FY29-82.

b. Poverty threshold and minimum taxable level, by number in family, under Virginia and Federal laws and 2 tax reform options, 1982.

c. State comparisons: capital gains treatment, personal exemptions, and standard deduction; rate structure for single individuals; tax rate for married couple with 2 dependents, by adjusted gross income (AGI) level; tax per capita and per $1,000 personal income, and Advisory Commission on Intergovernmental Relations (ACIR) tax effort index; and individual income tax revenue as percent of total tax revenue; all by State, various years 1980-82.

d. Reform options: tax system features; and hypothetical tax rates and liabilities, by taxpayer filing status, number of dependents, and AGI level, with detail for taxpayers at poverty threshold; for Virginia's existing tax system and 6 reform options.

Also includes data on status of local personal income tax in 10 States and D.C., including rate range and structure, and number of taxing jurisdictions, as of Dec. 1982.

Data are derived from Virginia and Federal agencies, ACIR, and a variety of other sources. Data sources are specified for each table.

Contains foreword and listings of contents, tables, and charts (p. v-x); acknowledgments and executive summary (p. xi-xx); 6 narrative chapters, with text data, 6 charts, and 20 tables (p. 1-113); and bibliography (p. 114-124).

Availability: University of Virginia: Tayloe Murphy Institute, Dynamics Bldg., 4th Floor, 2015 Ivy Rd., Charlottesville, VA 22903-1780, $5.20; SRI/MF/complete.

U9080–16   TRANSPORTATION AND COMMUTING IN VIRGINIA, 1980

Monograph. July 1984.
iii+86 p.
1980 Census Analysis Series, Vol. 2.
LC 84-623368.
SRI/MF/complete

By Michael A. Spar. Report presenting 1980 census data on commuting patterns in Virginia, covering points of origin and destination for Virginia residents and for nonresidents employed in the State. Data are cross-tabulated among counties, SMSA components, and cities of Virginia and similar locations of neighboring States.

Also includes Virginia population, and estimated net effect of commuting on population, by type of location, 1980; and number of workers by means of transportation to work, 1960, 1970, and 1980.

Data are based on unpublished tabulations from Summary Tape File 4 of the 1980 Census of Population and Housing.

Contains contents listing (p. iii); narrative report in 5 sections, interspersed with 11 maps and 13 tables (p. 1-51); and appendices, with 2 extended tables (p. 53-86)

Availability: University of Virginia: Tayloe Murphy Institute, Dynamics Bldg., 4th Floor, 2015 Ivy Rd., Charlottesville VA 22903-1780, $10.40; SRI/MF/complete.

U9350
University of Wyoming:
Institute for Policy Research

U9350–2   WYOMING QUARTERLY UPDATE
Quarterly.   Approx. 50 p.
SRI/MF/complete

Quarterly report on Wyoming business conditions and economic activity, including employment, finance, and energy production. Data are from State and Federal agencies, and private data bases. Most data are current to 1-2 quarters preceding cover date.

Contents:

a. Economic outlook commentaries and industry profiles for agriculture, mineral, and selected other sectors, and sometimes 1 or more additional articles, occasionally with statistics.

b. 11 quarterly economic indicator tables, listed below, with accompanying notes and charts.

c. Quarterly cost-of-living index rankings, by city, for all items, food, housing, transportation, and medical. Indexes are shown for 3-day periods in quarter prior to cover date.

d. Annual and/or special tables, or supplemental annual data interspersed among quarterly economic indicator tables. Annual data usually show 12-year trends.

e. Table code keys and data sources.

Cost-of-living index rankings and quarterly economic indicator tables appear in all issues. All additional features with substantial statistical content are described, as they appear, under "Statistical Features." Nonstatistical features are not described.

A more detailed cost-of-living index, not covered by SRI, is available from the Dept of Administration and Fiscal Control, 302 Emerson Bldg., Cheyenne WY 82002.

Prior to the Summer 1984 issue, report also included county socioeconomic profiles, presented for 2-4 counties each quarter, with text statistics, charts, and 2 tables showing food stamp and AFDC payments and/or recipients, births, deaths, divorces, marriages, population, mineral production and valuation, personal income generated by industry division, and county detail for selected topics covered for State in quarterly economic indicator tables, various periods 1970s to current year. Beginning with the Summer 1984 issue, industry profiles replace county profiles.

Availability: University of Wyoming: Institute for Policy Research, University Station, PO Box 3925, Laramie WY 82071, †; SRI/MF/complete.

Issues reviewed during 1984: Winter-Fall 1984 (P) (Vol. 3, Nos. 2-4; Vol. 4, No. 1).

QUARTERLY ECONOMIC INDICATOR TABLES:
[Tables show data for 12 consecutive quarters, ending 1-2 quarters prior to cover date, unless otherwise noted. Data are for Wyoming, with selected U.S. comparisons. Table numbering and sequence may vary as annual or special tables are included.]

[1] Energy and mineral production [including coal, oil, and natural gas].

[2] Agriculture [including national forest timber harvesting, and farm price indexes].

[3] Tourism [including national park visits by site and gasoline sales].

[4] Employment and labor [including unemployment insurance claims, nonfarm job openings and placements, and mining earnings and hours].

[5] Business conditions [including new domestic and foreign incorporations, number and value of business failures, and personal bankruptcies].

[6] Construction [including building values and permits].

[7] Utilities [including electricity and natural gas consumption].

[8] Consumers [including new motor vehicle registrations, liquor sales, and personal income].

[9] Government [including sales/use tax revenues and percent of crimes cleared].

[10] Banking and finance [including bank loans, total and noninterest bearing deposits, and savings and loan mortgage loans and deposits].

[11] Average rents by city [apartment and trailer lot rents in 23 Wyoming cities, for quarter ending 2 quarters prior to cover date; table begins in Summer 1984 issue].

STATISTICAL FEATURES:

U9350–2.501: Winter 1984 (Vol. 3, No. 2)
WINTER MINERALS OUTLOOK: COAL, RECURRING FEATURE
(p. 6-7) Recurring article, by Richard W. Jones, on Wyoming coal activity. Data are from Wyoming Geological Survey. Includes 1 table showing coal production, by county; and total contracted production; 1981-90.

STATE REVENUE OUTLOOK
(p. 11-14) Article summarizing State revenue source projections, with focus on mineral industry tax base. Data are from Wyoming Legislative Service Office. Includes 2 tables showing projections by 3-4 State agencies for oil, gas, coal, and uranium production and valuation, 1983-87.

GOVERNMENT: SUPPLEMENTAL DATA
(p. 46-50) Supplement to quarterly government table, showing the following, all by county: cigarette tax distribution, gasoline gallonage sold, State Board of Equalization and locally assessed property valuations, and sales/use tax collections, FY71-83. 5 tables.

CENSUS RETRIEVAL INFORMATION SERVICE: HOW WYOMING RANKS AMONG THE 50 STATES
(p. 52-53) Table showing selected demographic and socioeconomic data for Wyoming and U.S., with State ranking for Wyoming. Data are shown for most recent available year, primarily late 1970s-82, with some trends.

Includes approximately 70 items within the following categories: population characteristics, land area, vital statistics, health care, housing, crime, education, employment, income and poverty, government finances, voter participation, motor vehicle use, traffic fatalities, energy consumption, weather, farms, mineral production, construction, manufacturing shipments, and retail sales.

Data were compiled by the Census Bureau.

U9350–2.502: Spring 1984 (Vol. 3, No. 3)
SPRING MINERALS OUTLOOK: COAL, RECURRING FEATURE
(p. 5-6) Recurring article, by Richard W. Jones, on Wyoming coal activity. Data are from the State Inspector of Mines. Includes 1 table showing Wyoming coal production, mines, and employment, by county arranged by basin, 1983.

SPRING MINERALS OUTLOOK: OIL AND GAS
(p. 6-7) By Alan J. VerPloeg. Article, with 1 table showing Wyoming oil and gas well completions, for new field wildcat and all wells, 1982-83. Data are from Petroleum Information Corp.

FORECASTING STATE SALES TAX REVENUES
(p. 12-17) By Dan Rickman. Article, with 5 tables showing estimation variables, and actual and/or forecast sales tax collections by county, 1982-85. Data are based on State agency statistics.

U9350–2.503: Summer 1984 (Vol. 3, No. 4)
SUMMER MINERALS OUTLOOK: COAL, RECURRING FEATURE
(p. 7-8) Recurring article, by Richard W. Jones, on Wyoming coal activity. Data are from Wyoming Geological Survey. Includes 1 map showing consumption of Wyoming coal in 23 States, 1983.

INDUSTRY PROFILE: WYOMING COAL REVIEW
(p. 16-25) Article, with 1 map and 2 tables showing Wyoming coal production and employment, by company and mine, 1983, with aggregate trends annually from 1865. Data are from U.S. Geological Survey and Wyoming Inspector of Mines.

U9350–2.504: Fall 1984 (Vol. 4, No. 1)
FALL MINERALS OUTLOOK
(p. 4-10) Article, with 2 tables showing valuation and actual and projected production of oil, natural gas, coal, trona, and uranium, with aggregate valuation for all other minerals, various years 1981-88. Data are from Wyoming Geological Survey.

INDUSTRY PROFILE: WYOMING TRAVEL REVIEW
(p. 16-25) Article, with 4 tables showing national, State, and historic site visitor days, for 4 State regions, 1980-83. Data are from Wyoming Recreation Commission, U.S. Forest Service, and National Park Service.

U9640
Washington University:
Center for the
Study of American Business

**U9640–1   HAZARDS OF "PURSE
STRINGS" REGULATORY
REFORM: Regulatory
Spending and Staffing Under
the Reagan Administration,
1981-85**
Annual. Apr. 1984. 2+20 p.
Rpt. No. OP34.
SRI/MF/complete

Annual report, by Kenneth W. Chilton and Ronald J. Penoyer, on Federal regulation, with data on expenditures and staff of 55 major agencies, selected years FY70-83 and estimated FY84-85. Regulatory areas covered are consumer and job safety, environment/energy, finance/banking, industry-specific, and general business.

Data are from *Budget of the U.S. Government.*

Contains highlights, and contents and table listings (2 p.); analysis of regulatory budget and staffing trends, interspersed with 4 tables (p. 1-14); and 2 detailed tables (p. 15-20).

Report updates *Next Step in Regulatory Reform: Updating the Statutes, 1983 Report on Regulatory Budgets,* described in SRI 1983 Annual under this number.

Availability: Washington University: Center for the Study of American Business, Campus Box 1208, St. Louis MO 63130, ‡; SRI/MF/complete.

U9660
Wayne State University:
School of Business
Administration

U9660–2   MICHIGAN ECONOMY
Bimonthly. Approx. 8 p.
ISSN 0730-272X.
SRI/MF/complete

Bimonthly report on Michigan business activity and economic indicators, including manufacturing hours and earnings, consumer and farm price indexes, construction, and personal income, with selected comparisons to total U.S. Month of coverage for most bimonthly data is 1-2 months prior to cover date.

Data are from Census Bureau, BLS, State Crop Reporting Service, and other government and private sources.

Issues contain feature articles, usually statistical; 2 bimonthly tables; and 1 recurring table.

Bimonthly and recurring tables are listed below. All additional features with substantial statistical content are described, as they appear, under "Statistical Features;" page locations and latest periods of coverage for recurring table are also noted. Nonstatistical features are not covered.

Availability: Wayne State University: School of Business Administration, Bureau of Business Research, 209 Prentis Bldg., Detroit MI 48202, †; SRI/MF/complete.

Issues reviewed during 1984: Sept./Oct. 1983-May/June 1984 (P) (Vol. 2, Nos. 6-7; Vol. 3, Nos. 1-3).

TABLES:

BIMONTHLY TABLES

[1] Michigan economic indicators [State and U.S. average hours and earnings in manufacturing, electricity consumption, and raw steel production; CPI for Detroit area and U.S.; U.S. motor vehicle production and PPI; and State farm price index; mostly for month of coverage, previous month, and same month of preceding year].

[2] Permit authorized construction [residential, industrial, office, and mercantile] in [21] selected counties [and the State, current and previous year through month of coverage].

RECURRING TABLE

[1] Quarterly personal income in Michigan [includes labor/proprietors income, by type and industry division; and other types of income, including transfer payments and unemployment insurance benefits; for 7-8 quarters, through quarter ending 3-5 months prior to cover date].

STATISTICAL FEATURES:

U9660–2.501: Sept./Oct. 1983 (Vol. 2, No. 6)

FORECAST UPDATE

(p. 8) By George A. Fulton and Donald R. Grimes. Article, with 1 table showing forecast vs. actual Michigan employment for 11 outstate (excludes Detroit area) SMSAs and 2 outstate regions, 1st half 1983. Data are from Michigan Employment Security Commission.

U9660–2.502: Nov./Dec. 1983 (Vol. 2, No. 7)

RECURRING TABLE

[1] Personal income in Michigan, for 2nd quarter 1983. (p. 6)

NORTHWEST MICHIGAN: AN ECONOMIC REVIEW AND OUTLOOK

(p. 1-3, 8) Article, with 3 charts and 3 tables showing employment shares for manufacturing, nonmanufacturing, and government sectors (no date); average annual migration rate, and percent change in employment, various periods 1970-83; and population projections, 1984-90; all for northwest Michigan, with selected comparisons to Grand Traverse Area, total State, and U.S.

YEAR-TO-YEAR CHANGE IN SELECTED ECONOMIC INDICATORS, RECURRING FEATURE

(p. 5) Recurring table on percent changes in selected U.S. and Michigan economic indicators, including civilian employment, nonagricultural wage/salary jobs, and retail sales, with detail for Detroit SMSA; and motor vehicle production, with State detail by company; Oct. 1982-Oct. 1983.

Data are from various government agencies and private sources. Table last appeared in the Nov. 1982 issue (for description, see SRI 1983 Annual, under U9660-2).

QUARTERLY MOTOR VEHICLE EMPLOYMENT AND ASSEMBLY, RECURRING FEATURE

(p. 7) Recurring table, showing Michigan and U.S. employment for 3 major motor vehicle manufacturers; motor vehicle production at 14 Michigan plants; and passenger car and bus/truck production in Michigan, U.S., and Canada; quarterly 1981-3rd quarter 1983.

Data are from motor vehicle industry sources. This is the 1st appearance of the table.

U9660–2.503: Jan. 1984 (Vol. 3, No. 1)

STEEL INDUSTRY UPDATE

(p. 3, 7-8) By David I. Verway. Article, with 2 tables showing raw steel production, and shipments of selected steel mill products, for U.S. and Michigan, various years 1951-83. Data are from Census Bureau.

NUMBER AND HOURLY EARNINGS OF AUTOMOTIVE WORKERS: SELECTED OCCUPATIONS

(p. 5-6) Table showing automotive industry employment and average hourly earnings, by detailed occupation, for U.S. and Michigan, selected months 1963-83. Data are from BLS.

U9660–2.504: Mar./Apr. 1984 (Vol. 3, No. 2)

AUTOPACT UPDATE

(p. 1-3, 5-8) By David I. Verway. Article on trends in U.S.-Canada motor vehicle trade and production. Data are from Dept of Commerce, Motor Vehicle Manufacturers Assn, and other sources. Includes 3 tables showing the following:

a. U.S. and Canada: value of bilateral trade in vehicles and parts; and volume of auto and truck/bus factory sales by destination (domestic, U.S.-Canada exports, and other exports); 1964-83.

b. Michigan, U.S., and Canadian shares of total employment in North American vehicle assembly and parts/accessories industries, 1977-83.

U9660–2.505: May/June 1984 (Vol. 3, No. 3)

RECURRING TABLE

[1] Personal income in Michigan, for 1st quarter 1984. (p. 5)

BRIEF

(p. 7-8) Article on R&D expenditures and patents granted in Michigan, 1963-81. Data are from NSF, U.S. Commissioner of Patents and Trademarks, and Census Bureau.

Includes 3 tables showing top 10 companies ranked by number of patents with Michigan origin, 1980; Federal and company R&D expenditures in Michigan, and patents with Michigan origin, 1963-81; and Michigan employment in 5 high-technology occupations, 1970 and 1980; all with comparisons to total U.S.